EARLY AMERICAN WRITINGS

GENERAL EDITOR
Carla Mulford

ASSOCIATE EDITORS
Angela Vietto
Amy E. Winans

New York   Oxford
OXFORD UNIVERSITY PRESS
2002

Oxford University Press

Oxford   New York
Athens   Auckland   Bangkok   Bogotá   Buenos Aires   Cape Town
Chennai   Dar es Salaam   Delhi   Florence   Hong Kong   Istanbul   Karachi
Kolkata   Kuala Lumpur   Madrid   Melbourne   Mexico City   Mumbai   Nairobi
Paris   São Paulo   Shanghai   Singapore   Taipei   Tokyo   Toronto   Warsaw

and associated companies in
Berlin   Ibadan

Copyright © 2002 by Oxford University Press, Inc.

Published by Oxford University Press, Inc.
198 Madison Avenue, New York, New York 10016
http://www.oup-usa.org

Oxford is a registered trademark of Oxford University Press

Library of Congress Cataloging-in-Publication Data

Early American writings / general editor, Carla Mulford ; associate editors, Angela
Vietto, Amy E. Winans.
      p. cm.
   Includes bibliographical references.
   ISBN 0-19-511840-5 (alk. paper) — ISBN 0-19-511841-3 (pbk. : alk. paper)
   1. United States—History—Colonial period, ca. 1600–1775—Sources. 2. America—Early
works to 1800. 3. America—History—To 1810—Sources. 4. United
States—History—Revolution, 1775–1783—Sources. 5. United
States—History—1783–1815—Sources. I. Mulford, Carla, 1955– II. Vietto, Angela. III.
Winans, Amy E.

E173 .E28 2001
973—dc21   2001016384

Printing number: 9 8 7 6 5 4 3 2 1

Printed in the United States of America
on acid-free paper

CONTENTS

3. THE STORIES OF THE PEOPLE: STRANGERS IN THE LAND   140

4. BRITAIN'S FIRST CENTURY IN AMERICA   159

5. NEW SPAIN IN NORTH AMERICA   358

6. NEW FRANCE IN NORTH AMERICA   426

7. THE BRITISH COLONIES OF NORTH AMERICA, THE EARLIER COLONIAL YEARS   479

11. THE NATIVE PEOPLES OF EASTERN NORTH AMERICA AND THE SETTLERS WHO REMAINED   1109

PREFACE

Early American Writings attempts to convey the cultural richness and cultural complexities of the Atlantic world, roughly from the fifteenth century through the late eighteenth century. The texts included in this volume cover the era of colonialism from the beginnings in South America and the northern areas of North America to the formation of the American Republic in English-speaking North America. Although it represents far more materials by British and European peoples who came to the Americas, this anthology also includes materials from the indigenous cultures. The ultimate emphasis upon the cultural formation that became the United States of America derives from the editors' assumption that their readers will be seeking a full sense of the literatures that form the background to what has come to be called American literature in North America.

To select a finite number of texts as a just example of an entire corpus of work is a great challenge, so to compile this anthology, the editors devised a general rationale for inclusion, well aware as they did so that any rationale must allow for exceptions. The three main (and overlapping) goals involved representing (1) the writings that were known and admired in the writers' own day, (2) the diversity of interests and peoples represented in those writings, and (3) the range of cross-cultural references that early readers regularly experienced. All three goals signal the editors' concern to represent the many cultures of the Americas while providing texts addressing those matters that had the greatest impact upon English-speaking North America.

The first goal was to provide readers today with a fuller understanding of what readers in the earlier eras were reading. Relatively speaking, readers today know fewer languages than readers did during the fifteenth, sixteenth, seventeenth, and even the eighteenth centuries. One goal of the editors, then, involved the extent to which writers and readers of that day were multilingual and had a broader sense of multicultural issues than we might today assume. For instance, as he does in many of his writings, Cotton Mather mentions Spanish writers in *The Negro Christianized,* his essay related to slavery. Joel Barlow nearly a century later constructed his poetic epic about the Americas from information gathered from a range of sources, several of which were based in writings about South America. French writers also knew the Spanish ones of their day, and English speakers knew the writings of the French and later the Dutch and Germans in their midst. *Early American Writings* includes several writers of the Spanish colonial era in South America to indicate the richness of the reading culture that people like Mather and the first generations of British and European colonists shared. Similarly, in keeping with the idea of a representation of readings *in their time* that were well known, the editors made some determinations related to several writers of prose whose novels and autobiographies are now familiar but who might have been more generally known in their own day through their newspaper writings. The volume offers some of Franklin's published newspaper essays, which in their day were known (and Franklin's autobiography generally unknown), for instance. Also, the selections provided from eighteenth-century novels or essay collections (such as Crevecoeur's *Letters from an American Farmer*) are typically selections that editors offered readers of newspapers in the eighteenth century. The goal is to provide an understanding of written commerce *then,* so readers will be able to make appropriate assessments about the reading and writing culture of that day. In general, with regard especially to eighteenth-century literary culture, the balance of representation has gone to English speakers under the assumption that the collection will be used mostly by readers who are interested in the cultural formation of the early United States of America in North America.

The efforts to represent cultural diversity derive from the sense that, historically, there was no unified culture of the Americas, and so the diversity of cultures is an important feature of the book. Before they came to the Americas, people considered themselves definable by territory; after they arrived, they continued, frequently, to do so. There was no "Spain" as it is currently conceived but, rather, different "Hispanic" peoples, peoples from an area they called Hispania—New Castilians, Aragonese, Catalans, and others—all of whom sailed for different reasons and who set up in territories that revealed the orientation of their leadership. Several areas were called New Spain, just as several areas were called New France. Indeed, although when readers think of France in the Americas, they think primarily of the work of the Jesuits (who were Catholics) in what is now Canada, they often do so without recognizing that the Jesuits operated all along the Hudson and Mississippi Rivers, and where they were not operating, other Catholic or Protestant groups were seeking residence, whether in Louisiana or in South America. Jean de Léry, Marie Guyart Martin (Marie l'Incarnation), and Marie Madeleine Hachard (Sister St. Stanislaus) thus provide important counterpoints to the writings of the Jesuits of Canada.

Generally, the editors have attempted to create a collection of readings that "talk" to one another in their own day and across time. Thus, for instance, materials from Native America begin and conclude the volume as significant contrasts to writings of conquest and settlement created by Europeans. The texts make thematic and comparative reflections upon one another, even as they reveal the extent to which there really existed no cultural unification, even at the time of the confederation of the states that would become the (English-speaking) United States. Thematic comparisons are available, perhaps the most notable being a range of texts imaging different kinds of captivity, whether Spanish or English people's captivity among Native peoples (selections by Garcilaso de la Vega, Cabeza de Vaca, and Mary Rowlandson), French people's captivity among Native peoples (Radisson), English captivity among French and Native peoples (J. Williams), Africans' captivity in the hands of Europeans or Native peoples (Equiano, Marrant, Wheatley), or women's captivity by men (Ashbridge). Generic comparisons are also possible. Readers can compare the many autobiographical writings across and within cultures and can similarly examine the different poetic forms and norms.

The texts included represent the cultures of Portuguese, Spanish, French, Dutch, Swedish, German, and English speakers. By necessity, then, *Early American Writings* includes texts in translation. The editors are aware of the language-power dimensions of offering works in translation, but they also recognize that most readers of this volume will not be familiar with all the languages represented herein. With regard to issues in translation, the editors have sought to represent some of the interesting cross-cultural dimensions faced by writers in their own day, so as to reveal the cultural complexities of intercolonial political and linguistic tension. For instance, the selection by Pierre-Esprit Radisson, a native French speaker, was written in English because Radisson was involved in making an alliance with England's Charles II. Radisson's account of his captivity among Mohawk peoples of Iroquoia is written in his own mixed English, something that can show readers the multilingual situation of North America in the seventeenth century. When providing work in translation, the editors have attempted to use reliable translations. When possible, as in the instance of Le Page du Pratz, the editors selected translations that were circulated in the writers' own day. In other cases, contemporary translations are nonexistent or too difficult to locate, so later translations were used. And in two cases—Christoph Saur and Henricus Selyns—the editors offer first-time translations made by scholars Patrick Erben and David Shields. By providing works in translation, the editors avoid the problem inherent in presenting texts written only in English. English speakers in their day were well aware of the cultures around them. English speakers came late, and their settlements were less widely dispersed than those of the Spanish and the French. To provide only English speakers' texts might give a false impression about the English-speaking culture, as if it understood itself as monolinguistic and monocultural. Indeed, English speakers' culture was severely tested during the eighteenth century, when many Germans came to the middle colonies in North America, thus testing the strength and solidarity of what Franklin called the British Empire there. English colonists in the colonial period cannot stand in for all "America," even though we understand today that the English speakers' culture was the dominant cultural force behind the forming of the North American nation called the United States of America.

Finally, the editors are continuing to supply additional texts at an electronic text website that complements the publication of this volume. At the Electronic Text Center of the Alderman Library of the University of Virginia, at *http://etext.lib.virginia.edu/,* readers will find supplemental materials that will serve more comprehensively to flesh out what already appears—we think, generously—in this volume. The website, called "Early American Writings," is an ongoing project, and those interested in finding out more about the electronic site being maintained should feel free to contact General Editor Carla Mulford.

The editors hope that readers will find the present volume interesting and useful, and they will personally welcome comments on it, asking, as Franklin phrased it in his autobiography, "the Advantage Authors have in a second Edition to correct some Faults of the first."

ACKNOWLEDGMENTS

Selecting texts to include is the anthologist's most difficult task, given the great number of interesting materials available. For their many excellent suggestions and advice on possible texts to include, the editors wish to thank several colleagues who responded to their calls for suggestions, beginning in early 1997. Several of these colleagues engaged in extended conversations with one another and the general editor on one or more discussion listserves or in person, and several sent syllabuses of courses they offered. We thank for their assistance: Jonathan M. Barz (Concordia University), Charles Boewe, Michelle Burnham (Santa Clara University), Ted Burrows (Brooklyn College), Jon Butler (Yale University), Emily Clark (Tulane University), David Curtis (Belmont University), Lois Dean (U.S. Department of Housing and Urban Development), Michael G. Ditmore (Pepperdine University), Jim Egan (Brown University), Gregory J. Eiselein (Kansas State University), Edward Gallagher (Lehigh University), Alan Gallay (Western Washington University), Joanne Gaudio (University of Wyoming), Elizabeth Swanson Goldberg (Miami University of Ohio), Allan Greer (University of Toronto), Sharon M. Harris (Texas Christian University), Madelon Jacoba (California University of Pennsylvania), Helen Jaskoski (California State University, Fullerton), Cynthia A. Kierner (University of North Carolina, Charlotte), Austin Meredith (University of California, Irvine), Charles Mignon (University of Nebraska), Dennis Moore (Florida State University), Anne Myles (University of Northern Iowa), Steven Neuwirth (Western Connecticut State University), Ross J. Pudaloff (Wayne State University), Jeffrey Richards (Old Dominion University), A. Gregg Roeber (Pennsylvania State University), John Saillant (Western Michigan University), Mary Schweitzer (Villanova University), David S. Shields (The Citadel), E. Thomson Shields, Jr. (East Carolina University), Alan Silva (Hamline University), Timothy Sweet (West Virginia University), Michael Vella (Indiana University of Pennsylvania), Daniel Walden (Pennsylvania State University), Germaine Warkentin (Victoria College, University of Toronto), Michael Warner (Rutgers University), David Williams (George Mason University), Bridgett Williams-Searle (University of Iowa), and Rafia Zafar (Washington University at St. Louis). The editors are grateful to Suzanne Begnoche for her research and assistance in the preparation of material on colonial Spanish literature.

Assistance with specific editorial tasks has been essential to the completion of the volume. Latin translations within the Cotton Mather selections were offered by Marianne Messmer (Georg-August University, Göttingen, Germany), Caleb Crain (senior editor, *Lingua Franca*), Elizabeth A. Latshaw (University of South Florida), and Phil Foti. The editors used Messmer's Latin translations in completing the Mather selection. Patrick Erben (Emory Universitiy) provided a new translation for a first-time printing of one of Christoph Saur's dialogues from his newspaper. Erben drafted the editorial matter for the Saur, Francis Daniel Pastorius, and Gottlieb Mittelberger selections. The editors turned to Gordon Sayre (University of Oregon) for his expertise in colonial French materials. Sayre drafted the editorial matter for the selections of Jean de Léry, Jean de Brébeuf, Marie Guyart Martin (Marie de l'Incarnation), and Antoine le Page du Pratz. Finally, David S. Shields offered the original translations, in verse, of the poems by Henricus Selyns, along with drafting the accompanying editorial matter for the Selyns selection. The editors remain grateful for the selections provided them by Erben, Sayre, and Shields.

The editors received assistance from several people. Angela Vietto thanks Alan Bilansky for his support and assistance; and Amy E. Winans extends her thanks to Crystal Van Horn and Amy Kimball, and she wishes especially to thank Windsor Morgan, who assisted her work in many ways. Carla Mulford is grateful to Louis Cellucci, who knows just how much he helped her all along the way.

Oxford University Press has been exemplary in its attention to all aspects of the development and production of this book. The editors wish to thank Yarisa Paulino and Christine D'Antonio for their assistance with all areas of production, and they especially thank the copyeditor, Wendy Almeleh, who read the manuscript with attention. D. Anthony English, senior acquisitions editor for the New York Oxford office at the time we began this project, was delightful to work with. Tony waited with interest and patience as we faced the many challenges of creating the volume, and he assisted us throughout the publication process. After his departure, Janet M. Beatty became our editor and helped us through the final stages of the project with consummate professionalism. We remain grateful for both editors' thorough attention to the project.

1

❧

THE STORIES OF THE PEOPLE
Creation, Emergence, Transformation

The stories told by the generations of people whose ancestral ties lie anciently in the lands of the Americas are like stories by indigenous people in most places: They tell how the people reached their present locations; why there are different kinds of people, plants, and animals on the earth's surface; how the people learned what should be their food and how to care for themselves; and how the people learned what would be their dwelling places. The stories often provide specific cultural directives, and they give a sense of coherence to daily living. Like important stories in most cultures, the stories of Native American peoples also include instructions about behaviors personal and interpersonal. That is, the stories indicate taboos and rituals that one should adhere to; they provide guidance about perseverance and the consequences of hasty actions; they illustrate the importance of understanding the phenomena of life and death and the uncertainty of one's here-and-now existence; and they give instruction about the group's social formation and polity.

Often stories that treat Native peoples' subsistence (such as stories about planting, hunting, and fishing) and their lifeways (particularly birth, puberty, and death) fall into cycles of stories that are told as a part of the cultural ritual moments, when the groups are together and relating the stories of their ancient past and their present circumstances. At other times, groups and individuals relate stories as explanations of current experiences and in informal situations, while engaging in day-to-day activities. In other words, just as stories do in most cultures around the world, the stories of Native American people can serve both ritual and personal functions. Each group has its own stories, and even within each group, there are different versions of the stories, as they have been passed down through the generations via different family or cultural connections. Differences occur because Native peoples conveyed their stories through oral channels, not in writing, and so variations in the telling of stories occurred across time. In the case where materialist memory systems were in use—the Incas (inhabitants of the area now called Peru), employed the *quipu,* a reckoning system of ropes, with colored knots, to retain cultural knowledge, and the Mayas (inhabitants of present-day Mexico) used hieroglyphic writing—cultural narratives were preserved with greater uniformity in the telling, but even within these cultures, slight differences emerged in their stories. Some of these differences are available in the records made by Europeans, who used their own systems of letters to speak about these peoples and record their stories. The reliability of Europeans' records, of course, should be questioned, but without any such records, general information about many Native peoples would be scanty because in many cultures, the telling of cultural narratives was suppressed with the infiltration of the Europeans.

The number and kinds of stories told by the first peoples of the Americas are too numerous to detail closely. The selections that follow are some of the narratives told by different groups in different parts of North America. They are representations of some Native peoples' stories of their origin and emergence, their cultural heroes, and their trickster figures. Origin and emergence stories are complicated and symbolic stories about how the people reached the earth's surface. In some story cycles, the people came from an ancestor who came down in some fashion from the Sky World, and in other cycles of stories, the people came from ancestors who emerged from the center of the earth. Generally speaking, in the eastern and woodland areas of North America, origin stories tend to feature people falling from the sky or experiencing floods and ultimately being saved by the animals who find sufficient earth to assist the people from a catastrophic fall or from floundering in the too-great waters. In western portions of North America and in more arid areas, stories of emergence tend to feature a dark underworld from which the people, again with the assistance of animals and plants, emerge and reach the surface. Stories of culture heroes dramatize the people's reverence for particular individuals (sometimes having ancestry from the gods), who acted in ways that would significantly change the people's world or their social order. Cultural heroes, in some Native cultures, are the foundation of particular cultural beliefs, values, and practices. Their actions determined why the people live and act in certain ways, affiliate themselves with some groups, and avoid particular places or kinds of people. Trickster stories—stories typically about Raven or Coyote or Rabbit—are stories that explain the otherwise unexplainable, dramatize the reasons behind certain taboos, or simply provide some humor about daily activities. Trickster figures often seek food by stealing it or trying to swindle people out of it, and they frequently seek sexual gratification by transforming themselves into animals or people. Typically, they become the dupes of their own misdeeds, and their outcomes serve as instruction regarding behavior and the acceptance of cultural rituals.

A final word about the stories presented. It is useful to remember that the stories told by Native peoples have come down across generations, for centuries, as oral stories, and they have been told ritually within Native groups. Even within groups, versions of the stories can differ. It is impossible to offer "authentic" stories *as they existed* in what (in the West) is considered historical time because the stories are themselves products of cultures that have changed and adapted across time. Thus, in some stories, references to white people or French people, references to non-Native people generally, give a sense that the stories have changed as the different groups adapted to or explained the occurrence of newcomers, non-Native people, to the earth's surface and the group's location. These adaptations of what might have been original Native American cultural stories represent the resilience of Native peoples in light of the immense change that occurred as a result of the arrival of strangers to their ancestral lands.

Penobscot

The Penobscots form part of the Eastern Abenaki (Wabanaki) peoples, Algonquians, of the area today called Maine. Historically, the languages employed by the Eastern Abenakis were part of the Eastern Algonquian language system that about four hundred years ago extended from northeastern North Carolina to Nova Scotia. The Penobscots have survived as an enclave within their traditional homeland.

To Native American peoples of the northeastern and southwestern parts of North America, corn is a sacred food, an all-nourishing and life-sustaining force within the communities. Corn is the subject of many stories of the people from these regions. Although the stories may differ in content and form, the effect of the sacred importance of corn to the people is quite clear.

CORN MOTHER[1]

When Kloskurbeh, the All-maker, lived on earth, there were no people yet. But one day when the sun was high,

---

1. This story is a modern version by Richard Erdoes and Alfonso Ortiz, based on nineteenth-century sources about the Penobscots and their culture.

a youth appeared and called him "Uncle, brother of my mother." This young man was born from the foam of the waves, foam quickened by the wind and warmed by the sun. It was the motion of the wind, the moistness of water, and the sun's warmth which gave him life—warmth above all, because warmth is life. And the young man lived with Kloskurbeh and became his chief helper.

Now, after these two powerful beings had created all

manner of things, there came to them, as the sun was shining at high noon, a beautiful girl. She was born of the wonderful earth plant, and of the dew, and of warmth. Because a drop of dew fell on a leaf and was warmed by the sun, and the warming sun is life, this girl came into being—from the green living plant, from moisture, and from warmth.

"I am love," said the maiden. "I am a strength giver, I am the nourisher, I am the provider of men and animals. They all love me."

Then Kloskurbeh thanked the Great Mystery Above for having sent them the maiden. The youth, the Great Nephew, married her, and the girl conceived and thus became First Mother. And Kloskurbeh, the Great Uncle, who teaches humans all they need to know, taught their children how to live. Then he went away to dwell in the north, from which he will return sometime when he is needed.

Now the people increased and became numerous. They lived by hunting, and the more people there were, the less game they found. They were hunting it out, and as the animals decreased, starvation came upon the people. And First Mother pitied them.

The little children came to First Mother and said: "We are hungry. Feed us." But she had nothing to give them, and she wept. She told them: "Be patient. I will make some food. Then your little bellies will be full." But she kept weeping.

Her husband asked: "How can I make you smile? How can I make you happy?"

"There is only one thing that will stop my tears."

"What is it?" asked her husband.

"It is this: you must kill me."

"I could never do that."

"You must, or I will go on weeping and grieving forever."

Then the husband traveled far, to the end of the earth, to the north he went, to ask the Great Instructor, his uncle Kloskurbeh, what he should do.

"You must do what she wants. You must kill her," said Kloskurbeh. Then the young man went back to his home, and it was his turn to weep. But First Mother said: "Tomorrow at high noon you must do it. After you have killed me, let two of our sons take hold of my hair and drag my body over that empty patch of earth. Let them drag me back and forth, back and forth, over every part of the patch, until all my flesh has been torn from my body. Afterwards, take my bones, gather them up, and bury them in the middle of this clearing. Then leave that place."

She smiled and said, "Wait seven moons and then come back, and you will find my flesh there, flesh given out of love, and it will nourish and strengthen you forever and ever."

So it was done. The husband slew his wife and her sons, praying, dragged her body to and fro as she had commanded, until her flesh covered all the earth. Then they took up her bones and buried them in the middle of it. Weeping loudly, they went away.

When the husband and his children and his children's children came back to that place after seven moons had passed, they found the earth covered with tall, green, tasseled plants. The plants' fruit—corn—was First Mother's flesh, given so that the people might live and flourish. And they partook of First Mother's flesh and found it sweet beyond words. Following her instructions, they did not eat all, but put many kernels back into the earth. In this way her flesh and spirit renewed themselves every seven months, generation after generation.

And at the spot where they had buried First Mother's bones, there grew another plant, broad-leafed and fragrant. It was First Mother's breath, and they heard her spirit talking: "Burn this up and smoke it. It is sacred. It will clear your minds, help your prayers, and gladden your hearts."

And First Mother's husband called the first plant *Skarmunal,* corn, and the second plant *utarmur-wayeh,* tobacco.

"Remember," he told the people, "and take good care of First Mother's flesh, because it is her goodness become substance. Take good care of her breath, because it is her love turned into smoke. Remember her and think of her whenever you eat, whenever you smoke this sacred plant, bcause she has given her life so that you might live. Yet she is not dead, she lives: in undying love she renews herself again and again."

ALGONQUIAN

The Micmacs and Passamaquoddy peoples of the Northeast coast are, like the Penobscots, Eastern Abenaki (Wabanaki) peoples. They tell traditional Algonquian stories like this trickster story about Rabbit. Mahtigwess, the Rabbit, is a trickster who has *m'téoulin,* great powers. The intrusion of French missionaries on Abenaki culture is evident in this version of the story, thus dating the narrative that became this version at least to the time when French Jesuits lived among the Abenakis.

A STORY ABOUT GREAT RABBIT[1]

Wildcat is mean and ferocious. He has a short tail and big, long, sharp fangs, and his favorite food is rabbit. One day when Wildcat was hungry, he said to himself: "I'm going to catch and eat Mahtigwess, Great Rabbit, himself. He's plump and smart, and nothing less will do for my dinner." So we went hunting for Great Rabbit.

Now, Great Rabbit can sense what others are thinking from a long way off, so he already knew that Wildcat was after him. He made up his mind that he would use his magic power against Wildcat's strength. He picked up a handful of wood chips, threw them ahead of himself, and jumped after them, and because Great Rabbit is *m'téoulin,* every jump was a mile. Jumping that far, of course, he left very few tracks to follow.

Wildcat swore a mighty oath that he would catch Great Rabbit, that he would find him even if Mahtigwess had fled to the end of the world. At that time Wildcat had a beautiful long tail, and he swore by it: "Let my tail fall off—may I have just a little stump for a tail—if I fail to catch Great Rabbit!"

After a mile he found Rabbit's tracks. After another mile he found some more tracks. Wildcat was not altogether without magic either, and he was persevering. So mile by mile, he kept on Rabbit's trail.

In fact, Wildcat was drawing closer and closer. It grew dark and Great Rabbit grew tired. He was on a wide, empty plain of snow, and there was nothing to hide behind except a little spruce tree. He stomped on the snow and made himself a seat and bed of spruce boughs.

When Wildcat came to that spot, he found a fine, big wigwam and stuck his head through the door. Sitting inside was an old, gray-haired chief, solemn and mighty. The only strange thing about him was that he had two long ears standing up at each side of his head.

"Great Chief," said Wildcat, "have you by any chance seen a biggish rabbit running like mad?"

"Rabbits? Why of course, there are hundreds, thousands of rabbits hereabouts, but what's the hurry? It's late and you must be tired. If you want to hunt rabbits, start in the morning after a good night's sleep. I'm a lonely man and enjoy the company of a respected personage like you. Stay overnight; I have a fine rabbit stew cooking here."

Wildcat was flattered. "Big Chief, I am honored," he said. He ate a whole kettle full of tasty rabbit stew and then fell asleep before the roaring fire.

Wildcat awoke early because he was freezing. He found himself alone in the midst of a huge snowfield. Nothing was there, no wigwam, no fire, no old chief; all he could see were a few little spruce boughs. It had been a dream, an illusion created by Great Rabbit's magic. Even the stew had been an illusion, and Wildcat was ravenous.

Shivering in the icy wind, Wildcat howled: "Rabbit has tricked me again, but I'll get even with him. By my tail, I swear I'll catch, kill, and eat him!"

Again Great Rabbit traveled with his mile-wide jumps, and again Wildcat followed closely. At nightfall Rabbit said to himself: "Time to rest and conjure something up." This time he trampled down a large area and spread many pine boughs around.

When Wildcat arrived, he found a large village full of busy people, though of what tribe he couldn't tell. He also saw a big wooden church painted white, the kind the French Jesuits were putting up among some tribes. Wildcat went up to a young man who was about to enter the church. "Friend, have you seen a biggish rabbit hereabouts, running away?"

---

1. This story is a modern version by Richard Erdoes and Alfonso Ortiz, based on a nineteenth-century source, Charles G. Leland, *Algonquin Legends of New England; or, Myths and Folklore of the Micmac, Passamaquoddy, and Penobscot Tribes* (1884).

"Quiet," said the young man, "we're having a prayer meeting. Wait until the sermon is over." The young man went into the church, and Wildcat followed him. There were lots of people sitting and listening to a gray-haired preacher. The only strange thing was the two long ears sticking up at each side of the priest's cap. He was preaching a very, very long sermon about the wickedness of ferocious wild beasts who tear up victims with their big, sharp fangs and then devour them. "Such savage fiends will be punished for their sins," said this preacher over and over.

Wildcat didn't like the long sermon, but he had to wait all the same. When the preaching was over at last, he went up to the priest with the long ears and asked: "Sir, have you seen a very sacred, biggish rabbit hereabouts?"

"Rabbits!" exclaimed the preacher. "We have a wet, foggy cedar swamp nearby with thousands of rabbits."

"I don't mean just any rabbit; I'm speaking of Great Rabbit."

"Of him I know nothing, friend. But over there in that big wigwam lives the wise old chief, the Sagamore. Go and ask him; he knows everything."

Wildcat went to the wigwam and found the Sagamore, an imposing figure, gray-haired like the preacher, with long white locks sticking up on each side of his head. "Young man," said the Sagamore gravely, "what can I do for you?"

"I'm looking for the biggish Great Rabbit."

"Ah! Him! He's hard to find and hard to catch. Tonight it's too late, but tomorrow I'll help you. Sit down, dear man. My daughters will give you a fine supper."

The Sagamore's daughters were beautiful. They brought Wildcat many large wooden bowls of the choicest food, and he ate it all up, because by now he was very hungry. The warmth of the fire and his full stomach made him drowsy, and the Sagamore's daughters brought him a thick white bearskin to sleep on. "You people really know how to treat a guest," said Wildcat as he fell asleep.

When he awoke, he found himself in a dismal, wet, foggy cedar swamp. Nothing was there except mud and icy slush and a lot of rabbit tracks. There was no village, no church, no wigwam, no Sagamore, no beautiful daughters. They had all been a mirage conjured up by Great Rabbit. The fine food had been a mirage too, and Wildcat's stomach was growling. He was ankle-deep in the freezing swamp. The fog was so thick he could hardly see anything. Enraged, he vowed to find and kill Great Rabbit even if he should die in the attempt. He swore by his

tail, his teeth, his claws—by everything dear to him. Then he hastened on.

That night Wildcat came to a big longhouse. Inside, it was like a great hall, and it was full of people. On a high seat sat the chief, who wore two long white feathers at each side of his head. This venerable leader also had beautiful daughters who fed all comers, for Wildcat had stumbled into the midst of a great feast.

Exhausted and panting, he gasped, "Has any one seen the bi-big-biggish G-G-Great Ra-Rab-Rabbit?"

"Later, friend," said the chief with the two white feathers. "We are feasting, dancing, singing. You seem exhausted, poor man! Sit down; catch your breath. Rest. Eat."

Wildcat sat down. The people were having a singing contest, and the chief on his high seat pointed at Wildcat and said, "Our guest here looks like a fine singer. Perhaps he will honor us with a song."

Wildcat was flattered. He arose and sang:

> Rabbits!
> How I hate them!
> How I despise them!
> How I laugh at them!
> How I kill them!
> How I scalp them!
> How I eat them!

"A truly wonderful song," said the chief. "I must reward you for it. Here's what I give you." And with that the chief jumped up from his high seat, jumped over Wildcat's head, struck him a blow with his tomahawk, kept on jumping with mile-long leaps—and all was gone. The longhouse, the hall, the people, the daughters: none remained. Once more Wildcat found himself alone in the middle of nowhere, worse off than ever, for he had a gash in his scalp where Great Rabbit had hit him with the tomahawk. His feet were sore, his stomach empty. He could hardly crawl. But he was more infuriated than ever. "I'll kill him!" he growled, "I'll give my life! And the tricks are over; he won't fool me again!"

That night Wildcat came to two beautiful wigwams. In the first was a young woman, obviously a chief's daughter. In the other was someone whom Wildcat took for her father, an elderly, gray-haired, gentle-looking man with two scalp locks sticking up at the sides of his head.

"Come in, come in, poor man," said the gray-haired host. "You're wounded! My daughter will wash and cure that cut. And we must build up your strength. I have a fine broth here and a pitcher full of wine, the drink Frenchmen make. It has great restorative powers."

But Wildcat was suspicious. "If this is Great Rabbit in disguise again, he won't fool me," he promised himself.

"Dear sir," said Wildcat, "I hesitate to mention it, but the two scalp locks sticking up at the sides of your head look very much like rabbit's ears."

"Rabbit's ears? How funny!" said the old man. "Know, friend, that in our tribe we all wear our scalp locks this way."

"Ah," said Wildcat, "but your nose is split exactly like a rabbit's nose."

"Don't remind me, friend. Some weeks ago I was hammering wampum beads, and the stone I was using to pound them on broke in half. A sharp piece flew up and split my nose—a great misfortune, because it does disfigure me."

"It does indeed. A pity. But why are your soles so yellow, like a rabbit's soles?"

"Oh, that's nothing. I prepared some tobacco yesterday, and the juice stained my palms yellow."

Then Wildcat said to himself: "This man is no rabbit."

The old man called his daughter, who washed Wildcat's wound, put a healing salve into it, and bathed his face. Then the old man gave him a wonderfully strengthening broth and a large pitcher of sweet wine.

"This wine is really good," said Wildcat, "the first I ever tasted."

"Yes, these white people, these Frenchmen, are very clever at making good things to drink."

When Wildcat awoke, he found, of course, that he had been tricked again. The food he had eaten was rabbit pellets, the wine was stale water in a half-wilted pitcher plant. Now it was only his great hatred that kept Wildcat going, but go he did, like a streak, on Rabbit's tail.

Mahtigwess, Great Rabbit, had only enough *m'téoulin,* enough magic power, left for one more trick. So he said to himself: "This time I'd better make it good!"

Great Rabbit came to a big lake and threw a chip of wood into the water. Immediately it turned into a towering ship, the kind white men build, with tall sides, three masts, white sails, and colored flags. That ship was pierced on each side with three rows of heavy cannon.

When Wildcat arrived at this lake, he saw the big ship with its crew. On deck was the captain, a gray-haired man with a large, gold-trimmed, cocked hat that had fluffy white plumes right and left.

"Rabbit!" cried Wildcat, "I know you! You're no French captain; you're Great Rabbit. I know you, Mahtigwess! I am the mighty Wildcat, and I'm coming to scalp and kill you now!"

And with that, Wildcat jumped into the lake and swam toward the ship. Then the captain, who indeed was Mahtigwess, the Great Rabbit, ordered his men to fire their muskets and the three rows of heavy cannon. Bullets went whistling by Wildcat; cannonballs flew toward him; the whole world was spitting thunder and fire.

Wildcat had never before faced white men's firearms; they were entirely new to him. It didn't matter that ship, cannon, muskets, cannon-balls, bullets, fire, noise, and smoke were merely illusions conjured up by Rabbit. To Wildcat they were real, and he was scared to death. He swam back to shore and ran away. And if he hasn't died, he is running still.

And yes, as Wildcat had sworn by his tail to catch and kill Rabbit, his tail fell off, and ever since then this kind of big wildcat has a short, stumpy tail and is called a bobcat.

IROQUOIS

The Haudenosaunee peoples, called the Iroquois by the French and the Five Nations (later the Six Nations, when the Tuscaroras joined them) by the English, consider their homeland the area that is today called New York State. Traditionally, the peoples called the Iroquois included—as situated from the eastern to the western area of Iroquoia—the Mohawks (keepers of the eastern gate), the Oneidas, the Onandagas, the Cayugas, and the Senecas (keepers of the western gate). According to tradition, the Haudenosaunees formed a league to bring peace to the area because of factionalism and wars among the competing groups. At different times during the course of their history, the Iroquois negotiated with, traded with, and fought with other American Indian peoples of the Northeast, the French in Canada, the various English colonists, and the Dutch on the Hudson River. They were very important during the eighteenth-century era of wars among the European powers in North America, and, according to Iroquoian traditions, they were influential in providing a model for peace during the era of the English colonies' confederation.

Many Native Americans of the northern and eastern regions tell stories of the world's creation on the back of a giant sea turtle. The following story is just one version of many that circulate about the creation, one of the earliest to be written down (thus explaining the somewhat old-fashioned terminology used). This account was recorded by John Norton in about 1816. Norton, the son of Scottish and Cherokee parents and an adopted Mohawk, was prominent at the time this story was recorded, and he had a special interest in recording the narratives of the Iroquois people. Norton traveled widely among the Native Americans of the East, and he traveled to England to speak on Indian affairs there. While in England in 1805, Norton delivered an abbreviated version of the story he later recorded in his journal, the version reprinted here.

THE CREATION OF THE WORLD[1]

The tradition of the Nottowegui or Five Nations says, "that in the beginning before the formation of the earth; the country above the sky was inhabited by Superior Beings, over whom the Great Spirit presided. His daughter having become pregnant by an illicit connection, he pulled up a great tree by the roots, and threw her through the cavity thereby formed; but, to prevent her utter destruction, he previously ordered the Great Turtle, to get from the bottom of the waters, some slime on its back, and to wait on the surface of the water to receive her on it. When she had fallen on the back of the Turtle, with the mud she found there, she began to form the earth, and by the time of her delivery had increased it to the extent of a little island. Her child was a daughter, and as she grew up the earth extended under their hands. When the young woman had arrived at the age of discretion, the Spirits who roved about, in human forms, made proposals of marriage for the young woman: the mother always rejected their offers, until a middle aged man, of a dignified appearance, his bow in his hand, and his quiver on his back, paid his addresses. On being accepted, he entered the house, and seated himself on the birth[2] of his intended spouse; the mother was in a birth on the other side of the fire. She observed that her son-in-law did not lie down all night; but taking two arrows out of his quiver, he put them by the side of his bride: at the dawn of day he took them up, and having replaced them in his quiver, he went out.

"After some time, the old woman perceived her daughter to be pregnant, but could not discover where the father had gone, or who he was. At the time of delivery, the twins disputed which way they should go out of the womb; the wicked one said, let us go out of the side; but the other said, not so, lest we kill our mother; then the wicked one pretending to acquiesce, desired his brother to go out first: but as soon as he was delivered, the wicked one, in attempting to go out at her side, caused the death of his mother.

"The twin brothers were nurtured and raised by their Grandmother; the eldest was named Teharonghyawago, or the Holder of Heaven; the youngest was called Tawiskaron, or Flinty rock, from his body being entirely covered with such a substance. They grew up, and with their bows and arrows, amused themselves throughout the island, which encreased in extent, and they were favoured with various animals of Chace. Tawiskaron was the most fortunate hunter, and enjoyed the favour of his Grandmother. Teharonghyawago was not so successful in the Chace, and suffered from their unkindness. When he was a youth, and roaming alone, in melancholy mood, through the island, a human figure, of noble aspect, appearing to him, addressed him thus. 'My son, I have seen your distress, and heard your solitary lamentations; you are unhappy in the loss of a mother, in the unkindness of your Grandmother and brother. I now come to comfort you, I am your father, and will be your Protector; therefore take courage, and suffer not your spirit to sink. Take this (giving him an ear of *maize*) plant it, and attend it in the manner, I shall direct; it will yield you a certain support, independent of the Chace, at the same time that it will render more palatable the viands, which you may thereby obtain. I am the Great Turtle which supports the earth, on which you move. Your brother's ill treatment will increase with his years; bear it with patience till the time appointed, before which you shall hear further.'

"After saying this, and directing him how to plant the corn, he disappeared. Teharonghyawago planted the corn, and returned home. When its verdant sprouts began to flourish above the ground, he spent his time in clearing

---

1. The text is from *The Journal of Major John Norton, 1816,* ed. Carl F. Klinck and James J. Talman (1970).

2. An old spelling for *berth,* a bed or bunk.

from it all growth of grass and weeds, which might smother it or retard its advancement while yet in its tender state, before it had acquired sufficient grandeur to shade the ground. He now discovered that his wicked brother caught the timid deer, the stately elk with branching horns, and all the harmless inhabitants of the Forest; and imprisoned them in an extensive cave, for his own particular use, depriving mortals from having the benefit of them that was originally intended by the Great Spirit. Teharonghyawago discovered the direction his brother took in conducting these animals captive to the Cave; but never could trace him quite to the spot, as he eluded his sight with more than common dexterity!

"Teharonghyawago endeavoured to conceal himself on the path that led to the cave, so that he might follow him imperceptibly; but he found it impossible to hide himself from the penetrating Tawiskaron. At length he observed, that altho' his brother saw, with extraordinary acuteness, every surrounding object, yet he never raised his eyes to look above: Teharonghyawago then climbed a lofty tree, which grew near to where he thought the place of confinement was situated: in the meantime, his brother passed, searching with his eyes the thickest recesses of the Forest, but never casting a glance above. He then saw his brother take a straight course, and when he was out of sight, Teharonghyawago descended, and came to the Cave, a short time after he had deposited his charge; and finding there an innumerable number of animals confined, he set them free, and returned home.

"It was not long before Tawiskaron, visiting the Cave, discovered that all his captives, which he had taken so much pains to deprive of their liberty, had been liberated: he knew this to be an act of his brother, but dissembling his anger, he mediated revenge, at some future period.

"Teharonghyawago laboured to people the earth with inhabitants, and to found Villages in happy situations, extending the comforts of men. Tawiskaron was equally active in destroying the works his brother had done; and in accumulating every evil in his power on the heads of ill fated mortals. Teharonghyawago saw, with regret, his brother persevere in every wickedness; but waited with patience the result of what his father had told him.

"At one time, being in conversation with his brother, Tawiskaron said 'Brother, what do you think there is on earth, with which you might be killed?' Teharonghyawago replied, 'I know of nothing that could affect my life, unless it be the foam of the billows of the Lake or the downy topped[3] reed.' 'What do you think would take your life?' Tawiskaron answered, 'Nothing except horn or flint.' Here their discourse ended.

"Teharonghyawago returning from hunting, heard a voice singing a plaintive air: he listened and heard it name his Mother, who was killed by Tawiskaron; he immediately hastened towards the spot from whence the voice proceeded, crying, 'Who is that, who dares to name my deceased mother in my hearing?' When he came there, he saw the track of a fawn, which he pursued, without overtaking it, till the autumn, when it dropped its first horns; these he took up, and fixed upon the forked branches of a tree.

"He continued the pursuit seven years; and every autumn, when its horns fell, he picked them up, and placed them as he had done the first. At last, he overtook the deer, now grown to be a stately buck: it begged its life, and said, 'Spare me, and I will give you information that may be great service to you.' When he had promised it its life, it spoke as follows, 'It was to give you the necessary information that I have been subjected to your pursuit, and that which I shall now tell you was the intended reward of your perseverance and clemency. Your brother, in coming into the world, caused the death of your Mother; if he was then wicked in his infancy, his malice has grown with his stature; he now premeditates evil against you; be therefore on your guard: as soon as he assaults you, exert yourself, and you will overcome him.'

"He returned home; and not long after this adventure, was attacked by his brother. They fought; the one made use of the horn and flint stone which he had provided: the other sought for froth and the reed, which made little impression on the body of Teharonghyawago. They fought a long time, over the whole of the island, until at last Tawiskaron fell under the conquering hand of his brother. According to the varied tones of their voices in the different places through which they passed during the contest, the people, who afterwards sprung up there, spoke different languages."

---

3. "It is called Fox-tail, in America; from the resemblance it bears to it. It is a reed or strong grass that grows in wild, low meadows,—the top containing a down, almost like cotton." [Norton's note]

IROQUOIS

The Haudenosaunee or Iroquois confederacy, as it has come to be called, has particular importance to the history of English-speaking and French-speaking peoples in North America. Historians have determined that the confederation of the five groups—Mohawks, Oneidas, Onandagas, Cayugas, and Senecas—occurred shortly before Columbus landed in areas to the south, probably around 1450. Degonawida or Dekanawida, probably a Huron, and Hiawatha, a Mohawk, are central to the story of the making of the confederation of the tribes.

The text of this story was transcribed about 1850 by Ely S. Parker, a Seneca who was born on the Tonawanda Seneca Reservation in New York State. Parker was educated at an Indian mission school established by the French and was sent to Canada to live, but he returned to New York, learned English, and studied law. Parker was prevented from practicing law because he was Indian, so he worked on the Genesee Valley canal operation. His leadership and negotiating skills brought him significant recognition, and he was appointed to supervise the construction of the Custom House and marine hospital at Galena, Illinois, where he met Ulysses S. Grant. Parker served as secretary under General Grant during the Civil War, and he was later appointed by Grant to be commissioner of Indian affairs. Parker died in 1895. He was serving as a member of the New York City police department at the time.

In speaking of this narrative, Parker said, "I cannot tell how much reliance can be placed upon this tradition, which is more of an allegory than real. The main facts of its origin may be embodied in the allegory, while it has been painted up by the imagination of the Indians." Parker was trying to explain to a non-Indian audience the difference between the way that Iroquoian peoples tell their stories compared to the way Europeans form narratives of their events and exploits.

IROQUOIS, OR THE CONFEDERACY OF THE FIVE NATIONS[1]

By the tradition of the Five Nations it appears that in their early history, they were frequently engaged in petty wars one with another, as well also with tribes living north of the lakes. The Five Nations, on account of their small numbers, suffered more by these wars than their neighbors, until there sprang up among the Onondagas a man more formidable in war than a whole tribe or nation. He consequently became the terror of all the surrounding nations, especially of the Cayugas and Senecas. This man, so formidable and whose cabin was as impregnable as a tower, is said to have had a head of hair, the ends of each terminating in a living snake; the ends of his fingers, and toes, his ears, nose & lips, eye brows & eye lashes all terminated in living snakes. He required in war, no bow and arrow, no battle axe or war club, for he had but to look

upon his enemies, & they fell dead—so great was the power of the snakes that enshrouded him. He was a warrior by birth, and by his great power he had become the military despot of all the surrounding nations. And when he marched against his enemies they fled before his fatal sight.

Among the Onondagas there lived a man renowned for his wisdom, and his great love of peace. For a long time he had watched with great anxiety the increasing power of this military despot who on account of his snakey habiliaments, was known by the applicable name Tadodahoh, or Atotahoh, signifying tangled because the snakes seemed to have tangled themselves into his hair; he saw bands of noble warriors fall before his fatal look. He revolved in his mind by what means he could take from the Tadodahoh his power, and also to divest him of his snakey appendages. He well knew that he could not wrest his power from him, unless he could put into his hands some means by which he could still exercise power and influence. He therefore concluded to call a general council, of the Five Nations, and to invite to this council the Tadodahoh, at which council he proposed to lay before the wise men a plan of Union that would secure not only amity and

---

1. The story was transcribed around 1850 by Ely S. Parker and retold by Arthur C. Parker in the early part of the twentieth century.

peace among themselves, and a perpetual existence as a confederacy but they would render themselves formidable & superior in power to any nation on the Continent. He accordingly called a council to be held upon the east bank of the Onondaga Lake, and to this council the Tadodahoh was invited, who it is said lived near the shores of Lake Ontario a short distance from Irondequoit Bay. He accepted the invitation and proceeded to the place. He occupied the council grounds alone, for no one would approach near to him, although great numbers had come to attend. The projector of the alliance alone proceeded to the grounds and into the presence of the Tadodahoh. He proceeded to divulge his plan when he was informed that his daughter had died whom he had left at home sick. He drew his robe about him, covering himself completely, and mourned for her. (His style of mourning was afterwards adopted by the Confederacy as the custom to mourn for sachems just before another was to be installed in his place.) He mourned night and day, and in his mourning which he did in a kind of song, he repeated the whole plan of Union. And when he had finished, no one of the wise men seemed to understand or comprehend his meaning and objects. Daganowedah, the projector of the plan of alliance, being provoked at their dullness of comprehension, which resulted more from their ignorance of civil matters than dullness of comprehension, arose in the night and travelled towards the east. He had not travelled far when he struck a small lake, and anyone could go around it sooner than to cross it in a canoe. Yet he chose to make a canoe of bark and go across it. It seems that he did not wish to deviate from a straight line. While he was crossing the lake, his canoe ran upon what he supposed to be a sand bar; he put his paddle down into the water to ascertain the cause of the stopping of the boat; in taking out his paddle he found a quantity of small shells, he took pains to put a sufficient quantity into his canoe, and after going ashore, he made a pouch of a young deer skin, and put these shells into it, after having first made a number of belts, and put the rest into strings of equal lengths. To this he gave the name of wampum, and the belts and strings he had made of the shells, he converted into the records of his wise sayings & the entire plan of his project of alliance.

He then proceeded on his journey, and he had not travelled far when he came to an Indian castle. Without calling a council he began to rehearse his plan of alliance, by means of his belts and strings of wampum. But the people of this castle were unable to comprehend the benefits of his project, and talked of him as crazy. When he heard

what they were saying concerning him, he proceeded on his journey, sorrowing that he could not find a people who would listen to the words of wisdom. He at length came to another settlement, which was one of the Mohawk castles. Here again he rehearsed his plan of Union. Still his sayings were incomprehensible to that people. They however listened carefully for the purpose of ascertaining what it was that he could talk so long upon. All that they could understand of it, was the manner in which councils were to be called. A council was accordingly called and he invited to attend. They invited him for the purpose of giving him an opportunity to say in council and before a large number what he had been so long saying in the open fields. But after he had taken his seat in council and nothing was said or done, no exchange of wampum belts (for he had lent them a belt with which to call a council), he arose and again went into the fields and there repeated his speeches. He concluded by saying that they too were ignorant, and knew nothing about transacting civil matters. This was reported to the Grand Chief of the Mohawks and again he called another council and invited Daganowedah. When the council was opened and the wise man had taken his seat, the Mohawk Chief presented to him a belt of wampum, with a request that whatever he should have to say, should be said in open council. If he was a messenger from another tribe, they would hear in open council what were their wishes. He merely replied that he was the messenger of no one; that he had conceived a noble plan of alliance, but had not found a nation wise enough to comprehend its benefits, and thus he had travelled and should continue so to travel until he found support. He then rehearsed in open council his plan of Union, which though they could not comprehend it, was pronounced by all to be a noble project. Daganowedah the Onondaga wise man was immediately adopted into the Mohawk Nation, nor could the Onondagas afterwards claim him, since they first rejected his project of Alliance. He was also made a chief of the Mohawk Nation, and was to exercise equal power with the original Mohawk chief. They were to live in the same lodge, and to be, in every respect, equals.

But he had lived with the original chief but a short time, when he was ordered about as though he had been a mere servant. To this a free spirit will ever revolt, he therefore left him, and again went into the fields. He was asked why he left the house of his friend. He replied that he had not been treated as a friend or visitor, but as a slave. The original chief begged his pardon, and solicited him to return. He did, and was thenceforth treated with great regard. Daganowedah at length suggested the propriety of sending runners to the west, from whence he had come, to ascertain what may be doing from whence he had come. He wanted runners to go and seek the smoke of the council fire. The chief of the Mohawks at once called upon some runners to go towards the west in search of the smoke of a council fire. The guardian bird of the runners was the heron; they accordingly took upon themselves the form of herons. They went towards the west, but flying too high they did not see the smoke of the council fire of Onondaga. They proceeded as far west as Sandusky in Ohio, where they were unable to transform or change themselves again into men. Another set of runners were then sent out, who took upon them the form or shape of crows. They found the smoke of the council fire at Onondaga and so reported.

Daganowedah then proposed to send a few runners to the council to inform them that they had found a wise man of the Onondaga nation, who had conceived a plan of Union, and to request that he might be heard before the Great Tadodahoh. This was done; and as soon as the council at Onondaga heard where their wise man had gone, they sent a deputation to recall him. Daganowedah had in the mean time made arrangement with the Mohawk Chief to act as his spokesman when they should be in council. He was also to take the lead in the file, and to perform all the duties necessary to the completion of the Alliance, but he was to act as Daganowedah should direct. His reason for choosing a spokesman, was that he had not been heard when the council first opened, and that probably they might listen to a wise man of the Mohawks. To this arrangement the Mohawk agreed. He agreed also to divest Tadodahoh of his snakes, and to make him as other men, except that he should clothe him in civil power as the Head of the Confederacy that should be formed. They then proceeded with a delegation of the Mohawks to the council grounds at Onondaga. When they had arrived they addressed Todadahoh the great military despot. The Mohawk divested him of his snakes, and for this reason he was styled Hayowenthah, or one who takes away or divests.

The plan of alliance was at first simple. It provided for the establishment of a confederacy, enjoying a democratic form of government. The civil and legislative power was to be vested in a certain number of wise men who should be styled civil sachems, and the military and executive power in another set of men who should be styled military sachems. The Union was to be established as a family organization, the Mohawks, Onondagas and Senecas to compose the Fathers and the Cayugas and Oneidas the children. This plan was adopted.

SENECA

The theme of the origination of stories is common in many Native American traditions. Stories tell how the people came here, and they provide the sustenance of ceremony and ritual, so that the people can continue to examine their situation in the earth world. That the stories originated in the earth or came from somewhere else and were related to human beings in dreams or by magical agents indicates American Indian peoples' revitalizing belief in the importance of the stories as signals regarding the peoples' original relationship with the land, its water, its animals and insects, and the sky. The concept of giving gifts in order to hear stories or giving gifts to the earth for such stories marks the symbolic importance of stories to the continuance of the people. In many cultures, it is a wanderer or a despised one, often an orphan, who becomes the receiver and keeper of sacred knowledge, the teller of the stories of the people.

THE ORIGIN OF STORIES[1]

There was once a boy who had no home. His parents were dead and his uncles would not care for him. In order to live this boy, whose name was Gaqka, or Crow, made a bower of branches for an abiding place and hunted birds and squirrels for food.

He had almost no clothing but was very ragged and dirty. When the people from the village saw him they called him Filth-Covered-One, and laughed as they passed by, holding their noses. No one thought he would ever amount to anything, which made him feel heavy-hearted. He resolved to go away from his tormentors and become a great hunter.

One night Gaqka found a canoe. He had never seen this canoe before, so he took it. Stepping in he grasped the paddle, when the canoe immediately shot into the air, and

---

1. The text is from Arthur C. Parker, *Seneca Myths and Folktales* (1923).

he paddled above the clouds and under the moon. For a long time he went always southward. Finally the canoe dropped into a river and then Gaqka paddled for shore.

On the other side of the river was a great cliff that had a face that looked like a man. It was at the forks of the river where this cliff stood. The boy resolved to make his home on the top of the cliff and so climbed it and built a bark cabin.

The first night he sat on the edge of the cliff he heard a voice saying, "Give me some tobacco." Looking around the boy, seeing no one, replied, "Why should I give tobacco?"

There was no answer and the boy began to fix his arrows for the next day's hunt. After a while the voice spoke again, "Give me some tobacco."

Gaqka now took out some tobacco and threw it over the cliff. The voice spoke again: "Now I will tell you a story."

Feeling greatly awed the boy listened to a story that seemed to come directly out of the rock upon which he was sitting. Finally the voice paused, for the story had ended. Then it spoke again saying, "It shall be the custom hereafter to present me with a small gift for my stories." So the boy gave the rock a few bone beads. Then the rock said, "Hereafter when I speak, announcing that I shall tell a story you must say, 'Nio,' and as I speak you must say 'Hĕ'',' that I may know that you are listening. You must never fall asleep but continue to listen until I say 'Dā'neho nigagā'is.' (So thus finished is the length of my story). Then you shall give me presents and I shall be satisfied."[2]

The next day the boy hunted and killed a great many birds. These he made into soup and roasts. He skinned the birds and saved the skins, keeping them in a bag.

That evening the boy sat on the rock again and looked westward at the sinking sun. He wondered if his friend would speak again. While waiting he chipped some new arrow-points, and made them very small so that he could use them in a blow gun. Suddenly, as he worked, he heard the voice again. "Give me some tobacco to smoke," it said. Gaqka threw a pinch of tobacco over the cliff and the voice said, "Hau'nio'," and commenced a story. Long into the night one wonderful tale after another flowed from the rock, until it called out, "So thus finished is the length of my story." Gaqka was sorry to have the stories

ended but he gave the rock an awl made from a bird's leg and a pinch of tobacco.

The next day the boy hunted far to the east and there found a village. Nobody knew who he was but he soon found many friends. There were some hunters who offered to teach him how to kill big game, and these went with him to his own camp on the high rock. At night he allowed them to listen to the stories that came forth from the rock, but it would speak only when Gaqka was present. He therefore had many friends with whom to hunt.

Now after a time Gaqka made a new suit of clothing from deer skin and desired to obtain a decorated pouch. He, therefore, went to the village and found one house where there were two daughters living with an old mother. He asked that a pouch be made and the youngest daughter spoke up and said, "It is now finished. I have been waiting for you to come for it." So she gave him a handsome pouch.

Then the old mother spoke, saying, "I now perceive that my future son-in-law has passed through the door and is here." Soon thereafter, the younger woman brought Gaqka a basket of bread and said, "My mother greatly desires that you should marry me." Gaqka looked at the girl and was satisfied, and ate the bread. The older daughter was greatly displeased and frowned in an evil manner.

That night the bride said to her husband, "We must now go away. My older sister will kill you for she is jealous." So Gaqka arose and took his bride to his own lodge. Soon the rock spoke and began to relate wonder stories of things that happened in the old days. The bride was not surprised, but said, "This standing rock, indeed, is my grandfather. I will now present you with a pouch into which you must put a trophy for every tale related."

All winter long the young couple stayed in the lodge on the great rock and heard all the wonder tales of the old days. Gaqka's bag was full of stories and he knew all the lore of former times.

As springtime came the bride said, "We must now go north to your own people and you shall become a great man." But Gaqka was sad and said, "Alas, in my own country I am an outcast and called by an unpleasant name."

The bride only laughed, saying, "Nevertheless we shall go north."

Taking their pelts and birdskins, the young couple descended the cliff and seated themselves in the canoe. "This is my canoe," said the bride. "I sent it through the air to you."

The bride seated herself in the bow of the canoe and

---

2. The speaker here describes conventions common in many oral literatures.

Gaqka in the stern. Grasping a paddle he swept it through the water, but soon the canoe arose and went through the air. Meanwhile the bride was singing all kinds of songs, which Gaqka learned as he paddled.

When they reached the north, the bride said, "Now I shall remove your clothing and take all the scars from your face and body." She then caused him to pass through a hollow log, and when Gaqka emerged from the other end he was dressed in the finest clothing and was a handsome man.

Together the two walked to the village where the people came out to see them. After a while Gaqka said, "I am the boy whom you once were accustomed to call 'Cia'' dō dă'.' I have now returned." That night the people of the village gathered around and listened to the tales he told, and he instructed them to give him small presents and tobacco. He would plunge his hand in his pouch and take out a trophy, saying, "Ho ho! So here is another one!" and then looking at his trophy would relate an ancient tale.

Everybody now thought Gaqka a great man and listened to his stories. He was the first man to find out all about the adventures of the old-time people. That is why there are so many legends now.

CREEK

The Creeks of the southeastern part of North America have, like other Native American groups, their own traditions regarding how the people came into their homelands—how they emerged, migrated to their current location, and formed relationships with other Indians in the area. The story of the Creeks speaks of a confederacy among the Indian nations in the southeastern areas of present-day Georgia. The Creeks' story of origin encompasses details of the arrival of English-speaking people in their homelands, thus dating this story to the early era of contact with the English. The story related here was originally recorded on a buffalo skin that evidently reached the Georgia Trustees in London sometime after it was made. It was first printed in Germany in 1739.

Governor James Oglethorpe of Georgia traveled to England in 1734, taking with him a group of Creeks, including Tomochichi, a leader from the Yamacraw village near Savannah. Tomochichi had successfully begun trading with Oglethorpe and his people, and as a result of their trading relationship, Tomochichi asked to have Christian teaching brought to the Creeks. On the journey, Tomochichi was accompanied by his wife, Senaukey, and his nephew, Toonahowi. While they were in England, they met King George II and several leaders of state, including the Lords Trustees of the Colony of Georgia. It might have been that from the standpoint of the British settlers, they were bringing a curiosity back to England. Taking into account what Tomochichi might have thought of his visit, he probably considered that he was a sovereign leader of his people meeting another sovereign leader over the people alongside whom he had been living. Tomochichi died five years after his return from London. His nephew was killed in fighting against the Spanish in 1753.

ORIGINS OF THE PEOPLE[1]

What Chekilli, the head-chief of the upper and lower Creeks said, in a talk held at Savannah, Anno 1735, and which was handed over by the interpreter, written upon a buffalo-skin was, word for word, as follows:

At a certain time the Earth opened in the West, where its mouth is. The Earth opened and the Kasihtas came out of its mouth, and settled nearby. But the Earth became angry and ate up their children; therefore they moved farther West. A part of them, however, turned back, and came again to the same place where they had been, and settled there. The greater number remained behind, because they thought it best to do so. Their children, nevertheless, were eaten by the Earth, so that, full of dissatisfaction, they journeyed toward the sunrise.

They came to a thick, muddy, slimy river—came there, camped there, rested there, and stayed overnight there. The next day they continued their journey and came, in one day, to a red, bloody river. They lived by this river, and ate of its fishes for two years; but there were low

---

1. The text is from Albert S. Gatschet, *A Migration Legend of the Creek Indians* (1884).

springs there; and it did not please them to remain. They went toward the end of this bloody river, and heard a noise as of thunder. They approached to see whence the noise came. At first they perceived a red smoke, and then a mountain which thundered; and on the mountain was a sound as of singing. They sent to see what this was; and it was a great fire which blazed upward, and made this singing noise. This mountain they named the King of Mountains. It thunders to this day; and men are very much afraid of it.

They here met a people of three different Nations. They had taken and saved some of the fire from the mountain; and, at this place, they also obtained a knowledge of herbs and of other things.

From the East, a white fire came to them; which, however, they would not use. From the South came a fire which was [blue?]; neither did they use it. From the West, came a fire which was black; nor would they use it. At last, came a fire from the North, which was red and yellow. This they mingled with the fire they had taken from the mountain; and this is the fire they use today; and this, too, sometimes sings. On the mountain was a pole which was very restless and made a noise, nor could any one say how it could be quieted. At length they took a motherless child, and struck it against the pole; and thus killed the child. They then took the pole, and carry it with them when they go to war. It was like a wooden tomahawk, such as they now use, and of the same wood.

Here they also found four herbs or roots, which sang and disclosed their virtues: first, Pasaw, the rattlesnake root; second Micoweanochaw, red-root; third Sowatchko, which grows like wild fennel; and fourth, Eschalapootchke, little tobacco. These herbs, especially the first and third, they use as the best medicine to purify themselves at their Busk.[2] At this Busk, which is held yearly, they fast, and make offerings of the first fruits. Since they have learned the virtues of these herbs, their women, at certain times, have a separate fire, and remain apart from the men five, six, and seven days, for the sake of purification. If they neglected this, the power of the herbs would depart; and the women would not be healthy.

About this time a dispute arose, as to which was the oldest, and which should rule; and they agreed, as they were four Nations, they would set up four poles, and make them red with clay which is yellow at first, but becomes red by burning. They would go to war; and whichever Nation should first cover its pole, from top to bottom, with the scalps of their enemies, should be oldest.

They all tried, but the Kasihtas covered their pole first, and so thickly that it was hidden from sight. Therefore, they were looked upon, by the whole Nation, as the oldest. The Chickasaws covered their pole next; then the Alabamas; but the Abihkas did not cover their pole higher than to the knee.[3]

At that time there was a bird of large size, blue in color, with a long tail, and swifter than an eagle, which came every day and killed and ate their people. They made an image in the shape of a woman, and placed it in the way of this bird. The bird carried it off, and kept it a long time, and then brought it back. They left it alone, hoping it would bring something forth. After a long time, a red rat came forth from it, and they believed the bird was the father of the rat. They took council with the rat how to destroy its father. Now the bird had a bow and arrows; and the rat gnawed the bowstring, so that the bird could not defend itself, and the people killed it. They called this bird the King of Birds. They think the eagle is a great King; and they carry its feathers when they go to War or make Peace; the red mean War; the white, Peace. If an enemy approaches with white feathers and a white mouth, and cries like an eagle, they dare not kill him.

After this they left that place, and came to a white footpath. The grass and everything around were white; and they plainly perceived that people had been there. They crossed the path, and slept near there. Afterward they turned back to see what sort of path that was, and who the people were who had been there, in the belief that it might be better for them to follow that path. They went along it to a creek called Coloose-hutche, that is, Coloose-creek, because it was rocky there and smoked.

They crossed it, going toward the sunrise, and came to a people and a town named Coosa.[4] Here they remained four years. The Coosas complained that they were preyed upon by a wild beast, which they called man-eater or lion, which lived in a rock.

The Kasihtas said they would try to kill the beast. They dug a pit and stretched over it a net made of hickory-bark. They then laid a number of branches, crosswise, so that the lion could not follow them, and, going to the place

---

2. The busk, the Green Corn Festival, is a major ritual among southeastern peoples.

3. The Chickasaws appear in this legend, although they were not originally part of the Creek Confederacy.

4. The main town, the "mother town," of the Upper Creeks.

where he lay, they threw a rattle into his den. The lion rushed forth in great anger, and pursued them through the branches. Then they thought it better that one should die rather than all; so they took a motherless child, and threw it before the lion as he came near the pit. The lion rushed at it, and fell in the pit, over which they threw the net, and killed him with blazing pine-wood. His bones, however, they keep to this day; on one side, they are red, on the other blue.

The lion used to come every seventh day to kill the people; therefore, they remained there seven days after they had killed him. In remembrance of him, when they prepare for War, they fast six days and start on the seventh. If they take his bones with them, they have good fortune.

After four years they left the Coosas, and came to a river which they called Nowphawpe, now Callasi-hutche. There they tarried two years; and, as they had no corn, they lived on roots and fishes, and made bows, pointing the arrows with beaver teeth and flint-stones, and for knives they used split canes.

They left this place, and came to a creek, called Wat-toola-hawka-hutche, Whooping-creek, so called from the whooping of cranes, a great many being there; they slept there one night. They next came to a river, in which there was a waterfall; this they named the Owatunka-river. The next day they reached another river, which they called the Aphoosa pheeskaw.

The following day they crossed it, and came to a high mountain, where were people who, they believed, were the same who made the white path. They, therefore, made white arrows and shot at them, to see if they were good people. But the people took their white arrows, painted them red, and shot them back. When they showed these to their chief, he said that it was not a good sign; if the arrows returned had been white, they could have gone there and brought food for their children, but as they were red they must not go. Nevertheless, some of them went to see what sort of people they were; and found their houses deserted. They also saw a trail which led into the river; and, as they could not see the trail on the opposite bank, they believed that the people had gone into the river, and would not again come forth.

At that place is a mountain, called Moterelo, which makes a noise like beating on a drum; and they think this people live there. They hear this noise on all sides when they go to war.

They went along the river, till they came to a waterfall, where they saw great rocks, and on the rocks were bows lying; and they believed the people who made the white path had been there.

They always have, on their journeys, two scouts who go before the main body. These scouts ascended a high mountain and saw a town. They shot white arrows into the town; but the people of the town shot back red arrows. Then the Kasihtas became angry, and determined to attack the town, and each one have a house when it was captured.

They threw stones into the river until they could cross it, and took the town (the people had flattened heads) and killed all but two persons. In pursuing these they found a white dog, which they slew. They followed the two who escaped, until they came again to the white path, and saw the smoke of a town, and thought that this must be the people they had so long been seeking. This is the place where now the tribe of Apalachicolas live, from whom Tomochichi is descended.

The Kasihtas continued bloody-minded; but the Apalachicolas gave them black drink, as a sign of friend-ship,[5] and said to them: "Our hearts are white, and yours must be white, and you must lay down the bloody toma-hawk, and show your bodies as a proof that they shall be white." Nevertheless, they were for the tomahawk; but the Apalachicolas got it by persuasion, and buried it under their beds. The Apalachicolas likewise gave them white feathers, and asked to have a chief in common. Since then they have always lived together.

Some settled on one side of the river, some on the other. Those on one side are called Kasihtas, those on the other, Cowetas; yet they are one people, and the principal towns of the Upper and Lower Creeks. Nevertheless, as the Kasihtas first saw the red smoke and the red fire, and make bloody towns, they cannot yet leave their red hearts, which, though white on one side, are red on the other. They now know that the white path was the best for them: for, although Tomochichi was a stranger, they see he has done them good; because he went to see the great King with Esquire Oglethorpe, and hear his talk, and had related it to them, and they had listened to it, and believed it.

---

5. "Black drink," a strong tea, was made to induce vomiting for purification rituals.

SALISH

The Salishan linguistic groups of the northern Rockies include the Flatheads, the Kalispels, and the Coeur D'Alênes. In language and culture, these groups of present-day Idaho, Montana, and Washington resemble the Salishan groups of the plateau area, including the Spokanes, the Sanpoils, the Okanogans, and others. Early in the era of contact, the Flatheads, the Kalispels, and the Coeur D'Alênes were converted to Catholicism by Jesuit missionaries, and they were particularly influenced by a young Belgian priest of the Jesuit orders, Jean De Smet.

The following Salishan story, a story told among the Flatheads of their beginning, was sent to George Gibbs, an ethnographer, by Father Gregory Mengarini. According to Mengarini, these people believed at the time that the earth was flat and surrounded by water like an island. They considered the sky a huge hollow mountain covering the earth. Mengarini reported that "When the Salish Indians saw the whites the first time, they thought them the sons of Amotken and hence immortal, until one of them was killed by Blackfeet."

THE BEGINNING[1]

Before the world was created, a son was born to a very powerful woman, Skomeltem. The son's name is Amotken, which means "he who sits on top of the mountain," for his home is on the summit of the covering of the earth. Amotken created heaven and earth and mankind. He created other worlds also, worlds under and above and around us. His mother lives alone on one of those worlds beyond the waters.

The first human beings that Amotken created became very wicked and turned a deaf ear to his teachings and his warnings. Angry with them, he drowned all of them in a great flood. Then he created a second tribe, twice as tall as the first. But they became even more wicked than the first people, and so Amotken destroyed them by fire from heaven. He created a third tribe; when they became as wicked as the first, he destroyed them by a pestilence. The fourth tribe would have been destroyed also had not Amotken's mother begged him to let them live. She so softened the anger of Amotken that he promised never to destroy his creations again.

Until the time of the fourth tribe, the world was in darkness, for there was no sun. Believing that the sole cause of their wickedness was the darkness, the people held a council to discuss the matter. These were the animal people—animals that could reason and talk. All of them refused to be the sun except Sinchlep, or Coyote. He was the smartest and most powerful of the animal people. But when Coyote was the sun and passed over the land,

he saw what everyone was doing. And he called out, so that all might hear, even the secret doings of people. The evildoers angrily took Coyote by the tail, which at that time was very long, and brought him back to the ground. They told him that he could no longer be the sun.

Crow then offered to be the sun. But as he was really black all over, he gave very little light. People laughed at him. Unable to endure their ridicule, Crow gave up the task in shame.

Amotken, though invisible, had several sons, one of whom was Spokani. Seeing the people's need for light, he sent Spokani down to be the sun. Spokani, wishing to marry a woman from the earth, landed in a camp of Flatheads. People thought him very handsome but so different from themselves that they refused to admit him to their lodges.

Disappointed, Spokani left the place. Nearby, he saw a family of frogs to whom he complained about the treatment their neighbors had given him. One of the frogs, very large and fat, said that she was willing to marry him; she would be happy to become the wife of Amotken's son. With a jump she attached herself to one cheek of Spokani.

The neighboring people, seeing the disfigured cheek, were so angry that they tried to kill the frog with sticks, but they could not. She remained on Spokani's cheek. She begged him to leave the earth and become the sun at once.

And so Spokani became the sun. To revenge himself for the contempt of the people, he does not allow them to see him closely during the day but covers himself with a shining robe. As night approaches, he removes his robe, crosses the waters under the earth, and then only shows himself as he is. Then he is the moon. The spots on the moon are the frog on his cheek.

---

1. The text is from *Indian Legends from the Northern Rockies,* comp. Ella E. Clark (1966).

16

GROS VENTRES

The creation story of the Gros Ventres, an Arapaho group of the Plains area, has striking resemblances to creation stories shared among Algonquian-speaking peoples, especially stories told by the Iroquois and the Hurons of eastern North America. The divers of the stories vary among the groups, but the roots of the stories reveal similar watershed beginnings that have traditionally been honored by these peoples. Sacred among these people are flat pipes, corn, and turtles, as evidenced by the following story of their beginning.

THE CREATION OF THE WORLD[1]

The people before the present people were wild and did not know how to do anything. Because the Creator did not like the way they lived, he thought, "I will make a new world." He had the chief pipe. He went outdoors, hung the pipe on three sticks, and picked up four buffalo chips. He put one under each of the three sticks supporting the pipe, and took the fourth chip for his own seat.

The Creator said to himself, "I will sing three times and shout three times. Then I will kick the earth. There will be a heavy rain, and soon water will cover the earth."

So he sang three times, he shouted three times, and he kicked the earth. The earth cracked, and water came out. Then it rained many days and many nights, until water was deep over the earth. Because of the buffalo chips, he and the pipe floated. Then the rain stopped. For days he drifted, floating where the wind and water took him. All the animals and birds had drowned except Crow.

Above the Creator, Crow flew around, crying. When it became tired, it cried, "My father, I am tired. I want to rest."

Three times Crow said these words. After the third time, the Creator replied, "Alight on the pipe and rest."

At last the Creator became tired from sitting in one position, and he cried. For a long time he did not know what to do. Then he remembered to unwrap the pipe. It contained all the animals. He took out all those that have a long breath and thus are able to dive through water. Large Loon, which he selected first, was not alive, but its body was wrapped up in the pipe. The Creator sang to it and then commanded it to dive and try to bring up some mud. Not half way down, Large Loon lost its breath and turned

back. Almost drowned, it reached the place where the Creator sat.

Then the Creator took Small Loon's body from the pipe, unwrapped it, sang, and commanded it to dive for mud. Small Loon nearly reached the bottom before it lost its breath and turned back. It was almost dead when it came back to the surface. Then the Creator took Turtle from the pipe, sang until it became alive, and sent it down after some mud.

Meanwhile, Crow flew about, crying for rest. The Creator paid no attention. After a long time Turtle came up from the water, nearly dead.

"Did you reach the mud?" asked the Creator.

"Yes," answered Turtle. "I had much of it in my feet and along my sides, but it was washed away before I reached you."

"Come to me." The Creator looked in the cracks along its sides and in its feet. There he found a little earth, which he scraped into his hand. Then he began to sing. Three times he sang, and three times he shouted.

"I will throw this little dust in my hand into the water," he said. "Little by little, let there be enough to make a strip of land large enough for me."

He began to drop it, little by little, opening and closing his hand carefully. When he had finished, there was a small strip of land, big enough for him to sit on. Then the Creator said to Crow, "Come down and rest. I have made a piece of land for myself and for you."

Crow came down and rested, and then flew up again. The Creator took from his pipe two long wing feathers, held one in each hand, and began to sing. Three times he sang, and three times he shouted, "Youh, hou, hou!" Then he spread out his arms, closed his eyes, and said to himself, "Let there be land as far as my eyes can see around me."

When he opened his eyes, the water was gone and there was land as far as he could see. He walked over the earth with his pipe and with Crow. When he became

---

1. The text follows the story as reported by Alfred Kroeber in 1907.

thirsty, he did not know what to do to get water. Then he thought, "I will cry." So he closed his eyes and cried until his tears, dropping on the ground, formed a large spring in front of him. Soon a stream ran from out the spring. When the Creator stopped crying, a large river was flowing. In this way he made all the streams.

When he became tired of being alone with Crow and his pipe, he decided to make persons and animals. First he took earth and made it into the shape of a man. Then he took another piece of earth and made it into the shape of a woman. He molded more figures out of earth until he had created many men and women. People are dark because the earth is dark.

When the Creator thought he had enough people, he made animals of all kinds, in pairs. Then he gave names to the tribes of people and names to all kinds of animals. He sang three times, shouted three times, and kicked the ground. When he had finished, many pairs of living creatures stood before him, persons and animals.

He called the world "Turtle" because Turtle had helped him create it. Then he made bows and arrows, and he taught men how to use them. The pipe, he gave to a tribe called *Haa-ninin.* White people call them Gros Ventres.

He said to the people, "If you are good, there will be no more water and no more fire. Long before the flood came, the world had been burned. This now is the third life."

Then he showed people the rainbow and said, "This rainbow is the sign that the earth will not be covered with water again. Whenever you have had rain, you will see the rainbow. It will mean that the rain has gone. There will be another world after this one."

He told the people to go off in pairs and to find homes for themselves. That is why human beings are scattered.

ACOMA

Along with Oraibi, a Hopi town, the ancient pueblo, Acoma, or Sky-line Village, is considered the oldest continuously inhabited area in the present-day United States. Already well established when Spanish explorers saw it in 1540, Acoma has remained central among the series of pueblos in the area of New Mexico between Albuquerque and Taos. The Acomans are the indigenous peoples the Spanish wrote about continually during the sixteenth and seventeenth centuries.

Acoma pueblo has a long-standing history of retaining its own sovereignty, and although Acomans follow some of the similar patterns of living of other Keresan-speaking groups in the area, their religious and cultural practices differ to some extent. Acoma lacks any significant influence of Spanish dwellers in the area, and its extended kinship system is matrilineal, so that rituals and leadership descend according to the mother's family line. As this story indicates, Ia'tik, the All-Mother, herself makes the gods that she will believe in.

EMERGENCE INTO THE UPPER WORLD[1]

In the beginning two female human beings were born. There was land already, but no one knows how long it had existed. The two girls were born underground at a place called Cipapu. There was no light, but as they grew up they became aware of each other through touch. Being in the dark, they grew slowly.

When they had reached adulthood, a spirit, Tsitctinako, spoke to them and gave them nourishment. Slowly they began to think for themselves. One day they asked the spirit to appear to them and say whether it was male or female. But Tsitctinako replied only that it was not allowed to meet them.

The women asked the spirit why they had to live in the dark without knowing each other by name. It told them that they were under the earth (*nuk'timi*), and that they must be patient until everything was ready for them to go up into the light. During the long time that they waited, Tsitctinako taught them their language.

One day the sisters found two baskets full of presents: seeds of all kinds, and little images of many animals. Tsitctinako told them that the baskets had been sent by their father, whose name was Utc'tsiti, and that he wanted them to take his gifts up into the light.

---

1. The text is a modern version by Richard Erdoes and Alfonso Ortiz, based on a legend reported by C. Daryll Forde in 1930 and on various oral accounts.

Tsitctinako said, "You have the seeds of four types of trees. Plant them; you will use the trees to climb up." Because the sisters could not see, they felt each object in their baskets and asked, "Is this it?" and Tsitctinako answered yes or no. In that way they identified the four seeds and then buried them in their underground world. All sprouted, but the trees grew very slowly in the dark. The women themselves slept for a long time, and whenever they woke, they felt the trees to find out how tall they were. A certain pine grew faster than the others, and after a very long while it pushed a hole through the earth and let in a little light.

However, the hole was not large enough for the women to pass through. With Tsitctinako's help they found the image of an animal called *dyu·p* (badger) in their baskets. Commanding the badger to come alive, the sisters asked him to climb the tree and dig around the edges of the hole. They warned him not to go out in the light, so he climbed up, enlarged the hole, and returned directly. Thanking him, they said, "As a reward, you will come up with us into the light and live in happiness."

Next Tsitctinako helped them sort through the baskets until they found *tawai'nu* (the locust). They gave him life, asked him to smooth the hole by plastering it, and warned him not to go into the light. But the locust, having smoothed the hole, was curious and slipped out to look around before he returned. Three times the women asked him if he had gone out, and three times the locust said no. When they asked a fourth time, he admitted that he had.

"What is it like?" they asked him. "It's just *tsi'iti,* laid out flat," he replied. "From now on," they said, "you will be known as Tsi·k'a. You may come up with us, but for your disobedience you will be allowed to see the light for only a short time. Your home will be in the ground. You will soon die, but you will be reborn each season."

A shaft of light now reached into the place where the two sisters lived. "It is time for you to go out," Tsitctinako said. "When you come to the top, wait for the sun to rise. That direction is called *ha'nami,* east. Pray to the sun with pollen and sacred cornmeal, which you will find in your baskets. Thank it for bringing you to the light. Ask for long life and happiness, and for success in the purpose for which you were created."

Tsitctinako taught them the prayers to say and the creation song to sing. Then the humans, followed by the badger and the locust, climbed the pine tree. Stepping out into the light, the sisters put down their baskets and for the first time saw what they contained. Gradually the sky grew lighter, and finally the sun came up. As they faced it

their eyes hurt, for they were not accustomed to strong light.

Before they began to pray, Tsitctinako told them that their right side, the side their best arm was on, would be known as south, and the left north. At their backs was west, the direction in which the sun would go down. Underground they had already learned the direction *nuk'um',* down. (Later they asked where their father was, and Tsitctinako said, "*Tyunami*—four skies above.")

As they waited to pray to the sun, the girl on the right moved her best hand and was named Ia'tik, which means "Bringing to life." "Now name your sister," Tsitctinako told her. Ia'tik was perplexed at first, but then she noticed that her sister's basket was fuller than her own. So she called her sister Nao'tsiti—"More of everything in the basket."

They prayed and sang the creation song, and for the first time they asked Tsitctinako why they had been created. The spirit replied, "It was not I but your father, Utc'tsiti, who made you. He made the world, the sun, the sky, and many other things, but he is not yet satisfied. For this reason he has made you in his image. You will rule over the world and create the things he has given you in the baskets."

"And who are you?" they asked Tsitctinako. "And why don't you become visible to us so that we can see you and live together?"

"I am female like you," the spirit replied. "But I don't know how to live like a human being. Your father has sent me to teach you, and I will always look after you."

When it became dark at the end of the first day, the sisters were frightened. They thought that Tsitctinako had betrayed them, but she explained, "This is the way it will always be. The sun will go down and a new sun will come up in the east tomorrow. Rest and sleep while it is dark." So the sisters slept, and the next day the sun rose. Happy to feel its warmth, they prayed to it as they had been taught.

Tsitctinako asked Nao'tsiti which clan she wished to belong to. Nao'tsiti said, "I see the sun; my clan will be the Sun clan." The spirit asked Ia'tik what clan she wanted. It'tik had noticed that her basket contained the seed from which the sacred meal was made, and she said, "My clan will be Ya'ka-Hano, the Red Corn clan."

The sun was too bright for Ia'tik; it hurt her eyes. She tilted her head sideways so that her hair hung as a sunscreen, producing a reddish shade on her face. "The sun has not appeared for you," Tsitctinako observed. "See how it shines on Nao'tsiti, and how white she looks."

Hastily Ia'tik also bared her face to the sun. But it did not make her as white as Nao'tsiti, and Ia'tik's mind was slowed down, while Nao'tsiti's was made quick. Even so, both always remembered to do everything Tsitctinako taught them.

"From now on," Tsitctinako told the sisters, "you will rule in every direction, north, west, south, and east. Bring everything in your baskets to life for Utc'tsiti has created you to help him complete the world. Now is the time to plant the seeds."

So far the sisters had not eaten food, and they did not understand what the seeds in their baskets were for. "First plant the corn, and when it grows, it will produce a part that you can eat," Tsitctinako said. Highly interested, the two women watched the growing corn every day. The spirit showed them where the pollen formed so that they could continue to offer pollen and cornmeal every morning to the sun. And they always did, though sometimes Nao'tsiti was a little lazy.

After a while the corn turned hard and ripe. Ia'tik carefully picked two ears without hurting the plant; Nao'tsiti yanked two off, and Ia'tik told her to handle it more gently. Tsitctinako had said that the corn must be cooked, but the sisters did not understand what "cooked" meant until a red light dropped from the sky that evening. Explaining that it was fire, the spirit taught them to scoop some of the flames up on a flat rock and feed them with branches from the pine tree.

Following Tsitctinako's directions, they roasted the corn and seasoned it with salt from their baskets. Nao'tsiti grabbed some and ate it, exclaiming how good it was. Then she gave a piece to Ia'tik, and so it was that the two women had their first meal. "You have been fasting for a long time, and your father has nourished you," the spirit told them. "Now you will eat in order to live."

The sisters learned to give life to their salt by praying to the earth, whereupon salt appeared in each of the four directions. Then Tsitctinako taught them their first song for creating an animal—a mouse. When they had sung it, they said, "Come to life, mouse," and their mouse image breathed. "Go and increase," they told it, and it ran away and soon bred many offspring. Tsitctinako showed them how to take one back, kill it, and roast it with the corn and salt. They prayed to their father and offered him little pieces of the meal before they ate. There was not much food on the mouse, but they thought it was good.

Looking into their baskets for larger animals to eat, the women found images of a rat, a mole, and a prairie dog. "Before you give life to them," Tsitctinako said, "you must plant grass for their food." The sisters took grass seed and scattered it north, west, south, and east—and grass immediately covered the ground. Then they gave life to the animals, telling each its name as it began to breathe. Before commanding them to run away and increase, they told the three creatures to live in the ground, because there was no shade on earth.

"Now we are going to make the mountains," Tsitctinako said, and showed them how to throw a certain stone from the basket toward the north while speaking certain words. There a large mountain arose. They did the same in the other directions, and mountains appeared all around them. "Now that you have the mountains," the spirit said, "you must clothe them with growing things." From the trees they had planted underground the sisters took seeds which they scattered in all the directions. "These will be tall trees," Tsitctinako said, "and large enough to form the logs you will use to build houses."

There were many seeds left in their baskets. The women planted the food-yielding trees—piñon, cedar, oak, and walnut—with the prayer, "Grow on this mountain and yield fruit for food. Your places are in the mountains. You will grow and be useful." They planted other seeds, such as pumpkin, squash, and beans, that Tsitctinako said would be important to them. As these crops ripened, she showed them which parts to eat.

The sisters too were growing, and they needed more food. They began to bring the larger animals to life: first rabbits, jackrabbits, antelope, and water deer; then deer, elk, mountain sheep, and buffalo. They told the buffalo to live in the plains, the elk and deer in the mountains, and the sheep on the very high mountain slopes. They ate their meat and enjoyed the new tastes, and always they prayed to their father before they began a meal.

The sisters made mountain lions, wolves, wildcats, and bears—strong beasts that hunted the same game the humans used. They made birds—eagles and hawks, which hunted small game, and little birds whose bright colors beautified the country. They made the wild turkey, and told it not to fly. They told the smaller birds to eat various seeds on the mountains and plains.

Tsitctinako pointed out that there were still fish, snakes, and turtles to be created, and the sisters gave life to all these and tried them for food. They found that some were good to eat and others were not, but whenever they ate they prayed first to their father. So it happened that many animals came alive in the world.

Ia'tik was always ready to use her seeds and images, but Nao'tsiti was selfish about the things in her basket.

Now Nao'tsiti had many left, and she said she wanted a chance to give life to more of her images. "I am the elder," Ia'tik replied. "You are younger than I." "Is that true?" Nao'tsiti said. "I thought we were created at the same time. Let's put it to the test: tomorrow let's see for which of us the sun rises first."

Ia'tik agreed to the test, but she was afraid that her sister would get the better of her in some way. She went to a white bird she knew called *co'eka* (the magpie) and asked it to fly quickly into the east and use its wings to shade the sun from Nao'tsiti. The magpie flew fast and far, for Ia'tik had told it not to stop. But it began to feel hungry, and when it passed over a lion's kill, it could not resist landing. The carcass, a deer, had a hole in its side. The bird put its head into the gash to eat the intestines, and then flew on without noticing that its white feathers were soiled and bloody.

The magpie did reach the east before the sun had risen. It spread its wings on the sun's left side, creating shade over Nao'tsiti. In this way it happened that the sun struck Ia'tik first, and Nao'tsiti was very angry. Ia'tik whispered to the magpie that it must never tell. Then she saw its filthy plumage and said, "Because you stopped and ate, from this day on you will eat carrion, and your feathers will be spotted instead of white."

Both sisters were now having selfish thoughts. Nao'tsiti was full of plans to outwit Ia'tik, but Ia'tik watched her and anticipated everything. Nao'tsiti saw that Ia'tik was not happy; Ia'tik noticed that Nao'tsiti wandered off alone.

Tsitctinako had told them that their father forbade them to think about having children. She promised that other humans would be born to them at the appropriate time. But now Nao'tsiti met a snake who said, "Why are you sad? If you bore a child in your likeness, you wouldn't have to be lonely just because you and your sister don't get along."

"What can I do?" Nao'tsiti asked.

"Go to the rainbow; he will show you."

Soon afterward Nao'tsiti was sitting alone on a rock when it rained. It was so hot that the rain cracked on the ground, and she lay on her back to receive the drops. As the water dripped into her, the rainbow did his work and she conceived without knowing it. Ia'tik noticed that her sister was growing very fat, and after a time Nao'tsiti bore two children, both boys.

Very angry, Tsitctinako came to them. "Why have you disobeyed your father?" she said. "For your sin, he is taking me away. You are alone now."

Tsitctinako left them, but instead of feeling sorry, the two sisters found that they were happier. It turned out that Nao'tsiti disliked one of her children, so Ia'tik took him and brought him up. The two women still did not get along, but they were so busy with the children that it hardly mattered.

When the children were almost grown, Nao'tsiti said to her sister, "We aren't really happy together. Let's divide what remains in our baskets and separate. I still have many things, though they require a lot of work." Nao'tsiti pulled out sheep and cows, seeds for wheat and vegetables, and many metals. But Ia'tik refused them, saying they would be too difficult to take care of. Nao'tsiti looked again in her basket and found something written. She offered it, but Ia'tik did not want the gift of writing either. "You should have taken some of the things I offered," Nao'tsiti said. "In a long time we will meet again, and then you will desire my possessions. We'll still be sisters, but I'll have the better of you again."

Taking the boy she had brought up, Nao'tsiti disappeared into the east. Ia'tik said to the other boy, "We will continue to live here with everything our father has given us." The years passed, and Tia'muni, as she called him, grew up to become her husband. Ia'tik bore him a girl who was entered into the clan of her sister, the Sun clan. After the fourth day of the baby's birth, Ia'tik put some pollen and sacred cornmeal into its hands and took it to pray to the sun. And with the many children that Ia'tik bore afterwards, she followed this same ritual that she herself had been taught when she came up into the light.

Ia'tik's children lived together and began to increase. Their mother ruled over them, for she had her own power now that Tsitctinako was gone. But Ia'tik wished to create some other rulers, so she made the spirits of the seasons by taking earth from her baskets and giving it life. First she made the spirit of winter, which she told, "You will live in the north mountain and give life to everything in the wintertime." Next she created the spirit of spring and sent him to the west mountain. The spirit of summer she sent to the south mountain and the spirit of autumn to the east mountain. These four spirits were ugly, not at all like the children she had borne. She taught each one what to do: winter was to bring snow, spring would warm up the world, summer would heat the world, and autumn would dislike the smell of plants and fruits and work to destroy them. And Ia'tik taught her children how to pray to these spirits for moisture, warmth, ripening, and frost.

Taking dirt from her basket, Ia'tik next gave life to the gods. The first one she created she named Tsitsenuts.

"You are very handsome," she said, "but I will give you a mask that makes you different from us humans." She fashioned it from buffalo skin, colored it with different kinds of earth, and decorated it with feathers. Around Tsitsenuts' neck she hung a wildcat skin, and she painted his body. She gave him a skirt, a belt, and moccasins, put cords on each wrist, and painted buffalo skins on his arms. On his calves she bound spruce branches.

"You see that I have created many other gods," she told him. "I appoint you their ruler; you will initiate the others."

She gave him weeds of the soapwood plant for the initiation and then spoke to them all: "From now on, wear the costumes I have made for you. You are rain gods, created to call the rain when you dance before my people. They will worship you for all time." And after she had instructed each of the gods and given each his costume and a prayer, she told them that they would have a sacred chamber in each of the four mountains. And so everything was as it should be.

2

EUROPEANS' NEW WORLD
The First Century

At the time when Portuguese, Dutch, Italian, Spanish, and French sailors laid their courses for distant lands, whether in the Mediterranean or across the Atlantic, they were experiencing changes that eventually would lead Europe from medieval to modern impulses. Theirs was an era marked by interethnic and territorial wars among city-states; an era rife with unspeakable famine, disease, and dislocation; an era of hierarchical social structures that meant one's birthplace status would determine one's level of freedom and possibility. The changes that Europeans set afoot in the Atlantic world from the twelfth through the fourteenth century had a significant effect upon their own lives and others' for centuries to come. By the end of the fifteenth century, surprising findings in the areas of mechanical arts and sciences, geography, the physical sciences, and the fine arts brought outcomes that would forever change the way Europeans looked at the world they lived in.

The beginning of the changes emerged as a result of a series of wars, wars that were anciently ongoing in terms of ethnic and cultural dimensions but that are now characterized as taking place between Muslims and Christians over who would dominate the territorial spaces today called Western Europe, the Mediterranean, and northern Africa. For the peoples who inhabited the territories now called Portugal and Spain—Castilians, Leonese, Basques, Galicians, Navarrese, Aragonese, Catalans, and Portuguese—the *Reconquista* and *Repoblación* (the era of reconquering and repopulation) of what they considered to be Hispania (or Iberia) was conceived as an epic war of Christianity over Islam. Assisted by Frankish and, later, Norman peoples, the people inhabiting the northern areas of present-day Spain began to consolidate forces to drive the Muslims (who had controlled the European regions for centuries) away from the Iberian peninsula, from areas of Italy and France, and from much of the territory that would become known generally as Europe. The wars over territory became known to Europeans as the Crusades, and the peoples the European Christians (who were themselves ethnically and regionally divided) fought were called by their ethnic names, Saracens or Moors, Turks or Tartars. To be sure, their Muslim rivals in the Ottoman empire considered the so-called Christian Crusaders as infidels and barbarians who were attacking the world of Islam. The conflict in the area was a conflict over both land and cultural identity: Would Christians or Muslims predominantly live in and control the land? While these two major identities were themselves unstable (because of the different ethnic populations in the areas), so that neither Christians nor Muslims were homogeneous peoples, the wars the Christians called the *Reconquista* assisted in the creation of more common ways of looking at the world, whether one was Christian or Muslim. Identity was informed by what one was not and by those with whom one associated in cultural matters. Ethnicity combined with cultural practices to determine which lands one would fight for and inhabit.

The fifteenth-century voyages to the Americas made by European sailors, sailing in behalf of Spain and Portugal, were outcomes of the momentum provided by the retaking of the Iberian peninsula and the repopulation of southern European territories by Christians during the previous centuries. If sailors were willing to venture over the Atlantic, they were willing to do so, in part, because of their successful navigation and cultural infiltration in Hispania; in Sicily, Naples, and Greece; and in Africa and the Atlantic islands just to the west of Africa's coast. These peoples had recent successful experience in the conquest and colonization of alien lands; continued conquest fostered a sense of privilege in their cultural values and institutions. They would set sail for the "Indies" (as the Americas came to be called) to spread their culture around the globe. As Francisco López de Gómora wrote in the middle of the sixteenth century, "The Conquest of the Indies began when that of the Moors was over, for the Spanish have always fought against infidels." In the context of the era of the Iberian *Reconquista* and *Repoblación,* then, the move to find other worlds to conquer for Christendom was merely an extension of ongoing activities that had gained momentum from successes in Europe.

How the "other world" that we today call the Americas struck Europeans' consciousness as news filtered back into different court powers in different city-states and regions becomes the key concern for those who are interested in understanding the writings of the era. Some writers made of the Europeans' "new world" an old one, aligning it with a biblical past and making of the indigenous peoples, called "Indians" because Columbus said he had found the "Indies," those who had belonged to the ten lost tribes of Israel. Others, among them Columbus himself by the time of his third voyage, looked less to ancient biblical history than to Christian prophecy and found in the Americas the earthly paradise just over the next hill. Still others, and they were many, saw the Americas solely in terms of what its commodities—flora, fauna, and peoples—could offer in terms of acquiring personal wealth and status.

Almost all who wrote about their new world experiences spoke in terms of existing discourse about peoples and places in an attempt to configure the strange in a language of the familiar. They revered ancient knowledge and attached themselves to the idea that they were fulfilling anciently inspired patterns by writing present-day narratives and formal letters recording their own experiences in history, epic poetry, and songs. Whether they adopted a language that celebrated *as* new the newness and strangeness of the newfound lands and peoples or whether their language detailed the new in the cloak of already familiar categories—and most writers did both these things—the European writers on the Americas were compelled by the ancient and ritualized necessity of creating records of their experiences.

They often adopted a colonizing rhetoric of superiority, a rhetoric that was even then common in conquest writings. In so doing, they were repeating a colonizing gesture common to most groups who seek to differentiate themselves from those unlike themselves. In establishing for readers the differences between their group and those about whom they wrote, writers highlighted several key factors. They wrote of how the strangers looked, typically discussing physique, facial expression, hairstyle and ornamentation, clothing, and sexual organs (if these were visually available and, if not, what covered them). They offered commentary about evidence of belief systems, typically concluding that none existed if tokens of the speaker's beliefs were not evident. If the strangers seemed not to follow the speaker's faith, then frequently the commentary would discuss relative cleanliness, including remarks ranging on topics from bathing techniques to food preparation. The writers remarked about matters of polity, covering such matters as how the people lived with one another in the social formation, how they got along together, how rulership was determined, how partnerships and marital unions were publicized, and who gathered the foodstuffs and took care of the children.

Thus, the Europeans employed a language that defined events and peoples in terms of their relative similarity to their own ways of living. When clear differences occurred, they shifted to a language of colonialism marked by terms, such as *savagism* and *civility, barbarity* and *Christianity.* The tropes of difference such language established would characterize European writings on the Americas for centuries. The peoples the Europeans came across were savages, infidels, heathens, or barbarians, simply because they did not practice Christianity and did not come from Europe. Readers today will note the cultural insensitivity, indeed the arrogance, of such a colonizing rhetoric of difference, but it was a common means of defining culture in that day: Infidels needed to be ousted, and barbarians needed to be subjected to civilized sway. Evidence of the common use of such colonial discursive framing occurs across many cultures, and if the colonists seem harsh in their evaluations of Native Americans as "savages" or "barbarians," it is useful to remember that such characterizations were typical in their day and had been used, for instance, by Muslims as well, in their descriptions of Christians. The Christian Europeans were regularly called barbaric infidels by the Muslims of the Ottoman Empire. An impression of the so-called Christian crusaders is available in the writings of a traveler, Ibn Jubayr, a Muslim native of Valencia in Spain, who visited Syria in 1184 and traveled through several cities held by the Christians. Of Acre, the central port of the Christians, Ibn Jubayr wrote: "The city of Acre, may God destroy it and return it to Islam. This is the chief city of the Franks in Syria . . . the meeting place of Muslim and Christian merchants from all parts. Its streets and roads are thronged with such crowds of people, that one can hardly walk. But it is a land of unbelief and impiety, swarming with pigs and crosses, full of filth and ordure, all of it filled with uncleanliness." Ibn Jubayr was engaging a discourse of alterity, using the Christians' difference from himself and his people's lifeways to define what he—and they—valued. When they turned their own pens to describe those others whom they considered to be infidels, whether they were Muslims or Native Americans, the European Christian commentators were employing a common discourse of colonialism that, in their day, was central to identifying friend and foe.

Yet cultural complexities emerged, almost from the moment of contact, making the use of colonialist discourse difficult in some cases, impossible in others. For some writers, the key difference about their situation in the Americas was that in recognizing the differences between Native peoples and themselves, they recognized some important similarities in attitudes and a potential for better living than that they had known before. That is to say that some Christians, such as Cabeza de Vaca and Bartholomé de Las Casas, remarked about the hospitality and peacefulness of the peoples among whom they lived and traveled. Hospitality and peacefulness also entered into colonialist discourse of alterity, but when these words were used to describe, by contrast, the atrocities furthered by so-called Christian conquerors, a new dimension in the cultural discussion arose. A signal complexity of the colonizing process in the Americas was that although the peoples were considered alien, they were sometimes understood to have a better, more "civilized" lifestyle than that practiced by the Europeans who were engaged in taking their lands, enslaving them, maiming them, and killing them, simply for the sake of gaining greater wealth. Alongside procolonializing rhetoric, anticolonialist discourse emerged from the pens of several of the writers. The competing discourses of colonialism—savagism versus civility and barbarism versus humanity—inverted the traditional European cultural norms, so that the supposedly civilized Christian conquerer was a more vividly hateful and cruel barbarian than the people whose very humanity was being called into question. Anticolonial writings centered the question of whether conquering and enslaving the peoples indigenous to the Americas was right, was warranted, and was possible. Both procolonialist and anticolonialist writings emerged, in uneasy tension, almost from the moment Columbus landed on an island in the present-day Bahamas on October 12, 1492.

So that the European world would know the reasons behind such voyages, sailors and the courts they represented adopted language appropriate to their undertakings. Distinctive legalistic language, language that revealed the maneuvers that "justice" could make in behalf of empire, emerged during the era of colonialism. The monarchies competing to colonize the Americas sought to maximize their chances to consolidate and expand their interests and holdings. The determinates for the legitimacy of the colonial takeover occurred under several different conditions, understood as what we might today call legal concepts, that, in effect, predated European contact with indigenous peoples of the Americas.

Four key concepts regarding land functioned in the Europeans' feudal and medieval world. The first was the taking of land by right of original occupation, or "discovery." When different early European American writers provide written records of someone from their party "taking" the land by planting a flag upon it, or a cross, or a shield, for instance, the goal is to assure the European community reading the text that the lands were being claimed for their enterprise by right of "discovery." Sometimes these "discoveries" were made when no one was present, thus indicating that no ownership could be disputed. If the claims were made in the presence of others and were not disputed despite the presence of those others, then the writers would be providing evidence that the territory was taken by agreement or cession. They did not necessarily address the issue of whether agreement could occur if the Native group did not understand the words being spoken, of course; they just assumed that an agreement or understanding had been reached because no dispute arose. Later, they sometimes called such "meetings" of dispute "treaties," a method that would haunt legal theorists for years to come. Still a third way of claiming territorial acquisition was—and was frequently—by right of conquest. If one could claim one was making a "just war and holy war" against the infidels (as in the so-called Christian crusades), one could claim territory if the opponents were defeated and their lands and persons acquired. Finally, claims to territory made within groups dominated by the Holy Roman Empire were also accorded by right of papal donation, that is, a granting of land by the pope. Such donation occurred, for instance, when the Treaty of Tordesillas (1494), signed by Spain, Portugal, and Pope Alexander VI, gave to Portugal a dominance of Africa and Brazil in exchange for Spain's freedom of operation in the rest of the Americas. These four concepts—rights to lands by way of "discovery," by agreement or cession, by conquest, or by papal donation—entered the writings on colonialism, whether we speak of Spanish, Portuguese, French, Dutch, Swedish, or English texts, demarcating for writers from each group an essential anxiety about their group's right of exclusivity to operate among Native Americans and their lands by establishing particular spheres of influence solely within their own cultural framing. Spheres of influence were cultural spheres, covered by legal concepts understood in Europe and legitimated in European court practices.

Europeans have been described as if they were homogeneous groups, but, of course, they were not. The term has been used generally to indicate certain peoples from certain areas of the world. Like the American Indians they met in the Americas, the Europeans were from different tribal groups, having different ethnicities and lifeways. They were consolidated by regional orientation and subsistence and by adherence to principles of feudal culture, which was in the middle of a transformation into more modern monarchic and nascently dynastic political forms. The newcomers to the Indians' world included Jews, Christians, and Muslims, and they came from many different parts of the area we today call Europe, as well as from Africa and the Middle East. The Christians who came to the Americas divided according to the different forms of their Christian practice, whether it was adherence to different forms of Roman Catholicism or, slightly later, to different forms of Protestantism. Europe in the fifteenth and sixteenth centuries was overwhelmed by religious wars over the nature and forms of Christian worship and Christian polity. Religious wars in all areas pitted Christians against one another as they fought over which Christian practices should dominate.

In some cases, the Europeans fought their intercultural wars and their intracultural wars in the American territories in much the same way, though perhaps in a more vicious fashion, as they did back in their homelands. Yet in their homelands, a monarch might make firm and decisive what in the Americas was unstable and worth battling over by beheading offending members of the opposing group. Of Catholics, the Dominicans, Mercedarians, Franciscans, Jansenists, Augustinians, and, later, Jesuits dominated the scene, in religious terms, sometimes competing against each other in the same or nearby territories for the opportunity to lay claim to the saving of souls. After the Reformation, the sixteenth-century separation of the Roman Catholic Church into Protestant and Catholic groups, different Protestant groups competed with one another and with Catholics to have the opportunity to save the souls, as they would have it, of Native peoples. The presence of French Huguenots (French Protestant followers of Jean Calvin of Geneva) in the territories still under duress by different Spanish and French Catholic groups provides an additional indication of the driving assumptions of all religious orders.

To members of each different religious group, the Native peoples somehow needed saving, not just from the indigenous religious practices that Christian religious peoples considered pagan, but from particular Christian practices taught by members of any of the other groups. Missionary leaders needed to assume that their work was beneficial, and their records of successes in their efforts are compelling testimony to both the will to believe in the validity of their efforts and the desire to convince others of their successful work. Yet American Indian people practiced an amalgamated series of religions, retaining what they could of their own rituals while participating as necessary and perhaps as desired by whichever orders were practicing among them at the time. Many missionaries from many of the different groups developed a respect for the resilience of Native Americans in the face of what the Europeans would have implemented as a total cultural erasure.

When Bartholomé de Las Casas published his *Short Account of the Destruction of the Indies* in 1552, he was launching a telling indictment against methods used by religious people to support what had become a wholesale conquest of the bodies and souls of the indigenous population. Outraged by the actions of his missionary colleagues, he specifically targeted one of the first and then most noted friars, Fray Toribio de Benavente in New Spain. Toribio de Benavente had taken upon himself the name Motolonía, from an Indian word meaning "poor," and under the assumption that the era was apocalyptic because so many Indians were dying, he took to baptizing as many as forty thousand people in a week's time. Motolonía's response, in a letter explaining himself to Charles V, was that Las Casas must be a lunatic because when Cortés "entered these lands, God was very offended and the people suffered many cruel deaths, and the Devil, our enemy, was served here with the worst idolatries and murders that ever were."

It is difficult to discern, at this distance in time, what missionary people really thought about their work, whether they really considered it to be justified by an angry God or whether they—even the ones who defended their missionary activities—saw it for what it ended up being, an obliteration of Native American lifeways as they had been known anciently among the indigenous peoples. What we do know is that by the end of the first century of European activity in the Americas, Spanish expeditions and settlements had gone westward from the Caribbean islands through Mexico, southward into South America (to and through present-day Chile), and northward into the southwestern part of North America (to and through present-day New Mexico). Many of the exploits were bloody, as evidenced by the expeditions of Cortés against the Aztecs of Mexico (1519–21) and of Pizarro against the Incas (the 1520s and early 1530s). The Spanish were seeking, as Bernal Díaz del Castillo phrased it, "to bring light to those in darkness and also to get rich, which is what all of us men commonly seek." Today we deplore the methods used, but it is useful to keep in mind that the Spanish were not alone in their efforts, and their attitudes were not unlike those held by other Europeans who came at the time.

The Portuguese and French peoples used similar justifications—God and gold—to effect their own colonial projects. The Portuguese conquered Brazil and created sugar plantations there, using Indian laborers, at the time that Spain claimed, by the Treaty of Tordesillas (1494), the rest of South America and territory in North America. The French, following Cartier's landing in northeastern North America (present-day Canada) and following efforts in the Floridas by both Catholics and Protestants who were working for France, sought outcomes similar to those of the Spanish conquistadors. As René Goulaine de Laudonnière said in his history of the expedition to Florida in 1576, French people were in the Americas for two reasons: They had a "naturall desire" to "search out the commodities to live happily, plentifully, and at ease," thus relieving the homeland of its overpopulation, and they had an obligation to Rome (Catholicism) to fulfill. Because of difficulties with Spain, which claimed the Florida territory because of the Treaty of Tordesillas, and because the trade in fur from Canada proved more lucrative, by the end of their first century in the Americas, the French concentrated their efforts on Canada, where they worked successfully with Indian peoples in trading furs and where they would settle with increasing regularity numerous Jesuit missionaries, Black Robes, among the Algonquian peoples of the St. Lawrence throughway.

While the written record of the Europeans' takeover of the Americas gives evidence of America's legacy as one built upon a troubling, indeed disgraceful conquest of peoples, that record has also provided restorative witness to the immense resilience of people—especially Native people, but Europeans as well—in the face of tremendous odds and obstacles to their survival. The record shows, too, that not all Europeans understood the extent of the devastation they were wreaking, and not all were willing to participate in parties of conquest, just as they were unwilling to create written records in promotional behalf of monarchies and civil leaders they could no longer support. The favorable experiences that many Europeans had living among Native peoples during their first century of contact in the Americas compromised

Europeans' narrow visions of their "deserved fruits" of conquest, as well as their cultural assumptions about Christianity, civility, and humanity. For many settlers, the opportunity was not one to establish an old world in the new but to reconceive a civilization that was not encumbered by a European past. What they did with this opportunity is also the record, the testament, so to speak, made in the various first writings by Europeans of early America.

SOUTHERN EXPERIENCES

CHRISTOPHER COLUMBUS (1451–1506)

Christopher Columbus, the son of Domenico Columbus, a weaver, and Susanna Fontanarossa, was born in Genoa in 1451. Apprenticed while still a young man as a wool carder, Columbus set his mind to the sea and joined a shipping firm with interests in the Mediterranean. In 1474, Columbus sailed to the Greek island of Chios, but his fleet was attacked by French pirates during its return to Portugal. Columbus escaped by swimming to shore. He later made voyages to West Africa, and he grew interested in making an Atlantic voyage. His 1488 proposal for a voyage to "the Indies" was rejected by the king of Portugal, so Columbus sought the support of the Spanish monarchy, which represented Aragon and Castille. Columbus's second proposal was accepted by Ferdinand and Isabella in 1492.

On August 3, 1492, Columbus set sail on the first of the four voyages he would take between 1492 and 1504. He arrived at an island the native peoples called Guanahaní, which he promptly named San Salvador. He then traveled to the Bahamas, Cuba, and Hispaniola. On Hispaniola he left behind colonists to establish a settlement and to search for gold. Upon his return in 1493, all the Europeans were dead, presumably killed by the Taino Indians.

Columbus hoped that his second voyage in 1493 would provide the opportunity to establish successful colonies on some of the islands, which could then be used as bases for further exploration. Yet conflicts with Indians, unfamiliar diet, tensions among the crew and settlers, and limited discoveries of gold disappointed his schemes. Although he traveled to Puerto Rico, Jamaica, Cuba, the Virgin Islands, and the Lesser Antilles, his search for riches proved unsuccessful. Criticism of the administration of the colony of Española and the introduction of Indian slavery further complicated the situation. In response to criticism, Columbus returned to Spain in 1496 to defend himself before the royal court.

His third voyage in 1498 was taken to explore the South American mainland. From the lush landscape there, he concluded he had found an earthly paradise. When he returned to Hispaniola, he found that Spanish settlers were challenging his authority. Columbus was later arrested and sent back to Spain in 1500 to answer further charges, including a dereliction of duty to the monarchy. Although Queen Isabella ordered Columbus released, she had been persuaded by other colonists that there were significant problems with Columbus's administration of the colony and that Columbus should no longer be viceroy of the colony. Columbus's attempts to improve his reputation by making a final voyage resulted in shipwreck in Jamaica. After Columbus was rescued, he returned, disillusioned, to Europe, where he soon died.

Columbus kept a journal of his first voyage to America and presented it to Ferdinand and Isabella upon his return to Spain. Both the original and a copy made for Columbus are now lost. What survives is a partially quoted and partially summarized version made by Bartolomé de Las Casas, a cleric and friend of the family, in the 1530s. An account of his first voyage is also available in one of Columbus's letters. When he arrived in Portugal after completing his first voyage, he wrote to Ferdinand and Isabella in a letter dated March 14, 1493. Editions were printed in Italy and Spain, with the different versions appearing in Italian, Latin, German, and Spanish.

Although Columbus made four journeys to the Americas, throughout his life he denied having discovered a new continent. As evidence from others' journeys increasingly cast doubt upon his having found a new path to the Indies, Columbus declared that he had instead found the location of an earthly paradise. Columbus's move to defend an old vision of the globe, rather than to hypothesize a new one based in his experience, reveal his familiarity with the geography of the ancient astronomer, Ptolemy (fl. A.D. 190). Ptolemy believed that the sun, the planets, and the stars revolved around the earth. His calculations, based on these scientific misunderstandings, made the earth's circumference about one-third smaller than its actual length. Following Ptolemy's calculations, Columbus set sail, only to discover, in the experience, the error. Columbus's writings reveal his strong reliance upon the Ptolemaic system, his belief in the Bible, and his desire to discover the pathway of Marco Polo to China.

from THE *DIARIO* OF CHRISTOPHER COLUMBUS'S FIRST VOYAGE TO AMERICA, 1492–1493[1]

[Thursday 11 October][2]

After sunset he steered on his former course to the west. They made about 12 miles each hour and, until two hours after midnight, made about 90 miles, which is twenty-two leagues and a half. And because the caravel *Pinta* was a better sailer and went ahead of the Admiral[3] it found land and made the signals that the Admiral had ordered. A sailor named Rodrigo de Triana[4] saw this land first, although the Admiral, at the tenth hour of the night, while he was on the sterncastle, saw a light, although it was something so faint that he did not wish to affirm that it was land. But he called Pero Gutiérrez, the steward of the king's dais, and told him that there seemed to be a light, and for him to look: and thus he did and saw it. He also told Rodrigo Sánchez de Segovia, whom the king and queen were sending as *veedor*[5] of the fleet, who saw nothing because he was not in a place where he could see

it. After the Admiral said it, it was seen once or twice; and it was like a small wax candle that rose and lifted up, which to few seemed to be an indication of land. But the Admiral was certain that they were near land, because of which when they recited the *Salve*[6] which sailors in their own way are accustomed to recite and sing, all being present, the Admiral entreated and admonished them to keep a good lookout on the forecastle and to watch carefully for land; and that to the man who first told him that he saw land he would later give a silk jacket in addition to the other rewards that the sovereigns had promised, which were ten thousand *maravedis*[7] as an annuity to whoever should see it first. At two hours after midnight the land appeared, from which they were about two leagues distant. They hauled down all the sails and kept only the *treo*, which is the mainsail without bonnets, and jogged on and off[8] passing time until daylight Friday, when they reached an islet of the Lucayas[9] which was called Guanahani in the language of the Indians. Soon they saw naked people; and the Admiral went ashore in the armed launch, and Martín Alonso Pinzón[10] and his brother Vicente Anes, who was captain of the *Niña*. The Admiral brought out the royal banner and the captains two flags with the green cross, which the Admiral carried on all the ships as a standard, with an **F** and a **Y,** and over each letter a crown, one on one side of the ✠ and the other on the other. Thus put ashore they saw very green trees and many ponds and fruits of various kinds. The Admiral called to the two captains and to the others who had jumped ashore and to Ro-

---

1. The original *Diario* was presented to Ferdinand and Isabella in 1493 but has since been lost. The text is taken from *The Diario of Christopher Columbus's First Voyage to America, 1492–1493,* abstracted by Fray Bartolomé de las Casas, and translated and edited by Oliver Dunn and James E. Kelly, Jr. (1989).

2. Earlier entries in Columbus's *Diario* describe his first months at sea.

3. Columbus.

4. This name does not appear on the ship's lists. Rodrigo's name might have been Juan Rodriguez Bermeo.

5. Appointed by the monarchs, a veedor makes a record of the wealth that is found in order to protect against stealing.

6. A prayer to the Virgin Mary.

7. 375 maravedís (copper coins) were worth one gold ducat.

8. Tacked back and forth.

9. This geographic reference, like many in Columbus's *Diario,* is the object of significant dispute. Many scholars have proposed that Guanahaní refers to Watlings Island.

10. Captain of the Pinta.

drigo Descobedo, the *escrivano*[11] of the whole fleet, and to Rodrigo Sánchez de Segovia;[12] and he said that they should be witnesses that, in the presence of all, he would take, as in fact he did take, possession of the said island for the king and for the queen his lords, making the declarations that were required, and which at more length are contained in the testimonials made there in writing. Soon many people of the island gathered there. What follows are the very words of the Admiral in his book about his first voyage to, and discovery of, these Indies. I, he says, in order that they would be friendly to us—because I recognized that they were people who would be better freed [from error] and converted to our Holy Faith by love than by force—to some of them I gave red caps, and glass beads which they put on their chests, and many other things of small value, in which they took so much pleasure and became so much our friends that it was a marvel. Later they came swimming to the ships' launches where we were and brought us parrots and cotton thread in balls and javelins and many other things, and they traded them to us for other things which we gave them, such as small glass beads and bells. In sum, they took everything and gave of what they had very willingly. But it seemed to me that they were a people very poor in everything. All of them go around as naked as their mothers bore them; and the women also, although I did not see more than one quite young girl. And all those that I saw were young people, for none did I see of more than 30 years of age. They are very well formed, with handsome bodies and good faces. Their hair [is] coarse—almost like the tail of a horse—and short. They wear their hair down over their eyebrows except for a little in the back which they wear long and never cut. Some of them paint themselves with black, and they are of the color of the Canarians, neither black nor white; and some of them paint themselves with white, and some of them with red, and some of them with whatever they find. And some of them paint their faces, and some of them the whole body, and some of them only the eyes, and some of them only the nose. They do not carry arms nor are they acquainted with them, because I

showed them swords and they took them by the edge and through ignorance cut themselves. They have no iron. Their javelins are shafts without iron and some of them have at the end a fish tooth and others of other things. All of them alike are of good-sized stature and carry themselves well. I saw some who had marks of wounds on their bodies and I made signs to them asking what they were; and they showed me how people from other islands nearby came there and tried to take them, and how they defended themselves; and I believed and believe that they come here from *tierra firme* to take them captive. They should be good and intelligent servants, for I see that they say very quickly everything that is said to them; and I believe that they would become Christians very easily, for it seemed to me that they had no religion. Our Lord pleasing, at the time of my departure I will take six of them from here to Your Highnesses in order that they may learn to speak. No animal of any kind did I see on this island except parrots. All are the Admiral's words.

Saturday 13 October

As soon as it dawned, many of these people came to the beach—all young as I have said, and all of good stature—very handsome people, with hair not curly but straight and coarse, like horsehair; and all of them very wide in the forehead and head, more so than any other race that I have seen so far. And their eyes are very handsome and not small; and none of them are black, but of the color of the Canary Islanders. Nor should anything else be expected since this island is on an east-west line with the island of Hierro in the Canaries. All alike have very straight legs and no belly but are very well formed. They came to the ship with dugouts that are made from the trunk of one tree, like a long boat, and all of one piece, and worked marvelously in the fashion of the land, and so big that in some of them 40 and 45 men came. And others smaller, down to some in which came one man alone. They row with a paddle like that of a baker and go marvelously. And if it capsizes on them they then throw themselves in the water, and they right and empty it with calabashes[13] that they carry. They brought balls of spun cotton and parrots and javelins and other little things that it would be tiresome to write down, and they gave everything for anything that was given to

---

11. The ship's clerk or purser, who had significant responsibility for maintaining the ship's register and serving as the ship's general business manager.

12. Both Rodrigo Descobedo and Rodrigo Sánchez de Segovia remained on Española and were subsequently killed by Indians.

---

13. A calabash is a bowl or container made from a dried, hollow gourd.

them. I was attentive and labored to find out if there was any gold; and I saw that some of them wore a little piece hung in a hole that they have in their noses. And by signs I was able to understand that, going to the south or rounding the island to the south, there was there a king who had large vessels of it and had very much gold. I strove to get them to go there and later saw that they had no intention of going. I decided to wait until the afternoon of the morrow and then depart for the southwest, for, as many of them showed me, they said there was land to the south and to the southwest and to the northwest and that these people from the northwest came to fight them many times. And so I will go to the southwest to seek gold and precious stones. This island is quite big and very flat and with very green trees and much water and a very large lake in the middle and without any mountains; and all of it so green that it is a pleasure to look at it. And these people are very gentle, and because of their desire to have some of our things, and believing that nothing will be given to them without their giving something, and not having anything, they take what they can and then throw themselves into the water to swim. But everything they have they give for anything given to them, for they traded even for pieces of bowls and broken glass cups, and I even saw 16 balls of cotton given for three Portuguese *çeotis,*[14] which is a Castilian *blanca.*[15] And in them there was probably more than an *arroba*[16] of spun cotton. This I had forbidden and I did not let anyone take any of it, except that I had ordered it all taken for Your Highnesses[17] if it were in quantity. It grows here on this island, but because of the short time I could not declare this for sure. And also the gold that they wear hung in their noses originates here; but in order not to lose time I want to go to see if I can find the island of Cipango. Now, since night had come, all the Indians went ashore in their dugouts.

Sunday 14 October

As soon as it dawned I ordered the ship's boat and the launches of the caravels made ready and went northnortheast along the island in order to see what there was

14. A copper coin.

15. A copper coin worth half a maravedí.

16. An arroba is a unit of measurement equivalent to 25 pounds.

17. Columbus addressed his account to the patrons of his voyage, Spanish monarchs Isabella and Ferdinand.

in the other part, which was the eastern part. And also to see the villages, and I soon saw two or three, as well as people, who all came to the beach calling to us and giving thanks to God. Some of them brought us water; others, other things to eat; others, when they saw that I did not care to go ashore, threw themselves into the sea swimming and came to us, and we understood that they were asking us if we had come from the heavens. And one old man got into the ship's boat, and others in loud voices called to all the men and women: Come see the men who came from the heavens. Bring them something to eat and drink. Many men came, and many women, each one with something, giving thanks to God, throwing themselves on the ground; and they raised their hands to heaven, and afterward they called to us in loud voices to come ashore. But I was afraid, seeing a big stone reef that encircled that island all around. And in between the reef and shore there was depth and harbor for as many ships as there are in the whole of Christendom, and the entrance to it is very narrow. It is true that inside of this belt of stone there are some shallows, but the sea is no more disturbed than inside a well. And I bestirred myself this morning to see all of this, so that I could give an account of everything to Your Highnesses, and also to see where a fort could be made. And I saw a piece of land formed like an island, although it was not one, on which there were six houses. This piece of land might in two days be cut off to make an island, although I do not see this to be necessary since these people are very naive about weapons, as Your Highnesses will see from seven that I caused to be taken in order to carry them away to you and to learn our language and to return them. Except that, whenever Your Highnesses may command, all of them can be taken to Castile or held captive in this same island; because with 50 men all of them could be held in subjection and can be made to do whatever one might wish. And later [I noticed], near the said islet, groves of trees, the most beautiful that I saw and with their leaves as green as those of Castile in the months of April and May, and lots of water. I looked over the whole of that harbor and afterward returned to the ship and set sail, and I saw so many islands that I did not know how to decide which one I would go to first. And those men whom I had taken told me by signs that they were so very many that they were numberless. And they named by their names more than a hundred. Finally I looked for the largest and to that one I decided to go and so I am doing. It is about five leagues distant from this island of San Salvador, and the others of them some more, some less. All are very flat without mountains and very fertile and all populated and they make war on one another, even though these men are very simple and very handsome in body.

Monday 15 October

I had killed time this night for fear of reaching land to anchor before morning, because of not knowing whether the coast was clear of shoals, and as soon as it dawned I spread sail; and as the island was farther than five leagues, rather about seven, and the tide detained me, it was around noon when I reached the said island and I found that the face which is in the direction of San Salvador runs north-south and that there are in it five leagues; and the other, which I followed, runs east-west, and there are in it more than ten leagues. And since from this island I saw another larger one to the west, I spread sail to go forward all that day until night because [otherwise] I would not yet have been able to reach the western cape of the island, to which island I gave the name Santa María de la Concepción.[18] And close to sundown I anchored near the said cape in order to find out if there was gold there, because these men that I have had taken on the island of San Salvador kept telling me that there they wear very large bracelets of gold on their legs and on their arms. I well believe that all they were saying was a ruse in order to flee. Nevertheless, my intention was not to pass by any island of which I did not take possession, although if it is taken of one, it may be said that it is taken of all. And I anchored and remained here until today, Tuesday, and at dawn went ashore with the armed launches. I got out, and the natives, who were numerous and naked and of the same character as those of the other island of San Salvador, let us go around on the island and gave us what was asked of them. And because the wind increased and blew toward shore from the southeast, I did not wish to stay and departed for the ship; and a large dugout was alongside the caravel *Niña*. And one of the men from the island of San Salvador who was in the *Niña* threw himself into the sea and went away in the dugout. And the night before at mid-. . . .[19] thrown the other and went after the dugout, which fled [so speedily] that there

was never ship's launch that could overtake it even if we had a big head start. However, the dugout made land, the natives left the dugout, and some of the men of my company went ashore after them; and they all fled like chickens. And the dugout that they had left we brought alongside the *Niña,* to which now from another cape came another small dugout with one man who came to trade a ball of cotton; and some sailors jumped into the sea because the man did not want to enter the caravel and they laid hold of him. And I, who was on the poop[20] of the ship and saw all this, sent for him and gave him a red bonnet, and some small green glass beads which I put on his arm, and two bells which I put on his ears, and I ordered his dugout, which I also had in the ship's launch, returned to him and sent him to land. And then I set sail to go to the other large island that I had in view to the west. And I also ordered the other dugout, which the caravel *Niña* was bringing along at her stern, let loose. And later I saw, on land, at the time of arrival of the other man—[the man] to whom I had given the things aforesaid and whose ball of cotton I had not wanted to take from him, although he wanted to give it to me—that all the others went up to him. He considered it a great marvel, and indeed it seemed to him that we were good people and that the other man who had fled had done us some harm and that for this we were taking him with us. And the reason that I behaved in this way toward him, ordering him set free and giving him the things mentioned, was in order that they would hold us in this esteem so that, when Your Highnesses some other time again send people here, the natives will receive them well. And everything that I gave him was not worth four *maravedís*. And so I departed when it was about the tenth hour, with the wind southeast and shifting to the south, in order to pass to this other island, which is exceedingly large and where all these men that I am bringing from San Salvador make signs that there is very much gold and that they wear rings of it on their arms and on their legs and in their ears and on their noses and on their chests. And from this island of Santa María to this other island it is nine leagues east-west, and all this part of the island runs northwest-southeast. And it appears that there may well be on this coast more than 28 leagues on this side. And it is very flat without any mountains, just like San Salvador and Santa María. And all the beaches are without rocks, except that at all of them there are some big rocks near land under the water, where it is necessary to keep your eyes open when

---

18. Perhaps Rum Cay.

19. Las Casas appears to have omitted something here. Perhaps this passage should read: "And the night before, at midnight, the other man had thrown himself into the sea and fled. Men of my company went after the dugout. . . ."

20. A deck above the open deck of a ship.

you wish to anchor and not to anchor close to land, although the waters are always very clear and one sees the bottom. And two lombard shots [away] from land in all of these islands the bottom is so deep that you cannot reach it. These islands are very green and fertile and with sweet-smelling breezes; and there may be many things that I do not know about because I do not want to stop, so I can investigate and go to many islands in order to find gold. And since these people make signs that they wear it on their arms and on their legs—and it is gold because I showed them some pieces that I have of it—I cannot fail with the help of Our Lord to find out where it originates. And when we were mid-sea between these two islands, that is, Santa María and this big one to which I gave the name Fernandina,[21] I found a man who was passing alone in a dugout from the island of Santa María to Fernandina and who was bringing a small amount of their bread, which was about the size of a fist, and a calabash of water and a piece of red earth made into dust and then kneaded and some dry leaves, which must be something highly esteemed among them, because earlier, in San Salvador, they brought some of them to me as a present. And he was bringing a little native basket in which he had a string of small glass beads and two *blancas;* because of which I recognized that he was coming from the island of San Salvador and had passed to that of Santa María and was passing to Fernandina. He came up to the ship and I had him enter, which was what he asked, and I had his dugout put in the ship and all that he brought watched over, and I ordered him given bread and honey and something to drink, and so I will transport him to Fernandina and I will give him all of his belongings in order that, through good reports of us—Our Lord pleasing—when Your Highnesses send [others] here, those who come will receive courteous treatment and the natives will give us of all that they may have.

Tuesday and Wednesday 16 October

I departed from the island of Santa María de la Concepción, when it was already about noon, for the island of Fernandina, which showed up very large to the west, and I sailed all that day in a very light wind. I could not arrive in time to be able to see the bottom in order to anchor in the clear, because in doing this it is important to have great diligence so as not to lose the anchors. And so I lay to all this night until day, when I came to a village where I anchored and to which had come that man whom I found

mid-sea yesterday in that dugout. He had given so many good reports about us that during the whole night there was no lack of dugouts alongside the ship, to which they brought us water and of what they had. I ordered something given to each one, that is to say ten or twelve little glass beads on a thread, and some brass jingles of the sort that in Castile are worth a *maravedi* each, and some metal lace-ends, all of which they considered of the greatest excellence. And also I ordered them given food, in order that they might eat when they came to the ship, and molasses. And later, at the hours of tierce,[22] I sent the ship's boat to shore for water. And the natives very willingly showed my people where the water was, and they themselves brought the filled barrels to the boat and delighted in pleasing us. This island is exceedingly large and I have decided to sail around it, because according to my understanding, on or near it there is a gold mine. This island is distant from that of Santa María eight leagues almost east-west, and this cape to which I came and all this coast runs north-northwest and south-southwest, and I saw quite 20 leagues of it but it did not end there. Now, writing this, I set sail with a south wind to strive to go around the whole island and to keep trying until I find Samoet, which is the island or city where the gold is; for so say all these men who come here in the ship, and so told us the men of the island of San Salvador and of Santa María. These people are like those of the said islands in speech and customs except that these now appear somewhat more civilized and given to commerce and more astute. Because I see that they have brought cotton here to the ship and other little things for which they know better how to bargain payment than the others did. And in this island I even saw cotton cloths made like small cloaks, and the people are more intelligent, and the women wear in front of their bodies a little thing of cotton that scarcely covers their genitals. It is a very green and flat and exceedingly fertile island and I have no doubt that all year they sow millet[23] and harvest it and likewise all other things. And I saw many trees very different from ours, and among them many which had branches of many kinds, and all on one trunk. And one little branch is of one kind, and another of another, and so different that it is the greatest wonder in the world how much diversity there is between one kind and another; that is to say, one branch has leaves like those of cane, and another like those of

---

21. Perhaps Long Island.

22. Approximately 9 A.M.

23. Columbus is probably referring to maize.

mastic, and thus on a single tree [there are] five or six of these kinds, and all very different. Nor are they grafted, because one might say that grafting does it. Rather, these trees are wild, nor do these people take care of them. I do not detect in them any religion and I believe that they would become Christians very quickly because they are of very good understanding. Here the fish are so different from ours that it is a marvel. There are some shaped like dories,[24] of the finest colors in the world: blues, yellows, reds, and of all colors; and others colored in a thousand ways. And the colors are so fine that there is no man who would not marvel and take great delight in seeing them. There are also whales. On land I saw no animals of any kind except parrots and lizards. A boy told me that he saw a large snake. I saw neither sheep nor goats nor any other beast, although I have been here very little time, for it is now midday, but if there were any of them I would not fail to see some. The circuit of this island I will write about after I have gone around it.

Wednesday 17 October

At midday I departed from the village where I was anchored and where I took on water in order to go around this island of Fernandina, and the wind was southwest and south. And since my intention had been to follow this coast of this island where I was to the southeast, because it all ran north-northwest and south-southeast, and I wanted to follow the said course to the south and southeast because in that region, according to all these Indians that I am bringing and another from whom I had information, in this southern region is the island those men call Samoet, where the gold is. And Martín Alonso Pinzón, captain of the caravel *Pinta,* in which I had sent three of these Indians, came to me and told me that one of them very positively had given him to understand that by way of the north-northwest I would go around the island much more quickly. I saw that the wind was not helping me on the course I wanted to follow and that it was good for the other; so I set sail to the north-northwest and when I was two leagues distant from the end of the island, I found a very wonderful harbor with one entrance, although one might say with two, because it has an *isleo*[25] in the middle and the entrances are both very narrow; and inside it would be wide enough for a hundred ships if it were deep

and clean-bottomed and deep at the entrance. There seemed to me good reason to look at it well and to take soundings, and so I anchored outside and went into it with all the ships' launches and we saw that it had no depth. And because I thought when I saw it that it was the mouth of some river, I had ordered barrels taken in order to get water, and on land I found some eight or ten men who soon came to us and showed us nearby the village where I sent the men for water: one group with arms and others with barrels; and so they got it. And because it was a bit far I stopped for a period of two hours and in this time I also walked among those trees, which were more beautiful to see than any other thing that has ever been seen, seeing as much verdure and in such degree as in the month of May in Andalusia. And all the trees are as different from ours as day from night; and also the fruits and grasses and stones and everything. It is true that some trees are of the same character as others in Castile; nevertheless, there was a very great difference. And the other trees of other kinds were so many that there is no one who can tell it or compare them with others of Castile. All the people are the same as the others already mentioned—of the same qualities and likewise naked and of the same stature—and they gave what they had for anything the men gave them. And here I saw that some ships' boys traded a few small pieces of broken pottery and glass for javelins. And the others who went for the water told me how they had been in their houses and that inside they were well swept and clean and that their beds and furnishings were made of things like cotton nets. The houses are all made like Moorish campaign tents, very high and with good smoke holes,[26] but I did not see among the many villages that I saw any that surpassed 12 to 15 houses. Here they found that the married women wore cotton shorts; the young girls did not, except some who were already 18 years of age. And there there were dogs, mastiffs and terriers. And there they found a man who had in his nose a piece of gold which was something like half of a *castellano,*[27] on which they saw letters. I rebuked them because they did not trade for it and give as much as he asked in order to see what it was and whose money it was; and they an-

---

24. Dories are a type of small, saltwater fish.

25. A small island next to a coast or a larger island.

---

26. Las Casas makes the following note in the margin: "These chimneys do not serve to let out the smoke, but are cornices which they have on their thatch roofs. To let out the smoke, they just leave an opening in the roof."

27. A castellano is a gold coin worth 480 maravedís or somewhat more than one gold ducat.

swered that they never dared to trade with him for it. After getting the water I returned to the ship and set sail and went northwest so far that I viewed all that part of the island as far as the coast that runs east-west. And later all these Indians said again that this island was smaller than the island of Samoet and that it would be well to turn back so as to be there more quickly. The wind there soon died on us and commenced to blow west-northwest, which was contrary to the direction in which we had been coming. And so I turned about and steered all this past night to the east-southeast and sometimes due east and sometimes southeast; and this was so as to keep away from land because it was heavily overcast and the weather very dirty. There was little [time] and it did not let me reach land to anchor. Also tonight it rained very hard after midnight until almost day and it still is cloudy and looks like rain. And we [will head] for the southeast cape of the island where I hope to anchor until the weather clears in order to see the other islands where I have to go. And so it has rained a lot, or a little, every day since I have been in these Indies. May Your Highnesses believe that this land is the best and most fertile and temperate and level and good that there is in the world.

Thursday 18 October

After the weather cleared I followed the wind and went around the island as much as I could and anchored when the time was not good for navigation; but I did not go ashore, and when dawn came I set sail.

[Monday 26 November]

On all of this coast he saw no populated places from the sea, [although] it may be that there were some and there were signs of them because, wherever they went ashore, they found indications of people and many fires. He judged that the land that he saw today southeast of the Cabo de Campana[28] was the island that the Indians called Bohío, and it seemed so because the said cape is separated from that land. All the people that he has found up to today, he says, have extreme fear of the men of Caniba, or Canima, and they say that they live on this island of Bohío, which must be very large, as it seems to him; and they believe that they are going to take them to their lands and houses since they are very cowardly and know noth-

ing about weapons. And because of this it appears to him that those Indians he has with him do not usually settle on the seacoast because of being neighbors to this land. He says that after they saw him take the route to this land they could not speak, fearing that they would have them to eat; and he could not take away their fear. And they say that they have but one eye and the face of a dog; and the Admiral thought they were lying and felt that those who captured them must have been under the rule of the Grand Khan.[29]

Tuesday 27 November

Yesterday at sunset he arrived near a cape that he called Campana and because the sky [was] clear and the wind faint he did not want to go [close] to land to anchor, although downwind he had five or six admirable harbors; he was delaying more than he wished because of the desire and delight that he had and received from seeing and looking at the beauty and freshness of those lands wherever he entered. And so as not to delay in furthering his purpose, for these reasons that night was spent jogging on and off and killing time until day. And because the tidal flows and currents that night had set him five or six leagues southeast,[30] beyond the place where he had been at nightfall, and where the land of Campana had appeared to him, and where beyond that cape there appeared a large opening that indicated a division of one land from another, and where something like an island was formed in between, he decided to turn back with a southwest wind and go where the opening had appeared. He found that it was but a large bay and at the southeast end of it [there was] a cape on which there was a high square mountain[31] that appeared to be an island. The wind shifted quickly to north and he again took a course to the southeast to run along the coast and to survey everything that might be there. And he soon saw at the foot of that Cabo de Campana an admirable harbor and a big river; and a quarter of a league away, another river; and from there a half league, another river; and beyond, at another half league, another river; and beyond, a league further, another river; and an-

---

28. Perhaps Punta Plata or Punta Baez.

29. Columbus uses his knowledge of Marco Polo's journey to interpret his surroundings.

30. Evidence suggests they might have drifted northwest rather than southeast.

31. The mountain is named El Yunque and is a landmark because of its visibility from significant distances.

other league beyond that, another river; and after another quarter league, another river; and another league beyond that, another big river, from which to the Cabo de Campana was about 20 miles to the southeast. And most of these rivers had big and wide and clear entrances with admirable harbors for the very largest ships, without sandbanks or stony shallows or reefs. Coming thus along the coast to the southeast of the last river mentioned, he found a great settlement, the largest that he had found up until now; and he saw a great number of men come to the seashore shouting, all naked, with their javelins in their hands. He desired to speak with them, and hauled down the sails and anchored; and he sent the launches of the ship and of the caravel with orders that they should do no harm to the Indians, but not receive any either, and commanding that they give them some little things from the trade goods. The Indians made gestures threatening to resist them and not to let them land, but seeing that the launches were approaching land more closely and that the Spaniards were not afraid of them, they withdrew from the sea. Believing that if only two or three men got out of the launches the Indians would not be afraid, three Christians got out, saying in their language not to be afraid, because they knew a bit of it through association with those they brought with them; but finally all took to flight and neither grown-ups nor little ones remained. The three Christians went to the houses, which are of straw, made the same way as the others they had seen; and they did not find anyone or anything in any of them. They returned to the ships and raised sail at noon to go to a beautiful cape that lay to the east eight leagues distant. Having gone half a league along the same bay, the Admiral saw to the south a most singular harbor and to the southeast some marvelously beautiful fields like a fertile rolling plain within the mountains; and there appeared much smoke and large settlements in them and the fields were very well tended. Because of this he decided to go down to this harbor and to see if he could talk or deal with them. The harbor was such that, if he had praised the other harbors, this one, he says, he praised more, with its fields and temperate climate and surrounding region and settlement. He says marvelous things of the beauty of the land and of the trees, where there are pines and palms, and of the great plain, which, although it is not entirely flat where it goes to the south-southeast but is rolling with gentle and low hills, is the most beautiful thing in the world. And there run through it many streams of water that descend from these mountains. After the ship anchored, the Admiral got into the launch in order to sound the harbor, which is shaped like a soup bowl, and when he was opposite the mouth he found to the south an entrance to a river which was wide enough for a galley to enter through it and of such a sort that it could not be seen until one reached it. And having gone into it as far as the length of the launch, it had a depth of five to eight *brazas*.[32] Going through it was a wonderful thing [because of] the groves of trees, the freshness, and the extremely clear water, and the birds, and its attractiveness. He says that it seemed to him that one might not wish to leave that place. He kept telling the men who were in his company that, in order to report to the sovereigns the things they were seeing, a thousand tongues would not suffice to tell it or his hand to write it; for it seemed to him that it was enchanted. He wished that many other prudent and creditable persons would see it, of whom he says he is certain that they would praise these things no less than he. Moreover, the Admiral says here these words: How great the benefit will be that can be obtained from this place I do not write. It is certain, Lord Princes, that where there are such lands there should be a vast number of profitable things. But I am not delaying in any harbor because I would like to see all the lands that I can in order to report on them to Your Highnesses. Also I do not know the language, and the people of these lands do not understand me nor do I, nor anyone else that I have with me, them. And many times I understand one thing said by these Indians that I bring for another, its contrary; nor do I trust them much, because many times they have tried to flee. But now, pleasing Our Lord, I will see the most that I can and little by little I will progress in understanding and acquaintance, and I will have this tongue taught to persons of my household because I see that up to this point it is a single language. And later the benefits will be known and efforts will be made to make all these peoples Christian; because it will be done easily, since they have no false religion nor are they idolaters. And Your Highnesses will order made in these regions a city and fortress; and these lands will be converted. And I assure Your Highnesses that it seems to me that under the sun there can be no better lands: in fertility and mildness of cold and heat, in abundance of good and healthful water, not like the rivers of Guinea, which are all pestilential, because, praise be to Our Lord, up until now of all my people there has been no one who has had a headache or been in bed with illness except one old man, from the pain of the stone which he has suffered all his life; and

---

32. *Braza:* fathom.

then he recovered after two days. This that I tell is [true] of all three ships. So that it will please God that Your Highnesses will send, or that there will come, learned men and then they will see the truth of everything. And although, further back, I have spoken of the site of a town and fortress in the harbor of the Rio de Mares, because of the good harbor and the region—and certainly all that I said is true—there is no comparing that place with this nor [the Puerto de Mares] with the Mar de Nuestra Señora: here, inland, there should be great settlements and innumerable people and things of great profit, since here, and in all else discovered and that I have hope of discovering before I go to Castile, I say that the whole of Christendom will do business in these lands; and how much more so Spain, to which everything should be subject. And I say that Your Highnesses ought not to consent that any foreigner set foot or trade here except Catholic Christians, since the beginning and end of the enterprise was the increase and glory of the Christian Religion, nor [consent that] anyone come to these regions who is not a good Christian. All these are his words. He went up the river and found some of its branches, and going around the harbor he found at the mouth of the river some attractive groves of trees like a delightful garden; and there he found a handsome dugout, or canoe, made of one timber, as big as a *fusta*[33] of 12 rowing benches, drawn up under a shelter or shed made of wood and covered with big palm leaves, so that neither sun nor water could damage it. And he says that there was the very place to make a town or city and fortress because of the good harbor, the good water, good lands, the good region, and much firewood.

Tuesday 25 December, Christmas Day

Yesterday, sailing with little wind from the Mar de Santo Thomás toward the Punta Santa,[34] off which at a distance of one league they stood until the first watch was over—which would be about the eleventh hour of the night—the Admiral decided to go to sleep because there had been two days and a night when he had not slept. As there had been little wind, the sailor who was steering the ship decided to go away to sleep and left the tiller to a ship's boy, something the Admiral had always strictly prohibited on the whole voyage, whether there was wind or whether it

was calm: that is, they did not let the ship's boys steer. The Admiral was safe from banks and rocks because on Sunday, when he sent the launches to the king, they had passed to the east of the said Punta Santa quite three and a half leagues and the sailors had seen all the coast and the shoals that lie from the said Punta Santa to the east-southeast quite three leagues; and they saw where they could pass, which was something he did not do in the whole voyage.[35] It pleased Our Lord that at the twelfth hour of night when they had seen the Admiral lie down and rest and saw that it was dead calm and the sea as smooth as water in a bowl, all lay down to sleep and left the tiller in the hands of that boy; and the currents of water carried the ship upon one of those banks, which, even though it was at night, could be seen, and which made a sound that from a full league off could be heard; and the ship went upon it so gently that it was hardly felt. The boy who felt the rudder[36] and heard the sound of the sea cried out, at which the Admiral came out, and it was so quick that still no one had sensed that they were aground. Then the master of the ship, whose watch it was, came out, and the Admiral told him and the others to haul in the boat that they were pulling astern and to take an anchor and throw it astern. And he with many others jumped into the boat, and the Admiral thought that they would do what he had ordered. But they cared for nothing but to flee to the caravel, which was upwind half a league. The caravel, dutifully, did not want to receive them, and for this reason they returned to the ship, but the caravel's launch got there first. When the Admiral saw that it was his men who were fleeing, that the waters were diminishing, and that the ship already lay crosswise to the seas, seeing no other remedy, he ordered the mast cut and the ship lightened of as much as they could to see if they could get her off; and as the waters still continued to diminish they could not remedy matters; and she listed toward the cross sea, although there was little or no sea running. And then the planking opened up, but not the ship. The Admiral went to the caravel [*Niña*] in order to put the men from the ship in safety. And since now a small land breeze was blowing and also because much of the night remained, and they did not know how far the banks extended, he jogged on and off until it was day and then went to the ship from inside the reef in the shoal. Previously he had sent the boat

---

33. A small galley, often propelled by oars.

34. Perhaps Pointe Nicolet or Pointe St. Honoré.

35. In other words, Columbus had not previously relied on the sailors' information during the journey.

36. He felt the rudder touch ground.

to land with Diego de Arana of Cordova,[37] bailiff of the fleet, and Pero Gutiérrez, a steward of the royal household, to inform the king, who on Saturday had sent to invite and beg him to come with the ships to his harbor. He had his town farther on, about a league and a half from the said shoal; and when he learned of it, they said that he cried and sent all his people from the town with many large canoes to unload everything from the ship. And thus it was done and in a very brief time everything from the decks was unloaded, so great was the care and diligence that that king exercised. And he himself and his brothers and relatives were as diligent [unloading] the ship as in guarding what was taken to land in order that everything would be well cared for. From time to time he sent one of his relatives to the Admiral, weeping, to console him, saying that he should not be sorrowful or annoyed because he would give him all that he had. The Admiral assures the sovereigns that in no part of Castile could they have taken such good care of everything, so that not a lace-end would be missing. The king ordered it put all together near some houses that he wished to provide, which were being emptied, where everything might be put and kept. He placed armed men around everything and ordered that they keep watch all night. He and the whole town were weeping; to such a degree, the Admiral says, are they loving people, and without greed, and docile in everything. And I assure Your Highnesses that I believe that in the world there are no better people or a better land. They love their neighbors as themselves, and they have the sweetest speech in the world; and [they are] gentle and are always laughing. They go about as naked, men and women, as their mothers bore them, but may Your Highnesses believe that among themselves they have very good customs, and the king [observes a] very wonderful estate in such a dignified manner that it is a pleasure to see everything. And the memory that they have! They want to see everything and ask what it is and what it is for! All of this the Admiral says.

Wednesday 26 December

Today at sunrise the king of that land, who was in that place, came to the caravel *Niña,* where the Admiral was, and almost weeping said to him not to be downhearted for he would give him all that he had, and that he had given

the Christians who were on land two very large houses, and that he would give them more if there were need, and as many canoes as could load and unload the ship and put ashore as many people as he wished, and that he had done so yesterday without a crumb of bread or any other thing at all being taken; to such a degree, says the Admiral, are they faithful and without greed for what is another's and, above all, so was that virtuous king. While the Admiral was talking to him, another canoe came from another place bringing certain pieces of gold which they wished to give for one bell, because they desired nothing else as much as bells, for the canoe was not yet alongside when they called and showed the pieces of gold, saying *chuq chuque* for bells, for they are on the point of going crazy for them. After having seen this—the canoes from other places departing—the Indians called to the Admiral and begged him to order one bell kept until the next day, because they would bring four pieces of gold as large as a hand. The Admiral rejoiced to hear this and later a sailor who came from land told the Admiral it was a thing to marvel at, the pieces of gold that the Christians who were ashore traded for a trifle. For a lace-end they gave pieces that would be more than two *castellanos,* and that [such trade] was nothing compared to what it would be after a month. The king rejoiced to see the Admiral happy, and he understood that he wanted a lot of gold; and he told him by signs that he knew where, nearby, there was very much, a great quantity of it, and to be of good heart, that he would give him as much gold as he might want. And, about this [gold], the Admiral says that the king gave him a report and, in particular, [said] that there was gold in Cipango, which they call Cybao, in such degree that they hold it in no regard and that he would bring it there; but also that in the island of Hispaniola, which they call Bohío, and in that province of Caribata, there was much more of it. The king had dinner on the caravel with the Admiral and afterward left with him to go ashore, where they did the Admiral much honor and gave him refreshments of two or three kinds of yams and shrimp and game and other foods that they had and some of their bread, which they call cassava.[38] They took him to see some groves of trees near the houses, and there walked with him quite a thousand persons, all naked. The lord was still wearing the shirt and gloves that the Admiral had given him; and he was pleased more with the gloves than with

---

37. Diego de Arana was left in charge of the fort at Navidad (on Hispaniola). Subsequently, he and his men were killed by Indians.

---

38. A cassava is a tropical plant whose starchy roots are used to make tapioca and bread.

anything else that they gave him. In his table manners, his urbanity, and [his] attractive cleanliness, he quite showed himself to be of noble lineage. After having eaten, for they spent quite a while at table, they brought certain herbs with which they rubbed their hands (the Admiral thought they did it to soften them), and they gave him water for washing his hands. After they finished [eating], the king took the Admiral to the beach, and the Admiral sent for a Turkish bow and a handful of arrows; and he had one of the men of his company who was familiar with it shoot it; and to the lord, since he did not know what weapons are, because they do not have and do not use them, it appeared a great thing, although he says that [at] the beginning [there] was some talk about the men of Caniba, whom they call Caribs, who come to capture them and who carry bows and arrows without iron points, for in all of those lands they have no knowledge of iron or of steel or of any other metal except gold and copper, although of copper the Admiral had seen but little. The Admiral told him by signs that the sovereigns of Castile would order the Caribs destroyed, and they would order all of them to be brought with hands tied. The Admiral ordered a lombard[39] and a spingard[40] to be fired, and when the king saw the effect of their force and what they penetrated, he was astonished. And when his people heard the shots they all fell to the ground. They brought the Admiral a large mask that had large pieces of gold in the ears and eyes and on other places. The king gave it to him with other gold jewels that he himself had put on the Admiral's head and neck; and to the other Christians who were with him he also gave many things. The Admiral received much pleasure and consolation from these things that he saw; and the anguish and sorrow that he had received and felt because of the loss of the ship were tempered; and he recognized that Our Lord had caused the ship to ground there so that he would found a settlement there. And for this purpose, he says, so many things came to hand that truly it was not disaster, but great luck. Because it is certain, he says, that if I had not gone aground I would have passed at a distance without anchoring at this place, because it is located here inside a large bay, and in it [there are] two or three reefs and shoals; nor on this voyage would I have left people here; nor, even if I had wished to leave them, could I have given them such good supplies or so many tools or so much foodstuff or equipment for a

fortress. And it is quite true that many people of those who are here have begged me and have had others beg me to be willing to give them license to stay. Now I have ordered them to build a tower and a fort, all very well constructed, and a big moat, not that I believe it to be necessary because of these Indians, for it is obvious that with these men that I bring I could subdue all of this island, which I believe is larger than Portugal and double or more in [number of] people, since they are naked and without arms and cowardly beyond remedy. But it is right that this tower be made and that it be as it should be (being so far from Your Highnesses) in order that the Indians may become acquainted with the skills of Your Highnesses' people and what they can do, so that with love and fear they will obey them. And thus they have timbers from which to build the whole fortress, and bread and wine for more than a year, and seeds to sow, and the ship's launch, and a caulker, and a carpenter, and a gunner, and a barrel maker; and many among them [are] men who greatly desire to serve Your Highnesses and to please me by finding out about the mine where gold is taken. So everything has worked out opportunely for this beginning to be made, especially since when the ship ran aground, it was so softly that it was not felt, nor was there wave nor wind. All of this the Admiral says. And he adds more to show that it was great luck and the particular will of God that the ship ran aground so that he would leave people there. He says that if it had not been for the treachery of the master and of the men, all or most of whom were from [his] region [in Spain], not wanting to cast the anchor astern to get the ship off, as the Admiral ordered them, the ship would have been saved and thus he would not have been able to learn about the country, he says, as he did [during] those days when he stayed there and [as] those who undertook to stay will do in future, because he always went with the intention to explore and not to stop anywhere more than one day, if it were not for lack of wind, because the ship, he says, was very sluggish and not suited for the work of exploration; and in taking such a ship, he says, the men of Palos failed to comply with their promise to the king and queen to provide suitable vessels for that trip, and they did not do it. The Admiral concludes saying that of everything that was in the ship not even a lace-end was lost, neither plank nor nail, because she remained in as good condition as when she left [Spain], except that she was cut and opened up somewhat to get out the storage jars and all the merchandise. And they put it all on land and guarded it well, as has been said. And he says that he hopes in God that on the return that he would undertake from Castile he

---

39. Type of cannon.

40. A muzzle-loaded firearm.

would find a barrel of gold that those who were left would have acquired by exchange; and that they would have found the gold mine and the spicery, and those things in such quantity that the sovereigns, before three years [are over], will undertake and prepare to go conquer the Holy Sepulcher; for thus I urged Your Highnesses to spend all the profits of this my enterprise on the conquest of Jerusalem, and Your Highnesses laughed and said that it would please them and that even without this profit they had that desire. These are the Admiral's words.

___

LETTER OF COLUMBUS, DESCRIBING THE RESULTS OF HIS FIRST VOYAGE[1]

SIR:[2] Since I know that you will be pleased at the great victory with which Our Lord has crowned my voyage, I write this to you, from which you will learn how in thirty-three days I passed from the Canary Islands to the Indies, with the fleet which the most illustrious King and Queen, our Sovereigns, gave to me. There I found very many islands, filled with innumerable people, and I have taken possession of them all for their Highnesses, done by proclamation and with the royal standard unfurled, and no opposition was offered to me.

To the first island which I found I gave the name "San Salvador,"[3] in remembrance of the Divine Majesty, Who had marvellously bestowed all this; the Indians call it "Guanahani." To the second, I gave the name the island of "Santa Maria de Concepcion,"[4] to the third,

"Fernandina,"[5] to the fourth, "Isabella,"[6] to the fifth island, "Juana,"[7] and so each received from me a new name.

When I came to Juana, I followed its coast to the westward, and I found it to be so extensive that I thought that it must be the mainland, the province of Cathay.[8] And since there were neither towns nor villages on the seashore, but small hamlets only, with the people of which I could not have speech because they all fled immediately, I went forward on the same course, thinking that I could not fail to find great cities or towns. At the end of many leagues, seeing that there was no change and that the coast was bearing me northwards, which I wished to avoid, since winter was already approaching and I proposed to make from it to the south, and as, moreover, the wind was carrying me forward, I determined not to wait for a change in the weather and retraced my path as far as a remarkable harbour known to me. From that point, I sent two men inland to learn if there were a king or great cities. They travelled three days' journey, finding an infinity of small hamlets and people without number, but nothing of importance. For this reason, they returned.

I understood sufficiently from other Indians, whom I had already taken, that this land was nothing but an island, and I therefore followed its coast eastward for one hundred and seven leagues to the point where it ended. From that point, I saw another island, distant about eighteen leagues from the first, to the east, and to it I at once gave the name "Española."[9] I went there and followed its northern coast, as I had followed that of Juana, to the eastward for one hundred and eighty-eight great leagues in a straight line. This island and all the others are very fertile to a limitless degree, and this island is extremely so. In it there are many harbours on the coast of the sea, beyond comparison with others that I know in Christendom, and many rivers, good and large, which is marvellous. Its lands are high; there are in it many sierras and very lofty mountains, beyond comparison with that of Tenerife.[10] All are most beautiful, of a thousand shapes; all are accessible and are filled with trees of a thousand

___

1. The letter was originally printed in Barcelona in 1493, shortly after Columbus returned from his first voyage. This text is taken from *The Journal of Columbus,* translated by Cecil Jane (1960).

2. The earliest published version of the letter was often addressed to either Gabriel Sánchez or Luis de Santangel, high officials of the Kingdom of Aragon. Columbus used essentially the same text when he wrote to Ferdinand and Isabella, the duke of Medinaceli, and the Cordoba town council.

3. Although the identity of the island Columbus named San Salvador is the subject of dispute, many believe it was Watlings Island.

4. Perhaps Rum Cay.

5. Perhaps Long Island.

6. Perhaps Crooked Island.

7. Cuba.

8. China.

9. Hispaniola, which currently comprises the countries of Haiti and the Dominican Republic.

10. The largest Canary Island.

kinds and tall, so that they seem to touch the sky. I am told that they never lose their foliage, and this I can believe, for I saw them as green and lovely as they are in Spain in May, and some of them were flowering, some bearing fruit, and some at another stage, according to their nature. The nightingale was singing and other birds of a thousand kinds, in the month of November, there where I went. There are six or eight kinds of palm, which are a wonder to behold on account of their beautiful variety, but so are the other trees and fruits and plants. In it are marvellous pine groves; there are very wide and fertile plains, and there is honey; and there are birds of many kinds and fruits in great diversity. In the interior, there are mines of metals, and the population is without number.

Española is a marvel. The sierras and the mountains, the plains, the champaigns, are so lovely and so rich for planting and sowing, for breeding cattle of every kind, for building towns and villages. The harbours of the sea here are such as cannot be believed to exist unless they have been seen, and so with the rivers, many and great, and of good water, the majority of which contain gold. In the trees, fruits and plants, there is a great difference from those of Juana. In this island, there are many spices and great mines of gold and of other metals.

The people of this island and of all the other islands which I have found and of which I have information, all go naked, men and women, as their mothers bore them, although some of the women cover a single place with the leaf of a plant or with a net of cotton which they make for the purpose. They have no iron or steel or weapons, nor are they fitted to use them. This is not because they are not well built and of handsome stature, but because they are very marvellously timorous. They have no other arms than spears made of canes, cut in seeding time, to the ends of which they fix a small sharpened stick. Of these they do not dare to make use, for many times it has happened that I have sent ashore two or three men to some town to have speech with them, and countless people have come out to them, and as soon as they have seen my men approaching, they have fled, a father not even waiting for his son. This is not because ill has been done to any one of them; on the contrary, at every place where I have been and have been able to have speech with them, I have given to them of that which I had, such as cloth and many other things, receiving nothing in exchange. But so they are, incurably timid. It is true that, after they have been reassured and have lost this fear, they are so guileless and so generous with all that they possess, that no one would believe it who has not seen it. They refuse nothing that they possess, if it be asked of them; on the contrary, they invite any one to share it and display as much love as if they would give their hearts. They are content with whatever trifle of whatever kind that may be given to them, whether it be of value or valueless. I forbade that they should be given things so worthless as fragments of broken scraps of broken glass and lace tips, although when they were able to get them, they fancied that they possessed the best jewel in the world. So it was found that for a thong a sailor received gold to the weight of two and a half castellanos,[11] and others received much more for other things which were worth less. As for new blancas,[12] for them they would give everything which they had, although it might be two or three castellanos' weight of gold or an arroba[13] or two of spun cotton. They took even the pieces of the broken hoops of the wine barrels and, like savages, gave what they had, so that it seemed to me to be wrong and I forbade it. I gave them a thousand handsome good things, which I had brought, in order that they might conceive affection for us and, more than that, might become Christians and be inclined to the love and service of Your Highnesses and of the whole Castilian nation, and strive to collect and give us of the things which they have in abundance and which are necessary to us.

They do not hold any creed nor are they idolaters; but they all believe that power and good are in the heavens and were very firmly convinced that I, with these ships and men, came from the heavens, and in this belief they everywhere received me after they had mastered their fear. This belief is not the result of ignorance, for they are, on the contrary, of a very acute intelligence and they are men who navigate all those seas, so that it is amazing how good an account they give of everything. It is because they have never seen people clothed or ships of such a kind.

As soon as I arrived in the Indies, in the first island which I found, I took some of the natives by force, in order that they might learn and might give me information of whatever there is in these parts. And so it was that they soon understood us, and we them, either by speech or signs, and they have been very serviceable. At present, those I bring with me are still of the opinion that I come

---

11. A castellano is a gold coin worth somewhat more than one gold ducat.

12. 750 blancas (small coins) were worth one gold ducat.

13. An arroba is a unit of measurement equivalent to 25 pounds.

from Heaven, for all the intercourse which they have had with me. They were the first to announce this wherever I went, and the others went running from house to house, and to the neighbouring towns, with loud cries of, "Come! Come! See the men from Heaven!" So all came, men and women alike, when their minds were set at rest concerning us, not one, small or great, remaining behind, and they all brought something to eat and drink, which they gave with extraordinary affection.

In all the islands, they have very many canoes, which are like rowing fustas,[14] some larger and some smaller; some are greater than a fusta of eighteen benches. They are not so broad, because they are made of a single log of wood, but a fusta would not keep up with them in rowing, since their speed is an incredible thing. In these they navigate among all those islands, which are innumerable, and carry their goods. I have seen one of these canoes with seventy or eighty men in it, each one with his paddle.

In all these islands, I saw no great diversity in the appearance of the people or in their manners and language. On the contrary, they all understand one another, which is a very curious thing, on account of which I hope that their Highnesses will determine upon their conversion to our holy faith, towards which they are very inclined.

I have already said how I went one hundred and seven leagues in a straight line from west to east along the seashore of the island of Juana, and as a result of this voyage I can say that this island is larger than England and Scotland together, for, beyond these one hundred and seven leagues, there remain to the westward two provinces to which I have not gone. One of these provinces they call "Avan,"[15] and there people are born with tails. These provinces cannot have a length of less than fifty or sixty leagues, as I could understand from those Indians whom I have and who know all the islands.

The other island, Española, has a circumference greater than all Spain from Collioure by the seacoast to Fuenterabia in Vizcaya, for I voyaged along one side for one hundred and eighty-eight great leagues in a straight line from west to east. It is a land to be desired and, when seen, never to be left. I have taken possession of all for their Highnesses, and all are more richly endowed than I know how or am able to say, and I hold all for their Highnesses, so that they may dispose of them as they do of the kingdoms of Castile and as absolutely. But especially, in this Española, in the situation most convenient and in the best position for the mines of gold and for all trade as well with the mainland here as with that there, belonging to the Grand Khan, where will be great trade and profit, I have taken possession of a large town, to which I gave the name "Villa de Navidad," and in it I have made fortifications and a fort, which will now by this time be entirely completed. In it I have left enough men for such a purpose with arms and artillery and provisions for more than a year, and a fusta, and one, a master of all seacraft, to build others, and I have established great friendship with the king of that land, so much so, that he was proud to call me "brother" and to treat me as such. And even were he to change his attitude to one of hostility towards these men, he and his do not know what arms are. They go naked, as I have already said, and they are the most timorous people in the world, so that the men whom I have left there alone would suffice to destroy all that land, and the island is without danger for their persons, if they know how to govern themselves.

In all these islands, it seems to me that all men are content with one woman, and to their chief or king they give as many as twenty. It appears to me that the women work more than do the men. I have not been able to learn if they hold private property; it seemed to me to be that all took a share in whatever any one had, especially of eatable things.

In these islands I have so far found no human monstrosities, as many expected, but on the contrary the whole population is very well formed, nor are they negroes as in Guinea, but their hair is flowing and they are not born where there is intense force in the rays of the sun. It is true that the sun there has great power, although it is distant from the equinoctial line twenty-six degrees. In these islands, where there are high mountains, the cold was severe this winter, but they endure it, being used to it and with the help of meats which they consume with many and extremely hot spices. Thus I have found no monsters, nor had a report of any, except in an island "Carib," which is the second at the coming into the Indies, and which is inhabited by a people who are regarded in all the islands as very fierce and who eat human flesh. They have many canoes with which they range through all the islands of India and pillage and take whatever they can. They are no more malformed than are the others, except that they have the custom of wearing their hair long like women, and they use bows and arrows of the same cane stems, with a small piece of wood at the end, owing to their lack of iron which they do not possess. They are fe-

---

14. A *fusta* is a small galley, often propelled by oars.

15. The name of the northern part of Cuba.

rocious among these other people who are cowardly to an excessive degree, but I make no more account of them than of the rest. These are they who have intercourse with the women of "Matinino," which is the first island met on the way from Spain to the Indies, in which there is not a man.[16] These women engage in no feminine occupation, but use bows and arrows of cane, like those already mentioned, and they arm and protect themselves with plates of copper, of which they have much.

In another island, which they assure me is larger than Española, the people have no hair. In it there is incalculable gold, and from it and from the other islands I bring with me Indians as evidence.

In conclusion, to speak only of what has been accomplished on this voyage, which was so hasty, their Highnesses can see that I will give them as much gold as they may need, if their Highnesses will render me very slight assistance; presently, I will give them spices and cotton, as much as their Highnesses shall command; and mastic, as much as they shall order to be shipped and which, up to now, has been found only in Greece, in the island of Chios, and the Seignory[17] sells it for what it pleases; and aloe, as much as they shall order to be shipped; and slaves, as many as they shall order, and who will be from the idolaters. I believe also that I have found rhubarb and cinnamon, and I shall find a thousand other things of value, which the people whom I have left there will have discovered, for I have not delayed at any point, so far as the wind allowed me to sail, except in the town of Navidad, in order to leave it secured and well established, and in truth I should have done much more if the ships had served me as reason demanded.

---

16. Martinique.

17. The Genoan government.

This is enough. And thus the eternal God, Our Lord, gives to all those who walk in His way triumph over things which appear to be impossible, and this was notably one. For, although men have talked or have written of these lands, all was conjectural, without ocular evidence, but amounted only to this, that those who heard for the most part listened and judged rather by hearsay than from even a small something tangible. So that, since Our Redeemer has given the victory to our most illustrious King and Queen, and to their renowned kingdoms, in so great a matter, for this all Christendom ought to feel delight and make great feasts and give solemn thanks to the Holy Trinity, with many solemn prayers for the great exaltation which they shall have in the turning of so many peoples to our holy faith, and afterwards for the temporal benefits, because not only Spain but all Christendom will have hence refreshment and gain.

This is an account of the facts, thus abridged.

Done in the caravel, off the Canary Islands, on the fifteenth day of February, in the year one thousand four hundred and ninety-three.

At your orders.
The Admiral.

After having written this, and being in the sea of Castile, there came upon me so great a south and southeast wind that I was obliged to ease the ship. But I ran here to-day into this port of Lisbon, which was the greatest marvel in the world, whence I decided to write to their Highnesses. In all the Indies, I have always found weather like May. There I went in thirty-three days and I should have returned in twenty-eight, save for these storms which have detained me for fourteen days, beating about in this sea. Here all the sailors say that never has there been so bad a winter nor so many ships lost.

Done on the fourth day of March.

AMERIGO VESPUCCI (1452?–1512)

An Italian merchant and navigator, Amerigo Vespucci was born into the Florentine professional class to Ser Nastagio di Amerigo Vespucci and Lisa di Giovanni Mini, a family with significant links to the ruling Medici family. He grew up among artists, poets, and intellectuals, and he was tutored alongside Piero Soderini, who would become the head of the Florentine Republic and to whom he would write one of his most famous letters. After serving as secretary during a diplomatic mission to France, in 1492 he traveled to Spain to oversee the management of the Medici banking interests and later became associated with the financing of Columbus's second expedition. As an astronomer and navigator, Vespucci was particularly curious about the ways of determining a ship's position more easily and accurately. In the years that followed, he undertook his own journeys to the Americas.

Vespucci's extant writings offer conflicting accounts of the locations and timing of his voyages. Although his two public letters, *Mundus Novus* (1503) and *Lettera di Amerigo Vespucci* (1505) refer to four journeys across the Atlantic, three unpublished letters uncovered during the eighteenth century called these earlier accounts into question. His voyages from Spain to Cape Verde, Venezuela, and Brazil in 1499 and from Portugal to Brazil and Patagonia in 1501 are unquestioned. However, on the basis of his claims regarding two additional journeys—one in 1497 from Spain to Venezuela and Haiti and another in 1503 from Portugal to Brazil—Vespucci was accused by people, such as Bartolomé de Las Casas, of being a fake. The nature and timing of his voyages appear to have been finessed in order to substantiate claims that Vespucci was the first to discover the Europeans' new world.

One of Vespucci's most famous letters, written to Piero Soderini in 1504, was published in Florence in 1505, quickly reprinted in France and Germany, and later translated into Latin, titled "Mondus Novus" or "New World." Vespucci's 1501 voyage to Brazil and Patagonia was particularly significant because it proved the basis for his assertion that he had discovered a "New World," rather than a part of Asia. Martin Waldseemüller (1470?–1513?), a geographer who was preparing a map of the Europeans' new world, proposed that the new continent should be named for its apparent discoverer. In fact, Waldseemüller attached Vespucci's name only to the southern hemisphere on his famous 1507 map. Later cartographers used the name in their maps of the northern hemisphere as well. Although many disputed the claim that Vespucci had, in fact, "discovered" the continent prior to Columbus, the Europeans' new world continued to be called "America."

LETTER TO PIERO SODERINI, GONFALONIERE OF THE REPUBLIC OF FLORENCE, 1504[1]

Magnificent Lord. After humble reverence and due commendations, etc. It may be that your Magnificence will be surprised by [*this conjunction of*] my rashness and your customary wisdom, in that I should so absurdly bestir myself to write to your Magnificence the present so-prolix letter: knowing [*as I do*] that your Magnificence is continually employed in high councils and affairs concerning the good government of this sublime Republic. And will hold me not only presumptuous, but also idly-meddlesome in setting myself to write things, neither suitable to your station, nor entertaining, and written in barbarous style, and outside of every canon of polite literature: but my confidence which I have in your virtues and in the truth of my writing, which are things [*that*] are not found written neither by the ancients nor by modern writers, as your Magnificence will in the sequel perceive, makes me bold. The chief cause which moved [*me*] to write to you, was at the request of the present bearer, who

is named Benvenuto Benvenuti our Florentine [*fellow-citizen*], very much, as it is proven, your Magnificence's servant, and my very good friend: who happening to be here in this city of Lisbon, begged that I should make communication to your Magnificence of the things seen by me in divers regions of the world, by virtue of four voyages which I have made in discovery of new lands: two by order of the King of Castile, King Don Ferrando VI.,[2] across the great gulph of the Ocean-sea towards the west: and the other two by command of the puissant King Don Manuel King of Portugal,[3] towards the south: Telling me that your Magnificence would take pleasure thereof, and that herein he hoped to do you service: wherefore I set me to do it: because I am assured that your Magnificence holds me in the number of your servants, remembering that in the time of our youth I was your friend, and now [*am your*] servant: and [*remembering our*] going to hear the rudiments of grammar under the fair example and instruction of the venerable monk friar of Saint Mark Fra Giorgio Antonio Vespucci[4]: whose counsels and teaching would to God that I had followed: for as saith

1. Originally written in 1504, the letter was first published in 1505. This text is taken from *The First Four Voyages of Amerigo Vespucci. Translated . . . by M. K.* (1885). Bracketed words are insertions by the original editor and translator.

2. In fact, the order was given not by Ferdinand VI but by Ferdinand V.

3. Manuel I (1469–1521) reigned from 1495 until his death.

4. Vespucci's paternal uncle, Giorgio Antonio Vespucci (1434–1514), was a famous monk and a Greek and Latin scholar.

Petrarch, I should be another man than what I am.[5] How-beit soever, I grieve not: because I have ever taken delight in worthy matters: and although these trifles of mine may not be suitable to your virtues, I will say to you as said Pliny to Mæcenas, you were sometime wont to take pleasure in my prattlings[6]: even though your Magnificence be continuously busied in public affairs, you will take some hour of relaxation to consume a little time in frivolous or amusing things: and as fennel is customarily given atop of delicious viands to fit them for better digestion, so may you, for a relief from your so heavy occupations, order this letter of mine to be read: so that they may withdraw you somewhat from the continual anxiety and assiduous reflection upon public affairs: and if I shall be prolix, I crave pardon, my Magnificent Lord. Your Magnificence shall know that the motive of my coming into this realm of Spain was to traffic in merchandise: and that I pursued this intent about four years: during which I saw and knew the inconstant shiftings of Fortune: and how she kept changing those frail and transitory benefits: and how at one time she holds man on the summit of the wheel, and at another time drives him back from her, and despoils him of what may be called his borrowed riches: so that, knowing the continuous toil which man undergoes to win them, submitting himself to so many anxieties and risks, I resolved to abandon trade, and to fix my aim upon something more praiseworthy and stable: whence it was that I made preparation for going to see part of the world and its wonders: and herefor the time and place presented themselves most opportunely to me: which was that the King Don Ferrando of Castile being about to despatch four ships to discover new lands towards the west, I was chosen by his Highness to go in that fleet to aid in making discovery: and we set out from the port of Cadiz on the 10 day of May 1497, and took our route through the great gulph of the Ocean-sea: in which voyage we were 18 months [*engaged*]: and discovered much continental land and innumerable islands, and great part of them inhabited: whereas there is no mention made by the ancient writers of them: I believe, because they had no knowledge thereof: for, if I remember well, I have read in some one [*of those writers*] that he considered that this Ocean-sea

was an unpeopled sea: and of this opinion was Dante our poet in the xxvi. chapter of the Inferno,[7] where he feigns the death of Ulysses: in which voyage I beheld things of great wondrousness, as your Magnificence shall understand. As I said above, we left the port of Cadiz four consort ships: and began our voyage in a direct course to the Fortunate Isles, which are called to-day *la gran Canaria,*[8] which are situated in the Ocean-sea at the extremity of the inhabited west, [*and*] set in the third climate: over which the North Pole has an elevation of 27 and a half degrees beyond their horizon: and they are 280 leagues distant from this city of Lisbon, by the wind between *mezzo di* and *libeccio:*[9] where we remained eight days, taking in provision of water, and wood, and other necessary things: and from here, having said our prayers, we weighed anchor, and gave the sails to the wind, beginning our course to westward, taking one quarter by south-west: and so we sailed on till at the end of 37 days we reached a land which we deemed to be a continent: which is distant westwardly from the isles of Canary about a thousand leagues beyond the inhabited region within the torrid zone: for we found the North Pole at an elevation of 16 degrees above its horizon, and [*it was*] westward, according to the shewing of our instruments, 75 degrees from the isles of Canary: whereat we anchored with our ships a league and a half from land: and we put out our boats freighted with men and arms: we made towards the land, and before we reached it, had sight of a great number of people who were going along the shore: by which we were much rejoiced: and we observed that they were a naked race: they shewed themselves to stand in fear of us: I believe [*it was*] because they saw us clothed and of other appearance [*than their own*]: they all withdrew to a hill, and for whatsoever signals we made to them of peace and of friendliness, they would not come to parley with us: so that, as the night was now coming on, and as the ships were anchored in a dangerous place, being on a rough and shelterless coast, we decided to remove from there the next day, and to go in search of some harbour or bay, where we might place our ships in safety: and we sailed with the maestrale wind, thus running along the coast with the land ever in sight, continually in our course observing people along the shore: till after having navigated for two

---

5. See Petrarch, *Rerumum Vulgarium Fragmenta I:* "when I was in part another man from what I am now."

6. Actually Vespucci echoes the language of Catullus to Cornelius Nepos in his *libellum:* "for you have been accustomed / to think that there is something in my trifles."

---

7. Dante, *Inferno* XXVI: "of the world that is unpeopled."

8. The Canary Islands.

9. Between south and southwest.

days, we found a place sufficiently secure for the ships, and anchored half a league from land, on which we saw a very great number of people: and this same day we put to land with the boats, and sprang on shore full 40 men in good trim: and still the land's people appeared shy of converse with us, and we were unable to encourage them so much as to make them come to speak with us: and this day we laboured so greatly in giving them of our wares, such as rattles and mirrors, beads, *spalline,* and other trifles, that some of them took confidence and came to discourse with us: and after having made good friends with them, the night coming on, we took our leave of them and returned to the ships: and the next day when the dawn appeared we saw that there were infinite numbers of people upon the beach, and they had their women and children with them: we went ashore, and found that they were all laden with their worldly goods which are suchlike as, in its [*proper*] place, shall be related: and before we reached the land, many of them jumped into the sea and came swimming to receive us at a bowshot's length [*from the shore*], for they are very great swimmers, with as much confidence as if they had for a long time been acquainted with us: and we were pleased with this their confidence. For so much as we learned of their manner of life and customs, it was that they go entirely naked, as well the men as the women, without covering any shameful part, not otherwise than when they issued from their mother's womb. They are of medium stature, very well proportioned: their flesh is of a colour that verges into red like a lion's mane: and I believe that if they went clothed, they would be as white as we[10]: they have not any hair upon the body, except the hair of the head which is long and black, and especially in the women, whom it renders handsome: in aspect they are not very good-looking, because they have broad faces, so that they would seem Tartar-like: they let no hair grow on their eyebrows, nor on their eyelids, nor elsewhere, except the hair of the head: for they hold hairiness to be a filthy thing: they are very light-footed in walking and in running, as well the men as the women: so that a woman recks nothing of running a league or two, as many times we saw them do: and herein

they have a very great advantage over us Christians: they swim [*with an expertness*] beyond all belief, and the women better than the men: for we have many times found and seen them swimming two leagues out at sea without any thing to rest upon. Their arms are bows and arrows very well made, save that [*the arrows*] are not [*tipped*] with iron nor any other kind of hard metal: and instead of iron they put animals' or fishes' teeth, or a spike of tough wood, with the point hardened by fire: they are sure marksmen, for they hit whatever they aim at: and in some places the women use these bows: they have other weapons, such as fire-hardened spears, and also clubs with knobs, beautifully carved. Warfare is used amongst them, which they carry on against people not of their own language, very cruelly, without granting life to any one, except [*to reserve him*] for greater suffering. When they go to war, they take their women with them, not that these may fight, but because they carry behind them their worldly goods: for a woman carries on her back for thirty or forty leagues a load which no man could bear: as we have many times seen them do. They are not accustomed to have any Captain, nor do they go in any ordered array, for every one is lord of himself: and the cause of their wars is not for lust of dominion, nor of extending their frontiers, nor for inordinate covetousness, but for some ancient enmity which in by-gone times arose amongst them: and when asked why they made war, they knew not any other reason to give us than that they did so to avenge the death of their ancestors, or of their parents: these people have neither King, nor Lord, nor do they yield obedience to any one, for they live in their own liberty: and how they be stirred up to go to war is [*this*] that when the enemies have slain or captured any of them, his oldest kinsman rises up and goes about the highways haranguing them to go with him and avenge the death of such his kinsman: and so are they stirred up by fellow-feeling: they have no judicial system, nor do they punish the ill-doer: nor does the father, nor the mother chastise the children: and marvellously [*seldom*] or never did we see any dispute among them: in their conversation they appear simple, and they are very cunning and acute in that which concerns them: they speak little and in a low tone: they use the same articulations as we, since they form their utterances either with the palate, or with the teeth, or on the lips: except that they give different names to things. Many are the varieties of tongues: for in every 100 leagues we found a change of language, so that they are not understandable each to the other. The manner of their living is very barbarous, for they do not eat at certain hours, and as

10. Here and in subsequent passages, Vespucci clearly echoes Columbus's *Diario.* In his entry of December 16, 1492, Columbus wrote "they are the handsomest men and women I have found until now. They are exceedingly white, and if they wore clothing and were protected from the sun and the air they would be almost as white as the people in Spain."

often-times as they will: and it is not much of a boon to them that the will may come more at midnight than by day, for they eat at all hours: and they eat upon the ground without a table-cloth or any other cover, for they have their meats either in earthen basins which they make themselves, or in the halves of pumpkins: they sleep in certain very large nettings made of cotton, suspended in the air: and although this their [*fashion of*] sleeping may seem uncomfortable, I say that it is sweet to sleep in those [*nettings*]: and we slept better in them than in the counterpanes. They are a people smooth and clean of body, because of so continually washing themselves as they do: when, saving your reverence, they evacuate the stomach they do their utmost not to be observed: and as much as in this they are cleanly and bashful, so much the more are they filthy and shameless in making water: since, while standing speaking to us, without turning round or shewing any shame, they let go their nastiness, for in this they have no shame: there is no custom of marriages amongst them: each man takes as many women as he lists: and when he desires to repudiate them, he repudiates them without any imputation of wrong-doing to him, or of disgrace to the woman: for in this the woman has as much liberty as the man: they are not very jealous and are immoderately libidinous, and the women much more so than the men, so that for decency I omit to tell you the artifice they practice to gratify their inordinate lust: they are very prolific women, and do not shirk any work during their pregnancies: and their travails in childbed are so light that, a single day after parturition, they go abroad everywhere, and especially to wash themselves in the rivers, and are [*then*] as sound and healthy as fishes: they are so void of affection and cruel, that if they be angry with their husbands they immediately adopt an artificial method by which the embryo is destroyed in the womb, and procure abortion, and they slay an infinite number of creatures by that means: they are women of elegant persons very well proportioned, so that in their bodies there appears no ill-shaped part or limb: and although they go entirely naked, they are fleshy women, and, of their sexual organ, that portion which he who has never seen it may imagine, is not visible, for they conceal with their thighs everything except that part for which nature did not provide, which is, speaking modestly, the pectignone.[11] In fine, they have no shame of their shameful parts, any more than we have in displaying the nose and the mouth: it is marvellously

[*rare*] that you shall see a woman's paps hang low, or her belly fallen in by too much childbearing, or other wrinkles, for they all appear as though they had never brought forth children: they shewed themselves very desirous of having connexion with us Christians. Amongst those people we did not learn that they had any law, nor can they be called Moors nor Jews, and [*they are*] worse than pagans: because we did not observe that they offered any sacrifice: nor even had they a house of prayer: their manner of living I judge to be Epicurean: their dwellings are in common: and their houses [*are*] made in the style of huts, but strongly made, and constructed with very large trees, and covered over with palm-leaves, secure against storms and winds: and in some places [*they are*] of so great breadth and length, that in one single house we found there were 600 souls: and we saw a village of only thirteen houses where there were four thousand souls: every eight or ten years they change their habitations: and when asked why they did so: [*they said it was*] because of the soil which, from its filthiness, was already unhealthy and corrupted, and that it bred aches in their bodies, which seemed to us a good reason: their riches consist of birds' plumes of many colours, or of rosaries which they make from fish-bones, or of white or green stones which they put in their cheeks and in their lips and ears, and of many other things which we in no wise value: they use no trade, they neither buy nor sell. In fine, they live and are contented with that which nature gives them. The wealth that we enjoy in this our Europe and elsewhere, such as gold, jewels, pearls, and other riches, they hold as nothing: and although they have them in their own lands, they do not labour to obtain them, nor do they value them. They are liberal in giving, for it is rarely they deny you anything: and on the other hand, liberal in asking, when they shew themselves your friends: the greatest sign of friendship which they shew you is that they give you their wives and their daughters, and a father or a mother deems himself [*or herself*] highly honored, when they bring you a daughter, even though she be a young virgin, if you sleep with her: and hereunto they use every expression of friendship. When they die, they use divers manners of obsequies, and some they bury with water and victuals at their heads: thinking that they shall have [*whereof*] to eat: they have not nor do they use ceremonies of torches nor of lamentation. In some other places, they use the most barbarous and inhuman burial, which is that when a suffering or infirm [*person*] is as it were at the last pass of death, his kinsmen carry him into a large forest, and attach one of those nets of theirs, in which they sleep, to two trees, and then put him in it, and

---

11. Pubic bone.

dance around him for a whole day: and when the night comes on they place at his bolster, water with other victuals, so that he may be able to subsist for four or six days: and then they leave him alone and return to the village: and if the sick man helps himself, and eats, and drinks, and survives, he returns to the village, and his [*friends*] receive him with ceremony: but few are they who escape: without receiving any further visit they die, and that is their sepulture: and they have many other customs which for prolixity are not related. They use in their sicknesses various forms of medicines, so different from ours that we marvelled how any one escaped: for many times I saw that with a man sick of fever, when it heightened upon him, they bathed him from head to foot with a large quantity of cold water: then they lit a great fire around him, making him turn and turn again every two hours, until they tired him and left him to sleep, and many were [*thus*] cured: with this they make much use of dieting, for they remain three days without eating, and also of blood-letting, but not from the arm, only from the thighs and the loins and the calf of the leg: also they provoke vomiting with their herbs which are put into the mouth: and they use many other remedies which it would be long to relate: they are much vitiated in the phlegm and in the blood because of their food which consists chiefly of roots of herbs, and fruits and fish: they have no seed of wheat nor other grain: and for their ordinary use and feeding, they have a root of a tree, from which they make flour, tolerably good, and they call it Iuca,[12] and another which they call Cazabi,[13] and another Ignami[14]: they eat little flesh except human flesh: for your Magnificence must know that herein they are so inhuman that they outdo every custom [*even*] of beasts: for they eat all their enemies whom they kill or capture, as well females as males with so much savagery, that [*merely*] to relate it appears a horrible thing: how much more so to see it, as, infinite times and in many places, it was my hap to see it: and they wondered to hear us say that we did not eat our enemies: and this your Magnificence may take for certain, that their other barbarous customs are such that expression is too weak for the reality: and as in these four voyages I have seen so many things diverse from our customs, I prepared to write a common-place-book which I name LE QUAT-

TRO GIORNATE[15]: in which I have set down the greater part of the things which I saw, sufficiently in detail, so far as my feeble wit has allowed me: which I have not yet published, because I have so ill a taste for my own things that I do not relish those which I have written, notwithstanding that many encourage me to publish it: therein everything will be seen in detail: so that I shall not enlarge further in this chapter: as in the course of the letter we shall come to many other things which are particular: let this suffice for the general. At this beginning, we saw nothing in the land of much profit, except some show of gold: I believe the cause of it was that we did not know the language: but in so far as concerns the situation and condition of the land, it could not be better: we decided to leave that place, and to go further on, continuously coasting the shore: upon which we made frequent descents, and held converse with a great number of people: and at the end of some days we went into a harbour where we underwent very great danger: and it pleased the Holy Ghost to save us: and it was in this wise. We landed in a harbour, where we found a village built like Venice upon the water: there were about 44 large dwellings in the form of huts erected upon very thick piles, and they had their doors or entrances in the style of drawbridges: and from each house one could pass through all, by means of the drawbridges which stretched from house to house: and when the people thereof had seen us, they appeared to be afraid of us, and immediately drew up all the bridges: and while we were looking at this strange action, we saw coming across the sea about 22 canoes, which are a kind of boats of theirs, constructed from a single tree: which came towards our boats, as they had been surprised by our appearance and clothes, and kept wide of us: and thus remaining, we made signals to them that they should approach us, encouraging them with every token of friendliness: and seeing that they did not come, we went to them, and they did not stay for us, but made to the land, and, by signs, told us to wait, and that they should soon return: and they went to a hill in the background, and did not delay long: when they returned, they led with them 16 of their girls, and entered with these into their canoes, and came to the boats: and in each boat they put 4 of the girls. That we marvelled at this behaviour your Magnificence can imagine how much, and they placed themselves with their canoes among our boats, coming to speak with us:

_____

12. Yucca.

13. Cassava.

14. Yams.

_____

15. *The Four Journeys* would be published in 1507.

insomuch that we deemed it a mark of friendliness: and while thus engaged, we beheld a great number of people advance swimming towards us across the sea, who came from the houses: and as they were drawing near to us without any apprehension: just then there appeared at the doors of the houses certain old women, uttering very loud cries and tearing their hair to exhibit grief: whereby they made us suspicious, and we each betook ourselves to arms: and instantly the girls whom we had in the boats, threw themselves into the sea, and the men of the canoes drew away from us, and began with their bows to shoot arrows at us: and those who were swimming each carried a lance held, as covertly as they could, beneath the water: so that, recognizing the treachery, we engaged with them, not merely to defend ourselves, but to attack them vigorously, and we overturned with our boats many of their almadie or canoes, for so they call them, we made a slaughter [*of them*], and they all flung themselves into the water to swim, leaving their canoes abandoned, with considerable loss on their side, they went swimming away to the shore: there died of them about 15 or 20, and many were left wounded: and of ours 5 were wounded, and all, by the grace of God, escaped [*death*]: we captured two of the girls and two men: and we proceeded to their houses, and entered therein, and in them all we found nothing else than two old women and a sick man: we took away from them many things, but of small value: and we would not burn their houses, because it seemed to us [*as though that would be*] a burden upon our conscience: and we returned to our boats with five prisoners: and betook ourselves to the ships, and put a pair of irons on the feet of each of the captives, except the little girls: and when the night came on, the two girls and one of the men fled away in the most subtle manner possible: and next day we decided to quit that harbour and go further onwards: we proceeded continuously skirting the coast, [*until*] we had sight of another tribe distant perhaps some 80 leagues from the former tribe: and we found them very different in speech and customs: we resolved to cast anchor, and went ashore with the boats, and we saw on the beach a great number of people amounting probably to 4000 souls: and when we had reached the shore, they did not stay for us, and betook themselves to flight through the forests, abandoning their things: we jumped on land, and took a pathway that led to the forest: and at the distance of a bow-shot we found their tents, where they had made very large fires, and two [*of them*] were cooking their victuals, and roasting several animals, and fish of many kinds: where we saw that they were roasting a certain animal[16] which seemed to be a serpent, save that it had no wings, and was in its appearance so loathsome that we marvelled much at its savageness: Thus went we on through their houses, or rather tents, and found many of those serpents alive, and they were tied by the feet and had a cord around their snouts, so that they could not open their mouths, as is done [*in Europe*] with mastiff-dogs so that they may not bite: they were of such savage aspect that none of us dared to take one away, thinking that they were poisonous: they are of the bigness of a kid, and in length an ell and a half: their feet are long and thick, and armed with big claws: they have a hard skin, and are of various colours: they have the muzzle and face of a serpent: and from their snouts there rises a crest like a saw which extends along the middle of the back as far as the tip of the tail: in fine we deemed them to be serpents and venomous, and [*nevertheless, those people*] ate them: we found that they made bread out of little fishes which they took from the sea, first boiling them, [*then*] pounding them, and making thereof a paste, or bread, and they baked them on the embers: thus did they eat them: we tried it, and found that it was good: they had so many other kinds of eatables, and especially of fruits and roots, that it would be a large matter to describe them in detail: and seeing that the people did not return, we decided not to touch nor take away anything of theirs, so as better to reassure them: and we left in the tents for them many of our things, placed where they should see them, and returned by night to our ships: and the next day, when it was light, we saw on the beach an infinite number of people: and we landed: and although they appeared timorous towards us, they took courage nevertheless to hold converse with us, giving us whatever we asked of them: and shewing themselves very friendly towards us, they told us that those were their dwellings, and that they had come hither for the purpose of fishing: and they begged that we would visit their dwellings and villages, because they desired to receive us as friends: and they engaged in such friendship because of the two captured men whom we had with us, as these were their enemies: insomuch that, in view of such importunity on their part, holding a council, we determined that 28 of us Christians in good array should go with them, and in the firm resolve to die if it should be necessary: and after we had been here some three days, we

---

16. An iguana.

went with them inland: and at three leagues from the coast we came to a village of many people and few houses, for there were no more than nine [*of these*]: where we were received with such and so many barbarous ceremonies that the pen suffices not to write them down: for there were dances, and songs, and lamentations mingled with rejoicing, and great quantities of food: and here we remained the night: where they offered us their women, so that we were unable to withstand them: and after having been here that night and half the next day, so great was the number of people who came wondering to behold us that they were beyond counting: and the most aged begged us to go with them to other villages which were further inland, making display of doing us the greatest honour: wherefore we decided to go: and it would be impossible to tell you how much honour they did us: and we went to several villages, so that we were nine days journeying, so that our Christians who had remained with the ships were already apprehensive concerning us: and when we were about 18 leagues in the interior of the land, we resolved to return to the ships: and on our way back, such was the number of people, as well men as women, that came with us as far as the sea, that it was a wondrous thing: and if any of us became weary of the march, they carried us in their nets very refreshingly: and in crossing the rivers, which are many and very large, they passed us over by skilful means so securely that we ran no danger whatever, and many of them came laden with the things which they had given us, which consisted in their sleeping-nets, and very rich feathers, many bows and arrows, innumerable popinjays of divers colours: and others brought with them loads of their household goods, and of animals: but a greater marvel will I tell you, that, when we had to cross a river, he deemed himself lucky who was able to carry us on his back: and when we reached the sea, our boats having arrived, we entered into them: and so great was the struggle which they made to get into our boats, and to come to see our ships, that we marvelled [*thereat*]: and in our boats we took as many of them as we could, and made our way to the ships, and so many [*others*] came swimming that we found ourselves embarrassed in seeing so many people in the ships, for there were over a thousand persons all naked and unarmed: they were amazed by our [*nautical*] gear and contrivances, and the size of the ships: and with them there occurred to us a very laughable affair, which was that we decided to fire off some of our great guns, and when the explosion took place, most of them through fear cast themselves [*into the sea*] to swim, not otherwise than

frogs on the margins of a pond, when they see something that frightens them, will jump into the water, just so did those people: and those who remained in the ships were so terrified that we regretted our action: however we reassured them by telling them that with those arms we slew our enemies: and when they had amused themselves in the ships the whole day, we told them to go away because we desired to depart that night, and so separating from us with much friendship and love, they went away to land. Amongst that people and in their land, I knew and beheld so many of their customs and ways of living, that I do not care to enlarge upon them: for Your Magnificence must know that in each of my voyages I have noted the most wonderful things, and I have indited it all in a volume after the manner of a geography: and I intitle it LE QUATTRO GIORNATE: in which work the things are comprised in detail, and as yet there is no copy of it given out, as it is necessary for me to revise it. This land is very populous, and full of inhabitants, and of numberless rivers, [*and*] animals: few [*of which*] resemble ours, excepting lions, panthers, stags, pigs, goats, and deer: and even these have some dissimilarities of form: they have no horses nor mules, nor, saving your reverence, asses nor dogs, nor any kind of sheep or oxen: but so numerous are the other animals which they have, and all are savage, and of none do they make use for their service, that they could not be counted. What shall we say of others [*such as*] birds? which are so numerous, and of so many kinds, and of such various-coloured plumages, that it is a marvel to behold them. The soil is very pleasant and fruitful, full of immense woods and forests: and it is always green, for the foliage never drops off. The fruits are so many that they are numberless and entirely different from ours. This land is within the torrid zone, close to or just under the parallel described by the Tropic of Cancer: where the pole of the horizon has an elevation of 23 degrees, at the extremity of the second climate. Many tribes came to see us, and wondered at our faces and our whiteness: and they asked us whence we came: and we gave them to understand that we had come from heaven, and that we were going to see the world, and they believed it. In this land we placed baptismal fonts, and an infinite [*number of*] people were baptized, and they called us in their language Carabi, which means men of great wisdom. We took our departure from that port: and the province is called Lariab: and we navigated along the coast, always in sight of land, until we had run 870 leagues of it, still going in the direction of the maestrale [*north-west*] making in our course many halts, and holding intercourse with many peoples: and in several places we obtained gold by barter but not much in quantity, for we had done enough in discovering the land and learning that they had gold. We had now been thirteen months on the voyage: and the vessels and the tackling were already much damaged, and the men worn out by fatigue: we decided by general council to haul our ships on land and examine them for the purpose of stanching leaks, as they made much water, and of caulking and tarring them afresh, and [*then*] returning towards Spain: and when we came to this determination, we were close to a harbour the best in the world: into which we entered with our vessels: where we found an immense number of people: who received us with much friendliness: and on the shore we made a bastion with our boats and with barrels and casks, and our artillery, which commanded every point: and our ships having been unloaded and lightened, we drew them upon land, and repaired them in everything that was needful: and the land's people gave us very great assistance: and continually furnished us with their victuals: so that in this port we tasted little of our own, which suited our game well: for the stock of provisions which we had for our return-passage was little and of sorry kind: where [*i.e., there*] we remained 37 days: and went many times to their villages? where they paid us the greatest honour: and [*now*] desiring to depart upon our voyage, they made complaint to us how at certain times of the year there came from over the sea to this their land, a race of people very cruel, and enemies of theirs: and [*who*] by means of treachery or of violence slew many of them, and ate them: and some they made captives, and carried them away to their houses, or country: and how they could scarcely contrive to defend themselves from them, making signs to us that [*those*] were an island-people and lived out in the sea about a hundred leagues away: and so piteously did they tell us this that we believed them: and we promised to avenge them of so much wrong: and they remained overjoyed herewith: and many of them offered to come along with us, but we did not wish to take them for many reasons, save that we took seven of them, on condition that they should come [*i.e., return home*] afterwards in [*their own*] canoes because we did not desire to be obliged to take them back to their country: and they were contented: and so we departed from those people, leaving them very friendly towards us: and having repaired our ships, and sailing for seven days out to sea between north-east and east: and at the end of the seven days we came upon the islands, which were many, some [*of them*] inhabited, and others deserted: and we anchored at one of them: where

we saw a numerous people who called it Iti[17]: and having manned our boats with strong crews, and [*taken ammunition for*] three cannon-shots in each, we made for land: where we found [*assembled*] about 400 men, and many women, and all naked like the former [*peoples*]. They were of good bodily presence, and seemed right warlike men: for they were armed with their weapons, which are bows, arrows, and lances: and most of them had square wooden targets: and bore them in such wise that they did not impede the drawing of the bow: and when we had come with our boats to about a bowshot of the land, they all sprang into the water to shoot their arrows at us and to prevent us from leaping upon shore: and they all had their bodies painted of various colours, and [*were*] plumed with feathers: and the interpreters who were with us told us that when [*those*] displayed themselves so painted and plumed, it was to betoken that they wanted to fight: and so much did they persist in preventing us from landing, that we were compelled to play with our artillery: and when they heard the explosion, and saw some of them fall dead, they all drew back to the land: wherefore, forming our council, we resolved that 42 of our men should spring on shore, and, if they waited for us, fight them: thus having leaped to land with our weapons, they advanced towards us, and we fought for about an hour, for we had but little advantage of them, except that our arbalasters and gunners killed some of them, and they wounded certain of our men: and this was because they did not stand to receive us within reach of lance-thrust or sword-blow: and so much vigour did we put forth at last, that we came to sword-play, and when they tasted our weapons, they betook themselves to flight through the mountains and the forests, and left us conquerors of the field with many of them dead and a good number wounded: and for that day we took no other pains to pursue them, because we were very weary, and we returned to our ships, with so much gladness on the part of the seven men who had come with us that they could not contain themselves [*for joy*]: and when the next day arrived, we beheld coming across the land a great number of people, with signals of battle, continually sounding horns, and various other instruments which they use in their wars: and all [*of them*] painted and feathered, so that it was a very strange sight to behold them: wherefore all the ships held council, and it was resolved that since this people desired hostility with us, we should proceed to encounter them and try by every means

---

17. Haiti.

to make them friends: in case they would not have our friendship, that we should treat them as foes, and so many of them as we might be able to capture should all be our slaves: and having armed ourselves as best we could, we advanced towards the shore, and they sought not to hinder us from landing, I believe from fear of the cannons: and we jumped on land, 57 men in four squadrons, each one [*consisting of*] a captain and his company: and we came to blows with them: and after a long battle [*in which*] many of them [*were*] slain, we put them to flight, and pursued them to a village, having made about 250 of them captives, and we burnt the village, and returned to our ships with victory and 250 prisoners, leaving many of them dead and wounded, and of ours there were no more than one killed, and 22 wounded, who all escaped [*i.e., re-covered*], God be thanked. We arranged our departure, and the seven men, of whom five were wounded, took an island-canoe, and, with seven prisoners that we gave them, four women and three men, returned to their [*own*] country full of gladness, wondering at our strength: and we thereon made sail for Spain with 222 captive slaves: and reached the port of Calis [*Cadiz*] on the 15 day of October 1498, where we were well received and sold our slaves. Such is what befel me, most noteworthy, in this my first voyage.

BARTOLOMÉ DE LAS CASAS (1474–1566)

An early critic of Spanish colonization, Bartolomé de Las Casas initially lived in the Americas as a Spanish soldier and colonist and later became an activist and defender of the Indians he himself had once enslaved. Las Casas was born in Seville in 1474 to the merchant Pedro de Las Casas and his wife, who died when her son was a child. The family had enough wealth to allow their son to study Latin, rather than join the family merchant business. Surely his father's taking sail, with three of his uncles, on Columbus's second journey had an impact upon the young man's interest in the Americas. In 1502, as a part of the largest Spanish expedition ever to the Americas, Las Casas left Spain in the 2,500-man fleet of Nicolas de Ovando. Ovando was charged with reestablishing royal authority in Hispaniola and ensuring that what became known as the *encomienda* system, a system of tribute equivalent to forced labor, was enforced.

After several years in the Americas, Las Casas returned to Europe and was ordained in Rome as a deacon before he returned to the Indies. In 1511 he traveled as chaplain with Diego de Velasquez and Pámphilo de Narváez when they set out to conquer Cuba. The land and Indian labor he received as a reward for his work during this conquest moved him into a comfortable, content life as a landowner. Gradually, however, Las Casas's feelings about the Spanish treatment of Native Americans changed significantly, and in 1514 he shocked many people by preaching a sermon that condemned the ill treatment of the indigenous peoples. After freeing his own Indian slaves, he returned to Spain in 1515, seeking an audience with the king so that he could describe the wrongs perpetuated against the Indians. Las Casas's early discussions with King Ferdinand in 1515 and Charles V in 1520 met with sympathy, but they achieved no action. After a failed attempt to establish a peaceful settlement in Venezuela in 1520, Las Casas temporarily withdrew from his life as an activist and became a monk of the Dominican order. While in the monastery, he began his *Apologetica Historias de Las Indies* and the *Historia de Las Indies,* both of which would be published after his death. He also wrote about the advisability of peacefully converting the Native Americans, rather than simply conquering them militarily.

Las Casas accepted Spain's authority over the Americas without question, but was sharply critical of the *encomenderos'* treatment of the native populations. (*Encomenderos* implemented the *encomienda* system.) He believed that the basis for Spain's rights in the Americas lay in the 1493 Bulls of Donation in which Pope Alexander VI "donated" sovereignty over the Americas to Isabella and Ferdinand, on the assumption that they would convert native inhabitants to Christianity. Thus Las Casas did not challenge church or state in his argument in favor of the rights and humanity of Native Americans. Nor did he believe that the Spanish colonizers should simply leave the inhabitants of the Americas alone. The Spanish had an obligation to expose Indians to Christianity, Las Casas asserted, but they did not have a right to ownership of their persons or their labor. In his eyes, the Indians were Spanish subjects, whose poor treatment under Spanish rule gave them the right to wage "just war" against the Spanish.

Las Casas devoted the rest of his life to arguing for the humanity of Native Americans and their legal rights as Spanish subjects. Gradually his efforts seemed to bear fruit. In 1537 Pope Paul III created a bull, *Sublimis Deus,* which established Indians as people with souls whose lives and property deserved protection. After Las Casas presented his *Very Brief Relation of the Devastation of the Indies* to the Royal Court in 1542, he helped bring about the Crown's New Laws, which phased out Indian slavery and the *encomienda* system. In the end, however, Spain's New Laws proved so unpopular and difficult to enforce that they were partially repealed. Indeed, when Las Casas returned to the Americas in 1544 as the bishop of Chiapas, a particularly poor area of New Spain, he was confronted head-on with the difficulty of enforcing the New Laws and changing the model of Spanish colonialism that had brought wealth to so many. After his return to Spain in 1547, he continued his writings on the cause of Native Americans.

When his *Brief Relation* was published in Seville, Spain, in 1552, it provoked dramatic reactions. Some people were horrified to learn of the conquistadores' actions in New Spain; others were shocked that Las Casas would make those actions public knowledge. Although Las Casas's immediate audience was Charles V, whom he sought to petition for justice, he also wished to reach the royal administration and the international community as well. When the *Brief Relation* was soon translated into Dutch, French, and English, Las Casas reached the broad audience he sought, though with somewhat unintended consequences. Other nations, particularly Protestant nations, saw the text as offering evidence of the uniquely Spanish evils in the New World. Las Casas's *Brief Relation* became the basis for the Protestant "Black Legend," which vilified the Spanish national character. Las Casas's most lasting reputation, however, is based upon his fifty-year career as a defender of the rights of indigenous peoples.

from A SHORT ACCOUNT OF THE DESTRUCTION OF THE INDIES[1]

Prologue

of Bishop Brother Bartolomé de Las Casas, or Casaus, to the most high and most mighty Prince of Spain, our Lord the Prince Philip[2]

Most high and most mighty Lord:

As Divine Providence has ordained that the world shall, for the benefit and proper government of the human race, be divided into kingdoms and peoples and that these shall be ruled by kings, who are (as Homer[3] has it) fathers and shepherds to their people and are, accordingly, the noblest and most virtuous of beings, there is no doubt, nor could there in all reason be any such doubt, but that these kings entertain nothing save that which is morally unimpeachable. It follows that if the commonwealth suffers from some defect, or shortcoming, or evil, the reason can only be that the ruler is unaware of it; once the matter is brought to his notice, he will work with the utmost diligence to set matters right and will not rest content until the evil has been eradicated. This would appear to be the sense of the words of Solomon in the Bible: 'A king that sitteth in the throne of judgement scattereth away all evil with his eyes'.[4] For, granted the innate and natural virtue of the ruler, it follows that the simple knowledge that something is wrong in his kingdom is quite sufficient to ensure that he will see that it is corrected, for he will not tolerate any such evil for a moment longer than it takes him to right it.

Contemplating, therefore (most mighty Lord), as a man with more than fifty years' experience of seeing at first hand the evil and the harm, the losses and diminutions suffered by those great kingdoms, each so vast and so wonderful that it would be more appropriate to refer to them as the New World of the Americas—kingdoms granted and entrusted by God and His Church to the Spanish Crown so that they might be properly ruled and governed, converted to the Faith, and tenderly nurtured to

---

1. *A Short Account of the Destruction of the Indies* was originally published in Spain in 1552. This version is the translation by Nigel Griffin (1992).

2. Philip, prince of Spain, heir to the throne occupied by his father, Emperor Charles V, until 1556.

3. The epic poet Homer wrote during the eighth century B.C.

4. Proverbs 20:8.

full material and spiritual prosperity—[5] I am persuaded that, if Your Highness had been informed of even a few of the excesses which this New World has witnessed, all of them surpassing anything that men hitherto have imagined even in their wildest dreams, Your Highness would not have delayed for even one moment before entreating His Majesty to prevent any repetition of the atrocities which go under the name of 'conquests': excesses which, if no move is made to stop them, will be committed time and again, and which (given that the indigenous peoples of the region are naturally so gentle, so peace-loving, so humble and so docile) are of themselves iniquitous, tyrannical, contrary to natural, canon, and civil law, and are deemed wicked and are condemned and proscribed by all such legal codes. I therefore concluded that it would constitute a criminal neglect of my duty to remain silent about the enormous loss of life as well as the infinite number of human souls despatched to Hell in the course of such 'conquests', and so resolved to publish an account of a few such outrages (and they can be only a few out of the countless number of such incidents that I could relate) in order to make that account the more accessible to Your Highness.

Thus it was that, when the then bishop of Cartagena and tutor to your Highness, the archbishop of Toledo,[6] asked me for a copy of my *Account,* I duly gave him one and this he presented to Your Highness. But Your Highness has been fully occupied with journeys, by land and sea, as well as other pressing royal business,[7] and it may well be that Your Highness has never found the time to read the *Account,* or has perhaps allowed it to slip to the back of your mind. Meanwhile, the boldness and the unreason of those who count it as nothing to drench the Americas in human blood and to dispossess the people who are the natural masters and dwellers in those vast and marvellous kingdoms, killing a thousand million of them, and stealing treasures beyond compare, grow by the day, and, masquerading under false colours, they do everything within their power to obtain further licence to continue their conquests (licence that cannot be granted without infringing natural and divine law and thereby conniving at the gravest of mortal sins, worthy of the most terrible and everlasting punishment). I therefore determined to present Your Highness with this *Short Account,* which is but a brief digest of the many and various outrages and depredations which could and should be recorded. I implore Your Highness to accept it and to read it in that spirit of clemency and royal benevolence with which Your Highness traditionally approaches the works of those of Your Highness's subjects and servants whose only desire is to serve the public good and the interests of the Crown. It is my fervent hope that, once Your Highness perceives the extent of the injustices suffered by these innocent peoples and the way in which they are being destroyed and crushed underfoot, unjustly and for no other reason than to satisfy the greed and ambition of those whose purpose it is to commit such wicked atrocities, Your Highness will see fit to beg and entreat His Majesty to refuse all those who seek royal licence for such evil and detestable ventures, and to put a stop once and for all to their infernal clamour in such a way that nobody will henceforth dare to make such a request nor even to mention ventures of this kind.

This, Your Royal Highness, is a matter on which action is both urgent and necessary if God is to continue to watch over the Crown of Castile and ensure its future well-being and prosperity, both spiritual and temporal. Amen.

[Preface]

The Americas were discovered in 1492, and the first Christian settlements established by the Spanish the following year. It is accordingly forty-nine years now since Spaniards began arriving in numbers in this part of the world.[8] They first settled the large and fertile island of Hispaniola,[9] which boasts six hundred leagues of coastline and is surrounded by a great many other large islands, all of them, as I saw for myself, with as high a native population as anywhere on earth. Of the coast of the mainland, which, at its nearest point, is a little over two hundred and fifty leagues from Hispaniola, more than ten

---

5. A reference to the 1493 Bulls of Donation, whereby Pope Alexander VI "donated" any lands newly discovered in the Americas to the Catholic sovereigns Ferdinand and Isabella.

6. Juan Martínez de Silíco emerged from a laboring background to assume prominent academic and religious positions.

7. Perhaps a reference to Philip's 1549 trip to the Netherlands.

---

8. Las Casas wrote the *Short Account* in 1542.

9. Today, Hispaniola comprises the Dominican Republic and Haiti.

thousand leagues[10] had been explored by 1541, and more are being discovered every day. This coastline, too, was swarming with people and it would seem, if we are to judge by those areas so far explored, that the Almighty selected this part of the world as home to the greater part of the human race.

God made all the peoples of this area, many and varied as they are, as open and as innocent as can be imagined. The simplest people in the world—unassuming, long-suffering, unassertive, and submissive—they are without malice or guile, and are utterly faithful and obedient both to their own native lords and to the Spaniards in whose service they now find themselves. Never quarrelsome or belligerent or boisterous, they harbour no grudges and do not seek to settle old scores; indeed, the notions of revenge, rancour, and hatred are quite foreign to them. At the same time, they are among the least robust of human beings: their delicate constitutions make them unable to withstand hard work or suffering and render them liable to succumb to almost any illness, no matter how mild. Even the common people are no tougher than princes or than other Europeans born with a silver spoon in their mouths and who spend their lives shielded from the rigours of the outside world. They are also among the poorest people on the face of the earth; they own next to nothing and have no urge to acquire material possessions. As a result they are neither ambitious nor greedy, and are totally uninterested in worldly power. Their diet is every bit as poor and as monotonous, in quantity and in kind, as that enjoyed by the Desert Fathers. Most of them go naked, save for a loincloth to cover their modesty; at best they may wrap themselves in a piece of cotton material a yard or two square. Most sleep on matting, although a few possess a kind of hanging net, known in the language of Hispaniola as a hammock. They are innocent and pure in mind and have a lively intelligence, all of which makes them particularly receptive to learning and understanding the truths of our Catholic faith and to being instructed in virtue; indeed, God has invested them with fewer impediments in this regard than any other people on earth. Once they begin to learn of the Christian faith they become so keen to know more, to receive the Sacraments, and to worship God, that the missionaries who instruct them do truly have to be men of exceptional patience and forbearance; and over the years I have time and again met Spanish laymen who have been so struck by the natural good-

ness that shines through these people that they frequently can be heard to exclaim: 'These would be the most blessed people on earth if only they were given the chance to convert to Christianity.'

It was upon these gentle lambs, imbued by the Creator with all the qualities we have mentioned, that from the very first day they clapped eyes on them the Spanish fell like ravening wolves upon the fold, or like tigers and savage lions who have not eaten meat for days. The pattern established at the outset has remained unchanged to this day, and the Spaniards still do nothing save tear the natives to shreds, murder them and inflict upon them untold misery, suffering and distress, tormenting, harrying and persecuting them mercilessly. We shall in due course describe some of the many ingenious methods of torture they have invented and refined for this purpose, but one can get some idea of the effectiveness of their methods from the figures alone. When the Spanish first journeyed there, the indigenous population of the island of Hispaniola stood at some three million; today only two hundred survive. The island of Cuba, which extends for a distance almost as great as that separating Valladolid from Rome, is now to all intents and purposes uninhabited; and two other large, beautiful and fertile islands, Puerto Rico and Jamaica, have been similarly devastated. Not a living soul remains today on any of the islands of the Bahamas, which lie to the north of Hispaniola and Cuba, even though every single one of the sixty or so islands in the group, as well as those known as the Isles of Giants and others in the area, both large and small, is more fertile and more beautiful than the Royal Gardens in Seville and the climate is as healthy as anywhere on earth. The native population, which once numbered some five hundred thousand, was wiped out by forcible expatriation to the island of Hispaniola, a policy adopted by the Spaniards in an endeavour to make up losses among the indigenous population of that island. One God-fearing individual was moved to mount an expedition to seek out those who had escaped the Spanish trawl[11] and were still living in the Bahamas and to save their souls by converting them to Christianity, but, by the end of a search lasting three whole years, they had found only the eleven survivors I saw with my own eyes.[12] A further thirty or so islands in the region of Puerto Rico are also now uninhabited and

---

10. One Spanish league is roughly equivalent to 2.6 miles.

11. A strong fishing net.

12. Las Casas later described these expeditions in the *History of the Indies.*

left to go to rack and ruin as a direct result of the same
practices. All these islands, which together must run
to over two thousand leagues, are now abandoned and
desolate.

On the mainland, we know for sure that our fellow-
countrymen have, through their cruelty and wickedness,
depopulated and laid waste an area which once boasted
more than ten kingdoms, each of them larger in area than
the whole of the Iberian Peninsula. The whole region,
once teeming with human beings, is now deserted over a
distance of more than two thousand leagues: a distance,
that is, greater than the journey from Seville to Jerusalem
and back again.

At a conservative estimate, the despotic and diabolical
behaviour of the Christians has, over the last forty years,
led to the unjust and totally unwarranted deaths of more
than twelve million souls, women and children among
them, and there are grounds for believing my own estimate of more than fifteen million to be nearer the mark.

There are two main ways in which those who have
travelled to this part of the world pretending to be Christians have uprooted these pitiful peoples and wiped them
from the face of the earth. First, they have waged war on
them: unjust, cruel, bloody and tyrannical war. Second,
they have murdered anyone and everyone who has shown
the slightest sign of resistance, or even of wishing to escape the torment to which they have subjected him. This
latter policy has been instrumental in suppressing the native leaders, and, indeed, given that the Spaniards normally spare only women and children, it has led to the annihilation of all adult males, whom they habitually
subject to the harshest and most iniquitous and brutal
slavery that man has ever devised for his fellow-men,
treating them, in fact, worse than animals. All the many
and infinitely varied ways that have been devised for oppressing these peoples can be seen to flow from one or
other of these two diabolical and tyrannical policies.

The reason the Christians have murdered on such a
vast scale and killed anyone and everyone in their way is
purely and simply greed. They have set out to line their
pockets with gold and to amass private fortunes as
quickly as possible so that they can then assume a status
quite at odds with that into which they were born. Their
insatiable greed and overweening ambition know no
bounds; the land is fertile and rich, the inhabitants simple,
forbearing and submissive. The Spaniards have shown
not the slightest consideration for these people, treating
them (and I speak from first-hand experience, having
been there from the outset) not as brute animals—indeed,

I would to God they had done and had shown them the
consideration they afford their animals—so much as piles
of dung in the middle of the road. They have had as little
concern for their souls as for their bodies, all the millions
that have perished having gone to their deaths with no
knowledge of God and without the benefit of the Sacraments. One fact in all this is widely known and beyond
dispute, for even the tyrannical murderers themselves acknowledge the truth of it: the indigenous peoples never
did the Europeans any harm whatever; on the contrary,
they believed them to have descended from the heavens,
at least until they or their fellow-citizens had tasted, at the
hands of these oppressors, a diet of robbery, murder, violence, and all other manner of trials and tribulations.

from New Spain

New Spain was discovered in 1517 and, at the time, great
atrocities were committed against the indigenous people
of the region and some were killed by members of the expedition. In 1518 the so-called Christians set about stealing from the people and murdering them on the pretence
of settling the area.[13] And from that year until this—and
it is now 1542—the great iniquities and injustices, the
outrageous acts of violence and the bloody tyranny of
these Christians have steadily escalated, the perpetrators
having lost all fear of God, all love of their sovereign, and
all sense of self-respect. The heinous outrages and acts of
barbarity have been so vile, the violence so intense, the
murders so frequent, other acts of despotism so extreme,
and the havoc and devastation so widespread throughout
the kingdoms of the Mainland that what we have so far set
down in this account is as nothing compared with what
went on in New Spain, and the scale and nature of the
atrocities committed without a break from 1518 right up
to this day beggars description. Even now, in September
1542, the atrocities get worse by the day, it being the case,
as we have said, that the infernal brutality and utter inhumanity of the acts committed have steadily increased as
time has gone on.

From the very first day they set foot in New Spain,
which was the eighteenth of April 1518, until 1530, there
was no respite whatever in the carnage and mayhem
provoked by these cruel and bloodthirsty Spaniards.

---

13. The first expedition to Mexico was led by Francisco
Hernández de Córdoba in 1517. Juan de Grijalva followed him
in 1518. Both were on trading as opposed to colonizing missions.

Throughout those twelve long years they pillaged their way over an area of some four hundred and fifty leagues around Mexico City, putting those who lived there to the sword and committing all manner of barbarities against them. This area had originally boasted four or five great kingdoms, each of them as large as Spain and a good deal better favoured, and each of them inhabited, as the Almighty had ordained, by more people than the combined population of Toledo, Seville, Valladolid, Saragossa and Barcelona, even when these Spanish cities were at the very height of their fortunes. The whole area veritably teemed with humanity, even though if one were to walk its frontier one would travel over one thousand eight hundred leagues. Yet, over the twelve years of which we are speaking, and during the course of what they term the 'conquest' (which is really and truly nothing other than a series of violent incursions into the territory by these cruel tyrants: incursions condemned not only in the eyes of God but also by law, and in practice far worse than the assaults mounted by the Turk in his attempt to destroy Christendom), the Europeans have, throughout these four hundred and fifty leagues, butchered, burned alive or otherwise done to death four million souls, young and old alike, men, women and children. And this figure does not include those killed and still being killed today as a direct result of the tyrannical slavery and the oppression and privation its victims are forced to endure on a daily basis.

And no account, no matter how lengthy, how long it took to write, nor how conscientiously it was compiled, could possibly do justice to the full horror of the atrocities committed at one time or another in various parts of this region by these mortal enemies of the human race. Even if one were simply to select one or two outrages from among the many, it would still be nigh on impossible to describe them in all their bloody and terrible detail. That said, and even though I am well aware that I can hardly recount one atrocity in a thousand, I will endeavour to say something about a few of these incidents.

Among other massacres was one which took place in Cholula,[14] a great city of some thirty thousand inhabitants. When all the dignitaries of the city and the region came out to welcome the Spaniards with all due pomp and ceremony, the priests to the fore and the high priest at the head of the procession, and then proceeded to escort them into the city and lodge them in the houses of the lord and the leading citizens, the Spaniards decided that the moment had come to organize a massacre (or 'punishment' as they themselves express such things) in order to inspire fear and terror in all the people of the territory. This was, indeed, the pattern they followed in all the lands they invaded: to stage a bloody massacre of the most public possible kind in order to terrorize those meek and gentle peoples. What they did was the following. They requested the local lord to send for all the nobles and leading citizens of the city and of all the surrounding communities subject to it and, as soon as they arrived and entered the building to begin talks with the Spanish commander, they were seized without anyone outside getting wind of what was afoot. Part of the original request was that they should bring with them five or six thousand native bearers and these were mustered in the courtyards when and as they arrived. One could not watch these poor wretches getting ready to carry the Spaniards' packs without taking pity on them, stark naked as they were with only their modesty hidden from view, each with a kind of little net on his shoulders in which he carried his own modest store of provisions. They all got down on their haunches and waited patiently like sheep. Once they were all safely inside the courtyard, together with a number of others who were also there at the time, armed guards took up positions covering the exits and Spanish soldiers unsheathed their swords and grasped their lances and proceeded to slaughter these poor innocents. Not a single soul escaped. After a day or two had gone by, several victims surfaced, soaked from head to foot in the blood of their fellows beneath whose bodies they had sheltered (so thick was the carpet of corpses in the courtyard) and, with tears in their eyes, pleaded for their lives; but the Spaniards showed them no mercy nor any compassion, and no sooner did they crawl out from under the pile of corpses than they were butchered. The Spanish commander gave orders that the leading citizens, who numbered over a hundred and were roped together, were to be tied to stakes set in the ground and burned alive. One of these dignitaries, however, who may well have been the first among them and the king of that whole region, managed to get free and took refuge, along with twenty or thirty or forty others, in the great temple of the city, which was fortified and was known in the local language as *quu*.[15] There they put up a stout defence against the

---

14. Hernán Cortés (1484?–1547) was responsible for this notorious massacre in the wealthy town of Cholula.

15. Temple.

Spaniards which lasted for the best part of the day. But the Spaniards, against whom no resistance is really possible, especially when it is mounted by unarmed civilians, set fire to the temple, burning those inside alive,[16] the victims shouting all the time: 'Oh, wicked men! What harm had we done to you? Why do you kill us? Wait till you get to Mexico City, for there our great king, Montezuma,[17] will avenge our deaths.' It is said that, while the Spaniards were slaughtering the five or six thousand men gathered in the courtyard, their commander regaled his men with snatches of:

> Nero watched from Tarpey's height
> the flames engulf Rome's awesome might;
> children and ancients shout in pain,
> he all regards with cold disdain.[18]

They were responsible also for another huge massacre in Tepeaca, a city bigger than Cholula and one with a larger population. Here the Spaniards put countless thousands to the sword in the cruellest possible manner.[19]

From Cholula they made their way to Mexico City.[20] On their journey, they were showered with thousands of gifts from the great king Montezuma who also sent some of his men to stage entertainments and banquets for them on the way. When they reached the Great Causeway which runs for some two leagues right up to the city itself, they were greeted by Montezuma's own brother[21] and many local dignitaries bearing valuable gifts of gold, silver and apparel from the great lord. At the city gates, Montezuma himself came out to meet them, carried on a litter of gold and surrounded by the entire court. He escorted them into the city to the great houses where he had directed they should be lodged. Yet that same day, or so I am reliably informed by a number of eye-witnesses, the Spaniards seized the great king unawares by means of a trick and held him under armed guard of eighty soldiers,

eventually putting him in irons.[22] But, leaving aside all of this, although much passed of consequence and one could dwell upon it at length, I should like to relate just one incident contrived by these tyrants. It happened that the Spanish commander[23] had occasion to go to the sea-port to deal with one of his captains[24] who was planning an attack on him, and he left another of his henchmen,[25] with a hundred or so men at his command, to guard King Montezuma while he was away. The garrison decided to stage a show of strength and thereby boost the fear they inspired in the people of this kingdom, a classic Spanish tactic in these campaigns, as we have had occasion to remark before. All the local citizens, great and small, as well as all the members of the court, were wholly taken up with entertaining their imprisoned lord. To this end, they organized fiestas, some of which involved staging traditional dances every afternoon and evening in squares and residential quarters throughout the city. These dances are called in the local language *mitotes* (those typical of the islands being known as *areitos*); and since these dances are the principal form of public entertainment and enjoyment among the people, they deck themselves out in all their best finery. And the entertainments were organized with close attention to rank and station, the noblest of the citizens dancing nearest the building where their lord was being held. Close by this building, then, danced over two thousand youths of quality, the flower of the nobility of Montezuma's whole empire. Thither the Spanish captain made his way, accompanied by a platoon of his men, under pretence of wanting to watch the spectacle but in fact carrying orders to attack the revellers at a pre-arranged time, further platoons with identical orders having been despatched to the other squares where entertainments were being staged. The nobles were totally absorbed in what they were doing and had no thought for their own safety when the soldiers drew their swords and shouting: 'For Saint James, and at 'em, men!'[26] proceeded to slice open the lithe and naked bodies of the dancers and to spill their noble blood. Not one dancer was left alive, and the same story was repeated in the other squares throughout the city. This series of events caused

---

16. This account is questionable because the temples, made of stone, were not flammable.

17. Montezuma (of Motecuçoma) was the Aztec ruler from 1503 until his death in 1520.

18. Excerpt from a traditional Spanish ballad.

19. Cortés offers his own account of the attack in *Letters from Mexico* (1522).

20. Mexico City was typically identified as Temixtitán or Tenochtitlán.

21. Montezuma's brother was Cuitlahuac, lord of Yztapalapa, a city through which Cortés traveled.

22. In *Letters from Mexico,* Cortés states that Montezuma was captured more than one week later than Las Casas suggests.

23. Cortés.

24. Pámphilo de Narváez (1480?–1528), governor of Cuba.

25. Pedro de Alvarado, second-in-command to Cortés.

26. A traditional Spanish battle cry.

horror, anguish and bitterness throughout the land; the whole nation was plunged into mourning and, until the end of time, or at least as long as a few of these people survive, they will not cease to tell and re-tell, in their *areitos* and dances, just as we do at home in Spain with our ballads, this sad story of a massacre which wiped out their entire nobility, beloved and respected by them for generations and generations.

Once the native population learned of this barbaric and unprecedented outrage, perpetrated against innocent individuals who had done nothing whatever to deserve such cruelty, the whole city, which had up to then tolerated the equally unmerited imprisonment of its lord and master simply because he himself had issued orders that no one was to fight the Christians nor to offer any resistance to them, took up arms and attacked them. Many Spaniards were wounded and only narrowly managed to make good their escape. They ordered Montezuma out on to the terrace at dagger point and forced him to order his men not to attack the house and to cease their insurrection. But the people ceased altogether at that juncture to obey such orders and there was a feeling that they should elect another lord in Montezuma's place who would be able and willing to lead them in battle. At this point, it became known that the Spanish commander was on his way back from the coast after his victory over the rebel forces and that he was not far off and was bringing reinforcements. There followed a lull in the fighting which lasted until he arrived some three or four days later; meanwhile, the number of protesters had swollen with the influx of people from all over the territory. Once the commander arrived, the natives attacked with such unrelenting ferocity that it seemed to the garrison that not one of them would be left alive, and they decided to abandon the city in secret and at night. The locals got wind of this, catching up with many as they fled across the causeways that span the lake and killing them in great numbers, as, indeed, they had every right to, given the attacks we have described that had been made on them: a reasonable and fair-minded man will see that theirs was a defensive action and a just one. The Spaniards then regrouped and there followed a battle for the city in which terrible and bizarre outrages were committed against the indigenous population, vast numbers of whom were killed and many others, several leaders among them, burned alive.[27]

After the vile outrages and abominations perpetrated by the Spaniards, both in Mexico City itself and throughout the whole region (an area or ten or fifteen or twenty leagues all round the city saw countless natives perish at their hands), they transferred their pestilential attentions to the densely populated Pánuco province, where once again they swept through the territory, pillaging and murdering on the grand scale as they went. They then moved on to the provinces of Tuxtepec,[28] Impilcingo,[29] and finally Colima,[30] each one of them greater in extent than the kingdoms of Castile and León, and in each they wrought the same destruction as they had in Mexico City and its province. It would be impracticable to compile a complete dossier of all the atrocities, foul murders and other barbarities they committed, and any such account would be so lengthy it would prove impossible for the reader to take in.

It should be recalled that the pretext upon which the Spanish invaded each of these provinces and proceeded to massacre the people and destroy their lands—lands which teemed with people and should surely have been a joy and a delight to any true Christian—was purely and simply that they were making good the claim of the Spanish Crown to the territories in question. At no stage had any order been issued entitling them to massacre the people or to enslave them. Yet, whenever the natives did not drop everything and rush to recognize publicly the truth of the irrational and illogical claims that were made, and whenever they did not immediately place themselves completely at the mercy of the iniquitous and cruel and bestial individuals who were making such claims, they were dubbed outlaws and held to be in rebellion against His Majesty. This, indeed, was the tenor of the letters that were sent back to the Spanish court, and everybody involved in the administration of the New World was blind to the simple truth enshrined in the first principles of law and government that nobody who is not a subject of a civil power in the first place can be deemed in law to be in rebellion against that power. Any reasonable person who knows anything of God, of rights and of civil law can imagine for himself what the likely reaction would be of any people living peaceably within their own frontiers, unaware that

---

27. Las Casas combines two separate events: the 1520 retreat and Cortés's 1521 attack on the city.

28. Also referred to as Tatutepeque, Tuchitebeque, Tutuepec, or Tuxtepeque.

29. Also referred to as Ipilcingo.

30. A Mexican state located on the Pacific coast. It is also referred to as Colimán or Alimán.

they owe allegiance to anyone save their natural lords, were a stranger suddenly to issue a demand along the following lines: 'You shall henceforth obey a foreign king, whom you have never seen nor ever heard of and, if you do not, we will cut you to pieces'—especially when they discover that these strangers are indeed quite prepared to carry out this threat to the letter. Even more shocking is the fact that when the local people do obey such commands they are harshly treated as common slaves, put to hard labour and subjected to all manner of abuse and to agonizing torments that ensure a slower and more painful death than would summary execution. Indeed, for them, the end result is the same: they, their wives and their children all perish and the whole of their nation is wiped from the face of the earth. And so blinded by ambition and driven by greed are the devils who advocate such treatment of these people that they cannot see that, when their victims come to obey under duress this foreign overlord and publicly recognize his authority over them, simply because of their fear of what will happen to them if they do not, such a recognition of suzerainty has no standing in law whatever, any such prerogative obtained by menaces from any people anywhere in the world being invalid. In practice, the only rights these perfidious crusaders have earned which can be upheld in human, divine, or natural law are the right to eternal damnation and the right to answer for the offences and the harm they have done the Spanish Crown by utterly ruining every one of these kingdoms and (as far as it is within their power) invalidating all claims the Spanish Crown may have to the territories of the New World. These, then, are the true services they have performed and continue to perform for their sovereign in this part of the world. . . .

ÁLVAR NÚÑEZ CABEZA DE VACA (1490?–1577?)

Álvar Núñez Cabeza de Vaca, a Spanish nobleman, was born around 1490 in Jerez de la Frontera, Spain, to Francisco de Vera, an alderman of Jerez, and Teresa Cabeza de Vaca. His paternal grandfather, Pedro de Vera Mendoza, had conquered the Guanache people of the Grand Canary Islands, and one of his relatives had been a hero in the wars against the Moors. The eldest of four children, Núñez Cabeza de Vaca joined the Spanish army in Italy in 1511, fighting in the bloody battle of Ravenna. He continued to distinguish himself militarily, first when he served the duke of Medina Sidonia after his return to Seville and later when he served Spain's Charles I at Puente la Reina in Navarre against the French. Little else is known about Núñez Cabeza de Vaca until he joined the Pámphilo de Narváez expedition to the Gulf coast in 1527. Charles I appointed Núñez Cabeza de Vaca the royal treasurer and chief constable of the enterprise. His official duties largely financial, Núñez Cabeza de Vaca was also asked to support royal interests by observing the Spanish treatment of the Indians.

In 1527, the conquistador Pámphilo de Narváez led six hundred men on an expedition to take possession of Florida. The results were disastrous: after seven years, only four survived. The expedition lost two ships in a hurricane and over one hundred men to desertion. Narváez stranded many of the remaining men in Florida by sending the remaining ships ahead. These ships never returned. In makeshift rafts, the men made a treacherous journey from the coast of Florida to Texas, traveling through storms and with little food. While en route, the men were abandoned by Narváez, probably in the area of the Mississippi delta. The rafts eventually wrecked on what is today known as Galveston Island in 1528. The small number of survivors dwindled until only Núñez Cabeza de Vaca; fellow Spaniards Andrés Dorantes and Alonso del Castillo Maldonado; and Dorante's slave Estéban (sometimes Estévan or Estevanico) remained. For the next six years, the men lived among groups of Indians in Texas, often in captivity as prisoners and slaves.

The men survived by finding a place within and between tribes and were eventually able to move among different tribes, even those at war with each other, trading and assuming the role of shamans (healers). Núñez Cabeza de Vaca's reputation as a healer began to precede him as he traveled north and west, and over time his reception among various Indian groups improved. Between 1528 and 1535, the men traveled approximately six thousand miles from Florida to the western coast of Mexico. After years of living among the Indians and searching for Spanish settlements, Núñez Cabeza de Vaca's eventual meeting with Spaniards in 1535 proved a mixed blessing. After his group and his Indian escorts encountered Captain Diego de Alcaraz's party searching for Indians to enslave in western Mexico, conflict ensued and Alcaraz sought to enslave hundreds of Núñez Cabeza de Vaca's followers. Núñez Cabeza de Vaca was sent to Mexico City, and in 1537 he returned to Spain to present his reports to Emperor Charles V.

Núñez Cabeza de Vaca wrote his first account of the Narváez expedition to explain its apparent failure and to help secure another royal office. He also sought to explain his conclusions about Spanish colonization in the Americas and to support further exploration and settlement. The first edition of *La Relación* was published in Zamora in 1542. Part captivity narrative, part hagiography (life of a saint), his accounts of the expedition offer detailed descriptions of the cultural practices of many of the Indian groups he had seen and demonstrated his growing acculturation into tribal life over the course of the eight-year journey.

Although Núñez Cabeza de Vaca was unable to convince the king to allow him to lead a new expedition to Florida—Hernando de Soto was named the commander—in 1539, the king drew on Núñez Cabeza de Vaca's experience living among native peoples by sending him to address catastrophic conditions in the Spanish settlements in Buenos Aires and Asunción. On this return to South America, Núñez Cabeza de Vaca had numerous disagreements with the standing officials regarding the treatment of native peoples, and he was soon forcibly removed from his position as governor and returned to Spain in chains. He was subjected to a lengthy trial in Spain, and he lost his position as governor of the Río de la Plata and was forbidden to return to the Americas. Limited information is available about Cabeza de Vaca's final years; he died in Seville after 1760. He worked on a second edition of *La Relación,* expanding it to include information about his time in South America, and published it under the title *Naufragios* (Shipwrecks) in 1555.

from THE *RELATION* OF ÁLVAR NÚÑEZ CABEZA DE VACA[1]

from CHAPTER 7 • The Character of the Country[2]

The country where we came on shore to this town and region of Apalachen, is for the most part level, the ground of sand and stiff earth. Throughout are immense trees and open woods, in which are walnut, laurel and another tree called liquidamber, cedars, savins, evergreen oaks, pines, red-oaks and palmitos like those of Spain. There are many lakes, great and small, over every part of it; some troublesome of fording, on account of depth and the great number of trees lying throughout them. Their beds are sand. The lakes in the country of Apalachen are much larger than those we found before coming there.

In this Province are many maize fields; and the houses are scattered as are those of the Gelves.[3] There are deer of three kinds, rabbits, hares, bears, lions[4] and other wild beasts. Among them we saw an animal with a pocket on its belly, in which it carries its young until they know how to seek food;[5] and if it happen that they should be out feeding and any one come near, the mother will not run until she has gathered them in together. The country is very cold. It has fine pastures for herds. Birds are of various kinds. Geese in great numbers. Ducks, mallards, royal-ducks, fly-catchers, night-herons and partridges abound. We saw many falcons, gerfalcons, sparrow-hawks, merlins, and numerous other fowl.

Two hours after our arrival at Apalachen, the Indians who had fled from there came in peace to us, asking for their women and children, whom we released; but the detention of a cacique[6] by the Governor[7] produced great excitement, in consequence of which they returned for battle early the next day [June 26], and attacked us with such promptness and alacrity that they succeeded in setting fire to the houses in which we were. As we sallied they fled to the lakes near by, because of which and the large maize fields, we could do them no injury, save in the single in-

---

1. The *Relation* was originally published in Seville in 1542. This text is based upon the *Relation of Alvar Nuñez Cabeza de Vaca,* trans. Buckingham Smith (1871).

2. At this point in the expedition, June 1528, Núñez Cabeza de Vaca was in northern Florida, perhaps near present-day Tallahassee.

3. Gelves likely refers to a town in Andalusia in Spain.

4. Probably the Florida panther.

5. An opossum.

6. Chief or ruler.

7. Pámphilo de Narváez was governor.

stance of one Indian, whom we killed. The day following, others came against us from a town on the opposite side of the lake, and attacked us as the first had done, escaping in the same way, except one who was also slain.

We were in the town twenty-five days [July 19], in which time we made three incursions, and found the country very thinly peopled and difficult to travel for the bad passages, the woods and lakes. We inquired of the cacique we kept and the natives we brought with us, who were the neighbors and enemies of these Indians, as to the nature of the country, the character and condition of the inhabitants, of the food and all other matters concerning it. Each answered apart from the rest, that the largest town in all that region was Apalachen; the people beyond were less numerous and poorer, the land little occupied, and the inhabitants much scattered; that thenceforward were great lakes, dense forests, immense deserts and solitudes. We then asked touching the region towards the south, as to the towns and subsistence in it. They said that in keeping such a direction, journeying nine days, there was a town called Aute,[8] the inhabitants whereof had much maize, beans and pumpkins, and being near the sea, they had fish, and that those people were their friends.

In view of the poverty of the land, the unfavorable accounts of the population and of everything else we heard, the Indians making continual war upon us, wounding our people and horses at the places where they went to drink, shooting from the lakes with such safety to themselves that we could not retaliate, killing a lord of Tescuco,[9] named Don Pedro,[10] whom the Commissary brought with him, we determined to leave that place and go in quest of the sea, and the town of Aute of which we were told. . . .

The Indians we had so far seen in Florida are all archers. They go naked, are large of body, and appear at a distance like giants. They are of admirable proportions, very spare and of great activity and strength. The bows they use are as thick as the arm, of eleven or twelve palms in length, which they will discharge at two hundred paces with so great precision that they miss nothing.

---

8. An Indian community close to present-day Tallahassee, Florida.

9. Tezcoco, in Mexico City.

10. Buckingham Smith indicates that Don Pedro was, in fact, Pedro Tetlahuehuezquiziti, the brother of King Ixtilxochitl, heir to the Aztec throne.

Having got through this passage, at the end of a league we arrived at another of the same character, but worse, as it was longer, being half a league in extent. This we crossed freely, without interruption from the Indians, who, as they had spent on the former occasion their store of arrows, had nought with which they dared venture to engage us. Going through a similar passage the next day [July 21], I discovered the trail of persons ahead, of which I gave notice to the Governor, who was in the rear guard, so that though the Indians came upon us, as we were prepared they did no harm. After emerging upon the plain they followed us, and we went back on them in two directions. Two we killed, and they wounded me and two or three others. Coming to woods we could do them no more injury, nor make them further trouble. . . .

from CHAPTER 8 • We Go from Aute

The next morning we left Aute, and traveled all day before coming to the place I had visited. The journey was extremely arduous. There were not horses enough to carry the sick, who went on increasing in numbers day by day, and we knew of no cure. It was piteous and painful to witness our perplexity and distress. We saw on our arrival how small were the means for advancing farther. There was not any where to go; and if there had been, the people were unable to move forward, the greater part being ill, and those were few who could be on duty. I cease here to relate more of this, because any one may suppose what would occur in a country so remote and malign, so destitute of all resource, whereby either to live in it or go out of it; but most certain assistance is in God, our Lord, on whom we never failed to place reliance. One thing occurred, more afflicting to us than all the rest, which was, that of the persons mounted, the greater part commenced secretly to plot, hoping to secure a better fate for themselves by abandoning the Governor and the sick, who were in a state of weakness and prostration. But, as among them were many hidalgos and persons of gentle condition, they would not permit this to go on, without informing the Governor and the officers of your Majesty; and as we showed them the deformity of their purpose, and placed before them the moment when they should desert their captain, and those who were ill and feeble, and above all the disobedience to the orders of your Majesty, they determined to remain, and that whatever might happen to one should be the lot of all, without any forsaking the rest.

After the accomplishment of this, the Governor called them all to him, and of each apart he asked advice as to what he should do to get out of a country so miserable, and seek that assistance elsewhere which could not here be found, a third part of the people being very sick, and the number increasing every hour; for we regarded it as certain that we should all become so, and could pass out of it only through death, which from its coming in such a place was to us all the more terrible. These, with many other embarrassments being considered, and entertaining many plans, we coincided in one great project, extremely difficult to put in operation, and that was to build vessels in which we might go away. This appeared impossible to every one: we knew not how to construct, nor were there tools, nor iron, nor forge, nor tow, nor resin, nor rigging; finally, no one thing of so many that are necessary, nor any man who had a knowledge of their manufacture; and, above all, there was nothing to eat, while building, for those who should labor. Reflecting on all this, we agreed to think of the subject with more deliberation, and the conversation dropped from that day, each going his way, commending our course to God, our Lord, that he would direct it as should best serve Him. . . .

During this time some went gathering shell-fish in the coves and creeks of the sea, at which employment the Indians twice attacked them and killed ten men in sight of the camp, without our being able to afford succor. We found their corpses traversed from side to side with arrows; and for all some had on good armor, it did not give adequate protection or security against the nice and powerful archery of which I have spoken. According to the declaration of our pilots under oath, from the entrance to which we had given the name *Bahía de la Cruz*[11] to this place, we had traveled two hundred and eighty leagues or thereabout. Over all that region we had not seen a single mountain, and had no information of any whatsoever.

Before we embarked[12] there died more than forty men of disease and hunger, without enumerating those destroyed by the Indians. By the twenty-second of the month of September, the horses had been consumed, one

only remaining; and on that day we embarked in the following order: In the boat of the Governor went forty-nine men; in another, which he gave to the Comptroller and the Commissary, went as many others; the third, he gave to Captain Alonzo del Castillo and Andrés Dorantes, with forty-eight men; and another he gave to two captains, Tellez and Peñalosa, with forty-seven men. The last was given to the Assessor and myself, with forty-nine men. After the provisions and clothes had been taken in, not over a span of the gunwales remained above water; and more than this, the boats were so crowded[13] that we could not move: so much can necessity do, which drove us to hazard our lives in this manner, running into a turbulent sea, not a single one who went, having a knowledge of navigation.

from CHAPTER 10 • The Assault from the Indians

[November 2] I found myself in thirty fathoms. . . . [The Governor] asked me what I thought we should do. I told him we ought to join the boat which went in advance, and by no means to leave her; and, the three being together, we must keep on our way to where God should be pleased to lead. He answered saying that could not be done, because the boat was far to sea and he wished to reach the shore. . . . [B]ut the Governor having in his boat the healthiest of all the men, we could not by any means hold with or follow her. Seeing this, I asked him to give me a rope from his boat, that I might be enabled to keep up with him; but he answered me that he would do no little, if they, as they were, should be able to reach the land that night. I said to him, that since he saw the feeble strength we had to follow him, and do what he ordered, he must tell me how he would that I should act. He answered that it was no longer a time in which one should command another; but that each should do what he thought best to save his own life; that he so intended to act; and saying this, he departed with his boat. . . .[14]

Near the dawn of day [November 5] . . . a wave

---

11. Bay of the Cross.

12. The men had constructed five rafts.

13. Two hundred and forty-two men were traveling on five rafts.

14. The governor in effect abandoned the rest of the men at the mouth of the Mississippi River.

took us, that knocked our boat out of the water the distance of the throw of a crowbar, and from the violence with which she struck, nearly all the people who were in her like dead, were roused to consciousness. Finding themselves near the shore, they began to move on hands and feet, crawling to land into some ravines.

from CHAPTER 11 • Of What Befel Lope de Oviedo with the Indians

As it appeared to us [Oviedo] was gone a long time, we sent two men that they should look to see what might have happened. They met him near by, and saw that three Indians with bows and arrows followed and were calling to him, while he, in the same way, was beckoning them on. Thus he arrived where we were, the natives remaining a little way back, seated on the shore. Half an hour after, they were supported by one hundred other Indian bowmen, who if they were not large, our fears made giants of them. . . . We gave them beads and hawk-bells, and each of them gave me an arrow, which is a pledge of friendship. They told us by signs that they would return in the morning and bring us something to eat, as at the time they had nothing.

from CHAPTER 21 • Our Cure of Some of the Afflicted[15]

That same night of our arrival, some Indians came to Castillo and told him that they had great pain in the head, begging him to cure them. After he made over them the sign of the cross, and commended them to God, they instantly said that all the pain had left, and went to their houses bringing us prickly pears, with a piece of venison, a thing to us little known. As the report of Castillo's performances spread, many came to us that night sick, that we should heal them, each bringing a piece of venison, until the quantity became so great we knew not where to dispose of it. We gave many thanks to God, for every day went on increasing his compassion and his gifts. After the sick were attended to, they began to dance and sing, making themselves festive, until sunrise; and because of our arrival, the rejoicing was continued for three days.

When these were ended, we asked the Indians about the country farther on, the people we should find in it, and of the subsistence there. They answered us, that throughout all the region prickly pear plants abounded; but the fruit was now gathered and all the people had gone back to their houses. They said the country was very cold, and there were few skins. Reflecting on this, and that it was already winter, we resolved to pass the season with these Indians.

Five days after our arrival, all the Indians went off, taking us with them to gather more prickly pears, where there were other peoples speaking different tongues. After walking five days in great hunger, since on the way was no manner of fruit, we came to a river and put up our houses. We then went to seek the product of certain trees,[16] which is like peas. As there are no paths in the country, I was detained some time. The others returned, and coming to look for them in the dark, I got lost. Thank God I found a burning tree, and in the warmth of it passed the cold of that night. In the morning, loading myself with sticks, and taking two brands with me, I returned to seek them. In this manner I wandered five days, ever with my fire and load; for if the wood had failed me where none could be found, as many parts are without any, though I might have sought sticks elsewhere, there would have been no fire to kindle them. This was all the protection I had against cold, while walking naked as I was born. Going to the low woods near the rivers, I prepared myself for the night, stopping in them before sunset. I made a hole in the ground and threw in fuel which the trees abundantly afforded, collected in good quantity from those that were fallen and dry. About the whole I made four fires, in the form of a cross, which I watched and made up from time to time. I also gathered some bundles of the coarse straw that there abounds, with which I covered myself in the hole. In this way I was sheltered at night from cold. On one occasion while I slept, the fire fell upon the straw, when it began to blaze so rapidly that notwithstanding the haste I made to get out of it, I carried some marks on my hair of the danger to which I was exposed. All this while I tasted not a mouthful, nor did I find anything I could eat. My feet were bare and bled a good deal. Through the mercy of God, the wind did not blow from the north in all this time, otherwise I should have died.

At the end of the fifth day I arrived on the margin of a

---

15. After being shipwrecked on Galveston Island, the other survivors were taken into captivity by the Karankawa Indians in September 1528.

16. Mesquite trees.

river, where I found the Indians, who with the Christians, had considered me dead, supposing that I had been stung by a viper. All were rejoiced to see me, and most so were my companions. They said that up to that time they had struggled with great hunger, which was the cause of their not having sought me. At night, all gave me of their prickly pears, and the next morning we set out for a place where they were in large quantity, with which we satisfied our great craving, the Christians rendering thanks to our Lord that he had ever given us his aid.

from CHAPTER 24 • Customs of the Indians of That Country

From the Island of Malhado[17] to this land, all the Indians whom we saw have the custom from the time in which their wives find themselves pregnant, of not sleeping with them until two years after they have given birth. The children are suckled until the age of twelve years, when they are old enough to get support for themselves. We asked why they reared them in this manner; and they said because of the great poverty of the land, it happened many times, as we witnessed, that they were two or three days without eating, sometimes four, and consequently, in seasons of scarcity, the children were allowed to suckle, that they might not famish; otherwise those who lived would be delicate having little strength.

If any one chance to fall sick in the desert, and cannot keep up with the rest, the Indians leave him to perish, unless it be a son or a brother; him they will assist, even to carrying on their back. It is common among them all to leave their wives when there is no conformity, and directly they connect themselves with whom they please. This is the course of the men who are childless; those who have children, remain with their wives and never abandon them. When they dispute and quarrel in their towns, they strike each other with the fists, fighting until exhausted, and then separate. Sometimes they are parted by the women going between them; the men never interfere. For no disaffection that arises do they resort to bows and arrows. After they have fought, or had out their dispute, they take their dwellings and go into the woods, living apart from each other until their heat has subsided. When no longer offended and their anger is gone, they return. From that time they are friends as if nothing had happened; nor is it necessary that any one should mend their

friendships, as they in this way again unite them. If those that quarrel are single, they go to some neighboring people, and although these should be enemies, they receive them well and welcome them warmly, giving them so largely of what they have, that when their animosity cools, and they return to their town, they go rich.

They are all warlike, and have as much strategy for protecting themselves against enemies as they could have were they reared in Italy in continual feuds. When they are in a part of the country where their enemies may attack them, they place their houses on the skirt of a wood, the thickest and most tangled they can find, and near it make a ditch in which they sleep. The warriors are covered by small pieces of stick through which are loop holes; these hide them and present so false an appearance, that if come upon they are not discovered. They open a very narrow way, entering into the midst of the wood, where a spot is prepared on which the women and children sleep. When night comes they kindle fires in their lodges, that should spies be about, they may think to find them there; and before daybreak they again light those fires. If the enemy comes to assault the houses, they who are in the ditch make a sally; and from their trenches do much injury without those who are outside seeing or being able to find them. When there is no wood in which they can take shelter in this way, and make their ambuscades, they settle on open ground at a place they select, which they invest with trenches covered with broken sticks, having apertures whence to discharge arrows. These arrangements are made for night.

While I was among the Aguenes,[18] their enemies coming suddenly at midnight, fell upon them, killed three and wounded many, so that they ran from their houses to the fields before them. As soon as these ascertained that their assailants had withdrawn, they returned to pick up all the arrows the others had shot, and following after them in the most stealthy manner possible, came that night to their dwellings without their presence being suspected. At four o'clock in the morning the Aguenes attacked them, killed five, and wounded numerous others, and made them flee from their houses, leaving their bows with all they possessed. In a little while came the wives of the Quevenes to them and formed a treaty whereby the parties became friends. The women, however, are sometimes the cause of war. All these nations, when they have personal enmities,

---

17. Galveston Island.

18. The Quevenes.

and are not of one family, assassinate at night, waylay, and inflict gross barbarities on each other.

from CHAPTER 27 • We Moved Away and Were Well Received

. . . At sunset we reached a hundred Indian habitations. Before we arrived, all the people who were in them came out to receive us, with such yells as were terrific, striking the palms of their hands violently against their thighs. They brought us gourds bored with holes and having pebbles in them, an instrument for the most important occasions, produced only at the dance or to effect cures, and which none dare touch but those who own them. They say there is virtue in them, and because they do not grow in that country, they come from heaven: nor do they know where they are to be found, only that the rivers bring them in their floods. So great were the fear and distraction of these people, some to reach us sooner than others, that they might touch us, they pressed us so closely that they lacked little of killing us; and without letting us put our feet to the ground, carried us to their dwellings. We were so crowded upon by numbers, that we went into the houses they had made for us. On no account would we consent that they should rejoice over us any more that night. The night long they passed in singing and dancing among themselves; and the next day they brought us all the people of the town, that we should touch and bless them in the way we had done to others among whom we had been. After this performance they presented many arrows to some women of the other town who had accompanied theirs.

The next day we left, and all the people of the place went with us: and when we came to the other Indians we were as well received as we had been by the last. They gave us of what they had to eat, and the deer they had killed that day. Among them we witnessed another custom, which is this: they who were with us took from him who came to be cured, his bow and arrows, shoes and beads if he wore any, and then brought him before us that we should heal him. After being attended to, he would go away highly pleased, saying that he was well. So we parted from these Indians, and went to others by whom we were welcomed. They brought us their sick, which, we having blessed, they declared were sound; he who was healed, believed we could cure him; and with what the others to whom we had administered would relate, they

made great rejoicing and dancing, so that they left us no sleep. . . .

from CHAPTER 32 • The Indians Give Us the Hearts of Deer

. . . We were in this town three days. A day's journey farther was another town, at which the rain fell heavily while we were there, and the river became so swollen we could not cross it, which detained us fifteen days. In this time Castillo saw the buckle of a sword-belt on the neck of an Indian and stitched to it the nail of a horse shoe. He took them, and we asked the native what they were: he answered that they came from heaven. We questioned him further, as to who had brought them thence: they all responded, that certain men who wore beards like us, had come from heaven and arrived at that river; bringing horses, lances, and swords, and that they had lanced two Indians. In a manner of the utmost indifference we could feign, we asked them what had become of those men: they answered us that they had gone to sea, putting their lances beneath the water, and going themselves also under the water; afterwards that they were seen on the surface going towards the sunset. For this we gave many thanks to God our Lord. We had before despaired of ever hearing more of Christians. Even yet we were left in great doubt and anxiety, thinking those people were merely persons who had come by sea on discoveries. However, as we had now such exact information, we made greater speed, and as we advanced on our way, the news of the Christians continually grew. We told the natives that we were going in search of that people, to order them not to kill nor make slaves of them, nor take them from their lands, nor do other injustice. Of this the Indians were very glad.

We passed through many territories and found them all vacant: their inhabitants wandered fleeing among the mountains, without daring to have houses or till the earth for fear of Christians. The sight was one of infinite pain to us, a land very fertile and beautiful, abounding in springs and streams, the hamlets deserted and burned, the people thin and weak, all fleeing or in concealment. As they did not plant, they appeased their keen hunger by eating roots, and the bark of trees. We bore a share in the famine along the whole way; for poorly could these unfortunates provide for us, themselves being so reduced they looked as though they would willingly die. They brought shawls of those they had concealed because of the Christians, presenting them to us; and they related how the Christians, at other times had come through the land destroying and burning the towns, carrying away half the men, and all the women and the boys, while those who had been able to escape were wandering about fugitives. We found them so alarmed they dared not remain anywhere. They would not, nor could they till the earth; but preferred to die rather than live in dread of such cruel usage as they received. Although these showed themselves greatly delighted with us, we feared that on our arrival among those who held the frontier and fought against the Christians, they would treat us badly, and revenge upon us the conduct of their enemies; but when God our Lord was pleased to bring us there, they began to dread and respect us as the others had done, and even somewhat more, at which we no little wondered. Thence it may at once be seen, that to bring all these people to be Christians and to the obedience of the Imperial Majesty, they must be won by kindness, which is a way certain, and no other is. . . .

from CHAPTER 33 • We See Traces of Christians

When we saw sure signs of Christians, and heard how near we were to them, we gave thanks to God our Lord, for having chosen to bring us out of a captivity so melancholy and wretched. The delight we felt let each one conjecture, when he shall remember the length of time we were in that country, the suffering and perils we underwent. That night I entreated my companions that one of them should go back three days' journey after the Christians who were moving about over the country, where we had given assurance of protection. Neither of them received this proposal well, excusing themselves because of weariness and exhaustion; and although either might have done better than I, being more youthful and athletic, yet seeing their unwillingness, the next morning I took the negro[19] with eleven Indians, and following the Christians by their trail, I traveled ten leagues, passing three villages, at which they had slept.

The day after I overtook four of them on horseback,

who were astonished at the sight of me, so strangely habited as I was, and in company with Indians. They stood staring at me a length of time, so confounded that they neither hailed me nor drew near to make an inquiry. I bade them take me to their chief: accordingly we went together half a league to the place where was Diego de Alcaraz, their captain.[20]

After we had conversed, he stated to me that he was completely undone; he had not been able in a long time to take any Indians; he knew not which way to turn, and his men had well begun to experience hunger and fatigue. I told him of Castillo and Dorantes, who were behind, ten leagues off, with a multitude that conducted us. He thereupon sent three cavalry to them, with fifty of the Indians who accompanied him. The negro returned to guide them, while I remained. I asked the Christians to give me a certificate of the year, month and day, I arrived there,[21] and of the manner of my coming, which they accordingly did. From this river[22] to the town of the Christians, named San Miguel, within the government of the province called New Galicia, are thirty leagues.

from CHAPTER 34 • Of Sending for the Christians

Five days having elapsed, Andrés Dorantes and Alonzo del Castillo arrived with those who had been sent after them. They brought more than six hundred persons of that community, whom the Christians had driven into the forests, and who had wandered in concealment over the land. Those who accompanied us so far, had drawn them out, and given them to the Christians, who thereupon dismissed all the others they had brought with them. Upon their coming to where I was, Alcaraz begged that we would summon the people of the towns on the margin of the river, who straggled about under cover of the woods, and order them to fetch us something to eat. This last was unnecessary, the Indians being ever diligent to bring us all they could. Directly we sent our messengers to call them,

---

19. Estéban, Estévan, or Estévanico, the Moroccan slave of Andrés Dorantes.

20. Diego de Alcaraz went on to become an officer in Francisco Vásquez de Coronado's expedition.

21. The precise date is uncertain; however, scholars estimate it as March 1536.

22. San Miguel de Culicán, Mexico.

when there came six hundred souls, bringing us all the maize in their possession. They fetched it in certain pots, closed with clay, which they had concealed in the earth. They brought us whatever else they had; but we, wishing only to have the provision, gave the rest to the Christians, that they might divide among themselves. After this we had many high words with them; for they wished to make slaves of the Indians we brought.

In consequence of the dispute, we left at our departure many bows of Turkish shape we had along with us and many pouches. The five arrows with the points of emerald were forgotten among others, and we lost them. We gave the Christians a store of robes of cowhide and other things we brought. We found it difficult to induce the Indians to return to their dwellings, to feel no apprehension and plant maize. They were willing to do nothing until they had gone with us and delivered us into the hands of other Indians, as had been the custom; for if they returned without doing so, they were afraid they should die, and going with us, they feared neither Christians nor lances. Our countrymen became jealous at this, and caused their interpreter to tell the Indians that we were of them, and for a long time we had been lost; that they were the lords of the land who must be obeyed and served, while we were persons of mean condition and small force. The Indians cared little or nothing for what was told them; and conversing among themselves said the Christians lied: that

we had come whence the sun rises, and they whence it goes down: we healed the sick, they killed the sound; that we had come naked and barefooted, while they had arrived in clothing and on horses with lances; that we were not covetous of anything, but all that was given to us, we directly turned to give, remaining with nothing; that the others had the only purpose to rob whomsoever they found, bestowing nothing on any one.

In this way they spoke of all matters respecting us, which they enhanced by contrast with matters concerning the others, delivering their response through the interpreter of the Spaniards. To other Indians they made this known by means of one among them through whom they understood us. Those who speak that tongue we discriminately call Primahaitu, which is like saying Vasconyados.[23] We found it in use over more than four hundred leagues of our travel, without another over that whole extent. Even to the last, I could not convince the Indians that we were of the Christians; and only with great effort and solicitation we got them to go back to their residences. We ordered them to put away apprehension, establish their towns, plant and cultivate the soil. . . .

---

23. The author suggests that these Indians (possibly Pimas) spoke a language that was similar to the Basque language, spoken in northern Spain.

PEDRO DE CASTAÑEDA (1510?–1570?)

Little is known of Pedro de Castañeda, a native of northern Spain, aside from his role as the retrospective chronicler of the 1540 Spanish expedition into northern Mexico and as far north and east as present-day Kansas. Led by Francisco Vásquez de Coronado, the expedition had been commissioned by Viceroy Antonio de Mendoza to search for a series of settlements that were said to be richer than those of the Incas. Rumors of the "Seven Cities of Cíbola" had reached Núñez Cabeza de Vaca, and even more enticing reports were offered by Fray Marcos de Niza, who claimed to have seen the great riches of Cíbola, in effect, Zuni Pueblo.

Coronado's party, in which Castañeda engaged as a private soldier, was large even for an expedition of its kind, including some three hundred Spaniards (mostly adventurers, but also some women and several Franciscans, including Fray Marcos) and an estimated one thousand Indian allies. When the party reached "Cíbola," they found a much smaller settlement than they had been led to expect, without the great mineral wealth Fray Marcos had reported. Coronado sent the friar back to Mexico City in disgrace but took the pueblo by force. The army established a base of operation there, later moving some distance away on the Rio Grande.

From this base Coronado sent out scouting parties in various directions. He and his group spent the winter on the Rio Grande, where they clashed repeatedly with the Pueblo peoples, on whose scarce food supply the Spaniards were a tremendous drain. In the spring of 1541, Coronado and his force followed an Indian guide who promised to lead them to a fabulously wealthy land, Quivira. This guide later admitted that the Pueblos had asked him to lead the Spaniards astray and strand them in a place where they would starve. The Spaniards killed their guide, and the expedition returned to the Rio Grande for a second winter. In the spring of 1542, the expedition returned to Mexico City, where Coronado was cleared of charges of mismanagement.

Castañeda wrote his account of the 1540–42 expedition two decades later, apparently in response to doubts and questions that had arisen over the facts of the expedition. It is not clear which "noble lord" Castañeda addressed or whether his motive in writing the document was to support a claim for remuneration for his service. His wife and eight children did later present such a claim to the Spanish crown. Regardless of his reasons for writing, however, Castañeda's narrative has been recognized as the most complete account of Coronado's expedition.

from CASTAÑEDA'S NARRATIVE[1]

Account of the expedition to Cibola which took place in the year 1540, in which all those settlements, their ceremonies & customs, are described.

from PART I

from Preface

To me it seems very certain, my very noble lord, that it is a worthy ambition for great men to desire to know and wish to preserve for posterity correct information concerning the things that have happened in distant parts, about which little is known. I do not blame those inquisitive persons who, perchance with good intentions, have many times troubled me not a little with their requests that I clear up for them some doubts which they have had about different things that have been commonly related concerning the events and occurrences that took place during the expedition to Cibola, or the New Land, which the good viceroy—may he be with God in His glory—Don Antonio de Mendoza, ordered and arranged, and on which he sent Francisco Vazquez de Coronado[2] as captain-general.

In truth, they have reason for wishing to know the truth, because most people very often make things of which they have heard, and about which they have perchance no knowledge, appear either greater or less than they are. They make nothing of those things that amount to something, and those that do not they make so remarkable that they appear to be something impossible to believe. This may very well have been caused by the fact that, as that country was not permanently occupied, there has not been anyone who was willing to spend his time in writing about its peculiarities, because all knowledge was lost of that which it was not the pleasure of God—He alone knows the reason—that they should enjoy.

In truth, he who wishes to employ himself thus in writing out the things that happened on the expedition, and the things that were seen in those lands, and the ceremonies and customs of the natives, will have matter enough to test his judgment, & I believe that the result can not fail to be an account which, describing only the truth, will be so remarkable that it will seem incredible.

And besides, I think that the twenty years and more since that expedition took place have been the cause of some stories which are related. For example, some make it an uninhabitable country, others have it bordering on Florida, and still others on Greater India, which does not appear to be a slight difference. They are unable to give

1. Castañeda's narrative was written in the 1560s. The text is taken from the English translation by George Parker Winship, first published in 1896.

2. Antonio de Mendoza (1485–1552) served as governor (viceroy) of Mexico from 1530 to 1550. Francisco Vazquez de

Coronado (1510–54), a younger son of a Spanish nobleman, was at this time governor of "New Galicia," the northernmost province of Spain's holdings in present-day Mexico.

any basis upon which to found their statements. There are those who tell about some very peculiar animals, who are contradicted by others who were on the expedition, declaring that there was nothing of the sort seen. Others differ as to the limits of the provinces and even in regard to the ceremonies and customs, attributing what pertains to one people to others. All this has had a large part, my very noble lord, in making me wish to give now, although somewhat late, a short general account for all those who pride themselves on this noble curiosity, and to save myself the time taken up by these solicitations. Things enough will certainly be found here which are hard to believe. All or most of these were seen with my own eyes, and the rest is from reliable information obtained by inquiry of the natives themselves.

Understanding as I do that this little work would be nothing in itself, lacking authority, unless it were favored and protected by a person whose authority would protect it from the boldness of those who, without reverence, give their murmuring tongues liberty, and knowing as I do how great are the obligations under which I have always been, & am, to Your Grace, I humbly beg to submit this little work to your protection. May it be received as from a faithful retainer and servant. . . .

May it please our lord to so favor me that with my slight knowledge and small abilities I may be able, by relating the truth, to make my little work pleasing to the learned and wise readers, when it has been accepted by Your Grace. For my intention is not to gain the fame of a good composer or rhetorician, but I desire to give a faithful account and to do this slight service to Your Grace, who will, I hope, receive it as from a faithful servant and soldier who took part in it. Although not in a polished style, I write that which happened—that which I heard, experienced, saw, and did.

I always notice, and it is a fact, that for the most part when we have something valuable in our hands, and deal with it without hindrance, we do not value or prize it as highly as if we understood how much we would miss it after we had lost it, and the longer we continue to have it the less we value it; but after we have lost it and miss the advantages of it, we have a great pain in the heart, and we are all the time imagining and trying to find ways and means by which to get it back again. It seems to me that this has happened to all or most of those who went on the expedition which, in the year of our Savior Jesus Christ 1540, Francisco Vazquez de Coronado led in search of the Seven Cities.

Granted that they did not find the riches of which they had been told, they found a place in which to search for them and the beginning of a good country to settle in, so as to go on farther from there. Since they came back from the country which they conquered and abandoned, time has given them a chance to understand the direction and locality in which they were, and the borders of the good country they had in their hands, and their hearts weep for having lost so favorable an opportunity. Just as men see more at the bullfight when they are upon the seats than when they are around in the ring, now when they know and understand the direction and situation in which they were, and see, indeed, that they can not enjoy it nor recover it, now when it is too late they enjoy telling about what they saw, and even of what they realize that they lost, especially those who are now as poor as when they went there. They have never ceased their labors and have spent their time to no advantage. I say this because I have known several of those who came back from there who amuse themselves now by talking of how it would be to go back and proceed to recover that which is lost, while others enjoy trying to find the reason why it was discovered at all. And now I will proceed to relate all that happened from the beginning. . . .

CHAPTER 2

How Francisco Vazquez de Coronado came to be governor, and the second account which Cabeza de Vaca[3] gave.

Eight years after Nuño de Guzman made this expedition, he was put in prison by a *juez de residencia,*[4] named the licentiate Diego de la Torre, who came from Spain with sufficient powers to do this. After the death of the judge, who had also managed the government of that country himself,

---

3. Álvar Núñez Cabeza de Vaca (1490?–1577?) had been part of a lost exploring party that traveled extensively in the present-day Southwest and northern Mexico in 1528.

4. A judge appointed to review a royal official's finances and affairs.

the good Don Antonio de Mendoza, viceroy of New Spain, appointed as governor of that province Francisco Vazquez de Coronado, a gentleman from Salamanca, who had married a lady in the City of Mexico, the daughter of Alonso de Estrada, the treasurer and at one time governor of Mexico, and the son, most people said, of His Catholic Majesty Don Ferdinand, and many stated it as certain. As I was saying, at the time Francisco Vazquez was appointed governor, he was traveling through New Spain as an official inspector, and in this way he gained the friendship of many worthy men who afterward went on his expedition with him.

It happened that just at this time three Spaniards, named Cabeza de Vaca, Dorantes, and Castillo Maldonado, and a negro, who had been lost on the expedition which Pamfilo de Narvaez led into Florida, reached Mexico. They came out through Culiacan, having crossed the country from sea to sea, as anyone who wishes may find out for himself by an account which this same Cabeza de Vaca wrote and dedicated to Prince Don Philip, who is now King of Spain and our sovereign. They gave the good Don Antonio de Mendoza an extended account of some powerful villages, four and five stories high, of which they had heard a great deal in the countries they had crossed, and other things very different from what turned out to be the truth. The noble viceroy communicated this to the new governor, who gave up the visits he had in hand, on account of this, and hurried his departure for his government, taking with him the negro who had come with three friars of the order of Saint Francis, one of whom was named Friar Marcos de Niza, a regular priest, and another Friar Daniel, a lay brother, and the other Friar Antonio de Santa Maria. When he reached the province of Culiacan he sent the friars just mentioned and the negro, who was named Stephen, off in search of that country, because Friar Marcos offered to go and see it, because he had been in Peru at the time Don Pedro de Alvarado went there overland.

It seems that, after the friars I have mentioned and the negro had started, the negro did not get on well with the friars, because he took the women that were given him and collected turquoises, and got together a stock of everything. Besides, the Indians in those places through which they went got along with the negro better, because they had seen him before. This was the reason he was sent on ahead to open up the way and pacify the Indians, so that when the others came along they had nothing to do except keep an account of the things for which they were looking.

CHAPTER 3

Of how they killed the negro Stephen at Cibola, and Friar Marcos returned in flight.

After Stephen had left the friars, he thought he could get all the reputation and honor himself, and that if he should discover those settlements with such famous high houses, alone, he would be considered bold and courageous. So he proceeded with the people who had followed him, and attempted to cross the wilderness which lies between the country he had passed through and Cibola. He was so far ahead of the friars that, when these reached Chichilticalli, which is on the edge of the wilderness, he was already at Cibola, which is 80 leagues beyond. It is 220 leagues from Culiacan to the edge of the wilderness, and 80 across the desert, which makes 300, or perhaps 10 more or less. As I said, Stephen reached Cibola laden with the large quantity of turquoises they had given him and some beautiful women whom the Indians who followed him and carried his things were taking with them and had given him. These had followed him from all the settlements he had passed, believing that under his protection they could traverse the whole world without any danger.

But as the people in this country were more intelligent than those who followed Stephen, they lodged him in a little hut they had outside their village, and the older men and the governors heard his story and took steps to find out the reason he had come to that country. For three days they made inquiries about him and held a council. The account which the negro gave them of two white men who were following him, sent by a great lord, who knew about the things in the sky, and how these were coming to instruct them in divine matters, made them think that he must be a spy or a guide from some nations who wished to come and conquer them, because it seemed to them unreasonable to say that the people were white in the country from which he came and that he was sent by them, he being black. Besides these other reasons, they thought it was hard of him to ask them for turquoises and women, and so they decided to kill him. They did this, but they did not kill any of those who went with him, although they kept some young fellows and let the others, about 60 persons, return freely to their own country. As these, who were badly scared, were returning in flight, they happened to come upon the friars in the desert 60 leagues from Cibola, and told them the sad news, which frightened them so much that they would not even trust these folks who had been with the negro, but opened the packs they were carrying and gave away everything they had except the holy vestments for saying mass. They returned from here by double marches, prepared for anything, without seeing any more of the country except what the Indians told them.

from CHAPTER 9

Of how the army started from Culiacan and the arrival of the general at Cibola and of the army at Señora and of other things that happened.

The general, as has been said, started to continue his journey from the valley of Culiacan somewhat lightly equipped, taking with him the friars, since none of them wished to stay behind with the army. After they had gone three days, a regular friar who could say mass, named Friar Antonio Victoria, broke his leg, and they brought him back from the camp to have it doctored. He stayed with the army after this, which was no slight consolation for all. The general and his force crossed the country without trouble, as they found everything peaceful, because the Indians knew Friar Marcos and some of the others who had been with Melchior Diaz when he went with Juan de Saldivar[5] to investigate.

After the general had crossed the inhabited region and came to Chichilticalli, where the wilderness begins, and saw nothing favorable, he could not help feeling somewhat downhearted, for, although the reports were very fine about what there was ahead, there was nobody who had seen it except the Indians who went with the negro, and these had already been caught in some lies. Besides all this, he was much affected by seeing that the fame of Chichilticalli was summed up in one tumble-down house without any roof, although it appeared to have been a strong place at some former time when it was inhabited, and it was very plain that it had been built by a civilized and warlike race of strangers who had come from a distance. This building was made of red earth. From here they went on through the wilderness, and in fifteen days came

to a river about eight leagues from Cibola, which they called Red River, because its waters were muddy and reddish. In this river they found mullets like those of Spain. The first Indians from that country were seen here—two of them, who ran away to give the news. During the night following the next day, about two leagues from the village, some Indians in a safe place yelled so that, although the men were ready for anything, some were so excited that they put their saddles on hind-side before; but these were the new fellows. When the veterans had mounted and ridden round the camp, the Indians fled. None of them could be caught because they knew the country.

The next day they entered the settled country in good order, and when they saw the first village, which was Cibola, such were the curses that some hurled at Friar Marcos that I pray God may protect him from them.

It is a little, crowded village, looking as if it had been crumpled all up together. There are ranch houses in New Spain which make a better appearance at a distance. It is a village of about 200 warriors, is three and four stories high, with the houses small and having only a few rooms, and without a courtyard. One yard serves for each section. The people of the whole district had collected here, for there are seven villages in the province, and some of the others are even larger and stronger than Cibola. These folk waited for the army, drawn up by divisions in front of the village. When they refused to have peace on the terms the interpreters extended to them, but appeared defiant, the Santiago[6] was given, and they were at once put to flight. The Spaniards then attacked the village, which was taken with not a little difficulty, since they held the narrow and crooked entrance. During the attack they knocked the general down with a large stone, and would have killed him but for Don Garcia Lopez de Cardenas and Hernando de Alvarado, who threw themselves above him and drew him away, receiving the blows of the stones, which were not few. But the first fury of the Spaniards could not be resisted, and in less than an hour they entered the village and captured it. They discovered food there, which was the thing they were most in need of. After this the whole province was at peace.

The army which had stayed with Don Tristan de Arellano[7] started to follow their general, all loaded with pro-

---

5. Díaz and Saldivar had been sent by Mendoza to verify Fray Marcos's report before Coronado's expedition left; they returned without conclusive information.

6. The Santiago was an invocation to St. James, used by the Spaniards as a battle cry.

7. Arellano had stayed behind with a detachment of men at Culiacan.

visions, with lances on their shoulders, and all on foot, so as to have the horses loaded. With no slight labor from day to day, they reached a province which Cabeza de Vaca had named Corazones (Hearts), because the people here offered him many hearts of animals. He founded a town here and named it San Hieronimo de los Corazones (Saint Jerome of the Hearts). After it had been started, it was seen that it could not be kept up here, and so it was afterward transferred to a valley which had been called Señora. The Spaniards call it Señora, and so it will be known by this name. . . .

from PART II

CHAPTER 3

Of Chichilticalli & the desert, of Cibola, its customs and habits, and of other things.

Chichilticalli is so called because the friars found a house at this place which was formerly inhabited by people who separated from Cibola. It was made of colored or reddish earth. The house was large and appeared to have been a fortress. It must have been destroyed by the people of the district, who are the most barbarous people that have yet been seen. They live in separate cabins and not in settlements. They live by hunting. The rest of the country is all wilderness, covered with pine forests. There are great quantities of the pine nuts. The pines are two or three times as high as a man before they send out branches. There is a sort of oak with sweet acorns, of which they make cakes like sugar plums with dried coriander seeds. It is very sweet, like sugar. Watercress grows in many springs, and there are rosebushes, and pennyroyal, and wild marjoram.

There are barbels and *picones,* like those of Spain, in the rivers of this wilderness. Gray lions and leopards were seen. The country rises continually from the beginning of the wilderness until Cibola is reached, which is 85 leagues, going north. From Culiacan to the edge of the wilderness the route had kept the north on the left hand.

Cibola is seven villages. The largest is called Maçaque. The houses are ordinarily three or four stories high, but in Maçaque there are houses with four and seven stories. These people are very intelligent. They cover their privy parts and all the immodest parts with cloths made like a sort of table napkin, with fringed edges & a tassel at each corner, which they tie over the hips. They wear

long robes of feathers and of the skins of hares and cotton blankets. The women wear blankets, which they tie or knot over the left shoulder leaving the right arm out. These serve to cover the body. They wear a neat well-shaped outer garment of skin. They gather their hair over the two ears, making a frame which looks like an old-fashioned headdress.

This country is in a valley between mountains in the form of isolated cliffs. They cultivate the corn, which does not grow very high, in patches. There are three or four large fat ears having each eight hundred grains on every stalk growing upward from the ground, something not seen before in these parts. There are large numbers of bears in this province, and lions, wild-cats, deer, and otter. There are very fine turquoises, although not so many as was reported. They collect the pine nuts each year, and store them up in advance. A man does not have more than one wife. There are *estufas* or hot rooms in the villages, which are the courtyards or places where they gather for consultation. They do not have chiefs as in New Spain, but are ruled by a council of the oldest men. They have priests who preach to them, whom they call "papas." These are the elders. They go up on the highest roof of the village and preach to the village from there, like public criers, in the morning while the sun is rising, the whole village being silent & sitting in the galleries to listen. They tell them how they are to live, and I believe that they give certain commandments for them to keep, for there is no drunkenness among them nor sodomy nor sacrifices, neither do they eat human flesh nor steal, but they are usually at work. The *estufas* belong to the whole village. It is a sacrilege for the women to go into the *estufas* to sleep. They make the cross as a sign of peace. They burn their dead, and throw the implements used in their work into the fire with the bodies.

It is 20 leagues to Tusayan, going northwest.[8] This is a province with seven villages, of the same sort, dress, habits, and ceremonies as at Cibola. There may be as many as 3,000 or 4,000 men in the fourteen villages of these two provinces. It is 40 leagues or more to Tiguex,[9] the road trending toward the north. The rock of Acuco, which we described in the first part, is between these.

---

8. Present-day northern Arizona.

9. Present-day New Mexico, the region of the pueblo settlements.

JEAN DE LÉRY (1534–1613)

Jean de Léry's *History of a Voyage to the Land of Brazil (Histoire d'un voyage fait en la terre du Bresil)* has been taken by many anthropologists and cultural critics as a model for the modern social science of ethnography, the systematic written description of cultures. Léry had lived for almost a year among the Tupi people at the site of present-day Rio de Janiero, and he wrote with keen observation of the flora and fauna of Brazil and of the food, festivals, wars, and laws of its indigenous peoples. Among Europeans, Brazil received its name from the brazilwood tree, source of a red dye that was sought after in Europe. Indeed, Léry said that he wrote notes there in brazilwood ink. A Portuguese sailor first landed in the area in 1500, but during the sixteenth century, the French, Spanish, and Dutch contended with the Portugese for trade and dominance of the region—and for the alliance of native peoples of the Tupi-Guarani culture.

Léry's special perspective on the Tupi is, in part, a consequence of his being a Protestant from Catholic France: the signs of religious conflict are evident in his book. Léry was born in the Burgundy region of France in 1534. When he was a young child there, Jean Calvin, the second major leader of Protestantism after Martin Luther, was writing, preaching, and establishing a theocratic city-state in Geneva. As a young man Léry traveled to Geneva to study to be a Calvinist minister. But in 1556 Calvin ordered a group of his followers to sail to Brazil with an expedition led by Nicolas Durand, Chevalier de Villegaignon (1510–71). Léry suspended his studies to join the group. French Protestants (called Huguenots), together with the Genevan Calvinists, were interested in the Americas for missionary work and as a possible refuge from persecution in Europe. Villegaignon, an acquaintance of Calvin, was thought to be sympathetic to the Protestants, but once in Brazil he turned hostile toward them. Indeed, he ordered the execution of three Huguenots on a charge of mutiny. Léry's first published work after he returned from Brazil was a eulogy of the three for a Protestant martyrology (a book designed as a hagiography of those martyred to the cause of religion).

As the pages of Léry's *History of a Voyage to the Land of Brazil* reveal, Léry conceived a rivalry in Brazil with André Thévet, a Catholic friar and the royal cosmographer to King Charles IX of France. Thévet had passed ten months in Brazil just prior to Léry's visit, had published *The Singularities of the Southern France (Les Singularitez de la France Antarctique)* in 1556, and reused the same material in his *Cosmographie Universelle,* a kind of atlas and encyclopedia then gaining renown, in 1575. Léry opens his book by attempting to destroy Thévet's status as the French expert on Brazil.

Léry's opposition to his Catholic rivals was based on tragic experience. In the twenty years between his return from Brazil and the publication of his book about it, France became embroiled in the Wars of Religion, and Léry was on the front lines. For eight months in 1573, he was stranded in the beseiged town of Sancerre, where residents turned to eating rats, shoe leather, and finally their dead relatives. His experiences enabled Léry to put the cannibalism of the Tupi, the topic of his chapter 14, in perspective. On that account, as with his consideration of Tupi religion reprinted next, Léry emerged with complex, ambivalent conclusions. He pondered whether the Native Americans had already been exposed to the Christian God and, if not, whether they would be damned for their ignorance. Convinced of the humanity of these people, who had given him refuge in flight from Villegaignon's persecution, Léry tried to fit New World native peoples into biblical frameworks that had originally left little space for such additions.

from HISTORY OF A VOYAGE TO THE LAND OF BRAZIL, OTHERWISE CALLED AMERICA

from Preface[1]

One might well be amazed that, having made the voyage to America eighteen years ago, I have waited so long to bring this history out: therefore it has seemed only proper that I explain what has impeded me. Early on, after I came back to France, I would show people my memoirs, most of them written with brazilwood ink, and in America itself, containing the notable things that I observed during my voyage, and I would give spoken accounts to those who wanted to know yet more; but I had not intended to go any further with them than that. However, some of those with whom I often spoke maintained that, rather than let so many things worthy of memory remain buried, I should set them down in writing at more length, and in a more orderly fashion.

Upon their entreaties and solicitations, in the year 1563 I wrote a rather full report of them. As I was leaving the place where I had been living at that time, I lent it to a reliable person; it so happened that, as the people to whom he had given it to return to me were passing through Lyon, it was taken from them at the city gate, and was so utterly lost that in spite of all my efforts, I could not recover it. Since I was distressed by the loss of this book, a while later, when I retrieved the rough draft that I had left with the person who had transcribed it for me, I managed to have another fair copy made (except for the colloquy of the savage language, which you will see in the twentieth chapter, and of which neither I nor anyone else had a copy). I finished it at a time when I was living in the town of La Charité-sur-Loire; violence was descending in France on those who were of the Religion, and I was constrained, in order to avoid that fury, to leave in haste all my books and papers and take refuge in Sancerre.

Immediately after my departure everything was ransacked, and this second American collection disappeared; so I was a second time deprived of the fruits of my labors.

However, one day I was recounting to a notable Seigneur the first loss in Lyon, and mentioned to him the name of the person to whom, I had been told, my work had been given. He was so taken with this matter, and gave it so much attention that he finally recovered it, and last year (1576), as I was passing by his house, he returned it to me. So that is how it has come about that what I had written about America, which had kept slipping out of my hands, could not until now see the light of day.

But to tell the truth, there was another reason. I had felt that I did not have the necessary qualities to take pen in hand. The same year that I returned from that land, which was in 1558, I saw the book entitled *Of the Singularities of America,* which M. de la Porte, following the tales and memoirs of the friar André Thevet, had prepared for publication. Although I was not unaware of what M. Fumée,[2] in his preface to the *General History of the West Indies* has justly remarked—that the *Singularities* are singularly stuffed with lies—, if the author had been content with that and had gone no further, I might still have suppressed the whole thing.

But in this present year 1577, reading Thevet's *Cosmography,* I saw that he has not only revived and augmented his early errors, but what is more (perhaps supposing that we were all dead, or that if one of us were still alive he would not dare contradict him), with no other pretext than the desire to backbite and, with false, stinging, and abusive digressions, to slander the ministers and those—of whom I was one—who in 1556 accompanied them to go join Villegagnon in Brazil, he has imputed to us crimes. Therefore, in order to refute these falsehoods of Thevet, I have been compelled to set forth a complete report of our voyage. And before I go on, lest you think that I am complaining about this new "cosmographer" without just cause, I will record here the libels that he has put forth against us, contained in Volume II, Book 21, Chapter 2, page 908:

> Moreover I had forgotten to tell you that shortly before, there had been some sedition among the French, brought about by the divisiveness and partiality of the four ministers of the new religion, whom Calvin had sent in order

---

1. Léry published five editions of his history between 1578 and 1611. The selection is from the second edition (Geneva, 1580) translated by Janet Whatley as *History of a Voyage to the Land of Brazil* (1990).

2. Martin Fumée translated Francisco Lopez de Gómara's *General History of the West Indies* from Spanish into French and published it in 1569. At many subsequent points in his book, Léry turns to Gómara for information about native peoples in other parts of the New World. Book and chapter numbers of that lengthy work are cited in Léry's notes.

to plant his bloody Gospel. Chief among them was a seditious minister named Richier,[3] who had been a Carmelite
and a Doctor of Paris a few years before his voyage.
These gallant preachers, who were trying only to get rich
and seize whatever they could, created secret leagues and
factions, and wove plots which led to the death of some
of our men. But some of these mutineers were caught and
executed, and their carcasses went to feed the fishes: the
others escaped, one of whom was the said Richier, who
soon after went to be minister at La Rochelle, where I believe he still is. The savages, incensed by such a tragedy,
nearly rushed upon us to put to death all who were left.

Those are Thevet's very words, which I ask the reader
to note well. For since he never saw us in America, nor we
him, and since even less was he (as he says) in danger for
his life because of us, I want to show that he has been in
this respect a bold-faced liar and a shameless calumnia-
tor. Therefore, to anticipate what he might want to say in
order to save face—that his report does not refer to the
time when he was in that country, but that he means to be
recounting an act that took place since his return—I ask
him in the first place whether this deliberate expression
that he uses, "The savages, incensed by such a tragedy,
nearly rushed upon us to put to death, etc.," can be meant
otherwise than, by this "us," to include himself in this
supposed danger. However, if he wanted to quibble further, and still deny that his intention was something other
than to have it believed that he really saw, in America, the
ministers that he speaks of, then let us listen to the language he uses in another passage:

> Moreover (says this Cordelier) if I had stayed longer in
> that land, I would have tried to win the lost souls of this
> poor people, rather than endeavoring to dig in the earth
> and seek the riches that nature has hidden there. But since
> I was not yet well versed in their language, and since the
> ministers that Calvin had sent there to plant his new
> Gospel were undertaking this charge and were envious of
> my resolution, I abandoned this enterprise of mine.

"Believe the bearer," goes the saying that mocks such
paid liars.[4] Therefore, if this good Roman Catholic has
given no other evidence of having abandoned the world
(as required by the order of Saint Francis, to which he be-

longs)[5] than by, as he says, "having scorned the riches
hidden in the bowels of the earth in Brazil," nor performed any other miracle than the conversion of the
American savages living there, "whose souls" he says "he
had meant to to win, if the ministers hadn't prevented
him"—when I have shown that such is not the case—he
is in great danger of

> neither being put on the Pope's calendar to be canonized,
> nor being hailed after his death as Monsieur Saint
> Thevet. . . .

Let me speak now of my own concerns, and first, of religion, since that is one of the principal issues that can and
must be attended to among men. Even though later,
throughout Chapter XVI, I will explain what the religion
of the savage American Tupinamba is (as far as I have
been able to understand it), still, seeing that I begin that
discussion with a problem which I continually wonder at,
and can by no means resolve as well as one might wish, I
will now touch on it in passing.

Those who have spoken best, according to common
feeling, have not only said but also recognized that being
human and having the intuition of dependence on a
greater Being than oneself, indeed, than any created
thing, are so conjoined with each other that, however different may be the ways of serving God, there remains the
fundamental fact that man must naturally have some religion, true or false. Nonetheless, having thus soberly
judged of the matter, when it is a question of understanding what the nature of man most willingly submits to regarding religious duty, they have also admitted that we all
recognize the truth of what the Latin poet said:

> Man's own cupidity
> Is his chief deity.[6]

If we then apply these two testimonies to our American savages: in the first place, regardless of what is particular to them, one certainly cannot deny that as natural
men they have that disposition and inclination common to
all, which is to understand something greater than man,
on which depends good and evil—or such at least as they
imagine good and evil to be. And to that is related the

---

3. Pierre Richier, a former Catholic priest, converted to
Calvinism and joined the Protestant colonization effort in Brazil.

4. "Volume II, Book 21, Chapter 8 (p. 925)." [Au.]

5. Thévet was a member of the Franciscan religious order,
which, following the model of St. Francis of Assisi, took vows
of poverty.

6. "Virgil, *Aeneid,* Book IX." [Au.]

honor they pay to those whom they call *caraïbes*,[7] whom we will speak of later, who, they believe, bring them good or bad fortune at certain times.

But the goal that they hold as their happiness and sovereign point of honor is the pursuit and vengeance on their enemies (as I shall show later when I speak of their wars); deeming this so great a glory, both in this life and after (just as it was, in part, by the ancient Romans), they hold such vengeance and victory to be their chief good. In short, as will be seen in this history, with respect to what one calls religion among other peoples, it must be said frankly that these poor savages have none whatsoever, and that if there is a nation in the world that exists and lives without God, it is truly this one. However, on this point they are perhaps not utterly condemnable: in admitting and confessing somewhat their misfortune and blindness—although they do not understand it in such a way as to be troubled by it, nor to seek a remedy even when one is presented to them—they do not pretend to be other than what they are. . . .

I do not endorse the fabulous tales found in the books of certain people who, trusting to hearsay, have written things that are completely false; yet I am not ashamed to confess that since I have been in this land of America, where everything to be seen—the way of life of its inhabitants, the form of the animals, what the earth produces—is so unlike what we have in Europe, Asia, and Africa that it may very well be called a "New World" with respect to us, I have revised the opinion that I formerly had of Pliny and others when they describe foreign lands, because I have seen things as fantastic and prodigious as any of those—once thought incredible—that they mention.

As for style and language, beyond what I have already said—that I recognize my incapacity in that regard—still, I know very well that, because I will not have used phrases and terms precise enough to explain and represent the art of navigation and various other things that I mention, there will be some who will not be satisfied—in particular our Frenchmen, who have such delicate ears and are so enamored of fine flowers of rhetoric that they will not approve or receive any writing without new-fangled and high-flown words. Even less will I please those who deem all books not only puerile, but also sterile, unless they are enriched with stories and examples taken from elsewhere: for although I could have put forth

a great number of them concerning the matters that I treat of, nevertheless except for the historian of the West Indies,[8] whom I cite often because he has written several things about the Indians of Peru that are consistent with what I say about our American savages, I have only rarely used others.

And indeed, in my modest judgment, a history that is not bedecked with the plumes of others is rich enough when it is full of its own subject; furthermore, the readers, who then do not stray from the goal proposed by the author that they have in hand, understand all the better his intention. I ask those who read the books that are printed every day, about wars and other things, whether the multitude of quotations taken from elsewhere, even if adapted to the matters being treated, do not weary them.

However, one might well object that, having rebuked Thevet on that point, and now reproving others, I am myself committing the same faults. If someone finds it ill that hereafter, when I speak of savage customs, I often use this kind of expression—"I saw," "I found," this happened to me," and so on (as if I wanted to show myself off)—I reply that not only are these things within my own subject but also I am speaking out of my own knowledge, that is, from my own seeing and experience; indeed, I will speak of things that very likely no one before me has ever seen, much less written about.[9] I mean this, however, not about all of America in general, but only about the place where I lived for about a year: that is, under the tropic of Capricorn among the savages called the *Tupinamba*. Finally, I assure those who prefer the truth simply stated over the adorned and painted lie of fine language, that they will find the things put forth by me in this history not only true, but also, since they have been hidden to those who lived before our age, worthy of wonder. And I pray the Eternal Author and Preserver of this whole universe and of all the beautiful creatures contained therein, that this little work of mine may redound to the glory of His Holy Name. Amen.

---

7. A Tupi word for their shamans.

8. Gómara.

9. In fact, Léry's book was hardly the only published account of Brazil at the time. Thévet's works, of course, Léry dismissed. But there were also several Portuguese works and one by a German, Hans Staden, who had been held captive by the Tupi in the years just prior to Léry's visit and had published his *True History* in 1557. In 1580 Léry did not yet know of that book.

CHAPTER 16

What one might call religion among the Savage Americans: of the errors in which certain charlatans called caraïbes hold them in thrall; and of the great ignorance of God in which they are plunged

Although the adage of Cicero is held by all as an indubitable maxim—that there is no people so brutish, nor any nation so barbarous and savage, as to have no feeling that there is a divinity[10]—nonetheless when I consider closely our Tupinamba of America, I find myself somewhat at a loss in applying it to them. Not only are they utterly ignorant of the sole and true God; what is more, in contrast to the custom of all the ancient pagans, who had many gods (as do the idolaters of today, even the Indians of Peru—a land adjacent to theirs and about five hundred leagues beyond it—who sacrifice to the sun and moon), they neither confess nor worship any gods, either of heaven or of earth. Consequently, having no rites nor any designated place of assembly for holding any ordinary service, they do not pray by any religious form to anything whatsoever, either in public or in private. Likewise, being ignorant of the creation of the world, they do not distinguish the days by names, nor do they give one day preference over another, any more than they count weeks, months or years; they only number and retain time by moons.

They know nothing of writing, either sacred or secular; indeed, they have no kind of characters that signify anything at all. When I was first in their country, in order to learn their language I wrote a number of sentences which I then read aloud to them. Thinking that this was some kind of witchcraft, they said to each other, "Is it not a marvel that this fellow, who yesterday could not have said a single word in our language, can now be understood by us, by virtue of that paper that he is holding and which makes him speak thus?"

And this is the same idea that the savages of Hispaniola had of the Spaniards who were first there: for he who wrote its history said that the Indians, knowing that the Spaniards understood each other without seeing or speaking to each other but only by sending letters from place to place, believed either that they had the spirit or

prophecy, or that the missives spoke. The savages, he said, fearing that they would be caught red-handed, were by this means so firmly held to their duty that they no longer dared to lie to the Spaniards or steal from them.[11]

Here is a fine subject for anyone who would like to enlarge upon it: both to praise and to exalt the art of writing, and to show how the nations that inhabit these three parts of the world—Europe, Asia, and Africa—have reason to praise God more than do the savages of that fourth part, called "America." For while they can communicate nothing except by the spoken word, we, on the other hand, have this advantage, that without budging from our place, by means of writing and the letters that we send, we can declare our secrets to whomever we choose, even to the ends of the earth. So even aside from the learning that we acquire from books, of which the savages seem likewise completely destitute, this invention of writing, which we possess and of which they are just as utterly deprived, must be ranked among the singular gifts which men over here have received from God.[12]

To return to our Tupinamba. In our conversations with them, when it seemed the right moment, we would say to them that we believed in a sole and sovereign God, Creator of the World, who, as He made heaven and earth with all the things contained therein, also now governs and disposes of the whole as it pleases Him to do. Hearing us hold forth on this subject, they would look at each other, saying "Teh!"—their customary interjection of astonishment—and be struck with amazement. As I will recount at more length, when they hear thunder, which they call *Toupan,* they are much afraid. Adapting ourselves to their crudeness, we would seize the occasion to say to them that this was the very God of whom we were speaking, who to show his grandeur and power made heavens and earth tremble; their resolution and response was that since he frightened them in that way, he was good for nothing.

And that, sad to say, is where these poor people are now. "What!" someone will now say, "can it be that, like brute beasts, these Americans live without any religion at all?" Indeed they do, or with almost none; I think that

---

10. Cicero's well-known belief was also held by Léry's spiritual mentor, John Calvin, who had written the same line in his *Institutes of the Christian Religion.*

---

11. "Gómara, *History,* Book I, Chapter 34." [Au.]

12. Léry was mistaken about the Americas being destitute of writing. The Aztec and Mayan civilizations, and arguably others as well, employed sophisticated writing systems centuries before European contact. However, not until the twentieth century was this fact widely recognized by European or American anthropologists.

there is no nation on earth that is further from it. Still, let me begin by declaring what light I perceived that they do, nevertheless, possess in the midst of the dense shadows of ignorance where they lie in bondage: in the first place, not only do they believe in the immortality of souls, but they also firmly maintain that after the death of bodies, the souls of those who have lived virtuously (that is, according to them, those who have properly avenged themselves and have eaten many of their enemies) go off behind the high mountains where they dance in beautiful gardens with the souls of their forebears (these are the Elysian Fields of the poets)[13] while on the contrary, the souls of the effeminate and worthless, who have neglected the defense of their fatherland, go with Aygnan (for so they call the devil in their language), by whom, they say, these unworthy ones are incessantly tormented.

And here it must be noted that these poor people are so afflicted throughout their lives with this evil spirit (whom they also call *Kaagerre*) that when the torment comes upon them, they cry out suddenly as if in a fit of madness—as I have seen them do several times even while they were speaking to us, saying, "Alas, defend us from Aygnan, who is beating us." In fact, they would say that they actually saw him, sometimes in the guise of a beast or bird or in some other strange form. They marveled to see that we were not assaulted by him. When we told them that such exemption came from the God of whom we spoke so often and who, being incomparably stronger than Aygnan, kept him from molesting or harming us, it sometimes happened that, feeling hard-pressed, they would promise to believe in Him as we did. But, as the proverb says, "When danger is past we mock the saint," so as soon as they were delivered, they no longer remembered their promises. Nevertheless, to show that what they endure is no child's play: I have often seen them so apprehensive of this hellish fury that when they remembered what they had suffered in the past, they would strike their thighs with their hands, the sweat of anguish beading their brow, and lament to me or to another of our company, saying, "*Mair Atouassap, acequeiey Aygnan Atoupavé,*" that is, "Frenchman, my friend—my perfect ally—, I fear the devil (or the evil spirit) more than any other thing." On the other hand, if the one they addressed said to them, "*Nacequeiey Aygnan,*" that is, "I do not fear him," then, bewailing their state, they would answer, "Alas, how happy we would be if we were saved as you are!" "You would have to believe and trust, as we do, in Him who is stronger and mightier," we would reply. But although at times, as they saw the evil approaching or already present, they declared they would do so, afterwards it all vanished from their brain.

Before going on, I will add something more to the remark I have made, that our American Brazilians consider the soul immortal. The historian of the West Indies said that the savages of Cuzco, the principal city of Peru, and those of that region, likewise confess the immortality of the soul. What is more (despite the maxim, which has always been commonly held by theologians, that all the philosophers, pagans, and other Gentiles and barbarians had been ignorant of and denied the resurrection of the flesh), they even believe in the resurrection of the body. And here is the example he offers: The Indians, upon seeing that the Spaniards who were opening the sepulchres to get at the gold and riches were scattering the bones of the dead all about, entreated them not to disperse them that way, lest it prevent them from being brought back to life; for they (the savages of that country) believe in the resurrection of the body and the immortality of the soul.[14] There is also another secular author who affirmed that in former times a certain pagan nation had arrived at this belief: "Afterwards Caesar vanquished Ariovistus and the Germans, who were great men beyond measure and fearless; for they attacked boldly and had no fear of death, confident that they would come back to life."[15]

I have wished expressly to recount all of this here, to demonstrate that if those worse-than-devil-ridden atheists, with whom our part of the earth is now covered, share with the Tupinamba the delusion—indeed, even stranger and more bestial in their case—that there is no God, they may at least learn from them, in the first place that even in this world there are devils to torment those who deny God and His power. They may reply that since there are no devils except the evil impulses of men, the belief in them is but a fantasy harbored by these savages about things that are not. To this I answer that if one considers what I have truly recounted—that the Americans are visibly and actually tormented by evil spirits—it will be easy to judge

---

13. The Tupi belief in an afterlife in a land toward the West resembled stories told by other Native American groups. Léry compares it to the classical Greek myth of an abode of the blessed after death.

---

14. "Gomara, *History,* Book 4, chapter 124." [Au.]

15. "Appian, *Of the Celtic War,* Chapter 1." [Au.]

how wrong it is to attribute these things to human impulses. For however violent those passions might be, how could they afflict men in this way? I will not bother to mention our own experience of these things over here in Europe; and were it not that I would be throwing pearls before swine, I could cite what is said in the Gospel about those possessed by demons who were cured by the Son of God.

In the second place, since these atheists, who, denying all principles, are utterly unworthy of having cited for them what the Scriptures say so magnificently about the immortality of souls, I will rather offer to them the example of our poor Brazilians, who, blind as they are, can yet teach them that there is in man a spirit which not only lives after the body dies, but also, when separated from the body, is susceptible of perpetual felicity or wretchedness.

And in the third place, regarding the resurrection of the flesh: inasmuch as these atheist dogs delude themselves by thinking that when the body is dead it never rises again, I cite the testimony of the Indians of Peru, who, in the midst of their false religion (indeed, having almost no knowledge other than natural feeling) will give the lie to the accursed atheists, and rise up in judgment against them. But since they are worse than the devils themselves—who, as St. James says, believe that there is a God, and tremble[16]—I do them too much honor in offering them these barbarians as theologians. Without speaking further at present of such abominable creatures, I send them straight to Hell, where they will taste the fruits of their monstrous errors.

Let me return to my principal subject, and pursue the consideration of what might be called religion among the savages of America. If one examines closely what I have already touched on—that is, that they would desire to live in repose but are nevertheless forced, when they hear thunder, to tremble under a power they cannot resist—one can gather that Cicero's adage is verified through them after all: indeed, there is no people that does not have the feeling that there is a divinity. Moreover, one can see that this fear they have of Him whom they refuse to acknowledge will render them utterly without excuse. And indeed, it is said by the Apostle that although God in former times let all the Gentiles go their own way, nevertheless, He did not leave himself without witness, in that He did good to everyone, and gave us rain from heaven and the fruitful

seasons:[17] this clearly shows us that when men do not recognize their Creator, it is a result of their own wickedness. For further proof, it is said elsewhere that the invisible things of God are clearly seen in the creation of the world.[18]

So although our Americans do not confess it with their lips, nonetheless inasmuch as they are convinced within themselves that there is some divinity, I concluded that just as they will not be exempt from judgment, so, too, they will not be able to plead ignorance. But beyond what I have said about their belief in the immortality of the soul, about the thunder that terrifies them, about the devils and evil spirits that beat them and torment them (three points to note), I will show in the fourth place how, despite the utter darkness in which they are plunged, the seed of religion (if, after all, what they do deserves that name) germinates in them and cannot be extinguished.

To proceed further into this matter, you must know that there are among them certain false prophets that they call *caraïbes,* who, going and coming from village to village like popish indulgence-bearers,[19] would have it believed that by their communication with spirits they can give to anyone they please the strength to vanquish enemies in war, and, what is more, can make grow the big roots and the fruits (which I have described elsewhere) produced by this land of Brazil.

Now I had heard from the Norman interpreters who had lived a long time in that country that our Tupinamba held a solemn assembly every three or four years; since I once found myself by chance attending one of these, and here is what I can truthfully report. Another Frenchman named Jacques Rousseau and I, with an interpreter, were traveling through the country, and had spent one night in a village named *Cotiva.* The next morning very early, as we were about to move on, we saw the savages from the neighboring regions arriving from all directions, and being met by people of the village, who were coming out of their houses; five or six hundred were soon assembled in a large open place. We stopped and turned back to find out the purpose of this assembly, and saw them suddenly separate into three groups: all the men in one house, the women in another, and the children in a third. Seeing ten

---

16. James 2.19.

17. Acts 14.17.

18. Romans 1.20.

19. Léry expresses his contempt for the Tupi shamans by comparing them to Catholic priests and their practice of selling parishioners indulgences, or forgiveness from sins.

or twelve of these *caraïbe* gentlemen who had joined the men, and suspecting that they would do something extraordinary, I urged my companions to stay with me to see this mystery, and they agreed.

The *caraïbes,* before leaving the women and children, had strictly forbidden them to go out of their houses; rather they were to listen attentively to the singing from there. They also ordered us to confine ourselves to the house where the women were. While we were having our breakfast, with no idea as yet of what they intended to do, we began to hear in the men's house (not thirty feet from where we stood) a very low murmur, like the muttering of someone reciting his hours. Upon hearing this, the women (about two hundred of them) all stood up and clustered together, listening intently. The men little by little raised their voices and were distinctly heard singing all together and repeating this syllable of exhortation, *He, he, he, he;* the women, to our amazement, answered them from their side, and with a trembling voice; reiterating that same interjection *He, he, he, he,* they let out such cries, for more than a quarter of an hour, that as we watched them we were utterly disconcerted. Not only did they howl, but also, leaping violently into the air, they made their breasts shake and they foamed at the mouth—in fact, some, like those who have the falling-sickness[20] over here, fell in a dead faint; I can only believe that the devil entered their body and that they fell into a fit of madness. We heard the children similarly shaken and tormented in the house where they were kept, which was quite near us. Although I had been among the savages for more than half a year and was already fairly well used to their ways, nonetheless (to be frank) being somewhat frightened and not knowing how the game might turn out, I wished I were back at our fort. However, after these chaotic noises and howls had ended and the men had taken a short pause (the women and children were now silent), we heard them once again singing and making their voices resound in a harmony so marvelous that you would hardly have needed to ask whether, since I was now somewhat easier in my mind at hearing such sweet and gracious sounds, I wished to watch them from nearby.

When I was about to go out and draw near, the women held me back; also, our interpreter said that in the six or seven years that he had been in that country, he had never dared be present among the savages at such a ceremony:

so that, he added, if I went over there I would be behaving imprudently and exposing myself to danger. For a moment I was undecided; however, as I sounded out the case further, it seemed to me that he gave me no good reason for what he said. Besides, I knew I could count on the friendship of certain kindly elders who lived in this village, which I had visited four or five times; so, willy-nilly, I ventured forth.

I drew near the place where I heard the chanting; the houses of the savages are very long and of a roundish shape (like the trellises of gardens over here). Since they are covered with grasses right down to the ground, in order to see as well as I might wish, I made with my hands a little opening in the covering. I beckoned to the two Frenchmen who were watching me; emboldened by my example, they drew near without any hindrance or difficulty, and we all three entered the house. Seeing that our entering did not disturb the savages as the interpreter thought it would, but rather, maintaining admirably their ranks and order, they continued their chants, we quietly withdrew into a corner to drink in the scene.

Now since I promised earlier, when I spoke of the dancing at their drinking bouts and *caouinages,*[21] that I would also tell of their other way of dancing, the more fully to represent them, I will describe the solemn poses and gestures that they used here. They stood close to each other, without holding hands or stirring from their place, but arranged in a circle, bending forward, keeping their bodies slightly stiff, moving only the right leg and foot, with the right hand placed on the buttocks, and the left hand and arm hanging: in that posture they sang and danced.

Because there were so many of them, there were three circles, and in the middle of each circle there were three or four of these *caraïbes,* richly decked in robes, headdresses, and bracelets made of beautiful natural feathers of various colors, holding in each hand a *maraca* or rattle[22] made of a fruit bigger than an ostrich-egg (of which I have spoken elsewhere). So that (as they said) the spirit might thereafter speak through these rattles, to dedicate them to this use they made them sound incessantly. And

20. Epilepsy.

21. In chapter 9 of the *History,* Léry described how the Tupi make an intoxicating beverage, *caouin,* and the festival of drinking it.

22. The word has been adopted into English for a musical instrument made from a gourd filled with beans or stones.

you could find no better comparison than to the bell-ringers that accompany those impostors who, exploiting the credulity of our simple folk over here, carry from place to place the reliquaries of Saint Anthony or Saint Bernard, and other such instruments of idolatry.[23] In addition to this description, I have tried to illustrate all this for you by the accompanying figure of a dancer and a *maraca*-player.

Moreover, these *caraïbes,* advancing and leaping forward, then drawing back, did not always stay in one place as the others did. I noticed that they would frequently take a wooden cane four or five feet long, at the end of which was burning some of the dried herb *petun*[24] (which I have mentioned elsewhere); turning and blowing the smoke in all directions on the other savages, they would say to them, "So that you may overcome your enemies, receive all of you the spirit of strength." And thus these master *caraïbes* did several times.

These ceremonies went on for nearly two hours, with the five or six hundred men dancing and singing incessantly; such was their melody that—although they do not know what music is—those who have not heard them would never believe that they could make such harmony. At the beginning of this witches' sabbath, when I was in the women's house, I had been somewhat afraid; now I received in recompense such joy, hearing the measured harmonies of such a multitude, and especially in the cadence and refrain of the song, when at every verse all of them would let their voices trail, saying *Heu, heuaure, heura, heuraure, heura, heura, oueh*—I stood there transported with delight. Whenever I remember it, my heart trembles, and it seems their voices are still in my ears. When they decided to finish, each of them struck his right foot against the earth more vehemently than before, and spat in front of him; then all of them with one voice uttered hoarsely two or three times the words *He, hua, hua, hua,* and then ceased.

Since I did not understand their language perfectly at that time, they had said several things that I had not been able to comprehend, and I asked the interpreter to explain them to me. He told me that at the beginning of the songs they had uttered long laments for their dead ancestors, who were so valiant, but in the end, they had taken com-fort in the assurance that after their death they would go join them behind the high mountains, where they would dance and rejoice with them. Likewise, they had pronounced violent threats against the Ouetaca (a nation of enemy savages, who, as I have said elsewhere, are so warlike that they have never been able to subdue them), to capture and eat them, as their *caraïbes* had promised. Moreover, mingled in their songs there was mention of waters that had once swelled so high above their bounds that all the earth was covered, and all the people in the world were drowned, except for their ancestors, who took refuge in the highest trees. This last point, which is the closest they come to the Holy Scriptures, I have heard them reiterate several times since. And, indeed, it is likely that from father to son they have heard something of the universal flood that occurred in the time of Noah.[25] In keeping with the habit of men, which is always to corrupt the truth and turn it into falsehood, together with what we have already seen—that, being altogether deprived of writing, it is hard for them to retain things in their purity—they have added this fable (as did the poets), that their ancestors took refuge in the trees.

To return to our *caraïbes.* They were cordially received that day by all the other savages, who entertained them magnificently with the best food they could find, not forgetting to make them drink and *caouiner,* according to their custom. My two French companions and I, who as I said had found ourselves unexpectedly present at this bacchanalia, were also well feasted by our *moussacats* (that is, by the generous householders who give food to people who are passing through). In addition to all this, after these solemn days have passed (during which, every three or four years, all the mummery you have heard about takes place again among our Tupinamba), and even sometimes before, the *caraïbes* go from one village to another, and have each family adorn three or four of these big rattles that they call *maracas,* using the finest plumes they can find. When the *maracas* are thus decked out, they stick the long end of the rod that runs through them into the earth, and arrange them along the middles of the houses; they then demand that the *maracas* be given food and drink. So these impostors make those poor simpletons believe that these fruits and gourds, hollowed out, adorned, and consecrated, will then eat and drink at night.

---

23. Another expression of Léry's anti-Catholicism; he derides the belief that the relics of saints held miraculous powers.

24. Tobacco. The word was later used by French explorers in North America.

25. Many indigenous cultures around the world have legends of a primordial flood, but Léry believed that this must be a distorted version of the story in Genesis.

Since each head of a household credits this, he never fails to put out beside his *maracas* not only flour with meat and fish, but also some of their *caouin*. They usually leave them planted in the earth for two or three weeks, always attended to in the same way; and they have a strange belief concerning these *maracas* (which they almost always have in hand): attributing a certain sanctity to them once this bewitchment has been accomplished, they say that whenever they make them sound, a spirit speaks.

As we passed through their longhouses, if we saw some fine morsels presented to these *maracas* and took and ate them (as we often did), our Americans, duped as they were, and judging that such a deed would bring some misfortune down upon us, were no less offended than those superstitious ones, successors of the priests of Baal, at seeing someone take the offerings brought to their puppets—on which offerings, however, to the dishonor of God, they themselves feed gluttonously and idly with their whores and bastards. If, when we seized the occasion to point out their errors, we told them that the *caraïbes,* who gave it out that the *maracas* ate and drank, were deceiving them; and also, that it was not the *caraïbes* (as they falsely boasted) who caused their fruits and their big roots to grow, but rather the God in whom we believe and whom we were making known to them— well, that had about as much effect as speaking against the Pope over here, or saying in Paris that the reliquary of St. Genevieve doesn't make it rain.[26] Therefore these *caraïbe* charlatans hated us no less than the false prophets of Israel (fearing to lose their fat morsels) hated Elijah, the true servant of God, who similarly revealed their abuses,[27] they began to hide from us, fearing even to approach or to sleep in the villages where they knew we were lodging.

Pursuing what I said at the beginning of this chapter: our Tupinamba (all their ceremonies notwithstanding) do not worship either their *caraïbes* or their *maracas* or any creatures whatsoever by kneeling or by any other external gesture; much less do they pray to them or invoke them. Nonetheless, I will cite another example of what I have perceived in them concerning religion. I was with some compatriots in a village named *Ocarentin,* two leagues from Cotiva. As we were having our dinner in an open area, the savages of that place assembled—not to eat with us but to view us. For if they want to do honor to a per-

sonage they do not take their meal while he does (not even the old men, who were proud to see us in their village, and showed us all possible signs of friendship). Each one had in his hand the nosebone of a certain fish, two or three feet long and saw-shaped. Rather like our footmen archers, they stood around us to chase away the children, saying to them in their language: "Get out of here, you little rascals! The likes of you are not to come near these people."

After this whole crowd had let us dine in peace without interrupting a single word of our conversation, an old man who had observed that we had prayed to God at the beginning and end of our meal asked us, "What does this mean, this way of doing things, taking off your hat twice, and remaining silent except for one speaker? To whom was all that addressed, those things he was saying? Is it to you who are here, or to others who are absent?" Seizing the occasion that he offered us to speak of the true religion, and considering that this village of Ocarentin is one of the biggest and most populated of that country, and that the savages seemed more attentive than usual and more ready to listen to us, I enlisted our interpreter to help me make them understand what I was about to say.

I first answered the old man's question by telling him that it was to God that we had addressed our prayers, and that although He was not visible, nonetheless He not only heard us but He knew what we were thinking and what was in our hearts. I then began to speak to them about the creation of the world. Above all, I insisted on their understanding that if God had made man excellent above all other creatures, it was so that he might all the more glorify his Creator. I added that, because we served Him, He preserved us as we crossed the sea, even as we lived on that sea continually for four or five months without putting foot to ground, just so that we might seek them out. We did not fear, as they did, being tormented by Aygnan, neither in this life nor in the other: so, I said, if they were willing to turn away from the errors in which their lying and deceiving *caraïbes* held them captive, and leave their barbarity and no longer eat the flesh of their enemies, they would receive the same grace whose effects they had seen in us. In short, so that we might prepare them to receive Jesus Christ, having told them of man's perdition, we spent more than two hours on the matter of the Creation, constantly making comparisons with things that were known to them (on which, however, for the sake of brevity, I will speak no further).

All of them, lending ear, listened attentively and with great wonder. Amazed at what they had heard, another old man spoke up: "Certainly you have told us of marvels that

---

26. Anti-Catholic expressions.

27. "I Kings 19.19." [Au.]

we had never heard of. Still, your discourse has recalled to me something we often heard our grandfathers tell of: a long time ago, so many moons ago that we cannot count them, a *Mair*[28] (that is, a Frenchman or a stranger) dressed and bearded like some of you, came into this country, and, thinking to bring them to an obedience to your God, spoke to them in the same manner that you have just done. But, as we have also heard from father to son, they refused to believe. And so there came another who, as a sign of a curse, left them the sword with which we have been killing each other ever since. And we have entered so far into our possession of it that if we were to desist and abandon our custom, all neighboring nations would mock us." We replied vehemently that, far from concerning themselves with the jibes of others, they had only to worship and serve the sole and true God of heaven and earth, whom we were making known to them; then if their enemies came and attacked them, they would overcome and vanquish them all. In short, by the efficacy that God gave to our words, our Tupinamba were so stirred that several of them promised to live as we had taught them, and even to leave off eating the human flesh of their enemies. After this colloquy (which, as I have said, lasted a long time), they got down on their knees with us, and one of our company, giving thanks to God, offered aloud in the midst of this people a prayer, which was then explained by the interpreter. Then they bedded us down in their style, in cotton beds suspended in the air. But before we fell asleep, we heard them singing together, that in order to avenge themselves on their enemies, they must capture and eat more of them than they ever had before.

And there you have the inconstancy of this poor people, a fine example of the corrupt nature of man. Still, I am of the opinion that if Villegagnon had not revolted from the Reformed Religion, and if we had stayed longer in that country, we would have drawn and won some of them to Jesus Christ.

Since that time I have reflected on what they had said they had learned from their forebears: that many centuries earlier a *Mair,* that is, a man from our part of the world (whether French or German hardly matters), had come into their land and had told them of the true God; I have wondered whether he could have been one of the Apos-

tles.[29] Now by no means do I approve of the fanciful books which people have written about the voyages and peregrinations of the Apostles, which go beyond what the Word of God has said on the matter. However, Nicephorus,[30] recounting the story of St. Matthew, says expressly that he preached the Gospel in the country of man-eating cannibals,[31] a people not so different from our Brazilian Americans. But I put much more trust in the passage of St. Paul, taken from the Nineteenth Psalm, which some good expositors apply to the Apostles: "Their sound went into the earth, and their words unto the ends of the world."[32] Considering that they have certainly been in many far-off lands unknown to us, why may we not believe that one of them, or even several, have been in the land of these barbarians? This would serve as an illumination and general exposition of the saying of Jesus Christ, that the Gospel would be preached throughout the world.[33] While I make no claim concerning what happened in the time of the Apostles, I will maintain nonetheless, as I have shown in this history, that in our day I have seen and heard the Gospel proclaimed even to the Antipodes. So that not only will any objection about that passage from the Gospel be answered by this, but also, it will make the savages all the more inexcusable on the Last Day.

As for the other remark of our Americans, that since their ancestors refused to believe him who tried to lead them into the right path, there came another, who, because of this refusal, cursed them and gave them the sword with which they still kill each other every day: we read in the Apocalypse that to him who sat on the red horse—which according to some signifies persecution by fire and by war—was given power "to take peace from the earth, and that they should kill one another; and there was

---

28. This word, which the Tupi used as a general term for their heroes, came to be applied to European colonists (according to the colonists) and implied an awe of their powers.

29. Following upon the New Testament's claim that the faith of Jesus spread around the world, there arose many legends that the apostles had appeared in distant lands, including India and America.

30. Léry cites the *Scriptoris vere catholici ecclesisaticae historiae* by Byzantine historian Nicephorus Callistus Xanthopoulos (1256?–1335?) for one of the legends of the travels of the apostles.

31. "Book 2, chapter 41." [Au.]

32. "Psalms 19.5; Romans 10.18." [Au.]

33. "Matthew 24.14." [Au.]

to him given a great sword."[34] There is the text that, to the letter, corresponds to what the Tupinamba say and practice; still, since I am wary of distorting its true sense, and do not want to think that my interpretations are far-fetched, I will leave the application of this text to others.

I do recall, however, another example that I will put forth here, showing that these nations of savage living in the land of Brazil are teachable enough to be drawn to the knowledge of God, if one were to take the trouble to instruct them. One day, going from our island to the mainland to get provisions, I was accompanied by two of our Tupinikin savages and by another of the nation called *Oueanen* (which is their ally), who had come with his wife to visit his friends and was returning to his own land. As I was passing with them through a great forest, contemplating so many different trees, grasses, and flowers, all green and fragrant, and hearing the songs of the countless birds warbling through the woods in the sunlight, I felt impelled to praise God, and feeling gay of heart, I began to sing aloud Psalm 104, "Bless the Lord, O my soul." My three savages and the woman who walked behind me took such delight in it (that is, in the sound, for they understood nothing of the rest) that when I had finished, the Oueanen, stirred with joy, his face beaming, came forward and said to me, "Truly you have sung wonderfully; your resounding song has recalled to me that of a nation that is our neighbor and ally, and I have been filled with joy at hearing you. But we understand their language, and not yours: therefore I entreat you to tell us what your song was about." So I explained to him as best I could (I was on my way to join two of my countrymen at the place where I was to spend the night, and I was the only Frenchman present) that I had in general praised my God for the beauty and governance of his creatures, and in particular I had attributed to him this: that it was he alone who nourished all men and all animals, and made the trees, fruits, and plants grow throughout the whole world; moreover, that this song I had just sung, dictated by the spirit of this magnificent God whose name I had celebrated, had first been sung more than ten thousand moons ago (for that is their way of counting) by one of our great prophets, who had left it to posterity to be used to that same end. They are wonderfully attentive to what

you say to them, and will never interrupt you, so that, as they made their way, it was more than half an hour after hearing this discourse that—using their interjection of amazement, "Teh!"—they said, "O you *Mairs* (that is, Frenchmen) how fortunate you are to know so many secrets that are hidden from us poor wretches!" And to compliment me, saying "Here, because you have sung so well," he made me a present of an *agouti*[35] that he was carrying, which I have described along with other animals in Chapter X.

I have insisted on making this digression to prove that these nations of America, however barbarous and cruel they may be toward their enemies, are not so fierce that they do not consider what is said to them in a reasonable way. And indeed, as far as the natural quality of man is concerned, I maintain that they hold forth better than most of our peasants, and indeed than some others back over here who think they are very clever fellows.

To conclude now, let me touch on a question that one might ask about this whole subject I am treating: that is, from whom are these savages descended? In the first place, they certainly issued from one of the three sons of Noah; but to affirm which one, especially since it could not be proved by Holy Scripture nor yet by secular history, is not easy. It is true that Moses, mentioning the children of Japhet, said that they inhabited the islands; but since, as everyone agrees, what is meant is the countries of Greece, Gaul, Italy, and other regions over here (which, since the sea separates them from Judaea, are called "islands" by Moses), there would be no good reason to take this to mean America or the adjacent lands.

Similarly, to say that they are descended from Shem, from whom issued the blessed seed and the Jews: although the latter too have so corrupted themselves that they have finally been rightly rejected by God, nonetheless for several reasons one could cite, no one, I think, would admit such a thing.

As for blessedness and eternal bliss (which we believe in and hope for through Jesus Christ alone), in spite of the glimpse and the intimation of it that I have said they have, this is a people accursed and abandoned by God, if there be any such under the heavens. (As to this earthly life, I have already shown and will show again that, while most people over here, who are given over to the goods of this world, do nothing but languish, they on the contrary who

---

34. Revelations 6.4. This, and the curse of the *Mair* mentioned earlier, are versions of a widespread pattern of myths explaining the differences between European weapons and those the Americans were using at the time of contact.

---

35. A South American species of rodent still called by this name.

take things as they come, spend their days and live cheerfully, almost without care.) It seems, therefore, more likely that we should conclude that they are descended from Ham; that, I think, is the most plausible conjecture. For the Holy Scripture testifies that when Joshua began to enter and take possession of the land of Canaan according to the promises that God gave to the patriarchs and the commandment that he himself had received, the people who lived there were struck with such terror that their strength failed them.[36] It could have happened (I may be wrong in this) that the forebears and ancestors of our Americans, having been chased by the children of Israel from several regions of the land of Canaan, took ship and put themselves at the mercy of the sea, to be cast ashore in this land of America. And indeed, the Spaniard who wrote the *General History of the Indies*[37] (a man well versed in all kinds of knowledge, whatever else he may be) is of the opinion that the Indians of Peru, a land adjacent to that of Brazil, are descended from Ham, and have

inherited the curse that God laid on him[38]—a thing that I had also thought and written in the notes that I made for the present history more than sixteen years before I had seen his book. Still, since one could make many objections to all this, and as I do not want to pronounce on it here, I will let everyone believe what he pleases.

However that may be, I take it as resolved that these are poor people issued from the corrupt race of Adam. But having considered them thus void and deprived of any right sense of God, my faith has by no means been in the least shaken on that account. Even less have I concluded from all this, with the atheists and Epicureans, either that there is no God, or that He does not concern Himself in human affairs; on the contrary, having clearly recognized in their persons the difference between those who are illuminated by the Holy Spirit and the Holy Scripture, and those who are abandoned to their own faculties and left in their blindness, I have been greatly confirmed in the assurance of the truth of God.

---

36. "Joshua 2.9." [Au.]

37. "Book 5, Chapter 217." [Au.]

38. Léry cites Gómara's book once again. This curse was widely cited as justification for the enslavement of Africans, who were believed to be descended from Ham and his son Canaan. The biblical text is in Genesis 9.22–26.

René Goulaine de Laudonnière (1529–1574)

René Goulaine de Laudonnière was born in northern France to a Protestant family with connections to Gaspard de Coligny, a royal adviser and leader of the Huguenots (French Protestants). He experienced a diverse career, in war and in peace. In 1561 he was captured by a Spanish galleon off Catalonia in command of a ship that was carrying war materials to the natives of Algiers. The next year he became extensively involved in French efforts to establish colonies in Florida and the Carolinas, territory also claimed by Spain.

Laudonnière traveled to South Carolina in 1562, second in command of an expedition under the leadership of Jean Ribault (1520–65). There, on present-day Parris Island, a fort named for the French King Charles IX was erected. Ribault left some of his force behind to colonize the area, while he and the larger part of the expedition returned to France for reinforcements. Those who remained behind experienced severe food shortages and confusion, and their internal dissensions eventually led to their building a small ship and returning to France instead of waiting for reinforcements.

Laudonnière was sent to lead a second expedition in 1564, establishing Fort Caroline (near present-day Jacksonville, Florida). This group suffered difficulties like those faced by the first group of colonists, but they managed to remain until the arrival of a third expedition, under the command of Ribault, who had orders to take over in command at Fort Caroline. At the same time, however, in late August, Spanish forces had also arrived in Florida, with orders to drive the French Protestants out of the area. Under the command of Pedro Menéndez de Avilés, the Spanish defeated the garrison and killed almost all the French. Laudonnière was among the few survivors who escaped on two French ships.

In 1566, Laudonnière reported personally to the king. After his return to France, he continued working as a navigator. His preparations for a new voyage to America (a voyage never made) saved him from execution on August 24, 1572, as Huguenots in France were being persecuted for their faith and, worse, executed, with the tacit approval of the intolerant French Crown. Laudonnière's written accounts of the French expeditions to Florida and South Carolina were first printed in 1586 and in England the following year. The following selection reprints the Preface to that work and a portion of the description of the first expedition.

from A NOTABLE HISTORIE CONTAINING FOURE VOYAGES MADE BY CERTAINE FRENCH CAPTAINES UNTO FLORIDA[1]

from Preface

There are two thinges, which according to mine opinion have been the principall causes in consideration whereof as well they of auncient times, as those of our age have been enduced to travell into farre and remote regions. The first hath been the naturall desire which we have to fetch out the commodities to live happely, plentifully, and at ease: be it whether one abandon his naturall cuntrie altogether, to dwell in a better, or bee it that men make voiages thither, there to fetch out and bring from thence such thinges as are there to bee found, and are in greatest estimation and in most request in our cuntries. The second cause hath beene the multitude of people too frutefull in generation, which, being no longer able to dwell in their native soyles, have entred uppon their neighbours limites, and oftentimes passing further have pearced even unto the uttermost regions. After this sorte the north climate, a frutefull father of so many nations, hath oftentimes sent foorth this way and that way his valiant people, and by this meane hath peopled infinite countries: so that most of the nations of Europe drawe their original from these partes. Contrariwise the more southern regions, because they be too barraine by reason of their insupportable heate which raigneth in them, neede not any such sending foorth of their inhabitances, and have been oftentimes constrained to receave other people more often by force of armes then

willingly. All Africke, Spaine, and Italie, can also testifie the same, which never so abounded with people that they had neede to send them abroode to inhabit else where: as on the contrary Scythia, Norway, Gotland,[2] and France have done. The posterities of which nations remaineth yet not only in Italie, Spaine and Affricke, but also in frutefull and faire Asia. Neverthelesse I find that the Romains proceding farther, or rather adding unto these two chiefe causes aforesayd, (as being most curious to plant not only their ensignes and victories, but also their lawes, customes, and religion in those provinces which they had conquered by force of armes) have oftentimes by the decree of their soveraine Senate sent forth inhabitantes, which they called colonies, (thinking by this way to make their name immortall), even to the unfurnishing of their owne countrye of the forces which should have perserved the same in her perfection: a thing which hindred them much more, then advanced them to the possession of the universall monarchie, where unto their intention did aspyre. For it came to passe that their colonies here and there being miserably sacked by strang people did utterly ruine and overthrowe their empire. The brinkes of the river of Rine are yet red, those of Danubius are noe lesse bloodie, and our France be came fatte with their blood which they lost. These are the effectes and rewards of al such as being pricked forward with this Romaine and tirannicall ambition will goe aboute thus to subdue strange people: effectes, I say, contrarie to the profitte which those shall receave, which only are affectioned to the common benefitte, that is to say, to the generall pollicie of all men, and endevour to unite them one with another as well by traficke and forraine conversations, as also by militarie vertues, and force of armes, whenas the savages wil not yeeld unto their endevours so much tending unto their profite.

For this cause princes have sent foorth out of the dominions certaine men of good activitie, to plante them-

<hr />

1. The text is from *A Notabile History Containing Four Voyages Made by Certaine French Captains Unto Florida,* by René Laudonnière, ed. Martin Basonier and trans. Richard Hakluyt (London, 1587).

<hr />

2. Sweden.

selves in strang countries, there to make their profite to bring the countrie to civilitie, and, if it might be, to reduce the inhabitantes to the true knowledg of our God: an end so much more commendable, as it is farre from all tiranicall and cruell governmement: and so they have always thrived in their enterprises, and by lyttle and little gained the hartes of them which they have conquered or wonne unto them by any meanes. Hereof we may gather that sometimes it is good, yea very expedient to send foorth men to discover the pleasure and commoditie of strang countries: But so, that the country out of which these companies are to passe remayne not weakned, nor deprived of her forces: And againe in such sorte that the companie sent forth be of so juste and sufficient number, that it may not bee defeated by strangers, which every foote endevour nothing else but to surprise the same upon the suddaine. As within these fewe dayes past the french have proved to my great greife, being able by no means possible to withstand the same, considering that the elementes, men, and al the favours which might be hoped for of a faithful and Christian alliance fought against us: which thing I purpose to discover in this present historie with so evident truth, that the kings majestie my soverainge prince shall in parte be satisfied of the diligence which I have used in his service, and myne adversaries shall find themselves so discovered in their false reportes, that they shall have no place of refuge. But before I beginne, I will brefely set downe the situation and description of the land where unto we have sailed and where we have inhabited from the year 1561 unto sixtie five, to the ende that those thinges may the more easily be borne a way, which I meane to describe in this discourse. . . .

from The Historie of the First Voyage[3]

The next day in the morning, what time the weather waxing fayre and the Sea calme wee discouvered a River which we called Belle a veoir.[4] After we had sayled three or foure leagues, we began to espie our Pinnisses which came straight towardes us, and at their arivall they reported to the Captayne,[5] that, while the foule weather and fogges endured, they harbored themselves in a mightie

River which in bignesse and beautie exceeded the former: wherewithall the Captayne was exceeding joyfull, for his chiefe desire was to finde out an Haven to harboure his Shippes, and there to refresh our selves for a while. Thus making thitherwarde wee arrived athwarte the said River (which because of the fayrenesse and largenes thereof we named Port Royal) wee strooke our sayles and cast Anker at ten fathom of water: for the depth is such, namely when the Sea beginneth to flowe, that the greatest Shippes of Fraunce, yea, the Arguesses[6] of Venice may enter in there. Having cast Anker the Captayne with his Souldiers went on shore, and hee himselfe went first on land: where we found the place as pleasant as was possible, for it was all covered over with mightie high Okes and infinite store of Cedars, and with Lentisques[7] growing underneath them, smelling so sweetly that the very fragrant odour only made the place to seeme exceeding pleasant. As we passed throw these woods we saw nothing but Turkey-cockes flying in the forests, Partidges gray and redde, litle different from ours, but chiefly in bignesse. Wee heard also within the Woods, the voyces of Stagges, of Beares, of Luserns,[8] of Leopards and of divers other sorts of Beasts unknown unto us. Being delighted with this place we set our selves to fishing with nettes, and we caught such a number of fishe, that it was wonderfull. And amongst other we tooke a certayne kind of fish which we call Sallicoques,[9] which were no less than Crevises,[10] so that two draughts of the net were sufficient sometimes to feede all the company of our two Shippes for a whole day. The River at the mouth thereof from Cape to Cape is no lesse then three french leagues broad: it is devided into two great armes, whereof the one runneth toward the West, the other towards the North. And I beleeve in my judgment that the arme which stretcheth toward the North runneth up into the Countrey as farre as the river of Jordan,[11] the other arme runneth into the South Sea, as it was knowen and understood by those of our company, which were left behind to dwell in this place. These two armes are two great leagues broad: and in the middest of them there is an Ile, which is poynted towardes the opening of

---

3. This passage describes events a few days after the arrival of the first expedition, under the command of Jean Ribault, in the region of South Carolina.

4. Present-day Callibogue Sound.

5. Jean Ribault (1520–65).

6. Galleons.

7. Gum trees.

8. Wolves.

9. Shrimp.

10. Crayfish.

11. Probably the present-day Pee Dee River.

the great river, in which Ilande there are infinite numbers of all sorts of strange beasts. There are Simples growing there of so rare properties, and in so great quantitie, that it is an excellent thing to behold them. On every side there is nothing to be seene but Palme trees and other sortes of trees bearing blossoms and frute of very rare shape and very good smel. But seeing the evening approach, and that the Captayne determined to returne unto the shippes, we prayed him to suffer us to passe the night in this place. In our absence the Pilots and chiefe mariners advertised the Captayne that it was needful to bring the Shippes further up within the River, to avoyde the daungers of the windes which might anoy us by reason of our being so neere to the mouth of the River: and for this cause the Captayne sent for us. Being come to our Shippes we sayled three great leagues farther up within the River, and there wee cast Anker. A little while after, John Ribault accompanied with a good number of souldiers imbarked himselfe desirous to sayle further up into the arme that runneth toward the west, and to search the commodities of the place. Having sayled twelve leagues at the least wee perceaved a troupe of Indians, which as soon as ever they espied the Pinnisses, were so afrayd that they fledde into the woods, leaving behind them a young Lucerne which they were a turning upon a spitte: for which cause the place was called Lucerne Cape:[12] proceeding forth on our way, we found an other arme of the river, which ranne toward the East, up which, the Captain determined to sayle and to leave the great currant. A little while after they began to espie diverse other Indians both men and women half hidden within the woods: who knowing not that wee were such as desired their friendship, were dismayed at the first, but soone after were embouldned, for the Captayne caused store of marchandise to be shewed them openly, wherby they knew that we ment nothing but wel unto them: and then they made a signe that we should come on land, which we would not refuse. At our comming on shore diverse of them came to salute our Generall according to their barbarouse fashion. Some of them gave him skins of Chamoys,[13] others little baskets made of Palme leaves, some presented him with perles, but no great number. Afterwards they went about to make an arbour to defend us in that place from the parching heate of the sunne. But we would not stay as then. Wherefore the Captayne thanked them much for their good wil, and gave

presents to eche of them: wherewith he pleased them so well before hee went thence, that his suddaine departure was nothing pleasaunt unto them. For knowing him to be so liberall they would have wished him to have stayed a little longer, seking by all meanes, to give him occasion to stay, shewing him by signes that he should stay but that day onely, and that they desired to advertise a great Indian Lord which had perles in great aboundance, and silver also, all which things should be given unto him at that kings arival: saying farther that in the meane while that this great Lord came thether they wold lead him to their houses, and shew him there a thousand pleasures in shooting and seeing the Stag killed, therfore they prayed him not to deny them their request. Notwithstanding we returned to our ships, wher after we had been but one night the captayne in the morning commaunded to put into the Pinnisse a pillour of hard stone fashioned like a columne wherin the armes of the king of Fraunce were graven, to plant the same in the fayrest place that he could finde. This done we imbarked our selves and sayled three leagues towards the west where we discovered a litle river, up which we sayled so long, that in the ende we found it returned into the great currant, and in his returne to make a litle Iland separated from the firme land, where we went on shore: and by commaundement of the Captayne, because it was exceeding fayre and pleasaunt, there we planted the Pillour upon a hillocke open round about to the view, and environed with a lake halfe a fathom deepe of very good and sweete water. In which Ilande wee sawe two Stagges of exceeding bignesse, in respect of those which we had seene before, which wee might easily have killed with our harquebuses, if the Captayne had not forbidden us, moved with the singular fayrenes and bignesse of them. But before our departure we named the Little River which environed this Ile the River of Liborne. Afterward we imbarked our selves to search another Ile not farre distant from the former: wherein after we had gon a land we found nothing but tall Ceders, the fayrest that were seen in this Countrey. For this cause we called it the Ile of Ceders:[14] so we returned into our Pinnisse to goe towards our Shippes. A fewe dayes afterward John Ribault determined to returne once againe toward the Indians which inhabited that arme of the River which runneth toward the West, and to carry with him good store of souldiers. For his meaning was to take two Indians of this place to bring them into Fraunce, as the Queene had

----

12. Probably the present-day Horse Island.

13. Deer skins.

14. Possibly Pinckney Island.

commaunded him. With this deliberation againe we tooke
our former course, so farre foorth that at the last we came
to the selfesame place where at the first we found the Indians, from thence we tooke two Indians by the permission of the king, which thinking that they were more
favoured then the rest thought themselves very happie to
stay with us. But these two Indians seeing we made no
shew at all that we would goe on land, but rather that we
followed the middest of the courrant, began to be somewhat offended, and would by force have lepte into the
water, for they are so good swimmers that immediately
they woulde have gotten into the forrestes. Neverthelese
being acquainted with their humour, wee watched them
narrowly and sought by all meanes to appease them:
which wee could not by any meanes doe for that time,
though wee offered them thinges which they much esteemed, which thinges they disdayned to take, and gave
backe againe whatsoever was given them, thinking that
such giftes should have altogether bound them, and that
in restoring them they shoulde bee resored unto their libertie. In fine, perceiving that all that they did avayled them
nothing, they prayed us to give them those thinges which
they had restored, which wee did incontinent:[15] then they
approached one toward the other, and beganne to singe,
agreeing so sweetly together, that in hearing their songe it
seemed that they lamented for the absence of their frien-
des. They continued their songes alnight without ceass-
ing: al which time we were constrained to lie at anker by
reason of the tide which was against us, but wee hoysed
sayle the next day very early in the morning, and returned
to our ships. As soone as we were come to our shippes
everyone sought to gratifie these two Indians, and to shew
them the best countenaunce that was possible: to the intent that by such curtesies they might perceive the good
desire and affection which we had to remain their friends
in time to come. Then we offered them meate to eate, but
they refused it, and made us understande that they were
accustomed to wash their face, and to staye until the
sunnne were set before they did eate, which is a cere-
monie common to al the Indians of new Fraunce. Neverthelesse in the ende they were constrayned to forget their
superstitions, and to apply themselves to our nature,
which was somewhat strange unto them at the first. They
became therefore more joconde, and every houre made us
a thousande discourses, being marvellous sorie that we
could not understand them. A few dayes after they began
to beare good wil toward me, so heartie good will I say,
that, as I thinke, they would rather have perished with
hunger and thirst then have taken their refection at any
mans hand but mine. Seeing this their great good will, I
sought to learn some Indian wordes, and began to aske
them questions, shewing them the thing whereof I desired
to know the name, how they called it. They were very glad
to tell it me, and knowing the desire that I had to learne
their language, they incouraged me afterward to aske
them everye thing. So that putting downe in writing the
wordes and phrases of the Indian speech, I was able to understand the greatest part of their discourses. Every day
they did nothing but speake unto me of the desire that they
had to use me well, if we returned unto their houses, and
cause me to receive all the pleasures that they could devise, as well in hunting as in seeing their verye strange
and superstitious ceremonies at a certaine feast which
they call Toya. Which feast they observe as straightly as
we observe the Sunday. They gave me to understand, that
they would bring me to see the greatest Lord of this countrey which they called Chiquola, which exceedeth them in
height (as they tolde me) a good foote and a halfe. They
said unto me that he dwelt within the land in a very large
place and inclosed exceeding high, but I coulde not learne
wherewith. And as farre as I can judge, this place,
whereof they spake unto me, was a very faire citie. For
they sayde unto me that within the inclosure there was
great store of houses which were built very high, wherein
there was an infinite number of men like unto themselves,
which made none account of golde, or silver, nor of
pearles, seeing they had thereof in aboundance. I began
then to shew them al the parts of heaven to the intent to
learne in which quarter they dwelt. And straightway one
of them stretching forth his hand shewed me that they
dwelt toward the North, which maketh mee thinke that it
was in the river of Jordan. And now I remember, that in
the reigne of the Emperour Charles the fift, certaine
Spaniardes inhabitants of Saint Domingo, (which made a
voyage to get certaine slaves to worke in their mynes)
stole away by suttletie the inhabitants of this river, to the
number of fortie, thinking to carry them into their new
Spaine. But they lost their labour: for in despite they died
all for hunger, saving one that was brought to the Emperour, which a little while after he caused to be baptised,
and gave him his owne name and called him Charles of
Chiquola, because he spake so much of the Lorde of
Chiquola, whose subject he was. Also, (as men woorthy
credite have assured me) he reported continually, that

---

15. Immediately.

Chiquola made his abode within a very great inclosed citie. Besides this proofe, those which were left there in the first voyage have certified me, that the Indians shewed them by evident signes, that farther within the land on the foresaide part toward the North, there was a great enclosure or Citie, and within the same manye faire houses, wherein Chiquola dwelt. But not to digresse from my matter, I wil returne to the Indian, which took so great delight in speaking to me of this Chiquola, that there never passed anie one day, wherein hee did not discourse of some rare thing concerning the same. After they had stayed a while in our shippes, they beganne to be sorie, and still demaunded of me when they shoulde returne. I made them understande that the Captaines will was to sende them home againe, but that first we would bestow apparrel of them, which few dayes after was delivered unto them. But seeing he would not give them licence to depart, they resolved with themselves to steale away by night, and to get a little boate which we had, and by the helpe of the tide, to sayle homeward towarde their dwellinges, and by this means to save themselves. Which thing they failed not to doe, and put their enterprise in execution, yet leaving behind them the apparel which the Captaine had given them, and acarrying away nothing but that which was their owne, shewing wel hereby that they were not void of reason. The Captaine cared not greatly for their departure, considering they had not been used otherwise then well: and that therefore they woulde not estrange themselves from the Frenchmen. Captaine Ribault therefore knowing the singular fairnesse of this river desired by all meanes to encourage some of his men to dwell there, well foreseeing that this thing might be of greate importaunce for the Kinges service, and the reliefe of the common wealth of Fraunce. Therefore proceeding on with his intent, he commaunded the ankers to be weighted and to set things in order to returne unto the opening of the river, to the end that if the winde came faire he might passe out to accomplish the rest of his meaning. When therefore we were come to the mouth of the river, he made them cast anker, whereupon we stayed without discovering any thing all the rest of the day. The next day he commaunded that all the men of his ship should come up upon the decke, saying that he had somewhat to say unto them. They all came up, and immediately the Caytaine beganne to speake unto them in this manner. I thinke there is none of you that is ignorant of howe great consequence this our enterprise is, and also howe acceptable it is to our young king. Therefore, my friends, as one de-

sireing your honour and benefite, I woulde not fayle to advertise you all of the exceeding greate good hape which sholde fall to them, which, as men of valure and worthy courage, would make triall in this our first discoverie of the benefites and commodities of this newe lande: which shold be, as I assure my selfe, the greatest occasion that ever could happen unto them, to arise unto the title and degree of honour. And for this cause I was desirous to propose unto you and set downe before your eies the eternall memorie which of right they deserve, which forgetting both their parents and their countrey have had the courage to enterprise a thing of such importance, which even kinges themselves understanding to be men aspiring to so high degree of magnanimitie and increase of their majesties, doe not disdaine so wel to regarde, that afterwardes employing them in matters of weight and of high enterprise, they make their names immortal for ever. How beit, I woulde not have you perswade your selves, as manie do, that you shall never have such good fortune as not being knowen, neither to the king nor the Princes of the Realme, and besides descending of so poore a stock, that few or none of your parents, having ever made profession of armes, have been knowen unto the great estates. For albeit that from my tender yeeres I my self have applied al my industry to follow them, & have hazarded my life in so many dangers for the service of my Prince, yet could I never attaine therunto, (not that I did not deserve this title and degree of government,) as I have seen it happen to many others, only bicause they descended of a noble race, since more regarde is had of their birth than of their vertue. For well I nowe that if vertue were regarded, there would more be found better to deserve the title, and by good right to be named noble and valiant. I will therfore make sufficient answere to such propositions and suche thinges as you maye object against mee, laying before you the infinite examples which we have of the Romaines: which concerning the point of honour were the first that triumphed over the world. For how many find we among them, which for their so valiant enterprises, not for the greatnesse of their parentage, have obtayned the honour to triumph. If we have recourse unto their auncesters, wee shall finde that their parentes were of so meane condition, that by labouring with their handes they lived verie basely. As the father of Aelius Perinax, which was a poore artisant, his Grandfather likewise was a bonde man, as the historiographers do witnesse: and neverthelesse, being moved with a valiant courage, he was nothing dismayed for al this, but rather desirous to aspire unto high things, he began with a brave stomacke to learne feates of armes, and profited so well therein, that from stepe to step he became at length to be Emperour of the Romaines. For all this dignitie he despised not his parentes: but contrariwise, and in remembrance of them, hee causes his fathers shoppe to bee covered with a fine wrought marble, to serve for an example to men descended of base & poore linages, and to give them ocasion to aspire unto high things, not withstanding the meannes of their auncesters. I will not passe over in silence the excellencie and prowes of the valiant and renoumed Agathocles the sonne of a simple potter, and yet forgeting the contemptible estate of his father, he so applied himselfe to vertue in his tender yeeres, that by the favour of armes he came to be king of Sicilie: and for all this title he refused not to be counted the sonne of a Potter. But the more to eternise the memorie of his parents and to make his name renowmed, he commaunded that he should be served at the Table in Vessels of gold and silver and others of earth; declaring thereby, that the dignities wherein he was placed came not unto him by his parents, but by his owne vertue onely. If I shal speak of our time, I will lay before you onely Rusten Basha, which may be a sufficient example to all men: which though he were the sonne of a poore heardman, did so apply his youth in all vertue, that being brought up in the service of the great Turke he seemed so to aspire to great & high matters, in such sorte that growing in yeeres he increased also in courage, so farre foorth, that in fine for his excellent vertues he married the daughter of the great Turke his Prince. How much then ought so many worthy examples to move you to plant here? Considering also that hereby you shal be registered for ever as the first that inhabited this strange countrey. I pray you therefore all to advise your selves thereof and to declare your minds freely unto me, protesting that I will so well imprint your names in the kings eares, and the other princes, that your renowme shall hereafter shyne unquenchable through our Realme of Fraunce. He had scarcely ended his Oration, but the greatest part of our souldiers replyed, that a greater pleasure could never betide them, perceiving well the acceptable service which by this meane they should doe unto their prince: besides that this thing should be for the increase of their honors: therefore they besought the Captayne before he departed out of the place to beginne to build them a Fort, which they hoped afterward to finish, and to leave them munition necessary for their defence, shewing as it seemed that they were displeased, that it was so long, in doing. Whereupon John Ribault being as glad as might be to see his

men so well willing, determined the nexe day to search the most fit and convenient place to be inhabited. Wherefore he embarked himself very early in the morning and commaunded them to follow him that were desirous to inhabite there, to the intent that they might like the better of the place. Having sayled up the great river on the north side, in costing an Ile which endeth with a sharpe point toward the mouth of the river, and having sayled a while, he discovered a small river, which entred into the Ilande, which hee would not sayle to search out. Which done, and finding the same deepe inough to harbour therein Gallies and Galliots[16] in good number, proceeding further, hee found a very open place, joyning upon the brinke thereof, where he went on land, and seeing the place fit to builde a fortresse in, and commodious for them that were willing to plant there, he resolved incontinent to cause the bignes of the fortification to be measured out. And considering that there stayed but sixe and twentie there, hee caused the forte to bee made in length but sixteene fathome, and thirteene in breadth, with flankes according to the proposition thereof. The measure being taken by me and Captaine Salles, we sent unto the Shippes for me, and to bring Shovels, Pickaxes and other instruments necessary to make the fortification. We travelled so diligently that in a shorte space the fort was made in some sorte defensible. In which meane time John Ribault caused victuales and warre-like munition to be brought for the defence of the place. After he had furnished them with all such thinges as they had neede of, he determined to take his leave of them. But before his departure he pled this speach unto Captayne Albert, which hee lefte in this place: Captayne Albert, I have to request you in the presence of all men, that you would quite your selfe so wisely in your charge, and governe so modestly your small company which I leave you, which with so good cheere remayneth under your obedience, that I never have ocasion but to commend you, and to recount unto the king, as I am desirous, the faithful service which before us all you undertake to doe him in his new Fraunce: And you companions, quoth hee to the Souldiers, I beseech you also to esteeme of Captayne Albert as if it were my selfe that stayed here with you, yeelding him that obedience which a souldier oweth unto his Generall and Captayne, living as brethren one with another, without all dissention: and in so doing God will assist you and blesse your enterprises. Having ended his exhortation wee tooke

---

16. Smaller boats.

our leaves of eche of them, and sayled toward our Sippes, calling the Forte by the name of Charles Forte, and the River by the name of Chenonceau. The next day wee determined to depart from this place being as well contented as was possible that wee had so happily ended our businesse, with good hope, if occasion would permitte, to discover perfectely the River of Jordan. For this cause we hoysed our sayles about ten of the clocke in the morning: after wee were ready to depart Captaine Ribault comaunded to shoote of our Ordinance to give a farewell unto our Frenchmen, which sayled not to doe the like on their parte. This being done wee sayled towarde the North: and then wee named this River Porte Royall, because of the largeness and excellent fayreness of the same.

Garcilaso de la Vega, el Inca (1539–1616)

When in his later years he was seeking literary acceptance in Spain, Gómez Suárez de Figueroa dubbed himself Garcilaso de la Vega, el Inca, taking on the name of a renowned, distant Castilian ancestor while also proudly marking his indigenous origin by adding "the Inca" to his name. His parents were representatives of high-status groups, Spanish and Incan, that just fifteen years prior to the author's birth were unknown to one another. Garcilaso de la Vega, el Inca, was born in Cuzco, Peru, in 1539 to Chimpu (sometimes Chimpa) Ocllo, a blood relation of the last legitimate Inca ruler, Huayna Capac, and Don Sebastián Garcilaso de la Vega Vargas, a Spanish conquistador who fought against the indigenous peoples of Peru alongside Pedro de Alvarado and then Pizarro. In repayment for his military assistance, Don Sebastián was given a significant estate near Cuzco, where he lived with Chimpu Ocllo.

The area of Cuzco was an area that for two centuries had been the capital of the Inca empire. According to traditional Inca stories, Manco Capac and his three brothers and four sisters led ten clans into the fertile valley of Cuzco, conquering the people and taking the land for themselves. To establish a royal Inca bloodline, Manco Capac married one of his sisters, and descendants continued to dominate the area through marriage alliances and conquests, until the Inca territory extended along roughly 3,000 miles of coastline and united diverse peoples under one common language, Quechua, and a common manner of living. Inca culture, hierarchical in orientation and with land space divided into four quarters, was kept under relatively centralized control through the use of the *quipu,* a system of memory based in a series of colored knots on ropes that enabled the large territory, its numbers and peoples, to share knowledge. The Inca empire was undergoing stresses and strains at the time the Spanish conquistadors arrived in the area.

Raised by unmarried parents among other young men of similarly mixed ancestry, Garcilaso de la Vega, el Inca, was treated to two sets of equally important stories, some by his mother's family of their ancient traditions, noble lineage, and memorable actions and some by his father and his associates of the importance of Spain's imperial conquest of the Americas. When his father established a marital union, according the new laws of the "Indies," with a Creole woman from Panama and his mother married a local merchant, Garcilaso de la Vega, el Inca, a young teenager, was left to develop his own maturity. As a token of his father's interest in his future, he was willed, upon his father's death in 1559, a sum sufficient to travel to Spain. There, while in his early twenties, he sought a financial return or a political appointment for his father's service to the Crown, only to be rejected for such a request on the grounds that his father had behaved badly and that his mother was Indian. The rebuff stunned the young man. He joined the army for Spain, perhaps to gain acceptance, but his service went unnoticed. Having spent some time in Madrid and Seville, Garcilaso de la Vega, el Inca, settled at Montilla and then Córdova and continued to perfect his learning for the remainder of his life. Here he engaged in religious studies, translated popular Spanish and Italian writings, and wrote the two major works for which he is best known. Here, too, he took orders and served a minor official role as a steward of the hospital of the Limpia Concepción. He died in 1616.

Garcilaso de la Vega's best-known works, *The Florida of the Inca* (*La Florida del Ynca,* as originally published) and *Royal Commentaries and General History of Peru* (*Comentarios Reales* and *Historia Gen-*

eral del Perú), reveal the complexities of the author's mixed commitments to his Incan ancestors and his Spanish ones. The *Florida* is a celebratory story about Spanish efforts to "conquer" Florida, despite the failed enterprise of Hernando de Soto. Taken from various printed and oral accounts, most notably from association with Gonzalo Silvestre, whom he met at Los Posadas, the *Florida* evinces Garcilaso's clear sympathy for Hernando de Soto's efforts to take over Florida and shows as well his pride in Indian and especially his own Inca heritage, which he considered superior to that of the indigenous peoples of the Floridas. His story about Juan Ortiz, the captive among the Florida Indians, is an interesting reminder of his mixed sympathies.

Similar themes occupy the author in his two-volume set, known as the *Royal Commentaries (Comentarios Reales),* that treats the history of Peru from its origin in the Inca empire through its conquest by Spain. This long work reveals Garcilaso's excessive pride in his indigenous heritage, even as it celebrates the Spanish conquest of his ancestral lands. Yet despite the elaborate praise the author offered to Philip II, the *Royal Commentaries* did not bring him the fame he sought. Indeed, Part II was delayed in its publication and would be licensed not as "royal commentaries" but simply as a "general history of Peru," and its publication was withheld, for reasons unclear, until after the author's death in 1616.

from THE FLORIDA OF THE INCA

BOOK I

CHAPTER 3

Other explorers who have gone to Florida.[1]

Those Castilians who had sailed for Florida in the ships of the seven rich men of Santo Domingo told of what they had seen when they came again to that island; meanwhile, Miruelo's story was being circulated in the same place. Now when these accounts reached the ears of the Judge, Lucas Vázquez de Ayllón,[2] he came to Spain to petition the conquest and government of Chicoria,[3] one of the many provinces of Florida. Not only did the Emperor favor his request, but he honored him with knighthood in the order of Santiago. So returning to Santo Domingo, this man fitted out three large vessels in the year 1524, and taking Miruelo as his navigator, sailed for that land which the latter had discovered earlier, for it was rumored to be richer than Chicoria. But persistently as he tried, Miruelo could never locate the spot he had previously visited and as a result fell into such a melancholia that in a few days he lost his reason and expired.

The Licenciate Ayllón now proceeded in search of the province of Chicoria. At the river Jordan he lost his flagship, but with his two remaining vessels, he sailed toward the east and landed on the coast of a peaceful and delightful region near Chicoria where the natives received him with much festivity and praise. Believing that all now was in his power, he commanded two hundred Spaniards to disembark and inspect a village three leagues inland. The Indians directed these men to that place, but one night, after they had feasted them for three or four days and given assurances of loyalty, they slew them all. Then at dawn they made a sudden attack on the few who had remained at the coast to guard the ships, and when they had killed or wounded the majority, they forced the others, including the Judge, to embark and return, broken and de-

---

1. *The Florida of the Inca* was first published in Lisbon in 1605. The text is from the translation by John Grier Varner and Jeannette Johnson Verner (1951). Hernando de Soto was granted the authority to conquer, pacify, and populate all provinces of the "new world" previously assigned to Lucas Vázquez de Ayllón and to Pámphilo de Narváez. In the selection, Garcilaso places Hernando de Soto's efforts in the context of the failed efforts of other Spanish explorers and distinguishes the nobility of their efforts by showing the difficulties faced because of the duplicity of the indigenous peoples they encountered. See also the selections by the Gentleman of Elvas and Alvar Núñez Cabeza de Vaca.

2. Lucas Vázquez de Ayllón (1475–1526) sailed to the Florida coast from Hispaniola, landing in a place he called San Miguel, later called Jamestown by the English colonists, where he died of a fever.

---

3. Chicoria, probably in the area of present-day South Carolina.

feated, to Santo Domingo. Thus they avenged the Indians betrayed on the previous voyage. Among the few who managed to escape with Lucas Vázquez de Ayllón was a cavalier named Hernando Mogollón, a native of the city of Badajoz. This man, whom I knew personally, later came to Peru and told at length what we have given in resumé.

After Judge Lucas Vázquez de Ayllón, the next explorer in Florida was Pámphilo de Narváez, who went there in the year 1537. As Alvar Núñez Cabeza de Vaca, who accompanied him as Treasurer of the Royal Purse, tells us in his *Naufragios*,[4] this captain and all of his men except Cabeza de Vaca himself, three other Spaniards and one Negro,[5] were miserably lost. Our Lord God was so merciful to the five who escaped that they succeeded in performing miracles in His name and thus gained such a reputation and esteem among the Indians that they were worshipped as deities. Nevertheless they did not want to remain in this land, and as soon as they were able to do so, left very hastily and came to Spain to solicit new governorships. They succeeded in obtaining their desire, but many things occurred which were to bring them to a sad end, according to this same Alvar Núñez Cabeza de Vaca, who died in Valladolid after returning in chains from the Río de la Plata where he had gone as Governor.

When Pámphilo de Narváez went to Florida he took on the journey as navigator another Miruelo who was a relative of the aforementioned one and equally as unfortunate in his profession, for he never succeeded in finding the land his uncle had discovered. From his kinsman's account he had received information concerning that land, and it was for this reason that Pámphilo de Narváez had taken him with him.

After the unfortunate Pámphilo de Narváez, the Adelantado Hernando de Soto went to Florida, entering it in the year thirty-nine. It is our intention to record his history along with that of numerous other famous Spanish and Indian cavaliers, to give an account of the many great provinces he explored up until the termination of his life, and moreover to tell of what his captains and soldiers did after his death until they abandoned that land and came to a halt in Mexico.

---

4. *Naufragios,* "the shipwrecked" or "castaways."

5. Alternatively called by these writers Estéban, Estévan, or Estévanico.

CHAPTER 4

Still others who have made the same journey to Florida. The customs and common weapons of the natives of that country.

As soon as the news of the death of Hernando de Soto became known in Spain, many candidates appeared to ask for the governorship and conquest of Florida; but the Emperor Charles V refused them all, sending instead at his own cost in the year 1549 a group of Dominicans led by one of their order, Luis Cancer de Balbastro. These friars had offered to convert the Indians to the Evangelical faith with their preaching, but when they arrived in Florida and disembarked for the purpose, the natives, who had learned a lesson in their previous contact with the Spaniards, refused to listen. Instead they fell upon them and slew Friar Luis as well as two of his companions. The remainder of the brothers then took refuge in their ship and, returning to Spain, proclaimed that people so barbarous and inhuman as Indians had no desire to hear sermons.

In the year 1562, a son of the judge, Lucas Vázquez de Ayllón, asked for this same conquest and governorship, and his petition was granted. But this man died in Hispañola while searching for a crew, his sickness and death having been caused by sorrow and anxiety over an undertaking that had little possibility of completion and was consequently becoming more difficult each day. Since then, others have gone to Florida, among whom was the Adelantado Pedro Meléndez de Valdés; but I shall not write of these men because I do not have complete information relative to their accomplishments.

Although brief, this is the most accurate account that it has been possible to give concerning the land of Florida and those who have gone there to explore and conquer it. But before we continue, it will be well to describe some of the customs which in general the Indians of that great kingdom observe, at least those which the Adelantado Hernando de Soto discovered to be common to practically all of the provinces that he visited. And if in some other place in the process of our history customs differ, we shall take care to note the fact. In general, however, all Indians observe essentially the same mode of living.

The Indians are a race of pagans and idolaters; they worship the sun and the moon as their principal deities, but, unlike the rest of heathendom, without any ceremony of images, sacrifices, prayers, or other superstitions. They do have temples but they use them as sepulchres and not as houses of prayer. Moreover, because of the great size of these structures, they let them serve to hold the best and richest of their possessions. Their veneration for the temples and burial places, therefore, is most profound. On the doors of them they place the trophies of victories won over their enemies.

Among the common people a man marries only one woman and she is obliged to be faithful to her husband under penalty of laws that have been ordained for the punishment of adultery. In certain provinces this punishment is cruel death, and in others it is something very humiliating, as we shall show in its place. The lords, by royal prerogative, have license to take whatever women they please, and this law or liberty of the nobility is observed in all of the Indies of the New World, but ever with the distinction of the principal legitimate wife; the other women, who act as servants, are more concubines than wives, and their offspring, being illegitimate, are not equal in honor or inheritance to those of the principal wife.

Throughout Peru, the common man marries only one woman, and he who takes two does so under penalty of death. But the Incas, who are those of royal blood, and the curacas, who are lords of vassals, have license to possess all the women they desire or can maintain, although with the distinction stated above between the legitimate wife and the concubines. As heathens they claim that this dispensation is permitted because it is necessary that they have many wives in order to produce many children, for it being the nobility who are wasted and destroyed in battles, there is a need for additional people of this class to wage wars and to augment and govern the republic. There are more than enough of the base-born to carry burdens, till the soil and perform the duties of serfs, they say, for not being people who can be used as the nobility in times of peril, they increase extensively regardless of how few are born. Persons of this second class are of no value to the government, and it is unlawful and even an insult for them to offer their services for such work, since governing and administering justice are the duties of cavalier hidalgos and not plebeians. But let us return to the natives of Florida.

The basic food of these people is corn rather than wheat, and their general fare consists of beans, the type of squash known as Roman squash, and many of the fish indigenous to their rivers. There being no tame animals in large numbers, they have a scarcity of beef; but with their bows and arrows, they shoot much wild game such as stags, roedeer and bucks, which are larger and more numerous than those of Spain. They also kill a great variety of birds, first to eat the flesh, and then to obtain different colored feathers with which to decorate their heads; for the adornments they wear on their heads are sometimes half a fathom in height, and by means of them the nobles are differentiated from common people in time of peace, and the soldiers from non-combatants in time of war. Whatever meat and fish they do eat must be well baked and boiled, and their fruit must be very ripe. In no wise will they partake of green or half-ripe fruit, and they ridicule the Spaniards for eating green grapes. Their drink is clear water as nature gives it, without mixture of anything.

People who say that the Indians eat human flesh attribute this practice to them falsely, at least to those of the provinces our Governor discovered. They on the contrary abominate this practice, as Alvar Núñez Cabeza de Vaca notes in his *Naufragios,* chapters fourteen and seventeen. Here he states that certain Castilians who were camped apart died gradually of hunger and that those of them who remained alive devoured the dead until the last one of them had perished, there being none left to eat him.[6] Because of this incident, he says, the natives were scandalized and wanted to destroy all of the Spaniards who had remained in the other camp. It may be, however, that the Indians do eat human flesh in places where our men did not penetrate, for Florida is so broad and long that there is space enough within it for anything to happen.

The Indian men go naked, wearing only certain little cloths of varicolored chamois, something like extremely short pants, which modestly cover all parts of their bodies necessary to conceal, both in front and behind. Instead of cloaks they have robes which are fastened at the neck and extend to the middle of the legs. Some are made of very fine marten fur and smell of musk, whereas others are of cowhide and different small skins of such animals as bucks, roes, stags, bears, lions, and various species of cats. These skins they dress to the utmost perfection, preparing a cowhide or bearskin without removing the hair. Thus it remains soft and smooth, and can be worn as a cloak or can serve at night on their beds. Their hair they permit to grow, wearing it caught up in a large knot on the head. As an adornment, they use a thick skein of thread, of whatever color they wish, which encircles the head and

---

6. Hernando de Esquivel survived by eating the dried flesh of one Soto-Mayor, brother of the man who later became Hernando de Soto's lieutenant general in Florida, Vasco Porcallo de Figueroa.

falls over the forehead. In the ends of the skein they tie two half knots, so that each end hangs over a separate temple down to the bottom of the ears. The women dress in chamois, keeping their whole body modestly covered.

The weapon which the Indians commonly carry is the bow and arrow. It is true that they do possess and are skillful in the use of other arms such as pikes, lances, darts, halberds, slings, clubs, broadswords, sticks and the like, if there are more such weapons; but they do not understand and thus cannot use the arquebus and the crossbow. Yet with all their various types of arms, they generally employ only the bow and arrow, because it is more dressy and more ornamental for those who carry it. For this same reason ancient pagans painted their most beloved gods such as Apollo, Diana and Cupid with bows and arrows; for in addition to what such arms signified among them, they were very beautiful and increased both grace and elegance in the one who bore them. But the Indians have found also that they can obtain a better effect with this weapon either at a distance or near at hand, whether they are fleeing or attacking, or whether they are fighting or taking recreation in hunting. In all the New World, therefore, it is a very much used weapon.

The bows are of the same height as the men who carry them, and since the natives of Florida are generally tall, theirs are more than two yards in length and are thick in proportion. They make them of oak and of their other different woods which are strong and heavy. Thus they are so difficult to bend that no Spaniard, regardless of how much he persisted, was able to draw a bowstring back as far as his face. The Indians, on the other hand, because of their skill and constant use of this weapon, draw the cord with great ease, even to the back of the ear; and they make very fierce and frightful shots, as we shall see later.

The bowstrings are made with thongs of deerskin. Taking a strip two fingers wide from the tip of the tail to the head of the deer, the Indians after first removing the hair, wet and twist this strip firmly. Tying one end to the branch of a tree, they suspend from the other end a weight of one hundred or one hundred and twenty-five pounds and leave it thus until it becomes like one of the heavy cords of the bass-viol and is very strong. In order to shoot with safety, so that the bowstring on being loosened may not injure the left arm, they trim that arm on the inner side with a half bracer of heavy feathers, in this way protecting it from the wrist to the elbow. This bracer is secured with a deerskin thong which encircles the arm seven or eight times at the place where the bowstring quivers with the greatest force.

The above is what in sum may be said of the life and customs of the Indians of Florida. And now we return to Hernando de Soto, who has asked for the conquest and governorship of that great kingdom, a project which has been so unhappy and so costly to all those who have undertaken it.

BOOK II

CHAPTER 1

The Governor arrives in Florida and finds traces of Pámphilo de Narváez.

Governor Hernando de Soto, who, as we have said, was sailing in search of Florida, first sighted land in that kingdom on the last day of May. He had been nineteen days at sea because of unfavorable weather, but his ships now anchored in a good, deep bay which the Spaniards named the Bay of the Holy Spirit.[7] It being late afternoon when the armada arrived, no one disembarked, but on the following day, which was the first of June, some went ashore in small boats. They returned with their vessels loaded with grass for the horses and with many unripe grapes from vines found growing wild in the forests. The grape is not cultivated by the natives of this great kingdom of Florida, and they do not care as much for it as do people of other nations, but they will eat it when it is very ripe or has been dried. Our men were extremely happy over these fine specimens of the fruit, for they were similar to those grown in Spain, the like of which they had not found in Mexico or in the whole of Peru.

On the second of June, the Governor ordered three hundred foot-soldiers ashore to perform the solemn act of taking possession of Florida in the name of the Emperor Charles V, King of Spain. This procedure completed, these men passed the rest of the day walking along the coast, and that night slept on land. As yet they had seen nothing of the natives, but at the third or dawn watch, the Indians burst upon them with such audacity and force as to compel them to retreat to the edge of the water. Meanwhile, however, they sounded an alarm, and both men and

---

7. They first sighted land on May 25, 1539, the Feast of *Espíritu Santo,* and they landed in the area of present-day Tampa Bay on May 31.

horses came from the ships to aid them as quickly as if they too had been on land.

Lieutenant General Vasco Porcallo de Figueroa, who commanded the assistance, found these footsoldiers very much upset and confused, for like raw recruits, they had got in each other's way while fighting, and some already had been wounded by arrows. With the advent of help, however, all pursued the Indians for a good while and then returned to their quarters. But hardly had they arrived there when Vasco Porcallo's horse fell dead from the effects of an arrow. Striking above the saddle, the missile had passed through the cloth, saddle tree, and pack saddle; and more than a third of it had penetrated the ribs of the animal to the very cavity of its body. Vasco Porcallo, however, was exceedingly pleased that the first horse to be used in the conquest and the first lance to be employed in the first skirmish should have been his.

On this and the following day, the Spaniards disembarked both animals and men. Then when they had rested for eight or nine days and had put everything in order pertaining to their ships, they marched inland a little more than two leagues to the town of a cacique known as Hirrihigua. When Pámphilo de Narváez had gone to conquer that province, he had waged war with Hirrihigua and later he had converted the Indian to friendship; then for some unknown reason, he had committed certain abuses against the Cacique which are of too odious a nature to be told here. It suffices to say that because of those offenses, Hirrihigua was now so fearful of the Spaniards and so consumed with bitterness toward them that on learning of Hernando de Soto's arrival in his land, he left both his house and village unprotected and fled to the forest. And although the Governor sent him gifts, endearments and promises by means of certain of his vassals whom the Spaniards had captured, still he refused to come out and make peace or even listen to any messages. Instead his anger was aroused at those of his vassals serving as envoys, and he ordered them to refrain from doing so, since they were aware of the manner in which he had been hurt and offended by the Spanish nation. He would willingly receive the heads of these Castilians, he said, but he wanted to hear nothing more of their names and words.

All such things and more abuse can bring about, particularly if it is committed against someone who has given no offense. But in order to present a better picture of the rage Hirrihigua felt for the Castilians, it will be well to show here some of the cruelties and martyrdoms he himself had inflicted upon four of Pámphilo de Narváez' men whom he succeeded in capturing. To a certain extent

we may be digressing; yet we will not be leaving the main purpose of the story, and the digression will contribute much to the value of our history.

Know then that some days after Pámphilo de Narváez had done what we have mentioned and had departed from the land of Hirrihigua, one of his ships, which had stopped elsewhere, happened to call at this same bay in search of its captain.[8] On ascertaining the identity and purpose of the vessel, the Cacique resolved to seize every man aboard and burn him alive. Therefore, with the idea of instilling confidence in them, he pretended to be a friend of their captain, sending them word that Pámphilo de Narváez had indeed been in that place, and moreover had left a message with him as to what their ship should do if it too should call there. Then to persuade them to belief, he disclosed from land two or three sheets of white paper and some old letters which he had obtained from Spaniards in former times by friendly means, or however it may have been, and in the interim had guarded very carefully.

But in spite of all of Hirrihigua's manifestations, the men aboard ship were very cautious and refused to disembark. Then the Cacique sent out a canoe with four principal Indians, saying that he was offering these lords and cavaliers as hostages and security so that those Spaniards who wished to come ashore and learn of their captain, Pámphilo de Narváez, might do so. (It seems inappropriate to employ the term cavalier, or *caballero,* in referring to Indians because they possessed no horses, or *caballos,* from which word the name is deduced; but since in Spain this term implies a nobleman and since there is a nobility among the Indians, it may be used likewise in speaking of them.) And he added that if they were not reassured thereby, he would send more pledges. On witnessing the apparent good faith of the chieftain, four Spaniards set out in the canoe with those Indians who had brought the hostages. The Cacique had hoped for all of them; still when he saw that only these few were coming, he resolved not to insist on more lest the four be offended and return to their ship.

As soon as the Indian hostages saw the Christians on land and in the hands of their people, they plunged into the sea, and diving far below the surface, swam like fish to the shore, thus fulfilling the instructions of their chieftain. Meanwhile, the Spaniards on board ship, finding

---

8. According to the account by the Gentleman of Elvas, the ship had returned to Cuba after Narváez landed but was ordered back to Florida.

themselves fooled, sailed out of the bay before anything worse could befall them, very much grieved, however, at having lost their four companions so indiscreetly.

CHAPTER 2

The tortures which an Indian chief inflicted upon a Spaniard who was his slave.

The Cacique Hirrihigua now ordered that the four Spaniards be guarded most cautiously so that with their death his Indians might solemnize a great feast which according to the rites of paganism they expected to celebrate within a few days. Then with the arrival of that festival, he commanded that the captives be taken naked to the plaza and there made to run in turn from one side to the other while the Indians shot arrows at them as if they were wild beasts. But to delay further the death and increase the agonies of their victims, and at the same time to prolong and enliven their own festivity and enjoyment, they were to discharge only a few arrows at a time.

Three of the Spaniards were tortured in this manner, and Hirrihigua received a great amount of pleasure and delight as he watched them flee in all directions, searching for a refuge which they found only in death. But when the Indians wanted to bring out the fourth, a native of Seville named Juan Ortiz, who was scarcely eighteen years of age, the Cacique's wife came with her three daughters and, standing before her husband, begged that he be content with the death of the three captives and pardon the fourth, since he and his companions had not come to that land with Pámphilo de Narváez and therefore were guiltless of the wickedness perpetrated by their predecessors. This particular boy, she said, was deserving of forgiveness because of his tender age, which gave proof of his innocence and pled for compassion; and since he had committed no crime, it was therefore enough that he remain with them as a slave and not be destroyed so cruelly.

In an effort to make his wife and daughters happy, the Cacique for the time being spared the life of Juan Ortiz; but afterward he tortured him so grievously and bitterly that the boy frequently was moved to envy his three dead companions. The ceaseless labor of carrying firewood and water was so strenuous, the eating and sleeping were so infrequent, and the daily slaps, blows, and lashes as well as other torments given him on feast days were so

cruel that he many times would have sought relief in suicide had he not been a Christian. For in addition to daily tortures, Hirrihigua on numerous occasions of celebration, just as a diversion, ordered the boy to run continuously the entire day in the long plaza where his comrades had been slain. He himself went out to watch, taking his noblemen, who carried bows and arrows with which to kill the captive at any time he should pause. Thus Juan Ortiz began at sunrise and continued from one side of the plaza to the other until sunset, these being the time limits allotted by the Indians for him to run; and even when Hirrihigua went away to eat, he left his cavaliers to watch the youth so that they might slay him in the event he should stop. Then when the day was over, this sad boy lay extended on the ground, more dead than alive, as one can imagine. But on such occasions as these, he received the compassion of the chieftain's wife and daughters, who took him and clothed him and did other things which helped to sustain his life, although it would have been better had they deprived him of it and thereby freed him from his many tasks.

Hirrihigua now realized that such numerous and continuous torments were not sufficient to destroy Juan Ortiz, and his hatred for him increased by the hour. So to finish with the youth he gave the order on a certain feast day to kindle a great fire in the center of the plaza, and when he saw many live coals made, he commanded that they be spread out and that over them there be placed a grill-like wooden structure which stood a yard above the ground, and upon which they should put his captive in order to roast him alive. Thus it was done, and here the poor Spaniard, after being tied to the grill, lay stretched out on one side for a long time. But at the shrieks of the miserable youth, the wife and daughters of the Cacique rushed up, and, pleading with their lord and even scolding him for his cruelty, removed the boy from the fire, not, however, before he was half-baked and blisters that looked like halves of oranges had formed on one of his sides. Some of these blisters burst and much blood ran from them, so that they were painful to behold. Hirrihigua overlooked what his wife and daughters were doing because they were women whom he loved deeply, and possibly also because he wanted someone on whom he later might vent his wrath and exercise his vengeance. And although Juan Ortiz provided less occasion for vengeance than the chieftain desired, still he was amused with that little. Thus he many times expressed his regret that he had destroyed the other three Spaniards so precipitately. The women, on the contrary, had time and again repented of having saved Juan Ortiz from death on the first occasion, since they had seen how long and cruel his daily torments had been. But being moved to great compassion on beholding him in his present state, they took him to their lodging and treated him with the juices of herbs (for having no doctors, both Indian men and women are great herbalists). Hence after many days, Juan Ortiz recovered, although the burns from the fire left great scars.

Wishing to free himself from the sight of his captive as he now was and at the same time from the bother of the pleas of his wife and daughters, the Cacique ordered to be inflicted upon the youth another torment which, though not so grave as those in the past, would keep him from idleness. This was that day and night he should guard the remains of dead citizens placed in a designated section of a forest that lay at a distance from the town. These bodies had been put above the ground in some wooden chests which served as sepulchres. The chests had no hinges and could be closed only by covering them with boards and then placing rocks or beams of wood on top of the boards. Since the Indians were not cautious about guarding their dead, the lions, which are numerous in that country, sometimes robbed the chests and carried away the bodies, thus creating a situation which grieved and angered these people exceedingly. So it was that the Cacique now ordered Juan Ortiz to guard the place carefully, and he threatened and swore that should any corpse or any part of one be borne away, he would bake the Spaniard alive, this time without any remedy. Then as a means of protecting the sepulchres, he gave the youth four darts to throw at the lions or any other wild beasts that might come to desecrate the place.

Thanking God for having delivered him from the continuous presence of his master, Juan Ortiz now went to guard the dead, hoping to find with them a better life than he had found with the living. And he did watch these bodies with the utmost care, especially at night, since it was then that the risk was greater. But it happened that on one of these nights when he was thus occupied, he found himself unable to resist sleep and consequently succumbed in the dawn watch, this being the hour at which sleep ordinarily shows its greatest force against those who keep vigil. At this time a lion came to the place of the dead, and knocking down the covers of one of the chests, seized and bore away the body of a child which had been laid there only two days previously.

Juan Ortiz was awakened by the noise of the falling boards, and when on rushing to the chest he failed to find the body, he considered himself as good as dead. Never-

theless in his anxiety and anguish he did not waver in his duty and determined instead to go in search of the lion; for he vowed that on running across it, he would recover the remains of the child or die at the hands of the beast. At the same time, however, he commended himself to God, invoking His name and making his confessions, for he was confident that when the Indians came at dawn to visit the sepulchres and failed to find the body of the child, they would burn him alive. As he moved here and there through the forest, haunted by the fear of death, he came out upon a broad road and proceeded for a little while down the middle of it, for impossible as escape was, he had made up his mind to flee. Then in the woods not far from where he was walking, he heard a sound much like that of a dog gnawing bones. Listening carefully, he made certain of the sound, and suspecting that it might be the lion devouring the stolen corpse, groped his way through the underbrush toward the spot from whence it was coming. Presently in the light of the moon, which was shining, although dimly, he saw the beast nearby, feeding at its pleasure upon the remains of the child.

Calling upon God and mustering courage, Juan Ortiz hurled a dart. At the moment he did not see what kind of throw he had made because of the underbrush; still, he felt that his marksmanship had not been bad because his hand was salty, and there was a saying among hunters that one's hands were thus when he had made a successful shot at wild beasts in the night. Encouraged now by this hope, slight as it was, and by the fact that he had not heard the lion flee from the spot to which he had directed his dart, Juan Ortiz now awaited the coming of dawn, trusting in Our Lord to succor him in his necessity.

CHAPTER 3

A continuation of the miserable life of the captive.
How he fled from his master.

With the light of day, Juan Ortiz verified the good throw made blindly in the night, for he discovered the lion lying dead, pierced through the center of its heart and entrails (as was afterward seen when its carcass was opened). The sight was more than he could believe, so with a joy that can be imagined more easily than described, he gathered up the uneaten remnants of the child's body and returned them to the chest. Then seizing the dead beast by one foot, he dragged it to his master without removing the dart so that the Cacique could see the animal just as he himself had found it.

Hirrihigua and his whole village were greatly amazed at what Juan Ortiz had accomplished, for in that land it is generally considered miraculous to kill a lion, and he who happens to do so is treated thereafter with great veneration and respect. Since this creature is so savage, people everywhere should be held in high esteem for destroying it, especially if, as in the case of Juan Ortiz, they do so without benefit of arquebus or crossbow. It is true that the lions of Florida, Mexico and Peru are not so large or so wild as those of Africa, but after all they are lions and the name is enough. Even though there is a common saying to the effect that these animals are not so fierce as they are painted, nevertheless those who have found themselves in the proximity of them insist that live lions are much fiercer than painted ones, no matter how lifelike the painting may be.

With the good fortune of Juan Ortiz, the Cacique's wife and daughters became even more daring and courageous in their efforts to persuade their lord to exonerate the youth completely and give him tasks that would be both honorable and worthy of his strength and valor. And thenceforward for a few days, Hirrihigua did treat his slave better, being motivated as much by the admiration and esteem the people of his house and town had bestowed upon him as by the fact that he had performed a deed which was not only valiant but one that the Indians in their superstition had come to venerate as something sacred and even superhuman. Nevertheless outrage knows no forgiveness, and each time that Hirrihigua recalled that Spaniards had cast his mother to the dogs and permitted them to feed upon her body, and each time that he attempted to blow his nose and failed to find it, the Devil seized him with the thought of avenging himself on Juan Ortiz, as if that young man personally had deprived him of his nostrils. The very sight of this Spaniard always brought past offenses before his eyes, and such memories increased each day his anger and lust for retribution.

So although Hirrihigua for some time restrained these passions, he now was unable to resist them. Thus one day he informed his wife and daughters that he could no longer suffer the Christian to live. For, he said, he found the life of this man very odious and abominable and could not view him without experiencing a revival of past grievances and without feeling offended anew; and it was therefore his command that unless they were willing to share the same anger, they should in no manner intercede

further for the Christian. Then he added that in order to end completely with his slave he had made up his mind that on such and such a feast day soon to be celebrated, the Indians should shoot the Spaniard with arrows and slay him just as they had slain his companions. This, he said, was to be done in spite of Juan Ortiz' bravery, for such bravery being that of an enemy should be abhorred rather than esteemed.

Perceiving the anger of the Cacique, the women realized that further intercession was useless, and moreover that it had been rude for them to importune and pain their lord so extensively in behalf of his slave. So they ventured no word in contradiction, instead hastening with female astuteness to agree that he should by all means proceed with his plan since such was his pleasure. But a few days before the approaching celebration, the eldest daughter, in order to carry out an idea of her own, secretly notified Juan Ortiz of her father's decision against him, warning at the same time that neither she nor her mother and sisters would or could prevail upon Hirrihigua since he had imposed silence upon them in regard to his prisoner and had threatened them should they violate his restriction. To this sad news, however, the maiden in her desire to encourage the Spaniard added some words of quite another character.

"Lest you lose faith in me and despair of your life or doubt that I will do everything in my power to save you," she said, "I will assist you to escape and find refuge if you are a man and have the courage to flee. For tonight, if you will come at a certain hour to a certain place, you will find an Indian in whom I shall entrust both your welfare and mine. This man will guide you to a bridge two leagues distant; but when you arrive there, you must command him to go no further and instead to return before dawn to this village lest he be missed and by revealing my rashness as well as his own cause both of us to suffer for having given you aid. Six leagues beyond the bridge there is another town, the lord of which is Mucozo, a man who loves me exceedingly and desires my hand in marriage. You will tell him that I am sending you in my name so that he may help you in your need. I know that, being the person he is, he will do everything he can for you, as you shall see. And now commend yourself to your God, for there is no more that I can do in your behalf."

Juan Ortiz threw himself at the feet of the maiden in gratitude for this favor and benefit as well as for all of her kindnesses both past and present. Then he made preparations to flee during the coming night. At the appointed hour, when everyone in the Cacique's household was asleep, he sought out the promised guide and they departed from the town without being heard. When they reached the bridge and the youth learned that there was no further possibility of his losing his way before coming to the town of Mucozo, he instructed his companion to return at once with the utmost caution to his home.

CHAPTER 4

The magnanimity of the Curaca or Cacique Mucozo
to whom the captive was entrusted.

A fugitive now, Juan Ortiz arrived before dawn at the place he was seeking, but he dared not enter lest he create a disturbance. Then when it was day he saw two Indians coming out of the town by the same path he himself was pursuing. These men wanted to shoot at him, for the people of Florida are always armed; but Juan Ortiz, being armed also, put an arrow to his bow to defend himself and even to take the offense. Oh, how much a small favor can do, especially if it be the favor of a lady; for we now see that he who only a short time previously feared death and knew not where to hide, now dared mete it out with his own hands simply because he had seen himself assisted by a beautiful, discreet and generous young maiden. But such a favor does exceed all other human kindness.

Mustering his courage and strength and even his arrogance, Juan Ortiz disclosed that he was no enemy but merely a messenger sent by a lady to the lord of that land. On hearing him, the Indians withheld their arrows and then conducted him to the town where they informed their Cacique that Hirrihigua's slave had come with a message for him.

This news having been made known to Mucozo (or Mocozo, for it is the same name), he came to the plaza to receive the Christian's words. Then Juan Ortiz, after having saluted the chieftain as best he knew how according to native customs, gave a brief account of the martyrdoms he had suffered at the hands of his master, in testimony of which he revealed the scars from the burns, blows, and other injuries he had received. He told how Hirrihigua at last had determined to kill him for the purpose of enlivening a certain feast day that was approaching, and how that Cacique's wife and daughters, who had saved him so many times previously, dared not speak now in his behalf since they had been forbidden to do so under penalty of incurring their lord's wrath. "But the eldest daughter," he continued, "not wanting to see me perish, commanded and gave me courage as a last resort to flee. She provided a guide to direct me to your town and your lodging, and told me to present myself before you in her name, saying that she begs Your Lordship, for the love that you bear her, to receive me under your protection and, being the person you are, to favor me as something she herself has entrusted to you."

Mucozo received the Christian affably and listened with compassion to his account of the sufferings and torments he had experienced, evidences of which were clearly revealed by the scars on his body, for he was dressed as the Indians of that land in no more than some loin cloths. At this point in the story Alonso de Carmona adds that the Cacique embraced Juan Ortiz and kissed him on the face as a sign of peace. Moreover, he assured him of his welcome and urged him to make an effort to forget the fear of his former existence; for, he said, in his house and company he would find life very different from what he had known previously. "In order to serve the one who sent you as well as yourself who have come to me and my house for protection," he continued, "I will do all that I can, as you shall see by my actions; and you may be certain that so long as I shall live, no one will take the occasion to molest you."

All the promises this good Cacique made in favor of Juan Ortiz, he fulfilled; and he did much more, for immediately he appointed him his chamberlain and carried him in his company day and night. He bestowed many honors upon him and increased these honors exceedingly when he learned that Juan Ortiz had killed a lion with a single dart. In sum he treated him as his own brother, but as a very much beloved brother (for there are some brothers who love each other like fire and water).

Hirrihigua suspected that his slave had fled to his neighbor for protection, and he many times asked for his return; but on each occasion Mucozo excused himself, finally telling the Cacique among other things that the loss of a slave so odious to him was a small loss indeed and that he should cease molesting that slave now that he had sought protection in his neighbor's house. Then Hirrihigua asked the assistance of Urribarracuxi, a brother-in-law of Mucozo, but when that chieftain sent messages concerning the release of the captive, Mucozo gave the same reply. Furthermore, he did not vary in his decision when Urribarracuxi, after finding his messages futile, came to him in person. On the contrary, he angrily informed his brother-in-law that it was unjust for a kinsman to demand that he do a thing so unbefitting his honor and reputation. And he added that if performing his duty meant delivering up an afflicted person who had been entrusted to his care just so that person's enemy might torture and kill him like a wild beast solely for entertainment and pleasure, then he would continue remiss in his obligation. Indeed this Cacique defended Juan Ortiz with such generosity against the two chieftains who sought him so persistently and obstinately that rather than return the slave to be slaughtered by his former master, he chose to abandon all possibility of a marriage with Hirrihigua's daughter, whom he ardently desired and subsequently lost, and at the same time to forfeit his friendship and kinship with Urribarracuxi. Moreover, he continued to hold the Christian in high esteem and to regale him until the coming of Governor Hernando de Soto to Florida.

Juan Ortiz was ten years among those Indians. For a year and a half he was in the power of Hirrihigua; but the remainder of the time he spent with the good Mucozo, who although a barbarian, behaved toward this Christian in a manner far different from that of the famous Triumvirate of Laino (a place near Bologna), which made a never-sufficiently abominated proscription and agreement to exchange relatives, friends and protectors for enemies and adversaries. And too, his behavior was much more admirable than that of other Christian princes who since then have made bargains equally odious, if not more so, when one considers the innocence of those delivered up, the rank of some of them, and the fidelity which their deliverers should have had and respected. For the betrayed were infidels, whereas their betrayers took pride in the name and doctrines of Christianity. Violating the laws and statutes of pagan realms, disrespecting the very existence and rank of kings and great princes, and valuing even less their sworn and promised fidelity (a thing unworthy of such a name), these Christians, solely to avenge their anger, exchanged people who had not offended them for those who had, thus giving up the innocent for the guilty. To this fact, both ancient and modern histories testify, but we shall abandon this subject lest we offend powerful ears and grieve the pious.

It suffices to represent the magnanimity of an infidel so that princes of the Faith may make efforts to imitate and if possible surpass him—not in infidelity, as some do who are undeserving of the title of Christian, but in virtue and similar excellences; for being of a more lofty estate, they are under greater obligations. In fact, when one has considered well the circumstances of this Indian's valiant deed, the people for whom and against whom it was performed, and the great amount he was willing to forego and forfeit, even proceeding contrary to his own love and desire by denying the aid and favor asked of and promised by him, it will be seen that he was born with a most generous and heroic spirit and did not deserve to have come into the world and lived in the barbarous paganism of Florida. But God and human nature many times produce such souls in sterile and uncultivated deserts to the greater confusion and shame of people who are born and reared in lands that are fertile and abundant in all good doctrines and sciences, as well as the Christian religion.

---

from ROYAL COMMENTARIES OF THE INCAS AND GENERAL HISTORY OF PERU, PART I[1]

BOOK I

CHAPTER 6

What a certain author says about the name Peru.

Apart from what Cieza de León, Padre José de Acosta, and López de Gómara say about the name *Peru,*[2] I have the authority of another illustrious writer, a member of the Holy Society of Jesus, called Padre Blas Valera, who

---

1. *The Royal Commentaries of the Indies* (published in Lisbon, 1609) and its second volume, *The General History of Peru* (published posthumously, 1616–17), treat the civilization and history of the Incas until the civil wars between brothers Atahuallpa and Huáscar and continue with the arrival of the Spanish conquistadors and the takeover by Pizarro and his followers, concluding with the appointment of Francisco de Toledo as viceroy of Peru and the deaths of Incas and mestizos at his hands. The text is taken from the translation by Harold V. Livermore (1966).

2. Pedro Cieza de León (1518–60), José de Acosta (1540–1600), and Francisco López de Gómara (1510–60?), considered the leading experts on the history of Spain's conquests of "the Indies," especially Peru. The conflicting stories about the different attempts to conquer the Incas returned home with survivors, making the original naming of Peru and its lands—and the consequent status of the Incas whose land was overtaken by Spanish conquistadors—of particular importance to the Crown and to historians.

wrote a history of the Peruvian empire in very elegant Latin, and could have written it in many other languages, for he had that gift. But to the misfortune of my country, which did not deserve perhaps to be written about by so noble a hand, his papers were lost in the sack and destruction of Cádiz by the English in 1596, and he died soon after. I received the remains of the papers which were saved from the pillage, and they caused me great regret and grief at the loss of the rest, the importance of which can be deduced from what survived. What is missing is the greater and better part. I was presented with the papers by Padre Pedro Maldonado de Saavedra, of Seville, of the same society, who in the present year of 1600 reads Scripture in this city of Córdova. Speaking of the name *Peru,* he says in his polished Latin, the following, which I, as an Indian, have translated into my rough romance:

The kingdom of Peru, illustrious, famous, vast, contains a great quantity of gold, silver, and other rich metals, from the abundance of which arose the saying, "he possesses Peru," to say that a man is rich. This name was newly imposed on the empire of the Incas by the Spaniards, and imposed inappropriately and by chance. It is unknown to the Indians, who regard it as barbarous and so detest it that none of them will use it: only the Spaniards do so. Its recent imposition does not refer to wealth or to any great event. Its use with reference to riches is as new as the imposition of the name and has proceeded from the good fortune of events there. The name *pelú* is a word that means "a river" among the barbarous Indians who dwell between Panama and Guayaquil. It is also the name of a certain island, *Pelua* or *Pelú.* As the first Spanish conquerors sailed from Panama and reached these parts before the rest, the name *Peru* or *Pelua* pleased them so much that they applied it to anything they found as though it had meant some thing grand and noteworthy, and so they called the empire of the Incas *Peru.* There were many who disliked the name, and they called the country *New Castile.* The two names were imposed on that great kingdom, and are commonly used by the royal scribes and ecclesiastical notaries, though in Europe and in the other kingdoms they prefer the name *Peru* to the other. Many also affirm that this word is derived from *pirua,* a term of the Quechuas of Cuzco, meaning a granary for storing crops. I am quite willing to accept this opinion because the Indians of that kingdom do have a great many granaries for storing their crops. It was easy therefore for the Spaniards to use this foreign word and say *Pirú,* leaving off the final vowel and transferring the stress to the last syllable. This noun with

its two meanings was adopted by the first conquerors as the name of the empire they had conquered, and I shall use it also in the two forms, *Peru* and *Pirú,* indifferently. Nor should the introduction of this new word be rejected on the ground that it was usurped without rhyme or reason, since the Spaniards found no other generic native name applicable to the whole region. Before the Inca rule each province had its own name, such as Charca, Colla, Cuzco, Rímac, Quitu, and many others, without regard for or reference to other regions; but after the Incas had subjected them all to their empire, they gave them names according to the order of their conquest and as they submitted and acknowledge vassalage; and finally they were called *Tabuantinsuyu,* or "the four parts of the kingdom," or *Incap Rúnam,* "vassals of the Inca." The Spaniards, observing the variety and confusion of these names, wisely called it *Peru* or *New Castile,*

etc.

This is from Blas Valera, who, like Padre Acosta, says the name was given by the Spaniards and that the Indians did not have it in their language. Having thus quoted Padre Blas Valera's words, I should add that it is more likely that the name *Peru* should have originated from the proper name *Berú* or the noun *pelú,* meaning "a river" in the speech of that province, than that it should come from the word *birua,* "a granary." For, as has been said, the name was given by the followers of Vasco Núñez de Balboa,[3] who did not go inland where they would come across the word *pirua,* and not by the conquerors of Peru. Fifteen years before the latter set out on their conquest, the Spaniards living in Panama called all the coast south of the equator *Peru.* We are assured of this by Francisco López de Gómara in his *History of the Indies* (ch. cx), where he says: "Some say Balboa heard reports of how the land of Peru had gold and emeralds; whether this be true or not, it is certain that Peru had great fame in Panama when Pizarro and Almagro prepared to go there," etc. This is from López de Gómara, whence it is clear that the application of the name *Peru* occurred long before the departure of the conquerors who won the empire.

---

3. Vasco Núñez de Balboa (1475–1518?) learned of Peru and of the Pacific from native peoples with whom he traded while exploring in 1512.

CHAPTER 15

The origin of the Inca kings of Peru.

While these peoples were living or dying in the manner we have seen, it pleased our Lord God that from their midst there should appear a morning star to give them in the dense darkness in which they dwelt some glimmerings of natural law, of civilization, and of the respect men owe to one another. The descendants of this leader should thus tame those savages and convert them into men, made capable of reason and of receiving good doctrine, so that when God, who is the sun of justice, saw fit to send forth the light of His divine rays upon those idolaters, it might find them no longer in their first savagery, but rendered more docile to receive the Catholic faith and the teaching and doctrine of our Holy Mother the Roman Church, as indeed they have received it—all of which will be seen in the course of this history. It has been observed by clear experience how much prompter and quicker to receive the Gospel were the Indians subdued, governed, and taught by the Inca kings than the other neighboring peoples unreached by the Incas' teachings, many of which are still today as savage and brutish as before, despite the fact that the Spaniards have been in Peru seventy years. And since we stand on the threshold of this great maze, we had better enter and say what lay within.

After having prepared many schemes and taken many ways to begin to give an account of the origin and establishment of the native Inca kings of Peru, it seemed to me that the best scheme and simplest and easiest way was to recount what I often heard as a child from the lips of my mother and her brothers and uncles and other elders about these beginnings. For everything said about them from other sources comes down to the same story as we shall relate, and it will be better to have it as told in the very words of the Incas than in those of foreign authors. My mother dwelt in Cuzco, her native place, and was visited there every week by the few relatives, both male and female, who escaped the cruelty and tyranny of Atahuallpa (which we shall describe in our account of his life). On these visits the ordinary subject of conversation was always the origin of the Inca kings, their greatness, the grandeur of their empire, their deeds and conquests, their government in peace and war, and the laws they ordained so greatly to the advantage of their vassals. In short, there was nothing concerning the most flourishing period of their history that they did not bring up in their conversations.

From the greatness and prosperity of the past they turned to the present, mourning their dead kings, their lost empire, and their fallen state, etc. These and similar topics were broached by the Incas and Pallas on their visits, and on recalling their departed happiness, they always ended these conversations with tears and mourning, saying: "Our rule is turned to bondage" etc. During these talks, I, as a boy, often came in and went out of the place where they were, and I loved to hear them, as boys always do like to hear stories. Days, months, and years went by, until I was sixteen or seventeen. Then it happened that one day when my family was talking in this fashion about their kings and the olden times, I remarked to the senior of them, who usually related these things: "Inca, my uncle, though you have no writings to preserve the memory of past events, what information have you of the origin and beginnings of our kings? For the Spaniards and the other peoples who live on their borders have divine and human histories from which they know when their own kings and their neighbors' kings began to reign and when one empire gave way to another. They even know how many thousand years it is since God created heaven and earth. All this much more they know through their books. But you, who have no books, what memory have you preserved of your antiquity? Who was the first of our Incas? What was he called? What was the origin of his line? How did he begin to reign? With what men and arms did he conquer this great empire? How did our heroic deeds begin?"

The Inca was delighted to hear these questions, since it gave him great pleasure to reply to them, and turned to me (who had already often heard him tell the tale, but had never paid as much attention as then) saying:

"Nephew, I will tell you these things with pleasure: indeed it is right that you should hear them and keep them in your heart (this is their phrase for 'in the memory'). You should know that in olden times the whole of this region before you was covered with brush and heath, and people lived in those times like wild beasts, with no religion or government and no towns or houses, and without tilling or sowing the soil, or clothing or covering their flesh, for they did not know how to weave cotton or wool to make clothes. They lived in twos and threes as chance brought them together in caves and crannies in rocks and underground caverns. Like wild beasts they ate the herbs of the field and roots of trees and fruits growing wild and also human flesh. They covered their bodies with leaves and the bark of trees and animals' skins. Others went naked. In short, they lived like deer or other game, and even in their intercourse with women they behaved like beasts, for they knew nothing of having separate wives."

I must remark, in order to avoid many repetitions of the words "our father the Sun," that the phrase was used by the Incas to express respect whenever they mentioned the sun, for they boasted of descending from it, and none but Incas were allowed to utter the words: it would have been blasphemy and the speaker would have been stoned. The Inca said:

"Our father the Sun, seeing men in the state I have mentioned, took pity and was sorry for them, and sent from heaven to earth a son and a daughter of his to indoctrinate them in the knowledge of our father the Sun that they might worship him and adopt him as their god, and to give them precepts and laws by which they would live as reasonable and civilized men, and dwell in houses and settled towns, and learn to till the soil, and grow plants and crops, and breed flocks, and use the fruits of the earth like rational beings and not like beasts. With this order and mandate our father the Sun set these two children of his in Lake Titicaca, eighty leagues from here, and bade them go where they would, and wherever they stopped to eat or sleep to try to thrust into the ground a golden wand half a yard long and two fingers in thickness which he gave them as a sign and token: when this wand should sink into the ground at a single thrust, there our father the Sun wished them to stop and set up their court.

"Finally he told them: 'When you have reduced these people to our service, you shall maintain them in reason and justice, showing mercy, clemency, and mildness, and always treating them as a merciful father treats his beloved and tender children. Imitate my example in this. I do good to all the world. I give them my light and brightness that they may see and go about their business; I warm them when they are cold; and I grow their pastures and crops, and bring fruit to their trees, and multiply their flocks. I bring rain and calm weather in turn, and I take care to go round the world once a day to observe the wants that exist in the world and to fill and supply them as the sustainer and benefactor of men. I wish you as children of mine to follow this example sent down to earth to teach and benefit those men who live like beasts. And henceforward I establish and nominate you as kings and lords over all the people you may thus instruct with your reason, government, and good works.'

"When our father the Sun had thus made manifest his will to his two children he bade them farewell. They left Titicaca and travelled northwards, and wherever they stopped on the way they thrust the golden wand into the earth, but it never sank in. Thus they reached a small inn or rest-house seven or eight leagues south of this city. Today it is called Pacárec Tampu, 'inn or resthouse of the dawn.' The Inca gave it this name because he set out from it about daybreak. It is one of the towns the prince later ordered to be founded, and its inhabitants to this day boast greatly of its name because our first Inca bestowed it. From this place he and his wife, our queen, reached the valley of Cuzco which was then a wilderness."

CHAPTER 16

The foundation of Cuzco, the imperial city.

"The first settlement they made in this valley," said the Inca, "was in the hill called Huanacauri, to the south of this city. There they tried to thrust the golden wand into the earth and it easily sank in at the first blow and they saw it no more. Then our Inca said to his wife: 'Our father the Sun bids us remain in this valley and make it our dwelling place and home in fulfilment of his will. It is therefore right, queen and sister, that each of us should go out and call together these people so as to instruct them and benefit them as our father the Sun has ordained.' Our first rulers set out from the hill of Huanacauri, each in a different direction, to call the people together, and as that was the first place we know they trod with their feet and because they went out from it to do good to mankind, we made there, as you know, a temple for the worship of our father the Sun, in memory of his merciful beneficence towards the world. The prince went northwards, and the princess south. They spoke to all the men and women they found in that wilderness and said that their father the Sun had sent them from the sky to be teachers and benefactors to the dwellers in all that land, delivering them from the wild lives they led and in obedience to the commands given by the Sun, their father, calling them together and removing them from those heaths and moors, bringing them to dwell in settled valleys and giving them the food of men instead of that of beasts to eat. Our king and queen said these and similar things to the first savages they found in those mountains and heaths, and as the savages beheld two persons clad and adorned with the ornaments our father the Sun had given them—and a very different dress from their own—with their ears pierced and opened in the way we their descendants have, and saw that their words and countenances showed them to be children of the Sun, and that they came to mankind to give them towns to dwell in and food to eat, they wondered at what they saw and were at the same time attracted by the promises that were held out to them. Thus they fully credited all they were told and worshipped and venerated the strangers as children of the Sun and obeyed them as kings. These savages gathered others and repeated the wonders they had seen and heard, and a great number of men and women collected and set out to follow our king and queen wherever they might lead.

"When our princes saw the great crowd that had formed there, they ordered that some should set about supplying open-air meals for them all, so that they should not be driven by hunger to disperse again across the heaths. Others were ordered to work on building huts and houses according to plans made by the Inca. Thus our imperial city began to be settled: it was divided into two halves called Hanan Cuzco, which as you know, means upper Cuzco, and Hurin Cuzco, or lower Cuzco. The king wished those he had brought to people Hanan Cuzco, therefore called the upper, and those the queen had brought to people Hurin Cuzco, which was therefore called the lower. The distinction did not imply that the inhabitants of one half should excel those of the other in privileges and exemptions. All were equal like brothers, the children of one father and one mother. The Inca only wished that there should be this division of the people and distinction of name, so that the fact that some had been gathered by the king and others by the queen might have a perpetual memorial. And he ordered that there should be only one difference and acknowledgment of superiority among them, that those of upper Cuzco be considered and respected as first-born and elder brothers, and those of lower Cuzco be as younger children. In short they were to be as the right side and the left in any question of precedence of place and office, since those of the upper town had been gathered by the men and those of the lower by the women. In imitation of this, there was later the same division in all the towns, great or small, of our empire, which were divided by wards or by lineages, known as *hanan aillu* and *hurin aillu,* the upper and lower lineage, or *hanan suyu* and *hurin suyu,* the upper and lower district.

"At the same time, in peopling the city, our Inca showed the male Indians which tasks were proper to men: breaking and tilling the land, sowing crops, seeds, and vegetables which he showed to be good to eat and fruitful, and for which purpose he taught them how to make ploughs and other necessary instruments, and bade them and showed them how to draw irrigation channels from the streams that run through the valley of Cuzco, and even showed them how to make the footwear we use. On her side the queen trained the Indian women in all the feminine occupations: spinning and weaving cotton and wool, and making clothes for themselves and their husbands and children. She told them how to do these and other duties of domestic service. In short, there was nothing relating to human life that our princes failed to teach their first vassals, the Inca king acting as master for the men and the Coya queen, mistress of the women."

CHAPTER 17

The peoples subdued by the first Inca Manco Cápac.

The very Indians who had thus been recently subdued, discovering themselves to be quite changed and realizing the benefits they had received, willingly and joyfully betook themselves to the sierras, moors, and heaths to seek their inhabitants and give them news about the children of the Sun. They recounted the many benefits they had brought them, and proved it by showing their new clothes they wore and the new foods they ate, and telling how they lived in houses and towns. When the wild people heard all this, great numbers of them came to behold the wonders that were told and reported of our first fathers, kings, and lords. Once they had verified this with their own eyes, they remained to serve and obey them. Thus some called others and these passed the word to more, and so many gathered in a few years that after six or seven, the Inca had a force of men armed and equipped to defend themselves against any attackers and even to bring by force those who would not come willingly. He taught them how to make offensive weapons such as bows and arrows, lances, clubs, and others now in use.

"And to cut short the deeds of our first Inca, I can tell you that he subdued the region to the east as far as the river called Paucartampu, and to the west eight leagues up to the river Apurímac, and to the south for nine leagues to Quequesana. Within this area our Inca ordered more than a hundred villages to be settled, the biggest with a hundred houses and others with less, according to what the land could support. These were the first beginnings of our city toward being established and settled as you now see it. They were also the beginnings of our great, rich, and famous empire that your father and his friends deprived us of. These were our first Incas and kings, who appeared in the first ages of the world; and from them descend all the other kings we have had, and from these again we are all descended. I cannot inform you exactly how many years it is since our father the Sun sent us his first children, for it is so long no one has been able to remember: we believe it is above four hundred years. Our Inca was called Manco Cápac and our Coya Mama Ocllo Huaco. They were, as I have told you, brother and sister, children of the Sun and the Moon, our parents. I think I have expatiated at length on your enquiry and answered your questions, and in order to spare your tears, I have not recited this story with tears of blood flowing from my eyes as they flow from my heart from the grief I feel at seeing the line of our Incas ended and our empire lost."

This long account of the origin of our kings was given me by the Inca, my mother's uncle, of whom I asked it. I have tried to translate it faithfully from my mother tongue, that of the Inca, into a foreign speech, Castilian, though I have not written it in such majestic language as the Inca used, nor with the full significance the words of that language have. If I had given the whole significance, the tale would have been much more extensive than it is. On the contrary, I have shortened it, and left out a few things that might have been odious. However, it is enough to have conveyed its true meaning, which is what is required for our history. The Inca told me a few similar things, though not many, during the visits he paid to my mother's house; these I will include in their places later on, giving their source. I much regret not having asked many more questions so that I might now have information about them from so excellent an archive and write them here.

CHAPTER 18

On some fabulous accounts of the origin of the Incas.

Another fable about the origin of their Inca kings is told by the common people of Peru, the Indians of the region south of Cuzco called Collasuyu and those of the regions to the west called Cuntisuyu. They say that it occurred after the deluge, about which they have no more to say than that it took place, without making it clear whether this was the general deluge of Noah's time or some special one (for this reason, we shall omit what they say about it and similar matters, for by the way they have of telling them they make them seem more like dreams or disjointed fables than historical events). According to them, after the flood ended, there appeared a man at Tiahuanacu [Tiahuanaco], to the south of Cuzco, and he was so powerful that he divided the world into four parts and gave them to four men he called kings. The first was called Manco Cápac, the second Colla, the third Tócay and the fourth Pinahua. They say that he gave the northern part to Manco Cápac, the southern to Colla (whence the extensive province was afterward called Colla), the eastern to the third, Tócay, and the western to the fourth, called Pinahua. He ordered each to go to his district, and conquer and govern the people he found there. They do not, however, say if the deluge had drowned them or if the Indians had been resurrected to be conquered and instructed; and so it is with respect to everything they tell of these times. They say that this division of the world was the origin of that which the Incas made of their kingdom called Tahuantinsuyu. They say that Manco Cápac went northwards, reached the valley of Cuzco and founded the city there, and subdued and instructed the surrounding Indians. After this beginning their version of Manco Cápac is almost the same as the one we have given: they assert that the Inca kings were descended from him and cannot say what happened to the other three kings. This is the way with all the stories of those ancient times; and it is hardly to be wondered at that people without letters with which to preserve the memory of their antiquity should have so confused an idea of their beginnings, when the heathens of the Old World, though they had letters and displayed great skill in them, invented legends as laughable as the Indian stories, or more so—for example, there is the fable of Pyrrha and Deucalion, and a great many others we could mention. Moreover the fables of both of these ages of heathendom can be compared, and in many points they will be found to agree. Thus the Indians have something similar to the story of Noah, as some Spaniards have said: of this we shall deal later, and at the end I will say what I myself feel about the origin of the Incas.

Another version of the origin of the Incas similar to this is given by the Indians living to the east and north of the city of Cuzco. According to them, at the beginning of the world four men and four women, all brothers and sisters, came out of some "windows" in some rocks near that city at a place called Paucartampu. The windows are three in number and they came out of the middle one, called the "royal window." Because of this fable they lined this window on all sides with great gold plates and many precious stones. The side windows they decorated only with gold and not with stones. The first brother was called Manco Cápac and his wife Mama Ocllo. They say he founded the city and called it Cuzco, which means "navel" in the private language of the Incas, and that he subdued all those tribes and taught them how to be men, and that from him all the Incas are descended. The second brother they call Ayar Cachi, the third Ayar Uchu, and the fourth Ayar Sauca. The word *ayar* has no meaning in the ordinary tongue of Peru, though it must have had one in the special language of the Incas. The other words occur in the general language: *cachi* is the salt we eat; *uchu* is the condiment they season dishes with, which the Spaniards call "*pimento*" (the Peruvian Indians had no other spices). The other word, *sauca,* means "rejoicing," "satisfaction," or "delight." If we press the Indians for information about what the three brothers and three sisters of the first king did, they invent a thousand foolish tales and find no choice but to explain the fable by an allegory. Salt, which is one of the names, they declare to mean the teaching the Inca gave them about the natural life. The pepper is the relish they took in it, and the word "rejoicing" shows the joy and contentment in which they afterwards lived. Even this is told in such rambling, disjointed, and confused style that one understands what they mean by conjectures rather than by the sense and order of their words. The only thing they are clear about is that Manco Cápac was the first king and that the rest are descended from him. Thus all three accounts ascribe the beginnings and origins of the Incas to Manco Cápac, and say nothing of the other three brothers—on the contrary they are done away with in the allegory and only Manco Cápac remains. This seems likely since no king of this time was ever called by those names, nor has any tribe boasted of descending from them. Some Spanish scholars who have heard these legends think that the Indians heard of the story of Noah, his three sons, his wife, and daughters-in-law, and that the four men and women God spared from the deluge are the four in the fable and that the Indians mean the window of Noah's ark when they spoke of the window of Paucartampu; and the powerful man who, the first version says, appeared at Tiahuanaco and divided the world between the four men, they hold to have been God, who sent Noah and his three sons to people the earth. Other parts of this legend and the other seem to point to those of Holy Writ, which they are thought to resemble. I do not venture on such profound matters: I simply repeat the fabulous accounts I used to hear my family tell in my childhood; let each take them as he wishes and apply whatever allegory he thinks most appropriate. Just as the Incas have the fables we have mentioned, so the other peoples of Peru invent endless stories of the origin and beginning of their earliest ancestors, which distinguish them from one another, as we shall see in the course of this story. For the Indian does not consider himself honorable unless descended from a spring, river, or lake—or even from the sea—or from wild animals, such as the bear, lion, or tiger, or from the eagle, or the bird called *cuntur,* or other birds of prey, or from mountains, moors, peaks, or caverns, each according to his own family, to the greater praise and nobility of his name. This shall suffice for fables.

from CHAPTER 19

The author's declaration about his history.

Now that we have laid the first stone of our edifice, though it be fabulous, it will be proper to proceed from the origin of the Inca kings of Peru to the conquest and subjugation of the Indians, enlarging somewhat the brief account that my uncle the Inca gave me with the accounts of many other Incas and Indians born in the towns that the first Inca Manco Cápac founded, peopled, and added to his empire. I was brought up among these Indians, and as I frequented their society until I was twenty I was able to learn during that time something of all the subjects I am writing about, for in my childhood they used to recount their histories, just as stories are told for children. . . .

NORTHERN EXPERIENCES

JACQUES CARTIER (1491–1557)

"The voyage of this kingdom to the New Lands to discover certain islands and countries where there are said to be great quantities of gold and other riches": such was the charge that Francis I, king of France, gave to Jacques Cartier in 1534. Like navigators before and after him, Cartier hoped to find a passage through North America to Asia and its valued trade goods. Failing that, his task was to determine what valuable materials were available in the "new lands" of the Americas.

Born in Saint-Malo, a major French port, Cartier must have become an experienced navigator, although little is known of his early life. There is some evidence that suggests that he might have participated in Verrazzano's westward explorations in the 1520s. By 1534, Cartier apparently had garnered sufficient experience to be entrusted with the ambitious expedition to North America, an expedition that was supposed to lay the groundwork for French colonization of Canada. During this first voyage, Cartier's expedition explored the Gulf of St. Lawrence, made contact (and traded) with Micmac and Iroquois peoples, and claimed possession of territory for the French king by erecting a number of crosses. The expedition returned to France with two Iroquois men who described the St. Lawrence River, which the French hoped was a sea passage to the Indies.

Cartier made a second expedition in 1535, this time with a larger force. They traveled as far as Montreal, where they found an Iroquois village of approximately 2,000 people. An early winter, an epidemic of scurvy, and deteriorating relations with the Iroquois prevented the expedition from traveling farther west. They returned to France the following spring, once again taking with them a number of Iroquois people. In 1541, Cartier was sent back to Canada with the first colonization effort. This third expedition included 1,500 colonists on five vessels. The initial effort to found a colony at Cape Rouge (near present-day Quebec) was a dismal failure. Cartier took some survivors back to France in 1542; the colony itself was abandoned in 1543. After this voyage, Cartier retired in Saint-Malo, where he continued to advise navigators until his death in 1557.

Cartier's narratives, written as reports to the king, shed important light on the Algonquian peoples that the Europeans encountered in North America. They also serve as useful reminders that the first voyages to create settlements were not for the promotion of the Catholic faith in the North, as the later history of northeastern North America might suggest, but rather to compete with the newfound wealth of France's European neighbors, Portugal and Spain. Lapidaries (gem specialists) accompanied Cartier on his first voyage.

from THE FIRST RELATION[1]

Of the Baie called Saint Lunario, *and other notable baies, and Capes of lande, and of the qualitie, and goodnesse of those groundes.*

The next day being the second of July we discovered and had sight of land on the Northerne side towarde us, that dyd joyne unto the lande abovesayd, all compassed about, and we knew that it had about _____ in depth, and as much athwart, we named it Saint Lunarios Baie[2]. . . . All that night the weather was very ill, and great windes, so that we were constrained to beare a small sayle untill the next morning, being the thirde of July, that the winde came from the West: and we sayled Northwarde, to have

---

1. This text is the first English publication of Cartier's narratives, printed in London as *A shorte and briefe narration of the two navigations and discoveries to the northwest partes called Newe Fraunce* (London, 1580).

2. The large blank occurs in the original.

a sight of the lande that we had left on the Northeast side, above the lowe landes, among whiche high and lowe landes there is a Gulf, or Breache, in some places about five and twenty fahoms deepe, and fifteene leagues in breadth, with varietie of landes, hoping to find some passage thyther, we went even as the passage of the Castels. The sayde gulfe lyeth Easte Northeast, and West Southwest. The grounde that lyeth on the South side of the sayde gulfe, is as good and vaste to be Wroughte,[3] and full of as goodly fieldes and meadowes, as anye that ever we have, as plaine and smoothe as anye die:[4] and that which lyeth on the North, is a Countrey altogether hillie, full of woods, and very high and great trees of sundry sortes: among the rest there are as goodly Ceders, and Firre trees, as possibly can be seene, able to make mastes for ships of three hundered Tunne: Neyther did we see anye place that was not full of the sayde trees, excepted two onlye, that were full of goodly meadowes, with two very faire Lakes. The middest of the sayde Baie is seauen and fourtie degrees and halfe in latitude.

Of the Cape of Hope, *and of* Saint Martins *Creeke, & howe seven boats ful of wilde men, came to our boate; wold not retire themselves, but being terrified with our Colubrins and lanches we shot at them, they fled with great hast.*

The Cape of the said South land, was called The Cape of Hope, through the hope that there we had to finde some passage. The fourth of July we went along the coast of the sayd land on the Northerly side to finde some harborough, where we entred into a Creeke altogether open on the South, where there is no succour against the wind: we thought good to name it S. Martines Creeke. Ther we stayed from the fourth of July, until the twelfth: while we were there, on Monday being the fifth of the month, service being done, we with one of our boates went to discover a Cape and point of lande that on the Northerne side was about seauen or eight leagues from us, to see whiche way it did bend, and being within halfe a league of it, we saw two companies of boats of wilde men going from one land to the other: theyr boates were in number about five and fortie or fifty. One part of the whiche came to the

sayde pointe, and a great number of the men went on those, making a great noyse, beckning unto us that we shoulde come on lande, shewing us certaine skinnes uppon pieces of Woode, but bicause we hadde but one onely boate, we woulde not goe to them, but went to the other side, lying in the sea: they seeing us flee, prepared two of their boats to follow us, with which came also five more of them that were comming from the sea side, al which approached nere unto our boate, dauncing, and making many signes of love and myrth, as it were desiring our friendship, saying in their tongue Napev Tondamen Assurtah, with manye other that we understoode not. But bicause (as we have said) we had but one boate, we wold not stande to theyr curtesie, but made signes unto them, that they shoulde turne backe, which they would not do, but with great furye came toward us: and sodainely with their boates compassed us aboute: and bycause they woulde not awaye from us by any signes that we coulde make, we shotte of two pieces among them, whiche did so terrifie them, that they put themselves to flight towarde the sayde pointe, makyng a great noyse: and having stayde a while, they began a new, even as at the first, to come to us againe, and being come neere our boate, we strucke at them with two launces, which thing was so great a terrour unto them, that with greate hast they began to flee, and would no more follow us.

How the sayde men comming to our shippes, and our men going toward them, both parties went on land, and how the saide wilde men with great joye beganne to traficke with our men.

The next daye, part of the sayde wilde men with nine of their boates came to the point and entrance of the creek, where we with our ships were at rest. We being advertised of their coming, went to the point where they met with our boates: but so soone as they sawe us, they began to flee, making signes that they came to traficke with us, shewing us such skinnes as they cloth themselves withall, whiche are of small value. We likewise made signes unto them, that we wished them no evil: and in signe thereof two of our men ventured to go on lande to them, and carrie them knives with other Iron wares, and a red hat to give unto their Captain. Which when they saw, they also came on land, and broughte some of their skinnes, and so began to deale with us, seeming to be very glad to have our iron wares, and other things, stil dauncing with many other ceremonies, as with their handes to cast sea water on theyr heades. They gave us whatsoever they had, not

---

3. Cultivated.

4. An iron block on which ore is smashed.

keeping any thing, that they were constrained to go backe againe naked, and made us signes that the nexte day they would come againe, and bring more skinnes wyth them.

How that we having sent two of our men on lande with wares, there came about 300 wilde men with great gladnes. Of the quality of the Country, what it bringeth forth, and of the Baie called The Baie of heate.

Upon Thursday being the eight of the moneth, bicause the winde was not good to go out with our ships, we set our boates in a readinesse to go to discover the saide Baie, and with daye we went fifteene leagues within it. The nexte day, the winde and wether being faire, we sayled until noone, in which time we had notice of a great part of the sayd Baie, and how that upon the lowe landes, there were other lands, with high mountaines: but seeing that there was no passage at al, we began to turne backe again, taking our way along the coast, and sayling, we sawe certaine wilde men, that stoode upon the shore of a Lake, that is among the lowe groundes, who were making fires and smokes: we went thither, and founde that there was a Chanel of the sea, that did enter into the Lake, and setting our boates at one of the banckes of the Chanell, the wilde men with one of their boates came unto us, and brought us pieces of Seales readie fodde, putting them upon pieces of wood: then retyring themselves, they would make signes unto us, that they did give them us. We sente two men unto them with hatchets, knives, beades, and other such like ware, whereat they were very glad, and by and by in clusters they came to the shore where we wer with their boates, bringing with them skinnes, and other such things as they had, to have of our wares. They were more than three hundred men, women, and children: some of the women which came not over, we might see them stand up to the knees in water, singing and dauncing, the other that had passed the river where we were, came verye friendlye to us, rubbing our armes with their owne handes, then woulde they lifte them uppe towarde heaven, shewing manye signes of gladnesse: and in such wise were we assured one of another, that we very familiarly beganne to trafficke of whatsoever they had, till they had nothing but their naked bodies, for they gave us al whatsoever they had, and that was but of small value. We perceived that this people might verie easily be converted to our religion. They go from place to place. They live only with fishing. They have an ordinarie time to fish for their provision. The Countrey is hotter, than the Countrey of *Spaine,* and the fairest that can possibly be found, alto-

gether smooth, and leavel. There is no place, be it never so little, but it hathe some trees (yea albeit it be sandie) or else is ful of wilde corn, that hath an eare like unto Rie: the corn is like Dates, small pease as thicke as if they had bin sown and plowed, white and red gooseberies, strawberries, blackberies, white and red Roses, with many other flowres, of very sweete and plesant smel. Ther be also many goodly meadowes ful of grasse, and Lakes where gret plentie of Salmons be. They cal a Hatchet in their tong Cochi, and a knife Bacon: we named it The Bay of Heate.

Of another nation of wilde men: of their maners, living and clothing.

We being certified that there was no passage through the said Bay, we hoised saile, and went from S. Martines Creeke upon Sunday being the twelfth of July, to go and discover further in the said Baie and went along the sea coast Estward about eighteene leagues, till we came to the Cape of *Prato,* where we found the tide very greate, but shallow, and the sea stormie, so that we were constrained to draw toward shore, betweene the saide Cape and an Ilande lying Eastwarde, about halfe a league from the Cape, where we cast Ancker for that night. The next morning we hoised sayle to trend the said coaste about, which lyeth North Northeast. But there rose such a stormie and raging winde against us, that we were constrained to come to the place againe, from whence we were come: There did we stay all that daye till the nexte, that wee hoised up sayle, and came to the middest of a river five or sixe leagues from the Cape of *Prato* Northward, and being overthwart the said river, there arose againe a contrarie winde, with great fogges and stormes. So that we were constrayned upon Wednesday, being the fourteenth of the moneth, to enter into the river, and there did we stay til the fifteenth of the moneth, looking for faire weather to come out of it, on which day being Thursdaye, the winde became so raging, that one of our shippes lost an Ancker, and we were constrayned to go up higher into the river seaven or eighte leagues, into a good harborough and ground, that we with our boates found out, and through the evil weather, tempest, and darkenesse that was, we stayed in the saide harborough till the five and twentith of the month, that we coulde not come out: in the mean time we sawe a great multitude of wilde men that were fishing for Mackrels, whereof there is great store. Their boats wer about fortie, and the persons, what with men, women, and children, two hundred, which after they had haunted our companie a while, they came very familiarly with their boates to the sides of our ships. We gave them knives, combs, beades of glas, and other trifles of small value, for which they made many signes of gladnesse, lifting their handes up to Heaven, dauncing and singing in their boates. These men may very wel and truely be called Wilde, bicause there is no poorer people in the world. For I thinke al that they had together, besides their boates and nets, was not worth five sous. They go altogether naked, saving their privities, which covered with a little skinne, and certaine olde skinnes that they cast upon them. Neyther in nature nor in language, do they any whit agree with them we found first: Their heads be altogether shaven, except one bush of haire, they suffer to grow upon the toppe of theyr crowne, as long as a horsse taile, and then with certaine leather strings binde it in a knot upon their heades. They have no other dwelling but their boates, which they tourne upside down, and under them they lay themselves al along upon the bare ground. They eate their fleshe almost rawe, onely that they heate it a little uppon embers of coles, so doe they theyr fish. Upon Magdalens day we with our boates went to the bancke of the river, and freelye went on shore among them, whereat they made many signes of gladnesse, and al their men in two or three companies began to sing and daunce, seeming to be very glad of our comming. They had caused al the yong women to flee into the wood, two or three excepted, that stayed with them, to each of which we gave a combe, and a little bell made of Tinne, for which they were very glad, thanking our Captaine, rubbing his armes and breastes with theyr handes. When the men saw us give something unto those that had stayde, it caused all the rest to come out of the wood, to the ende they should have as muche as the others: These women were about twentie, who altogether in a knot fell upon our Captain, touching and rubbing him with their hands, according to their manner of cherishing and making muche of one, who gave to eache of them a little Tinne bell: then sodainely they began to daunce, and sing many songs. There we founde great store of Mackrels, that they had taken upon the shore, with certaine nettes that they make to fishe, of a kinde of hempe that groweth in that place where ordinarilye they abide, for they never come to the sea, but onlye in fishing time. As farre as I understand, ther groweth likewise a kinde of Millet as bigge as small pease, like unto that which groweth in Brasile, which they eat instead of bread. They had greate store of it. They call it Kaipage. They have also plums . . . which they dry for the winter as we do. They call them Honesta. They have also figges, nuttes, Apples, and other fruites and Beanes, that they call Sahv, their nuttes Cahehya. If we shewed them any thing that they have not, nor knowe not what it is, shaking their heads, they will say Nohda, whiche is as much to say, they have it not, nor they know it not. Of those things they have, they would with signes shew us the way how to dresse them, and how they grow. They eate nothing that hath any tast of salte. They are very great Theeves, for they will filch and steale whatsoever they can lay hold of, and all is fish that commeth to net.

How our men set up a great Crosse upon the poynt of the sayd Porte, and the Captayne of those wild men, after a long Oration, was by our Captayne appeased, and contented that two of his Children should goe with him.

Upon the 24 of the Moneth, we caused a faire high Crosse to be made of the height of thirtie foote, which was made in the presence of many of them, upon the poynt of the entrance of the Gulfe, in the middest whereof, we hanged up a Shield with three Floure de Luces in it, and in the toppe was carved in the wood with Anticke letters this poste, VIVE LE ROY DE FRANCE. Then before them all we set it up upon the sayd poynt. They with great heede beheld both the making and setting of it up. So soone as it was up, we altogether kneeled downe before them, with our hands towarde Heaven, yielding God thankes: and we made signes unto them, shewing them the Heavens, and that all our salvation dependeth only on him which in them dwelleth: whereat they shewed a great admiration, looking first one at another, and then upon the Crosse. And after we were returned to oure Shippes, their Captayne clad with an old Beares Skinne, with three of his Sonnes, and a Brother of his with him, came unto us in one of their Boates, but they came not so neere us as they were wont to do: there he made a long Oration unto us, shewing us the crosse we had set up, and making a crosse with two of his fingers, then did he shew us all the Countrey about us, as if he would say that all was his, and that we should not set up any Crosse without his leave. His talke being ended, we shewed him an Axe, fayning that we would give it him for his skinne, to whiche he listned, for by little and little he came neere our Ships. One of our fellowes that was in our boate, tooke holde on theirs, and suddaynely lept into it, with two or three more, who enforced him to enter into our Ships, whereat they were greatly astonished. But our Captaine did straightwayes assure them, that they should have no harme, nor any injury offered them at all, and entertained them very frendly, making them eate and drinke. Then did we shew them with signes, that the Crosse was but only set up to be as a light and leader which wayes to enter into the port, and that we would shortly come againe, and bring good store of iron wares and other things, but that we would take two of his children with us, and afterward bring them to the said port againe: and so we clothed two of them in shirtes, and coloured coates, with red cappes, and put about every ones necke a copper chaine, whereat they were greatly contented: then gave they their old clothes to their fellowes that wente back againe, and we gave to each one of

those three that went backe, a hatchet, and some knives, which made them very glad. After these were gone, and had told the newes unto their fellowes, in the after noone there came to our ships five boates of them, with five or six men in every one, to take their farewels of those two we had retained to take with us, and brought them some fish, uttering many words which we did not understand, making signes that they woulde not remove the Crosse we had set up.

SAMUEL DE CHAMPLAIN (1570?–1635)

Samuel de Champlain once wrote that navigation was the means by which "we attract and bring to our own land all kinds of riches; by it the idolatry of paganism is overthrown, and christianity proclaimed throughout all the regions of the earth." His background prepared him for the life of navigation he enjoyed. Champlain was born to a mariner in Brouage, France, and while still quite young, he accompanied his father on voyages. Although he served several years as a soldier in European wars, he made his first important voyage in 1599, to the West Indies and Mexico, where he collected the first significant information for the French about the holdings of New Spain in the Americas. As a result of this journey, Champlain received a pension and was appointed the royal geographer. In 1603, he accompanied a journey to Canada, during which he explored the St. Lawrence River. From that voyage until the end of his life, Champlain divided his time between New France and short visits home to France to recruit colonists or to request financial assistance for the continued development of New France.

In 1608, Champlain laid the foundation of Quebec. The next year, he joined the Hurons in a successful expedition against the Iroquois in New York. This collaborative effort between the French and the Hurons solidified an alliance that would make both groups enemies of the Iroquois for years to come. Within the first decade of the seventeenth century, when the British were just beginning to land on the eastern coast of North America, Champlain explored west as far as present-day Lake Huron, looking for water passages that might lead to the Pacific. From 1616 until 1629, when the colony was seized by the British, Champlain served as the leader of Quebec. Champlain was held prisoner in England until 1632, when Quebec was returned to France. From 1633 until his death Champlain retained the governorship of Quebec.

Champlain wrote several accounts of events in New France and his travels there, describing the territory he moved across, the natural commodities, and the native peoples with whom he and the other French interacted. The current selection is taken from his account of his voyage of 1615, in which he made his westernmost explorations to Georgian Bay and Lake Huron.

from VOYAGES AND DISCOVERIES IN NEW FRANCE[1]

To the King

Sire,
This is a third volume containing a narrative of what has transpired most worthy of note during the voyages I have

made to New France, and its perusal will, I think, afford your Majesty greater pleasure than that of those preceding, which only designate the ports, harbors, situations, declinations, and other particulars, having more interest for navigators and sailors than for other persons. In this narrative you will be able to observe more especially the manners and mode of life of these peoples both in particular and in general, their wars, ammunition, method of at-

---

1. Champlain's *Voyages and Discoveries in New France from the Year 1615 to the End of the Year 1618* was first printed in France in 1619. The current text reprints Charles Pomeroy Otis's 1882 English translation.

tack and of defence, their expeditions and retreats in various circumstances, matters about which those interested desire information. You will perceive also that they are not savages to such an extent that they could not in course of time and through association with others become civilized and cultivated. You will likewise perceive how great hopes we cherish from the long and arduous labors we have for the past fifteen years sustained, in order to plant in this country the standard of the cross, and to teach the people the knowledge of God and the glory of His holy name, it being our desire to cultivate a feeling of charity towards His unfortunate creatures, which it is our duty to practise more patiently than any other thing, especially as there are many who have not entertained such purposes, but have been influenced only by the desire of gain. Nevertheless, we may, I suppose, believe that these are the means which God makes use of for the greater promotion of the holy desire of others. As the fruits which the trees bear are from God, the Lord of the soil, who has planted, watered, and nourished them with an especial care, so your Majesty can be called the legitimate lord of our labors, and the good resulting from them, not only because the land belongs to you, but also because you have protected us against so many persons, whose only object has been by troubling us to prevent the success of so holy a determination, taking from us the power to trade freely in a part of your country, and striving to bring everything into confusion, which would be, in a word, preparing the way for the ruin of everything to the injury of your state. To this end your subjects have employed every conceivable artifice and all possible means which they thought could injure us. But all these efforts have been thwarted by your Majesty, assisted by your prudent council, who have given us the authority of your name, and supported us by your decrees rendered in our favor. This is an occasion for increasing in us our long-cherished desire to send communities and colonies there, to teach the people the knowledge of God, and inform them of the glory and triumphs of your Majesty, so that together with the French language they may also acquire a French heart and spirit, which, next to the fear of God, will be inspired with nothing so ardently as the desire to serve you. Should our design succeed, the glory of it will be due, after God, to your Majesty, who will receive a thousand benedictions from Heaven for so many souls saved by your instrumentality, and your name will be immortalized for carrying the glory and sceptre of the French as far to the Occident as your precursors have extended it to the Orient, and over the entire habitable earth. This will augment the quality of Most Christian belonging to you above all the kings of the earth, and show that it is as much your due by merit as it is your own of right, it having been transmitted to you by your predecessors, who acquired it by their virtues; for you have been pleased, in addition to so many other important affairs, to give your attention to this one, so seriously neglected hitherto, God's special grace reserving to your reign the publication of His gospel, and the knowledge of His holy name to so many tribes who had never heard of it. And some day may God's grace lead them, as it does us, to pray to Him without ceasing to extend your empire, and to vouchsafe a thousand blessings to your Majesty.

Sire,
Your most humble, most faithful,
and most obedient servant and subject,
Champlain.

Preface

As in the various affairs of the world each thing strives for its perfection and the preservation of its being, so on the other hand does man interest himself in the different concerns of others on some account, either for the public good, or to acquire, apart from the common interest, praise, and reputation with some profit. Wherefore many have pursued this course, but as for myself I have made choice of the most unpleasant and difficult one of the perilous navigation of the seas; with the purpose, however, not so much of gaining wealth, as the honor and glory of God in behalf of my King and country, and contributing by my labors something useful to the public good. And I make declaration that I have not been tempted by any other ambition, as can be clearly perceived, not only by my conduct in the past, but also by the narratives of my voyages, made by the command of His Majesty, in New France, contained in my first and second books, as may be seen in the same.

Should God bless our purpose, which aims only for His glory, and should any fruit result from our discoveries and arduous labors, I will return thanks to Him, and for Your Majesty's protection and assistance will continue my prayers for the aggrandizement and prolongation of your reign.

[Of the Hurons]

The regions towards the east are sufficiently well known, inasmuch as the ocean borders these places. These are the coasts of Labrador, Newfoundland, Cape Breton, La

Cadie, and the Almouchiquois,[2] places well known, as I have treated of them sufficiently in the narrative of my previous voyages, as likewise of the people living there, on which account I shall not speak of them in this treatise, my object being only to make a succinct and true report of what I have seen in addition.

The country of the nation of the Attigouantans[3] is in latitude 44° 30′, and extends two hundred and thirty leagues in length westerly, and ten in breadth. It contains eighteen villages, six of which are enclosed and fortified by palisades of wood in triple rows, bound together, on the top of which are galleries, which they provide with stones and water; the former to hurl upon their enemies and the latter to extinguish the fire which their enemies may set to the palisades. The country is pleasant, most of it cleared up. It has the shape of Brittany, and is similarly situated, being almost surrounded by the *Mer Douce*.[4] They assume that these eighteen villages are inhabited by two thousand warriors, not including the common mass, which amounts to perhaps thirty thousand souls.

Their cabins are in the shape of tunnels or arbors, and are covered with the bark of trees. They are from twenty-five to thirty fathoms long, more or less, and six wide, having a passage-way through the middle from ten to twelve feet wide, which extends from one end to the other. On the two sides there is a kind of bench, four feet high, where they sleep in summer, in order to avoid the annoyance of the fleas, of which there were great numbers. In winter they sleep on the ground on mats near the fire, so as to be warmer than they would be on the platform. They lay up a stock of dry wood, with which they fill their cabins, to burn in winter. At the extremity of the cabins there is a space, where they preserve their Indian corn, which they put into great casks made of the bark of trees and placed in the middle of their encampment. They have pieces of wood suspended, on which they put their clothes, provisions, and other things, for fear of the mice, of which there are great numbers. In one of these cabins there may be twelve fires, and twenty-four families. It smokes excessively, from which it follows that many receive serious injury to the eyes, so that they lose their sight towards the close of life. There is no window nor any opening, except that in the upper part of their cabins for the smoke to escape.

This is all that I have been able to learn about their mode of life; and I have described to you fully the kind of dwelling of these people, as far as I have been able to learn it, which is the same as that of all the tribes living in these regions. They sometimes change their villages at intervals of ten, twenty, or thirty years, and transfer them to a distance of one, two, or three leagues from the preceding situation, except when compelled by their enemies to dislodge, in which case they retire to a greater distance, as the Antouhonorons,[5] who went some forty to fifty leagues. This is the form of their dwellings, which are separated from each other some three or four paces, for fear of fire, of which they are in great dread.

Their life is a miserable one in comparison with our own; but they are happy among themselves, not having experienced anything better, and not imagining that anything more excellent is to be found. Their principal articles of food are Indian corn and Brazilian beans, which they prepare in various ways. By braying in a wooden mortar they reduce the corn to meal. They remove the bran by means of fans made of the bark of trees. From this meal they make bread, using also beans which they first boil, as they do the Indian corn for soup, so that they may be more easily crushed. Then they mix all together, sometimes adding blueberries or dry raspberries, and sometimes pieces of deer's fat, though not often, as this is scarce with them. After steeping the whole in lukewarm water, they make bread in the form of bannocks or pies, which they bake in the ashes. After they are baked they wash them, and from these they often make others by wrapping them in corn leaves, which they fasten to them, and then putting them in boiling water.

But this is not their most common kind. They make another, which they call *migan,* which is as follows: They take the pounded Indian corn, without removing the bran, and put two or three handfuls of it in an earthen pot full of water. This they boil, stirring it from time to time, that it may not burn nor adhere to the pot. Then they put into the pot a small quantity of fish, fresh or dry, according to the season, to give a flavor to the *migan,* as they call it. They make it very often, although it smells badly, especially in winter, either because they do not know how to prepare it rightly, or do not wish to take the trouble to do so. They make two kinds of it, and prepare it very well when they choose. When they use fish the *migan* does not smell

2. The New England coast.

3. The Hurons.

4. Lake Huron and the rivers connected to it.

5. The Onondagas.

badly, but only when it is made with venison. After it is all cooked, they take out the fish, pound it very fine, and then put it all together into the pot, not taking the trouble to remove the appendages, scales, or inwards, as we do, which generally causes a bad taste. It being thus prepared, they deal out to each one his portion. This *migan* is very thin, and without much substance, as may be well supposed. As for drink, there is no need of it, the *migan* being sufficiently thin of itself.

They have another kind of *migan,* namely, they roast new corn before it is ripe, which they preserve and cook whole with fish, or flesh when they have it. Another way is this: they take Indian corn, which is very dry, roast it in the ashes, then bray it and reduce it to meal as in the former case. This they lay up for the journeys which they undertake here and there. The *migan* made in the latter manner is the best according to my taste. Figure H shows the women braying their Indian corn. In preparing it, they cook a large quantity of fish and meat, which they cut into pieces and put into great kettles, which they fill with water and let it all boil well. When this is done, they gather with a spoon from the surface the fat which comes from the meat and fish. Then they put in the meal of the roasted corn, constantly stirring it until the *migan* is cooked and thick as soup. They give to each one a portion, together with a spoonful of the fat. This dish they are accustomed to prepare for banquets, but they do not generally make it.

Now the corn freshly roasted, as above described, is highly esteemed among them. They eat also beans, which they boil with the mass of the roasted flour, mixing in a little fat and fish. Dogs are in request at their banquets, which they often celebrate among themselves, especially in winter, when they are at leisure. In case they go hunting for deer or go fishing, they lay aside what they get for celebrating these banquets, nothing remaining in their cabins but the usual thin *migan,* resembling bran and water, such as is given to hogs to eat.

They have another way of eating the Indian corn. In preparing it, they take it in the ear and put it in water under the mud, leaving it two or three months in this state until they think it is putrefied. Then they remove it, and eat it boiled with meat or fish. They also roast it, and it is better so than boiled. But I assure you that there is nothing that smells so badly as this corn as it comes from the water all muddy. Yet the women and children take it and suck it like sugar-cane, nothing seeming to them to taste better, as they show by their manner. In general they have two meals a day. As for ourselves, we fasted all of Lent and longer, in order to influence them by our example. But it was time lost.

They also fatten bears, which they keep two or three years, for the purpose of their banquets. I observed that if this people had domestic animals they would be interested in them and care for them very well, and I showed them the way to keep them, which would be an easy thing for them, since they have good grazing grounds in their country, and in large quantities, for all kinds of animals, horses, oxen, cows, sheep, swine, and other kinds, for lack of which one would consider them badly off, as they seem to be. Yet with all their drawbacks they seem to me to live happily among themselves, since their only ambition is to live and support themselves, and they lead a more settled life than those who wander through the forests like brute beasts. They eat many squashes, which they boil, and roast in the ashes.

In regard to their dress, they have various kinds and styles made of the skins of wild beasts, both those which they capture themselves, and others which they get in exchange for their Indian corn, meal, porcelain, and fishing-nets from the Algonquins, Nipissings, and other tribes, which are hunters having no fixed abodes. All their clothes are of one uniform shape, not varied by any new styles. They prepare and fit very well the skins, making their breeches of deer-skin rather large, and their stockings of another piece, which extend up to the middle and have many folds. Their shoes are made of the skins of deer, bears, and beaver, of which they use great numbers. Besides, they have a robe of the same fur, in the form of a cloak, which they wear in the Irish or Egyptian style, with sleeves which are attached with a string behind. This is the way they are dressed in winter, as is seen in figure D. When they go into the fields, they gird up their robe about the body; but when in the village, they leave off their sleeves and do not gird themselves. The Milan trimmings for decorating their garments are made of glue and the scrapings of the before-mentioned skins, of which they make bands in various styles according to their fancy, putting in places bands of red and brown color amid those of the glue, which always keep a whitish appearance, not losing at all their shape, however dirty they may get. There are those among these nations who are much more skilful than others in fitting the skins, and ingenious in inventing ornaments to put on their garments. It is our Montagnais and Algonquins, above all others, who take more pains in this matter. They put on their robes bands of porcupine quills, which they dye a very fine scarlet color. They value these bands very highly, and detach them so that they may serve for other robes when they wish to make a change. They also make use of them to adorn the face, in order to give it a more graceful appearance whenever they wish particularly to decorate themselves.

Most of them paint the face black and red. These colors they mix with oil made from the seed of the sunflower, or with bear's fat or that of other animals. They also dye their hair, which some wear long, others short, others on one side only. The women and girls always wear their hair in one uniform style. They are dressed like men, except that they always have their robes girt about them, which extend down to the knee. They are not at all ashamed to expose the body from the middle up and from the knees down, unlike the men, the rest being always covered. They are loaded with quantities of porcelain, in the shape of necklaces and chains, which they arrange in the front of their robes and attach to their waists. They also wear bracelets and earrings. They have their hair carefully combed, dyed, and oiled. Thus they go to the dance, with a knot of their hair behind bound up with eel-skin, which they use as a cord. Sometimes they put on plates a foot square, covered with porcelain, which hang on the back. Thus gaily dressed and habited, they delight to appear in the dance, to which their fathers and mothers send them, forgetting nothing that they can devise to embellish and set off their daughters. I can testify that I have seen at dances a girl who had more than twelve pounds of porcelain on her person, not including the other bagatelles with which they are loaded and bedecked. In the illustration already cited, F shows the dress of the women, G that of the girls attired for the dance.

All these people have a very jovial disposition, although there are many of them who have a sad and gloomy look. Their bodies are well proportioned. Some of the men and women are well formed, strong, and robust. There is a moderate number of pleasing and pretty girls, in respect to figure, color, and expression, all being in harmony. Their blood is but little deteriorated, except when they are old. There are among these tribes powerful women of extraordinary height. These have almost the entire care of the house and work; namely, they till the land, plant the Indian corn, lay up a store of wood for the winter, beat the hemp and spin it, making from the thread fishing-nets and other useful things. The women harvest the corn, house it, prepare it for eating, and attend to household matters. Moreover they are expected to attend their husbands from place to place in the fields, filling the office of pack-mule in carrying the baggage, and

to do a thousand other things. All the men do is to hunt for deer and other animals, fish, make their cabins, and go to war. Having done these things, they then go to other tribes with which they are acquainted to traffic and make exchanges. On their return, they give themselves up to festivities and dances, which they give to each other, and when these are over they go to sleep, which they like to do best of all things.

They have some sort of marriage, which is as follows: when a girl has reached the age of eleven, twelve, thirteen, fourteen, or fifteen years she has suitors, more or less according to her attractions, who woo her for some time. After this, the consent of their fathers and mothers is asked, to whose will the girls often do not submit, although the most discreet and considerate do so. The lover or suitor presents to the girl some necklaces, chains, and bracelets of porcelain. If the girl finds the suitor agreeable, she receives the present. Then the lover comes and remains with her three or four nights, without saying anything to her during the time. They receive thus the fruit of their affections. Whence it happens very often that, after from eight to fifteen days, if they cannot agree, she quits her suitor, who forfeits his necklaces and other presents that he has made, having received in return only a meagre satisfaction. Being thus disappointed in his hopes, the man seeks another woman, and the girl another suitor, if it seems to them desirable. Thus they continue to do until a favorable union is formed. It sometimes happens that a girl thus passes her entire youth, having more than twenty mates, which twenty are not alone in the enjoyment of the creature, mated though they are; for when night comes the young women run from one cabin to another, as do also the young men on their part, going where it seems good to them, but always without any violence, referring the whole matter to the pleasure of the woman. Their mates will do likewise to their women-neighbors, no jealousy arising among them on that account, nor do they incur any reproach or insult, such being the custom of the country.

Now the time when they do not leave their mates is when they have children. The preceding mate returns to her, renews the affection and friendship which he had borne her in the past, asserting that it is greater than that of any other one, and that the child she has is his and of his begetting. The next says the same to her. In fine, the victory is with the stronger, who takes the woman for his wife. Thus it depends upon the choice of the woman to take and accept him who shall please her best, having meantime in her searching and loves gained much porcelain and, besides, the choice of a husband. The woman remains with him without leaving him; or if she do leave him, for he is on trial, it must be for some good reason other than impotence. But while with this husband, she does not cease to give herself free rein, yet remains always at home, keeping up a good appearance. Thus the children which they have together, born from such a woman, cannot be sure of their legitimacy. Accordingly, in view of this uncertainty, it is their custom that the children never succeed to the property and honors of their fathers, there being doubt, as above indicated, as to their paternity. They make, however, the children of their sisters, from whom they are known to have issued, their successors and heirs.

The following is the way they nourish and bring up their children: they place them during the day on a little wooden board, wrapping them up in furs or skins. To this board they bind them, placing them in an erect position, and leaving a little opening for the child to do its necessities. If it is a girl, they put a leaf of Indian corn between the thighs, which presses against its privates. The extremity of the leaf is carried outside in a turned position, so that the water of the child runs off on it without inconvenience. They put also under the children the down of certain reeds that we call hare's-foot, on which they rest very softly. They also clean them with the same down. As an ornament for the child, they adorn the board with beads, which they also put on its neck, however small it may be. At night they put it to bed, entirely naked, between the father and mother. It may be regarded as a great miracle that God should thus preserve it so that no harm befalls it, as might be expected, from suffocation, while the father and mother are in deep sleep, but that rarely happens. The children have great freedom among these tribes. The fathers and mothers indulge them too much, and never punish them. Accordingly they are so bad and of so vicious a nature, that they often strike their mothers and others. The most vicious, when they have acquired the strength and power, strike their fathers. They do this whenever the father or mother does anything that does not please them. This is a sort of curse that God inflicts upon them.

In respect to laws, I have not been able to find out that they have any, or anything that approaches them, inasmuch as there is not among them any correction, punishment, or censure of evil-doers, except in the way of vengeance when they return evil for evil, not by rule but

by passion, which produces among them conflicts and differences, which occur very frequently.

Moreover, they do not recognize any divinity, or worship any God and believe in anything whatever, but live like brute beasts. They have, however, some respect for the devil, or something so called, which is a matter of uncertainty, since the word which they use thus has various significations and comprises in itself various things. It is accordingly difficult to determine whether they mean the devil or something else, but what especially leads to the belief that what they mean is the devil is this: whenever they see a man doing something extraordinary, or who is more capable than usual, or is a valiant warrior, or furthermore who is in a rage as if out of his reason and senses, they call him *oqui,* or, as we should say, a great knowing spirit, or a great devil. However this may be, they have certain persons, who are the *oqui,* or, as the Algonquins and Montagnais call them, *manitous;* and persons of this kind are the medicine-men, who heal the sick, bind up the wounded, and predict future events, who in fine practice all abuses and illusions of the devil to deceive and delude them. These *oquis* or conjurers persuade their patients and the sick to make, or have made banquets and ceremonies that they may be the sooner healed, their object being to participate in them finally themselves and get the principal benefit therefrom. Under the pretence of a more speedy cure, they likewise cause them to observe various other ceremonies, which I shall hereafter speak of in the proper place. These are the people in whom they put especial confidence, but it is rare that they are possessed of the devil and tormented like other savages living more remote than themselves.

This gives additional reason and ground to believe that their conversion to the knowledge of God would be more easy, if their country were inhabited by persons who would take the trouble and pains to instruct them. But it is not enough to send to them friars, unless there are those to support and assist them. For although these people have the desire today to know what God is, to-morrow this disposition will change when they are obliged to lay aside and bring under their foul ways, their dissolute manners, and their savage indulgences. So that there is need of people and families to keep them in the way of duty, to constrain them through mildness to do better, and to move them by good example to mend their lives. Father Joseph and myself have many times conferred with them in regard to our belief, laws, and customs. They listen attentively in their assemblies, sometimes saying to us:

You say things that pass our knowledge, and which we cannot understand by words, being beyond our comprehension; but if you would do us a service come and dwell in this country, bringing your wives and children, and when they are here we shall see how you serve the God you worship, and how you live with your wives and children, how you cultivate and plant the soil, how you obey your laws, how you take care of animals, and how you manufacture all that we see proceeding from your inventive skill. When we see all this, we shall learn more in a year than in twenty by simply hearing you discourse; and if we cannot then understand, you shall take our children, who shall be as your own. And thus being convinced that our life is a miserable one in comparison with yours, it is easy to believe that we shall adopt yours, abandoning our own.

Their words seemed to me good common sense, showing the desire they have to get a knowledge of God. It is a great wrong to let so many men be lost, and see them perish at our door, without rendering them the succor which can only be given through the help of kings, princes, and ecclesiastics, who alone have the power to do this. For to them alone belongs the honor of so great a work; namely, planting the Christian faith in an unknown region and among savage nations, since we are well informed about these people, that they long for and desire nothing so much as to be clearly instructed as to what they should do and avoid. It is accordingly the duty of those who have the power, to labor there and contribute of their abundance, for one day they must answer before God for the loss of the souls which they allowed to perish through their negligence and avarice; and these are not few but very numerous. Now this will be done when it shall please God to give them grace to this end. As for myself, I desire this result rather to-day than to-morrow, from the zeal which I have for the advancement of God's glory, for the honor of my King, and for the welfare and renown of my country.

When they are sick the man or woman who is attacked with any disease sends for the *oqui,* who visits the patient and informs himself about the malady and the suffering. After this, the *oqui* sends for a large number of men, women, and girls, including three or four old women. These enter the cabin of the sick, dancing, each one having on his head the skin of a bear or some other wild beast, that of the bear being the most common as it is the most frightful. There are three or four other old women about the sick or suffering, who for the most part feign sickness, or are sick merely in imagination. But they are soon cured

of this sickness, and generally make banquets at the expense of their friends or relatives, who give them something to put into their kettle, in addition to the presents which they receive from the dancers, such as porcelain and other bagatelles, so that they are soon cured; for when they find that they have nothing more to look for, they get up with what they have secured. But those who are really sick are not readily cured by plays, dances, and such proceedings.

To return to my narrative: the old women near the sick person receive the presents each singing and pausing in turn. When all the presents have been made, they proceed to lift up their voices with one accord, all singing together and keeping time with sticks on pieces of dry bark. Then all the women and girls proceed to the end of the cabin, as if they were about to begin a ballet or masquerade. The old women walk in front with their bearskins on their heads, all the others following them, one after the other. They have only two kinds of dances with regular time, one of four steps and the other of twelve, as in the *trioli* of Brittany. They exhibit much grace in dancing. Young men often take part with them. After dancing an hour or two, the old women lead out the sick person to dance, who gets up dolefully and prepares to dance, and after a short time she dances and enjoys as much as the others. I leave it to you to consider how sick she was. Below is represented the mode of their dances.

The medicine-man thus gains honor and credit, his patient being so soon healed and on her feet. This treatment, however, does nothing for those who are dangerously ill and reduced by weakness, but causes their death rather than their cure; for I can testify that they sometimes make such a noise and hubbub from morning until two o'clock at night that it is impossible for the patient to endure it without great pain. Sometimes the patient is seized with the desire to have the women and girls dance all together, which is done in accordance with the direction of the *oqui.* But this is not all, for he and the *manitou,* accompanied by some others, make grimaces, perform magic arts, and twist themselves about so that they generally end in being out of their senses, seemingly crazy, throwing the fire from one side of the cabin to the other, eating burning coals, holding them in their hands for a while, and throwing red-hot ashes into the eyes of the spectators. Seeing them in this condition, one would say that the devil, the *oqui,* or *manitou,* if he is thus to be called, possesses and torments them. This noise and hubbub being over, they retire each to his own cabin.

But those who suffer especially during this time are the wives of those possessed, and all the inmates of their cabins, from the fear they have lest the raging ones burn up all that is in their homes. This leads them to remove everything that is in sight; for as soon as he arrives he is all in a fury, his eyes flashing and frightful, sometimes standing up, sometimes seated, as his fancy takes him. Suddenly a fit seizes him, and laying hold of everything he finds in his way he throws them to one side and the other. Then he lies down and sleeps for some time. Waking up with a jump, he seizes fire and stones, which he throws about recklessly on all sides. This rage passes off with the sleep which seizes him again. Then he rages and calls several of his friends to sweat with him. The latter is the best means they have for preserving themselves in health. While they are sweating, the kettle boils to prepare them something to eat. They remain, two or three hours or so, covered up with great pieces of bark and wrapped in their robes, with a great many stones about them which have been heated red-hot in the fire. They sing all the time while they are in the rage, occasionally stopping to take breath. Then they give them many draughts of water to drink, since they are very thirsty, when the demoniac, who was crazy or possessed of an evil spirit, becomes sober.

Thus it happens that three or four of these sick persons get well, rather by a happy coincidence and chance than in consequence of any intelligent treatment, and this confirms their false belief that they are healed by means of these ceremonies, not considering that, for two who are thus cured, ten others die on account of the noise, great hubbub and hissing, which are rather calculated to kill than cure a sick person. But that they expect to recover their health by this noise, and we on the contrary by silence and rest, shows how the devil does everything in hostility to the good.

There are also women who go into these rages, but they do not do so much harm. They walk on all fours like beasts. Seeing this, the magician, called *oqui,* begins to sing; then, with some contortions of the face, he blows upon her, directing her to drink certain waters, and make at once a banquet of fish or flesh, which must be procured although very scarce at the time. When the shouting is over and the banquet ended, they return each to her own cabin. At another time he comes back and visits her, blowing upon her and singing in company with several others, who have been summoned for this purpose, and who hold in the hand a dry tortoise-shell filled with little pebbles, which they cause to resound in the ears of the sick woman. They direct her to make at once three or four banquets with singing and dancing, when all the girls appear adorned and painted as I have represented in figure G. The *oqui* orders masquerades, and directs them to disguise themselves, as those do who run along the streets in France on Mardi-gras. Thus they go and sing near the bed of the sick woman and promenade through the village while the banquet is preparing to receive the maskers, who return very tired, having taken exercise enough to be able to empty the kettle of its *migan.*

According to their custom each household lives on what it gets by fishing and planting, improving as much land as it needs. They clear it up with great difficulty, since they do not have the implements adapted to this purpose. A party strip the trees of all their branches, which they burn at their base in order to kill them. They clear carefully the land between the trees, and then plant their corn at distances of a pace, putting in each place some ten kernels, and so on until they have made provision for three or four years, fearing that a bad year may befall them. The women attend to the planting and harvesting, as I have said before, and to procuring a supply of wood for winter. All the women aid each other in procuring this provision of wood, which they do in the month of March or April, in the order of two days for each. Every household is provided with as much as it needs; and if a girl marries, each woman and girl is expected to carry to the newly married one a parcel of wood for her provision, since she could not procure it alone, and at a season when she has to give her attention to other things.

The following is their mode of government: the older and leading men assemble in a council, in which they settle upon and propose all that is necessary for the affairs of the village. This is done by a plurality of voices, or in accordance with the advice of some one among them whose judgment they consider superior: such a one is requested by the company to give his opinion on the propositions that have been made, and this opinion is minutely obeyed. They have no particular chiefs with absolute command, but they show honor to the older and more courageous men, whom they name captains, as a mark of honor and respect, of which there are several in a village. But, although they confer more honor upon one than upon others, yet he is not on that account to bear sway, nor esteem himself higher than his companions, unless he does so from vanity. They make no use of punishments nor arbitrary command, but accomplish everything by the en-treaties of the seniors, and by means of addresses and re-monstrances. Thus and not otherwise do they bring every-thing to pass.

They all deliberate in common, and whenever any member of the assembly offers to do anything for the wel-fare of the village, or to go anywhere for the service of the community, he is requested to present himself, and if he is judged capable of carrying out what he proposes, they exhort him, by fair and favorable words, to do his duty. They declare him to be an energetic man, fit for under-takings, and assure him that he will win honor in accom-plishing them. In a word, they encourage him by flatter-ies, in order that this favorable disposition of his for the welfare of his fellow-citizens may continue and increase. Then, according to his pleasure, he refuses the responsi-bility, which few do, or accepts, since thereby he is held in high esteem.

When they engage in wars or go to the country of their enemies, two or three of the older or valiant captains make a beginning in the matter, and proceed to the ad-joining villages to communicate their purpose, and make presents to the people of these villages, in order to induce them to accompany them to the wars in question. In so far they act as generals of armies. They designate the place where they desire to go, dispose of the prisoners who are captured, and have the direction of other matters of espe-cial importance, of which they get the honor, if they are successful; but, if not, the disgrace of failure in the war falls upon them. These captains alone are looked upon and considered as chiefs of the tribes.

They have, moreover, general assemblies, with repre-sentatives from remote regions. These representatives come every year, one from each province, and meet in a town designated as the rendezvous of the assembly. Here are celebrated great banquets and dances, for three weeks or a month, according as they may determine. Here they renew their friendship, resolve upon and decree what they think best for the preservation of their country against their enemies, and make each other handsome presents, after which they retire each to his own district.

In burying the dead, they take the body of the de-ceased, wrap it in furs, and cover it very carefully with the bark of trees. Then they place it in a cabin, of the length of the body, made of bark and erected upon four posts. Others they place in the ground, propping up the earth on all sides, that it may not fall on the body, which they cover with the bark of trees, putting earth on top. Over this trench they also make a little cabin. Now it is to be un-derstood that the bodies remain in these places, thus in-humed, but for a period of eight or ten years, when the men of the village recommend the place where their cer-emonies are to take place; or, to speak more precisely, they hold a general council, in which all the people of the country are present, for the purpose of designating the place where a festival is to be held. After this they return each to his own village, where they take all the bones of the deceased, strip them and make them quite clean. These they keep very carefully, although they smell like bodies recently interred. Then all the relatives and friends of the deceased take these bones, together with their necklaces, furs, axes, kettles, and other things highly val-ued, and carry them, with a quantity of edibles, to the place assigned. Here, when all have assembled, they put the edibles in a place designated by the men of the village, and engage in banquets and continual dancing. The festi-val continues for the space of ten days, during which time other tribes, from all quarters, come to witness it and the ceremonies. The latter are attended with great outlays.

Now, by means of these ceremonies, including dances, banquets, and assemblies, as above stated, they renew their friendship to one another, saying that the bones of their relatives and friends are to be all put together, thus indicating by a figure that, as their bones are gathered to-gether, and united in one and the same place, so ought they also, during their life, to be united in one friendship and harmony, like relatives and friends, without separa-tion. Having thus mingled together the bones of their mu-tual relatives and friends, they pronounce many dis-courses on the occasion. Then, after various grimaces or exhibitions, they make a great trench, ten fathoms square, in which they put the bones, together with the necklaces, chains of porcelain, axes, kettles, sword-blades, knives, and various other trifles, which, however, are of no slight account in their estimation. They cover the whole with earth, putting on top several great pieces of wood, and placing around many posts, on which they put a covering. This is their manner of proceeding with regard to the dead, and it is the most prominent ceremony they have. Some of them believe in the immortality of the soul, while others have only a presentiment of it, which, how-ever, is not so very different; for they say that after their decease they will go to a place where they will sing like crows, a song, it must be confessed, quite different from that of angels. On the following page are represented their sepulchres and manner of interment.

It remains to describe how they spend their time in winter; namely, from the month of December to the end of March, or the beginning of our spring, when the snow melts. All that they might do during autumn, as I have before stated, they postpone to be done during winter; namely, their banquetings, and usual dances for the sake of the sick, which I have already described, and the assemblages of the inhabitants of various villages, where there are banquetings, singing, and dances, which they call *tabagies,* and where sometimes five hundred persons are collected, both men, women, and girls. The latter are finely decked and adorned with the best and most costly things they have.

On certain days they make masquerades, and visit each other's cabins, asking for the things they like, and if they meet those who have what they want, these give it to them freely. Thus they go on asking for many things without end; so that a single one of those soliciting will have robes of beaver, bear, deer, lynxes, and other furs, also fish, Indian corn, tobacco, or boilers, kettles, pots, axes, pruning-knives, knives, and other like things. They go to the houses and cabins of the village, singing these words, That one gave me this, another gave that, or like words, by way of commendation. But if one gives them nothing they get angry, and show such spite towards him that when they leave they take a stone and put it near this man or that woman who has not given them anything. Then, without saying a word, they return singing, which is a mark of insult, censure, and ill-will. The women do so as well as the men, and this mode of proceeding takes place at night, and the masquerade continues seven or eight days. There are some of their villages which have maskers or merry-makers, as we do on the evening of Mardi-gras, and they invite the other villages to come and see them and win their utensils, if they can. Meanwhile banquets are not wanting. This is the way they spend their time in winter.

Moreover, the women spin, and pound meal for the journeys of their husbands in summer, who go to other tribes to trade, as they decide to do at the above-mentioned councils, in which it is determined what number of men may go from each village, that it may not be deprived of men of war for its protection; and nobody goes from the country without the general consent of the chiefs, or if they should go they would be regarded as behaving improperly. The men make nets for fishing, which they carry on in summer, but generally in winter, when they capture the fish under the ice with the line or with the seine.

The following is their manner of fishing. They make several holes in a circular form in the ice, the one where they are to draw the seine being some five feet long and three wide. Then they proceed to place their net at this opening, attaching it to a rod of wood from six to seven feet long, which they put under the ice. This rod they cause to pass from hole to hole, when one or more men, putting their hands in the holes, take hold of the rod to which is attached an end of the net, until they unite at the opening of five to six feet. Then they let the net drop to the bottom of the water, it being sunk by little stones attached to the end. After it is down they draw it up again with their arms at its two ends, thus capturing the fish that are in it. This is, in brief, their manner of fishing in winter.

The winter begins in the month of November and continues until the month of April, when the trees begin to send forth the sap and show their buds.

Pierre-Esprit Radisson (1636–1710?)

Born in Saint-Malo, France, Pierre-Esprit Radisson was only fifteen in 1651, when he arrived in New France as a colonist with his parents at the area called by the French "Trois Rivières" (Three Rivers), where the St. Maurice and St. Lawrence Rivers meet. The next spring, he was taken prisoner by Mohawk people and adopted into a Mohawk family, where he remained for a year and a half, learning about and participating in Mohawk life. In the fall of 1653, Radisson escaped to the Dutch settlement at Fort Orange (now Albany, New York) and then to France.

The following year, Radisson returned to his family at Three Rivers, where he met his new brother-in-law, Medard Chouart, sieur des Groseilliers, with whom Radisson would frequently travel in the years that followed. Groseilliers took Radisson on a trip exploring lands to the west, a two-year voyage that began in 1654. In 1658–59, the two men took a more extensive western exploration trip, traveling as far as present-day southeastern Wisconsin. In 1659, the pair embarked on a circuitous journey heading south from Lake Michigan. During the course of this trip, they reached the upper portions of the Mississippi

River, probably the first time Europeans had done so. In 1660, the two persuaded a group of Hurons from Minnesota to return with them to Montreal. Their travels had been extensive, their experiences invaluable. Yet they were forbidden by the governor to continue their explorations. Perhaps they had discovered that the colonists had no monopoly on virtue.

In 1661, Radisson and Groseilliers journeyed west again, despite having been forbidden by the governor to do so. On this journey through present-day Wisconsin and Minnesota, they interacted with Ottawas and Sioux and gained commercially valuable firsthand information about the potential for fur trading in the southern Hudson Bay region. They returned to New France in 1663, only to be fined in punishment for taking their journey without permission. In France, Groseilliers was unable to persuade the crown to invest in the Hudson Bay fur trade. Instead, Radisson and his brother-in-law contracted with a private French merchant and made several abortive attempts to establish the trade themselves. In the mid-1660s and 1670s, the pair worked for England's Hudson's Bay Company, which did finally establish the Hudson Bay trade. Through the 1680s, Radisson, who married an Englishwoman, shifted political allegiances numerous times, working sometimes for the English and sometimes for the French. He received a pension from the Hudson's Bay Company until his death in 1710.

Before their formal alliance with the English, Radisson met with King Charles II to describe the commercial potential of the Hudson Bay area. In preparation for this meeting, he drafted his *Relation,* a manuscript describing his travels in Canada from 1652 to 1664. Although French was his first language, Radisson wrote in English. The selection printed here is from Radisson's first narrative of his life as a captive and adopted son among the Mohawks as a young man.

from THE RELATION OF MY VOYAGE

being in Bondage in the Lands of the Irokoits, which was the next yeare after my coming into Canada, in the yeare 1651, the 24th day of May[1]

Being persuaded in the morning by two of my comrades to go and recreat ourselves in fowling, I disposed myselfe to keepe them Company; wherfor I cloathed myselfe the lightest way I could possible, that I might be the nimbler and not stay behinde, as much for the prey that I hoped for, as for to escape the danger into which wee have ventered ourselves of an enemy the cruelest that ever was uppon the face of the Earth. It is to bee observed that the french had warre with a wild nation called Iroquoites, who for that time weare soe strong and so to be feared that scarce any body durst stirre out either Cottage or house without being taken or killed, saving that he had nimble limbs to escape their fury; being departed, all three well armed, and unanimiously rather die then abandon one another, notwithstanding these resolutions weare but young mens deboasting; being then in a very little assurance and lesse security.

At an offspring of a village of three Rivers we consult together that two should go the watter side, the other in a wood hardby to warne us, for to advertise us if he accidentaly should light [upon] or suspect any Barbars[2] in ambush, we also retreat ourselves to him if we should discover any thing upon the River. Having comed to the first river, which was a mile distant from our dwellings, wee mett a man who kept cattell, and asked him if he had knowne any appearance of Ennemy, and likewise demanded which way he would advise us to gett better fortune, and what part he spied more danger; he guiding us the best way he could, prohibiting us by no means not to render ourselves att the skirts of the mountains; for, said he, I discovered oftentimes a multitude of people which rose up as it weare of a sudaine from of the Earth, and that doubtless there weare some Enemys that way; which sayings made us looke to ourselves and charge two of our fowling peeces with great shot the one, and the other with

---

1. Radisson's manuscript was written in 1665; the text presented here is slightly modernized in spelling and punctuation.

2. Barbarians.

small. Priming our pistols, we went where our fancy first lead us, being impossible for us to avoid the destinies of the heavens; no sooner tourned our backs, but my nose fell ableeding without any provocation in the least. Certainly it was a warning for me of a beginning of a yeare and a half of hazards and of miseryes that weare to befall mee. We did shoot sometime and killed some Duks, which made one of my fellow travellers go no further. I seeing him taking such a resolution, I proferred some words that did not like him, giving him the character of a timourous, childish humor; so this did nothing prevaile with him, to the Contrary that had with him quite another issue then what I hoped for; for offending him with my words he prevailed so much with the others that he persuaded them to doe the same. I lett them goe, laughing them to scorne, beseeching them to helpe me to my fowles, and that I would tell them the discovery of my designes, hoping to kill meat to make us meate att my retourne.

I went my way along the wood some times by the side of the river, where I finde something to shute att, though no considerable quantitie, which made me goe a league off and more, so I could not go in all further then St. Peeter's, which is nine mile from the plantation by reason of the river Ovamasis, which hindered me the passage. I begun'd to think att my retourne how I might transport my fowle. I hide one part in a hollow tree to keep them from the Eagles and other devouring fowles, so as I came backe the same way where before had no bad incounter. Arrived within one halfe a mile where my comrades had left me, I rested awhile by reason that I was looden'd with three geese, tenn ducks, and one crane, with some teales.

After having laid downe my burden upon the grasse, I thought to have heard a noise in the wood by me, which made me to overlook my armes; I found one of my girdle pistols wette. I shott it off and charged it againe, went up to the wood the soffliest I might, to discover and defend myselfe the better against any surprise. After I had gone from tree to tree some 30 paces off I espied nothing; as I came back from out of the wood to an adjacent brooke, I perceived a great number of Ducks; my discovery imbouldened me, and for that there was a litle way to the fort, I determined to shute once more; coming nigh preparing meselfe for to shute, I found another worke: the two young men that I left some tenne houres before heere weare killed. Whether they came after mee, or weare brought thither by the Barbars, I know not. However weare murthered. Looking over them, I knew them albeit quite naked, and their hair standing up, the one being

shott through with three boulletts and two blowes of an hatchett on the head, and the other runne thorough in severall places with a sword and smitten with an hatchett. Att the same instance my nose begun'd to bleed, which made me afraid of my life; but with drawing myselfe to the water side to see if any body followed mee, I espied twenty or thirty heads in a long grasse. Mightily surprized att that view, I must needs passe through the midst of them or tourne backe into the woode. I slipped a boulett upon the shott and beate the paper into my gunne. I heard a noise, which made me looke on that side; hopeing to save meselfe, perswading myselfe I was not yet perceived by them that weare in the medow, and in the meane while some gunns weare lett off with an horrid cry.

Seeing myselfe compassed round about by a multitude of dogges, or rather devils, that rose from the grasse, rushes and bushes, I shott my gunne, whether unawares or purposly I know not, but I shott with a pistolle confidently, but was seised on all sides by a great number that threw me downe, taking away my arme without giving mee one blowe; for afterwards I felt no paine att all, onely a great guidinesse in my heade, from whence it comes I doe not remember. In the same time they brought me into the wood, where they shewed me the two heads all bloody. After they consulted together for a while, retired into their boats, which weare four or five miles from thence, and wher I have bin a while before. They laid mee hither, houlding me by the hayre, to the imbarking place; there they began to errect their cottages, which consisted only of some sticks to boyle their meate, whereof they had plenty, but [it] stuncke, which was strange to mee to finde such an alteration so sudaine. They made [me] sitt downe by. After this they searched me and tooke what I had, then stripped me naked, and tyed a rope about my middle, wherin I remained, fearing to persist, in the same posture the rest of the night. After this they removed me, laughing and howling like as many wolves, I knowing not the reason, if not for my skin, that was soe white in respect of theirs. But their gaping did soone cease because of a false alarme, that their scout who stayed behind gave them, saying that the French and the wild Algongins, friends to the French, came with all speed. They presently put out the fire, and tooke hould of the most advantageous passages, and sent 25 men to discover what it meant, who brought certaine tydings of assurance and liberty.

In the meanewhile I was garded by 50 men, who gave me a good part of my cloathes. After kindling a fire againe, they gott theire supper ready, which was sudenly don, for they dresse their meat halfe boyled, mingling

some yallowish meale in the broath of that infected stinking meate; so whilst this was adoing they combed my
head, and with a filthy grease greased my head, and
dashed all over my face with redd paintings. So then,
when the meat was ready, they feeded me with their hod-
pot, forcing me to swallow it in a maner. My heart did so
faint at this, that in good deede I should have given freely
up the ghost to be freed from their clawes, thinking every
moment they would end my life. They perceived that my
stomach could not beare such victuals. They tooke some
of this stinking meate and boyled it in a cleare watter, then
mingled a litle Indian meale put to it, which meale before
was tossed amongst bourning sand, and then made in
powder betwixt two rocks. I, to shew myselfe cheerfull att
this, swallowed downe some of this that seemed to me
very unsavoury and clammie by reason of the scume that
was upon the meat. Having supped, they untyed mee, and
made me lye betwixt them, having one end of one side
and one of another, and covered me with a red Coverlet,
through which I might have counted the starrs. I slept a
sound sleep, for they awaked me uppon the breaking of
the day. I dreamed that night that I was with the Jesuits at
Quebec drinking beere, which gave me hopes to be free
sometimes, and also because I heard those people lived
among Dutch people in a place called Menada, and fort of
Orang,[3] where without doubt I could drinke beere. I, after
this, finding meselfe somewhat altered, and my body
more like a devil then anything else, after being so
smeared and burst with their filthy meate that I could not
digest, but must suffer all patiently.

Finally they seemed to me kinder and kinder, giving
me of the best bitts where lesse wormes weare. Then they
layd [me] to the watter side, where there weare 7 and 30
boats, for each of them imbark'd himselfe. They tyed me
to the barre in a boat, where they tooke at the same instance the heads of those that weare killed the day before,
and for to preserve them they cutt off the flesh to the skull
and left nothing but skin and haire, putting of it into a litle
panne wherein they melt some grease, and gott it dry with
hot stones. They spread themselves from off the side of
the river a good way, and gathered together againe and
made a fearfull noise and shott some gunns off, after
which followed a kind of an incondit singing after notes,
which was an oudiousom noise. As they weare departing
from thence they injoyned silence, and one of the Company, wherein I was, made three shouts, which was an-

swered by the like maner from the whole flocke; which
done they tooke their way, singing and leaping, and so
past the day in such like. They offered mee meate; but
such victuals I reguarded it litle, but could drinke for
thirst. My sperit was troubled with infinite deale of
thoughts, but all to no purpose for the ease of my sicknesse; sometimes despairing, now againe in some hopes.
I allwayes indeavoured to comfort myselfe, though half
dead. My resolution was so mastered with feare, that at
every stroake of the oares of these inhumans I thought it
to be my end.

By sunsett we arrived att the Isles of Richelieu, a place
rather for victors than for captives most pleasant. There is
to be seen 300 wild Cowes together, a number of Elks and
Beavers, an infinit of fowls. There we must make cottages, and for this purpose they imploy all together their
wits and art, for 15 of these Islands are drowned in
Spring, when the floods begin to rise from the melting of
the snow, and that by reason of the lowness of the land.
Here they found a place fitt enough for 250 men that their
army consisted [of]. They landed mee & shewed mee
great kindnesse, saying Chagon, which is as much [as] to
say, as I understood afterwards, be cheerfull or merry; but
for my part I was both deafe and dumb. Their behaviour
made me neverthelesse cheerfull, or att least of a smiling
countenance, and constraine my aversion and feare to an
assurance, which proved not ill to my thinking; for the
young men tooke delight in combing my head, greasing
and powdering out a kinde of redd powder, then tying my
haire with a redd string of leather like to a coard, which
caused my haire to grow longer in a short time.

The day following they prepared themselves to passe
the adjacent places and shoote to gett victualls, where we
stayed 3 dayes, making great cheere and fires. I more and
more getting familiarity with them, that I had the liberty
to goe from cottage, having one or two by mee. They untyed mee, and tooke delight to make me speake words of
their language, and weare earnest that I should pronounce
as they. They tooke care to give me meate as often as I
would; they gave me salt that served me all my voyage.
They also tooke the paines to put it up safe for mee, not
taking any of it for themselves. There was nothing else
but feasting and singing during our abode. I tooke notice
that our men decreased, for every night one other boate
tooke his way, which persuaded mee that they went to the
warrs to gett more booty.

The fourth day, early in the morning, my Brother, viz.,
he that tooke me, so he called me, embarked me without
tying me. He gave me an oare, which I tooke with a good

_____

3. Manhattan and Albany.

will, and rowed till I sweate againe. They, perceaving, made me give over; not content with that I made a signe of my willingnesse to continue that worke. They consent to my desire, but shewed me how I should row without putting myselfe into a sweat. Our company being considerable hitherto, was now reduced to three score. Mid-day wee came to the River of Richlieu, where we weare not farre gone, but mett a new gang of their people in cottages; they began to hoop and hollow as the first day of my taking. They made me stand upright in the boat, as they themselves, saluting one another with all kindnesse and joy. In this new company there was one that had a minde to doe me mischiefe, but was prevented by him that tooke me. I taking notice of the fellow, I shewed him more friendshipe. I gott some meate roasted for him, and throwing a litle salt and flower over it, which he finding very good tast, gave it to the rest as a rarity, nor did afterwards molest mee.

They tooke a fancy to teach mee to sing; and as I had allready a beginning of their hooping, it was an easy thing for me to learne, our Algonquins making the same noise. They tooke an exceeding delight to heare mee. Often have I sunged in French, to which they gave eares with a deepe silence. We passed that day and night following with litle rest by reason of their joy and mirth. They lead a dance, and tyed my comrades both their heads att the end of a stick and hopt it; this done, every one packt and embarked himselfe, some going one way, some another. Being separated, one of the boats that we mett before comes backe againe and approaches the boat wherein I was; I wondered, a woman of the said company taking hould on my haire, signifying great kindnesse. Shee combs my head with her fingers and tyed my wrist with a bracelett, and sunged. My wish was that shee would proceed in our way. After both companys made a shout wee separated. I was sorry for this woman's departure, for having shewed me such favour att her first aspect, doubtlesse but shee might, if neede required, saved my life.

Our journey was indifferent good, without any delay, which caused us to arrive in a good and pleasant harbour. It was on the side of the sand where our people had any paine scarce to errect their cottages, being that it was a place they had sejourned before. The place round about full of trees. Here they kindled a fire and provided what was necessary for their food. In this place they cutt off my hair in the front and upon the crowne of the head, and turning up the locks of the haire they dab'd mee with some thicke grease. So done, they brought me a looking-glasse. I viewing myselfe all in a pickle, smir'd with redde

and black, covered with such a cappe, and locks tyed up with a peece of leather and stunked horridly, I could not but fall in love with myselfe, if not that I had better instructions to shun the sin of pride. So after repasting themselves, they made them ready for the journey with takeing repose that night. This was the time I thought to have escaped, for in vaine, for I being alone feared least I should be apprehended and dealt with more violently. And moreover I was desirous to have seene their country.

Att the sun rising I awaked my brother, telling him by signes it was time to goe. He called the rest, but non would stirre, which made him lye downe againe. I rose and went to the water side, where I walked awhile. If there weare another we might, I dare say, escape out of their sight. Heere I recreated myselfe running a naked sword into the sand. One of them seeing mee after such an exercise calls mee and shews me his way, which made me more confidence in them. They brought mee a dish full of meate to the water side. I began to eat like a beare.

In the mean time they imbark'd themselves, one of them tooke notice that I had not a knife, brings me his, which I kept the rest of the voyage, without that they had the least feare of me. Being ready to goe, saving my boat that was ammending, which was soone done. The other boats weare not as yett out of sight, and in the way my boat killed a stagg. They made me shoot att it, and not quite dead they runed it thorough with their swoords, and having cutt it in peeces, they devided it, and proceeded on their way. At 3 of the clock in the afternoone we came into a rappid streame, where we weare forced to land and carry our Equipages and boats thorough a dangerous place. Wee had not any encounter that day. Att night where we found cottages ready made, there I cutt wood as the rest with all dilligence. The morning early following we marched without making great noise, or singing as accustomed. Sejourning awhile, we came to a lake 6 leagues wide, about it a very pleasant country imbellished with great forests. That day our wild people killed 2 Bears, one monstrous like for its biggnesse, the other a small one. Wee arrived to a fine sandy bancke, where not long before many Cabbanes weare errected and places made where Prisoners weare tyed.

In this place our wild people sweated after the maner following: first heated stones till they weare redd as fire, then they made a lantherne with small sticks, then stoaring the place with deale[4] trees, saving a place in the mid-

---

4. Pine.

dle whereinto they put the stoanes, and covered the place with severall covers, then striped themselves naked, went into it. They made a noise as if the devil weare there; after they being there for an hour they came out of the watter, and then throwing one another into the watter, I thought veryly they weare insensed. It is their usual Custome. Being comed out of this place, they feasted themselves with the two bears turning the outside of the tripes inward not washed. They gave every one his share; as for my part I found them [neither] good, nor savory to the pallet. In the night they heard some shooting, which made them embark themselves speedily. In the mean while they made me lay downe whilst they rowed very hard. I slept securely till the morning, where I found meselfe in great high rushes. There they stayed without noise.

From thence wee proceeded, though not without some feare of an Algonquin army. We went on for some dayes that lake. Att last they endeavoured to retire to the woods, every one carrying his bundle. After a daye's march we came to a litle river where we lay'd that night. The day following we proceeded on our journey, where we mett 2 men, with whome our wild men seemed to be acquainted by some signes. These 2 men began to speake a longe while. After came a company of women, 20 in number, that brought us dry fish and Indian corne. These women loaded themselves, after that we had eaten, like mules with our baggage. We went through a small wood, the way well beaten, until the evening we touched a place for fishing, of 15 Cabbans. There they weare well received but myselfe, who was stroaken by a yong man. He, my keeper, made a signe I should to him againe. I tourning to him instantly, he to me, taking hould of my haire, all the wild men came about us, encouraging with their Cryes and hands, which encouraged me most that none helpt him more than mee. Wee clawed one another with hands, tooth, and nailes. My adversary being offended I have gotten the best, he kick't me; but my french shoes that they left mee weare harder than his, which made him [give up] that game againe. He tooke me about the wrist, where he found himselfe downe before he was awarre, houlding him upon the ground till some came and putt us asunder. My company seeing mee free, began to cry out, giving me watter to wash me, and then fresh fish to relish me. They encouraged me so much, the one combing my head, the other greasing my haire. There we stayed 2 dayes, where no body durst trouble me.

In the same Cabban that I was, there has bin a wild man wounded with a small shott. I thought I have seen him the day of my taking, which made me feare least I was the one that wounded him. He knowing it to be so had shewed me as much charity as a Christian might have given. Another of his fellowes (I also wounded) came to me att my first coming there, whom I thought to have come for reveng, contrarywise shewed me a cheerfull countenance; he gave mee a box full of red paintings, calling me his brother. I had not as yett caryed any burden, but meeting with an ould man, gave me a sacke of tobacco of 12 pounds' weight, bearing it uppon my head, as it's their usuall custome. We made severall stayes that day by reason of the severall encounters of their people that came from villages, as warrs, others from fishing and shooting. In that journey our company increased, among others a great many Hurrons that had bin lately taken, and who for the most part are as slaves. We lay'd in the wood because they would not goe into their village in the night time.

The next day we marched into a village where as wee came in sight we heard nothing but outcryes, as from one side as from the other, being a quarter of a mile from the village. They satt downe and I in the midle, where I saw women and men and children with staves and in array, which put me in feare, and instantly stripped me naked. My keeper gave me a signe to be gone as fast as I could drive. In the meane while many of the village came about us, among which a good old woman, and a boy with a hatchet in his hand came near mee. The old woman covered me, and the young man tooke me by the hand and lead me out of the company. The old woman made me step aside from those that weare ready to stricke att mee. There I left the 2 heads of my comrades, and that which comforted me that I escaped the blowes. Then they brought me into their Cottage; there the old woman shewed me kindnesse. Shee gave me to eate. The great terror I had a little before tooke my stomack away from me. I stayed an hour, where a great company of people came to see mee. Heere came a company of old men, having pipes in their mouthes, satt about me.

After smoaking, they lead me into another cabban, where there weare a company all smoaking; they made sitt downe by the fire, which made [me] apprehend they should cast me into the said fire. But it proved otherwise; for the old woman followed mee, speaking aloud, whom they answered with a loud ho, then shee tooke her girdle and about mee shee tyed it, so brought me to her cottage, and made me sitt downe in the same place I was before. Then shee began to dance and sing a while, after [she] brings downe from her box a combe, gives it to a maide that was neare mee, who presently comes to greas and combe my haire, and tooke away the paint that the fellows stuck to my face. Now the old woman getts me some Indian Corne toasted in the fire. I tooke paines to gether it out of the fire; after this shee gave me a blew coverlett, stokins and shoos, and where with to make me drawers. She looked in my cloathes, and if shee found any lice shee would squeeze them betwixt her teeth, as if they had ben substantiall meate. I lay'd with her son, who tooke me from those of my first takers, and gott at last a great acquaintance with many. I did what I could to gett familiarity with them, yet I suffered no wrong att their hands, taking all freedom, which the old woman inticed me to doe. But still they altered my face where ever I went, and a new dish to satisfy nature.

I tooke all the pleasures imaginable, having a small peece at my command, shooting patriges and squerells, playing most part of the day with my companions. The old woman wished that I would make meselfe more familiar with her 2 daughters, which weare tolerable among such people. They weare accustomed to grease and combe my haire in the morning. I went with them into the wilderness, there they would be gabling which I could not understand. They wanted no company but I was shure to be of the number. I brought all ways some guifts that I received, which I gave to my purse-keeper and refuge, the good old woman. I lived 5 weeks without thinking from whence I came. I learned more of their maners in 6 weeks then if I had bin in france 6 months. Att the end I was troubled in minde, which made her inquire if I was Anjonack, a Huron word. Att this I made as if I weare suported for speaking in a strang language, which shee liked well, calling me by the name of her son who before was killed, Orimha, which signifies ledd or stone, without difference of the words. So that it was my Lordshippe. Shee inquired [of] mee whether I was Asserony, a french. I answering no, saying I was Panugaga, that is, of their nation, for which shee was pleased.

My father feasted 300 men that day. My sisters made me clean for that purpos, and greased my haire. My mother decked me with a new cover and a redd and blew cappe, with 2 necklace of porcelaine.[5] My sisters tyed me with braceletts and garters of the same porcelaine. My brother painted my face, and feathers on my head, and tyed both my locks with porcelaine. My father was liberall to me, giving me a garland instead of my blew cap and a necklace of porcelaine that hung downe to my heels,

and a hattchet in my hand. It was hard for me to defend myselfe against any encounter, being so laden with riches. Then my father made a speech shewing many demonstrations of vallor, broak a kettle full of Cagamite[6] with a hattchett. So they sung, as is their usual coustom. They weare waited on by a sort of yong men, bringing downe dishes of meate of Oriniacke, of Castors,[7] and of red deer mingled with some flowers. The order of makeing was thus: the corne being dried between 2 stones into powder, being very thick, putt it into a kettle full of watter, then a quantity of Bear's grease. This banquett being over, they cryed to me Shagon, Orimha, that is, be hearty, stone or ledd. Every one withdrew into his quarters, and so did I.

But to the purpose of my history. As I went to the fields once, where I mett with 3 of my acquaintance, who had a designe for to hunt a great way off, they desired me to goe along. I lett them know in Huron language (for that I knew better then that of the Iroquoits) I was content, desiring them to stay till I acquainted my mother. One of them came along with mee, and gott leave for me of my kindred. My mother gott me presently a sack of meale, 3 paire of shoos, my gun, and tourned backe where the 2 stayed for us. My 2 sisters accompanied me even out of the wildernesse and carried my bundle, where they tooke leave.

We marched on that day through the woods till we came by a lake where we travelled without any rest. I wished I had stayed att home, for we had sad victualls. The next day about noone we came to a River; there we made a skiffe, so litle that we could scarce go into it. I admired their skill in doing of it, for in lesse then 2 hours they cutt the tree and pulled up the Rind, of which they made the boat. We embarked ourselves and went to the lower end of the river, which emptied it selfe into a litle lake of about 2 miles in length and a mile in breadth. We passed this lake into another river broader then the other; there we found a fresh track of a stagge, which made us stay heere a while. It was five of the clock att least when 2 of our men made themselves ready to looke after that beast; the other and I stayed behind. Not long after we saw the stagge crosse the river, which foarding brought him to his ending. So done, they went on their cours, and came backe againe att 10 of the clocke with 3 bears, a castor, and the stagge which was slaine att our sight. How did

---

wee rejoice to see that killed which would make the kettle boyle. After we have eaten, wee slept.

The next day we made trappes for to trapp castors, whilst we weare bussie, one about one thing, one about another. As 3 of us retourned homewards to our cottage we heard a wild man singing. He made us looke to our selves least he should prove an ennemy, but as we have seene him, called to him, who came immediately, telling us that he was in pursuite of a Beare since morning, and that he gave him over, having lost his 2 doggs by the same beare. He came with us to our cottage, where we mett our companion after having killed one beare, 2 staggs, and 2 mountain catts, being 5 in number. Whilst the meat was a boyling that wild man spoake to me the Algonquin language. I wondered to heare this stranger; he tould me that he was taken 2 years agoe; he asked me concerning the 3 rivers and of Quebuck, who wished himselfe there, and I said the same, though I did not intend it. He asked me if I loved the french. I inquired him also if he loved the Algonquins? Marry, quoth he, and so doe I my owne nation. Then replyed he, Brother, cheare up, lett us escape, the 3 rivers are not a farre off. I tould him my 3 comrades would not permitt me, and that they promissed my mother to bring me back againe. Then he inquired whether I would live like the Hurrons, who were in bondage, or have my owne liberty with the french, where there was good bread to be eaten. Feare not, quoth he, [we] shall kill them all 3 this night when they will bee a sleepe, which will be an easy matter with their owne hatchetts.

Att last I consented, considering they weare mortall ennemys to my country, that had cutt the throats of so many of my relations, burned and murdered them. I promissed him to succour him in his designe. They not understanding our language asked the Algonquin what is that that he said, but tould them some other story, nor did they suspect us in the least. Their belly full, their mind without care, wearyed to the utmost of the formost day's journey, fell a sleepe securely, leaning their armes up and downe without the least danger. Then my wild man pushed me, thinking I was a sleepe. He rises and sitts him downe by the fire, behoulding them one after an other, and taking their armes a side, and having the hattchetts in his hand gives me one; to tell the truth I was loathsome to do them mischif that never did me any. Yett for the above said reasons I tooke the hattchet and began the Execution, which was soone done. My fellow comes to him that was nearest to the fire (I dare say he never saw the stroake), and I have done the like to an other, but I hitting him with the edge of the hattchett could not disingage presently,

being so deep in his head, [he] rises upon his breast, butt fell back sudainly, making a great noise, which almost waked the third; but my comrade gave him a deadly blow of a hattchet, and presently after I shott him dead.

Then we prepared our selves with all speed, throwing their dead corps, after that the wild man took off their heads, into the watter. We tooke 3 guns, leaving the 4th, their 2 swoords, their hattchetts, their powder and shott, and all their proselaine; we tooke also some meale and meate. I was sorry for to have ben in such an incounter, but too late to repent. Wee tooke our journey that night alongst the river. The break of day we landed on the side of a rock which was smooth. We carryed our boat and equippage into the wood above a hundred paces from the watter side, where we stayed most sadly all that day tormented by the Maringoines;[8] we tourned our boat upside downe, we putt us under it from the raine. The night coming, which was the fitest time to leave that place, we goe without any noise for our safty. Wee travelled 14 nights in that maner in great feare, hearing boats passing by. When we have perceaved any fire, left off rowing, and went by with as litle noise as possible. Att last with many tournings by lande and by watter, wee came to the lake of St. Peeter's.

We landed about 4 of the clock, leaving our skiff in among rushes farr out of the way from those that passed that way and doe us injury. We retired into the wood, where we made a fire some 200 paces from the river. There we roasted some meat and boyled meale; after, we rested ourselves a while from the many labours of the former night.

So, having slept, my companion awaks first, and stirrs me, saying it was high time that we might by day come to our dweling, of which councel I did not approve. Tould him the Ennemys commonly weare lurking about the river side, and we should doe very well stay in that place till sunnsett. Then, said he, lett us begon, we passed all feare. Let us shake off the yoake of a company of whelps that killed so many french and black-coats, and so many of my nation. Nay, saith he, Brother, if you come not, I will leave you, and will go through the woods till I shall be over against the french quarters. There I will make a fire for a signe that they may fetch me. I will tell to the Governor that you stayed behind. Take courage, man, says he. With this he tooke his peece and things. Att this I considered how if [I] weare taken att the doore by meere

---

8. Mosquitoes.

rashnesse; the next, the impossibility I saw to go by my-selfe if my comrad would leave me, and perhaps the wind might rise, that I could come to the end of my journey in a long time, and that I should be accounted a coward for not daring to hazard myselfe with him that so much ventured for mee. I resolved to go along through the woods; but the litle constancy that is to be expected in wild men made me feare he should to his heels, which approved his unfortunate advice; for he hath lost his life by it, and I in great danger have escaped by the helpe of the Almight. I consent to goe by watter with him.

In a short time wee came to the lake. The watter very calme and cleare. No liklihood of any storme. We hazarded to the other side of the lake, thinking for more security. After we passed the third part of the lake, I being the foremost, have perceaved as if it weare a black shaddow, which proved a real thing. He at this rises and tells mee that it was a company of buzards, a kinde of geese in that country. We went on, where wee soone perceaved our owne fatall blindnesse, for they weare ennemys. We went back againe towards the lande with all speed to escape the evident danger, but it was too late; for before we could come to the russhes that weare within halfe a league of the waterside we weare tired. Seeing them approaching nigher and nigher, we threw the 3 heads in the watter. They meet with these 3 heads, which makes them to row harder after us, thinking that we had runn away from their country. We weare so neere the lande that we saw the bottom of the watter, but yett too deepe to step in. When those cruel inhumans came within a musquett shott of us, and fearing least the booty should gett a way from them, shott severall times att us, and deadly wounding my comrade, fell dead. I expected such another shott. The litle skiff was pierced in severall places with their shooting, that watter ran in a pace. I defended me selfe with the 2 arms. Att last they environed me with their boats, that tooke me just as I was a sinking. They held up the wild man and threw him into one of their boats and me they brought with all diligence to land. I thought to die without mercy.

They made a great fire and tooke my comrade's heart out, and choped off his head, which they put on an end of a stick and carryed it to one of their boats. They cutt off some of the flesh of that miserable, broyled it and ate it. If he had not ben so desperately wounded they had don their best to keepe him alive to make him suffer the more by bourning him with small fires; but being wounded in the chin, and bullet gon through the troat, and another in the shoulder that broake his arme, making him incurable,

they burned some parte of his body, and the rest they left there. That was the miserable end of that wretch.

Lett us come now to the beginning of my miseries and calamities that I was to undergo. Whilst they weare bussie about my companion's head, the others tyed me safe and fast in a strang maner; having striped me naked, they tyed me above the elbows behind my back, and then they putt a collar about me, not of porcelaine as before, but a rope wrought about my midle. So brought me in that pickle to the boat. As I was imbarqued they asked mee severall questions. I being not able to answer, gave me great blowes with their fists. Then pulled out one of my nailes, and partly untied me.

What displeasure had I, to have seen meselfe taken againe, being almost come to my journey's end, that I must now goe back againe to suffer such torments, as death was to be expected. Having lost all hopes, I resolved alltogether to die, being a folly to think otherwise. I was not the [only] one in the clawes of those wolves. Their company was composed of 150 men. These tooke about Quebucq and other places 2 frenchmen, one french woman, 17 Hurrons, men as [well as] women. They had Eleven heads which they sayd weare of the Algonquins, and I was the 33rd victime with those cruels.

The wild men that weare Prisners sang their fatal song, which was a mornfull song or noise. The 12 coulours (which weare heads) stood out for a show. We prisoners weare separated, one in one boat, one in an other. As for me, I was put into a boat with a Huron whose fingers weare cutt and bourned, and very [few] amongst them but had the markes of those inhuman devils. They did not permitt me to tarry long with my fellow prisoner, least I should tell him any news, as I imagine, but sent me to another boat, where I remained the rest of the voyage by watter, which proved somewhat to my disadvantage.

In this boat there was an old man, who having examined me, I answered him as I could best; tould him how I was adopted by such an one by name, and as I was hunting with my companions that wildman that was killed came to us, and after he had eaten went his way. In the evening came back againe and found us all a sleepe, tooke a hattchett and killed my 3 companions, and awaked me, and so embarked me and brought me to this place. That old man believed me in some measure, which I perceived in him by his kindnesse towards me. But he was not able to protect me from those that [had] a will to doe me mischief. Many slandred me, but I tooke no notice.

Some 4 leagues thence they erected cottages by a small river, very difficult to gett to it, for that there is litle watter on a great sand a league wide. To this very houre I tooke notice how they tyed their captives, though att my owne cost. They planted severall poastes of the bignesse of an arme, then layd us of a length, tyed us to the said poasts far a sunder from one another. Then tyed our knees, our wrists, and elbows, and our hairs directly upon the crowne of our heads, and then cutt 4 barrs of the bignesse of a legge & used thus. They tooke 2 for the necke, puting one of each side, tying the 2 ends together, so that our heads weare fast in a hole like a trappe; like-wayes they did to our leggs. And what tormented us most was the Maringoines and great flyes being in abundance; [we] did all night but puff and blow, that by that means we saved our faces from the sting of those ugly creatures; having no use of our hands, we are cruelly tormented. Our voyage was laborious and most miserable, suffering every night the like misery.

When we came neere our dwellings we mett severall gangs of men to our greatest disadvantage, for we weare forced to sing, and those that came to see us gave porcelaine to those that most did us injury. One cutt off a finger, and another pluck'd out a naile, and putt the end of our fingers into their bourning pipes, & burned severall parts in our bodyes. Some tooke our fingers and of a stick made a thing like a fork, with which [they] gave severall blowes on the back of the hands, which caused our hands to swell, and became att last insensible as dead. Having souffred all these crueltyes, which weare nothing to that they make usually souffer their Prisoners, we arrived att last to the place of execution, which is att the coming in to their village, which wheere not [long] before I escaped very neere to be soundly beaten with staves and fists. Now I must think to be no lesse traited by reason of the murder of the 3 men, but the feare of death takes away the feare of blowes.

Nineteen of us prisoners weare brought thither, and 2 left behind with the heads. In this place we had 8 coulours. Who would not shake att the sight of so many men, women, and children armed with all sorte of instruments: staves, hand Irons, heelskins wherein they putt halfe a score bullets? Others had brands, rods of thorne, and all suchlike that their Crueltie could invent to putt their Prisoners to greater torments. Heere, no help, no remedy. We must passe this dangerous passage in our extremity without helpe. He that is the fearfullest, or that is observed to stay the last, getts nothing by it butt more blowes, and putt him to more paine. For the meanest sort of people commonly is more cruell to the fearfullest then

to the others that they see more fearfull, being att last to suffer chearfuly and with constancy.

They begun to cry to both sides, we marching one after another, environed with a number of people from all parts to be witnesse to that hidious sight, which seriously may be called the Image of hell in this world. The men sing their fatall song, the women make horrible cryes, the victores cryes of joy, and their wives make acclamations of mirth. In a word, all prepare for the ruine of these poore victimes who are so tyed, having nothing saving only our leggs free, for to advance by litle and litle according [to] the will of him that leades; for as he held us by a long rope, he stayed us to his will, & often he makes us falle, for to shew them cruelty, abusing you so for to give them pleasure and to you more torment.

As our band was great, there was a greater crew of people to see the prisoners, and the report of my taking being now made, and of the death of the 3 men, which afflicted the most part of that nation, great many of which came through a designe of revenge and to molest me more then any other. But it was alltogether otherwise, for among the tumult I perceaved my father & mother with their 2 daughters. The mother pushes in among the Crew directly to mee, and when shee was neere enough, shee clutches hould of my haire as one desperat, calling me often by my name; drawing me out of my ranck, shee putts me into the hands of her husband, who then bid me have courage, conducting me an other way home to his Cabban, when he made me sitt downe. Said to me: You senselesse, thou was my son, and thou rendered thyself enemy, thou lovest not thy mother, nor thy father that gave thee thy life, and thou notwithstanding will kill me. Bee merry; Conharrassan, give him to eate. That was the name of one of the sisters. My heart shook with trembling and feare, which tooke away my stomach. Neverthelesse to signifie a bould countenance, knowing well a bould generous minde is allwayes accounted among all sort of nations, especially among wariors, as that nation is very presumptious and haughty. Because of their magnanimity and victories opposing themselves into all dangers and incounters what ever, running over the whole land for to make themselves appeere slaining and killing all they meete in exercising their cruelties, or else shewing mercy to whom they please to give liberty. God gave mee the grace to forgett nothing of my duty, as I tould my father the successe of my voyage in the best tearme I could, and how all things passed, mixturing a litle of their languag with that of the Hurrons, which I learned more fluently than theirs, being longer and more frequently with the Hurrons.

Every one attentively gave ears to me, hoping by this means to save my life. Uppon this heere comes a great number of armed men, enters the Cabban, where finding mee yett tyed with my cords, sitting by my parents, made their addresses to my father, and spak to him very loud. After a while my father made me rise and delivers me into their hands. My mother seeing this, cryes and laments with both my sisters, and I believing in a terrible motion to goe directly on to the place of execution. I must march, I must yeeld wheere force is predominant att the publique place.

I was conducted where I found a good company of those miserable wretches, alltogether beaten with blowes, covered with blood, and bourned. One miserable french-man, yett breathing, having now ben consumed with blowes of sticks, past so through the hands of this inraged crew, and seeing he could no more, cutt off his head and threw it into the fire. This was the end of this Execrable wofull body of this miserable.

They made me goe up the scaffold where weare 5 men, 3 women, and 2 children captives, and I made the Eleventh. There weare severall scaffolds nigh one an other, where weare these wretches, who with dolefull singings replenished the heavens with their Cryes. For I can say that an houre before the weather approved very faire, and in an instant the weather changed and rayned Extremely. The most part retired for to avoid this hayle, and now we must expect the full rigour of the weather by the retiration of those perfidious, except one part of the Band of hell who stayed about us for to learn the trade of barbary; for those litle devils seeing themselves all alone, continued thousand inventions of wickednesse. This is nothing strang, seeing that they are brought up, and suck the crueltie from their mother's brest.

I prolong a litle from my purpose of my adventure for to say the torments that I have seen suffred att Coutu, after that they have passed the sallett, att their entering in to the village, and the recounters that they meet ordinarily in the wayes, as above said. They tie the prisoners to a poast by their hands, their backs tourned towards the hangman, who hath a bourning fire of dry wood and rind of trees, which doth not quench easily. They putt into this fire hattchets, swords, and such like instruments of Iron. They take these and quench them on human flesh. They pluck out their nailes for the most part in this sort. They putt a redd coale of fire upon it, and when it is swolen bite it out with their teeth. After they stop the blood with a brand which by litle and litle drawes the veines the one after another from off the fingers, and when they draw all as much as they can, they cutt it with peeces of redd hott Iron; they squeeze the fingers between 2 stones, and so draw the marrow out of the boanes, and when the flesh is all taken away, they putt it in a dishfull of bourning sand. After they tye your wrist with a corde, putting two for this effect, one drawing him one way, another of another way. If the sinews be not cutt with a stick, putting it through & tourning it, they make them come as fast as they can, and cutt them in the same way as the others. Some others cutt peeces of flesh from all parts of the body & broyle them, gett you to eat it, thrusting them into your mouth, puting into it a stick of fire. They break your teeth with a stoane or clubbs, and use the handle of a kettle, and upon this do hang 5 or 6 hattchetts, red hott, which they hang about their neck and roast your leggs with brands of fire, and thrusting into it some sticks pointed, wherein they put ledd melted and gunnepowder, and then give it fire like unto artificiall fire,[9] and make the patient gather it by the stumps of his remaining fingers. If he cannot sing they make him quack like a henne.

I saw two men tyed to a rope, one att each end, and hang them so all night, throwing red coales att them, or bourning sand, and in such like bourne their feet, leggs, thighs, and breech. The litle ones doe exercise themselves about such cruelties; they deck the bodyes all over with hard straw, putting in the end of this straw, thornes, so leaves them; now & then gives them a litle rest, and sometimes gives them fresh watter and make them repose on fresh leaves. They also give them to eat of the best they have that they come to themselves againe, to give them more torments. Then when they see that the patient can no more take up his haire, they cover his head with a platter made of rind[10] full of bourning sand, and often getts the platter a fire. In the next place they cloath you with a suit made of rind of a tree, and this they make bourne out on your body. They cutt off your stones and the women play with them as with balles. When they see the miserable die, they open him and pluck out his heart; they drink some of his blood, and wash the children's heads with the rest to make them valient. If you have indured all the above said torments patiently and without moanes, and

---

9. A forge.

10. Bark.

have defied death in singing, then they thrust burning blades all along your boanes, and so ending the tragedie cutt off the head and putt it on the end of a stick and draw his body in quarters which they hawle about their village. Lastly throw him into the watter or leave in the fields to be eaten by the Crowes or doggs.

Now lett me come to our miserable poore captives that stayed all along [in] the raine upon the scaffold to the mercy of 2 or 300 rogues that shott us with litle arrowes, and so drew out our beards and the haire from those that had any. The showre of rayne being over, all come together againe, and having kindled fires began to burne some of those poore wretches. That day they plucked 4 nailes out of my fingers, and made me sing, though I had no mind att that time. I became speechlesse oftentimes; then they gave me watter wherin they boyled a certain herbe that the gunsmiths use to polish their armes. That liquor brought me to my speech againe. The night being come they made me come downe all naked as I was, & brought [me] to a strang Cottage. I wished heartily it had ben that of my parents. Being come, they tyed me to a poast, where I stayed a full houre without the least molestation.

A woman came there with her boy, inticed him to cutt off one of my fingers with a flint stoan. The boy was not 4 years old. This [boy] takes my finger and begins to worke, but in vaine, because he had not the strength to breake my fingers. So my poore finger escaped, having no other hurt done to it but the flesh cutt round about it. His mother made him suck the very blood that runn from my finger. I had no other torment all that day. Att night I could not sleep for because of the great paine. I did eat a litle, and drunk much watter by reason of a feaver I caught by the cruel torment I suffred.

The next morning I was brought back againe to the scaffold, where there were company enough. They made me sing a new, but my mother came there and made hold my peace, bidding me be cheerfull and that I should not die. Shee brought mee some meate. Her coming comforted me much, but that did not last long; for heare comes severall old people, one of which being on the scaffold, satt him downe by me, houlding in his mouth a pewter pipe burning, tooke my thumb and putt it on the burning tobacco, and so smoaked 3 pipes one after another, which made my thumb swell, and the nayle and flesh became as coales. My mother was allwayes by me to comfort me, but said not what I thought. That man having finished his hard worke, but I am sure I felt it harder to suffer it. He trembled, whether for feare or for so much

action I cannot tell. My mother tyed my fingers with cloath, and when he was gone shee greased my haire and combed my haire with a wooden comb, fitter to combe a horse's tayle than anything else. Shee goes back againe.

That day they ended many of those poore wretches, slinging some all alive into the midle of a great fire. They burned a frenchwoman; they pulled out her breasts and tooke a child out of her belly, which they broyled and made the mother eat of it; so, in short, [she] died. I was not abused all that day till the night. They bourned the soales of my feet and leggs. A souldier run through my foot a swoord red out of the fire, and plucked severall of my nailes. I stayed in that maner all night. I neither wanted in the meane while meate nor drinke. I was supplied by my mother and sisters. My father alsoe came to see me & tould me I should have courage. That very time there came a litle boy to gnaw with his teeth the end of my fingers. There appears a man to cutt off my thumb, and being about it leaves me instantly & did no harme, for which I was glad. I believe that my father dissuaded him from it.

A while after my father was gon 3 came to the scaffold who swore they would do me a mischiefe, as I thinke, for that he tied his leggs to mine, called for a brand of fire, and layd it between his leggs and mine, and sings: but by good lucke it was out on my side, and did no other effect then bourne my skin, but bourned him to some purpos. In this posture I was to follow him, & being not able to hould mee, draweth mee downe. One of the Company Cutt the rope that held us with his knife, and makes mee goe up againe the scaffold and then went their way.

There I stayed till midday alone. There comes a multitude of people who make me come downe and led mee into a cottage where there weare a number of sixty old men smoaking tobacco. Here they make mee sitt downe among them and stayed about halfe an houre without that they asked who and why I was brought thither, nor did I much care. For the great torments that I souffred, I knew not whether I was dead or alive. And albeit I was in a hott feavor & great pain, I rejoyced att the sight of my brother, that I have not seene since my arrivement. He comes in very sumptuously covered with severall necklaces of porcelaine, & a hattchett in his hand, satt downe by the company and cast an eye on me now and then. Presently and comes in my father with a new and long cover, and a new porcelaine about him, with a hatchett in his hands, likewise satt downe with the company. He had a calumet of red stoane in his hands, a cake[11] uppon his shoulders,

---

11. Medicine bag.

that hanged downe his back, and so had the rest of the old men. In that same cake are incloased all the things in the world, as they tould me often, advertising mee that I should [not] disoblige them in the least nor make them angry, by reason they had in their power the sun, and moone, and the heavans, and consequently all the earth. You must know in this cake there is nothing but tobacco and roots to heale some wounds or sores; some others keepe in it the bones of their deceased friends; most of them wolves' heads, squirrels', or any other beast's head. When there they have any debatement among them they sacrifice to this tobacco, that they throw into the fire, and make smoake, of that they puff out of their pipes; whether for peace or adversity or prosperity or warre, such ceremonies they make very often.

My father, taking his place, lights his pipe & smoaks as the rest. They held great silence. During this they bring 7 prisoners; to wit, 7 women and 2 men, more [than] 10 children from the age of 3 to 12 years, having placed them all by mee, who as yett had my armes tyed. The others all att liberty, being not tyed, which putt me into some despaire least I should pay for all. Awhile after one of the company rises and makes a long speech, now shewing the heavens with his hands, and then the earth, and fire. This good man putt himselfe into a sweate through the earnest discours. Having finished his panigerique, another begins, and also many, one after another.

They gave then liberty to some, butt killed 2 children with hattchetts, and a woman of 50 years old, and threw them out of the cottage (saving onely myselfe) att full liberty. I was left alone for a stake, they contested together [upon] which my father rose and made a speech which lasted above an houre, being naked, having nothing on but his drawers and the cover of his head, and putt himselfe all in a heate. His eyes weare hollow in his head; he appeared to me like mad, and naming often the Algonquins in their language which made me believe he spoake in my behalfe. In that very time comes my mother, with two necklaces of porcelaine, one in her armes, and another about her like a belt. As soone as shee came in shee began to sing and dance, and flings off one of her necklaces in the midle of the place, having made many tourns from one end to the other. Shee takes the other necklace and gives it mee, then goes her way. Then my brother rises and holding his hattchett in his hand sings a military song. Having finished departs. I feared much that he was first to knock me in the head; and happy are those that can escape so well, rather then be bourned. My father rises for a second time and sings; so done, retired himselfe. I thought all

their guifts, songs, and speeches should prevaile nothing with mee.

Those that stayed held a councell and spoake one to an other very long, throwing tobacco into the fire, making exclamations. Then the Cottage was open of all sides by those that came to view, some of the company retires, and place was made for them as if they weare Kings. Forty staye about me, and nigh 2000 about my cottage, of men, women, and children. Those that went their way retourned presently. Being sett downe, smoaked againe whilest my father, mother, brother, and sisters weare present. My father sings a while; so done, makes a speech, and taking the porcelaine necklace from off me throws it att the feet of an old man, and cuts the cord that held me, then makes me rise. The joy that I receaved att that time was incomparable, for suddenly all my paines and griefs ceased, not feeling the least paine. He bids me be merry, makes me sing, to which I consented with all my heart. Whilst I did sing they hooped and hollowed on all sides. The old man bid me "ever be cheerful, my son!" Having don, my mother, sisters, and the rest of their friends [sung] and danced.

Then my father takes me by the arme and leads me to his cabban. As we went along nothing was heard but hooping and hollowing on all parts, biding me to take great courage. My mother was not long after me, with the rest of her friends. Now I see myselfe free from death. Their care att this was to give me meate. I have not eaten a bitt all that day, and for the great joy I had conceaved, caused me to have a good stomach, so that I did eat lustily. Then my mother begins to cure my sores and wounds. Then begins my paines anew; for shee cleans my wounds and scrapes them with a knife, and often thrusts a stick in them, and then takes watter in her mouth, and spouts it to make them cleane. The meanwhile my father goes to seeke rootes, and my sister chaws them, and my mother applyes them to my sores as a plaster. The next day the swelling was gone, but worse than before; but in lesse than a fortnight my sores weare healed, saving my feete, that kept [me] more than a whole month in my Cabban. During this time my nailes grewed a pace. I remained onely lame of my midle finger, that they have squeezed between two stoanes. Every one was kind to mee as beforesaid, and wanted[12] no company to be merry with.

---

12. Lacked.

I should [be] kept too long to tell you the particulars that befell me during my winter. I was beloved of my Parents as before. My exercise was allwayes a hunting without that any gave me the least injury. My mother kept me most brave, and my sisters tooke great care of mee. Every month I had a white shirt, which my father sent for from the Flemings, who weare not a farr off our village. I could never gett leave to goe along with my brother, who went there very often. Finally, seeing myselfe in the former condition as before, I constituted as long as my father and fortune would permitt mee to live there. Dayly there weare military feasts for the South nations, and others for the Algonquins and for the French. The exclamations, hoopings and cryes, songs and dances, signifies nothing but the murdering and killing, and the intended victory that they will have the next yeare, which is in the beginning of Spring. In those feasts my father heaves up his hattchett against the Algonquins. For this effect makes great preparations for his next incamping. Every night never failes to instruct and encourage the young age to take armes and to reveng the death of so many of their ennemy that lived among the french nation. The desire that I had to make me beloved, for the assurance of my life made me resolve to offer myselfe for to serve, and to take party with them. But I feared much least he should mistrust me touching his advis to my resolution. Neverthelesse I finding him once of a good humour and on the point of honnour encourages his son to break the kettle and take the hattchett and to be gon to the forraigne nations, and that was of courage and of great renowne to see the father of one parte and the son of another part, & that he should not mispraise if he should seperat from him, but that it was the quickest way to make the world tremble, & by that means have liberty everywhere by vanquishing the mortall enemy of his nation; uppon this I venture to aske him what I was. [He] presently answers that I was a Iroquoite as himselfe. Lett me revenge, said I, my kindred. I love my brother. Lett me die with him. I would die with you, but you will not because you goe against the French. Lett me a gaine goe with my brother, the prisoners & the heads that I shall bring, to the joy of my mother and sisters, will make me undertake att my retourne to take up the hattchett against those of Quebecq, of the 3 rivers, and Monteroyall in declaring them my name, and that it's I that kills them, and by that you shall know I am your son, worthy to beare that title that you gave me when you adopted me. He sett a great crye, saying, have great courage, son Orimha, thy brother died in the warrs not in the Cabban; he was of a courage not of a woman. I goe to aveng his death. If I die, aveng you mine. That one word was my leave, which made me hope that one day I might escape, having soe great an opportunity; or att least I should have the happinesse to see their country, which I heard so much recommended by the Iroquoites, who brought wondrous stories and the facilitie of killing so many men.

Thus the winter was past in thoughts and preparing for to depart before the melting of the snow, which is very soone in that Country. I began to sett my witts together how I should resolve this my voyage; for my mother opposed against it mightily, saying I should bee lost in the woods, and that I should gett it [put] off till the next yeare. But at last I flattered with her and dissembled; besides, my father had the power in his hands. Shee daring not to deny him any thing because shee was not borne in my father's country, but was taken [when] little in the Huronit's Country. Notwithstanding well beloved of her husband, having lived together more then fourty years, and in that space brought him 9 children, 4 males and 5 females. Two girls died after a while, and 3 sons killed in the warrs, and one that went 3 years before with a band of 13 men to warre against a fiery nation which is farre beyonde the great lake. The 5th had allready performed 2 voyages with a greate deale of successe. My father was a great Captayne in warrs, having ben Commander in all his times, and distructed many villages of their Ennemy, having killed 19 men with his owne hands, whereof he was marked his right thigh for as many he killed. He should have as many more, but that you must know that the Commander has not amused himselfe to kille, but in the front of his army to encourage his men. If by chance he tooke any prisoners, he calles one of his men and gives him the captives, saying that it's honour enough to command the conquerors, and by his example shews to the yong men that he has the power as much as the honour. He receaved 2 gunn shots and 7 arrows shotts, and was runne through the shoulders with a lance. He was aged 3 score years old, he was talle, and of an excellent witt for a wild man. . . .

This voyage being ended,[13] albeit I came to this village, twice with feare & terror, the 3d time notwithstanding with joy & contentment. As we came neare the village, a multitude of people came to meete us with great exclamations, and for the most part for my sake, biding

---

13. After the attack, Radisson and his native "brothers" returned to their family, bringing with them prisoners and heads of those killed.

me to be cheerfull & qualifying me dodcon, that is, devil, being of great veneration in that country to those that shew any vallour. Being arrived within halfe a league of the village, I shewed a great modesty, as usually warriors use to doe. The whole village prepares to give the scourge to the captives, as you heard before, under which I my-selfe was once to undergoe. My mother comes to meet mee, leaping & singing. I was accompanied with both my sisters. Shee takes the woman slave that I had, and would not that any should medle with her. But my brother's pris-oner, as the rest of the captives, weare soundly beaten. My mother accepted of my brother's 2 heads. My brother's prisoner was burned the same day, and the day following I received the salary of my booty, which was of porcelaine necklaces, Tourns of beads, pendants, and girdles.

There was but banqueting for a while. The greatest part of both young men & women came to see me, & the women the choicest of meats, and a most dainty and cor-diall bit which I goe to tell you; doe not long for it, is the best that is among them. First when the corne is greene they gather so much as need requireth, of which leaves they preserve the biggest leaves for the subject that fol-lowes. A dozen more or lesse old women meet together alike, of whome the greatest part want teeth, and seeth not a jott, and their cheeks hange downe like an old hunting-dogg, their eyes full of watter and bloodshott. Each takes an eare of corne and putts in their mouths, which is prop-erly as milke, chawes it, and when their mouths are full, spitts it out in their hands, which possibly they wash not once one yeare; so that their hands are white inside by reason of the grease that they putt to their haire & rubbing of it with the inside of their hands, which keeps them pretty clean, but the outside in the rinknesse of their rin-kled hands there is a quarter of an ounze of filth and stink-ing grease.

And so their hands being full of that mince meate minced with their gumms and [enough] to fill a dish. So they chaw chesnutts; then they mingle this with bear's grease or oyle of flour (in french we call it Tourne Sol) with their hands. So made a mixture, they tye the leaves att one end & make a hodgepot & cover it with the same leaves and tye the upper end so that what is within these leaves becomes a round ball, which they boile in a kettle full of watter or brouth made of meate or fish. So there is the description of the most delicious bitt of the world. I leave you taste of their Salmi gondy, which I hope to tell you in my following discourses of my other voyages in that country, and others that I frequented the space of tenne years.

To make a period of this my litle voyage. After I stayed awhile in this village with all joy & mirth, for feasts, dances, and playes out of meere gladnesse for our small victorious company's hapy retourne, so after that their heads had sufficiently danced, they begin to talke [of going] to warre against the hollanders. Most of us are traited againe for the castors we bestowed on them. They resolve unanimously to goe on their designe. Every thing ready, we march along. The next day we arrived in a small brough[14] of the hollanders, where we masters them, with-out that those beere-bellies had the courage to frowne att us. Whether it was out of hope of lucre or otherwise, we with violence tooke the meate out of their potts, and open-ing their coubards we take and eat what we gett. For drinking of their wine we weare good fellowes. So much that they fought with swords among themselves without the least offer of any misdeed to me. I drunk more then they, but more soberly, letting them make their quarrells without any notice.

The 4th day we come to the fort of Orange, where we weare very well received, or rather our Castors, every one courting us; and was nothing but prunes and raisins and tobbacco plentifully, and all for ho, ho, which is thanks, adding *nianonnha*, thanke you. We went from house to house. I went into the fort with my brother, and have not yett ben knowne a french. But a french souldier of the fort speaks to me in Iroquois language, & demanded if I was not a stranger, and did veryly believe I was french, for all that I was all dabbled over with painting and greased. I answered him in the same language, that no; and then he speaks in swearing, desiring me how I fell in the hands of those people. And hearing him speake french, amazed, I answered him, for which he rejoyced very much. As he embraces me, he cryes out with such a stirre that I thought him senselesse. He made a shame for all that I was wild but to blush red. I could be no redder than what they painted me before I came there. All came about me, French as well as duch, every one makeing drink out of the bottles, offering me their service; but my time yett was not out, so that I wanted not their service, for the onely ru-mour of my being a frenchman was enough. The flemish women drawed me by force into their houses, striving who should give, one bread, other meate, to drinke and to eate, and tobacco. I wanted not for those of my nation, Iroquoise, who followed me in a great squadroon through

---

14. Town.

the streets, as if I had bin a monster in nature or a rare thing to be seen.

I went to see the Governor, & [he] talked with me a long time, and tould him the life that I lead, of which he admired. He offred me to buy me from them att what prise so ever, or else should save me, which I accepted not, for severall reasons. The one was for not to be behoulding to them, and the other being loathsome to leave such kind of good people. For then I began to love my new parents that weare so good & so favourable to me. The 3d reason was to watch a better opportunity for to retyre to the french rather than make that long circuit which after I was forced to doe for to retyre to my country more then 2,000 leagues; and being that it was my destiny to discover many wild nations, I would not to strive against destinie. I remitted myselfe to fortune and adventure of time, as a thing ordained by God for his greatest glorie, as I hope it will prove. Our treatis being done, overladend with bootyes abundantly, we putt ourselves in the way that we came to see againe our village, and to passe that winter with our wives, and to eat with them our Cagamitie in peece, hoping that nobody should trouble us during our wintering, and also to Expect or finde our fathers retourning home.

Leaving that place, many cryed to see me among a company of wolves, as that souldier tould me who knowed me the first houre; and the poore man made the tears come to my eyes. The truth is, I found many occasions to retire for to save me, but have not yett souffred enough to have merited my deliverence. In 2 dayes' journey we weare retourned to our cabbans, where every one of us rendered himself to his dearest kindred or master. My sisters weare charged of porcelaine, of which I was shure not to faile, for they weare too liberall to mee and I towards them. I was not 15 dayes retourned, but that nature itselfe reproached me to leade such a life, remembering the sweet behaviour and mildnesse of the french, & considered with meselfe what end should I expect of such a barbarous nation, enemy to God and to man. The great effect that the flemings shewed me, and the litle space was from us there; can I make that journey one day? The great belief that the people had in me should make them not to mistrust me, & by that I should have greater occasion to save me without feare of being pursued.

All these reasons made one deliberat to take a full resolution, without further delay, of saving meselfe to the flemings; for I could be att no safety among such a nation full of reveng. If in case the French & algonquins defeats that troupe of theirs, then what spite they will have will reveng it on my boanes; for where is no law, no faith to undertake to goe to the French. I was once interrupted, nor have I had a desire to venture againe for the second time. I should delight to be broyled as before in pitifull torments. I repented of a good occasion I lett slippe, finding meselfe in the place with offers of many to assist me. But he that is of a good resolution must be of strong hopes of what he undertakes; & if the dangers weare considered which may be found in things of importancy, you ingenious men would become cooks. Finally, without expecting my father's retourne, putting away all feare & apprehension, I constituted to deliver meselfe from their hands at what ever rate it would come too. For this effect I purposed to feign to goe a hunting about the brough; & for to dissemble the better, I cutt long sticks to make handles for a kind of a sword they use, that thereby they might not have the least suspition.

One day I tooke but a simple hattchett & a knife, if occasion presented to cutt some tree, & for to have more defence, if unhappily I should be rencountred, to make them believe that I was lost in the woods. Moreover, as the whole nation tooke me for proud, having allways great care to be guarnished with porcelaine, & that I would fly away like a beggar, a thing very unworthy, in this deliberation I ventured. I inquired my brother if he would keepe me company. I knewed that he never thought, seeing that he was courting of a young woman, who by the report of many was a bastard to a flemish. I had no difficulty to believe, seeing that the colour of her hayre was much more whiter then that of the Iroquoits. Neverthelesse, shee was of a great familie. I left them to their love. In shorte, that without any provision I tooke journey through the forests guided by fortune. No difficulty if I could keepe the highway, which is greatly beatten with the great concours of that people that comes & goes to trade with the flemings; but to avoid all encounters I must prolong a farre off. Soe being assisted by the best hope of the world, I made all diligence in the meene while that my mother nor kindred should mistrust me in the least.

I made my departure att 8 of the clock in the morning the 29th October, 1653. I marched all that journey without eating, but being as accustomed to that, without staying I contined my course att night. Before the breaking of the day I found myselfe uncapable because of my feeblenesse and faintnesse for want of food and repose after such constraint. But the feare of death makes vertu of necessity. The morning commanded me to goe, for it's faire and cold ayre, which [was] somewhat advantageous to keepe [me] more cheerfull. Finally the resolution reterning my courage, att 4 of the clocke att evening, the next daye I arrived in a place full of trees cutt, which made mee looke to myselfe, fearing to approach the habitation, though my designe was such. It is a strange thing that to save this life they abhorre what they wish, & desire which they apprehend. Approaching nigher and nigher untill I perceived an opening that was made by cutting of wood where was one man cutting still wood, I went nearer and called him. [He] incontinently leaves his work & comes to me, thinking I was Iroquoise. I said nothing to him to the contrary. I kept him in that thought, promising him to treat with him all my castors att his house, if he should promise me there should be non of my brother Iroquoise there, by reson we must be liberall to one another. He assured me there was none then there. I tould him that my castors were hidden and that I should goe for them tomorrow. So satisfied [he] leads me to his cabban & setts before me what good cheare he had, not desiring to loose time because the affaire concerned me much. I tould him I was savage, but that I lived awhile among the french, & that I had something valuable to communicate to the governor. That he would give me a peece of paper and Ink and pen. He wondered very much to see that, what he never saw before don by a wildman. He charges himself with my letter, with promise that he should tell it to nobody of my being there, and to retourne the soonest he could possible, having but 2 litle miles to the fort of Orange.

In the meane while of his absence shee shews me good countenance as much as shee could, hoping of a better imaginary profit by me. Shee asked me if we had so much libertie with the french women to lye with them as they; but I had no desire to doe anything, seeing myselfe so insnared att death's door amongst the terrible torments, but must shew a better countenance to a worse game. In the night we heard some wild men singing, which redoubled my torments and apprehension, which inticed me to declare to that woman that my nation would kill [me] because I loved the french and the flemings more than they, and that I resolved hereafter to live with the flemings. Shee perceiving my reason hid me in a corner behind a

sack or two of wheat. Nothing was to me but feare. I was scarcely there an houre in the corner, but the flemings came, 4 in number, whereof [one was] that french man [who] had knowne me the first, who presently getts me out & gives me a suite that they brought purposely to disguise me if I chanced to light upon any of the Iroquoits. I tooke leave of my landlady & landlord, yett [it] grieved me much that I had nothing to bestow upon them but thanks, being that they weare very poore, but not so much as I.

I was conducted to the fort of Orange, where we had no incounter in the way, where I have had the honnour to salute the Governor, who spoake french, and by his speech thought him a french man. The next day he caused an other habit to be given me, with shoos & stokins & also linnen. A minister that was a Jesuit gave me great offer, also a Marchand, to whom I shall ever have infinit obligations, although they weare satisfied when I came to france att Rochel. I stayed 3 days inclosed in the fort & hidden. Many came there to search me, & doubt not but my parents weare of the party. If my father had ben there he would venture hard, & no doubt but was troubled att it, & so was my mother, & my parents who loved me as if I weare their owne naturall Son. My poore sisters cryed out & lamented through the town of the flemings, as I was tould they called me by my name, for they came there the 3rd day after my flight. Many flemings wondered, & could not perceive how those could love me so well; but the pleasure caused it, as it agrees well with the Roman proverbe, "doe as they doe." I was imbarked by the governor's order; after taking leave, and thanks for all his favours, I was conducted to Menada, a towne faire enough for a new country, where after some 3 weeks I embarked in one of their shipps for holland, where arrived after many boisterous winds and ill weather, and, after some six weeks' sayle and some days, we landed att Amsterdam the 4th of January, 1654. Some days after I imbarked myselfe for france and came to Rochelle well & safe, not without blowing my fingers many times as well as I done before I arrived in holland. I stayed till spring, expecting the transporte of a shippe for new france.

3

THE STORIES OF THE PEOPLE
Strangers in the Land

Like their stories of the origin, emergence, and peopling of their lands, Native Americans' stories about contact with the Europeans, frequently described as "the white people" or "the pale ones," typically integrate moments of contact within the larger cultural narratives of the people. In Salishan cultures, for instance, the moment when Europeans first showed up in their lands—at the time of the Lewis and Clark expedition, in most cases—has, in many of their stories, been spliced into the ongoing narrative of the creation of the peoples. The story told by Flatheads of the creation of red and white races is an excellent example of such an integrative process of storytelling and life explanation, for it defines the differences of the races according to the existing cultural understandings of Coyote and Mountain Sheep. The Flatheads' story reveals the remarkable power of cultural stories both to record experiences and to explain experiences. Their story employs cultural narrative principles similar to those evident in the stories of eastern coastal peoples, who tend to speak of the strangers' arrivals on floating islands, logs, or sea foam. The newcomers, white people, are naturalized, their strangeness neutralized in the process, because they are associated with existing natural phenomena or existing culture figures. In most cases, American Indians' stories of the coming of white people to their lands work this way: They formulate the moment of contact as a record of the moment, making the record intelligible to the people by affiliating contact with other, ongoing narratives.

Just as the stories told by Europeans commented upon Native peoples' appearances, including skin color, relative hairiness or lack of hair, and general physique, so many of the stories told by Native Americans reveal curiosity about the appearances of Europeans. Likewise, several of the stories speak to cultural matters, such as evidence of faith practice and foods used. Because the Europeans came from the east when reaching several Native groups, they were sometimes, according to the integrative process just described, formulated in cultural narratives and cultural assumptions as having peculiar power. Indeed, several cultures of present-day Mexico and New Mexico considered Europeans to be their *bahana,* the deified cultural hero who would come from the east to prophecy peace and sanctify the people. Only in the later, more narrow descriptions made of the Europeans—and, often, only after aggression by the newcomers—did it become clear that Europeans were strange new people, not gods. Europeans' physical appearances, then, served often as the differentiation that Native peoples made between the spirit world and the world of the everyday, and experiences with Europeans made the everyday more complicated.

In most cases, the cultural stories told by American Indians were handed down, and continue to be handed down, as part of the oral cultural fabric of their peoples' existence because most groups did not use forms of writing. In the case of the Mayas, however, their tables of hieroglyphs reveal their culture's continued attempt to explain why the white people have come among them. The Mayas' records of their experiences present far from the rosy picture of marvel and wonder and awe that some scholars would have us consider the norm of experience among American Indian people. Rather, their written records reveal the complexities of the integrative process of cultural narrative formation: The Mayas believed the Spanish conquerors came as a result of their having lost the way provided them by their calendrical observations and linguistic uniformity. Their records also reveal the extent to which the differences of these Europeans from any other peoples they had known before, differences most evident in the process of worship and its linking to service to the strangers as enslaved peoples, marked the potential closing down of any future possibility of retaining cultural uniformity. In their fear of losing the way of the People forever, the elders wrote down their stories into a counsel book for the youths. They wrote about who the Mayas are, where they came from, how they lived together, and what was becoming of them. The *Book of Chumayel* (frequently called *The Book of Chilam Balam*) is a testimony of the resilience of peoples in the face of their perceptions of utter cultural destruction. The Mayas' case is perhaps the most stark, revealing the negative impact of European peoples upon American Indian culture. Yet other narratives also reveal Native peoples' disillusion with the strange ones who came to live among them. The stories of Native peoples are testaments to courage in the face of unaccountable adversity.

YUCATEC MAYA

During the second century A.D., elites among the Mayas centralized the cultures of the indigenous peoples of the regions called the Yucatan. Despite the relative instability of the different Indian cultures and the difficulty of the landscape—a lowland, tropical area, where independent horticultural production dominated—Mayan leaders developed highly intricate and successful city-states in which the peoples shared common rituals and religious beliefs, customs, crafts, and artistic forms of expression. Extending through the lowlands and densely populated rainforest areas, their political jurisdiction was cohesive, and they developed scientific astronomical calculations that the priests, whose ancestors were said to be the *Halach Unicob,* the "True People," found ways to incorporate into everyday life, from agricultural practice to cultural ceremonies. Many historians have suggested that their success in developing a coherent cultural system might lie, in part, in their use of a language system, based in hieroglyhs, that could be commonly known. Other contributing factors to cultural amalgamation included the Mayan calendar, based on observations of natural phenomena and of astronomy.

The Yucatec Mayas created manuscripts, generally known as the *Books of Chilam Balam,* or the *Book of Chumayal,* that reveal the expressions of an ancient dialogue between the peoples of the regions. *The Book of Chumayal,* the Counsel Book of the Yucatec Maya, records the ritual conversations of these people, created about four hundred years ago, spoken and recorded at the time when their very lives and culture faced significant duress from the incursions of Spanish people and their culture. Inhumane treatment of the Mayan peoples, along with disease, decimated the population, so that by some estimates 80 to 90 percent of the population was lost to the colonial takeover. At the center of their own analysis of their cultural demise, the Maya elders considered that their Calendar Stone—a central point of great ritual activity—had broken, along the way, breaking their path to unity because allowing for two different languages of the Calendar to be spoken "brokenly." This fracturing of the ancient Maya traditions and language brought about, the elders believed, the subjection of the Maya peoples to outside Indian elites (roughly from A.D. 900–1100). The fracturing of ancient unity had a tremendous psychological impact on the Mayas, and for this reason, when the Spanish conquistadors showed up in their lands beginning in 1539, they attributed the further destruction of the Maya peoples and culture to punishment for having allowed the unity of the Calendar to break.

The Counsel Book was created by the elders as a book of counsel and cultural recourse for the generations of Mayas to come, so that they would know their history and their culture and know what happened to the People. The elders' counsel book, in the words of the translator, Richard N. Luxton, "expresses a cry of remorse at the suffering imposed by a new political order come to the Yucatan peninsula." It is certainly, as Luxton indicates, "a remarkable act of spiritual and cultural foresight on the part of the Yucatec Mayan elders" that they created such a sacred counsel book for future generations.

THE FIRST SEATING OF THE LAND OWNERS

The chapter of the year:
The first katun,
11 Ahau the first seating of the land owners, truly.[1]

Figure of Katun lord with his eyes closed and a noose round his neck. The number '1' is written beside his right cheek.

First:
Katun 11 Ahau
[Is] the first origin of the counting and reading of the katun,
The first fold of the katun;
Skyborn Five is the seat of the katun
When the foreigners arrived.[2]
Red the beards of the sons of the sun,
The bearded ones from the east.
Those who came then arrived here in this land,
These foreigners in the world,
White men,
Red men . . .
    . . . the foundation of the Flower—
    . . . flower the foodstuffs . . . bitterness . . .

Oh, Itza . . . seized.[3]
[What is] coming to the town
[Is] a white circle 'O' from inside the sky.
The "White Ending Stone Child" comes from heaven.[4]
The White Standing Tree
Comes forth from the sky.
One shout,
From one resting place away He approaches.
You will see the dawning of the world.
You will see the news.
Yes, we were made to weep at their coming.
Their arrival united the gatherer[s] of stones,
United the gatherer[s] of trees,
[Against] the "white beans" of the town.[5]
Fire comes from the tips of their hands,
The poisoners of their fellow man
And enslavers
Who bring about the hanging of the fathers.
Yes, Oh Itza,
This is your worship—Nothing—
When you see this is the True God who descends here, truly.
One transgression of His word,
One transgression of His learning,
And impoverished will be the katun,
Impoverished the raingods.
Who will be the sun priest?
Who will be the prophet?
Who is going to understand
When Mayan tribute comes in the middle of the town

---

1. The selection is from the "Gathered Wisdom Stone," a ritual recital, the first recital of a cycle, a series of ritual stories, of Katan 11 Ahau 1539. The title-time identifies the first katun of the cycle, the first katun of Spanish settlement also. *Katan* here indicates the war period, of 256 years' duration according to the Counsel Book, thus ending in 1796. More than any other passage of the *Book of Chumayal*, the Gathered Wisdom Stone presents the elders' thoughts concerning the arrival of Christianity in their world. The text is from *The Book of Chumayal: The Counsel Book of the Yucatec Maya, 1539–1638*, trans. and ed. Richard N. Luxton (1995).

2. Skyborn Five (Merida) is the seat of the *yahuliloh*, the "Prophetically Wise Rulers."

3. The promotion of the new Christian word is directed at the Itza, one of the two ruling lineages of the Yucatan peninsula at the time of the arrival of the Spanish. "Flower" in this context can mean many things, including the Christians' conception of carnal sin, but also, poetry, sexual license, and the oral expression of the glyph.

4. Probably a reference to a halo encircling a vision, thus indicating that this will be a Christian cycle of stories, a cycle marked by the Spaniards' Christ, Jesus.

5. These seem to be white lima beans, and terms here are spoken in contempt.

To the Chichen Itza?
Yes, the brotherhood is declared
That comes from inside Katun 7 Ahau[6]
The enforcement through pain,
The duress of wretched labor,
From the obligation
Of putting on the first clothes,
As you bear
The remaining obligation tomorrow
And the day after tomorrow.
It will come, legitimate sons.
You will be seized to pay the burden of suffering
Which is to come first to the townspeople.
This is the katun that is seated, truly.
War.
The katun of wretched labor,
The katun of the aggravation of the devil is established
Inside Katun 11 Ahau.
Receive them.
Receive and welcome them,
The bearded ones,
The bringers of the sign of god.
Coming then is the settlement
Of your elder brothers,[7]
The people of "Front Stone."
Then will be the bewitching of your god
By them.
And this is the name of their sun priests:
Lord Misnilacpe.[8]
Crazy.
Antichrist.
[These are] the faces of the days
That are coming,
The days of payment by you.
Yes, your many miseries,
Engendered sons.
This is the Word of our Father:
"The earth will burn.
There will be a white circle in the sky

In the katun that will come."
It comes from the mouth of God the Father.
The command is no lie,
Yes.
Very painful is the burden of the katun
That is established within Christianity.
That which arises and comes
Is the enslavement of speech,
The enslavement . . . stone,
[And] the enslavement of people.
What comes will be god . . .
. . . you will see them
Coming to your town.
These are the True . . .
The Two-day thrones,
The Two-day mats,
In the greatly bewitched year,
In the days of enforced injuries by them.
In truth it is the end of the Word of God.
The eleventh measure is his gourd;
Gathered emptiness are the tidings
In the face of the prophet,
Gathered stone his learning,
Gathered stone the word.
You will die.[9]
[But] You will live.
Full-grown then your understanding
Of the word
Of the Living Glyph, truly.
The man from "Capital City" [comes].
You by yourself, engendered son, all alone,
Are justice.
That is the seizure in irons;
That is the binding up—
When he is tied,
When he is beaten.
So then next he is to be seated.
Then he is to speak the admonishment to his son.
He has a hat on his head
And sandals on his feet.
He has his rope tied around his waist.
In this way, perhaps, he is to come.[10]

---

6. Katun 7 Ahau began in 1579, ended in 1598. This katun saw an insurrection take place.

7. Perhaps a reference to a vision of the coming of a new people in the shaman's divining stone, held up to the flame.

8. An untranslatable word, perhaps signifying the antichrist, collectively identified as the faces of sun priests, Ah Mis, Ni Lac, and Pe Coh.

9. Perhaps a reference to the Christian promise of everlasting life.

10. That is, the new theology forms the basis for insurrection.

Aztec/Mexican

The Aztecs, having joined with the Tezcucans and the Tecpanecans by the middle of the fifteenth century, dominated the valley of Mexico in the sixteenth century, when Hernán Cortés came upon them in 1519. Cortés considered the groups too formidable to attempt to subdue with his own small force, so he won the assistance of an alienated group, the Texcocans, to overcome the Aztecs. The Texcocan king sent a group of men, under the leadership of one of his eight sons, to work with Cortés in defeating the Aztecs. This son, Tlacateccatl, an honored war leader, left his several wives in order to take part in the wars that ended in the decisive defeat of the Aztecs. Cortés and his followers sacked and destroyed Tenochtitlan (Mexico City) and razed all the Aztec monuments to their gods in the area.

Tlacateccatl, living among the Spanish, then fell under the tutelage of Franciscan missionaries who accompanied the Cortés party. Though of royal lineage, he gave up his place among the Texcocans and, it is said, in humility took on the name, Juan Diego. It is said that Juan Diego became a relative commoner, cast off the war honors of his own people, and entered into biblical study, surrounded by just one of his wives and their household. When Juan Diego in 1531 spoke of a visitation to him by the Catholics' Virgin Mary, he gained many followers among the Indian people of the region, who spread news of the miraculous apparition by word of mouth. It is no surprise that the Indian people were the first to be impressed by Juan Diego's story of his experience: The apparition took place on the hilly site of a former ancient temple honoring an Aztec fertility god, the female deity Tonanzin (sometimes Tonantzin). The story Juan Diego told thus had marked significance for the Indians because of the importance of the already sacred location, Tepeyac (sometimes Tepeyacac) hill, and the importance of Tonanzin to everyday life. While native peoples made journeys to the site, Spanish historians preferred not to record Juan Diego's story, in part, out of fear that Juan Diego was attempting to create a subversion of Spanish Catholic dominion by gathering the Indian people around him and, in part, because they feared that an apparition by an Indian might be the mark of the devil in their midst. They finally started recording what they considered to have been the appearance of their Virgin Mary to a poor, simple, humble Indian. Juan Diego remained at the site the rest of his life, a chaplain at the Chapel of Tepeyac and custodian and interpreter of the Tilma (shroud) on which the image of the Virgin had been painted.

The overall lines of the story (which Juan Diego related originally in his native tongue, Náhuatl) and the image as it was first painted as the story on what some consider to have been Juan Diego's Tilma indicate that the Virgin of Guadalupe was an amalgamated or syncretic religious figure. Her brown skin, her common depiction in a stance resembling an Aztec dancer, the colors and flowers associated with her—all are marks of an indigenous personage. Yet the insistence upon the message of peace and love that often figures into the stories surrounding her appearance signifies qualities associated with the Catholics' version of Mary's story. Here is a figure that for centuries has been one of the most highly valued by Mexicans for its mixture of Spanish and Indian worlds, its promise of love and peace. Indeed, during the eighteenth century, the figure of the Virgin of Guadalupe strengthened as an image of the *mestizo,* the mixed-race person, making her name and figure extremely important to cultural independence movements of that day. Today, the image of the Virgin of Guadalupe carries religious, cultural, and political significance to Mexican American peoples. It appears on home and church altars, on murals, and on automobiles, among other things, an icon of civil struggle for a better way of life.

HISTORY OF THE MIRACULOUS APPARITION OF THE VIRGIN OF GUADALUPE IN 1531[1]

Herein is told, in all truth, how by a great miracle the illustrious Virgin, Blessed Mary, Mother of God, Our Lady, appeared anew, in the place known as Tepeyacac.

She appeared first to an Indian named Juan Diego; and later her divine Image appeared in the presence of the first Bishop of Mexico, Don Fray Juan de Zumárraga; also there are told various miracles which have been done. It was ten years after the beginning of bringing water from the mountain of Mexico, when the arrow and the shield had been put away, when in all parts of the country there was tranquillity which was beginning to show its light, and faith and knowledge of Him was being taught through Whose favor we have our being, Who is the only true God.

In the year 1531, early in the month of December, it happened that an humble Indian, called Juan Diego, whose dwelling, it is said, was in Quahutítlan, although for divine worship he pertained to Tlatilolco, one Saturday very early in the morning, while he was on his way to divine worship according to his custom, when he had arrived near the top of the hill called Tepeyacac, as it was near dawn, he heard above the hill a singing like that when many choice birds sing together, their voices resounding as if echoing throughout the hills; he was greatly rejoiced; their song gave him rapture exceeding that of the bell-bird and other rare birds of song.

Juan Diego stopped to wonder and said to himself: *Is it I who have this good fortune to hear what I hear? Or am I perhaps only dreaming? Where am I? Perhaps this is the place the ancients, our forefathers, used to tell about—our grandfathers—the flowery land, the fruitful land? Is it perchance the earthly paradise?*

And while he was looking towards the hilltop, facing the east, from which came the celestial song, suddenly the singing stopped and he heard someone calling as if from the top of the hill, saying: *Juan.* Juan Diego did not dare to go there where he was being called; he did not move, perhaps in some way marvelling; yet he was filled with great joy and delight, and then, presently, he began to climb to the summit where he was called.

And, when he was nearing it, on the top of the peak he saw a lady who was standing there who had called him from a distance, and, having come into her presence, he was struck with wonder at the radiance of her exceeding great beauty, her garments shining like the sun; and the stones of the hill, and the caves, reflecting the brightness of her light were like precious gold; and he saw how the rainbow clothed the land so that the cactus and other things that grew there seemed like celestial plants, their leaves and thorns shining like gold in her presence. He made obeisance and heard her voice, her words, which rejoiced him utterly when she asked, very tenderly, as if she loved him:

Listen, xocoyote mio,[2] Juan, where are you going?

And he replied: *My Holy One, my Lady, my Damsel, I am on my way to your house at Mexico-Tlatilulco; I go in pursuit of the holy things which our priests teach us.*

Whereupon She told him, and made him aware of her divine will, saying: *You must know, and be very certain in your heart, my son, that I am truly the eternal Virgin, holy Mother of the True God, through Whose favor we live, the Creator, Lord of Heaven, and the Lord of the Earth. I very much desire that they build me a church here, so that in it I may show and may make known and give all my love, my mercy and my help and my protection—I am in truth your merciful mother—to you and to all the other people dear to me who call upon me, who search for me, who confide in me; here I will hear their sorrow, their words, so that I may make perfect and cure their illnesses, their labors, and their calamities. And so that my intention may be made known, and my mercy, go now to the episcopal palace of the Bishop of Mexico and tell him that I send you to tell him how much I desire to have a church built here, and tell him very well all that you have seen and all that you have heard; and be sure in your heart that I will*

---

1. Juan Diego's original Náhuatl story was circulated for decades and then published in 1649 by Bachiller Luis Lazo de Vega, the chaplain at the sanctuary at Tepeyac, over a century after the apparition was said to have occurred. The text he used is said to have been prepared by Antonio Valeriano, who was a contemporary of Juan Diego. But the story is maintained today in numerous different versions among Mexicans and Mexican American peoples, to whom it belongs as an important cultural story. The text is from *The Dark Virgin: The Book of Our Lady of Guadalupe,* ed. D. Demarest and C. Taylor (1956).

2. *Xocoyote,* a Náhuatl term that here may be rendered "my little son" or "my dearest son." *Xocoyota* is the form meaning "daughter."

pay you with glory and you will deserve much that I will repay you for your weariness, your work, which you will bear diligently doing what I send you to do, Now hear my words, my dear son, and go and do everything carefully and quickly.

Then he humbled himself before her and said: *My Holy One, my Lady, I will go now and fulfill your commandment.*

And straightway he went down to accomplish that with which he was charged, and took the road that leads straight to Mexico.

And when he had arrived within the city, he went at once to the episcopal palace of the Lord Bishop, who was the first [Bishop] to come, whose name was Don Fray Juan de Zumárraga, a religious of St. Francis. And having arrived there, he made haste to ask to see the Lord Bishop, asking his servants to give notice of him. After a good while they came to call him, and the Bishop advised them that he should come in; and when he had come into his presence, he knelt and made obeisance, and then after this he related the words of the Queen of Heaven, and told besides all that he had seen and all that he had heard. And [the Bishop] having heard all his words and the commandment as if he were not perfectly persuaded, said in response:

My son, come again another time when we can be more leisurely; and I will hear more from you about the origin of this; I will look into this about which you have come, your will, your desire.

And he departed with much sorrow because he had not been able to convince him of the truth of his mission.

Thereupon he returned that same day and went straightway to the hill where he had seen the Queen of Heaven, who was even then standing there where he had first seen Her, waiting for him, and he, having seen Her, made obeisance, kneeling upon the ground, and said:

My Holy One, most noble of persons, My Lady, my Xocoyota, my Damsel, I went there where You sent me; although it was most difficult to enter the house of the Lord Bishop, I saw him at last, and in his presence I gave him your message in the way You instructed me; he received me very courteously, and listened with attention; but he answered as if he could not be certain and did not believe; he told me: Come again another time when we can be at leisure, and I will hear you from beginning to end; I will look into that about which you come, what it is you want and ask me for. He seemed to me, when he answered, to be thinking perhaps that the church You desire to have

made here was perchance not Your will, but a fancy of mine. I pray You, my Holy One, my Lady, my Daughter, that any one of the noble lords who are well known, reverenced and respected be the one to undertake this so that Your words will be believed. For it is true that I am only a poor man; I am not worthy of being there where You send me; pardon me, my Xocoyota, I do not wish to make your noble heart sad; I do not want to fall into your displeasure.

Then the always noble Virgin answered him, saying: *Hear me, my son, it is true that I do not lack for servants or ambassadors to whom I could entrust my message so that my will could be verified, but it is important that you speak for me in this matter, weary as you are; in your hands you have the means of verifying, of making plain my desire, my will; I pray you, my xocoyote, and advise you with much care, that you go again tomorrow to see the Bishop and represent me; give him an understanding of my desire, my will, that he build the church that I ask; and tell him once again that it is the eternal Virgin, Holy Mary, the Mother of God, who sends you to him.*

And Juan Diego answered her, saying: *Queen of Heaven, my Holy One, my Damsel, do not trouble your heart, for I will go with all my heart and make plain Your voice, Your words. It is not because I did not want to go, or because the road is stony, but only because perhaps I would not be heard, and if I were heard I would not be believed. I will go and do your bidding and tomorrow in the afternoon about sunset I will return to give the answer to your words the Lord Bishop will make; and now I leave You, my Xocoyota, my Damsel, my Lady; meanwhile, rest You.*

With this, he went to his house to rest. The next day being Sunday, he left his house in the morning and went straightway to Tlatilulco, to attend Mass and the sermon. Then, being determined to see the Bishop, when Mass and the sermon were finished, at ten o'clock, with all the other Indians he came out of the church; but Juan Diego left them and went to the palace of the Lord Bishop. And having arrived there, he spared no effort in order to see him and when, after great difficulty, he did see him again, he fell to his knees and implored him to the point of weeping, much moved, in an effort to make plain the words of the Queen of Heaven, and that the message and the will of the most resplendent Virgin would be believed; that the church be built as She asked, where She wished it.

But the Lord Bishop asked Juan Diego many things, to know for certain what had taken place, questioning him:

Where did he see Her? What did the Lady look like whom he saw? And he told the Lord Bishop all that he had seen. But although he told him everything exactly, so that it seemed in all likelihood that She was the Immaculate Virgin, Mary most pure, the beloved Mother of Our Lord Jesus Christ, the Bishop said he could not be certain. He said: It is not only with her words that we have to do, but also to obtain that for which she asks. It is very necessary to have some sign by which we may believe that it is really the Queen of Heaven who sends you.

And Juan Diego, having heard him, said to the Lord Bishop: *My Lord, wait for whatever sign it is that you ask for, and I will go at once to ask the Queen of Heaven, who sent me.* And the Lord Bishop, seeing that he had agreed, and so that he should not be confused or worried, in any way, urged him to go; and then, calling some of his servants in whom he had much confidence, he asked them to follow and to watch where he went and see whomsoever it was that he went to see, and with whom he might speak. And this was done accordingly, and when Juan Diego reached the place where a bridge over the river, near the hill, met the royal highway, they lost him, and although they searched for him everywhere they could not find him in any part of that land. And so they returned, and not only were they weary, but extremely annoyed with him, and upon their return they abused him much with the Lord Bishop, over all that had happened, for they did not believe in him; they said that he had been deceiving him, and had imagined all that he had come to relate to him, or perhaps he had dreamed it, and they agreed and said that if he should come again they would seize him and chastise him severely so that he would not lie another time.

The next day, Monday, when Juan Diego was to bring some sign by which he might be believed, he did not return, since, when he arrived at his house, an uncle of his who was staying there, named Juan Bernardino, was very ill of a burning fever; Juan Diego went at once to bring a doctor and then he procured medicine; but there still was no time because the man was very ill. Early in the morning his uncle begged him to go out to bring one of the priests from Tlatilulco so that he might be confessed, for he was very certain that his time had come to die, now that he was too weak to rise, and could not get well.

And on Tuesday, very early in the morning, Juan Diego left his house to go to Tlatilulco to call a priest, and as he was nearing the hill on the road which lies at the foot of the hill towards the west, which was his usual way, he said to himself: *If I go straight on, without doubt I will see*

Our Lady and She will persuade me to take the sign to the Lord Bishop; let us first do our duty; I will go first to call the priest for my poor uncle; will he not be waiting for him?

With this he turned to another road at the foot of the slope and was coming down the other side towards the east to take a short cut to Mexico; he thought that by turning that way the Queen of Heaven would not see him, but She was watching for him, and he saw Her on the hilltop where he had always seen Her before, coming down that side of the slope, by the shortest way, and She said to him:

Xocoyote mio, where are you going? What road is this you are taking?

And he was frightened; it is not known whether he was disgusted with himself, or was ashamed, or perhaps he was struck with wonder; he prostrated himself before Her and greeted her, saying: *My Daughter, my Xocoyota, God keep You, Lady. How did You waken? And is your most pure body well, perchance? My Holy One, I will bring pain to your heart—for I must tell You, my Virgin, that an uncle of mine, who is Your servant, is very sick, with an illness so strong that without doubt he will die of it; I am hastening to Your house in Mexico to call one of Our Lord's dear ones, our priests, to come to confess him, and when I have done that, then I will come back to carry out Your commandment. My Virgin, my Lady, forgive me, be patient with me until I do my duty, and then tomorrow I will come back to You.*

And having heard Juan Diego's explanation, the most holy and immaculate Virgin replied to him:

Listen, and be sure, my dear son, that I will protect you; do not be frightened or grieve, or let your heart be dismayed; however great the illness may be that you speak of, am I not here, I who am your mother, and is not my help a refuge? Am I not of your kind?[3] *Do not be concerned about your uncle's illness, for he is not now going to die; be assured that he is now already well. Is there anything else needful?* (And in that same hour his uncle was healed, as later he learned.)

And Juan Diego, having heard the words of the Queen of Heaven, greatly rejoiced and was convinced, and besought Her that She would send him again to see the Lord Bishop, to carry him some sign by which he could believe, as he had asked.

---

3. The Virgin of Guadalupe thus identifies with the Indians.

Whereupon the Queen of Heaven commanded him to climb up to the top of the hill where he had always seen her, saying: *Climb up to the top of the hill, my xocoyote, where you have seen me stand, and there you will find many flowers; pluck them and gather them together, and then bring them down here in my presence.*

Then Juan Diego climbed up the hill and when he had reached the top he marvelled to see blooming there many kinds of beautiful flowers of Castile, for it was then very cold, and he marvelled at their fragrance and odor. Then he began to pluck them, and gathered them together carefully, and wrapped them in his mantle, and when he had finished he descended and carried to the Queen of Heaven all the flowers he had plucked. She, when she had seen them, took them into her immaculate hands, gathered them together again, and laid them in his cloak once more and said to him:

My xocoyote, all these flowers are the sign that you must take to the Bishop; in my name tell him that with this he will see and recognize my will and that he must do what I ask; and you who are my ambassador worthy of confidence, I counsel you to take every care that you open your mantle only in the presence of the Bishop, and you must make it known to him what is that you carry, and tell him how I asked you to climb to the top of the hill to gather the flowers. Tell him also all that you have seen, so that you will persuade the Lord Bishop and he will see that the church is built for which I ask.

And the Queen of Heaven having acquainted him with this, he departed, following the royal highway which leads directly to Mexico; he traveled content, because he was persuaded that now he would succeed; he walked carefully, taking great pains not to injure what he was carrying in his mantle; he went glorying in the fragrance of the beautiful flowers. When he arrived at the Bishop's palace, he encountered his majordomo and other servants and asked them to tell the Bishop that he would like to see him; but none of them would, perhaps because it was still very early in the morning or, perhaps recognizing him, they were vexed or, because they knew how others of their household had lost him on the road when they were following him. They kept him waiting there a long time; he waited very humbly to see if they would call him, and when it was getting very late, they came to him to see what it was he was carrying as a proof of what he had related. And Juan Diego, seeing that he could not hide from them what he was carrying, when they had tormented him

and jostled him and knocked him about, let them glimpse that he had roses, to deliver himself from them; and they, when they saw that they were roses of Castile, very fragrant and fresh, and not at all in their season, marvelled and wanted to take some of them. Three times they made bold to take them, but they could not because, when they tried to take them, they were not roses that they touched, but were as if painted or embroidered. Upon this, they went to the Lord Bishop to tell him what they had seen, and that the Indian who was there often before had come again and wanted to see him, and that they had kept him waiting there a long time.

The Lord Bishop, having heard this, knew that now this was the sign that should persuade him whether what the Indian had told him was true. He straightway asked that he be brought in to see him.

Having come into his presence, Juan Diego fell to his knees (as he had always done) and again related fully all that he had seen, and full of satisfaction and wonder he said: *My Lord, I have done that which you asked me; I went to tell my Holy One, the Queen of Heaven, the beloved Virgin Mary, Mother of God, how you asked me for some sign that you might believe that it was She who desired you to build Her the church for which She asked. And also I told Her how I had given my word that I would bring you some sign so that you could believe in what She had put in my care, and She heard with pleasure your suggestion and found it good, and just now, early this morning. She told me to come again to see you and I asked Her for the sign that I had asked Her to give me, and then She sent me to the hilltop where I have always seen Her, to pluck the flowers that I should see there. And when I had plucked them, I took them to the foot of the mountain where She had remained, and She gathered them into her immaculate hands and then put them again into my mantle for me to bring them to you. Although I knew very well that the hilltop was not a place for flowers, since it is a place of thorns, cactuses, caves and mezquites, I was not confused and did not doubt Her. When I reached the summit I saw there was a garden there of flowers with quantities of the fragrant flowers which are found in Castile; I took them and carried them to the Queen of Heaven and She told me that I must bring them to you, and now I have done it, so that you may see the sign that you ask for in order to do Her bidding, and so that you will see that my word is true. And here they are.*

Whereupon he opened his white cloak, in which he was carrying the flowers, and as the roses of Castile dropped out to the floor, suddenly there appeared the most pure image of the most noble Virgin Mary, Mother of God, just exactly as it is, even now, in Her holy house, in Her church which is named Guadalupe;[4] and the Lord Bishop, having seen this, and all those who were with him, knelt down and gazed with wonder; and then they grew sad, and were sorrowful, and were aghast, and the Lord Bishop with tenderness and weeping begged Her forgiveness for not having done Her bidding at once. And when he had finished, he untied from Juan Diego's neck the cloak on which was printed the figure of the Queen of Heaven. And then he carried it into his chapel; and Juan Diego remained all that day in the house of the Bishop, who did not want him to go. And the following day the Bishop said to him: *Come, show us where it is the Queen of Heaven wishes us to build Her church.* And when he had shown them where it was, he told them that he wanted to go to his house to see his uncle Juan Bernardino who had been very ill and he had set out for Tlatilulco to get a priest to confess him, but the Queen of Heaven had told him that he was already cured.

They did not let him go alone, but went with him to his house, and when they arrived there, they saw that his uncle was well and that nothing was now the matter with him; and the uncle wondered much when he saw such a company with his nephew, and all treating him with great courtesy, and he asked him: *How is it they treat you this way? And why do they reverence you so much?*

And Juan Diego told him that when he had gone from the house to call a confessor for him, he saw the Queen of Heaven on the hill called Tepeyacac and She had sent him to Mexico to see the Lord Bishop to have a church built for Her. And that She had also told him not to worry about his uncle, that he was now well.

Whereupon his uncle showed great joy and told him that it was true that at that very hour he had been healed, and that he himself had seen exactly that same Person, and that She had told him how She had sent him to Mexico to see the Bishop, and also that when he saw him again, to tell him all that he had seen also, and how, mirac-

ulously, he had been restored to health, and that the most holy Image of the Immaculate Virgin should be called Santa María de Guadalupe.

And after this they brought Juan Bernardino into the Lord Bishop's presence so that he might tell him under oath all that he had just related; and the Bishop kept the two men (that is, Juan Diego and Juan Bernardino) as his guests in his own house several days until the church for the Queen of Heaven was built where Juan Diego had shown them. And the Lord Bishop moved the sacred Image of the Queen of Heaven, which he had in his chapel, to the cathedral so that all the people could see it.

All the city was in a turmoil upon seeing Her most holy portrait; they saw that it had appeared miraculously, that no one in the world had painted it on Juan Diego's mantle; for this, on which the miraculous Image of the Queen of Heaven appeared, was *ayate,* a coarse fabric made of cactus fibre, rather like homespun, and well woven, for at that time all the Indian people covered themselves with *ayate,* except the nobles, the gentlemen and the captains of war, who dressed themselves in cloaks of cotton, or in cloaks made of wool.

The esteemed *ayate* upon which the Immaculate Virgin, Our Sovereign Queen, appeared unexpectedly is made of two pieces sewn together with threads of cotton; the height of Her sacred Image from the sole of Her foot to the top of Her head measures six hands, and one woman's hand. Her sacred face is very beautiful, grave, and somewhat dark; her precious body, according to this, is small; her hands are held at her breast; the girdle at her waist is violet; her right foot only shows, a very little, and her slipper is earthen in color; her robe is rose-colored; in the shadows it appears deeper red, and it is embroidered with various flowers outlined in gold; pendant at her throat is a little gold circlet which is outlined with a black line around it; in the middle it has a cross; and one discovers glimpses of another, inner vestment of white cotton, daintily gathered at her wrists. The outer mantle which covers her from her head almost to her feet is of heavenly blue; half-way down its fullness hangs in folds, and it is bordered with gold, a rather wide band of gold thread, and all over it there are golden stars which are in number forty-six. Her most holy head is turned towards the right and is bending down; and on her head above her mantle she wears a shining gold crown, and at her feet there is the new moon with its horns pointed upward; and exactly in the middle of it the Immaculate Virgin is standing, and, it would seem also, in the middle of the sun,

---

4. The image is clearly modeled on the Catholics' Virgin Mary, Queen of Heaven, featured in statues as the Virgin standing on a half-moon, crushing a serpent (the devil) with her right foot. The word *Guadalupe* may be an amalgamated term derived from both Náhuatl and Spanish, as *"coatl-llope"*: *coatl,* "snake" in Náhuatl, and *llope,* "crush" or "trample" in Spanish.

since its rays surround her everywhere. These rays number a hundred; some are large and others are small; those on each side of her sacred face and those above her head number twelve, in all they number fifty on each side. And outside the edges of this and her robes She is encircled with white clouds. This divine Image as it is described stands above an angel, half of whose body only appears, since he is in the midst of clouds. The angel's outstretched arms hold the edges of her outer robes as they hang in folds near her sacred feet. His garment is of rosy color with a gold ornament at his neck; his wings are made or composed of various sizes of feathers, and it seems as if he were very happy to be accompanying the Queen of Heaven.

HOPI

During the second century of conquest, sporadic attempts to reach and conquer the pueblos of the present-day Arizona and New Mexico territories brought difficulty for Pueblo peoples. The Hopis tell a story quite different from the poetic narrative of epic conquest memorialized by Gaspar Pérez de Villagrá (1555–1620). From the Hopi vantage point, the Franciscans behaved in despicable ways in cultural and interpersonal terms, taking not just the souls but the bodies of the people into their own covetous grasp. The Hopis found no use in giving up their cachinas and their religious practices in behalf of a people who would overwork them, starve them, and rape them. They found it difficult to believe in a god who would not prize their religious practices, which had secured them rain, food, and continuance for centuries. This story, told by Hopis, reveals the amalgamative process of the oral tradition in its nonlinear telling of events associated with the Spanish conquest of the Pueblos. It collapses history's typical linear chronology into one chronological level, making the different events of different centuries part of the same story, as if all occurred in the same real time.

THE COMING OF THE SPANISH AND THE PUEBLO REVOLT[1]

It may have taken quite a long time for these villages to be established. Anyway, every place was pretty well settled down when the Spanish came.[2] The Spanish were first heard of at Zuni and then at Awatovi. They came on to Shung-opovi, passing Walpi. At First Mesa, Siky-atki was the largest village then, and they were called Sikyatki, not Walpi. The Walpi people were living below the present village on the west side. When the Spaniards came, the Hopi thought that they were the ones they were looking for—their white brother, the Bahana, their savior.[3]

The Spaniards visited Shung-opovi several times before the missions were established. The people of Mishongovi welcomed them so the priest who was with the white men built the first Hopi mission at Mishongovi. The people of Shung-opovi were at first afraid of the priests but later they decided he was really the Bahana, the savior, and let him build a mission at Shung-opovi.

Well, about this time the Strap Clan were ruling at Shung-opovi and they were the ones that gave permission

---

1. This version of the Hopi narrative comes from Edmund Nequatewa, *Truth of a Hopi: Stories Relating to the Origin, Myths, and Clan Histories of the Hopi* (1936).

2. The Hopis had their own complex social and religious practices when they were first subjected to the efforts of missionary priests in 1629. Coronado had been the first to visit the Hopis, in 1540. As a result of subsequent expeditions, the Franciscans established themselves among the Hopis, beginning in the early seventeenth century. The Hopis joined the freedom movement, called by the Spanish settlers the Pueblo Revolt of 1680.

3. Belief in the *bahana,* or savior, a fair-skinned hero-savior was common to the Aztecs and the Hopis. Both the Aztecs and the Hopis believed that their hero would return from the east to bring peace and prosperity to the People. In Mexico, Hernán Cortés played upon his knowledge of this religious tradition, and the Franciscans at Hopi village used it as vehicle for their entrance into Hopi culture. By the time this narrative was told in 1936, it included significant implications related to Christianity.

to establish the mission. The Spaniards, whom they called Castilla, told the people that they had much more power than all their chiefs and a whole lot more power than the witches. The people were very much afraid of them, particularly if they had much more power than the witches. They were so scared that they could do nothing but allow themselves to be made slaves. Whatever they wanted done must be done. Any man in power that was in this position the Hopi called *Tota-achi,* which means a grouchy person that will not do anything himself, like a child. They couldn't refuse, or they would be slashed to death or punished in some way. There were two *Tota-achi.*

The missionary did not like the ceremonies. He did not like the Kachinas and he destroyed the altars and the customs. He called it idol worship and burned up all the ceremonial things in the plaza.

When the Priests started to build the mission, the men were sent away over near the San Francisco peaks to get the pine or spruce beams. These beams were cut and put into shape roughly and were then left till the next year when they had dried out. Beams of that size were hard to carry and the first few times they tried to carry these beams on their backs, twenty to thirty men walking side by side under the beam. But this was rather hard in rough places and one end had to swing around. So finally they figured out a way of carrying the beam in between them. They lined up two by two with the beam between the lines. In doing this, some of the Hopis were given authority by the missionary to look after these men and to see if they all did their duty. If any man gave out on the way he was simply left to die. There was great suffering. Some died for lack of food and water, while others developed scabs and sores on their bodies.

It took a good many years for them to get enough beams to Shung-opovi to build the mission. When this mission was finally built, all the people in the village had to come there to worship, and those that did not come were punished severely. In that way their own religion was altogether wiped out, because they were not allowed to worship in their own way. All this trouble was a heavy burden on them and they thought it was on account of this that they were having a heavy drought at this time. They thought their gods had given them up because they weren't worshiping the way they should.

Now during this time the men would go out pretending they were going on a hunting trip and they would go to some hiding place, to make their prayer offerings. So to-day, a good many of these places are still to be found where they left their little stone bowls in which they ground their copper ore to paint the prayer sticks. These places are called *Puwa-kiki,* cave places. If these men were caught they were severely punished.

Now this man, Tota-achi (the Priest)[4] was going from bad to worse. He was not doing the people any good and he was always figuring what he could do to harm them. So he thought out how the water from different springs or rivers would taste and he was always sending some man to these springs to get water for him to drink, but it was noticed that he always chose the men who had pretty wives. He tried to send them far away so that they would be gone two or three days, so it was not very long until they began to see what he was doing. The men were even sent to the Little Colorado River to get water for him, or to Moencopi. Finally, when a man was sent out he'd go out into the rocks and hide, and when the night came he would come home. Then, the priest, thinking the man was away, would come to visit his wife, but instead the man would be there when he came. Many men were punished for this.

All this time the priest, who had great power, wanted all the young girls to be brought to him when they were about thirteen or fourteen years old. They had to live with the priest. He told the people they would become better women if they lived with him for about three years. Now one of these girls told what the Tota-achi were doing and a brother of the girl heard of this and he asked his sister about it, and he was very angry. This brother went to the mission and wanted to kill the priest that very day, but the priest scared him and he did nothing. So the Shung-opovi people sent this boy, who was a good runner, to Awatovi to see if they were doing the same thing over there, which they were. So that was how they got all the evidence against the priest.

Then the chief at Awatovi sent word by this boy that all the priests would be killed on the fourth day after the full

---

4. Among the priests who served at Hopi village (Shung-gopovi) prior to the freedom movement the Spaniards called the Pueblo Revolt were Fr. José Trujillo, an intense, charismatic leader. Prior to the arrival of Trujillo, Fr. Salvador de Guerra served at Hopi village, but he was transferred to Jemez, much farther east, for having tortured the Indians under his dominion. Tota-achi is probably a conflated figure who embodies the misbehavior of several priests.

moon.[5] They had no calendar and that was the best way they had of setting the date. In order to make sure that everyone would rise up and do this thing on the fourth day the boy was given a cotton string with knots in it and each day he was to untie one of these knots until they were all out and that would be the day for the attack.

Things were getting worse and worse so the chief of Shung-opovi went over to Mishongnovi and the two chiefs discussed their troubles.[6] "He is not the savior and it is your duty to kill him," said the chief of Shung-opovi. The chief of Mishongnovi replied, "If I end his life, my own life is ended."

Now the priest would not let the people manufacture prayer offerings, so they had to make them among the rocks in the cliffs out of sight, so again one day the chief of Shung-opovi went to Mishongnovi with tobacco and materials to make prayer offerings. He was joined by the chief of Mishongnovi and the two went a mile north to a cave. For four days they lived there heartbroken in the cave, making *pahos*. Then the chief of Mishongnovi took the prayer offerings and climbed to the top of the Corn Rock and deposited them in the shrine, for according to the ancient agreement with the Mishongnovi people it was their duty to do away with the enemy.

He then, with some of his best men, went to Shung-opovi, but he carried no weapons. He placed his men at every door of the priest's house. Then he knocked on the door and walked in. He asked the priest to come out but the priest was suspicious and would not come out. The chief asked the priest four times and each time the priest refused. Finally, the priest said, "I think you are up to something."

The chief said, "I have come to kill you." "You can't kill me," cried the priest, "you have no power to kill me. If you do, I will come to life and wipe out your whole tribe."

The chief returned, "If you have this power, then blow me out into the air; my gods have more power than you have. My gods have put a heart into me to enter your home. I have no weapons. You have your weapons handy, hanging on the wall. My gods have prevented you from getting your weapons."

The old priest made a rush and grabbed his sword from the wall. The chief of Mishongnovi yelled and the doors were broken open. The priest cut down the chief and fought right and left but was soon overpowered, and his sword taken from him.

They tied his hands behind his back. Out of the big beams outside they made a tripod. They hung him on the beams, kindled a fire and burned him.

---

5. The reference is to the work of Tío Pépe and his associates, who planned the successful rebellion of the Pueblo peoples on August 13, 1680. Many soldiers and priests were killed in the uprising, and the remaining colonists retreated southward. The Spanish did not reestablish dominion in the area until 1692, when Don Diego de Vargas recaptured the pueblos.

6. This debate between the two chiefs reveals that the cultural import of this narrative for the Hopis is primarily religious rather than military. That is, to the Hopis, the indicator of Christianity's failure is the drought that followed the suppression of their kiva culture and the inability of the priest to live up to the sanctity of his own culture's Christ-like ideal or the ideal of the Hopis' *bahane*.

JOSEPH JEREMY, MICMAC

The Micmacs (whose traditional way of spelling their name is Mi'kmaq) were widely spread through the coastal areas of present-day Nova Scotia, Prince Edward Island, Cape Breton, and northern Maine, and they retain a rich narrative tradition of their Algonquian forebears. Like the Montagnais and other peoples in the upper northeastern section of North America, the Micmacs expressed astonishment at the arrival of European people in their lands, although it is likely, if Norse sagas are any indication, that these peoples witnessed sailing vessels on their seas long before any of those ships came in to harbor. Because they were living along all the waterways from the Gulf of the St. Lawrence to the Atlantic Ocean, they were the first peoples whom the Europeans came across. When Frenchman Jacques Cartier came to the land in 1534, it was the Micmacs who met him and entered into trade with his ship.

The following story about the floating island, the Europeans' ship, was related in the Micmac language by a Micmac named Joseph Jeremy, in 1869. Its traditional motif of the dream-relation foregrounds the importance of the event of contact in Micmac cultural traditions. To the Micmacs, dreams are the vehicle for interaction with the spirit world; they are to be respected and revered as glimpses of the future.

THE FLOATING ISLAND[1]

When there were no people in this country but Indians, and before any others were known, a young woman had a singular dream. She dreamed that a small island came floating in towards the land, with tall trees on it, and living beings,—among whom was a man dressed in rabbit-skin garments. The next day she related her dream, and sought for an interpretation. It was the custom in those days, when any one had a remarkable dream, to consult the wise men, and especially the magicians and soothsayers. These pondered over the girl's dream, but could make nothing of it. The next day an event occurred that explained all. Getting up in the morning, what should they see but a singular little island, as they supposed, which had drifted near to the land and become stationary there! There were trees on it, and branches to the trees, on which a number of bears, as they supposed, were crawling about. They all seized their bows, arrows, and spears, and rushed down to the shore, intending to shoot the bears; what was their surprise to find that these supposed bears were men, and that some of them were lowering down into the water a very singularly constructed canoe, into which several of them jumped and paddled ashore. Among them was a man dressed in white,—a priest with his white stole on,—who came towards them making signs of friendship, raising his hand towards heaven, and addressing them in an earnest manner, but in a language which they could not understand.

The girl was now questioned respecting her dream. Was it such an island as this that she had seen. Was this the man? She affirmed that they were indeed the same. Some of them, especially the necromancers, were displeased, they did not like it that the coming of these foreigners should have been intimated to this young girl, and not to them. Had an enemy of the Indian tribes with whom they were at war been about to make a descent upon them, they could have foreseen and foretold it by the power of their magic; but of the coming of this teacher of a new religion they could know nothing.

The new teacher was gradually received into favor, though the magicians opposed him. The people received his instructions, and submitted to the rites of baptism; the priest learned their tongue, and gave them the Prayer Book written in what they call *abootŭloeëgăsĭk'* (ornamental mark-writing); a mark standing for a word, and rendering it so difficult to learn that it may be said to be impossible.

1. This relation by Joseph Jeremy appears in Silas T. Rand, *Legends of the Micmacs* (1894).

YUCHI

Some of the peoples native to southeastern North America speak of their origin in an emergence from the center of the earth, while others attribute their origin to elements in the sky or the sea or to flora or fauna. The Yuchis call themselves the "Offspring of the Sun," perhaps because they originally lived high in the southern Appalachian mountains before they moved southward and eastward during the seventeenth and eighteenth centuries. This narrative of the arrival of white people resembles that of the Micmacs, in that the visual picture of white people lifted from the water by wood, in this case a floating log, dominates the scene of the narrative. As in the story told by the Hopis about the coming of the Spanish people and their own rebellion against them, the events in this Yuchi narrative have been collapsed into one, relatively sequential narrative time frame, the time of the story's telling.

CREATION OF THE WHITES[1]

It was out upon the ocean. Some sea-foam formed against a big log floating there. Then a person emerged from the sea-foam and crawled out upon the log. He was seen sitting there. Another person crawled up, on the other side of the log. It was a woman. They were whites. Soon the Indians saw them, and at first thought that they were sea-gulls, and they said among themselves, "Are they not white people?" Then they made a boat and went out to look at the strangers more closely.

Later on the whites were seen in their house-boat. Then they disappeared.

1. This tale appears in J.R. Swanton's *Early History of the Creek Indians* (1922).

In about a year they returned, and there were a great many of them. The Indians talked to them but they could not understand each other. Then the whites left.

But they came back in another year with a great many ships. They approached the Indians and asked if they could come ashore. They said, "Yes." So the whites landed, but they seemed to be afraid to walk much on the water. They went away again over the sea.

This time they were gone a shorter time; only three months passed and they came again. They had a box with them and asked the Indians for some earth to fill it. It was given to them as they desired. The first time they asked they had a square box, and when that was filled they brought a big shallow box. They filled this one too. Earth was put in them and when they were carried aboard the ship the white men planted seed in them and many things were raised. After they had taken away the shallow box, the whites came back and told the Indians that their land was very strong and fertile. So they asked the Indians to give them a portion of it that they might live on it. The Indians agreed to do it, the whites came to the shore, and they have lived there ever since.

Handsome Lake, Seneca

The Senecas, keepers of the western gate of Iroquoia, were the members of the Iroquois Confederacy of Five Nations responsible for working with the western Indian peoples. They came under the influence of French, Dutch, and English settlers later and less fully than the eastern peoples of the Iroquois (particularly the Onandagas, the keepers of the fire of Iroquoia, and the Mohawks, the keepers of the eastern gate). Their lack of proximity to the wars, famines, and disease of the colonists meant that their population was sustained and indeed increased (in comparison with the other Iroquoian peoples) during the eighteenth century, and their traditions were thus perhaps more easily preserved.

This traditional Seneca story reveals Seneca antipathy toward the Europeans and their Christian practices. It was told by Handsome Lake, a chief in the Iroquois League and a half brother to Cornplanter, the great Senecan leader caught up in the troubles caused by the colonists' Revolution against England. After the American Revolution, the Iroquois were not even named in the Treaty of Paris that resolved the land disputes among the European colonists in the area. Their land was, in effect, forfeited, despite the Iroquoian support for the British in several major battles and despite their losses at the hands of colonial militias as a result of their thus mixed alliances. Handsome Lake became the center of a strong movement to sustain Iroquois culture, after the time of the American Revolution. Handsome Lake said he had a vision in the spring of 1799. Three messengers of the great creator, he said, came to him in traditional Iroquoian dress and told him that the Peoples' ways must change back to the old ways, so that the People could be purified. Alcohol drinking was corrupting them, he was told, and the People needed to return to their seasonal festivals. The result of the vision was Handsome Lake's so-called Longhouse Religion, a revitalization movement that successfully restored Iroquois confidence in the face of increasing pressure by outsiders to interrupt their way of life. Handsome Lake's relation, printed next, was recorded by Arthur C. Parker, a Seneca of distinction who attempted to negotiate the difficult terrain between the Indian and white worlds at the time of the Civil War and later.

HOW AMERICA
WAS DISCOVERED[1]

According to Chief Cornplanter, Handsome Lake taught that America was discovered in the manner here related.

A great queen had among her servants a young minister. Upon a certain occasion she requested him to dust some books that she had hidden in an old chest. Now when the young man reached the bottom of the chest he found a wonderful book which he opened and read. It told that the white men had killed the son of the Creator and it said, moreover, that he had promised to return in three days and then again forty but that he never did. All his followers then began to despair but some said, "He surely will come again some time." When the young preacher

---

1. The text is from Arthur C. Parker, *Seneca Myths and Folktales,* ed. W. H. Fenton (1923).

read this book he was worried because he had discovered that he had been deceived and that his Lord was not on earth and had not returned when he promised. So he went to some of the chief preachers and asked them about the matter and they answered that he had better seek the Lord himself and find if he were not on the earth now. So he prepared to find the Lord and the next day when he looked out into the river he saw a beautiful island and marveled that he had never noticed it before. As he continued to look he saw a castle built of gold in the midst of the island and he marveled that he had not seen the castle before. Then he thought that so beautiful a palace on so beautiful an isle must surely be the abode of the son of the Creator. Immediately he went to the wise men and told them what he had seen and they wondered greatly and answered that it must indeed be the house of the Lord. So together they went to the river and when they came to it they found that it was spanned by a bridge of gold. Then one of the preachers fell down and prayed a long time and arising to cross the bridge turned back because he was afraid to meet his Lord. Then the other crossed the bridge and knelt down upon the grass and prayed but he became afraid to go near the house. So the young man went boldly over to attend to the business at hand and walking up to the door knocked. A handsome man welcomed him into a room and bade him be of ease. "I wanted you," he said. "You are bright young man; those old fools will not suit me for they would be afraid to listen to me. Listen to me, young man, and you will be rich. Across the ocean there is a great country of which you have never heard. The people there are virtuous, they have no evil habits or appetites but are honest and single-minded. A great reward is yours if you enter into my plans and carry them out. Here are five things. Carry them over to the people across the ocean and never shall you want for wealth, position or power. Take these cards, this money, this fiddle, this whiskey and this blood corruption and give them all to the people across the water. The cards will make them gamble away their goods and idle away their time, the money will make them dishonest and covetous, the fiddle will make them dance with women and their lower natures will command them, the whiskey will excite their minds to evil doing and turn their minds, and the blood corruption will eat their strength and rot their bones."

The young man thought this a good bargain and promised to do as the man had commanded him. He left the palace and when he had stepped over the bridge it was gone, likewise the golden palace and also the island. Now he wondered if he had seen the Lord but he did not tell the great ministers of his bargain because they might try to forstall him. So he looked about and at length found Columbus to whom he told the whole story. So Columbus fitted out some boats and sailed out into the ocean to find the land on the other side. When he had sailed for many days on the water the sailors said that unless Columbus turned about and went home they would behead him but he asked for another day and on that day land was seen and that land was America. Then they turned around and going back reported what they had discovered. Soon a great flock of ships came over the ocean and white men came swarming into the country bringing with them cards, money, fiddles, whiskey and blood corruption.

Now the man who had appeared in the gold palace was the devil and when afterward he saw what his words had done he said that he had made a great mistake and even he lamented that his evil had been so enormous.

LENAPE AND MAHICAN

The Mahicans and the Lenapes, Algonquian peoples, lived along the coast of present-day New Jersey and up into the Hudson River valley when the Dutch first arrived in 1609. The Lenapes, whose name in their own language means "The People," were given the name Delaware under the later colonial occupation of British Governor Lord de la Warr. Both Lenapes and Mahicans followed conciliatory methods with the European newcomers and engaged in treaty making in an effort to reach a peaceful solution to the stresses the people faced over the takeover of their lands. They continued to move northward and westward as new treaties and new relations with other Indian groups made such moves feasible.

The following account was recorded by John Heckewelder (1743–1823), a missionary of the Moravian faith, who traveled with David Zeisberger after 1768 to establish a mission among the Monsey Indians on the Allegheny River. Together, the missionaries worked to convert native peoples to the faith of the Moravians, a sectarian Protestant group. Heckewelder recorded the story "verbatim," he said, "as it was related to me by aged and respected" Lenapes and Mahicans in the 1760s.

ARRIVAL OF THE DUTCH[1]

A long time ago, when there was no such thing known to the Indians as people with a *white skin,* (their expression,) some Indians who had been out a-fishing, and where the sea widens, espied at a great distance something remarkably large swimming, or floating on the water, and such as they had never seen before. They immediately returning to the shore apprised their countrymen of what they had seen, and pressed them to go out with them and discover what it might be. These together hurried out, and saw to their great surprise the phenomenon, but could not agree what it might be; some concluding it either to be an uncommon large fish, or other animal, while others were of opinion it must be some very large house. It was at length agreed among those who were spectators, that as this phenomenon moved towards the land, whether or not it was an animal, or anything that had life in it, it would be well to inform all the Indians on the inhabited islands of what they had seen, and put them on their guard. Accordingly, they sent runners and watermen off to carry the news to their scattered chiefs, that these might send off in every direction for the warriors to come in. These arriving in numbers, and themselves viewing the strange appearance, and that it was actually moving towards them, (the entrance of the river or bay,) concluded it to be a large canoe or house, in which the great Mannitto (great or Supreme Being) *himself* was, and that he probably was coming to visit them. By this time the chiefs of the different tribes were assembled on York Island, and were counselling (or deliberating) on the manner they should receive their Mannitto on his arrival. Every step had been taken to be well provided with a plenty of meat for a sacrifice; the women were required to prepare the best of victuals; idols or images were examined and put in order; and a grand dance was supposed not only to be an agreeable entertainment for the Mannitto, but might, with the addition of a sacrifice, contribute towards appeasing him, in case he was angry with them. The conjurors were also set to work, to determine what the meaning of this phenomenon was, and what the result would be. Both to these, and to the chiefs and wise men of the nation, men, women, and children were looking up for advice and protection. Between hope and fear, and in confusion, a dance commenced. While in this situation fresh runners arrive declaring it a house of various colours, and crowded with living creatures. It now appears to be certain that it is the great Mannitto bringing them some kind of game, such as they had not before; but other runners soon after arriving, declare it a large house of various colours, full of people, yet of quite a different colour than they (the Indians) are of; that they were also dressed in a different manner from them, and that one in particular appeared altogether red, which must be the *Mannitto* himself. They are soon hailed from the vessel, though in a language they do not understand; yet they shout (or yell) in their way. Many are for running off to the woods, but are pressed by others to stay, in order not to give offence to their visiters, who could find them out, and might destroy them. The house (or large canoe, as some will have it,) stops, and a smaller canoe comes ashore with the red man and some others in it; some stay by this canoe to guard it. The chiefs and wise men (or councillors) had composed a large circle, unto which the red-clothed man with two others approach. He salutes them with friendly countenance, and they return the salute after their manner. They are lost in admiration, both as to the colour of the skin (or these whites) as also to their manner of dress, yet most as to the habit of him who wore the red clothes, which shone with something they could not account for. He *must* be the great Mannitto (Supreme Being,) they think, but why should he have a *white skin?* A large hockhack [Their word for gourd, bottle, decanter] is brought forward by one of the (supposed) Mannitto's servants, and from this a substance is poured out into a small cup (or glass) and handed to the Mannitto. The (expected) Mannitto drinks; has the glass filled again, and hands it to the chief next to him to drink. The chief receives the glass, but only smelleth at it, and passes it on to the next chief, who does the same. The glass thus passes through the circle without the contents being tasted by any one; and is upon the point of being returned again to the red-clothed man, when one of their number, a spirited man and great warrior jumps up—harangues the assembly on the impropriety of returning the glass with the contents in it; that the same was handed them by the Mannitto in order that they should drink it, as he himself had done before them; that this would please him; but to return what he had given to them might provoke him, and be the cause of their being destroyed by him. And that, since he believed it for the good of the nation that the contents offered them *should* be drank, and as no one was willing to

---

1. The text is from Heckewelder's account, as reprinted in the *Collections of the New York Historical Society,* 2d ser., vol. I (1841).

drink it *he would,* let the consequence be what it would; and that it was better for one man to die, than a whole nation to be destroyed. He then took the glass and bidding the assembly a farewell, *drank it off.* Every eye was fixed on their resolute companion to see what an effect this would have upon him, and he soon beginning to stagger about, and at last dropping to the ground, they bemoan him. He falls into a sleep, and they view him as expiring. He awakes again, jumps up, and declares that he never felt himself before so happy as after he had drank the cup. Wishes for more. His wish is granted; and the whole assembly soon join him, and become intoxicated. [The Delawares call this place (New-York Island) *Mannahattanink* or *Mannahachtanink* to this day. They have frequently told me that it derived its name from this general *intoxication,* and that the word comprehended the same as to say, *the island or place of general intoxication.* The Mahicanni, (otherwise called Mohiggans by the English, and Mahicanders by the Low Dutch,) call this place by the same name as the Delawares do; yet think it is owing or given in consequence of a kind of wood which grew there, and of which the Indians used to make their bows and arrows. This wood the latter (Mohiccani) call "*gawaak.*" The universal name the Monseys have for New-York, is *Laa-phawachking,* which is interpreted, *the place of stringing beads (wampum).* They say this name was given in consequence of beads being here distributed among them by the Europeans; and that after the European vessel had returned, wherever one looked, one would see the Indians employed in stringing the beads or wampum the whites had given them.]

After this general intoxication had ceased, (during which time the whites had confined themselves to their vessel,) the man with the red clothes returned again to them, and distributed presents among them, to wit, beads, axes, hoes, stockings, &c. They say that they had become familiar to each other, and were made to understand by signs; that they now would return home, but would visit them next year again, when they would bring them more presents, and stay with them awhile; but that, as they could not live without eating, they should then want a little land of them to sow some seeds in order to raise herbs to put in their broth. That the vessel arrived the season following, and they were much rejoiced at seeing each other; but that the whites laughed at them (the Indians,) seeing they knew not the use of the axes, hoes, &c., they had given them, they having had these hanging to their breasts as ornaments; and the stockings they had made use of as tobacco pouches. The whites now put handles (or helves) in the former, and cut trees down before their eyes, and dug the ground, and showed them the use of the stockings. Here (say they) a general laughter ensued among them (the Indians), that they had remained for so long a time ignorant of the use of so valuable implements; and had borne with the weight of such heavy metal hanging to their necks for such a length of time. They took every white man they saw for a Mannitto, yet inferior and attendant to the *supreme Mannitto,* to wit, to the one which wore the red and laced clothes. Familiarity daily increasing between them and the whites, the latter now proposed to stay with them, asking them only for so much land as the hide of a bullock would cover (or encompass,) which hide was brought forward and spread on the ground before them. That they readily granted this request; whereupon the whites took a knife, and beginning at one place on this hide, cut it up into a rope not thicker than the finger of a little child, so that by the time this hide was cut up there was a great heap. That this rope was drawn out to a great distance, and then brought round again, so that both ends might meet. That they carefully avoided its breaking, and that upon the whole it encompassed a large piece of ground. That they (the Indians) were surprised at the superior wit of the whites, but did not wish to contend with them about a little land, as they had enough. That they and the whites lived for a long time contentedly together, although these asked from time to time more land of them; and proceeding higher up the Mahicanittuk (Hudson river), they believed they would soon want all their country, and which at this time was already the case.

FLATHEAD

The Flathead Indians of the northwestern part of the present-day United States are a Salishan people who first saw the expedition party of Lewis and Clark in 1805. At the time they met with the Lewis and Clark party, they were not used to seeing white people, although they were aware that six days' travel eastward or northward would take them to areas where they might trade with these people. Given that contact between the Flatheads and whites was relatively recent, this story integrating the two races must be of recent origin, though it is now a traditional story among the people, according to Ella E. Clark, who recorded the narrative in the mid-twentieth century.

CREATION OF THE RED AND WHITE RACES[1]

Long, long ago when the world was young, Old Man in the Sky drained off the earth which he had made. When he had it crowded down into the big salt holes, the land became dry. About the same time, Old Man Coyote[2] became lonely and so went up into the Sky Land to talk to Old Man. Old Man questioned him.

"Why are you unhappy and crying? Have I not made much land for you to run about on? Are not Beaver, Otter, Bear, and Buffalo on the land to keep you company? Why do you not like Mountain Sheep? Did I not place him up in the hills, so that you need not fight? Why do you come up here so often, just to talk?"

Old Coyote sat down and cried many more tears. Old Man became very cross and began to scold. "Foolish old Coyote, you must not drop so much water upon the land. Have I not worked many days to dry it? Soon you will have it all covered with water again. What is the trouble with you? What more do you want to make you happy?"

"I am very lonely because I have no one to talk to," Coyote answered. "Beaver, Otter, Bear, and Buffalo are busy with their families. They do not have time to visit with me. I want a people of my own, so that I may watch over them."

Old Man replied: "If you will stop this shedding of water, and stop annoying me with your visits, I will make you a people. Take this rawhide bag, this parfleche, and carry it to the mountain where there is red earth. Fill it full and bring it back to me. Hurry!"

Old Coyote took the bag and traveled many days and nights. Finally he came to a mountain where there was much red soil. Though weary after his long journey, he managed to fill the parfleche. Then he was sleepy.

"I will lie down to sleep for a while. When I awaken I will run swiftly back to Old Man in the Sky."

Coyote slept so soundly that he did not hear Mountain Sheep come along and look at the red soil in the bag.

"Foolish Coyote has come a long distance to get such a load of red soil," Mountain Sheep said to himself. "I wonder what he wants it for. I will have fun with him."

He dumped the red soil out upon the mountain. Then he filled the lower half of the bag with white earth and put some red soil on the upper half. Laughing to himself, Mountain Sheep ran away to his hiding place.

When Old Coyote awakened, he tied the top of the parfleche and hurried with it to Old Man in the Sky. The sun was going to sleep when he arrived. It was so dark that they could scarcely see the soil in the bag. Old Man in the Sky took the dirt and said, "I will make the soil into the forms of two men and two women."

He did not see that half the soil was red and half white.

"Take them to the dry land below," he said to Coyote when he had finished shaping them. "They are your people, and you can talk with them. So do not come up here to trouble me."

Old Coyote put the new people in the parfleche and carried them to dry land. In the morning when he took them out to put breath into them, he was surprised to find one pair red and the other pair white. Instantly he knew the trick that had been played upon him.

"I see that Mountain Sheep came while I slept," Coyote said."What shall I do now? I know that I can not keep these two colors together."

So he carried the white ones to the land by the big salt hole. The red ones he kept in his own land, so that he could visit with them.

That is how Indians and white men came upon the earth. And that is why Coyote was a friend of the Indians.

---

1. The text is from Ella E. Clark, *Indian Legends from the Northern Rockies* (1966).

2. Salishan narratives configure Old Man Coyote as a figure of good and Mountain Sheep as the figure of evil.

4

BRITAIN'S FIRST CENTURY IN AMERICA

Britain came relatively late to imperial European colonization efforts in the Americas. Spain and Portugal had been in their new worlds since the late fifteenth century and France since the 1530s. Britain was a latecomer, then, but it had been profiting from efforts in other seas: It gained goods—especially dyes and furs—by trade, and it had relatively clear fisheries sailing in coastal areas off the British islands, Greenland, and Newfoundland. Yet it is worthwhile examining the reasons behind Britain's late appearance in the Americas, especially in light of the clear later success, a success so great that "America" would become known by the eighteenth century as that part of North America occupied primarily by English settlements. Numerous social problems within England can be adduced for Britain's late arrival on the colonial American scene, including residual feudal inequities that caused social unrest at home and other major problems, such as factionalism at court, disease, and warfare over territory and religion (particularly in Ireland).

This is not to say that Britain had not sponsored voyages for the empire, of course. Vessels taking off from the western coast of England had long been navigating the Atlantic in search of potential, permanent opportunity for Britons to settle and take greater advantage of the potential for dominating the fishery of the northern seas. Under British sails, the Genoese John Cabot had sailed around Newfoundland (1497), and Sebastian Cabot and Sir Thomas Pert traveled to the West Indies (1510s). The West Indian successes of John Hawkins and Sir Francis Drake in the mid-sixteenth century (1560s–1570s), as they marauded Spanish vessels attempting to return to Europe with goods, added sufficient impetus to English attempts to control the seas around England that Britain set sail against a Spanish fleet in 1588 and succeeded in defeating Spain's much-touted control of the maritime sea-lanes off its coast. Yet most historians agree that it was the accession of Elizabeth I, who reigned from 1558 to 1603, that brought a renewal within England of an imperial concept of nationhood and a special force and a form to Britain's colonial efforts overseas in the Americas.

Conditions within England assisted in spurring the court of Elizabeth I to confirm imperial interest in the Americas. First, as attested by the efforts of Hawkins and Drake and the eventual overtaking of Spanish ships in traditional English sea-lanes, Britain had significant concern about the trading successes of Spain and Portugal in Europe's "new world." Portugal and Spain, spending so much effort traversing the Atlantic for gains from their American colonies, spent less time sailing their traditional routes in the Mediterranean. From Britain's vantage point, their less frequent sailing in the Mediterranean would cause Britain difficulty in obtaining, through trade with their vessels, dyes and oils for England's renowned textile production. The ability to get dyes quickly and cheaply was a central factor in England's stable trade within Europe of a key English product, textiles. As a result of obtaining its own dyes and gaining access to wool from animals like llamas in the Indies and the sheep exported there, Spain was supplanting Britain in textile manufacture. Britain's domestic fiscal and social sustenance was at stake, then, with the shifting endeavors of the European groups away from the Mediterranean and across the Atlantic.

Britain's imperial efforts in the Americas were brought about by additional conditions related to trade, as well. Spain and Portugal were gaining significant raw wealth not only in minerals, but also in other imports—especially foodstuffs, such as potatoes, tomatoes, squash, and sugar—back to Europe. Under Elizabeth I, Britain discovered a need for such goods, thereby discovering a need to compete for the colonial trade. Elizabeth I strongly supported the 1590s efforts of Sir Walter Raleigh to mount expeditions to Guiana, a region within Spanish territory in the northern part of South America, even after Raleigh failed more than once to make a successful voyage. England wanted a part of the raw worth available to Portugal and Spain, and it originally sought to compete in exactly the territories held by these growing empires.

Yet another reason for Britain's concern about the strength of Portugal and Spain in the Americas was their spreading Catholicism there. Even if the propaganda was only partly correct, it seemed that Native Americans were welcoming a range of Catholic missionaries and were serving the Catholic Church, its pope, and its kings and queens. Britain had only relatively recently but successfully broken from the Roman Catholic Church under Henry VIII (Elizabeth I's father), and the spread of Catholicism to regions unknown but productive of wealth threatened to the very core the roots of Protestantism in England and the cultural norms still in the process of being tested and established. Concerned about old French alliances with Scotland and Ireland, as well about Catholicism specifically in Ireland, Elizabeth I could not tolerate the further spread of a religious practice that was, in effect, antithetical to the grounding of her own leadership—in Henry VIII's Act of Supremacy—as monarch of Britain. Britain jealously watched France as religious wars there between Catholics and Protestants for three decades (1560s–90s) brought turmoil and devastation to the population, thus bringing instability to the French crown and nation. But even the Edict of Nantes (1598), issued by Henry IV of France, putting Huguenots (French Protestants) on an equal political footing with Catholics, could not resolve the tensions among the French people. England had significant concern about retaining its Protestant status and thus the monarchy according to England's Act of Supremacy. These concerns only increased when Louis XIV gained the throne and, in 1685, revoked the Edict of Nantes.

Other conditions, however, also influenced Britain's entrance into colony building. Like France at about this time, England was troubled with overpopulation and vagrancy. A series of enclosure acts that permitted landowners to enclose their estates with fences brought about a crisis in the standard of living for many people—country people, beggars, vagrants who walked across the land seeking labor, indigents, and non-British nationals seeking to enter the labor market in England. For centuries, Britain and Europe had been populated by migrants who traveled daily or seasonally, looking for places to set up camp and look for work. The shift away from a feudal economy to a more open trade- and market-based economy ironically closed down domestic spaces for thousands of laborers who were used to traversing Britain and Europe for work and sustenance. Vagrants were workers seeking jobs, but they often traveled with their children and, as the years went on, lived in more squalid circumstances than ever before, thus having the potential for spreading disease. A growth in population in the sixteenth century compounded the problems people faced. Pamphleteers enlarged upon the difficulties of having nonlanded people, vagabonds, and vagrants—all masterless men and many, many children—around, and public concern about migrant peoples heightened as never before. Following the lead of earlier monarchs, Elizabeth I implemented several harsh laws against vagrants, laws that emerged, it is interesting to note, at precisely the time that the first calls for developing English plantations in the Americas were heard. Indeed, the first writings on the desirability of English plantations in the Americas—the elder Richard Hakluyt's "Inducements to the Liking of a Voyage Intended towards Virginia" (1585), the younger Richard Hakluyt's "Discourse of Western Planting" (1584), Thomas Harriot's "Brief and True Report of the New Found Land of Virginia" (1590), and Sir Walter Raleigh's "Of the Voyage to Guiana" (a manuscript circulated in 1596)—all included the "venting" (the removal) of skilled and unskilled laborers and of excess goods to the colonies as among the key reasons for developing plantations.

As Spain, Portugal, and France had done, Britain developed its own rhetoric of colonization. In Britain's case, colonialist impulses and language mimicked the work of European groups but was built upon Britain's own colonizing efforts, some more successful and some less so, in Wales, Scotland, and Ireland. England's move into Wales and Scotland met with some resistance, but in the main, England's relations with the Welsh and Scottish were much less troubled than those with Ireland. Over centuries, English people had made efforts to settle in Ireland. Some of the oldest ventures resulted in the Anglo-Norman settlers—the Old English, as they were called—adopting the ways of life of the ancestral Irish people. Newer ventures brought to Ireland a less adaptive population and a more willful and self-interested set of English planters. One of the fears of colonizing Ireland, a fear based on the past experiences of the Anglo-Norman settlers, was that one might lose one's "Englishness" and become Irish. Propaganda about colonization made clear that such assimilation was unacceptable. In the words of Sir William Herbert, an Irish landowner and administrator, "Colonies degenerate assuredly when the colonists imitate and embrace the habits, customs, and practices of the natives." Herbert's response to this assimilation "problem," which he labeled an "evil," was "to do away with and destroy completely the habits and practices of the natives" (from *Croftus Sive de Hibernia Liber,* written in the 1590s). The fear of "degeneration," or the falling away from English cultural norms, was a significant factor marking the discourse of English colonialism, based on what was a negative experience, from England's vantage point, of early English settlements in Ireland. Anxiety about degeneration is a distinguishing characteristic of English writings on colonial planting in the Americas.

In other areas, however, British writings on colonization fell into many of the same patterns already established by writings that came from others' colonial projects. The common tropes of savagism versus civility, barbarism versus humanity, appear in writings by English speakers. English writers, like others, also wrote about Native peoples in ways that described their looks, lifeways, and belief systems (typically an absence of belief because it was not Christianity), and they sometimes attempted, like their European counterparts, to place American Indians historically among the ten lost tribes of Israel. Also, almost from the start, English writings evidenced tensions regarding colonialist outcomes similar to writings from other colonies: Some writings were highly promotional, and some were entirely antipromotional; some supported colonial endeavors strongly, and some propagandized against such endeavors, saying that life was better back in old England. Finally, like their European counterparts, English writers attempted to create justifications for the taking of Indian lands, and these justifications tended to cluster around legal concepts known and used by neighbors in Europe. In English writings, as in writing by Europeans, claims to land rights by way of "discovery," by agreement with or cession by Indians, or, less frequently, by conquest mark the writers' goals of creating an indissoluble right to dominion. It was precisely this aspect, dominion, that troubled many writers (including Roger Williams) in the English colonies, for the literature of others' colonization had made them well aware of the outcomes for Native peoples when faced with unending aggression by Europeans in their own ancestral territories.

Britain's late start meant that the literature from English and European writers about colonial holdings was readily available to English readers long before they considered embarking on their own voyages. Of the literature about colonizing Ireland, Sir Thomas Herbert's *Croftus Sive de Hibernia Liber* would have been well known in aristocratic circles. Herbert located Irish colonization in the context of contemporary writers, such as Niccolò Machiavelli (*The Prince*), and classical writers, such as Tacitus, Livy, Thucydides, Sallust, and Plato, arguing for the necessity of colonizing lands so that indigenous inhabitants would benefit from the colonizers' "better" culture. English readers would also have been familiar with arguments justifying colonization by Sir Thomas More in his famous book, *The Best State of a Commonwealth and the New Island of Utopia,* published first in 1516. More centered his arguments in behalf of the Utopians (colonizers) squarely in the legal language of the day, indicating that because the Utopians had a "better" culture and knew best how to use lands wisely, they had a just claim to others' unoccupied and uncultivated land, and, if resistance by the indigenous population occurred, the Utopians could with justice wage war. Perhaps the most influential accounts written and published by English writers, however, were those by Richard Hakluyt the elder and Richard Hakluyt the younger, cousins, who created their own arguments for English "planting," recorded travel accounts from seafarers as they returned to Britain, and published translations of accounts by others in their circulated manuscripts and later in their books. Hakluyt the younger, in *Divers Voyages Touching the Discovery of America and the Islands*

Adjacent (London, 1582) and later in *Principall Navigations, Voyages, and Traffics of the English Nation* (London, 1589), was a central figure in Britain's promotional efforts, with writings countenanced—indeed encouraged and supported by—the court of Elizabeth I.

One of the influential accounts excerpted and published by Hakluyt the younger (in Latin) in 1587 was an account made by Peter Martyr d'Anghiera, who recorded voyagers' reports for the Spanish Crown. As early as 1516, Martyr published some of these voyage records, later collected in his book, *De Orbe Novo* (1530), which was soon translated into other languages, English among them. Selections of Martyr's *De Orbe Novo* reached print in English as early as 1577, and the book was fully printed in English in 1612. Martyr configured Native people as innocent but needing the guidance of colonizers from Europe. Featured in Martyr's work were lists of the resources found in the Americas, so his writings served as a significant impetus to colonization efforts of European and English groups. Of the West Indian peoples he wrote, "The inhabitants of these Ilands have been ever so used to live at liberty, in play and pastime, that they can hardly away with the yoke of servitude, which they attempt to shake off by all means they may. And surely if they had received our religion, I would think their life most happy of all men, if they might therewith enjoy their ancient liberty." Martyr's is an interesting argument in behalf of the colonization and religious instruction of indigenous peoples—but with freedom for them as well.

Yet this was not a common feature in most colonial Spanish writings (and indeed not always in Martyr's own writings). By the time the British set sail for Virginia, stories about atrocities against the Indians at the hands of the Spanish conquerors were well known in England—so well known that they had come to be called the "Black Legend" of Spain. A little book called *The Spanish Colony,* published in England in 1583, was based on Bartolomé de las Casas's *Brevísima Relación* (1552), the *Short Account of the Destruction of the Indies.* The impact of Las Casas upon the English was powerful, for in his report about the destruction of the Indian peoples, he underscored the slavery and killings of Indians, but also the proselytizing taking place in the name of the Roman Catholic Church. English readers imagined they would do a better job with colonization and with Indian peoples, and they feared the spread of the Catholicism that Las Casas spoke about. The Puritans who came to New England considered Las Casas's report a prime impetus for their efforts to bring the Protestant religion, specifically their Puritan faith practices, to North America in behalf of England.

By the time that English colonization took place—beginning with the failed attempt in 1584 (reported by Arthur Barlowe) at Roanoke Island, off the coast of present-day North Carolina—three goals of colonization were established for British colonials. In the words of Richard Hakluyt the elder, these goals were "1. To plant Christian religion; 2. To trafficke [i.e., to establish trade]; 3. To conquer." The English would bring their "better" civilization to the indigenous peoples, engage in trade with them, and build colonies among them so that the indigenous population would benefit from English culture. The goals of the English were not new among colonizers, of course. Yet English colonization and settlement efforts received significant impetus, first, from observations of the activities of those who had gone before to gain wealth for their nations and establish the Catholic faith among Indian peoples and, second, from the increasing movements of British laborers who migrated so as to avoid the penury resulting from overpopulation.

The English voyages across the Atlantic to the southern areas of North America, from the Caribbean through the Floridas and up into Virginia, like those to the northern area eventually dubbed "New England" by Captain John Smith, brought both adventurers, those seeking wealthy returns on labor and investments, and pious people of different Protestant faiths—Anglican, Separatist, and Puritan. Their collective goals were to preserve Protestant ways, to trade with Indian peoples, and to live among them, not necessarily conquering them, it turned out, but supplanting Indian culture in the establishment of their own. Their efforts would be for the English nation, and they would be distinctly opposed to the efforts by Spain in the southern areas and France in the north to establish territories, New Spain and New France, that would be Catholic and would compete with English interests in the natural productions and mineral wealth of North America.

The English settlers adopted the Europeans' original goals of colonization and the rhetoric of colonization, as well. But after only a decade of settlement, British settlers determined that their colonization would have a significant difference from that of their European neighbors. Britain's ultimate goal was firmly to plant colonies, as they phrased it, in North America, rather than merely to exhaust the land and lives of the peoples they were taking over. This key difference marks the first century of English writings, whether one reads the writings emanating from the Virginia colony or those from the later settlements to the north, Plymouth in 1620 and Massachusetts Bay in 1630. Convinced that theirs was a better culture, English people would work as they could to bring permanent change to Indian peoples, and they would work, too, to offset the changes already being wrought for Indians at the hands of Spanish and especially French settlers, in the case of New England. Adventurers and Anglicans sailed for Virginia on the basis of a charter granted to a company of adventurers (stockholders in a joint-stock company) called the Virginia Company in 1607. Adventurers and Separatists set sail, patented as the Plymouth Company, in 1620. They were followed by Puritans who sailed for Massachusetts Bay in 1630.

Some cultural historians argue that the clear distinction between English efforts and efforts by Spain, France, and the Netherlands (to a lesser extent) occurred because of the effects of the Protestant Reformation on English culture. When Henry VIII broke from the Catholic Church and declared himself, with the assistance of Parliament, supreme monarch, leader of both the church and the state of England, his actions paved the way for a liberation of what came to be understood as individual conscience from collective theological practice. The Anglican Church, established as England's Church, fostered similar rituals as the Catholic Church, but emptied the faith practice of any necessary allegiance to Catholic norms, especially to a pope whose interests were not centered in the English nation alone. The English Church would supplant the Roman Catholic one. During the sixteenth-century Protestant Reformation, English speakers came to know the work of Martin Luther, a German monk, and Jean Calvin, a Frenchman who fled to Geneva, Switzerland, and a growing number of them considered that the Anglican Church still retained too much of the ritual and theology of Catholicism. These nonconforming people dissented from the Anglican practice and formed clusters of followers of their own.

Some dissenters remained in England and attempted to practice their faith there, while others moved to Holland, which needed laborers and encouraged English people to settle there to practice their faith without interference from the Dutch or English authorities. But after a generation, these English people, known as Separatists, recognized that their children were no longer "English," and several groups decided it was worth the risk to sail with a company of adventurers to North America and establish themselves anew. They were followed within a decade by a group of people, several from England's aristocracy, who, though they were dissenters from Anglicanism, had remained in England in an attempt to "purify" the Anglican Church from within. Called Puritans by their detractors, this group benefited significantly from the assistance provided by the Plymouth settlers and became the envy of many people who marveled at their successes in light of so many failures that had gone before.

One who envied the successes of the New Englanders was Captain John Smith, who wanted the Virginia colony to succeed as Britain's prime colony in North America. In writing his *Description of New England,* Smith created an appeal that, for many generations of readers, has been credited as one of the first expressions of the English colonists' "American dream." "Who can desire more content," Smith wrote, "that hath small means, or but only his merit to advance his fortune, than to tread and plant that ground he hath purchased by the hazard of his life?" He continued,

> What so truly suits with honor and honesty as the discovering of things unknown? erecting towns, peopling countries, informing the ignorant, reforming things unjust, teaching virtue, and gain to our Native mother-country a kingdom to attend her, find employment for those that are idle, because they know not what to do— so far from the wronging any, as to cause posterity to remember thee, and remembering thee, even honor that remembrance with praise?

Smith was taking up, in this series of rhetorical questions, a discourse of colonialism, common among English-speaking writers, that held colony building to be the highest and most heroic achievement a person could offer the nation and the future. Such a rhetoric became a foundational rhetoric of the new American republic at the time when the British American colonies broke from England, and it still has—despite its obvious imperialist tenor—a strong appeal to many readers in the United States, but especially abroad.

To the Virginian Voyage
(Michael Drayton, 1563–1631)

You brave Heroique Minds,
Worthy your Countries Name,
   That Honour still pursue,
   Goe, and subdue,
Whilst loyt'ring Hinds
Lurke here at home, with shame.

Britans, you stay too long,
Quickly aboord bestow you,
   And with a merry Gale
   Swell your stretch'd Sayle,
With Vowes as strong,
As the Winds that blow you.

Your Course securely steere,
West and by South forth keepe,
   Rocks, Lee-shores, nor Sholes,
   When Eolus scowles,
You need not feare,
So absolute the Deepe.

And cheerefully at Sea,
Successe you still intice,
   To get the Pearle and Gold,
   And ours to hold,
Virginia,
Earth's onely Paradise.

Where Nature hath in store
Fowle, Venison, and Fish,
   And the fruitfull'st Soyle,
   Without your Toyle,
Three Harvests more,
All greater then your Wish.

And the ambitious Vine
Crownes with his purple Masse,
   The Cedar reaching hie
   To kisse the Sky,
The Cypresse, Pine
And use-full Sassafras.

To whose, the golden Age
Still Natures lawes doth give,
   No other Cares that tend,
   But Them to defend
From Winters age,
That long there doth not live.

When as the Lushious smell
Of that delicious Land,
   Above the Seas that flowes,
   The cleere Wind throwes,
Your Hearts to swell
Approching the deare Strand.

In kenning of the Shore
(Thanks to God first given,)
   O you the happy'st men,
   Be Frolike then,
Let Cannons roare,
Frighting the wide Heaven.

And in Regions farre
Such Heroes bring yee fooorth,
   As those from whom We came,
   And plant Our name,
Under that Starre
Not knowne unto our North.

And as there Plenty growes
Of Lawrell every where,
   Apollo's Sacred tree,
   You it may see,
A Poets Browes
To crowne, that may sing there.

Thy Voyages attend,
Industrious Hackluit,
   Whose Reading shall inflame
   Men to seeke Fame,
And much commend
To after-Times thy Wit.

SOUTHERN EXPERIENCES

ARTHUR BARLOWE (FLOURISHED 1584–1585)

What we know about Arthur Barlowe derives from his account of his voyage in 1584 to the region surrounding present-day Roanoke Island off the coast of North Carolina. Soon after Sir Walter Raleigh received a patent to colonize, he sent Barlowe and Philip Amadas on a reconnoitering mission to the coast of North America. Barlowe and Amadas were likely joined by the naturalist Thomas Harriot and the artist John White, who would later become well known for his drawings of Native Americans. Barlowe, like his fellow commander Amadas, was probably part of the large household of Raleigh prior to his voyage. Barlowe seems to have had sea experience at the time of the voyage. During the English wars to take over Ireland, 1580–81, Barlowe served in one of the companies under Raleigh's command. Prior to his North American voyage, he also traveled to the eastern Mediterranean.

Barlowe's account of the first voyage was written for Raleigh, sponsor of the voyage, probably around 1585. It is possible that Raleigh himself or Thomas Harriot played a role in revising the text. In any event, the glowing descriptions of the people and the land suggest that Barlowe was well aware of the role that accounts like his might play in furthering colonization. By adapting long-standing images of the Americas as paradise, Barlowe created memorable and appealing propaganda supporting future voyages to the Americas.

from THE FIRST VOYAGE MADE TO THE COASTS OF AMERICA[1]

The 27 day of Aprill, in the yeere of our redemption 1584, we departed the West of England,[2] with two barkes[3] well furnished with men and victuals, having received our last and perfect directions by your letters, confirming the former instructions, and commandements delivered by your selfe at our leaving the river of Thames. And I thinke it a matter both unnecessary, for the manifest discoverie of the Countrey, as also for tediousnesse sake, to remember unto you the diurnall of our course, sayling thither and re-

turning:[4] onely I have presumed to present unto you this briefe discourse, by which you may judge how profitable this land is likely to succeede,[5] as well to your selfe, (by whose direction and charge, and by whose servantes this our discoverie hath beene performed) as also to her Highnesse,[6] and the Common wealth, in which we hope your wisedome wilbe satisfied, considering that as much by us hath bene brought to light, as by those smal meanes, and number of men we had, could any way have bene expected, or hoped for.

The tenth of May we arrived at the Canaries, and the tenth of June in this present yeere, we were fallen with the Islands of the West Indies, keeping a more Southeasterly course then was needefull, because wee doubted[7] that the current of the Bay of Mexico, disbogging[8] betweene the Cape of Florida and Havana, had bene of greater force then afterwardes we found it to bee. At which Islands we

---

1. The text is based upon the first version of Barlowe's account, printed in Richard Hakluyt, *The Principall Navigations, Voiages, Traffiques, and Discoveries of the English Nation* (1589). Hakluyt's introduction read: "*The first voyage made to the coasts of America, with two barks, wherein were Captaines M. Philip Amadas, and M. Arthur Barlowe, who discovered part of the Countrey now called Virginia Anno 1584. Written by one of the said Captaines, and sent to sir Walter Ralegh knight, at whose charge and direction, the said voyage was set forth.*"

2. Plymouth was probably the point of departure.

3. Ship.

4. In other words, it was unnecessary to offer Raleigh the daily record of the journey.

5. Prove.

6. Queen Elizabeth I (1533–1603) reigned from 1558 until her death.

7. Suspected.

8. Discharging.

found the ayre[9] very unwholsome, and our men grew for the most part ill disposed: so that having refreshed our selves with sweet water, and fresh victuall, we departed the twelfth day of our arrivall there. These Islands, with the rest adjoyning, are so well knowen to your selfe, and to many others, as I will not trouble you with the remembrance of them.

The second of July, we found shole water, wher we smelt so sweet, and so strong a smel, as if we had bene in the midst of some delicate garden abounding with all kinde of odoriferous flowers, by which we were assured, that the land could not be farre distant: and keeping good watch, and bearing but slacke saile, the fourth of the same moneth we arrived upon the coast, which we supposed to be a continent and firme lande, and we sayled along the same a hundred and twentie English miles before we could finde any entrance, or river issuing into the Sea. The first that appeared unto us, we entred, though not without some difficultie, and cast anker about three harquebuz-shot[10] within the havens mouth, on the left hand of the same: and after thankes given to God for our safe arrivall thither, we manned our boats, and went to view the land next adjoyning, and to take possession of the same, in the right of the Queenes most excellent Majestie, as rightfull Queene, and Princesse of the same, and after delivered the same over to your use, according to her Majesties grant, and letters patents, under her Highnesse great seale.[11] Which being performed, according to the ceremonies used in such enterprises, we viewed the land about us, being, whereas we first landed, very sandie and low towards the waters side, but so full of grapes, as the very beating and surge of the sea overflowed them, of which we found such plentie, as well there as in all places else, both on the sand and on the greene soile on the hils, as in the plaines, as well on every little shrubbe, as also climing towards the tops of high Cedars, that I thinke in all the world the like abundance is not to be found: and my selfe having seene those parts of Europe that most abound, find such difference as were incredible to be written.

We passed from the Sea side towardes the toppes of those hilles next adjoyning, being but of meane higth, and from thence wee behelde the Sea on both sides to the North, and to the South, finding no ende any of both wayes. This lande lay stretching it selfe to the West, which after wee found to bee but an Island of twentie miles long, and not above sixe miles broade.[12] Under the banke or hill whereon we stoode, we behelde the vallyes replenished with goodly Cedar trees, and having discharged our harquebuz-shot, such a flocke of Cranes (the most part white) arose under us, with such a cry redoubled by many ecchoes, as if an armie of men had showted all together.

This Island had many goodly woodes full of Deere, Conies,[13] Hares, and Fowle, even in the middest of Summer in incredible abundance. The woodes are not such as you finde in Bohemia, Moscovia, or Hercynia,[14] barren and fruitles, but the highest and reddest Cedars of the world, farre bettering the Ceders of the Açores, of the Indies, or Lybanus, Pynes, Cypres, Sassaphras, the Lentisk, or the tree that beareth the Masticke, the tree that beareth the rine of blacke Sinamon, of which Master Winter brought from the streights of Magellan,[15] and many other of excellent smell and qualitie. We remained by the side of this Island two whole dayes before we saw any people of the Countrey: the third day we espied one small boate rowing towardes us having in it three persons: this boat came to the Island side, foure harquebuz-shot from our shippes, and there two of the people remaining, the third came along the shoreside towardes us, and wee being then all within boord, he walked up and downe upon the point of the land next unto us: then the Master and the Pilot of the Admirall, Simon Ferdinando,[16] and the Captaine Philip Amadas,[17] my selfe, and others rowed to the land, whose comming this fellow attended, never making any shewe of feare or doubt. And after he had spoken of many things not understood by us, we brought him with his owne good liking, aboord the ships, and gave him a

9. Air.

10. In other words, the distance was triple the distance that could be covered by the shot of a harquebus, a heavy gun.

11. Hakluyt's note in margin: "July 13, possession taken."

12. Hakluyt's note in margin: "Isle of Wokokon."

13. Rabbits.

14. Regions in central Europe known for their forests.

15. John Winter (fl. 1577–79) traveled with Sir Francis Drake (1540–96) on Drake's voyage around the world.

16. Simon Fernandes (1538–90), a native of Portugal, had served under Raleigh during a 1578–79 journey.

17. Philip Amadas (1565–86?), a member of a prominent merchant family, commanded the larger of the two ships bound for Virginia.

shirt, a hat and some other things, and made him taste of our wine, and our meat, which he liked very wel: and after having viewed both barks, he departed, and went to his owne boat againe, which hee had left in a little Cove or Creeke adjoyning: assoone as hee was two bow shoot into the water, he fell to fishing, and in lesse then halfe an houre, he had laden his boate as deepe, as it could swimme, with which hee came againe to the point of the lande, and there he divided his fish into two parts, pointing one part to the ship, and the other to the pinnesse;[18] which, after he had (as much as he might) requited the former benefites received, departed out of our sight.

The next day there came unto us divers[19] boates, and in one of them the Kings brother, accompanied with fortie or fiftie men, very handsome and goodly people, and in their behaviour as mannerly and civill as any of Europe. His name was Granganimeo, and the king is called Wingina,[20] the countrey Wingandacoa and now by her Majestie Virginia.[21] The maner of his comming was in this sort: hee left his boates altogether as the first man did a little from the shippes by the shore, and came along to the place over against the ships, followed with fortie men. When he came to the place his servants spread a long matte upon the ground, on which he sate downe, and at the other ende of the matte foure others of his companie did the like, the rest of his men stood round about him, somewhat a farre off: when we came to the shore to him with our weapons, hee never mooved from his place, nor any of the other foure, nor never mistrusted any harme to be offred from us, but sitting still he beckoned us to come and sit by him, which we performed: and being set hee made all signes of joy and welcome, striking on his head and his breast, and afterwardes on ours, to shew wee were all one, smiling and making shewe the best he could of all love, and familiaritie. After hee had made a long speech unto us, wee presented him with divers things, which hee received very joyfully, and thankefully. None of the companie durst speake one worde all the time: only the foure which were at the other ende, spake one in the others eare very softly.

The King is greatly obeyed, and his brothers and children reverenced: the King himselfe in person was at our being there, sore wounded in a fight which hee had with the King of the next countrey, called Wingina, and was shot in two places through the body, and once cleane through the thigh, but yet he recovered: by reason whereof and for that hee lay at the chiefe towne of the countrey, being six dayes journey off, we saw him not at all.

After we had presented this his brother with such things as we thought he liked, wee likewise gave somewhat to the other that satte with him on the matte: but presently he arose and tooke all from them and put it into his owne basket, making signes and tokens, that all things ought to bee delivered unto him, and the rest were but his servants, and followers. A day or two after this, we fell to trading with them, exchanging some things that we had, for Chamoys,[22] Buffe,[23] and Deere skinnes: when we shewed him all our packet of merchandize, of all things that he sawe, a bright tinne dish most pleased him, which hee presently tooke up and clapt it before his breast, and after made a hole in the brimme thereof and hung it about his necke, making signes that it would defend him against his enemies arrowes: for those people maintaine a deadly and terrible warre, with the people and King adjoyning. We exchanged our tinne dish for twentie skinnes, woorth twentie Crownes, or twentie Nobles:[24] and a copper kettle for fiftie skins woorth fiftie Crownes. They offered us good exchange for our hatchets, and axes, and for knives and would have given any thing for swordes: but wee would not depart with any. After two or three dayes the Kings brother came aboord the shippes, and dranke wine, and eat of our meat and of our bread, and liked exceedingly thereof: and after a fewe days overpassed, he brought his wife with him to the ships, his daughter and two or three children: his wife was very well favoured, of meane stature, and very bashfull: shee had on her backe a long cloake of leather, with the furre side next to her body, and before her a piece of the same: about her forehead shee had a bande of white Corall, and so had her husband many times: in her eares shee had bracelets of pearles hanging downe to her middle, (whereof wee delivered your worship a little bracelet) and those were of the

18. A pinnace is a small ship. Barlowe commanded the pinnace.

19. Several.

20. Wingina was chief of the Roanoke-area group.

21. The land was soon named "Virginia," in honor of the so-called virgin queen, Elizabeth I.

22. Perhaps dressed deerskins.

23. Buffalo skins.

24. English coins.

bignes of good pease. The rest of her women of the better sort had pendants of copper hanging in either eare, and some of the children of the kings brother and other noble men, have five or sixe in either eare: he himselfe had upon his head a broad plate of golde, or copper, for being unpolished we knew not what mettall it should be, neither would he by any meanes suffer us to take it off his head, but feeling it, it would bow very easily. His apparell was as his wives, onely the women weare their haire long on both sides, and the men but on one. They are of colour yellowish, and their hair black for the most part, and yet we saw children that had very fine aburne and chestnut coloured haire.

After that these women had bene there, there came downe from all parts great store of people, bringing with them leather, corall, divers kindes of dies, very excellent, and exchanged with us: but when Granganimeo the kings brother was present, none durst trade but himselfe: except such as weare red pieces of copper on their heads like himselfe: for that is the difference between the noble men, and the governours of countreys, and the meaner sort. And we both noted there, and you have understood since by these men, which we brought home,[25] that no people in the worlde cary more respect to their King, Nobilitie, and Governours, then these doe. The Kings brothers wife, when she came to us (as she did many times) was followed with forty or fifty women alwayes: and when she came into the shippe, she left them all on land, saving her two daughters, her nurse and one or two more. The Kings brother alwayes kept this order, as many boates as he would come withall to the shippes, so many fires would hee make on the shore a farre off, to the end we might understand with what strength and company he approached. Their boates are made of one tree, either of Pine or of Pitch trees: a wood not commenly knowen to our people, nor found growing in England. They have no edge-tooles to make them withall; if they have any they are very fewe, and those it seemes they had twentie yeres since, which, as those two men declared, was out of a wracke which happened upon their coast of some Christian ship, being beaten that way by some storme and outragious weather, whereof none of the people were saved, but only the ship, or some part of her being cast upon the sand, out of whose

sides they drew the nayles and the spikes, and with those they made their best instruments. The manner of making their boates is thus: they burne downe some great tree, or take such as are winde fallen, and putting gumme and rosen upon one side thereof, they set fire into it, and when it hath burnt it hollow, they cut out the coale with their shels, and ever where they would burne it deeper or wider they lay on gummes, which burne away the timber, and by this meanes they fashion very fine boates, and such as will transport twentie men. Their oares are like scoopes, and many times they set with long poles, as the depth serveth.

The Kings brother had great liking of our armour, a sword, and divers other things which we had: and offered to lay a great box of pearl in gage for them:[26] but we refused it for this time, because we would not make them knowe, that we esteemed thereof, untill we had understoode in what places of the countrey the pearle grew: which now your Worshippe doeth very well understand. . . .

Besides they had our ships in marvelous admiration, and all things els were so strange unto them, as it appeared that none of them had ever seene the like. When we discharged any piece, were it but an hargubuz, they would tremble threat for very feare, and for the strangenesse of the same: for the weapons which themselves use are bowes and arrowes: the arrowes are but of small canes, headed with a sharpe shell or tooth of a fish sufficient ynough to kill a naked man. Their swordes be of wood hardened: likewise they use wooden breastplates for their defence. They have besides a kinde of club, in the end whereof they fasten the sharpe hornes of a stagge, or other beast. When they goe to warres they cary about with them their idol, of whom they aske counsel, as the Romans were woont of the Oracle of Apollo.[27] They sing songs as they march towards the battell in stead of drummes and trumpets: their warres are very cruell and bloody, by reason whereof, and of their civill dissentions which have happened of late yeeres amongst them, the people are marvelously wasted, and in some places the countrey left desolate.

Adjoyning to this countrey aforesaid called Secotan beginneth a countrey called Pomooik,[28] belonging to an-

---

25. Barlowe and Amadas brought two Native Americans with them to England: Manteo, a Coatoan, who lived near present-day Cape Hatteras, and Wanchese, a Roanoke and a member of Wingina's group.

26. That is, he promised to exchange his pearls for Barlowe's items.

27. The Roman Emperor Augustus (63 B.C.–A.D. 14) constructed a temple in Rome to Apollo.

28. In the margin Haklyut added "Or Pananuaioc."

other king whom they call Piamacum, and this king is in league with the next king adjoyning towards the setting of the Sunne, and the countrey Newsiok, situate upon a goodly river called Neus: these kings have mortall warre with Wingina king of Wingandacoa: but about two yeeres past there was a peace made betweene the King Piemacum, and the Lord of Secotan, as these men which we have brought with us to England, have given us to understand: but there remaineth a mortall malice in the Secotanes, for many injuries and slaughters done upon them by this Piemacum. They invited divers men, and thirtie women of the best of his countrey to their towne to a feast: and when they were altogether merry, and praying before their Idol, (which is nothing els but a meer illusion[29] of the devill) the captaine or Lord of the town came suddenly upon them, and slewe them every one, reserving the women and children: and these two have oftentimes since perswaded us to surprize Piemacum his towne, having promised and assured us, that there will be found in it great store of commodities. But whether their perswasion be to the ende they may be revenged of their enemies, or for the love they beare to us, we leave that to the tryall hereafter.

Beyond this Island called Roanoak, are maine Islands very plentifull of fruits and other naturall increases, together with many townes, and villages, along the side of the continent, some bounding upon the Islands, and some stretching up further into the land.

When we first had sight of this countrey, some thought the first land we saw to bee the continent; but after we entred into the Haven, we saw before us another mighty long Sea: for there lyeth along the coast a tracte of Islands, two hundreth miles in length, adjoyning to the Ocean sea, and betweene the Islands, two or three entrances: when you are entred betweene them (these Islands being very narrow for the most part, as in most places sixe miles broad, in some places lesse, in fewe more) then there appeareth another great Sea, containing in bredth in some places, forty, and in some fifty, in some twenty miles over, before you come unto the continent: and in this inclosed Sea there are above an hundreth Islands of divers bignesses, whereof one is sixteene miles long, at which we were, finding it a most pleasant and fertile ground, replenished with goodly Cedars, and divers other sweete woods, full of Corrants[30] of flaxe, and many other notable commodities, which we at that time had no leasure to view. Besides this Island there are many, as I have sayd, some of two, or three, of foure, of five miles, some more, some lesse, most beautifull and pleasant to behold, replenished with Deere, Conies, Hares, and divers beasts, and about them the goodliest and best fish in the world, and in greatest abundance. . . .

We brought home also two of the Savages being lustie men, whose names were Wanchese and Manteo.

---

29. Image.

---

30. Small grapes.

JOHN SMITH (1580–1631)

Soldier, adventurer, and leader of early Jamestown, John Smith was born in Lincolnshire, England, the son of a farmer and his wife. After grammar school, Smith was apprenticed to a successful merchant in King's Lynn, Norfolk. When his father died in 1596, Smith inherited the family farm and left his apprenticeship. Instead of working the land, however, he became a volunteer soldier, fighting for the Dutch in their war for independence of the Netherlands from Spain. He went on to serve on a privateer in the Mediterranean, later joining the Austrian army in its war against the Ottoman Empire. His military successes led to his promotion to captain, though in 1602 he found himself wounded and sold into Turkish slavery. According to Smith's published accounts, the only source for much of his early biography, he later murdered his master, escaped, and traveled back to Romania and eventually to England. By the time he became involved in plans for the Virginia colony in 1605, Smith had already traveled through present-day Austria, Poland, France, Germany, Italy, Greece, the Balkans, and North Africa.

In December 1606, Smith and more than one hundred others set sail for Virginia under the sponsorship of the Virginia Company of London. Smith's military background and assertive temperament might have qualified him for his position among the Virginia colonists, yet his personality also seems to have caused significant tension. On the voyage to Virginia, Smith came into conflict with the expedition's leaders and was placed under arrest in February 1607, as the ships passed the Canary Islands, in effect, just as they were getting started on their Atlantic voyage. Yet when the list of the men who would become council members (leaders of the colony) was opened in June, Smith's name was included, and Smith later returned to a central position in the expedition. Once the colonists landed in what became Jamestown, Smith immediately went to work exploring the region.

Political and logistical difficulties overwhelmed the colony from its inception. The Jamestown colony was expected to amass immediate profit for Virginia Company stockholders, and the colonists, assuming their experiences would be like those of the first Europeans in South America, focused on searching for gold, rather than cultivating the crops they would need to survive. Tensions ran high between elite gentlemen and working-class men, supplies were limited, relations with the indigenous populations were troubled, and many colonists fell ill and died. The first president of the council, Edward Wingfield, struggled unsuccessfully to negotiate these challenges, and by 1608 Smith was elected leader of the colony. Although many of Smith's policies—such as "he who does not work shall not eat"—proved unpopular, they also ensured survival. Smith recognized the importance of retaining good trade relations with the Powhatans in the area, and he learned a significant amount of detail about their customs, language, and agricultural methods. His efforts were successful in elevating the colonists' survival rate to more than 90 percent, yet the group failed to produce the profits the stockholders desired. Discouraged by the colony's inability to bring home a wealthy return for their investments, the Virginia Company stockholders in 1609 decided to replace the colony's government and reorganize the settlement. Before Smith was replaced by the new president, however, he was severely injured in a gunpowder explosion and forced to return to England.

Smith's enthusiasm for the colonial enterprise continued unabated, and when he was back in England, he publicized materials about colonization and prepared himself for a return trip to the Americas. In 1614 he explored the coast of the region he later named New England. The information he gathered on this trip served as the basis for his later writings and for his plans for a colony in that northern location. Although the Plymouth Company made him admiral of New England, his attempts to return to New England proved futile. He devoted much of the rest of his life to writing about his experiences in the Americas and seeking sponsors who would enable him to return there. In writings, such as *A Description of New-England* (1616), Smith sought to recruit colonists, tempting those of "small meanes" with visions of a fertile land awaiting industrious settlers. Up until the time Smith died in 1631, he struggled to receive the recognition he felt he deserved for his colonization efforts.

Smith encouraged colonization, and his writings were intended to strengthen his reputation as a colonial leader. Although Smith's best-known works, such as *The Generall Historie of Virginia, New-England, and the Summer Isles* (1624), drew substantially from earlier writers, Smith consistently reminded readers that his accounts were uniquely reliable because of his firsthand experience as "a real Actor" in the Americas. For many readers today, Smith's best-known adventure in the *Generall Historie* remains his description of his captivity by Powhatan and his so-called rescue by Pocahontas. Questions about historical accuracy aside, Smith's romantic tale of rescue employed one of the existing conceptions about the ease of occupation and colonization. In Smith's narrative, as well as in numerous later accounts of Native American and British American relations, a noble Indian happily yields to the "superior" representative of European civilization. Smith's accounts of Virginia and New England offer episodic and chivalric portraits of a strong, adventuresome leader, who, misunderstood in his own day, rose above adversity to found a new-world community.

from PROCEEDINGS OF THE ENGLISH COLONIE IN VIRGINIA[1]

[Powhatan's Speech to Captain Smith]

Captaine Smith, you may understand that I having seene the death of all my people thrice, and not any one living of these three generations but my selfe; I know the difference of Peace and Warre better than any in my Country. But now I am old and ere long must die, my brethren, namely Opitchapam, Opechancanough, and Kekataugh, my two sisters, and their two daughters, are distinctly each others successors. I wish their experience no lesse then mine, and your love to them no lesse then mine to you. But this bruit from Nandsamund, that you are come to destroy my Country, so much affrighteth all my people as they dare not visit you. What will it availe you to take that by force you may quickly have by love, or to destroy them that provide you food. What can you get by warre, when we can hide our provisions and fly to the woods? whereby you must famish by wronging us your friends. And why are you thus jealous of our loves seeing us un-armed, and both doe, and are willing still to feede you, with that you cannot get but by our labours? Think you I am so simple, not to know it is better to eate good meate, lye well, and sleepe quietly with my women and children, laugh and be merry with you, have copper, hatchets, or what I want being your friend: then be forced to flie from all, to lie cold in the woods, feede upon Acornes, rootes, and such trash, and be so hunted by you, that I can neither rest, eate, nor sleepe; but my tyred men must watch, and if a twig but breake, every one cryeth there commeth Cap-taine Smith: then must I fly I know not whether: and thus with miserable feare, end my miserable life, leaving my pleasures to such youths as you, which through your rash unadvisednesse may quickly as miserably end, for want

of that, you never know where to finde. Let this therefore assure you of our loves, and every yeare our friendly trade shall furnish you with Corne; and now also, if you would come in friendly manner to see us, and not thus with your guns and swords as to invade your foes.

---

from A DESCRIPTION OF NEW ENGLAND[1]

And surely by reason of those sandy cliffes and cliffes of rocks, both which we saw so planted with Gardens and Corne fields, and so well inhabited with a goodly, strong and well proportioned people, besides the greatnesse of the Timber growing on them, the greatnesse of the fish and the moderate temper of the ayre (for of twentie five, not any was sicke, but two that were many yeares dis-eased before they went, notwithstanding our bad lodging and accidentall diet) who can but approove this a most excellent place, both for health and fertility? And of all the foure parts of the world that I have yet seene not in-habited, could I have but meanes to transport a Colonie, I would rather live here then any where: and if it did not maintaine it selfe, were wee but once indifferently well fitted, let us starve.

The maine Staple, from hence to bee extracted for the present to produce the rest, is fish; which however it may seeme a mean and a base commoditie: yet who will but tru-ely take the pains and consider the sequell, I thinke will allow it well worth the labour. It is strange to see what great adventures the hopes of setting forth men of war to rob the industrious innocent, would procure; or such massie promises in grosse: though more are choked then well fedde with such hastie hopes. But who doth not know that the poore Hollanders, chiefly by fishing, at a great charge and labour in all weathers in the open Sea, are made a peo-ple so hardy, and industrious? and by the venting this poore commodity to the Easterlings[2] for as meane, which is Wood, Flax, Pitch, Tarre, Rosin, Cordage, and such like (which they exchange againe, to the French, Spaniards, Portugales, and English, etc. for what they want) are made

---

1. Smith published the "Proceedings" first in 1612, to explain the circumstances of the settlement in Virginia. The Powhatan peoples, as they were called by the British settlers, had been integral to the survival of the colony in 1607, having supplied the newcomers with food and assistance. They became alienated from the colony when aggressive settlers dealt badly with them, and the uneasy friendship between the two groups fell into warlike hostilities by the year 1609. Powhatan's opening statement may refer to three epidemics, for which no records survive, although the reference is unclear.

1. *A Description of New England* was first published in London in 1616. This text, slightly modified, is taken from Philip L. Barbour, ed., *The Complete Works of Captain John Smith* (1986).

2. Eastern or Baltic coast Germans.

so mighty, strong and rich, as no State but Venice, of twice their magnitude, is so well furnished with so many faire Cities, goodly Townes, strong Fortresses, and that aboundance of shipping and all sorts of marchandize, as well of Golde, Silver, Pearles, Diamonds, Pretious stones, Silkes, Velvets, and Cloth of golde; as Fish, Pitch, Wood, or such grosse commodities? What Voyages and Discoveries, East and West, North and South, yea about the world, make they? What an Army by Sea and Land, have they long maintained in despite of one of the greatest Princes of the world? And never could the Spaniard with all his Mynes of golde and Silver, pay his debts, his friends, and army, halfe so truly, as the Hollanders stil have done by this contemptible trade of fish. Divers (I know) may alledge many other assistances: But this is their Myne; and the Sea the source of those silvered streames of all their vertue; which hath made them now the very miracle of industrie, the pattern of perfection for these affaires: and the benefit of fishing is that Primum mobile that turnes all their Spheres to this height of plentie, strength, honour and admiration.

Herring, Cod, and Ling, is that triplicitie that makes their wealth and shippings multiplicities, such as it is, and from which (few would thinke it) they yearly draw at least one million and a halfe of pounds starling; yet it is most certaine (if records be true): and in this faculty they are so naturalized, and of their vents so certainely acquainted, as there is no likelihood they will ever bee paralleld, having 2 or 3000 Busses, Flat bottomes, Sword pinks, Todes,[3] and such like, that breedes them Saylers, Mariners, Souldiers and Marchants, never to be wrought out of that trade, and fit for any other. I will not deny but others may gaine as well as they, that will use it, though not so certainely, nor so much in quantity; for want of experience. And this Herring they take upon the Coast of Scotland and England; their Cod and Ling, upon the Coast of Izeland[4] and in the North Seas.

Hamborough, and the East Countries, for Sturgion and Caviare, gets many thousands of pounds from England, and the Straites:[5] Portugale, the Biskaines,[6] and the Spaniards, make 40 or 50 Saile yearely to Cape-blank,[7] to hooke for Porgos,[8] Mullet, and make Puttargo,[9] and New found Land, doth yearely fraught neere 800 sayle of Ships with a sillie leane skinny Poore-John,[10] and Corfish, which at least yearely amounts to 3 or 400000 pound. If from all those parts such paines is taken for this poore gaines of fish, and by them hath neither meate, drinke, nor clothes, wood, iron, nor steele, pitch, tarre, nets, leades, salt, hookes, nor lines, for shipping, fishing, nor provision, but at the second, third, fourth, or fift hand, drawne from so many severall parts of the world ere they come together to be used in this voyage: If these I say can gaine, and the Saylers live going for shares, lesse then the third part of their labours, and yet spend as much time in going and comming, as in staying there, so short is the season of fishing; why should wee more doubt, then Holland, Portugale, Spaniard, French, or other, but to doe much better then they, where there is victuall to feede us, wood of all sorts, to build Boats, Ships, or Barks; the fish at our doores, pitch, tarre, masts, yards, and most of other necessaries onely for making? And here are no hard Landlords to racke us with high rents, or extorted fines to consume us, no tedious pleas in law to consume us with their many years disputations for Justice: no multitudes to occasion such impediments to good orders, as in popular States. So freely hath God and his Majesty bestowed those blessings on them that will attempt to obtaine them, as here every man may be master and owner of his owne labour and land; or the greatest part in a small time. If hee have nothing but his hands, he may set up this trade; and by industrie quickly grow rich; spending but halfe that time wel, which in England we abuse in idlenes, worse or as ill. Here is ground also as good as any lyeth in the height of forty one, forty two, forty three, etc. which is as temperate and as fruitfull as any other paralell in the world. As for example, on this side the line West of it in the South Sea, is Nova Albion, discovered as is said, by Sir Francis Drake.[11] East from it, is the most temperate part of Portugale, the ancient kingdomes of Galazia, Biskey, Navarre, Arragon, Catalonia, Castilia the olde, and the most moderatest of Castilia the new, and Valentia, which is the greatest part of Spain: which if the Spanish

---

3. Busses were two- or three-masted herring boats; flat-bottoms were a kind of barge; sword-pinks were pinks provided with leeboards; and tode-boats were small fishing vessels.

4. Iceland.

5. The "Straits" of Gibraltar.

6. People of Biscay, in northern Spain.

7. Cape Bianco is on the west coast of Africa.

---

8. A general reference to spiny fishes.

9. Puttargo or "botargo" is a relish made from the roe of mullet or tuna.

10. A name for hake or cod salted and dried for food.

11. Galicia.

Histories bee true, in the Romanes time abounded no lesse with golde and silver Mines, then now the West Indies; the Romanes then using the Spaniards to work in those Mines, as now the Spaniard doth the Indians.

. . . This is onely as God made it, when he created the worlde. Therefore I conclude, if the heart and intralls[12] of those Regions were sought: if their Land were cultured, planted and manured by men of industrie, judgement, and experience; what hope is there, or what neede they doubt, having those advantages of the Sea, but it might equalize any of those famous Kingdomes, in all commodities, pleasures, and conditions? seeing even the very edges doe naturally afford us such plenty, as no ship need returne away empty: and onely use but the season of the Sea, fish will returne an honest gaine, beside all other advantages; her treasures having yet never beene opened, nor her originalls wasted, consumed, nor abused.

And whereas it is said, the Hollanders serve the Easterlings themselves, and other parts that want, with Herring, Ling, and wet Cod; the Easterlings, a great part of Europe, with Sturgion and Caviare; Cape-blanke, Spaine, Portugale, and the Levant, with Mullet, and Puttargo; New found Land, all Europe, with a thin Poore John: yet all is so overlaide with fishers, as the fishing decayeth, and many are constrained to returne with a small fraught. Norway, and Polonia, Pitch, Tar, Masts, and Yardes; Sweathland, and Russia, Iron, and Ropes; France, and Spaine, Canvas, Wine, Steele, Iron, and Oyle; Italy and Greece, Silks, and Fruites. I dare boldly say, because I have seen naturally growing, or breeding in those parts the same materialls that all those are made of, they may as well be had here, or the most part of them, within the distance of 70 leagues for some few ages, as from all those parts; using but the same meanes to have them that they doe, and with all those advantages.

First, the ground is so fertill, that questionless it is capable of producing any Grain, Fruits, or Seeds you will sow or plant, growing in the Regions afore named: But it may be, not every kinde to that perfection of delicacy; or some tender plants may miscarie, because the Summer is not so hot, and the winter is more colde in those parts wee have yet tryed neere the Sea side, then we finde in the same height in Europe or Asia; Yet I made a Garden upon the top of a Rockie Ile in 43. $\frac{1}{2}$, 4 leagues from the Main, in May, that grew so well, as it served us for sallets in June and July. All sorts of cattell may here be bred and fed in

the Iles, or Peninsulaes, securely for nothing. In the Interim till they encrease if need be (observing the seasons) I durst undertake to have corne enough from the Salvages for 300 men, for a few trifles; and if they should bee untoward[13] (as it is most certaine they are) thirty or forty good men will be sufficient to bring them all in subjection, and make this provision; if they understand what they doe: 200 whereof may nine monethes in the yeare be imployed in making marchandable fish, till the rest provide other necessaries, fit to furnish us with other commodities.

In March, Aprill, May, and halfe June, here is Cod in abundance; in May, June, July, and August Mullet and Sturgion; whose roes doe make Caviare and Puttargo. Herring, if any desire them, I have taken many out of the bellies of Cods, some in nets; but the Salvages compare their store in the Sea, to the haires of their heads: and surely there are an incredible abundance upon this Coast. In the end of August, September, October, and November, you have Cod againe, to make Cor fish, or Poore John: and each hundred is as good as two or three hundred in the New-found Land. So that halfe the labour in hooking, splitting, and turning,[14] is saved: and you may have your fish at what Market you will, before they can have any in New-found Land; where their fishing is chiefly but in June and July: whereas it is heere in March, Aprill, May, September, October, and November, as is said. So that by reason of this plantation, the Marchants may have fraught both out and home: which yeelds an advantage worth consideration.

Your Cor-fish you may in like manner transport as you see cause, to serve the Ports in Portugale (as Lisbon, Avera, Porta port, and divers others, or what market you please) before your Ilanders[15] returne: They being tyed to the season in the open Sea; you having a double season, and fishing before your doors, may every night sleep quietly a shore with good cheare and what fires you will, or when you please with your wives and familie: they onely, their ships in the maine Ocean.

The Mullets heere are in that abundance, you may take them with nets, sometimes by hundreds, where at Cape blank they hooke them; yet those but one foot and a halfe

---

12. Entrails.

13. Disinclined, intractable.

14. Fisherman's jargon for the steps to be taken in drying cod for market.

15. Newfoundlanders.

in length; these two, three, or foure, as oft I have measured: much Salmon some have found up the Rivers, as
they have passed: and heer the ayre is so temperate, as all
these at any time may well be preserved.

Now, young boyes and girles Salvages, or any other,
be they never such idlers, may turne, carry, and return
fish, without either shame, or any great paine: hee is very
idle that is past twelve yeares of age and cannot doe so
much: and she is very olde, that cannot spin a thred to
make engines to catch them. . . .

Moos, a beast bigger then a Stagge; deere, red,
and Fallow; Bevers, Wolves, Foxes, both blacke and
other; Aroughconds,[16] Wildcats, Beares, Otters, Martins,
Fitches, Musquassus,[17] and diverse sorts of vermine,
whose names I know not. All these and diverse other good
things do heere, for want of use, still increase, and decrease with little diminution, whereby they growe to that
abundance. You shall scarce finde any Baye, shallow
shore, or Cove of sand, where you may not take many
Clampes, or Lobsters, or both at your pleasure, and in
many places lode your boat if you please; Nor Iles where
you finde not fruits, birds, crabs, and muskles, or all of
them, for taking, at a lowe water. And in the harbors we
frequented, a little boye might take of Cunners, and
Pinacks, and such delicate fish, at the ships sterne, more
then sixe or tenne can eate in a daie; but with a casting-
net, thousands when wee pleased: and scarce any place,
but Cod, Cuske, Holybut, Mackerell, Scate, or such like,
a man may take with a hooke or line what he will. And, in
diverse sandy Baies, a man may draw with a net great
store of Mullets, Bases, and diverse other sorts of such excellent fish, as many as his Net can drawe on shore: no
River where there is not plentie of Sturgion, or Salmon, or
both; all which are to be had in abundance observing but
their seasons. But if a man will goe at Christmasse to
gather Cherries in Kent, he may be deceived; though there
be plentie in Summer: so, heere these plenties have each
their seasons, as I have expressed. We for the most part
had little but bread and vineger: and though the most part
of July when the fishing decaied they wrought all day, laie
abroade in the Iles all night, and lived on what they found,
yet were not sicke: But I would wish none put himself
long to such plunges;[18] except necessitie constraine it: yet

worthy is that person to starve that heere cannot live; if he
have sense, strength and health: for, there is no such
penury of these blessings in any place, but that a hundred
men may, in one houre or two, make their provisions for
a day: and hee that hath experience to mannage well these
affaires, with fortie or thirtie honest industrious men,
might well undertake (if they dwell in these parts) to subject the Salvages, and feed daily two or three hundred
men, with as good corne, fish, and flesh, as the earth hath
of those kindes, and yet make that labor but their pleasure: provided that they have engins,[19] that be proper for
their purposes.

Who can desire more content, that hath small meanes;
or but only his merit to advance his fortune, then to tread,
and plant that ground hee hath purchased by the hazard of
his life? If he have but the taste of virtue, and magnanimitie, what to such a minde can bee more pleasant, then
planting and building a foundation for his Posteritie, gotte
from the rude earth, by Gods blessing and his owne industrie, without prejudice to any? If hee have any graine
of faith or zeale in Religion, what can hee doe lesse hurt-
full to any; or more agreeable to God, then to seeke to
convert those poore Salvages to know Christ, and human-
itie, whose labors with discretion will triple requite thy
charge and paines? What so truely sutes with honour and
honestie, as the discovering things unknowne? erecting
Townes, peopling Countries, informing the ignorant, reforming things unjust, teaching virtue; and gaine to our
Native mother-countrie a kingdom to attend her; finde imployment for those that are idle, because they know not
what to doe: so farre from wronging any, as to cause Posteritie to remember thee; and remembring thee, ever honour that remembrance with praise? Consider: What were
the beginnings and endings of the Monarkies of the
Chaldeans, the Syrians, the Grecians, and Romanes, but
this one rule; What was it they would not doe, for the
good of the commonwealth, or their Mother-citie? For example: Rome, What made her such a Monarchesse, but
onely the adventures of her youth, not in riots at home;
but in dangers abroad? and the justice and judgement out
of their experience, when they grewe aged. What was
their ruine and hurt, but this; The excesse of idlenesse, the
fondnesse of Parents, the want of experience in Magistrates, the admiration of their undeserved honours, the
contempt of true merit, their unjust jealosies, their poli-
ticke incredulities, their hypocriticall seeming goodnesse,

---

16. Raccoons.

17. Muskrat.

18. Stresses.

---

19. Contrivances, implements.

and their deeds of secret lewdnesse? finally, in fine, growing onely formall temporists, all that their predecessors got in many years, they lost in few daies. Those by their pains and vertues became Lords of the world; they by their ease and vices became slaves to their servants. This is the difference betwixt the use of Armes in the field, and on the monuments of stones; the golden age and the leaden age, prosperity and miserie, justice and corruption, substance and shadowes, words and deeds, experience and imagination, making Commonwealths and marring Commonwealths, the fruits of vertue and the conclusions of vice.

Then, who would live at home idly (or thinke in himselfe any worth to live) onely to eate, drink, and sleepe, and so die? Or by consuming that carelesly, his friends got worthily? Or by using that miserably, that maintained vertue honestly? Or, for being descended nobly, pine with the vaine vaunt of great kindred, in penurie? Or (to maintaine a silly shewe of bravery) toyle out thy heart, soule, and time, basely, by shifts,[20] tricks, cards, and dice? Or by relating newes of others actions, sharke[21] here or there for a dinner, or supper; deceive thy friends, by faire promises, and dissimulation, in borrowing where thou never intendest to pay; offend the lawes, surfeit with excesse, burden thy Country, abuse thy selfe, despaire in want, and then couzen thy kindred, yea even thine owne brother, and wish thy parents death (I will not say damnation) to have their estates? though thou seest what honours, and rewards, the world yet hath for them will seeke them and worthily deserve them.

I would be sory to offend, or that any should mistake my honest meaning: for I wish good to all, hurt to none. But rich men for the most part are growne to that dotage, through their pride in their wealth, as though there were no accident could end it, or their life. And what hellish care do such take to make it their owne miserie, and their Countries spoile, especially when there is most neede of their imployment? drawing by all manner of inventions, from the Prince and his honest subjects, even the vitall spirits of their powers and estates: as if their Bagges,[22] or Bragges, were so powerfull a defence, the malicious could not assault them; when they are the onely baite, to cause us not to be onely assaulted; but betrayed and murdered in our owne security, ere we well perceive it.

May not the miserable ruine of Constantinople, their impregnable walles, riches, and pleasures last taken by the Turke (which are but a bit, in comparison of their now mightines) remember[23] us, of the effects of private covetousness? at which time the good Emperour held himselfe rich enough, to have such rich subjects, so formall in all excesse of vanity, all kinde of delicacie, and prodigalitie. His povertie when the Turke besieged, the citizens (whose marchandizing thoughts were onely to get wealth, little conceiving the desperate resolution of a valiant expert enemy) left the Emperour so long to his conclusions,[24] having spent all he had to pay his young, raw, discontented Souldiers; that sodainly he, they, and their citie were all a prey to the devouring Turke. And what they would not spare for the maintenance of them who adventured their lives to defend them, did serve onely their enemies to torment them, their friends, and countrey, and all Christendome to this present day. Let this lamentable example remember you that are rich (seeing there are such great theeves in the world to robbe you) not grudge to lend some proportion, to breed them that have little, yet willing to learne how to defend you: for, it is too late when the deede is a-doing. The Romanes estate hath beene worse then this: for, the meere covetousnesse and extortion of a few of them, so mooved the rest, that not having any imployment, but contemplation; their great judgements grew to so great malice, as themselves were sufficient to destroy themselves by faction: Let this moove you to embrace imployment, for those whose educations, spirits, and judgements, want but your purses; not onely to prevent such accustomed dangers, but also to gaine more thereby then you have. And you fathers that are either so foolishly fond, or so miserably covetous, or so willfully ignorant, or so negligently carelesse, as that you will rather maintaine your children in idle wantonness, till they growe your masters; or become so basely unkinde, as they wish nothing but your deaths; so that both sorts growe dissolute: and although you would wish them any where to escape the gallowes, and ease your cares; though they spend you here one, two, or three hundred pound a yeer; you would grudge to give halfe so much in adventure with them, to obtaine an estate, which

---

20. Expedients.

21. Sponge.

22. "Bagges" of money.

23. Remind.

24. Fate.

in a small time but with a little assistance of your providence,[25] might bee better then your owne. But if an Angell should tell you, that any place yet unknowne can afford such fortunes; you would not beleeve him, no more then Columbus was beleeved there was any such Land as is now the well knowne abounding America; much lesse such large Regions as are yet unknowne, as well in America, as in Africa, and Asia, and Terra incognita; where were courses for gentlemen (and them that would be so reputed) more suiting their qualities, then begging from their Princes generous disposition, the labours of his subjects, and the very marrow of his maintenance.

I have not beene so ill bred, but I have tasted of Plenty and Pleasure, as well as Want and Miserie: nor doth necessity yet, or occasion of discontent, force me to these endeavors: nor am I ignorant what small thanke I shall have for my paines; or that many would have the Worlde imagine them to be of great judgement, that can but blemish these my designes, by their witty objections and detractions: yet (I hope) my reasons with my deeds, will so prevaile with some, that I shall not want imployment in these affaires, to make the most blinde see his owne senselesnesse, and incredulity; Hoping that gaine will make them affect that, which Religion, Charity, and the Common good cannot. It were but a poore device in me, To deceive my selfe; much more the King, and State, my Friends, and Countrey, with these inducements: which, seeing his Majestie hath given permission, I wish all sorts of worthie, honest, industrious spirits, would understand: and if they desire any further satisfaction, I will doe my best to give it: Not to perswade them to goe onely; but goe with them: Not leave them there; but live with them there. I will not say, but by ill providing and undue managing, such courses may be taken, may make us miserable enough: But if I may have the execution of what I have projected; if they want to eate, let them eate or never digest Me. If I performe what I say, I desire but that reward out of the gaines may sute my paines, quality, and condition. And if I abuse you with my tongue, take my head for satisfaction. If any dislike at the yeares end, defraying their charge, by my consent they should freely returne. I feare not want of companie sufficient, were it but knowne what I know of those Countries; and by the proofe of that wealth I hope yearely to returne, if God please to blesse me from such accidents, as are beyond my power in reason to prevent: For, I am not so simple, to thinke, that ever

any other motive then wealth, will ever erect there a Commonweale; or draw companie from their ease and humours at home, to stay in New England to effect my purposes. And lest any should thinke the toile might be insupportable, though these things may be had by labour, and diligence: I assure my selfe there are who delight extreamly in vaine pleasure, that take much more paines in England, to enjoy it, then I should doe heere to gaine wealth sufficient: and yet I thinke they should not have halfe such sweet content: for, our pleasure here is still gaines; in England charges and losse. Heer nature and liberty affords us that freely, which in England we want, or it costeth us dearely. What pleasure can be more, then (being tired with any occasion a-shore) in planting Vines, Fruits, or Hearbs, in contriving their owne Grounds, to the pleasure of their owne mindes, their Fields, Gardens, Orchards, Buildings, Ships, and other works, etc. to recreate themselves before their owne doores, in their owne boates upon the Sea, where man woman and childe, with a small hooke and line, by angling, may take diverse sorts of excellent fish, at their pleasures? And is it not pretty sport, to pull up two pence, six pence, and twelve pence, as fast as you can hale and veare a line? He is a very bad fisher, cannot kill in one day with his hooke and line, one, two, or three hundred Cods: which dressed and dryed, if they be sould there for ten shillings the hundred, though in England they will give more then twentie; may not both the servant, the master, and marchant, be well content with this gaine? If a man worke but three dayes in seaven, he may get more then hee can spend, unlesse he will be excessive. Now that Carpenter, Mason, Gardiner, Taylor, Smith, Sailer, Forgers, or what other, may they not make this a pretty recreation though they fish but an houre in a day, to take more then they eate in a weeke: or if they will not eate it, because there is so much better choice; yet sell it, or change it, with the fisher men, or marchants, for any thing they want. And what sport doth yeeld a more pleasing content, and lesse hurt or charge then angling with a hooke, and crossing the sweete ayre from Ile to Ile, over the silent streames of a calme Sea? wherein the most curious may finde pleasure, profit, and content. Thus, though all men be not fishers: yet all men, whatsoever, may in other matters doe as well. For necessity doth in these cases so rule a Commonwealth, and each in their severall functions, as their labours in their qualities may be as profitable, because there is a necessary mutuall use of all.

For Gentlemen, what exercise should more delight them, then ranging dayly those unknowne parts, using

---

25. Provision.

fowling and fishing, for hunting and hauking? and yet you shall see the wilde haukes give you some pleasure, in seeing them stoope[26] (six or seaven after one another) an houre or two together, at the skuls[27] of fish in the faire harbours, as those a-shore at a foule; and never trouble nor torment your selves, with watching, mewing, feeding, and attending them: nor kill horse and man with running and crying, See you not a hauk? For hunting also: the woods, lakes, and rivers, affoord not onely chase sufficient, for any that delights in that kinde of toyle, or pleasure; but such beasts to hunt, that besides the delicacy of their bodies for food, their skins are so rich, as may well recompence thy dayly labour, with a Captains pay.

For labourers, if those that sowe hemp, rape, turnups, parsnips, carrats, cabidge, and such like; give 20, 30, 40, 50 shillings yearely for an acre of ground, and meat drinke and wages to use it, and yet grow rich: when better, or at least as good ground, may be had and cost nothing but labour; it seemes strange to me, any such should there grow poore.

My purpose is not to perswade children from their parents; men from their wives; nor servants from their masters: onely, such as with free consent may be spared: But that each parish, or village, in Citie, or Countrey, that will but apparell their fatherlesse children, of thirteene or fourteene years of age, or young maried people, that have small wealth to live on; heere by their labour may live exceeding well: provided alwaies that first there bee a sufficient power to command them, houses to receive them, meanes to defend them, and meet provisions for them; for, any place may bee overlain[28] and it is most necessarie to have a fortresse (ere this grow to practice) and sufficient masters (as, Carpenters, Masons, Fishers, Fowlers, Gardiners, Husbandmen, Sawyers, Smiths, Spinsters,[29] Taylors, Weavers, and such like) to take ten, twelve, or twentie, or as ther is occasion, for Apprentices. The Masters by this may quicklie growe rich; these may learne their trades themselves, to doe the like; to a generall and an incredible benefit, for King, and Countrey, Master, and Servant.

---

26. Swoop down.

27. Schools.

28. Overpowered.

29. Spinners.

from THE GENERALL HISTORIE OF VIRGINIA, NEW ENGLAND AND THE SUMMER ISLES[1]

from THE THIRD BOOKE

The Proceedings And Accidents of The English Colony in Virginia, Extracted from the Authors following, by William Simons,[2] Doctour of Divinitie

from CHAPTER 1

It might well be thought, a Countrie so faire (as Virginia is) and a people so tractable, would long ere this have beene quietly possessed, to the satisfaction of the adventurers, & the eternizing of the memory of those that effected it. But because all the world doe see a defailement; this following Treatise shall give satisfaction to all indifferent Readers, how the businesse hath bin carried: where no doubt they will easily understand and answer to their question, how it came to passe there was no better speed and successe in those proceedings.

Captaine Bartholomew Gosnoll,[3] one of the first movers of this plantation, having many yeares solicited many of his friends, but found small assistants; at last prevailed with some Gentlemen, as Captaine John Smith, Mr. Edward-maria Wingfield,[4] Mr. Robert Hunt,[5] and divers others, who depended a yeare upon his projects, but nothing could be effected, till by their great charge and industrie, it came to be apprehended by certaine of the Nobilitie, Gentry, and Marchants, so that his Majestie by his letters patents, gave commission for establishing

---

1. *The Generall Historie of Virginia, New England, and the Summer Isles* was first published in London in 1624. This text is adapted from Edward Arber, ed., *The General Historie of Virginia* (1907).

2. William Simons, or the Rev. William Symonds (1556–1616?), edited *The Proceedings of the English Colonies in Virginia* (1612).

3. Captain Bartholomew Gosnold (c.1572–1607), an explorer who recruited colonists for the Virginia expedition.

4. Edward Maria Wingfield (1560?–1613?) became the first president of Jamestown.

5. Reverend Robert Hunt (c.1569–1608) was Jamestown's first preacher.

Councels, to direct here; and to governe, and to execute there. To effect this, was spent another yeare, and by that, three ships were provided, one of 100 Tuns, another of 40. and a Pinnace of 20. The transportation of the company was committed to Captaine Christopher Newport,[6] a Marriner well practised for the Westerne parts of America. But their orders for government were put in a box, not to be opened, nor the governours knowne untill they arrived in Virginia.

On the 19 of December, 1606, we set sayle from Blackwall, but by unprosperous winds, were kept six weekes in the sight of England; all which time, Mr. Hunt our Preacher, was so weake and sicke, that few expected his recovery. Yet although he were but twentie myles from his habitation (the time we were in the Downes) and notwithstanding the stormy weather, nor the scandalous imputations (of some few, little better then Atheists, of the greatest ranke amongst us) suggested against him, all this could never force from him so much as a seeming desire to leave the busines, but preferred the service of God, in so good a voyage, before any affection to contest with his godlesse foes, whose disasterous designes (could they have prevailed) had even then overthrowne the businesse, so many discontents did then arise, had he not with the water of patience, and his godly exhortations (but chiefly by his true devoted examples) quenched those flames of envie, and dissention.

We watered at the Canaries, we traded with the Salvages at Dominica; three weekes we spent in refreshing our selves amongst these west-India Isles; in Gwardalupa we found a bath so hot, as in it we boyled Porck as well as over the fire. And at a little Isle called Monica, we tooke from the bushes with our hands, neare two hogsheads full of Birds in three or foure houres. In Mevis,[7] Mona, and the Virgin Isles, we spent some time, where with a lothsome beast like a Crocodil, called a Gwayn, Tortoises, Pellicans, Parrots, and fishes, we daily feasted. Gone from thence in search of Virginia, the company was not a little discomforted, seeing the Marriners had 3 dayes passed their reckoning and found no land, so that Captaine Ratliffe[8] (Captaine of the Pinnace) rather

desired to beare up the helme to returne for England, then make further search. But God the guider of all good actions, forcing them by an extreame storme to hull all night, did drive them by his providence to their desired Port, beyond all their expectations, for never any of them had seene that coast. The first land they made they called Cape Henry; where thirtie of them recreating themselves on shore, were assaulted by five Salvages, who hurt two of the English very dangerously. That night was the box opened, and the orders read, in which Bartholomew Gosnoll, John Smith, Edward Wingfield, Christopher Newport, John Ratliffe, John Martin,[9] and George Kendall,[10] were named to be the Councell, and to choose a President amongst them for a yeare, who with the Councell should governe . . . Untill the 13 of May they sought a place to plant in, then the Councell was sworne, Mr. Wingfield was chosen President, and an Oration made, why Captaine Smith was not admitted of the Councell as the rest.

Now falleth every man to worke, the Councell contrive the Fort, the rest cut downe trees to make place to pitch their Tents; some provide clapbord to relade the ships, some make gardens, some nets, &c. The Salvages often visited us kindly. The Presidents overweening jealousie would admit no exercise at armes, or fortification, but the boughs of trees cast together in the forme of a halfe moone by the extraordinary paines and diligence of Captaine Kendall, Newport, Smith, and twentie others, were sent to discover the head of the river: by divers small habitations they passed, in six dayes they arrived at a Towne called Powhatan, consisting of some twelve houses, pleasantly seated on a hill; before it three fertile Isles, about it many of their cornefields, the place is very pleasant, and strong by nature, of this place the Prince is called Powhatan,[11] and his people Powhatans, to this place the river is navigable: but higher within a myle, by reason of the Rockes and Isles, there is not passage for a small Boat, this they call the Falles, the people in all parts kindly intreated them, till being returned within twentie myles of James towne, they gave just cause of jealousie, but had God not blessed the discoverers otherwise then those at the Fort, there had then beene an end of that plan-

---

6. Captain Christopher Newport (1560–1617) commanded the Virginia Company's fleet.

7. Nevis.

8. According to the Virginia Charter, Captain John Ratcliff was apparently the alias of John Sicklemore (fl. 1607–09).

9. Captain John Martin (c.1597–1632?) is remembered for his quarrelsome nature.

10. Captain George Kendall (fl. 1600–07) was executed in late 1607 for a mutiny.

11. Powhatan (1540s?–1618) was the ruler of the Algonquians in tidewater Virginia.

tation; for at the Fort, where they arrived the next day, they found 17 men hurt, and a boy slaine by the Salvages, and had it not chanced a crosse barre shot from the Ships strooke down a bough from a tree amongst them, that caused them to retire, our men had all beene slaine, being securely all at worke, and their armes in dry fats.[12]

Hereupon the President was contented the Fort should be pallisadoed, the Ordnance mounted, his men armed and exercised, for many were the assaults, and ambuscadoes of the Salvages, & our men by their disorderly stragling were often hurt, when the Salvages by the nimblenesse of their heeles well escaped. What toyle we had, with so small a power to guard our workemen adayes, watch all night, resist our enemies, and effect our businesse, to relade the ships, cut downe trees, and prepare the ground to plant our Corne, &c, I referre to the Readers consideration. Six weekes being spent in this manner, Captaine Newport (who was hired onely for our transportation) was to returne with the ships. Now Captaine Smith, who all this time from their departure from the Canaries was restrained as a prisoner upon the scandalous suggestions of some of the chiefe (envying his repute) who fained he intended to usurpe the government, murther the Councell, and make himselfe King, that his confederats were dispersed in all the three ships, and that divers of his confederats that revealed it, would affirme it, for this he was committed as a prisoner: thirteene weekes he remained thus suspected, and by that time the ships should returne they pretended out of their commisserations, to referre him to the Councell in England to receive a check, rather then by particulating his designes make him so odious to the world, as to touch his life, or utterly overthrow his reputation. But he so much scorned their charitie, and publikely defied the uttermost of their crueltie, he wisely prevented their policies, though he could not suppresse their envies, yet so well he demeaned himselfe in this businesse, as all the company did see his innocency, and his adversaries malice, and those suborned to accuse him, accused his accusers of subornation; many untruthes were alledged against him; but being so apparently disproved, begat a generall hatred in the hearts of the company against such unjust Commanders, that the President was adjudged to give him 200l. so that all he had was seized upon, in part of satisfaction, which Smith presently returned to the Store for the generall use of the Colony. Many were the mischiefes that daily sprung from their ignorant (yet ambitious) spirits; but the good Doctrine and exhortation of our Preacher Mr. Hunt reconciled them, and caused Captaine Smith to be admitted of the Councell; the next day all received the Communion, the day following the Salvages voluntarily desired peace, and Captaine Newport returned for England with newes; leaving in Virginia 100. the 15 of June 1607. . . .

from CHAPTER 2

What happened till the first supply

Being thus left to our fortunes, it fortuned that within ten dayes scarce ten amongst us could either goe, or well stand, such extreame weaknes and sicknes oppressed us. And thereat none need marvaile, if they consider the cause and reason, which was this; whilest the ships stayed, our allowance was somewhat bettered, by a daily proportion of Bisket, which the sailers would pilfer to sell, give, or exchange with us, for money, Saxefras, furres, or love. But when they departed, there remained neither taverne, beere house, nor place of reliefe, but the common Kettell. Had we beene as free from all sinnes as gluttony, and drunkennesse, we might have beene canonized for Saints; But our President[13] would never have beene admitted, for ingrossing to his private, Oatmeale, Sacke, Oyle, Aquavitæ, Beefe, Egges, or what not, but the Kettell; that indeed he allowed equally to be distributed, and that was halfe a pint of wheat, and as much barely boyled with water for a man a day, and this having fryed some 26. weekes in the ships hold, contained as many wormes as graines; so that we might truely call it rather so much bran then corne, our drinke was water, our lodgings Castles in the ayre: with this lodging and dyet, our extreame toile in bearing and planting Pallisadoes, so strained and bruised us, and our continuall labour in the extremitie of the heat had so weakned us, as were cause sufficient to have made us as miserable in our native Countrey, or any other place in the world. From May, to September, those that escaped, lived upon Sturgeon, and Sea-crabs, fiftie in this time we buried . . . But now was all our provision spent, the Sturgeon gone, all helps abandoned, each houre expecting the fury of the Salvages; when God the patron of all good indevours, in that desperate extremitie so changed the hearts of the Salvages,

---

12. A container for stacking guns.

13. Wingfield.

that they brought such plenty of their fruits, and provision, as no man wanted.

And now where some affirmed it was ill done of the Councell to send forth men so badly provided, this incontradictable reason will shew them plainely they are too ill advised to nourish such ill conceits; first, the fault of our going was our owne, what could be thought fitting or necessary we had, but what we should find, or want, or where we should be, we were all ignorant, and supposing to make our passage in two moneths, with victuall to live, and the advantage of the spring to worke; we were at Sea five moneths, where we both spent our victuall and lost the opportunitie of the time, and season to plant, by the unskilfull presumption of our ignorant transporters, that understood not at all, what they undertooke.

Such actions have ever since the worlds beginning beene subject to such accidents, and every thing of worth is found full of difficulties, but nothing so difficult as to establish a Common wealth so farre remote from men and meanes, and where mens mindes are so untoward as neither doe well themselves, nor suffer others. But to proceed.

The new president and Martin, being little beloved, of weake judgement in dangers, and lesse industrie in peace, committed the managing of all things abroad to Captaine Smith: who by his owne example, good words, and faire promises, set some to mow, others to binde thatch, some to build houses, others to thatch them, himselfe alwayes bearing the greatest taske for his owne share, so that in short time, he provided most of them lodgings, neglecting any for himselfe. This done, seeing the Salvages superfluitie beginne to decrease (with some of his workemen) shipped himselfe in the Shallop[14] to search the Country for trade. The want of the language, knowledge to mannage his boat without sailes, the want of a sufficient power, (knowing the multitude of the Salvages) apparell for his men, and other necessaries, were infinite impediments, yet no discouragement. Being but six or seaven in company he went downe the river to Kecoughtan, where at first they scorned him, as a famished man, and would in derision offer him a handfull of Corne, a peece of bread, for their swords and muskets, and such like proportions also for their apparell. But seeing by trade and courtesie there was nothing to be had, he made bold to try such conclusions as necessitie inforced, though contrary to his Commission: Let fly his muskets, ran his boat on shore,

whereat they all fled into the woods. So marching towards their houses, they might see great heapes of corne: much adoe he had to restraine his hungry souldiers from present taking of it, expecting as it hapned that the Salvages would assault them, as not long after they did with a most hydeous noyse. Sixtie or seaventie of them, some blacke, some red, some white, some party-coloured, came in a square order, singing and dauncing out of the woods, with their Okee (which was an Idoll made of skinnes, stuffed with mosse, all painted and hung with chaines and copper) borne before them: and in this manner being well armed, with Clubs, Targets, Bowes and Arrowes, they charged the English, that so kindly received them with their muskets loaden with Pistoll shot, that downe fell their God, and divers lay sprauling on the ground; the rest fled againe to the woods, and ere long sent one of their Quiyoughkasoucks to offer peace, and redeeme their Okee. Smith told them, if onely six of them would come unarmed and loade his boat, he would not only be their friend, but restore them their Okee, and give them Beads, Copper, and Hatchets besides: which on both sides was to their contents performed: and then they brought him Venison, Turkies, wild foule, bread, and what they had, singing and dauncing in signe of friendship till they departed. In his returne he discovered the Towne and Country of Warraskoyack.[15]

> Thus God unboundlesse by his power,
> Made them thus kind, would us devour.

Smith perceiving (notwithstanding their late miserie) not any regarded but from hand to mouth (the company being well recovered) caused the Pinnace to be provided with things fitting to get provision for the yeare following; but in the interim he made 3. or 4. journies and discovered the people of Chickahamania:[16] yet what he carefully provided the rest carelessly spent. Wingfield and Kendall living in disgrace, seeing all things at randome in the absence of Smith, the companies dislike of their presidents weaknes, and their small love to Martins never mending sicknes, strengthened themselves with the sailers, and other confederates to regaine their former credit and authority, or at least such meanes abord the Pinnace, (being fitted to saile as Smith had appointed for trade) to

---

14. An open boat.

15. A village south of the James River.

16. A region west of Jamestown, along the Chickahominy River.

alter her course and to goe for England. Smith unexpect-edly returning had the plot discovered to him, much trou-ble he had to prevent it, till with store of sakre and mus-ket shot he forced them stay or sinke in the river, which action cost the life of captaine Kendall. These brawles are so disgustfull, as some will say they were better forgotten, yet all men of good judgement will conclude, it were bet-ter their basenes should be manifest to the world, then the busines beare the scorne and shame of their excused dis-orders. The President and captaine Archer[17] not long after intended also to have abandoned the country, which proj-ect also was curbed, and suppressed by Smith. The Spaniard never more greedily desired gold then he vict-uall, nor his souldiers more to abandon the Country, then he to keepe it. But finding plentie of Corne in the river of Chickahamania where hundreds of Salvages in divers places stood with baskets expecting his comming. And now the winter approaching, the rivers became so covered with swans, geese, duckes, and cranes, that we daily feasted with good bread, Virginia pease, pumpions, and putchamins,[18] fish, fowle, and diverse sorts of wild beasts as far as we could eate them: so that none of our Tuftaffaty humorists desired to goe for England. But our Comædies never endured long without a Tragedie; some idle exceptions[19] being muttered against Captaine Smith, for not discovering the head of Chickahamania river, and taxed by the Councell, to be too slow in so worthy an at-tempt. The next voyage hee proceeded so farre that with much labour by cutting of trees in sunder he made his pas-sage, but when his Barge could passe no farther, he left her in a broad bay out of danger of shot, commanding none should goe a shore till his returne: himselfe with two English and two Salvages went up higher in a Canowe, but hee was not long absent, but his men went a shore, whose want of government, gave both occasion and op-portunity to the Salvages to surprise one George Cassen, whom they slew, and much failed not to have cut of the boat and all the rest. Smith little dreaming of that acci-dent, being got to the marshes at the rivers head, twentie myles in the desert, had his two men slaine (as is sup-posed) sleeping by the Canowe, whilst himselfe by fowl-ing sought them victuall, who finding he was beset with

200. Salvages, two of them hee slew, still defending him-selfe with the ayd of a Salvage his guid, whom he bound to his arme with his garters, and used him as a buckler,[20] yet he was shot in his thigh a little, and had many arrowes that stucke in his cloathes but no great hurt, till at last they tooke him prisoner. When this newes came to James towne, much was their sorrow for his losse, fewe expect-ing what ensued. Six or seven weekes those Barbarians kept him prisoner, many strange triumphes and conjura-tions they made of him, yet hee so demeaned himselfe amongst them, as he not onely diverted them from sur-prising the Fort, but procured his owne libertie, and got himselfe and his company such estimation amongst them, that those Salvages admired him more then their owne Quiyouckosucks. The manner how they used and deliv-ered him, is as followeth.

   The Salvages having drawne from George Cassen whether Captaine Smith was gone, prosecuting that op-portunity they followed him with 300. bowmen, con-ducted by the King of Pamaunkee, who in divisions searching the turnings of the river, found Robinson and Emry by the fire side, those they shot full of arrowes and slew. Then finding the Captaine, as is said, that used the Salvage that was his guide as his shield (three of them being slaine and divers other so gauld[21]) all the rest would not come neere him. Thinking thus to have returned to his boat, regarding them, as he marched, more then his way, slipped up to the middle in an oasie creeke & his Salvage with him, yet durst they not come to him till being neere dead with cold, he threw away his armes. Then according to their composition[22] they drew him forth and led him to the fire, where his men were slaine. Diligently they chafed his benummed limbs. He demanding for their Captaine; they shewed him Opechankanough,[23] King of Pamaunkee, to whom he gave a round Ivory double com-pass Dyall. Much they marvailed at the playing of the Fly[24] and Needle, which they could see so plainely, and yet not touch it, because of the glasse that covered them. But when he demonstrated by that Globe-like Jewell, the roundnesse of the earth, and skies, the sphaere of the

---

17. Captain Gabriel Archer (c.1575–1609?) was a strong opponent of Smith.

18. Persimmons.

19. Objections.

20. Shield.

21. Wounded.

22. Agreement for surrender.

23. Opechancanough (fl.1607–44) was Powhatan's younger half brother. In December 1607, he took Smith captive.

24. Compass.

Sunne, Moone, and Starres, and how the Sunne did chase the night round about the world continually; the greatnesse of the Land and Sea, the diversitie of Nations, varietie of complexions, and how we were to them Antipodes, and many other such like matters, they all stood as amazed with admiration. Notwithstanding, within an houre after they tyed him to a tree, and as many as could stand about him prepared to shoot him, but the King holding up the Compass in his hand, they all laid downe their Bowes and Arrowes, and in a triumphant manner led him to Orapaks,[25] where he was after their manner kindly feasted, and well used.

Their order in conducting him was thus; Drawing themselves all in fyle, the King in the middest had all their Peeces and Swords borne before him. Captaine Smith was led after him by three great Salvages, holding him fast by each arme: and on each side six went in fyle with their Arrowes nocked. But arriving at the Towne (which was but onely thirtie or fortie hunting houses made of mats, which they remove as they please, as we our tents) all the women and children staring to behold him, the souldiers first all in fyle performed the forme of a Bissom so well as could be, and on each flanke, officers as Serjeants to see them keepe their orders. A good time they continued this exercise, and then cast themselves in a ring, dauncing in such severall Postures, and singing and yelling out such hellish notes and screeches; being strangely painted, every one his quiver of Arrowes, and at his backe a club; on his arme a Fox or an Otters skinne, or some such matter for his vambrace; their heads and shoulders painted red, with Oyle and Pocones[26] mingled together, which Scarlet-like colour made an exceeding handsome shew; his Bow in his hand, and the skinne of a Bird with her wings abroad dryed, tyed on his head, a peece of copper, a white shell, a long feather, with a small rattle growing at the tayles of their snaks tyed to it, or some such like toy. All this while Smith and the King stood in the middest guarded, as before is said, and after three dances they all departed. Smith they conducted to a long house, where thirtie or fortie tall fellowes did guard him, and ere long more bread and venison was brought him then would have served twentie men, I thinke his stomacke at that time was not very good; what he left they put in baskets and tyed over his head. About midnight

they set the meate againe before him, all this time not one of them would eate a bit with him, till the next morning they brought him as much more, and then did they eate all the old, & reserved the new as they had done the other, which made him thinke they would fat him to eat him. Yet in this desperate estate to defend him from the cold, one Maocassater brought him his gowne, in requitall[27] of some beads and toyes Smith had given him at his first arrivall in Virginia.

Two dayes after a man would have slaine him (but that the guard prevented it) for the death of his sonne, to whom they conducted him to recover the poore man then breathing his last. Smith told them that at James towne he had a water would doe it, if they would let him fetch it, but they would not permit that; but made all the preparations they could to assault James towne, craving his advice, and for recompence he should have life, libertie, land, and women. In part of a Table booke[28] he writ his minde to them at the Fort, what was intended, how they should follow that direction to affright the messengers, and without fayle send him such things as he writ for. And an Inventory with them. The difficultie and danger, he told the Salvages, of the Mines, great-gunnes, and other Engins[29] exceedingly affrighted them, yet according to his request they went to James towne, in as bitter weather as could be of frost and snow, and within three dayes returned with an answer.

But when they came to James towne, seeing men sally out as he had told them they would, they fled; yet in the night they came againe to the same place where he had told them they should receive an answer, and such things as he had promised them, which they found accordingly, and with which they returned with no small expedition, to the wonder of them all that heard it, that he could either divine, or the paper could speake: then they led him to the Youthtanunds, the Mattapanients, the Payankatanks, the Nantaughtacunds, and Onawmanients[30] upon the rivers of Raphanock, and Patawomek, over all those rivers, and backe againe by divers other severall Nations, to the Kings habitation at Pamaunkee . . .

Not long after, early in a morning a great fire was made in a long house, and a mat spread on the one side,

---

25. A village farther inland, which later became Powhatan's residence.

26. A vegetable die.

27. Payment.

28. A pocket notebook.

29. Weaponry.

30. Powhatan's chiefdom extended over a tributary confederacy of several Indian groups in the area.

as on the other; on the one they caused him to sit, and all the guard went out of the house, and presently came skipping in a great grim fellow, all painted over with coale, mingled with oyle; and many Snakes and Wesels skins stuffed with mosse, and all their tayles tyed together, so as they met on the crowne of his head in a tassell; and round about the tassell was as a Coronet of feathers, the skins hanging round about his head, backe, and shoulders, and in a manner covered his face; with a hellish voyce and a rattle in his hand. With most strange gestures and passions he began his invocation, and environed the fire with a circle of meale; which done, three more such like devils came rushing in with the like antique tricks, painted halfe blacke, halfe red: but all their eyes were painted white, and some red stroakes like Mutchato's,[31] along their cheekes: roundabout him those fiends daunced a pretty while, and then came in three more as ugly as the rest; with red eyes, and white stroakes over their blacke faces, at last they all sat downe right against him; three of them on the one hand of the chiefe priest, and three on the other. Then all with their rattles began a song, which ended, the chiefe Priest layd downe five wheat cornes: then strayning his armes and hands with such violence that he sweat, and his veynes swelled, he began a short Oration: at the conclusion they all gave a short groane; and then layd down three graines more. After that, began their song againe, and then another Oration, ever laying downe so many cornes as before, till they had twice incirculed the fire; that done, they tooke a bunch of little stickes prepared for that purpose, continuing still their devotion, and at the end of every song and Oration, they layd downe a sticke betwixt the divisions of Corne. Till night, neither he nor they did either eate or drinke, and then they feasted merrily, with the best provisions they could make. Three dayes they used this Ceremony; the meaning whereof they told him, was to know if he intended them well or no. The circle of meale signified their Country, the circles of corne the bounds of the sea, and the stickes his Country. They imagined the world to be flat and round, like a trencher,[32] and they in the middest. After this they brought him a bagge of gunpowder, which they carefully preserved till the next spring, to plant as they did their corne; because they would be acquainted with the nature of that seede . . .

At last they brought him to Meronocomo, where was Powhatan their Emperor. Here more then two hundrd of those grim Courtiers stood wondering at him, as he had beene a monster; till Powhatan and his trayne had put themselves in their greatest braveries.[33] Before a fire upon a seat like a bedsted, he sat covered with a great robe, made of Rarowcun[34] skinnes, and all the tayles hanging by. On either hand did sit a young wench of 16 or 18 yeares, and along on each side the house, two rowes of men, and behind them as many women, with all their heads and shoulders painted red; many of their heads bedecked with the white downe of Birds; but every one with something: and a great chayne of white beads about their necks. At his entrance before the King, all the people gave a great shout. The Queene of Appamatuck was appointed to bring him water to wash his hands, and another brought him a bunch of feathers, in stead of a Towell to dry them: having feasted him after their best barbarous manner they could, a long consultation was held, but the conclusion was, two great stones were brought before Powhatan: then as many as could layd hands on him, dragged him to them, and thereon laid his head, and being ready with their clubs, to beate out his braines, Pocahontas[35] the Kings dearest daughter, when no intreaty could prevaile, got his head in her armes, and laid her owne upon his to save him from death: whereat the Emperour was contented he should live to make him hatchets, and her bells, beads, and copper; for they thought him aswell of all occupations as themselves. For the King himselfe will make his owne robes, shooes, bowes, arrowes, pots; plant, hunt, or doe any thing so well as the rest.

> They say he bore a pleasant shew,
> But sure his heart was sad.
> For who can pleasant be, and rest,
> That lives in feare and dread:
> And having life suspected, doth
> It still suspected lead.[36]

Two dayes after, Powhatan having disguised himselfe in the most fearefull manner he could, caused Capt. Smith to be brought forth to a great house in the woods, and there upon a mat by the fire to be left alone. Not long after

---

31. Mustaches.

32. A platter made of wood or metal.

33. Finery.

34. Raccoon.

35. Pocahontas (c.1591–1617) was the daughter of Powhatan.

36. Drawn from a translation of Euripides by Fotherby.

from behinde a mat that divided the house, was made the most dolefullest noyse he ever heard; then Powhatan more like a devill then a man with some two hundred more as blacke as himselfe, came unto him and told him now they were friends, and presently he should goe to James towne, to send him two great gunnes, and a gryndstone, for which he would give him the Country of Capahowosick, and forever esteeme him as his sonne Nantaquoud. So to James towne with 12 guides Powhatan sent him. That night they quarterd in the woods, he still expecting (as he had done all this long time of his imprisonment) every houre to be put to one death or other: for all their feasting. But almightie God (by his divine providence) had mollified the hearts of those sterne Barbarians with compassion. The next morning betimes they came to the Fort, where Smith having used the Salvages with what kindnesse he could, he shewed Rawhunt, Powhatans trusty servant two demi-Culverings[37] & a millstone to carry Powhatan: they found them somewhat too heavie; but when they did see him discharge them, being loaded with stones, among the boughs of a great tree loaded with Isickles, the yce and branches came so tumbling downe, that the poore Salvages ran away halfe dead with feare. But at last we regained some conference with them, and gave them such toyes; and sent to Powhatan, his women, and children such presents, as gave them in generall full content. Now in James Towne they were all in combustion, the strongest preparing once more to run away with the Pinnace; which with the hazzard of his life, with Sakre falcon and musket shot, Smith forced now the third time to stay or sinke. Some no better then they should be, had plotted with the president, the next day to have put him to death by the Leviticall law, for the lives of Robinson and Emry, pretending the fault was his that had led them to their ends: but he quickly tooke such order with such Lawyers, that he layd them by the heeles till he sent some of them prisoners for England. Now ever once in foure or five dayes, Pocahontas with her attendants, brought him so much provision, that saved many of their lives, that els for all this had starved with hunger.

Thus from numbe death our good God sent reliefe,
The sweete asswager of all other griefe.[38]

---

37. Large cannons.

38. The first line was likely written by Smith based upon Fotherby. The second line was taken from Fotherby's translation of a phrase of Euripides apearing in Plutarch.

His relation of the plenty he had seene, especially at Werawocomoco, and of the state and bountie of Powhatan, (which till that time was unknowne) so revived their dead spirits (especially the love of Pocahontas) as all mens feare was abandoned. Thus you may see what difficulties still crossed any good indevour: and the good successe of the businesse being thus oft brought to the very period of destruction; yet you see by what strange means God hath still delivered it. As for the insufficiency of them admitted in Commission, that error could not be prevented by the electors; there being no other choise, and all strangers to each others education, qualities, or disposition. And if any deeme it a shame to our Nation to have any mention made of those inormities, let them peruse the Histories of the Spanyards Discoveries and Plantations, where they may see how many mutinies, disorders, and dissentions have accompanied them, and crossed their attempts: which being knowne to be particular mens offences; doth take away the generall scorne and contempt, which malice, presumption, covetousnesse, or ignorance might produce; to the scandall and reproach of those, whose actions and valiant resolutions deserve a more worthy respect. . . .

from CHAPTER 3

The Arrivall of the first supply, with their Proceedings, and the Ships returne

All this time our care was not so much to abandon the Countrey; but the Treasurer and Councell in England, were as diligent & carefull to supply us. Two good ships they sent us, with neare a hundred men, well furnished with all things could be imagined necessary, both for them and us; The one commanded by Captaine Newport: the other by Captaine Francis Nelson, an honest man, and an expert Marriner. But such was the lewardnesse of his Ship (that though he was within the sight of Cape Henry) by stormy contrary winds was he forced so farre to Sea, that the West Indies was the next land, for the repaire of his Masts, and reliefe of wood and water. But Newport got in and arrived at James Towne, not long after the redemption of Captaine Smith. To whom the Salvages, as is sayd, every other day repaired, with such provisions that sufficiently did serve them from hand to mouth: part alwayes they brought him as Presents from their Kings, or Pocahontas; the rest he as their Market Clarke set the price himselfe, how they should sell: so he had inchanted these poore soules being their prisoner; and now Newport, whom he called his Father arriving, neare as directly as he foretold, they esteemed him as an Oracle, and had them at that submission he might command them what he listed. That God that created all things they knew he adored for his God: they would also in their discourses tearme the God of Captaine Smith.

Thus the Almightie was the bringer on,
The guide, path, terme, all which was God alone.[39]

But the President and Councell so much envied his estimation among the Salvages, (though we all in generall equally participated with him of the good thereof,) that they wrought it into the Salvages understandings (by their great bounty in giving foure times more for their commodities then Smith appointed) that their greatnesse and authoritie as much exceeded his, as their bountie and liberalitie. Now the arrivall of this first supply so overjoyed us, that wee could not devise too much to please the Marriners. We gave them libertie to trucke or trade at their pleasures. But in a short time it followed, that could not be had for a pound of Copper, which before was sould us for an ounce: thus ambition and sufferance cut the throat of our trade, but confirmed their opinion of the greatnesse of Capt. Newport, (wherewith Smith had possessed Powhatan) especially by the great presents Newport often sent him, before he could prepare the Pinnace to goe and visit him: so that this great Savage desired also to see him. A great coyle there was to set him forward. When he went he was accompanied with Captaine Smith, & Mr. Scrivener . . . with thirtie or fortie chosen men for their guard . . .

These . . . comming a-shore, landed amongst a many of creekes, over which they were to passe such poore bridges, onely made of a few cratches,[40] thrust in the ose, and three or foure poles laid on them, and at the end of them the like, tyed together onely with barkes of trees, that it made them much suspect those bridges were but traps. Which caused Smith to make diverse Salvages goe over first, keeping some of the chiefe as hostage till halfe his men were passed, to make a guard for himselfe and the rest. But finding all things well, by two or three hundred

Salvages they were kindly conducted to their towne. Where Powhatan strained himselfe to the utmost of his greatnesse to entertaine them, with great shouts of joy, Orations of protestations; and with the most plenty of victualls he could provide to feast them. Sitting upon his bed of mats, his pillow of leather imbrodered (after their rude manner with pearle and white Beads) his attyre a faire robe of skinnes as large as an Irish mantell: at his head and feete a handsome young woman: on each side his house sat twentie of his Concubines, their heads and shoulders painted red, with a great chaine of white beads about each of their neckes. Before those sat his chiefest men in like order in his arbour-like house, and more then fortie platters of fine bread stood as a guard in two fyles on each side the doore. Foure or five hundred people made a guard behinde them for our passage; and Proclamation was made, none upon paine of death to presume to doe us any wrong or discourtesie. With many pretty Discourses to renew their old acquaintance, this great King and our Captaine spent the time till the ebbe left our Barge aground. Then renewing their feasts with feates, dauncing and singing, and such like mirth, we quartered that night with Powhatan. The next day Newport came a shore and received as much content as those people could give him: a boy named Thomas Salvage[41] was then given unto Powhatan, whom Newport called his sonne; for whom Powhatan gave him Namontack his trustie servant, and one of a shrewd, subtill capacitie. Three or foure dayes more we spent in feasting, dauncing, and trading, wherein Powhatan carried himselfe so proudly, yet discreetly (in his salvage manner) as made us all admire his naturall gifts, considering his education. As scorning to trade as his subjects did; he bespake Newport in this manner.

Captaine Newport it is not agreeable to my greatnesse, in this pedling manner to trade for trifles; and I esteeme you also a great Werowance. Therefore lay me downe all your commodities together; what I like I will take, and in recompence give you what I thinke fitting their value. Captaine Smith being our interpreter, regarding Newport as his father, knowing best the disposition of Powhatan, tould us his intent was but onely to cheate us; yet Captaine Newport thinking to out brave this Salvage in ostentation of greatnesse, and so to bewitch him with his bountie, as to have what he listed, it so hapned, that Powhatan

---

39. Taken from a translation of Boethius by Fotherby.

40. Wooden frames or racks.

41. Thomas Savage (1594–before 1633) learned the language of the Powhatans and later served as an interpreter.

having his desire, valued his corne at such a rate, that I thinke it better cheape in Spaine: for we had not foure bushells for that we expected to have twentie hogsheads. This bred some unkindnesse betweene our two Captaines; Newport seeking to please the unsatiable desire of the Salvage, Smith to cause the Salvage to please him; but smothering his distast to avoyd the Salvages suspition, glanced in the eyes of Powhatan many trifles, who fixed his humor upon a few blew beades. A long time he importunately desired them, but Smith seemed so much the more to affect them, as being composed of a most rare substance of the coulour of the skyes, and not to be worne but by the greatest kings in the world. This made him halfe madde to be the owner of such strange Jewells: so that ere we departed, for a pound or two of blew beades, he brought over my king for 2. or 300. Bushells of corne; yet parted good friends. The like entertainment we found of Opechankanough king of Pamaunkee, whom also he in like manner fitted (at the like rates) with blew beads, which grew by this meanes, of that estimation, that none durst weare any of them but their great kings, their wives and children. And so we returned all well to James towne, where this new supply being lodged with the rest, accidentally fired their quarters and so the towne, which being but thatched with reeds, the fire was so fierce as it burnt their Pallisado's, (though eight or ten yards distant) with their Armes, bedding, apparell, and much private provision. Good Master Hunt our Preacher lost all his Library and all he had but the cloathes on his backe: yet none never heard him repine at his losse. This happned in the winter in that extreame frost, 1607. Now though we had victuall sufficient I meane onely of Oatmeale, meale and corne, yet the Ship staying 14. weekes when shee might as wel have beene gone in 14. dayes, spent a great part of that, and neare all the rest that was sent to be landed. When they departed what there discretion could spare us, to make a little poore meale or two, we called feastes, to relish our mouthes: of each somwhat they left us, yet I must confesse, those that had either money, spare clothes credit to give billes of paiment, gold rings, furrs, or any such commodities, were ever welcome to this removing taverne, such was our patience to obay such vile Commanders, and buy our owne provisions at 15 times the value, suffering them feast (we bearing the charge) yet must not repine, but fast, least we should incure the censure of factious and seditious persons: and then leakage, shiprats, and other casuallties occasioned them losse, but the vessels and remnants (for totals) we were glad to receave with all our hearts to make up the account, highly commending their providence for preserving that, least they should discourage any more to come to us. Now for all this plenty our ordynary was but meale and water, so that this great charge little releeved our wants, whereby with the extremitie of the bitter cold frost and those defects, more then halfe of us dyed; I cannot deny but both Smith and Skrivener did their best to amend what was amisse, but with the President went the major part, that there hornes were to short. But the worst was our guilded refiners with their golden promises made all men their slaves in hope of recompences; there was no talke, no hope, no worke, but dig gold, wash gold, refine gold, loade gold, such a bruit of gold, that one mad fellow desired to be buried in the sands least they should by there art make gold of his bones: little neede there was and lesse reason, the ship should stay, there wages run on, our victualls consume 14. weekes, that the Mariners might say, they did helpe to build such a golden Church that we can say the raine washed neere to nothing in 14. dayes. Were it that captaine Smith would not applaude all those golden inventions, because they admitted him not to the sight of their trialls nor golden consultations, I know not; but I have heard him oft question with Captaine Martin & tell him, except he could shew him a more substantiall triall, he was not inamoured with their durty skill, breathing out these and many other passions, never any thing did more torment him, then to see all necessary busines neglected, to fraught such a drunken ship with so much guilded durt . . .

> Oh cursed gold those, hunger-starved movers,
> To what misfortunes lead'st thou all those lovers!
> For all the China wealth, nor Indies can
> Suffice the minde of an av'ritious man.[42]

from CHAPTER 4

The Arrivall of the Phœnix; her returne; and other Accidents

The authoritie now consisting in Captaine Martin, and the still sickly President, the sale of the Stores commodities maintained his estate, as an inheritable revenew.

---

42. Smith quoted Fotherby and combined a couplet from Juvenal with a couplet from Virgil.

The spring approaching, and the Ship departing, Mr. Scrivener and Captaine Smith devided betwixt them the rebuilding James towne; the repairing our Pallizadoes; the cutting downe trees; preparing our fields; planting our corne, and to rebuild our Church, and recover our Store house. All men thus busie at their severall labours, Master Nelson arrived with his lost Phœnix; lost (I say) for that we all deemed him lost. Landing safely all his men, (so well he had mannaged his ill hap,) causing the Indian Isles to feede his company, that his victuall to that we had gotten, as is said before, was neare after our allowance sufficient for halfe a yeare. He had not any thing but he freely imparted it, which honest dealing (being a Marriner) caused us admire him: we would not have wished more then he did for us. Now to relade this ship with some good tydings, the President (not holding it stood with the dignitie of his place to leave the Fort) gave order to Captaine Smith to discover and search the commodities of the Monacans Countrey beyond the Falls. Sixtie able men was allotted them, the which within six dayes, Smith had so well trained to their armes and orders, that they little feared with whom they should incounter: yet so unseasonable was the time, and so opposit was Captaine Martin to any thing, but onely to fraught this ship also with his phantasticall gold, as Captaine Smith rather desired to relade her with Cedar, (which was a present dispatch) then either with durt, or the hopes and reports of an uncertaine discovery, which he would performe when they had lesse charge and more leisure.

> But, The God of Heav'n, He eas'ly can
> Immortalize a mortall man,
> With glory and with fame.
> The same God, ev'n as eas'ly may
> Afflict a mortall man, I say,
> With sorrow and with shame.[43]

Whilst the conclusion was a resolving, this hapned.

Powhatan (to expresse his love to Newport) when he departed, presented him with twentie Turkies, conditionally to returne him twentie swords, which immediately was sent him; now after his departure he presented Captaine Smith with the like luggage, but not finding his humor obeyed in not sending such weapons as he desired, he caused his people with twentie devices to obtaine them. At last by ambuscadoes at our very Ports they would take them perforce, surprise us at worke, or any way; which was so long permitted, they became so insolent there was no rule; the command from England was so strait not to offend them, as our authoritie-bearers (keeping their houses) would rather be any thing then peacebreakers. This charitable humor prevailed, till well it chanced they medled with Captaine Smith, who without farther deliberation gave them such an incounter, as some he so hunted up and downe the Isle, some he so terrified with whipping, beating, and imprisonment, as for revenge they surprised two of our forraging disorderly souldiers, and having assembled their forces, boldly threatned at our Ports to force Smith to redeliver seven Salvages, which for their villanies he detained prisoners, or we were all but dead men. But to try their furies he sallied out amongst them, and in lesse then an houre, he so hampred their insolencies, they brought them his two men, desiring peace without any further composition for their prisoners. Those he examined, and caused them all beleeve, by severall vollies of shot one of their companions was shot to death, because they would not confesse their intents and plotters of those villanies. And thus they all agreed in one point, they were directed onely by Powhatan to obtaine him our weapons, to cut our owne throats, with the manner where, how, and when, which we plainly found most true and apparant: yet he sent his messengers, and his dearest daughter Pocahontas with presents to excuse him of the injuries done by some rash untoward Captaines his subjects, desiring their liberties for this time, with the assurance of his love for ever. After Smith had given the prisoners what correction he thought fit, used them well a day or two after, & then delivered them Pocahontas, for whose sake onely he fayned to have saved their lives, and gave them libertie. The patient Councell that nothing would move to warre with the Salvages, would gladly have wrangled with Captaine Smith for his crueltie, yet none was slaine to any mans knowledge, but it brought them in such feare and obedience, as his very name would sufficiently affright them; where before, wee had sometime peace and warre twice in a day, and very seldome a weeke, but we had some trecherous villany or other.

The fraught of this Ship being concluded to be Cedar, by the diligence of the Master, and Captaine Smith, she was quickly rela   ded: Master Scrivener was neither idle nor slow to follow all things at the Fort; the Ship being ready to set sayle, Captaine Martin being alwayes very sickly, and unserviceable, and desirous to injoy the credit of his supposed Art of finding the golden Mine, was most willingly admitted to returne for England.

---

43. From a translation of Homer by Fotherby.

EDWARD MARIA WINGFIELD (1560?–1613?)

Edward Maria Wingfield, first president of the Virginia colony, was born into an aristocratic family in Britain the eldest son and heir of Thomas Wingfield and his second wife. Little is known of Wingfield's life. He served as a soldier during wars in Ireland and the Netherlands before entering into proceedings with the Virginia Company and its colony. On April 10, 1606, the Virginia Charter was granted to Wingfield, Sir Thomas Gates, George Somers, and Richard Hakluyt. Of that group, Wingfield was the only one who sailed for Virginia later that year. One of the original members of the Royal Council responsible for running the colony, Wingfield was soon elected the first leader of the Virginia colony of Jamestown.

The struggles the colony experienced regarding supplies, illness, and factionalism proved difficult for Wingfield to negotiate. Separated by their divergent status, backgrounds, and goals, the early colonists seemed less concerned with establishing a stable settlement and more interested in pursuing wealth and continuing their explorations. Wingfield's elite background distanced him from the colonists who were laborers, yet his treatment of the "gentlemen" colonists also failed to gain him the support of the other councillors. After approximately one year of conflict and strife, the colonists removed the unpopular Wingfield from office in September 1607. Wingfield was imprisoned for several months before he was returned to England in May 1608.

His account of his experiences in Jamestown, "A Discourse of Virginia" (1608), offers a defense of his actions in governing the colony and offers insight into the struggles he faced as a leader. Wingfield's refutation of the charges that had been lodged against him offers a counterpoint to John Smith's well-known account of the early Virginia settlement and helps illuminate the myriad challenges confronting early colonial leaders.

A DISCOURSE OF VIRGINIA[1]

Here Followeth What Happened in James Town,
in Virginia, after Captain Newport's Departure
for England.

Captain Newport,[2] having always his eyes and ears open to the proceedings of the Colony, three or four days before his departure asked the President[3] how he thought himself settled in the government—whose answer was that no disturbance could endanger him or the Colony but it must be wrought either by Captain Gosnold or Mr. Archer.[4] For the one was strong with friends and followers, and could if he would, and the other was troubled with an ambitious spirit, and would if he could. The Captain gave them both knowledge of this, the President's opinion, and moved them with many entreaties to be mindful of their duties to His Majesty and the Colony.

June, 1607, the 22nd: Captain Newport returned for England, for whose good passage and safe return we made many prayers to our Almighty God.

June the 25th, an Indian came to us from the great Powhatan[5] with the word of peace—that he desired greatly our friendship, that the werowances [chiefs] Pasyaheigh and Tapahanah should be our friends, that we should sow and reap in peace or else he would make wars upon them with us. This message fell out true; for both those werowances have ever since remained in peace and

---

1. Although Wingfield's *Discourse* was evidently written in 1608 and circulated at that time, it was not published until 1860. The text derives from that publication, in *Transactions and Collections of the American Antiquarian Society* (1860).

2. Captain Christopher Newport (1560–1617), one of the original councillors, commanded the Virginia Company fleet.

3. Wingfield typically refers to himself as "the President" throughout the *Discourse*.

4. Captain Bartholomew Gosnold (1572?–1607) and Captain Gabriel Archer (1575?–1609/10) were both members of the original Royal Council.

5. Powhatan (1540?–1618) was the tributary chief of the Powhatan confederacy, as the colonists called them, in tidewater Virginia.

trade with us. We rewarded the messenger with many trifles which were great wonders to him. This Powhatan dwelleth 10 miles from us, upon the River Pamunkey[6] which lies north from us. The Powhatan in the former journal mentioned (a dweller by Capt. Newport's faults) is a werowance and under this great Powhatan, which before we knew not.

July—the 3rd of July, seven or eight Indians presented the President a deer from Pamaonke, a werowance desiring our friendship. They inquired after our shipping, which the President said was gone to Croutoon.[7] They fear much our ships; and therefore he would not have them think it far from us. Their werowance had a hatchet sent him. They were well contented with trifles. A little after this came a deer to the President from the Great Powhatan. He and his messengers were pleased with the like trifles. The President likewise bought, diverse times, deer of the Indians [and] beavers and other flesh, which he always caused to be equally divided among the Colony.

About this time diverse of our men fell sick. We missed above forty before September did see us, amongst whom was the worthy and religious gentleman Capt. Bartholomew Gosnold, upon whose life stood a great part of the good success and fortune of our government and Colony. In his sickness time the President did easily foretell his own deposing from his command—so much differed the President and the other councillors in managing the government of the Colony.

July—the 7th of July, Tapahanah, a werowance [and a] dweller on Salisbury side,[8] hailed us with the word of peace. The President, with a shallop well manned, went to him. He found him sitting on the ground cross-legged, as is their custom, with one attending on him which did often say, "This is the werowance Tapahanah", which he did likewise confirm with stroking his breast. He was well enough known, for the President had seen him diverse times before. His countenance was nothing cheerful, for we had not seen him since he was in the field against us; but the President would take no knowledge thereof, and used him kindly, giving him a red waistcoat which he did desire. Tapahanah did inquire after our ship-

ping. He received [the same] answer as before. He said his old store was spent, that his new [one] was not a full growth by a foot, [and] that as soon as any was ripe he would bring it; which promise he truly performed.

The ——— of ———[9] Mr. Kendall[10] was put off from being [a member] of the Council and committed to prison, for [the reason] that it did manifestly appear he did practice to sow discord between the President and Council. Sickness had not now left us six able men in our town. God's only mercy did now watch and ward for us; but the President hid this our weakness carefully from the savages, never suffering them in all this time to come into our town.

September—the 6th of September, Pasyaheigh sent us a boy that was run from us. This was the first assurance of his peace with us; besides, we found them no cannibals. The boy observed the men and women to spend the most part of the night in singing or howling, and that every morning the women carried all the little children to the river side; but what they did there he did not know. The rest of the werowances do likewise send our men renegades to us home again, using them well during their being with them; so as now, they being well rewarded at home at their return, they take little joy to travel abroad without passports.

The Council demanded some larger allowance for themselves, and for some sick [persons], their favorites— which the President would not yield unto without their warrants. This matter was before propounded by Capt. Martin, but so nakedly as that he neither knew the quantity of the store to be but for 13 weeks and a half, under the captain-merchant's hand. He prayed them further to consider the long time before we expected Capt. Newport's return, the uncertainty of his return (if God did not favor his voyage), the long time before our harvest would be ripe, and the doubtful peace that we had with the Indians (which they would keep no longer than opportunity served to do us mischief).

It was then therefore ordered that every meal of fish or flesh should excuse the allowance for porridge, both against the sick and [against the] whole. The Council, therefore, sitting again upon this proposition [and being] instructed in the former reasons and order, did not think

---

6. York River.

7. Survivors of the disastrous Roanoke settlement were believed to have gone to the Indian town of Croatoon in 1587.

8. South shore of the James River.

9. Here and elsewhere in the *Discourse,* missing dates were not added to the original text.

10. Captain George Kendall (fl. 1600–07) was one of the original seven councillors.

fit to break the former order by enlarging their allowance, as will appear by the most voices ready to be showed under their hands. Now was the common store of oil, vinegar, sack, and aquavita all spent, saving two gallons of each. The sack [was] reserved for the Communion Table, [and] the rest for such extremities as might fall upon us, which the President had only made known to Capt. Gosnold, of which course he liked well. The vessels were, therefore, bunged up.[11] When Mr. Gosnold was dead, the President did acquaint the rest of the Council with the said remnant; but, Lord, how they then longed for [a chance] to sup up that little remnant! For they had now emptied all their own bottles, and all others that they could smell out.

A little while after this the Council did again fall upon the President for some better allowance for themselves and [for] some few [of] the sick, their privates. The President protested he would not be partial; but, if one had anything of him, every man should have his portion according to their places. Nevertheless [he said] that, upon [being shown] their warrants, he would deliver what [it] pleased them to demand. If the President had at that time enlarged the proportion according to their request, without doubt in [a]very short time he had starved the whole company. He would not join with them, therefore, in such ignorant murder without their own warrant.

The President, well seeing to what end their impatience would grow, desired them earnestly and oftentimes to bestow the Presidentship among themselves, [and said] that he would obey, [as] a private man, as well as they could command. But they refused to discharge him of the place, saying they might not do it; for [they said] that he did His Majesty good service in it. In this meantime the Indians did daily relieve us with corn and flesh, [so] that in three weeks the President had reared up 20 men able to work; for, as his store increased, he mended the common pot, [and] he had laid up, besides, provision for three weeks' wheat beforehand.

By this time the Council had fully plotted to depose Wingfield, their then President, and had drawn certain articles in writing amongst themselves, and took their oaths upon the Evangelists to observe them—the effect whereof was, first: to depose the then President; to make Mr. Ratcliffe[12] the next President; not to depose the one the other; not to take the deposed President into [the] Council again; not to take Mr. Archer into the Council, or any other, without the consent of every one of them. To these [articles] they had subscribed, as out of their own mouths at several times it was easily gathered. Thus had they forsaken His Majesty's government, [as] set [for] us down in the instructions, and made it a triumvirate. It seemeth [that] Mr. Archer was nothing acquainted with these articles. Though all the rest crept out of his notes and commentaries that were preferred against the President, yet it pleased God to cast him into the same disgrace and pit that he prepared for another, as will appear hereafter.

September—the 10th of September, Mr. Ratcliffe, Mr. Smith, and Mr. Martin[13] came to the President's tent, with a warrant subscribed under their hands, to depose the President, saying they thought him very unworthy to be either President or [a member] of the Council; and therefore [they] discharged him of both [positions]. He answered them that they had eased him of a great deal of care and trouble [and] that, long since, he had diverse times proffered them the place at an easier rate. And [he said] further, that the President ought to be removed (as appeareth in His Majesty's instructions for our government) by the greater number of 13 voices, [the] Concillors, [and] that they were but three;[14] and therefore [he] wished them to proceed advisedly. But they told him [that] if they did him wrong they must answer [for] it. Then said the deposed President, "I am at your pleasure. Dispose of me as you will, without further garboils."[15]

I will now write what followeth in my own name, and give the new President his title. I shall be the briefer, being thus discharged. I was committed to a sergeant, and sent to the pinnace; but I was answered with, "If they did me wrong, they must answer [for] it."

The 11th of September, I was sent for to come before the President and Council upon their court day. They had now made Mr. Archer [the] recorder of Virginia. The President made a speech to the Colony [for the reason] that he thought it fit to acquaint them why I was deposed. (I am now forced to stuff my paper with frivolous trifles, [in order] that our grave and worthy Council may the better strike those veins where the corrupt blood lieth, and

---

11. Stopped up with a cork.

12. One of the original seven councillors. He later succeeded Wingfield as president.

---

13. All members of the original Royal Council.

14. Ratcliff, Smith, and Martin.

15. Confusion.

that they may see in what manner of government the hope of the Colony now travaileth.) First, Master President said that I had denied him a penny-whistle, a chicken, a spoonful of beer, and [had] served him with foul corn; and with that [he] pulled some grain out of a bag, showing it to the company. Then started up Mr. Smith and said that I had told him plainly how he lied; and that I [had] said [that] though we were equal here, yet, if he were in England, he would think scorn his name should [he] be my companion. Mr. Martin followed with, "He reporteth that I do slack the service in the Colony, and do nothing but tend my pot, spit, and oven; but he hath starved my son and denied him a spoonful of beer. I have friends in England [who] shall be revenged on him, if ever he come in London."

I asked Mr. President if I should answer these complaints and whether he had aught else to charge me withal. With that he pulled out a paper book, loaded full with articles against me, and gave them [to] Mr. Archer to read. I told Mr. President and Council that, by the instructions for our government, our proceeding ought to be verbal, and [that] I was there ready to answer; but they said they would proceed in that order. I desired a copy of the articles and time given me to answer them likewise by writing; but that would not be granted. I bade them then please themselves. Mr. Archer then read some of the articles—when, on the sudden, Mr. President said, "Stay, stay! We know not whether he will abide [by] our judgment, or whether he will appeal to the King." [He continued], saying to me, "How say you: will you appeal to the King, or no?" I apprehended presently that God's mercy had opened [for] me a way, through their ignorance, to escape their malice; for I never knew how I might demand an appeal. Besides, I had secret knowledge how they had forejudged me to pay five-fold for anything that came to my hands, whereof I could not discharge myself by writing; and [I knew] that I should lie in prison until I had paid it.

The Captain Merchant had delivered me our merchandise, without any note of the particulars, under my hand; for [he] himself had received them in gross. I likewise, as occasion moved me, spent them in trade or by gift amongst the Indians. So likewise did Capt. Newport take [out]of them, when he went up to discover the King's river, what[ever] he thought good, without any note of his hand mentioning the certainty. And [he] disposed of them as was fit for him. Of these, likewise, I could make no account; only I was well assured I had never bestowed the value of three penny-whistles to my own use nor to the

private use of any other; for I never carried any favorite over with me, or entertained any there. I was all [to] one and one to all. Upon these considerations I answered Mr. President and the Council that His Majesty's hands were full of mercy and that I did appeal to His Majesty's mercy. Then they committed me [as a] prisoner again to the master of the pinnace, with these words, "Look to him well; he is now the King's prisoner."

Then Mr. Archer pulled out of his bosom another paper book full of articles against me, desiring that he might read them in the name of the Colony. I said [that] I stood there, ready to answer any man's complaint whom I had wronged; but no one man spoke one word against me. Then was he willed to read his book, whereof I complained; but I was still answered, "If they do me wrong, they must answer [for] it." I have forgotten the most of the articles, [for] they were so slight (yet he glorieth much in his penwork). I know well the last—and a speech that he then made savored well of a mutiny—for he desired that by no means I might lie prisoner in the town, lest both he and others of the Colony should not give such obedience to their command as they ought to do; which goodly speech of his they easily swallowed.

But it was usual and natural to this honest gentleman, Mr. Archer, to be always hatching of some mutiny in my time. He might have appeared an author of three several mutinies. And he (as Mr. Pearsy sent me word) had bought some witnesses' hands against me to diverse articles, with Indian cakes (which was no great matter to do after my deposal, and considering their hunger), persuasions, and threats. At another time he feared not to say, openly and in the presence of one of the Council, that, if they had not deposed me when they did, he had gotten twenty others to himself which should have deposed me. But this speech of his was likewise easily digested. Mr. Crofts feared not to say that, if others would join with him, he would pull me out of my seat and out of my skin too. Others would say (whose names I spare) that, unless I would amend their allowance, they would be their own carvers. For these mutinous speeches I rebuked them openly, and proceeded no further against them, considering therein of men's lives in the King's service there. One of the Council was very earnest with me to take a guard about me. I answered him [that] I would [have] no guard but God's love and my own innocence. In all these disorders was Mr. Archer a ringleader.

When Mr. President and Mr. Archer had made an end of their articles above mentioned, I was again sent prisoner to the pinnace; and Mr. Kendall, taken from thence, had his liberty, but might not carry arms. All this while the savages brought to the town such corn and flesh as they could spare. Pasyaheigh, by Tapahanah's mediation, was taken into friendship with us. The Councillors, Mr. Smith especially, traded up and down the river with the Indians for corn; which relieved the Colony well.

As I understand by a report, I am much charged with starving the Colony. I did always give every man his allowance faithfully, both of corn, oil, aquavita, etc., as was by the Council proportioned; neither was it bettered after my time, until, towards the end of March, a biscuit was allowed to every working man for his breakfast, by means of the provision brought us by Capt. Newport, as will appear hereafter. It is further said [that] I did much banquet and riot. I never had but one squirrel roasted, whereof I gave part to Mr. Ratcliffe, then sick—yet was that squirrel given [to] me. I did never heat a flesh-pot but when the common pot was so used likewise. Yet how often Mr. President's and the Councillor's spits have night and day been endangered to break their backs—so laden with swans, geese, ducks, etc.! How many times their flesh-pots have swelled, many hungry eyes did behold to their great longing. And what great thieves and thieving there hath been in the common store since my time—I doubt not but it is already made known to his Majesty's Council for Virginia.

The 17th day of September I was sent for to [come to] the Court to answer a complaint exhibited against me by Jehu Robinson; for [he charged] when I was President I did say [that] he with others had consented to run away with the shallop to Newfoundland. At another time I must answer Mr. Smith for [the charge] that I had said he did conceal an intended mutiny. I told Mr. Recorder [that] those words would bear no actions—that one of the causes was done without the limits mentioned in the patent granted to us. And therefore [I] prayed Mr. President that I might not be thus lugged with these disgraces and troubles; but he did wear no other eyes or ears than grew on Mr. Archer's head. The jury gave the one of them 100 pounds and the other 200 pounds damages for slander. Then Mr. Recorder did very learnedly comfort me, [saying] that if I had wrong I might bring my writ of error in London; whereat I smiled.

I, seeing their law so speedy and cheap, desired justice for a copper kettle which Mr. Croft did detain from me. He said I had given it [to] him. I did bid him bring his proof for that. He confessed he had no proof. Then Mr. President did ask me if I would be sworn [that] I did not

give it him. I said I knew no cause why to swear for mine own [property]. He asked Mr. Croft if he would make oath [that] I did give it him; which oath he took, and won my kettle from me, that was in that place and time worth half his weight in gold. Yet I did understand afterwards that he would have given John Capper the one half of the kettle to have taken the oath for him; but he would [have] no copper on that price. I told Mr. President I had not known the like law, and prayed they would be more sparing of law until we had more wit or wealth. [I said] that laws were good spies in a populous, peaceable, and plentiful country, where they did make the good men better and stayed the bad from being worse; yet we were so poor as they did but rob us of time that might be better employed in service in the Colony.

The ——— day of ——— the President did beat James Read, the smith. The smith struck him [back] again. For this he was condemned to be hanged; but before he was turned off the ladder he desired to speak with the President in private—to whom he accused Mr. Kendall of a mutiny, and so escaped himself. What indictment Mr. Recorder framed against the smith I know not; but I know it is familiar for the President, Councillors, and other officers, to beat men at their pleasure. One lieth sick till death, another walketh lame, the third crieth out of all his bones; which miseries they do take upon their consciences to come to them by this their alms of beating. Were this whipping, lawing, beating, and hanging in Virginia known in England, I fear it would drive many well-affected minds from this honorable action of Virginia.

This smith, coming aboard the pinnace with some others about some business two or three days before his arraignment, brought me commendations from Mr. Pearsy, Mr. Waller, Mr. Kendall, and some others, saying they would be glad to see me on shore. I answered him [that] they were honest gentlemen and had carried themselves very obediently to their governors. I prayed God that they did not think of any ill thing unworthy [of] themselves. I added further that upon Sunday if the weather were fair I would be at the sermon. Lastly, I said that I was so sickly, starved, [and] lame, and did lie so cold and wet in the pinnace, as I would be dragged thither before I would go thither any more. Sunday proved not fair; I went not to the sermon.

The ——— day of ——— Mr. Kendall was executed, being shot to death for a mutiny. In the arrest of his judgement he alleged to Mr. President that his name was Sicklemore, not Ratcliffe,[16] and so [he] had no authority to pronounce judgement. Then Mr. Martin pronounced judgement.

Somewhat before this time the President and Council had sent for the keys of my coffers, supposing that I had some writings concerning the Colony. I requested that the Clerk of the Council might see what they took out of my coffers; but they would not suffer him or any other. Under color hereof they took my books of accounts and all my notes that concerned the expenses of the Colony, and [the] instructions under the Captain Merchant's hand of the store of provisions, diverse other books, and trifles of my own proper goods, which I could never recover. Thus was I made good prize on all sides.

The ——— day of ——— the President commanded me to come on shore, which I refused [to do], as not rightfully deposed. And [I] desired that I might speak to him and the Council in the presence of ten of the best sort of the gentlemen. With much entreaty some of them were sent for. Then I told them [that] I was determined to go into England to acquaint our Council there with our weakness. I said further [that] their laws and government were such as I had no joy to live under them any longer, [and] that I did much mislike their triumvirate, having forsaken His Majesty's instructions for our government; and therefore [I] prayed there might be more made of the Council. I said further [that] I desired not to go into England, if either Mr. President or Mr. Archer would go, but was willing to take my fortune with the Colony; and [I] did also proffer to furnish them with £100 towards the fetching home [of] the Colony, if the action was given over. They did like of none of my proffers, but made diverse shot at me in the pinnace. I, seeing their resolutions, went ashore to them—where, after I had stayed a while in conference, they sent me to the pinnace again.

December—the 10th of December Mr. Smith went up the river of the Chickahominy to trade for corn. He was desirous to see the head of that river; and, when it was not possible with the shallop, he hired a canoe and an Indian to carry him up further. The river—the higher [he went]—grew worse and worse. Then he went on shore with his guide and left Robinson and Emmery, two of our men, in the canoe—which were presently slain by the Indians, Pa-

munkey's men. And he himself [was] taken prisoner, and by the means of his guide his life was saved. And Pamunkey, having him prisoner, carried him to his neighbors' wero-wances to see if any of them knew him for one of those which had been, some two or three years before us, in a river amongst them [to the] northward and [had] taken away some Indians from them by force. At last he brought him to the great Powhatan (of whom before we had no knowledge), who sent him home to our town the 8th of January.

During Mr. Smith's absence the President did swear [in] Mr. Archer [as] one of the Council, contrary to his oath taken in the articles agreed upon between themselves (before spoken of), and contrary to the King's instructions, and without Mr. Martin's consent; whereas there were no more but the President and Mr. Martin then of the Council.

Mr. Archer, being settled in his authority, sought how to call Mr. Smith's life in question, and had indicted him upon a chapter in Leviticus[17] for the death of his two men. He had had his trial the same day of his return and, I believe, his hanging the same or the next day—so speedy is our law there. But it pleased God to send Captain Newport unto us the same evening, to our unspeakable comfort; whose arrival saved Mr. Smith's life and mine, because he took me out of the pinnace and gave me leave to lie in the town. Also by his coming was prevented a parliament, which the new Councillor, Mr. Recorder, intended there to summon. Thus error begot error.

Captain Newport, having landed, lodged, and refreshed his men, employed some of them about a fair storehouse, others about a stove, and his mariners about a church—all which works they finished cheerfully and in short time.

January—the 7th of January our town was almost quite burnt with all our apparel and provision; but Captain Newport healed our wants, to our great comforts, out of the great plenty sent us by the provident and loving care of our worthy and most worthy Council.

This vigilant Captain, slacking no opportunity that might advance the prosperity of the Colony, having settled the company upon the former works, took Mr. Smith and Mr. Scrivener (another Councillor of Virginia, upon whose discretion liveth a great hope of the action) [and] went to discover the River Pamunkey on the further side

---

16. According to the Virginia Company charter, Captain John Ratcliff was apparently the alias of John Sicklemore (fl. 1607–09).

17. Leviticus 24.19–21.

whereof dwelleth the Great Powhatan, and to trade with him for corn. This river lieth north from us, and runneth east and west. I have nothing but by relation of that matter, and therefore dare not make any discourse thereof, lest I might wrong the great desert which Captain Newport's love to the action hath deserved—especially himself being present, and best able to give satisfaction thereof. I will hasten, therefore, to his return.

March—the 9th of March he returned to Jamestown with his pinnace well laden with corn, wheat, beans, and peas to our great comfort and his worthy commendations.

By this time the Council and Captain, having attentively looked into the carriage both of the Councillors and other officers, removed some officers out of the store, and [especially] Captain Archer, a Councillor whose insolency did look upon that little himself with great-sighted spectacles, derogating from others' merits by spewing out his venomous libels and infamous chronicles upon them, as doth appear in his own handwriting; for which, and other worse tricks, he had not escaped the halter, but that Captain Newport interposed his advice to the contrary.

Captain Newport, having now dispatched all his business and set the clock in a true course (if so the Council will keep it), prepared himself for England upon the 10th of April, and arrived at Blackwall on Sunday, the 21st of May, 1608.

LETTERS FROM VIRGINIA

Letters written back to the home country reveal much about the various concerns of the earliest colonists. In the earliest days of settlement, the Virginia colonists worried about the tensions evident among the leaders because if the tensions remained unresolved, all the colonists would be at risk of starvation, disease, and attacks by the Indian populations nearby. The leaders worried about the implications of their actions, as indicated by the letter that John Rolfe wrote to his friend, Sir Thomas Dale, regarding his decision to create a union with Pocahontas. Those in the serving classes, indentured servants and slaves, were expected to do much of the labor, yet their powerlessness within the community's structure left them little decision making about the bare necessities, such as food and clothing. Nor did they, like their masters, have items to trade with local peoples (outside the purview of the colony's leaders, of course). Richard Frethorne's letters written to his parents show the extent to which indentured servants, although they were putatively free, were not provided for by their masters, yet had to keep their bonds to work for the duration of their indenture period, regardless of personal volition to leave or hardship faced. To be sure, many indentured laborers ran off under such circumstances, but many, like Frethorne, sought a legal resolution to their personal difficulties, and many simply wanted to return home.

In the years following the relative successes of planting the colony of Virginia, the leaders were forced to reformulate their goals and visions of how the colony could best serve Britain. Wars with the Powhatans and other Indians in alliance with the tidewater peoples brought trouble for the colonists. As Powhatan said in a speech to Captain John Smith, the Indian people were ready to assist the colonists on fair terms. But the wildness of the country and the absence of familiar social forms of control made it impossible to monitor the behavior of colonists to assure consistency in their dealings with Native peoples, whom they sometimes considered good neighbors and sometimes considered so beneath them that they could engage in raiding parties with impugnity.

The Virginia Company's initial charter had been drawn up with an eye to the discovery of minerals and ores that could be mined, just as Spain and Portugal had mined areas of Mexico and South America. When it became clear that the soils of Virginia would not yield such wealth to stockholders, the purposes of the colonial endeavor shifted to agricultural concerns and to the exportation of produce that would interest merchants and their purchasers back in England. Concerns about farming, then, replaced concerns about mining, and small plantations began to emerge as the best means by which wealth could be wrested from the earth. The formation of a plantation culture in Virginia would change as sources of labor changed from indentured laborers to Indian and African slaves, many of whom were born in the Virginia area itself by the end of the century. In an effort to confirm the viability of continued expenditure in Virginia and to suggest to associates and patrons back in England the usefulness of owning plantations in the colony, the colonists sought affiliation with the Royal Society of London, and the society began to circulate letters from the colonies regarding scientific and social matters. In letters like colonist John Clayton's to the Royal Society, much can be learned about plantation culture and expectations for plantation owners. Clayton's letter also reveals the attitude of imperial England toward those in the colonies: Although laboring colonists who were working the land expected that they knew best what would serve them in the colony, those who were better educated and who retained connections in London assumed they knew best how to manage large estates in Virginia.

LETTER TO SIR THOMAS DALE (1614)[1]

JOHN ROLFE

The copy of the gentleman's letters to Sir Thomas Dale, that after married Powhatan's daughter, containing the reasons moving him there-unto.

Honorable Sir, and most worthy Governor:
When your leisure shall best serve you to peruse these lines, I trust in God the beginning will not strike you into a greater admiration than the end will give you good content. It is a matter of no small moment, concerning my own particular, which here I impart unto you, and which toucheth me so nearly as the tenderness of my salvation. How be it, I freely subject myself to your grave and mature judgement, deliberation, approbation, and determination, assuring myself of your zealous admonitions and godly comforts, either persuading me to desist or encouraging me to persist therein, with a religious fear and godly care—for which (from the very instant that this began to root itself within the secret bosom of my breast) my daily and earnest prayers have been, still are, and ever shall be produced forth with as sincere a godly zeal as I possibly may, to be directed, aided, and governed in all my thoughts, words, and deeds, to the glory of God, and for my eternal consolation. To persevere wherein I never had

more need, nor (till now) could ever imagine to have been moved with the like occasion.

But (my case standing as it doth) what better worldly refuge can I here seek than to shelter myself under the safety of your favorable protection? And did not my ease proceed from an unspotted conscience, I should not dare to offer to your view and approved judgement these passions of my troubled soul, so full of fear and trembling is hypocrisy and dissimulation. But knowing my own innocence and godly fervor in the whole prosecution hereof, I doubt not of your benign acceptance and clement construction. As for malicious depravers and turbulent spirits, to whom nothing is tasteful but what pleaseth their unsavory palate, I pass not for them, being well assured in my persuasion (by the often trial and proving of myself, in my holiest meditations and prayers) that I am called hereunto by the spirit of God; and it shall be sufficient for me to be protected by yourself in all virtuous and pious endeavors. And for my more happy proceeding herein, my daily oblations shall ever be addressed to bring to pass so good effects that your self and all the world may truly say: this is the work of God, and it is marvelous in our eyes.

But to avoid tedious preambles and to come nearer the matter: first suffer me, with your patience, to sweep and make clean the way wherein I walk from all suspicions and doubts which may be covered therein, and faithfully to reveal unto you what should move me hereunto.

Let therefore this, my well-advised protestation, which here I make between God and my own conscience, be a sufficient witness at the dreadful Day of Judgement (when the secret of all men's hearts shall be opened) to condemn me herein, if my chiefest intent and purpose be not to strive with all my power of body and mind in the undertaking of so mighty a matter—no way led (so far forth as man's weakness may permit) with the unbridled desire of carnal affection, but for the good of this plantation, for the honor of our country, for the glory of God, for my own salvation,

---

1. The letter John Rolfe (1585–1622) wrote in 1614 to Sir Thomas Dale details the concerns he experienced prior to his marriage to Pocahontas. After their marriage, Pocahontas was taken to England, but she died while there, and Rolfe returned to the colony alone. He died in 1622, fighting the same Powhatans with whom he had made a formal marriage tie. The text, slightly modernized, is from *Narratives of Early Virginia,* ed. Lyon G. Tyler (1907).

and for the converting to the true knowledge of God and Jesus Christ an unbelieving creature, namely Pocahontas, to whom my hearty and best thoughts are, and have a long time been, so entangled, and enthralled in so intricate a labyrinth, that I was even wearied to unwind myself thereout. But Almighty God, who never faileth His [followers] that truly invoke His Holy Name, hath opened the gate and led me by the hand that I might plainly see and discern the safe paths wherein to tread.

To you, therefore, most noble Sir, the patron and father of us in this country, do I utter the effects of this my settled and long-continued affection (which hath made a mighty war in my meditations); and here I do truly relate to what issue this dangerous combat is come unto, wherein I have not only examined but thoroughly tried and pared my thoughts even to the quick, before I could find any fit, wholesome, and apt applications to cure so dangerous an ulcer. I never failed to offer my daily and faithful prayers to God for His sacred and holy assistance. I forgot not to set before mine eyes the frailty of mankind, his proneness to evil, his indulgence of wicked thoughts, with many other imperfections wherein man is daily ensnared and oftentimes overthrown, and them compared to my present estate. Nor was I ignorant of the heavy displeasure which Almighty God conceived against the sons of Levi and Israel for marrying strange wives, nor of the inconveniences which may thereby arise, with other the like good motions which made me look about warily and with good circumspection into the grounds and principal agitations which thus should provoke me to be in love with one whose education hath been rude, her manners barbarous, her generation accursed, and so discrepant in all nurture from myself that oftentimes with fear and trembling I have ended my private controversy with this: surely these are wicked instigations, hatched by him who seeketh and delighteth in man's destruction. And so, with fervent prayers to be ever preserved from such diabolical assaults (as I took those to be), I have taken some rest.

Thus, when I had thought I had obtained my peace and quietness, behold, another but more gracious temptation hath made breaches into my holiest and strongest meditations, with which I have been put to a new trial in a straighter manner than the former. For besides the many passions and sufferings which I have daily, hourly, yea, and in my sleep endured, even awaking me to astonishment, taxing me with remissness and carelessness, refusing and neglecting to perform the duty of a good Christian, pulling me by the ear and crying, "why dost not thou endeavor to make her a Christian?" (and these have happened, to my greater wonder, even when she hath been furthest separated from me, which in common reason, were it not an undoubted work of God, might breed forgetfulness of a far more worthy creature)—besides, I say, the holy spirit of God hath often demanded of me, why I was created, if not for transitory pleasures and worldly vanities, but to labor in the Lord's vineyard, there to sow and plant, to nourish and increase the fruits thereof, daily adding with the good husband in the gospel somewhat to the talent, that in the end the fruits may be reaped, to the comfort of the laborer in this life and his salvation in the world to come? And if this be, as undoubtedly this is, the service Jesus Christ requireth of His best servant: woe unto him that hath these instruments of piety put into his hands and willfully despiseth to work with them. Likewise, adding hereunto her great appearance of love to me, her desire to be taught and instructed in the knowledge of God, her capableness of understanding, her aptness and willingness to receive any good impression; and also the spiritual, besides her own, incitements stirring me up hereunto.

What should I do? Shall I be of so untoward a disposition as to refuse to lead the blind into the right way? Shall I be so unnatural as not to give bread to the hungry? Or uncharitable as not to cover the naked? Shall I despise to actuate these pious duties of a Christian? Shall the base fear of displeasing the world overpower and withhold me from revealing unto man these spiritual works of the Lord, which in my meditations and prayers I have daily made known to Him? God forbid. I assuredly trust He hath thus dealt with me for my eternal felicity and for His glory; and I hope so to be guided by His heavenly grace that in the end, by my faithful pains and Christian-like labor, I shall attain to that blessed promise, pronounced by that holy prophet Daniel, unto the righteous that bring many unto the knowledge of God: namely, that they shall shine like the stars forever and ever. A sweeter comfort cannot be to a true Christian, nor a greater encouragement for him to labor all the days of his life in the performance thereof, nor a greater gain of consolation to be desired at the hour of death and in the Day of Judgement.

Again, by my reading and conference with honest and religious persons have I received no small encouragement—besides *serena mea conscientia,* the clearness of my conscience clean from the filth of impurity, *quae est instar muri ahenei,* which is unto me as a brazen wall. If I should set down at large the perturbations and godly motions which have stricken within me, I should but make a tedious and unnecessary volume. But I doubt not these shall be sufficient both to certify you of my true intents in discharging of my duty to God and to yourself, to whose gracious providence I humbly submit myself, for His glory, your honor, our country's good, the benefit of this plantation, and for the converting of one unregenerate to regeneration; which I beseech God to grant, for His dear son Christ Jesus, His sake.

Now if the vulgar sort, who square all men's actions by the base rule of their own filthiness, shall tax or taunt me in this my Godly labor, let them know it is not any hungry appetite to gorge myself with incontinency. [To be] sure, (if I would, and were so sensually inclined), I might satisfy such desire—though not without a seared conscience, yet with Christians more pleasing to the eye and less fearful in the offence unlawfully committed. Nor am I in so desperate an estate that I regard not what becometh of me. Nor am I out of hope but one day to see my country; nor so void of friends, nor mean in birth, but there to obtain a match to my great content. Nor have I ignorantly passed over my hopes there; nor regardlessly seek to lose the love of my friends by taking this course. I know them all, and have not rashly overslipped any.

But shall it please God thus to dispose of me (which I earnestly desire to fulfill my ends before set down), I will heartily accept of it as a Godly task appointed me. And I will never cease, (God assisting me), until I have accomplished and brought to perfection so holy a work, in which I will daily pray God to bless me, to mine and her eternal happiness. And thus desiring no longer to live, to enjoy the blessings of God, than this my resolution doth tend to such Godly ends as are by me before declared, not doubting of your favorable acceptance, I take my leave, beseeching Almighty God to rain down upon you such plenitude of His heavenly graces as your heart can wish and desire. And so I rest,

at your command, most willing
to be disposed of,
John Rolfe

LETTERS TO HIS PARENTS (1623)[1]

RICHARD FRETHORNE

Loving and kind father and mother:
My most humble duty remembered to you, hoping in God of your good health, as I myself am at the making hereof.

This is to let you understand that I your child am in a most heavy case by reason of the nature of the country, [which] is such that it causeth much sickness, [such] as the scurvy and the bloody flux and diverse other diseases, which maketh the body very poor and weak. And when we are sick there is nothing to comfort us; for since I came out of the ship I never ate anything but peas, and loblollie (that is, water gruel). As for deer or venison I never saw any since I came into this land. There is indeed some fowl, but we are not allowed to go and get it, but must work hard both early and late for a mess of water gruel and a mouthful of bread and beef. A mouthful of bread for a penny loaf must serve for four men which is most pitiful. [You would be grieved] if you did know as much as I [do], when people cry out day and night—Oh! that they were in England without their limbs—and would not care to lose any limb to be in England again, yea, though they beg from door to door. For we live in fear of the enemy every hour, yet we have had a combat with them on the Sunday before Shrovetide, and we took two alive and made slaves of them. But it was by policy, for we are in great danger; for our plantation is very weak by reason of the death and sickness of our company. For we came but twenty for the merchants, and they are half dead just; and we look every hour when two more should go. Yet there came some four other men yet to live with us, of which there is but one alive; and our Lieutenant is dead, and [also] his father and his brother. And there was some five or six of the last year's twenty, of which there is but three left, so that we are fain to get other men to plant with us; and yet we are but 32 to fight against 3000 if they should come. And the nighest help that we have is ten miles of us, and when the rogues overcame this place [the] last [time] they slew 80 persons. How then shall we do, for we lie even in their teeth? They may easily take us, but [for the fact] that God is merciful and can save with few as well as with many, as he showed to Gilead. And like Gilead's soldiers, if they lapped water, we drink water which is but weak.

And I have nothing to comfort me, nor there is nothing to be gotten here but sickness and death, except [in the event] that one had money to lay out in some things for profit. But I have nothing at all—no, not a shirt to my back but two rags (2), nor no clothes but one poor suit, nor but one pair of shoes, but one pair of stockings, but one

---

1. Richard Frethorne's extended letter—written March 20, April 2, and April 3, 1623—reveals fully the issues faced by a

young indentured man, about whom nothing is known except what appears in this letter. The text, edited to assist clarity, is from *The Records of the Virginia Company of London*, IV, ed. Susan M. Kingsbury (1935).

cap, [and] but two bands. My cloak is stolen by one of my own fellows, and to his dying hour [he] would not tell me what he did with it, but some of my fellows saw him have butter and beef out of a ship, which my cloak, I doubt [not], paid for. So that I have not a penny, nor a penny worth, to help me to either spice or sugar or strong waters, without the which one cannot live here. For as strong beer in England doth fatten and strengthen them, so water here doth wash and weaken these here [and] only keeps [their] life and soul together. But I am not half [of] a quarter so strong as I was in England, and all is for want of victuals; for I do protest unto you that I have eaten more in [one] day at home than I have allowed me here for a week. You have given more than my day's allowance to a beggar at the door; and if Mr. Jackson had not relieved me, I should be in a poor case. But he like a father and she like a loving mother doth still help me.

For when we go up to Jamestown (that is 10 miles of us) there lie all the ships that come to land, and there they must deliver their goods. And when we went up to town [we would go], as it may be, on Monday at noon, and come there by night, [and] then load the next day by noon, and go home in the afternoon, and unload, and then away again in the night, and [we would] be up about midnight. Then if it rained or blowed never so hard, we must lie in the boat on the water and have nothing but a little bread. For when we go into the boat we [would] have a loaf allowed to two men, and it is all [we would get] if we stayed there two days, which is hard; and [we] must lie all that while in the boat. But that Goodman Jackson pitied me and made me a cabin to lie in always when I [would] come up, and he would give me some poor jacks [to take] home with me, which comforted me more than peas or water gruel. Oh, they be very godly folks, and love me very well, and will do anything for me. And he much marvelled that you would send me a servant to the Company; he saith I had been better knocked on the head. And indeed so I find it now, to my great grief and misery; and [I] saith that if you love me you will redeem me suddenly, for which I do entreat and beg. And if you cannot get the merchants to redeem me for some little money, then for God's sake get a gathering or entreat some good folks to lay out some little sum of money in meal and cheese and butter and beef. Any eating meat will yield great profit. Oil and vinegar is very good; but, father, there is great loss in leaking. But for God's sake send beef and cheese and butter, or the more of one sort and none of another. But if you send cheese, it must be very old cheese; and at the cheesemonger's you may buy very good cheese for twopence farthing or halfpenny, that will be liked very well. But if you send cheese, you must have a care how you pack it in barrels; and you must put cooper's chips between every cheese, or else the heat of the hold will rot them. And look whatsoever you send me—be it never so much—look, what[ever] I make of it, I will deal truly with you. I will send it over and beg the profit to redeem me; and if I die before it come, I have entreated Goodman Jackson to send you the worth of it, who hath promised he will. If you send, you must direct your letters to Goodman Jackson, at Jamestown, a gunsmith. (You must set down his freight, because there be more of his name there.) Good father, do not forget me, but have mercy and pity my miserable case. I know if you did but see me, you would weep to see me; for I have but one suit. (But [though] it is a strange one, it is very well guarded.) Wherefore, for God's sake, pity me. I pray you to remember my love to all my friends and kindred. I hope all my brothers and sisters are in good health, and as for my part I have set down my resolution that certainly will be; that is, that the answer of this letter will be life or death to me. Therefore, good father, send as soon as you can; and if you send me any thing let this be the mark.

ROT

Richard Frethorne,
Martin's Hundred

The names of them that be dead of the company [that] came over with us to serve under our Lieutenants:

John Flower	George Goulding
John Thomas	Jos. Johnson
Thos. Howes	our lieutenant, his
John Butcher	father and brother
John Sanderford	Thos. Giblin
Rich. Smith	George Banum
John Olive	a little Dutchman
Thos. Peirsman	one woman
William Cerrell	one maid
	one child

All these died out of my master's house, since I came; and we came in but at Christmas, and this is the 20th day of March. And the sailors say that there is two-thirds of the 150 dead already. And thus I end, praying to God to send me good success that I may be redeemed out of Egypt. So *vale in Christo*.

Loving father, I pray you to use this man very exceeding kindly, for he hath done much for me, both on my journey and since. I entreat you not to forget me, but by any means redeem me; for this day we hear that there is 26 of [the] Englishmen slain by the Indians. And they have taken a pinnace of Mr. Pountis, and have gotten pieces, armor, [and] swords, all things fit for war; so that they may now steal upon us and we cannot know them from [the] English till it is too late—[till the time] that they be upon us—and then there is no mercy. Therefore if you love or respect me as your child, release me from this bondage and save my life. Now you may save me, or let me be slain with infidels. Ask this man—he knoweth that all is true and just that I say here. If you do redeem me, the Company must send for me to my Mr. Harrod; for so is this Master's name. April, the second day,

Your loving son,
Richard Frethorne

Moreover, on the third day of April we heard that after these rogues had gotten the pinnace and had taken all furnitures [such] as pieces, swords, armor, coats of mail, powder, shot and all the things that they had to trade withal, they killed the Captain and cut off his head. And rowing with the tail of the boat foremost, they set up a pole and put the Captain's head upon it, and so rowed home. Then the Devil set them on again, so that they furnished about 200 canoes with above 1000 Indians, and came, and thought to have taken the ship; but she was too quick for them—which thing was very much talked of, for they always feared a ship. But now the rogues grow very bold and can use pieces, some of them, as well or better than an Englishman; for an Indian did shoot with Mr. Charles, my master's kinsman, at a mark of white paper, and he hit it at the first, but Mr. Charles could not hit it. But see the envy of these slaves, for when they could not take the ship, then our men saw them threaten Accomack, that is the next plantation. And now there is no way but starving; for the Governor told us and Sir George that except the *Seaflower* come in or that we can fall foul of these rogues and get some corn from them, above half the land will surely be starved. For they had no crop last year by reason of these rogues, so that we have no corn but as ships do relieve us, nor we shall hardly have any crop this year; and we are as like to perish first as any plantation. For we have but two hogsheads of meal left to serve us this two months, if the *Seaflower* do stay so long before she come in; and that meal is but three weeks bread for us, at a loaf for four about the bigness of a penny loaf in England—that is but a halfpennyloaf a day for a man. Is it not strange to me, think you? But what will

it be when we shall go a month or two and never see a bit of bread, as my master doth say we must do? And he said he is not able to keep us all. Then we shall be turned up to the land and eat barks of trees or molds of the ground; therefore with weeping tears I beg of you to help me. Oh, that you did see my daily and hourly sighs, groans, and tears, and thumps that I afford mine own breast, and rue and curse the time of my birth, with holy Job. I thought no head had been able to hold so much water as hath and doth daily flow from mine eyes.

But this is certain: I never felt the want of father and mother till now; but now, dear friends, full well I know and rue it, although it were too late before I knew it.

I pray you talk with this honest man. He will tell you more than now in my haste I can set down.

Your loving son,
Virginia, 3rd April, 1623   Richard Frethorne

————————

LETTER TO
DR. RALPH SMITH (1686)[1]
WILLIAM FITZHUGH

Doctor Ralph Smith, April 22, 1686
In order to [facilitate] the exchange [which] you promised to make for me, and [which] I desired you to proceed therein—[that is] to say to exchange an estate of inheritance in land there of two or three hundred pounds a year, or in houses in any town of three or four hundred pounds a year—I shall be something particular in the relation of my concerns here, that is to go in return thereof. As, first, the plantation where I now live contains a thousand acres, at least 700 acres of it being rich thicket, the remainder good hearty plantable land, without any waste either by marshes or great swamps. The commodiousness, conveniency, and pleasantness your self well knows. Upon it

————————

1. William Fitzhugh (1650/51–1701) came to Virginia, with training in the law, about 1670, having been persuaded by friends that Virginia was an excellent place for a young attorney to practice law. His law practice in the colony took shape well, and Fitzhugh quickly became associated with some of the largest landed families in the colony. His letter to Ralph Smith reveals the land brokering that went on within the colony well before Britain's first century in Virginia was concluded. The text, slightly modernized, is from *William Fitzhugh and His Chesapeake World, 1676–1701,* ed. Richard Beale Davis (1963).

there is three quarters well furnished, with all necessary houses, ground, and fencing, together with a choice crew of Negroes at each plantation, most of them [in] this country born, the remainder as likely as most in Virginia, there being twenty-nine in all, with stocks of cattle and hogs at each quarter. Upon the same land is my own dwelling house, furnished with all accommodations for a comfortable and genteel living, [such] as a very good dwelling house, with 13 rooms in it, four of the best of them hung, nine of them plentifully furnished with all things necessary and convenient; and all houses for use well furnished with brick chimneys; four good cellars, a dairy, dovecoat, stable, barn, henhouse, kitchen, and all other conveniences, and all in a manner new; a large orchard of about 2500 apple trees (most [of them] grafted), well fenced with a locust fence which is as durable as most brick walls; a garden a hundred foot square, well paled in; a yard wherein is most of the foresaid necessary houses, pallisaded in with locust puncheons, which is as good as if it were walled in and more lasting than any of our bricks; together with a good stock of cattle, hogs, horses, mares, sheep, etc. and [the] necessary servants belonging to it for the supply and support thereof. About a mile and half distant [there is] a good water gristmill, whose toll I find sufficient to find my own family with wheat and Indian corn for our necessities and occasions. Up the river in this country [I have] three tracts of land more; one of them contains 21996 acres, another 500 acres, and one other 1000 acres—all good, convenient, and commodious seats, and which in a few years will yield a considerable annual income. [There is also] a stock of tobacco with the crops and good debts lying out of about 250000 lb., besides sufficient [quantity] of almost all sorts of goods to supply the family's and the quarter's occasions for two, if not three, years. Thus I have given you some particulars [from] which I thus deduce [that] the yearly crops of corn and tobacco together with the surplus of meat more than will serve the family's use will amount annually to 60000 lb. tobacco which at 10 shillings per Ct. is £300 per annum; and the Negroes' increase, [they] being all young, and a considerable parcel of breeders, will keep that stock good for ever. The stock of tobacco, managed with an inland trade, will yearly yield 60000 lb. [of] tobacco without hazard or risk, which will be both clear, without charge of housekeeping or disbursements for servants' clothing. The orchard in a very few years will yield a large supply to plentiful housekeeping, or, if better husbanded, [will] yield at least 15000 lb. tobacco annual income. What I have not particularly mentioned, your own knowledge in my affairs is able to supply. If any are so desirous to deal for the estate without the stock of tobacco, I shall be ready and willing; but I will make no fractions of that, either all or none at all shall go. I have so fully discoursed [to] you in the affair that I shall add no further instructions, but leave it to your prudent and careful management. And [I] would advise that if any overtures of such a nature should happen, immediately give an account thereof to Mr. Nicholas Hayward, Notary Public near the Exchange [in] London, both of the person treating, and the place, situation, quantity, and quality of the estate, who will take speedy and effectual care, to give me a full and ready account thereof, which I hope you will for all opportunities do.

To Doctor Ralph Smith, in Bristol,

Sir, Your
William Fitzhugh

———

LETTER TO THE ROYAL SOCIETY OF LONDON (1688)[1]
JOHN CLAYTON

Sir:

My last was the journal of Thomas Bats, Thomas Woods, and Robert Fallam. I know Colonel Byrd very well, that's mentioned to have been about that time as far as the Totemas. He's one of the intelligentest gentlemen in all Virginia, and knows more of Indian affairs than any man in the country. I discoursed [with] him about the River on

———

1. John Clayton (1657–1725) was an Anglican clergyman who was better known in his day for his scientific letters and his experiments than for writings on matters of religion. He was sent as a minister to the Jamestown colony, but he also seems to have been sent to create scientific experiments and to record notes on botanical and mechanical discoveries while in the colony. His stay lasted only two years, 1684–86, but he continued to correspond with the colonists and thereby contributed valuable information to the Royal Society, to which he was elected in 1688. Clayton became known to leading men in the colony, including Governor Lord Effingham and Secretary of State Nicholas Spencer, who once had acted as governor; William Sherwood, a wealthy planter; Ralph Wormeley; and John Banister, himself a rector and naturalist like Clayton. This letter, dated August 17, 1688, is from *The Reverend John Clayton, a Parson with a Scientific Mind,* ed. E. Berkeley and D. S. Berkeley (1965).

the other side of the mountains, said to ebb and flow, which he assured me was a mistake in them. For [he said] that it must run into a lake now called Lake Petite, which is fresh water. For since that time a colony of the French are come down from Canada and have seated themselves on the back of Virginia, where Fallam and the rest supposed there might be a bay; but [there] is a lake to which they have given the name of Lake Petite, there being several larger lakes between that and Canada. The French, possessing themselves of these lakes, no doubt will in short time be absolute masters of the beaver trade, the greatest number of beavers being caught there. The Colonel told me likewise that the common notion of the lake of Canada he was assured was a mistake; for the river supposed to come out of it had no communication with any of the lakes, nor the lakes one with another, but were distinct. But [it is well] not to ramble after hearsay and other matters.

But with them [?] [it is necessary] to return to the parts of Virginia inhabited by the English, which in general is a very fertile soil, far surpassing England, for there English wheat—as they call it to distinguish it from maize, commonly called Virginia wheat—yields generally between 15 and 30 fold, the ground only once plowed, whereas 'tis a good crop in England that yields above 8 fold, after all their toil and labor. And yet in truth 'tis only the barrenest parts that they have cultivated—tilling and planting only the high lands, leaving the richer vales unstirred because they understand not anything of draining. So that the richest meadow lands, which is one third of the country, is boggy marsh and swamp, whereof they make little advantage, but loose in them abundance of their cattle, especially at the first of the spring when the cattle are weak and venture too far after young grass. Whereas vast improvements might be made thereof, for the generality of Virginia is a sandy land with a shallow soil. So that after they have cleared a fresh piece of ground out of the woods, it will not bear tobacco past two or three years, unless cow-penned; for they manure the ground by keeping their cattle, as in the south you do keep your sheep, every night confining them within hurdles, which they remove when they have sufficiently dunged one spot of ground.

But, alas, they cannot improve much thus; besides, it produces a strong sort of tobacco in which the smokers say they can plainly taste the fulsomeness of the dung. Therefore every three or four years they must be [ready] for clearing a new piece of ground out of woods, which requires much labor and toil, it being so thick grown all over with massy timber. Thus their plantations run over vast tracts of ground, each ambitioning to engross as much as they can [in order] that they may be sure [to] have enough to plant, and [enough] for their stocks and herds of cattle to range and feed in; [so] that plantations of 1000, 2000, or 3000 acres are common, whereby the country is thinly inhabited, their living is solitary and unsociable, trading [is] confused and dispersed; besides other inconveniences. Whereas they might improve 200 or 300 acres to more advantage, and would make the country much more healthy; for those that have 3000 acres have scarce cleared 600 acres thereof, which is peculiarly termed the plantation, being surrounded with the 2400 acres of woods. So that there can be no free or even motion of the air; but the air is kept either stagnant, or the lofty sulphurous particles of the air, that are higher than the tops of the trees, which are above as high again as the generality of the woods in England, descending when they pass over the cleared spots of ground, must needs in the violent heat of summer raise a preternatural ferment and produce bad effects. Nor is it any advantage to their stocks or crops; for did they but drain their swamps and low lands they [would] have a very deep soil that would endure planting 20 or 30 years, and some would scarce ever be worn out, but be ever longer better. For they might lay them all winter or when they pleased in water, and the product of their labor would be double or treble, whether [for] corn or tobacco. And [I am certain] that this is no fond projection—though when I [have] discoursed the same to several and [have] in part shown them how their particular grounds might be drained at a very easy rate, they have either been so conceited of their old way, so sottish as not to apprehend, or so negligent as not to apply themselves thereto.

But on the plantation where I lived, I drained a good large swamp, which fully answered expectation. The gentlewoman where I lived was a very acute, ingenious lady, who one day [was] discoursing [with] the overseer of her servants about pitching the ensuing year's crop. The overseer was naming one place where he designed to plant 30000 plants, another place for 15000, another for 10000, and so forth—the whole crop designed to be about 100000 plants. Having observed the year before [that] he had one the like and [had] scattered his crop up and down the plantation at places a mile or a mile and a half asunder, which was very inconvenient and whereby they lost much time, I interposed and asked why they did not plant all their crop together. The fellow smiled, as it were at my ignorance, and said there was very good reason for it. I replied that was it [which] I inquired after. He returned [that] the plantation had been an old, planted plantation, and being but a small plot of ground [it] was almost worn out; so that they had not ground all together that would bring forth tobacco. I told him then [that] they had better ground than ever yet they had planted, and more than their hands could manage. He smiled again, and asked me where. I then named such a swamp. He then said scornfully [that] he thought what a planter I was, [and] that I understood better how to make a sermon than managing tobacco. I replied with some warmness: though I hoped so, that was impertinence, and no answer. He then said that the tobacco there would drown and the roots rot. I replied that the whole country would drown if the rivers were stopped, but it might be laid as dry as any land on the plantation. In short we discoursed [about] it very warmly, till he told me he understood his own business well enough and did not desire to learn of me.

But the gentlewoman attended somewhat better to my reasoning, and got me one day to go and show her how I projected the draining of the swamp, and thought it so feasible that she was resolved to have it done, and therefore desired me I would again discourse [with] her overseer, which I did several times. But he would by no means hearken thereto and was so positive that she was forced to turn him away to have her servants set about the work, and with three men in thirteen days I drained the whole swamp. It, being sandy land, soaks and drains admirably well, and, what I little expected, laid a well dry at a considerable distance. The gentlewoman was in England last year, and I think Dr. Moulin was by when she asked me. Now to teach her how she might make her tobacco that grew in the swamp less—for it produced so very large that it was suspected to be of the Aranoko kind—I told her [that] though the complaint was rare, yet there was an excellent remedy for that. In letting every plant bear eight or nine leaves instead of four or five she would have more tobacco and less leaves. Now you must know [that] they top their tobacco, that is, take away the little top bud when the plant has put forth as many leaves as they think the richness of the ground will bring to a substance, but generally when it has shot forth four or six leaves. And when the top bud is gone, it puts forth no more leaves, but side branches instead which they call suckers [and] which they are careful ever to take away that they may not impoverish the leaves.

I have been more tedious in the particulars, the fuller to evince how resolute they are and conceitedly bent to follow their old practice and custom, rather than to receive directions from others, though plain, easy, and advantageous. There are many other places [that] are as easy to drain as this, though of larger extent and richer soil, for some of which I have given directions and have only had the return perhaps of a flout afterwards. Even in Jamestown Island, which is much [?] of an oval figure, there's a swamp [which] runs diagonal-wise over the island, whereby is lost at least 150 acres of land that would be meadow which would turn to as good account as if it were in England. Besides, it is the great annoyance of the town and no doubt but makes it much more unhealthy. If therefore they but scoured the channel, and made a pretty ordinary trench all along the middle of the swamp, placed a sluice at the mouth where it opens into the Back Creek (for the mouth of the channel there is narrow, has a good hard bottom, and is not past two yards deep when the flood is out, as if nature had designed it beforehand), they might thus drain all the swamp absolutely dry or lay it under water at their pleasure. I have talked several times hereof to Mr. Sherwood, the owner of the swamp, yet nothing is essayed in order thereto.

And now, since we are speaking of Jamestown, give me leave to adjoin some reflections as to the situation and fortifications of the place. The natural situation of the place is such as perhaps the world has not a more commodious place for a town, where all things conspire for [the] advantage thereof. To give you some idea of the place, the river and island lie thus.[2]

Jamestown Island is rather a peninsula, being joined to the continent by a small neck of land, not past 20 or 30 yards over, and which at spring tides is overflowed and is then an absolute island. Now they have built a silly sort of a fort, that is a brick wall in the shape of a half moon, at the beginning of the swamp, because the channel of the river lies very nigh the shore, but it is the same as if a fort were built at Chelsea to secure London from being taken by shipping. Besides, ships passing up the river are secured from the guns of the fort till they come directly over against the fort, by reason [that] the fort stands in a vale; and all the guns directed down the river, that should play on the ships as they are coming up the river, will lodge their shot within ten, twenty, or forty yards in the rising bank, which is much above the level of the fort, so that if a ship gave but a good broadside, just when she comes to bear upon the fort, she might put the fort into that confusion as to have free passage enough. There was indeed an

---

2. Clayton included a map with his letter.

old fort of earth in the town, being a sort of tetragon with something like bastions at the four corners, as I remember; but the channel lying further off to the middle of the river there, they let it be demolished and built that new one [already] spoken of, of brick, which seems little better than a blind wall to shoot wild ducks or geese.

If they would build a fort for the security of the town and country, I conceive it should be on Archer's Hope Point, for that would stop the ships from passing up the river before they came to the town, and would secure the town from being blocked up by sea. The channel at Archer's Hope Point lies close by the shore and makes such an angle there (by reason of Hogg Island) that going up or down the river, let the wind be where it will, they must there bring the contrary tack on board; and generally when they about the ship, as they call it, they are so nigh the shore that a man may almost fling a finger-stone on board. How much this hinders the motion of a ship, and what confusion it must be to them to bring a contrary tack on board whilst they have all the guns of a fort playing so nigh upon them, may readily be conceived. Archer's Hope is a neck of land that runs down three miles long [and] not much past half a mile broad between the main river and Archer's Hope Creek, which has large marshes and swamps; so that a citadel built upon the point would almost be impregnable, being it could be attacked [in] no way but one (which is so narrow a slender neck of land that it would be difficult to take it that way). And it would secure Jamestown from being blocked, being it would not be past a mile by water to the point of Jamestown Island. The island is surrounded with water and marshy land that the town could never be bombed by land.

But now to return to the reflections of improving and manuring of land in Virginia: hitherto, as I have said, they have used none but that of cow-penning. Yet I suppose they might find very good marl in many places. I have seen both the red and blue marl at some breaks of hills. This would be the properest manure for their sandy land if they spread it not too thick—theirs being, as I have said, a shallow, sandy soil, which was the reason I never advised any to use lime, though they have very good lime of oyster shells, but that's the properest manure for cold clay land and not for a sandy soil. But as most lands have one swamp or another bordering on them, they may certainly get admirable slitch, wherewith to manure all their uplands. But this, say they, will not improve ground, but [rather] clods and grows hard. 'Tis true [that] it will do so for some time, a year or two at the first; but did they cast it in heaps and let it lie for two or three years after a frost or two had seized it and it

has been well pierced therewith, I doubt not [that] it would turn to good account. And for this too I have something more then bare conjecture; for discoursing [about] it once with a good, notable planter, we went to view a heap thereof that casually he had cast up between three and four years before, and we found it not very binding but rather a fine natural mold, whereupon he did confess [that] he then remembered that out of a ridge of the like mold he had had very large plants, which must have been of the like slime or slitch cast up before. But [he] said that himself and others despaired of this manure, because they had taken some of this slitch fresh and moist out of the swamp, and filled tobacco hills with it, and in the midst of it planted their plants, which so bound the roots of their plants that they never came to anything. But he said he then saw his error, yet I have not heard [that] he has remembered to correct it.

But 'tis strange in how many things besides they are remiss, which one would think Englishmen should not be guilty of. They neither house nor milk any of their cows in winter, having a notion that it would kill them; yet I persuaded the aforementioned lady where I lived to milk four cows the last winter that I stayed in the country (whereof she found so good effect that she assured me she would keep to my advice for the future), and also, as I had further urged, house them too—for which they have mighty conveniences, their tobacco houses being empty ever at that time of the year and may easily be [re-]fitted in two or three days' time without any prejudice, whereby their cattle would be much sheltered from those pinching, sharp frosts that some nights on a sudden become very severe. I had another project for the preservation of their cattle [which] proved very successful. I urged the lady to sow her wheat as early as possibly she could, so that before winter it might be well rooted, to be early and flourishing at the first of the spring—so that she might turn thereon her weak cattle and such as should at any time be swamped, whereby they might be recruited and saved and it would do the wheat good also. I advised her likewise to save and carefully gather her Indian corntops and blades and all her straw and whatever could be made [into] fodder for her cattle, for they got no hay (though I was urging her to [grow] that, too), and to sow sainfoin, for being a sandy soil I'm confident [that] it would turn to very good account. They have little or no grasses in winter, so that their cattle are pined and starved; and many that are brought low and weak, when the spring begins, venture too far into the swamps after the fresh grass, where they perish, so that several persons lose 10, 20, or 30 head of cattle in a year.

I observed [that] this was much owing to their inadvertancy and error in their way of managing and feeding them, for they get little fodder; but as they think [of] corn [as] being more nourishing, [they] feed them with their Indian corn, which they give them morning and evening. They spend thus a great quantity of corn; and when all's done, what signifies two or three heads of corn to a beast in a morning? It makes them only linger about the houses for more, and after that sweet food they are not so prompt to browse on the trees and the coarse grass which the country affords. So that thus their guts shrink up; they become belly-shot, as they call it. I advised therefore never to give them anything in a morning, whereby as soon as they were set forth of the cow pens they would fall a-feeding; and though they filled their bellies only with such coarse stuff as had little nourishment in it, yet it would keep out their bellies and they would have a better digestion. And then when they were come home at nights [I said] to fodder them, beginning with straw and their coarsest fodder, which they would learn to eat by degrees before they tasted that that was more delicate, and whilst their digestion was strong would yield them nourishment to keep them still so. Afterwards when the winter pinched, their fine fodder then would stand them instead; and hereby they might preserve their weakest cattle by these methods and [with] the help of the wheat patch. She, the gentlewoman where I lived, saved all her cattle and lost not one in two winters after that I stayed there. Besides, she saved about 20 barrels of corn, as I remember, that she told me she used to spend upon her stock. And a barrel of corn is commonly worth 10 shillings. Nay, further, the last spring she fed two beasts, a bullock and a cow, fat upon her wheat with the addition only of a little boiled corn; and yet the wheat was scarce eaten down enough.

But to return again to the nature of the earth, which may be pretty well gathered from what I have already said: I have observed that at five or six yards deep, at the breaks of some banks, I have found veins of clay, admirably good to make pots, pipes, or the like of—and whereof I suppose the Indians make their pipes and pots

to boil their meat in, which they make very handsomely, and [which] will endure the fire better than most crucibles. I took [some] of this clay, dried, powdered, and sifted it; powdered and sifted potsherds and glass; [and mixed the whole in a ratio of] 3 parts, 2 parts, and 1 part, as I remember, and therewith made a large crucible which was the best I yet tried in my life. I took it, once [it had become] red-hot, out of the fire and clapped it immediately into water, and it started not at all. The country abounds mightily with iron ore that, as I have been assured by some upon trial, has been found very good. There are rocks thereof [which] appear at the precipice of hills, at the foot whereof there runs a river fit for a forge; and there's wood enough to supply it with charcoal. As I have heard, there was formerly some persons [who] undertook the work, and when they had made but a small quantity of iron (which proved very good) the Indian Massacre happened. And they, being higher-seated than the then-inhabited part of the country, were all cut off, and the work demolished; so that it has frightened others, I think, from the like attempt. Besides, such a work requires a greater fund and bank of money to carry it on than any there are able to lay out; and for persons in England to meddle therewith is certainly to be cheated at such a distance. Some Indians brought Colonel Byrd some black lead, whereof he has told me there was great store. There's very curious talc towards the falls of [the] Rappahannock River, which they burn and make a delicate white wash of it. The Secretary of State, Colonel Spencer, has assured me there were vitriolic or alluminous earths on the banks of [the] Potomac.

And thus far, of what my memory supplies me, referring to the earth. In the next I shall give a short account of the Byrds. My humble respects and service to the honorable society, more peculiarly to my acquaintance and friend. I am,

Sir
yours to serve,
J. Clayton
Wakefield, August the 17th/88

RICHARD LIGON (1634–1703)

Very little is known about the life of Richard Ligon, author of one of the most important seventeenth-century accounts of a British Caribbean colony. Finding himself socially and financially adrift at the end of the English Civil War, Ligon set sail for the British West Indies. He arrived at Barbados in 1647. His work as an architect and plantation operator there did not improve his fortune as he had hoped, and he returned to England during the 1650s, where he was imprisoned at Newgate, a debtors' prison. It was during this time in prison that Ligon drafted his pamphlet, *A True and Exact History of the Island of Barbados,* which was published first in London in 1657.

Ligon's *History* describes the inhabitants, social structure, flora and fauna, and plantation system of Barbados. His explanation of the situation for indentured servants on the island is an important reminder of the different kinds of labor used for the original plantation of the colonies. Ligon's tale of Inkle and Yarico has been taken by many recent critics as an allegory of colonization. In the tale, Yarico, an Indian woman, saves the Englishman, Inkle, who later concludes to sell her as a slave after he is rescued. This tale became enormously popular during the eighteenth century. Versions of it appeared in English, French, and German.

from A TRUE AND EXACT HISTORY OF THE ISLAND OF BARBADOS[1]

Having been Censur'd by some (whose Judgements I cannot controll, and therefore am glad to allow) for my weakenesse and Indiscretion, that having never made proofe of the Sea's operation, and the severall faces that watry Element puts on, and the changes and chances that happen there, from Smooth to Rough, from Rough to Raging Seas, and High going Billowes, (which are killing to some Constitutions,) should in the last Scene of my life, undertake to run so long a Risco from *England* to the *Barbadoes;* And truly I should without their help conclude my selfe guilty of that Censure, had I not the refuge of an old proverb to fly to, which is, Need makes the old wife trot: for having lost (by a Barbarous Riot) all that I had gotten by the painfull travells and cares of my youth; by which meanes I was stript and rifled of all I had, left destitute of a subsistance, and brought to such an Exigent, as I must famish or fly; and looking about for friends, who are the best supporters in so staggering a condition, found none, or very few, whom griefs and afflictions had not deprest, or worne out, Banishment absented, or Death devour'd; so that in stead of these neere and Native comforters, I found my selfe a stranger in my owne Country, and therefore resolv'd to lay hold on the first opportunity that might convoy me to any other part of the World, how far distant soever, rather then abide here. I continued not many weekes in this expectation, when a friend, as willing to shift his ground as I, gave me an Overture which I accepted, and so upon the sixteenth day of *June 1647,* we

embark'd in the Downes, on the good Ship called the *Achilles;* a vessell of 350 tunnes the Master *Thomas Crowder* of *London;* and no sooner were we all aboard, but we presently weighed Anchor, and put to Sea.

[At Cape Verde Islands, They Are Entertained]

Dinner being ended, and the Padre well neere wearie of his wayting, we rose, and made roome for better Companie; for now the Padre, and his blacke mistresse were to take their turnes; A Negro of the greatest beautie and majestie together that ever I saw in one woman. Her stature large, and excellently shap't, well favour'd, full eye'd, & admirably grac't; she wore on her head a roll of green taffatie, strip't with white and Philiamort,[2] made up in manner of a Turban; and over that a sleight vayle, which she tooke off at pleasure. On her bodie next her linen, a Peticoate of Orange Tawny and Skye Colour; not done with Straite stripes, but wav'd; and upon that a mantle of purple silke, ingrayld with straw Colour. This Mantle was large, and tyed with a knot of verie broad black Ribbon, with a rich Jewell on her right shoulder, which came under her left arme, and so hung loose and carelesly, almost to the ground. On her Legs, she wore buskins of wetched Silke, deckt with Silver lace, and Fringe; Her shooes, of white Leather, lac't with skie colour; and pinkt between those laces. In her eares, she wore Large Pendants, about her neck; and on her armes, fayre Pearles. But her eyes were her richest Jewells: for they were the largest, and most orientall, that I have ever seene.

Seing all these perfections in her onely at passage, but not yet heard her Speake; I was resolv'd after dinner, to make an Essay what a present of rich silver silke and gold Ribbon would doe, to perswade her to open her lips:

---

1. The text is based on *A True and Exact History of the Island of Barbados* as first published in London (1657).

2. The color of a dead or faded leaf.

Partly out of a Curiositie, to see whether her teeth were exactly white, and cleane, as I hop'd they were; for 'tis a generall opinion, that all *Negroes* have white teeth; but that is a Common error, for the black and white, being so neere together, they set off one another with the greater advantage. But looke neerer to them, and you shall find those teeth, which at a distance appear'd rarely white, are yellow and foul. This knowledge wrought this Curiositie in me, but it was not the mayne end of my enquirie; for there was now, but one thing more, to set her off in my opinion, the rarest black swanne that I had ever seen, and that was her language, & gracefull delivery of that, which was to unite and confirme a perfection in all the rest. And to that end I took a Gentleman that spoke good Spanish with me, and awaited her comming out, which was with far greater majesty, and gracefulness, then I have seen Queen *Anne,* descend from the Chaire of State, to dance the Measures with a Baron of England, at a Maske in the Banquetting house. And truly, had her followers and friends, with other perquisits (that ought to be the attendants on such a state and beautie) wayted on her, I had made a stop, and gone no farther. But finding her but slightly attended and considering she was but the Padres Mistres, & therefore the more accessible, I made my addresses to her, by my interpreter; & told her, I had some Trifles made by the people of *England,* which for their value were not worthy her acceptance, yet for their Novelty, they might be of some esteem, such having bin worn by the great Queens of *Europe,* & intreated her to vouchsafe to receive them. She with much gravity, and reserv'dness, opened the paper; but when she lookt on them, the Colours pleased her so, as she put her gravity into the loveliest smile that I have ever seen. And then shewed her rowes of pearls, so clean, white, Orient, and well shaped, as *Neptunes* Court was never pav'd with such as these; & to shew whether was whiter, or more Orient, those or the whites of her eyes, she turn'd them up, & gave me such a look, as was a sufficient return for a far greater present, and withall wisht, I would think of somewhat wherein she might pleasure me, and I should finde her both ready and willing. And so with a gracefull bow of her neck, she took her way towards her own house; which was not above a stones cast from the *Padres.* Other addresses were not to be made, without the dislike of the *Padre,* for they are there as jealous of their Mistrisses, as the *Italians* of their wives.

In the afternoon we took leave, and went aboard, where we remained three or four days; about which time, some passengers of the ship, who had no great store of linnen for shift, desired leave to go ashoare and took divers women along with them, to wash their linnen. But (it seem'd) the *Portugalls,* and *Negroes* too, found them handsome and fit for their turnes, and were a little Rude, I cannot say Ravisht them; for the Major part of them, being taken from Bridewell, Turnboule street,[3] and such like places of education, were better natur'd then to suffer such violence; yet complaints were made, when they came aboard, both of such abuses, and stealing their linnen.

But such a praise they gave of the place, as we all were desirous to see it: for, after the Raine, every day gave an increase to the beauty of the place, by the budding out of new fruits and flowers.

This was the valley on the left side of the Hill, more spacious and beautifull by much than that on the right hand, where the *Padre* dwelt. The next day, a dozen Gentlemen of our company, resolv'd to go and see this so much admired valley, and when our Saylers with their long boat went to fetch water, (as dayly they did,) we went along with them and landed there, in as high going Billows, as I have ever seen, so near the land. Much adoe we had, to be carried to land though on mens backs, and yet the grapple came as near the shoare as they durst bring it, for bulging against the bottome.

No sooner were we landed, but the Captaine of the Castle, with one souldier with him; came towards us, with a slow formall pace; who desired to speake with one of us alone. Colonel *Modiford,* being the chiefe man in the Company, went with an Interpreter to meet him; and being at the distance of speech, desired to know his pleasure; which he told him was this. That he understood divers of our women had bin ashoare, the day before; and received some injury, from the people of the Iland, and that it was conceiv'd, we were come Arm'd to take revenge on those that did the affront. He therefore advised us, either to make speedy returne to the boate that brought us: or to send back our swords and pistols, and commit our selves to his protection; and if one of those were not presently put in act, we should in a very short time have all our throats Cut.

We told him we had no intention of revenge for any wrong done, and that the only cause of our landing, was to see the beauty of the place we had heard so much Commended, by our people that were ashore, of which they had given a very large testimony, both of the pleasantness

---

3. Places of prostitution in London.

and fruitfulness of it, and that our visit was out of love, both to the place and people. But for sending our weapons back to the boate, we desired his pardon; for this reason, that the Billows going so very high at that time, we could not send them to the boat without being dipt in the Sea water, which would spoyle them; and the most of them, being rich swords, and pistols, we were loath to have their beauty covered with rust, which the salt water would be the occasion of. We desired rather, that he would Command a souldier of his, to stay with a man of ours, and keep them safe, till our returne; which he being content to doe, we committed our selves to his protection, who put a guard upon us of 10 Souldiers, part *Portugalls* part *Negroes;* the most part of either kind, as proper men as I have seen, and as handsomely cloathed.

Their garments made with much Art, and all seem'd to be done by the Tayler; the Coverings for their heads, were not unlike Helmits; of blew and white strip't silke, some tawny, and yellow, others of other sorts of Colours; but all of one fashion, their doublets close to their bodies, with Cassocks, made of the fashion of the Kings guard: loose sleeves, which came to their elbowes, but large and gathered so as to fit loose from their armes; with foure large skirts, reaching down to the middle of their thighs; but these of a different colour from their suits, their breeches indifferently large, comming down below the knee; and the upper part, so wrought with Whalebones within, as to keep them hollow, from touching their backs; to avoid heat, which they were much troubled with; upon their leggs, buskins of the colour of their suits, yet some made a difference: their shoes Colour'd for the most part; some white, but very few blacke. Their weapons, as Swords, Pistols, Muskets, Pikes, and Partisans, kept very bright, and worne comelily and gracefully, which argued a decencie in the Commander, as their awfull respect did of his autheritie.

Being now under a Guard, we marcht into this valley, one of the delightfullest places that I have ever seen, for besides the high and loftie trees, as the *Palmeto, Royall, Coco, Cedar, Locust, Masticke, Mangrave, Bully, Redwood, Pickled yellow wood, Cassia, Fistula, Calabash, Cherry, Figg tree,* whose body is large inough for timber, *Cittrons, Custard apple, Gnavers, Macow, Cipres, Oranges, Limons, Lymes, Pomegrannat, Abotto, Prickled apple, Prickled peare, Papa,* these and more may be accounted wood: and yet a good part of them bearing excellent fruit; But then there are of a lesser sort, that beare the rarest fruit; whose bodyes cannot be accompted wood, as the Plantine, Pine, Bonano, Milon, water Milon, etc.

and some few grapes, but those inconsiderable, by reason they can never make wine: because they have no winter, and so by that meanes, they can never ripe together, but one is green, another ripe, another rotten, which reason will ever hold, that no wine can be made on Ilands, where there is no winter: or within twenty degrees of the line on either side. I have heard that wine is made in the *East Indies,* within lesse then fifteen Degrees; but tis of the Palme tree; out of whose body, they draw both wine and oyle; which wine will not keep above a day, but no wine of grapes, for the reasons afore said. Other kinds of trees, we found good to smell to, as Mirtle, Jesaman, Tamarisk, with a tree somewhat of that bignesse, bearing a very beautifull flower. The first halfe next the stalke, of a deep yellow or gold colour; the other halfe being the larger, of a rich Scarlet: shap'd like a Carnation, & when the flowers fall off, there grows a pod, with 7 or 8 seeds in it, divers of which, we carried to the *Barbados,* and planted there: and they grew and multiplied abundantly, and they call them there, the *St. Iago* flower, which is a beautifull, but not sweet flower.

From these woods of pleasant trees, we saw flying divers birds, some one way, some another, of the fairest, and most beautifull colours, that can be imagined in Nature: others whose Colours and shapes come short of these, did so except in sweetnesse, and loudness of voyce, as our Nightingals in England, are short of them, in either of those two properties; but in variety of tunes, our birds are beyond them, for in that they are defective.

In this valley of pleasure, adorn'd as you have heard, we march't with our Guard, faire and softly, near a quarter of a mile; before we came to the much praised fountaine; from whence we fetcht our water. The circle whereof, was about 60 foot, the Diameter about 20 from the ground to the top of the Well, (which was of freestone,) 3 foot and a halfe, from thence within, downe to the surface of the water, about 15 foot. The spring itselfe, not so much to be praised for the excellency of the taste, though cleare inough, as for the Nymphs that repaire thither. For whilst we stayed there seeing the Sayles fill their Casks; and withall Contemplating the glory of the place: there appeared to our view, many pretie young Negro Virgins, playing about the Well. But amongst those; two, that came downe with either of them a naturall Pitcher, a Calibash upon their arme, to fetch water from this fountaine. Creatures, of such shapes, as would have puzzel'd *Albert Durer,* the great Master of Proportion, but to have imitated; and *Tition,* or *Andrea de Sarta,* for softness of muscles, and Curiositie of Colouring, though with a studied diligence; and a love both to the partie and the worke. To expresse all the perfections of Nature, and Parts, these Virgins were owners of, would aske a more skillfull pen, or pencill then mine; Sure I am, though all were excellent, their motions were the highest, and that is a beautie no painter can expresse, and therefore my pen may well be silent; yet a word or two, would not be amisse, to expresse the difference between these and those of high. *Africa* as of Morcoco, Guinny,[4] Binny,[5] Cutchow, Angola, Æthiopia, and *Mauritania,* or those that dwell nere the *River* of *Gambia,* who are thick lipt, short nosd, and commonly low foreheads. But these, are compos'd of such features, as would marre the judgment of the best Paynters, to undertake to mend. Wanton, as the soyle that bred them, sweet as the fruites they fed on; for being come so neere, as their motions, and graces might perfectly be discern'd, I guest that Nature could not, without help of Art, frame such accomplisht beauties not onely of colours, and favour, but of motion too, which is the highest part of beautie. If dancing had bin in fashion in this *Iland,* I might have been perswaded, that they had bin taught those motions, by some who had studied that Art. But considering the *Padre's Musique* to be the best the *Iland* afforded, I could not but cast away that thought, and attribute all to pure nature; Innocent, as youthfull, their ages about 15.

Seing their beauties so fresh and youthfull, withall the perfections I have named, I thought good to trie, whether the uttering of their language, would be as sweet and harmonious, as their other partes were comely. And by the helpe of a Gentleman that spoke *Portugall,* I accosted them; and began to praise their beauties, shapes, and manner of dressings; which was extreamly prettie. Their haire not shorne as the *Negroes* in the places I have named, close to their heads; nor in quarters, and mases, as they use to weare it, which is ridiculous to all that see them, but themselves: But in a due proportion of length so as having their shortenings by the naturall Curles, they appeared as weirs, and artificiall, dressings to their faces. On the sides of their Cheeks, they plat little of it, of purpose to tie small Ribbon; or some small beads, of white Amber, or blew bugle, sometimes of the rare flowers that grow there; Their eares hung with Pendants, their necks and armes adorn'd with bracelets of Counterfeit pearles, and blew

bugle; such as the *Portugalls* bestow on them, for these are free *Negroes,* and weare upon the small of one of their legs, the badge of their freedome; which is a small peece of silver, or tinne, as big as the stale of a spoone; which comes round about the leg: and by reason of the smoothnes, and lightnes, is no impediment to their going. Their cloathes, were petticoates of Strip't silk, next to their linen, which reach to their midle leg: and upon that a mantle, of blew taffitie, tied with a Ribbon on the right shoulder: which coming under the left arme, hung downe carelesly somewhat lower then the petticoate, so as a great part of the naturall beautie, of their backes and necks before, lay open to the view, their breast round, firme, and beautifully shaped.

Upon my addresses to them, they appeared a little disturb'd; and whispered to one another, but had not the Confidence to speake aloud. I had in my hat, a piece of silver and silke Ribbon, which I perceiv'd their well shap't eyes, often to dart at; but their modesties would not give them Confidence to aske. I tooke it out, and divided it between them, which they accepted with much alacritie; and in returne, dranke to one another my health in the liquor of the pure fountaine, which I perceiv'd by their wanton smiles, and jesticulations, and casting their eyes towards me: when they thought they had exprest enough they would take in their Countenances, and put themselves in the modestest postures that could be, but we having brought a Case of bottles, of English spirits, with us; I cald for some, and drunke a health to them, in a small dramme cup; and gave it to one of them; which they smelt to, and finding it too strong for their temper, pour'd some of it into one of their Calibashes: and put to it as much water, as would temper it to their palats; they dranke againe, but all this would not give them the Confidence to speake, but, in mute language, and extream pretty motions, shewed, they wanted neither wit nor discretion, to make an answer. But it seem'd, it was not the fashion there, for young Maides to speak to strangers, in so publick a place.

I thought I had been sufficiently arm'd with the perfections I found in the *Padre's* Mistresse, as to be free from the darts of any other Beauty of that place, and in so short a time: But I found the difference between young fresh Beauties, and those that are made up with the addition of State and Majesty: For though they counsell and perswade our Loves; yet, young Beauties force, and so commit rapes upon our affections. In summe, had not my heart been fixed fast in my breast, and dwelt there above sixty years, and therefore loath to leave his long kept habitation, I had undoubtedly left it between them for a

---

4. Guinea, in West Africa.

5. Benin, in West Africa.

Legacy. For, so equall were there Beauties, and my Love, as it was not, nor could be, particular to either.

I have heard it a question disputed, whether if a Horse, being plac'd at an equall distance, between two bottles of hey, equally good; and his appetite being equally fix'd upon either: Whether that Horse must not necessarily starve. For, if he feed on either, it must argue, that his appetite was more fixt on that; or else, that bottle was better than the other. Otherwise, what should move him to chose one before the other?

In this posture was I, with my two Mistresses; or rather, my two halves of one Mistresse: for, had they been conjoyned, and so made one, the poynt of my Love had met there; but, being divided, and my affection not forked, it was impossible to fix, but in one Centre.

In this doubtfull condition, I took my leave, with an assurance, that I should never finde two such parallel Paragons, in my whole search through the World.

[Barbados Society]

The Iland is divided into three sorts of men, *viz.* Masters, Servants, and slaves. The slaves and their posterity, being subject to their Masters for ever; are kept and preserv'd with greater care then the servants, who are theirs but for five yeers, according to the law of the Iland. So that for the time, the servants have the worser lives, for they are put to very hard labour, ill lodging, and their dyet very sleight. When we came first on the Iland, some Planters themselves did not eate bone meat, above twice a weeke: the rest of the seven dayes, Potatoes, Loblolly[6] and Bonavist.[7] But the servants no bone meat at all, unlesse an Oxe dyed: and then they were feasted, as long as that lasted, And till they had planted good store of Plantines, the *Negroes* were fed with this kind of food; but most of it Bonavist, and Loblolly, with some eares of Mayes[8] toasted, which food (especially Loblolly,) gave them much discontent: But when they had Plantines enough to serve them, they were heard no more to complaine; for 'tis a food they take great delight in, and their manner of dressing and eating it, is this: 'tis gathered for them (somewhat before it be ripe, for so they desire to have it,) upon Saturday, by the keeper of the Plantine grove; who is an able *Negro,* and knowes well the number of those

that are to be fed with this fruite; and as he gathers, layes them all together, till they fetch them away, which is about five a clock in the afternoon, for that day they breake off worke sooner by an houre: partly for this purpose, and partly for that the fire in the furnaces is to be put out, and the Ingenio and the roomes made cleane; besides they are to wash, shave and trim themselves again on Sunday. But 'tis a lovely sight to see a hundred handsome *Negroes,* men and women, with every one a grasse-green bunch of these fruits on their heads, every bunch twice as big as their heads, all comming in a train one after another, the black and green so well becomming one another. Having brought this fruit home to their own houses, and pilling off the skin of so much as they will use, they boyl it in water, making it into balls, and so they eat it. One bunch a week is a *Negres* allowance. To this, no bread nor drink, but water. Their lodging at night a board, with nothing under, nor any thing a top of them. They are happy people, whom so little contents. Very good servants, if they be not spoyled by the English. But more of them hereafter.

As for the usage of the Servants, it is much as the Master is, mercifull or cruell; Those that are mercifull, treat their Servants well, both in their meat, drink, and lodging, and give them such work, as is not unfit for Christians to do. But if the Masters be cruell, the Servants have very wearisome and miserable lives. Upon the arrival of any ship, that brings servants to the Iland, the Planters go aboard; and having bought such of them as they like, send them with a guide to his Plantation; and being come, commands them instantly to make their Cabins, which they not knowing how to do, are to be advised by other of their servants, that are their seniors; but, if they be churlish, and will not shew them, or if materialls be wanting, to make them Cabins, then they are to lie on the ground that night. These Cabins are to be made of sticks, withes, and Plantine leaves, under some little shade that may keep the rain off; Their suppers being a few Potatoes for meat, and water or Mobbie[9] for drink. The next day they ar rung out with a Bell to work, at six a clock in the morning, with a severe Overseer to command them, till the Bell ring again, which is at eleven a clock; and then they return, and are set to dinner, either with a messe of Lob-lollie, Bonavist, or Potatoes. At one a clock, they are rung out again to the field, there to work till six, and then home again, to a supper of the same. And if it chance to rain, and wet them

---

6. Thick gruel.

7. A soup made from bonavist (hyacinth) beans.

8. Maize.

9. A spiritous liquor made from sweet potatoes.

through, they have no shift, but must lie so all night. If they put off their cloths, the cold of the night will strike into them; and if they be not strong men, this ill lodging will put them into a sicknesse: if they complain, they are beaten by the Overseer; if they resist, their time is doubled. I have seen an Overseer beat a Servant with a cane about the head, till the blood has followed, for a fault that is not worth the speaking of; and yet he must have patience, or worse will follow. Truly, I have seen such cruelty there done to Servants, as I did not think one Christian could have done to another. But, as discreeter and better natur'd men have come to rule there, the servants lives have been much bettered; for now, most of the servants lie in Hamocks, and in warm rooms, and when they come in wet, have shift of shirts and drawers, which is all the cloths they were,[10] and are fed with *bone meat* twice or thrice a week. Collonell *Walrond*[11] seeing his servants when they came home, toyled with their labour, and wet through with their sweating, thought that shifting of their linnen not sufficient refreshing, nor warmth for their bodies, their pores being much opened by their sweating; and therefore resolved to send into *England* for rug Gownes, such as poor people wear in Hospitalls, that so when they had shifted themselves, they might put on those Gowns, and lie down and rest them in their Hamocks: For the Hamocks being but thin, and they having nothing on but shirts and drawers, when they awak'd out of their sleeps, they found themselves very cold; and a cold taken there, is harder to be recovered, than in *England,* by how much the body is infeebled by the great toyle, and the Sun's heat, which cannot but very much exhaust the spirits of bodies unaccustomed to it. But this care and charity of Collonell *Walrond's,* lost him nothing in the conclusion; for, he got such love of his servants, as they thought all too little they could do for him; and the love of the servants there, is of much concernment to the Masters, not only in their diligent and painfull labour, but in fore seeing and preventing mischiefes that often happen, by the carelessnesse and slothfulnesse of recklesse servants; sometimes by laying fire so negligently, as whole lands of Canes and Houses too, are burnt down and consumed, to the utter ruine and undoing of their Masters: For, the materialls there being all combustible, and apt to take fire, a

little oversight, as the fire of a Tobacco-pipe, being knockt out against a drie stump of a tree, has set it on fire, and the wind fanning that fire, if a land of Canes be but neer, and they once take fire, all that are down the winde will be burnt up. Water there is none to quench it, or if it were, a hundred *Negres* with buckets were not able to do it; so violent and spreading a fire this is, and such a noise it makes, as if two Armies, with a thousand shot of either side, were continually giving fire, every knot of every Cane, giving as great a report as a Pistoll. So that there is no way to stop the going on of this flame, but by cutting down and removing all the Canes that grow before it, for the breadth of twenty or thirty foot down the winde, and there the *Negres* to stand and beat out the fire, as it creeps upon the ground, where the Canes are cut down. And I have seen some *Negres* so earnest to stop this fire, as with their naked feet to tread, and with their naked bodies to tumble, and roll upon it; so little they regard their own smart or safety, in respect of their Masters benefit. The year before I came away, there were two eminent Planters in the Iland, that with such an accident as this, lost at least £10000 sterling, in the value of the Canes that were burnt; the one, Mr. *James Holduppe,* the other, Mr. *Constantine Silvester:* And the latter had not only his Canes, but his house burnt down to the ground. This, and much more mischiefe has been done, by the negligence and wilfulnesse of servants. And yet some cruell Masters will provoke their Servants so, by extream ill usage, and often and cruell beating them, as they grow desperate, and so joyne together to revenge themselves upon them.

A little before I came from thence, there was such a combination amongst them, as the like was never seen there before. Their sufferings being grown to a great height, & their daily complainings to one another (of the intolerable burdens they labour'd under) being spread throughout the Iland; at the last, some amongst them, whose spirits were not able to endure such slavery, resolved to break through it, or die in the act; and so conspired with some others of their acquaintance, whose sufferings were equall, if not above theirs; and their spirits no way inferiour, resolved to draw as many of the discontented party into this plot, as possibly they could; and those of this perswasion, were the greatest numbers of servants in the Iland. So that a day was appointed to fall upon their Masters, and cut all their throats, and by that means, to make themselves not only freemen, but Masters of the Iland. And so closely was this plot carried, as no discovery was made, till the day before they were to put it in act: And then one of them, either by the failing of his

---

10. Wear.

11. Humphrey Waldrond (c. 1600–c.70) was a prominent Barbadian Royalist.

courage, or some new obligation from the love of his Master, revealed this long plotted conspiracy; and so by this timely advertisement, the Masters were saved: Justice *Hethersall* (whose servant this was) sending Letters to all his friends, and they to theirs, and so one to another, till they were all secured; and, by examination, found out the greatest part of them; whereof eighteen of the principall men in the conspiracy, and they the first leaders and con-trivers of the plot, were put to death, for example to the rest. And the reason why they made examples of so many, was, they found these so haughty in their resolutions, and so incorrigible, as they were like enough to become actors in a second plot; and so they thought good to secure them; and for the rest, to have a speciall eye over them.

It has been accounted a strange thing, that the Negres, being more then double the numbers of the Christians that are there, and they accounted a bloody people, where they think they have power or advantages; and the more bloody, by how much they are more fearfull than others: that these should not commit some horrid massacre upon the Christians, thereby to enfranchise themselves, and be-come Masters of the Island. But there are three reasons that take away this wonder; the one is, They are not suf-fered to touch or handle any weapons: The other, That they are held in such awe and slavery, as they are fearfull to appear in any daring act; and seeing the mustering of our men, and hearing their Gun-shot, (than which nothing is more terrible to them) their spirits are subjugated to so low a condition, as they dare not look up to any bold at-tempt. Besides these, there is a third reason, which stops all designes of that kind, and that is, They are fetch'd from severall parts of *Africa*, who speake severall languages, and by that means, one of them understands not another: For, some of them are fetch'd from *Guinny* and *Binny*, some from *Cutchew*, some from *Angola*, and some from the River of *Gambra*.[12] And in some of these places where petty Kingdomes are, they sell their Subjects, and such as they take in Battle, whom they make slaves; and some mean men sell their Servants, their Children, and sometimes their Wives; and think all good traffick, for such commodities as our Merchants sends them.

When they are brought to us, the Planters buy them out of the Ship, where they find them stark naked, and there-fore cannot be deceived in any outward infirmity. They choose them as they do Horses in a Market; the strongest, youthfullest, and most beautiful, yield the greatest prices. Thirty pound sterling is a price for the best man Negre; and

twenty five, twenty six, or twenty seven pound for a Woman; the Children are at easier rates. And we buy them so, as the sexes may be equall; for, if they have more men then women, the men who are unmarried will come to their Masters, and complain, that they cannot live without Wives, and desire him, they may have Wives. And he tells them, that the next ship that comes, he will buy them Wives, which satisfies them for the present; and so they ex-pect the good time: which the Master performing with them, the bravest fellow is to choose first, and so in order, as they are in place; and every one of them knowes his bet-ter, and gives him the precedence, as Cowes do one an-other, in passing through a narrow gate; for the most of them are as neer beasts as may be, setting their souls aside. Religion they know none; yet most of them acknowledge a God, as appears by their motions and gestures: For, if one of them do another wrong, and he cannot revenge him-selfe, he looks up to Heaven for vengeance, and holds up both his hands, as if the power must come from thence, that must do him right. Chast they are as any people under the Sun; for, when the men and women are together naked, they never cast their eyes towards the parts that ought to be covered; and those amongst us, that have Breeches and Petticoats, I never saw so much as a kisse, or embrace, or a wanton glance with their eyes between them. Jealous they are of their Wives, and hold it for a great injury and scorn, if another man make the least courtship to his Wife. And if any of their Wives have two Children at a birth, they conclude her false to his Bed, and so no more adoe but hang her. We had an excellent Negre in the Plantation, whose name was *Macow,* and was our chiefe Musitian; a very valiant man, and was keeper of our Plantine-groave. This Negres Wife was brought to bed of two Children, and her Husband, as their manner is, had provided a cord to hang her. But the Overseer finding what he was about to do, enformed the Master of it, who sent for *Mascow,* to dis-swade him from this cruell act, of murdering his Wife, and used all perswasions that possibly he could, to let him see, that such double births are in Nature, and that divers pres-idents were to found amongst us of the like; so that we rather praised our Wives, for their fertility, than blamed them for their falsenesse. But this prevailed little with him, upon whom custome had taken so deep an impression; but resolved, the next thing he did, should be to hang her. Which when the Master perceived, and that the ignorance of the man, should take away the life of the woman, who was innocent of the crime her Husband condemned her for, told him plainly, that if he hang'd her, he himselfe should be hang'd by her, upon the same bough; and there-

---

12. Gambia.

fore wish'd him to consider what he did. This threatning wrought more with him, then all the reasons of Philosophy that could be given him; and so let her alone; but he never car'd much for her afterward, but chose another which he lik'd better. For the Planters there deny not a slave, that is a brave fellow, and one that has extraordinary qualities, two or three Wives, and above that number they seldome go: But no woman is allowed above one Husband.

At the time the wife is to be brought abed, her husband removes his board (which is his bed) to another room (for many severall divisions they have, in their little houses, and none above six foot square). And leaves his wife to God, and her good fortune, in the room, and upon the board alone, and calls a neighbour to come to her, who gives little help to her deliverie, but when the child is borne, (which she calls her Pickaninnie) she helps to make a little fire nere her feet and that serves instead of Possets[13] Broaths, and Caudles.[14] In a fortnight, this woman is at worke with her Pickaninny at her back, as merry a soule as any there: If the overseer be discreet, shee is suffer'd to rest her selfe a little more than ordinary; but if not, shee is compelled to doe as others doe. Times they have of suckling their Children in the fields, and refreshing themselves; and good reason, for they carry burdens on their backs; and yet work too. Some women, whose Pickaninnies are three yeers old, will, as they worke at weeding, which is a stooping worke, suffer the hee Pickaninnie, to sit astride upon their backs, like St. *George* a horseback; and there spurre his mother with his heeles, and sings and crowes on her backe, clapping his hands, as if he meant to flye; which the mother is so pleas'd with, as shee continues her painfull stooping posture, longer than she would doe, rather than discompose her Joviall Pickaninnie of his pleasure, so glad she is to see him merry. The worke which the women doe, is most of it weeding, a stooping and painfull worke; at noon and night they are call'd home by the ring of a Bell, where they have two hours time for their repast at noone; and at night, they rest from sixe, till sixe a Clock next morning.

On Sunday they rest, and have the whole day at their pleasure; and the most of them use it as a day of rest and pleasure; but some of them who will make benefit of that dayes liberty, goe where the Mangrave trees grow, and gather the barke of which they make ropes, which they trucke[15] away for other Commoditie, as shirts and drawers.

In the afternoons on Sundayes, they have their musicke, which is of kettle drums, and those of severall sises; upon the smallest the best musitian playes, and the other come in as Chorasses: the drum all men know, has but one tone; and therefore varietie of tunes have little to doe in this musick; and yet so strangely they varie their time, as 'tis a pleasure to the most curious eares, and it was to me one of the strangest noyses that ever I heard made of one tone; and if they had the varietie of tune, which gives the greater scope in musick, as they have of time, they would doe wonders in that Art. And if I had not faln sicke before my comming away, at least seven months in one sickness, I had given them some hints of tunes, which being understood, would have serv'd as a great addition to their harmonie; for time without tune, is not an eighth part of the science of Musick.

[On the Indians. Yarico's Story]

As for the *Indians,* we have but few, and those fetcht from other Countries; some from the neighbouring Islands, some from the Main,[16] which we make slaves: the women who are better vers'd in ordering the Cassavie[17] and making bread, then the *Negroes,* we imploy for that purpose, as also for making Mobbie: the men we use for footmen, and killing of fish, which they are very good at; with their own bowes and arrows they will go out; and in a dayes time, kill as much fish, as will serve a family of a dozen persons, two or three dayes, if you can keep the fish so long. They are very active men, and apt to learn any thing, sooner than the *Negroes;* and as different from them in shape, almost as in colour; the men very broad shoulder'd, deep breasted, with large heads, and their faces almost three square, broad about the temples, and sharp at the chin, their skins some of them brown, some a bright Bay, they are much craftier, and subtiler then the *Negroes;* and in their nature falser; but in their bodies more active: their women have very small breasts, and have more of the shape of the *Europeans* than the *Negroes,* their hair black and long, a great part whereof hangs down upon their backs, as low as their hanches, with a large lock

---

13. Posset is a drink of hot milk curdled with ale or wine.

14. Caudle is a warm drink, often for the sick, usually made of ale or wine with eggs, meal, spices, and sugar.

15. Trade.

16. The mainland.

17. The tuberous root of the cassava is used to make bread as well as other foods.

hanging over either breast, which seldom or never curles: cloaths they scorn to wear, especially if they be well shap'd; a girdle they use of tape, covered with little smooth shells of fishes, white, and from their flank of one side, to their flank on the other side, a fringe of blew *Bugle;* which hangs so low as to cover their privities. We had an *Indian* woman, a slave in the house, who was of excellent shape and colour, for it was a pure bright bay; small breasts, with the niples of a porphyrie[18] colour, this woman would not be woo'd by any means to wear Cloaths. She chanc'd to be with Child, by a Christian servant, and lodging in the *Indian* house, amongst other women, women of her own Country, where the Christian servants, both men and women came; and being very great, and that her time was come to be delivered, loath to fall in labour before the men, walk'd down to a Wood, in which was a Pond of water, and there by the side of the Pond, brought her self a bed; and presently washing her Child in some of the water of the Pond, lap'd it up in such rags, as she had begg'd of the Christians; and in three hours time came home, with her Child in her arms, a lusty Boy, frolick and lively.

This *Indian* dwelling near the Sea-coast, upon the Main, an *English* ship put in to a Bay, and sent some of her men a shoar, to try what victuals or water they could find, for in some distress they were: But the *Indians* perceiving them to go up so far into the County, as they were sure they could not make a safe retreat, intercepted them in their return, and fell upon them, chasing them into a Wood, and being dispersed there, some were taken, and some kill'd: but a young man amongst them stragling from the rest, was met by this *Indian* Maid, who upon the first sight fell in love with him, and hid him close from her Country-men (the *Indians*) in a Cave, and there fed him, till they could safely go down to the shoar, where the ship lay at anchor, expecting the return of their friends. But at last, seeing them upon the shoar, sent the long-Boat for them, took them aboard, and brought them away. But the youth, when he came ashoar in the *Barbadoes,* forgot the kindness of the poor maid, that had ventured her life for his safety, and sold her for a slave, who was as free born as he: And so poor *Yarico* for her love, lost her liberty.

[Sugar Culture and Refining Sugarcane]

At the time we landed on this Iland, which was in the beginning of *September,* 1647, we were informed, partly by those Planters we found there, and partly by our own observations, that the great work of Sugar-making, was but newly practiced by the inhabitants there. Some of the most industrious men, having gotten Plants from *Fernamlock,* a place in *Brasill,* and made tryall of them at the *Barbadoes;* and finding them to grow, they planted more and more, as they grew and multiplyed on the place, till they had such a considerable number, as they were worth the while to set up a very small Ingenio and so make tryall what Sugar could be made upon that soyl. But, the secrets of the work being not well understood, the Sugars they made were very inconsiderable, and little worth, for two or three years. But they finding their errours by their daily practice, began a little to mend; and, by new directions from *Brasil,* sometimes by strangers, and now and then by their own people, (who being covetous of the knowledge of a thing, which so much concerned them in their particulars, and for the generall good of the whole Iland) were content sometimes to make a voyage thither, to improve their knowledge in a thing they so much desired. Being now made much abler to make their queries, of the secrets of that mystery, by how much their often failings, had put them to often stops and nonplusses in the work. And so returning with more Plants, and better Knowledge, they went on upon fresh hopes, but still short, of what they should be more skilfull in: for, at our arrivall there, we found them ignorant in three main points, that much conduced to the work; *viz.* The manner of Planting, the time of Gathering, and the right placing of their Coppers in their Furnaces; as also, the true way of covering their Rollers, with plates or Bars of Iron: All which being rightly done, advance much in the performance of the main work.

At the time of our arrivall there, we found many Sugar-works set up, and at work; but yet the Sugars they made, were but bare Muscavadoes[19] and few of them Merchantable commodities; so moist, and full of molosses, and so ill cur'd, as they were hardly worth the bringing home for *England.* But about the time I left the Iland, which was in 1650, they were much better'd; for then they had the skill to know when the Canes were ripe, which was not, till they were fifteen months old; and before, they gathered them at twelve, which was a main disadvantage to the making good Sugar; for, the liquor wanting of the sweetnesse it ought to have, caused the Sugars to be lean, and unfit to keep. Besides, they were grown greater proficients, both in boyling and curing them, and had learnt the

---

18. Purple.

19. Raw or unrefined sugar.

knowledge of making them white, such as you call Lump Sugars here in *England;* but not so excellent as those they make in *Brasill,* nor is there any likelyhood they can ever make such: the land there being better, and lying in a Continent, must needs have constanter and steadier weather, and the Aire much drier and purer, than it can be in so small an Iland, as that of *Barbadoes.* And now, seeing this commodity, Sugar, hath gotten so much the start of all the rest of those, that were held the staple Commodities of the Iland, and so much over-top't them, as they are for the most part sleighted and neglected. And, for that few in *England* know the trouble and care of making it, I think it convenient, in the first place, to acquaint you, as far as my memory will serve, with the whole processe of the work of Sugar-making, which is now grown the soul of Trade in this Iland. And leaving to trouble you and my self, with relating the errours our Predecessors so long wandred in, I will in briefe set down the right and best way they practised, when I left the Iland, which, I think, will admit of no greater or farther improvement.

But, before I will begin with that, I will let you see, how much the land there hath been advanc'd in the profit, since the work of Sugar began, to the time of our landing there, which was not above five or six years: For, before the work began, this Plantation of Major *Hilliards,* of five hundred acres, could have been purchased for four hundred pound sterling; and now the halfe of this Plantation, with the halfe of the Stock upon it, was sold for seven thousand pound sterling: and it is evident, that all the land there, which has been imployed to that work, hath found the like improvement. And, I believe, when the small Plantations in poor mens hands, often, twenty, or thirty acres, which are too small to lay to that work, be bought up by great men, and put together, into Plantations of five, six, or seven hundred acres, that two thirds of the Iland will be fit for Plantations of Sugar, which will make it one of the richest Spots of earth under the Sun. . . .

The manner of grinding them [i.e., sugarcanes], is this, the Horses and Cattle being put to their tackle: they go about, and by their force turne (by the sweeps) the middle roller; which being Cog'd to the other two, at both ends, turne them about; and they all three, turning upon their Centres, which are of Brass and Steele go very easily of themselves, and so easie, as a mans taking hold, of one of the sweeps, with his hand will turne all the rollers about with much ease. But when the Canes are put in between the rollers, it is a good draught for five Oxen or Horses; a *Negre* puts in the Canes of one side, and the rollers draw them through to the other side, where another *Negre*

stands, and receives them; and returnes them back on the other side of the middle roller, which drawes the other way. So that having past twice through, that is forth and back, it is conceived all the juyce is prest out; yet the Spaniards have a press, after both the former grindings, to press out the remainder of the liquor, but they having but small works in Spaine, make the most of it, whilst we having far greater quantities are loath to be at that trouble. The Canes having past to and againe, there are young Negre girles that carry them away, and lay them on a heap, at the distance of six score paces or there abouts; where they make a large hill, if the worke have continued long; under the rollers, there is a receiver, as big as a large Tray; into which the liquor falls, and stayes not there, but runs under ground in a pipe or gutter of lead cover'd over close, which pipe or gutter, carries it into the Cistern, which is fixt neer the staires, as you go down from the Mill-house to the boyling house. But it must not remaine in that Cisterne above one day, lest it grow sower; from thence it is to passe through a gutter, (fixt to the wall) to the Clarifying Copper, as there is occasion to use it, and as the work goes on, and as it Clarifies in the first Copper, and the skumme rises, it is conveyed away by a passage, or gutter for that purpose; as also of the second Copper, both which skimmings, are not esteem'd worth the labour of stilling; because the skum is dirtie and grosse: But the skimmings of the other three Coppers, are conveyed down to the Still-house, there to remaine in the Cisterns, till it be a little sower, for till then it will not come over the helme. This liquor is remov'd, as it is refin'd, from one Copper to another, and the more Coppers it passeth through, the finer and purer it is, being continually drawn up, and keel'd by ladles, and skim'd by skimmers, in the Negres hands, till at last it comes to the tach; where it must have much labour, in keeling and stirring, and as it boyles, there is thrown into the four last Coppers, a liquor made of water and Withs which they call Temper, without which, the Sugar would continue a Clammy substance and never kerne. The quantities they put in are small, but being of a tart quality it turnes the ripeness and clamminesse of the Sugar to curddle and separate: which you will find, by taking out some drops of it, to Candy, and suddenly to grow hard; and then it has inough of the fire.

[The Industrious Should Go to Barbados]

There are some that have heard of the pleasures of *Barbadoes,* but are loath to leave the pleasures of England behind them. These are of a sluggish humour, and are altogether unfit for so noble an undertaking; but if any such shall happen to come there, he shall be transmitted to the innumerable Armie of Pismires; and Ants, to sting him with such a reproof, as he shall wish himselfe any where rather than amongst them. So much is a sluggard detested in a Countrey, where Industry and Activity is to be exercised. The Dwarfe may come there, and twice a year vie in competition with the Giant: for set them both together upon a levell superficies,[20] and at noone, you shall not know by their shadowes who is the tallest man.

The Voluptuous man, who thinks the day not long enough for him to take his pleasure, Nor the sleepie man who thinks the longest night too short for him to dreame out his delights, are not fit to repose and solace themselves upon this Iland; for in the whole compasse of the Zodiacke, they shall neither find St. Barnabies day, or St. Lucies night. The Sun, running an eeven course, is there an indifferent Arbiter of the differences which are between those two Saints, and like a just and cleere sighted Judge, reconciles those extreams to a Medium, of 12 and 12 houres, which equality of time is utterly inconsistent to the humours and dispositions of these men.

But I speak this, to such as have their fancies so Aere-all, and refin'd as not to be pleased with ordinary delight; but think to build and settle a felicity here: above the ordinary levell of mankind. Such spirits, are too volatile to fixe on businesse; and therefore I will leave them out, as uselesse in this Common-wealth. But such as are made of middle earth: and can be content to wave those pleasures, which stand as Blocks, and Percullisses,[21] in their way; and are indeed, the main Remoras[22] in their passage to their profits. Such may here find moderate delights, with moderate labour, and those taken moderately will conduce much to their healths, and they that have industry, to imploy that well, may make it the Ladder to clyme to a high degree, of Wealth and opulencie, in this sweet Negotiation of Sugar, provided they have a competent stock to begin with; such I mean as may settle them in a Sugar-work, and lesse than £14000 sterling, will not do that: in a Plantation of 500 acres of land, with a proportionable stock of Servants, Slaves, Horses, Camels, Cattle, Assinigoes, with an Ingenio, and all other houseing, thereunto belonging; such as I have formerly nam'd.

But one wil say, why should any man that has 14000 l.

in his purse, need to runne so long a Risco, as from hence to the Barbadoes: when he may live with ease and plenty at home; to such a one I answer, that every drone can sit and eate the Honey of his own Hive: But he that can by his own Industry, and activity, (having youth and strength to friends,) raise his fortune, from a small beginning to a very great one, and in his passage to that, doe good to the publique, and be charitable to the poor, and this to be accomplished in a few years, deserves much more commendation and applause. And shall find his bread, gotten by his painfull and honest labour and industry, eate sweeter by much, than his that onely minds his ease, and his belly.

[The Return Voyage]

At last, a little Virgin, who was a passenger in the Ship, stood up upon the quarter deck, like a she-Worthy, and said, that if they would be rul'd by her, she would not only be the contriver, but the acter of our deliverance. At whose speech, we all gave a strict attention, as ready to contribute our help to all she commanded; which was, that the Ship-Carpenter should make her a Distaffe and Spindle, and the Saylers combe out some of the Occome: with which instruments and materialls, she doubted not, but to make such a quantity of thread, as to repair our then uselesse Sailes; which accordingly she did, and by her vertue (under God) we held our lives.

Though such an accident as this, and such a deliverance, deserve a gratefull commemoration; yet, this is not all the use we are to make of it, somewhat more may be considered, that may prevent dangers for the future; and that is, the great abuse of Captaines and Masters of Ships, who promise to their Passengers, such plenty of victualls, as may serve them the whole voyage: But, before they be halfe way, either pinch them of a great part, or give them that which is nastie and unwholsome. And therefore I could wish every man, that is to go a long voyage, to carry a reserve of his owne, of such viands, as will last, and to put that up safe; for, if it be not under lock and key, they are never the neer; for, the Saylers will as certainly take it, as you trust it to their honesties: Complaine to the Master, and you finde no remedy. One thing I have observed, let a Sayler steal any part of the Ships provision, he shall be sure to have severe punishment; but, if from a Passenger, though it concern him never so neerly, his remedy is to be laughed at. These enormities are fit to be complained on at the Trinity-house, that some redresse may be had; for, the abuses are grievous.

20. Surfaces.

21. Gates.

22. Obstacles or hindrances.

Out of this danger at Sea, it has pleased the God of all mercy to deliver me, as also from a grievous and tedious sicknesse on land, in a strange Country; For which, may his holy Name be eternally blessed and praised, for ever and ever.

I am now cast in Prison, by the subtle practices of some, whom I have formerly called Friends: But the eternall and mercifull God has been pleased to visit and comfort me, and to raise me up such friends, as have kept me from cold and hunger, whose charities in an Age, where cruelties and tyrannies are exercised in so high a measure, may be accounted a prodigie. But, I doubt not of my release out of this restraint, by the power of him, who is able to do all in all. For, as *David* said to *Saul,*[23] that God, who

had delivered him out of the paw of the Lion, and out of the paw of the Bear, would deliver him from that uncircumcised Philistine, *Goliah* of *Gath:* So may I now say; that God, which has delivered me from a sicknesse to death, on land, and from shipwrack and hazards at Sea, will also deliver me from this uncircumcised Philistine, the *Upper Bench,* than which, the

burning fire of a Feavour, nor the raging waves of the Sea,
are more formidable: But, we have seen and suffered
greater things. And when the great Leveller of the world, Death, shall run his progresse, all Estates will be laid eeven.

---

23. Compare with 1 Samuel 17:37.

CONFLICT IN THE CARIBBEAN AND IN VIRGINIA

Land and labor problems emerged in the British staple colonies—so called because they supplied Britain with staple crops for export, especially tobacco, cotton, indigo, sugar, and rice—well before the first century of settlement was concluded. In the earliest years of colony building in the Lesser Antilles through the Chesapeake area, service in the British colonies was provided by indentured laborers, workers who agreed to labor for a certain number of years to gain passage to America. These laborers' reasons for coming over were myriad: better working conditions, a greater degree of control over one's working life (because the supply was short, compared with the supply of workers in England), and an opportunity to purchase land and create a homestead of one's own at the time the indenture concluded. For indentured women, there tended to be a greater freedom and mobility than in the homeland because fewer women were willing to risk the crossing, yet women laborers were sought for domestic chores. Those who were interested in marrying, historians have argued, had a greater chance of finding suitable working partners in the Chesapeake than in many other areas because the number of women in that area was relatively low.

During the seventeenth century, the Caribbean and the Chesapeake regions received about 90 percent of Britain's servants. Around the midcentury, the supply of servants who were willing to indenture to the Caribbean diminished because of the difficulty of labor there and the lack of available land to purchase once the indenture period was over and one became one's own master. Slightly later, a similar situation arose in Virginia. A second phase in the labor and land situation arose, then, as fewer servants were making themselves available for colonial labor at precisely the time when the desire for colonial exports, especially of sugar, rice, and tobacco, was increasing. In the West Indies in particular, as willing laborers became harder to find, planters turned to schemes for involuntary servitude, and vagrants, debtors, convicts, and political prisoners were brought in to work the fields. During the latter part of the seventeenth century, then, involuntary laborers were brought from Britain, experiments in enslaving the Indian population continued, and the importation of African slaves increased. African slave laborers supplanted indentured laborers in the Caribbean by the end of the century. The transformation was most notable in the West Indies, where the laboring situation was difficult because of the tropical climate and the kind of labor exacted. Yet a similar transformation followed shortly in the Chesapeake area.

The shift of the laboring population from bonded but putatively free to enslaved increased concerns about resistance among the slaveholding classes in both the Caribbean and the Chesapeake. In Barbados,

Africans and African Americans outnumbered white people by the 1660s, making what had been a fascination about the resilience of the African laborer into a fear of what the African might do if freedom revolts occurred. Many of the larger Caribbean plantations were owned by landlords who remained in England, where they staunchly supported the enactment in 1667 of a very harsh slave code, the "Act to regulate the Negroes on the British Plantations," which said that the Africans of the Caribbean were "of wild, barbarous, and savage nature and to be controlled only with strict severity." As one writer put it, the islands were "of immense importance to the grandeur and prosperity of England," thus linking the argument for increased constraint upon slaves with establishing England's greater grandeur around the globe.

In the Chesapeake, to address what was becoming the absence of laboring people in the area, planters brought in Irish laborers and many more women than ever before, and they also brought in Africans by the end of the century. In Virginia, there seems to have been some initial resistance to basing the economy upon slave labor, so the colony first attempted alternative routes to obtaining labor before it turned almost exclusively to the slave system for its laborers by the eighteenth century. The result, with regard to problems in securing a captive labor force in both areas, was a social formation along lines of labor, class, and race and ethnicity, with planters concerned about controlling the increasing number of persons of unfree status—voluntary and involuntary laborers and chattel slaves.

The year 1676 brought uprisings in both the Caribbean and in Virginia, the first, a slave conspiracy supported by African slave laborers and the second, an uprising supported by people in western Virginia who turned their anger about displacement and lack of support into aggression against the elite in the east. In both cases, the growing population of laborers resisted dominance by a tiny elite of planters whose goals seemed to be to retain all goods, services, and social inequity for its own service and well-being. The key elements behind the armed resistances were economic and social, the results of the resisters' relative status as unfree people. But because British colonial society was by 1676 fractured by racial and ethnic boundaries and by spatial boundaries that placed the elite group in separate geographic spaces apart from most laborers, the literature related to these resistance movements is marked by racializing language that mystifies the concerns of the resisters in the white English readers' concern for social stability and freedom from fear of rebellion.

GREAT NEWS FROM THE BARBADOES (1676)[1]

Anonymous

The Relation of a Conspiracy in the *BARBADOES*

This *Conspiracy* first broke out and was hatched by the *Cormantee* or *Gold-Cost Negro's* about Three years since, and afterwards Cunningly and Clandestinely carried, and kept secret, even from the knowledge of their own Wifes. Their grand design was to choose them a King, one *Coffee* an Ancient Gold-Cost *Negro,* who should have been Crowned the 12th of *June* last past in a Chair of State exquisitely wrought and Carved after their Mode; with Bowes and Arrowes to be likewise carried in

State before his Majesty their intended King: Trumpets to be made of Elephants Teeth and Gourdes to be sounded on several Hills, to give Notice of their general Rising, with a full intention to fire the Sugar-Canes, and so run in and Cut their Masters the Planters Throats in their respective Plantations whereunto they did belong.

Some affirm, they intended to spare the lives of the Fairest and Handsomest Women (their Mistresses and their Daughters) to be Converted to their own use. But some others affirm the contrary; and I am induced to believe they intended to Murther all the White People there, as well Men as Women: for *Anna* a house Negro Woman belonging to Justice *Hall,* over-hearing a Young *Cormantee Negro* about 18 years of age, and also belonging to Justice *Hall,* as he was working near the Garden, and discoursing with another *Cormantee Negro* working with him, told him boldly and plainly, *He would have no hand in killing the* Baccararoes *or White Folks; And that he would tell his Master.* All which the aforesaid *Negro*

---

1. This pamphlet was first published in 1676.

Woman (being then accidentally in the Garden) over-heard, and called to him the aforesaid Young *Negro* Man over the Pales,[2] and enquired and asked of him *What it was they so earnestly were talking about?* He answered and told her freely, *That it was a general Design amongst them the* Cormantee Negro's, *to kill all the* Baccararoes *or White People in the Island within a fortnight.* Which she no sooner understood, but went immediately to her Master and Mistris, and discovered the whole truth of what she heard, saying withal, *That it was great Pity so good people as her Master and Mistriss were, should be destroyed.* Which was the first discovery that I can learn came to the knowledge of the worthy Inhabitants of that Noble and most flourishing Island.

Afterwards the Discreet and Prudent Justice sent presently for the young *Negro* Man, who discovered and impeached several, as well his own Master's *Negro's* as others belonging to the adjacent Plantations who had a hand in this Plot.

Of all which the said Justice sending the true Information to that Noble Person (now Governour there) Sir *Jonathan Atkins,* he with his Life-Guard presently came to the house of the aforesaid Justice *Hall,* and granted him and others Commissions to apprehend the guilty and impeached *Negroes,* with the Ring-leaders of this fatal Conspiracy; which is pursuance was put in Execution with much Celerity and Secrecy, that the Heads and Chief of these ungrateful wretches (who I have often heard confess to live better in Servitude there, then at Liberty in their own Native Country) were apprehended and brought to Tryal at a Court of *Oyer* and *Terminer* granted by the aforesaid Governour to a Dozen or more of the Colonels and Field-Officers as Judges of that Island; Who after strict and due Examination of the matter of Fact of their Conspiracy, at first Seventeen were found guilty and Executed, (*viz.*) Six burnt alive, and Eleven beheaded, their dead bodies being dragged through the Streets at *Spikes* a pleasant Port-Town in that Island, and were afterwards burnt with those that were burned alive.

One of those that were burned alive being chained at the stake, was perswaded by that honest Gentleman Mr. *George,* the Deputy Provost-Marshall, *That since he was going to suffer death, Ingeniously to Confess the depth of their design.* The *Negro* calling for water to drink (which is a Custome they use before they tell or discover any

thing) he just then going to speak and confess the truth of what he knew in this Matter; The next *Negro* Man chained to him (one *Tony,* a sturdy Rogue, a *Jew's Negro*) jogged him, and was heard to Chide him in these words, *Thou, Fool, are there not enough of our Country-men killed already? Art thou minded to kill them all?* Then the aforesaid *Negro* that was going to make Confession, would not speak one word more.

Which the spectators observing cryed out to *Tony, Sirrah, we shall see you fry bravely by and by.* Who answered undauntedly, *If you Roast me today you cannot Roast me tomorrow:* (all those *Negro's* having an opinion that after their death they go into their own Countrey). Five and Twenty more have been since Executed. The particulars of whose due Punishment are not yet come to my hands.

Five impeached Hanged themselves, because they would not stand Tryal.

Threescore and odd more are in Custody at the *Hole,* a fine Haven and small Town in the said Island, and are not as yet brought to Tryal.

Thus escaped from Eminent dangers, this flourishing and Fertile Island, or to say more properly Spatious and profitable Garden, one of the chiefest of his Majesties Nurseries for Seamen.

This little Spot imploying every year above 100 good Merchant Ships, to carry off its product, *viz.* Sugar, Ginger, Cotton, and Indigo; of which I have heard it affirmed, That that Earth and Rich soyl being so thinly placed on most part of the said Island, as not exceeding above half a foot in depth, the said product since its first manuring carried off in several years, much exceeds in bulk and weight the surface of the Island, it being only a Rock. So leaving to others the giving an account of the great plenty of fresh Fish there, though of different shapes and names from ours, which it exceeds in pleasantness and nourishment, especially the Turtles there caught; their admirable Pork, Poultry etc. Their Wood Pidgeons, Turtle-Doves of several kinds, wild Fowls, Plovers, Thrushes, Crabs, Lobsters, Prawns, and all other necessary and pleasant Provisions in abundance, both Fish and Flesh. But above all, admirable (considering it is so small an Island) is the Populousness thereof, for I have seen at a General Rendezvous in *Hethersals* Pasture 12000 well Armed fighting men, Horse and Foot, of the Train-Bands, besides *Negro's* that waited on their Masters: And I have lately seen a list taken by Authority that amounts to above 80000 Souls. 'Tis fortified (besides the stone Wall all along the places of most danger for Landing, near the Seaside) with sev-

---

2. A fence made of branches tied together in vertical formation.

eral strong uniform Forts Alla-Modern, well mounted with store of great Guns; so as considering the strength, Riches, Pleasant situation, Populousness and good Hospitality of those Noble Gentlemen there now inhabiting, I conclude it to be the finest and worthiest Island in the World.

————

MANIFESTO CONCERNING THE PRESENT TROUBLES IN VIRGINIA (1676)[1]
NATHANIEL BACON

If vertue be a sin, if Piety be guilt, all the Principles of morality goodness and Justice be perverted, Wee must confesse That those who are now called Rebells may be in danger of those high imputations, Those loud and severall Bulls would affright Innocents and render the defense of our Brethren and the enquiry into our sad and heavy oppressions, Treason. But if there bee as sure there is, a just God to appeal to, if Religion and Justice be a sanctuary here, if to plead ye cause of the oppressed, if

————

1. Nathaniel Bacon (1647–76), trained as a lawyer, emigrated to the Virginia colony, settled on the upper James River, and joined the governor's council. The resistance movement called "Bacon's Rebellion" was initiated because of attacks on isolated colonial homesteads by Susquehannock Indians who were experiencing displacement by other Indian peoples and by colonial settlers in their ancestral lands. Virginia Governor William Berkeley argued for modcration in dealings with the Indians, but the western Virginians sought retaliation against the Indians in their area, and they sought from the governor a commission for Bacon to lead a military attack against the Indians there. The governor, unpersuaded that military action was necessary, vacillated in granting such a commission, and in the upset that ensued from his decision, Berkeley declared Bacon a rebel. Bacon retaliated against the governor by leading his associates against Jamestown, the center of government. Bacon died of illness before prolonged serious civil war occurred, but the issues he had raised did not go away quickly, and they were exacerbated when Berkeley executed some of the known insurgents. In the ensuing activity, people from the western country came forward to complain about the lack of representation in government, the lack of support for their needs, and related problems, and they were joined by Africans and Indians in the vicinity, who had their own complaints about ill treatment. Bacon's manifesto was circulated widely in his own day.

sincerely to aime at his Majesties Honour and the Publick good without any reservation or by Interest, if to stand in the Gap after soe much blood of our dear Brethren bought and sold, if after the losse of a great part of his Majesties Colony deserted and dispeopled, freely with our lives and estates to indeavor to save the remaynders bee Treason, God Almighty Judge and let the guilty dye. But since wee cannot in our hearts find one single spott of Rebellion or Treason, or that wee have in any manner aimed at the subverting the setled Government, or attempting of the Person of any either magistrate or private man, notwithstanding the severall Reproaches and Threats of some who, for sinister ends, were disaffected to us and censured our inocent and honest designes; and since all people in all places where wee have yet bin can attest our civill quiet, peaseable behaviour—farre different from that of Rebellion and tumultuous persons—let Trueth be bold and all the world know the real Foundations of pretended giult. Wee appeale to the Country itselfe, what and of what nature their Oppressions have bin, or by what Caball and mistery the designs of many of those whom wee call great men have bin transacted and caryed on. But let us trace these men in Authority and Favour to whose hands the dispensation of the Countries wealth has been commited; let us observe the sudden Rise of their Estates compared with the Quality in which they first entered this Country, or the Reputation they have held here amongst wise and discerning men. And lett us see wither their extractions and Education have not bin vile, and by what pretence of learning and vertue they could soe soon into Imployments of so great Trust and consequence.

Let us consider their sudden advancement and let us also consider wither any Publick work for our safety and defence or for the Advancement and propogation of Trade, liberall Arts or sciences is here Extant in any way adequate to our vast chardg. Now let us compare these things together and see what spounges have suckt up the Publique Treasure, and wither it hath not bin privately contrived away by unworthy Favourites and juggling Parasites whose tottering Fortunes have bin repaired and supported at the Publique chardg. Now if it be so Judg, what greater guilt can bee then to offer to pry into these and to unriddle the misterious wiles of a powerful Cabal. Let all people Judge what can be of more dangerous Import then to suspect the soe long Safe proceedings of Some of our Grandees and wither People may with safety open their Eyes in soe nice a Concerne.

Another main article of our Guilt is our open and manifest aversion of all, not onely the Foreign but the protected and Darling Indians. This wee are informed is Rebellion of a deep dye For that both the Governour and Councell are by Colonell Coales Assertion bound to defend the Queen and the Appamatocks with their blood. Now whereas we doe declare and can prove that they have bin for these Many years enemies to the King and Country, Robbers and Theeves and Invaders of his Majesties Right and our Interest and Estates, but yet have by persons in Authority bin defended and protected even against His Majesties loyall Subjects; and that in soe high a Nature that even the Complaints and oaths of his Majesties Most loyall Subjects, in a lawfull Manner proffered by them against those barborous Outlawes, have bin by the right Honourable Governour rejected and the Delinquents from his presence dismissed, not only with pardon and indemnitye, but with all incouragement and favour, Their Fire Arms soe destructfull to us and by our lawes prohibited, Commanded to be restored them, and open Declaration before Witness made That they must have Ammunition, although directly contrary to our law. Now what greater guilt can be then to oppose and indeavour the destruction of these Honest quiet neighbours of ours?

Another main article of our Guilt is our Design not only to ruine and extirpate all Indians in Generall but all Manner of Trade and Commerce with them. Judge who can be innocent that strike at this tender Eye of Interest. Since the Right honourable the Governour hath bin pleased by his Commission to warrant this Trade, who dare oppose it, or opposing it can be innocent? Although Plantations be deserted, the blood of our dear Brethren Split, on all Sides or complaints, continually Murder upon Murder renewed upon us, who may or dare think of the generall Subversion of all Mannor of Trade and Commerce with our enemies who can or dare impeach any of the Traders at the Heades of the Rivers if, contrary to the wholesome provision made by lawes for the countries safety, they dare continue their illegall practises and dare asperse ye right honourable Governours wisdome and Justice soe highly to pretend to have his warrant to break that law which himself made? Who dare say That these Men at the Heads of the Rivers buy and sell our blood, and doe still notwithstanding the late Act made to the contrary, admit Indians painted and continue to Commerce? Although these things can be proved yet who dare bee soe giulty as to doe it.

Another Article of our Guilt is To Assert all those neighbour Indians as well as others to be outlawed, wholly unqualifyed for the benefitt and Protection of the law; For that the law does reciprocally protect and punish, and that all people offending must either in person or Estate make equivalent satisfaction or Restitution, according to the manner and merit of ye Offences Debts or Trespasses. Now since the Indians cannot, according to the tenure and forme of any law to us known, be prosecuted, Seised or Complained against, Their Persons being difficulty distinguished or known, Their many nations languages, and their subterfuges such as makes them incapeable to make us Restitution or satisfaction, would it not be very guilty to say They have bin unjustly defended and protected these many years?

If it should be said that the very foundation of all these disasters, the Grant of the Beaver trade to the Right Honourable Governour, was illegall and not granteable by any power here present as being a monopoly, were not this to deserve the name of Rebell and Traytor?

Judge therefore all wise and unprejudiced men, who may or can faithfully or truely with an honest heart attempt ye country's good, their vindication and libertie without the aspersion of Traitor and Rebell, since as soe doing they must of necessity gall such tender and dear concernes. But to manifest Sincerity and loyalty to the World, and how much wee abhorre those bitter names, may all the world know that we doe unanimously desire to represent our sad and heavy grievances to his most sacred Majestie as our Refuge and Sanctuary, where wee doe well know that all our Causes will be impartially heard and Equall Justice administered to all men.

BACON'S EPITAPH AND UPON THE DEATH OF G: BACON[1]
JOHN COTTON OF QUEEN'S CREEK

Bacons Epitaph, made by his Man[2]

Death why soe crewill what, no other way
To manifest thy splleene, but thus to slay

---

1. The two poems, "Bacon's Epitaph" and "Upon the Death of G: Bacon," are recorded in the "History of Bacon's and Ingram's Rebellion," written by John Cotton of Queen's Creek. The manuscript circulated in a number of hands until it was printed in *Collections of the Massachusetts Historical Society* in 1814 and then reprinted in 1866. Cotton, the son of an Anglican clergyman, was widely read, as the fuller manuscript indicates, and he seems to have been offended by both Bacon's and Berkeley's behavior.

2. The poems, written in sequence into the manuscript, are preceded by the following statement: "After he [Bacon] was

Our hopes of safety; liberty, our all
Which, through thy tyrany, with him must fall
5   To its late Caoss? Had thy riged force
Bin delt by retale, and not thus in gross
Griefe had bin silent: Now wee must complaine
Since thou, in him, hast more then thousand slane
Whose lives and safetys did so much depend
10 On him there lif, with him there lives must end.
     If't be a sin to thinke Death brib'd can bee
Wee must be guilty; say twas bribery
Guided the fatall shaft. Verginias foes,
To whom for secrit crimes just vengance owes
15 Disarved plagues, dreding their just disart
Corrupted Death by Parasscellcian art[3]

Him to destroy; whose well tride curage such,
There heartless harts, nor arms, nor strength could
    touch.
     Who now must heale those wounds, or stop that blood
20 The Heathen made, and drew into a flood?
Who i'st must please our Cause? nor Trump nor Drum
Nor Deputations; these alass are dumb,
And Cannot speake. Our Arms (though nere so strong)
Will want the aide of his Commanding tongue,
25 Which Conquer'd more than Ceaser: He orethrew
Onely the outward frame; this Could subdue
The ruged workes of nature. Soules repleate
With dull Child could,[4] he'd annemate with heate
Drawne forth of reasons Lymbick.[5] In a word
30 Marss and Minerva both in him Concurd
For arts, for arms, whose pen and sword alike,
As Catos did, may admireation strike
In to his foes; while they confess withall
It was there guilt stil'd him a Criminall.
35 Onely this difference doth from truth proceed:
They in the guilt, he in the name must bleed,
While none shall dare his Obseques to sing
In disarv'd measures, untill time shall bring

---

dead he was bemoaned in these following lines (drawne by the
Man that waited upon his person, as it is said) and who attended
his Corps to there Buriall place: . . . There was many coppes
of Verces made after his departure, calculated to the Lattitude of
there affections who composed them; as a relish taken from both
appetites I have here sent you a cuple."

3. Alchemical art, with reference to Paracelsus (1493–
1541), renowned Swiss physician and alchemist.

4. Chilled cold.

5. Alembic (as in "distilled" reasons).

Truth Crown'd with freedom, and from danger free,
To sound his praises to posterity.   40
    Here let him rest; while wee this truth report,
Hee's gon from hence unto a higher Court
To pleade his Cause: where he by this doth know
Whether to Ceaser hee was friend, or foe.

Upon the Death of G: B

Whether to Ceaser he was Friend or Foe?
Pox take such Ignorance, do you not know?
Can he be Friend to Ceaser, that shall bring
The Arms of Hell, to fight againt the King?
(Treason, Rebellion) then what reason have   5
Wee for to waite upon him to his Grave,
There to express our passions? Wilt not bee
Worss then his Crimes, to sing his Ellegie

In well tun'd numbers; where each Ella beares
(To his Flagitious name) a flood of teares?   10
A name that hath more soules with sorrow fed,
Then reched Niobe single teares ere shed;
A name that fil'd all hearts, all eares, with paine,
Untill blest fate proclaimed, Death had him slane.
Then how can it be counted for a sin   15
Though Death (nay though my selfe) had bribed bin,
To guide the fatall shaft? we honour all
That lends a hand unto a T[r]ators fall.
What though the well paide Rochit[6] soundly ply
And box the Pulpitt in to flatterey;   20
Urging his Rethorick, and straind elloquence,
T' adorne incoffin'd filth and excrements;
Though the Defunct (like ours) nere tride
A well intended deed untill he dide?
'Twill be nor sin, nor shame, for us, to say   25
A two fould Passion checker-workes this day
Of Joy and Sorrow; yet the last doth move
On feete impotent, wanting strength to prove
(Nor can the art of Logick yield releife)
How Joy should be surmounted, by our greife.   30
Yet that wee Grieve it cannot be denide,
But 'tis because he was, not cause he dide.
So wep the poore destressed Ilyum Dames[7]
Hereing those nam'd, there Citty put in flames,
And Country ruing'd; If wee thus lament   35
It is against our present Joyes consent.
For if the rule, in Phisick, trew doth prove,

---

6. A close-fit vestment worn by bishops.

7. The women of Ilium, Troy.

Remove the cause, th' effects will after move,
We have outliv'd our sorows, since we see
40   The Causes shifting, of our miserey.
     Nor is't a single cause, that's slipt away,
That made us warble out a well-a-day.
The Braines to plot, the hands to execute

Projected ills, Death Joyntly did nonsute
At his black Bar. And what no Baile could save   45
He hath commited Prissoner to the Grave;
From whence there's no reprieve. Death keep him close
We have too many Divells still goe loose.

NORTHERN EXPERIENCES

WILLIAM BRADFORD (1590–1657)

Born in Yorkshire, England, William Bradford was orphaned in childhood and raised by relatives in his yeoman farming family. While a young man, Bradford heard sermons by Richard Clyfton, a nonconformist minister, and found himself moved to lead a spiritual life. At the age of sixteen, despite his family's opposition, Bradford joined a group of Separatists led by Clyfton, who had established a community in the village of Scrooby. This group fled the official persecution of the Anglican Church in 1608 by relocating to Holland. They eventually settled in Leyden. There, Bradford learned to be a weaver.

In 1620, Bradford was part of the group that left Leyden for North America. The colonists wanted to establish a church and community that were free from both secular and religious influences in Europe. The emigrants sailed on the *Mayflower,* arriving in November off the coast of what is today Cape Cod, a point much farther north than the Virginia territory, which had been their destination. They made an initial settlement at Plymouth, where Bradford took on leadership roles almost from the first. The group was led in spiritual matters by William Brewster and in matters temporal by John Carver. When Carver died the year after they landed, Bradford was elected to succeed him and was reelected to that position almost continuously for the rest of his life, serving as governor for a total of thirty-three years.

In addition to serving as the settlement's leader in its formative years, Bradford also became its historian. He began writing his history, *Of Plymouth Plantation,* in 1630. Working on it at intervals over the years, by 1650, he had brought the account up to 1646. The manuscript was incomplete when he died in 1657, yet it stood as the colony's testament to the settlement of Separatists, a full ten years before the landing of the Puritans at Massachusetts Bay, and the record of their endeavors to live saintly lives in what they conceived as a wilderness suited to test the mettle of their God's people.

Of Plymouth Plantation records the events in the life of the colony and interprets those events in terms of the workings of divine providence. In the activities, the trials, and the successes of the Separatist congregation would lie the indications of God's presence or absence in the very lives of the congregants who settled in the community. In this respect, Bradford's history may usefully be compared with the genre of Puritan biography, with its intense concentration on the spiritual significance of events in an individual's life, and with hagiography, in its celebration of those saints who best reflected the sense of a divine intervention in the everyday experiences of his people.

From evidence in the text, it seems likely that Bradford envisioned a number of possible audiences for his history: members of the second and later generations at Plymouth, members of the Scrooby congregation who had not emigrated, and potential members of these groups who remained dissatisfied with their lives among Anglicans back in England. The manuscript of the history undoubtedly circulated among learned and pious congregants, and it also served as a telling reminder to the Puritans in Massachusetts Bay that the Separatist way had taken root in Plymouth well before the New England way conceived of itself and its future. The manuscript seems to have been consulted by numerous pious and learned historians of the colony, including Cotton Mather.

from OF PLYMOUTH PLANTATION[1]

THE FIRST BOOK

And first of the occasion and inducements thereunto; the which, that I may truly unfold, I must begin at the very root and rise of the same. The which I shall endeavour to manifest in a plain style, with singular regard unto the simple truth in all things; at least as near as my slender judgment can attain the same.

from CHAPTER 1 • [Why the Separatists Left England]

It is well known unto the godly and judicious, how ever since the first breaking out of the light of the gospel in our honourable nation of England, (which was the first of nations whom the Lord adorned therewith after the gross darkness of popery which had covered and overspread the Christian world), what wars and oppositions ever since, Satan hath raised, maintained and continued against the Saints,[2] from time to time, in one sort or other. Sometimes by bloody death and cruel torments; other whiles imprisonments, banishments and other hard usages; as being loath his kingdom should go down, the truth prevail and the churches of God revert to their ancient purity and recover their primitive order, liberty and beauty.

But when he could not prevail by these means against the main truths of the gospel, but that they began to take rooting in many places, being watered with the blood of the martyrs and blessed from Heaven with a gracious increase; he then began to take him to his ancient stratagems, used of old against the first Christians. That when by the bloody and barbarous persecutions of the heathen emperors he could not stop and subvert the course of the gospel, but that it speedily overspread, with a wonderful celerity, the then best known parts of the world; he then began to sow errours, heresies and wonderful dissensions amongst the professors[3] themselves, working upon their pride and ambition, with other corrupt passions incident to all mortal men, yea to the saints themselves in some measure, by which woeful effects followed. As not only bitter contentions and heartburnings, schisms, with other horrible confusions; but Satan took occasion and advantage thereby to foist in a number of vile ceremonies, with many unprofitable canons and decrees, which have since been as snares to many poor and peaceable souls even to this day.

So as in the ancient times, the persecutions by the heathen and their emperors was not greater than of the Christians one against other:—the Arians and other their complices against the orthodox and true Christians. As witnesseth Socrates in his second book.[4] His words are these:

> The violence truly (saith he) was no less than that of old practiced towards the Christians when they were compelled and drawn to sacrifice to idols; for many endured sundry kinds of torment, often rackings and dismembering of their joints, confiscating of their goods; some bereaved of their native soil, others departed this life under the hands of the tormentor, and some died in banishment and never saw their country again, etc.

The like method Satan hath seemed to hold in these later times, since the truth began to spring and spread after the great defection made by Antichrist, that man of sin.

For to let pass the infinite examples in sundry nations and several places of the world, and instance in our own, when as that old serpent could not prevail by those fiery flames and other his cruel tragedies, which he by his instruments put in ure[5] everywhere in the days of Queen Mary and before, he then began another kind of war and went more closely to work; not only to oppugn but even to ruinate and destroy the kingdom of Christ by more secret and subtle means, by kindling the flames of contention and sowing the seeds of discord and bitter enmity amongst the professors and, seeming reformed, them-

---

1. The manuscript was written in stages. Bradford wrote the first chapter in 1630, but he put the manuscript aside until 1644, when he finished up to chapter 11. Between 1646 and 1650, he wrote the segment taking the history up to the year 1646. The account circulated in manuscript during these years and later and was first published in 1856. The text is *Of Plymouth Plantation, 1620–1647,* ed. S.E. Morison (1952).

2. Church members, or God's chosen people.

3. Believers.

4. Socrates Scholasticus, a fifth-century Greek historian, author of *Ecclesiastical History*.

5. In practice.

selves. For when he could not prevail by the former means against the principal doctrines of faith, he bent his force against the holy discipline and outward regiment of the kingdom of Christ, by which those holy doctrines should be conserved, and true piety maintained amongst the saints and people of God.

Mr. Fox[6] recordeth how that besides those worthy martyrs and confessors which were burned in Queen Mary's days and otherwise tormented, "Many (both students and others) fled out of the land to the number of 800, and became several congregations, at Wesel, Frankfort, Basel, Emden, Markpurge, Strasburg and Geneva, etc." Amongst whom (but especially those at Frankfort) began that bitter war of contention and persecution about the ceremonies and service book, and other popish and antichristian stuff, the plague of England to this day, which are like the high places in Israel which the prophets cried out against, and were their ruin. Which the better part sought, according to the purity of the gospel, to root out and utterly to abandon. And the other part (under veiled pretences) for their own ends and advancements, sought as stiffly to continue, maintain and defend. As appeareth by the discourse thereof published in print, anno 1575; a book that deserves better to be known and considered.[7]

The one side laboured to have the right worship of God and discipline of Christ established in the church, according to the simplicity of the gospel, without the mixture of men's inventions; and to have and to be ruled by the laws of God's Word, dispensed in those offices, and by those officers of Pastors, Teachers and Elders, etc. according to the Scriptures. The other party, though under many colours and pretences, endeavoured to have the episcopal dignity (after the popish manner) with their large power and jurisdiction still retained; with all those courts, canons and ceremonies, together with all such livings, revenues and subordinate officers, with other such means as formerly upheld their antichristian greatness and enabled them with lordly and tyrannous power to persecute the poor servants of God. This contention was so great, as neither the honour of God, the common persecution, nor the mediation of Mr. Calvin and other worthies of the Lord in those places, could prevail with those

thus episcopally minded; but they proceeded by all means to disturb the peace of this poor persecuted church, even so far as to charge (very unjustly and ungodlily yet prelatelike) some of their chief opposers with rebellion and high treason against the Emperor, and other such crimes.

And this contention died not with Queen Mary, nor was left beyond the seas. But at her death these people returning into England under gracious Queen Elizabeth, many of them being preferred to bishoprics and other promotions according to their aims and desires, that inveterate hatred against the holy discipline of Christ in His church hath continued to this day. Insomuch that for fear it should prevail, all plots and devices have been used to keep it out, incensing the Queen and State against it as dangerous for the commonwealth; and that it was most needful that the fundamental points of religion should be preached in those ignorant and superstitious times. And to win the weak and ignorant they might retain divers harmless ceremonies; and though it were to be wished that divers things were reformed, yet this was not a season for it. And many the like, to stop the mouths of the more godly, to bring them on to yield to one ceremony after another, and one corruption after another; by these wiles beguiling some and corrupting others till at length they began to persecute all the zealous professors in the land (though they knew little what this discipline meant) both by word and deed, if they would not submit to their ceremonies and become slaves to them and their popish trash, which have no ground in the Word of God, but are relics of that man of sin. And the more the light of the gospel grew, the more they urged their subscriptions to these corruptions. So as (notwithstanding all their former pretences and fair colours) they whose eyes God had not justly blinded might easily see whereto these things tended. And to cast contempt the more upon the sincere servants of God, they opprobriously and most injuriously gave unto and imposed upon them that name of Puritans, which is said the Novatians[8] out of pride did assume and take unto themselves. And lamentable it is to see the effects which have followed. Religion hath been disgraced, the godly grieved, afflicted, persecuted, and many exiled; sundry have lost their lives in prisons and other ways. On the other hand, sin hath been countenanced; ignorance, profaneness and atheism increased, and the papists encouraged to hope again for a day. . . .

---

6. John Foxe (1516–1587), author of 1641 *Acts and Monuments* (also called the *Book of Martyrs*).

7. *Brieff Discours of the Troubles begonne at Franckford* by William Whittingham (d. 1579).

---

8. A third-century Christian sect.

This made that holy man Mr. Perkins[9] cry out in his exhortation to repentance, upon Zephaniah ii:

> Religion (saith he) hath been amongst us this thirty-five years; but the more it is published, the more it is contemned and reproached of many, etc. Thus not profaneness nor wickedness but religion itself is a byword, a mockingstock, and a matter of reproach; so that in England at this day the man or woman that begins to profess religion and to serve God, must resolve with himself to sustain mocks and injuries even as though he lived amongst the enemies of religion.

And this, common experience hath confirmed and made too apparent. But that I may come more near my intendment.

When as by the travail and diligence of some godly and zealous preachers, and God's blessing on their labours, as in other places of the land, so in the North parts, many became enlightened by the Word of God and had their ignorance and sins discovered unto them, and began by His grace to reform their lives and make conscience of their ways; the work of God was no sooner manifest in them but presently they were both scoffed and scorned by the profane multitude; and the ministers urged with the yoke of subscription; or else must be silenced. And the poor people were so vexed with apparitors and pursuivants[10] and the commissary courts, as truly their affliction was not small. Which, notwithstanding, they bore sundry years with much patience, till they were occasioned by the continuance and increase of these troubles, and other means which the Lord raised up in those days, to see further into things by the light of the Word of God. How not only these base and beggarly ceremonies were unlawful, but also that the lordly and tyrannous power of the prelates ought not to be submitted unto; which thus, contrary to the freedom of the gospel, would load and burden men's consciences and by their compulsive power make a profane mixture of persons and things in the worship of God. And that their offices and callings, courts and canons, etc. were unlawful and antichristian; being such as have no warrant in the Word of God, but the same that were used in popery and still retained. Of which a famous author thus writeth in his Dutch commentaries,[11] at the coming of King James into England:

> The new king (saith he) found there established the reformed religion according to the reformed religion of King Edward VI, retaining or keeping still the spiritual state of the bishops, etc. after the old manner, much varying and differing from the reformed churches in Scotland, France and the Netherlands, Emden, Geneva, etc., whose reformation is cut, or shapen much nearer the first Christian churches, as it was used in the Apostles' times.

So many, therefore, of these professors as saw the evil of these things in these parts, and whose hearts the Lord had touched with heavenly zeal for His truth, they shook off this yoke of antichristian bondage, and as the Lord's free people joined themselves (by a covenant of the Lord) into a church estate, in the fellowship of the gospel, to walk in all His ways made known, or to be made known unto them, according to their best endeavours, whatsoever it should cost them, the Lord assisting them. And that it cost them something this ensuing history will declare.

These people became two distinct bodies or churches, and in regard of distance of place did congregate severally; for they were of sundry towns and villages, some in Nottinghamshire, some of Lincolnshire, and some of Yorkshire where they border nearest together. In one of these churches (besides others of note) was Mr. John Smith a man of able gifts and a good preacher, who afterwards was chosen their pastor. But these afterwards falling into some errours in the Low Countries, there (for the most part) buried themselves and their names.

But in this other church (which must be the subject of our discourse) besides other worthy men, was Mr. Richard Clyfton, a grave and reverend preacher, who by his pains and diligence had done much good, and under God had been a means of the conversion of many. And also that famous and worthy man Mr. John Robinson, who afterwards was their pastor for many years, till the Lord took him away by death. Also Mr. William Brewster a reverend man, who afterwards was chosen an elder of the church and lived with them till old age.[12]

But after these things they could not long continue in any peaceable condition, but were hunted and persecuted on every side, so as their former afflictions were but as

---

9. William Perkins (1558–1602), English theologian. The quotation is from Perkins's *Exposition of Christ's Sermon Upon the Mount* (1618).

10. Officials of the Church of England whose job was to ensure conformity to church doctrine.

11. Emanuel van Meteren's *General History of the Netherlands* (1608).

12. Clyfton (d. 1616) and Robinson (1575?–1625) were both ministers to the Scrooby and later Plymouth congregations; Brewster (1566–1643) was an elder in Plymouth.

flea-bitings in comparison of these which now came upon them. For some were taken and clapped up in prison, others had their houses beset and watched night and day, and hardly escaped their hands; and the most were fain to flee and leave their houses and habitations, and the means of their livelihood.

Yet these and many other sharper things which afterward befell them, were no other than they looked for, and therefore were the better prepared to bear them by the assistance of God's grace and Spirit.

Yet seeing themselves thus molested, and that there was no hope of their continuance there, by a joint consent they resolved to go into the Low Countries, where they heard was freedom of religion for all men; as also how sundry from London and other parts of the land had been exiled and persecuted for the same cause, and were gone thither, and lived at Amsterdam and in other places of the land. So after they had continued together about a year, and kept their meetings every Sabbath in one place or other, exercising the worship of God amongst themselves, notwithstanding all the diligence and malice of their adversaries, they seeing they could no longer continue in that condition, they resolved to get over into Holland as they could. Which was in the year 1607 and 1608; of which more at large in the next chapter.

from CHAPTER 2

Of their Departure into Holland and their Troubles thereabout, with some of the many Difficulties they found and met withal. Anno 1608

Being thus constrained to leave their native soil and country, their lands and livings, and all their friends and familiar acquaintance, it was much; and thought marvelous by many. But to go into a country they knew not but by hearsay, where they must learn a new language and get their livings they knew not how, it being a dear place and subject to the miseries of war, it was by many thought an adventure almost desperate; a case intolerable and a misery worse than death. Especially seeing they were not acquainted with trades nor traffic (by which that country doth subsist) but had only been used to a plain country life and the innocent trade of husbandry. But these things did not dismay them, though they did sometimes trouble them; for their desires were set on the ways of God and to enjoy His ordinances; but they rested on His providence,

and knew Whom they had believed. Yet this was not all, for though they could not stay, yet were they not suffered to go; but the ports and havens were shut against them, so as they were fain to seek secret means of conveyance, and to bribe and fee the mariners, and give extraordinary rates for their passages. And yet were they often times betrayed, many of them; and both they and their goods intercepted and surprised, and thereby put to great trouble and charge . . .

But that I be not tedious in these things, I will omit the rest, though I might relate many other notable passages and troubles which they endured and underwent in these their wanderings and travels both at land and sea; but I haste to other things. Yet I may not omit the fruit that came hereby, for by these so public troubles in so many eminent places their cause became famous and occasioned many to look into the same, and their godly carriage and Christian behaviour was such as left a deep impression in the minds of many. And though some few shrunk at these first conflicts and sharp beginnings (as it was no marvel) yet many more came on with fresh courage and greatly animated others. And in the end, notwithstanding all these storms of opposition, they all gat over at length, some at one time and some at another, and some in one place and some in another, and met together again according to their desires, with no small rejoicing.

from CHAPTER 5

Showing What Means They Used for Preparation to This Weighty Voyage

And first after their humble prayers unto God for His direction and assistance, and a general conference held hereabout, they consulted what particular place to pitch upon and prepare for. Some (and none of the meanest) had thoughts and were earnest for Guiana, or some of those fertile places in those hot climates. Others were for some parts of Virginia, where the English had already made entrance and beginning. Those for Guiana alleged that the country was rich, fruitful, and blessed with a perpetual spring and a flourishing greenness, where vigorous nature brought forth all things in abundance and plenty without any great labour or art of man. So as it must needs make the inhabitants rich, seeing less provisions of clothing and other things would serve, than in more colder and less fruitful countries must be had. As also that the Spaniards (having much more than they could possess) had not yet planted there nor anywhere very near the same. But to this it was answered that out of question the country was both fruitful and pleasant, and might yield riches and maintenance to the possessors more easily than the other; yet, other things considered, it would not be so fit for them. And first, that such hot countries are subject to grievous diseases and many noisome impediments which other more temperate places are freer from, and would not so well agree with our English bodies. Again, if they should there live and do well, the jealous Spaniard would never suffer them long, but would displant or overthrow them as he did the French in Florida, who were seated further from his richest countries; and the sooner because they should have none to protect them, and their own strength would be too small to resist so potent an enemy and so near a neighbour.

On the other hand, for Virginia it was objected that if they lived among the English which were there planted, or so near them as to be under their government, they should be in as great danger to be troubled and persecuted for the cause of religion as if they lived in England; and it might be worse. And if they lived too far off, they should neither have succour nor defense from them.

But at length the conclusion was to live as a distinct body by themselves under the general Government of Virginia; and by their friends to sue to His Majesty that he would be pleased to grant them freedom of religion. And that this might be obtained they were put in good hope by some great persons of good rank and quality that were made their friends. Whereupon two were chosen and sent into England (at the charge of the rest) to solicit this matter, who found the Virginia Company very desirous to have them go thither and willing to grant them a patent, with as ample privileges as they had or could grant to any; and to give them the best furtherance they could.

from CHAPTER 9

Of their Voyage, and how they Passed the Sea; and of their Safe Arrival at Cape Cod

September 6. These troubles being blown over, and now all being compact together in one ship, they put to sea again with a prosperous wind, which continued divers days together, which was some encouragement unto them; yet, according to the usual manner, many were afflicted with seasickness. And I may not omit here a special work of God's providence. There was a proud and very profane young man, one of the seamen, of a lusty, able body, which made him the more haughty; he would alway be contemning the poor people in their sickness and cursing them daily with grievous execrations; and did not let to tell them that he hoped to help to cast half of them overboard before they came to their journey's end, and to make merry with what they had; and if he were by any gently reproved, he would curse and swear most bitterly. But it pleased God before they came half seas over, to smite this young man with a grievous disease, of which he died in a desperate manner, and so was himself the first that was thrown overboard. Thus his curses light on his own head, and it was an astonishment to all his fellows for they noted it to be the just hand of God upon him.

After they had enjoyed fair winds and weather for a season, they were encountered many times with cross winds and met with many fierce storms with which the ship was shroudly[13] shaken, and her upper works made very leaky; and one of the main beams in the midships was bowed and cracked, which put them in some fear that the ship could not be able to perform the voyage. So some of the chief of the company, perceiving the mariners to fear the sufficiency of the ship as appeared by their mutterings, they entered into serious consultation with the master and other officers of the ship, to consider in time of the danger, and rather to return than to cast themselves into a desperate and inevitable peril. And truly there was great distraction and difference of opinion amongst the mariners themselves; fain would they do what could be done for their wages' sake (being now near half the seas over) and on the other hand they were loath to hazard their lives too desperately. But in examining of all opinions, the master and others affirmed they knew the ship to be strong and firm under water; and for the buckling of the main beam, there was a great iron screw the passengers brought out of Holland, which would raise the beam into his place; the which being done, the carpenter and master affirmed that with a post put under it, set firm in the lower deck and otherways bound, he would make it sufficient. And as for the decks and upper works, they would caulk them as well as they could, and though with the working of the ship they would not long keep staunch, yet there

---

13. Wickedly, fiercely.

would otherwise be no great danger, if they did not over-press her with sails. So they committed themselves to the will of God and resolved to proceed.

In sundry of these storms the winds were so fierce and the seas so high, as they could not bear a knot of sail, but were forced to hull[14] for divers days together. And in one of them, as they thus lay at hull in a mighty storm, a lusty young man called John Howland, coming upon some occasion above the gratings was, with a seele of the ship, thrown into sea; but it pleased God that he caught hold of the topsail halyards which hung overboard and ran out at length. Yet he held his hold (though he was sundry fathoms under water) till he was hauled up by the same rope to the brim of the water, and then with a boat hook and other means got into the ship again and his life saved. And though he was something ill with it, yet he lived many years after and became a profitable member both in church and commonwealth. In all this voyage there died but one of the passengers, which was William Butten, a youth, servant to Samuel Fuller, when they drew near the coast.

But to omit other things (that I may be brief) after long beating at sea they fell with that land which is called Cape Cod; the which being made and certainly known to be it, they were not a little joyful. After some deliberation had amongst themselves and with the master of the ship, they tacked about and resolved to stand for the southward (the wind and weather being fair) to find some place about Hudson's River for their habitation. But after they had sailed that course about half the day, they fell amongst dangerous shoals and roaring breakers, and they were so far entangled therewith as they conceived themselves in great danger; and the wind shrinking upon them withal, they resolved to bear up again for the Cape and thought themselves happy to get out of those dangers before night overtook them, as by God's good providence they did. And the next day they got into the Cape Harbor[15] where they rid in safety.

A word or two by the way of this cape. It was thus first named by Captain Gosnold and his company, Anno 1602, and after by Captain Smith was called Cape James; but it retains the former name amongst seamen. Also, that point which first showed those dangerous shoals unto them they called Point Care, and Tucker's Terrour; but the French and Dutch to this day call it Malabar by reason of those perilous shoals and the losses they have suffered there.

Being thus arrived in a good harbor, and brought safe to land, they fell upon their knees and blessed the God of Heaven who had brought them over the vast and furious ocean, and delivered them from all the perils and miseries thereof, again to set their feet on the firm and stable earth, their proper element. And no marvel if they were thus joyful, seeing wise Seneca was so affected with sailing a few miles on the coast of his own Italy, as he affirmed, that he had rather remain twenty years on his way by land than pass by sea to any place in a short time, so tedious and dreadful was the same unto him.

But here I cannot but stay and make a pause, and stand half amazed at this poor people's present condition; and so I think will the reader, too, when he well considers the same. Being thus passed the vast ocean, and a sea of troubles before in their preparation (as may be remembered by that which went before), they had now no friends to welcome them nor inns to entertain or refresh their weatherbeaten bodies; no houses or much less towns to repair to, to seek for succour. It is recorded in Scripture as a mercy to the Apostle and his shipwrecked company, that the barbarians showed them no small kindness in refreshing them,[16] but these savage barbarians, when they met with them (as after will appear) were readier to fill their sides full of arrows than otherwise. And for the season it was winter, and they that know the winters of that country know them to be sharp and violent, and subject to cruel and fierce storms, dangerous to travel to known places, much more to search an unknown coast. Besides, what could they see but a hideous and desolate wilderness, full of wild beasts and wild men—and what multitudes there might be of them they knew not. Neither could they, as it were, go up to the top of Pisgah to view from this wilderness a more goodly country to feed their hopes; for which way soever they turned their eyes (save upward to the heavens) they could have little solace or content in respect of any outward objects. For summer being done, all things stand upon them with a weather-beaten face, and the whole country, full of woods and thickets, represented a wild and savage hue. If they looked behind them, there was the mighty ocean which they had passed and was now as a main bar and gulf to separate them from all

---

14. To drift with the wind.

15. Present-day Provincetown Harbor.

16. Acts 28:2.

the civil parts of the world. If it be said they had a ship to succour them, it is true; but what heard they daily from the master and company? But that with speed they should look out a place (with their shallop) where they would be, at some near distance; for the season was such as he would not stir from thence till a safe harbor was discovered by them, where they would be, and he might go without danger; and that victuals consumed apace but he must and would keep sufficient for themselves and their return. Yea, it was muttered by some that if they got not a place in time, they would turn them and their goods ashore and leave them. Let it also be considered what weak hopes of supply and succour they left behind them, that might bear up their minds in this sad condition and trials they were under; and they could not but be very small. It is true, indeed, the affections and love of their brethren at Leyden was cordial and entire towards them, but they had little power to help them or themselves; and how the case stood between them and the merchants at their coming away hath already been declared.

What could now sustain them but the Spirit of God and His grace? May not and ought not the children of these fathers rightly say: "Our fathers were Englishmen which came over this great ocean, and were ready to perish in this wilderness; but they cried unto the Lord, and He heard their voice and looked on their adversity,"[17] etc. "Let them therefore praise the Lord, because He is good: and His mercies endure forever." "Yea, let them which have been redeemed of the Lord, shew how He hath delivered them from the hand of the oppressor. When they wandered in the desert wilderness out of the way, and found no city to dwell in, both hungry and thirsty, their soul was overwhelmed in them. Let them confess before the Lord His lovingkindness and His wonderful works before the sons of men."[18]

from CHAPTER 10

*Showing How they Sought out a place of Habitation;
and What Befell them Thereabout*

Being thus arrived at Cape Cod the 11th of November, and necessity calling them to look out a place for habitation (as well as the master's and mariners' importunity);

they having brought a large shallop with them out of England, stowed in quarters in the ship, they now got her out and set their carpenters to work to trim her up; but being much bruised and shattered in the ship with foul weather, they saw she would be long in mending. Whereupon a few of them tendered themselves to go by land and discover those nearest places, whilst the shallop was in mending; and the rather because as they went into that harbor there seemed to be an opening some two or three leagues off, which the master judged to be a river. It was conceived there might be some danger in the attempt, yet seeing them resolute, they were permitted to go, being sixteen of them well armed under the conduct of Captain Standish,[19] having such instructions given them as was thought meet.

They set forth the 15th of November; and when they had marched about the space of a mile by the seaside, they espied five or six persons with a dog coming towards them, who were savages; but they fled from them and ran up into the woods, and the English followed them, partly to see if they could speak with them, and partly to discover if there might not be more of them lying in ambush. But the Indians seeing themselves thus followed, they again forsook the woods and ran away on the sands as hard as they could, so as they could not come near them but followed them by the track of their feet sundry miles and saw that they had come the same way. So, night coming on, they made their rendezvous and set out their sentinels, and rested in quiet that night; and the next morning followed their track till they had headed a great creek and so left the sands, and turned another way into the woods. But they still followed them by guess, hoping to find their dwellings; but they soon lost both them and themselves, falling into such thickets as were ready to tear their clothes and armor in pieces; but were most distressed for want of drink. But at length they found water and refreshed themselves, being the first New England water they drunk of, and was now in great thirst as pleasant unto them as wine or beer had been in foretimes.

Afterwards they directed their course to come to the other shore, for they knew it was a neck of land they were to cross over, and so at length got to the seaside and

---

17. Deuteronomy 26:5, 7.

18. Psalm 107:1–5, 8.

---

19. Myles Standish (1584–1656) had been hired to accompany the group that traveled on the Mayflower and to handle their military affairs.

marched to this supposed river, and by the way found a pond of clear, fresh water, and shortly after a good quantity of clear ground where the Indians had formerly set corn, and some of their graves. And proceeding further they saw new stubble where corn had been set the same year; also they found where lately a house had been, where some planks and a great kettle was remaining, and heaps of sand newly paddled with their hands. Which, they digging up, found in them divers fair Indian baskets filled with corn, and some in ears, fair and good, of divers colours, which seemed to them a very goodly sight (having never seen any such before). This was near the place of that supposed river they came to seek, unto which they went and found it to open itself into two arms with a high cliff of sand in the entrance but more like to be creeks of salt water than any fresh, for aught they saw; and that there was good harborage for their shallop, leaving it further to be discovered by their shallop, when she was ready. So, their time limited them being expired, they returned to the ship lest they should be in fear of their safety; and took with them part of the corn and buried up the rest. And so, like the men from Eshcol, carried with them of the fruits of the land and showed their brethren; of which, and their return, they were marvelously glad and their hearts encouraged.

After this, the shallop being got ready, they set out again for the better discovery of this place, and the master of the ship desired to go himself. So there went some thirty men but found it to be no harbor for ships but only for boats. There was also found two of their houses covered with mats, and sundry of their implements in them, but the people were run away and could not be seen. Also there was found more of their corn and of their beans of various colours; the corn and beans they brought away, purposing to give them full satisfaction when they should meet with any of them as, about some six months afterward they did, to their good content.

And here is to be noted a special providence of God, and a great mercy to this poor people, that here they got seed to plant them corn the next year, or else they might have starved, for they had none nor any likelihood to get any till the season had been past, as the sequel did manifest. Neither is it likely they had had this, if the first voyage had not been made, for the ground was now all covered with snow and hard frozen; but the Lord is never wanting unto His in their greatest needs; let His holy name have all the praise. . . .

So they ranged up and down all that day, but found no people, nor any place they liked. When the sun grew low, they hasted out of the woods to meet with their shallop, to whom they made signs to come to them into a creek hard by, the which they did at high water; of which they were very glad, for they had not seen each other all that day since the morning. So they made them a barricado as usually they did every night, with logs, stakes and thick pine boughs, the height of a man, leaving it open to leeward, partly to shelter them from the cold and wind (making their fire in the middle and lying round about it) and partly to defend them from any sudden assaults of the savages, if they should surround them; so being very weary, they betook them to rest. But about midnight they heard a hideous and great cry, and their sentinel called "Arm! arm!" So they bestirred them and stood to their arms and shot off a couple of muskets, and then the noise ceased. They concluded it was a company of wolves or such like wild beasts, for one of the seamen told them he had often heard such a noise in Newfoundland.

So they rested till about five of the clock in the morning; for the tide, and their purpose to go from thence, made them be stirring betimes. So after prayer they prepared for breakfast, and it being day dawning it was thought best to be carrying things down to the boat. But some said it was not best to carry the arms down, others said they would be the readier, for they had lapped them up in their coats from the dew; but some three or four would not carry theirs till they went themselves. Yet as it fell out, the water being not high enough, they laid them down on the bank side and came up to breakfast.

But presently, all on the sudden, they heard a great and strange cry, which they knew to be the same voices they heard in the night, though they varied their notes; and one of their company being abroad came running in and cried, "Men, Indians! Indians!" And withal, their arrows came flying amongst them. Their men ran with all speed to recover their arms, as by the good providence of God they did. In the meantime, of those that were there ready, two muskets were discharged at them, and two more stood ready in the entrance of their rendezvous but were commanded not to shoot till they could take full aim at them. And the other two charged again with all speed, for there were only four had arms there, and defended the barricado, which was first assaulted. The cry of the Indians was dreadful, especially when they saw their men run out of the rendezvous toward the shallop to recover their arms, the Indians wheeling about upon them. But some running out with coats of mail on, and cutlasses in their hands, they soon got their arms and let fly amongst them and quickly stopped their violence. Yet there was a lusty man, and no less valiant, stood behind a tree within half a musket shot, and let his arrows fly at them; he was seen [to] shoot three arrows, which were all avoided. He stood three shots of a musket, till one taking full aim at him and made the bark or splinters of the tree fly about his ears, after which he gave an extraordinary shriek and away they went, all of them. They left some to keep the shallop and followed them about a quarter of a mile and shouted once or twice, and shot off two or three pieces, and so returned. This they did that they might conceive that they were not afraid of them or any way discouraged.

Thus it pleased God to vanquish their enemies and give them deliverance; and by His special providence so to dispose that not any one of them were either hurt or hit, though their arrows came close by them and on every side [of] them; and sundry of their coats, which hung up in the barricado, were shot through and through. Afterwards they gave God solemn thanks and praise for their deliverance, and gathered up a bundle of their arrows and sent them into England afterward by the master of the ship, and called that place the First Encounter. . . .

Though the partners were thus plunged into great engagements and oppressed with unjust debts, yet the Lord prospered their trading, that they made yearly large returns and had soon wound themselves out of all if yet they had otherwise been well dealt withal as will more appear hereafter.

Also the people of the Plantation began to grow in their outward estates, by reason of the flowing of many people into the country, especially into the Bay of the Massachusetts. By which means corn and cattle rose to a great price, by which many were much enriched and commodities grew plentiful. And yet in other regards this benefit turned to their hurt, and this accession of strength to their weakness. For now as their stocks increased and the increase vendible, there was no longer any holding them together, but now they must of necessity go to their great lots. They could not otherwise keep their cattle, and having oxen grown they must have land for plowing and tillage. And no man now thought he could live except he had cattle and a great deal of ground to keep them, all striving to increase their stocks. By which means they were scattered all over the Bay quickly and the town in which they lived compactly till now was left very thin and in a short time almost desolate.

And if this had been all, it had been less, though too much; but the church must also be divided, and those that had lived so long together in Christian and comfortable fellowship must now part and suffer many divisions. First, those that lived on their lots on the other side of the Bay, called Duxbury, they could not long bring their wives and children to the public worship and church meetings here, but with such burthen as, growing to some competent number, they sued to be dismissed and become a body of themselves. And so they were dismissed about this time, though very unwillingly. But to touch this sad matter, and handle things together that fell out afterward; to prevent any further scattering from this place and weakening of the same, it was thought best to give out some good farms to special persons that would promise to live at Plymouth, and likely to be helpful to the church or commonwealth, and so tie the lands to Plymouth as farms for the same; and there they might keep their cattle and tillage by some servants and retain their dwellings here. And so some special lands were granted at a place general called Green's Harbor, where no allotments had been in the former division, a place very well meadowed and fit to keep and rear cattle good store. But alas, this remedy proved worse than the disease; for within a few years those that had thus got footing there rent themselves away, partly by force and partly wearing the rest with importunity and pleas of necessity, so as they must either suffer them to go or live in continual opposition and contention. And other still, as they conceived themselves straitened or to want accommodation, broke away under one pretence or other, thinking their own conceived necessity and the example of others a warrant sufficient for them. And this I fear will be the ruin of New England, at least of the churches of God there, and will provoke the Lord's displeasure against them.

THE SECOND BOOK

from CHAPTER 28 • Anno Dom: 1637
[The Pequot War]

In the fore part of this year, the Pequots fell openly upon the English at Connecticut, in the lower parts of the river, and slew sundry of them as they were at work in the fields, both men and women, to the great terrour of the rest, and went away in great pride and triumph, with many high threats. They also assaulted a fort at the river's mouth, though strong and well defended; and though they did not there prevail, yet it struck them with much fear and astonishment to see their bold attempts in the face of danger. Which made them in all places to stand upon their guard and to prepare for resistance, and earnestly to solicit their friends and confederates in the Bay of Massachusetts to send them speedy aid, for they looked for more forcible assaults. Mr. Vane, being then Governor, writ from their General Court to them here to join with them in this war. To which they were cordially willing, but took opportunity to write to them about some former things, as well as present, considerable hereabout. The which will best appear in the Governor's answer, which he returned to the same, which I shall here insert.[20]

In the meantime, the Pequots, especially in the winter before, sought to make peace with the Narragansetts, and used very pernicious arguments to move them thereunto: as that the English were strangers and began to overspread their country, and would deprive them thereof in time, if they were suffered to grow and increase. And if the Narragansetts did assist the English to subdue them, they did but make way for their own overthrow, for if they were rooted out, the English would soon take occasion to subjugate them. And if they would hearken to them they should not need to fear the strength of the English, for they would not come to open battle with them but fire their houses, kill their cattle, and lie in ambush for them as they went abroad upon their occasions; and all this they might easily do without any or little danger to themselves. The which course being held, they well saw the English could not long subsist but they would either be starved with hunger or be forced to forsake the country. With many the like things; insomuch that the Narragansetts were once wavering and were half minded to have made peace with them, and joined against the English. But again, when they considered how much wrong they had received from the Pequots, and what an opportunity they now had by the help of the English to right themselves; revenge was so sweet unto them as it prevailed above all the rest, so as they resolved to join with the English against them, and did.

The Court here agreed forthwith to send fifty men at their own charge; and with as much speed as possibly they could, got them armed and had made them ready under sufficient leaders, and provided a bark to carry them provisions and tend upon them for all occasions. But when they were ready to march, with a supply from the Bay, they had word to stay; for the enemy was as good as vanquished and there would be no need.

I shall not take upon me exactly to describe their proceedings in these things, because I expect it will be fully done by themselves who best know the carriage and circumstances of things. I shall therefore but touch them in general. From Connecticut, who were most sensible of the hurt sustained and the present danger, they set out a party of men, and another party met them from the Bay, at Narragansetts', who were to join with them. The Narragansetts were earnest to be gone before the English were well rested and refreshed, especially some of them which came last. It should seem their desire was to come upon the enemy suddenly and undiscovered. There was a bark of this place, newly put in there, which was come from Connecticut, who did encourage them to lay hold of the Indians' forwardness, and to show as great forwardness as they, for it would encourage them, and expedition might prove to their great advantage. So they went on, and so ordered their march as the Indians brought them to a fort of the enemy's (in which most of their chief men were) before day. They approached the same with great silence and surrounded it both with English and Indians, that they might not break out; and so assaulted them with great courage, shooting amongst them, and entered the fort with all speed. And those that first entered found sharp resistance from the enemy who both shot at and grappled with them; others ran into their houses and brought out fire and set them on fire, which soon took in their mat; and standing close together, with the wind all was quickly on a flame, and thereby more were burnt to death than was otherwise slain; It burnt their bowstrings and made them unserviceable; those that scaped the fire were slain with the sword, some hewed to pieces, others run through with their rapiers, so as they were quickly dispatched and very few escaped. It was conceived they thus destroyed about 400 at this time. It was a fearful sight to see them thus frying in the fire and the streams of blood quenching the same, and horrible was the stink and scent thereof; but the victory seemed a sweet sacrifice, and they gave the praise thereof to God, who had wrought so wonderfully for them, thus to enclose their enemies in their hands and give them so speedy a victory over so proud and insulting an enemy.

The Narragansett Indians all this while stood round about, but aloof from all danger and left the whole execution to the English, except it were the stopping of any that broke away. Insulting over their enemies in this their ruin and misery, when they saw them dancing in the flames,

---

20. This document was included in Bradford's manuscript but is not reproduced here.

calling them by a word in their own language, signifying "O brave Pequots!" which they used familiarly among themselves in their own praise in songs of triumph after their victories. After this service was thus happily accomplished, they marched to the waterside where they met with some of their vessels, by which they had refreshing with victuals and other necessaries. But in their march the rest of the Pequots drew into a body and accosted them, thinking to have some advantage against them by reason of a neck of land. But when they saw the English prepare for them they kept aloof, so as they neither did hurt nor could receive any.

After their refreshing, and repair together for further counsel and directions, they resolved to pursue their victory and follow the war against the rest. But the Narragansett Indians, most of them, forsook them, and such of them as they had with them for guides or otherwise, they found them very cold and backward in the business, either out of envy, or that they saw the English would make more profit of the victory than they were willing they should; or else deprive them of such advantage as themselves desired, by having them become tributaries unto them, or the like.

For the rest of this business, I shall only relate the same as it is in a letter which came from Mr. Winthrop to the Governor here, as followeth.[21]

That I may make an end of this matter, this Sassacus (the Pequots' chief sachem) being fled to the Mohawks, they cut off his head, with some other of the chief of them, whether to satisfy the English or rather the Narragansetts (who, as I have since heard, hired them to do it) or for their own advantage, I well know not; but thus this war took end. The rest of the Pequots were wholly driven from their place, and some of them submitted themselves to the Narragansetts and lived under them. Others of them betook themselves to the Mohegans under Uncas, their sachem, with the approbation of the English of Connecticut, under whose protection Uncas lived; and he and his men had been faithful to them in this war and done them very good service. But this did so vex the Narragansetts, that they had not the whole sway over them, as they have never ceased plotting and contriving how to bring them under; and because they cannot attain their ends, because of the English who have protected them, they have sought to raise a general conspiracy against the English, as will appear in another place.

---

21. This document was included in Bradford's manuscript but is not reproduced here.

from CHAPTER 32 • Anno Dom: 1642
[Wickedness Breaks Forth]

Marvelous it may be to see and consider how some kind of wickedness did grow and break forth here, in a land where the same was so much witnessed against and so narrowly looked unto, and severely punished when it was known, as in no place more, or so much, that I have known or heard of; insomuch that they have been somewhat censured even by moderate and good men for their severity in punishments. And yet all this could not suppress the breaking out of sundry notorious sins (as this year, besides other, gives us too many sad precedents and instances), especially drunkenness and uncleanness. Not only incontinency between persons unmarried, for which many both men and women have been punished sharply enough, but some married persons also. But that which is worse, even sodomy and buggery (things fearful to name) have broke forth in this land oftener than once.

I say it may justly be marveled at and cause us to fear and tremble at the consideration of our corrupt natures, which are so hardly bridled, subdued and mortified; nay, cannot by any other means but the powerful work and grace of God's Spirit. But (besides this) one reason may be that the Devil may carry a greater spite against the churches of Christ and the gospel here, by how much the more they endeavour to preserve holiness and purity amongst them and strictly punisheth the contrary when it ariseth either in church or commonwealth; that he might cast a blemish and stain upon them in the eyes of [the] world, who use to be rash in judgment. I would rather think thus, than that Satan hath more power in these heathen lands, as some have thought, than in more Christian nations, especially over God's servants in them.

2. Another reason may be, that it may be in this case as it is with waters when their streams are stopped or dammed up. When they get passage they flow with more violence and make more noise and disturbance than when they are suffered to run quietly in their own channels; so wickedness being here more stopped by strict laws, and the same more nearly looked unto so as it cannot run in a common road of liberty as it would and is inclined, it searches everywhere and at last breaks out where it gets vent.

3. A third reason may be, here (as I am verily persuaded) is not more evils in this kind, nor nothing near so many by proportion as in other places; but they are here

more discovered and seen and made public by due search, inquisition and due punishment; for the churches look narrowly to their members, and the magistrates over all, more strictly than in other places. Besides, here the people are but few in comparison of other places which are full and populous and lie hid, as it were, in a wood or thicket and many horrible evils by that means are never seen nor known; whereas here they are, as it were, brought into the light and set in the plain field, or rather on a hill, made conspicuous to the view of all. . . .

And after the time of the writing of these things befell a very sad accident of the like foul nature in this government, this very year, which I shall now relate. There was a youth whose name was Thomas Granger. He was servant to an honest man of Duxbury, being about 16 or 17 years of age. (His father and mother lived at the same time at Scituate.) He was this year detected of buggery, and indicted for the same, with a mare, a cow, two goats, five sheep, two calves and a turkey. Horrible it is to mention, but the truth of the history requires it. He was first discovered by one that accidentally saw his lewd practice towards the mare. (I forbear particulars.) Being upon it examined and committed, in the end he not only confessed the fact with that beast at that time, but sundry times before and at several times with all the rest of the forenamed in his indictment. And this his free confession was not only in private to the magistrates (though at first he strived to deny it) but to sundry, both ministers and others; and afterwards, upon his indictment, to the whole Court and jury; and confirmed it at his execution. And whereas some of the sheep could not so well be known by his description of them, others with them were brought before him and he declared which were they and which were not. And accordingly he was cast by the jury and condemned, and after executed about the 8th of September, 1642. A very sad spectacle it was. For first the mare and then the cow and the rest of the lesser cattle were killed before his face, according to the law, Leviticus xx.15; and then he himself was executed. The cattle were all cast into a great and large pit that was digged of purpose for them, and no use made of any part of them.

Upon the examination of this person and also of a former that had made some sodomitical attempts upon another, it being demanded of them how they came first to the knowledge and practice of such wickedness, the one confessed he had long used it in old England; and this youth last spoken of said he was taught it by another that had heard of such things from some in England when he

was there, and they kept cattle together. By which it appears how one wicked person may infect many, and what care all ought to have what servants they bring into their families.

But it may be demanded how came it to pass that so many wicked persons and profane people should so quickly come over into this land and mix themselves amongst them? Seeing it was religious men that began the work and they came for religion's sake? I confess this may be marveled at, at least in time to come, when the reasons thereof should not be known; and the more because here was so many hardships and wants met withal. I shall therefore endeavour to give some answer hereunto.

1. And first, according to that in the gospel, it is ever to be remembered that where the Lord begins to sow good seed, there the envious man will endeavour to sow tares.

2. Men being to come over into a wilderness, in which much labour and service was to be done about building and planting, etc., such as wanted help in that respect, when they could not have such as they would, were glad to take such as they could; and so, many untoward servants, sundry of them proved, that were thus brought over, both men and womenkind who, when their times were expired, became families of themselves, which gave increase hereunto.

3. Another and a main reason hereof was that men, finding so many godly disposed persons willing to come into these parts, some began to make a trade of it, to transport passengers and their goods, and hired ships for that end. And then, to make up their freight and advance their profit, cared not who the persons were, so they had money to pay them. And by this means the country became pestered with many unworthy persons who, being come over, crept into one place or other.

4. Again, the Lord's blessing usually following His people as well in outward as spiritual things (though afflictions be mixed withal) do make many to adhere to the People of God, as many followed Christ for the loaves' sake (John vi.26) and a "mixed multitude" came into the wilderness with the People of God out of Egypt of old (Exodus xii.38). So also there were sent by their friends, some under hope that they would be made better; others that they might be eased of such burthens, and they kept from shame at home, that would necessarily follow their dissolute courses. And thus, by one means or other, in 20 years' time it is a question whether the greater part be not grown the worser?

from CHAPTER 33 • Anno Dom: 1643
[The Life and Death of Elder Brewster]

I am to begin this year with that which was a matter of great sadness and mourning unto them all. About the 18th of April died their Reverend Elder and my dear and loving friend Mr. William Brewster, a man that had done and suffered much for the Lord Jesus and the gospel's sake, and had borne his part in weal and woe with this poor persecuted church above 36 years in England, Holland and in this wilderness, and done the Lord and them faithful service in his place and calling. And notwithstanding the many troubles and sorrows he passed through, the Lord upheld him to a great age. He was near fourscore years of age (if not all out) when he died. He had this blessing added by the Lord to all the rest; to die in his bed, in peace, amongst the midst of his friends, who mourned and wept over him and ministered what help and comfort they could unto him, and he again recomforted them whilst he could. His sickness was not long, and till the last day thereof he did not wholly keep his bed. His speech continued till somewhat more than half a day, and then failed him, and about nine or ten a clock that evening he died without any pangs at all. A few hours before, he drew his breath short, and some few minutes before his last, he drew his breath long as a man fallen into a sound sleep without any pangs or gaspings, and so sweetly departed this life unto a better. . . .

I should say something of his life, if to say a little were not worse than to be silent. But I cannot wholly forbear, though happily more may be done hereafter. After he had attained some learning, viz. the knowledge of the Latin tongue and some insight in the Greek, and spent some small time at Cambridge, and then being first seasoned with the seeds of grace and virtue, he went to the Court and served that religious and godly gentleman Mr. Davison, divers years when he was Secretary of State. Who found him so discreet and faithful as he trusted him above all other that were about him, and only employed him in all matters of greatest trust and secrecy; he esteemed him rather as a son than a servant, and for his wisdom and godliness, in private he would converse with him more like a friend and familiar than a master. He attended his master when he was sent in ambassage by the Queen into the Low Countries, in the Earl of Leicester's time, as for other weighty affairs of state; so to receive possession of the cautionary towns, and in token and sign thereof the keys of Flushing being delivered to him in Her Majesty's name, he kept them some time and committed them to this his servant who kept them under his pillow, on which he slept the first night. And at his return the States honoured him with a gold chain and his master committed it to him and commanded him to wear it when they arrived in England, as they rid through the country, till they came to the Court. He afterwards remained with him till his troubles, that he was put from his place about the death of the Queen of Scots; and some good time after doing him many faithful offices of service in the time of his troubles. Afterwards he went and lived in the country, in good esteem amongst his friends and the gentlemen of those parts, especially the godly and religious.

He did much good in the country where he lived in promoting and furthering religion, not only by his practice and example, and provoking and encouraging of others, but by procuring of good preachers to the places thereabout and drawing on of others to assist and help forward in such a work. He himself most commonly deepest in the charge, and sometimes above his ability. And in this state he continued many years, doing the best good he could and walking according to the light he saw, till the Lord revealed further unto him. And in the end, by the tyranny of the bishops against godly preachers and people in silencing the one and persecuting the other, he and many more of those times began to look further into things and to see into the unlawfulness of their callings, and the burthen of many antichristian corruptions, which both he and they endeavoured to cast off; as they also did as in the beginning of this treatise is to be seen.

After they were joined together in communion, he was a special stay and help unto them. They ordinarily met at his house on the Lord's Day (which was a manor of the bishop's) and with great love he entertained them when they came, making provision for them to his great charge, and continued so to do whilst they could stay in England. And when they were to remove out of the country he was one of the first in all adventures, and forwardest in any charge. He was the chief of those that were taken at Boston, and suffered the greatest loss, and of the seven that were kept longest in prison and after bound over to the assizes. After he came into Holland he suffered much hardship after he had spent the most of his means, having a great charge and many children; and in regard of his former breeding and course of life, not so fit for many employments as others were, especially such as were toilsome and laborious. But yet he ever bore his condition with much cheerfulness and contentation.

Towards the latter part of those twelve years spent in Holland, his outward condition was mended, and he lived well and plentifully; for he fell into a way (by reason he had the Latin tongue) to teach many students who had a desire to learn the English tongue, to teach them English; and by his method they quickly attained it with great facility, for he drew rules to learn it by after the Latin manner. And many gentlemen, both Danes and Germans, resorted to him as they had time from other studies, some of them being great men's sons. He also had means to set up printing by the help of some friends, and so had employment enough, and by reason of many books which would not be allowed to be printed in England, they might have had more than they could do.

But now removing into this country all these things were laid aside again, and a new course of living must be framed unto, in which he was no way unwilling to take his part, and to bear his burthen with the rest, living many times without bread or corn many months together, having many times nothing but fish and often wanting that also; and drunk nothing but water for many years together, yea till within five or six years of his death. And yet he lived by the blessing of God in health till very old age. And besides that, he would labour with his hands in the fields as long as he was able. Yet when the church had no other minister, he taught twice every Sabbath, and that both powerfully and profitably, to the great contentment of the hearers and their comfortable edification; yea, many were brought to God by his ministry. He did more in this behalf in a year than many that have their hundreds a year do in all their lives.

For his personal abilities, he was qualified above many. He was wise and discreet and well spoken, having a grave and deliberate utterance, of a very cheerful spirit, very sociable and pleasant amongst his friends, of an humble and modest mind, of a peaceable disposition, undervaluing himself and his own abilities and sometime overvaluing others. Inoffensive and innocent in his life and conversation, which gained him the love of those without as well as those within; yet he would tell them plainly of their faults and evils, both publicly and privately, but in such a manner as usually was well taken from him. He was tenderhearted and compassionate of such as were in misery, but especially of such as had been of good estate and rank and were fallen unto want and poverty either for goodness and religion's sake or by the injury and oppression of others; he would say of all

men these deserved to be pitied most. And none did more offend and displease him than such as would haughtily and proudly carry and lift up themselves, being risen from nothing and having little else in them to commend them but a few fine clothes or a little riches more than others.

In teaching, he was very moving and stirring of affections, also very plain and distinct in what he taught; by which means he became the more profitable to the hearers. He had a singular good gift in prayer, both public and private, in ripping up the heart and conscience before God in the humble confession of sin, and begging the mercies of God in Christ for the pardon of the same. He always thought it were better for ministers to pray oftener and divide their prayers, than be long and tedious in the same, except upon solemn and special occasions as in days of humiliation and the like. His reason was that the heart and spirits of all, especially the weak, could hardly continue and stand bent as it were so long towards God as they ought to do in that duty, without flagging and falling off.

For the government of the church, which was most proper to his office, he was careful to preserve good order in the same, and to preserve purity both in the doctrine and communion of the same, and to suppress any errour or contention that might begin to rise up amongst them. And accordingly God gave good success to his endeavours herein all his days, and he saw the fruit of his labours in that behalf. But I must break off, having only thus touched a few, as it were, heads of things.

I cannot but here take occasion not only to mention but greatly to admire the marvelous providence of God! That notwithstanding the many changes and hardships that these people went through, and the many enemies they had and difficulties they met withal, that so many of them should live to very old age! It was not only this reverend man's condition (for one swallow makes no summer as they say) but many more of them did the like, some dying about and before this time and many still living, who attained to sixty years of age, and to sixty-five, divers to seventy and above, and some near eighty as he did. It must needs be more than ordinary and above natural reason, that so it should be. For it is found in experience that change of air, famine or unwholesome food, much drinking of water, sorrows and troubles, etc., all of them are enemies to health, causes of many diseases, consumers of natural vigour and the bodies of men, and shorteners of life. And yet of all these things they had a large part and suffered deeply in the same. They went from England to Holland, where they found both worse air and diet than that they came from; from thence, enduring a long imprisonment as it were in the ships at sea, into New England; and how it hath been with them here hath already been shown, and what crosses, troubles, fears, wants and sorrows they had been liable unto is easy to conjecture. So as in some sort they may say with the Apostle, 2 Corinthians xi.26, 27, they were "in journeyings often, in perils of waters, in perils of robbers, in perils of their own nation, in perils among the heathen, in perils in the wilderness, in perils in the sea, in perils among false brethren; in weariness and painfulness, in watching often, in hunger and thirst, in fasting often, in cold and nakedness."

What was it then that upheld them? It was God's visitation that preserved their spirits. Job x.12: "Thou hast given me life and grace, and thy visitation hath preserved my spirit." He that upheld the Apostle upheld them. "They were persecuted, but not forsaken, cast down, but perished not." "As unknown, and yet known; as dying, and behold we live; as chastened, and yet not killed"; 2 Corinthians vi.9.

God, it seems, would have all men to behold and observe such mercies and works of His providence as these are towards His people, that they in like cases might be encouraged to depend upon God in their trials, and also to bless His name when they see His goodness towards others. Man lives not by bread only, Deuteronomy viii.3. It is not by good and dainty fare, by peace and rest and heart's ease in enjoying the contentments and good things of this world only that preserves health and prolongs life; God in such examples would have the world see and behold that He can do it without them; and if the world will shut their eyes and take no notice thereof, yet He would have His people to see and consider it. Daniel could be better liking with pulse than others were with the king's dainties. Jacob, though he went from one nation to another people and passed through famine, fears and many afflictions, yet he lived till old age and died sweetly and rested in the Lord, as infinite others of God's servants have done and still shall do, through God's goodness, notwithstanding all the malice of their enemies, "when the branch of the wicked shall be cut off before his day" (Job xv.32) "and the bloody and deceitful men shall not live [out] half their days"; Psalm lv.23. . . .

JOHN WINTHROP (1588–1649)

Born into a wealthy family in Groton, England, John Winthrop was trained in law at Trinity College, and during his life in England, he served as a justice of the peace, managed his father's manor, and practiced law in London. In his youth, Winthrop became interested in the Puritan movement and its efforts to reform the Anglican Church. With the ascension to the throne in 1625 of Charles I, who was sympathetic toward Catholicism, Winthrop, like many other Puritans, saw a doubtful future in England for those of their faith. In 1629, a group of them received permission to emigrate to New England, with a charter establishing them as the Massachusetts Bay Company. Before their departure, Winthrop was chosen to serve as the new colony's governor. In 1630, the group of approximately seven hundred emigrants sailed from England.

At some point during the voyage aboard the ship *Arbella,* Winthrop delivered the sermon called "A Model of Christian Charity," which outlined the principles by which the new colony should be run, stressing the overwhelming commitment they were making, in love for one another. Winthrop expressed an ideal of a community structured around its faith, a community that would serve as an example of how Puritan faith could construct an ideal society. In the famous phrase that Winthrop adapted from scripture, the Massachusetts settlers would be living in a "city upon a Hill" whose success or failure would be watched by the entire world. From this critical moment in the colony's early days until his death, Winthrop was among the most important leaders of the Massachusetts Bay colony. Elected governor twelve times, Winthrop defended the colony when it came under criticism in England. He also had to defend himself, at times, as when he faced charges of overstepping his authority and not following the doctrines of Puritanism closely enough. Negotiating these practical difficulties ably, Winthrop was remembered after his death as one of the colony's most important early leaders. Indeed, Cotton Mather identified Winthrop as the ideal earthly leader.

In addition to his sermon "A Model of Christian Charity," Winthrop's most important writing was his journal, which covers the years from the 1630 journey to Massachusetts until Winthrop's death. Some scholars have suggested that it was the knowledge of Winthrop's journal that prompted William Bradford to compose *Of Plymouth Plantation,* to confirm the integrity and originality of the Plymouth endeavor out of concern that the larger number of Massachusetts Bay settlers would overshadow the Plymouth group of Separatists. Whatever the case, both documents provide useful evidence of the importance of history writing to these early settlers. Winthrop's journal relates the story of the early years of Massachusetts Bay from the point of view of its leadership. The journal documents the various challenges faced by the fledgling colony, from practical difficulties, such as the 1634 smallpox epidemic, to political ones, as when dissenting members of the community, notably Roger Williams and Anne Hutchinson, were banished. Winthrop's journal reflects his clear sense of the religious and historical importance, for the present and for the future, of the settlement at Massachusetts Bay.

A MODEL OF
CHRISTIAN CHARITY[1]

I

A Model Hereof

God Almighty in His most holy and wise providence, hath so disposed of the condition of mankind, as in all times some must be rich, some poor, some high and eminent in power and dignity; others mean and in subjection.

The Reason Hereof

First, to hold conformity with the rest of His works, being delighted to show forth the glory of His wisdom in the variety and difference of the creatures; and the glory of His power, in ordering all these differences for the preservation and good of the whole; and the glory of His greatness, that as it is the glory of princes to have many officers, so this great King will have many stewards, counting Himself more honored in dispensing His gifts to man by man, than if He did it by His own immediate hands.

Secondly, that He might have the more occasion to manifest the work of His Spirit: first upon the wicked in moderating and restraining them, so that the rich and mighty should not eat up the poor, nor the poor and despised rise up against their superiors and shake off their yoke; secondly in the regenerate, in exercising His graces, in them, as in the great ones, their love, mercy, gentleness, temperance, etc., in the poor and inferior sort, their faith, patience, obedience, etc.

Thirdly, that every man might have need of other, and from hence they might be all knit more nearly together in the bonds of brotherly affection. From hence it appears plainly that no man is made more honorable than another or more wealthy, etc., out of any particular and singular respect to himself, but for the glory of his Creator and the common good of the creature, man. Therefore God still reserves the property of these gifts to Himself as [in] Ezekiel: 16.17. He there calls wealth His gold and His silver. [In] Proverbs: 3.9, he claims their service as His due: honor the Lord with thy riches, etc. All men being thus (by divine providence) ranked into two sorts, rich and poor; under the first are comprehended all such as are able to live comfortably by their own means duly improved; and all others are poor according to the former distribution.

There are two rules whereby we are to walk one towards another: justice and mercy. These are always distinguished in their act and in their object, yet may they both concur in the same subject in each respect; as sometimes there may be an occasion of showing mercy to a rich man in some sudden danger of distress, and also doing of mere justice to a poor man in regard of some particular contract, etc.

There is likewise a double law by which we are regulated in our conversation one towards another in both the former respects: the law of nature and the law of grace, or the moral law or the law of the Gospel, to omit the rule of justice as not properly belonging to this purpose otherwise than it may fall into consideration in some particular cases. By the first of these laws man as he was enabled so withal [is] commanded to love his neighbor as himself. Upon this ground stands all the precepts of the moral law, which concerns our dealings with men. To apply this to the works of mercy, this law requires two things: first, that every man afford his help to another in every want or dis-

---

1. Winthrop's sermon was delivered in 1630 aboard the *Arbella.* The text is an adaptation of the first printing, in 1838, of a surviving copy of the manuscript.

tress; secondly, that he performed this out of the same affection which makes him careful of his own goods, according to that of our Savior. Matthew: "Whatsoever ye would that men should do to you."[2] This was practiced by Abraham and Lot in entertaining the Angels and the old man of Gibeah.[3]

The law of grace or the Gospel hath some difference from the former, as in these respects: First, the law of nature was given to man in the estate of innocency; this of the Gospel in the estate of regeneracy. Secondly, the former propounds one man to another, as the same flesh and image of God; this as a brother in Christ also, and in the communion of the same spirit and so teacheth us to put a difference between Christians and others. *Do good to all, especially to the household of faith:* Upon this ground the Israelites were to put a difference between the brethren of such as were strangers though not of Canaanites. Thirdly, the law of nature could give no rules for dealing with enemies, for all are to be considered as friends in the state of innocency, but the Gospel commands love to an enemy. Proof. If thine Enemy hunger, feed him; Love your Enemies, do good to them that hate you. Matthew: 5.44.

This law of the Gospel propounds likewise a difference of seasons and occasions. There is a time when a Christian must sell all and give to the poor, as they did in the Apostles' times. There is a time also when a Christian (though they give not all yet) must give beyond their ability, as they of Macedonia, Corinthians: 2.8. Likewise community of perils calls for extraordinary liberality, and so doth community in some special service for the Church. Lastly, when there is no other means whereby our Christian brother may be relieved in his distress, we must help him beyond our ability, rather than tempt God in putting him upon help by miraculous or extraordinary means.

This duty of mercy is exercised in the kinds; *giving, lending* and *forgiving.*—

Quest. What rule shall a man observe in giving in respect of the measure?

Ans. If the time and occasion be ordinary, he is to give out of his abundance. Let him lay aside as God hath blessed him. If the time and occasion be extraordinary, he must be ruled by them; taking this withal, that then a man cannot likely do too much, especially if he may leave himself and his family under probable means of comfortable subsistence.

Objection. A man must lay up for posterity, the fathers lay up for posterity and children and he "is worse than an infidel" that "provideth not for his own."

Ans. For the first, it is plain that it being spoken by way of comparison, it must be meant of the ordinary and usual course of fathers and cannot extend to times and occasions extraordinary. For the other place, the Apostle speaks against such as walked inordinately, and it is without question, that he is worse than an infidel who through his own sloth and voluptuousness shall neglect to provide for his family.

Objection. "The wise man's eyes are in his head" saith Solomon, "and foreseeth the plague," therefore we must forecast and lay up against evil times when he or his may stand in need of all he can gather.

Ans. This very argument Solomon useth to persuade to liberality, Ecclesiastes: "Cast thy bread upon the waters," and "for thou knowest not what evil may come upon the land." Luke: 16.9. "Make you friends of the riches of iniquity."[4] You will ask how this shall be? very well. For first he that gives to the poor, lends to the Lord and He will repay him even in this life an hundred fold to him or his—The righteous is ever merciful and lendeth and his seed enjoyeth the blessing; and besides we know what advantage it will be to us in the day of account when many such witnesses shall stand forth for us to witness the improvement of our talent. And I would know of those who plead so much for laying up for time to come, whether they hold that to be Gospel, Matthew: 6.19: "Lay not up for yourselves treasures upon earth," etc. If they acknowledge it, what extent will they allow it? if only to those primitive times, let them consider the reason whereupon our Savior grounds it. The first is that they are subject to the moth, the rust, the thief. Secondly, they will

---

2. Matthew 7:12: "Therefore all things whatsoever ye would that men should do to you, do ye even so to them: for that is the law of the prophets."

3. In Genesis 18, Abraham entertained angels who appeared as wandering strangers; in Genesis 19, Lot escaped the destruction of Sodom because he defended two angels from a mob; in Judges 19:16–21, an old citizen of Gibeah sheltered and defended a traveling stranger.

4. In Luke 16, a servant unjustly accused of wasting his master's money goes to his master's debtors and cuts their bills in half. Luke 16:9: "And I say unto you, Make to yourselves friends of the mammon of unrighteousness; that, when ye fail, they may receive you into everlasting habitations." Also Luke 16:13: "No servant can serve two masters . . . Ye cannot serve God and mammon."

steal away the heart; where the treasure is there will the heart be also. The reasons are of like force at all times. Therefore the exhortation must be general and perpetual, with always in respect of the love and affection to riches and in regard of the things themselves when any special service for the church or particular distress of our brother do call for the use of them; otherwise it is not only lawful but necessary to lay up as Joseph did to have ready upon such occasions,[5] as the Lord (whose stewards we are of them) shall call for them from us. Christ gives us an instance of the first, when He sent his disciples for the ass, and bids them answer the owner thus, the Lord hath need of him. So when the tabernacle was to be built He sends to His people to call for their silver and gold, etc.; and yields them no other reason but that it was for His work. When Elisha comes to the widow of Sareptah and finds her preparing to make ready her pittance for herself and family, He bids her first provide for Him; he challengeth first God's part which she must first give before she must serve her own family. All these teach us that the Lord looks that when He is pleased to call for His right in anything we have, our own interest we have must stand aside till His turn be served. For the other, we need look no further than to that of John: 1: "He who hath this world's goods and seeth his brother to need and shuts up his compassion from him, how dwelleth the love of God in him," which comes punctually to this conclusion: if thy brother be in want and thou canst help him, thou needst not make doubt, what thou shouldst do, if thou lovest God thou must help him.

Quest. What rule must we observe in lending?

Ans. Thou must observe whether thy brother hath present or probable, or possible means of repaying thee, if there be none of these, thou must give him according to his necessity, rather than lend him as he requires. If he hath present means of repaying thee, thou art to look at him not as an act of mercy, but by way of commerce, wherein thou art to walk by the rule of justice; but if his means of repaying thee be only probable or possible, then is he an object of thy mercy, thou must lend him, though there be danger of losing it, Deuteronomy: 15.7: "If any of thy brethren be poor," etc., "thou shalt lend him sufficient." That men might not shift off this duty by the apparent hazard, He tells them that though the year of Ju-

bilee[6] were at hand (when he must remit it, if he were not able to repay it before) yet he must lend him and that cheerfully: "It may not grieve thee to give him" saith He; and because some might object; "why so I should soon impoverish myself and my family," He adds "with all thy work,"[7] etc.; for our Savior, Matthew: 5.42: "From him that would borrow of thee turn not away."

Quest. What rule must we observe in forgiving?

Ans. Whether thou didst lend by way of commerce or in mercy, if he have nothing to pay thee, [you] must forgive, (except in cause where thou hast a surety or a lawful pledge) Deuteronomy: 15.2. Every seventh year the creditor was to quit that which he lent to his brother if he were poor as appears—verse 8: "Save when there shall be no poor with thee." In all these and like cases, Christ was a general rule, Matthew: 7.22: "Whatsoever ye would that men should do to you, do ye the same to them also."

Quest. What rule must we observe and walk by in cause of community of peril?

Ans. The same as before, but with more enlargement towards others and less respect towards ourselves and our own right. Hence it was that in the primitive church they sold all, had all things in common, neither did any man say that which he possessed was his own. Likewise in their return out of the captivity, because the work was great for the restoring of the church and the danger of enemies was common to all, Nehemiah exhorts the Jews to liberality and readiness in remitting their debts to their brethren, and disposing liberally of his own to such as wanted, and stand not upon his own due, which he might have demanded of them. Thus did some of our forefathers in times of persecution in England, and so did many of the faithful of other churches, whereof we keep an honorable remembrance of them; and it is to be observed that both in Scriptures and later stories of the churches that such as have been most bountiful to the poor saints, especially in these extraordinary times and occasions, God hath left them highly commended to posterity, as Zacheus, Cornelius, Dorcas, Bishop Hooper, the Cuttler of Brussells and divers others. Observe again that the Scripture gives no caution to restrain any from being over liberal this

---

5. Genesis 41: Joseph stored grain in the seven years before the famine.

6. According to Old Testament law, during every seventh, "Jubilee" year, all debts were forgiven.

7. Deuteronomy 15:10: "Thou shalt surely give him, and thine heart shall not be grieved when thou givest unto him: because that for this thing the Lord thy God shall bless thee in all thy works, and in all that thou puttest thine hand unto."

way; but all men to the liberal and cheerful practice hereof by the sweetest promises; as to instance one for many, Isaiah: 58.6: "Is not this the fast I have chosen to loose the bonds of wickedness, to take off the heavy burdens, to let the oppressed go free and to break every yoke, to deal thy bread to the hungry and to bring the poor that wander into thy house, when thou seest the naked to cover them. And then shall thy light break forth as the morning, and thy health shall grow speedily, thy righteousness shall go before God, and the glory of the Lord shall embrace thee; then thou shalt call and the Lord shall answer thee" etc. [Verse] 10: "If thou pour out thy soul to the hungry, then shall thy light spring out in darkness, and the Lord shall guide thee continually, and satisfy thy soul in drought, and make fat thy bones; thou shalt be like a watered garden, and they shalt be of thee that shall build the old waste places" etc. On the contrary, most heavy curses are laid upon such as are straightened towards the Lord and His people, Judges: 5.[23]: "Curse ye Meroshe because ye came not to help the Lord," etc. Proverbs: [21.13]: "He who shutteth his ears from hearing the cry of the poor, he shall cry and shall not be heard." Matthew: 25: "Go ye cursed into everlasting fire" etc. "I was hungry and ye fed me not." 2 Corinthians: 9.6: "He that soweth sparingly shall reap sparingly."

Having already set forth the practice of mercy according to the rule of God's law, it will be useful to lay open the grounds of it also, being the other part of the commandment, and that is the affection from which this exercise of mercy must arise. The apostle tells us that this love is the fulfilling of the law, not that it is enough to love our brother and so no further; but in regard of the excellency of his parts giving any motion to the other as the soul to the body and the power it hath to set all the faculties on work in the outward exercise of this duty.[8] As when we bid one make the clock strike, he doth not lay hand on the hammer, which is the immediate instrument of the sound, but sets on work the first mover or main wheel, knowing that will certainly produce the sound which he intends. So the way to draw men to works of mercy, is not by force of argument from the goodness or necessity of the work; for though this course may enforce a rational mind to some present act of mercy, as is frequent in experience, yet it cannot work such a habit in a soul, as shall make it prompt upon all occasions to produce the same effect, but by framing these affections of love in the heart which will as

natively bring forth the other, as any cause doth produce effect.

The definition which the Scripture gives us of love is this: "Love is the bond of perfection." First, it is a bond or ligament. Secondly it makes the work perfect. There is no body but consists of parts and that which knits these parts together gives the body its perfection, because it makes each part so contiguous to others as thereby they do mutually participate with each other, both in strength and infirmity, in pleasure and pain. To instance in the most perfect of all bodies: Christ and His church make one body. The several parts of this body, considered apart before they were united, were as disproportionate and as much disordering as so many contrary qualities or elements, but when Christ comes and by His spirit and love knits all these parts to Himself and each to other, it is become the most perfect and best proportioned body in the world. Ephesians: 4.16: "Christ, by whom all the body being knit together by every joint for the furniture thereof, according to the effectual power which is the measure of every perfection of parts," "a glorious body without spot or wrinkle," the ligaments hereof being Christ, or His love, for Christ is love (1 John: 4.8). So this definition is right: "Love is the bond of perfection."

From hence we may frame these conclusions. 1. First of all, true Christians are of one body in Christ, 1 Corinthians: 12.12, 27: "Ye are the body of Christ and members of their part." Secondly: The ligaments of this body which knit together are love. Thirdly: No body can be perfect which wants its proper ligament. Fourthly. All the parts of this body being thus united are made so contiguous in a special relation as they must needs partake of each other's strength and infirmity; joy and sorrow, weal and woe. 1 Corinthians: 12.26: "If one member suffers, all suffer with it, if one be in honor, all rejoice with it." Fifthly. This sensibleness and sympathy of each other's conditions will necessarily infuse into each part a native desire and endeavor to strengthen, defend, preserve and comfort the other.

To insist a little on this conclusion being the product of all the former, the truth hereof will appear both by precept and pattern. 1 John: 3.10: "Ye ought to lay down your lives for the brethren." Galatians: 6.2: "bear ye one another's burthens and so fulfill the law of Christ." For patterns we have that first of our Savior who out of His good will in obedience to His father, becoming a part of this body, and being knit with it in the bond of love, found such a native sensibleness of our infirmities and sorrows

---

8. Paul, Epistle to the Romans 9:31.

as He willingly yielded Himself to death to ease the infirmities of the rest of His body, and so healed their sorrows. From the like sympathy of parts did the apostles and many thousands of the saints lay down their lives for Christ. Again, the like we may see in the members of this body among themselves. Romans: 9. Paul could have been contented to have been separated from Christ, that the Jews might not be cut off from the body. It is very observable what he professeth of his affectionate partaking with every member: "who is weak" saith he "and I am not weak? who is offended and I burn not;" and again, 2 Corinthians: 7.13. "therefore we are comforted because ye were comforted." Of Epaphroditus he speaketh, Philippians: 2.30. that he regarded not his own life to do him service. So Phoebe and others are called the servants of the church. Now it is apparent that they served not for wages, or by constraint, but out of love. The like we shall find in the histories of the church in all ages, the sweet sympathy of affections which was in the members of this body one towards another, their cheerfulness in serving and suffering together, how liberal they were without repining, harborers without grudging and helpful without reproaching; and all from hence, because they had fervent love amongst them, which only make the practice of mercy constant and easy.

The next consideration is how this love comes to be wrought. Adam in his first estate was a perfect model of mankind in all their generations, and in him this love was perfected in regard of the habit. But Adam rent himself from his creator, rent all his posterity also one from another; whence it comes that every man is born with this principle in him, to love and seek himself only, and thus a man continueth till Christ comes and takes possession of the soul and infuseth another principle, love to God and our brother. And this latter having continual supply from Christ, as the head and root by which he is united, gets the predomining in the soul, so by little and little expels the former. 1 John: 4.7. "love cometh of God and every one that loveth is borne of God," so that this love is the fruit of the new birth, and none can have it but the new creature. Now when this quality is thus formed in the souls of men, it works like the spirit upon the dry bones. Ezekiel: 37: "bone came to bone." It gathers together the scattered bones, of perfect old man Adam, and knits them into one body again in Christ, whereby a man is become again a living soul.

The third consideration is concerning the exercise of this love which is twofold, inward or outward. The outward hath been handled in the former preface of this discourse. For unfolding the other we must take in our way that maxim of philosophy *simile simili gaudet,* or like will to like; for as it is things which are turned with disaffection to each other, the ground of it is from a dissimilitude arising from the contrary or different nature of the things themselves; for the ground of love is an apprehension of some resemblance in things loved to that which affects it. This is the cause why the Lord loves the creature, so far as it hath any of His image in it; He loves His elect because they are like Himself, He beholds them in His beloved son. So a mother loves her child, because she thoroughly conceives a resemblance of herself in it. Thus it is between the members of Christ. Each discerns, by the work of the spirit, his own image and resemblance in another, and therefore cannot but love him as he loves himself. Now when the soul, which is of a sociable nature, finds anything like to itself, it is like Adam when Eve was brought to him. She must have it one with herself. This is flesh of my flesh (saith the soul) and bone of my bone. She conceives a great delight in it, therefore she desires nearness and familiarity with it. She hath a great propensity to do it good and receives such content in it, as fearing the miscarriage of her beloved she bestows it in the inmost closet of her heart. She will not endure that it shall want any good which she can give it. If by occasion she be withdrawn from the company of it, she is still looking towards the place where she left her beloved. If she heard it groan, she is with it presently. If she find it sad and disconsolate, she sighs and moans with it. She hath no such joy as to see her beloved merry and thriving. If she see it wronged, she cannot hear it without passion. She sets no bounds to her affections, nor hath any thought of reward. She finds recompense enough in the exercise of her love towards it. We may see this acted to life in Jonathan and David. Jonathan a valiant man endowed with the spirit of Christ, so soon as he discovers the same spirit in David had presently his heart knit to him by this lineament of love so that it is said he loved him as his own soul. He takes so great pleasure in him, that he strips himself to adorn his beloved. His father's kingdom was not so precious to him as his beloved David. David shall have it with all his heart, himself desires no more but that he may be near to him to rejoice in his good. He chooseth to converse with him in the wilderness even to the hazard of his own life, rather than with the great courtiers in his father's palace. When he sees danger towards him, he spares neither rare pains nor peril to direct it. When injury was offered his beloved David, he would not bear it, though from his own father; and when they must part for a season only, they thought their hearts would have broke for sorrow, had not their affections found vent by abundance of tears. Other instances might be brought to show the nature of this affection, as of Ruth and Naomi, and many others; but this truth is cleared enough.

If any shall object that it is not possible that love should be bred or upheld without hope of requital, it is granted; but that is not our cause; for this love is always under reward. It never gives, but it always receives with advantage; first, in regard that among the members of the same body, love and affection are reciprocal in a most equal and sweet kind of commerce. Secondly, in regard of the pleasure and content that the exercise of love carries with it, as we may see in the natural body. The mouth is at all the pains to receive and mince the food which serves for the nourishment of all the other parts of the body, yet it hath no cause to complain; for first the other parts send back by several passages a due proportion of the same nourishment, in a better form for the strengthening and comforting the mouth. Secondly, the labor of the mouth is accompanied with such pleasure and content as far exceeds the pains it takes. So is it in all the labor of love among Christians. The party loving, reaps love again, as was showed before, which the soul covets more than all the wealth in the world. Thirdly: Nothing yields more pleasure and content to the soul than when it finds that which it may love fervently, for to love and live beloved is the soul's paradise, both here and in heaven. In the state of wedlock there be many comforts to bear out the troubles of that condition; but let such as have tried the most, say if there be any sweetness in that condition comparable to the exercise of mutual love.

From former considerations arise these conclusions.

First: This love among Christians is a real thing, not imaginary.

Secondly: This love is as absolutely necessary to the being of the body of Christ, as the sinews and other ligaments of a natural body are to the being of that body.

Thirdly: This love is a divine, spiritual nature free, active, strong, courageous, permanent; undervaluing all things beneath its proper object; and of all the graces, this makes us nearer to resemble the virtues of our Heavenly Father.

Fourthly: It rests in the love and welfare of its beloved. For the full and certain knowledge of these truths concerning the nature, use, and excellency of this grace, that which the Holy Ghost hath left recorded, I Corinthians: 13, may give full satisfaction, which is needful for every true member of this lovely body of the Lord Jesus, to

work upon their hearts by prayer, meditation, continual exercise at least of the special [influence] of His grace, till Christ be formed in them and they in Him, all in each other, knit together by this bond of love.

II

It rests now to make some application of this discourse by the present design, which gave the occasion of writing of it. Herein are four things to be propounded: first the persons, secondly the work, thirdly the end, fourthly the means.

First, For the persons. We are a company professing ourselves fellow members of Christ, in which respect only though we were absent from each other many miles, and had our employments as far distant, yet we ought to account ourselves knit together by this bond of love, and live in the exercise of it, if we would have comfort of our being in Christ. This was notorious in the practice of the Christians in former times; as is testified of the Waldenses,[9] from the mouth of one of the adversaries *Æneas Sylvius*[10] "mutuo [ament] penè antequam norunt," they used to love any of their own religion even before they were acquainted with them.

Secondly, for the work we have in hand. It is by a mutual consent, through a special overvaluing providence and a more than an ordinary approbation of the Churches of Christ, to seek out a place of cohabitation and consortship under a due form of government both civil and ecclesiastical. In such cases as this, the care of the public must oversway all private respects, by which, not only conscience, but mere civil policy, doth bind us. For it is a true rule that particular estates cannot subsist in the ruin of the public.

Thirdly. The end is to improve our lives to do more service to the Lord; the comfort and increase of the body of Christ whereof we are members; that ourselves and posterity may be the better preserved from the common corruptions of this evil world, to serve the Lord and work out our salvation under the power and purity of His holy ordinances.

Fourthly, for the means whereby this must be effected. They are twofold, a conformity with the work and end we aim at. These we see are extraordinary, therefore we must

---

9. An early Christian reformist sect.

10. Aeneas Sylvius Piccolomini (1405–64), Pope Pius II.

not content ourselves with usual ordinary means. What-soever we did or ought to have done when we lived in England, the same must we do, and more also, where we go. That which the most in their churches maintain as a truth in profession only, we must bring into familiar and constant practice, as in this duty of love. We must love brotherly without dissimulation; we must love one an-other with a pure heart fervently. We must bear one an-other's burthens. We must not look only on our own things, but also on the things of our brethren, neither must we think that the Lord will bear with such failings at our hands as he doth from those among whom we have lived; and that for three reasons.

First, In regard of the more near bond of marriage be-tween Him and us, where-in He hath taken us to be His after a most strict and peculiar manner, which will make Him the more jealous of our love and obedience. So He tells the people of Israel, you only have I known of all the families of the earth, therefore will I punish you for your transgressions. Secondly, because the Lord will be sanc-tified in them that come near Him. We know that there were many that corrupted the service of the Lord, some setting up altars before His own, others offering both strange fire and strange sacrifices also; yet there came no fire from heaven or other sudden judgment upon them, as did upon Nadab and Abihu,[11] who yet we may think did not sin presumptuously. Thirdly. When God gives a spe-cial commission He looks to have it strictly observed in every article. When He gave Saul a commission to de-stroy Amaleck, He indented with him upon certain arti-cles, and because he failed in one of the least, and that upon a fair pretense, it lost him the kingdom which should have been his reward if he had observed his commis-sion.[12]

Thus stands the cause between God and us. We are en-tered into covenant with Him for this work. We have taken out a commission, the Lord hath given us leave to draw our own articles. We have professed to enterprise these actions, upon these and those ends, we have here-upon besought Him of favor and blessing. Now if the Lord shall please to hear us, and bring us in peace to the place we desire, then hath He ratified this covenant and sealed our commission, [and] will expect a strict perfor-mance of the articles contained in it; but if we shall neg-lect the observation of these articles which are the ends we have propounded, and, dissembling with our God, shall fall to embrace this present world and prosecute our carnal intentions, seeking great things for ourselves and our posterity, the Lord will surely break out in wrath against us; be revenged of such a perjured people and make us know the price of the breach of such a covenant.

Now the only way to avoid this shipwreck, and to pro-vide for our posterity, is to follow the counsel of Micah, to do justly, to love mercy, to walk humbly with our God. For this end, we must be knit together in this work as one man. We must entertain each other in brotherly affection, we must be willing to abridge ourselves of our super-fluities, for the supply of other's necessities. We must up-hold a familiar commerce together in all meekness, gen-tleness, patience and liberality. We must delight in each other, make other's conditions our own, rejoice together, mourn together, labor and suffer together, always having before our eyes our commission and community in the work, our community as members of the same body. So shall we keep the unity of the spirit in the bond of peace. The Lord will be our God, and delight to dwell among us as His own people, and will command a blessing upon us in all our ways, so that we shall see much more of His wisdom, power, goodness and truth, than formerly we have been acquainted with. We shall find that the God of Israel is among us, when ten of us shall be able to resist a thousand of our enemies; when He shall make us a praise and glory that men shall say of succeeding plantations, "the Lord make it like that of New England." For we must consider that we shall be as a city upon a hill.[13] The eyes of all people are upon us, so that if we shall deal falsely with our God in this work we have undertaken, and so cause Him to withdraw His present help from us, we shall be made a story and a by-word through the world. We shall open the mouths of enemies to speak evil of the ways of God, and all professors for God's sake. We shall shame the faces of many of God's worthy servants, and

---

11. Leviticus 10:1–2: Nadab and Abihu "offered strange fire before the Lord, which he commanded them not. And there went out fire from the Lord, and devoured them, and they died before the Lord."

12. I Samuel 15:1–34: Saul was told to destroy the Amalekites and all their possessions, but he did not destroy their livestock; because he did not do exactly as instructed, he was re-jected as the king.

13. Matthew 5:14–15: "Ye are the light of the world. A city that is set on a hill cannot be hid. Neither do men light a candle, and put it under a bushel, but on a candlestick; and it giveth light unto all that are in the house."

cause their prayers to be turned into curses upon us till we be consumed out of the good land whither we are agoing.

And to shut up this discourse with that exhortation of Moses, that faithful servant of the Lord, in his last farewell to Israel, Deuteronomy 30. Beloved, there is now set before us life and good, death and evil, in that we are commanded this day to love the Lord our God, and to love one another, to walk in His ways and to keep His commandments and His ordinance and His laws, and the articles of our covenant with Him, that we may live and be multiplied, and that our Lord our God may bless us in the land whither we go to possess it. But if our hearts shall turn away, so that we will not obey, but shall be seduced, and worship other gods, our pleasures and profits, and serve them; it is propounded unto us this day, we shall surely perish out of the good land whither we pass over this vast sea to possess it.

> Therefore let us choose life,
> that we and our seed
> may live by obeying His
> voice and cleaving to Him,
> for He is our life and
> our prosperity.

from THE JOURNAL OF JOHN WINTHROP[1]

[June 8, 1630] About 3 in the afternoon we had sight of land to the NW about 15 leagues, which we supposed was the Isles of Monhegen, but it proved Mount Mansell.[2] Then we tacked and stood WSW. We had now fair sunshine weather and so pleasant a sweet ether as did much refresh us, and there came a smell off the shore like the smell of a garden. There came a wild pigeon into our ship and another small land bird.

[July 5, 1632] At Watertown there was (in the view of divers witnesses) a great combat between a mouse and a snake, and after a long fight the mouse prevailed and killed the snake. The pastor of Boston, Mr. Wilson,[3] a very sincere, holy man, hearing of it gave this interpretation: that the snake was the devil, the mouse was a poor contemptible people which God had brought hither, which should overcome Satan here and dispossess him of his kingdom. Upon the same occasion he told the governor[4] that before he was resolved to come into this country he dreamed he was here, and that he saw a church arise out of the earth, which grew up and became a marvelous goodly church.

[December 27, 1633] The governor and assistants met at Boston and took into consideration a treatise which Mr. Williams[5] (then of Salem) had sent to them, and which he had formerly written to the governor and Council of Plymouth, wherein among other things he disputes their right to the lands they possessed here, and concluded that claiming by the King's grant they could have no title, nor otherwise except they compounded with the natives. For this, taking advice with some of the most judicious ministers (who much condemned Mr. Williams's error and presumption), they gave order that he should be convented[6] at the next Court to be censured, etc. There were 3 passages chiefly whereat they were much offended: 1. For that he chargeth King James to have told a solemn public lie, because in his patent he blessed God that he was the first Christian prince that had discovered this land; 2. For that he chargeth him and others with blasphemy for calling Europe Christendom or the Christian world; 3. For that he did personally apply to our present King Charles these 3 places in the Revelation, viz.

Mr. Endecott[7] being absent, the governor wrote to him to let him know what was done, and withal added divers arguments to confute the said errors, wishing him to deal

---

1. Winthrop kept his journal from 1630 to 1649, regularly recording events so as to create a narrative of the settlement. Selections from Winthrop's journal were first printed in *A Journal of the Transactions and Occurrences in the Settlement of Massachusetts and the Other New-England Colonies, from the Year 1630 to 1644* (1790). The text used here is from *The Journal of John Winthrop, 1630–1649,* ed. R. S. Dunn and L. Yeandles (1996).

2. Present-day Mount Desert Island, Maine.

3. John Wilson (1588–1667) was pastor in Boston for thirty-seven years.

4. Winthrop himself.

5. Roger Williams (1603–83) refused to become the preacher for the First Church of Boston because of doctrinal differences.

6. Summoned.

7. John Endecott (c. 1588–1665) was governor of Salem, the advance settlement for Massachusetts Bay, for two years before Winthrop's arrival.

with Mr. Williams to retract the same, etc. Whereunto he returned a very modest and discreet answer. Mr. Williams also wrote very submissively, professing his intent to have been only to have written for the private satisfaction of the governor, etc., of Plymouth without any purpose to have stirred any further in it if the governor here had not required a copy of him; withal offering his book or any part of it to be burnt, etc. So it was left and nothing done in it.

[January 20, 1634] Hall and the 2 others who went to Connecticut November 3 came now home, having lost themselves and endured much misery. They informed us that the smallpox was gone as far as any Indian plantation was known to the W., and much people dead of it, by reason whereof they could have no trade. At Narragansett by the Indians' report there died 700, but beyond Pascataquack none to the E.

[January 11, 1636] The governor[8] and assistants met at Boston to consult about Mr. Williams, for that they were credibly informed that notwithstanding the injunction laid upon him (upon the liberty granted him to stay till the spring) not to go about to draw others to his opinions, he did use to entertain company in his house and to preach to them, even of such points as he had been censured for; and it was agreed to send him into England by a ship then ready to depart. The reason was because he had drawn above 20 persons to his opinion and they were intended to erect a plantation about the Narragansett Bay,[9] from whence the infection would easily spread into these churches (the people being many of them much taken with the apprehension of his godliness). Whereupon a warrant was sent to him to come presently to Boston to be shipped, etc. He returned answer (and divers of Salem came with it) that he could not come without hazard of his life, etc., whereupon a pinnace was sent with commission to Captain Underhill,[10] etc., to apprehend him and carry him aboard the ship (which then rode at Nantasket), but when they came at his house they found he had been gone 3 days before, but whither they could not learn.

[October 21, 1636] . . . One Mrs. Hutchinson,[11] a member of the church of Boston, a woman of a ready wit and bold spirit, brought over with her two dangerous errors: 1. That the person of the Holy Ghost dwells in a justified person. 2. That no sanctification can help to evidence to us our justification.—From these two grew many branches; as, 1, Our union with the Holy Ghost, so as a Christian remains dead to every spiritual action, and hath no gifts nor graces, other than such as are in hypocrites, nor any other sanctification but the Holy Ghost Himself.

There joined with her in these opinions a brother of hers, one Mr. Wheelwright,[12] a silenced minister sometimes in England.

[October 25, 1636] The other ministers in the bay, hearing of these things, came to Boston at the time of a general court, and entered conference in private with them, to the end they might know the certainty of these things; that if need were, they might write to the church of Boston about them, to prevent (if it were possible) the dangers which seemed hereby to hang over that and the rest of the churches. At this conference, Mr. Cotton was present, and gave satisfaction to them, so as he agreed with them all in the point of sanctification, and so did Mr. Wheelwright; so as they all did hold that sanctification did help to evidence justification. The same he had delivered plainly in public, divers times; but, for the indwelling of the person of the Holy Ghost, he held that still, but not union with the person of the Holy Ghost, so as to amount to a personal union.

[November 1, 1637] . . . There was great hope that the late general assembly would have had some good effect in pacifying the troubles and dissensions about matters of religion; but it fell out otherwise. For though Mr. Wheelwright and those of his party had been clearly confuted and confounded in the assembly, yet they persisted in their opinions, and were as busy in nourishing contentions (the principal of them) as before. . . .

The court also sent for Mrs. Hutchinson, and charged her with divers matters, as her keeping two public lectures every week in her house, whereto sixty or eighty persons did usually resort, and for reproaching most of the minis-

---

8. The governor at this time was John Hays (1594–1654).

9. The settlement that eventually became Providence, Rhode Island.

10. John Underhill (c. 1597–1672), leader of the Massachusetts Bay militia.

11. Anne Hutchinson (1591–1643), originally a follower of John Cotton.

12. John Wheelright (c. 1592–1679) had been a minister in England but was removed from the ministry, probably for refusing to sign an oath of loyalty to the Church of England.

ters (viz., all except Mr. Cotton) for not preaching a covenant of free grace, and that they had not the seal of the spirit, nor were able ministers of the New Testament; which were clearly proved against her, though she sought to shift it off. And after many speeches to and fro, at last she was so full as she could not contain, but vented her revelations; amongst which this was one, that she had it revealed to her that she should come into New England, and she should here be persecuted, and that God would ruin us and our posterity and the whole state for the same. So the court proceeded and banished her; but because it was winter, they committed her to a private house where she was well provided, and her own friends and the elders permitted to go to her, but none else.

The court called also Capt. Underhill and some five or six more of the principal, whose hands were to the said petition; and because they stood to justify it they were disfranchised, and such as had public places were put from them.

The court also ordered, that the rest, who had subscribed the petition, (and would not acknowledge their fault, and which near twenty of them did,) and some others, who had been chief stirrers in these contentions, etc., should be disarmed. This troubled some of them very much, especially because they were to bring them in themselves; but at last, when they saw no remedy, they obeyed.

All the proceedings of this court against these persons were set down at large, with the reasons and other observations, and were sent into England to be published there, to the end that our godly friends might not be discouraged from coming to us, etc. . . . .

[March 1638] While Mrs. Hutchinson continued at Roxbury, divers of the elders and others resorted to her, and finding her to persist in maintaining those gross errors beforementioned and many others to the number of thirty or thereabout, some of them wrote to the church at Boston, offering to make proof of the same before the church, etc., [March] 15; whereupon she was called, (the magistrates being desired to give her license to come,) and the lecture was appointed to begin at ten. (The general court being then at Newtown, the governor and the treasurer, being members of Boston, were permitted to come down, but the rest of the court continued at Newtown.) When she appeared, the errors were read to her. The first was that the souls of men are mortal by generation, but after made immortal by Christ's purchase. This she maintained a long time; but at length she was so

clearly convinced by reason and scripture, and the whole church agreeing that sufficient had been delivered for her conviction, that she yielded she had been in an error. Then they proceeded to three other errors: That there was no resurrection of these bodies, and that these bodies were not united to Christ, but every person united hath a new body, etc. These were also clearly confuted, but yet she held her own; so as the church (all but two of her sons) agreed she should be admonished, and because her sons would not agree to it, they were admonished also.

Mr. Cotton pronounced the sentence of admonition with great solemnity, and with much zeal and detestation of her errors and pride of spirit. The assembly continued till eight at night, and all did acknowledge the special presence of God's spirit therein; and she was appointed to appear again the next lecture day. . . . .

[March 22, 1638] Mrs. Hutchinson appeared again; (she had been licensed by the court, in regard she had given hope of her repentance, to be at Mr. Cotton's house that both he and Mr. Davenport[13] might have the more opportunity to deal with her;) and the articles being again read to her, and her answer required, she delivered it in writing, wherein she made a retractation of near all, but with such explanations and circumstances as gave no satisfaction to the church; so as she was required to speak further to them. Then she declared that it was just with God to leave her to herself, as He had done, for her slighting His ordinances, both magistracy and ministry;[14] and confessed that what she had spoken against the magistrates at the court (by way of revelation) was rash and ungrounded; and desired the church to pray for her. This gave the church good hope of her repentance; but when she was examined about some particulars, as that she had denied inherent righteousness, etc., she affirmed that it was never her judgment; and though it was proved by many testimonies that she had been of that judgment, and so had persisted and maintained it by argument against divers, yet she impudently persisted in her affirmation, to the astonishment of all the assembly. So that after much time and many arguments had been spent to bring her to see her sin, but all in vain, the church with one consent cast her out. Some moved to have her admonished once more; but, it being for manifest evil in matter of conversation, it was agreed otherwise; and for that reason also

---

13. Minister John Davenport (1597–1670).

14. Both civil and church law.

the sentence was denounced by the pastor, matter of manners belonging properly to his place.

After she was excommunicated, her spirits which seemed before to be somewhat dejected revived again, and she gloried in her sufferings, saying that it was the greatest happiness next to Christ that ever befell her. Indeed it was a happy day to the churches of Christ here, and to many poor souls who had been seduced by her, who by what they heard and saw that day were (through the grace of God) brought off quite from her errors, and settled again in the truth.

At this time the good providence of God so disposed, divers of the congregation (being the chief men of the party, her husband being one) were gone to Narragansett to seek out a new place for plantation, and taking liking of one in Plymouth patent, they went thither to have it granted them; but the magistrates there, knowing their spirit, gave them a denial, but consented they might buy of the Indians an island in the Narragansett Bay.

After two or three days the governor sent a warrant to Mrs. Hutchinson to depart this jurisdiction before the last of this month, according to the order of court, and for that end set her at liberty from her former constraint, so as she was not to go forth of her own house till her departure; and upon the 28th she went by water to her farm at the Mount, where she was to take water with Mr. Wheelwright's wife and family to go to Pascataquack; but she changed her mind, and went by land to Providence, and so to the island in the Narragansett Bay which her husband and the rest of that sect had purchased of the Indians, and prepared with all speed to remove unto. For the court had ordered, that except they were gone with their families by such a time they should be summoned to the general court, etc.

[September 1638] . . . Mrs. Hutchinson, being removed to the Isle of Aquiday[15] in the Narragansett Bay, after her time was fulfilled that she expected deliverance of a child, was delivered of a monstrous birth. Hereupon the governor wrote to Mr. Clarke,[16] a physician and a preacher to those of the island, to know the certainty thereof, who returned him this answer: Mrs. Hutchinson, six weeks before her delivery, perceived her body to be greatly distempered and her spirits failing and in that regard doubtful of life, she sent to me etc., and not long after (in *immoderato fluore uterino*)[17] it was brought to light, and I was called to see it, where I beheld innumerable distinct bodies in the form of a globe, not much unlike the swims of some fish, so confusedly knit together by so many several strings (which I conceive were the beginning of veins and nerves) so that it was impossible either to number the small round pieces in every lump, much less to discern from whence every string did fetch its original, they were so snarled one within another. The small globes I likewise opened, and perceived the matter of them (setting aside the membrane in which it was involved) to be partly wind and partly water. The governor, not satisfied with this relation, spake after with the said Mr. Clarke, who thus cleared all the doubts: The lumps were twenty-six or twenty-seven, distinct and not joined together; there came no secundine[18] after them; six of them were as great as his fist, and the smallest about the bigness of the top of his thumb. The globes were round things, included in the lumps, about the bigness of a small Indian bean, and like the pearl in a man's eye. The two lumps which differed from the rest were like liver or congealed blood, and had no small globes in them, as the rest had.

[March 16, 1639] . . . At Aquiday also Mrs. Hutchinson exercised publicly, and she and her party (some three or four families) would have no magistracy. She sent also an admonition to the church of Boston; but the elders would not read it publicly because she was excommunicated. By these examples we may see how dangerous it is to slight the censures of the church; for it was apparent that God had given them up to strange delusions. . . . Mrs. Hutchinson and some of her adherents happened to be at prayer when the earthquake was at Aquiday, etc., and the house being shaken thereby, they were persuaded (and boasted of it) that the Holy Ghost did shake it in coming down upon them, as He did upon the apostles.

[September 1643] The Indians near the Dutch, having killed 15 men, began to set upon the English who dwelt under the Dutch. They came to Mrs. Hutchinson's[19] in way of friendly neighborhood, as they had been accustomed, and taking their opportunity, killed her and Mr. Collins, her son-in-law (who had been kept prisoner in Boston, as is before related), and all her family, and such

---

15. Aquidneck Island, Rhode Island.

16. John Clarke was one of those disarmed as an antinomian in 1637.

17. "In a heavy discharge from the womb."

18. Afterbirth.

19. In 1642, widowed, Hutchinson had moved to Dutch territory in what is today the Bronx in New York.

[other] families as were at home; in all sixteen, and put their cattle into their houses and there burnt them. These people had cast off ordinances and churches, and now at last their own people, and for larger accommodation had subjected themselves to the Dutch and dwelt scatteringly near a mile asunder. . . .

[July 3, 1645] . . . Then was the deputy governor[20] desired by the Court to go up and take his place again upon the bench, which he did accordingly. And the Court being about to rise, he desired leave for a little speech which was to this effect.

I suppose something may be expected from me upon this charge that is befallen me, which moves me to speak now to you. Yet I intend not to intermeddle in the proceedings of the Court, or with any of the persons concerned therein. Only I bless God that I see an issue of this troublesome business. I also acknowledge the justice of the Court, and for mine own part I am well satisfied. I was publicly charged, and I am publicly and legally acquitted, which is all I did expect or desire. And though this be sufficient for my justification before men, yet not so before the Lord, who hath seen so much amiss in any dispensations (and even in this affair) as calls me to be humbled. For to be publicly and criminally charged in this Court is matter of humiliation (and I desire to make a right use of it), notwithstanding I be thus acquitted. If her father had spit in her face (saith the Lord concerning Miriam), should she not have been ashamed 7 days? Shame had lain upon her whatever the occasion had been. I am unwilling to stay you from your urgent affairs, yet give me leave (upon this special occasion) to speak a little more to this assembly. It may be of some good use to inform and rectify the judgments of some of the people, and may prevent such distempers as have arisen amongst us. The great questions that have troubled the country are about the authority of the magistrates and the liberty of the people. It is yourselves who have called us to this office, and being called by you we have our authority from God in way of an ordinance, such as hath the image of God eminently stamped upon it, the contempt and violation whereof hath been vindicated with examples of divine vengeance. I entreat you to consider that when you choose magistrates you take them from among yourselves, men subject to like passions as you are. Therefore, when you see infir-

mities in us, you should reflect upon your own, and that would make you bear the more with us, and not be severe censurers of the failings of your magistrates when you have continual experience of the like infirmities in yourselves and others. We account him a good servant who breaks not his covenant. The covenant between you and us is the oath you have taken of us, which is to this purpose, that we shall govern you and judge your causes by the rules of God's laws and our own, according to our best skill. When you agree with a workman to build you a ship or house, etc., he undertakes as well for his skill as for his faithfulness, for it is his profession, and you pay him for both. But when you call one to be a magistrate, he doth not profess nor undertake to have sufficient skill for that office, nor can you furnish him with gifts, etc. Therefore you must run the hazard of his skill and ability. But if he fail in faithfulness, which by his oath he is bound unto, that he must answer for. If it fall out that the case be clear to common apprehension and the rule clear also, if he transgress here the error is not in the skill but in the evil of the will; it must be required of him. But if the case be doubtful, or the rule doubtful, to men of such understanding and parts as your magistrates are, if your magistrates should err here yourselves must bear it.

For the other point concerning liberty, I observe a great mistake in the country about that. There is a twofold liberty: natural (I mean as our nature is now corrupt), and civil or federal. The first is common to man with beasts and other creatures. By this, man as he stands in relation to man simply, hath liberty to do what he list. It is a liberty to evil as well as to good. This liberty is incompatible and inconsistent with authority, and cannot endure the least restraint of the most just authority. The exercise and maintaining of this liberty makes men grow more evil, and in time to be worse than brute beasts, *omnes sumus licentia deteriores.*[21] This is that great enemy of truth and peace, that wild beast which all the ordinances of God are bent against, to restrain and subdue it.

The other kind of liberty I call civil or federal. It may also be termed moral, in reference to the covenant between God and man in the moral law, and the politic covenants and constitutions amongst men themselves. This liberty is the proper end and object of authority and cannot subsist without it, and it is a liberty to that only which is good, just, and honest. This liberty you are to stand for, with the hazard not only of your goods but of

---

20. Winthrop himself. The following speech was delivered after Winthrop had been acquitted of overstepping his authority.

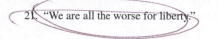
21. "We are all the worse for liberty."

your lives, if need be. Whatsoever crosseth this is not authority, but a distemper thereof. This liberty is maintained and exercised in a way of subjection to authority. It is of the same kind of liberty wherewith Christ hath made us free. The woman's own choice makes such a man her husband, yet being so chosen he is her lord and she is to be subject to him, yet in a way of liberty, not of bondage, and a true wife accounts her subjection her honor and freedom, and would not think her condition safe and free but in her subjection to her husband's authority. Such is the liberty of the church under the authority of Christ her King and husband. His yoke is so easy and sweet to her as a bride's ornaments, and if through frowardness or wantonness, etc., she shake it off at any time, she is at no rest in her spirit until she take it up again. And whether her Lord smiles upon her and embraceth her in His arms, or whether He frowns, or rebukes, or smites her, she apprehends the sweetness of His love in all and is refreshed, supported, and instructed by every such dispensation of His authority over her. On the other side, you know who they are that complain of this yoke and say: let us break their bands, etc.; we will not have this man to rule over us. Even so, brethren, it will be between you and your magistrates. If you stand for your natural corrupt liberties, and will do what is good in your own eyes, you will not endure the least weight of authority, but will murmur and oppose and be always striving to shake off that yoke. But if you will be satisfied to enjoy such civil and lawful liberties, such as Christ allows you, then will you quietly and cheerfully submit unto that authority which is set over you in all the administrations of it for your good; wherein if we fail at any time, we hope we shall be willing (by God's assistance) to hearken to good advice from any of you, or in any other way of God. So shall your liberties be preserved in upholding the honor and power of authority amongst you.

The deputy governor having ended his speech, the Court arose, and the magistrates and deputies retired to attend their other affairs. . . .

[July 1646] . . . A daughter of Mrs. Hutchinson was carried away by the Indians near the Dutch, when her mother and others were killed by them; and upon the peace concluded between the Dutch and the same Indians, she was returned to the Dutch governor, who restored her to her friends here. She was about 8 years old when she was taken, and continued with them about 4 years, and she had forgot her own language, and all her friends, and was loath to have come from the Indians.

THOMAS MORTON (1579?–1647)

Little is known of Morton's life before the period described in his single published book, *New English Canaan* (1637). It is likely that he was born in the West Country of England, where he became a lawyer. In 1621 he married Alice Miller, a widow, and the following year he sailed to New England aboard the *Unity*. Having no leanings toward Separatism or Puritanism, he settled in an area slightly apart from the Puritan community in Massachusetts. By living in the area called Passonagessit, present-day Quincy, Massachusetts, he could establish himself as a fur trader and the head of a trading post of the struggling settlement there, which he renamed "Ma-re Mount."

Unlike the neighboring Puritans, Morton believed that colonization should be undertaken primarily for financial profit. Although both Morton and the Puritans were very interested in the beaver trade, their approaches and goals differed significantly. Morton's goals were, he said, to strengthen Britain's empire. By contrast, he thought, the Puritans wanted to establish New England as their center and "city on a hill" apart from England itself. Morton and his Puritan neighbors clashed in 1627, when Indians joined the fur traders and planters at their May Day festivities, an episode that Morton would later recount in *New English Canaan*. The actions of the Anglican Morton proved offensive to the neighboring Puritans. The Puritans charged him with selling guns to the Indians and creating other disturbances antithetical to their way of living. After being arrested by Miles Standish, Morton was tried at Plymouth Plantation and returned to England, after spending one month imprisoned on the Isle of Shoals.

When Morton was acquitted the following year, he returned to Plymouth, only to continue having clashes with the Puritan leaders. In 1629, John Endicott and Morton had a significant controversy over whether fur traders had the right to remain independent of general partnerships or local management. When Morton's conflict with Massachusetts Bay officials grew, he was arrested again, tried in Charlestown, and banished from the Massachusetts Bay colony. His house was burned and his goods were confiscated. He returned to England, this time to work with anti-Puritan Anglicans to challenge the authority of the Massachusetts Bay Company. Although Morton and others successfully filed complaints against members of both the Massachusetts Bay and Plymouth companies, in the end the Massachusetts Bay Colony managed to retain its charter.

The reasons for Morton's final trip back to New England in 1643 are unclear, although he appears to have sought to examine land for himself or others. Soon after his return to the New England colonies, however, he was charged with slander for his campaign against the Massachusetts Bay Company and the 1637 publication of his book, *New English Canaan*. He was imprisoned in a Boston jail and later fined and released. He then traveled to Agamenticus, Maine, where he died in 1647.

His sole literary work was the promotional tract *New English Canaan*, first published in Amsterdam. His book, timed for publication at the height of his challenge to the Puritans' authority in the area they claimed as their own, quickly became well known for its satirical portrayal of Puritanism and what has come to be called the New England way. Written in a style that reflected a classical education, Morton's book argued that New England was ideal for colonization that could assist the British empire, yet it insisted that the Puritans were hindering the effective workings of trade with the Indians. During his years in New England, Morton traveled up and down the coast, collecting information that became the basis for his paradisical account of the land and its inhabitants. Perhaps because he was Anglican and wrote in a manner more typical of Anglican writers, Morton's work stands out among many early Massachusetts writers. His style and his approach to the land, the inhabitants, and colonization have much in common with British writers who settled in other areas, such as John Smith and William Byrd.

from NEW ENGLISH CANAAN[1]

from THE SECOND BOOK[2]

from CHAPTER 1 • The General Survey of the Country

In the month of June, *Anno Salutis*[3] 1622, it was my chance to arrive in the parts of New England with 30 servants and provision of all sorts fit for a plantation; and while our houses were building, I did endeavor to take a survey of the country. The more I looked, the more I liked it. And when I had more seriously considered of the beauty of the place, with all her fair endowments, I did not think that in all the known world it could be paralleled for so many goodly groves of trees, dainty fine round rising hillocks, delicate fair large plains, sweet crystal fountains, and clear running streams that twine in fine meanders through the meads,[4] making so sweet a murmuring noise to hear as would even lull the senses with delight asleep, so pleasantly do they glide upon the pebble stones, jetting most jocundly where they do meet, and hand in hand run down to Neptune's[5] court, to pay the yearly tribute which they owe to him as sovereign lord of all the springs. Contained within the volume of the land, [are] fowls in abundance, [and] fish in multitude. And [I] discovered, besides, millions of turtledoves on the green boughs, which sat pecking of the full ripe pleasant grapes

---

1. Morton's title reflects the ideological position taken by the Puritans, that they were founding a new community built upon biblical prophecy. "Canaan" refers to the Israelites' "promised land." *New English Canaan* was originally published in 1637. Text here is slightly modernized.

2. The title of the second book is "Containing a Description of the Beauty of the Country with Her Natural Endowments, Both in the Land and Sea; with the great Lake of Iroquois."

3. In the year of our prosperity.

---

4. Meadows.

5. God of the sea.

that were supported by the lusty[6] trees, whose fruitful load did cause the arms to bend: [among] which here and there dispersed, you might see lillies and of [*sic*] the Daphnean-tree, which made the land to me seem paradise. For in mine eye t'was Nature's masterpiece, her chiefest magazine[7] of all where lives her store. If this land be not rich, then is the whole world poor.

from THE THIRD BOOK[8]

[THE INCIDENT AT MERRY MOUNT]

CHAPTER 14 • Of the Revels of New Canaan

The inhabitants of Passonagessit[9] (having translated the name of their habitation from that ancient savage name to Ma-re Mount, and being resolved to have the new name confirmed for a memorial to after ages) did devise amongst themselves to have it performed in a solemn manner, with revels and merriment after the old English custom; [they] prepared to set up a Maypole upon the festival day of Philip and Jacob,[10] and therefore brewed a barrel of excellent beer and provided a case of bottles to be spent, with other good cheer, for all comers of that day. And because they would have it in a complete form, they had prepared a song fitting to the time and present occasion. And upon May Day they brought the Maypole to the place appointed, with drums, guns, pistols, and other fitting instruments for that purpose, and there erected it with the help of savages that came thither of purpose to see the manner of our revels. A goodly pine tree of 80 foot long was reared up, with a pair of buckhorns nailed on somewhat near unto the top of it, where it stood as a fair sea-

mark for directions how to find out the way to mine host[11] of Ma-re Mount.

And because it should more fully appear to what end it was placed there, they had a poem in readiness made, which was fixed to the Maypole, to show the new name confirmed upon that plantation, which, although it were made according to the occurrence of the time, it being enigmatically composed, puzzled the Separatists[12] most pitifully to expound it, which (for the better information of the reader) I have here inserted.

The Poem

Rise Oedipus,[13] and, if thou canst, unfold
What means Charybdis underneath the mold,
When Scylla solitary on the ground[14]
(Sitting in form of Niobe[15]) was found,
Till Amphitrite's darling did acquaint
Grim Neptune with the tenor of her plaint,[16]
And caused him send forth Triton[17] with the sound
Of trumpet loud, at which the seas were found
So full of protean forms that the bold shore
Presented Scylla a new paramour
So strong as Samson and so patient
As Job himself, directed thus, by fate,
To comfort Scylla so unfortunate.
I do profess, by Cupid's beauteous mother,[18]
Here's Scogan's choice[19] for Scylla, and none other;

---

6. When Apollo chased the nymph Daphne, she was saved by being changed into a laurel tree.

7. Warehouse.

8. The title of the third book is "Containing a Description of the People That Are Planted There, What Remarkable Accidents Have Happened There Since They Were Settled, What Tenets They Hold, Together with the Practice of Their Church."

9. Morton was the one who referred to Merry Mount as Ma-re Mount.

10. The feast day of Saints Philip and James, celebrated by the Church of England, was May 1.

11. Morton.

12. The Plymouth colonists had separated from the Church of England and were referred to as Separatists.

13. King of Thebes, Oedipus fulfilled the prophecy of his birth, killing his father and marrying his mother.

14. In Greek mythology, Scylla, a sea nymph turned into a monster by Circe, lived in a cave opposite Charybdis. She was said to have six heads, each with a triple row of teeth, and twelve feet.

15. After Niobe's fourteen children were slain and she was turned into stone by Zeus, she continued to weep for her children.

16. Complaint or lament.

17. Triton is the son of Poseidon, god of the sea.

18. Venus.

19. "Scogan's choice" implied that even an unappealing choice is better than no choice. John Scogan (1442–83), Edward IV's jester, was able to escape his sentence of hanging when he was unable to locate an appropriate tree; his chance to choose the tree saved him.

Though Scylla's sick with grief, because no sign
Can there be found of virtue masculine.
Asclepius[20] come; I know right well
His labor's lost when you may ring her knell.
The fatal sisters'[21] doom none can withstand,
Nor Cytherea's[22] power, who points to land
With proclamation that the first of May
At Ma-re Mount shall be kept holiday.

The setting up of this Maypole was a lamentable spectacle to the precise Separatists that lived at New Plymouth. They termed it an idol; yea, they called it the Calf of Horeb[23] and stood at defiance with the place, naming it Mount Dagon, threatening to make it a woeful mount and not a merry mount.

The riddle, for want of Oedipus, they could not expound, only they made some explication of part of it and said it was meant by Samson Job, the carpenter of the ship that brought over a woman to her husband that had been there long before and thrived so well that he sent for her and her children to come to him, where shortly after he died; having no reason but because of the sound of those two words, when as (the truth is) the man they applied it to was altogether unknown to the author.

There was likewise a merry song made which (to make their revels more fashionable) was sung with a chorus, every man bearing his part, which they performed in a dance, hand in hand about the Maypole, while one of the company sang and filled out the good liquor, like Ganymede and Jupiter.[24]

The Song

Chorus.

Drink and be merry, merry, merry boys;
Let all your delight be in the Hymen's[25] joys;
Io[26] to Hymen, now the day is come,
About the merry Maypole take a room.
  Make green garlands, bring bottles out

And fill sweet nectar freely about.
Uncover thy head and fear no harm,
For here's good liquor to keep it warm.
Then drink and be merry, &c.
Io to Hymen, &c.
  Nectar is a thing assigned
  By the Deity's own mind
  To cure the heart oppressed with grief,
  And of good liquors is the chief.
Then drink, &c.
Io to Hymen, &c.
  Give to the melancholy man
  A cup or two of't now and then;
  This physic will soon revive his blood,
  And make him be of a merrier mood.
Then drink, &c.
Io to Hymen, &c.
  Give to the nymph that's free from scorn
  No Irish stuff nor Scotch over worn.[27]
  Lasses in beaver coats come away,
  Ye shall be welcome to us night and day.
To drink and be merry, &c.
Io to Hymen, &c.

This harmless mirth made by young men (that lived in hope to have wives brought over to them, that would save them a labor to make a voyage to fetch any over) was much distasted of the precise Separatists that keep much ado about the tithe of mint and cummin,[28] troubling their brains more than reason would require about things that are indifferent, and from that time [they] sought occasion against my honest host of Ma-re Mount, to overthrow his undertakings and to destroy his plantation quite and clean. But because they presumed [that] with their imaginary gifts (which they have out of Phaon's box[29]) they could expound hidden mysteries, to convince them of blindness as well in this as in other matters of more consequence, I will illustrate the poem according to the true

---

20. Son of Apollo, Greek god of medicine and healing.

21. The three fates (in Greek and Roman mythology).

22. Also known as Aphrodite, goddess of love and beauty.

23. In Exodus 32, Moses destroys the Calf of Horeb because it was a false idol.

24. Ganymede is Jupiter's cupbearer.

25. Roman god of marriage.

26. Hurrah or hail.

27. Cloth.

28. Matthew 23:23: "Woe unto you, scribes and Pharisees, hypocrites! for ye pay tithe of mint, anise, and cummin, and have omitted the weightier matters of the law, judgment, mercy, and faith: these ought ye to have done, and not to leave the others undone."

29. The elderly boatman Phaon was rewarded by Aphrodite, goddess of love and beauty, with a chest containing an elixir promising youth.

intent of the authors of these revels, so much distasted by those moles.

Oedipus is generally received for the absolute reader of riddles, who is invoked; Scylla and Charybdis are two dangerous places for seamen to encounter, near unto Venice, and have been by poets formerly resembled to man and wife. The like license the author challenged for a pair of his nomination, the one lamenting for the loss of the other as Niobe for her children. Amphitrite is an arm of the sea, by which the news was carried up and down of a rich widow, now to be taken up or laid down. By Triton is the fame spread that caused the suitors to muster (as it had been to Penelope[30] of Greece), and, the coast lying circular, all our passage to and fro is made more convenient by sea than land. Many aimed at this mark, but he that played Proteus[31] best and could comply with her humor must be the man that would carry her; and he had need have Samson's strength to deal with a Delilah,[32] and as much patience as Job that should come there, for a thing that I did observe in the lifetime of the former.

But marriage and hanging (they say) come by destiny, and Scogan's choice is better [than] none at all. He that played Proteus (with the help of Priapus[33]) put their noses out of joint, as the proverb is.

And this the whole company of the revelers at Ma-re Mount knew to be the true sense and exposition of the riddle that was fixed to the Maypole which the Separatists were at defiance with. Some of them affirmed that the first institution thereof was in memory of a whore, not knowing that it was a trophy erected at first in honor of Maia.[34] The Lady of Learning which [sic] they despise, vilifying the two universities[35] with uncivil terms, accounting what is there obtained by study is but unnecessary learning, not considering that learning does enable men's minds to converse with elements of a higher nature than is to be found within the habitation of the mole.

CHAPTER 15 • Of a Great Monster Supposed to Be at Ma-re Mount; and the Preparation Made to Destroy It

The Separatists, envying the prosperity and hope of the plantation at Ma-re Mount (which they perceived began to come forward and to be in a good way for gain in the beaver trade), conspired together against mine host especially (who was the owner of that plantation) and made up a party against him and mustered up what aid they could, accounting of him as of a great monster.

Many threatening speeches were given out both against his person and his habitation, which they divulged should be consumed with fire. And taking advantage of the time when his company (which seemed little to regard their threats) were gone up unto the inlands to trade with the savages for beaver, they set upon my honest host at a place called Wessaguscus, where, by accident, they found him. The inhabitants there were in good hope of the subversion of the plantation at Ma-re Mount (which they principally aimed at) and the rather because mine host was a man that endeavored to advance the dignity of the Church of England, which they (on the contrary part) would labor to vilify with uncivil terms, inveighing against the sacred Book of Common Prayer[36] and mine host that used it in a laudable manner amongst his family as a practice of piety.

There he would be a means to bring sacks to their mill (such is the thirst after beaver) and [it] helped the conspirators to surprise mine host (who was there all alone), and they charged him (because they would [want to] seem to have some reasonable cause against him, to set a gloss upon their malice) with criminal things, which indeed had been done by such a person, but was of their conspiracy. Mine host demanded of the conspirators who it was that was author of that information that seemed to be their ground for what they now intended. And because they answered they would not tell him, he as peremptorily replied

---

30. Wife of Odysseus.

31. Son of Oceanus and Tethus, Proteus is a sea god known for his ability to prophesy and to assume different shapes.

32. Betrayer of Samson. See Judges 16.

33. God of fertility.

34. According to Morton, the Separatists claimed that the people at Merry Mount honored the licentious Flora, Roman goddess of flowers, instead of Maia, the goddess of the spring.

35. Oxford and Cambridge.

---

36. Rejected by Separatists, the Book of Common Prayer was used by Anglicans, members of the Church of England.

that he would not say whether he had or he had not done as they had been informed.

The answer made no matter (as it seemed) whether it had been negatively or affirmatively made, for they had resolved what he would suffer because (as they boasted) they were now become the greater number; they had shaken off their shackles of servitude and were become masters and masterless people.

It appears they were like bears' whelps in former time when mine host's plantation was of as much strength as theirs, but now (theirs being stronger) they (like overgrown bears) seemed monstrous. In brief, mine host must endure to be their prisoner until they could contrive it so that they might send him for England (as they said), there to suffer according to the merit of the fact which they intended to father upon him, supposing (belike) it would prove a heinous crime.

Much rejoicing was made that they had gotten their capital enemy (as they concluded him) whom they purposed to hamper in such sort that he should not be able to uphold his plantation at Ma-re Mount.

The conspirators sported themselves at my honest host, that meant them no hurt, and were so jocund that they feasted their bodies and fell to tippling as if they had obtained a great prize, like the Trojans when they had the custody of Epeios' pinetree horse.[37]

Mine host feigned grief and could not be persuaded either to eat or drink, because he knew emptiness would be a means to make him as watchful as the geese kept in the Roman Capital,[38] whereon, the contrary part, the conspirators would be so drowsy that he might have an opportunity to give them a slip instead of a tester.[39]

Six persons of the conspiracy were set to watch him at Wessaguscus. But he kept waking, and in the dead of the night (one lying on the bed for further surety), up gets mine host and got to the second door that he was to pass, which, notwithstanding the lock, he got open and shut it after him with such violence that it affrighted some of the conspirators.

The word which was given with an alarm was, "O he's gone, he's gone, what shall we do, he's gone!" The rest (half asleep) start up in amaze and like rams, ran their heads one at another full butt in the dark.

Their grand leader, Captain Shrimp,[40] took on most furiously and tore his clothes for anger, to see the empty nest and their bird gone.

The rest were eager to have torn their hair from their heads, but it was so short that it would give them no hold. Now Captain Shrimp thought in the loss of this prize (which he accounted his masterpiece) all his honor would be lost forever.

In the meantime mine host was got home to Ma-re Mount through the woods, eight miles round about the head of the river Monatoquit that parted the two plantations, finding his way by the help of the lightning (for it thundered as he went terribly), and there he prepared powder, three pounds dried, for his present employment, and four good guns for him and the two assistants left at his house, with bullets of several sizes, three hundred or thereabouts, to be used if the conspirators should pursue him thither; and these two persons promised their aids in the quarrel and confirmed that promise with health in good *rosa solis*.[41]

Now Captain Shrimp, the first captain in the land (as he supposed) must do some new act to repair this loss and to vindicate his reputation, who had sustained blemish by this oversight, begins now to study how to repair or survive his honor; in this manner, calling of council, they conclude.

He takes eight persons more to him, and (like the nine worthies of New Canaan) they embark with preparation against Ma-re Mount where this monster of a man, as their phrase was, had his den; the whole number, had the rest not been from home, being but seven, would have given Captain Shrimp (a *quondam* drummer) such a welcome as would have made him wish for a drum as big as Diogenes' tub,[42] that he might have crept into it out of sight.

Now the nine worthies are approached, and mine host prepared, having intelligence by a savage that hastened in love from Wessaguscus to give him notice of their intent.

---

37. The wooden horse built by Epeios was filled with Greek soldiers and used to conquer Troy.

38. The Gauls' attempted invasion of Rome was disrupted by hissing geese.

39. A fake coin, rather than a true British coin.

40. Captain Miles Standish (1584–1656).

41. A cordial.

42. Diogenes (c.412–323 B.C.), a Greek philosopher, was said to have lived in a tub.

One of mine host's men proved a craven; the other had proved his wits to purchase a little valor, before mine host had observed his posture.

The nine worthies coming before the den of this supposed monster (this seven-headed hydra, as they termed him) and began, like Don Quixote against the windmill, to beat a parley and to offer quarter if mine host would yield, for they resolved to send him to England and bade him lay by[43] his arms.

But he (who was the son of a soldier), having taken up arms in his just defense, replied that he would not lay by those arms because they were so needful at sea, if he should be sent over. Yet, to save the effusion of so much worthy blood as would have issued out of the veins of these nine worthies of New Canaan if mine host should have played upon them out at his portholes (for they came within danger like a flock of wild geese, as if they had been tailed one to another, as colts to be sold at a fair), mine host was content to yield upon quarter and did capitulate with them in what manner it should be for more certainty, because he knew what Captain Shrimp was.

He expressed that no violence should be offered to his person, none to his goods, nor any of his household but that he should have his arms and what else was requisite for the voyage, which their herald returns; it was agreed upon and should be performed.

But mine host no sooner had set open the door and issued out, but instantly Captain Shrimp and the rest of the worthies stepped to him, laid hold of his arms, and had him down; and so eagerly was every man bent against him (not regarding any agreement made with such a carnal man), that they fell upon him as if they would have eaten him; some of them were so violent that they would have a slice with scabbard, and all for haste, until an old soldier (of the Queen's, as the proverb is) that was there by accident, clapped his gun under the weapons and sharply rebuked these worthies for their unworthy practices. So the matter was taken into more deliberate consideration.

Captain Shrimp and the rest of the nine worthies made themselves (by this outrageous riot) masters of mine host of Ma-re Mount and disposed of what he had at his plantation.

This they knew (in the eye of the savages) would add to their glory and diminish the reputation of mine honest host, whom they practiced to be rid of upon any terms, as willingly as if he had been the very hydra of the time.

from CHAPTER 16 • How the Nine Worthies Put Mine Host of Ma-re Mount into the Enchanted Castle at Plymouth and Terrified Him with the Monster Briareus[44]

The nine worthies of New Canaan having now the law in their own hands (there being no general governor in the land, nor none of the separation that regarded the duty they owe their sovereign, whose natural born subjects they were, though translated out of Holland from whence they had learned to work all to their own ends and make a great show of religion but no humanity), for [*sic*] they were now to sit in council on the cause.

And much it stood mine honest host upon to be very circumspect and to take Eacus[45] to task for that his voice was more allowed of than both the other; and had not mine host confounded all the arguments that Eacus could make in their defense and confuted him that swayed the rest, they would have made him unable to drink in such manner of merriment any more. So that following this private counsel, given him by one that knew who ruled the roost, the hurrican ceased that else would split his pinnace.

A conclusion was made and sentence given that mine host should be sent to England a prisoner. But when he was brought to the ships for that purpose, no man dared be so foolhardly as to undertake to carry him. So these worthies set mine host upon an island, without gun, powder, or shot, or dog, or so much as a knife to get anything to feed upon, or any other clothes to shelter him with at winter than a thin suit which he had on at that time. Home he could not get to Ma-re Mount. Upon this island he stayed a month at least and was relieved by savages that took notice that mine host was a sachem of Passonages-

---

43. Put down.

---

44. In Greek mythology, Briareus was a monster with fifty heads and one hundred arms.

45. In Greek mythology, Eacus was a judge in the underworld. Morton was likely referring to Dr. Samuel Fuller of Plymouth.

sit, and would bring bottles of strong liquor to him and unite themselves into a league of brotherhood with mine host, so full of humanity are these infidels before those Christians.

From this place for England sailed mine host in a Plymouth ship (that came into the land to fish upon the coast) that landed him safe in England at Plymouth; and he stayed in England until the ordinary time for shipping to set forth for these parts, and then returned, no man being able to tax[46] him of anything.

But the worthies (in the meantime) hoped they had been rid of him. . . .

---

46. Charge.

ROGER WILLIAMS (1603–1683)

An early advocate of the separation of church and state and a supporter of the Narragansett Indian peoples, Roger Williams was born in Smithfield, London, where he reached adulthood. In 1627, he graduated from Cambridge, and two years later he married Mary Barnard, with whom he would have six children. At this time of great religious questioning in England, religion played a primary role in Williams's life, even though Williams served as household chaplain to Sir William Masham. His religious feelings developed more fully about the time the Massachusetts Bay colony started up. Williams and his wife traveled to Boston in 1631, aboard the *Lyon*. Because he was a committed Separatist, he turned down a position at the prestigious First Church of Boston, a non-Separatist church. He moved to Plymouth and later to a post in Salem.

Although Williams clearly supported English colonization according to religious principles, the Massachusetts Bay colony banished him in 1635, because many of his positions were antithetical to the colony's founding ideology. Williams challenged Puritan theocracy and the Massachusetts Bay charter by arguing for the separation of church and state; by arguing that all Puritans should be Separatists; and by asserting that although Indians should be christianized and thus colonization should take place, Puritans did not have a right to claim Indian lands. According to Williams, King Charles I had no right to bestow the Indian lands to the Puritans, so the Puritans had no right to claim control of those lands. When the Massachusetts General Court ordered Williams to return to England in 1635, he and a small group of followers traveled to Rhode Island, where they lived among Native peoples and founded the town of Providence. He was later joined by other exiles and dissenters, including Anne Hutchinson, and several Quakers, Baptists, and Jews.

In 1643, Williams traveled to England to obtain a charter for Providence Plantations. On his journey, he wrote *A Key into the Language of America*, which was published that year in London. In part a promotional tract and in part a cultural and linguistic introduction to the Narragansetts, the *Key* offered one of the few English studies of Native American languages. Organized as a dialogue between the English and the Narrangansetts, the *Key* suggested the importance of English speakers' attempts to convert the indigenous peoples to Christianity. The publication of this work encouraged the Massachusetts Bay colonists to work more actively as missionaries to the Indians, and it helped Williams obtain a charter for Rhode Island.

While in England, Williams also began a series of writings that clarified his differences with John Cotton and other Puritan leaders. He emphasized that Puritans must be Separatists and that true Christianity could be practiced only in those congregations in which both the individual and the parish had freedom to worship apart from the laws and guidance of civil magistrates. In one of his most famous works, *The Bloody Tenet of Persecution* (1644), Williams challenged Cotton's claim that one might justifiably be persecuted for personal beliefs and emphasized the importance of the separation of church and state, so that one's religious beliefs could not bring down upon one the power of the state. William's writings provoked extended public debates, particularly over his belief that civil government has power only when the people confer power to the leaders.

After Williams returned to Rhode Island in 1644 with the colony's charter, he was elected to the position of chief officer of the Providence Plantations. He returned to England in 1651, however, because the 1649 execution of King Charles I under the Puritan insurgence against Anglican authority challenged the validity of the colony's charter. Williams continued his writings, and when he returned to New England in 1654, he continued to work actively to shape the colony's policies. He composed his well-known letter "To the Town of Providence" (1655) to address a divisive dispute concerning religious autonomy, which some believed threatened political anarchy. One of Williams's final acts on behalf of the Indians occurred during the colonists' battles against the local Indians, which the colonists labeled King Philip's War (1675–76). To resolve the conflicts, Williams tried, unsuccessfully, to negotiate on behalf of the Narrangansetts. The Narragansetts instead entered into full and open warfare, and they were finally decimated.

Williams is often portrayed as one of the most liberal Puritan or Separatist leaders because he believed that religious practice should be separated from civil control. Yet liberalism is often associated with the belief that provisions for all kinds of freedom should be enforced by the government. Williams believed, to the contrary, that the government should have little say in an individual's life pursuits, a view that today tends to be associated with conservative social values. In terms of religious practice, Williams argued that religious beliefs are private and individual and should not be thwarted because of social pressure. In terms of the colonists' relations with the Indians, Williams sought measures of peaceful interaction. As readers of this volume will recognize, the desire to understand Native American cultures and language was not original or unique with Roger Williams; many colonists sought better relations with Native peoples and sought by means of pacific measures, rather than warfare, to accommodate the needs of the colonists and those of indigenous people. Yet Williams is frequently remembered for his principles, especially with regard to questions of conscience, because his model of dissent has been employed by many American writers, most notably Henry David Thoreau.

from A KEY INTO THE LANGUAGE OF AMERICA[1]

To My Dear and Well-Beloved Friends and Countrymen, in Old and New England

I present you with a key; I have not heard of the like, yet framed, since it pleased God to bring that mighty continent of America to light. Others of my countrymen have often, and excellently, and lately written of the country (and none that I know beyond the goodness and worth of it).

This key, respects the native language of it, and happily may unlock some rarities concerning the native themselves, not yet discovered.

I drew the materials in a rude lump at sea, as a private help to my own memory, that I might not, by my present absence, lightly lose what I had so dearly bought in some few years hardship, and charges among the barbarians.

Yet being reminded by some, what pity it were to bury those materials in my grave at land or sea; and withal, remembering how oft I have been importuned by worthy friends of all sorts, to afford them some helps this way. I resolved (by the assistance of The Most High) to cast those materials into this key, pleasant and profitable for all, but especially for my friends residing in those parts.

A little key may open a box, where lies a bunch of keys.

With this I have entered into the secrets of those countries, wherever English dwell about two hundred miles, between the French and Dutch plantations; for want of this, I know what gross mistakes myself and others have run into.

There is a mixture of this language north and south, from the place of my abode, about six hundred miles; yet within the two hundred miles (aforementioned) their dialects do exceedingly differ;[2] yet not so, but (within that

---

1. The text is derived from the 1643 edition, though the typography has been modernized.

2. Their dialects belonged to the Algonquian language family.

compass) a man may, by this help, converse with thousands of natives all over the country: and by such converse it may please the Father of Mercies to spread civility, (and in His own most holy season) Christianity. For one candle will light ten thousand, and it may please God to bless a little leaven to season the mighty lump of those peoples and territories.

It is expected, that having had so much converse with these natives, I should write some little of them.

Concerning them (a little to gratify expectation) I shall touch upon four heads:

First, by what names they are distinguished.

Secondly, their original[3] and descent.

Thirdly, their religion, manners, customs, etc.

Fourthly, that great point of their conversion.

To the first, their names are of two sorts:

First, those of the English giving: as natives, savages, Indians, wildmen, (so the Dutch call them *wilden*) Abergeny[4] men, pagans, barbarians, heathen.

Secondly, their names which they give themselves.

I cannot observe that they ever had (before the coming of the English, French or Dutch amongst them) any names to difference themselves from strangers, for they knew none; but two sorts of names they had, and have amongst themselves:

First, general, belonging to all natives, as Nínnuock, Ninnimissinnûwock, Eniskeetompaũwog, which signifies Men, Folk, or People.

Secondly, particular names, peculiar to several nations, of them amongst themselves, as Nanhigganĕuck, Massachusêuck, Cawasumsêuck, Cowwesêuck, Quintikóock, Qunnipiĕuck, Pequttóog, etc.

They have often asked me, why we call them Indians, natives, etc. And understanding the reason, they will call themselves Indians, in opposition to English, etc.

For the second head proposed, their original and descent:

From Adam and Noah that they spring, it is granted on all hands.

But for their later descent, and whence they came into those parts, it seems as hard to find, as to find the wellhead of some fresh stream, which running many miles out of the country to the salt ocean, hath met with many mixing streams by the way. They say themselves, that they have sprung and grown up in that very place, like the very trees of the wilderness.

They say that their great god Kautántowwìt created those parts, as I observed in the chapter of their religion. They have no clothes, books, nor letters, and conceive their fathers never had; and therefore they are easily persuaded that the God that made Englishmen is a greater God, because He hath so richly endowed the English above themselves. But when they hear that about sixteen hundred years ago, England and the inhabitants thereof were like unto themselves, and since have received from God, clothes, books, etc. they are greatly affected with a secret hope concerning themselves.

Wise and judicious men, with whom I have discoursed, maintain their original to be northward from Tartaria:[5] and at my now taking ship, at the Dutch plantation, it pleased the Dutch Governor, (in some discourse with me about the natives), to draw their line from Iceland, because the name Sackmakan (the name for an Indian prince, about the Dutch) is the name for a prince in Iceland.

Other opinions I could number up: under favor I shall present (not mine opinion, but) my observations to the judgment of the wise.

First, others (and myself) have conceived some of their words to hold affinity with the Hebrew.

Secondly, they constantly anoint their heads as the Jews did.

Thirdly, they give dowries for their wives, as the Jews did.

Fourthly (and which I have not so observed amongst other nations as amongst the Jews, and these:) they constantly separate their women (during the time of their monthly sickness) in a little house alone by themselves four or five days, and hold it an irreligious thing for either father or husband or any male to come near them.

They have often asked me if it be so with women of other nations, and whether they are so separated: and for their practice they plead nature and tradition. Yet again I have found a greater affinity of their language with the Greek tongue.

---

3. Tribal origin.

4. Aboriginal.

5. Mongolia.

2. As the Greeks and other nations, and ourselves call the seven stars (or Charles' Wain, the Bear,)[6] so do they Mosk or Paukunnawaw, the Bear.

3. They have many strange relations of one Wétucks, a man that wrought great miracles amongst them, and walking upon the waters, etc., with some kind of broken resemblance to the Son of God.

Lastly, it is famous that the Sowwest (Sowaniu) is the great subject of their discourse. From thence their traditions. There they say (at the southwest) is the court of their great god Kautántowwìt: at the southwest are their forefathers' souls: to the southwest they go themselves when they die; from the southwest came their corn, and beans out of their great god Kautántowwìt's field: and indeed the further northward and westward from us their corn will not grow, but to the southward better and better. I dare not conjecture in these uncertainties. I believe they are lost, and yet hope (in the Lord's holy season) some of the wildest of them shall be found to share in the blood of the Son of God. To the third head, concerning their religion, customs, manners etc. I shall here say nothing, because in those 32 chapters of the whole book,[7] I have briefly touched those of all sorts, from their birth to their burials, and have endeavored (as the nature of the work would give way) to bring some short observations and applications home to Europe from America.

Therefore fourthly, to that great point of their conversion, so much to be longed for, and by all New-English so much pretended,[8] and I hope in truth.

For myself I have uprightly labored to suit my endeavors to my pretenses: and of later times (out of desire to attain their language) I have run through varieties of intercourses[9] with them day and night, summer and winter, by land and sea, particular passages tending to this, I have related divers, in the chapter of their religion.

Many solemn discourses I have had with all sorts of nations of them, from one end of the country to another (so far as opportunity, and the little language I have could reach).

I know there is no small preparation in the hearts of multitudes of them. I know their many solemn confessions to myself, and one to another of their lost wandering conditions.

I know strong convictions upon the consciences of many of them, and their desires uttered that way.

I know not with how little knowledge and grace of Christ the Lord may save, and therefore, neither will despair, nor report much.

But since it hath pleased some of my worthy countrymen to mention (of late in print) Wequash, the Péquot captain,[10] I shall be bold so far to second their relations, as to relate mine own hopes of him (though I dare not be so confident as others).

Two days before his death, as I passed up to Qunníhticut[11] River, it pleased my worthy friend Mr. Fenwick, (whom I visited at his house in Saybrook Fort at the mouth of that river,) to tell me that my old friend Wequash lay very sick. I desired to see him, and himself was pleased to be my guide two miles where Wequash lay.

Amongst other discourse concerning his sickness and death (in which he freely bequeathed his son to Mr. Fenwick) I closed with him concerning his soul: he told me that some two or three years before he had lodged at my house, where I acquainted him with the condition of all mankind, & his own in particular; how God created man and all things; how man fell from God, and of his present enmity against God, and the wrath of God against him until repentance. Said he, "your words were never out of my heart to this present;" and said he "me much pray to Jesus Christ." I told him so did many English, French, and Dutch, who had never turned to God, nor loved Him. He replied in broken English: "Me so big naughty heart, me heart all one stone!" Savory expressions using to breathe from compunct and broken hearts, and a sense of inward hardness and unbrokenness. I had many discourses with him in his life, but this was the sum of our last parting until our General Meeting.[12]

Now, because this is the great inquiry of all men: what Indians have been converted? what have the English done in those parts? what hopes of the Indians receiving the knowledge of Christ?

And because to this question, some put an edge from the boast of the Jesuits in Canada and Maryland, and es-

---

6. The constellation Ursa Major (the Great Bear) or Charlemagne's wagon.

7. Williams's *Key.*

8. Asserted.

9. Discussions, conversations.

---

10. Wequash's conversion was described by Thomas Shepard in *New England's First Fruits* (1643).

11. Connecticut.

12. Judgment Day.

pecially from the wonderful conversions made by the Spaniards and Portugals in the West-Indies, besides what I have here written, as also, beside what I have observed in the chapter of their religion, I shall further present you with a brief additional discourse concerning this great point, being comfortably persuaded that that Father of Spirits, who was graciously pleased to persuade Japhet[13] (the Gentiles) to dwell in the tents of Shem[14] (the Jews), will, in His holy season (I hope approaching), persuade these Gentiles of America to partake of the mercies of Europe, and then shall be fulfilled what is written by the prophet Malachi,[15] from the rising of the sun (in Europe) to the going down of the same (in America), My name shall be great among the Gentiles. So I desire to hope and pray,

Your unworthy countryman,
Roger Williams

Directions for the Use of the Language

1. A dictionary or grammar way I had consideration of, but purposely avoided, as not so accommodate to the benefit of all, as I hope this form is.

2. A dialogue also I had thoughts of, but avoided for brevity's sake, and yet (with no small pains) I have so framed every chapter and the matter of it, as I may call it an implicit dialogue.

3. It is framed chiefly after the *Narragansett* dialect, because most spoken in the country, and yet (with attending to the variation of peoples and dialects) it will be of great use in all parts of the country.

4. Whatever your occasion be, either of travel, discourse, trading etc. turn to the table which will direct you to the proper chapter.

5. Because the life of all language is in the pronunciation, I have been at the pains and charges to cause the accents, tones or sounds to be affixed, (which some understand, according to the Greek language, acutes, graves, circumflexes) for example, in the second leaf[16] in the word *Ewò He:* the sound or tone must not be put on *E,* but *wò* where the grave accent is.

---

13. Noah's third son, sometimes understood as the progenitor of the Greeks and Medes. See Genesis 9:18.

14. Noah's eldest son.

15. See Malachi 1:11.

16. Page.

In the same leaf, in the word *Ascowequássin,* the sound must not be on any of the syllables, but on *quáss,* where the acute or sharp sound is.

In the same leaf in the word *Anspaumpmaûntam,* the sound must not be on any other syllable but *maûn,* where the circumflex or long sounding accent is.

6. The English for every Indian word or phrase stands in a straight line directly against the Indian: yet sometimes there are two words for the same thing (for their language is exceeding copious, and they have five or six words sometimes for one thing) and then the English stands against them both: for example in the second leaf:

Cowáunckamish &	I pray your favor.
Cuckquénamish	

An Help to the Native Language of That Part of America Called New England

from CHAPTER 21 • Of Religion, the Soul, etc.

Manìt-manittó, wock.	God, Gods.

Obs. He that questions whether God made the world, the Indians will teach him. I must acknowledge I have received in my converse[17] with them many confirmations of those two great points, Hebrews II. 6. viz:

1. That God is.
2. That He is a rewarder of all them that diligently seek Him.

They will generally confess that God made all, but them in special, although they deny not that Englishman's God made Englishmen, and the heavens and earth there! yet their Gods made them and the heaven, and earth where they dwell.

Nummusquauna-	God is angry with me?
múckqun manìt.	

Obs. I have heard a poor Indian lamenting the loss of a child at break of day, call up his wife and children, and all about him to lamentation, and with abundance of tears cry out! "O God thou hast taken away my child! thou art

---

17. Conversation.

angry with me: O turn Thine anger from me, and spare the rest of my children."

If they receive any good in hunting, fishing, harvest etc. they acknowledge God in it.

Yea, if it be but an ordinary accident, a fall, etc. they will say God was angry and did it, *musquàntum manit* God is angry. But herein is their misery:

First, they branch their God-head into many gods.

Secondly, attribute it to creatures.

First, many gods: they have given me the names of thirty seven which I have, all which in their solemn worships they invoke, as:

Kautántowwìt the great Southwest God, to whose house all souls go, and from whom came their corn, beans, as they say.

Wompanand.	The Eastern god.
Chekesuwànd.	The Western God.
Wunnanaméanit.	The Northern God.
Sowwanànd.	The Southern God.
Wetuómanit.	The House God.

Even as the papists have their he and she saint protectors as St. George, St. Patrick, St. Denis, Virgin Mary, etc.

Squáuanit.	The Woman's God.
Muckquachuckquànd.	The Children's God.

Obs. I was once with a native dying of a wound, given him by some murderous English who robbed him and ran him through with a rapier, from whom in the heat of his wound, he at present escaped from them, but dying of his wound, they suffered death at New Plymouth, in New England,[18] this native dying called much upon *Muck-quachuckquànd,* which of other natives I understood (as they believed) had appeared to the dying young man, many years before, and bid him whenever he was in distress call upon him.

Secondly, as they have many of these fained deities; so worship they the creatures in whom they conceive doth rest some deity:

Keesuckquànd.	The Sun God.
Nanepaûshat.	The Moon God.

Paumpágussit.	The Sea.
Yotáanit.	The Fire God.

Supposing that deities be in these, etc.

. . .

They have a modest religious persuasion not to disturb any man, either themselves English, Dutch, or any in their conscience, and worship, and therefore say:

Aquiewopwaũwash.	Peace, hold your peace.
Aquiewopwaũwock.	
Peeyàuntam.	He is at prayer.
Peeyaúntamwock	They are praying.
Cowwéwonck.	The soul.

Derived from *cowwene* to sleep, because say they, it works and operates when the body sleeps. *Míchachunck,* the soul, in a higher notion which is of affinity, with a word signifying a looking glass, or clear resemblance, so that it hath its name from a clear sight or discerning, which indeed seems very well to suit with the nature of it.

Wuhóck.	The body
Nohòck: cohòck	My body, your body
Awaunkeesitteoúwin-cohòck:	
Tunna-awwa commítchi-chunck-kitonckquèan?	Whether goes your soul when you die?
An. Sowánakitaúwaw.	It goes to the southwest.

Obs. They believe that the souls of men and women go to the southwest, their great and good men and women to Kautántowwìt, his house, where they have hopes (as the Turks have of carnal joys). Murderers, thieves and liars, their souls (say they) wander restless abroad.

Now because this book (by God's good providence) may come into the hand of many fearing God, who may also have many an opportunity of occasional discourse with some of these, their wild brethren and sisters, and may speak a word for their and our glorious Maker, which may also prove some preparatory mercy to their souls: I shall propose some proper expressions concerning the creation of the world, and man's estate, and in particular theirs also, which from myself many hundreds of times, great numbers of them have heard with great delight, and great convictions; which, who knows (in God's holy season), may rise to the exalting of the Lord Jesus Christ in their conversion, and salvation?

Nétop Kunnatótemous.	Friend, I will ask you a question.
Natótema:	Speak on.

---

18. In 1638 four runaway servants murdered a Narragansett.

Tocketunnûntum?	What think you?
Awaun Keesiteoûwin Kéesuck?	Who made the heavens?
Aûke Wechêkom?	The earth, the sea?
Míttauke.	The world.

Some will answer *Tattá*, I cannot tell, some will answer *Manittôwock,* the gods.

Tà suóg Maníttôwock	How many gods be there?
Maunaũog Mishaúna wock.	Many, great many.
Nétop machàge.	Friend, not so.
Paũsuck naũnt manìt.	There is only one God.
Cuppíssittone.	You are mistaken.
Cowauwaúnemun.	You are out of the way.

A phrase which much pleaseth them, being proper for their wandering in the woods, and similitudes greatly please them.

Kukkakótemous, wâchit-quáshouwe.	I will tell you, presently.
Kuttaunchemókous.	I will tell you news.
Paûsuck naũnt manit kéesittin keesuck, etc.	One only God made the heavens etc.
Napannetashèmittan naugecautúmmonab nshque.	Five thousand years ago and upwards.
Naũgom naũnt wukkesit tínnes wâme teâgun.	He alone made all things.
Wuche mateâg.	Out of nothing.
Quttatashuchuckqún-nacauskeesitínnes wâme.	In six days He made all things.
Nquittaqúnne.	The first day He made the light.
Wuckéesitin wequâi.	
Néesqunne.	The second day He made the firmament.
Wuckéestin Keésuck.	
Shúckqunnewuckéesitin Aũke kà wechêkom.	The third day He made the earth and sea.
Yóqunne wuckkéesitin Nippaũus kà Nane-. paũshat	The fourth day He made the sun and the moon.
Neenash-mamockíuwash wêquanantíganash.	Two great lights.

Kà wáme anócksuck.	And all the stars.
Napannetashúckqunne Wuckéesittin pus-suckseésuck wâme.	The fifth day He made all the fowl.
Keesuckquíuke	In the air, or heavens.
Ka wáme namaũsuck. Wechekommíuke.	And all the fish in the sea.
Quttatashúkqunne wuck-keésittin penashín-nvock wamè.	The sixth day He made all the beasts of the field.
Wuttàke wuchè wuckeesit-tin pausuck Enìn, or, Eneskéetomp.	Last of all he made one man.
Wuche mishquòck.	Of red earth,
Ka wesuonckgonna-kaûnes Adam, túp-pautea mishquòck.	And called him Adam, or red earth.
Wuttàke wuchè, Câwit míshquock,	Then afterward, while Adam, or red earth, slept,
Wuckaudnúmmenes manìt peetaũgon wuche Adam.	God took a rib from Adam, or red earth.
Kà wuchè peteaúgon. Wukkeesitínnes pausuck squàw.	And of that rib he made one woman.
Kà pawtouwúnnes Adûmuck	And brought her to Adam.
Nawônt Adam wuttúnna-waun nuppeteûgon ewò.	When Adam saw her, he said, "This is my bone."
Enadatashúckqunne, aquêi,	The seventh day He rested,
Nagaũ wuchè quttata-shúckqune ana-caûsuock English-mánuck.	And, therefore, Englishmen work six days.
Enadatashuckqunnóckat taubataũmwock.	On the seventh day they praise God.

Obs. At this relation they are much satisfied, with a reason why (as they observe) the English and Dutch, etc., labor six days, and rest and worship the seventh.

Besides, they will say, we never heard of this before: and then will relate how they have it from their fathers, that Kautántowwìt made one man and woman of a stone, which disliking, he broke them in pieces, and made another man and woman of a tree, which were the fountains of all mankind. . . .

from THE BLOODY TENET OF PERSECUTION, FOR CAUSE OF CONSCIENCE, IN A CONFERENCE BETWEEN TRUTH AND PEACE[1]

To every Courteous Reader.

While I plead the cause of *truth* and *innocency* against the bloody *doctrine* of *persecution* for cause of *conscience,* I judge it not unfit to give *alarm* to myself, and all men to prepare to be *persecuted* or hunted for cause of *conscience.*

Whether thou standest charged with ten or but two talents, if thou huntest any for cause of *conscience,* how canst thou say thou followest the *Lamb of God* who so abhorred that practice?

If Paul, if Jesus Christ, were present here at London, and the question were proposed what religion would they approve of: the Papists, Prelatists,[2] Presbyterians, Independents, etc. would each say, "Of mine, of mine."

But put the second question, if one of the several sorts should by major vote attain the sword of steel: what weapons doth Christ Jesus authorize them to fight with in His cause? Do not all men hate the persecutor, and every conscience true or false complain of cruelty, tyranny? etc.

Two mountains of crying guilt lie heavy upon the backs of all that name the name of Christ in the eyes of Jews, Turks and Pagans.

First, the blasphemies of their idolatrous inventions, superstitions, and most unchristian conversations.

Secondly, the bloody, irreligious and inhumane oppressions and destructions under the mask or veil of the name of Christ, etc.

O how like is the jealous Jehovah, the consuming fire to end these present slaughters in a greater slaughter of the holy witnesses? Revelation 11.

Six years preaching of so much truth of Christ (as that time afforded in King Edward's days) kindles the flames of Queen Mary's bloody persecutions.[3]

Who can now but expect that after so many scores of years preaching and professing of more truth, and amongst so many great contentions amongst the very best of Protestants, a fiery furnace should be heat, and who sees not now the fires kindling?

I confess I have little hopes till those flames are over, that this discourse against the doctrine of persecution for cause of conscience should pass current (I say not amongst the wolves and lions, but even amongst the sheep of Christ themselves) yet *liberavi animam meam,*[4] I have not hid within my breast my soul's belief; and although sleeping on the bed either of the pleasures or profits of sin thou thinkest thy conscience bound to smite at him that dares to waken thee? Yet in the midst of all these civil and spiritual wars[5] I hope we shall agree in these particulars.

First, however, the proud (upon the advantage of an higher earth or ground) overlook the poor and cry out schismatics, heretics, etc. shall blasphemers and seducers escape unpunished, etc. Yet there is a sorer punishment in the Gospel for despising of Christ than Moses, even when the despiser of Moses was put to death without mercy, Hebrews 10.28–29. "He that believeth not shall be damned," Mark 16.16.[6]

Secondly, whatever worship, ministry, ministration, the best and purest are practiced without faith and true persuasion that they are the true institutions of God, they are sin, sinful worships, ministries, etc. And however in civil things we may be servants unto men, yet in divine and spiritual things the poorest peasant must disdain the service of the highest prince: "Be ye not the servants of men," I Corinthians 14.[7]

Thirdly, without search and trial no man attains this faith and right persuasion, I Thessalonians 5. "Try all things."[8]

In vain have English Parliaments permitted English Bibles in the poorest English houses, and the simplest man or woman to search the Scriptures, if yet against their soul's persuasion from the Scripture, they should be

---

1. Written in response to the Puritan leader John Cotton, William's *Bloody Tenet of Persecution* was included on a list of books that Parliament ordered burned. The text is from *The Writings of Roger Williams* (1866–74).

2. Episcopalians.

3. Edward VI reigned from 1547 to 1553. Queen Mary I reigned from 1553 to 1558, during which time many Protestants were burned at the stake.

4. "I have freed my soul," as the clause following the Latin expression indicates.

5. The Civil Wars began in England in the year 1642.

6. Williams's citations are accurate unless otherwise noted.

7. The correct reference is 1 Corinthians 7:23, "Ye are bought with a price; be not ye the servants of men."

8. Compare with 1 Thessalonians 5:21, "Prove all things: hold fast that which is good."

forced (as if they lived in Spain or Rome itself without the sight of a Bible) to believe as the Church believes.

Fourthly, having tried, we must hold fast, I Thessalonians 5[9] upon the loss of a crown, Revelation 13.[10] we must not let go for all the flea bitings of the present afflictions, etc. having bought truth dear, we must not sell it cheap, not the least grain of it for the whole world, no not for the saving of souls, though our own most precious; least of all for the bitter sweetening of a little vanishing pleasure.

For a little puff of credit and reputation from the changeable breath of uncertain sons of men.

For the broken bags of riches on eagles' wings: For a dream of these, any or all of these which on our deathbed vanish and leave tormenting stings behind them: Oh, how much better is it from the love of truth, from the love of the Father of Lights, from whence it comes, from the love of the Son of God, who is the way and the truth, to say as He, John 18.37: "For this end was I born, and for this end came I into the world that I might bear witness to the truth."[11]

A LETTER TO THE TOWN OF PROVIDENCE[1]

That ever I should speak or write a tittle,[2] that tends to such an infinite liberty of conscience, is a mistake, and which I have ever disclaimed and abhorred. To prevent such mistakes, I shall at present only propose this case: There goes many a ship to sea, with many hundred souls in one ship, whose weal and woe is common, and is a true picture of a commonwealth, or a human combination or society. It hath fallen out sometimes, that both Papists and Protestants, Jews and Turks, may be embarked in one ship; upon which supposal I affirm, that all the liberty of conscience, that ever I pleaded for, turns upon these two hinges—that none of the Papists, Protestants, Jews, or Turks be forced to come to the ship's prayers or worship, nor compelled from their own particular prayers or worship, if they practice any. I further add, that I never denied, that notwithstanding this liberty, the commander of this ship ought to command the ship's course, yea, and also command that justice, peace, and sobriety be kept and practiced, both among the seamen and all the passengers. If any of the seamen refuse to perform their services, or passengers to pay their freight; if any refuse to help, in person or purse, towards the common charges or defence; if any refuse to obey the common laws and orders of the ship, concerning their common peace or preservation; if any shall mutiny and rise up against their commanders and officers; if any should preach or write that there ought to be no commanders or officers, because all are equal in Christ, therefore no masters nor officers, no laws nor orders, nor corrections nor punishments; I say, I never denied, but in such cases, whatever is pretended, the commander or commanders may judge, resist, compel, and punish such transgressors, according to their deserts and merits. This if seriously and honestly minded, may, if it so please the Father of Lights, let in some light to such as willingly shut not their eyes.

I remain studious of your common peace and liberty.
Roger Williams

---

9. See Thessalonians 5:21.

10. Williams's reference is unclear. Consider Revelation 3:11, "Behold, I come quickly: hold that fast which thou hast, that no man take thy crown."

11. Compare with John 18:37.

1. The letter was likely written in January 1654/55, after Williams returned from England to Providence. The text is taken from *The Writings of Roger Williams* (1866–74).

2. Dot.

JOHN ELIOT (1604–1690)

Born in England, John Eliot, who would become known as New England's "Apostle to the Indians," spent his early years in Essex. He graduated from Jesus College, Cambridge, in 1622 and went on to become a minister. Having allied himself with nonconforming clergy, he worked with Thomas Hooker at his small school, but when Hooker departed to Holland in 1630, Eliot joined the colonists in Massachusetts Bay. There he married Hannah Mumford in 1632, and there Eliot became a teacher and later a pastor at a new church in Roxbury. A much-loved minister recognized for his charity, Eliot was also admired for his 1645 founding of a grammar school, later called the Roxbury Latin School.

Eliot was among the first of the Puritan ministers to proselytize among the Indians. Believing that christianizing the Indians was a crucial step toward Christ's second coming, Eliot worked among the Algonquian-speaking peoples in eastern Massachusetts beginning in the 1640s. Although many Puritans described missionary work among Native peoples as a key part of the colonial project, few acted upon these words. Eliot received some support from other Massachusetts ministers, though his main financial backing came from the Society for Promoting and Propagating the Gospel of Jesus Christ in New England. Indian tutors taught him Algonquian, and by 1646 Eliot was able to preach to the Indian villages he visited. As support for his efforts grew, Eliot established an Indian College at Harvard and began to publish Algonquian translations of scripture. Publishing such translations was challenging because the Algonquian language was oral and so had not established orthography. Eliot created his own written version of the language and used it to teach reading, so the Indians would be able to use his biblical translations. He eventually translated the entire Bible, as well as the Bay Psalm book, into Algonquian. His biblical translation seems to have been used into the nineteenth century.

In addition to teaching Christianity to the Massachuetts and Wampanoag peoples, Eliot sought to influence their social structure by creating fourteen towns of what the colonists called "praying Indians" in Massachusetts. Inspired by the instructions Jethro offered to Moses in the biblical book of Exodus, Eliot organized towns with schools, churches, and governments, where he encouraged Indians to adopt English styles and customs to focus primarily on agriculture, leaving behind their semiagricultural and hunting activities. The Massachusetts retained their own language and played an important role in their Congregational churches, yet the new towns changed Indian lifestyles and social structure dramatically. In 1675, during the general war between Native people and British settlers in the region (known to the colonists as King Philip's War), the colonists grew distrustful of "praying Indian" loyalties and forced the Indians from their towns. Many of the Indian Bibles were burned, and numerous Indians were killed or died in exile. Concerned about what the colonists were doing, Eliot petitioned the Boston leaders to challenge the treatment of the Indians during King Philip's War and the selling of captives into slavery. At the end of the war, only a handful of villages were reconstructed. Yet Eliot continued his work, and he also engaged in tutoring African slaves. He died in 1690. Although his missionary work was not always supported during his lifetime, Eliot was praised highly by Cotton Mather, in Mather's 1702 *Magnalia Christi Americana,* as a "perfect and upright man" who sought, tirelessly, to "do good unto all."

Although Eliot is best known for his work among the Indians, he was a prolific author of biblical translations, catechisms, and other instructional materials. He wrote the *Indian Dialogues* (1671) in an attempt to expand the influence of his christianizing mission. He hoped the *Dialogues* would both assist Indian missionaries and demonstrate to Puritans that christianized Indian people could be responsible, obedient Christians. Although the *Dialogues* did not represent actual conversations, they reflect Eliot's decades of experience in his ministry.

from INDIAN DIALOGUES, FOR THEIR INSTRUCTION IN THAT GREAT SERVICE OF CHRIST[1]

DIALOGUE 1 • [A Dialogue between Pium bukhou and His Unconverted Relatives]

The church did sent forth sundry of the brethren to several parts of the country among their friends and relations, to instruct, exhort and persuade them to pray unto God, to turn from their lewd and lazy life to the living God, and to come forth from the dark dungeon of their lost and ruined condition, into the light of the Lord Jesus, whose glory in the gospel, like the rising sun, beginneth to be displayed among their dead countrymen, who begin to be clothed with sinews, flesh and skin upon their dried bones, by the power of the spirit of Jesus Christ, in the preaching of the gospel unto them.

Piumbukhou[2] was sent to Nashaurreg[3] among his kindred and friends there inhabiting: whose entertainment, discourse and success, was, or is, desired that it might be as followeth.

Near the town a kinsman of his met him; whose discourse was to such purpose as this.

Dialog. I

Kinsman Piumbukhou Speakers

KINSMAN: Well met, and welcome beloved cousin. I am glad you are still alive. Can you make shift to live in that new way of living that you have taken up at Natick?[4] I am glad of your coming, because I shall thereby have an opportunity to be informed truly of your ways and what your doings be, about which there be such various reports, some commending, some condemning, some deriding, some wondering. But so far as I see few desire to imitate you.

PIUM: I am very glad that God hath guided my way so well, as that I should meet you, whom I have longed to see. You are my friend whom I purposed first to look out, and lo God hath ordered us to meet each other, at my first coming to your town. Likewise I am glad that you are so desirous to speak with me about our religion, and praying to God, for that is the very errand I come upon, that I might persuade you to do as we do. I am like a friend that has found honey, and plenty of food, and I come to call my friends to come partake with me. But what noise is this that I hear?

KINSMAN: I perceive you have quite left off those delights and fashions that your countrymen use, and which in your young time accustomed to, because you have forgot the meaning of such noises. There is a great dancing, and sacrifice, and play, and that is the noise you hear.

PIUM: You say right. We have indeed quite left off and cast away those works of darkness. For we have great light shining among us which discovers the filth and folly of those things; as when a light is set up in a dark room in a dark night, it discovereth all the dirty corners of the house, and all the evil actions that are wont to be done in the dark, without discovery. We plainly see the sinfulness of our own former, and of your still continued ways, and I desire that God will help me to open among you some of the divine light which God hath showed us, that it may shame you from such filthy practices and shine them away forever, as the rising sun doth dissipate and drive away all the darkness of the night and maketh wolves, bears, and all other wild beasts hide themselves in thickets, and not dare to be seen in the day light.

KINSMAN: Will you go with me unto them, and see what they do? I will give you this one encouragement to persuade you to it, because you shall there see many of your friends and kindred.

PIUM: I cannot serve two masters. I have undertaken and promised to serve God, and therefore I cannot now go back again and serve the Devil. I have found that Jesus Christ is a good master, and I come to persuade you to come and be his servant. Far be it from me that now I am come among you, I should forsake my master, and serve

---

1. John Eliot's *Indian Dialogues, for Their Instruction in that great Service of Christ, in calling home their Country-men to the Knowledge of GOD, and of THEMSELVES and of JESUS CHRIST* was published in 1671 in Cambridge.

2. Piumbukhou's identity is uncertain. He might be Piambow of the praying town of Hassanamesitt or Piam Boohan of the praying town of Natick.

3. A Nipmuck Indian village, located in present-day Windham County, Connecticut.

4. Natick was founded by Eliot in 1650 and was designed to be a model praying town.

the Devil; or that I should so far grieve my master, as to go unto those games, which his soul hateth.

And whereas you say, that many of my friends are there, the more is my grief. I desire that I were able to pull you all out of that deep pit and filthy puddle; which to perform, I should utterly be disabled, if I should go in myself, and so be defiled with the same filth, which I persuade them to forsake and cast away.

KINSMAN: Let us go unto my house, that you make take there some refreshment of food after your weary journey, and there we shall have liberty to discourse fully of these matters. And while we are in the way, let me ask you of the estate and welfare of our friends and kindred at Natick. Doth your praying to God exempt you from sickness, poverty, nakedness? Will praying to God fill you with food, gladness, and garments?

PIUM: Our friends at Natick were when I left them in good state of health, peace, and comfort: for which we give God thanks, who is the father of all mercies.

Touching your question, whether praying to God doth exempt us from sickness, poverty, and fills us with food and garments. I answer, if praying to God did bring with it outward plenty and worldly prosperity, then all carnal people would pray to God, not because they love God, or praying to God, but because they love themselves, and love food, clothing, and worldly pleasures. But the benefits of praying are spiritual and heavenly, it teaches us to know God, and the evil of sin; it teacheth us to repent of sin, and seek for pardon, and it teacheth us to forsake sin forever. And if we are loth to part with sin, God will chastise us with sickness, poverty, and other worldly crosses, to call us to repentance, and therefore many times we fare worse in the world then wicked men do, that thereby we might be weaned from the world and brought and taught to love and long for heaven. And yet I further tell you, that religion doth teach the right way to be rich and prosperous in this world, and many, English especially, have learned that way. For religion teacheth us to be diligent in labor six days, and on the seventh day to rest, and keep it an holy sabbath; and God hath promised that *the diligent hand shall make rich.*[5] And when we walk with God in godliness and obedience, he will give us the blessing of this life, so far as it best for us. He will withhold no good thing from us. If any thing be withheld from us, or taken

away from us, it is because it is not good for us. Our father better knoweth what is good for us, then we ourselves know.

KINSMAN: If your praying to God do indeed teach you the true way of being rich, as you say, how then cometh it to pass you are so poor still? For you have prayed to God these twenty years and more, and I do not see that you have increased in riches very much. You are still poor. Where are your riches? Where be your flocks and herds of cattle? Where be your clothes? What great houses have you built? Where be your fields of corn, barns and orchards? Alas, you are not like the English; and therefore I doubt upon this point. It is not as you say, that praying to God teacheth you the right way to be rich.

PIUM: This is one of the least, the last, the lowest of those things that our religion teacheth us. There be two sorts of riches; earthly riches, of which only you speak, and heavenly riches, which God's word calleth true riches. These earthly riches are but temporary, and shall soon perish. But the true riches are heavenly, and eternal. They last forever. And we have spent these twenty years in seeking chiefly after heavenly riches, for so God commandeth us in his word, *Seek first the kingdom of heaven.* As for these earthly riches, *they shall be added to you,*[6] so much as you need. And the word of God commandeth us to *be content if we have food and clothes.*[7] Now we have food and clothes more then we were wont to have before we prayed to God, and we have contented ourselves therewith, and have bent our minds more to look after heavenly riches, and in those things we have increased more, than in earthly riches.

KINSMAN: I pray tell me what are those heavenly riches of which you speak so highly, and upon which you bestow your chief care and pains, and so much prefer before earthly riches, which we account so much of, and think to be the best things attainable in this world?

PIUM: The true riches which we spend our time to seek after, are, 1. The knowledge of the great God, who hath made this vast world, and governeth the same by his wisdom and power, and who hath made man, and gover-

---

5. Proverbs 10:4: "He becometh poor that dealeth with a slack hand; but the hand of the diligent maketh rich."

6. Luke 12:31: "But rather seek yet the kingdom of God; and all these things shall be added unto you."

7. Matthew 6:33: "Therefore, take no thought, saying, What shall we eat? or, What shall we drink? or, Wherewithal shall we be clothed?"

neth us by his holy laws and commandments. 2. The knowledge of ourselves, who be miserable sinners, and do daily offend and sin against God, provoking his wrath against us, to punish us for our transgressions against his holy laws and commandments. 3. The knowledge of Jesus Christ, the Redeemer of the world, who hath in unspeakable love took a course to deliver us from the wrath of God. For whereas we have by our sins deserved death and damnation, Christ became a man, and died for us, and thereby hath pacified the justice and wrath of God, and opened a way of salvation for us, obtaining a pardon for us, and offering grace unto us, whereby we may be saved, and be brought to eternal glory and happiness. 4. The knowledge of the grace of God in Jesus Christ, whereby he bringeth us to repent of our sins, to convert and turn from all our evil ways, and to believe in the Lord Jesus, and to walk with God in the ways of holiness and righteousness before him. 5. The knowledge of the means of grace, the ordinances of God; whereby we walk with God in ways of civil government, and good order. And in the ordinances of worshipping God, in the sanctifying of the sabbath, and walking in the communion of saints, by the Word of God, and prayer, and singing of Psalms. 6. In the knowledge of the estate of all men after death; how the godly men that penitently believe in Christ, go to heaven when they die; and the wicked, that refuse to repent and believe, they go to hell, and there abide till the day of judgement; at which day or time, when it cometh, all men shall rise again and be judged according to their deeds in this life. And then shall the godly go with Christ to eternal glory, and the wicked shall be cast into hell, soul and body, and there be tormented with the devils forever.

KINSMAN: These are great and strange things you speak of. I understand them not. But yet methinks there is a majesty and glory in them. I am amazed at what you say, though I do not understand them distinctly.

PIUM: You see then that we are grown rich with riches that are above your capacity; and these are the *true riches,* and about these things we spend most of our time. And as for these worldly riches, we less regard them, as being poor, low, little, small, contemptible things, in comparison of those heavenly riches about which we spend our time, and in which we have increased and gained, by God's grace in Christ, so much as doth make you admire at us, though we know but little of what is to be known, but you cannot perceive the glory and excellency thereof.

And indeed it is the wisdom and love of God unto us, that setteth us rather to grow in these riches, which the eyes of worldly men cannot see, than to grow rich in earthly and worldly riches, which the carnal world can see. Because if we should abound in earthly riches, we should be thronged with multitudes of carnal persons, who love the world, and love not God, who would be a cumber and temptation to us. And it is a sign that our ways are good and godly, and above the world, because so few (in comparison) come unto us, but rather fly from us; because they love to live in ways and deeds of darkness, and hate the light and glory that is in our ways. But I pray cousin, whose house that is before us, where I see so many going in and out, and standing about in every place?

KINSMAN: That is my house, and I am glad there be so many of our friends together, who may have the opportunity to hearing this good discourse.

[After their entrance into the house, there be four speakers: Kinsman, Kinswoman, All the Company, Piumbukhou]

KINSMAN: I had rather that my actions of love should testify how welcome you are, and how glad I am of this your kind visitation, than that I should say it in a multitude of words. But in one word, you are very welcome into my heart, and I account it among the best of the joys of this day, that I see your face, and enjoy your company in my habitation.

KINSWOMAN: It is an addition to the joys of this day, to see the face of my loving kinsman. And I wish you had come a little earlier, that you might have taken part with us in the joys of this day, wherein we have had all the delights that could be desired, in our merry meeting, and dancing.

And I pray cousin, how doth your wife, my loving kinswoman, is she yet living? And is she not yet weary of your new way of praying to God? And what pleasure have you in those ways?

PIUM: My wife doth remember her love to you. She is in good health of body, and her soul is in a good condition. She is entered into the light of the knowledge of God, and of Christ. She is entered into the narrow way of heavenly joys, and she doth greatly desire that you would turn from these ways of darkness in which you so much delight, and come taste and see how good the Lord is.

And whereas you wish I had come sooner, to have shared with you in your delights of this day. Alas, they are no delights, but griefs to me, to see that you do still delight in them. I am like a man that have tasted of sweet wine and honey, which have so altered the taste of my mouth, that I abhor to taste of your sinful and foolish pleasures, as the mouth doth abhor to taste the most filthy and stinking dung, the most sour grapes, or most bitter gall. Our joys in the knowledge of God, and of Jesus Christ, which we are taught in the Book of God, and feel in our heart, is sweeter to our soul, than honey is unto the mouth and taste.

KINSWOMAN: We have all the delights that the flesh and blood of man can devise and delight in, and we taste and feel the delights of them, and would you make us believe that you have found out new joys and delights, in comparison of which all our delights do stink like dung? Would you make us believe that we have neither eyes to see, nor ears to hear, nor mouth to taste? Ha, ha, he! I appeal to the sense and sight and feeling of the company present, whether this be so.

ALL: You say very true. Ha, ha, he!

PIUM: Hearken to me, my friends, and see if I do not give a clear answer unto this seeming difficulty. Your dogs take as much delight in these meetings, and the same kinds of delight as you do. They delight in each others company. They provoke each other to lust, and enjoy the pleasures of lust as you do. They eat and play and sleep as you do. What joys have you more than dogs have to delight the body of flesh and blood?

But all mankind have an higher and better part than the body. We have a soul, and that soul shall never die. Our soul is to converse with God, and to converse in such things as do concern God, and heaven, and an eternal estate, either in happiness with God, if we walk with him and serve him in this life, or in misery and torment with the Devil, if we serve him in this life. The service of God doth consist in virtue, and wisdom, and delights of the soul, which will reach to heaven, and abide forever.

But the service of the Devil is in committing sins of the flesh, which defile both body and soul, and reach to hell, and will turn all to fire and flame to torment your souls and bodies in all eternity.

Now consider, all your pleasures and delights are such as defile you with sin, and will turn to flame, to burn and torment you. They provoke God to wrath, who hath created the prison of hell to torment you, and the more you have took pleasure in sin, the greater are your offences against God, and the greater shall be your torments.

But we that pray to God repent of our old sins, and by faith in Christ we seek for, and find a pardon for what is past, and grace and strength to reform for time to come.

So that our joys are soul joys in godliness, and virtue, and hope of glory in another world when we die.

Your joys are bodily, fleshly, such as dogs have, and will all turn to flames in hell to torment you.

KINSMAN: If these things be so, we had need to cease laughing, and fall to weeping, and see if we can draw water from our mournful eyes to quench these tormenting flames. My heart trembles to hear these things. I never heard so much before, nor have I any thing to say to the contrary, but that these things may be so. But how shall I know that you say true? Our forefathers were (many of them) wise men, and we have wise men now living. They all delight in these our delights. They have taught us nothing about our soul, and God, and heaven, and hell, and joy and torment in the life to come. Are you wiser than our fathers? May not we rather think that *English* men have invented these stories to amaze us and fear us out of our old customs, and bring us to stand in awe of them, that they might wipe us of our lands, and drive us into corners, to seek new ways of living, and new places too? And be beholding to them for that which is our own, and was ours, before we knew them.

ALL: You say right.

PIUM: The Book of God is no invention of Englishmen. It is the holy law of God himself, which was given unto man by God, before Englishmen had any knowledge of God; and all the knowledge which they have, they have it out of the Book of God. And this book is given to us as well as to them, and it is as free for us to search the scriptures as for them. So that we have our instruction from a higher hand, than the hand of man. It is the great Lord God of heaven and earth, who teacheth us these great things of which we speak. Yet this is also true, that we have great cause to be thankful to the English, and to thank God for them. For they had a good country of their own, but by ships sailing into these parts of the world, they heard of us, and of our country, and of our nakedness, ignorance of God, and wild condition. God put it into their hearts to desire to come hither, and teach us the good knowledge of God; and their King gave them leave so to do, and in our country to have their liberty to serve God according to the word of God. And being come hither, we gave them leave freely to live among us. They have purchased of us a great part of those lands which they possess. They love us, they do us right, and no wrong willingly. If any do us wrong, it is without the consent of their rulers, and upon our complaints our wrongs are righted. They are (many of them, especially the ruling part) good men, and desire to do us good. God put it into the heart of one of their ministers (as you all know) to teach us the knowledge of God, by the word of God, and hath translated the holy Book of God into our language,[8] so that we can perfectly know the mind and counsel of God. And out of this book have I learned all that I say unto you, and therefore you need no more doubt of the truth of it, then you have cause to doubt that the heaven is over our head, the sun shineth, the earth is under our feet, we walk and live upon it, and breathe in the air. For as we see with our eyes these things to be so, so we read with our own eyes these things which I speak of, to be written in God's own book, and we feel the truth thereof in our own hearts.

KINSWOMAN: Cousin, you have wearied your legs this day with a long journey to come and visit us, and you weary your tongue with long discourses. I am willing to comfort and refresh you with a short supper.

ALL: Ha, ha, he. Though short, if sweet that has good favor to a man that is weary. Ha, ha, he.

KINSWOMAN: You make long and learned discourses to us which we do not well understand. I think our best answer is to stop your mouth, and fill your belly with a good supper, and when your belly is full you will be content to take rest yourself, and give us leave to be at rest from these gastering[9] and heart-trembling discourses. We are well as we are, and desire not to be troubled with these new wise sayings.

ALL: You say true. Ha, ha, he.

PIUM: It is good to be merry and wise. I am hungry and weary, and willing to eat. God hath appointed food to be a means of sustaining, relieving and repairing our spent strength. This being a work above the power of the food we eat, or of ourselves that eat it, and only in the power of God himself to bless it, for such great uses. Therefore God hath taught us, and it is our custom, among all that are godly, to pray to God for a blessing before we eat and therefore I entreat you to have so much patience and compliance, as to give me the quiet liberty to pray to God before we eat.

KINSMAN: I pray do, and we shall with quietness and silence attend to such a service unto God.

PIUM: Let us lift up our eyes and hearts to God in heaven, and say, almighty, glorious, merciful and heavenly Father, thou dwellest in the high heavens, and fillest both heaven and earth with thy presence. Thou takest care of, and governest us here on earth. We are poor worms under thy feet, thou feedest every living creature, and makest our food to be like a staff to sustain our faint and weary bodies. Thou renewest our strength every day and though we are sinners in thy sight, yet thou art merciful to us, and with long patience dost call us to repentance. We confess all our sins before thee, and pray thee for Jesus Christ, his sake, who died for sinners, to have mercy on us, and freely pardon and forgive us all our sins. Bless us at this time, and this food which is set before us. Let it be blessed to us. Make us wise to receive it at thy hand, and to use the strength we get by it to the glory of thy name, through Jesus Christ. And bless all our souls, feed them by thy word and truth, and guide our tongues to speak wise words, that may minister grace to the hearers, and help us all to rejoice in the Lord through Jesus Christ. Amen. Now let us eat and rejoice together, for God filleth our bodies with food, and our souls with gladness.

KINSMAN: When the body is full of meat, and the head full of wit, and the mouth full of words, there will be wise discourse.

PIUM: Add but one more thing. *If the heart be full of grace,* then the discourse will be both wise and godly.[10]

ALL: Ha, ha, he. They be not half full yet. Ha, ha, he.

KINSMAN: What news do the ships bring from beyond sea?

PIUM: They say wicked men are bold, and that good men who pray to God are hated, vexed, troubled, persecuted, and not suffered to pray to God according to the laws of God's word, but by the laws of men.

ALL: It is an ill time for you to come to persuade us to pray to God, when praying to God is so opposed, hated, and hindered. You may be more like to prevail with us, when praying to God is of credit, honor, and good esteem.

PIUM: Such as will turn to God only at such times when praying is in credit, leave themselves under a doubt, whether it be for the love of God and his ways, that

---

8. Eliot first published his Algonquian Indian Bible in 1663.

9. Frightening.

10. See Hebrews 13:9: "Be not carried about with divers and strange doctrines. For *it is* a good thing that the heart be established with grace; not with meats, which have not profited them that have been occupied therein."

they pray, or for the love of themselves and their own credit.

But when men will take up praying to God in evil times, when they must expect hard measure from the world for it, this is a sign that they love God, and love praying to God, better then they love themselves, and that they deny themselves, for Christ his sake. Therefore I have taken the fittest time to try you, and to sift you, to catch none but the good corn, and to let go and lose all the dust and chaff.

KINSMAN: Some speak of very many English people killed with thunder, and many burnt in their houses. Is it so indeed?

PIUM: It is so indeed, and in many parts of the country, at Boston, and in many other places. Very lately, there were in one winter eight or nine persons burnt to death in one house, five in another, one in another. Sicknesses are often sent of God among them, which kill many. Their corn is blasted, and they are punished by God many ways, by sea and land, in these late years.[11]

KINSWOMAN: These are but cold and weak arguments to persuade us to take up the English fashion, and to serve their God, when you tell us how sharply he dealt with his servants.

ALL: You say right. We are better as we are.

PIUM: We know there be many sins among the English, which provoke God to be angry with them, and to punish them, to the end he might bring them to repentance. When we exhort you to pray, and to serve the God of the English, we call you to imitate the virtues and good ways of the English, wherein you shall be acceptable to the Lord. We do not call you to imitate their sins, whereby they and you shall provoke the anger and displeasure of the Lord. And what though God doth chastise his people for their sins? It is his wisdom, faithfulness, and love so to do. A child will not run away from his wise and loving father, because he chastises him for his faults, but will love him the better, fear him the more, and learn thereby to be a good child. The wise English love God the more, for his wise chastisement of them for their sins. And why may not I use it as an argument to persuade you to choose him to be your God, who will love and encourage you in all virtue, and love and punish you for all sins, that he might bring you to repentance and amendment of life.

God's rods have more encouragement to a wise heart than discouragement to them.

KINSWOMAN: Cousin, had you not a great thunder and lightning today as you came, and were you not afraid? We had it so with us, and I was very much afraid, and especially since I have heard of so many English stricken and killed by it, and cannot restrain myself from fear.

PIUM: I perceived the thunder to be more this way, than it was in the place where I was at that time travelling. Touching the fear of thunder, the word of God saith it is terrible, and the brute beasts tremble at it. It is sometime called *The Voice of God,* by reason of the terribleness of it. And the reason of its terror to man is, because we are great sinners, and have deserved God's wrath, and it should move our hearts to repentance for our sins, and take heed of provoking the anger of that God, who is able to utter so terrible a voice, and can dash down destroying fire upon us worms, who are no ways able to defend our selves.

KINSMAN: Would you not lie down now you have eaten, and take some rest after your long journey?

PIUM: Nay, we must first return to God, and give thanks to him for our food, and health and strength by the same.

KINSMAN: I pray tell me why you are so careful to pray unto God before and after meat?

PIUM: Let us first give thanks, and then we will discourse that point. Attend all. We do give humble thanks unto thy holy name, O Lord our God, for our life, health, food, raiments, and for the present food whereby we are refreshed. We thank thee, O Lord, for the love we find among our friends, and for our freedom in good discourse for the good of our souls. We do pray for a blessing upon both, that our food may strengthen our bodies, and our discourse may do good to our souls. Help me so to declare thy word and thy works, that I may win their souls to love thee, and to forsake their sins, and turn unto the Lord by true repentance. These, and all other mercies we pray for, in the name, and for the sake of our Lord Jesus Christ. Amen.

ALL: Tabat, tabat, tabat.[12]

PIUM: Now my kinsmen and friends, let us discourse a little about the question propounded, why we pray unto God before and after meat? Our Lord Jesus Christ did so

---

11. Perhaps a reference to smut or rust.

12. According to Roger Williams's *Key into the Language of America* (1643), "taubot" means "I am glad."

before meat, as it is written of him in many examples, and we are not to doubt but he did the same after meat, because the Lord hath commanded the same so expressly, saying, *when thou hast eaten and art full, then beware lest thou forget the Lord.*[13]

And to show you what great reason we have thus to do, consider that God doth some of his chief works in this world, in the matter of our eating, which no creature can do. For take you a tray of meat, and ask, who can turn this into blood, and flesh, and sinews, and bones, and skin? And who can give every part of our body its due proportion, that one part shall not overgrow the other, but every part alike? Who but God can do this? And who but God can make our bodies grow to such an appointed stature, and then to grow no more? And who but God can preserve our health and turn away sickness? Now these marvelous things God doth for us every day, and every time we eat, and therefore is it not very good reason that we should pray and give thanks to God at such time as he doth such great and obliging things for us?

Again, God provideth all our food for us. He provideth corn, not we ourselves. We do but a little towards it. The great work is God's. All that we do is to put our corn into the ground, and keep the ground clean about it, but God makes it grow. He gives it a root, a blade, a stalk, and ears, whereby one corn shall become three or four or five hundred. Who but God can do this? Therefore corn is of his providing.

Again, who provideth water, and watereth the corn? Is it not God? For when springs and rivers are dried up, what can men do, but cry to God? And then God will bring clouds, like great bottles full of water, and drop them down upon the withered and parched earth, and thereby make the corn and grass and all fruits to grow. Who but God can do this?

Again, God provides flesh for us to feed upon, for he maketh the grass and herbs to grow, and when the beasts do feed thereon, he doth turn those leaves into blood, flesh, sinews and bones, and this he giveth us for food, and turneth it into blood, flesh, sinews, and bones in us. All these wonderful works God doth, in the matter of feeding us, and therefore is it not good reason we should then pray to him?

KINSMAN: I never heard so much before, nor thought of these things. But now you declare and teach them, my heart saith, that all is true which you say, and I now see great reason for this practice of you that pray to God, to pray and give thanks both before and after meat. And I see not but that there is good and just reason so to do, every time we drink, and take any sustenance, at least to lift up our hearts to God, who hath so eminent an hand in doing us good thereby, or hurt if he will.

PIUM: Your acceptance and approbation of what I say, and of what we do in this point, is a great argument that God doth bow your heart to pray unto God. For you acknowledge it to be our duty so to do, and the neglect of it would be against the light of your own reason, so that this conviction hath cast a chain upon your soul, to bind you to pray unto God. What say you my friends?

ALL: We cannot say any thing against what you say, but what we shall do, we cannot yet tell. We must first consider of it, for we are ignorant and foolish. We cannot do as you do.

PIUM: Bend your hearts to it, and God will teach you by his word. For we were at first as ignorant as you are, but God helped us to hear the word, and do what we could, and you see what God hath brought the matter unto. We now walk in the light, and now we call you to come into the light. Therefore I say, *awake you that sleep, stand up from the dead, and Christ will give you light.*[14]

KINSMAN: We shall tire you with these discourses after your long and weary journey. It is time for you to go to rest.

PIUM: This discourse is better to me than meat, drink and sleep, if I may do good to your souls, and turn you unto God.

But before we go to rest and sleep, we must pray unto God, for it is God that giveth rest and sleep unto his servants.

KINSMAN: Do all you praying Indians thus do when you are weary and tired with labor, or travel, or hunting, etc.? Do you pray before you go to rest? What is the reason of your so doing?

PIUM: We always do so, and if any should at any time through sloth or sleepiness fail so to do, we judge ourselves for our sin, and repent, and confess our sin unto God, and beg pardon and mercy for Christ his sake.

---

13. See Deuteronomy 6:11b–12a.

14. Ephesians 5:14: "Wherefore he saith, Awake thou that sleepest, and arise from the dead, and Christ shall give thee light."

And there is great reason thus to pray unto God before we go to rest. For besides what I said that God giveth us rest, and therefore it is fit humbly to ask it of him, there be many other reasons why we should thus do: for 1. We must give God thanks for all the mercies we have received all the day, which are more than the moments of the time that we live. 2. We must pray for God's protection of us when we are asleep. We lie like so many dead men, and how easily might mischief befall us, either by fire, or by an enemy, if God did not defend and keep us. But when God is our keeper we may rest quietly, in safety without fear, under the covert[15] of his hand. And by faith in God's protection we sleep quietly without fear, whereas you that do not pray, nor believe, nor commit your selves to God, you do always sleep in fear and terror. 3. Moreover, our sleep and rest is a great reparation of our strength and spirits, and preservation of our health. While we sleep our food is boiled up within us, and digested into all parts of our body, and new spirits are extracted out of our food, and sent up both to our head, heart, and all parts of our body, so that we are fresh and strong in the morning after a good night's rest. Now all this is the special work of God, beyond the power and skill of man to perform for us, and therefore it is great reason to pray for this blessing when we go to rest.

KINSMAN: What you say is plain, clear and true in every bodies experience, though I never heard nor considered so much of it before. If therefore you will pray we will attend you.

PIUM: Let us appear before God reverently and with godly fear. Let none lie along or sit, which are postures of unreverence, but either stand like servants, or kneel like sons and daughters before the Lord. And so let us pray. *O merciful Lord God,* etc.

KINSMAN: I perceive that you pray for all our countrymen, who do not yet pray unto God. It is your love so to do. But what is the effect of your prayers? There are not many, that I hear of, that pray unto God. And you that do pray unto God, what do you get by it? Wherein are you bettered by your praying to God?

PIUM: These are two great points which you have propounded. I am willing to speak to both. First, for the numbers that pray to God. At first this matter of praying

to God was a little thing, like a cloud in the west of the bigness of a man's hand. But now the cloud is great and wide, and spreadeth over all the country. Nop,[16] and Nantuket,[17] and Paumenuk islands,[18] Mahshepog,[19] and many parts of the mainland to the utmost bounds of this country eastward. And westward, not only all the Massachusets[20] pray, but also a large part of Nipmuk.[21] Yea and the fields are ripe unto the harvest in many places more, whom I will not name until they have given up themselves to the Lord, to forsake their vanities, and to pray unto God. The church at Natick have sent forth many into many parts of the country, to call them in unto Jesus Christ. I am sent unto you, and I have good hope that God will bow your hearts to pray unto God. So that the *praying Indians* are many, and like to be more every year. And our hope is the greater, because the Lord hath raised up sundry of our young men (who were children when we first prayed unto God) unto good knowledge in the scriptures, and are able to teach others the good knowledge of God, and are fit to be sent forth unto all parts of the country, to teach them to pray unto God.

KINSWOMAN: Husband, what do you mean to withhold our friend from rest so long, so late? Alas cousin, you had need to be at rest. I pray tire not yourself with these long discourses.

PIUM: I thank you for your care of me. There is but one thing more that I am to speak to, viz. the second part of your question, *what have we gained and got by praying to God?* Of which point we discoursed before we came into the house, and therefore I shall but touch on it now.

1. We are come into the light, and it is an heavenly light, which leadeth us to God, and to the eternal enjoyment of happiness by Jesus Christ.
2. We have attained to some measure of the true

---

15. Protection.

16. Martha's Vineyard.

17. Nantucket.

18. Indian name for eastern Long Island.

19. Mashpee.

20. Most of Eliot's converts were from the Massachuset tribe.

21. During the 1670s, Eliot built eight mission towns among the Nipmuck peoples.

riches, by faith in Jesus Christ, and love to God and his people.

3. We are content with that portion of food and raiment which God giveth us.

4. We enjoy the Lord's Sabbath days for our souls good, and communion with God.

5. We have government, and all God's ordinances in peace.

6. We can lie down in peace, and sleep quietly without fear.

In all which, and many more respects, our condition doth far exceed what we were and had afore we prayed to God, or what you have or enjoy unto this day. And now let us lie down in God's bosom, and take our rest.

LETTER TO THE HONORABLE COUNCIL SITTING AT BOSTON (1675)[1]

*To the Honorable Council sitting at Boston this
13th 6th 1675:—*
The humble petition of John Eliot showeth that the terror of selling away such Indians into the islands for perpetual slavery, who shall yield up themselves to your mercy, is like to be an effectual prolongation of the war. Such an exasperation of them as it may produce we know not what evil consequence upon all the land. Christ hath said: 'Blessed are the merciful, for they shall obtain mercy.'[2] This usage of them is worse than death. To put to death men that have deserved to die is an ordinance of God, and a blessing is promised for it. It may be done in faith. The design of Christ in these last days is not to extirpate nations, but to gospelize them. He will spread the gospel round the world about. Rev. xi. 15: 'The kingdoms of the world are become the kingdoms of our Lord and of his Christ.'[3] His sovereign hand and grace hath brought the gospel into these dark places of the earth. When we came we declared to the world, and it is recorded, yea, we are engaged by our Letters Patent from the King's Majesty, that the endeavor for the Indians' conversion, not their extirpation, were one great end of our enterprise in coming to these ends of the earth. The Lord hath so succeeded the work as that (by his grace) they have the Holy Scriptures, and sundry of themselves able to teach their countrymen the good knowledge of God. The light of the gospel is risen among those that sat in darkness and in the region of the shadow of death. And however some of them have refused to receive the gospel, and now are incensed in their spirits into a war against the English, yet by that good promise,—Psalm ii. 1,2,3,4,5,6,7,—I doubt not but the morning of Christ is to open a door for the free passage of the gospel among them, and that the Lord will publish the word. Ver. 6: 'Yet have I set my king, my anointed, upon the holy hill of Zion, though some rage at it.'[4]

My humble request is that you would follow Christ his designs in this matter to foster the passages of religion among them, and not to destroy them. To send into a place a slave away from spiritual direction, to the eternal ruin of their souls, is as I apprehend to act contrary to the mind of Christ. Christ's command is we should enlarge the kingdom of Jesus Christ. Isa. liv. 2: 'Enlarge the place of thy tent.'

It seemeth to me that to sell them away as slaves is to hinder the enlargement of his kingdom. How can a Christian sell [except?] to act in casting away their souls for which Christ hath in an eminent hand provided an offer of the gospel? To sell souls for money seemeth to me a dangerous merchandise. If they deserve to die, it is far better to be put to death under godly persons who will take religious care that means may be used that they may die penitently. To sell them away from all means of grace when Christ hath provided means of grace for them is the way for us to be active in destroying their souls, when we are highly obliged to seek their conversion and salvation, and have opportunity in our hand so to do. Deut. xxiii. 15, 16.[5] A fugitive servant from a Pagan master might not be de-

---

1. Eliot's petition, under the date of June 13, 1675 [13th 6th month 1675], was originally printed in *The Memorial History of Boston,* collected by Justin Winsor (Boston, 1880).

2. Matthew 5:7.

3. Eliot's quotation of part of Revelations 11:15 is generally accurate. Unless otherwise noted, his biblical citations are accurate.

4. Psalms 2:6 "Yet have I set my king upon my holy hill of Zion."

5. Deuteronomy 23:15–16: "Thou shalt not deliver unto his master the servant which is escaped from his master unto thee: He shall dwell with thee, *even* among you, in that place which he shall choose in one of thy gates, where it liketh him best: thou shalt not oppress him."

livered to this master, but be kept in Israel for the good of his soul. How much less lawful is it to sell away souls from under the light of the gospel into a condition where their souls shall be utterly lost so far as appeareth unto men! All men (of reading) condemn the Spaniard for cruelty upon this point in destroying men and depopulating the land. The country is large enough. Here is land enough for them and us too.

In the multitude of people is the King's honor. It will be more to the glory of Christ to have many brought in to worship his great name.

I beseech the honorable Council to pardon my boldness, and let the case of conscience be discussed orderly before the thing be acted. Pardon my weakness, and leave to reason and religion their liberty in this great case of conscience.

ANNE BRADSTREET (1612–1672)

In one of the several commendatory letters published with Anne Bradstreet's book of poems, *The Tenth Muse, Lately Sprung Up in America* (1650), her brother-in-law John Woodbridge wrote: "Now I believe tradition, which doth call/The Muses, Virtues, Graces, females all." The title of the volume and the letter referred to Bradstreet's status both as a woman and as an English colonist. In both these areas, Bradstreet was unusual: She was the first person in the British colonies to publish a book of poetry, and she was also the first published woman writer in British America.

Anne Dudley Bradstreet was born in England, the daughter of Dorothy Yorke and Thomas Dudley. Her mother came from a well-to-do family, and her father was steward to the earl of Lincoln. Bradstreet grew up in an atmosphere that fostered an unusually broad education for a woman. She had access to the libraries of her father and the earl, and as evidenced by her poetry, it is clear that she read widely. Her family were nonconformist Puritans, and in 1628, Anne Dudley married Simon Bradstreet, also a Nonconformist. The Bradstreets emigrated to New England along with her parents, with the group led by John Winthrop in 1630. In later life, she remembered that her "heart rose" at the "new world and new manners" she found in the wilderness of New England, but that she became reconciled to her new condition because she was convinced "it was the way of God."

Bradstreet's family was prominent in the life of early New England. Her father became the second governor of the Massachusetts Bay colony, a position her husband would also later hold. The Bradstreets lived first in Newtown (now Cambridge), then moved to Ipswich and finally to North Andover sometime after 1644, where Bradstreet lived the remainder of her life. While her husband pursued public service, Bradstreet bore and raised eight children. In the time left over from her domestic duties, Bradstreet also wrote poetry. The manuscript of what became her first volume of poems evidently circulated among her relations before her brother-in-law took it with him on a trip to England and had it published in London in 1650 under the title *The Tenth Muse Lately Sprung Up in America.* This first volume of poetry consisted primarily of poems dealing with historical and philosophical issues. It included a series called the "Quaternions," so called because they were four poems, each in four parts, describing the four elements, the four humors, the four ages of man, and the four seasons. Another four-part poem, "The Four Monarchies," put into verse the histories of four ancient kingdoms. These historical and philosophical poems were dedicated in an introductory poem to Bradstreet's father.

After *The Tenth Muse* was published, Bradstreet continued writing poetry. She also evidently made revisions to the poems that had been published, and she wrote a poem about the revision process, "The Author to Her Book," which asserted that her book had been published without her knowledge. She compared her published volume to a "rambling brat" who had strayed from its mother without permission. This poem and the revisions to the earlier poems were republished as *Several Poems* in Boston in 1678, six years after Bradstreet's death. This second published volume also included additional poems that were more personal than the earlier poetry, such as the religious meditation, "Contemplations," love poems to her husband, and laments on the death of grandchildren. In 1867, John Harvard Ellis reprinted the second edition and printed for the first time manuscript materials that had remained unpublished previously, including a set of prose religious meditations that Bradstreet addressed to her children and additional poetry.

The selections of Bradstreet's poetry presented here range from her earliest work to a late poem. The selections from "The Four Ages of Man" exemplify the concerns and style of the Quaternions. "Contemplations," one of Bradstreet's most admired poems, demonstrates the Puritan concern with understanding the natural world as a manifestation of God's will. The shorter poems presented here are examples of Bradstreet's personal poetry, much admired by twentieth-century critics and modernist poets like Adrienne Rich.

from THE TENTH MUSE, LATELY SPRUNG UP IN AMERICA

from **The Four Ages of Man**[1]

Loe now! four other acts upon the stage,[2]
Childhood, and Youth, and Manly, and Old-age.
The first: son unto Flegme, grand-child to water,[3]
Unstable, supple, moist, and cold's his Nature.
The second, frolick, claimes his pedigree,
From blood and aire, for hot, and moist is he.
The third, of fire, and choler is compos'd,
Vindicative, and quarelsome dispos'd.
The last, of earth, and heavy melancholly,
Solid, hating all lightnesse, and al folly.
Childhood was cloath'd in white, and given to show,
His spring was intermixed with some snow.
Upon his head a Garland Nature set:
Of Dazy, Primrose, and the Violet.
Such cold mean flowers (as these) blossome betime,
Before the Sun hath throughly warm'd the clime.
His hobby[4] striding, did not ride, but run,
And in his hand an hour-glasse new begun,
In dangers every moment of a fall,

And when tis broke, then ends his life and all.
But if he hold, til it have run its last,
Then may he live, til threescore years or past.
Next, youth came up, in gorgeous attire;
(As that fond age, doth most of al desire.)
His Suit of Crimson, and his Scarfe of Green:
In's countenance, his pride quickly was seen.
Garland of Roses, Pinks, and Gilliflowers,
Seemed to grow on's head (bedew'd with showers:)
His face as fresh, as is *Aurora*[5] faire,
When blushing first, she 'gins to red the Aire.
No wooden horse, but one of mettal try'd:
He seems to flye, or swim, and not to ride.
Then prauncing on the Stage, about he wheels;
But as he went, death waited at his heeles.
The next came up, in a more graver sort,
As one that cared, for a good report.
His Sword by's side, and choler in his eyes;
But neither us'd (as yet) for he was wise.
Of Autumne fruits a basket on his arme.
His golden god in's purse, which was his charm.
And last of al, to act upon this Stage;
Leaning upon his staffe, comes up old age.
Under his arme a Sheafe of wheat he bore,
A Harvest of the best, what needs he more.
In's other hand a glasse, ev'n almost run,
This writ about: *This out, then I am done.*
His hoary haires, and grave aspect made way;
And al gave eare, to what he had to say.
These being met, each in his equipage,
Intend to speak, according to their age:
But wise Old-age, did with all gravity,
To childish childhood, give precedency.
And to the rest, his reason mildly told;

---

1. First published in *The Tenth Muse, Lately Sprung Up In America* (London, 1650).

2. This poem is the third in a series of four, treating the four elements, the four humors, the four ages of man, and the four seasons.

3. In medieval physiology, human blood was characterized by qualities that were indicative of a person's temperment. The four humors were phlegm (cold and moist), blood (hot and moist), choler (hot and dry), and melancholy (cold and dry).

4. Hobby horse.

---

5. Greek goddess of the dawn.

That he was young, before he grew so old.
To do as he, the rest ful soon assents,
Their method was, that of the Elements,
That each should tel, what of himselfe he knew;
Both good and bad, but yet no more then's true.
With heed now stood, three ages of fraile man;
To hear the child, who crying, thus began.

Childhood.

Ah me! conceiv'd in sin, and born in sorrow,
A nothing, here to day, but gone to morrow.
Whose mean beginning, blushing cann't reveale,
But night and darkenesse, must with shame conceal.
My mothers breeding sicknes, I will spare;
Her nine months weary burden not declare.
To shew her bearing pangs, I should do wrong,
To tel that paine, which cann't be told by tongue;
With tears into this world I did arrive;
My mother stil did waste, as I did thrive:
Who yet with love, and all alacrity,
Spending was willing, to be spent for me;
With wayward cryes, I did disturbe her rest;
Who sought stil to appease me, with her brest,
With weary armes, she danc'd, and *By, By,* sung,
When wretched I (ungrate) had done the wrong.
When Infancy was past, my Childishnesse,
Did act al folly, that it could expresse.
My sillinesse did only take delight,
In that which riper age did scorn, and slight:
In Rattles, Bables, and such toyish stuffe.
My then ambitious thoughts, were low enough.
My high-borne soule, so straitly was confin'd:
That its own worth, it did not know, nor mind.
This little house of flesh, did spacious count:
Through ignorance, all troubles did surmount.
Yet this advantage, had mine ignorance,
Freedome from Envy, and from Arrogance.
How to be rich, or great, I did not carke;[6]
A Baron or a Duke, ne'r made my mark.
Nor studious was, Kings favours how to buy,
With costly presents, or base flattery.
No office coveted, wherein I might
Make strong my selfe, and turne aside weak right.
No malice bare, to this, or that great Peer,
Nor unto buzzing whisperors, gave ear.
I gave no hand, nor vote, for death, or life:
I'd nought to do, 'twixt prince, and peoples strife.

No Statist I: nor Marti'list i' th' field;
Where e're I went, mine innocence was shield.
My quarrells, not for Diadems did rise;
But for an Apple, Plumbe, or some such prize,
My stroks did cause no death, nor wounds, nor skars.
My little wrath did cease soon as my wars.
My duel was no challenge, nor did seek.
My foe should weltering, with his bowels reek.
I had no Suits at law, neighbours to vex.
Nor evidence for land, did me perplex.
I fear'd no stormes, nor al the windes that blows,
I had no ships at Sea, no fraughts to loose.
I fear'd no drought, nor wet, I had no crop,
Nor yet on future things did place my hope.
This was mine innocence, but oh the seeds,
Lay raked up; of all the cursed weeds,
Which sprouted forth, in my insuing age,
As he can tell, that next comes on the stage.
But yet let me relate, before I go,
The sins, and dangers I am subject to.
From birth stayned, with Adams sinfull fact;
From thence I 'gan to sin, as soon as act.
A perverse will, a love to what's forbid:
A serpents sting in pleasing face lay hid.
A lying tongue as soon as it could speak,
And fift Commandement[7] do daily break.
Oft stubborn, peevish, sullen, pout, and cry:
Then nought can please, and yet I know not why.
As many was my sins, so dangers too:
For sin brings sorrow, sicknesse, death, and woe.
And though I misse, the tossings of the mind:
Yet griefs, in my fraile flesh, I still do find.
What gripes of wind, mine infancy did pain?
What tortures I, in breeding teeth sustain?
What crudities my cold stomach hath bred?
Whence vomits, wormes, and flux have issued?
What breaches, knocks, and falls I daily have?
And some perhaps, I carry to my grave.
Some times in fire, sometimes in waters fall:
Strangely preserv'd, yet mind it not at all.
At home, abroad, my danger's manifold.
That wonder tis, my glasse till now doth hold.
I've done, unto my elders I give way.
For 'tis but little, that a childe can say. . . .

------

6. Take trouble over.

------

7. Exodus 20:12: "Honour thy father and thy mother: that thy days may be long upon the land which the Lord thy God giveth thee."

Old Age.

What you have been, ev'n such have I before,
And all you say, say I, and something more;
Babes innocence, Youths wildnes I have seen,
And in perplexed Middle-age have bin,
Sicknesse, dangers, and anxieties have past,
And on this Stage am come to act my last:
I have bin young, and strong, and wise as you,
But now, *Bis pueri senes,*[8] is too true;
In every Age i've found much vanitie,
An end of all perfection now I see.
It's not my valour, honour, nor my gold,
My ruin'd house, now falling can uphold;
It's not my Learning, Rhetorick, wit so large,
Now hath the power, Deaths Warfare, to discharge;
It's not my goodly house, nor bed of down,
That can refresh, or ease, if Conscience frown;
Nor from alliance now can I have hope,
But what I have done wel, that is my prop;
He that in youth is godly, wise, and sage,
Provides a staffe for to support his age.
Great mutations, some joyful, and some sad,
In this short Pilgrimage I oft have had;
Sometimes the Heavens with plenty smil'd on me,
Sometimes again, rain'd all adversity;
Sometimes in honour, sometimes in disgrace,
Sometime an abject, then again in place,
Such private changes oft mine eyes have seen,
In various times of state i've also been.
I've seen a Kingdom flourish like a tree,
When it was rul'd by that Celestial she;[9]
And like a Cedar, others so surmount,
That but for shrubs they did themselves account;
Then saw I *France,* and *Holland* sav'd, *Cales* won,
And *Philip,* and *Albertus,*[10] half undone;
I saw all peace at home, terror to foes,
But ah, I saw at last those eyes to close:
And then, me thought, the world at noon grew dark,
When it had lost that radiant Sun-like spark,
In midst of greifs, I saw some hopes revive,
(For 'twas our hopes then kept our hearts alive)

I saw hopes dasht, our forwardnesse was shent,
And silenc'd we, by Act of Parliament.
I've seen from *Rome,* an execrable thing,
A plot to blow up Nobles, and their King;[11]
I've seen designes at *Ree,* and *Cades* crost,[12]
And poor *Palatinate*[13] for ever lost;
I've seen a Prince, to live on others lands,
A Royall one, by almes from Subjects hands,
I've seen base men, advanc'd to great degree,
And worthy ones, put to extremity:
But not their Princes love, nor state so high;
Could once reverse, their shamefull destiny.
I've seen one stab'd, another loose his head;[14]
And others fly their Country, through their dread.
I've seen, and so have ye, for 'tis but late,
The desolation, of a goodly State.
Plotted and acted, so that none can tell,
Who gave the counsel, but the Prince of hell.
I've seen a land unmoulded with great paine.
But yet may live, to see't made up again:
I've seen it shaken, rent, and soak'd in blood,
But out of troubles, ye may see much good,
These are no old wives tales, but this is truth;
We old men love to tell, what's done in youth.
But I returne, from whence I stept awry,
My memory is short, and braine is dry.
My Almond-tree (gray haires) doth flourish now,
And back, once straight, begins apace to bow.
My grinders[15] now are few, my sight doth faile
My skin is wrinkled, and my cheeks are pale.
No more rejoyce, at musickes pleasant noyse,
But do awake, at the cocks clanging voyce.
I cannot scent, savours of pleasant meat,
Nor sapors[16] find, in what I drink or eat.

---

11. The Gunpowder plot (1605).

12. The Island of Rhé and Bay of Cadiz in Spain were both unsuccessfully attacked by the English in the 1620s.

13. Elector Palatine Frederick V ruled Bohemia for one year before being forced into exile. He was a supporter of the Nonconformist movement; his defeat ended that religious movement in Bohemia and was seen as a setback by English Nonconformists.

14. George Villiers, second duke of Buckingham (1592–1628), and Thomas Wentworth, earl of Strafford (1593–1641).

15. Teeth.

16. Flavors.

---

8. "Old men are children twice."

9. Queen Elizabeth I (1533–1603).

10. King Philip II of Spain and Albert, archduke of Austria, who governed the Netherlands under Philip II. The English attacked Cadiz in 1587 and again in 1596.

My hands and armes, once strong, have lost their might,
I cannot labour, nor I cannot fight:
My comely legs, as nimble as the Roe,
Now stiffe and numb, can hardly creep or go.
My heart sometimes as fierce, as Lions bold,
Now trembling, and fearful, sad, and cold;
My golden Bowl, and silver Cord, e're long,[17]
Shal both be broke, by wracking death so strong;
I then shal go, whence I shal come no more,
Sons, Nephews, leave, my death for to deplore;
In pleasures, and in labours, I have found,
That earth can give no consolation sound.
To great, to rich, to poore, to young, or old.
To mean, to noble, fearful, or to bold:
From King to begger, all degrees shal finde
But vanity, vexation of the minde;
Yea knowing much, the pleasant'st life of all,
Hath yet amongst that sweet, some bitter gall.
Though reading other Works, doth much refresh.
Yet studying much, brings wearinesse to th' flesh;
My studies, labours, readings, all are done,
And my last period now e'n almost run;
Corruption, my Father, I do call,
Mother, and sisters both; the worms, that crawl,
In my dark house, such kindred I have store,
There, I shal rest, til heavens shal be no more;
And when this flesh shal rot, and be consum'd,
This body, by this soul, shal be assum'd;
And I shal see, with these same very eyes,
My strong Redeemer, comming in the skies;
Triumph I shal, o're Sin, o're Death, o're Hel,
And in that hope, I bid you all farewel.

---

from SEVERAL POEMS[1]

Contemplations

Sometime now past in the Autumnal Tide,
When *Phœbus*[2] wanted but one hour to bed,

The trees all richly clad, yet void of pride,
Were gilded o're by his rich golden head.
Their leaves & fruits seem'd painted, but was true
Of green, of red, of yellow, mixed hew,
Rapt were my sences at this delectable view.

2

I wist not what to wish, yet sure thought I,
If so much excellence abide below;
How excellent is he that dwells on high?
Whose power and beauty by his works we know.
Sure he is goodness, wisdome, glory, light,
That hath this under world so richly dight:[3]
More Heaven then Earth was here, no winter & no night.

3

Then on a stately Oak I cast mine Eye,
Whose ruffling top the Clouds seem'd to aspire;
How long since thou wast in thine Infancy?
Thy strength, and stature, more thy years admire,
Hath hundred winters past since thou wast born?
Or thousand since thou brakest thy shell of horn,
If so, all these as nought, Eternity doth scorn.

4

Then higher on the glistering Sun I gaz'd,
Whose beams was shaded by the leavie Tree,
The more I look'd, the more I grew amaz'd,
And softly said, what glory's like to thee?
Soul of this world, this Universes Eye,
No wonder, some made thee a Deity:
Had I not better known, (alas) the same had I.

5

Thou as a Bridegroom from thy Chamber rushes,
And as a strong man, joyes to run a race,[4]
The morn doth usher thee, with smiles & blushes,
The Earth reflects her glances in thy face.
Birds, insects, Animals with Vegative,
Thy heat from death and dulness doth revive:
And in the darksome womb of fruitful nature dive.

6

Thy swift Annual, and diurnal Course,
Thy daily streight, and yearly oblique path,

---

17. Ecclesiastes 12:6: "Or ever the silver cord be loosed, or the golden bowl be broken, or the pitcher be broken at the fountain, or the wheel broken at the cistern."

1. The following poems were first published in *Several Poems* (Boston, 1678).

2. The Greek sun god, Apollo.

3. Dressed.

4. Psalm 19:4–5: "a bridegroom coming out of his chamber . . . rejoiceth as a strong man to run a race."

Thy pleasing fervor, and thy scorching force,
All mortals here the feeling knowledg hath.
Thy presence makes it day, thy absence night,
Quaternal Seasons caused by thy might:
Hail Creature, full of sweetness, beauty & delight.

7

Art thou so full of glory, that no Eye
Hath strength, thy shining Rayes once to behold?
And is thy splendid Throne erect so high?
As to approach it, can no earthly mould.
How full of glory then must thy Creator be?
Who gave this bright light luster unto thee:
Admir'd, ador'd for ever, be that Majesty.

8

Silent alone, where none or saw, or heard,
In pathless paths I lead my wandring feet,
My humble Eyes to lofty Skyes I rear'd
To sing some Song, my mazed Muse thought meet.
My great Creator I would magnifie,
That nature had, thus decked liberally:
But Ah, and Ah, again, my imbecility!

9

I heard the merry grashopper then sing,
The black clad Cricket, bear a second part,
They kept one tune, and plaid on the same string,
Seeming to glory in their little Art.
Shall Creatures abject, thus their voices raise?
And in their kind resound their makers praise:
Whilst I as mute, can warble forth no higher layes.

10

When present times look back to Ages past,
And men in being fancy those are dead,
It makes things gone perpetually to last,
And calls back moneths and years that long since fled
It makes a man more aged in conceit,
Then was *Methuselah,* or's grand-sire great:[5]
While of their persons & their acts his mind doth treat.

11

Sometimes in *Eden* fair, he seems to be,
Sees glorious *Adam* there made Lord of all,
Fancyes the Apple, dangle on the Tree,

That turn'd his Sovereign to a naked thral.
Who like a miscreant's driven from that place,
To get his bread with pain, and sweat of face:
A penalty impos'd on his backsliding Race.

12

Here sits our Grandame in retired place,
And in her lap, her bloody *Cain* new born,
The weeping Imp oft looks her in the face,
Bewails his unknown hap, and fate forlorn;
His Mother sighs, to think of Paradise,
And how she lost her bliss, to be more wise,
Believing him that was, and is, Father of lyes.

13

Here *Cain* and *Abel* come to sacrifice,
Fruits of the Earth, and Fatlings each do bring,
On *Abels* gift the fire descends from Skies,
But no such sign on false *Cain's* offering;
With sullen hateful looks he goes his wayes.
Hath thousand thoughts to end his brothers dayes,
Upon whose blood his future good he hopes to raise.

14

There *Abel* keeps his sheep, no ill he thinks,
His brother comes, then acts his fratricide,
The Virgin Earth, of blood her first draught drinks
But since that time she often hath been cloy'd;
The wretch with gastly face and dreadful mind,
Thinks each he sees will serve him in his kind,
Though none on Earth but kindred near then could he
    find.

15

Who fancyes not his looks now at the Barr,
His face like death, his heart with horror fraught,
Nor Male-factor ever felt like warr,
When deep dispair, with wish of life hath fought,
Branded with guilt, and crusht with treble woes,
A Vagabond to Land of *Nod* he goes,
A City builds, that wals might him secure from foes.

16

Who thinks not oft upon the Fathers ages.
Their long descent, how nephews sons they saw,
The starry observations of those Sages,
And how their precepts to their sons were law,
How Adam sigh'd to see his Progeny,
Cloath'd all in his black sinfull Livery,
Who neither guilt, nor yet the punishment could fly.

---

5. Methusaleh lived 969 years and his grandfather lived 962
years, according to Genesis 5:18–27.

17

Our life compare we with their length of dayes
Who to the tenth of theirs doth now arrive?
And though thus short, we shorten many wayes,
Living so little while we are alive;
In eating, drinking, sleeping, vain delight
So unawares comes on perpetual night,
And puts all pleasures vain unto eternal flight.

18

When I behold the heavens as in their prime,
And then the earth (though old) stil clad in green,
The stones and trees, insensible of time,
Nor age nor wrinkle on their front are seen;
If winter come, and greeness then do fade,
A Spring returns, and they more youthfull made;
But Man grows old, lies down, remains where once he's
    laid.

19

By birth more noble then those creatures all,
Yet seems by nature and by custome curs'd,
No sooner born, but grief and care makes fall
That state obliterate he had at first:
Nor youth, nor strength, nor wisdom spring again
Nor habitations long their names retain,
But in oblivion to the final day remain.

20

Shall I then praise the heavens, the trees, the earth
Because their beauty and their strength last longer
Shall I wish there, or never to had birth,
Because they're bigger, & their bodyes stronger?
Nay, they shall darken, perish, fade and dye,
And when unmade, so ever shall they lye,
But man was made for endless immortality.

21

Under the cooling shadow of a stately Elm
Close sate I by a goodly Rivers side,
Where gliding streams the Rocks did overwhelm;
A lonely place, with pleasures dignifi'd.
I once that lov'd the shady woods so well,
Now thought the rivers did the trees excel,
And if the sun would ever shine, there would I dwell.

22

While on the stealing stream I fixt mine eye,
Which to the long'd for Ocean held its course,
I markt, nor crooks, nor rubs that there did lye

Could hinder ought, but still augment its force:
O happy Flood, quoth I, that holds thy race
Till thou arrive at thy beloved place,
Nor is it rocks or shoals that can obstruct thy pace.

23

Nor is't enough, that thou alone may'st slide,
But hundred brooks in thy cleer waves do meet,
So hand in hand along with thee they glide
To *Thetis*[6] house, where all imbrace and greet:
Thou Emblem true, of what I count the best,
O could I lead my Rivolets to rest,
So may we press to that vast mansion, ever blest.

24

Ye Fish which in this liquid Region 'bide,
That for each season, have your habitation,
Now salt, now fresh where you think best to glide
To unknown coasts to give a visitation,
In Lakes and ponds, you leave your numerous fry,
So nature taught, and yet you know not why,
You watry folk that know not your felicity.

25

Look how the wantons frisk to task the air,
Then to the colder bottome streight they dive,
Eftsoon to *Neptun's* glassie Hall[7] repair
To see what trade they great ones there do drive,
Who forrage o're the spacious sea-green field,
And take the trembling prey before it yield,
Whose armour is their scales, their spreading fins their
    shield.

26

While musing thus with contemplation fed,
And thousand fancies buzzing in my brain,
The sweet-tongu'd Philomel[8] percht ore my head,
And chanted forth a most melodious strain
Which rapt me so with wonder and delight,
I judg'd my hearing better then my sight,
And wisht me wings with her a while to take my flight.

27

O merry Bird (said I) that fears no snares,
That neither toyles nor hoards up in thy barn,

---

6. Achilles' mother, Thetis, lived in the sea.

7. Neptune was the Roman god of the ocean.

8. The nightingale.

Feels no sad thoughts, nor cruciating cares
To gain more good, or shun what might thee harm
Thy cloaths ne're wear, thy meat is every where,
Thy bed a bough, thy drink the water cleer,
Reminds not what is past, nor whats to come dost fear.

28

The dawning morn with songs thou dost prevent,
Sets hundred notes unto thy feathered crew,
So each one tunes his pretty instrument,
And warbling out the old, begin anew,
And thus they pass their youth in summer season,
Then follow thee into a better Region,
Where winter's never felt by that sweet airy legion.

29

Man at the best a creature frail and vain,
In knowledg ignorant, in strength but weak,
Subject to sorrows, losses, sickness, pain,
Each storm his state, his mind, his body break,
From some of these he never finds cessation,
But day or night, within, without, vexation,
Troubles from foes, from friends, from dearest, near'st
    Relation.

30

And yet this sinfull creature, frail and vain,
This lump of wretchedness, of sin and sorrow,
This weather-beaten vessel wrackt with pain,
Joyes not in hope of an eternal morrow;
Nor all his losses, crosses and vexation,
In weight, in frequency and long duration
Can make him deeply groan for that divine
    Translation.

31

The Mariner that on smooth waves doth glide,
Sings merrily, and steers his Barque with ease,
As if he had command of wind and tide,
And now becomes great Master of the seas;
But suddenly a storm spoiles all the sport,
And makes him long for a more quiet port,
Which 'gainst all adverse winds may serve for fort.

32

So he that faileth in this world of pleasure,
Feeding on sweets, that never bit of th' sowre,
That's full of friends, of honour and of treasure,
Fond fool, he takes this earth ev'n for heav'ns bower.
But sad affliction comes & makes him see

Here's neither honour, wealth, or safety;
Only above is found all with security.

33

O Time the fatal wrack of mortal things,
That draws oblivions curtains over kings,
Their sumptuous monuments, men know them not,
Their names without a Record are forgot,
Their parts, their ports, their pomp's all laid in th' dust
Nor wit nor gold, nor buildings scape times rust;
But he whose name is grav'd in the white stone[9]
Shall last and shine when all of these are gone.

Before the Birth of One of Her Children

All things within this fading world hath end,
Adversity doth still our joyes attend;
No tyes so strong, no friends so clear and sweet,
But with deaths parting blow is sure to meet.
The sentence past is most irrevocable,
A common thing, yet oh inevitable;
How soon, my Dear, death may my steps attend,
How soon't may be thy Lot to lose thy friend,
We both are ignorant, yet love bids me
These farewell lines to recommend to thee,
That when that knot's unty'd that made us one,
I may seem thine, who in effect am none.
And if I see not half my dayes that's due,
What nature would, God grant to yours and you;
The many faults that well you know I have,
Let be interr'd in my oblivious grave;
If any worth or virtue were in me,
Let that live freshly in thy memory
And when thou feel'st no grief, as I no harms,
Yet love thy dead, who long lay in thine arms:
And when thy loss shall be repaid with gains
Look to my little babes my dear remains.
And if thou love thy self, or lov'd'st me
These O protect from step Dames injury.
And if chance to thine eyes shall bring this verse,
With some sad sighs honour my absent Herse;
And kiss this paper for thy loves dear sake,
Who with salt tears this last Farewel did take.

-----

9. Revelation 2:17: "To him that overcometh, will I give to
eat of the hidden manna, and will give him a white stone, and in
the stone a new name written, which no man knoweth saving
him that receiveth it."

In Memory of My Dear Grand-child Elizabeth Bradstreet, Who Deceased August, 1665 Being a Year and Half Old

Farewel dear babe, my hearts too much content,
Farewel sweet babe, the pleasure of mine eye,
Farewel fair flower that for a space was lent,
Then ta'en away unto Eternity.
Blest babe why should I once bewail thy fate,
Or sigh thy dayes so soon were terminate;
Sith thou art setled in an Everlasting state.

2

By nature Trees do rot when they are grown.
And Plumbs and Apples throughly ripe do fall,
And Corn and grass are in their season mown,
And time brings down what is both strong and tall.
But plants new set to be eradicate,
And buds new blown, to have so short a date,
Is by his hand alone that guides nature and fate.

HERE FOLLOWS SOME VERSES UPON THE BURNING OF OUR HOUSE JULY 10TH, 1666. COPIED OUT OF A LOOSE PAPER[1]

In silent night when rest I took
For sorrow near I did not look
I wakened was with thund'ring noise
And piteous shrieks of dreadful voice.
That fearful sound of "Fire!" and "Fire!"
Let no man know is my desire.
I, starting up, the light did spy,
And to my God my heart did cry
To strengthen me in my distress
And not to leave me succorless.
Then, coming out, beheld a space
The flame consume my dwelling place.
And when I could no longer look,

I blest His name that gave and took,
That laid my goods now in the dust.
Yea, so it was, and so 'twas just.
It was His own, it was not mine,
Far be it that I should repine;
He might of all justly bereft
But yet sufficient for us left.
When by the ruins oft I past
My sorrowing eyes aside did cast,
And here and there the places spy
Where oft I sat and long did lie:
Here stood that trunk, and there that chest,
There lay that store I counted best.
My pleasant things in ashes lie,
And them behold no more shall I.
Under thy roof no guest shall sit,
Nor at thy table eat a bit.
No pleasant tale shall e'er be told,
Nor things recounted done of old.
No candle e'er shall shine in thee,
Nor bridegroom's voice e'er heard shall be.
In silence ever shall thou lie,
Adieu, Adieu, all's vanity.
Then straight I 'gin my heart to chide,
And did thy wealth on earth abide?
Didst fix thy hope on mold'ring dust?
The arm of flesh didst make thy trust?
Raise up thy thoughts above the sky
That dunghill mists away may fly.
Thou hast an house on high erect,
Framed by that mighty Architect,
With glory richly furnished,
Stands permanent though this be fled.
It's purchased and paid for too
By Him who hath enough to do.
A price so vast as is unknown
Yet by His gift is made thine own;
There's wealth enough, I need no more,
Farewell, my pelf,[2] farewell my store.
The world no longer let me love,
My hope and treasure lies above.

---

1. First published in *Works of Anne Bradstreet,* ed. J. H. Ellis (1867).

2. Money.

LETTERS FROM NEW ENGLAND

Family members, friends, and well-wishers in England learned much about the New England colonies from letters and writings sent home by the Separatists of Plymouth and the Puritans of Massachusetts. Yet these religious peoples were not the sole interpreters of New England experiences, nor were they necessarily the most reliable witnesses of ongoing events because of their commitment to settle new religious communities in what they constantly wrote about as a "wilderness" filled with "savages." The rhetorical constructions of the religious writers were conditioned by their willingness to see in their isolated condition in New England a new version of the biblical exodus of God's chosen people into the lands where heathens dwelled, a land inhospitable to them that would test their religious mettle. In the letters of others who traveled with the Separatists and the Puritans in the 1620s and 1630s, complementary sets of experiences were recorded that had fewer markings of religious fascination with events undertaken.

The two letters that appear next were written by men who joined the communities of religious travelers but whose interests were defined by their goals of finding wealth and settling a colony for the British empire, rather than by any particular religious calling to become God's saints in a new world church of the holy. Emmanuel Altham was involved with the group of merchants, the Company of Adventurers for New Plymouth, who assisted in financing the Plymouth settlement, expecting a return of goods for trade in Europe that would bring wealth to the stockholders in the company. As Altham's relation in his letter indicates, some of the adventurers, as these financial and personal risk takers were called, grew impatient with the delays involved in settlement, and after being kept alive largely at the hands of the Separatists during the first year, they set up their own private, all-male colony at Wessagusset (present-day Weymouth, Massachusetts), expecting a rich trade with the Indians in the area. The concentration on the goods that could be wrought from the land also marks the letter of John Pond, who wrote in March 1631 to his parents back home about his arrival in Massachusetts Bay and what the country was like. As historian Richard S. Dunn has shown, Pond had arrived during a great survival crisis in Massachusetts Bay, and the ship he sailed on would take more than eighty disgruntled colonist passengers back to England. According to Pond, eighty more would have sailed for England in the ship's return, had they the wherewithal to afford the voyage. Governor John Winthrop was unhappy with the behavior of the colonists in such a crisis, and he wrote to his wife during the height of their troubles that he did not regret having come over, for he considered the sickness and mortality as God's test of the colonists' corruption. In February 1631, Winthrop had commented in his journal that "It hathe been allwayes observed here that suche as fell into discontente and lingered after their former Conditions in Englande, fell into the skirvye, and died." Pond had not reached a haven in the wilderness, and he would struggle for survival in the flegling community. Pond's letter, far from detailing the riches of what he found in the Watertown area, makes a plea for goods to be sent from England, for "here we may live if we have supplies every year from old England; otherwise, we cannot subsist." Letters like these by Altham and Pond, filled with promotional materials—and also with warnings and comments against promoting colonial settlement—serve as good vehicles for examining the full record of the writings from New England, since they comment upon turns of attitude and phrase common among more religious writers and suggest the multiple purposes behind the colonial efforts that were taking place in New England.

LETTER TO SIR EDWARD ALTHAM (1623)[1]

EMMANUEL ALTHAM

Most loving and kind brother,

My promise doth put me in remembrance, with the first opportunity of a messenger,[2] to write unto you. And if I were not by promise, yet that special nearness that is between us obliges me to the same, for as I have always to this time found your constant affections towards me, so have I, and shall continually, acknowledge the same.

And now, loving brother, since I have undertaken a voyage not altogether pleasing to some of my friends—and because of my forwardness in the same, I may be taxed with many censures—therefore, as it doth more nearly concern me, I will here lay down not what my ear hath heard, but what I have with my eyes seen to be true.

After our departure from the Cowes in the Isle of Wight, we recovered our desired passage three months and one day after, being the 5th of August, with many bitter a storm. And I have learned by this voyage that God hath made the seas more for use than pleasure, but I praise the Lord for his goodness that I never had my health better. And likewise by the blessings of God, I have and hope to learn that at sea which will prove for my extraordinary advantage. But everyone hath a time, although some sooner than others.

After our arrival in New England, we found all our plantation in good health, and neither man, woman or child sick. And here, likewise, we found the other ship set forth by the Company, who came from Portsmouth six days after us, and arrived here at New England ten days before, with all her people well—as we with our people did the like. And yet one good wife Jennings[3] was brought abed of a son aboard our ship and was very well. And then, we had an old woman in our ship about four score years of age, which was in good health—and this I speak not as needful to write of, but to show that God did give us our health when we looked not for it, and to those, likewise, that had not been well a year before on the shore.

And now to come more nearer to that I intend to write of, and first of the situation of the place—I mean the plantation at Patuxet.[4] It is well situated upon a high hill close unto the seaside, and very commodious for shipping to come unto them. In this plantation is about twenty houses, four or five of which are very fair and pleasant, and the rest (as time will serve) shall be made better. And this town is in such manner that it makes a great street between the houses, and at the upper end of the town there is a strong fort, both by nature and art, with six pieces of reasonable good artillery mounted thereon; in which fort is continual watch, so that no Indian can come near thereabouts but he is presently seen. This town is paled round about with pale of eight foot long, or thereabouts, and in the pale are three great gates. Furthermore, here is belonging to the town six goats, about fifty hogs and pigs, also divers hens. And lastly, the town is furnished with a company of honest men, that do, in what lies in them, to get profit to the adventurers.

And now to speak more at large of the country and what profit is to be raised here; and first, to speak of the fishing that is in this country. Indeed it is beyond belief, but I can assure you thus much: that if a man be well provided with all things necessary for to make a fishing voyage, he may easily make his voyage two for one. But lest this should seem incredible to some, I will give you an instance of the same. Before we got hither to Patuxet, we had many fogs at sea, insomuch that we were driven to lie at hull and to take down all our sails—and so went to fishing. In one hour we got 100 great cod, and if we would have but stayed after the fog broke up, we might quickly [have] loaded our ship—and, I am persuaded, had we been prepared with all things necessary for a fishing voy-

---

1. Emmanuel Altham (1600–35/36) was born into a mercantile family of gentry status at Latton, just north of London. Over objections of relatives, he became an investor in the Company of Adventurers for New Plymouth, serving for a time as company agent and sailing as the captain on one of the company's vessels, the *Little James,* in 1623. He admired the Separatist colonists, and he deplored the factionalism in the company that resulted in the Reverend John Clyfton's being sent to Plymouth. Yet he was an adventurer, and after working the coastal areas of New England, he set sail to return to England. He returned once more to New England, but finding his goals of securing wealth unfulfilled, joined the East India Company in 1630, as a factor and captain of a fort at Armagon (north of Madrid). He started to gain wealth in this post, but he died at Armagon before a return trip to England. The text is from *Three Visitors to Early Plymouth,* ed. S. V. James, Jr. (1963).

2. Edward Winslow, who sailed for England on the ship *Anne,* September 10, 1623. The *Anne* is the company's "other ship" mentioned later.

3. Perhaps the wife of John Jenny.

4. Patuxet is the Indians' name for the area the settlers called Plymouth.

age, we might have loaded our ship in a week. I think we got 1000 in all. And indeed, when we had nothing else to do, my people took delight to catch them, although we threw them away again, as I think we did 300. One fish we got, I think, weighed 100 pound: it was as big a cod as ever was seen. We got many turbots, likewise, and one turbot we got gave all our ship a meal and to spare. And to speak what voyages of fishing hath been found and made this year, here hath been at Monhegan, Damerill's Cove, Anquam, Pemaquid, Sagadahoc, and the Isles of Shoals[5]—all principal places for fishing—about 400 sail. And every one of them, by their confession, say that they have made good voyages, and now most of them are gone into Spain, to sell their fish where they have ready gold for it.

And now to speak what sorts of other fish are here to be had. Here are great store of sturgeon—I mean abundance; likewise great of salmon, bass, trout, eels—and lobsters such infinite that when we have them the very multitude of them cloys us. There are likewise great store of other fish which I cannot remember, as clams and oysters.

And now to speak somewhat of our store of beaver's skins that are round about us both to the norward and southward. And now at this present, we are going to the southward into Hudson's River, where the Dutchmen have all their skins of the savages. We hope there to get good store of beaver's, otter's and martin's skins, as also fox skins and raccoon skins—all which will yield money good store in England. And towards Christmas we are to return to our plantation again. And then, before the fishermen come in February to the norward, we mean to go trade for all the skins that are to be had thereabout, and then to take the best stage for fishing[6] in the country, and so to fish in the beginning of the year; and then about May, 1624, to go trading for furs again. And then it may be so, that we will come home about Christmas come twelvemonth, but look not for me before I come. Divers occasions of employments may fall out so that I may be hindered—and indeed, I shall not desire to come for England unless I bring good store of profit with me, which I make no doubt of, by God's help.

Thirdly, I will speak somewhat of the timber in the country, which will raise great profit to the Adventurers. We have here as good timber as ever I saw—of many sorts. We have here cedar, beech, pine, oak, and divers other sorts, of which we have here sent a sample of about two or three hundred pounds worth, and with it a good many beaver's skins and furs of divers sorts.

Fourthly, we will say somewhat of the sarsaparilla and sassafras—as also, alkermes berries[7]—all which are worth good store of money in England, and of which, when I come myself, God willing, I will bring a pattern to London. For when I was at London, sarsaparilla was of two shillings a pound, at the least, and we have here enough to load a ship.

Fifthly, to speak of the profit that may arise by salt—and I make no doubt we shall make much salt before I come for England. And if we could but have salt to sell to the fishing ships that come hither yearly, I think we might compare our plantation to the Spaniards' Indies. And we have good hopes of making salt about a mile from our plantation, and it shall be put in execution 'ere long.

Sixthly and lastly, here are many other things in this country to raise profit, as for example, at the place whereto we are now bound with our ship to the southward—the place is called Capawack[8]—there is a mountain of bole armeniac[9] and divers other metals. No English hath been there, but only one Captain Dermer whom was killed by the savages there;[10] for the savages in this place are very strong and are men of very able bodies. But notwithstanding, we mean to put it upon trial and to go well armed among them. We hope there to get store of skins.

---

7. Alkermes berries are actually insects that live on kerm oaks in the Mediterranean; Altham, like Captain John Smith, probably used the term to describe cranberries.

8. Present-day Martha's Vineyard, Massachusetts.

9. The term refers to an astringent earth, used as a styptic, typically found in Armenia at the time.

10. Thomas Dermer was a coastal explorer who sailed for Sir Ferdinando Gorges between Monhegan and Virginia in 1619 and 1620. In dealing with the Narragansetts (and while liberating some French mariners who had been taken captive), he seems to have created in the Narragansetts a distrust for English people. He was killed by Epenow, an Indian who had once been captive to Sir Ferdinando Gorges and who had been shown off, as a curiosity, in England.

---

5. Monhegan and Damerill's Cove (Damariscove) are islands off the coast of Maine; Pemaquid is a peninsula east of Boothbay, Maine; Sagadahoc is an extension of the Kennebec River; Anquam is probably Gloucester or Annisquam on Cape Ann, Massachusetts; the Isles of Shoals are off New Hampshire.

6. A scaffold for fishing.

And now, having spoken what is but the truth concerning the profit that may with small labor be got for the Company of Adventurers, I will now, as briefly as I can, show you what good will redound to those that live here. And first, of the fish in the country, which, as I said before, is of all sorts in infinite number; and two, for the fowl that are in the country. Here are eagles of many sorts, pigeons, innumerable turkeys, geese, swans, duck, teel, partridge divers sorts, and many others fowl, [so] that one man at six shoots hath killed 400. And then to speak of the healthfulness of the air. It lieth in 42 degrees of northerly latitude. We have here the wind come off the land all the day time, and in the night off the sea, which is wondrous wholesome. Some few have had agues at the first coming over, but not sick above a week—and myself was ill for three or four days, but I thank these good friends of mine at the plantation, I am recovered pretty well, thanks be to God. Thirdly, those that live here need never want wood, for here is great store. Four (fourthly), here is as good ground as ever I heard of, whenas the ground yield five or six hundred for one—nay, some 1400! And this year they have great store of corn—as goodly corn as ever I saw—of which I have sent you six ears. And if God will, when I come myself, you nor my worshipful friend, Sir John Leventhorpe, shall not want so much beaver's skins as will make each of you a hat. But to our purpose, I say that none of these commodities can be got without a little pains, and the most pains and cost is to be stowed at the beginning; for men must provide for the worst, that they may have provision for themselves a twelvemonth if these things fail—and then the[y] must take pains to build them houses and the like. And because I have spoken somewhat large of the country—and indeed I have good cause, because if I were well provided with all things necessary, as servants and the like, I could live here contentedly with great pleasure—but I shall better think and determine of such matters when more important business doth not call me aside.

And now I will speak somewhat of the savages in the country about—I mean the native Indians. The nearest that any dwell unto [Plymouth] is fourteen miles, and their town is called Manomet. Only without our pales dwells one Hobomok, his wives and his household (above ten persons), who is our friend and interpreter, and one whom we have found faithful and trusty.[11] He I carry away with me to the southward. And now, likewise, in this bay wherein we live, in former time hath lived about 2000 Indians. Here is not one living now, nor not one living which belonged to this plantation before we came, so that the ground on which we are planted belongs to nobody.

And now to speak of the king of the country, who is a great emperor among his people. Upon the occasion of the Governor's marriage,[12] since I came, Massasoit was sent for to the wedding, where came with him his wife, the queen, although he hath five wives. With him came four other kings and about six score men with their bows and arrows—where, when they came to our town, we saluted them with the shooting off of many muskets and training our men. And so all the bows and arrows was brought into the Governor's house, and he brought the Governor three or four bucks and a turkey. And so we had very good pastime in seeing them dance, which is in such manner, with such a noise that you would wonder. And at that time when we gave Massasoit his hat, coat, band and feather, I craved a boy of him for you, but he would not part with him; but I will bring you one hereafter.

And now to say somewhat of the great cheer we had at the Governor's marriage. We had about twelve pasty venisons, besides others, pieces of roasted venison and other such good cheer in such quantity that I could wish you some of our share. For here we have the best grapes that ever you say[13]—and the biggest, and divers sorts of plums and nuts which our business will not suffer us to look for.

And now to speak somewhat of Massasoit's stature. He is as proper a man as ever was seen in this country, and very courageous. He is very subtle for a savage, and he goes like the rest of his men, all naked but only a black wolf skin he wears upon his shoulder. And about the breadth of a span he wears beads about his middle. And these beads they make themselves, which they account as gold above silver before the beads we bring out of England.

Lastly, to speak a little in what peace and friendship we are with the savages, which peace we have had with Massasoit ever since our coming. And he never expressed his love more to us than of late; for in the Massachusetts there was a colony—I may rather say a company of idle persons, for they had no civil government among them-

---

11. Hobomok, a Wampanoag Indian from west of Plymouth, was one of the last Indians who were willing to live in proximity to English settlements. He died in 1622.

12. William Bradford married his second wife, Alice Carpenter Southworth, on August 14, 1623.

13. Saw.

selves, much less were they able to govern and rule Indians by them. And this plantation was begun about one year and one half since by one Mr. Weston,[14] who came this year to see his plantation. But by many notorious deeds among themselves, and also having in their necessity stolen corn from the Indians, the Indians began to condemn them and would have killed all the English, but they feared that when the English of Patuxet did hear what they had done, then they would set upon the squaw sachem in the Massachusetts and so kill all the Indians in the Massachusetts. Whereupon they determined another resolution: to cut the English at Patuxet, whom they stand in fear of now, and the English at Massachusetts both at one time. But in the mean time, the great Massasoit sent to Patuxet for some physic, because he was fallen very sick, and so, by God's help, he was cured. And upon his recovery, he made known the plot of the Indians of Massachusetts against us, and told us that if we would not go fight with them, he would. So at the return of our surgeon from Massasoit, came a messenger from Mr. Weston's plantation at Massachusetts, telling us that there was a plot against us by the Indians of Massachusetts. Whereupon the Governor, Mr. William Bradford (well worthy the place), sent Captain Standish with some six or seven others to the Massachusetts to bring away the head of him that made the broil. And so, by God's goodness, he killed our chief enemy and five or six others without any hurt to our part, and brought away the head of the chiefest of them.[15] And [it] is set on the top of our fort, and instead of an ancient,[16] we have a piece of linen cloth dyed in the same Indian's blood, which was hung out upon the fort when Massasoit was here. And now the Indians are most of them fled from us, but they now seek to us to make peace. But we are informed by Hobomok that eight shallops of Indians, well provided, are coming this way. They say themselves that they come to fight with other Indians

that have killed a friend of theirs, but if they come at us to offer any violence, I doubt they will never carry their shallops back again—it may be, not with their lives. And these Indians, we hear, have muskets and fowling pieces, with powder and shot, which they have bought of the Frenchmen in Canada and of the Englishmen at the Isle of Monhegan; but that trade is already stopped by the King's proclamations concerning the same trade.

And now, loving brother, I have little else to write of unto you—but only one thing I thank you kindly for, and that was for the last letter you sent me in England, wherein you desire [me] to hold fast to the truth and likewise to be diligent in my place. Of both which make no doubt—no! be persuaded that I will rather die a thousand deaths than once to shame God or my country. And now, seeing that I am entered into this place, doubt not but that I will always increase in knowledge. And indeed, when I undertook this voyage at first, I always held the art of navigation to be most hard and difficult, but now, through some practice and reading, I have attained to that I hope never to forget. And I hope by that time I see old England to be able to conduct a ship myself, safe into any harbor in New England. But God disposeth of all things. And truly, I never lived better to my content nor among those who can more respect me as the Company in old England and here likewise do, who think nothing too good for me. I praise God, I have my health 'till now that I wrote this letter—but I mended apace.

And now, loving brother, I must make an end, although I think no pains sufficient to express my love unto you. I doubt not but you will show yourself a friend to me in taking care for that little stock I have. I am desirous it should increase—and in your hands, if you think it profitable to you. I know you will deal the more providently for me, because of divers reasons well known to yourself. I pray let that same £100 be taken of my Mr. Hawes or his heirs when it is due (and that will be about March, 1624), and if you and my brother Hawtry[17] think good, take it into your own hands. I have wrote to my brother Hawtry to buy me the books of English voyages, which will do me great good. I pray look that they be bought me, and send by this messenger that is come from New England and hath lived there three years. And he comes away about December from London, that he may come with the fishermen, to be here in February. I pray let those books

---

14. Thomas Weston, a London merchant and original promoter of the Company of Adventurers for New Plymouth in 1620, desired profit from the enterprise and sent out the all-male contingent mentioned. The colony of men settled at Wessagusset (Weymouth, Massachusetts).

15. Miles Standish and his company went to the settlement to warn the settlers of the Indian conspiracy and ambushed several Indians, including Wituwamat, whose head he took back to Plymouth.

16. Flag.

---

17. Ralph Hawtry, husband of Altham's sister, Mary.

be of the same voyages that is lately put forth by Mr. Purchas, minister about Ludgate.[18]

Thus much I have thought good to let you understand
concerning the estate of myself and New England, and
now I will take my leave of you, desiring the God of hosts
to guide you and yours in your going out and coming, so
that all your labors may prosper under your hands, and
that your life in this world of misery may be such a life
that may prepare you to a better in the world to come.

And thus, my kindest love and best affections being
remembered to you, desiring you to accept of this mite
(being compared to my mind). Likewise, as I am bound to
respect, so let my love be remembered to my sister your
wife, and to my worthy friend, Sir John Leventhorpe, and
to his good lady, and all the rest of that noble house, as to
my Lady Fowle and Sir John Fowle, my brother Thomas,
and my sister Mary.[19] And I pray merrily tell her it will be
no tarrying for me because I know not when I shall come
into England. But I pray likewise tell [her] that I could
here give her much land if she will come and live among
this wild scene of Indians. I hope this will make her smile.
And now, I pray let my love be remembered to my aunt
Wolley, hoping that she will have me in her mind, although not in her eye; I mean I hope she will remember
me at her death, which must be one day. Pray remember
me likewise to Mr. Denn and his wife and old goodwife
Stracy, and to my worthy Adventurer Henry Stracy, who,
if he claims his money, let him have it, I pray you, for I
see it will come in with profit. Pray likewise remember
my love to Mr. Bland and William Watson, and pray tell
them thus much: that because a ship could not be got
when I had cattle in my hands, and likewise because I
could get nobody to join with me, I put that money into
the common stock; and it shall be answered in that,
which, if they be not contented, I will repay again. The
like, I pray, do to goodman Wells.[20] Remember me to him

and tell him I find great need of his cousin, the potter. I
pray, sir, let them read this letter—either the same or a
copy of the same—and so, likewise, I pray let my noble
friend, Sir John Leventhorpe; although I have wrote to
him, yet I refer him to particulars in your letters.

And so I take my leave of you; but I pray remember me
to my father Adee and mother Adee, and to all the rest of
my friends to whom I am by any way tied—as to Seth
Haggar and Edward Skoles, whose so long continuance
and good service in your house have caused me to speak
well of them.

And thus I end, desiring the Lord to direct you in all
your ways, words and actions, and to guide you by his
Holy Spirit and so to enable you, that in what you have
been wanting to glorify his name in this world among
men, your heart may be more and more touched with the
reverence of so great a God, and to labor more and more
to glorify him here, that so you may be glorified by him
in the world to come, where one day, if I see you not in
this world, I make no doubt but to meet you, which God,
for Christ Jesus' sake grant unto us. And so I bid you,
Farewell! Farewell in the Lord; and the God of heaven,
earth, seas and all things be with you and protect you in
your going forth and coming in. And so, being guided and
directed by God's holy angels, you may not be ashamed
to show yourself before God and the Lord Christ at that
great day of account when all things shall be made
known. And so, even from my heart and soul, I take my
leave of you and the rest of my other friends who are mentioned in my other letters. *Vale!*

I shall be glad to hear from you. In the beginning of
December, pray send your letters to Mr. Sherley's in
Crooked Lane.[21] Divers matters I could write, but only
this let me tell you: that I would entreat you to stir up a
few friends to venture four or five hundred pounds with
me when I come myself. For I then intend to make a voyage to fish, which I make no doubt but I can get two of one
in eight months. This thing I thought good to impart to
you, and do entreat you to provide such a course against I
come home, if you can.

Forth, this is a most ordinary voyage undertaken.
Thus I rest,

your most loving brother,
Emmanuel Altham.

18. Samuel Purchas, *Hakluytus Posthumus, or Purchas His
Pilgrimes* (1625), 4 vols. The books had been announced as
early as 1621.

19. The Leventhorpes, neighbors in England, were close
friends; Sir Edward Altham married one of Sir John Leventhorpe's daughters. Sir John Fowle had married another daughter. "My brother Thomas" is the son and heir of Sir John Leventhorpe; Mary Leventhorpe is another daughter.

20. Margaret Wolley listed Emmanuel Altham in her will.
Denn was rector at Latton; Stracy, a tenant on the Altham estate;
Bland, a minister and friend of the family; Watson, a London
gunsmith; Well, a tenant.

21. James Sherley, the goldsmith and treasurer of the company.

I have sent my sister Altham six ears of Indian corn and beans to sow in her garden. Also, I have sent you a tobacco pipe which I had of the Indians.

LETTER TO HIS PARENTS (1630)[1]
[JOHN] POND

Most loving and kind Father and Mother:

My humble duty [be] remembered unto you, trusting in God you are in good health. And, I pray, remember my love unto my brother Joseph, and thank him for his kindness that I found at his hand at London, which was not the value of a farthing. I know, loving father, and do confess that I was an undutiful child unto you when I lived with you and by you, for the which I am much sorrowful and grieved for it, trusting in God that He will guide me that I will never offend you so anymore; and I trust in God you will forgive me for it.

[The reason for] my writing this unto you is to let you understand what a country this New England is, where we live. Here are but few Indians; a great part of them died this winter; it was thought it was [because] of the plague. They are a crafty people, and they will cozen and cheat, and they are a subtle people. And whereas we did expect great store of beaver, here is little or none to be had; and their Sackemore John wastes it, and many of us truck with them, and it layeth us many times in eight shillings a pound. They are proper men and clean-jointed men, and many of them go naked with a skin about their loins, but now some of them get Englishmen's apparel. And the country is very rocky and hilly, and [there is] some champion ground, and the soil is very flete. And here is some good ground and marsh ground, but here is no Michael-mas.[2] Spring cattle thrive well here, but they give small store of milk. The best cattle for profit is swine, and a good swine is here at five pounds' price; a goose is worth two pounds, a good one got. Here is timber [in] good store, and acorns [in] good store; and here is good store of fish, if we had boats to go for [it] and lines to serve fishing. Here are good stores of wild fowl, but they are hard to come by. It is harder to get a shot than it is in old England. And people here are subject to disease, for here have died of the scurvy and of the burning fever nigh two hundred and odd. Besides, as many lyeth lame; and all Sudbury men are dead but three, and [some] women and some children; and provisions are here at a wonderful rate. Wheat meal is 14 shillings a bushel, and peas 10 shillings, and malt 10 shillings, and Einder seed wheat is 15 shillings, and their other wheat is 10 shillings. Butter [is] 12 pence a pound, and cheese is 8 pence a pound, and all kind of spices [are] very dear and [there are] almost none to be got.

If this ship had not come when it did, we had been put to a wonderful strait, but thanks be to God for sending of it in. I received from the ship a hogshead of meal, and the Governor telleth me of a hundred-weight of cheese, the which I have received part of it. I humbly thank you for it. I did expect two cows, the which I had none; nor I do not earnestly desire that you should send me any, because the country is not so [suitable] as we did expect it. Therefore, loving father, I would entreat you that you would send me a firkin of butter and a hogshead of malt unground, for we drink nothing but water; and a coarse cloth of four pounds price, so it [will] be thick. [As] for the freight, if you of your love will send them I will pay the freight. For here is nothing to be got without we had commodities to go up to the East parts amongst the Indians to truck; for here where we live, here is no beaver. Here is no cloth to be had to make no apparel; and shoes are at five shillings a pair for me; and that cloth that is worth two shillings [and] eight pence a yard is worth here five shillings. So I pray, father, send me four or five yards of cloth to make us some apparel. And, loving father, though I be far distant from you, yet I pray you remember me as your child. And we do not know how long we may subsist, for we cannot live here without provisions from old England. Therefore, I pray, do not put away your shop stuff, for I think that in the end, if I live, it must be my living. For we do not know

---

1. John Pond and his family arrived in Massachusetts Bay in February 1630/31, having sailed in the *Lyon,* a ship that brought supplies ordered by the colony Governor John Winthrop, along with Pond and about twenty other passengers. The family settled in Watertown, among a community of settlers who were disgruntled about the lack of representation in government. Pond's letter—headed with the instruction "To my loving father William Pond, at Etherston in Suffolk, give this"—probably went back with an acquaintance or a bundle of letters on the *Lyon,* which took back to England over eighty persons who did not wish to stay in the troubled colony. The text is from *Proceedings of the Massachusetts Historical Society,* Second Series, vol. 7 (1892–94).

2. Michaelmas is a feast typically held on September 29, in honor of archangel Michael (Michael's mass).

how long this plantation will stand, for some of the magnates that did uphold it have turned off their men and have given it over. Besides, God hath taken away the chiefest stud in the land, Mr. Johnson, and the lady Arabella, his wife, which was the chiefest man of estate in the land and one that would have done most good.[3]

Here came over 25 passengers, and there came back again four score and odd persons; and as many more would have come if they had where-withal to bring them home. For here are many that came over last year, which was worth two hundred pounds before they came out of old England, that between this [time] and Michaelmas will hardly be worth 30 pounds. So here we may live if we have supplies every year from old England; otherwise we cannot subsist. I may, as I will, work hard, set an acre of Einder wheat; and if we do not set it with fish (and that

---

3. Isaac Johnson and his wife, Arbella, variously called "the Lady Arrabella" or "the Lady Arbella," were the wealthiest of the first emigrants to Massachusetts Bay in 1630. Arbella Johnson, the daughter of the earl of Lincoln, came from the aristocracy. The flagship (on which John Winthrop had delivered his lay sermon, "A Model of Christian Charity") was named in her honor. Both she and her husband died within a month of the landing.

will cost 20 shillings), if we set it without fish, they shall have but a poor crop. So, father, I pray, consider of my case; for here will be but a very poor being—no being—without, loving father, your help with provisions from old England. I had thought to have come home in this ship, for my provisions were almost all spent; but [you should know] that I humbly thank you for your great love and kindness in sending me some provisions, or else I should and might have been half famished. But now I will—if it please God that I have my health—I will plant what corn I can; and if provisions be not cheaper between this [time] and Michaelmas, and [assuming] that I do not hear from you what I was best [advised] to do, I purpose to come home at Michaelmas.

My wife remembers her humble duty unto you and to my mother; and my love to my brother Joseph and to Sarah Myler. Thus I leave you to the protection of the Almighty God.

From Watertown in New England,
the 15 of March, 1630.
[no signature]

We were wonderful sick, as we came at sea, with the small pox. No man thought that I and my little child would have lived. My boy is lame and my girl too, and there died in the ship that I came in 14 persons.

EDWARD TAYLOR (1642?–1729)

Relatively little is known about Edward Taylor's life, particularly his youth in England. Taylor was born into a farming family in Leicestershire, England. Taylor's writings mention two brothers and a strictly religious mother. He might have studied at Cambridge for some period, beginning preparations for the ministry. Evidence suggests that in 1668, Taylor was dismissed from teaching school for refusing to sign a loyalty oath. Such dismissals were common occurrences for Puritans, and so it is to be assumed that he was engaged in Nonconformist practices antithetical to remaining in England. Taylor emigrated that year to New England, where he quickly enrolled at Harvard and was admitted with advanced standing. While there, he shared a room with Samuel Sewell, who remained a lifelong friend.

Taylor graduated from Harvard in 1671 and became the minister at Westfield, Massachusetts, where he would remain pastor for the rest of his life. The call to serve in Westfield, a border town in a less settled area, evidently caused Taylor some concern about isolation because he copied into his own manuscripts several books from the Harvard College library. In 1674, he married Elizabeth Fitch, a minister's daughter, with whom he had eight children, only three of whom survived to adulthood. During the English and Indian conflicts known then as King Philip's War (for the Wampanoag leader, Metacom, whom the colonists called "King Philip") between 1674 and 1676, Taylor, like others in Westfield, refused to retreat from their border-area community. With other town leaders, Taylor wrote a letter justifying the community's decision to remain in the area, addressing the concerns raised by leaders of churches and

militia in townships that called for their retreat. Instead of withdrawing, the town of Westfield pulled together as a community and created a stronghold according to guidelines set down by the General Court
of Massachusetts.

Taylor served as a minister for more than fifty years, during which time he must have preached hundreds of sermons. Among his surviving manuscripts are over sixty sermons. The corpus of sermonic prose
is accompanied by an extensive number of poems that worked through complementary themes and indeed
the same books of the Bible referenced in his sermons. Taylor's literary reputation during the twentieth
century was built on his extensive poetic productions—over four hundred manuscript pages of verse,
largely religious and sometimes personal as well—but his sermons are remarkable for their linguistic and
philosophical complexity and their sometimes twisted, sometimes lyrical turns.

Among the most important of Taylor's poetical works is *Gods Determinations,* probably written in the
early 1680s, a series of poems in the form of a dialogue among several parties—the human soul, God,
Christ, and Satan—that dramatizes God's various methods of bringing the elect church to salvation. Beginning in 1682, Taylor began writing two series of "Sacramental" or "Preparatory" meditations, poems
in a contemplative mood based on specific biblical texts. According to Taylor's description of these
poems, they were written as part of his preparation for his duties in delivering communion to his parishioners. Examination of the evidence reveals that Taylor wrote the Meditations at the time he was preparing his sermons, and the Meditations employ the same texts as the sermons he would preach. Taylor's life
was not without its personal concerns. Elizabeth Fitch Taylor, his much loved wife, died in 1689. He remarried in 1692 and he had six more children from this second marriage.

Taylor did not publish his poems during his lifetime, although two stanzas of his elegy for his first wife
appeared in the London printing of one of Cotton Mather's sermons. Although he probably circulated his
manuscripts among his closest friends, Taylor was disinclined to gain a reputation by his writings, prose
or poetic, and so he did not publish his voluminous writings in his own day and requested that his heirs
not publish his poems. As a result, the poetry was known only to those who had contact with the manuscripts until the twentieth century. Yet Taylor's poems are richly indicative of a temperament and an inclination to writing, and their very number reveals Taylor's preoccupation with language, both spoken and
written, and with the individual's having a significant emotional response to religious experience. In their
content, Taylor's Meditations reflect important questions of Puritan theology. In style, they reflect the
metaphysical school of poetry associated with British poet John Donne, in which widely disparate images
are often linked for surprising linguistic and thematic incongruity that can expose complicated insight. In
addition to these major poetic achievements in religion and philosophy, Taylor wrote a number of elegies
and other poems for specific occasions. In the early part of the eighteenth century, he wrote a long verse
history of Christianity. He continued writing preparatory meditations and other religious poetry until just
a few years before his death.

The following selections present one of Taylor's Meditations (number 44), along with his sermon addressing the same text. In addition, the selections offer a number of Taylor's poems that were highly appreciated during the twentieth century. Taylor presents an interesting case study in the shifting evaluations
of early American writers over time. Although his contemporaries probably knew him best as a faithful
shepherd of his church, an able leader in times of crisis, and an interesting and imaginative preacher of
God's work, Taylor's large body of poems are what garnered critical favor in the twentieth century, after
Thomas Johnson and then Donald Stanford presented much of Taylor's work in print for the first time.
Since that time, Taylor has been celebrated as one of early America's most prolific and creative poets, even
though he most likely wrote and was read by only a small and local audience during his lifetime.

from CHRISTOGRAPHIA

Meditation 44[1]

Joh. 1. 14. The word was made Flesh.

The Orator from Rhetorick gardens picks
    His Spangled Flowers of sweet-breathd Eloquence
Wherewith his Oratory brisk he tricks
    Whose Spicy Charms Eare jewells do commence.
    Shall bits of Brains be candid thus for eares?
    My Theme claims Sugar Candid far more cleare.

Things Styld Transcendent do transcende the Stile
    Of Reason, reason's stares neere reach so high.
But Jacob's golden Ladder rounds do foile
    All reasons Strides, wrought of THEANTHROPIE.
    Two Natures distance-standing, infinite,
    Are Onifide, in person, and Unite.

In Essence two, in Properties each are
    Unlike, as unlike can be. One All-Might,
A Mite the other; One Immortall fair:
    One mortall, this all Glory, that all night:
    One Infinite, One finite. So forever:
    Yet ONED are in Person. part'd never.

The Godhead personated in Gods Son
    Assum'd the Manhood to its Person known,
When that the Manhoods essence first begun
    That it did never Humane person own.
    Each natures Essence e're abides the same.
    In person joynd, one person each do claim.

Oh! Dignifide Humanity indeed:
    Divinely person'd, almost Deifide.
Nameing one Godhead person, in our Creed,
    The Word-made-Flesh. Here's Grace's 'maizing
stride.
    The vilst design, that villany e're hatcht
    Hath tap't Such Grace in God, that can't be matcht.

Our Nature Spoild: under all Curses groans,
    Is purg'd, tooke, grac'd with grace, united to
A Godhead person, Godhead-person owns.
    Its only person. Angells Lord its so.
    This Union ever lasts, if not relate

Which Cov'nant claims Christs Manhood, Sepa-
rate.
You Holy Angell, Morning-Stars, bright Sparks,
    Give place: and lower your top gallants. Shew
Your top-saile Conjues to our slender barkes:
    The highest honour to our nature's due.
    Its neerer Godhead by the Godhead made
    Than yours in you that never from God stray'd.

Here is good anchor hold: and argument
    To anchor here: Lord, make my Anchor stronge
And Cable, both of holy geer, out sent
    And in this anch'ring dropt and let at length.
    My bark shall Safely ride then tho' there fall
    On't th'strongest tempests hell can raise of all.

Unite my Soule, Lord, to thyselfe, and stamp
    Thy holy print on my unholy heart.
I'st nimble be when thou destroyst my cramp
    And take thy paths when thou dost take my part
    If thou wilt blow this Oaten Straw of mine,
    The sweetest piped praises Shall be thine.

---

from Sermon III[1]

John 1. 14. The Word was made flesh, etc.

We have Considered, and made out, that Our Redeemer is God: Hath a Divine Nature. And also that he is Man, and hath a Humane Nature. And now I am come to Consider the Union of these two Natures together in our Redeemer, and that it is a Personall Union: for that end I have fixt upon this portion of Scripture. Wherein we are to Consider 1. The Subject, or Person Spoken of, viz, the Word; i, e, not a Word Spoken: nor any Written. But, the Person of the Son of God So called, as in ver. 1. he is described to bee God: as thus the Word was God: and in our text the Son of God thus, the Word was made flesh—and we beheld his Glory, as the glory of the onely begotten Son. Hence the Onely begotten Son of God, who is God, is the Person Spoken of here. Now he is call'd the word, from

---

1. This meditation is dated December 1701 in Taylor's manuscript book, *Poetical Works.* It was first published in *Edward Taylor's Christographia,* ed. Norman S. Grabo (1962), from which the present text is taken.

1. This sermon is dated December 1701 in the manuscript book, *Christographia, or a Discourse touching Christ's Person, Natures, Qualifications, and Operations Opened, Confirmed, and Practically improoved in Several Sermons delivered upon Certain Sacrament Days unto the Church and people of God in Westfield.* It was first published in *Edward Taylor's Christographia,* ed. Norman S. Grabo (1962), from which the present text is taken.

the propheticall office that he attended: for as a word is the Conception of the minde, and being Spoken declares the minde to others: So Christ being Conceived in the Fathers minde comes forth of the Fathers bosom, and declares what is the minde of the Father unto others, i, e, unto the Children of men.

2. That which is Spoken of this person, and this describes him thus. Was made flesh. Not that the Divine Nature was made humane Nature: this was impossible. But that God, i, e, the Divine Nature, was born of man, i, e, assumed the nature of man, and was united to it, and in union with it in its birth: was made Flesh. By Flesh here we are not to understand with Apolinarius of Laodicea,[2] Simple flesh without the Soule, for he from this place saith: Christ took not a living Soule that had a Minde, and Reason, but flesh without a minde and without Reason, i, e, without a rationall Soule. But we are by a Synecdoche to understand the Whole by the part; the perfect humane Nature, and hence it was the Humane Nature thats intended thereby: as the Scripture uses to name Flesh and Soule or Spirit for the man compound. The word was made Flesh. It remaining Still what it was was made what it was not, i, e, It received flesh, as Heb. 2. 14. 16: took upon him the Seed of Abraham. Now it is said The Word was made Flesh to import that the Humane Nature was So joyned unto the Divine that neerer to Godhead nature it was impossible for Created nature to be advanced, and that the Godhead was so joyned to the Manhood, that it was impossible for Increated nature neerer to approach, and that their Union was Such, as in all true Predication, there is a right appropriation of the Properties of one nature to the other in the Person: and of Either to the person. And hence it must needs be a personall Union that is here intended, in saying, that the Word was made Flesh. For altho' it doth not import, that Christs Flesh was made of Godhead, nor that his Godhead was turned into Flesh; yet it notes that the Union was Such, as did rightly according to the Law of Right reason, argue the Properties of both natures were[3] properly the persons; and the Properties of the Person unto both natures; as firmly, and undeniably, as the Union between the Soule, and the Body, confers the

Properties of both unto the person, and of the Person to both. And hence I lay down from these words this Conclusion,

Doctrine. That the Divine Nature, and the Humane are Personally United in Christ. Or, that the Union between them is a personall Union.

The Word was made flesh. Hence Christ is called Immanuel, God with us Isai. 7. 14. Matt. 1. 23. And he is said to take part of them, i, e, Flesh, and blood, i, e, Manhood: to take upon him the Form of a Servant, Phili. 2. 7. To be an Holy thing Lu. 2. 35, and that God was manifested in the Flesh 1 Tim. 3. 16. etc. All which terms importing an Union between the two Natures in Christ, between the taking, and the taken Nature: and there being none other Union constituted by the act uniting, but a Personall Union, it must needs be a personall Union that is intended by these Scriptures. In my Speaking to this truth, I shall not Stande to shew what a person is; but shall do these things following:

First. What is this Personall Union of these two Natures?
Solution: It is a joyning of the Godhead, and the Manhood so together into an Oneness in the Person of Christ, as that they remain essentially the Same in Nature, united inseparably forever.

Here to proceed regularly we may consider

1. Something of the Name of the thing described, and this is Union, or making One of two or of more. *Unio* of UNUS, or ἕνωσις: it properly notes that act whereby things are united and made one. And hence there are Many kinds of Unions,

of which I may say they are $\begin{cases} \text{Physicall.} \\ \text{Not Physicall.} \end{cases}$

A Physicall is that whereby the Essentiall Parts of things are joyned together, that are endowed with animation as the Matter, and Form of Animal Nature. So the uniting of Soul and Body together makes the living Creatures Being: But this is not the Union that I am Concernd with here.

A Union, Not-Physicall, and this is either $\begin{cases} \text{Artificiall.} \\ \text{Not} \\ \text{Artificiall.} \end{cases}$

Artificiall. And this is that Union that joyns things together according to the Rules of any Art, whether Liberall as in Grammar by Grammar Rules; or in Rhetorick according to the Rules of Rhetorick, or in Logick, according to the Rules of right Reasoning, etc., but this Union our

---

2. Apollinaris the Younger of Laodicea (300?–390?) was associated with a group of early Christians who were branded heretics.

3. One illegible word in the manuscript.

Case is not affected with. Or else Mechanicall, and this Union is altogether by Contact as in raising a building, glewing a box, or Sewing a Glove, etc., but this affects not our case. Or else by Mixture, as in Salves, and Medicine, but Still this is far from our Case. Then

A Union Not Artificiall. Now this Union is Such a Uniting of things together as makes no essentiall alteration in the things thus United, but Constitutes a Speciall Relation between them. And this Sort of Union is either Common as in a Civill Covenant, and Marriage Compacts: or Supernaturall, as to the Institution of it, which is either Visible as our Solemn, and Visible Covenanting with God, according to Rules of the Covenant of Grace, and this is our Visible joyning With God in Covenant: Or it is Invisible, which is either Universall to all the Members of the Body of Christ Mysticall, and so it is a Mysticall Union, and it is that whereby Every Child of God is Savingly joyned to Christ in his Regeneration, and so a Christ like Spirit, and Disposition is comon to all these. 1 Cor. 6. 17. He that is joyned to the Lord is one Spirit. Yet this is not the Union I am Speaking to. But as there is a Union Common to all Members Mysticall: So there is an Union of our nature Speciall to the Head, and this is this Personall Union, whereby the two Natures in our Lord Christ are joyned together, and thus much touching the Name Union.

2. Something touching the thing, or Nature of this Personall Union of Christs Natures. And here I say

1. It is a joyning of them together. All Union being a making One of Severall, lyeth in joyning things together. Our Lord Styles marriage Union a joyning together. Matth. 19. 5. So the Mysticall Union is a joyning the Soule and Christ together. 1 Cor. 6. 17. and So this Personall Union, is a joyning the Godhead, and Manhood together.

2. Its Such a joyning them together as doth not make any essentiall alteration in the Natures joyned together, and herein it hath the property of all Sorts of Morall Unions, and so belongs in some Sort to that head of Unions. Hence tho' the Godhead σαρκωθεῖσα is made flesh, or fleshed οὐκ 'επιοτρεφθεῖσα εἰ σάρκα, it is not turned into flesh, and tho' the Manhood is united to the Word it is not made λόγος the Word. They are not changed in their Natures. The Godhead is Godhead Still, and hath all Godhead properties Still, and as to its essence onely Godhead properties. The Manhood remains Manhood Still, and hath all Manhood properties Still: and as to its essence onely Manhood properties inhering, and hence the Spirit of God as properly calls him, the Man

Christ Jesus 1 Tim. 2. 5, as he doth, God blessed forever. Rom. 9. 5.

3. This joyning of these two Natures is made primarily in the Person of the Son. It is not made between the Natures primarily, and then with the Person, for so great absurdities would follow: as that the Godhead did assume the Nature, and not the person: and that the Personality did result out of the Union of the Natures together, as the Effect or Consequent thereof, as mans personality flows from the union of Soule, and body together, whereas Christ was the Son of God, and so the Second person in the trinity before the world was. Further it would not then be a personall Union, but a Divine Union. But the Scripture all along makes it a personall Union, in ascribing the act of assuming the manhood to the person of the Son. He took upon him the form of a Servant. He took part, and he took upon him the Seed of Abraham. In our text the Word, i, e, the Person of the Son, was united to the Flesh. So the fulness of the Godhead dwelt in him, etc.; and in that its said, that God was manifested in the Flesh; it notes onely the Godhead of Christs person appeared in the Manhood of his person; nay and still if the Union was firstly in the Natures, and by that to the Person, it would be common to all the Persons, as the Godhead is, and then firstly to the Father, then to the person of the Son: and then to the Holy Ghost, whereas there is no Such thing to be found. The Father, and the Holy Ghost never had this Union to Manhood. So that its evident, that this Union of Godhead, and Manhood was made in the Person of the Son. Our Nature in the Assumption of it by the Sons person, was united to his person, and so to his Godhead in the person. Further it is not easily mentaind, that if the Union be made in the Natures first, and properly (as this Union is proper) that the Union is τουνθέτως not by way of Composition, or by Mistion. For I know no Union of Natures, that are not personall, but is by Composition, or Mixing together, unless it be purely artificiall. But to go on, this is indeed properly Personall, and there the Manhood is first United to the person: and then to the Godhead in the Person. Hence is a Personall Union.

4. This joyning of the Natures together in the Person is Such as Constitutes a Unity between them thereby, which is *aliquid tertium*[4] resulting out of the Union, as an undeniable Consequent, or effect of the Same, and this is something that by this Union is made Common to both Natures. This must be granted; otherwise there was no

---

4. "A third person."

need of this Union. But we see a necessity of this Union in order to the Work of Redemption, which according to divine Ordination, could not be effected any other way, and this thing that results out of this Union is the Fitness of his Person for his Worke as a Redeemer. There was a necessity upon the person, that should redeem the Elect, that he should be fitted, for his worke, and hence must be like his brethren in all things, Sin and the *modus Subsistendi,*[5] only excepted Heb. 2. 17. Such an High Priest becomes[6] that is holy etc. and Higher than the Heavens. C. 7. 25. So for this end serves Heb. 2. 12. Now this fitness is the thing which both are made one in: and is Comon to both, with all those necessary Conclusions touching the Same. And here I shall mention some few things, as follow:

1. The Person of the Son is Really the person of both Natures. As the Person of a man, is the person as well of the body, as of the Soule: So the Person of the Son of God is as well the Person of his Humane Nature, yet not personating it, hath no proper person properly as the person of the Divine. The Manhood hath as true, and as Reall a Right, and Propriety in it, as the Godhead hath. It ever was the person of his Godhead: and his Manhood never had any other person but this. Hence he is as frequently Styled the Son of man, as the Son of God. So that the Person is Really the person of both Natures. As truly the person of his manhood by propriety as of his Godhead. Yet the manhood hath no hand in the Constituting the Person nor any proper person of its own: but hath a true propriety in and Sustentation by the person of the Son of God.

2. That the Properties of both Natures are equally the properties of the Person. The Humane nature doth as much confer its properties to the person, as the Divine, and confers its usefulness thereto as the Divine doth its. Hence Christ is as truely Flesh, as Spirit: as properly Mortall as Immortall. No more rightly stiled God, than Man; Infinite than finite; Almighty, than Weake; Unchangeable, than changable; Omniscient, than nescient; Omnipresent, than confined, etc.

3. That the Fitness of the Person for his Office doth as really result from the One Nature as from the other.

4. That the Properties, and Actions of the Person are rightly applied to either of the Natures; tho' their inherence be but in one nature yet it may rightly be predicated of the other, because it is especially the persons propriety in which the Natures are united. Hence tho' to dy or to lay down blood is peculiarly proper onely to the Humane Nature, yet it being performed by the person of the Divine Nature it is appropriated to the Godhead Acts 20. 28, the Church of God which he hath purchased with his own blood.

5. A Communication of Influences from each nature to each nature answerable unto the Speciall Worke that is to be carried on proper thereto, by the person. Here is the offices of Prophet, Priest, and King to be Carried on in the Humane Nature, as peculiarly Proper to it. Yet all above the power thereof. And therefore necessary thereunto, is a Communication of Influences from the Divine Nature to it, or Light, Grace, Dignity, and Power of a Spirituall, and Sanctifying Nature, else the works carried on by the Person of this Sort will be ineffectuall. There is also the Efficaciousness of all the Offices of Christ to be attended on: but I will instance peculiarly in his interceding with the Father, which is the Worke more especially of the Divine Nature. But now Relitive influences of Propriety arising from the Humane are necessary thereunto, or else these Office acts, and Entercession of the Person will be exclusive of the Manhood from anything therein, or from any right in those workes that are peculiarly effected by the efficiency of the Godhead in the Person. But as to the Godhead absolutely considerd: altho' it wants not anything of the Manhood, yet here in the mediatory work of the Person it is always to be considered as acting joyntly with the whole of the Mediator and so as in relation to the Manhood. Now this Union that the Natures Stand in as made in the person of Christ, is thus a means comunicative of Such influences. And on this account the Communications from the Divine unto the Humane is Wonderfull: and beyond all Conception. Hence it pleased the Father, that in him Should all fulness dwell. Col: 1. 19, yea, the fulness of the Godhead bodily C. 2. 9.

6. It Constitutes a mutuall Propriety that each Nature hath one in the other. So that this individuall Manhood of Christ is the Manhood of Christs Godhead: and the Personated Godhead of Christ is, (as Such) especially the Godhead of Christs Manhood. These by this Union have a Speciall propriety in one another that neither the Godhead in any other Persons, nor the Manhood in any other individuall, can lay claim unto.

5. These two Natures in this union thus joyned together remain so inseparably, and forever. They are not onely uncompounded, and also Unaltered: but also not to be Divided, to make two persons, not to be Separated forever. Now I am to Consider them as abiding thus United forever, and for this take that one Scripture Heb. 13. 8:

---

5. "Manner of being."

6. One illegible word in the manuscript.

Jesus Christ the Same, yesterday, and today, and forever. Rev. 1. 4. But that these two natures shall remain thus United together forever, I thus evince.

1. Because the things United are of an Eternall duration. As for the Godhead, and the Person of Christ they are Eternall Rom. 9. 5, Who is God blessed forever, and also the Manhood of Christ is so too: for tho' it had a beginning it never shall have an end. For Such is the property of all Rationall Nature: Hence some shall enjoy Everlasting life, and some go to eternall torment. Matt. 25. 46. Christs Manhood then cannot be excepted: but must needs be Eternall much more than any. Now Such Natures as are of an Everlasting duration, when they are united together ever remain united, as the Soule, and body, and we have not another instance, below the Angells: and their Natures Consisting of *forma* and *formatum,* abide forever. And so also are the Natures united in the person of the Lord Christ.

2. Because the Humane Nature in the Person of Christ is the Head of the Church. Eph. 1. 20. 21. 22. The Father raised him from the Dead (Hence it is the Manhood of Christ thus advanced) and set him [at] his own right hand in heavenly places (and there he is to abide till the restitution of all things Act. 3. 21) far above all principalities and Powers, and Might, and Dominion, and every name that is named not onely in this World but in that to come— and hath given him to bee head over all things to the Church which is his body. So Col. 1. 18. He is the head of the body, the Church. Now this headship being the Headship of the Son, it is enjoyed in the person of the Son. For it is too great a matter for any mere man whatever to be head in: Head of the Body of Christ, i, e, the Church. It is too much for any Angell in Heaven. Christ now is mannaging this Headship, and will do it forever. 1 Thess. 4. *ult.* We Shall ever be with the Lord. Joh. 17. 24 and ever be his Body. He is the Head of the Church in an absolute sense, not with a limited duration: but to all eternity. Of his Kingdome there shall be no end Lu. 1. 33. Dan. 7. 14. Now when he shall carry on immediately this Kingdom, it is not in this world as Joh. 18. 36. Mat. 20. 21. 23. Hence then Christs Kingdom remains to be managed in Glory Matt. 25. 41. Come (saith he at the day of judgment to his subjects) inherit the Kingdome prepared for you. But now if the Union between the Godhead, and the Manhood in the Person of Christ be dissolved, then Christs Headship remains onely with the Godhead in the Person, and the Manhood that fitted the person for his Office work, and was with the Godhead invested with this Headship; is now deprived of it in the most glorious part of it, and the Church also will be without any head in its own nature. Now this Seems most absurd to imagine, and its altogether unlikly, that the Manhood that was placed in this Headship, and carried on the Satisfactory part of the Work, and the Suffering Service thereof, Should be deposed from the reigning Glory of this Headship. Nay further if the Union be dissolved to the deposing the Humane Nature from the Headship; the Headship, not onely of the Manhood, but of the Person, will likewise Cease. For the Humanity is necessary to the Headship: without it the Person hath onely a Godhead Sovereignity, and not so properly a relative Headship. But now to avoid such things, it is cleare that the Union in the person is eternall.

3. Because the Relation Constituted between Christ and his Church shall never cease. This will not be denied by any reason. Relats are eternall. Hence the Sort of Relation also remains. If a Son ever a Son. If a Servant of God by grace ever Such. If a Sinner, tho' this ought not to be, and therefore grace takes place to the Conquering and pardening Sin in the Elect, yet the Relation between the person, and his Sin remains; the denying of Peter, claims Peter for its author, and Peter cannot deny but that denyall was his Sin. But now if this Personall Union of the Natures in Christ, bee not eternall there will be an Evacuating, and an abolishing of Relation, constituted hereby between Christ, and his Church. For the Relation between Christ, the Head of it, and his Humane Nature, is destroyed. Further, the Naturall Relation between Christ and it, is destroyed. For there is not onely a Mysticall Relation between Christ, and his Church but also a Naturall, by this personall Union. The Spirit of God tells us Eph. 5. 30, that we are members of his Body, of his Flesh, and of his Bones. His Manhood is of our Manhood. He was as concerning the flesh of the Fathers. Rom. 9. 5, took upon him the Seed of Abraham. Heb. 2. 16: etc. Had not another Humane Nature made as Adams was, but it was of our Flesh; He is our גּוֹאֵל neer kinsman: so that there is a naturall relation between his Manhood, and Ours; and hence so long as his Humane Nature remains in personall Union to the Divine, there is this Naturall relation between Christ, and his Church. But if the Union should cease, then this relation also would cease. But Seing Relation to Christ shall not cease this Union shall not cease.

4. *Ab absurdis.* I argue the eternity of the Union, from the absurdities on the Contrary. That Doctrine is false, that cannot bee without the being of absurdities. For truth hath no absurdity in its hand. But here are many absurdities follow upon the Conclusion that the Personall Union of the Natures in Christ shall ever Cease. For resolve this

without absurdities if you can; What must become of Christs Manhood, or Humane Nature? . . .

Now an example ought to be perfect, and compleate. For wherein anything is not so it is not examplary. Hence saith Paul. 1 Cor. 11. 1: Follow me as I follow Christ, and therefore Christ is a perfect Example for all to live up unto. But whence should Christ be thus accomplisht for this exemplariness? But from his Godhead in personall Union with his Manhood? His life is the life of his person: his person led Such a life. The Godhead of his person acted the life of the Manhood of his person, fully, and Compleatly, internally, and externally, according to the minde of the Godhead. For it was and is impossible that his person should erre, in the least tittle. As the Rationall Soule in the body of man, acts the Sensitive body to live a rationall life, by means of its personall Union to it: So doth the Godhead of Christ act the Manhood of Christ by reason of its personall Union thereunto into a Divine and Godlike life in all things, and that compleatly, and that tho' the Union of the Soul and body be Physicall, and this rather as a Morall Union, yet it serves to explain this in some Sense. For the Influences and intimacie of the Godhead in the manhood is transendently more than that of the Soule is in the Body. And hence Christs examplariness in holiness, and living up to the minde of God is absolute, and perfect every way and in all things. Its impossible to have an higher Patern.

USE. 2. By way of Conviction, and Reproofe. Is it thus That the Humane, and the Divine Natures are united together in the Person of Christ? that both have one Person? then this convicteth some of Greate [evill] as

all Such as erre in $\begin{cases} \text{Doctrine.} \\ \text{Practice.} \end{cases}$

First. Some there are and ever have been whose Doctrine is not Consistent with, but destructive to, the Doctrine of Christs Personall Union in these two Natures, and these Some are ancient as the Arians, who denied Christ Godhead, the Apollinarians etc. who denied the reality of Christs Manhood in denying that he had a rationall Soule, and the Nestorians that asserted Christ to have a Humane Person, as well as a Divine, etc.: Now these that so assert, assert things inconsistent with this personall Union, and so oppose, and reject all the Grace of God containd therein, and that can be come at none other way, and hence overthrow all the Effect of this Holy Union, and render Christ an insufficient, and so an uncomfortable Saviour: nay, a Cheate. For if he be not Sufficient for his Work he is no Saviour: but will deceive all that rely upon

him or trust to him. Yea, and they rob Humane Nature of the highest Honour, and Glory that God ever Conferd upon it. Even Personall Union to the Godhead in his Son, and ought not Such as these to be rebuked that thus destroy the Workes,—nay the most Gracious, and Wisest Works of God?

But there are others that are of later date than these, nay that are but of yesterday, that harm this truth, as the Quakers etc. that Slight and Despise the Lord Christ, Stiling him a Carnal Christ, and what can the man that Sufferd at Jerusalem do for you? Look for a Christ within, and thus denying the onely Lord that bought them as Jude hath it. They put contempt upon that Individuall Manhood that is made Head of Angells, and the object of the Greatest Loves, Honour, and Design, and the Subject of the Greatest Glory, Preferment, Authority, and Concern, that ever any Creature was advanced to, or betrusted withall by God. Oh! these blasphemous mouths, and Wicked tongues act more to the Dishonour of God, and Christ, and the intrest of Grace, than ever the Pagan world did, who cast it in the teeth of Christians, for worshiping a Crucified God. Is that very man that was born of the Virgin Mary, that wrought miracles at Jerusalem, that preached the Gospell of Salvation: and that Sent it to the Gentiles, and was Crucified at Jerusalem, united to Godhead in the Person of the Son of God, to be Slighted and vilified by thy blasphemous tongues? God will confound all Such vilanous proceeding ere long.

Secondly. This Doctrine comes with rebuke to all Such as erre in Practice. This Union hath fitted Christ for, and hath brought him out with, the greatest examplariness of holy Living which is, as wholy living up to the minde of God. And dost thou profess Christ? then thou oughtest to walk as he walked 1 Joh. 2. 6, and is it thus that thou comest not up to imitate this example? wilt thou leave this so perfect and divine a Copy? dost thou run to other courses? and follow other things and such that this Example leads thee from? This is the best Example that can be: it is a Coppy written by the pen of perfect Manhood, in the Unerring hand of Godhead, in Christ and wilt thou not endeavour to Write by this Coppy? Consider what thou dost. Dost live a Sinfull Life? In Sensuality? in Pride? In Covetousness? In Unrighteousness? In Oppression? in Drunkeness? In Uncleaness? In Envy? In Lying? In Swearing? In Disorder? In Prophaness? In Blasphemie? In Scholding? In Discontent? etc.: oh! Consider it, did the Influences of the Godhead upon the Manhood of Christ run forth into Such a Life? Did Christ shew any instance of Such a Life? Is it not then a Discredit to this high Union in the Person of Christ, to live Such a life? It holds out that either thou hast nothing to do with Christ: no Saving intrest in him, nor Relation to him: and then thy State is woefull, and Damnable, or that Such a life is not unbeseeming this Personall Union. That this personall Union convayes no Influences inconsistent with a Sinfull Life: or that a Sinfull Life, is not unanswerable to a life of God, and this is Utterly false: a discredit to, and disgracing of both the Personall Union of Christ's natures: and the Mysticall Union unto Christ's Person, and hence our Doctrine Reprooves all that live not answerably to this Personall Union of Godhead, and Manhood in Christ.

USE 3. By way of Exhortation. Is the Godhead and the Manhood United personally together in Christ Jesus? This Use then let us make of this truth.

First, in Generall, all of us joyntly, and as one man

1. To Meditate, admire, and affectionatly to Adore God on the account of this Union. It is wonderfull; it is the greatest Mystery in all the Creation of God. It is the Wonderfullst advancement given to our Nature that created nature is, or Can be capable of: it lifts it up almost into Deity itselfe. It makes it partaker of Divine Efficiency, partaker in Divine Honour, and a Partner also of Divine Adoration. All men are [bound] to worship the Son, as they Worship the father Joh. 2. 23. Heb. 1. 6. Let all the Angells of God worship him. It is above the contemplation, and reach of Men, or Angells to describe this Union, as it is. That Small account above given of it is like unto our Shallow, and darke understandings, and tho' we conceive of it in Some respect thus, yet we canot come to it thereby, for tho' in some respect it seems to be like a Morall Union, yet there seems to be as reall an Inbeing of the two Natures united one in another, as there is of the Soul in the Body. Col. 2. 9. Oh! then how should it be Studied, be Admired, and God adored on this account.

2. To Admire, Prize, and Set by, the Lord Jesus Christ, that makes this Confession of himselfe, Ps. 139. 14. 15. Fearfully, and Wonderfully was I made—when I was made in Secret, and curiously wrought in the lowest parts of the Earth, and the Spirit of God Styles him Wonderfull also. Isai. 9. 6. We ought then to admire him, and Prize him. We are apt to admire Singular things, and there's not another person like him neither in Heaven, nor in earth. The brightest portraiture of Divine Wisdom, and the most transplendent luster of Divine Grace, that heaven itselfe can discover. So precious, that he is above all price. Hence ever prized too little: never prized enough. And

therefore we are bound to prize him. Our intrest lies in him.

3. To make Sure of him: a Saving intrest in him. He is made thus, that thou shouldst make him thine. Godhead Nature is in him, and his nature is in thee. His Nature is not without thine that thy nature might not be without him. He Honours thy Nature: do not thou dishonour his. Thy Nature is in his Person: His Nature is in thy person, that thy Person, and his person might make an Union of persons by his personal Union. O then Strive to be one with him. United to him in a Saving Union: if thou attainst to this, then the End of this personall Union, will be attain'd to by thee. Oh then thou wilt have Communion with the father, and with his Son Jesus Christ, 1 Joh. 1. 3: and that in Grace, in Spirit, in Life, and in Eternall glory. Joh: 1. 16. 1 Cor. 6. 17. 1 Joh. 2. 6. Rev. 3. 21.

Secondly. This truth cometh in a more particular way to call Upon all that have attain'd to a Saving intrest in Christ. Strive to hold forth the Glory of the Person of Christ in your Christian life, and Conversation. The Person of Christ is most Glorious. He is the King of Glory Psa: 24. *ult.* Now all the glory of his Person is derived to his Manhood by the way of this personall Union. And by the Mysticall Union to every Child of God. Hence then as the personall Union, gives the Manhood propriety in the Glory, and Efficiency of his person: So the Mysticall Union unto the person entitles every Member to the Same Glory, and the Influences thereof, and the duty of Every member to improove all the talents thus derived unto it, calls upon all to se to this: and the attendence upon this call will make the Shine of this Glory breake forth in an holy Life to the glory of the Unions, both Mysticall, and personall. Oh! then mentain the Glory of Christ by a Christ like life. It is your highest Honour, and it is your giving the Highest honour to Christ. It will be your greatest Comfort: and the most comfortable Communion with it. It will be the best improovment of your Union to Christ: and of Christ's Union to God. For the Personall Union is to Communicate the Godhead Excellency unto the Manhood to accomplish it to act gloriously. The Mysticall Union is to Communicate the Personall Excellency into the heart, and Life of every Member that the functions thereof may be mannaged with a Godlike glory upon them, and so then to act thus will be to the Glory of God, the Glory of the Personall Union, the Glory of Christs Person; the Glory of the Mysticall Union, to the Glory of Grace, to the glory of Profession, to the Glory of each Member of the Body, and to the glorious Consolation of the Soul and its eternall Salvation. Whereas greate

will be the Dishonour of all in case of failure so to live.
Oh! then let us all intrested in this person so imploy ourselves in improoving our Mysticall Union to him, as shall
be to the display of the Glory of this Personall Union of
the two Natures thro' the Mysticall Union of our Persons
to this Wonderfull Person, in every branch of our lives.

from GODS DETERMINATIONS

The Joy of Church Fellowship
Rightly Attended[1]

In Heaven soaring up, I dropt an Eare
    On Earth: and oh! sweet Melody:
And listening, found it was the Saints who were
      Encoacht for Heaven that sang for Joy.
      For in Christs Coach they sweetly sing;
    As they to Glory ride therein.
Oh! joyous hearts! Enfir'de with holy Flame!
    Is speech thus tassled with praise?
Will not your inward fire of Joy contain;
      That it in open flames doth blaze?
      For in Christ's Coach Saints sweetly sing,
    As they to Glory ride therein.

And if a string do slip, by Chance, they soon
    Do screw it up again: whereby
They set it in a more melodious Tune
      And a Diviner Harmony.
      For in Christs Coach they sweetly sing
    As they to Glory ride therein.

In all their Acts, publick, and private, nay
    And secret too, they praise impart.
But in their Acts Divine and Worship, they
      With Hymns do offer up their Heart.
      Thus in Christs Coach they sweetly sing
    As they to Glory ride therein.

Some few not in; and some whose Time, and Place
    Block up this Coaches way do goe
As Travellers afoot, and so do trace
      The Road that gives them right thereto
      While in this Coach these sweetly sing
    As they to Glory ride therein.

UPON A SPIDER CATCHING A FLY[1]

Thou sorrow, venom Elfe.
    Is this thy play,
To spin a web out of thyselfe
      To Catch a Fly?
      For Why?

I saw a pettish wasp
    Fall foule therein.
Whom yet thy Whorle pins[2] did not clasp
      Lest he should fling
      His sting.

But as affraid, remote
    Didst stand hereat
And with thy little fingers stroke
      And gently tap
      His back.

Thus gently him didst treate
    Lest he should pet,
And in a froppish, waspish heate
      Should greatly fret
      Thy net.

Whereas the silly Fly,
    Caught by its leg
Thou by the throate tookst hastily
      And 'hinde the head
      Bite Dead.

This goes to pot, that not
    Nature doth call.
Strive not above what strength hath got
      Lest in the brawle
      Thou fall.

This Frey seems thus to us.
    Hells Spider gets
His intrails spun to whip Cords thus
      And wove to nets
      And sets.

To tangle Adams race
    In's stratigems

---

1. This is the concluding poem from Taylor's long work, *Gods Determinations*. It was first published by Thomas H. Johnson in the *New England Quarterly* (1937).

---

1. Undated; first published in Thomas H. Johnson, *The Poetical Works of Edward Taylor* (1939).

2. On a spinning wheel, the pin that fastens together the whorl and spindle.

To their Destructions, spoil'd, made base
    By venom things
        Damn'd Sins.

But mighty, Gracious Lord
    Communicate
Thy Grace to breake the Cord, afford
    Us Glorys Gate
        And State.

We'l Nightingaile sing like
    When pearcht on high
In Glories Cage, thy glory, bright,
    And thankfully,
        For joy.

UPON A WASP CHILD WITH COLD[1]

The Bare[2] that breaths the Northern blast
Did numb, Torpedo like, a Wasp
Whose stiffend limbs encrampt, lay bathing
In Sol's warm breath and shine as saving,
Which with her hands she chafes and stands
Rubbing her Legs, Shanks, Thighs, and hands.
Her petty toes, and fingers ends
Nipt with this breath, she out extends
Unto the Sun, in greate desire
To warm her digits at that fire.
Doth hold her Temples in this state
Where pulse doth beate, and head doth ake.
Doth turn, and stretch her body small,
Doth Comb her velvet Capitall.
As if her little brain pan were
A Volume of Choice precepts cleare.
As if her sattin jacket hot
Contained Apothecaries Shop
Of Natures recepts, that prevails
To remedy all her sad ailes,
As if her velvet helmet high
Did turret[3] rationality.

She fans her wing up to the Winde
As if her Pettycoate were lin'de,
With reasons fleece, and hoises sails
And hu'ming flies in thankfull gails
Unto her dun Curld palace Hall
Her warm thanks offering for all.

    Lord cleare my misted sight that I
May hence view thy Divinity.
Some sparkes whereof thou up dost hasp
Within this little downy Wasp
In whose small Corporation wee
A school and a schoolmaster see
Where we may learn, and easily finde
A nimble Spirit bravely minde
Her worke in e'ry limb: and lace
It up neate with a vitall grace,
Acting each part though ne'er so small
Here of this Fustian animall.
Till I enravisht Climb into
The Godhead on this Lather doe.
Where all my pipes inspir'de upraise
An Heavenly musick furrd with praise.

HUSWIFERY[1]

Make me, O Lord, thy Spining Wheele compleate.
    Thy Holy Worde my Distaff make for mee.
Make mine Affections thy Swift Flyers neate
    And make my Soule thy holy Spoole to bee.
    My Conversation make to be thy Reele
    And reele the yarn thereon spun of thy Wheele.

Make me thy Loome then, knit therein this Twine:
    And make thy Holy Spirit, Lord, winde quills:
Then weave the Web thyselfe. The yarn is fine.
    Thine Ordinances make my Fulling Mills.
    Then dy the same in Heavenly Colours Choice,
    All pinkt with Varnisht Flowers of Paradise.

Then cloath therewith mine Understanding, Will,
    Affections, Judgment, Conscience, Memory

------

1. Undated; first published by Thomas H. Johnson in the *New England Quarterly* (1943).

2. Referring to the northern constellations, Ursa Major and Ursa Minor (Great Bear and Little Bear)

3. Enclose.

------

1. Undated; first published by Thomas H. Johnson in the *New England Quarterly* (1937).

My Words, and Actions, that their shine may fill
   My wayes with glory and thee glorify.
   Then mine apparell shall display before yee
   That I am Cloathd in Holy robes for glory.

UPON WEDLOCK, AND DEATH OF CHILDREN[1]

A Curious Knot God made in Paradise,
   And drew it out inamled neatly Fresh.
It was the True-Love Knot, more sweet than spice
   And set with all the flowres of Graces dress.
   Its Weddens Knot, that ne're can be unti'de.
   No Alexanders Sword[2] can it divide.

The slips here planted, gay and glorious grow:
   Unless an Hellish breath do sindge their Plumes.
Here Primrose, Cowslips, Roses, Lilies blow
   With Violets and Pinkes that voide perfumes.
   Whose beautious leaves ore laid with Hony Dew.
   And Chanting birds Cherp out sweet Musick true.

When in this Knot I planted was, my Stock
   Soon knotted, and a manly flower out brake.
And after it my branch again did knot
   Brought out another Flowre its sweet breathd mate.
   One knot gave one tother the tothers place.
   Whence Checkling smiles fought in each others face.

But oh! a glorious hand from glory came
   Guarded with Angells, soon did Crop this flowre
Which almost tore the root up of the same
   At that unlookt for, Dolesome, darksome houre.
   In Pray're to Christ perfum'de it did ascend,
   And Angells bright did it to heaven tend.

But pausing on't, this sweet perfum'd my thought,
   Christ would in Glory have a Flowre, Choice, Prime,
And having Choice, chose this my branch forth brought.
   Lord take't. I thanke thee, thou takst ought of mine,

It is my pledg in glory, part of mee
   Is now in it, Lord, glorifi'de with thee.

But praying ore my branch, my branch did sprout
   And bore another manly flower, and gay
And after that another, sweet brake out,
   The which the former hand soon got away.
   But oh! the tortures, Vomit, screechings, groans,
   And six weeks Fever would pierce hearts like stones.

Griefe o're doth flow: and nature fault would finde
   Were not thy Will, my Spell Charm, Joy, and Gem:

That as I said, I say, take, Lord, they're thine.
   I piecemeale pass to Glory bright in them.
   I joy, may I sweet Flowers for Glory breed,
   Whether thou getst them green, or lets them seed.

THE EBB AND FLOW[1]

When first thou on me Lord wrought'st thy Sweet Print,
   My heart was made thy tinder box.
   My 'ffections were thy tinder in't.
   Where fell thy Sparkes by drops.
Those holy Sparks of Heavenly Fire that came
Did ever catch and often out would flame.

But now my Heart is made thy Censar trim,
   Full of thy golden Altars fire,
   To offer up Sweet Incense in
   Unto thyselfe intire:
I finde my tinder scarce thy sparks can feel
That drop out from thy Holy flint and Steel.

Hence doubts out bud for feare thy fire in mee
   'S a mocking Ignis Fatuus[2]
   Or lest thine Altars fire out bee,
   Its hid in ashes thus.
Yet when the bellows of thy Spirit blow
Away mine ashes, then thy fire doth glow.

---

1. Undated; first published by Thomas H. Johnson in the *New England Quarterly* (1937).

2. Alexander the Great (356–323 B.C.) cut the Gordian knot, a challenge set by the king of Phrygia, in order to rule Asia.

1. Undated; first published by Thomas H. Johnson in the *New England Quarterly* (1937).

2. A light sometimes seen over marshes, popularly believed to be supernatural trickery designed to mislead travelers.

A FUNERALL POEM UPON THE DEATH OF MY EVER ENDEARED, AND TENDER WIFE MRS. ELIZABETH TAYLOR

Who Fell Asleep in Christ the 7th Day of July at Night about Two Hours after Sun Setting 1689 and in the 39 Years of Her Life[1]

Part. 1.

My Gracious Lord, I Licence of thee Crave,
Not to repine but drop upon the Grave
Of my Deare Wife a Teare, or two: or wash
Thy Milk White hand in tears that downward pass.
Thou summond hast her Noble part away:
And in Salt Tears I would Embalm her Clay.
Some deem Death doth the True Love Knot unty:
But I do finde it harder tide thereby.
My heart is in't and will be squeez'd therefore
To pieces if thou draw the Ends much more.
Oh strange Untying! it ti'th harder: What?
Can anything unty a True Love Knot?
Five Babes thou tookst from me before this Stroake.
Thine arrows then into my bowells broake,
But now they pierce into my bosom smart,
Do strike and stob me in the very heart.
I'de then my bosom Friend a Comfort, and
To Comfort: Yet my Lord, I kiss thy hand.
I Her resign'd, thou tookst her into thine,
Out of my bosom, yet she dwells in mine:
And though her Precious Soule now swims in bliss,
Yet while grim Death, that Dismall Sergeant is,
Between the Parts Essentiall now remote,
And hath this stately Tabernacle broke
My Harp is turnd to mourning: Organ sweet
Is turn'de into the Voice of them that weep.
Griefe swelling girds the Heart Strings where its purst,
Unless it Vent the Vessell sure will burst.
     My Gracious Lord, grant that my bitter Griefe
     Breath through this little Vent hole for reliefe.

Part. 2.

     My Dear, Deare Love, reflect thou no such thing,
Will Griefe permit you at my Grave to sing?
Oh! Black Black Theme! The Girths of Griefe alone

Do gird my heart till Gust of Sorrows groan
And dash a mournfull Song to pieces on
The Dolefull Face of thy Sepulcher Stone.
My Onely DOVE, though Harp and Harrow, loe,
Better agree than Songs and Sorrows doe,
Yet spare me thus to drop a blubber'd Verse
Out of my Weeping Eyes Upon thy Herse.
What shall my Preface to our True Love Knot
Frisk in Acrostick Rhimes? And may I not
Now at our parting, with Poetick knocks
Break a salt teare to pieces as it drops?
Did Davids bitter Sorrow at the Dusts
Of Jonathan raise such Poetick gusts?
Do Emperours interr'd in Verses lie?
And mayn't such Feet run from my Weeping Eye?
Nay, Dutie lies upon mee much; and shall
I in thy Coffin naile thy Vertues all?
How shall thy Babes, and theirs, thy Vertuous shine
Know, or Persue unless I them define?
Thy Grace will Grace unto a Poem bee
Although a Poem be no grace to thee.
Impute it not a Crime then if I weep
A Weeping Poem on thy Winding Sheet.
Maybe some Angell may my Poem sing
To thee in Glory, or relate the thing,
     Which if he do, my mournfull Poem may
     Advance thy Joy, and my Deep Sorrow lay.

Part. 3.

     Your Ears, Bright Saints, and Angells: them I
  Choose
To stough her Praises in: I'le not abuse.
Her Modesty would blush should you profess,
I in Hyperboles her praises dress.
Wherefore as Cramping Griefe permitts to stut
Them forth accept of such as here I put.
     Her Husbands Joy, Her Childrens Chiefe Content.
Her Servants Eyes, Her Houses Ornament.
Her Shine as Child, as Neighbour, flies abroad
As Mistress, Mother, Wife, her Walke With God.
As Child she was a Tender, Pious Bud
Of Pious Parents, sprang of Pious Blood
Two Grandsires, Gran'ams: one or two, she had
A Father too and Mother, that englad
The Gracious heart to thinke upon, they were
Bright Pillars in Gods Temple shining cleare.
Her Father, and her Mothers Father fix
As shining Stars in Golden Candlesticks.
She did Obedient, Tender, Meek Child prove
The Object of her Fathers Eye, and Love.

---

1. The exact date of the composition is unknown; first published by Thomas H. Johnson in *Publications of the Colonial Society of Massachusetts* (1942).

Her Mother being Dead, her heart would melt
When she her Fathers looks not pleasant felt.
His smile Would her enliven, Frown, down pull
Hence she became his Child most Dutifull.

    As Neighbour, she was full of Neighbourhood
Not Proud, or Strang; Grave, Courteous, ever good.
Compassionate: but unto none was Soure.
Her Fingers dropt with Myrrh, oft, to her power.

    As Mistress she order'd her Family
With all Discretion, and most prudently
In all things prompt: Dutie in this respect
Would to the meanest in it not neglect.
Ripe at her Fingers Ends, Would nothing flinch.
She was a neate good Huswife every inch.
Although her weakenesse made her let alone
Things so to go, as made her fetch a groan.
Remiss was not, nor yet severe unto
Her Servants: but i'th' golden mean did goe.

    As Mother, Oh! What tender Mother She?
Her bowells Boiled ore to them that bee
Bits of her tender Bowells. She a share
Of her affections ever made them ware.
Yet never chose to trick them, nor herselfe
In antick garbs; or Lavishness of Wealth.
But was a Lover much of Comeliness:
And with her Needle work would make their Dress.
The Law of Life within her Lips she would
Be dropping forth upon them as shee should.
Foolishly fond she was not but would give
Correction wisely, that their Soules might Live.

    As Wife, a Tender, Tender, Loving, Meet,
Meeke, Patient, Humble, Modest, Faithfull, Sweet
Endearing Help she was: Whose Chiefest Treasure
Of Earthly things she held her Husbands pleasure.
But if she spi'de displeasure in his face,
Sorrow would spoile her own, and marr its grace.

Dear Heart! She would his Joy, Peace, Honour, Name,
Even as her very Life, seeke to mentain.
And if an hasty word by chance dropt in:
She would in secret sigh it or'e with him.
She was not wedded unto him alone
But had his joy, and sorrow as her own.
She, where he chanc'd to miss, a Cover would lay
Yet would in Secret fore him all Display
In meekness of sweet wisdom, and by Art,
As Certainly would winde into the heart.
She laid her neck unto the Yoake he draws:
And was his Faithfull Yoake Mate, in Christ's Cause.

    As to her walk with God, she did inherit
The very Spirits of her Parents Spirit.
She was no gaudy Christian, or gilt Weed:
But was a Reall, Israelite indeed.
When in her Fathers house God toucht her Heart,
That Trembling Frame of Spirit, and that Smart,
She then was under very, few did know:
Whereof she somewhat to the Church did show.
Repentance now's her Work: Sin poyson is:
Faith, carries her to Christ as one of his.
Fear Temples in her heart; Love flowers apace
To God, Christ, Grace Saints, and the Means of Grace.
She's much in Reading, Pray're, Selfe-Application
Holds humbly up, a pious Conversation
In which she makes profession * * * * * * * *
Which unto Westfield Church she did disclose.
Holy in Health; Patient in Sickness long.
And very great. Yet gracious Speech doth throng:
She oft had up, An Alwise God Doth this.
And in a filiall way the Rod would kiss.
When Pains were Sore, Justice can do no wrong,
Nor Mercy Cruell be; became her Song.
The Doomsday Verses much perfum'de her Breath,
Much in her thoughts, and yet she fear'd not Death.

MARY WHITE ROWLANDSON (1637?–1711)

Mary White Rowlandson Talcott, author of a best-selling narrative of a captivity among Indians in New England, was born in England and was brought to New England while still a child. Little is known of her life beyond what is described in her narrative. She grew up in Massachusetts in a wealthy family that moved to Salem and then Wenham before settling in the tiny border town of Lancaster. In 1656, three years after her family moved to Lancaster, Mary White married Harvard-educated Joseph Rowlandson, the town's first minister.

Mary Rowlandson's narrative relates much information about life as a captive among the Indians who were raiding British colonial settlements during the years 1674–76. The 1676 raid of Lancaster by Narragansett Indians was part of an ongoing conflict between British colonists and Algonquian tribes in the area. It occurred approximately one year after the colonies of Rhode Island, Connecticut, Plymouth, and

Massachusetts declared war on the Algonquian tribes allied under Metacom (sometimes Metacomet), a Wampanoag leader the colonists dubbed "King Philip." Some historians have suggested that the encroachment of British settlers on Indian lands, both by purchase and by squatting, caused the violent retaliation by Wampanoag chief Metacom. Others have remarked that the settlers' squabbles among themselves and their lack of concern for the Indians in their midst, once treaties had been arranged, led Metacom to recognize that the territory that had ancestrally belonged to the Wampanoags, Nipmucks, and Narragansetts had been forever altered and that Indian peoples and lifeways had been displaced. Back in the 1630s or 1640s, settlers had outnumbered Indians in Plymouth territory. Indians were perforce adopting British cultural materials and lifeways in increasing numbers, and the old Wampanoag territory had become more English than it was Indian. The collaborative effort of the Nipmucks, Narragansetts, and Wampanoags—ancestral enemies—to lay waste to British settlements indicates these peoples' central recognition that they were fighting for an Indian way of life that was becoming unrecognizable to many Indians in the area.

The colonists interpreted the Indian attacks, which they called "King Philip's War," as the just punishment of an angry God against a wayward people who had fallen into corruption and fallen from the godliness of former generations of the godly. Rowlandson's narrative tension between an understanding of the scarcities of living in an Indian way and an all-out insistence upon the Puritan way reflects the complications of the kind of New England jeremiad rhetoric that emerged at the time of these wars. Rowlandson had been taken captive along with three of her children and other family and community members. Her husband was away in Boston at the time of the attack. She spent approximately eleven weeks in captivity among the Narragansetts and traveled 150 miles through western Massachusetts and southern New Hampshire. The narrative describes the twenty individual "removes" taken from Lancaster, but its rhetorical focus is upon the extent to which this physical journey was primarily a spiritual journey toward recognition of election in God's church and the consequent need for righteousness. Yet the Puritan-centered rhetorical method sometimes seems a too-conscious overstory that competes with what the narrative reveals about the Indians' situation among the Puritans.

To be sure, Rowlandson did suffer hardship in her journey. Although she was taken captive with three of her children, her six-year-old daughter Sarah died one week after being captured, and Rowlandson was soon separated from daughter Mary and son Joseph. She was eventually ransomed and was able to return to her family. Children Mary and Joseph were released the following month in June 1676. Because Lancaster had been destroyed, the family eventually settled in Wethersfield, Connecticut, where Joseph Rowlandson served as the minister. Joseph Rowlandson died shortly after this period of turmoil, and Mary Rowlandson later remarried Captain Samuel Talcott, a prominent community leader.

Rowlandson probably wrote her narrative, *A Narrative of the Captivity and Restauration of Mrs. Mary Rowlandson* (1682), after she moved to Wethersfield and before her first husband's death. The narrative appears to have been written for circulation among her family and friends. Later, with the encouragement and perhaps the collaboration of Increase Mather, a prominent minister and leader of the Massachusetts Bay colony, Rowlandson published her narrative in 1682, during an era when Congregational Church membership was on the wane. Most seventeenth-century editions of the narrative included Joseph Rowlandson's final sermon and a preface that was probably written by Increase Mather. The book circulated widely in New England and England, and within one year of its publication, four more editions appeared.

The immediate and extended popularity of the narrative might be explained by the well-publicized Lancaster raids and by Rowlandson's prominent position as a minister's wife. A variety of accounts describing captivity among Indian peoples had come out prior to the publication of Rowlandson's narrative, but because future English-speaking writers of captivities followed similar rhetorical and narrative conventions, Rowlandson's narrative has received significant critical attention. Part jeremiad, part spiritual autobiography, part adventure story, the captivity narrative genre was especially significant for Puritan readers because captives were viewed as a representatives of the Puritan community. As the captive was taken to the "howling wilderness" and challenged to reexamine her relationship with God, so, too, was the Puritan community taken and held hostage until it could recognize God's "soveraignty and goodness" in finding a means to test the faith of a fallen people. Although the conventions of the captivity narrative changed significantly over the century following Rowlandson's publication, her narrative has for many reasons remained popular from her day to this one.

NARRATIVE OF THE CAPTIVITY AND RESTAURATION OF MRS. MARY ROWLANDSON[1]

On the tenth of February 1675[2] came the Indians with great numbers upon Lancaster.[3] Their first coming was about sunrising. Hearing the noise of some guns, we looked out; several houses were burning and the smoke ascending to heaven. There were five persons taken in one house; the father and the mother and a sucking child they knocked on the head; the other two they took and carried away alive. There were two others, who being out of their garrison upon some occasion were set upon; one was knocked on the head, the other escaped. Another there was who running along was shot and wounded and fell down; he begged of them his life, promising them money (as they told me), but they would not hearken to him but knocked him in head, stripped him naked, and split open his bowels. Another, seeing many of the Indians about his barn, ventured and went out but was quickly shot down. There were three others belonging to the same garrison who were killed; the Indians, getting up upon the roof of the barn, had advantage to shoot down upon them over their fortification. Thus these murderous wretches went on, burning and destroying before them.

At length they came and beset our own house, and quickly it was the dolefullest day that ever mine eyes saw. The house stood upon the edge of a hill. Some of the Indians got behind the hill, others into the barn, and others behind anything that could shelter them; from all which places they shot against the house so that the bullets seemed to fly like hail; and quickly they wounded one man among us, then another, and then a third. About two hours (according to my observation in that amazing time) they had been about the house before they prevailed to fire it (which they did with flax and hemp which they brought out of the barn, and there being no defense about the house, only two flankers[4] at two opposite corners and one of them not finished). They fired it once, and one ventured out and quenched it, but they quickly fired it again and that took.

Now is that dreadful hour come that I have often heard of (in time of war as it was the case of others), but now mine eyes see it. Some in our house were fighting for their lives, others wallowing in their blood, the house on fire over our heads, and the bloody heathen ready to knock us on the head if we stirred out. Now might we hear mothers and children crying out for themselves and one another, "Lord, what shall we do?" Then I took my children[5] (and one of my sisters, hers) to go forth and leave the house, but as soon as we came to the door and appeared, the Indians shot so thick that the bullets rattled against the house as if one had taken an handful of stones and threw them so that we were fain to give back. We had six stout dogs belonging to our garrison, but none of them would stir although another time, if any Indian had come to the door, they were ready to fly upon him and tear him down. The Lord hereby would make us the more to acknowledge His hand and to see that our help is always in Him. But out we must go, the fire increasing and coming along behind us roaring, and the Indians gaping before us with their guns, spears, and hatchets to devour us. No sooner were we out of the house, but my brother-in-law[6] (being

---

1. Mary Rowlandson's narrative was appended to a publication of her husband Joseph's last sermon, together titled *The Soveraignty and Goodness of God, Together, with the Faithfulness of His Promises Displayed; Being a Narrative of the Captivity and Restauration of Mrs. Mary Rowlandson* in 1682. No copies are extant of the first 1682 edition. This text is taken from *Puritans among the Indians,* ed. A. T. Vaughan and E. W. Clark (1981), which contains a copy of the second edition, originally published in Cambridge in 1682 by Samuel Green, Sr.

2. Rowlandson was captured on February 10, 1675, according to the Julian calendar (used before 1752), and February 10, 1676, according to the calendar used today.

3. Lancaster, Massachusetts, a small frontier town thirty miles west of Boston.

4. Projection fortifications that defend another structure.

5. Joseph, Mary, and Sarah Rowlandson.

6. John Divoll was the husband of Rowlandson's sister Hannah.

before wounded, in defending the house, in or near the throat) fell down dead; whereat the Indians scornfully shouted, hallooed, and were presently upon him, stripping off his clothes. The bullets flying thick, one went through my side, and the same (as would seem) through the bowels and hand of my dear child[7] in my arms. One of my elder sister's children, named William, had then his leg broken, which the Indians perceiving, they knocked him on the head. Thus were we butchered by those merciless heathen, standing amazed, with the blood running down to our heels.

My eldest sister being yet in the house and seeing those woeful sights, the infidels hailing mothers one way and children another and some wallowing in their blood, and her elder son telling her that her son William was dead and myself was wounded, she said, "And, Lord, let me die with them." Which was no sooner said, but she was struck with a bullet and fell down dead over the threshold. I hope she is reaping the fruit of her good labors, being faithful to the service of God in her place. In her younger years she lay under much trouble upon spiritual accounts till it pleased God to make that precious scripture take hold of her heart, 2 Cor. 12:9, "And he said unto me, my grace is sufficient for thee."[8] More than twenty years after I have heard her tell how sweet and comfortable that place was to her. But to return: the Indians laid hold of us, pulling me one way and the children another, and said, "Come go along with us." I told them they would kill me. They answered, if I were willing to go along with them they would not hurt me.

Oh, the doleful sight that now was to behold at this house! "Come, behold the works of the Lord, what desolation He has made in the earth."[9] Of thirty-seven persons who were in this one house none escaped either present death or a bitter captivity save only one,[10] who might say as he, Job 1:15, "And I only am escaped alone to tell the news."[11] There were twelve killed, some shot, some stabbed with their spears, some knocked down with their hatchets. When we are in prosperity, oh, the little that we think of such dreadful sights, and to see our dear friends and relations lie bleeding out their heart-blood upon the ground! There was one who was chopped into the head with a hatchet and stripped naked, and yet was crawling up and down. It is a solemn sight to see so many Christians lying in their blood, some here and some there, like a company of sheep torn by wolves, all of them stripped naked by a company of hell-hounds, roaring, singing, ranting and insulting, as if they would have torn our very hearts out. Yet the Lord by his almighty power preserved a number of us from death, for there were twenty-four of us taken alive and carried captive.

I had often before this said that if the Indians should come I should choose rather to be killed by them than taken alive, but when it came to the trial, my mind changed; their glittering weapons so daunted my spirit that I chose rather to go along with those (as I may say) ravenous beasts than that moment to end my days. And that I may the better declare what happened to me during that grievous captivity, I shall particularly speak of the several removes[12] we had up and down the wilderness.

The First Remove

Now away we must go with those barbarous creatures with our bodies wounded and bleeding and our hearts no less than our bodies. About a mile we went that night up upon a hill within sight of the town where they intended to lodge. There was hard by a vacant house (deserted by the English before for fear of the Indians). I asked them whether I might not lodge in the house that night, to which they answered, "What, will you love English men still?" This was the dolefullest night that ever my eyes saw. Oh, the roaring and singing and dancing and yelling of those black creatures in the night, which made the place a lively resemblance of hell. And as miserable was the waste that was there made of horses, cattle, sheep, swine, calves, lambs, roasting pigs, and fowl (which they had plundered in the town), some roasting, some lying and burning, and some boiling to feed our merciless enemies who were joyful enough though we were disconsolate. To add to the dolefulness of the former day and the dismalness of the present night, my thoughts ran upon my losses and sad bereaved condition. All was gone: my husband gone (at least separated from me, he being in the

---

7. Sarah.

8. Rowlandson describes her sister's conversion experience. Rowlandson's biblical citations are generally accurate. Exceptions will be noted.

9. Psalm 46:8.

10. Ephraim Roper. Rowlandson did not realize that three children escaped as well.

11. Job 1:15: "and I only am escaped to tell thee."

12. Movements from one place to the next.

Bay,[13] and to add to my grief, the Indians told me they would kill him as he came homeward), my children gone, my relations and friends gone, our house and home and all our comforts within door and without, all was gone except my life, and I knew not but the next moment that might go too. There remained nothing to me but one poor wounded babe, and it seemed at present worse than death that it was in such a pitiful condition bespeaking compassion, and I had no refreshing for it nor suitable things to revive it. Little do many think what is the savageness and brutishness of this barbarous enemy, ay, even those that seem to profess more than others among them when the English have fallen into their hands.

Those seven that were killed at Lancaster the summer before upon a Sabbath day and the one that was afterward killed upon a week day were slain and mangled in a barbarous manner by one-eyed John[14] and Marlborough's praying Indians which Capt. Mosely[15] brought to Boston, as the Indians told me.

The Second Remove[16]

But now, the next morning, I must turn my back upon the town and travel with them into the vast and desolate wilderness, I knew not whither. It is not my tongue or pen can express the sorrows of my heart and bitterness of my spirit that I had at this departure, but God was with me in a wonderful manner, carrying me along and bearing up my spirit that it did not quite fail. One of the Indians carried my poor wounded babe upon a horse; it went moaning all along, "I shall die, I shall die." I went on foot after it with sorrow that cannot be expressed. At length I took it off the horse and carried it in my arms till my strength failed, and I fell down with it. Then they set me upon a horse with my wounded child in my lap. And there being no furniture upon the horse back, as we were going down a steep hill, we both fell over the horse's head, at which they like inhuman creatures laughed and rejoiced to see it, though I thought we should there have ended our days, as overcome with so many difficulties. But the Lord renewed my strength still and carried me along that I might

see more of His power; yea, so much that I could never have thought of had I not experienced it.

After this it quickly began to snow, and when night came on, they stopped. And now down I must sit in the snow by a little fire and a few boughs behind me, with my sick child in my lap and calling much for water, being now (through the wound) fallen into a violent fever. My own wound also growing so stiff that I could scarce sit down or rise up; yet so it must be that I must sit all this cold winter night upon the cold, snowy ground with my sick child in my arms, looking that every hour would be the last of its life, and having no Christian friend near me either to comfort or help me. Oh, I may see the wonderful power of God that my spirit did not utterly sink under my affliction! Still the Lord upheld me with His gracious and merciful spirit, and we were both alive to see the light of the next morning.

The Third Remove[17]

The morning being come, they prepared to go on their way. One of the Indians got up upon a horse, and they set me up behind him with my poor sick babe in my lap. A very wearisome and tedious day I had of it what with my own wound and my child's being so exceeding sick in a lamentable condition with her wound. It may be easily judged what a poor feeble condition we were in, there being not the least crumb of refreshing that came within either of our mouths from Wednesday night to Saturday night except only a little cold water. This day in the afternoon about an hour by sun we came to the place where they intended, viz.[18] an Indian town called Wenimesset, norward of Quabaug.[19] When we were come, oh, the number of pagans (now merciless enemies) that there came about me that I may say as David, Psal. 27:13, "I had fainted, unless I had believed," etc. The next day was the Sabbath. I then remembered how careless I had been of God's holy time, how many Sabbaths I had lost and misspent and how evilly I had walked in God's sight, which lay so close unto my spirit that it was easy for me to see how righteous it was with God to cut the thread of my life and cast me out of His presence forever. Yet the Lord still showed mercy to me and upheld me, and as He

13. Boston, the center of authority for Massachusetts Bay.

14. A Nipmuck leader also known as Monoco and Apequinsah.

15. Captain Samuel Mosley, leader of the New England forces.

16. To Princeton, Massachusetts.

17. To the Indian village, Menameset, on the Ware River (present-day New Braintree, Massachusetts).

18. Namely.

19. Present-day Brookfield, Massachusetts.

wounded me with one hand, so He healed me with the other.

This day there came to me one Robert Pepper (a man belonging to Roxbury) who was taken in Captain Beers his fight and had been now a considerable time with the Indians and up with them almost as far as Albany to see King Philip,[20] as he told me, and was now very lately come into these parts. Hearing, I say, that I was in this Indian town, he obtained leave to come and see me. He told me he himself was wounded in the leg at Captain Beers his fight and was not able some time to go, but, as they carried him, and as he took oaken leaves and laid to his wound, and through the blessing of God, he was able to travel again. Then I took oaken leaves and laid to my side, and, with the blessing of God, it cured me also. Yet before the cure was wrought, I may say, as it is in Psal. 38:5, 6, "My wounds stink and are corrupt, I am troubled, I am bowed down greatly, I go mourning all the day long." I sat much alone with a poor wounded child in my lap, which moaned night and day, having nothing to revive the body or cheer the spirits of her, but instead of that sometimes one Indian would come and tell me one hour that, "Your master[21] will knock your child in the head." And then a second, and then a third, "Your master will quickly knock your child in the head."

This was the comfort I had from them. "Miserable comforters are ye all," as He said.[22] Thus nine days I sat upon my knees with my babe in my lap till my flesh was raw again; my child being even ready to depart this sorrowful world, they bade me carry it out to another wigwam (I suppose because they would not be troubled with such spectacles), whither I went with a heavy heart, and down I sat with the picture of death in my lap. About two hours in the night my sweet babe like a lamb departed this life on Feb. 18, 1675, it being about six years and five months old. It was nine days from the first wounding in this miserable condition without any refreshing of one nature or other except a little cold water. I cannot but take notice how at another time I could not bear to be in the room where any dead person was, but now the case is changed; I must and could lie down by my dead babe side by side all the night after. I have thought since of the wonderful goodness of God to me in preserving me in the use of my reason and senses in that distressed time that I did not use wicked and violent means to end my own miserable life.

In the morning when they understood that my child was dead, they sent for me home to my master's wigwam. (By my master in this writing must be understood Quanopin who was a sagamore and married King Philip's wife's sister, not that he first took me, but I was sold to him by another Narragansett Indian who took me when first I came out of the garrison.) I went to take up my dead child in my arms to carry it with me, but they bid me let it alone. There was no resisting, but go I must and leave it. When I had been at my master's wigwam, I took the first opportunity I could get to go look after my dead child. When I came, I asked them what they had done with it. Then they told me it was upon the hill. Then they went and showed me where it was, where I saw the ground was newly digged, and there they told me they had buried it. There I left that child in the wilderness and must commit it and myself also in this wilderness condition to Him who is above all.

God having taken away this dear child, I went to see my daughter Mary who was at this same Indian town at a wigwam not very far off, though we had little liberty or opportunity to see one another. She was about ten years old and taken from the door at first by a praying Indian and afterward sold for a gun. When I came in sight, she would fall a-weeping at which they were provoked and would not let me come near her but bade me be gone, which was a heart-cutting word to me. I had one child dead, another in the wilderness I knew not where; the third they would not let me come near to. "Me," as he said, "have ye bereaved of my children, Joseph is not, and Simeon is not, and ye will take Benjamin also, all these things are against me."[23] I could not sit still in this condition but kept walking from one place to another. And as I was going along, my heart was even overwhelmed with the thoughts of my condition and that I should have children and a nation which I knew not ruled over them. Whereupon I earnestly entreated the Lord that He would consider my low estate and show me a token for good, and if it were His blessed will, some sign and hope of some relief.

And indeed quickly the Lord answered in some measure my poor prayers; for, as I was going up and down mourning and lamenting my condition, my son came to me and asked me how I did. I had not seen him before since the destruction of the town, and I knew not where he was till I was informed by himself that he was amongst a

---

20. Metacom or Metacomet, Wampanoag leader.

21. Indian captor of Rowlandson.

22. Job 16:1–2.

---

23. Genesis 42:36.

smaller parcel of Indians whose place was about six miles off. With tears in his eyes he asked me whether his sister Sarah was dead and told me he had seen his sister Mary and prayed me that I would not be troubled in reference to himself. The occasion of his coming to see me at this time was this. There was, as I said, about six miles from us a small plantation of Indians where it seems he had been during his captivity, and at this time there were some forces of the Indians gathered out of our company and some also from them (among whom was my son's master) to go to assault and burn Medfield.[24] In this time of the absence of his master his dame brought him to see me. I took this to be some gracious answer to my earnest and unfeigned desire.

The next day, *viz.* to this, the Indians returned from Medfield all the company, for those that belonged to the other small company came through the town that now we were at. But before they came to us, oh, the outrageous roaring and whooping that there was! They began their din about a mile before they came to us. By their noise and whooping they signified how many they had destroyed, which was at that time twenty-three. Those that were with us at home were gathered together as soon as they heard the whooping, and every time that the other went over their number, these at home gave a shout that the very earth rung again. And thus they continued till those that had been upon the expedition were come up to the sagamore's wigwam. And then, oh, the hideous insulting and triumphing that there was over some Englishmen's scalps that they had taken (as their manner is) and brought with them!

I cannot but take notice of the wonderful mercy of God to me in those afflictions in sending me a Bible. One of the Indians that came from Medfield fight had brought some plunder came to me and asked me if I would have a Bible; he had got one in his basket. I was glad of it and asked him whether he thought the Indians would let me read. He answered, "Yes." So I took the Bible, and in that melancholy time it came into my mind to read first the 28 chapter of Deut., which I did, and when I had read it, my dark heart wrought on this manner, that there was no mercy for me, that the blessings were gone and the curses come in their room, and that I had lost my opportunity. But the Lord helped me still to go on reading till I came to chapter 30, the seven first verses, where I found there was mercy promised again if we would return to him by repentance, and, though we were scattered from one end

of the earth to the other, yet the Lord would gather us together and turn all those curses upon our enemies. I do not desire to live to forget this scripture and what comfort it was to me.

Now the Indians began to talk of removing from this place, some one way and some another. There were now besides myself nine English captives in this place, all of them children except one woman. I got an opportunity to go and take my leave of them, they being to go one way and I another; I asked them whether they were earnest with God for deliverance. They told me they did as they were able, and it was some comfort to me that the Lord stirred up children to look to Him. The woman, *viz.* Goodwife Joslin,[25] told me she should never see me again and that she could find in her heart to run away; I wished her not to run away by any means, for we were near thirty miles from any English town and she very big with child and had but one week to reckon and another child in her arms, two years old, and bad rivers there were to go over, and we were feeble with our poor and coarse entertainment. I had my Bible with me; I pulled it out and asked her whether she would read. We opened the Bible and lighted on Psalm 27, in which psalm we especially took notice of that *ver. ult.,*[26] "Wait on the Lord, be of good courage, and He shall strengthen thine heart, wait I say on the Lord."

The Fourth Remove

And now I must part with that little company I had. Here I parted from my daughter Mary (whom I never saw again till I saw her in Dorchester, returned from captivity) and from four little cousins and neighbors, some of which I never saw afterward. The Lord only knows the end of them. Amongst them also was that poor woman before mentioned who came to a sad end, as some of the company told me in my travel. She, having much grief upon her spirit about her miserable condition, being so near her time, she would be often asking the Indians to let her go home; they, not being willing to that and yet vexed with her importunity, gathered a great company together about her and stripped her naked and set her in the midst of them. And when they had sung and danced about her (in their hellish manner) as long as they pleased, they knocked her on head and the child in her arms with her. When they had done that, they made a fire and put them

---

24. The assault took place on February 21, 1676.

25. Ann Joslin of Lancaster.

26. Last verse. The verse was Psalm 27:14.

both into it and told the other children that were with them that if they attempted to go home they would serve them in like manner. The children said she did not shed one tear but prayed all the while. But to return to my own journey, we traveled about half a day or little more and came to a desolate place in the wilderness where there were no wigwams or inhabitants before;[27] we came about the middle of the afternoon to this place, cold and wet, and snowy, and hungry, and weary, and no refreshing for man but the cold ground to sit on and our poor Indian cheer.

Heartaching thoughts here I had about my poor children who were scattered up and down among the wild beasts of the forest. My head was light and dizzy (either through hunger or hard lodging or trouble or all together), my knees feeble, my body raw by sitting double night and day that I cannot express to man the affliction that lay upon my spirit, but the Lord helped me at that time to express it to Himself. I opened my Bible to read, and the Lord brought that precious scripture to me, Jer. 31:16, "Thus saith the Lord, 'Refrain thy voice from weeping and thine eyes from tears, for thy work shall be rewarded, and they shall come again from the land of the enemy.'" This was a sweet cordial to me when I was ready to faint; many and many a time have I sat down and wept sweetly over this scripture. At this place we continued about four days.

The Fifth Remove[28]

The occasion (as I thought) of their moving at this time was the English army,[29] it being near and following them. For they went as if they had gone for their lives for some considerable way, and then they made a stop and chose some of their stoutest men and sent them back to hold the English army in play whilst the rest escaped. And then, like Jehu,[30] they marched on furiously with their old and with their young; some carried their old decrepit mothers; some carried one and some another. Four of them carried a great Indian upon a bier, but, going through a thick

wood with him, they were hindered and could make no haste; whereupon they took him upon their backs and carried him, one at a time, till they came to Bacquaug River. Upon a Friday a little after noon we came to this river. When all the company was come up and were gathered together, I thought to count the number of them, but they were so many and, being somewhat in motion, it was beyond my skill. In this travel because of my wound I was somewhat favored in my load; I carried only my knitting work and two quarts of parched meal. Being very faint, I asked my mistress to give me one spoonful of the meal, but she would not give me a taste. They quickly fell to cutting dry trees to make rafts to carry them over the river, and soon my turn came to go over. By the advantage of some brush which they had laid upon the raft to sit upon, I did not wet my foot (which many of themselves at the other end were mid-leg deep) which cannot but be acknowledged as a favor of God to my weakened body, it being a very cold time. I was not before acquainted with such kind of doings or dangers. "When thou passeth through the waters I will be with thee, and through the rivers they shall not overflow thee," Isai. 43:2. A certain number of us got over the river that night, but it was the night after the Sabbath before all the company was got over. On the Saturday they boiled an old horse's leg which they had got, and so we drank of the broth as soon as they thought it was ready, and when it was almost all gone, they filled it up again.

The first week of my being among them I hardly ate anything; the second week, I found my stomach grow very faint for want of something; and yet it was very hard to get down their filthy trash. But the third week, though I could think how formerly my stomach would turn against this or that and I could starve and die before I could eat such things, yet they were sweet and savory to my taste. I was at this time knitting a pair of white cotton stockings for my mistress and had not yet wrought upon a Sabbath day. When the Sabbath came, they bade me go to work; I told them it was the Sabbath day and desired them to let me rest and told them I would do as much more tomorrow, to which they answered me they would break my face. And here I cannot but take notice of the strange providence of God in preserving the heathen. They were many hundreds, old and young, some sick and some lame, many had papooses at their backs. The greatest number at this time with us were squaws, and they traveled with all they had, bag and baggage, and yet they got over this river aforesaid. And on Monday they set their wigwams on fire, and away they went. On that very

---

27. The camp was located near the Indian village of Nichewaug (present-day Petersham, Massachusetts).

28. Making this move entailed crossing the Baquag River in Orange, Massachusetts.

29. Captain Thomas Savage commanded the colonial militia of Massachusetts and Connecticut.

30. King of Israel (c.843–816 B.C.).

day came the English army after them to this river and saw the smoke of their wigwams, and yet this river put a stop to them. God did not give them courage or activity to go over after us; we were not ready for so great a mercy as victory and deliverance. If we had been, God would have found out a way for the English to have passed this river, as well as for the Indians with their squaws and children and all their luggage. "Oh that my people had hearkened to me, and Israel had walked in my ways, I should soon have subdued their enemies and turned my hand against their adversaries," Psal. 81:13, 14.

The Sixth Remove

On Monday (as I said) they set their wigwams on fire and went away. It was a cold morning, and before us there was a great brook with ice on it; some waded through it up to the knees and higher, but others went till they came to a beaver dam, and I amongst them, where through the good providence of God I did not wet my foot. I went along that day mourning and lamenting, leaving farther my own country and traveling into the vast and howling wilderness, and I understood something of Lot's wife's temptation when she looked back.[31] We came that day to a great swamp by the side of which we took up our lodging that night.[32] When I came to the brow of the hill that looked toward the swamp, I thought we had been come to a great Indian town (though there were none but our own company). The Indians were as thick as the trees: it seemed as if there had been a thousand hatchets going at once. If one looked before one, there was nothing but Indians and behind one nothing but Indians, and so on either hand, I myself in the midst, and no Christian soul near me, and yet how hath the Lord preserved me in safety. Oh, the experience that I have had of the goodness of God to me and mine!

The Seventh Remove

After a restless and hungry night there we had a wearisome time of it the next day. The swamp by which we lay was, as it were, a deep dungeon and an exceeding high and steep hill before it. Before I got to the top of the hill, I thought my heart and legs and all would have broken and failed me. What through faintness and soreness of body it was a grievous day of travel to me. As we went along, I saw a place where English cattle had been. That was comfort to me, such as it was. Quickly after that we came to an English path which so took with me that I thought I could have freely laid down and died. That day, a little after noon, we came to Squakeag where the Indians quickly spread themselves over the deserted English fields, gleaning what they could find; some picked up ears of wheat that were crickled down; some found ears of Indian corn; some found groundnuts, and others sheaves of wheat that were frozen together in the shock, and went to threshing of them out. Myself got two ears of Indian corn, and whilst I did but turn my back, one of them was stolen from me, which much troubled me. There came an Indian to them at that time with a basket of horse liver. I asked him to give me a piece. "What," says he, "can you eat horse liver?" I told him I would try if he would give a piece, which he did, and I laid it on the coals to roast, but before it was half ready they got half of it away from me so that I was fain to take the rest and eat it as it was with the blood about my mouth, and yet a savory bit it was to me: "For to the hungry soul every bitter thing is sweet."[33] A solemn sight methought it was to see fields of wheat and Indian corn forsaken and spoiled and the remainders of them to be food for our merciless enemies. That night we had a mess of wheat for our supper.

The Eighth Remove[34]

On the morrow morning we must go over the river, i.e. Connecticot, to meet with King Philip. Two canoesful they had carried over; the next turn I myself was to go, but as my foot was upon the canoe to step in, there was a sudden outcry among them, and I must step back. And instead of going over the river, I must go four or five miles up the river farther northward. Some of the Indians ran one way and some another. The cause of this rout was, as I thought, their espying some English scouts who were thereabout. In this travel up the river about noon the company made a stop and sat down, some to eat and others to rest them. As I sat amongst them musing of things past, my son Joseph unexpectedly came to me. We asked of each other's welfare, bemoaning our doleful condition and the change that had come upon us. We had husbands and father, and children, and sisters, and friends, and re-

---

31. When Lot's wife looked back at the city of Sodom, she was turned into a pillar of salt.

32. In Northfield, Massachusetts.

33. Proverbs 27:7.

34. To Coasett, in southern Vernon, Vermont.

lations, and house, and home, and many comforts of this life, but now we may say as Job, "Naked came I out of my mother's womb, and naked shall I return. The Lord gave, and the Lord hath taken away, blessed be the name of the Lord."[35] I asked him whether he would read; he told me he earnestly desired it, I gave him my Bible, and he lighted upon that comfortable scripture, Psal. 118:17, 18, "I shall not die but live and declare the works of the Lord: the Lord hath chastened me sore, yet he hath not given me over to death." "Look here, Mother," says he, "did you read this?" And here I may take occasion to mention one principal ground of my setting forth these lines, even as the psalmist says to declare the works of the Lord and His wonderful power in carrying us along, preserving us in the wilderness while under the enemy's hand and returning of us in safety again and His goodness in bringing to my hand so many comfortable and suitable scriptures in my distress.

But to return, we traveled on till night, and in the morning we must go over the river to Philip's crew. When I was in the canoe, I could not but be amazed at the numerous crew of pagans that were on the bank on the other side. When I came ashore, they gathered all about me, I sitting alone in the midst. I observed they asked one another questions and laughed and rejoiced over their gains and victories. Then my heart began to fail and I fell a-weeping, which was the first time to my remembrance that I wept before them. Although I had met with so much affliction and my heart was many times ready to break, yet could I not shed one tear in their sight but rather had been all this while in a maze and like one astonished. But now I may say as Psal. 137:1, "By the rivers of Babylon there we sat down; yea, we wept when we remembered Zion." There one of them asked me why I wept; I could hardly tell what to say, yet I answered they would kill me. "No," said he, "none will hurt you." Then came one of them and gave me two spoonfuls of meal to comfort me, and another gave me half a pint of peas which was more worth than many bushels at another time. Then I went to see King Philip. He bade me come in and sit down and asked me whether I would smoke it (a usual compliment nowadays among saints and sinners), but this no way suited me. For though I had formerly used tobacco, yet I had left it ever since I was first taken. It seems to be a bait the devil lays to make men lose their precious time. I remember with shame how formerly when I had taken two or three pipes I was presently ready for another, such a be-

witching thing it is. But I thank God He has now given me power over it; surely there are many who may be better employed than to lie sucking a stinking tobacco pipe.

Now the Indians gather their forces to go against Northampton. Overnight one went about yelling and hooting to give notice of the design, whereupon they fell to boiling of groundnuts and parching of corn (as many as had it) for their provision, and in the morning away they went. During my abode in this place Philip spoke to me to make a shirt for his boy, which I did, for which he gave me a shilling. I offered the money to my master, but he bade me keep it, and with it I bought a piece of horseflesh. Afterwards he asked me to make a cap for his boy, for which he invited me to dinner. I went, and he gave me a pancake about as big as two fingers; it was made of parched wheat, beaten and fried in bear's grease, but I thought I never tasted pleasanter meat in my life. There was a squaw who spoke to me to make a shirt for her *sannup*, for which she gave me a piece of bear. Another asked me to knit a pair of stockings, for which she gave me a quart of peas. I boiled my peas and bear together and invited my master and mistress to dinner, but the proud gossip, because I served them both in one dish, would eat nothing except one bit that he gave her upon the point of his knife.

Hearing that my son was come to this place, I went to see him and found him lying flat upon the ground. I asked him how he could sleep so. He answered me that he was not asleep but at prayer and lay so that they might not observe what he was doing. I pray God he may remember these things now he is returned in safety. At this place (the sun now getting higher) what with the beams and heat of the sun and the smoke of the wigwams, I thought I should have been blind. I could scarce discern one wigwam from another. There was here one Mary Thurston of Medfield who, seeing how it was with me, lent me a hat to wear, but as soon as I was gone, the squaw who owned that Mary Thurston came running after me and got it away again. Here was the squaw that gave one spoonful of meal. I put it in my pocket to keep it safe, yet notwithstanding somebody stole it but put five Indian corns in the room of it, which corns were the greatest provision I had in my travel for one day.

The Indians, returning from Northampton,[36] brought with them some horses, and sheep, and other things which they had taken. I desired them that they would carry me to

---

35. Job 1:21.

36. They had attacked Northampton, Massachusetts, on March 14, 1676, and were repulsed.

Albany upon one of those horses and sell me for powder, for so they had sometimes discoursed. I was utterly hopeless of getting home on foot the way that I came. I could hardly bear to think of the many weary steps I had taken to come to this place.

The Ninth Remove

But instead of going either to Albany or homeward, we must go five miles up the river and then go over it. Here we abode awhile.[37] Here lived a sorry Indian who spoke to me to make him a shirt. When I had done it, he would pay me nothing. But he living by the riverside where I often went to fetch water, I would often be putting of him in mind and calling for my pay; at last he told me if I would make another shirt for a papoose not yet born, he would give me a knife, which he did when I had done it. I carried the knife in, and my master asked me to give it him, and I was not a little glad that I had anything that they would accept of and be pleased with. When we were at this place, my master's maid came home; she had been gone three weeks into the Narragansett country to fetch corn where they had stored up some in the ground. She brought home about a peck and half of corn. This was about the time that their great captain, Naananto,[38] was killed in the Narragansett country. My son being now about a mile from me, I asked liberty to go and see him; they bade me go, and away I went. But quickly lost myself, traveling over hills and through swamps, and could not find the way to him. And I cannot but admire at the wonderful power and goodness of God to me in that though I was gone from home and met with all sorts of Indians, and those I had no knowledge of, and there being no Christian soul near me, yet not one of them offered the least imaginable miscarriage to me.

I turned homeward again and met with my master; he showed me the way to my son. When I came to him, I found him not well, and withall he had a boil on his side which much troubled him. We bemoaned one another awhile, as the Lord helped us, and then I returned again. When I was returned, I found myself as unsatisfied as I was before. I went up and down mourning and lamenting, and my spirit was ready to sink with the thoughts of my poor children. My son was ill, and I could not but think of his mournful looks, and no Christian friend was near him to do any office of love for him either for soul or body. And

my poor girl, I know not where she was nor whether she was sick or well, or alive or dead. I repaired under these thoughts to my Bible (my great comfort in that time) and that scripture came to my hand, "Cast thy burden upon the Lord, and He shall sustain thee," Psal. 55:22.

But I was fain to go and look after something to satisfy my hunger, and going among the wigwams I went into one and there found a squaw who showed herself very kind to me and gave me a piece of bear. I put it into my pocket and came home but could not find an opportunity to broil it for fear they would get it from me, and there it lay all that day and night in my stinking pocket. In the morning I went to the same squaw who had a kettle of groundnuts boiling; I asked her to let me boil my piece of bear in her kettle, which she did and gave me some groundnuts to eat with it, and I cannot but think how pleasant it was to me. I have sometime seen bear baked very handsomely among the English, and some like it, but the thoughts that it was bear made me tremble, but now that was savory to me that one would think was enough to turn the stomach of a brute creature.

One bitter cold day I could find no room to sit down before the fire. I went out and could not tell what to do, but I went into another wigwam where they were also sitting around the fire, but the squaw laid a skin for me, bid me sit down, gave me some groundnuts, bade me come again, and told me they would buy me if they were able, and yet these were strangers to me that I never saw before.

The Tenth Remove

That day a small part of the company removed about three-quarters of a mile, intending further the next day. When they came to the place where they intended to lodge and had pitched their wigwams, being hungry, I went again back to the place we were before at to get something to eat, being encouraged by the squaw's kindness who bade me come again when I was there. There came an Indian to look after me, who, when he had found me, kicked me all along. I went home and found venison roasting that night, but they would not give me one bit of it. Sometimes I met with favor and sometimes with nothing but frowns.

The Eleventh Remove

The next day in the morning they took their travel, intending a day's journey up the river.[39] I took my load at

---

37. In the Ashuelot valley, New Hampshire.
38. Better known as Canonchet.

39. This remove took Rowlandson to her northernmost location, near Chesterfield, New Hampshire.

my back, and quickly we came to wade over the river and passed over tiresome and wearisome hills. One hill was so steep that I was fain to creep up upon my knees and to hold by the twigs and bushes to keep myself from falling backward. My head also was so light that I usually reeled as I went, but I hope all these wearisome steps that I have taken are but a forewarning of me to the heavenly rest. "I know, O Lord, that Thy judgments are right, and that Thou in faithfulness hast afflicted me," Psal. 119:71.

The Twelfth Remove

It was upon a Sabbath-day morning that they prepared for their travel. This morning I asked my master whether he would sell me to my husband; he answered me *nux,* which did much rejoice my spirit. My mistress, before we went, was gone to the burial of a papoose, and, returning, she found me sitting and reading in my Bible. She snatched it hastily out of my hand and threw it out of doors; I ran out and catched it up and put it into my pocket and never let her see it afterward. Then they packed up their things to be gone and gave me my load. I complained it was too heavy, whereupon she gave me a slap in the face and bade me go. I lifted up my heart to God, hoping the redemption was not far off, and the rather because their insolency grew worse and worse.

But the thoughts of my going homeward (for so we bent our course) much cheered my spirit and made my burden seem light and almost nothing at all. But (to my amazement and great perplexity) the scale was soon turned, for when we had gone a little way, on a sudden my mistress gives out. She would go no further but turn back again and said I must go back again with her. And she called her *sannup* and would have had him gone back also, but he would not but said he would go on and come to us again in three days. My spirit was upon this, I confess, very impatient and almost outrageous. I thought I could as well have died as went back; I cannot declare the trouble that I was in about it, but yet back again I must go. As soon as I had an opportunity, I took my Bible to read, and that quieting scripture came to my hand, Psal. 46:10, "Be still and know that I am God," which stilled my spirit for the present. But a sore time of trial, I concluded, I had to go through, my master being gone, who seemed to me the best friend that I had of an Indian both in cold and hunger, and quickly so it proved. Down I sat with my heart as full as it could hold, and yet so hungry that I could not sit neither. But, going out to see what I could find and walking among the trees, I found six acorns and two chestnuts which were some refreshment to me. Towards

night I gathered me some sticks for my own comfort that I might not lie a-cold, but when we came to lie down they bade me go out and lie somewhere else, for they had company (they said) come in more than their own. I told them I could not tell where to go; they bade me go look. I told them if I went to another wigwam they would be angry and send me home again. Then one of the company drew his sword and told me he would run me through if I did not go presently. Then was I fain to stoop to this rude fellow and to go out in the night, I knew not whither. Mine eyes have seen that fellow afterwards, walking up and down Boston under the appearance of a friend-Indian and several others of the like cut.

I went to one wigwam, and they told me they had no room. Then I went to another, and they said the same; at last an old Indian bade me come to him, and his squaw gave me some groundnuts; she gave me also something to lay under my head, and a good fire we had. And through the good providence of God I had a comfortable lodging that night. In the morning another Indian bade me come at night, and he would give me six groundnuts, which I did. We were at this place and time about two miles from Connecticut River. We went in the morning to gather groundnuts to the river and went back again that night. I went with a good load at my back (for they, when they went though but a little way, would carry all their trumpery with them); I told them the skin was off my back, but I had no other comforting answer from them than this, that it would be no matter if my head were off too.

The Thirteenth Remove

Instead of going toward the Bay, which was that I desired, I must go with them five or six miles down the river into a mighty thicket of brush where we abode almost a fortnight.[40] Here one asked me to make a shirt for her papoose, for which she gave me a mess of broth which was thickened with meal made of the bark of a tree, and to make it the better she had put into it about a handful of peas and a few roasted groundnuts. I had not seen my son a pretty while, and here was an Indian of whom I made inquiry after him and asked him when he saw him. He answered me that such a time his master roasted him and that himself did eat a piece of him as big as his two fingers and that he was very good meat. But the Lord upheld my spirit under this discouragement, and I considered their horrible addictedness to lying and that there is not

---

40. Near present-day Hinsdale, New Hampshire.

one of them that makes the least conscience of speaking of truth. In this place on a cold night as I lay by the fire, I removed a stick that kept the heat from me; a squaw moved it down again at which I looked up, and she threw a handful of ashes in mine eyes. I thought I should have been quite blinded and have never seen more, but lying down, the water run out of my eyes and carried the dirt with it that by the morning I recovered my sight again. Yet upon this and the like occasions I hope it is not too much to say with Job, "Have pity upon me, have pity upon me, oh, ye my friends, for the hand of the Lord has touched me."[41]

And here I cannot but remember how many times sitting in their wigwams and musing on things past I should suddenly leap up and run out as if I had been at home, forgetting where I was and what my condition was. But when I was without and saw nothing but wilderness and woods and a company of barbarous heathens, my mind quickly returned to me, which made me think of that spoken concerning Sampson, who said, "I will go out and shake myself as at other times, but he wished not that the Lord was departed from him."[42]

About this time I began to think that all my hopes of restoration would come to nothing. I thought of the English army and hoped for their coming and being taken by them, but that failed. I hoped to be carried to Albany as the Indians had discoursed before, but that failed also. I thought of being sold to my husband, as my master spake, but instead of that my master himself was gone and I left behind so that my spirit was now quite ready to sink. I asked them to let me go out and pick up some sticks that I might get alone and pour out my heart unto the Lord. Then also I took my Bible to read, but I found no comfort here neither, which many times I was wont to find. So easy a thing it is with God to dry up the streams of scripture-comfort from us. Yet I can say that in all my sorrows and afflictions God did not leave me to have my impatience work towards Himself, as if His ways were unrighteous. But I knew that He laid upon me less than I deserved. Afterward, before this doleful time ended with me, I was turning the leaves of my Bible and the Lord brought to me some scriptures, which did a little revive me, as that Isai. 55:8, " 'For my thoughts are not your thoughts, neither are your ways my ways,' saith the Lord." And also that Psal. 37:5, "Commit thy way unto the Lord, trust also in Him, and He shall bring it to pass."

About this time they came yelping from Hadley where they had killed three Englishmen and brought one captive with them, *viz.* Thomas Read. They all gathered about the poor man, asking him many questions. I desired also to go and see him, and when I came he was crying bitterly, supposing they would quickly kill him. Whereupon I asked one of them whether they intended to kill him; he answered me they would not. He being a little cheered with that, I asked him about the welfare of my husband; he told me he saw him such a time in the Bay, and he was well but very melancholy. By which I certainly understood (though I suspected it before) that whatsoever the Indians told me respecting him was vanity and lies. Some of them told me he was dead, and they had killed him. Some said he was married again, and that the governor wished him to marry and told him he should have his choice, and that all persuaded I was dead. So like were these barbarous creatures to him who was a liar from the beginning.

As I was sitting once in the wigwam here, Philip's maid came in with the child in her arms and asked me to give her a piece of my apron to make a flap for it. I told her I would not. Then my mistress bode me give it, but still I said no. The maid told me if I would not give her a piece she would tear a piece off it. I told her I would tear her coat then; with that my mistress rises up and takes up a stick big enough to have killed me and struck at me with it, but I stepped out, and she struck the stick into the mat of the wigwam. But while she was pulling of it out, I ran to the maid and gave her all my apron, and so that storm went over.

Hearing that my son was come to this place, I went to see him and told him his father was well but very melancholy. He told me he was as much grieved for his father as for himself; I wondered at his speech, for I thought I had enough upon my spirit in reference to myself to make me mindless of my husband and everyone else, they being safe among their friends. He told me also that a while before his master, together with other Indians, were going to the French for powder,[43] but by the way the Mohawks met with them and killed four of their company which made the rest turn back again, for which I desire that myself and he may bless the Lord. For it might have been worse with him had he been sold to the French than it proved to be in remaining with the Indians.

I went to see an English youth in this place, one John Gilberd of Springfield. I found him lying without doors

---

41. Job 19:21.

42. Compare with Judges 16:20.

---

43. Despite laws forbidding colonists from selling guns to Indians, by 1676 Indians had obtained many firearms.

upon the ground; I asked him how he did. He told me he was very sick of a flux[44] with eating so much blood. They had turned him out of the wigwam and with him an Indian papoose almost dead (whose parents had been killed) in a bitter cold day without fire or clothes. The young man himself had nothing on but his shirt and waistcoat. This sight was enough to melt a heart of flint. There they lay quivering in the cold, the youth round like a dog, the papoose stretched out with his eyes, nose, and mouth full of dirt and yet alive and groaning. I advised John to go and get to some fire; he told me he could not stand, but I persuaded him still, lest he should lie there and die. And with much ado I got him to a fire and went myself home. As soon as I was got home, his master's daughter came after me to know what I had done with the Englishman; I told her I had got him to a fire in such a place. Now had I need to pray Paul's prayer, 2 Thess. 3:2, "That we may be delivered from unreasonable and wicked men." For her satisfaction I went along with her and brought her to him, but before I got home again, it was noised about that I was running away and getting the English youth along with me, that as soon as I came in they began to rant and domineer, asking me where I had been, and what I had been doing, and saying they would knock him on the head. I told them I had been seeing the English youth and that I would not run away. They told me I lied, and taking up a hatchet, they came to me and said they would knock me down if I stirred out again and so confined me to the wigwam. Now may I say with David, 2 Sam. 24:14, "I am in a great strait." If I keep in, I must die with hunger, and if I go out, I must be knocked in head. This distressed condition held that day and half the next. And then the Lord remembered me, whose mercies are great.

Then came an Indian to me with a pair of stockings that were too big for him, and he would have me ravel them out and knit them fit for him. I showed myself willing and bid him ask my mistress if I might go along with him a little way; she said yes, I might, but I was not a little refreshed with that news that I had my liberty again. Then I went along with him, and he gave me some roasted groundnuts which did again revive my feeble stomach.

Being got out of her sight, I had time and liberty again to look into my Bible, which was my guide by day and my pillow by night. Now that comfortable scripture presented itself to me, Isa. 54:7, "For a small moment have I forsaken thee, but with great mercies will I gather thee."

Thus the Lord carried me along from one time to another and made good to me this precious promise and many others. Then my son came to see me, and I asked his master to let him stay awhile with me that I might comb his head and look over him, for he was almost overcome with lice. He told me when I had done that he was very hungry, but I had nothing to relieve him but bid him go into the wigwams as he went along and see if he could get anything among them, which he did. And it seems tarried a little too long, for his master was angry with him and beat him, and then sold him. Then he came running to tell me he had a new master, and that he had given him some groundnuts already. Then I went along with him to his new master who told me he loved him and he should not want. So his master carried him away, and I never saw him afterward till I saw him at Pascataqua in Portsmouth.

That night they bade me go out of the wigwam again. My mistress's papoose was sick, and it died that night, and there was one benefit in it that there was more room. I went to a wigwam and they bade me come in and gave me a skin to lie upon, and a mess of venison and groundnuts, which was a choice dish among them. On the morrow they buried the papoose and afterward, both morning and evening, there came a company to mourn and howl with her though I confess I could not much condole with them. Many sorrowful days I had in this place, often getting alone "like a crane, or a swallow, so did I chatter; I did mourn as a dove, mine eyes fail with looking upward. Oh, Lord, I am oppressed; undertake for me," Isa. 38:14. I could tell the Lord as Hezekiah, ver. 3, "Remember now, O Lord, I beseech Thee, how I have walked before Thee in truth."[45]

Now had I time to examine all my ways. My conscience did not accuse me of unrighteousness toward one or other, yet I saw how in my walk with God I had been a careless creature. As David said, "Against Thee, Thee only, have I sinned,"[46] and I might say with the poor publican, "God be merciful unto me a sinner."[47] On the Sabbath days I could look upon the sun and think how people were going to the house of God to have their souls refreshed and then home and their bodies also, but I was destitute of both and might say as the poor prodigal, "He would fain have filled his belly with the husks that the swine did eat, and no man

---

44. Dysentery.

45. Isaiah 38:3.

46. Psalm 51:4.

47. Luke 18:13.

gave unto him," Luke 15:16. For I must say with him, "Father I have sinned against heaven and in thy sight," ver. 21.[48] I remembered how on the night before and after the Sabbath when my family was about me and relations and neighbors with us, we could pray and sing, and then refresh our bodies with the good creatures of God, and then have a comfortable bed to lie down on. But instead of all this I had only a little swill for the body and then like a swine must lie down on the ground. I cannot express to man the sorrow that lay upon my spirit; the Lord knows it. Yet that comfortable scripture would often come to my mind, "For a small moment have I forsaken thee, but with great mercies will I gather thee."[49]

The Fourteenth Remove

Now must we pack up and be gone from this thicket, bending our course toward the Bay towns,[50] I having nothing to eat by the way this day but a few crumbs of cake that an Indian gave my girls the same day we were taken. She gave it me, and I put it in my pocket; there it lay till it was so moldy (for want of good baking) that one could not tell what it was made of; it fell all to crumbs and grew so dry and hard that it was like little flints, and this refreshed me many times when I was ready to faint. It was in my thoughts when I put it into my mouth that if ever I returned I would tell the world what a blessing the Lord gave to such mean food. As we went along, they killed a deer with a young one in her; they gave me a piece of the fawn, and it was so young and tender that one might eat the bones as well as the flesh, and yet I thought it very good. When night came on we sat down. It rained, but they quickly got up a bark wigwam where I lay dry that night. I looked out in the morning, and many of them had laid in the rain all night I saw by their reeking.[51] Thus the Lord dealt mercifully with me many times, and I fared better than many of them. In the morning they took the blood of the deer and put it into the paunch and so boiled it; I could eat nothing of that, though they ate it sweetly. And yet they were so nice[52] in other things that when I had fetched water and had put the dish I dipped the water with into the kettle of water which I brought, they would say they would knock me down for they said it was a sluttish trick.

The Fifteenth Remove

We went on our travel. I having got one handful of groundnuts for my support that day, they gave me my load, and I went on cheerfully (with the thoughts of going homeward) having my burden more on my back than my spirit. We came to Baquaug River[53] again that day, near which we abode a few days. Sometimes one of them would give me a pipe, another a little tobacco, another a little salt which I would change for a little victuals. I cannot but think what a wolfish appetite persons have in a starving condition, for many times when they gave me that which was hot, I was so greedy that I should burn my mouth that it would trouble me hours after, and yet I should quickly do the same again. And after I was thoroughly hungry, I was never again satisfied. For though sometimes it fell out that I got enough and did eat till I could eat no more, yet I was as unsatisfied as I was when I began. And now could I see that scripture verified (there being many scriptures which we do not take notice of or understood till we are afflicted), Mic. 6:14, "Thou shalt eat and not be satisfied." Now might I see more than ever before the miseries that sin hath brought upon us. Many times I should be ready to run out against the heathen, but the scripture would quiet me again, Amos 3:6, "Shall there be evil in the city, and the Lord hath not done it?" The Lord help me to make a right improvement of His word and that I might learn that great lesson, Mic. 6:8, 9, "He hath showed thee (Oh Man) what is good, and what doth the Lord require of thee, but to do justly and love mercy and walk humbly with thy God? Hear ye the rod and who hath appointed it."

The Sixteenth Remove

We began this remove with wading over Baquag River; the water was up to the knees and the stream very swift and so cold that I thought it would have cut me in sunder. I was so weak and feeble that I reeled as I went along and thought there I must end my days at last after my bearing and getting through so many difficulties. The Indians stood laughing to see me staggering along, but in my distress the Lord

---

48. Luke 15:21.

49. Isaiah 54:7.

50. Towns near Boston.

51. Streaming.

52. Fastidious.

---

53. Miller's River, in Orange, Massachusetts.

gave me experience of the truth and goodness of that promise, Isai. 43:2, "When thou passest through the waters, I will be with thee, and through the rivers, they shall not overflow thee." Then I sat down to put on my stockings and shoes with the tears running down mine eyes and many sorrowful thoughts in my heart, but I got up to go along with them. Quickly there came up to us an Indian who informed them that I must go to Wachuset to my master, for there was a letter come from the council to the sagamores about redeeming the captives and that there would be another in fourteen days and that I must be there ready. My heart was so heavy before that I could scarce speak or go in the path and yet now so light that I could run. My strength seemed to come again and recruit my feeble knees and aching heart, yet it pleased them to go but one mile that night, and there we stayed two days. In that time came a company of Indians to us, near thirty, all on horseback. My heart skipped within me, thinking they had been Englishmen at the first sight of them, for they were dressed in English apparel, with hats, white neckcloths, and sashes about their waists, and ribbons upon their shoulders, but when they came near there was a vast difference between the lovely faces of Christians and the foul looks of those heathens which much damped my spirit again.

The Seventeenth Remove

A comfortable remove it was to me because of my hopes. They gave me a pack, and along we went cheerfully, but quickly my will proved more than my strength. Having little or no refreshing, my strength failed me, and my spirit were almost quite gone. Now may I say with David, Psal. 119:22, 23, 24, "I am poor and needy, and my heart is wounded within me. I am gone like the shadow when it declineth: I am tossed up and down like the locust; my knees are weak through fasting, and my flesh faileth of fatness."[54]

At night we came to an Indian town,[55] and the Indians sat down by a wigwam discoursing, but I was almost spent and could scarce speak. I laid down my load and went into the wigwam, and there sat an Indian boiling of horses' feet (they being wont to eat the flesh first, and when the feet were old and dried and they had nothing else, they would cut off the feet and use them). I asked him to give me a little of his broth or water they were boil-

ing in; he took a dish and gave me one spoonful of samp [corn mush] and bid me take as much of the broth as I would. Then I put some of the hot water to the samp and drank it up and my spirit came again. He gave me also a piece of the rough or ridding of the small guts, and I broiled it on the coals; and now may I say with Jonathan, "See, I pray you, how mine eyes have been enlightened because I tasted a little of this honey," 1 Sam. 14:29. Now is my spirit revived again, though means be never so inconsiderable; yet if the Lord bestow His blessing upon them, they shall refresh both soul and body.

The Eighteenth Remove

We took up our packs and along we went, but a wearisome day I had of it. As we went along I saw an Englishman stripped naked and lying dead upon the ground but knew not who it was. Then we came to another Indian town where we stayed all night.[56] In this town there were four English children, captives, and one of them my own sister's. I went to see how she did, and she was well, considering her captive condition. I would have tarried that night with her, but they that owned her would not suffer it. Then I went into another wigwam where they were boiling corn and beans, which was a lovely sight to see, but I could not get a taste thereof. Then I went to another wigwam where there were two of the English children. The squaw was boiling horses' feet; then she cut me off a little piece and gave one of the English children a piece also. Being very hungry, I had quickly eat up mine, but the child could not bite it, it was so touch and sinewy but lay sucking, gnawing, chewing, and slabbering of it in the mouth and hand. Then I took it of the child and ate it myself and savory it was to my taste. Then I may say Job, chap. 6:7, "The things that my soul refused to touch are as my sorrowful meat." Thus the Lord made that pleasant refreshing which another time would have been an abomination. Then I went home to my mistress' wigwam, and they told me I disgraced my master with begging, and if I did so anymore they would knock me in head. I told them they had as good knock me in head as starve me to death.

The Nineteenth Remove

They said when we went out that we must travel to Wachuset[57] this day. But a bitter weary day I had of it,

---

54. Here Rowlandson quotes Psalm 109:22–24, not Psalm 119:22–24.

55. Probably Nichewaug (Petersham).

56. Probably Wanimesset (present-day New Bedford, Massachusetts).

57. Princeton, Massachusetts.

traveling now three days together without resting any day between. At last, after many weary steps, I saw Wachuset Hills but many miles off. Then we came to a great swamp through which we traveled up to the knees in mud and water, which was heavy going to one tired before. Being almost spent, I thought I should have sunk down at last and never got out, but I may say, as in Psal. 94:18, "When my foot slipped, Thy mercy, O Lord, held me up." Going along, having indeed my life but little spirit, Philip, who was in the company, came up and took me by the hand and said, "Two weeks more and you shall be mistress again." I asked him if he spake true. He answered, "Yes, and quickly you shall come to your master again who has been gone from us three weeks." After many weary steps we came to Wachuset where he was, and glad I was to see him. He asked me when I washed me. I told him not this month. Then he fetched me some water himself and bid me wash and gave me the glass to see how I looked and bid his squaw give me something to eat. So she gave me a mess of beans and meat and a little groundnut cake. I was wonderfully revived with this favor showed me, Psal. 106:46, "He made them also to be pitied, of all those that carried them captives."

My master had three squaws, living sometimes with one and sometimes with another one. This old squaw at whose wigwam I was, my master had been those three weeks. Another was Wettimore with whom I had lived and served all this while. A severe and proud dame she was, bestowing every day in dressing herself neat as much time as any of the gentry of the land, powdering her hair and painting her face, going with necklaces, with jewels in her ears, and bracelets upon her hands. When she had dressed herself, her work was to make girdles of wampum and beads. The third squaw was a younger one by whom he had two papooses. By that time I was refreshed by the old squaw with whom my master was, Wettimore's maid came to call me home, at which I fell a-weeping. Then the old squaw told me, to encourage me, that if I wanted victuals I should come to her, and that I should lie there in her wigwam. Then I went with the maid and quickly came again and lodged there. The squaw laid a mat under me and a good rug over me; the first time I had any such kindness showed me. I understood that Wettimore thought that if she should let me go and serve with the old squaw, she would be in danger to lose not only my service but the redemption pay also. And I was not a little glad to hear this, being by it raised in my hopes that in God's due time there would be an end of this sorrowful hour. Then came an Indian and asked me to knit him three pair of stockings, for which I had a hat and a

silk handkerchief. Then another asked me to make her a shift, for which she gave me an apron.

Then came Tom and Peter[58] with the second letter from the council about the captives. Though they were Indians, I got them by the hand and burst out into tears; my heart was so full that I could not speak to them, but recovering myself, I asked them how my husband did and all my friends and acquaintances. They said they all very well but melancholy. They brought me two biscuits and a pound of tobacco. The tobacco I quickly gave away; when it was all gone, one asked me to give him a pipe of tobacco. I told him it was all gone. Then began he to rant and threaten. I told him when my husband came I would give some. "Hang rogue," says he, "I will knock out his brains if he comes here." And then again in the same breath they would say that if there should come a hundred without guns they would do them no hurt, so unstable and like madmen they were, so that fearing the worst, I durst not send to my husband though there were some thoughts of his coming to redeem and fetch me, not knowing what might follow. For there was little more trust to them than to the master they served.

When the letter was come, the sagamores met to consult about the captives and called me to them to inquire how much my husband would give to redeem me. When I came, I sat down among them as I was wont to do as their manner is. Then they bade me stand up and said they were the General Court.[59] They bid me speak what I thought he would give. Now knowing that all we had was destroyed by the Indians, I was in a great strait. I thought if I should speak of but a little, it would be slighted and hinder the matter; if of a great sum, I knew not where it would be procured. Yet at a venture, I said twenty pounds yet desired them to take less, but they would not hear of that but sent that message to Boston that for twenty pounds I should be redeemed. It was a praying Indian that wrote their letter for them. There was another praying Indian who told me that he had a brother that would not eat horse; his conscience was so tender and scrupulous (though as large as hell for the destruction of poor Christians). Then he said he read that scripture to him, 2 Kings, 6:25, "There was a famine in Samaria, and behold they

---

58. Tom Dublet (Nepanet) and Peter Conway (Tatatiquinea) were Christian Indians from Nashobah who were negotiating for the ransom.

59. They wanted Rowlandson to stand before their legislative assembly (as before the Colonial Assembly of Massachusetts).

besieged it, until an ass's head was sold for fourscore pieces of silver, and the fourth part of a kab of doves' dung for five pieces of silver." He expounded this place to his brother and showed him that it was lawful to eat that in a famine which is not at another time. And now, says he, he will eat horse with any Indian of them all.

There was another praying Indian who, when he had done all the mischief that he could, betrayed his own father into the English hands thereby to purchase his own life. Another praying Indian was at Sudbury fight, though, as he deserved, he was afterward hanged for it. There was another praying Indian so wicked and cruel as to wear a string about his neck strung with Christians' fingers. Another praying Indian, when they went to Sudbury fight, went with them and his squaw also with him with her papoose at her back.

Before they went to that fight, they got a company together to powwow; the manner was as followeth. There was one that kneeled upon a deerskin with the company round him in a ring, who kneeled, and striking upon the ground with their hands and with sticks, and muttering or humming with their mouths; besides him who kneeled in the ring, there also stood one with a gun in his hand. Then he on the deerskin made a speech, and all manifested assent to it, and so they did many times together. Then they bade him with the gun go out of the ring, which he did, but when he was out, they called him in again. But he seemed to make a stand; then they called the more earnestly till he returned again. Then they all sang. Then they gave him two guns, in either hand one. And so he on the deerskin began again, and at the end of every sentence in his speaking, they all assented, humming or muttering with their mouths and striking upon the ground with their hands. Then they bade him with the two guns go out of the ring again, which he did a little way. Then they called him in again, but he made a stand; so they called him with greater earnestness, but he stood reeling and wavering as if he knew not whether he should stand or fall or which way to go. Then they called him with exceeding great vehemency, all of them, one and another. After a little while he turned in, staggering as he went, with his arms stretched out, in either hand a gun. As soon as he came in, they all sang and rejoiced exceedingly awhile. And then he upon the deerskin made another speech unto which they all assented in a rejoicing manner, and so they ended their business and forthwith went to Sudbury fight.[60]

To my thinking they went without any scruple but that they should prosper and gain the victory. And they went out not so rejoicing, but they came home with as great a victory, for they said they had killed two captains and almost an hundred men. One Englishman they brought along with them; and he said it was too true for they had made sad work at Sudbury, as indeed it proved. Yet they came home without that rejoicing and triumphing over their victory which they were wont to show at other times but rather like dogs (as they say) which have lost their ears. Yet I could not perceive that it was for their own loss of men. They said they had not lost but above five or six, and I missed none except in one wigwam. When they went, they acted as if the devil had told them that they should gain the victory, and now they acted as if the devil had told them they should have a fall. Whither it were so or no, I cannot tell, but so it proved for quickly they began to fall and so held on that summer till they came to utter ruin.

They came home on a Sabbath day, and the powwow that kneeled upon the deerskin came home (I may say without abuse) as black as the devil. When my master came home, he came to me and bid me make a shirt for his papoose of a Holland lace pillowbeer.[61] About that time there came an Indian to me and bid me come to his wigwam at night, and he would give me some pork and groundnuts, which I did. And as I was eating, another Indian said to me, "He seems to be your good friend, but he killed two Englishmen at Sudbury, and there lie their clothes behind you." I looked behind me, and there I saw bloody clothes with bullet holes in them, yet the Lord suffered not this wretch to do me any hurt. Yea, instead of that, he many times refreshed me; five or six times did he and his squaw refresh my feeble carcass. If I went to their wigwam at any time, they would always give me something, and yet they were strangers that I never saw before. Another squaw gave me a piece of fresh pork and a little salt with it and lent me her pan to fry it in, and I cannot but remember what a sweet, pleasant and delightful relish that bit had to me to this day. So little do we prize common mercies when we have them to the full.

The Twentieth Remove[62]

It was their usual manner to remove when they had done any mischief, lest they should be found out, and so they

---

60. In the April 18 attack on Sudbury, Massachusetts, many in the English militia were killed.

61. Pillowcase.

62. The encampment was located near the southern end of Wachusett Lake, in Princeton, Massachusetts.

did at this time. We went about three or four miles, and there they built a great wigwam big enough to hold a hundred Indians, which they did in preparation to a great day of dancing. They would say now amongst themselves that the governor would be so angry for his loss at Sudbury that he would send no more about the captives, which made me grieve and tremble. My sister being not far from the place where we now were, and hearing that I was here, desired her master to let her come and see me, and he was willing to it and would go with her. But she, being ready before him, told him she would go before and was come within a mile or two of the place. Then he overtook her and began to rant as if he had been mad and made her go back again in the rain so that I never saw her till I saw her in Charlestown. But the Lord requited many of their ill doings, for this Indian, her master, was hanged afterward at Boston.

The Indians now began to come from all quarters, against their merry dancing day. Among some of them came one Goodwife Kettle.[63] I told her my heart was so heavy that it was ready to break. "So is mine, too," said she. But yet said, "I hope we shall hear some good news shortly." I could hear how earnestly my sister desired to see me, and I as earnestly desired to see her and yet neither of us could get an opportunity. My daughter was also now about a mile off, and I had not seen her in nine or ten weeks as I had not seen my sister since our first taking. I earnestly desired them to let me go and see them; yea, I entreated, begged, and persuaded them but to let me see my daughter, and yet so hardhearted were they that they would not suffer it. They made use of their tyrannical power whilst they had it, but through the Lord's wonderful mercy their time was now but short.

On a Sabbath day, the sun being about an hour high in the afternoon, came Mr. John Hoar[64] (the council permitting him and his own forward spirit inclining him) together with the two forementioned Indians, Tom and Peter, with their third letter from the council. When they came near, I was abroad; though I saw them not, they presently called me in and bade me sit down and not stir. Then they catched up their guns and away they ran as if an enemy had been at hand, and the guns went off apace. I manifested some great trouble, and they asked me what was the matter. I told them I thought they had killed the Englishman (for they had in the meantime informed me that an Englishman was come). They said, "No." They shot over his horse and under, and before his horse, and they pushed him this way and that way at their pleasure, showing what they could do. Then they let them come to their wigwams. I begged of them to let me see the Englishman, but they would not; but there was I fain to sit their pleasure. When they had talked their fill with him, they suffered me to go to him. We asked each other of our welfare, and how my husband did and all my friends. He told me they were all well and would be glad to see me. Amongst other things which my husband sent me, there came a pound of tobacco which I sold for nine shillings in money, for many of the Indians for want of tobacco smoked hemlock and ground ivy. It was a great mistake in any who thought I sent for tobacco, for through the favor of God that desire was overcome.

I now asked them whether I should go home with Mr. Hoar. They answered, "No," one and another of them. And it being night, we lay down with that answer. In the morning Mr. Hoar invited the sagamores to dinner, but when we went to get it ready, we found that they had stolen the greatest part of the provision Mr. Hoar had brought out of his bags in the night. And we may see the wonderful power of God in that one passage in that when there was such a great number of the Indians together and so greedy of a little good food and no English there but Mr. Hoar and myself that there they did not knock us in the head and take what he had, there being not only some provision but also trading cloth,[65] a part of the twenty pounds agreed upon. But instead of doing us any mischief, they seemed to be ashamed of the fact and said it were some *matchit* Indian that did it. Oh, that we could believe that there is nothing too hard for God! God showed His power over the heathen in this as He did over the hungry lions when Daniel was cast into the den.[66] Mr. Hoar called them betime to dinner, but they ate very little, they being so busy in dressing themselves and getting ready for their dance, which was carried on by eight of them—four men and four squaws, my master and mistress being two. He was dressed in his Holland shirt[67] with great laces sewed at the tail of it; he had his silver buttons, his white stockings, his garters were

---

63. Elizabeth Ward Kettle of Lancaster.

64. John Hoar, of Concord, Massachusetts, was delegated by Rowlandson's husband to represent him at the council for the Sagamore Indians in order to bargain for her redemption.

65. Cloth used for barter.

66. See Daniel 6:1–29.

67. Linen.

hung round with shillings, and he had girdles of wampum upon his head and shoulders. She had a kersey coat[68] and covered with girdles of wampum from the loins upward; her arms from her elbows to her hands were covered with bracelets; there were handfuls of necklaces about her neck and several sorts of jewels in her ears. She had fine red stockings and white shoes, her hair powdered and face painted red that was always before black. And all the dancers were after the same manner. There were two other singing and knocking on a kettle for their music. They kept hopping up and down one after another with a kettle of water in the midst, standing warm upon some embers, to drink of when they were dry. They held on till it was almost night, throwing out wampum to the standersby.

At night I asked them again if I should go home. They all as one said no except[69] my husband would come for me. When we were lain down, my master went out of the wigwam, and by and by sent in an Indian called James the Printer[70] who told Mr. Hoar that my master would let me go home tomorrow if he would let him have one pint of liquors. Then Mr. Hoar called his own Indians, Tom and Peter, and bid them go and see whether he would promise it before them three, and if he would, he should have it, which he did, and he had it. Then Philip, smelling the business, called me to him and asked me what I would give him to tell me some good news and speak a good word for me. I told him I could not tell what to give him. I would anything I had and asked him what he would have. He said two coats and twenty shillings in money and half a bushel of seed corn and some tobacco. I thanked him for his love, but I knew the good news as well as the crafty fox.

My master, after he had had his drink, quickly came ranting into the wigwam again and called for Mr. Hoar, drinking to him and saying he was a good man. And then again he would say, "Hang rogue." Being almost drunk, he would drink to him, and yet presently say he should be hanged. Then he called for me. I trembled to hear him, yet I was fain to go to him, and he drank to me, showing no incivility. He was the first Indian I saw drunk all the while that I was amongst them. At last his squaw ran out, and he after her round the wigwam with his money jingling at his knees, but she escaped him. But having an old squaw, he

ran to her, and so through the Lord's mercy, we were no more troubled that night.

Yet I had not a comfortable night's rest, for I think I can say I did not sleep for three nights together. The night before the letter came from the council I could not rest, I was so full of fears and troubles, God many times leaving us most in the dark when deliverance is nearest. Yea, at this time I could not rest night nor day. The next night I was overjoyed, Mr. Hoar being come and that with such good tidings. The third night I was even swallowed up with the thoughts of things, *viz.* that ever I should go home again and that I must go, leaving my children behind me in the wilderness so that sleep was now almost departed from mine eyes.

On Tuesday morning they called their General Court (as they call it) to consult and determine whether I should go home or no. And they all as one man did seemingly consent to it that I should go home except Philip who would not come among them.

But before I go any further, I would take leave to mention a few remarkable passages of providence which I took special notice of in my afflicted time.

1. Of the fair opportunity lost in the long march a little after the fort fight when our English army was so numerous and in pursuit of the enemy and so near as to take several and destroy them, and the enemy in such distress for food that our men might track them by their rooting in the earth for groundnuts while they were flying for their lives. I say that then our army should want provision and be forced to leave their pursuit and return homeward. And the very next week the enemy came upon our town like bears bereft of their whelps or so many ravenous wolves, rending us and our lambs to death. But what shall I say? God seemed to leave His people to themselves and order all things for His own holy ends. "Shall there be evil in the city and the Lord hath not done it?[71] They are not grieved for the affliction of Joseph, therefore shall they go captive with the first that go captive."[72] It is the Lord's doing, and it should be marvelous in our eyes.

2. I cannot but remember how the Indians derided the slowness and dullness of the English army in its setting out. For after the desolations at Lancaster and Medfield, as I went along with them, they asked me when I thought the English would come after them. I told them I could not tell. It may be they will come in May, said they. Thus

---

68. Made from coarse, woven wool.

69. Unless.

70. James, a "praying Indian" who helped the Reverend John Eliot print the Bible in Algonquian.

71. Amos 3:6.

72. Amos 6:6–7.

did they scoff at us, as if the English would be a quarter of a year getting ready.

3. Which also I have hinted before when the English army with new supplies were sent forth to pursue after the enemy, and they, understanding it, fled before them till they came to Baquaug River where they forthwith went over safely, that that river should be impassable to the English. I can but admire to see the wonderful[73] providence of God in preserving the heathen for further affliction to our poor country. They could go in great numbers over, but the English must stop. God had an overruling hand in all those things.

4. It was thought if their corn were cut down they would starve and die with hunger, and all their corn that could be found was destroyed, and they driven from that little they had in store into the woods in the midst of winter. And yet how to admiration did the Lord preserve them for His holy ends and the destruction of many still amongst the English! Strangely did the Lord provide for them that I did not see (all the time I was among them) one man, woman, or child die with hunger. Though many times they would eat that that a hog or dog would hardly touch, yet by that God strengthened them to be a scourge to His people.

The chief and commonest food was groundnuts. They eat also nuts and acorns, artichokes, lily roots, groundbeans, and several other weeds and roots that I know not.

They would pick up old bones and cut them to pieces at the joints, and if they were full of worms and maggots, they would scald them over the fire to make the vermin come out and then boil them and drink up the liquor and then beat the great ends of them in a mortar and so eat them. They would eat horses' guts and ears, and all sorts of wild birds which they could catch; also bear, venison, beaver, tortoise, frogs, squirrels, dogs, skunks, rattlesnakes, yea, the very bark of trees, besides all sorts of creatures and provision which they plundered from the English. I can but stand in admiration to see the wonderful power of God in providing for such a vast number of our enemies in the wilderness where there was nothing to be seen but from hand to mouth. Many times in a morning the generality of them would eat up all they had and yet have some further supply against they wanted. It is said, Psal. 81:13, 14, "Oh, that My people had hearkened to Me, and Israel had walked in My ways; I should soon have subdued their enemies and turned My hand against their adversaries." But now our perverse and evil carriages in the sight of the Lord have so offended Him that

instead of turning His hand against them the Lord feeds and nourishes them up to be a scourge to the whole land.

5. Another thing that I would observe is the strange providence of God in turning things about when the Indians at the highest and the English at the lowest. I was with the enemy eleven weeks and five days, and not one weeks passed without the fury of the enemy and some desolation by fire and sword upon one place or other. They mourned (with their black faces) for their own losses, yet triumphed and rejoiced in their inhuman and many times devilish cruelty to the English. They would boast much of their victories, saying that in two hours' time they had destroyed such a captain and his company at such a place, and such a captain and his company in such a place, and such a captain and his company in such a place, and boast how many towns they had destroyed; and then scoff and say they had done them a good turn to send them to heaven so soon. Again they would say this summer that they would knock all the rogues in the head, or drive them into the sea, or make them fly the country, thinking surely Agag-like,[74] "The bitterness of death is past."[75] Now the heathen begins to think all is their own, and the poor Christians' hopes to fail (as to man), and now their eyes are more to God, and their hearts sigh heavenward and to say in good earnest, "Help Lord, or we perish." When the Lord had brought His people to this that they saw no help in anything but Himself, then He takes the quarrel into His own hand, and though they had made a pit in their own imaginations as deep as hell for the Christians that summer, yet the Lord hurled themselves into it. And the Lord had not so many ways before to preserve them, but now He hath as many to destroy them.

But to return again to my going home where we may see a remarkable change of providence. At first they were all against it except my husband would come for me, but afterwards they assented to it and seemed much to rejoice in it. Some asked me to send them some bread, others some tobacco, others shaking me by the hand, offering me a hood and scarf to ride in, not one moving hand or tongue against it. Thus hath the Lord answered my poor desire and the many earnest requests of others put up unto God for me. In my travels an Indian came to me and told me if I were willing, he and his squaw would run away and go home along with me. I told him no. I was not willing to run away but desired to wait God's time that I might go home

---

73. Full of wonder.

74. King of Amalek thought himself spared after his defeat by Saul, but he was killed by Samuel. See 1 Samuel 15.

75. 1 Samuel 15:32.

quietly and without fear. And now God hath granted me my desire. O, the wonderful power of God that I have seen and the experience that I have had! I have been in the midst of those roaring lions and savage bears that feared neither God nor man nor the devil, by night and day, alone and in company, sleeping all sorts together, and yet not one of them ever offered me the least abuse of unchastity to me in word or action. Though some are ready to say I speak it for my own credit, I speak it in the presence of God and to His glory. God's power is as great now and as sufficient to save as when He preserved Daniel in the lion's den or the three children in the fiery furnace.[76] I may well say as his Psal. 107:12, "Oh, give thanks unto the Lord for He is good, for His mercy endureth forever." Let the redeemed of the Lord say so whom He hath redeemed from the hand of the enemy, especially that I should come away in the midst of so many hundreds of enemies quietly and peaceably and not a dog moving his tongue.

So I took my leave of them, and in coming along my heart melted into tears more than all the while I was with them, and I was almost swallowed up with the thoughts that ever I should go home again. About the sun going down, Mr. Hoar, myself, and the two Indians came to Lancaster, and a solemn sight it was to me. There had I lived many comfortable years amongst my relations and neighbors, and now not one Christian to be seen nor one house left standing. We went on to a farmhouse that was yet standing where we lay all night, and a comfortable lodging we had though nothing but straw to lie on. The Lord preserved us in safety that night and raised us up again in the morning and carried us along that before noon we came to Concord. Now was I full of joy and yet not without sorrow—joy to see such a lovely sight, so many Christians together and some of them my neighbors. There I met with my brother and my brother-in-law who asked me if I knew where his wife was. Poor heart! He had helped to bury her and knew it not, she being shot down the house was partly burned so that those who were at Boston at the desolation of the town and came back afterward and buried the dead did not know her. Yet I was not without sorrow to think how many were looking and longing and my own children amongst the rest to enjoy that deliverance that I had now received, and I did not know whether ever I should see them again.

Being recruited[77] with food and raiment, we went to Boston that day where I met with my dear husband, but the thoughts of our dear children, one being dead and the other we could not tell where, abated our comfort each to other. I was not before so much hemmed in with the merciless and cruel heathen but now as much with pitiful, tender-hearted, and compassionate Christians. In that poor and distressed and beggarly condition I was received in, I was kindly entertained in several houses; so much love I received from several (some of whom I knew and others I knew not) that I am not capable to declare it. But the Lord knows them all by name. The Lord reward them sevenfold into their bosoms of His spirituals for their temporals.

The twenty pounds, the price of my redemption, was raised by some Boston gentlemen and Mrs. Usher,[78] whose bounty and religious charity I would not forget to make mention of. Then Mr. Thomas Shepard of Charlestown[79] received us into his house where we continued eleven weeks, and a father and mother they were to us. And many more tenderhearted friends we met with in that place. We were now in the midst of love, yet not without much and frequent heaviness of heart for our poor children and other relations who were still in affliction. The week following after my coming in, the governor and council sent forth to the Indians again, and that not without success, for they brought in my sister and Goodwife Kettle.

Their not knowing where our children were was a sore trial to us still, and yet we were not without secret hopes that we should see them again. That which was dead lay heavier upon my spirit than those which were alive and amongst the heathen, thinking how it suffered with its wounds and I was no way able to relieve it, and how it was buried by the heathen in the wilderness from among all Christians. We were hurried up and down in our thoughts; sometime we should hear a report that they were gone this way, and sometimes that, and that they were come in in this place or that. We kept inquiring and listening to hear concerning them but no certain news as yet. About this time the council had ordered a day of public thanksgiving, though I thought I had still cause of mourning, and, being unsettled in our minds, we thought we would ride toward the eastward to see if we could hear anything concerning our children. And as we were riding along (God is the wise disposer of all things) between Ipswich and Rowly we met with Mr. William Hubbard,[80] who told us that our son

---

76. Daniel 3:13–30.

77. Refreshed.

78. The wife of Boston bookseller and selectman Hezekiah Usher.

79. Son of the Reverend Thomas Shepard (1604?–49) of Cambridge, a prominent, first-generation Puritan leader.

80. Minister at Ipswich, Massachusetts.

Joseph was come in to Major Waldren's,[81] and another with him which was my sister's son. I asked him how he knew it. He said the major himself told him so.

So along we went till we came to Newbury, and, their minister being absent, they desired my husband to preach the thanksgiving for them, but he was not willing to stay there that night but would go over to Salisbury to hear further and come again in the morning, which he did and preached there that day. At night when he had done, one came and told him that his daughter was come in at Providence. Here was mercy on both hands. Now hath God fulfilled that precious scripture which was such a comfort to me in my distressed condition. When my heart was ready to sink into the earth (my children being gone I could not tell whither), and my knees trembled under me, and I was walking through the valley of the shadow of death, then the Lord brought and now has fulfilled that reviving word unto me. Thus saith the Lord, "Refrain thy voice from weeping, and thine eyes from tears, for thy work shall be rewarded," saith the Lord, "and they shall come again from the land of the enemy."[82]

Now we were between them, the one on the east and the other on the west. Our son being nearest, we went to him first to Portsmouth where we met with him and with the major also who told us he had done what he could but could not redeem him under seven pounds, which the good people thereabouts were pleased to pay. The Lord reward the major and all the rest, though unknown to me, for their labor of love. My sister's son was redeemed for four pounds, which the council gave order for the payment of. Having now received one of our children, we hastened toward the other; going back through Newbury, my husband preached there on the Sabbath day, for which they rewarded him manyfold.

On Monday we came to Charlestown where we heard that the governor of Rhode Island[83] had sent over for our daughter to take care of her, being now within his jurisdiction, which should not pass without our acknowledgments. But she being nearer Rehoboth than Rhode Island, Mr. Newman[84] went over and took care of her and brought her to his own house. And the goodness of God was admirable to us in our low estate in that he raised up passionate friends on every side to us when we had noth-

ing to recompense any for their love. The Indians were now gone that way that it was apprehended dangerous to go to her, but the carts which carried provision to the English army, being guarded, brought her with them to Dorchester where we received her safe. Blessed be the Lord for it, for great is His power, and He can do whatsoever seemeth Him good.

Her coming in was after this manner. She was traveling one day with the Indians with her basket at her back; the company of Indians were got before her and gone out of sight, all except one squaw. She followed the squaw till night, and then both of them lay down, having nothing over them but the heavens and under them but the earth. Thus she traveled three days together, not knowing whither she was going, having nothing to eat or drink but water and green hirtleberries.[85] At last they came into Providence where she was kindly entertained by several of that town. The Indians often said that I should never have her under twenty pounds. But now the Lord hath brought her in upon free cost and given her to me the second time. The Lord make us a blessing indeed each to others. Now have I seen that scripture also fulfilled, Deut. 30:4, 7: "If any of thine be driven out to the outmost parts of heaven, from thence will the Lord thy God gather thee, and from thence will He fetch thee. And the Lord thy God will put all these curses upon thine enemies, and on them which hate thee which persecuted thee." Thus hath the Lord brought me and mine out of that horrible pit and hath set us in the midst of tenderhearted and compassionate Christians. It is the desire of my soul that we may walk worthy of the mercies received and which we are receiving.

Our family being now gathered together (those of us that were living), the South Church in Boston hired an house for us. Then we removed from Mr. Shepard's, those cordial friends, and went to Boston where we continued about three-quarters of a year. Still the Lord went along with us and provided graciously for us. I thought it somewhat strange to set up housekeeping with bare walls, but as Solomon says, "Money answers all things,"[86] and that we had through the benevolence of Christian friends, some in this town and some in that and others, and some from England, that in a little time we might look and see the house furnished with love. The Lord hath been exceeding good to us in our low estate in that when we had neither house nor home nor other necessaries, the Lord so moved the hearts of these and those towards us that we

---

81. Richard Waldron of Dover, New Hampshire.

82. Jeremiah 31:16.

83. William Coddington.

84. The Reverend Noah Newman of Rehoboth, Massachusetts.

---

85. Huckleberries.

86. Ecclesiastes 10:19.

wanted neither food nor raiment for ourselves or ours, Prov. 18:24, "There is a friend which sticketh closer than a brother." And how many such friends have we found and now living amongst? And truly such a friend have we found him to be unto us in whose house we lived, *viz.* Mr. James Whitcomb, a friend unto us near hand and afar off.

I can remember the time when I used to sleep quietly without workings in my thoughts whole nights together, but now it is other ways with me. When all are fast about me and no eye open but His who ever waketh, my thoughts are upon things past, upon the awful dispensation of the Lord towards us, upon His wonderful power and might in carrying of us through so many difficulties in returning us in safety and suffering none to hurt us. I remember in the night season how the other day I was in the midst of thousands of enemies and nothing but death before me. It then hard work to persuade myself that ever I should be satisfied with bread again. But now we are fed with the finest of the wheat, and, as I may say, with honey out of the rock.[87] Instead of the husk, we have the fatted calf.[88] The thoughts of these things in the particulars of them, and of the love and goodness of God towards us, make it true of me what David said of himself, Psal. 6:5. "I watered my couch with my tears." Oh, the wonderful power of God that mine eyes have seen, affording matter enough for my thoughts to run in that when others are sleeping mine eyes are weeping!

I have seen the extreme vanity of this world. One hour I have been in health and wealth, wanting nothing, but the next hour in sickness and wounds and death, having nothing but sorrow and affliction. Before I knew what affliction meant, I was ready sometimes to wish for it. When I lived in prosperity, having the comforts of the world about me, my relations by me, my heart cheerful, and taking little care for anything, and yet seeing many whom I preferred before myself under many trials and afflictions, in sickness, weakness, poverty, losses, crosses, and cares of the world, I should be sometimes jealous lest I should have my portion in this life, and that scripture would come to mind, Heb. 12:6, "For whom the Lord loveth he chasteneth and scourgeth every son whom He receiveth." But now I see the Lord had His time to scourge and chasten me. The portion of some is to have their afflictions by drops, now one drop and then another, but the dregs of the cup, the wine of astonishment, like a sweeping rain that leaveth no food, did the Lord prepare to be my portion. Affliction I wanted and affliction I had, full measure (I thought) pressed down and running over. Yet I see when God calls a person to anything and through never so many difficulties, yet He is fully able to carry them through and make them see and say they have been gainers thereby. And I hope I can say in some measure, as David did, "It is good for me that I have been afflicted."[89]

The Lord hath showed me the vanity of these outward things. That they are the vanity of vanities and vexation of spirit, that they are but a shadow, a blast, a bubble, and things of no continuance. That we must rely on God himself and our whole dependence must be upon Him. If trouble from smaller matters begin to arise in me, I have something at hand to check myself with and say, why am I troubled? It was but the other day that if I had had the world I would have given it for my freedom or to have been a servant to a Christian. I have learned to look beyond present and smaller troubles and to be quieted under them, as Moses said, Exod. 14:13, "Stand still and see the salvation of the Lord."

---

87. Psalm 81:16.
88. Luke 15:23.

89. Psalm 119:71.

John Williams (1664–1729)

A prominent minister and author of a best-selling Indian captivity narrative, John Williams was born to a shoemaker and his wife in Massachusetts Bay. Drawing on financial support from his maternal grandfather, Williams attended Roxbury Latin School and Harvard College, where he worked briefly as a teacher. In his early twenties, he moved to Deerfield, a small, recently settled town on the New England border area, to fill the position of Congregational minister. There he married Eunice Mather, a niece of the prominent minister Increase Mather, with whom he had seven surviving children.

Hostilities between the French and English had a long history, beginning during the seventeenth century, and each side relied upon its own Indian allies. By 1694, after Williams's arrival, the town of Deerfield had successfully challenged a combined attack of French and Indians. Ten years later, during what the British called Queen Anne's War, Deerfield proved unable to repel the attack ordered by Governor-General Vaudreuil of New France. In February 1704, Hertel de Rouville and his mixed force of Hurons, Abenakis, Caughnawaga Mohawks, and French Canadians, attacked the frontier town, killing many people, among them Williams's daughter Jerusha and his son John. Williams was himself a prime captive because of his leadership in the community as a minister. He was taken with his wife and five of their children, joined with approximately one hundred other townspeople, and forced to walk to Canada. During the two-year captivity that ensued, Williams was initially held by the Mohawks for about eight weeks and then was given over to the French.

Given Williams's prominence in the Deerfield community, he was a particularly valuable prisoner for the French, and he would be an even greater asset were he to accept conversion to Catholicism. While in Canada the Puritan minister struggled to protect his flock from the Jesuits' attempts to convert the entire group to Catholic ways. The threat to the Puritans, Williams believed, was both religious and cultural. Captivity changed Williams's family dramatically and permanently: His wife died during the march northward, and despite Williams's ongoing efforts to the contrary, his daughter Eunice remained with the Mohawks and converted to Catholicism.

Williams's release was eventually negotiated by William Dudley, son of the Massachusetts Bay governor, who agreed to exchange Frenchman Pierre Maisonnat, known as Captain Baptiste, imprisoned in Boston, for Williams. After returning to Deerfield in 1706, Williams resumed his post, worked for the release of English prisoners, and remarried. It is likely that he wrote his narrative during the winter of 1706–07. The first of six eighteenth-century editions of the narrative appeared during the following spring and sold approximately one thousand copies within one week of publication.

As the title of Williams's narrative, *The Redeemed Captive, Returning to Zion* (1707), suggests, Williams's return to the Puritan settlement was understood as an illustration of divine will. The religious implications of Williams's narrative held favorable meaning not only for Williams but for the community at large. Williams's narrative reveals many characteristics of the Puritans' jeremiad tradition. Most notably, it reminds Puritans of their covenant with God and cautions them of God's anger toward those who are unfaithful to Him. To the Puritans, captivity among Indians served as God's warning, yet it also offered people the opportunity to reflect upon their past failings and God's mercy. Captivity required their humble submission to their God. Drawing on the anti-Catholic sentiments of Protestant readers, the narrative also demonstrates Williams's fear and discomfort with a religion he viewed as a perversion of Christianity. The narrative thus offers both religious and historical insight into the Puritanism, Protestant versus Catholic tensions, and the wars that enveloped the English, French, and Indians in New England.

from THE REDEEMED CAPTIVE RETURNING TO ZION[1]

The Dedication
To His Excellency, Joseph Dudley, Esq.
Captain-General and Governor-in-Chief,
in and over her Majesty's Province of the
Massachusetts Bay in New England, etc.[2]

---

1. *The Redeemed Captive Returning to Zion* was originally published in 1707. The text is from *Puritans among the Indians: Accounts of Captivity and Redemption, 1676–1724,* ed. A. T. Vaughan and E. W. Clark (1981). The original editors' clarifying emendations have been retained in brackets.

2. Joseph Dudley (1647–1720), governor of the Massachusetts Bay colony from 1702 to 1715.

Sir,

It was a satirical answer, and deeply reproachful to mankind, which the Philosopher gave to that question, "What soonest grows old?" [He] replied, "Thanks." The reproach of it would not be so sensible, were there not sensible demonstrations of the truth of it in those that wear the character of the ingenuous. Such as are at first surprised at and seem to have no common relish of divine goodness, yet too soon lose the impression: "they sang God's praise, but soon forgot His works." That it should be thus with respect to our benefactors on earth is contrary to the ingenuity of human nature; but, that our grateful resentments of the signal favors of heaven should soon be worn off by time is to the last degree criminal and unpardonable.

It would be unaccountable stupidity in me not to maintain the most lively and awful sense of divine rebukes which the most holy God has seen meet in spotless sovereignty to dispense to me, my family and people in delivering us into the hands of those that hated us, who led us into a strange land: "my soul has these still in remembrance and is humbled in me;" however, God has given us plentiful occasion to sing of mercy as well as judgment. The wonders of divine mercy, which we have seen in the land of our captivity and deliverance therefrom, cannot be forgotten without incurring the guilt of the blackest ingratitude.

To preserve the memory of these, it has been thought advisable to publish a short account of some of those signal appearances of divine power and goodness for hoping it may serve to excite the praise, faith, and hope of all that love God, and may peculiarly serve to cherish a grateful spirit, and to render the impressions of God's mighty works indelible on my heart, and on those that with me have seen the wonders of the Lord and tasted of His salvation, that we may not fall under that heavy charge made against Israel of old, Psalms 78:11, 42: "They forgot His works and the wonders He showed them. They remembered not His hand, nor the day that He delivered them from the enemy."[3]

And I cannot, Sir, but think it most agreeable to my duty to God our supreme redeemer, to mention your Excellency's name with honor since heaven has honored you as the prime instrument in returning our captivity. Sure I am [that] the laws of justice and gratitude, which are the laws of God, do challenge from us the most public acknowledgments of your uncommon sympathy with us, your children, in our bonds expressed in all endearing methods of parental care and tenderness. All your people are cherished under your wings, happy in your government, and are obliged to bless God for you. And among your people those that are immediately exposed to the outrages of the enemy have peculiarly felt refreshment from the benign influences of your wise and tender conduct and are under the most sensible engagements to acknowledge your Excellency, under God, as the breath of their nostrils.

Your uncommon sagacity and prudence in contriving to loose the bonds of your captived children, your unwearied vigor and application in pursuing them to work our deliverance, can never be enough praised. It is most notorious that nothing was thought too difficult by you to effect this design in that you readily sent your own son, Mr. William Dudley, to undergo the hazards and hardships of a tedious voyage that this affair might be transacted with success, which must not be forgotten, as an expression of your great solicitude and zeal to recover us from the tyranny and oppression of our captivity.[4]

I doubt not but that the God, whom herein you have served, will remember and gloriously reward you, and may heaven long preserve you at our helm, a blessing so necessary for the tranquility of this province in this dark and tempestuous season; may the best of blessings from the Father of Lights be showered down upon your person, family, and government, which shall be the prayer of,

Your Excellency's
most humble, obedient,
and dutiful servant,
John Williams

The Redeemed Captive Returning to Zion

The history I am going to write proves that days of fasting and prayer, without reformation, will not avail to turn away the anger of God from a professing people. And yet witnesseth how very advantageous gracious supplications are to prepare particular Christians patiently to suffer the will of God in very trying public calamities! For some of us, moved with fear, set apart a day of prayer to ask of God, either to spare and save us from the hands of our enemies or to prepare us to sanctify and honor Him in what way soever He should come forth towards us. The places of Scripture from whence we were entertained were Gen. 32:10–11: "I am not worthy of least of all the mercies and of all the truth which thou hast showed unto thy servant.[5] Deliver me, I pray thee, from the hand of my brother, from the hand of Esau, for I fear him, lest he will come and smite me and the mother with the children" (in the forenoon). And Gen. 32:26: "And he said, 'Let me go, for the day breaketh'; and he said, 'I will not let thee go, except thou bless me'" (in the afternoon). From which we were called upon to spread the causes of fear relating to our own selves or families before God; as also how it becomes us with an undeniable importunity to be following

---

3. Williams's citations here and elsewhere are generally accurate. Exceptions will be noted.

4. William Dudley, the governor's son, traveled to Quebec with a delegation to negotiate the release of English captives. Although his mission was considered successful, many children and some adults remained in Canada.

5. Williams omits the second part of Genesis 32:10.

God with earnest prayers for His blessing in every condition. And it is very observable how God ordered our prayers in a peculiar manner to be going up to Him to prepare us with a right Christian spirit to undergo and endure suffering trials.

Not long after, the holy and righteous God brought us under great trials as to our persons and families which put us under a necessity of spreading before Him in a wilderness the distressing dangers and calamities of our relations; yea, that called on us notwithstanding seeming present frowns, to resolve by His grace not to be sent away without a blessing. Jacob in wrestling has the hollow of his thigh put out of joint, and it is said to him, "Let me go"; yet he is rather animated to an heroical Christian resolution to continue earnest for the blessing than discouraged from asking.[6]

On the twenty-ninth of February, 1703/4, not long before break of day, the enemy came in like a flood upon us, our watch being unfaithful: an evil, whose awful effects in a surprisal of our fort, should bespeak all watchmen to avoid, as they would not bring the charge of blood upon themselves. They came to my house in the beginning of the onset and, by their violent endeavors to break open doors and windows with axes and hatchets, awakened me out of sleep; on which I leaped out of bed, and running toward the door, perceived the enemy making their entrance into the house. I called to awaken two soldiers in the chamber and returned towards my bedside for my arms. The enemy immediately brake into the room, I judge to the number of twenty, with painted faces and hideous acclamations. I reached up my hands to the bed tester for my pistol, uttering a short petition to God for everlasting mercies for me and mine on the account of the merits of our Glorified Redeemer, expecting a present passage through the Valley of the Shadow of Death, saying in myself as Isaiah 38:10–11: "I said in the cutting off my days, 'I shall go to the gates of the grave. I am deprived of the residue of my years.' I said, 'I shall not see the Lord, even the Lord, in the land of the living. I shall behold man no more with the inhabitants of the world.'" Taking down my pistol, I cocked it and put it to the breast of the first Indian who came up, but my pistol missing fire, I was seized by three Indians who disarmed me and bound me naked, as I was in my shirt, and so I stood for near the space of an hour. Binding me, they told me they would carry me to Quebeck. My pistol missing fire was an occasion of my life's being preserved, since

which I have also found it profitable to be crossed in my own will. The judgment of God did not long slumber against one of the three which took me, who was a captain, for by sunrising he received a mortal shot from my next neighbor's house, who opposed so great a number of French and Indians as three hundred and yet were no more than seven men in an ungarrisoned house.

I cannot relate the distressing care I had for my dear wife, who had lain-in but a few weeks before, and for my poor children, family, and Christian neighbors. The enemy fell to rifling the house and entered in great numbers into every room of the house. I begged of God to remember mercy in the midst of judgment, that He would so far restrain their wrath as to prevent their murdering of us, that we might have grace to glorify His name, whether in life or death, and, as I was able, committed our state to God. The enemies who entered the house were all of them Indians and Macquas,[7] insulted over me awhile, holding up hatchets over my head threatening to burn all I had. But yet God beyond expectation made us in a great measure to be pitied, for though some were so cruel and barbarous as to take and carry to the door two of my children and murder them, as also a Negro woman,[8] yet they gave me liberty to put on my clothes, keeping me bound with a cord on one arm, till I put on my clothes to the other, and then changing my cord, they let me dress myself and then pinioned me again. [They] gave liberty to my dear wife to dress herself and our children.

About sun an hour high we were all carried out of the house for a march and saw many of the houses of my neighbors in flames, perceiving the whole fort, one house excepted, to be taken. Who can tell what sorrows pierced our souls when we saw ourselves carried away from God's sanctuary to go into a strange land exposed to so many trials, the journey being at least three hundred miles we were to travel, the snow up to the knees, and we never inured to such hardships and fatigues, the place we were to be carried to a popish country.

Upon my parting from the town, they fired my house and barn. We were carried over the [Deerfield] River to the foot of the mountain, about a mile from my house, where we found a great number of our Christian neighbors, men, women, and children, to the number of an hun-

---

6. See Genesis 32:24–28.

7. Williams refers to the Caughnawaga Indians or Christian Mohawks as "Macquas."

8. John Williams; Jerusha Williams; and Parthena, a slave woman, were killed.

dred, nineteen of which were afterward murdered by the way and two starved to death near Cowass[9] in a time of great scarcity or famine the savages underwent there. When we came to the foot of our mountain, they took away our shoes and gave us, in the room of them, Indian shoes[10] to prepare us for our travel. Whilst we were there, the English beat out a company that remained in the town and pursued them to the river, killing and wounding many of them, but the body of the army, being alarmed, they repulsed those few English that pursued them.

I am not able to give you an account of the number of the enemy slain, but I observed after this fight no great insulting mirth as I expected and saw many wounded persons, and for several days together, they buried [several] of their party and one of chief note among the Macquas. The governor of Canada[11] told me his army had that success with the loss but of eleven men, three Frenchmen, one of which was the lieutenant of the army, five Macquas, and three Indians; but after my arrival at Quebeck I spake with an Englishman who was taken the last war and married there and of their religion, who told me they lost above forty and that many were wounded. I replied the governor of Canada said they lost but eleven men. He answered, "'Tis true that there were but eleven killed outright at the taking of the fort, but that many others were wounded, among who was the ensign of the French." But, said, he, "They had a fight in the meadow, and that in both engagements they lost more than forty. Some of the soldiers, both French and Indians then present, told me so," said he, adding that, "The French always endeavor to conceal the number of their slain."

After this we went up the mountain and saw the smoke of the fires in the town and beheld the awful desolations of our town, and, before we marched any farther, they killed a sucking child of the English. There were slain by the enemy of the inhabitants of our town to the number of thirty-eight besides nine of the neighboring towns. We traveled not far the first day; God made the heathen so to pity our children that, though they had several wounded persons of their own to carry upon their shoulders for thirty miles before they came to the river, yet they carried our children, incapable of traveling, upon their shoulders and in their arms.

When we came to our lodging-place the first night, they dug away the snow and made some wigwams, cut down some of the small branches of spruce trees to lie down on, and gave the prisoners somewhat to eat, but we had but little appetite. I was pinioned and bound down that night, and so I was every night whilst I was with the army. Some of the enemy who brought drink with them from the town fell to drinking, and in their drunken fit they killed my Negro man,[12] the only dead person I either saw at the town or on the way. In the night an Englishman made his escape;[13] in the morning I was called for and ordered by the general to tell the English that, if any more made their escape, they would burn the rest of the prisoners.

He that took me was unwilling to let me speak with any of the prisoners as we marched; but on the morning of the second day, he being appointed to guard the rear, I was put into the hands of my other master who permitted me to speak to my wife when I overtook her and to walk with her to help her in her journey. On the way we discoursed of the happiness of them who had a right to an house not made with hands, eternal in the heavens and God for a father and a friend; as also that it was our reasonable duty quietly to submit to the will of God and to say the will of the Lord be done. My wife told me her strength of body began to fail and that I must expect to part with her, saying she hoped God would preserve my life and the lives of some, if not all of our children with us, and commended to me, under God, the care of them.[14] She never spake any discontented word as to what had befallen us, but with suitable expressions justified God in what had befallen us.

We soon made an halt in which time my chief surviving master came up, upon which I was put upon marching with the foremost, and so made to take my last farewell of my dear wife, the desire of my eyes and companion in many mercies and afflictions. Upon our separation from each other we asked, for each other, grace sufficient for what God should call us to. After our being parted from one another, she spent the few remaining minutes of her stay in reading the holy Scriptures, which she was wont personally every day to delight her soul in reading, praying, meditating of and over, by herself in her closet,

---

9. Cowass is close to present-day Newbury, Vermont.

10. Moccasins.

11. Phillippe de Rigaud de Vaudreuil (c. 1643–1725).

12. Frank, the husband of Parthena. His last name is unknown.

13. John Alexander escaped.

14. The eldest Williams child, Elcazar, was not in Deerfield during the attack.

over and above what she heard out of them in our family worship.

I was made to wade over a small river and so were all the English, the water above knee-deep, the stream very swift; and after that to travel up a small montain; my strength was almost spent before I came to the top of it. No sooner had I overcome the difficulty of that ascent, but I was permitted to sit down and be unburdened of my pack. I sat pitying those who were behind and entreated my master to let me go down and help up my wife, but he refused and would not let me stir from him. I asked each of the prisoners as they passed by me after her, and heard that in passing through the abovesaid river, she fell down and was plunged over head and ears in the water; after which she traveled not far, for at the foot of this mountain the cruel and bloodthirsty savage who took her, slew her with his hatchet at one stroke, the tidings of which were very awful; and yet such was the hardheartedness of the adversary that my tears were reckoned to me as a reproach.

My loss and the loss of my children was great; our hearts were so filled with sorrow that nothing but the comfortable hopes of her being taken away in mercy, to herself, from the evils we were to see, feel, and suffer under (and joined to the assembly of the spirits of just men made perfect, to rest in peace and joy unspeakable, and full of glory, and the good pleasure of God thus to exercise us) could have kept us from sinking under at that time. That Scripture, Job 1:21, "Naked came I out of my mother's womb, and naked shall I return thither. The Lord gave and the Lord hath taken away, blessed be the name of the Lord," was brought to my mind and from it that an afflicting God was to be glorified, with some other places of Scripture to persuade to a patient bearing [of] my afflictions.

We were again called upon to march with a far heavier burden on my spirits than on my back; I begged of God to overrule in His providence that the corpse of one so dear to me, and of one whose spirit He had taken to dwell with Him in glory, might meet with a Christian burial and not be left for meat to the fowls of the air and beasts of the earth, a mercy that God graciously vouchsafed to grant. For God put it into the hearts of my neighbors to come out as far as she lay to take up her corpse, recarry it to the town, and decently to bury it soon after. In our march they killed another sucking infant of one of my neighbors and before night a girl of about eleven years of age. I was made to mourn at the consideration of my flock's being so far a flock of slaughter, many being slain in town and so many murdered in so few miles from the town, and from fears

what we must yet expect from such who delightfully imbrued their hands in the blood of so many of His people.

When we came to our lodging-place, an Indian captain from the Eastward spake to my master about killing of me and taking off my scalp. I lifted up my heart to God to implore His grace and mercy in such a time of need. And afterwards I told my master if he intended to kill me I desired he would let me know of it, assuring him that my death after a promise of quarter would bring the guilt of blood upon him. He told me he would not kill me. We lay down and slept, for God sustained and kept us.

In the morning we were all called before the chief sachems of the Macquas and Indians that a more equal distribution might be made of the prisoners among them; at my going from the wigwam, my best clothing was taken from me. As I came nigh the place appointed, some of the captives met me and told me they thought the enemies were going to burn some of us for they had peeled off the bark from several trees and acted very strangely. To whom I replied they could act nothing against us but as they were permitted of God, and I was persuaded He would prevent such severities. When we came to the wigwam appointed, several of the captives were taken from their former masters and put into the hands of others, but I was sent again to my two masters who brought me from my house.

In our fourth day's march the enemy killed another of my neighbors, who being nigh the time of travail, was wearied with her journey. When we came to the great river,[15] the enemy took sleighs to draw their wounded, several of our children, and their packs, and marched a great pace. I traveled many hours in water up to the ankles. Near night I was very lame, having before my travel wronged my ankle bone and sinews; I thought, so did others, that I should not be able to hold out to travel far. I lifted up my heart to God (my only refuge) to remove my lameness and carry me through with my children and neighbors if He judged it best; however, I desired God would be with me in my great change if He called me by such a death to glorify Him, and that He would take care of my children and neighbors and bless them. And within a little space of time I was well of my lameness, to the joy of my children and neighbors who saw so great an alteration in my traveling.

On the Saturday the journey was long and tedious; we traveled with such speed that four women were tired and then slain by them who led them captive. On the Sabbath

---

15. The Connecticut River.

day we rested, and I was permitted to pray and preach to the captives. The place of Scripture spoken from was Lam. 1:18: "The Lord is righteous, for I have rebelled against his commandment. Hear, I pray you, all people, and behold my sorrow. My virgins and my young men are gone into captivity." The enemy, who said to us, "Sing us one of Zion's songs," were ready some of them to upbraid us because our singing was not so loud as theirs. When the Macquas and Indians were chief in power, we had this revival in our bondage to join together in the worship of God and encourage one another to a patient bearing of the indignation of the Lord till He should plead our cause. When we arrived to New France, we were forbidden praying one with another or joining together in the service of God.

The next day, soon after we marched, we had an alarm on which many of the English were bound; I was then near the front and my masters not with me so I was not bound. This alarm was occasioned by some Indians shooting at geese that flew over them that put them into a considerable consternation and fright, but, after they came to understand they were not pursued by the English, they boasted that the English would not come out after them as they had boasted before we began our journey in the morning. They killed this day two women who were so faint they could not travel.

The next day in the morning before we traveled, one Mary Brooks, a pious young woman, came to the wigwam where I was and told me she desired to bless God who had inclined the heart of her master to let her come to take her farewell of me. Said she, "By my falls on the ice yesterday I wronged myself, causing an abortion this night so that I am not able to travel far. I know they will kill me today, but," says she, "God has (praised be His name) by His spirit with His word strengthened me to my last encounter with death." And [she] mentioned to me some places of Scripture so seasonably sent in for her support. "And," says she, "I am not afraid of death; I can, through the grace of God, cheerfully submit to the will of God. Pray for me," said she at parting, "that God would take me to Himself." Accordingly she was killed that day. I mentioned it to the end I may stir up all in their young days to improve the death of Christ by faith to a giving them a holy boldness in the day of death.

The next day we were made to scatter one from another into smaller companies, and one of my children [was] carried away with Indians belonging to the Eastern parts.[16] At night my master came to me with my pistol in

his hand, and put it to my breast, and said, "Now I will kill you, for," said he, "at your house you would have killed me with it if you could." But by the grace of God I was not much daunted, and whatever his intention might be, God prevented my death.

The next day I was again permitted to pray with that company of captives with me, and we allowed to sing a Psalm together. After which I was taken from all the company of the English, excepting two children of my neighbors, one of which, a girl of four years of age, was killed by her Macqua master the next morning, the snow being so deep when we left the river that he could not carry the child and his pack too.

When the Sabbath came, one Indian stayed with me and a little boy nine years old while the rest went a-hunting. And when I was here, I thought with myself that God had now separated me from the congregation of His people who were now in His sanctuary where He commandeth the blessing, even life forever, and made to bewail my unfruitfulness under and unthankfulness for such a mercy. When my spirit was almost overwhelmed within me at the consideration of what had passed over me and what was to be expected, I was ready almost to sink in my spirit. But God spoke those words with a greater efficacy than man could speak them for my strengthening and support: Psalms 118:17: "I shall not die but live and declare the works of the Lord"; Psalms 42:11: "Why art thou cast down, o my soul? and why art thou disquieted within me? Hope thou in God, for I shall yet praise Him who is the health of my countenance and my God"; Nehem. 1:8–9: "Remember I beseech thee, the word thou commandedest thy servant Moses, saying, 'If ye transgress, I will scatter you abroad among the nations; but, if ye turn unto me, and keep my commandments and do them, though there were of you cast out unto the uttermost part of the heavens, yet will I gather them from thence and will bring them unto the place that I have chosen to set my Name there.'" Those three places of Scripture, one after another by the grace of God, strengthened my hopes that God would so far restrain the wrath of the adversary that the greatest number of us left alive should be carried through so tedious a journey. That though my children had no father to take care of them, that word quieted me to a patient waiting to see the end the Lord would make, Jer. 49:11: "Leave thy fatherless children, I will preserve them alive and let thy widows trust in me." Accordingly God carried them wonderfully through great difficulties and dangers.

My youngest daughter, aged seven years, was carried all the journey and looked after with a great deal of ten-

---

16. The Abenaki Indians.

derness. My youngest son, aged four years, was wonderfully preserved from death; for, though they that carried him or drawed him on sleighs were tired with their journeys, yet their savage cruel tempers were so overruled by God that they did not kill him, but in their pity he was spared and others would take care of him; so that four times on the journey he was spared and others would take care of him, till at last he arrived at Mont-Royal [Montreal] where a French gentlewoman, pitying the child, redeemed it out of the hands of the heathen. My son Samuel and my eldest daughter were pitied so as to be drawn on sleighs when unable to travel. And though they suffered very much through scarcity of food and tedious journeys, they were carried through to Mont-Royal. And my son Stephen, about eleven years of age, [was] wonderfully preserved from death in the famine whereof three English persons died and after eight months brought into Shamblee [Chambly].

My master returned on the evening of the Sabbath and told me he had killed five moose. The next day we removed to the place where he killed them. We tarried there three days till we had roasted and dried the meat. My master made me a pair of snowshoes, "For," said he, "you cannot possibly travel without, the snow being knee-deep." We parted from thence heavy laden; I traveled with a burden on my back, with snowshoes, twenty-five miles the first day of wearing them and again the next day till afternoon, and then we came to the French River.[17] My master at this place took away my pack and drew the whole load on the ice, but my bones seemed to be misplaced and I unable to travel with any speed. My feet were very sore, and each night I wrung blood out of my stockings when I pulled them off. My shins also were very sore, being cut with crusty snow in the time of my traveling without snowshoes. But finding some dry oak leaves by the river banks, I put them to my shins and in once applying of them they were healed. And here my master was very kind to me, would always give me the best he had to eat, and by the goodness of God, I never wanted a meal's meat during my captivity though some of my children and neighbors were greatly wounded (as I may say) with the arrows of famine and pinching want, having for many days nothing but roots to live upon and not much of them either. My master gave me a piece of a Bible, never disturbed me in reading the Scriptures, or in praying to God. Many of my neighbors also found that mercy in their journey to have Bibles, psalm books, catechisms, and good

books put into their hands with liberty to use them; and yet after their arrival at Canada all possible endeavors were used to deprive them of them. Some of them say their Bibles were demanded by the French priests and never re-delivered to them, to their great grief and sorrow.

My march on the French River was very sore, for, fearing a thaw, we traveled a very great pace; my feet were so bruised and my joints so distorted by my traveling in snowshoes that I thought it unpossible to hold out. One morning a little before break of day my master came and awakened me out of my sleep, saying, "Arise, pray to God, and eat your breakfast, for we must go a great way today." After prayer I arose from my knees, but my feet were so tender, swollen, bruised, and full of pain that I could scarce stand upon them without holding on the wigwam. And then the Indians said, "You must run today."

I answered, "I could not run."

My master, pointing out to his hatchet, said to me, "Then I must dash out your brains and take off your scalp."

I said, "I suppose then you will do so, for I am not able to travel with speed." He sent me away alone on the ice.

About sun half an hour high he overtook me for I had gone very slowly, not thinking it possible to travel five miles. When he came up, he called me to run; I told him I could go no faster; he passed by without saying one word more so that sometimes I scarce saw anything of him for an hour together. I traveled from about break of day till dark, never so much as set down at noon to eat warm victuals, eating frozen meat which I had in my coat pocket as I traveled. We went that day two of their day's journey as they came down. I judge we went forty or forty-five miles that day. God wonderfully supported me and so far renewed my strength that in the afternoon I was stronger to travel than in the forenoon. My strength was restored and renewed to admiration. We should never distrust the care and compassion of God who can give strength to them who have no might and power to them who are ready to faint.

When we entered on the lake [Champlain], the ice was very rough and uneven, which was very grievous to my feet that could scarce endure to be set down on the smooth ice on the river: I lifted up my cry to God in ejaculatory requests that He would take notice of my state and some way or other relieve me. I had not marched above half a mile before there fell a moist snow about an inch and a half deep that made it very soft for my feet to pass over the lake to the place where my master's family was—wonderful favors in the midst of trying afflictions!

17. The present-day Winooski River.

We went a day's journey from the lake to a small company of Indians who were a-hunting; they were after their manner kind to me and gave me the best they had, which was mooseflesh, groundnuts, and cranberries but not bread; for three weeks together I eat no bread. After our stay there and undergoing difficulties in cutting of wood, [I] suffered from lousiness having lousy old clothes of soldiers put upon me when they stripped me of mine to sell to the French soldiers of the army. We again began a march for Shamblee; we stayed at a branch of the lake and feasted two or three days on geese we killed there.

After another day's travel we came to a river where the ice was thawed; we made a canoe of elm bark in one day and arrived on a Saturday near noon at Shamblee, a small village where is a garrison and a fort of French soldiers. This village is about fifteen miles from Mont-Royal. The French were very kind to me; a gentleman of the place took me into his house and to his table and lodged me at night on a good feather bed. The inhabitants and officers were very obliging to me the little time I stayed with them and promised to write a letter to the governor-in-chief to inform him of my passing down the river. Here I saw a girl taken from our town, and a young man who informed me that the greatest part of the captives were come in and that two of my children were at Mont-Royal, and that many of the captives had been in three weeks before my arrival—mercy in the midst of judgment!

As we passed along the river towards [Fort] Sorel, we went into an house where was an Englishwoman of our town who had been left among the French in order to her conveyance to the Indian fort. The French were very kind to her and to myself and gave us the best provision they had, and she embarked with us to go down to St. Francois Fort.[18] When we came down to the first inhabited house at Sorel, a Frenchwoman came to the riverside and desired us to go into her house, and, when we were entered, she compassioned our state and told us she had in the last war[19] been a captive among the Indians and therefore was not a little sensible of our difficulties. She gave the Indians something to eat in the chimney-corner and spread a cloth on the table for us with napkins, which gave such offense to the Indians that they hasted away and would not call in at the fort. But wherever we entered into houses, the French were very courteous.

When we came to St. Francois River, we found some difficulty by reason of the ice, and, entering into a Frenchman's house, he gave us a loaf of bread and some fish to carry away with us; but we passed down the river till night, and there seven of us supped on the fish, called bullhead or pout, and did not eat it up, the fish was so very large. The next morning we met with such a great quantity of ice that we were forced to leave our canoe and travel on land. We went to a French officer's house, who took us into a private room out of the sight of the Indians, and treated us very courteously.

That night we arrived at the fort called St. Francois, where we found several poor children who had been taken from the Eastward the summer before, a sight very affecting, they being in habit very much like Indians and in manner very much symbolizing with them. At this fort lived two Jesuits, one of which was made superior of the Jesuits at Quebeck. One of these Jesuits met me at the fort gate and asked me to go into the church and give God thanks for preserving my life; I told him I would do that in some other place. When the bell rang for evening prayers, he that took me bid me go, but I refused.

The Jesuits came to our wigwam and prayed a short prayer and invited me to sup with them and justified the Indians in what they did against us, rehearsing some things done by Major Walden above thirty years ago,[20] and how justly God retaliated them in the last war, and inveighed against us for beginning this war with the Indians. And [then they] said we had before the last winter, and in the winter, been very barbarous and cruel in burning and killing Indians. I told them that the Indians in a very perfidious manner had committed murders on many of our inhabitants after the signing articles of peace, and, as to what they spake of cruelties, they were undoubtedly falsehoods, for I well knew the English were not approvers of inhumanity or barbarity towards enemies.

They said that an Englishman had killed one of St. Casteen's relations, which occasioned this war; for, say they, the nations in a general counsel had concluded not to engage in the war, on any side, till they themselves were first molested, and then all of them as one would engage against them that began a war with them; and that upon the killing of Casteen's kinsman, a post was dispatched to

---

18. An Abenaki stronghold.

19. King William's War, 1689–97.

20. Richard Waldron or Walderne (d. 1689) captured approximately two hundred Indians in 1689 but was subsequently tortured to death.

Canada to advertise the Macquas and Indians that the English had begun a war. On which they gathered up their forces, and the French joined with them to come down on the Eastern parts; and, when they came near New England, several of the Eastern Indians told them of the peace made with the English and the satisfaction given them from the English for that murder. But the Macquas told them it was now too late, for they were sent for and were now come and would fall on them if without their consent they made a peace with the English. [They] said also that a letter was shown them sent from the governor of Port Royal, which he said was taken in an English ship, being a letter from the queen of England to our governor writing how she approved his designs to ensnare and deceitfully to seize on the Indians; so that being enraged from that letter and being forced as it were, they began the present war. I told them the letter was a lie forged by the French.

The next morning the bell rang for Mass. My master bid me to go to church. I refused. He threatened me and went away in a rage. At noon the Jesuits sent for me to dine with them, for I eat at their table all the time I was at the fort. And after dinner they told me the Indians would not allow of any of their captives staying in their wigwams whilst they were at church and were resolved by force and violence to bring us all to church if we would not go without. I told them it was highly unreasonable so to impose upon those who were of a contrary religion, and to force us to be present at such service as we abhorred was nothing becoming Christianity. They replied they were savages and would not hearken to reason but would have their wills; [they] said also [that] if they were in New England themselves, they would go into the churches to see their ways of worship.

I answered the case was far different, for there was nothing (themselves being the judges) as to matter or manner of worship but what was according to the word of God in our churches; and therefore it could not be an offense to any man's conscience. But among them there were idolatrous superstitions in worship; they said, "Come and see and offer us conviction of what is superstitious in [our] worship." To which I answered that I was not to do evil that good might come on it, and that forcing in matters of religion was hateful. They answered the Indians were resolved to have it so, and they could not pacify them without my coming; and they would engage they should offer no force or violence to cause any compliance with their ceremonies.

The next Mass my master bid me go to church. I objected; he arose and forcibly pulled me out by head and shoulders out of the wigwam to the church that was nigh the door. So I went in and sat down behind the door, and there saw a great confusion instead of gospel order. For one of the Jesuits was at the altar saying Mass in a tongue unknown to the savages, and the other between the altar and the door saying and singing prayers among the Indians at the same time saying over their Pater Nosters and Ave Mary [Marias] by tale from their chaplets, or beads on a string. At our going out, we smiled at their devotion so managed, which was offensive to them, for they said we made a derision of their worship. When I was here, a certain savagess died; one of the Jesuits told me she was a very holy woman who had not committed one sin in twelve years.

After a day or two the Jesuits asked me what I thought of their way now [that] I saw it? I told them I thought Christ said of it as Mark 7:7–9: "Howbeit in vain do they worship me, teaching for doctrines the commandments of man. For laying aside the commandment of God, ye hold the tradition of men as the washing of pots and cups and many such like things ye do. And He said unto them, 'Full well ye reject the commandment of God that ye may keep your own tradition.'" They told me they were not the commandments of men but apostolical traditions of equal authority with the holy Scriptures. And that after my death I would bewail my not praying to the Virgin Mary, and that I should find the want of intercession for me with her Son, judging me to hell for asserting the Scriptures to be perfect rule of faith, and said I abounded in my own sense, entertaining explications contrary to the sense of the pope regularly sitting with a general council explaining Scripture and making articles of faith. I told them it was my comfort that Christ was to be my judge and not they at the Great Day, and, as for their censuring and judging of me, I was not moved with it.

One day a certain savagess taken prisoner in King Philip's War, who had lived at Mr. Buckley's at Wethersfield,[21] called Ruth, who could speak English very well, who had been often at my house but was now proselyted to the Romish faith, came into the wigwam. And with her [came] an English maid who was taken the last war,[22] who was dressed up in Indian apparel, could not speak one word of English, who said she could neither tell her own name or the name of the place from whence she was taken. These two talked in the Indian dialect with my

---

21. Possibly Reverend Gershom Bulkeley (1636–1712).

22. King William's War.

master a long time after which my master bade me to cross myself. I told him I would not; he commanded me several times, and I as often refused.

Ruth said, "Mr. Williams, you know the Scripture and therefore act against your own light, for you know the Scripture saith, 'Servants, obey your masters.' He is your master and you his servant."

I told her she was ignorant and knew not the meaning of the Scripture, telling her [that] I was not to disobey the great God to obey any master, and that I was ready to suffer for God if called thereto. On which she talked to my master; I suppose she interpreted what I said.

My master took hold of my hand to force me to cross myself, but I struggled with him and would not suffer him to guide my hand; upon this he pulled off a crucifix from his own neck and bade me kiss it, but I refused once again. He told me he would dash out my brains with his hatchet if I refused. I told him I should sooner choose death than to sin against God; then he ran and caught up his hatchet and acted as though he would have dashed out my brains. Seeing I was not moved, he threw down his hatchet, saying he would first bite off all my nails if I still refused; I gave him my hand and told him I was ready to suffer. He set his teeth in my thumbnails and gave a grip with his teeth, and then said, "No good minister, no love God, as bad as the devil," and so left off.

I have reason to bless God who strengthened me to withstand; by this he was so discouraged as nevermore to meddle with me about my religion. I asked leave of the Jesuits to pray with those English of our town that were with me, but they absolutely refused to give us any permission to pray one with another and did what they could to prevent our having any discourse together.

After a few days the Governor de Vaudreuil, governor-in-chief, sent down two men with letters to the Jesuits desiring them to order my being sent up to him to Mont-Royal, upon which one of the Jesuits went with my two masters and took me along with them, as also two more of Deerfield, a man and his daughter about seven years of age. When we came to the lake,[23] the wind was tempestuous and contrary to us so that they were afraid to go over; they landed and kindled a fire and said they would wait awhile to see whether the wind would fall or change.

I went aside from the company among the trees and spread our case with the temptations of it before God and pleaded that He would order the season so that we might not go back again but be furthered on our voyage that I might have opportunity to see my children and neighbors and converse with them and know their state. When I returned, the wind was more boisterous, and then a second time, and the wind was more fierce; I reflected upon myself for my unquietness and the want of a resigned will to the will of God. And a third time [I] went and bewailed before God my anxious cares and the tumultuous working of my own heart, begged a will fully resigned to the will of God, and thought that by the grace of God I was brought to say amen to whatever God should determine.

Upon my return to the company the wind was yet high; the Jesuit and my master said, "Come, we will go back again to the fort, for there is no likelihood of proceeding in our voyage, for very frequently such a wind continues three days, sometimes six."

After it continued so many hours, I said to them, "The will of the Lord be done," and the canoe was put again into the river and we embarked.

No sooner had my master put me into the canoe and put off from the shore, but the wind fell, and coming into the middle of the river they said, "We may go over the lake well enough." And so we did.

I promised if God gave me opportunity I would stir up others to glorify God in a continued persevering, committing their straits of heart to Him: He is a prayer-hearing God and the stormy winds obey Him. After we passed over the lake, the French wherever we came were very compassionate to us.

When I came to Mont-Royal, which was eight weeks after my captivity, the Governor de Vaudrel [Vaudreuil] redeemed me out of the hands of the Indians, gave me good clothing, took me to his table, gave me the use of a very good chamber, and was in all respects relating to my outward man courteous and charitable to admiration. At my first entering into his house, he sent for my two children who were in the city[24] that I might see them and promised to do what he could to get all my children and neighbors out of the hands of the savages. My change of diet after the difficulties of my journeys caused an alteration in my body; I was physicked, blooded, and very tenderly taken care of in my sickness.[25]

---

23. Lake St. Pierre.

24. Probably Esther and Warsham.

25. Bloodletting was standard medical treatment for most ailments during the seventeenth and eighteenth centuries.

The governor redeemed my eldest daughter[26] out of the hands of the Indians, and she was carefully tended in the hospital until she was well of her lameness and by the governor provided for with respect during her stay in the country. My youngest child was redeemed by a gentlewoman in the city as the Indians passed by.[27] After the Indians had been at their fort and discoursed with the priests, they came back and offered to the gentlewoman a man for the child, alleging that the child could not be profitable to her, but the man would, for he was a weaver and his service would much advance the design she had of making cloth. But God overruled so far that this temptation to the woman prevailed not for an exchange, for had the child gone to the Indian fort in an ordinary way, it had abode there still, as the rest of the children carried there do.

The governor gave orders to certain officers to get the rest of my children out of the hands of the Indians and as many of my neighbors as they could. After six weeks a merchant of the city obtained my eldest son[28] that was taken to live with him; he took a great deal of pains to persuade the savages to part with him. An Indian came to the city (Sagamore George of Pennacook) from Cowass and brought word of my son Stephen's being near Cowass, and some money was put into his hand for his redemption and a promise of full satisfaction if he brought him; but the Indian proved unfaithful, and I never saw my child till a year after.

The governor ordered a priest to go along with me to see my youngest daughter among the Macquas and endeavor her ransom.[29] I went with him; he was very courteous to me, and, from his parish which was near the Macqua fort, he wrote a letter to the Jesuit to desire him to send my child to see me and to speak with them that took her to come along with it [her]. But the Jesuit wrote back a letter that I should not be permitted to speak with or see my child; if I came, that my labor would be lost, and that the Macquas would as soon part with their hearts as my child. At my return to the city I with a heavy heart carried the Jesuit's letter to the governor who, when he read it, was very angry and endeavored to comfort me, assuring

me I should see it and speak with it, and he would to his utmost endeavor its ransom. Accordingly he sent to the Jesuits who were in the city and bade them improve their interest for the obtaining the child.

After some days he went with me in his own person to the fort. When we came thither, he discoursed with the Jesuits after which my child was brought into the chamber where I was. I was told I might speak with her but should be permitted to speak to no other English person there. My child was about seven years old; I discoursed with her near an hour; she could read very well and had not forgotten her catechism. And [she] was very desirous to be redeemed out of the hands of the Macquas and bemoaned her state among them, telling me how they profaned God's Sabbaths and said she thought that a few days before they had been mocking the devil, and that one of the Jesuits stood and looked on them.

I told her she must pray to God for His grace every day. She said she did as she was able and God helped her. But, says she, "They force me to say some prayers in Latin, but I don't understand one word of them; I hope it won't do me any harm." I told her she must be careful she did not forget her catechism and the Scriptures she had learned by heart. She told the captives after I was gone, as some of them have informed me, almost everything I spake to her and said she was much afraid she should forget her catechism, having none to instruct her. I saw her once a few days after in the city but had not many minutes of time with her, but what time I had I improved to give her the best advice I could.

The governor labored much for her redemption; at last he had a promise of it in case he would procure for them an Indian girl in her stead. Accordingly he sent up the river some hundreds of leagues for one,[30] but it was refused when offered by the governor: he offered them a hundred pieces of eight for her redemption, but it was refused. His lady went over to have begged her from them, but all in vain; it's there still and has forgotten to speak English. Oh! That all who peruse this history would join in their fervent requests to God, with whom all things are possible, that this poor child, and so many others of our children who have been cast upon God from the womb and are now outcast ready to perish, might be gathered from their dispersions and receive sanctifying grace from God!

---

26. Esther.

27. Warsham.

28. Samuel.

29. Eunice was not redeemed. She married a Caughnawaga Indian.

---

30. Up the Saint Lawrence River to the Great Lakes.

When I had discoursed with the child and was coming out of the fort, one of the Jesuits went out of the chamber with me and some soldiers to convey me to the canoe. I saw some of my poor neighbors who stood with longing expectations to see me and speak with me and had leave from their savage masters so to do. I was by the Jesuit himself thrust along by force and permitted only to tell them some of their relations they asked after were well in the city, and that with a very audible voice, being not permitted to come near to them.

After my return to the city I was very melancholy, for I could not be permitted so much as to pray with the English who dwelled in the same house. And the English who came to see me were most of them put back by the guard at the door and not suffered to come and speak with me. Sometimes the guard was so strict that I could scarce go aside on necessary occasions without a repulse; and whenever I went out into the city (a favor the governor himself never refused when I asked it of him) there were spies to watch me and to observe whether I spake to the English. Upon which I told some of the English they must be careful to call to mind and improve former instructions and endeavor to stand at a further distance for awhile, hoping that after a short time I should have more liberty of conversing with them. But some spies sent out found on a Sabbath day more than three (the number we by their order published were not to exceed together) of us in company, who informed the priest; the next day one of the priests told me I had a greater number of the English with me and that I had spoken something reflecting on their religion. I spake to the governor that no forcible means might be used with any of the captives respecting their religion; he told me he allowed no such thing. I am persuaded that the governor, if he might act as himself, would not have suffered such things to be done as have been done and that he never did know of several things acted against the English.

At my first coming to Mont-Royal, the governor told me I should be sent home as soon as Captain Baptiste was returned and not before,[31] and that I was taken in order to his redemption. The governor sought by all means to divert me from my melancholy sorrows and always showed a willingness for seeing my children. And one day I told

him of my design of walking into the city; he pleasantly answered, "Go, with all my heart." His eldest son went with me as far as the door and saw the guard stop me; he went in and informed his father, who came to the door and asked why they affronted the gentleman going out. They said it was their order. But with an angry countenance he said his orders were that I should not be stopped, but within a little time I had my orders to go down to Quebeck.

Another thing showing that many things are done without the governor's consent though his name be used to justify them: *viz.,* I asked the priest after I had been at Mont-Royal two days leave to go and see my youngest child; he said, "Whenever you would see it, tell me and I will bring it to you, for," says he, "the governor is not willing you should go thither." And yet not many days after when we were at dinner, the governor's lady (seeing me sad) spoke to an officer at the table who could speak Latin to tell me that after dinner I should go along with them and see my two children. And accordingly after dinner I was carried to see them, and, when I came to the house, I found three or four English captives who lived there, and I have leave to discourse with them. And not long after the governor's lady asked me to go along with her to the hospital to see one of my neighbors sick there.

One day one of the Jesuits came to the governor and told the company there that he never saw such persons as were taken from Deerfield. Said he, "The Macquas will not suffer any of their prisoners to abide in their wigwams whilst they themselves are at Mass but carry them with them to the church, and they can't be prevailed with to fall down on their knees to pray there, but no sooner are they returned to their wigwams, but they fall down on their knees to prayer." He said they could do nothing with the grown persons there, and they hindered the children's complying. Where-upon the Jesuits counseled the Macquas to sell all the grown persons from the fort—a stratgem to seduce poor children. Oh Lord! Turn the counsels of these Ahit[h]ophels[32] into foolishness, and make the counsels of the heathen of none effect!

Here I observed they were wonderfully lifted up with pride after the return of Captain Montinug from Northampton with news of success;[33] they boasted of their suc-

---

31. Captain Baptiste was Pierre Maisonnat (1663–1714), a privateer later captured by the British and exchanged for Williams.

32. False advisers. See 2 Samuel 15–17.

33. Probably Jacques Testard de Montigny (1663–1737),

cess against New England. And they sent out an army as they said of seven hundred men, if I mistake not, two hundred of which were French, in company of which army went several Jesuits, and said they would lay desolate all the places on Connecticut River. The superior of the priests told me their general was a very prudent and brave commander of undaunted courage, and he doubted not but they should have great success. This army went away in such a boasting, triumphant manner that I had great hopes God would discover and disappoint their designs; our prayers were not wanting for the blasting such a bloody design.

The superior of the priests said to me, "Don't flatter yourselves in hopes of a short captivity, for," said he, "there are two young princes contending for the kingdom of Spain, and a third that care is to be taken for his establishment on the English throne." And [he] boasted what they would do to Europe, and that we must expect not only [in] Europe but in New England the establishment of popery.

I said, "Glory not, God can make great changes in a little time and revive His own interest and yet save His poor afflicted people."

Said he, "The time for miracles is past, and in the time of the last war the King of France was, as it were, against all the world and yet did very great things, but now the kingdom of Spain is for him, and the Duke of Bavaria, and the Duke of Savoy, etc." And spake in a lofty manner of great things to be done by them and having the world, as I may say, in subjection to them.

I was sent down to Quebeck in company of Governor de Ramesey, governor of Mont-Royal,[34] and the superior of the Jesuits, and ordered to live with one of the council, from whom I received many favors for seven weeks. He told me it was the priest's doing to send me down before the governor came down, and that, if I went much to see the English, or they came much to visit me, I should yet certainly be sent away where I should have no converse with the English.

After my coming down to Quebeck, I was invited to dine with the Jesuits, and to my face they were civil enough. But after a few days a young gentleman came to my chamber and told me that one of the Jesuits (after we had done dinner) made a few distichs of verse and gave them to his scholars to translate into French. He showed them to me. The import of them was that the King of France's grandson had sent out his huntsmen, and that they had taken a wolf, who was shut up, and now he hopes the sheep would be in safety. I knew at the reading of them what he aimed at but held my peace as though I had been ignorant of the Jesuit's intention. Observing this reproaching spirit, I said in my heart [that] if God will bless, let men curse if they please, and I looked to God in Christ the great shepherd to keep his scattered sheep among so many Romish ravenous wolves and to remember the reproaches wherewith His holy name, ordinances, and servants were daily reproached. And upon an observation of the time of these verses being composed, I find that near the same time the bishop of Canada with twenty ecclesiastics were taken by the English as they were coming from France and carried into England as prisoners of war.[35]

One Sabbath day morning I observed many signs of approaching rain, a great moisture on the stones of the hearth and chimney jams. I was that day invited to dine with the Jesuits, and when I went up to dinner, it began to rain a small drizzling rain. The superior told me they had been praying for rain that morning, "And lo," says he, "it begins to rain." I told him I could tell him of many instances of God's hearing our prayers for rain. However, in the afternoon there was a general procession of all orders, priests, Jesuits, and friars, and the citizens in great pomp, carrying (as they said) as an holy relic one of the bones of St. Paul.

The next day I was invited to the priest's Seminary to dinner; "Oh," said they, "we went in procession yesterday for rain, and see what a plentiful rain followed." I answered we had been answered when praying for rain when no such signs of rain, and the beginnings of rain preceded, as now with them, before they appointed or began their procession, etc. However, they upbraided me that God did not approve of our religion in that He disregarded our prayers and accepted theirs. For, said they, "We hear you had days of fasting and prayer before the fleet came to Quebeck; God would not regard your

---

34. Governor de Ramesey, or Claude de Ramezay (1659–1724), mayor of Montreal and later acting governor of New France.

35. English warships captured a French ship, the *Seine*, which was bringing the bishop and several clergymen to Canada.

prayers but heard ours, and almost in a miraculous way preserved us when assaulted and refused to hear your fastday prayers for your preservation but heard ours for your desolation and our success."[36]

They boasted also of their king and his greatness and spake of him as though there could be no settlement of the world but as he pleased, reviling us as in a low and languishing case, having no king but being under the government of a queen.[37] And [they] spake as though the Duke of Bavaria would in a short time be emperor.

From this day forward God gave them to hear sorrowful tidings from Europe, that a war was commenced against the Duke of Savoy and so their enemies increased, their bishop taken and two millions of wealth with him. News every year more distressing and impoverishing of them; and the Duke of Bavaria so far from being emperor that he is dispossessed of his dukedom; and France so far from being strengthened by Spain that the kingdom of Spain [is] like to be an occasion of the weakening and impoverishing their own kingdom—they themselves reporting so. And their great army going against New England turned back ashamed, and they discouraged and disheartened and every year very exercising fears and cares as to the savages who live up the river. Before the return of that army they told me we were led up and down and sold by the heathen as sheep for the slaughter, and they could not devise what they should do with us, we should be so many prisoners when the army returned.

The Jesuits told me it was a great mercy that so many of our children were brought to them, and that, now especially since they were not like speedily to be returned, there was hope of their being brought over to the Romish faith. They would take the English children born among them and, against the consent of their parents, baptize them. One Jesuit came to me and asked whether all the English at Lorette, a place not far from Quebeck where the savages lived, were baptized. I told him they were. He said, "If they be not, let me know of it that I may baptize them for fear they should die and be damned if they died without baptism." Says he, "When the savages went against you, I charged them to baptize all children before they killed them, such was my desire of your eternal salvation though you were our enemies."

There was a gentleman called Monsieur de Beauville, a captain, the brother of the lord intendant, who was a good friend to me and very courteous to all the captives; he lent me an English Bible and, when he went to France, gave it me.

All means were used to seduce poor souls. I was invited one day to dine with one of chief note. As I was going, [I] met with the superior of the Jesuits coming out of the house, and he came in after dinner; and presently it was propounded to me, if I would stay among them and be of their religion, I should have a great and honorable pension from the king every year. The superior of the Jesuits turned to me and said, "Sir, you have manifested much grief and sorrow for your separation from so many of your neighbors and children; if you will now comply with this offer and proposal, you may have all your children with you, and here will be enough for an honorable maintenance for you and them."

I answered, "Sir, if I thought your religion to be true, I would embrace it freely without any such offer, but so long as I believe it to be what it is, the offer of the whole world is of no more value to me than a blackberry." And [I] manifested such as abhorrence of this proposal that I speedily went to take my leave and be gone.

"Oh! Sir," said he, "set down, why [are you] in such a hurry, you are alone in your chamber, divert yourself a little longer," and fell to other discourse. And within half an hour says again, "Sir, I have one thing earnestly to request of you. I pray pleasure me!"

I said, "Let your Lordship speak."

Said he, "I pray come down to the palace tomorrow morning and honor me with your company in my coach to the great church, it being then a saint's day."

I answered, "Ask me anything wherein I can serve you with a good conscience, and I am ready to gratify you, but I must ask your excuse here," and immediately went away from him. Returning unto my chamber, I gave God thanks for His upholding of me and also made an inquiry with myself whether I had by any action given encouragement for such a temptation.

Not many days after and a few days before Governor de Vaudrel coming down, I was sent away fifteen miles down the river that I might not have opportunity of converse with the English. I was courteously treated by the French and the priest of that parish; they told me he was one of the most learned men in the country; he was a very ingenious man, zealous in their way but yet very familiar. I

---

36. The reference is to Sir William Phips's failed 1690 attack on Quebec.

37. Queen Anne reigned from 1702 to 1714.

had many disputes with the priests who came thither, and, when I used their own authors to confute some of their positions, my books borrowed of them were taken away from me, for they said I made an ill use of them. They, many of them having boasted of their unity in doctrine and profession, were loath I should show them from their own best approved authors as many different opinions as they could charge against us.

Here again a gentleman in the presence of the old bishop and a priest offered me his house and whole living with assurance of honor, wealth, and employment if I would embrace their ways. I told them I had an indignation of soul against such offers on such terms as parting with what was more valuable than all the world, alleging, "What is a man profited if he gain the whole world and lose his own soul? Or what shall a man give in exchange for his soul?"

I was sometimes told I might have all my children if I would comply and must never expect to have them on any other terms; I told them my children were dearer to me than all the world, but I would not deny Christ and His truths for the having of them with me; I would still put my trust in God who could perform all things for me.

I am persuaded that the priest of that parish where I [was] kept abhorred their sending down the heathen to commit outrages against the English, saying it was more like committing murders than managing a war. In my confinement in this parish I had my undisturbed opportunities to be humbly imploring grace for ourselves, for soul and body, for His protecting presence with New England, and His disappointing the bloody designs of enemies, that God would be a little sanctuary to us in a land of captivity, and that our friends in New England might have grace to make a more thankful and fruitful improvement of means of grace than we had done, who by our neglects found ourselves out of God's sanctuary.

On the twenty-first of October 1704, I received some letters from New England with an account that many of our neighbors escaped out of the desolations in the fort, and that my dear wife was recarried and decently buried. and that my eldest son who was absent in our desolation was sent to college[38] and provided for, which occasioned

thanksgiving to God in the midst of afflictions and caused prayers even in Canada to be going daily up to heaven for a blessing upon benefactors showing such kindness to the desolate and afflicted.

The consideration of such crafty designs to ensnare young ones and to turn them from the simplicity of the gospel to Romish superstition was very exercising; sometimes they would tell me my children, sometimes my neighbors, were turned to be of their religion. Some made it their work to allure poor souls by flatteries and great promises, some threatened, some offered abusive carriages to such as refused to go to church and be present at Mass; for some they industriously contrived to get them married among them. A priest drew up a compendium of the Romish Catholic faith and pretended to prove it by the Scriptures, telling the English that all they required was contained in the Scriptures, which they acknowledged to be the rule of faith and manners, but it was by Scriptures horribly perverted and abused. I could never come to the sight of it, though I often earnestly entreated a copy of it, until I was ashipboard for our voyage for New England, but hearing of it I endeavored to possess the English with their danger of being cheated with such a pretense. I understood they would tell the English that I was turned that they might gain them to change their religion; these their endeavors to seduce to popery were very exercising to me.

And in my solitariness I drew up these following sorrowful, mournful considerations (though unused to and unskillful in poetry) yet in a plain style for the use of some of the captives who would sometimes make their secret visits to me, which at the desire of some of them are here made public.

Some Contemplations of the Poor and Desolate State of the Church at Deerfield

The sorrows of my heart enlarged are,
Whilst I my present state with past compare,
I frequently unto God's house did go,
With Christian friends, His praises forth to show,
But now I solitary sit, both sigh and cry,
Whilst my flock's misery think on do I.
  Many, both old and young, were slain outright,
Some in a bitter season take their flight.
Some burned to death, and others stifled were,
The enemy no sex or age would spare.
The tender children with their parents sad
Are carried forth as captives, some unclad.

---

38. Eleazar Williams (1668–1742) attended Harvard College (B.A., 1708).

Some murdered in the way unburied left,
And some through famine were of life bereft.
After a tedious journey some are sold,
Some kept in heathen hands; all from Christ['s] fold
By popish rage and heathenish cruelty
Are banished. Yea, some compelled to be
Present at Mass. Young children parted are
From parents and such as instructors were.
Crafty designs are used by papists all
In ignorance of truth them to enthrall.
Some threatened are unless they comply
In heathen hands again be made to lie.
To some large promises are made if they
Will truths renounce and choose their popish way.
    Oh Lord! mine eyes on Thee shall waiting be
Till Thou again turn our captivity.
Their Romish plots Thou canst confound, and save
This little flock, this mercy I do crave.
Save us from all our sins and yet again
Deliver us from them who truth disdain.
    Lord! for Thy mercy sake Thy covenant mind,
And in Thy house again rest let us find.
    So we Thy praises forth will show and speak
Of all Thy wondrous works, yea we will seek
The advancement of Thy great and glorious name,
Thy rich and sovereign grace we will proclaim.

The hearts of some were ready to be discouraged and sink, saying they were "out of sight and so out of mind." I endeavored to persuade them we were not forgotten, that undoubtedly many prayers were continually going up to heaven for us. Not long after came Capt. Livingston and Mr. Sheldon with letters from his excellency our governor to the governor of Canada about the exchange of prisoners, which gave a revival to many and raised expectations of a return. These visits from New England to Canada so often greatly strengthened many who were ready to faint and gave some check to the designs of the papists to gain proselytes.

But God's time of deliverance was not yet come; as to some particular persons their temptations and trials were increased, and some abused because they refused a compliance with their superstitions. A young woman of our town met with a new trial. For on a day a Frenchman came into the room where she was and showed her his beads and boasted of them, putting them near to her; she knocked them out of his hands on the floor, for which she was beaten and threatened with death and for some days imprisoned. I pleaded with God His overruling this first

essay for the deliverance of some as a pledge of the rest being delivered in due time.

I improved Capt. de Beauville, who had always been very friendly, to intercede with the governor for the return of my eldest daughter, and for his purchasing my son Stephen from the Indians at St. Francois Fort, and for liberty to go up and see my children and neighbors at Mont-Royal. Divine Providence appeared to a moderating [of] my affliction in that five English persons of our town were permitted to return with Capt. Livingston, among whom went my eldest daughter. And my son Stephen was redeemed and sent to live with me. He was almost quite naked and very poor; he had suffered much among the Indians. One of the Jesuits took upon him to come to the wigwam and whip him on some complaint that the squaws had made that he did not work enough for them.

As to my petition for going up to Mont-Royal to see my children and neighbors, it was denied, as my former desire of coming up to the city before Capt. Livingston's coming was. God granted me favor as to two of my petitions, but yet brought me by His grace to be willing that He should glorify Himself in disposing of me and mine as He pleased and knew to be most for His glory. And almost always before any remarkable favor I was brought to lie down at the foot of God and made to be willing that God should govern the world so as might be most for His own honor and brought to resign all to His holy sovereignty. A frame of spirit when wrought in me by the grace of God giving the greatest content and satisfaction, and very often a forerunner of the mercy asked of God or a plain demonstration that the not obtaining my request was best for me. I had no small refreshing in having one of my children with me for four months. And the English were many of them strengthened with hopes that the treaty between the governments would issue in opening a door of escape for all. . . .

I shall here give an account of what was done to one of my children, a boy between fifteen and sixteen years of age, two hundred miles distance from me, which occasioned grief and sorrow that I want words to utter, and yet kept under such awe that he never durst write anything to me for fear of being discovered in writing about religion. They threatened to put him to the Indians again if he would not turn, telling him he was never bought out of their hands but only sojourned with them, but, if he would turn, he should never be put into their hands anymore. The priests would spend whole days in urging of him.

He was sent to school to learn to read and write

French; the schoolmaster sometimes flattered him with promises if he would cross himself, then threatened him if he would not. But when he saw flattering promises of rewards and threatenings were ineffectual, he struck him with a stick he had in his hand; and when he saw that would not do, he made him get down on his knees about an hour and then came and bid him make the sign of the cross, and that without any delay; he still refused. Then he gave him a couple of strokes with a whip he had in his hand, which whip had three branches and about twelve great knots tied in it. And again bid him make the sign of the cross, and if it was any sin he would bear it himself. And said also, "You are afraid you shall be changed if you do it, but," said he, "you will be the same, your fingers won't be changed." And after he had made him shed many tears under his abuses and threatenings, he told him he would have it done; and so through cowardice and fear of the whip, he made the sign.

[He] did so for several days together; with much ado he was brought to cross himself. And then the master told him he would have it done without his particular bidding him. And when he came to say his lesson and crossed not himself, the master said, "Have you forgot what I bid you do?"

"No sir," said he.

Then the schoolmaster said, "Down on your knees." And so kept him for an hour and a half till school was done, and so did for about a week. When he saw this would not do, he took the whip, "What, won't you do it?" said he, "I will make you." And so again frightened him to a compliance.

After this [he] commanded him to go to the church; when he refused, he told him he would make him. And one morning [he] sent four of the biggest boys of the school to draw him by force to Mass. These with other severities and witty stratagems were used, and I utterly ignorant of any attempt made upon him to bring him to change his religion. His fear was such that he never durst write any of these things lest his letters should fall into their hands, and he should again be delivered to the Indians. Hearing of an opportunity of writing to him by one of the parish where I was, going up to Mont-Royal, I wrote a letter to him and had by him a letter from my son which I shall here insert.

Honored Father,

I have received your letter bearing date January 11th, 1705/6, for which I give you many thanks with my duty and my brother's. I am sorry you have not received all the letters I have writ to you, as I have not received all yours. According to your good counsel I do almost every day read something of the Bible and so strengthen my faith.

As to the captives newly brought, Lancaster is the place of two of them and Marlborough that of the third: the governor of Mont-Royal has them all three. There is other news that will seem more strange to you: that two English women who in their lifetime were dreadfully set against the Catholic religion did on their deathbed embrace it. The one Abigail Turbet,[39] the other of them Esther Jones,[40] both of them known to you.

Abigail Turbet sent for Mr. Meriel[41] the Sabbath before she died. [She] said (many a time upon several following days) that she committed her soul into his hands and was ready to do whatever he pleased. She desired him to go to the Chapel St. Anne and there to say a holy Mass for her that she might have her sins pardoned and the will of the Lord accomplished upon her. Her cousin Mrs. Badston, now Stilson, asked her whether she should be willing to do as she said; she answered, yes. And upon the Tuesday she was taken into the Catholic Church in the presence of John Laland, and Madam Grizalem, an Englishwoman, and Mrs. Stilson, also with many French people besides.

She was anointed with oil on the same day; according to her will then upon the Wednesday an image of Christ crucified was brought to her, she caused it to be set up over against her at the curtains of her bed and looked continually upon the same; and also a little crucifix brought unto her, she took it, and kissed it, and laid it upon her stomach. She did also make the sign of the cross upon herself when she took any meat or drink. She promised to God that if she should recover she would go to the Mass every day. She, having on her hand a crucifix, saying, "Oh my Lord that I should have known thee so late!"

She did also make a prayer to the Virgin Mary the two last days of the week. She could utter no word, but by kissing the crucifix, endeavoring the crossing herself, she gave every evidence of her faith; she died Saturday the 24th of November [1705] at three a clock in the afternoon. The next day the priest did commend that woman's soul to the prayers of the congregation in the Mass; in the afternoon she was honorably buried in the churchyard

---

39. Abigail Cass Turbet (1674–1705).

40. Esther Ingersoll Jones (1665–1705).

41. Father Henri-Antoine de Meriel, a Sulpican priest.

next to the church close to the body of the Justice Pese's wife, all the people being present at her funeral.

The same day in the evening Mr. Meriel with an Englishwoman went to Esther Jones; she did at first disdain, but a little after she confessed there were seven sacraments; Christ's body present, the sacrament of the Mass, the inequality of power among the pastors of the church; and, being returned to wait by her all night long, he read and expounded to her some part of the Catholic Confession of Faith to her satisfaction. About midnight he asked her whether she might not confess her sins. "I doubt not but I may," said she. And two hours after she made unto him a fervent confession of all the sins of her whole life. When he said he was to offer Christ to His Father for her, she liked it very well.

The superior of the nuns being come in to see her, she now desired that she might receive Christ's body before she died. She did also show Mrs. Stilson a great mind to receive the sacrament of extreme unction and said that if ever she should recover and get home she would have reproached the ministers for their neglecting that sacrament so plainly commanded by St. James. In the afternoon after she had begged pardon for her wavering and the Catholic Confession of Faith was read aloud to her in the hearing of Mr. Craston, Mrs. Stilson, and another Englishwoman, and she owned the same;[42] about seven a clock the same day she said to Mr. Dubison, "Shall not they give me the holy communion?" But her tongue was then so thick that she could hardly swallow anything. She was then anointed with holy oil, but before she said to Mr. Meriel, "Why have you not yet, sir, forgiven my sins?"

In the following night that priest and Mr. Dubison were continually by her and sometimes praying to God in her name and praying to the Virgin Mary and other saints. She said also, "I believe all. I am very glad Christ was offered to His Father for me." Six or seven hours before she died, a crucifix was showed to her by Mr. Dubison, she took it and laid it upon her heart and kissed it, and the nuns hung it with a pair of beads upon her neck. A little before she died Mr. Dubison asked her to pray for him in heaven; she promised him.

So she gave up the ghost at ten of the clock the 27th of November [1705] whilst the high Mass was saying; she was soon commended to the prayers. On the fourth day of the week following [she] was buried after the Mass had been said for her. She was laid by Abigail Turbet.

Jan. 23rd, 1705/6

I have here transcribed the letter in the very words of it without the least alteration: the same for substance was sent to several other captives. When I had this letter, I presently knew it to be of Mr. Meriel's composing, but the messenger who brought the letter brought word that my son had embraced their religion. Afterwards when some blamed him for letting me know of it because they said they feared my sorrow would shorten my days, he told me he thought with himself that if he was in my case he should be willing to know the worst and, therefore, told me as he would have desired to have known if in my place. I thanked him, acknowledging it a favor to let me know of it, but the news was ready to overwhelm me with grief and sorrow.

I made my complaint to God and mourned before Him; sorrow and anguish took hold upon me. I asked of God to direct me what to do and how to write and find out an opportunity of conveying a letter to him and committed this difficulty to His providence. I now found a greater opposition to a patient, quiet, humble resignation to the will of God than I should otherwise have known if not so tried. Here I thought of my afflictions and trials; my wife and two children killed and many of my neighbors; and myself and so many of my children and friends in a popish captivity separated from our children, not capable to come to instruct them in the way they ought to go, and cunning crafty enemies using all their subtlety to insinuate into young ones such principles as would be pernicious. I thought with myself how happy many others were, in that they had their children with them under all advantages to bring them up in the nurture and admonition of the Lord, while we were separated one from another and our children in great peril of embracing damnable doctrines.

Oh! That all parents who read this history would bless God for the advantages they have of educating their children and faithfully improve it! I mourned when I thought with myself that I had one child with the Macquas,[43] second turned to popery,[44] and a little child of six years of

---

42. In other words, Esther Jones also stated her belief in Catholic confession.

43. Eunice.

44. Samuel.

age in danger from a child to be instructed in popery,[45] and knew full well that all endeavors would be used to prevent my seeing or speaking with them. But in the midst of all these God gave me a secret hope that He would magnify His power and free grace and disappoint all their crafty designs. When I looked on the right hand and on the left, all refuge failed, and none showed any care for my soul. But God brought that word to uphold me who is able to do exceeding abundantly above what we can ask or think. As also that—is anything too hard for God? I prayed to God to direct me and wrote very short the first time and in general terms, fearing lest if I should write about things in controversy, my letters would not come to him. I therefore addressed him with the following letter:

Son Samuel,
Yours of January 23rd I received and with it had the tidings that you had made an abjuration of the Protestant faith for the Romish—news that I heard with the most distressing, afflicting, sorrowful spirit that ever I heard any news. Oh! I pity you; I mourn over you day and night! Oh, I pity your weakness that through the craftiness of man you are turned from the simplicity of the gospel! I persuade myself you have done it through ignorance. Oh! Why have you neglected to ask your father's advice in an affair of so great importance as the change of religion! God knows that the catechism in which I instructed you is according to the word of God and so will be found in the Day of Judgment. Oh! Consider and bethink yourself what you have done! And whether you ask me or not, my poor child, I cannot but pray for you that you may be recovered out of the snare you are taken in. Read the Bible, pray in secret, make Christ's righteousness your only plea before God for justification. Beware of all immorality and of prophaning God's Sabbaths.

Let a father's advice be asked for the future in all things of weight and moment. What is a man profited if he gain the whole world and lose his own soul? Or what shall a man give in exchange for his soul? I desire to be humbled under the mighty hand of God thus afflicting of me. I would not do as you have done for ten thousand worlds. My heart aches within me, but I will yet wait upon the Lord, to Him will I commit your case day and night. He can perform all things for me and mine and can yet again recover you from your fall. He is a God forgiving iniquity,

transgression, and sin; to the Lord our God belong forgivenesses though we have rebelled. I charge you not to be instrumental to ensnare your poor brother Warham, or any other, and to add sin to sin. Accept of my love and don't forsake a father's advice, who, above all things, desires that your soul may be saved in the day of the Lord.

What I mournfully wrote, I followed with my poor cries to God in heaven to make effectual, to cause in him a consideration of what he had done. God saw what a proud heart I had and what need I had to be so answered out of the whirlwind that I might be humbled before Him.

God, who is gloriously free and rich in His grace to vile sinners, was pleased to bless poor and weak means for the recovery of my child so taken and gave me to see that He did not say to the House of Jacob, "Seek you me in vain." Oh! That every reader would in every difficulty make Him their refuge; He is a hopeful stay. To alleviate my sorrow, I received the following letter in answer to mine.

Mont-Royal, May 12, 1706
Honored Father,
I received your letter which you sent by   , which good letter I thank you for and for the good counsel which you gave me; I desire to be thankful for it and hope it will be for the good of my soul. I may say as in the Psalms: "The sorrows of death compassed me, and the pains of hell got hold on me. I found trouble and sorrow, then called I upon the name of the Lord. O Lord, I beseech Thee deliver my soul! Gracious is the Lord and righteous, yea our God is merciful."

As for what you ask me about my making an abjuration of the Protestant faith for the Romish, I durst not write so plain to you as I would but hope to see and discourse with you. I am sorry for the sin I have committed in changing of religion, for which I am greatly to blame. You may know that Mr. Meriel, the schoolmaster, and others were continually at me about it; at last I gave over to it, for which I am very sorry.

As for that letter you had from me, it was a letter I transcribed for Mr. Meriel. And for what he said about Abigail Turbet and Esther Jones, nobody heard them but he as I understand. I desire your prayers to God for me to deliver me from my sins. Oh, remember me in your prayers! I am your dutiful son, ready to take your counsel.

Samuel Williams

This priest, Mr. Meriel, has brought many letters to him and bid him write them over and send them, and so

---

45. Warham.

he has done for many others. By this as also by Mrs. Stilson's saying she does not think that either of these women did change their religion before their death (she affirms also that oftentimes during their sickness, whilst they had the use of their reason, they protested against the Romish religion and faith), it's evident that these women never died papists, but that it was a wily stratagem of the priests to advance their religion, for letters were sent immediately after their death to use this as a persuasive argument to gain others. But God in His providence gave in farther conviction of their fallaciousness in this matter.

For the last summer one Biggilow[46] of Marlborough, a captive at Mont-Royal, was very sick in the hospital and in the judgment of all with a sickness to death. Then the priests and others gave out that he was turned to be of their religion and taken into their communion. But contrary to their expectation he was brought back from the gates of death and would comply with none of their rites, saying that whilst he had the use of his reason he never spake anything in favor of their religion. And that he never disowned the Protestant faith, nor would he now. So that they were silenced and put to shame. There is no reason to think that these two women were any more papists than he, but they are dead and cannot speak. One of the witnesses spoken of in the forementioned letter told me she knew of no such thing and said Mr. Meriel told her that he never heard a more fervent and affectionate prayer than one which Esther Jones made a little before her death. I am verily persuaded that he calls that [fervent] prayer [directed] to God [just before her death] so full of affection and confession, the confession made by her of the sins of her whole life. These two women always in their health, and so in their sickness, opposed all popish principles as all that knew them can testify so long as they could be permitted to go and speak with them. One of these women was taken from the Eastward, and the other, namely Esther Jones, from Northampton. . . .

In the latter end of summer they told me they had news from New England by one who had been a captive at Boston who said that the ministers at Boston had told the French captives that the Protestant religion was the only true religion, and that as a confirmation of it they would raise a dead person to life before their eyes for their conviction, and that, having persuaded one to feign himself dead, they came and prayed over him and then commanded him in the name of Christ (whose religion they

kept pure) to arise; they called and commanded, but he never arose, so that instead of raising the dead they killed the living, which the bereaved relations discovered. I told them it was an old lie and calumny against Luther and Calvin new vamped and that they only changed the persons and place, but they affirmed it to be a truth; I told them I wondered they were so fond of a faith propagated and then maintained by lying words.

We were always out of hopes of being returned before winter, the season proving so cold in the latter end of September, and were praying to God to prepare our hearts with all holy submission to His holy will to glorify His holy name in a way of passive obedience in the winter. For my own part I was informed by several who came from the city that the lord intendant said if more returned and brought word that Battis [Baptiste] was in prison, he would put me into prison and lay me in irons. They would not permit me to go into the city, saying I always did harm when I came to the city, and if at any time I was in the city, they would persuade the governor to send me back again.

In the beginning of last June the superior of the priests came to the parish where I was and told me he saw I wanted my friend Captain de Beauville and that I was ragged. "But" says he, "your obstinacy against our religion discourages [us] from providing better clothes." I told him it was better going in a ragged coat than with a ragged conscience.

In the beginning of last June went out an army of five hundred Macquas and Indians with an intention to have fallen on some English towns down Connecticut River, but lighting on a Scalacook Indian,[47] who ran away in the night, they were discouraged, saying he would alarm the whole country. About fifty as some say, or eighty as others, returned; thus, God restrained their wrath.

When they were promising themselves another winter to draw away the English to popery, came news of an English brigantine a-coming and that the honorable Captain Samuel Appleton, Esq., was coming ambassador to fetch off the captives, and Captain John Bonner with him. I cannot tell you how the clergy and others labored to stop many of the prisoners; to some liberty, to some money and yearly pensions were offered if they would stay. Some they urged to tarry at least till the spring of the year, telling them it was so late in the year they would be lost by shipwreck if they went now; some younger ones they told if they were home they would be damned and burn in hell forever, to affright them; day and night they were urg-

---

46. John Bigelow, a carpenter.

47. Probably a Scatacook Indian from Connecticut.

ing of them to stay. And I was threatened to be sent abroad without a permission to come ashore again if I should again discourse with any of the English who were turned to their religion.

At Mont-Royal especially, all crafty endeavors were used to stay the English. They told my child if he would stay he should have an honorable pension from the king every year and that his master, who was an old man and the richest in Canada, would give him a great deal, telling him if he returned he would be poor, for, said they, your father is poor, [he] has lost all his estate; it was all burned. But he would not be prevailed with to stay; and others were also in like manner urged to stay, but God graciously brake the snare and brought them out. They endeavored in the fall of the year to have prevailed with my son to have gone to France when they saw he would not come to their communion anymore.

One woman belonging to the Eastern parts, who had by their persuasions married an English captive taken the last war, came away with her husband, which made them say they were sorry they ever persuaded her to turn to their religion and then to marry. For, instead of advancing their cause by it, they had weakened it, for now they had not only lost her, but another they thought they had made sure of. Another woman belonging to the Eastward, who had been flattered to their religion, to whom a Bible was denied till she promised to embrace their religion and then had the promise of it for a little time, opening her Bible while in the church and present at Mass, she read the fourth chapter of Deuteronomy and received such conviction while reading that before her first communion she fell off from them and could never be prevailed with anymore to be of their religion.

We have reason to bless God who has wrought deliverance for so many, and yet to pray to God for a door of escape to be opened for the great number yet behind, not much short of an hundred, many of which are children, and of these not a few among the savages and having lost the English tongue, will be lost and turn savages in a little time unless something extraordinary prevent.

The vessel that came for us in its voyage to Canada struck on a bar of sands and there lay in very great hazard for four tides, and yet they saw reason to bless God for striking there, for had they got over the bar, they should at midnight in a storm of snow have run upon a terrible ledge of rocks.

We came away from Quebeck October twenty-five [1706] and by contrary winds and a great storm we were retarded, and then driven back nigh the city, and had a great deliverance from shipwreck, the vessel striking twice on a rock in that storm. But through God's goodness we all arrived in safety at Boston November twenty-one, the number of captives fifty-seven, two of which were my children. I have yet a daughter of ten years of age and many neighbors whose case bespeaks your compassion and prayers to God to gather them, being outcasts ready to perish.

At our arrival at Boston we found the kindnesses of the Lord in a wonderful manner in God's opening the hearts of many to bless God with us and for us wonderfully to give for our supplies in our needy state. We are under obligation to praise God for disposing the hearts of so many to so great charity and under great bonds to pray for blessing on the heads, hearts, and families of them who so liberally and plentifully gave for our relief. It's certain that the charity of the whole country of Canada, though moved with the doctrine of merit, does not come up to the charity of Boston alone, where notions of merit are rejected, but acts of charity [are] performed out of a right Christian spirit from a spirit of thankfulness to God out of obedience to God's command and unfeigned love and charity to them that are of the same family and household of faith. The Lord grant that all who devise such liberal things may find accomplishment of the promises made by God in their own person and theirs after them from generation to generation. . . .

A COLLECTION OF POEMS FROM NEW ENGLAND

For seventeenth-century British colonists, as for their contemporaries across the Atlantic, poetry represented the highest form of literary art. According to the aesthetic standards of the age, poetry was the genre best adapted to depicting drama, evoking emotion, and displaying wit. Popular misconceptions about the Puritans may suggest that such dour-seeming people would not take delight in the characteristic linguistic versatility that poetry could display, yet educated British Americans read and wrote a great deal of verse. Some wrote with the aim of circulation among friends to pass away time while contemplating matters of the spirit, and some wrote with the larger aim of publication in England, for circulation there and in New England.

Poetry was used to commemorate historical public events and private moments in daily experience, and it functioned within the public life of the English colonies and the private lives of individuals as testament to intellectual and emotional responses to living and working to establish Britain in America. The types of poems written varied widely and partook of the most commonly used forms of the day. Elegies were written for the most widely known public figures, but also for poets' relatives and friends of lesser social standing. While elegies were perhaps the most widely written poems, other forms were popular as well, including epics, lyrics, acrostics, puns, and anagrams. Common poetic subjects included discussions of courtship, love, and marriage; commentaries on war and political disputes; and observations upon nature, natural disasters, and natural science. Religious contemplation and spiritual life—of both individuals and their larger church—was a dominant subject, particularly in New England. (In the middle and southern colonies, mercantile and secular topics were more frequent.) Regardless of region, poetry was a highly valued genre by British New England settlers, and it was influenced by educated colonists' reading of classical Greek and Latin poetry; biblical psalms and other verse; and the work of contemporary writers from France, Italy, and England. Several poets wrote in the vein of British poetry called "metaphysical," with complicated displays of learned and linguistic "wit" and metaphors that brought together disparate images and ideas. The result in New England was a variety of form and style as noticeable as the variety of these in English poetry.

Poetry was a staple of literary culture in the British colonies, and it was a part of daily life for educated British colonists. With few exceptions, authors of verse did not see themselves as professional writers. Writing poetry was a polite accomplishment. Both men and women wrote verse, which might be published in book form; in the form of broadsides commemorating specific events; or in publications that featured other writings, such as sermons or memoirs. In addition, however, much verse was never printed but was circulated in manuscript form among the friends and family of the writer. The selections printed next offer a wide sampling of popular poetry of New England's in the seventeenth century.

from THE WHOLE BOOKE OF PSALMES FAITHFULLY TRANSLATED INTO ENGLISH METRE (1640)[1]

Just as access to vernacular translations of the Bible was an important concern of the Protestant Reformation, the establishment of vernacular texts for sacred singing was a question that received serious consideration among devout Puritans. The translation included in the Church of England's Book of Common Prayer, according to the Puritans, took liberties with the text that amounted to "corrupting" the purity of biblical text. A more acceptable translation had been made by Henry Ainsworth, minister of the English Church in Amsterdam, whose psalm book was used by the English colonists at Plymouth. The tunes indicated for singing in this edition, however, were apparently difficult. For a number of reasons, a dozen or so of New England's leading clergymen were unhappy enough with existing translations of the Psalms to conclude that they should create their own.

The Whole Booke of Psalmes Faithfully Translated into English Metre (1640), better known as the *Bay Psalm Book,* bears the distinction of being the first book written and printed in New England. In the preface to this first edition, John Cotton noted that the ministers' primary concern had been to translate the meaning of the Psalms as exactly as possible. Acknowledging that in some cases the verses might not be "so smoothe and elegant as some may desire or expect," Cotton explained that the translators had "attended Conscience rather than Elegance, fidelity rather than poetry . . . that so we may sing in Sion the Lord's songs of praise according to his own will." The *Bay Psalm Book* was the dominant psalter for more

---

1. *The Whole Booke of Psalmes,* also known as the *Bay Psalm Book,* was first published in Cambridge in 1640.

than half a century, and it continued to be used in New England well into the eighteenth century. It was revised several times over the years, to adapt to changes in singing practices and in language. With its strong focus on accuracy of meaning as opposed to what was understood as aesthetic "Elegance," the 1640 version of the *Bay Psalm Book* has been criticized as inferior poetry. The Puritan aesthetic, however, was shaped by spiritual concerns. The *Bay Psalm Book* thus provides an important insight into the Puritan approach to language, as well as the opportunity to explore a text that would have been part of everyday life for most New England colonists.

Psalme 1

O Blessed man, that in th' advice
   Of wicked doeth not walk:
Nor stand in sinners way, or sit
   In chayre of scornfull folk.
But in the law of Jehovah,
   Is his longing delight:
And in his law doth meditate,
   By day and eke by night.
And he shall be like to a tree
   Planted by water-rivers:
That in his season yeilds his fruit,
   And his leafe never withers.
And all he doth, shall prosper well,
   The wicked are not so:
But they are like unto the chaffe,
   Which winde drives to and fro.
Therefore shall not ungodly men,
   Rise to stand in the doome,
Nor shall the sinners with the just,
   In their assemblie *come*.
For of the righteous men, the Lord
   Acknowledgeth the way:
But the way of ungodly men,
   Shall utterly decay.

Psalme 19

To the chiefe musician a psalme of David

The heavens doe declare
   The majesty of God:
Also the firmament shews forth
   His handy-work abroad.
Day speaks to day, knowledge
   Night hath to night declar'd.
There neither speach nor language is,
   Where their voyce is not heard.
Through all the earth their line
   Is gone forth, and unto
The utmost end of all the world,
   Their speaches reach also:

A Tabernacle hee
   In them pitcht for the Sun.
Who Bridegroom like from's chamber goes
   Glad Giants-race to run.
From heavens utmost end,
   His course and compassing;
To ends of it, and from the heat
   Thereof is hid nothing.

2

The Lords law perfect is,
   The soule converting back:
Gods testimony faithfull is,
   Makes wise who-wisdome-lack.
The statutes of the Lord,
   Are right, and glad the heart:
The Lords commandement is pure,
   Light doth to eyes impart.
Jehovahs feare is cleane,
   And doth indure for ever:
The judgements of the Lord are true,
   And righteous altogether.
Then gold, then much fine gold,
   More to be prized are,
Then hony, and the hony-comb,
   Sweeter they are by farre.
Also thy servant is
   Admonished from hence:
And in the keeping of the same
   Is a full recompence.
Who can his errors know?
   From secret faults cleanse mee.
And from presumptuous-sins, let thou
   Kept back thy servant bee:
Let them not beare the rule
   In me, and then shall I
Be perfect, and shall cleansed bee
   From much iniquity.
Let the words of my mouth,
   And the thoughts of my heart,
Be pleasing with thee, Lord, my Rock
   Who my redeemer art.

Psalme 23

A Psalm of David

The Lord to me a shepherd is,
    want therefore shall not I.
He in the folds of tender grass,
    doth cause me down to lie:
To waters calm me gently leads
    Restore my soul doth he:
he doth in paths of righteousness:
    for his name's sake lead me.
Yea though in valley of death's shade
    I walk, none ill I'll fear:
because thou are with me, thy rod,
    and staff my comfort are.
For me a table thou has spread,
    in presence of my foes:
thou dost anoint my head with oil.
    my cup it overflows.
Goodness & mercy surely shall
    all my days follow me:
and in the Lord's house I shall dwell
    so long as days shall be.

Psalme 137

The rivers on of Babilon
    there when wee did sit downe:
yea even then wee mourned, when
    wee remembered Sion.

Our Harps wee did hang it amid,
    upon the willow tree.
Because there they that us away
    led in captivitee,
Requir'd of us a song, & thus
    askt mirth: us waste who laid,
sing us among a Sions song,
    unto us then they said.
The lords song sing can wee? being
    in strangers land. Then let
loose her skill my right hand, if I
    Jerusalem forget.
Let cleave my tongue my pallate on,
    if minde thee doe not I:
if chiefe joyes or'e I prize not more
    Jerusalem my joy.
Remember Lord, Edoms sons word,
    unto the ground said they,
it rase, it rase, when as it was
    Jerusalem her day.
Blest shall hee bee, that payeth thee,
    daughter of Babilon,
whom must be waste: that which thou hast
    rewarded us upon.
O happie hee shall surely bee
    that taketh up, that eke
thy little ones against the stones
    doth into pieces breake.

from THE NEW ENGLAND PRIMER (1683)

New Englanders prized literacy, particularly the ability to read the Bible in the vernacular. So important was literacy to their values that a 1642 law required town leaders to ensure that children could "read and understand the principles of Religion and the Capital laws of the country." One of the most important tools used to spread literacy was the *New England Primer.* Between 1683 and 1830, an estimated 5 million copies of the *Primer* were sold, making it one of the most widely spread books in early America, after the Bible.

The *Primer* was designed for teaching children to read, starting with learning the letters of the alphabet. In various versions of the *Primer,* the basic elements used to help children learn to read remained the same: an illustrated alphabet, sentences and poems containing moral messages, and a formal catechism. Over time, however, the specific content was revised and expanded. In addition, the *Primer* was adapted for different locales (becoming the *Pennsylvania Primer,* for example) and even for different audiences. A 1781 "Indian Primer" was produced in a dual-language edition for Mohawk children. Over time, the tone and style of the *Primer* changed. The punishments with which children were threatened if they misbehaved became gentler, as attitudes toward childhood and religion shifted. The following poetry selections, from early versions of the *Primer,* provide insight into the education of children in the earliest years of the English colonies.

Alphabet[1]

A	In *Adam's* Fall We Sinned all.	N	*Nightengales* sing In Time of Spring.
		O	The Royal *Oak* it was the Tree
B	Thy Life to Mend This *Book* Attend.		That sav'd His Royal Majestie.
C	The *Cat* doth play And after slay.	P	*Peter* denies His Lord and cries
D	A *Dog* will bite A Thief at night	Q	*Queen Esther* comes in Royal State To Save the JEWS from dismal Fate
E	An *Eagle's* flight Is out of sight.	R	*Rachel* doth mourn For her first born.
F	The Idle *Fool* Is whipt at School.	S	*Samuel* anoints Whom God appoints.
G	As runs the *Glass* Man's life doth pass.	T	*Time* cuts down all Both great and small.
H	My *Book* and *Heart* Shall never part.	U	*Uriah's* beauteous Wife Made David seek his Life.
J	*Job* feels the Rod Yet blesses GOD.	W	*Whales* in the Sea God's Voice obey.
K	Our KING the good No man of blood.	X	*Xerxes* the great did die And so must you & I.
L	The *Lion* bold The *Lamb* doth hold.	Y	*Youth* forward slips Death soonest nips.
M	The *Moon* gives light In time of night.	Z	*Zacheus* he Did climb the Tree His Lord to see,

Now the Child being entred in his Letters and Spelling, let him learn these and such like Sentences by Heart, whereby he will be both instructed in his Duty, and encouraged in his Learning.

The Dutiful Child's Promises[2]

I Will fear GOD, and honour the KING.

I will honour my Father & Mother.

I will Obey my Superiours.

I will Submit to my Elders,

I will Love my Friends.

I will hate no Man.

I will forgive my Enemies, and pray to God for them.

I will as much as in me lies keep all God's Holy Commandments.

I will learn my Catechism.

I will keep the Lord's Day Holy.

I will Reverence God's Sanctuary,

 For our GOD is a consuming Fire.

Verses

I in the Burying Place may see
 Graves shorter there than I;
From Death's Arrest no Age is free,
 Young Children too may die;
My God, may such an awful Sight,
 Awakening be to me!
Oh! that by early Grace I might
 For Death prepared be.

Good Children must,

Fear God all Day,	Love Christ alway,
Parents obey,	In Secret Pray,
No false thing say,	Mind little Play,
By no Sin stray,	Make no delay,

 In doing Good.

* * *

Awake, arise, behold thou hast
Thy Life a Leaf, thy Breath a Blast;
At Night lye down prepar'd to have
Thy sleep, thy death, thy bed, thy grave.

---

1. The alphabet probably appeared in the earliest versions of the *Primer*.

2. This verse, which originally appeared in Cotton Mather's 1713 "Instructions for Children," along with the "Verses" that follow, first appeared in the 1727 version of the *Primer*.

The Death of John Rogers[3]

Mr. *John Rogers*, Minister of the Gospel in *London*, was the first Martyr in Q *Mary's* Reign, and was burnt at *Smithfield, February* the fourteenth, 1554 His Wife, with nine small Children, and one at her Breast, following him to the Stake, with which sorrowful sight he was not in the least daunted, but with wonderful Patience died coragiously for the Gospel of Jesus Christ.

Some few Days before his Death, he writ the following Exhortation to his Children.

Give ear my Children to my words,
   whom God hath dearly bought,
Lay up his Laws within your heart,
   and print them in your thought,
5 I leave you here a little Book,
   for you to look upon;

That you may see your Fathers face,
   when he is dead and gone.
Who for the hope of heavenly things,
   while he did here remain,   10
Gave over all his golden Years
   to Prison and to Pain.
Where I among my Iron Bands,
   inclosed in the dark,
Not many days before my Death   15
   I did compose this Work.
And for Example to your Youth,
   to whom I wish all good;
I send you here God's perfect Truth,
   and seel it with my Blood   20
To you my Heirs of earthly Things,
   which I do leave behind,
That you may read and understand,
   and keep it in your mind.
That as you have been Heirs of thet   25
   which once shall wear away,
you also may possess that part,
   which never shall decay.
   . . .

---

3. "The Death of John Rogers," which featured a martyrdom for faith, was a popular English poem, first printed in 1559. It appeared in the *Primer* as early as 1683.

JOHN COTTON (1584–1652)

As a Nonconformist minister in Lincolnshire, England, John Cotton was called to court in 1632 for resisting Anglican doctrine. In 1633 he fled to Massachusetts Bay, where he became the teacher of the Church at Boston and was recognized as one of Boston's leading religious figures. Cotton engaged in a pamphlet debate with Roger Williams, and he was instrumental in expelling both Williams and Anne Hutchinson. Because he wrote the preface to the *Bay Psalm Book*, it seems likely that Cotton was one of the key organizers behind the collaborative production of that book. A number of Cotton's religious poems appeared in print on both sides of the Atlantic.

A Thankful Acknowledgment of God's Providence[1]

In mothers womb thy fingers did me mak,
And from the womb thou didst me safely take:
From breast thou hast me nurst my life throughout,
That I may say I never wanted ought.

In all my meals my table thou hast spread,
In all my lodgings thou hast [made my] bed:
Thou hast me clad with changes of array,
And chang'd my house for better far away.

In youthful wandrings thou didst stay my slide,
In all my journies thou hast been my Guide:
Thou hast me sav'd from many-an-unknown danger,
And shew'd me favour, even where I was a stranger.

In both my Callings thou hast heard my voice,
In both my matches thou hast made my choice:
Thou gav'st me sons, and daughters, them to peer,
And giv'st me hope thoul't learn them thee to fear.

Oft have I seen thee look with Mercy's face,
And through thy Christ have felt thy saving-grace.
This is the Heav'n on Earth, if any be:
For this, and all, my soul doth worship Thee.

---

1. This poem originally appeared in John Norton, *Abel Being Dead Yet Speaketh* (London, 1658).

NATHANIEL WARD (1578–1652)

Born in Suffolk, England, the son of a Puritan minister, Nathaniel Ward studied law at Cambridge but was ordained as a minister and served two churches in England before he was silenced in 1633 for nonconformity to the tenets of the Anglican Church. In 1634 he emigrated to New England, where he served as minister at Ipswich (known by Native Americans as Agawam), and in 1641 he helped to compile *The Body of Liberties,* Massachusetts Bay's first legal code. His major poetic work, *The Simple Cobbler of Aggawam in America* (1647), argued for stability in social and religious life. In 1647, Ward returned to England, where he was reestablished as a minister. He remained there for the rest of his life. When Anne Bradstreet's book of poetry, *The Tenth Muse,* was published in England in 1650, Ward may have been involved in ensuring that it was published. The following poem appeared among others as an endorsement of Bradstreet's poetic skill.

[Mercury shew'd *Apollo, Bartas* Book][1]

Mercury shew'd *Apollo, Bartas* Book,[2]
Minerva this, and wisht him well to look,
And tell uprightly, which did which excell,
He view'd and view'd, and vow'd he could not tel.
They did him Hemisphear his mouldy nose,
With's crackt leering-glasses, for it would pose
The best brains he had in's old pudding-pan,
Sex weigh'd, which best, the Woman, or the Man?
He peer'd, and por'd, and glar'd, and said for wore
I'me even as wise now, as I was before:
They both 'gan laugh, and said, it was no mar'l
The Auth'ress was a right *Du Bartas* Girle.
Good sooth quoth the old *Don,* tel ye me so,
I muse whither at length these Girls will go;
It half revives my chil frost-bitten blood,
To see a woman once do, ought, that's good;
And chode by *Chaucers* Boots, and *Homers* Furrs,
Let Men look to't, least Women wear the Spurrs.

----

1. This poem originally appeared in Anne Bradstreet's *The Tenth Muse* (London, 1650).

2. Guillaume du Bartas, the French poet whose work *La Semaine* appeared in English as *Divine Weeks and Works* (1605–07).

BENJAMIN WOODBRIDGE (1622–1684)

Born in England, Benjamin Woodbridge emigrated to New England in 1640, where he joined his minister brother. Woodbridge, one of the first graduates of Harvard, returned to England in 1647, where he served as a minister and wrote theological pamphlets. Although a resident of New England for only a portion of his life, Woodbridge seems to have assisted in the publication of Anne Bradstreet's poems in England, and he contributed a commendatory poem to that volume. He also wrote a well-known elegy for the famous John Cotton. Both these poems are reprinted next.

Upon the Author; by a Known Friend[1]

Now I believe Tradition, which doth call
The Muses, Virtues, Graces, Females all;
Only they are not nine, eleven nor three;
Our Auth'ress proves them but one unity.
Mankind take up some blushes on the score;
Monopolize perfection no more;
In your own Arts, confess your selves out-done,
The Moon hath totally eclips'd the Sun,
Not with her sable Mantle muffling him;
But her bright silver makes his gold look dim:
Just as his beams force our pale lamps to wink,
And earthly Fires, within their ashes shrink.

----

1. This poem originally appeared in Anne Bradstreet's *The Tenth Muse* (London, 1650).

Upon the TOMB of the most Reverend *Mr. John Cotton*, Late Teacher of the Church of Boston in *New-England*[2]

Here lies magnanimous Humility,
Majesty, Meekness; Christian Apathy
On soft Affections: Liberty in thrall;
A Noble Spirit, Servant unto all.
Learnings great Master-piece; who yet would sit
As a Disciple at his Schollars feet.
A simple Serpent, or Serpentine Dove,
Made up of Wisdome, Innocence, and Love.
Neatness Embroider's with *it self* alone;
And Civils Canonized in a Gown:
Embracing old and young, and low and high;
Ethicks imbodyed in Divinity:
Ambitious to be lowest, and to raise
His Brethrens Honour on his own Decayes.
Thus doth the *Sun* retire into his bed,
That being gone, the *Stars* may shew their head.
Could wound at Argument without Division;
Cut to the quick, and yet make no Incision;
Ready to Sacrifice Domestick Notions
To Churches Peace, and Ministers Devotions.
Himself indeed (and singular in that)
Whom all admired, he admired not.
Liv'd like an Angel of a Mortal Birth,
Convers'd in Heaven while he was on Earth:
Though not (as *Moses*) radiant with Light,
Whose Glory dazell'd the beholders sight;
Yet so divinely beautifi'd, youl'd count
He had been born and bred upon the Mount.
A living breathing Bible: Tables where
Both Covenants at large engraven were;
Gospel and *Law* in's Heart had each its Colume

His Head an Index to the Sacred Volume.
His very Name a *Title Page;* and next,
His Life a *Commentary* on the Text.
O what a Monument of glorious worth,
When in a *New Edition* he comes forth
Without *Errata's,* may we think hee'll be,
In *Leaves* and *Covers* of Eternitie!
A man of Might at Heavenly Eloquence,
To fix the Ear, and charm the Conscience,
As if *Apollos* were reviv'd in him,
Or he had learned of a *Seraphim.*
Spake many Tongues in one: one Voice and Sense
Wrought Joy and Sorrow, Fear and Confidence.
Rocks rent before him, Blinde receiv'd their sight,
Souls levell'd to the dunghil, stood upright.
Infernal Furies burst with rage to see
Their Pris'ners captiv'd into Libertie.
A *Star* that in our Eastern *England rose,*
Thence hurry'd by the Blast of stupid foes,
Whose foggy Darkness, and benummed Senses,
Brook'd not his daz'ling fervent Influences.
Thus did he move on Earth from East to West;
There he went down, and up to Heaven for Rest.
Nor from himself, whilst living doth he vary,
His death hath made him an *Ubiquitary:*
Where is his Sepulchre is hard to tell,
Who in a thousand Sepulchres doth dwell;
(Their *Hearts,* I mean, whom he hath left behind,)
In them his Sacred Relique's now Enshrin'd.
But let his Mourning Flock be comforted,
Though *Moses* be, yet *Joshua* is not dead:
I mean Renowned *NORTON;*[3] worthy hee
Successor to our *MOSES* is to bee,
O happy Israel in *AMERICA,*
In such a *MOSES* such a *JOSHUA.*

---

2. This poem originally appeared in Nathaniel Morton, *New Englands Memoriall* (Cambridge, 1669).

3. John Norton (1606–36) was, like John Cotton, a respected minister of the first generation of New England settlers.

JOHN JOSSELYN (1608?–1700?)

John Josselyn was born in England to an aristocratic family but traveled twice to New England and published accounts of his voyages as *New-Englands Rarities Discovered* (1672) and *An Account of Two Voyages to New-England* (1674). Josselyn's travel accounts are full of details about the natural environment, as well as stories of fantastic encounters, including an account of a merman. The following poem appeared in the first of Josselyn's travel narratives.

Verses Made Sometime since upon the Picture of a Young and Handsome Gypsie, Not Improperly Transferred upon the Indian Squa[1]

The Poem

Whether White or Black be best
Call your Senses to the quest;
And your touch shall quickly tell
The Black in softness doth excel,
And in smoothness; but the Ear,
What, can that a Colour hear?
No, but 'tis your Black ones Wit
That doth catch, and captive it.
And if Slut and Fair be one,
Sweet and Fair, there can be none:
Nor can ought so please the tast
As what's brown and lovely drest:
And who'll say, that that is best
To please one sense, displease the rest?
Maugre then all that can be sed
In flattery of White and Red:
Those flatterers themselves must say
That darkness was before the Day;
And such perfection here appears
It neither Wind nor Sun-shine fears.

---

1. This poem originally appeared in Josselyn's *New England's Rarities Discovered* (1672).

5

NEW SPAIN IN NORTH AMERICA

As the rhetoric of conquest indicates, Spain's first century in the Americas was characterized by a significant concern about the natural resources and peoples that could serve to increase the wealth and imperial prestige of Spain among European powers. Spain had been challenged by the Portuguese in the conquering of South America, but their territorial dispute had been settled by the Treaty of Tordesillas in 1494, giving Spain putative advantage over much of South America, outside Brazil, and all North America. Empire building was attempted in Florida, with some small success, but it was relinquished because of the too great difficulty in creating systematic settlements among unfriendly Native peoples and a difficult environment. Greater success for the Spanish empire in North America occurred in the outposts created and supported by the Franciscans (and later the Jesuits) beginning in the late sixteenth century and early seventeenth century in areas of northern Mexico, from present-day Texas to coastal Baja and Alta California.

Among the goals behind Spain's developing a presence in North America was to support the mines in Peru and Mexico. Mining was difficult, and the large enslaved population, composed primarily of Native peoples but also of Africans, was insufficient to the tasks expected of mining the gems, gold, silver, and ores so desired by the Crown and the rest of Europe. From settled areas to the north of the mines, a trade network could occur, it was thought, that would supply the mining areas with people, foodstuffs, and cloth for textiles. Slaving parties gained Indian slaves through trade with Native populations to the north and raiding parties headed by Spanish conquistadors. Goods, such as cloth, blankets, leather, and other products, were taken from Indian peoples in the north and used as commodities for trade in Mexico City and other southern areas. And foodstuffs—the corn, beans, and squash native to the area and wheat and other cereal grains introduced there—could be harvested in the north and taken to the south, since the southern Indian population, much of it enslaved, was being devoted to mining and other extraction activities.

In the eyes of civil officials, the settlements to the north, whether in Texas; the Pueblo country, extending from the mythological "Cíbola" (the Acoma area of present-day New Mexico) to the Pimería (land of the Pima Indians); or the semiagricultural country of the peoples living from "old" (Baja) California to "new" (Alta) California—all should be made to contribute to the ultimate goal of extending Spanish culture and the Spanish empire, while also enriching the individual local leaders in so doing. The wealth gained from the mines and commodity trading brought a brilliant court life to Mexico City, which served as the center of high culture, supporting the arts and sciences. The styles and manner of living rivaled the courts of Europe, and a literature of the high Renaissance—as evidenced by the secular writings of Sor Juana Inés de la Cruz—flourished.

Yet outside the arena of high literate culture, which was itself dependent upon the wealth of the empire of New Spain, the rhetoric of empire dominated the language of civil officials as they continued to have arguments with friars and priests who sought, after the most devastating years of conquest at the hands of Cortés (in Mexico, 1519–21) and Pizarro (in Peru, the early 1530s), more lenient treatment for the indigenous peoples of the Americas. Even in the late sixteenth century, long after appeals in behalf of Indian peoples like those made by Bartolomé de las Casas had received a good hearing in Spain, a conquest mentality and conquest language survived fully among the settlers who were pushing forward into the kingdom of New Mexico to the north of Mexico City, to gain control of alien Indian peoples, both their land and their persons, to benefit the system already set up in the capital city, Mexico City. Don Juan Perez de Oñate and his followers entered Pueblo lands as if they were reenacting the *reconquista* (reconquering) of the Iberian peninsula, using popular drama of the reconquest along the way, to symbolize for the Indian people their presumably permanent takeover. Although the Indian peoples surely understood something else entirely, Oñate was bringing settlers and war to Pueblo territory. Although Oñate was eventually found guilty of the mistreatment of Indian peoples, the devastation created in the name of the Spanish Crown was so memorable that the Pueblo peoples would for centuries work with a high degree of success (as evidenced by the Pueblo rebellions of the 1680s) to keep Spaniards and other settlers out of their ancestral homelands. Indeed, even after the late seventeenth-century "reconquest" of the territory, Spaniards were wary of settling among Pueblo peoples without significant military presence in the area. Too, the Spanish learned from their experiences with Pueblos that the military should always accompany any settler or missionary effort.

The rhetoric of conquest was complemented throughout Spain's second and third centuries in North America with a language of concern for the dignity, humanity, and civility of the Indian peoples. The 1573 Royal Orders for New Discoveries had given missionaries a central role in what was considered the exploration and pacification of new territory. According to those Royal Orders, "preaching the holy gospel . . . is the principal purpose for which we order new discoveries and settlements to be made." So the efforts by friars in behalf of Indian peoples met with some degree of interest by officials in Spain because the Royal Orders explicitly prohibited conquest or violence against Indian peoples. Such language, of course, served Spain's interest among other European powers because the language of pacifism also demarcated the "legal" taking of Indians' ancestral lands—for presumably "holy" reasons. In practice, however, the economic motives of the civilians often defined the quality of treatment the Indian peoples received.

In northern New Spain (present-day New Mexico), Franciscan friars worked, with some small success, to protect Indians from hardships that would result in the loss of life, even as they worked to create nucleated settlements, where missions and mission life would dominate the lives of Indian converts. Indian peoples were called upon by both friars and civil officials for labor, and thus the Indians were, in effect, unable to perform the necessary work on their own farms for their own sustenance, as letters from friars, such as Carlos José Delgado, would attest to civil magistrates. The *encomienda* system, a system of tribute whereby Indians would be expected to provide labor or goods to civil or military leaders, confined Indians to labor similar to slave labor, simply as a result of their willingness to join the friars' communities at the missions. The contest over the Indian body was high, and the friars, rarely in positions of power sufficient to have their attestations count against civil authorities, found their efforts in behalf of their Catholic Church and their order undermined by *encomenderos*. By the middle of the eighteenth century, missions in northern New Spain lost much of their vigor, and the number of Franciscans declined. What the Spanish Crown had referred to as the Church's "spiritual and temporal conquest" did not extend beyond El Paso and the narrow range of Pueblos along the Rio Grande. Although its settlement was older and more complex than the Texas area, New Mexico's Hispanic population was relatively scant by mid-century; the attempt to use the missions as supply forts for mining and other enterprises had lost its impetus.

As the Franciscans were in the process of diminishing in number in the New Mexico area, Jesuits moved into the territory. Under the leadership of Jesuits, such as Eusebio Francisco Kino, who must have been as strong in his faith as he was in physical ability, the Jesuits made significant efforts to work with the peoples of the Sonora and the Pimería Alta (in present-day Arizona). Driving cattle, horses, and pigs with him as he traveled from one Indian population to another, Kino worked conversions among peoples who had evaded or fought off the Franciscans. Part of Kino's success might have resulted from a distinct sense that Indian people were deserving of dignity and respect. Instead of insisting that the Indians build missions and develop nucleated settlements around them, Kino created only a few key missions and instead built up enclaves of Indians, most of whom were, by ancestral culture, hunters, nonagricultural people who were uninterested in settlement. It was Jesuits, rather than Franciscans, the earlier missionaries to the areas, who extended the mission frontier of Sonora northward into the land of the upper Pimas and explored the Gila and Colorado River areas.

The arrival of Kino accelerated missionary activity during the twenty-five years he served the area, from 1687 until his death in 1711, and the presence of the Jesuits brought renewed activity among the Franciscans to reestablish themselves in the territory of the Hopis, as the work of Carlos José Delgado in that area indicates. In reading Delgado's reports, one has a sense that the clear stress expressed regarding the mistreatment of the Indian peoples resulted, in part, from a knowledge of the successes of Jesuits in territories near these resistant peoples. The Franciscans eventually won in the competition for Indian souls, as a result of the 1767 order by Carlos III, king of Spain, that expelled Jesuits from Spain and all its dominions. The 2,500 Jesuits in New Spain at the time were rounded up if they failed to leave, and they were forcibly made to leave the areas they had worked so fully to settle. The Jesuits' self-sufficient Indian communities would revert to Franciscan control thereafter. The Jesuit Kino's efforts in California had simply made the way easier for Franciscans like Junípero Serra, who more than a half-century later would benefit from Kino's work in the area.

Carlos III had charged the Jesuits with sedition, but the charge was a pretext for his clear wish to rid the territories of that wealthy and organized religious order that, in the minds of the king's ministers, could thwart the secularization of Spain, preventing the enlightened reforms that Carlos III sought to implement. Under the leadership of people like Bernardo de Gálvez, viceroy of New Spain, the Spaniards' civil policy stabilized, and Indian leaders and many Spanish leaders alike began to see that more good might result from peace than from aggression. Gálvez, who saw himself as helping to sponsor the Spanish Enlightenment, did not care for missionaries, and he assisted his uncle, José de Gálvez, secretary of the Indies, in finding ways to stabilize the frontiers of New Spain while bringing the territory under greater secular control. It was Bernardo de Gálvez who received the various petitions of the scientists who were sent to effect the work for the Royal Scientific Expedition to New Spain (also called the Royal Botanical Expedition) in 1787. He took a great interest in the efforts to send important scientific findings back to Madrid, and he gave Longinos Martínez the orders that took him to Guatemala after the California expedition he had made.

Bernardo de Gálvez understood the global consequences of Spain's efforts to join the European community of enlightened scientists, philosophers, and members of state. Well aware of what he phrased as "the way in which the English and the French treat or have treated their Indians," making them dependent on them for European trade goods, Gálvez, like a few other high-ranking Spanish officials before him, proposed to the Spanish Crown that Indians be given guns and munitions in trade, thus bringing Spanish policy in line with that of England and France. His concerns were prophetic: During the wars that, taken collectively, are called the American Revolution, Gálvez had stunning and famous victories in the spring of 1781 against the British in the Florida area and on the Mississippi and Gulf of Mexico. Carlos III had ordered public prayers for the successes of his troops against the British, and Father Junípero Serra prescribed a weekly liturgy with the invocation, "That Thou [God] wouldst be pleased to humiliate the enemies of our Holy Church." Spain, while entering into the wartime arena in eastern North America, had moved philosophically into the European Enlightenment, even as it also would employ the support of Franciscans in New Spain to secure the reliability of the Indian peoples of North America.

———

Sor Juana Inés de la Cruz (1648?–1695)

Sor Juana Inés de la Cruz had an illustrious life at court before she entered a convent in 1669. Born in the hacienda of San Miguel Nepantla near Mexico City probably in 1648 (1651, according to some sources), she was given the name Juana Ramírez de Asbaje by her parents. Her mother, Isabel Ramírez, was a *criolla,* a mixed-race American-born woman of Spanish ancestry, and her father (who was not married to her mother) seems to have been Pedro Manuel de Asbaje, a Basque. Raised in her mother's household until she reached young adulthood, Juana Ramírez was a brilliant and precocious child who delighted in the books housed in the library of her grandfather, Pedro Ramírez. Her family's modest standing as small landowners gave Juana Ramírez opportunities that other young women might not so readily have had, but these opportunities increased as she entered young adulthood. When she was thirteen, she was moved to Mexico City, into the house of wealthy relatives, Juan de Mata and Doña María Ramírez. She was thereafter presented at the viceregal court, where she impressed all who met her. In 1664, she became a personal servant to Doña Leonor Carreto, marquesa de Mancera, the newly arrived vicereine, and she moved into court circles more frequently and received the patronage of several members of court. Most of her poetry, written after she entered the convent, gives clear evidence of Sor Juana's fascination with life at court, its intrigues, manners, flirtations, and sheer sensuality. Her poems on secular matters treat themes of hypocrisy, the shallowness of social forms, and the vulnerability of women to men and their demands. Many of these poems were commissioned by the most important people of her day, and many thus carry dedications to secular leaders and patrons.

When she entered into orders in 1669, Juana Ramírez was forced to lie about her parentage so as to claim legitimate birth. She first joined the Convent of the Barefoot Carmelites, but she soon moved to the Convent of Santa Paula of the Order of San Jerónimo, a convent that would have allowed greater freedom for her intellectual pursuits. The Convent of Santa Paula, founded primarily for *criolla* women, offered classes to young women in music, dance, and theater, and the sisters engaged in activities that included musical concerts, theatrical events, poetry tournaments, masquerades, and other social gatherings that today might seem unexpected for life in a convent of Sor Juana's day. Sor Juana flourished in such circumstances. She amassed what some scholars estimate to have been a library of between 2,000 and 4,000 volumes at a time when books were difficult to attain because of expense and importation problems and at one time seems to have owned a significant number of imported and indigenous musical instruments.

Evidence suggests that Sor Juana chafed at the gendered conventions of her day and the behaviors required of her both outside and inside the convent walls. She had numerous debates with renowned theologians, all men, regarding aspects of theology, such as the nature of Christ's love for humanity and the essence of pure Christian love. Although her numerous body of writings extends from plays to riddles for parlor guessing games, from odes and panegyric poems to sonnets, epigrams, and romances, Sor Juana was probably best known in her own day, as she seems to be today, for her writings that contested the Church authority, particularly the authority of the men who ruled in Church and secular affairs.

Her *Response to the Most Illustrious Poetess Sor Filotea de la Cruz* (1691) was written not to a woman (as the title suggests) but to a man, her sometime friend, Don Manuel Fernández de Santa Cruz y Sahagún, the bishop of Puebla. In the late 1680s, Fernández de Santa Cruz had circulated and then privately printed Sor Juana's treatise, the *Atenagórica (Athenagoric Letter),* written as a learned critique on current theology and church policy, with specific attention to the work of a Portuguese Jesuit, Father Antonio de Vieyra, a distinguished theologian of an earlier era. When her *Letter* became known, Sor Juana's name and her person were catapulted into a realm of inquiry, even infamy, reducing her privacy and constraining her activities. Although some praised Sor Juana's forthright and learned commentary, others feared the strength and learning behind her evaluations. As a result of the furor he had himself assisted in instigating, the bishop of Puebla ended up writing Sor Juana a letter of mild chastisement, suggesting she take up the proper roles of a nun in her convent, leaving questions of high theology to the theologians, so that she could spend her time contemplating her spiritual marriage to Christ. His letter seemed to address Sor Juana in respectful terms—he called her *Vuestra merced* (Your Reverence)—but because he wrote the letter not in his own name but under the name of a fictitious nun, Sor Filotea de la Cruz, he seems not to have taken authority for his role in creating Sor Juana's notoriety among the learned clergy. Although she surely knew who had penned the letter she received, Sor Juana accepted the subterfuge and addressed the bishop as Sor Filotea in a letter that shows, in its very learnedness, how silly it was to ask a learned woman to forget what she knew. Yet it seems that no amount of learning could protect a woman from attack in her day.

In the early 1690s, Mexico City was ravaged by heavy rains, floods, famine, plague, and violence, and fears of apocalyptic retribution were great. Sor Juana seems to have felt forced to accept a life of resignation, and she wrote statements (one signed in blood) of her full renunciation of worldly things, including humane letters, in 1694. These official documents of abjuration were declarations of loyalty to Catholicism, repentances for sinful actions, and requests for forgiveness by the Holy Spirit. She sold or gave away most of her books and nearly all her musical instruments. She did not live long after doing so. Sor Juana died in the convent in 1695 as she nursed several nuns during a devastating plague in Mexico City.

from RESPONSE TO THE MOST ILLUSTRIOUS POETESS SOR FILOTEA DE LA CRUZ[1]

My most illustrious *señora,* dear lady. It has not been my will, my poor health, or my justifiable apprehension that for so many days delayed my response. How could I write, considering that at my very first step my clumsy pen encountered two obstructions in its path? The first (and, for me, the most uncompromising) is to know how to reply to your most learned, most prudent, most holy, and most loving letter. For I recall that when Saint Thomas, the Angelic Doctor of Scholasticism, was asked about his silence regarding his teacher Albertus Magnus,[2] he replied that he had not spoken because he knew no words worthy of Albertus. With so much greater reason,

must not I too be silent? Not, like the Saint, out of humility, but because in reality I know nothing I can say that is worthy of you. The second obstruction is to know how to express my appreciation for a favor as unexpected as extreme, for having my scribblings printed, a gift so immeasurable as to surpass my most ambitious aspiration, my most fervent desire, which even as a person of reason never entered my thoughts. Yours was a kindness, finally, of such magnitude that words cannot express my gratitude, a kindness exceeding the bounds of appreciation, as great as it was unexpected—which is as Quintilian[3] said: *aspirations engender minor glory; benefices, major.* To such a degree as to impose silence on the receiver.

When the blessedly sterile—that she might miraculously become fecund—Mother of John the Baptist saw in her house such an extraordinary visitor as the Mother of the Word, her reason became clouded and her speech deserted her; and thus, in the place of thanks, she burst out with doubts and questions: *And whence is to me [that the mother of my Lord should come to me?]*[4] And whence cometh such a thing to *me?* And so also it fell to Saul when he found himself the chosen, the anointed, King of Israel: *Am I not a son of Jemini, of the least tribe of Israel,*

---

1. *La Repuesta de la poetisa a la muy ilustre Sor Filotea de la Cruz, Response to the Most Illustrious Poetess Sor Filotea de la Cruz,* was written and circulated widely in 1691. The text is from the translation by Margaret Sayers Peden, published in *Sor Juana Inés de la Cruz: Poems, Protest, and a Dream,* ed. Ilan Stavans, (1997).

2. Thomas Aquinas (1225?–74), the famous Italian theologian, sometimes called "Doctor Angelicus" and the "Father of Moral Philosophy," was a Dominican who studied with Albertus Magnus (1193?–1280), sometimes called "The Great" and "Doctor Universalis," the learned theologian who favored the work of Aristotle above that of Plato.

3. Quintilian (35?–95?), a celebrated Roman rhetorician and teacher of oratory.

4. Luke 1.43. Words in brackets have been added for clarification.

and my kindred the last among all the families of the tribe of Benjamin? Why then hast thou spoken this word to me?[5] And thus say I, most honorable lady. Why do I receive such favor? By chance, am I other than an humble nun, the lowliest creature of the world, the most unworthy to occupy your attention? "Wherefore then speakest thou so to me?" "And whence is this to me?"

Nor to the first obstruction do I have any response other than I am little worthy of your eyes; nor to the second, other than wonder, in the stead of thanks, saying that I am not capable of thanking you for the smallest part of that which I owe you. This is not pretended modesty, lady, but the simplest truth issuing from the depths of my heart, that when the letter which with propriety you called *Atenagórica* reached my hands, in print, I burst into tears of confusion (withal, that tears do not come easily to me) because it seemed to me that your favor was but a remonstrance God made against the wrong I have committed, and that in the same way He corrects others with punishment He wishes to subject me with benefices, with this special favor for which I know myself to be His debtor as for an infinitude of others from His boundless kindness. I looked upon this favor as a particular way to shame and confound me, it being the most exquisite means of castigation, that of causing me, by my own intellect, to be the judge who pronounces sentence and who denounces my ingratitude. And thus, when here in my solitude I think on these things, I am wont to say: Blessed art Thou, oh Lord, for Thou hast not chosen to place in the hands of others my judgment, nor yet in mine, but hast reserved that to Thy own, and freed me from myself, and from the necessity to sit in judgment on myself, which judgment, forced from my own intellect, could be no less than condemnation, but Thou hast reserved me to Thy mercy, because Thou lovest me more than I can love myself.

I beg you, lady, to forgive this digression to which I was drawn by the power of truth, and, if I am to confess all the truth, I shall confess that I cast about for some manner by which I might flee the difficulty of a reply, and was sorely tempted to take refuge in silence. But as silence is a negative thing, though it explains a great deal through the very stress of not explaining, we must assign some meaning to it that we may understand what the silence is intended to say, for if not, silence will say nothing, as that is its very office: *to say nothing.* The holy Chosen Vessel, Saint Paul, having been caught up into

paradise, and having heard the arcane secrets of God, *heard secret words, which it is not granted to man to utter.*[6] He does not say what he heard, he says that he cannot say it. So that of things one cannot say, it is needful to say at least that they cannot be said, so that it may be understood that not speaking is not the same as having nothing to say, but rather being unable to express the many things there are to say. Saint John says that if all the marvels our Redeemer wrought "were written every one, the world itself, I think, would not be able to contain the books that should be written."[7] And Vieyra[8] says on this point that in this single phrase the Evangelist said more than in all else he wrote; and this same Lusitanian Phoenix speaks well (but when does he not speak well, even when it is not well he speak?) because in those words Saint John said everything left unsaid and expressed all that was left to be expressed. And thus I, lady, shall respond only that I do not know how to respond; I shall thank you in saying only that I am incapable of thanking you; and I shall say, through the indication of what I leave to silence, that it is only with the confidence of one who is favored and with the protection of one who is honorable that I presume to address your magnificence, and if this be folly, be forgiving of it, for folly may be good fortune, and in this manner I shall provide further occasion for your benignity and you will better shape my appreciation.

Because he was halting of speech, Moses thought himself unworthy to speak with Pharaoh, but after he found himself highly favored of God, and thus inspired, he not only spoke with God Almighty but dared ask the impossible: *shew me thy face.*[9] In this same manner, lady, and in view of how you favor me, I no longer see as impossible the obstructions I posed in the beginning: for who was it who had my letter printed unbeknownst to me? Who entitled it, who bore the cost, who honored it, it being so unworthy in itself, and in its author? What will such a person not do, not pardon? What would he fail to do, or fail to pardon? And thus, based on the supposition that I speak under the safe-conduct of your favor, and with the assurance of your benignity and with the knowledge that like a

---

5. I Kings 9.21.

6. II Corinthians 12.4.

7. John 21.25.

8. The Portuguese Jesuit, Father Antonio de Vieyra, was a distinguished theologian whom Sor Juana had critiqued in her *Athenagoric Letter.*

9. Exodus 33.13.

second Ahasuerus[10] you have offered to me to kiss the top of the golden scepter of your affection as a sign of conceding to me your benevolent license to speak and offer judgments in your exalted presence, I say to you that I have taken to heart your most holy admonition that I apply myself to the study of the Sacred Books, which, though it comes in the guise of counsel, will have for me the authority of a precept, but with the not insignificant consolation that even before your counsel I was disposed to obey your pastoral suggestion, as your direction, which may be inferred from the premise and arguments of my Letter. For I know well that your most sensible warning is not directed against it, but rather against those worldly matters of which I have written. And thus I had hoped with the Letter to make amends for any lack of application you may (with great reason) have inferred from others of my writings; and, speaking more particularly, I confess to you with all the candor of which you are deserving, and with the truth and clarity which are the natural custom in me, that my not having written often of sacred matters was not caused by disaffection or by want of application, but by the abundant fear and reverence due those Sacred Letters, knowing myself incapable of their comprehension and unworthy of their employment. Always resounding in my ears, with no little horror, I hear God's threat and prohibition to sinners like myself. *Why dost thou declare my justices, and take my covenant in thy mouth?*[11] This question, as well as the knowledge that even learned men are forbidden to read the Canticle of Canticles until they have passed thirty years of age, or even Genesis—the latter for its obscurity, the former in order that the sweetness of those epithalamia not serve as occasion for imprudent youth to transmute their meaning into carnal emotion, as borne out by my exalted Father Saint Jerome, who ordered that these be the last verses to be studied, and for the same reason: *And finally, one may read without peril the Song of Songs, for if it is read early one may suffer harm through not understanding those Epithalamia of the spiritual wedding which is expressed in carnal terms.* And Seneca[12] says: *In the early years the faith is dim.* For how then would I have dared take in my unworthy hands these verses, defying gender, age, and,

above all, custom? And thus I confess that many times this fear has plucked my pen from my hand and has turned my thoughts back toward the very same reason from which they had wished to be born: which obstacle did not impinge upon profane matters, for a heresy against art is not punished by the Holy Office but by the judicious with derision, and by critics with censure, and censure, *just or unjust, is not to be feared,* as it does not forbid the taking of communion or hearing of mass, and offers me little or no cause for anxiety, because in the opinion of those who defame my art, I have neither the obligation to know nor the aptitude to triumph. If, then, I err, I suffer neither blame nor discredit: I suffer no blame, as I have no obligation; no discredit, as I have no possibility of triumphing—*and no one is obliged to do the impossible.* And, in truth, I have written nothing except when compelled and constrained, and then only to give pleasure to others; not alone without pleasure of my own, but with absolute repugnance, for I have never deemed myself one who has any worth in letters or the wit necessity demands of one who would write; and thus my customary response to those who press me, above all in sacred matters, is, what capacity of reason have I? what application? what resources? what rudimentary knowledge of such matters beyond that of the most superficial scholarly degrees? Leave these matters to those who understand them; I wish no quarrel with the Holy Office, for I am ignorant, and I tremble that I may express some proposition that will cause offense or twist the true meaning of some scripture. I do not study to write, even less to teach—which in one like myself were unseemly pride—but only to the end that if I study, I will be ignorant of less. This is my response, and these are my feelings.

I have never written of my own choice, but at the urging of others, to whom with reason I might say, *You have compelled me.*[13] But one truth I shall not deny (first, because it is well-known to all, and second, because although it has not worked in my favor, God has granted me the mercy of loving truth above all else), which is that from the moment I was first illuminated by the light of reason, my inclination toward letters has been so vehement, so overpowering, that not even the admonitions of others—and I have suffered many—nor my own meditations—and they have not been few—have been sufficient to cause me to forswear this natural impulse that God placed in me: the Lord God knows why, and for what pur-

---

10. Ahasuerus is Xerxes, who ruled 486–465 B.C., as discussed in Ezra 4.6 and throughout the book of Esther.

11. Psalms 49.16.

12. Lucius Annaeus Seneca (4 B.C.–A.D. 65), Roman stoic philosopher.

13. II Corinthians 12.11.

pose. And He knows that I have prayed that He dim the light of my reason, leaving only that which is needed to keep His Law, for there are those who would say that all else is unwanted in a woman, and there are even those who would hold that such knowledge does injury. And my Holy Father knows too that as I have been unable to achieve this (my prayer has not been answered), I have sought to veil the light of my reason—along with my name—and to offer it up only to Him who bestowed it upon me, and He knows that none other was the cause for my entering into Religion, notwithstanding that the spiritual exercises and company of a community were repugnant to the freedom and quiet I desired for my studious endeavors. And later, in that community, the Lord God knows—and, in the world, only the one who must know—how diligently I sought to obscure my name, and how this was not permitted, saying it was temptation: and so it would have been. If it were in my power, lady, to repay you in some part what I owe you, it might be done by telling you this thing which has never before passed my lips, except to be spoken to the one who should hear it. It is my hope that by having opened wide to you the doors of my heart, by having made patent to you its most deeply-hidden secrets, you will deem my confidence not unworthy of the debt I owe to your most august person and to your most uncommon favors.

Continuing the narration of my inclinations, of which I wish to give you a thorough account, I will tell you that I was not yet three years old when my mother determined to send one of my elder sisters to learn to read at a school for girls we call the *Amigas*. Affection, and mischief, caused me to follow her, and when I observed how she was being taught her lessons I was so inflamed with the desire to know how to read, that deceiving—for so I knew it to be—the mistress, I told her that my mother had meant for me to have lessons too. She did not believe it, as it was little to be believed, but, to humor me, she acceded. I continued to go there, and she continued to teach me, but now, as experience had disabused her, with all seriousness; and I learned so quickly that before my mother knew of it I could already read, for my teacher had kept it from her in order to reveal the surprise and reap the reward at one and the same time. And I, you may be sure, kept the secret, fearing that I would be whipped for having acted without permission. The woman who taught me, may God bless and keep her, is still alive and can bear witness to all I say.

I also remember that in those days, my tastes being those common to that age, I abstained from eating cheese because I had heard that it made one slow of wits, for in me the desire for learning was stronger than the desire for eating—as powerful as that is in children. When later, being six or seven, and having learned how to read and write, along with all the other skills of needlework and household arts that girls learn, it came to my attention that in Mexico City there were Schools, and a University, in which one studied the sciences. The moment I heard this, I began to plague my mother with insistent and importunate pleas: she should dress me in boy's clothing and send me to Mexico City to live with relatives, to study and be tutored at the University. She would not permit it, and she was wise, but I assuaged my disappointment by reading the many and varied books belonging to my grandfather, and there were not enough punishments, nor reprimands, to prevent me from reading: so that when I came to the city many marveled, not so much at my natural wit, as at my memory, and at the amount of learning I had mastered at an age when many have scarcely learned to speak well.

I began to study Latin grammar—in all, I believe, I had no more than twenty lessons—and so intense was my concern that though among women (especially a woman in the flower of her youth) the natural adornment of one's hair is held in such high esteem, I cut off mine to the breadth of some four to six fingers, measuring the place it had reached, and imposing upon myself the condition that if by the time it had again grown to that length I had not learned such and such a thing I had set for myself to learn while my hair was growing, I would again cut it off as punishment for being so slow-witted. And it did happen that my hair grew out and still I had not learned what I had set for myself—because my hair grew quickly and I learned slowly—and in fact I did cut it in punishment for such stupidity: for there seemed to me no cause for a head to be adorned with hair and naked of learning—which was the more desired embellishment. And so I entered the religious order, knowing that life there entailed certain conditions (I refer to superficial, and not fundamental, regards) most repugnant to my nature; but given the total antipathy I felt for marriage, I deemed convent life the least unsuitable and the most honorable I could elect if I were to insure my salvation. Working against that end, first (as, finally, the most important) was the matter of all the trivial aspects of my nature that nourished my pride, such as wishing to live alone, and wishing to have no obligatory occupation that would inhibit the freedom of my studies, nor the sounds of a community that would intrude upon the peaceful silence of my books. These desires caused me to falter some while in my decision, until certain learned persons enlightened me, explaining that they were temptation, and, with divine favor, I overcame them, and took upon myself the state which now so unworthily I hold. I believed that I was fleeing from myself, but—wretch that I am!—I brought with me my worst enemy, my inclination, which I do not know whether to consider a gift or a punishment from Heaven, for once dimmed and encumbered by the many activities common to Religion, that inclination exploded in me like gunpowder, proving how *privation is the source of appetite.*

I turned again (which is badly put, for I never ceased), I continued, then, in my studious endeavour (which for me was respite during those moments not occupied by my duties) of reading and more reading, of study and more study, with no teachers but my books. Thus I learned how difficult it is to study those soulless letters, lacking a human voice or the explication of a teacher. But I suffered this labor happily for my love of learning. Oh, had it only been for love of God, which were proper, how worthwhile it would have been! I strove mightily to elevate these studies, to dedicate them to His service, as the goal to which I aspired was to study Theology—it seeming to me debilitating for a Catholic not to know everything in this life of the Divine Mysteries that can be learned through natural means—and, being a nun and not a layperson, it was seemly that I profess my vows to learning through ecclesiastical channels; and especially, being a daughter of a Saint Jerome and a Saint Paula, it was essential that such erudite parents not be shamed by a witless daughter. This is the argument I proposed to myself, and it seemed to me well-reasoned. It was, however (and this cannot be denied) merely glorification and approbation of my inclination, and enjoyment of it offered as justification.

And so I continued, as I have said, directing the course of my studies toward the peak of Sacred Theology, it seeming necessary to me, in order to scale those heights, to climb the steps of the human sciences and arts; for how could one undertake the study of the Queen of Sciences if first one had not come to know her servants? How, without Logic, could I be apprised of the general and specific way in which the Holy Scripture is written? How, without Rhetoric, could I understand its figures, its tropes, its locutions? How, without Physics, so many innate questions concerning the nature of animals, their sacrifices, wherein exist so many symbols, many already declared, many still to be discovered? How should I know whether Saul's being refreshed by the sound of David's harp was due to the virtue and natural power of Music, or to a transcen-

dent power God wished to place in David? How, without Arithmetic, could one understand the computations of the years, days, months, hours, those mysterious weeks communicated by Gabriel to Daniel, and others for whose understanding one must know the nature, concordance, and properties of numbers? How, without Geometry, could one measure the Holy Arc of the Covenant and the Holy City of Jerusalem, whose mysterious measures are foursquare in all their dimensions, as well as the miraculous proportions of all their parts? How, without Architecture, could one know the great Temple of Solomon, of which God Himself was the Author who conceived the disposition and the design, and the Wise King but the overseer who executed it, of which temple there was no foundation without mystery no column without symbolism, no cornice without allusion, no architrave without significance; and similarly others of its parts, of which the least fillet was never intended solely for the service and complement of Art, but as symbol of greater things? How, without great knowledge of the laws and parts of which History is comprised, could one understand historical Books? Or those recapitulations in which many times what happened first is seen in the narrated account to have happened later? How, without great learning in Canon and Civil Law, could one understand Legal Books? How, without great erudition, could one apprehend the secular histories of which the Holy Scripture makes mention, such as the many customs of the Gentiles, their many rites, their many ways of speaking? How without the abundant laws and lessons of the Holy Fathers could one understand the obscure lesson of the Prophets? And without being expert in Music, how could one understand the exquisite precision of the musical proportions that grace so many Scriptures, particularly those in which Abraham beseeches God in defense of the Cities, asking whether He would spare the place were there but fifty just men therein; and then Abraham reduced that number to five less than fifty, forty-five, which is a ninth, and is as Mi to Re; then to forty, which is a tone, and is as Re to Mi; from forty to thirty, which is a diatessaron, the interval of the perfect fourth; from thirty to twenty, which is the perfect fifth, and from twenty to ten, which is the octave, the diapason; and as there are no further harmonic proportions, made no further reductions. How might one understand this without Music? And there in the Book of Job, God says to Job: *Shalt thou be able to join together the shining stars the Pleiades, or canst thou stop the turning about of Arcturus? Canst thou bring forth the day star in its time and make the evening star to rise upon the children of the earth?*[14] Which message, without knowledge of Astrology, would be impossible to apprehend. And not only these noble sciences; there is no applied art that is not mentioned. And, finally, in consideration of the Book that comprises all books, and the Science in which all sciences are embraced, and for whose comprehension all sciences serve, and even after knowing them all (which we now see is not easy, nor even possible), there is one condition that takes precedence over all the rest, which is uninterrupted prayer and purity of life, that one may entreat of God that purgation of spirit and illumination of mind necessary for the understanding of such elevated matters: and if that be lacking, none of the aforesaid will have been of any purpose.

Of the Angelic Doctor Saint Thomas the Church affirms: *When reading the most difficult passages of the Holy Scripture, he joined fast with prayer. And he was wont to say to his companion Brother Reginald that all he knew derived not so much from study or his own labor as from the grace of God.* How then should I—so lacking in virtue and so poorly read—find courage to write? But as I had acquired the rudiments of learning, I continued to study ceaselessly divers subjects, having for none any particular inclination, but for all in general; and having studied some more than others was not owing to preference, but to the chance that more books on certain subjects had fallen into my hands, causing the election of them through no discretion of my own. And as I was not directed by preference, nor, forced by the need to fulfill certain scholarly requirements, constrained by time in the pursuit of any subject, I found myself free to study numerous topics at the same time, or to leave some for others; although in this scheme some order was observed, for some I deigned study and others diversion, and in the latter I found respite from the former. From which it follows that though I have studied many things I know nothing, as some have inhibited the learning of others. I speak specifically of the practical aspect of those arts that allow practice, because it is clear that when the pen moves the compass must lie idle, and while the harp is played the organ is stilled, *et sic de caeteris.* And because much practice is required of one who would acquire facility, none who divides his interest among various exercises may reach per-

fection. Whereas in the formal and theoretical arts the contrary is true, and I would hope to persuade all with my experience, which is that one need not inhibit the other, but, in fact, each may illuminate and open the way to others, by nature of their variations and their hidden links, which were placed in this universal chain by the wisdom of their Author in such a way that they conform and are joined together with admirable unity and harmony. This is the very chain the ancients believed did issue from the mouth of Jupiter, from which were suspended all things linked one with another, as is demonstrated by the Reverend Father Athanasius Kircher in his curious book, *De Magnate.*[15] All things issue from God, Who is at once the center and the circumference from which and in which all lines begin and end. . . .

. . . It has been my fortune that, among other benefices, I owe to God a most tender and affable nature, and because of it my sisters (who being good women do not take note of my faults) hold me in great affection, and take pleasure in my company; and knowing this, and moved by the great love I hold for them—having greater reason than they—I enjoy even more *their* company. Thus I was wont in our rare idle moments to visit among them, offering them consolation and entertaining myself in their conversation. I could not help but note, however, that in these times I was neglecting my study, and I made a vow not to enter any cell unless obliged by obedience or charity; for without such a compelling constraint—the constraint of mere intention not being sufficient—my love would be more powerful than my will. I would (knowing well my frailty) make this vow for the period of a few weeks, or a month, and when that time had expired, I would allow myself a brief respite of a day or two before renewing it, using that time not so much for rest (for *not* studying has never been restful for me) as to assure that I not be deemed cold, remote, or ungrateful in the little-deserved affection of my dearest sisters.

In this practice one may recognize the strength of my inclination. I give thanks to God, Who willed that such an ungovernable force be turned toward letters and not to some other vice. From this it may also be inferred how obdurately against the current my poor studies have sailed

---

14. Job 38.31, 32.

15. Kircher's *Magnes sive de arte magnetica* seems to have been confused here with William Gilbert's *De magnete* (London, 1600).

(more accurately, have foundered). For still to be related is the most arduous of my difficulties—those mentioned until now, either compulsory or fortuitous, being merely tangential—and still unreported the more-directly aimed slings and arrows that have acted to impede and prevent the exercise of my study. Who would have doubted, having witnessed such general approbation, that I sailed before the wind across calm seas, amid the laurels of widespread acclaim. But our Lord God knows that it has not been so; He knows how from amongst the blossoms of this very acclaim emerged such a number of aroused vipers, hissing their emulation and their persecution, that one could not count them. But the most noxious, those who most deeply wounded me, have not been those who persecuted me with open loathing and malice, but rather those who in loving me and desiring my well-being (and who are deserving of God's blessing for their good intent) have mortified and tormented me more than those others with their abhorrence. "Such studies are not in conformity with sacred innocence; surely she will be lost; surely she will, by cause of her very perspicacity and acuity, grow heady at such exalted heights." How was I to endure? An uncommon sort of martyrdom in which I was both martyr and executioner.

And as for my (in me, twice hapless) facility in making verses, even though they be sacred verses, what sorrows have I not suffered? What sorrows not ceased to suffer? Be assured, lady, it is often that I have meditated on how one who distinguishes himself—or one on whom God chooses to confer distinction, for it is only He who may do so—is received as a common enemy, because it seems to some that he usurps the applause they deserve, or that he dams up the admiration to which they aspired, and so they persecute that person.

That politically barbaric law of Athens by which any person who excelled by cause of his natural gifts and virtues was exiled from his Republic in order that he not threaten the public freedom still endures, is still observed in our day, although not for the reasons held by the Athenians. Those reasons have been replaced by another, no less efficient though not as well founded, seeming, rather, a maxim more appropriate to that impious Machiavelli—which is to abhor one who excels, because he deprives others of regard. And thus it happens, and thus it has always happened. . . .

. . . And in my own behalf I can attest that calumny has often mortified me, but never harmed me, being that I hold as a great fool one who having occasion to receive credit suffers the difficulty and loses the credit, as it is with those who do not resign themselves to death, but, in the end, die anyway, their resistance not having prevented death, but merely deprived them of the credit of resignation and caused them to die badly when they might have died well. And thus, lady, I believe these experiences do more good than harm, and I hold as greater the jeopardy of applause to human weakness, as we are wont to appropriate praise that is not our own, and must be ever watchful, and carry graven on our hearts those words of the Apostle: *Or what hast thou that thou hast not received? And if thou hast received, why doest thou glory as if thou hadst not received it.*[16] so that these words serve as a shield to fend off the sharp barbs of commendations, which are as spears which when not attributed to God (whose they are), claim our lives and cause us to be thieves of God's honor and usurpers of the talents He bestowed on us and the gifts that He lent to us, for which we must give the most strict accounting. And thus, lady, I fear applause more than calumny, because the latter, with but the simple act of patience becomes gain, while the former requires many acts of reflection and humility and proper recognition so that it not become harm. And I know and recognize that it is by special favor of God that I know this, as it enables me in either instance to act in accord with the words of Saint Augustine: *One must believe neither the friend who praises nor the enemy who detracts.* Although, most often I squander God's favor, or vitiate with such defects and imperfections that I spoil what, being His, was good. And thus in what little of mine that has been printed, neither the use of my name, nor even consent for the printing, was given by my own counsel, but by the license of another who lies outside my domain, as was also true with the printing of the *Atenagórica* letter, and only a few *Exercises of the Incarnation* and *Offerings of the Sorrows* were printed for public devotions with my pleasure but without my name; of which I am sending some few copies that (if you so desire) you may distribute them among our sisters, the nuns of that holy community, as well as in that city. I send but one copy of the *Sorrows* because the others have been exhausted and I could find no other copy. I wrote them long ago, solely for the devotions of my sisters, and later they were spread

---

16. I Corinthians 4.7.

abroad; and their contents are disproportionate as regards my unworthiness and my ignorance, and they profited that they touched on matters of our exalted Queen; for I cannot explain what it is that inflames the coldest heart when one refers to the Most Holy Mary. It is my only desire, esteemed lady, to remit to you works worthy of your virtue and wisdom; as the poet said:

Though strength may falter, good will must be praised.
In this, I believe, the gods will be content.

If ever I write again, my scribbling will always find its way to the haven of your holy feet and the certainty of your correction, for I have no other jewel with which to pay you, and, in the lament of Seneca, he who has once bestowed benefices has committed himself to continue; and so you must be repaid out of your own munificence, for only in this way shall I with dignity be freed from debt and avoid that the words of that same Seneca come to pass: *It is contemptible to be surpassed in benefices.* For in his gallantry the generous creditor gives to the poor debtor the means to satisfy his debt. So God gave His gift to a world unable to repay Him: He gave His son that He be offered a recompense worthy of Him.

If, most venerable lady, the tone of this letter may not have seemed right and proper, I ask forgiveness for its homely familiarity, and the less than seemly respect in which by treating you as a nun, one of my sisters, I have lost sight of the remoteness of your most illustrious person; which, had I seen you without your veil, would never have occurred; but you in all your prudence and mercy will supplement or amend the language, and if you find unsuitable the *Vos* of the address I have employed, believing that for the reverence I owe you, Your Reverence seemed little reverent, modify it in whatever manner seems appropriate to your due, for I have not dared exceed the limits of your custom, nor transgress the boundary of your modesty.

And hold me in your grace, and entreat for me divine grace, of which the Lord God grant you large measure, and keep you, as I pray Him, and am needful. From this convent of our Father Saint Jerome in Mexico City, the first day of the month of March of sixteen hundred and ninety-one. Allow me to kiss your hand, your most favored

Juana Inés de la Cruz

from ROMANCES[1]

[Prologue to the Reader][2]

These poems, Dear Reader, I give you
with hopes your pleasure they ensure,
though all that may speak well of them
is that I know them to be poor;
　I do not wish to argue them,
nor of their worth give evidence,
for such attention to these lines
would seem to lend them consequence.
　Nor do I seek your good esteem,
for, after all, no one demands
you value what I never thought
would find its way into your hands.
　If you should wish to criticize,
I place you in full liberty,
as I am free now to conclude,
you may conclude that you are free.
　We know nothing as unbound
as our human intellect;
and what God never violates,
should I not honor and respect?
　Say of these verses what you will,
the more that you are inhumane,
and at them cruelly bite and gnaw,
the more my debtor you remain,
　for in the Court it is well known
that only through my Muse's grace
do you enjoy that richest dish,
the spiteful chatter you embrace.
　How well I serve you, at all times,
in pleasing you or pleasing not;
you are diverted if I please,
and gossip if I come to naught.
　In asking pardon, I might say
I hoped some poems to remedy,
but due to haste in copying,

---

1. The three poems collected here follow the conventions of poetic romances, Spanish ballads written (in Spanish) in octosyllabic verse, with even-numbered lines rhyming with the same assonance and odd-numbered lines left free. Sor Juana Inés de la Cruz did not title her works. The titles provided have been supplied by the editors.

2. The prologue appeared in Sor Juana's first book of poems. The text is a translation by Margaret Sayers Peden.

had little opportunity;
  they come in many different hands
and some, where little lads have erred,
do kill the sense, and you will see
cadavers made of living words,

  besides which, when I wrote these lines,
they were composed in those rare fêtes
when leisure called a holiday
amidst the duties of my state;

  for I suffer from ill-health,
my life, with obstacles is fraught,
so many, even as I write,
my pen is racing at a trot.

  But pay no heed to what I say,
lest you think I vaunt my rhymes,
suggesting that they would be good
had I but had sufficient time;

  I would not have you so believe,
for their life, their imminence,
the cause for bringing them to light,
was dutiful obedience.

  And so it is, think as you will,
I do not die to have them read,
and you are free to do with them
whatever comes into your head.

  Godspeed to you, all I do here
is show a piece, but not the whole:
so if you do not like the cloth,
the bolt were better left unrolled.

[In Reply to a Gentleman from Peru, Who Sent Her Clay Vessels While Suggesting She Would Better Be a Man][3]

  Kind Sir, while wishing to reply,
my Muses all have taken leave,
and none, even for charity,
will aid me now I wish to speak;

  and though we know these Sisters nine
good mothers are of wit and jest,
not one, once having heard your verse,
will dare to jest at my behest.

  The God Apollo listens, rapt,
and races on, so high aloft
that those who guide his Chariot

must raise their voices to a shout.

  To hear your lines, fleet Pegasus
his lusty breathing will retain,
that no one fear his thunderous neigh
as your verses are declaimed.

  Checking, against nature's order,
altering crystalline watercourse,
Helicon stays its gurgling water,
Agannipe, her murmuring source:

  for, having heard your murmuring,
the Nine Daughters all concede,
beside your verses they are wanting,
unfit to study at your feet.

  Apollo sets aside the wand
that he employs to mark the beat,
because, on seeing you, he knows
he cannot justly take the lead.

  And thus, acknowledge it I must,
I cannot scribe the verses owed
unless, perhaps, compassionate,
keen inspiration you bestow.

  Be my Apollo, and behold
(as your light illumines me)
how my lyre will then be heard
the length and breadth of land and sea.

  Though humble, oh, how powerful
my invocation's consequence,
I find new valor in my breast,
new spirit given utterance!

  Ignited with unfamiliar fervor,
my pen bursting into flame,
while giving due to famed Apollo
I honor Navarrete's name.

  Traveling where none has trod,
expression rises to new heights,
and, reveling in new invention,
finds in itself supreme delight.

  Stammering with such abundance
my clumsy tongue is tied with pain:
much is seen, but little spoken,
some is known, but none explained.

  You will think that I make mock;
no, nothing further from the truth,
to prophesy, my guiding spirit
is lacking but a fine hair's breadth.

  But if I am so little able
to offer you sufficient praise,
to form the kind of compliment
that only your apt pen may phrase,

---

3. A Señor Navarette sent Sor Juana some clay vessels from Chile, along with some original poems, saying "she would better be a man." The text is a translation by Margaret Sayers Peden.

what serve me then to undertake it?
to venture it, what good will serve?
if mine be pens that write in water,
recording lessons unobserved.

That they themselves elucidate,
I now leave your eulogies:
as none to their measure correspond,
none can match them in degree,

and I turn to giving thanks
for your fair gifts, most subtly made;
Art lifts a toast to appetite
in lovely Vessels of fragrant clay.

Earthenware, so exquisite
that Chile properly is proud,
though it is not gold or silver
that gives your gift its wide renown

but, rather, from such lowly matter
forms emerge that put to shame
the brimming Goblets made of gold
from which Gods their nectar drained.

Kiss, I beg, the hands that made them,
though judging by the Vessels' charm
—such grace can surely leave no doubt—
yours were the hands that gave them form.

As for the counsel that you offer,
I promise you, I will attend
with all my strength, although I judge
no strength on earth can en-Tarquin:

for here we have no Salmacis,
whose crystal water, so they tell,
to nurture masculinity
possesses powers unexcelled.

I have no knowledge of these things,
except that I came to this place
so that, if true that I am female,
none substantiate that state.

I know, too, that they were wont
to call wife, or woman, in the Latin
uxor, only those who wed,
though wife or woman might be virgin.

So in my case, it is not seemly
that I be viewed as feminine,
as I will never be a woman
who may as woman serve a man.

I know only that my body,
not to either state inclined,
is neuter, abstract, guardian
of only what my Soul consigns.

Let us renounce this argument,
let others, if they will, debate;
some matters better left unknown
no reason can illuminate.

Generous gentleman from Peru,
proclaiming such unhappiness,
did you leave Lima any art,
given the art you brought to us?

You must know that law of Athens
by which Aristides was expelled:
it seems that, even if for good,
it is forbidden to excel.

He was expelled for being good,
and other famous men as well;
because to tower over all
is truly unforgiveable.

He who always leads his peers
will by necessity invite
malicious envy, as his fame
will rob all others of the light.

To the degree that one is chosen
as the target for acclaim,
to that same measure, envy trails
in close pursuit, with perfect aim.

Now you are banished from Peru
and welcomed in my Native Land,
we see the Heavens grant to us
the blessing that Peru declined.

But it is well that such great talent
live in many different zones,
for those who are with greatness born
should live not for themselves alone.

[While by Grace I Am Inspired][4]

While by Grace I am inspired,
'tis then I near the precipice,
I would ascend unto the Sphere,
but am dragged down to the abyss.

Virtue and custom are at odds,
and deep within my heart contend,
my anguished heart will agonize
until the two their combat end.

I fear that virtue will be crushed,
though all know its just repute,
for custom is long flourishing,

---

4. The text is from *Obras completas de Sor Juana Inés de la Cruz,* ed. Alfonso Méndez Plancarte and translated by Margaret Sayers Peden.

and virtue, tender as a shoot.

My thinking often is obscured,
among dark shadows ill-defined,
then who is there to give me light,
when reason falters as if blind?

Of myself I am the gaoler,
I, executioner of me,
who can know the painful pain,
who can know the tragedy?

I cause displeasure to the One
I most desire to gratify,

and from displeasure that I give,
the one who suffers most is I.

I love and find myself in God,
but my will His grace transforms,
turning solace to a cross,
quitting port to seek the storm.

Then suffer, it is God's command,
but let this be the paradigm,
that though your sins cause suffering,
your suffering not be seen as sin.

GASPAR PÉREZ DE VILLAGRÁ (1555?–1620)

Gaspar Pérez de Villagrá, well known among early Spanish writers for his epic poem of the conquest of the New World, the first published history of the Spanish settlement of New Mexico, remains a relatively vague literary figure because relatively little is known about his life. He was born at Puebla de Los Angeles in New Spain, to a family situation sufficiently privileged that he traveled to Europe for his education. He earned a degree from the University of Salamanca and returned to New Spain sometime before 1596, when he became involved in Don Juan Perez de Oñate's New Mexican expedition, one of the final expeditions to expand the Spanish empire. Villagrá was appointed captain, legal officer, and ecclesiastical counsel for the expedition, which would establish the first permanent Spanish settlement in north central New Mexico.

When Oñate's expedition departed on January 26, 1598, thousands of horses, mules, pigs, goats, cattle, and sheep accompanied hundreds of colonists and soldiers. Limited food and water, significant heat, and difficult terrain made travel onerous for the group. Early meetings between Oñate's army and the Native peoples were peaceful, but it became clear that the Indians were fearful of Europeans, on the basis of their experiences during earlier exploring missions by Spaniards. Tensions among members of the exploring party emerged as the colonists, who were most interested in focusing on livestock and agriculture, fought pushing on with Oñate, who wanted to continue to survey the lands for mineral wealth. Although Oñate continued to focus on exploration of the territory, before winter came, the colonists were able to establish a village and, assisted by 1,500 Indians, build a church, San Juan Bautista. Oñate assigned the pueblos of New Mexico to eight Franciscan friars.

Villagrá's poem recounts the colonizing expedition, ending with the Spanish takeover of Acoma, an ancient pueblo set atop a mesa. Acoma is so high, in fact, that the Indians call it "skyline town." In a challenge to Spanish rule, the Acomans fought a small group of Spaniards who were exploring, among them Juan de Zaldívar, the commanding officer of Oñate's men. Oñate feared that the Acomans' victory might be the beginning of a rebellion of all the pueblos against Spanish rule. In January 1599, he organized a punitive expedition against Acoma, led by Vicente de Zaldivar y Bañuelos, brother of the slain officer. After a lengthy, difficult battle—eight hundred people were killed—the Spanish prevailed. As punishment to the Acomans, the Spaniards handed down strict measures against those who were unable to escape. Many were sentenced to twenty years of servitude, and men over age twenty-five were further punished by having one foot severed. Some of the colonists sympathized with the Indians as a result, and dissension grew among the colonists on the basis of Oñate's leadership and his treatment of the indigenous peoples. Several of the original Oñate party later brought charges against him for his excesses.

Villagrá remained with the colony until 1600, when Oñate sent him back to New Spain for reinforcements. But Oñate's request was refused, in part because of his behaviors toward his men and the Indian people. Villagrá was removed as the head of the expedition for its return trip to New Mexico, and he returned to Europe when charges were brought against Oñate for misconduct. Information about the remainder of Villagrá's life is limited. Villagrá seems to have spent much of the rest of his life in Spain after his return there (most likely in 1605), despite his desire to return to New Spain. His epic poem, *The History of New Mexico,* was published in Spain in 1610. In 1612, because of the formal charges filed against Oñate and his officers for their actions against the Acomans during the New Mexican expedition, Villagrá was tried and found guilty. He was banished for six years from New Mexico as part of his sentence. In 1620, while on a voyage to Guatemala, where he was to become mayor of Zapotitlán, he died in a shipwreck.

The History of New Mexico contextualizes Oñate's conquest historically, in part by recounting the journeys and narratives of earlier Spanish explorers, among them Cabeza de Vaca, Fray Marco de Niza, and Pedro de Casteñeda. But its form as an epic poem distinguishes the narrative structure and reveals Villagrá's reliance upon the classical model of Virgil's *Aeneid.* Although his poem was dedicated to Philip III, king of Spain, this dedication seems to have had little impact on Villagrá's relationship with the king. Indeed, his 1613 and 1615 petitions—to seek a new position—for hearings with the king remained unanswered. Many of the events described in the poem were events Villagrá had witnessed personally, yet some of the events in the poem, particularly those featuring Indians, partake of both epic conventions and Spanish romances and do not present any circumstances that Villagrá experienced. Yet the reality of the poem struck home, at the end, for Villagrá. Despite the blurry line separating fact from fiction, the closing cantos of the poem were judged reliable enough to be brought as evidence against Villagrá, Oñate, and others during their trial.

from THE HISTORY OF NEW MEXICO[1]

Canto 1

Which sets forth the outline of the history and the location of New Mexico, and the reports had of it in the traditions of the Indians, and of the true origin and descent of the Mexicans.

I sing of arms and the heroic man,
The being, courage, care, and high emprise
Of him whose unconquered patience,
Though cast upon a sea of cares,
5 In spite of envy slanderous,
Is raising to new heights the feats,
The deeds, of those brave Spaniards who,
In the far India of the West,
Discovering in the world that which was hid,
10 'Plus ultra'[2] go bravely saying

By force of valor and strong arms,
In war and suffering as experienced
As celebrated now by pen unskilled.
I beg of thee, most Christian Philip,[3]
Being the Phoenix of New Mexico   15
Now newly brought forth from the flames
Of fire and new produced from ashes
Of the most ardent faith, in whose hot coals
Sublime your sainted Father and our lord
We saw all burned and quite undone,   20
Suspend a moment from your back
The great and heavy weight which bears you down
Of this enormous globe which, in all right,
Is by your arm alone upheld,
And, lending, O great King, attentive ear,   25
Thou here shalt see the load of toil,
Of calumny, affliction, under which
Did plant the evangel holy and the Faith of Christ
That Christian Achilles whom you wished
To be employed in such heroic work.   30
And if in fortune good I may succeed
In having you, my Monarch, listener,

1. The text is from *Historia de la Nueva México, 1610 [History of New Mexico, 1610],* trans. and ed. M. Encinias, A. Rodriguez, and J. P. Sanchez (1992). It was originally published in 1610.

2. Farther on.

3. Villagrá dedicated his poem to Philip III, king of Spain, 1598–1621.

Who doubts that, with a wondering fear,
The whole round world shall listen too
35 To that which holds so high a King intent.
For, being favored thus by you,
It being no less to write of deeds worthy
Of being elevated by the pen
Than to undertake those which are no less
40 Worthy of being written by this same pen,
'Tis only needed that those same brave men
For whom this task I undertook
Should nourish with their great, heroic valor
The daring flight of this my pen,
45 Because I think that this time we shall see
The words well equaled by the deeds.
Hear me, great King, for I am witness
Of all that here, my Lord, I say to you.
Beneath the Arctic Pole, in height
50 Some thirty-three degrees, which the same
Are, we know, of sainted Jerusalem,
Not without mystery and marvel great,
Are spread, extended, sown, and overflow
Some nations barbarous, remote
55 From the bosom of the Church, where
The longest day of all the year contains and has
Some fourteen hours and a half when it arrives,
The furious sun, at the rising of Cancer,
Through whose zenith he doth usually pass
60 The image of Andromeda and Perseus,[4]
Whose constellation always influences
The quality of Venus and Mercury.
And shows to us its location in longitude,
According as most modern fixed meridian
65 Doth teach us and we practice,
Two hundred just degrees and seventy
Into the temperate zone and the fourth clime,[5]
Two hundred long leagues from the place
Where the Sea of the North[6] and Gulf of Mexico
70 Approach the most and nearest to the coast
On the southeast; and to the side
Toward the rough Californio[7] and Sea of the Pearls[8]
The distance in that direction is about the same
Toward where the southwest wind strikes the coast

4. Northern constellations.

5. The space between lines of latitude.

6. The Atlantic Ocean.

7. The Colorado River.

8. The Gulf of California.

And from the frozen zone its distance is   75
About five hundred full long leagues;
And in a circle round we see it hold,
Beneath the parallel, if we should take
The height of thirty-seven degrees,
Five thousand goodly Spanish leagues,   80
Whose greatness it is a shame it should be held
By so great sum of people ignorant
About the blood of Christ, whose holiness
It causes pain to think so many souls know not.
From these new regions 'tis notorious,   85
Of public voice and fame, that there descended
Those oldest folk of Mexico
Who to the famous city, Mexico,
Did give their name, that it might be
Memorial eternal of their name, and lasting,   90
In imitation of wise Romulus
Who put a measure to the walls of Rome,[9]
Whose truth is drawn from and is proved by
That extremely ancient painting
And hieroglyphic method which they have,   95
By which they deal and speak and are well understood,
Though not with the same excellent perfection
Of graceful conversation which is offered
When we converse with absent friends
By means of the excellence and greatness   100
Of the noble writing which we have.
And there reconfirms and corroborates this tradition
That prodigy immense which we did find
When taking road, uncertain and unknown,
For that New Mexico. It happened that   105
In the last towns of what is called New Spain,
And on the border of the Kingdom of Vizcaya,[10]
The whole camp having risen
To make a start upon the route,
Wild, rough, and difficult and hidden yet,   110
One thing we learned for very certain
And talked of through immortal memory
And which had come from hand to hand,
Just as midst us the coming here to Spain
Of those brave hearts who at the first   115
Came here to populate and conquer it.
They told us then, those native folk,

9. The legendary founder of Rome (with his brother Remus).

10. Area of present-day Mexico that borders on the Rio Grande.

Unanimous, agreed, and with one voice,
That from that land beyond, and pointing out
120 That section where the North doth hide
The hollow cavern, craggy,
Of vigorous and hasty Boreas,[11]
There came two most courageous brethren,
Of high and noble Kings descended,
125 Sons of a King, and king of highest lineage,
Desirous of esteem and elevation
By discovering the marvels of the world,
And all its kings illustrious and all its lords,
With noble triumph and with famous trophies,
130 By active force of arms, perhaps without them,
Like gentle lamblings to the fold,
Reduce, subject, and obedient
To the harsh yoke of their immense empire,
Proud lordship, great estate;
135 And that, arriving there with a great force
Of many soldiers and well armed,
Divided in two camps most large
Of mighty squadrons and well formed,
The elder of the two did lead the van
140 With number great of squadrons,
And the younger brother reinforced
The rear guard with a number just as great
And led it with great skill,
And in the middle of the force
145 Great sum of baggage and of apparatus,
Tents and pavilions shining bright
With which their Highnesses did make their camp,
And like to free and tender fawns
Infinity of children and of babes
150 Here, there, and elsewhere frolicking,
Surrounded by most pretty toys
Of simple, innocent infancy,
And with no sort of plan or concert.
And also in that proud camp
155 There showed themselves among the deadly arms,
As flowers beautiful are seen 'mid thorns,
Fair dames and ladies and bright damsels,
As dainty, lovely, and discreet
As noble, beautiful, and well-advised;
160 And, in the very flower of youth, young men,
And gentlemen and well dressed, all,
Each one competing with the rest
Such sum of finery and of livery

---

11. The mythological name for the north wind.

As in the finest and most lofty courts   165
Are customed to be worn on festal days
By the most conspicuous courtiers.
And then, also, the mighty squadrons
Showed in the midst of such gallantry
A number terrible, and fearful, too,   170
Of notable animal disguises:
One wore the hide of a manéd lion
With which he represented well
The face ferocious and the appearance of the proud
      animal;
Some the striped hide of fierce Hircanian tiger,   175
Of speedy ounce, astute monkey, and leopard,
There were the hungry wolf carnivorous,
The fox, the hare and the rabbit shy,
The fishes huge and lordly eagles, too,
With all the rest of the brute beasts   180
Which occupy the earth and sky and the broad seas.
There they appeared all, most natural,
A native, old invention, one that's used
Among all peoples and all nations
Which we have yet discovered in the Indies.   185
There were of arms, warlike and strong,
A shining, great, and goodly sum:
Bent Turkish bows, well strung,
Broad quivers, broad and of a capacious size,
Well stuffed with arrows light,   190
Light javelins and maces heavy,
Strong bucklers and cuirasses strong,
Well made, of knotted, woven work,
Mischievous slings, swung in the air,
Thick clubs with heavy stones   195
Imbedded in their strong wood,
And, lined with sharp flints,
Strong, well-wrought, wooden swords;
And lofted in air there fluttered,
With gallantry and grace bizarre,   200
A quantity of banners and of standards
Of different colors, many hued.
And the well-serried ranks of troops,
Each gripping fast his arms,
Kept marching over the great field   205
With greatest ease and gallant tread,
And, lashed by tread of many men,
The hard-baked earth sent high into the air
A cloud of dust so thick and dense
It seemed that the whole earth was there dissolved   210
In blinding dust, whirled on
By swift and sudden earthquake,

Which through the broad dome of the air
Spreads out in lofty whirlwinds.
215 Well, going thus and traveling carelessly,
There placed himself before them by intent,
In form of an old and haglike woman,
A valiant and cunning demon
Whose face ferocious dare I not,
220 If I must with some care depict it,
Set out to paint without new strength.

from Canto 29

*How the twelve companions scaled the first rock and
the battle they had with the Indians, and the council
held to raise Gicombo[12] as General, and his acceptance of the charge, and the conditions he expected to
exercise it.*

It is a thing clear, patent, manifest,
O powerful lord, if we but notice it,
That many times we see advantage won
Over discretion, wisdom, and learning
5 By a foolish reasoning, if prudently
It knows how to dissimulate, convince.
We see that this disguise was taken on
By the sagacious Sergeant here, astute, cunning,
For the barbarians, seeing that together
10 The Castilians had moved forward,
All rushing to the mighty wall,
And that no living soul remained
At our encampment, where the tents
Had all been struck, the better to conceal our plan,
15 All fearing that our threat was true,
They hastened, all in a great troop,
To guard the pass, the best guarded
That could, in all the world, be wished.
Seeing, then, that they left vacant
20 The whole first rock, those gallant men
Did sally out at once and to scaling,
Like the swift runners who do strive
For a rich prize, so together
Those twelve Castilians did set themselves,
25 And 'tis but just their names be writ
Since their deeds call for no silence:
The Sergeant Major and León de Isasti,
Marcos Cortés, Munuera, Antonio Hernández,
Also the secretary, Juan Velarde,
30 Cristóbal Sánchez and Cristóbal López,

Hernán Martín, Cordero, and that Pablo
They call de Aguilar, and I with them,
So that their true greatness be somewhat less
Complete and e'en perhaps somewhat lessened.
Now when these stalwart men attacked   35
The strongest wall and climbed up it,
The great Gicombo and Bempol were together,
And old Chumpo, noble Zutancalpo
With all their friends who did desire
And work for peace insistently,   40
For which the rest did all despise
Those poor, ruined barbarians.
And so, taking no thought of them,
Like a brute beast, without suspicion,
Zutacapán, with all the town,   45
Went to defend an entrance from the Castilians
That was reserved unto the birds alone,
Leaving that rock unoccupied.
Gicombo, noting the Spaniards
Were occupying the first rock   50
And that 'twas necessary they be slain,
Thinking that these were all his opponents,
Ordered that Bempol should attack at once
With four hundred barbarians. And, just when
They all attacked, all of the twelve   55
Had gained the summit of the rock,
And they did meet upon the neck
And, in a narrow place, they all
Did flesh their weapons in such wise
That, had I distinguished myself   60
Like them, 'tis certain the number
Of twelve would have been lost to France
And found in this narrow passage.
The Sergeant then, seeing such zeal
In arms so valiant and so courageous,   65
Said unto them: "Ye cavaliers of Christ,
This is the holy day of Saint Vincent,[13]
With whose most holy name I am honored,
And by this great, heroic, famous saint
I hope, ye valorous Spaniards,   70
That we are to come out of this affair
Triumphing like brave men over these folk,
Idolaters, lost, vile, and infamous."
We, all together, hearing this,
Gritting our teeth, did submit to   75
A furious rain of arrows and of rocks
That was cutting us to pieces

---

12. The Acoma leader who encouraged peace.

13. The feast of Saint Vincent was held on January 22.

Until our great chief struck Polco,
A valiant barbarian, dead to earth,
80 At which good luck the secretary,
Marcos Cortés, Cordero, and León de Isasti,
With every four bullets discharged
From their swift barrels, did strike down
Ten brave barbarians, after whom
85 Fourteen more were at once dispatched. . . .
Now great Gicombo, furious,
Went recklessly about, in every place
Encouraging the savage rabble there
135 With shout on shout, and then attacked
With all his troops in such manner
That the small Castilian squadron
Would there have been all overwhelmed
Had not the Sergeant Major suddenly,
140 With shot of musket, broken in pieces
His mighty arm high in the upper part.
At this good fortune, come by chance,
There ne'er was seen such bellowing
Nor spurting foam from out the mouth
145 From the fury and boundless savageness
Of raging bull that has been houghed
And whom we see attack in all directions
Dragging his severed hocks behind
And raising up his pointed horns,
150 As we did see Gicombo, furious,
Now here, now there, and bursting forth
With violent wrath and, thus, furious,
Encouraging his men, he ordered them
To send upon us from their ready arms
155 Such storm of arrows, clubs, and stones
As we see of great dust when thick
The powerful winds drive it at us. . . .
235 Those savages, seeing the death
And the fearful destruction, and how they
Were now conquered in fact and all destroyed,
Called all to council and, all being met,
They saw Gicombo and Zutancalpo
240 And brave Bempol had not come there.
For this reason they all did there agree
Mencal should go at once and call them in,
As he was a great friend of all the three.
And, going for this purpose, he observed
245 Poor Luzcoija making much lament
Over the shattered arm of her husband,
Whom by her life and soul she did implore
He would no more go into the battle
Since she would be an orphan without him.

Just then Mencal arrived and on the part   250
Of all the council he announced to them
That all were called and they should go,
For without them the much endangered fort
Would necessarily be lost and overcome.
And, finally, he knew so well how to treat them   255
That Bempol and Zutancalpo did go,
Though 'twas impossible that Gicombo
Should go with them. And if by chance
They should return to call him and should not
See him, he told Bempol he would retire   260
Unto a certain hidden spot upon that rock
Where he would wait for their return.
The two coming to the council,
When it was seen Gicombo had not come
They all asked of them with great insistence   265
That they should bring him there, for they must see
That without him that fort would, of necessity,
Forever be dishonored.
With this they gave other reasons
With which they obliged them to go   270
To that retired spot at which he was
And they told him so much that he then said:
"For you I go, and I would never go
If all the gods together should command."
And telling Luzcoija to remain   275
And stay in that place all alone,
She, all dissolved in sorry tears,
And much perturbed, replied to him:
"Now, if the sun should rise a thousand times and sink,
And all the stars as many times   280
Should bring and take away their lights,
I shall not fail you, lord, although I die
Upon my solitary post where you leave me."
Leaving her there, he came to the council
And, when they saw him, carefully   285
Zutacapán got to his feet
And said: "It will be well, ye noble men,
That ere anything be proposed
The powerful arm, now sore wounded,
Of Gicombo be tended to."   290
Hearing these words, he then replied:
"My arm would be entirely healed
If I had taken, as an enemy,
The first advice which you gave me,
Saying that in the shadow of your mace   295
My life would be entirely safe.
But let us leave this for the nonce,
For what I speak not of requires reply.

Let us now know what you, in council, wish
300 Of him who would have counseled you so ill
When I said 'twould be well we should not wait
For these Castilians in any way."
Now, upon this, they all replied:
"For this sole reason we all wish
305 To give our lives and to surrender them
To no more than your pleasure, and at once
We here do name you General of all,
All of us will obey you as such."
And after many great things had occurred
310 And the office was accepted perforce
By gallant Gicombo, it was
Under condition and compact, express and firm,
That if the said illustrious Gicombo
And noble Zutancalpo, brave Bempol,
315 Should in the present struggle and battles
Give up their lives, and beside them
Zutacapán, Cotumbo, and Tempal, also,
Together in one sepulcher, with all their arms,
Should be buried without discussion
320 So that in the next life the passions and
The mortal challenges they had
Most firmly fixed within themselves
Might be finished by all of them;
And that if they should win a victory
325 They should engage in battle and, that done,
The whole fortress should be governed
By only one General and no one
Should pretend to any dominion;
And that if they perchance should lose,
330 No one should give up until death,
But, after being conquered, they should kill
Each other, and thus nothing should
Remain alive for us within the fort.
With these conditions, valiant Gicombo
335 Began to exercise his new office,
And since we now have a new government,
Again let us cut a new pen.

from Canto 30

How the new General, having given orders to his sol-
diers, went to take leave of Luzcoija, and the battle he
had with the Spaniards, and the things that happened.

When man enkindles himself against right
And forces his desires to bend themselves

To undertake a thing that has no plan,
With what ease he doth mark and note
What is in favor, what against that thing   5
That he wills to undertake against justice.
Gicombo, then, fearing and foreseeing,
Being prudent, skillful, and cautious,
That Zutacapán and all the people
Together would fail him at any time,   10
Did make them bind themselves and take an oath
According to their laws, rites, and customs,
As Hannibal once swore upon the fanes
And altars of his gods that he would be
Ever a mortal foe to the Romans,   15
So that they would keep inviolate,
Subject to penalties, controls, and force,
The conditions made and agreed.
The ceremony done and done also
The vile and superstitious oath taking,   20
He, with his own hand, did select
Five hundred brave barbarian warriors
And ordered them to go in a body
Unto a great cavern, by nature made,
Near to the two ditches we have mentioned,   25
Purposing, when your men should pass that place,
That they should sally forth from their ambush and
Deprive them, then and there, of all their lives.
And when he'd posted them and entrusted
To brave Bempol, Chumpo, Zutancalpo,   30
To Calpo, Buzcoico, and Ezmicaio,
To each of these a squadron well-chosen,
The better to trap us into their hands
He carefully gave us to understand
That all the town was deserted.   35
And when the shining sun had gone to rest
And the dark bodies had been plunged
Into deep shadows, and in silence deep
All living things remained at rest,
From the sea came forth the night,   40
Enveloping the earth in a dark veil.
And before all the stars had run
The mighty course which they do take,
He went to take leave of Luzcoija,
Who was awaiting him in that same place   45
Where he had chosen to leave her, wounded
Deeply by that love which did burn in her.
And when she saw him, overcome,
Like a mild turtledove which, lost
From its sweet company, roosts not   50
Nor takes repose on flowering branches,

But on the dry and leafless trees,
And like a tender mother who carries
Her tender child about with her, hanging
55 About her lovely neck, and, filled with love,
Yearns over him and grows tender
In loving fire, and wastes away,
So this poor woman, conquered by her love,
Making two fountains of her tears,
60 Did there raise her discouraged voice:
"If the dear pure love I have had for you,
A thousand times more loving you than my own
    soul,
Deserveth that you give me some comfort,
I beg of you, my lord, not to permit
65 A flower so tender to wither
Which you have made me think was e'er
To you more pleasing, sweet, and beautiful
Than the life which you live and do enjoy.
By which dear gift I beg of you
70 That if you come, lord, but to go,
You take my life, for I cannot
Live without you a single hour."
And she became expectantly quiet,
Awaiting a reply, and then spoke out
75 The sad barbarian: "Madam, I swear
Now by the beauty of those eyes
Which are the peace and light of mine,
And by those lips with which you hide
Those lovely oriental pearls,
80 And by those soft, delicate hands
Which hold me in such sweet prison,
That now I cannot make excuse
From going to battle against Spain.
Wherefore you must rouse your courage
85 And strengthen mine, so this sad soul
May return but to look on you,
For though 'tis true it fears your loss
It has firm hope to enjoy you.
And though I die a thousand times I swear
90 I shall return to see and console you,
And that, dear love, you may understand this
I leave you as ransom my heart and soul."
And so he took his leave, for now
The morning light was appearing,
95 And, entering the cavern with his men,
The light came fast and embroidered
All of the sky with bright red clouds.
At this great time and conjuncture
The Father Fray Alonso, saying mass,

Did celebrate the day of his name saint,[14]   100
And having given communion to us all,
Turned from the altar and addressed us thus:
"Ye valiant cavaliers of Christ
And of our most holy laws defenders,
I have not to exhort you to the Church   105
For as her noble sons you have always
Taken great pains to serve and respect her.
By Jesus Christ I ask and beg of you,
And by His holy blood, that you restrain
Your keen swords, in so far as possible,   110
From shedding the blood of the enemy,
For thus the valor of the Spaniards is,
To conquer without blood and death whom they attack.
And since you carry God within your souls,
May He bless all of you and may His powerful hand   115
Protect you, and I, in His name,
Do bless you all." And having thus
Received the blessing from this holy Father there,
We then climbed to the lofty passageway,
Whence we all saw from afar off   120
That all the pueblo was deserted quite
And that no living soul was seen.
For this reason thirteen immediately
Did pass both ditches from the passageway
Without the Sergeant's order or his permission,   125
And hardly had they, all together, occupied
The further side when all at once
There charged from the horrible cave
The valiant Gicombo, roaring loud.
And, like the young whale which, wounded   130
By keen harpoon and deadly steel,
Projects on high thick clouds of spume
And lashes the sea with his tail and cleaves

The water here and there, rising
His spacious back, and, in anger   135
Snorting and restless, doth stir up
A thousand whirlpools in the deep, so he,
Enraged, his mighty weapons lifted high,
Attacked with them and struck at all.
Seeing the enemy so near at hand   140
Our men did, in a volley, fire
Their ready harquebuses and, though many
Were stricken down, they yet were forced,
Unable to load a second time,
To come to swords, and in the hot melee,   145

---

14. The feast of Saint Alphonse was held on January 26.

Mixed with each other, we could not
Give any aid to them because they had
Taken that beam by which they crossed
Unto the second ditch and did not note
150 They left the first without means of crossing.
All thus involved in such confusion,
Plunging their daggers and the sharp edges
Of their swift swords into a great slaughter
Of miserable, shattered bodies,
155 They made a fearful butchery. . . .

from Canto 31

*How the battle was carried forward until gaining vic-
tory and how fire was set to all the pueblo, and of
other things that happened.*

Always astute prevision, diligence,
A careful watchfulness and care
Never to lose a single point,
This, for a warrior in fight,
5 Is what most elevates and raises up
The clear resplendency and the greatness
Of deeds heroic and adventurous
That we see him embark upon. . . .
And round him, then, the battle raged so fierce
And was so bloody upon both the sides
50 That only immense God was there enough
For them to hold against the savage force.
Because of their great fury the astute
Sergeant did order that there be brought up
Two fieldpieces, and, in the interim,
55 Addressing his men, he thus spoke to them:
"Ye founders of manorial houses,[15]
Ye columns of the Church invincible,
Ye mirrors for brave men, whose breasts
Deserve with reason to be honored
60 With crosses red and white and green,[16]
Today your deeds attain the highest point
And to the highest homage that Spaniards
Have ever yet raised them on high.
Let them not fall, sustain the scale
65 That thus sustains and weighs the true greatness
Of the most honorable, gallant deed

---

15. The colonizers of Oñate's expedition attained the rank
of hidalgo.

16. The insignia of the Calatrava, Alcantara, and Santiago
military orders.

That noble arms were ever seen to do."
Just then the two pieces came up
And were set at the place and spot
Where an attack, by chance, was being made   70
By three hundred brave, furious barbarians,
All delivering terrible shouts.
And as they made their charge, at last,
The two pieces did suddenly belch forth
Two hundred spikes from each, at which,   75
Just as we see the magpies, terrorized,
Suspend their chirping and their cackling
At the charge of powder which scatters
Great store of small shot, and we see
A few escaping and others   80
Remain with shattered limbs, and others dead,
And others beating their wings on the ground,
Their black beaks gaping and their bowels
Pouring from out their torn bellies,
We then beheld, not otherwise than this,   85
A sudden great heap of the dead,
Mangled, without hands, legs, shattered,
Deep wounds opened into their breasts,
Their heads laid open and their arms,
Pierced a thousand times, their flesh   90
Pouring out blood in mortal agony,
Took leave of their immortal souls,
Leaving the bodies quivering there. . . .
The Sergeant, then, seeing the bravery,   160
Endurance and persistence with which all
Of the barbarians yet fought furiously,
That he might see no more of butchery,
Just as the clever, cautious pruner does
Who judges well the vine and looks and runs   165
His careful glance over each spreading bough,
And when he has surveyed, doth act and prune
The ill-shaped branches and the withered ones,
With all superfluous and useless ones,
And leaves with skill and good judgment   170
The stems with runners and new shoots
Which are considered fruitful ones,
That great soldier, surveying all the field,
Withdrawing all the soldiery
From their appointed stations,   175
He ordered that from him the foe be told
They should observe the slaughter, the destruction
Of all the miserable wretches that there were
Stretched out upon the ground and they should grieve
At such corpses and blood, and he gave them   180
The word and faith of noble gentleman

To do them justice and with clemency
To hear their case as if he were
Their own true father. And immediately
185 Loosing a great flight of arrows,
Like to mad dogs, they made reply
They would not speak of this, but they would take
Their arms and teeth and fists, as well,
Because they, their wives and children
190 Perforce would die and would give up
Their lives and souls and their honor
In this struggle. And, upon this,
They, fighting furiously, did charge
To die or conquer with such force
195 That they caused fear and terror to us all.
Now at this time, turned cowardly
And thinking to find safety here,
Zutacapán did come and beg for peace
Before the gallant Sergeant; he, content,
200 Not knowing who that traitor was,
Told him that he should give and hand over
Only the chief ones who had caused
The recent mutiny and that with this
He would do all that he well could.
205 The tender cinquefoil was never seen
To tremble so at single gentle touch
Of a soft hand as he then shook,
That brutal savage, at the word.
And so, hesitant, sad, suspicious,
210 Hardly had there driven to his settling,
In mighty and precipitous course,
The sun his beauteous chariot and hid
The light with which he lighted us,
When in the sorry town all was
215 Divided and set off in two parties,
Both one and the other being timorous
About the Spaniards' strength and their courage.
And when the light did grow once more
The barbarians, having discussed
220 All the grave matters of this peace,
Seeing Zutacapán had been the chief
Who had brought on the recent mutiny,
With all his friends and all his followers,
Like leafed forests that are rustled
225 By powerful Boreas, shaken,
So in a confused mass they move
Hither and thither, shaking off
Their dust, raising and altering
Their lofty tops, and all about
230 Are all moved to and fro and everywhere,

These poor barbarians, ruined,
Took refuge in their arms to such effect
That for three whole days the soldiers
Nor ate nor slept nor drank a drop,
Nor sat down nor laid aside   235
Their strong weapons from out their hands,
Shedding such store of blood they now
Were flooded, tired out with shedding it.
And now the fire kept sending up
A ruddy vapor, bit by bit,   240
Attacking all the sad houses,
And then in a short time it mustered up
Sufficient vigor and in the dry pine
Of the resinous houses and dwellings
It crackled in the roofs and in a thousand spots,   245
A very thick and dense and sluggish smoke,
Like great fleeces, was puffing out thickly
From windows here, there, and everywhere,
And like the most ardent of volcanoes
They poured out, whirling toward the sky   250
Great store of embers and of sparks.
And thus, those wild and mad barbarians,
Seeing themselves now conquered, 'gan to kill
Each other, and did so in such fashion
That sons from fathers, fathers from their loved children, 255
Took life away, and further, more than this,
Others in groups did give aid to the fire
So that it might leap up with more vigor,
Consume the pueblo and destroy it all.
Only Zutacapán and they his friends,   260
Fleeing as cowards lest they see themselves
Within Gicombo's hands, did hide themselves
Within the caves and hollows which there were
Upon the fortress rock, whose great extent
Did show itself a second Labyrinth[17]   265
Because of many caves and hiding holes,
Their entrances and exits and chambers.
The General and brave Bempol, seeing
That all did kill themselves and seal
Truly the pact which all had sworn   270
To suicide if they as conquered should
Come from the struggle with the Castilians,
Determined jointly they would kill themselves.
And so, fearful, because of this,
Of such incurable evil, not to see all   275
In death's own arms, some of their friends,

---

17. The labyrinth of Crete.

Sad, much dismayed, did speak to them,
Begging sincerely they would surrender
And so, together, they might save their lives.
280 At this appeal they instantly replied,
Those furious, obstinate barbarians:
"Tell us, ye Acomans unfortunate,
What state is this of Acoma today
To undertake so infamous a thing
285 As this you ask us? Tell us now
What refuge you do think that fate doth leave
As soon as peace might be secured
All firmly with these Castilians?
Do you not see that we have now arrived
290 At that last sorrow and that final point
Where we all must, without our liberty,
Live out our sorry life as infamous wretches?
Acoma was once, and upon the peak
We saw her name, heroic, lifted high,
295 And now the very gods who gave
Their hands to her, to raise and honor her,
We see only did so that her ruin
Might be more miserably felt
By those poor wretches who did hope
300 For such firmness in such feeble weakness.
For this reason, we, all of us, agreed,
If you are, as we two do feel you are,
Firm in the promise which we swore
That we would give our throats to happy death
305 and submit them since there remaineth not
Another greater remedy for this our health
Than to give up the hope that yet remains
For us to gain it and to secure it."
And when, with this, the haughty General
310 Had also told them other arguments
Maximian, Macrinus, Maxentius,
Procrustes, Diocletian, nor Tiberius,
Nero, nor all the rest of cruel men,[18]
Displayed upon no one ferocity
315 More harsh, atrocious, nor more terrible
Than these displayed upon their very selves,
Not only men, but the women as well.
Some, like to Dido,[19] took leave of

Their bodies and did perish in the flames,
And, like the Spartans, they also   320
Gave up their tender babes unto harsh death.
Others did hurl and cast their babes
Into the burning flames, and others, sad,
With them held tight, from off the wall
Hurled themselves dashing down, as we could see. 325
Others, like Portia,[20] quickly satisfied
With living coals, did end their lives.
Others, like Lucrece,[21] with a keen dagger
Piercing their tender breasts, did thus speed forth
Their miserable souls, and many more   330
By very many other sorts of death
Did end and render up their lives.
In the meantime, the fair sisters
Of Zutancalpo brave, in great distress
Beside themselves, went out to seek   335
Their brother, to end their sad lives with his.
Their bitter grief, their sad weeping,
I wish, lord, in a canto new to sing.

from Canto 32

How Zutancalpo was found by his four sisters and of
the end and death of Gicombo and Luzcoija.

What lofty rock or towering cliff
Can by the wrathful, haughty sea
Be battered harder, more atrociously,
Than our own sad and miserable life,
If we but note it, most mortals,   5
Whom cruel pride, exaggerated,
And vile ambition, raving, furious,
Could never satisfy: the great scepter,
The royal crown, and its brave throne,
The poorest commoner of lowliest estate?   10
Oh sad condition of our human life,
Subjected, prostrate, to such thirsty beasts,
From whose most greedy fountain, vile and infamous,
Never contented of their thirst inordinate,
Each one pretends to take satisfaction!   15
What did it serve noble Zutancalpo
To have opposed with such great strength
The furious designs of his father
Which had ended so many human lives

---

18. Maximian, Macrinus, Maxentius, Diocletian, Tiberius, and Nero were Roman emperors associated with extreme acts of cruelty and torture. Procrustes was an Attic assaulter renowned for his cruelty.

19. That is, they committed suicide. For the account of Dido, legendary queen of Carthage, see the *Aeneid* IV.

---

20. See the biography of Marcus Brutus in Plutarch's *Lives* for the account of Portia, Brutus's wife.

21. See *Livy* I.

20 And had consumed so many goodly men,
    And burned down so many noble homes?
    Cruel Zutacapán, why did you choose
    To go against the current that did bear
    The peaceful people who are now ruined
25 And that brave youth whom you begot!
    What profited the threats and bravado
    With which you did perturb so many innocents,
    And what the harsh, wild pride you showed
    In wishing the Castilians might come
30 In arms against your little strength?
    What profited to have broken the truce,
    Your word, and oath that you had given for the peace?
    By what vile fury were you dragged along
    That you with such lofty ideas
35 Did move an unjust war so carelessly? . . .
270 This tragedy prodigious being done,
    I think, lord, that we should return
    To the unhappy spot where yet remain
    The poor General and the brave Bempol,
    Who, as I say and said before,
275 Were like illustrious Brutus and Cassius,
    Who wished to take away their lives
    Because they saw themselves conquered.[22]
    Thus, never to live as subjects,
    The one departed to leap off the cliff,
280 The other to give undeserved death
    To his dear Luzcoija, lest he might see her
    In hands of Spaniards who could
    Enjoy her beauty, now wasted.
    Now, coming from the mighty labyrinth,
285 Desperate, reckless, furious,
    They then spoke to each other in this wise:
    "Oh how the harsh fates do now destroy us
    And violent tempest doth batter us
    And troubles us with living fire and blood,
290 Oppresses, subdues, conquers, ruins us!
    And you, infamous men of Acoma,
    Shall be most horribly punished,[23]
    With such penalty as 'tis well should come
    Upon such coward spirits as yours are.
295 And you, vile Zutacapán, who have been
    The instrument of such calamity,

Know that for you there are waiting, prepared,
Most cruel beatings, cruel punishments,
For this evil and this shameful disgrace,
And are entrusted to most fearsome gods,   300
Who for your monstrous crimes will give to you
A very late and profitless reward."
Having said this, the two did separate.
Gicombo made his way to his own house,
Which was enveloped in smoke and live flames,   305
And, forcing passage through the hostile coals
And embers, and through leaping flames,
He came into the very room where was
His most beloved wife, she lamenting
With a great store of matrons and maidens   310
Who, openmouthed, were all gasping
Most heated breath out of their lungs
And implanting sad kisses on the wall.
As he entered, it was impossible
Amid the confused cries and lamentings   315
And the thick smoke that hovered over all,
For him to find her, and because of this
He held the doorway so that all of them
Might there consume and be burnt up.
As the fire, gaining strength, approached   320
The miserable palace, unconsoled,
The Sergeant came in search of the barbarian
With a good squadron of our warriors,
And when the brute Arabian saw him
He fixed his eyes on him, inflamed with rage   325
And violent with insane anger.
Like a ferocious boar hemmed in
By speedy greyhounds and foxhounds,
Grinding foam freely from his mouth
And threatening with his curving tusks,   330
Thus did the General display his rage,
Obstructing the exit for those who were
Within that perilous dwelling.
And Luzcoija's beauteous face showing,
Like those who go by a shortcut   335
To shorten the course of the road,
So the poor, afflicted savage
Offered her broad, spacious forehead
To the force of the powerful mace
That caused her two most beauteous eyes   340
To spring from out her solid skull.
Never was seen in the eager hunter
Greater content when he possessed
His longed-for game, already caught,
Than this barbarian had having   345

---

22. After being conquered by Caesar, both men killed themselves. See their biographies in Plutarch's *Lives*.

23. The Acoman men were punished by having one foot severed and then being sentenced to twenty years of servitude.

Now quite destroyed his dearest pledge
And deprived her of all feeling.
The Sergeant, then, seeing the hardihood
Of that valiant, stern General,
350 Attempted to make a true friend of him
By dint of promises and reasoning,
Giving to him his word as a soldier
And faith as cavalier of noble birth
To settle his affairs in such fashion
355 That he alone should govern that fortress
For your Majesty, and no other one
Except Don Juan should give commands in it.
As he himself had been a living coal,
Which at its time of dying, going out,
360 Doth kindle its light higher and show it,
The furious, bloody idolater,
Smiling disdainfully, thus replied to him:
"You now can give me no greater sorrow
Than life, this woman being now dead.
365 But if you wish to do me a favor,
Then allow me to fight with six or seven
Of the best soldiers found within your camp,

And then kill me yourself, for 'tis unjust
To refuse such a trifling favor
To me whom you see now so bound for death.　370
I shall do more for you, as you must see
That all these women must be burnt,
Let them all be freed from this fire
And not one of them stay on my account."
Seeing that his cause was hopeless,　375
By this and other things which had happened,
He ordered Simón Pérez to shoot him
Right quickly and with certain aim,
And, without being seen nor understood,
He struck the unhappy General to the earth,　380
His face all tainted in ugly yellow.
When he had ended and was quite lifeless,
Those savage women, amazed, whom he kept
In killing heat, almost unconscious,
Pouring out streams of sweat, boiling,　385
All their closed pores now open wide
And their hot mouths and their nostrils
Being satisfied by air alone,
Did then escape in greatest haste. . . .

PUEBLO CONFLICT IN NEW SPAIN (1680–1692)

From the time when Coronado first arrived in Pueblo territory through the ordeal faced by the Pueblos at Oñate's hands (a story recorded in Spanish epic form by Gaspar Pérez de Villagrá), Pueblo peoples of the *Gran Chichimeca,* the area of upper northern Mexico now called New Mexico, experienced an uneasy occupation of their lands by Spanish settlers and their African and Indian slaves. The Spanish settlers attempted to maintain a colonial system in which Native peoples were required to show allegiance to both royal officials (civil and military authorities) and to missionary leaders. Native peoples were placed in great jeopardy because of the multiple demands they faced: They were expected to pay tribute to royal officials (often through labor or the giving of goods, such as blankets) and to follow the Catholic teachings of the Franciscans who were working to convert them. Native lifeways were forcibly suppressed by violence, and whether dancing traditional dances, or keeping cachina cultural symbols, or meeting partners privately and outside accepted social jurisdictions, Native peoples were regularly punished.

During the seventeenth century, the Pueblos mounted small-scale rebellions against Spanish authority several times, but in the late 1670s, a variety of factors combined to increase the pressures on the Pueblos. A full-scale revolt occurred in 1680, spearheaded by leaders among the Hopis (also called at the time Moquis). The tensions that led to open and unified revolt came from a combination of environmental and political sources. Drought conditions during the 1660s and 1670s led to a severe famine. Forced to work for the Spanish civil and religious authorities, who competed with each other for attention and duty, the Pueblos were unable to maintain open trade with the Navajos and Apaches, who began to raid Pueblo food supplies. In such a stressful time, the Pueblos looked to traditional religious leaders for guidance, and the Spanish settlers reacted with harsh suppression, even hanging several Pueblo priests. In the midst of this escalating cycle of stress and reaction against the Spanish settlers who seemed to want control of Pueblo resources, persons, and religious practices, the Pueblos made a concerted effort and struck a decisive blow against the Spaniards. They united under two Pueblo religious leaders, San Juan Puebloan Tío Pépe, whom the Spaniards called Popé, and Catiti, of the Santo Domingo Pueblo. On August 10, the Pueblos attacked Spaniards throughout the settlement, killing over four hundred (nearly a sixth of the Spanish settlers) in the first days and killing twenty-one of the thirty-three priests in the area. In Santa Fe, Governor Antonio de Otermín, with a small armed force and a number of civilians, held out under siege for a short time before fleeing south to El Paso. In just a few weeks, the Pueblos had driven the Spanish out of New Mexico, at least for a time.

During the next decade, Spanish civilians and military forces in New Mexico remained mostly in El Paso, struggling to maintain control over the areas they still inhabited. Meanwhile, the French, from their settlements in the Great Lakes regions, were strategically developing trade relationships with native peoples north of Spanish territory. Spanish officials worried that they might lose New Mexico altogether. In 1691, a new royal governor was appointed. Diego de Vargas (?–1740) made a short exploratory campaign in 1692 before undertaking a campaign of reconquest in 1693–94. After an initial success, Vargas quelled another rebellion in 1696. The conflicts with the Pueblos between 1680 and 1700 were decisive factors in New Spain's overall program to conquer indigenous peoples: No longer could authorities assume that the *Gran Chichimeca* could be easily enslaved to serve the needs of the Spanish Mexican military in terms of food and slaves for the mines; instead, Spanish settlements in the area would be retained primarily as border-strengthening and territorial demarcations against encroaching imperial neighbors.

The letters printed next were written by two governors of New Mexico. The first, by Antonio de Otermín, written September 8, 1680, describes the devastation wreaked on the Spanish at the hands of the combined Pueblo peoples. The second, by Don Diego de Vargas, describes the work of the Spaniards who reclaimed the territory in the name of New Spain. From these letters, one gains a sense of the strength of the Pueblos' determination to oust the intruders and learns as well the anxieties and complicated motives behind colonial settlement in New Spain.

LETTER ON THE PUEBLO REVOLT OF 1680[1]

ANTONIO DE OTERMÍN

My very reverend father, Sir, and friend, most beloved Fray Francisco de Ayeta

The time has come when, with tears in my eyes and deep sorrow in my heart, I commence to give an account of the lamentable tragedy, such as has never before happened in the world, which has occurred in this miserable kingdom and holy *custodia*,[2] His Divine Majesty having thus permitted it because of my grievous sins. Before beginning my narration I desire, as one obligated and grateful, to give your reverence the thanks due for the demonstrations of affection and kindness which you have given in your solicitude in ascertaining and inquiring for definite notices about both my life and those of the rest in this miserable kingdom, in the midst of persistent reports which had been circulated of the deaths of myself and the others, and for sparing neither any kind of effort nor large expenditures. For this only Heaven can reward your reverence, though I do not doubt that his Majesty (may God keep him) will do so.

After I sent my last letter to your reverence by the *maese de campo*,[3] Pedro de Leyba, while the necessary things were being made ready alike for the escort and in the way of provisions, for the most expeditious despatch of the returning carts and their guards, as your reverence had enjoined me, I received information that a plot for a general uprising of the Christian Indians was being formed and was spreading rapidly. This was wholly contrary to the existing peace and tranquillity in this miserable kingdom, not only among the Spaniards and natives,

---

1. Otermín's letter is available in *Historical Documents Relating to New Mexico, Nueva Vizcaya, and Approaches Thereto, to 1773,* 3 vols., ed. C. W. Hackett (1937).

2. Area of protection.

3. Officer.

but even on the part of the heathen enemy, for it had been a long time since they had done us any considerable damage. It was my misfortune that I learned of it on the eve of the day set for the beginning of the said uprising, and though I immediately, at that instant, notified the lieutenant-general on the lower river and all the other *alcaldes mayores*[4]—so that they could take every care and precaution against whatever might occur, and so that they could make every effort to guard and protect the religious ministers and the temples—the cunning and cleverness of the rebels were such, and so great, that my efforts were of little avail. To this was added a certain degree of negligence by reason of the [report of the] uprising not having been given entire credence, as is apparent from the ease with which they captured and killed both those who were escorting some of the religious, as well as some citizens in their houses, and, particularly, in the efforts that they made to prevent my orders to the lieutenant-general passing through. This was the place where most of the forces of the kingdom were, and from which I could expect some help, but of three orders which I sent to the said lieutenant-general, not one reached his hands. The first messenger was killed and the others did not pass beyond Santo Domingo, because of their having encountered on the road the certain notice of the deaths of the religious who were in that convent, and of the *alcalde mayor,* some other guards, and six more Spaniards whom they captured on that road. Added to this is the situation of this kingdom which, as your reverence is aware, makes it so easy for the said [Indian] alcaldes to carry out their evil designs, for it is entirely composed of *estancias,*[5] quite distant from one another.

On the eve [of the day] of the glorious San Lorenzo, having received notice of the said rebellion from the governors of Pecos and Tanos, [who said] that two Indians had left the Theguas, and particularly the pueblo of Thesuque,[6] to which they belonged, to notify them to come and join the revolt, and that they [the governors] came to tell me of it and of how they were unwilling to participate in such wickedness and treason, saying that they now regarded the Spaniards as their brothers, I thanked them for their kindness in giving the notice, and told them to go to their pueblos and remain quiet. I busied myself immedi-

ately in giving the said orders which I mentioned to your reverence, and on the following morning as I was about to go to mass there arrived Pedro Hidalgo, who had gone to the pueblo of Thesuque, accompanying Father Fray Juan Pio, who went there to say mass. He told me that the Indians of the said pueblo had killed the said Father Fray Pio and that he himself had escaped miraculously. [He told me also] that the said Indians had retreated to the sierra with all the cattle and horses belonging to the convent, and with their own.

The receipt of this news left us all in the state that may be imagined. I immediately and instantly sent the *maese de campo,* Francisco Gómez, with a squadron of soldiers sufficient to investigate this case and also to attempt to extinguish the flame of the ruin already begun. He returned here on the same day, telling me that [the report] of the death of the said Fray Juan Pio was true. He said also that there had been killed that same morning Father Fray Tomás de Torres, *guardián* of Nambé, and his brother, with the latter's wife and a child, and another resident of Thaos, and also Father Fray Luis de Morales, *guardián* of San Ildefonso, and the family of Francisco de Anaya; and in Poxuaque Don Joseph de Goitia, Francisco Ximénez, his wife and family, and Doña Petronila de Salas with ten sons and daughters; and that they had robbed and profaned the convents and [had robbed] all the haciendas of those murdered and also all the horses and cattle of that jurisdiction and La Cañada.

Upon receiving this news I immediately notified the *alcalde mayor* of that district to assemble all the people in his house in a body, and told him to advise at once the *alcalde mayor* of Los Taos to do the same. On this same day I received notice that two members of a convoy had been killed in the pueblo of Santa Clara, six others having escaped by flight. Also at the same time the *sargento mayor,* Bernabe Márquez, sent to ask me for assistance, saying that he was surrounded and hard pressed by the Indians of the Queres and Tanos nations. Having sent the aid for which he asked me, and an order for those families of Los Cerrillos to come to the villa, I instantly arranged for all the people in it and its environs to retire to the *casas reales.*[7] Believing that the uprising of the Tanos and Pecos might endanger the person of the reverend father custodian, I wrote him to set out at once for the villa, not feeling reassured even with the escort which the lieutenant took, at my orders, but when they arrived with the letter

---

4. A civil official; in this case, *alcalde mayore* is used to refer both to a Spanish and to a Pueblo official.

5. Farms.

6. In the northern part of the Rio Grande valley.

7. Public buildings, including the governor's palace.

they found that the Indians had already killed the said father custodian; Father Fray Domingo de Vera; Father Fray Manuel Tinoco, the minister *guardián* of San Marcos, who was there; and Father Fray Fernando de Velasco, *guardián* of Los Pecos, near the pueblo of Galisteo, he having escaped that far from the fury of the Pecos. The latter killed in that pueblo Fray Juan de la Pedrosa, two Spanish women, and three children. There died also at the hands of the said enemies in Galisteo Joseph Nieto, two sons of *Maestre de Campo* Leiba, Francisco de Anaya, the younger, who was with the escort, and the wives of *Maestre de Campo* Lieba and Joseph Nieto, with all their daughters and families. I also learned definitely on this day that there had died in the pueblo of Santo Domingo fathers Fray Juan de Talabán, Fray Francisco Antonio Lorenzana, and Fray Joseph de Montesdoca, and the *alcalde mayor,* Andrés de Peralta, together with the rest of the men who went as escort.

Seeing myself with notices of so many and such untimely deaths, and that not having received any word from the lieutenant-general was probably due to the fact that he was in the same exigency and confusion, or that the Indians had killed most of those on the lower river, and considering also that in the pueblo of Los Taos the fathers *guardianes* of that place and of the pueblo of Pecuries might be in danger, as well as the *alcalde mayor* and the residents of that valley, and that at all events it was the only place from which I could obtain any horses and cattle—for all these reasons I endeavored to send a relief of soldiers. Marching out for that purpose, they learned that in La Cañada, as in Los Taos and Pecuries, the Indians had risen in rebellion, joining the Apaches of the Achos nation. In Pecuries they had killed Francisco Blanco de la Vega, a *mulata* belonging to the *maese de campo,* Francisco Xavier, and a son of the said *mulata.* Shortly thereafter I learned that they also killed in the pueblo of Taos the father *guardián,* Fray Francisco de Mora, and Father Fray Mathías Rendón, the *guardián* of Pecuries, and Fray Antonio de Pro, and the *alcalde mayor,* as well as another fourteen or fifteen soldiers, along with all the families of the inhabitants of that valley, all of whom were together in the convent. Thereupon I sent an order to the *alcalde mayor,* Luis de Quintana, to come at once to the villa with all the people whom he had assembled in his house, so that, joined with those of us who were in the *casa reales,* we might endeavor to defend ourselves against the enemy's invasions. It was necessarily supposed that they would join all their forces to take our lives, as was seen later by experience.

On Tuesday, the thirteenth of the said month, at about nine o'clock in the morning, there came in sight of us in the suburb of Analco, in the cultivated field of the hermitage of San Miguel, and on the other side of the river of the villa, all the Indians of the Tanos and Pecos nations and the Querez of San Marcos, armed and giving warwhoops. As I learned that one of the Indians who was leading them was from the villa and had gone to join them shortly before, I sent some soldiers to summon him and tell him on my behalf that he could come to see me in entire safety, so that I might ascertain from him the purpose for which they were coming. Upon receiving this message he came to where I was, and, since he was known, as I say, I asked him how it was that he had gone crazy too—being an Indian who spoke our language, was so intelligent, and had lived all his life in the villa among the Spaniards, where I had placed such confidence in him—and was now coming as a leader of the Indian rebels. He replied to me that they had elected him as their captain, and that they were carrying two banners, one white and the other red, and that the white one signified peace and the red one war. Thus if we wished to choose the white it must be [upon our agreeing] to leave the country, and if we chose the red, we must perish, because the rebels were numerous and we were very few; there was no alternative, inasmuch as they had killed so many religious and Spaniards.

On hearing his reply, I spoke to him very persuasively, to the effect that he and the rest of his followers were Catholic Christians, [asking] how they expected to live without the religious; and said that even though they had committed so many atrocities, still there was a remedy, for if they would return to the obedience of his Majesty they would be pardoned; and that thus he should go back to his people and tell them in my name all that had been said to him, and persuade them to [agree to] it and to withdraw from where they were; and that he was to advise me of what they might reply. He came back from there after a short time, saying that his people asked that all classes of Indians who were in our power be given up to them, both those in the service of the Spaniards and those of the Mexican nation of that suburb of Analco. He demanded also that his wife and children be given up to him, and likewise that all the Apache men and women whom the Spaniards had captured in war [be turned over to them], inasmuch as some Apaches who were among them were asking for them. If these things were not done they would declare war immediately, and they were unwilling to leave the place where they were because they were awaiting the Taos, Pecuries, and Theguas nations, with whose aid they would destroy us.

Seeing his determination, and what they demanded of us, and especially the fact that it was untrue that there were any Apaches among them, because they were at war with all of them, and that these parleys were intended solely to obtain his wife and children and to gain time for the arrival of the other rebellious nations to join them and besiege us, and that during this time they were robbing and sacking what was in the said hermitage and the houses of the Mexicans, I told him (having given him all the preceding admonitions as a Christian and a Catholic) to return to his people and say to them that unless they immediately desisted from sacking the houses and dispersed, I would send to drive them away from there. Whereupon he went back, and his people received him with peals of bells and trumpets, giving loud shouts in sign of war.

With this, seeing after a short time that they not only did not cease the pillage but were advancing toward the villa with shamelessness and mockery, I ordered all the soldiers to go out and attack them until they succeeded in dislodging them from that place. Advancing for this purpose, they joined battle, killing some at the first encounter. Finding themselves repulsed, they took shelter and fortified themselves in the said hermitage and the houses of the Mexicans, from which they defended themselves a part of the day with the firearms that they had and with arrows. Having set fire to some of the houses in which they were, thus having them surrounded and at the point of perishing, there appeared on the road from Thesuque a band of the people whom they were awaiting, who were all the Teguas. Thus it was necessary to go to prevent these latter from passing on to the villa, because the *casas reales* were poorly defended; whereupon the said Tanos and Pecos fled to the mountains and the two parties joined together, sleeping that night in the sierra of the villa. Many of the rebels remained dead and wounded, and our men retired to the *casas reales* with one soldier killed and the *maese de campo,* Francisco Gómez, and some fourteen or fifteen soldiers wounded, to attend them and entrench and fortify ourselves as best we could.

On the morning of the following day, Wednesday, I saw the enemy come down all together from the sierra where they had slept, toward the villa. Mounting my horse, I went out with the few forces that I had to meet them, above the convent. The enemy saw me and halted, making ready to resist the attack. They took up a better position, gaining the eminence of some ravines and thick

timber, and began to give war-whoops, as if daring me to attack them.

I paused thus for a short time, in battle formation, and the enemy turned aside from the eminence and went nearer the sierras, to gain the one which comes down behind the house of the *maese de campo,* Francisco Gómez. There they took up their position, and this day passed without our having any further engagements or skirmishes than had already occurred, we taking care that they should not throw themselves upon us and burn the church and the houses of the villa.

The next day, Thursday, the enemy obliged us to take the same step as on the day before of mounting on horseback in fighting formation. There were only some light skirmishes to prevent their burning and sacking some of the houses which were at a distance from the main part of the villa. I knew well enough that these dilatory tactics were to give time for the people of the other nations who were missing to join them in order to besiege and attempt to destroy us, but the height of the places in which they were, so favorable to them and on the contrary so unfavorable to us, made it impossible for us to go and drive them out before they should all be joined together.

On the next day, Friday, the nations of the Taos, Pecuries, Hemes, and Querez having assembled during the past night, when dawn came more than 2,500 Indians fell upon us in the villa, fortifying and entrenching themselves in all its houses and at the entrances of all the streets, and cutting off our water, which comes through the *arroyo* and the irrigation canal in front of the *casas reales.* They burned the holy temple and many houses in the villa. We had several skirmishes over possession of the water, but seeing that it was impossible to hold even this against them, and almost all the soldiers of the post being already wounded, I endeavored to fortify myself in the *casas reales* and to make a defense without leaving their walls. [The Indians were] so dexterous and so bold that they came to set fire to the doors of the fortified tower of Nuestra Señora de las Casas Reales, and, seeing such audacity, and the manifest risk that we ran of having the *casas reales* set on fire, I resolved to make a sally into the plaza of the said *casas reales* with all my available force of soldiers, without any protection, to attempt to prevent the fire which the enemy was trying to set. With this endeavor we fought the whole afternoon, and, since the enemy, as I said above, had fortified themselves and made embrasures in all the houses, and had plenty of arquebuses, powder, and balls. They did us much damage. Night overtook us thus and God was pleased that they

should desist somewhat from shooting us with arquebuses and arrows. We passed this night, like the rest, with
much care and watchfulness, and suffered greatly from
thirst because of the scarcity of water.

On the next day, Saturday, they began at dawn to press
us harder and more closely with gunshots, arrows, and
stones, saying to us that now we should not escape them,
and that besides their own numbers, they were expecting
help from the Apaches whom they had already summoned. They fatigued us greatly on this day, because all
was fighting, and above all we suffered from thirst, as we
were already oppressed by it. At nightfall, because of the
evident peril in which we found ourselves by their gaining the two stations where cannon were mounted, which
we had at the doors of the *casas reales,* aimed at the entrances of the streets, in order to bring them inside it was
necessary to assemble all the forces that I had with me,
because we realized that this was their [the Indians'] intention. Instantly all the said Indian rebels began a chant
of victory and raised war-whoops, burning all the houses
of the villa, and they kept us in this position the entire
night, which I assure your reverence was the most horrible that could be thought of or imagined, because the
whole villa was a torch and everywhere were war chants
and shouts. What grieved us most were the dreadful
flames from the church and the scoffing and ridicule
which the wretched and miserable Indian rebels made of
the sacred things, intoning the *alabado*[8] and the other
prayers of the church with jeers.

Finding myself in this state, with the church and the
villa burned, and with the few horses, sheep, goats, and
cattle which we had without feed or water for so long that
many had already died, and the rest were about to do so,
and with such a multitude of people, most of them children and women, so that our numbers in all came to about
a thousand persons, perishing with thirst—for we had
nothing to drink during these two days except what had
been kept in some jars and pitchers that were in the *casas
reales*—surrounded by such a wailing of women and children, with confusion everywhere, I determined to take
the resolution of going out in the morning to fight with the
enemy until dying or conquering. Considering that the
best strength and armor were prayers to appease the Divine wrath, though on the preceding days the poor women
had made them with fervor, that night I charged them to
do so increasingly, and told the father *guardián* and the

other two religious to say mass for us at dawn, and exhort
all alike to repentance for their sins and to conformance
with the Divine will, and to absolve us from guilt and
punishment. These things being done, all of us who could
mounted our horses, and the rest [went] on foot with their
arquebuses, and some Indians who were in our service
with their bows and arrows, and in the best order possible
we directed our course toward the house of the *maese de
campo,* Francisco Xavier, which was the place where (apparently) there were the most people and where they had
been most active and boldest. On coming out of the entrance to the street it was seen that there was a great number of Indians. They were attacked in force, and though
they resisted the first charge bravely, finally they were put
to flight, many of them being overtaken and killed. Then
turning at once upon those who were in the streets leading to the convent, they also were put to flight with little
resistance. The houses in the direction of the house of the
said *maestre de campo,* Francisco Xavier, being still full
of Indians who had taken refuge in them, and seeing that
the enemy with the punishment and deaths that we had inflicted upon them in the first and second assaults were
withdrawing toward the hills, giving us a little room, we
laid siege to those who remained fortified in the said
houses. Though they endeavored to defend themselves,
and did so, seeing that they were being set afire and that
they would be burned to death, those who remained alive
surrendered and much was made of them. The deaths of
both parties in this and the other encounters exceeded
three hundred Indians.

Finding myself a little relieved by this miraculous
event, though I had lost much blood from two arrow
wounds which I had received in the face and from a remarkable gunshot wound in the chest on the day before, I
immediately had water given to the cattle, the horses, and
the people. Because we now found ourselves with very
few provisions for so many people, and without hope of
human aid, considering that our not having heard in so
many days from the people on the lower river would be
because of their all having been killed, like the others in
the kingdom, or at least of their being or having been in
dire straits, with the view of aiding them and joining with
them into one body, so as to make the decisions most conducive to his Majesty's service, on the morning of the
next day, Monday, I set out for La Isleta, where I judged
the said comrades on the lower river would be. I trusted in
Divine Providence, for I left without a crust of bread or a
grain of wheat or maize, and with no other provisions for
the convoy of so many people except four hundred ani-

---

8. A sacred hymn.

mals and two carts belonging to private persons, and, for food, a few sheep, goats, and cows.

In this manner, and with this fine provision, besides a few small ears of maize that we found in the fields, we went as far as the pueblo of La Alameda, where we learned from an old Indian whom we found in a maize-field that the lieutenant-general with all the residents of his jurisdictions had left some fourteen or fifteen days before to return to El Paso to meet the carts. This news made me very uneasy, alike because I could not be persuaded that he would have left without having news of me as well as of all the others in the kingdom, and because I feared that from his absence there would necessarily follow the abandonment of this kingdom. On hearing this news I acted at once, sending four soldiers to overtake the said lieutenant-general and the others who were following him, with orders that they were to halt wherever they should come up with them. Going in pursuit of them, they overtook them at the place of Fray Cristóbal. The lieutenant-general, Alonso Garcia, overtook me at the place of Las Nutrias, and a few days' march thereafter I encountered the *maese de campo,* Pedro de Leiba, with all the people under his command, who were escorting these carts and who came to ascertain whether or not we were dead, as your reverence had charged him to do, and to find me, ahead of the supply train. I was so short of provisions and of everything else that at best I should have had a little maize for six days or so.

Thus, after God, the only succor and relief that we have rests with your reverence and in your diligence. Wherefore, and in order that your reverence may come immediately, because of the great importance to the service of God and the king of your reverence's presence here, I am sending the said *maese de campo,* Pedro de Leyba, with the rest of the men whom he brought so that he may come as escort for your reverence and the carts or mule-train in which we hope you will bring us some assistance of provisions. Because of the haste which the case demands I do not write at more length, and for the same reason I cannot make a report at present concerning the above to the señor viceroy, because the *autos*[9] are not verified and there has been no opportunity to conclude them. I shall leave it until your reverence's arrival here. For the rest I refer to the account which will be given to your reverence by the father secretary, Fray Buene Ventura de Berganza. I am slowly overtaking the other party,

which is sixteen leagues from here, with the view of joining them and discussing whether or not this miserable kingdom can be recovered. For this purpose I shall not spare any means in the service of God and of his Majesty, losing a thousand lives if I had them, as I have lost my estate and part of my health, and shedding my blood for God. May He protect me and permit me to see your reverence in this place at the head of the relief. September 8, 1680. Your servant, countryman, and friend kisses your reverence's hand.

Don Antonio de Otermin.

---

from LETTER ON THE RECONQUEST OF NEW MEXICO (1692)[1]
DIEGO DE VARGAS

Excellent Sir:

I scarcely arrived from my happy conquest, on the twentieth of December last, when two hours later the courier arrived with the answer to that which, with testimony of the records, I sent to your Excellency from the villa of Santa Fe, notifying your Highness through them and the letter of transmittal of what had been conquered up to the said day. A happy day, luck, and good fortune were attained, your Excellency, through the impulse which, fervently, spurred by the faith and as a loyal vassal of his Majesty, led me to undertake the said enterprise, considering that it is a region so large as to be a kingdom, all of which was in rebel hands for the past twelve years, and only on the confines of which was it known that they had been visited. For their safety, they were living on the mesas, the approaches to which made it difficult to invade them without their being assured of victory. All these conditions could have justly embarrassed me, but, realizing that the defense of my faith and my king were of greater importance, I scorned them and put into execution the said enterprise. . . .

I acknowledge the command and order of your Excellency, made in agreement with the real junta de hacienda,[2]

---

9. Official reports.

1. Vargas's letter is available in *Coronado Cuarto Centennial Publications, 1540–1940* (1940).

2. The royal administration.

in which you say, order, and command that I should continue in the region. I wrote your Excellency, telling you that upon my return from subduing and conquering the Pecos, the Keres tribes living on various mesas, and the Jémez, I would make entry to the rock of Acoma and the provinces of Zuñi and Moqui, should I consider it possible for the horses to travel two hundred leagues. I answer that despite great obstacles, as attested in the records, I made the said entry which I had previously proposed to your Excellency with doubt; having also succeeded in obtaining some *almagre* earth, or vermilion, which is believed to contain quicksilver ore,[3] and having made known the new route which might be used for transit from the said kingdom, for his Majesty, should it contain quicksilver. With great interest I embarked upon the discovery of the said route and crossing, and, having come out at the pueblo of Socorro on the tenth of December last, there was such continuous snow and ice that on the following day we found the river frozen over. And we found that to return to the said villa and its surrounding pueblos by this route would be a waste of time and unfruitful, for it entailed the danger of the enemy Apaches as well as their partisans in this region of El Paso. I decided to hasten there so that the inhabitants would have the defense and garrison of the arms of their presidio and in order that the horses might gain strength and recuperate in order that I might carry out your Excellency's orders.

With regard to the transportation of the families which may be found at this pueblo of El Paso, I decided to visit them in order to make a census list, which I am sending to your Excellency so that your Highness may have record of the exact number of children and other persons who are under the care of each family. Those who can be taken unburdened will go, trusting that your Excellency will take into consideration my report which I referred to in the letter of remission adjoined to the said census. As for the return of the inhabitants who have withdrawn and who live in the kingdoms of [New] Vizcaya and [New] Galicia, I have decided to go in person in order effectively to persuade them, for I shall endeavor to find those who are living in haciendas and known localities, and in the settlements, announcing your Excellency's order and command to the royal authorities, and with their assistance they also will be made known by the proclamation

which I will have published. And I shall make known therein that all those who desire to come and colonize the said kingdom will be promised all that which is contained in your Excellency's order. I will enlist them all with their privileges, paying the expenses of those who are to be transported, not only to this pueblo of El Paso, but as far as the villa of Santa Fe. In order that your Excellency may be entirely without anxiety with regard to the said colonization, I shall at all costs set out from this pueblo of El Paso with both groups of settlers upon my return from the said kingdoms, providing that your Excellency, in view of this, will send me the necessary sum, in response to the same and with the same courier. He will find me at the camp of Sombrerete collecting the twelve thousand pesos which your Excellency has placed to my account, if it is not obtainable at Guadiana. For I shall also visit that place for the purpose of enlisting some people, as those obtained for these parts must be of good quality, campaigners and persons agile in the pursuit of this war. . . .

As for the settlement of the region, the soldiers needed for its presidio, its defense and safety, and that of the lives of the religious, I repeat to your Excellency my opinion that five hundred families are necessary for the settlement of the villa and the following districts, not counting the one hundred soldiers necessary for the presidio at the villa of Santa Fe.

While I was there I examined and appraised the land. And, nine days after its conquest, having taken the road to the pueblo of Galisteo, which is the wagon road, and having entered the pueblo of the Pecos tribe, I returned to the said villa by way of the short road through the mountains, which the said tribes travel on foot and on horseback. I then went to the pueblos of the Tegua and Tano tribes, continued to that of Picuríes, and from there to that of Taos. Having seen the said thirteen pueblos and inspected the character of their lands, pastures, water supply, and wood, I find that the only place adequate for the founding of the said villa is its existing site, setting it up and establishing it on this side of the arroyo where it overlooks and dominates the pueblo and stronghold occupied there by the Tegua and Tano tribes, which comprises what was formerly the major portion of the palace and royal houses of the governor, and those of the inhabitants of the said villa who left as a result of their rebellion. They have extended and raised the walls, and fortified them, so that the said pueblo is walled. Besides, in La Ciénega and its lowland, the waters gather from the surrounding mountains and mesas, and the said stronghold being near by, it is in the shade, and for that reason it is hidden from the sun in the

_____

3. Mercury (quicksilver) was valuable because it was essential to refining silver.

morning, and in the afternoon it also is without the sun's
rays. And, due to the climate and temperature of the said
kingdom, which is extremely cold, cloudy, and abounding in water, with heavy frosts and ice, and due to its
shade and thick fog and mists of known and evident detriment, the said place is unsatisfactory.

The favor granted to the said natives, which I promised
them at the time of their conquest, is not prejudicial to the
said colonists, rather it is to their interest to settle at the
place where I established my encampment on the day of
my entry there. It is located a musket shot distance away.
Its land dominates and overlooks the said stronghold, the
place having sufficient height so that the artillery may
control and cause much respect from the enemy. Also the
surrounding country is well supplied with wood, farm
lands, and pastures. These can be reserved, setting aside
and reserving from the entrance at Las Bocas along the
road to Santo Domingo, a distance of seven leagues. And
as for the pueblo of La Ciénega, which I found abandoned, if some Keres Indians should repopulate it, it will
be with the *tasación*[4] of five hundred varas, from the door
of the church to the four cardinal points, and no more.
Also with regard to the abandoned hacienda of El Alamo,
to whomsoever lays claim to it will be given the lands
with limits, but without liability claims with regard to the
said horses.

With regard to the abandoned hacienda which is located a distance of two leagues from there, beyond the arroyo or river called the Seco, also to its owner, in the same
manner, if he wishes to settle it, and the aforesaid length
and distance, with its entrances and exits, will be reserved
as the common land not only for the horses and mules of
the inhabitants who settle there, but also for those of the
soldiers of the presidio. And also, the said place should be
settled because it has dry land, with very little gravel, and
is clear, getting the sun all day, and enjoying the winds
from every direction.

With regard to its settlers, as many as one hundred and
fifty families may enter and settle the said villa, as well as
the one hundred presidial soldiers, who may cover the
land with their arms by being established at this central
point which controls a distance of ninety leagues in the
following manner: thirty-two long leagues to the pueblo
of Taos, to the north, thirty leagues to the pueblos of the
Jémez and the Keres of Sia, which are between the south

and west, and thirty leagues to the pueblo of Isleta, which
is to the west. At the said place they will be assured of
having provisions, whether or not the weather is good,
and should the population be augmented such that they
will need additional sources of supply, the one hundred
and fifty families may settle part of the land; for, the said
kingdom having the protection of the arms of the presidio, many will decide to settle on the haciendas which
they formerly had and which they abandoned at the time
of the uprising. The number of those which are occupied
will be shared with the families hailing from other parts.

It is my wish, with those with whom I enter, including
the soldiers, that they should, first and foremost, personally build the church and holy temple, setting up in it before all else the patroness of the said kingdom and villa,
who is the one that was saved from the ferocity of the savages, her title being Our Lady of the Conquest. And so,
with the aid of the soldiers and settlers, the foundations
will be laid and the walls of the holy temple raised, bringing at the same time, by means of the oxen that will be
taken, the timber necessary. At the same time the said
construction will be hastened, so that by our example the
conquered will be moved to build gladly their churches in
their pueblos, which I hope will be accomplished. . . .

With regard to the settlement at the pueblo of Taos,
which is on the frontier, and the most distant one of the
kingdom, where the Apaches continually make their
entry, it will be necessary to place one hundred settlers
there. This pueblo has a site even more favorable for settlement, because its valleys are very broad, and it has
many arroyos, wood, and pastures, and the land is very
fertile and will yield good crops and is very suitable for
the raising of all types of livestock, large and small. The
said number of settlers, backed by the strength of the arms
of the presidio of the said villa, will make it impossible
for the enemy easily to swoop down on the pueblos of the
said tribes; and also those who rebuild and resettle their
haciendas may live in safety, for on the way to this pueblo
there are many abandoned sites which were pointed out to
me and named by their previous owners.

At the pueblo of Pecos, a distance of eight leagues
from Santa Fe, fifty families may be settled, for it is also
an Apache frontier and is surrounded by very mountainous country, very adaptable to ambush. And so, if it is settled, and with the said arms at the said villa, it will be possible to prevent the thefts and deaths otherwise facilitated
by easy entry. It is very fertile land, which responds with
great abundance to all the types of seeds that are planted.

---

4. Measure.

Between the pueblos of Santo Domingo and Cochití, the original inhabitants of this kingdom who so desire may settle, should the Indians of the Keres tribe not come down to occupy the said pueblos. Those of Cochití are living on the mesa and mountain of La Cieneguilla, a distance of four leagues away; and those of Santo Domingo are living on the mesa of the Cerro Colorado with the Keres Indians of Captain Malacate who were absent from their pueblo of Sia at the time General Don Domingo Jironza, my predecessor, burned it and captured those who escaped from fire and arms. And so the people of this Keres tribe are living on the said mesas, which are those of the said two pueblos and the one of Sia. From what they told me on the mesa of the Cerro Colorado, where they again have their pueblo, it is doubtful that they will return to resettle the one of Sia, which was burned by General Don Domingo. They said that they would not return to the pueblo for the additional reason that the land is nitrous, lacks sufficient water, is without wood, and is very sterile, and that if they should descend they would settle in the canyon between the pueblo of Sia and that of abandoned Santa Ana.

In the vicinity of this pueblo of Santa Ana, another fifty settlers may be established, because it has good lands and also because they are necessary to close the way to the enemy Apache; and so that the fathers who minister to the Keres Indians, and those of the Jémez tribe, may have the said settlers near by for their protection, and may, without fear of risking their lives, minister to them, punish them, and reprehend them as the case might be.

In the abandoned pueblo of Jémez, the walls of the church and most of the houses of the dwellings are standing, in which pueblo, should the Indians who are living on the mesa of the canyon remain there, one hundred residents can be settled. It has plenty of lands for planting and pastures, with water and very fertile, and the settlement of the said place would be very important because the Apaches make entry there, by virtue of which some of the Indians are rebellious in spirit and are our enemies.

From the hacienda of "La Angostura," two leagues from the pueblo of "La Angostura," that is, San Felipe, to the abandoned pueblo of Sandía, and one league from the abandoned pueblo of Puaray, at the said first one of Sandía Spaniards also may be settled. The walls of the church and some houses, although badly damaged, may be repaired. The lands are good, with their irrigation ditches. The said pueblos are on the camino real, and it would be very desirable to settle the region with another one hundred colonists, who will be able to live very comfortably and prosperously. It is a distance of twenty leagues from the said villa and will be of great value for the protection of the haciendas which extend from "Las Huertas."

At a distance of ten leagues, on the said camino real, on the other side of the river, there is situated the pueblo of Isleta, which is abandoned. The walls of the church are in good condition, as are most of the houses of the Indians of the Tegua nation who were withdrawn by General Don Antonio de Otermín when he made the entry in the year of 'eighty-one, at the expense of his Majesty, in the time of his Excellency, the viceroy, Conde de Paredes. The natives of the said tribe now live in some miserable huts in the pueblo of Isleta, in this district of El Paso, and so it will be desirable to restore them to their pueblo. They will be assured success in cultivating the fields which they plant at the pueblo, because the lands are extensive, in a good climate, and can be easily irrigated. And they will be protected if the said intervening haciendas called "Las Huertas" are settled, along with those extending from Las Barrancas, and those toward the abandoned pueblos of Alamillo and Sevilleta, whose natives are scattered and restless, and with the settlement of the said haciendas and the pueblo referred to, it will be possible to restore them to their pueblos.

Continuing a distance of ten leagues, Socorro is found, which may be settled with the Indians who at present occupy this one of Socorro in this district of El Paso, and they may be joined by the Piros, who are few, and who live in the pueblo of Senecú in this district, for it is a vast and fertile land; it has its irrigation ditches, and some of the walls of the convent are in good condition. Senecú, which the Piros occupied previously, a distance of ten leagues away, should not be settled because the river has damaged the land, and furthermore it is on a frontier infested with many Apaches. If it is the wish of some to settle the abandoned haciendas, it will be useful for the protection of the said Indians, and it will also prepare the way for the filling in and occupying of the land. The above is only the form in which the settlement should be made, in order that the natives of the said tribes, aware of the neighboring settlers and of the armed strength of the presidio, may be kept in submission, and so that our holy faith may be spread among them, and their children may join it with full obedience, and the missionaries, their teachers of Christian doctrine, may not find themselves alone and afraid to teach them, as I repeat, the doctrines of our holy faith.

As for the natives of the rock of Acoma, since they are a distance of twenty-four leagues from Isleta, and also those of the province of Zuñi, they may be left as they are. But as for those of the province of Moqui, in case the said vermilion earth is found not to contain quicksilver ore, it is my opinion that they should be removed from their pueblos to the abandoned ones of Alamillo and Sevilleta and the region between them, for in this way they will be safe and their missionaries will have control over them, for otherwise they would undergo great risk.

FRAY CARLOS JOSÉ DELGADO (1677–POST-1750)

Throughout the course of his missionary work in the southwestern area today called New Mexico, Carlos José Delgado retained a reputation for piety and humility in his efforts to evangelize among the Puebloan peoples in behalf of the order of St. Francis. Of the many who expressed concern about the situation of the Indians at the hands of civil authorities, Delgado was among the first and most stalwart in speaking for just treatment of the Pueblo Indians among whom he worked and prayed throughout his adult life. He spent most of his career, aside from his journeys to seek converts, as the resident missionary at the Pueblo of San Agustín de Isleta.

When it seemed that the Jesuits, another Catholic order, would be likely to gain converts among Indian peoples earlier met by the Franciscans, Delgado was among the missionary leaders who were sent to work among the Pueblos—specifically with the Hopis, who led rebellions during the previous century—to seek converts for the Franciscans. Delgado and another missionary, Ignacio Pino, rode to the Hopi mesas in the summer of 1742 and preached to several Hopi villagers. Although Hopi leaders resolutely refused to have their peoples again take on the Spanish way, Delgado and Pino found several willing listeners among some of the peoples who had fled the pueblos during the rebellion of 1680. They brought back to the Rio Grande area 441 followers, expressing dismay that they had had to leave behind some young children and older people for whom the journey would have been too difficult. Two years later, in March 1744, Delgado initiated another missionary effort among the Navajos. In a letter to Father Commissary General Fray Juan Fogueras, Delgado reported that with gifts, exhortations, and good treatment, he and his assistant had persuaded five thousand Navajos to come in to the missionaries' care. Another trip to the Hopis in 1745 met with fewer converts, and Delgado thereafter concentrated his efforts among the Pueblos of central and north central New Mexico.

Delgado seems to have been tireless in his concern for the situation of the Indians. He wrote to Fray Fogueras in the 1740s that more living space for the Indian converts was necessary, as well as more missionaries, if their work was to succeed because to secure the Indians against outside pressure, separate housing would be useful. In many cases, requests by missionaries concentrated on what the missionaries themselves needed; in Delgado's case, the requests most frequently concerned the stability of mission life and the needs of the Indian peoples who had converted. For himself, in one letter after the trip to Navajo country in 1744, Delgado asked only that he be sent clothing and shoes because the journey had left him "without a habit, or sandals, or anything else, on account of the country's being so rough. . . . I ask, not a new habit or new sandals, but something old that may be spared there." In this letter, he typifies his successful conversion of the Navajos as the outcome of a life of following St. Francis:

> God and our holy father, Saint Francis, have permitted—for few of us would consider ourselves worthy—that I, the least individual shall have commenced these enterprises and won in them such good will among all the heathen, and even among the Christians, that in every pueblo they desired to have me as their minister, but I cannot because I am one only.

Part of Delgado's missionary zeal arose from concern about the Jesuits entering the territory originally traversed by the Franciscans, and part of it arose from his significant concern that civil leaders were creating great difficulties for the Indian peoples. He believed that the success of his efforts would come, despite his being in his sixties, because "judging by the strength that I feel in myself I would say that I have seven and sixty spiritual arms to defend this *custodia* [this realm] from so many enemies. They will be conquered, for envy and greed never prevail." Delgado's letter to the Reverend Father Ximeno, printed next, reveals the strength of his commitments to the Indian peoples whom he spent his life converting and attempting to protect from the hardships that Spanish colonial life might otherwise have brought them. The *alcaldes mayores,* local civil constables, received no outright pay for their military station, so they relied upon Indian labor to bring them food and goods for their own sustenance and for a lucrative trade to the south. The Indian peoples were, as Delgado attests, subject to intrusions by the *alcaldes mayores* in their private and their spiritual lives, and this problem, in addition to the accepted colonial system of *repartimiento,* a form of rotational labor required of the Puebloans for the sustenance of the Spanish villagers, was creating such hardship for the Indians that they were not surviving well among the Spanish people. Letters about the *alcaldes'* abuses were sent in later years by Fray Andrés Varo in 1751, Fray Juan Sanz de Lezaún in 1760, Fray Pedro Serrano in 1761, and Fray Juan Agustín de Morfi in 1778. Delgado's was among the first to designate clearly the exact nature of the abuses the Indians were subjected to. The tenor of the Franciscans' combined efforts to effect a change in the system of civil authority is well captured in a letter by another correspondent, Fray Varo, in 1751. "Oh land and kingdom of New Mexico!" wrote Varo. "So long oppressed, humiliated, and persecuted, so often not governed, but tyrannized over by these unworthy chiefs." Their combined efforts to speak of the outrages against the Indians eventually resulted in King Charles III's dispatching the Spanish Royal Corps of Engineers in 1765 to map the areas thoroughly in an effort not just to fortify the frontier and create a trade network, but to prevent further abuse of the Indians at the hands of civil leaders who were taking too great advantage of them.

REPORT MADE BY REV. FATHER FRAY CARLOS DELGADO TO OUR REV. FATHER XIMENO . . . THE YEAR 1750[1]

Very Reverend Father and our Minister Provincial: I, Fray Carlos José Delgado, preacher general, commissary, notary, and censor of the Holy Office, apostolic notary, and missionary in the *custodia*[2] of the conversion of San Pablo of this province of El Santo Evangelio in the kingdom of New Mexico, appear before your reverence only for the purpose of lamenting before your paternal love the grave extortions that we, the ministers of these missions, are suffering, at the hands of the governors and alcaldes of that kingdom. I declare, that of the eleven governors and many *alcaldes mayores* whom I have known in the long period of forty years that I have served at the mission called San Agustín de la Isleta, most of them have hated, and do hate to the death, and insult and persecute the missionary religious, causing them all the troubles and annoyances that their passion dictates, without any other reason or fault than the opposition of the religious to the very serious injustices which the said governors and alcaldes inflict upon the helpless Indians recently received into the faith, so that the said converts shall not forsake our holy law and flee to the heathen, to take up anew their former idolatries. This is experienced every day, not without grave sorrow and heartfelt tears on the part of those evangelical sowers, who, on seeing that their work is wasted and that the fecund seed of their preaching to those souls is lost and bears no fruit, cry out to heaven and sorrowfully ask a remedy for this great evil. In order that your reverence's exalted understanding may regard as just the reasons which support the said missionaries in their opposition to the aforesaid extortions, even though it should be at the cost of their lives, and also in order that you may come to their aid with the measures best fitted

---

1. The whole title of the letter reads: *Report Made by Rev. Father Fray Carlos Delgado to Our Rev. Father Ximeno Concerning the Abominable Hostilities and Tyrannies of the Governors and Alcaldes Mayores toward the Indians, to the Consternation of the Custodia. The Year 1750.* The text is from *Historical Documents Relating to New Mexico, Nueva Vizcaya, and Approaches Thereto, to 1773,* ed. C. W. Hackett (1937).

2. Guardianship.

for the total abolition of the said injuries and injustices, I shall specify them in the following manner:

The first annoyance with which the persons mentioned molest the Indians is to send agents every year (contrary to the royal ordinances, and especially to a decree of the most excellent señor, Don Francisco Fernández de la Cueva Henríquez, Duke of Albuquerque, and viceroy of New Spain, issued in this City of Mexico on May 18, 1709, whose content I present, the original being kept in the archive of the *custodia* mentioned) at the time of the harvest, to all the pueblos of the kingdom, under the pretext of buying maize for the support of their households, though most of it is really to be sold in the nearest villages. The said agents take from all the pueblos and missions eight hundred or a thousand *fanegas*,[3] and compel the Indians to transport them to the place where the governor lives. Besides not paying them anything for the said transportation, they do not pay them for the maize at once, and when the date arrives which they have designated for the payment, if the maize is worth two pesos a *fanega* they give them only one. Even this amount is not in coin or in any article that can be useful to the Indians, but in baubles, such as *chuchumates,* which are glass beads, ill-made knives, relics, awls, and a few handfuls of common tobacco, the value of which does not amount even to a tenth part of what the maize is worth which they extract from them by force, and this even though as has been said, they pay them only half the proper price that is charged throughout the kingdom. From this manifest injustice two very serious evils result: first, the unhappy Indians are left without anything to eat for the greater part of the year; and second, in order not to perish of hunger they are forced to go to the mountains and hunt for game or to serve on the ranches or farms for their food alone, leaving the missions abandoned.

The second oppression that the Indians frequently suffer at the hands of the governors is being compelled arbitrarily and by force, for the small price of an awl or other similar trifle, to work on the buildings that they need, whatever they may be and whether they require little or much time. The Indians also are required to drive cattle as far as the villa of Chihuahua,[4] which is more than two hundred leagues distant from the place where the governors live. They receive in payment for this service only a little ground corn, which they call *pinole,* and the Indian cattle drivers are compelled to pay for those [animals] that are lost or die for want of care or by any other accident. A pernicious evil arises from this cattle driving, for the Indians must abandon their families and leave their lands uncultivated, and, as a consequence, be dying of hunger during the greater part of the year.

The third oppression, and the most grievous and pernicious, from which originate innumerable evils and sins against God, and manifest injuries against the missionaries and Indians, is the wicked dissimulation of the governors in regard to the acts of the *alcaldes mayores,* for it is publicly known throughout the realm that when they give them their *varas,* or wands of office, they tell and advise them to make the Indians work without pity.

With such express license, your reverence can imagine how many disturbances will be caused by men who usually take the employment of *alcaldes mayores* solely for the purpose of advancing their own interests and acquiring property with which to make presents to the governors, so that the latter will countenance their unjust proceedings, even though they be denounced before them, and perhaps will even promote them in office. Every year they make the Indians weave four hundred blankets, or as many woolen sheets; they take from all the pueblos squads of thirty or forty Indians and work them the greater part of the year in planting maize and wheat, which they care for until it is placed in the granaries; they send them among the heathen Indians to trade indigo, knives, tobacco, and *chuchumates,* for cattle and for deer hides. Not even the women are exempt from this tyranny, for if the officials cannot make use of their work in any other way they compel them to spin almost all the wool needed for the said sheets and blankets. And the most lamentable thing about all this is that they recompense them for these tasks with only a handful of tobacco, which is divided among eighteen or twenty.

The most grievous thing for the heathen Indians is that the alcaldes and even some of the governors, mix with their wives and daughters, often violating them, and this so openly that with a very little effort the violation of their consorts comes to the knowledge of the husbands, and as a result it often happens that they repudiate their wives and will not receive them until the missionary fathers labor to persuade them. The shameless way in which the officials conduct themselves in this particular is proved by an occasion when a certain governor was in conversation with some missionaries, and an Indian woman came

---

3. Bushels.

4. The major trading town of Neuva Vizcaya (northern New Mexico), where the *alcaldes mayores,* local civil constables, exchanged Indian goods to their own personal benefit.

into their presence to charge him with the rape of her daughter, and he, without changing countenance, ordered that she should be paid by merely giving her a buffalo skin that he had at hand.

Yet all that I have hitherto related does not drive the Indians to the limits of desperation or cause them to fall away from our holy faith so much as when the said alcaldes compel them to deliver to them a quantity of deer skins, lard, sheaves [of grain], chickens, and other things that their desires dictate, saying that they are for the governors, who ask for them. The Indian has to submit to this injustice, for they either take it from him without asking, or, if he does not have what the alcaldes ask for or does not give it promptly enough when he has it, he suffers either spoliation or punishment.

These punishments are so cruel and inhuman that sometimes for a slight offence, sometimes because the Indian resists the outrages that they inflict upon him, or sometimes because they are slow in doing what the alcaldes order, they are put in jail for many days, are confined in the stocks, or—and I cannot say it without tears—the officials flog them so pitilessly that, their wrath not being appeased by seeing them shed their blood, they inflict such deep scars upon them that they remain for many years. It is a proof of this second point that when I went among the heathen to reduce the apostates there were among them some who, with an aggrieved air, showed me their scars, thus giving me to understand that the reason why they fled and did not return to the pale of the church was their fear of these cruel punishments.

A further distressing proof of this practice is what was done in the past year at El Paso by a captain to a Catholic Indian of the Zuma nation, sacristan of the mission of El Real. A servant of the captain of El Paso had hidden three ears of corn which he had stolen from his master. The sacristan took them from him, and, without any more proof or reason than having found him with them in his hands, and because the said servant, to escape punishment, said that the innocent Indian often stole corn from the granaries, the said captain became so angered that, in violation of all natural and divine laws, he ordered six soldiers to take the Indian out and kill him in the fields.

They carried out the order, and when the unfortunate Zuma cried aloud for confession they did not yield to his entreaties, but gave him a violent death, perhaps being fearful that the missionary religious, whose duty it was to administer the holy sacrament to him, would prevent the execution of that unjust order, even though it might be at the cost of his life.

The outrage did not stop here, for when the Zuma In-

dians of the mission of El Real learned of the death of their countryman, they began to rise up, all crying out: "Why, since we are Christians, do they not permit us to confess at the hour of death? Let us flee to the mountains!" They did not flee, our father, either because the soldiers restrained them or because the fathers appealed to them. A still greater injury, however, arose from the remedy, for the governor having ordered a large troop of Zumas of both sexes to come to this city, simply because an Indian woman and two men were not able to travel as fast as the others, having crippled feet, the corporal who was leading them ordered them to be beheaded at a place called El Gallego, where he left the bodies unburied, to the intense grief of their companions and relatives, whose sorrow was not lessened on seeing that the said corporal and the rest of the escort robbed them of their little children in order to sell them as slaves in various places along the road.

Nor is it only the said alcaldes and governors that ill-treat the Indians in the manner described, but even the judges who enter to conduct the *residencias* of the alcaldes and governors who have completed their terms of office, inflict upon the Indians as much injury and hardship as may conduce to the advancement of their own interests and the success of their ambitious desires. It is public knowledge throughout the kingdom that such persons seek to conduct these *residencias* more for what they gain by unjust and violent spoliation of the Indians than for what they receive from the office that they exercise.

Finally, to such an extreme do the iniquities reach that are practiced against the Indians by governors and *alcaldes mayores,* as well as by the judges of *residencia,*[5] that, losing patience and possessed by fear, they turn their backs to our holy mother, the Church, abandon their pueblos and missions, and flee to the heathen, there to worship the devil, and, most lamentable of all, to confirm in idolatries those who have never been illumined by the light of our holy faith, so that they will never give ear or credit to the preaching of the gospel. Because of all this, every day new conversions become more difficult, and the zealous missionaries who in the service of both Majesties are anxiously seeking the propagation of the gospel, most often see their work wasted and do [not] accomplish the purpose of their extended wanderings.

Although it cannot be denied that those barbarous na-

---

5. Other official constables living in the Spanish settlements.

tions are stiffnecked, yet there have been many instances where thousands of them have entered joyfully through the requisite door of the holy sacrament of baptism, and most of the apostates would return to the bosom of the Church if they did not fear, with such good reason, the punishments and extortions that I have already spoken of. They have told me this on most of the occasions when I have entered in fulfillment of my obligation to reduce apostates and convert the heathen. In the year 1742, when, at the cost of indescribable labor and hardships, I reduced four hundred and forty odd among apostates and heathen in the province of Moqui, innumerable souls would have come to the bosom of our holy Church had they not been deterred by the reason that I have stated.

Although the missionary religious ought to oppose themselves to these grave injuries and their pernicious consequences, they often do not do it; first, because they never succeed in attaining their purpose, but on the contrary are insulted, disrespected, and held to be disturbers of the peace; second, because the governors and alcaldes impute and charge them with crimes that they have never committed, which they proceed to prove with false witnesses whom they have suborned before the father custodian, and compel the latter to proceed against the religious whom they calumniate. And although the said custodians know very well that the denunciations are born of hatred, they proceed against the missionaries, changing them from one mission to another, in order to prevent the said governors from committing the excess of using their power to expel the missionaries from the kingdom, as has often happened; and also because, when the custodians do not agree to what the governors ask, the latter refuse to certify the allowance for the administration of the religious, which certification is necessary in order that the most excellent señor viceroy may issue the honorariums that his Majesty (whom may God preserve) assigns for the maintenance of the missionary religious. It has seemed to me that all that I have said ought to be presented before the charitable zeal of your reverence, so that, having it before you as father of those faithful sons, your apostolic missionaries, you may put into execution the means that your discretion may decide upon, with the purpose of ending this great abuse, of redeeming all those helpless people, and consoling your sorrowing sons. It is indisputable that whatever I have said is public, notorious, certain and true, as I swear *in verbo sacerdotis tacto pectore,* at this hospice of Santa Bárbara of the pueblo of Tlatelolco,[6] on March 27, 1750. Our very reverend father, your humblest subject, Fray CARLOS JOSE DELGADO, who venerates you, places himself at your feet.

---

6. A town just north of Mexico City in the eighteenth century.

EUSEBIO FRANCISCO KINO (1644–1711)

Jesuit missionary Father Eusebio Francisco Kino is credited with having created the first accurate map of the whole Pimería Alta, the area now called southern Arizona and northern Sonora, lands drained by the Gila and Colorado Rivers, and for writing what for over a century became a trusted resource regarding the Indians of the area. During his nearly twenty-five-year residence (1687–1711) at his central mission Nuestra Señora de los Dolores, which he founded, Kino made roughly fifty trips by horseback and mule, traversing anywhere from 100 to 1,000 miles in such trips, to explore and map the territory in behalf of the Jesuits and Spain and to find indigenous groups who were willing to become Christians under Jesuit teachings. Few missionaries of that area, whether Franciscan or Jesuit, had his skills or endurance in the face of the physical difficulties and hardship caused by unfamiliar terrain and peoples.

Francisco Eusebio Kino, as he called himself, was born near Trent, in the Austrian province of Tyrol, in August 1644. Although his name seems Italian, it might have been Kühn at his birth, and it was sometimes given in the records as Chinus, Chino, and Quino. His situation provides a useful reminder, then, that the missionaries who came to North America, from whatever orders, were not necessarily bound by birthright to the nation-states for which they would serve as functionaries. Indeed, Kino was not unusual among the early Jesuit missionaries in Arizona, Sonora, and California, many of whom were in the service of Spain but whose ethnic or national roots were not in Spain. Kino was trained at Ala, in Tyrol, and later studied at the universities of Ingolstädt and Freiburg, where he distinguished himself in astronomy and mathematics. But at age twenty-five—in 1669—he became severely ill. Despaired of by physicians, he evidently had a conversion experience that brought him thoroughly into the leanings and teaching of the Jesuits, whom he joined evidently in the early 1670s. Kino traveled to Mexico in 1681, sailing from Genoa. With his arrival in Mexico and his unflagging missionary activities, the Jesuits secured for the Catholic Church an area that had, for the most part, been forsaken by the Spaniards and Franciscans who had come before.

Kino worked among the peoples of the Sonora and Pimería Alta, including the Pimas (today called the O'odham), the Papagos (the Tohona O'odham), the Yumas (also known as Quechans), the Sobaipuris, the Cocomaricopas, and the Cocopas. Of these peoples, only the Pimas and Papagos were culturally attuned to the use of agriculture and lived in dense settlements. At the time he first visited the Pimas, Kino wrote that he found the lower Gila River watering groves of cottonwoods and sustaining the peoples there with "abundant fish and with their maize, beans, and calabashes." The other Indian peoples he worked with preferred to remain free of a settled existence because in so doing they might evade the raids by their nearby neighbors, the Apaches. These peoples ancestrally relied upon hunting and gathering for their cultural and subsistence needs. Kino introduced cattle and horses to their cultures, brought them fruit trees, different European beans, wheat, and other cereal grains to plant and encouraged them to live in nucleated settlements in order to farm and to herd their new animal acquisitions. By the time his work was completed, he established more than twenty *pueblos de visita* (nucleated enclaves) in the region.

Kino's concern for the welfare of his Indian converts was well known. Unlike many of his missionary colleagues, he seems to have understood that providing the means to sustenance and security for the future would encourage those peoples who were used to moving across the terrain to settle in one area and develop agricultural lifeways. In working with the Indian peoples, giving them food and gifts and assisting them with herding (he was an expert cattleman and horseman), Kino showed an alternative way of living that was attractive and settled, even as he showed them a form of Catholicism they might accept. Over the course of his stay in the Sonora and Pimería Alta, he baptized an estimated 4,500 people. His writings suggest he might have baptized many more, but he was unwilling to engage in sacramental baptisms (which did not require prior instruction) and instead insisted upon careful preparatory instruction and catechism. In 1700, Kino participated in founding the mission San Xavier del Bac (near present-day Tucson, Arizona). He and three associates also established the missions San Gabriel de Guevavi and San Cayetano de Tumacácori.

Kino's experiences of the terrain and its peoples and his understanding of the imperial attempts by Russia, England, and France against the coast of California made him come to the important recognition that if Spain wished to defend its claim to California, it should lay claim to principal harbors along the seaboard. Although he explored lower California, Kino found the Pimería Alta more beautiful and more conducive to the kinds of independent ranching and agricultural settlements that were appropriate to the Indian peoples he worked among. Because of his explorations and production of numerous accurate maps, he was able to prove to European cartographers and officials in Mexico City—because it had been inaccurately disclosed for decades—that lower California was a peninsula, rather than an island. Kino's maps and other documents proved useful to scientific explorers, army and navy officers, and others for a full century following his death.

For many years, scholars knew that Kino wrote a manuscript history of his work among the Indian peoples because it was often cited in important works, but the manuscript was not located until the early twentieth century, when it was first translated and made generally available by Herbert Eugene Bolton. The original folio manuscript of 433 pages consisted of text in five parts. Part I contained a record of the work of his explorations, conversions, and Indian concerns, with significant attention to California, from the time of his arrival in the area in March 1687 to November 1699. The succeeding parts covered similar topics for the years 1700–07, except that attention in these books was given to discussions of Pimería Alta, along the Gila and Colorado Rivers, and the Gulf coast of California. Kino, a learned scholar, wrote from and referred to two hundred sources, some in their entirety. Known well in his own day as the "apostle of Sonora and Arizona," Kino died in 1711.

from THE CELESTIAL FAVORS OF JESUS[1]

To the Very Catholic Majesty of Our Sovereign, Philip V
When, six years ago,[2] I received from our Father General, Thirso Gonsales,[3] a most paternal letter of the preceding year, very urgently charging me to continue to write the "Celestial Favors Experienced in These New Conquests and New Conversions," at the same time the father provincial, Francisco de Arteaga (who without my meriting it named me rector of these missions), sent me the very Catholic royal *cédula* of your Majesty, dated July 17, 1701, in printed form, and inserted in the report which, upon request of the Royal Audiencia of Guadalaxara and by order of your Majesty, was made and printed by Father Francisco Maria Picolo, missionary of California, concerning the prosperous condition of that apostolic conquest and conversion. And since the royal, very Catholic, and most Christian *cédula* of your Majesty so greatly favors all these new conversions, both of California and of this mainland of Cinaloa and Sonora, and of this Pimeria, through your Majesty's so piously ordering that they be maintained, extended, and encouraged by all possible means, and through your Majesty's so tenderly granting the benign license which, in the year 1697, the Señor

Viceroy Don Joseph Sarmiento de Valladares gave to Father Rector Juan Maria de Salvatierra and me to go to California to seek the conversion of those heathen, charging his Royal Audiencia of Guadalaxara with preparing the necessary reports, in order that in view of them such provisions should be made as might be considered proper in order to perfect the work which had been undertaken so many years before, and which is of such great service to God and to the increase of our holy Catholic faith, resolving that there should be assigned six thousand *pesos* each year from this treasury, etc., in view of all this I recognize this royal *cédula* of Your Majesty to be one of the chief celestial favors which our Lord bestows upon us, and about which I have here to write.

And having present this royal and Catholic *cédula* of your Majesty, and the said report of the prosperous condition of California and of the neighboring friends, lovers of the new conversions, a religious pen[4] answered me that it was even more important to report and write of these new conversions of this province of Sonora and of this Pimeria, since they have more profitable and fertile lands, and are of less expense to the royal estate.

Because of this very Catholic royal *cédula* of your Majesty, these conquests in this very extensive North America might be called the New Philippines of America, with the same and with even greater propriety than that with which the conquered islands of the East Indies in Asia were named Philippines in consideration of the great Catholic zeal of Philip III;[5] unless your Royal Majesty prefers, as has been and is the opinion of various persons very zealous in the service of both Majesties, that these new conquests, which are more than two hundred leagues in extent, should be decorated with the name of the New Kingdom of Nueva Navarra, as others are called king-

---

1. The *Favores Celestiales de Iesus y de Maria Ssma. . . . ,* in English, *Celestial Favors of Jesus, Most Holy Mary, and the Most Glorious Apostle of the Indies, San Francisco Xavier, Experienced in the New Conquests and New Conversions . . . of this Unknown North America . . . Dedicated to the Royal Majesty of Philip V, Very Catholic King and Grand Monarch of the Spains and the Indies,* was circulated in manuscript at the time it was written (the late seventeenth and early eighteenth centuries), but was not printed until the twentieth century. The text is *Kino's Historical Memoir of Pimería Alta, 1683–1711,* ed. H. E. Bolton (1919).

2. In 1702. Philip V was king of Spain, 1700–46.

3. Father Tirso Gonzáles, a general of the Jesuits, 1687–1705.

---

4. Father Agustín Campos, missionary at San Ignacio.

5. Philip III reigned 1598–1621. The Philippines were named to honor the prince who became Philip II, as a result of an expedition in 1543 by Villalobos.

doms of Nueva Biscaya, Nueva Galisia, etc. For this New Kingdom of the American Nueva Navarra might unite still other neighboring kingdoms which are being conquered with those already conquered, just as the kingdom of Navarra in Europe lies between and unites the crowns and realms of France and Spain.

With all my heart, I wish that now I might have a small part of the good fortune which Father Andres Peres de Rivas had when he dedicated to Philip, the fourth of this so happy name, and your Majesty's immediate predecessor, the notable volume or history of the Triumphs of the Faith among barbarous nations[6] (which were the new conquests and the new conversions of Cinaloa and of surrounding tribes) from the year 1590 to that of 1645, now that since then we have penetrated more than one hundred leagues further this way, as far as this province of Sonora, and more than one hundred and fifty other leagues to the Taraumares,[7] and now that I, with only my servants and fifty or sixty or more mules and horses, in more than fifty journeys inland, made through the great mercy of our Lord during these twenty years, some of which have been fifty, sixty, and one hundred leagues and some one hundred and fifty and two hundred leagues in extent, have penetrated to the north, to the west, and to the northeast, and particularly to the most unknown regions of the northwest, as far as the land passage to California, which I discovered in the years 1698 and 1699, and which is in the latitude of thirty-five degrees, where I discovered also the very large, extremely fertile, and most densely populated Colorado River (the true Rio del Norte of the ancients), which flows into the head of the Sea of California and reaches to the neighborhood of the hither borders of Gran Quivira.

By means of these many and repeated journeys and missions which I have made to all parts, without special expense to the royal estate, there remain reduced to our friendship and to obedience to the royal crown, and with a desire to receive our holy faith, more than thirty thousand souls in this vicinity, both in this Pima nation, which has more than sixteen thousand souls, and in the neighboring lands of the Cocomaricopas, Yumas, Quiquimas,

Cutganes, Bagiopas, Hoabonomas,[8] etc. And there are many more tribes with more souls and people, where one can enter with all ease; for I have already sent them messages and discourses concerning Christian doctrine, and they have informed me, and we know, that if missionary fathers come they will follow and imitate these other nations already reduced.

In these twenty-one years, after having been missionary of California in the expedition made at a cost of more than half a million to the royal estate by the Admiral Don Ysidro de Atondo y Antillon, whom I aided in taking possession of California (passing to the opposite coast and the South Sea in the latitude of twenty-six degrees, and holding the offices of first rector of that new conversion, vicar of the Señor Bishop of Guadalaxara, and cosmographer of his Majesty), I have baptized here in these new conquests and new conversions about four thousand five hundred souls,[9] and could have baptized twelve or fifteen thousand if we had not suspended further baptisms until our Lord should bring us missionary fathers to aid us in instructing and ministering to so many new subjects of your Majesty and parishioners of our Holy Mother Church.

Since afterwards the conquest and conversion of California was suspended, I asked for and obtained permission to come to these neighboring coasts and the heathen people of this province of Sonora, which begins in the latitude of thirty-two degrees. And the father provincial, Anbrosio Oddon,[10] having named me rector of these new missions and of those of San Francisco Xavier de Sonora, and Father Juan Maria de Salvatierra as visitor of Cinaloa and Sonora, when, in the year 1691, his Reverence came to visit these new conversions of this Pimeria, we went inland for the space of a whole month and more than fifty leagues of travel. And, seeing these lands so pleasant, so rich, so fertile and able so easily to lend aid to the scanty lands of California, the said father visitor, Juan Maria de

---

6. That is, Andrés Pérez de Ribas's *History of the Triumphs of Our Santa Fe,* published in Spanish in Madrid, 1645.

7. The Tarahumares peoples, related to the Pimas, lived east of the Sierra Madres, mainly in the present state of Chihuahua.

8. Indian peoples living near the Lower Gila River and the Lower Colorado.

9. In the 1750s, José de Ortega reported in a publication that Kino had baptized 40,000, based perhaps on a misreading of Kino's manuscripts.

10. Father Ambrosio Oddon succeeded Pather Bernabé de Soto in 1689. He became rector of the Colegio Máximo of Mexico.

Salvatierra,[11] and I agreed to foster so far as we could the continuation of that new conquest and conversion of California, his Reverence at once making for that purpose a very favorable report. When, seven years afterwards, we obtained the desired license, which is cited in the said royal *cédula* of your Majesty, my going was prevented by the reports which the royal officials of this province of Sonora dispatched to Mexico, saying that I was needed in this extensive Pimeria, and Father Francisco Maria Picolo was sent in my place. But I, always encouraged to that end by our father general, Thirso Gonzales, and by the father visitor, Orasio Polise,[12] from here have tried to promote the welfare of both conquests, and of their new conversions, in this most extensive and unknown North America, which seems to give thanks to the Lord by offering such an opportunity for its complete conquest and conversion, that, God helping, we shall be able to write new treatises and volumes. One of them may be called:

THE SEVEN NEW KINGDOMS. "The seven ancient, heathen, and fallen cities[13] of this unknown North America, which are being changed and reduced under the most Christian protection of the very Catholic King and great [monarch] of the Spains and the Indies, Philip V., may God preserve him."

These seven new kingdoms, in place of the seven ancient cities, might be: I, Nueva Biscaya, which lies to the south and southeast; II, Nuevo Mexico, which is northeast of us; III, California Baja, which lies to the southwest and west of us, and extends as far as the latitude of thirty-five degrees, with the Gulf of California between; IV, this new kingdom of Nueva Navarra, scene of these new conquests and new conversions, which are between the other new kingdoms, and about in the center or heart of all this North America; V, California Alta,[14] which lies to the west and northwest of us, from the latitude of thirty-five degrees to that of forty-five or forty-six; VI, Gran

Quivira,[15] which lies to the northwest of us, where the pirate English captain placed his pretended Sea of California; VII, Gran Teguayo,[16] or Nueva Borboña, which is to the north of us, beyond the Moqui, and extends from thirty-seven or thirty-eight degrees north latitude to the Sea of the North, which Hudson discovered in the year 1612, in the latitude of fifty-two, fifty-three, and fifty-four degrees.

COSMOGRAPHIC PROOF that California is not an Island, but a Peninsula. I have just written another small treatise called "Cosmographic Proof that California is not an Island, but a Peninsula, and is continuous with this New Spain, the Gulf of California ending in the latitude of thirty-five degrees,"[17] and, with its map, I am sending it to Mexico to the father provincial, Juan de Estrada,[18] as his Reverence asks me to do.

The purposes of these new conquests and new conversions and of the celestial favors that we experience in them are very much and very particularly promoted by the holy, paternal letter which I have just received from our most reverend father general, Miguel Angel Tamburini,[19] who, at the same time that he furnishes a copy of most of these writings of mine, which, by order of his predecessor, Father Thirso Gonzales, went to Rome, among other paternal, most excellent, and holy things, writes me the following:

LETTER OF OUR FATHER GENERAL. Hearing of the new discoveries and of their condition, I find much to praise in the mercies of God towards those nations that are being discovered and brought to the knowledge of Him; and our Company owes special thanks to His Divine Majesty, in that he chooses its sons as instruments of so great glory to Him. I await the other two parts of the *Celestial Favors* which your Reverence promises. All these reports are such as fill me with joy and with a desire to respond to the zeal of your Reverence and of your com-

---

11. Father Juan María Salvatierra led the Jesuits in missionary activity in Baja California, 1697–1717, and held the office of provincial of New Spain.

12. Oracio Polici was a visitor in 1696. In that year and the next, Kino made several trips into present-day Arizona, at Polici's orders.

13. Perhaps an allusion to the mythical Seven Cities of Cíbola, really the pueblos of present-day New Mexico.

14. The upper parts of present-day California and lower Oregon.

15. Originally sought in upper northeastern New Mexico, this area was later named on maps as the northwestern area.

16. Gran Teguayo seems to be the name Spaniards gave to the Tewa (Tegua) country of New Mexico.

17. The manuscript does not survive, though Kino was credited with creating the analysis and a map to show the locations in a way that corrected earlier misapprehensions.

18. Estrada became acting provincial in 1707. He had served an administrative position at the Casa Profesa of Mexico.

19. Succeeding Father Tirso González, Father Michele Angelo Tamburini was general of the Jesuit Order from 1706 to 1730.

panions. But just as there are obstacles there, we regret that here wars, lack of intercourse, and the dangers of the seas detain our missionaries. But we all trust with great confidence in the loving providence of God; for since it has been His will, in such troubled times as these, to disclose those new regions, and to reveal to us the many souls that are scattered outside of His flock, it can not be in order that we may see them perish, but instead to give us means and power to draw them from their forests and reduce them to pueblos and churches. Thus, I beg his divine Majesty to guard your Reverence the many years which I desire.

Your Reverence's servant, MIGUEL ANGEL TAMBURINI. Rome, September 5, 1705.

Thus far the letter of our father general, from Rome, so laden with celestial favors. Here follow the means and forces which he says our Lord will give us to reduce so many souls to pueblos and churches. They are those which by divine grace we already have, and are as follows:

MEANS FOR THESE NEW CONVERSIONS. I. The very rich and fertile lands, abounding in wheat, maize, beans, good rivers, groves, etc. We already have made many crops, fields, and abundant harvests. II. We already have prepared many ranches of cattle, sheep, goats, and horses, not only in these new pueblos, but also very far inland, at distances of twenty, thirty, forty, fifty, and more leagues. III. We already have very good orchards and vineyards to supply wine for the masses. IV. The temperature of these new lands is similar to that of Europe. V. These new conquests are inhabited by industrious Indians. VI. The lands are mineral bearing. VII. We already have conquered these Pima Indians, who are able and accustomed to win continual victories over the enemies who infest this province of Sonora, etc. VIII. These natives on the neighboring California Gulf have very good salines, and fisheries of all kinds of palatable fish, oysters, and shrimps. They also have bezoar, the medicinal fruit called *jojoba,* blankets, cotton fabrics, curious and very showy baskets or pitchers, macaws, and feathers; and further inland there must be other means, advantages, and conveniences. IX. The harvest of the very many souls is now so ripe that all the year they come from distances of fifty, one hundred, one hundred and fifty, and more leagues, to see me and to ask me to go and baptize them, or to procure for them priests who shall go to assist, care for, and minister to them.

And although these extensive conquests will require about fifty missionary fathers, all with their customary alms or necessary supplies, your Majesty can furnish them, without its causing any new expense to the royal estate, by merely ordering that some amounts which are now being spent by it without securing the ends for which your Royal Majesty intends them, and which are therefore not profitable, be assigned to the said fifty missionary fathers of these new conquests and new conversions, who, God willing, will better achieve both purposes, as I will state in another and separate memorial.

I conclude with what, so much to our purpose and to the purposes of all, our Holy Mother Church says, prays, and sings on the first feast day in May, that of San Felipe and Santiago, namely, *Gentiles Salvatorem videre cupientes ad Philipum accesserunt,* that is, the Gentiles who wished to see the Saviour of the world drew near to Philip. And thus we see and happily experience with the very Catholic, very pious, and most Christian royal *cédula* of your Majesty, that all the innumerable Gentiles of these new conversions and new conquests of this very extensive and formerly unknown North America and Nueva Navarra, etc., in order to see, know, and love the Saviour of the world and to save themselves eternally, draw near to the most pious protection, happy obedience, and fortunate vassalage of Philip V, the very Catholic and most happy king and grand monarch of the Spains and the Indies, whose royal life may the Sovereign Divine Majesty preserve and prosper through long and most happy years with His celestial favors, for the temporal and eternal happiness of the European and American worlds, and of the universe of the heavens and of the earth, for evermore, amen. Nuestra Señora de los Dolores, of these new conquests and new conversions of Nueva Navarra,

November 21, 1708.

From your very Catholic and humble Chaplain,
Eusebio Francisco Kino.

BOOK I

CHAPTER 3 • My Arrival at These Missions of Sonora, and My First Entry into This Pimeria, with the Father Visitor, Manuel Gonzales

With this royal provision and royal *cédula,* which by its admirable Catholic zeal might well and should astonish and edify the whole world, I came in February of 1687 to these missions of Sonora, and went to Opossura to see and talk with the father visitor, who then was Father

Manuel Gonzales.[20] I found in his Reverence such charity and so holy a zeal for the welfare of souls, that his Reverence in person came at once more than fifty leagues' journey to this pueblo of Nuestra Señora de los Dolores, which is five leagues from the old mission of Cucurpe, of the rectorate of San Francisco Xavier de Sonora. On the way we passed by the mining town of San Juan[21] and saw the Señor alcalde mayor, who, with the great respectfulness that characterizes him, gave obedience to the royal *cédula* and to the royal provision. Coming by the valley of Sonora we saw the father rector of the mission or rectorate, who then was Father Juan Muños de Burgos, and by the valley and pueblo of Opodepe, Tuape, and Cocorpe,[22] divisions or pueblos then administered by Father Josep[h] de Aguilar; and on the thirteenth of March, 1687, we three Fathers together came to Nuestra Señora de los Dolores del Bamotze, or de Cosari, having the day before notified the natives. Their governor was absent, but, nevertheless, they received us with all love, for, months and years before they had asked for fathers and holy baptism.

The following day the father visitor, leaving us fathers and the children with a very paternal goodbye, returned toward Oposura to the necessary occupations of Holy Week, etc., suggesting to Father Aguilar and me that we should see later if there was opportunity to go somewhat further inland to seek and find a place where a second pueblo might be founded.

CHAPTER 4 • Expedition to San Ygnacio de Caborica, San Joseph de Los Himiris, and Nuestra Señora de Los Remedios

Upon this advice of the father visitor we at once, the very same day, went inland to the west, and after going ten leagues found the very good post of Caborica, inhabited by affable people, which by order of the father visitor we named San Ygnacio. Then, turning to the north, we found another good post, with plenty of docile and domesticated people. This place we named San Joseph de los Himires. To the east we found another, likewise of industrious In-

dians, which we named Nuestra Señora de los Remedios. It is distant from Nuestra Señora de los Dolores seven leagues, to the north.[23] In all places they received with love the Word of God for the sake of their eternal salvation. We returned, thanks to the Lord, safe and rejoicing, to Nuestra Señora de los Dolores. Father Aguilar went on to Cucurpe, and I began to catechize the people and to baptize children. The governor of Nuestra Señora de los Dolores came from inland and by him and others I sent to various and even remote parts of this Pimeria divers messages and friendly invitations, requesting that they should endeavor likewise to become Christians, saying that for them would be the good and the advantage, for I had come to aid them in order that they might be eternally saved.

CHAPTER 5 • First Opposition Experienced in This New Conversion

Being always very much aided in everything by the great charity of Father Joseph de Aguilar, by Divine grace everything went, on the part of the natives, with entire prosperity, pleasantness, and satisfaction, and there were welcome additions,[24] but on the part of others there was no lack of hostility, which has endured up to the present day. A false report was despatched to the Señor alcalde-mayor of the mining town of San Juan, that these natives, on the coming of the father missionary, had moved far away. These serious but false reports reached the father visitor, Manuel Gonzales, troubling his Reverence greatly, and he wrote to Tuape, where the three fathers, Joseph de Aguilar, Antonio de Roxas, and I were holding Holy Week,[25] with more than one hundred Pimas of this new pueblo of Nuestra Señora de los Dolores. Of the Pimas there were about forty recently baptized infants and children, whom the Spanish ladies of the mining town of Opodepe dressed richly and adorned with their ornaments and best jewels, like new Christians, for the Procession of the Blessed Sacrament, to the great delight

---

20. Kino probably went to the Ures, arriving in 1687, and obtained interpreters from these peoples.

21. The Real de San Juan was the seat of government of the *alcalde mayore* of Sonora.

22. Cucurpe was the border mission at this time, situated south of the site of mission Dolores, in the San Miguel River Valley.

23. All the missions named are in the region of the mission Dolores.

24. Records indicate that Kino baptized thirty young people at Dolores, including the children of the Indians' religious leader.

25. His Holy Week that year was March 23–30, 1687. Kino took the newly baptized from Dolores to Tuape to celebrate Holy Week, probably because the mission was incomplete.

of all; nor was there the least truth in the pretended withdrawal of the natives, which so falsely was reported to the mining town of San Juan. All this we wrote to the father visitor for his consolation, we three fathers signing the letter.

CHAPTER 6 • Second Opposition and Discord Sown in Pimeria

Returning from Holy Week and Easter at Tuape to Nuestra Señora de los Dolores, I went inland to San Ygnacio and San Joseph de los Himires, where in all places things were going very well, in spiritual and temporal matters, in Christian teaching, beginnings of baptisms, buildings, planting of crops, etc., but in Nuestra Señora de los Remedios I found the people so disconsolate that they said to me openly that they neither wished to be Christians nor to have a missionary father. On asking them why, they answered me, first, because they had heard it said that the fathers ordered the people hanged and killed; second, because they required so much labor and sowing for their churches that no opportunity was left the Indians to sow for themselves; third, because they pastured so many cattle that the watering places were drying up; fourth, because they killed the people with the holy oils; fifth, because they deceived the Indians with false promises and words, and because I had falsely said that I had a letter or royal *cédula* of the king our Sovereign, whereas I had no such letter, for if I had I would have shown it to

the Señor lieutenant of Bacanuche. These chimeras, discords, and altercations disturbed me very much, but I recognized at once whence they might have come; and although the father visitor and I had shown the royal provision which I carried, with the royal *cédula* inserted, to the Señor alcalde-mayor in the mining town of San Juan, which was sufficient there, within two days (on the tenth of May) I went with the justices[26] of Nuestra Señora de los Dolores to the mining town of Bacanuche,[27] which is twenty leagues away. I showed the royal provision and the royal *cédula* to the Señor lieutenant, Captain Francisco Pacheco Zevallos, in whom I found all kindness, and told him of what had happened in Nuestra Señora de los Remedios because of the untruths which had been spread so falsely during the preceding days against the fathers. And gradually things were remedied and the calumnies of the malicious and of the common enemy hushed, and although there was no lack of stories and pretended dangers from persons of little loyalty, the natives of this Pimeria became so inclined to our holy faith that from places further inland, from El Tupo, El Tubutama, and other parts, they asked for fathers and holy baptism.

---

26. These were Native officials.

27. Bacanuche was a *real* or mining camp, situated on the Bacanuche River, a branch of the Sonora.

FRANCISCO PALÓU (1723–1789)

Like the missionary whose life he memorialized, Francisco Palóu was born at Majorca, Spain. He entered the Franciscan order in 1739, where he studied under the tutelage of Junípero Serra, and received his ordination in 1743. When he learned of Serra's plans to join the missionary effort in New Spain, Palóu joined the small cluster of men who were sailing for the Americas. They reached Vera Cruz, Mexico, in 1749. For several years, these Franciscans engaged in missionary work in Mexico, but after Charles III expelled the Jesuit missionaries from New Spain's original dominions in 1767, Palóu joined Serra in traveling northward to work with the Indians in the areas Christianized by the Jesuits, where they benefited from the work of Kino and other Jesuits who had, fifty years in advance of this renewed Franciscan effort, mapped the geographic and religious terrain. They went first to Baja California and established missions there, but then started moving northward. They reached Loreto in the spring of 1768. When Serra was assigned to travel the next year to Alta California, Palóu remained behind to continue the missionary effort in Baja Calfornia.

Palóu evidently missed his teacher and friend and so decided to join Serra in serving the chain of missions he was establishing in Alta California. Palóu went first to San Diego, then on to Monterey-Carmel, where Serra had established a sort of headquarters for the Alta California effort. Palóu assisted in placing friars in missionary locations and collected historical data that survives today as some of the only historical records of these early California years at the time of European settlement there. Like Serra, Palóu argued that the missions needed to be maintained because the Indian converts were not ready to survive in the Spanish world. The missionaries sought to retain a guardianship of the missions in the face of encroachments by civil authorities who, eying their successes, wished to take advantage of the settlements they had created. By the time Serra died in Carmel in 1784, Palóu could count the Franciscans' progress in terms of sustained missions: New California (as Alta California had come to be called) had nine missions with eighteen Franciscans in residence. Taken together, the missions were producing a surplus from their agricultural endeavors, and their success brought more converts as the years continued. Palóu served the mission of San Francisco from 1776 to 1784. After Serra's death, he entered the presidency of Alta California, as Serra's replacement, but he lasted only a year in the post. Ailing health prevented him from fulfilling his duties well, and he stepped down in 1785. He traveled back to Mexico, where he lived the remainder of his life and completed his biography of Serra, written for the most part during his missionary stay in San Francisco.

Palóu's two key works are the *Noticias de la Nueva California* (circulated in manuscript and published in the mid-nineteenth century) and the biography of Serra, titled *Relación Histórica de la Vida y Apostólicas Tareas del Venerable Padre Fray Junípero Serra* (published in 1787). Along with only a few other documents, these two books are cornerstones in an understanding of the lives of Europeans and Indians in California at the time of Spanish settlement during the eighteenth century. Although Palóu had written much of the life of Serra while in San Francisco, he relied upon the library at San Fernando to assist his final work on the manuscript before publishing it in Mexico City in 1787. The manuscript was sent to the missions at Sonora and California, as well as to the royal palace in Madrid, Spain, and to Majorca. Palóu wrote of Serra's life as a model saint, and the form of the detailed biography falls into the genre of hagiography, the life of a saint on earth. The narrative blends epistolary documentation, re-created dialogue, impassioned exposition, and moral *sententiae*, and it serves as a useful counterpoint to similar kinds of work written by other religious groups, such as the Puritans, whose religious missions were well recorded by Cotton Mather in *Magnalia Christi Americana*.

from LIFE OF JUNÍPERO SERRA[1]

from CHAPTER 22 • The Expeditions Arrive at the Port of Monterey—The Mission and Presidio of San Carlos Are Founded

What this chapter proposes will be taken care of by the following letter which the Venerable Father wrote to me, in which he announces his arrival at Monterey and what occurred at that port.

Live Jesus Mary and Joseph!
Reverend Father Lector and
President Fray Francisco Palóu

Most dear friend and esteemed Sir:
On May 31, by God's help, after a somewhat distressful sea voyage of a month and a half, this packet-boat, the

San Antonio, with Don Juan Pérez as captain, arrived and anchored in this beautiful Port of Monterey. It is exactly the same in substance and features as the expedition of Don Sebastián Vizcaíno left it in the year 1603.[2] I was exceedingly comforted when that very night we learned that the over-land expedition had arrived fully eight days before. Father Fray Juan traveled with it. All are enjoying good health. I was further comforted when on the holyday of Pentecost, June 3, in the presence of all the officers of land and sea, together with all their subordinates, near the very same ravine and oak where the [Carmelite] Fathers of the said expedition had celebrated Mass, the altar was prepared, the bells were hung up and rung, the hymn *Veni, Creator* was sung, water was blessed, the large cross and

---

1. The text is from *Palóu's Life of Junípero Serra,* trans. and ed. Maynard J. Geiger (1955).

2. Spanish and other ships had sailed along the coast of California for some time, but the Bay of Monterey was not noted until Vizcaíno sent an expedition to the area in 1602. Plans were made at the time to settle the area, but nothing was done until Junípero Serra established a mission there.

the royal standards were set up and blessed, and I sang the first Mass known to have been celebrated here since that time. Afterwards we sang the *Salve Regina* to Our Lady before a statue given by His Excellency, which stood on the altar. During the Mass I preached to the men. We concluded the ceremonies by singing the *Te Deum.* Thereupon the civil officials performed the formal act of taking possession of the land in the name of the King, our Sovereign (may God save him!). After this we all ate together in the shade by the beach. The entire celebration was accompanied by frequent salvos from the guns aboard ship and ashore. . . .

I beg Your Reverence and earnestly request that two of the group be assigned to these missions, so as to make six with the four who are here, and to establish the Mission of San Buenaventura along the Santa Barbara Channel. It is a section of greater value than that of San Diego or Monterey or of the entire territory thus far discovered. Provisions for that mission have already been sent on two occasions. Up till now, no one has been able to blame the friars for not having established it; nor would I wish such blame to be attached once the guard is at hand for founding it. The truth is that as long as Father Fray Juan and I are on our feet, it shall not be delayed, because we shall then separate, each one going to his mission. For me it will be the greatest trial to remain alone, with the nearest priest at a distance of eighty leagues. Wherefore I beg Your Reverence to see to it that this utter loneliness of mine does not last too long a time. Father Lasuén ardently desires to come to these missions, and hence Your Reverence may keep him in mind when you have the opportunity to decide on the matter of assigning missionaries.

We are very short of wax for Mass-candles, both here and at San Diego. Nevertheless, tomorrow we are going to celebrate the feast and hold the procession of Corpus Christi, even though it be done in a poor fashion, in order to drive away whatever little devils there may be in this land. If it is possible to send some wax, it will be very helpful to us. Also the incense which I asked for on another occasion. Let Your Reverence not fail to write to His Illustrious Lordship, congratulating him on the discovery of this port and writing whatever may seem proper to you. Cease not to commend us to God. May He preserve Your Reverence for many years in His holy love and grace.

Mission San Carlos de Monterey
June [13], the feast of St. Anthony of Padua, 1770
Your most affectionate friend, companion and
servant kisses the hand of Your Reverence.
Fray Junípero Serra

On the very day they took possession of the port, they began the Royal Presidio of San Carlos and founded the mission of the same name. Adjoining the presidio they built a chapel of palings to serve as a temporary church; likewise living quarters with their respective rooms or compartments for the use of the fathers, and the necessary workshops. Both establishments were surrounded by a stockade for their protection. The natives did not show themselves during those days, since the many volleys of artillery and muskets fired by the soldiers had frightened them. But they began to approach after a little while, and the Venerable Father began to offer them gifts to bring about their entrance into the fold of Holy Church and gain their souls, which was the principle purpose of his presence. . . .

The lieutenant of the Catalonian volunteers, Don Pedro Fages, remained in charge of the New Presidio of San Carlos in Monterey. In consideration of the few soldiers he had at his disposal, in accord with the Venerable President he determined to suspend the founding of Mission San Buenaventura until a captain and nineteen soldiers should arrive. These had gone to Old California in February to return with some cattle. However, the captain with the soldiers and cattle returned only as far as San Diego, without sending to Monterey any notice of the fact. The news came only the following year by a ship, as will be seen a little further on. Since for this reason the third mission could not be established, our Venerable Father with his former pupil Fray Juan Crespí applied himself to the conversion of the Indians of Monterey, trying to attract with small gifts those who came to visit him. But since there was no one who knew their language, the missionaries experienced great difficulties in the beginning and up until the time when God desired to open the door to them by means of an Indian boy, a neophyte who had been brought along from Old California. Because of the association which the Venerable Father Junípero ordered him to maintain with the pagans for this precise purpose, he began to understand them and to pronounce some words in their tongue. So by means of this interpreter, Father Junípero was able to explain to the Indians the reason for his coming into their country, which was to guide their souls on the way to heaven.

On December 26 of that year he performed his first baptism in that pagan nation. For the fervent and ardent soul of our Venerable Father, this was the source of inexpressible joy. In time he succeeded in gaining others, and the number of Christians increased, so that three years afterwards, when I arrived at that mission, he had already baptized 165. By the time the Venerable Founder Fray Junípero closed his glorious career, he had baptized 1,014, of whom many had already died, to enjoy God in eternal life through the incessant efforts of that apostolic man.

What greatly aided these conversions, or better, what constituted the principal basis of this important conquest, were the singular marvels and prodigies which God our Lord wrought on behalf of the pagans to make them fear and love the Catholics: fear, so as to restrain them in order that so great a multitude might not treat with impudence so small a number of Christians; and love, that they might listen willingly to the evangelical doctrines which the missionaries had come to teach them, that they might embrace the sweet yoke of our holy law.

In his diary of the second over-land expedition to the Port of Monterey, Father Crespí states on May 24 (as the reader may see for himself) the following:

> After marching about three leagues, at one o'clock in the afternoon we arrived at the lagoons of salt water by the Point of Pines, toward the northeast, where on the first expedition a second cross had been erected. Before we dismounted, the governor, a soldier and I went to inspect the cross, in order to determine whether we could find any sign of the arrival of the ship there; but we found none. We beheld the cross entirely surrounded by arrows and sticks with many feathers which had been stuck in the ground by the pagans. Also there was a string of sardines, still quite fresh, hanging from a pole at one side of the cross, and another stick with a piece of meat at the foot of the cross; also a little mound of mussels.

That was a source of great wonder to all, but since they did not know the explanation, they suspended judgment.

Once the newly baptized began to converse in Spanish and the Lower California neophyte understood the Indians' language, the natives on several occasions declared the following: the very first time they saw our people the Indians noticed that all the Spaniards bore on their breasts a very resplendent cross; and when the Spaniards went away from there, leaving that large cross by the beach, the Indians were filled with such fear that they did not dare to approach so sacred an emblem. For they saw the cross shining with bright rays at a time when the rays of the sun which illumined the day were gone and were replaced by the shadows of night. They noticed, however, that the light of the cross grew so bright that it seemed to them to reach the very heavens. On beholding it during the day without these phenomena, and in its natural size, they approached it and tried to win its favor lest they suffer any

harm, and in deference to it they made their offerings of meat, fish and mussels. When to their surprise it did not consume what they offered, they placed before it feathers and arrows, showing thereby they desired peace with the Holy Cross and with the people who had erected it there.

Various Indians made this statement at different times (as I have said), and again in the year 1774 when the Venerable Father President returned from Mexico City, before whom they repeated, without the slightest variation, what they had told me the preceding year. This the servant of God, for purposes of edification, wrote to His Excellency the Viceroy, in order to increase his fervor and to encourage him at the same time in the happy realization of this spiritual enterprise. Because of this prodigy and many others which the Lord showed, the conversion of these pagans has continued with all peacefulness and without the conflict of arms. Blessed be God, to Whom be all glory and praise.

from CHAPTER 58 • The Exemplary Death of the Venerable Father Junípero

. . . I arrived on August 18 at his Mission San Carlos. There I found His Paternity in a very weakened condition, although he was up and around, and with great congestion of the chest. This condition, however, did not prevent him from going to church in the afternoon to recite the catechism and prayers with the neophytes. He concluded the devotions with the tender and pious hymns and versicles composed by the Venerable Father Margil in honor of the Assumption of the Blessed Virgin, whose octave we were celebrating. When I heard him sing with his voice as strong as usual, I remarked to a soldier who was talking to me: "It does not seem that the Father President is very sick." The soldier, who had known him since 1769, answered me: "Father, there is no basis for hope: he is ill. This saintly priest is always well when it comes to praying and singing, but he is nearly finished." . . .

We spoke leisurely on the matters for which he had called me, until the ship arrived. However, I was always in fear he would shortly die, for whenever I would enter into his little room or cell of adobes, I always found him quite interiorly recollected, although his companion told me he had acted this way ever since his faculty to confirm had expired. This, as I have stated before, was on the very day the ship anchored at these missions [of San Francisco]. Five days after I arrived at Monterey, the packet-boat anchored at that port. Immediately the royal surgeon went over to the mission to visit the Reverend Father

President. Finding his chest in so bad a condition, he suggested hot poultices to expel the phlegm that had accumulated in the chest. The Father President told him to apply whatever remedy he chose. He did, but with no effect other than to cause further pain to that already worn-out body. But he did not show the least sign of pain, either at this strong application or at the agonies he was suffering. He acted as if he were not sick at all, always up and about as if he were well. When some of the cloth from the supplies of the ship was brought over, with his own hands he began to cut it up and distribute it to the neophytes to cover their nakedness.

On August 25 he told me he was disappointed that the fathers from Missions San Antonio and San Luis Obispo had not arrived, and that possibly the letters he had written them were delayed. I immediately sent word to the presidio, and the letters were brought over with the information that they had been overlooked. As soon as I saw their contents, an invitation to the fathers for a final farewell, I sent a courier with these letters, adding a message that the fathers should come posthaste, for I feared that our beloved superior would not be long with us because of his very weakened condition. And although the priests set out as soon as they received those letters, they did not arrive in time. The one from Mission San Antonio, which was twenty-five leagues away, arrived after his death and could assist only at his burial. The one from San Luis Obispo, fifty leagues away, arrived three days later and was able to be present at the commemorative services only on the seventh day after his death, as I shall point out later.

On August 26 he arose, weaker still. He told me he had passed a bad night. As a result, he desired to prepare himself for whatever God might decree with regard to him. He remained secluded the entire day, admitting not a single distraction. That night he made his general confession to me amid many tears, and with a clear mind just as if he were well. When this was over, after a brief period of reflection he took a cup of broth and then went to rest, his wish being that no one remain with him in his little room.

As soon as morning dawned on the 27th, I went to visit him and found him saying his breviary, since it was his custom always to commence Matins before daybreak. On the road he always began it as soon as morning dawned. When I asked him how he had spent the night, he answered: "As usual." Nevertheless, he asked me to consecrate a Host and reserve It, and he would let me know when he wanted to receive. I did, and after finishing Mass I returned to tell him, and then he said he would like to receive the Most Holy Viaticum, and that for this he would go to the church. When I told him that was not necessary, that his cell could be fixed up in the best way possible and that the divine Majesty would come to visit him, he said, "No," that he wanted to receive Him in church, since if he could walk there, there was no need for the Lord to come to him. I had to give in and grant his holy desires. He went by himself to the church (more than a hundred yards distant), accompanied by the commandant of the presidio, who came to the ceremony with part of the soldiers (who were joined by the soldiers of the mission); and all the Indians of the town or mission accompanied the sick and devout priest to the church, all of them with great tenderness and piety.

When His Paternity reached the step of the sanctuary, he knelt down before a little table prepared for the ceremony. I came out of the sacristy vested, and on arriving at the altar, as soon as I prepared the incense to begin the devotional ceremony, the fervent servant of God intoned in his natural voice, as sonorous as when he was well, the verse *Tantum ergo Sacramentum,* singing it with tears in his eyes. I gave him the Holy Viaticum, according to the ceremonies of the ritual. When this very devotional function was over, which I had never seen in such circumstances, His Paternity remained in the same posture, kneeling, giving thanks to the Lord. When he was finished, he returned to his little cell accompanied by all the people. Some shed tears from devotion and tenderness, others out of sadness and sorrow because they feared they would be left without their beloved father. He remained alone in his cell in meditation, seated on the chair at the table. When I beheld him thus absorbed, I saw no reason to enter to talk to him. . . .

During the night he felt worse, and he asked to be anointed. This holy sacrament he received seated on an *equipal,* a little stool made of rushes. He recited with us the Litany of All Saints and the Penitential Psalms. He spent the entire night without sleep, the greater part of it on his knees, while he pressed his chest against the boards of his bed. When I suggested that he lie down awhile, he answered that in that position he felt more relieved. Other short periods of the night he spent seated on the floor, leaning against the lap of some of the neophytes. All night long his little cell was filled with these neophytes, drawn there by the great love they had for him as for the father who had begotten them anew in the Lord. When I saw him in this state of exhaustion and leaning against the arms of the Indians, I asked the surgeon how he thought he was. He answered (since the father appeared to be in a very critical state): "It seems to me that this blessed father wants to die on the floor."

I went in soon after and asked him if he wished absolution and the application of the plenary indulgence. He answered "Yes," and prepared himself. On his knees he received the plenary absolution, and I gave him also the plenary indulgence of the Order, with which he was most happy. He passed the entire night in the manner described. The feast of the Doctor of the Church St. Augustine dawned, August 28, and he appeared relieved. He did not experience so much congestion in his chest. During the whole night he had not slept or taken anything. He spent the morning seated on the rush stool, leaning against the bed. This bed consisted of some roughhewn boards, covered by a blanket serving more as a covering than as an aid to rest, for he never used even a sheepskin covering, such as was customary at our college. Along the road he used to do the same thing. He would stretch the blanket and a pillow on the ground, and he would lie down on these to get his necessary rest. He always slept with a crucifix upon his breast, in the embrace of his hands. It was about a foot in length. He had carried it with him from the time he was in the novitiate at the college, nor did he ever fail to have it with him. On all his journeys he carried it with him, together with the blanket and pillow. At his mission and whenever he stopped, as soon as he got up from bed he placed the crucifix upon the pillow. Thus he had it on this occasion when he did not wish to go to bed during the entire night or next morning, on the day when he was to deliver his soul to his Creator.

About ten o'clock in the morning on that feast of St. Augustine, the officers of the frigate came to visit him. . . .

After listening to them, he said: "Well, gentlemen, I thank you that after such a long time, during which we have not seen each other, and after making such a long voyage, you have come from so far off to this port to throw a little earth upon me." On hearing this, the gentlemen and all the rest of us present were surprised, seeing him seated on the little rush stool and hearing him answer everything with full mental faculties. But, scarcely concealing their tears which they could not restrain, they said: "No, Father, we trust that God will still make you well and enable you to continue this conquest." The servant of God (who, if he did not have a foreknowledge of the hour of his death, could not but know that it was near at hand) answered them: "Yes, yes, do me this favor and work of mercy; throw a little bit of earth upon my body, and I shall be greatly indebted to you." And casting his eyes upon me, he said: "I desire you to bury me in the church, quite close to Father Fray Juan Crespí for the present; and when the stone church is built, they may put me wherever they want."

When my tears allowed me to speak, I said to him: "Father President, if God is pleased to call you to Himself, it will be done as Your Paternity wishes. In that case, I ask Your Paternity out of love and the great affection you have always had for me, that when you arrive in the presence of the Most Blessed Trinity, you adore the Same in my name, and that you be not unmindful of me; and do not forget to pray for all the dwellers in these missions, particularly for those here present." He answered: "I promise, if the Lord in His infinite mercy grants me that eternal happiness, which I do not deserve because of my faults, that I shall pray for all and for the conversion of so many pagans whom I leave unconverted."

Within a short time he asked me to sprinkle his little room with holy water, and I did. When I asked him if he felt some pain, he said "No"; but he asked me to do it so he would have none. He remained in profound silence. All of a sudden, very frightened, he said to me: "Great fear has come upon me; I have a great fear. Read me the Commendation for a Departing Soul, and say it aloud so I can hear it." I did as he asked, while all the gentlemen from the ship assisted. Also present were his priest companion, Fray Matías Noriega, and the surgeon, and many others both from the ship and from the mission. I read for him the Commendation for a Departing Soul, to which the Venerable Father, though dying, responded as if he were well, just sitting there on his little rush stool, moving the hearts of us all to tenderness.

As soon as I finished, he broke out in words full of joy, saying: "Thanks be to God, thanks be to God, all fear has now left me. Thanks be to God, I have no more fear, and so let us go outside." All of us retired to a little outside room with His Paternity. When we noticed this change, we were at one and the same time surprised and happy. . . .

He sat on the chair by the table, picked up his diurnal and began to pray. As soon as he was finished, I told him it was already after one o'clock in the afternoon, and asked him if he would like a cup of broth. He said "Yes." He took it and, after giving thanks, said: "Now, let us go to rest." He walked to his little room where he had his bed. He took off only his mantle and lay down over the boards covered with a blanket, with his holy crucifix mentioned above, in order to rest. We all thought he was going to sleep, as during the whole night he had not slept any. The gentlemen went out to eat. Since I was a little uneasy, after a short time I returned and approached his bed to see if he was sleeping. I found him just as we had left him a little before, but now asleep in the Lord, without having given any sign or trace of agony, his body showing no other sign of death than the cessation of breathing; on the contrary, he seemed to be sleeping. We piously believe that he went to sleep in the Lord a little before two in the afternoon, on the feast of St. Augustine in the year 1784, and that he went to receive in heaven the reward of his apostolic labors.

He ended his laborious life when he was seventy years, nine months and four days old. He lived in the world sixteen years, nine months and twenty-one days; as a religious fifty-three years, eleven months and thirteen days, of which he spent thirty-five years, four months and thirteen days as apostolic missionary. During this time he performed the glorious deeds of which we have read, in which his merits were more numerous than his steps. He lived in continuous activity, occupied in virtuous and holy exercises and in outstanding deeds, all directed to the greater glory of God and the salvation of souls. And would not one who labored so much for them, not labor much more for his own? Much there is that I could say, but this demands more time and more leisure. If God grants me this, and it is His most holy will, I shall not refuse the task of writing something about his heroic virtues for the sake of edification and good example.

As soon as I satisfied myself that we were now orphans, bereft of the amiable company of our venerable superior, that he was not sleeping but actually dead, I ordered the neophytes who were standing there to ring the bells in order to make the news known. As soon as the double peal rang out the sad news, the whole town assembled, weeping over the death of their beloved father who had begotten them anew in the Lord and who was more esteemed by them than if he had been their natural father. All wanted to see him in order to give vent to the sorrow that filled their hearts, and to express it in tears. So great was the crowd of people, including Indians and soldiers and sailors, that it was necessary to close the door in order to place him in the coffin that His Paternity had ordered to be made the day before. And in order to prepare his shroud, we had to do nothing else than to take off his sandals (which the captain of the packet-boat and the Father Chaplain, who were present, received as keepsakes).

He remained in the shroud in which he died, that is, the habit, the cowl and the cord, but no inner tunic, for the two which he had for use on his journeys he had sent out to be washed six days before, together with a change of underclothing, which he did not care to use, for he wanted to die wearing only the habit, cowl and cord.

When the venerable corpse was placed in the coffin, and six burning candles were placed about it, the door of his cell was opened, which his saddened sons, the neophytes, immediately entered with their wreaths of wild flowers of varied hues, in order to grace the remains of the deceased Venerable Father. The remains were kept in the cell until nightfall, a continuous concourse of people entering and coming out. They were praying to him and touching rosaries and medals to his venerable hands and face, openly calling him "Holy Father," "Blessed Father," and other names dictated by the love they bore him, and by the heroic virtues which they had witnessed in him during life.

At nightfall we carried the remains to the church in procession. This was composed of the town of neophytes and the soldiers and sailors who remained. The remains were placed on a table surrounded by six lighted candles, and the ceremony was concluded with a response. They asked me to leave the church open in order to keep guard over the remains, and alternately to recite the Rosary for the soul of the deceased. They renewed the watch at set intervals, thus passing the whole night in continual prayer. I consented to this and left two soldiers as a guard to prevent any kind of indiscreet piety or theft, for all desired to obtain some little thing which the deceased had used. Chiefly the seamen and the soldiers, who had known him better and who had a great opinion of the virtue and sanctity of the deceased Venerable Father and who had dealt with him at sea and on land, asked me for some little article from among the things he had used. Although I promised all I would satisfy them after his burial, this was not enough to prevent them from cutting away small pieces of his habit from below, so it would not be noticed, and part of the hair of his tonsure, the guard being unable to restrain them, if it was not that he abetted them and participated in the pious theft. All wanted to obtain some memorial of the deceased, although such was the opinion they had of him that they called such items relics. I tried to correct them and explain it to them.

JOSÉ LONGINOS MARTÍNEZ (?–1803)

José Longinos Martínez, the naturalist assigned to Spain's Royal Scientific Expedition to New Spain (also called the Royal Botanical Expedition) in 1787, was certainly the most singular of the men who were sent to explore, in the name of scientific enlightenment, the territories held by New Spain. A native of Cala-horra, on the upper Ebro River, Longinos Martínez studied in Madrid under Don Casimiro Gómez Ortega, director of the Royal Botanical Garden there, gaining a practical, rather than a formal, university training in the natural sciences, but particularly in the arts of taxidermy and surgery. The source of Longinos Martínez's education and its association with the practical, not the theoretical, sciences, in addition to the affiliation of surgery and taxidermy with the kind of work done by barbers, rather than physicians—all probably contributed to the particular disregard in which Longinos Martínez was held by his major asso-ciate in the royal scientific enterprise, Dr. Martíde Sessé y Lacasta. Although the disputes between the two scientists caused a breakdown in the original plans of the Royal Scientific Expedition, they resulted in Longinos Martínez's setting off on his own and creating a scientific document unique among the records of early California.

Longinos Martínez had considerable skill in collecting and interpreting specimens, particularly animal specimens. For this reason, he experienced difficulty with the orders given him during the first expedition trip, in 1788, by the expedition party's leader, Sessé. While Sessé preferred that the exploring party re-main together while traveling—such an approach would ensure collaboration among the botanists col-lecting plant specimens—Longinos Martínez tended to stray from the group so as to collect items, in-cluding animals, that were of particular importance to his own interests. As the end of their first expeditionary mission neared, Longinos Martínez petitioned to remain behind with one of the expedi-tion's painters, in Mexicalzingo, while the botanists returned to Mexico City. He remained apart, by de-sign it seems, from the second excursion as well, probably because he was preparing to set up his own museum of stuffed specimens in Mexico City. Longinos Martínez planned to open his museum in the summer of 1790, offering this announcement about its prospects to the public: "The Naturalist . . . will explore and investigate everything produced on the surface of the Earth, as well as in her Bowels, exam-ining valleys, hills, quarries, mines, and the loftiest peaks, and deserts and volcanoes, descending to the rivers and the seas, and collecting everywhere the varied products of Nature. He will send to the Royal Museum of Madrid all the more important specimens, reserving the duplicates for the enrichment of this Museum, which in the course of time will not be inferior to that of Spain, now competing with the best of Europe." This move to go out on his own while taking advantage of the auspices of the Royal Botanical Expedition infuriated the expedition party leaders so much that, upon petition, the two scientists, Longi-nos Martínez and Sessé, would thereafter engage in their own separate excursions.

The next year, 1791–92, Longinos Martínez, set off on the memorable scientific excursion he recorded in a journal and sent, on demand for it, to Viceroy Conde de Revillagigedo, in Mexico City. On his own—partly because he preferred it that way, partly because no one with education was willing to travel with him, and partly because the one "student" who was sent with him was of no assistance to him—Longinos Martínez traveled an immense amount of territory, from Mexico City to San Blas on the coast, then across the Gulf of California to Loreto, and then around the whole peninsula from Cabo (Cape) San Lucas north-ward. He crossed into Alta California at San Diego and visited the mission there and went on to the mis-sions at San Capistrano and San Gabriel. After an interesting stop at Rancho Brea (within present-day Los Angeles), he continued his journey northward to Santa Barbara and then Monterey. He returned to San Blas by sail and then trekked inland to Mexico City after a year of further exploration—not recorded in the journal—in Mexico. Longinos Martínez finally returned to Mexico City in early 1794, but he was un-happy there because of accusations and counteraccusations among the scientists regarding their relative successes in the field. He left Mexico City on an authorized excursion to Guatemala, never returning to the capital city. Arriving in Guatemala City in the summer of 1796, Longinos Martínez proceeded to establish a Museum of Natural History under the auspices of Jacobo de Villa Urrutia, director of the Economics Society of the Friends of the Country. Reports about his museum highly complimented the naturalist, and Longinos Martínez finally seems to have received the praise he had sought for his efforts all along. He died of tuberculosis while on a journey to Yucatán in 1803.

Although he was sometimes given to pomposity, Longinos Martínez was well aware that he was fulfilling for Spain an obligation to present, for the world to view, Spain's accomplishments in behalf of Enlightenment. Spain had long been accused by Western European powers of being backward in its ways, in part because of the "Black Legend" of Spain that emanated from the first century of Spain's conquest of the Americas. Longinos Martínez's journal, written with the expectation that it would be made public, contains lively descriptions of the natural phenomena he saw and the peoples he visited, records of scientific calculations, and observations upon Spain's potential for export from and manufacture within areas of Baja and Alta California. With an eye to joining the ranks of the most renowned natural philosophers of his day—Buffon, Raynal, de Pauw, Linnaeus, and Humboldt—Longinos Martínez created the first explicitly "scientific" record that would, he hoped, be circulated around the globe as a symbol of Spain's expeditionary and observational achievements in the Americas.

from THE JOURNAL OF JOSÉ LONGINOS MARTÍNEZ[1]

from PART TWO • JOURNEY THROUGH OLD CALIFORNIA, CAPE SAN LUCAS TO MISSION SAN MIGUEL

Customs, Arms, and Clothing

From Lat. 23 (Cape San Lucas) to Lat. 28 (San Ignacio), there are hardly any Indians left, as I have said, and the few who remain have kept none of their ancient customs except only their language. Those of the Cape, Santiago, and Todos Santos are Guaicuros and Pericos. In the rest of [Old] California, comprising more than fifty language groups, the Indians are given only the name of the place or mission where they live. The few Indians who are left in the missions from the Cape to San Ignacio, men as well as women, have very good features, are fairly lively and fond of music, particularly the violin. They practice none of their ancient dances, which are said to have been very obscene. When they are allowed to dance they perform those they have learned from the whites, or those that have become established in the missions. The only one they practice in their own style is called *la pescola*,[2] in

which a man comes out with clappers and dances alone with very violent movements.

They are addicted to gambling and, those who associate with the whites, to the chances of cards. But pelota is their most common game. They play it very dextrously with the shoulder, arm, hand, and foot, although the most usual way is with the hand alone. Pelota and the manner of playing it are the same as with us. The thing is to knock the ball over a board dividing the two sides, the side upon which the ball dies losing the point. Women as well as men play it, and they [all] do so with such enthusiasm that on the feast days when it is permitted they become very fatigued and out of breath with the continuous exercise. This game is such a vice with them that on such feast days, from the time they hear Mass at seven or eight in the morning until they go to prayers at six in the evening, they are to be found playing in the sunniest spots, even in the hottest season, rarely changing players.

They have another game which is played with four small sticks, white on one side and black on the other, of about a span in length and a finger in thickness. These they toss, the game going to the player who tosses the greatest number of sticks with the white or the black side up.

These nations are generally much given to the vice of lechery. They watch over their women very little, and it frequently happens that the husbands themselves offer their wives to travelers.

They are fairly enduring in work, women as well as men, and those of the coast are skillful at fishing and diving. They fish with tridents, harpoons, and hooks, and they get around in a sort of raft made of rushes or canes and shaped like a small boat. They put out to sea in this

---

1. The text is from *Journal of José Longinos Martínez,* trans. and ed. Lesley Byrd Simpson (1961).

2. *La pascola,* a ritual dance still practiced by the Yaqui and Sinaloa Indians.

rudimentary craft, one man in each manipulating a double paddle, half-kneeling or squatting, and are lost to sight for many hours.

They endure hunger and thirst very well, but on occasion they are voracious eaters, one of them alone being capable of eating as much as a dozen ordinary men, without its having any ill effect on them. They are also fond of wine and rum and, if given the opportunity, they will drink until intoxicated. They like to smoke, gathering a kind of wild tobacco with which to satisfy their vice, because of the difficulty they have in procuring that of the tobacco monopoly.

The Indians of this part of California have no weapon but the arrow, which they use with great skill in hunting and war.

The Indians of the missions wear cotton shirts and pantaloons, but for working they wear only a breechclout. The women also wear cotton shirts and skirts, with kerchiefs or blankets. From Mission San Borja to the boundary of El Rosario they live in rancherías like the gentiles, with the single difference that the men wear a breechclout and have to go to Mass at the Mission every fortnight.

Those of the rancherías live in great poverty, because the missionaries do not look after them with the careful attention that they give to those settled in the [mission] villages. So the men [of the rancherías] wear nothing but a breechclout, and most of the women only a small apron made of many strings of cane joints, like bunches of rosaries; behind, they wear a deer or *berrendo*[3] skin. Their dwellings consist only of a few branches thrown together to give them a little shade. The men occupy themselves in catching an occasional deer (those who have the skill for it, who are very few), or a squirrel, mouse, gopher, rabbit, or any other small animal, whatever it may be, because, as I have said, they will eat anything, and weeds as well as seeds. They are so disgusting and naturally vile that this is the only place in California where they have been observed to pick up dried human excrement, prepare it in the form of pinole, and eat it. This they call "second crop."[4] Another bit of filth current among them is called *maroma.* When they find a piece of meat to their liking, five, six, eight, or more of them will gather in a circle and tie a piece of string to the meat, which each swallows in turn, after which it is pulled up again when it has rested a while in the esophagus or gullet, and makes the round of the cir-

cle until it is consumed. This practice, which I have witnessed, proves how barbarous they are and how voracious in eating. Even those of the coast prefer sea lions and turtles to more palatable fish, and if a whale gets stranded they eat its blubber and other parts, considering them great delicacies, even though the whale has been stranded for several days and stinks. Such is the nastiness of these people that the basket (*cora*) the women wear on their heads is also made to serve as a urinal and a dish for their food.

The form of the arrow, which is their only weapon, varies little among the Indians of Old California. The only differences occur in the points, which they make from stone or flint, the hardest, toughest, and most pleasing to the eye. I used this evidence to determine the presence of any useful rocks, such as crystal, carnelian, etc., as I did several times.

All these recently conquered Indians have been extremely docile, making little resistance at the time of their conquest. It is said that only two or three rancherías of Calamajué conspired for a time to molest the soldiers who approached them. Today all of them as far [north] as this mission [of Calamajué] are reduced to the brotherhood of the Church and not the slightest unrest has been noticed among them.

The stretch from San Borja [rather, San Fernando Velicatá] to San Diego, known by the name of Fronteras among the missions that lie between, is much more populous, and many gentiles live in the vicinity of all the missions. From San Borja to the mouth of the Colorado River, which lies at the parallel of Mission Santo Tomás, their principal diet is *mescal tatemado*[5] and seeds. Those of the coast eat fish; those of the brush, the numerous rabbits which they hunt with great zeal for the women's *tápalos,* made with the skins, as the coast dwellers make them of otter skins.

The gentiles of this whole stretch of 200 leagues between the two missions, together with the Indians of Missions San Miguel, Santo Tomás, San Vicente, El Rosario, and San Fernando, speak some fourteen different languages in that short distance, and one has the annoyance of having to pass one's questions or conversation through three or four captured interpreters.

Among these gentiles the men generally go completely naked, and have not the slightest shame at appear-

---

3. *Berrend,* a pronghorned antelope.

4. The undigested seeds excreted, probably of *pitaya* fruit.

5. The roasted head of the agave (*tatemar,* in Mexico, means "roast").

ing in this fashion at any time before a person they have never seen before. In some parts of the mountains of the Colorado River [country] many women go about in the same way, or at most they wear a straw apron, or an apron of other materials, such as rows of canes worn like a long fringe, and over the buttocks a piece of untanned deer or *berrendo* skin. They also wear over their shoulders a blanket or shawl made of twisted strips of rabbit, otter, or fox skin—this last in the mountains. They weave a kind of oblong shawl of the twisted cords, the corners tied together, the head and one arm thrust through the upper opening.

Their marriage ceremony consists of [the bridegroom's] bringing gifts of food three times to the closest relatives of the bride, such as the father, mother, etc. On the day they receive the third gift, without further contract they deliver their daughter to her husband. Some are able to have as many as three wives, the number being determined by the husband's ability as a hunter, fisherman, or warrior. Divorce occurs when either party has a just complaint for any reason whatever. Although divorce is easy, it happens very infrequently.

All the rancherías have a chief to whom they yield the utmost obedience. The chieftainship always passes from father to son, or to the nearest relative. Some rancherías join with others to make war on common enemies. These wars always originate, either in their trespassing on each other's territories to gather seeds, or in disputes over women. They are very expert with the arrow, sling, and a curved stick they use for hunting rabbits.

They burn their dead in a great fire, fanning the ashes repeatedly. If a sick man is old and considered incurable they usually burn him alive. If an enemy dies in battle he is not burned but, as an insult, is flayed and thrown out for the beasts to eat.

Women in the last stage of pregnancy are buried in a hole up to the waist and, after the birth of the child, their bellies are entirely covered with ashes and damp earth, and hot stones are placed upon them for several hours.

Their dwellings are nothing but small inclosures of stones placed one upon the other, without clay or mortar of any kind, being hardly more than shelters made of branches. Farther north very small houses are erected against the winter, half buried in the ground, the roof covered with branches, straw, and earth. If water is available near by they remove their rancherías frequently, in order to get rid of the fleas and other vermin that infest them.

In most of the rancherías there is a man venerated for his mystery who, as if he were a prophet, predicts famine, sickness, war, and other calamities. This fellow is usually the greatest rascal among them and always fabricates another lie when his predictions turn out to be false. Thus he keeps them all in fear of him, and all contribute what they can to his support in order to keep him happy and friendly, for no one can shake their belief in the childish things they attribute to him.

In spite of their ferocity and skill in war, all these nations are very docile in their acceptance of a new religion. What some of the gentiles fear most before their conversion is the punishment and daily work stints in the missions. Another thing that makes them fearful is the wrong that is done them in forcing them to abandon their own land, which they love exceedingly. Nothing, therefore, can be done with the new Christians unless they are given permission now and then to visit their relatives for a few days.

Their games are very innocent. The most common one is played every evening after work in the missions; it is called *panimai*. They take two sticks in their hands, which they hide [behind their backs]; then, with a thousand jingles, grimaces, and gestures, they bring them out again closed and their opponents have to guess what hand the sticks are concealed in. Another game of theirs is a continual running back and forth over a short course of eight or ten paces. From either end they throw two small sticks, the winner being the one who throws them the greatest number of times in the form of a cross. But the game that exhausts them and prostrates many for days is one in which they drive a ball with their feet, to see who can kick it most rapidly two or three leagues to a goal and bring it back to the starting point in the same fashion.

Among all the gentile peoples it is the women who do most of the work. They gather the seeds, clean them, make the pinoles, carry the firewood, and do all the household chores. During removals it is the women who carry the burdens, together with their children and all their possessions. They make baskets of every size and shape from the root of the rush; in them they carry their seeds. With yarn spun from the fibers of certain plants they weave a handsome fabric, which they make into a kind of purse or round sack.

The only occupation of the men is to roam the brush with bow and arrow, which they do for sport, to see if they might kill something.

All the gentiles in general are extremely reserved when one tries to get them to explain their customs.

The cords (*mecate*) and their other yarns are made from a species of *Asclepia* and mallows, and from their own hair; their bow strings, of the tendons of deer and certain fishes. The seeds they use in their pinoles are those of the *Quenopodium Fretido* [*Chenopodium Fetidum*] which they call *quaich;* the California sage (*Salvia Californica*), called *ucasan;* another species of sage (*pasinor*); a small variety called *panch;* a species of *Geranco* [*Geranio?*], called *gabat.* This last usually causes baldness, and for this reason they use it very little. They gather great crops of these and other seeds, as well as pine nuts, acorns, etc., by which many millions [*sic*] of gentiles are sustained. When the crops are good they celebrate the end of the harvest with dances, festivities, and merrymaking.

Dances are performed for various reasons. The one they perform for grief is done with a costume, that is, a kind of blanket adorned with hair, odd figures, and other gewgaws which they hang upon it. They call this dance *cabellera.* The one they perform as a votive offering is done with great merriment, with several live birds of prey and other animals placed in the center of the circle of dancers. The marriage dance is performed with obscene and lascivious gestures.

In the high mountains of Fronteras, near the Colorado River, the dancing place is ornamented with the most pleasing and curious possessions of those who attend. All their dances are performed by many at the same time, accompanying themselves with rattles and loud singing, in which the bystanders participate.

For these dances and gatherings some of the men and boys paint their bodies to look like soldiers [soldiers' uniforms], whom some of them have seen. They paint on a black coat, white waistcoat, white stockings, red pantaloons, black shoes with buckles, and they [even] paint buttons and buttonholes of a different color on the coat and waistcoat. The women paint their bodies with red ochre, their faces black from the nose down, the rest white. Others do the contrary: the upper part black, the lower white. The rancherías have distinctive patterns of painting by which they can be recognized in any gathering.

Men and women both pierce their ears and the central cartilage of the nose. The girl who seems to have some beauty is marked with a crosshatch of lines and other figures on her cheeks, nose, lips, forehead, and chin. These lines, which are permanent, are made with the thorn of bishop's weed (*Ammi Visnaga*), or the point of a vitreous stone. They are rubbed afterward with black earth or ground charcoal and she thus remains marked for life.

Girls of twelve to fifteen come eagerly to the missions and become Christians, doubtless because at that age the men begin to pursue them and because they see what a burdensome thing matrimony will be, with the trouble it brings in caring for their husbands and children, and their other duties. Hence they seek the easier life of the missions. Parents willingly give up their children to the missions and have them converted; this they do without reluctance for some slight gift, such as food, glass beads, and thread. With gifts such as these I obtained seven girls in different gentile rancherías and left them in the adjacent missions. The old women are the greatest enemies of religion and the ones who object to giving up the children.

The general appearance of the Indians of Fronteras is as follows: They are rather large, well formed, strong, not very ugly, without hair on their chins or any other part of their body, save the head. This is not because they are born that way, but because they carefully pluck it out hair by hair as soon as it appears, with the aid of a small stick, leaving half of it [on the head] uncut *para que goznee.*[6] The coast dwellers make use of a certain bivalve shell, of the best shape and fineness, for small tweezers, and [with it] they leave not a hair on their bodies.

No idolatry has been noted among these Indians [of Fronteras], their only belief being that there is some Deity who rules over everything, although they do not represent Him with images. Nor does their belief arise from principle, for they recognize Him only in their minds, following in this what their witch doctors tell them, taking it on faith.

When I arrived in Fronteras I heard a story from a new Christian to the effect that a rebellion had occurred a short time before in the missions, and it was confirmed by the missionaries at San Fernando, El Rosario, and Santo Domingo. These three missions share the Indians of the highlands of the Valley of San Rafael, and in all of them the neophytes are [now] contented.

They told me that on the summit of the range there is a great water, which is their way of indicating a lagoon which, like the ocean, has fish and otters in it. They said that whoever should be immersed in it or drank the water died at once. In spite of their solemnity and mystery, I suspected that it was only one of their many superstitions. At the same time, in case there might be something to the story which was beyond their comprehension, and because they assured me that the lake was in a beautiful spot, I decided to make an expedition to that land of gentiles—this in spite of the rough appearance of the mountains, for I wished to explore the country as far as the Port

---

6. Perhaps the hair was cut down the middle.

of San Felipe de Jesús (where, they said, the configuration of the coast formed a port), and because I wished to see the end of the Gulf which I had touched at so many places.

I left Mission Santo Domingo on July 17, 1792, with an escort of five soldiers, three servants from the Mission, and twelve Indians, including new Christians and friendly gentiles. Between daybreak and noon I covered seven leagues over a bad road of hills and canyons to a place called Valladares, where it crosses the early route of the conquest. The way was thick with roses of Castile, rosemary, poppies (*Papaver Californicus*), juniper, alder (*Betula*), willow, sage (both the apothecary's and *Salvia Californica*), etc. We passed several gentile rancherías with few people in them, for it seems they were still out harvesting their seeds. Valladares is very green, with a large creek [Arroyo de Valladares] flowing through it from the mountains. After eating we followed the creek to its source, arriving there a little before sundown, having covered five leagues in the shade of the plants mentioned, and some others, without encountering any more rancherías, although there were many signs of gentiles. We set out up a very steep slope, which we had to climb on foot because of the grade, and about an hour after nightfall we stopped half way up on a shelf or small plain. This night we met no gentiles either. The following morning I continued up the slope, reaching the summit at eight.

Scattered pines began to appear toward the middle of the ascent, and the summit was covered with a thick forest of several kinds of immense pines. We traversed this forest ENE, crossing hills and ravines flowing with little crystalline streams. About ten in the morning we came to a level place perhaps half a league long and half a block (*cuarto*) wide, thickly covered with cynodon (*grama*) [possibly couch grass, *Triticum Repens*], free of trees or shrubs, surrounded by pine forests, very high ranges of mountains, and outcroppings of living rock. This flat is crossed by a narrow creek a half or three-quarters of a vara wide and two varas [*sic*] deep, which is the greatest size it attains there, carrying about a vara of clear sweet water. The creek has its source at the base of the very high mountain north of the valley, where we found several rancherías with a fair number of gentiles in them. Continuing in the same direction, over plateaus and ravines, at about eleven I came to a beautiful valley, some two leagues long and half a league wide, also free of trees and covered with cynodon. The pines surrounding it are astonishingly large; I measured several of them which were fourteen to sixteen varas in circumference. This forest ex-

tends to the foot of several ranges of steep, high, and rocky peaks.

In the thick grassy meadows of this valley, which could afford pasturage for every kind of cattle, I noticed small patches of the flax that is cultivated in Spain. There is a great deal of sage on the hills and in the surrounding valleys, together with madroño, tobacco, rose of Castile, larkspur, etc. The valley is well watered by five large streams flowing in from different directions, and at its entrance, through which all these streams discharge, it is somewhat marshy and has a deep pond, the source of the river flowing through Mission Santo Domingo. In spite of its sandy bed, most of the year it reaches the sea.

One of the most famous chiefs of the mountains has his ranchería in the woods near this valley, and many others surround his. The valley is about in the center of the mountains.

Continuing in the same direction, I crossed other creeks, hills, and ravines, and at about two in the afternoon arrived at the "great water." When we sighted it the new Christians and gentile friends of the escort, along with others who had joined them, began to drop behind and take up positions on the highest spots, from which they could watch us when we reached the lake, thinking they would see us fall dead. Notwithstanding my conviction that it was one of their superstitious beliefs, I did not allow the soldiers of my escort to taste the water until I had analyzed it, in case the belief originated in its being impregnated with minerals or particles that might have caused the death of some person. I performed this operation and found that the water was one of the finest that could be drunk, for it had its source in the forest and carried not the slightest trace of mineral. Then we all drank of it, and the neophytes and gentiles were forced to drink and bathe in it, to show them their error.

They said that the animals they imagined they had seen in the lake from a distance were only trees. Among other superstitions, they venerated a high hill near the lake, saying that whoever slept with his back toward it, or performed his necessities there, died immediately. We destroyed this belief by obliging them to present their bare behinds to the said hill, by way of ridiculing their superstition. After our exposure of the "great water" it was easy to get them to perform this act of disrespect.

The two valleys we had seen [before] were excellent, but they were not to be compared with this last one, to which we gave the name of El Carmen. It is an enclosed valley with a beautiful view from every point. It is free of trees and shrubs; it is surrounded by level woods of very large pines, and has several outlets to smaller valleys. It is watered by three large streams, by which the whole floor of the valley could be irrigated. It was so covered with flax, more so than the one already described, that it seemed to have been sown with it. All the streams flow into the enchanted lake, which in turn feeds a river that I followed. That afternoon I had a load of flax picked in order to have it worked at the Mission. We spent the night in this valley, unmolested by gentiles, who were all at their rancherías, driven away to a league round about by their fear of the lake.

The next day, after making a careful reconnaissance of the surroundings, I continued my journey by a wide ravine in the same ENE direction. At the mouth of the ravine we emerged upon the descent to the Valley of San Rafael [probably the Valley of San Felipe, since the Valley of San Rafael is 20 leagues to the NW]. The descent is very difficult. From it to the Port of San Felipe de Jesús is somewhat over three leagues across the narrows of the Valley of San Rafael [San Felipe, as above]. Continuing NE, I could see at low tide the mouth of the Colorado River about eight leagues distant. This whole stretch is thickly populated with gentiles, whose great numbers forced me to turn back without examining the mouth of the said river as I had desired.

The gentiles of the valley [of San Felipe] are warlike and have the bad habit of eating human flesh. A few days before my arrival they had killed, with the intention of eating him, a neophyte who had carelessly come down from the mountains to visit his relatives. When we approached the ranchería the slayer, with great arrogance, sent us a message to the effect that if we were coming for him he would await us with horse and lance.

This whole valley abounds in mescal, which is the principal food of the Indians, although in the vicinity of the Colorado the gentiles are now raising maize, squashes, and watermelons. The squash is of good quality; dried in halves (*orejones*) and cooked, it tastes like conserve.

We returned by way of the same valley, intending to cross the whole range. In fact, at a place near the central valley of the range called Las Animas, we had a very bad climb to the summit, where we spent the night in the severe cold, notwithstanding it was the end of July. The gentiles did not bother us. The following day we continued our ascent through almost impassable spots, where at times we had to put down logs in order to get across. We found no locality in these uplands fit for the support of a mission or the raising of cattle. From the summit we de-

scended very steeply to a flat more frequented by gentiles, so we slept that night with some vigilance.

This whole range, which we traversed from south to north, is thickly wooded with pines of a different species from those in the lower mountains. All of it is without grass, there being hardly any cynodon, even at the summit. At the beginning of our ascent I noted several veins or argentine talc (*talc argentino*).[7]

Reaching the end of the range the following day, I began my descent on this side [i.e., the west side, from which Longinos is writing] which, although longer than the ascent, was gentle and free of stones. I saw the fires from several rancherías on the flat below, but far from the place where I intended to stop. My greatest danger now lay behind me, so I did not make camp where they might molest us, and we lay down to sleep without the least uneasiness, but about midnight a great crowd came shouting and making the hubbub they usually set up when attacking. The corporal and the rest of the soldiers of my escort, all veterans of the conquest of Monterey, had taken the precaution of leaving their horses saddled. Thus prepared, they rushed upon the gentiles who, when they saw we were not off guard as they had supposed, retreated under cover of darkness. Only a few arrows, which we found the next morning, reached us.

La Concepción, as this place is called, should not be overlooked. When measures are taken to halt the raids of the Indians of the Valley of San Rafael, it will be suitable for the establishment of a mission. It is a plain of considerable size, with water and irrigable land, and facilities for stock, lumber, firewood, and the like.

The distance from La Concepción to Mission Santo Domingo is ten or twelve leagues, by a fair road through hills and valleys, with the same kind of vegetation as that met on the ascent by way of Valladares. The road passes many rancherías of gentiles, but, since about half way down it crosses the road to the mission, I traversed it that day without further incident.

from PART THREE • Journey through New California, San Diego to Monterey

New California is a narrow strip of land extending from the Presidio of San Diego to that of San Francisco; from Lat. 34 to Lat. 39, some 300 leagues. Its breadth at its widest is sixteen to twenty leagues, and at its narrowest

---

7. The reference is unclear, perhaps indicating talc, although more commonly in Longinos's day, talc referred to magnesium.

three or four. Old California is a very broken country, but New California is formed of several plains, free of stones, except those that roll down from the hills and mountain slopes, or those washed up by the sea. This strip is bounded on the west by the Pacific Ocean; on the north by an arm of the sea [San Francisco Bay], which penetrates some forty leagues inland; on the east by a chain of mountains [the Coast Range] inhabited by many gentiles which is a continuation of the range that traverses Old California; on the south by Fronteras of Old California.

This country enjoys a fine climate. Although it lies at a latitude where the cold should be severely felt, this does not happen, because it is all on the coastal plain, protected on the north by the trend of the mountains. Every year it snows a little, but it never freezes except in the mountains, and only in the highest of them does the snow last for more than a few days. The winter is very rainy, with strong northwest winds, but no thunder or lightning. Rain is rare in summer. From the month of February to June and July fogs are frequent, although in the past few years it has been observed that they are diminishing. The four seasons of the year are very like those of Spain, and all the trees and grains that have been introduced from that country flourish in the same abundance and quality.

New California is among the most healthful countries that I have visited. No endemic disease has been noted except syphilis, which makes more rapid progress among the Indians than among the other inhabitants, although in time these too will succumb to the virus, as has occurred in Old California, unless some remedy is provided for it.

Its situation, climate, temperature, and other circumstances make this land of California most suitable for the production of grain, fruit, and every kind of cattle. The virgin soil has very few trees and no great variety of plants. Cynodon (*grama*) abounds in the valleys and along the water courses. Willows, alders (*Betula,* which is called *aliso*), live oaks, oaks, mesquite, etc., are plentiful, as are pines in the mountains and foothills, from which all the missions are well provided with timber and logs. During the past few years grains have been planted at the missions and it has been discovered that, however slight the increase, they have more grain than they know what to do with. If there were a few farmers here of an industrious people like the Catalans, within a few years this land would flourish like no other. I have noted that for the settlement of a country like this it has often been proposed to gather up criminals guilty of grave offenses and other troublesome people, and bring them to these lands, as it were, for punishment. If one considers the matter, however, one sees that such plans are mistaken. If anyone doubts it I refer him to the natives of the Santa Barbara Channel, who have imbibed the maxims of civilization and retained them. There are plenty of people in this land; what is needed is someone to teach them.

In Old California the Jesuits always procured German missionaries, as the most useful settlers, and thus they accomplished all they could desire. The two or three missions of New California under Catalan missionaries are far superior to the others, although much smaller. One of them is San Diego, which, together with the Presidio, suffered a thousand privations from lack of water; but, since the Catalans came, they have had water and such an abundance of everything that they are no longer able to dispose of their grain, livestock, fruit, etc.

All the crops introduced from Spain yield in the greatest profusion. Flax and hemp would be profitable commercial ventures. With them, and with tallow, flour, and furs, the Spaniards could make a beginning; other activities would follow: people would come, mines would be opened, and the nations that frequent that coast for the single purpose of fur trading would be frightened off, because their numbers would be inferior to ours. I cannot conceive the reason for the neglect of this activity in our domain, when the advantages of this coast over Nootka and places farther north are incomparable. No fewer than thirty to forty vessels have sailed to those stormy and little-known waters [of Nootka], where trade must be carried on with unfriendly gentiles and otter skins must be paid for in copper plates and other goods. The cost of each pelt there is from six to eight pesos, while the few that have been procured in Fronteras and New California cost no more than two, and, because even at this price there are no buyers, I have seen great lots of them allowed to spoil. For that reason not many men go in for hunting otters, although according to my information otters are more plentiful in some parts of California than in the north. . . .

Near Los Ojitos, between Missions San Luis and San Antonio, there are several very hot springs, each forming a delightful bathing place, since the land is level and the soil soft and clayey. No medicinal use is made of these waters, which could serve for the relief of many diseases. The gentiles possess these and many other waters, but they lack even the dictates of instinct that would allow them to take advantage of the gifts that Nature freely offers them.

I have also observed a different kind of spring, rare in Nature, of petroleum, pitch, and other volcanic substances. At the parallel of San Juan Capistrano one finds several pitch springs on the eastern slope of the mountains. In the vicinity of San Gabriel are other pitch springs, and near the Pueblo de Los Angeles more than twenty springs of liquid petroleum, pitch, etc. To the west of the said town, in the middle of a great plain of more than fifteen leagues in circumference, there is a large lake of pitch,[8] with many pools in which bubbles or blisters are constantly forming and exploding. They are shaped like conical bells and make a little report when they burst at the apex. I tried to examine the holes left by the bubbles, but they explode in such rapid succession that they give one no opportunity to do so.

The variety of these great masses of tar, the movement that one sees in all of them at once, the pitchy smell, the sight of that great lake of strange matter, and all these phenomena together present an astonishing and frightful picture, reminding one of those painted of the infernal caverns. If one stands upon the more solid masses of pitch one seems to be rising insensibly from the ground. The plain where one stands sinks in the form of a cone with the apex downward. In hot weather animals have been seen to sink in it, unable to free themselves because their feet were stuck, and the lake swallowed them. After many years their bones come up through the holes, as if petrified. I brought away several specimens of them.

For a great distance around these volcanoes there is no water, and when the heat of the sun forces birds to seek it they alight upon the lake, mistaking it for water. All the birds that do so are caught by the feet and wings until they die of hunger and thirst. Rabbits, squirrels, and other animals are deceived in the same way, and for this reason the gentiles keep a careful watch at such places in order to hunt without effort. Off the road near San Buenaventura there are several other springs of bituminous petroleum, and near them deposits of the same pitch, hardened.

Near the coast of the Santa Barbara Channel occur many springs of these substances, which flow into the sea and are carried by the tides all along the shore. One also finds such springs from Monterey to San Francisco. The odd thing about all these eruptions is that they occur in such immense plains, there not being a high hill within twenty leagues.

The same thing is true of a fire volcano[9] on the coast between Santa Barbara and La Purísima that I explored.

The singular thing about it is that when the sea is rough and it is covered by water at high tide, then are its eruptions of fire and ashes the greater—so much so that one can observe it only from a distance. Even after an eruption the ground is so covered with ashes that one cannot approach it without being half-buried. I was able to observe the craters only because the wind blew [the smoke away] and the tide had receded. The craters were varnished with sticky pitch mixed with sulphur, alum, and other substances. The ground all about the circumference was so hot that one could not remain standing half a minute without getting the soles of his feet burned. Small flames issued from the mouths from time to time, together with smoke so sulphurous that I could not breathe and was forced to abandon the place before I wished. All that day and the day following I suffered from a violent cough that gave me some concern.

Neither Buffon[10] nor any other authority mentions a volcano on a plain where there is not another close by on an elevation, much less on a beach. A spectator witnessing its violence would say that all the waters of the sea would not suffice to extinguish it; but Naturalists, perceiving that the principal agent of these eruptions is water, and that without it the fire does not become active, know that its activity depends upon the amount of sea water that washes into it. This is a natural effect and one that astonished the natives very much.

Few veins of ore have been discovered in New California as yet, because the places where they are probably situated (that is, the mountains and foothills) are so infested with gentiles that it is impossible to explore them. In the mountains adjacent to the Santa Barbara Channel, where I heard there is a vein of silver, two soldiers who had gone to examine it were killed, and for this reason the project was abandoned. I went to the place myself and, in fact, saw several veins of silver whose matrix and appearance indicated an excellent quality of ore, but the warlike nature of these gentiles discourages any enthusiastic miner from attempting to work it. . . .

The mineral kingdom in New California would be very profitable if the mountains were cleared of the many gentiles who take refuge in them and make traveling dangerous.

Most of the coast of New California affords anchorage. The beaches are accessible, although, according to

---

8. The asphalt springs and lake at Rancho La Brea (Brea Park, Los Angeles).

9. Other early voyagers mentioned this "volcano," probably a burning oil spring of an undetermined location.

10. Georges Louis Leclerc, comte de Buffon (1707–88), a French naturalist and author of one of the earliest attempts to create a natural history of the world.

what the natives say, the sea during the past few years has covered them with loose round stones, leaving only short stretches of beach free of them.

On the whole coast of New California no port is known other than that of San Diego,[11] which is one of the best. Another, close by, called the False Port, would be better than San Diego if it had a good approach. There are several on the coast of Old California that may be utilized some day, but because of their lack of [fresh] water they have not been explored from the sea, still less by land.

The plains of New California are inhabited by an infinite number of gentiles, and the mountains even more so. They speak so many different languages that they are understood with difficulty in the missions, for questions and answers have to pass through as many as three interpreters. What is more noteworthy among these natives is that their customs, character, vigor, and talent should vary so greatly in the single district of the Santa Barbara Channel, which extends from San Buenaventura to San Luis [Obispo] and from the coast to the mountains. They differ from the nations farther to the south and north in the following characteristics:

These Indians[12] live in communities and have a fixed domicile. They arrange their houses in groups. The houses are very well constructed, round like an oven, spacious and fairly comfortable; light enters through a hole in the center of the roof. Their beds are made on frames (*tapestes*) and they cover themselves with skins and shawls (*tápalos*). The beds have divisions between them like the cabins of a ship, so that even if many people sleep in one house they do not see one another. In the middle of the floor they make a fire for cooking seeds, fish, and other foods, for they eat everything boiled or roasted. Next their houses they build smaller ones in which to store seeds, dried fish, sardines, and other things against the winter, when the cold, rain, and roughness of the sea prevent foraging.

Outside the ranchería they have a cemetery for burying all their dead. Above each grave they erect a board, some three varas long and half a vara wide, painted in black and white squares, and a pole three or four times as tall as the board, painted in the same colors, on top of which they usually place trophies: if the dead man was a

fisherman, hooks and lines; if a hunter, bow and arrows, etc. They also lay lengthwise over the grave the rib of a whale, bent like a bow. The cemetery is enclosed by a high stockade.

Each of the villages has one or more sweat houses (*temescales*), depending upon the number of inhabitants. Men and women both enter them twice a day [and emerge] streaming with sweat, after which they plunge into pools or streams of cold water which they always have at hand. This rite, which truly seems repugnant to our way of life, they perform daily, even in the severest cold, which on some days is considerable. I attribute to this bad practice of theirs, which they follow from birth, their want of hardiness, unlike the nations that do not do such violence to Nature. But these people are so addicted to it that the missionary fathers, even in the missions, allow them to have their sweat houses and ponds of cold water for the daily ablutions that they all perform because of their cleanliness and their fondness for soaping themselves at all hours.

Although these Indians are warlike, skillful with the bow, intrepid, and of a proud nature, their fixed domicile makes them accept the yoke of obedience and religion with greater readiness and constancy than do the other nations. These are the only ones among whom the practice of idolatry has been noted. All the rancherías alike, without exception, plant a stake about a vara and a quarter high in the clearest and most elevated spot, and on top of it they place a bunch of feathers plucked indiscriminately from the first bird they catch. When the stake is destroyed by the weather, rain, or otherwise, they replace it in a new clearing. I have also observed that even when their idol is taken from them several times and their belief in it is ridiculed, they do not take offense or manifest the slightest annoyance. Hence I infer that their idolatry is inward and that they erect this reminder or symbol so that they may gaze upon it from a distance and fix their thoughts upon the Deity they worship, [invoking Him] for the happy outcome of their enterprises. On the coast they try to place it where it can be seen from out at sea when they go fishing, for the prayers of all these gentiles are addressed to the One they hold as Author, so that He will give them the seeds, fish, and the other foodstuffs they need for their sustenance.

They gather their harvests of seeds with more skill than the other nations. In this operation the women go alone about the country, many leagues if necessary, carrying a large basket on their back and another in one hand. Then with a kind of long-handled fan which has a net at

---

11. This comment indicates that Longinos Martínez did not get to San Francisco, which was known well as a port at the time.

12. The Chumash peoples lived in ancestral lands between San Buenaventura and San Luis Obispo.

one end they knock the seeds from the plants into their baskets, which are thus filled with little effort.

The dress and adornment of the women is graceful. From the waist down they usually wear two very soft pieces of buckskin, the edges of which are cut into fringes and ornamented with strings of beads, snail shells, and others of various colors, which give a very pretty effect. One of these skins is worn in front, the other behind. From the waist up they wear what they call a *tápalo*[13] of fox, otter, squirrel, or rabbit fur, oblong in shape and very comfortable. Tying the opposite corners together, they thrust their head and one arm through the upper aperture, arranging it gracefully so as to cover their flesh.

They adorn their heads tastefully with necklaces and earrings. Their hair is worn in bangs, cut short and combed forward, which gives it the appearance of a brush. They trim it daily by singeing it hair by hair with a piece of pine bark, so that no hair protrudes. If by chance their forehead or hair line is ill-shaped, they correct it with black pitch, as true as if done with compass and ruler. They wear side locks (*balcarrotas*), but the rest of their back hair is worn loose, slicked down on top as much as possible. Their headdress or coiffure gives the women a neat and graceful appearance and makes them less horribly ugly than the rest of the gentile women, giving them some attraction for the Spaniards.

The women bestow the same care on their handicrafts that they use on their persons. Everything they see they imitate in their basketwork, which they make with the utmost delicacy from the root of the rush. Their instinct leads them to manufacture their pots and pans of a kind of mica stone,[14] which is so resistant to heat that it never wears out or becomes unserviceable. We consider this substance to be unaffected by the hottest fire, and for this reason the pots are handed down forever, from father to son to grandson.

Their canoes are of a singular construction and extremely light, made of a number of pieces, fashioned without nails or glue, or any tools other than flints, but with such precision and neatness that they look like the work of our best master carpenter, with all his tools and rules. Their bows and arrows are different from those of the other nations, excelling them in workmanship, beauty, and effectiveness. They also make war clubs, somewhat

curved, and sticks which they use with great skill for hunting rabbits and other small game. Their fishhooks are of shell or bone, which they sometimes prefer to our iron ones. They fish also with tridents (*fisgas*) and harpoons of shell or flint. They hunt sea otters in the same manner as the Indians of Old California.

All these Indians are fond of trafficking and commerce. They trade frequently with the mountain people, bringing fish and beadwork and exchanging them for seeds, *tápalos* of fox skin, and a kind of blanket made of the fibers of a plant resembling cotton, preferring it to their own made of otter. In their trading they use beads for money. The beads are strung on long threads, arranged according to their value. The unit of exchange is a *ponco* of beads, which is two turns of the strings about the wrist and the extended third finger. The value of a *ponco* depends upon the fineness and color of the beads, ours being held in the greatest esteem; it also depends upon their abundance and their price relative to ours. In everything they keep as careful an account as the most scrupulous magnate does of his money. Their currency is fashioned from a kind of snail shell, broken up and shaped one piece at a time into lentil-like beads, which they drill with our needles and then string, polishing them to the fineness they consider most desirable. The men wear strings of their beads and ours on their heads and around their necks, woven in various patterns. Each man displays his wealth on his head, from which he removes it for gambling or trafficking.

These Channel Indians are exceedingly addicted to gambling. The game they play most is one in which they conceal a stick in one hand; he wins who guesses in what hand the stick is held—which, in substance, is all there is to it. They make use of a thousand tricks and grimaces [to deceive their opponents] and are delighted when their opponents fail, as if it were owing to their cleverness with their mysteries and pantomimes.

They are also very fond of *perpibate,*[15] a paste made of the tobacco found in the hills, mixed with ground shells. When fermented this paste has a powerful effect. Shortly after chewing it they become as drunken as if with the strongest liquor. I tested them by giving them brandy and wine, but they liked neither of these beverages [so well]. Dr. Hernández tells us that the Mexican Indians used to make little balls of tobacco and ground sea shells in order

---

13. Actually a Spanish word indicating "cover."

14. Mica stone, but really the well-known soapstone or steatite pots.

15. *Perpibate,* from *per-pivat* (sometimes *ves-pibat*), the southern California Shoshonean name for tobacco.

to endure thirst and hunger for a long time; these they placed under their tongue and with the juice sustained themselves, for the little balls made the saliva flow sufficiently to allay their hunger over a considerable period.

The liveliness of these Indians makes them more prone to thievery than those of other parts, and to the possession of things of value, to acquire which they trade with our soldiers and sailors. The men become pimps, even for their own wives, for any miserable profit.

The men of this nation have only one wife, who is acquired through the simple formula of "You love me and I love you." Adultery is not considered a grave offense among them.

There is in this nation a class of effeminate men who perform all the duties of women: they dress like women; they go out with the women to gather seeds, firewood, etc.; they cannot marry. It is a serious crime for one of them to take a mistress, whether she is single or married.

Both men and women pierce their ears and the central cartilage of the nose. They commonly paint their bodies with red ochre and other colors, their faces and all parts. Each ranchería has a distinctive pattern, so that they can be recognized whenever they gather for a dance or other function.

The women are as strong as men and are very fecund by nature, but they engage in certain practices so abominable that they seem to have degenerated below the point of rationality. In this region they have the notion that unless they have an abortion at their first pregnancy, or if the child does not die immediately, they will never conceive again. Hence they murder many babies with the efforts they make, the blows they give themselves, and the barbarous medicines they take in order to induce an abortion, so that some of the women die and others are badly injured.

As soon as the child is born it is secured to a small hand ladder, of the same form as ours, somewhat longer than the child's body, the steps protruding on both sides. A bed of soft fibers and small bits of grass is made in the middle. The child is wrapped and then secured with rope wound from one side to the other, as if it were a bundle. Where the shoulders of the child project, an arch is made of some woven stuff, or of the material used in baskets, forming a kind of niche, which is adorned about the edges with shells and strings of beads, as is done here [in Mexico City] with the images carried by beggars. Once the child is arranged in this fashion it is kept most of the day in its prison. The mother attends to it and gives it the breast without picking it up, but goes to the place where

the ladder stands, usually in a vertical position. It [the ladder] is never carried on the mother's back, but is dragged from one place to the next. The mother keeps the child in this fashion most of the day, not freeing it even for cleaning, because in the middle of the frame they leave a hole for the baby's member, so that it will have no occasion to wet or scald itself. The same device is used in the straw behind for evacuation. Until a baby is able to walk it lives in a state of total inaction. I do not think that other nations should follow this example, for it is evident that these natives are less robust than those that do not make use of such oppression in childhood, or of the daily sweating and cold baths.

Although customs vary only slightly in the forty or fifty leagues of this district, there is a great difference in languages. I have observed as many as five. Some of them are fairly alike and the Indians understand each other to a certain extent, but the rest are entirely distinct. The confusion resulting from there being so many languages in such a short distance would make a dictionary of them of little utility for history. What indeed is worthy of note is that at La Purísima they use the Latin word *homo* for "man"; "come here" is *aguna,* which in Chichimec is the same. At San Borja meat is called *jehi,* the same as among the Apaches; the same is true of "fire," which they call *que,* the word used for it by that nation [the Apaches]. The Apaches indicate the number of seven by *saipi,* which the Basques use with the same meaning. These widely scattered words, at such great distances from their origins, present a vast amount of material for speculating upon the causes of these strange phenomena.

It is also wonderful to consider the great differences between the nations of the [Santa Barbara] Channel and those of other conquered parts, because, although in their mat-weaving, their physiognomy, and certain customs their common Asiatic origin is manifest, in all other respects they are entirely dissimilar. All who have speculated upon the matter are of the opinion that these people landed here from the wreck of some Asiatic ship, but my opinion is that these nations came from families that were scattered by wars and sought safety in distance and in uninhabited places. Thus one sees that each ranchería or small district of adjoining rancherías has its own chief, and that those a short distance away have different languages and customs, according to the family or families that congregated at their formation.

In this part of the Santa Barbara Channel, in my opinion, a Chinese landed, or some person of great skill in his own crafts and other things, and because of this initial superiority the nation has gone on progressing as it has increased, although its customs have not passed beyond its borders, owing to the scanty commerce and trade among these nations. If a chief merely makes an attempt to pass through another's jurisdiction, fighting and quarreling result, so great is the distrust that these nations have of one another.

With this in mind, a commandant made a study of their fighting habits [and observed that] if one should make an effort to win their friendship it would be easy to dominate the whole country even with a small force, and, in my opinion, all the gentile lands to the north, because most of the natives are of an amiable disposition, the greatest docility, and unequaled humility. The most warlike are those of Fronteras, who have had some traffic and contact with our soldiers; but there is nothing to fear from the rest, to judge by our experience in the conquests. We should not be astonished at the exploits of Hernán Cortés, which to some read like fiction or something supernatural. In my opinion their explanation lies in what I have just said, namely, in the bitter quarrels these nations carry on with each other. Their wars are frequent and always originate over rights to seed-gathering grounds, or in disputes over concubines.

All the other nations in the north and south of New California are practically the same as those of Fronteras of Old California: in customs, appearance, and laziness; in having no fixed domicile, cremating their dead, having their women go about naked, and in building their houses half underground against the rain and cold. But their houses are badly constructed and, when summer comes, the Indians burn them and live in shelters made of branches, which they remove on the slightest pretext, or whenever the notion strikes them. In winter the Indians of the coast suffer from hunger, when storms and bad weather prevent their going out to fish, their apathy being such that they store nothing.

The gentiles living between San Diego and San Buenaventura store up against the winter the plants that bear the most seeds, many rancherías displaying great skill in it; but when the rains are long and the cold is severe these natives also suffer from hunger, because their scanty supplies give out and their sources of food are cut off. Their necessities have obliged them to accustom themselves to consume everything that Nature offers: weeds, seeds, roots, etc.

The same differences may be observed among these nations of gentiles as among those of Old California. In the vicinity of San Diego they are warlike and proud, and are to be feared because of their treachery. In the country around San Juan Capistrano they are affable and learn Castilian readily. Most of them sleep on the ground on bed frames (*tapestes*); their houses, though portable, are comfortable, being constructed of several poles joined at the top, forming a pyramid like a bell tent. When this framework has been erected, they make the walls by weaving reeds, rushes, and other materials, as if they were mats. In this fashion they put up their houses with as much speed as [military] encampments. . . .

These nations [north of Santa Barbara] continually keep on hand small baskets of seeds and other foodstuffs. From this point [northward] they also wear strings of beads about their necks and adorn their ears and heads with them, giving some value to these ornaments, although not in the same way as the Channel Indians. Some of these gentiles wear a kind of waistcoat or jacket of bearskin, the hair side out, which reaches only to their middle and gives them a ridiculous appearance. Their headdress, made of the net used for hunting quail, makes them look like Turks. They also wear feathers and false hair put up in braids. Over all this promontory [Point Concepcion] they wear a kind of thrust sword with a hilt as long as the blade and of almost the same shape, usually a third of a vara in length and one or two inches wide, made of whatever pieces of iron they are able to acquire from the neophytes of the missions and from the soldiers, in exchange for their handicrafts. They prefer barrel hoops for this purpose, although some make their swords of copper.

In all New California from Fronteras northward the gentiles have the custom of burning the brush, this for two purposes: one, for catching rabbits (brush-burning being a form of hunting); two, so that with the first light rain or dew the shoots will come up which they call *pelillo* [little hair] and upon which they feed like cattle when the weather prevents their seeking other food.

They hunt deer by disguising themselves as does, wearing a deer head. Painted with ashes, they pretend to graze, calling to the males until these come within bowshot. With this stratagem and their ease and speed in traversing woods and crossing precipices, they kill many deer for the meat and skins. They are very dextrous in killing little animals, either with arrows or by patiently digging them out of their burrows. With the skins they make wallets (*bolsitas*) in which they carry whatever they please, most of them made with great skill. They use the skins of smaller animals, the weasel, for example, for tobacco pouches, leaving the pelt entire, with head, feet, etc., except for a single opening between the thighs. These little purses, like all their portable possessions, are worn in the hair.

The nations in the vicinity of San Gabriel have the custom of carrying small stones, which they acquire at a high price from the Indians who bring them from the Island of Los Angeles[16] [Santa Catalina]. These stones are galena *ferulata*,[17] with silver. It is noteworthy that they are not prized because of the metals, of which no use is made, but because of the current belief that he who has one with him thereby acquires valor and bravery—a belief which enables the gentiles of that island to sell the stones at a good price.

I sent one of my Indians, accompanied by another from Mission San Gabriel to act as interpreter, to that island to collect all its products for me. The interpreter did very well with the chief, assuring him that I had been sent by the Great Chief (which is their way of referring to our King). The chief, with his natural intelligence, sent me everything which to his way of thinking was of value in his dominion: two seal skins, two otter skins, several strings of abalones and limpets, one string of the small stones of silver and lead that I have described, and several

of quartz, sardonyx, and jasper. My Indians brought back some other shells also. The chief sent all this by his eldest son, accompanied by two other Indians whom he trusted; he also sent me an expressive message, regretting that he could not come himself and putting himself at my orders, offering me this modest gift of the only things the island produced which they held of value.

I thanked him and sent him by his messengers several varas of striped cloth, some strings of beads, and several cheeses and pieces of the tobacco in paste which they esteem so highly. The soldiers of my escort informed me that these goods of ours are what they most appreciate. Thereupon the Indians departed very contentedly, after a hearty meal. I was assured [later] on the coast that the chief of the island had made many fine expressions of thanks and affection for our Great Chief. The news traveled very quickly among the rancherías all along the coast, and I was everywhere well received. The novelty [of my procedure] caused no alarm, nor did they make the slightest hostile movement which might have been expected of them, given their nature and character. To judge by what the soldiers told me, it would not have been strange if the gentiles had played one of their tricks on me, because they do not like to have their lands and customs examined, especially with the thoroughness which my commission requires in such reconnaissances.

---

16. Elsewhere referred to as San Gabriel Island.

17. Probably galena.

6

꿈※쫑

NEW FRANCE IN NORTH AMERICA

The approach taken by religious and civil officials in France was distinctive among the groups—Spanish, British, and others—that were seeking to take control of the lands and peoples in North America. Unlike the Spanish Crown and its related civil officials who sought quick gain from the mineral and agricultural products rendered available to Spanish people by the enslavement of Indians, the French Crown did not push for total conquest of the Indians, even though it did initially seek significant wealth from mining and trade, especially in fur. Unlike the British Crown and British officials who relied upon nucleated settlements of laboring and middling-level people, both men and women, France initially sent over men as *engagés* (contracted laborers) to build forts, missions, and small towns and set up fur trade routes and as missionaries to proselytize among the Native peoples. And unlike the Dutch, who (like the English) created nucleated settlements and who made funding arrangements for Dutch groups through companies set up by wealthy burghers, the French Crown relied upon wealthy individuals or the Church to support settlement efforts, after the initial efforts funded by the Crown failed to win general public support and the formation of a Company of the Indies did not succeed in bringing home the immediate wealthy return that was sought. Indeed, by the seventeenth century, various groups within the Catholic Church—particularly the Récollets, Jesuits, Ursulines, and Capuchins, but others as well—were the most successful at sending over novitiates and learned missionaries. Given the nature of their missionary endeavors and the belief system (which included celibacy) under which they were practicing, the Catholics who came over were not positioned to create French American settlements like those established by other European groups. French colonial literature, as a result, bears some similarity to the colonial literatures of, for instance, Portugal, Spain, and Britain, but it also differs markedly from some of the colonial writings of those groups as well. An understanding of France's imperial situation assists in understanding its colonial literary output.

Despite the fact that the Treaty of Tordesillas (1494) gave to Spain the Atlantic coastal areas of North America, both English and French sailors scouted along the Atlantic seaboard (Spain, France, and England were all then Catholic). Verrazano, an Italian backed by Italian bankers but sailing for France in 1523, was the first to navigate the coastline from Florida (at present-day Cape Fear) to Maine. The territory, which he called *Nouvelle-France* (New France), did not yield the passage to Asia hoped for by the expedition, but it did enable France to claim a territorial right to the entire length of the North American coastline. French place names appeared on maps, and Francis I (challenged by both Spain and Britain in his efforts) sent Jacques Cartier on an expedition in 1534 that effected France's claim to navigate the waters from present-day Newfoundland inland to the Gulf of the St. Lawrence. Cartier had brought with him two lapidaries (specialists in gems), but the general search for mineral wealth did not meet with the successes the French king had hoped for. Religious wars in France from the middle of the century to its end precluded the Crown's sponsoring a continued search for minerals in the North Atlantic coastal areas, but the newly named lands for France made it possible for French people, both Protestants and Catholics, to consider traveling to New France to establish their own communities, as the selections presented earlier in this volume attest.

France did not sponsor settlements in the way that its competitors did. Instead, during the seventeenth and eighteenth centuries, expeditions that included mostly men came over, scouted, and claimed the territories especially in the area of the St. Lawrence, built forts, and returned home. *Engagés,* as these contracted laborers were called, tended to have shorter work assignments than their British counterparts, and their passage back to France was typically a condition for their signing on to labor in New France, whether in the St. Lawrence area or Louisiana. Family migration to New France was rare. The Société de Montréal recruited some families in 1649, and John Law's Compagnie de la Louisiane (1717–20), generally known as the Louisiana Company, sought families for the southern colony. But for the most part, individuals or families rarely accepted redemption contracts explicitly associated with emigration, and most—up to two-thirds of the St. Lawrence Valley *engagés*—returned home after the contracted labor period was completed. Because the labor was not in mineral wealth, which brought speedy returns back in Europe, laboring in New France was not conceived as a good alternative to remaining at home. The writings suggest that the lack of available European women and the danger posed by repeated Indian attacks offset any attractions that available land held for these men. It is interesting, too, that the concept that there was land available to French people was not circulated in public prints as it was in other countries, especially in the Netherlands, Germany, and Britain. Printed propaganda was rare, so those in the lower classes who might most readily have agreed to travel to North America relied upon hearsay for information about the Americas, and they often heard bad reports: Canada was cold, the Iroquois were fierce, and the French colonies in the St. Lawrence and Louisiana (particularly the latter) were primarily places where undesirable people and criminals went.

A remarkable sign of this hearsay appears in the writings of the Récollets, Jesuits, and Ursulines, who consistently expressed concern about the effects upon their work among Native peoples of having those whom they considered less desirable living among their prospective converts. The dominance of the writings of French missionary people is a characteristic difference of French colonial writings from the writings of other groups. Travel narratives from France, like those of other groups, emphasize the opportunities of the territories for France, but French people, tending to be laborers rather than settlers, did not create the body of writings more typically found among colonial writings from other countries. In addition, because France did not locate within its own territories the vast mineral wealth available in Spain, the French writings are not characterized by a sense of the necessary (and God-ordained) conquest of the indigenous peoples. Indeed, quite to the contrary, the French writings by religious people show again and again a tendency to attempt to understand Native people but not to overpower them.

The Récollets, mendicant brothers of a reform branch of the Franciscans, were the first to come to New France. Some traveled with Champlain on his first ventures among the Hurons in 1615–16 and again in 1623–24. As Spain's example makes clear, Franciscan missionary policy depended heavily upon European colonization (making the Indian people the laborers in European-controlled settlements). Because the French trading companies did not encourage permanent settlements, the Franciscans were less interested in missionary activity in French territories. A new and different missionary effort began in 1625, then, when three Jesuit volunteers, among them Jean de Brébeuf, began to work in upper New France. Unlike other missionary groups (except for a few British protestant missionaries, somewhat later), the Jesuits engaged in what have come to be called "flying missions." They would go out to live among the Native peoples, rather than expect them (as the Franciscans had) to come to a nuclear center that they themselves were expected to build and maintain. The Jesuits sought to convert the Native peoples to Christianity and a European Christian's sense of morality, but without necessarily erasing the essentials of precontact indigenous civilization. This approach meant less interference in Indian ways, and it assisted fur traders' and fishery activities because it meant that the fur and freshwater fishing trades would not be interrupted by the imposition of a European way of life that would displace traditional Indian hunting and fishing goals. Indian peoples came to be affiliated with the Black Robes, as they called the Jesuits, but they were free to go, then, after visiting awhile, typically accepting baptism and catechism, and trading with nearby traders.

Largely through the efforts of Jesuits and other missionaries and fur traders, France extended its northern territory inland along the key waterways that were ancestrally used by Indian peoples for trade and communication. By the middle of the eighteenth century, missions and forts extended from the St. Lawrence Valley through the Great Lakes, into Illinois territory and, sporadically, down the Mississippi River to the Missouri. By the late seventeenth century, these posts extended finally to the area of Louisiana, a new colony created by Louis XIV in 1699 to keep the British from moving inland from the areas of Virginia, the Carolinas, and Georgia and thereby harassing New Spain's territories in Mexico and the West. Louisiana developed fitfully at first, perhaps because the Jesuits were perceived to have independent ways and were made to feel less welcome than other religious groups, including the Franciscans and especially the Capuchins, a stricter reformed branch of the Franciscans.

The population of Louisiana remained sparse until John Law's Compagnie des Indes (Company of the Indies) developed in 1717, and the company began shipping people—about seven thousand Europeans (French, but also Swedes, Germans, and others) and an equal number of African slaves—with most arriving before 1721. As capitals were developing at Mobile (1711–19), Biloxi (1719–22), and finally New Orleans (1722), wars were waged against the Natchez, Fox, and Chickasaw peoples of the Mississippi area, and labor resources were thus dispersed for protection of the small enclaves of colonists in the areas. The conditions of living for laborers, and indeed all those but the elite, were terrible in Louisiana, reports went. Estimates indicate that by 1730, only 5,300 inhabitants were there, about half of them African slaves.

The Jesuits might have been less welcome in Louisiana because their own more wealthy status among Catholics brought with it a certain degree of independent thinking that might not have easily coalesced with the goals of political, military, and economic sponsors who had hoped for conquest and mineral wealth. The Franciscans, who settled in mission communities with slaves and indentured laborers to do related subsistence work, fared better. Yet the scarceness of European women in French settlements throughout New France put tremendous stress upon the Native and mixed-race women, even as it gave them an unusual form of power among European settlers and their own people, whether one considers northern New France in the St. Lawrence River area or the Wisconsin and Illinois territory or the territory of Louisiana. The Jesuits' and others missionaries' comments about the importance of the Virgin Mary— an adaptation of Catholicism's cult of the Virgin appropriate to the circumstances—brought a significant number of indigenous women to the Catholic faith. The presence of an increasing number of indigenous women to proselytize attracted the Ursulines, an official Roman Catholic teaching order, the order of Saint Ursula, to settlement in New France. Founded in Italy in 1535 by St. Angela Merici of Brescia, the Ursulines were a cloistered teaching order that settled in Avignon, Paris, and Bordeaux and eventually in New France, the last movement as a missionary arm of the order. The Ursulines founded in Louisiana in 1727 one of the first schools for women in North America, and their efforts turned from schools to hospitals in the area soon after their founding, as the writings of Marie Hachard show. In 1739, the Ursulines established a mission school at Montreal, as well, complementing the congregational schools already established there for young women. The emphasis upon women's education, which also served to assist the Europeans' ultimate goals of conversion and eventual assimilation, brought a relatively high rate of literacy among women to the colonies. The women living in colonial New France had a similar or slightly higher rate of literacy than did the men in the earliest years, matching the situation in New England during New England's second century.

The literary output of New France is marked by different colonial conditions. Like its British and European counterparts, France had a significant amount of travel and promotional literature resulting from its initial expeditions to North America. Yet after the period of initial contact and exploration of Natives' lands ceased, the literature of French settlements was as sporadic as the settlements themselves and not marked by patterns of materials frequently found in the settlement literature. Because company workers were not expected to remain, their letters have less of the promotional effects and less of the frustrated complaints raised in letters by workers from other colonial settlements. French high literature of the seventeenth and eighteenth centuries favored poetry and drama. Theatrical activity was widespread in the Jesuits' Quebec, where French drama and some locally written plays were staged with some degree of regularity. Historians have suggested that the popularity of theatrical activity (not represented in the following selections) derived from the Jesuits' college exercises, brought to New France, in activities called the *réception,* a ritualized set of addresses like recitatives or responsive addresses. In terms of published and private writings available to people in New France and old, the Jesuit *Relations* and publications, like those of Marie Hachard's letters home from her Ursuline habitation in Louisiana, are more frequent among the writings emanating from New France. Unlike New Spain, where conquest is a major factor of the literary record, and unlike New England and the other British colonies, where writings explaining oneself (whether in religious or civil terms) to those back home dominate the literary records, New France had literary productions of a cross-cultural but Catholic kind, whether Capuchin or Jesuit or Ursuline, and these writings, along with letters and travel narratives, dominate the literary output of the French colonies much more than either a rhetoric of conquest or one promoting or forestalling settlement.

JEAN DE BRÉBEUF (1593–1649)

Jean de Brébeuf was a man of extraordinary zeal, even in an era of deep religious commitment. Born in Normandy, France, in 1593, he was ordained a Jesuit priest in 1625 and went to New France, in present-day Canada. He lived for three years as the lone missionary among the Huron peoples, near the lake that bears their name. The French colony at Quebec was still a fragile outpost in 1634 when Brébeuf decided to establish a permanent mission in Huronia. Brébeuf and his Jesuit brethren believed that they had a better chance to win converts among a stationary, agricultural people than among the peoples who relied upon hunting and gathering, as those did near Quebec. The Hurons, like their Iroquois neighbors to the south, were a confederacy of peoples who lived prosperously on corn, beans, and squash, as well as on game. As Brébeuf explained to prospective missionaries in the third chapter presented here, the Jesuits needed to immerse themselves in Huron society, traveling by canoe, sleeping in smoky longhouses, and occasionally accepting adoption into individual families.

Such missionary fervor was customary for the men who belonged to the Society of Jesus, or Jesuits. Founded by Ignatius Loyola in 1534, the order established no monasteries, and its members did not lead lives of prayer and contemplation but instead worked largely in schools and missions, trying to spread Catholicism at a time when Protestants were gaining converts across Europe. From China and Japan to Canada and Paraguay, the Jesuits proved adept at learning indigenous languages and adapting to local ways. Their intense academic training in numerous cultures around the world prepared them to approach members of different cultures on their own terms, as well as for the goal of conversion. Understanding the importance of their missionary efforts, the Jesuits often attempted to learn the language of the peoples among whom they lived. Brébeuf himself translated the catechism into the Huron language, for use among those peoples.

To publicize their missionary efforts and appeal for contributions from the faithful in Europe, the Jesuits wrote annual *Relations,* reports forwarded from the field to the superior (in Brébeuf's case in 1636, Paul Le Jeune at Quebec) and sent on to Paris for publication. These texts sometimes included little more than a count of new converts and a few edifying anecdotes about pious, obedient, so-called primitives. But in the hands of Brébeuf and other skilled observers, the *Relations* offered insightful portraits of Native American culture, along with cross-cultural reflections on the essence of spirituality, family, wealth, or mourning. For instance, Brébeuf's account in the *Relation of 1636* of the Huron "Feast of the Dead"—in which the bones of tribal ancestors were exhumed and reburied—is equal to the best work of modern anthropologists and shows an understanding of the importance of accepting others' behaviors.

The Huron mission was the crowning achievement of the Jesuit effort in Canada, but it came to an unhappy end. Contact with the French introduced diseases, such as smallpox, which took a severe toll on the Indians who had had no previous exposure to such germs. As many passages in the *Relations* show, the Hurons wondered if the rite of baptism transmitted the illness or might protect against it. Their strength reduced by disease and incursions by other Europeans, the Hurons struggled to retain their culture and their land, especially the latter. They were losing ground in an ongoing war against the Iroquois as well. This war brought an end to the Jesuit mission among the Hurons and an end to its founder. Brébeuf was captured by an Iroquois war party and tortured to death, alongside another missionary, Gabriel Lalemant, in 1649. According to an account in the *Relation of 1649,* the Iroquois mutilated him and poured boiling water on his head in mockery of baptism, but Brébeuf showed no signs of his pain and continued preaching to his torturers. The Huron dispersed as refugees, to live with other Indian peoples or as converts at mission settlements near Quebec and Montreal. Brébeuf's bones were sent to Quebec as relics, and in 1930, he and seven other martyrs—five other Jesuits and two lay servants—were canonized by the Catholic Church as saints.

from RELATION OF WHAT OCCURRED IN THE COUNTRY OF THE HURONS IN THE YEAR 1636[1]

[Dedicatory Letter to Paul Le Jeune]

My Reverend Father,

Having learned from your letters, and from the statements of the Fathers who arrived here fortunately last year, how old France is burning with ardent desires for the New; that our Reverend Father General cherishes this Mission as the apple of his eye; that the Father Provincial is inclined to it with his whole heart; that the ardor in our Colleges[2] is so great that it is more difficult to check the tears of those who are turned away, and refused permission to come to our assistance, than to find those who will work; that a very great number of persons, Religious and secular, are continually offering their prayers and their vows to God for the con-

version of the poor Barbarians of this whole country; and that in the House of Montmartre,[3] not to speak of others, a Nun is prostrated night and day before the Holy Sacrament, praying for this result; all this makes us hope and believe that God will now open the treasures of his grace and favor upon these poor Peoples, and unseal the eyes of their souls to know the truth. For he would not incite so many devout persons to ask, if he had not the inclination to grant their prayers. Besides, we learn that the colony of Kebec is rapidly increasing, through the efforts of Messieurs the Associates of the Company of New France, who spare no pains on their side; and we hope the good example of our Frenchmen will greatly aid not only to bring together and encourage to work the idle and wandering Savages, but to incite them to do for God what they shall find practicable. Moreover, I can say with reason that if divine Goodness continues to scatter his favors and blessings on our Hurons, and on us who labor among them, as freely as he has done since our arrival, we ought, without doubt, to expect here some day an abundant harvest of souls. It is true, there are among these Tribes many errors, superstitions, vices, and utterly evil customs to uproot,—more than we had imagined at first, as will be seen in the course of this Relation; but with God nothing is impossible. It is by his aid that we have already planted the Cross in the midst of this Barbarism, and are beginning and will continue, if it please him, to make known the name and marvelous works of him who by the Cross has redeemed the world. But enough has been said in a general way; it is time to enter into particulars, which I shall willingly and fully

---

1. Brébeuf's *Relation* was first published in French by Sebastien Cramoisy (Paris, 1636). The text is from *The Jesuit Relations and Allied Documents,* vol. 10, ed. Reuben Gold Thwaites (1897). Thwaites was a prolific editor of colonial exploration literature, and this seventy-three-volume series, which prints the English translation opposite the original French or Latin, is the standard source. The Canadian *Relations* were published in Paris from 1632 to 1673, but Thwaites added to these other missionary writings, dating back to 1612 and ahead into the eighteenth century.

2. The Jesuit schools that trained candidates for the priesthood.

3. A convent in Paris.

do, assuring you that I shall state nothing that I have not seen myself or have not learned from persons worthy of credence.

from PART 1

CHAPTER 1

Of the Conversion, Baptism, and Happy Death of Some Hurons; and of the Condition of Christianity amid this Barbarism

During the present year, eighty-six have been baptized, and, adding to these the fourteen of last year, there are a hundred souls in all who, we believe, have been rescued from the service of the devil in this country since our return. Of this number God has called ten to Heaven,—six while they were young, and four more advanced in age. One of these, named François *Sangwati,* was Captain of our village. He had a naturally good disposition, and consented very willingly to be instructed and to receive Holy Baptism, a course he had previously praised and approved in others. I admired the tender Providence of God in the conversion of a woman, who is one of the four deceased. I baptized her this Autumn at the village of *Scanonaenrat,*[4] when returning from the house of Louys de saincte Foy, where we had gone to instruct his parents. The deafness of this sick woman, and the depths of the mysteries I brought to her notice, prevented her from sufficiently understanding me; and, besides, the accent of that Nation is a little different from that of the Bears,[5] with whom we live. My own imperfect acquaintance with the language rendered me still less intelligible, and increased my difficulties. But Our Lord, who willed to save this soul, immediately sent us a young man, who served us as interpreter. He had been with us in the Cabin of Louys, and had heard us talking of our mysteries, so that he already knew a considerable part of them, and understood very well what I said. It is said that this woman, who was named Marie, in the midst of her greatest weakness foretold that she would not die for eight days; and so it happened.

They seek Baptism almost entirely as an aid to health. We try to purify this intention, and to lead them to receive from the hand of God alike sickness and health, death and life; and teach them that the life-giving waters of Holy Baptism principally impart life to the soul, and not to the body. However, they have the opinion so deeply rooted that the baptized, especially the children, are no longer sickly, that soon they will have spread it abroad and published it everywhere. The result is that they are now bringing us children to baptize from two, three, yes, even seven leagues away.

Moreover, the divine Goodness which acts in us according to the measure of our Faith, has thus far preserved these little ones in good health; so that the death of those who have passed away has been attributed to incurable and hopeless maladies contracted beforehand; and, if another has occasionally suffered from some trifling ailment, the parents, although still unbelieving, have attributed it to the neglect and irreverence they have shown toward the service of God.

There is in our village a little Christian girl named Louyse, who at six months began to walk alone; the parents declare they have seen nothing like it, and attribute it to the efficacy of Holy Baptism. Another person told us one day, with great delight, that his little boy, who had always been sick and much emaciated before Baptism, had been very well since then. This will suffice to show how Our Lord is inspiring them with a high opinion of this divine Sacrament, which is strengthened by the perfect health God gives us, and which he has given to all the French who have been in this country; for, they say, it is very strange that, except a single man who died here from natural causes, all the others, during the twenty-five years or thereabout in which the French have been frequenting this region, have scarcely ever been sick.

From all this may be easily gathered the present state of the young Christianity of this country, and the hope for the future. Two or three things besides will help to the same end. The first is the method we pursue in the instruction of the Savages. We gather together the men as often as we can; for their councils, their feasts, their games, and their dances do not permit us to have them here at any hour, nor every day. We pay especial attention to the Old Men, inasmuch as they are the ones who determine and decide all matters, and everything is ordered by their advice. All come willingly to hear us; all, without exception, say they have a desire to go to Heaven and fear the fiery torments of hell. They have hardly anything to answer us with; we could wish sometimes that they would bring forward more objections, which would always afford us better opportunity to explain our holy Mysteries in detail. Of a truth, the Commandments of God are very

---

4. This and the other villages of the Hurons were located between Lake Simcoe and Georgian Bay in present-day Ontario.

5. One of the clans of the Hurons.

just and reasonable, and they must be less than men who find therein anything to censure. Our Hurons, who have as yet only the light of nature, have found them so noble, so agreeable to reason, that after having heard the explanation of them they would say, in admiration, *ca chia attwain aa arrihwaa,* "Certainly these are important matters, and worthy of being discussed in our councils; they speak the truth, they say nothing but what is to the purpose; we have never heard such discourse." Among other things which made them acknowledge the truth of one God, Creator, Governor, and Preserver of all things, was the illustration I employed of the child conceived in its mother's womb. "Who," said I, "but God forms the body of this child; who out of one and the same material forms the heart, the liver, the lungs,—in short, an infinite variety of members, all necessary, all well-proportioned, and joined one to another? Not the father, for these wonders take place in his absence, and sometimes after his death. Nor is it the mother, for she does not know what takes place in her womb. If it be the father or the mother that forms this body at discretion, why is not a son or a daughter begotten at will? Why do they not produce children, handsome, tall, strong, and active? And, if parents give the soul to their children, why do they not impart to all of them great minds, a retentive memory, and all sorts of noble and praiseworthy qualities, seeing that there is no one who would not desire to have such children if this were in his power?" To all this the Hurons, full of wonder, make no reply. They confess that we speak the truth, and that indeed there is a God; they declare that henceforth they will recognize, serve, and honor him; and, desiring to be promptly instructed, they ask us to teach them the Catechism every day; but, as I have said, their occupations and amusements do not permit that.

Moreover, the harmony of all points of Christian Doctrine pleases them wonderfully; "For," they say, "you always speak connectedly, and consistently with what you have said; you never wander off, you never speak save to the purpose; we, on the contrary, speak heedlessly, not knowing what we say." It is a characteristic of falsehood to embarrass itself in a multitude of contradictions.

The evil is, they are so attached to their old customs that, knowing the beauty of truth, they are content to approve it without embracing it. Their usual reply is, *oniondechouten,* "Such is the custom of our country." We have fought this excuse and have taken it from their mouths, but not yet from their hearts; our Lord will do that when it shall please him.

Thus, then, we deal with the Old Men. As the women and children caused us much trouble, we have hit upon this plan, which succeeds fairly well. Father Antoine Daniel[6] and the other Fathers go every day through the Cabins, teaching the children, whether baptized or not, Christian doctrine,—namely, the sign of the Cross, the *Pater, the Ave, the Credo,*[7] the Commandments of God, the Prayer to the Guardian Angel, and other brief prayers, all in their own tongue, because these Peoples have a natural inaptitude for learning any other.

On Sundays, we assemble all these young people twice in our Cabin, which serves as a Chapel. In the morning we get them to assist at Mass, even to the offertory, before which we solemnly bless the holy water; then I make them say all together, after me, the *Pater, the Ave,* and other prayers they know. In the afternoon I propose to them some little question from the Catechism, and make them give account of what they have learned during the week, giving to each some little prize according to his merit.

This method, along with the little rewards, has wonderful results. For, in the first place, it has kindled among all the children so great a desire to learn that there is not even one who, if it can stammer out words at all, does not desire to be instructed; and, as they are almost all fairly intelligent, they make rapid progress, for they even teach one another.

I cannot tell you the satisfaction and consolation these little children give us. When we consider their Fathers, still plunged in their superstitions, although recognizing sufficiently the truth, we are afraid that God, provoked by their sins, has rejected them for a time; but, as for the children, without doubt he holds out his arms to them and draws them to himself. The eagerness they show to learn the duties of a Christian keeps us from doubting it. The smallest ones throw themselves into our arms, as we pass through the Cabins, and do not require to be urged to talk and to learn. Father Daniel hit upon the plan of quieting a little child, crying in its mother's arms, by having it make the sign of the Cross. And indeed, one day when I had just been teaching the Catechism to them in our Cabin, this child made us laugh; its mother was carrying it in her

---

6. Father Daniel was a missionary in Huronia from 1634 until his death at the hands of the Iroquois in 1648.

7. Three Latin prayers: the Lord's prayer, the Hail Mary, and a teaching of St. Augustine. These prayers would have been part of the catechism taught to the Hurons.

arms, and was going out; but, as soon as she reached the door, it began to cry so that she was compelled to turn back. She asked it what was the matter. "Let me begin again," it said, "let me begin again, I want to say more." I then got it to make again the sign of the Cross, and it immediately began to laugh and to jump for joy. I saw the same child, another time, crying hard because it had had its finger frozen; but it quieted down and laughed, as soon as they had it make the sign of the Cross. I dwell willingly upon this matter, as I am sure pious souls take pleasure in hearing all these particulars. In the beginnings of this infant Church, what can we speak about if not the stammerings of our spiritual children? We have one little girl, among others, named Marie *Aoesiwa,* who has not her equal. Her whole satisfaction seems to be in making the sign of the Cross and in saying her *Pater* and *Ave.* Scarcely have we set foot in her Cabin, when she leaves everything to pray to God. When we assemble the children for prayers or for Catechism, she is always among the first, and hastens there more cheerfully than many would to play. She does not stir from our Cabin, and does not omit making the sign of the Cross, and saying over and over fifty times a day the *Pater* and *Ave.* She gets others to do the same; and, one of our Frenchman having newly come, her only greeting was to take his hand, and have him make the sign of the Cross. Often she is in the field when our Fathers recite their Office there; she stands in the road, and, almost every time they return, she begins to make the sign of the Cross, and to pray to God in a loud voice.

Another little girl named Catherine had often been wayward about receiving instruction, and so had not been rewarded like the others. Some days afterward, one of her companions brought her to one of our Fathers, giving him to understand that she was quite disposed to learn; but, when it came to the point, she acted as usual. The little girl who had brought her became annoyed, and used all her little natural rhetoric to make her open her lips and to get her to speak,—sometimes using threats, sometimes holding out a reward from me if she spoke properly; she was so earnest that she succeeded, to the great satisfaction of those of our Fathers who were listening to her.

Another benefit that results from this practice—which is in conformity with our Institute[8]—is, that even the adults become instructed by this means; for the desire of the fathers and mothers that their children should be praised and rewarded leads them to be instructed themselves, in order to teach their children; particularly many older girls take pleasure in imitating the younger ones. When they are returning from the forest, they often stop the first of our Fathers whom they meet, and say to him, *ta arrihwaienstan sen,* "Teach me, I pray thee;" and although they may be well laden, they are not satisfied unless he has them say the *Pater* and the *Ave.* Sometimes they anticipate us, and, from as far as they can see one of our Fathers, they begin to recite what they know. What a consolation to hear these districts resound with the name of Jesus, where the devil has been, so to speak, adored and recognized as God during so many ages.

This exercise also enables us to improve greatly in the use and knowledge of the language, which is no small gain. Generally speaking they praise and approve the Christian Religion, and blame their wicked customs; but when will they leave them off entirely? Some say to us: "Do you think you are going to succeed in overturning the Country?" Thus do they style the change from their Pagan and Barbarous life to one that is civilized and Christian. We reply that we are not so presumptuous, but that what is impossible to man is not only possible but easy to God. Here is another indication of their good will toward the Faith. Monsieur de Champlain and Monsieur the General du Plessis Bochart[9] rendered us great service last year, by exhorting the Hurons in full council to embrace the Christian Religion, and by telling them that it was the only means not only of being some day truly happy in Heaven, but also of cementing in the future a very close alliance with the French,—who, if this were done, would readily come into their Country, marry their daughters, teach them different arts and trades, and assist them against their enemies; and that, if they would bring some of their children next year, to be instructed at Kébec, our Fathers would take good care of them. And, inasmuch as the Captains of the country were not there, they asked them to hold a general council on their return, concerning the points mentioned; also to give me the letters with which

---

8. That is, consistent with the constitution of the Jesuit order, which implored the teaching of the catechism to uninformed pagans.

9. Samuel de Champlain (1567?–1635), a Frenchman who explored North America and the founder of the colony at Quebec in 1608. Du Plessis Bochart was an officer under Champlain and later commandant of the fort at Trois Rivières (Three Rivers).

they were pleased to honor me, in which these Gentlemen informed us of what had been said, in order that we might be present at the Huron Council, and be able to avail ourselves of what they had done. In accordance with this, in the month of April last, having been invited to an Assembly or Council, where all the Old Men and Chiefs of the Nation of the Bear met to deliberate on their great feast of the dead, I took occasion to show them the letters of these Gentlemen, and asked them to decide, after careful deliberation, what they wished to answer thereto. I told them that every man, as possessing an immortal soul, would at last, after this life, go to one or the other of two places, Paradise or Hell, and that forever; but that these places were widely different, since Paradise is a place abounding in blessings of all kinds, and free from all manner of ills; Hell, a place where no blessing comes, and where ills of all kinds abound; that it is a fiery furnace, in the midst of which the damned would be forever tormented, and burned without ever being consumed; that they must now consider to which of these two places they preferred to go some day, forever, and to do this while they were still in this life, because the matter was decided so far as it concerned all the dead for whom they had made or were going to make feasts; that all those who had slighted God and broken his commandments had followed the path to Hell, where they now were tormented by punishments that could not be imagined, and for which there was no remedy. I told them that, if they wished to go to Heaven, we would teach them the way; and, inasmuch as all affairs of importance are managed here by presents, and as the Porcelain[10] that takes the place of gold and silver in this Country is all-powerful, I presented in this Assembly a collar of twelve hundred beads of Porcelain, telling them that it was given to smooth the difficulties of the road to Paradise. It is customary to employ such terms, when they make presents to succeed in some difficult enterprise. Then all, in turn expressing their opinions, said that they dreaded these glowing fires of Hell, and that they preferred the road to Heaven. There was, nevertheless, one who—either seriously, or more probably in jest—said it was very fine that all should wish to go to Heaven, and be happy; but that, as far as he was concerned, it did not matter even if he should be burned in Hell. I replied that God gave us all the choice of the one or the other; that he did

not know what Hell fire was, and that I hoped he would change his mind when he was better informed.

You see the inclination of the Hurons, and especially of the Nation of the Bear, to receive Christianity; and this will be greatly increased by the fact that we have already baptized many of their children. For they say, "We do not wish to be separated from our children, we desire to go to Heaven with them. You can judge," they say, "how much we approve your talk, seeing we willingly listen to it, without contradiction, and permit you to baptize our children." I must not forget to express on this occasion the satisfaction which Louys de saincte Foy[11] gives us; he certainly performs his duties as a Christian as much to our edification and pleasure as formerly he failed therein. In this month of September he had a desire to return to our house at Kébec for the winter, in order to resume quietly the good instructions he had had formerly from our Fathers in France, and to devote himself again to the practice of virtue and Christian piety. We strongly approved this design, the more so as he could have taken with him some young relative who might have been instructed and baptized there; but as some difficulty came in the way of his resolution, he concluded that he would pass a good part of the Winter with us. This he has done with much satisfaction and profit, both to himself and to us; for he has resumed attendance upon the Sacraments, and the habit of prayer. At Christmas he made a very good general Confession for the period since his Baptism. Besides, in our Catechizing and teaching of the Savages, he served as Interpreter, and has translated several things into the Huron language for us, wherein we admired the facility with which he understood our language, and comprehended and explained the most difficult mysteries. In short, he gives evidence that truly he has the fear of God before his eyes.

To conclude this chapter, we hope to send you Fathers Antoine Daniel and Ambroise Davot[12] with a band of honest little Hurons, to make a beginning for the Seminary, from which we can reasonably expect much fruit in the conversion of these Peoples. If there were Nuns at Kébec, I believe we might be able to send also girls for a Seminary. There are here a number of fine little girls, who, if they were well brought up, would not yield in any respect to our young French girls. It makes our hearts

---

10. Known as wampum in English colonies, these beads made from shells had both monetary and ceremonial value among the Natives of the interior Northeast.

11. The baptismal name of a Huron convert.

12. Also spelled "Davost," another of the Jesuits who first established the mission to the Hurons.

ache to see these innocent young girls so soon defile their purity of body and beauty of soul, for lack of a good example and good instruction. I doubt not at all that the divine Goodness will crown with great blessings those in particular whom he inspires to contribute to the foundation of these Seminaries, and to the education of these young plants of this infant Church. . . .

CHAPTER 3

Important advice for those whom it shall please God to call to New France, and especially to the country of the Hurons

We have learned that the salvation of so many innocent souls, washed and made white in the Blood of the Son of God, is stirring very deeply the hearts of many, and is exciting new desires in them to leave old France that they may come to the New. God be forever blessed that he, as this shows us, has at last opened to these Tribes the bowels of his infinite pity. I wish not to chill the ardor of this generous resolution. Alas! it is those hearts after God's own heart whom we are expecting; but I only wish to give one word of advice.

It is true that *fortis ut mors dilectio,* the love of God has power to do what death does,—that is to say, to detach us entirely from creatures and from ourselves; nevertheless, these desires that we feel of working for the safety of Infidels are not always sure signs of that pure love. There may be sometimes a little self-love and regard for ourselves, if we look only at the blessing and satisfaction of putting souls in Heaven without considering fully the pains, the labors and the difficulties which are inseparable from these Evangelical functions.

On this account, in order that no one may be deceived in regard to this, *ostendam illi quanta hic oporteat pro nomine Jesu pati.*[13] True, the two who came last, Fathers Mercier and Pijart, had no such trouble in their journey as those of us who came here the year before. They did not paddle, their men were not sick, as ours were; they had not to bear the heavy loads. Yet notwithstanding this, easy as may be a trip with the Savages, there is always enough to greatly cast down a heart not well under subjection. The readiness of the Savages does not shorten the road,

does not smooth down the rocks, does not remove the dangers. Be with whom you like, you must expect to be, at least, three or four weeks on the way, to have as companions persons you have never seen before; to be cramped in a bark Canoe in an uncomfortable position, not being free to turn yourself to one side or the other; in danger fifty times a day of being upset or of being dashed upon the rocks. During the day, the Sun burns you; during the night, you run the risk of being a prey to Mosquitoes. You sometimes ascend five or six rapids in a day; and, in the evening, the only refreshment is a little corn crushed between two stones and cooked in fine clear water; the only bed is the earth, sometimes only the rough, uneven rocks, and usually no roof but the stars; and all this in perpetual silence. If you are accidentally hurt, if you fall sick, do not expect from these Barbarians any assistance, for whence could they obtain it? And if the sickness is dangerous, and if you are remote from the villages, which are here very scattered, I would not like to guarantee that they would not abandon you, if you could not make shift to follow them.

When you reach the Hurons, you will indeed find hearts full of charity; we will receive you with open arms as an Angel of Paradise, we shall have all the inclination in the world to do you good; but we are so situated that we can do very little. We shall receive you in a Hut, so mean that I have scarcely found in France one wretched enough to compare it with; that is how you will be lodged. Harassed and fatigued as you will be, we shall be able to give you nothing but a poor mat, or at most a skin, to serve you as a bed; and, besides, you will arrive at a season when miserable little insects that we call here *Taouhac,* and, in good French, *pulces,*[14] will keep you awake almost all night, for in these countries they are incomparably more troublesome than in France; the dust of the Cabin nourishes them, the Savages bring them to us, we get them in their houses; and this petty martyrdom, not to speak of Mosquitoes, Sandflies, and other like vermin, lasts usually not less than three or four months of the Summer.

Instead of being a great master and great Theologian as in France, you must reckon on being here a humble Scholar, and then, good God! with what masters!—women, little children, and all the Savages,—and exposed to their laughter. The Huron language will be your saint Thomas and your Aristotle; and clever man as you are, and speaking glibly among learned and capable persons,

---

13. "I will show him what he ought to suffer here for the name of Jesus." Brébeuf sometimes provided translations of his Latin phrases, sometimes, as here, he did not.

14. Fleas, today spelled "pouces."

you must make up your mind to be for a long time mute among the Barbarians. You will have accomplished much, if, at the end of a considerable time, you begin to stammer a little.

And then how do you think you would pass the Winter with us? After having heard all that must be endured in wintering among the Montagnets[15] Savages, I may say that that is almost the life we lead here among the Hurons. I say it without exaggeration, the five and six months of Winter are spent in almost continual discomforts,—excessive cold, smoke, and the annoyance of the Savages; we have a Cabin built of simple bark, but so well jointed that we have to send some one outside to learn what kind of weather it is; the smoke is very often so thick, so annoying, and so obstinate that, for five or six days at a time, if you are not entirely proof against it, it is all you can do to make out a few lines in your Breviary. Besides, from morning until evening our fireplace is almost always surrounded by Savages,—above all, they seldom fail to be there at mealtimes. If you happen to have anything more than usual, let it be ever so little, you must reckon on most of these Gentlemen as your guests; if you do not share with them, you will be considered mean. As regards the food, it is not so bad, although we usually content ourselves with a little corn, or a morsel of dry smoked fish, or some fruits, of which I shall speak further on.

For the rest, thus far we have had only roses; henceforth, as we have Christians in almost every village, we must count upon making rounds through them at all seasons of the year, and of remaining there, according to necessity, for two or three whole weeks, amid annoyances that cannot be described. Add to all this, that our lives depend upon a single thread; and if, wherever we are in the world, we are to expect death every hour, and to be prepared for it, this is particularly the case here. For not to mention that your Cabin is only, as it were, chaff, and that it might be burned at any moment, despite all your care to prevent accidents, the malice of the Savages gives especial cause for almost perpetual fear; a malcontent may burn you down, or cleave your head open in some lonely spot. And then you are responsible for the sterility or fecundity of the earth, under penalty of your life; you are the cause of droughts; if you cannot make rain, they speak of nothing less than making away with you. I have only to mention, in addition, the danger there is from our enemies; it is enough to say that, on the thirteenth of this month of June, they killed twelve of our Hurons near the village of Contarrea, which is only a day's journey from us; that a short time before, at four leagues from our village, some Iroquois were discovered in the fields in ambuscade, only waiting to strike a blow at the expense of the life of some passer-by. This Nation is very timid,—they take no precautions against surprise, they are not careful to prepare arms or to inclose their villages with palisades; their usual recourse, especially when the enemy is powerful, is flight. Amid these alarms, which affect the whole Country, I leave you to imagine if we have any grounds for a feeling of safety.

After all, if we had here the exterior attractions of piety, as they exist in France, all this might pass. In France the great multitude and the good example of Christians, the solemnity of the Feasts, the majesty of the Churches so magnificently adorned, preach piety to you; and in the Houses of our order the fervor of our brethren, their modesty, and all the noble virtues which shine forth in all their actions, are so many powerful voices which cry to you without ceasing, *respice, et fac similiter.*[16] You have the consolation of celebrating every day the holy Mass; in a word, you are almost beyond the danger of falling,—at least, the falls are insignificant, and you have help immediately at hand. Here we have nothing, it seems, which incites towards good; we are among Peoples who are astonished when you speak to them of God, and who often have only horrible blasphemies in their mouths. Often you are compelled to deprive yourself of the holy Sacrifice of the Mass; and, when you have the opportunity to say it, a little corner of your Cabin will serve you for a Chapel, which the smoke, the snow, or the rain hinders you from ornamenting and embellishing, even if you had the means. I pass over the small chance of seclusion there is among Barbarians, who scarcely ever leave you, who hardly know what it is to speak in a low tone. Especially I would not dare to speak of the danger there is of ruining oneself among their impurities, in the case of any one whose heart is not sufficiently full of God to firmly resist this poison. But enough of this; the rest can only be known by experience.

"But is that all?" some one will exclaim. "Do you think by your arguments to throw water on the fire that consumes me, and lessen ever so little the zeal I have for

---

15. Father Paul Le Jeune had passed a winter with the Montagnais Indians north of Quebec and written about it in one of the first Jesuit *Relations,* in 1634.

16. "Go thou, and do likewise."

the conversion of these Peoples? I declare that these things have served only to confirm me the more in my vocation; that I feel myself more carried away than ever by my affection for New France, and that I bear a holy jealousy towards those who are already enduring all these sufferings; all these labors seem to me nothing, in comparison with what I am willing to endure for God; if I knew a place under Heaven where there was yet more to be suffered, I would go there." Ah! whoever you are to whom God gives these sentiments and this light, come, come, my dear Brother, it is workmen such as you that we ask for here; it is to souls like yours that God has appointed the conquest of so many other souls whom the Devil holds yet in his power; apprehend no difficulties,—there will be none for you, since it is your whole consolation to see yourself crucified with the Son of God; silence will be sweet to you, since you have learned to commune with God, and to converse in the Heavens with Saints and Angels; the victuals would be very insipid if the gall endured by our Lord did not render them sweeter and more savory to you than the most delicious viands of the world. What a satisfaction to pass these rapids, and to climb these rocks, to him who has before his eyes that loving Savior, harassed by his tormentors and ascending Calvary laden with his Cross; the discomfort of the Canoe is very easy to bear, to him who considers the crucified one. What a consolation!—for I must use such terms, as otherwise I could not give you pleasure—what a consolation, then, to see oneself even abandoned on the road by the Savages, languishing with sickness, or even dying with hunger in the woods, and of being able to say to God, "My God, it is to do your holy will that I am reduced to the state in which you see me,"—considering above all that God-man who expires upon the Cross and cries to his Father, *Deus meus, Deus meus, ut quid dereliquisti me.* If God among all these hardships preserve you in health, no doubt you will arrive pleasantly in the Huron country with these holy thoughts. *Suaviter navigat quem gratia Dei portat.*[17]

And now, as regards a place of abode, food, and beds,—shall I dare to say to a heart so generous, and that mocks at all that of which I have already spoken, that truly, even though we have hardly more of those necessities than the Savages have, still, I know not how, the divine Goodness renders every difficult thing easy; and all

and every one of us find everything almost as comfortable as life is in France. The sleep we get lying on our mats seems to us as sweet as if we were in a good bed; the food of the Country does not disgust us, although there is scarcely any other seasoning than that which God has put into it; and, notwithstanding the cold of a winter six months long, passed in the shelter of a bark Cabin open to the daylight, we have still to experience its evil effects; no one complains of his head or his stomach; we do not know what diarrhoea, colds, or catarrh are. This leads me to say that delicate persons do not know, in France, how to protect themselves from the cold; those rooms so well carpeted, those doors so well fitted, and those windows closed with so much care, serve only to make its effects more keenly felt; it is an enemy from whom one wins almost more by holding out one's hands to him than by waging a cruel war upon him. As to our food, I shall say this further, that God has shown his Providence very clearly to our eyes; we have obtained in eight days our provision of corn for a whole year, without making a single step beyond our Cabin. They have brought us dried fish in such quantities that we are constrained to refuse some of it, and to say that we have sufficient; you might say that God, seeing we are here only for his service, in order that all our work may be for him, wishes to act himself as our provider. This same Goodness takes care to give us from time to time a change of provisions in the shape of fresh fish. We live on the shore of a great Lake, which affords as good fish as I have ever seen or eaten in France; true, as I have said, we do not ordinarily procure them, and still less do we get meat, which is even more rarely seen here. Fruits even, according to the season, provided the year be somewhat favorable, are not lacking to us; strawberries, raspberries, and blackberries are to be found in almost incredible quantities. We gather plenty of grapes, which are fairly good; the squashes last sometimes four and five months, and are so abundant that they are to be had almost for nothing, and so good that, on being cooked in the ashes, they are eaten as apples are in France. Consequently, to tell the truth, as regards provisions, the change from France is not very great; the only grain of the Country[18] is a sufficient nourishment, when one is somewhat accustomed to it. The Savages prepare it in more than twenty ways and yet employ only fire and water; it is true that the best sauce is that which it carries with it.

---

17. "He sails smoothly who is carried along by the grace of God."

18. Corn or maize.

As for the dangers of the soul, to speak frankly, there are none for him who brings to the Country of the Hurons the fear and love of God; on the contrary, I find unparalleled advantages for acquiring perfection. Is it not a great deal to have, in one's food, clothing, and sleep, no other attraction than bare necessity? Is it not a glorious opportunity to unite oneself with God, when there is no creature whatsoever that gives you reason to spend your affection upon it? when the exercises you practice constrain you without force to inward meditation? Besides your spiritual exercises, you have no other employment than the study of the language, and conversation with the Savages. Ah! how much pleasure there is for a heart devoted to God to make itself the little Scholar of a Savage and of a little child, thereby to gain them for God, and to render them Disciples of our Lord! How willingly and liberally God communicates himself to a soul which practices from love to him these heroic acts of humility! The words he learns are so many treasures he amasses, so many spoils he carries off from the common enemy of the human race; so that he has reason to say a hundred times a day, *Lætabor super eloquia tua tanquam qui invenit spolia multa.* Viewed in this light, the visits of the Savages, however frequent, cannot be annoying to him. God teaches him the beautiful lesson he taught formerly to Saint Catherine of Sienna,[19] to make of his heart a room or temple for him, where he will never fail to find him, as often as he withdraws into it; that, if he encounters Savages there, they do not interfere with his prayers, they serve only to make them more fervent; from this he takes occasion to present these poor wretches to this sovereign Goodness, and to entreat him warmly for their conversion.

Certainly we have not here that exterior solemnity which awakens and sustains devotion. Only what is essential in our Religion is visible, the holy Sacrament of the Altar, to the marvels of which we must open the eyes of our Faith without being aided by any sensible mark of its grandeur, any more than the Magi were in the stable. But it seems that God, supplying what we lack,—and as a recompense of grace that he has given us in transporting it, so to speak, beyond so many seas, and in finding a place for it in these poor Cabins,—wishes to crown us with the same blessings, in the midst of these infidel Peoples, with which he is accustomed to favor persecuted Catholics in the Countries of heretics.[20] These good people scarcely ever see either Church or Altar; but the little they see is worth double what they would see in full liberty. What consolation would there be, in your opinion, in prostrating ourselves at times before a Cross in the midst of this Barbarism! to turn our eyes toward, and to enter, in the midst of our petty domestic duties, even into the room which the Son of God has been pleased to take in our little dwelling. Is it not to be in Paradise day and night, that we are not separated from this Well-beloved of the Nations except by some bark or the branch of a tree? *En ipse stat post parietem nostrum. Sub umbra illius quem desideraveram, sedi.*[21] See what we have within. If we go outside our cabin, Heaven is open to us; and those great buildings which lift their heads to the clouds, in large cities, do not conceal it from our view; so that we can say our prayers in full liberty before the noble Oratory that saint François Xavier loved better than any other. If the question is of the fundamental virtues, I will glory not in myself, but in the share which has fallen to me; or, if I must, acknowledge it humbly beside the Cross which our Lord in his grace gives us to bear after him. Certain it is that this Country, or our work here, is much more fitted to feed the soul with the fruits of Heaven than with the fruits of earth. I may be deceiving myself, but I imagine that here is a grand means of increasing the soul in Faith, in Hope, and in Charity. Should we scatter the seeds of the Faith without ourselves profiting by them? Could we put our confidence anywhere but in God in a Region where, as far as man is concerned, everything is lacking to us? Could we wish a nobler opportunity to exercise Charity than amid the roughness and discomfort of a new world, where no human art or industry has yet provided any conveniences? and to live here that we may bring back to God men who are so unlike men that we must live in daily expectation of dying by their hand, should the fancy take them, should a dream suggest it to them, or should we fail to open or close the Heavens to them at discretion, giving them rain or fine weather at command. Do they not make us responsible for the state of the weather? And if God does not inspire us, or if we cannot work miracles by faith, are we not continually in danger, as they have threatened us, of seeing them fall upon those who have done no wrong? Indeed, if he who is

---

19. Saint Catherine of Sienna (1347?–80) was a Dominican nun.

20. The Protestant countries of Europe.

21. "Behold he standeth behind our wall. I sat down under his shadow, whom I desired." From the Song of Solomon 2.9 and 2.3.

the Truth itself had not declared that there is no greater love than to lay down one's life, verily and once for all, for one's friends, I should conceive it a thing equally noble, or even more so, to do what the Apostle said to the Corinthians, *Quotidie morior per vestram gloriam, fratres, quam habeo in Christo Jesu Domino nostro,*[22] than to drag out a life full of misery, amid the frequent and ordinary dangers of an unforeseen death, which those whom you hope to save will procure for you. I call to mind occasionally what Saint François Xavier once wrote to Father Simon, and wish that it may please God to so act that at least the same thing may be said or written one day even of us, although we may not be worthy of it. Here are the words: *Optimi è Moluco perferuntur nuntii, quippe in maximis ærumnis perpetuísque vitæ discriminibus, Joannes Beira eiúsque socii versantur, magno cum Christianæ Religionis incremento.*[23]

There seems to be one thing here which might give apprehension to a Son of the Society, to see himself in the midst of a brutal and sensual People, whose example might tarnish the luster of the most and the least delicate of all the virtues, unless especial care be taken—I mean Chastity.

In order to obviate this difficulty, I make bold to say that if there is any place in the world where this so precious virtue is safe, for a man among us who wishes to be on his guard, it is here. *Nisi Dominus custodierit civitatem, frustrà vigilat qui custodit eam. Scivi quoniam aliter non possem esse continens, nisi Deus det. Et hoc ipsum erat sapientia, scire cujus esset hoc donum.*[24] It is said that the victories which this Daughter of Heaven gains over her enemies, are gained by flight; but I believe

it is God and no one else who puts to flight this very enemy in the most severe encounters, before those who, fearing nothing so much as his approaches, go with bowed heads, and hearts full of confidence in his Goodness, where his glory calls them. And where should we seek this glory? I should say, where find it more fully purified and disentangled from our own interests, than in a place where there is nothing more to be hoped for than the reward of having left all for the love of him of whom St. Paul said, *Scio cui credidi.*[25] You remember that plant, named "the fear of God," with which it is said our Fathers at the beginning of our Society charmed away the spirit of impurity; it does not grow in the land of the Hurons, but it falls there abundantly from Heaven, if one has but a little care to cultivate that which he brings here. Barbarism, ignorance, poverty, and misery, which render the life of these Savages more deplorable than death, are a continual reminder to us to mourn Adam's fall, and to submit ourselves entirely to him who still chastises disobedience in his children, in so remarkable a way, after so many centuries. Saint Theresa[26] said once that she never found her meditations more profitable than in the mysteries in which she found our Lord apart and alone, as if she had been in the garden of Olives; and she called this a part of her simplicity. You may reckon this among my follies, if you like; but it seems to me that we have here so much the more leisure to caress, so to speak, and to entertain our Lord with open heart, in the midst of these uninhabited lands, because there are so few people who trouble themselves about him. And, on account of this favor, we can boldly say, *Non timebo mala, quoniam tu mecum es.*[27] In short, I imagine that all the Guardian Angels of these neglected and abandoned Nations are continually endeavoring and laboring to save us from these dangers. They know well that if there were anything in the world that ought to give us wings, to fly back whence we came both by obedience and by our own inclination, it would be this misfortune, if we were not shielded from it by the protection of Heaven. This is what excites them to procure for us the means to guard against it, that they may not lose the brightest hope they have ever had, by the grace of God, of the conversion of these Peoples.

---

22. I Corinithians 15.31: "I die daily, I protest by your glory, brethren, which I have in Christ Jesus our Lord."

23. "I have received thrilling news . . . regarding the great things that have been accomplished . . . for Christianity in Malacca. You will learn of all this from their letters. . . . Juan de Beira and his companions labor constantly under great difficulties and reap an increase for Christianity." The passage is indeed quoted from a letter from Francis Xavier to Simon Rodriguez regarding missionary efforts in the Malucca, in the East Indies. Xavier was a founding member of the Jesuit order and a successful missionary in the Far East. Brébeuf wishes to show that the mission to the Hurons might have equal success.

24. "Unless the Lord build the house, they labour in vain to build it. I know full well that I could not live a chaste life without the help of God. It is in itself wisdom to know who is one's benefactor." The first sentence is from Psalm 126.1

---

25. "He who knows, believes."

26. St. Teresa of Avila (1515–82), a Spanish nun and mystic.

27. "I will fear no evil, for thou art with me." Psalm 22.4.

I finish this discourse and this Chapter with this sentence: If, at the sight of the difficulties and Crosses that are here prepared for us, some one feels himself so fortified from above that he can say it is too little, or like St. François Xavier, *Ampliùs, ampliùs,*[28] I hope that our Lord will also draw from his lips this other confession, in the midst of the consolations he will give him, that it will be too much for him, that he cannot endure more. *Satis est, Domine, satis est.*[29]

---

28. "More, more." That is, one begs God for further suffering.

29. "Enough, O Lord, enough."

Marie Guyart Martin, "Marie de l'Incarnation" (1599–1672)

One night around Christmas in 1633, Marie Guyart Martin had a dream: She traveled with a companion through great difficulties to a small house atop a precipice, where she saw the Blessed Virgin Mary and the baby Jesus. Some months later, she determined that the companion must have been St. Joseph and the place, Quebec, a tiny French settlement founded by Samuel de Champlain in 1608. She interpreted her dream as a call to go to Canadian New France and join the efforts of missionaries who were bent upon bringing the Catholic faith to the Native Americans.

Martin had lived all her life until then in Tours, in central France. She had married Claude Martin, a silk worker, in 1619, with whom she had had a son, also named Claude. Her husband died after two years, however, and the widow Marie Martin had a series of visions and became increasingly devout, even as she gained worldly wealth and responsibility in managing her brother-in-law's mercantile business. She entered the Ursuline convent in Tours in 1631. Four years after the dream about seeing the Virgin Mary, Marie Martin met an even wealthier widow named Mme. de la Peltrie. Together they laid plans to found a seminary for converted Native American girls in Quebec. They sailed in May 1639, and although Mme. de la Peltrie soon left to join the new settlement at Montreal, Marie de l'Incarnation (that is, "Marie of the Incarnation") became superior of the new Ursuline school. She remained there until her death, enduring cold, hunger, fires, an earthquake, and self-imposed isolation and self-torture. As a cloistered nun, she could talk to men only through a grille. Yet her long residence in the colony enabled her to write much of its history and major personalities. She shared with the more famous Jesuit missionaries a zeal that envisioned the converted Huron and Algonquian Indians as pious and primitive people, free of the detriments that lives of European luxury had wrought in white people. Such devout people as these embraced the possibility of death at the hands of Iroquois, their enemies.

The population of Quebec was comprised of French civil and military officials, farmers, fur traders (called *habitants*), Native Americans, and the religious community. The religious people there were Jesuit and Sulpician missionaries and nuns of the Hospitalière order, as well as the Ursulines. Marie de l'Incarnation wrote of all these worlds, and although she published nothing in her lifetime, she was aware of her role in documenting the activities of the colony and the religious people there. The first letter presented next recounts the martyrdoms of leading missionaries, martyrdoms also celebrated in the Jesuit *Relations*. The last letter reprinted here indicates an important reminder about the records the Jesuits were creating: the *Relations* do not tell of all that transpired in Quebec.

Marie wrote two spiritual autobiographies, only one of which is known to exist today. Her letters evidently numbered nearly 20,000, yet only 278 survive—a significant amount of letters, certainly, despite the number evidently originally written. Marie Martin's son, Claude Martin, rose to a position of influence in the Church in France. Although he never saw his mother after she joined the Ursulines, he grew close to her through their correspondence. He published a memoir about her life in 1677, followed by a collection of her letters. These works promoted an image of his mother just short of saintly, but they also provided an unsurpassed record of the work of Catholic women in New France, an appropriate balance to the voluminous records of the Jesuits and other missionaries there.

LETTERS TO HER SON[1]

[The Deaths of Daniel, Brébeuf, and
Gabriel Lalemant]

To the Community of the Ursulines of Tours

Quebec, 1649

My reverend Mother, and very dear Sisters:
I informed you last year that we had had news that the Iroquois had martyred the Reverend Father de Brébeuf. It is true that the cruelty of those barbarians had made a martyr, but Father de Brébeuf's time had not yet arrived, as it has since. The one that was so richly requited last year was the Reverend Father Antoine Daniel.[2]

While he was on mission to the Hurons in the month of July, the town in which he was [Saint-Joseph II] was attacked by the Iroquois. He was still in his sacerdotal robes when he heard the tumult of the enemies and, without taking time to remove his alb, he ran from cabin to cabin seeking the sick, the old, the children, and all who had not yet received baptism.[3] He prepared them for the sacrament with apostolic zeal and, gathering them all together in the church, baptized them by sprinkling.

When he saw the enemy approach, he said to his flock, 'Escape, brothers, and leave me alone in the confusion.'

Then this saintly man faced the enemy with a majestic bearing, which terrified them completely. He spoke to them of God, preached the Faith in a loud voice, and reproached them for their treacherousness. But at length the barbarians lost the fear they had conceived at his appearance. They covered him with arrows, and when he did not fall, a group of musketeers fired a salvo upon him, from which he fell dead on the spot. They carried his body into his church and set it afire, and thus, like a victim of good odour, he was consumed at the foot of the altar with the altar itself. They put everything to fire and carnage, sparing neither the children nor the women nor anyone whatsoever. Those that could flee to other nations escaped their cruelty, failing which everyone would have been destroyed.

This holy martyr appeared a little time after his death to a Father of the Company and the mission.[4]

The latter, recognizing him, said, 'Ah, my dear Father, how has God permitted that your body should be treated so unworthily after your death that we could not gather up your ashes?'

The holy martyr replied, 'My very dear Father, God is great and wonderful. He beheld this reproach and, like a great God, rewarded the labours of his servant. After my death he gave me a great many souls in purgatory that I might take them with me to accompany my triumph in heaven.'

He also appeared at a council as if presiding at it and inspiring the resolutions that had to be taken for the glory of God.

The martyrdom of the Reverend Fathers Jean de Brébeuf and Gabriel Lalemant came to pass on the eve of

---

1. Marie de l'Incarnation's letters were first edited by her son and published in 1681. The standard French text of these materials was edited by Dom Albert Jamet (Paris, 1929–39). The text here is taken from *Word from New France: The Selected Letters of Marie de l'Incarnation,* trans. and ed. Joyce Marshall (1967).

2. Daniel, who had served the Huron mission since 1634, was killed on July 4, 1648. That Marie should describe this fate as "richly requited" shows her zeal for martyrdom and suffering in the name of religion.

3. The missionaries believed that once baptized, even an uninstructed heathen could go to heaven, so Daniel sought to baptize those who might soon be killed by the Iroquois.

4. The Jesuit *Relation* for 1648–49 also reported that Daniel appeared in a vision to Father Pierre Joseph Marie Chaumonot (1611–93).

St Joseph of this year 1649[5] while they were on mission together. The first had grown white in the apostolic missions and the conquest of the souls of the Savages, of whom he had had the consolation of seeing as many as seven or eight thousand baptized. The second was the nephew of the Reverend Father Superior of the missions[6] who preceded him here. He was the frailest and most delicate man one could see, and yet God, by a miracle of his grace, wished to make visible in his person what an instrument, however feeble, could do when he chose it for his glory and his service. He was fifteen entire hours in horrible torments. The Reverend Father de Brébeuf was but three. But note that ever since he had been in these regions, where he had preached the Gospel since the year 1628[7] (except for a space of time while he was in France, the English having made themselves masters of the country), his life had been a continual martyrdom.

This, then, is how the martyrdom of these holy Fathers came to pass.

When the village in which they were was taken by the Iroquois, they did not wish to flee or abandon their flock, as they could have done as easily as several others, both Christians and pagans, who begged them to go with them. Having remained then to prepare the victims for the sacrifice, they began to baptize those that were not baptized and to confess those that were. On this occasion a miracle of God's all-powerful hand was seen, for several persons that would not hear any word of baptism, because of their attachment to their superstitions, were the most eager to request and receive it.

Our good Fathers continued these holy practices till the barbarians pounced upon them like enraged wolves and, after stripping them naked, beat them with clubs in a very cruel manner, urged on by some renegade Hurons in detestation of the Faith. They were taken to the place of their execution[8] where they at once prostrated themselves upon the ground, kissing it with a particular devotion and rendering thanks to Our Lord for the honour he was granting them by making them worthy to suffer for his love.

They were attached to stakes to be more conveniently tortured. Then each barbarian had the power to do the worst he could.

They began with the older, for whom the renegades bore a mortal hatred. Some cut off their feet and hands, others removed the flesh from their arms, legs, and thighs, part of which they boiled and part roasted so as to eat it in their presence. While they were still alive, they drank their blood. After this brutal cruelty, they drove blazing firebrands into their wounds. They reddened the blades of their hatchets and made collars of them, which they hung around their necks and under their armpits.

Then, in derision of our holy Faith, the barbarians poured boiling water upon their heads, saying, 'We are greatly obliging you. We are giving you great pleasure. We are baptizing you so that you will be very happy in heaven, for that is what you teach.'

After these blasphemies and a thousand like taunts, they removed their scalps, which is a fairly common torture among the Savages that they make their captives suffer.

To this extent the torture was common to both these saints but, in addition, Father Lalemant's head was cleft by a hatchet so that the substance of his brain could be seen. Meanwhile he kept his eyes raised to heaven, suffering all these outrages without any complaint or saying a word. It was not thus with the Reverend Father de Brébeuf. He continually preached the grandeurs of God, which caused his torturers such vexation that they cut away his entire mouth in rage and pierced his tongue. The Reverend Father Lalemant was fifteen hours in these torments and the Reverend Father de Brébeuf but three, and so he preceded his companion into glory as he had preceded him in the labours of the mission.

This is how the martyrdom of our holy Fathers concluded. I wished to make you a little abridgement until you see it at greater length in the *Relation*,[9] where you will also see the great calamities of this Church and the great risks the workers of the Gospel run. Those in the Huron mission have been obliged to leave their residence at Sainte-Marie and take refuge on an island with the remainder of the Christians, with the intention of building a fort there.

I ask the intercession of your prayers for the maintenance of Christianity in these new lands. Make mention

---

5. March 16, 1649.

6. Jerome Lalemant (1593–1673) was superior from 1645 to 1650.

7. Brébeuf was actually in Canada from 1625 to 1629 and from 1633 until his death in 1649.

8. The mission named Saint-Ignace, after the founder of the Jesuit order, Ignatius Loyola, canonized in 1622.

---

9. A narrative of the martyrdom did appear in the Jesuit *Relation* of 1649.

of me in particular, I beseech you, and excuse me, if you please, if I do not write to each one of you in particular. I have the desire to do so, but the affairs with which I am charged and the little time I have deprives me of the power. Be persuaded nevertheless that I am for time and for eternity, to each in particular as well as to all in general, yours etc.

[A New Language to Learn]

To Her Son

Quebec, 17 March 1650

My very dear son:
The circumstance that the Quebec frigate is going to fish at Île-Percée, where there are fishing vessels that return to France sooner than the vessels here are ready to depart, gives me the opportunity to write you this little word. In giving myself this consolation it seems to me that I am giving it to you, since you and I are but one in Our Lord.

I shall tell you, then, that since the letters I wrote to you in the month of October last, all has been at peace in this region. We do not yet know what has happened among the Hurons, except that our Reverend Fathers completed their fort which has good walls, in the month of November. We learned this from a Huron that journeyed three hundred leagues through underbrush and by uncleared trails for fear of being stopped. This fort is to shelter the Hurons that are pursued by their enemies, as well as the Reverend Fathers of the mission. As for those that are still in the open country, only God can protect them.

As for us, as I have said, we have been at peace. But a fortnight ago the Iroquois appeared. Some of them were captured and the others put to flight. Some of them, nevertheless, have done what they have never dared do till now. They have never approached nearer than forty leagues of us but on this occasion they came to within three leagues of Quebec, where they attacked the habitation of one our habitants, killed two of his domestics, put his whole family to flight, and pillaged his house and his goods. Then they went to burn the house of a worthy gentleman, which is a little more distant. These raids terrified all the habitants, who are scattered here and there the better to carry on their affairs. It is said that the Iroquois are arming in great number to come to attack Quebec, but have no fear for us. Our house, as well as being very good, is safe under the cannon of the fort. But our confidence

and strength is not in these things but entirely in our good Jesus.

The Reverend Father Bressani,[10] who set out to go on mission in the month of September, retraced his steps when he had not yet made fifty leagues of the journey. He spent the winter here with a group of Hurons that he was instructing. Our three religious houses, and some charitable persons, joined together to nourish these poor exiles, who have just departed to fetch the other members of their families from their country so as to settle close to us. These new habitants oblige us to study the Huron tongue, to which I had not previously applied myself, having contented myself with knowing only that of the Algonkins and Montagnais who are always with us. You will perhaps laugh that at the age of fifty years I am beginning to study a new tongue, but one must undertake all things for the service of God and the salvation of one's neighbour. I commenced this study a week after the octave of All Saints, and the Reverend Father Bressani has been my master till the present with an entire charity. As we can only study tongues in winter, I hope that someone else will come down this autumn who will render us the same assistance. Pray to Our Lord that it may please him to open my mind for his glory that it may render him some little service. . . .

I do not risk writing to you more fully. I am merely entrusting this letter to chance, not having yet tried this way. If you receive it, let me know, so that we may neglect no means of sending our news to one another. We are awaiting your news and that of all our friends—God in his mercy grant that it be good.

As I finish this letter, I learn that the young men are being gathered together to go against the Iroquois, who are quite close. Everyone fears them, because they hide in the underbrush and pounce upon people when no-one is thinking of them. They are real assassins that cannot be extinguished and laugh at the most skilful.

-----

10. Francesco Giuseppe Bressani (1612–72), a Jesuit missionary from Rome, was captured by the Iroquois in 1644 and tortured, but was ransomed by the Dutch and returned to France. In 1653 he published an account of his captivity in Italian, a translation of which is included in the Jesuit *Relations*.

[The End of the Huron Mission]

To Her Son

Quebec, 30 August 1650

My very dear and well-loved son:
The life and love of Jesus be your life and love for eternity.

It is a great evidence of your affection for me that you wish me the same portion as our Reverend Fathers. But, alas, I am unworthy of such an honour and so high a grace, although it seems very close to us. For since I told you something of the great and extraordinary persecution of the Iroquois, there has been yet another great clash between the French and those barbarians in an encounter near Trois-Rivières, when our men went in search of nine Frenchmen that the Iroquois had captured and carried off. Today they have the intention of storming Trois-Rivières and you will note that with them they have several Hollanders that are helping them.[11] One was recognized during the battle and a Huron that escaped has also assured us of it.

They are resolved (so we are told) to come, after they have taken Trois-Rivières, to attack us. Although in appearance there is not so much reason for fear in our houses, which are strong, still what has happened in all the Huron villages, which were laid waste by fire and arms (for assuredly they are powerful), should make the French apprehend a like disaster if prompt help does not come to us. This is the belief of the wisest and most experienced, such as the Reverend Fathers who have come down from the Hurons after bearing the weight of the tyranny of those barbarians.

This help can only come to us from France, for there are not enough forces in all the country to resist them. If France fails us, then, we must shortly either leave or die. But because all the French, who are to the number of more than two thousand, will not be able to find means to withdraw, they will be forced to perish, either through poverty or through the cruelty of their enemies; and, also, the fact that they would have to leave the goods they have

acquired in this country and be deprived of all means of support in France will make them choose death in this country rather than misery in another.

We ourselves have other motives, through the mercy of Our Lord. It is not worldly goods that keep us here but rather the remnant of our good Christians, with whom we should deem ourselves happy to die a million times if it were possible. These are our treasures, our brothers, our spiritual children, whom we cherish more than our lives and all the worldly goods under heaven. Rejoice, then, if we die and if news is brought to you that our blood and ashes are mingled with theirs. There is likelihood that this will happen if the thousand Iroquois that have separated to go to the Neutral nation rejoin those that are at our gates.

The Reverend Father Daran, whom I have charged to give you this letter, is one of those that have come from the Hurons. He has suffered all it is possible to suffer without dying, so he will be able to converse with you at leisure about all that has happened these last years in this new Church, and I promise myself that you will be very edified to hear him. He is going to make a tour of duty in France while waiting to be recalled here in case the affairs of the country improve, for he is extremely regretted here. I regret him like the others and you must soothe my regrets by welcoming him as he deserves. Others, such as the Reverend Fathers Ragueneau and Pijart, are going to France also, to ask help of His Majesty.[12] The former is more interested, because he is the Superior of the Huron mission. He is one of the great personages and most zealous missionaries of New France, but I esteem him more for his great holiness than for all his great natural talents and abundant graces. We hope to see him again next year.

Just when I had finished speaking to you of the Reverend Father Ragueneau, I was informed that he was asking for me to say good-bye. He has promised to see you and, to this end, he has taken your name in writing. He is one of the best friends of our seminary and has great knowledge of the graces divine Goodness pours upon it. He has assured me again, out of his experience of the fury and strength of the Iroquois, that if we do not have prompt help from France or if it does not please God to succour this country in some extraordinary way, all is lost. This is

---

11. The Dutch established a colony in the Hudson River valley and allied with the Iroquois against the French and Hurons. Trois-Rivières (Three Rivers), the next major settlement up the St. Lawrence River from Quebec, was at the mouth of the St. Maurice River, where it met the St. Lawrence.

12. Paul Ragueneau (1608–80) was the superior of the Jesuit mission to the Hurons in 1649, when the attacks of the Iroquois forced a retreat to Quebec. Wars between the two peoples had been raging for at least a decade.

not an exaggeration. I tell you the same thing from my little knowledge.

You see by this that as we await help we are in the pure providence of God. For myself personally, my very dear son, I feel as well here and my spirit and my heart are as content as they could be. If it should happen that you are brought news of my death next year, praise God thereafter and offer the holy sacrifice of the Mass for me. . . .

I replied in another letter to the methods you propose for rearing some Savages so they will be able to win their compatriots to the Faith. In addition to what I have written to you, discuss this with the Reverend Father Daran. He will tell you that, even if the country recovers, it will always be necessary to depend on Europe for the workers for the Gospel, the nature of the American Savages (even the most holy and spiritual) not being at all suited to ecclesiastical functions but only to being taught and led gently along the way to heaven, which makes one suspect, in this reversal of affairs, that God wishes only a transient Church here.

It is true that the Reverend Father de Brébeuf had received the sacred gift of which I spoke.[13] The Reverend Father Garnier, one of those that won the crown this year, had it eminently. You will never know this by study, my very dear son, nor by the force of speculation, but only in humble prayer and submission of the soul at the feet of the crucifix. . . . It would need a very large book to describe the life of this Reverend Father. . . . He was eminently humble, gentle, obedient, and full of virtues acquired by great travail. It was pleasant to see the effect of his virtues in practical affairs. He was in continual colloquy and familiar converse with God. Pierced by wounds, he was seen still engaged in the practice of charity, making an effort to drag himself towards a poor woman who had been struck several times by a hatchet and was in the last extremity and in need of help to die well.

The Reverend Father Chabanel, one of those that was massacred this year, had by nature the greatest possible aversion to living in the cabins of the Savages. For this reason it was often wished to exempt him from this by sending him to other missions where he would not have had to engage in this sort of life. But, with unusual courage and driven by the spirit of which we are speaking, he made a vow to remain there and die there, if it pleased God to grant him this mercy. His Superior, however, knowing that he was extremely fatigued from the travails of his mission, recalled him and it was on this journey that he was captured and massacred, though it is not known by what enemies nor what was done to his body. Whatever may be, he died in the act of obedience.

The other Reverend Fathers that have retired here from the distant missions have suffered so terribly that no human tongue could express it. . . .

I am of your sentiment that lack of money may well prevent the expedition of our bull at Rome.[14] I see, moreover, that the troubles of this country will hold many things in suspense. For there are three things one must consider in the present state of affairs. The first, that neither we nor all Canada can subsist two years longer without help. The second, that if this help is lacking, we must, in the opinion of the more judicious, either die or return to France. I believe, however, that if the enemy has a war with the Neutral nation and the Andastoué,[15] this will be a diversion of arms that will enable us to subsist a little longer. But if he continues in his conquests and victories, there will be nothing for the French to do here. It will not be possible to carry on trade. If there is no trade, no more ships will come here. If ships no longer come, we shall lack all things necessary for life, such as cloth, linens, and the greater part of our food, including the bacon and flour that the garrison and religious houses cannot do without. It is not that people do not work hard and that food is not produced, but the country does not yet provide what it needs to maintain itself. The third thing that retards our affairs is that if trade fails because of continuation of the war, the Savages, who stop here only to trade, will scatter in the woods. Thus there will be no more need for a bull, as there will be no more work for those of us that are here only to lead the Savages to the Faith and gain them for God. You can judge from this whether a bishop would come here in a time so full of calamity, aside from the fact that, the Church having been only transient, there is no more need for a pastor—I am speaking in the supposition that God permits the extremity that is feared.

---

13. Charles Garnier (1600–49) had "won the crown" of martyrdom by being killed by the Iroquois on December 7, 1649. In 1930 he, Brébeuf, Lalemant, Daniel, Chabanel, and other Jesuit martyrs were canonized.

14. Marie de l'Incarnation was seeking a papal bull affirming the union of the Ursuline congregation at Quebec.

15. The Susquehanna Indians. This name appears again later in variant spellings.

This new Church being in so manifest a peril, do me the charity of making a devotion before the very blessed Virgin that it may please her to take it under her protection. Pray to her also for me and for our election, which we shall hold in Pentecost week.[16]

This peril and these fears, however, do not diminish the worship the Christians, both French and Savage, are in the habit of rendering to God. You would have felt a very sensible devotion to see the procession that was held on the Feast of the Assumption of the Mother of Goodness. Two Fathers of the Company[17] carried her image in relief on a beautifully ornamented litter to the three religious houses, which had been assigned to be the stations. As these houses are somewhat far from each other, two other Fathers were prepared to succeed the first two and relieve them in this sacred charge. In addition to the greater number of the French, there were about six hundred Savages marching in order. The devotion of these good converts was so great that it brought tears to the eyes of those that looked upon them. I had the curiosity to watch them from a place where I could not be seen, and I assure you that I have never seen a procession in France in which there was so much order and, in appearance, so much devotion. Where the Savages are concerned, this is always new to me, for the thought of what they were before they knew God, and of what they are now that they know him, touches me far more than I can tell you. From this you may judge how much I suffer to see the tyranny that the barbarous Iroquois practise towards them. Ah, my very dear son, how happy I should be if all this persecution should terminate upon me! Present this desire of mine to the Blessed Virgin, to whom I willingly present yours.

I have already written this letter in several snatches, and in the intervals some news always comes. The captive that escaped from the Iroquois reports that the Andoouestéronon [Susquehannah] and Neutral warriors have taken two hundred Iroquois prisoners. If this is true, they will be treated in a terrible way and this will be so much burden for us. This captive will be here fully a fortnight more before he has told everything he knows, for it is the custom of the Savages to tell what they know only little by little and on different days, which makes our Frenchmen impatient, for they have lively spirits and would like to know things once for all, especially when they involve matters of consequence and are reported by only one messenger.

Since the above, two more Hurons have escaped the captivity of the Iroquois. They are both good Christians in their hearts and catechumens in effect. Desire for Holy Baptism caused them to make great efforts, by long journeys through the woods and without any provision. They reported that our ten Algonkins from Sillery that were captured in the month of June last were burned alive in sentiments of faith and religion. One of them, for love of whom I write this note, was especially marked by zeal and fervour. He was twenty-two years old or thereabouts and was my spiritual son, loving me as much as or more than his mother. He was in very terrible torture for three days and three nights, in derision of the Faith, which he confessed in a loud voice till his last breath.

The barbarians said to him in mockery, 'Where is your God? He does not help you.' Then they would begin to torture him again and also to mock him, saying, 'Pray to your God and see if he will help you.'

Meanwhile this courageous servant of God redoubled his prayers and his praises of the One for love of whom he suffered, for naturally he sang very well, and this enraged the barbarians. He was named Joseph [Onahari] and he had been raised in the Faith almost from childhood by the Reverend Father Le Jeune.[18] Have I not, in your opinion, a good son? He is rather my father and my advocate with God. I am overjoyed, because of the love I bore him, at the high grace he has received by persevering so courageously. He was a perfectly formed young man and extremely modest, but I praise him only for his fidelity. Ah, if I were told as much of you, my very dear son, how could I express the joy this would bring me? But these signal favours are not in the province of our election. They are among the treasures of God, who bestows them upon chosen souls. I had to close this letter with this final wish, which is one of the greatest evidences of my affection for the person in the world that is dearest to me. . . .

---

16. Marie was again elected superior of the Ursuline mission.

17. The Company of Jesus, or Jesuits.

18. Paul Le Jeune (1591–1664) was among the first Jesuits to establish a mission in Canada in 1632, and was the author of the first installments of the Jesuit *Relations*.

[The Coming of Bishop Laval]

To Her Son

Quebec, 1659

My very dear and well-loved son:

It was a great privation to me to see a ship arrive and not receive any letters from you. I was always persuaded, however, that you had written to me; but I believed, and was not mistaken, that your letters were in the first vessel, which brought us news that we should have a bishop this year but did not appear until a long time after the others.

This delay meant that we received the Bishop sooner than the news that promised him to us. But that was an agreeable surprise in every respect. For in addition to the happiness that returns to the whole country at having an ecclesiastical superior, it is a consolation to have a man whose personal qualities are rare and extraordinary. Without speaking of his birth, which is very illustrious—for he is of the house of Laval—he is a man of high merit and singular virtue.[19]

I quite understood what you wished to tell me about his election but, one may say what one wishes, it was not men that chose him. I do not say that he is a saint—that would be to say too much—but I shall say with truth that he lives like a saint and an apostle. He does not know the meaning of deference to public opinion. He is for speaking the truth to everyone and speaks it freely when necessary. We needed a man of this strength here to eradicate the gossipmongering that was rife and taking profound roots. In a word, his life is so exemplary that he holds all the country in admiration. He is an intimate friend of Monsieur de Bernières,[20] with whom he lived out of devoutness for four years. So one should not be astonished if, having frequented that school, he has reached the sublime state of prayer in which we see him.

A nephew of Monsieur de Bernières was pleased to accompany him. He is a young gentleman that delights everyone with his modesty. He wishes to give everything to God, in imitation of his uncle, and to consecrate himself to the service of this new Church; and so, the better to succeed in this, he is preparing himself to receive the order of priesthood from our new prelate.

I told you we did not expect a bishop this year. In consequence there was nothing ready to welcome him when he arrived. We have lent him our seminary, which is at one corner of our enclosure and quite close to the parish church. There he will have the use and pleasure of a beautiful garden and, so that he and we may be lodged according to the Canons, he has had a wall of separation built. We shall be inconvenienced by this as we have to lodge our seminarians in our apartments; but the occasion merits it and we shall bear this inconvenience with pleasure until his episcopal residence is built.

As soon as he was consecrated Bishop in Paris, he requested the Reverend Father General of the Jesuits that Father Lalemant, who for the last three months had been rector of La Flèche, might accompany him.[21] This is a boon for all the country and for us in particular—and for me more than any other. For I shall tell you in confidence that I was suffering from the lack of a person to whom I could communicate from within. All year I felt an intimation within me that Our Lord would send me help. He has done so when it was time—for this may his holy name be eternally praised!

You know what has happened these last years concerning Monsieur l'Abbé de Queylus.[22] He is at present the director of a seminary of the priests of St Sulpice of Paris, which Monsieur de Bretonvilliers undertook to build at Montreal, with a very beautiful church. The Abbé de Queylus came down from Montreal to greet our prelate. He was established Grand Vicar here by Monseigneur the Archbishop of Rouen, but today all that no longer holds and his authority ceases.

However, the progress of the mission is great there. Some Hospitalières of La Flèche have come. Thirty families are to be established at one go, the last vessel having brought a great number of girls for this purpose. We are also urged to establish ourselves there,[23] but we are not in a state to do so.

---

19. The new bishop, Francois-Xavier Laval-Montmorency (1623–1708) was of a noble family. Laval University in Quebec is named for him.

20. Jean de Bernières was a gentleman from Caen, Normandy, who had assisted Marie de l'Incarnation and Mme. de la Peltrie to come to Canada by posing as Mme. de la Peltrie's husband.

21. Jerome Lalemant had returned to France in 1656 and had become rector at a Jesuit college in Paris.

22. Gabriel de Thubière de Levy de Queylus (1612–77) had been named superior of the Sulpician missions in Canada and became a rival of Laval, who as bishop outranked him.

23. At Montreal.

Monseigneur our Prelate will have authority over all this, though he is here only under the title of Bishop of Petraea and not of Quebec or of Canada. This title has caused a great deal of talk, but it came about because of a disagreement between the courts of Rome and France. The King desires that the Bishop of Canada depend upon him and owe the oath of fealty to him as do the bishops of France, and the Holy Father claims to have a special right in foreign nations. Because of this, he has sent us a bishop not as bishop of the country but as Apostolic Delegate with the foreign title of Bishop of Petraea.

You are anxious about the affairs of this country. They are as they were before the Iroquois made peace, for they have disrupted it and have already captured (or killed) nine Frenchmen on an occasion when they were not expected and no-one even knew they had evil designs against the French. They have already burned one of their prisoners alive; it will be a marvel if the others have better treatment. Since then our Frenchmen have killed eleven of their men and are on guard against others, for it has been learned from an escaped Huron captive that they are preparing a powerful army to come to carry off our new Christians and, as I believe, as many of the French as they can.

The Huron escaped in this way. Some Iroquois in the canoe he was travelling in, seeing a canoe of Hurons going to harpoon eels, allowed it to pass so they could pounce upon the Hurons when they were no longer together and in a state to defend themselves. Moved by tenderness for these people of his nation, the captive escaped from his masters, who had disembarked, and retraced his steps to warn his compatriots of the Iroquois design and of the danger they were in. They embarked as soon as possible, he with them, and all came in haste to Quebec where they gave warning of the enterprises of the Iroquois. Without this there would have been many heads broken, and not only among the Hurons, who could not have escaped their rage, for they would have stolen among the harvesters who, under the good faith of peace, were working without fear or distrust. That indeed is what happened at Trois-Rivières, where the Iroquois captured the nine Frenchmen of whom I spoke earlier.

As I write, Monsieur our Governor[24] is in the field pursuing and perhaps capturing some of them. What made him set out is that the Iroquois he held captive between two

good walls secured with iron doors, having learned that their nation had broken the peace and believing they would certainly be burned alive, forced their stronghold last night and leaped over the walls of the fort. The sentinel, who perceived them, gave the warning signal and immediately they were pursued. I do not know yet whether they have been captured, for those people run like deer.

You astonish me by saying that our Mothers wish to recall us. May God preserve us from such a calamity! If we did not leave after our fire and all our other losses, we shall not leave for the Iroquois, unless all the country does or a superior obliges us to do so, for we are daughters of obedience and must prefer it to all else. However, I shall be much surprised if this happens. It is certainly said that an army of enemies is making ready to come here, but now that their design is discovered, this will not be easy for them. If Our Lord had permitted it, they would have destroyed us long ago, but his goodness reverses their designs, giving us warning of them so we may put ourselves on guard. If there were danger, I should be the first to advise you of it so that you might look after our safety, since our Mothers confide their feelings to you. But thanks be to God, we do not see or believe that this is so. However, if matters transpired contrary to our opinions, should we not be happy to terminate our lives in the service of our Master and restore them to the One that gave us them? Such are my feelings, which you will make known to our Mothers if you judge it fitting.

My own feeling is that if we suffer in Canada for our persons it will be from poverty rather than from the sword of the Iroquois. And as for the country in general, its destruction in my opinion will come less from the barbarians than from certain persons who, through envy or otherwise, write to the gentlemen of the Company[25] a number of false things about the most saintly and virtuous and even rend with their calumnies those that maintain justice here and enable the country to subsist by their prudence. As this mischief is done in secret, it cannot be warded off and, as corrupt nature inclines to believe evil rather than good, these slanders are readily believed. Thence it transpires that when we think of it least, we receive very irritating commands and hindrances. God is

---

24. Pierre de Voyer d'Argenson (1612–1709?), governor of New France, 1658–61.

25. The Company of One Hundred Associates was a consortium of fur traders and merchants who controlled the colony of New France until it was taken over by the French Crown in 1663.

very grievously wronged in all this, and he would grant us a great grace if he were to purge the country of these carping and contrary spirits.

The last vessel was infected with purpural and pestilential fevers. It carried two hundred people, almost all of whom were sick. Eight died at sea and others on land. Almost all the country has been infected and the hospital is full of the sick. Monseigneur our Prelate[26] is there continually, caring for the sick and making their beds. Every effort has been made to prevent him and to conserve his person, but there is no eloquence that can turn him from these acts of humility.

The Reverend Father de Quen took this malady in his great charity and is dead from it. This is a notable loss for the mission, for he is the former missionary of the Algonkins, among whom he toiled for twenty-five years with incredible fatigue. Finally, quitting the charge of Superior of missions, he lost his life in the exercise of charity.

Two Hospitalière religious have been very sick with this malady. By the grace of God our Community has not been attacked. We are in a very healthful place here and exposed to great winds that cleanse the air.

My own health is very good. I do not cease to sigh powerfully after eternity, though I am prepared to live as long as will be pleasing to Our Lord.

[New France a Crown Colony]

To Her Son

Quebec, 1663

My very dear son:
A vessel that has just arrived and is making ready for a prompt return obliges me to write you a word, although I have not received news from you or from any of our monasteries in France. I believe you know that the King is now master of this country. When the Gentlemen of the Company learned he had the intention of taking it from them, they voluntarily offered it to him. He took them at their word and promised to indemnify them, and so the change took place without a great deal of difficulty.

The King's ships have brought back Monseigneur our Prelate, who we are told had a great deal of contention in France about the liquors that are given to the Savages and have almost destroyed this new Church. He made the voyage in the company of a new Governor,[27] whom His Majesty has sent us, his predecessor, who had been here only two years, having departed before his arrival.

With them the King has also sent an Intendant, who since his arrival has regulated all the affairs of the country. He has set up officers to administer justice according to the prescription of the law. He has also established regulations to take care of trade and maintain civil society. All the inhabitants of the country without exception have rendered faith and homage to him, declaring themselves dependent upon the King because of his château at Quebec. In the regulations that have been set up, Quebec is named a city and New France a province or kingdom. A mayor and aldermen have been elected and without exception all the officers, who are people of honour and probity, have been chosen by election. A great unity between them all is noted. Monseigneur the Bishop and Monsieur the Governor have been named heads of the Council. There is talk of building a palace for the administering of justice and prisons for criminals, the premises used for this purpose being too small and inconvenient.

Monsieur our Governor, whose name is Monsieur de Mézy, is a very pious and upright gentleman from Normandy, an intimate friend of the late Monsieur de Bernières, who in his lifetime did not a little to win him to God.

The levy of tithes has likewise been established, this money being assigned for the maintenance of a seminary founded by our Bishop, who must by its means have churches built wherever necessary and support priests to serve in them. These churches will be parishes, but those that preside in them will be called, instead of curés, superiors, of which the Bishop will be the chief. The surplus tithes are to go towards the relief of the poor. The worthy prelate has already had a house built, to serve as bishop's residence and to lodge the greater part of the seminary.

In a word, all this has an impressive sound and is beginning well, but only God sees what will be the issues, experience having shown us that the outcome is often very different from the ideas conceived.

---

26. Bishop Laval.

27. King Louis XIV named Augustin de Saffray de Mézy governor of New France.

The dreadful earthquakes experienced throughout Canada[28] contribute greatly to the unity of persons, for, as they kept everyone in fear and humiliation, everyone also dwells in peace. It would be impossible to believe the great number of conversions God has wrought—both among infidels, who have embraced the Faith, and among Christians, who have abandoned their wicked lives. One would have said that, even while God shook the mountains and marble rocks of these regions, he took pleasure in shaking consciences. The days of carnival were changed into days of penitence and sadness; public prayers, processions, and pilgrimages were continual, fasts on bread and water very frequent, and general confessions more sincere than they would have been in the extremity of sickness.

A single ecclesiastic, who administers the parish of Château-Richer, assured us that he alone heard more than eight hundred general confessions. I leave you to imagine how many were heard by the Reverend Fathers, who were in the confessional day and night. I do not believe there was a single inhabitant of the whole country that did not make a general confession. Some inveterate sinners, to satisfy their conscience, began theirs over again more than three times. Wonderful reconciliations were seen, enemies kneeling before one another to ask pardon, with so much grief that it was easy to see these transformations were bolts of heaven and God's mercy rather than of his justice.

At Fort St François-Xavier, which is in the parish of Sillery, there was a soldier of the garrison, come from France in the King's ships, who was the most wicked and abominable man alive. He boasted impudently of his crimes as another man might of an action worthy of praise.

When the earthquake began, he was seized with such utter fear that he cried out before everyone, 'Don't search for any other cause of what you see. This is God wishing to punish my crimes.'

He then began to confess his sins in a loud voice, being unaware of anything but God's justice, which was about, so he believed, to precipitate him into hell. The fort is a quarter of a league from Sillery, and he had to be borne there prostrate to make his confession, fear having made him almost paralysed. God made so happy and so entire a conversion in him that today he is a model of virtue and good works.

This, then, is the state of Canada, as regards both spiritual and temporal matters. To this I shall add that the King has not sent us troops, as he had permitted us to hope, to destroy the Iroquois. We are informed that this is because of his contentions in Italy.[29] Instead he has sent a hundred families, which are five hundred persons. He is defraying their expenses for a year so they can easily establish themselves and subsist afterwards without inconvenience. For when one can have a year paid in advance in this country, one can clear the land and make oneself a foundation for the years to come. . . .

[An Answer to Criticism]

To Her Son

Quebec, 9 August 1668

My very dear son:
Here is the reply to your third letter. I thank you as much as I possibly can for the holy and precious relic you have sent me; it will be kept in a beautiful reliquary from which we removed the relics to place them in the altar of our church when its consecration was held. You have obliged me by sending me the attestations, because the relic is to be exposed to the public. When I saw this holy relic, my heart was moved by devotion and I thanked this great saint for honouring this country with his venerable remains. I thank you once again, my very dear son.

You believe I am going to die. I do not know when that happy moment will arrive that will give me entirely to our divine Saviour. My health is in a sense better than it has been of late years but, since my strength is greatly diminished, it would take very little to carry me off, especially as I am not entirely quit of that hepatic flux that has lasted for so long and still have that bitterness in my mouth that gives the taste of wormwood to all the food I take. I am accustomed to this, otherwise I should die of weakness. Yet my spirit is content amidst this infirmity, which makes me continually remember Our Lord's bitterness on the cross. Despite these discomforts I keep my Rules. I fasted in Lent and on the other fast-days of the Church

---

28. The earthquake struck on February 5, 1666, and was felt as far away as New England. Although it inspired much religious anxiety, as Marie described, there were no deaths.

29. King Louis XIV had been attempting to assert the independence of the French Catholic Church by provoking confrontations with the papal forces in Rome.

and the Rule; in a word, I fulfil my charge, thanks to Our Lord. I sing so low that I can scarcely be heard, but I still have enough strength to recite in *recto tono*. I can scarcely remain on my knees throughout a Mass; I am weak in this respect, and it is astonishing that I am not more so, considering the nature of the illness from which I have suffered for so long, with high fever.

We hope to have by this voyage my dear Mother Cécile de Reuville de l'Enfant-Jésus, a religious of Rouen, and I am preparing myself to teach her the Algonkin tongue, being persuaded that she would be fitted for this and will have firmness, for these barbarous tongues are difficult and, to apply oneself to them, one needs a constant mind. My occupation on winter mornings is to teach them to my young sisters: there are some that have got as far as knowing the rules and being able to analyse the words, provided I translate the Savage for them into French. But to learn a number of words from the dictionary—this is difficult for them, this is thorny. Of our young sisters, there is but one that presses on with vigour. The Assistant Mother and Mother de Sainte-Croix are quite skilled in these tongues, for in the beginning we learned the dictionary by heart.

As these matters are very difficult, I am resolved that before my death I shall leave as much writing as I can. Between the beginning of last Lent and Ascension Day, I wrote a big book in Algonkin about sacred history and holy things, and also an Iroquois dictionary and an Iroquois catechism that is a treasure. Last year I wrote a big dictionary in the French alphabet; I have another in the Savage alphabet. I tell you this to show you that divine Goodness gives me strength in my weakness to leave my sisters something to work with in its service for the salvation of souls. To teach the French girls, we need no other study than our Rules, but, after we have done everything we can, we must still believe ourselves useless servants and little grains of sand at the base of the edifice of this new Church.

I wrote to you by all the ways, but as my letters may perish, I shall repeat here what I have said elsewhere about our employment, since you desire that I should discuss it with you.

Firstly, we have seven choir religious employed every day in the instruction of the French girls, not including two lay sisters who are for the day-girls. The Savage girls lodge and eat with the French girls, but it is necessary to have a special mistress for their instruction, and sometimes more, depending upon how many we have. I have just refused seven Algonkin seminarians to my great regret because we lack food, the officers having taken it all away for the King's troops, who were short. Never since we have been in Canada have we refused a single seminarian, despite our poverty, and the necessity of refusing these has caused me a very sensible mortification; but I had to submit and humble myself in our helplessness, which has even obliged us to return a few French girls to their parents. We are limited to sixteen French girls and three Savages, of whom two are Iroquois and one a captive to whom it is desired that we should teach the French tongue. I do not speak of the poor, who are in very great number and with whom we must share what we have left. But let us return to our boarding pupils.

Great care is taken in this country with the instruction of the French girls, and I can assure you that if there were no Ursulines they would be in continual danger for their salvation. The reason is that there are a great many men, and a father and mother who would not miss Mass on a feast-day or a Sunday are quite willing to leave their children at home with several men to watch over them. If there are girls, whatever age they may be, they are in evident danger, and experience shows they must be put in a place of safety.

In a word, all I can say is that the girls in this country are for the most part more learned in several dangerous matters than those of France. Thirty girls give us more work in the boarding-school than sixty would in France. The day-girls give us a great deal also, but we do not watch over their habits as if they were confined. These girls are docile, they have good sense, and they are firm in the good when they know it, but as some of them are only boarders for a little time, the mistresses must apply themselves strenuously to their education and must sometimes teach them in a single year reading, writing, calculating, the prayers, Christian habits, and all a girl should know.

Some of them are left with us by their parents till they are of an age to be provided, either for the world or for religion. We have eight, both professed and novices, who did not wish to return to the world and do very well, having been reared in great innocence, and we have others that do not wish to return to their parents since they feel comfortable in God's house. Two of these are granddaughters of Monsieur de Lauson, who is very well known in France. They are awaiting only the return of Monsieur de Lauson de Charny[30] to enter the noviciate.

---

30. Jean de Lauson (1584–1666) had been governor of New France from 1651 to 1656. Monsieur de Lauson de Charny was the guardian of the two girls, his nieces.

Some are given to us to be prepared for their First Communion; for this purpose they spend two or three months in the seminary.

In the case of Savage girls, we take them at all ages. It will happen that a Savage, either Christian or pagan, wishes to carry off a girl of his nation and keep her contrary to God's law; she is given to us, and we instruct her and watch over her till the Reverend Fathers come to take her away. Others are here only as birds of passage and remain with us only until they are sad, a thing the Savage nature cannot suffer; the moment they become sad, their parents take them away lest they die. We leave them free on this point, for we are more likely to win them over in this way than by keeping them by force or entreaties. There are still others that go off by some whim or caprice; like squirrels, they climb our palisade, which is high as a wall, and go to run in the woods.

Some persevere and we bring them up to be French; we then arrange their marriages and they do very well. One was given to Monsieur Boucher,[31] who has since been Governor of Trois-Riviéres. Others return to their Savage kinsmen; they speak French well and are skilled at reading and writing.

Such are the fruits of our little labour, of which I wished to give you some particulars as a reply to the rumours you say are put about that the Ursulines are useless in this country and that the *Relations* do not speak of their accomplishing anything. Our Reverend Fathers and Monseigneur our Prelate are delighted with the education we give the young girls. They let our girls receive communion as soon as they are eight years old, finding them as well instructed as they could be. If it is said that we are useless here because the *Relations* do not speak of us, it would have to be said that Monseigneur our Prelate is useless, that his Seminary is useless, that the Seminary of the Reverend Fathers is useless, that Messieurs the Ecclesiastics of Montreal are useless, and finally that the Hospitalières are useless because the *Relations* say nothing of all this. And yet they provide the support, the strength, and even the honour of the whole country.

If the *Relations* say nothing of us or of the Companies and Seminaries I have just named, it is because they only make mention of the progress of the Gospel and of what is concerned with this, and also, when the originals are sent from here, many things are struck out of them in France. Madame the Duchess de Senécey,[32] who does me the honour of writing to me every year, informed me last year of the displeasure she had felt about something that had been removed, and she told me about something similar this year. Monsieur Cramoisy,[33] who prints the *Relations* and exceedingly loves the Hospitalières of Quebec, inserted on his own account a letter their Superior wrote to him, and this has caused a great stir in France.

My very dear son, what we accomplish in this new Church is seen by God and not by men; our enclosure covers all, and it is difficult to speak of what one does not see. It is quite otherwise with the Hospitalière Mothers; the hospital being open and the good done there seen by everyone, their exemplary charities can be rightly praised. But ultimately they and we await recompense for our services from the One that penetrates into the most hidden places and sees as clearly in the shadows as in the light; that is sufficient for us.

---

31. Pierre Boucher (1622–1717) was, in his youth, a servant to the Jesuit missionaries to the Hurons. He was governor of the settlement of Trois Riviéres from 1652 to 1667 and author of a short treatise about New France.

32. Catherine de la Rochefoucauld, marquess de Senécey, was lady-in-waiting to the queen of France. The missions in Canada attracted the interest of some of the most powerful people in France.

33. The publishing house of Sebastien Cramoisy in Paris published the *Relations* from 1633 to 1672.

Marie Madeleine Hachard, "Sister Saint Stanislaus" (1704–1760)

Of the numerous writings that came from New Orleans during the eighteenth century, few can touch the letters of novitiate Marie Madeleine Hachard (also Hauchard), known in later life as Sister St. Stanislaus, for their vivacity, level of detail, and psychological complexity. Hachard clearly loved her home country, and she spent her first year in New Orleans attempting to grasp all the changes that would be wrought in her life as a result of her having entered the Order of Saint Ursula, the teaching order devoted to the education of girls. While at times Hachard seems quite determined that her life of dedication to the Ursulines was an inevitable calling, she also shows signs of homesickness, worry about her mission, and insecurity about what exactly the Ursulines were doing in such a culturally mixed and different place as New Orleans. Despite the doubts that occasionally surface in her letters, Hachard phrases a pride of birthplace uncommon in most colonial writings. She foregrounds her Norman heritage and her pleasure that New Orleans, founded by people from Rouen, could become a leading city in New France, even though it clearly was not Paris, she affirmed. She seems to have understood her mission well, and she seems to have been very happy to be working with the Ursulines to found what would become one of the first institutions of learning for women in what is now the United States.

Hachard was born into what seems to have been a large family in Rouen, France, in 1704. Her five known letters mention two brothers, one already a priest and one whom she wished would become a missionary, and four sisters, three of whom were already on their way to becoming nuns. Her father, procurator in charge of accounts for Rouen, seems to have had significant concern about his daughter's well-being, as indicated by Hachard's frequent reassurances to him of her good health and personal security. Hachard's evident disposition to work hard brought her the high regard of her superior, Mother Tranchepain. In addition to taking on teaching duties as the Ursulines developed their institution in New Orleans, Sister Saint Stanislaus became the secretary for the community. She died in her sleep at age fifty-six.

Hachard's father saw that her letters were printed in Rouen in 1727–28. Surely, Hachard's pride in her Norman heritage contributed to the popularity of her letters in her own day. The letters were reprinted during the nineteenth century, and they were translated and edited yet again during the twentieth century.

LETTERS WRITTEN AT NEW ORLEANS TO HER FATHER

October 27, 1727[1]

My dear father,

I had the honor of receiving your letter dated the sixth of April last; I received it the twentieth of this month, the eve of Saint Ursula's feast,[2] upon coming out of retreat. Judge for yourself, my very dear Father, what was my joy to have news of you, of my dear Mother and of all my sisters. You must have received both my letters: one written the eve of our embarkation at L'Orient, city in lower Brittany, the other written in Quay Saint Louis, one of the ports of the Island of Santo Domingo. In the first, dated the twenty-second of February 1727, I told you all that had happened on our way from Rouen to our embarkation

and in the second, on the fourteenth of May, I wrote of our arrival on that island. You see, my dear Father, I do not miss a single opportunity to show you the perfect gratitude that I have for the goodness that you have always shown me, but particularly for the blessed consent which you gave to my departure, against the advice of so many persons who opposed the plans of God. Of all the debts I owe you, I regard this last as the greatest, the most agreeable to God and I pray that He will reward you and keep you in perfect health.

Those who told you that we were in peril of our lives for fifteen days at the anchorage of L'Orient are quite mistaken. It is true that for an hour we did have difficulties, but after that we shook our ears as students do and resumed our course. Nothing more occurred except that the vessel did take on a little water so that the pumps were manned every two hours and occasionally more often. It could be that the inhabitants of L'Orient thought we were lost, but if that had happened, we would have been lost, with the Grace of God, only to the world. But Our Lord would not have it so. He is not content with just our good intentions: He wants to see our results.

You inform me that my sister Louison is a postulant at the Convent of the Val de Grace. I hope with all my heart

---

1. The texts for all three letters derive from *The Letters of Marie Madeleine Hachard, 1727–28,* trans. Myldred M. Costa (1974).

2. The letters arrived on October 20, the eve of St. Ursula's feast day, October 21, honoring the martyrdom of Ursula.

that she will be able to become a Nun in that holy Religious Order. There she will have the advantage of living with a person whom I greatly honor because of her merit and virtue, Madame de Quevreville.[3] The Lord gave to her, as to me, a vocation for our establishment in Louisiana. I was greatly looking forward to making the voyage with so amiable a companion, but family reasons have kept her in France. If my sister believes in my advice, she shall follow exactly the advice of Reverend Father de Houppeville, my past Director and hers now, for I am sure that his advice will be as helpful to her as it has been to me.

I shall be most happy also if my sister Elizabeth continues to remain at Saint Francis, what happiness for her to be a Nun in the same Convent with my eldest sister! Do I flatter myself to hope that you will instruct me in the progress that my dear brother is making in science? The most ardent desire of my heart is that he will some day be either a good holy Priest or a fervent Jesuit Missionary. I am, however, a little angry with my brother because he has not yet written to me. If he lacks a pen, let him advise me of this confidentially and I shall send him one, or, if it is that he has forgotten how to write, that is another story and I beg him to relearn it quickly and at the first opportunity to write to me of his welfare. I await the same favor from my sister Dorothy whom I embrace with all my heart.

As for my brother, the Religious, he has not yet done me the honor of writing either. Is he angry with me or does he think I am angry with him? It is true that to make me change my plans, he told me many things just before my departure that couldn't give me any pleasure however I took everything he said as a proof of his affection. But, my dear Father, when one is assured of doing the will of God, one values as nothing the arguments of men. Many people have considered our project as foolishness, but what is foolishness in the eyes of the world, is wisdom in the eyes of the Lord. So if my dear brother is still angry with me because I did not blindly follow his advice, I beg of you to make my peace with him, and if I have not written to him, it is only that, naturally timid, I do not dare take that liberty when he has not previously given me his permission. However, I believe that he did not forget me during the voyage; I seem to have felt the effect of his fervent prayers in many instances in which I assure you we

might well have perished. Everyone on our vessel, which was called *La Gironde,* said that out of any ten ships meeting the same difficulties as ours, not another would have escaped and that there must have been many good souls praying for us. At the head of these good souls I always thought of my dear brother and I pray you to assure him that I still maintain for him the most sincere of affections.

While I do not yet know the country of Louisiana perfectly, I shall however, my dear Father, give you a few details. I can assure you that I can hardly believe that I am at the Mississippi; there is as much politeness and magnificence here as in France and the use of cloth of gold and velvet is very common, even though it is three times as expensive here as in Rouen. Bread costs ten sols per pound here and is made of Indian, or sometimes Turkish, corn meal. Eggs are forty-five to fifty sols a dozen and milk is fourteen sols for a pot of half the measure of France. We eat meat, fish, peas, and wild beans and many fruits and vegetables, like pineapples, which are the most excellent of fruit, watermelons, sweet potatoes, apples, which are very much like the russets of France, figs, pecans, cashew nuts, which when eaten stick in the throat, and "giranmons," a kind of pumpkin. Even so there are a thousand other fruits which have not yet come to my knowledge.

In fact, we live on wild beef, deer, swans, geese and wild turkeys, rabbits, chickens, ducks, teals, pheasants, partridges, quail and other fowl and game of different kinds. The rivers are teeming with enormous fish, especially the brill, which is an excellent fish, rays, carps, salmon and an infinity of other fish which are unknown in France. Milk chocolate and coffee are much used here. A lady of this country gave us a goodly supply and we take some every day. We eat meat here three days a week during Lent and during the rest of the year meat can be eaten on Saturdays here, just as on the Island of Santo Domingo. We are getting remarkably used to the wild food of this country. We eat a bread which is half rice and half wheat. There is here a wild grape that is larger than our French grape and does not grow in a bunch. It is served in a dish like a prune. Rice cooked in milk is very common and we eat it often along with sagamite, which is made from Indian corn that has been ground in a mortar and then boiled in water with butter or bacon fat.[4] Everyone in Louisiana considers this an excellent dish.

---

3. The Convent of the Val de Grace, where Hachard evidently lived with Mme. De Quevreville, is unknown.

4. This cornmeal pudding was common fare among all Indian peoples.

I was curious to find out about the state of the terrain of this country so that, my dear Father, I could give you some small idea of it. At times this place is called Louisiana and at others Mississippi, but it is to be definitely called Louisiana because this is the name which was given it by Monsieur Robert Cavelier, Sieur de la Salle, native of Rouen, when he came here with Sieur de Joustel and several others of that same city to first discover it in 1676 and to again explore in 1685.[5] In consideration of Louis the Great during whose reign it was discovered, the name of Louisiana has remained. The word Mississippi refers to the river which is so called, however Sieur de la Salle had given it the name of Colbert, because Monsieur Colbert was at that time Minister of State,[6] but that name somehow is not being used for the river is still being called Mississippi even though many at present call it the Saint Louis River. It is the largest river in all America except for the Saint Lawrence. An infinity of rivers are joined to the Mississippi and it is seven to eight hundred leagues from its source to the Gulf of Mexico into which it empties. It however is not navigable by large ships—only small sloops which carry but twelve to fifteen persons can go up or down it. Inasmuch as it is bordered with forests of huge trees, the rapidity of the water digs into the banks causing them to cave in. Because of the thus weakened banks, the trees often fall in so that sometimes so many are gathered in one place that they close the passage of the river. It would cost a great deal, both in money and in labor to remove all the trees and make the river navigable and in condition to allow ships to sail up and down. Morever, there are many sand banks and an embankment would have to be built.

We are closer to the sun here than at Rouen without, however, experiencing very great heat. Winter is rather moderate lasting about three months; we never have more than a slight white frost. We are told that the country of Louisiana is four times as large as that of France and that the lands are very fertile, yielding several crops a year. This land, however, is not along the river banks for here are found forests of oaks and other trees of prodigious height and breadth, and reeds and canes which grow from fifteen to twenty feet high. But a few leagues from here are prairies, fields, and plains where grow a number of trees including cottonwoods, which, in spite of their name, do not bear cotton, sycamores, mulberries, chestnuts, figs, almonds, walnuts, lemons and oranges, pomegranates and others, all which add to the beauty of the country. If the land were cultivated there would be no better in the world, but for that it would have to be otherwise inhabited and France would have to send workmen of all trades. A man working only two days a week digging the ground and planting wheat would harvest more than he would need to feed himself all year, but, the majority of the people here live in idleness and apply themselves only to hunting and fishing. The Company of the Indies does much business in furs, beavers and other merchandise with the savages, the majority of whom are very sociable.[7] This is all I have been able to learn of this country but I shall inform you more fully when I have learned more.

You have stated, my dear Father, that you bought two large maps of the state of Mississippi and that you could not find New Orleans on them. These maps are apparently old or else they would have not omitted the Capital City of the country. I am sorry that after having spent one hundred ten sols you were still unable to find the place of our residence but I am sure that new maps will soon be made on which the city will be marked.[8]

We made an eight day retreat before the feast of Saint Ursula, the Reverend Father de Beaubois making three talks each day.[9] Our postulant, a young lady from Tours,

---

5. René-Robert-Cavalier, sieur de La Salle (1643–87), like the sieur de Joustel mentioned, evidently was a native of Rouen. La Salle navigated the Mississippi waterway and its tributaries in the 1670s and 1680s, traveling from the Illinois territory down to the delta, naming the area "Louisiane" for the French King Louis XIV.

6. Jean-Baptiste Colbert, marquis de Seignelay (1619–83).

7. John Law's Company of the Indies sent indentured Swedes, Germans, French, and other Europeans to labor for four years in the colony.

8. The map probably featured Biloxi, but not New Orleans, a relatively new capital. Biloxi, in present-day Mississippi, was the original site of the Company of the Indies. Jean-Baptiste Le Moyne, sieur de Bienville (1680–1767) was comandant of old Biloxi, beginning in 1700, and governor from 1706 to 1712 and then again after 1715. He experienced much opposition from the company when he sought in 1721 to remove the company center to New Orleans. He succeeded in his petition to move to New Orleans in 1723.

9. Father Nicolas-Ignatius de Beaubois, considered the founder of the Jesuit Mission in New Orleans, was appointed vicar-general for his district. It was Beaubois who brought both Jesuits and Ursulines to the city, having been commissioned by Bienville to obtain sisters of some order to assume charge of a hospital and school.

took the Habit on the feast day of Saint Ursula and my Sister Frances will take it on All Saints Day. We are as well lodged as one could wish while waiting for our Convent to be finished being built; there were surely no other Religious Communities so well off in their beginning.

When we arrived here, the Reverend Father de Beaubois told us that he had just lost nine Negroes who had all perished at one time from a North Wind; this was a loss of nine thousand livres. Fifteen days ago, the Company gave us eight, two of which have already escaped into the woods or elsewhere. Fourteen or fifteen ran away from the Company on that same day. We kept a handsome woman to wait on us and the rest we sent to our plantation which is only about a league from here to cultivate the land. We also have over there an overseer and his wife who are careful to protect our interests.

We are cloistered here with as much regularity as in the Convents of France, and if we had the misfortune of Father de Beaubois falling ill and not being able to say Mass, we would miss it on Easter Sunday or even for six months rather than leave the Convent and attend the Parish Church.

The Reverend Fathers Tartarin and Doutrelo left here six weeks ago to find their posts near the Illinois.[10] Our Reverend Father Superior is now alone here with Brother Parisel.[11]

I shall not speak to you, my dear Father, of the morals of the lay people of this country. I do not know them very well and have no desire to meet them, but it is said that they are quite corrupt and scandalous. There are also a great number of honest folks. One does not see any of these girls who were said to have been deported here; none seem to have come as far as this. You say, my dear Father, that all the devoted parishioners of the Reverend Father de Houppeville are entering the Religious Life. We have great need of this Reverend Father here—not to inspire women to become Nuns but to gather faithful followers because, as one of the Reverend Capuchin Fathers assured us the other day, there are none in all the country or its environs.

All of our Mothers are in perfect health except our Reverend Mother Superior, whom we have had the grief of seeing almost always ill since we arrived here.[12] She is however a little better than she was and sends you her greeting, as indeed does all of our Community.

I assure you, my dear Father, that they have always been most kind to me, our admirable Mother Superior in particular. The longer I am under her guidance, the more I grow to love her. Every day I receive new signs of her tenderness. The only sorrow I have is to realize that I do not deserve it. I could not be more content, that is, I am as happy as anyone can be in this world, yet who would not be in the company of such holy women? One can readily see that God Himself has chosen His subjects because not one of His Mothers is without infinite merit and perfect devotion, especially Reverend Mother Superior and Mother Saint Francis Xavier, mistress of the Novices, who was with the Ursulines at Le Havre and with whom I left Rouen. I would not be surprised if these two could perform miracles. It is up to me to walk in their footsteps, follow their example and imitate them in every way that I can.

I suppose that my eldest sister is well. I am greatly surprised that she has not written to me. I embrace her with all my heart and recommend myself to her holy prayers.

I forgot to tell you, my dear Father, that while we were in peril on *La Gironde* I promised to have six Masses said for the souls in Purgatory because I was both certain that you would have the goodness to have them said and persuaded of your good will I know you will not refuse me this.

This package will leave on the *Prince de Conty* which has just brought us Negroes from Guinea. *La Gironde* will be leaving here at the same time, the *Dromedary,* too, but I hope that the *Prince de Conty* is the best sailing ship and that it will be the first to arrive in France and that, at the moment it drops anchor at L'Orient, this packet will be put in the post for you.

I assure you, my dear Father, that my separation in no way diminishes the esteem and respect which I have always had for you. If I were not as happy as I am in my vocation, the distance of your dear selves would be a very great sorrow to me.

I am very well, thanks to the Lord, and I hope that your health is also good. I was not in the least bit seasick even though our crossing was quite long and very difficult—

---

10. Fathers Tartarin and Doutreleau had accompanied the Ursulines, who came over under the leadership of their Mother Mary Trancepain of St. Augustine, Hachard's mother superior. Father Tartarin worked with Father Le Boulenger among the Illinois at Kaskaskia; Doutreleau, on the Wabash, at Vincennes.

11. Father Nicholas-Ignatius de Beaubois was the founder of the Jesuit mission in New Orleans and vicar-general for his district.

12. Mother Mary Trancepain of St. Augustine.

caused by winds almost constantly against us. I am sending you an account of our entire voyage; it will no doubt please you. I shall close for fear of boring you. Farewell, my very dear Father, I embrace you a thousand times— but no, I cannot for you are too far away for that; I hope that my dear Brother will discharge this amiable commission for me. I am, with all my heart, filled with a profound respect and a perfect gratitude,

My dear father,
Your very humble and very obedient
Daughter and Servant,
Marie Madelaine HACHARD of Saint Stanislas.

January 1, 1728

My dear father,
I have just learned that the ship called *The Two Brothers* is leaving for France; I take advantage of this occasion to wish you, as well as my dear Mother, Brothers and Sisters, a good and happy year. I pray each day to the Lord to keep you in perfect health.

You must have received a packet of my letters with an Account of our whole voyage, which I sent to you the twenty-seventh of October last by the ship called the *Prince de Conty.* Your recommend in all your letters that I never let an opportunity pass without writing to you. It is my duty. I obey you and take great care to completely satisfy your request.

All our Community is in perfect health. We have at present nine boarders, and a like number will come to us after Epiphany. We also instruct a number of day students.

They are working very hard on our home.[13] Monsieur Perier, our Commandant, always interested in whatever may give us pleasure, promises that it will be finished within the year. The engineer came yesterday to show us the plans. We desire nothing more than to be in that home so that we can also occupy ourselves at the Hospital serving the sick. We learn every day of the terrible condition there; the majority of the sick die from want of any medical care.

The intention of Monsieur the Commandant and the principal inhabitants of the city is that we should also take charge of the girls and women of ill-repute. We have not yet agreed to this, but they keep telling us that it would be of great service to the Colony. To this end they plan to build a special building at the end of our enclosure to lock up these people.

We also conduct a class to instruct Negro and savage women and girls; they come every day from one to two thirty in the afternoon. You see, my dear Father, we are not useless in this country. I assure you that every moment is accounted for and that we have none to ourselves. A short time ago we took in a little orphan girl who had been serving in a house which was not setting a very good example. It is moreover the intention of Reverend Father de Beaubois that we take charge of orphan girls out of charity and that he and Monsieur Perier take full charge of all orphan boys.

We are determined to in no way spare ourselves in anything that may be for the greater glory of God. I sometimes occupy myself with the day students. I cannot express to you what joy I find in instructing these little souls and teaching them to know and love God. I pray that the Lord gives me the grace to succeed in this.

In a few years, it may well be that we shall need to have more women come from France, as we may not be able to take care of everything, but we shall not ask for them until it is absolutely necessary.

Our Reverend Mother Superior still has for me a thousand kindnesses. She sends you her greetings as does Mother Saint Francis Xavier whom you saw in Rouen.

All our Community feels a contentment that one can hardly express. We are following, all at the same time, the functions of four different Communities, that of the Ursulines, which is our first and principal Order, that of Hospitalier, that of Saint Joseph and that of Refuge and we shall try to discharge each of these as faithfully as possible.

I beg you to believe that I still retain for you a very sincere and very respectful attachment,

My dear father,
Your very humble and very obedient
Daughter and Servant,
HACHARD of Saint Stanislas.

April 24, 1728

My very dear father,
I received with much pleasure the two letters you had the goodness to write to me dated the twelfth and the twenty-ninth of August 1727. You ask me for an explanation of the state of the country, the location of our city and

---

13. Bienville, then governor of New Orleans, had given the Ursulines his own home until their establishment was built, followed by their hospital.

finally all that I can learn of these parts. I hope to have sufficiently foreseen your requests in the accurate Account of the little adventures of our entire voyage and our arrival here which I sent to you in October of 1727 and in several other letters that I have had the honor of writing to you.

I believe that I have already told you that our city, named New Orleans, Capital of all Louisiana, is located on the banks of the Mississippi on the eastern side. The river is at this spot wider than is the Seine at Rouen. On our side of the river there is a well-cared for embankment to protect us from floods. All the length of the bank on the city side there is a large ditch to catch any water that might come over the top of the embankment. Palisades of wood close off this area.

On the other side of the river is a wilderness of forest in which there are a few cabins where the slaves of the Company of the Indies lodge. By that you can see that the map which you told me you bought showing the city of New Orleans on the banks of a lake named Pontchartrain, a distance of six leagues from the Mississippi River, is not correct. Our city is positively not located on the shore of a lake, but on the very banks of the Mississippi River. It is true however that the full strength of the river does not pass here because above the city the river separates and forms three branch rivers which rejoin below the city and empty into the Gulf of Mexico.

Our city is very pretty, well constructed and regularly built, from what I know and saw of it the day we first arrived in this country. Since that day we have remained in our Cloister. Before our arrival we had been given a very bad impression of the city, but I admit that those who spoke so had not seen it for several years. The people have worked and still work to perfect it. The streets are very wide and are laid out in straight lines. The main street is nearly a league in length. The houses are very well built of "collombage et mortier." They are white-washed, paneled and filled with sunlight. The roofs of the houses are covered with tiles which are little pieces of wood in the shape of slate. One must see this to believe it, for this covering has all the beauty and appearance of slate.

It suffices to say that there is a song sung openly here in which the words proclaim that this city is as beautiful as Paris. Does that not explain to you how the people feel? In fact, it is very beautiful, but if I do not have enough eloquence to convince you of all the beauty claimed in the song, it is because I find that there is a difference between this city and the city of Paris. While the song may persuade people who have never seen the Capital of France,

I have seen it and the song does not persuade me to believe this opinion. It is true however that it grows daily and could therefore become as beautiful and large as one of the principal cities of France—if more workmen come over and it becomes populated in proportion to its size.

While the women ignore facts pertaining to their salvation, they ignore nothing when it comes to vanity. The luxury in this city is such that one can distinguish no one; everyone is of equal magnificence. Most of the women and their families are reduced to living only on sagamite, a sort of gruel. However, notwithstanding the expense, they are dressed in velvets and damasks covered with ribbons, materials which are regularly sold in this country for three times their cost in France. The women here, as elsewhere, use red and white paint and patches, too, to cover the wrinkles in their faces. The devil here possesses a large empire, but this does not discourage us from the hope of destroying him, with God's love. There are certainly an infinite number of examples for His strength to show through our weakness. The more powerful the enemy, the more we are encouraged to engage him in combat. What pleases us here particularly is the docility of the children whom one can mold as one wishes. The Negroes also are easy to instruct once they know how to speak French. It is not the same with the savages. They are baptized with grave doubts as they are so prone to sin, especially the women, who, under a modest air, hide the passions of beasts.

Our residence since our arrival here is the finest house in the city. It has two stories and a garret.[14] We have all the apartments we need with six doors to enter those on the ground floor. There are large windows everywhere, however they do not have any panes. Instead a fine, thin cloth which lets in as much light as glass is pulled taut inside the window frames. Our residence is located at one end of the city. We have a poultry yard and a garden bounded on one side and end by large wilderness trees of prodigious height and breadth. Because our home is so close to this forest we have the honor of being the first to be visited by an infinite number of Maringouins, Frappes d'abord and another specie of fly or midge which I have not yet met. I know these last by neither name nor surname, but only by sight and there are at this very moment several flying around me: they would like to assassinate me. These wicked animals sting without mercy. We are assailed every night. Happily they appear only between sunset and

---

14. This was the governor's house.

sunrise—at which time they return to the forest. This obliges us to be sure our doors and windows are securely locked, otherwise they would positively visit us in our beds. No matter what precaution we take we are never without their marks.

The house they are building for us is located at the other end of the city. Reverend Father de Beaubois and the engineer of the Company made the plans, following the ideas that we gave them, and they frequently bring them for our inspection. It will be all of brick and large enough to lodge even a large Community. There will be all the rooms that we could wish for, all regularly built and well paneled, with large windows and panes in the frames. However its construction is not advancing at all. Monsieur Perier, our Governor and Commandant, had given us cause to hope that it would be ready at the end of this year, but, with the scarcity of workmen, we should be happy to be lodged therein and take possession of our Hospital by Easter 1729. So we shall once again have need of the Lord's help and I pray that He will send us good workmen.

Monsieur Perier and Madame his wife, who is most amiable and very pious, do us the honor of visiting us often. The Lieutenant of the King is also a perfect gentleman and a past Officer. The people smother us with all sorts of presents. We have been given two cows with their calves, a sow with her little ones, some chickens and Muscovy ducks. All of these have helped to start up our barnyard. We also have some turkeys and geese in it. The inhabitants, seeing that we do not wish to take money to instruct our day students, are filled with gratitude and help us in every way they can. The marks of protection that we receive from the important people of the colony make us respected by everyone. Of course none of this would continue if we did not nourish with our actions the great esteem that they have for us.

During Lent we eat meat four days a week as allowed by the Church, but at all other times we fast only on Fridays. We drink beer. Our most common food is rice with milk, little wild beans, meat and fish. In summer however, we eat little meat as it is slaughtered only twice a week and is not easy to preserve. Hunting is done about ten leagues from our city and lasts all winter which here begins in October. Many wild oxen are taken and brought here to New Orleans and nearby areas. We buy this meat for three sols a pound, the same as deer, which is better than the beef and mutton you eat in Rouen.

Wild ducks are very cheap. Teals, water-hen, geese and other fowl and game are also very common, but we do not buy it as we do not wish to indulge in delicacies. Really, it is a charming country all winter and in summer the fish are plentiful and good. There are oysters and carps of prodigious size and delicious flavor. As for the other fish, there are none in France like them. They are large monster fish that are fairly good. We also eat watermelons and French melons and sweet potatoes which are large roots that are cooked in the coals like chestnuts. They even taste somewhat like chestnuts but are much sweeter, very soft and very good. All this, my dear Father, is exactly like I am telling you—I do not tell you anything that I have not yet personally experienced. Many other kinds of meat, fish and vegetables are eaten here but I have not yet tasted them so I cannot tell you of their goodness.

Regarding the fruits of the country, there are many that we do not care for but the peaches and figs are very excellent and abundant. We are sent so many of them from the nearby plantations that we make them into preserves and jelly. Blackberry jelly is particularly good. Reverend Father de Beaubois has the finest garden in the city. It is full of orange trees which bear as beautiful and as sweet an orange as those of Cape Francis. He gave us about three hundred sour ones which we preserved. Thanks to God, we have never yet lacked anything. Our Reverend Father carefully sees to it that we are provided with food. We are better off than we would ever have believed, but this is neither the intention nor the wish of our enterprise. Our principal aim is to attract souls to the Lord and He accords us graces so that we can perform this duty. Our Reverend Father aids us well in this. He says Mass for us daily and gives us public conferences. If we had the misfortune of losing him, either by illness or otherwise, we would be much saddened and greatly to be pitied.

Reverend Father conducted a retreat for us and our boarders during Holy Week. Several ladies of the city followed it assiduously; sometimes at the sermons and exhortations they numbered up to two hundred. Each day we had the Tenebrae in music and a Miserere accompanied by instruments. Our assistant Mother, Madame Boullenger,[15] was in charge of these occasions. Easter Day, at Mass and Benediction, we sang Motets in four parts and on the last of the Easter Holy Days we sang the entire Mass to music. The Convents of France with all their splendor could not have done any better.

---

15. The sister of Father Boulenger, sent to the Kaskaskia mission.

All this is very impressive and helps to draw in the public, some out of a beginning of devotion, some out of curiosity. There is always a sermon at the end, because our Reverend Father is of such an admirable zeal it seems that he has taken it upon himself to convert everyone here and is determined to accomplish his goal. But I assure you, my dear Father, that he will have a lot of work to do before he succeeds because not only do debauchery, lack of faith and all other vices reign here more than elsewhere, but they reign with an immeasurable abundance! As for the girls of bad conduct, they are watched closely and severely punished by being placed on a wooden horse and flogged by all the soldiers of the Regiment that guards our city. In spite of all this there are still just too many of these women to be put in a house of refuge. A thief is brought to trial in two days and is either hung or broken on the wheel. Whether he be White, Indian or Negro, there is neither distinction nor mercy.

Our little Community increases each day. We have twenty boarders, eight of whom made their first Communion today, three ladies who are also boarders and three orphan girls whom we took in out of charity. We also have seven slave boarders to instruct for Baptism and first Communion, a large number of day students and Negresses and Indian girls who come two hours each day for instruction. The custom here is to marry girls of twelve to fourteen years of age. Before our arrival a great number of these girls had been married without even knowing that there was a God (you can imagine how everything else is here) but since we are here, girls are only married if they have come to our instructions.

We are accustomed to seeing black people. We were given a short time ago two Negress boarders, one of six and the other of seventeen years, to instruct them in our Religion. They will stay to serve us. If it were the custom here for Negresses to wear patches, they would have to be given white ones, which would be rather funny.

You see, my dear Father, all the different ways we exercise our zeal. I cannot express the pleasure that we get from instructing all this youth, especially when we remember the great need they have. These boarders of twelve and fifteen years of age have never been to Confession, nor even to Mass. They were brought up on their plantations, a distance of five to six leagues from the city, and consequently had received no spiritual help. In short, they had never even heard of God. For them the most ordinary things we tell them become oracles out of our mouths. We have the consolation of finding in them much docility and a great interest in learning. All of them would like to become Nuns. This is not at all to the liking of Reverend Father de Beaubois, our very worthy Superior. He finds that it would be better for them to become Christian mothers and thereby establish Religion in this country through their good examples.

I am still very happy to be in this country and following my vocation. My joy redoubles with the approach of my Final Vows, to be made in a foreign land where Christianity is nearly unheard of. It is true that there are many honest people in this country, but there is not the slightest indication of devotion, nor even of Christianity. How happy we would be if we could establish it here. With the aid of our Reverend Father Superior and a few Capuchin Religious who are also dedicated to this cause and do everything in their power to accomplish it, I assure you that we spare nothing.

I cannot help telling you the sad adventure which befell our two Reverend Fathers Tartarin and Doutrelo, the worthy leaders of our voyage. We have just learned by their letters that, at twenty leagues from the Illinois, the canoe of Reverend Father Doutrelo was lost in crossing the river. He saved himself and the shirt on his back by swimming, but he lost everything for his Chapel, his clothes and all his equipment. He had gone over five hundred leagues safely only to be shipwrecked almost in sight of port. Nothing happened to Reverend Father Tartarin who was in another canoe. He very charitably gave one of his two cassocks to Father Doutrelo, as well as half of all the rest of his goods.

Since I have been led to speak of the Illinois, I shall tell you, my dear Father, that the Reverend Father Boullenger,[16] who is stationed there, is asking for some Nuns to make an establishment there. He wrote to Madame Boullenger, his sister, about this but she answered that she did not feel that her vocation was yet strong enough to go that far away from New Orleans, but that it might be in a few years hence. Even if she becomes zealous enough to teach Christianity to those poor savage Illinois, the majority of whom, like the savages here, have never heard of God, I hope that she will not leave us since we have here quite enough to exercise her charity. We are not too many, and I assure you that we are all occupied from morning till night. We have not a moment to ourselves; the time I take writing to you is taken from my night's rest.

Monsieur Perier, our Commandant, a few days ago made use of our home as a prison to confine in it one of

---

16. Boulenger worked with Tartarin at the Kaskaskia mission.

our lady boarders, whom he had himself given us previously, because she was separated from her husband. This lady began to be bored at the Convent and wanted to have secret relations with a layman. Monsieur Perier, therefore, had her imprisoned, with her husband's consent, until she could be sent back to France. Such is the manner in which they act here.

I have already noted in one of my preceding letters that Monsieur Robert Cavelier, Sieur de la Salle, native of Rouen, had come in 1676 and 1685, by order of the King Louis XIV, to this country of Louisiana, in the capacity of Viceroy of the Mississippi, with a number of other people from the same city of Rouen, to explore the country before anyone else. That is all that I knew at that time, but I have since learned certain circumstances that I think will interest you.[17]

After the first discovery made by Monsieur de la Salle of the lands of the Mississippi in the year 1676, the King learned of the esteem which he, Monsieur de la Salle, had acquired with the savages, that he was loved by the Illinois, the Hurons and the majority of the other Indian nations of the Mississippi, and that he had found a means to make the Iroquois, the most cruel and barbarous nation of all American (they eat the Whites), fear and respect him. The King therefore named Monsieur de la Salle, in 1684, Viceroy of all Louisiana, permitted him to raise troops and gave him four vessels commanded by Captain Beaujeu. The embarkation took place at La Rochelle around the month of July of the said year, 1684.

Monsieur de la Salle took with him workmen of all trades to establish a colony, and also six Apostolic Missionaries—actually three Ecclesiastics and three Religious Recollects. The priests were Monsieur Jean Cavelier, Monsieur de la Salle's brother, Monsieur Francois de Chefdeville, his relative who had been trained at Saint Sulpice in Paris, and Monsieur d'Aimanville, who also came from Saint Sulpice; the three Recollects were the Fathers Zenoble, Anastase and Maxime. He also brought with him a large number of volunteers who offered to come with him, all handpicked young men, children of families native of Rouen. Among these were the Sieurs Cavelier and Crevel du Moranger, his nephews, Henry de

Chefdeville, brother of the Ecclesiastic of the same name, and Desloges, his relatives, Oris, Bihorel, de Clere, Planterose, le Carpentier, Thibault, Tessier, le Gras, Minet, de Ville Perdry, Davault, Hurie, Tallon, Gayen, le Noir, l'Archeveque, Liotot, de Marle, Hians, Munier, Joustel, the brothers Duhault, des Liettes, le Clere, Dumesnil, Saget and many others amounting to about two hundred and fifty, including one hundred soldiers and their Officers, of which Monsieur de la Sablonniere was the Lieutenant. The Sieur Henry de Chefdeville, eighteen years of age, died of disease on board, after three months of navigation.

Monsieur de la Salle had planned to land at the mouth of the Mississippi River, but some disagreement which occurred during the voyage between Monsieur de la Salle and Sieur Beaujeu, Captain of the vessel of the King, prevented them from finding the river's mouth. Monsieur de la Salle found it necessary to disembark with his troops about one hundred and fifty leagues further down on the western coast, between the river and New Spain. That territory of America is occupied by the Spaniards and has several gold and silver mines which produce a very considerable profit for the Spanish King every year. Sieur Beaujeu abandoned Monsieur de la Salle there and returned to France with his vessel.

Monsieur de la Salle and his troops marched north and, after having crossed a number of rivers, forests and plains, found themselves near a fort of the Illinois, at a spot now called Little Rock. They did not even approach our district. Of course, at that time there was no city of New Orleans, only a deserted and wild place—until the time of the Regency of the Duke of Orleans, when the foundations of this city were first laid. It is for this reason that the city is called New Orleans. Not until 1723 did New Orleans begin to take on the appearance of a city—before that work depended on the availability of workers.

But let us return to Monsieur de la Salle. Since this brave Captain knew how to make himself feared and esteemed by the savages, it seemed that everything favored his undertaking; but in the month of March 1687, the very day he was preparing to send Monsieur Cavelier, the priest and his brother, to France to inform the King of the state of his expedition, he was assassinated by the sinister plot of five of his own men, due to some sort of jealousy. The crime of Duhault, the man who dealt the cruel death blow, did not remain unpunished. A short time later Hians reproached him of his perfidy and killed him. The four accomplices have since died miserably in this country, not daring to return to France.

---

17. Hachard relates in the following passage a record of La Salle's murder by disgruntled men in his own party as they sought their way back to the Mississippi in order to head upriver to Quebec.

After the troops had lost their brave Captain, who alone knew the country, they became disoriented and desolate; they dispersed. Monsieur Cavelier, the priest, Sieur Cavelier, his nephew, sixteen years old, Father Anastase, the Recollect, and the Sieurs Joustel and Tessier resolved to return to France. Passing through a village of the Accanas, they found a dwelling in which lived a carpenter named Couture and a cook named Delaunay, both natives of Rouen. Monsieur Tonti, at that time the Commander of the Fort Saint Louis in the Illinois had left them at the Accanas post to watch it. The party finally made their way to Canada, passing through Fort Saint Louis and Montreal. At Quebec they embarked for France.

The Sieurs Desloges, Oris, Thibault, le Gras, Liotot and le Carpentier were killed by the savages. The remainder of the troop escaped one by one. Monsieur de Chefdeville, the Missionary, stayed at the same spot, Little Rock, until April 1688. He then advanced on the side of the Illinois toward the Iroquois where he baptized and converted a great number of souls to God. He died in their village in great sanctity—to be crowned in Heaven as a reward for the ardent zeal which he showed for the salvation of the souls of those poor savages. He had been one of the first who had the consolation of opening Heaven to the first Christians and Saints of this nation.

It is thus that the noble and glorious expedition of Monsieur de la Salle failed. Without that perfidy he would have explored all the country of the Mississippi, which he had named Louisiana, and an infinity of families would have come from France and Canada to settle here and plant the faith. One of those in the company of Monsieur de la Salle at Little Rock, a man named des Liettes told the above story in the manner I have had the honor of telling it to you. Des Liettes stayed at Little Rock until he died, only two years ago. There you have all that I could learn of these events.

Is not your city of Rouen proud, my dear Father, of the honor which it has received from Monsieur de la Salle and his company, almost all natives of your city, who first discovered the Mississippi, from Monsieur de Chefdeville, Missionary, who first established the faith here and finally from the Priests and Ursuline Nuns of the same city who today do everything possible to instruct and save the souls of these poor savages? This is surely something to excite your citizens and to encourage them to commit themselves to the continued discovery of still more unknown lands and the bringing of Christianity to them. I do not know if it is for this reason or some other that the savages of Louisiana have so much esteem for the Normans.

They have more regard for people from that province than for anyone from any other and recognize them as capable of succeeding in all their enterprises. If they were told of the conquests of the Dukes of Normandy, the bravery of the Normans in the Holy Land during the Crusades, their conquest of the kingdom of England and of others, they would be even more convinced. We are not here for that, however. It they want to know these facts, let them get them from others or read them in history books.

I should be curious to know and I pray you to inquire of what family is this Monsieur Francois de Chefdeville, the Missionary. I had heard my grandfather and our cousin Autin, the Capuchin, often say that we were related to Monsieur Chefdeville, a merchant of Rouen, who had, I believe, two sons, both Capuchins, and one daughter, a Saint Francis Nun. I believe it is she whom I have the honor of knowing, as she was Mother Vicar when I left Rouen. We could be of the same family. It would be easy for you to find out from Reverend Father Autin, Prior of the Monks of Saint Antoine, if he is still living. Or you can consult the Genealogy that you have of our family. If we are related, it must be on the side of Monsieur Autin or of Monsieur Dumontier, the present Master of Accounts. If it is as I think, have the goodness to let me know by your first letter. I greatly hope to be related to this holy Missionary, and to share more fully in the holy prayers he addresses to the Lord in Heaven for the greater good of, first of all, his relatives and, secondly, all others.

You will find enclosed a letter which our very Reverend and amiable Mother Superior writes to you. I assure you, my dear Father, that she, as well as all our Mothers, still has a thousand attentions for me. It is not for me to tell them all to you. I cannot however neglect to say that the more I proceed, the more I find happiness in having listened to the voice of the Lord when He called me to so holy a vocation. I would wish that all my sisters would do the same. I rejoice to learn that my sister Elizabeth continues to stay at Saint Francis with my sister the Nun. The longer she stays there, the better she will find herself. Religion seems to present to our eyes nothing but thorns, but after having experienced them, these thorns are changed into roses. In regard to my sister Louison, I pray each day that the Lord allows me to learn in your very next letter that she has pronounced her Vows at the Val de Grace. That would bring me great joy.

I had written this letter up to this point so that, my dear Father, it would be ready to be sent by the first ship leaving for France, but none have left before today, the eighth of May, 1728. I have just learned that there is one ready to set sail so I am now finishing it. I have nothing new to tell you except that I have for several days now had an attack of fever. Yesterday, as a cure, I took an emetic. It is the usual medicine of the country.

Our reverend Mother and dear Superior is still ill but our other Mothers are in perfect health. They have all asked me to assure you of their regards.

We have gotten rid of the lady who had been prisoner in our house. A Counselor of the country let it slip out that he would be willing to take her into his home so Monsieur Perier, our Commandant, had her conducted there and charged the Counselor with her guard.

I pray each day that the Lord keep you all in perfect health and am, from the bottom of my heart, very respectfully,

My dear father,
Your very humble and very obedient
Daughter and Servant,
HACHARD of Saint Stanislas.

LOUIS VIVIER (1714–1756)

Father Louis Vivier was born perhaps in Rouen, France, on October 7, 1714. He became a novice with the Jesuits at the age of seventeen and remained in France working with the order until about 1749, when he evidently crossed over to Canada. His name first appears on the rolls in Canada for that year, where he is listed, in the fall of the year, as among the Illinois peoples, along with the Reverend Father Alexandre Xavier de Guyenne, the superior; three other priests, Joseph Julien Fourré, Philippe Watrin, and Sébastien Louis Meurin; and a lay teacher, Charles Magendie. Vivier remained in the Kaskaskia area for about four years, when he was transferred to Vincennes, late in 1753 or early in 1754. He died there in October 1756.

The Jesuits' stations in the Kaskaskia area, as Vivier's letters attest, had, around the turn into the eighteenth century, been strengthened by numerous requests for baptism. The peoples indigenous to the Illinois area, facing depopulation for a number of reasons, were coming into the missions for security and for an opportunity to affiliate with traders and trappers who had networked throughout the waterways and forests. As historian Richard White has indicated, when one looks at the imbalance of women to men (roughly four women to one man), one has a better sense of why Indian women complained to the Jesuits about harsh treatment by Indian men and why they were happy to form partnerships with other men in the area, particularly the trappers and traders who formed relationships according to what they called "the custom of the country," outside the forms of Catholic marriage. The Jesuits, under the leadership of Father Jacques Gravier in the 1690s, began to emphasize in their teachings, especially of young women, the cult of the Virgin Mary and the importance of chastity. This approach to the Indian people, more of whom were women, would have provided an avenue for the women to achieve greater power among their people, whether they chose to work inside the Jesuits' teachings and remain celibate themselves or whether they sought partnerships with influential men, both Indians or Europeans. This period of warfare (probably the cause of the population decline of men); cultural incursions by Jesuits; and, if Jesuit accounts are accurate, widespread violence against women finally produced for the Jesuits what they considered to be happy returns on their flying mission among the Illinois peoples.

By the middle of the eighteenth century, however, the strength of the Jesuit missionary effort in the greater Louisiana territory had fallen off, as Vivier's letters suggest. Squabbling among superior organizations over who actually had ecclesiastical jurisdiction in the Louisiana territory caused occasional friction among the missionaries—Jesuits, Capuchins, and Récollets—in the area, and it was unclear who actually should resolve the mission-territorial concerns, the Jesuits' bishop of Quebec, the Congregation de Propaganda Fide in Rome, or the Society of Foreign Missions. More important, continued fighting among Indians and Europeans over the territory surrounding the waterways and the control of the watering system contributed to a sense of France's loss of imperial potential underlying the discussion that Vivier offers of the Illinois area. Vivier's reports to two different Jesuits from his location in the Illinois country provide an important insight into the Jesuits' conception of their mission among Indian peoples, even as they likewise indicate his strong, secularized awareness of the excellent imperial positioning of the Illinois missions should France seek fully to squeeze the English to the east of the Mississippi. The Company of the Indies, designed originally in the 1710s and 1720s to develop French holdings in the Mississippi Valley, had long given up the idea of supporting linked colonies peopled by various Europeans but in support of the French treasury. If Vivier was frustrated by the evident lack of interest shown in his work by the Indian peoples and by the lack of responsiveness of the French government to creating systematic settlement of the region, perhaps this was a result of a misapprehension of the impact of the imperial wars on both Indian peoples and Europeans in the area. The ceding of the greater Louisiana territory to Spain in the late 1760s brought an end to concentrated French effort in the territory. When Vivier's Jesuit colleague, Sébastien Louis Meurin, died in 1777, the death effectually marked the end of the long line of Black Robe evangelists who served in the northcentral French colonies.

LETTERS WRITTEN AMONG THE ILLINOIS

June 8, 1750[1]

My dear friend,
Pax Christi.
When one leaves France for distant countries, it is not difficult to make promises to one's friends; but, when the time comes, it is no slight task to keep them, especially during the first years. We have here but a single opportunity, once a year, for sending our letters to France. It is therefore necessary to devote an entire week to writing, without interruption, if one wish to fulfill all one's promises. Moreover, what we have to write of this country is so little curious and so little edifying that it is hardly worth while to take up a pen. It is less for the purpose of gratifying your curiosity than of responding to the friendship that you display for me, that I write to you to-day. Let us try, nevertheless, to give you some idea of the country, of its inhabitants, and of our occupations. The Illinois country lies about the 39th degree of north latitude, about 9 degrees from new Orleans, the capital of the whole Colony. The climate is very much like that of France, with this difference, that the winter here is not so long and is less continuous, and the heat in summer is a little greater. The country is general is covered with an alternation of plains and forests, and is watered by very fine rivers. Wild cattle, deer, elk, bears, and wild turkeys abound everywhere,

in all seasons, except near the inhabited portions. It is usually necessary to go one or two leagues to find deer, and seven or eight to find oxen. During a portion of the autumn, through the winter, and during a portion of the spring, the country is overrun with swans, bustards, geese, ducks of three kinds, wild pigeons, and teal. There are also certain birds as large as hens, which are called pheasants in this country, but which I would rather name "grouse;" they are not, however, equal in my opinion to the European grouse. I speak not of partridges or of hares, because no one condescends to shoot at them. The plants, trees, and vegetables that have been brought from France or from Canada, grow fairly well. As a rule, the country can produce all things needed to support life, and even to make it agreeable.

There are three classes of inhabitants: French, Negroes, and Savages; to say nothing of Half-breeds born of the one or the other,—as a rule, against the Law of God. There are 5 French Villages and 3 Villages of Savages within a distance of 21 leagues, between the Mississippi and another river called the Kaskaskias. In the five French Villages there may be eleven hundred white people, three hundred black, and about sixty red slaves, otherwise Savages. The three Illinois Villages do not contain more than eight hundred Savages, of all ages. The majority of the French settled in this country devote themselves to the cultivation of the soil. They sow quantities of wheat; they rear cattle brought from France,[2] also pigs and horses in great numbers. This, with hunting, enables them to live very comfortably. There is no fear of famine in this country; there is always three times as much food as can be

---

1. The recipient of this letter is unknown. The text is from *The Jesuit Relations and Allied Documents,* vol. 69, ed. Reuben Gold Thwaites (1900).

2. Domestic cattle were introduced in the area around 1712.

consumed. Besides wheat, maize—otherwise "Turkish corn"—grows plentifully every year, and quantities of flour are conveyed to new Orleans. Let us consider the Savages in particular. Nothing but erroneous ideas are conceived of them in Europe; they are hardly believed to be men. This is a gross error. The Savages, and especially the Illinois, are of a very gentle and sociable nature. They have wit, and seem to have more than our peasants,—as much, at least, as most Frenchmen. This is due to the freedom in which they are reared; respect never makes them timid. As there is neither rank nor dignity among them, all men seem equal to them. An Illinois would speak as boldly to the King of France as to the lowest of his subjects. Most of them are capable of sustaining a conversation with any person, provided no question be treated of that is beyond their sphere of knowledge. They submit to raillery very well; they know not what it is to dispute and get angry while conversing. They never interrupt you in conversation. I found in them many qualities that are lacking in civilized peoples. They are distributed in cabins; a cabin is a sort of room in common, in which there are generally from 15 to 20 persons. They all live in great peace, which is due, in a great measure, to the fact that each one is allowed to do what he pleases. From the beginning of October to the middle of March, they hunt at a distance of forty or fifty leagues from their Village; and, in the middle of March, they return to their Village. Then the women sow the maize. As to the men, with the exception of a little hunting now and then, they lead a thoroughly idle life; they chat and smoke, and that is all. As a rule, the Illinois are very lazy and greatly addicted to brandy; this is the cause of the insignificant results that we obtain among them. Formerly, we had Missionaries in the three Villages. The Gentlemen of the Missions étrangères have charge of one of the three. We abandoned the second through lack of a Missionary, and because we obtained but scanty results. We confined ourselves to the third, which alone is larger than the two others. We number two Priests there, but the harvest does not correspond to our labors. If these Missions have no greater success, it is not through the fault of those who have preceded us, for their memory is still held in veneration among French and Illinois. It is perhaps due to the bad example of the French, who are continually mingled with these people; to the brandy that is sold to them, and above all to their disposition which is certainly opposed to all restraint, and consequently to any Religion. When the first Missionaries came among the Illinois, we see, by the writings which they have left us, that they counted five thousand persons of all ages in that Nation. To-day we count but two thousand. It should be observed that, in addition to these three Villages which I have mentioned, there is a fourth one of the same Nation, eighty leagues from here, almost as large as the three others. You may judge by this how much they have diminished in the period of sixty years. I commend myself to your holy sacrifices, in the union whereof I have the honor to be, etc.

Among the Illinois, this 8th of June, 1750.

November 17, 1750[3]

My reverend father,
The peace of Our Lord.
I accept with pleasure the proposal which you make me. The slight merits I may acquire by my labors I consent willingly to share with you, on the assurance that you give me of assisting me with your holy prayers. I gain too much from this association not to be desirous of entering into it with all my heart.

There is another point which you desire, and on which I will satisfy you; and that is, the description of our Missions. We have three in this quarter: one consisting of Savages; one of French; and a third, partly of French and partly of Savages.

The first is composed of over six hundred Illinois, all baptized excepting five or six; but the brandy sold by the French, especially by the soldiers, in spite of the King's repeated prohibitions, and that which is sometimes distributed to them under the pretext of maintaining them in our interest, has ruined this Mission, and has caused the majority of them to abandon our holy Religion. The Savages—and especially the Illinois, who are the gentlest and most tractable of men—become, when intoxicated, madmen and wild beasts. Then they fall upon one another, stab with their knives, and tear one another. Many have lost their ears, and some a portion of their noses, in these tragic encounters. The greatest good that we do among them consists in administering baptism to dying children. I usually reside in this Mission of Savages with Father Guienne, who acts as my Master in the study of the Illinois language.[4]

---

3. The text is from *The Jesuit Relations and Allied Documents,* vol. 69, ed. Reuben Gold Thwaites (1900).

4. The Reverend Father Alexandre Xavier de Guyenne (that is, Xavier of present-day Aquitaine) was listed in 1749 as the mission's superior.

The French Cure under Father Vattrin's charge is composed of more than four hundred French people, of all ages, and more than two hundred and fifty Negroes. The third Mission is seventy leagues from here. It is much smaller; Father Meurin[5] has charge of it. The remainder of our Louisiana Mission consists of a residence at New Orleans, where the Superior-general of the Mission resides with another of our Fathers, and two Brethren. We have there a considerable settlement, which is in very good condition. The revenues of this settlement, added to the pensions given us by the King, supply the needs of the Missionaries.

When the Mission is sufficiently provided with laborers (who in this Colony should be twelve in number), one is maintained among the Akansas, another among the Tchactas and a third among the Alibamons.[6] Reverend Father Baudouin, the present Superior-general of the Mission, formerly resided among the Tchactas; he dwelt eighteen years among those barbarians. When he was on the eve of deriving some fruit from his labors, the disturbances excited by the English in that Nation, and the danger to which he was manifestly exposed, compelled Father Vitri, then Superior-general, in concert with Monsieur the Governor, to recall him to New Orleans.[7] Now that the troubles are beginning to subside, they are thinking of reëstablishing this Mission. Father Moran was among the Alibamons some years ago. The impossibility of exercising his Ministry, as regards both the Savages and the French, induced the Superior to recall him and confide to him the direction of the Nuns and of the King's hospital, which is in our charge.

The English, as well as the French, trade among the Alibamon Savages. You can imagine what an obstacle this may be to the progress of Religion. The English are ever ready to preach controversy. Would a poor Savage be in a position to make a choice? At present we have no one among the Akansas. Such, my Reverend Father, is the state of our Mission. The remainder of my letter will be a short description of this country. I shall give particulars which will perhaps be of little interest to you, but which would become useful to this country if the Government would take into consideration a portion of what is herein contained.

The mouth of the Mississipi lies on the 29th degree of north latitude. The King maintains a small garrison there, and also a Pilot to meet vessels and bring them into the river. The multitude of islands and of banks—not of sand, but of mud—which fill it, make its entrance very difficult for those who have never been there. The question is, to find the channel; and there is only one Pilot who is accustomed to the place and knows it thoroughly. Vessels experience difficulty in ascending the Mississipi. Besides the fact that the tide of the sea is not felt in it, it winds continually; so that it is necessary either to tow, or to have at one's command wind from all points of the compass. From the twenty-ninth to the thirty-first degree of latitude, it did not seem to me wider than the Seine in front of Rouen, but it is infinitely deeper. As one ascends, it becomes wider, but is shallower in proportion. Its length from the North to the South is known to be more than seven hundred leagues. According to the reports of the latest travelers, its source—which is more than three hundred leagues to the North of the Illinois—is formed by the discharge of some lakes and swamps.

Mississipi, in the Illinois language, means "the great river." It seems to have usurped that name from the Missouri. Before its junction with that river, the Mississipi is of no great size. Its current is slight, while the Missouri is wider, deeper, more rapid, and takes its rise much farther away. Several rivers of considerable size empty into the Mississipi; but the Missouri alone seems to pour into it more water than all these rivers together. Here is the proof of it: the water of most—I might say, of all—of the rivers that fall into the Mississipi is only passably good, and that of several is positively unwholesome; that of the Mississipi itself, above its junction with the Missouri, is not of the best; on the contrary, that of the Missouri is the best water in the world. Now that of the Mississipi, from its junction with the Missouri to the sea, becomes excellent; the water of the Missouri must therefore predominate. The first travelers who came through Canada discovered the Mississipi; that is the reason why the latter has acquired the name of "great," at the expense of the glory of the other.

---

5. According to the mission record of 1749, Philippe Watrin and Sébastien Louis Meurin were both originally from the Champagne area of France. The mission served by Meurin was near present-day Peoria, Illinois.

6. Early in the eighteenth century, French officials established fairly good relations with the principal peoples in the area, including several whom Vivier named here, the Arkansas, Choctaws, and Alibamus.

7. Pierre de Vitry (1700–49), who joined the Jesuits in 1719, went to Louisiana in 1732, where he spent the rest of his life, mostly at New Orleans, where he was mission superior between 1739 and 1749.

Both banks of the Mississipi are bordered, throughout nearly the whole of its course, by two strips of dense forests, the depth of which varies more or less from half a league to four leagues. Behind these forests the country is more elevated, and is intersected by plains and groves, wherein the trees are almost as thinly scattered as in our public promenades. This is partly due to the fact that the Savages set fire to the prairies toward the end of the autumn, when the grass is dry; the fire spreads everywhere and destroys most of the young trees. This does not happen in the places nearer the river, because, the land being lower, and consequently more watery, the grass remains green longer, and is less susceptible to the attacks of fire.

The plains and forests contain wild cattle, which are found in herds; deer, elk, and bears; a few tigers; numbers of wolves, which are much smaller than those of Europe, and much less daring; wildcats; wild turkeys and pheasants; and other animals, less known and of smaller size. This river, with all those that flow into it, as well as the lakes,—of which there are a great number, but which, individually, are quite small in extent,—are the abode of beavers; of a prodigious number of ducks, of three kinds; of teal, bustards, geese, swans, snipe; and of some other aquatic birds, whose names are unknown in Europe, to say nothing of the fish of many kinds in which they abound.

It is only at fifteen leagues above the mouth of the Mississipi that one begins to see the first French settlements, as the land lower down is not habitable. They are situated on both sides of the river as far as the Town. The lands throughout this extent, which is fifteen leagues, are not all occupied; many await new settlers. New Orleans, the Metropolis of Louisiana, is built on the east bank of the river; it is of medium size, and the streets are in straight lines; some of the houses are built of brick, and others of wood. It is inhabited by French, Negroes, and some Savages who are slaves; all these together do not, it seemed to me, number more than twelve hundred persons.

The climate, although infinitely more bearable than that of the islands, seems heavy to one who has recently landed. If the country were less densely wooded, especially on the side toward the sea, the wind coming thence would penetrate inland and greatly temper the heat. The soil is very good, and nearly all kinds of vegetables grow very well in it. There are splendid orange-trees; the people cultivate indigo, maize in abundance, rice, potatoes, cotton, and tobacco. The vine might succeed there; at least I have seen some very good muscatel grapes. The

climate is too hot for wheat. Buckwheat, millet, and oats grow very well. Poultry of all kinds are raised, and horned cattle have multiplied considerably. The forests are at present the chief and surest source of revenue of many habitans;[8] they obtain from them quantities of lumber for building purposes, which they manufacture easily and at slight expense in the sawmills, which several persons have erected.

You will observe that the land, thirty leagues below the Town and for nearly the same distance above it, is of peculiar formation. Throughout nearly the whole country, the bank of a river is the lowest spot; here, on the contrary, it is the highest. From the river to the beginning of the Cypress forests, several arpents behind the settlements, there is a slope of as much as fifteen feet. Do you wish to irrigate your land? Dig a drain to the river, with a dyke at the end of the drain; and in a short time it will be covered with water. To work a mill, it is only necessary to have an opening to the river. The water flows through the Cypress forests to the sea. Care must be taken, however, not to abuse this facility anywhere; as the water could not always flow away easily, it would, in the end, inundate the settlements.

At New Orleans there is nothing scarcer than stones; you might give a louis to get one belonging to the country, and you would not find it; bricks made on the spot are substituted for it. Lime is made from shells, which are obtained at a distance of three or four leagues on the shores of lake Pontchartrain. Hills of shells are found there,—a singular thing for that region; they are also found far inland, at a depth of two or three feet below the surface. The following articles are sent down to New Orleans from the upper country and adjacent territories: salt beef, tallow, tar, fur, bear's grease, and, from the Illinois especially, flour and pork. In this vicinity, and still more toward Mobile, grow in abundance the trees called "wax-trees," because means have been found to extract from their seeds a wax, which, if properly prepared, would be almost equal to French wax. If the use of this wax could be introduced into Europe, it would be a very considerable branch of trade for the Colony. You will see, by all these details, that some trade can be carried on at New Orleans. In former years, when eight to ten ships entered the Mississipi, that was considered a great number; this year over

---

8. Typically used to indicate fur traders, the word *habitants* by midcentury came to identify any persons living in the woods as opposed to living in towns.

forty entered, mostly from Martinique and San Domingo; they came to load cargoes chiefly of timber and bricks, to rebuild the houses destroyed by two fires, which are said to have been caused in those two islands by fire from Heaven.

Ascending the river, one finds French settlements above as well as below New Orleans. The most notable establishment is a small German Colony, ten leagues above it. La Pointe coupée is thirty-five leagues from the German settlement.[9] A palisaded fort has been built there, in which a small garrison is maintained. There are sixty residences, spread over an extent of five or six leagues, along the west bank of the river. Fifty leagues from la pointe coupée are the Natchez. We now have there only a garrison,—which is kept imprisoned, as it were, in a fort, through fear of the Chicachats[10] and other Savage enemies. Formerly there were at that place about sixty dwellings, and a savage Nation of considerable numbers called the Natchez, who were greatly attached to us and rendered us great services. The tyranny which a French Commandant undertook to exercise over them drove them to extremities. One day they killed all the French, excepting a few who sought safety in flight. One of our Fathers, who was descending the Mississipi and was asked to tarry there to say Mass on Sunday, was included in the massacre. Since that time the blow has been avenged by the almost total destruction of the Natchez Nation; only a few remain scattered among the Chicachats and Chéraquis, where they live precariously and almost as slaves.[11]

At la Pointe coupée, and still more at Natchez, excellent tobacco is grown. If, instead of obtaining from strangers the tobacco that is consumed in France, we obtained it here, we would get a better quality, and save the money that goes out of the Kingdom for that product; and the colony would be settled.

One hundred leagues above the Natchez are the Akansas, a savage Nation of about four hundred warriors. We have near them a fort with a garrison, where the convoys ascending to the Illinois stop to rest.[12] There were some settlers there but in the month of May, 1748, the Chicachats, our irreconcilable foes, aided by some other barbarians, suddenly attacked the post; they killed several persons, and carried off thirteen into captivity. The rest escaped into the fort, in which there were at the time only a dozen soldiers. They made an attempt to attack it, but no sooner had they lost two of their people than they retreated. Their Drummer was a French deserter from the Akansas garrison itself.

The distance from the Akansas to the Illinois is estimated at nearly one hundred and fifty leagues. Throughout all that extent of country, not a single hamlet exists. Nevertheless, in order to secure our possession of it, it would be very advisable that we should have a good fort on the Ouabache,[13] the only place by which the English can enter into the Mississipi.

The Illinois are on the parallel of 38 degrees 15 minutes of latitude. The climate, which is very different from that of New Orleans, is almost similar to that of France; the great heats make themselves felt there a little earlier and more intensely; but they are neither so constant nor so lasting. The severe cold comes later. In winter, when the North wind blows, ice forms on the Mississipi sufficiently thick to bear the heaviest carts; but such cold weather does not last long. The winter here is an alternation of severe cold and quite mild weather, according as the winds blow from the North or from the South; and they succeed each other with fair regularity. This alternation is very injurious to the fruit-trees. The weather may be very mild, a little warm even, as early as mid-February; the sap ascends in the trees, which become covered with blossoms; then a wind from the North springs up, and destroys the brightest hopes.

The soil is fertile, and vegetables of all kinds would grow in it almost as well as in France, if they were cultivated with care. Nevertheless wheat, as a rule, yields only from five to eightfold; but it must be observed that the

---

9. Germans, many of them Lutheran, had been recruited to come over between 1717 and 1720 as *engagés* to France's Company of the Indies, to work at developing the colony of Louisiana. Populations during this migration, in which many of the people were forced to take part, concentrated around New Orleans and Point Coupee, where planters used slaves to grow small amounts of tobacco, along with refining indigo and timber, for export.

10. Chickasaws.

11. The Natchez people were defeated after they engaged in a destructive uprising in 1729. Many joined with Chickasaws and Cherokees, thus moving away from their ancestral territory along the Mississippi.

---

12. The French had a trading post (*Poste aux Akansas,* the Arkansas Post) on the Arkansas River as early as 1685. Marquette had visited Indians along the river at an even earlier date.

13. The Wabash.

lands are tilled in a very careless manner, and that they have never been manured during the thirty years while they have been cultivated. This poor success in growing wheat is due still more to the heavy fogs and too sudden heats. But, on the other hand, maize—which in France is called Turkish corn—grows marvelously; it yields more than a thousandfold; it is the food of domestic cattle, of the slaves, and of most of the natives of the country, who eat it as a treat. The country produces three times as much food as can be consumed in it. Nowhere is game more abundant; from mid-October to the end of March the people live almost entirely on game, especially on the wild ox and deer.

The horned cattle have multiplied exceedingly; most of them cost nothing, either for care or for food. The working animals graze on a vast common around the village; others, in much larger numbers, which are intended for breeding, are shut up throughout the year on a peninsula over ten leagues in extent, formed by the Mississipi and the river of the Tamarouas. These animals, which are seldom approached, have become almost wild, and artifice must be employed in order to catch them. If a habitant needs a pair of oxen, he goes to the peninsula. When he sees a bull large enough to be trained, he throws a handful of salt to him, and stretches out a long rope with a noose at the end; then he lies down. The animal which is eager for salt, draws near; as soon as its foot is in the noose the man on the watch pulls the rope, and the bull is captured. The same is done for horses, calves, and colts; this is all that it costs to get a pair of oxen or of horses. Moreover, these animals are not subject to any diseases; they live a long time, and, as a rule, die only of old age.

In this part of Louisiana there are five French and three Illinois villages within a distance of twenty-two leagues; they are situated upon a long prairie bounded on the East by a chain of mountains and the river of the Tamarouas, and on the West by the Mississipi. The five French villages contain in all about one hundred and forty families. The three villages of Savages may furnish three hundred men capable of bearing arms. There are several salt-springs in this country, one of which, two leagues from here, supplies all the salt consumed in the surrounding country, and in many posts which are dependencies of Canada. There are mines without number, but as no one is in a position to incur the expense necessary for opening and working them, they remain in their original condition. Certain individuals content themselves with obtaining lead from some of these, because it lies almost at the surface of the ground. They supply this country, all the

Savage Nations of the Missouri and Mississipi, and several posts of Canada. Two men who are here, a Spaniard and a Portuguese, who claim to know something about mines and minerals, assert that these mines in no wise differ from those of Mexico and Peru; and that, if slightly deeper excavations were made, silver ore would be found under the lead ore. This much is certain: that the lead is very fine, and that a little silver is obtained from it. Borax has also been found in these mines, and in some places gold, but in very small quantities. Beyond a doubt, there are copper mines; because, from time to time, very large pieces of it are found in the streams.

There is not, in all America, any special Officer who has such a province as has he who commands for the King among the Illinois. On the North and Northwest, the extent is unlimited; it spreads through the vast country watered by the Missouri and the rivers that fall into it,—the finest country in the world. How many Savage Nations in these immense regions offer themselves to the Missionaries' zeal! They belong to the district of the Gentlemen of the Missions étrangères, to whom Monseigneur the Bishop of Quebec allotted them many years ago. There are three of these Gentlemen here, who have charge of two French Cures. Nothing can be more amiable than their character, or more edifying than their conduct. We live with them as if we were members of the same body.

Among the Nations of the Missouri are some who seem to be specially disposed to receive the Gospel: as, for instance, the Panismahas.[14] One of the Gentlemen of whom I have just spoken wrote one day to a Frenchman who traded among the Savages, and asked him in his letter to baptize dying children. When the chief of the village perceived the letter, he said to the Frenchman: "What is the news?" "There is none," replied the latter. "How," retorted the Savage, "because our color is red, can we not know the news?" "It is the black Chief," replied the Frenchman, "who writes, recommending me to baptize dying children, in order to send them to the great Spirit." The Savage chief, thoroughly satisfied, said to him:"Be not anxious; I myself undertake to notify thee whenever a child is in danger of death." He gathered his people together and said to them: "What think ye of this black Chief?" (for that is the name which they give to the Missionaries.) "We have never seen him; we have never done him any good; he dwells far from us, beyond the sun. And

---

14. A group affiliated with the Pawnees living near the Arkansas River.

yet he thinks of our village; he desires to do good to us; and, when our children die, he wishes to send them to the great Spirit. This black Chief must be very good."

Some traders who came from his village have mentioned to me instances which prove that, savage as he is, he none the less possesses intelligence and good sense. At the death of his predecessor all the suffrages of his Nation were in his favor. At first, he excused himself from accepting the position of Chief; but at last, on being compelled to acquiesce, he said to them: "You desire then that I should be your Chief; I consent, but you must bear in mind that I wish to be your Chief in reality, and that I must be faithfully obeyed in that capacity. Hitherto the widows and orphans have been left destitute. I intend that in future their wants shall be provided for; and, in order that they may not be forgotten, I desire and intend that they be the first to get their share." Accordingly, he gave orders to his Escapia—who is, as it were, his Steward—to set aside, whenever a hunt should take place, a quantity of meat sufficient for the widows and orphans. These people have as yet but very few guns. They hunt on horseback with arrows and spears; they surround a herd of cattle, and but few escape them. When the animals fall to the ground, the Chief's Escapia touches a certain number of them with his hand; these are the share of the widows and orphans, and no one else can take any portion of them. One of the hunters,—through inadvertence, no doubt,—having begun to cut a piece from one of these, the Chief killed him on the spot with a shot from his gun. This Chief receives the French with great distinction; he makes them eat with him alone, or with the chief of another Nation, if such happen to be present. He honors with the title of "sun" the most wretched Frenchman who may happen to be in his village; and he says, therefore, that the sky is always serene while the Frenchman sojourns there. Only a month ago he came to pay his respects to our commandant. I proceeded to fort de Chartres,[15] six leagues from here, for the express purpose of seeing him. He is a thoroughly fine man. He was polite to me, in his own fashion; and invited me to go to give his people sense,—that is, to instruct them. According to the reports of the Frenchmen who have been there, his village can furnish nine hundred men capable of bearing arms.

For the rest, this country is of far greater importance than is imagined. Through its position alone, it deserves that France should spare nothing to retain it. It is true that it has not yet enriched the King's coffers, and that convoys to and fro are costly; but it is none the less true that the tranquillity of Canada and the safety of the entire lower part of the Colony depend upon it. Assuredly, without this post there can be no communication by land between Louisiana and Canada. There is another consideration: several regions of the same Canada and all those on the lower part of the river would be deprived of the provisions they obtain from the Illinois, which are often a great resource to them. By founding a solid establishment here, prepared to meet all these troubles, the King would secure the possession of the most extensive and the finest country in north America. To be convinced of this one has but to glance at the well-known map of Louisiana, and to consider the situation of the Illinois country and the multitude of Nations against whom the post usually serves as a barrier. In union with your holy sacrifices, I remain, etc.

---

15. Fort Chartres was built just northwest of Kaskaskia in 1720 by Pierre Dugué, sieur de Boisbriant, royal commandant in the Illinois country. First built at the expense of the Company of the Indies, it was rebuilt in stone masonry between 1753 and 1756.

Antoine-Simon Le Page du Pratz (1695?–1775?)

The so-called cajun culture of Louisiana preserves a strong French influence, surviving as one small part of the concentration of French interests in the southeastern part of North America. During the eighteenth century, the Louisiana territory encompassed all the Mississippi Valley, extending vaguely toward the Spanish colonies in the West. The area was little explored by Europeans, but it held great potential for agriculture and trade and for consolidating French control of North America. The writings of Antoine-Simon Le Page du Pratz record much about the early conditions in the colony and the culture of Native Americans along the Mississippi.

Le Page du Pratz had training as a military engineer, and he arrived in North America in 1718 as part of a large group of emigrés who were responding to the speculative land scheme set up in Paris by the

Scottish financier, John Law. He stayed in the Louisiana until 1734, living half of that time among the Natchez Indians at the site of the town of that name in modern Mississippi. He formed a household with the Chitimacha woman he introduces in the excerpt presented next, and a few slaves of African descent. Le Page du Pratz had great respect for the Indians, whom he called "Naturels" in French, rather than "Sauvages," the usage typical among French writers. He became especially close to the Natchez, befriending their Great Sun, who was in his eighties; the temple guardian quoted later; and Stung Serpent, a promising young chief whose death and funeral inspired one of the most interesting ethnographic passages in Le Page's book. In 1728 he returned downstream to New Orleans, just in time to avoid probable death in the uprising called the Natchez massacre. Several hundred French colonists were killed in the attack by the area's Indians. The military backlash took the lives of many more Natchez, and Le Page du Pratz's account of the incident sympathizes with the Native peoples and explains the injustices that motivated the rebellion. He credits them with curing him of illness.

After returning to France, Le Page du Pratz wrote a series of articles about Louisiana for the *Journal Oeconomique* between 1751 and 1752. He expanded these articles into the three-volume *Histoire de la Louisiane* in 1758. In spite of its title, the work is more than a history of the colony because it includes a memoir of his time there, an invitation to colonists, sections of natural history, and an ethnography of the Natchez and other Indian tribes.

Le Page du Pratz was eager to promote emigration to the Louisiana territory, and he described its fertile soils and friendly natives in somewhat exaggerated terms. Yet most of his information is accurate, and his expertise was invaluable to those who traveled to the area. In 1763, when England defeated France in the Seven Years War and claimed title to the French colonies in America, a translation of the book appeared in London. A lengthy preface explained that Le Page du Pratz offered a guide for exploiting the vast resources of the Mississippi and Ohio River basin, which was now under English control. The translator even retitled the book to connect Louisiana to the English colonies to the east. The following excerpt, taken from that contemporaneous English version, provides a sense of the way Le Page du Pratz's narrative was circulated among English people of that time.

from THE HISTORY OF LOUISIANA[1]

from BOOK 4

CHAPTER 1 • *The Origin of the* Americans

The remarkable difference I observed between the Natchez, including in that name the nations whom they treat as brethren, and the other people of Louisiana, made me extremely desirous to know whence both of them might originally come. We had not then that full information which we have since received from the voyages and discoveries of M. De Lisle[2] in the eastern parts of the Russian empire. I therefore applied myself one day to put the keeper of the temple[3] in good humour, and having succeeded in that without much difficulty, I then told him, that from the little resemblance I observed between the Natchez and the neighbouring nations, I was inclined to believe that they were not originally of the country which they then inhabited; and that if the ancient speech taught him any thing on that subject, he would do me a great pleasure to inform me of it. At these words he leaned his

---

1. Le Page du Pratz originally published his book as *Histoire de la Louisiane* in 1758. The English translation, *History of Louisiana, or of the Western Parts of Virginia and Carolina,* which abridged and rearranged the French original, was published in 1763, with a second edition in 1774. The text is taken from the 1774 edition.

2. Joseph-Nicolas De Lisle (or Delisle), from an esteemed family of French explorers and geographers, published in the early 1750s maps that showed Asia and America connected at the Northern latitudes. The area had not yet been well explored.

3. Le Page Du Pratz quotes at great length in the book his conversations with the Natchez "gardien du temple" or temple guardian.

head on his two hands, with which he covered his eyes, and having remained in that posture about a quarter of an hour, as if to recollect himself, he answered to the following effect:

"Before we came into this land we lived yonder under the sun, (pointing with his finger nearly south-west, by which I understood that he meant Mexico;) we lived in a fine country where the earth is always pleasant; there our Suns had their abode, and our nation maintained itself for a long time against the ancients of the country, who conquered some of our villages in the plains, but never could force us from the mountains. Our nation extended itself along the great water where this large river loses itself;[4] but as our enemies were become very numerous, and very wicked, our Suns sent some of their subjects who lived near this river, to examine whether we could retire into the country through which it flowed. The country on the east side of the river[5] being found extremely pleasant, the Great Sun, upon the return of those who had examined it, ordered all his subjects who lived in the plains, and who still defended themselves against the antients of the country, to remove into this land, here to build a temple, and to preserve the eternal fire.

"A great part of our nation accordingly settled here, where they lived in peace and abundance for several generations. The Great Sun, and those who had remained with him, never thought of joining us, being tempted to continue where they were by the pleasantness of the country, which was very warm, and by the weakness of their enemies, who had fallen into civil dissentions, in consequence of the ambition of one of their chiefs, who wanted to raise himself from a state of equality with the other chiefs of the villages, and to treat all the people of his nation as slaves. During those discords among our enemies, some of them even entered into an alliance with the Great Sun, who still remained in our old country, that he might conveniently assist our other brethren who had settled on the banks of the Great Water to the east of the large river, and extended themselves so far on the coast and among the isles, that the Great Sun did not hear of them sometimes for five or six years together.

"It was not till after many generations that the Great Suns came and joined us in this country, where, from the fine climate, and the peace we had enjoyed, we had mul-

tiplied like the leaves of the trees. Warriors of fire, who made the earth to tremble, had arrived in our old country, and having entered into an alliance with our brethren, conquered our ancient enemies;[6] but attempting afterwards to make slaves of our Suns, they, rather than submit to them, left our brethren who refused to follow them, and came hither attended only with their slaves."

Upon my asking him who those warriors of fire were, he replied, that they were bearded white men, somewhat of a brownish colour, who carried arms that darted out fire with a great noise, and killed at a great distance; that they had likewise heavy arms which killed a great many men at once, and like thunder made the earth tremble; and that they came from the sun-rising in floating villages.

The antients of the country he said were very numerous, and inhabited from the western coast of the great water to the northern countries on this side the sun, and very far upon the same coast beyond the sun. They had a great number of large and small villages, which were all built of stone, and in which there were houses large enough to lodge a whole village. Their temples were built with great labour and art, and they made beautiful works of all kinds of materials.

But ye yourselves, said I, whence are ye come? The ancient speech, he replied, does not say from what land we came; all that we know is, that our fathers, to come hither, followed the sun, and came with him from the place where he rises; that they were a long time on their journey, were all on the point of perishing, and were brought into this country without seeking it.

To this account of the keeper of the temple, which was afterwards confirmed to me by the Great Sun, I shall add the following passage of Diodorus Siculus,[7] which seems to confirm the opinion of those who think the eastern Americans are descended from the Europeans, who may have been driven by the winds upon the coasts of Guiana or Brasil.

"To the west of Africa, he says, lies a very large island, distant many days sail from that part of our continent. Its

---

4. The Gulf of Mexico.

5. That is, the east bank of the Mississippi, where modern Natchez is located.

6. An apparent reference to the Spanish conquest of the Aztec empire in Mexico. The Aztecs may be the Natchez's "ancient enemies," although their empire did not extend as widely as the subsequent paragraph suggests.

7. A Greek historian of the first century B.C., author of a three-part *Bibliotheca Historica,* or Historical Dictionary. The description of the western land that Le Page du Pratz quotes from this work comes from Greek myths of Atlantis and of the Golden Age.

fertile soil is partly plain, and partly mountainous. The plain country is most sweet and pleasant, being watered every where with rivulets, and navigable rivers; it is beautified with many gardens, which are planted with all kinds of trees, and the orchards particularly are watered with pleasant streams. The villages are adorned with houses built in a magnificent taste, having parterres[8] ornamented with arbours covered with flowers. Hither the inhabitants retire during the summer to enjoy the fruits which the country furnishes them with in the greatest abundance. The mountainous part is covered with large woods, and all manner of fruit trees, and in the vallies, which are watered with rivulets, the inhabitants meet with every thing that can render life agreeable. In a word, the whole island, by its fertility and the abundance of its springs, furnishes the inhabitants not only with every thing that may flatter their wishes, but with what may also contribute to their health and strength of body. Hunting furnishes them with such an infinite number of animals, that in their feasts they have nothing to wish for in regard either to plenty or delicacy. Besides, the sea, which surrounds the island, supplies them plentifully with all kinds of fish, and indeed the sea in general is very abundant. The air of this island is so temperate that the trees bear leaves and fruit almost the whole year round. In a word, this island is so delicious, that it seems rather the abode of the gods than of men.

"Anciently, on account of its remote situation, it was altogether unknown; but afterwards it was discovered by accident. It is well known, that from the earliest ages the Phenicians[9] undertook long voyages in order to extend their commerce, and in consequence of those voyages established several colonies in Africa and the western parts of Europe. Every thing succeeding to their wish, and being become very powerful, they attempted to pass the pillars of Hercules and enter the ocean. They accordingly passed those pillars, and in their neighbourhood built a city upon a peninsula of Spain, which they named Gades. There, amongst the other buildings proper for the place, they built a temple to Hercules, to whom they instituted splendid sacrifices after the manner of their country. This temple is in great veneration at this day, and several Ro-

mans who have rendered themselves illustrious by their exploits, have performed their vows to Hercules for the success of their enterprizes.

"The Phenicians accordingly having passed the Streights of Spain, sailed along Africa, when by the violence of the winds they were driven far out to sea, and the storm continuing several days, they were at length thrown on this island. Being the first who were acquainted with its beauty and fertility, they published them to other nations. The Tuscans, when they were masters at sea, designed to send a colony thither, but the Carthaginians[10] found means to prevent them on the two following accounts; first, they were afraid lest their citizens, tempted by the charms of that island, should pass over thither in too great numbers, and desert their own country; next they looked upon it as a secure asylum for themselves, if ever any terrible disaster should befal their republic."

This description of Diodorus is very applicable in many circumstances to America, particularly in the agreeable temperature of the climate to Africans, the prodigious fertility of the earth, the vast forests, the large rivers, and the multitude of rivulets and springs. The Natchez may then justly be supposed to be descended from some Phenicians or Carthaginians, who had been wrecked on the shores of South America, in which case they might well be imagined to have but little acquaintance with the arts, as those who first landed would be obliged to apply all their thoughts to their immediate subsistence, and consequently would soon become rude and barbarous. Their worship of the eternal fire likewise implies their descent from the Phenicians; for every body knows that this superstition, which first took its rise in Egypt, was introduced by the Phenicians into all the countries that they visited. The figurative style,[11] and the bold and Syriac expressions in the language of the Natchez, is likewise another proof of their being descended from the Phenicians.

As to those whom the Natchez, long after their first establishment, found inhabiting the western coasts of America, and whom we name Mexicans, the arts which they possessed and cultivated with success, obliged me to

---

8. Geometric garden plots, in the French garden style of the time.

9. An ancient kingdom—more commonly spelled "Phoenician"—at the east end of the Mediterranean, in present-day Lebanon and Syria, noted for its maritime power.

10. The Tuscans inhabited central Italy, and the Carthaginians present-day Tunisia in northern Africa.

11. The author might have mentioned a singular custom, in which both nations agree; for it appears from Polybius, book I, chapter 6, that the Carthaginians practiced scalping. [English translator's note in the original]

give them a different origin. Their temples, their sacrifices, their buildings, their form of government, and their manner of making war, all denote a people who have transmigrated in a body, and brought with them the arts, the sciences, and the customs of their country. Those people had the art of writing, and also of painting. Their archives consisted of cloths of cotton, whereon they had painted or drawn all those transactions which they thought, worthy of being transmitted to prosperity. It were greatly to be wished that the first conquerors of this new world had preserved to us the figures of those drawings; for by comparing them with the characters used by other nations, we might perhaps have discovered the origin of the inhabitants. The knowledge which we have of the Chinese characters, which are rather irregular drawings than characters, would probably have facilitated such a discovery; and perhaps those of Japan would have been found greatly to have resembled the Mexican; for I am strongly of opinion that the Mexicans are descended from one of those two nations.[12]

In fact, where is the impossibility, that some prince in one of those countries, upon failing in an attempt to raise himself to the sovereign power, should leave his native country with all his partizans, and look for some new land, where, after he had established himself, he might drop all foreign correspondence? The easy navigation of the South-Sea renders the thing probable; and the new map of the eastern bounds of Asia, and the western of North America, lately published by Mr. De Lisle, makes it still more likely. This map makes it plainly appear, that between the islands of Japan, or northern coasts of China, and those of America, there are other lands, which to this day have remained unknown; and who will take upon him to say there is no land, because it has never yet been discovered? I have therefore good grounds to believe, that the Mexicans came originally from China or Japan, especially when I consider their reserved and uncommunicative disposition, which to this day prevails among the people of the eastern parts of Asia. The great antiquity of the Chinese nation likewise makes it possible that a colony might have gone from thence to America early enough to be looked upon as *the Ancients of the country,* by the first of the Phenicians who could be supposed to arrive there. As a further corroboration of my conjectures, I was in-

formed by a man of learning in 1752, that in the king's library there is a Chinese manuscript, which positively affirms that America was peopled by the inhabitants of Corea. . . .

from CHAPTER 2, SECTION 1 • [Of the Natives of Louisiana]

The Natchez in former times appear to have been one of the most respectable nations in the colony, not only from their own tradition, but from that of the other nations, in whom their greatness and civilized customs raised no less jealousy than admiration. I could fill a volume with what relates to this people alone; but as I am now giving a concise account of the people of Louisiana, I shall speak of them as of the rest, only enlarging a little upon some important transactions concerning them.

When I arrived in 1720 among the Natchez, that nation was situated upon a small river of the same name; the chief village where the Great Sun resided was built along the banks of the river, and the other villages were planted round it. They were two leagues above the confluence of the river, which joins the Mississippi at the foot of the great precipices of the Natchez. From thence are four leagues to its source, and as many to fort Rosalie, and they were situated within a league of the fort.

Two small nations lived as refugees among the Natchez. The most ancient of these adopted nations were the Grigras, who seem to have received that name from the French, because when talking with one another they often pronounce those two syllables, which makes them be remarked as strangers among the Natchez, who, as well as the Chickasaws, and all the nations that speak the Chickasaw language, cannot pronounce the letter R.

The other small nation adopted by the Natchez, are the Thioux, who have also the letter R in their language. These were the weak remains of the Thioux[13] nation, formerly one of the strongest in the country. However, according to the account of the other nations, being of a turbulent disposition, they drew upon themselves the resentment of the Chickasaws, which was the occasion of their ruin; for by their many engagements they were at length so weakened that they durst not face their enemy,

---

12. Although the Mexican civilizations did employ a form of hieroglyphic writing, it is not so similar to Chinese as Le Page du Pratz believes.

13. Some of the smaller Indian nations Le Page du Pratz writes of, such as the Thioux and the Grigras below, are mentioned only in a few other sources, and thus little is known about them.

and consequently were obliged to take refuge among the Natchez.

The Natchez, the Grigras, and the Thioux, may together raise about twelve hundred warriors; which is but a small force in comparison of what the Natchez could formerly have raised alone; for according to their traditions they were the most powerful nation of all North America, and were looked upon by the other nations as their superiors, and on that account respected by them. To give an idea of their power, I shall only mention, that formerly they extended from the river Manchac, or Iberville, which is about fifty leagues from the sea, to the river Wabash,[14] which is distant from the sea about four hundred and sixty-leagues; and that they had about five hundred Suns or princes. From these facts we may judge how populous this nation formerly has been; but the pride of their Great Suns, or sovereigns, and likewise of their inferior Suns, joined to the prejudices of the people, has made greater havock among them, and contributed more to their destruction, than long and bloody wars would have done.

As their sovereigns were despotic, they had for a long time past established the following inhuman and impolitic custom, that when any of them died, a great number of their subjects, both men and women, should likewise be put to death. A proportionable number of subjects were likewise killed upon the death of any of the inferior Suns; and the people on the other hand had imbibed a belief that all those who followed their princes into the other world, to serve them there, would be eternally happy. It is easy to conceive how ruinous such an inhuman custom would be among a nation who had so many princes as the Natchez.[15]

It would seem that some of the Suns, more humane than the rest, had disapproved of this barbarous custom, and had therefore retired to places at a remote distance from the centre of their nation. For we have two branches of this great nation settled in other parts of the colony, who have preserved the greatest part of the customs of the Natchez. One of these branches is the nation of the Taen-sas on the banks of the Mobile, who preserve the eternal fire,[16] and several other usages of the nation from whom they are descended. The other branch is the nation of the Chitimachas, whom the Natchez have always looked upon as their brethren. . . .

from CHAPTER 3, SECTION 2 • [Of Their Language, Government, Religion, Ceremonies, and Feasts]

During my residence among the Natchez I contracted an intimate friendship, not only with the chiefs or guardians of the temple, but with the Great Sun, or the sovereign of the nation, and his brother the Stung Serpent, the chief of the warriors;[17] and by my great intimacy with them, and the respect I acquired among the people, I easily learned the peculiar language of the nation.

This language is easy in the pronunciation, and expressive in the terms. The natives, like the Orientals, speak much in a figurative stile, the Natchez in particular more than any other people of Louisiana. They have two languages, that of the nobles and that of the people, and both are very copious. I will give two or three examples to shew the difference of these two languages. When I call one of the common people, I say to him *aqucnan,* that is, *hark ye:* if, on the other hand, I want to speak to a Sun, or one of their nobles, I say to him, magani, which signifies, *hark ye.* If one of the common people call at my house, I say to him, *tacbte-cabanacte, are you there,* or I am glad to see you, which is equivalent to our good-morrow. I express the same thing to a Sun by the word *apapegouaiché.* Again, according to their custom, I say to one of the common people, *petchi, sit you down;* but to a Sun, when I desire him to sit down, I say, *cabam.* The two languages are nearly the same in all other respects; for the difference of expression seems only to take place in matters relating to the persons of the Suns and nobles, in distinction from those of the people.

Tho' the women speak the same language with the men, yet, in their manner of pronunciation, they soften and smooth the words, whereas the speech of the men is

---

14. The modern Wabash River flows along the present-day Illinois and Indiana border into the Ohio River, but Le Page du Pratz applied the name Wabash to the Ohio downstream from this confluence. The Manchac river or bayou was between New Orleans and Baton Rouge.

15. This custom is termed "retainer death" by anthropologists.

16. These peoples inhabited the western side of the Mississippi River and shared many cultural similarities with the Natchez.

17. Elsewhere in his *History,* Le Page du Pratz tells of the death of his friend Serpent Piqué and his efforts to forestall the killing of many Natchez in tribute to this leader.

more grave and serious. The French, by chiefly frequenting the women, contracted their manner of speaking, which was ridiculed as an effeminacy by the women, as well as the men, among the natives.

From my conversations with the chief of the guardians of the temple, I discovered that they acknowledged a supreme being, whom they called *Coyococop-Chill,* or *Great Spirit.* The *Spirit infinitely great,* or the *Spirit* by way of excellence. The word *chill,* in their language, signifies the most superlative degree of perfection, and is added by them to the word which signifies *fire,* when they want to mention the Sun; thus *Oua is fire,* and *Oua-chill* is the *supreme fire,* or the *Sun;* therefore, by the word *Coyocop-Chill* they mean a spirit that surpasses other spirits as much as the sun does common fire.

"God," according to the definition of the guardian of the temple, "was so great and powerful, that, in comparison with him, all other things were as nothing; he had made all that we see, all that we can see, and all that we cannot see; he was so good, that he could not do ill to any one, even if he had a mind to it. They believe that God had made all things by his will; that nevertheless the little spirits, who are his servants, might, by his orders, have made many excellent works in the universe, which we admire; but that God himself had formed man with his own hands."

The guardian added, that they named those little spirits, *Coyocop-techou,* that is, a *free servant,* but as submissive and as respectful as a slave; that those spirits were always present before God, ready to execute his pleasure with an extreme diligence; that the air was filled with other spirits, some good some wicked; and that the latter had a chief, who was more wicked than them all; that God had found him so wicked, that he had bound him for ever, so that the other spirits of the air no longer did so much harm, especially when they were by prayers entreated not to do it; for it is one of the religious customs of those people to invoke the spirits of the air for rain or fine weather, according as each is needed. I have seen the Great Sun fast for nine days together, eating nothing but maiz-corn, without meat or fish, drinking nothing but water, and abstaining from the company of his wives during the whole time. He underwent this rigorous fast out of complaisance to some Frenchmen, who had been complaining that it had not rained for a long time. Those inconsiderate people had not remarked, that notwithstanding the want of rain, the fruits of the earth had not suffered, as the dew is so plentiful in summer as fully to supply that deficiency.

The guardian of the temple having told me that God had made man with his own hands, I asked him if he knew how that was done. He answered, "that God had kneaded some clay, such as that which potters use, and had made it into a little man; and that after examining it, and finding it well formed, he blew up his work, and forthwith that little man had life, grew, acted, walked, and found himself a man perfectly well shaped." As he made no mention of the woman, I asked him how he believed she was made; he told me, "that probably in the same manner as the man; that their *antient speech* made no mention of any difference, only told them that the man was made first, and was the strongest and most courageous, because he was to be the head and support of the woman, who was made to be his companion."

Here I did not omit to rectify his notions on the subjects we had been talking about, and to give him those just ideas which religion teaches us, and the sacred writings have transmitted to us. He hearkened to me with great attention, and promised to repeat all that I had told him to the old men of his nation, who certainly would not forget it; adding, that we were very happy in being able to retain the knowledge of such fine things by means of the speaking cloth, so they name books and manuscripts.

I next proceeded to ask him, who had taught them to build a temple; whence had they their eternal fire, which they preserved with so much care; and who was the person that first instituted their feasts? He replied, "The charge I am entrusted with obliges me to know all these things you ask of me; I will therefore satisfy you: hearken to me. A great number of years ago there appeared among us a man and his wife, who came down from the sun. Not that we believe that the sun had a wife who bore him children, or that there were the descendants of the sun; but when they first appeared among us they were so bright and luminous that we had no difficulty to believe that they came down from the sun. This man told us, that having seen from on high that we did not govern ourselves well; that we had no master; that each of us had presumption enough to think himself capable of governing others, while he could not even conduct himself; he had thought fit to come down among us to teach us to live better.

"He moreover told us, that in order to live in peace among ourselves, and to please the supreme Spirit, we must indispensably observe the following points; we must never kill any one but in defence of our own lives; we must never know any other woman besides our own; we must never take any thing that belongs to another; we must never lye nor get drunk; we must not be avaricious, but must give liberally, and with joy, part of what we have to others who are in want, and generously share our subsistence with those who are in need of it."[18]

"The words of this man deeply affected us, for he spoke them with authority, and he procured the respect even of the old men themselves, tho' he reprehended them as freely as the rest. Next day we offered to acknowledge him as our sovereign. He at first refused, saying that he should not be obeyed, and that the disobedient would infallibly die; but at length he accepted the offer that was made him on the following condition:

"That we would go and inhabit another country, better than that in which we were, which he would shew us; that we would afterwards live conformable to the instructions he had given us; that we would promise never to acknowledge any other sovereigns but him and his descendants; that the nobility should be perpetuated by the women after this manner; if I, said he, have male and female children, they being brothers and sisters cannot marry together; the eldest boy may chuse a wife from among the people, but his sons shall be only nobles; the children of the eldest girl, on the other hand, shall be princes and princesses, and her eldest son be sovereign; but her eldest daughter be the mother of the next sovereign, even tho' she should marry one of the common people; and, in defect of the eldest daughter, the next female relation to the person reigning shall be the mother of the future sovereign; the sons of the sovereign and princes shall lose their rank, but the daughters shall preserve theirs."[19]

"He then told us, that in order to preserve the excellent precepts he had given us, it was necessary to build a temple, into which it should be lawful for none but the princes and princesses to enter, to speak to the Spirit. That in the temple they should eternally preserve a fire, which he

would bring down from the sun, from whence he himself had descended; that the wood with which the fire was supplied should be pure wood without bark; that eight wise men of the nation should be chosen for guarding the fire night and day; that those eight men should have a chief, who should see them do their duty, and that if any of them failed in it he should be put to death. He likewise ordered another temple to be built in a distant part of our nation, which was then very populous, and the eternal fire to be kept there also, that in case it should be extinguished in the one it might be brought from the other; in which case, till it was again lighted, the nation would be afflicted with a great mortality."

"Our nation having consented to these conditions, he agreed to be our sovereign; and in presence of all the people he brought down the fire from the sun, upon some wood of the walnut-tree which he had prepared, which fire was deposited in both the temples. He lived a long time, and saw his children's children. To conclude, he instituted our feasts such as you see them."

The Natchez have neither sacrifices, libations, nor offerings: their whole worship consists in preserving the eternal fire, and this the Great Sun watches over with a peculiar attention. The Sun, who reigned when I was in the country, was extremely solicitous about it, and visited the temple every day. His vigilance had been awakened by a terrible hurricane which some years before had happened in the country, and was looked upon as an extraordinary event, the air being generally clear and serene in that climate. If to that calamity should be joined the extinction of the eternal fire, he was apprehensive their whole nation would be destroyed.

One day, when the Great Sun called upon me, he gave me an account of a dreadful calamity that had formerly befallen the nation of the Natchez, in consequence, as he believed, of the extinction of the eternal fire. He introduced his account in the following manner: "Our nation was formerly very numerous and very powerful; it extended more than twelve days journey from east to west, and more than fifteen from south to north. We reckoned then 500 Suns, and you may judge by that what was the number of the nobles, of the people of rank, and the common people. Now in times past it happened, that one of the two guardians, who were upon duty in the temple, left it on some business, and the other fell asleep, and suffered the fire to go out. When he awaked and saw that he had incurred the penalty of death, he went and got some profane fire, as tho' he had been going to light his pipe, and with

---

18. The resemblance of this story to traditional Jewish and Christian stories about Jesus and Moses may be an effect of Le Page du Pratz's desire to portray the Natchez as potential converts, or perhaps an effect of the temple gardian's desire to please the colonists.

19. This account of clan structure among the Natchez has been the focus of great interest among anthropologists. Le Page du Pratz explains it more fully in another place. There were four castes: Suns, Nobles, Honored, and Stinkards ("Puants" in French). Only the Stinkards were allowed to marry within their caste.

that he renewed the eternal fire. His transgression was by that means concealed; but a dreadful mortality immediately ensued, and raged for four years, during which many Suns and an infinite number of the people died.

The guardian at length sickened, and found himself dying, upon which he sent for the Great Sun, and confessed the heinous crime he had been guilty of. The old men were immediately assembled, and, by their advice, fire being snatched from the other temple, and brought into this, the mortality quickly ceased." Upon my asking him what he meant by "snatching the fire," he replied, "that it must always be brought away by violence, and that some blood must be shed, unless some tree on the road was set on fire by lightning, and then the fire might be brought from thence; but that the fire of the sun was always preferable.[20] . . .

The Natchez are brought up in a most perfect submission to their sovereign; the authority which their princes exercise over them is absolutely despotic, and can be compared to nothing but that of the first Ottoman emperors.[21] Like these, the Great Sun is absolute master of the lives and estates of his subjects, which he disposes of at his pleasure, his will being the only law; but he has this singular advantage over the Ottoman princes, that he has no occasion to fear any seditious tumults, or any conspiracy against his person. If he orders a man guilty of a capital crime to be put to death, the criminal neither supplicates, nor procures intercession to be made for his life, nor attempts to run away. The order of the sovereign is executed on the spot, and nobody murmurs. But however absolute the authority of the Great Sun may be, and although a number of warriors and others attach themselves to him, to serve him, to follow him wherever he goes, and to hunt for him, yet he raises no stated impositions; and what he receives from those people appears given, not so much as a right due, as a voluntary homage, and a testimony of their love and gratitude.

---

20. In the following scene, not included in the selection, Le Page du Pratz brings fire down from the sun using a magnifying glass, a feat that amazes the Natchez, who offer him great wealth in exchange for the glass.

21. The Ottoman Empire of Muslim peoples arose in the 1300s in the area of modern Turkey. At its height during the Renaissance, this empire conquered much of southeastern Europe. Europeans typically referred to it as unusually despotic and capricious.

7

THE BRITISH COLONIES OF NORTH AMERICA, THE EARLIER COLONIAL YEARS

Writings from Britain's first empire in North America and the Caribbean evoke the concerns relevant to the regions in which they were produced. They indicate the range of attitudes that colonials experienced as they faced shifts in Britain's state policy as the British government attempted to manage the distant colonies from the metropolitan center in London. The writings emanating from Britain's colonies as they began to get established in North America and the Caribbean tend to reflect three intertwined issues—commerce and its regulation according to Britain's changing mercantile system; state power and its relevance to the lived experiences of the settlers; and social relations, especially with regard to other settling peoples, Native peoples, and Africans in the Americas, but also with regard to the relationships between women and men. These three themes—commerce, state power, and social relations—are the preoccupations in the writings of Britain's first empire in North America.

Britain's staple colonies, that is, colonies upon which Britain relied for staple commodities, such as sugar, tobacco, rice, cotton, and indigo, included the colonies that extended from Virginia to Jamaica. These colonies were fostered under different charters as part of a mercantile system that protected Britain's trade monopolies by employing governmental controls on manufacturing. The staple system brought an immense amount of unfamiliar raw produce and materials into Britain, either for trade from there to other European countries or for manufacture within Britain of finished goods that would then be sold outside Britain, including back to the people who were living in the British colonies. The market in sugar was the most lucrative, especially as Europeans developed a greater desire for manufactured sweets and raw sugar. Having gained access to the Caribbean through settlements on St. Christopher's island (later called St. Kitts) in 1623, British colonial settlers and plantation owners sought additional islands in order to gain control of overseas trade in sugar commodities. Britain took the Spanish colony of Jamaica by force in 1655, and British privateers sailed the seas, harassing Spanish vessels in the Caribbean. Spain signed the Treaty of Madrid in 1670, giving Britain relatively free sailing in the Caribbean area and some colonies central to the production of sugar.

Plantation culture brought a need for laborers in the staple colonies. The colonies of the first British empire were first worked by indentured laborers who came primarily from Britain but also from European countries, yet the conditions of laboring in the Caribbean were so difficult that after awhile, few indentured laborers were willing to sign on to work in the West Indies if they could get work just as easily—and they could—in Britain's colonies to the north. Britain formed the Royal African Company in 1672 to address and to profit from the labor shortage by bringing a large number of enslaved Africans to the West Indian plantations. By the end of the seventeenth century, enslaved Africans and Native Americans significantly outnumbered free British and European settlers and laborers.

Writings from the staple colonies emphasized the raw products and the peoples of the colonies, their relationship to Britain and the growing British commercial system, and the importance of the West Indies to sustaining Britain's international presence. The poetic writings often celebrated the commercial potential of Britain's staples and the people involved in settling and laboring in the colonies. The prose writings discussed the relations between the colonies and the system in which they were run, depending on the kind of charters under which the colonies were operating. The colony of Georgia was special in this regard, since it was chartered as a philanthropic trusteeship. The high ideals expressed in writings by the trustees and the rhetoric of paradise that they employed were undermined when reports sent back expressed in clear terms that the lived experiences of those who were brought over were distinctly different from what the trustees announced. Settlers in Georgia chafed at their circumstances, and especially that they could not own slaves. Thus it is that Georgia's writings differ markedly from writings from other colonies that produced staples. Even within regions, in other words, the writings from Britain's first empire differ from one another, depending on issues related to commerce, state power, and the social relations within the specific colonies. For the most part, a discourse of commodities was the most significant discourse available in the staple colonies, while concerns about religion found their way into writings of more northerly colonials who were situated among a greater number of disparate people who found ways to enter the British colonies.

The middle Atlantic colonies of Maryland, Pennsylvania, New Jersey, and New York all had different founding principles and different purposes according to the purposes for and means by which they were chartered. These colonies, highly productive of wheat, served as what has been called Britain's breadbasket. These colonies, too, were the recipients of a great number of persecuted peoples from Europe, whether Catholics (welcomed in Maryland) or Protestants (all welcomed, especially in Pennsylvania). Germans, Swiss, Dutch, Swedish, and some French people came to these colonies, settling alongside a great number of laboring British people, whether those serving out indentures or those working in established family businesses or farms.

As in the writings of Britain's staple colonies, a propaganda of plenty occurred in writings from the middle Atlantic. Yet the writings from Britain's middle Atlantic reflect social issues, including ethnic and racial tensions, religious turmoil, and class differentials. Perhaps because these middle colonies had a greater number of indentured laborers and persons who came over because they experienced a lack of freedom in Europe, the writings produced here evidenced increasing concerns about relationships between people, especially between those who were enslaved and indentured and those who were more wealthy and free.

The philosophy of members of the Society of Friends who settled in West Jersey and in Philadelphia is particularly noteworthy in this regard. These people (called Quakers in their day, as a form of derision) came to Penn's colony from all parts of Britain and northern Europe, seeking a place where they could practice their unchurched methods without interference from state or religious officials. The first movements to rid the British colonies of slavery would occur in West Jersey and Philadelphia through the efforts of Quakers, some from the Rhineland (Germany) and some from Britain, in the 1680s. The first challenge to the freedom of the press would occur, too, in Philadelphia, in the early 1690s, when printer William Bradford was charged with sedition for publishing the writings of George Keith. Keith questioned whether members of the Society of Friends should hold public office and questioned, too, the consistency of Quakers who said they believed in liberty even when they owned slaves. The commercial successes of Quakers in the area conflicted, some thought, with their testimony of peace and inward light.

Religious issues dominated the writings of England's colonies known as New England, yet here, as elsewhere, the issues of commerce and state power intertwined with social and particularly religious concerns. The first generation of Puritans had come to question the relationship between the authority of individuals and the authority of the state in examining John Winthrop for overstepping his power as a magistrate. Toward the end of the seventeenth century, the social formation in Massachusetts Bay was troubled by numerous factors, including unsettling wars against Native peoples and a diminishing land base for a growing population. Severe generational tensions, tensions from what ministers considered a declension (falling away) from true faith, and problems from economic shortfalls—all seem to have combined to fracture communities, breaking up any sense of communal purpose that had historically defined the New England Way. A key sign for us today of trouble within Massachusetts Bay is the hanging of nineteen persons and the crushing to death of another—all because they were accused of being witches. Anxieties about the community and its purpose mark the writings of Puritans during the late seventeenth and early eighteenth centuries, during the notorious Salem witch trials of 1692 and during the later religious revivals of the 1730s and 1740s.

Like their counterparts in the middle Atlantic, New Englanders began to wonder whether people who professed religious attitudes featuring personal liberty and liberty of conscience, attitudes that centered an individual's direct relationship with divinity, could in good conscience keep slaves. Some expressed a position that was gaining favor in England that persons who were baptized were free before God and so should be free before all mankind. Others argued that Christianizing Africans was God's will and would bring the Christian into a better relationship with God. The debates over slavery, over whether Christianity should be taught to enslaved people or to putatively "pagan" people like Native Americans, and over the rights of ancient Britons newly "planted" in New England—all hinged on arguments related to commerce, state power, and social relations.

Whether in Britain's staple colonies, the middle Atlantic colonies, or the New England colonies, then, similar themes dominate the written record that has come down from a settler population who were interested in finding ways to secure permanent settlements of English speakers in Britain's American colonies.

THE STAPLE COLONIES
EDWARD "NED" WARD (1667–1731)

A prolific writer of articles for the popular press and for London newspapers, Edward Ward was likely born in Oxfordshire, England. Sometime in his young adulthood, Ward left his family home and moved to London where, during the early 1690s, he began to write, initially with limited success. He struggled to support himself amid mounting debts, but he proved unsuccessful at getting ahead and decided to embark for Port Royal, Jamaica, on board the Andalucia, in 1697. Finding his financial situation in Jamaica no better than what he left behind in London, he remained abroad for less than a year. But his Jamaica journey proved a success for Ward, after all, when he discovered that, back in London, his writings about Jamaica would bring him his earliest pamphlet success.

Soon after he returned to England, Ward wrote and published anonymously *A Trip to Jamaica* (1698), a parody of the promotional tracts often used to recruit settlers to the Americas. His popular account appeared in at least seven editions, and Ward's future publications bore his name, followed by the inscription, "By the Author of A Trip To Jamaica." Drawing upon the success of *A Trip to Jamaica,* Ward wrote and published *A Trip to New England* (1699) the following year. His claim to have traveled to New England remains unsubstantiated, though, and scholars suggest that he drew his information from John Josselyn's accounts of his 1638 and 1663 voyages to that area. Ward built upon and exaggerated Josselyn's description of the people, customs and laws, climate, and natural life of New England.

Ward's satiric accounts of the Americas struck a nerve with London readers, and a series of imitators attempted time and again to gain similar publishing successes. Ward also turned his satiric pen on his homeland and published a well-received series of sketches of London life, published in *The Spy* between 1698 and 1700. He remained a popular and prolific journalist throughout the first decade of the eighteenth century. Yet by about 1712, Ward seems to have turned to trade as his primary means of support. Working first at an alehouse, he later spent more than a decade working at Bacchus Tavern in Moorfields. Although he wrote comparatively little during the last fifteen years of his life, his name remained familiar to writers, such as Alexander Pope, who referred to him critically in works like the *Dunciad* (1728) and the *Dunciad Variorum* (1729). Ward died in Fulwood's Rents in 1731.

A TRIP TO JAMAICA[1]

To the Reader

The Condition of an Author, *is much like that of a* Strumpet, *both exposing our* Reputations *to supply our* Necessities, *till at last we contract such an ill habit, thro' our Practices, that we are equally troubl'd with an* Itch *to be always* Doing; *and if the Reason be requir'd, Why we betake our selves to so Scandalous a Profession as* Whoring *or* Pamphleteering, *the same excusive Answer will serve us both, viz. That the unhappy circumstances of a Narrow Fortune, hath forc'd us to do that for our Subsistance, which we are much asham'd of.*

The chiefest and most commendable Talent, admir'd in either, is the knack of Pleasing; and He or She amongst us that happily arives to a Perfection in that sort of Witchcraft, may in a little time (to their great Honour) enjoy the Pleasure of being Celebrated by all the Coxcombs *in the Nation.*

The only difference between us is, in this particular, wherein the Jilt *has the Advantage, We do our Business First, and stand to the Courtesie of our Benefactors to Reward us After; whilst the other, for her Security, makes her* Rider *pay for his* Journey, *before he mounts the* Saddle.

It is necessary I should say something in relation to the following Matter: I do not therein present you with a formal Journal *of my Voyage, or* Geographical *Description of the* Island *of* Jamaica, *for that has been already done by Persons better qualifi'd for such a Task. I only Entertain you with what I intend for your* Diversion, *not* Instruction; *Digested into such a Stile as might move your* Laughter, *not merit your* Esteem. *I question not but the* Jamaica *Coffee-House will be much affronted at my* Character *of their* Sweating Chaos, *and if I was but as well assur'd of Pleasing every body else, as I am of Displeasing those who have an Interest in that Country, I should not question but the* Printer *would gain his End, which are the Wishes of the* Author.

A Trip to Jamaica

In the times of *Adversity* when *Poverty* was held no *Shame* and *Piety* no *Virtue;* When *Honesty* in a Trades-

man's Conscience, and *Money* in his Counting-House, were as scarce as *Health* in an Hospital, or *Charity* in a Clergyman. The *Sword* being advanc'd, and the *Pen* silenc'd; *Printers* being too Poor to Pay down *Copy-Money,* and *Authors* too Poor to Trust' em: *Fools* getting more by hazarding their *Carcasses,* than *Ingenious Men* by imploying their *Wits;* which was well enough observed by a Gentleman, in these following Lines:

When Pens *were valu'd less than* Swords,
And Blows got Money more than Words
When Am'rous Beaux *and Campaign* Bully,
Thriv'd by their Fighting *and their* Folly;
Whilst Men of Parts, as Poor as Rats,
With Mourning Swords *and Flapping Hats,*
Appear by Night like Owles *and* Bats:
With Hungry hast pursuing way,
To Sir John Lend, *or 'Squire* Pay.
Till Wit *in* Rags *and* Fool *in* Feather,
Were join'd by Providence together.
The one o'er Bottle breaks his Jest,
Like Country Parson at a Feast;
For which he's Treated and Exalted,
By his Dear Friend Sir Looby Dolthead.
Unhappy Age, which so in Vice surpasses,
That Men of Worth must Worship Golden Asses.

I being influenc'd by my Stars, with an unhappy propensity to the Conversation of those unlucky kind of *Fortune-Hunters,* till at last, tho' I had no more Wit to boast of than another Man, yet I shar'd the Fate of those that had; and to bear them Company, straglad so far from the Paths of *Profit* and *Preferment,* into a Wilderness of *Pleasure* and *Enjoyment,* that I had like to have been struck fast in a Thicket of Brambles, before I knew where abouts I was; to clear my Self of which, I bustled like a *Fox* in a *Gin,* or a Hare in a *Patridge Net:* But before I could free my self from this Entanglement, I had so wounded my Feet, and stuck so many Thorns in my Side, that I halted homewards like a *Gouty Puritan* to an *Election,* or a *Lame Beggar* to a *Misers Funeral.*

These little Afflictions mov'd me to reflect upon my Mis-spent Time; and like a *Thief* in a *Goal,*[2] or a *Whore* in a *Flux,* I Resolv'd for the future to Reform my Life, change my Measures, and push my self upon something that might recover those lost Moments I had hitherto con-

---

1. Ned Ward's *A Trip to Jamaica: with a True Character of the People and Island,* was published in London in 1698. This is the earliest extant edition.

2. Gaol or jail.

verted to the use of others, and not my self. I now began to peep into the *Business* of the World, and chang'd the Company of those who had nothing to do but *Spend Money,* for the conversation of such whose practice was to *Get it.*

But I, thro' inadvertency, neglecting to consult Doctor *Trotter,* or some other infallible Predicting *Wisaker,* began my Reformation in an Unfortunate Minute, when *Usurers* were unbinding their *Fetter'd Trunks* and breaking up their *Deified Bags* and *Consecrated Sums,* for the Security of *Religion* and the further establishment of *Liberty of Conscience,* without which [*Liberty*]³ join'd, *Conscience* to them would be of no use. *Tradesmen* Grumbling at the *Taxes, Merchants* at their *Losses,* most Men complaining for want of *Business,* and all Men in *Business,* for want of *Money;* Every Man upon *Change*⁴ looking with as peevish a Countenance, as if he had unluckily stumbled upon his *Wifes Failings,* and unhappily become a Witness to his own *Cuckoldome.* These I thought but slender Encouragements to a *New Reformist,* who had forsaken *Liberty* for *Restraint, Ease* for *Trouble, Laziness* for *Industry, Wine* for *Coffee,* and the *Pleasures* of *Witty Conversation,* for the *Plagues* of a *Muddy-Brain'd Society,* who could talk of nothing but *Prime Cost* and *Profit,* the *Good Humour* of their *Wives,* the *Wittiness* of their *Children,* and the *Unluckiness* of their *Prentices;* and knew no more how *Handsomely* to Spend their Money, than *Honestly* to Get it.

The *Complaints* of these *Philodenarians,*⁵ the *Declination* of *Trade,* and the *Scarcity* of *Money,* gave me no more hopes of mending my Condition, by pursuing my intended measures, than a *Good Husband* has of mending a *Bad Wife* by winking at her *Vices.* I now found my self in great danger of a Relapse, to prevent which, after two or three Gallons of *Derby-Ale* had one day sent my *Wits* a *Wooll-gathering,* and generated as many *Maggots* in my *Brains,* as there are *Crotchets* in the *Head* of a *Musician,* or *Fools* in the *Million Lottery,* I e'en took up a Resolution to Travel, and Court the Blinking Gipsy *Fortune* in another Country. I then began to Consider what Climate might best suit with my *Constitution,* and what Part of the World with my *Circumstances;* and upon mature Deliberation, found a *Warm Latitude* would best agree with *Thin*

Apparel, and a *Money'd Country* with a *Narrow Fortune;* and having often heard such extravagant Encomiums of that Blessed Paradise, *Jamaica,* where *Gold* is more plentiful than *Ice, Silver* than *Snow, Pearle* than *Hailstones,* I at last determin[e]d to make a trial of my Stars in that Island, and see whether they had the same Unlucky Influence upon me there, as they had, hitherto, in the Land of my Nativity.

In order to proceed my *Voyage,* I took a Passage in the good Ship the *Andalucia;* and about the latter end of *January,* 1697 upon the dissolution of the hard Frost, I passed, with many others, by the Night Tide, in a *Wherry* to *Gravesend,* where our *Floating Receptacle* lay ready to take in *Goods* and *Passengers;* but our Lady *Thames* being put into a Passion, by the rude Kisses of an *Easterly Wind,* drew her Smooth Face into so many Wrinckles that her illfavour'd Aspect and Murmurings, were to me as Terrible as the Noise of *Thieves* to a *Miser,* or *Bailiffs* to a *Bankrupt;* and being pent up with my Limbs, in an awkward Posture, lying Heads and Tails, like *Essex* Calves in a *Rumford* Waggon, I was forc'd to endure the Insolence of every Wave, till I was become as Wet as a New Pump'd *Kidnapper.*

In this Condition I Embark'd about two a Clock in the Morning, where the chief Mate, as Master of the Ceremonies, conducted me to a wellcome Collation of *Cheese* and *Bisket,* and presented me with a Magnificent *Can* of Soveraign *Flip,*⁶ prepar'd with as much Art as an *Apothecary* can well shew in the mixing of a Cordial. After this Refreshment, I betook my self to a *Cabin,* which fitted me so well, it sat as tite as a *Jacket* to a *Dutchman,* where I Slept till Morning, as close as *a Snaile* in a *Shell,* or a *Maggot* in an *Apple-Kernel.* Then Rising, and after I had survey'd our Wooden Terretories, I began to Contemplate upon things worthy of a serious Consideration, which stir'd up in me that Malignant Spirit of *Poetry,* with which I am oft times unhappily possess'd: And what my *Muse* dictated to me, her *Emanuensis,* I here present unto the *Reader.*

A Farewell to England

I.

Farewell my Country, *and my* Friends,
My Mistress, *and my* Muse;
In distant Regions, diff'rent Ends

---

3. Brackets appeared in the original.

4. The stock exchange.

5. Lovers of money.

6. A type of alcoholic drink, sometimes spiced and sweetened.

My Genius *now pursues.*
Those Blessings which I held most dear,
Are, by my stubborn Destiny,
(That uncontroul'd Necessity)
Abandon'd from me, and no more appear.

II.

Despair of Fortune makes me bold,
I can in Tempests Sleep,
And fearless of my Fate, behold
The Dangers of the Deep.
No Covetous desire of Life,
Can now my Careless Thoughts imploy,
Banish'd from Friendship, Love, and Joy,
To view the Waves and Winds at equal Strife.

III.

O'er threatning Billows can I fly,
And, unconcern'd, conceive,
'Tis here less difficult to Die,
Than 'twas on Land to Live.
To me 'tis equal, Swim or Sink,
I smiling to my Fate can bow,
Bereft of Joy, I think it now
No more to Drown, than 'twas before to Drink.

IV.

Dear Friends with Patience bear the Load
Of troubles, still to come,
You Pitty us who range Abroad,
We Pitty you at Home.
Let no Oppression, Fears, or Cares,
Make us our Loyalty Disband,
Which like a well built Arch, should stand
The more secure, the greater Weight it bears.

V.

Farewell Applause, *that vain Delight*
The Witty *fondly seek;*
He's Blest who like a Dunce *may* Write,
Or like a Fool *may* Speak;
What ever Praise *we gain to day,*
Whether deservedly or no,
We to the Worlds Opinion owe,
Who does as oft Miss-take *the same away.*

VI.

Something there is, which touches near,
I scarce can bid Adieu;
'Tis all my Hope, my Care, my Fear,

And all that I pursue:
'Tis what I Love, yet what I Fly;
But what I dare not, must not Name;
Angels Protect the Sacred Frame,
Till I to England *shall Return, or Die.*

Towards the Evening the Captain came on Board, with the rest of our Fellow-Travellours, who, when we were altogether, patch'd up as pretty a Society, as a Man under my Circumstances would desire to tumble into: There was three of the *Troublesome Sex,* as some call them, (tho' I never thought 'em so) whose Curteous Affabillity, and Complaisancy of Temper, admitted of no other Emulation, but to strive who (within the bounds of Modesty) should be most Obliging. One *Unfortunate Lady* was in pursuit of a *Stray'd Husband,* who, in *Jamaica,* had Feloniously taken to Wife (for the sake of a Plantation) A *Lacker-Fac'd Creolean,* to the great dissatisfaction of his Original Spouse, who had often declar'd (thro' the sweetness of her Disposition) That if he had Marry'd another Handsomer than her self, it would never have Vex'd her; but to be Rival'd by a *Gipsy,* a Tawny Fac'd *Moletto*[7] Strumpet, a Pumpkin colour'd Whore; no, her Honour would not suffer her to bear with Patience so coroding an Indignity. The other two were a pretty *Maid,* and a comely *Widow;* so that in these three, we had every Honourable State of the whole Sex: One in the *State of Innocency,* another of *Fruition,* the third of *Deprivation;* and if we'd had but one in the *State* of *Corruption,* a Man might have pleas'd himself as well in our *Little World,* as you *Libertines* can do in the *Great One.*

I shall be too tedious if I at large Particularize the whole Company, I shall therefore *Hustle* them together, as a *Morefields*[8] *Sweetener* does *Luck in a Bag,*[9] and then you may Wink and Choose, for the Devil a Barrel the better Herring amongst us. We had one (as I told you before) *Cherubimical Lass,* who I fear, had *Lost her self,* two more, of the same *Gender,* who had lost their *Husbands;* two *Parsons,* who had lost their *Livings;* three *Broken Tradesmen,* who had lost their *Credit;* and several, like me, that had lost their *Wits;* a *Creolean Captain,* a *Superanuated Mariner,* an *Independant Merchant,* and *Irish*

---

7. Mulatto.

8. A London market.

9. "Luck in a bag" likely refers to a bag of assorted goods purchased before being viewed.

Kidnapper, and a *Monmothean Sythes-Man,*[10] all going with one Design, to patch up their *Decay'd Fortunes.*

Every thing being in Order for *Sailing,* the *Pilot* came on *Board,* who put on such a commanding Countenance, that he look'd as Stern as a *Sarazens*[11] *Head* and the *Sins* of his *Youth* having crep't into his *Pedestals,* he Limp'd about the *Quarter-Deck,* like a *Cripple* in *Forma Pauperis*[12] upon a *Mountebanks Stage,* making as great a Noise in his *Tarpaulin Cant,* as a *Young Counsel* in a *Bad Cause,* or a *Butcher* at a *Bear-Garden.* As soon as we had weigh'd *Anchor,* under the doleful Cry and hard Service of *Haul Cat haul,* there was nothing heard till we reach'd the *Downs,* but *About Ship my Lads, bring your Fore Tack on Board, haul Fore-Sail haul, Brace about the Main-Yard,* and the Devil to do; that I was more Amaz'd than a *Mouse* at a *Throsters*[13] *Mill,* or the *Russian Embassador* at a *Clap* of *Thunder.*

By the help of *Providence,* the *Pilots* Care, and *Seamens* Industry, we pass'd safe to *Deal,* where we Anchor'd three or four Days for a fair Wind. In which interim, the *Prince* of the *Air* had puff'd up an unwelcome Blast in the Night, which forc'd a Vessel upon the *Goodwin.* The next Morning the *Salvages* Man'd out a fleet of their *Deal Skimming-dishes,* and made such unmerciful work with the poor distressed *Bark,* that a *Gang* of *Bailiffs* with an *Execution,* or a *Kennel* of *Hounds* upon a *Dead Horse,* could not have appear'd more *Ravenous.* From thence, with a prosperous Gale, we made the best of our way into the wide *Ocean,* which *Mariners* say, is of such Profundity, that, like a *Misers Conscience,* or a *Womans Concupiscence* 'tis never to be Fathom'd.

'Twas in the midst of Winter, and very Cold Weather when we set out; but in a Fortnights time we were got into a comfortable Climat, which yielded us so pleasant a warmth, that a Man might pluck off his Shirt upon Deck, and commit *Murther* upon his own *Flesh* and *Blood* till he was weary, without the danger of an Ague.

I happen'd one Morning to hear two *Tar-jackets*[14] in a very high Dispute; I went to them, and ask'd the reason of the Difference. *Why, Sir,* says one, *I'll tell you, there was my Master* Whistlebooby, *an old* Boatswain *in one of his Majesties Ships, who was* Superhanded, *and past his Labour, and the* Ambaraltie Divorc'd *him from his Ship, and the* King *allow'd him a* Suspension, *and this Lubberly Whelp here says I talk like a Fool; and sure I have not used the Sea this Thirty Years but I can* Argufie *any thing as proper as he can.*

The chief *Sports* we had on Board, to pass away the tedious Hours, were *Hob, Spie the Market, Shove the Slipper, Dilly-Dally,* and *Back-Gammon;* the latter of which prov'd as serviceable to me, as a *Book* of *Heraldry* to a *Gentleman Mumper,*[15] or a *Pass*[16] to a *Penniless Vagabond:* For (like the *Whore* who boasted of her *Industry*) I us'd to make my Days Labour worth *Two Shillings,* or *Half a Crown,* at *Two Pence* or a *Groat* a Bout. The most Powerful Adversary I engag'd with, was a *Parson,* who, when the Bell Rung to Prayers, would start up in the middle of a Hit, desire my Patience whilst he step'd into the *Great Cabbin,* and gave his Sinful Congregation a *Dram* of Evangelical *Comfort,* and he would wait upon me presently. But that *Recreation* in which we took a more peculiar delight, was the Harmony we made, but the assistance of the two *Heaven-drivers,* in Lyricking over some *Antiquated Sonnets,* and for varieties sake now and then a *Psalm,* which our Canonical *Vice-Whippers* Sung with as Penitential a grace, as a Sorrowful Offender in his *Last Night-Cap.*

To please my self at a Spare-Hour, I had taken with me a *Flute,* and there being on Board a *Spanniel-Dog,* who (*Seaman-like*) had no great kindness for *Wind Musick,* for when ever he heard me *Tooting,* he'd be *Howling,* which, together made a Noise so surprising, that it frighted away a *Quotidian Ague,* from a Young Fellow who had been three Weeks under the Hands of our Doctor.

One Night after we had well Moisten'd our Drouthy Carcasses with an Exhilerating Dose of Right Honourable *Punch,* there arose a *Storm,* for which I had often wish'd, that I might not be a stranger to any Surprising Accident the Angry Elements, when at Variance, might afford me. The Heavens all round us (in as little time as a *Girl* might lose her *Maidenhead*) had put on such a Malignant Aspect, as if it threaten'd our Destruction; and *Æolus*[17] gave us such unmerciful Puffs and Whiffs, that I

---

10. A Scythe-man or farm laborer from Monmouthshire, a county in east Wales.

11. Sarazen or Saracen: a Muslim or Arab.

12. In the form of a poor person.

13. A throwster makes silk thread.

14. Sailors.

15. Beggar.

16. A pass allowed a poor person to return to his parish of birth in order to receive charitable support.

17. Ruler of the wind.

was fearful to stand upon the *Quarter Deck,* least before my Time I should be snatch'd up to Heaven in a Whirle-Wind. From all the Corners of the Sky there darted forth such Beams of *Lightning,* that I Vow and Protest the *Fire-Works in* St. *James's-Square,* were no more to be compar'd to't, than a *Gloworms Arse* to a *Cotton Candle,* which were instantly succeeded with such Volly's of *Thunder,* from every side, that you would have thought the *Clouds* had been fortifi'd with *Whole Cannon,* and weary of being tost about with every Wind, were Fighting their way into a Calmer Region to enjoy their Rest. Then fell such an excessive *Rain,* that as we had one Sea under us, we fear'd another had been tumbling upon our Heads; for my part, I fear'd the very *Falling* of the *Sky,* and thought of nothing but *Catching* of *Larks.* My Spirits being a little deprest, by the apprehensions of the Danger we were under, I went down into the *Gun-room,* to consult my *Brandy-Cask* about taking of a *Dram;* where one of our *Ladies,* thro' want of better Accommodation, was forc'd to be Content with a *Cradle,* in which she was *Praying* with as much Sincerity for *Fair Weather,* as a *Farmer* for a *Kind Harvest,* or an *Old Maid* for a *Good Husband:* And I being greatly pleas'd at her most Importunate Solicitations, have given you a Repetition of one part, *viz. And if Thou hast Decreed, that we shall Perish in this* Tempest, *I most humbly beseech Thee to Punish with* Pox, Barrenness, *and* Dry-Belly-Ach, *that* Adultrous Strumpet, *who, by Robbing me of my* Husband, *hath been a means of bringing me to this untimely End; may her whole Life be a continued course of* Sin *without a Moments* Repentance, *that she may* Die *without* Forgiveness, *and be* Damn'd *without* Mercy. In which Interim a Sea wash'd over our *Fore-Castle,* run *Aft,* and came down the *Whip-scuttle;* she concluding we were going to the Bottom, Shreek'd out, and fell into a *Fit;* whilst I, thro' my *Fear,* together with my *Modesty,* scorn'd to take the Advantage of so fair an Opportunity.

In a doubtful Condition, between this World and the next, we labour'd till near Morning, about which time the Storm abated: But as soon as Day-light appear'd, and the Serenity of the Weather had turn'd our Frightful Apprehensions into a little Alacrity, some of the Men, from Aloft, espi'd a Sail bearing after us with all Expedition; and being no great distance from the Coast of *Sally,*[18] a jealousy arose amongst our Officers, of her being a Man

of War belonging to that Country, they having upon the Conclusion of the late Peace with *France,*[19] Proclaim'd a War with *England;* so that we thought our selves now in as great Danger of being knock'd on the Head, or made Slaves, as we were before of being Drown'd. This Alarm kindled up amongst us new fears of approaching Danger, more Terrible than the former we had so happily surviv'd.

Command was given by our Captain, to prepare for a Fight; down Chests, up Hammocks, bring the small Arms upon the Quarter-Deck, and every Man directed to his Post, by orders fix'd upon the *Mizzen-mast* in the *Steerage;* the *Bulkhead* and *Cabins* knock'd down, the *Deck* clear'd *Fore* and *Aft,* for every Man to have free access to his Business. When all things were in a readiness to receive an Enemy, I took a walk on purpose to look about me, and was so animated with the Seamans Activity and Industry, together with the smell of Sweat, Match, and Gunpowder, that like 'Squire *Witherington* in *Chivy Chase,* I could have Fought upon my Stumps. By this time our suppos'd Enemy was almost come up with us, under *English* Colours, but his keeping close upon our *Quarter,* and not bearing off, gave us still reason to mistrust him; but seeing him a small Ship, and ours a Vessel of 400 Tuns, 28 Guns, and about 50 Men, we Furl'd our *Main Sail* with all our Hands at once, as a Stratagem to seem well Man'd; put our *Top-Sails* aback, and lay by, to let 'em see we were *no more Afraid than Hurt.* We had on Board an *Irishman* going over a Servant, who I suppose was *Kidnap'd;* I observ'd this Fellow, being quarter'd at a Gun, look'd as pale as a *Pick-Pocket* new taken: I ask'd him why he put on such a *Cowardly* look; and told him 'twas a shame for a Man to shew so much Fear in his Countenance. *Indeed Sir* (said he) *I cannot halp et, I love the bate of a Drum, the Pop of a Pistol, or the Bounch of a Mushket wall enough, but by my Shoul, the Roaring of a Great Gun always makesh me start.* I ask'd him whose Servant he was. *By my Fait,* said he, *I cannot tell; I wash upon Change looking for a good Mashter, and a brave Gentleman came to me and ask'd me who I wash; and I told him I was myn nown shelf, and he gave me some good Wine and good Ale, and brought me on Board, and I have not sheen him sinch.* By this time our Adversary was come within hearing, and upon our Hailing of him, prov'd

---

18. Sally or Salé, an independent republic and seaport in northwestern Morocco.

19. The Treaty of Ryswick ended the war with France in 1697.

a little Ship bound to *Guinea,* which put an end to our Fears, and made us fly to the *Punch-Bowl* with as much Joy as the *Mob* to a *Bonfire* upon a States *Holyday.*

After we had chas'd away the remembrance of our past Dangers, with a reviving Draught of our Infallible Elixir, we began to be *Merry* as so many *Beggars* (and indeed were before as *Poor*) beginning to turn that into Ridicule, which so lately had chang'd our Jollitry into Fear and Sadness. When we had thus refresh'd our Bodies, and strengthen'd our Spirits, by passing round a Health to our noble Selves, *&c.* 'twas thought high time by our Reverend Pastors, to return Thanks for our great Deliverance from the Hands of our Enemies tho' we had none near us, which was accordingly perform'd with all the Solemnity a parcel of *Merry Juvenal* Wags could compose themselves to observe.

By this time we were got into so warm a Latitude, that (God be thanked) a *Louse* would not live in it. We now began to thin our Dress, and, had not Decency forbid it, could have gladly gone Naked as our first Parents. Kissing here grew out of Fashion; there's no joyning of Lips, but your Noses would drop Sweat into your Mouths. The Sea, and other Elements, began now to Entertain us with Curiosities in Nature worth observing, as *Crampos, Sharks, Porpus, Flying-Fish, Albacores Bonettas, Dolphin, Bottlenoses, Turtle Blubber, Stingrays, Sea-Adders,* and the Devil and all of *Monsters* without Names, and some without Shape. As for Birds, *Noddys, Boobies, Shear-waters, Shags, Pitternels, Men of War, Tropick Birds, Pellicans, &c.* I shall not undertake here to describe these Creatures, because some of them are so Frightfully Ugly, that if any Friends Wife with Child should long for the Reading of my Book, it should chance to make her Miscarry. But that which I thought most worthy of Observation, were the *Clouds,* whose various Forms, and Beautious Colours, were Inimitable by the Pencil of the greatest Artist in the Universe, *Cities, Palaces, Groves, Fields,* and *Gardens; Monuments, Castles, Armies, Bulls, Bears,* and *Dragons. &c.* as if the Air above us had been Frozen into a *Looking-Glass,* and shew'd us by Reflection, all the Rarities in Nature.

By this time we had gain'd the Tropick, and come into a Trade-Wind; the greatest of our Fears being now a Calm, which is fine Weather to please fearful Tempers; but it brings us more in danger of being *Starv'd,* than a *Storm* does of being Drown'd: Tho' it was our Fortune in a few Days after, to make the *Leward-Islands,* and put us past the dread of so terrible a *Catastrophe,* those we

pass'd in sight of were, *Descado,*[20] a rare place for a Bird-Catcher to be Governour of, Birds being the only Creatures by which 'tis inhabited; *Montserat, Antego,*[21] *Mevis,*[22] possess'd by the *English;* St. *Christophers,* by half *English* half *French; Rodunda,*[23] an uninhabitable high Rock. From amongst these *Caribbe* Islands, in a few days, we got to *Hispaniola,* without any thing remarkable; and from thence in 24 Hours, with a fresh Gale, within sight of *Jamaica,* which (without Malice or Partiallity) I shall proceed to give you some Account of.

A Character of JAMAICA

The Dunghill of the Universe, the Refuse of the whole Creation, the Clippings of the Elements, a shapeless Pile of Rubbish confusd'ly jumbl'd into an Emblem of the *Chaos,* neglected by Omnipotence when he form'd the World into its admirable Order. The Nursery of Heavens Judgments, where the Malignant Seeds of all Pestilence were first gather'd and scatter'd thro' the Regions of the Earth, to Punish Mankind for their Offences. The place where *Pandora* fill'd her Box, where *Vulcan* Forg'd *Joves* Thunder-bolts, and that *Phaeton,*[24] by his rash misguidance of the Sun, scorch'd into a Cinder. The Receptacle of Vagabonds, the Sanctuary of Bankrupts, and a Close-stool for the Purges of our Prisons. As Sickly as an Hospital, as Dangerous as the Plague, as Hot as Hell, and as Wicked as the Devil. Subject to Turnadoes, Hurricanes and Earthquakes, as if the Island, like the People, were troubled with the *Dry Belly-Ach.*

Of Their Provisions

The chiefest of their Provisions is *Sea-Turtle,* or *Toad in a shell,* stew'd in its own Gravy; its lean is as White as a Green-sickness Girl, its Fat of a Calves-turd Colour; and is excellently good to put a Stranger into a Flux, and purge out part of those ill-humours it infallibly Creates. The Belly is call'd *Caillipee,* the Back *Callipach;* and is

---

20. Desiradé, an island east of Guadeloupe.

21. Antigua.

22. Nevis.

23. Redonda, a rocky island belonging to Antigua.

24. Phaëton, the son of Apollo, lost control of his father's chariot, driving it dangerously close to the earth.

serv'd up to the Table in its own Shell, instead of a Platter. They have *Guanas,*[25] *Hickeries,* and *Crabs;* the first being an Amphibeous *Serpent,* shap'd like a *Lizard,* but black and larger; the second a *Land-Tortoise,* the last needs no Description, but are as numerous as *Frogs* in *England,* and burrow in the Ground like *Rabbets,* so that the whole *Island* may be justly call'd, a *Crab-Warren.* They are Fattest near the *Pallasadoes,* where they will make a Skeleton of a Corps in as little time as a *Tanner* will Flea a Colt, or a *Hound* after Hunting devour a Shoulder of *Mutton.* They have *Beef* without Fat, Lean *Mutton* without Gravy, and *Fowles* as dry as the Udder of an Old Woman, and as tough as a Stake from the Haunches of a Superanuated *Car-Horse.*

Milk is so plenty, you may buy it for Fifteen Pence a Quart; but Cream so very scarce, that a Firkin of Butter, of their own making, would be so costly a Jewel, that the Richest Man in the Island would be unable to purchase it. They value themselves greatly upon the sweetness of their Pork, which is indeed Lushious, but as flabby as the Flesh of one just risen from a Flux, and ought to be forbid in all hot Countries (as amongst the *Jews*) for the prevention of *Leprosie, Scurvy,* and other Distempers, of which it is a great occasion.

There is very little Veal, and that Lean; for in *England* you may Nurse four Children much cheaper than you can one Calf in *Jamaica.* They have course *Teal,* almost as big as *English Ducks;* and *Muscovy Ducks* as big as *Geese;* But as for their *Geese,* they may be all *Swans,* for I never see one in the Island.

There are sundry sorts of *Fish,* under *Indian* Names, without Scales, and of a *Serpentine Complection;* they Eat as dry as a *Shad,* and much stronger than stale *Herrings* or *Old Ling;* with Oyl'd *Butter* to the Sauce, as Rank as *Goose-Grease,* improv'd with the Palatable Relish of a stinking *Anchovie.*

They make a rare *Soop* they call *Pepper-pot;* its an excellent Breakfast for a *Salamander,* or a good preparative for a *Mountebanks Agent,* who Eats Fire one day, that he may get better Victuals the next. Three Spoonfuls so Inflam'd my Mouth, that had I devour'd a Peck of *Horse-Radish,* and Drank after it a Gallon of *Brandy* and *Gunpowder,* (*Dives* like) I could not have been more importunate for a Drop of Water to cool my Tongue.

They greatly abound in a Beautiful Fruit, call'd, a *Cussue,* not unlike an *Apple,* but longer; its soft and very

Juicy, but so great an Acid, and of a Nature so Restringent, that by Eating of one, it drew up my mouth like a *Hens Fundament,* and made my Palate as Rough, and Tongue as Source, as if I had been Gargling it with *Allom-Water:* From whence I conjecture, they are a much fitter Fruit to recover *Lost Maiden-heads,* properly apply'd, than to be Eaten. Of *Water-Mellons* and *Mus-Mellons* they have plenty; the former is of as cold a quality as a *Coucumber,* and will dissolve in your *Mouth* like *Ice* in a hot *Frying-pan,* being as *Pleasant* to the *Eater* (and, I believe, as *Wholesome*) as *Cup* of *Rock-Water* to a Man in a *Hectick Feavour:* The latter are Large and Lushious, but much too watery to be good.

Coco-Nuts, and *Physick-Nuts* are in great esteem amongst the Inhabitants; the former they reckon *Meat, Drink,* and *Cloth,* but the Eatable part is secur'd within so strong a Magazeen, that it requires a lusty *Carpenter,* well Arm'd with *Ax* and *Handsaw,* to hew a passage to the *Kernel,* and when he has done, it will not recompence his Labour. The latter is as big as a *Filbert,* but (like the *Beautiful Woman* well Drest, and *Infectious*), if you venture to Taste, is of ill consequence: Their Shell is Black, and *Japan'd* by Nature, exceeding Art; the Kernel White, and extream Pleasant to the Palat, but of so powerful an Operation, that by taking two, my Guts were Swept as clean, as ever *Tom-T—d-man* made a *Vault,* or any of the *Black Fraternity*[26] a Chimney.

They have *Oranges, Lemons, Limes,* and several other Fruits, as *Sharp* and *Crabbed* as themselves, not given them as a *Blessing,* but a *Curse;* for Eating so many sower things, Generates a *Corroding Slime* in the Bowels, and is one great occasion of that Fatal and Intolerable Distemper, *The Dry Belly-Ach;* which in a Fortnight, or Three Weeks, takes away the use of their Limbs, that they are forc'd to be led about by *Negro's.* A Man under this Misery, may be said to be the '*Scutchion* of the *Island,* the Complection of the Patient, being the *Field,* bearing *Or,* charg'd with all the Emblems of Destruction, *proper,* supported by *Two Devils, Sables;* and *Death* the *Crest, Argent.*[27] Many other Fruits there are, that are neither worth Eating, Nameing, or Describing: Some that are never Tasted but in a *Drouth,* and others in a *Famine.*

---

25. Iguanas.

26. Chimney sweeps.

27. These are a series of heraldic terms.

Of Port Royal

It is an Island distinct from the Main of *Jamaica,* tho' before the *Earthquake,*[28] it joyn'd by a Neck of Land to the *Palisados,* but was seperated by the Violence of an Inundation (thro' God's Mercy) to prevent the Wickedness of their Metropolis diffusing it self, by Communication, over all the Parts of the Country, and so call that Judgment upon the Whole, which fell more particularly upon the Sinfulest part.

From a Spacious fine Built-Town (according to Report) it is now reduc'd, by the Encroachments of the Sea, to a little above a quarter of a Mile in Length, and about half so much the Breadth, having so few remains left of its former splendour, I could think no otherwise, but that every Travellour who had given its Description, made large use of his *License.* The Houses are low, little, and irregular; and if I compare the Best of their Streets in *Port-Royal,* to the Fag-End of *Kent-street,* where the *Broom-men*[29] Live, I do them more than Justice.

About Ten a Clock in the Morning, their Nostrils are saluted with a *Land-Breeze,* which Blowing o'er the Island, searches the Bowels of the Mountains (being always crack'd and full of Vents, by reason of excessive Heat) bringing along with it such *Sulpherous Vapours,* that I have fear'd the whole Island would have burst out into a Flaming *Ætna,*[30] or have stifled us with Suffocating Fumes, like that of the melted Mineral and Brimstone.

In the Afternoon, about Four a Clock, they might have the refreshment of a *Sea-Breeze,* but suffering the *Negroes* to carry all their *Nastiness* to *Windward* of the Town, that the Nauseous Effluvias which arise from their stinking Dunghills, are blown in upon them; thus what they might enjoy as a Blessing, they Ingratefully pervert by their own ill Management.

They have a Church, 'tis true, but built rather like a *Market-House;* and when the *Flocks* are in their *Pens* and the *Pastor* Exalted to over-look his *Sheep,* I took a Survey around me, and saw more variety of *Scare-Crows* than ever was seen at the Feast of *Ugly-Faces.*

Every thing is very Dear, and an Ingenious or an Honest Man may meet with this Encouragement, To spend a Hundred Pounds before he shall get a Penny. *Madera-Wine* and *Bottle-Beer* are Fifteen Pence the Bottle; nasty *Clarat,* Half a Crown; *Rhennish,* Five Shillings; and their best *Canary,* Ten Bits, or Six and Three Pence. They have this Pleasure in Drinking, That what they put into their Bellies, they may soon stroak out of their Fingers Ends; for instead of *Exonerating,* they *Fart;* and *Sweat* instead of *Pissing.*

Of the People

The generality of the Men look as if they had just knock'd off their Fetters, and by an unexpected Providence, escap'd the danger of a near Mis-fortune; the dread of which, hath imprinted that in their *Looks,* which they can no more alter than an *Ethiopian* can his *Colour.*

They are all *Colonels, Majors, Captains, Lieutenants,* and *Ensigns,* the two last being held in such disdain, that they are look'd upon as a Bungling *Diver*[31] amongst a Gang of *Expert Picket-Pockets; Pride* being their *Greatness,* and *Impudence* their *Virtue.*

They regard nothing but Money, and value not how they get it; there being no other Felicity to be enjoy'd but purely Riches. They are very Civil to Strangers who bring over considerable Effects; and will try a great many ways to Kill him fairly, for the Lucre of his Cargo: And many have been made Rich by such Wind-falls.

A Broken *Apothecary* will make there a Topping *Physician;* a *Barbers Prentice,* a good *Surgeon;* a *Bailiffs Follower,* a passable *Lawyer:* and an *English Knave,* a very *Honest Fellow.*

They have so great a veneration for *Religion,* That *Bibles* and *Common-Prayer-Books* are as good a Commodity amongst them, as *Muffs* and *Warming-pans.*

A little Reputation among the *Women,* goes a great way; and if their Actions be answerable to their Looks, they may view *Wickedness* with the *Devil:* An *Impudent Air,* being the only *Charms* of their *Countenance,* and a *Lewd Carriage,* the *Study'd Grace* of their *Deportment.* They are such who have been *Scandalous* in *England* to the utmost degree, either *Transported* by the *State,* or led by their *Vicious Inclinations;* where they may be *Wicked* without *Shame,* and *Whore* on without *Punishment.*

They are Stigmatiz'd with *Nick-Names,* which they bear, not with *Patience* only, but with *Pride;* as *Unconscionable Nan, Salt-Beef Peg, Buttock-de-Clink Jenny,*

---

28. Port Royal, Jamaica, was the site of a very destructive earthquake on June 7, 1692.

29. Street sweepers.

30. Mount Etna, a volcano in Sicily.

---

31. A pickpocket lacking experience.

&c. *Swearing, Drinking,* and *Obscene Talk* are the Principal Qualifications that render them acceptable to *Male Conversation;* and she that wants a perfection in these admirable acquirements, shall be as much Ridicul'd for her *Modesty,* as a *Plain-Dealing Man* amongst a Gang of *Knaves,* for his *Honesty.*

In short, *Virtue* is so *Despis'd,* and all sorts of *Vice Encourag'd* by both *Sexes,* that the Town of *Port-Royal* is the very *Sodom* of the Universe.

FINIS

JOHN LAWSON (1670?–1711?)

John Lawson came from England to North America in 1700, but little is known about his life prior to that event. He might have received some training in London as an apothecary before departing for the British colonies, but even this remains a mystery. After his arrival in Charleston, South Carolina, Lawson was commissioned to undertake a survey of the interior of Carolina, an area relatively unknown to British colonials before that time. He made the survey during the winter of 1700 to 1701, and he wrote an account of his travels that was first published in a collection of such narratives in 1708. *A New Voyage to Carolina* describes Lawson's journey itself; the topography, geology, and natural products of North Carolina; the current settlement of the area; and the lives and languages of the Indian peoples of the region.

Following his survey, Lawson became a Carolina landholder and participated in the founding of Bath, North Carolina. In 1709, he made a journey back to England, at least partly to secure the publication of his travel narrative as a separate book. While in London, he met Baron Christoph von Graffenried, who was interested in establishing a settlement of Palatine Germans in the Carolinas. Lawson agreed to help von Graffenried with the project. He drew the plans for the New Bern settlement and participated in its founding in 1710. In 1711, Lawson and von Graffenried made an expedition to find a more convenient route to Virginia at a time when hostilities broke out between the Tuscarora Indians and white colonists. Lawson's party was captured, and Lawson himself was tortured and killed.

Lawson's narrative of his travels in Carolina remained the most important account of the region and its people for decades. The selections from that text presented here are from the second section of the narrative, which describes the geography and the flora and fauna of North Carolina, and the fifth section, which describes the indigenous peoples of the region.

from A NEW VOYAGE TO CAROLINA[1]

from A Description of North-Carolina

The Province of *Carolina* is separated from *Virginia* by a due West-Line, which begins at *Currituck*-Inlet, in 36 Degrees, 30 Minutes, of Northern-Latitude, and extends indefinitely to the Westward, and thence to the Southward, as far as 29 Degrees; which is a vast Tract of Sea-Coast. But having already treated, as far as is necessary, concerning South-*Carolina,* I shall confine myself, in the ensuing Sheets, to give my Reader a Description of that Part of the Country only, which lies betwixt *Currituck* and *Cape-Fair,* and is almost 34 Deg. North. And this is commonly call'd *North Carolina.*

This part of *Carolina* is faced with a Chain of Sand-Banks, which defends it from the Violence and Insults of the *Atlantick* Ocean; by which Barrier, a vast Sound is hemm'd in, which fronts the Mouths of the Navigable and Pleasant Rivers of this Fertile Country, and into which they disgorge themselves. Thro' the same are Inlets of several Depths of Water. Some of their Channels admit only of Sloops, Brigantines, small Barks, and Ketches; and such are *Currituck, Ronoak,* and up the Sound above *Hatteras:* Whilst others can receive Ships of Burden, as

---

1. *A New Voyage to Carolina* was originally published in *A New Collection of Voyages and Travels* (London, 1708).

Ocacock, Topsail-Inlet, and *Cape-Fair;* as appears by my Chart.

The first Discovery and Settlement of this Country was by the Procurement of Sir *Walter Raleigh,* in Conjunction with some publick-spirited Gentlemen of that Age, under the Protection of Queen *Elizabeth;* for which Reason it was then named *Virginia,* being begun on that Part called *Ronoak*-Island, where the Ruins of a Fort[2] are to be seen at this day, as well as some old *English* Coins which have been lately found; and a Brass-Gun, a Powder-Horn, and one small Quarter deck-Gun, made of Iron Staves, and hoop'd with the same Metal; which Method of making Guns might very probably be made use of in those Days, for the Convenience of Infant-Colonies.

A farther Confirmation of this we have from the *Hatteras Indians,* who either then lived on *Ronoak*-Island, or much frequented it. These tell us, that several of their Ancestors were white People, and could talk in a Book, as we do; the Truth of which is confirm'd by gray Eyes being found frequently amongst these *Indians,* and no others. They value themselves extremely for their Affinity to the *English,* and are ready to do them all friendly Offices. It is probable, that this Settlement miscarry'd for want of timely Supplies from *England;* or thro' the Treachery of the Natives, for we may reasonably suppose that the *English* were forced to cohabit with them, for Relief and Conversation; and that in process of Time, they conform'd themselves to the Manners of their *Indian* Relations. And thus we see, how apt Humane Nature is to degenerate.

I cannot forbear inserting here, a pleasant Story that passess for an uncontested Truth amongst the Inhabitants of this Place; which is, that the Ship which brought the first Colonies, does often appear amongst them, under Sail, in a gallant Posture, which they call Sir *Walter Raleigh*'s Ship; And the truth of this has been affirm'd to me, by Men of the best Credit in the Country.

A second Settlement of this Country was made about fifty Years ago, in that part we now call *Albemarl*-County, and chiefly in *Chuwon* Precinct, by several substantial Planters, from *Virginia,* and other Plantations; Who finding mild Winters, and a fertile Soil, beyond Expectation, producing every thing that was planted, to a prodigious Increase; their Cattle, Horses, Sheep, and Swine, breeding very fast, and passing the Winter, without any Assistance from the Planter; so that every thing seem'd to come by Nature, the Husbandman living almost void of Care,

and free from those Fatigues which are absolutely requisite in Winter-Countries, for providing Fodder and other Necessaries; these Encouragements induc'd them to stand their Ground, altho' but a handful of People, seated at great Distances one from another, and amidst a vast number of *Indians* of different Nations, who were then in *Carolina.* Nevertheless, I say, the Fame of this new-discover'd Summer-Country spread thro' the neighbouring Colonies, and, in a few Years, drew a considerable Number of Families thereto, who all found Land enough to settle themselves in, (had they been many Thousands more) and that which was very good and commodiously seated, both for Profit and Pleasure. And indeed, most of the Plantations in *Carolina* naturally enjoy a noble Prospect of large and spacious Rivers, pleasant Savanna's, and fine Meadows, with their green Liveries, interwoven with beautiful Flowers, of most glorious Colours, which the several Seasons afford; hedg'd in with pleasant Groves of the ever-famous Tulip-tree, the stately Laurel, and Bays, equalizing the Oak in Bigness and Growth; Myrtles, Jessamines, Wood-bines, Honeysuckles, and several other fragrant Vines and Ever-greens, whose aspiring Branches shadow and interweave themselves with the loftiest Timbers, yielding a pleasant Prospect, Shade and Smell, proper Habitations for the Sweet-singing Birds, that melodiously entertain such as travel thro' the Woods of *Carolina.*

The Planters possessing all these Blessings, and the Produce of great Quantities of Wheat and *Indian* Corn, in which this Country is very fruitful, as likewise in Beef, Pork, Tallow, Hides, Deer-Skins, and Furs; for these Commodities the *New-England*-Men and *Bermudians* visited *Carolina* in their Barks and Sloops, and carry'd out what they made, bringing them, in Exchange, Rum, Sugar, Salt, Molosses, and some wearing Apparel, tho' the last at very extravagant Prices.

As the Land is very fruitful, so are the Planters kind and hospitable to all that come to visit them; there being very few Housekeepers, but what live very nobly, and give away more Provisions to Coasters and Guests who come to see them, than they expend amongst their own Families. . . .

We have, amongst the Inhabitants, a Water, that is, inwardly, a great Apersive, and, outwardly, cures Ulcers, Tettars, and Sores, by washing therewith.

There has been a Coal-Mine lately found near the *Mannakin* Town, above the Falls of *James*-River in *Virginia,* which proves very good, and is us'd by the *Smiths,* for their Forges; and we need not doubt of the same

---

2. Fort Raleigh.

amongst us, towards the Heads of our Rivers; but the Plenty of Wood (which is much the better Fuel) makes us not inquisitive after Coal-Mines. Most of the *French,* who lived at that Town on *James*-River, are remov'd to *Trent*-River, in *North-Carolina,* where the rest were expected daily to come to them, when I came away, which was in *August,* 1708. They are much taken with the Pleasantness of that Country, and, indeed, are a very industrious People. At present, they make very good Linnen-Cloath and Thread, and are very well vers'd in cultivating Hemp and Flax, of both which they raise very considerable Quantities; and design to try an Essay of the Grape, for making of Wine.

As for those of our own Country in *Carolina,* some of the Men are very laborious, and make great Improvements in their Way; but I dare hardly give 'em that Character in general. The easy Way of living in that plentiful Country, makes a great many Planters very negligent, which, were they otherwise, that Colony might now have been in a far better Condition than it is, (as to Trade, and other Advantages) which an universal Industry would have led them into.

The Women are the most industrious Sex in that Place, and, by their good Houswifry, make a great deal of Cloath of their own Cotton, Wool and Flax; some of them keeping their Families (though large) very decently apparel'd, both with Linnens and Woollens, so that they have no occasion to run into the Merchant's Debt, or lay their Money out on Stores for Cloathing.

The *Christian* Natives of *Carolina* are a straight, clean-limb'd People; the Children being seldom or never troubled with Rickets, or those other Distempers, that the *Europeans* are visted withal. 'Tis next to a Miracle, to see one of them deform'd in Body. The Vicinity of the Sun makes Impression on the Men, who labour out of doors, or use the Water. As for those Women, that do not expose themselves to the Weather, they are often very fair, and generally as well featur'd, as you shall see any where, and have very brisk charming Eyes, which sets them off to Advantage. They marry very young; some at Thirteen or Fourteen; and She that stays till Twenty, is reckon'd a stale Maid; which is a very indifferent Character in that warm Country. The Women are very fruitful; most Houses being full of Little Ones. It has been observ'd, that Women long marry'd, and without Children, in other Places, have remov'd to *Carolina,* and become joyful Mothers. They have very easy Travail in their Childbearing, in which they are so happy, as seldom to miscarry. Both Sexes are generally spare of Body, and not

Cholerick, nor easily cast down at Disappointments and Losses, seldom immoderately grieving at Misfortunes, unless for the Loss of their nearest Relations and Friends, which seems to make a more than ordinary Impression upon them. Many of the Women are very handy in Canoes, and will manage them with great Dexterity and Skill, which they become accustomed to in this watry Country. They are ready to help their Husbands in any servile Work, as Planting, when the Season of the Weather requires Expedition; Pride seldom banishing good Houswifry. The Girls are not bred up to the Wheel, and Sewing only; but the Dairy and Affairs of the House they are very well acquainted withal; so that you shall see them, whilst very young, manage their Business with a great deal of Conduct and Alacrity. The Children of both Sexes are very docile, and learn any thing with a great deal of Ease and Method; and those that have the Advantages of Education, write good Hands, and prove good Accountants, which is most coveted, and indeed most necessary in these Parts. The young Men are commonly of a bashful, sober Behaviour; few proving Prodigals, to consume what the Industry of their Parents has left them, but commonly improve it. The marrying so young, carries a double Advantage with it, and that is, that the Parents see their Children provided for in Marriage, and the young married People are taught by their Parents, how to get their Living; for their Admonitions make great Impressions on their Children. I had heard (before I knew this new World) that the Natives of *America* were a short-liv'd People, which, by all the Observations I could ever make, proves quite contrary; for those who are born here, and in other colonies, live to as great Ages as any of the *Europeans,* the Climate being free from Consumptions, which Distemper, fatal to *England,* they are Strangers to. And as the Country becomes more clear'd of Wood, it still becomes more healthful to the Inhabitants, and less addicted to the Ague; which is incident to most new Comers into *America* from *Europe,* yet not mortal. A gentle Emetick seldom misses of driving it away, but if it is not too troublesome, 'tis better to let the Seasoning have its own Course, in which case, the Party is commonly free from it ever after, and very healthful.

And now, as to the other Advantages the Country affords, we cannot guess at them at present, because, as I said before, the best Part of this Country is not inhabited by the *English,* from whence probably will hereafter spring Productions that this Age does not dream of, and of much more Advantage to the Inhabitants than any things we are yet acquainted withal: And as for several Productions of other Countries, much in the same Latitude, we may expect, with good Management, they will become familiar to us, as Wine, Oil, Fruit, Silk, and other profitable Commodities, such as Drugs, Dyes, &c. And at present the Curious may have a large Field to satisfy and divert themselves in, as Collections of strange Beasts, Birds, Insects, Reptiles, Shells, Fishes, Minerals, Herbs, Flowers, Plants, Shrubs, intricate Roots, Gums, Tears,[3] Rozins, Dyes, and Stones, with several other that yield Satisfaction and Profit to those, whose Inclinations tend that Way. And as for what may be hop'd for, towards a happy Life and Being, by such as design to remove thither, I shall add this; That with prudent Management, I can affirm, by Experience, not by Hear-say, That any Person, with a small Beginning, may live very comfortably, and not only provide for the Necessaries of Life, but likewise for those that are to succeed him; Provisions being very plentiful, and of good Variety, to accommodate genteel House-keeping; and the neighbouring *Indians* are friendly, and in many Cases serviceable to us, in making us Wares to catch Fish in, for a small matter, which proves of great Advantage to large Families, because those Engines take great Quantities of many Sorts of Fish, that are very good and nourishing: Some of them hunt and fowl for us at reasonable Rates, the Country being as plentifully provided with all Sorts of Game, as any Part of *America;* the poorer Sort of Planters often get them to plant for them, by hiring them for that Season, or for so much Work, which commonly comes very reasonable. Moreover, it is remarkable, That no Place on the Continent of *America,* has seated an *English* Colony so free from Blood-shed, as *Carolina;* but all the others have been more damag'd and disturb'd by the *Indians,* than they have; which is worthy Notice, when we consider how oddly it was first planted with Inhabitants.

The Fishing-Trade in *Carolina* might be carried on to great Advantage, considering how many Sorts of excellent Fish our Sound and Rivers afford, which cure very well with Salt, as has been experienced by some small Quantities, which have been sent abroad, and yielded a good Price. As for the Whale-fishing, it is no otherwise regarded than by a few People who live on the Sand-Banks; and those only work on dead Fish cast on shoar, none being struck on our Coast, as they are to the Northward; altho' we have Plenty of Whales there. Great Plenty is generally the Ruin of Industry. Thus our Merchants are not many, nor have those few there be, apply'd themselves to the *European* Trade. The Planter sits contented at home, whilst his Oxen thrive and grow fat, and his Stocks daily increase; The fatted Porkets and Poultry are easily rais'd to his Table, and his Orchard affords him Liquor, so that he eats, and drinks away the Cares of the World, and desires no greater Happiness, than that which he daily enjoys. Whereas, not only the *European,* but also the *Indian*-Trade, might be carried on to a great Profit, because we lie as fairly for the Body of *Indians,* as any Settlement in *English-America;* And for the small Trade that has been carried on in that Way, the Dealers therein have throve as fast as any Men, and the soonest rais'd themselves of any People I have known in *Carolina.*

Lastly, As to the Climate, it is very healthful; our Summer is not so hot as in other places to the Eastward in the same Latitude; neither are we ever visited by Earthquakes, as many places in *Italy* and other Summer-Countries are. Our Northerly Winds, in Summer, cool the Air, and free us from pestilential Fevers, which *Spain, Barbary,* and the neighbouring Countries in *Europe,* &c. are visited withal. Our Sky is generally serene and clear, and the Air very thin, in comparison of many Parts of *Europe,* where Consumptions and Catarrhs reign amongst the Inhabitants. The Winter has several Fitts of sharp Weather, especially when the Wind is at N. W. which always clears the Sky, though never so thick before. However, such Weather is very agreeable to *European* Bodies, and makes them healthy. The N. E. Winds blowing in Winter, bring with them thick Weather, and, in the Spring, sometimes, blight the Fruits; but they very seldom endure long, being blown away by Westerly Winds, and then all becomes fair and clear again. Our Spring, in *Carolina,* is very beautiful, and the most pleasant Weather a Country can enjoy. The Fall is accompanied with cool Mornings, which come in towards the latter end of *August,* and so continue (most commonly) very moderate Weather till about *Christmas;* then Winter comes on apace. Tho' these Seasons are very piercing, yet the Cold is of no continuance. Perhaps, you will have cold Weather for three or four days at a time; then pleasant warm Weather follows, such as you have in *England,* about the latter end of *April* or beginning of *May.* In the Year 1707. we had the severest Winter in *Carolina,* that ever was known since the *English* came to settle there; for our Rivers, that were not above half a Mile wide, and fresh Water, were frozen over; and some of them, in the North-part of this Country, were passable for People to walk over.

---

3. Tars.

One great Advantage of *North-Carolina* is, That we are not a Frontier, and near the Enemy; which proves very chargeable and troublesome, in time of War, to those Colonies that are so seated. Another great Advantage comes from its being near *Virginia,* where we come often to a good Market, at the Return of the *Guinea*-Ships for Negro's, and the Remnant of their Stores, which is very commodious for the *Indian*-Trade; besides, in War-time, we lie near at hand to go under their Convoy, and to sell our Provisions to the Tobacco-fleets; for the Planting of Tobacco generally in those Colonies, prevents their being supplyed with Stores, sufficient for victualling their Ships.

As for the Commodities, which are necessary to carry over to this Plantation, for Use and Merchandize, and are, therefore, requisite for those to have along with them, that intend to transport themselves thither; they are Guns, Powder and Shot, Flints, Linnens of all sorts, but chiefly ordinary Blues, *Osnabrugs,*[4] *Scotch* and *Irish* Linnen, and some fine: Mens and Womens Cloaths ready made up, some few Broad-Cloaths, Kerseys and Druggets; to which you must add *Haberdashers*-Wares, Hats about Five or Six Shillings apiece, and a few finer; a few Wiggs, not long, and pretty thin of Hair; thin Stuffs for Women; Iron-Work, as Nails, Spades, Axes, broad and narrow Hoes, Frows, Wedges, and Saws of all sorts, with other Tools for Carpenters, Joiners, Coopers, Shoemakers, Shave-locks, &c. all which, and others which are necessary for the Plantations, you may be inform'd of, and buy at very reasonable Rates, of Mr. *James Gilbert,* Ironmonger, in *Mitre-Tavern-Yard,* near *Aldgate.* You may also be used very kindly, for your Cuttlery-Ware, and other advantageous Merchandizes, and your Cargo's well sorted, by Capt. *Sharp,* at the *Blue gate* in *Cannon-street;* and for Earthen-Ware, Window-Glass, Grind-Stones, Mill-Stones, Paper, Ink-Powder, Saddles, Bridles, and what other things you are minded to take with you, for Pleasure or Ornament.

And now, I shall proceed to the rest of the Vegetables, that are common in *Carolina,* in reference to the Place where I left off, which is the *Natural History* of that Country.

An Account of the Indians of North-Carolina

The *Indians,* which were the Inhabitants of *America,* when the *Spaniards* and other *Europeans* discover'd the several Parts of that Country, are the People which we reckon the Natives thereof; as indeed they were, when we first found out those Parts, and appear'd therein. Yet this has not wrought in me a full Satisfaction, to allow these People to have been the Ancient Dwellers of the New-World, or Tract of Land we call *America.* The Reasons that I have to think otherwise, are too many to set down here; but I shall give the Reader a few, before I proceed; and some others he will find scatter'd in my Writings elsewhere.

In *Carolina* (The Part I now treat of) are the fairest Marks of a Deluge, (that at some time has probably made strange Alterations, as to the Station that Country was then in) that ever I saw, or, I think, read of, in any History. Amongst the other Subterraneous Matters, that have been discover'd, we found, in digging of a Well that was twenty six foot deep, at the Bottom thereof, many large Pieces of the Tulip-Tree, and several other sorts of Wood, some of which were cut and notch'd, and some squared, as the Joices of a House are, which appear'd (in the Judgment of all that saw them) to be wrought with Iron Instruments; it seeming impossible for any thing made of Stone, or what they were found to make use of, to cut Wood in that manner. It cannot be argu'd, that the Wood so cut, might float from some other Continent; because Hiccory and the Tulip-Tree are spontaneous in *America,* and in no other Places, that I could ever learn. It is to be acknowledg'd, that the *Spaniards* give us Relations of magnificent Buildings, which were raised by the *Indians* of *Mexico* and other Parts, which they discover'd, and conquer'd; amongst whom no Iron Instruments were found: But 'tis a great Misfortune, that no Person in that Expedition was so curious, as to take an exact Draught of the Fabricks of those People, which would have been a Discovery of great Value, and very acceptable to the Ingenious; for, as to the Politeness[5] of Stones, it may be effected by Collision, and Grinding, which is of a contrary Nature, on several Accounts, and disproves not my Arguments, in the least.

The next is, the Earthen Pots that are often found under Ground, and at the Foot of the Banks where the Water has wash'd them away. They are for the most part broken in pieces; but we find them of a different sort, in Comparison of those the *Indians* use at this day, who have had no other, ever since the *English* discover'd *America.* The Bowels of the Earth cannot have alter'd them, since

---

4. A coarse linen, named for Osnaburg, Germany, where it was produced.

5. Polishing.

they are thicker, of another Shape, and Composition, and nearly approach to the Urns of the Ancient *Romans.*

Again, the Peaches, which are the only tame Fruit, or what is Foreign, that these People enjoy, which is an Eastern Product, and will keep and retain its vegetative and growing Faculty, the longest of any thing of that Nature, that I know of. The Stone, as I elsewhere have remark'd, is thicker than any other sort of the Peaches in *Europe,* or of the *European* sort, now growing in *America,* and is observed to grow if planted, after it has been for several Years laid by; and it seems very probable, that these People might come from some Eastern Country; for when you ask them whence their Fore-Fathers came, that first inhabited the Country, they will point to the Westward and say, *Where the Sun sleeps, our Forefathers came thence,* which, at that distance, may be reckon'd amongst the Eastern Parts of the World. And to this day, they are a shifting, wandring People; for I know some *Indian* Nations, that have chang'd their Settlements, many hundred Miles; sometimes no less than a thousand, as is prov'd by the *Savanna Indians,* who formerly lived on the Banks of the *Messiasippi,* and remov'd thence to the Head of one of the Rivers of South-*Carolina;* since which, (for some Dislike) most of them are remov'd to live in the Quarters of the *Iroquois* or *Sinnagars,*[6] which are on the Heads of the Rivers that disgorge themselves into the Bay of *Chesapeak.* I once met with a young *Indian* Woman, that had been brought from beyond the Mountains, and was sold a Slave into *Virginia.* She spoke the same Language, as the *Coranine*[7] *Indians,* that dwell near Cape-*Look-out,* allowing for some few Words, which were different, yet no otherwise, than that they might understand one another very well.

The *Indians* of North-*Carolina* are a well-shap'd clean-made People, of different Statures, as the *Europeans* are, yet chiefly inclin'd to be tall. They are a very streight People, and never bend forwards, or stoop in the Shoulders, unless much overpower'd by old Age. Their Limbs are exceeding well-shap'd. As for their Legs and Feet, they are generally the handsomest in the World. Their Bodies are a little flat, which is occasion'd, by being laced hard down to a Board, in their Infancy. This is all the Cradle they have, which I shall describe at large elsewhere. Their Eyes are black, or of a dark Hazle; The White is marbled with red Streaks, which is ever common to these People, unless when sprung from a white Father or Mother. Their Colour is of a tawny, which would not be so dark, did they not dawb themselves with Bears Oil, and a Colour like burnt Cork. This is begun in their Infancy, and continued for a long time, which fills the Pores, and enables them better to endure the Extremity of the Weather. They are never bald on their Heads, although never so old, which, I believe, proceeds from their Heads being always uncover'd, and the greasing their Hair (so often as they do) with Bears Fat, which is a great Nourisher of the Hair, and causes it to grow very fast. Amongst the Bears Oil (when they intend to be fine) they mix a certain red Powder, that comes from a Scarlet Root which they get in the hilly Country, near the Foot of the great Ridge of Mountains, and it is no where else to be found. They have this Scarlet Root in great Esteem, and sell it for a very great Price, one to another. The Reason of its Value is, because they not only go a long way for it, but are in great Danger of the *Sinnagars* or *Iroquois,* who are mortal Enemies to all our *Indians,* and very often take them Captives, or kill them, before they return from this Voyage. The *Tuskeruros* and other *Indians* have often brought this Seed with them from the Mountains; but it would never grow in our Land. With this and Bears Grease they anoint their Heads and Temples, which is esteem'd as ornamental, as sweet Powder to our Hair. Besides, this Root has the Virtue of killing Lice, and suffers none to abide or breed in their Heads. For want of this Root, they sometimes use *Pecoon* Root, which is of a Crimson Colour, but it is apt to die the Hair of an ugly Hue.

Their Eyes are commonly full and manly, and their Gate sedate and majestick. They never walk backward and forward as we do, nor contemplate on the Affairs of Loss and Gain; the things which daily perplex us. They are dexterous and steady both as to their Hands and Feet, to Admiration. They will walk over deep Brooks, and Creeks, on the smallest Poles, and that without any Fear or Concern. Nay, an *Indian* will walk on the Ridge of a Barn or House and look down the Gable-end, and spit upon the Ground, as unconcern'd, as if he was walking on *Terra firma.* In Running, Leaping, or any such other Exercise, their Legs seldom miscarry, and give them a Fall; and as for letting any thing fall out of their Hands, I never yet knew one Example. They are no Inventers of any Arts or Trades worthy mention; the Reason of which I take to be, that they are not possess'd with that Care and Thoughtfulness, how to provide for the Necessaries of Life, as the *Europeans* are; yet they will learn any thing

---

6. Senecas.

7. Coree.

very soon. I have known an *Indian* stock Guns better than most of our *Joiners,* although he never saw one stock'd before; and besides, his Working-Tool was only a sorry Knife. I have also known several of them that were Slaves to the *English,* learn Handicraft-Trades very well and speedily. I never saw a Dwarf amongst them, nor but one that was Hump-back'd. Their Teeth are yellow with Smoaking Tobacco, which both Men and Women are much addicted to. They tell us, that they had Tobacco amongst them, before the *Europeans* made any Discovery of that Continent. It differs in the Leaf from the sweet-scented, and *Oroonoko,* which are the Plants we raise and cultivate in *America.* Theirs differs likewise much in the Smell, when green, from our Tobacco, before cured. They do not use the same way to cure it as we do; and therefore, the Difference must be very considerable in Taste; for all Men (that know Tobacco) must allow, that it is the Order-ing thereof which gives a Hogoo[8] to that Weed, rather than any Natural Relish it possesses, when green. Al-though they are great Smokers, yet they never are seen to take it in Snuff, or chew it.

They have no Hairs on their Faces (except some few) and those but little, nor is there often found any Hair under their Arm-Pits. They are continually plucking it away from their Faces, by the Roots. As for their Privities, since they wore Tail-Clouts, to cover their Nakedness, several of the Men have a deal of Hair thereon. It is to be observ'd, that the Head of the *Penis* is cover'd (through-out all the Nations of the *Indians* I ever saw) both in Old and Young. Although we reckon these a very smooth Peo-ple, and free from Hair; yet I once saw a middleaged Man, that was hairy all down his Back; the Hairs being above an Inch long.

As there are found very few, or scarce any, Deformed, or Cripples, amongst them, so neither did I ever see but one blind Man; and then they would give me no Account how his Blindness came. They had a Use for him, which was to lead him with a Girl, Woman, or Boy, by a String; so they put what Burdens they pleased upon his Back, and made him very serviceable upon all such Occasions. No People have better Eyes, or see better in the Night or Day, than the *Indians.* Some alledge, that the Smoke of the Pitch-Pine, which they chiefly burn, does both preserve and strengthen the Eyes; as, perhaps, it may do, because that Smoak never offends the Eyes, though you hold your Face over a great Fire thereof. This is occasion'd by the volatile Part of the Turpentine, which rises with the Smoke, and is of a friendly, balsamick Nature; for the Ashes of the Pine-Tree afford no fix'd Salt in them.

They let their Nails grow very long, which, they reckon, is the Use Nails are design'd for, and laugh at the *Europeans* for pairing theirs, which, they say, disarms them of that which Nature design'd them for.

They are not of so robust and strong Bodies, as to lift great Burdens, and endure Labour and slavish Work, as the *Europeans* are; yet some that are Slaves, prove very good and laborious: But, of themselves, they never work as the *English* do, taking care for no farther than what is absolutely necessary to support Life. In Travelling and Hunting, they are very indefatigable; because that carries a Pleasure along with the Profit. I have known some of them very strong; and as for Running and Leaping, they are extraordinary Fellows, and will dance for several Nights together, with the greatest Briskness imaginable, their Wind never failing them.

Their Dances are of different Natures; and for every sort of Dance, they have a Tune, which is allotted for that Dance; as, if it be a War-Dance, they have a warlike Song, wherein they express, with all the Passion and Vehemence imaginable, what they intend to do with their Enemies; how they will kill, roast, sculp, beat, and make Captive, such and such Numbers of them; and how many they have destroy'd before. All these Songs are made new for every Feast; nor is one and the same Song sung at two several Festivals. Some one of the Nation (which has the best Gift of expressing their Designs) is appointed by their King, and War-Captains, to make these Songs.

Others are made for Feasts of another Nature; as, when several Towns, or sometimes, different Nations have made Peace with one another; then the Song suits both Nations, and relates, how the bad Spirit made them go to War, and destroy one another; but it shall never be so again; but that their Sons and Daughters shall marry to-gether, and the two Nations love one another, and become as one People.

They have a third sort of Feasts and Dances, which are always when the Harvest of Corn is ended, and in the Spring. The one, to return Thanks to the good Spirit, for the Fruits of the Earth; the other, to beg the same Bless-ings for the succeeding Year. And, to encourage the young Men to labour stoutly, in planting their Maiz and Pulse, they set a sort of an Idol in the Field, which is dress'd up exactly like an *Indian,* having all the *Indians* Habit, be-sides abundance of *Wampum,* and their Money, made of

---

8. Relish.

Shells, that hangs about his Neck. The Image none of the young Men dare approach; for the old ones will not suffer them to come near him, but tell them, that he is some famous *Indian* Warriour, that died a great while ago, and now is come amongst them, to see if they work well, which if they do, he will go to the good Spirit, and speak to him to send them Plenty of Corn, and to make the young Men all expert Hunters and mighty Warriours. All this while, the King and old Men sit round the Image, and seemingly pay a profound Respect to the same. One great Help to these *Indians,* in carrying on these Cheats, and inducing Youth to do what they please, is, the uninterrupted Silence, which is ever kept and observ'd, with all the Respect and Veneration imaginable.

At these Feasts, which are set out with all the Magnificence their Fare allows of, the Masquerades begin at Night, and not before. There is commonly a Fire made in the middle of the House, which is the largest in the Town, and is very often the Dwelling of their King, or War-Captain; where sit two Men on the Ground, upon a Mat; one with a Rattle, made of a Gourd, with some Beans in it; the other with a Drum, made of an earthen Pot, cover'd with a dress'd-Deer-Skin, and one Stick in his Hand to beat thereon; and so they both begin the Song appointed. At the same time, one drums, and the other rattles, which is all the artificial Musick of their own making I ever saw amongst them. To these two Instruments they sing, which carries no Air with it, but is a sort of unsavoury Jargon; yet their Cadences and Raising of their Voices are form'd with that Equality and Exactness, that (to us *Europeans*) it seems admirable, how they should continue these Songs, without once missing to agree, each with the others Note and Tune.

As for their Dancing, were there Masters of that Profession amongst them, as there are with us, they would dearly earn their Money; for these Creatures take the most Pains at it, that Men are able to endure. I have seen thirty odd together a dancing, and every one dropp'd down with Sweat, as if Water had been poured down their Backs. They use those hard Labours, to make them able to endure Fatigue, and improve their Wind, which indeed is very long and durable, it being a hard matter, in any Exercise, to dispossess them of it.

At these Feasts, they meet from all the Towns within fifty or sixty Miles round, where they buy and sell several Commodities, as we do at Fairs and Markets. Besides, they game very much, and often strip one another of all they have in the World; and what is more, I have known several of them play themselves away, so that they have remain'd the Winners Servants, till their Relations or themselves could pay the Money to redeem them; and when this happens, the Loser is never dejected or melancholy at the Loss, but laughs, and seems no less contented than if he had won. They never differ at Gaming, neither did I ever see a Dispute, about the Legality thereof, so much as rise amongst them.

Their chiefest Game is a sort of Arithmetick, which is managed by a Parcel of small split Reeds, the Thickness of a small Bent; these are made very nicely, so that they part, and are tractable in their Hands. They are fifty one in Number, their Length about seven Inches; when they play, they throw part of them to their Antagonist; the Art is, to discover, upon sight, how many you have, and what you throw to him that plays with you. Some are so expert at their Numbers, that they will tell ten times together, what they throw out of their Hands. Although the whole Play is carried on with the quickest Motion it's possible to use, yet some are so expert at this Game, as to win great *Indian* Estates by this Play. A good Sett of these Reeds, fit to play withal, are valued and sold for a dress'd Doe-Skin.

They have several other Plays and Games; as, with the Kernels or Stones of Persimmons, which are in effect the same as our Dice, because Winning or Losing depend on which side appear uppermost, and how they happen to fall together.

Another Game is managed with a Batoon and a Ball, and resembles our Trap-ball; besides, several Nations have several Games and Pastimes, which are not used by others.

These Savages live in *Wigwams,* or Cabins built of Bark, which are made round like an Oven, to prevent any Damage by hard Gales of Wind. They make the Fire in the middle of the House, and have a Hole at the Top of the Roof right above the Fire, to let out the Smoke. These Dwellings are as hot as Stoves, where the *Indians* sleep and sweat all Night. The Floors thereof are never paved nor swept, so that they have always a loose Earth on them. They are often troubled with a multitude of Fleas, especially near the Places where they dress their Deer-Skins, because that Hair harbours them; yet I never felt any ill, unsavory Smell in their Cabins, whereas, should we live in our Houses, as they do, we should be poison'd with our own Nastiness; which confirms these *Indians* to be, as they really are, some of the sweetest People in the World.

CHARLES WOODMASON (1720?–POST-1776)

Charles Woodmason emigrated from England in 1752 to South Carolina, where he settled beyond the Peedee River. He became a planter and merchant in the area, and he served several elected posts—warden in 1756, vestryman in 1757, and lay preacher in Prince Frederick parish—in the decade following his arrival. He moved to Charleston in 1762, where he served several civic posts, including the clerkship of the Assembly. In 1765, he sought the position of stamp distributor, the official who would enforce the provisions of the controversial Stamp Act. This action turned public opinion against him, and Woodmason traveled briefly to England that year. In England, he was ordained an Anglican minister in 1766, and upon his return to South Carolina, he settled in the interior, where he was admired as a leader and became a spokesperson regarding local affairs. From 1766 to 1768, Woodmason traveled over 9,000 miles in the course of his itinerant ministry. He kept a journal of his experience in the unsettled areas and among his rural parishioners. Although he considered the settlements to have great potential, Woodmason considered the country settlers disorderly, dirty, poor, and sinful. In 1774, with the Revolution about to begin, Woodmason returned to England and remained loyal to the British Crown and Parliament. He died sometime after 1776, the year he petitioned for compensation as a Loyalist refugee.

As a planter and a minister, Woodmason maintained a high level of intellectual activity, and he sought a career as a man of letters. In the early years, when he was a planter, Woodmason wrote poetry that was later published in the London *Gentleman's Magazine,* and he likewise published in that magazine an essay on cultivating and manufacturing indigo, a much-desired plant grown for its blue extracts that were used for dye, under cultivation in the West Indies and South Carolina. Woodmason published a proposal in 1757 for a volume of poetry, but the proposals evidently never acquired enough subscribers, and the proposed volume remained unpublished.

During his years as an itinerant minister, Woodmason took on leadership in the Regulator movement, a movement that gathered together men who would serve the border area as vigilantes. The Regulators claimed that they were the only source of order on the frontier. As their spokesman, Woodmason wrote a number of articles and letters, along with a petition entitled "A Remonstrance Presented to the Commons House of Assembly of South Carolina" (1767) that described the lawlessness on the frontier. In addition, he wrote sermons and letters to many people of renown in the colonies and England. The journal of Woodmason's trips as a minister was published in the twentieth century and is recognized as one of the best descriptions of the colonial South Carolina interior.

The poems reprinted next reveal Woodmason's wide reading in the well-received classical and contemporary writings of his day. Woodmason's clear neoclassical inclinations are evident in the opening to the poem addressed to Franklin and in the pastoral implications underlying the production of indigo. His poem, "Indico," is in the tradition of the poetic treatment of agriculture that goes back to Virgil's *Georgics.* Like Virgil, Woodmason portrays agriculture as an essential part of empire building, as the bringing of civilization to a wilderness. Only two portions of this poem survive; the portions used here advertise Woodmason's proposed book.

TO BENJAMIN FRANKLIN ESQ; OF PHILADELPHIA, ON HIS EXPERIMENTS AND DISCOVERIES IN ELECTRICITY[1]

Cooper River, S. Carolina, Sept. 20, 1753

Let others muse on sublunary things,
The rise of empires and the fall of kings;
Thine is the praise, with bolder flight to soar,
And airy regions, yet untrack'd, explore;
To dictate science with imperial nod,
And save not ruin by an *iron rod*.[2]

If for thy birth, when latest times draw nigh,
As now for Homer's, rival cities vie;
This spot perhaps unmov'd may hear the strife,
Content to claim the vigour of thy life;
To shew thy tomb, like Virgil's shewn before,
With laurel, proof to lightning, covered o'er.

Happy that here we boast the guardian friend,
Where most the hostile elements contend:
This hour tremendous thunders strike my ear,
Keen light'nings dart, and threat'ning clouds appear:
Now fly the negroes from the impending storm!
The air how cold! this moment mild and warm.
Now down it pours! the tempest shakes the skies,
On flashes flashes, clouds on clouds arise;
The noxious rattle snake with fear deprest,
Now creeps for safety to his poisonous nest;
Bears, foxes, lynxes, seek the thickest brake,
Wolves, tygers, panthers in their caverns quake:
Now allegators diving quit the strand,
And birds unknown, in flocks repair to land;

Small riv'lets swell to streams, and streams to floods,
Loud whirlwinds rush impetuous thro' the woods,
Huge oaks midst foaming torrents fiercely burn,
And tall pines blasted from their roots are torn:
The bolt descends and harrows up the ground,
And stones and sand are widely scatter'd round;
How near the welkin breaks! now nearer still!
But now askance, it drives o'er yonder hill;

The rain abates, the gloomy clouds retreat,
And all is light, serenity and heat:
The change how sudden! but how frequent too!
The change, at length, without one fear I view:
Sedate, composed, I hear the tempest roll,
Which once with terror shook my boding soul!
No fire I fear my dwelling shou'd invade,
No bolt transfix me, in the dreadful shade;
No falling steeple trembles from on high,
No shivered organs now in fragments fly,[3]
The guardian point erected high in air,
Nature disarms, and teaches storms to spare.
So through the sultry deep unmov'd I sail,
When the wave whitens with a boding gale;
A fire ball strikes the mast a silent blow,
Then thunder speaks—no further shalt thou go;
Quick it descends the wire, around the shrouds,
Which checks the fury of the flaming clouds.
With hallow'd wands strange circles once were made,
To gull an ign'rant crowd, the jugglers trade;
Within the line no blue infernal fire,
Could pierce, but hence, malignant powers, retire;
What these pretended, Franklin, thou hast wrought,
And truth is own'd what once was fiction thought;
Within thy magic circle calm I sit,
Nor friends nor business in confusion quit;
Whate'er explosions dreadful break around,
Or fiery meteors sweep the crackling ground.

O friend, at once to science, and to man,
Persue each noble and each gen'rous plan;
With all the bliss beneficence obtains,
Be thine whate'er from gratitude it gains,
Be thine those honours that are virtue's meed,
Whate'er to genius wisdom has decreed!

Accept this off'ring of an humble mind,
By sickness weaken'd—long to cares confin'd:
Tho' yet untasted the Pierian spring,
In lonely woods she thus attempts to sing,
Where seldom muse before e'er tun'd a lay,
Where yet the graces slowly find their way:
Wild as the fragrant shrubs and blooming flow'rs
Which nature scatters round o'er artless bow'rs.
More soft and sweet will be her future strain,
Should this rude note thy approbation gain.

C. W.

---

1. The poem was published in *Gentleman's Magazine* 24 (February 1754), and it was thereafter reprinted in *Scot's Magazine* (Edinburgh, June 1754), the *Boston Post Boy* (July 1754), and the *New York Gazette* (July 1754).

2. "By the application of a rod of iron, or a wire, the effect of thunder and lightning is prevented." [Au.]

3. "The steeple and organ of St. Philip's church at Charles Town, have twice been damaged by lightning." [Au.]

INDICO[1]

The Means and Arts that to Perfection bring,
The richer Dye of INDICO, I sing.
Kind Heav'n! whose wise and providential Care
5 Has granted us another World to share,
These happy Climes to Antients quite unknown,
And fields more fruitful than *Britannia's* own;
Who for Man's Use has blest with Herbs the Soil,
Who crowns with Joy the wary Planter's Toil,
Do thou propitious grant the Help I need,
10 Success shall follow and my Labours speed.

IF Time permits, the Shady Forest clear,
And turn the Fallow for the following Year;
Beneath the noxious Pine the Soil is sour,
And spreading Oaks prevent the genial Pow'r
15 Of mellowing Suns; but yet, Experience shews,
In these hot climes that rich Herbage grows,
The following Summer, where in Winter past
The hungry Swine had found a Winter Mast.

Begin when first bleak Winter strips the Trees,
20 When Herds first shudder at the Northern
'Tis time the Walnut and the Cypress tall
And tow'ring Pride of Verdant Pines to fall.
Arm'd with destructive Steel thy Negroes bring,
With Blows repeated let the Woodlands ring;
25 With winged Speed, the tim'rous Deer from far
Shall fly the Tumult of the Sylvan War,
When rattling Oaks and Pines promisc'ous bound,
And distant Groves re-eccho to the Sound.
Whilst the bright Flames shall seize the useless Log
30 For brush and trunks thy fertile Acres clog
Then peaceful sleep—secure thy Herds shall be,
And live to feast they Country Friends and thee.
When midnight Wolves, impell'd by Hunger's Pow'r,
With fiercest Rage the darken'd Forest scow'r,
35 Scar'd by the dreaded Flames, they'll turn away,

---

1. Woodmason's georgic poem "Indico" was printed in two different pieces during his lifetime but never published in its entirety. If a manuscript of the complete poem ever existed, that manuscript remains undiscovered. The sections published here appeared in the *South Carolina Gazette,* August 25, 1757 (the segment to line 95 in the current selection) and December 1, 1758 (line 96 to the end). Although the *Gazette* publisher announced in November 1759 that the "The Poem on INDICO, for which subscriptions have been on foot for abot two years, being in our hands, will be put to press as soon as possible," the complete poem never appeared.

And hideous howl when baulk'd of whist for Prey.
Most skilful Planters in the Judgement rest,
That rotten Soil for INDICO's the best:
But let not that thy Hopes of Crops impair,
Some stiffer Soils great Droughts may better bear.   40
I've seen a Crop of Weed, like Thicket grown,
From stubborn Clay, on some Plantations mown.
Such Lands with double Exercise prepare,
And double Harvest shall reward thy Care.
Laborious Toil!—But all is Toil below,   45
Since Heav'n pronounc'd to mortal Man this Woe.
Immediate Want, or Dread of Future, can
With pow'rful Influence sway the Mind of Man.
Hence urging Poverty is justly stild
Mother of Arts, Invention's call's her Child.   50
All hail, great Source of Industry! of Yore
A Goddess deem'd, when fam'd *Fabricus* bore
The Sway in *Rome,* and yet content to share
But one small Field, to plant his rural Fare.
Here from a State's tempestuous Troubles free,   55
Amidst the Sweets of honest Poverty,
In Freedom, Privacy, and calm Content,
He reap'd those Bounties Providence has sent:
She first inspir'd the *Mantuan* Bard, who sung
The Care of Flocks, and of their tender Young;   60
Who taught the lab'ring Hind to plough and sow,
The various Seasons of the Year to know,
To prune his Vines, to plant, to graft his Trees,
And reap the Labour of sagacious Bees.
Nor Rage of Seas, nor distant Worlds affright,   65
Nor native Soil, or Nature's Ties, our Flight
From them retard; if she her dire Commands
Impose on Man: She calls unnumber'd Bands
Of valiant Youth to War, she fires the Cold,
Spurs on the Drone, and makes the Coward bold.   70
All-conquering Rome to thee first owes her Birth,
How universal is thy Pow'r on Earth!
She peopled this new World, she still explores
Angola's Coast, and savage *Gambia's* Shores,
In Search of Slaves, a Race in Numbers great,   75
Whose Constitutions, temper'd to the Heat
By situation of their native Soil,
Best bear the scorching Suns, and rustic Toil:

But joyful Spring returns, the Winter's past,
The trees bud forth nor dread the Northern Blast,   80
Break off Delays, and thus prepare the Plain,
Let Two Feet void 'twixt every Trench remain.
Tho' some, imprudently, their Room confine,
Allowing half that Space to every Line.

85 Give Room, one Stem as much shall yield,
    And richer far the Weed: So shall thy Field
    With greater Ease from noxious Herbs be freed,
    And knotty Grass that choaks the tender Weed,
    So shall the Root by larger Banks be fed,
90 Nor fear the Rays from piercing Phoebus shed.
    Cautious of this, in Lines direct and true
    (For Order's best, and pleases best the View)
    Extend thy long-stretch'd Furrows o'er the Plain
    Then invocating Heav'n for speedy Rain
95 *Sprinkle the Seed, &c.*

    YET[2] Summer Fallows[3] best your Crops ensure,
    And far exceed all Species of Manure.

    By this the nitrous Particles of Air
    When loose the Surface, and the Passage fair,
    With Ease descend, and to the Soil Adhere.   100
    By this, malignant Vapours find a Vent,
    And genial Salts by earthly Bodies pent,
    When freed from Chains with which before th'are
        bound
    Exert their Pow'r and spread their Virtues round.
    Rich Emanations that from Phoebus flow   105
    (The Life and Soul of all the Plants that grow),
    Search latent Parts, correct the Humours sow'r,
    And raise, and fix the vegative Pow'r.
    How much less Toil would then our Planter have?
    How much Expence in weeding might they save?   110
    If 'ere the Grass to Shed its Seed begun,
    The Roots were turn'd, and parched in the Sun.
    But more than all the *Golden Weed*[4] requires
    Such Husbandry, for as it first aspires
    To spread, and branch on sudden stops to grow,   115
    And all its Force employs to root below.
    Cautious of future Heat, for Thirsty Days
    It's uppward Growth, by rooting deep delays.
    Mean Time the Weeds their baneful Summits rear,
    And Fennel wild, and Crab-Grass domineer.   120

---

2. When this second part of the poem was printed on December 1, 1758, it appeared under the following heading: "'TIS Observable that the Planters of *Carolina,* in the Months of *May, June,* and *July,* (when Farmers in *England* have more Leisure than any other Part of the Year), are then in the greatest Hurry; when without great Care and Labour in weeding their Crops, they would be entirely lost. This must be attributed to bad Husbandry, wich the following Verses were intended to remedy. They are an Extract of the Poem INDICO, mentioned in your Gazette about *Twelve* Months ago; which can't be published 'till Subscriptions arrive from London, expected in the Spring, those here not amounting to the Expence of the Press. I have found it beneficial to me to follow the Method prescribed by the Verses, and (with the Author's Leave) I send them to you, to be referred to the Judgement of my Brother-Planters, whether his Reasoning is not agreeable to Philosophy and good Husbandry." Agricola was probably Woodmason himself.

3. "*Plowing the Ground you intend to sow next Summer.*" [Au.]

---

4. "Indico." [Au.]

JAMES GRAINGER (1721?–1766)

James Grainger was probably born in Scotland in 1721. Although little is known of his youth, records indicate that he entered the University at Edinburgh to study medicine and served in Scotland and Holland as an army surgeon before completing his medical degree in 1753. After this service, Grainger settled in London, where he struggled to support himself as a doctor and ended up relying upon his literary wit to keep himself going. By writing poems, translations of classical poetry, and contributions to the *Monthly Review,* Grainger supplemented his income. Grainger was well connected in London, and his circle of prominent literary friends included such writers as Samuel Johnson, Oliver Goldsmith, William Shenstone, and Robert Dodsley. Eventually, however, Grainger decided to accept the offer of his wealthy friend John Bourryau, a plantation owner, to accompany him on his travels as his paid companion. On their journey to St. Christopher's island (now St. Kitts) in 1759, Grainger met his future wife, the daughter of a prominent plantation family. After the marriage, Grainger terminated his employment with Bourryau and assumed a position as manager of several of his wife's family's estates. He also continued his medical practice and published *Essay on the More Common West-Indian Diseases* in 1764.

Grainger's poem, *The Sugar-Cane*, published in Britain in 1764, reflects his detailed knowledge of the history, culture, flora and fauna, and sugar plantations of the Caribbean. Inspired by his experiences in the West Indies, Grainger sought to expand the parameters of poetry. As Grainger explained, his reasons for writing the poem "were, not only the importance and novelty of the subject, but more especially this consideration; that, as the face of this country was wholly different from that of *Europe,* so whatever hand copied its appearances, however rude, could not fail to enrich poetry with many new picturesque images." He also sought to instruct his readers, in part by including lengthy, detailed footnotes about topics, such as plants, animals, and disease, information that Grainger drew from his medical background and gleaned through his research.

Grainger's poem is distinctive because of the way it adapted his medical knowledge and Caribbean subject matter to the neoclassical form of the georgic poem to create what he described in his preface as a "West-Indian georgic." Traditionally, georgic poems sought to instruct an idealized farmer. Grainger drew upon the classical model of Virgil, yet adapted the classical precedent to his own purposes. The unusual concrete approach of Grainger's writing was off-putting to some readers who were troubled not by the topic of his poem but by Grainger's use of West Indian words and technical or scientific terms within his poetry. Yet the poem was generally well received by Grainger's English readers. Dr. Johnson reviewed it favorably, saying of Grainger, "we have been destitute till now of an American poet, that could bear any degree of competition."

The Sugar-Cane is divided into four books, the first three of which address planting, obstacles to planters' success, harvesting, and planters themselves. The final book, presented here, describes slaves and the slave system that supported the sugar plantations. It illustrates an early justification for slavery in the British West Indies, one that links productivity in the colonies with patriotism for Britain.

from THE SUGAR CANE. A POEM. IN FOUR BOOKS. WITH NOTES[1]

BOOK IV • "THE GENIUS OF AFRICA"

Argument

Invocation to the Genius of Africa. Address. Negroes when bought should be young, and strong. The Congo-negroes are fitter for the house and trades, than for the field. The Gold-Coast, but especially the Papaw-negroes, make the best field-negroes: but even these, if advanced in years, should not be purchased. The marks of a sound negroe at a negroe sale. Where the men do nothing but hunt, fish or fight, and all field drudgery is left to the women; these are to be preferred to their husbands. The Minnahs[2] make good tradesmen, but addicted to suicide. The Mundingos,[3] in particular, subject to worms; and the Congas, to dropsical disorders. How salt-water, or new negroes should be seasoned. Some negroes eat dirt. Negroes should be habituated by gentle degrees to field labour. This labour, when compared to that in lead-mines, or of those who work in the gold and silver mines of South America, is not only less toilsome, but far more healthy. Negroes should always be treated with humanity. Praise of freedom. Of the dracunculus, or dragon-worm. Of chigres. Of the yaws. Might not this disease be imparted by inoculation? Of worms, and their multiform appearance. Praise of commerce. Of the imaginary disorders of negroes, especially those caused by their conjurers or Obia-men. The composition and supposed virtues of a magicphiol.

---

1. The text is James Grainger's *The Sugar-Cane,* first published in London in 1764.

2. The Minnahs come from the area surrounding Minna, a central Nigerian city.

3. The Mandingo or Mande of West Africa.

*Field-negroes should not begin to work before six in
the morning, and should leave off between eleven and
twelve; and beginning again at two, should finish
before sun-set. Of the weekly allowance of negroes.
The young, the old, the sickly, and even the lazy,
must have their victuals prepared for them. Of
negroe-ground, and its various productions. To be
fenced in, and watched. Of an American garden. Of
the situation of the negroe-huts. How best defended
from fire. The great negroe-dance described.
Drumming, and intoxicating spirits not to be allowed.
Negroes should be made to marry in their masters
plantation. Inconveniences arising from the contrary
practice. Negroes to be cloathed once a year, and
before Christmas. Praise of Lewis XIV.[4] for the Code
Noir. A body of laws of this kind recommended to the
English sugar colonies. Praise of the river Thames. A
moon-light landscape and vision.*

The Sugar Cane
Book IV

  GENIUS of Africk! whether thou bestrid'st
The castled elephants; or at the source,
(While howls the desart fearfully around,)
Of thine own Niger, sadly thou reclin'st
5 Thy temples shaded by the tremulous palm,
Or quick papaw,[5] whose top is necklac'd round
With numerous rows of party-colour'd fruit:
Or hear'st thou rather from the rocky banks
Of Rio Grandê, or black Sanaga?[6]
10 Where dauntless thou the headlong torrent brav'st
In search of gold, to brede thy wooly locks,
On with bright ringlets ornament thine ears,
Thine arms, and ankles: O attend my song.
A muse that pities thy distressful state;
15 Who sees, with grief, thy sons in fetters bound;
Who wishes freedom to the race of man;
Thy nod assenting craves: dread Genius, come!

  YET vain thy presence, vain thy favouring nod;
Unless once more the muses, that erewhile
20 Upheld me fainting in my past career,

Through Caribbe's cane-isles; kind condescend
To guide my footsteps, through parch'd Libya's wilds;
And bind my sun-burnt brow with other bays,
Than ever deck'd the Sylvan bard before.

  SAY, will my Melvil,[7] from the public care,   25
Withdraw one moment, to the muses shrine?
Who smit with thy fair fame, industrious cull
An Indian wreath to mingle with thy bays,
And deck the hero, and the scholar's brow!
Wilt thou, whose mildness smooths the face of war, 30
Who round the victor-blade the myrtle twin'st,
And mak'st subjection loyal and sincere;
O wilt thou gracious hear the unartful strain,
Whose mild instructions teach, no trivial theme,
What care the jetty African requires?   35
Yes, thou wilt deign to hear; a man thou art
Who deem'st nought foreign that belongs to man.

  IN mind, and aptitude for useful toil,
The negroes differ: muse that difference sing.

  WHETHER to wield the hoe, or guide the plane;[8] 40
Or for domestic uses thou intend'st
The sunny Libyan: from what clime they spring,
It not imports; if strength and youth be theirs.

  YET those from Congo's wide-extended plains,
Through which the long Zaire winds with chrystal 45
   stream,
Where lavish Nature sends indulgent forth
Fruits of high favour, and spontaneous seeds
Of bland nutritious quality, ill bear
The toilsome field; but boast a docile mind,
And happiness of features. These, with care, 50
Be taught each nice mechanic art: or train'd
To houshold offices: their ductile souls
Will all thy care, and all thy gold repay.

  BUT, if the labours of the field demand
Thy chief attention; and the ambrosial cane 55
Thou long'st to see, with spiry frequence, shade
Many an acre: planter, chuse the slave,
Who sails from barren climes; where art alone,
Offspring of rude necessity, compells
The sturdy native, or to plant the soil, 60
Or stem vast rivers, for his daily food.

---

4. King Louis XIV of France (1638–1715) reigned from
1643 until 1715.

5. The papaya tree.

6. The Senegal River in West Africa.

---

7. Count de Melvil appears in Tobias Smollett's novel *The
Adventures of Ferdinand Count Fathom* (1753).

8. Plough.

SUCH are the children of the Golden Coast;
Such the Papaws, of negroes far the best:
And such the numerous tribes, that skirt the shore,
65 From rapid Volta to the distant Rey.[9]

BUT, planter, from what coast soe'er they sail,
Buy not the old: they ever sullen prove;
With heart-felt anguish, they lament their home;
They will not, cannot work; they never learn
70 Thy native language; they are prone to ails;
And oft by suicide their being end.—

MUST thou from Africk reinforce thy gang?—
Let health and youth their every sinew firm;
Clear roll their ample eye; their tongue be red;
75 Broad swell their chest; their shoulders wide
        expand;
Not prominent their belly; clean and strong
Their thighs and legs, in just proportion rise.
Such soon will brave the fervours of the clime;
And free from ails, that kill thy negroe-train,
80 A useful servitude will long support.

YET, if thine own, thy childrens life, be dear;
Buy not a Cormantee,[10] tho' healthy, young.
Of breed too generous for the servile field;
They, born to freedom in their native land,
85 Chuse death before dishonourable bonds:
Or, fir'd with vengeance, at the midnight hour,
Sudden they seize thine unsuspecting watch,
And thine own poinard[11] bury in thy breast.

AT home, the men, in many a sylvan realm,
90 Their rank tobacco, charm of sauntering minds,
From clayey tubes inhale; or, vacant, beat
For prey the forest; or, in war's dread ranks,
Their country's foes affront: while, in the field,
Their wives plant rice, or yams, or lofty maize,
95 Fell hunger to repel. Be these thy choice:
They, hardy, with the labours of the Cane
Soon grow familiar; while unusual toil,
And new severities their husbands kill.

THE slaves from Minnah are of stubborn breed:
100 But, when the bill, or hammer, they affect;

They soon perfection reach. But fly, with care,
The Moco-nation;[12] they themselves destroy.

WORMS lurk in all: yet, pronest they to worms,
Who from Mundingo sail. When therefore such
Thou buy'st, for sturdy and laborious they,   105
Straight let some learned leach[13] strong medicines give,
Till food and climate both familiar grow.
Thus, tho' from rise to set, in Phoebus' eye,[14]
They toil, unceasing; yet, at night, they'll sleep,
Lap'd in Elysium;[15] and, each day, at dawn,   110
Spring from their couch, as blythsome as the sun.

ONE precept more, it much imports to know.—
The Blacks, who drink the Quanza's lucid stream,[16]
Fed by ten thousand springs, are prone to bloat,
Whether at home or in these ocean-isles;   115
And tho' nice art the water may subdue,
Yet many die; and few, for many a year,
Just strength attain to labour for their lord.

WOULD'ST thou secure thine Ethiop from those ails,
Which change of climate, change of waters breed,   120
And food unusual? let Machaon[17] draw
From each some blood, as age and sex require;
And well with vervain,[18] well with sempre-vive,[19]
Unload their bowels.—These, in every hedge,
Spontaneous grow.—Nor will it not conduce   125
To give what chemists, in mysterious phrase,
Term the white eagle; deadly foe to worms.
But chief do thou, my friend, with hearty food,
Yet easy of digestion, likest that
Which they at home regal'd on; renovate   130
Their sea-worn appetites. Let gentle work,
Or rather playful exercise, amuse
The novel gang: and far be angry words;

---

12. A people probably originating from modern-day Nigeria.

13. A doctor.

14. The sun.

15. In classical mythology, the dwelling place of happy souls after death.

16. The River Kwanza in Angola.

17. During the Trojan War, Machaon served as doctor to the Greeks.

18. An herbaceous plant.

19. The houseleek, a common European succulent with pink flowers.

---

9. Rivers in present-day Ghana, West Africa.

10. Slaves (or their descendants) from present-day Kromanti in Ghana were referred to as "Cormantee."

11. A poiniard, a type of dagger.

Far ponderous chains; and far disheartening blows.—
135 From fruits restrain their eagerness; yet if
The acajou, haply, in thy garden bloom,
With cherries,[20] or of white or purple hue,
Thrice wholesome fruit in this relaxing clime!
Safely thou may'st their appetite indulge.
140 Their arid skins will plump, their features shine:
No rheums, no dysenteric ails torment:
The thirsty hydrops[21] flies.—'Tis even averr'd,
(Ah, did experience sanctify the fact;
How many Lybians now would dig the soil,
145 Who pine in hourly agonies away!)
This pleasing fruit, if turtle join its aid,
Removes that worst of ails, disgrace of art,
The loathsome leprosy's infectious bane.

THERE are, the muse hath oft abhorrent seen,
150 Who swallow dirt; (so the chlorotic fair
Oft chalk prefer to the most poignant cates:[22])
Such, dropsy bloats, and to sure death consigns;
Unless restrain'd from this unwholesome food,
By soothing words, by menaces, by blows:
155 Nor yet will threats, or blows, or soothing words,
Perfect their cure; unless thou, Paean,[23] design'st
By medicine's power their cravings to subdue.

TO easy labour first inure thy slaves;
Extremes are dangerous. With industrious search,

Let them fit grassy provender[24] collect   160
For thy keen stomach'd herds.—But when the earth
Hath made her annual progress round the sun,
What time the conch[25] or bell resounds, they may
All to the Cane-ground, with thy gang, repair.

NOR, Negroe, at thy destiny repine,   165
Tho' doom'd to toil from dawn to setting sun.
How far more pleasant is thy rural task,
Than theirs who sweat, sequester'd from the day,
In dark tartarean caves, sunk far beneath
The earth's dark surface, where sulphureous flames,   170
Oft from their vapoury prisons bursting wild,
To dire explosion give the cavern'd deep,
And in dread ruin all its inmates whelm?—
Nor fateful only is the bursting flame;
The exhalations of the deep-dug mine,   175
Tho' slow, shake from their wings as sure a death.
With what intense severity of pain
Hath the afflicted muse, in Scotia, seen
The miners rack'd, who toil for fatal lead?
What cramps, what palsies shake their feeble limbs,   180
Who, on the margin of the rocky Drave,[26]
Trace silver's fluent ore? Yet white men these!

HOW far more happy ye, than those poor slaves,
Who, whilom,[27] under native, gracious chiefs,
Incas and emperors, long time enjoy'd   185
Mild government, with every sweet of life,
In blissful climates? See them dragg'd in chains,
By proud insulting tyrants, to the mines
Which once they call'd their own, and then despis'd!
See, in the mineral bosom of their land,   190
How hard they toil! how soon their youthful limbs
Feel the decrepitude of age! how soon
Their teeth desert their sockets! and how soon
Shaking paralysis unstrings their frame!
Yet scarce, even then, are they allow'd to view   195
The glorious God of day, of whom they beg,
With earnest hourly supplications, death;
Yet death slow comes, to torture them the more!

WITH these compar'd, ye sons of Afric, say,

---

20. "The tree which produces this wholesome fruit is tall, shady, and of quick growth. Its Indian name is *Acajou;* hence corruptly called *Cashew* by the English. The fruit has no resemblance to a cherry, either in shape or size; and bears, at its lower extremity, a nut (which the Spaniards name *Anacardo,* and physicians *Anacardium*) that resembles a large kidney-bean. Its kernel is as grateful as an almond, and more easy of digestion. Between its rhinds is contained a highly caustic oil; which, being held to a candle, emits bright, salient sparkles, in which the American fortune-tellers pretended they saw spirits who gave answers to whatever questions were put to them by their ignorant followers. This oil is used as a cosmetic by the ladies, to remove freckles and sun-burning; but the pain they necessarily suffer makes its use not very frequent. This tree also produces a gum not inferior to Gum-Arabic; and its bark is an approved astringent. The juice of the cherry stains exceedingly. The long citron, or amber-coloured, is the best. The cashew-nuts, when unripe, are of a green colour; but, ripe, they assume that of a pale olive. This tree bears fruit but once a year." [Au.]

21. Edema.

22. Choice foods.

23. A title for Apollo, a Greek god.

24. Feed for domestic animals.

25. "Plantations that have no bells, assemble their Negroes by sounding a conch-shell." [Au.]

26. "A river in Hungary, on whose banks are found mines of quicksilver." [Au.]

27. Formerly.

200 How far more happy is your lot? Bland health,
Of ardent eye, and limb robust, attends
Your custom'd labour; and, should sickness seize,
With what solicitude are ye not nurs'd!—
Ye Negroes, then, your pleasing task pursue;
205 And, by your toil, deserve your master's care.

    WHEN first your Blacks are novel to the hoe;
Study their humours: Some, soft-soothing words;
Some, presents; and some, menaces subdue;
And some I've known, so stubborn is their kind,
210 Whom blows, alas! could win alone to toil.

    YET, planter, let humanity prevail.—
Perhaps thy Negroe, in his native land,
Possest large fertile plains, and slaves, and herds:
Perhaps, whene'er he deign'd to walk abroad,
215 The richest silks, from where the Indus rolls,
His limbs invested in their gorgeous pleats:
Perhaps he wails his wife, his children, left
To struggle with adversity: Perhaps
Fortune, in battle for his country fought,
220 Gave him a captive to his deadliest foe:
Perhaps, incautious, in his native fields,
(On pleasurable scenes his mind intent)
All as he wandered; from the neighbouring grove,
Fell ambush dragg'd him to the hated main.—
225 Were they even sold for crimes; ye polish'd, say!
Ye, to whom Learning opes her amplest page!
Ye, whom the knowledge of a living God
Should lead to virtue! Are ye free from crimes?
Ah pity, then, these uninstructed swains;
230 And still let mercy soften the decrees
Of rigid justice, with her lenient hand.

    OH, did the tender muse possess the power,
Which monarchs have, and monarchs oft abuse:
'Twould be the fond ambition of her soul,
235 To quell tyrannic sway; knock off the chains
Of heart-debasing slavery; give to man,
Of every colour and of every clime,
Freedom, which stamps him image of his God.
Then laws, Oppression's scourge, fair Virtue's prop,
240 Offspring of Wisdom! should impartial reign,
To knit the whole in well-accorded strife:
Servants, not slaves; of choice, and not compell'd;
The Blacks should cultivate the Cane-land isles.

    SAY, shall the muse the various ills recount,
245 Which Negroe-nations feel? Shall she describe
The worm that subtly winds into their flesh,
All as they bathe them in their native streams?

There, with fell increment, it soon attains
A direful length of harm. Yet, if due skill,
And proper circumspection are employed,   250
It may be won its volumes to wind round
A leaden cylinder: But, O, beware,
No rashness practise; else 'twill surely snap,
And suddenly, retreating, dire produce
An annual lameness to the tortured Moor.   255

    NOR only is the dragon worm to dread:
Fell, winged insects,[28] which the visual ray
Scarcely discerns, their sable feet and hands
Oft penetrate; and, in the fleshy nest,
Myriads of young produce; which soon destroy   260
The parts they breed in; if assiduous care,
With art, extract not the prolific foe.

    Or, shall she sing, and not debase her lay,
The pest peculiar to the Æthiop-kind,
The yaw's[29] infectious bane?—The infected far   265
In huts, to leeward, lodge; or near the main.
With heartening food, with turtle, and with conchs;
The flowers of sulphur, and hard niccars[30] burnt,
The lurking evil from the blood expel,
And throw it on the surface: There in spots   270
Which cause no pain, and scanty ichor[31] yield,
It chiefly breaks about the arms and hips,
A virulent contagion!—When no more

---

28. "These, by the English, are called *Chigoes* or *Chigres*.
They chiefly perforate the toes, and sometimes the fingers; occasioning an itching, which some people think not unpleasing, and are at pains to get, by going to the copper-holes, or mill-round, where chigres most abound. They lay their nits in a bag, about the size of a small pea, and are partly contained therein themselves. This the Negroes extract without bursting, by means of a needle, and filling up the place with a little snuff; it soon heals, if the person has a good constitution. One species of them is supposed to be poisonous; but, I believe, unjustly. When they bury themselves near a tendon, especially if the person is in a bad habit of body, they occasion troublesome sores. The South-Americans call them *Miguas*." [Au.]

29. A tropical skin disease.

30. "The botanical name of this medicinal shrub is *Guilandina*. The fruit resembles marbles, though not so round. Their shell is hard and smooth, and contains a farinaceous nut, of admirable use in seminal weaknesses. They are also given to throw out the yaws." [Au.]

31. Watery or blood-tinged discharge from a wound.

Round knobby spots deform, but the disease
275 Seems at a pause: then let the learned leach
Give, in due dose, live-silver[32] from the mine;
Till copious spitting the whole taint exhaust.—
Nor thou repine, tho' half-way round the sun,
This globe, her annual progress shall absolve;
280 Ere, clear'd, thy slave from all infection shine.
Nor then be confident; successive crops
Of defoedations[33] oft will spot the skin:
These thou, with turpentine and guaiac pods,
Reduc'd by coction to a wholesome draught,
285 Total remove, and give the blood its balm.

    SAY, as this malady but once infests
The sons of Guinea, might not skill ingraft
(Thus, the small-pox are happily convey'd;)
This ailment early to thy Negroe-train?

290   YET, of the ills which torture Libya's sons,
Worms tyrannize the worst. They, Proteus-like,[34]
Each symptom of each malady assume;
And, under every mask, the assassins kill.
Now, in the guise of horrid spasms, they writhe
295 The tortured body, and all sense o'er-power.
Sometimes, like Mania, with her head downcast,
They cause the wretch in solitude to pine;
Or frantic, bursting from the strongest chains,
To frown with look terrific, not his own.
300 Sometimes like Ague, with a shivering mien,
The teeth gnash fearful, and the blood runs chill:
Anon the ferment maddens in the veins,
And a false vigour animates the frame.
Again, the dropsy's bloated mask they steal;
305 Or, "melt with minings of the hectic fire."[35]

    SAY, to such various mimic forms of death;
What remedies shall puzzled art oppose?—
Thanks to the Almighty, in each path-way hedge,
Rank cow-itch[36] grows, whose sharp unnumber'd stings,
310 Sheath'd in Melasses, from their dens expell,
Fell dens of death, the reptile lurking foe.—
A powerful vermifuge, in skilful hands,

The worm-grass proves; yet, even in hands of skill,
Sudden, I've known it dim the visual ray
For a whole day and night. There are who use   315
(And sage Experience justifies the use)
The mineral product of the Cornish mine;[37]
Which in old times, ere Britain laws enjoyed,
The polish'd Tyrians, monarchs of the main,
In their swift ships convey'd to foreign realms: 320
The sun by day, by night the northern star,
Their course conducted—Mighty commerce, hail!
By thee the sons of Attic's sterile land,
A scanty number, laws impos'd on Greece:
Nor aw'd they Greece alone; vast Asia's King,   325
Tho' girt by rich arm'd myriads, at their frown
Felt his heart whither on his farthest throne.
Perennial source of population thou!
While scanty peasants plough the flowery plains
Of purple Enna; from the Belgian fens,   330
What swarms of useful citizens spring up,
Hatch'd by thy fostering wing. Ah where is flown
That dauntless free-born spirit, which of old,
Taught them to shake off the tyrannic yoke
Of Spains insulting King; on whose wide realms,   335
The sun still shone with undiminished beam?
Parent of wealth! in vain, coy nature hoards
Her gold and diamonds; toil, thy firm compeer,
And industry of unremitting nerve,
Scale the cleft mountain, the loud torrent brave,   340
Plunge to the center, and thro' Nature's wiles,
(Led on by skill of penetrative soul)
Her following close, her secret treasures find,
To pour them plenteous on the laughing world.
On thee Sylvanus,[38] thee each rural god,   345

---

32. Mercury.

33. Defilements.

34. Like the classical sea god, Proteus, who could change his shape.

35. See John Armstrong's *The Art of Preserving Health, A Poem* (1744).

36. "See notes in Book II." [Au.]

---

37. "Tin-filings are a better vermifuge than tin in powder. The western parts of Britain, and the neighbouring isles, have been famous for this useful metal from the remotest antiquity; for we find from Strabo, that the Phænicians made frequent voyages to those parts (which they called *Cassiterides* from Κασσττερον, stannum) in quest of that commodity, which turned out so beneficial to them, that a pilot of that nation stranded his vessel, rather than show a Roman ship, that watched him, the way to those mines. For this public spirited action, he was amply rewarded, says that accurate writer, upon his return to his country. The Romans, however, soon made themselves masters of the secret, and shared with them in the profit of that merchandize." [Au.]

38. The Roman god of the woods and fields.

On thee chief Ceres,[39] with unfailing love
And fond distinction, emulously gaze.
In vain hath nature pour'd vast seas between
Far-distant kingdoms; endless storms in vain
350 With double night brood o'er them; thou dost throw,
O'er far-divided nature's realms, a chain
To bind in sweet society mankind.
By thee white Albion,[40] once a barbarous clime,
Grew fam'd for arms, for wisdom, and for laws;
355 By thee she holds the balance of the world,
Acknowledg'd now sole empress of the main.
Coy though thou art, and mutable of love,
There may'st thou ever fix thy wandering steps;
While Eurus[41] rules the wide atlantic foam!
360 By thee, thy favorite, great Columbus found
That world, where now thy praises I rehearse
To the resounding main and palmy shore;
And Lusitania's[42] chiefs those realms explor'd,
Whence negroes spring, the subject of my song.

365   NOR pine the Blacks, alone, with real ills,
That baffle oft the wisest rules of art:
They likewise feel imaginary woes;
Woes no less deadly. Luckless he who owns
The slave, who thinks himself bewitch'd; and whom,
370 In wrath, a conjuror's snake-mark'd[43] staff hath
      struck!
They mope, love silence, every friend avoid;
They inly pine; all aliment reject;
Or insufficient for nutrition take:
Their features droop; a sickly yellowish hue

------

39. The Roman goddess of agriculture.

40. A poetic name for England.

41. The Roman god of the southeast wind.

42. An ancient name for Portugal.

43. "The negroe-conjurers, or Obia-men, as they are called, carry about them a staff, which is marked with frogs, snakes, &c. The blacks imagine that its blow, if not mortal, will at least occasion long and troublesome disorders. A belief in magic is inseparable from human nature, but those nations are most addicted thereto, among whom learning, and of course, philosophy have least obtained. As in all other countries, so in Guinea, the conjurers, as they have more understanding, so are they almost always more wicked than the common herd of their deluded countrymen; and as the negroe-magicians can do mischief, so they can also do good on a plantation, provided they are kept by the white people in proper subordination." [Au.]

Their skin deforms; their strength and beauty fly.   375
Then comes the feverish fiend, with firy eyes,
Whom drowth, convulsions, and whom death surround,
Fatal attendants! if some subtle slave
(Such, Obia-men are stil'd) do not engage,
To save the wretch by antidote or spell.   380

   IN magic spells, in Obia, all the sons
Of sable Africk trust:—Ye, sacred nine!
(For ye each hidden preparation know)
Transpierce the gloom, which ignorance and fraud
Have render'd awful; tell the laughing world   385
Of what these wonder-working charms are made.

   FERN root cut small, and tied with many a knot;
Old teeth extracted from a white man's skull;
A lizard's skeleton; a serpent's head:
These mix'd with salt, and water from the spring,   390
Are in a phial pour'd; o'er these the leach
Mutters strange jargon, and wild circles forms.

   OF this possest, each negroe deems himself
Secure from poison; for to poison they
Are infamously prone: and arm'd with this,   395
Their sable country dæmons they defy,
Who fearful haunt them at the midnight hour,
To work them mischief. This, diseases fly;
Diseases follow: such its wonderous power!
This o'er the threshold of their cottage hung,   400
No thieves break in; or, if they dare to steal,
Their feet in blotches, which admit no cure,
Burst loathsome out: but should its owner filch,
As slaves were ever of the pilfering kind,
This from detection screens;—so conjurors swear.   405

   'TILL morning dawn, and Lucifer withdraw
His beamy chariot; let not the loud bell
Call forth thy negroes from their rushy couch:
And ere the sun with mid-day fervour glow,
When every broom-bush[44] opes her yellow flower;   410
Let thy black labourers from their toil desist:

------

44. "This small plant, which grows in every pasture, may, with propriety, be termed an American clock; for it begins every forenoon at eleven to open its yellow flowers, which about one are fully expanded, and at two closed. The jalap, or marvel of Peru, unfolds its petals between five and six in the evening, which shut again as soon as night comes on, to open again in the cool of the morning. This plant is called four o'clock by the natives, and bears either a yellow or purple-coloured flower." [Au.]

Nor till the broom her every petal lock,
Let the loud bell recall them to the hoe.
But when the jalap her bright tint displays,
415 When the solanum[45] fills her cup with dew,
And crickets, snakes, and lizards 'gin their coil;
Let them find shelter in their cane-thatch'd huts:
Or, if constrain'd unusual hours to toil,
(For even the best must sometimes urge their gang)
420 With double nutriment reward their pains.

HOWE'ER insensate some may deem their slaves,
Nor 'bove the bestial rank; far other thoughts
The muse, soft daughter of humanity!
Will ever entertain.—The Ethiop knows,
425 The Ethiop feels, when treated like a man;
Nor grudges, should necessity compell,
By day, by night, to labour for his lord.

NOT less inhuman, than unthrifty those;
Who, half the year's rotation round the sun,
430 Deny subsistence to their labouring slaves.
But would'st thou see thy negroe-train encrease,
Free from disorders; and thine acres clad
With groves of sugar: every week dispense
Or English beans, or Carolinian rice;
435 Iërne's[46] beef, or Pensilvanian flour;
Newfoundland cod, or herrings from the main
That howls tempestuous round the Scotian isles!

YET some there are so lazily inclin'd,
And so neglectful of their food, that thou,
440 Would'st thou preserve them from the jaws of death;
Daily, their wholesome viands must prepare:
With these let all the young, and childless old,
And all the morbid share;—so heaven will bless,
With manifold encrease, thy costly care.

445 SUFFICE not this; to every slave assign
Some mountain-ground: or, if waste broken land
To thee belong, that broken land divide.
This let them cultivate, one day, each week;

And there raise yams, and there cassada's root:[47]
From a good dæmon's staff cassada sprang,   450
Tradition says, and Caribbees[48] believe;
Which into three the white-rob'd genius broke,
And bade them plant, their hunger to repel.
There let angola's bloomy bush supply,[49]
For many a year, with wholesome pulse their board.   455
There let the bonavist,[50] his fringed pods
Throw liberal o'er the prop; while ochra[51] bears
Aloft his slimy pulp, and help disdains.
There let potatos[52] mantle o'er the ground;

---

47. "To an ancient Caribbean, bemoaning the savage uncomfortable life of his countrymen, a deity clad in white apparel
appeared, and told him, he would have come sooner to have
taught him the ways of civil life, had he been addressed before.
He then showed him sharp-cutting stones to fell trees and build
houses; and bade him cover them with the palm leaves. Then he
broke his staff in three; which, being planted, soon after produced cassada. See Ogilvy's America." [Au.]

48. Carib Indians.

49. "This is called the *Pidgeon-pea,* and grows on a sturdy
shrub, that will last for years. It is justly reckoned among the
most wholesome legumens. The juice of the leaves, dropt into
the eye, will remove incipient films. The botanic name is
Cytisus." [Au.]

50. "This is the Spanish name of a plant, which produces an
excellent bean. It is a parasitical plant. There are five sorts of
bonavist, the green, the white, the moon-shine, the small or common; and, lastly, the black and read. The flowers of all are white
and papilionaceous; except the last, whose blossoms are purple.
They commonly bear in six weeks. Their pulse is wholesome,
though somewhat flatulent; especially those from the black and
the read. The pods are flattish, two or three inches long; and contain from three to five seeds in partitional cells." [Au.]

51. "Or *Ockro.* This shrub, which will last for years, produces a not less agreeable, than wholesome pod. It bears all the
year round. Being of a slimy and balsamic nature, it becomes a
truly medicinal aliment in dysenteric complaints. It is of the
Malva species. It rises to about four or five feet high, bearing, on
and near the summit, many yellow flowers; succeeded by green,
conic, fleshy pods, channelled into several grooves. There are as
many cells filled with small round seeds, as there are channels."
[Au.]

52. "I cannot positively say, whether these vines are of Indian original or not; but as in their fructification, they differ from
potatos at home, they probably are not European. They are
sweet. There are four kinds, the red, the white, the long, and
round: The juice of each may be made into a pleasant cool drink;
and, being distilled, yield an excellent spirit." [Au.]

---

45. "So some authors name the fire-weed, which grows
every where, and is the *datura* of Linnæus; whose virtues Dr.
Stork, at Vienna, has greatly extolled in a late publication. It
bears a white monopetalus flower, which opens always about
sun-set." [Au.]

46. Ireland's.

460 Sweet as the cane-juice is the root they bear.
　　There too let eddas[53] spring in order meet,
　　With Indian cale,[54] and foodful calaloo:[55]
　　While mint, thyme, balm, and Europe's coyer herbs,
　　Shoot gladsome forth, not reprobate the clime.

465   THIS tract secure, with hedges or of limes,
　　Or bushy citrons, or the shapely tree[56]
　　That glows at once with aromatic blooms,
　　And golden fruit mature. To these be join'd,
　　In comely neighbourhood, the cotton shrub;

470 In this delicious clime the cotton bursts
　　On rocky soils.—The coffee also plant;
　　White as the skin of Albion's lovely fair,
　　Are the thick snowy fragrant blooms it boasts:
　　Nor wilt thou, cocô, thy rich pods refuse;

475 Tho' years, and heat, and moisture they requires,
　　Ere the stone grind them to the food of health.
　　Of thee, perhaps, and of thy various sorts,
　　And that kind sheltering tree, thy mother nam'd,[57]
　　With crimson flowerets prodigally grac'd;

480 In future times, the enraptur'd muse may sing:
　　If public favour crown her present lay.

　　　　BUT let some antient, faithful slave erect
　　His sheltered mansion near; and with his dog,
　　His loaded gun, and cutlass, guard the whole:

485 Else negroe-fugitives, who skulk 'mid rocks
　　And shrubby wilds, in bands will soon destroy
　　Thy labourer's honest wealth; their loss and yours.

　　　　Perhaps, of Indian gardens I could sing,
　　Beyond what bloom'd on blest Phæacia's isle,

490 Or eastern climes admir'd in days of yore:
　　How Europe's foodful, culinary plants;

How gay Pomona's[58] ruby-tinctured births;
And gawdy Flora's[59] various-vested train;
Might be instructed to unlearn their clime,
And by due discipline adopt the sun.   495
The muse might tell what culture will entice
The ripened melon, to perfume each month;
And with the anana[60] load the fragrant board.
The muse might tell, what trees will best exclude
("Insuperable height of airiest shade")[61]   500
With their vast umbrage the noon's fervent ray.
Thee, verdant mammey,[62] first, her song should praise:
Thee, the first natives of these Ocean-isles,
Fell anthropophagi,[63] still sacred held;
And from thy large high-flavour'd fruit abstain'd, 505
With pious awe; for thine high-flavour'd fruit,
The airy phantoms of their friends deceas'd
Joy'd to regale on.—Such their simple creed.
The tamarind[64] likewise should adorn her theme,
With whose tart fruit the sweltering fever loves 510
To quench his thirst, whose breezy umbrage soon
Shades the pleas'd planter, shades his children long.
Nor, lofty cassia,[65] should she not recount
Thy woodland honours! See, what yellow flowers

---

53. "See notes on Book I. The French call this plant *Tayove*. It produces eatable roots every four months, for one year only." [Au.]

54. "This green, which is a native of the New World, equals any of the greens in the Old." [Au.]

55. "Another species of Indian pot-herb, no less wholesome than the preceding. These, with mezamby, and the Jamaica prickle-weed, yield to no esculent plants in Europe. This is an Indian name." [Au.]

56. "The orange tree." [Au.]

57. "See Book I. p.43." [Au.]

---

58. The Roman goddess of fruit.

59. The Roman goddess of flowers.

60. Pineappple.

61. See Milton, *Paradise Lost* IV. 138.

62. "This is a lofty, shady, and beautiful tree. Its fruit is as large as the largest melon, and of an exquisite smell, greatly superior to it in point of taste. Within the fruit are contained one or two large stones, which when distilled, give to spirits a ratafia flavour, and therefore the French call them *Les apricots de St. Domingue:* accordingly, *l'eaux des noiaux,* one of the best West-Indian cordials, is made from them. The fruit, eaten raw, is of an aperient quality; and made into sweet-meats, &c. is truly exquisite. This tree, contrary to most others in the New World, shoots up to a pyramidal figure: the leaves are uncommonly green; and it produces fruit, but once a year. The name is Indian. The English commonly call it *Mammey-sapota*. There are two species of it, the sweet, and the tart. The botanical name is *Achras*." [Au.]

63. Cannibals. Native Carib Indians were commonly assumed to be cannibals.

64. "See Book I. p. 44." [Au.]

65. "Both this tree and its mild purgative pulp are sufficiently known." [Au.]

515 Dance in the gale, and scent the ambient air;
While thy long pods, full-fraught with nectared sweets,
Relieve the bowels from their lagging load.
Nor chirimoia,[66] though these torrid isles
Boast not thy fruit, to which the anana yields
520 In taste and flavour, wilt thou coy refuse
Thy fragrant shade to beautify the scene.
But, chief of palms, and pride of Indian-groves,
Thee, fair palmeto,[67] should her song resound:
What swelling columns, form'd by Jones or Wren,[68]
525 Or great Palladio,[69] may with thee compare?
Not nice-proportion'd, but of size immense,
Swells the wild fig-tree, and should claim her lay:
For, from its numerous bearded twigs proceed
A filial train, stupendous as their fire,
530 In quick succession; and, o'er many a rood,
Extend their uncouth limbs; which not the bolt
Of heaven can scathe; nor yet the all-wasting rage
Of Typhon, or of hurricane, destroy.

Nor should, tho' small, the anata[70] not be sung:
Thy purple dye, the silk and cotton fleece   535
Delighted drink; thy purple dye the tribes
Of Northern-Ind,[71] a fierce and wily race,
Carouse, assembled; and with it they paint
Their manly make in many a horrid form,
To add new terrors to the face of war.   540
The muse might teach to twine the verdant arch,
And the cool alcove's lofty room adorn,
With ponderous granadillas,[72] and the fruit
Call'd water-lemon; grateful to the taste:
Nor should she not pursue the mountain-streams,   545
But pleas'd decoy them from their shady haunts,
In rills, to visit every tree and herb;
Or fall o'er fern-clad cliffs, with foaming rage;
Or in huge basons float, a fair expanse;
Or, bound in chains of artificial force,   550
Arise thro' sculptured stone, or breathing brass.—
But I'm in haste to furl my wind-worn sails,
And anchor my tir'd vessel on the shore.

IT much imports to build thy Negroe-huts,
Or on the sounding margin of the main,   555
Or on some dry hill's gently-sloping sides,
In streets, at distance due.—When near the beach,
Let frequent coco cast its wavy shade;

---

66. A small, tropical, fruit-bearing tree.

67. "This being the most beautiful of palms, nay, perhaps, superior to any other known tree in the world, has with propriety obtained the name of *Royal*. The botanical name is *Palma Maxima*. It will shoot up perpendicularly to an hundred feet and more. The stem is perfectly circular; only towards the root, and immediately under the branches at top, it bulges out. The bark is smooth, and of an ash-brown colour, except at the top where it is green. It grows very fast, and the seed from whence it springs is not bigger than an acorn. In this, as in all the palm-genus, what the natives call *Cabbage* is found; but it resembles in taste an almond, and is in fact the pith of the upper, or greenish part of the stem. But it would be the most unpardonable luxury to cut down so lovely a tree, for so mean a gratification; especially as the wild, or mountain cabbage tree, sufficiently supplies the table with that esculent. I never ride past the charming vista of royal palms on the Cayon-estate of Daniel Mathew, Esq; in St. Christopher, without being put in mind of the pillars of the Temple of the Sun at Palmyra. The tree grows on the tops of hills, as well as in valleys; its hard cortical part makes very durable laths for houses. There is a smaller species not quite so beautiful." [Au.]

68. Inigo Jones (1573–1652) and Sir Christopher Wren (1632–1723) were important English architects.

69. Andrea Palladio (1508–80), a prominent Italian architect.

70. "Or *Anotto*, or *Arnotta;* thence corruptly called *Indian Otter*, by the English. The tree is about the size of an ordinary apple-tree. The French call it *Rocou;* and send the farina home as a paint, &c. for which purpose the tree is cultivated by them in their islands. The flower is pentapetalous, of a bluish and spoon-like appearance. The yellow filaments are tipped with purplish apices. The style proves the rudiment of the succeeding pod, which is of a conic shape, an inch and a half long. This is divided into many cells, which contain a great number of small seeds, covered with a red farina." [Au.]

71. North American Indians.

72. "This is the Spanish name, and is a species of the *passiflora*, or passion-flower, called by Linnæus *Musa*. The seeds and pulp, through which the seeds are dispersed, are cooling, and grateful to the palate. This, as well as the water-lemon, bell-apple, or honeysuckle, as it is named, being parasitical plants, are easily formed into cooling arbors, than which nothing can be more grateful in warm climates. Both fruits are wholesome. The granadilla is commonly eat with sugar, on account of its tartness, and yet the pulp is viscid. Plumier calls it *Granadilla, latefolia, fructu maliformi*. It grows best in shady places. The unripe fruit makes an excellent pickle." [Au.]

'Tis Neptune's tree; and, nourish'd by the spray,
560 Soon round the bending stem's aerial height,
Clusters of mighty nuts, with milk and fruit
Delicious fraught, hang clattering in the sky.
There let the bay-grape,[73] too, its crooked limbs
Project enormous; of impurpled hue
565 Its frequent clusters grow. And there, if thou
Woud'st make the sand yield salutary food,
Let Indian millet[74] rear its corny reed,
Like arm'd battalions in array of war.
But, round the upland huts, bananas plant;
570 A wholesome nutriment bananas yield,
And sun-burnt labour loves its breezy shade.
Their graceful screen let kindred plantanes join,
And with their broad vans shiver in the breeze;
So flames design'd, or by imprudence caught,
575 Shall spread no ruin to the neighbouring roof.

YET nor the sounding margin of the main,
Nor gently sloping side of breezy hill,
Nor streets, at distance due, imbower'd in trees;
Will half the health, or half the pleasure yield,
580 Unless some pitying naiad deign to lave,
With an unceasing stream, thy thirsty bounds.

ON festal days; or when their work is done;
Permit thy slaves to lead the choral dance,
To the wild banshaw's[75] melancholy sound.

Responsive to the sound, head feet and frame   585
Move aukwardly harmonious; hand in hand
Now lock'd, the gay troop circularly wheels,
And frisks and capers with intemperate joy.
Halts the vast circle, all clap hands and sing;
While those distinguish'd for their heels and air,   590
Bound in the center, and fantastic twine.
Meanwhile some stripling, from the choral ring,
Trips forth; and, not ungallantly, bestows
On her who nimblest hath the greensward beat,
And whose flush'd beauties have inthrall'd his soul,   595
A silver token of his fond applause.
Anon they form in ranks; nor inexpert
A thousand tuneful intricacies weave,
Shaking their sable limbs; and oft a kiss
Steal from their partners; who, with neck reclin'd,   600
And semblant scorn, resent the ravish'd bliss.
But let not thou the drum their mirth inspire;
Nor vinous spirits: else, to madness fir'd,
(What will not bacchanalian frenzy dare?)
Fell acts of blood, and vengeance they pursue.   605

COMPEL by threats, or win by soothing arts,
Thy slaves to wed their fellow slaves at home;
So shall they not their vigorous prime destroy,
By distant journeys, at untimely hours,
When muffled midnight decks her raven-hair   610
With the white plumage of the prickly vine.[76]

WOULD'ST thou from countless ails preserve thy
gang;
To every Negroe, as the candle-weed[77]
Expands his blossoms to the cloudy sky,
And moist Aquarius melts in daily showers;   615
A woolly vestment give, (this Wiltshire weaves)
Warm to repel chill Night's unwholesome dews:

---

73. "Or sea-side grape, as it is more commonly called. This is a large, crooked, and shady tree, (the leaves being broad, thick, and almost circular;) and succeeds best in sandy places. It bears large clusters of grapes once a year; which, when ripe, are not disagreeable. The stones, seeds, or *acini,* contained in them, are large in proportion; and, being reduced to a powder, are an excellent astringent. The bark of the tree has the same property. The grapes steept in water and fermented with sugar, make an agreeable wine." [Au.]

74. "Or maise. This is commonly called *Guinea-corn,* to distinguish it from the great or Indian-corn, that grows in the southern parts of North-America. It soon shoots up to a great height, often twenty feet high, and will ratoon like the other; but its blades are not so nourishing to horses as those of the great corn, although its seeds are more so, and rather more agreeable to the taste. The Indians, Negroes, and poor white people, make many (not unsavoury) dishes with them. It is also called *Turkey wheat.* The turpentine tree will also grow in the sand, and is most useful upon a plantation." [Au.]

75. "This is a sort of rude guitar, invented by the Negroes. It produces a wild pleasing melancholy sound." [Au.]

76. "This beautiful white rosaceous flower is as large as the crown of one's hat, and only blows at midnight. The plant, which is prickly and attaches itself firmly to the sides of houses, trees, &c. produces a fruit, which some call *Wythe Apple,* and others with more propriety, *Mountain strawberry.* But though it resembles the large Chili-strawberry in looks and size; yet being inelegant of taste, it is seldom eaten. The botanical name is *Cereus scandens minor.* The rind of the fruit is here and there studded with tufts of small sharp prickles." [Au.]

77. "This shrub, which produces a yellow flower somewhat resembling a narcissus, makes a beautiful hedge, and blows about November. It grows wild every where. It is said to be a diuretic, but this I do not know from experience." [Au.]

While strong coarse linen, from the Scotian loom,
Wards off the fervours of the burning day.

620   THE truly great, tho' from a hostile clime,
The sacred Nine embalm; then, Muses, chant,
In grateful numbers, Gallic Lewis'[78] praise:
For private murder quell'd; for laurel'd arts,
Invented, cherish'd in his native realm;
625 For rapine punish'd; for grim famine fed;
For sly chicane expell'd the wrangling bar;
And rightful Themis[79] seated on her throne:
But, chief, for those mild laws his wisdom fram'd,
To guard the Æthiop from tyrannic sway!

630   DID such, in these green isles which Albion claims,
Did such obtain; the muse, at midnight-hour,
This last brain-racking study had not ply'd:
But, sunk in slumbers of immortal bliss,
To bards had listned on a fancied Thames!

635   ALL hail, old father Thames! tho' not from far
Thy springing waters roll; nor countless streams,
Of name conspicuous, swell thy watery store;
Tho' thou, no Plata,[80] to the sea devolve
Vast humid offerings; thou art king of streams:
640 Delighted Commerce broods upon thy wave;
And every quarter of this sea-girt globe
To thee due tribute pays; but chief the world
By great Columbus found, where now the muse
Beholds, transported, slow vast fleecy clouds,
645 Alps pil'd on Alps romantically high,
Which charm the sight with many a pleasing form.
The moon, in virgin-glory, gilds the pole,
And tips yon tamarinds, tips yon Cane-crown'd vale,
With fluent silver; while unnumbered stars
650 Gild the vast concave with their lively beams.
The main, a moving burnish'd mirror, shines;

No noise is heard, save when the distant surge
With drouzy murmurings breaks upon the shore!—

AH me, what thunders roll! the sky's on fire!
Now sudden darkness muffles up the pole!   655
Heavens! what wild scenes, before the affrighted sense,
Imperfect swim!—See! in that flaming scroll,
Which Time unfolds, the future germs bud forth,
Of mighty empires! independent realms!—
And must Britannia, Neptune's favorite queen,   660
Protect'ress of true science, freedom, arts;
Must she, ah! must she, to her offspring crouch?
Ah, must my Thames, old Ocean's favourite son,
Resign his trident to barbaric streams;
His banks neglected, and his waves unsought,   665
No bards to sing them, and no fleets to grace?—
Again the fleecy clouds amuse the eye,
And sparkling stars the vast horizon gild—
She shall not crouch; if Wisdom guide the helm,
Wisdom that bade loud Fame, with justest praise,   670
Record her triumphs! bade the lacquaying winds
Transport, to every quarter of the globe,
Her winged navies! bade the scepter'd sons
Of earth acknowledge her pre-eminence!—
She shall not crouch; if these Cane ocean-isles,   675
Isles which on Britain for their all depend,
And must for ever; still indulgent share
Her fostering smile: and other isles be given,
From vanquish'd foes.—And, see, another race!
A golden aera dazzles my fond sight!   680
That other race, that long'd-for aera, hail!

THE BRITISH GEORGE[81] NOW REIGNS, THE PA-
   TRIOT KING!
BRITAIN SHALL EVER TRIUMPH O'ER THE
   MAIN.

---

78. King Louis XIV of France.

79. A Greek goddess, guardian of divine law and order.

80. "One of the largest rivers of South America." [Au.]

81. King George III (1738–1820) reigned from 1760 until 1820.

ROBERT BEVERLEY (1673–1722)

Robert Beverley was born in Virginia and inherited several plantations at the time his father died. Like many large landholders, he divided his energies between his plantation and public service. In his early adulthood, he served in a number of important public posts, including clerk of the General Court, clerk of Council, clerk of the General Assembly, and burgess from Jamestown. During his years in public life, Beverley was often critical of the royal management of Virginia because it took control out of the hands of the colonials whose livelihoods were dependent upon their plantations and a mercantile system that was run from England.

In 1703, while in England on business, Beverley was asked to "correct" for publication a manuscript of John Oldmixon's *British Empire in America*. Saying that Oldmixon was too flawed to be worth correcting, he refused to edit Oldmixon's narrative, which used material on Virginia provided by Beverley's brother-in-law, William Byrd II. Reading Oldmixon's history inspired Beverley to write his own *History and Present State of Virginia* (1705). He used his history as a means by which to examine the work of several royal governors, who, in Beverley's view, used their posts to infringe on Virginians' liberties. This was a theme he was fond of during these years. While he was in England, Beverley discovered what he considered to be a plot by the current governor, Francis Nicholson, to curtail the rights of Virginians. He wrote his thoughts in letters to friends back in Virginia, and his comments were uncovered by those sympathetic to the royal governor. Nicholson removed Beverley from the office of clerk of the court of King and Queen County. For the rest of his life, Beverley focused his energies on his own plantation, where he attempted to grow grapes and establish wine making in Virginia, redesigned his estate into what he considered to be a model of Indian simplicity, and revised his *History,* softening much of the political commentary. The revised version was published in the year of his death, 1722.

Beverley's *History,* like many accounts of colonial areas, was a mixture of colonial history, natural science, and ethnography, all merged with speculation on the future potential for Europeans and British people who engaged in colonization. For the history of the earliest settlement of Virginia, Beverley relied heavily on John Smith's *General History of Virginia* (1624). Yet Beverley's interpretation of the colony's history was strongly influenced by his Whig views, which emphasized English liberties based on so-called ancient charters and charter rights while directly criticizing perceived infringements by the Crown on indissoluble liberties. In addition to including political commentary, however, the *History* included highly laudatory descriptions of local Indians and their culture. Beverley's closing section predicted a bright future for Virginia, on the basis of ideals of liberty that were affiliated with John Locke's conception of the social contract, an agreement among people so that they could engage in mutual self-protection but have their personal liberty preserved.

from HISTORY AND PRESENT STATE OF VIRGINIA (1705)[1]

from BOOK I • SHEWING WHAT HAPPEN'D IN THE FIRST ATTEMPTS TO SETTLE VIRGINIA, BEFORE THE DISCOVERY OF CHESAPEAK BAY

from CHAPTER 2 • Containing an Account of the First Settlement of Chesapeak Bay

. . . [A]nd the first great River they search'd, whose *Indian* Name was *Powhatan,* they call'd *James* River, after the King's own Name.[2]

----

1. Beverley's *History and Present State of Virginia,* originally published in 1705, serves as the basis for this selection. In the 1722 revision of the *History,* Beverley lessened both the severity of his critique of British leaders and the enthusiasm of his praise of the Indians.

2. This section of the narrative refers to the exploring and settlement activities of John Smith and his party in 1606.

C.15. Before they would make any Settlement here, they made a full Search of *James* River; and then by an unanimous Consent pitched upon a *Peninsula* about Fifty Miles up the River; which, besides the Goodness of the Soil, was esteem'd as most fit, and capable to be made a Place both of Trade and Security, Two Thirds thereof being environ'd by the main River, which affords good Anchorage all along; and the other Third by a small narrow River, capable of receiving many Vessels of an Hundred Tun, quite up as high as till it meets within Thirty Yards of the main River again, and where generally in Spring-Tides it overflows into the main River: By which Means the Land they chose to pitch their Town upon, has obtain'd the Name of an Island. In this back River Ships and small Vessels may ride lashed to one another, and moor'd a Shore secure from all Wind and Weather whatsoever.

The Town, as well as the River, had the Honour to be called by King *James's* Name. The whole Island thus enclosed contains about Two Thousand Acres of high Land, and several Thousands of very good and firm Marsh, and is an extraordinary good Pasture as any in that Country.

By Means of the narrow Passage, this Place was of great Security to them from the *Indian* Enemy: And if they had then known of the Biting of the Worm in the Salts, they would have valued this Place upon that Account also, as being free from that Mischief.[3]

C.16. They were no sooner settled in all this Happiness and Security, but they fell into Jars and Dissentions among themselves, by a greedy Grasping at the *Indian* Treasures, envying and overreaching one another in that Trade.

After Five Weeks Stay before this Town, the Ships return'd Home again, leaving One Hundred and Eight Men settled in the Form of Government before spoken of.

After the Ships were gone, the same sort of Feuds and Disorders happen'd continually among them, to the unspeakable Damage of the Plantation.

The *Indians* were the same there as in all other Places; at first very fair and friendly, tho' afterwards they gave great Proofs of their Deceitfulness. However, by the Help of the *Indian* Provisions, the *English* chiefly subsisted till the Return of the Ships the next Year; when Two Vessels were sent thither full freighted with Men and Provisions for Supply of the Plantation, one of which only arriv'd directly, and the other being beat off to the *Carribbee* Islands, did not arrive till the former was sail'd hence again.

C.17. In the Interval of these Ships returning from *England,* the *English* had a very advantageous Trade with the *Indians;* and might have made much greater Gains of it, and managed it both to the greater Satisfaction of the *Indians,* and the greater Ease and Security of themselves; if they had been under any Rule, or subject to any Method in Trade, and not left at Liberty to outvie or outbid one another; by which they not only cut short their own Profit, but created Jealousies and Disturbances among the *Indians,* by letting one have a better Bargain than another: For they being unaccustom'd to barter, such of them as had been hardest dealt by in their Commodities, thought themselves cheated and abused; and so conceiv'd a Grudge against the *English* in general, making it a National Quarrel: And this seems to be the original Cause of most of their subsequent Misfortunes by the *Indians.*

What also gave a greater Interruption to this Trade, was an Object that drew all their Eyes and Thoughts aside, even from taking the necessary Care for their Preservation, and for the Support of their Lives; which was this; They found in a Neck of Land, on the Back of *James-Town-Island,* a fresh Stream of Water springing out of a small Bank, which wash'd down with it a yellow sort of Dust-Isinglass,[4] which being cleansed by the fresh streaming of the Water, lay shining in the Bottom of that limpid Element, and stirr'd up in them an unseasonable and inordinate Desire after Riches: For they, taking all to be Gold that glister'd, run into the utmost Distraction, neglecting both the necessary Defence of their Lives from the *Indians,* and the Support of their Bodies by securing of Provisions; absolutely relying, like *Midas,* upon the Almighty Power of Gold,[5] thinking, that where this was in plenty nothing could be wanting: But they soon grew sensible of their Error; and found that if this gilded Dirt had been real Gold, it could have been of no Advantage to them. For, by their Negligence, they were reduced to an exceeding Scarcity of Provisions, and that little they had, was lost by the Burning of their Town, while all Hands were employ'd upon this imaginary Golden Treasure; so that they were forced to live for sometime upon the wild Fruits of the Earth, and upon Crabs, Muscles, and such like, not having a Day's Provision before-hand; as some of the laziest *Indians,* who have no Pleasure in Exercise, and won't be at the Pains to fish and hunt: And, indeed, not so well as they neither; For by this careless neglecting of their Defence against the *Indians,* many of 'em were destroy'd by that cruel People; and the Rest durst not venture abroad, but were forced to be content with what fell just into their Mouths.

C.18. In this Condition they were, when the first Ship of the Two before-mention'd came to their Assistance, but their Golden Dreams overcame all Difficulties: They spoke not, nor thought of any thing but Gold, and that was all the Lading that most of them were willing to take Care for; accordingly they put into this Ship all the yellow Dirt they had gathered, and what Skins and Furs they had trucked for; and filling her up with Cedar, sent her away.

After she was gone, the other Ship arrived, which they stow'd likewise with this supposed Gold-Dust, designing never to be poor again; filling her up with Cedar and Clapboard.

---

3. Elsewhere Beverley described "seedling-worms" in the rivers feeding into Chesapeake Bay that in summer attacked the timber of ships and boats.

4. A powdered muscovite (a crystalline mineral).

5. In Greek mythology, Dionysus gave Midas his wish that everything he touch turn to gold.

Those Two Ships being thus dispatched, they made several Discoveries in *James* River, and up *Chesapeak* Bay, by the Undertaking and Management of Capt. *John Smith:* And the Year 1608 was the first Year in which they gather'd *Indian* Corn of their own planting.

While these Discoveries were making by Capt. *Smith,* Matters run again into Confusion in *James* Town; and several uneasie People, taking Advantage of his Absence, attempted to desert the Settlement, and run away with the small Vessel that was left to attend upon it; for Capt. *Smith* was the only Man among them that could manage the Discoveries with Success, and he was the only Man too that could keep the Settlement in Order. Thus the *English* continued to give themselves as much Perplexity by their own Distraction, as the *Indians* did by their Watchfulness and Resentments. . . .

C.21. While these Things were acting in *Bermudas,*[6] Capt. *Smith* being very much burnt by the accidental Firing of some Gun-Powder, as he was upon a Discovery in his Boat, was forced for his Cure sake, and the Benefit of a Surgeon, to take his Passage for *England* in a Ship that was then upon the Point of Sailing.

Several of the Nine Ships that came out with the Three Governours arrived, with many of the Passengers; some of which in their Humours wou'd not submit to the Government there, pretending the New Commission destroy'd the Old one; that Governours were appointed instead of a President, and that they themselves were to be of the Council; and so wou'd assume an independent Power, inspiring the People with Disobedience; by which Means they became frequently exposed in great Parties to the Cruelty of the *Indians;* all sorts of Discipline was laid aside, and their necessary Defence neglected; so that the *Indians* taking Advantage of those Divisions, form'd a Stratagem to destroy them Root and Branch, and indeed they did cut many of 'em off, by massacring whole Companies at a time; so that all the Out-Settlements were deserted, and the People that were not destroy'd took Refuge in *James-Town,* except the small Settlement at *Kiquotan,* where they had built themselves a little Fort, and call'd it *Algernoon* Fort: And yet, for all this, they

continued their Disorders, wasting their old Provisions, and neglecting to gather others; so that they who remain'd alive were all near famish'd, having brought themselves to that Pass, that they durst not stir from their own Doors to gather the Fruits of the Earth, or the Crabs and Mussels from the Water-side: Much less to hunt or catch wild Beasts, Fish or Fowl, which were found in great Abundance there. They continued in these scanty Circumstances till they were at last reduced to such Extremity, as to eat the very Hides of their Horses, and the Bodies of the *Indians* they had killed; and sometimes also upon a Pinch they wou'd not disdain to dig them up again to make a homely Meal of after they had been buried. And that Time is to this Day remember'd by the Name of the *Starving Time.*

Thus a few Months indiscreet Management brought such an Infamy upon the Country, that to this Day it cannot be wiped away: And the Sicknesses occasion'd by this bad Diet, or rather want of Diet are unjustly remember'd to the Disadvantage of the Country, as a Fault in the Climate; which was only the Foolishness and Indiscretion of those who assumed the Power of Governing. I call it assumed because the New Commission mention'd, by which they pretended to be of the Council, was not in all this time arrived, but remain'd in *Bermudas* with the new Governours.

Here I can't but admire the Care, Labour, Courage and Understanding that Capt. *John Smith* show'd in the Time of his Administration; who not only founded, but also preserved all these Settlements in good Order, while he was amongst them. And without him, they had certainly all been destroy'd, either by Famine, or the Enemy long before; tho' the Country naturally afforded Subsistence enough, even without any other Labour than that of Gathering and Preserving its Spontaneous Provisions.

For the first Three Years that Capt. *Smith* was with them, they never had in that whole Time above Six Months *English* Provisions. But as soon as he had left 'em to themselves, all went to Ruine; for the *Indians* had no longer any Fear for themselves, or Friendship for the *English.* And Six Months after this Gentleman's Departure, the 500 Men that he left were reduced to Threescore; and they too must of Necessity have starved, if their Relief had been with-held a Week longer.

C.22. In the mean time, the Three Governours put to Sea from *Bermudas* in their Two small Vessels, with their Company, to the Number of One Hundred and Fifty, and in Fourteen Days, *viz.* the 25th of *May,* 1610. they arrived

---

6. The island was Bermuda. A hurricane stranded the ship, the *Sea Venture,* which carried Gates, Somers, and Newport with 500 new emigrants sailing for Virginia in the summer of 1609. The passengers constructed two new vessels and reached Virginia in May 1610.

both together in *Virginia;* and went with their Vessels up to *James-Town,* where they found the small Remainder of the Five Hundred Men, in that melancholy Way I just now hinted.

C.23. Sir *Thomas Gates,*[7] Sir *George Summers,*[8] and Capt. *Newport,*[9] the Governours, were very compassionate of their Condition; and call'd a Council, wherein they inform'd them, that they had but Sixteen Days Provision Aboard; and therefore desired to know their Opinion, whether they would venture to Sea under such a Scarcity: Or if they resolved to continue in the Settlement, and take their Fortunes; they would stay likewise, and share the Provisions among them; but desired that their Determination might be speedy. They soon came to the Conclusion of returning for *England:* But because their Provisions were short, they resolved to go by the Banks of *New-foundland,* in Hopes of meeting with some of the Fishermen, (this being now the Season) and dividing themselves among their Ships for the greater Certainty of Provision, and for their better Accommodation.

According to this Resolution, they all went aboard, and fell down to *Hog-Island* the 9th of *June* at Night, and the next Morning to *Mulberry-Island* Point, which is Eighteen Miles below *James-Town,* and Thirty above the Mouth of the River; and there they spied a Long-Boat, which the Lord *Delawar* (who was just arrived with Three Ships)[10] had sent before him up the River sounding the Channel.

---

7. Thomas Gates (d. after 1621) went back to Britain and returned with another group of 300 emigrants in 1611. He served as governor, 1611–1612.

8. Somers was the mariner in charge of the voyage in 1609. The islands were dubbed Somers Islands and placed into the third Virginia charter (1612), when another group of English settlers arrived for permanent settlement.

9. Christopher Newport (1565?–1617) was originally placed in charge of the Virginia expedition in 1607, and he led the group in 1608 and again in 1610, as they traveled from Bermuda to Virginia.

10. Thomas West, Third Baron De La Warr (1577–1618), was a member of the council of the Virginia Company. He arrived at Jamestown with three ships and 150 settlers, equipped at his own expense, just in time to bring desperately needed supplies to the original colonists and dissuade them from returning to England. He rebuilt Jamestown, built forts, and brought order to the colony. In 1611 he returned to England, where he attempted to promote colonization. He died on a return voyage to Virginia.

His Lordship was made sole Governour, and was accompanied by several Gentlemen of Condition. He caused all the Men to return again to *James-Town;* resettled them with Satisfaction, and staid with them till *March* following; and then being very sick, he return'd for *England,* leaving about Two Hundred in the Colony. . . .

C.30. This Account[11] was presented to her Majesty, and graciously received: But before Captain *Smith* sail'd for *New-England,* the *Indian* Princess arrived at *London,* and her Husband took Lodgings for her at *Branford,* to be a little out of the Smoak of the City, whither Capt. *Smith,* with some of her Friends, went to see her, and congratulate her Arrival, letting her know the Address he had made to the Queen in her Favour.

Till this Lady arrived in *England,* she had all along been inform'd that Capt. *Smith* was dead, because he had been diverted from that Colony by making Settlements in the Second Plantation, now call'd *New-England:* For which Reason, when she see him, she seem'd to think herself much affronted, for that they had dared to impose so gross an Untruth upon her, and at first Sight of him turn'd away. It cost him a great deal of Intreaty, and some Hours Attendance, before she would do him the Honour to speak to him: But at last she was reconcil'd, and talk'd freely to him. She put him in mind of her former Kindnesses, and then upbraided him for his Forgetfulness of her, shewing by her Reproaches, that even a State of Nature teaches to abhor Ingratitude.

She had in her Retinue a Great Man of her own Nation, whose Name was *Uttamaccomack.* This Man had Orders from *Powhatan,* to count the People in *England,* and give him an Account of their Number. Now the *Indians* having no Letters among them, he at his going ashore provided a Stick, in which he was to make a Notch for every Man he see; but this Accomptant soon grew weary of that tedious Exercise, and threw his Stick away: And at his return, being asked by his King, *How many People there were; He desired him to count the Stars in the Sky, the Leaves upon the Trees, and the Sand on the Seashore, for so many People* (he said) *were in* England.

C.31. *Pocahontas* had many Honours done her by the Queen upon Account of Capt. *Smith's* Story; and being

---

11. John Smith's letter to Queen Anne describing the life of Pocahontas. This section details Pocahontas's situation.

introduced by the Lady *Delawarr,* she was frequently admitted to wait on her Majesty, and was publickly treated as a Prince's Daughter; she was carried to many Plays, Balls, and other publick Entertainments, and very respectfully receiv'd by all the Ladies about the Court. Upon all which Occasions she behaved her self with so much Decency, and show'd so much Grandure in her Deportment, that she made good the brightest Part of the Character Capt. *Smith* had given of her. In the mean while she gain'd the good Opinion of every Body, so much that the poor Gentleman her Husband had like to have been call'd to an Account for presuming to marry a Princess Royal without the King's Consent; because it had been suggested that he had taken Advantage of her being a Prisoner, and forc'd her to marry him. But upon a more perfect Representation of the Matter, his Majesty was pleased at last to declare himself satisfied.

Every Body paid this young Lady all imaginable Respect; and it is supposed, she wou'd have sufficiently acknowledged those Favours, had she lived to return to her own Country, by bringing the *Indians* to have a kinder Disposition towards the *English.* But upon her Return she was unfortunately taken ill at *Gravesend,* and died in a few Days after, giving great Testimony all the Time she lay sick, of her being a very good Christian. She left Issue one Son, nam'd *Thomas Rolfe,* whose Posterity is at this Day in good Repute in *Virginia.* . . .

C.95. These were the Afflictions[12] that Country labour'd under, when the Fourth Accident happen'd, *viz.* The Disturbance offer'd by the *Indians* to the Frontiers.

This was occasion'd, First, By the *Indians* on the Head of the Bay. Secondly, By the *Indians* on their own Frontiers.

First, The *Indians* at the Head of the Bay drove a constant Trade with the *Dutch* in *Monadas,* now call'd *New-York;* and, to carry on this, they used to come and return every Year by their Frontiers of *Virginia,* to purchase Skins and Furs of the *Indians* to the Southward. This Trade was carried on peaceably while the *Dutch* held *Monadas;* and the *Indians* used to call on the *English,* to whom they would sell part of their Furs, and with the rest go on to *Monadas.* But after the *English* came to possess

that Place, and understood the Advantages the *Virginians* made by the Trade of their *Indians,* they inspired them with such a Hatred to the Inhabitants of *Virginia,* that, instead of coming peaceably to trade with them, as they had done for several Years before, they afterwards never came, but only to commit Robberies and Murders upon the People.

Secondly, The *Indians* upon their own Frontiers were likewise inspir'd with ill Thoughts of 'em. For their *Indian* Merchants had lost a considerable Branch of their Trade they knew not how; and apprehended the Consequences of Sir *William Berkeley's* intended Discoveries, which were espoused by the Assembly, might take away the remaining Part of their Profit.[13] This made them very troublesome to the Neighbour *Indians;* who on their part, observing an unusual Uneasiness in the *English,* and being terrified by their rough Usage, immediately suspected some wicked Design against their Lives, and so fled to their remoter Habitations. This confirm'd the *English* in the Belief, that they had been the Murderers, till at last they provoked them to be so in Earnest.

C.96. This Addition of Mischief to Minds already full of Discontent, made People ready to vent all their Resentment against the poor *Indians.* There was nothing to be got by Tobacco; neither could they turn any other Manufacture to Advantage; so that most of the poorer Sort were willing to quit their unprofitable Employments, and go Voluntiers against the *Indians.*

At first they flock'd together tumultuously, running in Troops from one Plantation to another without a Head; till at last the seditious Humour of Colonel *Nath. Bacon,* led him to be of the Party. This Gentleman had been brought up at one of the Inns of Court in *England,* and had a moderate Fortune. He was young, bold, active, of an inviting Aspect, and powerful Elocution. In a Word, he was every way qualified to head a giddy and unthinking Multitude. Before he had been Three Years in the Country, he was, for his extraordinary Qualifications, made one of the Council, and in great Honour and Esteem among the People. For this Reason he no sooner gave Countenance to this riotous Mob, but they all presently fix'd their Eyes

---

12. The preceding passages describe "afflictions" suffered by planters: they had difficulty making money on tobacco; they experienced heavy taxes on their products and purchases; and they had to work despite conflict with the Indians.

13. Sir William Berkeley (1606–77) governed Virginia during a difficult time because of the shift from the monarchy to Cromwell's interregnum and then back again. Problems in the Virginia colony emerged on border areas with Indian peoples, and many colonists considered him unresponsive to their needs.

upon him for their General, and accordingly made their Addresses to him. As soon as he found this, he harangued them publickly. He aggravated the *Indian* Mischiefs, complaining, that they were occasion'd for want of a due Regulation of their Trade. He recounted particularly the other Grievances and Pressures they lay under; and pretended, that he accepted of their Command with no other Intention, but to do them and the Country Service, in which he was willing to encounter the greatest Difficulties and Dangers. He farther assured them, he would never lay down his Arms, till he had revenged their Sufferings upon the *Indians,* and redress'd all their other Grievances.

C.97. By these Insinuations he wrought his Men into so perfect a Unanimity, that they were one and all at his Devotion. He took care to exasperate them to the utmost, by representing all their Misfortunes. After he had begun to muster them, he dispatch'd a Messenger to the Governour, by whom he aggravated the Mischiefs done by the *Indians,* and desired a Commission of General to go out against them. This Gentleman was in so great Esteem at that Time with the Council, that the Governour did not think fit to give him a flat Refusal: But sent him Word, he would consult the Council, and return him a further Answer.

C.98. In the mean time, *Bacon* was expeditious in his Preparations, and having all Things in Readiness, began his March, depending on the Authority the People had given him. He would not lose so much Time, as to stay for his Commission; but dispatched several Messengers to the Governour to hasten it. On the other Hand, the Governour, instead of a Commission, sent positive Orders to him to disperse his Men, and come down in Person to him, upon Pain of being declared a Rebel.

from BOOK III • OF THE INDIANS, THEIR RELIGION, LAWS, AND CUSTOMS, IN WAR AND PEACE

from CHAPTER 1 • Of the Persons of the Indians, and Their Dress

C.1. The *Indians* are of the middling and largest stature of the *English:* They are straight and well proportion'd, having the cleanest and most exact Limbs in the World: They are so perfect in their outward frame, that I never heard of one single *Indian,* that was either dwarfish, crooked, bandy-legg'd, or otherwise mis-shapen. But if they have any such practice among them, as the *Romans* had, of exposing such Children till they dyed, as were weak and mis-shapen at their Birth, they are very shy of confessing it, and I could never yet learn that they had.

Their Colour, when they are grown up, is a Chesnut brown and tawny; but much clearer in their Infancy. Their Skin comes afterwards to harden and grow blacker, by greasing and Sunning themselves. They have generally coal black Hair, and very black Eyes, which are most commonly grac'd with that sort of Squint which many of the *Jews* are observ'd to have. Their Women are generally Beautiful, possessing an uncommon delicacy of Shape and Features, and wanting no Charm, but that of a fair Complexion.

C.2. The Men wear their Hair cut after several fanciful Fashions, sometimes greas'd, and sometimes painted. The Great Men, or better sort, preserve a long Lock behind for distinction. They pull their Beards up by the roots with a Muscle-shell; and both Men and Women do the same by the other parts of their Body for Cleanliness sake. The Women wear the Hair of the Head very long, either hanging at their Backs, or brought before in a single Lock, bound up with a Fillet of Peak, or Beads; sometimes also they wear it neatly tyed up in a Knot behind. It is commonly greased, and shining black, but never painted.

The People of Condition of both Sexes, wear a sort of Coronet on their Heads, from 4 to 6 inches broad, open at the top, and composed of Peak, or Beads, or else of both interwoven together, and workt into Figures, made by a nice mixture of the Colours. Sometimes they wear a Wreath of Dyed Furrs; as likewise Bracelets on their Necks and Arms. The Common People go bareheaded, only sticking large shining Feathers about their Heads, as their fancies lead them.

CHAPTER 5 • Of the Travelling, Reception, and Entertainment of the Indians

C.19. Their Travels they perform altogether on foot, the fatigue of which they endure to admiration. They make no other provision for their Journey, but their Gun or Bow, to supply them with Food for many hundreds miles together. If they carry any Flesh in their marches, they barbicue it, or rather dry it by degrees, at some distance, over the clear Coals of a Wood fire; just as the *Charibees* are said, to preserve the Bodies of their Kings and Great men from Corruption. Their Sauce to this dry Meat, (if they have any besides a good Stomach) is only a little Bears Oyl, or Oyl of Acorns; which last they force out, by boyling the Acorns in a strong Lye. Sometimes also in their Travels, each man takes with him a pint or quart of *Rockahomonie,* that is, the finest *Indian* Corn, parched, and beaten to powder. When they find their Stomach empty, (and cannot stay for the tedious Cookery of other things), they put about a spoonful of this into their Mouths, and drink a draught of Water upon it, which stays their Stomachs, and enables them to pursue their Journey without delay. But their main dependence is upon the Game they kill by the way, and the natural Fruits of the Earth. They take no care about Lodging in these Journeys: but content themselves with the shade of a Tree, or a little High Grass.

When they fear being discover'd, or follow'd by an Enemy in their Marches; they, every morning, having first agreed where they shall rendezvouze at night, disperse themselves into the Woods, and each takes a several way, that so the Grass or Leaves being but singly prest, may rise again, and not betray them. For the *Indians* are very artful in following a track, even where the Impressions are not visible to other People, especially if they have any advantage from the looseness of the Earth, from the stiffness of the Grass, or the stirring of the Leaves, which in the Winter Season lye very thick upon the ground; and likewise afterwards, if they do not happen to be burned.

When in their Travels, they meet with any Waters, which are not fordable, they make Canoas of Birch Bark, by slipping it whole off the Tree, in this manner. First, they gash the Bark quite round the Tree, at the length they wou'd have the Canoe of, then slit down the length from end to end; when that is done, they with their *Tomahawks* easily open the Bark, and strip it whole off. Then they force it open with Sticks in the middle, slope the underside of the ends, and sow them up, which helps to keep the Belly open; or if the Birch Trees happen to be small, they sow the Bark of two together; The Seams they dawb with Clay or Mud, and then pass over in these Canoes, by two, three, or more at a time, according as they are in bigness. By reason of the lightness of these Boats, they can easily carry them over Land, if they foresee that they are like to meet with any more Waters, that may impede their March; or else they leave them at the Water-side, making no farther account of them; except it be to repass the same Waters in their return. . . .

C.20. They have a peculiar way of receiving Strangers, and distinguishing whether they come as Friends or Enemies; tho they do not understand each others Language: and that is by a singular method of smoaking Tobacco; in which these things are always observ'd.

1. They take a Pipe much larger and bigger than the common Tobacco Pipe, expressly made for that purpose, with which all Towns are plentifully provided; they call them the Pipes of Peace.

2. This Pipe they always fill with Tobacco, before the Face of the Strangers, and light it.

3. The chief Man of the *Indians,* to whom the Strangers come, takes two or three Whiffs, and then hands it to the chief of the Strangers.

4. If the Stranger refuses to Smoke in it, 'tis a sign of War.

5. If it be Peace, the chief of the Strangers takes a Whiff or two in the Pipe, and presents it to the next Great Man of the Town, they come to visit; he, after taking two or three Whiffs, gives it back to the next of the Strangers, and so on alternately, until they have past all the persons of Note on each side, and then the Ceremony is ended.

After a little discourse, they march together in a friendly manner into the Town, and then proceed to explain the Business upon which they came. This Method is as general a Rule among all the *Indians* of those parts of *America,* as the Flag of Truce is among the *Europeans.* And tho the fashion of the Pipe differ, as well as the ornaments of it, according to the humour of the several Nations, yet 'tis a general Rule, to make these Pipes remarkably bigger, than those for common use, and to adorn them with beautiful Wings, and Feathers of Birds, as likewise with Peak, Beads, or other such Foppery. Father *Lewis Henepin*[14] gives a particular description of one, that he took notice of, among the *Indians,* upon the Lakes wherein he Travell'd. He describes it by the Name of *Calumet* of Peace, and his words are these, . . .

"This *Calumet* is the most mysterious thing in the World, among the Salvages of the Continent of the Northern *America;* for it is used in all their important transactions: However, it is nothing else but a large Tobacco pipe, made of red, black or white Marble: The Head is finely polished, and the Quill, which is commonly two

---

14. Louis Hennepin (1626–1705?), a Belgian Récollet, explored for France the Great Lakes and upper Mississippi River. He published three books about his work among the Indians and his travels.

foot and an half long, is made of a pretty strong Reed, or Cane, adorn'd with Feathers of all Colours, interlac'd with Locks of Womens Hair. They tye it to two Wings of the most curious Birds they can find, which makes their *Calumet* not much unlike *Mercury's* Wand, or that Staff Ambassadors did formerly carry, when they went to treat of Peace. They sheath that Reed into the Neck of Birds they call *Huars,* which are as big as our Geese, and spotted with black and white; or else of a sort of Ducks, which make their Nests upon Trees, tho the Water be their ordinary element; and whose Feathers be of many different colours. However, every Nation adorns their *Calumet* as they think fit, according to their own genius, and the Birds they have in their Country.

"Such a Pipe is a Pass and Safe Conduct among all the Allies of the Nation who has given it. And in all Embassies, the Ambassador carries that *Calumet,* as the Symbol of Peace, which is always respected: For, the Salvages are generally perswaded, that a great misfortune would befall them, if they violated the Publick Faith of the *Calumet.*

"All their Enterprizes, Declarations of War, or Conclusions of Peace, as well as all the rest of their Ceremonies, are Seal'd, (if I may be permitted to say so) with this *Calumet:* They fill that Pipe with the best Tobacco they have, and then present it to those, with whom they have concluded any great affair; and Smoke out of the same after them." . . .

℄.21. They have a remarkable way of entertaining all Strangers of Condition, which is perform'd after the following manner. First, the King or Queen, with a Guard, and a great Retinue, march out of the Town, a quarter or half a mile, and carry Mats for their accommodation; when they meet the Strangers, they invite them to sit down upon those Mats. Then they pass the Ceremony of the Pipe, and afterwards, having spent about half an hour in grave discourse, they get up all together, and march into the Town. Here the first Complement, is to wash the Courteous Travellers Feet; then he is treated at a Sumptuous Entertainment, serv'd up by a great number of Attendants. After which he is diverted with Antique *Indian* Dances, perform'd both by Men and Women, and accompany'd with great variety of Wild Musick. At this rate he is regal'd till Bed time; when a Brace of young Beautiful Virgins are chosen, to wait upon him that night, for his particular refreshment. These Damsels are to Undress this happy Gentleman, and as soon as he is in Bed, they gently lay themselves down by him, one on one side of him,

and the other on the other. They esteem it a breach of Hospitality, not to submit to every thing he desires of them. This kind Ceremony is us'd only to Men of great Distinction: And the Young Women are so far from suffering in their Reputation for this Civility, that they are envy'd for it by all the other Girls, as having had the greatest Honour done them in the World.

After this manner perhaps many of the Heroes were begotten in old time, who boasted themselves to be the Sons of some Way-faring God.

CHAPTER 6 • Of the Learning, and Languages of the Indians

℄.22. These *Indians* have no sort of Letters to express their words by, but when they would communicate any thing, that cannot be deliver'd by Message, they do it by a sort of Hieroglyphick, or representation of Birds, Beasts or other things, shewing their different meaning, by the various forms describ'd, and by the different position of the Figures.

Baron *Lahontan* in his second Volume of new Voyages,[15] has two extraordinary Chapters, concerning the Heraldry and Hieroglyphicks of the *Indians:* but I having had no opportunity of conversing with our *Indians,* since that Book came to my hands, nor having ever suspected them, to be acquainted with Heraldry, I am not able to say any thing upon that subject.

The *Indians* when they travel never so small a way, being much embroil'd in War one with another, use several marks painted upon their Shoulders, to distinguish themselves by, and show what Nation they are of. The usual mark is one, two or three Arrows; one Nation paints these Arrows upwards, another downwards, a third sideways, and others again use other distinctions, as in Tab. 2. from whence it comes to pass, that the *Virginia* Assembly took up the humour, of making Badges of Silver, Copper or Brass, of which they gave a sufficient number, to each Nation in amity with the *English,* and then made a Law, that the *Indians* should not travel among the *English* Plantations, without one of these Badges in their Company to

---

15. Louis-Armand de Lom d'Arce, Baron de Lahontan, published *Nouveau Voyages de M. Le Baron de Lahontan, dans l'Amerique Septentrionale,* a three-volume book of "travels" in French in 1703. It was translated into English that year and circulated widely.

show that they are Friends. And this is all the Heraldry, that I know is practis'd among the *Indians.*

C.23. Their Language differs very much, as antiently in the several parts of *Britain;* so that Nations at a moderate distance, do not understand one another. However, they have a sort of general Language, like what *Lahontan* calls the *Algonkine,* which is understood by the Chief men of many Nations, as *Latin* is in most parts of *Europe,* and *Lingua Franca* quite thro the *Levant.*

The general Language here us'd, is said to be that of the *Occaneeches,* tho they have been but a small Nation, ever since those parts were known to the *English:* but in what this Language may differ from that of the *Algonkines,* I am not able to determin.

WILLIAM BYRD II (1674–1744)

William Byrd II, of Westover, published few writings in his day, preferring instead to act like other members of the British colonial gentry (such as Dr. Alexander Hamilton of Maryland) and circulate his manuscripts widely among clusters of friends. During his lifetime, Byrd collected one of the most complete and diverse libraries of any British colonial, according to book historian Kevin Hayes, including a significant number of books in law and medicine, history and travel, and the arts and letters. In the London where he spent his youth and young adulthood, coffeehouse culture was at its height, and Byrd conceived of himself as a colonial gentleman even then, writing cryptic diary notes that revealed his every activity, from the morning milk he drank to his coffeehouse reading to his using prostitutes in the evening.

Byrd's father, William Byrd I, a goldsmith, had emigrated from London at age eighteen and inherited from an uncle the large estate of Westover in Virginia. He conceived that his son should be a gentleman, and saw that he was educated to take on a significant estate by preparing him to enter the planter class in the Virginia colony. Except for one short visit home, William Byrd II—having been sent to England for schooling when he was seven—remained in England until he was twenty-one. His private writings reveal much confusion at this time and much preoccupation with the role he was expected to play all his life. While still a young man, Byrd was invited to join the Royal Society (the most important association for scientists). He became a lawyer and associated with prominent members of British society as well as London literary society. When his father died in 1705, he returned to Virginia. In addition to managing his father's large plantations, Byrd took his father's place in two public offices, as a member of the House of Burgesses and receiver-general of Virginia. He would remain in the House of Burgesses for the rest of his life. Between 1715 and 1725, Byrd again lived in England, representing the House of Burgesses in England, often in opposition to the royal governor, Alexander Spotswood.

In 1726 Byrd returned to Virginia, where he restored his father's mansion and built his impressive library. In 1728, he was appointed as the head of Virginia's commission to establish the border between North Carolina and Virginia. Byrd kept a diary during the surveying expedition and later revised that diary into two written works, the first today called *The Secret History of the Dividing Line* and second, *The History of the Dividing Line.* The *Secret History* used humorous "character" names for the members of the commission and recounted the surveyors' private exploits during the trip, including their drinking, gambling, and amorous intentions and encounters. Perhaps more than any other writing from this era, the *Secret History* reveals the cultural mentality of Virginia's planter elite, its assumptions about the use of land and people, and its self-understanding regarding its own urbanity, culture, and sophistication.

Byrd used his diaries and his *Secret History* (which he circulated among friends) to complete a different narrative about the dividing-line expedition, one that he could circulate among a wider readership without bringing personal embarrassment to those who had actually participated in the venture. He restored the correct names of the surveyors, increased the natural history observations, added material from a history of Virginia that he had written in his youth, and de-emphasized the private escapades of the surveyors. The goal seems to have been to prepare a public document that would record the history of Virginia while clarifying why the expedition to create a dividing line between Virginia and the neighboring

North Carolina was, in Byrd's view, necessary. This second long manuscript, *The History of the Dividing Line,* Byrd circulated among his friends in England, but it was not published until the nineteenth century.

Byrd's two histories of the dividing line constitute his longest works, but like most highly educated British Americans, Byrd wrote a significant amount throughout his life in the genres typical of his day, including letters, diaries, travel narratives, and poetry. His diaries, like many eighteenth-century men's diaries, tracked his health and sense of personal morality. They are notable for the number of records of sexual encounters they relate, as well as for the information they provide regarding his visits to the plantation slave headquarters that were distant from the estate center. Because Byrd spent considerable amounts of time both in Virginia and England and maintained friendships in both places, his letters often attempted to depict one society to members of the other. The following letters were all written to friends in England.

from THE HISTORY OF THE DIVIDING LINE RUN IN THE YEAR 1728[1]

Before I enter upon the Journal of the Line between Virginia and North Carolina, it will be necessary to clear the way to it, by shewing how the other British Colonies on the Main have, one after the other, been carved out of Virginia, by Grants from his Majesty's Royal Predecessors. All that part of the Northern American Continent now under the Dominion of the King of Great Britain, and Stretching quite as far as the Cape of Florida, went *at first under the General Name of Virginia.*

The only Distinction, in those early Days, was, that all the Coast to the Southward of Chesapeake Bay was called South Virginia, and all to the Northward of it, North Virginia.

The first Settlement of this fine Country was owing to that great Ornament of the British Nation, Sir Walter Raleigh, who obtained a Grant thereof from Queen Elizabeth of ever-glorious Memory, by Letters Patent, dated March the 25th, 1584.

But whether that Gentleman ever made a Voyage thither himself is uncertain; because those who have favour'd the Public with an Account of His Life mention nothing of it. However, thus much may be depended on, that Sir Walter invited sundry persons of Distinction to Share in his Charter, and join their Purses with his in the laudable project of fitting out a Colony to Virginia.

Accordingly, 2 Ships were Sent away that very Year, under the Command of his good Friends Amidas and Bar-

low, to take possession of the Country in the Name of his Roial Mistress, the Queen of England.

These worthy Commanders, for the advantage of the Trade Winds, shaped their Course first to the Charibbe Islands, thence stretching away by the Gulph of Florida, drop Anchor not far from Roanoak Inlet. They ventured ashoar near that place upon an Island now called Colleton island, where they set up the Arms of England, and Claimed the Adjacent Country in Right of their Sovereign Lady, the Queen; and this Ceremony being duly performed, they kindly invited the neighbouring Indians to traffick with them.

These poor people at first approacht the English with great Caution, having heard much of the Treachery of the Spaniards, and not knowing but these Strangers might be as treacherous as they. But, at length, discovering a kind of good nature in their looks, they ventured to draw near, and barter their Skins and Furs, for the Bawbles and Trinkets of the English.

These first Adventurers made a very profitable Voyage, raising at least a Thousand per cent. upon their Cargo. Amongst other Indian Commodities, they brought over Some of the bewitching Vegetable, Tobacco. And this being the first that ever came to England, Sir Walter thought he could do no less than make a present of Some of the brightest of it to His Roial Mistress, for her own Smoaking.

The Queen graciously accepted of it, but finding her Stomach sicken after two or three Whiffs, it was presently whispered by the earl of Leicester's Faction, that Sir Walter had certainly Poison'd Her. But Her Majesty soon recovering her Disorder, obliged the Countess of Nottingham and all her Maids to Smoak a whole Pipe out amongst them.

As it happen'd some Ages before to be the fashion to Santer to the Holy Land, and go upon other Quixot Ad-

---

1. *The History of the Dividing Line, Run in the Year 1728* was originally published in *The Westover Manuscripts* (1841).

ventures, so it was now grown the Humour to take a Trip to America. The Spaniards had lately discovered Rich Mines in their Part of the West Indies, which made their Maritime Neighbours eager to do so too. This Modish Frenzy being still more Inflam'd by the Charming Account given of Virginia, by the first Adventurers, made many fond of removeing to such a Paradise.

Happy was he, and still happier She, that cou'd get themselves transported, fondly expecting their Coarsest Utensils, in that happy place, would be of Massy Silver.

This made it easy for the Company to procure as many Volunteers as they wanted for their new Colony; but, like most other Undertakers who have no Assistance from the Public, they Starved the Design by too much Frugality; for, unwilling to Launch out at first into too much Expense, they Ship't off but few People at a Time, and Those but Scantily provided. The Adventurers were, besides, Idle and extravagant, and expected they might live without work in so plentiful a Country.

These Wretches were set Ashoar not far from Roanoak Inlet, but by some fatal disagreement, or Laziness, were either Starved or cut to Pieces by the Indians.

Several repeated Misadventures of this kind did, for some time, allay the Itch of Sailing to this New World; but the Distemper broke out again about the Year 1606. Then it happened that the Earl of Southampton and several other Persons, eminent for their Quality and Estates, were invited into the Company, who apply'd themselves once more to People the then almost abandon'd Colony. For this purpose they embarkt about an Hundred men, most of them Riprobates of good Familys, and related to some of the company, who were men of Quality and Fortune.

The Ships that carried them made a Shift to find a more direct way to Virginia, and ventured thro the Capes into the Bay of Chesapeak. The same Night they came to an Anchor at the Mouth of Powatan, the same as James River, where they built a Small Fort at a Place call'd Point Comfort.

This Settlement stood its ground from that time forward in spite of all the Blunders and Disagreement of the first Adventurers, and the many Calamitys that befel the Colony afterwards.

The six gentlemen who were first named of the company by the crown, and who were empowered to choose an annual President from among themselves, were always engaged in Factions and Quarrels, while the rest detested Work more than Famine. At this rate the Colony must have come to nothing, had it not been for the vigilance and Bravery of Capt. Smith, who struck a Terrour into all the Indians round about. This Gentleman took some pains to perswade the men to plant Indian corn, but they look upon all Labor as a Curse. They chose rather to depend upon the Musty Provisions that were sent from England: and when they fail'd they were forct to take more pains to Seek for Wild Fruits in the Woods, than they would have taken in tilling the Ground. Besides, this Exposed them to be knockt on the head by the Indians, and gave them Fluxes into the Bargain, which thind the Plantation very much. To Supply this mortality, they were reinforct the year following with a greater number of People, amongst which were fewer Gentlemen and more Labourers, who, however, took care not to kill themselves with Work.

These found the First Adventurers in a very starving condition, but relieved their wants with the fresh Supply they brought with them. From Kiquotan they extended themselves as far as James-Town, where like true Englishmen, they built a Church that cost no more than Fifty Pounds, and a Tavern that cost Five hundred.

They had now made peace with the Indians, but there was one thing wanting to make that peace lasting. The Natives coud, by no means, perswade themselves that the English were heartily their Friends, so long as they disdained to intermarry with them. And, in earnest, had the English consulted their own Security and the good of the Colony—Had they intended either to Civilize or Convert these Gentiles, they would have brought their Stomachs to embrace this prudent Alliance.

The Indians are generally tall and well-proportion'd, which may make full Amends for the Darkness of their Complexions. Add to this, that they are healthy & Strong, with Constitutions untainted by Lewdness, and not enfeebled by Luxury. Besides, Morals and all considered, I cant think the Indians were much greater Heathens than the first Adventurers, who, had they been good Christians, would have had the Charity to take this only method of converting the Natives to Christianity. For, after all that can be said, a sprightly Lover is the most prevailing Missionary that can be sent amongst these, or any other Infidels.

Besides, the poor Indians would have had less reason to Complain that the English took away their Land, if they had received it by way of Portion with their Daughters. Had such Affinities been contracted in the Beginning, how much Bloodshed had been prevented, and how populous would the Country have been, and, consequently, how considerable? Nor wou'd the Shade of the Skin have been any reproach at this day; for if a Moor may be washt white in 3 Generations, Surely an Indian might have been blancht in two.

The French, for their Parts, have not been so Squeamish in Canada, who upon Trial find abundance of Attraction in the Indians. Their late Grand Monarch thought it not below even the Dignity of a Frenchman to become one flesh with this People, and therefore Ordered 100 Livres for any of his Subjects, Man or Woman, that would intermarry with a Native.

By this piece of Policy we find the French Interest very much Strengthen'd amongst the Savages, and their Religion, such as it is, propagated just as far as their Love. And I heartily wish this well-concerted Scheme don't hereafter give the French an Advantage over his Majesty's good Subjects on the Northern Continent of America.

About the same time New England was pared off from Virginia by Letters Patent, bearing date April the 10th, 1608.[2] Several Gentlemen of the Town and Neighbourhood of Plymouth obtain'd this Grant, with the Ld Chief Justice Popham at their Head.

Their Bounds were Specified to Extend from 38 to 45 Degrees of Northern Latitude, with a Breadth of one Hundred Miles from the Sea Shore. The first 14 Years, this Company encounter'd many Difficulties, and lost many men, tho' far from being discouraged, they sent over Numerous Recruits of Presbyterians, every year, who for all that, had much ado to stand their Ground, with all their Fighting and Praying.

But about the year 1620, a Large Swarm of Dissenters fled thither from the Severities of their Stepmother, the Church. These Saints conceiving the same Aversion to the Copper Complexion of the Natives, with that of the first Adventurers to Virginia, would, on no Terms, contract Alliances with them, afraid perhaps, like the Jews of Old, lest they might be drawn into Idolatry by those Strange Women.

Whatever disgusted them I cant say, but this false delicacy creating in the Indians a Jealousy that the English were ill affected towards them, was the Cause that many of them were cut off, and the rest Exposed to various Distresses.

This Reinforcement was landed not far from Cape Codd, where, for their greater Security they built a Fort, and near it a Small Town, which in Honour of the Proprietors, was call'd New Plymouth. But they Still had many discouragements to Struggle with, tho' by being well Supported from Home, they by Degrees Triumph't over them all.

Their Bretheren, after this, flockt over so fast, that in a few Years they extended the Settlement one hundred Miles along the Coast, including Rhode Island and Martha's Vineyard.

Thus the Colony throve apace, and was throng'd with large Detachments of Independents and Presbyterians, who thought themselves persecuted at home.

Tho' these People may be ridiculd for some Pharisaical Particularitys in their Worship and Behaviour, yet they were very useful Subjects, as being Frugal and Industrious, giving no Scandal or bad Example, at least by any Open and Public Vices. By which excellent Qualities they had much the Advantage of the Southern Colony, who thought their being Members of the Establish't Church sufficient to Sanctifie very loose and Profligate Morals. For this Reason New England improved much faster than Virginia, and in Seven or Eight Years New Plimouth, like Switzerland, seemed too Narrow a Territory for its Inhabitants.

For this Reason, several Gentlemen of Fortune purchas'd of the Company that Canton of New England now called Massachuset colony. And King James confirm'd the Purchase by his Royal Charter, dated March the 4th, 1628. In less than 2 years after, above 1000 of the Puritanical Sect removed thither with considerable Effects, and these were followed by such Crowds, that a Proclamation was issued in England, forbidding any more of his Majesty's Subjects to be Shipt off. But this had the usual Effect of things forbidden, and serv'd only to make the Wilful Independents flock over the faster. And about this time it was that Messrs. Hampden and Pym, and (some say) Oliver Cromwell, to show how little they valued the King's Authority, took a Trip to New England.

In the Year 1630, the famous City of Boston was built, in a Commodious Situation for Trade and Navigation, the same being on a Peninsula at the Bottom of Massachuset Bay.

This Town is now the most considerable of any on the British Continent, containing at least 8,000 houses and 40,000 Inhabitants. The Trade it drives, is very great to Europe, and to every Part of the West Indies, having near 1,000 Ships and lesser Vessels belonging to it. . . .

The Quakers flockt over to this Country in Shoals, being averse to go to Heaven the same way with the Bishops. Amongst them were not a few of good Substance, who went Vigorously upon every kind of Improvement; and thus much I may truly say in their Praise, that by Dili-

---

2. The Plymouth Company was actually chartered in 1606.

gence and Frugality, For which this Harmless Sect is remarkable, and by having no Vices but such as are Private, they have in a few Years made Pensilvania a very fine Country.

The truth is, they have observed exact Justice with all the Natives that border upon them; they have purchased all their Lands from the Indians; and tho they paid but a Trifle for them, it has procured them the Credit of being more righteous than their Neighbours. They have likewise had the Prudence to treat them kindly upon all Occasions, which has savd them from many Wars and Massacres wherein the other Colonies have been indiscreetly involved. The Truth of it is, a People whose Principles forbid them to draw the Carnal Sword, were in the Right to give no Provocation.

Both the French and the Spaniards had, in the Name of their Respective Monarchs, long ago taken Possession of that Part of the Northern Continent that now goes by the Name of Carolina; but finding it Produced neither Gold nor Silver, as they greedily expected, and meeting such returns from the Indians as their own Cruelty and Treachery deserved, they totally abandond it. In this deserted Condition that country lay for the Space of 90 Years, till King Charles the 2d, finding it a DERELICT, granted it away to the Earl of Clarendon and others, by His Royal Charter, dated March the 24th, 1663. The Boundary of that Grant towards Virginia was a due West Line from Luck-Island, (the same as Colleton Island), lying in 36 degrees N. Latitude, quite to the South Sea.

But afterwards Sir William Berkeley, who was one of the Grantees and at that time Governour of Virginia, finding a Territory of 31 Miles in Breadth between the Inhabited Part of Virginia and the above-mentioned Boundary of Carolina, advisd the Lord Clarendon of it. And His Lordp had Interest enough with the King to obtain a Second Patent to include it, dated June the 30th, 1665.

This last Grant describes the Bounds between Virginia and Carolina in these words: "To run from the North End of Corotuck-Inlet, due West to Weyanoke Creek, lying within or about the Degree of Thirty-Six and Thirty Minutes of Northern Latitude, and from thence West, in a direct Line, as far as the South-Sea." Without question, this Boundary was well known at the time the Charter was Granted, but in a long Course of years Weynoke Creek lost its name, so that it became a Controversy where it lay. Some Ancient Persons in Virginia affirmd it was the same with Wicocon, and others again in Carolina were as Positive it was Nottoway River.

In the mean time, the People on the Frontiers Entered for Land, & took out Patents by Guess, either from the King or the Lords Proprietors. But the Crown was like to be the loser by this Incertainty, because the Terms both of taking up and seating Land were easier much in Carolina. The Yearly Taxes to the Public were likewise there less burdensom, which laid Virginia under a Plain disadvantage.

This Consideration put that Government upon entering into Measures with North Carolina, to terminate the Dispute, and settle a Certain Boundary between the two colonies. All the Difficulty was, to find out which was truly Weyanoke Creek. The Difference was too Considerable to be given up by either side, there being a Territory of 15 Miles betwixt the two Streams in controversy.

However, till that Matter could be adjusted, it was agreed on both sides, that no Lands at all Should be granted within the disputed Bounds. Virginia observed this Agreement punctually, but I am sorry I cant say the Same of North-Carolina. The great Officers of that Province were loath to lose the Fees accrueing from the Grants of Land, and so private Interest got the better of Public Spirit; and I wish that were the only Place in the World where such politicks are fashionable.

All the Steps that were taken afterwards in that Affair, will best appear by the Report of the Virginia-Commissioners, recited in the Order of Council given at St. James's, March the 1st, 1710, set down in the Appendix.

It must be owned, the Report of those Gentlemen was Severe upon the then commissioners of North-Carolina, and particularly upon Mr. Moseley. I wont take upon me to say with how much Justice they said so many hard things, tho it had been fairer Play to have given the Parties accused a Copy of such Representations, that they might have answered what they could for themselves.

But since that was not done, I must beg leave to say thus much in behalf of Mr. Moseley, that he was not much in the Wrong to find fault with the Quadrant produced by the Surveyors of Virginia because that Instrument plact the Mouth of Notoway River in the Latitude of 37 Degrees; whereas, by an Accurate Observation made Since, it Appears to line in 36° 30′ ½′, so that there was an Error of near 30 minutes, either in the Instrument or in those who made use of it.

Besides, it is evident the Mouth of Notoway River agrees much better with the Latitude, wherein the Carolina Charter supposed Wyanoak Creek, (namely, in or about 36 Degrees and 30 minutes,) than it does with Wicocon Creek, which is about 15 Miles more Southerly.

This being manifest, the Intention of the King's Grant will be pretty exactly answered, by a due West Line drawn from Corotuck Inlet to the Mouth of Notaway River, for which reason tis probable that was formerly calld Wyanoak-Creek, and might change its Name when the Nottoway Indians came to live upon it, which was since the Date of the last Carolina Charter.

The Lievt Governor of Virginia, at that time Colo Spotswood, searching into the Bottom of this Affair, made very Equitable Proposals to Mr. Eden, at that time Governour of North Carolina, in Order to put an End to this Controversy. These, being formed into Preliminaries, were Signd by both Governours, and transmitted to England, where they had the Honour to be ratifyed by his late Majesty and assented to by the Lords Proprietors of Carolina.

Accordingly an Order was sent by the late King to Mr. Gooch, afterwards Lievt Governor of Virginia, to pursue those Preliminaries exactly. In Obedience thereunto, he was pleased to appoint Three of the Council of that colony to be Commissioners on the Part of Virginia, who, in Conjunction with others to be named by the Governor of North Carolina, were to settle the Boundary between the 2 Governments, upon the Plan of the above-mentioned Articles. . . .[3]

Thus we finish'd our Spring Campaign, and having taken leave of our Carolina-Friends, and agreed to meet them again the Tenth of September following, at the same Mr. Kinchin's, in order to continue the Line, we crost Meherin River near a Quarter of a Mile from the House. About ten Miles from that we halted at Mr. Kindred's Plantation, where we Christen'd two Children.

It happen'd that some of Isle of Wight militia Were exercising in the Adjoining Pasture, and there were Females enough attending that Martial Appearance to form a more invincible corps.

Ten miles farther we passed Nottoway River at Bolton's Ferry, and took up our Lodgings about three Miles from thence, at the House of Richard Parker, an honest Planter, whose Labours were rewarded with Plenty, which, in this country is the Constant Portion of the Industrious.

The Next day being Sunday, we order'd Notice to be sent to all the Neighbourhood that there wou'd be a Sermon at this Place, and an Opportunity of Christening their

Children. But the Likelihood of Rain got the better of their Devotion, and what perhaps, Might Still be a Stronger motive of their Curiosity. In the Morning we despacht a runner to the Nottoway Town, to let the Indians know we intend them a Visit that Evening, and our honest Landlord was so kind as to be our Pilot thither, being about 4 Miles from his House.

Accordingly in the Afternoon we marcht in good Order to the Town, where the Female Scouts, station'd on an Eminence for that purpose, had no sooner spy'd us, but they gave Notitce of our Approach to their Fellow-Citizens by continual Whoops and Cries, which cou'd not possibly have been more dismal at the Sight of their most implacable Enemys.

This Signal Assembled all their Great Men, who receiv'd us in a Body, and conducted us into the Fort. This Fort was a Square Piece of Ground, inclos'd with Substantial Puncheons, or Strong Palisades, about ten feet high, and leaning a little outwards, to make a Scalade more difficult.

Each side of the Square might be about 100 Yards long, with Loopholes at proper Distances, through which they may fire upon the Enemy.

Within this Inclosure we found Bark Cabanes Sufficient to lodge all their people, in Case they should be obliged to retire thither. These Cabanes are no other but Close Arbours made of Saplings, arched at the top, and cover'd so well with Bark as to be proof against all Weather. The fire is made in the Middle, according to the Hibernian Fashion, the Smoak whereof finds no other Vent but at the Door, and so keeps the whole family Warm, at the Expense both of their Eyes and Complexion.

The Indians have no standing Furniture in their Cabanes but Hurdles to repose their Persons upon, which they cover with Mats or Deer-skins. We were conducted to the best Appartments in the Fort, which just before had been made ready for our Reception, and adorn'd with new Mats, that were sweet and clean.

The Young Men had Painted themselves in a Hideous Manner, not so much for Ornament as Terror. In that frightful Equipage they entertain'd us with Sundry War-Dances, wherein they endeavour'd to look as formidable as possible. The Instrument they danct to was an Indian-drum, that is, a large Gourd with a Skin bract tort over the Mouth of it. The Dancers all Sang to this Musick, keeping exact Time with their feet, while their Heads and Arms were screw'd into a thousand Menacing Postures.

Upon this occasion the Ladies had array'd themselves in all their finery. They were Wrapt in their Red and Blue

---

3. The remainder of this selection recounts events that occurred during the surveying expedition itself.

Match-Coats, thrown so Negligently about them, that their Mehogony Skins appear'd in Several Parts, like the Lacedaemonian Damsels of Old. Their Hair was breeded with white and Blue Peak, and hung gracefully in a large Roll upon their Shoulders.

This peak Consists of Small Cylinders cut out of a Conque-Shell, drill'd through and Strung like Beads. It serves them both for Money and Jewels, the Blue being of much greater Value than the White, for the same reason that Ethiopian Mistresses in France are dearer than French, because they are more Scarce. The Women wear Necklaces and Bracelets of these precious Materials, when they have a mind to appear lovely. Tho' their complexions be a little Sad-Colour'd, yet their Shapes are very Strait and well porportion'd. Their Faces are Seldom handsome, yet they have an Air of Innocence and Bashfulness, that with a little less dirt wou'd not fail to make them desirable. Such Charms might have had their full Effect upon Men who had been so long deprived of female conversation, but that the whole Winter's Soil was so crusted on the Skins of those dark Angels, that it requir'd a very strong Appetite to approach them. The Bear's oyl, with which they anoint their Persons all over, makes their skins Soft, and at the Same time protects them from every Species of Vermin that use to be troublesome to other uncleanly People.

We were unluckily so many, that they cou'd not well make us the Complement of Bed-fellows, according to the Indian Rules of Hospitality, tho' a grave Matron whisper'd one of the Commissioners very civily in the Ear, that if her Daughter had been but one year Older, she should have been at his Devotion.

It is by no means a loss of Reputation among the Indians, for Damsels that are Single to have Intrigues with the Men; on the contrary, they count it an Argument of Superior Merit to be liked by a great Number of Gallants. However, like the Ladys that Game they are a little Mercenary in their Amours, and seldom bestow their Favours out of Stark Love and Kindness. But after these Women have once appropriated their Charms by Marriage, they are from thencefourth faithful to their Vows, and will hardly ever be tempted by an Agreeable Gallant, or be provokt by a Brutal or even by a fumbling Husband to go astray.

The little Work that is done among the Indians is done by the poor Women, while the men are quite idle, or at most employ'd only in the Gentlemanly Diversions of Hunting and Fishing.

In this, as well as in their Wars, they now use nothing but Fire-Arms, which they purchase of the English for Skins. Bows and Arrows are grown into disuse, except only amongst their Boys. Nor is it ill Policy, but on the contrary very prudent, thus to furnish the Indians with Fire-Arms, because it makes them depend entirely upon the English, not only for their Trade, but even for their subsistence. Besides, they were really able to do more mischief, while they made use of Arrows, of which they wou'd let Silently fly Several in a Minute with Wonderful Dexterity, whereas now they hardly ever discharge their Firelocks more than once, which they insidiously do from behind a Tree, and then retire as nimbly as the Dutch Horse us'd to do now and then formerly in Flanders.

We put the Indians to no expense, but only of a little Corn for our Horses, for which in Gratitude we cheer'd their hearts with what Rum we had left, which they love better than they do their Wives and Children.

Tho' these Indians dwell among the English, and see in what Plenty a little Industry enables them to live, yet they chuse to continue in their Stupid Idleness, and to Suffer all the Inconveniences of Dirt, Cold, and Want, rather than to disturb their hands With care, or defile their Hands with labour.

The whole Number of People belonging to the Nottoway Town, if you include Women and Children, amount to about 200. These are the only Indians of any consequence now remaining within the Limits of Virginia. The rest are either removed, or dwindled to a very inconsiderable Number, either by destroying one another, or else by the Small-Pox and other Diseases. Tho' nothing has been so fatal to them as their ungovernable Passion for Rum, with which, I am sorry to say it, they have been but too liberally supply'd by the English that live near them.

And here I must lament the bad Success Mr. Boyle's Charity[4] has hitherto had towards converting any of these poor Heathens to Christianity. Many children of our Neighbouring Indians have been brought up in the College of William and Mary. They have been taught to read and write, and have been carefully Instructed in the Principles of the Christian Religion, till they came to be men. Yet after they return'd home, instead of civilizeing and converting the rest, they have immediately Relapt into Infidelity and Barbarism themselves.

And some of them too have made the worst use of the Knowledge they acquir'd among the English, by employing it against their Benefactors. Besides, as they unhap-

---

4. English chemist Robert Boyle made an endowment to the College of William and Mary for the education and conversion of Indians.

pily forget all the good they learn, and remember the Ill, they are apt to be more vicious and disorderly than the rest of their Countrymen.

I ought not to quit this Subject without doing Justice to the great Prudence of Colo Spotswood in this Affair. That Gentleman was lieut Governor of Virginia when Carolina was engaged in a Bloody War with the Indians. At that critical Time it was thought expedient to keep a Watchful Eye upon our Tributary Savages, who we knew had nothing to keep them to their Duty but their Fears.

Then it was that he demanded of each Nation a Competent Number of their great Men's Children to be sent to the College, where they serv'd as so many Hostages for the good Behaviour of the Rest, and at the same time were themselves principled in the Christian Religion. He also Plac'd a School-Master among the Saponi Indians, at the salary of Fifty Pounds P Annum, to instruct their Children. The Person that undertook that Charitable work was Mr. Charles Griffin, a Man of good Family, who by the Innocence of his Life, and the Sweetest of his Temper, was perfectly well qualify'd for that pious undertaking. Besides, he had so much the Secret of mixing Pleasure with instruction, that he had not a Scholar, who did not love him affectionately.

Such Talents must needs have been blest with a Proportionable Success, had he not been unluckily remov'd to the College, by which he left the good work he had begun unfinisht. In short, all the Pains he had undertaken among the Infidels had no other Effect but to make them something cleanlier than other Indians are.

The Care Colo Spotswood took to tincture the Indian Children with Christianity produc'd the following Epigram, which was not publisht during his Administration, for fear it might then have lookt like flattery.

> Long has the Furious Priest assay'd in Vain,
> With Sword and Faggot, Infidels to gain,
> But now the Milder Soldier wisely tryes
> By Gentler Methods to unveil their Eyes.
> Wonders apart, he knew 'twere vain t' engage
> The fix'd Preventions of Misguided Age.
> With fairer Hopes he forms the Indian Youth
> To early Manners, Probity and Truth.
> The Lyon's whelp thus on the Lybian Shore
> Is tam'd and Gentled by the Artful Moor,
> Not the Grim Sire, inured to Blood before.

I am sorry I can't give a Better Account of the State of the Poor Indians with respect to Christianity, altho' a great deal of Pains has been and still continues to be taken with them. For my Part, I must be of Opinion, as I hinted before, that there is but one way of Converting these poor Infidels, and reclaiming them from Barbarity, and that is, Charitably to intermarry with them, according to the Modern Policy of the most Christian King in Canada and Louisiana.

Had the English done this at the first Settlement of the Colony, the Infidelity of the Indians had been worn out at this Day, with their Dark Complexions, and the Country had swarm'd with People more than it does with Insects.

It was certainly an unreasonable Nicety, that prevented their entering into so good-Natur'd an Alliance. All Nations of men have the same Natural Dignity, and we all know that very bright Talents may be lodg'd under a very dark Skin. The principal Difference between one People and another proceeds only from the Different Opportunities of Improvement.

The Indians by no means want understanding, and are in their Figure tall and well-proportion'd. Even their Copper-colour'd Complexion wou'd admit of Blanching, if not in the first, at the farthest in the Second Generation.

I may safely venture to say, the Indian Women would have made altogether as Honest Wives for the first Planters, as the Damsels they us'd to purchase from aboard the Ships. It is Strange, therefore, that any good Christian Shou'd have refused a wholesome, Straight Bed-fellow, when he might have had so fair a Portion with her, as the Merit of saving her Soul.

We rested on our clean Mats very comfortably, tho' alone, and the next Morning went to the Toilet of some of the Indian Ladys, where, what with the Charms of their Persons and the Smoak of their Apartments, we were almost blinded. They offer'd to give us Silk-Grass Baskets of their own making, which we Modestly refused, knowing that an Indian present, like that of a Nun, is a Liberality put out to Interest, and a Bribe plac'd to the greatest Advantage.

Our Chaplain observ'd with concern, that the Ruffles of Some of our Fellow Travellers were a little discolour'd with pochoon,[5] wherewith the good Man had been told those Ladies us'd to improve their invisible charms.

About 10 a Clock we marched out of Town in good order, & the War Captains saluted us with a Volley of Small-Arms. From thence we proceeded over Blackwater Bridge to colo' Henry Harrisons, where we congratulated each other upon our Return into Christendom.

---

5. Also called bloodroot, a plant used to make face and body paint.

Thus ended our Progress for this Season, which we may justly say was attended with all the Success that could be expected. Besides the Punctual Performance of what was Committed to us, we had the Pleasure to bring back every one of our Company in perfect Health. And this we must acknowledge to be a Singular Blessing, considering the Difficulties and Dangers to which they had been expos'd.

We had reason to fear the many Waters and Sunken Grounds, thro' which We were oblig'd to wade, might have thrown the men into Sundry Acute distempers; especially the Dismal, where the Soil was so full of Water, and the Air so full of Damps, that nothing but a Dutchman cou'd live in them.

Indeed the Foundation of all our Success was the Exceeding dry Season. It rain'd during the whole Journey but rarely, and then, as when Herod built his Temple, only in the Night or upon the Sabbath, when it was no hindrance at all to our progress. . . .

This being Sunday, we rested from our Fatigue, and had leisure to reflect on the signal Mercies of Providence.

The great Plenty of Meat herewith Bearskin furnisht us in these lonely Woods made us once more Shorten the men's allowance of Bread, from 5 to 4 Pounds of bisket a week. This was the more necessary, because we knew not yet how long our Business might require us to be out.

In the Afternoon our Hunters went forth, and return'd triumphantly with three brace of wild Turkeys. They told us they cou'd see the Mountains distinctly from every Eminence, tho' the Atmosphere was so thick with Smoak that they appear'd at a greater Distance than they really were.

In the Evening we examin'd our Friend Bearskin, concerning the Religion of his Country and he explain'd it to us, without any of that Reserve to which his Nation is Subject.

He told us he believ'd there was one Supreme God, who had Several Subaltern Deities under Him. And that this Master-God made the World a long time ago. That he told the Sun, the Moon, and Stars, their Business in the Beginning, which they, with good looking after, have faithfully perform'd ever Since.

That the same Power that made all things at first has taken care to keep them in the same Method and Motion ever since.

He believ'd God had form'd many Worlds before he form'd this, that those Worlds either grew old and ruinous, or were destroyed for the Dishonesty of the Inhabitants.

That God is very just and very good—ever well pleas'd with those men who possess those God-like Qualities. That he takes good People into his safe Protection, makes them very rich, fills their Bellies plentifully, preserves them from sickness, and from being surpriz'd or Overcome by their Enemies.

But all such as tell Lies, and Cheat those they have Dealings with, he never fails to punish with Sickness, Poverty and Hunger, and, after all that, Suffers them to be knockt on the Head and scalpt by those that fight against them.

He believ'd that after Death both good and bad People are conducted by a strong Guard into a great Road, in which departed Souls travel together for some time, till at a certain Distance this Road forks into two Paths, the one extremely Levil, and the other Stony and Mountainous.

Here the good are parted from the Bad by a flash of Lightening, the first being hurry'd away to the Right, the other to the Left. The Right hand Road leads to a charming warm Country, where the Spring is everlasting, and every Month is May; and as the year is always in its Youth, so are the People, and particularly the Women are bright as Stars, and never Scold.

That in this happy Climate there are Deer, Turkeys, Elks, and Buffaloes innumerable, perpetually fat and gentle, while the Trees are loaded with delicious Fruit quite throughout the four Seasons.

That the Soil brings forth Corn Spontaneously, without the Curse of Labour, and so very wholesome, that None who have the happiness to eat of it are ever Sick, grow old, or dy.

Near the Entrance into this Blessed Land Sits a Venerable Old Man on a Mat richly woven, who examins Strictly all that are brought before Him, and if they have behav'd well, the Guards are order'd to open the Crystal Gate, and let them enter into the Land of Delights.

The left Hand Path is very rugged and uneaven, leading to a dark and barren Country, where it is always Winter. The Ground is the whole year round cover'd with Snow, and nothing is to be seen upon the Trees but Icicles.

All the People are hungry, yet have not a Morsel of any thing to eat, except a bitter kind of Potato, that gives them the Dry-Gripes, and fills their whole Body with loathsome Ulcers, that Stink, and are unsupportably painfull.

Here all the Women are old and ugly, having Claws like a Panther, with which they fly upon the Men that

Slight their Passion. For it seems these haggard old Furies are intolerably fond, and expect a vast deal of Cherishing. They talk much and exceedingly Shrill, giving exquisite Pain to the Drum of the Ear, which in that Place of the Torment is so tender, that every Sharp Note wounds it to the Quick.

At the End of this Path sits a dreadful old Woman on a monstrous Toad-Stool, whose head is cover'd with Rattle-Snakes instead of Tresses, with glaring white Eyes, that strike a Terror unspeakable into all that behold her.

This Hag pronounces Sentence of Woe upon all the miserable Wretches that hold up their hands at her Tribunal. After this they are deliver'd over to huge Turkey-Buzzards, like harpys, that fly away with them to the Place above mentioned.

Here, after they have been tormented a certain Number of years, according to their several Degrees of Guilt, they are again driven back into this World, to try if they will mend their Manners, and merit a place the next time in the Regions of Bliss.

This was the Substances of Bearskin's Religion, and was as much to the purpose as cou'd be expected from a meer State of Nature, without one Glimpse of Revelation or Philosophy.

It contain'd, however, the three Great Articles of Natural Religion: The Belief of a God; The Moral Distinction betwixt Good and Evil; and the Expectation of Rewards and Punishments in Another World.

Indeed, the Indian Notion of a Future Happiness is a little Gross and Sensual, like Mahomet's Paradise. But how can it be otherwise, in a People that are contented with Nature as they find Her, and have no other Lights but what they receive from purblind Tradition?

———

LETTERS TO CHARLES BOYLE, EARL OF ORRERY[1]

Virginia, the 5th of July, 1726
My Lord
Soon after my arrival I had the honour to write to your Lordship to acquaint you that we had happily escaped all the dangers of the sea, and were safely landed at my own house. There was nothing frightfull in the whole voyage

---

1. The text is from *The Correspondence of the Three William Byrds of Westover*, ed. Marion Tinling (1977).

but a suddain puff that carried away our top-mast, which in the falling gave a very loud crack, but we received no other damage, neither were our women terrified at it.

The beautifull bloom of our spring when we came ashore, gave Mrs. Byrd a good impression of the country. But since that the weather is grown warm, and some days have been troublesome enough to make her wish herself in England. However she now begins to be seasoned to the heat, and to think more favorably of our climate. She comforts herself with the thought that a warm sun is necessary to ripen our fine fruit, and so pays herself with the pleasure of one sense, for the inconveniences that attend the others. I must own to your Lordship that we have about three months that impatient people call warm, but the colonel would think them cool enough for a pair of blankets, and perhaps a comfortable counterpain into the bargain. Yet there are not above ten days in a whole summer that your Lordship would complain of, and they happen when the breazes fail us, and it is a dead calm. But then the other nine months are most charmingly delightfull, with a fine air, and a serene sky, that keeps us in good health, and good-humour. Spleen, and vapours are as absolute rarities here as a winters-sun, or a publick spirit in England. A man may eat beef, be as lazy as Captain Hardy, or even marry in this clymate without having the least inclination to hang himself. It would cure all Mr. Hutchinson's distempers if the ministry would transport him hither, unless they sent lady G   along with him.

Your Lordship will allow it to be a fair commendation of a country, that it reconciles a man to himself, and makes him suffer the weight of his misfortunes, with the same tranquility he bears with his own frailtys.

After your September is over, I shall wish your Lordship a little of our sunshine, to disperse all that fogg and smoak with which your atmosphere is loaded. 'Tis miraculus that any lungs can breath in an air compounded of so many different vapours and exhalations, like that of dirty London. For my part mine were never of a texture to bear it in winter without great convulsions, so that nothing could make me amends for that uneasiness, but the pleasure of being near your Lordship.

Besides the advantages of a pure air, we abound in all kinds of provisions, without expence (I mean we who have plantations). I have a large family of my own, and my doors are open to every body, yet I have no bills to pay, and half-a-crown will rest undisturbed in my pocket for many moons together.

Like one of the patriarchs, I have my flocks and my herds, my bond-men, and bond-women, and every soart of trade amongst my own servants, so that I live in a kind of independance on every one, but Providence. However tho' this soart of life is without expence yet it is attended with a great deal of trouble. I must take care to keep all my people to their duty, to set all the springs in motion, and to make every one draw his equal share to carry the machine forward. But then tis an amusement in this silent country, and a continual exercise of our patience and economy.

Another thing my Lord, that recommends this country very much, we sit securely under our vines, and our fig-trees without any danger to our property. We have neither publick robbers nor private, which your Lordship will think very strange, when we have often needy governours, and pilfering convicts sent over amongst us. The first of these it is suspected have some-times an inclination to plunder, but want the power, and tho' they may be tyrants in their nature, yet they are tyrants without guards, which makes them as harmless as a scold would be without a tongue. Neither can they do much injustice by being partial in judgment, because in a supream court, the Council have each an equal vote with them. Thus both the teeth and the claws of the lion are secured, and he can neither bite nor tear us, except we turn him loose upon ourselves. I wish this was the case of all His Majesty's good subjects, and I dare say your Lordship has the goodness to wish so too.

Then we have no such trades carried on amongst us, as that of house-breakers, highway-men, or beggers. We can rest securely in our beds with all our doors and windows open, and yet find every thing exactly in place the next morning. We can travel all over the country, by night and by day, unguarded and unarmed, and never meet with any person so rude as to bid us stand. We have no vagrant mendicants to seize and deaften us wherever we go, as in your island of beggars.

Thus my Lord we are very happy in our Canaan, if we could but forget the onions, and flesh-pots of Egypt. There are so many temptations in England to inflame the appetite, and charm the senses, that we are constant to run all risques to enjoy them. They always had I must own too strong an influence upon me, as your Lordship will belive when they could keep me so long from the more solid pleasures of innocence, and retirement.

I doubt not but my Lord Boyle learn't at Paris to perform all his exercises in perfection, and is become an absolute master of the French language. I wish every secretary of state could write it as perfectly as his Lordship

does, that their performances might not be subjected to the correction of Mr. De-La-Fay. I am sure that Lord Boyle will in every respect answer the affectionate care your Lordship has taken of him; and I suppose it will not be long before I shall have the pleasure to hear that he is happily married, for it now seems wholy to depend upon him to furnish heirs to all the noble familys of his name.

I most heartily long to hear from your Lordship, and shall rejoice at every happy accident that befalls you, for I am as much as any man alive, my Lord yours &c. W. Byrd.

Virginia, the 2d of February, 1726/7
My Lord
Tis near a month since I had the honour of your Lordships commands bearing date the 21st of October: but those from Lord Boyle are not yet come to hand. I was so well entertained with his first letter, that I long for the arrival of a second.

I must own London has its charms, now you are returned from your travels; notwithstanding all the smoak, and noise, and dirt that disgrace it: but I did penance there all the time your Lordship was doing penance at Paris, only I did not purchase my penance quite so dear. England without doubt appears to some advantage after spending so many months in a less agreable place, and besides its own native charms, has those of novelty, which are no small recommendation. This is a pleasure we need not learn from the ladys, we love change at least as well as they, and if they are pleased with it too, they do but take after their fathers. Even this country seems to have new beautys after I have been smoaking myself into bacon at London. Each of the four elements seems to have more youth and excellence than in your northern climate, and the whole face of nature smiles with quite another air. Our heavens put on a cheerfull countenance, while yours lowre and look as dogged as those miserable people who are out of humour they know not why, and out of order they know not where. From hence our air receives a springiness and purity very friendly to our lungs, and beneficiall to the circulation both of our blood, and spirits. Nobody coughs himself into a consumption here, as your Lordship may remember I almost did every winter in England, and I had been long since surveying the wonders of the other world, if your skill had not prevented me. Neither have I half that passion for an elbow-chair, which my friends discovered me to have at Oxford.

Were your Lordship to see or smell our ground, you would think it almost as fresh, as if it newly came out of it's makers hands, while yours has been tortured, and torn to peices some thousands of years, and like a battered constitution, must be cherished and revived with restoratives to keep it in heart. Our waters too have a spirit and a sweetness, far beyond those of your island: which is the reason our Indians never thought it worth their while to provide any stronger drink; but are content to toast their copper beautys, and shew their wit, over their flowing crystal. Nay our very fire, besides being clearer, and more kindly for respiration, receives force and vigour from the neighbourhood of the sun, and casts its heat to a wider distance. If then our elements are more perfect in their kind, one would expect that every thing that is compounded of them should be so too. Our plants have juices more refined and better digested, our fruits are more sprightly flavoured, our meats are more savoury, and I doubt not but when we come to find them, our metals will prove all ripened into gold and silver. Thus nature is very indulgent to us, and produces it's good things almost spontaneously. Our men evade the original curse of hard labour, and sweat as much with eating their bread, as with geting it. The sentence seems to be executed too with less rigour upon the women, who bring forth children with little sorrow, and hardly any danger. We may safely belive as the Turks do, that all the women who die in childbed in this happy country, go directly to Paradise. The Indian women of our continent make so little of this affair, that they never will have any assistance. They are so far from needing the skill of a man-midwife, that they will not suffer a woman to be present at their labour. They retire into some lonely place, when they find their pains comeing on, and leaning upon a crutch, leave all to the midwifery of nature. Our ground likewise instead of thorns and thistles, brings forth pleasant fruits and wholesome grain, with little cultivation, and our poor Negros are free-men in comparison of the slaves who till your ungenerous soil; at least if slavery consists in scarcity, and hard work. Our land produces all the fine things of Paradise, except innocence and the tree of life; and these we should have in some measure, if we had the grace to use our other good things temperatly. If we could content ourselves with a farinacious dyet, and not devour our fellow-creaturs so unmercifully. If we could prohibit the juice of the sugarcane, and use the blood of the grape with moderation. If plenty and a warm sun did not make us lazy, and hate motion and exercise as much as the colonel, if we lived not

for ever, we might at least approach to the years of a patriarch.

Pardon me my Lord that I am so lavish in the praises of my country, it is only to convince you, that tho' I have received all these fine things in exchange for your Lordships company, yet I must say it with concern, I am a looser by the bargain. Neither could I sit down quietly under so great a disadvantage, but for the good of my children. There are so many expences in England, that there is no laying up any thing for them. But here I can live in great luxury, without being any thing out of pocket, and can save great part of what my effects produce on this side the water. Thus prudence has for once got the better of a very strong inclination, which has happened so seldome to me, that I may be allowed to boast of it.

I wonder they are so long in providing us with a lieutenant-governour, sure the post is not considerable enough for a violent competition. I was in hopes the duke and his noble brother[2] would have spoke a good word for an old acquaintance, who gave them timely notice of the vacancy, but it was his misfortune that he was born on the wrong side of Tweed. I have yet no account of any body named, but am informed by the bye that Sir Robert[3] reserves it for a friend of his. I am a little sorry for it, because I fear that his dependance being on so powerfull an interest, he may expect his gains to be proportionable to his merit. If such be his expectations, the gentleman will be sadly disappointed, because we are here so frugal of the publick money, that we are neither to be flatter'd nor frightened out of one penny more than the established salary. We give nothing more to one who uses us ill, nor are we more liberal to one who uses us well, having learnt from our mother country, how easy it is to draw publick liberalitys into presedent.

I long to hear, whether our strong squadrons of men of war, have been the proper ambassadors of peace, or whether they have hastened on the war. Bullys make a despicable figure when their blustring don't succeed. I confess ships of the line bully with the best grace in the world, and with the most noise, yet I know not by what fate it happens, ours commonly do ourselves more harm by the expence, than they do the enemy by their execution. The squadron sent to the West-Indies under the

---

2. Byrd considered the duke of Argyll and his brother, the earl of Islay, to be his patrons.

3. Sir Robert Walpole, First Lord of the Admiralty.

command of Admiral Hosier, has had a great mortality amongst the men, so that this peaceable campaign is like to cost abundance of brave fellows lives, as well as treasure. However the ministers will have the same excuse for it, that the pope has for licenceing some women to be harlots, to prevent greater mischif amongst the rest.

Mrs. Byrd begs your Lordship to accept of her humble service, and so do my daughters, who for want of the diversions of the town, amuse themselves with housewifery of every kind, that if ever they are married, they may be of some use to their husbands. I wish your Lordship as happy as health, innocence, and a son who copys all your fine qualitys can make you, being with the greatest respect your Lordships most humble servant W. Byrd.

LETTER TO JOHN BOYLE, BARON BOYLE OF BROGHILL[1]

Virginia, the 28th of July, 1730
My Lord

I read your Lordships entertaining letter of the 3d of September with exceeding great pleasure. You describe the happiness of the married state so naturally, that every word seems to flow from your heart, like the preaching of some divines, who at the same time they tell us our duty, convince us they practice it themselves. It is a great advantage to matrimony when it comes recommended by a person of your Lordships rank and good tast. So many are shipwreckt in that sea, that it has now quite lost the name of the Pacifick Ocean, in which they say there are no storms or intemperate weather, but all is smooth, calm, and undisturbed. But if I may be permitted to carry on the comparison, marriage, as it is commonly managed is more like the Bay of Biscay, where the sea is perpetually disturbed, and the waves run mountain-high, making every body sick that comes near it.

Tho' I shall never want temptations to return to England while Lord Orrery and your Lordship are there, yet I have as many reasons as I have children, which are no less than six, to stay where I am. Besides when it grows time for a man to think of quiting the world, he should do it by degrees, therefore retiring into the country, especially so lonely a country as this is, is a fair step towards dying, at least in the language of fine ladys, who call it being buryed alive. One great danger for them, is, least their tongues should grow to the roof of their mouths, in so silent a place. We have no musick but that of the innocent birds, no publick places to shew their charms, or masquerades to conceal their frailtys. Alass here are no pretty fellows to flatter their vanity, and make them belive they are angels, as the first step towards making them devils. Here they are forced to produce their beauties to fair daylight, which is not so friendly to their blemishes as candles, which make your ladies like bats turn night into day, and chuse darkness rather than light. This at least may be said of a country life, that one of the sexes are not so absolutely useless as it is in towne. There their whole business is to give pain to the men, and pleasure to themselves, tho' the dear creatures are very often mistaken, and the pain comes home to their own doors. But here for want of more agreable employment, they are forced to assist in the management and superintendency of their familys. The differance then is this, that here the women are the bees who help to make the honey, and your ladys the drones who eat it. Indeed I cannot say that our men are so well employed as they are with you. We do not exercize our wits, and our fingers in the slights and mysterys of gaming, to build our fortunes on the ruins of our friends, and acquaintance. We do not improve ourselves in politiques at coffee-houses, so as to be able to decide the pretensions and interests of all the princes of Europe. We know not how to hold the ballance of power, and weigh to a grain the strength and riches of all our neighbouring nations. We study not the gentle art of love, nor can flatter the women into a good oppinion of their undoers. We have no court where we might improve in our honesty and sincerity, no senate to teach us publick spirit, and the love of our country. These my Lord are huge disadvantages, which I must be content to lye under in this solitary part of the world.

I am glad Mr. Southwell is so happily married, I dare say he will do honour to the holy state. I have not heard from him, or any of the family these three years, but shall always rejoice at their felicity. They rank me among the dead, as a fresh-water philosopher used to say of all those who were at sea, but like them I have a chance of coming to life again some time or another. In the mean time, I wish Lord and Lady Boyle perfect health and content, and am, my Lord your Lordships most obediant humble servant W. Byrd.

---

1. The text is from *The Correspondence of the Three William Byrds of Westover,* ed. Marion Tinling (1977).

LETTER TO JOHN PERCEVAL, EARL OF EGMONT[1]

Virginia, the 12th of July, 1736
My Lord

I had the honour of your Lordships commands of the 9th of September, and since that have the pleasure of conversing a great deal with your picture. It is incomparably well done & the painter has not only hit your ayr, but some of the vertues too which used to soften and enliven your features. So that every connoisseur that sees it, can see t'was drawn for a generous, benevolent, & worthy person. It is no wonder perhaps that I could discern so many good things in the portrait, when I knew them so well in the original, just like those who pick out the meaning of the Bible, altho' in a strange language, because they were aquainted with the subject before. But I own I was pleased to find some strangers able to read your Lordships character on the canvas, as plain as if they had been physiognomists by profession.

Your Lordships opinion concerning rum & Negros is certainly very just, and your excludeing both of them from your colony of Georgia will be very happy; tho' with respect to rum, the saints of New England I fear will find out some trick to evade your Act of Parliament. They have a great dexterity at palliating a perjury so well as to leave no tast of it in the mouth, nor can any people like them slip through a penal statute. They will give some other name to their rum, which they may safely do, because it gos by that of kill-devil in this country from its banefull qualitys. A watchfull eye must be kept on these foul traders or all the precautions of the trustees will be vain.

I wish my Lord we coud be blesst with the same prohibitions. They import so many Negros hither, that I fear this colony will some time or other be confirmed by the name of New Guinea. I am sensible of many bad consequences of multiplying these Ethiopians amongst us. They blow up the pride, & ruin the industry of our white people, who seing a rank of poor creatures below them, detest work for fear it shoud make them look like slaves. Then that poverty which will ever attend upon idleness, disposes them as much to pilfer, as it dos the Portuguese, who account it much more like a gentleman to steal, than to dirty their hands with labour of any kind.

Another unhappy effect of many Negros, is, the necessity of being severe. Numbers make them insolent, & then foul means must do, what fair will not. We have however nothing like the inhumanity here, that is practiced in the islands, & God forbid we ever shoud. But these base tempers require to be rid with a tort rein, or they will be apt to throw their rider. Yet even this is terrible to a good naturd man, who must submit to be either a fool or a fury. And this will be more our unhappy case, the more Negros are increast amongst us.

But these private mischeifs are nothing if compard to the publick danger. We have already at least 10,000 men of these descendants of Ham fit to bear arms, & their numbers increase every day as well by birth as importation. And in case there shoud arise a man of desperate courage amongst us, exasperated by a desperate fortune, he might with more advantage than Cataline, kindle a sevile war. Such a man might be dreadfully mischeivous before any opposition coud be formed against him, and tinge our rivers as wide as they are with blood. Besides the calamitys which woud be brought upon us by such an attempt, it woud cost our mother country many a fair million to make us as profitable as we are at present.

It were therefore worth the consideration of a British Parliament, my Lord, to put an end to this unchristian traffick of makeing merchandize of our fellow creatures. At least the farther importation of them into our colonys shoud be prohibited lest they prove as troublesome & dangerous every where, as they have been lately in Jamaica, where besides a vast expence of mony, they have cost the lives of many of His Majestys subjects. We have mountains in Virginia too, to which they may retire as safely, and do as much mischeif as they do in Jamaica. All these matters duly considerd, I wonder the legislature will indulge a few ravenous traders to the danger of the publick safety, and such traders as woud freely sell their fathers, their elder brothers, & even the wives of their bosomes, if they coud black their faces & get any thing by them.

I intirely agree with your Lordship in the detestation you seem to have for that diabolical liquor rum, which dos more mischeif to peoples industry & morals than any thing except gin and the pope. And if it were not a little too poetical, I shoud fancy, as the Gods of old were said to quaff nectar, so the devils are fobbd off with rumm. Tho' my dear country men woud think this unsavory spirit much too good for devils, because they are fonder of it than they are of their wives & children, for they often sell the bread out of their mouths, to buy rumm to put in their own. Thrice happy Georgia, if it be in the power of any

---

1. The text is from *The Correspondence of the Three William Byrds of Westover*, ed. Marion Tinling (1977).

law to keep out so great an enimy to health industry & vertue! The new setlers there had much better plant vinyards like Noah, & get drunk with their own wine.

I wish Mr. Oglethorp after he has put his generous scheme in execution in that favorite colony, woud make the tour of the continent, & then I shoud hope for the pleasure of seing him in some of his planetary motions. I was acquainted with him formerly, when I coud see he had the seeds of vertue in him, which have since grown up into fruit. Heaven give both your Lordship & him success in your disinterested endeavours for makeing Georgia a very flourishing & happy place. And methinks if he were governour of Carolina, with a power of appointing a lieutenant governour of Georgia, he might do more service by far, than by visiting it only sometimes. Because things are apt to run into strange abuses in this part of the world, without an uninterrupted vigilance.

I have met with disappointment in the little colony I expected from Switzerland. Some body deluded them to Carolina, where most of them I understand are dead. They woud probably have had better luck at the place I intended for them, which is as healthy as any in America, the soil very good, & full of cool & delightful streams.

Not a syllable have I heard this long time of any of the Southwell family. They are so unkind as to drop me, distance being in their reckoning the same as death; but I must be dead indeed not to remember them and wish them all the health & prosperity in the world. If your Lordship will be so good as to give them a place in the much coveted account of your own family, it will be entertaining in a high degree to your Lordship's &c.

Lord Egmont

PATRICK TAILFER, HUGH ANDERSON, DAVID DOUGLAS (FLOURISHED 1741)

A True and Historical Narrative of the Colony of Georgia in America, first published in Charleston and then in London in 1741, is a wonderfully satirical account of Georgia governor James Oglethorpe and his colony. The narrative reveals the remarkable penchant for writers in the early eighteenth century to work collaboratively, in what might be called "coffeehouse style," in creating a publication of lasting renown.

James Edward Oglethorpe, the leader of the Georgia colonization movement and the target of the accumulated abuse raised in the *True and Historical Narrative,* was born in London in 1696. An English general and philanthropist, he projected the colony of Georgia for the settlement of England's and other countries' insolvent debtors and persecuted Protestants. He personally conducted the colonizing expedition for Georgia's settlement in 1733 and remained there a decade, returning to England in 1743, where he remained until his death in Essex in 1785. Oglethorpe conceived of Georgia as a haven for those who had nowhere to go but upward, in social and financial standing, and he considered that having people who otherwise were not contributing to England's commonwealth leave and make their own contribution from afar was a reasonable way to solve problems at home and in the southern colonies of North America.

Georgia's charter was granted to Oglethorpe, Lord Perceval (later Lord Egmont), and nineteen others by the king on June 9, 1732. The charter for "settling poor persons of London" in a colony to the southwest of Carolina was an outgrowth of Dr. Bray's associates of London, a philanthropic group interested in education and missionary activity. Unlike other charters that were more typically for corporations to settle with an idea of gaining a return on their venture, this charter provided for a governing council to serve as a trust for twenty-one years. The council was enabled by Georgia's charter to make rules of behavior and activity for the colony, and the idea was that the colony would be self-sustaining after its preliminary period and would, in fact, bring a return to England thereafter, with no need for interference (or expenditure) by the Crown or Parliament. Oglethorpe, Perceval, and Benjamin Martyn (the secretary throughout the life of the governing board) ruled through so-called regulations (rather than enacting laws, as in other British colonies), and these regulations were not subject to the king's veto. Their goal was to create a new society of impoverished misfits and otherwise persecuted peoples, and the colony attracted a number of different kinds of peoples, from criminals and ne'er-do-wells to poor law-abiders to clusters of Swiss Germans known as Salzburgers (Lutherans who were persecuted in their mountainous homeland in central Europe). In the propaganda circulated about Georgia, the colony was described as a utopian place, a haven for people under duress, with a climate and soil close to that in paradise.

In effect, though, the colony was to serve as a buffer state between South Carolina—Tailfer's and the others' "land of liberty" then becoming even more prized for its growing wealth from slavery and the production of staples—and the Spanish, French, and Indians on the interior to the south of Charleston and other central ports. The goal, from the point of view of imperial Britain, was to gain a buffer territory while also gaining potential produce for the staple-commodity marketplace of Britain and Europe. The intense conviction by the trustees that they were doing good seems to have blinded them to living conditions in the colony, though, to be sure, their utopian goal of collective land ownership (no individuals could own land in fee simple) and their lack of interest in the rum trade (it was harmful to Indians and Indian relations) and in permitting Georgia to become a slave colony (which undermined the attempt to develop an ethic of hard work) was in keeping with their philanthropic humanist goals.

What troubled Tailfer, Anderson, Douglas, and "the others" on the title page of Peter Timothy's publication of *A True and Historical Narrative of the Colony of Georgia in America* (Charleston, 1741) was that the goals were in excess of the possibilities of the land and the people who had settled in the area. In typical Grub Street style, they burlesqued Georgia propaganda literature (some of it written by Martyn and perhaps Oglethorpe himself), indicating that the paradise they spoke of was a mismanaged and uncontrolled wilderness. Using irony and invective, the authors targeted the overseas management of the colony (after the initial period of settlement, the trustees remained in England), all the while uncovering the true problems of the colony: its philanthropic goals conflicted with its military ones, and the persons permitted to be in the colony were unprepared for the kind of labor and manner of living expected of them.

The tract's authors were men of an elite-group station, ready to settle a colony under a more liberal government, such as that of South Carolina or North Carolina. Dr. Patrick Tailfer, born and educated in Scotland, arrived in Georgia in August 1734 with a land patent for 500 acres, the largest grant an individual was permitted to hold in the colony. His land, seventy miles inland from Savannah, was in his view, not agriculturally sound, and it was far from the kind of intellectual community he expected to be near. He set up a medical practice in Savannah, instead of working his land, and hired out his indentured servants at a profit. Disgruntled, perhaps because he considered himself a better potential leader for the colony than the absent trustees and landlords, he left the colony for Charleston, where he set up a medical practice, in 1741. His collaborators, Hugh Anderson and David Douglas, likewise were of a higher station than the typical settlers were expected to be in Georgia. Anderson was given a land grant and town lot in Savannah itself because, according to his petition, his wife was the granddaughter of an earl and had been "tenderly brought up, and would require some society." He arrived with his family (his wife, five children, and five servants) in 1737 and commenced overseeing the mulberry plantation that had been assigned to his care (he received a stipend for the work), but Anderson concluded that although Georgia might flourish in the future, it took too much work at present. In 1741, he was, like Tailfer, in Charleston, the head of a school there. David Douglas's background and reasons for settling in Georgia are less well known. In 1736, he was granted a town lot in Savannah. Four years later, he petitioned for land on Wilmington Island, a grant evidently given him at the time so that he, too, ended up in the more attractive "land of Liberty," Charleston.

from A TRUE AND HISTORICAL NARRATIVE OF THE COLONY OF GEORGIA IN AMERICA[1]

*To His Excellency James Oglethorpe, Esq;
General and Commander in Chief of His
Majesty's Forces in South Carolina and Georgia;
and one of the Honourable Trustees for
Establishing the Colony of GEORGIA in
AMERICA, &c.*

May it please Your Excellency,
As the few surviving Remains of the Colony of *Georgia* find it necessary to present the World (and in particular *Great-Britain*) with a true State of that Province, from its first Rise, to its present Period; Your Excellency (of all Mankind) is best entitled to the Dedication, as the principal Author of its present Strength and Affluence, Freedom and Prosperity: And tho' incontestable Truths will recommend the following *NARRATIVE* to the patient and attentive Reader; yet your Name, *SIR,* will be no little Ornament to the Frontispiece, and may possibly engage some courteous Perusers a little beyond it.

THAT Dedication and Flattery are synonimous, is the Complaint of every Dedicator, who concludes himself ingenuous and fortunate, if he can discover a less trite and direct Method of flattering than is usually practised; but we are happily prevented from the least Intention of this kind, by the repeated Offerings of the *Muses* and *News-Writers* to Your Excellency, in the publick Papers: 'Twere presumptuous even to dream of equalling or encreasing them: We therefore flatter ourselves, that Nothing we can advance will in the least shock Your Excellency's Modesty; not doubting but your Goodness will pardon any Deficiency of Elegance and Politeness, on account of our Sincerity, and the serious Truths we have the Honour to approach you with.

WE have seen the ancient Custom of sending forth Colonies, for the Improvement of any distant Territory, or new Acquisition, continued down to ourselves: but to Your Excellency alone it is owing, that the World is made acquainted with a Plan, highly refined from those of all former Projectors. They fondly imagin'd it necessary to communicate to such young Settlements the fullest

Rights and Properties, all the Immunities of their Mother Countries, and Privileges rather more extensive: By such Means, in deed, these Colonies flourish'd with early Trade and Affluence; but Your Excellency's Concern for our perpetual Welfare could never permit you to propose such transitory Advantages for us: You considered Riches like a Divine and Philosopher, as the *Irritamenta Malorum,*[2] and knew that they were disposed to inflate weak Minds with Pride; to pamper the Body with Luxury, and introduce a long Variety of Evils. Thus have you *Protected us from ourselves,* as Mr. *Waller* says,[3] by keeping all Earthly Comforts from us: You have afforded us the Opportunity of arriving at the Integrity of the *Primitive Times,* by intailing a more than *Primitive Poverty* on us: The Toil, that is necessary to our bare Subsistence, must effectually defend us from the Anxieties of any further Ambition: As we have no Properties, to feed Vain-Glory and beget Contention; so we are not puzzled with any System of Laws, to ascertain and establish them: The valuable Virtue of Humility is secured to us, by your Care to prevent our procuring, or so much as seeing any *Negroes* (the only human Creatures proper to improve our Soil) lest our Simplicity might mistake the poor *Africans* for greater Slaves than ourselves: And that we might fully receive the Spiritual Benefit of those wholesome Austerities; you have wisely denied us the Use of such Spiritous Liquors, as might in the least divert our Minds from the Contemplation of our Happy Circumstances.

OUR Subjects swells upon us; and did we allow ourselves to indulge our Inclination, without considering our weak Abilities, we should be tempted to launch out into many of Your Excellency's extraordinary Endowments, which do not so much regard the Affair in Hand: But as this would lead us beyond the Bounds of a Dedication; so would it engross a Subject too extensive for us, to the Prejudice of other Authors and Panegyrists; We shall therefore confine ourselves to that remarkable Scene of Your Conduct, whereby *Great-Britain* in general, and the Settlers of *Georgia,* in particular, are laid under such inexpressible Obligations.

BE pleased then, *Great SIR,* to accompany our heated Imaginations, in taking a View of this Colony of *Georgia!* this Child of your auspicious Politicks! arrived at the ut-

---

1. The pamphlet was first published by Peter Timothy in Charleston, South Carolina, early in 1741. It was printed in London in December of that year. The text is adapted from the original publication in London.

2. *Irritamenta Malorum,* incitements to evil.

3. "Protect us from ourselves, and from the foe," a line from a poem by Edmund Waller (1606–87), "A Panegyrick to My Lord Protector, of the Present Greatness, and Joint Interest, of His Highness, and This Nation."

most Vigor of its Constitution, at a Term when most for-
mer States have been struggling through the Convulsions
of their Infancy. This early Maturity, however, lessens our
Admiration, that Your Excellency lives to see (what few
Founders ever aspired after) the great Decline and almost
final Termination of it. So many have finish'd their
Course during the Progress of the Experiment, and such
Numbers have retreated from the Fantoms of Poverty and
Slavery which their cowardly Imaginations pictur'd to
them; that you may justly vaunt with the boldest Hero of
them all,

—Like Death you reign
O'er silent Subjects and a desart Plain.
　　　　　B u s i r i s.[4]

YET must your Enemies (if you have any) be reduced
to confess, that no ordinary Statesman could have digested, in the like Manner, so capacious a Scheme, such a
copious Jumble of Power and Politicks. We shall content
ourselves with observing, that all those beauteous Models
of Government which the little States of *Germany* exercise, and those extensive Liberties which the Boors of
Poland enjoy, were design'd to concenter in your System;
and were we to regard the Modes of Government, we
must have been strangely unlucky to have miss'd of the
best, where there was an Appearance of so great a Variety;
for under the Influence of our *Perpetual Dictator,* we have
seen something like *Aristocracy, Oligarchy,* as well as the
Triumvirate, Decemvirate, and *Consular Authority* of famous Republicks, which have expired many Ages before
us: What Wonder then we share the same Fate? Do their
Towns and Villages exist but in Story and Rubbish? We
are all over Ruins; our Publick-Works, Forts, Wells, High-
Ways, Light-House, Store and Water-Mills, &c. are dignified like theirs, with the same venerable Desolation.
The Logg-House, indeed, is like to be the last forsaken
Spot of Your Empire; yet even this, through the Death, or
Desertion of those who should continue to inhabit it, must
suddenly decay; the Bankrupt Jailor himself shall be soon
denied the Privilege of human Conversation; and when
this last Moment of the Spell expires, the whole shall vanish like the Illusion of some *Eastern Magician.*

---

4. "Like Death, a solitary King I'll reign, / O'er silent Subjects, and a desart Plain," a line from the verse drama *Busiris*
(1719), by Edward Young (1683–1765). Busiris, in Greek
mythology, was an Egyptian king, the son of Poseidon, who
slaughtered on Zeus's altar all foreigners who entered Egypt.
Heracles was said to have come to Egypt to kill the king and his
followers.

BUT let not this solitary Prospect impress Your Excellency with any Fears of having your Services to Mankind,
and to the Settlers of *Georgia* in particular, buried in
Oblivion; for it we diminutive Authors are allow'd to
prophesy (as you know Poets in those Cases formerly did)
we may confidently presage, That while the Memoirs of
America continue to be read in *English, Spanish,* or the
Language of the *Scots* High-Landers, Your Excellency's
Exploits and Epocha will be transmitted to Posterity.

SHOULD your Excellency apprehend the least Tincture
of Flattery in any Thing already hinted, we may sincerely
assure you, we intended nothing that our Sentiments did
not very strictly attribute to your Merit; and, in such Sentiments, we have the Satisfaction of being fortified by all
Persons of Impartiality and Discernment.

BUT to trespass no longer on those Minutes, which
Your Excellency may suppose more significantly employ'd on the Sequel; let it suffice at present, to assure
you, that we are deeply affected with your Favours; and
tho' unable of ourselves properly to acknowledge them,
we shall embrace every Opportunity of Recommending
you to higher Powers, who (we are hopeful) will reward
Your Excellency according to your MERIT.

May it please Your Excellency,
Your Excellency's
Most devoted Servants,
The Land-Holders of Georgia,
Authors of the following Narrative

Preface

The colony of Georgia has afforded so much subject of
conversation to the world, that it is not to be questioned,
but a true and impartial account of it, from its first settlement, to its present period, will be generally agreeable;
and the more so, that the subject has hitherto been so
much disguised and misrepresented in pamphlets, poems,
gazettes, and journals.

If it is asked, Why this NARRATIVE has not been published to the world sooner? we assign two reasons, which
(we doubt not) will be satisfactory.

First, a number of honourable gentlemen accepted the
charge of Trustees for executing the purposes in His
Majesty's most gracious Charter; gentlemen, whose honour and integrity we never did, or yet do, call in question:
But, to our great misfortune, none of that honourable
body (excepting Mr. Oglethorpe) ever had opportunity of
viewing the situation and circumstances of the colony,
and judging for themselves as to the necessities thereof.
How far Mr. Oglethorpe's schemes were consistent with

the welfare or prosperity of it, will best appear from the following NARRATIVE.

When experience gradually unfolded to us the alterations we found absolutely requisite to our subsisting, we made all dutiful and submissive applications to these our patrons, in whom we placed so much confidence: This course we judged the most proper and direct, and therefore repeated these our dutiful applications, both to the body of the Trustees and to Mr. Oglethorpe; but alas! our miseries could not alter his views of things, and therefore we could obtain no redress from him; and the honourable board we found were prejudiced against our petitions (no doubt) through misinformations and misrepresentations; and this (we are confident) a further enquiry and time will convince them of.

The inviolable regard we paid to the honourable board, kept us from applying to any other power for redress, whilst the least hopes could be entertained of any from them: And we make no doubt, but that our moderation, in this respect, will recommend us to all persons of humanity.

A *second* reason is, that as we had daily occasion of seeing our supreme magistrates, who ruled over us with unlimited power, exercising illegal acts of authority, by threatenings, imprisonments, and other oppressions; therefore had just reason to apprehend, that any further steps, to obtain relief, might subject us to the like effects of arbitrary power; so, until now, that a handful of us have made our escape to a LAND OF LIBERTY[5] (after having made shipwreck of our time and substance in that unhappy colony) we had it not in our power to represent the state of that settlement to the world, or to make our application to higher powers for redress.

We are hopeful, that the perusal of the following sheets will rectify two sorts of readers in their surprize in relation to the colony of Georgia, viz. those of Great Britain, who have never known this part of the world but by description; and those of America: The first are no doubt surprized, to think it possible, that so pleasant and temperate a clime; so fruitful a soil; such extensive privileges; all which were publickly given out; and such considerable sums of publick and private benefactions, have not satisfied and enriched us: Them we refer to the following Narrative for satisfaction. The American reader,

on the other hand, must be equally surprized to find that such numbers should have been so fooled and blindfolded, as to expect to live in this part of America by cultivation of lands without Negroes, and much more without titles to their lands, and laid under a load of grievances and restrictions: And though these were redressed, how could persons in their senses ever imagine, that fifty acres of pine-barren, not value fifty six pences in property (and whereof many thousands may be purchased at half that rate in the neighbouring province) could maintain a family of white people, and pay such duties and quit-rents in a few years, as the richest grounds in Carolina, or other provinces in America will never bear? To these last we shall only beg leave to observe, that such fatal artifice was used (we shall not say by whom) such specious pretences were made use of, and such real falsities advanced, and the smallest foundations of truth magnified to hyperbole; that we, who had no opportunity of knowing other ways, or means of learning the real truth, and being void of all suspicion of artifice or design, easily believed all these, and fell into the decoy.

The mind of man is naturally curious and enterprizing; we easily feed our wishes into realities, and affect and look upon every novelty in the most favourable light; how easy then is it, for cunning and artifice to lay hold on the weak sides of our fellow-creatures, as we catch fish with a hook baited to their particular gout?

To prove this charge, we shall only transcribe some passages from a piece of prose, and some from a piece of poesy; by which specimens, the reader may judge of some considerable number which were dispersed and vended of the same stamp.

The first are from a pamphlet printed at London, 1733, entitled *A New and Accurate Account of the Provinces of South Carolina and Georgia*.[6] The author has not thought fit to favour us with his name; but it is easy to conceive, that we, who suspected no artifice or design, must conclude, that it came from the best authority, from the circumstances of its being dispersed publickly, and not being contradicted, and from the author's intimate acquaintance (at least so pretended) with all the Trustees'

---

5. South Carolina is the "land of liberty."

6. The title, regularly attributed at the time to Oglethorpe, was first published in London in 1732 and then again in 1733. It was probably written by Oglethorpe's associate, Benjamin Martyn.

measures and designs. After a high encomium upon the Trustees, page 7, he says, 'The air of Georgia is healthy, being always serene and pleasant, never subject to excessive heat or cold, or sudden changes of weather; the winter is regular and short, and the summer cooled with refreshing breezes; it neither feels the cutting north-west wind that the Virginians complain of, nor the intense heats of Spain, Barbary, Italy, and Egypt. The soil will produce anything with very little culture.' Page 19, 'All sorts of corn yield an amazing increase; one hundred fold is the common estimate; though their husbandry is so slight that they can only be said to scratch the earth, and meerely to cover the seed: All the best sort of cattle and fowls are multiplied without number, and therefore without a price: Vines are natives here.' Page 21, 'The woods near Savannah are not hard to be cleared; many of them have no under-wood, and the trees do not stand generally thick on the ground, but at considerable distances asunder; when you fall the timber for the use, or to make tar, the root will rot in four or five years; and in the mean time you may pasture the ground; but, if you would only destroy the timber, it is done by half a dozen strokes of an ax surrounding each tree a little above the root; in a year or two the water getting into the wound rots in the timber, and a brisk gust of wind fells many acres for you in an hour, of which you may make one bright bonfire. Such will be frequently here the fate of the pine, the wallnut, the cypress, the oak, and the cedar. Such an air and soil can only be described by a poetical pen, because there is no danger of exceeding the truth; therefore take Waller's description of an island in the neighbourhood of Carolina, to give you an idea of this happy climate:

'The Spring, which but salutes us here,
Inhabits there, and courts them all the Year;
Ripe Fruits and Blossoms on the same Tree live;
At once they promise what at once they give.
So sweet the Air, so moderate the Clime,
None sickly lives, or dies before his Time.
Heav'n sure has kept this Spot of Earth uncurst,
To shew how all Things were created first.'[7]

---

7. A quotation of lines from the first canto of Edmund Waller's *The Battle of the Summer Islands.*

Page 27, 'The Indians bring many a mile the whole deer's flesh, which they sell to the people who live in the country, for the value of sixpence sterling; and a wild turkey of forty pounds weight, for the value of two pence.' In page 32, the author when recommending the Georgia adventure to gentlemen of decayed circumstances, who must labour at home or do worse, states the following objection, viz. 'If such people can't get bread here for their labour, how will their condition be mended in Georgia?' Which he solves in the following manner, 'The answer is easy; part of it is well attested, and part self-evident; they have land there for nothing, and that land so fertile, that, as is said before, they receive a hundredfold increase, for taking a very little pains: Give here in England ten acres of good land to one of those helpless persons, and I doubt not his ability to make it sustain him, and by his own culture, without letting it to another; but the difference between no rent, and rack'd rent, is the difference between eating and starving.' Page 32, 'These Trustees not only give land to the unhappy who go thither, but are also impowered to receive the voluntary contributions of charitable persons, to enable to furnish the poor adventurers with all necessaries for the expense of their voyage, occupying the land, and supporting them, till they find themselves comfortably settled; so that now the unfortunate will not be obliged to bind themselves to a long servitude to pay for their passage; for they may be carried *gratis* into a land of liberty and plenty, where they immediately find themselves in the possession of a competent estate, in an happier climate than they knew before, and they are unfortunate indeed, if here they cannot forget their sorrows.' Nay, as if such assertions as these were not powerful enough to influence poor people, calculations are subjoined, to demonstrate, that a family consisting of one poor man, his wife, and child of seven years old, may in Georgia earn sixty pounds sterling per annum, and this abstracted from silk, wine, &c. Page 41, 'Now this very family in Georgia, by raising rice and corn sufficient for its occasions, and by attending the care of their cattle and land (which almost every one is able to do in some tolerable degree for himself) will easily produce in gross value the sum of sixty pounds sterling per annum, nor is this to be wondered at, because of the valuable assistance it has from a fertile soil and a stock given gratis; which must always be remembered in this calculation.'

'The calculation of one hundred such families when formally extended, stands thus',—Page 43,

	l.	*s.*	*d.*
'In London one hundred poor men earn,	500	00	0
One hundred women, and one hundred children,	500	00	0
	1000	00	0
In Georgia an hundred families earn,			
One hundred men for labour,	1200	00	0
Ditto for care of their stock at leisure hours,	1200	00	0
One hundred women and one hundred children.	2400	00	0
Land and stock in themselves,	1200	00	0
Total,	6000	00	0

Q.E.D.'

But we must conclude this head, lest we tire the reader. We shall now beg leave to quote a few poetical accounts of this paradise of the world, and of the fatherly care and protection we might depend on from Mr. Oglethorpe. An hundred hackney Muses might be instanced; but we shall confine ourselves to the celebrated performance of the Rev. Mr. Samuel Wesly, where we might well expect a sufficient stock of truth and religion, to counter-balance a poetical licence. *Vide* a poem entitled *Georgia, and Verses upon Mr. Oglethorpe's Second Voyage to Georgia.* Printed London, 1736.[8]

'See where beyond the spacious Ocean lies
A wide waste Land beneath the Southern Skies;
Where kindly Suns for Ages roll'd in vain,
Nor e'er the Vintage saw, or rip'ning Grain,
Where all Things into wild Luxuriance ran,
And burthen'd Nature ask'd the Aid of Man.
In this sweet Climate and prolifick Soil,
He bids the eager Swain indulge his Toil;
In free Possession to the Planter's Hand,
Consigns the rich uncultivated Land.
Go you, the Monarch cries, go settle there,
Whom *Britain* from her Plenitude can spare:
Go, your old wonted Industry pursue;
Nor envy *Spain* the Treasures of *Peru.*'[9]

'But not content in Council here to join,
A further Labour, OGLETHORPE, is thine:
In each great Deed thou claim'st the foremost Part,
And Toil and Danger charm thy gen'rous Heart:
But chief for this thy warm Affections rise;
For oh! thou view'st it with a Parent's Eyes:
For this thou tempt'st the vast tremendous Main,
And Floods and Storms oppose their Threats in vain.'[10]

'He comes, whose Life, while absent from your View,
Was one continued Ministry for you;
For you were laid out all his Pains and Art,
Won ev'ry Will and soften'd ev'ry Heart.
With what paternal Joy shall he relate,
How views its Mother Isle your little State:
Think while he strove your distant Coast to gain,
How oft he sigh'd and chid the tedious Main,
Impatient to survey, by Culture grac'd,
Your dreary Wood-Land and your rugged Waste.
Fair were the Scenes he feign'd, the Prospects fair;
and sure, ye *Georgians,* all he feign'd was there,
A Thousand Pleasures crowd into his Breast;
But one, one mighty Thought absorbs the rest,
And gives me Heav'n to see, the Patriot cries,
Another BRITAIN in the Desart rise.'[11]

Again,
'With nobler Products see they GEORGIA teems,
Chear'd with the genial Sun's director Beams;
There the wild Vine to Culture learns to yield,
And purple Clusters ripen through the Field.
Now bid thy Merchants bring thy Wine no more
Or from the *Iberian* or the *Tuscan* Shore;
No more they need th' *Hungarian* Vineyards drain,
And *France* herself may drink her best *Champain.*
Behold! at last, and in a subject Land,
Nectar sufficient for thy large Demand:
Delicious Nectar, powerful to improve
Our hospitable Mirth and social Love:
This for thy jovial Sons.—Nor less the Care
Of thy young Province, to oblige the FAIR;
Here tend the Silk Worm in the verdant Shade,
The frugal Matron and the blooming Maid.'[12]

From the whole, we doubt not, the reader will look upon us as sufficiently punished for our credulity: And in-

---

8. *Georgia, A Poem,* was published in London in 1736 with companion publications, "Tomo Chachi, an Ode" and "A Copy of Verses on Mr. Oglethorpe's Second Voyage to Georgia." The poems were long attributed to Samuel Wesley, but all were probably written by Wesley's friend, Thomas Fitzgerald (1695?–1752).

9. The lines match a series of lines in *Georgia, A Poem.*

10. The lines match a series of lines in *Georgia, A Poem.*

11. These lines are taken from "A Copy of Verses on Mr. Oglethorpe's Second Voyage to GEORGIA," published with *Georgia, A Poem.*

12. The lines match a series of lines in *Georgia, A Poem.*

deed, who would not have been catched with such promises, such prospects? What might not the poor man flatter himself with, from such an alteration in his situation? And how much more might a gentleman expect from a plentiful stock of his own, and numbers of servants to set up with? Could a person, with the least faith, have questioned the committing his interests to such guardians, and such a tender father as Mr. Oglethorpe was believed to be? Whether he has acted that generous, that human[e], that fatherly part, the following NARRATIVE must determine.

As for those poetical licences touching the wine and silk; we do not transcribe them as a reflection upon the author; but as a satyr upon the mismanagement of those manufactures; since no measures were taken that seemed really intended for their advancement.

We no wise question the possibility of advancing such improvements in Georgia, with far less sums of money, properly applied, than the publick has bestowed. But not even the flourishing of wine and silk can make a colony of British subjects happy, if they are deprived of the liberties and properties of their birthright.

We have endeavoured to the utmost to be tender of characters; but as we undertake to write an account of facts and truths; there is no help for it, when those facts and truths press home.

It is a common satisfaction to sufferers, to expose to the publick the rocks upon which they split, and the misfortunes by which they suffered; and it may well be allowed us, to publish the causes to which we attribute the ruin of that settlement and ourselves; and more especially as we are prosecutors for justice from higher powers; which we doubt not receiving as the case deserves.

We hope the truth of the following NARRATIVE will recommend itself to the perusal of the candid reader. The fatal truth of this tragedy hath already been sealed with the death of multitudes of our fellow-creatures; but still (thanks to the providence of the Almighty) some survive to attest and confirm the truth of what is herein contained, against any persons or names, however great, however powerful. Our circumstances and sincerity will excuse our want of that politeness and accuracy of stile, which might have represented our case to greater advantage, to the courteous reader, whom we shall no longer detain from the subject in hand.

A True and Historical Narrative, &c.

Nothing is more difficult for authors, than to divest themselves of byass and partiality, especially when they themselves are parties or sufferers in the affair treated of.

It is possible, this may be supposed the case with us the publishers of this *Narrative;* it may be imagined, that the hardships, losses, and disappointments we have met with in the colony of Georgia, will naturally sour our humours, and engage us to represent everything in the worst light.

As the probability of those surmises is very obvious to us, we have, to the utmost of our power, guarded against the weak side of ourselves; and, to convince the world of our sincerity, shall no further descend into the grievances of particular persons, than is absolutely requisite for making our *General Narrative* intelligible; and to a faithful detail of publick vouchers, records, extracts, missives, memorials and representations, shall only adjoin so much of history, as may be necessary to recount the most material events, and complete the connexion.

We are hopeful, that an information, founded upon the strictest truth, will effectually introduce any further steps that Providence shall enable us to take towards procuring the redress of our grievances. While we had the least hopes of redress from our immediate superiors and patrons, we would not; and when we began to despair of relief by that channel, we durst not, make application to any other tribunal, unless we would expose ourselves to the dreadful effects of the resentment of those who had before reduced us to poverty by oppression: And indeed, in all the applications we made for redress, we were browbeat, obstructed, threatened, and branded with opprobrious names, such as proud, idle, lazy, discontented and mutinous people, and several other appellations of that kind; and were always afterwards harrassed by all means whatsoever; several instances of which will appear to the reader in the sequel.

Our late retreat from that confinement, to a *Land of Liberty,* puts it in our power to speak the truth; and though our endeavours are too late to relieve the dead, the dying, and those many now dispersed in all the corners of His Majesty's dominions; yet they may be the means of ushering in sympathy and assistance to the survivors, and to multitudes of widows and orphans of the deceased, from the human[e] and generous.

As our sole design is to give a *plain narrative of the establishment and progress of the colony of Georgia, from its rise to its present period;* we shall court no other ornaments than those of truth and perspicuity; and shall endeavour to carry the reader's attention regularly, from the first to the last motions we make mention of. . . .

GEORGIA lies in the 30 and 31 degrees of north latitude: The air generally clear, the rains being much shorter as well as heavier than in England; the dews are very great; thunder and lightning are expected almost every day in

May, June, July, and August; they are very terrible, especially to a stranger: During those months, from ten in the morning to four in the afternoon, the sun is extremely scorching; but the sea-breeze sometimes blows from ten till three or four: The winter is nearly the same length as in England; but the mid-day sun is always warm, even when the mornings and evenings are very sharp, and the nights piercing cold.

The land is of four sorts; pine barren, oak land, swamp, and marsh. The pine land is of far the greatest extent, especially near the seacoasts: The soil of this is a dry whitish sand, producing shrubs of several sorts, and between them a harsh coarse kind of grass, which cattle do not love to feed upon; but here and there is a little of a better kind, especially in the Savannahs, (so they call the low watery meadows which are usually intermixed with pine lands:) It bears naturally two sorts of fruit; hurtle-berries much like those in England, and chinquopin nuts, a dry nut about the size of a small acorn: A laborious man may in one year clear and plant four or five acres of this land; it will produce, the first year, from two to four bushels of Indian corn, and from four to eight of Indian pease, per acre; the second year it usually bears much about the same; the third, less; the fourth, little or nothing: Peaches it bears well; likewise the white mulberry, which serves to feed the silk worms; the black is about the size of a black cherry, and has much the same flavour.

The oak land commonly lies in narrow streaks between pine land and swamps, creeks or rivers: The soil is a blackish sand, producing several kinds of oak, bay, laurel, ash, wallnut, sumach and gum trees, a sort of sycamore, dog trees and hickory: In the choicest part of this land grow parsimon trees, and a few black mulberry and American cherry trees: The common wild grapes are of two sorts, both red; the fox grape grows two or three only on a stalk, is thick-skinned, large stoned, of a harsh taste, and of the size of a small cherry; the cluster grape is of a harsh taste too, and about the size of a white currant. This land requires much labour to clear; but, when it is cleared, it will bear any grain, for three, four, or five years sometimes without laying any manure upon it: An acre of it generally produces ten bushels of Indian corn, besides five of pease, in a year; so that this is justly esteemed the most valuable land in the province, white people being incapable to clear and cultivate the swamps.

A swamp is any low watery place, which is covered with trees or canes: They are here of three sorts, cypress, river, and cane swamps. Cypress swamps are mostly large ponds, in and round which cypresses grow: Most river swamps are overflown on every side by the river which

runs through or near them; if they were drained, they would produce good rice; as would the cane swamps also, which in the meantime are the best feeding for all sorts of cattle.

The marshes are of two sorts; soft wet marsh, which is all a quagmire, and absolutely good for nothing, and hard marsh, which is a firm sand; but however at some seasons is good for feeding cattle: Marshes of both sorts abound on the sea islands, which are very numerous, and contain all sorts of land; and upon these chiefly, near creeks and runs of watar, cedar trees grow. . . .

We must likewise observe, that the proportion of pine barren to either good swamp or oak and hickory land, is at least six to one; that the far greater number of the small lots have none or very little oak land; and if they had swamp that would bear rice, white people are unable to clear them if they are covered with trees, and though only with canes, which is the easiest to cultivate; it were simply impossible to manufacture the rice by white men; the exercise being so severe, that no Negro can be employed in any other work or labour comparable to it, and many hundreds of them (notwithstanding all the care of their masters) yearly lose their lives by that necessary work.

SAVANNAH stands on a flat bluff (so they term a high land hanging over a creek or river) which rises about forty feet perpendicular from the river, and commands it several miles both upwards and downwards, and if it was not for a point of woods which, for about four miles down the river, stretches itself out towards the south-east, one might have a view of the sea, and the island of Tybee: The soil is a white sand for above a mile in breadth south-east and north-west; beyond this, eastward, is a river swamp; westward, a small body of wood-land (in which was the old Indian town) separated by a creek from a large tract of land, which runs upwards along the side of the river, for the space of about five miles; and being, by far, the best near the town, is reserved for the Indians, as General Oglethorpe declares, as are also some of the islands in the river Savannah, and the three most valuable islands upon all the coast of that province, viz. Ossiba, St. Katherine, and Sapula. South-west of the town is a pine barren, that extends about fourteen miles to Vernon river.

On the east side of the own is situated the publick garden, (being ten acres inclosed) on a barren piece of land, where it is hardly possible for what is planted to live, but impossible to thrive; and from this garden were all the planters to have been furnished with mulberry trees. &c.

The plan of the town was beautifully laid out in wards, tythings, and publick squares left at proper distances for markets and publick buildings; the whole making an agreeable uniformity.

The publick works in this town are, 1st, a court house, being one handsome room, with a piache on three sides: This likewise serves for a church for divine service, none having been ever built, notwithstanding the Trustees, in their publick acts, acknowledge the receipt of about seven hundred pounds sterling, from charitable persons for that express purpose.

2dly, Opposite to the *court house* stands the *log house* or prison (which is the only one remaining of five or six that have been successively built in Savannah) that place of terror, and support of *absolute* power in Georgia.

3dly, Nigh thereto is a house built of logs, at a very great charge, as was said, for the Trustees' Steward; the foundation below ground is already rotten [In August, 1740, a new foundation was begun], as the whole fabrick must be in a short time; for, the roof being flat, the rain comes in at all parts of it.

4thly, The *store-house,* which has been many times altered and amended at a very great charge; and it now serves as a store for the private benefit of one or two, as before mentioned.

5thly, The *guard-house,* which was first built on the bluff, soon decayed; as did a second through improper management; this, now standing, being the third. Several flagg-staffs were likewise erected, the last of which, according to common report, cost *5ol.* sterling.

6thly, A *publick mill* for grinding corn, was first erected at a considerable expence, in one square of the own; but in about three years time (without doing the least service) it fell to the ground: In another square of the town, a second was set up, at a far greater expence, but never finished; and is now erased, and converted into a house for entertaining the Indians, and other such like uses.

7thly, Wells and pumps were made at a great charge; but they were immediately choaked up, and never rendered useful, though this grievance was frequently represented both to the General and magistrates; the want of wells obliging the inhabitants to use the river water, which all the summer over is polluted with putrid marshes, and the numberless insects that deposit their ova there, together with putrefied carcasses of animals and corrupted vegetables; and this, no doubt, occasioned much of the sickness that swept off many.

Several of the houses which were built by freeholders, for want of heirs male, are fallen to the Trustees (even to the prejudice of the lawful creditors of the deceased) and are disposed of as the General thinks proper.

At least two hundred lots were taken up in Savannah,

about one hundred and seventy of which were built upon [Several of these had more than one house upon them]; a great many of these are now ruinous, and many more shut up and abandoned; so that the town appears very desolate, scarce one quarter part of its inhabitants being left, and most of those in a miserable condition, for want of the proper necessaries of life.

Having thus brought this Historical NARRATIVE within the compass proposed, and endeavoured to dispose the materials in as distinct a method and series as the necessary conciseness would allow: We readily admit that the design is far from being complete. To have acquainted the world with all the hardships and oppressions which have been exercised in the colony of Georgia must have required both a larger volume than we were capable of publishing, and more time than we could bestow: We therefore satisfy ourselves, that we have, with care and sincerity, executed so much of the design, as may pave the way to any others who can descend more minutely to particulars; and those, who are best acquainted with the affairs of that colony, will be most capable of judging how tenderly we have touched both persons and things.

It only remains, that we in a few paragraphs endeavour to exhibit to the view of the reader, the REAL causes of the ruin and desolation of the colony; and those briefly are the following.

1. The representing the climate, soil, &c. of Georgia in false and too flattering colours; at least, the not contradicting those accounts when publickly printed and dispersed, and satisfying the world in a true and genuine discription thereof.

2. The restricting the tenure of lands, from a fee simple to tail-male, cutting off daughters and all other relations.

3. The restraining the proprietor from selling, disposing of, or leasing any possesion.

4. The restricting too much the extent of possessions; it being impossible that fifty acres of good land, much less pine barren, could maintain a white family.

5. The laying the planter under a variety of restraints in clearing, fencing, planting, &c. which was impossible to be complied with.

6. The exacting a much higher quit-rent than the richest grounds in North America can bear.

7. But chiefly the denying the use of Negroes, and persisting in such denial after, by repeated applications, we had humbly remonstrated the impossibility of making improvements to any advantage with white servants.

8. The denying us the privilege of being judged by the

laws of our mother country; and subjecting the lives and fortunes of all people in the colony, to one person or set of men, who assumed the privilege, under the name of a Court of Chancery, of acting according to their own will and fancy.

9. General Oglethorpe's taking upon him to nominate magistrates, appoint justices of the peace, and to do many other such things, without ever exhibiting to the people any legal commission or authority for so doing.

10. The neglecting the proper means for encouraging the silk and wine manufactures, and disposing of the liberal sums contributed by the publick, and by private persons, in such ways and channels as have been of little or no service to the colony.

11. The misapplying or keeping up sums of money which have been appointed for particular uses, such as

building a church, &c. several hundreds of pounds sterling (as we are informed) having been lodged in Mr. Oglethorpe's hands for some years by past, for that purpose, and not one stone of it yet laid.

12. The assigning certain fixed tracts of land to those who came to settle in the colony, without any regard to the quality of the ground, occupation, judgment, ability, or inclination of the settler, &c. &c., &c.

By these and many other such hardships, the poor inhabitants of Georgia are scattered over the face of the earth; her plantations a wild; her towns a desart; her villages in rubbish; her improvements a by-word; and her liberties a jest: An object of pity to friends, and of insult, contempt and ridicule to enemies.

HENRY TIMBERLAKE (1730?–1765)

Henry Timberlake's narrative of his activities among the western Cherokees while a soldier for Britain during Europe's Seven Years War in North America, sometimes called the French and Indian War (1755–63), is an important record for many reasons. Timberlake narrated the interactions of British soldiers and traders with the "Over-hill" Cherokees who lived along the Little Tennessee River, revealing the complicated situation of the Cherokees as they faced incursions from the French and their Indian allies, especially the Shawnees, from the west and southwest and from the English to the east. He detailed the lives of these peoples, even as he made a rare record of the treaty-making talks between the British and the western Cherokees, a record that Cherokee peoples would remember and work from as they negotiated with the U.S. federal government a half-century and more later. While providing a significant amount of insight into the life of the soldiery in border areas, Timberlake also recounted stories told by the Cherokees and created a record of their concerns and their culture in the postcontact era, when the impact of European settlements on the ancestral lands of Indian peoples was clear to the Europeans whose lifeways and material goods were being adopted.

That Timberlake produced a "memoir" of his life among the Indians indicates the extent to which nostalgia was already well developed in Britain and Europe for anything remotely connected to "primitive" Indians, that is, Indians who were represented as if they were living in a precontact era. "Indian" poems, plays, and fictions were extremely popular during this midcentury colonial era, and they competed with domestic drama and fiction for a growing readership. For this readership, who was fascinated by anything purportedly "authentic" that was remotely connected to "primitive" Indian peoples, Timberlake included numerous items that would be of interest: a record of Cherokees' speeches, including a decidedly "Englished" poetic rendering of a purported Cherokee war song; discussions of the western Cherokees' dress, habitat, and religion; and stories of the dangers of border life and the battles and negotiations he had witnessed. As an added piece of interest, Timberlake included the Indians' comments and "wonder" at the remarkable things they witnessed when they came to England with him. Timberlake was well aware that even a bare mention of George Washington, already a renowned hero of Britain's wartime effort to control the waterways being challenged by the French, would assist his work, so he brought up Washington and the "Patriot Blues" within the first pages of his narrative to entice his readers into buying the book so as to read more about his experiences.

Beyond seeking a wide public readership for the sake of becoming an author, Timberlake had practical reasons for publishing his narrative, which reached print in London in 1765 as *The Memoirs of Lieut. Henry Timberlake, (Who accompanied the Three Cherokee Indians to England in the Year 1762): Containing Whatever he observed remarkable, or worthy of public Notice, during his Travels to and from that Nation; wherein the Country, Government, Genius, and Customs of the Inhabitants, are authentically described. Also the Principal Occurences during their Residence in London. . . .* At his own effort, risk, and expense, Timberlake volunteered to go as an ensign of peace to live among the western Cherokees as an official sign of amity, peace, and alliance between the British and the Cherokees. Again at his own expense, he traveled with several Cherokees to Williamsburg and then took key Cherokee leaders to England. Little did he know that some who went with him were charging English people fees to see the Cherokees, and he evidently suffered ridicule and abuse as a result of what happened while they were in England. Timberlake wrote the memoir, then, to explain his side of what had actually transpired and thus to restore his reputation and to clarify why he was seeking financial remuneration for engaging in what he considered to be patriotic efforts to create and continue amicable ties between Britain and the Cherokee peoples.

Of Timberlake's personal background, little is known beyond what appeared in his memoir. A native Virginian, Timberlake evidently received a rudimentary education before his father died. He entered the military after his father's death because, as he phrases it, "after my minorship was elapsed, my genius burst out. Arms had been my delight from my infancy, and I now resolved to gratify that inclination, by entering into the service." He began serving in the middle 1750s, when the interest of working to attach the Cherokees—whose ancestral and confederated territories covered about 10 million acres, extending from present-day Virginia to Alabama—to the British rather than the French was heightened by French encroachment on proclaimed British territory, from areas of present-day western Pennsylvania down to Alabama and Louisiana. To Timberlake, the extent of his labors in border areas and as a soldier served as full justification for his request for due remuneration; indeed, perhaps he even hoped to attain a commission as an officer for Britain's interior Indian affairs. What happened as a result of the publication of his "memoir," however, would be something he would not live to witness. Timberlake died in 1765, perhaps even before the book was published.

from THE MEMOIRS OF LIEUT. HENRY TIMBERLAKE[1]

After smoking and talking some time, I delivered a letter from Colonel Stephen, and another from Captain M'Neil,[2] with some presents from each, which were gratefully accepted by Ostenaco and his consort.[3] He gave me a general invitation to his house, while I resided in the country; and my companions found no difficulty in

---

1. The text is from *The Memoirs of Lieut. Henry Timberlake* (London, 1765).

2. The Cherokees affiliated with British military forces during the border wars brought on by Europe's Seven Years War in North America, but upon their return home from the Ohio territory and Fort DuQuesne (which the British later called Pittsburgh), Cherokee fighters raided British homesteads for replacement horses and goods. The colonials retaliated harshly, risking the Cherokees' alliance and bringing on the weakened British

army an attack by Cherokees who had previously been friendly. Once an agreement for peace was reached after this attack, November 19, 1761, Timberlake was sent as a mark of peace and amity between the two nations, British and Cherokee. He was serving the regiment under William Byrd III (of Westover) and Adam Stephen. John McNeill was left at Fort Robinson on Holston's River with the regiment after the truce was reached.

3. Ostenaco (also Ostanaco, Ostonoco, Ustenaca), a well-regarded leader who took part with the British in Virginia's battles against the French in the north in 1756. He was also called Outacity (Mankiller), and was known alternatively as Jud's (or Judd's) Friend. Timberlake took Ostenaco and other Cherokee leaders to London for an interview with George III.

getting the same entertainment, among an hospitable, tho' savage people, who always pay a great regard to any one taken notice of by their chiefs.

Some days after, the headmen of each town were assembled in the town-house of Chote,[4] the metropolis of the country, to hear the articles of peace read, whither the interpreter and I accompanied Ostenaco.

The town-house, in which are transacted all public business and diversions, is raised with wood, and covered over with earth, and has all the appearance of a small mountain at a little distance. It is built in the form of a sugar loaf, and large enough to contain 500 persons, but extremely dark, having, besides the door, which is so narrow that but one at a time can pass, and that after much winding and turning, but one small aperture to let the smoak out, which is so ill contrived, that most of it settles in the roof of the house. Within it has the appearance of an ancient amphitheatre, the seats being raised one above another, leaving an area in the middle, in the center of which stands the fire; the seats of the head warriors are nearest it.

They all seemed highly satisfied with the articles. The peace-pipe was smoaked, and Ostenaco made an harangue to the following effect:

"The bloody tommahawke, so long lifted against our brethren the English, must now be buried deep, deep in the ground, never to be raised again;[5] and whoever shall act contrary to any of these articles, must expect a punishment equal to his offence.[6] Should a strict observance of them be neglected, a war must necessarily follow, and a second peace may not be so easily obtained. I therefore once more

recommend to you, to take particular care of your behaviour towards the English, whom we must now look upon as ourselves; they have the French and Spaniards to fight, and we enough of our own colour, without medling with either nation. I desire likewise, that the white warrior, who has ventured himself here with us, may be well used and respected by all, wherever he goes amongst us."

The harrangue being finished, several pipes were presented me by the headsmen, to take a whiff. This ceremony I could have waved, as smoaking was always very disagreeable to me; but as it was a token of their amity, and they might be offended if I did not comply, I put on the best face I was able, though I dared not even wipe the end of the pipe that came out of their mouths; which, considering their paint and dirtiness, are not of the most ragoutant, as the French term it.

After smoaking, the eatables were produced, consisting chiefly of wild meat; such as venison, bear, and buffalo; tho' I cannot much commend their cookery, every thing being greatly overdone: there were likewise potatoes, pumpkins, homminy, boiled corn, beans, and pease, served up in small flat baskets, made of split canes, which were distributed amongst the croud; and water, which, except the spirituous liquor brought by the Europeans, is their only drink, was handed about in small goards. What contributed greatly to render this feast disgusting, was eating without knives and forks, and being obliged to grope from dish to dish in the dark. After the feast there was a dance; but I was already so fatigued with the ceremonies I had gone through, that I retired to Kanagatucko's hot-house;[7] but was prevented taking any repose by the smoke, with which I was almost suffocated, and the croud of Indians that came and sat on the bedside; which indeed was not much calculated for repose to any but Indians, or those that had passed an apprenticeship to their ways, as I had done: it was composed of a few boards, spread with bear-skins, without any other covering; the house being so hot, that I could not endure the weight of my own blanket. . . .

The country being situated between thirty-two and thirty-four degrees north latitude, and eighty-seven de-

---

4. The ancestral meeting town of the different groups of Cherokees, Echota, in present-day Georgia, in early texts variously named Chota, Chote, Chotah, choto, Chotee, Chotih, Choate, and Chotte.

5. "As in this speech several allusions are made to the customs of the Indians, it may not be impertinent to acquaint the reader, that their way of declaring war, is by smoaking a pipe as a bond among themselves, and lifting up a hatchet stained in blood, as a menace to their enemies; at declaring peace this hatchet is buried, and a pipe smoaked by both parties, in token of friendship and reconciliation." [Au.]

6. "The chiefs can inflict no punishment; but, upon the signing of the peace, it was agreed by both nations, that offenders on either side should be delivered up to be punished by the offended party, and it is to this the Chief alludes." [Au.]

---

7. "This Hot-House is a little hut joined to the house, in which a fire is continually kept, and the heat so great, that cloaths are not to be borne the coldest day in the winter." [Au.] Elsewhere in his memoir, Timberlake called Kanagatucko "the nominal chief of the Cherokees." A well-reputed chief, Kanagatucko was commonly called "Old Hop" by the British.

grees thirty minutes west longitude from London, as near as can be calculated, is temperate, inclining to heat during the summer-season, and so remarkably fertile, that the women alone do all the laborious tasks of agriculture, the soil requiring only a little stirring with a hoe, to produce whatever is required of it; yielding vast quantities of pease, beans, potatoes, cabbages, Indian corn, pumpions, melons, and tobacco, not to mention a number of other vegetables imported from Europe, not so generally known amongst them, which flourish as much, or more here, than in their native climate; and, by the daily experience of the goodness of the soil, we may conclude, that, with due care, all European plants might succeed in the same manner.

Before the arrival of the Europeans, the natives were not so well provided, maize, melons, and tobacco, being the only things they bestow culture upon, and perhaps seldom on the latter. The meadows or savannahs produce excellent grass; being watered by abundance of fine rivers, and brooks well stored with fish, otters and beavers; having as yet no nets, the Indians catch the fish with lines, spears, or dams; which last, as it seems particular to the natives of America, I shall trouble the reader with a description of. Building two walls obliquely down the river from either shore, just as they are near joining, a passage is left to a deep well or reservoir; the Indians then scaring the fish down the river, close the mouth of the reservoir with a large bush, or bundle made on purpose, and it is no difficult matter to take them with baskets, when inclosed within so small a compass.

North America, being one continual forest, admits of no scarcity of timber for every use: there are oaks of several sorts, birch, ash, pines, and a number of other trees, many of which are unknown in Europe, but already described by many authors. The woods likewise abound with fruits and flowers, to which the Indians pay little regard. Of the fruits there are some of an excellent flavour, particularly several sorts of grapes, which, with proper culture, would probably afford an excellent wine. There are likewise plumbs, cherries, and berries of several kinds, something different from those of Europe; but their peaches and pears grow only by culture: add to these several kinds of roots, and medicinal plants, particularly the plant so esteemed by the Chinese, and by them called gingsang, and a root which never fails curing the most inveterate venereal disease, which, however, they never had occasion for, for that distemper, before the arrival of Europeans among them. There are likewise an incredible number of buffaloes, bears, deer, panthers, wolves, foxes,

racoons, and opossums. The buffaloes, and most of the rest, have been so often described, and are so well known, that a description of them would be but tedious; the opossum, however, deserves some attention, as I have never seen it properly described. It is about the size of a large cat, short and thick, and of a silver colour. It brings forth its young, contrary to all other animals, at the teat, from whence, when of a certain size, and able to walk, it drops off, and goes into a false belly, designed by providence in its dam for its reception, which, at the approach of danger, will, notwithstanding this additional load, climb rocks and trees with great agility for its security.

There are a vast number of lesser sort of game, such as rabbits, squirrels of several sorts, and many other animals, beside turkeys, geese, ducks of several kinds, partridges, pheasants, and an infinity of other birds, pursued only by the children, who, at eight or ten years old, are very expert at killing with a sarbacan, or hollow cane, through which they blow a small dart, whose weakness obliges them to shoot at the eye of the larger sort of prey, which they seldom miss.

There are likewise a great number of reptiles, particularly the copper-snake, whose bite is very difficult to cure, and the rattle-snake, once the terror of Europeans, now no longer apprehended, the bite being so easily cured; but neither this, nor any other species, will attempt biting unless disturbed or trod upon; neither are there any animals in America mischievous unless attacked. The flesh of the rattle-snake is extremely good; being once obliged to eat one through want of provisions, I have eat several since thro' choice.

Of insects, the flying stag is almost the only one worthy of notice; it is about the shape of a beetle, but has very large beautiful branching horns, like those of a stag, from whence it took its name.

The Indians have now a numerous breed of horses, as also hogs, and other of our animals, but neither cows nor sheep; both these, however, might be supplied by breeding some tame buffaloes, from which, I have been informed, some white prisoners among them have procured both butter and cheese; and the fine long shag on its back could supply all the purposes of wool.

The mountains contain very rich mines of gold,[8] sil-

---

8. Gold was found in the Over-hill Cherokees' towns, in the western ancestral territory held by the Cherokee peoples.

ver, lead, and copper, as may be evinced by several accidentally found out by the Indians, and the lumps of valuable ore washed down by several of the streams, a bag of which sold in Virginia at a considerable price; and by the many salt springs, it is probable there are many mines of that likewise, as well as of other minerals. The fountains too may have many virtues, that require more skilful persons than the Cherokees or myself to find out.

They have many beautiful stones of different colours, many of which, I am apt to believe, are of great value;[9] but their superstition has always prevented their disposing of them to the traders, who have made many attempts to that purpose; but as they use them in their conjuring ceremonies, they believe their parting with them, or bringing them from home, would prejudice their health or affairs. Among others, there is one in the possession of a conjurer, remarkable for its brilliancy and beauty, but more so for the extraordinary manner in which it was found. It grew, if we may credit the Indians, on the head of a monstrous serpent, whose retreat was, by its brilliancy, discovered; but a great number of snakes attending him, he being, as I suppose by his diadem, of a superior rank among the serpents, made it dangerous to attack him. Many were the attempts made by the Indians, but all frustrated, till a fellow, more bold than the rest, casing himself in leather, impenetrable to the bite of the serpent or his guards, and watching a convenient opportunity, surprised and killed him, tearing this jewel from his head, which the conjurer has kept hid for many years, in some place unknown to all but two women, who have been offered large presents to betray it, but steadily refused, lest some signal judgment or mischance should follow. That such a stone exists, I believe, having seen many of great beauty; but I cannot think it would answer all the encomiums the Indians bestow upon it. The conjurer, I suppose, hatched the account of its discovery; I have however given it to the reader, as a specimen of an Indian story, many of which are much more surprising.

The Cherokees are of a middle stature, of an olive colour, tho' generally painted, and their skins stained with gun-powder, pricked into it in very pretty figures. The hair of their head is shaved, tho' many of the old people have it plucked out by the roots, except a patch on the hinder part of the head, about twice the bigness of a crown-piece, which is ornamented with beads, feathers, wampum, stained deers hair, and such like baubles. The

ears are slit and stretched to an enormous size, putting the person who undergoes the operation to incredible pain, being unable to lie on either side for near forty days. To remedy this, they generally slit but one at a time; so soon as the patient can bear it, they are wound round with wire to expand them, and are adorned with silver pendants and rings, which they likewise wear at the nose. This custom does not belong originally to the Cherokees, but taken by them from the Shawnese, or other northern nations.

They that can afford it wear a collar of wampum, which are beads cut out of clamshells, a silver breast-plate, and bracelets on their arms and wrists of the same metal, a bit of cloth over their private parts, a shirt of the English make, a sort of cloth-boots, and mockasons, which are shoes of a make peculiar to the Americans, ornamented with porcupine-quills; a large mantle or match-coat thrown over all compleats their dress at home; but when they go to war they leave their trinkets behind, and the mere necessaries serve them.

The women wear the hair of their head, which is so long that it generally reaches to the middle of their legs, and sometimes to the ground, club'd, and ornamented with ribbons of various colours; but, except their eyebrows, pluck it from all the other parts of the body, especially the looser part of the sex. The rest of their dress is now become very much like the European; and, indeed, that of the men is greatly altered. The old people still remember and praise the ancient days, before they were acquainted with the whites, when they had but little dress, except a bit of skin about their middles, mockasons, a mantle of buffalo skin for the winter, and a lighter one of feathers for the summer. The women, particularly the half-breed, are remarkably well featured; and both men and women are streight and well-built, with small hands and feet.

The warlike arms used by the Cherokees are guns, bows and arrows, darts, scalpping-knives, and tommahawkes, which are hatchets; the hammer-part of which being made hollow, and a small hole running from thence along the shank, terminated by a small brass-tube for the mouth, makes a compleat pipe. There are various ways of making these, according to the country or fancy of the purchaser, being all made by the Europeans; some have a long spear at top, and some different conveniencies on each side. This is one of their most useful pieces of field-furniture, serving all the offices of hatchet, pipe, and sword; neither are the Indians less expert at throwing it than using it near, but will kill at a considerable distance.

They are of a very gentle and amicable disposition to those they think their friends, but as implacable in their enmity, their revenge being only compleated in the entire de-

---

9. Amethysts, rubies, and aquamarines were found in the area.

struction of their enemies. They were pretty hospitable to all white strangers, till the Europeans encouraged them to scalp; but the great reward offered has led them often since to commit as great barbarities on us, as they formerly only treated their most inveterate enemies with. They are very hardy, bearing heat, cold, hunger and thirst, in a surprizing manner; and yet no people are given to more excess in eating and drinking, when it is conveniently in their power: the follies, nay mischief, they commit when inebriated, are entirely laid to the liquor; and no one will revenge any injury (murder excepted) received from one who is no more himself: they are not less addicted to gaming than drinking, and will even lose the shirt off their back, rather than give over play, when luck runs against them.

They are extremely proud, despising the lower class of Europeans; and in some athletick diversions I once was present at, they refused to match or hold conference with any but officers.

Here, however, the vulgar notion of the Indians uncommon activity was contradicted by three officers of the Virginia regiment, the slowest of which could outrun the swiftest of about 700 Indians that were in the place: but had the race exceeded two or three hundred yards, the Indians would then have acquired the advantage, by being able to keep the same pace a long time together; and running being likewise more general among them, a body of them would always greatly exceed an equal number of our troops.

They are particularly careful of the superannuated, but are not so till of a great age; of which Ostenaco's mother is an instance. Ostenaco is about sixty years of age, and the youngest of four; yet his mother still continues her laborious tasks, and has yet strength enough to carry 200 weight of wood on her back near a couple of miles. I am apt to think some of them, by their own computation, are near 150 years old.

They have many of them a good uncultivated genius, are fond of speaking well, as that paves the way to power in their councils; and I doubt not but the reader will find some beauties in the harangues I have given him, which I assure him are entirely genuine. Their language is not unpleasant, but vastly aspirated, and the accents so many and various, you would often imagine them singing in their common discourse. As the ideas of the Cherokees are so few, I cannot say much for the copiousness of their language.

They seldom turn their eyes on the person they speak of, or address themselves to, and are always suspicious when people's eyes are fixed upon them. They speak so low, except in council, that they are often obliged to re-peat what they were saying; yet should a person talk to any of them above their common pitch, they would immediately ask him, if he thought they were deaf?

They have likewise a sort of loose poetry, as the war-songs, love-songs, &c. Of the latter many contain no more than that the young man loves the young woman, and will be uneasy, according to their own expression, if he does not obtain her. Of the former I shall present the following specimen, without the original in Cherokee, on account of the expletive syllables, merely introduced for the music, and not the sense, just like the toldederols of many old English songs.

A Translation of the War-Song[10]

Caw waw noo dee, &c.

Where'er the earth's enlighten'd by the sun,
Moon shines by night, grass grows, or waters run,
Be't known that we are going, like men, afar,
In hostile fields to wage destructive war;
Like men we go, to meet our country's foes,
Who, woman-like, shall fly our dreaded blows;
Yes, as a woman, who beholds a snake,
In gaudy horror, glisten thro' the brake,
Starts trembling back, and stares with wild surprize,
Or pale thro' fear, unconscious, panting, flies.
Just so these foes, more tim'rous than the hind,[11]
Shall leave their arms and only cloaths behind;
Pinch'd by each blast, by ev'ry thicket torn,
Run back to their own nation, now its scorn:
Or in the winter, when the barren wood
Denies their gnawing entrails nature's food,
Let them sit down, from friends and country far,
And wish, with tears, they ne'er had come to war.

We'll leave our clubs, dew'd with their country
   show'rs,[12]

---

10. Scholars have suggested that Timberlake learned the substance of this song from an interpreter. If so, he then placed it into typical English verse form, and the merit of the song stands on its appeal to English-speaking readers, not on its supposed representation of Cherokee culture.

11. "As the Indians fight naked, the vanquished are constrained to endure the rigours of the weather in their flight, and live upon roots and fruit, as they throw down their arms to accelerate their flight thro' the woods." [Au.]

12. "It is the custom of the Indians, to leave a club, something of the form of a cricket-bat, but with their warlike exploits engraved on it, in their enemy's country, and the enemy accepts the defiance, by bringing this back to their country." [Au.]

And, if they dare to bring them back to our's,
Their painted scalps shall be a step to fame,
And grace our own and glorious country's name.
Or if we warriors spare the yielding foe,
Torments at home the wretch must undergo.[13]

But when we go, who knows which shall return,
When growing dangers rise with each new morn?
Farewel, ye little ones, yet tender wives,
For you alone we would conserve our lives!
But cease to mourn, 'tis unavailing pain,
If not fore-doom'd, we soon shall meet again.
But, O ye friends! in case your comrades fall,
Think that on you our deaths for vengeance call;
With uprais'd tommahawkes pursue our blood,
And stain, with hostile streams, the conscious wood,
That pointing enemies may never tell
The boasted place where we, their victims, fell.[14]

Both the ideas and verse are very loose in the original, and they are set to as loose a music, many composing both tunes and song off hand, according to the occasion; tho' some tunes, especially those taken from the northern Indians, are extremely pretty, and very like the Scotch.

The Indians being all soldiers, mechanism can make but little progress; besides this, they labour under the disadvantage of having neither proper tools, or persons to teach the use of those they have: Thus, for want of saws, they are obliged to cut a large tree on each side, with great labour, to make a very clumsy board; whereas a pair of sawyers would divide the same tree into eight or ten in much less time: considering this disadvantage, their modern houses are tolerably well built. A number of thick posts is fixed in the ground, according to the plan and di-

mensions of the house, which rarely exceeds sixteen feet in breadth, on account of the roofing, but often extend to sixty or seventy in length, beside the little hot-house. Between each of these posts is placed a smaller one, and the whole wattled with twigs like a basket, which is then covered with clay very smooth, and sometimes whitewashed. Instead of tiles, they cover them with narrow boards. Some of these houses are two story high, tolerably pretty and capacious; but most of them very inconvenient for want of chimneys, a small hole being all the vent assigned in many for the smoak to get out at.

Their canoes are the next work of any consequence; they are generally made of a large pine or poplar, from thirty to forty feet long, and about two broad, with flat bottoms and sides, and both ends alike; the Indians hollow them now with the tools they get from the Europeans, but formerly did it by fire: they are capable of carrying about fifteen or twenty men, are very light, and can by the Indians, so great is their skill in managing them, be forced up a very strong current, particularly the bark canoes; but these are seldom used but by the northern Indians.

They have of late many tools among them, and, with a little instruction, would soon become proficients in the use of them, being great imitators of any thing they see done; and the curious manner in which they dress skins, point arrows, make earthen vessels, and basket-work, are proofs of their ingenuity, possessing them a long time before the arrival of Europeans among them. Their method of pointing arrows is as follows: Cutting a bit of thin brass, copper, bone, or scales of a particular fish, into a point with two beards, or some into an acute triangle, they split a little of their arrow, which is generally of reeds; into this they put the point, winding some deers sinew round the arrow, and through a little hole they make in the head; then they moisten the sinew with their spittle, which, when dry, remains fast glewed, nor ever untwists. Their bows are of several sorts of wood, dipped in bears oil, and seasoned before the fire, and a twisted bear's gut for the string.

They have two sorts of clay, red and white, with both which they make excellent vessels, some of which will stand the greatest heat. They have now learnt to sew, and the men as well as women, excepting shirts, make all their own cloaths; the women, likewise, make very pretty belts, and collars of beads and wampum, also belts and garters of worsted. In arts, however, as in war, they are greatly excelled by their northern neighbours.

Their chief trade is with those Europeans with whom they are in alliance, in hides, furs, &c. which they barter by the pound, for all other goods; by that means supply-

---

13. "The prisoners of war are generally tortured by the women, at the party's return, to revenge the death of those that have perished by the wretch's countrymen. This savage custom has been so much mitigated of late, that the prisoners were only compelled to marry, and then generally allowed all the privileges of the natives. This lenity, however, has been a detriment to the nation; for many of these returning to their countrymen, have made them acquainted with the country-passes, weakness, and haunts of the Cherokees; besides that it gave the enemy greater courage to fight against them." [Au.]

14. "Their custom is generally to engrave their victory on some neighboring tree, or set up some token of it near the field of battle; to this their enemies are here supposed to point to, as boasting their victory over them, and the slaughter that they made." [Au.]

ing the deficiency of money. But no proportion is kept to their value; what cost two shillings in England, and what cost two pence, are often sold for the same price; besides that, no attention is paid to the goodness, and a knife of the best temper and workmanship will only sell for the same price as an ordinary one. The reason of this is, that, in the beginning of the commerce, the Indians themselves greatly imposed upon, fixed a price on each article, according to their own judgment; powder, balls, and several other goods, are by this means set so low, that few people would bring them, but that the Indians refuse to trade with any person who has not brought a proportionable quantity, and the traders are cautious of losing a trade in which 5 or 600 per cent. in many articles fully recompences their loss in these.

As to religion, every one is at liberty to think for himself; whence flows a diversity of opinions amongst those that do think, but the major part do not give themselves that trouble. They generally concur, however, in the belief of one superior Being, who made them, and governs all things, and are therefore never discontent at any misfortune, because they say, the Man above would have it so. They believe in a reward and punishment, as may be evinced by their answer to Mr. Martin, who, having preached scripture till both his audience and he were heartily tired, was told at last, that they knew very well, that, if they were good, they should go up; if bad, down; that he could tell no more; that he had long plagued them with what they no ways understood, and that they desired him to depart the country. This, probably, was at the instigation of their conjurers, to whom these people pay a profound regard; as christianity was entirely opposite, and would soon dispossess the people of their implicit belief in their juggling art, which the professors have brought to so great perfection as to deceive Europeans, much more an ignorant race, whose ideas will naturally augment the extraordinary of any thing the least above their comprehension, or out of the common tract. After this I need not say that in every particular they are extremely superstitious, that and ignorance going always hand in hand. . . .

BRITAIN'S MIDDLE ATLANTIC: MARYLAND, PENNSYLVANIA, NEW JERSEY, NEW YORK

GEORGE ALSOP (1636–POST-1673)

George Alsop's *Character of the Province of Mary-Land* (1666) announces that it will not be like those pamphlets that, in promoting colonial development, base remarks entirely upon "tedious" bits of detail that their authors have not witnessed, the "several sorts of vegetables that flourishingly grows here," making such works "more fit for an Herbal, than a small Manuscript or History." Alsop's *Character,* the author attests, avoids the pedantic and exaggerated writing of the armchair naturalist because it presents what he actually witnessed: "What I present I know to be true, *Experientia docet.*" By insisting upon his own honesty, the author presents himself as reliable and forthright. The irony is that in declaiming against those who have written promotional pamphlets that are too good to be true, Alsop positions himself to be able to create an even richer—especially because authentic—propaganda piece than any that has gone before, all the while presenting himself as the humble truth teller who learned all he knows about Maryland while experiencing the "narrow walks of a four years Servitude." The result is a wonderfully witty piece of literature that rivals the best seventeeth-century satires of his day.

Alsop drew upon his four years as an indentured servant in Maryland to create his "character" of the province. His writing evidences a high degree of learning for someone of his station, suggesting that had the political situation been different in England at the time he was a young man, he might have chosen a different path from servitude in the colonies. The son of a tailor, Alsop was an Anglican, and during the reign of the Puritan Oliver Cromwell, he remained loyal to the crown. To escape persecution as a Royalist, Alsop fled to Maryland in 1658. Like many people who could not afford to pay for passage, Alsop signed indenture papers indicating that he would work, while in the colony, to pay off the cost of his transportation to Maryland. He worked four years in the Baltimore County household of Thomas Stockett, a planter and fur trader who was also an Anglican.

When his period of indenture expired, Alsop remained in Maryland as a trader with Indians and a factor (merchant), but he returned to England in 1663, safe from Puritan harassment because of the Restoration of the British monarchy in 1660. Back in England, Alsop wrote and published his witty, bawdy, and satiric pamphlet, *A Character of the Province of Mary-Land* (1666), celebrating his years in the colony and his return to his homeland. He served as a curate in Norfolk in the late 1660s and then as a rector in Essex from 1670 to 1673.

from A CHARACTER OF THE PROVINCE OF MARYLAND[1]

To the Right Honorable Cæcilius Lord Baltemore, Absolute Lord and Proprietary of the Provinces of Mary-Land and Avalon in America.
My Lord,

I HAVE adventured on your Lordships acceptance by guess; if presumption has led me into an Error that deserves correction, I heartily beg Indempnity, and resolve to repent soundly for it, and do so no more. What I present I know to be true, *Experientia docet;*[2] It being an infallible Maxim, That there is no Globe like the occular and experimental view of a Countrey. And had not Fate by a necessary imployment, confin'd me within the narrow walks of a four years Servitude, and by degrees led me through the most intricate and dubious paths of this Countrey, by a commanding and undeniable Enjoynment, I could not, nor should I ever have undertaken to have written a line of this nature.

If I have wrote or composed any thing that's wilde and confused, it is because I am so my self, and the world, as far as I can perceive, is not much out of the same trim; therefore I resolve, if I am brought to the Bar of Common Law for any thing I have done here, to plead *Non compos mentis,* to save my Bacon.

There is an old Saying in English, He must rise betimes that would please every one. And I am afraid I have lain so long a bed, that I think I shall please no body; if it must be so, I cannot help it. But as Feltham in his *Resolves*[3] says, In things that must be, 'tis good to be resolute; And therefore what Destiny has ordained, I am resolved to wink, and stand to it. So leaving your Honour to more serious meditations, I subscribe my self,

> *My Lord,*
> *Your Lordship most*
> *Humble Servant*
> *George Alsop.*

To all the Merchant Adventurers for Mary-Land, together with those Commanders of Ships that saile into that Province.
Sirs,

YOU are both Adventurers, the one of Estate, the other of Life: I could tell you I am an Adventurer too, if I durst presume to come into your Company. I have ventured to come abroad in Print, and if I should be laughed at for my good meaning, it would so break the credit of my Understanding, that I should never dare to shew my face upon the Exchange of (conceited) Wits again.

This dish of Discourse was intended for you at first, but it was manners to let my Lord have the first cut, the Pye being his own. I beseech you accept of the matter as 'tis drest, only to stay your stomachs, and I'le promise you the next shall be better done. 'Tis all as I can serve you in at present, and it may be questionable whether I have served you in this or no. Here I present you with *A Character of Mary-Land,* it may be you will say 'tis weakly done, if you do I cannot help it, 'tis as well as I could do it, considering the several Obstacles that like

---

1. Alsop dedicated *A Character of the Province of Mary-Land* to Cecilius Calvert, second Baron Baltimore (1605–75), the older son of Charles Calvert, the first baron and charter recipient of Maryland. Cecilius (also Cecil) Calvert is considered Maryland's central founder because settlements of Roman Catholics, Anglicans, and others prospered under his sponsorship of the colony, though he never visited it. His younger brother, Leonard Calvert (1606?–47) supervised Maryland's affairs. The text is from the original printing, 1666.

2. "Experience teaches."

3. Owen Felltham, *Resolves, Divine, Moral, and Political* (London, 1628).

blocks were thrown in my way to hinder my proceeding: The major part thereof was written in the intermitting time of my sickness, therefore I hope the afflicting weakness of my Microcosm may plead a just excuse for some imperfections of my pen. I protest what I have writ is from an experimental knowledge of the Country, and not from any imaginary supposition. If I am blamed for what I have done too much, it is the first, and I will irrevocably promise it shall be the last. There's a Maxim upon Tryals at Assizes, That if a thief be taken upon the first fault, if it be not to hainous, they only burn him in the hand and let him go: So I desire you to do by me, if you find any thing that bears a criminal absurdity in it, only burn me for my first fact and let me go. But I am affraid I have kept you too long in the Entry, I shall desire you therefore to come in and sit down.

G. Alsop.

The Preface to the Reader

THE REASON why I appear in this place is, lest the general Reader should conclude I have nothing to say for my self; and truly he's in the right on't, for I have but little to say (for my self) at this time: For I have had so large a Journey, and so heavy a Burden to bring Mary-Land into England, that I am almost out of breath: I'le promise you after I am come to my self, you shall hear more of me. Good Reader, because you see me make a brief Apologetical excuse for my self, don't judge me; for I am so self-conceited of my own merits, that I almost think I want none. *De Lege non judicandum ex solâ linea,* saith the Civilian; We must not pass judgement upon a Law by one line: And because we see but a small Bush at a Tavern door, conclude there is no Canary. For as in our vulgar Resolves 'tis said, A good face needs no Band, and an ill one deserves none: So the French Proverb sayes, *Bon Vien il n'a faut point de Ensigne,* Good Wine needs no Bush. I suppose by this time some of my speculative observers have judged me vainglorious; but if they did but rightly consider me, they would not be so censorious. For I dwell so far from Neighbors, that if I do not praise my self, no body else will: And since I am left alone, I am resolved to summon the *Magna Charta* of Fowles to the Bar for my excuse, and by their irrevocable Statutes plead my discharge, For its an ill Bird will befoule her own Nest: Besides, I have a thousand Billingsgate[4] Collegians that will give in their testimony, That they never knew a Fish-woman cry stinking Fish. Thus leaving the Nostrils of the Citizens Wives to demonstrate what they please as to that, and thee (Good Reader) to say what thou wilt, I bid thee Farewel.

Geo. Alsop.

A CHARACTER OF THE PROVINCE OF MARY-LAND

CHAPTER 1

Of the situation and plenty of the Province of Mary-Land.

Mary-Land is a Province situated upon the large extending bowels of America, under the Government of the Lord Baltemore, adjacent Northwardly upon the Confines of New-England and neighbouring Southwardly upon Virginia, dwelling pleasantly upon the Bay of Chæsapike, between the Degrees of 36 and 38,[5] in the Zone temperate, and by Mathematical computation is eleven hundred and odd Leagues in Longitude from England, being within her own imbraces extraordinary pleasant and fertile. Pleasant, in respect of the multitude of Navigable Rivers and Creeks that conveniently and most profitably lodge within the armes of her green, spreading, and delightful Woods; whose natural womb (by her plenty) maintains and preserves the several diversities of Animals that rangingly inhabit her Woods; as she doth otherwise generously fructifie this piece of Earth with almost all sorts of Vegetables, as well Flowers with their varieties of colours and smells, as Herbes and Roots with their several effects and operative virtues, that offer their benefits daily to supply the want of the Inhabitant whene're their necessities shall *Sub-pæna* them to wait on their commands. So that he, who out of curiosity desires to see the Landskip of the Creation drawn to the life, or to read Natures universal Herbal without book, may with the Opticks of a discreet discerning, view Mary-Land drest in her green and fragrant Mantle of the Spring. Neither do I think there is any place under the Heavenly altitude, or that has footing or room upon the circular Globe of this world, that can parallel this fertile and pleasant piece of ground in its multiplicity, or rather Natures extravagancy of a superabounding plenty. For so much doth this Country increase in a swelling Spring-tide of rich variety and diversities of all things, not only com-

---

4. A London fish market.

5. Maryland was located between 38 and 40 degrees latitude.

mon provisions that supply the reaching stomach of man with a satisfactory plenty, but also extends with its liberality and free convenient benefits to each sensitive faculty, according to their several desiring Appetites. So that had Nature made it her business, on purpose to have found out a situation for the Soul of profitable Ingenuity, she could not have fitted herself better in the traverse of the whole Universe, nor in convenienter terms have told man, Dwell here, live plentifully and be rich.

The Trees, Plants, Fruits, Flowers, and Roots that grow here in Mary-Land, are the only Emblems or Hieroglyphicks of our Adamitical or Primitive situation, as well for their variety as odoriferous smells, together with their vertues, according to their several effects, kinds and properties, which still bear the Effigies of Innocency according to their original Grafts; which by their dumb vegetable Oratory, each hour speaks to the Inhabitant in silent acts, That they need not look for any other Terrestrial Paradice, to suspend or tyre their curiosity upon, while she is extant. For within her doth dwell so much of variety, so much of natural plenty, that there is not any thing that is or may be rare, but it inhabits within this plentious soyle: So that those parts of the Creation that have borne the Bell away (for many ages) for a vegetable plentiousness, must now in silence strike and vayle all, and whisper softly in the auditual parts of Mary-Land, that None but she in this dwells singular; and that as well for that she doth exceed in those Fruits, Plants, Trees and Roots, that dwell and grow in their several Clymes or habitable parts of the Earth besides, as the rareness and super-excellency of her own glory, which she flourishly abounds in, by the abundancy of reserved Rarities, such as the remainder of the World (with all its speculative art) never bore any occular testimony of as yet. I shall forbear to particularize those several sorts of vegetables that flourishingly grows here, by reason of the vast tediousness that will attend upon the description, which therefore makes them much more fit for an Herbal, than a small Manuscript or History.

As for the wilde Animals of this Country, which loosely inhabits the Woods in multitudes, it is impossible to give you an exact description of them all, considering the multiplicity as well as the diversity of so numerous an extent of Creatures: But such as has fallen within the compass or prospect of my knowledge, those you shall know of; *videlicet,* the Deer, because they are oftner seen, and more participated of by the Inhabitants of the Land, whose acquaintance by a customary familiarity becomes much more common than the rest of Beasts that inhabit the Woods by using themselves in Herds about the Chris-

tian Plantations. Their flesh, which in some places of this Province is the common provision the Inhabitants feed on, and which through the extreme glut and plenty of it, being daily killed by the Indians, and brought in to the English, as well as that which is killed by the Christian Inhabitant, that doth it more for recreation, than for the benefit they reap by it. I say, the flesh of Venison becomes (as to food) rather denyed, than any way esteemed or desired. And this I speak from an experimental knowledge; For when I was under a Command, and debarr'd of a four years ranging Liberty in the Province of Mary-Land,[6] the Gentleman whom I served my conditional and prefixed time withall, had at one time in his house fourscore Venisons, besides plenty of other provisions to serve his Family nine months, they being but seven in number; so that before this Venison was brought to a period by eating, it so nauseated our appetites and stomachs, that plain bread was rather courted and desired than it.

The Deer here neither in shape nor action differ from our Deer in England: The Park they traverse their ranging and unmeasured walks in, is bounded and impanell'd in with no other pales then the rough and billowed Ocean: They are also mighty numerous in the Woods, and are little or not at all affrighted at the face of a man, but (like the Does of Whetstons Park)[7] though their hydes are not altogether so gaudy to extract an admiration from the beholder, yet they will stand (all most) till they be scratcht.

As for the Wolves, Bears, and Panthers of this Country, they inhabit commonly in great multitudes up in the remotest parts of the Continent; yet at some certain time they come down near the Plantations, but do little hurt or injury worth noting, and that which they do is of so degenerate and low a nature, (as in reference to the fierceness and heroick vigour that dwell in the same kind of Beasts in other Countries), that they are hardly worth mentioning: For the highest of their designs and circumventing reaches is but cowardly and base, only to steal a poor Pigg, or kill a lost and half starved Calf. The Effigies of a man terrifies them dreadfully, for they no sooner espy him but their hearts are at their mouths, and their spurs upon their heels, they (having no more manners than Beasts) gallop away, and never bid them farewell that are behind them.

The Elke, the Cat of the Mountain, the Rackoon, the Fox, the Beaver, the Otter, the Possum, the Hare, the

---

6. Referring to Alsop's period of indenture.

7. A London neighborhood.

Squirril, the Monack,[8] the Musk-Rat, and several others (whom I'le omit for brevity sake) inhabit here in Mary-Land in several droves and troops, ranging the Woods at their pleasure.

The meat of most of these Creatures is good for eating, yet of no value nor esteem here, by reason of the great plenty of other provisions, and are only kill'd by the Indians of the Country for their Hydes and Furrs, which become very profitable to those that have the right way of traffiquing for them, as well as it redounds to the Indians that take the pains to catch them, and to flay and dress their several Hydes, selling and disposing them for such Commodities as their Heathenish fancy delights in.

As for those Beasts that were carried over at the first seating of the Country, to stock and increase the situation, as Cows, Horses, Sheep and Hogs, they are generally tame, and use near home, especially the Cows, Sheep and Horses. The Hogs, whose increase is innumerable in the Woods, do disfrequent home more than the rest of Creatures that are look'd upon as tame, yet with little trouble and pains they are slain and made provision of. Now they that will with a right Historical Survey, view the Woods of Mary-Land in this particular, as in reference to Swine, must upon necessity judge this Land lineally descended from the Gadarean Territories.[9]

Mary-Land (I must confess) cannot boast of her plenty of Sheep here, as other Countries; not but that they will thrive and increase here, as well as in any place of the World besides, but few desire them, because they commonly draw down the Wolves among the Plantations, as well by the sweetness of their flesh, as by the humility of their nature, in not making a defensive resistance against the rough dealing of a ravenous Enemy. They who for curiosity will keep Sheep, may expect that after the Wolves have breathed themselves all day in the Woods to sharpen their stomachs, they will come without fail and sup with them at night, though many times they surfeit themselves with the sawce that's dish'd out of the muzzle of a Gun, and so in the midst of their banquet (poor Animals) they often sleep with their Ancestors.

Fowls of all sorts and varieties dwell at their several times and seasons here in Mary-Land: The Turkey, the Woodcock, the Pheasant, the Partrich, the Pigeon, and others, especially the Turkey, whom I have seen in whole hundreds in flights in the Woods of Mary-Land, being an extraordinary fat Fowl, whose flesh is very pleasant and sweet. These Fowls that I have named are intayled from generation to generation to the Woods. The Swans, the Geese and Ducks (with other Water-Fowl) derogate in this point of setled residence; for they arrive in millionous multitudes in Mary-Land about the middle of September, and take their winged farewell about the midst of March: But while they do remain, and beleagure the borders of the shoar with their winged Dragoons, several of them are summoned by a Writ of *Fieri facias,*[10] to answer their presumptuous contempt upon a Spit.

As for Fish, which dwell in the watry tenements of the deep, and by a providential greatness of power, is kept for the relief of several Countries in the world (which would else sink under the rigid enemy of want), here in Mary-Land is a large sufficiency, and plenty of almost all sorts of Fishes, which live and inhabit within her several Rivers and Creeks, far beyond the apprehending or crediting of those that never saw the same, which with very much ease is catched, to the great refreshment of the Inhabitants of the Province.

All sorts of Grain, as Wheat, Rye, Barley, Oates, Pease, besides several others that have their original and birth from the fertile womb of this Land (and no where else), they all grow, increase, and thrive here in Mary-Land, without the chargable and laborious manuring of the Land with Dung; increasing in such a measure and plenty, by the natural richness of the Earth, with the common, beneficial and convenient showers of rain that usually wait upon the several Fields of Grain (by a natural instinct), so that Famine (the dreadful Ghost of penury and want) is never known with his pale visage to haunt the Dominions of Mary-Land.

> Could'st thou (O Earth) live thus obscure, and now
> Within an Age, shew forth thy plentious brow
> Of rich variety, gilded with fruitful Fame,
> That (Trumpet-like) doth Heraldize thy Name,
> And tells the World there is a Land now found,
> That all Earth's Globe can't parallel its Ground?
> Dwell, and be prosperous, and with thy plenty feed
> The craving Carkesses of those Souls that need.

---

8. Woodchucks.

9. Luke 8:26–33: In the country of the Gadarenes, Jesus drove demons named Legion out of a possessed man into a herd of swine.

10. A writ authorizing a sheriff to obtain satisfaction on a court judgment out of the defendant's goods.

CHAPTER 3

The necessariness of Servitude proved, with the common usage of Servants in Mary-Land, together with their Priviledges.

As there can be no Monarchy without the Supremacy of a King and Crown, nor no King without Subjects, nor any Parents without it be by the fruitful off-spring of Children; neither can there be any Masters, unless it be by the inferior Servitude of those that dwell under them, by a commanding enjoyment: And since it is ordained from the original and superabounding wisdom of all things, That there should be Degrees and Diversities amongst the Sons of men, in acknowledging of a Superiority from Inferiors to Superiors; the Servant with a reverent and befitting Obedience is as liable to this duty in a measurable performance to him whom he serves, as the loyalest of Subjects to his Prince. Then since it is a common and ordained Fate, that there must be Servants as well as Masters, and that good Servitudes are those Colledges of Sobriety that checks in the giddy and wild-headed youth from his profuse and uneven course of life, by a limited constrainment, as well as it otherwise agrees with the moderate and discreet Servant: Why should there be such an exclusive Obstacle in the minds and unreasonable dispositions of many people, against the limited time of convenient and necessary Servitude, when it is a thing so requisite, that the best of Kingdoms would be unhing'd from their quiet and well setled Government without it. Which levelling doctrine we here of England in this latter age (whose womb was truss'd out with nothing but confused Rebellion) have too much experienced, and was daily rung into the ears of the tumultuous Vulgar by the Bell-weather Sectaries of the Times: But (blessed be God) those Clouds are blown over, and the Government of the Kingdom couch under a more stable form.

There is no truer Emblem of Confusion either in Monarchy or Domestick Governments, then when either the Subject, or the Servant, strives for the upper hand of his Prince, or Master, and to be equal with him, from whom he receives his present subsistance: Why then, if Servitude be so necessary that no place can be governed in order, nor people live without it, this may serve to tell those which prick up their ears and bray against it, That they are none but Asses, and deserve the Bridle of a strict commanding power to reine them in: For I'me certainly confident, that there are several Thousands in most Kingdoms of Christendom, that could not at all live and subsist, unless they had served some prefixed time, to learn either some Trade, Art, or Science, and by either of them to extract their present livelihood.

Then methinks this may stop the mouths of those that will undiscreetly compassionate them that dwell under necessary Servitudes: for let but Parents of an indifferent capacity in Estates, when their Childrens age by computation speak them seventeen or eighteen years old, turn them loose to the wide world, without a seven years working Apprenticeship (being just brought up to the bare formality of a little reading and writing) and you shall immediately see how weak and shiftless they'le be towards the maintaining and supporting of themselves; and (without either stealing or begging) their bodies like a Sentinel must continually wait to see when their Souls will be frighted away by the pale Ghost of a starving want.

Then let such, where Providence hath ordained to live as Servants, either in England or beyond Sea, endure the prefixed yoak of their limited time with patience, and then in a small computation of years, by an industrious endeavour, they may become Masters and Mistresses of Families themselves. And let this be spoke to the deserved praise of Mary-Land, That the four years I served there were not to me so slavish, as a two years Servitude of a Handicraft Apprenticeship was here in London; *Volenti enim nil difficile:*[11] Not that I write this to seduce or delude any, or to draw them from their native soyle, but out of a love to my Countrymen, whom in the general I wish well to, and that the lowest of them may live in such a capacity of Estate, as that the bare interest of their Livelihoods might not altogether depend upon persons of the greatest extendments.

Now those whose abilities here in England are capable of maintaining themselves in any reasonable and handsom manner, they had best so to remain, lest the roughness of the Ocean, together with the staring visages of the wilde Animals, which they may see after their arrival into the Country, may alter the natural dispositions of their bodies, that the stay'd and solid part that kept its motion by Doctor Trigs purgationary operation, may run beyond the byas of the wheel in a violent and laxative confusion.

Now contrarywise, they who are low, and make bare shifts to buoy themselves up above the shabby center of beggarly and incident casualties, I heartily could wish the removal of some of them into Mary-Land, which would make much better for them that stay'd behind, as well as it would advantage those that went.

---

11. "Nothing is difficult to the willing."

They whose abilities cannot extend to purchase their own transportation over into Mary-Land, (and surely he that cannot command so small a sum for so great a matter, his life must needs be mighty low and dejected) I say they may for the debarment of a four years sordid liberty, go over into this Province and there live plentiously well. And what's a four years Servitude to advantage a man all the remainder of his dayes, making his predecessors happy in his sufficient abilities, which he attained to partly by the restrainment of so small a time?

Now those that commit themselves unto the care of the Merchant to carry them over, they need not trouble themselves with any inquisitive search touching their Voyage; for there is such an honest care and provision made for them all the time they remain aboard the Ship, and are sailing over, that they want for nothing that is necessary and convenient.

The Merchant commonly before they go aboard the Ship, or set themselves in any forwardness for their Voyage, has Conditions of Agreements drawn between him and those that by a voluntary consent become his Servants, to serve him, his Heirs or Assigns, according as they in their primitive acquaintance have made their bargain, some two, some three, some four years; and whatever the Master or Servant tyes himself up to here in England by Condition, the Laws of the Province will force a performance of when they come there: Yet here is this Priviledge in it when they arrive, If they dwell not with the Merchant they made their first agreement withall, they may choose whom they will serve their prefixed time with; and after their curiosity has pitcht on one whom they think fit for their turn, and that they may live well withall, the Merchant makes an Assignment of the Indenture over to him whom they of their free will have chosen to be their Master, in the same nature as we here in England (and no otherwise) turn over Covenant Servants or Apprentices from one Master to another. Then let those whose chaps are always breathing forth those filthy dregs of abusive exclamations, which are Lymbeckt from their sottish and preposterous brains, against this Country of Mary-Land, saying, That those which are transported over thither, are sold in open Market for Slaves, and draw in Carts like Horses; which is so damnable an untruth, that if they should search to the very Center of Hell, and enquire for a Lye of the most antient and damned stamp, I confidently believe they could not find one to parallel this: For know, That the Servants here in Mary-Land of all Colonies, distant or remote Plantations, have the least cause to complain, either for strictness of Servitude, want of Provisions, or need of Apparel: Five dayes and a half in the Summer weeks is the alotted time that they work in; and for two months, when the Sun predominates in the highest pitch of his heat, they claim an antient and customary Priviledge, to repose themselves three hours in the day within the house, and this is undeniably granted to them that work in the Fields.

In the Winter time, which lasteth three months (*viz.*) December, January, and February, they do little or no work or imployment, save cutting of wood to make good fires to sit by, unless their Ingenuity will prompt them to hunt the Deer, or Bear, or recreate themselves in Fowling, to slaughter the Swans, Geese, and Turkeys (which this Country affords in a most plentiful manner:) For every Servant has a Gun, Powder and Shot allowed him, to sport him withall on all Holidayes and leasurable times, if he be capable of using it, or be willing to learn.

Now those Servants which come over into this Province, being Artificers, they never (during their Servitude) work in the Fields, or do any other imployment save that which their Handicraft and Mechanick endeavours are capable of putting them upon, and are esteem'd as well by their Masters, as those that imploy them, above measure. He that's a Tradesman here in Mary-Land (though a Servant), lives as well as most common Handicrafts do in London, though they may want something of that Liberty which Freemen have, to go and come at their pleasure; yet if it were rightly understood and considered, what most of the Liberties of the several poor Tradesmen are taken up about, and what a care and trouble attends that thing they call Liberty, which according to the common translation is but Idleness, and (if weighed in the Ballance of a just Reason) will be found to be much heavier and cloggy then the four years restrainment of a Mary-Land Servitude. He that lives in the nature of a Servant in this Province, must serve but four years by the Custom of the Country; and when the expiration of his time speaks him a Freeman, there's a Law in the Province, that enjoyns his Master whom he hath served to give him Fifty Acres of Land, Corn to serve him a whole year, three Sutes of Apparel, with things necessary to them, and Tools to work withall; so that they are no sooner free, but they are ready to set up for themselves, and when once entred, they live passingly well.

The Women that go over into this Province as Servants, have the best luck here as in any place of the world besides; for they are no sooner on shoar, but they are courted into a Copulative Matrimony, which some of them (for aught I know) had they not come to such a Market with their Virginity, might have kept it by them until it had been mouldy, unless they had let it out by a yearly rent to some of the Inhabitants of Lewknors-lane,[12] or made a Deed of Gift of it to Mother Coney, having only a poor stipend out of it, untill the Gallows or Hospital called them away. Men have not altogether so good luck as Women in this kind, or natural preferment, without they be good Rhetoricians, and well vers'd in the Art of perswasion, then (probably) they may ryvet themselves in the time of their Servitude into the private and reserved favour of their Mistress, if Age speak their Master deficient.

In short, touching the Servants of this Province, they live well in the time of their Service, and by their restrainment in that time, they are made capable of living much better when they come to be free; which in several other parts of the world I have observed, That after some servants have brought their indented and limited time to a just and legal period by Servitude, they have been much more incapable of supporting themselves from sinking into the Gulf of a slavish, poor, fettered, and intangled life, then all the fastness of their prefixed time did involve them in before.

Now the main and principal Reason of those incident casualties, that wait continually upon the residencies of most poor Artificers, is (I gather) from the multiplicity or innumerableness of those several Companies of Tradesmen, that dwell so closely and stiflingly together in one and the same place, that like the chafing Gum in Watered-Tabby,[13] they eat into the folds of one anothers Estates. And this might easily be remedied, would but some of them remove and disperse distantly where want and necessity calls for them; their dwellings (I am confident) would be much larger, and their conditions much better, as well in reference to their Estates, as to the satisfactoriness of their minds, having a continual imployment, and from that imployment a continual benefit, without either begging, seducing, or flattering for it, encroaching that one month from one of the same profession, that they are heaved out themselves the next. For I have observed on the other side of Mary-Land, that the whole course of most Mechanical endeavours, is to catch, snatch, and undervalue one another, to get a little work, or a Customer; which when they have attained by their lowbuilt and sneaking circumventings, it stands upon so flashy, mutable, and transitory a foundation, that the best of his hopes is commonly extinguisht before the poor undervalued Tradesman is warm in the enjoyment of his Customer.

Then did not a cloud of low and base Cowardize eclipse the Spirits of these men, these things might easily be diverted; but they had as live take a Bear by the tooth, as think of leaving their own Country, though they live among their own National people, and are governed by the same Laws they have here, yet all this wont do with them; and all the Reason they can render to the contrary is, There's a great Sea betwixt them and Mary-Land, and in that Sea there are Fishes, and not only Fishes but great Fishes, and then should a Ship meet with such an inconsiderable encounter as a Whale, one blow with his tayle, and then *Lord have Mercy upon us:* Yet meet with these men in their common Exchange, which is one story high in the bottom of a Celler, disputing over a Blackpot, it would be monstrously dreadful here to insert the particulars, one swearing that he was the first that scaled the Walls of Dundee, when the Bullets flew about their ears as thick as Hail-stones usually fall from the Sky; which if it were but rightly examined, the most dangerous Engagement that ever he was in, was but at one of the flashy battels at Finsbury, where commonly there's more Custard greedily devoured, then men prejudiced by the rigour of the War. Others of this Company relating their several dreadful exploits, and when they are just entring into the particulars, let but one step in and interrupt their discourse, by telling them of a Sea Voyage, and the violency of storms that attends it, and that there are no back-doors to run out at, which they call, a handsom Retreat and Charge again; the apprehensive danger of this is so powerful and penetrating on them, that a damp sweat immediately involves their Microcosm, so that Margery the old Matron of the Celler, is fain to run for a half-Peny-worth of Angelica to rub their nostrils; and though the Port-hole of their bodies has been stopt from a convenient Evacuation some several months, they'le need no other suppository to open the Orifice of their Esculent faculties than this Relation, as their Drawers or Breeches can more at large demonstrate to the inquisitive search of the curious.

Now I know that some will be apt to judge, that I have written this last part out of derision to some of my poor Mechanick Country-men: Truly I must needs tell those to their face that think so of me, that they prejudice me extremely, by censuring me as guilty of any such crime: What I have written is only to display the sordidness of their dispositions, who rather than they will remove to another Country to live plentiously well, and give their Neighbors more Elbowroom and space to breath in, they

---

12. A disreputable London neighborhood.

13. Gum arabic was used in making watered silk.

will crowd and throng upon one another, with the pressure of a beggarly and unnecessary weight.

That which I have to say more in this business, is a hearty and desirous wish, that the several poor Tradesmen here in London that I know, and have borne an occular testimony of their want, might live so free from care as I did when I dwelt in the bonds of a four years Servitude in Mary-Land.

Be just (Domestick Monarchs) unto them
That dwell as Household Subjects to each Realm;
Let not your Power make you be too severe,
Where there's small faults reign in your sharp Career:
So that the Worlds base yelping Crew
May'nt bark what I have wrote is writ untrue,
So use your Servants, if there come no more,
They may serve Eight, instead of serving Four.

CHAPTER 4

*Upon Trafique, and what Merchandizing
Commodities this Province affords, also how
Tobacco is planted and made fit for Commerce.*

Trafique, Commerce, and Trade, are those great wheeles that by their circular and continued motion, turn into most Kingdoms of the Earth the plenty of abundant Riches that they are commonly fed withall: For Trafique in his right description, is the very soul of a Kingdom; and should but Fate ordain a removal of it for some years, from the richest and most populous Monarchy that dwells in the most fertile clyme of the whole Universe, he would soon find by a woful experiment, the miss and loss of so reviving a supporter. And I am certainly confident, that England would as soon feel her feebleness by withdrawment of so great an upholder; as well in reference to the internal and healthful preservative of her Inhabitants, for want of those Medicinal Drugs that are landed upon her Coast every year, as the external profits, Glory and beneficial Graces that accrue by her.

Paracelsus might knock down his Forge, if Trafique and Commerce should once cease, and grynde the hilt of his Sword into Powder, and take some of the Infusion to make him so valorous, that he might cut his own Throat in the honor of Mercury: Galen might then burn his Herbal, and like Joseph of Arimathea, build him a Tomb in his Garden, and so rest from his labours: Our Physical Collegians of London would have no cause then to thun-

der Fire-balls at Nich. Culpeppers Dispensatory:[14] All Herbs, Roots, and Medicines would bear their original christening, that the ignorant might understand them: *Album grecum* would not be *Album grecum* then, but a Dogs turd would be a Dogs turd in plain terms, in spight of their teeth.

If Trade should once cease, the Custom-house would soon miss her hundreds and thousands Hogs-heads of Tobacco, that use to be throng in her every year, as well as the Grocers would in their Ware-houses and Boxes, the Gentry and Commonalty in their Pipes, the Physician in his Drugs and Medicinal Compositions: The (leering) Waiters[15] for want of imployment, might (like so many Diogenes) intomb themselves in their empty casks, and rouling themselves off the Key into the Thames, there wander up and down from tide to tide in contemplation of Aristotles unresolved curiosity, until the rottenness of their circular habitation give them a *Quietus est,* and fairly surrender them up into the custody of those who both for the profession, disposition and nature, lay as near claim to them, as if they both tumbled in one belly, and for name they jump alike, being according to the original translation both Sharkes.

Silks and Cambricks, and Lawns to make sleeves, would be as soon miss'd at Court, as Gold and Silver would be in the Mint and Pockets: The Low-Country Soldier would be at a cold stand for Outlandish Furrs to make him Muffs, to keep his ten similitudes warm in the Winter, as well as the Furrier for want of Skins to uphold his Trade.

Should Commerce once cease, there is no Country in the habitable world but would undoubtedly miss that flourishing, splendid and rich gallantry of Equipage, that Trafique maintained and drest her up in, before she received that fatal Eclipse: England, France, Germany and Spain, together with all the Kingdoms——

But stop (good Muse) lest I should, like the Parson of Pancras, run so far from my Text in half an hour, that a two hours trot back again would hardly fetch it up: I had best while I am alive in my Doctrine, to think again of Mary-Land, lest the business of other Countries take up so much room in my brain, that I forget and bury her in oblivion.

The three main Commodities this Country affords for

---

14. Nicholas Culpeper (1616–54) published an unauthorized English translation of the Latin *London Pharmacopoeia* (1618), which established the legal standards for medications.

15. Customs inspectors.

Trafique, are Tobacco, Furrs, and Flesh. Furrs and Skins, as Beavers, Otters, Musk-Rats, Rackoons, Wild-Cats, and Elke or Buffeloe, with divers others, which were first made vendible by the Indians of the Country, and sold to the Inhabitant, and by them to the Merchant, and so transported into England and other places where it becomes most commodious.

Tobacco is the only solid Staple Commodity of this Province: The use of it was first found out by the Indians many Ages agoe, and transferr'd into Christendom by that great Discoverer of America Columbus. It's generally made by all the Inhabitants of this Province, and between the months of March and April they sow the seed (which is much smaller than Mustard-seed) in small beds and patches digg'd up and made so by art, and about May the Plants commonly appear green in those beds: In June they are transplanted from their beds, and set in little hillocks in distant rowes, dug up for the same purpose; some twice or thrice they are weeded, and succoured from their illegitimate Leaves that would be peeping out from the body of the Stalk. They top the several Plants as they find occasion in their predominating rankness: About the middle of September they cut the Tobacco down, and carry it into houses, (made for that purpose) to bring it to its purity: And after it has attained, by a convenient attendance upon time, to its perfection, it is then tyed up in bundles, and packt into Hogs-heads, and then laid by for the Trade.

Between November and January there arrives in this Province Shipping to the number of twenty sail and upwards, all Merchant-men loaden with Commodities to Trafique and dispose of, trucking with the Planter for Silks, Hollands, Serges, and Broad-clothes, with other necessary Goods, priz'd at such and such rates as shall be judg'd on is fair and legal, for Tobacco at so much the pound, and advantage on both sides considered; the Planter for his work, and the Merchant for adventuring himself and his Commodity into so far a Country: Thus is the Trade on both sides drove on with a fair and honest Decorum.

The Inhabitants of this Province are seldom or never put to the affrightment of being robb'd of their money, nor to dirty their Fingers by telling of vast sums: They have more bags to carry Corn, then Coyn; and though they want, but why should I call that a want which is only a necessary miss? the very effects of the dirt of this Province affords as great a profit to the general Inhabitant, as the Gold of Peru doth to the straight-breecht Commonalty of the Spaniard.

Our Shops and Exchanges of Mary-Land, are the Merchants Store-houses, where with few words and protestations Goods are bought and delivered; not like those Shop-keepers Boys in London, that continually cry, What do ye lack Sir? What d'ye buy? yelping with so wide a mouth, as if some Apothecary had hired their mouths to stand open to catch Gnats and Vagabond Flyes in.

Tobacco is the currant Coyn of Mary-Land, and will sooner purchase Commodities from the Merchant, then money. I must confess the New-England men that trade into this Province, had rather have fat Pork for their Goods, then Tobacco or Furrs, which I conceive is, because their bodies being fast bound up with the cords of restringent Zeal, they are fain to make use of the lineaments of this Non-Canaanite creature physically to loosen them; for a bit of a pound upon a two-peny Rye loaf, according to the original Receipt, will bring the costiv'st red-ear'd Zealot in some three hours time to a fine stool, if methodically observed.

Medera-Wines, Sugars, Salt, Wickar-Chairs, and Tin Candle-sticks, is the most of the Commodities they bring in: They arrive in Mary-Land about September, being most of them Ketches and Barkes, and such small Vessels, and those dispersing themselves into several small Creeks of this Province, to sell and dispose of their Commodities, where they know the Market is most fit for their small Adventures.

Barbadoes, together with the several adjacent Islands, has much Provision yearly from this Province: And though these Sun-burnt Phaetons think to outvye Mary-Land in their Silks and Puffs, daily speaking against her whom their necessities makes them beholding to, and like so many Don Diegos that becackt Pauls, cock their Felts and look big upon't; yet if a man could go down into their infernals, and see how it fares with them there, I believe he would hardly find any other Spirit to buoy them up, then the ill-visaged Ghost of want, that continually wanders from gut to gut to feed upon the undigested rynes of Potatoes.

Trafique is Earth's great Atlas, that supports
The pay of Armies, and the height of Courts,
And makes Mechanicks live, that else would die
Meer starving Martyrs to their penury:
None but the Merchant of this thing can boast,
He, like the Bee, comes loaden from each Coast,
And to all Kingdoms, as within a Hive,
Stows up those Riches that doth make them thrive:
Be thrifty, Mary-Land, keep what thou hast in store,
And each years Trafique to thy self get more.

EBENEZER COOK (1667–1733)

Ebenezer Cook's best-known work, his poem *The Sot-Weed Factor* (1708), targeted know-it-all visitors to the colonies who sought to get rich quickly while belittling the laborers who made their wealth possible, even as it criticized the "country bumpkin" quality of living the laborers themselves experienced. Through this double-directed satire, Cook was able to evaluate the attitudes of smugness of English and European readers and to mock their avidity for wealth from the colonial people they held in disregard. The poem employed the mock-heroic style popularized by British poet Samuel Butler (1612–80) in his poem *Hudibras* (1663–78), which satirized Puritanism and the kinds of people who became Puritans. It also imitated the literature of promotion and the literature against promotion flourishing in the British American colonies and England.

Cook knew well the kinds of people he was writing about, for he saw them in England and in Maryland. Born in England, the son of a merchant who dealt in Maryland tobacco, Cook evidently received a reasonably good education before he entered the mercantile business in London. Having taken up his father's business, he landed in Maryland as a tobacco factor (merchant), and he occasionally acted as a lawyer in Maryland, settling local disputes. Although he seems to have traveled back and forth between London and Maryland, he spent much time in his later years in Maryland, where he had inherited his father's plantation in 1712 and where he worked as a local official in Baltimore County.

Probably on one of his trips back to England, Cook published his poem, *The Sot-Weed Factor,* in London, 1708. He evidently considered the absence of a printer in Maryland a serious drawback, and so with others he persuaded printer William Parks to come to Annapolis to do government and other printing. After Parks's arrival in 1726, Cook was able to publish other writings in Maryland. In 1730, Parks published Cook's *Sotweed Redivivus,* which featured the same speaker as *The Sot-Weed Factor* but focused somewhat more seriously on problems confronting Maryland. The next year, Parks brought out another volume by Cook, *The Maryland Muse,* which contained a poem on Bacon's Rebellion and a revised version of *The Sot-Weed Factor.* Cook wrote a number of elegies on the deaths of prominent local figures, but he is known for the longer poems, rather than the occasional pieces. He clearly enjoyed writing poetry as a sideline to his more pressing business concerns, and he probably took considerable pleasure in signing some of his works as written by the "Poet Laureate of Maryland."

THE SOT-WEED FACTOR; OR, A VOYAGE TO MARYLAND, &C.[1]

Condemn'd by Fate to way-ward Curse,
Of Friends unkind, and empty Purse;
Plagues worse than fill'd *Pandora's* Box,
I took my leave of *Albion's* Rocks:
With heavy Heart, concern'd that I
Was forc'd my Native Soil to fly,
And the *Old World* must bid good-buy.
But Heav'n ordain'd it should be so,
And to repine is vain we know:
Freighted with Fools, from *Plymouth* sound,
To *Mary-Land* our Ship was bound;
Where we arriv'd in dreadful Pain,
Shock'd by the Terrours of the Main;
For full three Months, our wavering Boat,
Did thro' the surely Ocean float,
And furious Storms and threat'ning Blasts,
Both tore our Sails and sprung our Masts:
Wearied, yet pleas'd, we did escape
Such Ills, we anchor'd at the[2] *Cape,*
But weighing soon, we plough'd the *Bay,*
To[3] Cove it in[4] *Piscato-way,*

---

1. "Sot-weed" is tobacco, a "weed" that makes one become a "sot" (intoxicated); a factor is a merchant. The poem was first published in London.

2. "By the *Cape,* is meant the *Capes of Virginia,* the first Land on the Coast of *Virginia* and *Mary-Land.*" [Au.]

3. "To *Cove* is to lie at Anchor safe in Harbour." [Au.]

4. "The Bay of *Piscato-way,* the usual place where our Ships come to an Anchor in *Mary-Land.*" [Au.]

Intending there to open Store,
I put myself and Goods a-shore:
Where soon repair'd a numerous Crew,
In Shirts and Drawers of[5] *Scotch-cloth* Blue.
With neither Stockings, Hat, nor Shooe.
These *Sot-weed* Planters Crowd the Shoar,
In Hue as tawny as a Moor:
Figures so strange, no God design'd,
To be a part of Humane Kind:
But wanton Nature, void of Rest,
Moulded the brittle Clay in Jest,
At last a Fancy very odd
Took me, this was the Land of *Nod;*
Planted at first, when Vagrant *Cain,*
His Brother had unjustly slain:
Then conscious of the Crime he'd done,
From Vengeance dire, he hither run;
And in a Hut supinely dwelt,
The first in *Furs* and *Sot-weed* dealt.
And ever since his Time, the Place,

Has harbour'd a detested Race;
Who when they cou'd not live at Home,
For Refuge to these Worlds did roam;
In hopes by Flight they might prevent,
The Devil and his fell intent;
Obtain from Tripple Tree[6] repreive,
And Heav'n and Hell alike deceive:
But e're their Manners I display,
I think it fit I open lay
My Entertainment by the way;
That Strangers well may be aware on,
What homely Diet they must fare on.
To touch that Shoar, where no good Sense is found,
But Conversation's lost, and Maners drown'd.
I crost unto the other side,
A River whose impetuous Tide,
The Savage Borders does divide;
In such a shining odd invention,
I scarce can give its due Dimention.
The *Indians* call this watry Waggon
[7]*Canoo,* a Vessel none can brag on;
Cut from a *Popular-Tree,* or *Pine,*
And fashion'd like a Trough for Swine:
In this most noble Fishing-Boat,

I boldly put myself a-float;
Standing Erect, with Legs stretch'd wide,
We paddled to the other side:
Where being Landed safe by hap,
As *Sol* fell into *Thetis* Lap.
A ravenous Gang bent on the stroul,
Of[8] Wolves for Prey, began to howl;
This put me in a pannick Fright,
Least I should be devoured quite:
But as I there a musing stood,
And quite benighted in a Wood,[9]
A Female Voice pierc'd thro' my Ears,
Crying, *You Rogue drive home the Steers.*
I listen'd to th' attractive sound,
And straight a Herd of Cattel found
Drove by a Youth, and homewards bound:
Cheer'd with the sight, I straight thought fit,
To ask where I a Bed might get.
The surley Peasant bid me stay,
And ask'd from whom[10] I'de run away.
Surprized at such a saucy Word,
I instantly lugg'd out my Sword;
Swearing I was no Fugitive,
But from *Great-Britain* did arrive,
In hopes I better there might Thrive.
To which he mildly made reply,
I beg your Pardon, Sir, *that I*
Should talk to you Unmannerly;
But if you please to go with me,
To yonder House, you'll welcome be.
Encountering soon the smoaky Seat,
The Planter old did thus me greet:
"Whether you come from Goal or Colledge,
"You're welcome to my certain Knowledge;
"And if you please all Night to stay,
"My Son shall put you in the way.
Which offer I most kindly took,
And for a Seat did round me look;
When presently amongst the rest,
He plac'd his unknown *English* Guest,
Who found them drinking for a whet,[11]

---

5. "The Planters generally wear Blue *Linnen.*" [Au.]

6. The gallows.

7. "A *Canoo* is an *Indian* Boat, cut out of the body of a Popler-Tree." [Au.]

8. "Wolves are very numerous in *Mary-Land.*" [Au.]

9. In the English story "The Babes of the Wood," two children die of exposure in the forest.

10. "'Tis supposed by the Planters, that all unknown Persons are run away from some Master." [Au.]

11. Appetizer.

A Cask of[12] Syder on the Fret,[13]
Till Supper came upon the Table,
On which I fed whilst I was able.
So after hearty Entertainment,
Of Drink and Victuals without Payment;
For Planters Tables, you must know,
Are free for all that come and go.
While[14] Pon and Milk, with[15] Mush well stoar'd,
In wooden Dishes grac'd the Board;
With[16] Homine and Syder-pap,
(Which scarce a hungry Dog wou'd lap)
Well stuff'd with Fat, from Bacon fry'd,
Or with *Molossus* dulcify'd.
Then out our Landlord pulls a Pouch,
As greasy as the Leather Couch
On which he sat, and straight begun,
To load with Weed his *Indian* Gun;[17]
In length, scarce longer than ones Finger,
Or that for which the Ladies linger.
His Pipe smoak'd out with aweful Grace,
With aspect grave and solemn pace;
The reverend Sire walks to a Chest,
Of all his Furniture the best,
Closely confin'd within a Room,
Which seldom felt the weight of Broom;
From thence he lugs a Cag of Rum,
And nodding to me, thus begun:
I find, says he, you don't much care,
For this our *Indian* Country Fare;
But let me tell you, Friend of mine,
You may be glad of it in time,
Tho' now your Stomach is so fine;
And if within this Land you stay,
You'll find it true what I do say.
This said, the Rundlet up he threw,
And bending backwards strongly drew:
I pluck'd as stoutly for my part,
Altho' it made me sick at Heart,
And got so soon into my Head

I scarce cou'd find my way to Bed;
Where I was instantly convey'd
By one who pass'd for Chamber-Maid;
Tho' by her loose and sluttish Dress,
She rather seem'd a *Bedlam-Bess:*[18]
Curious to know from whence she came,
I prest her to declare her Name.
She Blushing, seem'd to hide her Eyes,
And thus in Civil Terms replies;
In better Times, e'er to this Land,
I was unhappily Trapann'd;
Perchance as well I did appear,
As any Lord or Lady here,
Not then a Slave for twice two[19] Year.
My Cloaths were fashionably new,
Nor were my Shifts of Linnen Blue;
But things are changed now at the Hoe,
I daily work, and Bare-foot go,
In weeding Corn or feeding Swine,
I spend my melancholy Time.
Kidnap'd and Fool'd, I hither fled,
To shun a hated Nuptial[20] Bed,
And to my cost already find,
Worse Plagues than those I left behind.
Whate'er the Wanderer did profess,
Good-faith I cou'd not choose but guess
The Cause which brought her to this place,
Was supping e'er the Priest said Grace.
Quick as my Thoughts, the Slave was fled,
(Her Candle left to shew my Bed)
Which made of Feathers soft and good,
Close in the[21] Chimney-corner stood;
I threw me down expecting Rest,
To be in golden Slumbers blest:
But soon a noise disturb'd my quiet,
And plagu'd me with nocturnal Riot;
A Puss which in the ashes lay,
With grunting Pig began a Fray;
And prudent Dog, that Feuds might cease,
Most strongly bark'd to keep the Peace.

---

12. "Syder-pap is a sort of Food made of Syder and small Homine, like our Oatmeal." [Au.]

13. Fermenting.

14. "Pon is Bread made of *Indian Corn*." [Au.]

15. "Mush is a sort of Hasty-Pudding made with Water and *Indian* Flower." [Au.]

16. "Homine is a Dish that is made of boiled *Indian* Wheat, eaten with Molossus, or Bacon-Fat." [Au.]

17. Tobacco pipe.

---

18. Bedlam was a famous insane asylum.

19. "'Tis the Custom for Servants to be obliged for four Years to very servile Work; after which time they have their Freedom." [Au.]

20. "These are the general Excuses made by *English* Women, which are sold, or sell themselves to *Mary-Land*." [Au.]

21. "Beds stand in the Chimney-corner in this Country." [Au.]

This Quarrel scarcely was decided,
By stick that ready lay provided;
But *Reynard* arch and cunning Loon,
Broke into my Appartment soon;
In hot pursuit of Ducks and Geese,
With fell intent the same to seize:
Their Cackling Plaints with strange surprize,
Chac'd Sleeps thick Vapours from my Eyes:
Raging I jump'd upon the Floar,
And like a Drunken Saylor Swore;
With Sword I fiercly laid about,
And soon dispers'd the Feather'd Rout:
The Poultry out of Window flew,
And *Reynard* cautiously withdrew:
The Dogs who this Encounter heard,
Fiercly themselves to aid me rear'd,
And to the Place of Combat run,
Exactly as the Field was won.
Fretting and hot as roasting Capon,
And greasy as a Flitch of Bacon;
I to the Orchard did repair,
To Breathe the cool and open Air;
Expecting there the rising Day,
Extended on a Bank I lay;
But Fortune here, that saucy Whore,
Disturb'd me worse and plagu'd me more,
Than she had done the night before.
Hoarse croaking[22] Frogs did 'bout me ring,
Such Peals the Dead to Life wou'd bring,
A Noise might move their Wooden King.[23]
I stuff'd my Ears with Cotten white
For fear of being deaf out-right,
And curst the melancholy Night:
But soon my Vows I did recant,
And Hearing as a Blessing grant;
When a confounded Rattle-Snake,
With hissing made my Heart to ake:
Not knowing how to fly the Foe,
Or whether in the Dark to go;
By strange good Luck, I took a Tree,
Prepar'd by Fate to set me free;

Where riding on a Limb astride,
Night and the Branches did me hide,
And I the Devil and Snake defy'd.
Not yet from Plagues exempted quite,
The curst Muskitoes did me bite;
Till rising Morn' and blushing Day,
Drove both my Fears and Ills away;
And from Night's Errors set me free.
Discharg'd from hospitable Tree;
I did to Planters Booth repair,
And there at Breakfast nobly Fare,
On rashier broil'd of infant Bear:
I thought the Cub delicious Meat,
Which ne'er did ought but Chesnuts eat;
Nor was young Orsin's flesh the worse,
Because he suck'd a Pagan Nurse.[24]
Our Breakfast done, my Landlord stout,
Handed a Glass of Rum about;
Pleas'd with the Treatment I did find,
I took my leave of Oast so kind;
Who to oblige me, did provide,
His eldest Son to be my Guide,
And lent me Horses of his own,
A skittish Colt, and aged Rhoan,
The four-leg'd prop of his Wife *Joan*.
Steering our Barks in Trot or Pace,
We sail'd directly for a place
In *Mary-Land* of high renown,
Known by the Name of *Battle-Town*.
To view the Crowds did there resort,
Which Justice made, and Law their sport,
In that sagacious County Court:
Scarce had we enter'd on the way,
Which thro' thick Woods and Marshes lay;
But *Indians* strange did soon appear,
In hot persuit of wounded Deer;
No mortal Creature can express,
His wild fantastick Air and Dress;
His painted Skin in colours dy'd,
His sable Hair in Satchel ty'd,
Shew'd Savages not free from Pride:
His tawny Thighs, and Bosom bare,
Disdain'd a useless Coat to wear,
Scorn'd Summer's Heat, and Winters Air;
His manly Shoulders such as please,

---

22. "Frogs are called Virginea Bells, and make, (both in that Country and Mary-Land) during the Night, a very hoarse un-grateful Noise." [Au.]

23. In Aesop's fables, the frogs ask for a king and are given a log.

---

24. In the tale of Valentine and Orson, two infants are aban-doned in the forest and one, Orson, is nursed by a bear.

Widows and Wives, were bath'd in Grease
Of Cub and Bear, whose supple Oil,
Prepar'd his Limbs 'gainst Heat or Toil.
Thus naked Pict in Battel faught,
Or undisguis'd his Mistress sought;
And knowing well his Ware was good,
Refus'd to screen it with a Hood;
His Visage dun, and chin that ne'er
Did Raizor feel or Scissers bear,
Or knew the Ornament of Hair,
Look'd sternly Grim, surpriz'd with Fear,
I spur'd my Horse, as he drew near:
But Rhoan who better knew than I,
The little Cause I had to fly;
Seem'd by his solemn steps and pace,
Resolv'd I shou'd the Specter face,
Nor faster mov'd, tho' spur'd and lick'd,
Than *Balaam's* Ass by Prophet kick'd.
Kekicknitop[25] the Heathen cry'd;
How is it *Tom.* my Friend reply'd:
Judging from thence the Brute was civel,
I boldly fac'd the Courteous Devil;
And lugging out a Dram of Rum,
I gave his Tawny worship some:
Who in his language as I guess,
(My Guide informing me no less,)
Implored the[26] Devil, me to bless.
I thank'd him for his good Intent,
And forwards on my Journey went,
Discoursing as along I rode,
Whether this Race was framed by God
Or whether some Malignant pow'r,
Contriv'd them in an evil hour

And from his own Infernal Look,
Their Dusky form and Image took:
From hence we fell to Argument
Whence Peopled was this Continent.
My Friend suppos'd *Tartarians* wild,
Or *Chinese* from their Home exiled;
Wandering thro' Mountains hid with Snow,
And Rills did in the Vallies flow,
Far to the South of *Mexico:*
Broke thro' the Barrs which Nature cast,
And wide unbeaten Regions past,
Till near those Streams the humane deludge roll'd,
Which sparkling shin'd with glittering Sands of Gold,
And fetch[27] *Pizarro* from the[28] *Iberian* Shoar,
To Rob the Natives of their fatal Stoar.
I Smil'd to hear my young Logician,
Thus Reason like a Politician;
Who ne're by Fathers Pains and Earning
Had got at Mother *Cambridge* Learning;
Where Lubber youth just free from birch
Most stoutly drink to prop the Church;
Nor with[29] *Grey Groat* had taken Pains
To purge his Head and Cleanse his Reines:
And in obedience to the Colledge,
Had pleas'd himself with carnal Knowledge:
And tho' I lik'd the youngester's Wit,
I judg'd the Truth he had not hit;
And could not choose but smile to think
What they could do for Meat and Drink,
Who o'er so many Desarts ran,
With Brats and Wives in *Caravan;*
Unless perchance they'd got the Trick.
To eat no more than Porker sick;
Or could with well contented Maws,
Quarter like[30] Bears upon their Paws.
Thinking his Reasons to confute,
I gravely thus commene'd Dispute,
And urg'd that tho' a *Chinese* Host,

---

25. "Kekicknitop is an Indian Expression, and signifies no more than this, How do you do?" [Au.]

26. "These Indians worship the Devil, and pray to him as we do to God Almighty. 'Tis suppos'd, That America was peopl'd from Scythia or Tartaria, which Borders on China, by reason the Tartarians and Americans very much agree in their Manners, Arms, and Government. Other Persons are of Opinion, that the Chinese first peopled the West Indies; imagining China and the Southern part of America to be contiguous. Others believe that the Phoenicians who were very skilful Mariners, first planted a Colony in the Isles of America, and supply'd the Persons left to inhabit there with Women and all other Necessaries; till either the Death or Shipwreck of the first Discovers, or some other Misfortune occasioned the loss of the Discovery, which had been purchased by the Peril of the first Adventurers." [Au.]

27. "Pizarro was the Person that conquer'd Peru; a Man of a most bloody Disposition, base, treacherous, covetous, and revengeful." [Au.]

28. "Spanish Shoar." [Au.]

29. "There is a very bad Custom in some Colledges, of giving the Students A Groat and purgandus Rhenes, which is usually employ'd to the use of the Donor." [Au.]

30. "Bears are said to live by sucking of their Paws, according to the Notion of some Learned Authors." [Au.]

Might penetrate this *Indian* Coast;
Yet this was certainly most true,
They never cou'd the Isles subdue;
For knowing not to steer a Boat,
They could not on the Ocean float,
Or plant their Sunburnt Colonies,
In Regions parted by the Seas:
I thence inferr'd[31] *Phoenicians* bol,
Discover'd first with Vessels bold
These Western Shoars, and planted here,
Returning once or twice a Year,

With *Naval Stoars* and Lasses kind,
To comfort those were left behind;
Till by the Winds and Tempest toar,
From their intended Golden Shoar;
They suffer'd Ship-wreck, or were drown'd,
And lost the World so newly found.
But after long and learn'd Contention,
We could not finish our dissention;
And when that both had talk'd their fill,
We had the self same Notion still.
Thus Parson grave well read and Sage,
Does in dispute with Priest engage;
The one protests they are not Wise,
Who judge by[32] Sense and trust their Eyes;
And vows he'd burn for it at Stake,
That Man may God his Maker make;
The other smiles at his Religion,
And vows he's but a learned Widgeon:
And when they have empty'd all their stoar
From Books and Fathers, are not more
Convinc'd or wiser than before.

   Scarce had we finish'd serious Story,
But I espy'd the Town before me,
And roaring Planters on the ground,
Drinking of Healths in Circle round:
Dismounting Steed with friendly Guide,
Our Horses to a Tree we ty'd,
And forwards pass'd amongst the Rout,
To chuse convenient *Quarters* out:
But being none were to be found,

We sat like others on the ground
Carousing Punch in open Air
Till Cryer did the Court declare;
The planting Rabble being met,
Their Drunken Worships likewise set:
Cryer proclaims that Noise shou'd cease,
And streight the Lawyers broke the Peace:
Wrangling for Plaintiff and Defendant,
I thought they ne'er would make an end on't:
With nonsense, stuff and false quotations,
With brazen Lyes and Allegations;
And in the splitting of the Cause,
They us'd such Motions with their Paws,
As shew'd their Zeal was strongly bent,
In Blows to end the Argument.
A reverend Judge, who to the shame
Of all the Bench, cou'd write his[33] Name;
At Petty-fogger took offence,
And wonder'd at his Impudence.
My Neighbour *Dash* with scorn replies,
And in the Face of Justice flies:
The Bench in fury streight divide,
And Scribbles take, or Judges side;
The Jury, Lawyers, and their Clyents,
Contending, fight like earth-born Gyants:
But Sheriff wily lay perdue,
Hoping Indictments wou'd ensue,
And when————
A Hat or Wig fell in the way,
He seiz'd them for the *Queen* as stray:
The Court adjourn'd in usual manner,
In Battle Blood, and fractious Clamour:
I thought it proper to provide,
A Lodging for myself and Guide,
So to our Inn we march'd away,
Which at a little distance lay;
Where all things were in such Confusion,
I thought the World at its conclusion:
A Herd of Planters on the ground,
O'er-whelm'd with Punch, dead drunk we found:
Others were fighting and contending,
Some burnt their Cloaths to save the mending.
A few whose Heads by frequent use,
Could better bare the potent Juice,
Gravely debated State Affairs.
Whilst I most nimbly trip'd up Stairs;

---

31. "The Phoenicians were the best and boldest Saylors of Antiquity, and indeed the only Persons, in former Ages, who durst venture themselves on the Main Sea." [Au.]

32. "The Priests argue, That our Senses in the point of Transubstantiation ought not to be believed, for tho' the Consecrated Bread has all the accidents of Bread, yet they affirm, 'tis the Body of Christ, and not Bread but Flesh and Bones." [Au.]

---

33. "In the County-Court of Maryland, very few of the Justices of the Peace can write or read." [Au.]

Leaving my Friend discoursing oddly,
And mixing things Prophane and Godly:
Just then beginning to be Drunk,
As from the Company I slunk,
To every Room and Nook I crept,
In hopes I might have somewhere slept;
But all the bedding was possest
By one or other drunken Guest:
But after looking long about,
I found an antient Corn-loft out,
Glad that I might in quiet sleep,
And there my bones unfractur'd keep.
I lay'd me down secure from Fray,
And soundly snoar'd till break of Day;
When waking fresh I sat upright,
And found my Shoes were vanish'd quite,
Hat, Wig, and Stockings, all were fled

From this extended *Indian* Bed:
Vext at the Loss of Goods and Chattel,
I swore I'd give the Rascal battel,
Who had abus'd me in this sort,
And Merchant Stranger made his Sport.
I furiously descended Ladder;
No Hare in *March* was ever madder:
In vain I search'd for my Apparel,
And did with Oast and Servants Quarrel;
For one whose Mind did much aspire
To[34] Mischief, threw them in the Fire;
Equipt with neither Hat nor Shooe, ⎤
I did my coming hither rue, ⎬
And doubtful thought what I should do: ⎦
Then looking round, I saw my Friend
Lie naked on a Tables end;
A Sight so dismal to behold,
One wou'd have judg'd him dead and cold;
When wringing of his bloody Nose,
By fighting got we may suppose;
I found him not so fast asleep,
Might give his Friends a cause to weep:
Rise[35] *Oronooko,* rise, said I,
And from this *Hell* and *Bedlam* fly.
My Guide starts up, and in amaze,
With blood-shot Eyes did round him gaze;

At length with many a sigh and groan,
He went in search of aged Rhoan;
But Rhoan, tho' seldom us'd to faulter,
Had fairly this time slipt his Halter;
And not content all Night to stay
Ty'd up from Fodder, ran away:
After my Guide to ketch him ran,
And so I lost both Horse and Man;
Which Disappointment, tho' so great,
Did only Mirth and Jests create:
Till one more Civil than the rest,
In Conversation for the best,
Observing that for want of Rhoan,
I should be left to walk alone;
Most readily did me intreat,
To take a Bottle at his Seat;
A Favour at that time so great,
I blest my kind propitious Fate;
And finding soon a fresh supply,
Of Cloaths from Stoar-house kept hard by,
I mounted streight on such a Steed,
Did rather curb, than whipping need;
And straining at the usual rate, ⎤
With spur of Punch which lay in Pate, ⎬
E'er long we lighted at the Gate: ⎦
Where in an antient *Cedar* House,
Dwelt my new Friend, a[36] Cokerouse;
Whose Fabrick, tho' 'twas built of Wood,
Had many Springs and Winters stood;
When sturdy Oaks, and lofty Pines
Were level'd with[37] Musmelion Vines,
And Plants eradicated were,
By Hurricanes into the air;
There with good Punch and apple Juice,
We spent our Hours without abuse:
Till Midnight in her sable Vest,
Persuaded Gods and Men to rest;
And with a pleasing kind surprize,
Indulg'd soft Slumbers to my Eyes.
Fierce[38] *Æthon* courser of the Sun,
Had half his Race exactly run;
And breath'd on me a fiery Ray, ⎤
Darting hot Beams the following Day, ⎬
When snug in Blanket white I lay: ⎦

---

34. "'Tis the Custom of the Planters, to throw their own, or any other Persons Hat, Wig, Shooes, or Stockings in the Fire." [Au.]

35. "Planters are usually call'd by the Name of Oronooko, from their Planting Oronooko-Tobacco." [Au.]

36. "Cockerouse, is a Man of Quality." [Au.]

37. "Musmilleon Vines are what we call Muskmilleon Plants." [Au.]

38. "Æthon is one of the Poetical Horses of the Sun." [Au.]

But Heat and[39] *Chinces* rais'd the Sinner,
Most opportunely to his Dinner;
Wild Fowl and Fish delicious Meats,
As good as *Neptune's* Doxy eats,
Began our Hospitable Treat;
Fat Venson follow'd in the Rear,
And Turkies[40] wild Luxurious Chear:
But what the Feast did most commend,
Was hearty welcom from my Friend.
Thus having made a noble Feast,
And eat as well as pamper'd Priest,
Madera strong in flowing Bowls,
Fill'd with extream, delight our Souls;
Till wearied with a purple Flood,
Of generous Wine (the Giant's blood,
As Poets feign) away I made,
For some refreshing verdant Shade;
Where musing on my Rambles strange,
And Fortune which so oft did change;

In midst of various Contemplations
Of Fancies odd, and Meditations,
I slumber'd long————
Till hazy Night with noxious Dews,
Did Sleep's unwholsom Fetters lose:
With Vapours chil'd, and misty air,
To fire-side I did repair:
Near which a jolly Female Crew,
Were deep engag'd at *Lanctre-Looe,*[41]
In Nightrails[42] white, with dirty Mein,
Such Sights are scarce in *England* seen:
I thought them first some Witches bent,
On Black Designs in dire Convent.
Till one who with affected air,
Had nicely learn'd to Curse and Swear:
Cry'd Dealing's lost is but a Flam,[43]
And vow'd by G—d she'd keep her *Pam.*[44]
When dealing through the board had run,
They ask'd me kindly to make one;
Not staying often to be bid,
I sat me down as others did:

We scarce had play'd a Round about,
But that these *Indian* Froes[45] fell out.
D—m you, says one, tho' now so brave,
I knew you late a Four-Years Slave;
What if for Planters Wife you go,
Nature design'd you for the Hoe.
Rot you replies the other streight,
The Captain kiss'd you for his Freight;
And if the Truth was known aright,
And how you walk'd the Streets by night,
You'd blush (if one cou'd blush) for shame,
Who from *Bridewell* or *Newgate* came.
From Words they fairly fell to Blows,
And being loath to interpose,
Or meddle in the Wars of Punk,[46]
Away to Bed in hast I slunk.
Waking next day, with aking Head,
And Thirst, that made me quit my Bed;
I rigg'd myself, and soon got up,
To cool my Liver with a Cup
Of[47] *Succahana* fresh and clear,
Not half so good as *English* Beer;
Which ready stood in Kitchin Pail,
And was in fact but *Adam's* Ale;
For Planters Cellars you must know,
Seldom with good *October*[48] flow,
But Perry Quince and Apple Juice,
Spout from the Tap like any Sluce;
Untill the Cask's grown low and stale,
They're forc'd again to[49] Goad and Pail:
The soathing drought scarce down my Throat,
Enough to put a Ship a float,
With Cockerouse as I was sitting,
I felt a Feaver Intermitting;
A fiery Pulse beat in my Veins,
From Cold I felt resembling Pains:
This cursed seasoning I remember,
Lasted from *March* to cold *December;*
Nor would it then its *Quarters* shift,
Until by *Cardus*[50] turn'd a drift,

---

39. "Chinces are a sort of Vermin like our Bugs in England." [Au.]

40. "Wild Turkies are very good Meat, and prodigiously large in Maryland." [Au.]

41. A card game, more commonly called loo.

42. Dressing gowns.

43. A trick.

44. The highest card in loo.

45. Ill-tempered women.

46. Prostitutes.

47. "Succahana is Water." [Au.]

48. Ale brewed in October.

49. "A Goad grows upon an Indian Vine, resembling a Bottle, when ripe it is hollow; this the Planters make use of to drink water out of." [Au.]

50. Herbal medicine.

And had my Doctress wanted skill,
Or Kitchin Physick at her will,
My Father's Son had lost his Lands,
And never seen the *Goodwin-Sands:*
But thanks to Fortune and a Nurse
Whose Care depended on my Purse,
I saw myself in good Condition,
Without the help of a Physitian:
At length the shivering ill relieved,
Which long my Head and Heart had grieved;
I then began to think with Care,
How I might sell my *British* Ware,
That with my Freight I might comply,
Did on my Charter party lie:
To this intent, with Guide before,
I tript it to the Eastern Shoar;
While riding near a Sandy Bay,
I met a *Quaker, Yea* and *Nay;*
A Pious Conscientious Rogue,
As e'er woar Bonnet or a Brogue,
Who neither Swore nor kept his Word,
But cheated in the Fear of God;
And when his Debts he would not pay,
By Light within he ran away.
With this sly Zealot soon I struck
A Bargain for my *English* Truck,
Agreeing for ten thousand weight,
Of *Sot-weed* good and fit for freight,
Broad *Oronooko* bright and sound,
The growth and product of his ground;
In Cask that should contain compleat,
Five hundred of Tobacco neat.
The Contract thus betwixt us made,
Not well acquainted with the Trade,
My Goods I trusted to the Cheat,
Whose crop was then aboard the Fleet;
And going to receive my own,
I found the Bird was newly flown:
Cursing this execrable Slave,
This damn'd pretended Godly Knave;
On due Revenge and Justice bent,
I instantly to Counsel went,
Unto an ambodexter[51] *Quack,*
Who learnedly had got the knack
Of giving Glisters,[52] making Pills,
Of filling Bonds, and forging Wills;

And with a stock of Impudence,
Supply'd his want of Wit and Sense;
With Looks demure, amazing People,
No wiser than a Daw in Steeple;
My Anger flushing in my Face,
I stated the preceeding Case:
And of my Money was so lavish,
That he'd have poyson'd half the Parish,
And hang'd his Father on a Tree,
For such another tempting Fee;
Smiling, said he, the Cause is clear,
I'll manage him you need not fear;
The Case is judg'd, good Sir, but look
In *Galen,* No—in my Lord *Cook,*[53]
I vow to God I was mistook:
I'll take out a Provincial Writ,
And Trounce him for his Knavish Wit;
Upon my Life we'll win the Cause,
With all the ease I cure the[54] *Yaws:*
Resolv'd to plague the holy Brother,
I set one Rogue to catch another;
To try the Cause then fully bent,
Up to[55] *Annapolis* I went,
A City Situate on a Plain,
Where scarce a House will keep out Rain;
The Buildings fram'd with Cyprus rare,
Resembles much our *Southwark* Fair:[56]
But Stranger here will scarcely meet
With Market-place, Exchange, or Street;
And if the Truth I may report,
'Tis not so large as *Tottenham Court.*[57]
St. *Mary's*[58] once was in repute,
Now here the Judges try the Suit,
And Lawyers twice a Year dispute.
As oft the Bench most gravely meet,
Some to get Drunk, and some to eat
A swinging share of Country Treat.
But as for Justice right or wrong,

---

51. "This Fellow was an Apothecary, and turn'd an Attorney at Law." [Au.]

52. Enemas.

53. A popular handbook of medicine was named after the ancient Greek physician Galen; Edward Coke's *Institutes* was a well-known book on law.

54. "The Yaws is the Pox." [Au.]

55. "The chief of Mary-land containing about twenty four Houses." [Au.]

56. A London fair where tents and temporary shacks were set up.

57. A small London neighborhood.

58. The capital of Maryland before Annapolis.

Not one amongst the numerous throng,
Knows what they mean, or has the Heart,
To give his Verdict on a Stranger's part:
Now Court being call'd by beat of Drum,
The Judges left their Punch and Rum,
When Pettifogger Doctor draws,
His Paper forth, and opens Cause:
And least I shou'd the better get,
Brib'd *Quack* supprest his Knavish Wit.
So Maid upon the downy Field,
Pretends a Force, and Fights to yield:
The Byast Court without delay,
Adjudg'd my Debt in Country Pay;
In[59] Pipe staves, Corn, or Flesh of Boar,
Rare Cargo for the *English* Shoar:
Raging with Grief, full speed I ran,

To joyn the Fleet at[60] *Kicketan;*[61]
Embarqu'd and waiting for a Wind,
I left this dreadful Curse behind.
    May Canniballs transported o'er the Sea
Prey on these Slaves, as they have done on me;
May never Merchant's, trading Sails explore
This Cruel, this Inhospitable Shoar;
But left abandon'd by the World to starve,
May they sustain the Fate they well deserve:
May they turn Savage, or as *Indians* Wild,
From Trade, Converse, and Happiness exil'd;
Recreant to Heaven, may they adore the Sun,
And into Pagan Superstitions run
For Vengence ripe————
May Wrath Divine then lay those Regions wast
Where no Man's[62] Faithful, nor a Woman Chast.

---

59. "There is a Law in this Country, the Plantiff may pay his Debt in Country pay, which consists in the produce of his Plantation." [Au.]

60. "The homeward bound Fleet meets here." [Au.]

61. Hampton, Virginia.

62. "The Author does not intend by this, any of the English Gentlemen resident there." [Au.]

RICHARD LEWIS (1700–1734)

Richard Lewis, a Maryland schoolmaster and member of the Maryland Assembly, was probably born in Wales. Before emigrating to Maryland, he seems to have spent a short period studying at Oxford. He displayed his classical education in his first book, *The Mouse-Trap* (1728), and in his translation of *Muscipula,* a Latin poem written by Edward Holdsworth (1684–1746). Between 1728 and 1734, Lewis published two book-length volumes of his own poetry, and a number of his poems appeared in literary magazines. According to his biographer, Lewis's poetry was the most widely reprinted of any poet on American topics.

    The most admired poems in Lewis's day were those that drew upon the popular mode of the pastoral to describe and praise the American landscape. English pastorals, based upon classical models replete with nymphs and shepherds, idealized rural life and rural scenery, in a verse form of regular line and meter that emulated the order and harmony of nature. At the hands of the poet Alexander Pope and writers like him, the pastoral during the eighteenth century in England began to show the realities of rural life in a specifically English countryside. In applying himself to the English pastoral model while filling his poems with peculiarly "American" natural phenomena, Lewis was celebrating the singularity of poetic vision that one could gain while in Britain's middle colonies.

    In his "Journey from Patapsco to Annapolis," Lewis employed the allegorical model of the voyage of a day being like the voyage of life. In "Food for Criticks," Lewis approached similar material but focused more on the relationship between people and their environment. In a third major poem not reprinted here, "Upon Prince Madoc's Expedition to the Country now called America," written between 1733 and 1734, Lewis created an epic figure in the form of Madoc, a twelfth-century Welsh king who wanted to found an empire in the Western hemisphere. While the form of this poem differed from the pastorals printed here, the interest in uniquely American subject matter remained consistent throughout Lewis's work.

A JOURNEY FROM PATAPSKO TO ANNAPOLIS, APRIL 4, 1730[1]

Me vero primum dulces ante omnia Musae,
Quarum sacra fero ingenti perculsus amore,
Accipiant; Coelique vias & Sydera *monstrent;*———
Sin has ne possim Naturae accedere partes
Frigidus obstiterit circum praecordia Sanguis,
Rura *mihi,* & rigui *placeant in Vallibus* Amnes,
Flumina *amem,* Sylvasque *inglorius.*

VIRG. GEOR. 2[2]

At length the *wintry* Horrors disappear,
And *April* views with Smiles the infant Year;
The grateful Earth from frosty Chains unbound,
Pours out its *vernal* Treasures all around,
Her Face bedeckt with Grass, with Buds the Trees are
   crown'd.
In this soft Season, 'ere the Dawn of Day,
I mount my Horse, and lonely take my Way,
From woody Hills that shade *Patapsko's* Head,
(In whose deep Vales he makes his stony Bed,
From whence he rushes with resistless Force,
Tho' hug rough Rocks retard his rapid Course,)
Down to *Annapolis,* on that smooth Stream[3]
Which took from fair *Anne-Arundel* its Name.
And now the *Star* that ushers in the Day,[4]
Begins to pale her ineffectual Ray.
The *Moon,* with blunted Horns, now shines less bright,
Her fading Face eclips'd with growing Light;
The fleecy Clouds with streaky Lustre glow,
And Day quits Heav'n to view the Earth below.
Oe'r you tall *Pines* the *Sun* shews half his Face,
And fires their floating Foliage with his Rays;
Now sheds aslant on Earth his lightsome Beams,

That trembling shine in many-colour'd Streams:
Slow-rising from the Marsh, the Mist recedes,
The Trees, emerging, rear their dewy Heads;
Their dewy Heads the *Sun* with Pleasure views,
And brightens into Pearls the pendent Dews.
   The *Beasts* uprising, quit their leafy Beds,
And to the cheerful *Sun* erect their Heads;
All joyful rise, except the filthy *Swine,*
On obscene Litter stretch'd they snore supine:
In vain the Day awakes, Sleep seals their Eyes,
Till Hunger breaks the Bond and bids them rise.
Mean while the *Sun* with more exalted Ray,
From cloudless Skies distributes riper Day;
Thro' sylvan Scenes my Journey I pursue,
Ten thousand Beauties rising to my View;
Which kindle in my Breast poetic Flame,
And bid me my CREATOR'S praise proclaim;
Tho' my low Verse ill-suits the noble Theme.
   Here various Flourets grace the teeming Plains,
Adorn'd by Nature's Hand with beauteous Stains;
First-born of *Spring,* here the *Pacone*[5] appears,
Whose golden Root a silver Blossom rears.
In spreading Tufts, see there the *Crowfoot* blue,
On whose green Leaves still shines a globous Dew;
Behold the *Cinque-foil,* with its dazling Dye
Of flaming Yellow, wounds the tender Eye:
But there, enclos'd the grassy *Wheat* is seen,
To heal the aching Sight with cheerful Green.
   Safe in yon Cottage dwells the *Monarch-Swain,*
His *Subject-Flocks,* close-grazing, hide the Plain;
For him they live;——and die t'uphold his Reign.
Viands unbought his well-till'd Lands afford,
And smiling *Plenty* waits upon his Board;
Health shines with sprightly Beams around his Head,
And *Sleep,* with downy Wings, o'er-shades his Bed;
His *Sons* robust his daily Labours share,
Patient of Toil, Companions of his Care:
And all their Toils with sweet Success are crown'd.
In graceful Ranks there *Trees* adorn the Ground,
The *Peach,* the *Plum,* the *Apple,* here are found;
Delicious Fruits!——Which from their Kernels rise,
So fruitful is the Soil—so mild the Skies.
The lowly *Quince* yon sloping Hill o'er-shades.
Here lofty *Cherry-Trees* erect their Heads;
High in the Air each spiry Summit waves,
Whose Blooms thick-springing yield no Space for
   Leaves;

---

1. Patapsco was the name of a settlement at the site of present-day Baltimore. The poem was first published in the London *Weekly Register* in January 1731.

2. "But as for me—first above all, may the sweet Muses whose holy emblems, under the spell of a mighty love, I bear, take me to themselves, and show me heaven's pathways, [and] the stars. . . . But if the chill blood about my heart bar me from reaching those realms of nature, let my delight be the country, and the running streams amid the dells—may I love the waters and the woods, though fame be lost" (Virgil, *Georgics,* 2:745–77, 483–86).

3. The Severn River.

4. "Venus." [Au.]

---

5. Tumeric root. It is not possible to identify with certainty the plants named in the following lines.

Evolving Odours fill the ambient Air,
The *Birds* delighted to the Grove repair:
On ev'ry Tree behold a tuneful Throng,
The vocal Vallies echo to their Song.
    But what is *He*,[6] who perch'd above the rest,
Pours out such various Musick from his Breast!
His Breast, whose Plumes a cheerful White display,
His quiv'ring Wings are dress'd in sober Grey.
Sure, all the *Muses,* this their Bird inspire!
And *He,* alone, is equal to the Choir
Of warbling Songsters who around him play,
While, Echo like, *He* answers ev'ry Lay.
The chirping *Lark* now sings with sprightly Note,
Responsive to her Strain *He* shapes his Throat:
Now the poor widow'd *Turtle* wails her Mate,
While in soft Sounds *He* cooes to mourn his Fate.
Oh, sweet Musician, thou dost far excel
The soothing Song of pleasing *Philomel!*
Sweet is her Song, but in few Notes confin'd;
But thine, thou *Mimic* of the feath'ry Kind,
Runs thro' all Notes!——*Thou* only know'st them *All,*
At once the *Copy,*——and th'*Original.*
    My *Ear* thus charm'd, mine *Eye* with Pleasure sees,
Hov'ring about the Flow'rs, th'industrious *Bees.*
Like them in Size, the *Humming-Bird* I view,
Like them, *He* sucks his Food, the Honey-Dew,
With nimble Tongue, and Beak of jetty Hue.
He takes with rapid Whirl his noisy Flight,
His gemmy Plumage strikes the Gazer's Sight;
And as he moves his ever-flutt'ring Wings,
Ten thousand Colours he around him flings.
Now I behold the Em'rald's vivid Green,
Now scarlet, now a purple Die is seen;
In brightest Blue, his Breast *He* now arrays,
Then strait his Plumes emit a golden Blaze.
Thus whirring round he flies, and varying still,
He mocks the *Poet*'s and the *Painter*'s Skill;
Who may forever strive with fruitless Pains,
To catch and fix those beauteous changeful Stains;
While Scarlet now, and now the Purple shines,
And Gold, to Blue its transient Gloss resigns.
Each quits, and quickly each resumes its Place,
And ever-varying Dies each other chase.
Smallest of Birds, what Beauties shine in thee!
A living *Rainbow* on thy Breast I see.
    Oh had that *Bard*[7] in whose heart-pleasing Lines,

The *Phoenix* in a Blaze of Glory shines,
Beheld those Wonders which are shewn in Thee,
That Bird had lost his Immortality!
Thou in His Verse hadst stretch'd thy flutt'ring Wing
Above all other Birds,—their beauteous King.
    But now th'enclos'd Plantation I forsake,
And onwards thro' the Woods my Journey take;
The level Road, the longsome Way beguiles,
A blooming Wilderness around me smiles;
Here hardy *Oak,* there fragrant *Hick'ry* grows,
Their bursting Buds the tender Leaves disclose;
The tender Leaves in downy Robes appear,
Trembling, they seem to move with cautious Fear,
Yet new to Life, and Strangers to the Air.
Here stately *Pines* unite their whisp'ring Heads,
And with a solemn Gloom embrown the Glades.
See there a green *Savane* opens wide,
Thro' which smooth Streams in wanton Mazes glide;
Thick-branching Shrubs o'er-hang the silver Streams,
Which scarcely deign t'admit the solar Beams.
    While with Delight on this soft Scene I gaze,
The *Cattle* upward look, and cease to graze,
But into covert run thro' various Ways.
And now the Clouds in black Assemblage rise,
And dreary Darkness overspreads the Skies,
Thro' which the Sun strives to transmit his Beams,
"But sheds his sickly Light in straggling Streams."[8]
Hush'd is the Musick of the wood-land Choir,
Fore-knowing of the Storm, the Birds retire
For Shelter, and forsake the shrubby Plains,
And dumb Horror thro' the Forest reigns;
In that lone House which opens wide its Door,
Safe may I tarry till the Storm is o'er.
    Hark how the *Thunder* rolls with solemn Sound!
And see the forceful *Lightning* dart a Wound,
On yon toll Oak!——Behold its Top laid bare!
Its Body rent, and scatter'd thro' the Air
The Splinters fly!——Now—now the *Winds* arise,
From different Quarters of the lowring Skies;
Forth-issuing fierce, the *West* and *South* engage,
The waving Forest bends beneath their Rage:
But where the winding Valley checks their Course,
They roar and ravage with redoubled Force;
With circling Sweep in dreadful Whirlwinds move
And from its Roots tear up the gloomy Grove,

---

6. "The Mock Bird." [Au.]

7. "Claudian." [Au.]

8. The quotation seems to refer to Dryden's translation of
Virgil: "Or if thro' mists he shoots his sullen beams, / Frugal of
light, in loose and straggling streams."

Down-rushing fall the Trees, and beat the Ground,
In Fragments file the shatter'd Limbs around;
Tremble the Under-woods, the Vales resound.
    Follows, with patt'ring Noise, the icy *Hail,*
And *Rain,* fast falling, floods the lowly Vale.
Again the *Thunders* roll, the *Lightnings* fly,
And as they first disturb'd, now clear the Sky;
For lo, the *Gust* decreases by Degrees,
The dying *Winds* but sob amidst the Trees;
With pleasing Softness falls the silver Rain,
Thro' which at first faint-gleaming o'er the Plain,
The Orb of Light scarce darts a watry Ray
To gild the Drops that fall from ev'ry Spray;
But soon the dusky Vapours are dispell'd,
And thro' the Mist that late his Face conceal'd,
Bursts the broad *Sun,* triumphant in a Blaze
Too keen for Sight—Yon Cloud refracts his Rays,
The mingling Beams compose th'*ethereal Bow,*
How sweet, how soft, its melting Colours glow!
Gaily they shine, by heav'nly Pencils laid,
Yet vanish swift,——How soon does *Beauty* fade!
    The *Storm* is past, my Journey I renew,
And a new Scene of Pleasure greets my View:
Wash'd by the copious Rain the gummy *Pine,*
Does cheerful, with unsully'd Verdure shine;
The *Dogwood* Flow'rs assume a snowy white,
The *Maple* blushing gratifies the Sight:
No verdant leaves the lovely *Red-Bud* grace,
Cornation blossoms now supply their Place.
The *Sassafras* unfolds its fragrant Bloom,
The *Vine* affords an exquisite Perfume;
These grateful Scents wide-wafting thro' the Air
The smelling Sense with balmy Odours cheer.
And now the *Birds,* sweet singing, stretch their Throats,
And in one Choir unite their various Notes,
Nor yet unpleasing is the *Turtle*'s Voice,
Tho' he complains while other Birds rejoice.
    These vernal Joys, all restless Thoughts controul,
And gently-soothing calm the troubled Soul.
    While such Delights my Senses entertain,
I scarce perceive that I have left the *Plain;*
'Till now the Summit of a *Mount* I gain:
Low at whose sandy Base the *River* glides,
Slow-rolling near their Height his languid Tides;
Shade above Shade, the Trees in rising Ranks,
Cloath with eternal Green his steepy Banks:
The Flood, well pleas'd, reflects their verdant Gleam
From the smooth Mirror of his limpid Stream.
    But see the *Hawk,* who with acute Survey,
Towring in Air predestinates his Prey

Amid the Floods!——Down dropping from on high,
He strikes the *Fish,* and bears him thro' the Sky.
The Stream disturb'd, no longer shews the Scene
That lately stain'd its silver Waves with green;
In spreading Circles roll the troubled Floods,
And to the Shores bear off the pictur'd Woods.
    Now looking round I view the out-stretch'd *Land,*
O'er which the Sight exerts a wide Command;
The fertile Vallies, and the naked Hills,
The Cattle feeding near the chrystal Rills;
The Lawns wide-op'ning to the sunny Ray,
And mazy Thickets that exclude the Day.
A-while the Eye is pleas'd these Scenes to trace,
Then hurrying o'er the intermediate Space,

Far-distant Mountains drest in Blue appear,
And all their Woods are lost in empty Air.
    The *Sun* near setting now arrays his Head
In milder Beams and lengthens ev'ry Shade.
The rising Clouds usurping on the Day
A bright Variety of Dies display;
About the wide Horizon swift they fly,
"And chase a Change of Colours round the Sky:
And now I view but half the *flaming Sphere,*
Now one faint Glimmer shoots along the Air,
And all his golden Glories disappear.[9]
    Onwards the *Ev'ning* moves in Habit grey,
And for her Sister *Night* prepares the Way.
The plumy People seek their secret Nests,
To Rest repair the ruminating Beasts.
Now deep'ning Shades confess th' Approach of Night,
Imperfect Images elude the Sight:
From earthly Objects I remove mine Eye,
And view with Look erect the vaulted Sky;
Where dimly-shining now the Stars appear,
At first thin-scatt'ring thro' the misty Air;
Till Night confirm'd, her jetty Throne ascends,
On her the *Moon* in clouded State attends,
But soon unveil'd her lovely Face is seen,
And *Stars* unnumber'd wait around their Queen;
Rang'd by their MAKER's Hand in just Array,
They march majestic thro' th'ethereal Way.
    Are these bright Luminaries hung on high
Only to please with twinkling Rays our Eye?
Or may we rather count each *Star* a *Sun,*
Round which *full peopled Worlds* their Courses run?

9. Despite the quotation marks, these four lines are loose
adaptations from James Thomson's *The Seasons* (1628–29),
"Summer" ll. 635–38.

Orb above Orb harmoniously they steer
Their various voyages thro' Seas of Air.
   Snatch me some *Angel* to those high Abodes,
The Seats perhaps of *Saints* and *Demigods!*
Where such as bravely scorn'd the galling Yoke
Of *vulgar Error,* and her Fetters broke;
Where *Patriots* who fix the publick Good,
In Fields of Battle sacrific'd their Blood;
Where *pious Priests* who Charity proclaim'd,
And *Poets* whom a *virtuous Muse* enflam'd;
Philosophers who strove to mend our Hearts,
And such as polish'd Life with *useful Arts,*
Obtain a Place; when by the Hand of Death
Touch'd, they retire from this poor Speck of Earth;
Their *Spirits* freed from bodily Alloy
Perceive a Fore-taste of that endless Joy,
Which from Eternity hath been prepar'd,
To crown their labours with a vast Reward.
While to these Orbs my wand'ring Thoughts aspire,
A falling *Meteor* shoots his lambent Fire;
Thrown from the heav'nly Space he seeks the Earth,
From whence he first deriv'd his humble Birth.
   The *Mind* advis'd by this instructive Sight,
Descending sudden from th'aerial Height,
Obliges me to view a different Scene,
Of more importance to myself, tho' mean.
These distant Objects I no more pursue,
But turning inward my reflective View,
My working Fancy helps me to survey,
In the just Picture of this *April Day,*
My Life o'er past,———a Course of thirty *Years*
Blest with few Joys, perplex'd with num'rous Cares.
   In the dim Twilight of our *Infancy,*
Scarce can the Eye surrounding Objects see;
Then thoughtless *Childhood* leads us pleas'd and gay,
In Life's fair Morning thro' a flow'ry Way:
The *Youth* in Schools inquisitive of Good,
Science pursues thro' *Learning's* mazy Wood;
Whose lofty Trees, he, to his Grief perceives,
Are often bare of *Fruit,* and only fill'd with *Leaves:*
Thro' lonely Wilds his tedious Journey lies,
At last a brighter Prospect cheers his Eyes;
Now the gay Fields of *Poetry* he views,
And joyous listens to the *tuneful Muse;*
Now *History* affords him vast Delight,
And opens lovely Landscapes to his Sight:
But ah too soon this Scene of Pleasure flies!
And o'er his Head tempestous Troubles rise.

He hears the Thunders roll, he feels the Rains,
Before a friendly Shelter he obtains;
And thence beholds with Grief the furious Storm
The *noon-tide* Beauties of his *Life* deform:
He views the *painted Bow* in distant Skies;
Hence, in his Heart some Gleams of Comfort rise;
He hopes the *Gust* has almost spent its Force,
And that he safely may pursue his Course.
   Thus far *my Life* does with the *Day* agree,
Oh may its coming Stage from Storms be free!
While passing thro' the World's most private Way,
With Pleasure I my MAKER's Works survey;
Within my Heart let *Peace* a Dwelling find,
Let my *Goodwill* extend to *all Mankind:*
Freed from *Necessity,* and blest with *Health;*
Give me *Content,* let others toil for *Wealth:*
In *busy* Scenes of Life let me exert
A *careful Hand,* and wear an *honest Heart;*
And suffer me my *leisure* Hours to spend,
With chosen *Books,* or a well-natur'd *Friend.*
Thus journeying on, as I advance in Age
May I look back with Pleasure on my Stage;
And as the setting *Sun* withdrew his Light
To rise on other Worlds serene and bright,
Cheerful may I resign my vital Breath,
Nor anxious tremble at th' Approach of *Death;*
Which shall (I hope) but strip me of *my Clay,*
And to a better World my Soul convey.
   Thus musing, I my silent Moments spend,
Till to the *River's* margin I descend,
From whence I may discern my *Journey's* End:
Annapolis adorns its further Shore,
To which the *Boat* attends to bear me o'er.
   And now the moving *Boat* the Flood divides,
While the *Stars* "tremble on the floating Tides;"[10]
Pleas'd with the Sight, again I raise mine Eye
To the bright Glories of the azure Sky;
And while these Works of God's creative Hand,
The *Moon* and *Stars,* that move at his Command,
Obedient thro' their circling Course on high,
Employ my Sight,——struck with amaze I cry,
ALMIGHTY LORD! whom Heav'n and Earth proclaim,
The *Author* of their universal Frame,
Wilt thou vouchsafe to view the *Son of Man,*

---

10. Pope, *Rape of the Lock,* II 48.

Thy Creature, who but Yesterday began,
Thro' animated Clay to draw his Breath,
To-morrow doom'd a Prey to ruthless Death!
    TREMENDOUS GOD! May I not justly fear,
That I, unworthy Object of thy Care,
Into this World from thy bright Presence tost,
Am in th'Immensity of Nature lost!
And that my Notions of the World above,
Are but Creations of my own Self-Love;
To feed my coward Heart, afraid to die,
With fancied Feasts of Immortality!
    These Thoughts, which thy amazing Works suggest,
Oh glorious FATHER, rack my troubled Breast.
    Yet, GRACIOUS GOD, reflecting that my Frame
From Thee deriv'd in animating Flame,
And that what e'er I am, however mean,
By thy Command I enter'd on this Scene
Of Life,——thy wretched Creature of a Day,
Condemn'd to travel thro' a tiresome Way;
Upon whose Banks (perhaps to cheer my Toil)
I see thin Verdures rise, and Daisies smile:
Poor Comforts these, my Pains t'alleviate!
While on my Head tempestuous Troubles beat.
And must I, when I quit this earthly Scene,
Sink total into Death, and never rise again?
    No sure,——These Thoughts which in my Bosom
    roll
Must issue from a never-dying Soul;
These active Thoughts that penetrate the Sky,
Excursive into dark Futurity;
Which hope eternal Happiness to gain,
Could never be bestow'd on Man in vain.
To Thee, OH FATHER, fill'd with fervent Zeal,
And sunk in humble Silence I appeal;
Take me, my great CREATOR to Thy Care.
And gracious listen to my ardent Prayer!
    SUPREME OF BEINGS, omnipresent Power!
My great Preserver from my natal Hour,
Fountain of Wisdom, boundless Deity,
OMNISCIENT GOD, my Wants are known to THEE,
With Mercy look on mine Infirmity!
Whatever State thou shalt for me ordain,
Whether my Lot in Life by Joy or Pain;
Patient let me sustain thy wise Decree,
And learn to know myself, and honour Thee.

FOOD FOR CRITICKS[1]

Hic sunt gelidi sontes, hic mollia prata, Lycori
Hic nemus, hic tecum toto consumerer avo.

VIRG.[2]

Of ancient streams presume no more to tell,
The fam'd castalian or pierian well;
SKUYLKIL[3] superior, must those springs confess,
As Pensilvania yields to Rome or Greece.
More limpid water can no fountain show,
A fairer bottom or a smoother brow.
A painted world its peaceful gleam contains
The heav'nly arch, the bord'ring groves and plains:
Here in mock silver Cynthia seems to roll.
And trusty pointers watch the frozen pole.
Here sages might observe the wandring stars,
And rudest swains commence astrologers.
Along the brink the lonely plover stalks,
And to his visionary fellow talks:
Amid the wave the vagrant blackbird sees,
And tries to perch upon the imag'd trees:
On flying clouds the simple bullocks gaze,
Or vainly reach to crop the shad'wy grass:
From neighb'ring hills the stately horse espies
Himself a feeding, and himself envies:
Hither pursu'd by op'ning hounds, the hare
Blesses himself to see a forest near;
The waving shrubs he takes for real wood,
And boldly plunges in the yielding flood.
Here bending willows hem the border round,
There graceful trees the promontory crown,
Whose mingled tufts and outspread arms compose
A shade delightful to the lawrel'd brows.
Here mossy couches tempt to pleasing dreams

---

1. The poem was probably in the *Maryland Gazette* for May 1730, but no copies of that issue survive. The poem also appeared in the *New England Weekly Journal* in June 1731 and in the *Pennsylvania Gazette* in July 1732, from which this text is taken.

2. "Here are cool springs, soft mead and grove, Lycoris; / here might our lives with time have worn away" (Virgil, *Eclogues* X).

3. The river referred to in the poem was changed, depending on where the poem was printed; in the original version set in Maryland, it is the Severn River.

The love-sick soul; and ease the weary limbs.
No noxious snake disperses poison here,
Nor screams of night-bird rend the twilight air,
Excepting him, who when the groves are still,
Hums am'rous tunes, and whistles whip poor will;
To hear whose carol, elves in circles trip,
And lovers hearts within their bosoms leap;
Whose savage notes the troubled mind amuse,
Banish despair, and hold the falling dews.
   If to the west you turn your ravish'd eyes,
There shaggy hills prop up the bending skies,
And smoaky spires, from lowly cots arise
Tow'rds the northwest the distant mountains wear
In May a green, in June a whit'ning ear,
Or all alive with woolly flocks appear.
Beneath their feet a wide extended plain,
Or rich in cider, or in swelling grain;
Does to the margin of the water stretch,
Bounded by meadows and rushy beach.
The rest a motley mixture, hill and dale,
There open fields here mingled woods prevail:
Here lasting oaks, the hope of navies, stand,
There beauteous poplars hide th'unsightly strand:
In autumn there the full-ripe clusters blush
Around the walnut or the hawthorn bush.
Here fruitful orchards bend their aged boughs,
There sweats the reaper, here the peasant mows.
Each smiling month diversifies the view,
Ev'n hoary winter teams with something new:
A milkwhite fleece does then the lawns o'erspread,
The stream becomes a looking-glass indeed.
A polish'd surface spreads across the deep.
O'er which the youth with rapid vigour slip.
But now the groves the gayest liv'ries wear,
How pleas'd, could it be spring throughout the year!
And in these walks eternity be spent,
Atheists would then to immortality consent.
   The grateful shifting of the colour'd scene,
The rich embroid'ry of the level green;
The trees, and rusling of the branches there,
The silent whispers of the passing air;
Of falling cataracts the solemn roar,
By murmuring eccho sent from shore to shore,
Mix'd with the musick of the winged choir,
Awake the fancy and the poet's fire.
Here rural Maro might attend his sheep,
And the Maeonian with advantage sleep.
Hither ye bards for inspiration come,
Let ev'ry other fount but this be dumb.
With way soe'er your airy genius leads,

Receive your model from these vocal shades.
Wou'd you in homely pastoral excel,
Take patterns from the merry piping quail;
Observe the bluebird for a roundelay,
The chatt'ring pie, or ever babling jay:
The plantive dove the soft love verse can teach,
And mimick thrash to imitators preach.
In Pindar's strain the lark salutes the dawn,
The lyrick robin chirps the ev'ning on:
For poignant satyr mind the movis well,
And hear the sparrow for a madrigal;
For every verse a pattern here you have,
From strains heroic down to humble stave.
Not Phoebus self, altho' the god of verse,
Could hit more fine, more entertaining airs;
Nor the fair maids who round the fountain sate,
Such artless heavenly music modulate.
Each thicket seems a paradise renew'd,
The soft vibrations fire the moving blood:
Each sense its part of sweet delusion shares,
The scenes bewitch the eye, the song the ears:
Pregnant with the scent, each wind regales the smell,
Like cooling sheets th' enwrapping breezes feel.
During the dark, if poets eyes we trust,
These lawns are haunted by some swarthy ghost,
Some indian prince, who fond of former joys,
With bow and quiver thro' the shadow flies;
He can't in death his native groves forget,
But leaves elyzium for his ancient seat.
O happy stream! hadst thow in Grecia flow'd,
The bounteous blessing of some wat'ry god
Thou'dst been; or had some Ovid sung thy rise
Distill'd perhaps from slighted virgins eyes.
Well is thy worth in indian story known,
Thy living lymph and fertile borders shown.
The shining roach and yellow bristly breme,
The pick'rel rav'nous monarch of the stream;
The pearch whose back a ring of colours shows;
The horned pout who courts the slimy ooze;
The eel serpentine, some of dubious race;
The tortoise with his golden spotted case;
Thy hairy musk-rat, whose perfume defies
The balmy odours of arabian spice;
The various flocks who shores alternate shun,
Drove by the fowler and the fatal gun.
   Young philadelphians know thy pleasures well,
Joys too extravagant perhaps to tell.
Hither oftimes th'ingenious youth repair,
When Sol returning warms the growing year:
Some take the fish with a delusive bait,

Or for the fowl beneath the arbors wait;
And arm'd with fire, endanger ev'ry shade,
Teaching ev'n unfledg'd innocence a dread.
To gratify a nice luxurious taste
How many pretty songsters breath their last:
Spite of his voice they fire the linnet down,
And make the widow'd dove renew his moan.
But some more humane seek the shady gloom,
Taste nature's bounty and admire her bloom:

In pensive thought revolve long vanish'd toil,
Or in soft song the pleasing hours beguile;
What Eden was, by every prospect told,
Strive to regain the temper of that age of gold;
No artful harms for simple brutes contrive,
But scorn to take a being they cannot give;
To leafy woods resort for health and ease,
Not to disturb their melody and peace.

Dr. Alexander Hamilton (1712–1756)

Dr. Alexander Hamilton (not to be mistaken with statesman Alexander Hamilton) was born in Edinburgh, Scotland, the center of British culture outside the imperial center of London during the eighteenth century. Hamilton's father, the Reverend William Hamilton, held a prestigious position with the University of Edinburgh and saw that his sons were well educated and aware of their own cultured station. Along with his brother, Dr. John Hamilton, Alexander Hamilton studied medicine at the university. He emigrated to Maryland in 1739 and established a medical practice in Annapolis. From his earliest days in his new home, Hamilton experienced poor health, and alternatives were limited to finding a way to adapt to life in Maryland or returning to Britain. In an effort to restore himself, he determined to leave Maryland during the heat of the summer, when the weather was damp and least fresh, and travel through the British colonies to the north.

The result of one such trip is Hamilton's journal, which he called *Itinerarium,* written as an account of his travels from his home in Annapolis to York, Maine, and back. Hamilton recorded his thoughts during this four-month trip (May 30–September 7, 1744) in a sometimes lightly humorous and sometimes bitingly satiric vein, employing the typical mode of travel diary as a means to organize his comments on people, culture, topography, and nature. The *Itinerarium* reveals that its author was fascinated with language and manners of expression, with people who were unlike himself, and with humorous episodes that might be turned into stories of foibles or disquisitions upon "characters," renderings of people's activities as representative of their being certain "characters types." Hamilton used his *Itinerarium* as a means by which he could demonstrate to himself and his readers his own urbanity, his own sense of "culture," and his own abilities in perception, which, if well rendered in his readers' eyes, would constitute his "wit." While readers today might think such a diary as this a private text, readers and writers then considered diaries like Hamilton's to be public texts. They circulated their diaries frequently among friends, not just to reveal the details of their trips, but to reveal themselves as appropriate commentators on the peoples seen and the actions undertaken as part of the journeys. Hamilton circulated his diary, just as scholars assume Sarah Kemble Knight circulated hers: as a mark of the writer's culture, observational skill, and wit. As a sign of the public nature of Hamilton's *Itinerarium,* the travel diary was dedicated to an Italian nobleman, Onorio Razolini, the friend to whom he sent the manuscript. Razolini would have circulated Hamilton's work among his associates and friends, thus bringing Hamilton a particularly cultured form of "publicity," given the assumptions of Hamilton's class and his day.

When Jonas Green established the *Maryland Gazette* in 1745, Hamilton began contributing to his friend's newspaper, along with several of their other friends. Hamilton's contributions were humorous and satirical, and Hamilton took part in lighthearted literary debates with other Annapolis and Baltimore writers. At the same time, Hamilton organized a gentlemen's club, called the Tuesday Club of Annapolis. Members of the club and their visitors were prominent Maryland citizens, including clergymen, physicians, judges, merchants, politicians, scientists, writers, musicians, and painters—in short, the people who considered themselves the most important to the life and culture of the colony. The club met for eleven years, disbanding shortly before Hamilton's death. During the eleven years of his club's existence, Hamilton kept its minutes, fictionalizing the goings-on of the club members into a fourteen-volume mock-epic, *The History of the Tuesday Club of Annapolis.* Tracing the supposed decline of clubbing from its origins in an ideal of simplicity to its current miring in degenerate luxuriousness, Hamilton's *History of the Tuesday Club* parodied jeremiad laments about the falling away of present times from former glories, taking up this common literary trope while reversing its import precisely in the form offering the lament: Hamilton's *History* is, for people like Hamilton and his associates, the best representative of the very ideal whose loss is being lamented.

from ITINERARIUM[1]

Thursday, May 31. I got up by times this morning pour prendre le frais[2] as the French term it, and found it heavy and cloudy, portending rain. Att 9 o'clock I took my leave of Mr. H———t his wife and sister, and took horse. A little before I reached Patapscoe Ferry, I was overtaken by a certain captain of a tobacco ship, whose name I know not, nor did I inquire concerning it lest he should think me impertinent.

Patapscoe Ferry

We crossed the ferry together att 10 o'clock. He talked inveterately against the clergy and particularly the Maryland clerks of the holy cloth, but I soon found that he was a prejudiced person, for it seems he had been lately cheated by one of our parsons.

Baltimore Town—Gunpowder Ferry—Joppa

This man accompanied me to Baltimore Town, and after I parted with him, I had a solitary journey till I came within three miles of Gunpowder Ferry where I met one Mathew Baker, a horse jockey.

Crossing the ferry I came to Joppa, a village pleasantly situated and lying close upon the river. There I called att one Brown's, who keeps a good taveren in a large brick house. The landlord was ill with intermitting fevers, and understanding from some there who knew me that I professed physick, he asked my advice, which I gave him.

Here I encountered Mr. D———n the minister of the parish, who (after we had dispatched a bowl of sangaree) carried me to his house. There passed between him, his wife, and I some odd rambling conversation which turned chiefly upon politicks. I heard him read, with great patience, some letters from his correspondents in England, written in a gazett stile, which seemed to be an abridgement of the politicall history of the times and a dissection of the machinations of the French in their late designs upon Great Brittain. This reverend gentleman and his wife seemed to express their indignation with some zeal against certain of our st—sm—n and c———rs att Annapolis who, it seems, had opposed the interest of the clergy by attempting to reduce the number of the taxables. This brought the proverb in my mind, The shirt is nearest the skin. Touch a man in his private interest, and you immediately procure his ill will.

Leaving Joppa I fell in company with one Captain Waters and with Mr. D———gs, a virtuoso in botany. He affected some knowledge in naturall philosophy, but his learning that way was but superficiall.

Description of the Gensing[3]

He showed me a print or figure of the gensing which, he told me, was to be found in the rich bottoms near Susquehanna. The plant is of one stemm, or stalk, and jointed. From each joint issues four small branches. At the extremity of each of these is a cinquefoil, or 5 leaves, somewhat oblong, notched and veined. Upon the top of the stemm, it bears a bunch of red berries, but I could not learn if it had any apparent flower, the colour of that flower, or att what season of the year it blossomed or bore fruit. I intended, however, to look for it upon the branches of Susquehanna; not that I imagined it of any singular virtue, for I think it has really no more than what may be in the common liquorice root mixed with an aromatick or

---

1. Written in 1744, the *Itinerarium* was dedicated to Onorio Razolini, and the manuscript remained in the possession of his family until the end of the ninetheenth century, when it was sold and first printed as *Hamilton's Itinerarium,* ed. Albert Bushnell Hart (1907).

2. To take the air.

3. Ginseng.

spicy drug, but I had a curiosity to see a thing which has been so famous.

After parting with this company, I put up att one Tradaway's about 10 miles from Joppa. The road here is pritty hilly, stonny, and full of a small gravell. I observed some stone which I thought looked like limestone.

Just as I dismounted att Tradaway's, I found a drunken club dismissing. Most of them had got upon their horses and were seated in an oblique situation, deviating much from a perpendicular to the horizontal plan[e], a posture quite necessary for keeping the center of gravity within its proper base for the support of the superstructure; hence we deduce the true physicall reason why our heads overloaded with liquor become too ponderous for our heels. Their discourse was as oblique as their position; the only thing intelligible in it was oaths and God dammes; the rest was an inarticulate sound like Rabelais' frozen words a thawing, interlaced with hickupings and belchings. I was uneasy till they were gone, and my landlord, seeing me stare, made that trite apology—that indeed he did not care to have such disorderly fellows come about his house; he was always noted far and near for keeping a quiet house and entertaining only gentlemen or such like, but these were country people, his neighbours, and it was not prudent to dissoblige them upon slight occasions. "Alas, sir!" added he, "we that entertain travellers must strive to oblige every body, for it is our dayly bread." While he spoke thus, our Bacchanalians, finding no more rum in play, rid off helter skelter as if the devil had possessed them, every man sitting his horse in a see-saw manner like a bunch of rags tyed upon the saddle.

I found nothing particular or worth notice in my landlord's character or conversation, only as to his bodily make. He was a fat pursy man and had large bubbies like a woman. I supped upon fry'd chickens and bacon, and after supper the conversation turned upon politicks, news, and the dreaded French war;[4] but it was so very lumpish and heavy that it disposed me mightily to sleep. This learned company consisted of the landlord, his overseer and miller, and another greasy thumb'd fellow who, as I understood, professed physick and particularly surgery. In the drawing of teeth, he practiced upon the house maid,

a dirty piece of lumber, who made such screaming and squalling as made me imagine there was murder going forwards in the house. However, the artist got the tooth out att last with a great clumsy pair of black-smith's forceps; and indeed it seemed to require such an instrument, for when he showed it to us, it resembled a horsenail more than a tooth.

The miller, I found, professed musick and would have tuned his crowd[5] to us, but unfortunatly the two middle strings betwixt the bass and treble were broke. This man told us that he could play by the book. After having had my fill of this elegant company, I went to bed att 10 o'clock.

Friday, June 1st. The sun rose in a clear horizon, and the air in these highlands was, for two hours in the morning, very cool and refreshing. I breakfasted upon some dirty chocolate, but the best that the house could afford, and took horse about half an hour after six in the morning. For the first thirteen miles the road seemed gravelly and hilly, and the land but indifferent.

Susquehanna Ferry

When I came near Susquehanna, I looked narrowly in the bottoms for the gensing but could not discover it. The lower ferry of Susquehanna, which I crossed, is above a mile broad. It is kept by a little old man whom I found att vittles with his wife and family upon a homely dish of fish without any kind of sauce. They desired me to eat, but I told them I had no stomach. They had no cloth upon the table, and their mess was in a dirty, deep, wooden dish which they evacuated with their hands, cramming down skins, scales, and all. They used neither knife, fork, spoon, plate, or napkin because, I suppose, they had none to use. I looked upon this as a picture of that primitive simplicity practiced by our forefathers long before the mechanic arts had supplyed them with instruments for the luxury and elegance of life. I drank some of their syder, which was very good, and crossed the ferry in company with a certain Scots-Irish-man by name Thomas Quiet. The land about Susquehanna is pritty high and woody, and the channell of the river rockey.

Mr. Quiet rid a little scrub bay mare which he said was sick and ailing and could not carry him, and therefor he 'lighted every half mile and ran a couple of miles att a footman's pace to spell the poor beast (as he termed it). He in-

---

4. Hostilities that became what in Europe was called the Seven Years War (in the American colonies, often the French and Indian Wars) had been formally declared between Great Britain and France in March 1744. The French attacked British holdings in Canada almost immediately.

---

5. Possibly referring to a medieval Welsh stringed instrument that, when played, could be both bowed and plucked; also used in some English dialects to refer to a violin.

formed me he lived att Monocosy and had been out three weeks in quest of his creatures (horses), four of which had strayed from his plantation. I condoled his loss and asked him what his mare's distemper was, resolving to prescribe for her, but all that I could gett out of him was that the poor silly beast had choaked herself in eating her oats; so I told him that if she was choaked, she was past my art to recover.

This fellow, I observed, had a particular down hanging look which made me suspect he was one of our New Light biggots. I guessed right, for he introduced a discourse concerning Whitfield[6] and inlarged pritty much and with some warmth upon the doctrines of that apostle, speaking much in his praise. I took upon me, in a ludicrous manner, to impugn some of his doctrines, which, by degrees, put Mr. Quiet in a passion. He told me flatly that I was damnd without redemption. I replyed that I thought his name and behaviour were very incongruous and desired him to change it with all speed, for it was very improper that such an angry, turbulent mortall as he should be called by the name of Thomas Quiet. . . .

Pensylvania—Newcastle

Tuesday, June 5th. I took horse a little after 5 in the morning, and after a solitary ride thro stonny, unequall road, where the country people stared att me like sheep when I enquired of them the way, I arrived att Newcastle upon Delaware att 9 a'clock in the morning and baited my horses att one Curtis's att the Sign of the Indian King, a good house of entertainment.

This town stands upon stonny ground just upon the water, there being from thence a large prospect eastward towards the Bay of Delaware and the province of the Jerseys. The houses are chiefly brick, built after the Dutch modell, the town having been originally founded and inhabited by the Dutch when it belonged to New York government. It consists chiefly of one great street which makes an elbow att right angles. A great many of the houses are old and crazy. There is in the town two publick buildings, viz., a court house and church.

Att Curtis's I met company going to Philadelphia and was pleased att it, being my self an utter stranger to the roads. This company consisted of three men: Thomas Howard, Timothy Smith, and William Morison. I treated

them with some lemmon punch and desired the favour of their company. They readily granted my request and stayed some time for me till I had eat breakfast. Smith, in his hat and coat, had the appearance of a Quaker, but his discourse was purged of thee's and thou's tho his delivery seemed to be solemn and slow paced. Howard was a talkative man, abounding with words and profuse in compliments which were generally blunt and came out in an awkward manner. He bestowed much panegyrick upon his own behaviour and conduct.

Morison (who, I understood, had been att the Land Office in Annapolis enquiring about a title he had to some land in Maryland) was a very rough spun, forward, clownish blade, much addicted to swearing, att the same time desirous to pass for a gentleman; notwithstanding which ambition, the conscientiousness of his naturall boorishness obliged him frequently to frame ill tim'd apologys for his misbehaviour, which he termed frankness and freeness. It was often, "Damn me, gentlemen, excuse me; I am a plain, honest fellow; all is right down plain dealing, by God." He was much affronted with the landlady att Curtis's who, seeing him in a greasy jacket and breeches and a dirty worsted cap, and withall a heavy, forward, clownish air and behaviour, I suppose took him for some ploughman or carman and so presented him with some scraps of cold veal for breakfast, he having declared that he could not drink "your damnd washy tea." As soon as he saw his mess he swore, "Damn him, if it wa'n't out of respect to the gentleman in company," (meaning me) he would throw her cold scraps out at the window and break her table all to pieces should it cost him 100 pounds for dammages. Then taking off his worsted night cap, he pulled a linnen one out of his pocket and clapping it upon his head, "Now," says he, "I'm upon the borders of Pensylvania and must look like a gentleman; 'tother was good enough for Maryland, and damn my blood if ever I come into that rascally province again if I don't procure a leather jacket that I may be in a trim to box the saucy jacks there and not run the hazard of tearing my coat." This showed, by the bye, that he payed more regard to his coat than his person, a remarkable instance of modesty and self denyall.

He then made a transition to politicks and damnd the late Sr. R——— w——— for a rascall.[7] We asked him his reasons for cursing Sr. R———, but he would give us no other but this, that he was certainly informed by some very good gentlemen, who understood the thing right well, that

6. George Whitefield (1714–70) and the Wesley brothers were among the central founders of Methodism. Whitefield traveled and preached in America on several extended trips beginning in the 1730s.

7. Robert Walpole (1676–1745), prime minister of England (1721–42).

the said Sr. R——— was a damnd rogue. And att the conclusion of each rodomontade, he told us that tho he seemed to be but a plain, homely fellow, yet he would have us know that he was able to afford better than many that went finer: he had good linnen in his bags, a pair of silver buckles, silver clasps, and gold sleeve buttons, two Holland shirts, and some neat night caps; and that his little woman att home drank tea twice a day; and he himself lived very well and expected to live better so soon as that old rogue B———t dyed and he could secure a title to his land.

The chief topic of conversation among these three Pensylvanian dons upon the road was the insignificancy of the neighbouring province of Maryland when compared to that of Pensylvania. They laid out all the advantages of the latter which their bungling judgement could suggest and displayed all the imperfections and dissadvantages of the first. They inlarged upon the immorality, drunkeness, rudeness and immoderate swearing so much practised in Maryland and added that no such vices were to be found in Pensylvania. I heard this and contradicted it not, because I knew that the first part of the proposition was pritty true. They next fell upon the goodness of the soil as far more productive of pasturage and grain. I was silent here likewise, because the first proposition was true, but as to the other relating to grain, I doubted the truth of it. But what appeared most comical in their criticisms was their making a merit of the stonnyness of the roads. "One may ride," says Howard, "50 miles in Maryland and not see as many stones upon the roads as in 50 paces of road in Pensylvania." This I knew to be false, but as I thought there was no advantage in stonny roads, I even let them take the honour of it to themselves and did not contradict them. . . .

Albany

Tuesday, June 26th. Early this morning I went with Mr. M———s to Albany, being a pleasant walk of two miles from the island. We went a small mile out of town to the house of Jeremiah Ranslaer, who is dignified here with the title of Patroon. He is the principal landed man in these parts, having a large mannor, 48 miles long and 24 broad, bestowed upon his great grandfather by K. Charles the Second after his restoration. The old man, it seems, had prophesied his recovering of his kingdoms ten years before it happened. The King had been his lodger when he was in Holland, and thereby he had an opportunity to ingratiate himself and procure the royall favour. This mannor is divided into two equall halves by Hudson's River, and the city of Albany stands in the middle of it.

This city pays him a good yearly rent for the liberty of cutting their fire wood. The Patroon is a young man of good mein and presence. He is a batchellor, nor can his friends perswade him to marry. By paying too much hommage to Bacchus, he has acquired a hypochondriac habit. He has a great number of tennants upon his mannor, and he told me himself that he could muster 600 men fit to bear arms. Mr. M———s and I dined att his house and were handsomly entertained with good viands and wine. After dinner he showed us his garden and parks, and M———s got into one of his long harangues of farming and improvement of ground.

Att 4 a'clock M———s and I returned to town where M———s, having a generall acquaintance, for he had practised physick ten years in the city and was likewise the Church of England minister there, he introduced me into about 20 or 30 houses where I went thro' the farce of kissing most of the women, a manner of salutation which is expected (as M———s told me) from strangers coming there. I told him it was very well, if he led the way I should follow, which he did with clericall gravity. This might almost pass for a pennance, for the generality of the women here, both old and young, are remarkably ugly.

Att night we went to the island, where we supped. While we were att supper we smelt something very strong like burnt oatmeal which they told me was an animall called a schunk, the urine of which could be smelt att a great distance, something of the nature of the polecat but not quite so dissagreeable.

Cohoos

Wednesday, June 27. I went this morning with the Patroon's brother, Stephen Renslaer, to see the Cochoos,[8] a great fall of water 12 miles above Albany. The water falls over a rock almost perpendicular, 80 foot high and 900 foot broad, and the noise of it is easily heard att 4 miles' distance; but in the spring of the year when the ice breaks, it is heard like great guns all the way att Albany. There is a fine mist scattered about where it falls for above half a mile below it, upon which when the sun shines opposite, appears a pritty rainbow. Near the fall the noise is so great that you cannot discern a man's voice unless he hollows pritty loud. Below the fall the river is very narrow and very deep, running in a rockey channell about 200 foot wide, att each side of which channell there is a bank of sollid rock about 3 or 400 foot wide, as smooth and levell as a table.

---

8. Present-day Cohoes Falls.

In this journey we met a Mohook Indian and his family going a hunting. His name was Solomon. He had a squaw with him over whom he seemed to have an absolute authority. We travelled for two miles thro impenetrable woods, this Indian being our guide, and when we came to the banks of the river near the falls, we were obliged to leave our horses and descend frightfull precipices. One might walk across the river on foot upon the top of the rock whence the water falls was it not for fear of being carried down by the force of the water, and Solomon told us that the Indians sometimes run across it when the water is low.

Mohooks Town

We rid att a pritty hard rate 15 or 16 miles farther to the Mohooks town[9] standing upon the same river. In it there are severall wooden and brick houses, built after the Dutch fashion, and some Indian wigwams or huts, with a church where one Barclay preaches to a congregation of Indians in their own language, for the bulk of the Mohooks up this way are Christians.

Returning from here we dined att Coll. Skuyler's[10] about 4 a'clock in the afternoon, who is naturalized among the Indians, can speak severall of their languages, and has lived for years among them. We spent part of the evening att the Patroon's, and going to town att night I went to the tavern with Mr. Livingston, a man of estate and interest there, where we had a mixed conversation. . . .

Oversleigh

Att seven o'clock we reach the Oversleigh and there run aground again. In the meantime a Dutch gentleman, one Volckert Douw, came on board a passenger, and I flattered myself I should not be quite alone but enjoy some conversation; but I was mistaken, for the devil a word but Dutch was bandied about betwixt the saylors and he, and in generall there was such a medley of Dutch and English as would have tired a horse. We heaved out our anchor and got off the shoal att half an hour after seven, so got clear of the Oversleigh, the only troublesom part in the whole voyage. We sailed four miles below it, the wind north east and the night very rainy and dark. We dropt anchor at nine at night and went to bed.

The city of Albany lyes on the west side of Hudson's River upon a rising hill about 30 or 40 miles below where the river comes out of the lake and 160 miles above New York. The hill whereon it stands faces the south east. The city consists of three pritty compact streets, two of which run paralell to the river and are pritty broad, and the third cuts the other two att right angles, running up towards the fort, which is a square stone building about 200 foot square with a bastion att each corner, each bastion mounting eight or ten great guns, most of them 32 pounders. In the fort are two large, brick houses facing each other where there is lodging for the souldiers. There are three market houses in this city and three publick edifices, upon two of which are cupolos or spires, vizt., upon the Town House and the Dutch church. The English church is a great, heavy stone building without any steeple, standing just below the fort. The greatest length of the streets is half a mile. In the fort is kept a garrison of 300 men under the King's pay, who now and then send reinforcements to Oswego, a frontier garrison and trading town lying about 180 miles south[11] and by west of Albany. This city is inclosed by a rampart or wall of wooden palisadoes about 10 foot high and a foot thick, being the trunks of pine trees rammed into the ground, pinned close together, and ending each in a point att top. Here they call them stockadoes. Att each 200 foot distance round this wall is a block house, and from the north gate of the city runs a thick stone wall down into the river, 200 foot long, att each end of which is a block house. In these block houses about 50 of the city militia keep guard every night, and the word all's well walks constantly round all night long from centry to centry and round the fort. There are 5 or 6 gates to this city, the chief of which are the north and the south gates. In the city are about 4,000 inhabitants, mostly Dutch or of Dutch extract.

The Dutch here keep their houses very neat and clean, both without and within. Their chamber floors are generally laid with rough plank which, in time, by constant rubbing and scrubbing becomes as smooth as if it had been plained. Their chambers and rooms are large and handsom. They have their beds generally in alcoves so that you may go thro all the rooms of a great house and see never a bed. They affect pictures much, particularly scripture history, with which they adorn their rooms. They set out their cabinets and bouffetts much with china. Their kitchens are likewise very clean, and there they hang

---

9. Present-day Schenectady.

10. Peter Schuyler (1710–62) was a commander during the French and Indian Wars.

---

11. Actually north.

earthen or delft plates and dishes all round the walls in manner of pictures, having a hole drilled thro the edge of the plate or dish and a loop of ribbon put into it to hang it by. But notwithstanding all this nicety and cleanliness in their houses, they are in their persons slovenly and dirty. They live here very frugally and plain, for the chief merit among them seems to be riches, which they spare no pains or trouble to acquire, but are a civil and hospitable people in their way but, att best, rustick and unpolished. I imagined when I first came there that there were some very rich people in the place. They talked of 30, 40, 50 and 100 thousand pounds as of nothing, but I soon found that their riches consisted more in large tracts of land than in cash. They trade pritty much with the Indians and have their manufactorys for wampum, a good Indian commodity. It is of two sorts—the black, which is the most valuable, and the white wampum. The first kind is a bead made out of the bluish black part of a clam shell. It is valued att 6 shillings York money per 100 beads. The white is made of a conch shell from the W. Indies and is not so valuable. They grind the beads to a shape upon a stone, and then with a well tempered needle dipt in wax and tallow, they drill a hole thro' each bead. This trade is apparently triffling but would soon make an estate to a man that could have a monopoly of it, for being in perpetuall demand among the Indians from their custome of burying quantitys of it with their dead, they are very fond of it, and they will give skins or money or any thing for it, having (tho they first taught the art of making it to the Europeans) lost the art of making it themselves.

They live in their houses in Albany as if it were in prisons, all their doors and windows being perpetually shut. But the reason of this may be the little desire they have for conversation and society, their whole thoughts being turned upon profit and gain which necessarily makes them live retired and frugall. Att least this is the common character of the Dutch every where. But indeed the excessive cold winters here obliges them in that season to keep all snug and close, and they have not summer sufficient to revive heat in their veins so as to make them uneasy or put it in their heads to air themselves. They are a healthy, long lived people, many in this city being in age near or above 100 years, and 80 is a common age. They are subject to rotten teeth and scorbutick gumms which, I suppose, is caused by the cold air and their constant diet of salt provisions in the winter, for in that season they are obliged to lay in as for a sea voyage, there being no stirring out of doors then for fear of never stirring again. As to religion they have little of it among them and of enthu-

siasm not a grain. The bulk of them, if any thing, are of the Lutheran church. Their women in generall, both old and young, are the hardest favoured ever I beheld. Their old women wear a comicall head dress, large pendants, short petticoats, and they stare upon one like witches. They generally eat to their morning's tea raw hung beef sliced down in thin chips in the manner of parmezan cheese. Their winter here is excessive cold so as to freeze their cattle stiff in one night in the stables.

To this city belongs about 24 sloops about 50 tons burden that go and come to York. They chiefly carry plank and rafters. The country about is very productive of hay and good grain, the woods not much cleared.

The neighbouring Indians are the Mohooks to the north west, the Canada Indians to the northward, and to the southward a small scattered nation of the Mohackanders.

The young men here call their sweethearts luffees, and a young fellow of 18 is reckoned a simpleton if he has not a luffee; but their women are so homely that a man must never have seen any other luffees else they will never entrap him. . . .

Newport

We arrived att Newport att 12 o'clock. Rhode Island is a pleasant, open spot of land, being an intire garden of farms, 12 or 13 miles long and 4 or 5 miles broad att its broadest part. The town Newport is about a mile long, lying pritty near north and south. It stands upon a very levell spot of ground and consists of one street, narrow but so streight that standing att one end of it you may see to the other. It is just close upon the water. There are severall lanes going from this street on both sides. Those to the landward are some of them pritty long and broad. There is one large market house near the south end of the main street. The Town House stands a little above this market house away from the water and is a handsom brick edifice, lately built, having a cupola at top. There is, besides, in this town two Presbyterian meetings, one large Quaker meeting, one Anabaptist, and one Church of England. The church has a very fine organ in it, and there is a publick clock upon the steeple as also upon the front of the Town House. The fort is a square building of brick and stone, standing upon a small island which makes the harbour. This place is famous for privateering, and they had about this time brought in severall prizes, among which was a large Spanish snow near 200 ton burden which I saw in the harbour with her bowsplitt shot off.

This town is as remarkable for pritty women as Albany

is for ugly ones, many of whom one may see sitting in the shops in passing along the street. I dined att a taveren kept by one Nicolls att the Sign of the White Horse where I had put up my horses, and in the afternoon Dr. Moffat, an old acquaintance and schoolfellow of mine, led me a course thro' the town. He carried me to see one Feykes, a painter, the most extraordinary genius ever I knew, for he does pictures tollerably well by the force of genius, having never had any teaching. I saw a large table of the Judgement of Hercules copied by him from a frontispiece of the Earl of Shaftesburry's which I thought very well done. This man had exactly the phizz of a painter, having a long pale face, sharp nose, large eyes with which he looked upon you stedfastly, long curled black hair, a delicate white hand, and long fingers.

I went with Moffet in the evening to Dr. Keith's, another countryman and acquaintance, where we spent the evening very agreeably in the company of one Dr. Brett, a very facetious old man. I soon found that Keith passed for a man of great gallantry here, being frequently visited by the young ladies in town who are generally very airy and frolicksome. He showed me a drawer full of the trophys of the fair, which he called his cabinet of curiositys. They consisted of tore fans, fragments of gloves, whims, snuff boxes, girdles, apron strings, laced shoes and shoe heels, pin cussions, hussifs, and a deal of other such trumpery. I lay this night att Dr. Moffets's lodging. . . .

Boston

I left my horses att Barker's stables and drank tea with my landlady, Mrs. Guneau. There was in the company a pritty young lady. The character of a certain Church of England clergiman in Boston was canvassed, he having lost his living for being too sweet upon his landlady's daughter, a great belly being the consequence. I pitied him only for his imprudence and want of policy. As for the crime, considered in a certain light it is but a peccadillo, and he might have escaped unobserved had he had the same cunning as some others of his bretheren who doubtless are as deep in the dirt as he in the mire. I shall not mention the unfortunate man's name (absit foeda calumnia),[12] but I much commiserated his calamity and regretted the loss, for he was an execellent preacher; but the wisest men have been led into silly scrapes by the attractions of that vain sex, which, I think, explains a certain enigmatic verse.

Diceti grammatici, cur mascula nomina cunnus
Et cur Famineum mentula nomen habet[13]

The first is masculine, because it attracts the male, the latter feminine, because it is an effeminate follower of the other.

I had the opportunity this night of seeing Mons. la Moinnerie, my fellow lodger. He was obliged to keep the house close for fear of being made a prisoner of war. He was the strangest mortal for eating ever I knew. He would not eat with the family but always in his own chamber, and he made a table of his trunk. He was always a chawing except some little intervals of time in which he applied to the study of the English language.

Sunday, August 5. I went this morning into Monsieur's chamber and asked him how he did. He made answer in French but asked me in maimd English if I had made un bon voyage, what news, and many other little questions culled out of his grammar. I was shy of letting him know I understood French, being loath to speak that language as knowing my faultiness in the pronounciation. He told me that hier a soir he had de mos' excellen' soupé and wished I had been to eat along with him. His chamber was strangely set out: here a bason with the relicts of some soup, there a fragment of bread, here a paper of salt, there a bundle of garlick, here a spoon with some pepper in it, and upon a chair a saucer of butter. The same individual bason served him to eat his soup out of and to shave in, and in the water, where a little before he had washed his hands and face, he washed likewise his cabbages. This, too, served him for a punch-bowl. He was fond of giving directions how to dress his vittles and told Nanny, the cook maid, "Ma foy, I be de good cock, Madame Nannie," said he. The maid put on an air of modest anger and said she did not understand him. "Why, here you see," says he, "my cock be good, can dress de fine viandes."

This morning I went and heard Mr. Hooper and dined with Mr. Grey. I went to meeting again in the afternoon. He (Mr. Hooper) is one of the best preachers I have heard in America, his discourse being sollid sense, strong connected reasoning, and good language. I drank tea with Mrs. Guneau in the afternoon and staid at home this night reading a little of Homer's first Iliad.

Monday, August 6. I was visited this morning by Mons. de la Moinnerie, who spoke bad English and I in-

---

12. Let me not falsely accuse.

13. Grammatically, why is the word for the female sexual organs masculine while the word for the male sexual organs is feminine?

different French; so we had recourse to Latin and did somewhat better. He gave me an account of his own country, their manners and goverment, and a detail of his own adventures since he came abroad. He told me that he had studied the law and showed me a deploma granted him by the University of Paris. He had practised as a chamber councel in Jamaica for two months and was coming into pritty business, but intermeddling in some political matters procured the ill will of the grandees there and, being obliged to go away, took to merchandizing; but his vessel being cast away att sea, he took passage for Bostton in a sloop before the French war was declared, intending from thence to old France.

I dined this day att Withered's and spent the evening with Dr. Clerk, a gentleman of a fine naturall genius, who, had his education been equivalent, would have outshone all the other physitians in Boston. Dr. D———;[14] was there, and Mr. Light-foot, and another gentleman, a lawer, a professed connoiseur.

Dr. D——— talked very slightingly of Boerhaave[15] and upon all occasions, I find, sets himself up as an enimy to his plan of theory and laughs att all practise founded upon it. He called him a mere helluo librorum,[16] an indefatigable compiler that dealt more in books than in observation or αὐτοψια.[17] I asked his pardon and told him that I thought he was by far the greatest genius that ever appeared in that way since the days of Hippocrates. He said his character was quite eclipsed in England. "Pardon me, sir," said I, "you are mistaken. Many of the English physitians who have studied and understand his system admire him. Such as have not, indeed, never understood him, and in England they have not as yet taught from his books, but till once they embrace his doctrines they will always, like the French, be lagging behind a century or two in the improvements of physick." I could not learn his reasons for so vilifying this great man, and most of the physitians here (the young ones I mean) seem to be awkward imitators of him in this railing faculty. They are all mighty nice and mighty hard to please, and yet are mighty raw and uninstructed (excepting D——— himself and Clerk) in even the very elements of physick. I must say it raised my spleen to hear the character of such a man as Boerhaave picked att by a parcell of pigmies, mere homuncios in

physick, who shine no where but in the dark corner allotted them like a lamp in a monk's cell, obscure and unknown to all the world excepting only their silly hearers and imitators, while the splendour of the great character which they pretend to canvass eclipses all their smaller lights like the sun, enlightens all equally, is ever admired when looked upon, and is known by every one who has any regard for learning or truth; so that all their censure was like the fable of the dog barking att the moon. I found, however, that Dr. D——— had been a disciple of Pitcairn's, and as some warm disputes had subsisted betwixt Pitcairn and Boerhave at his leaving the professional chair of Leyden when turned out by the interest of K: William (for Pitcairn was a strenuous Jacobite) he bore Boerhaave a mortall grudge afterwards and endeavoured all he could to lessen his interest and deminish his character. I left the company att eleven a'clock and went home.

Tuesday, August 7th. I was visited this morning by Monsieur, whose address was, "Eh bien, Monsieur, comment se porte, monsieur, votre vit, a't'il erigé ou Badiné ce matin?" "Oui monsieur," repartis je, "et comment se porte, monsieur, le votre?" "Perfaitment bien, monsieur. Il vous rendit graces."

I dined att Withered's and called att Mr. Hooper's after dinner to know when he intended to go for Cambridge; we agreed upon to morrow afternoon. Coming home again I had the other volley of French from Monsieur, accompanied with a deal of action.

Att night I went to the Scots' Quarterly Society which met att the Sun Taveren. This is a charitable society and act for the relief of the poor of their nation, having a considerable summ of money att interest which they give out in small pensions to needy people. I contributed for that purpose 3 pounds New England currency and was presented with a copy of their laws. When the bulk of the company were gone I sat sometime with Dr. Dowglass, the president, and two or three others and had some chat on news and politicks. Att half an hour after ten I went home and had some more French from Monsieur who was applying strenuously to learn English.

Wednesday, August 8. This proving a very rainy day, I was frustrated in my design of going to Cambridge and was obliged to stay att home most of the day. I had severall dialogues with La Moinnerie relating to the English language. Mr. Hughes and I eat some of his soup. By way of whet he made us some punch, and rinsing the bowl with water, tossed it out upon the floor without any ceremony. The French are generally the reverse of the Dutch in this respect. They care not how dirty their chambers

---

14. Dr. William Douglass.

15. Herman Boerhave (1668–1738), a Dutch physician.

16. A devourer of books.

17. An actual experience.

and houses are but affect neatness much in their dress when they appear abroad. I cannot say cleanliness, for they are dirty in their linnen wear. Mr. Hughes and I dined with Mrs. Guneau and went to Withered's. After dinner we walked out upon the Long Wharf. The rain still continuing, I went home att 4 o'clock and stayed att home all that evening.

Thursday, August 9th. I went with Mr. Hughes before dinner to see my countrywoman Mrs. Blackater (here Blackadore, for our Scots names generally degenerate when transplanted to England or English America, loseing their propper orthography and pronounciation). She is a jolly woman with a great, round, red face. I bought of her a pound of chocolate and saw one of her daughters, a pritty buxom girl in a gay tawdry deshabille, having on a robe de chambre of cherry coloured silk laced with silver round the sleeves and skirts and neither hoop nor stays. By this girl's phisiognomy, I judged she was one of that illustrious class of the sex commonly called coquetts. She seemed very handsom in every respect and, indeed, needed neither stays nor hoop to set out her shapes which were naturally elegant and good. But she had a vile cross in her eyes which spoilt in some measure the beauty and symmetry of her features. Before we went away the old woman invited Hughes and I to drink tea any afternoon when att leisure.

I dined with Mr. Fletcher in the company of two Philadelphians, who could not be easy because forsooth they were in their night-caps seeing every body else in full dress with powdered wigs; it not being customary in Boston to go to dine or appear upon Change in caps as they do in other parts of America. What strange creatures we are, and what triffles make us uneasy! It is no mean jest that such worthless things as caps and wigs should disturb our tranqulity and disorder our thoughts when we imagin they are wore out of season. I was my self much in the same state of uneasiness with these Philadelphians, for I had got a great hole in the lappet of my coat, to hide which employed so much of my thoughts in company that, for want of attention, I could not give a pertinent answer when I was spoke to.

I visited Mr. Smibert in the afternoon and entertained my self an hour or two with his paintings. Att night I was visited by Messrs. Parker and Laughton, who did not tarry long. Dr. Clerk came and spent the evening with me, and as we were a discussing points of philosophy and physick, our enquirys were interrupted by La Moinnerie who entered the room with a dish of roasted mutton in his hand. "Messieurs, votre serviteur," says he. "Voila de

mouton rotie. Voulez vous manger une peu avec moi?" Dr. Clerk could not refrain laughing, but I payed a civil compliment or two to Monsieur, and he retired, bowing, carrying his mutton with him.

I had occasion to see a particular diversion this day which they call *hawling the fox*. It is practised upon simple clowns. Near the town there is a pond of about half a quarter of a mile broad. Across this they lay a rope, and two or three strong fellows, concealed in the bushes, hold one end of it. To a stump in view, there is tied a large fox. When they can lay hold of an ignorant clown on the opposite side of the pond, they inviegle him by degrees into the scrape—two people pretending to wager, one upon the fox's head and the other upon the clown's, twenty shillings or some such matter that the fox shall not or shall pull him thro' the water in spight of his teeth. The clown easily imagines himself stronger than the fox and, for a small reward, allows the rope to be put around his waste. Which done, the sturdy fellows on the other side behind the bush pull lustily for their friend the fox who sits tied to his stump all the time of the operation, being only a mere spectator, and haul poor pill-garlick with great rapidity thro' the pond, while the water hisses and foams on each side of him as he ploughs the surface, and his coat is well wet. I saw a poor country fellow treated in this manner. He run thro the water upon his back like a log of wood, making a frothy line across the pond, and when he came out he shook himself and swore he could not have believed the fox had so much strength. They gave him 20 shillings to help to dry his coat. He was pleased with the reward and said that for so much a time he would allow the fox to drag him thro' the pond as often as he pleased. . . .

Charlestown Ferry—Castle of Boston—Lighthouse

Thursday, August 16. I stayed att home most of the forenoon and had a deal of chat with La Moinnerie. I regretted much that I should be obliged to leave this facetious companion so soon, upon the account of losing his diverting conversation and the opportunity of learning to speak good French, for he used to come to my room every morning and hold forth an hour before breakfast.

I intended to begin my journey homeward to morrow. I dined with Hughes att Dr. Gardiner's,[18] and our table talk was agreeable and instructing, divested of these trif-

---

18. Sylvester Gardiner, a Boston physician and merchant.

fles with which it is commonly loaded. We visited att Mrs. Blackater's in the afternoon and had the pleasure of drinking tea with one of her fair daughters, the old woman and the other daughter being gone to their country farm.

I went in the evening with Mr. Hughes to a club att Withered's where we had a deal of discourse in the disputatory way. One Mr. Clackenbridge (very propperly so named upon account of the volubility of his tongue) was the chief disputant as to verbosity and noise but not as to sense or argument. This was a little dapper fellow full of the opinion of his own learning. He pretended to argue against all the company, but like a confused logician, he could not hold an argument long but wandered from one topic to another, leading us all into confusion and loud talking. He set up for a woman hater and, preferring what he called liberty before every other enjoyment in life, he therefor decryed marriage as a politicall institution destructive of human liberty.

My head being quite turned this night with this confused dispute and the thoughts of my journey to morrow, I got into a strange fit of absence, for having occasion to go out of the company two or three times to talk with Mr. Withered, I heedlessly every time went into a room where there was a strange company as I returned and twice sat down in the midst of them, nor did I discover I was in the wrong box till I found them all staring att me. For the first slip I was obliged to form the best apology I could, but att the second hitt I was so confused and saw them so inclinable to laugh that I run out at the door precipitatly without saying any thing and betook me to the right company. I went to my lodging att 12 o'clock.

I need scarce take notice that Boston is the largest town in North America, being much about the same extent as the city of Glasgow in Scotland and having much the same number of inhabitants, which is between 20 and 30 thousand. It is considerably larger than either Philadelphia or New York, but the streets are irregularly disposed and, in generall, too narrow. The best street in the town is that which runs down towards the Long Wharff which goes by the name of King's Street. This town is a considerable place for shipping and carrys on a great trade in time of peace. There were now above 100 ships in the harbour besides a great number of small craft tho now, upon account of the war, the times are very dead. The people of this province chiefly follow farming and merchandise. Their staples are shipping, lumber, and fish. The goverment is so far democratic as that the election of the Governour's Council and the great officers is made by the members of the Lower House, or representatives of the people. Mr. Shirly,[19] the present Governour, is a man of excellent sense and understanding and is very well respected there. He understands how to humour the people and, att the same time, acts for the interest of the Goverment. Boston is better fortified against an enimy than any port in North America, not only upon account of the strength of the Castle but the narrow passage up into the harbour which is not above 160 foot wide in the channell att high water.

There are many different religions and perswasions here, but the chief sect is that of the Presbyterians. There are above 25 churches, chapells, and meetings in the town, but the Quakers here have but a small remnant, having been banished the province att the first settlement upon account of some disturbances they raised. The people here have lately been, and indeed are now, in great confusion and much infested with enthusiasm from the preaching of some fanaticks and New Light teachers, but now this humour begins to lessen. The people are generally more captivated with speculative than with practicall religion. It is not by half such a flagrant sin to cheat and cozen one's neighbour as it is to ride about for pleasure on the sabbath day or to neglect going to church and singing of psalms.

The middling sort of people here are to a degree dissingenuous and dissembling, which appears even in their common conversation in which their indirect and dubious answers to the plainest and fairest questions show their suspicions of one another. The better sort are polite, mannerly, and hospitable to strangers, such strangers, I mean, as come not to trade among them (for of them they are jealous). There is more hospitality and frankness showed here to strangers than either att York or at Philadelphia. And in the place there is abundance of men of learning and parts; so that one is att no loss for agreeable conversation nor for any sett of company he pleases. Assemblys of the gayer sort are frequent here; the gentlemen and ladys meeting almost every week att consorts of musick and balls. I was present att two or three such and saw as fine a ring of ladys, as good dancing, and heard musick as elegant as I had been witness to any where. I must take notice that this place abounds with pritty women who appear rather more abroad than they do att York and dress elegantly. They are, for the most part, free and affable as well as pritty. I saw not one prude while I was here.

---

19. William Shirley (1693–1771), governor of Massachusetts from 1741 to 1745.

The paper currency of these provinces is now very much depreciated, and the price or value of silver rises every day, their money being now 6 for one upon sterling. They have a variety of paper currency in the provinces; viz., that of New Hampshire, the Massachusets, Rhode Island, and Connecticut, all of different value, divided and subdivided into old and new tenors so that it is a science to know the nature and value of their moneys, and what will cost a stranger some study and application. Dr. Dowglass has writ a compleat treatise upon all the different kinds of paper currencys in America, which I was att the pains to read.[20] It was the expense of the Canada expedition that first brought this province in debt and put them upon the project of issuing bills of credit. Their money is chiefly founded upon land security, but the reason of its falling so much in value is their issuing from time to time such large summs of it and their taking no care to make

payments att the expiration of the stated terms. They are notoriously guilty of this in Rhode Island colony so that now it is dangerous to pass their new moneys in the other parts of New England, it being a high penalty to be found so doing. This fraud must light heavy upon posterity. This is the only part ever I knew where gold and silver coin is not commonly current.

Friday, August 17. I left Boston this morning att half an hour after nine o'clock, and nothing I regretted so much as parting with La Moinnerie, the most livily and merry companion ever I had met with, always gay and chearfull, now dancing and then singing tho every day in danger of being made a prisoner. This is the peculiar humour of the French in prosperity and adversity. Their temper is always alike, far different from the English who, upon the least misfortune, are for the most part cloggd and overclouded with mellancholly and vapours and, giving way to hard fortune, shun all gaiety and mirth. La Moinnerie was much concerned att my going away and wished me again and again *une bon voyage* and *bon santé,* keeping fast hold of my stirrup for about a quarter of an hour.

---

20. William Douglass, *A Discourse Concerning the Currencies of the British Plantations in America* (1739).

WILLIAM PENN (1644–1718)

The founder and namesake of Pennsylvania, then considered by Europeans a haven of toleration for all peoples, elite and nonelites of many European countries, William Penn was born into an aristocratic family in London in 1644. His father, Sir William Penn (1621–70), well connected at the courts of the Stuart kings, was an admiral who assisted the British navy in regaining sea control off England. Penn studied a traditional program at Oxford University but was ousted when he defied Anglican authorities there by associating with freethinkers and dissenters and protesting compulsory attendance at chapel. Sent for a brief time to study at a French protestant university, Penn returned to England in 1664 and entered Lincoln's Inn to study law.

For much of his youth, Penn had struggled against the concept of having a combined authority in church and state. He appreciated the writings of Christian humanists and those who followed, in their daily living, practices of toleration and peace. Penn found the teachings of George Fox and the Society of Friends, denigratingly called Quakers, attractive for the simplicity of their faith practice and their conceptions of the directness of the individual's relationship with divinity (not configured as devolving from Christ or the Christian Trinity) and of freedom of conscience. Like most followers of Fox, Penn believed that persons ought to be able to express themselves freely, without interference from the state, and he acted upon these beliefs by joining the Society of Friends and speaking in their behalf. Such an emphasis as freedom of religious expression brought him into direct opposition to the authorities who implemented the Conventicle Act, passed by Parliament in behalf of the state's suppression of dissent from state practices. Penn was jailed several times working with Friends and for speaking and writing on their behalf. He used well the lessons of the law regarding trial action and worked to undermine the system that would incarcerate persons—and entire juries—that refused to practice the law in the way the state wished to see power administered. That he suffered at the hands of the state for his beliefs is no question, but this experience only seemed to spur his actions and commitments to developing a colony whose central tenets would include freedom of conscience and toleration.

Penn recognized that toleration would not occur as he wished it would in England, and, now a leading speaker for the Friends, he traveled to Holland and Germany to visit and assist the work of Friends there. By the 1670s, he became convinced that removing to North America would save the lives of Quakers and other persecuted people, and he became part proprietor, in 1675, in the province of West Jersey. Favoring the proprietary system but looking to establish his own colony, he sought (1680) and received a charter from British King Charles II, in March 1681, to plan and settle a colony in territory west of the Delaware River and north of Maryland. The Lenapes and their German, Dutch, and Swedish neighbors were already there, but Penn's charter granted him this territory as his own proprietary, where he would own the land of the original grant. Penn traveled to the area, settling there and working with the Lenapes to gain more land, and siting and situating the city of Philadelphia (Greek for city of brotherly love) at a crucial trading point on a confluence of waterways meeting the Delaware River.

While Penn is often and justifiably associated with issues in the liberty of conscience and religious toleration, it is also useful to recall that his colony was a colony in need of the financial backing of traders. He had great philosophical purposes, in other words, but he had the purposes of most colonists of his status in his day: to secure to himself and backers of his endeavor a reasonable return on their investments. Penn's pamphlet, *Some Account of the Province of Pennsylvania,* was the first in a series of immigration pamphlets that were designed to entice laborers to the new colony, as well as those who were wealthy enough to seek to settle larger tracts. First Purchasers, as they were called, received special privileges as to their land allotments, and they were largely well-off Quakers in London and Bristol. These people or their representatives joined some of the first representatives of the settlement group that would organize and run the Pennsylvania colony. After arranging for their lands to be distributed, Penn turned to the real business of establishing a colony, and he formed the Free Society of Traders in 1682 to gain the financial backing necessary to launch a laboring and trading initiative with those already settled on his lands and with the Lenapes in the surrounding areas. He set sail with some members of the Society in 1682, arriving in Pennsylvania for the first time in October of that year. When he sat down to write the *Letter to the Free Society of Traders,* Penn was full of details about his new colony, having just examined its territory. He was excited about the colony's prospects and self-satisfied about what he conceived as his own plans for ethical dealings with Native peoples in the region. A steady stream of immigrants was pouring into his colony, and he hoped to establish a tolerant and successful community. Penn's *Letter* has been considered by many scholars the most important and interesting of his Pennsylvania pamphlets. It was published in London the year it was written, republished there, and in 1684 published in three languages—Dutch (two editions, Amsterdam), German (Hamburg), and French (Hague).

Penn returned to England in 1684 to continue his endeavors to find settlers for his proprietary colony. After the peaceful revolution of 1688 in England, which brought the monarchy back into Protestantism with the accession of William III of Orange, Penn was soon accused of intriguing to restore the British monarchy to the Stuarts, the line of monarchs with whom his family had long associations, but a line that had again turned Catholic under James II. Under an accusation of intrigue against the state, Penn was deprived of his estates and the province of Pennsylvania in 1692, but the province was returned to him two years later, at a time when he was living in what was, for him, penury and being assisted by his friend, the philosopher John Locke. He visited his province again in 1699 but returned to England, to remain there, in 1701. Penn faced problems with managers of the province and of his estates thereafter, but he continued to promote his colony. In the fall of 1712, while he was writing yet another pamphlet about Pennsylvania and its future, he had a stroke. He died in 1718, having established a colony that attracted many more than his persecuted English coreligionists, including Welsh, Dutch, Germans, French, Swedes, and others.

LETTER FROM WILLIAM PENN TO THE COMMITTEE OF THE FREE SOCIETY OF TRADERS[1]

My Kind Friends;

The Kindness of yours by the Ship *Thomas and Anne,* doth much oblige me; for by it I perceive the Interest you take in my Health and Reputation, and the prosperous Beginnings of this Province, which you are so kind as to think may much depend upon them. In return of which, I have sent you a long Letter, and yet containing as brief an Account of My self, and the Affairs of this Province, as I have been able to make.

In the first place, I take notice of the News you sent me, whereby I find some Persons have had so little Wit, and so much Malice, as to report my Death, and to mend the matter, dead a Jesuit too. One might have reasonably hop'd, that this Distance, like Death, would have been a protection against Spite and Envy; and indeed, Absence being a kind of Death, ought alike to secure the Name of the Absent as the Dead; because they are equally unable as such to defend themselves: But they that intend Mischief, do not use to follow good Rules to effect it. However, to the great Sorrow and Shame of the Inventors, I am still Alive, and No Jesuit, and I thank God, very well: And without Injustice to the Authors of this, I may venture to infer, That they that wilfully and falsly Report, would have been glad it had been So. But I perceive, many frivolous and Idle Stories have been Invented since my Departure from England, which perhaps at this time are no more Alive, than I am Dead.

But if I have been Unkindly used by some I left behind me, I found Love and Respect enough where I came; an universal kind Welcome, every sort in their way. For here are some of several Nations, as well as divers Judgments: Nor were the Natives wanting in this, for their Kings, Queens and Great Men both visited and presented me; to whom I made suitable Returns, etc.

For the Province, the general Condition of it take as followeth.

---

1. The title page, too long to quote in full, employs the main title, *A Letter from William Penn, Proprietary and Governor of Pennsylvania in America, to the Committee of the Free Society of Traders of that Province, residing in London,* as published in the London 1683 first edition.

I. The Country it self in its Soyl, Air, Water, Seasons and Produce both Natural and Artificial is not to be despised. The Land containeth divers sorts of Earth, as Sand Yellow and Black, Poor and Rich: also Gravel both Loomy and Dusty; and in some places a fast fat Earth, like to our best Vales in England, especially by Inland Brooks and Rivers, God in his Wisdom having ordered it so, that the Advantages of the Country are divided, the Back-Lands being generally three to one Richer than those that lie by Navigable Waters. We have much of another Soyl, and that is a black Hasel Mould, upon a Stony or Rocky bottom.

II. The Air is sweet and clear, the Heavens serene, like the South-parts of France, rarely Overcast; and as the Woods come by numbers of People to be more clear'd, that it self will Refine.

III. The Waters are generally good, for the Rivers and Brooks have mostly Gravel and Stony Bottoms, and in Number hardly credible. We have also Mineral Waters, that operate in the same manner with Barnet[2] and Northhall,[3] not two Miles from Philadelphia.

IV. For the Seasons of the Year, having by God's goodness now lived over the Coldest and Hottest, that the Oldest Liver in the Province can remember, I can say something to an English Understanding.

1*st,* Of the Fall, for then I came in: I found it from the 24th of October, to the beginning of December, as we have it usually in England in September, or rather like an English mild Spring. From December to the beginning of the Moneth called March, we had sharp Frosty Weather; not foul, thick, black Weather, as our North-East Winds bring with them in England; but a Skie as clear as in Summer, and the Air dry, cold, piercing and hungry; yet I remember not, that I wore more Clothes than in England. The reason of this Cold is given from the great Lakes that are fed by the Fountains of Canada. The Winter before was as mild, scarce any Ice at all; while this for a few dayes Froze up our great River Delaware. From that Moneth to the Moneth called June, we enjoy'd a sweet Spring, no Gusts, but gentle Showers, and a fine Skie. Yet this I observe, that the Winds here as there, are more Inconstant Spring and Fall, upon that turn of Nature, than in Summer or Winter. From thence to this present Moneth, which endeth the Summer (commonly speaking) we have had ex-

---

2. Chipping (sometimes called High) Barnet, in Hertfordshire, north of London, had a mineral spring.

3. Northaw, also in Hertfordshire, had a salt spring.

traordinary Heats, yet mitigated sometimes by Cool Breezese. The Wind that ruleth the Summer-season, is the South-West; but Spring, Fall and Winter, 'tis rare to want the wholesome North Wester seven dayes together: And whatever Mists, Fogs or Vapours foul the Heavens by Easterly or Southerly Winds, in two Hours time are blown away; the one is alwayes followed by the other: A Remedy that seems to have a peculiar Providence in it to the Inhabitants; the multitude of Trees, yet standing, being liable to retain Mists and Vapours, and yet not one quarter so thick as I expected.

V. The Natural Produce of the Country, of Vegetables, is Trees, Fruits, Plants, Flowers. The Trees of most note are, the black Walnut, Cedar, Cyprus, Chestnut, Poplar, Gumwood, Hickery, Sassafrax, Ash, Beech and Oak of divers sorts, as Red, White and Black; Spanish Chestnut and Swamp, the most durable of all: of All which there is plenty for the use of man.

The Fruits that I find in the Woods, are the White and Black Mulberry, Chestnut, Wallnut, Plumbs, Strawberries, Cranberries, Hurtleberries and Grapes of divers sorts. The great Red Grape (now ripe) called by Ignorance, the Fox-Grape (because of the Relish it hath with unskilful Palates) is in it self an extraordinary Grape, and by Art doubtless may be Cultivated to an excellent Wine, if not so sweet, yet little inferior to the Frontimack, as it is not much unlike in taste, Ruddiness set aside, which in such things, as well as Mankind, differs the case much. There is a white kind of Muskedel, and a little black Grape, like the cluster-Grape of England, not yet so ripe as the other; but they tell me, when Ripe, sweeter, and that they only want skilful Vinerons to make good use of them: I intend to venture on it with my French man[4] this season, who shews some knowledge in those things. Here are also Peaches, and very good, and in great quantities, not an Indian Plantation without them; but whether naturally here at first, I know not, however one may have them by Bushels for little; they make a pleasant Drink and I think not inferior to any Peach you have in England, except the true Newington. 'Tis disputable with me, whether it be best to fall to Fining the Fruits of the Country, especially the Grape, by the care and skill of Art, or send for forreign Stems and Sets, already good and approved. It seems most reasonable to believe, that not only a thing groweth

best, where it naturally grows; but will hardly be equalled by another Species of the same kind, that doth not naturally grow there. But to solve the doubt, I intend, if God give me Life, to try both, and hope the consequence will be as good Wine as any European Countries of the same Latitude do yield.

VI. The Artificial Produce of the Country, is Wheat, Barley, Oats, Rye, Pease, Beans, Squashes, Pumkins, Water-Melons, Mus-Melons, and all Herbs and Roots that our Gardens in England usually bring forth.[5]

VII. Of living Creatures; Fish, Fowl, and the Beasts of the Woods, here are divers sorts, some for Food and Profit, and some for Profit only: For Food as well as Profit, the Elk, as big as a small Ox, Deer bigger than ours, Beaver, Racoon, Rabbits, Squirrels, and some eat young Bear, and commend it. Of Fowl of the Land, there is the Turkey (Forty and Fifty Pound weight) which is very great; Phesants, Heath-Birds, Pidgeons and Partridges in abundance. Of the Water, the Swan, Goose, white and gray, Brands, Ducks, Teal, also the Snipe and Curloe, and that in great Numbers; but the Duck and Teal excel, nor so good have I ever eat in other Countries. Of Fish, there is the Sturgeon, Herring, Rock, Shad, Catshead, Sheepshead, Ele, Smelt, Pearch, Roach; and in Inland Rivers, Trout, some say Salmon, above the Falls. Of Shelfish, we have Oysters, Crabbs, Cockles, Concks, and Mushels; some Oysters six Inches long, and one sort of Cockles as big as the Stewing Oysters, they make a rich Broth. The Creatures for Profit only by Skin or Fur, and that are natural to these parts, are the Wild Cat, Panther, Otter, Wolf, Fox, Fisher, Minx, Musk-Rat; and of the Water, the Whale for Oyl, of which we have good store, and two Companies of Whalers, whose Boats are built, will soon begin their Work,[6] which hath the appearance of

4. Andrew Doz, a French Huguenot served as Penn's vine keeper.

5. "Note, that Edward Jones, Son-in Law to Thomas Wynn, living on the Sckulkil, had with ordinary Cultivation, for one Grain of English Barley, seventy Stalks and Ears of Barley; And 'tis common in this Coutnry from one Bushel sown, to reap forty, often fifty, and sometimes sixty. And three Pecks of Wheat sows an Acre here." [Au.]

Dr. Edward Jones was one of the leaders of the first company of Welsh settlers; Thomas Wynne came over with Penn originally in 1682 and became speaker of the provincial assembly.

6. Whalers centered their activity on the entrance to the Delaware Bay.

a considerable Improvement. To say nothing of our reasonable Hopes of good Cod in the Bay.

VIII. We have no want of Horses, and some are very good and shapely enough; two Ships have been freighted to Barbadoes with Horses and Pipe-Staves, since my coming in. Here is also Plenty of Cow-Cattle, and some Sheep; the People Plow mostly with Oxen.

IX. There are divers Plants that not only the Indians tell us, but we have had occasion to prove by Swellings, Burnings, Cuts, etc., that they are of great Virtue, suddenly curing the Patient: and for smell, I have observed several, especially one, the wild Mirtle; the other I know not what to call, but are most fragrant.

X. The Woods are adorned with lovely Flowers, for colour, greatness, figure, and variety: I have seen the Gardens of London best stored with that sort of Beauty, but think they may be improved by our Woods: I have sent a few to a Person of Quality this Year for a tryal.

Thus much of the Country, next of the Natives or Aborigines.

XI. The *Natives* I shall consider in their Persons, Language, Manners, Religion and Government, with my sence of their Original. For their Persons, they are generally tall, streight, well-built, and of singular Proportion; they tread strong and clever, and mostly walk with a lofty Chin: Of Complexion, Black, but by design, as the Gypsies in England: They grease themselves with Bears-fat clarified, and using no defence against Sun or Weather, their skins must needs be swarthy; Their Eye is little and black, not unlike a straight-look't Jew: The thick Lip and flat Nose, so frequent with the East-Indians and Blacks, are not common to them; for I have seen as comely European-like faces among them of both, as on your side the Sea; and truly an Italian Complexion hath not much more of the White, and the Noses of several of them have as much of the Roman.

XII. Their Language is lofty, yet narrow, but like the Hebrew; in Signification full, like Short-hand in writing; one word serveth in the place of three, and the rest are supplied by the Understanding of the Hearer: Imperfect in their Tenses, wanting in their Moods, Participles, Adverbs, Conjunctions, Interjections: I have made it my business to understand it, that I might not want an Interpreter on any occasion: And I must say, that I know not a Language spoken in Europe, that hath words of more sweetness or greatness, in Accent and Emphasis, than theirs; for Instance, *Octorockon, Rancocas, Ozicton, Shakamacon, Poquerim,* all of which are names of

Places,[7] and have Grandeur in them: Of words of Sweetness, *Anna,* is Mother, *Issimus,* a Brother, *Netap,* Friend, *usque ozet,* very good; *pone,* Bread, *metse,* eat, *matta,* no, *hatta,* to have, *payo,* to come; *Sepassen,*[8] *Passijon,* the Names of Places; *Tamane,*[9] *Secane,*[10] *Menanse, Secatereus,* are the names of Persons. If one ask them for anything they have not, they will answer, *mattá ne hattá,* which to translate is, not I have, instead of I have not.

XIII. Of their Customs and Manners there is much to be said; I will begin with Children. So soon as they are born, they wash them in Water, and while very young, and in cold Weather to chuse, they Plunge them in the Rivers to harden and embolden them. Having wrapt them in a Clout, they lay them on a straight thin Board, a little more than the length and breadth of the Child, and swadle it fast upon the Board to make it straight; wherefore all Indians have flat Heads; and thus they carry them at their Backs. The Children will go very young, at nine Moneths commonly; they wear only a small Clout round their Waste, till they are big; if Boys, they go a Fishing till ripe for the Woods, which is about Fifteen; then they Hunt, and after having given some Proofs of their Manhood, by a good return of Skins, they may Marry, else it is a shame to think of a Wife. The Girls stay with their Mothers, and help to hoe the Ground, plant Corn and carry Burthens; and they do well to use them to that Young, they must do when they are Old; for the Wives are the true Servants of their Husbands: otherwise the Men are very affectionate to them.

XIV. When the Young Women are fit for Marriage, they wear something upon their Heads for an Advertise-

---

7. Octorara Creek, an eastern tributary to the Susquehanna; Rancocas Creek, in Burlington County, New Jersey; Orectons was near the falls of the Delaware and Penn's country estate, Pennsbury, in Bucks County; Shackamaxon, now Kensington area, Philadelphia, was where Penn lived with the household of Thomas Fairman early in 1683.

8. Sepassing Land was the name given to the area of Bucks County, where Penn's manor was located.

9. Tamany (sometimes spelled by colonials Tamene, Tamine, Tamina, Tamanee, Tamanen, Tamanend, and Taminent) was a leading negotiating chief of the Lenapes for the area now called Bucks County. He became a figure of legend, especially during the era of the American Revolution against England, as John Leacock's popular song of that time indicates.

10. Siccane or Secane, sometimes called Shikane, was one of the two chiefs who agreed to grant land between the Schuylkill River and Chester Creek to Penn in 1683.

ment, but so as their Faces are hardly to be seen, but when they please: The Age they Marry at, if Women, is about thirteen and fourteen; if Men, seventeen and eighteen; they are rarely elder.

XV. Their Houses are Mats, or Barks of Trees set on Poles, in the fashion of an English Barn, but out of the power of the Winds, for they are hardly higher than a Man; they lie on Reeds or Grass. In Travel they lodge in the Woods about a great Fire, with the Mantle of Duffills they wear by day, wrapt about them, and a few Boughs stuck round them.

XVI. Their Diet is Maze, or Indian Corn, divers ways prepared: sometimes Roasted in the Ashes, sometimes beaten and Boyled with Water, which they call *Homine;* they also make Cakes, not unpleasant to eat: They have likewise several sorts of Beans and Pease that are good Nourishment; and the Woods and Rivers are their Larder.

XVII. If an European comes to see them, or calls for Lodging at their House or *Wigwam* they give him the best place and first cut. If they come to visit us, they salute us with an *Itah* which is as much as to say, Good be to you, and set them down, which is mostly on the Ground close to their Heels, their Legs upright; may be they speak not a word more, but observe all Passages: If you give them any thing to eat or drink, well, for they will not ask; and be it little or much, if it be with Kindness, they are well pleased, else they go away sullen, but say nothing.

XVIII. They are great Concealers of their own Resentments, brought to it, I believe, by the Revenge that hath been practised among them; in either of these, they are not exceeded by the Italians. A Tragical Instance fell out since I came into the Country; A King's Daughter thinking her self slighted by her Husband, in suffering another Woman to lie down between them, rose up, went out, pluck't a Root out of the Ground, and ate it, upon which she immediately dyed; and for which, last Week he made an Offering to her Kindred for Attonement and liberty of Marriage; as two others did to the Kindred of their Wives, that dyed a natural Death: For till Widdowers have done so, they must not marry again. Some of the young Women are said to take undue liberty before Marriage for a Portion; but when marryed, chaste; when with Child, they know their Husbands no more, till delivered; and during their Moneth, they touch no Meat, they eat, but with a Stick, least they should defile it; nor do their Husbands frequent them, till that time be expired.

XIX. But in Liberality they excell, nothing is too good for their friend; give them a fine Gun, Coat, or other thing, it may pass twenty hands, before it sticks; light of Heart, strong Affections, but soon spent; the most merry Creatures that live, Feast and Dance perpetually; they never have much, nor want much: Wealth circulateth like the Blood, all parts partake; and though none shall want what another hath, yet exact Observers of Property. Some Kings have sold, others presented me with several parcels of Land; the Pay or Presents I made them, were not hoarded by the particular Owners, but the neighbouring Kings and their Clans being present when the Goods were brought out, the Parties chiefly concerned consulted, what and to whom they should give them? To every King then, by the hands of a Person for that work appointed, is a proportion sent, so sorted and folded, and with that Gravity, that is admirable. Then that King sub-divideth it in like manner among his Dependents, they hardly leaving themselves an Equal share with one of their Subjects: and be it on such occasions, at Festivals, or at their common Meals, the Kings distribute, and to themselves last. They care for little, because they want but little; and the Reason is, a little contents them: In this they are sufficiently revenged on us; if they are ignorant of our Pleasures, they are also free from our Pains. They are not disquieted with Bills of Lading and Exchange, nor perplexed with Chancery-Suits and Exchequer-Reckonings. We sweat and toil to live; their pleasure feeds them, I mean, their Hunting, Fishing and Fowling, and this Table is spread every where; they eat twice a day, Morning and Evening; their Seats and Table are the Ground. Since the European came into these parts, they are grown great lovers of strong Liquors, Rum especially, and for it exchange the richest of their Skins and Furs: If they are heated with Liquors, they are restless till they have enough to sleep; that is their cry, Some more, and I will go to sleep; but when Drunk, one of the most wretchedst Spectacles in the world.

XX. In sickness impatient to be cured, and for it give any thing, especially for their Children, to whom they are extreamly natural; they drink at those times a *Teran* or Decoction of some Roots in spring Water; and if they eat any flesh, it must be of the Female of any Creature; If they dye, they bury them with their Apparel, be they Men or Women, and the nearest of Kin fling in something precious with them, as a token of their Love: Their Mourning is blacking of their faces, which they continue for a year; They are choice of the Graves of their Dead; for least they should be lost by time, and fall to common use, they pick off the Grass that grows upon them, and heap up the fallen Earth with great care and exactness.

XXI. These poor People are under a dark Night in things relating to Religion, to be sure, the Tradition of it; yet they believe a God and Immortality, without the help of Metaphysicks; for they say, There is a great King that made them, who dwells in a glorious Country to the Southward of them, and that the Souls of the good shall go thither, where they shall live again. Their Worship consists of two parts, Sacrifice and *Cantico.* Their Sacrifice is their first Fruits; the first and fattest Buck they kill, goeth to the fire, where he is all burnt with a Mournful Ditty of him that performeth the Ceremony, but with such marvellous Fervency and Labour of Body, that he will even sweat to a foam. The other part is their *Cantico,* performed by round-Dances, sometimes Words, sometimes Songs, then Shouts, two being in the middle that begin, and by Singing and Drumming on a Board direct the Chorus: Their Postures in the Dance are very Antick and differing, but all keep measure. This is done with equal Earnestness and Labour, but great appearance of Joy. In the Fall, when the Corn cometh in, they begin to feast one another; there have been two great Festivals already, to which all come that will: I was at one my self; their Entertainment was a green Seat by a Spring, under some shady Trees, and twenty Bucks, with hot Cakes of new Corn, both Wheat and Beans, which they make up in a square form, in the leaves of the Stem, and bake them in the Ashes: And after that they fell to Dance, But they that go, must carry a small Present in their Money, it may be six Pence, which is made of the Bone of a Fish; the black is with them as Gold, the white, Silver; they call it all *Wampum.*

XXII. Their Government is by Kings, which they call *Sachema,* and those by Succession, but always of the Mothers side; for Instance, the Children of him that is now King, will not succeed, but his Brother by the Mother, or the Children of his Sister, whose Sons (and after them the Children of her Daughters) will reign; for no Woman inherits; the Reason they render for this way of Descent, is, that their Issue may not be spurious.

XXIII. Every King hath his Council, and that consists of all the Old and Wise men of his Nation, which perhaps is two hundred People: nothing of Moment is undertaken, be it War, Peace, Selling of Land or Traffick, without advising with them; and which is more, with the Young Men too. 'Tis admirable to consider, how Powerful the Kings are, and yet how they move by the Breath of their People. I have had occasion to be in Council with them upon Treaties for Land, and to adjust the terms of Trade; their

Order is thus: The King sits in the middle of an half Moon, and hath his Council, the Old and Wise on each hand; behind them, or at a little distance, sit the younger Fry, in the same figure. Having consulted and resolved their business, the King ordered one of them to speak to me; he stood up, came to me, and in the Name of his King saluted me, then took me by the hand, and told me, That he was ordered by his King to speak to me, and that now it was not he, but the King that spoke, because what he should say, was the King's mind. He first pray'd me, To excuse them that they had not complied with me the last time; he feared, there might be some fault in the Interpreter, being neither Indian nor English; besides, it was the Indian Custom to deliberate, and take up much time in Council, before they resolve; and that if the Young People and Owners of the Land had been as ready as he, I had not met with so much delay. Having thus introduced his matter, he fell to the Bounds of the Land they had agreed to dispose of, and the Price, (which now is little and dear, that which would have bought twenty Miles, not buying now two.) During the time that this Person spoke, not a man of them was observed to whisper or smile; the Old, Grave, the Young, Reverend in their Deportment; they do speak little, but fervently, and with Elegancy: I have never seen more natural Sagacity, considering them without the help, (I was agoing to say, the spoil) of Tradition; and he will deserve the Name of Wise, that Outwits them in any Treaty about a thing they understand. When the Purchase was agreed, great Promises past between us of Kindness and good Neighbourhood, and that the Indians and English must live in Love, as long as the Sun gave light. Which done, another made a Speech to the Indians, in the Name of all the *Sachamakers* or Kings, first to tell them what was done; next, to charge and command them, To Love the Christians, and particularly live in Peace with me, and the People under my Government: That many Governours had been in the River, but that no Governour had come himself to live and stay here before; and having now such a one that had treated them well, they should never do him or his any wrong. At every sentence of which they shouted, and said, Amen, in their way.

XXIV. The Justice they have is Pecuniary: In case of any Wrong or evil Fact, be it Murther it self, they Attone by Feasts and Presents of their *Wampon,* which is proportioned to the quality of the Offence or Person injured, or of the Sex they are of: for in case they kill a Woman, they pay double, and the Reason they render, is, That she breedeth Children, which Men cannot do. 'Tis rare that they fall out, if Sober; and if Drunk, they forgive it, saying, It was the Drink, and not the Man, that abused them.

XXV. We have agreed, that in all Differences between us, Six of each side shall end the matter: Don't abuse them, but let them have Justice, and you win them: The worst is, that they are the worse for the Christians, who have propagated their Vices, and yielded them Tradition for ill, and not for good things. But as low an Ebb as they are at, and as glorious as their Condition looks, the Christians have not out-liv'd their sight with all their Pretensions to an higher Manifestation: What good then might not a good People graft, where there is so distinct a Knowledge left between Good and Evil? I beseech God to incline the Hearts of all that come into these parts, to out-live the Knowledge of the Natives, by a fixt Obedience to their greater Knowledge of the Will of God, for it were miserable indeed for us to fall under the just censure of the poor Indian Conscience, while we make profession of things so far transcending.

XXVI. For their Original, I am ready to believe them of the Jewish Race, I mean, of the stock of the Ten Tribes,[11] and that for the following Reasons; first, They were to go to a Land not planted or known, which to be sure Asia and Africa were, if not Europe; and he that intended that extraordinary Judgment upon them, might make the Passage not uneasie to them, as it is not impossible in it self, from the Easter-most parts of Asia, to the Wester-most of America. In the next place, I find them of like Countenance and their Children of so lively Resemblance, that a man would think himself in Dukes-place or Berry-street in London, when he seeth them. But this is not all, they agree in Rites, they reckon by Moons: they offer their first Fruits, they have a kind of Feast of Tabernacles; they are said to lay their Altar upon twelve Stones; their Mourning a year, Customs of Women, with many things that do not now occur.

So much for the Natives, next the Old Planters will be considered in this Relation, before I come to our Colony, and the Concerns of it.

XXVII. The first Planters in these parts were the Dutch, and soon after them the Sweeds and Finns. The Dutch applied themselves to Traffick, the Sweeds and Finns to Husbandry. There were some Disputes between them some years, the Dutch looking upon them as Intruders upon their Purchase and Possession, which was finally ended in the Surrender made by John Rizeing, the Sweeds Governour, to Peter Styvesant, Governour for the States of Holland, *Anno* 1655.

XXVIII. The Dutch inhabit mostly those parts of the Province, that lie upon or near to the Bay, and the Sweeds the Freshes of the River Delaware. There is no need of giving any Description of them, who are better known there then here; but they are a plain, strong, industrious People, yet have made no great progress in Culture or propagation of fruit-Trees, as if they desired rather to have enough, than Plenty or Traffick. But I presume, the Indians made them the more careless, by furnishing them with the means of Profit, to wit, Skins and Furs, for Rum, and such strong Liquors. They kindly received me, as well as the English, who were few, before the People concerned with me came among them; I must needs commend their Respect to Authority, and kind Behaviour to the English; they do not degenerate from the Old friendship between both Kingdoms. As they are People proper and strong of Body, so they have fine Children, and almost every house full; rare to find one of them without three or four Boys, and as many Girls; some six, seven and eight Sons: And I must do them that right, I see few Young men more sober and laborious.

XXIX. The Dutch have a Meeting-place for Religious Worship at New Castle, and the Sweedes three, one at Christina, one at Tenecum,[12] and one at Wicoco, within half a Mile of this Town.

XXX. There rests, that I speak of the Condition we are in, and what Settlement we have made, in which I will be as short as I can; for I fear, and not without reason, that I have tryed your Patience with this long Story. The Country lieth bounded on the East, by the River and Bay of Delaware, and Eastern Sea; it hath the Advantage of many Creeks or Rivers rather, that run into the main River or Bay; some Navigable for great Ships, some for small Craft: Those of most Eminency are Christina, Brandywine, Skilpot,[13] and Skulkill; any one of which have room to lay up the Royal Navy of England, there being from four to eight Fathom Water.

---

11. Penn is repeating an explanation for the presence of American Indians that was popular among some colonial writers—that they derived from the Ten Lost Tribes of Israel.

12. Tinicum Island. Wicaco was the Swedish settlement at present-day Front Street and Washington Avenue.

13. Shelpot Creek.

XXXI. The lesser Creeks or Rivers, yet convenient for Sloops and Ketches of good Burthen, are Lewis, Mespilion,[14] Cedar, Dover, Cranbrook, Feversham, and Georges, below, and Chichester, Chester, Toacawny, Pemmapecka, Portquessin, Neshimenck and Pennberry in the Freshes; many lesser that admit Boats and Shallops. Our People are mostly settled upon the upper Rivers, which are pleasant and sweet, and generally bounded with good Land. The Planted part of the Province and Territories is cast into six Counties, Philadelphia, Buckingham,[15] Chester, New Castle, Kent and Sussex, containing about Four Thousand Souls. Two General Assemblies have been held, and with such Concord and Dispatch, that they sate but three Weeks, and at least seventy Laws were past without one Dissent in any material thing. But of this more hereafter, being yet Raw and New in our Geer: However, I cannot forget their singular Respect to me in this Infancy of things, who by their own private Expences so early consider'd Mine for the Publick, as to present me with an Impost upon certain Goods Imported and Exported: Which after my Acknowledgements of their Affection, I did as freely Remit to the Province and the Traders to it. And for the well Government of the said Counties, Courts of Justice are establisht in every County, with proper Officers, as Justices, Sheriffs, Clarks, Constables, etc., which Courts are held every two Moneths: But to prevent Law-Suits, there are three Peace-makers chosen by every County-Court, in the nature of common Arbitrators, to hear and end Differences betwixt man and man; and Spring and Fall there is an Orphan's Court in each County, to inspect, and regulate the Affairs of Orphans and Widdows.

XXXII. Philadelphia, the Expectation of those that are concern'd in this Province, is at last laid out to the great Content of those here, that are any wayes Interested therein; The Scituation is a Neck of Land, and lieth between two Navigable Rivers, Delaware and Skulkill, whereby it hath two Fronts upon the Water, each a Mile, and two from River to River. Delaware is a glorious River, but the Skulkill being an hundred Miles Boatable above the Falls, and its Course North-East toward the Fountain of Susquahannah (that tends to the Heart of the Province, and both sides our own) it is like to be a great part of the Settlement of this Age. I say little of the Town it self, because a *Plat-form*[16] will be shewn you by my Agent, in which those who are Purchasers of me, will find their Names and Interests: But this I will say for the good Providence of God, that of all the many Places I have seen in the World, I remember not one better seated; so that it seems to me to have been appointed for a Town, whether we regard the Rivers, or the conveniency of the Coves, Docks, Springs, the loftiness and soundness of the Land and the Air, held by the People of these parts to be very good. It is advanced within less than a Year to about four Score Houses and Cottages, such as they are, where Merchants and Handicrafts, are following their Vocations as fast as they can, while the Country-men are close at their Farms; Some of them got a little Winter-Corn in the Ground last Season, and the generality have had a handsom Summer-Crop, and are preparing for their Winter-Corn. They reaped their Barley this Year in the Moneth called May; the Wheat in the Moneth following; so that there is time in these parts for another Crop of divers Things before the Winter-Season. We are daily in hopes of Shipping to add to our Number; for blessed be God, here is both Room and Accommodation for them; the Stories of our Necessity being either the Fear of our Friends, or the Scare-Crows of our Enemies; for the greatest hardship we have suffered, hath been Salt-Meat, which by Fowl in Winter, and Fish in Summer, together with some Poultery, Lamb, Mutton, Veal, and plenty of Venison the best part of the year, hath been made very passable. I bless God, I am fully satisfied with the Country and Entertainment I can get in it; for I find that particular Content which hath always attended me, where God in his Providence hath made it my place and service to reside. You cannot imagin, my Station can be at present free of more than ordinary business, and as such, I may say, It is a troublesom Work; but the Method things are putting in, will facilitate the Charge, and give an easier Motion to the Administration of Affairs. However, as it is some mens Duty to plow, some to sow, some to water, and some to reap; so it is the Wisdom as well as Duty of a man, to yield to the mind of Providence, and chearfully, as well as carefully imbrace and follow the Guidance of it.

---

14. Mispillion Creek. The following are place-names that Penn and his group attached to the area of waterways between present-day Philadelphia and Newcastle, Delaware.

15. Bucks County.

16. That is, a map. The map was made by Thomas Holme in 1683 and published with the pamphlet as "A Portraiture of the City of Philadelphia."

XXXIII. For your particular Concern, I might entirely refer you to the Letters of the President of the Society;[17] but this I will venture to say, Your Provincial Settlements both within and without the Town, for Scituation and Soil, are without Exception; Your City-Lot is an whole Street, and one side of a Street, from River to River, containing near one hundred Acers, not easily valued, which is besides your four hundred Acers in the City Liberties, part of your twenty thousand Acers in the Countery. Your Tannery hath such plenty of Bark, the Saw-Mill for Timber, the place of the Glass-house so conveniently posted for Water-carriage, the City-Lot for a Dock, and the Whalery for a sound and fruitful Bank, and the Town Lewis by it to help your People, that by Gods blessing the Affairs of the Society will naturally grow in their Reputation and Profit.

I am sure I have not turned my back upon any Offer that tended to its Prosperity; and though I am ill at Projects, I have sometimes put in for a Share with her Officers, to countenance and advance her Interest. You are already informed what is fit for you further to do, whatsoever tends to the Promotion of Wine, and to the Manufacture of Linnen in these parts, I cannot but wish you to promote it; and the French People are most likely in both respects to answer that design: To that end, I would advise you to send for some Thousands of Plants out of France, with some able Vinerons, and People of the other Vocation: But because I believe you have been entertained with this and some other profitable Subjects by your President, I shall add no more, but to assure you, that I am heartily inclined to advance your just Interest, and that you will always find me

Your Kind Cordial Friend,
William Penn.
Philadelphia, the 16th of the
6th Moneth, call'd August,
1683.

---

17. The Free Society of Traders, a joint stock company Penn developed between 1680 and 1682, received a liberal charter from Penn. They purchased twenty-thousand acres in the province. Dr. Nicholas More of London was the society's first president.

GEORGE KEITH (1639–1716)

In his own day in Philadelphia, George Keith became known as a troublemaker and a turncoat, someone who wanted to disrupt the good beginnings made in developing a Philadelphia community of the Society of Friends (known as Quakers) and someone who turned his back on practicing a fruitful and individualized inward light theology in order to denigrate Friends who were holding public office. Trouble for Keith started when, in pursuing his understanding of liberty as established by George Fox (1624–91), the founder of the Society of Friends, Keith expressed his doubts about whether Quakers should hold public office because inward light theology seemed to contradict the public use and display of power. Keith also wished to see a more regular service emerge for the Quakers in the community because the disparate peoples of Europe practiced their faith in different ways. Keith sought a more regular practice in keeping with his understanding of inward light principles, a practice marked by some degree of learning and ordered according to a creed and discipline that most Quakers disliked.

Keith was born in Scotland in 1639, and he originally trained for the Presbyterian ministry, before listening to the calling of the Philadelphia community to establish a city of brotherly love. He traveled to Philadelphia in 1689, where he began to teach school. Soon after his arrival, Keith developed his own cluster of followers, the "Christian Friends," and he started running into serious trouble with the authorities beginning in 1690. By 1693, the local Philadelphia Quakers had disowned him. Keith left Philadelphia and found his way to London to complain about the treatment he had received. The London Meeting disavowed support for Keith. By 1700, Keith joined the Anglican Church, and in 1702, he was sent back to the British American colonies by the Church as one of the first missionaries for the Society for the Propagation of the Gospel in Foreign Parts. Keith returned to England in 1704 and was made a rector of a church in Sussex, where he remained the rest of his life.

Keith developed a small following of "Christian Quakers" in Philadelphia who were concerned, as he was, about the disparate practices employed by the Society of Friends and by Friends in the community who were taking public office and, it seemed, bettering their own lives as a result. Keith's published pamphlets attacking the local Quakers and their systematic political office keeping brought down upon him the opprobrium of the well-to-do in his community, and his publications were considered to be seditious libel. Keith's publisher, William Bradford (1663–1752), the first printer in the colony, was arrested in 1692 for printing Keith's works. Bradford's press and all his type were confiscated, causing him to leave the colony in 1693 and to set up a printing business in New York, instead. In sailing back to London at about this time, Keith hoped to win English Friends over to his way of thinking. Before he left Philadelphia for London, he made a public statement against slave-holding, one of the practices that well-to-do Quakers, including William Penn and his associates, did not consider unreconcilable with their conceptions of liberty. Keith, considering the inward light philosophy based upon an innate and inviolable conception of personal liberty, denounced the Quaker practice of keeping slaves. He was partaking in an ongoing argument against slavery that was first made by German Quakers, including Francis Daniel Pastorius, in West Jersey and Philadelphia, an argument that continued in the later work of John Woolman and others who sought emancipation for all Africans brought into the British colonies.

AN EXHORTATION AND CAUTION TO FRIENDS CONCERNING BUYING OR KEEPING OF NEGROES[1]

Seeing our Lord Jesus Christ hath tasted Death for every Man, and given himself a Ransom for all, to be testified in due time, and that his Gospel of Peace, Liberty and Redemption from Sin, Bondage and all Oppression, is freely to be preached unto all, without Exception, and that *Negroes, Blacks* and *Taunies* are a real part of Mankind, for whom Christ hath shed his precious Blood, and are capable of Salvation, as well as *White Men;* and Christ the Light of the World hath (in measure) enlightened them, and every Man that cometh into the World, and that all such who are sincere *Christians* and true Believers in Christ Jesus, and Followers of him, bear his Image, and are made conformable unto him in Love, Mercy, Goodness and Compassion, who came not to destroy mens Lives, but to save them, nor to bring any part of Mankind into outward Bondage, Slavery or Misery, nor yet to detain them, or hold them therein, but to ease and deliver the Oppressed and Distressed, and bring into Liberty both inward and outward.

Therefore we judge it necessary that all faithful Friends should discover themselves to be true *Christians*

by having the Fruits of the Spirit of Christ, which are *Love, Mercy, Goodness, and Compassion* towards all in Misery, and that[2] Oppression and severe Usage, so far as in them is possible to ease and relieve them, and set them free of their hard Bondage, whereby it may be hoped, that many of them will be gained by their beholding these good Works of sincere *Christians,* and prepared thereby, through the Preaching the Gospel of Christ, to imbrace the true Faith of Christ. And for this cause it is, as we judge, that in some places in *Europe* Negroes cannot be bought and sold for Money, or detained to be Slaves, because it suits not with the Mercy, Love & Clemency that is essential to *Christianity,* nor to the Doctrine of Christ, nor to the Liberty the Gospel calleth all men unto, to whom it is preached. And to buy Souls and Bodies of men for Money, to enslave them and their Posterity to the end of the World, we judge is a great hinderance to the spreading of the Gospel, and is occasion of much War, Violence, Cruelty and Oppression, and Theft & Robery of the highest Nature; for commonly the Negroes that are sold to white Men, are either stollen away or robbed from their Kindred, and to buy such is the way to continue these evil Practices of Manstealing, and transgresseth that Golden Rule and Law, *To do to others what we would have others do to us.*

Therefore, in true *Christian Love,* we earnestly recommend it to all our Friends and Brethren, Not to buy any Negroes, unless it were on purpose to set them free, and that such who have bought any, and have them at present,

---

1. The pamphlet was first published by William Bradford in New York in 1693. The printed version carried the captioned title, "Given forth by our monethly meeting in Philadelphia, the 13th day of the 8th moneth, 1693."

---

2. The print is unclear after "that," perhaps reading "further. . . ."

after some reasonable time of moderate Service they have had of them, or may have of them, that may reasonably answer to the Charge of what they have laid out, especially in keeping Negroes Children born in their House, or taken into their House when under Age, that after a reasonable time of service to answer that Charge, they may set them at Liberty, and during the time they have them, to teach them to read, and give them a Christian Education.

Some Reasons and Causes of Our Being against Keeping of Negroes for Term of Life

First, Because it is contrary to the Principles and Practice of the *Christian Quakers* to buy Prize or stollen Goods, which we bore a faithful Testimony against in our Native Country; and therefore it is our Duty to come forth in a Testimony against stollen Slaves, it being accounted a far greater Crime under *Moses's* Law than the stealing of Goods; for such were only to restore four fold, *but he that stealeth a Man and selleth him, if he be found in his hand, he shall surely be put to Death, Exod.* 21. 16. Therefore as we are not to buy stollen Goods, (but if at unawares it should happen through Ignorance, we are to restore them to the Owners, and seek our Remedy of the Thief) no more are we to buy stollen Slaves; neither should such as have them keep them and their Posterity in perpetual Bondage and Slavery, as is usually done, to the great scandal of the *Christian Profession.*

Secondly, Because Christ commanded, saying, *All things whatsoever ye would that men should do unto you, do ye even so to them.* Therefore as we and our Children would not be kept in perpetual Bondage and Slavery against our Consent, neither should we keep them in perpetual Bondage and Slavery against their Consent, it being such intollerable Punishment to their Bodies and Minds, that none but notorious Criminal Offendors deserve the same. But these have done us no harme; therefore how inhumane is it in us so grievously to oppress them and their Children from one Generation to another.

Thirdly, Because the Lord hath commanded, saying, *Thou shalt not deliver unto his Master the Servant that is escaped from his Master unto thee, he shall dwell with thee, even amongst you in that place which he shall chuse in one of thy Gates, where it liketh him best; thou shalt not oppress him, Deut.* 23. 15, 16. By which it appeareth, that those which are at Liberty and freed from their Bondage, should not by us be delivered into Bondage again, neither by us should they be oppressed, but being escaped from

his Master, should have the Liberty to dwell amongst us, where it liketh him best. Therefore, if God extend such Mercy under the legal Ministration and Dispensation to poor Servants, he doth and will extend much more of his Grace and Mercy to them under the clear Gospel Ministration; so that instead of punishing them and their Posterity with cruel Bondage and perpetual Slavery, he will cause the Everlasting Gospel to be preached effectually to all Nations, to them as well as others; *And the Lord will extend Peace to his People like a River, and the Glory of the* Gentiles *like a flowing Stream; And it shall come to pass, saith the Lord, that I will gather all Nations and Tongues, and they shall come and see my Glory, and I will set a sign among them, and I will send those that escape of them unto the Nations, to Tarshish, Pull and Lud that draw the Bow, to Tuball and Javan, to the Isles afar off that have not heard my Fame, neither have seen my Glory, and they shall declare my Glory among the* Gentiles, *Isa.* 66. 12–18.

Fourthly, Because the Lord hath commanded, saying, *Thou shalt not oppress an hired Servant that is poor and needy, whether he be of thy Brethren, or of the Strangers that are in thy Land within thy Gates, least he cry against thee unto the Lord, and it be sin unto thee; Thou shalt neither vex a stranger nor oppress him, for ye were strangers in the Land of* Egypt, *Deut.* 24. 14, 15. *Exod.* 12. 21. But what greater Oppression can there be inflicted upon our Fellow Creatures, than is inflicted on the poor Negroes! they being brought from their own Country against their Wills, some of them being stollen, others taken for payment of Debt owing by their Parents, and others taken Captive in War, and sold to Merchants, who bring them to the *American* Plantations, and sell them for Bond-Slaves to them that will give most for them; the Husband from the Wife, and the Children from the Parents; and many that buy them do exceedingly afflict them and oppress them, not only by continual hard Labour, but by cruel Whippings, and other cruel Punishments, and by short allowance of Food, some Planters in *Barbadoes* and *Jamaica,* 'tis said, keeping one hundred of them, and some more, and some less, and giving them hardly any thing more than they raise on a little piece of Ground appointed them, on which they work for themselves the seventh days of the Week in the after-noon, and on the first days, to raise their own Provisions, to wit, Corn and Potatoes, and other Roots, etc. the remainder of their time being spent in their Masters service; which doubtless is far worse usage than is practiced by the *Turks* and *Moors* upon their Slaves. Which tends to the great Reproach of the *Christian Profession;* therefore it would be better for all such as fall short of the Practice of those *Infidels,* to refuse the Name of a *Christian,* that those *Heathen* and *Infidels* may not be provoked to blaspheme against the blessed Name of Christ, by reason of the unparallel'd Cruelty of these cruel and hard hearted pretended *Christians.* Surely the Lord doth behold their Oppressions & Afflictions, and will further visit for the same by his righteous and just Judgments, except they break off their sins by Repentance, and their Iniquity by shewing Mercy to these poor afflicted, tormented miserable Slaves!

Fifthly, Because Slaves and Souls of Men are some of the *Merchandize of Babylon* by which the Merchants of the Earth are made Rich; but those Riches which they have heaped together, through the cruel Oppression of these miserable Creatures, will be a means to draw Gods Judgments upon them; therefore, *Brethren,* let us hearken to the Voice of the Lord, who saith, *Come out of* Babylon, *my People, that ye be not partakers of her Sins, and that ye receive not her Plagues; for her Sins have reached unto Heaven, and God hath remembered her Iniquities; for he that leads into Captivity shall go into Captivity, Rev.* 18. 4, 5. & 13. 10.

Given forth by our Monethly Meeting in Philadelphia, *the 13th day of the 8th Moneth,* 1693. *and recommended to all our Friends and Brethren, who are one with us in our Testimony for the Lord Jesus Christ, and to all others professing Christianity.*

ELIZABETH ASHBRIDGE (1713–1755)

Despite her prominence in Britain and Britain's American colonies as a Quaker preacher, Elizabeth Ashbridge left few clues beyond what she reveals in her autobiography about her earliest years. She was born in Middlewich, in Cheshire, England, the only child of a ship's surgeon, Thomas Sampson, and his wife, Mary, a devout Anglican. When she was just fourteen years old, Elizabeth Sampson eloped with a poor weaver, only to be widowed several months later. Now irreparably separated from her parents, Elizabeth resided at various times with two different relatives. During this time, she first encountered members of the Society of Friends, called Quakers by their detractors, just before deciding to leave for the North American colonies. Although she escaped one woman's efforts to kidnap and sell her as an indentured servant, Ashbridge nonetheless ended up sold upon her ship's 1732 landing in New York, where the ship's captain claimed her as his indentured passenger. Three years later, she paid off her indenture and married Mr. Sullivan. As she recounts the story in her autobiography, this was a complicated and difficult time for her. She met some Friends and felt moved to be near them and associate with them as they pursued their testimony of peace in the world. Her Quaker leanings brought her significant abuse from her new husband, who, himself confused, struggled to prevent his wife from acting on her newly identified spiritual beliefs. Sullivan, however, began to understand the ways of the Society of Friends, as a result of his wife's influence, but he died shortly thereafter, in 1741.

Five years later, Elizabeth married Aaron Ashbridge, a Quaker from a successful Pennsylvania family and soon circulated among the Quaker elite in the Pennsylvania colony. Hers became an important and public role in the Quaker community, which authorized her to speak at local and regional meetings of Friends. Ashbridge spoke aloud her testimony and won significant acclaim. In 1753, after receiving the approval of the Quaker community, she decided to sail to England and Ireland to preach, leaving her husband and her comfortable life in Pennsylvania behind her. Her trip proved successful, and her reputation among the transatlantic Quaker community grew. Before she could return to Pennsylvania, however, Ashbridge fell ill. She died in Ireland in 1755.

The publication of Ashbridge's spiritual autobiography reflects a significant accomplishment among the Society of Friends who responded so warmly to Ashbridge's testimony. In order for any society member's writings to be published, the manuscript had to be reviewed by a rigorous committee of readers who determined whether the author offered sufficient didactic materials to warrant publication. Ashbridge's narrative was not only praised by the committee, but was published, circulated, and republished throughout the eighteenth, nineteenth, and early twentieth centuries. Aaron Ashbridge sent a copy of the manuscript to the prominent Quaker, John Woolman, who had requested a copy. (Woolman's own journal was published in 1774.) Today Ashbridge's autobiography offers readers a fascinating glimpse into the life of a former indentured servant and immigrant who assumed a prominent public role within the Quaker community, a role uncommon for many women of her day.

SOME ACCOUNT OF THE EARLY PART OF THE LIFE OF ELIZABETH ASHBRIDGE[1]

My life having been attended with many uncommon occurrences, I have thought proper to make some remarks on the dealings of divine goodness with me. I have often had cause, with David, to say, "It is good for me that I have been afflicted;"[2] and most earnestly I desire that they who read the following lines may take warning, and shun the evils into which I have been drawn.

I was born at Middlewich, in Cheshire, in the year 1713, of honest parents, named Thomas and Mary Sampson. My father bore a good character, but he was not so strictly religious as my mother, who was a pattern of virtue to me. I was my father's only child; but my mother had a son and a daughter by a former husband. Soon after I was born, my father went to sea, and, following his profession, which was that of a surgeon, made many long voyages. He continued in his sea-faring course of life till I was twelve years old, so that the care of the early part of my education, devolved upon my mother; and she discharged her duty, in endeavouring to imbue my mind with the principles of virtue. I have had reason to be thankful that I was blest with such a parent; her good advice and counsel to me have been as bread cast upon the waters.[3] She was an instructive example to all who knew her, and generally beloved; but, alas! as soon as the time came, when she might reasonably expect the benefit from her

labours, and have had comfort in me, I deserted her. In my childhood I had an awful regard for religion and religious people, particularly for ministers, all of whom I believed to be good men and beloved of God, which I earnestly wished to be my own case. I had also great tenderness for the poor, remembering that I had read they were beloved of the Lord. This I supposed to mean such as were poor in temporal things; whom I often visited in their cottages, and used to think that they were better off than myself; yet, if I had money, or any thing suitable for a gift, I bestowed it on them, recollecting that they who gave to such, lent unto the Lord. I made remarks on those who pretended to religion; and, when I heard people swear, I was troubled; for my mother told me that, if I used any naughty words, God would not love me.

I observed that there were several different religious societies; this I often thought of, and wept with desires that I might be directed to the one which it would be best for me to join. In this frame of mind passed my younger years. I was sometimes guilty of the faults common among children, but was always sorry, for what I had done amiss; and, till I was fourteen years of age, I was as innocent as most children. About this time, my sorrows (which have continued, for the greatest part of my life, ever since) began, by my giving way to a foolish passion, in setting my affections on a young man, who, without the leave of my parents, courted me till I consented to marry him; and, with sorrow of heart, I relate, that I suffered myself to be carried off in the night. We were married. My parents made all possible search for me, as soon as I was missing, but it was in vain. This precipitate act plunged me into much sorrow. I was soon smitten with remorse for thus leaving my parents, whose right it was to have disposed of me to their content, or who, at least, ought to have been consulted. But I was soon chastised for my disobedience, and convinced of my error. In five months, I was stripped of the darling of my heart, and left a young and disconsolate widow. I was now without a home. My husband had derived his livelihood only from his trade, which was that of a stocking weaver; and my father was so displeased that he would do nothing for me. My dear mother had some compassion for me, and kept me among

---

1. Ashbridge's *Some Account of the Fore-Part of the Life of Elizabeth Ashbridge* was first published in Nantwich, England (1774). The original manuscript of that edition is now lost. The text reprinted here is taken from the first American publication (Philadelphia, 1807) of *Some Account of the Early Part of the Life of Elizabeth Ashbridge.*

2. Psalms 119:71: "It is good for me that I have been afflicted, that I may learn thy statutes."

3. Ecclesiastes 11:1: "Cast thy bread upon the waters: for thou shalt find it after many days."

the neighbours. Afterwards, by her advice, I went to a relation of hers, at Dublin. We hoped that my absence would soften my father's rigour; but he continued inflexible; he would not send for me back, and I dared not to return unless he did.

The relation I went to reside with was one of the people called Quakers. His habits were so very different to what I had been accustomed to, that the visit proved disagreeable to me. I had been brought up in the way of the Church of England, and though, as I have said, I had a religious education, yet I was allowed to sing and dance, which my cousin would not permit. The great vivacity of my natural disposition would not, in this instance, suffer me to give way to the gloomy sense of sorrow and conviction; and therefore my present restraints had a wrong effect. I became more wild and airy than ever; my cousin often reproved me; but I then thought his conduct was the result of singularity, and would not bear it, or be controlled. Having a distant relation in the West of Ireland, I went to him. I now enjoyed all the liberty I wished; for, what rendered me disagreeable to my other kinsman, was quite pleasing to this. Between these two relations I spent three years and three months.

While I was in Ireland, I contracted an intimate acquaintance with a widow and her daughter, who were papists. We conversed very frequently about religion, each of us defending our peculiar tenets; and, though I was much given to gaiety, our discussions often made me thoughtful. The old woman told me of such mighty miracles, done by their priests, that I began to be shaken in my own belief; and thought that, if these things were so, they must, of a truth, be the apostles' successors. She perceived the state of my mind, and, one day, exclaimed with rapture, "Oh! if I can, under God, be the happy instrument of converting you to the holy Catholic Faith, all the sins that ever I committed will be forgiven." Sometimes I frequented her place of worship, but none of my relations knew what was the motive. The affair went so far, that the priest came to converse with me. Being young, and my judgment weak, I was ready to believe what he said; yet resolved not blindly to adopt their creed. I thought that, if their articles of faith were sound, they would not be against my knowing them; and, therefore, the next time I saw the priest, I told him, that I had some intention of becoming one of his flock, but wished first to know what I must agree to. He answered, that I must first confess my sins to him; and gave me till the next day to consider of them. I was not averse to this, conscious of having done nothing for which any one could harm me; and thinking

that, if what he had said was true, the confession would be for my good. When he came again, I told all that I could remember; which, for my part, I thought bad enough; but he considered me, he said, the most innocent creature that ever made confession to him. When I had done, he took a book, which he read, and told me, I was to swear I believed, if I joined them. I shall not trouble my reader with the recital of its ridiculous contents. What principally made me sick of my new intention, was, that I was to swear I considered the Pretender[4] to be king James's son, and the true heir of the crown of England; and that all who died out of the pale of the popish church, would be damned. These doctrines startled me; I hesitated, and desired time to take them into consideration; but, before I saw the priest again, a change of circumstances freed me from the necessity of giving him an answer.

My father still keeping me at such a distance, I thought myself quite excluded from his affections, and therefore resolved not to return home. I became acquainted with a gentlewoman, lately arrived from Pennsylvania; she was intending to return, and, as I had an uncle (my mother's brother) in this province, I soon agreed with her for my passage. I was ignorant of the nature of an indenture, and suffered myself to be bound. This was done privately, that it might not be found out. As soon as it was over, she invited me to see the vessel in which I was to sail. I readily consented, and we went on board, where there was another young woman, who, as I afterwards found, was of a respectable family, and had been brought there in the same way as myself. I was pleased with the thought that I should have such an agreeable companion in my voyage. While we were busy conversing, my conductor went on shore, and, when I wished to go, I was not permitted. I now saw I was kidnapped. I was kept a prisoner in the ship three weeks, at the end of which time my companion was found out by her friends, who fetched her away; and, by her information, my friends sent the water-bailiff, who took me on shore. I was kept close for two weeks, but at length found means to get away. I was so filled with the thoughts of going to America that I could not give up the design; and, meeting the captain, I inquired when he sailed; he told me, and I went on board.

There was, in the ship, sixty Irish servants, and several English passengers. The latter were unacquainted with

---

4. James Edward Stuart, heir to Catholic English king James II, who was exiled following the Revolution of 1689 and replaced by the Protestant William and Mary.

the Irish language, which I had taken much pains to learn, and understood pretty well. Twenty of the servants belonged to the gentlewoman above-mentioned, who, with a young man, (her husband's brother,) went with us. While we were on the coast of Ireland, where the wind kept us some weeks, I overheard the Irish contriving how they should be free, when they got to America. To accomplish their design, they concluded to rise and kill the ship's crew, and all the English, and to appoint the above-mentioned young man to navigate the vessel. But, overhearing their conversation, I discovered their barbarous intention to the captain, who acquainted the English with it. The next day, we bore for the shore, and, at a short distance from the cove of Cork, lowered sail and dropt anchor, under pretence that the wind was not fair for us to stand our course. The boat was hoisted out, and the passengers were invited to go and divert themselves on shore. Along with others went the ringleader of the Irish. This was all that was desired. The rest left him, and came on board. The captain immediately ordered his men to weigh anchor, and hoist sail. There were great outcries for the young man on shore, but he said that the wind had freshened up, and he would not stay for his own son. Thus were the designs of those Irish servants rendered abortive, in a way they did not suspect, and which it was thought advisable to keep a secret, lest they should injure me. At length, however, they discovered that I understood their speech, by my smiling at a story they were telling. From this time they divised many ways to do me a mischief, for which several of them were punished.

On the 15th of the 7th month, which was nine weeks after we left Dublin, we arrived at New York. Here I was betrayed by the very men whose lives I had preserved. The captain caused an indenture to be made, and threatened me with a gaol, if I refused to sign it. I told him that I could find means to satisfy him for my passage without becoming bound. He replied, that I might take my choice, either to sign the indenture he showed me, or the one I had signed in Ireland should be in force. In a fright, I signed the former; for I had, by this time, learned the character of the woman who first induced me to think of going to America; she was a vile creature, and I feared that, if I fell into her hands, I should be used ill.

In two weeks I was sold. At first I had not much reason to complain of the treatment I received; but, in a short time, a difference, in which I was innocent, happened, that set my master against me, and rendered him inhuman. It will be impossible for me to convey an adequate idea of the sufferings of my servitude. Though my father was not rich, yet, in his house, I lived well, and I had been used to little but my school; but, now, I found it would have been better for me if I had been brought up with less indulgence. I was not allowed decent clothes; I was obliged to perform the meanest drudgery, and even to go barefoot in the snow. I suffered the utmost hardship that my body was able to bear, and the effect produced on my mind had nearly been my ruin for ever.

My master seemed to be a very religious man, taking the sacrament (so called)[5] regularly, and praying every night in his family; unless his prayer-book could not be found, for he never prayed without it to my knowledge. His example, however, made me sick of his religion: for, though I had but little religion myself, I had some idea of what religious people ought to be. Respecting religion, my opinions began to waver; I even doubted whether there was any such thing; and began to think that the convictions I had felt, from my infancy, were only the prejudices of education. These convictions seemed now to be lost; and, for some months, I do not remember to have felt them. I became hardened, and was ready to conclude that there was no God. The veneration I had felt for religious men, in my infancy, was entirely gone; I now looked upon them in a very different manner. My master's house was a place of great resort for the clergy; and, sometimes, those who came from a distance lodged with him. The observations I made on their conduct confirmed me in my atheistical opinions. They diverted themselves, in the evening, with cards and songs, and, a few moments after, introduced prayers and singing psalms to Almighty God. Often did I say to myself, "If there be a God, he is a pure Being, and will not hear the prayers of polluted lips."

But he who hath, in an abundant manner, shown mercy to me, (as will be seen in the sequel,) did not long suffer my mind to be perplexed with doubts; but, in a moment, when my feet were on the brink of the bottomless pit, plucked me back.

To one woman, and to no other, I told the nature of the difference which had happened, two years before, between my master and me. By her means, he heard of it, and, though he knew it was true, he sent for the town's whipper to correct me. I was called in. He never asked me whether I had told any such thing, but ordered me to strip. My heart was ready to burst. I would as freely have given up my life as have suffered such ignominy. "If," said I,

---

5. Ashbridge refers here to the Sacrament of the Lord's Supper (Communion).

"there be a God, be graciously pleased to look down on one of the most unhappy creatures, and plead my cause; for thou knowest that, what I have related, is the truth;" and, had it not been for a principle more noble than he was capable of, I would have told it to his wife. Then, fixing my eyes on the barbarous man, I said, "Sir, if you have no pity on me, yet, for my father's sake, spare me from this shame; (for he had heard several ways of my parents;) and, if you think I deserve such punishment, do it yourself." He took a turn over the room, and bade the whipper go about his business. Thus I came off without a blow; but my character seemed to be lost. Many reports of me were spread, which I bless God were not true. I suffered so much cruelty that I could not bear it; and was tempted to put an end to my miserable life. I listened to the temptation, and, for that purpose, went into the garret to hang myself. Now it was I felt convinced that there was a God. As I entered the place, horror and trembling seized me; and, while I stood as one in amazement, I seemed to hear a voice saying, "There is a hell beyond the grave." I was greatly astonished, and cried, "God be merciful, and enable me to bear whatsoever thou, in thy providence, shall bring or suffer to come upon me." I then went down stairs, but let no one know what I had been about.

Soon after this I had a dream; and, though some make a ridicule of dreams, this seemed very significant to me, and therefore I shall mention it. I thought I heard a knocking at the door, by which, when I had opened it, there stood a grave woman, holding in her right hand a lamp burning, who, with a solid countenance, fixed her eye upon me and said, "I am sent to tell thee that, if thou wilt return to the Lord thy God, who created thee, he will have mercy on thee, and thy lamp shall not be put out in obscurity." Her lamp then flamed, in an extraordinary manner; she left me, and I awoke.

But, alas! I did not give up to the "heavenly vision," as I think I may call it. I was nearly caught in another snare, of the most dangerous nature. I was esteemed skilful at singing and dancing, in which I took great delight. Once, falling in with a company of players, who were then in New York, they took a great fancy, as they said, to me, and invited me to become an actress amongst them. They added, that they would find means to release me from my cruel servitude, and I should live like a lady. The proposal pleased me, and I took no small pains to qualify myself for them, in reading their play-books, even when I should have slept. Yet, on reflection, I demurred at taking this new step, when I came to consider what my father would think of it, who had forgiven my disobedience in marry-

ing, and had sent for me home, earnestly desiring to see me again. But my proud heart would not suffer me to return, in so mean a condition, and I preferred bondage. However, when I had served about three years, I bought out the remainder of my time, and worked at my needle, by which I could maintain myself handsomely. But, alas! I was not sufficiently punished. I released myself from one cruel servitude, and, in the course of a few months, entered into another for life, by marrying a young man who fell in love with me for my dancing; a poor motive for a man to chuse a wife, or a woman a husband. For my part, I was in love with nothing I saw in him; and it seems unaccountable to me, that after refusing several offers, both in this country and Ireland, I should at last marry one I did not esteem. My husband was a schoolmaster. A few days after we were married, we went from New York to a place called Westerly, in Rhode Island, where he had engaged to keep a school. With respect to religion he was much like myself, without any; and, when intoxicated, would use the worst of oaths. I do not mention this to expose him, but to show the effect it had on myself. I saw myself ruined, as I thought, in being joined to a man I did not love, and who was a pattern of no good to me. We thus seemed hastening towards destruction, when I concluded, if I was not forsaken of heaven, to alter my course of life. To fix my affection on the divine being, and not to love my husband, seemed inconsistent. I daily desired, with tears, that my affections might be directed in a right manner, and can say that, in a little time, my love was sincere. I resolved to do my duty to God, and, expecting I must come to the knowledge of it by the scriptures, I read these sacred writings with a determination to follow their directions. The more I read, the more uneasy I grew,—especially about baptism. I had reason to believe I had been sprinkled[6] in my infancy, because, at the age of thirteen, I was confirmed by the bishop; yet I could not discover a precedent for the practice. In the course of reading, I came to the passage where it is said, "He that believes and is baptized,"[7] & c.—Here I observed that belief, of which I was not capable when sprinkled, went before baptism. I conversed frequently with the seventh day baptists that lived in the neighbourhood, and, at length, thinking it only a real duty, was, in the winter, baptized by one of their teachers. I did not strictly join with them, though I

---

6. Baptized with holy water.

7. Mark 16:16: "He that believeth and is baptized shall be saved; but he that believeth not shall be damned."

began to think the seventh day[8] the true sabbath, and, for a time, kept it. My husband did not oppose me, for he saw I grew more affectionate to him; and, as yet, I did not refuse to sing and dance, when he asked me, though this way of amusing myself did not yield me so much satisfaction as formerly.

My husband and I now formed the plan of going to England, and, for this purpose, we went to Boston, where we found a vessel bound to Liverpool. We agreed for our passage, and expected to sail in about two weeks; but, in the mean time, a gentleman hired the vessel to carry himself and his attendants to Fayal, and take no other passengers. There being no other ship near sailing, we, for that time, gave up our design, though we continued at Boston several weeks. My mind was still not satisfied, with regard to religion. I had reformed my conduct, so as to be accounted, by those who knew me, a sober woman; yet I was not content, for I expected to find the sweets of such a change; and, though several thought me religious, I dared not to think so myself. I conversed with people of all societies, as opportunity offered, several of whom thought I was of their persuasion; however, I joined strictly with none, but resolved never to leave off searching till I found the truth. This was in the twenty-second year of my age. While we were in Boston, I went, one day, to the Quaker's meeting, where I heard a woman friend speak, at which I was a little surprised. I had been told of women's preaching, but had never heard it before; and I looked upon her with pity for her ignorance, and contempt for her practice; saying to myself, "I'm sure you're a fool, and, if ever I turn Quaker, (which will never be,) I will never be a preacher." Thus was my mind occupied while she was speaking. When she had done, a man stood up, who I could better bear. He spoke sound doctrine on good Joshua's resolution, "As for me and my house we will serve the Lord."[9] After sitting down, and remaining silent awhile, he went to prayer, which was attended with something so awful and affecting, that it drew tears from my eyes.

After leaving Boston, my husband being given to rambling, which was very disagreeable to me, we went to Rhode Island, and from thence to the east end of Long Island, where he hired to keep a school. This place was principally settled by Presbyterians, and I soon became acquainted with the most religious among them. My poverty was no bar to my reception with people of the best credit, with whom I frequently conversed; but, the more I became acquainted with them, the worse I liked their opinions. Many temptations, in the mean time, assaulted my unsettled mind. Having been abroad one day, I perceived that the people, in whose house we had a room, had left some flax in an apartment through which I was to pass; at the sight of it, I was tempted to steal some to make thread. I went to it, and took a small bunch in my hand, upon which I was smitten with such remorse that I laid it down again, saying, "Lord keep me from so vile an action." But the temptation to steal became stronger than before; and I took the bunch of flax into my room; when I came there, horror seized me, and, with tears, I cried out, "O, thou God of mercy, enable me to abstain from this vile action." I then took the flax back, and felt that pleasure which is only known to those who have resisted temptation.

My husband having hired further up the Island, we changed our residence, and the nearest place of worship belonging to a congregation of the Church of England, which, on the whole, I liked best, I attended it.

A fresh exercise, of a very peculiar kind, now came upon me. It was in the second month:[10] I thought myself sitting by a fire, in company with several others, among whom was my husband; when there arose a thunder gust, and a noise, loud as from a mighty trumpet, pierced my ears with these words: "OH ETERNITY! ETERNITY, THE ENDLESS TERM OF LONG ETERNITY! I was exceedingly astonished, and, while I was sitting as in a trance, I beheld a long roll, written in black characters, hearing, at the same time, a voice saying, "These are thy sins," and afterwards adding, "And the blood of Christ is not sufficient to wash them out. This is shown thee that thou mayest confess thy damnation to be just, and not in order that thou shouldst be forgiven." I sat speechless; at last I got up trembling, and threw myself on the bed. The company thought my indisposition proceeded from a fright occasioned by the thunder; but it was of another kind. For several months I was almost in a state of despair, and if, at any time, I endeavoured to hope, or lay hold of any gracious promise, the Tempter would insinuate that it was now too late; that the day of mercy was over; and that I should only add to my sins by praying for pardon, and

---

8. Saturday. Quakers referred to both days of the week and months of the year by numbers in order to avoid using the conventional names, which were associated with pagan gods.

9. Joshua 24:15.

---

10. April.

provoke divine vengeance to make of me a monument of wrath. I was, at it were, already in torment. I could not sleep, and ate but little. I became extremely melancholy, and took no delight in any thing. Had all the world been mine, I would have given it gladly for one glimpse of hope.

My husband was shocked to see me so changed. I, who once used to divert him with singing and dancing, in which he greatly delighted, could not, since I grew religious, do it any longer. My singing was turned into mourning, and my dancing into lamentation.

My nights and days were one continued scene of sorrow; but I let no one know the state of my mind. In vain did my husband use all the means in his power to divert my melancholy. The wound was too deep to be healed with any thing short of the true balm of Gilead.[11] For fear of evil spirits I dared not, nor would my husband suffer me, to go much alone; and, if I took up the bible, he would take it from me, exclaiming, "How you are altered; you used to be agreeable company, but now I've no comfort in you." I endeavoured to bear all with patience, expecting that I should soon have to bear more than man could inflict.

I went to the priest, to see if he could relieve me; but he was a stranger to my case. He advised me to take the sacrament, and amuse myself with innocent diversions. He also lent me a book of prayers, which he said were suited to my condition. But all was to no purpose; as to the sacrament, I thought myself in a very unfit state to receive it worthily; as for prayers, it appeared to me that, when I could pray acceptably, I should be enabled to do it without form; and diversions were burthensome. My husband, with a view to alleviate my grief, persuaded me to go to what is called the raising of a building, where much company was collected, but it had a contrary effect. An officer came to summons a jury to sit on the body of a man who had hanged himself; on receiving which information a voice within me seemed to address me thus:— Thou shalt be the next to come to a like end; for thou art not worthy to die a natural death. For two months, I was daily tempted to destroy myself, often so strongly that I could scarcely resist. Before I ventured to walk out alone I left behind me every article which, in an unguarded moment, I might use for this purpose; fervently desiring, at

the same time, that God would preserve me from taking that life which he had given, and which he would have made happy, if I had accepted the offers of his grace, by regarding the convictions he had favoured me with from my youth. During all this agony of mind, I could not shed a tear. My heart was hardened, and my life was miserable; but God, in his infinite mercy, delivered my soul from this thraldom. One night, as I lay in bed, bemoaning my condition, I cryed "Oh my God, in thy mercy, I beseech thee, look down upon me for Christ's sake, who hath promised that all manner of sins and blasphemies shall be forgiven. Lord, if thou wilt be graciously pleased to extend this promise to me, an unworthy creature, trembling before thee, in all that thou shalt command I will obey thee." In an instant my heart was tendered, and I dissolved in a flood of tears. I abhorred my past offences, and admired the mercies of my God. I could now hope in Christ my redeemer, and look upon him with an eye of faith. I experienced what I believed when the priest lent me his book, that, when my prayers would be acceptable, I should not need a form, which I used no more. I now took the sacrament, and can say I did it with reverence and fear.

Being thus released from my deep distress, I seemed like another creature, and went often alone without fear. Once, as I was abhorring myself, in great humility of mind, I seemed to hear a gracious voice, full of love, say to me, "I will never forsake thee, only obey in what I shall make known unto thee." I answered, "My soul doth magnify the God of mercy. If thou wilt dispense thy grace, the rest of my days shall be devoted to serve thee; and, if it be thy will that I should beg my bread, I will submit, with content, to thy providence."

I now began to think of my relations in Pennsylvania, whom I had not yet seen. My husband gave me liberty to visit them, and I obtained a certificate from the priest, in order that, if I made any stay, I might be received as a member of the church wherever I came. My husband accompanied me to the Blazing-star Ferry, saw me safely over, and then returned. In my way, I fell from my horse, and, for several days, was unable to travel. I abode at the house of an honest Dutchman, who, with his wife, paid me the utmost attention, and would have no recompence for their trouble. I left them with deep sentiments of gratitude for their extraordinary kindness, and they charged me, if ever I came that way again, to lodge with them. I mention this, because I shall have occasion to allude to it hereafter.

When I came to Trent-town Ferry, I felt no small mor-

---

11. The "balm of Gilead" refers to a spiritual anointing or the solace of grace. See references in Jeremiah 8:22 and 46:11.

tification on hearing that my relations were all Quakers, and, what was worst of all, that my aunt was a preacher. I was exceedingly prejudiced against this people, and often wondered how they could call themselves Christians. I repented my coming, and was almost inclined to turn back; yet, as I was so far on my journey, I proceeded, though I expected but little comfort from my visit. How little was I aware it would bring me to the knowledge of the truth!

I went from Trent-town to Philadelphia by water, and from thence to my uncle's on horseback. My uncle was dead, and my aunt married again; yet, both she and her husband received me in the kindest manner. I had scarcely been three hours in the house, before my opinion of these people began to alter. I perceived a book lying upon the table, and, being fond of reading, took it up; my aunt observed me, and said, "Cousin, that is a Quaker's book." She saw I was not a Quaker, and supposed I would not like it. I made her no answer, but queried with myself, what can these people write about? I have heard that they deny the scriptures, and have no other bible than George Fox's Journal.[12] . . . denying, also, all the holy ordinances. But, before I had read two pages, my heart burned within me, and, for fear I should be seen, I went into the garden. I sat down, and, as the piece was short, read it before I returned, though I was often obliged to stop to give vent to my tears. The fulness of my heart produced the involuntary exclamation of, "My God, must I, if ever I come to the knowledge of thy truth, be of this man's opinion, who has sought thee as I have done; and must I join this people, to whom, a few hours ago, I preferred the papists. O, thou God of my salvation, and of my life, who hath abundantly manifested thy long suffering and tender mercy, in redeeming me as from the lowest hell, I beseech thee to direct me in the right way, and keep me from error; so will I perform my covenant, and think nothing too near to part with for thy name's sake. O, happy people, thus beloved of God!" After having collected myself, I washed my face, that it might not be perceived I had been weeping. In the night I got but little sleep; the enemy of mankind haunted me with his insinuations, by suggesting that I was one of those that wavered, and not stead-fast in faith; and advancing several texts of scripture against me,

as that, in the latter days, there should be those who would deceive the very elect;[13] that of such were the people I was among, and that I was in danger of being deluded. Warned in this manner, (from the right source as I thought,) I resolved to be aware of those deceivers, and, for some weeks, did not touch one of their books. The next day, being the first of the week, I was desirous of going to church, which was distant about four miles; but, being a stranger, and having no one to go with me, I gave up all thoughts of that, and, as most of the family were going to meeting, I went there with them. As we sat in silence, I looked over the meeting, and said to myself, "How like fools these people sit; how much better would it be to stay at home, and read the Bible, or some good book, than come here and go to sleep." As for me I was very drowsy; and, while asleep, had nearly fallen down. This was the last time I ever fell asleep in a meeting. I now began to be lifted up with spiritual pride, and to think myself better than they; but this disposition of mind did not last long. It may seem strange that, after living so long with one of this society at Dublin, I should yet be so much a stranger to them. In answer, let it be considered that, while I was there, I never read any of their books, nor went to one meeting; besides, I had heard such accounts of them, as made me think that, of all societies, they were the worst. But he who knows the sincerity of the heart, looked on my weakness with pity; I was permitted to see my error, and shown that these were the people I ought to join.

A few weeks afterwards, there was an afternoon meeting at my uncle's, at which a minister named William Hammans was present. I was highly prejudiced against him when he stood up, but I was soon humbled; for he preached the gospel with such power that I was obliged to confess it was the truth. But, though he was the instrument of assisting me out of many doubts, my mind was not wholly freed from them. The morning before this meeting I had been disputing with my uncle about baptism, which was the subject handled by this minister, who removed all my scruples beyond objection, and yet I seemed loath to believe that the sermon I had heard proceeded from divine revelation. I accused my aunt and uncle of having spoken of me to the friend; but they

---

12. George Fox (1624–91) founded the Society of Friends. Fox's journal, first published in 1694, was a central text for Quakers.

---

13. Matthew 24:24: "For there shall arise false Christs, and false prophets, and shall shew great signs and wonders; insomuch that, if it were possible, they shall deceive the very elect."

cleared themselves, by telling me, that they had not seen him, since my coming, until he came into the meeting. I then viewed him as the messenger of God to me, and, laying aside my prejudices, opened my heart to receive the truth; the beauty of which was shown to me, with the glory of those who continued faithful to it. I had also revealed to me the emptiness of all shadows and types, which, though proper in their day, were now, by the coming of the Son of God, at an end, and everlasting righteousness, which is a work in the heart, was to be established in the room thereof. I was permitted to see that all I had gone through was to prepare me for this day; and that the time was near, when it would be required of me, to go and declare to others what the God of mercy had done for my soul; at which I was surprised, and desired to be excused, lest I should bring dishonour to the truth, and cause his holy name to be evil spoken of.

Of these things I let no one know. I feared discovery, and did not even appear like a friend.

I now hired to keep school, and, hearing of a place for my husband, I wrote, and desired him to come, though I did not let him know how it was with me.

I loved to go to meetings, but did not love to be seen going on week-days, and therefore went to them, from my school, through the woods. Notwithstanding all my care, the neighbours, (who were not friends,) soon began to revile me with the name of Quaker; adding, that they supposed I intended to be a fool, and turn preacher. Thus did I receive the same censure, which, about a year before, I had passed on one of the handmaids of the Lord in Boston. I was so weak, that I could not bear the reproach. In order to change their opinion, I went into greater excess of apparel than I had freedom to do, even before I became acquainted with friends. In this condition I continued till my husband came, and then began the trial of my faith.

Before he reached me, he heard I was turned Quaker; at which he stamped, and said, "I had rather have heard she was dead, well as I love her; for, if it be so, all my comfort is gone." He then came to me; it was after an absence of four months; I got up and said to him, "My dear, I am glad to see thee." At this, he flew into a great range, exclaiming, "The devil thee, thee, thee, don't thee me."[14] I endeavoured, by every mild means, to pacify him; and,

at length, got him fit to speak to my relations. As soon after this as we were alone, he said to me, "And so I see your Quaker relations have made you one;" I replied, that they had not, (which was true,) I never told them how it was with me. He said he would not stay amongst them; and, having found a place to his mind, hired, and came directly back to fetch me, walking, in one afternoon, thirty miles to keep me from meeting the next day, which was first day.[15] He took me, after resting this day, to the place where he had hired, and to lodgings he had engaged at the house of a churchwarden. This man was a bitter enemy of Friends, and did all he could to irritate my husband against them.

Though I did not appear like a friend, they all believed me to be one. When my husband and he used to be making their diversions and reviling, I sat in silence, though now and then an involuntary sigh broke from me; at which he would say, "There, did not I tell you your wife was a Quaker, and she will become a preacher." On such an occasion as this, my husband once came up to me, in a great rage, and shaking his hand over me, said, "You had better be hanged in that day." I was seized with horror, and again plunged into despair, which continued nearly three months. I was afraid that, by denying the Lord, the heavens would be shut against me. I walked much alone in the woods, and there, where no eye saw, or ear heard me, lamented my miserable condition. Often have I wandered, from morning till night, without food. I was brought so low that my life became a burden to me; and the devil seemed to vaunt that, though the sins of my youth were forgiven me, yet now I had committed an unpardonable sin, and hell would inevitably be my portion, and my torments would be greater than if I had hanged myself at first.

In the night, when, under this painful distress of mind, I could not sleep, if my husband perceived me weeping, he would revile me for it. At length, when he and his friend thought themselves too weak to overset me, he went to the priest at Chester, to inquire what he could do with me. This man knew I was a member of the Church, for I had shown him my certificate. His advice was, to take me out of Pennsylvania, and settle in some place where there were no Quakers. My husband replied, he did not care where we went, if he could but restore me to my natural liveliness of temper. As for me, I had no resolution to oppose their proposals, nor much cared where I went.

---

14. The Quakers' use of the personal addresses "thee" and "thou" reflected the belief that there was "something of God" in all people.

15. Sunday.

I seemed to have nothing to hope for. I daily expected to be made a victim of divine wrath, and was possessed with the idea that this would be by thunder.

When the time of removal came, I was not permitted to bid my relations farewell; and, as my husband was poor, and kept no horse, I was obliged to travel on foot. We came to Wilmington, fifteen miles, and from thence to Philadelphia by water. Here we stopt at a tavern, where I became the spectacle and discourse of the company. My husband told them his wife had become a Quaker, and he designed, if possible, to find out a place where there was none: (thought I,) I was once in a condition to deserve that name, but now it is over with me. O that I might, from a true hope, once more have an opportunity to confess the truth; though I was sure of all manner of cruelties, I would not regard them. Such were my concerns, while he was entertaining the company with my story, in which he told them that I had been a good dancer, but now he could get me neither to dance or sing. One of the company then started up, and said, "I'll fetch a fiddle, and we'll have a good dance;" a proposal with which my husband was pleased. When the fiddle was brought, my husband came and said to me, "My dear, shake off that gloom, and let us have a civil dance; you would, now and then, when you were a good churchwoman, and that's better than a stiff Quaker." I had taken up the resolution not to comply with his request, whatever might be the consequence; this I let him know, though I durst say little, for fear of his choleric temper. He pulled me round the room, till the tears fell from my eyes, at the sight of which the musician stop, and said "I'll play no more; let your wife alone." There was a person in company that came from Freehold, in East Jersey, who said, "I see your wife's a Quaker, but, if you'll take my advice you need not go so far as you intend; come and live with us; we'll soon cure her of her Quakerism, and we want a schoolmaster and schoolmistress too." He consented, and a happy turn it was for me, as will shortly be seen. The answer of peace was afforded me, for refusing to dance; I rejoiced more than if I had been made mistress of much riches, and, with tears, prayed, "Lord, I dread to ask, and yet without thy gracious pardon, I am miserable. I therefore fall down before thy throne, imploring mercy at thy hand. O Lord, once more, I beseech thee, try my obedience, and then, in whatsoever thou commandest, I will obey thee, and not fear to confess thee before men." My cries were heard, and it was shown to me, that he delights not in the death of a sinner. My soul was again set at liberty, and I could praise him.

In our way to Freehold, we visited the kind Dutchman, whom I have mentioned in a former part of this narrative. He made us welcome, and invited us to pass a day or two with him. During our stay, we went to a large meeting of Presbyterians, held not only for worship, but business, in particular, the trial of one of their priests, who had been charged with drunkenness, was to come on. I perceived such great divisions among the people, respecting who should be their shepherd, that I pitied them. Some insisted on having the old offender restored; others wished to have a young man they had on trial for some weeks; others, again, were for sending to New England for a minister. In reply, one who addressed himself to the chief speaker observed, "Sir, when we have been at the expense (which will not be trilling) of fetching this gentleman from New England, perhaps he'll not stay with us." "Don't you know how to make him stay?" said another. "No Sir." "I'll tell you; give him a large salary, and I'll engage he'll stay." I listened attentively to the debate, and most plainly it appeared to me, that these mercenary creatures were all actuated by one and the same motive, which was, not the regard for souls, but the love of money. One of these men, called a reverend divine, whom these people almost adored, had, to my knowledge, left his flock in Long Island, and removed to Philadelphia, where he could get more money. I have myself heard some on the Island say that they had almost empoverished themselves in order to keep him; but, being unable to equal what he was offered at Philadelphia, he left them. Surely these are the shepherds who regard the fleece more than the flock, and in whose mouths are lies, when they say that they are the ambassadours of Christ, whose command it is, "Freely ye have received, freely give."[16]

In our way to Freehold, as we came to Stony Brook, my husband turned towards me, and tauntingly said, "Here's one of Satan's synagogues, don't you long to be in it; I hope to see you cured of your new religion." A little further on, we came to a large run of water, over which there was no bridge, and, being strangers, we knew no way to avoid passing through it. He carried over our clothes, which we had in bundles; and, taking off my shoes, I walked through in my stockings. It was in the 12th month;[17] the weather was very cold, and a fall of snow lay on the ground. It was the concern of my heart, that the Lord would sanctify all my afflictions to me, and give me patience to bear them. After walking nearly a

---

16. Matthew 10:8.

17. February.

mile, we came to a house, which proved to be a sort of tavern. My husband called for some spirituous liquors, and I got some weakened cider mulled, which rendered me extremely sick; so that, after we were a little past the house, being too faint to proceed, I fell down. "What's the matter now?" said my husband, "what, are you drunk? Where's your religion now?" He knew I was not drunk and, at that time, I believe he pitied me, although he spoke in this manner. After I was a little recovered, we went on, and came to another tavern, where we lodged. The next day. as we journied, a young man, driving an empty cart, overtook us. We asked him to let us ride, and he readily granted the request. I had known the time when I would not have been seen in a cart, but my proud heart was humbled, and I did not now regard the look of it. This cart belonged to a man in Shrewsbury, and was to go through the place of our destination. We soon had the care of the team to ourselves, through a failure of the driver, and arrived with it at Freehold. My husband would have had me stay here, while he went to see the team safe home; I told him, No; since he had led me through the country like a vagabond, I would not stay behind him. We therefore went together, and lodged, that night, at the house of the owner of the cart. The next day, on our return to Freehold, we met a man riding full speed, who, stopping, said to my husband, "Sir, are you a schoolmaster?" He answered, "Yes." "I am come," replied the stranger, "to tell you of two new schoolhouses, two miles apart, each of which wants a master." How this person came to hear of us, who arrived but the night before, I never knew. I was glad he was not called a Quaker, lest it should have been thought a plot by my husband, to whom I turned and said,—"My dear, look on me with pity, if thou, hast any affection left for me, which I hope thou hast, for I am not conscious of having done any thing to alienate it. Here is an opportunity to settle us both, and I am willing to do all in my power, towards getting an honest livelihood." After a short pause, he consented to go with the young man. In our way, we came to the house of a worthy Friend, who was a preacher, though we did not know it. I was surprised to see the people so kind to us. We had not been long in the house, till we were invited to lodge there for the night, being the last of the week. My husband accepted the invitation, saying, "My wife has had a tedious travel, and I pity her." These kind expressions affected me, for I heard them very seldom. The friend's kindness could not proceed from my appearing like a Quaker, because I had not yet altered my dress. The woman of the house, after we had concluded to stay, fixed her eyes upon

me, and said, "I believe thou hast met with a deal of trouble," to which I made but little answer. My husband observing they were of that sort of people, whom he had so much endeavoured to shun, gave us no opportunity for discourse that night; but, the next morning, I let my friend know a little of my situation.

When meeting-time came I longed to go, but dared not to ask my husband's leave. As the Friends were getting ready themselves, they asked him if he would accompany them, observing, that they knew those who were to be his employers, and, if they were at meeting, would speak to them. He consented. The woman Friend then said, "And wilt thou let thy wife go too;" which request he denied; but she answered his objections so prudently that he could not be angry, and at last consented. I went with joy, and a heavenly meeting it was. My spirit did rejoice in the God of my salvation. May I ever, in humility, preserve the remembrance of his tender mercies to me.

By the end of the week, we got settled in our new situation. We took a room, in a friend's house, one mile from each school, and eight from the meeting-house. I now deemed it proper to let my husband see I was determined to join with friends. When first day came, I directed myself to him in this manner: "My dear, art thou willing to let me go to meeting?" He flew into a rage, and replied "No you sha'n't." Speaking firmly, I told him, "That, as a dutiful wife, I was ready to obey all his lawful commands; but, when they imposed upon my conscience, I could not obey him. I had already wronged myself, in having done it too long; and though he was near to me, and, as a wife ought, I loved him, yet God, who was nearer than all the world to me, had made me sensible that this was the way in which I ought to go. I added, that this was no small cross to my own will; but I had given up my heart, and I trusted that He who called for it would enable me, for the remainder of my life, to keep it steadily devoted to his service; and I hoped I should not, on this account, make the worse wife." I spoke, however, to no purpose;—he continued inflexible.

I had now put my hand to the plough, and resolved not to draw back; I therefore went without leave. I expected he would immediately follow and force me back, but he did not. I called at the house of one of the neighbours, and, getting a girl to show me the way, I went on rejoicing, and praising God in my heart.

Thus, for some time, I had to go eight miles on foot to meeting, which I never thought hard. My husband had a horse, but he would not suffer me to ride on it; nor, when my shoes were worn out, would he let me have a new pair;

but, though he hoped, on this account, to keep me from meeting, it did not hinder me:—I have tied them round with strings to keep them on.

Finding that all the means he had yet used could not alter my resolutions, he several times struck me with severe blows. I endeavoured to bear all with patience, believing that the time would come when he would see I was in the right. Once he came up to me, took out his penknife, and said, "If you offer to go to meeting tomorrow, with this knife I'll cripple you, for you shall not be a Quaker." I made him no answer. In the morning, I set out as usual; he did not attempt to harm me. Having despaired of recovering me himself, he fled, for help, to the priest, whom he told, that I had been a very religious woman, in the way of the Church of England, of which I was a member, and had a good certificate from Long Island; that I was now bewitched, and had turned Quaker, which almost broke his heart; and, therefore, he desired that, as he was one who had the care of souls, he would come and pay me a visit, and use his endeavours to reclaim me, which he hoped, by the blessing of God, would be done. The priest consented, and fixed the time for his coming, which was that day two weeks, as he said he could not come sooner. My husband came home extremely pleased, and told me of it. I replied, with a smile, I trusted I should be enabled to give a reason for the hope within me; yet I believed, at the same time, that the priest would never trouble himself about me, which proved to be the case. Before the day he appointed came, it was required of me, in a more public manner, to confess to the world what I was. I felt myself called to give up to prayer in meeting. I trembled, and would freely have given up my life to be excused. What rendered the required service harder on me was, that I was not yet taken under the care of friends; and was kept from requesting to be so, for fear I should bring a scandal on the society. I begged to be excused till I had joined, and then I would give up freely. The answer was, "I am a covenant-keeping God, and the word that I spake to thee, when I found thee in distress, even that I would never forsake thee, if thou wouldst be obedient to what I should make known unto thee, I will assuredly make good. If thou refusest, my spirit shall not always strive. Fear not, I will make way for thee through all thy difficulties, which shall be many, for my name's sake; but, be faithful, and I will give thee a crown of life." To this language I answered "Thy will, O God, be done; I am in thy hand, do with me according to thy word;" and I then prayed.

This day, as usual, I had gone to meeting on foot.

While my husband (at he afterwards told me) was lying on the bed, these words crossed his mind: "Lord, where shall I fly to shun thee,"[18] &c. upon which he arose, and, seeing it rain, got the horse and set off to fetch me, arriving just as the meeting broke up. I got on horseback as quickly as possible, lest he should hear I had been speaking; he did hear of it nevertheless, and, as soon as we were in the woods, began with saying, "Why do you mean thus to make my life unhappy? What, could you not be a Quaker, without turning fool in this manner?" I answered in tears, "My dear, look on me with pity, if thou hast any; canst thou think that I, in the bloom of my days, would bear all that thou knowest of, and much that thou knowest not of, if I did not feel it my duty." These words touched him, and he said, "Well, I'll e'en give you up; I see it wont avail to strive; if it be of God I cannot overthrow it; and, if of yourself, it will soon fall." I saw the tears stand in his eyes, at which I was overcome with joy, and began already to reap the fruits of my obedience. But my trials were not yet over. The time appointed for the priest to visit me arrived, but no priest appeared. My husband went to fetch him, but he refused, saying he was busy, which so displeased my husband that he never went to hear him again, and, for some time, went to no place of worship.

My faith was now assaulted in another way, so strongly, that all my former trials were but trifling to it. This exercise came upon me unexpectedly, by hearing a woman speak of a book she had read, in which it was asserted that Christ was not the Son of God. A voice within me seemed to answer "No more he is, it's all a fancy, and the contrivance of men." Thus again was I filled with inexpressible trouble, which continued three weeks; and again did I seek desolate places, where I might make my moan. I have lain whole nights without sleep. I thought myself deserted of God, but did not let go my trust in him. I kept alive a hope that He who had delivered me as it were out of the paw of the bear, and the jaws of the lion, would in his own good time, deliver me from this temptation also. This was, at length, my experience; and I found the truth of his words, that all things shall work together for the good of those who love and fear him. My present exercises were to prepare me for further services in his cause; and it is necessary for his ministers to experience

18. Psalm 139:7.

all conditions, that they may thereby be abler to speak to them.

This happened just after my first appearance as a minister, and friends had not been to talk with me. They did not well know what to do, till I had appeared again, which was not for some time, when the Monthly Meeting appointed four friends to pay me a visit. They left me well satisfied with the conference, and I joined the society. My husband still went to no place of worship. One day he said to me, "I would go to meeting, only I'm afraid I shall hear your clack, which I cannot bear." I used no persuasions. When meeting-time came, he got the horse, took me behind him, and went. For several months, if he saw me offer to rise, he went out; till, one day, I rose before he was aware and then, as he afterwards owned, he was ashamed to do it.

From this time, he left off the practice, and never hindered me from going to meeting. Though he did not take up the cross, yet his judgment was convinced; and, sometimes, melting into tears, he would say to me, "My dear, I have seen the beauty there is in the truth, and that thou hast followed the right way, in which I pray God to preserve thee." I told him, that I hoped He who had given me strength would also favour him, "O," said he, "I cannot bear the reproach thou dost, to be called turn-coat, and become a laughing-stock to the world; but I'll no longer hinder thee." This I considered a favour, and a little hope remained that my prayers, on his account, would be heard.

We lived in a small house by ourselves, which, though mean, and though we had little to put in it, our bed being no better than chaff, I was truly content. The only desires I had were for my own preservation, and to be blessed with the reformation of my husband. He was connected with a set of men whom he feared would make game of him, which indeed they already did; asking him when he designed to commence preacher, for they saw he intended to turn Quaker, and seemed to love his wife better since she became one than before. They used to come to our house, and provoked him to sit up and drink with them, sometimes till near day, while I have been sorrowing in a stable. Once as I sat in this condition, I heard him say to his company, "I can't bear any longer to afflict my poor wife in this manner; for, whatever you may think of her, I do believe she's a good woman." He then came to me and said, "Come in, my dear, God has given thee a deal of patience: I'll put an end to this practice." This was the last time they sat up at night.

My husband now thought that if he was in any place where it was not known he had been so bitter against

friends, he could do better. I objected to this, fearing it would not be for his benefit. Frequently, in a broken and affectionate manner, he condemned his ill usage of me. I answered, that I hoped it had been for my good, and therefore desired he would not be afflicted on that account. According to the measure of grace received, I did what I could, both by example and precept, for his good. My advice was for him to stay where he was, as I was afraid he would grow weaker in his good resolutions, if he removed.

All I could say would not avail. Hearing of a place at Borden-town, he went thither, but was not suited. He next removed to Mount Holly, where he settled. We had each of us a good school; we soon got our house pretty well furnished, and might have done very well. Nothing seemed wanting to complete my happiness, except the reformation of my husband, which I had much reason to doubt I should not see soon. It fell out according to my fears. He addicted himself much to drinking, and grew worse than before. Sorrow was again my lot, I prayed for patience to bear my afflictions, and to submit to the dispensations of Providence. I murmured not; nor do I recollect that I ever uttered any harsh expressions except on one occasion. My husband coming home a little intoxicated, (a state in which he was very fractious,) and, finding me at work by a candle, he put it out, fetching me, at the same time, a box on the ear, and saying, "You don't earn your light." At this unkind usage, which I had not been used to for the last two years, I was somewhat angry, and said, "Thou art a vile man." He struck me again; but my anger had cooled, and I received the blow without so much as a word in return. This also displeased him, and he went on in a distracted like manner, uttering such expressions of despair as, he believed he was predestined to damnation, and he did not care how soon God struck him dead. I said very little, till, at length, in the bitterness of my soul, I broke out into these expressions: "Lord, look down on my afflictions, and deliver me by some means or other." My prayer was granted, but in such a manner that I thought it would have killed me. He went to Burlington, where he got drunk, and inlisted to go as a common soldier to Cuba, in the year 1740. I had drunk many bitter cups, but this seemed the bitterest of them all. A thousand times I blamed myself for making such a request, which I was afraid had displeased God, who had, in displeasure, granted it for my punishment.

I have since had cause to believe that he was benefited by his rash act, as, in the army, he did what he could not at home;—he suffered for the testimony of truth. When they came to prepare for an engagement, he refused to fight; he was whipt, and brought before the general, who asked him, why he inlisted if he would not fight. "I did it," said he, "in a drunken frolic, when the devil had the better of me; but now my judgment is convinced I ought not to fight, neither will I, whatever I suffer. I have had one life, and you may take that if you please, for I'll never take up arms." He adhered to this resolution. By their cruel usage of him in consequence, he was so much disabled that the general sent him to Chelsen Hospital, near London. Within nine months afterwards, he died at this place, and I hope made a good end.

Having been obliged to say much of his ill usage to me, I have thought it my duty to say what I could in his favour. Although he was so bad, I never thought him the worst of men. If he had suffered religion to have had its perfect work, I should have been happy in the lowest sit-uation of life. I have had cause to bless God, for enabling me, in the station of a wife, to do my duty, and now that I am a widow, I submit to his will. May I still be preserved by the arm of Divine Power; may I never forget the tender mercies of my God, the remembrance of which often boweth my soul in humility before his throne, and I cry, "Lord! what was I, that thou shouldst have revealed to my soul the knowledge of thy truth, and have done so much for one who deserved thy displeasure? Mayst thou, O God, be glorified, and I abased. It is thy own works that praise thee; and, of a truth, to the humble soul, thou makest every bitter thing sweet.[19]

---

19. This concludes the text written by Elizabeth Ashbridge. The 1807 edition of her autobiography also includes additional biographical information about Ashbridge written by her third husband, Aaron Ashbridge, and by other Quakers.

John Woolman (1720–1772)

John Woolman was one of thirteen children born to Quakers Samuel and Elizabeth Burr Woolman on their farm in Burlington County, New Jersey. Although Woolman's formal education was limited, he was an avid reader who turned frequently to his father's library. He spent about five years as a clerk, but his primary work while still a youth was as an apprentice tailor. When he reached his maturity, he established himself in an independent business as a retailer and tailor in Mount Holly, New Jersey. During Woolman's years in Mount Holly, he found in his increasing inward motions of spirit that his spiritual life was developing a growing and lasting significance. Distressed with the system of values all around him, Woolman believed he was moved to a life of simplicity and a life of ministry. He began to speak from his newly identified sense of spirit at local meetings, focusing on his inward life. He began to travel about that time as an itinerant visitant at other groups' meetings, as well. During the two years between 1746 and 1748, Woolman traveled extensively throughout New England, Pennsylvania, New Jersey, New York, Maryland, Virginia, and North Carolina. Shortly after he returned from his travels, he married Sarah Ellis from neighboring Chesterfield in New Jersey.

Woolman struggled to reconcile his business life with his spiritual beliefs. As an apprentice Woolman had been asked to write up a bill of sale for a slave. Although he felt troubled by this request, he did as he was requested to do. When he later found himself facing a similar situation with his employer, he spoke to the employer about his beliefs and refused thereafter to participate in actions that assisted slave keeping. He felt a similar degree of concern about success in business. He discovered that his business could make him wealthy, but such involvement in worldly matters hindered his sense of leading a spiritual life. Thus he decided to limit his business activities, believing that withdrawing from the business world would help him focus on inward and spiritual matters. Woolman devoted much of his life to encouraging others to examine their daily lives for actions that conflicted with living a life that was sufficiently pure.

Woolman's commitment to his beliefs was manifest in his itinerant preaching, his work on the frontier among Native Americans, and his challenges to war taxation, military conscription, and slavery. In 1754, Woolman published the first part of his long essay, *Some Considerations on the Keeping of Negroes*. Four years later, he spoke out against slavery during the Philadelphia Yearly Meeting. The meeting ended up adopting abolitionist resolutions. Woolman continued his itinerant ministry until his death, even traveling to England. In 1772, while visiting England to work among the poor, Woolman fell ill from smallpox and died.

Woolman began his *Journal* in 1756 and continued it until his death. His *Journal* has remained in print since its original 1774 publication, which took place just after his death. Woolman's journal is well known for its simple, direct style and for the emulable life of humility and commitment that the journal describes. In all his writings, Woolman's cautions—whether they are implicit, as in the journal, or explicit, as in his published essays—emphasize the worth of living an examined life, one in which actions and spoken words are deliberate, ethical, and clear of any taint of self-interest and worldly concern. Woolman's spiritual autobiography and his essays on slavery quietly encourage readers to examine the impetus and impact of their actions on the world.

from SOME CONSIDERATIONS ON THE KEEPING OF NEGROES

Recommended to the Professors of Christianity of Every Denomination[1]

Introduction

Customs generally approved and opinions received by youth from their superiors become like the natural produce of a soil, especially when they are suited to favourite inclinations. But as the judgments of God are without partiality, by which the state of the soul must be tried, it would be the highest wisdom to forego customs and popular opinions, and try the treasures of the soul by the infallible standard: Truth.

Natural affection needs a careful examination. Operating upon us in a soft manner, it kindles desires of love and tenderness, and there is danger of taking it for something higher. To me it appears an instinct like that which inferior creatures have; each of them, we see, by the ties of nature love self best. That which is a part of self they love by the same tie or instinct. In them it in some measure does the offices of reason, by which, among other things, they watchfully keep and orderly feed their helpless offspring. Thus natural affection appears to be a branch of self-love, good in the animal race, in us likewise with proper limitations, but otherwise is productive of evil by exciting desires to promote some by means prejudicial to others.

Our blessed Saviour seems to give a check to this irregular fondness in nature and, at the same time, a precedent for us: "Who is my mother, and who are my brethren?"—thereby intimating that the earthly ties of relationship are, comparatively, inconsiderable to such who, through a steady course of obedience, have come to the happy experience of the Spirit of God bearing witness with their spirits that they are his children: "And he stretched forth his hands towards his disciples and said, 'Behold my mother and my brethren; for whosoever shall do the will of my Father which is in heaven (arrives at the more noble part of true relationship)[2] the same is my brother, and sister, and mother.'" Mt. 12:48 [–50].

This doctrine agrees well with a state truly complete, where love necessarily operates according to the agreeableness of things or principles unalterable and in themselves perfect. If endeavouring to have my children eminent amongst men after my death be that which no reasons grounded on those principles can be brought to support, then to be temperate in my pursuit after gain and to keep always within the bounds of those principles is an indispensable duty, and to depart from it a dark unfruitful toil.

In our present condition, to love our children is needful; but except this love proceeds from the true heavenly principle which sees beyond earthly treasures, it will rather be injurious than of any real advantage to them. Where the fountain is corrupt, the streams must necessarily be impure.

That important injunction of our Saviour (Mt. 6:33),[3] with the promise annexed, contains a short but comprehensive view of our duty and happiness. If then the busi-

---

1. *Some Considerations on the Keeping of Negroes* was first published in 1754. The text is taken from *The Journal and Major Essays of John Woolman,* ed. Phillips Moulton (1971).

2. Woolman inserted this phrase into the biblical quotation.

3. Matthew 6:3, "But when thou doest alms, let not thy left hand know what thy right hand doeth."

ness of mankind in this life is to first seek another, if this cannot be done but by attending to the means, if a summary of the means is not to do that to another which (in like circumstances) we would not have done unto us, then these are points of moment and worthy of our most serious consideration.

What I write on this subject is with reluctance, and the hints given are in as general terms as my concern would allow. I know it is a point about which in all its branches men that appear to aim well are not generally agreed, and for that reason I chose to avoid being very particular. If I may happily have let drop anything that may excite such as are concerned in the practice to a close thinking on the subject treated of, the candid amongst them may easily do the subject such further justice as, on an impartial enquiry, it may appear to deserve; and such an enquiry I would earnestly recommend.

Some Consideration on the Keeping of Negroes

"Forasmuch as ye did it to the least of these my brethren, ye did it unto me."

MT. 25:40.

As many times there are different motives to the same actions, and one does that from a generous heart which another does for selfish ends, the like may be said in this case.

There are various circumstances amongst them that keep Negroes, and different ways by which they fall under their care; and, I doubt not, there are many well-disposed persons amongst them who desire rather to manage wisely and justly in this difficult matter than to make gain of it. But the general disadvantage which these poor Africans lie under in an enlightened Christian country having often filled me with real sadness, and been like undigested matter on my mind, I now think it my duty, through divine aid, to offer some thoughts thereon to the consideration of others.

When we remember that all nations are of one blood (Gen. 3:20),[4] that in this world we are but sojourners; that we are subject to the like afflictions and infirmities of body, the like disorders and frailties in mind, the like temptations, the same death and the same judgment; and that the All-wise Being is judge and Lord over us all, it seems to raise an idea of a general brotherhood and a disposition easy to be touched with a feeling of each other's afflictions. But when we forget those things and look chiefly at our outward circumstances, in this and some ages past, constantly retaining in our minds the distinction betwixt us and them with respect to our knowledge and improvement in things divine, natural, and artificial, our breasts being apt to be filled with fond notions of superiority, there is danger of erring in our conduct toward them.

We allow them to be of the same species with ourselves; the odds is we are in a higher station and enjoy greater favours than they. And when it is thus that our Heavenly Father endoweth some of his children with distinguished gifts, they are intended for good ends. But if those thus gifted are thereby lifted up above their brethren, not considering themselves as debtors to the weak nor behaving themselves as faithful stewards, none who judge impartially can suppose them free from ingratitude. When a people dwell under the liberal distribution of favours from heaven, it behooves them carefully to inspect their ways and consider the purposes for which those favours were bestowed, lest through forgetfulness of God and misusing his gifts they incur his heavy displeasure, whose judgments are just and equal, who exalteth and humbleth to the dust as he seeth meet.

It appears by Holy Record that men under high favours have been apt to err in their opinions concerning others. Thus Israel, according to the description of the prophet (Is. 65:5), when exceedingly corrupted and degenerated, yet remembered they were the chosen people of God and could say, "Stand by thyself, come not near me, for I am holier than thou." That this was no chance language, but their common opinion of other people, more fully appears by considering the circumstances which attended when God was beginning to fulfil his precious promises concerning the gathering of the Gentiles.

The Most High, in a vision, undeceived Peter, first prepared his heart to believe, and at the house of Cornelius showed him of a certainty that God was no respecter of persons. The effusion of the Holy Ghost upon a people with whom they, the Jewish Christians, would not so much as eat was strange to them. All they of the circumcision were astonished to see it, and the apostles and brethren of Judea contended with Peter about it, till he having rehearsed the whole matter and fully shown that the Father's love was unlimited, they are thereat struck with admiration and cry out, "Then hath God also to the Gentiles granted repentance unto life!" [Acts 11:18].

---

4. Genesis 3:20, "And Adam called his wife's name Eve; because she was the mother of all living."

The opinion of peculiar favours being confined to them was deeply rooted, or else the above instance had been less strange to them, for these reasons: First, they were generally acquainted with the writings of the prophets, by whom this time was repeatedly spoken of and pointed at. Secondly, our blessed Lord shortly before expressly said, "I have other sheep, not of this fold; them also must I bring," etc. [Jn. 10:16]. Lastly, his words to them after his resurrection, at the very time of his ascension, "Ye shall be witnesses to me not only in Jerusalem, Judea, and Samaria, but to the uttermost parts of the earth" [Acts 1:8].

Those concurring circumstances, one would think, might have raised a strong expectation of seeing such a time. Yet when it came, it proved matter of offense and astonishment.

To consider mankind otherwise than brethren, to think favours are peculiar to one nation and exclude others, plainly supposes a darkness in the understanding. For as God's love is universal, so where the mind is sufficiently influenced by it, it begets a likeness of itself and the heart is enlarged towards all men. Again, to conclude a people froward,[5] perverse, and worse by nature than others (who ungratefully receive favours and apply them to bad ends), this will excite a behavior toward them unbecoming the excellence of true religion.

To prevent such error let us calmly consider their circumstances, and, the better to do it make their case ours. Suppose, then, that our ancestors and we have been exposed to constant servitude in the more servile and inferior employments of life; that we had been destitute of the help of reading and good company; that amongst ourselves we had had few wise and pious instructors; that the religious amongst our superiors seldom took notice of us; that while others in ease have plentifully heaped up the fruit of our labour, we had received barely enough to relieve nature, and being wholly at the command of others had generally been treated as a contemptible, ignorant part of mankind. Should we, in that case, be less abject than they now are? Again, if oppression be so hard to bear that a wise man is made mad by it (Eccles. 7:7), then a series of those things altering the behaviour and manners of a people is what may reasonably be expected.

When our property is taken contrary to our mind by means appearing to us unjust, it is only through divine influence and the enlargement of heart from thence proceeding that we can love our reputed oppressors. If the Negroes fall short in this, an uneasy, if not a disconsolate, disposition will be awakened and remain like seeds in their minds, producing sloth and many other habits appearing odious to us, with which being free men they perhaps had not been chargeable. These and other circumstances, rightly considered, will lessen that too great disparity which some make between us and them.

Integrity of heart hath appeared in some of them, so that if we continue in the world of Christ (previous to discipleship, Jn. 8:31)[6] and our conduct towards them be seasoned with his love, we may hope to see the good effect of it, the which, in a good degree, is the case with some into whose hands they have fallen. But that too many treat them otherwise, not seeming conscious of any neglect, is, alas! too evident.

When self-love presides in our minds our opinions are biased in our own favour. In this condition, being concerned with a people so situated that they have no voice to plead their own cause, there's danger of using ourselves to an undisturbed partiality till, by long custom, the mind becomes reconciled with it and the judgment itself infected.

To humbly apply to God for wisdom, that we may thereby be enabled to see things as they are and ought to be, is very needful; hereby the hidden things of darkness may be brought to light and the judgment made clear. We shall then consider mankind as brethren. Though different degrees and a variety of qualifications and abilities, one dependent on another, be admitted, yet high thoughts will be laid aside, and all men treated as becometh the sons of one Father, agreeable to the doctrine of Christ Jesus.

He hath laid down the best criterion by which mankind ought to judge of their own conduct, and others judge for them of theirs, one towards another—viz., "Whatsoever ye would that men should do unto you, do ye even so to them." I take it that all men by nature are equally entitled to the equality of this rule and under the indispensable obligations of it. One man ought not to look upon another man or society of men as so far beneath him but that he should put himself in their place in all his actions towards them, and bring all to this test—viz., How should I approve of this conduct were I in their circumstances and

---

5. Contrary.

6. John 8:31, "And many of the people believed on him, and said, When Christ cometh, will he do more miracles than these which this *man* hath done?"

they in mine?—Arscott's Considerations, *Part III, Fol.*
107.[7]

This doctrine, being of a moral unchangeable nature, hath been likewise inculcated in the former dispensation: "If a stranger sojourn with thee in your land, ye shall not vex him; but the stranger that dwelleth with you shall be as one born amongst you, and thou shalt love him as thyself." Lev. 19:33, 34. Had these people come voluntarily and dwelt amongst us, to have called them strangers would be proper. And their being brought by force, with regret and a languishing mind, may well raise compassion in a heart rightly disposed. But there is nothing in such treatment which upon a wise and judicious consideration will any ways lessen their right of being treated as strangers. If the treatment which many of them meet with be rightly examined and compared with those precepts, "Thou shalt not vex him nor oppress him; he shall be as one born amongst you, and thou shalt love him as thyself" (Lev. 19:33; Deut. 27:19), there will appear an important difference betwixt them.

It may be objected there is cost of purchase and risk of their lives to them who possess 'em, and therefore needful that they make the best use of their time. In a practice just and reasonable such objections may have weight; but if the work be wrong from the beginning, there's little or no force in them. If I purchase a man who hath never forfeited his liberty, the natural right of freedom is in him. And shall I keep him and his posterity in servitude and ignorance? How should I approve of this conduct were I in his circumstances and he in mine? It may be thought that to treat them as we would willingly be treated, our gain by them would be inconsiderable; and it were, in diverse respects, better that there were none in our country.

We may further consider that they are now amongst us, and those of our nation the cause of their being here, that whatsoever difficulty accrues thereon we are justly chargeable with, and to bear all inconveniences attending it with a serious and weighty concern of mind to do our duty by them is the best we can do. To seek a remedy by continuing the oppression because we have power to do it

and see others do it, will, I apprehend, not be doing as we would be done by.

How deeply soever men are involved in the most exquisite difficulties, sincerity of heart and upright walking before God, freely submitting to his providence, is the most sure remedy. He only is able to relieve not only persons but nations in their greatest calamities. David, in a great strait when the sense of his past error and the full expectation of an impending calamity as the reward of it were united to the aggravating his distress, after some deliberation saith, "Let me fall now into the hands of the Lord, for very great are his mercies; let me not fall into the hand of man." I Chron. 21:13.

To act continually with integrity of heart above all narrow or selfish motives is a sure token of our being partakers of that salvation which God hath appointed for walls and bulwarks (Is. 5:26; Rom. 15:8), and is, beyond all contradiction, a more happy situation than can ever be promised by the utmost reach of art and power united, not proceeding from heavenly wisdom.

A supply to nature's lawful wants, joined with a peaceful, humble mind, is the truest happiness in this life. And if here we arrive to this and remain to walk in the path of the just, our case will be truly happy. And though herein we may part with or miss of some glaring shows of riches and leave our children little else but wise instructions, a good example, and the knowledge of some honest employment, these, with the blessing of providence, are sufficient for their happiness, and are more likely to prove so than laying up treasures for them which are often rather a snare than any real benefit, especially to them who, instead of being exampled to temperance, are in all things taught to prefer the getting of riches and to eye the temporal distinctions they give as the principal business of this life. These readily overlook the true happiness of man as it results from the enjoyment of all things in the fear of God, and miserably substituting an inferior good, dangerous in the acquiring and uncertain in the fruition, they are subject to many disappointments; and every sweet carries its sting.

It is the conclusion of our blessed Lord and his apostles, as appears by their lives and doctrines, that the highest delights of sense or most pleasing objects visible ought ever to be accounted infinitely inferior to that real intellectual happiness suited to man in his primitive innocence and now to be found in true renovation of mind, and that the comforts of our present life, the things most grateful to us, ought always to be received with temperance and never made the chief objects of our desire, hope, or

---

7. A slightly altered version of this passage appears in Alexander Arscott, *Some Considerations Relating to the Present State of the Christian Religion, wherein the Nature, End, and Design of Christianity, as well as the Principle Evidence of the Truth of it, are Explained and Recommended out of the Holy Scriptures; with a General Appeal to the Experience of all Men for Confirmation thereof,* Part III (London, 1734).

love, but that our whole heart and affections be principally looking to that city "which hath foundations, whose maker and builder is God" [Heb. 11:10].

Did we so improve the gifts bestowed on us that our children might have an education suited to these doctrines, and our example to confirm it, we might rejoice in hopes of their being heirs of an inheritance incorruptible. This inheritance, as Christians, we esteem the most valuable; and how then can we fail to desire it for our children? Oh, that we were consistent with ourselves in pursuing means necessary to obtain it!

It appears by experience that where children are educated in fullness, ease, and idleness, evil habits are more prevalent than is common amongst such who are prudently employed in the necessary affairs of life. And if children are not only educated in the way of so great temptation, but have also the opportunity of lording it over their fellow creatures and being masters of men in their childhood, how can we hope otherwise than that their tender minds will be possessed with thoughts too high for them?—which by continuance, gaining strength, will prove like a slow current, gradually separating them from (or keeping from acquaintance with) that humility and meekness in which alone lasting happiness can be enjoyed. . . .

from THE JOURNAL OF JOHN WOOLMAN[1]

[Early Life and Vocation]

I have often felt a motion of love to leave some hints in writing of my experience of the goodness of God, and now, in the thirty-sixth year of my age, I begin this work. I was born in Northampton, in Burlington County in West Jersey, A.D. 1720, and before I was seven years old I began to be acquainted with the operations of divine love. Through the care of my parents, I was taught to read near as soon as I was capable of it, and as I went from school one Seventh Day,[2] I remember, while my companions went to play by the way, I went forward out of sight; and sitting down, I read the twenty-second chapter of the Revelations: "He showed me a river of water, clear as crystal, proceeding out of the throne of God and the Lamb, etc."[3] And in reading it my mind was drawn to seek after that pure habitation which I then believed God had prepared for His servants. The place where I sat and the sweetness that attended my mind remains fresh in my memory.

This and the like gracious visitations[4] had that effect upon me, that when boys used ill language it troubled me, and through the continued mercies of God I was preserved from it. The pious instructions of my parents were often fresh in my mind when I happened amongst wicked children, and was of use to me. My parents, having a large family of children, used frequently on First Days after meeting[5] to put to read in the Holy Scriptures or some religious books, one after another, the rest sitting by without much conversation, which I have since often thought was a good practice. From what I had read and heard, I believed there had been in past ages people who walked in uprightness before God in a degree exceeding any that I knew, or heard of, now living; and the apprehension of there being less steadiness and firmness amongst people in this age than in past ages often troubled me while I was a child.

I had a dream about the ninth year of my age as follows: I saw the moon rise near the west and run a regular course eastward, so swift that in about a quarter of an hour she reached our meridian, when there descended from her a small cloud on a direct line to the earth, which lighted on a pleasant green about twenty yards from the door of my father's house (in which I thought I stood) and was immediately turned into a beautiful green tree. The moon appeared to run on with equal swiftness and soon set in the east, at which time the sun arose at the place where it commonly does in the summer, and shining with full radiance in a serene air, it appeared as pleasant a morning as ever I saw.

---

1. Woolman's journal was first published in 1774; the text is from *The Journal and Major Essays of John Woolman,* ed. Phillips Moulton (1971).

2. Saturday. Quakers used numbers rather than names (which reflected pagan gods) to identify the calendrical days.

3. Revelation 21:1.

4. Moments when he felt God's presence.

5. Quaker worship took place at a "meeting," which was typically silent unless someone felt moved by God to speak.

All this time I stood still in the door in an awful[6] frame of mind, and I observed that as heat increased by the rising sun, it wrought so powerfully on the little green tree that the leaves gradually withered; and before noon it appeared dry and dead. There then appeared a being, small of size, full of strength and resolution, moving swift from the north, southward, called a sun worm.[7]

Another thing remarkable in my childhood was that once, going to a neighbor's house, I saw on the way a robin sitting on her nest; and as I came near she went off, but having young ones, flew about and with many cries expressed her concern for them. I stood and threw stones at her, till one striking her, she fell down dead. At first I was pleased with the exploit, but after a few minutes was seized with horror, as having in a sportive way killed an innocent creature while she was careful for her young. I beheld her lying dead and thought those young ones for which she was so careful must now perish for want of their dam to nourish them; and after some painful considerations on the subject, I climbed up the tree, took all the young birds and killed them, supposing that better than to leave them to pine away and die miserably, and believed in this case that Scripture proverb was fulfilled, "The tender mercies of the wicked are cruel."[8] I then went on my errand, but for some hours could think of little else but the cruelties I had committed, and was much troubled.

Thus He whose tender mercies are over all His works hath placed a principle in the human mind which incites to exercise goodness toward every living creature; and this being singly attended to, people become tenderhearted and sympathizing, but being frequently and totally rejected, the mind shuts itself up in a contrary disposition.

About the twelfth year of my age, my father being abroad, my mother reproved me for some misconduct, to which I made an undutiful reply; and the next First Day as I was with my father returning from meeting, he told me he understood I had behaved amiss to my mother and advised me to be more careful in future. I knew myself blameable, and in shame and confusion remained silent. Being thus awakened to a sense of my wickedness, I felt remorse in my mind, and getting home I retired and prayed to the Lord to forgive me, and do not remember that I ever after that spoke unhandsomely to either of my parents, however foolish in other things.

Having attained the age of sixteen years, I began to love wanton company, and though I was preserved from profane language or scandalous conduct, still I perceived a plant in me which produced much wild grapes. Yet my merciful Father forsook me not utterly, but at times through His grace I was brought seriously to consider my ways, and the sight of my backsliding affected me with sorrow. But for want of rightly attending to the reproofs of instruction, vanity was added to vanity, and repentance to repentance; upon the whole my mind was more and more alienated from the Truth, and I hastened toward destruction. While I meditate on the gulf toward which I travelled and reflect on my youthful disobedience, for these things I weep; mine eye runneth down with water.

Advancing in age the number of my acquaintance increased, and thereby my way grew more difficult. Though I had heretofore found comfort in reading the Holy Scriptures and thinking on heavenly things, I was now estranged therefrom. I knew I was going from the flock of Christ and had no resolution to return; hence serious reflections were uneasy to me and youthful vanities and diversions my greatest pleasure. Running in this road I found many like myself, and we associated in that which is reverse to true friendship.

But in this swift race it pleased God to visit me with sickness, so that I doubted of recovering. And then did darkness, horror, and amazement with full force seize me, even when my pain and distress of body was very great. I thought it would have been better for me never to have had a being than to see the day which I now saw. I was filled with confusion, and in great affliction both of mind and body I lay and bewailed myself. I had not confidence to lift up my cries to God, whom I had thus offended, but in a deep sense of my great folly I was humbled before Him, and at length that Word which is as a fire and a hammer broke and dissolved my rebellious heart. And then my cries were put up in contrition, and in the multitude of His mercies I found inward relief, and felt a close engagement that if He was pleased to restore my health, I might walk humbly before Him.

After my recovery this exercise[9] remained with me a considerable time; but by degrees giving way to youthful vanities, they gained strength, and getting with wanton

6. Full of awe.

7. He imagines this happening.

8. Proverbs 12:10.

9. Religious experience.

young people I lost ground. The Lord had been very gracious and spoke peace to me in the time of my distress, and I now most ungratefully turned again to folly, on which account at times I felt sharp reproof but did not get low enough to cry for help. I was not so hardy as to commit things scandalous, but to exceed in vanity and promote mirth was my chief study. Still I retained a love and esteem for pious people, and their company brought an awe upon me.

My dear parents several times admonished me in the fear of the Lord, and their admonition entered into my heart and had a good effect for a season, but not getting deep enough to pray rightly, the tempter when he came found entrance. I remember once, having spent a part of the day in wantonness, as I went to bed at night there lay in a window near my bed a Bible, which I opened, and first cast my eye on the text, "We lie down in our shame, and our confusion covers us."[10] This I knew to be my case, and meeting with so unexpected a reproof, I was somewhat affected with it and went to bed under remorse of conscience, which I soon cast off again.

Thus time passed on; my heart was replenished with mirth and wantonness, while pleasing scenes of vanity were presented to my imagination till I attained the age of eighteen years, near which time I felt the judgments of God in my soul like a consuming fire, and looking over my past life the prospect was moving. I was often sad and longed to be delivered from those vanities; then again my heart was strongly inclined to them, and there was in me a sore conflict. At times I turned to folly, and then again sorrow and confusion took hold of me. In a while I resolved totally to leave off some of my vanities, but there was a secret reserve in my heart of the more refined part of them, and I was not low enough to find true peace. Thus for some months I had great trouble, there remaining in me an unsubjected will which rendered my labours fruitless, till at length through the merciful continuance of heavenly visitations I was made to bow down in spirit before the Lord.

I remember one evening I had spent some time in reading a pious author, and walking out alone I humbly prayed to the Lord for His help, that I might be delivered from all those vanities which so ensnared me. Thus being brought low, He helped me; and as I learned to bear the cross I felt refreshment to come from His presence; but not keeping in that strength which gave victory, I lost ground

again, the sense of which greatly affected me; and I sought deserts and lonely places and there with tears did confess my sins to God and humbly craved help of Him. And I may say with reverence He was near to me in my troubles, and in those times of humiliation opened my ear to discipline.

I was now led to look seriously at the means by which I was drawn from the pure Truth, and learned this: that if I would live in the life which the faithful servants of God lived in, I must not go into company as heretofore in my own will, but all the cravings of sense must be governed by a divine principle. In times of sorrow and abasement these instructions were sealed upon me, and I felt the power of Christ prevail over selfish desires, so that I was preserved in a good degree of steadiness. And being young and believing at that time that a single life was best for me, I was strengthened to keep from such company as had often been a snare to me.

I kept steady to meetings, spent First Days after noon chiefly in reading the Scriptures and other good books, and was early convinced in my mind that true religion consisted in an inward life, wherein the heart doth love and reverence God the Creator and learn to exercise true justice and goodness, not only toward all men but also toward the brute creatures; that as the mind was moved on an inward principle to love God as an invisible, incomprehensible being, on the same principle it was moved to love Him in all His manifestations in the visible world; that as by His breath the flame of life was kindled in all animal and sensitive creatures, to say we love God as unseen and at the same time exercise cruelty toward the least creature moving by His life, or by life derived from Him, was a contradiction in itself.

I found no narrowness respecting sects and opinions, but believed that sincere, upright-hearted people in every Society who truly loved God were accepted of Him.

As I lived under the cross and simply followed the openings of Truth,[11] my mind from day to day was more enlightened; my former acquaintance was left to judge of me as they would, for I found it safest for me to live in private and keep these things sealed up in my own breast.

While I silently ponder on that change wrought in me, I find no language equal to it nor any means to convey to another a clear idea of it. I looked upon the works of God in this visible creation and an awfulness covered me; my heart was tender and often contrite, and a universal love

---

10. Jeremiah 3:25.

11. He awaited messages from God or "openings."

to my fellow creatures increased in me. This will be understood by such who have trodden in the same path. Some glances of real beauty may be seen in their faces who swell in true meekness. There is a harmony in the sound of that voice to which divine love gives utterance, and some appearance of right order in their temper and conduct whose passions are fully regulated. Yet all these do not fully show forth that inward life to such who have not felt it, but this white stone and new name is known rightly to such only who have it.[12]

Now though I had been thus strengthened to bear the cross, I still found myself in great danger, having many weaknesses attending me and strong temptations to wrestle with, in the feelings whereof I frequently withdrew into private places and often with tears besought the Lord to help me, whose gracious ear was open to my cry.

All this time I lived with my parents and wrought[13] on the plantation, and having had schooling pretty well for a planter, I used to improve in winter evenings and other leisure times. And being now in the twenty-first year of my age, a man in much business shopkeeping and baking asked me if I would hire with him to tend shop and keep books. I acquainted my father with the proposal, and after some deliberation it was agreed for me to go.

At home I had lived retired, and now having a prospect of being much in the way of company, I felt frequent and fervent cries in my heart to God, the Father of Mercies, that He would preserve me from all taint and corruption, that in this more public employ I might serve Him, my gracious Redeemer, in that humility and self-denial with which I had been in a small degree exercised in a very private life.

The man who employed me furnished a shop in Mount Holly, about five miles from my father's house and six from his own, and there I lived alone and tended his shop. Shortly after my settlement here I was visited by several young people, my former acquaintance, who knew not but vanities would be as agreeable to me now as ever; and at these times I cried to the Lord in secret for wisdom and strength, for I felt myself encompassed with difficulties and had fresh occasion to bewail the follies of time past in contracting a familiarity with a libertine people. And as I had now left my father's house outwardly, I found my Heavenly Father to be merciful to me beyond what I can express.

By day I was much amongst people and had many trials to go through, but in evenings I was mostly alone and may with thankfulness acknowledge that in those times the spirit of supplication was often poured upon me, under which I was frequently exercised and felt my strength renewed.

In a few months after I came here, my master bought several Scotch menservants from on board a vessel and brought them to Mount Holly to sell,[14] one of which was taken sick and died. The latter part of his sickness he, being delirious, used to curse and swear most sorrowfully, and after he was buried I was left to sleep alone the next night in the same chamber where he died. I perceived in me a timorousness. I knew, however, I had not injured the man but assisted in taking care of him according to my capacity, and was not free to ask anyone on that occasion to sleep with me. Nature was feeble, but every trial was a fresh incitement to give myself up wholly to the service of God, for I found no helper like Him in times of trouble.

After a while my former acquaintance gave over expecting me as one of their company, and I began to be known to some whose conversation was helpful to me. And now, I had experienced the love of God through Jesus Christ to redeem me from many pollutions and to be a succour to me through a sea of conflicts, with which no person was fully acquainted, and as my heart was often enlarged in this heavenly principle, I felt a tender compassion for the youth who remained entangled in snares like those which had entangled me. From one month to another this love and tenderness increased, and my mind was more strongly engaged for the good of my fellow creatures.

I went to meetings in an awful frame of mind and endeavoured to be inwardly acquainted with the language of the True Shepherd. And one day being under a strong exercise of spirit, I stood up and said some words in a meeting, but not keeping close to the divine opening, I said more than was required of me; and being soon sensible of my error, I was afflicted in mind some weeks without any light or comfort, even to that degree that I could take sat-

---

12. Compare with Revelation 2:17, "To him that overcometh will I give to eat of the hidden manna, and will I give him a white stone, and in the stone a new name written, which no man knoweth saving he that receiveth it."

13. Worked.

---

14. Woolman's employer had paid for the indentures of the Scottish men and then sought to resell them.

isfaction in nothing. I remembered God and was troubled, and in the depth of my distress He had pity upon me and sent the Comforter. I then felt forgiveness for my offense, and my mind became calm and quiet, being truly thankful to my gracious Redeemer for His mercies. And after this, feeling the spring of divine love opened and a concern to speak, I said a few words in a meeting, in which I found peace. This I believe was about six weeks from the first time, and as I was thus humbled and disciplined under the cross, my understanding became more strengthened to distinguish the language of the pure Spirit which inwardly moves upon the heart and taught [me] to wait in silence sometimes many weeks together, until I felt that rise which prepares the creature to stand like a trumpet through which the Lord speaks to His flock.

From an inward purifying, and steadfast abiding under it, springs a lively operative desire for the good of others. All faithful people are not called to the public ministry, but whoever are, are called to minister of that which they have tasted and handled spiritually. The outward modes of worship are various, but wherever men are true ministers of Jesus Christ it is from the operation of His spirit upon their hearts, first purifying them and thus giving them a feeling sense of the conditions of others. This truth was early fixed in my mind, and I was taught to watch the pure opening and to take heed lest while I was standing to speak, my own will should get uppermost and cause me to utter words from worldly wisdom and depart from the channel of the true gospel ministry.

In the management of my outward affairs I may say with thankfulness I found Truth to be my support, and I was respected in my master's family, who came to live in Mount Holly within two year after my going there.

About the twenty-third year of my age, I had many fresh and heavenly openings in respect to the care and providence of the Almighty over his creatures in general, and over man as the most noble amongst those which are visible. And being clearly convinced in my judgment that to place my whole trust in God was best for me, I felt renewed engagements that in all things I might act on an inward principle of virtue and pursue worldly business no further than as Truth opened my way therein.

About the time called Christmas I observed many people from the country and dwellers in town who, resorting to the public houses, spent their time in drinking and vain sports, tending to corrupt one another, on which account I was much troubled. At one house in particular there was much disorder, and I believed it was a duty laid on me to go and speak to the master of that house. I considered I was young and that several elderly Friends in town had opportunity to see these things, and though I would gladly have been excused, yet I could not feel my mind clear.

The exercise was heavy, and as I was reading what the Almighty said to Ezekiel[15] respecting his duty as a watchman, the matter was set home more clearly; and then with prayer and tears I besought the Lord for His assistance, who in lovingkindness gave me a resigned heart. Then at a suitable opportunity I went to the public house, and seeing the man amongst a company, I went to him and told him I wanted to speak with him; so we went aside, and there in the fear and the dread of the Almighty I expressed to him what rested on my mind, which he took kindly, and afterward showed more regard to me than before. In a few years after, he died middle-aged, and I often thought that had I neglected my duty in that case it would have given me great trouble, and I was humbly thankful to my gracious Father, who had supported me herein.

My employer, having a Negro woman, sold her and directed me to write a bill of sale, the man being waiting who bought her. The thing was sudden, and though the thoughts of writing an instrument of slavery for one of my fellow creatures felt uneasy, yet I remembered I was hired by the year, that it was my master who directed me to do it, and that it was an elderly man, a member of our Society, who bought her; so through weakness I gave way and wrote it, but at the executing it, I was so afflicted in my mind that I said before my master and the Friend that I believed slavekeeping to be a practice inconsistent with the Christian religion. This in some degree abated my uneasiness, yet as often as I reflected seriously upon it I thought I should have been clearer if I had desired to be excused from it as a thing against my conscience, for such it was. And some time after this a young man of our Society spake to me to write an instrument of slavery, he having lately taken a Negro into his house. I told him I was not easy to write it, for though many kept slaves in our Society, as in others, I still believed the practice was not right, and desired to be excused from writing [it]. I spoke to him in good will, and he told me that keeping slaves was not altogether agreeable to his mind, but that the slave being a gift made to his wife, he had accepted of her. . . .

---

15. The priest and prophet Ezekial delivered warnings from God to the Israelites. Ezekial 3:17.

[Travels through North Carolina]

About this time believing it good for me to settle, and thinking seriously about a companion, my heart was turned to the Lord with desires that He would give me wisdom to proceed therein agreeable to His will; and He was pleased to give me a well-inclined damsel, Sarah Ellis, to whom I was married the 18th day, 8th month, 1749.[16]

In the fall of the year 1750 died my father Samuel Woolman with a fever, aged about sixty years.[17] In his lifetime he manifested much care for us his children, that in our youth we might learn to fear the Lord, often endeavouring to imprint in our minds the true principles of virtue, and particularly to cherish in us a spirit of tenderness, not only toward poor people, but also towards all creatures of which we had the command.

After my return from Carolina I made some observations on keeping slaves, which I had some time before showed him, and he perused the manuscript, proposed a few alterations, and appeared well satisfied that I found a concern on that account. And in his last sickness as I was watching with him one night, he being so far spent that there was no expectation of his recovery, but had the perfect use of his understanding, he asked me concerning the manuscript, whether I expected soon to offer it to the Overseers of the Press, and after some conversation thereon said, "I have all along been deeply affected with the oppression of the poor Negroes, and now at last my concern for them is as great as ever."[18]

By his direction I had wrote his will in a time of health, and that night he desired me to read it to him, which I did, and he said it was agreeable to his mind. He then made mention of his end, which he believed was now near, and signified that though he was sensible of many imperfections in the course of his life, yet his experience of the power of Truth and of the love and goodness of God from time to time, even till now, was such that he had no doubt but that in leaving this life he should enter into one more happy.

The next day his sister Elizabeth came to see him and told him of the decease of their sister Anne, who died a few days before. He then said, "I reckon sister Anne was free to leave this world." Elizabeth said she was. He then said, "I also am free to leave it," and being in great weakness of body said, "I hope I shall shortly go to rest." He continued in a weighty frame of mind and was sensible till near the last.

2nd day, 9th month, 1751. Feeling drawings in my mind to visit Friends at the Great Meadows, in the upper part of West Jersey, with the unity of our Monthly Meeting I went there and had some searching laborious exercise amongst Friends in those parts, and found inward peace therein.

In the 9th month, 1753, in company with my well-esteemed friend John Sykes,[19] and with unity of Friends, we traveled about two weeks visiting Friends in Bucks County.[20] We laboured in the love of the gospel according to the measure received, and through the mercies of Him who is strength to the poor who trust in Him, we found satisfaction in our visit. And in the next winter, way opening to visit Friends' families within the compass of our Monthly Meeting, partly by the labors of two friends from Pennsylvania, I joined some in it, having had a desire some time that it might go forward amongst us.

About this time a person at some distance lying sick, his brother came to me to write his will. I knew he had slaves, and asking his brother, was told he intended to leave them slaves to his children. As writing is a profitable employ, as offending sober people is disagreeable to my inclination, I was straitened in my mind; but as I looked to the Lord, He inclined my heart to His testimony, and I told the man that I believed the practice of continuing slavery to this people was not right and had a scruple in mind against doing writings of that kind: that though many in our Society kept them as slaves, still I was not easy to be concerned in it and desired to be excused from going to write the will. I spake to him in the fear of the Lord, and he made no reply to what I said, but went away; he also had some concerns in the practice, and I thought he was displeased with me.

In this case I had a fresh confirmation that acting contrary to present outward interest from a motive of divine love and in regard to truth and righteousness, and thereby

---

16. Sarah Ellis (1721–87), a childhood friend of Woolman.

17. Samuel Woolman (1690–1750) had lived on a farm in Burlington County, New Jersey.

18. Woolman published *Some Considerations on the Keeping of Negroes* in 1754.

---

19. John Sykes (1682–1771), a Quaker missionary who often traveled with Woolman.

20. Pennsylvania.

incurring the resentments of people, opens the way to a treasure better than silver and to a friendship exceeding the friendship of men.

On the 7th day, 2nd month, 1754, at night, I dreamed that I was walking in an orchard, it appeared to be about the middle of the afternoon; when on a sudden I saw two lights in the east resembling two suns, but of a dull and gloomy aspect. The one appeared about the height of the sun at three hours high, and the other more northward and one-third lower. In a few minutes the air in the east appeared to be mingled with fire, and like a terrible storm coming westward the streams of fire reached the orchard where I stood, but I felt no harm. I then found one of my acquaintance standing near me, who was greatly distressed in mind at this unusual appearance. My mind felt calm, and I said to my friend, "We must all once die, and if it please the Lord that our death be in this way, it is good for us to be resigned." Then I walked to a house hard by, and going upstairs, saw people with sad and troubled aspects, amongst whom I passed into another room where the floor was only some loose boards. There I sat down alone by a window, and looking out I saw in the south three great red streams standing at equal distance from each other, the bottom of which appeared to stand on the earth and the top to reach above the region of the clouds. Across those three streams went less ones, and from each end of such small stream others extended in regular lines to the earth, all red and appeared to extend through the whole southern firmament. There then appeared on a green plain a great multitude of men in a military posture, some of whom I knew. They came near the house, and passing on westward some of them, looking up at me, expressed themselves in a scoffing, taunting way, to which I made no reply; soon after, an old captain of the militia came to me, and I was told these men were assembled to improve in the discipline of war. . . .

Until the year 1756 I continued to retail goods, besides following my trade as a tailor, about which time I grew uneasy on account of my business growing too cumbersome. I began with selling trimmings for garments and from thence proceeded to sell clothes and linens, and at length having got a considerable shop of goods, my trade increased every year and the road to large business appeared open; but I felt a stop in my mind.

Through the mercies of the Almighty I had in a good degree learned to be content with a plain way of living. I had but a small family, that on serious consideration I believed Truth did not require me to engage in much cumbrous affairs. It had been my general practice to buy and sell things really useful. Things that served chiefly to please the vain mind in people I was not easy to trade in, seldom did it, and whenever I did I found it weaken me as a Christian.

The increase of business became my burden, for though my natural inclination was toward merchandise, yet I believed Truth required me to live more free from outward cumbers and there was now a strife in my mind between the two; and in this exercise my prayers were put up to the Lord, who graciously heard me and gave me a heart resigned to His holy will. Then I lessened my outward business, and as I had opportunity told my customers of my intentions that they might consider what shop to turn to, and so in a while wholly laid down merchandise, following my trade as a tailor, myself only, having no apprentice. I also had a nursery of apple trees, in which I employed some of my time—hoeing, grafting, trimming, and inoculating.

In merchandise it is the custom where I lived to sell chiefly on credit, and poor people often get in debt, and when payment is expected, not having wherewith to pay, their creditors often sue for it at law. Having often observed occurrences of this kind, I found it good for me to advise poor people to take such goods as were most useful and not costly.

In the time of trading, I had an opportunity of seeing that too liberal a use of spirituous liquors and the custom of wearing too costly apparel lead some people into great inconveniences, and these two things appear to be often connected one with the other. For by not attending to that use of things which is consistent with universal righteousness, there is an increase of labor which extends beyond what our Heavenly Father intends for us. And by great labor, and often by much sweating in the heat, there is even amongst such who are not drunkards a craving of some liquors to revive the spirits: that partly by the wanton, luxurious drinking of some, and partly by the drinkings of others led to it through immoderate labor, very great quantities of rum are every year expended in our colonies, the greater part of which we should have no need did we steadily attend to pure wisdom.

Where men take pleasure in feeling their minds elevated with strong drink and so indulge their appetite as to disorder their understandings, neglect their duty as members in a family or civil society, and cast off all pretense to religion, their case is much to be pitied. And where such whose lives are for the most part regular, and whose examples have a strong influence on the minds of others, adhere to some customs which strongly draw toward the use of more strong liquor than pure wisdom directs to the use of, this also, as it hinders the spreading of the spirit of meekness and strengthens the hands of the more excessive drinkers, is a case to be lamented.

As the least degree of luxury hath some connection with evil, for those who profess to be disciples of Christ and are looked upon as leaders of the people, to have that mind in them which was also in Him, and so stand separate from every wrong way, is a means of help to the weaker. As I have sometimes been much spent in the heat and taken spirits to revive me, I have found by experience that in such circumstance the mind is not so calm nor so fitly disposed for divine meditation as when all such extremes are avoided, and have felt an increasing care to attend to that Holy Spirit which sets right bounds to our desires and leads those who faithfully follow it to apply all the gifts of divine providence to the purposes for which they were intended. Did such who have the care of great estates attend with singleness of heart to this Heavenly Instructor, which so opens and enlarges the mind that men love their neighbors as themselves, they would have wisdom given them to manage without finding occasion to employ some people in the luxuries of life or to make it necessary for others to labor too hard. But for want of steadily regarding this principle of divine love, a selfish spirit takes place in the minds of people, which is attended with darkness and manifold confusions in the world. . . .

When I was at Newbegun Creek,[21] a Friend was there who labored for his living, having no Negroes, and had been a minister many years. He came to me the next day, and as we rode together he signified that he wanted to talk with me concerning a difficulty he had been under, and related it near as follows, to wit: That as monies had of late years been raised by a tax to carry on the wars, he had a scruple in his mind in regard to paying it and chose rather to suffer distraint of goods than pay it. And as he was the only person who refused it in them parts and knew not that anyone else was in the like circumstance, he signified that it had been a heavy trial upon him, and the more so for that some of his brethren had been uneasy with his conduct in that case, and added that from a sympathy he felt with me yesterday in meeting, he found a freedom thus to open the matter in the way of querying concerning Friends in our parts; whereupon I told him the state of Friends amongst us as well as I was able, and also that I had for some time been under the like scruple. I believed him to be one who was concerned to walk uprightly before the Lord and esteemed it my duty to preserve this memorandum.

From hence I went back into Virginia and had a meeting near James Copeland's; it was a time of inward suffering, but through the goodness of the Lord I was made content. Then to another meeting where through the renewings of pure love we had a very comfortable meeting.

Traveling up and down of late, I have renewed evidences that to be faithful to the Lord and content with his will concerning me is a most necessary and useful lesson for me to be learning, looking less at the effects of my labor than at the pure motion and reality of the concern as it arises from heavenly love. In the Lord Jehovah is everlasting strength, and as the mind by a humble resignation is united to Him and we utter words from an inward knowledge that they arise from the heavenly spring, though our way may be difficult and require close attention to keep in it, and though the manner in which we may be led may tend to our own abasement, yet if we continue in patience and meekness, heavenly peace is the reward of our labors.

From hence I went to Curles Meeting, which, though small, was reviving to the honest-hearted. Thence to Black Creek and Caroline Meetings, from whence, accompanied by William Stanley[22] before-mentioned, we rode to Goose Creek, being much through the woods and about one hundred miles. We lodged the first night at a public house, the second in the woods, and the next day we reached a Friend's house at Goose Creek. In the woods we lay under some disadvantage, having no fireworks, nor bells for our horses, but we stopped some before night and let them feed on wild grass, which was plenty, we the meantime cutting with our knives a store against night, and then tied them; and gathering some bushes under an oak we lay down, but the mosquitoes being plenty and the ground damp, I slept but little.

Thus lying in the wilderness and looking at the stars, I was led to contemplate the condition of our first parents when they were sent forth from the garden, and consid-

---

21. North Carolina.

22. William Stanley (1729–1807) from Cedar Creek, Virginia.

ered that they had no house, no tools for business, no garments but what their Creator gave them, no vessels for use, nor any fire to cook roots or herbs. But the Almighty, though they had been disobedient, was a father to them; way opened in process of time for all the conveniences of life. And He who by the gracious influence of His spirit illuminated their understand and showed them what was acceptable to Him and tended to their felicity as intelligent creatures, did also provide means for their happy living in this world as they attended to the manifestations of His wisdom. . . .

CADWALLADER COLDEN (1688–1776)

Over the course of more than fifty years, Cadwallader Colden became a prominent leader in Britain's New York colony. While holding high office, under royal appointments, Colden wrote a significant amount of material in several fields, including imperial political relations, botany, medicine, mathematics, physics, moral philosophy, and history. In his own day, Colden's political and scientific writings, along with his *History of the Five Indian Nations Depending on the Province of New York* (published first in 1727 and then significantly revised and enlarged for publication in 1747), all contributed to his gaining wide renown as a learned expert in politics, Indian relations, and science.

Cadwallader Colden was born in Scotland into a Presbyterian minister's family. He grew up in Berwickshire and was educated for church ministry. After graduating from the University at Edinburgh, Colden determined against becoming a minister and traveled instead to London, where he spent the next five years studying medicine. In 1710 he emigrated to North America, like many young Scottish professionals. He settled first in Philadelphia, practicing medicine and engaging in commercial activity. In 1718, on a visit to New York, Colden met the state's governor, Robert Hunter, who, evidently impressed with Colden's abilities, found offices for him in New York. Colden moved to New York in 1720 and shortly thereafter became the most trusted adviser of the new royal governor, William Burnet, who found him a position on the provincial council in 1721. Over the years, Colden was to serve the prestigious roles of surveyor-general (thirty years), provincial councilor (forty years), and lieutenant-governor (his last fifteen years). During this time, Colden conducted a scientific career that gained him transatlantic respect as a botanist and mathematician.

His early years as surveyor-general brought him into contact with the Iroquois peoples, a loose confederation of (at that time) five separate peoples—the Mohawks, Oneidas, Onandagas, Cayugas, and Senecas (as they were situated in their ancestral places in the New York area, east to west). Because Colden was situated near New York City and because he was taking part in political affairs in the eastern part of the state (which involved an understanding of Dutch and French relations with the trading centers at Albany), he knew best the Mohawk peoples along the waterways to the eastern part of present-day New York. During the 1720s, as he was writing his *History of the Five Indian Nations,* Colden came to understand well the poor relations the British had with the Indian peoples in their midst and how, comparatively speaking, the British were undermining their own imperial efforts in the area by neglecting to cement relationships with the Iroquois and especially the Mohawks, who conceived of themselves (as they continue to do today) as keepers of the eastern gate of Iroquoia. Colden pointed out in his *History* that previous writing on the Iroquois peoples had been dominated by the French, who were often engaged in outright hostilities against the Iroquois and the British and who thus portrayed the Iroquois in an unfair light. In the 1727 edition of the *History,* Colden described the first European contacts with the Iroquois, up to 1688. In an expanded 1747 edition, he added a description of events that took place in the area up to the year 1697.

Colden's *History* established themes that continued to be important in British writings about Indian peoples. He explained his understanding of the Iroquois culture by employing "noble savage" tropes that were typical in his day but not typically associated with these New York area peoples. Thus Colden's *His-*

tory stressed the Iroquois' nobility, courage, and potential for loyalty. Colden took great care to reproduce speeches by Iroquois leaders. His goals were to strengthen his claim that the Iroquois represented a model of what ancient Greek and Roman civilization and oratory must have been like, but his *History* reveals for readers today a much richer picture than this, for in his records of the oral agreements made between the Iroquois and the British are useful reminders of mutual negotiations taking place between Indian peoples and British and European settlers in the region.

from THE HISTORY OF THE FIVE INDIAN NATIONS[1]

To His Excellency WILLIAM BURNET, Esq;
Captain General and Governor in Chief of the
Provinces of New-York, New-Jersey, and
Territories thereone depending, in America, and
Vice-Admiral of the same, etc.

Sir;
The Indian Affairs of this Province have appear'd to your Excellency of such Importance to the Welfare of the People here, that you have carefully apply'd your Thoughts to them, in which I hope your Excellency will have such Success, that not only the present Generation shall enjoy the Benefit of your Care, but our latest Posterity likewise may bless your Memory under their Happiness, the Foundation of which may be laid under your Excellency's Administration, if the People here, who's Interest is chiefly concern'd, do on their parts second your Endeavours, as their Duty requires, towards securing the Peace and advancing the Prosperity of their Country.

The following Account of the Five Nations will show what Dangerous Neighbours the Indians have been, what Pains a Neighbouring Colony (who's Interest is Opposit to ours) has taken to withdraw their Affections from Us, and how dreadful the Consequences may be, if that Colony should succeed in their Designs: and therefore how much we ought to be on our Guard. If we only consider the Riches which a People, who have under no apprehensions from the Indians themselves) it may be thought imprudent in Us to suffer such People to grow Rich and Powerful, while it is in our Power to prevent it,

with much less Charge and Trouble than it is in theirs to accomplish their designs.

These Considerations are sufficient to make the Indian Affairs deserve the most serious Thoughts of the Governor of New-York. But I know your Excellency's Views are not confin'd to the Interest of your own Country only.

The Five Nations are a poor Barbarous People, under the darkest Ignorance, and yet a bright and noble Genius shines thro' these black Clouds. None of the greatest Contempt to Death than these Barbarians have done, when Life and Liberty came in Competition: Indeed, I think our Indians have out-done the Romans in this particular; for some of the greatest Romans have Murder'd themselves to avoid Shame or Torments,[2] Whereas our Indians have refused to Dye meanly with the least Pain, when they thought their Country's Honour would be at stake, by it, but gave their Bodies willingly up to the most cruel Torments of their Enemies, to shew, that the Five Nations consisted to Men whose Courage and Resolution could not be shaken. They sully, however, these noble Vertues by that cruel Passion Revenge, which they think not only lawful, but Honourable to exert without Mercy on their Country's Enemies, and for this only they deserve the Name of Barbarians.

But what have we Christians done to make them better? Alas! we have reason to be ashamed, that these Infidels, by our Conversation and Neighborhood, are become worse than they were before they knew us. Instead of Vertues we have only taught them Vices, that they were entirely free of before that time. The narrow Views of private Interest have occasioned this, and will occasion greater, even Publick Mischiefs, if the Governors of the People do not, like true Patriots, exert themselves, and put a stop to these growing Evils. If these Practices be winked at instead of faithful Friends that have Manfully fought

---

1. Colden addressed his *History of the Five Indian Nations Depending on the Province of New York* (1727) to the new royal governor, William Burnet, the son of the famous bishop and historian Gilbert Burnet, who had befriended him. The text is from the expanded *History* published in 1747.

2. "This will appear by several Instances in the second Part of this History." [Au.]

our Battles for us, the Five Nations will become faithless Thieves and Robbers, and joyn with every Enemy that can give them the hopes of Plunder.

If care were taken to plant in them, and cultivate that general Benevolence to Mankind, which is the true Principle of Vertue, it would effectually eradicate those horrid Vices occasioned by their Unbounded Revenge; and then the Five Nations would no longer deserve the name of Barbarians, but would become a People whose Friendship might add Honour to the British Nation, tho' they be now too generally despised.

The Greeks & Romans, once as much Barbarians as our Indians now are, deified the Hero's that first taught them the Vertues, from whence the Grandeur of those Renowned Nations wholly proceeded; but a good Man will feel more real Satisfaction and Pleasure from the Sense of having any way forwarded the Civilizing of Barbarous Nations, or of having Multiplied the Number of good Men, than from the fondest hopes of such extravagant Honour.

These Considerations, I believe, would make your Excellency think a good History of the Five Nations worthy of your Patronage. As to this, I only hope, that you will look on my offering the following Account, however meanly perform'd, to proceed from the Desire I have of making some Publick Profession of that Gratitude, which is so much the Duty of

SIR,
Your Most Obliged
And Most Obedient
Humble Servant,
Cadwallader Colden.

The Preface

Though every one that is in the least acquainted with the Affairs of North-America, knows of what Consequence the Indians, commonly known to the people of New-York by the Name of the Five Nations, are both in Peace and War, I know of no Accounts of them Published in English, but what are meer Translations of French Authors. This seems to throw some Reflection on the Inhabitants of this Province, as if we wanted Curiosity to enquire into our own Affairs, and that we were willing to rest satisfied with the Accounts the French give us of our own Indians, notwithstanding that the French in Canada are always in a different Interest, and sometimes in open Hostility with us. This Consideration, I hope, will justify my attempting to write an History of the Five Nations at this time; and my endeavouring to remove that Blame with which we

may be charged, perhaps will attone for many Faults which the want of Capacity may have occasioned.

Having had the Perusal of the Minutes of the Commissioners for Indian Affairs, I have been enabled to collect many Materials for this History, which are not to be found any where else: And this Collection will, at least, be useful to any Person of more Capacity, who shall afterwards undertake this Task. When a History of these Nations shall be well wrote, it will be of great use to all the British Colonies in North-America; for it may enable them to learn Experience at the Expence of others; and if I can contribute anything to so good a Purpose, I shall not think my Labour lost.

It will be necessary to Excuse two things in the following Performance, which, I am afraid, will be found fault with by those that are the best Judges. The First is, My filling up so great part of the Work with the Adventures of small Parties, and sometimes with those of one single Man. The Second is, The inserting so many Speeches at length. I must confess, that I have done both these designedly.

As to the First, The History of Indians would be very lame without an Account of these Private Adventures; for their War-like Expeditions are almost always carried on by Surprizing each other, and their whole Art of War consists in managing small Parties. The whole Country being one continued Forrest, gives great Advantages to these Sculking Parties, and has obliged the Christians to imitate the Indians in this Method of making War. I believ'd likewise, that some would be curious to know the Manners and Customs of the Indians, in their Publick Treaties especially, who could not be satisfied without taking Notice of several minute Circumstances, and some things otherwise of no Consequence. We are fond of searching into Remote Antiquity, to know the Manners of our Earliest Progenitors: if I be not mistaken, the Indians are living Images of them.

My Design in the Second was, That thereby the Genius of the Indians might better appear. An Historian may paint Mens Actions in lively Colours, or in faint Shades, as he likes best, and in both cases preserve a perfect Likeness: But it will be a difficult Task to show the Wit, and Judgment, and Art, and Simplicity, and Ignorance of the several Parties, managing a Treaty, in other Words than their own. As to my part, I thought myself uncapable of doing it, without depriving the judicious Observer of the Opportunity of discovering much of the Indian Genius, by my Contracting or Paraphrasing their Harrangues, and without committing often gross Mistakes. For, on these Occasions, a skilful Manager often talks Confusedly and

Obscurely with design; which if an Historian should endeavour to amend, the Reader would receive the History in a false Light.

The Reader will find a great Difference between some of the Speeches made at Albany, and those taken from the French Authors. The first are genuine, and truly related, as delivered by the Sworn Interpreters, and where Truth only is required; a rough Stile with it, is preferable to Eloquence without it. But I must own, that I suspect our Interpreters may not have done Justice to the Indian Eloquence. For, the Indians having but few words, and few complex ideas, use many Metaphors in their Discourse, which interpreted by an hesitating Tongue, may appear mean, and strike our Imagination faintly, but under the Pen of a skilful Interpreter may strongly move our Passions by their lively Images. I have heard an old Indian Sachem speak with much Vivacity and Elocution, so that the Speaker pleas'd and moved the Auditors with the manner of delivering his Discourse; which, however, as it came from the Interpreter, disappointed us in our Expectations. After the Speaker had employ'd a considerable time in Haranguing with much Elocution, the Interpreter often explained the whole by one single Sentence. I believe the Speaker in that time imbellished and coloured his Figures, that they might have their full force on the Imagination, while the Interpreter contented himself with the Sense, in as few words as it could be exprest.

He that first writes the History of Matters which are not generally known, ought to avoid, as much as possible, to make the Evidence of the Truth depend entirely on his own Veracity and Judgment: For this reason I have often related several Transactions in the Words of the Registers. When this is once done, he that shall write afterwards need not act with so much Caution.

The History of Indians well wrote, would give an agreeable Amusement to many, every one might find something therein suited to his own Pallat; but even then, every Line would not please every Man; on the contrary, one will praise what another condemns, and one desires to know what another thinks not worth the Trouble of Reading: And therefore, I think, it is better to run the Risque of being sometimes Tedious, than to omit anything that may be Useful.

I have sometimes thought that the Histories wrote with all the Delicacy of a fine Romance, are like French Dishes, more agreeable to the Pallat than the Stomach, and less wholsom than more common and courser Dyet.

An Historian's Views must be various and extensive, and the History of different People and different Ages, requires different Rules, and often different Abilities to write it: I hope, therefore, the Reader will receive this first Attempt of the kind, in this Country, with more than usually Favourable Allowances.

The Inhabitants of New-York have been much more concern'd in the Transactions which followed the year 1688, than in those which preceeded that year. As it requires uncommon Courage and Resolution to engage willingly in the Wars of Cruel and Barbarous Enemies; I should be sorry to forget any that may deserve to be remembred by their Country with gratitude. The First Part of this History going abroad by it self, may give those that have any Memoirs of their Friends who have distinguished themselves, an opportunity of Communicating them, and may thereby enable the Writer hereof to do some Justice to their Merit.

They likewise that are better acquainted with the Indian Affairs may, perhaps, find some Mistakes in what is now Published, and may know some things which I know not, if they will be so kind as to Communicate them, I shall gladly Amend and Insert them in what is to follow.

C.C.

A Short View of the Form of Government of the Five Nations

It is necessary to know something of the Form of Government of the People whose History one reads. A few words will serve to give the Reader a general Notion of that of the Five Nations, because it still remains under Original Simplicity, free from those complicated Contrivances which have become necessary to those Nations where Deceit and Cunning have increased as much as their Knowledge and Wisdom.

The Five Nations (as their Name denotes) consist of so many Tribes or Nations joyn'd together by a League or Confederacy, like the United Provinces, without any Superiority of any one over the other. This Union has continued so long that the Christians know nothing of the Original of it.

They are known to the English under the Names of Mohawks, Oneydoes, Onnondagas, Cayugas and Sennekas;[3] but it is probable that this Union at first consisted only of three Nations, *viz.* the Mohawks, Onnondagas and Sennekas, and that the Oneydoes and Cayugas were af-

---

3. That is, Mohawks, Oneidas, Onandagas, Cayugas, and Senecas. Colden employs the typical English name for these peoples, more frequently then, as now, called the Iroquois (but who today often call themselves the Haudenosaunee peoples).

terwards adopted or received into this League; for the Oneydoes acknowledge the Mohawks to be their Fathers, as the Cayugas do the Sennekas to be theirs.

Each of the Nations are distinguished into 3 Tribes or Families, who distinguish themselves by three different sorts of Arms or Ensigns, *viz.* the Tortoise, the Bear & the Wolfe. The Sachems of these Families, when they sign any Publick Papers, put the Mark or Ensign of their Family to it.

Each Nation is an absolute Republick by its self, govern'd in all Publick Affairs of War and Peace by the Sachems or Old Men, whose Authority and Power is gain'd by and consists wholly in the Opinion the rest of the Nation have of their Wisdom and Integrity. They never execute their Resolutions by Compulsion or Force upon any of their People. Honour and Esteem are their Principal Rewards, as Shame & being Despised are their Punishments. They have certain Customs which they observe in their Publick Affairs with other Nations, and in their Private Affairs among themselves, which it is scandalous for any one not to observe, and draw after them publick or private Resentment when they are broke.

Their Generals and Captains obtain their Authority likewise by the general Opinion of their Courage and Conduct, and loose it by a Failure in those Vertues.

Their Great Men, both Sachems and Captains, are generally poorer than the common People, for they affect to give away and distribute all the Presents or Plunder they get in their Treaties or War, so as to leave nothing to themselves. If they should once be suspected of Selfishness, they would grow mean in the opinion of their Countrymen, and would consequently loose their Authority.

Their Affairs of Great Consequence, which concern all the Nations, are Transacted in a General Meeting of the Sachems of every Nation. These Conventions are generally held at Onnondaga, which is nearly in the Center of all the Five Nations. But they have fixed upon Albany to be the Place for their Solemn Treaties with the English Colonies.

The Tuscaroras, since the War they had with the People of Carolina, fled to the Five Nations, and are now incorporated with them,[4] so that they now properly consist of Six Nations (tho' they still retain the old Name among the English.) The Tuscaroras, since they came under the Government of New-York, behave themselves well, and remain peaceable and quiet. By which may be seen the advantage of using the Indians well; and, I believe, if they were still better used, (as there is room enough to do it) the Indians would be proportionably more Useful to us.

As I am fond to think, that the present state of the Indian Nations exactly shows the most Ancient and Original Condition of almost every Nation; so I believe, here we may with more certainty see the Original Form of all Government, than in the most curious Speculations of the Learned; and that the Patriarchal, and other Schemes in Politicks are no better than Hypotheses in Philosophy, and as prejudicial to real Knowledge.

I shall only add the Character which Mons. De la Poterie[5] gives of the Five Nations in his History of North-America, *viz.*

"When one talks (says he) of the Five Nations in France, they are thought, by a common Mistake, to be meer Barbarians, always thirsting after Human Blood; but their true Character is very different: They are the Fiercest and most Formidable People in North America, and at the same time as Politick and Judicious as well can be conceiv'd. This appears from their Management of the Affairs which they Transact, not only with the French and English, but likewise with almost all the Indian Nations of this vast Continent." . . .

---

4. The Tuscaroras joined the Iroquois confederation, as Colden reports, largely because they had ancestral roots to the Iroquoian peoples. The Tuscaroras' territory in the Carolinas was being invaded by British and European settlers at the time they recombined with the Iroquois to the north.

5. Claude-Charles Le Roy de Bacqueville de La Potherie, *Histoire de l'Amérique Septentrionale,* 4 vols. (Paris, 1722).

NEW ENGLAND
COTTON MATHER (1663–1728)

Among the most prolific writers of early New England, Cotton Mather was born into two of the most learned and influential colonial families. Both his grandfathers, John Cotton and Richard Mather, had been important religious leaders in the earliest days of New England. Cotton Mather's father, Increase Mather, was pastor of the Old North Church, president of Harvard College, and a central force in colony politics. As a young man, Cotton Mather showed promise of following in the footsteps of his father and grandfathers. Considered a prodigy, he graduated from Harvard at the age of sixteen and was ordained pastor of the Old North Church at the age of twenty-two. He held that prestigious position for the rest of his life, over four decades.

Cotton Mather never became the major political force that his family expected him to be. In 1692, he supported the Salem witch trials, out of concern that the Devil was among the congregations of New England. His actions at that time became a source of later embarrassment, but Mather never went as far as his colleague and friend, Samuel Sewall, in publicly renouncing his own behaviors. As a writer and scientist, Mather was most accomplished. During his lifetime, he published over four hundred pamphlets and books. Mather's *Wonders of the Invisible World* (1692) described the witchcraft trials and has remained an important source of information on what may be considered the low point of Puritan rationality. On the other hand, Mather's substantial scientific writings earned him election to the elite Royal Society in 1713. Mather's notable scientific writings included *Curiosa Americana* (1712–24), a study of natural phenomena in the Americas, and *The Christian Philosopher* (1721), primarily a work linking theology to naturalism. As part of his lifelong interest in medicine, Mather advocated inoculation against smallpox and suffered much criticism for doing so from a populace who were worried about being forced into undergoing what they conceived as deadly medical practices by the ruling elite in their community. The issue was so controversial that when Mather inoculated his own son, a bomb was thrown through his window.

Mather wrote religious and social works, such as *The Negro Christianized* (1706) and *India Christiana* (1721), in which he advocated missionary work among African slaves and Native Americans. He wrote biographies and essays to inspire virtuous action. Mather's longest and most admired work, *Magnalia Christi Americana: or, the Ecclesiastical History of New England* (1702), presented the life stories of prominent New Englanders. His *Bonifacius or Essays to Do Good* (1710) described the work of reforming societies. In his own day, despite his early conservatism reflected in his Christian fanaticism over the witch trials, Mather was a significant force of social and scientific reform, even if his attitudes about slavery did not lend themselves to what readers today consider the moral rectitude of liberation theology.

Selecting the works to present from such a prolific writer is a difficult task. The following texts represent Mather's concern for good social and moral order, an order centered in Mather's understanding of the dominant status of British American Christians in New England. As a group, these biographies told New England's history; each biography also presented a life that was meant to be exemplary for the reader, including an early Christian conversion experience and a religious deathbed scene. The biographies in *Magnalia Christi Americana* offer Mather's understanding of the mission of founding a New Canaan in the North American wilderness, and thus his life of William Bradford, the leader of the Plymouth Colony, signals Mather's understanding of the importance of the Separatist endeavor to found a colony in New England. Mather's *The Negro Christianized* argued not for freedom for slaves, as readers today might have hoped, but for Christian education for them.

from MAGNALIA CHRISTI AMERICANA[1]

Galeacius Secundus:[2] The Life of William Bradford, Esq., Governor of Plymouth Colony

Omnium Somnos illius vigilantia defendit; omnium otium, illius Labor; omnium Delicias, illius Industria; omnium vacationem, illius occupatio.[3]

It has been a matter of some observation, that although Yorkshire be one of the largest shires in England; yet for all the fires of martyrdom which were kindled in the days of Queen Mary,[4] it afforded no more fuel than one poor leaf; namely, John Leaf, an apprentice, who suffered for the doctrine of the Reformation at the same time and stake with the famous John Bradford.[5] But when the reign of Queen Elizabeth[6] would not admit the reformation of worship to proceed unto those degrees, which were proposed and pursued by no small number of the faithful in those days, Yorkshire was not the least of the shires in England that afforded suffering witnesses thereunto. The churches there gathered were quickly molested with such a raging persecution, that if the spirit of separation in them did carry them unto a further extreme than it should have done, one blamable cause thereof will be found in the extremity of that persecution. Their troubles made that cold country too hot for them, so that they were under a necessity to seek a retreat in the Low Countries;[7] and yet the watchful malice and fury of their adversaries rendered it almost impossible for them to find what they sought. For them to leave their native soil, their lands and their friends, and go into a strange place, where they must hear foreign language, and live meanly and hardly, and in other employments than that of husbandry, wherein they had been educated, these must needs have been such discouragements as could have been conquered by none, save those who sought first the kingdom of God, and the righteousness thereof. But that which would have made these discouragements the more unconquerable unto an ordinary faith, was the terrible zeal of their enemies to guard all ports, and search all ships, that none of them should be carried off. I will not relate the sad things of this kind then seen and felt by this people of God; but only exemplify those trials with one short story. Divers of these people having hired a Dutchman, then lying at Hull, to carry them over to Holland, he promised faithfully to take them in, between Grimsby and Hull; but they coming to the place a day or two too soon, the appearance of such a multitude alarmed the officers of the town adjoining, who came with a great body of soldiers to seize upon them. Now it happened that one boat full of men had been carried aboard, while the women were yet in a bark that lay aground in a creek at low water. The Dutchman perceiving the storm that was thus beginning ashore, swore by the sacrament that he would stay no longer for any of them; and so taking the advantage of a fair wind then blowing, he put out to sea for Zeeland.[8] The women thus left near Grimsby-common, bereaved of their husbands, who had been hurried from them, and forsaken of their neighbors, of whom none durst in this fright stay with them, were a very rueful spectacle; some crying for fear, some shaking for cold, all dragged by troops of armed and angry men from one Justice to another, till not knowing what to do with them, they even dismissed them to shift as well as they could for themselves. But by their singular afflictions, and by their Christian behaviors, the cause for which they exposed themselves did gain considerably. In the meantime, the men at sea found reason to be glad that their families were not with them, for they were surprised with an horrible tempest, which held them for fourteen days together, in seven whereof they saw not sun,

---

1. First published in London in 1702, the full title was *Magnalia Christi Americana: The ecclesiastical History of New England from its first planting, in the year 1620, unto the year of our Lord, 1698*. The Latin title may be translated as "History of the Wonderful Works of Christ in America." The *Magnalia* includes seven books, covering the founding of New England, the lives of the governors (including Bradford and Winthrop), the lives of famous divines, a history of Harvard College, a record of the synods' church ordinances, and a record of "illustrious" or "wondrous" events witnessed in New England. The text is from the 1853–55 edition by Thomas Robbins.

2. "The second Galeazzo": Galeazzo Caraccoli (1517–86) was an Italian nobleman who converted to Calvinism.

3. "His vigilance defends the sleep of all; his labor, their rest; his industry, their pleasures; and his dilgence, their leisure."

4. Mary Tudor (1516–58) ruled England from 1553 to 1558, during which time an effort was made to restore the Catholic Church as the national church.

5. John Bradford (1510?–55) and Leaf were burned at the stake on July 1, 1555.

6. Elizabeth I (1533–1603) ruled England from 1558 to 1603 and as queen prescribed church ritual for the Church of England.

7. Holland.

8. The Netherlands.

moon or star, but were driven upon the coast of Norway. The mariners often despaired of life, and once with doleful shrieks gave over all, as thinking the vessel was foundered: but the vessel rose again, and when the mariners with sunk hearts often cried out, "We sink! we sink!" the passengers, without such distraction of mind, even while the water was running into their mouths and ears, would cheerfully shout, "Yet, Lord, thou canst save! Yet, Lord, thou canst save!" And the Lord accordingly brought them at last safe unto their desired haven: and not long after helped their distressed relations thither after them, where indeed they found upon almost all accounts a new world, but a world in which they found that they must live like strangers and pilgrims.

Among these devout people was our William Bradford, who was born *Anno* 1588, in an obscure village called Austerfield, where the people were as unacquainted with the Bible, as the Jews do seem to have been with part of it in the days of Josiah;[9] a most ignorant and licentious people, and like unto their priest. Here, and in some other places, he had a comfortable inheritance left him of his honest parents, who died while he was yet a child, and cast him on the education, first of his grandparents, and then of his uncles, who devoted him, like his ancestors, unto the affairs of husbandry. Soon a long sickness kept him, as he would afterwards thankfully say, from the vanities of youth, and made him the fitter for what he was afterwards to undergo. When he was about a dozen years old, the reading of the Scriptures began to cause great impressions upon him; and those impressions were much assisted and improved, when he came to enjoy Mr. Richard Clifton's illuminating ministry,[10] not far from his abode; he was then also further befriended, by being brought into the company and fellowship of such as were then called professors; though the young man that brought him into it did after become a profane and wicked apostate. Nor could the wrath of his uncles, nor the scoff of his neighbors, now turned upon him, as one of the Puritans, divert him from his pious inclinations.

At last, beholding how fearfully the evangelical and apostolical churchform, whereinto the churches of the primitive times were cast by the good spirit of God, had been deformed by the apostacy of the succeeding times; and what little progress the Reformation had yet made in many parts of Christendom towards its recovery, he set himself by reading, by discourse, by prayer, to learn whether it was not his duty to withdraw from the communion of the parish-assemblies, and engage with some society of the faithful, that should keep close unto the written Word of God, as the rule of their worship. And after many distresses of mind concerning it, he took up a very deliberate and understanding resolution, of doing so; which resolution he cheerfully prosecuted, although the provoked rage of his friends tried all the ways imaginable to reclaim him from it, unto all whom his answer was:

> Were I like to endanger my life, or consume my estate by any ungodly courses, your counsels to me were very seasonable; but you know that I have been diligent and provident in my calling, and not only desirous to augment what I have, but also to enjoy it in your company; to part from which will be as great a cross as can befall me. Nevertheless, to keep a good conscience, and walk in such a way as God has prescribed in His Word; is a thing which I must prefer before you all, and above life itself. Wherefore, since 'tis for a good cause that I am like to suffer the disasters which you lay before me, you have no cause to be either angry with me, or sorry for me; yea, I am not only willing to part with every thing that is dear to me in this world for this cause, but I am also thankful that God has given me an heart so to do, and will accept me so to suffer for Him.

Some lamented him, some derided him, all dissuaded him: nevertheless, the more they did it, the more fixed he was in his purpose to seek the ordinances of the Gospel, where they should be dispensed with most of the commanded purity; and the sudden deaths of the chief relations which thus lay at him, quickly after convinced him what a folly it had been to have quitted his profession, in expectation of any satisfaction from them. So to Holland he attempted a removal.

Having with a great company of Christians hired a ship to transport them for Holland, the master perfidiously betrayed them into the hands of those persecutors, who rifled and ransacked their goods, and clapped their persons into prison at Boston,[11] where they lay for a month together. But Mr. Bradford being a young man of about eighteen, was dismissed sooner than the rest, so that within a while he had opportunity with some others to get over to Zeeland, through perils, both by land and sea not inconsiderable; where he was not long ashore ere a viper seized on his hand—that is, an officer—who carried him

---

9. 2 Kings 22. Josiah, king of Judah, worshiped false gods out of ignorance of God's law.

10. A Puritan minister (?–1616) who accompanied the Separatists to Amsterdam.

11. Boston, England.

unto the magistrates, unto whom an envious passenger had accused him as having fled out of England. When the magistrates understood the true cause of his coming thither, they were well satisfied with him; and so he repaired joyfully unto his brethren at Amsterdam, where the difficulties to which he afterwards stooped in learning and serving of a Frenchman at the working of silks, were abundantly compensated by the delight wherewith he sat under the shadow of our Lord, in His purely dispensed ordinances. At the end of two years, he did, being of age to do it, convert his estate in England into money; but setting up for himself, he found some of his designs by the Providence of God frowned upon, which he judged a correction bestowed by God upon him for certain decays of internal piety, whereinto he had fallen; the consumption of his estate he thought came to prevent a consumption in his virtue. But after he had resided in Holland about half a score years, he was one of those who bore a part in that hazardous and generous enterprise of removing into New England, with part of the English church at Leyden, where, at their first landing, his dearest consort[12] accidently falling overboard, was drowned in the harbor; and the rest of his days were spent in the services, and the temptations, of that American wilderness.

Here was Mr. Bradford, in the year 1621, unanimously chosen the governor of the plantation; the difficulties whereof were such, that if he had not been a person of more than ordinary piety, wisdom and courage, he must have sunk under them. He had, with a laudable industry, been laying up a treasure of experiences, and he had now occasion to use it; indeed, nothing but an experienced man could have been suitable to the necessities of the people. The potent nations of the Indians, into whose country they were come, would have cut them off, if the blessing of God upon his conduct had not quelled them; and if his prudence, justice and moderation had not overruled them, they had been ruined by their own distempers. One specimen of his demeanor is to this day particularly spoken of. A company of young fellows that were newly arrived were very unwilling to comply with the governor's order for working abroad on the public account; and therefore on Christmas Day, when he had called upon them, they excused themselves, with a pretense that it was against their conscience to work such a day. The governor gave them no answer, only that he would spare them till they were better informed; but by and by he found them all at play in the street, sporting themselves with various diversions; whereupon commanding the instruments of their games to be taken from them, he effectually gave them to understand that it was against his conscience that they should play whilst others were at work, and that if they had any devotion to the day, they should show it at home in the exercises of religion, and not in the streets with pastime and frolics; and this gentle reproof put a final stop to all such disorders for the future.

For two years together after the beginning of the colony, whereof he was now governor, the poor people had a great experiment of "man's not living by bread alone";[13] for when they were left all together without one morsel of bread for many months, one after another, still the good Providence of God relieved them, and supplied them, and this for the most part out of the sea. In this low condition of affairs, there was no little exercise for the prudence and patience of the governor, who cheerfully bore his part in all; and, that industry might not flag, he quickly set himself to settle propriety among the new planters, foreseeing that while the whole country labored upon a common stock, the husbandry and business of the plantation could not flourish, as Plato and others long since dreamed that it would if a community were established. Certainly, if the spirit which dwelt in the old Puritans, had not inspired these new planters, they had sunk under the burden of these difficulties; but our Bradford had a double portion of that spirit.

The plantation was quickly thrown into a storm that almost overwhelmed it, by the unhappy actions of a minister sent over from England by the adventurers[14] concerned for the plantation; but by the blessing of Heaven on the conduct of the governor, they weathered out that storm. Only the adventurers, hereupon breaking to pieces, threw up all their concernments with the infant colony; whereof they gave this as one reason, that the planters dissembled with his Majesty and their friends in their petition, wherein they declared for a church discipline, agreeing with the French and others of the reforming churches in Europe.[15] Whereas 'twas now urged, that they had admitted into their communion a person who at his admission utterly re-

---

12. Bradford's wife went overboard.

13. Luke 4:4.

14. Investors.

15. The French Edict of Nantes (1598) allowed French people to remain in France, even if they held Protestant leanings. Other countries forced inhabitants into the state church or to leave.

nounced the churches of England, (which person, by the way, was that very man who had made the complaints against them) and therefore, though they denied the name of Brownists,[16] yet they were the thing. In answer hereunto, the very words written by the governor were these:

> Whereas you tax us with dissembling about the French discipline, you do us wrong, for we both hold and practice the discipline of the French and other Reformed Churches (as they have published the same in the Harmony of Confessions) according to our means, in effect and substance. But whereas you would tie us up to the French discipline in every circumstance, you derogate from the liberty we have in Christ Jesus. The Apostle Paul would have none to follow him in any thing, but wherein he follows Christ; much less ought any Christian or church in the world to do it. The French may err, we may err, and other churches may err, and doubtless do in many circumstances. That honor therefore belongs only to the infallible Word of God, and pure Testament of Christ, to be propounded and followed as the only rule and pattern for direction herein to all churches and Christians. And it is too great arrogancy for any man or church to think that he or they have so sounded the Word of God unto the bottom, as precisely to set down the church's discipline without error in substance or circumstance, that no other without blame may digress or differ in any thing from the same. And it is not difficult to show that the reformed churches differ in many circumstances among themselves.

By which words it appears how far he was free from that rigid spirit of separation, which broke to pieces the Separatists themselves in the Low Countries, unto the great scandal of the reforming churches. He was indeed a person of a well-tempered spirit, or else it had been scarce possible for him to have kept the affairs of Plymouth in so good a temper for thirty-seven years together; in every one of which he was chosen their governor, except the three years wherein Mr. Winslow,[17] and the two years wherein Mr. Prince, at the choice of the people, took a turn with him.

The leader of a people in a wilderness had need be a Moses; and if a Moses had not led the people of Plymouth Colony, where this worthy person was the governor, the people had never with so much unanimity and importu-

nity still called him to lead them. Among many instances thereof, let this one piece of self-denial be told for a memorial of him, wheresoever this history shall be considered: the patent of the colony was taken in his name, running in these terms: "To William Bradford, his heirs, associates, and assigns," but when the number of the freemen was much increased, and many new townships erected, the General Court there desired of Mr. Bradford that he would make a surrender of the same into their hands, which he willingly and presently assented unto, and confirmed it according to their desire by his hand and seal, reserving no more for himself than was his proportion, with others, by agreement. But as he found the Providence of Heaven many ways recompensing his many acts of self-denial, so he gave this testimony to the faithfulness of the Divine Promises: that he had forsaken friends, houses and lands for the sake of the Gospel, and the Lord gave them him again. Here he prospered in his estate; and besides a worthy son which he had by a former wife, he had also two sons and a daughter by another, whom he married in this land.

He was a person for study as well as action; and hence, notwithstanding the difficulties through which he passed in his youth, he attained unto a notable skill in languages: the Dutch tongue was become almost as vernacular to him as the English; the French tongue he could also manage; the Latin and the Greek he had mastered; but the Hebrew he most of all studied, because he said he would see with his own eyes the ancient oracles of God in their native beauty. He was also well skilled in history, in antiquity, and in philosophy; and for theology he became so versed in it, that he was an irrefragable disputant against the errors, especially those of Anabaptism,[18] which with trouble he saw rising in his colony; wherefore he wrote some significant things for the confutation of those errors. But the crown of all was his holy, prayerful, watchful, and fruitful walk with God, wherein he was very exemplary.

At length he fell into an indisposition of body, which rendered him unhealthy for a whole winter; and as the spring advanced, his health yet more declined; yet he felt himself not what he counted sick, till one day, in the night after which, the God of Heaven so filled his mind with ineffable consolations, that he seemed little short of Paul, rapt up unto the unutterable entertainments of Paradise.[19]

---

16. Robert Browne (c. 1550–1633), a Separatist identified with Congregationalism, in which each church is independent of any national church.

17. Edward Winslow (1595–1655) and Thomas Prince (1600–73).

18. Anabaptists believed that baptism should be reserved for adults and argued for the separation of church and state.

19. 2 Corinthians 12:2–4.

The next morning he told his friends that the good spirit of God had given him a pledge of his happiness in another world, and the first fruits of his eternal glory; and on the day following he died, May 9, 1657, in the 69th year of his age—lamented by all the colonies of New England as a common blessing and father to them all.

O mihi si Similis Contingat Clausula Vitae![20]

Plato's brief description of a governor, is all that I will now leave as his character, in an

Epitaph

Νομευ. Τροψο. ἀγελη. ανθρωπινη.[21]
Men are but flocks: Bradford beheld their need,
And long did them at once both rule and feed.

THE NEGRO CHRISTIANIZED[1]

It is a *Golden Sentence,* that has been sometimes quoted from *Chrysostom; That for a man to know the Art of Alms, is more than for a man to be Crowned with the Diadem of Kings: But to Convert one Soul unto God, is more than to pour out Ten Thousand Talents into the Baskets of the Poor.*[2] Truly, to Raise a *Soul,* from a dark State of Ignorance and Wickedness, to the Knowledge of GOD, and the Belief of CHRIST, and the practice of our Holy and Lovely RELIGION; 'Tis the noblest Work, that ever was undertaken among the Children of men. An Opportunity to Endeavour the CONVERSION of a Soul, from a Life of *Sin,* which is indeed a woful *Death,* to Fear God, and Love CHRIST, and by a Religious Life to Escape the *Paths of the Destroyer;* it cannot but be Acceptable to all that have themselves had in themselves Experience of such a *Conversion.* And such an Opportunity there is in your Hands, O all you that have any Negroes in your Houses; an Opportunity to try, Whether you may not be the Happy *Instruments,* of Converting, the *Blackest* Instances of *Blindness* and *Baseness,* into admirable *Candidates* of Eternal Blessedness. Let not this Opportunity be Lost; if you have any concern for *Souls,* your Own or Others; but, make a Trial, Whether by your Means, the most *Bruitish* of Creatures upon Earth may not come to be disposed, in some Degree, like the *Angels* of Heaven; and the *Vassals* of Satan, become the *Children* of God. Suppose these Wretched *Negroes,* to be the Offspring of *Cham*[3] (which yet is not so very certain,) yet let us make a Trial, Whether the CHRIST who *dwelt in the Tents of Shem,*[4] have not some of His Chosen among them; Let us make a Trial, Whether they that have been Scorched and Blacken'd by the Sun of *Africa,* may not come to have their Minds Healed by the more Benign *Beams* of the *Sun of Righteousness.*

It is come to pass by the *Providence* of God, without which there comes nothing to pass, that Poor *Negroes* are cast under your Government and Protection. You take them into your *Families;* you look on them as part of your *Possessions;* and you Expect from their Service, a Support, and perhaps an Increase, of your other *Possessions.* How agreeable would it be, if a Religious Master or Mistress thus attended, would now think with themselves! *Who can tell but that this Poor Creature may belong to the Election of God! Who can tell, but that God may have sent this Poor Creature into my Hands, that so One of the Elect may by my means be Called; & by my Instruction be made Wise unto Salvation! The glorious God will put an unspeakable Glory upon me, if it may be so!* The Considerations that would move you, To Teach your *Negroes* the *Truths* of the Glorious Gospel, as far as you can, and bring them, if it may be, to Live according to those *Truths,* a *Sober,* and a *Righteous,* and a *Godly* Life; They are *Innumerable;* And, if you would after a *Reasonable* manner consider, the Pleas which we have to make on the behalf of *God,* and of the *Souls* which He has made, one would wonder that they should not be *Irresistible. Show your*

------

20. "Oh, that I might meet such a death!"

21. "Shepherd and provider of the human flock."

1. Originally published in 1706 under the title *The Negro Christianized. An Essay to Excite and Assist that Good Work, The Instruction of Negro-Servants in Christianity.*

2. "Although thou give countless treasure unto the poor, thou wilt do no such work as he who converteth one soul": John Chrysostom (c. 347–407), *Homilies on First Corinthians,* Homily III.

3. Genesis 9:22–27. Cham, or Ham, Noah's son, is cursed by his father to be a "servant of servants" for the offense of looking on his father's nakedness. Defenders of slavery cited this passage; Africans were, it was claimed, descendants of Ham and subject to his curse.

4. In Genesis 9:27, Noah declares that God shall dwell in the tents of his son Shem, and "Canaan shall be his servant."

selves *Men,* and let *Rational Arguments* have their Force upon you, to make you treat, not as *Bruits* but as *Men,* those *Rational Creatures* whom God has made your *Servants.*

For,

First; The Great GOD *Commands* it, and *Requires* it of you; to do what you can that *Your Servants,* may also be *His.* It was an Admonition once given; Eph. 5.9.[5] *Masters, Know that your Master is in Heaven.* You will confess, That the God of Heaven is your *Master.* If your *Negroes* do not comply with your *Commands,* into what Anger, what Language, Perhaps into a misbecoming *Fury,* are you transported? But you are now to attend unto the *Commands* of your more Absolute *Master;* and they are His *Commands* concerning your *Negroes* too. What can be more Expressive; than those words of the Christian Law? Col. 4.1. *Masters, give unto your Servants, that which is Just & Equal, knowing that ye also have a Master in Heaven.* Of what *Servants* is this Injunction to be understood? Verily, of *Slaves.* For *Servants* were generally such, at the time of Writing the New Testament. Wherefore, *Masters,* As it is *Just & Equal,* that your *Servants* be not *Over-wrought,* and that while they *Work* for you, you should *Feed* them, and *Cloath* them, and afford convenient *Rest* unto them, and make their Lives comfortable; So it is *Just* and *Equal,* that you should Acquaint them, as far as you can, with the way to Salvation by JESUS CHRIST. You deny your *Master in Heaven,* if you do nothing to bring your *Servants* unto the Knowledge and Service of that glorious *Master.* One Table of the *Ten Commandments,* has this for the Sum of it; *Thou shalt Love thy Neighbour as thy self.* Man, Thy *Negro* is thy *Neighbour.* T'were an Ignorance, unworthy of a *Man,* to imagine otherwise. Yea, if thou dost grant, *That God hath made of one Blood, all Nations of men,* he is thy *Brother* too. Now canst thou *Love* thy *Negro,* and be willing to see him ly under the Rage of Sin, and the Wrath of God? Canst thou *Love* him, and yet refuse to do any thing, that his miserable Soul may be rescued from Eternal miseries? Oh! Let thy *Love* to that Poor *Soul,* appear in thy concern, to make it, if thou canst, as happy as thy own! We are Commanded, Gal. 6.10. *As we have opportunity let us Do Good unto all men, especially unto them, who are of the Houshold of Faith.* Certainly, we have *Opportunity,* to *Do Good* unto our *Servants,* who are of our *own Houshold;*

certainly, we may do something to *make them Good,* and bring them to be of the *Houshold of Faith.* In a word, All the Commandments in the Bible, which bespeak our *Charity* to the *Souls* of others, and our *Endeavour* that the *Souls* of others may be delivered from the Snares of Death; every one of these do oblige us, to do what we can, for the *Souls* of our *Negroes.* They are more nearly *Related* unto us, than many others are; we are more fully *capable* to do for them, than for many others.

To deal yet more plainly with you; Secondly; With what Face can you call yourselves *Christians,* if you do nothing that your *Servants* also may become *Christians?.* A *Face* that has been *Baptized* into the Name of the One GOD, in Three Persons, may Blush to continue unconcerned, Whether the Name of that God, be ever Known or no, in the very *Families* that belong unto them. Are they Worthy to be counted *Christians,* who are content tho' a part of their *Families* remain *Heathen,* who do *not know God,* nor *call upon His Name?.* We read, I Tim. 5.3. *If any provide not for his own, and especially those of his own house, he has denied the Faith, and is worse than an Infidel.* And what is he, who does *Provide* nothing for the Souls of those whom God has made *his own;* that their Souls may be *fed* with the *Bread of Life,* and *cloath'd* with the *Garments of Righteousness,* and *Heal'd* of the Deadly Wounds which their Fall from God has brought upon them! What is he, who is willing that those of *his own House* remain Strangers to the *Faith,* and Wretched *Infidels?* Housholder, Call thy self any thing but a *Christian!* As for that *Worthy Name,*———*Nomen Depone,* Do not pretend unto it; Thou art not *Worthy* of it, If thou wilt *Name the Name of* CHRIST, in denominating thy self a *Christian,* then *Depart from this Iniquity,* of leaving thy Servants, to continue the *Servants of Iniquity.* It will be found a Maxim that Fails not; That no man can Really and Heartily be of any *Religion,* without some Desire to have that *Religion* Propagated. For a man to Profess a Religion, and care not a Straw, Whether any body besides himself be of it; certainly, That mans *Profession* is not worth a Straw; it can be no *Sincere Profession.* It is *Natural* for men, to promote their own Religion. Shall *Christians* fall short of *Mahametans,* or of *Idolaters?* The Pagan *Sapenians,* were too much in the right on it, when they concluded a certain Worldly Generation of *Europeans,* to be no *Christians;* Because they declined *the doing of any thing for the Propagation of Christianity.* The *Christians,* who have no concern upon their Minds to have *Christianity Propagated,* never can justify themselves. *They say they are* Christians, *but they are not;* What they are, we know not. All along the Pagans themselves, have made it the main Stroke in the Definition of, *A Good Man; He is One who does all the Good that he can.* The greatest *Good* that we can do for any, is to bring them unto the fullest Acquaintance with *Christianity.* Will *Christianity* allow him then to be, A *Good Man,* or, which is the same thing, A *Christian,* who refuses to do this *Good,* for the *Servants* that are under his influence? All genuine *Christians* are to be look'd on as the *Children* of the Faithful *Abraham,* who is therefore called, *The Father of the Faithful.* Now of this our Father, did Heaven take it for granted; Gen. 18.19. *I know him, that he will Command his Children, and his Houshold, and they shall keep the way of the Lord.* He had some Hundreds of *Servants* belonging to his *Houshold:* He obtained, that the *Slaves* of his *Houshold* should *Know* the *Way of the Lord; He* then *Commanded,* that they should *Keep* that *Way.* Now, *Christianity* is, *The Way of the Lord.* Housholder, There are *Servants* pertaining to thy *Houshold.* It is a mighty Power which thou hast over them; A *Despotick Power* which gives thee numberless Advantages, to call them, and lead them into *the Way of the Lord.* Are thou Regardless of bringing them into *Christianity?* Then thou doest not *Walk in the Steps of our Father Abraham,* and are not like to call him thy *Father,* any otherwise than the *Rich Man in the place of Torment.* We are very sure, That where the *Spirit of Christianity* has had its true operation, it has from the Beginning Shone forth in most *Lively Essayes,* to diffuse the Light of the *Glorious Gospel,* unto such as have been *Perishing* for the *Lack of that Vision.* All Ecclesiastical History, down from the Book of *The Acts of the Apostles,* to this Time, are fill'd with admirable Examples, of a *Zeal* flaming in the Hearts of *Christians,* to *Christianize* the rest of the World. *Christianity,* Whither art thou fled! *Return, Return, that we may look upon thee.* What shall we then see, but a vast company of *Christian Housholders,* filled with zealous contrivance and agony, to see their *Houses* become *Christian Temples,* and a glorious CHRIST worshipped and obeyed by all their *Housholds!* Yea, we read concerning some of the *Primitive Christians,* that with a *Prodigie* of *Charity,* they have bound themselves in the Quality of *Servants,* to Pagan *Families,* meerly that they might be in a way to *Christianize* the *Families;* And their successes were Wonderful. But what shall we say of it, When *Masters* that would be thought *Christians* already shall even refuse to have the *Servants* in their *Families* duely *Christianized?* Pray, deal faithfully; Don't mince the matter; say of it, as it is; It is a *Prodigy* of *Wickedness;* It is a prodigious In-

consistency, with true *Christianity!* Householder, art thou a *Christian?* Then the *Glory* of a precious CHRIST is of such Account with thee, that it afflicts thee to think, that any one Person in the World should be without the Sight of it. And how can it be, that thou shouldest be negligent about bringing to a sight of the *Glory of God, in the Face of* JESUS CHRIST, the *Folks of thy own House,* upon whom thou art able to do a great deal more than upon the rest of the World? Art thou a *Christian?* Then thou dost *Pray* for thy *Servants,* that they may become the *Servants* of the Lord Jesus Christ, and the *Children* of God, and not *fall short of entering into Rest.* What! *Pray* for this; and yet never *do* any thing for it! It is impossible, or, such *Praying,* is but *Mocking* of God? Art thou a *Christian?* Then thou art apprehensive of a dreadful Danger, attending the *Souls* of them who *know not God and obey not His Gospel:* Tis thy perswasion, *That if our Gospel be hid, it is hid from them that are left;* and the *Ungospelized Souls* are in danger of an Eternal *Banishment* from the *Favour* and the *City* of God. Can a *Christian* see his own *Servants* in this condition, and not be sollicitous to have them saved out of it? No; When such *Christians* appear before the Glorious LORD, it will be in vain for them to plead, that they calld him LORD, and own'd Him for their LORD. If they did it why did they not bring their *Servants* under the Government of the LORD? *Verily,* He will say to such *Christians, I knew you not?* Suppose that Language were heard from the mouth of a Master concerning a Servant; *If I can have the Labour of the Slave, that's all I care for: Let his Soul go and be damn'd for all me!* would not every Christian say, This were Language for the Mouth of a *Devil,* rather than for the Mouth of a *Christian!* Would not every Christian cry out, *Let him not be call'd a Master, but a Monster that shall speak so!* Consider, Syrs, whether *Deeds* have not a Language in them, as well as *Words;* a plainer Language than *Words.*

But we were saying; the *Condition* of the *Servants!* This invites us to say, Thirdly: The *condition* of your *Servants* does loudly sollicit your pains to *Christianize* them; and you cannot but hear the cry of it, if you have not put off all *Christian Compassion,* all Bowels of *Humanity.* When you see how laboriously, how obsequiously your *Negros* apply themselves, to serve you, to content you, to enrich you, What? have you abandoned all principles of Gratitude, or of Generosity? A generous Mind cannot but entertain such sentiments as these: *Well, what shall I do, to make this poor creature happy? What shall I do, that this poor creature may have cause, to bless God forever, for falling into my Hands!* The very *First Thought* which will arise in a Mind thus disposed, will form a Resolution, to get these poor *Negroes* well instructed in *the things of their Everlasting Peace;* It cannot be otherwise! The State of your *Negroes* in this World, must be low, and mean, and abject; a State of Servitude. No *Great Things* in this World, can be done for them. Something then, let there be done, towards their welfare in the *World to Come.* Even a Papist calls upon us; ['tis *Acosta:*] *Barbaris pro libertate erepta fidem Jesu Christi, et vitem hominubus diguam recdamus.*[6] In the mean time; tis a most horrid and cursed *Condition,* wherein your *Servants* are languishing, until *Christianity* has made saving impressions upon them. *A roaring Lion who goes about seeking whom he may devour,* hath made a seizure of them: Very many of them do with Devilish Rites actually worship *Devils,* or maintain a magical conversation with *Devils:* And all of them are more *Slaves* to *Satan* than they are to *You,* until a Faith in the *Son of God* has made them *Free indeed.* Will you do nothing to pluck them out of the Jaws of *Satan* the *Devourer?* Especially since you may justly imagine them crying to you in terms like those of the Child whom a *Lion* was running away withal; *Help! Help! I am yet alive!* O Souls deaf to the cry of Souls, Pitty, Pitty the Souls of your *Negroes,* which cry unto you *Have pitty on us, O our Masters, have pitty on us, whom the holy God has justly delivered over into a woful Slavery to the Powers of Darkness: And, Oh! do something, that the light of Salvation by the glorious Lord JESUS CHRIST may arrive unto me.* A SOUL, Ignorant of God and His Christ, and vicious in all the affections of it, and that neither knows nor likes the Things that are Holy and Just and Good, and that has no illuminations from Heaven ever visiting of it but is, in *Great Folly wandering down to the Congregation of the Dead;* Such a Soul is a terrible sight! It can be no other than such a Soul, who does not count it so. Neighbours, you have such a sight, in all your *Negroes,* as long as they are left a *People of no understanding.* The uninstructed *Negroes* about your houses, appear like so many *Ghosts* and *Spectres.* You may, without being Fanciful, imagine that like so many Murdered *Ghosts,* they look very Ghastly upon you, and summon you to answer before the Tribunal of God, for suffering them to perish in their mis-

erable Circumstances. Most certainly, Syrs; The *Blood* of the *Souls* of your poor *Negroes,* lies upon you, and the guilt of their Barbarous Impieties, and superstitions, and their neglect of God and their *Souls:* If you are willing to have nothing done towards the Salvation of their Souls. We read of, *People destroy'd for lack of knowledge.* If you withhold *Knowledge* from your *Black People,* they will be *Destroy'd.* But their *Destruction* must very much ly at *Your* door; *You* must answer for it. It was a *Black charge* of old brought in against the *Jewish Nation;* Jer. 2.34. *In thy skirts is found the Blood of Souls.* It were to be wish'd, that in the *Skirts,* the outborders, the Colonies and Plantations of the *English Nation,* there might be no room for such a charge. But surely, Things look very *Black* upon us. You have your selves renounced *Christianity,* if you do not receive that *Faithful saying* of it, and most *Awful* one: *Every one of us shall give account of himself to God.* But then Remember, that one Article of your *Account* will be this: *You had poor* Negroes *under you, and you expected and exacted Revenues of profit from them. Did you do any thing to save them from their Blindness and Baseness, and that the Great God might have Revenues of glory from them.* Alas, if you have not thought and car'd and *Watch'd for the Souls* of your *Negroes,* as *they that must give an Account,* You will give up your *Account* with *Grief,* and not with *Joy;* very *Grievous* will be the consequences. A *Prophet* of God, might without putting any *Disguise* upon the matter, thus represent it; God has brought a *Servant* unto thee, and said, *Keep that Soul, Teach it, and Help it, that it may not be lost; if thou use no means to save that Soul, thy soul shall certainly smart for it.* Vain Dreamer; canst thou suppose that the *Negroes* are made for nothing but only to serve thy Pleasures, or that they owe no Homage to their *Maker?* Do thy part, that they may become a *People of so much Understanding,* as to Understand who is their *Maker* and their *Saviour,* and what Homage they owe unto Him: Else, *He that made them will not have mercy on them.* Yea, but *Thy* claim to His *Mercy* will be less than *Theirs.* More *Stripes* will belong unto thee.

On the other side, Fourthly: Oh! That our neighbours would consider the incomparable *Benefits* that would follow upon your *Endeavours* to *Christianize* your *Negroes,* and bring them to a share with your selves in the *Benefits* of the Heavenly *Inheritance.* If your care and cost about the cultivation of your *Negroes,* be laid out upon such a Stony and Barren Soil, that you can see no Fruit of it, yet it is not all thrown away. The blessed God will approve and reward what you have done; Think, *Tho' my* Negroes

6. Mather is evidently quoting from a work by José de Acosta that in translation reads: "In exchange for taking away their freedom, we shall give the barbarians (i.e., heathens) the faith of Jesus Christ and a life worthy of human beings."

will not prove a part of the Israel of God, and will not be gathered unto the Lord, yet my work is with my God, and what I do is glorious in the Eyes of the Lord. But it is very probable, You may see some good *Success* of your Travail. And *then!* Oh! the *Consolations* that will belong unto you! *Christianity* does Marvellously befriend and enrich and advance Mankind. The greatest *Kindness* that can be done to any Man is to make a *Christian* of him. Your *Negroes* are immediately Raised unto an astonishing Felicity, when you have *Christianized* them. They are become amiable spectacles, & such as the *Angels* of God would gladly repair unto the Windows of Heaven to look upon. Tho' they remain your *Servants,* yet they are become the *Children* of God. Tho' they are to enjoy no *Earthly Goods,* but the small Allowance that your Justice and Bounty shall see proper for them, yet they are become *Heirs* of God, and *Joint-Heirs* with the Lord Jesus Christ. Tho' they are your *Vassals,* and must with a profound subjection wait upon you, yet the *Angels* of God now take them under their Guardianship and vouchsafe to tend upon them. Oh! what have you done for them! Happy *Masters,* who are Instrumental to raise their *Servants* thus from the *Dust,* and make them objects for the *Nobels* of *Heaven* to take Notice of! But it will not be long before you and they come at length to be together in the *Heavenly City. Lazarus* there lies down at the same Feast, with his Master *Abraham.* There was *Joy in Heaven,* when your *Servants* first came to *taste that the Lord is Gracious:* and it cannot but be a vast Accession unto your *Joy in Heaven,* to meet your *Servants* there, and hear them forever blessing the gracious God, for the Day when He first made them your *Servants.* If these *Consolations of God* be *small* unto a Man, truly, he has very Bad Symptoms upon him.

Yea, the pious *Masters,* that have instituted their *Servants* in Christian Piety, will even in this Life have a sensible *Recompence.* The more *Serviceable,* and Obedient and obliging Behaviour of their *Servants* unto them, will be a sensible & a notable *Recompence.* Be assured, Syrs; Your *Servants* will be the *Better Servants,* for being made *Christian Servants.* To *Christianize* them aright, will be to *fill them with all Goodness. Christianity* is nothing but a very Mass of Universal *Goodness.* Were your *Servants* well tinged with the Spirit of *Christianity,* it would render them exceeding *Dutiful* unto their *Masters,* exceeding *Patient* under their *Masters,* exceeding faithful in their Business, and afraid of speaking or doing any thing that may justly displease you. It has been observed, that those *Masters* who have used their *Negroes* with most of *Humanity,*

in allowing them all the Comforts of Life, that are necessary and *Convenient* for them, (Who have remembered, that by the Law of God, even an *Ass* was to be relieved, When *Sinking under his Burden,*[7] and an *Ox* might not be *Muzzled* when *Treading out the Corn;*[8] and that if a *Just man will regard the Life of his Beast,* he will much more allow the comforts of life to and not hide himself *from his own Flesh:*) have been better *Serv'd,* had more work done for them, and better done, than those *Inhumane Masters,* who have used their *Negroes* worse than their *Horses.* And those *Masters* doubtless, who use their *Negroes* with most of *Christianity,* and use most pains to inform them in, and conform them to, *Christianity,* will find themselves no losers by it. *Onesimus* was doubtless a *Slave:*[9] but this poor *Slave,* on whose behalf a great Apostle of God was more than a little concerned; yea, one Book in our Bible was Written on his behalf! When he was *Christianized,* it was presently said unto his *Master,* Philem. 11. *In time past he was unprofitable to thee, but now he will be profitable.* But many *Masters* whose *Negroes* have greatly vexed them, with miscarriages, may do well to examine, Whether Heaven be not chastising of them, for their failing in their Duty about their *Negroes.* Had they done more, to make their *Negroes* the knowing and willing *Servants* of God, it may be, God would have made their *Negroes* better *Servants* to them. Syrs, you may Read your *Sin* in the *Punishment.*

And now, what *Objection* can any Man Living have, to refund the force of these *Considerations?* Produce the cause, O Impiety, *Bring forth thy strong reasons,* and let all men see what Idle and silly cavils, are thy best *Reasons* against this Work of God.

It has been cavilled, by some, that it is questionable Whether the *Negroes* have *Rational Souls,* or no. But let that *Bruitish* insinuation be never Whispered any more. Certainly, their *Discourse,* will abundantly prove, that they have *Reason. Reason* showes it self in the *Design* which they daily act upon. The vast improvement that *Education* has made upon *some* of them, argues that there is a *Reasonable Soul* in *all* of them. An old Roman, and Pagan, would call upon the Owner of such Servants,

---

7. Exodus 23:5.

8. Deuteronomy 25:4.

9. In his Epistle to Philemon, Paul asks for a pardon for the slave boy Onesimus, whom he converted and who was his companion in prison.

Homines tamen esse memento.[10] They are *Men,* and not *Beasts* that you have bought, and they must be used accordingly. 'Tis true; They are *Barbarous.* But so were our own *Ancestors.* The *Britons* were in many things as *Barbarous,* but a little before our Saviours Nativity, as the *Negroes* are at this day if there be any Credit in *Cæsars Commentaries. Christianity* will be the best cure for this *Barbarity.* Their *Complexion* sometimes is made an Argument, why nothing should be done for them. A *Gay* sort of argument! As if the great God went by the *Complexion* of Men, in His *Favours* to them! As if none but *Whites* might hope to be Favoured and Accepted with God! Whereas it is well known, That the *Whites,* are the least part of Mankind. The biggest part of Mankind, perhaps, are *Copper-Coloured;* a sort of *Tawnies.* And our *English* that inhabit some Climates, do seem growing apace to be not much unlike unto them. As if, because a people, from the long force of the African *Sun & Soil* upon them, (improved perhaps, to further Degrees by maternal imaginations, and other accidents,) are come at length to have the small *Fibres* of their *Veins,* and the Blood in them, a little more Interspersed thro their Skin than other People, this must render them less valuable to Heaven then the rest of Mankind? Away with such Trifles. The God who *looks on the Heart,* is not moved by the colour of the *Skin;* is not more propitious to one *Colour* than another. Say rather, with the Apostle; Acts 10.34, 35. *Of a truth I perceive, that God is no respecter of persons; but in every Nation, he that feareth Him and worketh Righteousness, is accepted with Him.* Indeed their *Stupidity* is a *Discouragement.* It may seem, unto as little purpose, to *Teach,* as to *wash an Æthopian.* But the greater their *Stupidity,* the greater must be our *Application.* If we can't learn them so much as we *Would,* let us learn them as much as we *Can.* A little divine *Light* and *Grace* infused into them, will be of great account. And the more *Difficult* it is, to fetch such *forlorn things* up out of the perdition whereinto they are fallen, the more *Laudable* is the undertaking: There will be the more of a *Triumph,* if we prosper in the undertaking. Let us encourage our selves from that word; Mat. 3.9 *God is able to these Stones, to raise up Children unto Abraham.*

Well; But if the *Negroes* are *Christianized,* they will be *Baptized;* and their *Baptism* will presently entitle them to their *Freedom;* so our *Money* is thrown away.

Man, If this were true; that a *Slave* bought with thy *Money,* were by thy means brought unto the *Things that accompany Salvation,* and thou shouldest from this time have no more Service from him, yet thy *Money* were not thrown away. That Mans *Money will perish with him,* yet he had rather the *Souls* in his Family should *Perish,* than that he should lose a little *Money.* And suppose it were so, that *Baptism* gave a legal Title to *Freedom.* Is there no guarding against this Inconvenience? You may by sufficient *Indentures,* keep off the things, which you reckon so Inconvenient. But it is all a Mistake. There is no such thing. What *Law* is it, that Sets the *Baptized Slave* at *Liberty?* Not the *Law of Christianity:* that allows of *Slavery;* Only it wonderfully Dulcifies, and Mollifies, and Moderates the Circumstances of it. *Christianity* directs a *Slave,* upon his embracing the *Law of the Redeemer,* to satisfy himself, *That he is the Lords Free-man,* tho' he continues a *Slave.* It supposes, (Col. 3.11.) That there are *Bond* as well as *Free,* among those that have been *Renewed in the Knowledge and Image of Jesus Christ.* Will the *Canon-law* do it? No; The *Canons* of Numberless *Councils,* mention, the *Slaves* of *Christians,* without any contradiction. Will the *Civil Law* do it? No: Tell, if you can, any part of *Christendom,* wherein *Slaves* are not frequently to be met withal. But is not *Freedom* to be claim'd for a *Baptised Slave,* by the *English* Constitution? The English *Laws,* about *Villains,*[11] or, *Slaves,* will not say so; for by those *Laws,* they may be granted *for Life,* like a *Lease,* and passed over with a *Mannor,* like other *Goods or Chattels.* And by those *Laws,* the Lords may sieze the Bodies of their *Slaves* even while a Writt, *De libertate probanda,*[12] is depending. These English *Laws* were made when the *Lords* & the *Slaves,* were both of them *Christians;* and they stand still unrepealed. If there are not now such *Slaves* in *England* as formerly, it is from the *Lords,* more than from the *Laws.* The *Baptised* then are not thereby entitled unto their *Liberty.* Howbeit, if they have arrived unto such a measure of *Christianity,* that *some are forbid Water for the Baptising of them,* it is fit, that they should enjoy those *comfortable circumstances* with us, which are due to them, not only as the *Children* of *Adam,* but also as our *Brethren,* on the same level with us in the expectations of a blessed Immortality, thro' the *Second Adam.* Whatever Slaughter the Assertion may make among the pretensions which are made unto *Christianity,* yet while

---

10. "But remember that they are men."

11. During feudal times, a serf.

12. "Proving freedom."

the *sixteenth* Chapter of *Matthew* is in the Bible,[13] it must be asserted; the *Christian,* who cannot so far *Deny himself,* can be no *Disciple* of the Lord JESUS CHRIST. But, O Christian, thy *Slave* will not Serve thee one jot the worse for that *Self denial.*

The way is now cleared, for the work that is proposed: that excellent WORK, The Instruction of the Negroes in the Christian Religion.

A CATECHISM shall be got ready for them; first a *Shorter,* then a *Larger;* Suited unto their poor Capacities.

They who cannot themselves *Personally* so well attend the *Instruction* of the *Negroes,* may employ and reward those that shall do it for them. In many *Families,* the *Children* may help the *Negroes,* to Learn the *Catechism,* or their well-instructed and well-disposed *English Servants* may do it: And they should be *Rewarded* by the *Masters,* when they do it.

In a Plantation of many *Negroes,* why should not a *Teacher* be hired on purpose, to instil into them the principles of the *Catechism?*

Or, if the *Overseers* are once *Catechised* themselves, they may soon do the Office of *Catechisers* unto those that are under them.

However, Tis fit for the *Master* also *Personally* to enquire into the progress which his *Negroes* make in *Christianity,* and not leave it *Entierly* to the management of others.

There must be *Time* allow'd for the *Work.* And why not The Lords-Day? The precept of God concerning the *Sabbath,* is very positive; *Remember the SABBATH-DAY, to keep it Holy. Thou shalt not then do any work, thou nor thy Son, nor thy Daughter, thy Man-Servant, nor thy Maid-Servant.*[14] By virtue of this precept, we do even demand, The Lords-Day, for the *Negroes:* that they may be permitted the Freedom of The Lords-Day, and not be then unnecessarily diverted from attending on such *means of Instruction,* as may be afforded unto them.

To quicken them unto the learning of the *Catechism,* it would be very well to propose unto the *Negroes, Agreeable Recompences, & Priviledges,* to be receiv'd and enjoy'd by them, when they shall have made a good progress in it. Syrs, A *Mahometan* will do as much as this

comes to, for any one that will embrace his *Alcoran.* Oh, Christians, will not you do more for *your Generation,* than the *Children of this World* for theirs. And it is to be desired, that the *Negroes* may not learn to say their *Catechism* only by rote, like *Parrots;* but that their Instructors, may put unto them such other *Questions* relating to the points of the *Catechism,* that by their *Answers,* (at least of YES, or, NO,) it may be perceived, that they *Know* what they *Say.*

But it will be also needful and useful, to uphold a more particular *Conference* often with the *Negroes;* and in conferring with them, to inculcate on them such *Admonitions of Piety;* as may have a special tendency to *Form & Mould* their Souls for the Kingdom of God.

Having told them, *Who Made* them, and *Why* He made them, and that they have *Souls,* which will be *Wretched* or *Happy* forever, according as they mind *Religion;* then tell them;

That by their sin against God, they are fallen into a dreadful condition.

Show them, That the Almighty *God is Angry* with them, and that, if they Dy under the *Anger of God,* they will after *Death,* be cast among *Devils;* and that all the *Stripes,* and all the *Wants,* and all the sad things they ever suffered in this World, are nothing, to the *many Sorrows,* which they shall suffer among the Damned, in the *Dungeon of Hell.*

Tell them; *That JESUS CHRIST is a Saviour for them as well as others, and as willing to save them out of their dreadful condition, as any others.*

Show them, That JESUS CHRIST, who is both *God* and *Man* in One Person, came, and Kept the *Law* of God, and then Offer'd up His *Life* to God, on the *Cross,* to make amends for our *Sin;* and that JESUS CHRIST invites *Them* as well as others, to *Look* to Him, and *Hope* in Him, for Everlasting Life; and that if they come to JESUS CHRIST, they shall be as Welcome to Him, as any People; Tho' He be the *King of Kings,* and *Lord of Lords,* yet He will cast a Kind Look upon Sorry *Slaves* and *Blacks* that Believe on Him, and will prepare a *Mansion* in Heaven for them.

Tell them; *That if they Serve God patiently and cheerfully in the Condition which he orders for them, their condition will very quickly be infinitely mended, in Eternal Happiness.*

Show them, That it is GOD who has caused them to be *Servants;* and that they Serve JESUS CHRIST, while they are at work for their *Masters,* if they are *Faithful* and *Honest Servants,* and if they do cheerfully what they do, be-

---

13. Matthew 16:24: "If any man will come after me, let him deny himself, and take up his cross, and follow me."

14. Exodus 20:8, 10.

cause the Lord JESUS CHRIST has bid them to do it; and that, if they give themselves up to JESUS CHRIST, and keep always afraid of Sinning against Him, it won't be *Long* before they shall be in a most *Glorious Condition;* It can't be *Long* before they Dy, and *then!* they shall *Rest* from all their Labours, and all their Troubles, and they shall be Companions of *Angels* in the Glories of a *Paradise.*

Discourse with them, on these things, till their *Hearts burn within them.* In Discourse with them, at length put it unto them;

Well; Do you desire to Know the Only true God, and Jesus Christ, whom He hath sent?

Is it your Desire, that JESUS CHRIST may Save you from the Guilt of Sin, and the Curse of God?

Are you willing to put your self into the Gracious Hands of JESUS CHRIST, and be Ruled by all His Holy Laws?

Do you wish that the Blessed Spirit of the Lord, may Enter your Hearts, and make you Know and Love and Chuse the things that please Him?

Who can tell, but that while you are propounding such things to the poor *Negroes,* their conquered *Souls* may Consent unto them, and by that *Consent* open a *Well* that shall Spring up, & Spread out, unto *Everlasting Life?*

But in a Special manner Teach them to Pray. Teach them and Charge them every Day to fall down on their Knees before the Lord; with Supplications of this Importance.

Heavenly Father; Give me thy CHRIST; Give me they SPIRIT; Pardon my Sins; Make me thy Servant; Bring me to Heaven. Amen.

Or, As they get further on, they may Pray after this Manner.

O Great GOD; Thou hast made me, and all the World. Make me truly Sorry for my Sinning against my Maker.

Let thy Glorious CHRIST Save me: and help me to Know, and to Take His Great Salvation. Teach me to Serve Thee, O Lord. And make me a Blessing unto those that have me for their Servant.

Bring me to a part in Heaven among thy Children for ever more. Amen.

SAMUEL SEWALL (1652–1730)

Samuel Sewall belonged to a remarkable group of Harvard College graduates involved with measures that they considered would secure the stability, theological purity, and bright prospects of the New England colony as it moved into the eighteenth century. Born at Bishop Stoke, England, in 1652, Sewall was brought by his parents to settle in Newbury, Massachusetts, when he was nine years old. He graduated from Harvard in 1671 and in the middle of that decade married into one of the most wealthy families in the colony, when he married Hannah Hull. He became a merchant at that time, and by the early 1680s, he was one of the most influential men in Boston when he was appointed by the General Court to run the colony's only licensed press (1681–84). Sewall was a well-known and prolific writer for his day, and he used his press to publish his own works, as well of those of the government. In 1683, he became deputy to the General Court for the town of Westfield, and in the following year, he was named a magistrate for Massachusetts Bay colony. From then until the year 1725, Sewall served a number of positions affiliated with the Governor's Council.

Sewall's most memorable actions involve two major social issues of his day, the Salem witch trials and the slave-keeping controversy in New England. In both areas, Sewall fulfilled what he considered to be his obligation to his conscience and his God. During his tenure as a judge at the Salem witch trials, as a member of Governor Phips's Court of Oyer and Terminer appointed in 1692, Sewall participated, along with Cotton Mather and others, with little evident concern about the justice of their cause against the presumed witches. As his diary at that time indicates, he considered those who were "move[d]" by the so-called witches' protestations of innocence "unthinking persons." Yet Sewall thought more deeply about his actions, once they were over, and in rereading his diary from those days, ended up writing into its margin "Dolefull! Witchcraft." Within five years of his condemning to death twenty persons for witchcraft, however, Sewall declared his personal reservations about the trials. At the end of 1696, Sewall wrote a proclamation for a fast day of penance and reparation by the government for its activities against the supposed witches, and on January 15, 1697, he publicly apologized for his role in the trials, setting aside one day each year to fast and pray for his own sinful participation in those events of 1692. He was the only Salem trial judge to declare public repentance for his role.

Sewall's other well-known social proclamation came in the form of a pamphlet written in behalf of the abolition of slavery. The Massachusetts Puritans had enacted a Body of Liberties in 1641, and from then onward, the laws permitted slave keeping within New England. Slavery concerned Sewall for many years, at least as early as 1673, when his diary entries reveal the beginnings of his sense of the injustice of slavery. The immediate impulse behind Sewall's pamphlet, *The Selling of Joseph* (published in 1700), seems to have been a petition by a friend named Belknap to free an African slave and his wife. The slave was named Adam, owned by John Saffin, a merchant and slave trafficker. After having promised Adam his freedom once a term of labor had been served, Saffin revoked that promise and hired Adam out for work. Sewall published his pamphlet in response to a number of circumstances surrounding slavery and slave keeping in New England, however. Several people in Boston were, like Sewall, concerned about whether slaves should be permitted in the colony, and some were agitating to create a special impost on slaves, to keep people from purchasing or trading them. Sewall understood that Cotton Mather was contemplating a pamphlet regarding not emancipation but the Christianizing of Africans and those of African descent. (Mather published his pamphlet, *The Negro Christianized,* in 1706.) Primarily, though, with regard to his own conscience, Sewall was concerned about the relations between masters and servants according to biblical testaments regarding slavery. All these issues contributed to his publishing his statement about slavery, a standard exposition in the form similar to that of sermons. Sewall states the text; offers an elaboration of the text, replete with biblical and Latin citations; creates objections to examine; and draws conclusions based on the examination. Although for a reader today, Sewall's statement may seem to lack the rhetorical fervor one may expect, his pamphlet nonetheless was a most compelling document in his own day. Adam was finally freed, with Sewall's assistance, in 1703.

from THE DIARY OF SAMUEL SEWALL[1]

Augt. 19ᵗʰ 1692. . . .

This day [*in the margin,* Dolefull! Witchcraft] George Burrough, John Willard, Jnᵒ Procter, Martha Carrier and George Jacobs were executed at Salem, a very great number of Spectators being present. Mr. Cotton Mather was there, Mr. Sims, Hale, Noyes, Chiever, &c. All of them said they were innocent, Carrier and all. Mr. Mather says they all died by a Righteous Sentence. Mr. Burrough by his Speech, Prayer, protestation of his Innocence, did much move unthinking persons, which occasions their speaking hardly concerning his being executed.

Augt. 25. Fast at the old [*First*] Church, respecting the Witchcraft, Drought, &c.

Monday, Sept. 19, 1692. About noon, at Salem, Giles Corey was press'd to death for standing Mute; much pains was used with him two days, one after another, by the Court and Capt. Gardner of Nantucket who had been of his acquaintance: but all in vain.[2]

Sept. 20. Now I hear from Salem that about 18 years agoe, he was suspected to have stampd and press'd a man to death, but was cleared. Twas not remembred till Anne Putnam was told of it by said Corey's Spectre the Sabbath-day night before Execution.[3]

Sept. 20, 1692. The Swan brings in a rich French Prize of about 300 Tuns, laden with Claret, White Wine, Brandy, Salt, Linnen Paper, &c.

Sept. 21. A petition is sent to Town in behalf of Dorcas Hoar, who now confesses: Accordingly an order is sent to the Sheriff to forbear her Execution, notwithstanding her being in the Warrant to die to morrow. This is the first condemned person who has confess'd.

---

1. Sewall's diary began on December 3, 1673, and concluded on December 25, 1728. The text is from *The Diary of Samuel Sewall,* ed. M. Halsey Thomas (1973).

2. Giles Corey was eighty years old in 1692.

3. Anne Putnam was twelve years old when she became a witness against presumed witches.

Nov. 5. No disturbance at night by Bonfires.

Nov. 6. Joseph threw a knop of Brass and hit his Sister Betty on the forhead so as to make it bleed and swell; upon which, and for his playing at Prayer-time, and eating when Return Thanks, I whipd him pretty smartly. When I first went in (call'd by his Grandmother) he sought to shadow and hide himself from me behind the head of the Cradle: which gave me the sorrowfull remembrance of Adam's carriage.

Monday, April 29, 1695. The morning is very warm and Sunshiny; in the Afternoon there is Thunder and Lightening, and about 2 P.M. a very extraordinary Storm of Hail, so that the ground was made white with it, as with the blossoms when fallen; 'twas as bigg as pistoll and Musquet Bullets; It broke of the Glass of the new House about 480 Quarrels [*squares*] of the Front; of Mr. Sergeant's about as much; Col. Shrimpton, Major General, Gov'r Bradstreet, New Meetinghouse, Mr. Willard, &c. Mr. Cotton Mather dined with us, and was with me in the new Kitchen when this was; He had just been mentioning that more Ministers Houses than others proportionably had been smitten with Lightening; enquiring what the meaning of God should be in it. Many Hail-Stones broke throw the Glass and flew to the middle of the Room, or farther: People afterward Gazed upon the House to see its Ruins. I got Mr. Mather to pray with us after this awfull Providence; He told God He had broken the brittle part of our house, and prayd that we might be ready for the time when our Clay-Tabernacles should be broken. Twas a sorrowfull thing to me to see the house so far undon again before twas finsih'd. It seems at Milton on the one hand, and at Lewis's [*the ordinary at Lynn*] on the other, there was no Hail.

I mentioned to Mr. Mather that Monmouth made his discent into England about the time of the Hail in '85, Summer, that much cracked our South-west windows. Col. Archdell, Governour of Carolina comes to Town from Portsmouth this night.

Jany 15. [1697]. . . .

Copy of the Bill I put up on the Fast day; giving it to Mr. Willard as he pass'd by, and standing up at the reading of it, and bowing when finished; in the Afternoon.

Samuel Sewall sensible of the reiterated strokes of God upon himself and family;[4] and being sensible, that as

to the Guilt contracted, upon the opening of the late Commission of Oyer and Terminer at Salem (to which the order for this Day relates) he is, upon many accounts, more concerned than any that he knows of, Desires to take the Blame and Shame of it, Asking pardon of Men, And especially desiring prayers that God, who has an Unlimited Authority, would pardon that Sin and all other his Sins; personal and Relative: And according to his infinite Benignity, and Soveraignty, Not Visit the Sin of him, or of any other, upon himself or any of his, nor upon the Land: But that He would powerfully defend him against all Temptations to Sin, for the future; and vouchsafe him the Efficacious, Saving Conduct of his Word and Spirit.

July, 15. 1698. Mr. Edward Taylor comes to our house from West-field.

Monday July 18. I walk'd with Mr. Edward Taylor upon Cotton Hill, thence to Becon Hill, the Pasture, along the Stone-wall: As came back, we sat down on the great Rock, and Mr. Taylor told me his courting his first wife,[5] and Mr. Fitch his story of Mr. Dod's prayer to God to bring his Affection to close with a person pious, but hard-favoured. Has God answered me in finding out one Godly and fit for me, and shall I part for fancy? When came home, my wife gave me Mr. Tappan's Letter concerning Eliza,[6] which caus'd me to reflect on Mr. Taylor's Discourse. And his Prayer was for pardon of error in our ways—which made me think whether it were not best to overlook all, and go on. This day John Ive, fishing in great Spiepond, is arrested with mortal sickness which renders him in a manner speechless and senseless; dies next day; buried at Charlestown on the Wednesday. Was a very debauched, atheistical man. I was not at his Funeral. Had Gloves sent me, but the knowledge of his notoriously wicked life made me sick of going; and Mr. Mather, the president, came in just as I was ready to step out, and so I staid at home, and by that means lost a Ring:[7] but hope had no loss. Follow thou Me, was I suppose more complied with, than if had left Mr. Mather's company to go to such a Funeral. [*In margin:* Cambridge Mr. Ive's son Dies suddenly]

Fourth-day, June, 19. 1700. Mr. Jn° Eyre is entombed in the new burying place. Nine of his children are laid there

---

4. Sewall lost two children in 1696: one child was born dead, and the other, a daughter, died in December.

5. Elizabeth Fitch, who died July 7, 1689.

6. Elizabeth Tappan, Sewall's niece.

7. The ring would have been a memorial token. Invitations to funerals were made by the presentation of gloves.

to handsel the new Tomb: Bearers, Sewall, Addington, Townsend, Byfield, Dummer, Davis: Scarvs and Rings. Lt Govr and many of the Council there. Mr. Thomas Brattle led his mourning widowed Sister. When I parted, I pray'd God to be favourably present with her, and comfort her in the absence of so near and dear a Relation. Having been long and much dissatisfied with the Trade of fetching Negros from Guinea; at last I had a strong Inclination to Write something about it; but it wore off. At last reading Bayne, Ephes.[8] about servants, who mentions Blackamoors; I began to be uneasy that I had so long neglected doing any thing. When I was thus thinking, in came Bro^r Belknap to shew me a Petition he intended to present to the Genl Court for the freeing a Negro and his wife, who were unjustly held in Bondage. And there is a Motion by a Boston Committee to get a Law that all Importers of Negros shall pay 40^s *per* head, to discourage the bringing of them. And Mr. C. Mather resolves to publish a sheet to exhort Masters to labour their Conversion. Which makes me hope that I was call'd of God to Write this Apology for them; Let his Blessing accompany the same.

Lord's Day, June, 10. 1705. The Learned and pious Mr. Michael Wigglesworth dies at Malden about 9. m. Had been sick about 10. days of a Fever; 73 years and 8 moneths old. He was the Author of the Poem entituled The Day of Doom, which has been so often printed: and was very useful as a Physician.

Febr. 6. [1718]. This morning wandering in my mind whether to live a Single or a Married Life; I had a sweet and very affectionat Meditation Concerning the Lord Jesus; Nothing was to be objected against his Person, Parentage, Relations, Estate, House, Home! Why did I not resolutely, presently close with Him! And I cry'd mightily to God that He would help me so to doe![9] Govr sent Col. Brown and me in to the Deputies, to call them into the Council Chamber. Govr makes his Speech; are but just 40. Mr. Wadsworth preaches Excellently from

Gal. 6. 4. Let every one prove his own Work. Madam Dudley was present, and by a Note desired Thanks for her Recovery. Mr. Speaker, Mr. Airs, Stanton dine with us. Capt. Dwight dies on Friday night Jany 31. Mrs. Dwight today.

March, 14. Deacon Marion comes to me, sits with me a great while in the evening; after a great deal of Discourse about his Courtship—He told [*me*] the Olivers said they wish'd I would Court their Aunt.[10] I said little, but said twas not five Moneths since I buried my dear Wife. Had said before 'twas hard to know whether best to marry again or no; whom to marry. Gave him a book of the Berlin Jewish Converts.

Septr 5. [1720]. Mary Hirst goes to Board with Madam Oliver and her Mother Loyd. Going to Son Sewall's I there meet with Madam Winthrop, told her I was glad to meet her there, had not seen her a great while; gave her Mr. Homes's Sermon.

7^r 30. Mr. Colman's Lecture: Daughter Sewall acquaints Madam Winthrop that if she pleas'd to be within at 3. p. m. I would wait on her. She answer'd she would be at home.

8^r 1. Satterday, I dine at Mr. Stoddard's: from thence I went to Madam Winthrop's just at 3. Spake to her, saying, my loving wife died so soon and suddenly, 'twas hardly convenient for me to think of Marrying again; however I came to this Resolution, that I would not make my Court to any person without first Consulting with her. Had a pleasant discourse about 7 Single persons sitting in the Fore-seat 7^r 29th, viz. Mad^m Rebekah Dudley, Catharine Winthrop, Bridget Usher, Deliverance Legg, Rebekah Loyd, Lydia Colman, Elizabeth Bellingham. She propounded one and another for me; but none would do, said Mrs. Loyd was about her Age.[11]

Octob^r 3. 2. Waited on Madam Winthrop again; 'twas a little while before she came in. Her daughter Noyes being there alone with me, I said, I hoped my Waiting on her Mother would not be disagreeable to her.[12] She answer'd she should not be against that that might be for her

---

8. Sewall read Paul Baynes's *A commentary upon the First Chapter of the Epistle of St. Paul. Written to the Ephesians* (London, 1618) and decided to write *The Selling of Joseph,* published June 24, 1700.

9. Sewall was distressed over the loss of his beloved wife, Hannah Hull Sewall, who died on October 19, 1717. Sewall married Abigail Tilley on October 29, 1719, but she died within the year. In the fall of 1720, a few months after the death of his second wife, he began attempting to court Katherine Winthrop.

10. Katherine Brattle Winthrop, widow of Sewall's friend, Chief Justice Wait Still Winthrop.

11. The front pews of churches were typically reserved for widows.

12. Katherine Winthrop Jeffries Noyes, the first child of Katherine Brattle Winthrop. Katherine Winthrop was fifty-six at this time.

Comfort. I Saluted her, and told her I perceiv'd I must shortly wish her a good Time; (her mother had told me, she was with Child, and within a Moneth or two of her Time). By and by in came Mr. Airs, Chaplain of the Castle,[13] and hang'd up his Hat, which I was a little startled at, it seeming as if he was to lodge there. At last Madam Winthrop came in. After a considerable time, I went up to her and said, if it might not be inconvenient I desired to speak with her. She assented, and spake of going into another Room; but Mr. Airs and Mrs. Noyes presently rose up, and went out, leaving us there alone. Then I usher'd in Discourse from the names in the Fore-seat; at last I pray'd that Katharine [*Mrs. Winthrop*] might be the person assign'd for me. She instantly took it up in way of Denyal, as if she had catch'd at an Opportunity to do it, saying she could not do it before she was asked. Said that was her mind unless she should Change it, which she believed she should not; could not leave her Children. I express'd my Sorrow that she should do it so Speedily, pray'd her Consideration, and ask'd her when I should wait on her agen. She setting no time, I mention'd that day Sennight.[14] Gave her Mr. Willard's Fountain open'd with the little print and verses; saying, I hop'd if we did well read that book, we should meet together hereafter, if we did not now. She took the Book, and put it in her Pocket. Took Leave.

THE SELLING OF JOSEPH

A Memorial[1]

For as much as Liberty *is in real value next unto* Life: *None ought to part with it themselves, or deprive others of it, but upon most mature Consideration.*[2]

---

13. Obadiah Ayers, chaplain of Castle William in Boston Harbor.

14. "That day, seven nights," one week later.

1. The text is from the first printing in Boston by printers Green and Allen, June 24, 1700.

2. Sewall translates William Ames's "quia Libertas ex naturali æstimatione proxime accedit ad vitam ipsam," cited in the final sentence of his tract, as quoted from Ames's *De conscientia, et eius iure, vel casibus* (London, 1623). Dr. William Ames (1576–1633), a well-known Puritan, had fled to Holland in 1610 but died before he could make the anticipated crossing to New England.

The Numerousness of Slaves at this day in the Province, and the Uneasiness of them under their Slavery, hath put many upon thinking whether the Foundation of it be firmly and well laid; so as to sustain the Vast Weight that is built upon it. It is most certain that all Men, as they are the Sons of *Adam*, are Coheirs; and have equal Right unto Liberty, and all other outward Comforts of Life. GOD *hath given the Earth* [with all its Commodities] *unto the Sons of* Adam, *Psal 115.16. And hath made of One Blood, all Nations of Men, for to dwell on all the face of the Earth, and hath determined the Times before appointed, and the bounds of their habitation: That they should seek the Lord. Forasmuch then as we are the Offspring of GOD &c. Act* 17.26,27,29. Now although the Title given by the last ADAM, doth infinitely better Mens Estates, respecting GOD and themselves; and grants them a most beneficial and inviolable Lease under the Broad Seal of Heaven, who were before only Tenants at Will: Yet through the Indulgence of GOD to our First Parents after the Fall, the outward Estate of all and every of their Children, remains the same, as to one another. So that Originally, and Naturally, there is no such thing as Slavery. *Joseph* was rightfully no more a Slave to his Brethren than they were to him: and they had no more Authority to *Sell* him, than they had to *Slay* him. And if *they* had nothing to do to Sell him; the *Ishmaelites* bargaining with them, and paying down Twenty pieces of Silver, could not make a Title. Neither could Potiphar have any better Interest in him than the *Ishmaelites* had. *Gen.* 37.20,27,28. For he that shall in this case plead *Alteration of Property*, seems to have forfeited a great part of his own claim to Humanity. There is no proportion between Twenty Pieces of Silver, and LIBERTY. The Commodity it self is the Claimer. If *Arabian* Gold be imported in any quantities, most are afraid to meddle with it, though they might have it at easy rates; lest if it should have been wrongfully taken from the Owners, It should kindle a fire to the Consumption of their whole Estate. Tis pity there should be more Caution used in buying a horse, or a little lifeless dust; than there is in purchasing Men and Women: Whenas they are the Offspring of GOD and their Liberty is,

Auro pretiosior Omni.[3]

---

3. "More precious than all gold." Isaiah 13.12 reads, "I will make a man more precious than fine gold, even a man above the wedge of gold of Ophir."

And seeing GOD hath said, *He that Stealeth a Man and Selleth him, or if he be found in his hand, he shall surely be put to Death.* Exod. 21.16. This Law being of Everlasting Equity, wherein Man Stealing is ranked amongst the most atrocious of Capital Crimes: What louder Cry can there be made of that Celebrated Warning,

CAVEAT EMPTOR![4]

And all things considered, it would conduce more to the Welfare of the Province, to have White Servants for a Term of Years, than to have Slaves for Life. Few can endure to hear of a Negro's being made free; and indeed they can seldom use their freedom well; yet their continued aspiring after their forbidden Liberty, renders them Unwilling Servants. And there is such a disparity in their Conditions, Colour & Hair, that they can never embody with us, and grow up into orderly Families, to the Peopling of the Land: but still remain in our Body Politick as a kind of extravasat Blood.[5] As many Negro men as there are among us, so many empty places there are in our Train Bands, and the places taken up of Men that might make Husbands for our Daughters. And the Sons and Daughters of *New England* would become more like *Jacob,* and *Rachel,* if this Slavery were thrust quite out of doors. Moreover it is too well know what Temptations Masters are under, to connive at the Fornication of their Slaves; lest they should be obliged to find them Wives, or pay their Fines. It seems to be practically pleaded that they might be Lawless; 'tis thought much of, that the Law should have Satisfaction for their Thefts, and other Immoralities; by which means, *Holiness to the Lord,* is more rarely engraven upon this sort of Servitude. It is likewise most lamentable to think, how in taking Negros out of *Africa,* and Selling of them here, That which GOD ha's joyned together men do boldly rend asunder; Men from their Country, Husbands from their Wives, Parents from their Children. How horrible is the Uncleanness, Mortality, if not Murder, that the Ships are guilty of that bring great Crouds of these miserable Men, and Women. Methinks, when we are bemoaning the barbarous Usage of our Friends and Kinsfolk in *Africa:* it might not be unseasonable to enquire whether we are not culpable in forcing the *Africans* to become Slaves amongst our

selves. And it may be a question whether all the Benefit received by *Negro* Slaves, will balance the Accompt of Cash laid out upon them; and for the Redemption of our own enslaved Friends out of *Africa.* Besides all the Persons and Estates that have perished there.

Obj. I. *These Blackamores are of the Posterity of* Cham, *and therefore are under the Curse of Slavery.* Gen. 9.25,26,27.

Answ. Of all Offices, one would not begg this; viz. Uncall'd for, to be an Executioner of the Vindictive Wrath of God; the extent and duration of which is to us uncertain. If this ever was a Commission; How do we know but that it is long since out of Date? Many have found it to their Cost, that a Prophetical Denunciation of Judgment against a Person or People, would not warrant them to inflict that evil. If it would, *Hazael* might justify himself in all he did against his Master, and the *Israelites,* from 2 *Kings* 8.10,12.

But it is possible that by cursory reading, this Text may have been mistaken. For *Canaan* is the Person Cursed three times over, without the mentioning of *Cham.* Good Expositors suppose the Curse entaild on him, and that this Prophesie was accomplished in the Extirpation of the *Canaanites,* and in the Servitude of the *Gibeonites. Vide Pareum.*[6] Whereas the Blackmores are not descended of *Canaan,* but of *Cush.* Pial. 68.31, *Princes shall come out of Egypt* [Mizraim] *Ethiopia* [Cush] *shall soon stretch out her hands unto God.* Under which Names, all *Africa* may be comprehended; and their Promised Conversion ought to be prayed for. *Jer.* 13.23. *Can the Ethiopian change his Skin?* This shews that Black Men are the Posterity of Cush: Who time out of mind have been distinguished by their Colour. And for want of the true, *Ovid* assigns a fabulous cause of it.

Sanguine tum credunt in corpora fumma vocate Æthiopum populos nigrum traxisse colorem.
METAMORPH. LIB. 2.[7]

Obj. 2. *The* Nigers *are brought out of a Pagan Country, into places where the Gospel is Preached.*

---

4. "Let the buyer beware!"

5. Extravast blood, blood forced out of its proper vessels. Sewall seems to be concerned about the mixing of races.

---

6. That is, "see Pareus." David Pareus (1548–1635) was a well-known Protestant theologian of Heidelberg.

7. Ovid's *Metamorphoses,* book 2, includes a passage from the myth of Phæton: "It was then, as men think, that the peoples of Ethiopia became black-skinned, since the blood was drawn to the surface of their bodies by the heat."

Answ. Evil must not be done, that good may come of it. The extraordinary and comprehensive Benefit accruing to the Church of God, and to *Joseph* personally, did not rectify his brethrens Sale of him.

Obj. 3. *The* Africans *have Wars one with another: Our Ships bring lawful Captives taken in those Wars.*

Answ. For ought is known, their Wars are much such as were between *Jacob's* Sons and their Brother *Joseph.* If they be between Town and Town; Provincial, or National: Every War is upon one side Unjust. An Unlawful War can't make lawful Captives. And by Receiving, we are in danger to promote, and partake in their Barbarous Cruelties. I am sure, if some Gentlemen should go down to the *Brewsters* to take the Air, and Fish: And a stronger party from *Hull* should Surprise them, and Sell them for Slaves to a Ship outward bound: they would think themselves unjustly dealt with; both by Sellers and Buyers. And yet 'tis to be feared, we have no other kind of Title to our *Nigers. Therefore all things whatsoever ye would that men should do to you, do ye even so to them: for this is the Law and the Prophets.* Matt. 7.12.

Obj. 4. Abraham *had Servants bought with his Money, and born in his House.*

Answ. Until the Circumstances of *Abraham's* purchase be recorded, no Argument can be drawn from it. In the mean time, Charity obliges us to conclude, that He knew it was lawful and good.

It is Observable that the *Israelites* were strictly forbidden the buying, or selling one another for Slaves. *Levit.* 25.39,46. *Jer.* 34.8 . . . 22. And GOD gaged His Blessing in lieu of any loss they might conceipt they suffered thereby. *Deut.* 15.18.

And since the partition Wall is broken down, inordinate Self love should likewise be demolished. GOD expects that Christians should be of a more Ingenuous and benign frame of spirit. Christians should carry it to all the World, as the *Israelites* were to carry it one towards another. And for men obstinately to persist in holding their Neighbours and Brethren under the Rigor of perpetual Bondage, seems to be no proper way of gaining Assurance that God ha's given them Spiritual Freedom. Our Blessed Saviour ha's altered the Measures of the ancient Love Song, and set it to a most Excellent New Tune, which all ought to be ambitious of Learning. *Matt.* 5.43,44. *John* 13.34. These *Ethiopians,* as black as they are; seeing they are the Sons and Daughters of the First *Adam,* the Brethren and Sisters of the Last ADAM, and the Offspring of GOD; They ought to be treated with a Respect agreeable.

Servitus perfecta voluntaria, inter Christianum & Christianum, ex parte servi patientis sæpe est licita, quia est necessaria: sed ex parte domini agentis, & procurando & exercendo, vix potest esse licita: quia non convenit regulæ illi generali: Quæcunque volueritis ut factant vobis homines, ita & vos facite eis. Matt. 7.12.

Perfecta servitus pænæ, non potest jure locum habere, nisi ex delicto gravi quod ultimum supplicium aliquo modo meretur: quia Libertas ex naturali æstimatione proxime accedit ad vitam ipsam, & eidem a multis præferri solet.

AMES. CAS. CONS. LIB. 5. CAP. 23.
THES. 2,3.[8]

———

MY VERSES UPON THE NEW CENTURY[1]

Once more! Our GOD, vouchsafe to Shine:
Tame Thou the Rigour of our Clime.
Make haste with thy Impartial Light,
And terminate this long dark Night.

Let the transplanted *English* Vine   5
Spread further still: still Call it Thine.

———

8. The passage comes from William Ames's *De conscientia, et eius iure, vel casibus,* book 5, chap. 23, theses 2 and 3 (London, 1623). A translation of Ames, published in London, titled *Conscience with the Power and Cases Thereof* reads for this selection: "2.2 Perfect servitude, so it be voluntary, is on the patients part often lawfull betweene Christian and Christian, because indeed it is necessary: but on the Masters part who is the agent, in procuring and exercising the authority, it is scarce lawfull; in respect, it thwarts that generall Canon, *What you would have men doe unto you, even do doe unto them; Matth.* 17.12. 3.3, Perfect servitude, by way of punishment, can have no place by right, unless for some hainous offence, which might deserve the severest punishment, to wit, death: because our liberty in the naturall account, is the very next thing to life it selfe, yea by many is preferred before it."

1. Sewall had his verses printed as a broadside, a single sheet of long paper, which he hand delivered to friends as a gift to ring in the new year and new century, January 1, 1701. On January 1, several trumpeters met on Boston Common, and, Sewall wrote in his diary, "sounded there till about sunrise." The broadside poem was printed with the heading, "Wednesday, January 1. 1701. A little before Break-a-Day, at Boston of the Massachusetts."

Prune it wtih Skill: for yield it can
More Fruit to Thee the Husbandman.

Give the poor *Indians* Eyes to see
10 The Light of Life: and set them free;
That they Religion may profess,
Denying all Ungodliness.

From hard'ned *Jews* the Vail remove,
Let them their Martyr'd JESUS love;
15 And Homage unto Him afford,
Because He is their Rightfull LORD.

So false Religions shall decay,
And Darkness fly before bright Day:
So Men shall GOD in CHRIST adore;
And worship Idols vain, no more.   20

As *Asia,* and *Africa,*
Europa, with *America;*
All Four, in Consort join'd, shall Sing
New Songs of Praise to CHRIST our KING.

JOHN SAFFIN (1632–1710)

Like Samuel Sewall, the Massachusetts Bay leader he challenged, John Saffin was born in England (in Devonshire) and brought to Scituate, Massachusetts, as a very young man. He was educated well, and he trained as a lawyer, in preparation for a career of colonial leadership. Saffin amassed a large fortune from a range of commercial ventures, including trafficking in slaves, and he held several properties, farms, which he let out to those who wished to pay rentals for farming. Saffin conceived it his right to own slaves. Indeed, as historian John Demos has shown, Saffin's household was, next to only one other person's, the largest slave-owning household in the town of Bristol. Also like Sewall, Saffin held a number of prestigious posts, some of them similar to Sewall's. He was a justice of the peace, and he served the same courts as Sewall.

Saffin was enraged when Sewall came out in support of abolishing slavery, based on his own situation with his slave, Adam. In 1694, Saffin let out a farm, including its herds of cattle and sheep and a slave, Adam, to serve the leasee, Thomas Shepard. Adam created work difficulties, leaving Shepard unhappy with his service, and Saffin revoked his promise to free Adam after having promised to free him. Adam created a legal problem for Saffin, and his case came up before Judge Sewall in 1701 and continued to the Superior Court, to which Saffin had been appointed. Sewall argued that Saffin should have stepped down from the bench and then that Saffin had tampered with the jury for his case. Saffin, enraged, created a rejoinder to Sewall's *Selling of Joseph,* publishing his pamphlet in Boston in 1701 as *A Brief and Candid Answer to a Late Printed Sheet, Entituled, The Selling of Joseph.* . . . Saffin argued that Sewall was mistaken to assume that man stealing, the selling of Joseph, and slavery were parallel situations. The effort, by way of logic, seemed sound, and Sewall's efforts to reduce slavery in Massachusetts reached little fruition. Yet Adam was freed in 1703, thanks to the efforts of Samuel Sewall.

A BRIEF AND CANDID ANSWER[1]

That Honourable and Learned Gentleman, the Author of a Sheet, Entituled, *The Selling of Joseph,* A Memorial, seems from thence to draw this conclusion, that because

the Sons of *Jacob* did very ill in selling their Brother *Joseph* to the *Ishmaelites,* who were Heathens, therefore it is utterly unlawful to Buy and Sell Negroes, though among Christians; which Conclusion I presume is not well drawn from the Premises, nor is the case parallel; for it was unlawful for the *Israelites* to Sell their Brethren upon any account, or pretence whatsoever during life. But it was not unlawful for the Seed of *Abraham* to have Bond men, and Bond women either born in their House, or bought with their Money, as it is written of *Abraham, Gen. 14. 14. & 21. 10. & Exod.* 21. 16 & *Levit.* 25. 44. 45,

---

1. The text is from the 1701 publication of Saffin's *A Brief and Candid Answer to a Late Printed Sheet, Entituled, The Selling of Joseph.* . . .

46 v. After the giving of the Law: And in *Josh.* 9. 23. That famous Example of the *Gibeonites* is a sufficient proof where there no other.

To speak a little to the Gentlemans first Assertion: *That none ought to part with their Liberty themselves, or deprive others of it but upon mature consideration;* a prudent exception, in which he grants, that upon some consideration a man may be deprived of his Liberty. And then presently in his next Position or Assertion he denies it, *viz.: It is most certain, that all men as they are the Sons of* Adam *are Coheirs, and have equal right to Liberty, and all other Comforts of Life,* which he would prove out of *Psal.* 115. 16. *The Earth hath he given to the Children of Men.* True, but what is all this to the purpose, to prove that all men have equal right to Liberty, and all outward comforts of this life; which Position seems to invert the Order that God hath set in the World, who hath Ordained different degrees and orders of men, some to be High and Honourable, some to be Low and Despicable; some to be Monarchs, Kings, Princes and Governours, Masters and Commanders, others to be Subjects, and to be Commanded; Servants of sundry sorts and degrees, bound to obey; yea, some to be born Slaves, and so to remain during their lives, as hath been proved. Otherwise there would be a meer parity among men, contrary to that of the Apostle, I *Cor.* 12 *from the* 13 *to the* 26 *verse,* where he sets forth (by way of comparison) the different sorts and offices of the Members of the Body, indigitating that they are all of use, but not equal, and of like dignity. So God hath set different Orders and Degrees of Men in the World, both in Church and Common weal. Now, if this Position of parity should be true, it would then follow that the ordinary Course of Divine Providence of God in the World should be wrong, and unjust, (which we must not dare to think, much less to affirm) and all the sacred Rules, Precepts and Commands of the Almighty which he hath given to the Son of Men to observe and keep in their respective Places, Orders and Degrees, would be to no purpose; which unaccountably derogate from the Divine Wisdom of the most High, who hath made nothing in vain, but hath Holy Ends in all his Dispensations to the Children of men.

In the next place, this worthy Gentleman makes a large Discourse concerning the Utility and Conveniency to keep the one, and inconveniency of the other; respecting white and black Servants, which conduceth most to the welfare and benefit of this Province: which he concludes to be white men, who are in many respects to be preferred before Blacks; who doubts that? Doth it therefore follow, that it is altogether unlawful for Christians to buy and keep Negro Servants (for this is the Thesis) but that those that have them ought in Conscience to set them free, and so lose all the money they cost (for we must not live in any known sin) this seems to be his opinion; but it is a Question whether it ever was the Gentleman's practice? But if he could perswade the General Assembly to make an Act, That all that have Negroes, and do set them free, shall be Reimbursed out of the Publick Treasury, and that there shall be no more Negroes brought into the Country; 'tis probable there would be more of his opinion; yet he would find it a hard task to bring the Country to consent thereto; for then the Negroes must be all sent out of the Country, or else the remedy would be worse than the Disease; and it is to be feared that those Negroes that are free, if there be not some strict course taken with them by Authority, they will be a plague to this Country.

Again, If it should be unlawful to deprive them that are lawful Captives, or Bondmen of their Liberty for Life being Heathens; it seems to be more unlawful to deprive our Brethren, of our own or other Christian Nations of the Liberty, (though but for a time) by binding them to Serve some Seven, Ten, Fifteen, and some Twenty Years, which oft times proves for their whole Life, as many have been; which in effect is the same in Nature, though different in the time, yet this was allow'd among the *Jews* by the Law of God; and is the constant practice of our own and other Christian Nations in the World: the which our Author by his Dogmatical Assertions doth condemn as Irreligious; which is Diametrically contrary to the Rules and Precepts which God hath given the diversity of men to observe in their respective Stations, Callings, and Conditions of Life, as hath been observed.

And to illustrate his Assertion our Author brings in by way of Comparison the Law of God against man Stealing, on pain of Death: Intimating thereby, that Buying and Selling of Negro's is a breach of that Law, and so deserves Death: A severe Sentence: But herein he begs the Question with a *Caveat Emptor.* For, in that very Chapter there is a Dispensation to the People of *Israel,* to have Bond men, Women and Children, even of their own Nation in some case; and Rules given therein to be observed concerning them; Verse the 4*th.* And in the before cited place, *Levit.* 25.44, 45, 46. Though the *Israelites* were forbidden (ordinarily) to make Bond men and Women of their own Nation, but of Strangers they might: the words run thus, verse 44. *Both thy Bond men, and thy Bond maids which thou shalt have shall be of the Heathen, that are round about you: of them shall you Buy Bond men and Bond* maids, &c. See also, I Cor. 12.13. Whether we be Bond or Free, which shows that in the times of the New Testament, there were Bond men also, &c.

In fine, The sum of this long Haurange, is no other, than to compare the Buying and Selling of Negro's unto the Stealing of Men, and the Selling of *Joseph* by his Brethren, which bears no proportion therewith, nor is there any congruiety therein, as appears by the foregoing Texts.

Our Author doth further proceed to answer some Objections of his own framing, which he supposes some might raise.

Object. I. *That these Blackamores are of the Posterity of* Cham, *and therefore under the Curse of Slavery. Gen.* 9.25, 26, 27. The which the Gentleman seems to deny, saying, *they ware the Seed of Canaan that were Cursed, &c.*

Answ. Whether they were so or not, we shall not dispute: this may suffice, that not only the seed of *Cham* or *Canaan,* but any lawful Captives of other Heathen Nations may be made Bond men as hath been proved.

Obj. 2. *That the Negroes are brought out of Pagan Countreys into places where the Gospel is Preached.* To which he Replies, *that we must not doe Evil that Good may come of it.*

Ans. To which we answer, That it is no Evil thing to bring them out of their own Heathenish Country, where they may have the Knowledge of the True God, be Converted and Eternally saved.

Obj. 3. *The* Africans *have Wars one with another;* our Ships bring lawful Captives taken in those Wars.

To which our Author answers Conjecturally, and Doubtfully, *for ought we know,* that which may or may not be; which is insignificant, and proves nothing. He also compares the Negroes Wars, one Nation with another, with the Wars between *Joseph* and his Brethren. But where doth he read of any such War? We read indeed of a Domestick Quarrel they had with him, they envyed and hated *Joseph;* but by what is Recorded, he was meerly passive and meek as a Lamb. This Gentleman farther adds, *That there is not any War but is unjust on one side, &c.* Be it so, what doth that signify: We read of lawful Captives taken in the Wars, and lawful to be Bought and Sold without contracting the guilt of the *Agressors;* for which we have the example of *Abraham* before quoted; but if we must stay while both parties Warring are in the right, there would be no lawful Captives at all to be Bought; which seems to be rediculous to imagine, and contrary to the tenour of Scripture, and all Humane Histories on that subject.

Obj. 4. *Abraham had Servants bought with his Money,*

and born in his House. Gen. 14.14. To which our worthy Author answers, *until the Circumstances of Abraham's purchase be recorded, no Argument can be drawn from it.*

Ans. To which we Reply, this is also Dogmatical, and proves nothing. He farther adds, *In the mean time Charity Obliges us to conclude, that he knew it was lawful and good.* Here the gentleman yields the case; for if we are in Charity bound to believe *Abrahams* practice, in buying and keeping *Slaves* in his house to be lawful and good: then it follows, that our Imitation of him in this his Moral Action, is as warrantable as that of his Faith; *who is the Father of all them that believe. Rom.* 4.16.

In the close of all, Our Author Quotes two more places of Scripture, *viz.; Levit.* 25.46, and *Jer.* 34, from the 8. to the 22. *v.* To prove that the people of Israel were strictly forbidden the Buying and Selling one another for *Slaves:* who questions that? and what is that to the case in hand? What a strange piece of Logick is this? Tis unlawful for Christians to Buy and Sell one another for slaves. *Ergo,* It is unlawful to Buy and Sell Negroes that are lawful Captiv'd Heathens.

And after a Serious Exhortation to us all to Love one another according to the Command of Christ. *Math.* 5.43, 44. This worthy Gentleman concludes with this Assertion, *That these Ethiopeans as Black as they are, seeing they are the Sons and Daughters of the first* Adam; *the Brethren and Sisters of the Second* Adam, *and the Offspring of God; we ought to treat them with a respect agreeable.*

Ans. We grant it for a certain and undeniable verity, That all Mankind are the Sons and Daughters of *Adam,* and the Creatures of God: But it doth not therefore follow that we are bound to love and respect all men alike; this under favour we must take leave to deny; we ought in charity, if we see our Neighbour in want, to relieve them in a regular way, but we are not bound to give them so much of our Estates, as to make them equal with our selves, because they are our Brethren, the Sons of *Adam,* no, not our own natural Kinsmen: We are Exhorted *to do good unto all, but especially to them who are of the Household of Faith, Gal.* 6.10. And we are to love, honour and respect all men according to the gift of God that is in them: I may love my Servant well, but my Son better; Charity begins at home, it would be a violation of common prudence, and a breach of good manners, to treat a Prince like a Peasant. And this worthy Gentleman would deem himself much neglected, if we should show him no more Defference than to an ordinary Porter: And therefore these florid expressions, the Sons and Daughters of the First *Adam,* the Brethren and Sisters of the Second *Adam,* and the Offspring of God, seem to be misapplied to import and insinuate, that we ought to tender Pagan Negroes with all love, kindness, and equal respect as to the best of men.

By all which it doth evidently appear both by Scripture and Reason, the practice of the People of God in all Ages, both before and after the giving of the Law, and in the times of the Gospel, that there were Bond men, Women and Children commonly kept by holy and good men, and improved in Service; and therefore by the Command of God, *Lev.* 25, 44, and their venerable Example, we may keep Bond men, and use them in our Service still; yet with all candour, moderation and Christian prudence, according to their state and condition consonant to the Word of God.

The Negroes Character

Cowardly and cruel are those Blacks Innate,
Prone to Revenge, Imp of inveterate hate.
He that exasperates them, soon espies
Mischief and Murder in their very eyes.
Libidinous, Deceitful, False and Rude,
The spume Issue of Ingratitude.
The Premises consider'd, all may tell,
How near good Joseph they are parallel.

SARAH KEMBLE KNIGHT (1666–1727)

Sarah Kemble Knight's reputation as a writer today rests on the strength of one narrative, a journal of her five-month journey from Boston to New York and back between 1704 and 1705. Knight's journal is humorous and self-consciously literary, drawing on elements of the mock epic and picaresque traditions, with verses interspersed throughout the entries. Its character and method of development suggest that this was not a journal intended to be kept private, but was instead a narrative that Knight circulated among her friends when she returned, for their entertainment. Since the nineteenth century, critics have recognized the journal as a rare narrative that provides a significant amount of insight into literary culture and social attitudes in the northern British colonies.

Born on April 19, 1666, in Boston, Sarah Kemble married Richard Knight in 1689. Both before and after her husband's death (probably in 1706), Sarah Kemble Knight was active in a number of business capacities. Like many women in the British colonies, she assisted her husband with office duties. Knight copied and witnessed public documents, ran their shop, and took in boarders at the house she had inherited from her father. Also like many women in New England, she evidently ran a school. When her only daughter married and moved to Connecticut in 1713, Knight moved as well. Knight continued a number of business activities—speculating in Indian lands, running several farms, and innkeeping—in New London, Connecticut, where she died on September 25, 1727.

Knight's literary skill, personality, and self-confidence come to the fore in her journal. She made the trip to New York in 1704, following the death of her cousin, Caleb Trowbridge, to settle his estate. She first traveled to New Haven in October and then made an additional trip to New York in December. Returning to New Haven at the end of that month, Knight spent nearly two more months working to settle the estate before she returned home to Boston in March. Brief references in the journal suggest that the settlement of the estate was protracted and contentious, and Knight seems to have demonstrated considerable tenacity in refusing to settle on an agreement that she did not consider fair for her cousin's young widow.

Yet because her journal was evidently written for the women in her circle, rather than merely for family, the settlement of the estate received little attention in the journal, which reveals Knight's narrative skill. In episodic style, Knight recounts her daily travel and her search for lodging each night. Knight clearly delighted in story telling, creating interesting and occasionally detailed accounts of the people at the inns and homes where she and her guides were accommodated. She creates the effect of humor for her contemporaries by featuring the dialects of her speakers and making of them rather stereotypical stock characters, such as the country bumpkin. Knight's highly literary treatment of the people and places she encountered differentiates this journal from other travel narratives of the time, thus indicating that the narrative's purpose went beyond a mere recording of the events she experienced.

THE JOURNAL OF
SARAH KEMBLE KNIGHT[1]

Monday, Octb'r. ye Second, 1704.—About three o'clock afternoon, I begun my Journey from Boston to New-Haven; being about two Hundred Mile. My Kinsman, Capt. Robert Luist, waited on me as farr as Dedham, where I was to meet ye Western post.

I vissitted the Reverd. Mr. Belcher,[2] ye Minister of ye town, and tarried there till evening, in hopes ye post would come along. But he not coming, I resolved to go to Billingses where he used to lodg, being 12 miles further. But being ignorant of the way, Mad^m Billings,[3] seing no persuasions of her good spouses or hers could prevail with me to Lodg there that night, Very kindly went wyth me to ye Tavern, where I hoped to get my guide, And desired the Hostess to inquire of her guests whether any of them would go with mee. But they being tyed by the Lipps to a pewter engine, scarcely allowed themselves time to say what clownish. . . . [4] Peices of eight, I told her no, I would not be accessary to such extortion.

Then John shan't go, sais shee. No, indeed, shan't hee; And held forth at that rate a long time, that I began to fear I was got among the Quaking tribe, beleeving not a Limbertong'd sister among them could out do Madm. Hostes.

Upon this, to my no small surprise, son John arrose, and gravely demanded what I would give him to go with me? Give you, sais I, are you John? Yes, says he, for want of a Better; And behold! this John look't as old as my Host, and perhaps had bin a man in the last Century. Well, Mr. John, sais I, make your demands. Why, half a pss. of eight and a dram, sais John. I agreed, and gave him a Dram (now) in hand to bind the bargain.

My hostess catechis'd John for going so cheep, saying

his poor wife would break her heart. . . .[5] His shade on his Hors resembled a Globe on a Gate post. His habitt, Hors and furniture, its looks and goings Incomparably answered the rest.

Thus Jogging on with an easy pace, my Guide telling mee it was dangero's to Ride hard in the Night, (wh^ch his horse had the sence to avoid,) Hee entertained me with the Adventurs he had passed by late Rideing, and eminent Dangers he had escaped, so that, Remembring the Hero's in Parismus and the Knight of the Oracle, I didn't know but I had mett wth a Prince disguis'd.[6]

When we had Ridd about an how'r, wee come into a thick swamp, wch. by Reason of a great fogg, very much startled mee, it being now very Dark. But nothing dismay'd John: Hee had encountered a thousand and a thousand such Swamps, having a Universall Knowledge in the woods; and readily Answered all my inquiries wch. were not a few.

In about an how'r, or something more, after we left the Swamp, we come to Billinges, where I was to Lodg. My Guide dismounted and very Complasantly help't me down and shewd the door, signing to me wth his hand to Go in; wch I Gladly did—But had not gone many steps into the Room, ere I was Interogated by a young Lady I understood afterwards was the Eldest daughter of the family, with these, or words to this purpose, (viz.) Law for mee—what in the world brings You here at this time a night?—I never see a woman on the Rode so Dreadfull late, in all the days of my versall[7] life. Who are You? Where are You going? I'me scar'd out of my witts—with much now of the same Kind. I stood aghast, Prepareing to reply, when in comes my Guide—to him Madam turn'd, Roreing out: Lawfull heart, John, is it You?—how de do! Where in the world are you going with this woman? Who is she? John made no Ansr. but sat down in the corner, fumbled out his black Junk,[8] and saluted that instead of Debb; she then turned agen to mee and fell anew into her silly questions, without asking me to sitt down.

I told her shee treated me very Rudely, and I did not

1. The first printing of Knight's journal occurred in 1825, more than a century after Knight wrote it and well after it was getting circulated among her friends. In its original published title, *The Journal of Madam Knight,* along with that of Reverend Thomas Buckingham, was originally published by Timothy Dwight (New York, 1825). The manuscript no longer exists. The current text is taken from Dwight's edition.

2. Joseph Belcher (1669–1723).

3. Knight must have meant to write Mrs. Belcher here.

4. Here half a page of the manuscript was missing when Dwight first printed the journal.

5. Here half a page of the manuscript was missing when Dwight first printed the journal.

6. *Parismus, the Renowned Prince of Bohemia* (1598) and *The Famous History of Montelion, Knight of the Oracle* (earliest surviving edition 1633) were popular romances by Emanuel Ford.

7. Entire.

8. Tobacco.

think it my duty to answer her unmannerly Questions. But to get ridd of them, I told her I come there to have the post's company with me to-morrow on my Journey, &c. Miss star'd awhile, drew a chair, bid me sitt, And then run up stairs and putts on two or three Rings, (or else I had not seen them before,) and returning, sett herself just before me, showing the way to Reding, that I might see her Ornaments, perhaps to gain the more respect. But her Granam's new Rung sow,[9] had it appeared, would affected me as much. I paid honest John wth money and dram according to contract, and Dismist him, and pray'd Miss to shew me where I must Lodg. Shee conducted me to a parlour in a little back Lento, wch was almost fill'd wth the bedsted, wch was so high that I was forced to climb on a chair to gitt up to ye wretched bed that lay on it; on wch having Stretcht my tired Limbs, and lay'd my head on a Sad-colourd pillow, I began to think on the transactions of ye past day.

Tuesday, October ye Third, about 8 in the morning, I with the Post proceeded forward without observing any thing remarkable; And about two, afternoon, Arrived at the Post's second stage, where the western Post mett him and exchanged Letters. Here, having called for something to eat, ye woman bro't in a Twisted thing like a cable, but something whiter; and laying it on the bord, tugg'd for life to bring it into a capacity to spread; wch having wth great pains accomplished, shee serv'd in a dish of Pork and Cabage, I suppose the remains of Dinner. The sause was of a deep Purple, wch I tho't was boil'd in her dye Kettle; the bread was Indian,[10] and every thing on the Table service Agreeable to these. I, being hungry, gott a little down; but my stomach was soon cloy'd, and what cabbage I swallowed serv'd me for a Cudd the whole day after.

Having here discharged the Ordnary[11] for self and Guide, (as I understood was the custom,) About Three afternoon went on with my Third Guide, who Rode very hard; and having crossed Providence Ferry, we come to a River wch they Generally Ride thro'. But I dare not venture; so the Post got a Ladd and Cannoo to carry me to tother side, and hee rid thro' and Led my hors. The Can-

noo was very small and shallow, so that when we were in she seem'd redy to take in water, which greatly terrified mee, and caused me to be very circumspect, sitting with my hands fast on each side, my eyes stedy, not daring so much as to lodg my tongue a hair's breadth more on one side of my mouth then tother, nor so much as think on Lott's wife, for a wry thought would have oversett our wherey: But was soon put out of this pain, by feeling the Cannoo on shore, wch I as soon almost saluted with my feet; and Rewarding my sculler, again mounted and made the best of our way forwards. The Rode here was very even and ye day pleasant, it being now near Sunsett. But the Post told mee we had neer 14 miles to Ride to the next Stage, (where we were to Lodg.) I askt him of the rest of the Rode, foreseeing wee must travail in the night. Hee told mee there was a bad River we were to Ride thro', wch was so very firce a hors could sometimes hardly stem it: But it was but narrow, and wee should soon be over. I cannot express The concern of mind this relation sett me in: no thoughts but those of the dang'ros River could entertain my Imagination, and they were as formidable as varios, still Tormenting me with blackest Ideas of my Approaching fate—Sometimes seing my self drowning, otherwhiles drowned, and at the best like a holy Sister Just come out of a Spiritual Bath in dripping Garments.

Now was the Glorious Luminary, wth his swift Coursers arrived at his Stage, leaving poor me wth the rest of this part of the lower world in darkness, with which *wee* were soon Surrounded. The only Glimering we now had was from the spangled Skies, Whose Imperfect Reflections rendered every Object formidable. Each lifeless Trunk, with its shatter'd Limbs, appear'd an Armed Enymie; and every little stump like a Ravenous devourer. Nor could I so much as discern my Guide, when at any distance, which added to the terror.

Thus, absolutely lost in Thought, and dying with the very thoughts of drowning, I come up wth the post, who I did not see till even with his Hors: he told mee he stopt for mee; and wee Rode on Very deliberately a few paces, when we entred a Thickett of Trees and Shrubbs, and I perceived by the Hors's going, we were on the descent of a Hill, w^ch, as wee come neerer the bottom, 'twas totaly dark wth the Trees that surrounded it. But I knew by the Going of the Hors wee had entred the water, wch my Guide told mee was the hazzardos River he had told me off; and hee, Riding up close to my Side, Bid me not fear—we should be over Imediatly. I now ralyed all the Courage I was mistriss of, Knowing that I must either Venture my fate of drowning, or be left like ye Children in

---

9. A sow with a ring through its snout.

10. Indian bread was unleavened bread made with cornmeal, which the English generally considered inferior to white bread.

11. Paid the dinner bill (an ordinary was an eating establishment where meals were served at a fixed price).

the wood.[12] So, as the Post bid me, I gave Reins to my Nagg; and sitting as Stedy as Just before in the Cannoo, in a few minutes got safe to the other side, which hee told mee was the Narragansett country.

Here We found great difficulty in Travailing, the way being very narrow, and on each side the Trees and bushes gave us very unpleasent welcomes wth their Branches and bow's, w[ch] wee could not avoid, it being so exceeding dark. My Guide, as before so now, putt on harder than I, wth my weary bones, could follow; so left mee and the way beehind him. Now Returned my distressed aprehensions of the place where I was: the dole-some woods, my Company next to none, Going I knew not whither, and encompased wth Terrifying darkness; The least of which was enough to startle a more Masculine courage. Added to which the Reflections, as in the afternoon of y[e] day that my Call was very Questionable,[13] w[ch] till then I had not so Prudently as I ought considered. Now, coming to y[e] foot of a hill, I found great difficulty in ascending; But being got to the Top, was there amply recompenced with the friendly Appearance of the Kind Conductress of the night, Just then Advancing above the Horisontall Line. The Raptures w[ch] the Sight of that fair Planett produced in mee, caus'd mee, for the Moment, to forgett my present wearyness and past toils; and Inspir'd me for most of the remaining way with very divirting tho'ts, some of which, with the other Occurances of the day, I reserved to note down when I should come to my Stage. My tho'ts on the sight of the moon were to this purpose:

Fair Cynthia,[14] all the Homage that I may
Unto a Creature, unto thee I pay;
In Lonesome woods to meet so kind a guide,
To Mee's more worth than all the world beside.
Some Joy I felt just now, when safe got or'e
Yon Surly River to this Rugged shore,
Deeming Rough welcomes from these clownish Trees,
Better than Lodgings wth Nereidees.[15]
Yet swelling fears surprise; all dark appears—
Nothing but Light can disipate those fears.
My fainting vitals can't lend strength to say,

But softly whisper, O I wish'twere day.
The murmer hardly warm'd the Ambient air,
E're thy Bright Aspect rescues from dispair:
Makes the old Hagg her sable mantle loose,
And a Bright Joy do's through my Soul diffuse.
The Boistero's Trees now Lend a Passage Free,
And pleasent prospects thou giv'st light to see.

From hence wee kept on, with more ease y[n] before: the way being smooth and even, the night warm and serene, and the Tall and thick Trees at a distance, especially w[n] the moon glar'd light through the branches, fill'd my Imagination wth the pleasent delusion of a Sumpteous citty, fill'd wth famous Buildings and churches, wth their spiring steeples, Balconies, Galleries and I know not what: Granduers w[ch] I had heard of, and w[ch] the stories of foreign countries had given me the Idea of.

Here stood a Lofty church—there is a steeple,
And there the Grand Parade—O see the people!
That Famouse Castle there, were I but nigh,
To see the mote and Bridg and walls so high—
They'r very fine! sais my deluded eye.

Being thus agreably entertain'd without a thou't of any thing but thoughts themselves, I on a suden was Rous'd from these pleasing Imaginations, by the Post's sounding his horn, which assured mee hee was arrived at the Stage, where we were to Lodg: and that musick was then most musickall and agreeable to mee.

Being come to mr. Havens', I was very civilly Received, and courteously entertained, in a clean comfortable House; and the Good woman was very active in helping off my Riding clothes, and then ask't what I would eat. I told her I had some Chocolett, if shee would prepare it; which with the help of some Milk, and a little clean brass Kettle, she soon effected to my satisfaction. I then betook me to my Apartment, w[ch] was a little Room parted from the Kitchen by a single bord partition; where, after I had noted the Occurrances of the past day, I went to bed, which, tho' pretty hard, Yet neet and handsome. But I could get no sleep, because of the Clamor of some of the Town tope-ers in next Room, Who were entred into a strong debate concerning y[e] Signifycation of the name of their Country, (viz.) *Narraganset*. One said it was named so by y[e] Indians, because there grew a Brier there, of a prodigious Highth and bigness, the like hardly ever known, called by the Indians Narragansett; And quotes an Indian of so Barberous a name for his Author, that I could not write it. His Antagonist Replyed no—It was from a

---

12. "The Children in the Wood" was an English Ballad about a brother and sister abandoned in the woods to die.

13. Knight suggests uncertainty about the state of her soul.

14. A poetic name for the moon.

15. Sea nymphs.

Spring it had its name, wch hee well knew where it was, which was extreem cold in summer, and as Hott as could be imagined in the winter, which was much resorted too by the natives, and by them called Narragansett, (Hott and Cold,) and that was the originall of their places name— with a thousand Impertinances not worth notice, wch He utter'd with such a Roreing voice and Thundering blows with the fist of wickedness on the Table, that it peirced my very head. I heartily fretted, and wish't 'um tongue tyed; but wth as little succes as a freind of mine once, who was (as shee said) kept a whole night awake, on a Jorny, by a country Left.[16] and a Sergent, Insigne and a Deacon, contriving how to bring a triangle into a Square. They kept calling for tother Gill,[17] wch while they were swallowing, was some Intermission; But presently, like Oyle to fire, encreased the flame. I set my Candle on a Chest by the bed side, and setting up, fell to my old way of composing my Resentments, in the following manner:

I ask thy Aid, O Potent Rum!
To Charm these wrangling Topers Dum.
Thou hast their Giddy Brains possest—
The man confounded wth the Beast—
And I, poor I, can get no rest.
Intoxicate them with thy fumes:
O still their Tongues till morning comes!

And I know not but my wishes took effect; for the dispute soon ended w^th 'tother Dram; and so Good night!

Wedensday, Octob^r 4th. About four in the morning, we set out for Kingston (for so was the Town called) with a french Docter in our company. Hee and ye Post put on very furiously, so that I could not keep up with them, only as now and then they'd stop till they see mee. This Rode was poorly furnished wth accommodations for Travellers, so that we were forced to ride 22 miles by the post's account, but neerer thirty by mine, before wee could bait so much as our Horses, wch I exceedingly complained of. But the post encourag'd mee, by saying wee should be well accommodated anon at mr. Devills, a few miles further. But I questioned whether we ought to go to the Devil to be helpt out of affliction. However, like the rest of Deluded souls that post to ye Infernal denn, Wee made all possible speed to this Devil's Habitation; where alliting, in full assurance of good accommodation, wee were going in. But meeting his two daughters, as I suposed twins, they so

neerly resembled each other, both in features and habit, and look't as old as the Divel himselfe, and quite as Ugly, We desired entertainm't, but could hardly get a word out of 'um, till with our Importunity, telling them our necesity, &c. they call'd the old Sophister, who was as sparing of his words as his daughters had bin, and no, or none, was the reply's hee made us to our demands. Hee differed only in this from the old fellow in to'ther Country: hee let us depart. However, I thought it proper to warn poor Travailers to endeavour to Avoid falling into circumstances like ours, wch at our next Stage I sat down and did as followeth:

May all that dread the cruel feind of night
Keep on, and not at this curs't Mansion light.
'Tis Hell; 'tis Hell! and Devills here do dwell:
Here dwells the Devill—surely this's Hell.
Nothing but Wants; a drop to cool yo'r Tongue
Cant be procur'd these cruel Feinds among.
Plenty of horrid Grins and looks sevear,
Hunger and thirst, But pitty's bannish'd here—
The Right hand keep, if Hell on Earth you fear!

Thus leaving this habitation of cruelty, we went forward; and arriving at an Ordinary about two mile further, found tollerable accommodation. But our Hostes, being a pretty full mouth'd old creature, entertain'd our fellow travailer, ye french Docter, wth Inumirable complaints of her bodily infirmities; and whisperd to him so lou'd, that all ye House had as full a hearing as hee: which was very diviting to ye company, (of which there was a great many,) as one might see by their sneering. But poor weary I slipt out to enter my mind in my Jornal, and left my Great Landly with her Talkative Guests to themselves.

From hence we proceeded (about ten forenoon) through the Narragansett country, pretty Leisurely; and about one afternoon come to Paukataug River, wch was about two hundred paces over, and now very high, and no way over to to'ther side but this. I darid not venture to Ride thro, my courage at best in such cases but small, And now at the Lowest Ebb, by reason of my weary, very weary, hungry and uneasy Circumstances. So takeing leave of my company, tho' wth no little Reluctance, that I could not proceed wth them on my Jorny, Stop at a little cottage Just by the River, to wait the Waters falling, wch the old man that lived there said would be in a little time, and he would conduct me safe over. This little Hutt was one of the wretchedest I ever saw a habitation for human creatures. It was suported with shores enclosed with Clapboards, laid on Lengthways, and so much asunder, that the Light come throu' every where; the doore tyed on

---

16. Lieutenant.

17. A drinking vessel holding a quarter pint.

wth a cord in ye place of hinges; The floor the bear earth; no windows but such as the thin covering afforded, nor any furniture but a Bedd wth a glass Bottle hanging at ye head on't; an earthan cupp, a small pewter Bason, A Bord wth sticks to stand on, instead of a table, and a block or two in ye corner instead of chairs. The family were the old man, his wife and two Children; all and every part being the picture of poverty. Notwithstanding both the Hutt and its Inhabitance were very clean and tydee: to the crossing the Old Proverb, that bare walls make giddy hows-wifes.

I Blest myselfe that I was not one of this misserable crew; and the Impressions their wretchedness formed in me caused mee on ye very Spott to say:

Tho' Ill at ease, A stranger and alone,
All my fatigu's shall not extort a grone.
These Indigents have hunger with their ease;
Their best is wors behalfe then my disease.
Their Misirable hutt wch Heat and Cold
Alternately without Repulse do hold;
Their Lodgings thyn and hard, their Indian fare,
The mean Apparel which the wretches wear,
And their ten thousand ills wch can't be told,
Makes nature er'e 'tis midle age'd look old.
When I reflect, my late fatigues do seem
Only a notion or forgotten Dreem.

I had scarce done thinking, when an Indian-like Animal come to the door, on a creature very much like himselfe, in mien and feature, as well as Ragged cloathing; and having 'litt, makes an Awkerd Scratch wth his Indian shoo, and a Nodd, sitts on ye block, fumbles out his black Junk, dipps it in ye Ashes, and presents it piping hott to his muscheeto's,[18] and fell to sucking like a calf, without speaking, for near a quarter of an hower. At length the old man said how do's Sarah do? who I understood was the wretches wife, and Daughter to ye old man: he Replyed— as well as can be expected, &c. So I remembred the old say, and suposed I knew Sarah's case. Butt hee being, as I understood, going over the River, as ugly as hee was, I was glad to ask him to show me ye way to Saxtons, at Stoningtown; wch he promising, I ventur'd over wth the old mans assistance; who having rewarded to content, with my Tattertailed guide, I Ridd on very slowly thro' Stoningtown, where the Rode was very Stony and uneven. I asked the fellow, as we went, divers questions of the place and way, &c. I being arrived at my country Sax-

tons, at Stonington, was very well accommodated both as to victuals and Lodging, the only Good of both I had found since my setting out. Here I heard there was an old man and his Daughter to come that way, bound to N. London; and being now destitute of a Guide, gladly waited for them, being in so good a harbour, and accordingly, Thirsday, Octob^r ye 5th, about 3 in the afternoon, I sat forward with neighbour Polly and Jemima, a Girl about 18 Years old, who hee said he had been to fetch out of the Narragansetts, and said they had Rode thirty miles that day, on a sory lean Jade, wth only a Bagg under her for a pillion, which the poor Girl often complain'd was very uneasy.

Wee made Good speed along, wch made poor Jemima make many a sow'r face, the mare being a very hard trotter; and after many a hearty and bitter Oh, she at length Low'd out: Lawful Heart father! this bare mare hurts mee Dingeely, I'me direfull sore I vow; with many words to that purpose: poor Child sais Gaffer—she us't to serve your mother so. I don't care how mother us't to do, quoth Jemima, in a pasionate tone. At which the old man Laught, and kik't his Jade o' the side, which made her Jolt ten times harder.

About seven that Evening, we come to New London Ferry: here, by reason of a very high wind, we mett with great difficulty in getting over—the Boat tos't exceedingly, and our Horses capper'd at a very surprizing Rate, and set us all in a fright; especially poor Jemima, who desired her father to say so jack to the Jade, to make her stand. But the careless parent, taking no notice of her repeated desires, She Rored out in a Passionate manner: Pray suth father, Are you deaf? Say so Jack to the Jade, I tell you. The Dutiful Parent obey's; saying so Jack, so Jack, as gravely as if hee'd bin to saying Catechise after Young Miss, who with her fright look't of all coullers in ye Rain Bow.

Being safely arrived at the house of Mrs. Prentices in N. London, I treated neighbour Polly and daughter for their divirting company, and bid them farewell; and between nine and ten at night waited on the Rev^d Mr. Gurdon Saltonstall,[19] minister of the town, who kindly Invited me to Stay that night at his house, where I was very handsomely and plentifully treated and Lodg'd; and made good the Great Character I had before heard concerning him: viz. that hee was the most affable, courteous, Genero's and best of men.

---

18. Mustache.

19. Gurdon Saltonstall (1666–1724), minister at New London, Connecticut, and later governor of Connecticut.

Friday, Octo[r] 6th. I got up very early, in Order to hire somebody to go with mee to New Haven, being in Great parplexity at the thoughts of proceeding alone; which my most hospitable entertainer observing, himselfe went, and soon return'd wth a young Gentleman of the town, who he could confide in to Go with mee; and about eight this morning, wth Mr. Joshua Wheeler my new Guide, takeing leave of this worthy Gentleman, Wee advanced on towards Seabrook. The Rodes all along this way are very bad, Incumbred wth Rocks and mountainos passages, w[ch] were very disagreeable to my tired carcass; but we went on with a moderate pace w[ch] made y[e] Journy more pleasent. But after about eight miles Rideing, in going over a Bridge under w[ch] the River Run very swift, my hors stumbled, and very narrowly 'scaped falling over into the water; w[ch] extreemly frightened mee. But through God's Goodness I met with no harm, and mounting agen, in about half a miles Rideing, come to an ordinary, were well entertained by a woman of about seventy and vantage,[20] but of as Sound Intellectuals as one of seventeen. Shee entertain'd Mr. Wheeler wth some passages of a Wedding awhile ago at a place hard by, the Brides-Groom being about her Age or something above, Saying his Children was dredfully against their fathers marrying, w[ch] shee condemned them extreemly for.

From hence wee went pretty briskly forward, and arriv'd at Saybrook ferry about two of the Clock afternoon; and crossing it, wee call'd at an Inn to Bait, (foreseeing we should not have such another Opportunity till we come to Killingsworth.) Landlady come in, with her hair about her ears, and hands at full pay scratching. Shee told us shee had some mutton w[ch] shee would broil, w[ch] I was glad to hear; But I supose forgot to wash her scratchers; in a little time shee brot it in; but it being pickled, and my Guide said it smelt strong of head sause, we left it, and p[d] sixpence a piece for our Dinners, w[ch] was only smell.

So wee putt forward with all speed, and about seven at night come to Killingsworth, and were tollerably well with Travillers fare, and Lodgd there that night.

Saturday, Oct. 7th, we sett out early in the Morning, and being something unaquainted wth the way, having ask't it of some wee mett, they told us wee must Ride a mile or two and turne down a Lane on the Right hand; and by their Direction wee Rode on, but not Yet comeing to y[e] turning, we mett a Young fellow and ask't him how farr it was to the Lane which turn'd down towards Guilford. Hee said wee must Ride a little further, and turn down by the Corner of uncle Sams Lott. My Guide vented his Spleen at the Lubber; and we soon after came into the Rhode, and keeping still on, without any thing further Remarkabell, about two a clock afternoon we arrived at New Haven, where I was received with all Posible Respects and civility. Here I discharged Mr. Wheeler with a reward to his satisfaction, and took some time to rest after so long and toilsome a Journey; And Inform'd myselfe of the manners and customs of the place, and at the same time employed myselfe in the afair I went there upon.

They are Govern'd by the same Laws as wee in Boston, (or little differing,) thr'out this whole Colony of Connecticot, And much the same way of Church Government, and many of them good, Sociable people, and I hope Religious too: but a little too much Independant in their principalls, and, as I have been told, were formerly in their Zeal very Riggid in their Administrations towards such as their Lawes made Offenders, even to a harmless Kiss or Innocent merriment among Young people. Whipping being a frequent and counted an easy Punishment, about w[ch] as other Crimes, the Judges were absolute in their Sentances. They told mee a pleasant story about a pair of Justices in those parts, w[ch] I may not omit the relation of.

A negro Slave belonging to a man in y[e] Town, stole a hogs head from his master, and gave or sold it to an Indian, native of the place. The Indian sold it in the neighbourhood, and so the theft was found out. Thereupon the Heathen was Seized, and carried to the Justices House to be Examined. But his worship (it seems) was gone into the feild, with a Brother in office, to gather in his Pompions.[21] Whither the malefactor is hurried, And Complaint made, and satisfaction in the name of Justice demanded. Their Worships cann't proceed in form without a Bench: whereupon they Order one to be Imediately erected, which, for want of fitter materials, they made with pompions—which being finished, down setts their Worships, and the Malefactor call'd, and by the Senior Justice Interrogated after the following manner. You Indian why did You steal from this man? You sho'dn't do so—it's a Grandy wicked thing to steal. Hol't Hol't, cryes Justice Jun[r] Brother, You speak negro to him. I'le ask him. You sirrah, why did You steal this man's Hoggshead? Hoggshead? (replys the Indian,) me no stomany.[22] No? says

---

20. Over seventy.

21. Pumpkins.

22. Stomany: understand.

his Worship; and pulling off his hatt, Patted his own head with his hand, sais, Tatapa[23]—You, Tatapa—you; all one this. Hoggshead all one this. Hah! says Netop,[24] now me stomany that. Whereupon the Company fell into a great fitt of Laughter, even to Roreing. Silence is comanded, but to no effect: for they continued perfectly Shouting. Nay, sais his worship, in an angry tone, if it be so, *take mee off the Bench.*

Their Diversions in this part of the Country are on Lecture days and Training days mostly: on the former there is Riding from town to town.

And on training dayes The Youth divert themselves by Shooting at the Target, as they call it, (but it very much resembles a pillory,) where hee that hitts neerest the white has some yards of Red Ribbin presented him, w[ch] being tied to his hattband, the two ends streeming down his back, he is Led away in Triumph, wth great applause, as the winners of the Olympiack Games. They generally marry very young: the males oftener as I am told under twentie than above; they generally make public wedings, and have a way something singular (as they say) in some of them, viz. Just before Joyning hands the Bridegroom quitts the place, who is soon followed by the Bridesmen, and as it were, dragg'd back to duty—being the reverse of y[e] former practice among us, to steal m[s] Pride.

There are great plenty of Oysters all along by the sea side, as farr as I Rode in the Collony, and those very good. And they Generally lived very well and comfortably in their famelies. But too Indulgent (especially y[e] farmers) to their slaves: sufering too great familiarity from them, permitting y[m] to sit at Table and eat with them, (as they say to save time,) and into the dish goes the black hoof as freely as the white hand. They told me that there was a farmer lived nere the Town where I lodgd who had some difference wth his slave, concerning something the master had promised him and did not punctualy perform; w[ch] caused some hard words between them; But at length they put the matter to Arbitration and Bound themselves to stand to the award of such as they named—w[ch] done, the Arbitrators Having heard the Allegations of both parties, Order the master to pay 40[s] to black face, and acknowledge his fault. And so the matter ended: the poor master very honestly standing to the award.

There are every where in the Towns as I passed, a Number of Indians the Natives of the Country, and are the

most salvage of all the salvages of that kind that I had ever Seen: little or no care taken (as I heard upon enquiry) to make them otherwise. They have in some places Landes of their owne, and Govern'd by Law's of their own making;—they marry many wives and at pleasure put them away, and on the y[e] least dislike or fickle humour, on either side, saying *stand away* to one another is a sufficient Divorce. And indeed those uncomely *Stand aways* are too much in Vougue among the English in this (Indulgent Colony) as their Records plentifully prove, and that on very trivial matters, of which some have been told me, but are not proper to be Related by a Female pen, tho some of that foolish sex have had too large a share in the story.

If the natives committ any crime on their own precincts among themselves, y[e] English takes no Cognezens of. But if on the English ground, they are punishable by our Laws. They mourn for their Dead by blacking their faces, and cutting their hair, after an Awkerd and frightfull manner; But can't bear You should mention the names of their dead Relations to them: they trade most for Rum, for w[ch] they[d] hazzard their very lives; and the English fit them Generally as well, by seasoning it plentifully with water.

They give the title of merchant to every trader; who Rate their Goods according to the time and spetia they pay in: viz. Pay, mony, Pay as mony, and trusting. *Pay* is Grain, Pork, Beef, & c. at the prices sett by the General Court that Year; *mony* is pieces of Eight, Ryalls, or Boston or Bay shillings (as they call them,) or Good hard money, as sometimes silver coin is termed by them; also Wampom, viz[t]. Indian beads w[ch] serves for change. *Pay as mony* is provisions, as afores[d] one Third cheaper then as the Assembly or Gene[l] Court sets it; and *Trust* as they and the merch[t] agree for time.

Now, when the buyer comes to ask for a comodity, sometimes before the merchant answers that he has it, he sais, *is Your pay redy?* Perhaps the Chap Reply's Yes: what do You pay in? say's the merchant. The buyer having answered, then the price is set; as suppose he wants a sixpenny knife, in pay it is 12d—in pay as money eight pence, and hard money its own price, viz. 6d. It seems a very Intricate way of trade and what Lex Mercatoria[25] had not thought of.

Being at a merchants house, in comes a tall country fellow, wth his alfogeos[26] full of Tobacco; for they seldom Loose their Cudd, but keep Chewing and Spitting as long as they'r eyes are open,—he advanc't to the middle of the

---

23. Tatapa: the same as.

24. *Netop* was an Algonquian word meaning "adult male"; English settlers probably used it to mean "Indian man."

25. Lex Mercatoria: the mercantile law.

26. Alfogeos (*alforjas*), Spanish for "saddlebags."

Room, makes an Awkward Nodd, and spitting a Large deal of Aromatic Tincture, he gave a scrape with his shovel like shoo, leaving a small shovel full of dirt on the floor, made a full stop, Hugging his own pretty Body with his hands under his arms, Stood staring rown'd him, like a Catt let out of a Baskett. At last, like the creature Balaam Rode on, he opened his mouth and said: have You any Ribinen for Hatbands to sell I pray? The Questions and Answers about the pay being past, the Ribon is bro't and opened. Bumpkin Simpers, cryes its confounded Gay I vow; and beckning to the door, in comes Jone Tawdry, dropping about 50 curtsees, and stands by him: hee shows her the Ribin. *Law, You,* sais shee, *its right Gent,* do You, take it, *tis dreadfull pretty.* Then she enquires, *have You any hood silk I pray?* wch being brought and bought, Have You any *thred silk to sew it w^th* says shee, wch being accomodated wth they Departed. They Generaly stand after they come in a great while speachless, and sometimes dont say a word till they are askt what they want, which I Impute to the Awe they stand in of the merchants, who they are constantly almost Indebted too; and must take what they bring without Liberty to choose for themselves; but they serve them as well, making the merchants stay long enough for their pay.

We may Observe here the great necessity and bennifitt both of Education and Conversation; for these people have as Large a portion of mother witt, and sometimes a Larger, than those who have bin brought up in Citties; But for want of emprovements, Render themselves almost Ridiculos, as above. I should be glad if they would leave such follies, and am sure all that Love Clean Houses (at least) would be glad on't too.

They are generaly very plain in their dress, throuout all ye Colony, as I saw, and follow one another in their modes; that You may know where they belong, especially the women, meet them where you will.

Their Cheif Red Letter day is St. Election, wch is annualy Observed according to Charter, to choose their Goven^r: a blessing they can never be thankfull enough for, as they will find, if ever it be their hard fortune to loose it. The present Govenor in Conecticott is the Honble John Winthrop Esq.[27] A Gentleman of an Ancient and Honourable Family, whose Father was Govenor here sometimes before, and his Grand father had bin Govr of the Massachusetts. This gentleman is a very curteous and afable person, much Given to Hospitality, and has by his Good services Gain'd the affections of the people as much as any who had bin before him in that post.

Decr 6th. Being by this time well Recruited and rested after my Journy, my business lying unfinished by some concerns at New York depending thereupon, my Kinsman, Mr. Thomas Trowbridge[28] of New Haven, must needs take a Journy there before it could be accomplished, I resolved to go there in company wth him, and a man of the town wch I engaged to wait on me there. Accordingly, Dec. 6th we set out from New Haven, and about 11 same morning came to Stratford ferry; wch crossing, about two miles on the other side Baited our horses and would have eat a morsell ourselves, But the Pumpkin and Indian mixt Bred had such an Aspect, and the Bare-legg'd Punch so awkerd or rather Awfull a sound, that we left both, and proceeded forward, and about seven at night come to Fairfield, where we met with good entertainment and Lodg'd; and early next morning set forward to Norowalk, from its halfe Indian name *North-walk,* when about 12 at noon we arrived, and Had a Dinner of Fryed Venison, very savoury. Landlady wanting some pepper in the seasoning, bid the Girl hand her the spice in the little *Gay* cupp on ye shelfe. From hence we Hasted towards Rye, walking and Leading our Horses neer a mile together, up a prodigios high Hill; and so Riding till about nine at night, and there arrived and took up our Lodgings at an ordinary, wch a French family kept. Here being very hungry, I desired a fricasee, wch the Frenchman undertaking, mannaged so contrary to my notion of Cookery, that I hastned to Bed superless; And being shewd the way up a pair of stairs wch had such a narrow passage that I had almost stopt by the Bulk of my Body; But arriving at my apartment found it to be a little Lento Chamber furnisht amongst other Rubbish with a High Bedd and a Low one, a Long Table, a Bench and a Bottomless chair,—Little Miss went to scratch up my Kennell wch Russelled as if shee'd bin in the Barn amongst the Husks, and supose such was the contents of the tickin—nevertheless being exceeding weary, down I laid my poor Carkes (never more tired) and found my Covering as scanty as my Bed was hard. Annon I heard another Russelling noise in Y^e Room—called to know the matter—Little miss said shee was making a bed for the men; who, when they were in Bed, complained their leggs lay out of it by reason of its

---

27. Fitz-John Winthrop (1639–1707), governor of Connecticut from 1698 to 1707.

28. The brother of Caleb Trowbridge, whose estate Knight was helping to settle.

shortness—my poor bones complained bitterly not being used to such Lodgings, and so did the man who was with us; and poor I made but one Grone, which was from the time I went to bed to the time I Riss, which was about three in the morning, Setting up by the Fire till Light, and having discharged our ordinary wch was as dear as if we had had far Better fare—wee took our leave of Monsier and about seven in the morn come to New Rochell a french town, where we had a good Breakfast. And in the strength of that about an how'r before sunsett got to York. Here I applyd myself to Mr. Burroughs, a merchant to whom I was recommended by my Kinsman Capt. Prout, and received great Civilities from him and his spouse, who were now both Deaf but very agreeable in their Conversation, Diverting me with pleasant stories of their knowledge in Brittan from whence they both come, one of which was above the rest very pleasant to me viz. my Lord Darcy had a very extravagant Brother who had mortgaged what Estate hee could not sell, and in good time dyed leaving only one son. Him his Lordship (having none of his own) took and made him Heir of his whole Estate, which he was to receive at the death of his Aunt. He and his Aunt in her widowhood held a right understanding and lived as become such Relations, shee being a discreat Gentlewoman and he an Ingenios Young man. One day Hee fell into some Company though far his inferiors, very freely told him of the Ill circumstances his fathers Estate lay under, and the many Debts he left unpaid to the wrong of poor people with whom he had dealt. The Young gentleman was put out of countenance—no way hee could think of to Redress himself—his whole dependance being on the Lady his Aunt, and how to speak to her he knew not—Hee went home, sat down to dinner and as usual sometimes with her when the Chaplain was absent, she desired him to say Grace, wch he did after this manner:

Pray God in Mercy take my Lady Darcy
   Unto his Heavenly Throne,
That Little John may live like a man,
   And pay every man his own.

The prudent Lady took no present notice, But finishd dinner, after wch having sat and talk't awhile (as Customary) He Riss, took his Hatt and Going out she desired him to give her leave to speak to him in her Clossett, Where being come she desired to know why hee prayed for her Death in the manner aforesaid, and what part of her deportment towards him merritted such desires. Hee Reply'd, none at all, But he was under such disadvantages

that nothing but that could do him service, and told her how he had been affronted as above, and what Impressions it had made upon him. The Lady made him a gentle reprimand that he had not informed her after another manner, Bid him see what his father owed and he should have money to pay it to a penny, And always to lett her know his wants and he should have a redy supply. The Young Gentleman charm'd with his Aunts Discrete management, Beggd her pardon and accepted her kind offer and retrieved his fathers Estate, &c. and said Hee hoped his Aunt would never dye, for shee had done better by him than hee could have done for himself.—Mr. Burroughs went with me to Vendue[29] where I bought about 100 Rheem of paper wch was retaken in a flyboat from Holland and sold very Reasonably here—some ten, some Eight shillings per Rheem by the Lott wch was ten Rheem in a Lott. And at the Vendue I made a great many acquaintances amongst the good women of the town, who curteosly invited me to their houses and generously entertained me.

The Cittie of New York is a pleasant, well compacted place, situated on a Commodius River wch is a fine harbour for shipping. The Buildings Brick Generaly, very stately and high, though not altogether like ours in Boston. The Bricks in some of the Houses are of divers Coullers and laid in Checkers, being glazed look very agreeable. The inside of them are neat to admiration, the wooden work, for only the walls are plasterd, and the Sumers and Girt are plained and kept very white scowr'd as so is all the partitions if made of Bords. The fire places have no Jambs (as ours have) But the Backs run flush with the walls, and the Hearth is of Tyles and is as farr out into the Room at the Ends as before the fire, wch is Generally Five foot in the Low'r rooms, and the peice over where the mantle tree should be is made as ours with Joyners work, and as I supose is fasten'd to iron rodds inside. The House where the Vendue was, had Chimney Corners like ours, and they and the hearths were laid wth the finest tile that I ever see, and the stair cases laid all with white tile which is ever clean, and so are the walls of the Kitchen wch had a Brick floor. They were making Great preparations to Receive their Govenor, Lord Cornbury[30] from the

---

29. A market where auctions where held.

30. Edward Hyde, Viscount Cornbury, governor of New York and New Jersey from 1702 to 1708.

Jerseys, and for that End raised the militia to Gard him on shore to the fort.

They are Generaly of the Church of England and have a New England Gentleman for their minister, and a very fine church set out with all Customary requsites. There are also a Dutch and Divers Conventicles as they call them, viz. Baptist, Quakers, &c. They are not strict in keeping the Sabbath as in Boston and other places where I had bin, But seem to deal with great exactness as farr as I see or Deall with. They are sociable to one another and Curteos and Civill to strangers and fare well in their houses. The English go very fasheonable in their dress. But the Dutch, especially the middling sort, differ from our women, in their habitt go loose, were French muches wch are like a Capp and a head band in one, leaving their ears bare, which are sett out wth Jewells of a large size and many in number. And their fingers hoop't with Rings, some with large stones in them of many Coullers as were their pendants in their ears, which You should see very old women wear as well as Young.

They have Vendues very frequently and make their Earnings very well by them, for they treat with good Liquor Liberally, and the Customers Drink as Liberally and Generally pay for't as well, by paying for that which they Bidd up Briskly for, after the sack has gone plentifully about, tho' sometimes good penny worths are got there. Their Diversions in the Winter is Riding Sleys about three or four Miles out of Town, where they have Houses of entertainment at a place called the Bowery, and some go to friends Houses who handsomely treat them. Mr. Burroughs cary'd his spouse and Daughter and myself out to one Madame Dowes, a Gentlewoman that lived at a farm House, who gave us a handsome Entertainment of five or six Dishes and choice Beer and metheglin, Cyder, &c. all which she said was the produce of her farm. I believe we mett 50 or 60 slays that day—they fly with great swiftness and some are so furious that they'le turn out of the path for none except a Loaden Cart. Nor do they spare for any diversion the place affords, and sociable to a degree, they'r Tables being as free to their Naybours as to themselves.

Having here transacted the affair I went upon and some other that fell in the way, after about a fortnight's stay there I left New-York with no Little regrett, and Thursday, Dec. 21, set out for New Haven wth my Kinsman Trowbridge, and the man that waited on me about one afternoon, and about three come to half-way house about ten miles out of town, where we Baited and went forward, and about 5 come to Spiting Devil, Else Kings

bridge, where they pay three pence for passing over with a horse, which the man that keeps the Gate set up at the end of the Bridge receives.

We hoped to reach the french town and Lodg there that night, but unhapily lost our way about four miles short, and being overtaken by a great storm of wind and snow which set full in our faces about dark, we were very uneasy. But meeting one Gardner who lived in a Cottage thereabout, offered us his fire to set by, having but one poor Bedd, and his wife not well, &c. or he would go to a House with us, where he thought we might be better accommodated—thither we went, But a surly old shee Creature, not worthy the name of woman, who would hardly let us go into her Door, though the weather was so stormy none but shee would have turnd out a Dogg. But her son whose name was gallop, who lived Just by Invited us to his house and shewed me two pair of stairs, viz. one up the loft and tother up the Bedd, wch was as hard as it was high, and warmed it with a hott stone at the feet. I lay very uncomfortably, insomuch that I was so very cold and sick I was forced to call them up to give me something to warm me. They had nothing but milk in the house, wch they Boild, and to make it better sweetened wth molasses, which I not knowing or thinking oft till it was down and coming up agen wch it did in so plentifull a manner that my host was soon paid double for his portion, and that in specia. But I believe it did me service in Cleering my stomach. So after this sick and weary night at East Chester, (a very miserable poor place,) the weather being now fair, Friday the 22^d Dec. we set out for New Rochell, where being come we had good Entertainment and Recruited ourselves very well. This is a very pretty place well compact, and good handsome houses, Clean, good and passable Rodes, and situated on a Navigable River, abundance of land well fined and Cleerd all along as wee passed, which caused in me a Love to the place, wch I could have been content to live in it. Here wee Ridd over a Bridge made of one entire stone of such a Breadth that a cart might pass with safety, and to spare—it lay over a passage cutt through a Rock to convey water to a mill not farr off. Here are three fine Taverns within call of each other, very good provision for Travailers.

Thence we travailed through Merrinak, a neet, though little place, wth a navigable River before it, one of the pleasantest I ever see—Here were good Buildings, Especialy one, a very fine seat, wch they told me was Col. Hethcoats, who I had heard was a very fine Gentleman. From hence we come to Hors Neck, where wee Baited, and they told me that one Church of England parson officiated in all these three towns once every Sunday in turns throughout the Year; and that they all could but poorly maintaine him, which they grudg'd to do, being a poor and quarelsome crew as I understand by our Host; their Quarelling about their choice of Minister, they chose to have none—But caused the Government to send this Gentleman to them. Here wee took leave of York Government, and Descending the Mountainos passage that almost broke my heart in ascending before, we come to Stamford, a well compact Town, but miserable meeting house, wch we passed, and thro' many and great difficulties, as Bridges which were exceeding high and very tottering and of vast Length, steep and Rocky Hills and precipices, (Buggbears to a fearful female travailer.) About nine at night we come to Norrwalk, having crept over a timber of a Broken Bridge about thirty foot long, and perhaps fifty to ye water. I was exceeding tired and cold when we come to our Inn, and could get nothing there but poor entertainment, and the Impertinant Bable of one of the worst of men, among many others of which our Host made one, who, had he bin one degree Impudenter, would have outdone his Grandfather. And this I think is the most perplexed night I have yet had. From hence, Saturday, Dec. 23, a very cold and windy day, after an Intolerable night's Lodging, wee hasted forward only observing in our way the Town to be situated on a Navigable river wth indiferent Buildings and people more refind than in some of the Country towns wee had passed, tho' vicious enough, the Church and Tavern being next neighbours. Having Ridd thro a difficult River wee come to Fairfield where wee Baited and were much refreshed as well with the Good things wch gratified our appetites as the time took to rest our wearied Limbs, wch Latter I employed in enquiring concerning the Town and manners of the people, &c. This is a considerable town, and filld as they say with wealthy people—have a spacious meeting house and good Buildings. But the Inhabitants are Litigious, nor do they well agree with their minister, who (they say) is a very worthy Gentleman.

They have aboundance of sheep, whose very Dung brings them great gain, with part of which they pay their Parsons sallery, And they Grudg that, prefering their Dung before their minister. They Lett out their sheep at so much as they agree upon for a night; the highest Bidder always caries them, And they will sufficiently Dung a Large quantity of Land before morning. But were once Bitt by a sharper who had them a night and sheared them all before morning—From hence we went to Stratford, the next Town, in which I observed but few houses, and

those not very good ones. But the people that I conversed with were civill and good natured. Here we staid till late at night, being to cross a Dangerous River ferry, the River at that time full of Ice; but after about four hours waiting with great difficulty wee got over. My fears and fatigues prevented my here taking any particular observation. Being got to Milford, it being late in the night, I could go no further; my fellow travailer going forward, I was invited to Lodg at Mrs.——, a very kind and civill Gentlewoman, by whom I was handsomely and kindly entertained till the next night. The people here go very plain in their apparel (more plain than I had observed in the towns I had passed) and seem to be very grave and serious. They told me there was a singing Quaker lived there, or at least had a strong inclination to be so, His Spouse not at all affected that way. Some of the singing Crew come there one day to visit him, who being then abroad, they sat down (to the woman's no small vexation) Humming and singing and groneing after their conjuring way—Says the woman are you singing quakers? Yea says They—Then take my squalling Brat of a child here and sing to it says she for I have almost split my throat wth singing to him and cant get the Rogue to sleep. They took this as a great Indignity, and mediately departed. Shaking the dust from their Heels left the good woman and her Child among the number of the wicked.

This is a Seaport place and accomodated with a Good Harbour, But I had not opportunity to make particular observations because it was Sabbath day—This Evening.

December 24. I set out with the Gentlewomans son who she very civilly offered to go with me when she see no parswasions would cause me to stay which she pressingly desired, and crossing a ferry having but nine miles to New Haven, in a short time arrived there and was Kindly received and well accommodated amongst my Friends and Relations.

The Government of Connecticut Collony begins westward towards York at Stanford (as I am told) and so runs Eastward towards Boston (I mean in my range, because I dont intend to extend my description beyond my own travails) and ends that way at Stonington—And has a great many Large towns lying more northerly. It is a plentiful Country for provisions of all sorts and its Generally Healthy. No one that can and will be dilligent in this place need fear poverty nor the want of food and Rayment.

January 6th. Being now well Recruited and fitt for business I discoursed the persons I was concerned with, that we might finnish in order to my return to Boston. They delay^d as they had hitherto done hoping to tire my Patience. But I was resolute to stay and see an End of the matter let it be never so much to my disadvantage—So January 9th they come again and promise the Wednesday following to go through with the distribution of the Estate which they delayed till Thursday and then come with new amusements. But at length by the mediation of that holy good Gentleman, the Rev. Mr. James Pierpont, the minister of New Haven, and with the advice and assistance of other our Good friends we come to an accommodation and distribution, which having finished though not till February, the man that waited on me to York taking the charge of me I sit out for Boston. We went from New Haven upon the ice (the ferry being not passable thereby) and the Rev. Mr. Pierpont[31] wth Madam Prout Cuzin Trowbridge and divers others were taking leave wee went onward without any thing Remarkabl till wee come to New London and Lodged again at Mr. Saltonstalls—and here I dismist my Guide, and my Generos entertainer provided me Mr. Samuel Rogers of that place to go home with me—I stayed a day here Longer than I intended by the Commands of the Hon[ble] Govenor Winthrop to stay and take a supper with him whose wonderful civility I may not omitt. The next morning I Crossed y[e] Ferry to Groton, having had the Honor of the Company, of Madam Livingston[32] (who is the Govenors Daughter) and Mary Christophers and divers others to the boat—And that night Lodg[d] at Stonington and had Rost Beef and pumpkin sause for supper. The next night at Haven's and had Rost fowle, and the next day wee come to a river which by Reason of Y[e] Freshetts coming down was swell'd so high wee fear[d] it impassable and the rapid stream was very terryfying—However we must over and that in a small Cannoo. Mr. Rogers assuring me of his good Conduct, I after a stay of near an how'r on the shore for consultation went into the Cannoo, and Mr. Rogers paddled

about 100 yards up the Creek by the shore side, turned into the swift stream and dexterously steering her in a moment wee come to the other side as swiftly passing as an arrow shott out of the Bow by a strong arm. I staid on y[e] shore till Hee returned to fetch our horses, which he caused to swim over himself bringing the furniture in the Cannoo. But it is past my skill to express the Exceeding fright all their transactions formed in me. Wee were now in the colony of the Massachusetts and taking Lodgings at the first Inn we come too had a pretty difficult passage the next day which was the second of March by reason of the sloughy ways then thawed by the Sunn. Here I mett Capt. John Richards of Boston who was going home, So being very glad of his Company we Rode something harder than hitherto, and missing my way in going up a very steep Hill, my horse dropt down under me as Dead; this new surprize no little hurt me meeting it Just at the Entrance into Dedham from whence we intended to reach home that night. But was now obliged to gett another Hors there and leave my own, resolving for Boston that night if possible. But in going over the Causeway at Dedham the Bridge being overflowed by the high waters comming down I very narrowly escaped falling over into the river Hors and all w[ch] twas almost a miracle I did not—now it grew late in the afternoon and the people having very much discouraged us about the sloughy way w[ch] they said wee should find very difficult and hazardous it so wrought on mee being tired and dispirited and disapointed of my desires of going home that I agreed to Lodg there that night w[ch] wee did at the house of one Draper, and the next day being March 3d wee got safe home to Boston, where I found my aged and tender mother and my Dear and only Child in good health with open arms redy to receive me, and my Kind relations and friends flocking in to welcome mee and hear the story of my transactions and travails I having this day bin five months from home and now I cannot fully express my Joy and Satisfaction. But desire sincearly to adore my Great Benefactor for thus graciously carying forth and returning in safety his unworthy handmaid.

---

31. James Pierpont (1660–1714), minister at New Haven from 1685 until his death.

32. Mary Winthrop Livingston.

JONATHAN EDWARDS (1703–1758)

The grandson of Solomon Stoddard, a New England minister of significant renown in his day, Jonathan Edwards was raised in a pious household, where he was made well aware of the stature of his forebears. Edwards became a central figure in the New England religious revivals that occurred during the 1730s and 1740s, when commerce was becoming very important to people, perhaps, Edwards and others thought, more important than religious reflection. The cluster of revivals that Edwards and others assisted in fomenting came to be known during the nineteenth century as the Great Awakening in New England. In his own day, and as a result of his revivalist preaching and philosophical attitudes about the place of emotional agitation in religious experience, Edwards became a controversial figure who attracted criticism from opponents of his theology and even some persons within his own parish.

Educated at Yale for the ministry, Edwards's first position was a brief one in New York City, followed by a short period of teaching at Yale. In 1726, he became the assistant minister to Solomon Stoddard in Northampton. The following year he married Sarah Pierpont. In 1729, after Stoddard's death, Edwards assumed primary responsibility for the ministry at Northampton. As he developed his ministry in the 1730s, Edwards began to preach about the experience of conversion, which according to his theology was a passive experience on the part of the saved person, an experience totally reliant upon the will of an all-powerful God. This view was contrary to what some ministers were contending about the ability of the soul to effect its own salvation and contrary, too, to the gradual relinquishing that had taken place of Puritan dogma about the experience of grace and its effect on church membership. Edwards's theology allowed for conversion to be an emotive and sensual experience, in part so that it could be described and communicated to others.

The unusual number of conversions that occurred in Edwards's Northampton congregation in 1735 led fellow minister Benjamin Colman to request that Edwards describe the events in his church. Edwards did so in a letter to Colman, which he later expanded and published as a pamphlet, *A Faithful Narrative of the Surprising Work of God* (1736). This narrative, which included the stories of three conversions (one of them that of his wife Sarah), established Edwards's reputation as a central figure in this series of revivals. The religious fervor that seemed to have started in Northampton only increased in 1739 and 1740, when George Whitefield, a central figure in the emerging Methodist movement, traveled throughout the British colonies, generating thousands of conversions.

In 1741, Edwards preached what has become—even though it is not his most characteristic—his most famous sermon, *Sinners in the Hands of an Angry God*. After delivering it at Enfield, Massachusetts, Edwards preached this sermon a second time in Northampton and published it in the same year. With its emphasis on the helplessness of man and the arbitrary and almighty but gracious will of God, Edwards spoke a theology reminiscent of the older Puritan dogma, but with a special emphasis upon the experience of the senses in an effort to get his meaning across. The rhetoric of the sermon may seem to lend its delivery as highly oratorical, but Edwards actually preferred a quiet delivery, one in which he did not look parishioners in the eye but instead looked off into the distance or down toward the floor. Such an approach, by depersonalizing the presence of the minister, was itself moving to his congregations, for it would have reminded listeners that their relationship with their God was up to their soul-searching alone.

In the 1740s, the series of revivals taking place across New England provoked a great deal of debate among Congregational ministers. Edwards contributed to the debates in print with a *Treatise Concerning Religious Affections* (1746), which attempted to clarify the role of emotion in religion. In 1748, also inspired by the changes brought about by the revival, he attempted to introduce a change in his church's membership rules. Since his grandfather's time, the original Puritan rules about church membership had been relaxed, and anyone who had been baptized was allowed to receive communion. Edwards attempted to return to the original policy of requiring a formal profession of a conversion experience first. Over this issue and the growing controversy about his religious practices, his congregation voted to remove him in 1750.

Rather than accept the ministerial positions that were offered to him, Edwards moved to Stockbridge, in the border area between British settlements and what was considered Indian country to the west. He administered a mission to the Housatonick Indians and continued his writings about faith, philosophy, and religious practice. In 1754 he published *A Careful and Strict Enquiry,* a major contribution to the debate over free will, which became a standard theological textbook. In 1757, Edwards accepted a position as president of the College of New Jersey (present-day Princeton University). Shortly after arriving there, he took part in an inoculation against smallpox, but he became ill and died as a result.

Before his death, Edwards published over two dozen original works of science, philosophy, and theology. The selections here represent only a small sample of that work. Edwards's *Personal Narrative* demonstrates many of the generic conventions of many conversion narratives. It is a personal expression of Edwards's search for divinity, one that shows the particularly critical part that self-examination plays in the Puritan experience of grace. Edwards's sermon, *Sinners in the Hands of an Angry God,* exemplifies Edwards's emphasis upon parishioners' understanding God as an almighty God, one whom they need to accept, even if only out of fear. A different theology, more characteristic of Edwards's growing sense of the necessity to distinguish between the real affections deriving from grace and merely emotional responses to sermons, is articulated in *The Distinguishing Marks of a Work of the Spirit.* Edwards was responding to attacks against the sheer emotionalism and evidently charismatic tendencies of the revivals. His *Distinguishing Marks* was an attempt to approach the question of the validity of the felt experience of faith by developing a systematic, almost scientific analysis of what he called the work of the spirit. Although his personal influence was not as widely felt as George Whitefield's and his appointment at Northampton ended unhappily, Edwards's writings established him as a central figure in the first great wave of religious enthusiasm in the American colonies.

PERSONAL NARRATIVE

An Account of his CONVERSION,
EXPERIENCES, and RELIGIOUS EXERCISES,
given by himself[1]

I had a variety of Concerns and Exercises about my Soul from my Childhood; but had two more remarkable Seasons of Awakening, before I met with that Change, by which I was brought to those new Dispositions, and that new Sense of Things, that I have since had. The first Time was when I was a Boy, some Years before I went to College, at a Time of remarkable Awakening in my Father's Congregation. I was then very much affected for many Months, and concerned about the Things of Religion, and my Soul's Salvation; and was abundant in Duties. I used to pray five times a Day in secret, and to spend much Time in religious Talk with other Boys; and used to meet with them to pray together. I experienced I know not what Kind of Delight in Religion. My Mind was much engaged in it; and had much self-righteous Pleasure; and it was my Delight to abound in religious Duties. I, with some of my School-mates joined together, and built a Booth in a Swamp, in a very secret and retired Place, for a place of Prayer. And besides, I had particular secret Places of my own in the Woods, where I used to retire by my self; and used to be from time to time much affected. My Affections seemed to be lively and easily moved, and I seemed to be in my Element, when engaged in religious Duties. And I am ready to think, many are deceived with such Affections, and such a kind of Delight, as I then had in Religion, and mistake it for Grace.

But in process of Time, my Convictions and Affections wore off; and I entirely lost all those Affections and Delights, and left off secret Prayer, at least as to any constant Performance of it; and returned like a Dog to his Vomit, and went on in Ways of Sin.

---

1. First published in Samuel Hopkins, *The Life and Character of . . . Jonathan Edwards* (Boston, 1765), from which the present text is taken.

Indeed, I was at some Times very uneasy, especially towards the latter Part of the Time of my being at College. 'Till it pleas'd GOD, in my last Year at College, at a Time when I was in the midst of many uneasy Thoughts about the State of my Soul, to seize me with a Pleurisy; in which he brought me nigh to the Grave, and shook me over the Pit of Hell.

But yet, it was not long after my Recovery, before I fell again into my old Ways of Sin. But God would not suffer me to go on with any Quietness; but I had great and violent inward Struggles: 'till after many Conflicts with wicked Inclinations, and repeated Resolutions, and Bonds that I laid my self under by a kind of Vows to God, I was brought wholly to break off all former wicked Ways, and all Ways of known outward Sin; and to apply my self to seek my Salvation, and practise the Duties of Religion: But without that kind of Affection and Delight, that I had formerly experienced. My Concern now wrought more by inward Struggles and Conflicts, and Self-reflections, I made seeking my Salvation the main Business of my Life. But yet it seems to me, I sought after a miserable manner: Which had made me some times since to question, whether ever it issued in that which was saving; being ready to doubt, whether such miserable seeking was ever succeeded. But yet I was brought to seek Salvation, in a manner that I never was before. I felt a Spirit to part with all Things in the World, for an Interest in Christ. My Concern continued and prevailed, with many exercising Thoughts and inward Struggles; but yet it never seemed to be proper to express my Concern that I had, by the Name of Terror.

From my Childhood up, my Mind had been wont to be full of Objections against the Doctrine of GOD's Sovereignty, in choosing whom he would to eternal Life, and rejecting whom he pleased; leaving them eternally to perish, and be everlastingly tormented in Hell. It used to appear like a horrible Doctrine to me. But I remember the Time very well, when I seemed to be convinced, and fully satisfied, as to this Sovereignty of God, and his Justice in thus eternally disposing of Men, according to his sovereign Pleasure. But never could give an Account, how, or by what Means, I was thus convinced; not in the least imagining, in the Time of it, nor a long Time after, that there was an extraordinary Influence of God's Spirit in it: but only that now I saw further, and my Reason apprehended the Justice and Reasonableness of it. However, my Mind rested in it; and it put an end to all those Cavils and Objections, that had 'till then abode with me, all the preceeding part of my Life. And there has been a wonderful Alteration in my Mind, with respect to the Doctrine of God's Sovereignty, from that Day to this; so that I scarce ever have found so much as the rising of an Objection against God's Sovereignty, in the most absolute Sense, in shewing Mercy to whom he will shew Mercy, and hardening and eternally damning whom he will. God's absolute Sovereignty, and Justice, with respect to Salvation and Damnation, is what my Mind seems to rest assured of, as much as of any Thing that I see with my Eyes; at least it is so at Times. But I have often times since that first Conviction, had quite another Kind of Sense of God's Sovereignty, than I had then. I have often since, not only had a Conviction, but a *delightful* Conviction. The Doctrine of God's Sovereignty has very often appeared, an exceeding pleasant, bright and sweet Doctrine to me: and absolute Sovereignty is what I love to ascribe to God. But my first Conviction was not with this.

The first that I remember that ever I found any thing of that Sort of inward, sweet Delight in GOD and divine Things, that I have lived much in since, was on reading those Words, I *Tim.* i. 17. "Now unto the King eternal, immortal, invisible, the only wise GOD, be Honor and Glory for ever and ever, Amen." As I read the Words, there came into my Soul, and was as it were diffused thro' it, a Sense of the Glory of the Divine Being; a new Sense, quite different from any Thing I ever experienced before. Never any Words of Scripture seemed to me as these Words did. I thought with my self, how excellent a Being that was; and how happy I should be, if I might enjoy that GOD, and be wrapt up to GOD in Heaven, and be as it were swallowed up in Him. I kept saying, and as it were singing over these Words of Scripture to my self; and went to Prayer, to pray to GOD that I might enjoy him; and prayed in a manner quite different from what I used to do; with a new sort of Affection. But it never came into my Thought, that there was any thing spiritual, or of a saving Nature in this.

From about that Time, I began to have a new kind of Apprehensions and Ideas of Christ, and the Work of Redemption, and the glorious Way of Salvation by him. I had an inward, sweet Sense of these Things, that at times came into my Heart; and my Soul was led away in pleasant Views and Contemplations of them. And my Mind was greatly engaged, to spend my Time in reading and meditating on Christ; and the Beauty and Excellency of his Person, and the lovely Way of Salvation, by free Grace in him. I found no Books so delightful to me, as those that treated of these Subjects. Those Words *Cant.* ii. I. used to be abundantly with me: *I am the Rose of Sharon, the Lilly of the Valleys.* The Words seemed to me, sweetly to represent, the Loveliness and Beauty of Jesus Christ. And the whole Book of Canticles used to be pleasant to me; and I used to be much in reading it, about that time. And found, from Time to Time, an inward Sweetness, that used, as it were, to carry me away in my Contemplations; in what I know not how to express otherwise, than by a calm, sweet Abstraction of Soul from all the Concerns of this World; and a kind of Vision, or fix'd Ideas and Imaginations, of being alone in the Mountains, or some solitary Wilderness, far from all Mankind, sweetly conversing with Christ, and wrapt and swallowed up in GOD. The Sense I had of divine Things, would often of a sudden as it were, kindle up a sweet burning in my Heart; an ardor of my Soul, that I know not how to express.

Not long after I first began to experience these Things, I gave an Account to my Father, of some Things that had pass'd in my Mind. I was pretty much affected by the Discourse we had together. And when the Discourse was ended, I walked abroad alone, in a solitary Place in my Father's Pasture, for Contemplation. And as I was walking there, and looked up on the Sky and Clouds; there came into my Mind, a sweet Sense of the glorious Majesty and Grace of GOD, that I know not how to express. I seemed to see them both in a sweet Conjunction: Majesty and Meekness join'd together: It was a sweet and gentle, and holy Majesty; and also a majestick Meekness; an awful Sweetness; a high, and great, and holy Gentleness.

After this my Sense of divine Things gradually increased, and became more and more lively, and had more of that inward Sweetness. The Appearance of every thing was altered: there seem'd to be, as it were, a calm, sweet Cast, or appearance of divine Glory, in almost every Thing. God's Excellency, his Wisdom, his Purity and Love, seemed to appear in every Thing; in the Sun, Moon and Stars; in the Clouds, and blue Sky; in the Grass, Flowers, Trees; in the Water, and all Nature; which used greatly to fix my Mind. I often used to sit & view the Moon, for a long time; and so in the Day time, spent much time in viewing the Clouds & Sky, to behold the sweet Glory of GOD in these Things: in the mean Time, singing forth with a low Voice, my Contemplations of the Creator & Redeemer. And scarce any Thing, among all the Works of Nature, was so sweet to me as Thunder and Lightning. Formerly, nothing had been so terrible to me. I used to be a Person uncommonly terrified with Thunder: and it used to strike me with Terror, when I saw a Thunder-storm rising. But now, on the contrary, it rejoyced me. I felt GOD at the first Appearance of a Thunder-storm. And used to

take the Opportunity at such Times, to fix my self to view the Clouds, and see the Lightnings play, and hear the majestick & awful Voice of God's Thunder: which often times was exceeding entertaining, leading me to sweet Contemplations of my great and glorious GOD. And while I viewed, used to spend my time, as it always seem'd natural to me, to sing or chant forth my Meditations; to speak my Thoughts in Soliloquies, and speak with a singing Voice.

I felt then a great Satisfaction as to my good Estate. But that did not content me. I had vehement Longings of Soul after GOD and CHRIST, and after more Holiness; wherewith my Heart seemed to be full, and ready to break: which often brought to my Mind, the Words of the Psalmist, Psal. cxix. 28. *My Soul breaketh for the Longing it hath.* I often felt a mourning and lamenting in my Heart, that I had not turned to GOD sooner, that I might have had more time to grow in Grace. My Mind was greatly fix'd on divine Things; I was almost perpetually in the Contemplation of them. Spent most of my Time in thinking of divine Things, Year after Year. And used to spend abundance of my Time, in walking alone in the Woods, and solitary Places, for Meditation, Soliloquy and Prayer, and Converse with GOD. And it was always my Manner, at such times, to sing forth my Contemplations. And was almost constantly in ejaculatory Prayer, wherever I was. Prayer seem'd to be natural to me; as the Breath, by which the inward Burnings of my Heart had vent.

The Delights which I now felt in Things of Religion, were of an exceeding different Kind, from those forementioned, that I had when I was a Boy. They were totally of another Kind; and what I then had no more Notion or Idea of, than one born blind has of pleasant and beautiful Colours. They were of a more inward, pure, Soul-animating and refreshing Nature. Those former Delights, never reached the Heart; and did not arise from any Sight of the divine Excellency of the Things of GOD; or any Taste of the Soul-satisfying and Life-giving Good, there is in them.

My sense of divine Things seem'd gradually to increase, 'till I went to preach at *New-York;* which was about a Year and a half after they began. While I was there, I felt them, very sensibly, in a much higher Degree, than I had done before. My Longings after GOD & Holiness, were much increased. Pure and humble, holy and heavenly Christianity, appeared exceeding amiable to me. I felt in me a burning Desire to be in every Thing a compleat Christian; and conformed to the blessed Image of Christ: and that I might live in all Things, according to the pure, sweet and blessed Rules of the Gospel. I had an eager thirsting after Progress in these Things. My Longings after it, put me upon pursuing and pressing after them. It was my continual Strife Day and Night, and constant Inquiry, How I should be more holy, and live more holily, and more becoming a Child of God, and Disciple of Christ. I sought an encrease of Grace and Holiness, and that I might live an holy Life, with vastly more Earnestness, than ever I sought Grace, before I had it. I used to be continually examining my self, and studying and contriving for likely Ways and Means, how I should live holily, with far greater diligence and earnestness, than ever I pursued any thing in my Life: But with too great a Dependence on my own Strength; which afterwards proved a great Damage to me. My Experience had not then taught me, as it has done since, my extream Feebleness and Impotence, every manner of Way; and the innumerable and bottomless Depths of secret Corruption and Deceit, that there was in my Heart. However, I went on with my eager pursuit after more Holiness; and sweet conformity to Christ.

The Heaven I desired was a Heaven of Holiness; to be with GOD, and to spend my Eternity in divine Love, and holy Communion with Christ. My Mind was very much taken up with Contemplations on Heaven, and the Enjoyments of those there; and living there in perfect Holiness, Humility and Love. And it used at that Time to appear a great Part of the Happiness of Heaven, that there the Saints could express their Love to Christ. It appear'd to me a great Clog and Hindrance and Burden to me, that what I felt within, I could not express to GOD, and give vent to, as I desired. The inward ardor of my Soul, seem'd to be hinder'd and pent up, and could not freely flame out as it would. I used often to think, how in Heaven, this sweet Principle should freely and fully vent and express it self. Heaven appeared to me exceeding delightful as a World of Love. It appear'd to me, that all Happiness consisted in living in pure, humble, heavenly, divine Love.

I remember the Thoughts I used then to have of Holiness. I remember I then said sometimes to my self, I do certainly know that I love Holiness, such as the Gospel prescribes. It appeared to me, there was nothing in it but what was ravishingly lovely. It appeared to me, to be the highest Beauty and Amiableness, above all other Beauties: that it was a *divine* Beauty; far purer than any thing here upon Earth; and that every thing else, was like Mire, Filth and Defilement, in Comparison of it.

Holiness, as I then wrote down some of my Contemplations on it, appeared to me to be of a sweet, pleasant, charming, serene, calm Nature. It seem'd to me, it brought an inexpressible Purity, Brightness, Peacefulness & Ravishment to the Soul: and that it made the Soul like a Field or Garden of GOD, with all manner of pleasant Flowers; that is all pleasant, delightful & undisturbed; enjoying a sweet Calm, and the gently vivifying Beams of the Sun. The Soul of a true Christian, as I then wrote my Meditations, appear'd like such a little white Flower, as we see in the Spring of the Year; low and humble on the Ground, opening it's Bosom, to receive the pleasant Beams of the Sun's Glory; rejoycing as it were, in a calm Rapture; diffusing around a sweet Fragrancy; standing peacefully and lovingly, in the midst of other Flowers round about; all in like Manner opening their Bosoms, to drink in the Light of the Sun.

There was no Part of Creature-Holiness, that I then, and at other Times, had so great a Sense of the Loveliness of, as Humility, Brokenness of Heart and Poverty of Spirit: and there was nothing that I had such a Spirit to long for. My Heart as it were panted after this, to lie low before GOD, and in the Dust; that I might be nothing, and that GOD might be all; that I might become as a little Child.

While I was there at *New-York,* I sometimes was much affected with Reflections on my past Life, considering how late it was, before I began to be truly religious; and how wickedly I had lived till then: and once so as to weep abundantly, and for a considerable time together.

On *January* 12. 1722,3. I made a solemn Dedication of my self to GOD, and wrote it down; giving up my self, and all that I had to GOD; to be for the future in no Respect my own; to act as one that had no right to himself, in any Respect. And solemnly vowed to take GOD for my whole Portion and Felicity; looking on nothing else as any Part of my Happiness, nor acting as if it were: and his Law for the constant Rule of my Obedience: engaging to fight with all my Might, against the World, the Flesh and the Devil, to the End of my Life. But have Reason to be infinitely humbled, when I consider, how much I have fail'd to answering my Obligation.

I had then abundance of sweet religious Conversation in the Family where I lived, with Mr. *John Smith,* and his pious Mother. My Heart was knit in Affection to those, in whom were Appearances of true Piety; and I could bear the Thoughts of no other Companions, but such as were holy, and the Disciples of the blessed JESUS.

I had great Longings for the Advancement of Christ's Kingdom in the World. My secret Prayer used to be in great Part taken up in praying for it. If I heard the least hint of any thing that happened in any Part of the World, that appear'd to me, in some Respect or other, to have a favourable Aspect on the Interest of Christ's Kingdom, my Soul eagerly catch'd at it; and it would much animate and refresh me. I used to be earnest to read publick News-Letters, mainly for that End; to see if I could not find some News favourable to the Interest of Religion in the World.

I very frequently used to retire into a solitary Place, on the Banks of *Hudson's* River, at some Distance from the City, for Contemplation on Divine Things, and secret Converse with GOD; and had many sweet Hours there. Sometimes Mr. *Smith* and I walked there together, to converse of the Things of GOD; and our Conversation used much to turn on the Advancement of Christ's Kingdom in the World, and the glorious Things that GOD would accomplish for his Church in the latter Days.

I had then, and at other Times, the greatest Delight in the holy Scriptures of any Book whatsoever. Often-times in reading it, every Word seemed to touch my Heart. I felt an Harmony between something in my Heart, and those sweet and powerful Words. I seem'd often to see so much Light, exhibited by every Sentence, and such a refreshing ravishing Food communicated, that I could not get along in reading. Used often-times to dwell long on one Sentence, to see the Wonders contained in it; and yet almost every Sentence seemed to be full of Wonders.

I came away from *New-York* in the Month of *April,* 1723, and had a most bitter parting with Madam *Smith* and her Son. My Heart seemed to sink within me, at leaving the Family and City, where I had enjoyed so many sweet and pleasant Days. I went from *New-York* to *Weathersfield* by Water. As I sail'd away, I kept Sight of the City as long as I could; and when I was out of Sight of it, it would affect me much to look that Way, with a kind of Melancholly mixed with Sweetness. However, that Night after this sorrowful parting, I was greatly comforted in GOD at *Westchester,* where we went ashore to lodge: and had a pleasant Time of it all the Voyage to *Saybrook.* It was sweet to me to think of meeting dear Christians in Heaven, where we should never part more. At *Saybrook* we went ashore to lodge on Saturday, and there kept Sabbath; where I had a sweet and refreshing Season, walking alone in the Fields.

After I came home to *Windsor,* remained much in a like Frame of my Mind, as I had been in at *New-York;* but only some times felt my Heart ready to sink, with the Thoughts of my Friends at New-York. And my Refuge and Support was in Contemplations on the heavenly State; as I find in my Diary of *May* 1. 1723. It was my Comfort to think of that State, where there is fulness of Joy; where reigns heavenly, sweet, calm and delightful Love, without Alloy; where there are continually the dearest Expressions of this Love; where is the Enjoyment of the Persons loved, without ever parting; where these Persons that appear so lovely in this World, will really be inexpressibly more lovely, and full of love to us. And how sweetly will the mutual Lovers join together to sing the Praises of GOD and the LAMB! How full will it fill us with Joy, to think, that this Enjoyment, these sweet Exercises will never cease or come to an End; but will last to all Eternity!

Continued much in the same Frame in the general, that I had been in at *New-York,* till I went to *New-Haven,* to live there as Tutor of the College; having one special Season of uncommon Sweetness: particularly once at *Bolton,* in a Journey from *Boston,* walking out alone in the Fields. After I went to *New-Haven,* I sunk in Religion; my Mind being diverted from my eager and violent Pursuits after Holiness, by some Affairs that greatly perplexed and distracted my Mind.

In *September,* 1725, was taken ill at *New-Haven;* and endeavouring to go home to *Windsor,* was so ill at the North Village, that I could go no further: where I lay sick for about a Quarter of a Year. And in this Sickness, GOD was pleased to visit me again with the sweet Influences of his Spirit. My Mind was greatly engaged there on divine, pleasant Contemplations, and Longings of Soul. I observed that those who watched with me, would often be looking out for the Morning, and seemed to wish for it. Which brought to my Mind those Words of the Psalmist, which my Soul with Sweetness made it's own Language. *My Soul waiteth for the Lord, more than they that watch for the Morning.* And when the Light of the Morning came, and the Beams of the Sun came in at the Windows, it refreshed my Soul from one Morning to another. It seemed to me to be some Image of the sweet Light of GOD's Glory.

I remember, about that Time, I used greatly to long for the Conversion of some that I was concerned with. It seem'd to me, I could gladly honor them, and with Delight be a Servant to them, and lie at their Feet, if they were but truly holy.

But some Time after this, I was again greatly diverted in my Mind, with some temporal Concerns, that exceedingly took up my Thoughts, greatly to the wounding of my Soul: and went on through various Exercises, that it would be tedious to relate, that gave me much more Experience of my own Heart, than ever I had before.

Since I came to this Town,[2] I have often had sweet Complacency in GOD, in Views of his glorious Perfections, and the Excellency of Jesus Christ. GOD has appeared to me, a glorious and lovely Being, chiefly on the account of his Holiness. The Holiness of GOD has always appeared to me the most lovely of all his Attributes. The Doctrines of God's absolute Sovereignty, and free Grace, in shewing Mercy to whom he would shew mercy; and Man's absolute Dependance on the Operations of God's Holy Spirit, have very often appeared to me as sweet and glorious Doctrines. These Doctrines have been much my Delight. GOD's Sovereignty has ever appeared to me, as great Part of his Glory. It has often been sweet to me to go to GOD, and adore Him as a sovereign GOD, and ask sovereign Mercy of Him.

I have loved the Doctrines of the Gospel: They have been to my Soul like green Pastures. The Gospel has seem'd to me to be the richest Treasure; the Treasure that I have most desired, and longed that it might dwell richly in me. The Way of Salvation by Christ, has appeared in a general Way, glorious and excellent, and most pleasant and beautiful. It has often seem'd to me, that it would in a great Measure spoil Heaven, to receive it in any other Way. That Text has often been affecting and delightful to me, Isai. xxxii. 2. *A Man shall be an hiding Place from the Wind, and a Covert from the Tempest Etc.*

It has often appear'd sweet to me, to be united to CHRIST: to have Him for my Head, and to be a Member of his Body: and also to have CHRIST for my Teacher and Prophet. I very often think with Sweetness and Longings and Pantings of Soul, of being a little Child, taking hold of CHRIST, to be led by Him through the Wilderness of this World. That Text, *Matth.* xviii. at the Beginning, has often been sweet to me, *Except ye be converted, and become as little Children Etc.* I love to think of coming to CHRIST, to receive Salvation of him, poor in Spirit, and quite empty of Self; humbly exalting Him alone; cut en-

tirely off from my own Root, and to grow into, and out of CHRIST: to have GOD in CHRIST to be all in all; and to live by Faith on the Son of GOD, a Life of humble, unfeigned Confidence in Him. That Scripture has often been sweet to me, Psal. cxv. I. *Not unto us, O LORD, not unto us, but unto thy Name give Glory, for thy Mercy, and for thy Truth's sake.* And those Words of Christ, *Luk* x. 21. *In that Hour Jesus rejoyced in Spirit, and said, I thank thee, O Father, Lord of Heaven and Earth, that thou hast hid these Things from the wise and prudent, and hast revealed them unto Babes: Even so Father, for so it seemed good in thy Sight.* That Sovereignty of GOD that Christ rejoyced in, seemed to me to be worthy to be rejoyced in; and that rejoycing of CHRIST, seemed to me to shew the Excellency of CHRIST, and the Spirit that he was of.

Sometimes only mentioning a single Word, causes my Heart to burn within me: or only seeing the Name of CHRIST, or the Name of some Attribute of GOD. And GOD has appeared glorious to me, on account of the TRINITY. It has made me have exalting Thoughts of GOD, that he subsists in three Persons; FATHER, SON, and HOLY GHOST.

The sweetest Joys and Delights I have experienced, have not been those that have arisen from a Hope of my own good Estate; but in a direct View of the glorious Things of the Gospel. When I enjoy this Sweetness, it seems to carry me above the Thoughts of my own safe Estate. It seems at such Times a Loss that I cannot bear, to take off my Eye from the glorious, pleasant Object I behold without me, to turn my Eye in upon my self, and my own good Estate.

My Heart has been much on the Advancement of Christ's Kingdom in the World. The Histories of the past Advancement of Christ's Kingdom, have been sweet to me. When I have read Histories of past Ages, the pleasantest Thing in all my reading has been, to read of the Kingdom of Christ being promoted. And when I have expected in my reading, to come to any such thing, I have lotted upon it all the Way as I read. And my Mind has been much entertained and delighted, with the Scripture Promises and Prophecies, of the future glorious Advancement of Christ's Kingdom on earth.

I have sometimes had a Sense of the excellent Fulness of Christ, and his Meetness and Suitableness as a Saviour; whereby he has appeared to me, far above all, the chief of ten Thousands. And his Blood and Atonement has appeared sweet, and his Righteousness sweet; which is always accompanied with an Ardency of Spirit, and inward Strugglings and Breathings and Groanings, that cannot be

_____

2. "Northampton" [Au.]

uttered, to be emptied of my self, and swallowed up in CHRIST.

Once, as I rid out into the Woods for my Health, *Anno* 1737; and having lit from my Horse in a retired Place, as my Manner commonly has been, to walk for divine Contemplation and Prayer; I had a View, that for me was extraordinary, of the Glory of the SON OF GOD; as Mediator between GOD and Man; and his wonderful, great, full, pure and sweet Grace and Love, and meek and gentle Condescention. This Grace, that appear'd to me so calm and sweet, appear'd great above the Heavens. The Person of CHRIST appear'd ineffably excellent, with an Excellency great enough to swallow up all Thought and Conception. Which continued, as near as I can judge, about an Hour; which kept me, the bigger Part of the Time, in a Flood of Tears, and weeping aloud. I felt withal, an Ardency of Soul to be, what I know not otherwise how to express, than to be emptied and annihilated; to lie in the Dust, and to be full of Christ alone; to love him with a holy and pure Love; to trust in him; to live upon him; to serve and follow him, and to be totally wrapt up in the Fullness of Christ; and to be perfectly sanctified and made pure, with a divine and heavenly Purity. I have several other Times, had Views very much of the same Nature, and that have had the same Effects.

I have many Times had a Sense of the Glory of the third Person in the Trinity, in his Office of Sanctifier; in his holy Operations communicating divine Light and Life to the Soul. GOD in the Communications of his Holy Spirit, has appear'd as an infinite Fountain of Divine Glory and Sweetness; being full and sufficient to fill and satisfy the Soul: pouring forth it self in sweet Communications, like the Sun in its Glory, sweetly and pleasantly diffusing Light and Life.

I have sometimes had an affecting Sense of the Excellency of the Word of GOD, as a Word of Life; as the Light of Life; a sweet, excellent, Life-giving Word: accompanied with a thirsting after that Word, that it might dwell richly in my Heart.

I have often since I lived in this Town, had very affecting Views of my own Sinfulness and Vileness; very frequently so as to hold me in a kind of loud Weeping, sometimes for a considerable time together: so that I have often been forced to shut my self up. I have had a vastly greater Sense of my own Wickedness, and the Badness of my Heart, since my Conversion, than ever I had before. It has often appeared to me, that if GOD should mark Iniquity against me, I should appear the very worst of all Mankind; of all that have been since the beginning of the World to this time: and that I should have by far the lowest Place in Hell. When others that have come to talk with me about their Soul Concerns, have expressed the Sense they have had of their own Wickedness, by saying that it seem'd to them, that they were as bad as the Devil himself; I thought their Expressions seemed exceeding faint and feeble, to represent my Wickedness. I thought I should wonder, that they should content themselves with such Expressions as these, if I had any Reason to imagine, that their Sin bore any Proportion to mine. It seemed to me, I should wonder at my self, if I should express *my* Wickedness in such feeble Terms as they did.

My Wickedness, as I am in my self, has long appear'd to me perfectly ineffable, and infinitely swallowing up all Thought and Imagination; like an infinite Deluge, or infinite Mountains over my Head. I know not how to express better, what my Sins appear to me to be, then by heaping Infinite upon Infinite, and multiplying Infinite by Infinite. I go about very often, for this many Years, with these Expressions in my Mind, and in my Mouth, "Infinite upon Infinite. Infinite upon Infinite!" When I look into my Heart, and take a view of my Wickedness, it looks like an Abyss infinitely deeper than Hell. And it appears to me, that were it not for free Grace, exalted and raised up to the infinite Height of all the fulness and glory of the great JEHOVAH, and the Arm of his Power and Grace stretched forth, in all the Majesty of his Power, and in all the Glory of his Sovereignty; I should appear sunk down in my Sins infinitely below Hell it self, far beyond Sight of every Thing, but the piercing Eye of God's Grace, that can pierce even down to such a Depth, and to the bottom of such an Abyss.

And yet, I ben't in the least inclined to think, that I have a greater Conviction of Sin than ordinary. It seems to me, my Conviction of Sin is exceeding small, and faint. It appears to me enough to amaze me, that I have no more Sense of my Sin. I know certainly, that I have very little Sense of my sinfulness. That my Sins appear to me so great, don't seem to me to be, because I have so much more Conviction of Sin than other Christians, but because I am so much worse, and have so much more Wickedness to be convinced of. When I have had these Turns of weeping and crying for my Sins, I thought I knew in the Time of it, that my Repentance was nothing to my Sin.

I have greatly longed of late, for a broken Heart, and to lie low before GOD. And when I ask for Humility of GOD, I can't bear the Thoughts of being no more humble, than other Christians. It seems to me, that tho' their Degrees of Humility may be suitable for them; yet it would be a vile Self-exaltation in me, not to be the lowest in Humility of all Mankind. Others speak of their longing to be humbled to the Dust. Tho' that may be a proper Expression for them, I always think for my self, that I ought to be humbled down below Hell. 'Tis an Expression that it has long been natural for me to use in Prayer to God. I ought to lie infinitely low before GOD.

It is affecting to me to think, how ignorant I was, when I was a young Christian, of the bottomless, infinite Depths of Wickedness, Pride, Hypocrisy and Deceit left in my Heart.

I have vastly a greater Sense, of my universal, exceeding Dependence on God's Grace and Strength, and meer good Pleasure, of late, than I used formerly to have; and have experienced more of an Abhorrence of my own Righteousness. The Thought of any Comfort or Joy, arising in me, on any Consideration, or Reflection on my own Amiableness, or any of my own Performances or Experiences, or any Goodness of Heart or Life, is nauseous and detestable to me. And yet I am greatly afflicted with a proud and self-righteous Spirit; much more sensibly, than I used to be formerly. I see that Serpent rising and putting forth it's Head, continually, every where, all around me.

Tho' it seems to me, that in some Respects I was a far better Christian, for two or three Years after my first Conversion, than I am now; and lived in a more constant Delight and Pleasure: yet of late Years, I have had a more full and constant Sense of the absolute Sovereignty of GOD, and a delight in that Sovereignty; and have had more of a Sense of the Glory of CHRIST, as a Mediator, as revealed in the Gospel. On one Saturday Night in particular, had a particular Discovery of the Excellency of the Gospel of CHRIST, above all other Doctrines; so that I could not but say to my self; "This is my chosen Light, my chosen Doctrine:" and of Christ, "This is my chosen Prophet." It appear'd to me to be sweet beyond all Expression, to follow Christ, and to be taught and enlighten'd and instructed by him; to learn of him, and live to him.

Another Saturday Night, *January* 1738,9. had such a Sense, how sweet and blessed a Thing it was, to walk in the Way of Duty, to do that which was right and meet to be done, and agreeable to the holy Mind of GOD; that it caused me to break forth into a kind of a loud weeping, which held me some Time; so that I was forced to shut my self up, and fasten the Doors. I could not but as it were cry out, "How happy are they which do that which is right in the Sight of GOD! They are blessed indeed, they are the happy ones!" I had at the same time, a very affecting

Sense, how meet and suitable it was that GOD should govern the World, and order all Things according to his own Pleasure; and I rejoyced in it, that GOD reigned, and that his Will was done.

SINNERS IN THE HANDS OF AN ANGRY GOD[1]

Their foot shall slide in due time.

DEUT. 32.35

In this verse is threatened the vengeance of God on the wicked unbelieving Israelites, who were God's visible people, and who lived under the means of grace, but who, notwithstanding all God's wonderful works towards them, remained (as in verse 28.) void of counsel, having no understanding in them. Under all the cultivations of heaven, they brought forth bitter and poisonous fruit, as in the two verses next preceding the text.[2] The expression I have chosen for my text, "Their foot shall slide in due time," seems to imply the following things, relating to the punishment and destruction to which these wicked Israelites were exposed.

1. That they were always exposed to destruction; as one that stands or walks in slippery places is always exposed to fall. This is implied in the manner of their destruction coming upon them, being represented by their foot sliding. The same is expressed, Psalm 73.18: "Surely thou didst set them in slippery places; thou castedst them down into destruction."

2. It implies that they were always exposed to sudden unexpected destruction. As he that walks in slippery places is every moment liable to fall, he cannot foresee one moment whether he shall stand or fall the next; and when he does fall, he falls at once without warning. Which is also expressed in Psalm 73. 18–19: "Surely thou didst set them in slippery places; thou castedst them down

---

1. This sermon was delivered at Enfield, Massachusetts, and first published in Boston in 1741, the edition from which the present text is taken.

2. Deuteronomy 32:32–33. "For their vine is of the vine of Sodom, and the fields of Gomorrah: their grapes are grapes of gall, their clusters are bitter: their wine is the poison of dragons, and the cruel venom of asps."

into destruction: How are they brought into desolation as in a moment!"

3. Another thing implied is, that they are liable to fall of themselves, without being thrown down by the hand of another; as he that stands or walks on slippery ground needs nothing but his own weight to throw him down.

4. That the reason why they are not fallen already, and do not fall now, is only that God's appointed time is not come. For it is said, that when that due time or appointed times comes, their foot shall slide. Then they shall be left to fall, as they are inclined by their own weight. God will not hold them up in these slippery places any longer, but will let them go; and then, at that very instant, they shall fall into destruction; as he that stands on such slippery declining ground, on the edge of a pit, he cannot stand alone, when he is let go he immediately falls and is lost.

The observation from the words that I would now insist upon is this. "There is nothing that keeps wicked men at any one moment out of hell, but the mere pleasure of God." By the mere pleasure of God, I mean His sovereign pleasure, His arbitrary will, restrained by no obligation, hindered by no manner of difficulty, any more than if nothing else but God's mere will had in the least degree, or in any respect whatsoever, any hand in the preservation of wicked men one moment. The truth of this observation may appear by the following considerations.

1. There is no want of power in God to cast wicked men into hell at any moment. Men's hands cannot be strong when God rises up. The strongest have no power to resist Him, nor can any deliver out of His hands. He is not only able to cast wicked men into hell, but He can most easily do it. Sometimes an earthly prince meets with a great deal of difficulty to subdue a rebel, who has found means to fortify himself, and has made himself strong by the numbers of his followers. But it is not so with God. There is no fortress that is any defense from the power of God. Though hand join in hand, and vast multitudes of God's enemies combine and associate themselves, they are easily broken in pieces. They are as great heaps of light chaff before the whirlwind; or large quantities of dry stubble before devouring flames. We find it easy to tread on and crush a worm that we see crawling on the earth; so it is easy for us to cut or singe a slender thread that any thing hangs by: thus easy is it for God, when he pleases, to cast His enemies down to hell. What are we, that we should think to stand before him, at whose rebuke the earth trembles, and before whom the rocks are thrown down?

2. They deserve to be cast into hell; so that divine justice never stands in the way, it makes no objection against God's using His power at any moment to destroy them. Yea, on the contrary, justice calls aloud for an infinite punishment of their sins. Divine justice says of the tree that brings forth such grapes of Sodom, Cut it down, why cumbereth it the ground? Luke 13.7. The sword of divine justice is every moment brandished over their heads, and it is nothing but the hand of arbitrary mercy, and God's will, that holds it back.

3. They are already under a sentence of condemnation to hell. They do not only justly deserve to be cast down thither, but the sentence of the law of God, that eternal and immutable rule of righteousness that God has fixed between Him and mankind, is gone out against them, and stands against them: so that they are bound over already to hell. John 3.18: "He that believeth not is condemned already." So that every unconverted man properly belongs to hell; that is his place, from thence he is, John 8.23: "Ye are from beneath." And thither he is bound; it is the place that justice, and God's word, and the sentence of his unchangeable law assign to him.

4. They are now the objects of that very same anger and wrath of God that is expressed in the torments of hell. And the reason why they do not go down to hell at each moment is not because God, in whose power they are, is not then very angry with them as He is with many miserable creatures now tormented in hell, who there feel and bear the fierceness of His wrath. Yea, God is a great deal more angry with great numbers that are now on earth: yea, doubtless, with many that are now in this congregation, who it may be are at ease, than He is with many of those who are now in the flames of hell.

So that it is not because God is unmindful of their wickedness, and does not resent it, that He does not let loose His hand and cut them off. God is not altogether such an one as themselves, though they may imagine Him to be so. The wrath of God burns against them, their damnation does not slumber, the pit is prepared, the fire is made ready, the furnace is now hot, ready to receive them; the flames do now rage and glow. The glittering sword is whet, and held over them, and the pit hath opened its mouth under them.

5. The devil stands ready to fall upon them, and seize them as his own, at what moment God shall permit him. They belong to him; he has their souls in his possession, and under his dominion. The scripture represents them as

his goods. Luke 11.12.[3] The devils watch them; they are ever by them at their right hand; they stand waiting for them, like greedy hungry lions that see their prey, and expect to have it, but are for the present kept back. If God should withdraw His hand, by which they are restrained, they would in one moment fly upon their poor souls. The old serpent is gaping for them; hell opens it mouth wide to receive them; and if God should permit it, they would be hastily swallowed up and lost.

6. There are in the souls of wicked men those hellish principles reigning that would presently kindle and flame out into hell fire, if it were not for God's restraints. There is laid in the very nature of carnal men a foundation for the torments of hell. There are those corrupt principles, in reigning power in them, and in full possession of them, that are seeds of hell fire. These principles are active and powerful, exceeding violent in their nature, and if it were not for the restraining hand of God upon them, they would soon break out, they would flame out after the same manner as the same corruptions, the same enmity does in the hearts of damned souls, and would beget the same torments as they do in them. The souls of the wicked are in scripture compared to the troubled sea, Isaiah 57.20. For the present, God restrains their wickedness by His mighty power, as He does the raging waves of the troubled sea, saying, "Hitherto shalt thou come, but no further:" but if God should withdraw that restraining power, it would soon carry all before it. Sin is the ruin and misery of the soul; it is destructive in its nature; and if God should leave it without restraint, there would need nothing else to make the soul perfectly miserable. The corruption of the heart of man is immoderate and boundless in its fury; and while wicked men live here, it is like fire pent up by God's restraints, whereas if it were let loose, it would set on fire the course of nature; and as the heart is now a sink of sin, so if sin was not restrained, it would immediately turn the soul into a fiery oven, or a furnace of fire and brimstone.

7. It is no security to wicked men for one moment that there are no visible means of death at hand. It is no security to a natural man that he is now in health and that he does not see which way he should now immediately go out of the world by any accident, and that there is no visible danger in any respect in his circumstances. The manifold and continual experience of the world in all ages, shows this is no evidence that a man is not on the very brink of eternity, and that the next step will not be into another world. The unseen, unthought of ways and means of persons going suddenly out of the world are innumerable and inconceivable. Unconverted men walk over the pit of hell on a rotten covering, and there are innumerable places in this covering so weak that they will not bear their weight, and these places are not seen. The arrows of death fly unseen at noonday;[4] the sharpest sight cannot discern them. God has so many different unsearchable ways of taking wicked men out of the world and sending them to hell, that there is nothing to make it appear that God had need to be at the expense of a miracle, or go out of the ordinary course of His providence, to destroy any wicked man at any moment. All the means that there are of sinners going out of the world are so in God's hands, and so universally and absolutely subject to His power and determination, that it does not depend at all the less on the mere will of God whether sinners shall at any moment go to hell than if means were never made use of or at all concerned in the case.

8. Natural men's prudence and care to preserve their own lives, or the care of others to preserve them, do not secure them a moment. To this, divine providence and universal experience do also bear testimony. There is this clear evidence that men's own wisdom is no security to them from death; that if it were otherwise we should see some difference between the wise and politic men of the world, and others, with regard to their liableness to early and unexpected death: but how is it in fact? Ecclesiastes 2.16: "How dieth the wise man? even as the fool."

9. All wicked men's pains and contrivance which they use to escape hell, while they continue to reject Christ, and so remain wicked men, do not secure them from hell one moment. Almost every natural[5] man that hears of hell, flatters himself that he shall escape it; he depends upon himself for his own security, he flatters himself in what he has done, in what he is now doing, or what he intends to do. Every one lays out matters in his own mind how he shall avoid damnation, and flatters himself that he contrives well for himself, and that his schemes will not fail. They hear indeed that there are but few saved, and that the greater part of men that have died heretofore are gone to hell; but each one imagines that he lays out matters better for his own escape than others

---

3. "Or if he shall ask an egg, will he offer him a scorpion?"

4. Psalm 91:5. "Thou shalt not be afraid for the terror by night; nor for the arrow that flieth by day."

5. Unsaved, not in a state of grace.

have done. He does not intend to come in that place of torment; he says within himself that he intends to take effectual care, and to order matters so for himself as not to fail.

But the foolish children of men miserably delude themselves in their own schemes, and in confidence in their own strength and wisdom; they trust to nothing but a shadow. The greater part of those who heretofore have lived under the same means of grace, and are now dead, are undoubtedly gone to hell; and it was not because they were not as wise as those who are now alive: it was not because they did not lay out matters as well for themselves to secure their own escape. If we could speak with them, and inquire of them, one by one, whether they expected, when alive, and when they used to hear about hell, ever to be the subjects of that misery, we doubtless, should hear one and another reply, "No, I never intended to come here: I had laid out matters otherwise in my mind; I thought I should contrive well for myself. I thought my scheme good. I intended to take effectual care, but it came upon me unexpected; I did not look for it at that time, and in that manner; it came as a thief: Death outwitted me: God's wrath was too quick for me. Oh, my cursed foolishness! I was flattering myself, and pleasing myself with vain dreams of what I would do hereafter; and when I was saying, peace and safety, then suddenly destruction came upon me."

10. God has laid Himself under no obligation by any promise to keep any natural man out of hell one moment. God certainly has made no promises either of eternal life or of any deliverance or preservation from eternal death but what are contained in the covenant of grace, the promises that are given in Christ, in whom all the promises are yea and amen. But surely they have no interest in the promises of the covenant of grace who are not the children of the covenant, who do not believe in any of the promises, and have no interest in the Mediator of the covenant.[6]

So that, whatever some have imagined and pretended about promises made to natural men's earnest seeking and knocking, it is plain and manifest that whatever pains a natural man takes in religion, whatever prayers he makes, till he believes in Christ, God is under no manner of obligation to keep him a moment from eternal destruction.

---

6. According to Puritan theology, the original Covenant of Works was invalidated by Adam and Eve's disobedience; Christ brought the Covenant of Grace, available to those who believed in him, through his crucifixion.

So that, thus it is that natural men are held in the hand of God, over the pit of hell, they have deserved the fiery pit, and are already sentenced to it; and God is dreadfully provoked, His anger is as great towards them as to those that are actually suffering the executions of the fierceness of His wrath in hell, and they have done nothing in the least to appease or abate that anger, neither is God in the least bound by any promise to hold them up one moment; the devil is waiting for them, hell is gaping for them, the flames gather and flash about them, and would fain lay hold on them, and swallow them up; the fire pent up in their own hearts is struggling to break out; and they have no interest in any Mediator, there are no means within reach that can be any security to them. In short, they have no refuge, nothing to take hold of; all that preserves them every moment is the mere arbitrary will, and uncovenanted, unobliged forbearance of an incensed God.

Application

The use of this awful subject may be for awakening unconverted persons in this congregation. This that you have heard is the case of every one of you that are out of Christ. That world of misery, that lake of burning brimstone is extended abroad under you. There is the dreadful pit of the glowing flames of the wrath of God; there is hell's wide gaping mouth open; and you have nothing to stand upon, nor any thing to take hold of: there is nothing between you and hell but the air; it is only the power and mere pleasure of God that holds you up.

You probably are not sensible of this; you find you are kept out of hell, but do not see the hand of God in it; but look at other things, as the good state of your bodily constitution, your care of your own life, and the means you use for your own preservation. But indeed these things are nothing: if God should withdraw His hand, they would avail no more to keep you from falling, than the thin air to hold up a person that is suspended in it.

Your wickedness makes you as it were heavy as lead, and to tend downwards with great weight and pressure towards hell; and if God should let you go, you would immediately sink and swiftly descend and plunge into the bottomless gulf, and your healthy constitution, and your own care and prudence, and best contrivance, and all your righteousness, would have no more influence to uphold you and keep you out of hell, than a spider's web would have to stop a fallen rock. Were it not for the sovereign pleasure of God, the earth would not bear you one moment; for you are a burden to it; the creation groans with you; the creature is made subject to the bondage of your corruption, not willingly; the sun does not willingly shine upon you to give you light to serve sin and Satan; the earth does not willingly yield her increase to satisfy your lusts; nor is it willingly a stage for your wickedness to be acted upon; the air does not willingly serve you for breath to maintain the flame of life in your vitals, while you spend your life in the service of God's enemies. God's creatures are good, and were made for men to serve God with, and do not willingly subserve to any other purpose, and groan when they are abused to purposes so directly contrary to their nature and end. And the world would spew you out, were it not for the sovereign hand of Him who hath subjected it in hope. There are black clouds of God's wrath now hanging directly over your heads, full of the dreadful storm, and big with thunder; and were it not for the restraining hand of God, it would immediately burst forth upon you. The sovereign pleasure of God, for the present, stays His rough wind; otherwise it would come with fury, and your destruction would come like a whirlwind, and you would be like the chaff of the summer threshing floor.

The wrath of God is like great waters that are dammed for the present; they increase more and more, and rise higher and higher, till an outlet is given; and the longer the stream is stopped, the more rapid and mighty is its course when once it is let loose. It is true that judgment against your evil works has not been executed hitherto: the floods of God's vengeance have been withheld; but your guilt in the meantime is constantly increasing, and you are every day treasuring up more wrath; the waters are constantly rising, and waxing more and more mighty; and there is nothing but the mere pleasure of God that holds the waters back, that are unwilling to be stopped, and press hard to go forward. If God should only withdraw His hand from the floodgate, it would immediately fly open, and the fiery floods of the fierceness and wrath of God, would rush forth with inconceivable fury, and would come upon you with omnipotent power; and if your strength were ten thousand times greater than it is, yea, ten thousand times greater than the strength of the stoutest, sturdiest devil in hell, it would be nothing to withstand or endure it.

The bow of God's wrath is bent, and the arrow made ready on the string, and justice bends the arrow at your heart, and strains the bow, and it is nothing but the mere pleasure of God, and that of an angry God, without any promise or obligation at all, that keeps the arrow one moment from being made drunk with your blood. Thus all you that never passed under a great change of heart, by the mighty power of the Spirit of God upon your souls, all you that were never born again, and made new creatures, and raised from being dead in sin, to a state of new, and before altogether unexperienced light and life, are in the hands of an angry God. However you may have reformed your life in many things, and may have had religious affections, and may keep up a form of religion in your families and closets, and in the house of God, it is nothing but His mere pleasure that keeps you from being this moment swallowed up in everlasting destruction. However unconvinced you may now be of the truth of what you hear, by and by you will be fully convinced of it. Those that are gone from being in the like circumstances with you see that it was so with them; for destruction came suddenly upon most of them; when they expected nothing of it and while they were saying, peace and safety: now they see that those things on which they depended for peace and safety, were nothing but thin air and empty shadows.

The God that holds you over the pit of hell, much as one holds a spider or some loathsome insect over the fire, abhors you, and is dreadfully provoked: His wrath towards you burns like fire. He looks upon you as worthy of nothing else but to be cast into the fire; He is of purer eyes than to bear to have you in His sight; you are ten thousand times more abominable in His eyes than the most hateful venomous serpent is in ours. You have offended Him infinitely more than ever a stubborn rebel did his prince; and yet it is nothing but His hand that holds you from falling into the fire every moment. It is to be ascribed to nothing else, that you did not go to hell the last night; that you was suffered to awake again in this world, after you closed your eyes to sleep. And there is no other reason to be given, why you have not dropped into hell since you arose in the morning, but that God's hand has held you up. There is no other reason to be given why you have not gone to hell, since you have sat here in the house of God, provoking His pure eyes by your sinful wicked manner of attending His solemn worship. Yea, there is nothing else that is to be given as a reason why you do not this very moment drop down into hell.

O sinner! Consider the fearful danger you are in: it is a great furnace of wrath, a wide and bottomless pit, full of the fire of wrath, that you are held over in the hand of that God, whose wrath is provoked and incensed as much against you, as against many of the damned in hell. You hang by a slender thread, with the flames of divine wrath flashing about it, and ready every moment to singe it, and burn it asunder; and you have no interest in any Mediator, and nothing to lay hold of to save yourself, nothing to keep off the flames of wrath, nothing of your own, nothing that you ever have done, nothing that you can do, to induce God to spare you one moment. And consider here more particularly,

1. Whose wrath it is? It is the wrath of the infinite God. If it were only the wrath of man, though it were of the most potent prince, it would be comparatively little to be regarded. The wrath of kings is very much dreaded, especially of absolute monarchs, who have the possessions and lives of their subjects wholly in their power, to be disposed of at their mere will. Proverbs 20.2: "The fear of a king is as the roaring of a lion: Whoso provoketh him to anger, sinneth against his own soul." The subject that very much enrages an arbitrary prince, is liable to suffer the most extreme torments that human art can invent, or human power can inflict. But the greatest earthly potentates in their greatest majesty and strength, and when clothed in their greatest terrors, are but feeble, despicable worms of the dust, in comparison of the great and almighty Creator and King of heaven and earth. It is but little that they can do, when most enraged, and when they have exerted the utmost of their fury. All the kings of the earth, before God, are as grasshoppers; they are nothing, and less than nothing; both their love and their hatred is to be despised. The wrath of the great King of kings, is as much more terrible than theirs, as His majesty is greater. Luke 12.4–5: "And I say unto you, my friends, Be not afraid of them that kill the body, and after that, have no more that they can do. But I will forewarn you whom you shall fear: fear him, which after he hath killed, hath power to cast into hell: yea, I say unto you, Fear him."

2. It is the fierceness of His wrath that you are exposed to. We often read of the fury of God; as in Isaiah 59.18: "According to their deeds, accordingly he will repay fury to his adversaries." So Isaiah 66.15: "For behold, the Lord will come with fire, and with his chariots like a whirlwind, to render his anger with fury, and his rebuke with flames of fire." And in many other places. So, Revelation 19.15: we read of "the wine press of the fierceness and wrath o' Almighty God." The words are exceeding terrible. If it had only been said, "the wrath of God," the words would have implied that which is infinitely dreadful: but it is "the fierceness and wrath of God." The fury of God! the fierceness of Jehovah! Oh, how dreadful must that be! Who can utter or conceive what such expressions carry in them! But it is also "the fierceness and wrath of Almighty God." As though there would be a very great manifestation of His almighty power in what the fierceness of His wrath should inflict, as though omnipo-

tence should be as it were enraged, and exerted, as men are wont to exert their strength in the fierceness of their wrath. Oh! then, what will be the consequence! What will become of the poor worms that shall suffer it! Whose hands can be strong? And whose heart can endure? To what a dreadful, inexpressible, inconceivable depth of misery must the poor creature be sunk who shall be the subject of this!

Consider this, you that are here present that yet remain in an unregenerate state. That God will execute the fierceness of His anger implies that He will inflict wrath without any pity. When God beholds the ineffable extremity of your case, and sees your torment to be so vastly disproportioned to your strength, and sees how your poor soul is crushed, and sinks down, as it were, into an infinite gloom: He will have no compassion upon you, He will not forbear the executions of His wrath, or in the least lighten His hand; there shall be no moderation or mercy, nor will God then at all stay His rough wind: He will have no regard to your welfare, nor be at all careful lest you should suffer too much in any other sense, than only that you shall not suffer beyond what strict justice requires. Nothing shall be withheld because it is so hard for you to bear. Ezekiel 8.18: "Therefore will I also deal in fury; mine eye shall not spare, neither will I have pity; and though they cry in mine ears with a loud voice, yet I will not hear them." Now God stands ready to pity you; this is a day of mercy; you may cry now with some encouragement of obtaining mercy. But when once the day of mercy is past, your most lamentable and dolorous cries and shrieks will be in vain; you will be wholly lost and thrown away of God as to any regard to your welfare. God will have no other use to put you to, but to suffer misery; you shall be continued in being to no other end; for you will be a vessel of wrath fitted to destruction; and there will be no other use of this vessel, but to be filled full of wrath. God will be so far from pitying you when you cry to Him, that it is said He will only "laugh and mock." Proverbs 1.25–26, etc.[7]

How awful are those words, Isaiah 63.3. which are the words of the great God: "I will tread them in mine anger, and will trample them in my fury, and their blood shall be sprinkled upon my garments, and I will stain all my raiment." It is perhaps impossible to conceive of words that

---

7. "But ye have set at nought all my counsel, and would none of my reproof: I also will laugh at your calamity: I will mock you when your fear cometh."

carry in them greater manifestations of these three things, viz., contempt, and hatred, and fierceness of indignation. If you cry to God to pity you, He will be so far from pitying you in your doleful case, or showing you the least regard or favor, that instead of that, He will only tread you under foot. And though He will know that you cannot bear the weight of omnipotence treading upon you, yet He will not regard that, but He will crush you under His feet without mercy; He will crush out your blood, and make it fly and it shall be sprinkled on His garments, so as to stain all His raiment. He will not only hate you, but He will have you in the utmost contempt: no place shall be thought fit for you, but under His feet to be trodden down as the mire of the streets.

3. The misery you are exposed to is that which God will inflict to that end, that He might show what that wrath of Jehovah is. God hath had it on His heart to show to angels and men both how excellent His love is, and also how terrible His wrath is. Sometimes earthly kings have a mind to show how terrible their wrath is, by the extreme punishments they would execute on those that would provoke them. Nebuchadnezzar, that mighty and haughty monarch of the Chaldean empire, was willing to show his wrath when enraged with Shadrach, Meshech, and Abednego; and accordingly gave orders that the burning fiery furnace should be heated seven times hotter than it was before; doubtless, it was raised to the utmost degree of fierceness that human art could raise it. But the great God is also willing to show His wrath, and magnify His awful majesty and mighty power in the extreme sufferings of His enemies. Romans 9.22: "What if God, willing to show his wrath, and to make his power known, endure with much long-suffering the vessels of wrath fitted to destruction?" And seeing this in His design, and what He has determined, even to show how terrible the restrained wrath, the fury and fierceness of Jehovah is, He will do it to effect. There will be something accomplished and brought to pass that will be dreadful with a witness. When the great and angry God hath risen up and executed His awful vengeance on the poor sinner, and the wretch is actually suffering the infinite weight and power of His indignation, then will God call upon the whole universe to behold that awful majesty and mighty power that is to be seen in it. Isaiah 33.12–14: "And the people shall be as the burnings of lime, as thorns cut up shall they be burnt in the fire. Hear ye that are far off, what I have done; ye that are near, acknowledge my might. The sinners in Zion are afraid; fearfulness hath surprised the hypocrites," etc.

Thus it will be with you that are in an unconverted state, if you continue in it; the infinite might, and majesty, and terribleness of the omnipotent God shall be magnified upon you, in the ineffable strength of your torments. You shall be tormented in the presence of the holy angels, and in the presence of the Lamb: and when you shall be in this state of suffering, the glorious inhabitants of heaven shall go forth and look on the awful spectacle, that they may see what the wrath and fierceness of the Almighty is; and when they have seen it, they will fall down and adore that great power and majesty. Isaiah 66.23–24: "And it shall come to pass, that from one new moon to another, and from one sabbath to another, shall flesh come to worship before me, saith the Lord. And they shall go forth and look upon the carcasses of the men that have transgressed against me; for their worm shall not die, neither shall their fire be quenched, and they shall be an abhorring unto all flesh."

4. It is everlasting wrath. It would be dreadful to suffer this fierceness and wrath of Almighty God one moment: but you must suffer it to all eternity. There will be no end to this exquisite horrible misery. When you look forward, you shall see a long forever, a boundless duration before you, which will swallow up your thoughts, and amaze your soul; and you will absolutely despair of ever having any deliverance, any end, any mitigation, any rest at all. You will know certainly that you must wear out long ages, millions of millions of ages, in wrestling and conflicting with this almighty merciless vengeance; and then when you have so done, when so many ages have actually been spent by you in this manner, you will know that all is but a point to what remains. So that your punishment will indeed be infinite. Oh, who can express what the state of a soul in such circumstances is! All that we can possibly say about it gives but a very feeble, faint representation of it; it is inexpressible and inconceivable: For "who knows the power of God's anger?"[8]

How dreadful is the state of those that are daily and hourly in the danger of this great wrath and infinite misery! But this is the dismal case of every soul in this congregation that has not been born again, however moral and strict, sober and religious, they may otherwise be. Oh that you would consider it, whether you be young or old!

---

8. Psalm 90:11. "Who knoweth the power of thine anger? even according to thy fear, so is thy wrath."

There is reason to think that there are many in this congregation now hearing this discourse that will actually be the subjects of this very misery to all eternity. We know not who they are, or in what seats they sit, or what thoughts they now have. It may be they are now at ease, and hear all these things without much disturbance, and are now flattering themselves that they are not the persons, promising themselves that they shall escape. If they knew that there was one person, and but one, in the whole congregation, that was to be the subject of this misery, what an awful thing would it be to think of! If we knew who it was, what an awful sight would it be to see such a person! How might all the rest of the congregation lift up a lamentable and bitter cry over him! But, alas! instead of one, how many is it likely will remember this discourse in hell? And it would be a wonder, if some that are now present should not be in hell in a very short time, even before this year is out. And it would be no wonder if some persons, that now sit here, in some seats of this meeting-house, in health, quiet and secure, should be there before tomorrow morning. Those of you that finally continue in a natural condition, that shall keep out of hell longest will be there in a little time! your damnation does not slumber; it will come swiftly, and, in all probability, very suddenly upon many of you. You have reason to wonder that you are not already in hell. It is doubtless the case of some whom you have seen and known, that never deserved hell more than you, and that heretofore appeared as likely to have been now alive as you. Their case is past all hope; they are crying in extreme misery and perfect despair; but here you are in the land of the living and in the house of God, and have an opportunity to obtain salvation. What would not those poor damned hopeless souls give for one day's opportunity such as you now enjoy!

And now you have an extraordinary opportunity, a day wherein Christ has thrown the door of mercy wide open, and stands in calling and crying with a loud voice to poor sinners; a day wherein many are flocking to Him, and pressing into the kingdom of God. Many are daily coming from the east, west, north and south; many that were very lately in the same miserable condition that you are in are now in a happy state, with their hearts filled with love to Him who has loved them, and washed them from their sins in His own blood, and rejoicing in hope of the glory of God. How awful is it to be left behind at such a day! To see so many others feasting, while you are pining and perishing! To see so many rejoicing and singing for joy of heart, while you have cause to mourn for sorrow of heart,

and howl for vexation of spirit! How can you rest one moment in such a condition? Are not your souls as precious as the souls of the people at Suffield,[9] where they are flocking from day to day to Christ?

Are there not many here who have lived long in the world, and are not to this day born again? and so are aliens from the commonwealth of Israel, and have done nothing ever since they have lived, but treasure up wrath against the day of wrath? Oh, sirs, your case, in an especial manner, is extremely dangerous. Your guilt and hardness of heart is extremely great. Do you not see how generally persons of your years are passed over and left, in the present remarkable and wonderful dispensation of God's mercy? You had need to consider yourselves, and awake thoroughly out of sleep. You cannot bear the fierceness and wrath of the infinite God. And you, young men, and young women, will you neglect this precious season which you now enjoy, when so many others of your age are renouncing all youthful vanities, and flocking to Christ? You especially have now an extraordinary opportunity; but if you neglect it, it will soon be with you as with those persons who spent all the precious days in youth in sin, and are now come to such a dreadful pass in blindness and hardness. And you, children, who are unconverted, do not you know that you are going down to hell, to bear the dreadful wrath of that God, who is now angry with you every day and every night? Will you be content to be the children of the devil, when so many other children in the land are converted, and are become the holy and happy children of the King of kings?

And let every one that is yet of Christ, and hanging over the pit of hell, whether they be old men and women, or middle-aged, or young people, or little children, now hearken to the loud calls of God's word and providence. This acceptable year of the Lord, a day of such great favors to some, will doubtless be a day of as remarkable vengeance to others. Men's hearts harden, and their guilt increases apace at such a day as this, if they neglect their souls; and never was there so great danger of such person being given up to hardness of heart and blindness of mind. God seems now to be hastily gathering in His elect in all parts of the land; and probably the greater part of adult persons that ever shall be saved, will be brought in now in a little time, and that it will be as it was on the

---

9. "A town in the neighborhood." [Au.]

great outpouring of the Spirit upon the Jews in the apostles' days; the election will obtain, and the rest will be blinded. If this should be the case with you, you will eternally curse this day, and will curse the day that ever you was born, to see such a season of the pouring out of God's Spirit, and will wish that you had died and gone to hell before you had seen it. Now undoubtedly it is, as it was in the days of John the Baptist, the axe is in an extraordinary manner laid at the root of the trees, that every tree which brings not forth good fruit, may be hewn down and cast into the fire.

Therefore, let everyone that is out of Christ, now awake and fly from the wrath to come. The wrath of Almighty God is now undoubtedly hanging over a great part of this congregation: Let everyone fly out of Sodom: "Haste and escape for your lives, look not behind you, escape to the mountain, lest you be consumed."

---

from THE DISTINGUISHING MARKS OF A WORK OF THE SPIRIT[1]

The subjects of these uncommon appearances, have been of two sorts; either those who have been in great distress from an apprehension of their sin and misery; or those who have been overcome with a sweet sense of the greatness, wonderfulness, and excellency of divine things. Of the multitude of those of the former sort, that I have had opportunity to observe, there have been very few, but their distress has arisen apparently from real proper conviction, and being in a degree sensible of that which was the truth. And though I do not suppose, when such things were observed to be common, that persons have laid themselves under those violent restraints to avoid outward manifestations of their distress, that perhaps they otherwise would have done; yet there have been very few in whom there has been any appearance of feigning or affecting such manifestations, and very many for whom it would have been undoubtedly utterly impossible for them to avoid them. Generally, in these agonies they have appeared to be in the perfect exercise of their reason; and those of them who could speak, have been well able to give an account of the circumstances of their mind, and the cause of their distress, at the time, and were able to remember, and give an account of it afterwards. I have known a very few instances of those, who, in their great extremity, have for a short space been deprived, in some measure, of the use of reason; and among the many hundreds, and it may be thousands, that have lately been brought to such agonies, I never yet knew one lastingly deprived of their reason. In some that I have known, melancholy has evidently been mixed; and when it is so, the difference is very apparent; their distresses are of another kind, and operate quite after another manner, than when their distress is from mere conviction. It is not truth only that distresses them, but many vain shadows and notions that will not give place either to Scripture or reason. Some in their great distress have not been well able to give an account of themselves, or to declare the sense they have of things, or to explain the manner and cause of their trouble to others, that yet I have had no reason to think were not under proper convictions, and in whom there has been manifested a good issue. But this will not be at all wondered at, by those who have had much to do with souls under spiritual difficulties: some things of which they are sensible, are altogether new to them; their ideas and inward sensations are new, and what they therefore know not how to express in words. Some who, on first inquiry, said they knew not what was the matter with them, have on being particularly examined and interrogated, been able to represent their case, though of themselves they could not find expressions and forms of speech to do it.

Some suppose, that terrors producing such effects are only a fright. But certainly there ought to be a distinction made between a very great fear, or extreme distress arising from an apprehension of some dreadful truth—a cause fully proportionable to such an effect—and a needless, causeless fright. The latter is of two kinds; either, first, when persons are terrified with that which is not the truth (of which I have seen very few instances unless in case of melancholy); or, secondly, when they are in a fright from some terrible outward appearance and noise, and a general notion thence arising. These apprehend, that there is something or other terrible, they know not what; without having in their minds any particular truth whatever. Of such a kind of fright I have seen very little appearance, among either old or young.

Those who are in such extremity, commonly express a great sense of their exceeding wickedness, the multitude

---

1. This sermon was delivered at New Haven on September 10, 1741, and printed in Boston the same year, the printing from which the present text is taken.

and aggravations of their actual sins; their dreadful pollution, enmity, and perverseness; their obstinacy and hardness of heart; a sense of their great guilt in the sight of God; and the dreadfulness of the punishment due to sin. Very often they have a lively idea of the horrible pit of eternal misery; and at the same time it appears to them, that the great God who has them in his hands, is exceedingly angry, and his wrath appears amazingly terrible to them. God appears to them so much provoked, and his great wrath so increased; that they are apprehensive of great danger, and that he will not bear with them any longer; but will now forthwith cut them off, and send them down to the dreadful pit they have in view; at the same time seeing no refuge. They see more and more of the vanity of every thing they used to trust to, and with which they flattered themselves, till they are brought wholly to despair in all, and to see that they are at the disposal of the mere will of that God who is so angry with them. Very many, in the midst of their extremity, have been brought to an extraordinary sense of their fully deserving that wrath, and the destruction which was then before their eyes. They feared every moment, that it would be executed upon them; they have been greatly convinced that this would be altogether just, and that God is indeed absolutely sovereign. Very often, some text of Scripture expressing God's sovereignty, has been set home upon their minds, whereby they have been calmed. They have been brought, as it were, to lie at God's feet; and after great agonies, a little before light has arisen, they have been composed and quiet, in submission to a just and sovereign God; but their bodily strength much spent. Sometimes their lives, to appearance, were almost gone; and then light has appeared, and a glorious Redeemer, with his wonderful, all-sufficient grace, has been represented to them often, in some sweet invitation of Scripture. Sometimes the light comes in suddenly, sometimes more gradually, filling their souls with love, admiration, joy, and self-abasement; drawing forth their hearts after the excellent lovely Redeemer, and longings to lie in the dust before him; and that others might behold, embrace, and be delivered by him. They had longings to live to his glory; but were sensible that they can do nothing of themselves, appearing vile in their own eyes, and having much jealousy over their own hearts. And all the appearances of a real change of heart have followed; and grace has acted, from time to time, after the same manner that it used to act in those that were converted formerly, with the like difficulties, temptations, buffetings, and comforts;

excepting that in many, the light and comfort have been in higher degrees than ordinary. Many very young children have been thus wrought upon. There have been some instances very much like those (Mark i. 26, and chap. ix. 26,) of whom we read, that "when the devil had cried with a loud voice, and rent them sore, he came out of them." And probably those instances were designed for a type of such things as these. Some have several turns of great agonies, before they are delivered; and others have been in such distress, which has passed off, and no deliverance at all has followed.

Some object against it as great confusion, when there is a number together in such circumstances making a noise; and say, God cannot be the author of it; because he is the God of order, not of confusion. But let it be considered, what is the proper notion of confusion, but the breaking that order of things, whereby they are properly disposed, and duly directed to their end, so that the order and due connection of means being broken, they fail of their end. Now the conviction of sinners for their conversion is the obtaining of the end of religious means. Not but that I think the persons thus extraordinarily moved, should endeavour to refrain from such outward manifestations, what they well can, and should refrain to their utmost, at the time of their solemn worship. But if God is pleased to convince the consciences of persons, so that they cannot avoid great outward manifestations, even to interrupting and breaking off those public means they were attending, I do not think this is confusion, or an unhappy interruption, any more than if a company should meet on the field to pray for rain, and should be broken off from their exercise by a plentiful shower. Would to God that all the public assemblies in the land were broken off from their public exercises with such confusion as this the next Sabbath day! We need not be sorry for breaking the order of means, by obtaining the end to which that order is directed. He who is going to fetch a treasure, need not be sorry that he is stopped, by meeting the treasure in the midst of his journey.

Besides those who are overcome with conviction and distress, I have seen many of late, who have had their bodily strength taken away with a sense of the glorious excellency of the Redeemer, and the wonders of his dying love; with a very uncommon sense of their own littleness and exceeding vileness attending it, with all expressions and appearances of the greatest abasement and abhorrence of themselves. Not only new converts, but many who were, as we hope, formerly converted, have had their love and joy attended with a flood of tears, and a great appearance of contrition and humiliation, especially for their having lived no more to God's glory since their conversion. These have had a far greater sight of their vileness, and the evil of their hearts, than ever they had; with an exceeding earnestness of desire to live better for the time to come, but attended with greater self-diffidence than ever; and many have been overcome with pity to the souls of others, and longing for their salvation.—And many other things I might mention, in this extraordinary work, answering to every one of those marks which have been insisted on. So that if the apostle John knew how to give signs of a work of the true Spirit, this is such a work.

Providence has cast my lot in a place where the work of God has *formerly* been carried on. I had the happiness to be settled in that place two years with the venerable Stoddard, and was then acquainted with a number who, during that season, were wrought upon under his ministry. I have been intimately acquainted with the experiences of many others who were wrought upon under his ministry, before that period, in a manner agreeable to the doctrine of all orthodox divines. And of late, a work has been carried on there, with very much of uncommon operations; but it is evidently the same work that was carried on there, in different periods, though attended with some new circumstances. And certainly we must throw by all talk of conversion and Christian experience; and not only so, but we must throw by our Bibles, and give up revealed religion; if this be not in general the work of God. Not that I suppose the degree of the Spirit's influence is to be determined by the degree of effect on men's bodies; or, that those are always the best experiences which have the greatest influence on the body.

And as to the imprudencies, irregularities, and mixture of delusion that has been observed; it is not at all to be wondered at, that a reformation, after a long continued and almost universal deadness, should at first, when the revival is new, be attended with such things. In the first creation God did not make a complete world at once; but there was a great deal of imperfection, darkness, and mixture of chaos and confusion, after God first said, "Let there be light," before the whole stood forth in perfect form. When God at first began his great work for the deliverance of his people, after their long-continued bondage in Egypt, there were false wonders mixed with the true for a while; which hardened the unbelieving Egyptians, and made them to doubt of the divinity of the whole work. . . .

The imprudencies and errors that have attended this work, are the less to be wondered at, if it be considered, that chiefly young persons have been the subjects of it, who have less steadiness and experience, and being in the heat of youth, are much more ready to run to extremes. Satan will keep men secure as long as he can; but when he can do that no longer, he often endeavors to drive them to extremes, and so to dishonor God, and wound religion in that way. And doubtless it has been one occasion of much misconduct, that in many places, people see plainly that their ministers have an ill opinion of the work; and therefore, with just reason, durst not apply themselves to them as their guides in it; and so are without guides.—No wonder then that when a people are as sheep without a shepherd, they wander out of the way. A people in such circumstances, stand in great and continual need of guides, and their guides stand in continual need of much more wisdom than they have of their own. And if a people have ministers that favor the work, and rejoice in it, yet it is not to be expected that either the people or ministers should know so well how to conduct themselves in such an extraordinary state of things—while it is new, and what they never had any experience of before, and time to see their tendency, consequences, and issue. The happy influence of experience is very manifest at this day, in the people among whom God has settled my abode. The work which has been carried on there this year, has been much purer than that which was wrought there six years before: it has seemed to be more purely spiritual; free from natural and corrupt mixtures, and any thing savoring of enthusiastic wildness and extravagance.

. . . Those who are now waiting to see the issue of this work, think they shall be better able to determine by and by; but probably many of them are mistaken. The Jews that saw Christ's miracles, waited to see better evidences of his being the Messiah; they wanted a sign from heaven; but they waited in vain; their stumbling-blocks did not diminish, but increase. They found no end to them, and so were more and more hardened in unbelief. Many have been praying for that glorious reformation spoken of in Scripture, who knew not what they have been praying for (as it was with the Jews when they prayed for the coming of Christ), and who, if it should come, would not acknowledge or receive it.

This pretended prudence, in persons waiting so long before they acknowledged this work, will probably in the end prove the greatest imprudence. Hereby they will fail of any share of so great a blessing, and will miss the most precious opportunity of obtaining divine light, grace, and comfort, heavenly and eternal benefits, that God ever gave in New England. While the glorious fountain is set open in so wonderful a manner, and multitudes flock to it and receive a rich supply for the wants of their souls, they stand at a distance, doubting, wondering, and receiving nothing, and are like to continue thus till the precious season is past.—It is indeed to be wondered at, that those who have doubted of the work, which has been attended with such uncommon external appearances, should be easy in their doubts, without taking thorough pains to inform themselves, by going where such things have been to be seen, narrowly observing and diligently inquiring into them; not contenting themselves with observing two or three instances, nor resting till they were fully informed by their own observation. I do not doubt but that if this course had been taken, it would have convinced all whose minds are not shut up against conviction. How greatly have they erred, who only from the uncertain reproofs of others, have ventured to speak slightly of these things! That caution of an unbelieving Jew might teach them more prudence, Acts v. 38, 39: "Refrain from these men, and let them alone; for if this counsel or this work be of men, it will come to nought; but if it be of God, ye cannot overthrow it; lest haply ye be found to fight against God." Whether what has been said in this discourse be enough to produce conviction, that this is the work of God, or not; yet I hope that for the future, they will at least hearken to the caution of Gamaliel, now mentioned; so as not to oppose it, or say any thing which has even an indirect tendency to bring it into discredit, lest they should be found opposers of the Holy Ghost. There is no kind of sins so hurtful and dangerous to the souls of men, as those committed against the Holy Ghost. We had better speak against God the Father, or the Son, than to speak against the Holy Spirit in his gracious operations on the hearts of men. Nothing will so much tend forever to prevent our having any benefit of his operations on our own souls.

If there be any who still resolutely go on to speak contemptibly of these things, I would beg of them to take heed that they be not guilty of the unpardonable sin. When the Holy Spirit is much poured out, and men's lusts, lukewarmness, and hypocrisy are reproached by its powerful operations, then is the most likely time of any, for this sin to be committed. If the work goes on, it is well if among the many that show an enmity against it, some be not guilty of this sin, if none have been already. Those who maliciously oppose and reproach this work, and call it the work of the devil, want but one thing of the unpardonable sin, and that is, doing it against inward conviction. And though some are so prudent, as not openly to oppose and reproach this work, yet it is to be feared—at this day, when the Lord is going forth so gloriously against his enemies—that many who are silent and inactive, especially ministers, will bring that curse of the angel of the Lord upon themselves, Judg. v. 23: "Curse ye Meroz, said the angel of the Lord, curse ye bitterly the inhabitants thereof: because they came not to the help of the Lord, to the help of the Lord against the mighty."

CHARLES CHAUNCY (1705–1787)

Minister of Boston's First Church for six decades, Charles Chauncy experienced a literary and intellectual life that embraced the growing rationalism of his era as it found expression in religious practice and theology. Born in Boston, the son of a leading merchant and grandson of a controversial London minister, Chauncy was educated at Harvard and served as the pastor of the First Church of Boston from 1727 to 1787. In the early 1740s, Chauncy began to preach against the passionate emotional appeals of ministers, such as George Whitefield and Jonathan Edwards. Chauncy argued that excessive feeling in converts, often accompanied by pride in successful conversion, proved that the supposed religious experience was not genuine.

Chauncy's first full-scale argument on this subject appeared in his sermon *Enthusiasm Describ'd and Caution'd Against* (1742), which established Chauncy as a leading spokesman against revivalist movements. Whereas "New Light" preachers like Edwards considered emotional illumination to be part of the working of holy spirit, "Old Lights" like Chauncy declared that such emotionalism disrupted the orderly experiences of divinity, wherein emotions are subject to a rational understanding of the godhead. Chauncy opposed the emotionalism and concern for obtaining a sense of "religious affections," as Jonathan Edwards called the experience of grace. Instead, he associated himself closely with "enlightened" approaches to religion, approaches that placed religious affections subsidiary to reason. In opposition to Edwards's insistence upon the place of human emotion in religious experience, Chauncy conceived of religious perceptions as the subduing of imagination and will to reason and judgment.

In 1743, Chauncy published *Seasonable Thoughts Concerning the Revival of Religion,* partially in response to Jonathan Edwards's *Some Thoughts Concerning the Revival of Religion* (1742). Edwards had argued that there were inextricable connections among the understanding, the will, and the emotions, so that touching people's hearts became the key to conversion. In reply, Chauncy argued that the mind, not the emotions, should guide men in all matters, including religion.

As the furor of the New England revivals began to subside, Chauncy started to focus his writings on a number of other issues. In several writings, he warned ministers against competition and other inappropriate behavior. He also argued forcefully against the establishment of an Anglican bishop in the British colonies, fearing the oppressions of a state-run church. Chauncy played a significant role in opposing the Stamp Act and in developing colonial strategies to thwart British invasion during the Revolution. Chauncy's later religious writings developed a theology that became part of the Universalist movement, a theology that stressed God's benevolence, humankind's free will, and the possibility of salvation for anyone with true faith.

from ENTHUSIASM DESCRIBED AND CAUTION'D AGAINST[1]

If any Man among you think himself to be a PROPHET, *or* SPIRITUAL, *let him acknowledge that the Things that I write unto you are the Commandments of the* LORD.
I COR. XIV. XXXVII.

MANY Things were amiss in the *Church* of *Corinth,* when *Paul* wrote this Epistle to them. There were envyings, strife and divisions among them, on account of their ministers. Some cried up one, others another: one said, I am of PAUL, another I am of APOLLOS. They had form'd themselves into parties, and each party so admired the teacher they followed, as to reflect unjust contempt on the other.

Nor was this their only fault. A spirit of pride prevailed exceedingly among them. They were conceited of their gifts, and too generally dispos'd to make an ostentatious shew of them. From this vain glorious temper proceeded the forwardness of those that had the *gift* of *tongues,* to speak in languages which others did not understand, to the disturbance, rather than edification of the church: And

from the same principle it arose, that they spake not by turns, but several at once, in the same place of worship, to the introducing such confusion, that they were in danger of being tho't mad.

Nor were they without some pretence to justify these disorders. Their great plea was, that in these things they were guided by the Spirit, acted under his immediate influence and direction. This seems plainly insinuated in the words I have read to you. *If any man think himself to be a prophet, or spiritual, let him acknowledge that the things that I write unto you are the commandments of the Lord.* As if the apostle had said, you may imagine your selves to be *spiritual* men, to be under a divine afflatus in what you do; but 'tis all imagination, meer pretence, unless you pay a due regard to the *commandments* I have here *wrote to you;* receiving them not as the *word of man, but of* GOD. Make trial of your spiritual pretences by this rule: If you can submit to it, and will order your conduct by it, well; otherwise you only cheat yourselves, while you think yourselves to be *spiritual* men, or *prophets:* You are nothing better than Enthusiasts; your being acted by SPIRIT, immediately guided and influenced by him, is meer pretence; you have no good reason to believe any such thing.

From the words thus explained, I shall take occasion to discourse to you upon the following Particulars.

I. I shall give you some account of *Enthusiasm,* in its *nature* and *influence.*

II. Point you to a rule by which you may judge of

---

1. The sermon was delivered on the Sunday following Harvard's commencement in 1742 and published the same year in Boston.

persons, whether they are under the influence of *Enthusiasm.*

III. Say what may be proper to guard you against this unhappy turn of mind.

The whole will then be follow'd with some suitable Application

I. I am in the first place, to give you some account of *Enthusiasm.* And as this a thing much talk'd of at present, more perhaps than at any other time that has pass'd over us, it will not be tho't unseasonable, if I take some pains to let you into a true understanding of it.

The word, from it's Etymology, carries in it a good meaning, as signifying *inspiration from* GOD: in which sense, the prophets under the old testament, and the apostles under the new, might properly be called *Enthusiasts.* For they were under a divine influence, spake as moved by the HOLY GHOST, and did such things as can be accounted for in no way, but by recurring to an immediate extraordinary power, present with them.

But the word is more commonly used in a bad sense, as intending an *imaginary,* not a *real* inspiration: according to which sense, the *Enthusiast* is one, who has a conceit of himself as a person favoured with the extraordinary presence of the *Deity.* He mistakes the workings of his own passions for divine communications, and fancies himself immediately inspired by the SPIRIT of GOD, when all the while, he is under no other influence than that of an over-heated imagination.

The cause of this *enthusiasm* is a bad temperament of the blood and spirits; 'tis properly a disease, a sort of madness: And there are few; perhaps none at all, but are subject to it, tho' none are so much in danger of it as those, in whom *melancholy* is the prevailing ingredient in their constitution. In these it often reigns; and sometimes to so great a degree, that they are really beside themselves, acting as truly by the blind impetus of a wild fancy, as tho' they had neither reason nor understanding.

And various are the ways in which their *enthusiasm* discovers itself.

Sometimes, it may be seen in their countenance. A certain wildness is discernable in their general look and air; especially when their imaginations are mov'd and fired.

Sometimes, it strangely loosens their tongues, and gives them such an energy, as well as fluency and volubility in speaking, as they themselves, by their utmost efforts, can't so much as imitate, when they are not under the enthusiastick influence.

Sometimes, it affects their bodies, throws them into convulsions and distortions, into quakings and tremblings. This was formerly common among the people called *Quakers.* I was myself, when a Lad, an eye witness to such violent agitations and foamings, in a boisterous female speaker, as I could not behold but with surprize and wonder.

Sometimes, it will unaccountably mix itself with their conduct, and give it such a tincture of that which is freakish or furious, as none can have an idea of, but those who have seen the behaviour of a person in a phrenzy.

Sometimes, it appears in their imaginary peculiar intimacy with heaven. They are, in their own opinion, the special favourites of GOD, have more familiar converse with him than other good men, and receive immediate, extraordinary communications from him. The tho'ts, which suddenly rise up in their minds, they take for suggestions of the SPIRIT; their very fancies are divine illuminations; nor are they strongly inclin'd to any thing, but 'tis an impulse from GOD, a plain revelation of his will.

And what extravagances, in this temper of mind, are they not capable of, and under the specious pretext too of paying obedience to the authority of GOD? Many have fancied themselves acting by immediate warrant from heaven, while they have been committing the most undoubted wickedness. There is indeed scarce any thing so wild, either in *speculation* or *practice,* but they have given into it: They have, in many instances, been blasphemers of GOD, and open disturbers of the peace of the world.

But in nothing does the *enthusiasm* of these persons discover it self more, than in the disregard they express to the Dictates of *reason.* They are above the force of argument, beyond conviction from a calm and sober address to their understandings. As for them, they are distinguish'd persons; GOD himself speaks inwardly and immediately to their souls. "They see the light infused into their understandings, and cannot be mistaken; 'tis clear and visible there, like the light of bright sunshine; shews it self and needs no other proof but its own evidence. They feel the hand of GOD moving them within, and the impulses of his SPIRIT; and cannot be mistaken in what they feel. Thus they support themselves, and are sure reason hath nothing to do with what they see and feel. What they have a sensible experience of, admits no doubt, needs no probation".[2] And in vain will you endeavour to convince

---

2. John Locke, *An Essay Concerning Human Understanding,* Book IV, Chap. 19.

such persons of any mistakes they are fallen into. They are certainly in the right, and know themselves to be so. They have the SPIRIT opening their understandings and revealing the truth to them. They believe only as he has taught them: and to suspect they are in the wrong is to do dishonour to the SPIRIT; 'tis to oppose his dictates, to set up their own wisdom in opposition to his, and shut their eyes against that light with which he has shined into their souls. They are not therefore capable of being argued with; you had as good reason with the wind.

And as the natural consequence of their being thus sure of every thing, they are not only infinitely stiff and tenacious, but impatient of contradiction, censorious and uncharitable: they encourage a good opinion of none but such as are in their way of thinking and speaking. Those, to be sure, who venture to debate with them about their errors and mistakes, their weaknesses and indiscretions, run the hazard of being stigmatiz'd by them as poor unconverted wretches, without the SPIRIT, under the government of carnal reason, enemies to GOD and religion, and in the broad way to hell.

They are likewise positive and dogmatical, vainly fond of their own imaginations, and invincibly set upon propagating them: And in the doing of this, their Powers being awakened, and put as it were, upon the stretch, from the strong impressions they are under, that they are authorized by the immediate command of GOD himself, they sometimes exert themselves with a sort of *extatic* violence: And 'tis this that gives them the advantage, among the less knowing and judicious, of those who are modest, suspicious of themselves, and not too assuming in matters of conscience and salvation. The extraordinary fervour of their minds, accompanied with uncommon bodily motions, and an excessive confidence and assurance gains them great reputation among the populace; who speak of them as *men of* GOD in distinction from all others, and too commonly hearken to, and revere their dictates, as tho' they really were, as they pretend, immediately communicated to them from the DIVINE SPIRIT.

This is the nature of *Enthusiasm,* and this its operation, in a less or greater degree, in all who are under the influence of it. 'Tis a kind of religious Phrenzy, and evidently discovers it self to be so, whenever it rises to any great height.

And much to be pitied are the persons who are seized with it. Our compassion commonly works towards those, who, while under distraction, fondly imagine themselves to be Kings and Emperors: And the like pity is really due

to those, who, under the power of *enthusiasm,* fancy themselves to be *prophets; inspired of God,* and *immediately called and commissioned by him to deliver his messages to the world:* And tho' they should run into disorders, and act in a manner that cannot but be condemned, they should notwithstanding be treated with tenderness and lenity; and the rather, because they don't commonly act so much under the influence of a *bad mind,* as a *deluded imagination.* And who more worthy of christian pity than those, who, under the notion of serving GOD and the interest of religion, are filled with zeal, and exert themselves to the utmost, while all the time they are hurting and wounding the very cause they take so much pains to advance. 'Tis really a pitiable case: And tho' the honesty of their intentions won't legitimate their bad actions, yet it very much alleviates their guilt: We should think as favourably of them as may be, and be dispos'd to judge with mercy, as we would hope to obtain mercy.

But I come

II. In the second place, to point you to a *rule* by which you may judge of persons, whether they are *enthusiasts,* meer pretenders to the immediate guidance and influence of the SPIRIT. And this is, in general, *a regard to the bible, an acknowledgement that the things therein contained are the commandments of GOD.* This is the rule in the text. And 'tis an infallible rule of tryal in this matter: We need not fear judging amiss, while we keep closely to it.

'Tis true, it wont certainly follow, that a man, pretending to be a *prophet,* or *spiritual,* really is so, if he owns the *bible,* and receives the truths therein revealed as the mind of GOD: But the conclusion, on the other hand, is clear and certain; if he pretends to be conducted by the SPIRIT, and disregards the scripture, pays no due reverence to *the things there delivered as the commandments of GOD,* he is a meer pretender, be his pretences ever so bold and confident, or made with ever so much seeming seriousness, gravity, or solemnity.

And the reason of this is obvious; viz. that the things contained in the scripture were wrote by holy men as they were moved by the HOLY GHOST: they were received from GOD, and committed to writing under his immediate, extraordinary influence and guidance. And the divine, everblessed SPIRIT is consistent with himself. He cannot be suppos'd to be the author of any *private* revelations that are contradictory to the *public standing* ones, which he has preserved in the world to this day. This would be to set the SPIRIT of truth at variance with himself; than which a greater reproach can't be cast upon him. 'Tis therefore as true, that those are *enthusiastical,* who pretend to the SPIRIT, and at the same time express a disregard to the scripture, as that the SPIRIT is the great revealer of the things therein declared to us. And we may depend upon the certainty of this conclusion. We have warrant to do so from the *inspired Paul;* and we have the more reason to rely upon the rule he has given us, as he has made it evident to the world, that he was a *prophet,* and *spiritual,* by signs and wonders which he did before the people, by the power of the SPIRIT of GOD.

But the *rule* in the text is yet more particular. It refers especially to *the things wrote by the apostle* PAUL, and which he wrote to the *church of Corinth,* to rectify the *disorders* that had crept in among them. And whoever the person be, that pretends to be *spiritual,* to be under the extraordinary guidance of the SPIRIT and yet acts in contradiction to what the apostle has here wrote, he vainly imagines himself to be under the special guidance of the SPIRIT; he is a downright *enthusiast.*

And here suffer me to make particular mention of some of the things, the apostle has wrote in *this Epistle,* which, whoever will not acknowledge, in *deed* as well as *word,* to be the *commandments of GOD,* they are not guided by the SPIRIT but vainly pretend to be so.

The first thing, in this kind, I would mention, is that which relates to *Ministers;* condemning an undue preference of one to another, the holding one in such admiration as to reflect disgrace on another. This was one of the disorders the Apostle takes notice of, as prevailing in the *church* of *Corinth;* and he is particular in his care to give check to this unchristian spirit, which had crumbled them into parties, and introduced among them faction and contention.

Now, whoever, under the pretence of being guided by the spirit, set up one minister in opposition to another, glory in this minister to the throwing undue contempt on that, thereby obstructing his usefulness, and making way for strife and divisions, they are not really acted by the SPIRIT whatever they may pretend. For they evidently contradict what the apostle has wrote upon this very head: And if *he* was inspired, the spirit *they* are influenced by, cannot be the SPIRIT of GOD.

Not that one minister may not be preferr'd to another; this is reasonable: But no minister ought to be regarded, as tho' he was the author of our faith; nor, let his gifts and graces be what they will, is he to be so esteemed, as that others must be neglected, or treated in an unbecoming

manner. But I shall not enlarge here, having spoken fully to this point, in a Sermon you may, some of you, have in your hands.

Another thing the apostle is particular in writing upon, is the *commandment* of *charity.* And this he declares to be a matter of such essential importance in true christianity, that if a man is really destitute of it, he is nothing, in the sight of GOD: Nay, tho' his pretences, his attainments, his gifts, be ever so extraordinary or miraculous; still, if he is without charity he will certainly be rejected of GOD and the LORD JESUS CHRIST. This is beautifully represented in the three first verses of the 13th chapter of this Epistle, in some of the boldest figures. "Tho' I speak, says the apostle, with the tongues of men and of angels, and have not charity, I am become as sounding brass, or a tinkling cymbal. And tho' I have the gift of prophecy, and understand all mysteries and all knowledge; and tho' I have all faith, so that I could remove mountains, and have not charity, I am nothing. And tho' I bestow all my goods to feed the poor, and tho' I give my body to be burned, and have not charity, it profiteth me nothing." As if the apostle had said, tho' a man had the languages of all nations, and could speak with the eloquence of angels; tho', like an inspired prophet, he had understanding in the deep counsels of GOD, and knew even all things sacred and divine; tho' he had the faith of miracles, and could do impossibilities; tho' he had the zeal of a martyr, and should give his body to be burned; tho' he had a disposition to almsgiving, and should bestow upon the poor his whole substance; still, if he was without charity, "that charity which suffereth long, and is kind; that charity which envyeth not, vaunteth not it self, is not puffed up; that charity which behaveth not it self unseemly, seeketh not her own, is not easily provoked, thinketh no evil, rejoiceth not in iniquity, but rejoiceth in the truth; that charity, in fine, which beareth all things, believeth all things, hopeth all things, endureth all things": I say, if he was without this charity, this love of his neighbour, these things would be all nothing; he would notwithstanding be out of favour with GOD, without any interest in CHRIST, and in such circumstances, as that unless there was a change in them, he would certainly perish.

This, in sum, is what the apostle has, in a distinct and peremptory manner, delivered concerning charity.

And in vain may any pretend to be under the extraordinary guidance of the SPIRIT while in their practice they trample upon this law of christian love. Men may talk of their *impulses* and *impressions,* conceive of them as the call of GOD, and go about, as moved by them, from place to place, imagining they are sent of GOD, and immediately commissioned by him: But if they are censorious and uncharitable; if they harbour in their minds evil surmisings of their brethren; if they slander and reproach them; if they claim a right to look into their hearts, make it their business to judge of their state, and proclaim them hypocrites, carnal unregenerate sinners, when at the same time they are visibly of a good conversation in CHRIST; I say, when this is the practice of any, they do not acknowledge what the inspired PAUL has here *wrote as the commandment of GOD:* They are not therefore acted by the same SPIRIT with which he spake; but are evidently under a spirit of delusion: And this is so obviously the case, that there is no reasonable room to doubt upon the matter.

Charity, my brethren, is the commandment of the gospel by way of eminence. 'Tis the grand mark by which christians are to distinguish themselves from all others. *By this,* says our SAVIOUR,[3] *shall all men know that ye are my disciples, if ye have love to one another:* Yea, this is the grand criterion by which we are to judge, whither GOD *dwelleth in us by his SPIRIT. If we love one another, GOD dwelleth in us.*[4] And in the following Verse, Hereby, i.e. by our loving one another, *we know that we dwell in him, and he in us, because he hath given us of his SPIRIT.* To pretend therefore that we are led by the SPIRIT and are under his extraordinary influence, when, in contradiction to the plain laws of JESUS CHRIST, revealed by the SPIRIT we *judge our brother,* and *set at naught our brother,* and plead a right to do so, and are in a disposition TO THANK GOD, THAT WE ARE ENABLED TO DO SO; there is not a more sure mark, in all the revelations of GOD, of a BAD HEART, or a DISTEMPERED MIND. If any thing will evidence a man to be a *prophet* and *spiritual,* only in his own conceit, this must do it: And if this is not allow'd to be sufficient proof, there is no knowing, when a man is under the influence of *enthusiastick* heat and zeal.

Another thing the apostle bespeaks this church upon, is that *self-conceit* which appear'd among them in the exercise of *spiritual gifts:* And 'tis more than probable, there were those among them, who being vainly puffed up in their minds, behaved as tho' they were *apostles,* or *prophets,* or *teachers;* leaving their own station, and doing the work that was proper to others. It was to rectify such disorders, that the apostle, in the 12th chapter, ad-

dresses to them in that language, v. 29. *Are all apostles? Are all prophets? Are all teachers?* The question carries with it it's own answer, and means the same thing, as when he affirms in the foregoing verse *God hath set some in the church, first apostles, secondarily prophets, thirdly teachers,* and so on. 'Tis evident from what the apostle here writes, and indeed from the current strain of this whole chapter, that there is in the body of CHRIST, the Church, a distinction of members; some intended for one use, others for another; and that it would bring confusion into the *body mystical,* for one member to be employed in that service which is adapted to another, and is its proper business.

'Tis not therefore the pretence of being moved by the *SPIRIT,* that will justify *private christians* in quitting their own proper station, to act in that which belongs to another. Such a practice as this naturally tends to destroy that order, GOD has constituted in the church; and may be followed with mischiefs greater than we may be aware of.

'Tis indeed a powerful argument with many, in favour of these persons, their pretending to *impulses,* and a call from GOD; together with their insatiable thirst to do good to souls. And 'tis owing to such pretences as these, that encouragement has been given to the rise of such numbers of *lay-exhorters* and *teachers,* in one place and another, all over the land. But if 'tis one of the things wrote by the apostle as the *commandment of* GOD, that there should be *officers* in the church, an *order of men* to whom it should belong, as their *proper, stated work,* to exhort and teach, this cannot be the business of others: And if any who think themselves to be *spiritual,* are under *impressions* to take upon them *this ministry,* they may have reason to suspect, whether their *impulses* are any other than the workings of their own imaginations: And instead of being under any divine extraordinary influence, there are just grounds of fear, whether they are not acted from the vanity of their minds: Especially, if they are but beginners in religion; men of weak minds, babes in understanding: as is most commonly the case. The apostle speaks of *novices,* as in danger of being *lifted up with pride, and falling into the contamination of the devil:* And it is a seasonable caution to this kind of person. They should study themselves more, and they will see less reason to think their disposition to exhort and teach to be from the SPIRIT OF GOD. And indeed, if the SPIRIT has bid men to *abide in their own callings,* 'tis not conceivable he should influence them to *leave their callings:* And if he has set a mark of disgrace upon *busy-bodies in other men's matters,* 'tis impossible he should put men upon

---

3. "John 13.35." [Au.]

4. "I John 4.12." [Au.]

wandring about from house to house, speaking the things they ought not.

And it deserves particular consideration, whether the suffering, much more the encouraging WOMEN, yea, GIRLS to speak in the assemblies for religious worship, is not a plain breach of that *commandment of the* LORD,[5] wherein it is said, *Let your* WOMEN *keep silence in the churches; for it is not permitted to them to speak—It is a shame: for* WOMEN *to speak in the church.* After such an express constitution, designedly made to restrain WOMEN from speaking in the church, with what face can such a practice be pleaded for? They may pretend, they are moved by the SPIRIT and such a tho't of themselves may be encouraged by others; but if the apostle *spake by the* SPIRIT when he delivered *this commandment,* they can't *act by the* SPIRIT when they break it. 'Tis a plain case, these FEMALE EXHORTERS are condemned by the apostle; and if 'tis the *commandment of the* LORD, that they should not speak, they are *spiritual* only in their own tho'ts, while they attempt to do so.

The last thing I shall mention as written by the apostle, is that which obliges to a *just decorum in speaking* in the *house of* GOD. It was an extravagance these *Corinthians* had fallen into, their speaking many of them together, and upon different things, while in the same place of worship. *How is it, brethren,* says the apostle? *When ye come together, every one hath a psalm; hath a doctrine; hath a tongue; hath a revelation; hath an interpretation.* It was this that introduced the confusion and noise, upon which the apostle declares, if an unbeliever should come in among them, he would take them to be mad.[6] And the *commandment* he gives them to put a stop to this disorder, is, that they should *speak in course, one by one,* and so as that *things might be done to edifying.*[7]

And whoever the persons are, who will not acknowledge what the apostle has here said is the *commandment of* GOD, and act accordingly, are influenced by another spirit than that which moved in him, be their impressions or pretences what they will. The disorder of EXHORTING, and PRAYING, and SINGING, and LAUGHING, *in the same house of worship, at one and the same time,* is as great as was that, the apostle blames in the *church of Corinth:* And whatever the persons, guilty of such gross irregularity may imagine, and however they may plead their being

under the influence of the SPIRIT and mov'd by him, 'tis evidently a breach upon common order and decency; yea, a direct violation of the *commandment of* GOD, written on purpose to prevent such disorders: And to pretend the direction of the SPIRIT in such a flagrant instance of extravagant conduct, is to reproach the blessed SPIRIT who is not, as the apostle's phrase is, *the author of confusion, but of peace, as in all the churches of the saints.*

In these, and all other instances, let us compare men's pretences to the SPIRIT by the SCRIPTURE: And if their conduct is such as can't be reconcil'd with an *acknowledgment of the things therein revealed, as the commandments of* GOD, their pretences are vain, they are *prophets* and *spiritual,* only in their own proud imaginations. I proceed now to

III. The third thing, which is to caution you against giving way to *enthusiastic impressions.* And here much might be said, I might warn you from the *dishonour* it reflects upon the SPIRIT of GOD. And perhaps none have more reproach'd the blessed SPIRIT than men pretending to be under his extraordinary guidance and direction. The veryest fancies, the vainest imaginations, the strongest delusions, they have father'd on him. There is scarce any absurdity in *principle,* or irregularity in *practice,* but he has been made the patron of it.—And what a stone of stumbling has the wildness of *Enthusiasm* been to multitudes in the world? What prejudices have been hereby excited in their minds against the very being of the SPIRIT? What temptations have been thrown in their way to dispute his OFFICE as the SANCTIFIER and COMFORTER of GOD's people? And how have they been over-come to disown HIS WORK, when it has been really wro't in the hearts of men?

I might also warn you from the damage it has done in the world. No greater mischiefs have arisen from any quarter. It is indeed the genuine source of infinite evil. POPERY it self han't been the mother of more and greater blasphemies and abominations. It has made strong attempts to destroy all property, to make all things common, *wives* as well as *goods.*—It has promoted faction and contention; filled the church often-times with confusion, and the state sometimes with general disorder.—It has, by its pretended spiritual interpretations, made void the most undoubted laws of GOD. It has laid aside the *gospel sacraments* as weak and carnal things; yea, this *superior light within* has, in the opinion of thousands, render'd the *bible a useless dead letter.*—It has made men fancy themselves to be *prophets* and *apostles;* yea, some

5. "Context, v. 35, 26." [Au.]

6. "v. 23." [Au.]

7. "26, 27." [Au.]

have taken themselves to be CHRIST JESUS; yea, the blessed GOD himself. It has, in one word, been a pest to the church in all ages, as great an enemy to real and solid religion, as perhaps the grossest *infidelity*.[8]

---

from SEASONABLE THOUGHTS ON THE STATE OF RELIGION[1]

The true Account to be given of the *many* and *great* Mistakes of the present Day, about the *SPIRIT's* Influence, is not the *Newness* of the Thing, the not having *felt it before;* but a *notorious* Error generally prevailing, as to the *Way* and *Manner* of judging in this Matter. People, in order to know, whether the Influences they are under, are from the SPIRIT, don't carefully examine them by the *Word of GOD,* and view the *Change* they produce in the *moral State* of their *Minds* and of their *Lives,* but hastily conclude such and such *internal Motions* to be *divine Impressions,* meerly from the *Perception* they have of them. They are ready, at once, if this is *unusual,* or *strong,* to take it for some Influence from above, to speak of it as such, and to act accordingly. This is the Error of the present Day; and 'tis indeed the *proton Pseudos,* the first and grand Delusion: And where this prevails, we need not be at a loss to know the *true Spring* of other Errors.—As to the *Multitudes* who are bro't into such *new,* and (to them) *unheard of Circumstances,* 'tis true, they are *illiterate,* and *young* People; but this notwithstanding, if the *Newness* of their Circumstances is such as is proper to *new Creatures,* they will, in their *general Behaviour,* discover the *true Spirit* and *Genius* of this Sort of Persons. 'Tis a great Mistake to think, that the *new Nature,* or those *Influences* that produce it, however extraordinary, are apt to put Men upon making *wrong* and *strange* Judgments, either of *Persons* or *Things:* They have a contrary Tendency: and 'tis a Reproach to them both, to suppose otherwise. A *meer passionate* Religion, 'tis true, has always led to this, and always will; but not that, which enlightens the Understanding, renews the Will, and makes the Heart good and honest.—How far 'tis a Truth, that *this People* have *scarce* heard of such a Thing as the *Outpouring* of

the SPIRIT of GOD, or had *no Notion* of it, may admit of Dispute; but that the *Outpouring* of the SPIRIT should introduce *such a State of Things,* as that those *upon whom* he has been *poured out,* should *not know how to behave,* will, I think, admit of no good Plea in its Defence. 'Tis a plain Case, one of the *main Ends* of the *Out-pouring* of the SPIRIT, is to dispose and enable People to behave as *Christians,* in their various *Stations, Relations* and *Conditions* of Life; and if instead of this, they are thrown into such a *strange State,* as that they can't behave as they ought to do, not in here and there a perplext Case, but in some of the most *obvious* and *essential* Points of Practice; let who will call this an *Out-pouring* of the SPIRIT, 'tis not such an one as the *Bible* knows any Thing of. And 'tis nothing short of a gross Reflection on the *blessed SPIRIT,* to speak of *him* as *wonderfully* poured out upon a People, and, at the same Time, to suppose such a State of Things arising therefrom, as that People may run into *very ill Conduct,* and it not be thought *strange,* if they do so.— What is observ'd of People's *Readings* to hearken to those, who have been the *Instruments* of bringing them into their present Circumstances, I own, is no other than might be expected: Nor have I any Doubt, upon my Mind, whether the *Disorders,* so *general* in this Land, had their *Rise* from these Persons. But *Schism,* and *Confusion,* and other *evil Works,* won't change their Nature, be their *Origin* in *People* themselves, or their *Leaders.*

It is still urged, "That when Persons are *extraordinarily* affected with a recent Discovery of the Greatness and Excellency of the divine Being, the Certainty and infinite Importance of eternal Things, the Preciousness of Souls, and the dreadful Danger and Madness of Mankind, together with a great Sense of GOD's distinguishing Kindness and Love to them; no Wonder that now they think they must exert themselves, and do something extraordinary, for the Honour of God, and the Good of Souls, and know not how to forbear speaking and acting with uncommon Earnestness and Vigour. And in these circumstances, if they ben't Persons of uncommon Steadiness and Discretion, or han't some Persons of Wisdom to direct them, 'tis a Wonder, if they don't proceed without due Caution, and do Things that are irregular, and will, in the Issue, do more Hurt than Good." 'Tis readily granted, Persons under a just and strong Sense of divine Things, will exert themselves with an awaken'd Activity in the Business of Religion. 'Twould be no Wonder, if those who had *extraordinary* Discoveries of GOD, were, to an *extraordinary* Degree, filled with Lowliness and Humility, and such an Awe and Reverence of the divine Majesty,

---

8. "Undoubted instances of these, and many other things of a like nature, are well known to such as are, in any measure, acquainted with the *history* of the *church.*" [Au.]

1. This sermon was first published in Boston in 1743.

as would make them *eminently* circumspect in their whole Deportment towards him; if from the *uncommon* View they had of his Perfections, they were, in an *uncommon* Manner, transformed into his Likeness, appearing in the World *lively Images* of that Goodness, Righteousness, Faithfulness, Kindness, Mercy, Patience and Long-suffering, which are the *moral Glory* of the infinitely perfect Being. 'Twould be no Wonder, if those, who had upon their Minds an *extraordinary* Sense of the *Preciousness of Souls,* discovered extraordinary Care and Pains in working out the Salvation of their *own Souls;* if they were observably *diligent* in *adding to their Faith, Vertue; to Vertue, Knowledge; to Knowledge, Temperance; to Temperance, Patience; to Patience, Godliness; to Godliness, Brotherly-Kindness; and to Brotherly-Kindness, Charity: For they that lack these Things are blind* to the Worth of their *own Souls;* whereas, they *that do them* make it evident that they regard their Souls: *For so an Entrance shall be ministred to them abundantly, into the everlasting Kingdom of our* LORD *and* SAVIOUR JESUS CHRIST. In like Manner, 'twould be no Wonder, if those who had an *extraordinary* View of the *Danger* and *Madness* of those who neglect their Souls, were *proportionably* active, within their *proper Sphere,* in Endeavours to do them all the Service they could; if they were ready with their Advice, their Counsel, their Prayers, their Intreaties, to beget in them a just Concern about Salvation: Nor would they be "worthy of *Indignation,* and be beyond *Compassion,*" if, through an *indiscreet Zeal* they should, now and then, be betray'd into Weaknesses and Excesses. These are Things, not to be wondered at; they are no other than might reasonably be expected. But the Wonder is, how an *extraordinary* Discovery of the Greatness and Excellency of GOD, the Importance of eternal Things, and the Preciousness of Souls, and the Danger of their perishing, should make Men vain and conceited, full of themselves, and apt to throw Contempt on others; how it should loosen Men's Tongues to utter such Language as would not be seemly, even in those who profess no Sense of GOD, or divine Things; how it should lead them into wrong Sentiments in Religion, blind their Eyes as to some of the most plain Points of Doctrine; and in a Word, dispose them to such Things as are called in Scripture, the *Works of the Flesh.*

These don't look like the Fruit of *extraordinary* Discoveries of GOD; but they are the very Things which may be expected, where Men's *Passions* are rais'd to an *extraordinary* Height, without a proportionable Degree of Light in their Understandings.

Such *high Affections,* I know, are freely spoken of as owing to the Influence of the SPIRIT of GOD; and this, when there is not given "*Strength* of *Understanding* in *Proportion;* and by Means hereof, the *Subjects* of these Affections may be driven, through Error, into an *irregular* and *sinful Conduct.*" But it may justly be question'd, whether *extraordinary Warmth* in the *Passions,* when there is not *answerable Light* in the *Mind,* is so much owing to the SPIRIT of GOD, as some may be ready to imagine. For is it reasonable to think, that the *Divine SPIRIT,* in dealing with Men in a Way of Grace, and in Order to make them good Christians, would give their *Passions* the *chief* Sway over them? Would not this be to invert their Frame? To place the Dominion in those Powers, which were made to be kept in Subjection? And would the alwise GOD introduce such a State of Things in the human Mind? Can this be the Effect of the *Outpouring* of his SPIRIT? It ought not to be supposed. One of the most *essential* Things necessary in the *new-forming* Men, is the Reduction of their *Passions* to a proper Regimen, i.e. The Government of a *sanctified Understanding:* And 'till this is effected, they may be called *New-Creatures,* but they are far from deserving this Character. *Reasonable* Beings are not to be guided by *Passion* or *Affection,* though the Object of it should be GOD, and the Things of another World: They need, even in this Case, to be under the Government of a *well instructed Judgment:* Nay, when Men's *Passions* are raised to an *extraordinary* Height, if they have not, at the same Time, a due Ballance of *Light* and *Knowledge* in their Minds, they are so far from being in a more desirable State on this Account, that they are in Circumstances of extreme Hazard. There is no Wildness, but they are liable to be hurried into it; there is no Temptation, but they are expos'd to be drawn aside by it: Nor has the Devil ever greater Advantage against them, to make a Prey of them, and lead them captive at his Will. And this has often been verified by sad Experience. Who can boast of greater Transports of Affection, than the wildest Enthusiasts? Who have had their Passions excited to a higher Pitch, than those of the ROMISH Communion? Who have been more artful in their Addresses to the *Passions,* than *Popish Priests?* And who more successful, by *heating* the *Affections* of People, to establish Error and Delusion? Nay, what Engine has the *Devil* himself ever made Use of, to more fatal Purposes, in all Ages, than the *Passions* of the *Vulgar* heightened to such a Degree, as to put them upon acting without Thought and Understanding? The plain Truth is, an *enlightened Mind,* and not *raised Affections,* ought always to be the Guide of those who call themselves Men; and this, in the Affairs of Religion, as well as other Things: And it will be so, where GOD really works on their Hearts, by his SPIRIT. 'Tis true, "the End of the Influence of the SPIRIT of GOD is not to increase Men's natural Capacities:" But 'tis to fit their Powers for religious Exercise, and preserve them in a State of due Subordination. 'Tis as much intended to *open the Understanding,* as to *warm the Affections;* and not only so, but to keep the *Passions* within their proper Bounds, restraining them from usurping Dominion over the *reasonable* Nature. 'Tis true likewise, "GOD has not oblig'd himself immediately to increase *civil Prudence,* in Proportion to the Degrees of *spiritual Light.*" But if it shall please GOD to visit Men with the Influences of his SPIRIT, it may justly be expected, that he should increase their *moral* or *religious* Prudence; that, if he should give them *spiritual Light,* it should be for their Instruction in the Knowledge of what is *Sin,* and what is *Duty.* . . .

I have hitherto considered *Ministers* as the Persons, more especially obliged to discountenance the bad Things, prevailing in the Land; and now go on to observe.

That this is the Duty of *all in general.* Not that I would put any upon acting out of their *proper Sphere.* This would tend rather to Confusion than Reformation.— Good Order is the Strength and Beauty of the World.— The Prosperity both of *Church* and *State* depends very much upon it. And can there be Order, where Men transgress the Limits of their Station, and intermeddle in the Business of others? So far from it, that the only effectual Method, under GOD, for the Redress of *general Evils,* is, for *every one* to be faithful, in doing what is *proper* for him in his *own Place:* And even *all* may *properly* bear a Part, in *rectifying the Disorders* of this Kind, at this Day.

Civil Rulers may do a great deal, not only by their *good Example,* but a wise Use of their *Authority,* in their various Places, for the Suppression of every Thing hurtful to Society, and the Encouragement of whatever has a Tendency to make Men happy in the Enjoyment of their Rights, whether *natural* or *Christian.* And herein chiefly lies, (as I humbly conceive) the Duty of Rulers, at this Day. 'Tis true, as *private Men,* they are under the same Obligations with others, to make their Acknowledgments to CHRIST; and doubtless, if HE was *visibly* and *externally* (according to the Custom among *Kings* and *Governors*) to make his solemn Entry into the Land, as their SAVIOUR and LORD, "it would be expected they should, as *public Officers,* make their Appearance, and attend him as their *Sovereign* with sutable Congratulations, and Manifestations of Respect and Loyalty; and if they should stand at

a Distance, it would be much more taken Notice of, and awaken his Displeasure much more, than such a Behaviour in the common People."[2] But the Case is widely different, where his supposed Entry is in a *spiritual Sense only, and after such a Manner* even in this Sense, as that there is a *great Variety of Sentiments* about it, among the *best Sort* of Men, of all Ranks and Conditions: Nor does it appear to me, when the Case is thus circumstanc'd, that it is either the *Duty* of *Rulers,* or would be Wisdom in them, by any *authoritative Acts* to determine, whose Sentiments were the most agreable to Truth. And as to their Appointment of Days of *Thanksgiving,* or *fasting,* on this Account, there must be an Impropriety in it, so long as that Complaint of GOD against the *Jews* is to be seen in the *Bible, Behold ye fast for Strife and Debate!* Their *Duty* rather lies in keeping Peace between those, who unhappily differ in their Thoughts about the State of our religious Affairs: And their Care in this Matter ought to be *impartial.* Each Party, without Favour or Affection, should be equally restrain'd from Out-rage and Insult. Those, who may think themselves Friends to a *Work of GOD,* should be protected in the Exercise of all their *just Rights,* whether as *Men,* or *Christians:* So on the other Hand, those who may be Enemies to *Error* and *Confusion,* have the same Claim to be protected.

And if, on either Side, they invade the Rights of others, or throw out Slander, at Random, to the Hurt of their Neighbour's Reputation and Usefulness, and the bringing forward a State of Tumult and Disorder; I see not but the *civil Arm* may justly be stretched forth for the Chastisement of such Persons; and this, though their Abuses should be offered in the Name of the LORD, or under the Pretext of the most flaming Zeal for the REDEEMER's *Honour,* and serving the Interest of *his Kingdom:* For it ought always to be accounted an Aggravation of the Sin of *Slander,* rather than an Excuse for it, its being committed under the *Cloak of Religion,* and Pretence for the *Glory of GOD;* as it will, under these Circumstances, be of more pernicious Tendency. I am far from thinking, that any Man ought to suffer, either for his *religious Principles,* or *Conduct* arising from them, while he is no Disturber of the *civil Peace;* but when Men, under the Notion of appearing zealous for GOD and *his Truths,* insult their Betters, vilify their Neighbours, and spirit People to Strife and Faction, I know of no Persons more sutable to be

---

2. "Vid. Mr. EDWARDS's Book of the *late Revival of Religion.*" [Au.]

taken in Hand by *Authority:* And if they suffer 'tis for their own Follies; nor can they reasonably blame any Body but themselves: Nor am I asham'd, or afraid, to profess it as my Opinion, that it would probably have been of good Service, if those, in these Times, who have been publickly and out-ragiously reviled, had, by their Complaints, put it properly in the *Magistrates* Power, to restrain some Men's *Tongues* with *Bit* and *Bridle.*

Private Christians also, of all Ranks and Conditions, may do something towards the Suppression of these *Errors,* by mourning before the LORD the Dishonour which has hereby been reflected on the name of CHRIST, and Injury done to Souls; by being much in Prayer to GOD for the Out-pouring of his SPIRIT, in all desirable Influences of Light, and Love, and Peace; by taking good Heed that they ben't themselves drawn aside, avoiding to this End, the Company and familiar Converse of those, who, by *good Words* and *fair Speeches,* might be apt to deceive their Hearts, but especially an Attendance on religious Exercises, where the *Churches* and *Ministry* are freely declaimed against by those who have gone out from them, under the vain Pretence of being more holy than they; and in fine, by a faithful Performance of those Duties, which arise from the various Relations they sustain towards each other: As thus, if they are *Children,* by hearkening to the Advice of their *Parents,* and obeying and honouring them in the LORD; and if they are *Parents,* by counseling, reproving, warning, restraining, and commanding their *Children,* as there may be Occasion: If they are *Servants,* by pleasing their *Masters* well in all Things, not defrauding them of their Time or Labour, but accounting them worthy of all Honour, that the Name of GOD be not blasphemed; and, if they are *Masters,* not only by providing for their *Servants* Things honest and good, but by keeping them within the Rules of Order and Decorum, not suffering them to neglect the Religion of the Family at home, under Pretence of carrying it on elsewhere; especially, when they continue abroad 'till late in the Night, and so as to unfit themselves for the Services of the following Day.

In these, and such like Ways, *all* may exert themselves in making a Stand against the Progress of Error: And *all* are oblig'd to do so; and for this Reason, among others I han't Room to mention, because the *last Days* are particularly mark'd out in the *Prophecies of Scripture,* as the Times wherein may be expected, the Rise of SEDUCERS. . . .

'Tis true, we read of the coming on of a *glorious State* of Things in the LAST DAYS: Nor will the *Vision fail.*—We may rely upon it, the Prophesies, foretelling the Glory of the REDEEMER's *Kingdom,* will have their Accomplishment to the making this Earth of *Paradise,* in Compare with what it now is. But for the *particular Time* when this will be, it *is not for us to know it, the Father having put it in his own Power:* And whoever pretend to such Knowledge, they are wise above what is written; and tho' they may think they know much, they really know nothing as to this Matter.

8

DUTCH, SWEDES, AND GERMANS
IN NORTH AMERICA

Writings from the areas then called New Netherland, New Sweden, and Germantown are like colonial writings from many different European and British colonial enterprises: Writers speak about the trip across the Atlantic; the lands and peoples encountered; the difficulties of establishing the settlement, including obstructions to success or, sometimes, "divine providences" marking the "special" concern behind the settlements being established; and how much and what kind of assistance would most secure the colonial efforts under way. While Dutch, Swedish, and German speakers took part in colonial enterprises in other areas (the Germans most notably in enterprises in Charleston, South Carolina, and in Louisiana), the largest clusters of these populations landed and settled in the eastern Atlantic seaboard areas extending from present-day, Albany, New York, to present-day Wilmington, Delaware.

What makes the writings of New Netherland and New Sweden particularly distinctive among colonial writings are the clear signs of preoccupation with soothing the presumably troubled minds of the burghers back home and of Dutch West India Company officials and other individuals, such as Kiliaen van Rensselaer, who sponsored the voyages in the first place. Whether they are religious people or people whose activities are primarily secular, writers sending letters and reports to Amsterdam are very particular in their expressions of regard and respect for company officials and others, indicating that a high degree of social stratification marked their home communities. The writers are also clear about the accomplishments being made or, in the absence of successes, say where the blame should fall. Such characteristic concerns, especially about Dutch West India Company interests, derive from the founding conceptions of these colonies as fulfilling part of the larger scheme of the Dutch West India Company, but the concern is also evident in the letters of someone like Maria van Cortlandt van Rensselaer, who endeavors to account for every bit of money spent to further the interests of her patroon family.

During the seventeenth century, the Dutch West India Company was formulated as part of a move for global control of trade initiated by the successes of the Dutch East India Company (incorporated by the States General of the Netherlands in 1602). In the East, the Dutch controlled the area extending from the Cape of Good Hope eastward to the Strait of Magellan. The goal was to create a network of outposts in the West that would share commodities and peoples, thus establishing a global monopoly of trade that would counter the successes particularly of Spain during the sixteenth century. The Dutch West India Company was established in 1621 to create colonies in the Americas. In the West, it was granted by the States General of the Netherlands, in return for subsidies from the state, a monopoly on trade in the Americas and in Africa, in addition to primary rights to colonization and to maintain armed forces within colonies, as needed. The company sponsored colonizing efforts in Surinam, Curaçao, and the areas along the eastern North Atlantic seaboard, where trade in furs could rival the French trade and where colonies could more easily settle and survive because of the fine opportunities for growing self-sustaining foodstuffs.

The Dutch West India Company first sent settlers to the area called Hudson's Valley, based on examinations of the area made by Englishman Henry Hudson, who navigated the waterways for the Dutch, from the New York harbor to the region around Albany. Contesting French claims to the area (the French had extended into northern New York through the efforts of Samuel de Champlain and fur traders), the company sent settlers who created establishments at Fort Orange (Albany) beginning in 1624 and New Amsterdam (Manhattan) in 1626 after the colony governor, Director-General Peter Minuit, created a "purchase" of land there. New Netherland was never supported by the company in the way that its plantations in the West Indies received support, because it was clear that the sugar plantation economy of the Caribbean would bring a greater return on investment than the development of farms in the middle Atlantic. Instead of continuing to finance large operations in the area called New Netherland, the company decided in 1629 to offer its members large estates, called patroonships, with the understanding that the patroons, with some assistance from the company, would sponsor settlers to the colony. The patroonships worked, but they could not bring the immediate return that company officials—or indeed, as in Maria van Rensselaer's case, family members—expected. When the company appointed Willem Kieft director-general of New Netherland, Kieft, incompetent at establishing a new colony, drove the colony into war with the neighboring Indians, and the colony lost its favored fur-trade status, thus compromising what had been the colony's distinctive offering to global trade.

The arrival of Peter Stuyvesant in 1647 brought a more peaceful leadership, but one nonetheless authoritarian. The new director-general vigorously pursued encroaching British neighbors to the east and north and the Swedish settlers to the south of New Netherland. Stuyvesant stalled the exhorbitant claims of officers at Rensselaerwyck, the patroonship established by Kiliaen van Rensselaer above and below Fort Orange. He established more formal plans for defense and suppressed illegal trading with the Indians, especially the trade of firearms. The costs of establishing a firm administration were heavy, however, and the company situation required that the costs be borne by the inhabitants. Stuyvesant's new taxes far outweighed the colonists' abilities to pay. One means by which Stuyvesant kept unrest at bay was to permit new settlers, with different notions about forms of settlement, in the colony. This brought a degree of plurality to the colony as an increasing number of English speakers arrived. English ministers, unhappy with the situation in neighboring Connecticut, entered the colony and, as long as they agreed to follow Stuyvesant's administrative policy, were permitted to remain. This is how, for instance, Adriaen Van Der Donck met Mary Doughty, daughter of the dissenting minister Francis Doughty.

By the 1650s, under a failing administrative system and with increasing encroachments by British settlers from Connecticut, Stuyvesant began to consider what to do about the faltering colony of New Netherland. He was outraged and wanted to strike back when New Amsterdam was invaded by a small British force led by Richard Nicolls in the fall of 1664. Nicolls had been commissioned to take over New Amsterdam by King Charles II, who claimed for England the right of prior discovery of the region, based on examinations of the territory made in behalf of England by John Cabot in 1497 and 1498. This action contested the already faltering Dutch establishment, and Stuyvesant was persuaded to let the takeover be peaceful, rather than enter into a war the Dutch could not sustain. Stuyvesant capitulated, and Nicolls governed the colony as a deputy for James, duke of York, who later became James II of England. When Nicolls left the colony in the 1660s, it nonetheless remained under British control.

New Sweden was settled, resettled, and then taken over in much the same way as New Netherland. Swedish colonists were the first to settle Christinahamn (in the area of present-day Wilmington, Delaware) in 1638, under the leadership of Peter Minuit, who had successfully founded New Amsterdam, before being recalled by the Dutch West India Company. Minuit, concerned about fortifications, built Fort Christina near the site of the original settlement. Although they were sponsored, in part, by the Dutch West India Company, the Swedes who settled the area considered that their efforts were being made in behalf of Sweden because the Swedish government had also sponsored the settlement.

Yet New Sweden was dominated by Dutch concerns because the Dutch continued to claim the area as part of their original claim, which extended from Fort Nassau, built in 1623 (at present-day Gloucester,

New Jersey), to Fort Christina. The Swedes and the Dutch continued an uneasy alliance because of the Thirty Years' War in Europe, but when the Treaty of Westphalia of 1648 was concluded, the Dutch West India Company became significantly concerned about the trading successes of the Swedes in the region, jealous that these successes would redound to Dutch interests and not to a strengthening of the Crown of Sweden. The Dutch West India Company sent Peter Stuyvesant, director-general of New Amsterdam, to attack New Sweden in 1655, and New Sweden fell under the control of New Netherland.

For a brief time, then, New Netherland extended in pockets of settlements of Europeans sponsored by the Dutch West India Company all along the Atlantic seaboard, from present-day Albany, New York, to present-day Wilmington, Delaware. This situation did not last long, however. The English took over control of the area of New Sweden in 1664, when they took the leadership away from Stuyvesant in New Amsterdam and the larger territory of New Netherland. Within twenty years' time, the entire area between New York and Christiana was overtaken by English-speaking settlers. In 1682, William Penn gained possession of the region around New Sweden, and the claim to activity in the area was secured to Britain. The area called Pennsylvania became peopled by many different groups of northern Europeans thereafter.

Although much of the territory of Pennsylvania had been granted in the London Company's original patent for Virginia in 1606, the area had remained unexamined by Britain and was instead claimed competitively by the French and the Dutch, who had navigated the waterways extending through the eastern part of the region. Dutch West India Company interests, supported by the Swedish residents of New Sweden, were secured by a trading post on the Schuylkill River in 1633.

When William Penn arrived with his chartered rights, the area officially fell back into British claims, and immigration to the territory increased dramatically. Penn, a member of the Society of Friends, traveled among pious and working people in many parts of northern and western Europe, seeking artisans and agricultural workers to take part in his Holy Experiment. Middling people everywhere—English, Dutch, Welsh, Scottish, Scotch-Irish, and Germans—all found the idea of such an experiment far more attractive than the lives of manorial labor and penury they led back home, with no chance to own land and no say in governance. Part of the attraction to migrate lay in Penn's claim that all would have equal opportunity before the law. (Penn, a lawyer, was interested in cases of conscience, from his own experience of incarceration for dissent from the state and state church in England.) But an even larger attraction was the idea of owning one's own parcel and freely practicing one's religion without harassment from church or secular authorities. Pennsylvania became the magnet for all kinds of religious dissenters and practitioners of many of the different mystical and pietist faiths.

Followers of different radical Protestant sects arrived from different parts of Europe in larger and larger numbers in each decade after Penn's first landing in 1682, but no group surpassed the numbers of Germans and German speakers who arrived during the first six decades of the eighteenth century. As historians A. Gregg Roeber and Marianne Wockeck have indicated, the dissenters from Bern-Emmental, the Kraichgau, the Palatinate, and the lower Rhine developed an antipathy for established churches and for princes and sought freedom from their interference in determining what they considered should be matters of conscience, such as baptizing one's children and taking of oaths or being forced to make expressions of liege loyalty. These people determined that individuals did not require the attentions of a learned ministry hired by the state and did not need to have all decisions made for them by outsiders to their community. There had been migrations of German speakers earlier than the great migrations to Pennsylvania, when they traveled to areas in the southern Connecticut River valley and New York and to different places in the Carolinas. But William Penn's promises of toleration proved particularly attractive to German speakers, wracked as they were by poverty, overpopulation in the Rhineland, and increasing oppression at the hands of princes.

During the height of German immigration in the middle of the eighteenth century, German-speaking people flooded into Pennsylvania, reputed in Europe to be the most tolerant and hospitable of the British colonies in North America. Before the decade of 1750 was out, so many newcomers had arrived that a distinctly German community emerged, with Philadelphia and Germantown serving as central clearing stations for all German speakers, the place where they learned about life in Pennsylvania and where they could most readily labor and settle. In the areas outside Germantown, which was overpopulated by the middle of the eighteenth century, distinctly German communities had emerged, tied to different faiths, including Schwenkfelders, Rosicrucians, Protestant monastics, and Labadists and radical pietists like those at Ephrata cloister. These more radical groups joined earlier migrants, including the more staid German Lutheran and Dutch Reformed settlements in Virginia, and they themselves were joined by additional Lutherans and Reformed Church members, as well as by Moravians. Pennsylvania, but especially Philadelphia, was fast becoming a German community, which worried English speakers and British provincial and local officials almost as much as it evidently worried leaders back in Germany: In 1768, an imperial edict from Joseph II (1741–90), Holy Roman Emperor after 1765, forbade emigration to places that were not directly tied to the empire, thus curtailing further German emigration to the North American colonies held by Britain.

JOHANNES MEGAPOLENSIS, JR. (1603?–1669)

As a director of the West India Company and an absentee patroon of one of the largest estates in New Netherland, Kiliaen Van Rensselaer (1595–1644) held much in his hands as a promulgator and promoter of trading and agricultural interests in the Dutch colony. His large land grant, called Rensselaerwyck by the settlers, dominated the outlying areas of Fort Orange (near present-day Albany) and was the cultural and civic center of the community of people who were sent to settle this northern area of the colony. As patroon, according to the agreements made with the company and governing bodies of the United Netherlands, Van Rensselaer was responsible for three key aspects of daily life on his estate. He was required to make sure that the business of his estate was carried out according to the agreements with the company. For this position of responsibility, he sent his young relative, Arent Van Curler. He needed to trust that the estate would be run lawfully, that its people would behave lawfully, and that its agricultural production and trade would operate in keeping with the company's stipulations. For this position, the office of *schout,* he found the young lawyer, Adriaen Van Der Donck. And finally, Van Rennselaer was responsible for making sure that people would behave in what was conceived by members of the Dutch Reformed Church as a godly fashion. Until a clergyman arrived, this responsibility fell to Van Der Donck. But in June 1642, the Reverend Johannes Megapolensis, Jr., with his wife and four children, boarded the ship *De Houttuyn,* setting sail for New Amsterdam as the new minister for Rensselaerwyck.

Megapolensis was evidently born with the surname Van Grootstede, but following Church traditions adopted the same Latinized name used by his father, also a minister. He had been raised a Catholic while a boy, according to his own testimony, but the family lost their estate when they relinquished Catholicism to follow Protestantism. Megapolensis trained at the university and served in several ministerial positions in North Holland. He was a well-respected preacher, known for his piety, scholarship, energy, and stability. From the time he arrived at Rensselaerwyck in late 1642, he anticipated that a church would be built for him, but the church structure itself never materialized. Nonetheless, Megapolensis settled on the east side of the Hudson River, opposite Fort Orange, and began preaching to the settlers and to the Indians, whom he attempted to learn about from the moment of his arrival.

Megapolensis was required by contract to remain at Rensselaerwyck for six years. He served his post faithfully and fully, and he was preparing to return home to the Netherlands when he was approached by the Council at New Amsterdam and asked to serve the pulpit there because their minister had just recently resigned his position. Rather than leave an outpost unattended, and with the approval of the West India Company and the Dutch classis, Megapolensis decided to remain in the ministry in New Amsterdam, where he stayed the rest of his life. He proved to be narrow in his beliefs regarding Lutherans and members of the Society of Friends, rigidly wishing to keep to the traditions of the Dutch Reformed Church, but his steadiness in other matters was admirable. Indeed, Megapolensis was one of Peter Stuyvesant's advisers at the time the English invaded New Amsterdam in 1644, and he played a significant role in convincing Stuyvesant to submit to the English authorities.

Yet it is the minister's stay at Rensselaerwyck that has proved the most durable of his experiences across the centuries. What Megapolensis learned about the Mohawks in his first year of preaching there he wrote up in a brief pamphlet, *Een kort Ontwerp vande Mahakvase Indiaenen,* or in English, *A Short Account of the Mohawk Indians,* which was published at Alkmaar, the Netherlands, in 1644. His *Short Account* was recirculated in a collection of materials related to Virginia, New Netherland, and New England, compiled by Joost Hartgers and published in Amsterdam in 1651. Megapolensis gave his book to many people, including Adriaen Van Der Donck, who relied upon some of Megapolensis's comments as he wrote his own *A Description of the New Netherlands,* published over a decade later. Megapolensis's record of the lifeways of the Mohawks provides some glimpses into their perceptions of the Dutch Christians, even as it clarifies the colonialist perspective from which Megapolensis was writing.

A SHORT ACCOUNT OF THE MOHAWK INDIANS[1]

The country here is in general like that in Germany. The land is good, and fruitful in everything which supplies human needs, except clothes, linen, woollen, stockings, shoes, etc., which are all dear here. The country is very mountainous, partly soil, partly rocks, and with elevations so exceeding high that they appear to almost touch the clouds. Thereon grow the finest fir trees the eye ever saw. There are also in this country oaks, alders, beeches, elms, willows, etc. In the forests, and here and there along the water side, and on the islands, there grows an abundance of chestnuts, plums, hazel nuts, large walnuts of several sorts, and of as good a taste as in the Netherlands, but they have a somewhat harder shell. The ground on the hills is covered with bushes of bilberries or blueberries; the ground in the flat land near the rivers is covered with strawberries, which grow here so plentifully in the fields, that one can lie down and eat them. Grapevines also grow here naturally in great abundance along the roads, paths, and creeks, and wherever you may turn you find them. I have seen whole pieces of land where vine stood by vine and grew very luxuriantly, climbing to the top of the largest and loftiest trees, and although they are not culti-

vated, some of the grapes are found to be as good and sweet as in Holland. Here is also a sort of grapes which grow very large, each grape as big as the end of one's finger, or an ordinary plum, and because they are somewhat fleshy and have a thick skin we call them *Speck Druyven.*[2] If people would cultivate the vines they might have as good wine here as they have in Germany or France. I had myself last harvest a boat-load of grapes and pressed them. As long as the wine was new it tasted better than any French or Rhenish Must, and the color of the grape juice here is so high and red that with one wine-glass full you can color a whole pot of white wine. In the forests is great plenty of deer, which in autumn and early winter are as fat as any Holland cow can be. I have had them with fat more than two fingers thick on the ribs, so that they were nothing else than almost clear fat, and could hardly be eaten. There are also many turkies, as large as in Holland, but in some years less than in others. The year before I came here,[3] there were so many turkies and deer that they came to feed by the houses and hog pens, and were taken by the Indians in such numbers that a deer was sold to the Dutch for a loaf of bread, or a knife, or even for a tobacco pipe; but now one commonly has to give for a good deer six or seven guilders. In the forests here there are also many partridges, heath-hens and pigeons that fly together in thousands, and sometimes ten, twenty, thirty and even forty and fifty are killed at one shot. We have here, too, a great number of all kinds of fowl, swans, geese, ducks, widgeons, teal, brant, which sport upon the river in thou-

---

1. The complete title of the 1644 pamphlet published in Dutch in Alkmaar reads in English: A *Short Account of the Mohawk Indians, their Country, Language, Stature, Dress, Religion and Government, thus described and recently, August 26, 1644, sent out of New Netherland, by Johannes Megapolensis the younger, Preacher there.* The text is from *Narratives of New Netherland, 1609–1664,* ed. J. Franklin Jameson (1909).

2. Probably the so-called hog grape.

3. 1641.

sands in the spring of the year, and again in the autumn fly away in flocks, so that in the morning and evening any one may stand ready with his gun before his house and shoot them as they fly past. I have also eaten here several times of elks, which were very fat and tasted much like venison; and besides these profitable beasts we have also in this country lions,[4] bears, wolves, foxes, and particularly very many snakes, which are large and as long as eight, ten, and twelve feet. Among others, there is a sort of snake, which we call rattlesnake, from a certain object which it has back upon its tail, two or three fingers' breadth long, and has ten or twelve joints, and with this it makes a noise like the crickets. Its color is variegated much like our large brindled bulls. These snakes have very sharp teeth in their mouth, and dare to bite at dogs; they make way for neither man nor beast, but fall on and bite them, and their bite is very poisonous, and commonly even deadly too.

As to the soil of this country, that on the mountains is a reddish sand or rock, but in the low flat lands, and along the rivers, and even in the jutting sides of the mountains for an hundred or two hundred paces up, there is often clay. I have been on hills here, as high as a church, to examine the soil, and have found it to be clay. In this ground there appears to be a singular strength and capacity for bearing crops, for a farmer here[5] told me that he had raised fine wheat on one and the same piece of land eleven years successively without ever breaking it up or letting it lie fallow. The butter here is clean and yellow as in Holland. Through this land runs an excellent river, about 500 or 600 paces wide. This river comes out of the Mahakas Country, about four leagues north of us. There it flows between two high rocky banks, and falls from a height equal to that of a church, with such a noise that we can sometimes hear it here with us.[6] In the beginning of June twelve of us took a ride to see it. When we came there we saw not only the river falling with such a noise that we could hardly hear one another, but the water boiling and dashing with such force in still weather, that it seemed all the time as if it were raining; and the trees on the hills near by (which are as high as Schoorler Duyn[7]) had their

leaves all the time wet exactly as if it rained. The water is as clear as crystal, and as fresh as milk. I and another with me saw there, in clear sunshine, when there was not a cloud in the sky, especially when we stood above upon the rocks, directly opposite where the river falls, in the great abyss, the half of a rainbow, or a quarter of a circle, of the same color with the rainbow in the sky. And when we had gone about ten or twelve rods farther downwards from the fall, along the river, we saw a complete rainbow, like a half circle, appearing clearly in the water just as if it had been in the clouds, and this is always so according to the report of all who have ever been there. In this river is a great plenty of all kinds of fish—pike, eels, perch, lampreys, suckers, cat fish, sun fish, shad, bass, etc. In the spring, in May, the perch are so plenty, that one man with a hook and line will catch in one hour as many as ten or twelve can eat. My boys have caught in an hour fifty, each a foot long. They have three hooks on the instrument with which they fish, and draw up frequently two or three perch at once. There is also in the river a great plenty of sturgeon, which we Christians do not like, but the Indians eat them greedily. In this river, too, are very beautiful islands, containing ten, twenty, thirty, fifty and seventy morgens of land. The soil is very good, but the worst of it is, that by the melting of the snow, or heavy rains, the river readily overflows and covers that low land. This river ebbs and flows at ordinary low water as far as this place, although it is thirty-six leagues inland from the sea.

As for the temperature in this country, and the seasons of the year, the summers are pretty hot, so that for the most of the time we are obliged to go in just our shirts, and the winters are very cold. The summer continues long, even until All Saints' Day; but when the winter does begin, just as it commonly does in December, it freezes so hard in one night that the ice will bear a man. Even the rivers, in still weather when there is no strong current running, are frozen over in one night, so that on the second day people walk over it. And this freezing continues commonly three months; for although we are situated here in 42 degrees of latitude, it always freezes so. And although there come warm and pleasant days, the thaw does not continue, but it freezes again until March. Then, commonly, the rivers first begin to open, and seldom in February. We have the greatest cold from the northwest, as in Holland from the northeast. The wind here is very seldom east, but almost always south, southwest, northwest, and north; so also the rain.

Our shortest winter days have nine hours sun; in the summer, our longest days are about fifteen hours. We lie

---

4. Panthers.

5. Brant Peelen, who lived on Castle Island, a little below Fort Orange.

6. Cohoes Falls.

7. The dune, or sand mounds, on the coast of North Holland, near Schoorl, where Megapolensis had lived.

so far west of Holland that I judge you are about four hours in advance of us, so that when it is six o'clock in the morning with us it is ten in the forenoon with you, and when it is noon with us, it is four o'clock in the afternoon with you.

The inhabitants of this country are of two kinds: first, Christians—at least so called; second, Indians. Of the Christians I shall say nothing; my design is to speak of the Indians only. These among us are again of two kinds: first, the Mahakinbas, or, as they call themselves, *Kajinga-haga;* second, the Mahakans, otherwise called *Agotza-gena.*[8] These two nations have different languages, which have no affinity with each other, like Dutch and Latin. These people formerly carried on a great war against each other, but since the Mahakanders were subdued by the Mahakobaas, peace has subsisted between them, and the conquered are obliged to bring a yearly contribution to the others. We live among both these kinds of Indians; and when they come to us from their country, or we go to them, they do us every act of friendship. The principal nation of all the savages and Indians hereabouts with which we have the most intercourse, is the Mahakuaas,[9] who have laid all the other Indians near us under contribution. This nation has a very difficult language, and it costs me great pains to learn it, so as to be able to speak and preach in it fluently. There is no Christian here who understands the language thoroughly; those who have lived here long can use a kind of jargon just sufficient to carry on trade with it, but they do not understand the fundamentals of the language. I am making a vocabulary of the Mahakuaas' language, and when I am among them I ask them how things are called; but as they are very stupid, I sometimes cannot make them understand what I want. Moreover when they tell me, one tells me the word in the infinitive mood, another in the indicative; one in the first, another in the second person; one in the present, another in the preterit. So I stand oftentimes and look, but do not know how to put it down. And as they have declensions and conjugations also, and have their augments like the Greeks, I am like one distracted, and frequently cannot tell what to do, and there is no one to set me right. I shall have to speculate in this alone, in order to become in time an Indian grammarian. When I first observed that they pronounced their words so differently, I asked the commissary of the company[10] what it meant. He answered me that he did not know, but imagined they changed their language every two or three years; I argued against this that it could never be that a whole nation should change its language with one consent;—and, although he has been connected with them here these twenty years, he can afford me no assistance.

The people and Indians here in this country are like us Dutchmen in body and stature; some of them have well formed features, bodies and limbs; they all have black hair and eyes, but their skin is yellow. In summer they go naked, having only their private parts covered with a patch. The children and young folks to ten, twelve and fourteen years of age go stark naked. In winter, they hang about them simply an undressed deer or bear or panther skin; or they take some beaver and otter skins, wild cat, raccoon, martin, otter, mink, squirrel or such like skins, which are plenty in this country, and sew some of them to others, until it is a square piece, and that is then a garment for them; or they buy of us Dutchmen two and a half ells of duffel, and that they hang simply about them, just as it was torn off, without sewing it, and walk away with it. They look at themselves constantly, and think they are very fine. They make themselves stockings and also shoes of deer skin, or they take leaves of their corn, and plait them together and use them for shoes. The women, as well as the men, go with their heads bare. The women let their hair grow very long, and tie it together a little, and let it hang down their backs. The men have a long lock of hair hanging down, some on one side of the head, and some on both sides. On the top of their heads they have a streak of hair from the forehead to the neck, about the breadth of three fingers, and this they shorten until it is about two or three fingers long, and it stands right on end like a cock's comb or hog's bristles; on both sides of this cock's comb they cut all the hair short, except the aforesaid locks, and they also leave on the bare places here and there small locks, such as are in sweeping-brushes, and then they are in fine array.

They likewise paint their faces red, blue, etc., and then they look like the Devil himself. They smear their heads with bear's-grease, which they all carry with them for this purpose in a small basket; they say they do it to make their hair grow better and to prevent their having lice. When they travel, they take with them some of their maize, a

---

8. Mohawks and Mohicans.

9. *Maquas* or *Maquasaan* are terms often used to indicate Mohawks.

10. Probably Sebastian Jansen Krol, who had been at Fort Orange most times from 1626 on.

kettle, a wooden bowl, and a spoon; these they pack up and hang on their backs. Whenever they are hungry, they forthwith make a fire and cook; they can get fire by rubbing pieces of wood against one another, and that very quickly.

They generally live without marriage; and if any of them have wives, the marriage continues no longer than seems good to one of the parties, and then they separate, and each takes another partner. I have seen those who had parted, and afterwards lived a long time with others, leave these again, seek their former partners, and again be one pair. And, though they have wives, yet they will not leave off whoring; and if they can sleep with another man's wife, they think it a brave thing. The women are exceedingly addicted to whoring; they will lie with a man for the value of one, two, or three *schillings,*[11] and our Dutchmen run after them very much.

The women, when they have been delivered, go about immediately afterwards, and be it ever so cold, they wash themselves and the young child in the river or the snow. They will not lie down (for they say that if they did they would soon die), but keep going about. They are obliged to cut wood, to travel three or four leagues with the child; in short, they walk, they stand, they work, as if they had not lain in, and we cannot see that they suffer any injury by it; and we sometimes try to persuade our wives to lie-in so, and that the way of lying-in in Holland is a mere fiddle-faddle. The men have great authority over their concubines, so that if they do anything which does not please and raises their passion, they take an axe and knock them in the head, and there is an end of it. The women are obliged to prepare the land, to mow, to plant, and do everything; the men do nothing, but hunt, fish, and make war upon their enemies. They are very cruel towards their enemies in time of war; for they first bite off the nails of the fingers of their captives, and cut off some joints, and sometimes even whole fingers; after that, the captives are forced to sing and dance before them stark naked; and finally, they roast their prisoners dead before a slow fire for some days, and then eat them up. The common people eat the arms, buttocks and trunk, but the chiefs eat the head and the heart.

Our Mahakas carry on great wars against the Indians of Canada, on the River Saint Lawrence, and take many captives, and sometimes there are French Christians among them. Last year, our Indians got a great booty from the French on the River Saint Lawrence, and took three Frenchmen, one of whom was a Jesuit.[12] They killed one, but the Jesuit (whose left thumb was cut off, and all the nails and parts of his fingers were bitten,) we released, and sent him to France by a yacht which was going to our country. They spare all the children from ten to twelve years old, and all the women whom they take in war, unless the women are very old, and then they kill them too. Though they are so very cruel to their enemies, they are very friendly to us, and we have no dread of them. We go with them into the woods, we meet with each other, sometimes at an hour or two's walk from any houses, and think no more about it than as if we met with a Christian. They sleep by us, too, in our chambers before our beds. I have had eight at once lying and sleeping upon the floor near my bed, for it is their custom to sleep simply on the bare ground, and to have only a stone or a bit of wood under their heads. In the evening, they go to bed very soon after they have supped; but early in the morning, before day begins to break, they are up again. They are very slovenly and dirty; they wash neither their face nor hands, but let all remain upon their yellow skin, and look like hogs. Their bread is Indian corn beaten to pieces between two stones, of which they make a cake, and bake it in the ashes: their other victuals are venison, turkies, hares, bears, wild cats, their own dogs, etc. The fish they cook just as they get them out of the water without cleansing; also the entrails of deer with all their contents, which they cook a little; and if the intestines are then too tough, they take one end in their mouth, and the other in their hand, and between hand and mouth they separate and eat them. So they do commonly with the flesh, for they carve a little piece and lay it on the fire, as long as one would need to walk from his house to church, and then it is done; and then they bite into it so that the blood runs along their mouths. They can also take a piece of bear's-fat as large as two fists, and eat it clear without bread or anything else. It is natural to them to have no beards; not one in an hundred has any hair about his mouth.

They have also naturally a very high opinion of themselves; they say, *Ihy Othkon,* ("I am the Devil") by which they mean that they are superior folks. In order to praise themselves and their people, whenever we tell them they are very expert at catching deer, or doing this and that, they say, *Tkoschs ko, aguweechon Kajingahaga kouaane*

12. The event occurred on August 2, 1642. The Jesuit was Father Isaac Jogues, whose captivity lasted until August 1643.

Jountuckcha Othkon; that is, "Really all the Mohawks are very cunning devils." They make their houses of the bark of trees, very close and warm, and kindle their fire in the middle of them. They also make of the peeling and bark of trees, canoes or small boats, which will carry four, five and six persons. In like manner they hollow out trees, and use them for boats, some of which are very large. I have several times sat and sailed with ten, twelve and fourteen persons in one of these hollowed logs. We have in our colony[13] a wooden canoe obtained from the Indians, which will easily carry two hundred *schepels*[14] of wheat. Their weapons in war were formerly a bow and arrow, with a stone axe and mallet; but now they get from our people guns, swords, iron axes and mallets. Their money consists of certain little bones, made of shells or cockles, which are found on the sea-beach; a hole is drilled through the middle of the little bones, and these they string upon thread, or they make of them belts as broad as a hand, or broader, and hang them on their necks, or around their bodies. They have also several holes in their ears, and there they likewise hang some. They value these little bones as highly as many Christians do gold, silver- and pearls; but they do not like our money, and esteem it no better than iron. I once showed one of their chiefs a rix-dollar; he asked how much it was worth among the Christians; and when I told him, he laughed exceedingly at us, saying we were fools to value a piece of iron so highly; and if he had such money, he would throw it into the river. They place their dead upright in holes, and do not lay them down, and then they throw some trees and wood on the grave, or enclose it with palisades. They have their set times for going to catch fish, bears, panthers, beavers and eels. In the spring, they catch vast quantities of shad and lampreys, which are exceedingly large here; they lay them on the bark of trees in the sun, and dry them thoroughly hard, and then put them in *notasten,* or bags, which they plait from hemp which grows wild here, and keep the fish till winter. When their corn is ripe, they take it from the ears, open deep pits, and preserve it in these the whole winter. They can also make nets and seines in their fashion; and when they want to fish with seines, ten or twelve men will go together and help each other, all of whom own the seine in common.

---

13. Rensselaerwyck.

14. A *schepel* was about three pecks, or three-quarters of a bushel.

They are entire strangers to all religion, but they have a *Tharonhijouaagon,* (whom they also otherwise call *Athzoock-kuatoriaho,*) that is, a Genius, whom they esteem in the place of God; but they do not serve him or make offerings to him. They worship and present offerings to the Devil, whom they call *Otskon,* or *Aireskuoni.* If they have any bad luck in war, they catch a bear, which they cut in pieces, and roast, and that they offer up to their *Aireskuoni,* saying in substance, the following words: "Oh! great and mighty Aireskuoni, we confess that we have offended against thee, inasmuch as we have not killed and eaten our captive enemies;—forgive us this. We promise that we will kill and eat all the captives we shall hereafter take as certainly as we have killed, and now eat this bear." Also when the weather is very hot, and there comes a cooling breeze, they cry out directly, *Asoronusi, asoronusi, Otskon aworouhsi reinnuha;* that is, "I thank thee, I thank thee, devil, I thank thee, little uncle!" If they are sick, or have a pain or soreness anywhere in their limbs, and I ask them what ails them they say that the Devil sits in their body, or in the sore places, and bites them there; so that they attribute to the Devil at once the accidents which befall them; they have otherwise no religion. When we pray they laugh at us. Some of them despise it entirely; and some, when we tell them what we do when we pray, stand astonished. When we deliver a sermon, sometimes ten or twelve of them, more or less, will attend, each having a long tobacco pipe, made by himself, in his mouth, and will stand awhile and look, and afterwards ask me what I am doing and what I want, that I stand there alone and make so many words, while none of the rest may speak. I tell them that I am admonishing the Christians, that they must not steal, nor commit lewdness, nor get drunk, nor commit murder, and that they too ought not to do these things; and that I intend in process of time to preach the same to them and come to them in their own country and castles (about three days' journey from here, further inland), when I am acquainted with their language. Then they say I do well to teach the Christians; but immediately add, *Diatennon jawij Assirioni, hagiouisk,* that is, "Why do so many Christians do these things?" They call us *Assirioni,* that is, clothmakers, or *Charistooni,* that is, iron-workers, because our people first brought cloth and iron among them.

They will not come into a house where there is a menstruous woman, nor eat with her. No woman may touch their snares with which they catch deer, for they say the deer can scent it.

The other day an old woman came to our house, and told my people that her forefathers had told her "that *Tharonhij-Jagon,* that is, God, once went out walking with his brother, and a dispute arose between them, and God killed his brother." I suppose this fable took its rise from Cain and Abel. They have a droll theory of the Creation, for they think that a pregnant woman fell down from heaven, and that a tortoise, (tortoises are plenty and large here, in this country, two, three and four feet long, some with two heads, very mischievous and addicted to biting) took this pregnant woman on its back, because every place was covered with water; and that the woman sat upon the tortoise, groped with her hands in the water, and scraped together some of the earth, whence it finally happened that the earth was raised above the water. They think that there are more worlds than one, and that we came from another world.

The Mohawk Indians are divided into three tribes, which are called *Ochkari, Anaware, Oknaho,* that is, the Bear, the Tortoise and the Wolf. Of these, the Tortoise is the greatest and most prominent; and they boast that they are the oldest descendants of the woman before mentioned. These have made a fort of palisades, and they call their castle *Asserué.*[15] Those of the Bear are the next to these, and their castle is called by them *Banagiro.*[16] The last are a progeny of these, and their castle is called *Thenondiogo.*[17] These Indian tribes each carry the beast after which they are named (as the arms in their banner) when they go to war against their enemies, and this is done as well for the terror of their enemies, as for a sign

---

15. Assereawe was on the north side of the Mohawk River, not far up.

16. Sometimes spelled in contemporary documents Banagiro or Canagero, located on the south side of the Mohawk River.

17. Also called t'Iounontego.

of their own bravery. Lately one of their chiefs came to me and presented me with a beaver, an otter, and some cloth he had stolen from the French, which I must accept as a token of good fellowship. When he opened his budget he had in it a dried head of a bear, with grinning teeth. I asked him what that meant? He answered me that he fastened it upon his left shoulder by the side of his head, and that then he was the devil, who cared for nothing, and did not fear any thing.

The government among them consists of the oldest, the most intelligent, the most eloquent and most warlike men. These commonly resolve, and then the young and warlike men execute. But if the common people do not approve of the resolution, it is left entirely to the judgment of the mob. The chiefs are generally the poorest among them, for instead of their receiving from the common people as among Christians, they are obliged to give to the mob; especially when any one is killed in war, they give great presents to the next of kin of the deceased; and if they take any prisoners they present them to that family of which one has been killed, and the prisoner is then adopted by the family into the place of the deceased person. There is no punishment here for murder and other villainies, but every one is his own avenger. The friends of the deceased revenge themselves upon the murderer until peace is made by presents to the next of kin. But although they are so cruel, and live without laws or any punishments for evil doers, yet there are not half so many villainies or murders committed amongst them as amongst Christians; so that I oftentimes think with astonishment upon all the murders committed in the Fatherland, notwithstanding their severe laws and heavy penalties. These Indians, though they live without laws, or fear of punishment, do not (at least, they very seldom) kill people, unless it may be in a great passion, or a hand-to-hand fight. Wherefore we go wholly unconcerned along with the Indians and meet each other an hour's walk off in the woods, without doing any harm to one another.

JOHANNES MEGAPOLENSIS.

Adriaen Van Der Donck (1620–1655)

Adriaen Van Der Donck was twenty years old, with degrees in the canon and civil law from the University at Leyden, when he interviewed with Kiliaen Van Rensselaer, the patroon of Rensselaerwyck, for the position as *schout,* or legal officer, in the large colony on the banks of the Hudson. Van Der Donck sailed for New Amsterdam in 1641 and was settled on Castle Island at Rensselaerwyck by the fall of the year. His post as legal overseer of the large colony was not easy. People were unhappy because of the poor leadership by Director-General Willem Kieft, invasions by English-speaking settlers, and backbiting by leaders who distrusted one another. Distrustful of university-trained men, they created conflicting reports about Van Der Donck's competence and skill. When the Reverend Johannes Megapolensis, Jr., arrived in the colony as Rensselaer's clergyman, it was with orders from the patroon to watch Van Der Donck carefully, "for he shows many signs of ambition."

Van Der Donck's ambition, if such it may be called, was to have his own estate, rather than run someone else's. Van Der Donck first selected land on the Hudson, in the Catskills below Rensselaerwyck, but when spies informed Van Rensselaer of Van Der Donck's decision to purchase, Van Rensselaer saw that the land was purchased in his own name. Although his period of service for Rensselaer concluded around 1644, Van Der Donck remained in the area, probably to avoid violence from the unnecessary, indeed foolish, war that Kieft had incited against the Indian peoples in and surrounding New Amsterdam. Kieft concluded the war during the summer of 1645 by making a treaty with the Mohawks at Fort Orange, using gifts purchased from money that Van Der Donck loaned him. In return for his service, Van Der Donck sought and was granted the opportunity to purchase a large tract of land—about 24,000 acres—in the general area of New Amsterdam, on the eastern bank of the Hudson, where he set up his own patroonship. There, at the area he called Colen Donck, he built a sawmill and grew corn and wheat. Taking on the title of *Jonkheer,* "gentleman," Van Der Donck provided the place-name for the area, present-day Yonkers, New York.

At age twenty-six, Van Der Donck had literally established a place and a name for himself. He was elected to a position on the new Director-General Peter Stuyvesant's council, and he started speaking his thoughts about good government, requesting, with a cluster of others who were interested in seeing the colony develop, that Stuyvesant bring the West India Company into line with its founding promises. The new leaders advised Stuyvesant and the company that a significant number of colonists and laborers were needed; that trade with the Indians should be improved; that customs fees were too high, thus making trade with other colonies impractical; and that local and colonial taxes, which had recently been raised, should be reduced. Van Der Donck started keeping a record of the problems that he and the other leaders were planning to send to Amsterdam, and Stuyvesant had him arrested for crimes against the state. The group nonetheless prepared a text they called a remonstrance, and they sent it to Amsterdam in the summer of 1649, along with Van Der Donck and some other representatives.

Although the group was relatively successful in getting their case against Stuyvesant's government heard by West India Company officers, Van Der Donck was held in Holland under state's authority and was prevented from returning to his colony. His wife, Mary Doughty, joined him in Holland with their family, but Van Der Donck was still kept from going back to his colonial home. While he waited for hearings on their complaints to continue, he whiled away his time in Holland by writing his "little book," *Beschrijvinge van Nieuw-Nederlant,* or *A Description of the New Netherlands,* which in 1653 received the copyright needed for its printing. Van Der Donck was permitted to set sail for home, and he landed in New Amsterdam in the fall of that year. The conditions that led to his early death are unclear, but he seems to have been harassed by Stuyvesant upon his return to the colony, so much so that he sought and received a protection order from the city. He died in 1655 at age thirty-five, perhaps even before he saw a copy of his little book, published that year in Amsterdam. His popular book reached a second edition, also in Amsterdam, in 1656.

from A DESCRIPTION OF THE NEW NETHERLANDS[1]

On the Patrons and the History of New Netherlands

Still Amstel's faithful Burgher-Lords do live,
  Who East and West extend their faithful care;
To lands and men good laws they wisely give,
  That like the beasts ran wild in open air.
With aged care Holland's gardens still they save—
  And in New Netherlands their men will ne'er be
    slaves.

Why mourn about Brazil, full of base Portugese?
  When Van der Donck shows so far much better fare;
Where wheat fills golden ears, and grapes abound in
    trees;
  Where fruit and kine are good with little care;
Men may mourn a loss, when vain would be their voice,
But when their loss brings gain, they also may rejoice.

Then, reader, if you will, go freely there to live,
  We name it *Netherland,* though it excels it far;
If you dislike the voyage, pray due attention give,
  To *Van der Donck,* his book, which, as a leading star,
Directs toward the land where many people are,
Where lowland Love and Laws all may freely share.
                  Evert Nieuwenhof[2]

. . . New Netherlands is a fine, acceptable, healthy, extensive and agreeable country, wherein all people can more easily gain a competent support, than in the Netherlands, or in any other quarter of the globe, which is known to me or which I have visited.

When, and by Whom, New Netherlands Was First Discovered

This country was first found and discovered in the year of our Lord 1609; when, at the cost of the incorporated East India Company, a ship named the *Half-Moon* was fitted out to discover a westerly passage to the kingdom of China. This ship was commanded by Hendrick Hudson, as captain and supercargo, who was an Englishman by birth, and had resided many years in Holland, during which he had been in the employment of the East India Company. This ship sailed from the Canary Islands, steering a course north by west; and after sailing twenty days with good speed, land was discovered, which, by their calculation, lay 320 degrees by west. On approaching the land, and observing the coast and shore convenient, they landed, and examined the country as well as they could at the time, and as opportunity offered; from which they were well satisfied that no Christian people had ever been there before, and that they were the first who by Providence had been guided to the discovery of the country.

Why This Country Is Called New Netherlands

We have before related, that the Netherlanders, in the year 1609, had first discovered this country, of which they took possession as their own in right of their discovery, and finding the country fruitful and advantageously situated, possessing good and safe havens, rivers, fisheries, and many other worthy appurtenances corresponding with the Netherlands, or in truth excelling the same; for this good reason it was named New Netherlands, being as much as to say, another or a new-found Netherlands. Still the name depended most upon the first discovery, and upon the corresponding temperatures of the climates of the two countries, which to strangers is not so observable. We notice also that the French in the same quarter of the new world, have named their territory Canada or Nova Francia, only because they were the first Europeans who possessed the lands in those parts, for the temperature of the climate is so cold and wintry, that the snow commonly lies on the earth four or five months in succession and from four to five feet deep, which renders it costly to keep domestic animals there; and although this country lies no farther than fifty degrees north, still the air in winter is so fine, clear and sharp there, that when the snow once falls, which it commonly does about the first of December, it does not thaw away except by the power of the sun in April. If a shower of rain happens to fall in winter (which is seldom), then it forms a hard crust on the surface of the snow, that renders the travelling difficult for man and beast. The air there is clear and dry, and the snow seldom melts or thaws away suddenly.

The Swedes also have a possession on the south (Delaware) river, which they name New Sweden. The climate of this place by no means corresponds with that of

---

1. *A Description of the New Netherlands* was first published in 1655 in Amsterdam. The text is a translation of the second edition made by Jeremiah Johnson in 1833, published in *Collections of the New-York Historical Society,* 1841.

2. Nieuwenhof was the publisher and bookseller of the *Description.* He supplied his own poem in the second edition, in place of a longer poem by G. Vebiest printed in the first edition.

Sweden, as it lies in latitude 39 degrees north. But, although they have formed a settlement there, still their title is disputed, for they can show no legal right or claim to their possessions.

The country having been first found or discovered by the Netherlanders, and keeping in view the discovery of the same, it is named the New Netherlands. That this country was first found or discovered by the Netherlanders, is evident and clear from the fact, that the Indians or natives of the land, many of whom are still living, and with whom I have conversed, declare freely, that before the arrival of the Lowland ship, the *Half-Moon,* in the year 1609, they (the natives) did not know that there were any other people in the world than those who were like themselves, much less any people who differed so much in appearance from them as we did. Their men on the breasts and about the mouth were bare, and their women like ours, hairy; going unclad and almost naked, particularly in summer, while we are always clothed and covered. When some of them first saw our ship approaching at a distance, they did not know what to think about her, but stood in deep and solemn amazement, wondering whether it were a ghost or apparition, coming down from heaven, or from hell. Others of them supposed her to be a strange fish or sea monster. When they discovered men on board, they supposed them to be more like devils than human beings. Thus they differed about the ship and men. A strange report was also spread about the country concerning our ship and visit, which created great astonishment and surprise amongst the Indians. These things we have frequently heard them declare, which we hold as certain proof that the Netherlanders were the first finders or discoverers and possessors of the New Netherlands. There are Indians in the country, who remember a hundred years, and if there had been any other people here before us, they would have known something of them, and if they had not seen them themselves, they would have heard an account of them from others. There are persons who believe that the Spaniards have been here many years ago, when they found the climate too cold to their liking, and again left the country; and that the maize or Turkish corn, and beans found among the Indians, were left with them by the Spaniards. This opinion or belief is improbable, as we can discover nothing of the kind from the Indians. They say that their corn and beans were received from the southern Indians, who received their seed from a people who resided still farther south, which may well be true, as the Castilians have long since resided in Florida. The maize may have been among the Indians in the warm climate long ago; however, our Indians say that they did eat roots and the bark of trees instead of bread, before the introduction of Indian corn or maize.

Of the Limits of the New Netherlands, and How Far the Same Extend

New Netherlands is bounded by the ocean or great sea, which separates Europe from America, by New England and the Fresh (Connecticut) river, in part by the river of Canada (the St. Lawrence), and by Virginia. Some persons who are not well informed, name all North America *Virginia,* because Virginia from her tobacco trade is well known. These circumstances, therefore, will be observed as we progress, as admonitions to the readers. The coast of New Netherlands extends and stretches mostly northeast and southwest. The sea shore is mostly formed of pure sand, having a dry beach. On the south side, the country is bounded by Virginia. Those boundaries are not yet well defined, but in the progress of the settlement of the country, the same will be determined without difficulty. On the northeast the New Netherlands abut upon New England, where there are differences on the subject of boundaries which we wish were well settled. On the north, the river of Canada stretches a considerable distance, but to the northwest it is still undefined and unknown. Many of our Netherlanders have been far into the country, more than seventy or eighty miles from the river and seashore. We also frequently trade with the Indians, who come more than ten and twenty days' journey from the interior, and who have been farther off to catch beavers, and they know of no limits to the country, and when spoken to on the subject, they deem such enquiries to be strange and singular. Therefore we may safely say, that we know not how deep, or how far we extend inland. There are however many signs, which indicate a great extent of country, such as the land winds, which domineer much, with severe cold, the multitudes of beavers, and land animals which are taken, and the great numbers of water fowl, which fly to and fro, across the country in the spring and fall seasons. From these circumstances we judge that the land extends several hundred miles into the interior; therefore the extent and greatness of this province are still unknown. . . .

Of the Wood, the Natural Productions, and Fruits of the Land

The New Netherlands, with other matters, is very fruitful, and fortunate in its fine woods; so much so, that the whole country is covered with wood, and in our manner of speaking, there is all too much of it, and in our way. Still it comes to hand to build vessels and houses, and to enclose the farms &c. The oak trees are very large; from sixty to seventy feet high without knots, and from two to three fathoms thick, being of various sizes. There are several kinds of oak, such as white, smooth bark, rough bark, grey bark and black bark. It is all durable wood, being as good as the oak of the Rhine or the Weser when properly worked, according to the opinion of our woodcutters, who are judges of timber and are sawyers. The nut-wood grows as tall as the oak, but not so heavy. It is probable that this kind of wood will be useful for many purposes, it grows straight and is tough and hard. We now use it for cogs and rounds in our mills and for threshing-flails, swivel-trees, and other farming purposes. It also is excellent firewood, surpassing every other kind, and setting at naught our old adage, "The man is yet to come, who can find better wood to burn than oak." This wood is far better as well for heat as duration. It possesses a peculiar sap, which causes it to burn freely, whether green or dry. If we draw it up out of the fresh water where it has lain a long time, still, on account of its hardness, it is even then uncommonly durable on the fire. We all agree, that no turf, or other common fuel is equal to nut-wood. When it is dry, it keeps fire and sparkles like matches. Our women prefer nut-coals to turf for their stoves, because they last longer, and are not buried in ashes. This kind of wood is found all over the New Netherlands in such abundance, that it cannot become scarce in the first hundred years with an increased population. There also is oak and ash enough to supply its place for many purposes. The land also is so natural to produce wood, that in a few years large trees will be grown, which I can say with certainty from my own observation; and that unless there be natural changes or great improvidence, there can be no scarcity of wood in this country.

It has happened when I have been out with the natives (*Wilden,* for so we name those who are not born of Christian parents), that we have come to a piece of young woodland. When I have told them, in conversation, that they would do well to clear off such land, because it would bear good corn, that they said, "it is but twenty years since we planted corn there, and now it is woods again." I asked them severally if it were true, when they all answered in the affirmative. This relation was also corroborated by others. To return to the subject: this woodland was composed of oak, nut, and other kinds of wood, but principally of oak and nut; and there were several

trees in the same which were a fathom in circumference. The wood was so closely grown that it was difficult to pass through it on horseback. As the wood appeared young and thrifty, I give credit to the relation of the natives. I have also observed that the youngest woodlands are always covered closest with wood, and where the growth is small, the woods are so thick as to render walking through the same difficult. But where the woods are old, the timber is large and heavy, whereby the underwood is shaded, which causes it to die and perish.

The Indians have a yearly custom (which some of our Christians have also adopted) of burning the woods, plains and meadows in the fall of the year, when the leaves have fallen, and when the grass and vegetable substances are dry. Those places which are then passed over are fired in the spring in April. This practice is named by us and the Indians, "bush-burning," which is done for several reasons: First, to render hunting easier, as the bush and vegetable growth renders the walking difficult for the hunter, and the crackling of the dry substances betrays him and frightens away the game. Secondly, to thin out and clear the woods of all dead substances and grass, which grow better the ensuing spring. Thirdly, to circumscribe and enclose the game within the lines of the fire, when it is more easily taken, and also, because the game is more easily tracked over the burned parts of the woods.

The bush burning presents a grand and sublime appearance. On seeing it from without, we would imagine that not only the dry leaves, vegetables and limbs would be burnt, but that the whole woods would be consumed where the fire passes, for it frequently spreads and rages with such violence, that it is awful to behold; and when the fire approaches houses, gardens, and wooden enclosures, then great care and vigilance are necessary for their preservation, for I have seen several houses which have recently been destroyed, before the owners were apprized of their danger.

Notwithstanding the apparent danger of the entire destruction of the woodlands by the burning, still the green trees do not suffer. The outside bark is scorched three or four feet high, which does them no injury, for the trees are not killed. It however sometimes happens that in the thick pine woods, wherein the fallen trees lie across each other, and have become dry, that the blaze ascends and strikes the tops of the trees, setting the same on fire, which is immediately increased by the resinous knots and leaves, which promote the blaze, and is passed by the wind from tree to tree, by which the entire tops of the trees are sometimes burnt off, while the bodies remain standing. Frequently great injuries are done by such fires, but the burning down of entire woods never happens. I have seen many instances of wood-burning in the colony of Rensselaerwyck, where there is much pine wood. Those fires appear grand at night from the passing vessels in the river, when the woods are burning on both sides of the same. Then we can see a great distance by the light of the blazing trees, the flames being driven by the wind, and fed by the tops of the trees. But the dead and dying trees remain burning in their standing positions, which appear sublime and beautiful when seen at a distance.

Hence it will appear that there actually is such an abundance of wood in the New Netherlands, that, with ordinary care, it will never be scarce there. There always are, however, in every country, some people so improvident, that even they may come short here, and for this reason we judge that it should not be destroyed needlessly. There, however, is such an abundance of wood, that they who cultivate the land for planting and sowing can do nothing better than destroy it, and thus clear off the land for tillage, which is done by cutting down the trees and collecting the wood into great heaps and burning the same, to get it out of their way. Yellow and white pine timber, in all their varieties, is abundant here, and we have heard the Northerners say (who reside here) that the pine is as good here as the pine of Norway. But the pine does not grow as well near the salt water, except in some places. Inland, however, and high up the rivers, it grows in large forests, and it is abundant, and heavy enough for masts and spars for ships. There also are chestnuts here, like those of the Netherlands, which are spread over the woods. Chestnuts would be plentier if it were not for the Indians, who destroy the trees by stripping off the bark for covering for their houses. They, and the Netherlanders also, cut down the trees in the chestnut season, and cut off the limbs to gather the nuts, which also lessens the trees. We also find several kinds of beech trees, but those bear very little. Amongst the other trees, the water-beeches grow very large along the brooks, heavier and larger than most of the trees of the country. When those trees begin to bud, then the bark becomes a beautiful white, resembling the handsomest satin. This tree retains the leaves later than any other tree of the woods. Trees of this kind are considered more ornamental and handsomer than the linden trees for the purpose of planting near dwelling-houses. We can give no comparison with this species of trees, and can give the same no better name to make the

wood known.[3] There also is wild ash, some trees large; and maple trees, the wood resembling cedar; white-wood trees, which grow very large—the Indians frequently make their canoes of this wood, hence we name it *Canoe-wood;*[4] we use it for flooring, because it is bright and free of knots. There are also two kinds of ash, with linden, birch, yew, poplar, sapine, alder, willow, thorn trees, sassafras, persimmon, mulberry, wild cherry, crab, and several other kinds of wood, the names of which are unknown to us, but the wood is suitable for a variety of purposes. Some of the trees bear fruit. The oak trees in alternate years bear many acorns of the chestnut species. The nuts grow about as large as our persimmons, but they are not as good as ours. The mulberries are better and sweeter than ours, and ripen earlier. Several kinds of plums, wild or small cherries, juniper, small kinds of apples, many hazelnuts, black currants, gooseberries, blue India figs, and strawberries in abundance all over the country, some of which ripen at half May, and we have them until July; blueberries, raspberries, black-caps, &c., with artichokes, ground-acorns, ground beans, wild onions, and leeks like ours, with several other kinds of roots and fruits, known to the Indians, who use the same which are disregarded by the Netherlanders, because they have introduced every kind of garden vegetables, which thrive and yield well. The country also produces an abundance of fruits like the Spanish capers, which could be preserved in like manner. . . .

---

from OF THE MANNERS AND PECULIAR CUSTOMS OF THE NATIVES OF THE NEW NETHERLANDS

First—*Of Their Bodily Form and Appearance, and Why We Named Them (Wilden) Wild Men*

Having briefly remarked on the situation and advantages of the country, we deem it worth our attention to treat concerning the nature of the original native inhabitants of the land; that after the Christians have multiplied and the na-

---

3. The sycamore.
4. Tulip poplar.

tives have disappeared and melted away, a memorial of them may be preserved.

Their appearance and bodily form, as well of the men as of the women, are well proportioned, and equal in height to the Netherlanders, varying little from the common size. Their limbs are properly formed, and they are sprightly and active. They can run very fast for a long time, and they can carry heavy packs. To all bodily exertions they are very competent, as far as their dispositions extend; but to heavy slavish labour the men have a particular aversion, and they manage their affairs accordingly, so that they need not labour much. Misshapen or ill-formed persons are very rare amongst them. During the whole time of my residence in the country, I have not seen more than one who was born deformed. Cripples, hunchbacked, or other bodily infirmities, are so rare, that we may say that there are none amongst them; and when we see or hear of one who is crippled or lame, we on inquiry find the same to have originated by accident or in war. They are all properly formed and well proportioned persons. None are gross or uncommonly heavy. Although nature has not given them abundant wisdom, still they exercise their talents with discretion. No lunatics or fools are found amongst them, nor any mad or raving persons of either sex. The men and women commonly have broad shoulders and slender waists. Their hair, before old age, is jet black, sleek and uncurled, and nearly as coarse as a horse's tail. Hair of any other colour they dislike and despise. On the skin, the breast, under the arms, and on other parts of the body, they have little or no hair, and if any appear on their chins they pluck it out by the roots, and it seldom sprouts again. Their old men sometimes have a little stubble on their chins. The men and women all have fine brown eyes and snow-white teeth. Purblind or cross-eyed persons are rare objects, and I have never heard of a native who was born blind, and they seldom lose their sight by accident. One I have seen who had lost his eyesight by the smallpox; and when they become old, their sight does not fail so early in life as ours. The colour of their skin is not so white as ours; still we see some of them who have a fine skin, and they are mostly born with good complexions; otherwise they have a yellowish colour like the Tartars, or heathen who are seen in Holland, or like the Outlanders who keep in the fields and go uncovered as they do. Their yellowness is no fault of nature, but it is caused by the heat of the scorching sun, which is hotter and more powerful in that country than in Holland, which from generation to generation has been

shining on that people, and exhibits its effects stronger. Although this yellowness of the skin appears more or less on all this race, still we find very comely men and women amongst them. It is true that they appear singular and strange to our nation, because their complexion, speech and dress are so different, but this, on acquaintance, is disregarded. Their women are well favoured and fascinating. Several of our Netherlanders were connected with them before our women came over, and remain firm in their attachments. Their faces and countenances are as various as they are in Holland, seldom very handsome, and rarely very ugly, and if they were instructed as our women are, there then would be little or no difference in their qualifications.

The original natives of the country (for now there are native-born Christians also), although they are composed of different tribes, and speak different tongues, all pass by the appellation of (*Wilden*) wild men; and this name was given them as far as we can learn, at the first discovery of the country, which for various reasons seems very appropriate. First, on account of their religion, of which they have very little, and that is very strange; and secondly, on account of their marriages, wherein they differ from civilized societies; thirdly, on account of their laws, which are so singular as to deserve the name of wild regulations. And the Christians hold different names necessary to distinguish different nations, such as Turks, Mamelukes, and Barbarians; and as the name of Heathen is very little used in foreign lands, therefore they would not distinguish the native Americans by either of these names; and as they trade in foreign countries with dark and fair coloured people, and with those who resemble ourselves, in distinction from negroes, and as the American tribes are bordering on an olive colour, the name of *wild men* suits them best. Thus without deliberation, and as it were by chance at the first word (as we suppose), they were called Wild Men. And as unlearned persons never reflect much but speak their first thoughts, in this manner it has probably happened that this people received their national name, because they seemed to be wild and strangers to the Christian religion.

Of the Food and Subsistence of the Indians

In eating and drinking the Indians are not excessive, even in their feast-days. They are cheerful and well satisfied when they have a sufficiency to support nature, and to satisfy hunger and thirst. It is not with them as it is here in Holland, where the greatest, noblest, and richest live more luxuriously than a *Calis,* or a common man; but with them meat and drink are sufficient and the same for all. Their common drink is water from a living spring or well, when it can be had, wherein they seldom fail, as in days of old. Sometimes in the season of grapes, and when they have fresh meat or fish, and are well pleased, they will press out the juice of the grapes and drink it new. They never make wine or beer. Brandy or strong drink is unknown to them, except to those who frequent our settlements, and have learned that beer and wine taste better than water.

In the Indian languages, which are rich and expressive, they have no word to express drunkenness. Drunken men they call fools. When they associate much with our people, and can obtain liquor, they will drink to excess, when they become insolent and troublesome, and are malicious. To prevent this, the government has forbidden the sale of spirituous liquors to the Indians. Most of them however will not taste liquor. Before they are accustomed to spirituous liquor, they are easily made drunk, for which a small glass or two is sufficient; but in time they become accustomed to it, and bear it as well as our own people do. The rheumatic gout, red and pimpled noses, are snares unknown to them; nor have they any diseases or infirmities which are caused by drunkenness. . . .

How Men and Animals Came on the American Continent

There are various opinions on this subject, and many persons have endeavoured to show how those whom we name Indians first came to this part of the world, which is separated from the other parts by the great seas, and which appears always to have been thus separated. Some are of the opinion that they were planted as a colony; others ask, by whom? and how lions, bears, wolves, foxes, serpents, with poisonous reptiles, and other ravenous beasts came on the continent, because such are never carried or transported in ships. When we speak to the natives of the creation, we can never satisfy them on the subject, or receive from them any affirmation that they believe in the doctrine. Many remark that an unknown chronicle writer has observed, that in former days, when, according to some *Rationes Gentium,* people were accustomed to adventures, some persons well equipped and provided, sailed from a part of Norway or Sweden in search of a better country, under the command of a certain chief named *Sachema,* and that they had never been heard from after they sailed; and as all the native chiefs of the New Netherlands who reside along the rivers and the sea-shore are called *sachems,* they conclude that

the country was peopled by those adventurers. We, however, do not concur in this opinion, although the subject seems mysterious. Others go much farther, and inquire whether the natives of the new world have descended from Adam, and whether there has not been a separate creation of men and creatures for the same. This theory they endeavour to support by various reasons. They assert that there has been no deluge over America, and speak of the same as a separate and entire new world, being entirely different in formation and condition from the old world, and by connecting other matters in support of their proposition, they render their subject plausible. They also doubt whether the new world will be judged at the judgment day with the old world. In support of their doctrine they affirm that the period is not long since sinners came there; that the natives were innocent; that the land had not been cursed on their account; and that no righteous punishment can be inflicted on them with the other inhabitants of the old world. A more probable opinion is advanced by others, who affirm that many years ago the sea between Cape de Verds and America was as narrow or of less breadth than the strait between Calais and Dover, and that by the help of the adjacent and intervening islands, people and animals could pass and re-pass from Africa to America. If the communication was not there (which is not to be credited), it must have been elsewhere; and as memorials of Chinese origin are found at the Brazils, it is evident that the Chinese have formerly been there, and that they came to the country along the broken coast of the Strait of Magellan, or overland from the shore of the Pacific Ocean; or that they had driven a trade in the country. It is necessary that we support the planting of a colony, and the removal of people from the old world, and not a separate creation, as by the latter the doctrines of the Holy Scriptures would be subverted and ruined. Those who hold other opinions ask if at any time people could see across from Cape de Verds to America whether, in such a case, Columbus or Americus can have found a country which was never lost? It is not our intention to follow those disputations, but we will leave every person to the enjoyment of his own opinion on the subject, and proceed in our work.

Of the Different Nations and Languages

The nations, tribes, and languages are as different in America as they are in Europe. All those who are of one tribe or nation form one separate society, and usually keep together; every tribe or nation has its own chief, and is a separate government, subject to its own laws and regulations. They however all appear to have descended from one parent-stock, but they seldom marry out of their own tribes. They always are jealous of each other as it respects their national power; and every tribe endeavours to increase its own strength. As they have chiefs over their nations, tribes, and settlements, so also every family has its head, who is regarded as the most eminent and famous by descent, from which their rank in the tribe is usually settled. Their languages and dialects are very different, as unlike each other as the Dutch, French, Greek, and Latin are. Their declensions and conjugations have an affinity with the Greek and accord to it. Their declensions, augmentations, cases, and adverbs are like the Greek; but to reduce their language to any of ours, would be impossible, for there is no resemblance between the same. Before we have acquired a knowledge of any of their languages or dialects, we know no more of what they say than if a dog had barked. In some of their languages the letter *r* is not sounded, and in others scarcely a syllable is spoken without it; otherwise they are not very different, and the tribes usually can understand their dialects. Their various tongues may be classed into four distinct languages, namely, *Manhattan, Minquas, Savanoos,* and *Wappanoos.* With the Manhattans, we include those who live in the neighbouring places along the North River, on Long Island, and at the Neversink. With the Minquas we include the Senecas, the Maquaas, and other inland tribes. The Savanoos are the southern nations, and the Wappanoos are the eastern nations. Their languages are seldom learned perfectly by any of our people, and those who by long and continued intercourse and conversation with the Indians learn to speak their language are not men of education and are unable to compose grammatical rules for the same and of course are unable to instruct others.

Of Their Money or Circulating Medium

That there should be no miserly desire for the costly metals among the natives, few will believe; still it is true, the use of gold and silver or any metallic coin is unknown among them. The currency which they use in their places to which they resort is called *wampum,* the making and preparing of which is free to all persons. The species are black and white, but the black is worth more by one half than the white. The black wampum is made from conch shells, which are to be taken from the sea, or which are cast ashore from the sea twice a year. They strike off the thin parts of those shells and preserve the pillars or standards, which they grind smooth and even and reduce the

same according to their thickness, and drill a hole through every piece and string the same on strings, and afterwards sell their strings of wampum in that manner. This is the only article of moneyed medium among the natives, with which any traffic can be driven; and it is also common with us in purchasing necessaries and carrying on our trade; many thousand strings are exchanged every year for peltries near the seashores where the wampum is only made, and where the peltries are brought for sale. Among the Netherlanders gold and silver begin to increase and are current, but still the amount differs much from that of the Netherlands. . . .

Of Their Religion, and Whether They Can Be Brought over to the Christian Faith

The natives are all heathen and without any religious devotions. Idols are neither known nor worshipped among them. When they take an oath they swear by the sun, which, they say, sees all things. They think much of the moon, and believe it has great influence over vegetation. Although they know all the planets from the other stars, by appropriate names, still they pay no idolatrous worship to the same, yet by the planets and other signs they are somewhat weatherwise. The offering up of prayers, or the making of any distinction between days, or any matter of the kind, is unknown among them. They neither know or say any thing of God; but they possess great fear of the devil, who they believe causes diseases, and does them much injury. When they go on a hunting or fishing excursion they usually cast a part of what is first taken into the fire, without using any ceremony on the occasion, then saying, "stay thou devil, eat thou that." They love to hear us speak of God and of our religion, and are very attentive and still during divine service and prayers, and apparently are inclined to devotion; but in truth they know nothing about it, and live without any religion, or without any inward or outward godly fear, nor do they know of any superstition or idolatry; they only follow the instilled laws of nature, therefore some suppose they can easily be brought to the knowledge and fear of God. Among some nations the word Sunday is known by the name of *Kintowen.* The oldest among them say that in former times the knowledge and fear of God had been known among them, and they remark, that since they can neither read nor write, in process of time the Sunday will be forgotten, and all knowledge of the same lost. Their old men, when we reason earnestly with them on the matter, seem to feel pensive or sorrowful, but manifest no other emotions or agitations—when we reprove them for bad conduct and reason with them on its impropriety, and say that there is a God in heaven above whom they offend, their common answer is, "We do not know that God, we have never seen him, we know not who he is—if you know him and fear him, as you say you do, how does it then happen that so many thieves, drunkards, and evil-doers are found among you. Certainly that God will punish you severely, because he has warned you to beware of those deeds, which he has never done to us. We know nothing about it, and therefore we do not deserve such punishment." Very seldom do they adopt our religion, nor have there been any political measures taken for their conversion. When their children are young some of them are frequently taken into our families for assistants, who are, according to opportunity, instructed in our religion, but as soon as they are grown up, and turn lovers and associate again with the Indians, they forget their religious impressions and adopt the Indian customs. The Jesuits have taken great pains and trouble in Canada to convert the Indians to the Roman Church, and outwardly many profess that religion; but inasmuch as they are not well instructed in its fundamental principles, they fall off lightly and make sport of the subject and its doctrine.

In the year 1639, when a certain merchant, who is still living with us, went into that country to trade with an Indian chief who spoke good French, after he had drank two or three glasses of wine, they began to converse on the subject of religion. The chief said that he had been instructed so far that he often said mass among the Indians, and that on a certain occasion the place where the altar stood caught fire by accident, and our people made preparations to put out the fire, which he forbade them to do, saying that God, who stands there, is almighty, and he will put out the fire himself; and we waited with great attention, but the fire continued till all was burned up, with your almighty God himself and with all the fine things about him. Since that time I have never held to that religion, but regard the sun and moon much more, as being better than all your Gods are; for they warm the earth and cause the fruits to grow, when your lovely Gods cannot preserve themselves from the fire. In the whole country I know no more than one Indian who is firm in his religious profession, nor can any change be expected among them, as long as matters are permitted to remain as heretofore. If they are to be brought over to the Christian faith, then the public hand must be extended to them and continued; we must establish good schools at convenient places among them, for the instruction of their children; let them learn to write our catechism, and let them be thoroughly instructed in the fundamental principles of our religion, so that in process of time they may be enabled to instruct each other and become attached thereto. It certainly would be attended with some trouble and expense to the government, still, without such means and measures, it will be difficult to do any good among them. Our negligence on those matters is very reprehensible, for the Indians themselves say that they are very desirous to have their children instructed in our language and religion.

HENRICUS SELYNS (1636–1701)

Born to Jan Selyns and Agneta Kock, Henricus Selyns studied theology at the University of Amsterdam, his native city. Upon graduation he was called by the Dutch West India Company to be minister to the Dutch Reformed Church in New Amsterdam, in the area of present-day Brooklyn, New York. Selyns accepted, was found fit to minister by the classis of Amsterdam, and installed in February 1660. He emigrated to the colony that summer and assumed his pulpit, pastoring a church of twenty-seven persons, on September 7, 1660. Shortly thereafter he married Machtelt Specht.

Selyns was an eloquent and energetic minister, from all accounts. He expanded his congregation fourfold in four years. At Director-General Peter Stuyvesant's request, Selyns supplemented his usual pastoral work by preaching for forty manumitted Africans, originally slaves of the West India Company, at the Stuyvesant's farm. In a report to the Amsterdam classis of June 9, 1664, Selyns described the difficulty of catechizing older Africans and explained that most of his efforts found greatest use in Christianizing youths. Selyns was disgruntled by the English conquest of the Dutch colony in 1664. Yearning for closer contact with the world of learning and desiring to be near his aging parents, he returned to Holland. He spent sixteen years serving the congregation of the rural village of Waverveen. Eventually, provincial life palled for Selyns, and in 1682 he accepted the call to serve as pastor in New York City. His was the largest Dutch congregation in North America.

Selyns spent much of his later career attempting to create a church polity apart from the English style. The English regime, used to appointing Church of England ministers, disliked the idea of having a congregational call for ministers in New York City. Selyns defended his church from having to follow English practice, thus freeing the Dutch church from having to conform to the political imposition of ministers. He achieved the independence of Dutch church polity in 1696. He opposed Jacob Leisler during the revolutionary leader's short-lived presidency over New York. He condoned Leisler's execution, thereafter, thus contributing to the divisive spirit that troubled New York at the turn of the century. At Selyns's death in 1701, he was the most powerful Dutch Reformed clergyman in North America, with great influence in both ecclesiastical and political spheres.

Selyns was a prolific writer of verse, minting epigrams and composing epigraphs and occasional verses, humorous odes, and occasional songs in Latin. Like people in many of the learned circles in Europe and North America, he circulated his verse among friends and family members. In Selyns's day, circulating verses privately among friends was the best way to achieve publicity, respect, and renown, so Selyns saw that his poetry reached New York's Dutch literati, a network of government officials, schoolmasters, merchants, and clergymen. The wit of mid-seventeenth-century university verse dominates his performances, seen in the ingenious interplay of pagan mythology with Christian sentiment in several of his poems. His most elaborate composition and the wittiest surviving poem from New Netherland is his epithalamium for the marriage of his friend, The Reverend Aegidius Luyck.

BRIDAL TORCH FOR REV. ÆGIDIUS LUYCK,

Rector of the Latin School at New Amsterdam, and Judith Van Isendoorn, Ignited Shortly after the Esopus Massacre Committed by the Indians at Wiltwyck in New Netherland, 1663[1]

How soon war's flame the fire of love consumes!
Maliciously Mars comes to hurt the innocent;
And Cupid, who loves peace and life, fumes
In hiding, startled by the sight of armament.
5 He sees the unsuspected, calculated treachery:
"Can it be right to come so stealthily?
To hide behind a friendly smile their mind's hostility?
It's right to fear Absalom's and Joab's trickery."[2]

His words still hang in air—Can he believe the ravages?
House after house draped thick, alas, with savages?   10
Children roasted, man after man struck down to die?
Barns enflamed where pregnant women fry?
They scatter, each where he can. "From Wiltwyck I came,"
The sad sprite sighs, "seeking refuge in the woods and hills."
He looks for bow and arrow, but they became   15
Easy plunder for the wild men, hiding where they will.
Deprived of these, he's weaponless.
"How would it have been," he asked, "if I'd not fled?
"A slave to sachems[3] . . . toiling at some savage fortress?
"Taken captive . . . wounded . . . dead?   20
He plopped down on a Catskill mountainside and moaned:
'Til Hymen[4] heeds my wish, and Wedlock works my will!
"May you never feel the blessings of home!
"Curses canker you, whose wanton thoughts and ill

---

1. On June 7, 1663, the Esopus Indians, from the regions west of the Hudson valley, attacked Wiltwyck (Kingston) in the Hudson Valley. Twenty-one Dutch settlers were killed and fifty-five were taken captive. The houses and outbuildings were torched. One expectant mother was found among the dead. This poem is a new verse translation, prepared by David S. Shields.

2. The sons of King David of Israel who plotted the usurpation of his rule.

3. Leaders, or captains of Native bands.

4. Greek divinity of marriage.

"Inspire this country's three heart-sins and bring its
25   doom:
"Uncleanness, drunkenness, and vaunting pride—
"They drive this country's peace and happiness to the
    tomb.
"For brute indulgences, punishment's assigned,
"Warnings given often and often just ignored."
30 Then he said, "Remember when the earth did quake!
"When the heavens rained fire, and small-pox scourged"
"Go seek those lives whose lives are taken!
"Stupidly all profit and pleasure perish,
"And day by day wickedness begets more evil.
35 "That Wind?"—he mused, "it's filled with anguish,
"Repentant sighs, for in the end, all's due the devil.
    With such complaints the rascal made time go,
And then flew back to town, to civilization speeding.
    Where're he went, for lack of barb and bow
40 He did his job so-so, the lack impeding.
By luck he quickly came across his missile
Fallen in the path smack dab where Natives dropped it
It's not too long before he's sharpened it to sizzle
In doing so, his passion and his pique grow quiet,
45 (Despite the former and latter being quite unlike.)
"Who's entranced by Love? Who's he whom love
    entangles?
"Whatever Love may be, it doesn't put turf on the dyke;[5]
"Not strong—weak; its arrows, toys with angles.
"If this is the reason fewer folks now marry,
50 "And give themselves to travel, it's worth pondering,
"Unless the reason be that brazen sorts perversely carry
"Out a scheme to undermine the right of property.
"Who force on force exert and thirst for Christian blood
"(When patience would have served), and scant Christ's
    flock,
55 "Although the fool performs not bad nor good
"It's better to let Native kids sleep round the clock.
"Whoever takes his time, doesn't spend it, whatever else
    he spends;
"Why is it, then, too late to wait the proper hour?
"Since that is wisely suited to the country's ends,
60 "The right of higher law, the potency of higher power!
[But Cupid's true plan doesn't matter here.]
Finally our pains and punishments abate!
Random hostages wander back from the grave
The wild beast is dead; gone his kids and mate

His boscy[6] fortress burnt, likewise his maize.   65
His guns we've got; his seewan stuffs our treasury.
They fly through the forest, stray across the plain
If you can't stop a straggler, you won't get glory.
Using interpreters, Indians plead with main and might
For surrender terms that grant safe haven.   70
When Cupid hears of this, he comes in a fuss,
Asking, "My bow! Who has it!" and wailin'
"Where's my quiver! Villains! Soundrels!" Hear him
    cuss.
"What have I ever done to you, that you should screw
me so? Unless my barbs did bite you with love's pain.   75
But I only did to you what you-all do."
They give the boy his weapons back, and mum remain
Hoping to avoid his anger by a humble restitution.
He grabs them, bends the bow back toward the sky
As if he wished to pierce some target high above him   80
The fort (New Amsterdam) is all intact and nigh.
Luyck looks from the window while Judith stands
    beyond
Before either one can move, the arrow pierces Luyck's
    breast.
One shaft won't do—two are right for bliss's bond.
"Where did he shoot," the people squawk, "Towards east
    or west?"   85
Luyck quiet keeps; his heart feels foreign
As everyone stares up at Luyck (yes, Judith too)
Cupid cocks another time and plunges Isendooren,
Which sparks a joyous hub-bub the whole land through,
He's dumb, while countryside takes up the shout,   90
"A thousand blessings make their days a bliss!
"Now and forever, joy in their house and sorrow keep
    out!
"Body and soul, the next world and this!
"Who happiness gives, receive the same gift!"
    Well—we can't hope to understand the imp—   95
Child of Mars? Or Child of Venus?[7] Which?
Nor can we apprehend the fate of mortal men,
Except what leads to marriage and keeps us safe!
Wish them posterity and a happy house.
May the newlyweds know peace and saving grace!   100
Let Luyck's hopes bloom, and the worth of his spouse
Increasing over time at such a rate
That in the end they both pass heaven's gate.

———

5. A Dutch proverb, somewhat like the American saying, "It
doesn't put dinner on the table."

———

6. Woody.

7. In Roman mythology, Mars, the Roman god of War, was
married to Venus, the goddess of Love.

TO MY FRIEND CAPTAIN GERARD DOUW,

Living at His Plantation Near New York, Who Should Have Been Invited to the Lord's Supper, but Was Not for Lack of a Wagon to Send the Invitation

Douw! You're invited, now as ever,
It's not because time did sever,
Or will, except when the Apostles' horses ride,[1]
Too far for man on foot to hoof it,
5   Easier to urge him no than try it;
When each one spares his steed, his feet are spared besides.

Once they rode, and each came for the best.
They don't ride now, and each is for the less.
The sun sinks—is it a wonder?
10 Everyone grubs, grinds, gripes and grabs for himself
And to his loss, pursues just pelf;[2]
The world rises, God's church and Godliness go under.

O pen! Don't run on this too far!
No one has a wagon, horse, or car.
15 I come to you and everyone together.
You are welcome to this feast
Where you can't be too frequently a guest
Where Christ is your portion, and God our father.

Hush, my soul!—complain no more,
20 You draw near the threshold of the Lord!
Who wouldn't come, except to enter in?
I come, and could I higher go

I'd Jesus see and heaven know
In chariots aflame, and come to Him.

Come Douw, see my great regret.   25
That soul that has a wagon, or does not,
No longer needs to make request.
Are Jesus and his tribulations nothing?
O Douw, behold my aching breast.
Though insignificant, it God in his register will jot.[3]   30

Faith, which destroys both sin and death,
Is mightier than human law and mortal flesh;
To heaven it both you and us shall raise.
Godliness enables this and more
From faith and prayer salvation pours,   35
Confirming God's love both here and forevermore.

———

EPITAPH FOR PETER STUYVESANT,

Late General of New Netherland[1]

Sift not that sand, for there lies Stuyvesant,
Who once was overlord of all New Netherland.
Against his will, this land he handed to the foe;
If rue and aggravation trouble hearts, his heart
A thousand deaths did die, suffering insufferable smart.
At first too high and rich; at last, too poor and low.

———

1. The Apostles' horses support the rides of Apocalypse. Selyns means the end of time. This poem is a new verse translation, prepared by David S. Shields.
2. Material riches.

3. In Revelations, the book of life, where a person's good and bad deeds are recorded.

1. Stuyvesant, the last Dutch Governor of New Netherland, handed the colony over to the English in 1664. He remained a resident in New York, living on his private farm, the Bouwerie, until his death in 1672. This poem is a new verse translation, prepared by David S. Shields.

MARIA VAN CORTLANDT VAN RENNSELAER (1645–1689)

Maria Van Cortlandt was born in New Amsterdan in 1645 to Oloff Stevensen Van Cortlandt, a Dutch merchant settler, and Anna Loockermans Van Cortlandt. As her writings attest, she must have received early training in writing and accounts, and she was raised evidently with an eye to efficient domestic and mercantile economy. When she was not quite seventeen years old, Maria Van Cordlandt married Jeremias Van Rennselaer, who in 1658 had succeeded to the directorship of Rensselaerwyck, one of the largest Dutch patroonships in New York. She bore six children after the marriage, two daughters and four sons, the last son, his father's namesake, born shortly after the death of her husband in the fall of 1674. She was thus left alone at the estate, relatively far from her own birthplace, with much responsibility; little assistance from adult family members; and her own ailing health, which required that she use crutches to get around.

These were difficult times at Rensselaerwyck, and not particularly because Maria Van Rensselaer had to run the estate alone. Indeed, she managed the estate exceedingly well, as the available evidence indicates. The issue was the very foundation and nature of the estate. When Peter Stuyvesant capitulated to Richard Nicholls in 1664, the understanding was that patroonship landholdings would remain intact but be governed by British law. This formulation was confirmed by the Treaty of Westminster, which formally required the surrender of the colony by the Dutch to the British. As a result of the treaty, Edmund Andros was sent over to serve as governor of New York.

Yet by later agreements, churches practicing within the synods of the Dutch Reformed Church could bring Dutch ministers over from the Netherlands to serve the local parishes. Andros, in fact, encouraged this action for the area near Rensselaerwyck. When he came to the colony, he brought over with him Nicholaes Van Rensselaer, Maria van Cortlandt Van Rensselaer's brother-in-law. Van Rensselaer was given the ministry of the church at Albany, to serve with the Reverend Gideon Schaets. Nicholaes Van Rensselaer arrived in 1675 and petitioned Andros to be made director of Rensselaerwyck. But in the mind of Maria Van Rensselaer, the estate had a director, herself, and it needed no assistance from the Dutch Van Rensselaers. While her challenge (assisted by her brother, Stephanus Van Cortlandt) to the legality of the situation of Andros's creating such appointments remained in legal papers, the Dutch Van Rensselaers themselves appointed Maria's brother-in-law Nicholaes the estate's director, thus undercutting her efforts to retain the estate for herself and her family. They finally reached an agreement that Nicholaes might retain the directorship, but Maria would become Rensselaerwyck's treasurer and her brother, its accountant.

In essence, Maria Van Rensselaer was expected to operate the estate at a profit not only for her own family (herself and her six children), but for the Dutch Van Rensselaers, who had been given the ultimate right of disposition in most affairs. She made the best of the agreement, nonetheless, and the situation worked out well enough, it seems. Nicholaes Van Rensselaer died in 1678. Maria's brother then succeeded to the directorship, but because he was in New York City, Maria effectively had sole run of the operations. Her distance from the two men required that Van Rensselaer write numerous letters, giving accounts both to her brother and to Rygert Van Rensselaer, her Dutch brother-in-law and the sole surviving son of founder Kiliaen Van Rensselaer, who had come over to reside at Rensselaerwyck between 1664 and 1670 but who remained in Holland thereafter.

Although little legal authority had been granted her and although she had to struggle to retain what authority she did have over the estate, Maria Van Rensselaer kept the colony intact during a difficult time of transition in New York, seeing to it that, after all her effort, the estate would pass on to her own children upon her death. Her letters to her Dutch relatives provide ample evidence of her skills of observation, even as they indicate the level of frustration she must have experienced over the confusing legal situation when Dutch estates were passing into British legal jurisdiction and when women had no estate rights before the law.

LETTERS TO RYGART VAN RENSSELAER

December 1675?[1]

Dear Brother:

Your agreeable and long awaited letter of July 5th, stating that you were heartily sorry to learn of the death of your brother, my husband,[2] was duly received by me on the 18th of November, new style. I doubt not but it has caused a great sorrow, but as it has pleased the Lord to afflict me with such a great sorrow, I must put my [trust] in God's will. May He make me patient and strengthen me in all adversity and in my infirmity, from which at present I suffer great pain, through Jesus Christ, who gives me strength and who through His mercy will further [sustain] me.

As to the coming over of brother Nicolaes, you will have learned about that from my preceding letter. I had expected more from him. If it had pleased God to spare my husband, deceased, a while longer, things would not go so [badly]. And as to the colony, matters still stand as they did when my husband, deceased, was living. Could he have spoken with his Excellency, it would have gone better. I trust that before the receipt of this letter you will already have learned everything from my letter to brother Jan Baptist,[3] to which I refer. That I should have liked to see you come over, is true, as you know the situation better than a stranger [and also know] the circumstances in which I am placed. I doubt not but you would have helped me in everything. But as it has pleased God to provide you with a family there, I can not advise you in the matter, as the situation of the country is well known to you.

As to the government here in this country, (it is, as far as I know) good. Trade is carried on as heretofore to Boston and the West Indies and the trading with the Indians goes on as while you were here. The past summer there was a lively trade. As to agriculture, it has during the last two years become so much worse on account of high water and the increase of weeds that the farmers demand a reduction [in the rent]. The honorable governor has prohibited the exportation of wheat flour for six months, but allowed that of bread.

As to my house and the land across [the river?], they are in the same condition as when my late husband was living. May it please the Lord that we may [possess] them in peace and have the grist-mill and sawmill also, in order that I may be able to support myself. But we live here in great fear on account of the great war between the English and the Indians around the north and of New England,[4] although, thank God, we do not yet hear of any calamities. The Indians have plundered many villages and killed many [people?]. It seems that it pleases the Lord to visit us also in this region. May God Almighty preserve us and prevent that they receive reinforcement from other nations, for they are very bold, and that they may not proceed farther. The state of religion in this country is still the same, for which mercy we can not sufficiently thank God Almighty. Wherewith, with hearty greetings from myself and my son Kiliaen and Anna to you and your wife, I commend you to God.

September? 1680

Dear Brother:

Your favor of the 12th of July came duly to hand and from it I saw that you duly received the account of my husband, deceased, your brother, regarding the colony, and that you and your sister were quite shocked when you saw the balance of the account. In answer thereto I shall say that if my husband, deceased, had made up the account himself, there would have been quite a bit more due. Do not think, dear brother, that it is an account which is made up out of my head. God preserve me from doing that. We have taken it from his own writings and if I should include all

---

1. A fire destroyed some of the Van Rensselaer papers, and those pages that the fire did not touch have been marked by time, leaving several of Maria Van Rensselaer's letters quite incomplete. Materials in brackets are either editorial surmises based on available textual evidence or else omissions of material that is illegible. Other lengthy ellipses indicate unavailable words in the manuscripts. The texts of all the letters are from *Correspondence of Maria Van Rensselaer, 1669–1689,* trans. and ed. A. J. F. Van Laer (1935).

2. Jeremias Van Rensselaer died on October, 12, 1674.

3. Jan Baptist Van Rensselaer was director of Rensselaerwyck prior to his brother Jeremias Van Rensselaer, Maria's husband.

4. A reference to the 1675–78 wars between British colonists and Native peoples of New England commonly called King Philip's War because Metacom, whom the English called "King Philip," was one of the leaders of the attacks on English settlements.

the expenditures which have been made and charge for all the extraordinary meals, a great deal more would be coming to me. Dear brother, you well know yourself how it went, first upon the arrival of the English, then upon the arrival of the Dutch, and then again upon the arrival of the English, and how, whenever any one of importance came from New York, he had to be entertained to keep up the dignity of the colony. You also well know that brother Jan Baties[t] wrote that one should not be particular about 1000 gl. or two. For whom, then, was it done, except for the colony? For ourselves we did not need it; we could have got along very well with one authority.

And as to what brother writes about loss on grain, seawan, etc., you also know how the grain has gone up in schepels, to 5 and 6½ schepels to the beaver, which is a great loss to the colony, and the seawan from 20 to 25, 30 and 36 gl. to the beaver. What would have become of us, then, if we had not had something else besides? If you examine the receipts of the colony, you will see that one year with another it could not produce enough to cover the expenses. One has to pay the schout, the secretary, the governor, the councilors, and in addition pay all expenses. If brother will take that into consideration, he can only say that it is true.

And as to what you write about my deceased husband's [capital] having been great when he went to New Netherland and that [the business] which he afterwards did on commission [as well] as in brewing did not leave anything, I will not deny it, and therefore, brother, be pleased to consider also how the goods sent to him by [Jan] Batiest, deceased, and others have dwindled in the colony and that now little [is left] to me. . . .

That the friends in Holland through the war have suffered great loss makes us heartily sorry, God knows, but consider, dear brother, whether to lose my health and in addition to lose my property and my dearest partner and to be left with six children and such an encumbered estate is not hard on me either, especially, to sit here and not to know what I have and to get further and further into debt, for as long as I remain thus in possession of the undivided estate it will be nothing but loss to me and to the friends. And as to there being some items in the account which, as you write, have been entered twice, I shall in the spring write about it to my brother and find out what there is to it and if there is anything that is not right I shall be glad to see it straightened out. Therefore, dear brother, do me the favor to examine the account and talk it over with the friends and if, please God, you intend to come over, we can inform each other of everything and settle all ac-

counts as to one thing and another, in order that for once we may know where we stand. And if the friends do not at the same time resolve to do something about the colony, things will run entirely wild.

You also complain that nothing is being sent over. How can anything be sent over when so many outlays had to be made and must still be made? On the farm called Turckeyen a new house has been built. On the farm of the Vlaming[5] a new house must be built. On the farm of Thunis Dircx a new house must be built. Gerrit Gysbert, at Bettlem,[6] will in the spring build a barn. Jonge Jan must build. Hen[drick] Mase must build. Hendrick van Nes must build a dwelling house and the old grist-mill must be completely torn down. One hears of nothing but expenses and at present there is such a poor harvest that many will not have any grain for bread. Furthermore, much money has been spent on the new mill, as I thought that it would produce some revenue, but now bolting is also prohibited,[7] so that I am at a loss to know where a stiver is to come from to be sent over. Yes, if 700 schepels of wheat did not have to be paid and if they were private farms, every one would sell his grain with a profit and send over his. I shall keep all the farmers waiting as long as I can, in order that I may learn whether it is possible for you to come over so that you may see things for yourself sometime.

I have written before this about the farm of Broer Cornelis and the old grist-mill, which you may think at present. . . .[8]

Further, I recommend my affairs to you most highly, in order that I may know how matters stand. . . .

November 12, 1684

Dear Brother:
Your letter of the 11th of May I duly received. This, then, will serve for answer. That you have not written to Levingston strengthens his position and I should have been pleased to hear that the account of my husband, deceased, had been settled. I therefore beg, no, not beg, but pray,

---

5. "The Fleming" Pieter Winne.

6. Bethlehem.

7. By a January 1680 order of the governor and council (published in Albany in March), flour could be bolted and packed for export only at New York City.

8. The last part of this sentence was crossed out.

that the matter of the account may come to an end. I am sorry that you are still in litigation with the young patroon, but from what I have heard I fear that you will get involved in even more serious litigation with the co-participants, since one Blommert and Bessels have sent a power of attorney to Sr Steenwyck to take their share out of the colony and to sell it, and van Beeck and Musart have written to Livingston. What they wrote I do not know, but as to [the power of attorney] to Sr Steenwyck, that is true. They write that they want to have an accounting from the year 1630, and that they have never received one stiver out of the colony from the sale of farms. All this writing is to the advantage of Levingston, who is also the cause of all the trouble that is impending, of which D^e Dellius has some knowledge, so that we need not expect anything else but that the colony is at an end.

And as to my brother Steeven's [chance of] obtaining something from the governor with reference to the limits of the colony, brother says that the governor will write about it to the Duke, but what shall I say, it is not. . . .[9] So that you can see now how matters stand with us, for here we have no friends at New York, so that Livingston will have his way, for he has the governor on his side and the governor himself told me that he would not benefit the Rensselaers who are in Holland, as appears to be the case, for when recently he was up here he placed a quitrent on all the [houses] in the Fuyck and also imposed a quitrent on our colony and attached all [the grain?].

As to [. . .], when brother Steven requested that we might have a patent thereof, he asked in whose name it was to be put. He said in the name of the family van Renselaer, and if it could not be put in the name of a family, then in that of my son Kieliaen. No, said he, the Rensselaers have names enough, but if you like to have it, I shall do it. Think, therefore, how things stand. And here you are so embarrassed about the house of Schuyler. They are no longer our friends and you need not spare them; whatever they can do to stand in our way they will not fail to do.

As to your having written to my father, deceased, about the land, [namely,] that if I was satisfied with it, I should keep it still a while, I wrote to my brother Steven for a copy of father's letter, but did not get it, and although I do not know what you wrote to father, I shall, please God, keep the land. And as to your writing that if you had known that I wished to buy the land you would not have put a price on it, you would even then not have sold it to

me, but to such an interloper (*onderkruyper*), who does not even pay tithes. It was on his advice that I had the land cleared. You write that Philip offered you fl.2000, and that you leave it to him for fl.2500, but if he does not want to give that, you will let him have it for fl.2000. The *joffrou*[10] no sooner hears that I wish to keep the land but she says: I will give the fl.2500. I think that my father's money is as good as hers and that you would rather sell the land to me for fl.2000 than to her for fl.2500, because it takes that much off the debt due to father and also because it is for your brother's children. But it seems that you are in need [of money] to pay brother Batist's debts and to keep up his reputation and that he who is out of sight can not get anything for himself, but is passed by.

As to what you write about cultivating the land . . . that is only jealousy, for even if it should cost her fl.2000 more, she would still want to have it or do something else.

As you were in need of money, I sold the farm of Piter Winne to Myndert Harmense, for which at the first opportunity you were to receive fl.1000, but as in your letter you say nothing about this, I take it that the letter has not reached you. I therefore send you now the third bill of exchange on *Joff.* Sybinck and . . . . . . , so that you may receive 2000 guilders. So that I took care that you would get money and I the land. As to what brother Steven writes about the land being detrimental to the island, that is not so, but they have something else in mind, namely, three or four of them to buy the island and then to take possession of the land with it.

Barent, the miller, has been to see me. He was very angry that you had withheld his money on account of the money which was said to be due [by him] here in this country. He gave me several accounts, about which we had harsh words and which he will send to you himself. As to the water rights, that [question] must remain until it is known under whose jurisdiction he resides. As to the account in the colony's book, he has a counter claim for boards delivered by him, so that we had to agree that if, after we had adjusted accounts, it turned out that he owed money, he would pay it at once, as you can see.

As to Lysbet Bankeren[11] having asked you for fl.100 in seawan[12] on account of old van Nes, that was paid long ago by Jacop Sanderse, who has a receipt for it.

---

9. The last part of this sentence was crossed out.

---

10. Margareta Schuyler, widow of Philip Pietersen Schuyler.

11. Lysbet, wife of Gerrit Banker.

12. A Dutch word for the Mohawks' "money," wampum.

That I have written several times that I should like to own the land and the grist-mill is true, but as you can not consent to it, I shall keep possession of them, for it might happen within a short time that you would not get a stiver for them and that some one else got hold of them. As to your thinking that because the mill stands so near the town it must yield much revenue, that is not so, for there are mills everywhere, so that there is no specially large amount of grinding. Moreover, those of Albany are not allowed to have their grain ground outside, so that it goes badly with us. The other mill stands idle. The old mill must be repaired and it needs two new millstones, for the stones are so old that they are broken and held together by an iron band. Neither I, nor my father and brother doubted but that you would have granted me the mill, as I have no other [means of support and] we can not [live] in Holland with our father's family. For this reason brother Steven has sent me a pair of stones, which are already up here for my personal use, but which now must be left lying around, for there is no need to repair the mill for a stranger. I must say one thing more, namely, that the governor and others have told me that my husband, deceased, had entered into Jacop Janse Flodder's contract, for the grist-mill belonged to Flodder himself, as he had had it built, but as the patroon's mills, which stood on the strand, were carried away by the ice, he had to deliver another mill, which my husband did. I never knew that.

Therefore, I beg you, sell me the small grist-mill which stands next to Spitsenberg's mill, on appraisal by impartial persons. It is conveniently located; I only want it for a stiver on Sundays for the poor, for as you know I can do nothing and I am daily getting weaker. I could manage it with a Negro if there was anything to grind, for I must live and my children are growing up and father, deceased, founded the colony with that idea in mind.

As to your trusting that no one would try to overreach me with respect to the land of Broer Cornelis, I can not with the pen express the falseness of the people, which at present is so great that it cries unto heaven. I shall therefore be on my guard. As soon as Livingston and the others begin, I shall look out for myself and see to it that I also get some security, for whatever belongs to the Rensselaers they will attach until the account is settled.

I have heard that Sr Steenwyck would first write back to Holland for further answer. You can therefore speak with them[13] yourself. I have also written [him] that the [participants] had no power to sell any land if they wanted to have their share. What there is to it we must wait to see when the time comes.

Harmen, the brewer,[14] would like to buy the place of Jonge Jan for cash in Holland. It is a poor place and there is no barn on it and there is no income from it to erect one on it.

[As to] our inheritance from the estate of brother, deceased, I am much surprised that you take such care to settle his estate, for which even the money must come from the colony. Whence, then, is the other money to come? And if I am to send you a considerable sum of money to satisfy me, where, then, is the rest to come from? Therefore, I beg you to let me have what I have asked for; then the work of sending [money] back and forth will be avoided. You may be quite sure, dear brother, that I should like to see the estate of your brother, my deceased husband, settled just as much as your deceased brother Jan's estate. He left one son and your brother [Jeremias] six children and a sorrowful widow, who with God's help and in honor seeks to bring up her children and tries to satisfy every one, which in the sorrowful state in which I am at present often makes me sigh.

On the 5th of April it pleased God suddenly to take out of this world my dear father, while he was in his prayers and in good health, in the presence of myself and of my dear mother, who would have liked so much to keep me with her a while longer, but I had to go up the river. Having been home but a short time, I received a letter that I must come down again. I therefore went down again in all haste. God granted us a favorable wind, so that we arrived at New York the next day, but I found my dear mother in the place where my father's bier had stood. She had died on the 12th of May. You can imagine how I felt and still feel, being a widow with six children and having neither father nor mother, who were such a support to me in all things, but now I have no one. My father took care while he was alive that after his death I should have some property. Should I now not take care to know how my affairs stand, I should be worse than a heathen, for now I have no one and every one looks out for himself. I never thought that my br[other Stev]en would have deserted us so. [According to] father's and mother's will no [accounting was to be demanded of] him whether he had carried out his father's will.

As it seems strange to you that I wrote that I feared that there might be some dispute, I shall [explain] this. As I had

---

13. Nicolaes Van Beeck and other partners in the colony of Rennselaerwyck.

14. Harmen Mermensen Gansevoort.

understood from my [brother] that his mother[15] wanted to have the land even if she had to give more for it than it was worth, I, thinking that you needed money and would pay more attention to the contract than to me (she will be satisfied with other land, as you write), was determined not to give it out of my hands, as my father advised me, for he was taking care that the innocent after his death would have some property and if the rear land is separated from the fore-land, the fore-land is worth nothing. Therefore, there would no doubt have arisen a dispute. That brother did not know that I had written to have the farm and the island is strange, unless the letters did not reach him.

As to your writing that what was still due to my husband, deceased, by inheritance from his father, deceased, his mother, deceased, and his sister, has diminished by the war, that is sad, but you can understand that one would like to have an account of it and to know what one has. Brother Jan Baptist and uncle, deceased, wrote to my husband, deceased, about the real estate and other things which mother had bequeathed to him and about what was

further coming to him from the estate. Furthermore, brother and uncle, deceased, wrote to me that what one had received more than another would be paid to the latter with the interest thereof; also, that the agates and loose pearls were still undivided, that the large house was sold for 18,500 gl., that brother, deceased, had taken over the small house for 7000 gl., and that Slangevelt was still unsold. That Kraloo was divided among the four brothers and two sisters I agreed to. That I wrote about the houses may well be, but you are mistaken that I advised you to have them sold. However, I shall not trouble you any more about that. What seems even stranger to me is that what is due to me from the estate of father and mother is to be paid out of the estate of brother Jan Baptist, deceased. What is the use of my sending over a considerable sum in order that the inheritance may be paid to me in cash. Truly it is a hard letter which I have from you. . . . I doubt not but God will again rejoice us with His spirit and grace, for the Lord chastises whom He loves and punishes every son whom He adopts. If this had not been my joy and strength, I should long ago have perished in my sorrow.

This 12 9b[r] 1684

---

15. Meaning his mother-in-law, Margareta Schuyler.

Francis Daniel Pastorius (1651–1720)

In 1699, William Penn described Francis Daniel Pastorius as "a man sober, upright, wise, and pious, of a reputation approved on all hands and unimpeached." He might well have appreciated Pastorius's skills, since Pastorius became one of his earliest and most stalwart supporters during the period of founding in Pennsylvania. Pastorius was born in Sommerhausen, Germany, where he received an exemplary education as a youth and then in college. He studied law at the University of Altdorf, receiving there and at three additional institutions a broad training in the law, humanities, and modern and classical languages. He finished his law degree in 1676 and moved to Windsheim to practice as an attorney, a profession he later described as "nothing but work for Repentence." Seeking a more intellectually stimulating climate, Pastorius moved to Frankfurt in 1679 and eventually came in contact with Dr. Jacob Spener and his circle of Pietists. Spener found Pastorius work as a tutor, and Pastorius went on tour with a young German nobleman, as his guide, visiting Holland, England, France, Switzerland, and Italy and returning to his Frankfurt Pietist friends in 1682. Pastorius later wrote of the Pietists that he strongly desired "to continue in their society, and with them to lead a quiet, godly and honest life in a howling wilderness." His growing relationship with them would be his life's calling.

The Frankfurt Pietists who followed Spener were interested in reviving a practice of spiritual devotion that recentered the individual's spiritual reflections, so as to move away from the sacramental and creed-driven German Lutheran practice. When William Penn visited the Pietists in 1677, explaining his plans to develop a proprietorship that would enable freedom of religious practice, the opportunity drew significant interest from members of this mystical group of believers. By 1682, they determined to purchase fifteen thousand acres of land in Pennsylvania and eventually settle in the colony themselves. They formed the Frankfurt Land Company and vested Pastorius with their power of attorney in all transactions. Pastorius left Frankfurt in the spring of 1683, visited a group of Crefeld Mennonites, and left the coast of England on the ship *America* in June 1683.

As his writings attest, Pastorius liked what he saw when he arrived in Pennsylvania. He negotiated with Penn to obtain land for both the Crefeld settlers and the Frankfurt Land Company. Penn designated six thousand acres on the Schuylkill River for the German settlement, which Pastorius surveyed and named "Germantown." Pastorius set about his duties, and he found his new life sufficiently attractive that he determined to marry and remain. Pastorius married Ennecke Klostermanns in 1688. He was disappointed by his Pietist friends, however, who never joined Pastorius in Pennsylvania but maintained their land holdings for financial gain. When he learned they would remain in Germany, Pastorius sought release from his obligations to the Frankfurt Land Company, but its members ignored his request, retaining him as their agent until 1700. Pastorius realized that the young German settlement would need support, and he remained to assist in developing a community for German speakers. Taking advantage of his education in the law, Pastorius became a member of the Pennsylvania Assembly in 1687 and 1691 and a naturalized citizen in 1709. In 1696, Pastorius published a primer for the English language, and he also instructed his students in English at the Germantown school, thus helping the children of German immigrants cope with the unfamiliar environment and language. Pastorius taught at the school sponsored by members of the Society of Friends in Philadelphia from 1697 to 1700 and at the Germantown school from 1702 until 1718.

The desire to pursue a quietest and spiritual life had brought Pastorius to Pennsylvania, but conditions in the colony constantly required that he make public explanations regarding faith practice and governance. He was troubled about the controversy over George Keith's group of "Christian Friends," but he hoped to remain neutral in the squabbles that were taking place. When Henry Bernhard Koster, one of Keith's followers, violently disturbed a Friends meeting, Pastorius issued an unequivocal repudiation of the Keithians in his pamphlet, *Four Boasting Disputers of This World Briefly Rebuked.* In 1688, Pastorius and four other Germantown residents submitted protests against slavery to three different Friends meetings, arguing that it was as wrong to hold Africans enslaved as it would be any other group of people. The remonstrance, written in Pastorius's hand and signed by him and three others, was dismissed by both the Monthly Meeting and Quarterly Meeting of the Philadelphia Friends, as well at the Yearly Meeting at Burlington, New Jersey. The Germantown protest nonetheless was an important step in recognizing the difficulty in reconciling religious practices and social inequities and injustices.

The pamphlet related to the Keith controversy and the primer, both published in Pennsylvania, are only a small part of a large amount of writing by Francis Daniel Pastorius. Pastorius wrote on many subjects, including law, medicine, agriculture, and especially gardening. His *Description of Pennsylvania,* published in Frankfurt and Leipzig in 1700, was one of the most widely read accounts of the colony in Germany at the time. The narrative that frames the opening of the *Description* is a reworking of information that Pastorius had included in letters written to friends, family, and the Frankfurt Land Company. Pastorius appended many of these letters to the *Description,* thus making it an eclectic compilation of materials related to his experiences as a German in the new colony. One of his letters, *Positive Information from America, Concerning the Country of Pennsylvania, from a German who has migrated thither,* was issued separately as a pamphlet.

While his writings about Pennsylvania clearly mark Pastorius as a promoter of the new colony, his private writings circulated among family and friends are impressive for their learning and literary dexterity. Pastorius's "Hive or Bee Stock," generally called *The Beehive* by scholars, was dedicated to his two sons. Pastorius began work on this commonplace book and encyclopedia of contemporary knowledge in 1696 and continued to add to it until his death. He composed poetry in English, as well as in German, Dutch, Latin, French, Italian, and Greek. *The Beehive* is several hundred handwritten folio pages in length and contains thousands of entries of Pastorius's thoughts on a large variety of subjects. Pastorius also added a bibliography of the books he had used or consulted, thereby allowing insight into the scope of his reading and the titles available in early Pennsylvania. The present selection draws from the many original poems Pastorius composed for his *Beehive.*

PETITION OF THE GERMANTOWN QUAKERS,

"Reasons Why We Are Against the Traffic of Menbody"[1]

This is to the monthly meeting held at Richard Worrell's:

These are the reasons why we are against the traffic of menbody, as followeth: Is there any that would be done or handled at this manner? viz., to be sold or made a slave for all the time of his life? How fearful and faint-hearted are many at sea, when they see a strange vessel, being afraid it should be a Turk, and they should be taken, and sold for slaves into Turkey. Now, what is *this* better done, than Turks do? Yea, rather it is worse for them, which say they are Christians; for we hear that the most part of such negers are brought hither against their will and consent, and that many of them are stolen. Now, though they are black, we cannot conceive there is more liberty to have them slaves, as [than] it is to have other white ones. There is a saying, that we should do to all men like as we will be done ourselves; making no difference of what generation, descent, or colour they are. And those who steal or rob men, and those who buy or purchase them, are they not all alike? Here is liberty of conscience, which is right and reasonable; here ought to be likewise liberty of the body, except of evil-doers, which is another case. But to bring men hither, or to rob and sell them against their will, we stand against. In Europe, there are many oppressed for conscience-sake; and here there are those oppressed which are of a black colour. And we who know that men must not commit adultery—some do commit adultery *in* others, separating wives from their husbands, and giving them to others: and some sell the children of these poor creatures to other men. Ah! do consider well this thing, you who do it, if you would be done at this manner—and if it is done according to Christianity! You surpass Holland and Germany in this thing. This makes an ill report in all those countries of Europe, where they hear of [it,] that the Quakers do here handel men as they handel there the cattle. And for that reason some have no mind or inclination to come hither. And who shall maintain this your cause, or plead for it? Truly, we cannot do so, except you shall inform us better hereof, viz.: that Christians have liberty to practise these things. Pray, what thing in the world can be done worse towards us, than if men should rob or steal us away, and sell us for slaves to strange countries; separating husbands from their wives and children. Being now this is not done in the manner we would be done at, [by]; therefore, we contradict, and are against this traffic of menbody. And we who profess that it is not lawful to steal, must, likewise, avoid to purchase such things as are stolen, but rather help to stop this robbing and stealing, if possible. And such men ought to be delivered out of the hands of the robbers, and set free as in Europe. Then is Pennsylvania to have a good report, instead, it hath now a bad one, for this sake, in other countries: Especially whereas the Europeans are desirous to know in what manner *the Quakers* do rule in *their* province; and most of them do look upon us with an envious eye. But if this is done well, what shall we say is done evil?

If once these slaves (which they say are so wicked and stubborn men,) should join themselves—fight for their freedom, and handel their masters and mistresses, as they did handel them before; will these masters and mistresses take the sword at hand and war against these poor slaves, like, as we are able to believe, some will not refuse to do? Or, have these poor negers not as much right to fight for their freedom, as you have to keep them slaves?

Now consider well this thing, if it is good or bad. And in case you find it to be good to handel these blacks in that manner, we desire and require you hereby lovingly, that you may inform us herein, which at this time never was done, viz., that Christians have such a liberty to do so. To the end we shall be satisfied on this point, and satisfy likewise our good friends and acquaintances in our native country, to whom it is a terror, or fearful thing, that men should be handelled so in Pennsylvania.

This is from our meeting at Germantown, held ye 18th of the 2d month, 1688, to be delivered to the monthly meeting at Richard Worrell's.

> *Garret Henderich,*
> *Derick op de Graeff,*
> *Francis Daniel Pastorius,*
> *Abram op de Graeff.*

At our monthly meeting, at Dublin, ye 30th 2d mo., 1688, we having inspected ye matter, above mentioned, and considered of it, we find it so weighty that we think it not expedient for us to meddle with it *here,* but do rather

---

1. The protest was first printed in 1844 by Nathan Kite in the (Philadelphia) *Friend* and published that year by George H. Moore in *Notes on the History of Slavery in Massachusetts,* the source of the present text.

commit it to yᵉ consideration of yᵉ quarterly meeting; yᵉ tenor of it being related to yᵉ truth.

On behalf of yᵉ monthly meeting,
Jo. Hart.

This abovementioned, was read in our quarterly meeting, at Philadelphia, the 4th of yᵉ 4th mo., '88, and was from thence recommended to the yearly meeting, and the above said Derrick, and the other two mentioned therein, to present the same to yᵉ above said meeting, it being a thing of too great weight for this meeting to determine.

Signed by order of yᵉ meeting.
Anthony Morris.

from POSITIVE INFORMATION FROM AMERICA, CONCERNING THE COUNTRY OF PENNSYLVANIA[1]

To fulfill my duty as well as my promise made at my departure I will somewhat more circumstantially state what I have found and noted of these lands; and since I am not unaware that by imperfect relations many of you have been misinformed, I give my assurance beforehand that I with impartial pen and without deceptive additions will set forth faithfully both the inconveniences of the journey and the defects of this province, as well as that plentifulness of the same which has been praised by others almost to excess; for I desire nothing more in my little place than to walk in the footsteps of Him who is the way, and to follow His holy teachings, because He is the truth, in order that I may ceaselessly enjoy with Him eternal life.

I. Accordingly I will begin with the voyage, which is certainly on the one hand dangerous on account of the terror of shipwreck; and on the other hand very burdensome on account of the bad and hard fare, so that I now from my own experience understand in a measure what David says in the 107th Psalm, that on the sea one may observe and perceive not only the wonderful works of God but also the spirit of the storm. As to my voyage hither; I sailed from Deal the tenth of June with four men servants, two maid servants, two children and one young boy. We had the whole way over, for the most part, contrary winds, and never favorable for twelve hours together, many tempests and thunderstorms, also the foremast broke twice, so that it was ten weeks before we arrived here; yet *sat citò, si sat bene;*[2] considering that it seldom happens that any persons arrive here much more quickly. The Crefelders,[3] who arrived here on October 6, were also ten weeks upon the ocean, and the ship that set out with ours from Deal was fourteen days longer on the voyage, and several people died in it. The Crefelders lost a grown girl between Rotterdam and England, which loss however was made up between England and Pennsylvania by the birth of two children. On our ship, on the other hand, no one died and no one was born. Almost all the passengers were seasick for some days, I however for not more than four hours. On the other hand I underwent other accidents, namely, that the two carved lugs over the ship's bell fell right upon my back, and on the 9th of July during a storm in the night I fell so severely upon my left side that for some days I had to keep to my bed. These two falls reminded me forcibly of the first fall of our original parents in Paradise, which has come down upon all their posterity, and also of many of those falls which I have undergone in this vale of misery of my exile. *Per varios casus,*[4] etc. But praised be the fatherly hand of the divine mercy which lifts us up again so many times and holds us back that we fall not entirely into the abyss of the evil one. Georg Wertmüller also fell down extremely hard, Thomas Gasper had an eruption of the body, the English maid had the erysipelas, and Isaac

---

1. The pamplet is actually the report that Pastorius wrote to the Frankfurt Land Company. The complete title of this pamphlet is *Positive Information from America, concerning the Country of Pennsylvania, from a German who has migrated there; dated Philadelphia, March 7, 1684.* It was originally published in Zurich in a unique imprint, *Sichere Nachricht.* The text is from *Narratives of Early Pennsylvania, West New Jersey, and Delaware, 1630–1707,* trans. J. F. Jameson, ed. A. C. Myers (1912).

2. Quickly enough, if well enough.

3. Pastorius had stayed among the Crefelders as he traveled to Deal, England, to make his departure for Pennsylvania.

4. *Aeneid,* I. 204: "Through various accidents, through so many hazards, we go on toward Latium."

Dilbreck,[5] who according to outward appearance was the strongest, succumbed for the greatest length of time. So I had a small ship-hospital, although I alone of the Germans had taken my berth among the English. That one of the boatmen became insane and that our ship was shaken by the repeated assaults of a whale, I set forth at length in my last letter. The rations upon the ship were very bad. We lived *medice ac modice*.[6] Every ten persons received three pounds of butter a week, four cans of beer and two cans of water a day, two platters full of peas every noon, meat four dinners in the week and fish three, and these we were obliged to prepare with our own butter. Also we must every noon save up enough so that we might get our supper from it. The worst of all was, that both the meat and the fish were salted to such an extent and had become so rancid that we could hardly eat half of them. And had I not by the advice of good friends in England provided myself with various kinds of refreshment, it might perhaps have gone very badly. Therefore all those who hereafter intend to make the voyage hither should take good heed that they either, if there are many of them, procure their own provisions, or else agree distinctly with the captain as to both quantity and quality, how much food and of what sort they are to receive each day; and to hold him down the more completely to this agreement, one should reserve some small part of the passage money, to be paid on this side. Also when possible one should arrange with a ship which sails up to this city of Philadelphia, since in the case of the others which end their voyage at Upland, one is subjected to many inconveniences.

My company consisted of many sorts of people. There was a doctor of medicine with his wife and eight children, a French captain, a Low Dutch cake-baker, an apothecary, a glass-blower,[7] a mason, a smith, a wheelwright, a cabinet-maker, a cooper, a hat-maker, a cobbler, a tailor, a gardener, farmers, seamstresses, etc., in all about eighty persons besides the crew. They were not only different in respect to age (for our oldest woman was sixty years of age and the youngest child only twelve weeks) and in respect to their occupations, as I have mentioned, but were also of such different religions and behaviors that I might not unfittingly compare the ship that bore them hither with Noah's Ark, but that there were more unclean than clean (rational) animals to be found therein. In my household I have those who hold to the Roman, to the Lutheran, to the Calvinistic, to the Anabaptist, and to the Anglican church, and only one Quaker. On the 11th of August we cast the lead for the first time and perceived that we were close to the great sand bank, and so had to sail back and around and consequently to run more than a hundred leagues out of our course.

On the 16th we came with joy in sight of America and on the morning of the 18th arrived in Delaware Bay, which is thirty English miles long and fifteen wide and is of such unequal depth that since our ship drew thirteen feet of water we sometimes stuck upon the sand.

On the 20th we sailed past Neu Castle, Upland and Dunicum[8] and arrived at evening, praise God, safely at Philadelphia; where I on the following day delivered to William Penn the letters that I had, and was received by him with amiable friendliness; of that very worthy man and famous ruler I might properly

II. write many things; but my pen (though it is from an eagle, which a so-called savage lately brought to my house) is much too weak to express the high virtues of this Christian—for such he is indeed. He often invites me to his table and has me walk and ride in his always edifying company; and when I lately was absent from here a week, in order to fetch provisions from Neu Castle, and he had not seen me for that space of time, he came himself to my little house and besought me that I should at least once or twice a week be his guest. He heartily loves the [Germans],[9] and once said openly in my presence to his councillors and those who were about him, I love the [Germans] and desire that you also should love them. Yet

---

5. The servants of the Frankfurt Land Company accompanying Pastorius on the ship *America*. Wertmüller was Swiss, probably from Bern. The "English maid" was Frances Simson. Dilbrek or Dilbeek traveled with his wife Marieke and their two sons. "Erysipelas," a streptococcal infection, is characterized by large raised patches on the skin, with fever and severe general illness.

6. Medically and moderately.

7. The doctor was Thomas Lloyd (1640–94), deputy governor of Pennsylvania from 1691 to 1693. The cake baker was Cornelius Bom (d. 1688). Two letters by Bom and Georg Wertmüller were published in Dutch as *Twee Missiven geschreven uyt Pensilvania* (1684). The glassblower, Joshua Tittery, was a servant for the Free Society of Traders.

8. Tinicum; island on the west shore of the Delaware below the mouth of the Schuylkill.

9. All references to "Germans," "Frankfurters," and specific members of the Frankfurt Land Company in square brackets were inserted by the translator for the blanks given in the printed original.

in any other matter I have never heard such a command from him. This however pleased me so much the better because it was entirely conformable with the command of God (see John xiii. 23).[10] I can at present say no more than that William Penn is a man who honors God and is honored by Him, who loves what is good and is rightly beloved by all good men. I doubt not that some of them will come here and by their own experience learn, that my pen has in this case not written enough.

III. Of the nature of the land I can write with certainty only after one or more years of experience. The Swedes and Low Dutch who have occupied it for twenty years and more are in this as in most other things of divided opinions; *laudatur ab his, culpatur ab illis.*[11] Certain it is that the soil does not lack fruitfulness and will reward the labor of our hands as well as in Europe if one will duly work and manure it, both which things are for the most part lacking. For the above mentioned old inhabitants are poor agriculturists. Some of them have neither barns nor stables, and leave their grain for years together un-threshed and lying in the open air, and allow their cattle, horses, cows, swine, etc., to run in the woods summer and winter, so that they derive little profit from them. Certainly the penance with which God punished the disobedience of Adam, that he should eat his bread in the sweat of his brow, extends also to his posterity in these lands, and those who think to spare their hands may remain where they are. *Hic opus, hic labor est,* and it is not enough to bring money hither, without the inclination to work, for it slips out of one's hands, and I may well say with Solomon: It has wings. Inasmuch as in the past year very many people came hither both out of England and Ireland and also from Barbadoes and other American islands, and this province does not yet produce sufficient provisions for such a multitude, therefore all victuals are somewhat dear, and almost all the money goes out of the land to pay for them. Yet we hope in time to have a greater abundance of both things, because William Penn will coin money and agriculture will be better managed. Working people and husbandmen are in the greatest demand here, and I certainly wish that I had a dozen strong Tyrolese to cut down the thick oak trees, for in whatever direction one

turns, one may say: *Itur in antiquam sylvam.* It is nothing but forest, and very few cleared places are to be found, in which respect as also in some others the hope I had previously formed is deceived, namely, that in these wild orchards no apples or pears are to be found, and this winter (which indeed has been very cold) no deer, turkeys, etc., were to be had. The wild grapes are very small and better suited to make into vinegar than into wine. The walnuts have very thick shells, and few thick kernels within, so that they are scarcely worth the trouble of cracking. The chestnuts, however, and hazelnuts are somewhat more palatable; also the peaches, apples and pears are very good, no fault is to be found with them, except that there are not so many of them as some desire. On the other hand there are more rattlesnakes (whose bite is fatal) in the land than is agreeable to us. I must also add this, *tanquam testis oculatus,*[12] that on October 16 I found fine (March) violets in the bushes; also that, after I had on October 24 laid out the town of Germantown, and on the 25th had gone back there with seven others, we on the way found a wild grape-vine, running over a tree, on which were some four hundred clusters of grapes; wherefore we then hewed down the tree and satisfied all eight of us, and took home with us a hatfull apiece besides. Also as I on August 25 was dining with William Penn, a single root of barley was brought in which had grown in a garden here and had fifty grains upon it. But all grains do not bear so much and it is as we say in the proverb, one swallow does not make a summer. Yet I doubt not that in the future more fruitful examples of this sort will present themselves, when we shall put the plow to the land in good earnest. I lament the vines which I brought with me, for when we were already in Delaware Bay they were drenched with seawater and all but two were spoiled. The abovementioned William Penn has a fine vineyard of French vines planted; its growth is a pleasure to behold and brought into my reflections, as I looked upon it, the fifteenth chapter of John.[13]

IV. Philadelphia daily increases in houses and inhabitants and presently a house of correction will be built in order that those who are not willing to live in a Philadelphian manner may be disciplined, for some such are to be found, to whom fittingly applies what our dear friend

---

10. John 13: 23: "Now there was leaning on Jesus' bosom one of his disciples, whom Jesus loved."

11. Horace, *Satires,* I.2, 11: "It is praised by these, it is re-proached by those."

12. As an eyewitness.

13. John 15: "I am the true vine, and my Father is the husbandman. . . ."

[Van de Walle][14] mentions in his letter, that we have here more distress from the spoiled Christians than from the Indians. Furthermore here and there other towns are laid out; for the Society is beginning to build about an hour and a half from here[15] one bearing the name of Franckfurt, where they have erected a mill and a glass factory. Not far from there, namely two hours from here, lies our Germantown, where already forty-two people are living in twelve dwellings. They are mostly linen weavers and not any too skilled in agriculture. These good people laid out all their substance upon the journey, so that if William Penn had not advanced provisions to them, they must have become servants to others. The way from here to Germantown they have now, by frequent going to and fro, trodden out into good shape. Of that town I can say no more at present than that it lies on black fruitful soil and is half surrounded with pleasant streams like a natural defence. The chief street therein is sixty feet wide and the cross street forty. Every family has a house lot of three acres.

V. As to the inhabitants, I cannot better classify them than into the native and the engrafted. For if I were to call the former savages and the latter Christians, I should do great injustice to many of both varieties. Of the latter sort, I have already mentioned above, that the incoming ships are not altogether to be compared with Noah's Ark. The Lutheran preacher, who ought as a *statua Mercurialis*[16] to show the Swedes the way to heaven, is, to say it in one word, a drunkard. Also there are coiners of false money and other vicious persons here whom nevertheless, it may be hoped, the wind of God's vengeance will in his own time drive away like chaff. On the other hand there is no lack of pious, God-fearing people, and I can with truth affirm that I have nowhere in Europe seen the notice posted up, as here in our Philadelphia, that such an one has found this or that, and that the loser may call for it at his house; often however the converse, Lost this or that; he who returns it again shall receive a reward, etc.

Of these new engrafted strangers I will for the present say no more than that among them some High Germans are to be found who have lived already twenty years in this land and consequently are, so to speak, naturalized, namely, Silesians, Brandenburgers, Holsteiners, Swiss, etc., also a Nuremberg man named Jan Jaquet;[17] but will briefly give my account of those who are erroneously called savages. The first who came before my eyes were those two who at Upland came in a canoe to our ship. I presented them with a dram of brandy. They attempted to pay me for it with a sixpence, and when I refused the money they gave me their hands, and said, Thank you, brother. They are strong of limb, swarthy of body, and paint their faces, red, blue, etc., in various ways. In the summer they go quite naked, except that they cover their private parts with a piece of cloth, and now in winter hang duffels upon themselves. They have coal-black hair, while the Swedish children born here have hair snow-white. I was once dining with William Penn where one of their kings sat at table with us. William Penn, who can speak their language fairly fluently, said to him that I was a German, etc. He came accordingly on the third of October, and on the twelfth of December another king and queen came to my house. Also many common persons over-run me very often, to whom however I almost always show my love with a piece of bread and a drink of beer, whereby an answering affection is awakened in them and they commonly call me "Teutschmann," also "Carissimo" (that is, brother). N. B. Their language is manly and in my opinion is little inferior to the Italian in gravity, etc. As to their manners and nature, one must so to speak sub-distinguish them into those who have associated for some time with the so-called Christians and those who are just beginning to come forth out of their burrows. For the former are crafty and deceitful, which they owe to the above-mentioned nominal Christians. *Semper enim aliquid hæret.*[18] Such an one lately pledged me his strap as security that he would bring me a turkey, but in its place he brought an eagle and wished to persuade me that it was a turkey. When however I showed him that I had seen many eagles he acknowledged to a Swede who stood by that he had done it out of deception, in the belief that because we had lately come into the land I should not know such birds so accurately. Another at my fireside tested the brandy thus: he stuck his finger into it and then put the latter into the fire to see whether water had been mingled with the liquor. Those of the second

---

14. Jacob van de Walle, one of the Frankfurt Pietists and one of the principal stockholders in the Frankfurt Land Company.

15. The Free Society of Traders. "Here" means Philadelphia.

16. "Statue of Mercury," god and guide of travelers. The Lutheran preacher is the Reverend Jacob Fabritius.

---

17. Jean Paul Jaquet (c. 1615–85), a native of Nuremberg whose father came from Geneva.

18. For always something adheres.

class, on the contrary, are of a reasonable spirit, injure no-body, and we have nothing whatever to fear from them. One thing lately struck deeply into my heart when I pondered the sincere admonition of our Saviour, that we His disciples should take no thought for the morrow, because thus do the Gentiles. Ah, thought I to myself, how entirely has all been now perverted! When we Christians are not provided for a month and more how displeased are we, while these heathen in so wonderful a spirit of resignation refer their sustenance to God. Just at that time I saw four of them eating together. The earth was at once their table and their bench. A pumpkin, cooked in plain water, without butter or spice, was all their food. Their spoons were mussel-shells, with which they supped the warm water. Their plates were oak leaves, which they had no need to clean after the meal, nor, when they needed others, to give themselves much trouble about them. Now, dear friend, let us not hesitate to learn contentment from these people, that they may not hereafter shame us before the judgment-seat of Jesus Christ. . . .[19]

Concerning the fifteen thousand acres, two chief difficulties arose, namely, that William Penn did not wish to give them all together in one piece in order that so very large a space in the land might not lie uncultivated and empty, nor on the Delaware River, where indeed everything had already been taken up by others. But after I had repeatedly represented to him both orally and in writing that it would be very prejudicial to us and our German successors to be so completely wedged in among the English, and likewise that B. Fürly[20] had communicated to the [Frankfurters] his, William Penn's, letter in which he had promised otherwise to our nation, etc., he finally gave me a warrant, to have our land in one tract, provided that we within a year would settle thirty families upon the fifteen thousand acres, namely, three townships, each of ten households, among which might be reckoned the three which are already here (but in case thirty families do not come he will not be bound to give the land in one piece). I for my small part could indeed wish that we might have

a small separate province, and so might the better protect ourselves against all oppression. Now if one of you could be free to come hither and bring that number of families[21] your own best interests would be incomparably furthered thereby, for he, William Penn, only the day before yesterday told me that in that case he would give you the preference over all the English who though they had bought earlier had not yet arrived here, and would give you certain privileges in our new Franckenland (for so he called the tract of land destined for us). If, however, it is too difficult for you to transport so many families in so short a time, it would in my opinion, which of course is not binding, be well that the friends of [Frankfurters] should take from you a few thousand acres and, out of the abundance with which they have been blessed, send certain households hither, in order that the fifteen thousand acres may come to us undivided and without English neighbors intervening; especially as he will give these lands not too far away from this town, namely, on the Scollkill above the falls, where he himself intends to build a house and to lay out a small manse for himself. The land near the river is quite hilly, and not ill-suited to the cultivation of the vine. Farther in, however, it is level and fertile. The worst of it is, however, that one cannot go in a boat over the falls and the ledges, except when it has rained heavily and even then not without danger. Now since I could not know what you might conclude to do in these circumstances, and yet it was very important, and since moreover these often-mentioned fifteen thousand acres would cost 28 pounds sterling to survey, namely, 5 shillings of the local money for every hundred acres, which money however I did not have in hand, I was obliged to let the matter stand until I had received your decision, in order not to step over the limits of a faithful agent. In order, however, that I might settle the three families who had arrived upon their six hundred acres I have, in conjunction with the Crefelders (who have bought eighteen thousand acres, and though all here present cannot obtain the whole in one piece) taken up six thousand acres for a township, of which they have three thousand and we three thousand. This town I laid out on October 24, and called it Germantown. It lies only two hours' walk from here, on fertile soil, and near pleasant springs, which I have mentioned above. This I was obliged to do because William Penn will not give any man his portion separately but all must

---

19. In the section omitted, Pastorius provided a brief account of the health of the servants who accompanied him to Pennsylvania and of the Crefelders, the first Germantown settlers. He also described the land he purchased for the company and himself, as well as the first house he built in Philadelphia.

20. Benjamin Furly (1636–1714), Penn's chief agent for the sale of land and general promoter of immigration to Pennsylvania in Europe.

---

21. None of the members of the Frankfurt Land Company ever joined Pastorius in Pennsylvania.

dwell together in townships or towns, and this not without weighty reasons. Among these the chief is that in that way the children can be kept at school and much more conveniently brought up well. Neighbors also can better offer each other loving and helpful hands and with united mouths can in public assemblies praise and extol the goodness of God. N. B. You might accordingly assign only a hundred acres to the families that you bring over here in the future and yet obtain almost as large an estate.

As for my domestic establishment, I very much wished to arrange it in the good High German manner and Jacob Schuemacher and the old Swiss[22] are very serviceable to me toward this purpose. But the Hollanders whom I have with me adapt themselves but ill to this, especially the maid, who cannot get on well with the English one,[23] so that I, to preserve the peace, must send the latter away because the former with her two children cannot so easily remove or attach herself to another master. I greatly desire to obtain as soon as possible a High German maid whom I can trust better than, I am sorry to say, I now can do. If you wish not to be deceived in your hopes, send only Germans, for the Hollanders, as troublesome experience teaches me, are not so pleasant, which in this new land is a highly necessary quality. I have no carpenter among my servants, so a few ought to be sent over hither for the building of houses. In the making of the contract with them it may serve for your information that their daily wages are now much diminished, and beyond their board they receive not more than [two][24] shillings a day, though most of them for this reason do not work and are preferring to leave the country. N. B. A fixed price is set for all hand-workers, also not more than fifty per cent. gain must be made on merchant wares, though indeed perhaps three or four years from now there will be little profit to be made on these, as the Society is sufficiently aware. For (1) every newcomer brings so much clothing and provisions with him that he for some years needs nothing. (2) There is very little money here, although the desire for it is in the case of many persons so much the greater. On November 16 occurred the annual fair in our Philadelphia, where however I hardly took in a few pounds sterling. (3) One can not yet obtain from this land any return-goods to send to England. William Penn, to be sure, intends to establish weaving and wine-making and for this reason on several opportunities sends us good vines on whose prospering one can count. Also [send] all sorts of field and garden seeds, especially of lentils, millet, etc. Also, N. B., some great iron cooking-pots and nests of kettles. Also an iron stove, because the winter here is usually as cold as with you and the rough north winds much harsher. Also some coverlets or mattresses, because I did not bring more with me than I immediately needed yet have already got an additional manservant. Finally, if you would also send me some pieces of fustian and Osnabrück,[25] linen cloth, it can be sold to good advantage.

A tanner can undertake his work with great profit, since here and in the neighboring lands we can obtain hides enough and indeed two raw for one dressed. Also the very best for a pair of shoes. But a certain capital must be employed for this, but since these sums of money thus expended would in a short time bring a rich revenue, I leave the matter to your riper reflection. The two most necessary things are: (1) upon the lots in this town to build suitable houses, which are expensive to rent and from which twelve per cent. per annum can be obtained; (2) to establish a brick-kiln, for which William Penn has promised to give us an excellent place, for so long as we make no bricks our house-building is only of wood. Other artisans may well wait at home a few years yet. . . .

from THE BEEHIVE[1]

[When I Solidly Do Ponder]

When I solidly do ponder,
How *Thoughts wander;* I must wonder,
  And for Shame exclaim, and own,
  Mine are ranging up and down.
Now on Eagle's Wings ascending   5
Far above the Skies, there spending
  Some good Minutes in a Song;

---

22. Schuemacher (d. 1722) was a servant Pastorius had brought over from Mainz. The "old Swiss" is Georg Wertmüller.
23. Marieke Dilbeck and Frances Simson.
24. The original text is illegible here.

25. A coarse linen cloth from the German city of Osnabrück.

1. Pastorius made entries in his common-place book, affectionately called *The Beehive,* from 1669 until his death. The unpublished manuscript is located in the Rare Book and Manuscript Library of the University of Pennsylvania. The texts reproduced are from *Seventeenth-Century American Poetry,* ed. Harrison T. Meserole (1968).

But, alas! this lasts not long.
Unawares they are departing,
10 And themselves (like Arrows,) darting
    In the very Depth of Hell,
    Where the Damned wail and yell.
Weari'd with this frightful Crying,
They in haste from thence are flying,
15   And as giddy-headed hurl'd
    Fore- and back-ward in the World.
Thro' Great Britain, France and Holland,
Denmark, Moscovy, Spain, Polland,
    Portugal and Italy,
20   Oft'ner yet thro' Germany.
Hence returning to Braganza,[2]
To the Cape of Bon Speranza;
    So, by way of Africa,
    Home to Penn Silvania.
25 Here I bid them to be quiet,
They deny: however try it,
    Go to bed, and sleep almost;
    But soon starting, take the Post,
And afresh begin to travel,
30 Not regarding Mire nor Gravel,
    River, Valley, Swamps nor hill,
    Presently light where they will.
Tripping, traping still the faster
Like a Cur, that lost his Master,
35   To and fro, from place to place,
    Stir their Stumps, and run a Race.
Some times in the Garden ramble
From the Tulip to the Bramble:
    From the Rose and Eglantine
40   To the Nep or Columbine.
Then retiring leave these Flowers,
Sit a while in Shady Bowers,
    With a Book to meditate,
    And, as if it were, abate.
45 In a moment, loath to tarry,
Swiftly, as their feet can carry
    Their small Bodies, whip away
    In the Woods to seek a Stray.
Here they hith'r and thither straggle,
50 Gad, fig, f[r]isk, stir, waver, waggle
    Course and roam, and rove about,
    Till there is no Coming out.

---

2. Bragança, city in northern Portugal and seat of the ruling Portuguese dynasty from 1640 to 1710.

Justly I may call them Gropers,
Gypsies, Runnagates, Landlopers,
    Vagrants, Fugitives and Rogues,   55
    That deserve the Stocks and Strokes.
Animus sine pondere velox.   *Horat.*[3]

If any be pleased to walk into my poor Garden, I heartily bid him or her welcome, thus

Friend, Coming in a friendly wise,
From East, West, North or South,
Take here the Owner's own advice:
Put nothing in thy mouth;
But freely Fill thy Nose and Eyes   5
With all my Garden's growth.
For, if thou imitate the Apes,
And Clandestinely steal my grapes,
One wishes thee the Belly-Gripes,
An other hundred Scaffold-Stripes, &c.   10
Therefore, Pray, Curb thy appetite,
And mind what I hereunder write:
    Do not Covet,
    Though thou Love it;
    But without any Bluster,   15
    Go Buy a lusty Cluster.
Now, On those Terms, I give thee leave to Enter,
And Penetrate from both Ends to the Center:
But do not Break, nor Take Stalks, Fruit, or Seed,
For We hereby are Otherwise agreed.   20
Such-like Contracts bind without Seal and hand,
A good man's Word exceeds a bad ones Bond.

[When one or other rambles]

When one or other rambles,
To Fishermen and Shambles,
To Pothecaries Shops:
For Physick and for Vittles,
Which they cut with their Whittles,   5
And play the dainty Fops,
Then I go to my Garden,
But no flesh, nor Pope's Pardon,
Now in the time of Lent;
But herbs and Eggs there gather,   10
Whereon I'm feeding rather

---

3. Horace, *Epistles* I.xii. 3: "miramur, si Democrati pecus edit agellos / cultaque, dum peregre est animus sine corpore velox." That is, "We wonder that Democritus' herds ate up his fields and meadows, while his fast-moving mind wandered off by itself without his body."

Than on such graisement.
How be it a good Cony,
Young Chickens, Chees and honey,
15 I heartily do own,
Distasting likewise never
What Roots and Fruits soever
In Fields are sown and grown.
The best things for my Palat
20 Are parsnips, Corn and Sallet,
And sugar'd Apple-pyes,
For Med'cine I use Lillies:
They cure most all what ill is
In man's heart, brain, and Eyes.
25 Next Sage with hyssop rises,
Preferred to those Spices,
Fetcht from the East and West.
My pen now waxing weary,
I leave off to be airy:
30 Short Follies are the best.

[As often as some where before my Feet]

As often as some where before my Feet
I with a fine, rare, and fair Object meet,
I shut my Outward Eyes,
And bid my Inward rise
To Him, who made, and does uphold that Thing
So that my heart (whilst I His praises sing,)
To the Creator cleaves
And that quaint Creature leaves.
Concluding thus: If this, which is but vain,

Appears to men so handsom, deft and clean,
How beautiful must he
Pure, Bright, and Glorious be
Whose wondrous works I see.

[Extract the Quint-essence]

Extract the Quint-essence
Of *Time* and *Patience*
Which grow not in all Gardens;
It makes hard cases soft,
And when applied oft,
Faint, weak and soft hearts harden's.
None of the World's Produce
Hath such a gen'ral Use
As this quaint Quint Essence
Of Time and Patience.

[Delight in Books from Evening]

Delight in Books from Evening
Till mid-night when the Cocks do sing;
Till Morning when the day doth spring:
Till Sun-set when the Bell doth ring.
Delight in Books, for Books do bring
Poor men to learn most every thing;
The Art of true Levelling:
Yea even how to please the king.
Delight in Books, they're carrying
Us so far, that we know to fling
On waspish men (who taking wing
Surround us) that they can not sting.

CHRISTOPH SAUR (1695–1758)

Of the printing business he had just started in Philadelphia, Christoph Saur wrote in the fall of 1740, "My small printing shop . . . is dedicated to God, and I hope that during my and my son's lives nothing shall be printed except that which is to the glory of God and for the physical or eternal good of my neighbors. What ever does not meet this standard, I will not print." Saur's printing press, the first successful press established by a German entirely for German speakers in Pennsylvania, adhered to this motto. Saur published numerous religious works, including many hymnals, a Bible, a German-language newspaper, and an almanac.

Christoph Saur (in the Pennsylvania colony, the name was often spelled Christopher Sauer) was born in 1695 in Ladenburg, a small town in the Palatinate, but his family moved to Wittgenstein in Westphalia after his father's death in 1701. In the tolerant religious climate of this area, Saur came in contact with various religious groups who dissented from standard church practice, and he followed the thinking that led away from the support of established churches. After his marriage in 1720 and the birth of his only child, Christoph II, Saur and his wife Marie Christine decided to emigrate to Pennsylvania in 1724. They most likely followed the prospect of economic opportunity and religious freedom, especially as the situation for nonorthodox Christians in Wittgenstein became increasingly oppressive. Upon his arrival in Pennsylvania, Saur provided a glowing report of his new home, calling it "a very good and blessed land, like an earthly Paradise." The Saurs initially took up farming in the Conestoga area, but when Marie Christine abandoned her family to join Conrad Beissel's Ephrata Society, Saur moved with his son to Germantown.

Skilled artisans were desperately needed in the Philadelphia and Germantown areas of Pennsylvania. Saur quickly gained a reputation for his many trades, and he worked in many trades, from a clockmaker to an herbal healer, until in 1735, he became seriously interested in establishing a printing business that would lend itself to assisting the community of German speakers in the area. Saur trusted his own ingenuity in building a press, but he understood the usefulness of printing forms and types that would be familiar to Germans from back home, so he ordered his type from a prominent foundry in Frankfurt. Saur produced his own ink; taught himself bookbinding; and, in order to circumvent Benjamin Franklin's paper monopoly, established his own paper mill. He began by printing religious materials in 1738 (a translation of an English religious broadside), and he continued this line of work throughout his career. His first book project, an 800-page hymnal for the Ephrata Society, gained him a reputation as one who was accepting and understanding of the different radical religious movements in the colony.

The majority of Saur's publications between 1738 and his death in 1758 were of a religious nature, yet Saur also recognized the demand for more practical information. Both his almanac, *Der Hoch-Deutsch Americanische Calender,* and his newspaper, *Der Hoch-Deutsch Pensylvanische Geschichts-Schreiber,* were widely read by Germans, who saw that Saur's imprints circulated throughout German settlements as far as away South Carolina and Georgia. The almanac included the typical practical features—a calendar, weather prognostications, astronomical tables, and medicinal information—as well as articles written by Saur himself. A key secret behind Saur's success lay in his use of the German Gothic type because the majority of German immigrants could not read the Roman type employed by British printers. The newspaper, later renamed *Germantowner Zeitung,* was equally widely read as his other publications.

Saur was challenging the printing dominance of the successful printing house of Benjamin Franklin and his partners, but the challenges he was making to established churches were perhaps even more significant. In 1743, Saur completed a monumental but controversial Bible-printing project. Based on Martin Luther's translation, Saur's edition also included an apocryphal section from the Pietist Berleburg Bible. Saur's Bible was harshly criticized by leaders of the orthodox churches because they saw such radical faith practices as potentially troubling to good social and political structure, and they worried about the consequences of fractures among the immigrant populations. Yet Saur's Bible was highly sought after, even well after its initial publication—so much so that Saur's son published two further editions by 1776, after he took over his father's printing business.

Saur himself never secured a religious affiliation, even though he sympathized with individual sectarian groups, such as the Brethren and the Schwenkfelders. As a Pietist, Saur stressed the importance of an inner light of faith and rejected all material greed. He advocated a strict pacifism and attempted to translate his faith into political action. During the elections in the 1750s, Saur urged the Germans to cast their votes in favor of the pacifist Quakers and against the Proprietory party's attempt to raise money for a military defense of the colony. When Benjamin Franklin advocated a voluntary militia called the "Association" in his pamphlet, *Plain Truth,* Saur used his own newspaper for a countercampaign. He was also instrumental in fighting the Charity School movement, designed by authorities to assist German speakers in acculturating to the British-led colony because he regarded the whole affair as an attempt to anglicize the Germans.

The present selection is taken from the first in a series of annual installments in Saur's almanac, entitled "A Dialogue between a Newcomer and a Settler In Pennsylvania." Saur first included the dialogues in 1751, and he continued them until 1757. Designed as instructions that would assist those new to the colony, Saur's dialogues presented an older and wiser settler who offered both spiritual and practical advice to a young and inexperienced newcomer. Like himself at one time, and like many newcomers, in fact, Saur's newcomer left a small rural community in southwestern Germany to find a "comfortable place" to settle down and to lead a "more peaceful life."

from A DIALOGUE BETWEEN A NEWCOMER AND A SETTLER IN PENNSYLVANIA[1]

NEWCOMER: Can I lodge at your place tonight?

SETTLER: Yes! Where are you coming from, and where are you going?

NEWCOMER: Actually, I have come from Germany, but now I am looking around for a comfortable place for myself, where I can live and settle down. I have been told that if one was independent, one should not hurry but first consider well before buying something. In this good country there is supposedly also some bad land, which requires much work but yields little. I also hear that the best lots in the vicinity have long been chosen, and in more remote areas where there are still good places available, it is hard for a foreigner and beginner. I have already been moving around for several weeks, and I have seen many different places and have spoken with many different people.

SETTLER: How do you like it in this country compared to your *Vatterland?*

NEWCOMER: In my country people spoke of the New World, and it is certainly a *New World* to me, for almost everything is completely different than where I lived before.

SETTLER: Why? Is it better or worse?

NEWCOMER: On the one hand it is better, but on the other hand it is worse.

SETTLER: In what way is it better?

NEWCOMER: First of all, I really like that wherever you may go in this country, people are so modest that they offer one a piece of bread and gladly provide a meal and shelter; furthermore, I see that one has been spared large financial duties. There is no need to think about what to pay the landlord; whatever someone builds and plants [if his land is paid for] is his own; one pays neither customs nor tolls or tithes. One does not have to hunt or drudge for the sovereign, nor does one have to hold vigil, do socage service,[2] or pay taxes for the outfitting of the princess. I remember well all the different kinds of taxes one has to pay in the Palatinate, only so that the ruler and his courtiers can direct and exploit their great state. Now I see that the established inhabitants in this country live like noblemen, if not even better than some noblemen in Germany, because here many a person worth 10–20,000 guilders barely pays 5 to 10 guilders in taxes a year and some years nothing at all. And if someone gives one guilder or two for a poor tax, it is merely to provide for the needy or to keep beggars from one's door. And there are many other things I like in this country that I cannot think of right now.

However, there are many things that I don't like at all, and some things appear so completely unfamiliar to me that I cannot get used to them.

SETTLER: Wherever you may go in the whole world, you will always dislike some things and others will seem unfamiliar until you get used to them; a deeply rooted habit is like a tyrant, which is hard to overcome; and it is often nothing but an empty illusion that it would always have to be the way we are used to. And other things may be good in themselves, even though you cannot get accustomed to them at once. But what is it you do not like or what can you not get used to yet? Maybe I can rob you of some of your illusions.

NEWCOMER: First of all, I do not like that people live so far apart and that one has to go so far through the woods to get to the churches. I also do not like that there are so few preachers in this country, and many people either have to send their children to a school far away, or keep them at home and let them learn nothing at all; or, when someone lies on the deathbed, one can scarcely find a preacher who can console that person or preach a funeral sermon. There are so many different religions in this country that sometimes I do not know what to think of

---

1. The original text is from *Der Hoch-Deutsch Americanische Calender, Auf das Jahr Nach der Gnadenreichen Geburt unsers Herrn und Heylandes Jesu Christi 1751 (The High-German American Calendar, For the Year After the Blessed Birth of our Lord and Savior Jesus Christ 1751)* published in Germantown by Christoph Saur. The text has been translated from the original, for a first-time publication in this volume, by Patrick M. Erben. This translation retains the German sentence structure and punctuation, except for instances in which this practice would considerably obscure the meaning of the text. Saur's usage of the word *Vatterland,* an archaic form of the German word, *Vaterland,* has been retained throughout. In direct English translation, the word would be "fatherland," meaning "homeland." All insertions in square brackets are Saur's own.

2. A feudal tenure of land involving the payment of rent or other nonmilitary services to a superior.

that, and I still cannot get used to it. Also, I don't like that some people have so much trouble to keep their cattle together and that someone who falls ill or has some other kind of accident has to go so far to the doctor or the barber [surgeon].[3] I made the strenuous journey across the ocean so that I might improve my situation and establish for myself a more peaceful life than I had before. For that reason, I moved about in this country to choose the best place I could find according to my abilities. While I can still work, I hope to set myself up in order to have some provisions for old age and so that when I can no longer work so hard, I don't need to and may afterwards serve God so that I might be blessed in death.

SETTLER: It is the common course for most human beings to strive first for many temporal goods and think not at all of God's kingdom, or they live in an uncertain hope that heaven may fall to them. When Christ says: First seek God's kingdom and his justice, and all the rest will come to you, most people turn it around and look for a rope to which the enemy can tie them and make themselves a hobble [guy rope][4] so that they have to walk slowly and wearily. Even though Christ teaches: Be on your guard that your hearts are not burdened with gluttonous eating and drinking and cares for nourishment,[5] people often buy more than they can pay off in a long time and load many debts and worries on themselves. And instead of striving forcefully for the heavenly kingdom,[6] they violate the earthly kingdom until they have everything in plenty and abundance and provisions for many years; then, usually follows overly indulgent eating and drinking; and so for many a person death comes before he has begun to strive for the kingdom of God. As the old hymn says: When someone lies in his last misery, he wants to become righteous. One builds this, the other that, but his poor soul he will forget, as long as he lives on earth. And when he is unable to live any longer [becomes

deadly ill], then he starts a great lament and wants to give himself up to God; I am truly afraid that God's grace, which he has always ridiculed, will hardly be with him. But many people die before they have reached their purpose. You said that you desire a more comfortable life and that you would like to leave something to your children and afterwards quietly serve God and die in grace. That is not only your goal, but it is the way of many 1000 people; it would be better if all these people would believe and follow the loving warning of Christ and would not so foolhardily ignore and forfeit the best, as is written of such people: I have bought a field or a plantation, oxen, cows and horses; I don't have time to come, because I have to take care of this errand; I have something else to do; or, I have taken a wife, and, therefore, cannot come.

NEWCOMER: It is true! Christ knew that those invited guests would not taste his Eucharist,[7] and maybe the eternal salvation is meant by that; but how should one act in this country? Circumstances are often that one cannot find a place with the little money one is able to pay.

SETTLER: First of all it remains true what Christ says: First strive after the kingdom of God.[8] Let this be your most important thing; if you do that, you will stay away from heavy debt and foolhardiness, and your heart will say: Hey! do I have to have this or that; is it really necessary? Could it not be something smaller? Or, can I not dispense with it altogether? What really matters, are the needs of the body or food and clothing! And the more you strive for the heavenly kingdom, the less you will need and desire of the earthly kingdom; but if you don't have any sense for that, you may do whatever you wish. I know, however, that the more temporal goods you gather, the bigger your burden and your troubles will be, so that if you want to turn your mind away from these concerns afterwards, you will find one sign after the other that you have built an obstacle for yourself; but if God's grace pulls you away, follow faithfully and everything else will come about.

NEWCOMER: I have heard people say that you could probably have a large estate, but that when you own it,

---

3. All insertions in square brackets are Saur's own.

4. A rope or strap used to fasten together the legs of horses or cows to keep them from straying.

5. Mt. 6.25: Therefore I tell you, do not worry about your life, what you will eat or drink; or about your body, what you will wear. Is not life more important than food, and the body more important than clothes?

6. Mt. 11.12: From the days of John the Baptist until now, the kingdom of heaven has been forcefully advancing, and forceful men lay hold of it.

7. Mt. 22.2–14: The kingdom of heaven is like a king who prepared a wedding banquet for his son. He sent his servants to those who had been invited to the banquet to tell them to come, but they refused to come. . . .

8. Mt. 6.33: But seek first his kingdom and his righteousness, and all these things will be given to you as well.

you must treat it as if you did not own it, and it must not be close to your heart.

SETTLER: It is true, but rare, and the example makes it evident: the crown in France is worth much money, but, for all I care, whoever wants it may take it; I am not opposed to it; and a person who can let something go which he has, as easily as something which he does not have, owns it in the same way as if he did not own it.

NEWCOMER: I think it does not matter whether someone has much or little, he will always find displeasure or worries.

SETTLER: As long as one loves and seeks the world and worldly things, one will find a vexation in all things, whatever it may be; if one converts to God and loves heavenly things, on the other hand, then all things will certainly be to one's benefit.

NEWCOMER: If it would happen to me as it has happened to many people in this country, and I could not pay everything in cash and had to go into debt, would that be a big issue?

SETTLER: As long as you have its value in your estate and you do not impede your neighbor when he needs his money back; or you have to know whether your neighbor is content if the payment is delayed further. For when you borrow something for a certain term and do not pay it back on time, but in turn apply his money for your own benefit, you lied and did not keep your promise; and, at the same time, you effect that not everyone will trust you when you should be in need in the future. And if someone works for you, pay him; but if you cannot, then ask him ahead of time whether he may loan you the amount and for how long; there is a strict law against debts and debts have already kept many a person from living quietly. Even though it is quite common among bad people, it is not praiseworthy that one person has another person's money in his pocket against his will. Both honesty and Godliness do not allow it, which would have to be quite wicked and distinctly different from the sense and teachings of Christ if they did condone it.

NEWCOMER: I have to admit that Christ's teachings are the truth; I cannot imagine that He might have lied; but I have already told you that I do not at all like that people in this country live so far apart and many a person has to go so far to the church that he may, therefore, be kept from the kingdom of God.

SETTLER: In Germany there are churches in almost every village and certainly in every town and people live close to them, but don't be offended if I should ask: What has become of that and what is the good that has risen from it? Are the kings, the princes, the counts, the noblemen, the public officers and aldermen pious, god-fearing, meek, patient, kind, humble, chaste, sober and modest on account of that? Or can you find the virtues of Christ among those students who want to instruct others about these virtues? Or are they virtuous when they become preachers and hold the office of preaching? Or are their wives and children better if they live next to the church? Do the merchants and grocers walk in truth and justice? Or are the citizens, the artisans and apprentices and journeymen or the peasants doing so? Or are the soldiers? Which one of them is striving for the kingdom of God? Which one of them has Christ's spirit and mind? In whom can you discern the fruits of the spirit? Who has the kingdom of God, which is peace and joy in the Holy Ghost? Is there not in all the classes, professions, and trades pride, anger, quarrel, discord, struggle, avarice and voluptuousness in Satan and in the natural life?

NEWCOMER: I did not see what was going on at the royal courts, but I have heard of it; and in my *Vatterland,* the kitchen clerk of the elector[9] supposedly calculated once that an evening meal cost around 2000 guilders. And I have heard that one of the elector's kitchen boys with a narrow conscience threw himself at the electors feet in front of the church door and complained to him about the injustices going on in the kitchen; councilors and other high servants often have someone bring them whole roasts, geese and capons and such from the kitchen and do not pay for anything, and that it was weighing on his conscience like a rock; he had to notify him and could no longer witness the injustice. The heirless elector, however, did nothing about it and said: Just do the same. And everything comes from the sweat and blood of his subjects. Furthermore, a certain widow supposedly desired an answer to her supplication,[10] and she was told there were still well over 2000 supplications that had not been read yet on a heap, and the officer in charge did not know when they would be read and whether they would be read at all. What the government officials are doing must not be talked about in public. The students are frolicking worse than all wild and tame animals. The preachers live

---

9. One of the German princes entitled to elect the Holy Roman Emperor.

10. A written or formal petition.

rather honestly provided one brings them their set tribute alongside their gifts and their extras,[11] and makes one's deepest compliments and reverences. In their wives, sons, and daughters, however, their listeners hardly have a good example, and it seems as if they did not know how to be the heads of their own households. One must not say a word about that; otherwise, the father shall bring a jury trial against you and rob you of all your possessions. And one does well to remain silent about the lawyers, because they may find out and twist your words. The merchants and grocers walk in the truth in such a manner that when one asks: How much do you charge for the ell,[12] the piece, or the pound, one already knows for certain that the first word is a lie, and the second and third are not much better. The buyer also speaks one word and does not stick to it; he says: I won't pay any more, and once again, and then does it anyway. For lying does not count for much with most people. Citizens and artisans have a heavy burden, and some of them have but a small wage; some of them don't have much to do, and so one vies for the other one's bread; the envy among artisans is notorious and some of them go to the tavern or find some company out of anger and discontentment, others for their pleasure; they drink, play with dice or cards, and when the money is wasted, the wife or the servants have to pay for it. The apprentices, when they have worked to exhaustion all week, look forward to Sunday, so they can walk about, drink, dance and gamble; and that is permissible notwithstanding the preacher's railing against it in his sermon. When the peasants curse the authorities for their heavy taxes and on Sundays get intoxicated out of discontentment, they are not blamed for it. The volunteer soldiers are generally [after the beggars] the scum of all bad people, and so what can you ask of them? That's the extent of what I have witnessed in my *Vatterland*. But since so many people have no respect for the word of God and only little for the preacher's words, they probably sleep throughout the entire sermon and among those who are awake, only a few still remember a word after the sermon, unless it is in jest or for ridicule. What do you think should happen if the same people are supposed to walk as far for a sermon as in this country, if they didn't have to

go? Things are already bleak, but what would they be like after this?

SETTLER: Here it is still easier for the people than elsewhere. While some people do not travel for their pleasure, at this occasion they still sometimes hear a word that can serve them as testimony; and I would not want to tell or advise a person who likes to go to church not to go, even if he was 10 miles away. And we ought to thank God when there are still honorable preachers, for the sake of those people who are in need of them; for if there was no preaching among frivolous people, the name of God and Christ would finally be forgotten altogether, and the raw bunch would become all devilish: One would actually do well giving money to a publicly wicked babbler in order to silence him, instead of him abusing the covenant of God, as he hates discipline Ps. 50. and through wicked examples induces the people to sin, and instead have a better one in his place, someone who wants to do his best with good intentions. Therefore, I first and foremostly advise you, my dear Newcomer, to go to the sermon or to church diligently, and don't do it out of boredom; also, do not sleep during it, but beg God that he may enlighten your mind. Be serious about it and pay attention to all words you hear sung, preached or prayed, and ask yourself whether your heart is constituted accordingly. If not, ask God that he may create and give you a different, new mind, a new will, and a new heart; and do not slacken until you have it and until you are assured that you have a desire for all good and a loathing for all evil, until you love God for God's sake and more than everything visible, and until you love your neighbor as yourself for God's sake. Once you are coming to church or to a meeting in a state of unfeigned conversion, all truths will be sweet, lovely, and joyful: And you will be able to see a distinction in what is being preached; whether it is the pure truth or mixed up with the weakness of the human mind. Whether it explains or twists what is right and wrong, and whether it is falsified with human laws based on human selfishness. Whether the preacher is informed by the flesh or by the spirit, which means by God Joh. 6,45 or whether he has taken in human truths. Or whether they have grown in his heart in the manner of regeneration? Whether the preacher is concerned with the honor of God and the salvation of the soul; or whether he is only interested in his stipend so that, on lazy days, he may feed himself by chatting and still would like to be honored. Whether his art of babbling is inborn or whether he has learned it in school, or whether his tongue is being stirred

---

11. The German *accidentien* implies unregulated ("accidental") fees or donations to a government or church official. Obsolete in present-day German.

12. An obsolete measure of length.

by embers from the altar and moved by the Holy Ghost: Isaiah. 6,6–9. Because if you have to accept everything just as it is poured out in front of you, and if you don't know the chaff from the wheat, you will receive poor nourishment for your soul.

NEWCOMER: But what if I will be living so far away from churches that I could not possibly get there? Some people evidently have half a day's journey to church.

SETTLER: If you really have your mind set on a matter, the way won't be too long: I know people who set out the day before in order to get to a meeting on time. However, if the preacher did indeed present such poor things that it was not worth such an effort, go into your chamber or into the forest all by yourself and pour out your whole heart before God, remain before God in silence, and pray for the Holy Ghost, and do not slacken, whether you are idle or at work; and, thus, you will learn to recognize whether it is worth the effort or not.

NEWCOMER: But what if a preacher takes his text from the Bible and preaches on that passage; how could you call that a bad thing?

SETTLER: If he interprets those true words in a false sense: Because there are people who know how to interpret the Bible in such a manner that the listeners are kept from their salvation. I would like to give you a 1000 examples but for this time I only want to tell you a crude example, so you may see how human laws can be made biblical, as if they were God's word.

In Rotterdam, a pious Polish nobleman named Striska was eating lunch at a tavern on a Friday; 2 officers, oriented toward Roman Catholicism, were sitting with him. When they were almost done eating the meat, one officer said to the other: Brother! what are we doing? is not today a fast day? The other one threw his knife on the table quite harshly and said: I'll be d . . . . d;[13] I did not think of that. The pious nobleman said: eat it, because it is better to eat meat on a Friday than having a secret desire for it; it is not God's law but human law. The officer said: Yes, it is God's law; I want to prove it to him with the Bible. Doesn't it say in the 8th Psalm: all sheep and oxen, the wild animals; the fowl under the skies. The fish in the water, and whatsoever is astir in the sea. The nobleman said: But what is

this supposed to prove? He answered: the meat of sheep and oxen is for Monday and Tuesday. The wild animals and fowl are for Wednesday and Thursday. The fish in the water and whatsoever is astir in the sea are for Friday and Saturday. Sunday is the day of the Lord, and then you may eat whatever you want. Striska was thinking: The man is serious and fired up and believes in this error so stubbornly that he may challenge you with the sword and kill you on account of that matter, or even die himself. You have to restrain yourself and with all modesty make him ponder a little. And he said: So we have to eat lamb on Mondays, beef on Tuesdays, venison on Wednesdays, fowl on Thursdays, and fish on Fridays and Saturdays and nothing else if it is indeed one of God's commandments. Now see, my dear *Newcomer,* how anyone can interpret the Bible and twist it according to his own opinion; and it goes the same way with respect to the most important parts of what we call worship. Thus, it is an absolute necessity that you and everyone should ask God with all your heart for the Holy Ghost, who alone leads to all truth. And when you have received the Holy Ghost, the anointing will thereupon teach you sundry things, and whatever it will teach you, will be right. I Joh. 2,27.

NEWCOMER: I have heard people say that one should examine all spirits whether they are from God.

SETTLER: Therefore, it is necessary that one first knows God and his son Jesus and oneself. Only through the true light of God can one know others; how can someone who has been blind all his life distinguish different colors or tell what is black and what is white. And how can someone who has drunk water all his life know what Burgundy, Champagne, Renish, Hungarian or crab apple wine is?

NEWCOMER: While I was traveling through this country, I saw and heard many people talk who did not belong to the three common religions.[14] When I wanted to get advice on where I might find a good place or piece of land, they certainly did say something, but, in their household and with me, they rather wanted to talk of such things as how to find God in your heart, how to renounce the world, and how to reach the heavenly kingdom with all your might. I am not used to such things, because in

---

13. Saur used the expression, "Hol mich der T . . . l" (for "Hol mich der Teufel") at this point, which translates literally as "May the devil get me."

14. "Religions" most certainly refers to Christian denominations. It is unclear whether Germany or Pennsylvania serves as a reference point for the newcomer.

my *Vatterland* and in my religion such a practice is generally disparaged. It is usually only one man, the pastor, who only speaks on the pulpit of such things; otherwise, even at home and in public he speaks very little of such matters, except for when someone lies on his deathbed and when the children are soon to receive the Lord's Supper; except for that, one speaks about the household and about food. Most social circles have an amusing conversation as their pastime: They talk about a good glass of wine, they play cards, dice, or bowling for a while, and such things. In our country, it is shameful to discuss something from the Bible, except for a jest, as one would immediately be considered a Pietist. They are not well liked and people say strange things about them. Maybe the ones with whom I talked were such people.

SETTLER: I can't really say what kind of people they were, as there are simply not many who talk about the kingdom of God in their house; however, there are also not few of those who would like to be better and who have refrained from the crudest and most apparent drinking, dancing, cards and similar games.

NEWCOMER: The people who talk about such strange things in this country are still not all of one opinion; one certainly notices that sometimes one person speaks against another person and one party opposes another party; and everyone believes to know it best.

SETTLER: It partly comes from weakness, as the reasonable ones in all parties and outside of the parties watch out mostly for themselves; they tolerate in others what they cannot improve and wish only the best for all of mankind. When they see that others are committing sins or doing evil, they think: OH LORD! If you did not hold me I would have done it worse, so forgive them and save me. The others, like young soldiers, often think they are the best.

NEWCOMER: I have already heard in Germany and in this country about separatists and pietists. What kind of people are they?

SETTLER: "To separate" comes from Latin and means in German "to part from one another," "to sever," etc. A separatist is a person who was formerly attached to something and has become free from it or has parted from it; it may be from something good or something evil. Thus, Lucifer had been one with God before his fall; and, after he had cut himself off from God's light and love, he was separate from God. Accordingly, Adam was in his

essence one with God before his fall; but he turned his mind away from God, his animalistic nature appeared, and he turned towards that nature and, thus, paid more attention to the serpent's words than to God. As a consequence, he was separated from God to such a degree that it is still a misery for mankind. Thus, many people have again separated themselves from the kingdom of the devil and have turned to God and his kingdom. Thus, John the Baptist separated himself from the entire depraved Jewish society and their old worship, which had long since been rejected by God. Because there was nothing good left to be learned from the scribes and their worn out ceremonies, he listened to the indwelling spirit of God and had a much better opportunity to do so in the desert than among the scribes.

Christ, who had already been listening to the scribes when he was 12 years of age and disputed with them, soon realized that they had no true understanding of the kingdom of God and of the restoration of humankind. Thus, he separated himself from them and stayed with his parents and his carpentry until he was meant to preach; Marc. 6,3. Then, he even separated himself from all people, went to the desert and there withstood all the attempts of Satan to try him and did not yield to any one of these temptations; thus, he was afterwards able to preach openly about everything he had experienced. Had he not persevered in his utter poverty and starvation, and had he taken on an office or service for the sake of the perishable bread, he could not have preached more powerfully than all the scribes could. And, had He enjoyed the kingdoms of the world and their glory, then he would have let the people make him king and he would not have fled from them. And had he been satisfied with suffering through poverty and despising the wealth of the world, and had he trusted that Satan had been completely overcome and that he could cast himself from the pinnacle of the temple so that everyone could see what an eminent preacher had come, in fact, God's son from above, then he would have begun to fly; but, He separated himself from pride and remained humble. It would take much time for me to tell how Paul separated himself from the high priests and obeyed Christ's voice, and how many thousand people separated themselves from the idols and their temples and with their souls converted to the living word. Thus, **Luther** separated from papacy and **Calvin** from the pope and from Lutheranism and **Schwenckfeld** from these three parties and **Meno Simon** from these four and the **Quakers** from these five.[15] And, therefore, a person is a separatist who does not agree with everyone's opinion or who is not part of a group or community, but probably also someone who renounced himself and separated himself from willfulness or willfulness parted from him.

NEWCOMER: What exactly is a Pietist; I have heard of such people in my *Vatterland*.

SETTLER: Just as in Luther's time the high establishment of the papacy was so deeply depraved so that true godliness had become a mockery, likewise, something truly extraordinary happened at the time when Doctor Spener[16] was in Leipzig. Through the brilliant teachings of the blessed Spener numerous students were awakened to a godly life; afterwards, they lived in silence and seclusion and no longer according to the blatantly evil way of life of the students. . . . Later on, when Professor Francke[17] of Halle and other godly men were leading the Colegium Pietatis [conference of Godliness], it happened that when a student was leading a pious or only a righteous life, the wild students contemptuously called him a Pietist. Afterwards, this beautiful name was given to many people as an insult in order to scold or ridicule them. No truly godly person, however, has ever given himself this name, because humility does not allow a person to assume to be pious.

NEWCOMER: I have heard strange things about those people, as for example: they had fed each other pieces of paper and as a result they had become so learned that they no longer respected the preachers. When they were examined by their preachers, they were able to answer all questions in such a manner that the preachers were unable to do anything against them. Then, they supposedly had come together, blown out the lights, and lived ignominiously.

SETTLER: I want to tell you impartially the pure truth about the origin of this myth. When people have been awakened from their sleep of sinfulness either through the mediation of pious preachers and good books or directly through the chastening grace in their heart, they have abandoned their old, vain company and have congregated with their own kind, as in all of nature birds of a feather flock together. Instead of playing cards together as they had done before, some of them kept next to their good books a small chest with pieces of paper, on which were printed fine verses from the Bible and poems that applied to many different states of humankind. And when someone in this company started some vain talk, someone came with the treasure chest and everyone took a small letter from it, which was then read aloud. Generally, it happened that on one of the pieces of paper was a saying that explained the condition of the person's heart. In this manner, idle talk was completely interrupted. And this is the origin of the lie of the paper eating. . . .

NEWCOMER: When I come by again and have some time, I would further like to find out where other parties before and during our time had their origin, why some of them no longer exist, and what kind of lesson one could learn from that. Now, however, I would like to have some good advice on how to act when one intends to go to a new place to settle down.

SETTLER: First of all, you have to know for certain that the piece of land has not already been taken and that it does not have an owner yet. Afterwards, you get a warrant in Philadelphia. If the place has a lot of meadows, do not build so closely to the swamp, because a very wet house causes fever and other illnesses. If you are planting an orchard, look for the best fruit trees; or, graft your young trees and they will bear fruit earlier and better. I would like to teach you grafting, but maybe you already know it or your neighbor can show it to you better than one can describe it or write it down. Only make sure that the inner, sappy bark of the tree and of the branch are straight on top of each other and that they are not being moved again. You may mix lye with cow dung and connect the bark with that or you could stir in linseed oil. Or you could make a plaster out of one part wax, one part turpentine, and one part fat melted together, and if it is too stiff, add more oil or fat. If you buy cattle, buy it from people you know and who tell you the truth about the animals. . . .

---

15. Martin Luther (1483–1546), German Reformation leader and translator of the Bible; John Calvin (1509–64), French-Swiss theologian and Protestant reformer; Caspar Schwenckfeld (1490–1561), Silesian reformer (in 1734, a group of Schwenckfelders emigrated to Pennsylvania); Meno Simon (sometimes Menno Simons, 1492–1559), Frisian theologian and founder of the Mennonites; Quakers or Society of Friends, founded by George Fox (1624–91).

16. Philip Jacob Spener (1635–1705), founder of Lutheran Pietism, believed that only persons inspired by the Holy Ghost could understand the Scriptures. He began the organization of Pietists in local chapters, the "Collegia Pietatis."

17. August Herman Francke (1663–1727), Pietist leader in Halle, Germany.

NEWCOMER: Every day, one hears many complaints among the people that their cattle are running away and that they have to look for them all the time, which is a very wearisome thing. In Germany there are herdsmen for pigs, horses, cows, and sheep, so that one has no trouble with that at all.

SETTLER: It would be much worse than it already is, if people in their wicked natural state did not have any burdens. They would do other things that would be much more harmful for them. We do not read about the rich man that he had any vice other than that he lived every day magnificently and happily. That means he lived comfortably the proud and lustful life of a rich man and attended to the lust of his eyes and did whatever his flesh desired and not what pleased God and profited his neighbor. Therefore, physical afflictions are beneficial for a person if he can endure them with patience. If, however, he becomes impatient, they become a misery for him. It does not go with all people the same way. Some people treat their cattle so sensibly that the animals like to come back home, and there are two kinds of these people. People of the first kind have a natural sense of giving their cattle their due at the right time and govern them reasonably. The other kind are God-loving people: they do not know how to thank God enough for everything and for the cattle he has provided for their subsistence. Thus, they are very compassionate and merciful toward God's creatures. As Solomon says: the righteous person takes pity on his animals, but the heart of the wicked is merciless. Righteous people would rather go without food themselves than their animals; they would rather not have the use and profit of their animals than overburdening or driving them too hard, all out of gratefulness to God for his kindness. They know that he gave and gives them the animals for their need and not for their greed and wantonness, much less for their cruelty. The other kind of people are either unreasonable by nature, or godless, or cruel and merciless. Thus, many poor creatures have to suffer and often do not know where to turn. All creatures have enough sense to know what they like to eat and where the pasture is best, and they are drawn back there. Sometimes it happens, though, that when an evil rascal is looking for his cows on his horse and he finds them, he drives them with his whip so hard that they have to run, which very much hurts the cows, especially if they have to carry their udders full of milk. Or he is walking and really angry, because he had to search so long that he throws rocks and wooden sticks at his cows the whole way home, where he keeps on raging. The next day, the cows run even further away to be safe from their evil driver as long as they can. I know a man who would usually leave a few hours before nightfall, and he would sometimes come home at eleven or twelve midnight with his cows. When he sold the whole place including the cows to another man, the new owner's wife took something from the garden, poured salt water or salt over it, spread bran over it, and, at the same time, she milked the cows as gently as possible. Then, the same cows came home every night, and during the whole year his wife did not have to look for them but once, when she found them with a bull. That was the whole difference. The reason was not to be sought with the animals but with the human beings. Moreover, not only did they save the trouble of searching, but the cows also gave much more milk than before. Now the pasture has certainly become worse at many places due to the amount of inhabitants, but it is because the cattle are being pushed, beaten, and kicked at home that they rather enjoy their freedom far away. . . .[18]

---

18. In the remainder of the dialogue, the Settler gives advice on treating snakebites, baking sourdough bread, and preparing and tanning deer hide.

GOTTLIEB MITTELBERGER (1715–1779?)

Gottlieb Mittelberger joined the large-scale migration to Pennsylvania in 1750, one of the nearly five hundred passengers aboard the ship *Osgood,* aiming to settle in the region that had, according to much of the propaganda spread in Germany about Penn's Woods, become the single place where German speakers were welcome and would thrive and prosper. But Mittelberger ended up returning home because the conditions were quite unlike anything he had expected. He disliked the Pennsylvanians' disregard for people of rank and status, their lack of earnestness in religion, and the relativity of mannered behavior in Pennsylvania's interior. After he returned, he published a book on his experiences, *Journey to Pennsylvania,* meant to deter Germans from coming over. Describing the hazards of the ocean passage and the fate of German immigrants in Pennsylvania, Mittelberger's account became one of the most widely known antipromotional accounts available in southwestern Germany at the time.

Mittelberger was born in the Duchy of Württemberg (not Enzweihingen, as he claimed) in 1715. His family later moved to Enzweihingen, where Mittelberger became a schoolteacher and organist at the parish church. He married Elisabetha Theodor in 1742, but of their four children, only one survived infancy. When in 1749 Mittelberger's affair with the daughter of the local pastor was discovered, the Lutheran authorities immediately terminated his position as a teacher. Facing social ostracism and lacking a source of income, Mittelberger accepted an offer to travel to Philadelphia in order to supervise the moving and setting up of a church organ in a local Lutheran church. Mittelberger seized this opportunity to escape his social predicament. After Mittelberger landed in Philadelphia in October 1750, he assembled the new organ and accepted a post as organist and teacher at the Lutheran parish in New Providence. He supplemented his income by working privately as a private tutor and arranging for additional organs to reach Pennsylvania.

Mittelberger would not be welcome long in the community, however. In July 1753, he was discovered engaging in what Heinrich Melchior Mühlenberg, renowned pastor of the Providence church, called lewd conduct against a woman in the school building. The indiscretion brought his incipient career to an abrupt end and led to his return to Germany in 1754. Mittelberger connected again with his wife and child in Germany and moved the family to Ludwigsburg, where he became a city employee. After the death of his wife, he remarried in 1769 and died in obscurity some time before or during 1779.

It is difficult to determine the extent to which Mittelberger's dislike of his Pennsylvania experiences was influenced by his disgrace in the German community, but the information he reports does indeed reflect an honest characterization of life in the colony that contradicts conventional propaganda about Pennsylvania. When he returned to Germany and began speaking of his unhappiness with colonial life, Mittelberger found an eager patron in the duke of Württemberg, who was desperately struggling to diminish, if not stop altogether, the stream of emigrants leaving his territory. The duke encouraged Mittelberger to publish his account, so as to warn prospective emigrants of the perils awaiting them at sea and of the treatment they would receive as indentured servants. Mittelberger completed his *Journey to Pennsylvania* in 1755, and after some correction and annotation by an unknown editor, the little book was published in Stuttgart in 1756.

from JOURNEY TO PENNSYLVANIA[1]

[Preface][2]

Esteemed Reader,

The value of this little book does not lie in its elegant and elaborate composition, but in its remarkable contents. The former should not be expected from the author who is not a scholar. But his narrative, which, by the way, may be easily read, serves as testimony of his sincerity and, in addition, of the fact that he writes for the most part as an eyewitness. Inasmuch as he did not aim strictly to narrate all subjects of the same kind consecutively, his work has some variety—which is, perhaps, more agreeable to the reader. For the most part the author's artless and unornamented account of the habits of various Europeans and of the American savages, of their laws, their customs, their domestic and religious institutions, is new, and of such a nature that the reflective reader will be delighted to perceive in it a peculiar mixture of the European and the American environment, of the customs of the Old and the New World, and of a people living partly in civilization and partly in a state of natural freedom.

---

1. Mittelberger's book was originally published in Stuttgart in 1756 under the title, which reads in English, *Gottlieb Mittelberger's Journey to Pennsylvania in the Year 1750 and Return to Germany in the Year 1754, Containing not only a description of the country in its present condition, but also a detailed account of the sad and unfortunate circumstances of most of the Germans who have moved to that country or are about to do so.* The volume included Mittelberger's long dedicatory notice: "To the Most Illustrious Prince and Lord Carl, Duke of Württemberg and Teck, Count of Mömpelgard, Lord of Heidenshein, and Justingen &c. Knight of the Golden Fleece, and Field Marshal of the Illustrious Swabian Circle &c. To my most gracious Prince and Lord I dedicate in the most profound submission in its present revised form the humble publications parts of which Your Illustrious Princely Highness graciously deigned to peruse in manuscript, and I commend myself to a continuance of your high princely grace and favor." The text is from *Gottlieb Mittelberger's Journey to Pennsylvania,* trans. and ed. Oscar Handlin and John Clive. Cambridge, Mass.: Harvard University Press, 1960.

2. The preface was by the unknown editor of Mittelberger's *Journey.* All notes added by this eighteenth-century editor are marked [Ed.]. The editor not only elaborated but at times even commented on Mittelberger's narrative.

The information the book contains about the kingdom of nature—about animals, plants, etc.—should attract the attention of the reader no less, inasmuch as the wise Creator has in this land placed an entirely new arena to display his miracles before the eyes of rational men.

But the most important part of this publication undoubtedly lies in the account of the fate that awaits most of those unfortunate people who leave Germany in order to seek an uncertain fortune in the New World; and who find instead, if not death, surely oppressive servitude and slavery.

Nothing has been changed in the author's work, except that some notes taken from other writers of repute and confirming the author's narrative have been added to the text; and the spelling has been made to conform to that in general use. The little work is hereby warmly recommended to the reader.

from PART I • The Crossing to Pennsylvania

In the month of May 1750 I left my birthplace Enzweihingen in the district of Vaihingen for Heilbronn, where an organ was waiting for me, ready to be shipped to Pennsylvania. With this organ I took the usual route down the Neckar and the Rhine to Rotterdam in Holland. From Rotterdam I sailed with a transport of approximately 400 souls—Württemberger, Durlacher, Palatines, and Swiss, etc.—across the North Sea to Cowes in England; and, after a nine-day stopover there, across the Atlantic, until at last on the tenth of October 1750 I landed in Philadelphia, the capital of Pennsylvania.[3]

The trip from home to Rotterdam including the sojourn there, took fully seven weeks because of the many delays encountered both in going down the Rhine and in Holland. Without these one could have completed the journey more quickly. The voyage from Rotterdam to Philadelphia took fifteen weeks. I spent nearly four years in America and, as my testimonials show, held the post of organist and school-teacher in the German St. Augustine's Church in Providence. Besides that I gave private

---

3. Mittelberger inconsistently used "new style" and "old style" dating. This date is "new style." In Philadelphia, the arrival of the ship was dated September 29, according to the "old-style" calendar still in effect in the colonies.

music and German lessons in the house of Captain von Diemer,[4] as attested by the following certificate:

> Whereas the bearer Mr. Mittelberger, music master, has resolved to return from this province to his native land, which is in the Duchy of Württemberg in Germany, I have at his request granted these lines to certify that the above named Mr. Mittelberger has behaved himself honestly, diligently, and faithfully in the offices of schoolmaster and organist during the space of three years in the Township of New-Providence, County of Philadelphia and Province of Pennsylvania, &c. So that I and all his employers were entirely satisfied, and would willingly have him to remain with us. But as his call obliges him to proceed on his long journey, we would recommend the said Mr. Mittelberger to all persons of dignity and character; and beg their assistance, so that he may pass and repass until he arrives at his respective abode; which may God grant, and may the benediction of Heaven accompany him in his journey. *Deus benedicat susceptis ejus ferat eum ad amicos suos maxima prosperitate.*[5] *Dabam, Providentiae Philadelphiae*
>
> *Comitatu Pennsylvania in America,*
> *die 25. Apr. A. D. 1754*[6]
>
> > *John Diemer, Cap.*
> > *Sam. Kennedy, M.D.*
> > *Henry Pawling, Esqr.*
>
> *T.*[7]
> *Henry Marsteller*
> *Matthias Gmelin.*

I made careful inquiries into the conditions of the country. And what I am going to describe in this book I partly found out for myself, and partly heard from reliable people who know what they were talking about. I should no doubt have been able to report and to recount more if, at the time, I had ever considered publishing anything about Pennsylvania. But I always thought myself far too feeble to do that sort of thing. It was only the misfortunes I encountered on my voyage to and fro (for in the country itself things went well with me, because I was able to earn a living right away, and could easily support myself well)

and the nasty tricks the Newlanders[8] wanted to play on me and my family, as I shall relate further on, that first gave me the idea not to keep what I knew to myself.

But what really drove me to write this little book was the sad and miserable condition of those traveling from Germany to the New World, and the irresponsible and merciless proceedings of the Dutch traders in human beings and their man-stealing emissaries—I mean the so-called Newlanders. For these at one and the same time steal German people under all sorts of fine pretexts, and deliver them into the hands of the great Dutch traffickers in human souls. From this business the latter make a huge profit, and the Newlanders a smaller one.

This, as I say, is the principal reason for my publishing this little book. In fact, I had to take a solemn oath to write it. For before I left Pennsylvania, when it became known that I wanted to return to Württemberg, numerous Württemberger, Durlacher, and Palatines (a great many of whom live there and spend their days moaning and groaning about ever having left their native country) begged me with tears and uplifted hands, and even in the name of God, to publicize their misery and sorrow in Germany. So that not only the common people but even princes and lords might be able to hear about what happened to them; and so that innocent souls would no longer leave their native country, persuaded to do so by the Newlanders, and dragged by them into a similar kind of slavery. And so I vowed to the great God, and promised those people to reveal the entire truth about it to people in Germany, according to the best of my knowledge and ability.

I hope, therefore, that my dear countrymen and indeed all of Germany will be no less concerned to get news and factual information about how far it is to Pennsylvania and how long it takes to get there; about what the journey costs, and what discomforts and dangers one has to undergo in the bargain; about what happens when the people arrive in America well or ill; about how they are sold and scattered around; and, finally, about what conditions in general are like. I conceal neither good nor bad aspects; and thus I hope that the world, liking an honest man, will look on me as impartial and truthful. Once people have read all this I have no doubt that those who might still have some desire to go over there will stay at home and

---

4. No information is available about Diemer or the other signers of the following document.

5. May God bless his undertaking and bring him to his friends with the greatest dispatch.

6. Given at Providence in the County of Philadelphia, Pennsylvania in America on April 25, 1754.

7. *Testes* (Witnesses).

8. Newlanders (*Neuländer*) were German immigrants already living in Pennsylvania, who on trips to Germany worked as agents for land speculators. They attracted prospective German immigrants with hyperbolic tales of abundance in Pennsylvania.

will carefully avoid this long and difficult voyage and the misfortunes connected with it; since such a journey will mean for most who undertake it the loss of all they possess, of freedom and peace, and for some the loss of their very lives and, I can even go so far as to say, of the salvation of their souls.

To travel from Durlach or Württemberg as far as Holland and the open sea one must reckon on a trip of 200 hours. From there across the sea to England as far as Cowes, where all ships drop anchor before they finally begin the great ocean crossing, another 150 hours. From there over 100 hours until one completely loses sight of England. Then across the Atlantic, that is from land to land, as the sailors put it, 1,200 hours. Finally from the first sight of land in Pennsylvania to Philadelphia, over 40 hours. Altogether such a journey adds up to 1,700 hours or 1,700 French miles.

This journey lasts from the beginning of May until the end of October, that is, a whole six months, and involves such hardships that it is really impossible for any description to do justice to them. The reason for this is that the Rhine boats must pass by thirty-six different customs houses between Heilbronn and Holland. At each of these all the ships must be examined, and these examinations take place at the convenience of the customs officials. Meanwhile, the ships with the people in them are held up for a long time. This involves a great deal of expense for the passengers; and it also means that the trip down the Rhine alone takes from four to six weeks.

When the ships with their passengers arrive in Holland they are there held up once again for from five to six weeks. Because everything is very expensive in Holland the poor people must spend nearly all they own during this period. In addition various sad accidents are likely to occur here. I have, for instance, seen with my own eyes two of the children of a man trying to board ship near Rotterdam meet sudden death by drowning.

In Rotterdam, and to some extent also in Amsterdam, the people are packed into the big boats as closely as herring, so to speak. The bedstead of one person is hardly two feet across and six feet long, since many of the boats carry from four to six hundred passengers, not counting the immense amount of equipment, tools, provisions, barrels of fresh water, and other things that also occupy a great deal of space.

Because of contrary winds it sometimes takes the boats from two to four weeks to make the trip from Holland to Cowes. But, given favorable winds, that voyage can be completed in eight days or less. On arrival everything is examined once more and customs duties paid. It can happen that ships have to ride at anchor there from eight to fourteen days, or until they have taken on full cargoes. During this time everyone has to spend his last remaining money and to consume the provisions that he meant to save for the ocean voyage, so that most people must suffer tremendous hunger and want at sea where they really feel the greatest need. Many thus already begin their sufferings on the voyage between Holland and England.

When the ships have weighed anchor for the last time, usually off Cowes in Old England, then both the long sea voyage and misery begin in earnest. For from there the ships often take eight, nine, ten, or twelve weeks sailing to Philadelphia, if the wind is unfavorable. But even given the most favorable winds, the voyage takes seven weeks.

During the journey the ship is full of pitiful signs of distress—smells, fumes, horrors, vomiting, various kinds of sea sickness, fever, dysentery, headaches, heat, constipation, boils, scurvy, cancer, mouth-rot, and similar afflictions, all of them caused by the age and the highly-salted state of the food, especially of the meat, as well as by the very bad and filthy water, which brings about the miserable destruction and death of many. Add to all that shortage of food, hunger, thirst, frost, heat, dampness, fear, misery, vexation, and lamentation as well as other troubles. Thus, for example, there are so many lice, especially on the sick people, that they have to be scraped off the bodies. All this misery reaches its climax when in addition to everything else one must also suffer through two to three days and nights of storm, with everyone convinced that the ship with all aboard is bound to sink. In such misery all the people on board pray and cry pitifully together.

In the course of such a storm the sea begins to surge and rage so that the waves often seem to rise up like high mountains, sometimes sweeping over the ship; and one thinks that he is going to sink along with the ship. All the while the ship, tossed by storm and waves, moves constantly from one side to the other, so that nobody aboard can either walk, sit, or lie down and the tightly packed people on their cots, the sick as well as the healthy, are thrown every which way. One can easily imagine that these hardships necessarily affect many people so severely that they cannot survive them.

I myself was afflicted by severe illness at sea, and know very well how I felt. These people in their misery are many times very much in want of solace, and I often entertained and comforted them with singing, praying, and encouragement. Also, when possible, and when wind and waves permitted it, I held daily prayer meetings with them on deck, and, since we had no ordained clergyman on board, was forced to administer baptism to five children. I also held services, including a sermon, every Sunday, and when the dead were buried at sea, commended them and our souls to the mercy of God.

Among those who are in good health impatience sometimes grows so great and bitter that one person begins to curse the other, or himself and the day of his birth, and people sometimes come close to murdering one another. Misery and malice are readily associated, so that people begin to cheat and steal from one another. And then one always blames the other for having undertaken the voyage. Often the children cry out against their parents, husbands against wives and wives against husbands, brothers against their sisters, friends and acquaintances against one another.

But most of all they cry out against the thieves of human beings! Many groan and exclaim: "Oh! If only I were back at home, even lying in my pig-sty!" Or they call out: "Ah, dear God, if I only once again had a piece of good bread or a good fresh drop of water." Many people whimper, sigh, and cry out pitifully for home. Most of them become homesick at the thought that many hundreds of people must necessarily perish, die, and be thrown into the ocean in such misery. And this in turn makes their families, or those who were responsible for their undertaking the journey, often-times fall almost into despair—so that it soon becomes practically impossible to rouse them from their depression. In a word, groaning, crying, and lamentation go on aboard day and night; so that even the hearts of the most hardened, hearing all this, begin to bleed.

One can scarcely conceive what happens at sea to women in childbirth and to their innocent offspring. Very few escape with their lives; and mother and child, as soon as they have died, are thrown into the water. On board our ship, on a day on which we had a great storm, a woman about to give birth and unable to deliver under the circumstances, was pushed through one of the portholes into the sea because her corpse was far back in the stern and could not be brought forward to the deck.

Children between the ages of one and seven seldom survive the sea voyage; and parents must often watch their off-spring suffer miserably, die, and be thrown into the ocean, from want, hunger, thirst, and the like. I myself, alas, saw such a pitiful fate overtake thirty-two children on board our vessel, all of whom were finally thrown into the sea. Their parents grieve all the more, since their children do not find repose in the earth, but are devoured by the predatory fish of the ocean. It is also worth noting that children who have not had either measles or smallpox usually get them on board the ship and for the most part perish as a result.

On one of these voyages a father often becomes infected by his wife and children, or a mother by her small children, or even both parents by their children, or sometimes whole families one by the other, so that many times numerous corpses lie on the cots next to those who are still alive, especially when contagious diseases rage on board.

Many other accidents also occur on these ships, especially falls in which people become totally crippled and can never be completely made whole again. Many also tumble into the sea.

It is not surprising that many passengers fall ill, because in addition to all the other troubles and miseries, warm food is served only three times a week, and at that is very bad, very small in quantity, and so dirty as to be hardly palatable at all. And the water distributed in these ships is often very black, thick with dirt, and full of worms. Even when very thirsty, one is almost unable to drink it without loathing. It is certainly true that at sea one would often spend a great deal of money just for one good piece of bread, or one good drink of water—not even to speak of a good glass of wine—if one could only obtain them. I have, alas, had to experience that myself. For toward the end of the voyage we had to eat the ship's biscuit, which had already been spoiled for a long time, even though in no single piece was there more than the size of a thaler that was not full of red worms and spiders' nests. True, great hunger and thirst teach one to eat and drink everything—but many must forfeit their lives in the process. It is impossible to drink sea water, since it is salty and bitter as gall. If this were not the case, one could undertake such an ocean voyage with far less expense and without so many hardships.

When at last after the long and difficult voyage the ships finally approach land, when one gets to see the headlands for the sight of which the people on board had longed so passionately, then everyone crawls from below to the deck, in order to look at the land from afar. And people cry for joy, pray, and sing praises and thanks to God. The glimpse of land revives the passengers, especially those who are half-dead of illness. Their spirits, however weak they had become, leap up, triumph, and rejoice within them. Such people are now willing to bear all ills patiently, if only they can disembark soon and step on land. But, alas, alas!

When the ships finally arrive in Philadelphia after the long voyage only those are let off who can pay their sea freight or can give good security. The others, who lack the money to pay, have to remain on board until they are purchased and until their purchasers can thus pry them loose from the ship. In this whole process the sick are the worst off, for the healthy are preferred and are more readily paid for. The miserable people who are ill must often still remain at sea and in sight of the city for another two or three weeks—which in many cases means death. Yet many of them, were they able to pay their debts and to leave the ships at once, might escape with their lives.

Before I begin to describe how this commerce in human beings takes place I must report what the voyage to Philadelphia or Pennsylvania costs. Any one older than ten years has to pay £10, or 60 florins, for the passage from Rotterdam to Philadelphia. Children between five and ten pay half fare, that is to say £5, or 30 florins.[9] All children under the age of five get free passage. In return the passengers are transported across the ocean; and as long as they are at sea, they get their board, however bad it is (as I reported above).

All this covers only the sea voyage; the cost of land transportation from home to Rotterdam, including the Rhine passage, comes to at least 40 florins no matter how economically one tries to live on the way. This does not include the expenses of any extraordinary contingencies. I can assure readers of this much—that many travelers on the journey from their homes to Philadelphia spent 200 florins, even with all possible thrift.

This is how the commerce in human beings on board ship takes place. Every day Englishmen, Dutchmen, and High Germans come from Philadelphia and other places, some of them very far away, sometime twenty or thirty or forty hours' journey, and go on board the newly arrived vessel that has brought people from Europe and offers them for sale. From among the healthy they pick out those suitable for the purposes for which they require them. Then they negotiate with them as to the length of the period for which they will go into service in order to pay off their passage, the whole amount of which they generally still owe. When an agreement has been reached, adult persons by written contract bind themselves to serve for three, four, five, or six years, according to their health and

age. The very young, between the ages of ten and fifteen, have to serve until they are twenty-one, however.

Many parents in order to pay their fares in this way and get off the ship must barter and sell their children as if they were cattle. Since the fathers and mothers often do not know where or to what masters their children are to be sent, it frequently happens that after leaving the vessel, parents and children do not see each other for years on end, or even for the rest of their lives.

People who arrive without the funds to pay their way and who have children under the age of five, cannot settle their debts by selling them. They must give away these children for nothing to be brought up by strangers; and in return these children must stay in service until they are twenty-one years old. Children between five and ten who owe half-fare, that is, thirty florins, must also go into service in return until they are twenty-one years old, and can neither set free their parents nor take their debts upon themselves. On the other hand, the sale of children older than ten can help to settle a part of their parents' passage charges.

A wife must be responsible for her sick husband and a husband for his sick wife, and pay his or her fare respectively, and must thus serve five to six years not only for herself or himself, but also for the spouse, as the case may be. If both should be ill on arrival, then such persons are brought directly from the ship into a hospital, but not until it is clear that no purchaser for them is to be found. As soon as they have recovered, they must serve to pay off their fare, unless they have the means immediately to discharge the debt.

It often happens that whole families—husband, wife, and children—being sold to different purchasers, become separated, especially when they cannot pay any part of the passage money. When either the husband or the wife has died at sea, having come more than halfway, then the surviving spouse must pay not only his or her fare, but must also pay for or serve out the fare of the deceased.

When both parents have died at sea, having come more than halfway, then their children, especially when they are still young and have nothing to pawn or cannot pay, must be responsible for their own fares as well as those of their parents, and must serve until they are twenty-one years old. Once free of service, they receive a suit of clothing as a parting gift, and if it has been so stipulated the men get a horse and the women a cow.

When a servant in this country has the opportunity to get married he has to pay £5 to £6, that is, 30 to 36 florins

---

9. A gold or silver coin valid at the time in Europe. A guilder.

for every year that he would still have had to serve. But many who must purchase and pay for their brides in this manner come to regret their purchases later. They would just as soon surrender their damnably expensive wares again and lose their money into the bargain.

No one in this country can run away from a master who has treated him harshly and get far. For there are regulations and laws that ensure that runaways are certainly and quickly recaptured. Those who arrest or return a fugitive get a good reward. For every day that someone who runs away is absent from his master he must as a punishment do service an extra week, for every week an extra month, and for every month a half year. But if the master does not want to take back the recaptured runaway, he is entitled to sell him to someone else for the period of as many years as he would still have had to serve.

Occupations vary, but work is strenuous in this new land; and many who have just come into the country at an advanced age must labor hard for their bread until they die. I will not even speak of the young people. Most jobs involve cutting timber, felling oak trees, and levelling, or as one says there, clearing, great tracts of forest, roots and all. Such forest land, having been cleared in this way, is then laid out in fields and meadows. From the best wood that has been felled people construct railings or fences around the new fields. Inside these, all meadows, all lawns, gardens, and orchards, and all arable land are surrounded and enclosed by thickly cut wood planks set in zigzag fashion one above the other. And thus cattle, horses, and sheep are confined to pasture land.

Our Europeans who have been purchased must work hard all the time. For new fields are constantly being laid out; and thus they learn from experience that oak tree stumps are just as hard in America as they are in Germany. In these hot regions there is particularly fulfilled in them that with which the Lord God afflicted man in the first book of Moses, on account of his sin and disobedience, namely: "Thou shalt eat thy bread in the sweat of thy brow." Thus let him who wants to earn his piece of bread honestly and in a Christian manner and who can only do this by manual labor in his native country stay *there* rather than come to America.

For, in the first place, things are no better in Pennsylvania. However hard one may have had to work in his native land, conditions are bound to be equally tough or even tougher in the new country. Furthermore the emigrant has to undertake the arduous voyage, which means not only that he must suffer more misery for half a year

than he would have to suffer doing the hardest labor, but also that he must spend approximately two hundred florins which no one will refund to him. If he has that much money, he loses it; if he does not have it, he must work off his debt as a slave or as a miserable servant. So let people stay in their own country and earn their keep honestly for themselves and their families. Furthermore, I want to say that those people who may let themselves be talked into something and seduced into the voyage by the thieves of human beings are the biggest fools if they really believe that in America or Pennsylvania roasted pigeons are going to fly into their mouths without their having to work for them.

How sad and miserable is the fate of so many thousand German families who lost all the money they ever owned in the course of the long and difficult voyage, many of whom perished wretchedly and had to be buried at sea and who, once they have arrived in the new country, saw their old and young separated and sold away into places far removed one from the other! The saddest aspect of all this is that in most instances parents must give away their young children getting nothing in return. For such children are destined never to see or recognize parents, brothers, and sisters again, and, after they have been sold to strangers, are not brought up in any sort of Christian faith.

In Pennsylvania there exist so many varieties of doctrines and sects that it is impossible to name them all. Many people do not reveal their own particular beliefs to anyone. Furthermore there are many hundreds of adults who not only are unbaptized, but who do not even want baptism. Many others pay no attention to the Sacraments and to the Holy Bible, or even to God and His Word. Some do not even believe in the existence of a true God or Devil, Heaven or Hell, Salvation or Damnation, the Resurrection of the Dead, the Last Judgment and Eternal Life, but think that everything visible is of merely natural origin. For in Pennsylvania not only is everyone allowed to believe what he wishes; he is also at liberty to express these beliefs publicly and freely.

Thus when young people not raised in the fundamentals of religion must go into service for many years with such freethinkers and unbelievers and are not permitted by these people to attend any church or school, especially when they live far away from them, then such innocent souls do not reach a true knowledge of the Divine and are brought up like heathen or Indians.

The ocean voyage is sometimes dangerous for those people who bring money and effects with them from home, because at sea much is often spoiled by inrushing water. And sometimes they are robbed on board by dishonest people. Thus such once-wealthy folk are to have really unhappy experiences. . . .

from PART II • DESCRIPTION OF THE PROVINCE OF PENNSYLVANIA

There are many sugar trees[10] in this country, as thick and tall as oaks. In the spring, when they are in full sap, it is possible to tap the syrup. I tried this myself, and in March, when the trees began to flow, I bored a hole at the bottom of one through the bark and inserted a small tube made from a quill through which the syrup began to flow, just as when one is purifying brandy. Within a quarter of an hour I had a full glass of sugar-water. The people who collect that kind of syrup fill a kettle with it, and let the water boil till thick. When it cools off, it becomes like a kind of thick honey. Sugar trees are usually found in forests near brooks, and grow wild.

Many beautiful tulip trees[11] grow there. During the month of May when they are in blossom, they bear many flowers, colored a blazing yellow and red; and as natural as those grown from bulbs. The trees are as thick and tall as big cherry trees. I have observed yet another sort of tulip trees with their blooms. These are planted in gardens, but are no larger than dwarfed fruit trees. They do not bloom until August and are colored a blazing white and red. No blossoms appear on the first and large kind of tulip tree for a period of twenty or more years.

Many other kinds and species of trees, flowers, and herbs, as well as of grain, are to be found in America. Among others, for example, there is the daisy, so common and for that reason so little esteemed at home. But in Pennsylvania it is as rare as the most beautiful and rarest flowers can be in Europe. For they plant it as a rare flower in their gardens. The juniper shrub is equally rare there, being held in higher esteem than rosemary with us. And juniper berries are sold for higher prices than peppercorns. Juniper shrubs are also cultivated in gardens. All other European flowers and shrubs are equally rare. So,

what is of little value in Germany is very expensive and rare in America. On the other hand, what is not valued highly there is valuable in Germany. The Germans who have emigrated to America mourn after the good things they have lost by doing so, especially the Württemberger and the Rhinelander who miss the noble juice of the grape.

In all of Pennsylvania not a single meadow-saffron or "timeless flower," so-called, is to be seen in autumn time in the gardens and meadows. Wood grows quickly in the province; and it is much taller, though not as durable, as it is at home. This is a matter for great surprise, especially since the forests are very dense and consist of such beautiful, smooth, thick, and tall trees. Many kinds of trees grow there, mostly oaks that, however, are not as fruitful as those in Germany. Then there are also beech trees, but not many. One rarely sees birches. But I did see some birch trees that were as tall and as thick as a sturdy oak tree.

I have already mentioned the poplars. Their wood is soft, and it looks as white as snow inside. There are many of them. Walnut trees are indescribably plentiful. Their beautiful wood, hard and the color of brown coffee, is both precious and useful. All sorts of fine and beautiful household furniture are made from it. When it has been cut, much of it is sent overseas to Holland, England, Ireland, and similar places, where it fetches a good price. These walnut trees bear nuts every year. They are the size of a medium-sized apple. A great deal of oil is made from them. Their bark and leaves are similar to those of our large nut trees.

One finds few German or large walnut trees planted there as yet. In the forests there are few hazelnut shrubs. But on the other hand, there is a great mass of chestnut trees. There are also many hickory nuts, larger than hazel nuts, but not highly valued. One does not see many Indian or wild cherry trees. I myself have gathered and eaten Indian cherries. They are, however, not as good as the European cherries. There are no thorn and sloe hedges in the Pennsylvania forests, and no hedge berries or the like.

Beautiful and excellent cedar trees are the greatest ornament of the forests. They grow mostly in the high mountains. Their wood has a strong smell, is as light as foam, and is especially valuable for the construction of organ pipes. For organ pipes made of cedar wood have a far finer and purer tone than those made of tin. I saw enough evidence of this fact. All houses in Philadelphia are roofed with shingles made of cedar wood. Pelted by

---

10. This species of tree has been described under the name of maple in the *History and Transactions of the French Colonies in North America* (p. 213). De Dièreville calls them wild fig trees. [Ed.]

11. The French in Louisiana call these tulip trees *Tulipier,* a species of laurel tree. See the book quoted above, p. 334. [Ed.]

heavy rain, this wooden roof sounds like one made of copper or brass.

In springtime you do not see many May bugs in this country. But every five years there appears a horrible army of vermin called locusts, or *lockis*.[12] They are slightly bigger than May bugs and can do great damage in the fields and the forests. One does not see red and white snails here. And frogs make a totally different sound. They don't quack; they yelp. And this yelping begins as early as March.

American birds are quite different from those in Europe. Only ravens, swallows, and little hedge sparrows are exactly like European birds. American birds are very wonderful. It is impossible to overpraise their beautiful colors and their lovely songs. First of all, there are yellow birds with black wings; secondly, red birds with black wings; thirdly, completely yellow birds; fourthly, starlings, bigger than ours, blue all over with red wings; fifthly, brilliantly red ones with plumes on their heads; sixthly, entirely blue ones; seventhly, white ones with black wings; eighthly, multi-colored ones; ninthly, grass-green ones, with red heads; tenthly, there is a pied species colored black and white. These birds can imitate the song and the whistling of all other birds; within a half-hour such a bird can imitate thirty birds one after the other.

There is also a kind of bird who during the summer calls very clearly all day long: "Get you gone. Get you gone." Another kind, heard mainly at night, calls: "Whip-poor-Will. Whip-poor-Will"; and is known by that name. In Pennsylvania one doesn't find storks, magpies, cuckoos, larks, yellow-hammers, nightingales, quail, thistle-birds, goldfinches, canaries, blackbirds, tomtits, robin-redbreasts, redwings, and sparrows. It is possible that some Pennsylvanian birds bear some resemblance to the birds I just mentioned. But they are not completely similar, differing either in size, color, song, or something else. For instance, it is conceivable that one might take for a quail the Pennsylvanian bird who cries "Get you gone!" in almost the same cadence in which our quails call. But he has one thing our quail does not have, a little tail.

The most marvelous bird of all, not only in Pennsylvania but perhaps in the entire world, is a little bird rarely to be seen. This little bird is not even the size of a May bug. It is no bigger than a gold-crested wren. It glitters

like gold, and sometimes it appears to be green, blue, and red. Its beak is a little long, and sharp as a needle; its feet are like very fine wire. It sips nothing but honey out of flowers, and that is why it is known as the sugar-bird.[13] It

---

13. Father Charlevoix describes the bird under the name of fly bird, and demonstrates that it is even more beautiful than the hummingbird. See the *History and Transactions of the French Colonies in North America* (published by Mezler), p. 248. But let us hear what yet another author has to say about this rare bird. This is M. de Dièreville in his *Voyage to Acadia,* which may be found in the Collection of Voyages published in Göttingen. On p. 237 he writes as follows:

Let us now discuss small birds, whose eggs do not stand in danger of pilfering since they are no bigger than hempseed. These are the eggs belonging to the hummingbirds or fly birds, the most beautiful birds in the whole world, with colors so brilliant that it seems as if certain portions—and especially the males under the throat—emit flashes of fire. It is impossible to imagine anything more varied and at the same time more brilliant than these colors. But these birds are only to be seen at that time of the year when flowers are in season. For like the bees they fly from one flower to the next, in order to sip the sweet nectar from the pale as well as the reddish ones.

They carry out all these different movements with the utmost speed; no other bird resembles them in this. And one can hardly see them as they whir through the air. They show the same nimbleness in everything they do. They do not, for example, land on the flowers in order to suck out the sweet nectar hidden in their delicate tubes. All they do is flap their wings around the flower incessantly and with such swiftness that it is impossible to describe it. The way in which nature, that wise artificer, formed the beak and tongue of these small birds is truly admirable. The beak, black and thin, and pointed almost perfectly straight, is about a finger's breadth in length; and the delicate, split tongue is perhaps twice as long. In inserting this into a flower and moving it constantly, they fill it with the sweet nectar contained in each calyx. This juice is subsequently brought to their little stomachs by means of a force peculiar to the tongue. It constitutes their sole nourishment.

They have a light grey [sic.] belly, a silver green back, and a black tail shot through with white. Their black wings and feet are perfectly proportioned to their small body, which is not thicker than the tip of a child's finger.

And this same bird is described in the following manner in the *Description of New Scotland* (8 vols., Frankfurt, 1750, p. 174):

---

12. This creature seems to be a species of grasshopper. Perhaps the word *Lockis* is derived from *Locusta*. [Ed.]

builds its nest in some such place as the flower pots in a garden. And though the nest is no bigger than a cupping glass, there are generally four or five young in it. This bird moves its wings incredibly quickly, and makes a loud hissing sound with them. When these birds are not in flight, one can hear them singing most gracefully and prettily, if one is lucky enough to be quite close to them. I won't say how much great people are sometimes willing to pay for these birds. But they do not live long, as it is impossible to give them the food they require.

In Pennsylvania masses of fish may be caught every spring in the Delaware and Schuylkill rivers. And lots of wild pigeons can be shot twice a year, that is, in spring when they migrate north, and late in the fall when they return to migrate south.[14] The fish ascend from the sea at their proper seasons; and those not caught return to sea again toward the end of May. These fish are one ell in length, and nearly one half-ell in breadth. Often so many are caught that some people salt a whole barrel or tub full of them, enough to last an entire year. When one wants to eat these fish, one puts them into fresh water over night. Then they are washed once more, and fried. The pigeons that have been shot are salted in the same manner and brought to the table in winter time.

Among all the birds to be found here the most curious is the *murmur* (hummingbird), of which there are two species. One is extraordinarily small, with all its feathers no larger than a small fly. The other makes a loud noise in one's ears, like the humming of a big gnat, which is not much louder. Its claws which are the length of a thumb, seem to be fine needles, as is its beak, which is merely the sheath of another beak that it extends and puts in the midst of flowers in order to extract honey from them. This is its nourishment.

In short, this creature deserves to be called the ornament of nature. This bird wears a black plume on its crest, which is of an extraordinary beauty. Its breast resembles the most beautiful rose color one can see anywhere, and its belly is as white as milk. Its back, wings and tail are colored the most beautiful grey, which can well be compared with roses, and they are shaded all around with a brilliant gold. Its down which can barely be seen and which covers its whole plumage, gives it so delicate an appearance that it resembles a flower. It resembles a wave. All this is so delicate and pretty that it beggars description. [Ed.]

14. About these pigeons, see the book just cited, p. 306. [Ed.]

There is no longer as great a quantity of wildfowl and game around Philadelphia as there used to be, since everybody is allowed to shoot what he wants. But the further one penetrates into the country, the less inhabited it is, and the more game of all kinds one encounters, especially birds. Many people in this province support themselves by hunting.

One comes across many kinds of snakes as well as many kinds of vermin in Pennsylvania, especially in the Blue Mountains. There, many a snake ten, twelve, fifteen to eighteen feet long has been observed and many people as well as animals have been fatally bitten by these terrible and vicious creatures. There are black and white snakes, grass-green ones, grey ones, and then again black ones with yellow stripes. Among all these rattlesnakes are the biggest and most dangerous. But in some ways black snakes (twelve to fifteen feet long and thick as an arm) can do even more harm, since they have a marvelous power to charm through their steady glance, which, once fixed upon it, forces any creature crossing their path, be it hare, bird or squirrel, down from the trees and towards them. Then they pounce upon it and devour it.[15]

They can climb the tallest oaks as well as other trees. They are also able to charm little children, who are compelled to stand stock-still in front of them. The children then begin to cry pitifully. And so it often happens that one can still save them, while the large snakes are still coiled in front of them. Some of the rattlesnakes are even bigger than the species hitherto mentioned. Many of them are over eighteen feet long, and as thick as a haypole. This kind of snake has a rattling tail at its rear end. With this it can rattle; and one can hear it from afar. These snakes also rattle when they are angry or when they catch sight of anyone. Each year the rattle-tail develops a new ring. These creatures have fishlike scales—black, blue, and green—and they look like mother-of-pearl. It has often happened to people living in the forests that snakes have crawled into their houses, even under their beds, until the people lying on the beds became too heavy for the snakes and the latter grew restless. Then one could chase them out and beat them to death.

---

15. This account sounds rather strange, and I should be inclined to regard it as a fable palmed off on the author, had I not read the same account in the *Description of New Scotland,* which I cited above, pp. 213, 214. In this latter account, however, the power to charm is ascribed to the rattle-snakes, whereas our author attributes it to the black snakes. [Ed.]

Among the beauties of Pennsylvania are the fireflies that fly about in such numbers during the summertime that it appears to be snowing fire. Some years ago a newly arrived German got into a great fright over this. For when he was working late in the fields one evening at firefly time and several of the fireflies flew to and fro about him (he was not familiar with them) our Honest Hans was scared out of his wits, dropped everything, and rushed home. When, full of fright, he got home to his family, he said in fear and trembling, "O, God, guard and protect us. How many fiery spirits are abroad in this country. O, God, if only I were back in Germany!"

The Blue Mountains of Pennsylvania are located about thirty hours' journey from Philadelphia. These mountains begin at the Delaware River and extend to the left of this clear across the country, reaching as far as the great Ohio River. The mountains are very high. One can already catch sight of them from Delaware Bay, before one has even reached Philadelphia. These Blue Mountains extend over forty hours' journey.

There are a great many savages or Indians who are in peaceful communication with the English. These live even beyond the Ohio and beyond the Hudson River on which Albany lies, that is, on both sides, right and left, of Pennsylvania. These two large rivers are about a hundred hours' journey from Philadelphia. These savages live in the bush in huts, away from the above-mentioned rivers, and indeed so far inland that no one is able to find the point to which their habitations extend. The further one penetrates into the bush the more savages one encounters. They get their food by various means. Some shoot game, others dig roots, still others raise tobacco, as well as Indian corn, or maize, which they eat raw or boiled. Besides that they trade in hides, beaver skins, and costly furs.

Those savages living close to the Europeans are frequently to be seen; some of them even understand a little English. I myself have several times seen Indian families. Once I also had the opportunity of playing the organ for a savage family at the request of Captain von Diemer. Its effect on them was that they became very merry and showed their joy and admiration by gestures and by kneeling down. Those Indians who walk about among other people only wear horse blankets instead of clothes next to their body. These are neither cut nor sewn. They wear nothing on their heads or on their feet.

Their bodies look like ours, except that they are black-yellow in color. This is not their natural color, but the Indians smear and stain themselves. Yet they are born as white as we ourselves are.[16] Both men and women wear their hair long and smooth. The men don't like beards and when in their youth their hair begins to grow, they pull it out at once. Therefore, they have smooth faces like the women. Because of this, and because they wear the same dress, it is difficult to tell men from women. When these savages want to appear beautiful, they paint their foreheads and cheeks red, and hang their ears with strings of false beads an ell long. Under their rugs they wear neither shirts nor breeches nor skirts.

In the wilderness where they live, old and young run around naked during the summer. Every fall they come to Philadelphia in huge numbers, bringing with them various kinds of baskets which they can weave neatly and beautifully, different kinds of hides, as well as precious furs. Besides bringing these things they trade off to the governor, when they are assembled, a tract of land more than a thousand morgen in extent, and still all forest.

In the name of the province and the city they annually receive presents of many kinds, specifically blankets, rifles, rum or brandy and the like. Then they celebrate with their strange native songs, especially when they are drunk. It is impossible to understand their language. Some few of them who have had much contact with Englishmen are able to speak a little English. Among the Indians one finds some who are very strong, tall, and courageous. They "thou" and "thee" everybody in their language, even the governor himself; and they can run as fast as deer.

When one talks to them about the true and eternal God, the Creator of Heaven and Earth, they do not understand anything at all, but only answer as follows: they believe that there are two men, one good, one evil. The good man made everything that is good, and the bad man made everything that is bad. Thus it is unnecessary to worship the good man, since he is doing no one any harm. But one must pray to the bad man, so that he should do no harm to anyone. They wish to hear nothing of the Resurrection of the Dead, Salvation, Heaven or Hell. They bury their dead where they die.

Reliable people told me several times that the savages kill and bury those of their old people who are unable to move on account of age or break down on the road. But

---

16. Cf. Pastorius, *Description of Pennsylvania:* "They also besmear the children with grease, and let them creep about in the heat of the sun, so that they become the color of a nut, although they were at first white enough by Nature."

should a savage kill another human being (if it does not happen in war or on account of old age), then the murderer must die without fail, whether the dead person was one of ours or one of theirs. First they conduct the evildoer to their Indian king to be tried, thence back again to the place where the murder was committed. Then they kill him all of a sudden, bury him on the spot, and cover his grave with lots of wood and stones. On the other hand, they must receive satisfaction from us in similar cases. Otherwise they would treat an innocent white man in the same manner.

When the savages come into the city of Philadelphia and see the beautiful and marvelous buildings there, they are amazed and laugh at the Europeans for expending so much care and cost on their houses, saying: "That was quite unnecessary. After all, one could exist without such houses." They are especially amazed about European garments and finery. Indeed, they will even go so far as to spit when they see them.

When two savages get married or take their vows, then the bridegroom puts a piece of deer's leg into the bride's hand, meaning that he will nourish his future wife with meat. In return, his bride presents him with an ear of corn, to show that in future she will supply bread for her husband and children. Thus they take care of each other and remain together until death parts them.

Old savages have often been questioned about their descent and origin and have replied in this fashion: that they neither knew nor could say anything else but this— that their great-grandfathers had lived in the same wilderness, and that it was unjust of the Europeans to take their land away from them. That, however, was why they had to go further and further back into the wilderness in order to find game for their sustenance.

These savages use a remarkable weapon, a round bow. Into this they place front and center a sharp and pointed stone of a finger's length. This is a little more than an inch broad in back and as sharp as a knife on both sides. They take good aim with it; and when they hit an animal that will not fall, they run after it till they get it, for they can run faster than a horse. As evidence for this I myself brought such a stone with me, used by the Indians or savages to kill game. This was their sole weapon before they obtained guns from the Europeans. . . .

One could travel around Pennsylvania for an entire year without spending a kreuzer.[17] For it is the custom in this country that when a traveler comes on horseback to a house, he is asked whether he wishes to have anything to eat. Then the stranger is given a piece of cold meat, generally something left over from a meal. In addition he is given plenty of bread, butter or cheese, as well as drink. If he wants to stay overnight, he and his horse can do so, free of charge. When someone arrives at a house while a meal is in progress, he must sit down to the table at once and take pot luck. But there are also inns where one can obtain just what one wants.

Englishwomen in Pennsylvania and in all English colonies have the same qualities and privileges as do their sisters in Old England. They are exceptionally handsome and well formed, generally cheerful, friendly, very free in demeanor, plucky, smart and clever, but at the same time very haughty. They are fond of dress, and demand a great deal of attention from men. Englishmen do indeed make much of them, and respect them very highly. A man must not think of marrying a woman if he is not able to support her without her having to work. Otherwise she would make him very unhappy or even run away from him. For women must not be asked to do any work except such as they will do of their own free will.

The women are fond of receiving visits and attending parties. Whether the husband likes this or not, he must not even pull a face about it. I'd rather get into a fight with three men in England than give an Englishwoman a single slap in the face. When her own husband boxes her ears, and she complains to the neighboring women, his life is no longer safe. If it happens several times, he had better put a safe distance between himself and her; or she can see to it that he is put into prison for a long time or even sent to the galleys. And no one can force her to take her husband back. It is no wonder that Englishwomen are generally very good-looking. They are tenderly cared for from childhood on, they partake of no coarse foods or beverages, they are not allowed to work, and they spend little time in the sun. In court the evidence of one Englishwoman is worth that of three male witnesses. It is said that Englishwomen received this great privilege from Queen Elizabeth.

Concerning the size of America, people in Pennsylvania say that this part of the world is supposed to be far larger than Europe, and that it would be impossible to explore it completely on account of the lack of roads, and because of the forests, and the rivers, great and small. Pennsylvania is not an island, as some simpletons in Germany believe it to be. I took the opportunity of talking about the size of this part of the world with an English

---

17. A small silver or copper coin, originally stamped with a cross and formerly current in parts of Germany and in Austria.

traveler, who had been with the savages far inland. He told me that he had been with the Indians in the country, trading for skins and furs, more than 700 miles from Philadelphia, that is a journey of 233 Swabian hours. He had spoken about this topic with a very aged Indian who gave him to understand in English that he and his brother had at one time traveled straight across country and through the bush toward the setting sun, starting out from the very place where the meeting with the English traveler took place. And according to their calculation they had journeyed 1,600 English miles. But when they realized that they had no hope of reaching the end of the country they had turned back again. . . .

9

CULTURAL CONSOLIDATIONS IN
BRITISH NORTH AMERICA

Benjamin Franklin remarked in his *Observations Concerning the Increase of Mankind* (1751) that the settler population in the British colonies of North America doubled every twenty years. "What an Accession of Power to the British Empire by Sea as well as Land!" he concluded. Historians of demographics in the colonies have determined that Franklin was correct: The numbered persons (Native Americans, Africans, and African-descended persons were not counted) within the British colonies nearly doubled every twenty years. British Americans, settlers or those born of settlers, enjoyed a significantly higher life expectancy than their counterparts in Britain. They were living longer, their children were surviving childhood and reaching maturity, and they were generally fed and clothed sufficiently to maintain reasonably good health. Free white laborers, in shorter supply in the colonies, were better paid, and they had a greater diversity of foodstuffs and, as the century reached the midway point, more goods to choose from. The population density along the eastern seaboard diminished, making life in eastern towns more healthy than towns and cities in England or Western Europe.

Settlers in British North America were moving outward into other areas that had been acquired from Native peoples (in a variety of ways), and the outward migration meant a greater commingling of peoples—Scots, Scotch-Irish, Irish, Germans, Dutch, French, and others—across the colonies. Ethnic ties remained strong among different white groups in all the colonies throughout the century, and as the century wore on, a greater number of non-English speakers reached the shores in the East. The greatest influx of non-English speakers came from the slave system, which increased the importation of slaves from different cultural regions of Africa in the first half of the eighteenth century. And the so-called natural increase of slaves occurred as well. But other populations came over in great numbers as well, particularly Germans, and they found ways to live alongside English speakers while retaining their own lifeways.

Given the diversity of the population and its constant migratory shifting, how might Franklin have assumed that the people in the British colonies would contribute to the *British* empire, if so many different people were entering and living in the British colonies? British colonists found ways to secure their own cultural dominance in those colonies claimed and founded according to English charters during the late sixteenth and the seventeenth centuries. Several factors converged that assisted cultural consolidations among all groups that lived within the British colonies of North America. The most important factors include the rapid development and use of print technology, increased literacy, and the formation of cultural communities based on interests, gender, or race.

Print technology and the increased access to print was a significant contributor to the cultural consolidations experienced by English speakers in the British colonies. Compared with other provincial areas, the British colonies were remarkably well served with newspapers by about 1740, with about thirteen newspapers that circulated throughout the colonies. Post riders would bring newspapers with the "latest" news from other colonies, and many newspapers were served locally, on a subscription basis, directly to households. The readership of newspapers was multiplied by the number of readers within households who would have access to newspapers. In addition, printers took up the publication of handbills, broadsides, pamphlets, and books, as interest or need warranted, and readers thus gained access to information and cultural fare beyond what was available in newspapers. Print technology was used in various ways, then, to afford a greater extension of general knowledge about British laws and culture, peoples in other British colonies in North America, and goods being shipped to the British colonies. Benjamin Franklin, a major force behind the proliferation of newspapers into all the colonies, clearly understood the potentially culturally unifying capacities of print.

The sheer number and greater availability of newspapers indicates that there was a readership ready to use newspapers and other printed matter. The earliest newspapers in the colonies were formed almost entirely to provide the latest shipping news and, typically, political or legal news from England and other European polities. By the early 1720s, however, editors like James and Benjamin Franklin of the *New England Courant* began to assume that their readers would enjoy additional cultural fare, and they started publishing belletristic materials, essays, poems, and other materials that could serve to define and enhance the quality of the imaginative lives led by middling-level readers. The cultural impetus was normative in orientation, providing readers with a sense of what was considered good taste or decorous behavior, sometimes through characters who were themselves eminently people of sense and sometimes through characters who had foibles one would be advised to avoid acquiring. Such reading material was didactic, even if humorous, and it reveals an understanding on the part of editors that print could serve to unify or consolidate a cultural marketplace and a cultural value system that was being tested by the presence of diverse peoples in North America.

By midcentury, the gap between male and female literacy was nearly closed. That is, both men and women were being trained to read, and many men were being trained to write. When young men were sent off to writing masters to learn the skills of writing, young women were set to learning needlework and domestic arts. But this does not mean—as the number of women writers in the colonies at midcentury attests—that women did not write. Frequently, women were not taught formally to write in the way that men were, but they attained (often by teaching themselves or learning from other women) the rudimentary skills of writing. Native Americans, males particularly, were, like settler men, trained to read and to write if they were in one of the mission schools attempting to Christianize them (primarily in New England). Africans and African-descended people were, with less frequency, trained, but African schools were developed in communities in nearly all the colonies, typically sponsored by members of the Society of Friends (Quakers) and, later, Methodist schoolmasters. Many Africans and African-descended Americans well understood the importance of literacy in a community where knowledge of print had a high value, and many Africans trained themselves or found opportunities to receive training. Few reached the level of Phillis Wheatley, who received some formal training, or Benjamin Banneker, who taught himself mathematics and astronomy, but given the kind of labor they were expected to perform in sites off plantations, more Africans and African-descended people than one might assume had rudimentary skills of counting and letters. Literacy became a commodity one could use, and sell, among nonliterate peoples who wished to gain access to education. By the second half of the eighteenth century, schoolmasters appeared in greater numbers in the colonies, typically young graduates from families that could not afford to train them further in the law or sciences.

Given the high degree of ethnic and racial diversity, the constant movements of the population, and perhaps especially the desire of elites to retain their elite status in the face of the increasing successes of middling-level people like Franklin, the colonies experienced a proliferation of cultural communities that consolidated and secured cultural boundaries. In some ways, newspapers could be considered social levelers that might enable all to be relatively equal if they could read. At this time, additional cultural communities formed, among both elites and nonelites, that conveyed a sense of separate purpose within a narrower framing, whether it was based on gender, race, type of labor, belletristic goals, or any number of other factors. Among elites, the cultural clustering worked to counteract (or, at least, keep at bay) the leveling tendencies that increased print access made possible. Among nonelites, especially among those who were racially segregated as nonwhite, the cultural solidarity that emerged was profoundly important to strengthening a sense of communal purpose amid adversity.

Elite and middling-level men relied on a tradition of men's clubbing, based on models set in London and Edinburgh, centers for metropolitan clubs that enabled differentiations of status and culture to emerge. Sometimes the men's clubs formed for purposes of enlightenment—Franklin's Junto is a good example—and sometimes they would occur around particular forms of reading or social entertainment or special kinds of labor. Men's Masonic lodges developed throughout the colonies, and by the end of the century, these lodges were useful instruments, especially for Africans and African-descended men, for social organization and cultural consolidation. Prince Hall, the central force behind the African lodges, was intent upon bringing Africans into the center of the social and cultural marketplace that Africans had, through their labors, made significantly possible in most colonies. For Native Americans, cultural consolidation would occur only within communities of Christianized Indians like those sponsored by Samson Occom and, later, his son-in-law Joseph Johnson. For the most part, Native peoples remained justifiably dubious about joining with the settlers, for such affiliations required of them a total rejection of Indian lifeways. Unlike Africans, who were forcibly taken away from their homelands, Native peoples of North America lived between two worlds, Indian and white, and the demands of both worlds often conflicted and brought confusion and turmoil that was difficult for individuals to resolve.

Just as men sought solidarity, so did women. Women's circles developed in association primarily with women's domestic education, but also to sponsor their social and intellectual development, particularly their literary skills. What is today called higher education was not available to women, so women formed alternative communities that fostered the intellectual and social accomplishments of diverse groups of women, from the salons sponsored at the homes of Elizabeth Graeme Ferguson and Annis Boudinot Stockton to the Bible-reading and spiritual circles frequently available in most rural communities. Phillis Wheatley became the center of one such community of Africans and African Americans, a community interested in education and mutual aid, and one centered as well on spiritual assistance. Writing circles emerged in the New England and middle colonies particularly, sponsored by literate women who were interested in forming stronger bonds with other women who practiced certain social and literary arts. These women's societies became strong advocates of relief efforts during the Revolution against Great Britain, and they formed communities that worked across colonial boundaries to consolidate their labor and send assistance where it was most needed.

A range of interests and concerns, then, were sponsored by the growing number of internal communities—social, frequently but not exclusively gender based, and intraculturally supportive—within and across the First British Empire in North America. These communities worked to consolidate a sense of community that assisted in defining community members as special people within the larger local, regional, and indeed imperial colonial network. Print culture and increased literacy worked to frame for people within all the British colonies a greater sense of combined purpose and a greater sense of the value of being within the First British Empire of North America. More localized communities—whether based on gender, race, skills and interests, or a combination of these elements—also enabled people to form a sense of self-worth that might have been difficult to establish without the assistance of literacy and especially of print, given the long distances people regularly traveled. The cultural consolidations of the earlier eighteenth century importantly set the British colonies up for a level of intra- and intercolonial trade, establishing a sense of potential self-sufficiency that would eventuate in the political and cultural contest called the American Revolution against Great Britain. The lives of the writers in this cluster of readings greatly overlapped with those in the cluster related to the era of confederation, so the readings here should be considered in light of those other readings, as well.

BENJAMIN FRANKLIN (1706–1790)

Born into modest conditions and largely self-taught, Benjamin Franklin became, even in his lifetime, the person whose life came to represent for many in the British American colonies and the new United States the range of possibilities one could achieve if one worked hard enough, sought a healthy manner of living, and founded actions upon principles, rather than passions. Franklin's pithy aphorisms from his early and popular *Poor Richard's Almanac* suggest Franklin's wide reading, understanding of different kinds of people, and fondness for conscious self-scrutiny. "Reading makes a full Man, Meditation a profound Man, discourse a clear Man," he wrote in 1738, and in 1742, the year he began sponsoring John Bartram's botanical and scientific collecting and made plans to found a group that became the American Philosophical Society, "He that hath a Trade, hath an Estate." Franklin was fond of reminding people, even in the court circles in France, where he donned everyday clothes and indeed sometimes fur, that he was a printer by trade in order to be understood as a representative of the "common" people.

He was born on January 17, 1706 (January 6, 1705, Old Style) into the large family of Josiah Franklin, a tallow chandler and soap boiler who had emigrated from England in 1683, and his second wife, Abiah Folger Franklin. As the youngest son of a laborer in a family that would finally have fifteen children, Franklin would normally have been expected to be a laborer like his father, and he was trained while still young in soap making, cutlery, and printing. Having scant formal schooling—he studied at Boston Grammar School (1714–15) and George Brownell's English school (1715–16)—Franklin thought seriously about becoming a sailor, a dangerous trade, but he quickly was apprenticed to his brother James's printing house, where he worked on various publications, including the newspaper, *The New-England Courant.* In the meantime, he began writing his own verse, plays, and prose, which he published anonymously within his first essays, the Silence Dogood essays, in his brother's newspaper. Franklin and his brother were critical of Puritan authorities, and they found themselves in trouble when James Franklin was imprisoned for angering authorities by testing a printer's freedom to publish materials critical of town and government officials. During this time, early in 1722, Franklin became the publisher of James's newspaper. When James returned to active publishing, Franklin broke his indenture and left home for good. He sought his own fortunes as a publisher in Philadelphia. He was duped by Pennsylvania Governor William Keith into thinking he might be helped to set up on his own as a printer, and he made his way to London, expecting letters of support from Keith. Keith did not make good on his offer, so Franklin was stranded with a friend in London, aged eighteen and having no London friends. His printing trade and his evident inquisitiveness and ability to learn languages (he eventually taught himself Latin, French, German, Spanish, and Italian) and scientific arts brought him employment and friends in many circles, from tradesmen to philosophers, beginning with these years in London. Franklin remained in England until 1726, when he returned to Philadelphia with a friend, John Denham, who employed him as a shopkeeper and bookkeeper.

Franklin's years in Philadelphia brought him prosperity and some degree of fame in literary, religious, scientific, philanthropic, and political circles. During these Philadelphia years, roughly from 1726 through 1757, Franklin wrote some of his most memorable stories and essays, founded several newspapers, and assisted other printers in other colonies in founding newspapers, in an effort to form a chain of newspapers across the English colonies. Among his endeavors from these years are his support for many useful projects: an ecumenical place of worship for Philadelphians; a paper currency to assist the economic stagnation in the colonies; Masonic societies to benefit tradesmen and their families; a library for Philadelphians; newspapers to assist German-speaking emigrants arriving with greater frequency in the Pennsylvania colony; a system for a night watch and street lighting in the city; a fire company; improvements in scientific and mechanical arts, such as in printing, in fireplace design and stove making, and in discovering the sources and workings of electricity and thermal atmospheric currents; the formal establishment of a group of learned men who would exchange information (which became the American Philosophical Society); an academy (which became the University of Pennsylvania); and an intracolonial postal system.

Also during these years, Franklin took on increasingly important roles in government, attempting to find workable solutions to the growing factionalism between recent and long-standing emigrants; between the Pennsylvania Proprietary (the colonial government that was in the hands of the Penn family) and the colonists; and between the more eastern town dwellers of Pennsylvania and their rural, often more recently arrived neighbors in the west. He was elected a member of the Royal Society of London in 1756. Because of his obvious talents, Franklin achieved leadership roles in social, scientific, and key political issues and was sent, as an agent for the Pennsylvania Assembly, to England to attempt to resolve some of the problems in the governance of Pennsylvania.

His second period in London—roughly 1757 to 1775, with a return to the colonies for two years in 1762—brought Franklin continued prosperity but brought him notoriety as well, as he attempted to negotiate the difficulties of the rapidly growing Pennsylvania colony with many well-to-do people who little understood the range and nature of the difficulties the colonists were facing. During these years, Franklin went from having royalist opinions (in support of the monarchy, Britain, and the king) to one who held more liberal views of state formation, especially as he became increasingly aware that the British authorities were in disagreement about the methods of administering the colonies. Repeated attacks on border settlers by French military and settler groups and by their Native American allies brought continued duress to those living in the British colonies, German Swiss, Swedish, Welsh, Scottish, Irish, and Scotch-Irish peoples, as well as those from England. Franklin received numerous insults by British ministers and commoners before he came to the treasonous and, in his view, unhappy conclusion that the colonies would do better independent of British parliamentary control.

Franklin's writings during this period of his life were in all areas of the arts and sciences, mechanical arts, and social and political philosophy. When in England, he traveled to Scotland and Ireland and to other parts of Europe, where he met the most important and influential scientists, philanthropists, and European explorers of his time. He was granted an honorary doctor of laws degree from the University of St. Andrews in Scotland and the honorary degree of doctor of civil law from Oxford University and was elected to the Royal Academy of Sciences in Göttingen, Germany, and a similar Academy in Paris. Franklin enjoyed England and Europe immensely, but the political situation caused him great inner turmoil. He finally concluded "That Rebellion to Tyrants is Obedience to God" (published December 14, 1775), although the writings suggest that he reached this position with some degree of personal sorrow. He had been publicly humiliated before the king's Privy Council in January 1774, and none of his friends stepped up to defend him. Franklin's son, William, remained a loyalist throughout the war, and the two were estranged for the rest of their lives, despite two attempted reconciliations.

Franklin returned to the British colonies in May 1775, with a clear sense that France would assist their rebellion against England, and he was elected a representative to the second Continental Congress, serving on the committee to draft the Declaration of Independence. In 1776, he was sent to France to negotiate treaties of alliance between the two countries, and he remained there until 1785 as a negotiator over wartime and peacetime proceedings and as something like a cult hero to the French. Upon his return to Philadelphia, Franklin was celebrated for his political, philanthropic, and scientific achievements. In 1787, he helped found the Society for Political Enquiries, dedicated to improving knowledge about government, and served as Pennsylvania's delegate to the Constitutional Convention, but perhaps his most treasured appointment that year was as president of the newly reorganized Society for Promoting the Abolition of Slavery. His last public writing was a satire on the defense of holding slaves. He died quietly at home on April 17, 1790.

Franklin was a prolific writer on all aspects of life, from the mechanical arts to arts of virtue, from slavery to freedom, from the rights of women and women's education to the rights of citizens to revolt against authorities. Presented here are a cross-section of his writings, from his earliest public writing ("Silence Dogood, No. 1") to his last public writing on slavery. Franklin long had an interest in culture and in the ways in which women were unaccountably held to different educational and social expectations from men, in the cultivation of virtue and deterrence of vice, and in the importance of peaceable commerce between peoples. Although his autobiography is perhaps the best known of Franklin's writings to readers in the twenty-first century, it was not widely known in Franklin's own day; it was circulated among his close friends at the time, but not published until it started appearing in various bits and pieces and in French translations, copied from here and there without his knowledge or consent. Franklin actually wrote sparingly about himself in public and published materials. Some of these texts appear next, with the first two parts of the autobiography. The selections offered give only a small indication of the range and learned qualities of his writings.

SILENCE DOGOOD, NO. 1[1]

To the Author of the New-England Courant.
Sir,

It may not be improper in the first Place to inform your Readers, that I intend once a Fortnight to present them, by the Help of this Paper, with a short Epistle, which I presume will add somewhat to their Entertainment.

And since it is observed, that the Generality of People, now a days, are unwilling either to commend or dispraise what they read, until they are in some measure informed who or what the Author of it is, whether he be *poor* or *rich, old* or *young, a Schollar* or a *Leather Apron Man,* &c. and give their Opinion of the Performance, according to the Knowledge which they have of the Author's Circumstances, it may not be amiss to begin with a short Account of my past Life and present Condition, that the Reader may not be at a Loss to judge whether or no my Lucubrations are worth his reading.

At the time of my Birth, my Parents were on Shipboard in their Way from *London* to *N. England.* My Entrance into this troublesome World was attended with the Death of my Father, a Misfortune, which tho' I was not then capable of knowing, I shall never be able to forget; for as he, poor Man, stood upon the Deck rejoycing at my Birth, a merciless Wave entred the Ship, and in one Moment carry'd him beyond Reprieve. Thus was the *first Day* which I saw, the *last* that was seen by my Father; and thus was my disconsolate Mother at once made both a *Parent* and a *Widow.*

When we arrived at *Boston* (which was not long after) I was put to Nurse in a Country Place, at a small Distance from the Town, where I went to School, and past my Infancy and Childhood in Vanity and Idleness, until I was bound out Apprentice, that I might no longer be a Charge to my Indigent Mother, who was put to hard Shifts for a Living.

My Master was a Country Minister, a pious good-natur'd young Man, & a Batchelor: He labour'd with all his Might to instil vertuous and godly Principles into my tender Soul, well knowing that it was the most suitable Time to make deep and lasting Impressions on the Mind, while it was yet untainted with Vice, free and unbiass'd. He endeavour'd that I might be instructed in all that Knowledge and Learning which is necessary for our Sex, and deny'd me no Accomplishment that could possibly be attained in a Country Place; such as all Sorts of Needle-Work, Writing, Arithmetick, &c. and observing that I took a more than ordinary Delight in reading ingenious Books, he gave me the free Use of his Library, which tho' it was but small, yet it was well chose, to inform the Understanding rightly, and enable the Mind to frame great and noble Ideas.

Before I had liv'd quite two Years with this Reverend Gentleman, my indulgent Mother departed this Life, leaving me as it were by my self, having no Relation on Earth within my Knowledge.

I will not abuse your Patience with a tedious Recital of all the frivolous Accidents of my Life, that happened from this Time until I arrived to Years of Discretion, only in-

---

1. Published anonymously and without a title in *The New-England Courant,* April 2, 1722. The pseudonym, Silence Dogood, imitated Cotton Mather's two serious titles about self-improvement, *Silentarius* (1721) and his better-known essay series, *Bonifacius, or Essays to Do Good* (1710). Franklin's autobiography indicates that the essay piqued the curiosity of James Franklin and his friends, who could not identify its author. When he published it, James printed at the conclusion of the essay, "As the Favour of Mrs. Dogood's Correspondence is acknowledged by the Publisher of this Paper, les any of her Letters should miscarry, he desires they may for the future be deliver'd at his Printing-House, or at the Blue Ball in Union-Street, and no Questions shall be ask'd of the Bearer."

form you that I liv'd a chearful Country Life, spending my leisure Time either in some innocent Diversion with the neighbouring Females, or in some shady Retirement, with the best of Company, *Books*. Thus I past away the Time with a Mixture of Profit and Pleasure, having no Affliction but what was imaginary, and created in my own Fancy; as nothing is more common with us Women, than to be grieving for nothing, when we have nothing else to grieve for.

As I would not engross too much of your Paper at once, I will defer the Remainder of my Story until my next Letter; in the mean time desiring your Readers to exercise their Patience, and bear with my Humours now and then, because I shall trouble them but seldom. I am not insensible of the Impossibility of pleasing all, but I would not willingly displease any; and for those who will take Offence where none is intended, they are beneath the Notice of

Your Humble Servant,
SILENCE DOGOOD.

SILENCE DOGOOD, NO. 2[1]

To the Author of the New-England Courant.
SIR,
Histories of Lives are seldom entertaining, unless they contain something either admirable or exemplar: And since there is little or nothing of this Nature in my own Adventures, I will not tire your Readers with tedious Particulars of no Consequence, but will briefly, and in as few Words as possible, relate the most material Occurrences of my Life, and according to my Promise, confine all to this Letter.

My Reverend Master who had hitherto remained a Batchelor, (after much Meditation on the Eighteenth verse of the Second Chapter of *Genesis,*)[2] took up a Resolution to marry; and having made several unsuccessful fruitless Attempts on the more topping Sort of our Sex, and being tir'd with making troublesome Journeys and Visits to no Purpose, he began unexpectedly to cast a lov-

ing Eye upon Me, whom he had brought up cleverly to his Hand.

There is certainly scarce any Part of a Man's Life in which he appears more silly and ridiculous, than when he makes his first Onset in Courtship. The aukward Manner in which my Master first discover'd his Intentions, made me, in spite of my Reverence to his Person, burst out into an unmannerly Laughter: However, having ask'd his Pardon, and with much ado compos'd my Countenance, I promis'd him I would take his Proposal into serious Consideration, and speedily give him an Answer.

As he had been a great Benefactor (and in a Manner a Father to me) I could not well deny his Request, when I once perceived he was in earnest. Whether it was Love, or Gratitude, or Pride, or all Three that made me consent, I know not; but it is certain, he found it no hard Matter, by the Help of his Rhetorick, to conquer my Heart, and perswade me to marry him.

This unexpected Match was very astonishing to all the Country round about, and served to furnish them with Discourse for a long Time after; some approving it, others disliking it, as they were led by their various Fancies and Inclinations.

We lived happily together in the Heighth of conjugal Love and mutual Endearments, for near Seven years, in which Time we added Two likely Girls and a Boy to the Family of the *Dogoods*: But alas! When my Sun was in its meridian Altitude, inexorable unrelenting Death, as if he had envy'd my Happiness and Tranquility, and resolv'd to make me entirely miserable by the Loss of so good an Husband, hastened his Flight to the Heavenly World, by a sudden unexpected Departure from this.

I have now remained in a State of Widowhood for several Years, but it is a State I never much admir'd, and I am apt to fancy that I could be easily perswaded to marry again, provided I was sure of a good-humour'd, sober, agreeable Companion: But one, even with these few good Qualities, being hard to find, I have lately relinquish'd all Thoughts of that Nature.

At present I pass away my leisure Hours in Conversation, either with my honest Neighbour *Rusticus* and his Family, or with the ingenious Minister of our Town, who now lodges at my House, and by whose Assistance I intend now and then to beautify my Writings with a Sentence or two in the learned Languages, which will not only be fashionable, and pleasing to those who do not understand it, but will likewise be very ornamental.

I shall conclude this with my own Character, which (one would think) I should be best able to give. *Know*

---

1. Published anonymously and without a title in *The New-England Courant,* April 16, 1722.

2. Genesis 18.2: "And the Lord God said, It is not good that the man should be alone: I will make him an help meet for him."

then, That I am an Enemy to Vice, and a Friend to Vertue. I am one of an extensive Charity, and a great Forgiver of *private* Injuries: A hearty Lover of the Clergy and all good Men, and a mortal Enemy to arbitrary Government & unlimited Power. I am naturally very jealous for the Rights and Liberties of my Country; & the least appearance of an Incroachment on those invaluable Priviledges, is apt to make my Blood boil exceedingly. I have likewise a natural Inclination to observe and reprove the Faults of others, at which I have an excellent Faculty. I speak this by Way of Warning to all such whose Offences shall come under my Cognizance, for I never intend to wrap my Talent in a Napkin. To be brief; I am courteous and affable, good-humour'd (unless I am first provok'd,) and handsome, and sometimes witty, but always,

> *SIR,*
>
> *Your Friend, and Humble Servant,*
> *SILENCE DOGOOD*

THE SPEECH OF
MISS POLLY BAKER[1]

The SPEECH of Miss Polly Baker, before a Court of Judicature, at Connecticut in New England, where she was prosecuted the fifth Time for having a Bastard Child; which influenced the Court to dispense with her Punishment, and induced one of her Judges to marry her the next Day.

May it please the Honourable Bench to indulge me a few Words: I am a poor unhappy Woman; who have no Money to Fee Lawyers to plead for me, being hard put to it to get a tolerable Living. I shall not trouble your Honours with long Speeches; for I have not the presumption to expect, that you may, by any Means, be prevailed on to deviate in your Sentence from the Law, in my Favour. All I humbly hope is, that your Honours would charitably move the Governor's Goodness on my Behalf, that my Fine may be remitted. This is the Fifth Time, Gentlemen, that I have been dragg'd before your Courts on the same Account; twice I have paid heavy Fines, and twice have been brought to public Punishment, for want of Money to pay those Fines. This may have been agreeable to the Laws; I do not dispute it: But since Laws are sometimes unreasonable in themselves, and therefore repealed; and others bear too hard on the Subject in particular Circumstances; and therefore there is left a Power somewhere to dispense with the Execution of them; I take the Liberty to say, that I think this Law, by which I am punished, is both unreasonable in itself, and particularly severe with regard to me, who have always lived an inoffensive Life in the Neighbourhood where I was born, and defy my Enemies (if I have any) to say I ever wrong'd Man, Woman, or Child. Abstracted from the Law, I cannot conceive (may it please your Honours) what the Nature of my Offence is. I have brought Five fine Children into the World, at the Risque of my Life: I have maintained them well by my own Industry, without burthening the Township, and could have done it better, if it had not been for the heavy Charges and Fines I have paid. Can it be a Crime (in the Nature of Things I mean) to add to the Number of the King's Subjects, in a new Country that really wants People? I own I should think it rather a Praise worthy, than a Punishable Action. I have debauch'd no other Woman's Husband, nor inticed any innocent Youth: These Things I never was charged with; nor has any one the least cause of Complaint against me, unless, perhaps the Minister, or the Justice, because I have had Children without being Married, by which they have miss'd a Wedding Fee. But, can even this be a Fault of mine? I appeal to your Honours. You are pleased to allow I don't want Sense; but I must be stupid to the last Degree, not to prefer the honourable State of Wedlock, to the Condition I have lived in. I always was, and still am, willing to enter into it; I doubt not my Behaving well in it, having all the Industry, Frugality, Fertility, and Skill in Oeconomy, appertaining to a good Wife's Character. I defy any Person to say I ever Refused an Offer of that Sort: On the contrary, I readily Consented to the only Proposal of Marriage that ever was made me, which was when I was a Virgin; but too easily confiding in the Person's Sincerity that made it, I unhappily lost my own Honour, by trusting to his; for he got me with Child, and then forsook me: That very Person you all know; he is now become a Magistrate of this Country; and I had hopes he would have appeared this Day on the Bench, and have endeavoured to moderate the Court in my Favour; then I should have scorn'd to have mention'd it; but I must Complain of it as unjust and unequal, that my Betrayer and Undoer, the first Cause of all my Faults and Miscarriages (if they must be deemed such) should be

---

1. First published in *The Gentleman's Magazine* in April 15, 1747, this version is from the *Maryland Gazette*, August 11, 1747.

advanced to Honour and Power, in the same Government that punishes my Misfortunes with Stripes and Infamy. I shall be told, 'tis like, that were there no Act of Assembly in the Case, the Precepts of Religion are violated by my Transgressions. If mine, then, is a religious Offence, leave it, Gentlemen, to religious Punishments. You have already excluded me from all the Comforts of your Church Communion: Is not that sufficient? You believe I have offended Heaven, and must suffer eternal Fire: Will not that be sufficient? What need is there, then, of your additional Fines and Whippings? I own, I do not think as you do; for, if I thought, what you call a Sin, was really such, I would not presumptuously commit it. But how can it be believed, that Heaven is angry at my having Children, when, to the little done by me towards it, God has been pleased to add his divine Skill and admirable Workmanship in the Formation of their Bodies, and crown'd it by furnishing them with rational and immortal Souls? Forgive me Gentlemen, if I talk a little extravagantly on these Matters; I am no Divine: But if you, great Men,[2] must be making Laws, do not turn natural and useful Actions into Crimes, by your Prohibitions. Reflect a little on the horrid Consequences of this Law in particular: What Numbers of procur'd Abortions! and how many distress'd Mothers have been driven, by the Terror of Punishment and public Shame, to imbrue, contrary to Nature, their own trembling Hands in the Blood of their helpless Offspring! Nature would have induc'd them to nurse it up with a Parent's Fondness. 'Tis the Law therefore, 'tis the Law itself that is guilty of all these Barbarities and Murders. Repeal it then, Gentlemen; let it be expung'd for ever from your Books: And on the other hand, take into your wise Consideration, the great and growing Number of Batchelors in the Country, many of whom, from the mean Fear of the Expence of a Family, have never sincerely and honourably Courted a Woman in their Lives; and by their Manner of Living, leave unproduced (which I think is little better than Murder) Hundreds of their Posterity to the Thousandth Generation. Is not theirs a greater Offence against the Public Good, than mine? Compel them then, by a Law, either to Marry, or pay double the Fine of Fornication every Year. What must poor young Women do, whom Custom has forbid to sollicit the Men, and who cannot force themselves upon Husbands, when the Laws take no Care to provide them any, and yet severely punish

if they do their Duty without them? Yes, Gentlemen, I venture to call it a Duty; 'tis the Duty of the first and great Command of Nature, and of Nature's God, *Increase and multiply:* A Duty, from the steady Performance of which nothing has ever been able to deter me; but for it's Sake, I have hazarded the Loss of the public Esteem, and frequently incurr'd public Disgrace and Punishment; and therefore ought, in my humble Opinion, instead of a Whipping, to have a Statue erected to my Memory.

AN EDICT BY THE KING OF PRUSSIA[1]

For the Public Advertiser.
The SUBJECT of the following Article of
FOREIGN INTELLIGENCE

being exceeding EXTRAORDINARY, is the Reason of its being separated from the usual Articles of *Foreign News.*

Dantzick, September 5

We have long wondered here at the Supineness of the English Nation, under the Prussian Impositions upon its Trade entering our Port. We did not till lately know the *Claims,* antient and modern, that hang over that Nation, and therefore could not suspect that it might submit to those Impositions from a Sense of *Duty,* or from Principles of *Equity.* The following *Edict,* just made public, may, if serious, throw some Light upon this Matter.

'FREDERICK, *by the Grace of God, King of Prussia, &c.*[2]

---

2. "Turning to some Gentlemen of the Assembly, then in Court." [Au.]

1. Of the "Edict," Franklin wrote to his son, William, on October 6, 1773, that he designed it "to expose the conduct of this country [England, where he was living at the time] toward the colonies in a short, comprehensive, and striking view, and stated therefore in out-of-the-way forms, as most likely to take the general attention." The "Edict" did take the general attention, as people flocked to the printing office to buy up all the copies the printer had. Franklin's satire touched on people's own concerns about being overrun in England by Germans who could claim a right to prior authority over the British throne. He published it anonymously and was flattered when he heard people praise the essay as "the keenest and severest piece that has appeared here a long time." The text is from the original publication, the London *Public Advertiser,* September 22, 1773.

2. Frederick II, Frederick the Great, king of Prussia (1740–86), ruled in the territories Franklin names below.

&c. &c. to all present and to come,[3] HEALTH. The Peace now enjoyed throughout our Dominions, having afforded us Leisure to apply ourselves to the Regulation of Commerce, the Improvement of our Finances, and at the same Time the easing our *Domestic Subjects* in their Taxes: For these Causes, and other good Considerations us thereunto moving, We hereby make known, that after having deliberated these Affairs in our Council, present our dear Brothers, and other great Officers of the State, Members of the same, WE, of our certain Knowledge, full Power and Authority Royal, have made and issued this present Edict, viz.

'WHEREAS it is well known to all the World, that the first German Settlements made in the Island of *Britain,* were by Colonies of People, Subjects to our renowned Ducal Ancestors, and drawn from *their* Dominions, under the Conduct of *Hengist, Horsa, Hella, Uffa, Cerdicus, Ida,* and others; and that the said Colonies have flourished under the Protection of our august House, for Ages past, have never been *emancipated* therefrom, and yet have hitherto yielded little Profit to the same. And whereas We Ourself have in the last War fought for and defended the said Colonies against the Power of *France,* and thereby enabled them to make Conquests from the said Power in *America,* for which we have not yet received adequate Compensation. And whereas it is just and expedient that a Revenue should be raised from the said Colonies in *Britain* towards our Indemnification; and that those who are Descendants of our antient Subjects, and thence still owe us due Obedience, should contribute to the replenishing of our Royal Coffers, as they must have done had their Ancestors remained in the Territories now to us appertaining: WE do therefore hereby ordain and command, That from and after the Date of these Presents, there shall be levied and paid to our Officers of the Customs, on all Goods, Wares and Merchandizes, and on all Grain and other Produce of the Earth exported from the said Island of *Britain,* and on all Goods of whatever Kind imported into the same, a *Duty* of *Four and an Half* per Cent. *ad Valorem,* for the Use of us and our Successors.—And that the said Duty may more effectually be collected, We do hereby ordain, that all Ships or Vessels bound from *Great Britain* to any other Part of the World, or from any other Part of the World to *Great Britain,* shall in their respective

Voyages touch at our Port of KONINGSBERG, there to be unladen, searched, and charged with the said Duties.

'AND WHEREAS there have been from Time to Time discovered in the said Island of *Great Britain* by our Colonists there, many Mines or Beds of Iron Stone; and sundry Subjects of our antient Dominion, skilful in converting the said Stone into Metal, have in Times past transported themselves thither, carrying with them and communicating that Art; and the Inhabitants of the said Island, *presuming* that they had a natural Right to make the best Use they could of the natural Productions of their Country for their own Benefit, have not only built Furnaces for smelting the said Stone into Iron, but have erected Plating Forges, Slitting Mills, and Steel Furnaces, for the more convenient manufacturing of the same, thereby endangering a Diminution of the said Manufacture in our antient Dominion. WE *do therefore* hereby farther ordain, that from and after the Date hereof, no Mill or other Engine for Slitting or Rolling of Iron, or any Plating Forge to work with a Tilt-Hammer, or any Furnace for making Steel, shall be erected or continued in the said Island of *Great Britain:* And the Lord Lieutenant of every County in the said Island is hereby commanded, on Information of any such Erection within his County, to order and by Force to cause the same to be abated and destroyed, as he shall answer the Neglect thereof to Us at his Peril.—But We are nevertheless graciously pleased to permit the Inhabitants of the said Island to transport their Iron into *Prussia,* there to be manufactured, and to them returned, they paying our Prussian Subjects for the Workmanship, with all the Costs of Commission, Freight and Risque coming and returning, any Thing herein contained to the contrary notwithstanding.

'WE do not however think fit to extend this our Indulgence to the Article of *Wool,* but meaning to encourage not only the manufacturing of woollen Cloth, but also the raising of Wool in our antient Dominions, and to prevent *both,* as much as may be, in our said Island, We do hereby absolutely forbid the Transportation of Wool from thence even to the Mother Country *Prussia;* and that those Islanders may be farther and more effectually restrained in making any Advantage of their own Wool in the Way of Manufacture, We command that none shall be carried *out of one County into another,* nor shall any Worsted-Bay, or Woollen-Yarn, Cloth, Says, Bays, Kerseys, Serges, Frizes, Druggets, Cloth-Serges, Shalloons, or any other Drapery Stuffs, or Woollen Manufactures whatsoever, made up or mixt with Wool in any of the said Counties, be carried into any other County, or be Water-borne even

---

3. "*A tous present & à venir.* Orig." [Au.]

across the smallest River or Creek, on Penalty of Forfeiture of the same, together with the Boats, Carriages, Horses, &c. that shall be employed in removing them. *Nevertheless* Our loving Subjects there are hereby permitted, (if they think proper) to use all their Wool as *Manure for the Improvement of their Lands.*

'AND WHEREAS the Art and Mystery of making *Hats* hath arrived at great Perfection in *Prussia,* and the making of Hats by our remote Subjects ought to be as much as possible restrained. And forasmuch as the Islanders before-mentioned, being in Possession of Wool, Beaver, and other Furs, have *presumptuously* conceived they had a Right to make some Advantage thereof, by manufacturing the same into Hats, to the Prejudice of our domestic Manufacture, WE do therefore hereby strictly command and ordain, that no Hats or Felts whatsoever, dyed or undyed, finished or unfinished, shall be loaden or put into or upon any Vessel, Cart, Carriage or Horse, to be transported or conveyed *out of one County* in the said Island *into another County,* or to *any other Place whatsoever,* by any Person or Persons whatsoever, on Pain of forfeiting the same, with a Penalty of *Five Hundred Pounds* Sterling for every Offence. Nor shall any Hat-maker in any of the said Counties employ more than two Apprentices, on Penalty of *Five Pounds* Sterling per Month: We intending hereby that such Hat-makers, being so restrained both in the Production and Sale of their Commodity, may find no Advantage in continuing their Business.—But lest the said Islanders should suffer Inconveniency by the Want of Hats, We are farther graciously pleased to permit them to send their Beaver Furs to *Prussia;* and We also permit Hats made thereof to be exported from *Prussia* to *Britain,* the People thus favoured to pay all Costs and Charges of Manufacturing, Interest, Commission to Our Merchants, Insurance and Freight going and returning, as in the Case of Iron.

'And lastly, Being willing farther to favour Our said Colonies in *Britain,* We do hereby also ordain and command, that all the Thieves, Highway and Street-Robbers, House-breakers, Forgerers, Murderers, So——tes,[4] and Villains of every Denomination, who have forfeited their Lives to the Law in *Prussia,* but whom We, in Our great Clemency, do not think fit here to hang, shall be emptied out of our Gaols into the said Island of *Great Britain for the* BETTER PEOPLING *of that Country.*

'We flatter Ourselves that these Our Royal Regulations and Commands will be thought *just* and *reasonable* by Our much-favoured Colonists in *England,* the said Regulations being copied from their own Statutes of 10 and 11 Will. III. C. 10.—5 Geo. II. C. 22.—23 Geo. II. C. 29.—4 Geo. I. C. 11.[5] and from other equitable Laws made by their Parliaments, or from Instructions given by their Princes, or from Resolutions of both Houses entered into for the GOOD *Government* of their own Colonies in *Ireland* and *America.*

'And all Persons in the said Island are hereby cautioned not to oppose in any wise the Execution of this Our Edict, or any Part thereof, such Opposition being HIGH TREASON, of which all who are *suspected* shall be transported in Fetters from *Britain* to *Prussia,* there to be tried and executed according to the *Prussian Law.*

'Such is our Pleasure.

'Given at *Potsdam* this twenty-fifth Day of the Month of August, One Thousand Seven Hundred and Seventy-three, and in the Thirty-third Year of our Reign.

'By the KING in his Council.

'*RECHTMÆSSIG, Secr.*'[6]

Some take this Edict to be merely one of the King's *Jeux d'Esprit:*[7] Others suppose it serious, and that he means a Quarrel with England: But all here think the Assertion it concludes with, "that these Regulations are copied from Acts of the English Parliament respecting their Colonies," a very *injurious* one: it being impossible to believe, that a People distinguished for their *Love of Liberty,* a Nation so *wise,* so *liberal in its Sentiments,* so *just and equitable* towards its *Neighbours,* should, from mean and *injudicious* Views of *petty immediate Profit,* treat *its own Children* in a Manner so *arbitrary* and TYRANNICAL!

---

4. Sodomites. One of the colonials' complaints involved Britain's sending felons and ne'er-do-wells to the North American colonies.

5. Franklin names successors to the throne of Britain: William III (reigned 1689–1702); George I (reigned 1714–27); George II (reigned 1727–60).

6. The legally authorized (German) secretary.

7. "A game of spirit," a joke.

SPEECH IN THE CONVENTION AT THE CONCLUSION OF ITS DELIBERATIONS[1]

I confess that I do not entirely approve of this Constitution at present, but Sir, I am not sure I shall never approve it: For having lived long, I have experienced many Instances of being oblig'd, by better Information or fuller Consideration, to change Opinions even on important Subjects, which I once thought right, but found to be otherwise. It is therefore that the older I grow the more apt I am to doubt my own Judgment and to pay more Respect to the Judgment of others. Most Men indeed as well as most Sects in Religion, think themselves in Possession of all Truth, and that wherever others differ from them it is so far Error. Steele, a Protestant, in a Dedication tells the Pope, that the only Difference between our two Churches in their Opinions of the Certainty of their Doctrine, is, the Romish Church is infallible, and the Church of England is never in the Wrong. But tho' many private Persons think almost as highly of their own Infallibility, as that of their Sect, few express it so naturally as a certain French lady, who in a little Dispute with her Sister, said, I don't know how it happens, Sister, but I meet with no body but myself that's *always* in the right. *Il n'y a que moi qui a toujours raison.*

In these Sentiments, Sir, I agree to this Constitution, with all its Faults, if they are such: because I think a General Government necessary for us, and there is no *Form* of Government but what may be a Blessing to the People if well administered; and I believe farther that this is likely to be well administered for a Course of Years, and can only end in Despotism as other Forms have done before it, when the People shall become so corrupted as to need Despotic Government, being incapable of any other. I doubt too whether any other Convention we can obtain, may be able to make a better Constitution: For when you assemble a Number of Men to have the Advantage of their joint Wisdom, you inevitably assemble with those Men all their Prejudices, their Passions, their Errors of Opinion, their local Interests, and their selfish Views. From such an Assembly can a perfect Production be expected? It therefore astonishes me, Sir, to find this System approaching so near to Perfection as it does; and I think it will astonish our Enemies, who are waiting with Confidence to hear that our Councils are confounded, like those of the Builders of Babel, and that our States are on the Point of Separation, only to meet hereafter for the Purpose of cutting one another's Throats. Thus I consent, Sir, to this Constitution because I expect no better, and because I am not sure that it is not the best. The Opinions I have had of its Errors, I sacrifice to the Public Good. I have never whisper'd a Syllable of them abroad. Within these Walls they were born, & here they shall die. If every one of us in returning to our Constituents were to report the Objections he has had to it, and endeavour to gain Partizans in support of them, we might prevent its being generally received, and thereby lose all the salutary Effects & great Advantages resulting naturally in our favour among foreign Nations, as well as among ourselves, from our real or apparent Unanimity. Much of the Strength and Efficiency of any Government, in procuring & securing Happiness to the People depends on Opinion, on the general Opinion of the Goodness of that Government as well as of the Wisdom & Integrity of its Governors. I hope therefore that for our own Sakes, as a Part of the People, and for the Sake of our Posterity, we shall act heartily & unanimously in recommending this Constitution, wherever our Influence may extend, and turn our future Thoughts and Endeavours to the Means of having it well administered.—

On the whole, Sir, I cannot help expressing a Wish, that every Member of the Convention, who may still have Objections to it, would with me on this Occasion doubt a little of his own Infallibility, and to make *manifest* our *Unanimity,* put his Name to this Instrument.—

Then the Motion was made for adding the last Formula, viz Done in Convention by the unanimous Consent &c—which was agreed to and added—accordingly.

———

1. Franklin's speech was recorded at the time it was spoken, September 17, 1787. The transcript is in the Library of Congress; the text is from *The Writings of Benjamin Franklin,* ed. Albert Henry Smyth (1907).

SIDI MEHEMET IBRAHIM ON THE SLAVE TRADE[1]

To the Editor of the Federal Gazette

March 23d, 1790

SIR,

Reading last night in your excellent Paper the speech of Mr. Jackson in Congress[2] against their meddling with the Affair of Slavery, or attempting to mend the Condition of the Slaves, it put me in mind of a similar One made about 100 Years since by Sidi Mehemet Ibrahim, a member of the Divan of Algiers, which may be seen in Martin's Account of his Consulship, anno 1687. It was against granting the Petition of the Sect called *Erika,* or Purists, who pray'd for the Abolition of Piracy and Slavery as being unjust. Mr. Jackson does not quote it; perhaps he has not seen it. If, therefore, some of its Reasonings are to be found in his eloquent Speech, it may only show that men's Interests and Intellects operate and are operated on with surprising similarity in all Countries and Climates, when under similar Circumstances. The African's Speech, as translated, is as follows.

> *"Allah Bismillah, &c.*
> *God is great, and Mahomet is his Prophet.*

"Have these *Erika* considered the Consequences of granting their Petition? If we cease our Cruises against the Christians, how shall we be furnished with the Commodities their Countries produce, and which are so necessary for us? If we forbear to make Slaves of their People, who in this hot Climate are to cultivate our Lands? Who are to perform the common Labours of our City, and in our Families? Must we not then be our own Slaves? And is there not more Compassion and more Favour due to us as Mussulmen, than to these Christian Dogs? We have now above 50,000 Slaves in and near Algiers. This Number, if not kept up by fresh Supplies, will soon diminish, and be gradually annihilated. If we then cease taking and plundering the Infidel Ships, and making

Slaves of the Seamen and Passengers, our Lands will become of no Value for want of Cultivation; the Rents of Houses in the City will sink one half; and the Revenues of Government arising from its Share of Prizes be totally destroy'd! And for what? To gratify the whims of a whimsical Sect, who would have us, not only forbear making more Slaves, but even to manumit those we have.

"But who is to indemnify their Masters for the Loss? Will the State do it? Is our Treasury sufficient? Will the *Erika* do it? Can they do it? Or would they, to do what they think Justice to the Slaves, do a greater Injustice to the Owners? And if we set our Slaves free, what is to be done with them? Few of them will return to their Countries; they know too well the greater Hardships they must there be subject to; they will not embrace our holy Religion; they will not adopt our Manners; our People will not pollute themselves by intermarrying with them. Must we maintain them as Beggars in our Streets, or suffer our Properties to be the Prey of their Pillage? For Men long accustom'd to Slavery will not work for a Livelihood when not compell'd. And what is there so pitiable in their present Condition? Were they not Slaves in their own Countries?

"Are not Spain, Portugal, France, and the Italian states govern'd by Despots, who hold all their Subjects in Slavery, without Exception? Even England treats its Sailors as Slaves; for they are, whenever the Government pleases, seiz'd, and confin'd in Ships of War, condemn'd not only to work, but to fight, for small Wages, or a mere Subsistence, not better than our Slaves are allow'd by us. Is their Condition then made worse by their falling into our Hands? No; they have only exchanged one Slavery for another, and I may say a better; for here they are brought into a Land where the Sun of Islamism gives forth its Light, and shines in full Splendor, and they have an Opportunity of making themselves acquainted with the true Doctrine, and thereby saving their immortal Souls. Those who remain at home have not that Happiness. Sending the Slaves home then would be sending them out of Light into Darkness.

"I repeat the Question, What is to be done with them? I have heard it suggested, that they may be planted in the Wilderness, where there is plenty of Land for them to subsist on, and where they may flourish as a free State; but they are, I doubt, too little dispos'd to labour without Compulsion, as well as too ignorant to establish a good government, and the wild Arabs would soon molest and destroy or again enslave them. While serving us, we take care to provide them with every thing, and they are treated

---

1. Under the pseudonym, "Historicus," this essay was printed in *The Federal Gazette,* March 25, 1790.

2. James Jackson (1757–1806) represented Georgia in the first Congress, 1789–91.

with Humanity. The Labourers in their own Country are, as I am well informed, worse fed, lodged, and cloathed. The Condition of most of them is therefore already mended, and requires no further Improvement. Here their Lives are in Safety. They are not liable to be impress'd for Soldiers, and forc'd to cut one another's Christian Throats, as in the Wars of their own Countries. If some of the religious mad Bigots, who now teaze us with their silly Petitions, have in a Fit of blind Zeal freed their Slaves, it was not Generosity, it was not Humanity, that mov'd them to the Action; it was from the conscious Burthen of a Load of Sins, and Hope, from the supposed Merits of so good a Work, to be excus'd Damnation.

"How grossly are they mistaken in imagining Slavery to be disallow'd by the Alcoran! Are not the two Precepts, to quote no more, '*Masters, treat your Slaves with kindness; Slaves, serve your Masters with Cheerfulness and Fidelity,*' clear Proofs to the contrary? Nor can the Plundering of Infidels be in that sacred Book forbidden, since it is well known from it, that God has given the World, and all that it contains, to his faithful Mussulmen, who are to enjoy it of Right as fast as they conquer it. Let us then hear no more of this detestable Proposition, the Manumission of Christian Slaves, the Adoption of which would, by depreciating our Lands and Houses, and thereby depriving so many good Citizens of their Properties, create universal Discontent, and provoke Insurrections, to the endangering of Government and producing general Confusion. I have therefore no doubt, but this wise Council will prefer the Comfort and Happiness of a whole Nation of true Believers to the Whim of a few *Erika,* and dismiss their Petition."

The Result was, as Martin tells us, that the Divan came to this Resolution; "The Doctrine, that Plundering and Enslaving the Christians is unjust, is at best *problematical;* but that it is the Interest of this State to continue the Practice, is clear; therefore let the Petition be rejected."

And it was rejected accordingly.

And since like Motives are apt to produce in the Minds of Men like Opinions and Resolutions, may we not, Mr. Brown,[3] venture to predict, from this Account, that the Petitions to the Parliament of England for abolishing the Slave-Trade, to say nothing of other Legislatures, and

the Debates upon them, will have a similar Conclusion? I am, Sir, your constant Reader and humble Servant,

HISTORICUS.

---

from AUTOBIOGRAPHY

PART ONE[1]

Twyford, at the Bishop of St Asaph's

1771

Dear Son,[2]

I have ever had a Pleasure in obtaining any little Anecdotes of my Ancestors. You may remember the Enquiries I made among the Remains of my Relations when you were with me in England; and the Journey I took for that purpose. Now imagining it may be equally agreable to you to know the Circumstances of *my* Life, many of which you are yet unacquainted wi; and expecting a Weeks uninterrupted Leisure in my present Country Retirement, I sit down to write them for you. To which I have besides some other Inducements. Having emerg'd from the Poverty & Obscurity in which I was born & bred, to a State of Affluence & some Degree of Reputation in the World, and having gone so far thro' Life with a considerable Share of Felicity, the conducing Means I made use of, which, with the Blessing of God, so well succeeded, my Posterity may like to know, as they may find some of them suitable to their own Situations, & therefore fit to be

---

3. Andrew Brown (1744?–797) published *The Federal Gazette.*

1. Franklin began his memoir of his life, never published during his lifetime, while visiting with friends in England in 1771. Between July 30 and August 13, 1771, he composed what became the first part at Twyford, the country home of Jonathan Shipley, Bishop of St. Asaph, situated fifty miles north of London. He composed the second part in 1784, at Passy, France. He began the third part in 1788, at his home in Philadelphia, and continued working on it through May 1789. He began what became the fourth part around mid-November 1789. He died before completing the work. The text, based on the original manuscript in Franklin's hand, is taken from *Benjamin Franklin: Writings,* ed. J. A. Leo Lemay (1987).

2. William Franklin (1731–1813) had been governor of New Jersey since 1762.

imitated.—That Felicity, when I reflected on it, has induc'd me sometimes to say, that were it offer'd to my
Choice, I should have no Objection to a Repetition of the
same Life from its Beginning, only asking the Advantage
Authors have in a second Edition to correct some Faults
of the first. So would I if I might, besides corr^g the Faults,
change some sinister Accidents & Events of it for others
more favourable, but tho' this were deny'd, I should still
accept the Offer. However, since such a Repetition is not
to be expected, the Thing most like living one's Life over
again, seems to be a *Recollection* of that Life; and to make
that Recollection as durable as possible, the putting it
down in Writing.—Hereby, too, I shall indulge the Inclination so natural in old Men, to be talking of themselves
and their own past Actions, and I shall indulge it, without
being troublesome to others who thro' respect to Age
might think themselves oblig'd to give me a Hearing,
since this may be read or not as any one pleases. And
lastly, (I may as well confess it, since my Denial of it will
be believ'd by no body) perhaps I shall a good deal gratify my own *Vanity.* Indeed I scarce ever heard or saw the
introductory Words, *Without Vanity I may say,* &c. but
some vain thing immediately follow'd. Most People dislike Vanity in others whatever Share they have of it themselves, but I give it fair Quarter wherever I meet with it,
being persuaded that it is often productive of Good to the
Possessor & to others that are within his Sphere of Action: And therefore in many Cases it would not be quite
absurd if a Man were to thank God for his Vanity among
the other Comforts of Life.—

And now I speak of thanking God, I desire with all Humility to acknowledge, that I owe the mention'd Happiness of my past Life to his kind Providence, which led me
to the Means I us'd & gave them Success.—My Belief of
This, induces me to *hope,* tho' I must not *presume,* that the
same Goodness will still be exercis'd towards me in continuing that Happiness, or in enabling me to bear a fatal
Reverso, which I may experience as others have done, the
Complexion of my future Fortune being known to him
only: and in whose Power it is to bless to us even our
Afflictions.

The Notes one of my Uncles (who had the same kind
of Curiosity in collecting Family Anecdotes) once put
into my Hands, furnish'd me with several Particulars, relating to our Ancestors. From those Notes I learnt that the
Family had liv'd in the same Village, Ecton in Northamptonshire, for 300 Years, & how much longer he knew not,
(perhaps from the Time when the Name *Franklin* that before was the Name of an Order of People, was assum'd by

them for a Surname, when others took Surnames all over
the Kingdom.—[3]) on a Freehold of about 30 Acres, aided
by the Smith's Business which had continued in the Family till his Time, the eldest Son being always bred to that
Business. A Custom which he & my Father both followed
as to their eldest Sons.—When I search'd the Register at
Ecton, I found an Account of their Births, Marriages and
Burials, from the Year 1555 only, there being no Register
kept in that Parish at any time preceding.—By that Register I perceiv'd that I was the youngest Son of the
youngest Son for 5 Generations back. My Grandfather
Thomas, who was born in 1598, lived at Ecton till he grew
too old to follow Business longer, when he went to live
with his Son John, a Dyer at Banbury in Oxfordshire,
with whom my Father serv'd an Apprenticeship. There
my Grandfather died and lies buried. We saw his Grave-
stone in 1758. His eldest Son Thomas liv'd in the House
at Ecton, and left it with the Land to his only Child, a
Daughter, who with her Husband, one Fisher of Welling-
borough sold it to Mr Isted, now Lord of the Manor there.
My Grandfather had 4 Sons that grew up, viz. Thomas,
John, Benjamin and Josiah. I will give you what Account
I can of them at this distance from my Papers, and if those
are not lost in my Absence, you will among them find
many more Particulars. Thomas was bred a Smith under
his Father, but being ingenious, and encourag'd in Learning (as all his Brothers like wise werre,) by an Esquire
Palmer then the principal Gentleman in that Parish, he

---

3. "As a proof that FRANKLIN was anciently the common
name of an order or rank in England, see Judge Fortescue, *De
laudibus Legum Angliae,* written about the year 1412, in which
is the following passage, to show that good juries might easily
be formed in any part of England. . . . 'Moreover, the same
country is so filled and replenished with landed menne, that
therein so small a Thorpe cannot be found wherein dweleth not
a knight, an esquire, or such a householder, as is there commonly
called a *Franklin,* enriched with great possessions; and also
other freeholders and many yeomen able for their livelihoods to
make a jury in form aforementioned'—(*Old Translation.*)

Chaucer too calls his Country Gentleman, a *Franklin,* and
after describing his good housekeeping thus characterises him:

"'This worthy Franklin bore a purse of silk,
Fix'd to his girdle, white as morning milk.
Knight of the Shire, first Justice at th' Assize,
To help the poor, the doubtful to advise.
In all employments, generous, just, he proved;
Renown'd for courtesy, by all beloved.'" [Au.]

qualify'd himself for the Business of Scrivener, became a considerable Man in the County Affairs, was a chief Mover of all publick Spirited Undertakings, for the County or Town of Northampton & his own Village, of which many Instances were told us at Ecton and he was much taken Notice of and patroniz'd by the then Lord Halifax. He died in 1702 Jan. 6. old Stile,[4] just 4 Years to a Day before I was born. The Account we receiv'd of his Life & Character from some old People at Ecton, I remember struck you as something extraordinary from its Similarity to what you knew of mine. Had he died on the same Day, you said one might have suppos'd a Transmigration.—John was bred a Dyer, I believe of Woollens. Benjamin, was bred a Silk Dyer, serving an Apprenticeship at London. He was an ingenious Man, I remember him well, for when I was a Boy he came over to my Father in Boston, and lived in the House with us some Years. He lived to a great Age. His Grandson Samuel Franklin now lives in Boston. He left behind him two Quarto Volumes, M.S. of his own Poetry, consisting of little occasional Pieces address'd to his Friends and Relations, of which the following sent to me, is a Specimen.

Sent to My Name upon a Report of his Inclination to Martial affaires

7 July 1710

Beleeve me Ben. It is a Dangerous Trade
The Sword has Many Marr'd as well as Made
By it doe many fall Not Many Rise
Makes Many poor few Rich and fewer Wise
Fills Towns with Ruin, fields with blood beside
Tis Sloths Maintainer, And the Shield of pride
Fair Cities Rich to Day, in plenty flow
War fills with want, Tomorrow, & with woe
Ruin'd Estates, The Nurse of Vice, broke limbs & scarss
   Are the Effects of Desolating Warrs

Sent to B. F. in N. E. 15 July 1710

B   e to thy parents an Obedient Son
E   ach Day let Duty constantly be Done
N   ever give Way to sloth or lust or pride
I   f free you'd be from Thousand Ills beside
A   bove all Ills be sure Avoide the shelfe
M   ans Danger lyes in Satan sin and selfe
I   n vertue Learning Wisdome progress Make
N   ere shrink at Suffering for thy saviours sake
F   raud and all Falshood in thy Dealings Flee
R   eligious Always in thy station be
A   dore the Maker of thy Inward part
N   ow's the Accepted time, Give him thy Heart
K   eep a Good Conscience 'tis a constant Frind
L   ike Judge and Witness This Thy Acts Attend
I   n Heart with bended knee Alone Adore
N   one but the Three in One Forevermore.

He had form'd a Shorthand of his own, which he taught me, but never practicing it I have now forgot it. I was nam'd after this Uncle, there being a particular Affection between him and my Father. He was very pious, a great Attender of Sermons of the best Preachers, which he took down in his Shorthand and had with him many Volumes of them.—He was also much of a Politician, too much perhaps for his Station. There fell lately into my Hands in London a Collection he had made of all the principal Pamphlets relating to Publick Affairs from 1641 to 1717. Many of the Volumes are wanting, as appears by the Numbering, but there still remains 8 Vols. Folio, and 24 in 4to & 8vo.[5]—A Dealer in old Books met with them, and knowing me by my sometimes buying of him, he brought them to me. It seems my Uncle must have left them here when he went to America, which was above 50 Years since. There are many of his Notes in the Margins.—

This obscure Family of ours was early in the Reformation, and continu'd Protestants thro' the Reign of Queen Mary, when they were sometimes in Danger of Trouble on Account of their Zeal against Popery.[6] They had got an English Bible, & to conceal & secure it, it was

---

4. England adopted the Gregorian calendar on September 13, 1752. Until then, the old Julian calendar was used, in which new years began on March 25, with the old calendar, by the eighteenth century, eleven days behind the new. Franklin's birthday, January 6, Old Style, advanced eleven days to January 17, New Style.

5. Franklin makes reference to "folio," "quarto," and "octavo" volumes, indicating the size of the books according to the number of sheets it took (two, four, and eight), printed on each side, to make up the book.

6. At a time when England had been Protestant, Queen Mary I (reigned 1553–58) attempted to restore Catholicism to England.

fastned open with Tapes under & within the Frame of a Joint Stool. When my Great Great Grandfather read in it to his Family, he turn'd up the Joint Stool upon his Knees, turning over the Leaves then under the Tapes. One of the Children stood at the Door to give Notice if he saw the Apparitor coming, who was an Officer of the Spiritual Court.[7] In that Case the Stool was turn'd down again upon its feet, when the Bible remain'd conceal'd under it as before. This Anecdote I had from my Uncle Benjamin.— The Family continu'd all of the Church of England till about the End of Charles the 2ds Reign,[8] when some of the Ministers that had been outed for Nonconformity, holding Conventicles[9] in Northamptonshire, Benjamin & Josiah adher'd to them, and so continu'd all their Lives. The rest of the Family remain'd with the Episcopal Church.

Josiah, my Father, married young, and carried his Wife with three Children unto New England, about 1682. The Conventicles having been forbidden by Law, & frequently disturbed, induced some considerable Men of his Acquaintance to remove to that Country, and he was prevail'd with to accompany them thither, where they expected to enjoy their Mode of Religion with Freedom.— By the same Wife he had 4 Children more born there, and by a second Wife ten more, in all 17, of which I remember 13 sitting at one time at his Table, who all grew up to be Men & Women, and married;—I was the youngest Son and the youngest Child but two, & was born in Boston, N. England.

My Mother the 2d Wife was Abiah Folger, a Daughter of Peter Folger, one of the first Settlers of New England, of whom honourable mention is made by Cotton Mather, in his Church History of that Country, (entitled Magnalia Christi Americana) as a *godly learned Englishman,* if I remember the Words rightly.—I have heard that he wrote sundry small occasional Pieces, but only one of them was printed which I saw now many Years since. It was written in 1675, in the homespun Verse of that Time & People, and address'd to those then concern'd in the Government there. It was in favour of Liberty of Conscience, & in behalf of the Baptists, Quakers, & other Sectaries, that had been under Persecution; ascribing the Indian Wars & other Distresses, that had befallen the Country to that Persecution, as so many Judgments of God, to punish so heinous an Offence; and exhorting a Repeal of those uncharitable Laws. The whole appear'd to me as written with a good deal of Decent Plainness & manly Freedom. The six last concluding Lines I remember, tho' I have forgotten the two first of the Stanza, but the Purport of them was that his Censures proceeded from *Goodwill,* & therefore he would be known as the Author,

because to be a Libeller, (says he)
    I hate it with my Heart.
From Sherburne Town[10] where now I dwell,
    My Name I do put here,
Without Offence, your real Friend,
    It is Peter Folgier.

My elder Brothers were all put Apprentices to different Trades. I was put to the Grammar School at Eight Years of Age, my Father intending to devote me as the Tithe of his Sons to the Service of the Church. My early Readiness in learning to read (which must have been very early, as I do not remember when I could not read) and the Opinion of all his Friends that I should certainly make a good Scholar, encourag'd him in this Purpose of his. My Uncle Benjamin too approv'd of it, and propos'd to give me all his Shorthand Volumes of Sermons I suppose as a Stock to set up with, if I would learn his Character.[11] I continu'd however at the Grammar School not quite one Year, tho' in that time I had risen gradually from the Middle of the Class of that Year to be the Head of it, and farther was remov'd into the next Class above it, in order to go with that into the third at the End of the Year. But my Father in the mean time, from a View of the Expence of a College Education which, having so large a Family, he could not well afford, and the mean Living many so educated were afterwards able to obtain, Reasons that he gave to his Friends in my Hearing, altered his first Intention, took me from the Grammar School, and sent me to a School for Writing & Arithmetic kept by a then famous Man, Mr Geo. Brownell, very successful in his Profession generally, and that by mild encouraging Methods. Under him I acquired fair Writing pretty soon, but I fail'd in the Arithmetic, & made no Progress in it.—At Ten Years old, I was taken home to assist my Father in his Business, which was that of a Tallow Chandler and Sope-Boiler.[12] A Busi-

---

7. An ecclesiastical court, established to eliminate heresy against the state religion.

8. Charles II reigned between 1660 and 1685.

9. Conventicles were private religious meetings of those who would not conform to the established church in England.

10. "In the Island of Nantucket." [Au.]

11. That is, learn his writing method for shorthand.

12. That is, a maker of candles and soap.

ness he was not bred to, but had assumed on his Arrival in New England & on finding his Dying Trade would not maintain his Family, being in little Request. Accordingly I was employed in cutting Wick for the Candles, filling the Dipping Mold, & the Molds for cast Candles, attending the Shop, going of Errands, &c.—I dislik'd the Trade and had a strong Inclination for the Sea; but my Father declar'd against it; however, living near the Water, I was much in and about it, learnt early to swim well, & to manage Boats, and when in a Boat or Canoe with other Boys I was commonly allow'd to govern, especially in any case of Difficulty; and upon other Occasions I was generally a Leader among the Boys, and sometimes led them into Scrapes, of wch. I will mention one Instance, as it shows an early projecting public Spirit, tho' not then justly conducted. There was a Salt Marsh that bounded part of the Mill Pond, on the Edge of which at Highwater, we us'd to stand to fish for Minews. By much Trampling, we had made it a mere Quagmire. My Proposal was to build a Wharf there fit for us to stand upon, and I show'd my Comrades a large Heap of Stones which were intended for a new House near the Marsh, and which would very well suit our Purpose. Accordingly in the Evening when the Workmen were gone, I assembled a Number of my Playfellows, and working with them diligently like so many Emmets,[13] sometimes two or three to a Stone, we brought them all away and built our little Wharff.—The next Morning the Workmen were surpriz'd at Missing the Stones; which were found in our Wharff; Enquiry was made after the Removers; we were discovered & complain'd of; several of us were corrected by our Fathers; and tho' I pleaded the Usefulness of the Work, mine convinc'd me that nothing was useful which was not honest.—

I think you may like to know something of his Person & Character. He had an excellent Constitution of Body, was of middle Stature, but well set and very strong. He was ingenious, could draw prettily, was skill'd a little in Music and had a clear pleasing Voice, so that when he play'd Psalm Tunes on his Violin & sung withal as he some times did in an Evening after the Business of the Day was over, it was extreamly agreable to hear. He had a mechanical Genius too, and on occasion was very handy in the Use of other Tradesmen's Tools. But his great Excellence lay in a sound Understanding, and solid Judgment in prudential Matters, both in private & publick

Affairs. In the latter indeed he was never employed, the numerous Family he had to educate & the Straitness of his Circumstances, keeping him close to his Trade, but I remember well his being frequently visited by leading People, who consulted him for his Opinion on Affairs of the Town or of the Church he belong'd to & show'd a good deal of Respect for his Judgment and Advice. He was also much consulted by private Persons about their Affairs when any Difficulty occur'd, & frequently chosen an Arbitrator between contending Parties.—At his Table he lik'd to have as often as he could, some sensible Friend or Neighbour, to converse with, and always took care to start some ingenious or useful Topic for Discourse, which might tend to improve the Minds of his Children. By this means he turn'd our Attention to what was good, just, & prudent in the Conduct of Life; and little or no Notice was ever taken of what related to the Victuals on the Table, whether it was well or ill drest, in or out of season, of good or bad flavour, preferable or inferior to this or that other thing of the kind; so that I was bro't up in such a perfect Inattention to those Matters as to be quite Indifferent what kind of Food was set before me; and so unobservant of it, that to this Day, if I am ask'd I can scarce tell, a few Hours after Dinner, what I din'd upon.—This has been a Convenience to me in travelling, where my Companions have been sometimes very unhappy for want of a suitable Gratification of their more delicate because better instructed Tastes and Appetites.—

My Mother had likewise an excellent Constitution. She suckled all her 10 Children. I never knew either my Father or Mother to have any Sickness but that of which they dy'd, he at 89 & she at 85 Years of age. They lie buried together at Boston, where I some Years since plac'd a Marble stone over their Grave with this Inscription

Josiah Franklin
And Abiah his Wife
Lie here interred.
They lived lovingly together in Wedlock
Fifty-five Years.—
Without an Estate or any gainful Employment,
By constant Labour and Industry,
With God's Blessing,
They maintained a large Family
Comfortably;
And brought up thirteen Children,
And seven Grandchildren
Reputably.
From this Instance, Reader,

---

13. Ants.

Be encouraged to Diligence in thy Calling,
And distrust not Providence.
He was a pious & prudent Man,
She a discreet and virtuous Woman.
Their youngest Son,
In filial Regard to their Memory,
Places this Stone.
J. F. born 1655—Died 1744. Ætat[14] 89
A. F. born 1667—died 1752—85

By my rambling Digressions I perceive my self to be grown old. I us'd to write more methodically.—But one does not dress for private Company as for a publick Ball. 'Tis perhaps only Negligence.—

To return. I continu'd thus employ'd in my Father's Business for two Years, that is till I was 12 Years old; and my Brother John, who was bred to that Business having left my Father, married and set up for himself at Rhodeisland, there was all Appearance that I was destin'd to supply his Place and be a Tallow Chandler. But my Dislike to the Trade continuing, my Father was under Apprehensions that if he did not find one for me more agreeable, I should break away and get to Sea, as his Son Josiah had done to his great Vexation. He therefore sometimes took me to walk with him, and see Joiners, Bricklayers, Turners, Braziers, &c. at their Work,[15] that he might observe my Inclination, & endeavour to fix it on some Trade or other on Land.—It has ever since been a Pleasure to me to see good Workmen handle their Tools; and it has been useful to me, having learnt so much by it, as to be able to do little Jobs my self in my House, when a Workman could not readily be got; & to construct little Machines for my Experiments while the Intention of making the Experiment was fresh & warm in my Mind. My Father at last fix'd upon the Cutler's Trade, and my Uncle Benjamin's Son Samuel who was bred to that Business in London being about that time establish'd in Boston, I was sent to be with him some time on liking. But his Expectations of a Fee with me displeasing my Father, I was taken home again.—

From a Child I was fond of Reading, and all the little Money that came into my Hands was ever laid out in Books. Pleas'd with the Pilgrim's Progress, my first Collection was of John Bunyan's Works, in separate little Volumes.[16] I afterwards sold them to enable me to buy R. Burton's Historical Collections; they were small Chapmen's Books and cheap, 40 or 50 in all.—My Father's little Library consisted chiefly of Books in polemic Divinity, most of which I read, and have since often regretted, that at a time when I had such a Thirst for Knowledge, more proper Books had not fallen in my Way, since it was now resolv'd I should not be a Clergyman. Plutarch's Lives[17] there was, in which I read abundantly, and I still think that time spent to great Advantage. There was also a Book of Defoe's called an Essay on Projects and another of Dr Mather's call'd Essays to do Good,[18] which perhaps gave me a Turn of Thinking that had an Influence on some of the principal future Events of my Life.

This Bookish Inclination at length determin'd my Father to make me a Printer, tho' he had already one Son, (James) of that Profession. In 1717 my Brother James return'd from England with a Press & Letters[19] to set up his Business in Boston. I lik'd it much better than that of my Father, but still had a Hankering for the Sea.—To prevent the apprehended Effect of such an Inclination, my Father was impatient to have me bound to my Brother. I stood out some time, but at last was persuaded and signed the Indentures, when I was yet but 12 Years old.—I was to serve as an Apprentice till I was 21 Years of Age, only I was to be allow'd Journeyman's Wages[20] during the last Year. In a little time I made great Proficiency in the Business, and became a useful Hand to my Brother. I now had Access to better Books. An Acquaintance with the Apprentices of Booksellers, enabled me sometimes to borrow a small one, which I was careful to return soon & clean. Often I sat up in my Room reading the greatest Part of the Night, when the Book was borrow'd in the Evening & to be return'd early in the Morning lest it should be miss'd or wanted.—And after some time an ingenious

---

14. Aged.

15. Franklin was taken to see woodworkers, bricklayers, lathe workers, and brass workers.

16. John Bunyan (1628–88) wrote *The Pilgrim's Progress* (1678).

17. The writings of Plutarch (A.D. 46?–120?), a Greek biographer, saw a resurgence of interest during the seventeenth and eighteenth centuries. Plutarch's *Parallel Lives* were of forty-six Greek and Roman figures honored in history.

18. Daniel Defoe's *Essay Upon Projects* (1697) and Cotton Mather's *Bonifacius, or Essays to Do Good* (1710), offered advice about personal, economic, and moral improvements.

19. Types, for printing.

20. That is, wages appropriate to a day's (journey's) labor.

Tradesman[21] who had a pretty Collection of Books, & who frequented our Printing House, took Notice of me, invited me to his Library, & very kindly lent me such Books as I chose to read. I now took a Fancy to Poetry, and made some little Pieces. My Brother, thinking it might turn to account encourag'd me, & put me on composing two occasional Ballads. One was called the *Light House Tragedy,* & contain'd an Acc^t of the drowning of Capt. Worthilake with his Two Daughters; the other was a Sailor Song on the Taking of *Teach* or Blackbeard the Pirate. They were wretched Stuff, in the Grubstreet Ballad Stile,[22] and when they were printed he sent me about the Town to sell them. The first sold wonderfully, the Event being recent, having made a great Noise. This flatter'd my Vanity. But my Father discourag'd me, by ridiculing my Performances, and telling me Verse-makers were generally Beggars; so I escap'd being a Poet, most probably a very bad one. But as Prose Writing has been a great Use to me in the Course of my Life, and was a principal Means of my Advancement, I shall tell you how in such a Situation I acquir'd what little Ability I have in that Way.

There was another Bookish Lad in the Town, John Collins by Name, with whom I was intimately acquainted. We sometimes disputed, and very fond we were of Argument, & very desirous of confuting one another. Which disputacious Turn, by the way, is apt to become a very bad Habit, making People often extreamly disagreable in Company, by the Contradiction that is necessary to bring it into Practice, & thence, besides souring & spoiling the Conversation, is productive of Disgusts & perhaps Enmities where you may have occasion for Friendship. I had caught it by reading my Father's Books of Dispute about Religion. Persons of good Sense, I have since observ'd, seldom fall into it, except Lawyers, University Men, and Men of all Sorts that have been bred at Edinborough. A Question was once some how or other started between Collins & me, of the Propriety of educating the Female Sex in Learning, & their Abilities for Study. He was of Opinion that it was improper; & that they were naturally unequal to it. I took the contrary Side, perhaps a little for Dispute sake. He was naturally more eloquent, had a ready Plenty of Words, and sometimes as I thought bore me down more by his Fluency than by the Strength of his Reasons. As we parted without settling the Point, & were not to see one another again for some time, I sat down to put my Arguments in Writing, which I copied fair & sent to him. He answer'd & I reply'd. Three or four Letters of a Side had pass'd, when my Father happen'd to find my Papers, and read them. Without entring into the Discussion, he took occasion to talk to me about the Manner of my Writing, observ'd that tho' I had the Advantage of my Antagonist in correct Spelling & pointing[23] (which I ow'd to the Printing House) I fell far short in elegance of Expression, in Method and in Perspicuity, of which he convinc'd me by several Instances. I saw the Justice of his Remarks, & thence grew more attentive to the *Manner* in Writing, and determin'd to endeavour at Improvement.—

About this time I met with an odd Volume of the Spectator.[24] I had never before seen any of them. I bought it, read it over and over, and was much delighted with it. I thought the Writing excellent, & wish'd if possible to imitate it. With that View, I took some of the Papers, & making short Hints of the Sentiment in each Sentence, laid them by a few Days, and then without looking at the Book, try'd to compleat the Papers again, by expressing each hinted Sentiment at length & as fully as it had been express'd before, in any suitable Words that should come to hand.

Then I compar'd my Spectator with the Original, discover'd some of my Faults & corrected them. But I found I wanted a Stock of Words or a Readiness in recollecting & using them, which I thought I should have acquir'd before that time, if I had gone on making Verses, since the continual Occasion for Words of the same Import but of different Length, to suit the Measure,[25] or of different Sound for the Rhyme, would have laid me under a constant Necessity of searching for Variety, and also have tended to fix that Variety in my Mind, & make me Master of it. Therefore I took some of the Tales & turn'd them into Verse: And after a time, when I had pretty well forgotten the Prose, turn'd them back again. I also sometimes jumbled my Collections of Hints into Confusion, and after some Weeks, endeavour'd to reduce them into the best Order, before I began to form the full Sentences

---

21. "Mr. Matthew Adams." [Au.]

22. That is, in a "low" style, like the style of literary hacks, rather than fine writers.

23. Punctuation.

24. *The Spectator,* a literary miscellany including essays on literature and morality, was published from 1711 to 1712 and 1714.

25. The meter.

& compleat the Paper. This was to teach me Method in the Arrangement of Thoughts. By comparing my Work afterwards with the original, I discover'd many faults and amended them; but I sometimes had the Pleasure of Fancying that in certain Particulars of small Import, I had been lucky enough to improve the Method or the Language and this encourag'd me to think I might possibly in time come to be a tolerable English Writer, of which I was extreamly ambitious.

My Time for these Exercises & for Reading, was at Night after Work, or before Work began in the Morning; or on Sundays, when I contrived to be in the Printing House alone, evading as much as I could the common Attendance on publick Worship, which my Father used to exact of me when I was under his Care:—And which indeed I still thought a Duty; tho' I could not, as it seemed to me, afford the Time to practise it.

When about 16 Years of Age, I happen'd to meet with a Book written by one Tryon,[26] recommending a Vegetable Diet. I determined to go into it. My Brother being yet unmarried, did not keep House, but boarded himself & his Apprentices in another Family. My refusing to eat Flesh occasioned an Inconveniency, and I was frequently chid for my singularity. I made my self acquainted with Tryon's Manner of preparing some of his Dishes, such as Boiling Potatoes, or Rice, making Hasty Pudding, & a few others, and then propos'd to my Brother, that if he would give me Weekly half the Money he paid for my Board, I would board my self. He instantly agreed to it, and I presently found that I could save half what he paid me. This was an additional Fund for buying Books: But I had another Advantage in it. My Brother and the rest going from the Printing House to their Meals, I remain'd there alone, and dispatching presently my light Repast, (which often was no more than a Bisket or a Slice of Bread, a Handful of Raisins or a Tart from the Pastry Cook's, and a Glass of Water) had the rest of the Time till their Return, for Study, in which I made the greater Progress from that greater Clearness of Head & quicker Apprehension which usually attend Temperance in Eating & Drinking. And now it was that being on some Occasion made asham'd of my Ignorance in Figures, which I had twice fail'd in learning when at School, I took Cocker's Book of Arithmetick,[27] & went thro' the whole

by my self with great Ease.—I also read Seller's & Sturmy's Books of Navigation,[28] & became acquainted with the little Geometry they contain, but never proceeded far in that Science.—And I read about this Time Locke on Human Understanding and the Art of Thinking by Messrs du Port Royal.[29]

While I was intent on improving my Language, I met with an English Grammar (I think it was Greenwood's) at the End of which there were two little Sketches of the Arts of Rhetoric and Logic, the latter finishing with a Specimen of a Dispute in the Socratic Method.[30] And soon after I procur'd Xenophon's Memorable Things of Socrates,[31] wherein there are many Instances of the same Method. I was charm'd with it, adopted it, dropt my abrupt Contradiction, and positive Argumentation, and put on the humble Enquirer & Doubter. And being then, from reading Shaftsbury & Collins,[32] become a real Doubter in many Points of our Religious Doctrine, I found this Method safest for my self & very embarassing to those against whom I used it, therefore I took a Delight in it, practis'd it continually & grew very artful & expert in drawing People even of superior Knowledge into Concessions the Consequences of which they did not foresee, entangling them in Difficulties out of which they could not extricate themselves, and so obtaining Victories that neither my self nor my Cause always deserved.—I continu'd this Method some few Years, but gradually left it, retaining only the Habit of expressing my self in Terms of modest Diffidence, never using when I advance any thing that may possibly be disputed, the Words, *Certainly, undoubtedly,* or any others that give the Air of Positiveness to an Opinion; but rather say, *I conceive,* or *I apprehend* a Thing to be so or so, *It appears to me,* or *I should think it*

26. Thomas Tryon, *The Way to Health, Long Life and Happiness, or a Discourse of Temperance* (1683).

27. Edward Cocker, *Arithmetic* (1677).

28. John Seller, *An Epitome of the Art of Navigation* (1681), and Samuel Sturmy, *The Mariner's Magazine; or Sturmy's Mathematical and Practical Arts* (1669).

29. John Locke, *Essays Concerning Human Understanding* (1690); Antoine Arnauld and Pierre Nicole of Port-Royal translated *Logic: or the Art of Thinking* (1662) from Latin into English (1685).

30. James Greenwood, *An Essay towards a Practical English Grammar* (1711).

31. Xenophon, *The Memorable Things of Socrates,* trans. Edward Bysshe (1712).

32. Anthony Ashley Cooper, third earl of Shaftesbury (1671–1713), was a religious skeptic, and Anthony Collins (1676–1729) was a deist.

so or so for such & such Reasons, or *I imagine* it to be so, or *it is so* if *I am not mistaken.*—This Habit I believe has been of great Advantage to me, when I have had occasion to inculcate my Opinions & persuade Men into Measures that I have been from time to time engag'd in promoting.—And as the chief Ends of Conversation are to *inform,* or to be *informed,* to *please* or to *persuade,* I wish well meaning sensible Men would not lessen their Power of doing Good by a Positive assuming Manner that seldom fails to disgust, tends to create Opposition, and to defeat every one of those Purposes for which Speech was given us, to wit, giving or receiving Information, or Pleasure: For If you would *inform,* a positive dogmatical Manner in advancing your Sentiments, may provoke Contradiction & prevent a candid Attention. If you wish Information & Improvement from the Knowledge of others and yet at the same time express your self as firmly fix'd in your present Opinions, modest sensible Men, who do not love Disputation, will probably leave you undisturb'd in the Possession of your Error; and by such a Manner you can seldom hope to recommend your self in *pleasing* your Hearers, or to persuade those whose Concurrence you desire.—Pope says,[33] judiciously,

Men should be taught as if you taught them not,
And things unknown propos'd as things forgot,—

farther recommending it to us,

To speak tho' sure, with seeming Diffidence.

And he might have couple'd with this Line that which he has coupled with another, I think less properly,

For want of Modesty is want of Sense.

If you ask why *less properly,* I must repeat the Lines;

"Immodest Words admit of *no* Defence;
"*For* Want of Modesty is Want of Sense."[34]

Now is not *Want of Sense,* (where a Man is so unfortunate as to want it) some Apology for his *Want of Modesty?* and would not the Lines stand more justly thus?

Immodest Words admit *but this* Defence,
That Want of Modesty is Want of Sense.

This however I should submit to better Judgments.—

My Brother had in 1720 or 21, begun to print a Newspaper. It was the second that appear'd in America, & was called *The New England Courant.* The only one before it, was *the Boston News Letter.*[35] I remember his being dissuaded by some of his Friends from the Undertaking, as not likely to succeed, one Newspaper being in their Judgment enough for America.—At this time 1771 there are not less than five & twenty.—He went on however with the Undertaking, and after having work'd in composing the Types & printing off the Sheets I was employ'd to carry the Papers thro' the Streets to the Customers.—He had some ingenious Men among his Friends who amus'd themselves by writing little Pieces for this Paper, which gain'd it Credit, & made it more in Demand; and these Gentlemen often visited us.—Hearing their Conversations, and their Accounts of the Approbation their Papers were receiv'd with, I was excited to try my Hand among them. But being still a Boy, & suspecting that my Brother would object to printing any Thing of mine in his Paper if he knew it to be mine, I contriv'd to disguise my Hand, & writing an anonymous Paper[36] I put it in at Night under the Door of the Printing House. It was found in the Morning & communicated to his Writing Friends when they call'd in as Usual. They read it, commented on it in my Hearing, and I had the exquisite Pleasure, of finding it met with their Approbation, and that in their different Guesses at the Author none were named but Men of some Character among us for Learning & Ingenuity.—I suppose now that I was rather lucky in my Judges: And that perhaps they were not really so very good ones as I then esteem'd them. Encourag'd however by this, I wrote and convey'd in the same Way to the Press several more Papers, which were equally approv'd, and I kept my Secret till my small Fund of Sense for such Performances was pretty well exhausted, & then I discovered it; when I began to be considered a little more by my Brother's Acquaintance, and in a manner that did not quite please him, as he thought, probably with reason, that it tended to

---

33. Alexander Pope (1688–1744), *An Essay on Criticism* (1711), with slight alterations of lines 574–75 and 567: "Men must be taught as if you taught them not" and "And speak, tho' sure, with seeming diffidence."

34. Using "Decency," rather than "Modesty," Wentworth Dillon, earl of Roscommon, published these lines in *An Essay on Translated Verse* (1684), lines 113–14.

35. *The Boston News-Letter* began publishing in 1704; *The Boston Gazette,* in 1719; *The American Weekly Mercury* (Philadelphia), later in 1719; and *The New-England Courant* in 1721.

36. A reference to "Silence Dogood, No. 1."

make me too vain. And perhaps this might be one Occasion of the Differences that we began to have about this Time. Tho' a Brother, he considered himself as my Master, & me as his Apprentice; and accordingly expected the same Services from me as he would from another; while I thought he demean'd me too much in some he requir'd of me, who from a Brother expected more Indulgence. Our Disputes were often brought before our Father, and I fancy I was either generally in the right, or else a better Pleader, because the Judgment was generally in my favour: But my Brother was passionate & had often beaten me, which I took extreamly amiss;[37] and thinking my Apprenticeship very tedious, I was continually wishing for some Opportunity of shortening it, which at length offered in a manner unexpected.

One of the Pieces in our News-Paper, on some political Point which I have now forgotten, gave Offence to the Assembly.[38] He was taken up, censur'd and imprison'd for a Month by the Speaker's Warrant, I suppose because he would not discover his Author. I too was taken up & examin'd before the Council; but tho' I did not give them any Satisfaction, they contented themselves with admonishing me, and dismiss'd me; considering me perhaps as an Apprentice who was bound to keep his Master's Secrets. During my Brother's Confinement, which I resented a good deal, notwithstanding our private Differences, I had the Management of the Paper, and I made bold to give our Rulers some Rubs in it, which my Brother took very kindly, while others began to consider me in an unfavourable Light, as a young Genius that had a Turn for Libelling & Satyr. My Brother's Discharge was accompany'd with an Order of the House, (a very odd one) *that James Franklin should no longer print the Paper called the New England Courant*. There was a Consultation held in our Printing House among his Friends what he should do in this Case. Some propos'd to evade the

Order by changing the Name of the Paper; but my Brother seeing Inconveniences in that, it was finally concluded on as a better Way, to let it be printed for the future under the Name of *Benjamin Franklin*. And to avoid the Censure of the Assembly that might fall on him, as still printing it by his Apprentice, the Contrivance was, that my old Indenture should be return'd to me with a full Discharge on the Back of it, to be shown on Occasion; but to secure to him the Benefit of my Service I was to sign new Indentures for the Remainder of the Term, W^{ch}. were to be kept private. A very flimsy Scheme it was, but however it was immediately executed, and the Paper went on accordingly under my Name for several Months. At length a fresh Difference arising between my Brother and me, I took upon me to assert my Freedom, presuming that he would not venture to produce the new Indentures. It was not fair in me to take this Advantage, and this I therefore reckon one of the first Errata of my Life: But the Unfairness of it weigh'd little with me, when under the Impressions of Resentment, for the Blows his Passion too often urg'd him to bestow upon me. Tho' He was otherwise not an ill-natur'd Man: Perhaps I was too saucy & provoking.—

When he found I would leave him, he took care to prevent my getting Employment in any other Printing-House of the Town, by going round & speaking to every Master, who accordingly refus'd to give me Work. I then thought of going to New York as the nearest Place where there was a Printer: and I was the rather inclin'd to leave Boston, when I reflected that I had already made my self a little obnoxious, to the governing Party; & from the arbitrary Proceedings of the Assembly in my Brother's Case it was likely I might if I stay'd soon bring my self into Scrapes; and farther that my indiscrete Disputations about Religion began to make me pointed at with Horror by good People, as an Infidel or Atheist; I determin'd on the Point: but my Father now siding with my Brother, I was sensible that if I attempted to go openly, Means would be used to prevent me. My Friend Collins therefore undertook to manage a little for me. He agreed with the Captain of a New York Sloop for my Passage, under the Notion of my being a young Acquaintance of his that had got a naughty Girl with Child, whose Friends would compel me to marry her, and therefore I could not appear or come away publickly. So I sold some of my Books to raise a little Money, Was taken on board privately, and as we had a fair Wind, in three Days I found my self in New York near 300 Miles from home, a Boy of but 17, without the least Recommendation to or Knowledge of any Person in the Place, and with very little Money in my Pocket.—

---

37. "I fancy his harsh & tyrannical Treatment of me, might be a means of impressing me with that Aversion to arbitrary Power that has stuck to me thro' my whole Life." [Au.]

38. James Franklin twice had trouble with the authorities. He was imprisoned for nearly a month, from June 12 to July 7, 1722, and he hid from the sheriff from January 24 to February 12, 1722/3. On January 16, 1722/3, the General Court resolved to forbid James Franklin to publish his paper "except it be first supervised by the Secretary of the Province." The *Courant* first appeared with Benjamin Franklin as its publisher on February 12, 1722/3.

My Inclinations for the Sea, were by this time worne out, or I might now have gratify'd them.—But having a Trade, & supposing my self a pretty good Workman, I offer'd my Service to the Printer of the Place, old Mr W^m. Bradford.[39]—He could give me no Employment, having little to do, and Help enough already: But, says he, my Son at Philadelphia has lately lost his principal Hand, Aquila Rose, by Death. If you go thither I believe he may employ you.—Philadelphia was 100 Miles farther. I set out, however, in a Boat for Amboy;[40] leaving my Chest and Things to follow me round by Sea. In crossing the Bay we met with a Squall that tore our rotten Sails to pieces, prevented our getting into the Kill,[41] and drove us upon Long Island. In our Way a drunken Dutchman, who was a Passenger too, fell over board; when he was sinking I reach'd thro' the Water to his shock Pate & drew him up so that we got him in again.—His Ducking sober'd him a little, & he went to sleep, taking first out of his Pocket a Book which he desir'd I would dry for him. It prov'd to be my old favourite Author Bunyan's Pilgrim's Progress in Dutch, finely printed on good Paper with copper Cuts,[42] a Dress better than I had ever seen it wear in its own Language. I have since found that it has been translated into most of the Languages of Europe, and suppose it has been more generally read than any other Book except perhaps the Bible.—Honest John was the first that I know of who mix'd Narration & Dialogue, a Method of Writing very engaging to the Reader, who in the most interesting Parts finds himself as it were brought into the Company, & present at the Discourse. De foe in his Cruso, his Moll Flanders, Religious Courtship, Family Instructor, & other Pieces, has imitated it with Success. And Richardson has done the same in his Pamela, &c.—[43]

When we drew near the Island we found it was at a Place where there could be no Landing, there being a great Surff on the stony Beach. So we dropt Anchor & swung round towards the Shore. Some People came down to the Water Edge & hallow'd to us, as we did to them. But the Wind was so high & the Surff so loud, that we could not hear so as to understand each other. There were Canoes on the Shore, & we made Signs & hallow'd that they should fetch us, but they either did not understand us, or thought it impracticable. So they went away, and Night coming on, we had no Remedy but to wait till the Wind should abate, and in the mean time the Boatman & I concluded to sleep if we could, and so crouded into the Scuttle with the Dutchman who was still wet, and the Spray beating over the Head of our Boat, leak'd thro' to us, so that we were soon almost as wet as he. In this Manner we lay all Night with very little Rest. But the Wind abating the next Day, we made a Shift to reach Amboy before Night, having been 30 Hours on the Water without Victuals, or any Drink but a Bottle of filthy Rum:—The Water we sail'd on being salt.—

In the Evening I found my self very feverish, & went ill to Bed. But having read somewhere that cold Water drank plentifully was good for a Fever, I follow'd the Prescription, sweat plentifully most of the Night, my Fever left me, and in the Morning crossing the Ferry, proceeded on my Journey, on foot, having 50 Miles to Burlington,[44] where I was told I should find Boats that would carry me the rest of the Way to Philadelphia.

It rain'd very hard all the Day, I was thoroughly soak'd, and by Noon a good deal tir'd, so I stopt at a poor Inn, where I staid all Night, beginning now to wish I had never left home. I cut so miserable a Figure too, that I found by the Questions ask'd me I was suspected to be some runaway Servant, and in danger of being taken up on that Suspicion.—However I proceeded the next Day, and got in the Evening to an Inn within 8 or 10 Miles of Burlington, kept by one Dr Brown.[45]—

He entred into Conversation with me while I took some Refreshment, and finding I had read a little, became very sociable and friendly. Our Acquaintance continu'd as long as he liv'd. He had been, I imagine, an itinerant Doctor, for there was no Town in England, or Country in Europe, of which he could not give a very particular Account. He had some Letters, & was ingenious, but much of an Unbeliever, & wickedly undertook some Years after

39. William Bradford (1663–1752), American printer, father of Franklin's competitor, Andrew Bradford (1686–1742).

40. Perth Amboy, New Jersey.

41. Narrow channel between Staten Island, New York, and New Jersey.

42. That is, copper engravings.

43. Franklin refers to Daniel Defoe's *Robinson Crusoe* (1719), *Moll Flanders* (1722), *Religious Courtship* (1722), and *The Family Instructor* (1715–18) and to Samuel Richardson's *Pamela, or Virtue Rewarded* (1740).

44. In western New Jersey, about twenty miles from Philadelphia.

45. John Browne (1667?–1737), a Burlington physician, innkeeper, and religious skeptic.

to travesty the Bible in doggrel Verse as Cotton had done Virgil.[46]—By this means he set many of the Facts in a very ridiculous Light, & might have hurt weak minds if his Work had been publish'd:—but it never was.—At his House I lay that Night, and the next Morning reach'd Burlington.—But had the Mortification to find that the regular Boats were gone, a little before my coming, and no other expected to go till Tuesday, this being Saturday. Wherefore I return'd to an old Woman in the Town of whom I had bought Gingerbread to eat on the Water, & ask'd her Advice; she invited me to lodge at her House till a Passage by Water should offer; & being tired with my foot Travelling, I accepted the Invitation. She understanding I was a Printer, would have had me stay at that Town & follow my Business, being ignorant of the Stock necessary to begin with. She was very hospitable, gave me a Dinner of Ox Cheek with great Goodwill, accepting only of a Pot of Ale in return. And I tho't my self fix'd till Tuesday should come. However walking in the Evening by the Side of the River a Boat came by, which I found was going towards Philadelphia, with several People in her. They took me in, and as there was no Wind, we row'd all the Way; and about Midnight not having yet seen the City, some of the Company were confident we must have pass'd it, and would row no farther, the others knew not where we were, so we put towards the Shore, got into a Creek, landed near an old Fence with the Rails of which we made a Fire, the Night being cold, in October, and there we remain'd till Daylight. Then one of the Company knew the Place to be Cooper's Creek a little above Philadelphia, which we saw as soon as we got out of the Creek, and arriv'd there about 8 or 9 a Clock, on the Sunday morning,[47] and landed at the Market street Wharff.—

I have been the more particular in this Description of my Journey, & shall be so of my first Entry into that City, that you may in your Mind compare such unlikely Beginning with the Figure I have since made there. I was in my working Dress, my best Cloaths being to come round by Sea. I was dirty from my Journey; my Pockets were stuff'd out with Shirts & Stockings; I knew no Soul, nor where to look for Lodging. I was fatigu'd with Travelling, Rowing & Want of Rest. I was very hungry, and my whole Stock of Cash consisted of a Dutch Dollar and about a Shilling in Copper. The latter I gave the People of the Boat for my Passage, who at first refus'd it on Acc[t] of my Rowing; but I insisted on their taking it, a Man being sometimes more generous when he has but a little Money than when he has plenty, perhaps thro' Fear of being thought to have but little. Then I walk'd up the Street, gazing about, till near the Market House I met a Boy with Bread. I had made many a Meal on Bread, & inquiring where he got it, I went immediately to the Baker's he directed me to in second Street; and ask'd for Bisket, intending such as we had in Boston, but they it seems were not made in Philadelphia, then I ask'd for a threepenny Loaf, and was told they had none such: so not considering or knowing the Difference of Money & the greater Cheapness nor the Names of his Bread, I bad him give me three pannyworth of any sort. He gave me accordingly three great Puffy Rolls. I was surpriz'd at the Quantity, but took it, and having no Room in my Pockets, walk'd off, with a Roll under each Arm, & eating the other. Thus I went up Market Street as far as fourth Street, passing by the Door of Mr Read, my future Wife's Father, when she standing at the Door saw me, & thought I made as I certainly did a most awkward ridiculous Appearance. Then I turn'd and went down Chestnut Street and part of Walnut Street, eating my Roll all the Way, and coming round found my self again at Market street Wharff, near the Boat I came in, to which I went for a Draught of the River Water, and being fill'd with one of my Rolls, gave the other two to a Woman & her Child that came down the River in the Boat with us and were waiting to go farther. Thus refresh'd I walk'd again up the Street, which by this time had many clean dress'd People in it who were all walking the same Way; I join'd them, and thereby was led into the great Meeting House of the Quakers near the Market. I sat down among them, and after looking round a while & hearing nothing said, being very drowzy thro' Labour & want of Rest the preceding Night, I fell fast asleep, and continu'd so till the Meeting broke up, when one was kind enough to rouse me. This was therefore the first House I was in or slept in, in Philadelphia.—

Walking again down towards the River, & looking in the Faces of People, I met a young Quaker Man whose Countenance I lik'd, and accosting him requested he would tell me where a Stranger could get Lodging. We were then near the Sign of the Three Mariners. Here, says he, is one Place that entertains Strangers, but it is not a reputable House; if thee wilt walk with me, I'll show thee a better. He brought me to the Crooked Billet in Water-Street. Here I got a Dinner. And while I was eating it, several sly Questions were ask'd me, as it seem'd to be sus-

---

46. Charles Cotton (1630–87) parodied Virgil in *Scarronides, or the First Book of Virgil Travestied* (1664).

47. October 6, 1723.

pected from my youth & Appearance, that I might be some Runaway. After Dinner my Sleepiness return'd: and being shown to a Bed, I lay down without undressing, and slept till Six in the Evening; was call'd to Supper; went to Bed again very early and slept soundly till the next Morning. Then I made my self as tidy as I could, and went to Andrew Bradford the Printer's.—I found in the Shop the old Man his Father, whom I had seen at New York, and who travelling on horse back had got to Philadelphia before me.—He introduc'd me to his Son, who receiv'd me civilly, gave me a Breakfast, but told me he did not at present want a Hand, being lately supply'd with one. But there was another Printer in town lately set up, one Keimer,[48] who perhaps might employ me; if not, I should be welcome to lodge at his House, & he would give me a little Work to do now & then till fuller Business should offer.

The old Gentleman said, he would go with me to the new Printer: And when we found him, Neighbour, says Bradford, I have brought to see you a young Man of your Business, perhaps you may want such a One. He ask'd me a few Questions, put a Composing Stick in my Hand to see how I work'd, and then said he would employ me soon, tho' he had just then nothing for me to do. And taking old Bradford whom he had never seen before, to be one of the Towns People that had a Good Will for him, enter'd into a Conversation on his present Undertaking & Prospects; while Bradford not discovering that he was the other Printer's Father; on Keimer's Saying he expected soon to get the greatest Part of the Business into his own Hands, drew him on by artful Questions and starting little Doubts, to explain all his Views, what Interest he rely'd on, & in what manner he intended to proceed.—I who stood by & heard all, saw immediately that one of them was a crafty old Sophister, and the other a mere Novice. Bradford left me with Keimer, who was greatly surpriz'd when I told him who the old Man was.

Keimer's Printing House I found, consisted of an old shatter'd Press, and one small worn-out Fount of English,[49] which he was then using himself, composing in it an Elegy on Aquila Rose before-mentioned, an ingenious young Man of excellent Character much respected in the Town, Clerk of the Assembly, & a pretty Poet. Keimer

made Verses, too, but very indifferently.—He could not be said to write them, for his Manner was to compose them in the Types directly out of his Head; so there being no Copy, but one Pair of Cases,[50] and the Elegy likely to require all the Letter, no one could help him.—I endeavour'd to put his Press (which he had not yet us'd, & of which he understood nothing) into Order fit to be work'd with; & promising to come & print off his Elegy as soon as he should have got it ready, I return'd to Bradford's who gave me a little Job to do for the present, & there I lodged & dieted. A few Days after Keimer sent for me to print off the Elegy. And now he had got another Pair of Cases, and a Pamphlet to reprint, on which he set me to work.—

These two Printers I found poorly qualified for their Business. Bradford had not been bred to it, & was very illiterate; and Keimer tho' something of a Scholar, was a mere Compositor, knowing nothing of Presswork. He had been one of the French Prophets[51] and could act their enthusiastic Agitations. At this time he did not profess any particular Religion, but something of all on occasion; was very ignorant of the World, & had, as I afterwards found, a good deal of the Knave in his Composition. He did not like my Lodging at Bradford's while I work'd with him. He had a House indeed, but without Furniture, so he could not lodge me: But he got me a Lodging at Mr Read's before-mentioned, who was the Owner of his House. And my Chest & Clothes being come by this time, I made rather a more respectable Appearance in the Eyes of Miss Read, than I had done when she first happen'd to see me eating my Roll in the Street.—

I began now to have some Acquaintance among the young People of the Town, that were Lovers of Reading with whom I spent my Evenings very pleasantly and gaining Money by my Industry & Frugality, I lived very agreably, forgetting Boston as much as I could, and not desiring that any there should know where I resided except my Friend Collins who was in my Secret, & kept it when I wrote to him.—At length an Incident happened that sent me back again much sooner than I had intended.—

I had a Brother-in-law, Robert Holmes, Master of a Sloop,[52] that traded between Boston and Delaware. He

---

48. Samuel Keimer (1688?–1742) employed Franklin for a time, though once Franklin left him, Keimer became unsuccessful and left Philadelphia in 1730.

49. English type, oversized type.

50. Type trays, filled with upper- and lower-case letters.

51. Camisards, Protestants famous for their emotional practices, resided in the Cevennes region of France.

52. Robert Holmes (d. before 1743), was a ship's captain married to Franklin's sister, Mary.

being at New Castle 40 Miles below Philadelphia, heard there of me, and wrote me a Letter, mentioning the Concern of my Friends in Boston at my abrupt Departure, assuring me of their Goodwill to me, and that every thing would be accommodated to my Mind if I would return, to which he exhorted me very earnestly.—I wrote an Answer to his Letter, thank'd him for his Advice, but stated my Reasons for quitting Boston fully, & in such a Light as to convince him I was not so wrong as he had apprehended.—Sir William Keith[53] Governor of the Province, was then at New Castle, and Capt. Holmes happening to be in Company with him when my Letter came to hand, spoke to him of me, and show'd him the Letter. The Governor read it, and seem'd surpriz'd when he was told my Age. He said I appear'd a young Man of promising Parts, and therefore should be encouraged: The Printers at Philadelphia were wretched ones, and if I would set up there, he made no doubt I should succeed; for his Part, he would procure me the publick Business, & do me every other Service in his Power. This my Brother-in-Law afterwards told me in Boston. But I knew as yet nothing of it; when one Day Keimer and I being at Work together near the Window, we saw the Governor and another Gentleman (which prov'd to be Col. French, of New Castle) finely dress'd, come directly across the Street to our House, & heard them at the Door. Keimer ran down immediately, thinking it a Visit to him. But the Governor enquir'd for me, came up, & with a Condescension & Politeness I had been quite unus'd to, made me many Compliments, desired to be acquainted with me, blam'd me kindly for not having made my self known to him when I first came to the Place, and would have me away with him to the Tavern where he was going with Col. French to taste as he said some excellent Madeira. I was not a little surpriz'd, and Keimer star'd like a Pig poison'd. I went however with the Governor & Col. French, to a Tavern the Corner of Third Street, and over the Madeira he propos'd my Setting up my Business, laid before me the Probabilities of Success, & both he & Col French, assur'd me I should have their Interest & Influence in procuring the Publick Business of both Governments. On my doubting whether my Father would assist me in it, Sir William said he would give me a Letter to him, in which he would state the Advantages,—and he did not doubt of prevailing with him. So it was concluded I should return to Boston in the first Vessel with the Governor's Letter recommending me to my Father. In the mean time the Intention was to be kept secret, and I went on working with Keimer as usual, the Governor sending for me now & then to dine with him, a very great Honour I thought it, and conversing with me in the most affable, familiar, & friendly manner imaginable. About the End of April 1724. a little Vessel offer'd for Boston. I took Leave of Keimer as going to see my Friends. The Governor gave me an ample Letter, saying many flattering things of me to my Father, and strongly recommending the Project of my setting up at Philadelphia, as a Thing that must make my Fortune.—We struck on a Shoal in going down the Bay & sprung a Leak, we had a blustering time at Sea, and were oblig'd to pump almost continually, at which I took my Turn.—We arriv'd safe however at Boston in about a Fortnight.—I had been absent Seven Months and my Friends had heard nothing of me, for my Br. Holmes was not yet return'd; and had not written about me. My unexpected Appearance surpriz'd the Family; all were however very glad to see me and made me Welcome, except my Brother. I went to see him at his Printing-House: I was better dress'd than ever while in his Service, having a genteel new Suit from Head to foot, a Watch, and my Pockets lin'd with near Five Pounds Sterling in Silver. He receiv'd me not very frankly, look'd me all over, and turn'd to his Work again. The Journey-Men were inquisitive where I had been, what sort of a Country it was, and how I lik'd it? I prais'd it much, & the happy Life I led in it; expressing strongly my Intention of returning to it; and one of them asking what kind of Money we had there, I produc'd a handful of Silver, and spread it before them, which was a kind of Raree-Show[54] they had not been us'd to, Paper being the Money of Boston. Then I took an Opportunity of letting them see my Watch: and lastly, (my Brother still grum & sullen) I gave them a Piece of Eight to drink[55] & took my Leave.—This Visit of mine offended him extreamly. For when my Mother some time after spoke to him of a Reconciliation, & of her Wishes to see us on good Terms together, & that we might live for the future as Brothers, he said, I had insulted him in such a Manner before his People that he could never forget or forgive it.—In this however he was mistaken.—

My Father receiv'd the Governor's Letter with some apparent Surprize; but said little of it to me for some

---

53. Sir William Keith (1680–1749) governed Pennsylvania from 1717 to 1726.

54. A sideshow, like a peep show.

55. He gave them a Spanish dollar, for drinks.

Days; when Capt. Homes returning, he show'd it to him, ask'd if he knew Keith, and what kind of a Man he was: Adding his Opinion that he must be of small Discretion, to think of setting a Boy up in Business who wanted yet 3 Years of being at Man's Estate. Homes said what he could in fav^r of the Project; but my Father was clear in the Impropriety of it; and at last gave a flat Denial to it. Then he wrote a civil Letter to Sir William thanking him for the Patronage he had so kindly offered me, but declining to assist me as yet in Setting up, I being in his Opinion too young to be trusted with the Management of a Business so important; & for which the Preparation must be so expensive.—

My Friend & Companion Collins, who was a Clerk at the Post-Office, pleas'd with the Account I gave him of my new Country, determin'd to go thither also:—And while I waited for my Fathers Determination, he set out before me by Land to Rhodeisland, leaving his Books which were a pretty Collection of Mathematicks & Natural Philosophy, to come with mine & me to New York where he propos'd to wait for me. My Father, tho' he did not approve Sir William's Proposition was yet pleas'd that I had been able to obtain so advantageous a Character from a Person of such Note where I had resided, and that I had been so industrious & careful as to equip my self so handsomely in so short a time: therefore seeing no Prospect of an Accommodation between my Brother & me, he gave his Consent to my Returning again to Philadelphia, advis'd me to behave respectfully to the People there, endeavour to obtain the general Esteem, & avoid lampooning & libelling to which he thought I had too much Inclination;—telling me, that by steady Industry and a prudent Parsimony, I might save enough by the time I was One and Twenty to set me up, & that if I came near the Matter he would help me out with the Rest.— This was all I could obtain, except some small Gifts as Tokens of his & my Mother's Love, when I embark'd again for New-York, now with their Approbation & their Blessing.—

The Sloop putting in at Newport, Rhodeisland, I visited my Brother John, who had been married & settled there some Years. He received me very affectionately, for he always lov'd me.—A Friend of his, one Vernon, having some Money due to him in Pensilvania, about 35 Pounds Currency, desired I would receive it for him, and keep it till I had his Directions what to remit it in. Accordingly he gave me an Order.—This afterwards occasion'd me a good deal of Uneasiness.—At Newport we took in a Number of Passengers for New York: Among which were two young Women, Companions, and a grave, sensible Matron-like Quaker-Woman with her Attendants.—I had shown an obliging Readiness to do her some little Services which impress'd her I suppose with a degree of Good-will towards me.—Therefore when she saw a daily growing Familiarity between me & the two Young Women, which they appear'd to encourage, she took me aside & said, Young Man, I am concern'd for thee, as thou has no Friend with thee, and seems not to know much of the World, or of the Snares Youth is expos'd to; depend upon it those are very bad Women, I can see it in all their Actions, and if thee art not upon thy Guard, they will draw thee into some Danger: they are Strangers to thee,—and I advise thee in a friendly Concern for thy Welfare, to have no Acquaintance with them.—As I seem'd at first not to think so ill of them as she did, she mention'd some Things she had observ'd & heard that had escap'd my Notice; but now convinc'd me she was right. I thank'd her for her kind Advice, and promis'd to follow it.—When we arriv'd at New York, they told me where they liv'd, & invited me to come and see them: but I avoided it. And it was well I did: For the next Day, the Captain miss'd a Silver Spoon & some other Things that had been taken out of his Cabbin, and knowing that these were a Couple of Strumpets, he got a Warrant to search their Lodgings, found the stolen Goods, and had the Thieves punish'd.—So tho' we had escap'd a sunken Rock which we scrap'd upon in the Passage, I thought this Escape of rather more Importance to me. At New York I found my Friend Collins, who had arriv'd there some Time before me. We had been intimate from Children, and had read the same Books together. But he had the Advantage of more time for Reading, & Studying and a wonderful Genius for Mathematical Learning in which he far outstript me. While I liv'd in Boston most of my Hours of Leisure for Conversation were spent with him, & he continu'd a sober as well as an industrious Lad; was much respected for his Learning by several of the Clergy & other Gentlemen, & seem'd to promise making a good Figure in Life: but during my Absence he had acquir'd a Habit of Sotting[56] with Brandy; and I found by his own Account & what I heard from others, that he had been drunk every day since his Arrival at New York, & behav'd very oddly. He had gam'd too and lost his Money,

---

56. Sotting, becoming drunk.

so that I was oblig'd to discharge[57] his Lodgings, & defray his Expences to and at Philadelphia:—Which prov'd extreamly inconvenient to me.—The then Governor of N York, Burnet,[58] Son of Bishop Burnet hearing from the Captain that a young Man, one of his Passengers, had a great many Books, desired he would bring me to see him. I waited upon him accordingly, and should have taken Collins with me but that he was not sober. The Govr. treated me with greet Civility, show'd me his Library, which was a very large one, & we had a good deal of Conversation about Books & Authors. This was the second Governor who had done me the Honour to take Notice of me, which to a poor Boy like me was very pleasing.—We proceeded to Philadelphia. I received on the Way Vernon's Money, without which we could hardly have finish'd our Journey.—Collins wish'd to be employ'd in some Counting House; but whether they discover'd his Dramming by his Breath, or by his Behaviour, tho' he had some Recommendations, he met with no Success in any Application, and continu'd Lodging & Boarding at the same House with me & at my Expence. Knowing I had that Money of Vernon's he was continually borrowing of me, still promising Repayment as soon as he should be in Business. At length he had got so much of it, that I was distress'd to think what I should do, in case of being call'd on to remit it.—His Drinking continu'd, about which we sometimes quarrel'd, for when a little intoxicated he was very fractious. Once in a Boat on the Delaware with some other young Men, he refused to row in his Turn: I will be row'd home, says he. We will not row you, says I. You must says he, or stay all Night on the Water, just as you please. The others said, Let us row; What signifies it? But my Mind being soured with his other Conduct, I continu'd to refuse. So he swore he would make me row, or throw me overboard; and coming along stepping on the Thwarts towards me, when he came up & struck at me, I clapt my Hand under his Crutch, and rising pitch'd him head-foremost into the River. I knew he was a good Swimmer, and so was under little Concern about him; but before he could get round to lay hold of the Boat, we had with a few Strokes pull'd her out of his Reach.—And ever when he drew near the Boat, we ask'd if he would row, striking a few Strokes to slide her away from him.—He was ready to die with Vexation, & obstinately would not

promise to row; however seeing him at last beginning to tire, we lifted him in; and brought him home dripping wet in the Evening. We hardly exchang'd a civil Word afterwards; and a West India Captain who had a Commission to procure a Tutor for the Sons of a Gentleman at Barbadoes, happening to meet with him, agreed to carry him thither. He left me then, promising to remit me the first Money he should receive in order to discharge the Debt. But I never heard of him after.—The Breaking into this Money of Vernon's was one of the first great Errata of my Life. And this Affair show'd that my Father was not much out in his Judgment when he suppos'd me too Young to manage Business of Importance. But Sir William, on reading his Letter, said he was too prudent. There was great Difference in Persons, and Discretion did not always accompany Years, nor was Youth always without it. And since he will not set you up, says he, I will do it my self. Give me an Inventory of the Things necessary to be had from England, and I will send for them. You shall repay me when you are able; I am resolv'd to have a good Printer here, and I am sure you must succeed. This was spoken with such an Appearance of Cordiality, that I had not the least doubt of his meaning what he said.—I had hitherto kept the Proposition of my Setting up a Secret in Philadelphia, & I still kept it. Had it been known that I depended on the Governor, probably some Friend that knew him better would have advis'd me not to rely on him, as I afterwards heard it as his known Character to be liberal of Promises which he never meant to keep.—Yet unsolicited as he was by me, how could I think his generous Offers insincere? I believ'd him one of the best Men in the World.—

I presented him an Inventory of a little Print^g. House, amounting by my Computation to about 100£ Sterling. He lik'd it, but ask'd me if my being on the Spot in England to chuse the Types & see that every thing was good of the kind, might not be of some Advantage. Then, says he, when there, you may make Acquaintances & establish Correspondencies in the Bookselling, & Stationary Way. I agreed that this might be advantageous. Then says he, get yourself ready to go with Annis:[59] which was the annual Ship, and the only one at that Time usually passing between London and Philadelphia. But it would be some Months before Annis sail'd, so I continu'd working with Keimer, fretting about the Money Collins had got from

---

57. Discharge, pay for.

58. William Burnet (1688–1729) governed New Jersey and New York from 1720 to 1728.

59. Thomas Annis, captain of the ship sailing between Philadelphia and England.

me, and in daily Apprehensions of being call'd upon by Vernon, which however did not happen for some Years after.—

I believe I have omitted mentioning that in my first Voyage from Boston, being becalm'd off Block Island,[60] our People set about catching Cod & hawl'd up a great many. Hitherto I had stuck to my Resolution of not eating animal Food; and on this Occasion, I consider'd with my Master Tryon, the taking every Fish as a kind of unprovok'd Murder, since none of them had or ever could do us any Injury that might justify the Slaughter.—All this seem'd very reasonable.—But I had formerly been a great Lover of Fish, & when this came hot out of the Frying Pan, it smelt admirably well. I balanc'd some time between Principle & Inclination: till I recollected, that when the Fish were opened, I saw smaller Fish taken out of their Stomachs:—Then, thought I, if you eat one another, I don't see why we mayn't eat you. So I din'd upon Cod very heartily and continu'd to eat with other People, returning only now & then occasionally to a vegetable Diet. So convenient a thing it is to be a *reasonable Creature,* since it enables one to find or make a Reason for every thing one has a mind to do.—

Keimer & I liv'd on a pretty good familiar Footing & agreed tolerably well: for he suspected nothing of my Setting up. He retain'd a great deal of his old Enthusiasms, and lov'd an Argumentation. We therefore had many Disputations. I us'd to work him so with my Socratic Method, and had trapann'd him so often by Questions apparently so distant from any Point we had in hand, and yet by degrees led to the Point, and brought him into Difficulties & Contradictions, that at last he grew ridiculously cautious, and would hardly answer me the most common Question, without asking first, *What do you intend to infer from that?* However it gave him so high an Opinion of my Abilities in the Confuting Way, that he seriously propos'd my being his Colleague in a Project he had of setting up a new Sect. He was to preach the Doctrines, and I was to confound all Opponents. When he came to explain with me upon the Doctrines, I found several Conundrums[61] which I objected to, unless I might have my Way a little too, and introduce some of mine. Keimer wore his Beard at full Length, because somewhere in the Mosaic Law it is said, *thou shalt not mar the Corners of*

thy Beard.[62] He like-wise kept the seventh day Sabbath; and these two Points were Essentials with him.—I dislik'd both, but agreed to admit them upon Condition of his adopting the Doctrine of using no animal Food. I doubt, says he, my Constitution will not bear that. I assur'd him it would, & that he would be the better for it. He was usually a great Glutton, and I promis'd my self some Diversion in half-starving him. He agreed to try the Practice if I would keep him Company. I did so and we held it for three Months. We had our Victuals dress'd and brought to us regularly by a Woman in the Neighbourhood, who had from me a List of 40 Dishes to be prepar'd for us at different times, in all which there was neither Fish Flesh nor Fowl, and the Whim suited me the better at this time from the Cheapness of it, not costing us above 18^d Sterling each, per Week.—I have since kept several Lents most strictly, Leaving the common Diet for that, and that for the common, abruptly, without the least Inconvenience: So that I think there is little in the Advice of making those Changes by easy Gradations.—I went on pleasantly, but Poor Keimer suffer'd grievously, tir'd of the Project, long'd for the Flesh Pots of Egypt,[63] and order'd a roast Pig; He invited me & two Women Friends to dine with him, but it being brought too soon upon table, he could not resist the Temptation, and ate it all up before we came.—

I had made some Courtship during this time to Miss Read, I had a great Respect & Affection for her, and had some Reason to believe she had the same for me: but as I was about to take a long Voyage, and we were both very young, only a little above 18. it was thought most prudent by her Mother to prevent our going too far at present, as a Marriage if it was to take place would be more convenient after my Return, when I should be as I expected set up in my Business. Perhaps too she thought my Expectations not so well founded as I imagined them to be.—

My chief Acquaintances at this time were, Charles Osborne, Joseph Watson, & James Ralph; All Lovers of Reading. The two first were Clerks to an eminent Scrive-

---

60. Off the coast of Rhode Island.

61. Puzzles.

---

62. Leviticus 19.27: "Ye shall not round the corners of your heads, neither shalt thou mar the corners of thy beard."

63. Exodus 16.2-3: "And the whole congregation of the children of Israel murmured against Moses and Aaron in the wilderness: and the children of Israel said unto them, Would to God that we had died by the hands of the Lord in the land of Egypt, when we sat by the flesh pots, and when we did eat bread to the full."

ner or Conveyancer[64] in the Town, Charles Brogden;[65] the other was Clerk to a Merchant. Watson was a pious sensible young Man, of great Integrity.—The others rather more lax in their Principles of Religion, particularly Ralph, who as well as Collins had been unsettled by me, for which they both made me suffer.—Osborne was sensible, candid, frank, sincere, and affectionate to his Friends; but in litterary Matters too fond of Criticising. Ralph, was ingenious, genteel in his Manners, & extreamly eloquent; I think I never knew a prettier Talker.— Both of them great Admirers of Poetry, and began to try their Hands in little Pieces. Many pleasant Walks we four had together, on Sundays into the Woods near Skuylkill,[66] where we read to one another & conferr'd on what we read. Ralph was inclin'd to pursue the Study of Poetry, not doubting but he might become eminent in it and make his Fortune by it, alledging that the best Poets must when they first began to write, make as many Faults as he did.— Osborne dissuaded him, assur'd him he had no Genius for Poetry, & advis'd him to think of nothing beyond the Business he was bred to; that in the mercantile way tho' he had no Stock, he might by his Diligence & Punctuality recommend himself to Employment as a Factor,[67] and in time acquire wherewith to trade on his own Account. I approv'd the amusing one's Self with Poetry now & then, so far as to improve one's Language, but no farther. On this it was propos'd that we should each of us at our next Meeting produce a Piece of our own Composing, in order to improve by our mutual Observations, Criticisms & Corrections. As Language & Expression was what we had in View, we excluded all Considerations of Invention, by agreeing that the Task should be a Version of the 18th Psalm, which describes the Descent of a Deity. When the Time of our Meeting drew nigh, Ralph call'd on me first, & let me know his Piece was ready. I told him I had been busy, & having little Inclination had done nothing.—He then show'd me his Piece for my Opinion; and I much approv'd it, as it appear'd to me to have great Merit. Now, says he, Osborne never will allow the least Merit in any thing of mine, but makes 1000 Criticisms out of mere Envy. He is not so jealous of you. I wish therefore you would take this Piece, & produce it as yours. I will pretend not to have had time, & so produce nothing: We shall then see what he will say to it.—It was agreed, and I immediately transcrib'd it that it might appear in my own hand. We met. Watson's Performance was read: there were some Beauties in it: but many Defects. Osborne's was read: It was much better. Ralph did it Justice, remark'd some Faults, but applauded the Beauties. He himself had nothing to produce. I was backward, seem'd desirous of being excus'd, had not had sufficient Time to correct; &c. but no Excuse could be admitted, produce I must. It was read and repeated; Watson and Osborne gave up the Contest; and join'd in applauding it immoderately. Ralph only made some Criticisms & propos'd some Amendments, but I defended my Text. Osborne was against Ralph, & told him he was no better a Critic than Poet; so he dropt the Argument. As they two went home together, Osborne express'd himself still more strongly in favour of what he thought my Production, having restrain'd himself before as he said, lest I should think it Flattery. But who would have imagin'd, says he, that Franklin had been capable of such a Performance; such Painting, such Force! such Fire! he has even improv'd the Original! In his common Conversation, he seems to have no Choice of Words; he hesitates and blunders; and yet, good God, how he writes!—When we next met, Ralph discover'd the Trick we had plaid him, and Osborne was a little laught at. This Transaction fix'd Ralph in his Resolution of becoming a Poet. I did all I could to dissuade him from it, but He continu'd scribbling Verses, till *Pope* cur'd him.[68]—He became however a pretty good Prose Writer. More of him hereafter. But as I may not have occasion again to mention the other two, I shall just remark here, that Watson died in my Arms a few Years after, much lamented, being the best of our Set. Osborne went to the West Indies, where he became an eminent Lawyer & made Money, but died young. He and I had made a serious Agreement, that the one who happen'd first to die, should if possible make a friendly Visit to the other, and acquaint him how he found things in that separate State. But he never fulfill'd his Promise.

The Governor, seeming to like my Company, had me frequently to his House; & his Setting me up was always mention'd as a fix'd thing. I was to take with me Letters recommendatory to a Number of his Friends, besides the

---

64. Someone who writes up legal notes, such as leases and deeds.

65. Charles Brockden (1683–1769).

66. The Schuylkill River, near Philadelphia.

67. Factor, business agent.

---

68. Alexander Pope belittled James Ralph's poetry in his long poem, *The Dunciad* (1728).

Letter of Credit, to furnish me with the necessary Money for purchasing the Press & Types, Paper, &c. For these Letters I was appointed to call at different times, when they were to be ready, but a future time was still named.— Thus we went on till the Ship whose Departure too had been several times postponed was on the Point of sailing. Then when I call'd to take my Leave & receive the Letters, his Secretary, Dr Bard,[69] came out to me and said the Governor was extreamly busy, in writing, but would be down at Newcastle[70] before the Ship, & there the Letters would be delivered to me.

Ralph, tho' married & having one Child, had determined to accompany me in this Voyage. It was thought he intended to establish a Correspondence, & obtain Goods to sell on Commission. But I found afterwards, that thro' some Discontent with his Wifes Relations, he purposed to leave her on their Hands, & never return again.—Having taken leave of my Friends, & interchang'd some Promises with Miss Read, I left Philadelphia in the Ship, which anchor'd at Newcastle. The Governor was there. But when I went to his Lodging, the Secretary came to me from him with the civillest Message in the World, that he could not then see me being engag'd in Business of the utmost Importance, but should send the Letters to me on board, wish'd me heartily a good Voyage and a speedy Return, &c. I return'd on board, a little puzzled, but still not doubting.—

Mr Andrew Hamilton, a famous Lawyer of Philadelphia,[71] had taken Passage in the same Ship for himself and Son: and with Mr Denham a Quaker Merchant, & Messrs Onion & Russel Masters of an Iron Work in Maryland, had engag'd the Great Cabin; so that Ralph and I were forc'd to take up with a Birth in the Steerage:—And none on board knowing us, were considered as ordinary Persons.—But Mr Hamilton & his Son (it was James,[72] since Governor) return'd from New Castle to Philadelphia, the Father being recall'd by a great Fee to plead for a seized Ship.—And just before we sail'd Col. French coming on board, & showing me great Respect, I was more taken Notice of, and with my Friend Ralph invited by the other Gentlemen to come into the Cabin, there being now Room. Accordingly we remov'd thither.

Understanding that Col. French had brought on board the Governor's Dispatches, I ask'd the Captain for those Letters that were to be under my Care. He said all were put into the Bag together; and he could not then come at them; but before we landed in England, I should have an Opportunity of picking them out. So I was satisfy'd for the present, and we proceeded on our Voyage. We had a sociable Company in the Cabin, and lived uncommonly well, having the Addition of all Mr Hamilton's Stores, who had laid in plentifully. In this Passage Mr Denham[73] contracted a Friendship for me that continued during his Life. The Voyage was otherwise not a pleasant one, as we had a great deal of bad Weather.—

When we came into the Channel, the Captain kept his Word with me, & gave me an Opportunity of examining the Bag for the Governor's Letters. I found none upon which my Name was put, as under my Care; I pick'd out 6 or 7 that by the Handwriting I thought might be the promis'd Letters, especially as one of them was directed to Basket the King's Printer,[74] and another to some Stationer. We arriv'd in London the 24th of December, 1724.—I waited upon the Stationer who came first in my Way, delivering the Letter as from Gov. Keith. I don't know such a Person, says he: but opening the Letter, O, this is from Riddlesden;[75] I have lately found him to be a compleat Rascal, and I will have nothing to do with him, nor receive any Letters from him. So putting the Letter into my Hand, he turn'd on his Heel & left me to serve some Customer.—I was surprized to find these were not the Governor's Letters. And after recollecting and comparing Circumstances, I began to doubt his Sincerity.—I found my Friend Denham, and opened the whole Affair to him. He let me into Keith's Character, told me there was not the least Probability that he had written any Letters for me, that no one who knew him had the smallest Dependence on him, and he laught at the Notion of the Governor's giving me a Letter of Credit, having as he said no Credit to give.—On my expressing some Concern about what I should do: He advis'd me to endeavour getting some Employment in the Way of my Business. Among the Printers here, says he, you will improve yourself; and

---

69. Patrick Baird, a surgeon.

70. Newcastle, Delaware.

71. Andrew Hamilton (1678?–1783).

72. James Hamilton (1710?–83) governed Pennsylvania four times between 1748 and 1773.

73. Thomas Denham (d. 1728) was a Philadelphia merchant.

74. John Baskett (d. 1742).

75. William Riddlesden (d. before 1733) was known as a notorious swindler in Maryland.

when you return to America, you will set up to greater Advantage.—

We both of us happen'd to know, as well as the Stationer, that Riddlesden the Attorney, was a very Knave. He had half ruin'd Miss Read's Father by drawing him in to be bound for him. By his Letter it appear'd, there was a secret Scheme on foot to the Prejudice of Hamilton, (Suppos'd to be then coming over with us,) and that Keith was concern'd in it with Riddlesden. Denham, who was a Friend of Hamilton's, thought he ought to be acquainted with it. So when he arriv'd in England, which was soon after, partly from Resentment & Ill-Will to Keith & Riddlesden, & partly from Good Will to him: I waited on him, and gave him the Letter. He thank'd me cordially, the Information being of Importance to him. And from that time he became my Friend, greatly to my Advantage afterwards on many Occasions.

But what shall we think of a Governor's playing such pitiful Tricks, & imposing so grossly on a poor ignorant Boy! It was a Habit he had acquired. He wish'd to please every body; and having little to give, he gave Expectations.—He was otherwise an ingenious sensible Man, a pretty good Writer, & a good Governor for the People, tho' not for his Constituents the Proprietaries,[76] whose Instructions he sometimes disregarded.—Several of our best Laws were of his Planning, and pass'd during his Administration.—

Ralph and I were inseparable Companions. We took Lodgings together in Little Britain[77] at 3/6 per Week, as much as we could then afford.—He found some Relations, but they were poor & unable to assist him. He now let me know his Intentions of remaining in London, and that he never meant to return to Philad[a].—He had brought no Money with him, the whole he could muster having been expended in paying his Passage.—I had 15 Pistoles:[78] So he borrowed occasionally of me, to subsist while he was looking out for Business.—He first endeavoured to get into the Playhouse, believing himself qualify'd for an Actor; but Wilkes,[79] to whom he apply'd, advis'd him candidly not to think of that Employment, as it was impossible he should succeed in it.—Then he propos'd to Roberts, a Publisher in Paternoster Row,[80] to write for him a Weekly Paper like the Spectator, on certain Conditions, which Roberts did not approve. Then he endeavour'd to get Employm[t]. as a Hackney Writer to copy for the Stationers[81] & Lawyers about the Temple:[82] but could find no Vacancy.—

I immediately got into Work at Plamer's then a famous Printing House in Bartholomew Close;[83] and here I continu'd near a Year. I was pretty diligent; but spent with Ralph a good deal of my Earnings in going to Plays & other Places of Amusement. We had together consum'd all my Pistoles, and now just rubb'd on from hand to mouth. He seem'd quite to forget his Wife & Child, and I by degrees my Engagements wth Miss Read, to whom I never wrote more than one Letter, & that was to let her know I was not likely soon to return. This was another of the great Errata of my Life, which I should wish to correct if I were to live it over again.—In fact, by our Expences, I was constantly kept unable to pay my Passage.

At Palmer's I was employ'd in Composing for the second Edition of Woollaston's Religion of Nature.[84] Some of his Reasonings not appearing to me well-founded, I wrote a little metaphysical Piece, in which I made Remarks on them. It was entitled, *A Dissertation on Liberty & Necessity, Pleasure and Pain*.[85]—I inscrib'd it to my Friend Ralph.—I printed a small Number. It occasion'd my being more consider'd by Mr Palmer, as a young Man of some Ingenuity, tho' he seriously expostulated with me upon the Principles of my Pamphlet which to him appear'd abominable. My printing this Pamphlet was another Erratum.

While I lodg'd in Little Britain I made an Acquaintance with one Wilcox a Bookseller, whose Shop was at the next Door. He had an immense Collection of second-hand Books. Circulating Libraries were not then in Use;

---

76. The Penn family was the Proprietary in Pennsylvania.

77. Near St. Paul's Cathedral, London.

78. Pistoles, Spanish gold coins, each worth eighteen English Shillings.

79. Robert Wilks (1665?–1732), a London actor.

80. The printing district of London.

81. Copyists.

82. Inner and Middle Temples were names given to two of the four sets of buildings central to London's legal profession.

83. A small square in London, important to the printing trade.

84. William Wollaston's *The Religion of Nature Delineated* was published in its third edition by Samuel Palmer in 1725.

85. The pamphlet, published in 1725, argued against the existence of virtue and vice, which laid Franklin open to complaints about atheism.

but we agreed that on certain reasonable Terms which I have now forgotten, I might take, read & return any of his Books. This I esteem'd a great Advantage, & I made as much Use of it as I could.—

My Pamphlet by some means falling into the Hands of one Lyons, a Surgeon, Author of a Book intituled *The Infallibility of Human Judgment,* it occasioned an Acquaintance between us; he took great Notice of me, call'd on me often, to converse on these Subjects, carried me to the Horns a pale Ale-House in Lane, Cheapside, and introduc'd me to Dr Mandevile, Author of the Fable of the Bees[86] who had a Club there, of which he was the Soul, being a most facetious entertaining Companion. Lyons too introduc'd me to Dr Pemberton, at Batson's Coffee House, who promis'd to give me an Opportunity some time or other of seeing Sir Isaac Newton, of which I was extreamly desirous; but this never happened.

I had brought over a few Curiosities among which the principal was a Purse made of the Asbestos, which purifies by Fire. Sir Hans Sloane[87] heard of it, came to see me, and invited me to his House in Bloomsbury Square; where he show'd me all his Curiosities, and persuaded me to let him add that to the Number, for which he paid me handsomely.—

In our House there lodg'd a young Woman; a Millener, who I think had a Shop in the Cloisters.[88] She had been genteelly bred; was sensible & lively, and of most pleasing Conversation.—Ralph read Plays to her in the Evenings, they grew intimate, she took another Lodging, and he follow'd her. They liv'd together some time, but he being still out of Business, & her Income not sufficient to maintain them with her Child, he took a Resolution of going from London, to try for a Country School, which he thought himself well qualify'd to undertake, as he wrote an excellent Hand, & was a Master of Arithmetic & Accounts.—This however he deem'd a Business below him, & confident of future better Fortune when he should be unwilling to have it known that he once was so meanly employ'd, he chang'd his Name, & did me the Honour to assume mine.—For I soon after had a Letter from him, acquainting me, that he was settled in a small Village in Berkshire, I think it was, where he taught reading & writ-

ing to 10 or a dozen Boys at 6 pence each per Week, recommending Mrs T. to my Care, and desiring me to write to him directing for Mr Franklin Schoolmaster at such a Place. He continu'd to write frequently, sending me large Specimens of an Epic Poem, which he was then composing, and desiring my Remarks & Corrections.—These I gave him from time to time, but endeavour'd rather to discourage his Proceeding. One of Young's Satires was then just publish'd.[89] I copy'd & sent him a great Part of it, which set in a strong Light the Folly of pursuing the Muses with any Hope of Advancement by them. All was in vain. Sheets of the Poem continu'd to come by every Post. In the mean time Mrs T. having on his Account lost her Friends & Business, was often in Distresses, & us'd to send for me, and borrow what I could spare to help her out of them. I grew fond of her Company, and being at this time under no Religious Restraints, & presuming on my Importance to her, I attempted Familiarities, (another Erratum) which she repuls'd with a proper Resentment, and acquainted him with my Behaviour. This made a Breach between us, & when he return'd again to London, he let me know he thought I had cancel'd all the Obligations he had been under to me.—So I found I was never to expect his Repaying me what I lent to him or advanc'd for him. This was however not then of much Consequence, as he was totally unable.—And in the Loss of his Friendship I found my self reliev'd from a Burthen. I now began to think of getting a little Money beforehand; and expecting better Work, I left Palmer's to work at Watts's[90] near Lincoln's Inn Fields, a still greater Printing House. Here I continu'd all the rest of my Stay in London.

At my first Admission into this Printing House, I took to working at Press, imagining I felt a Want of the Bodily Exercise I had been us'd to in America, where Presswork is mix'd with Composing. I drank only Water; the other Workmen, near 50 in Number, were great Guzzlers of Beer. On occasion I carried up & down Stairs a large Form of Types in each hand, when others carried but one in both Hands. They wonder'd to see from this & several Instances that the Water-American as they call'd me was *stronger* than themselves who drunk *strong* Beer. We had an Alehouse Boy who attended always in the House to supply the Workmen. My Companion at the Press, drank

---

86. Bernard Mandeville wrote *Fable of the Bees, or Private Vices Public Benefits* (1714).

87. Sir Hans Sloane (1660–1753) presided over the Royal Society after Sir Isaac Newton.

88. That is, near St. Bartholomew's Church.

89. Probably Edward Young's *The Universal Passion* (1725–28).

90. The printing house was owned by John Watts (1678?–1763).

every day a Pint before Breakfast, a Pint at Breakfast with his Bread and Cheese; a Pint between Breakfast and Dinner; a Pint at Dinner; a Pint in the Afternoon about Six o'clock, and another when he had done his Day's-Work. I thought it a detestable Custom.—But it was necessary, he suppos'd, to drink *strong* Beer that he might be *strong* to labour. I endeavour'd to convince him that the Bodily Strength afforded by Beer could only be in proportion to the Grain or Flour of the Barley dissolved in the Water of which it was made; that there was more Flour in a Pennyworth of Bread, and therefore if he would eat that with a Pint of Water, it would give him more Strength than a Quart of Beer.—He drank on however, & had 4 or 5 Shillings to pay out of his Wages every Saturday Night for that muddling Liquor; an Expence I was free from.—And thus these poor Devils keep themselves always under.

Watts after some Weeks desiring to have me in the Composing-Room, I left the Pressmen. A new *Bienvenu*[91] or Sum for Drink, being 5/, was demanded of me by the Compostors. I thought it an Imposition, as I had paid below. The Master thought so too, and forbad my Paying it. I stood out two or three Weeks, was accordingly considered as an Excommunicate, and had so many little Pieces of private Mischief done me, by mixing my Sorts, transposing my Pages, breaking my Matter, &c. &c.[92] if I were ever so little out of the Room, & all ascrib'd to the Chapel Ghost, which they said ever haunted those not regularly admitted, that notwithstanding the Master's Protection, I found myself oblig'd to comply and pay the Money; convinc'd of the Folly of being on ill Terms with those one is to live with continually. I was now on a fair Footing with them, and soon acquir'd considerable Influence. I propos'd some reasonable Alterations in their Chapel[93] Laws, and carried them against all Opposition. From my Example a great Part of them, left their muddling Breakfast of Beer & Bread & Cheese, finding they could with me be supply'd from a neighbouring House with a large Porringer of hot Water-gruel, sprinkled with Pepper, crumb'd with Bread, & a Bit of Butter in it, for the Price of a Pint of Beer, viz, three halfpence. This was a more comfortable as well as cheaper Breakfast, & kept

their Heads clearer.—Those who continu'd sotting with Beer all day, were often, by not paying, out of Credit at the Alehouse, and us'd to make Interest with me to get Beer, *their Light,* as they phras'd it, *being out.* I watch'd the Pay table on Saturday Night, & collected what I stood engag'd for them, having to pay some times near Thirty Shillings a Week on their Accounts.—This, and my being esteem'd a pretty good Riggite, that is a jocular verbal Satyrist, supported my Consequence in the Society.—My constant Attendance, (I never making a St. Monday[94]), recommended me to the Master; and my uncommon Quickness at Composing, occasion'd my being put upon all Work of Dispatch which was generally better paid. So I went on now very agreably.—

My Lodging in Little Britain being too remote, I found another in Duke-street opposite to the Romish Chapel. It was two pair of Stairs backwards at an Italian Warehouse. A Widow Lady kept the House; she had a Daughter & a Maid Servant, and a Journey-man who attended the Warehouse, but lodg'd abroad.—After sending to enquire my Character at the House where I last lodg'd, she agreed to take me in at the same Rate 3/6 per Week, cheaper as she said from the Protection she expected in having a Man lodge in the House. She was a Widow, an elderly Woman, had been bred a Protestant, being a Clergyman's Daughter, but was converted to the Catholic Religion by her Husband, whose Memory she much revered, had lived much among People of Distinction, and knew a 1000 Anecdotes of them as far back as the Times of Charles the second. She was lame in her Knees with the Gout, and therefore seldom stirr'd out of her Room, so sometimes wanted Company; and hers was so highly amusing to me; that I was sure to spend an Evening with her whenever she desired it. Our Supper was only half an Anchovy each, on a very little Strip of Bread & Butter, and half a Pint of Ale between us.—But the Entertainment was in her Conversation. My always keeping good Hours, and giving little Trouble in the Family, made her unwilling to part with me; so that when I talk'd of a Lodging I had heard of, nearer my Business, for 2/ a Week, which, intent as I now was on saving Money, made some Difference; she bid me not think of it, for she would abate me two Shillings a Week for the future, so I remain'd with her at 1/6 as long as I staid in London.—

---

91. Welcome, in French.

92. That is, they caused Franklin problems by mixing up his types, putting the manuscript pages in the wrong order, and breaking up the type he had already set.

93. "A Printing House is always called a Chappel by the Workmen.—" [Au.]

94. That is, Franklin never took off on a Monday to observe any religious holiday.

In a Garret of her House there lived a Maiden Lady of 70 in the most retired Manner, of whom my Landlady gave me this Account, that she was a Roman-Catholic, had been sent abroad when young & lodg'd in a Nunnery with an Intent of becoming a Nun: but the Country not agreeing with her, she return'd to England, where there being no Nunnery, she had vow'd to lead the Life of a Nun as near as might be done in those Circumstances: Accordingly She had given all her Estate to charitable Uses, reserving only Twelve Pounds a Year to live on, and out of this Sum she still gave a great deal in Charity, living her self on Watergruel only, & using no Fire but to boil it.— She had lived many Years in that Garret, being permitted to remain there gratis by successive catholic Tenants of the House below, as they deem'd it a Blessing to have her there. A Priest visited her, to confess her every Day. I have ask'd her, says my Landlady, how she, as she liv'd, could possibly find so much Employment for a Confessor? O, says she, it is impossible to avoid *vain Thoughts*. I was permitted once to visit her: She was chearful & polite, & convers'd pleasantly. The Room was clean, but had no other Furniture than a Matras, a Table with a Crucifix & Book, a Stool, which she gave me to sit on, and a Picture over the Chimney of St. *Veronica,* displaying her Handkerchief with the miraculous Figure of Christ's bleeding Face on it, which she explain'd to me with great Seriousness. She look'd pale, but was never sick, and I give it as another Instance on how small an Income Life & Health may be supported.—

At Watts's Printinghouse I contracted an Acquaintance with an ingenious young Man, one Wygate, who having wealthy Relations, had been better educated than most Printers, was a tolerable Latinist, spoke French, & lov'd Reading. I taught him, & a Friend of his, to swim, at twice going into the River, & they soon became good Swimmers. They introduc'd me to some Gentlemen from the Country who went to Chelsea by Water to see the College[95] and Don Saltero's Curiosities.[96] In our Return, at the Request of the Company, whose Curiosity Wygate had excited, I stript & leapt into the River, & swam from near Chelsea to Blackfryars,[97] performing on the Way many Feats of Activity both upon & under Water, that sur-

priz'd & pleas'd those to whom they were Novelties.—I had from a Child been ever delighted with this Exercise, had studied & practis'd all Thevenot's Motions & Positions,[98] added some of my own, aiming at the graceful & easy, as well as the Useful.—All these I took this Occasion of exhibiting to the Company, & was much flatter'd by their Admiration.—And Wygate, who was desirous of becoming a Master, grew more & more attach'd to me, on that account, as well as from the Similarity of our Studies. He at length propos'd to me travelling all over Europe together, supporting ourselves every where by working at our Business. I was once inclin'd to it. But mentioning it to my good Friend Mr Denham, with whom I often spent an Hour, when I had Leisure. He dissuaded me from it; advising me to think only of return^g. to Pensilvania, which he was now about to do.—

I must record one Trait of this good Man's Character. He had formerly been in Business at Bristol, but fail'd in Debt to a Number of People, compounded[99] and went to America. There, by a close Application to Business as a Merchant, he acquir'd a plentiful Fortune in a few Years. Returning to England in the Ship with me, He invited his old Creditors to an Entertainment, at which he thank'd them for the easy Composition they had favour'd him with, & when they expected nothing but the Treat, every Man at the first Remove,[100] found under his Plate an Order on a Banker for the full Amount of the unpaid Remainder with Interest.

He now told me he was about to return to Philadelphia, and should carry over a great Quantity of Goods in order to open a Store there: He propos'd to take me over as his Clerk, to keep his Books (in which he would instruct me) copy his Letters, and attend the Store. He added, that as soon as I should be acquainted with mercantile Business he would promote me by sending me with a Cargo of Flour & Bread &c to the West Indies, and procure me Commissions from others; which would be profitable, & if I manag'd well, would establish me handsomely. The Thing pleas'd me, for I was grown tired of London, remember'd with Pleasure the happy Months I had spent in Pennsylvania, and wish'd again to see it. Therefore I immediately agreed, on the Terms of Fifty Pounds a Year Pensilvania

---

95. Chelsea Hospital was erected at the former site of Chelsea College.

96. James Salter's curiosities had dubious authenticity.

97. He swam over three miles.

98. A reference to *The Art of Swimming* (1699) by Melchisedec Thevenot.

99. Settled part of his debt.

100. That is, at the first clearing of the plates.

Money; less indeed than my then present Gettings as a Compostor, but affording a better Prospect.—

I now took Leave of Printing, as I thought for ever, and was daily employ'd in my new Business; going about with Mr Denham among the Tradesmen, to purchase various Articles, & see them pack'd up, doing Errands, calling upon Workmen to dispatch, &c. and when all was on board, I had a few Days Leisure. On one of these Days I was to my Surprize sent for by a great Man I knew only by Name, a Sir William Wyndham[101] and I waited upon him. He had heard by some means or other of my Swimming from Chelsey to Blackfryars, and of my teaching Wygate and another young Man to swim in a few Hours. He had two Sons about to set out on their Travels; he wish'd to have them first taught Swimming; and propos'd to gratify me handsomely if I would teach them.—They were not yet come to Town and my Stay was uncertain, so I could not undertake it. But from this Incident I thought it likely, that if I were to remain in England and open a Swimming School, I might get a good deal of Money.— And it struck me so strongly, that had the Overture been sooner made me, probably I should not so soon have returned to America.—After Many Years, you & I had something of more Importance to do with one of these Sons of Sir William Wyndham, become Earl of Egremont, which I shall mention in its Place.—

Thus I spent about 18 Months in London. Most Part of the Time, I work'd hard at my Business, & spent but little upon my self except in seeing Plays, & in Books.—My Friend Ralph had kept me poor. He owed me about 27 Pounds; which I was now never likely to receive; a great Sum out of my small Earnings. I lov'd him notwithstanding, for he had many amiable Qualities.—tho' I had by no means improv'd my Fortune.—But I had pick'd up some very ingenious Acquaintance whose Conversation was of great Advantage to me, and I had read considerably.

We sail'd from Gravesend on the 23^d of July 1726.— For The Incidents of the Voyage, I refer you to my Journal, where you will find them all minutely related. Perhaps the most important Part of that Journal is the *Plan*[102] to be found in it which I formed at Sea, for regulating my future Conduct in Life. It is the more remarkable, as being form'd when I was so young, and yet being pretty faithfully adhered to quite thro' to old Age.—We landed in Philadelphia the 11th of October, where I found sundry Alterations. Keith was no longer Governor, being superceded by Major Gordon: I met him walking the Streets as a common Citizen.[103] He seem'd a little asham'd at seeing me, but pass'd without saying any thing. I should have been as much asham'd at seeing Miss Read, had not her Fr.^{ds} despairing with Reason of my Return, after the Receipt of my Letter, persuaded her to marry another, one Rogers, a Potter, which was done in my Absence. With him however she was never happy, and soon parted from him, refusing to cohabit with him, or bear his Name It being now said that he had another Wife. He was a worthless Fellow tho' an excellent Workman which was the Temptation to her Friends. He got into Debt, and ran away in 1727 or 28, went to the West Indies, and died there. Keimer had got a better House, a Shop well supply'd with Stationary, plenty of new Types, a number of Hands tho' none good, and seem'd to have a great deal of Business.

Mr Denham took a Store in Water Street, where we open'd our Goods. I attended the Business diligently, studied Accounts, and grew in a little Time expert at selling.—We lodg'd and boarded together, he counsell'd me as a Father, having a sincere Regard for me: I respected & lov'd him: and we might have gone on together very happily: But in the Beginning of Feby. 172 $\frac{6}{7}$ when I had just pass'd my 21st Year, we both were taken ill. My Distemper was a Pleurisy, which very nearly carried me off:—I suffered a good deal, gave up the Point in my own mind, & was rather disappointed when I found my self recovering; regretting in some degree that I must now sometime or other have all that disagreable Work to do over again.—I forget what his Distemper was. It held him a long time, and at length carried him off.[104] He left me a small Legacy in a nuncupative Will,[105] as a Token of his Kindness for me, and he left me once more to the wide World. For the Store was taken into the Care of his Executors, and my Employment under him ended:—My Brother-in-law Homes, being now at Philadelphia, advis'd my Return to my Business. And Keimer tempted me

101. Sir William Wyndham (1687–1740), an English politician.

102. Presumably, a reference to Franklin's "Plan of Conduct," although the longer journal from which it was taken seems to have been lost.

103. Patrick Gordon (1644–1736) governed Pennsylvania from 1726 to 1736.

104. Franklin's friend, John Denham, died July 4, 1728, after a long illness.

105. In an oral will, Franklin was formally given the ten pounds he still owed to Denham for the return trip from London.

with an Offer of large Wages by the Year to come & take the Management of his Printing-House that he might better attend his Stationer's Shop.—I had heard a bad Character of him in London, from his Wife & her Friends, & was not fond of having any more to do with him. I try'd for farther Employment as a Merchant's Clerk; but not readily meeting with any, I clos'd again with Keimer.—

I found in *his* House these Hands; Hugh Meredith[106] a Welsh-Pensilvanian, 30 Years of Age, bred to Country Work: honest, sensible, had a great deal of solid Observation, was something of a Reader, but given to drink:— Stephen Potts,[107] a young Country Man of full Age, bred to the Same:—of uncommon natural Parts, & great Wit & Humour, but a little idle.—These he had agreed with at extream low Wages, per Week, to be rais'd a Shilling every 3 Months, as they would deserve by improving in their Business, & the Expectation of these high Wages to come on hereafter was what he had drawn them in with.—Meredith was to work at Press, Potts at Bookbinding, which he by Agreement, was to teach them, tho' he knew neither one nor t'other. John——a wild Irishman brought up to no Business, whose Service for 4 Years Keimer had purchas'd from the Captain of a Ship. He too was to be made a Pressman. George Webb,[108] an Oxford Scholar, whose Time for 4 Years he had likewise bought, intending him for a Compositor: of whom more presently. And David Harry,[109] a Country Boy, whom he had taken Apprentice. I soon perceiv'd that the Intention of engaging me at Wages so much higher than he had been us'd to give, was to have these raw cheap Hands form'd thro' me, and as soon as I had instructed them, then, they being all articled to him, he should be able to do without me.—I went on however, very chearfully; put his Printing House in Order, which had been in great Confusion, and brought his Hands by degrees to mind their Business and to do it better.

It was an odd Thing to find an Oxford Scholar in the Situation of a bought Servant. He was not more than 18 Years of Age, & gave me this Account of himself; that he was born in Gloucester, educated at a Grammar School there, had been distinguish'd among the Scholars for some apparent Superiority in performing his Part when they exhibited Plays; belong'd to the Witty Club there, and had written some Pieces in Prose & Verse which were printed in the Gloucester Newspapers.—Thence he was sent to Oxford; there he continu'd about a Year, but not well-satisfy'd, wishing of all things to see London & become a Player. At length receiving his Quarterly Allowance of 15 Guineas, instead of discharging his Debts, he walk'd out of Town, hid his Gown in a Furz Bush,[110] and footed it to London, where having no Friend to advise him, he fell into bad Company, soon spent his Guineas, found no means of being introduc'd among the Players, grew necessitous, pawn'd his Cloaths & wanted Bread. Walking the Street very hungry, & not knowing what to do with himself, a Crimp's Bill[111] was put into his Hand, offering immediate Entertainment & Encouragement to such as would bind themselves to serve in America. He went directly, sign'd the Indentures, was put into the Ship & came over; never writing a Line to acquaint his Friends what was become of him. He was lively, witty, good-natur'd and a pleasant Companion; but idle, thoughtless & imprudent to the last Degree.

John the Irishman soon ran away. With the rest I began to live very agreably; for they all respected me, the more as they found Keimer incapable of instructing them, and that from me they learnt something daily. We never work'd on a Saturday, that being Keimer's Sabbath. So I had two Days for Reading. My Acquaintance with ingenious People in the Town, increased. Keimer himself treated me with great Civility & apparent Regard; and nothing now made me uneasy but my Debt to Vernon, which I was yet unable to pay being hitherto but a poor Oeconomist.—He however kindly made no Demand of it.

Our Printing-House often wanted Sorts, and there was no Letter Founder in America. I had seen Types cast at James's in London,[112] but without much Attention to the Manner: However I now contriv'd a Mould, made use of the Letters we had, as Puncheons,[113] struck the Matrices[114] in Lead, and thus supply'd in a pretty tolerable way

---

106. Hugh Meredith (1696?–1749?) later became Franklin's business partner.

107. Stephen Potts (d. 1758), became a bookseller and tavern keeper.

108. George Webb (1709?), a printer.

109. David Harry (1708–60) later became a printer in Barbados.

110. That is, he hid his academic robe in an evergreen bush.

111. An advertisement for passage to the colonies in exchange for a promise of labor.

112. Thomas James's foundry was the largest in London.

113. Stamping tools.

114. Molds for casting type.

all Deficiencies. I also engrav'd several Things on occasion. I made the Ink, I was Warehouse-man & every thing, in short quite a Factotum.[115]—

But however serviceable I might be, I found that my Services became every Day of less Importance, as the other Hands improv'd in the Business. And when Keimer paid my second Quarter's Wages, he let me know that he felt them too heavy, and thought I should make an Abatement. He grew by degrees less civil, put on more of the Master, frequently found Fault, was captious and seem'd ready for an Out-breaking. I went on nevertheless with a good deal of Patience, thinking that his incumber'd Circumstances were partly the Cause. At length a Trifle snapt our Connexion. For a great Noise happening near the Courthouse, I put my Head out of the Window to see what was the Matter. Keimer being in the Street look'd up & saw me, call'd out to me in a loud Voice and angry Tone to mind my Business, adding some reproachful Words, that nettled me the more for their Publicity, all the Neighbours who were looking out on the same Occasion being Witnesses how I was treated. He came up immediately into the Printing-House, continu'd the Quarrel, high Words pass'd on both Sides, he gave me the Quarter's Warning we had stipulated, expressing a Wish that he had not been oblig'd to so long a Warning: I told him his Wish was unnecessary for I would leave him that Instant; and so taking my Hat walk'd out of Doors; desiring Meredith[116] whom I saw below to take care of some Things I left, & bring them to my Lodging.—

Meredith came accordingly in the Evening, when we talk'd my Affair over. He had conceiv'd a great Regard for me, & was very unwilling that I should leave the House while he remain'd in it. He dissuaded me from returning to my native Country which I began to think of. He reminded me that Keimer was in debt for all he possess'd, that his Creditors began to be uneasy, that he kept his Shop miserably, sold often without Profit for ready Money, and often trusted without keeping Account. That he must therefore fail; which would make a Vacancy I might profit of.—I objected my Want of Money. He then let me know, that his Father had a high Opinion of me, and from some Discourse that had pass'd between them, he was sure would advance Money to set us up, if I would enter into Partnership with him.—My Time, says he, will be out with Keimer in the Spring. By that time we may

have our Press & Types in from London:—I am sensible I am no Workman. If you like it, Your Skill in the Business shall be set against the Stock I furnish; and we will share the Profits equally.—The Proposal was agreable, and I consented. His Father was in Town, and approv'd of it, the more as he saw I had great Influence with his Son, had prevail'd on him to abstain long from Dramdrinking,[117] and he hop'd might break him of that wretched Habit entirely, when we came to be so closely connected. I gave an Inventory to the Father, who carry'd it to a Merchant; the Things were sent for; the Secret was to be kept till they should arrive, and in the mean time I was to get Work if I could at the other Printing House.—But I found no Vacancy there, and so remain'd idle a few Days, when Keimer, on a Prospect of being employ'd to print some Paper-money, in New Jersey, which would require Cuts & various Types that I only could supply, and apprehending Bradford might engage me & get the Jobb from him, sent me a very civil Message, that old Friends should not part for a few Words the Effect of sudden Passion, and wishing me to return. Meredith persuaded me to comply, as it would give more Opportunity for his Improvement under my daily Instructions.—So I return'd, and we went on more smoothly than for some time before.—The New Jersey Jobb was obtain'd. I contriv'd a Copper-Plate Press for it, the first that had been seen in the Country.—I cut several Ornaments and Checks for the Bills. We went together to Burlington, where I executed the Whole to Satisfaction, & he received so large a Sum for the Work, as to be enabled thereby to keep his Head much longer above Water.—

At Burlington I made an Acquaintance with many principal People of the Province. Several of them had been appointed by the Assembly a Committee to attend the Press, and take Care that no more Bills were printed than the Law directed. They were therefore by Turns constantly with us, and generally he who attended brought with him a Friend or two for Company. My Mind having been much more improv'd by Reading than Keimer's, I suppose it was for that Reason my Conversation seem'd to be more valu'd. They had me to their Houses, introduc'd me to their Friends and show'd me much Civility, while he, tho' the Master, was a little neglected. In truth he was an odd Fish, ignorant of common Life, fond of rudely opposing receiv'd Opinions, slovenly to extream dirtiness, enthusiastic in some Points of Religion, and a

---

115. A factotum, jack of all trades.

116. Simon Meredith (d. 1745?).

117. Drams are small measures, in this case, of alcohol.

little Knavish withal. We continu'd there near 3 Months, and by that time I could reckon among my acquired Friends, Judge Allen, Samuel Bustill, the Secretary of the Province, Isaac Pearson, Joseph Cooper & several of the Smiths, Members of Assembly, and Isaac Decow the Surveyor General. The latter was a shrewd sagacious old Man, who told me that he began for himself when young by wheeling Clay for the Brickmakers, learnt to write after he was of Age, carry'd the Chain for Surveyors, who taught him Surveying, and he had now by his Industry acquir'd a good Estate; and says he, I foresee, that you will soon work this Man out of his Business & make a Fortune in it at Philadelphia. He had not then the least Intimation of my Intention to set up there or any where.—These Friends were afterwards of great Use to me, as I occasionally was to some of them.—They all continued their Regard for me as long as they lived.—

Before I enter upon my public Appearance in Business, it may be well to let you know the then State of my Mind, with regard to my Principles and Morals, that you may see how far those influenc'd the future Events of my Life. My Parent's had early given me religious Impressions, and brought me through my Childhood piously in the Dissenting Way.[118] But I was scarce 15 when, after doubting by turns of several Points as I found them disputed in the different Books I read, I began to doubt of Revelation it self. Some Books against Deism fell into my Hands; they were said to be the Substance of Sermons preached at Boyle's Lectures.[119] It happened that they wrought an Effect on me quite contrary to what was intended by them: For the Arguments of the Deists which were quoted to be refuted, appeared to me much Stronger than the Refutations. In short I soon became a thorough Deist. My Arguments perverted some others, particularly Collins & Ralph: but each of them having afterwards wrong'd me greatly without the least Compunction, and recollecting Keith's Conduct towards me, (who was another Freethinker) and my own towards Vernon & Miss Read which at Times gave me great Trouble, I began to suspect that this Doctrine tho' it might be true, was not very useful.—My London Pamphlet, which had for its Motto those Lines of Dryden

——Whatever is, is right
Tho' purblind Man / Sees but a Part of
The Chain, the nearest Link,
His Eyes not carrying to the equal Beam,
That poizes all, above.[120]

And from the Attributes of God, his infinite Wisdom, Goodness & Power concluded that nothing could possibly be wrong in the World, & that Vice & Virtue were empty Distinctions, no such Things existing: appear'd now not so clever a Performance as I once thought it; and I doubted whether some Error had not insinuated itself unperceiv'd, into my Argument, so as to infect all that follow'd, as is common in metaphysical Reasonings.—I grew convinc'd that *Truth, Sincerity & Integrity* in Dealings between Man & Man, were of the utmost Importance to the Felicity of Life, and I form'd written Resolutions, (w[ch]. still remain in my Journal Book) to practise them ever while I lived. Revelation had indeed no weight with me as such; but I entertain'd an Opinion, that tho' certain Actions might not be bad *because* they were forbidden by it, or good *because* it commanded them; yet probably those Actions might be forbidden *because* they were bad for us, or commanded *because* they were beneficial to us, in their own Natures, all the Circumstances of things considered. And this Persuasion, with the kind hand of Providence, or some guardian Angel, or accidental favourable Circumstances & Situations, or all together, preserved me (thro' this dangerous Time of Youth & the hazardous Situations I was sometimes in among Strangers, remote from the Eye & Advice of my Father,) without any *wilful* gross Immorality or Injustice that might have been expected from my Want of Religion.—I say *wilful,* because the Instances I have mentioned, had something of *Necessity* in them, from my Youth, Inexperience, & the Knavery of others.—I had therefore a tolerable Character to begin the World with, I valued it properly, & determin'd to preserve it.—

We had not been long return'd to Philadelphia, before the New Types arriv'd from London.—We settled with Keimer, & left him by his Consent before he heard of it.— We found a House to hire near the Market, and took it. To lessen the Rent, (which was then but 24£ a Year tho' I have since known it let for 70) We took in Tho[s] Godfrey

---

118. That is, as a Congregationalist, a dissenter from the Church of England.

119. English scientist Robert Boyle (1627–91) endowed a series of lectures to defend religious practice against "notorious Infidels."

120. John Dryden's *Oedipus* (1679), III.i.244–48, although the first line is taken from Alexander Pope's *An Essay on Man* (1733–34), Epistle I.294.

a Glazier,[121] & his Family, who were to pay a considerable Part of it to us, and we to board with them. We had scarce opened our Letters & put our Press in Order, before George House, an Acquaintance of mine, brought a Countryman to us; whom he had met in the Street enquiring for a Printer. All our Cash was now expended in the Variety of Particulars we had been obliged to procure, & this Countryman's Five Shillings, being our First Fruits & coming so seasonably, gave me more Pleasure than any Crown I have since earn'd; and from the Gratitude I felt towards House, has made me often more ready than perhaps I should otherwise have been to assist young Beginners.—

There are Croakers in every Country always boding its Ruin. Such a one then lived in Philadelphia, a Person of Note, an elderly Man, with a wise Look and very grave Manner of Speaking. His Name was Samuel Mickle. This Gentleman, a Stranger to me, stopt one Day at my Door, and ask'd me if I was the young Man who had lately opened a new Printing-house: Being answer'd in the Affirmative; He said he was sorry for me; because it was an expensive Undertaking, & the Expence would be lost, for Philadelphia was a sinking Place, the People already half Bankrupts or near being so; all Appearances of the contrary such as new Buildings & the Rise of Rents, being to his certain Knowledge fallacious, for they were in fact among the Things that would soon ruin us. And he gave me such a Detail of Misfortunes now existing or that were soon to exist, that he left me half-melancholy. Had I known him before I engag'd in this Business, probably I never should have done it.—This Man continu'd to live in this decaying Place, & to declaim in the same Strain, refusing for many Years to buy a House there, because all was going to Destruction, and at last I had the Pleasure of seeing him give five times as much for one as he might have bought it for when he first began his Croaking.—

I should have mention'd before, that in the Autumn of the preceding Year,[122] I had form'd most of my ingenious Acquaintance into a Club, for mutual Improvement, which we call'd the Junto. We met on Friday Evenings. The Rules I drew up, requir'd that every Member in his Turn should produce one or more Queries on any Point of Morals, Politics or Natural Philosophy, to be discuss'd by the Company, and once in three Months produce and read an Essay of his own Writing on any Subject he pleased. Our Debates were to be under the Direction of a President, and to be conducted in the sincere Spirit of Enquiry after Truth, without fondness for Dispute, or Desire of Victory; and to prevent Warmth, all Expressions of Positiveness in Opinion, or of direct Contradiction, were after some time made contraband & prohibited under small pecuniary Penalties. The first Members were, Joseph Brientnal, a Copyer of Deeds for the Scriveners; a good-natur'd friendly middle-ag'd Man, a great Lover of Poetry, reading all he could meet with, & writing some that was tolerable; very ingenious in many little Nicknackeries, & of sensible Conversation. Thomas Godfrey, a self-taught Mathematician, great in his Way, & afterwards Inventor of what is now call'd Hadley's Quadrant. But he knew little out of his way, and was not a pleasing Companion, as like most Great Mathematicians I have met with, he expected unusual Precision in every thing said, or was forever denying or distinguishing upon Trifles, to the Disturbance of all Conversation.—He soon left us.—Nicholas Scull, a Surveyor, afterwards Surveyor-General, Who lov'd Books, & sometimes made a few Verses. William Parsons, bred a Shoemaker, but loving Reading, had acquir'd a considerable Share of Mathematics, which he first studied with a View to Astrology that he afterwards laught at. He also became Surveyor General.—William Maugridge, a Joiner, & a most exquisite Mechanic, & a solid sensible Man. Hugh Meredith, Stephen Potts, & George Webb, I have Characteris'd before. Robert Grace, a young Gentleman of some Fortune, generous, lively & witty, a Lover of Punning and of his Friends. And William Coleman, then a Merchant's Clerk, about my Age, who had the coolest clearest Head, the best Heart, and the exactest Morals, of almost any Man I ever met with. He became afterwards a Merchant of great Note, and one of our Provincial Judges: Our Friendship continued without Interruption to his Death, upwards of 40 Years. And the Club continu'd almost as long and was the best School of Philosophy, Morals & Politics that then existed in the Province; for our Queries which were read the Week preceding their Discussion, put us on reading with Attention upon the several Subjects, that we might speak more to the purpose: and here too we acquired better Habits of Conversation, every thing being studied in our Rules which might prevent our disgusting each other. From hence the long Continuance of the Club, which I shall have frequent Occasion to speak farther of hereafter; But my giving this Account of it here, is to show something of the Interest I had, every one of these exerting

---

121. A glazier, one who sets windows into frames, creating windowpanes.

122. That is, in the fall of 1727.

themselves in recommending Business to us.—Brientnal particularly procur'd us from the Quakers, the Printing 40 Sheets of their History, the rest being to be done by Keimer: and upon this we work'd exceeding hard, for the Price was low. It was a Folio, Pro Patria Size, in Pica with Long Primer Notes.[123] I compos'd of it a Sheet a Day, and Meredith work'd it off at Press. It was often 11 at Night and sometimes later, before I had finish'd my Distribution[124] for the next days Work: For the little Jobbs sent in by our other Friends now & then put us back. But so determin'd I was to continue doing a Sheet a Day of the Folio, that one Night when having impos'd my Forms, I thought my Days Work over, one of them by accident was broken and two Pages reduc'd to Pie,[125] I immediately distributed & compos'd it over again before I went to bed. And this Industry visible to our Neighbours began to give us Character and Credit; particularly I was told, that mention being made of the new Printing Office at the Merchants Every-night-Club, the general Opinion was that it must fail, there being already two Printers in the Place, Keimer & Bradford; but Doctor Baird (whom you and I saw many Years after at his native Place, St. Andrews in Scotland) gave a contrary Opinion; for the Industry of that Franklin, says he, is superior to any thing I ever saw of the kind: I see him still at work when I go home from Club; and he is at Work again before his Neighbours are out of bed. This struck the rest, and we soon after had Offers from one of them to supply us with Stationary. But as yet we did not chuse to engage in Shop Business.

I mention this Industry the more particularly and the more freely, tho' it seems to be talking in my own Praise, that those of my Posterity who shall read it, may know the Use of that Virtue, when they see its Effects in my Favour throughout this Relation.—

George Webb, who had found a Friend that lent him wherewith to purchase his Time of Keimer, now came to offer himself as a Journeyman to us. We could not then imploy him, but I foolishly let him know, as a Secret, that I soon intended to begin a Newspaper, & might then have Work for him.—My Hopes of Success as I told him were founded on this, that the then only Newspaper,[126] printed by Bradford was a paltry thing, wretchedly manag'd, no way entertaining; and yet was profitable to him.—I therefore thought a good Paper could scarcely fail of good Encouragem.t I requested Webb not to mention it, but he told it to Keimer, who immediately, to be beforehand with me, published Proposals for Printing one himself,—on which Webb was to be employ'd.—I resented this, and to counteract them, as I could not yet begin our Paper, I wrote several Pieces of Entertainm.t for Bradford's Paper, under the Title of the Busy Body[127] which Breintnal continu'd some Months. By this means the Attention of the Publick was fix'd on that Paper, & Keimers Proposals which we burlesqu'd & ridicul'd, were disregarded. He began his Paper however, and after carrying it on three Quarters of a Year, with at most only 90 Subscribers, he offer'd it to me for a Trifle, & I having been ready some time to go on with it, took it in hand directly and it prov'd in a few Years extreamly profitable to me.[128]—

I perceive that I am apt to speak in the singular Number, though our Partnership still continu'd. The Reason may be, that in fact the whole Management of the Business lay upon me. Meredith was no Compostor, a poor Pressman, & seldom sober. My Friends lamented my Connection with him, but I was to make the best of it.

Our first Papers made a quite different Appearance from any before in the Province, a better Type & better printed: but some spirited Remarks[129] of my Writing on the Dispute then going on between Gov.r Burnet[130] and the Massachusetts Assembly, struck the principal People, occasion'd the Paper & the Manager of it to be much talk'd of, & in a few Weeks brought them all to be our Subscribers. Their Example was follow'd by many, and our Number went on growing continually.—This was one of

---

123. A large volume, printed in twelve-point type, with notes in ten-point type.

124. That is, after he had returned the letters to their cases after the day's work.

125. Pie, a mixed-up pile of types.

126. *The American Weekly Mercury,* begun December 22, 1719.

127. Franklin's "Busy Body" series appeared in Bradford's *American Weekly Mercury* from February 4, 1728, through September 25, 1729.

128. *The Universal Instructor in All Arts and Sciences: and Pennsylvania Gazette* became Franklin's in October 1729. Franklin made it, simply, *The Pennsylvania Gazette.*

129. In the manuscript, Franklin made a note to himself to insert these "spirited Remarks" at this point. He had printed his remarks in *The Pennsylvania Gazette,* on October 9, 1729.

130. William Burnet (1688–1729), governor of Massachusetts.

the first good Effects of my having learnt a little to scribble.—Another was, that the leading Men, seeing a News Paper now in the hands of one who could also handle a Pen, thought it convenient to oblige & encourage me.—Bradford still printed the Votes & Laws & other Publick Business. He had printed an Address of the House to the Governor in a coarse blundering manner; We reprinted it elegantly & correctly, and sent one to every Member. They were sensible of the Difference, it strengthen'd the Hands of our Friends in the House, and they voted us their Printers for the Year ensuing.

Among my Friends in the House I must not forget Mr Hamilton before mentioned, who was then returned from England & had a Seat in it. He interested himself for me strongly in that Instance, as he did in many others afterwards, continuing his Patronage till his Death.[131] Mr Vernon about this time put me in mind of the Debt I ow'd him:—but did not press me.—I wrote him an ingenuous Letter of Acknowledgments, crav'd his Forbearance a little longer which he allow'd me, & as soon as I was able I paid the Principal with Interest & many Thanks.—So that *Erratum* was in some degree corrected.—

But now another Difficulty came upon me, which I had never the least Reason to expect. Mr. Meredith's Father, who was to have paid for our Printing House according to the Expectations given me, was able to advance only one Hundred Pounds, Currency, which had been paid, & a Hundred more was due to the Merchant; who grew impatient & su'd us all. We gave Bail, but saw that if the Money could not be rais'd in time, the Suit must come to a Judgment & Execution, & our hopeful Prospects must with us be ruined, as the Press & Letters must be sold for Payment, perhaps at half-Price.—In this Distress two true Friends whose Kindness I have never forgotten nor ever shall forget while I can remember any thing, came to me separately unknown to each other, and without any Application from me, offering each of them to advance me all the Money that should be necessary to enable me to take the whole Business upon my self if that should be practicable, but they did not like my continuing the Partnership with Meredith, who as they said was often seen drunk in the Streets, & playing at low Games in Alehouses, much to our Discredit. These two Friends were *William Coleman* & *Robert Grace*.[132] I told them I could

not propose a Separation while any Prospect remain'd of the Merediths fulfilling their Part of our Agreement. Because I thought my self under great Obligations to them for what they had done & would do if they could. But if they finally fail'd in their Performance, & our Partnership must be dissolv'd, I should then think myself at Liberty to accept the Assistance of my Friends. Thus the matter rested for some time. When I said to my Partner, perhaps your Father is dissatisfied at the Part you have undertaken in this Affair of ours, and is unwilling to advance for you & me what he would for you alone: If that is the Case, tell me, and I will resign the whole to you & go about my Business. No—says he, my Father has really been disappointed and is really unable; and I am unwilling to distress him farther. I see this is a Business I am not fit for. I was bred a Farmer, and it was a Folly in me to come to Town & put my self at 30 Years of Age an Apprentice to learn a new Trade. Many of our Welsh People are going to settle in North Carolina where Land is cheap: I am inclin'd to go with them, & follow my old Employment. You may find Friends to assist you. If you will take the Debts of the Company upon you, return to my Father the hundred Pound he has advanc'd, pay my little personal Debts, and give me Thirty Pounds & a new Saddle, I will relinquish the Partnership & leave the whole in your Hands. I agreed to this Proposal. It was drawn up in Writing, sign'd & seal'd immediately. I gave him what he demanded & he went soon after to Carolina; from whence he sent me next Year two long Letters, containing the best Account that had been given of that Country, the Climate, Soil, Husbandry, &c. for in those Matters he was very judicious. I printed them in the Papers, and they gave grate Satisfaction to the Publick.[133]

As soon as he was gone, I recurr'd to my two Friends; and because I would not give an unkind Preference to either, I took half what each had offered & I wanted, of one, & half of the other; paid off the Company Debts, and went on with the Business in my own Name, advertising that the Partnership was dissolved. I think this was in or about the Year 1729.—[134]

About this Time there was a Cry among the People for more Paper-Money, only 15,000£ being extant in the Province & that soon to be sunk. The wealthy Inhabitants oppos'd any Addition, being against all Paper Currency,

---

131. "I got his son once 500 l." [Au.]

132. William Coleman (1704–69) and Robert Grace (1709–66), original members of the Junto.

133. The letters appeared in *The Pennsylvania Gazette* on May 6 and May 13, 1731.

134. The partnership was dissolved in July 1730.

from an Apprehension that it would depreciate as it had done in New England to the Prejudice of all Creditors.— We had discuss'd this Point in our Junto, where I was on the Side of an Addition, being persuaded that the first small Sum struck in 1723 had done much good, by increasing the Trade Employment, & Number of Inhabitants in the Province, since I now saw all the old Houses inhabited, & many new ones building, where as I remember'd well, that when I first walk'd about the Streets of Philadelphia, eating my Roll, I saw most of the Houses in Walnut street between Second & Front streets with Bills on their Doors, to be let; and many likewise in Chesnut Street, & other Streets; which made me then think the Inhabitants of the City were one after another deserting it.—Our Debates possess'd me so fully of the Subject, that I wrote and printed an anonymous Pamphlet on it, entituled, *The Nature & Necessity of a Paper Currency.* It was well receiv'd by the common People in general; but the Rich Men dislik'd it; for it increas'd and strengthen'd the Clamour for more Money; and they happening to have no Writers among them that were able to answer it, their Opposition slacken'd, & the Point was carried by a Majority in the House. My Friends there, who conceiv'd I had been of some Service, thought fit to reward me, by employing me in printing the Money, a very profitable Jobb, and a great Help to me.—This was another Advantage gain'd by my being able to write. The Utility of this Currency became by Time and Experience so evident, as never afterwards to be much disputed, so that it grew soon to 55000£, and in 1739 to 80,000£ since which it arose during War to upwards of 350,000£. Trade, Building & Inhabitants all the while increasing. Tho' I now think there are Limits beyond which the Quantity may be hurtful.—

I soon after obtain'd, thro' my Friend Hamilton, the Printing of the NewCastle Paper Money,[135] another profitable Jobb, as I then thought it; small Things appearing great to those in small Circumstances. And these to me were really great Advantages, as they were great Encouragements.—He procured me also the Printing of the Laws and Votes of that Government which continu'd in my Hands as long as I follow'd the Business.—

I now open'd a little Stationer's Shop. I had in it Blanks of all Sorts the correctest that ever appear'd among us, being assisted in that by my Friend Brientnal; I had also Paper, Parchment, Chapmen's Books, &c. One

Whitemash a Compositor I had known in London, an excellent Workman now came to me & work'd with me constantly & diligently, and I took an Apprentice the Son of Aquila Rose. I began now gradually to pay off the Debt I was under for the Printing-House.—In order to secure my Credit and Character as a Tradesmen, I took care not only to be in *Reality* Industrious & frugal, but to avoid all *Appearances* of the Contrary. I drest plainly; I was seen at no Places of idle Diversion; I never went out a-fishing or shooting; a Book, indeed, sometimes debauch'd me from my Work; but that was seldom, snug, & gave no Scandal: and to show that I was not above my Business, I sometimes brought home the Paper I purchas'd at the Stores, thro' the Streets on a Wheelbarrow. Thus being esteem'd an industrious thriving young Man, and paying duly for what I bought, the Merchants who imported Stationary solicited my Custom, others propos'd supplying me with Books, & I went on swimmingly.—In the mean time Keimer's Credit & Business declining daily, he was at last forc'd to sell his Printing-house to satisfy his Creditors. He went to Barbadoes, & there lived some Years, in very poor Circumstances.

His Apprentice David Harry, whom I had instructed while I work'd with him, set up in his Place at Philadelphia having bought his Materials. I was at first apprehensive of a powerful Rival in Harry, as his Friends were very able, & had a good deal of Interest. I therefore propos'd a Partnership to him; which he, fortunately for me, rejected with Scorn. He was very proud, dress'd like a Gentleman, liv'd expensively, took much Diversion & Pleasure abroad, ran in debt, & neglected his Business, upon which all Business left him; and finding nothing to do, he follow'd Keimer to Barbadoes; taking the Printinghouse with him. There this Apprentice employ'd his former Master as a Journeyman. They quarrel'd often. Harry went continually behind-hand, and at length was forc'd to sell his Types, and return to his Country Work in Pensilvania. The Person that bought them, employ'd Keimer to use them, but in a few years he died. There remain'd now no Competitor with me at Philadelphia, but the old one, Bradford, who was rich & easy, did a little Printing now & then by straggling Hands, but was not very anxious about the Business. However, as he kept the Post Office, it was imagined he had better Opportunities of obtaining News, his Paper was thought a better Distributer of Advertisements than mine, & therefore had many more, which was a profitable thing to him & a Disadvantage to me. For tho' I did indeed receive & send Papers by the Post, yet the publick Opinion was otherwise; for what I

---

135. New Castle Kent, and Sussex counties had the same governor as Pennsylvania but a separate legislature.

did send was by Bribing the Riders who took them privately: Bradford being unkind enough to forbid it: which occasion'd some Resentment on my Part; and I thought so meanly of him for it, that when I afterwards came into his Situation,[136] I took care never to imitate it.

I had hitherto continu'd to board with Godfrey who lived in Part of my House with his Wife & Children, & had one Side of the Shop for his Glazier's Business, tho' he work'd little, being always absorb'd in his Mathematics.—Mrs Godfrey projected a Match for me with a Relation's Daughter, took Opportunities of bringing us often together, till a serious Courtship on my Part ensu'd the Girl being in herself very deserving. The old Folks encourag'd me by continual Invitations to Supper, & by leaving us together, till at length it was time to explain. Mrs Godfrey manag'd our little Treaty. I let her know that I expected as much Money with their Daughter as would pay off my Remaining Debt for the Printing-house, which I believe was not then above a Hundred Pounds. She brought me Word they had no such Sum to spare. I said they might mortgage their House in the Loan Office.—The Answer to this after some Days was, that they did not approve the Match; that on Enquiry of Bradford they had been inform'd the Printing Business was not a profitable one, the Types would soon be worn out & more wanted, that S. Keimer & D. Harry had fail'd one after the other, and I should probably soon follow them; and therefore I was forbidden the House, & the Daughter shut up.—Whether this was a real Change of Sentiment, or only Artifice, on a Supposition of our being too far engag'd in Affection to retract, & therefore that we should steal a Marriage, which would leave them at Liberty to give or withold what they pleas'd, I know not: But I suspected the latter, resented it, and went no more. Mrs Godfrey brought me afterwards some more favourable Accounts of their Disposition, & would have drawn me on again: But I declared absolutely my Resolution to have nothing more to do with that Family. This was resented by the Godfreys, we differ'd, and they removed, leaving me the whole House, and I resolved to take no more Inmates. But this Affair having turn'd my Thoughts to Marriage, I look'd round me, and made Overtures of Acquaintance in other Places; but soon found that the Business of a Printer being generally thought a poor one, I was not to expect Money with a Wife unless with such a one, as I should not otherwise think agreable.—In the mean time, that hard-to-be-govern'd Passion of Youth, had hurried me frequently into Intrigues with low Women that fell in my Way, which were attended with some Expence & great Inconvenience, besides a continual Risque to my Health by a Distemper which of all Things I dreaded, tho' by great good Luck I escaped it.—

A friendly Correspondence as Neighbours & old Acquaintances, had continued between me & Mrs Read's Family who all had a Regard for me from the time of my first Lodging in their House. I was often invited there and consulted in their Affairs, wherein I sometimes was of Service.—I pity'd poor Miss Read's unfortunate Situation, who was generally dejected, seldom chearful, and avoided Company. I consider'd my Giddiness & Inconstancy when in London as in a great degree the Cause of her Unhappiness; tho' the Mother was good enough to think the Fault more her own than mine, as she had prevented our Marrying before I went thither, and persuaded the other Match in my Absence. Our mutual Affection was revived, but there were now great Objections to our Union. That Match was indeed look'd upon as invalid, a preceding Wife being said to be living in England; but this could not easily be prov'd, because of the Distance &c. And tho' there was a Report of his Death, it was not certain. Then, tho' it should be true, he had left many Debts which his Successor might be call'd upon to pay. We ventured however, over all these Difficulties, and I took her to Wife Sept. 1. 1730.[137] None of the Inconveniencies happened that we had apprehended, she prov'd a good & faithful Helpmate, assisted me much by attending the Shop, we throve together, and have ever mutually endeavour'd to make each other happy.—Thus I corrected that great *Erratum* as well as I could.

About this Time our Club meeting, not at a Tavern, but in a little Room of Mr Grace's set apart for that Purpose; a Proposition was made by me, that since our Books were often referr'd to in our Disquisitions upon the Queries, it might be convenient to us to have them all together where we met, that upon Occasion they might be consulted; and By thus clubbing our Books to a common Library, we should, while we lik'd to keep them together, have each of us the Advantage of using the Books of all the other Members, which would be nearly as beneficial as if each owned the whole. It was lik'd and agreed to, & we fill'd one End of the Room with such Books as we could best spare. The

---

136. Franklin became deputy postmaster-general for the colonies in 1753.

137. Because she could not prove the death of her husband, John Rogers, Deborah Read was not free to marry Benjamin Franklin. They thus had a "common law" marriage without having a civil or church ceremony.

Number was not so great as we expected; and tho' they had been of great Use, yet some Inconveniencies occurring for want of due Care of them, the Collection after about a Year was separated, & each took his Books home again.

And now I set on foot my first Project of a public Nature, that for a Subscription Library.[138] I drew up the Proposals, got them put into Form by our great Scrivener Brockden, and by the help of my Friends in the Junto, procur'd Fifty Subscribers of 40/ each to begin with & 10/ a Year for 50 Years, the Term our Company was to continue. We afterwards obtain'd a Charter, the Company being increas'd to 100. This was the Mother of all the N American Subscription Libraries now so numerous. It is become a great thing itself, & continually increasing.— These Libraries have improv'd the general Conversation of the Americans, made the common Tradesmen & Farmers as intelligent as most Gentlemen from other Countries, and perhaps have contributed in some degree to the Stand so generally made throughout the Colonies in Defence of their Privileges.—

Mem°.

Thus far was written with the Intention express'd in the Beginning and therefore contains several little family Anecdotes of no Importance to others. What follows was written many Years after in compliance with the Advice contain'd in these Letters, and accordingly intended for the Publick. The Affairs of the Revolution occasion'd the Interruption.

PART TWO[139]

Letter from Mr. Abel James, with Notes on my Life,
(received in Paris.)

My dear & honored Friend.

I have often been desirous of writing to thee, but could not be reconciled to the Thought that the Letter might fall into the Hands of the British, lest some Printer or busy Body should publish some Part of the Contents & give our Friends Pain & myself Censure.

Some Time since there fell into my Hands to my great Joy about 23 Sheets in thy own hand-writing containing an Account of the Parentage & Life of thyself, directed to thy Son ending in the Year 1730 with which there were Notes likewise in thy writing, a Copy of which I inclose in Hopes it may be a means if thou continuedst it up to a later period, that the first & latter part may be put together; & if it is not yet continued, I hope thou wilt not delay it, Life is uncertain as the Preacher tells us, and what will the World say if kind, humane & benevolent Ben Franklin should leave his Friends & the World deprived of so pleasing & profitable a Work, a Work which would be useful & entertaining not only to a few, but to millions.

The Influence Writings under that Class have on the Minds of Youth is very great, and has no where appeared so plain as in our public Friends' Journals. It almost insensibly leads the Youth into the Resolution of endeavouring to become as good and as eminent as the Journalist. Should thine for Instance when published, and I think it could not fail of it, lead the Youth to equal the Industry & Temperance of thy early Youth, what a Blessing with that Class would such a Work be. I know of no Character living nor many of them put together, who has so much in his Power as Thyself to promote a greater Spirit of Industry & early Attention to Business, Frugality and Temperance with the American Youth. Not that I think the Work would have no other Merit & Use in the World, far from it, but the first is of such vast Importance, that I know nothing that can equal it.

The foregoing letter and the minutes accompanying it being shewn to a friend, I received from him the following:

Letter from Mr. Benjamin Vaughan

Paris, January 31, 1783

MY DEAREST SIR,

When I had read over your sheets of minutes of the principal incidents of your life, recovered for you by your Quaker acquaintance; I told you I would send you a letter expressing my reasons why I thought it would be useful to complete and publish it as he desired. Various concerns have for some time past prevented this letter being written, and I do not know whether it was worth any expectation: happening to be at leisure however at present, I shall

---

138. The Library Company of Philadelphia was formed on July 1, 1731.

139. Franklin again took up the project of composing his autobiography at the instigation of his friends, Abel James (1724–90) and Benjamin Vaughan (1751–1835), as the letters he wanted to have inserted in his manuscript indicate. James was an old friend from Franklin's midcentury Philadelphia years; Vaughan, one of Franklin's many protégés, had been Lord Sherburn's private secretary, and he was Franklin's emissary during the peace talks in Paris, 1782–83.

by writing at least interest and instruct myself; but as the terms I am inclined to use may tend to offend a person of your manners, I shall only tell you how I would address any other person, who was as good and as great as yourself, but less diffident. I would say to him, Sir, I *solicit* the history of your life from the following motives.

Your history is so remarkable, that if you do not give it, somebody else will certainly give it; and perhaps so as nearly to do as much harm, as your own management of the thing might do good.

It will moreover present a table of the internal circumstances of your country, which will very much tend to invite to it settlers of virtuous and manly minds. And considering the eagerness with which such information is sought by them, and the extent of your reputation, I do not know of a more efficacious advertisement than your Biography would give.

All that has happened to you is also connected with the detail of the manners and situation of *a rising* people; and in this respect I do not think that the writings of Caesar and Tacitus can be more interesting to a true judge of human nature and society.

But these, Sir, are small reasons in my opinion, compared with the chance which your life will give for the forming of future great men; and in conjunction with your *Art of Virtue,* (which you design to publish) of improving the features of private character, and consequently of aiding all happiness both public and domestic.

The two works I allude to, Sir, will in particular give a noble rule and example of *self-education.* School and other education constantly proceed upon false principles, and shew a clumsy apparatus pointed at a false mark; but your apparatus is simple, and the mark a true one; and while parents and young persons are left destitute of other just means of estimating and becoming prepared for a reasonable course in life, your discovery that the thing is in many a man's private power, will be invaluable!

Influence upon the private character late in life, is not only an influence late in life, but a weak influence. It is in *youth* that we plant our chief habits and prejudices; it is in youth that we take our party as to profession, pursuits, and matrimony. In youth therefore the turn is given; in youth the education even of the next generation is given; in youth the private and public character is determined; and the term of life extending but from youth to age, life ought to begin well from youth; and more especially *before* we take our party as to our principal objects.

But your Biography will not merely teach self-education, but the education of *a wise man;* and the wis-

est man will receive lights and improve his progress, by seeing detailed the conduct of another wise man. And why are weaker men to be deprived of such helps, when we see our race has been blundering on in the dark, almost without a guide in this particular, from the farthest trace of time. Shew then, Sir, how much is to be done, *both to sons and fathers;* and invite all wise men to become like yourself; and other men to become wise.

When we see how cruel statesmen and warriors can be to the humble race, and how absurd distinguished men can be to their acquaintance, it will be instructive to observe the instances multiply of pacific acquiescing manners; and to find how compatible it is to be great and *domestic;* enviable and yet *good-humoured.*

The little private incidents which you will also have to relate, will have considerable use, as we want above all things, *rules of prudence in ordinary affairs;* and it will be curious to see how you have acted in these. It will be so far a sort of key to life, and explain many things that all men ought to have once explained to them, to give them a chance of becoming wise by foresight.

The nearest thing to having experience of one's own, is to have other people's affairs brought before us in a shape that is interesting; this is sure to happen from your pen. Your affairs and management will have an air of simplicity or importance that will not fail to strike; and I am convinced you have conducted them with as much originality as if you had been conducting discussions in politics or philosophy; and what more worthy of experiments and system, (its importance and its errors considered) than human life!

Some men have been virtuous blindly, others have speculated fantastically, and others have been shrewd to bad purposes; but you, Sir, I am sure, will give under your hand, nothing but what is at the same moment, wise, practical, and good.

Your account of yourself (for I suppose the parallel I am drawing for Dr. Franklin, will hold not only in point of character but of private history), will shew that you are ashamed of no origin; a thing the more important, as you prove how little necessary all origin is to happiness, virtue, or greatness.

As no end likewise happens without a means, so we shall find, Sir, that even you yourself framed a plan by which you became considerable; but at the same time we may see that though the event is flattering, the means are as simple as wisdom could make them; that is depending upon nature, virtue, thought, and habit.

Another thing demonstrated will be the propriety of

every man's waiting for his time for appearing upon the stage of the world. Our sensations being very much fixed to the moment, we are apt to forget that more moments are to follow the first, and consequently that man should arrange his conduct so as to suit the *whole* of a life. Your attribution appears to have been applied to your *life,* and the passing moments of it have been enlivened with content and enjoyment, instead of being tormented with foolish impatience or regrets. Such a conduct is easy for those who make virtue and themselves their standard, and who try to keep themselves in countenance by examples of other truly great men, of whom patience is so often the characteristic.

Your Quaker correspondent, Sir, (for here again I will suppose the subject of my letter resembling Dr. Franklin,) praised your frugality, diligence, and temperance, which he considered as a pattern for all youth: but it is singular that he should have forgotten your modesty, and your disinterestedness, without which you never could have waited for your advancement, or found your situation in the mean time comfortable; which is a strong lesson to shew the poverty of glory, and the importance of regulating our minds.

If this correspondent had known the nature of your reputation as well as I do, he would have said; your former writings and measures would secure attention to your Biography, and Art of Virtue; and your Biography and Art of Virtue, in return, would secure attention to them. This is an advantage attendant upon a various character, and which brings all that belongs to it into greater play; and it is the more useful, as perhaps more persons are at a loss for the *means* of improving their minds and characters, than they are for the time or the inclination to do it.

But there is one concluding reflection, Sir, that will shew the use of your life as a mere piece of biography. This style of writing seems a little gone out of vogue, and yet it is a very useful one; and your specimen of it may be particularly serviceable, as it will make a subject of comparison with the lives of various public cut-throats and intriguers, and with absurd monastic self-tormentors, or vain literary triflers. If it encourages more writings of the same kind with your own, and induces more men to spend lives fit to be written; it will be worth all Plutarch's Lives put together.

But being tired of figuring to myself a character of which every feature suits only one man in the world, without giving him the praise of it; I shall end my letter, my dear Dr. Franklin, with a personal application to your proper self.

I am earnestly desirous then, my dear Sir, that you should let the world into the traits of your genuine character, as civil broils may otherwise tend to disguise or traduce it. Considering your great age, the caution of your character, and your peculiar style of thinking, it is not likely that any one besides yourself can be sufficiently master of the facts of your life, or the intentions of your mind.

Besides all this, the immense revolution of the present period, will necessarily turn our attention towards the author of it; and when virtuous principles have been pretended in it, it will be highly important to shew that such have really influenced; and, as your own character will be the principal one to receive a scrutiny, it is proper (even for its effects upon your vast and rising country, as well as upon England and upon Europe), that it should stand respectable and eternal. For the furtherance of human happiness, I have always maintained that it is necessary to prove that man is not even at present a vicious and detestable animal; and still more to prove that good management may greatly amend him; and it is for much the same reason, that I am anxious to see the opinion established, that there are fair characters existing among the individuals of the race; for the moment that all men, without exception, shall be conceived abandoned, good people will cease efforts deemed to be hopeless, and perhaps think of taking their share in the scramble of life, or at least of making it comfortable principally for themselves.

Take then, my dear Sir, this work most speedily into hand: shew yourself good as you are good, temperate as you are temperate; and above all things, prove yourself as one who from your infancy have loved justice, liberty, and concord, in a way that has made it natural and consistent for you to have acted, as we have seen you act in the last seventeen years of your life. Let Englishmen be made not only to respect, but even to love you. When they think well of individuals in your native country, they will go nearer to thinking well of your country; and when your countrymen see themselves well thought of by Englishmen, they will go nearer to thinking well of England. Extend your views even further; do not stop at those who speak the English tongue, but after having settled so many points in nature and politics, think of bettering the whole race of men.

As I have not read any part of the life in question, but know only the character that lived it, I write somewhat at hazard. I am sure however, that the life, and the treatise I allude to (on the *Art of Virtue*), will necessarily fulfil the chief of my expectations; and still more so if you take up the measure of suiting these performances to the several views above stated. Should they even prove unsuccessful in all that a sanguine admirer of yours hopes from them, you will at least have framed pieces to interest the human mind; and whoever gives a feeling of pleasure that is innocent to man, has added so much to the fair side of a life otherwise too much darkened by anxiety, and too much injured by pain.

In the hope therefore that you will listen to the prayer addressed to you in this letter, I beg to subscribe myself, my dearest Sir, &c. &c.

Signed BENJ. VAUGHAN.

Continuation of the Account of my Life. Begun at Passy 1784[140]

It is some time since I receiv'd the above Letters, but I have been too busy till now to think of complying with the Request they contain. It might too be much better done if I were at home among my Papers, which would aid my Memory, & help to ascertain Dates. But my Return being uncertain, and having just now a little Leisure, I will endeavour to recollect & write what I can; If I live to get home, it may there be corrected and improv'd.

Not having any Copy here of what is already written, I know not whether an Account is given of the means I used to establish the Philadelphia publick Library, which from a small Beginning is now become so considerable, though I remember to have come down to near the Time of that Transaction, 1730. I will therefore begin here, with an Account of it, which may be struck out if found to have been already given.—

At the time I establish'd my self in Pensylvania, there was not a good Bookseller's Shop in any of the Colonies to the Southward of Boston. In New-York & Philad^a the Printers were indeed Stationers, they sold only Paper, &c. Almanacks, Ballads, and a few common School Books. Those who lov'd Reading were oblig'd to send for their Books from England.—The Members of the Junto had each a few. We had left the Alehouse where we first met, and hired a Room to hold our Club in. I propos'd that we should all of us bring our Books to that Room, where they would not only be ready to consult in our Conferences, but become a common Benefit, each of us being at Liberty to borrow such as he wish'd to read at home. This was accordingly done, and for some time contented us. Finding the Advantage of this little Collection, I propos'd to render the Benefit from Books more common by commencing a Public Subscription Library. I drew a Sketch of the Plan and Rules that would be necessary, and got a skilful Conveyancer Mr Charles Brockden to put the whole in Form of Articles of Agreement to be subscribed, by which each Subscriber engag'd to pay a certain Sum down for the first Purchase of Books and an annual Contribution for encreasing them.—So few were the Readers at that time in Philadelphia, and the Majority of us so poor, that I was not able with great Industry to find more than Fifty Persons, mostly young Tradesmen, willing to pay down for this purpose Forty shillings each, & Ten Shillings per Annum. On this little Fund we began. The Books were imported. The Library was open one Day in the Week for lending them to the Subscribers, on their Promisory Notes to pay Double the Value if not duly returned. The Institution soon manifested its Utility, was imitated by other Towns and in other Provinces, the Librarys were augmented by Donations, Reading became fashionable, and our People having no publick Amusements to divert their Attention from Study became better acquainted with Books, and in a few Years were observ'd by Strangers to be better instructed & more intelligent than People of the same Rank generally are in other Countries.—

When we were about to sign the above-mentioned Articles, which were to be binding on us, our Heirs, &c for fifty Years, Mr Brockden, the Scrivener, said to us, "You are young Men, but it is scarce probable that any of you will live to see the Expiration of the Term fix'd in this Instrument." A Number of us, however, are yet living: But the Instrument was after a few Years rendred null by a Charter that incorporated & gave Perpetuity to the Company.—

The Objections, & Reluctances I met with in Soliciting the Subscriptions, made me soon feel the Impropriety of presenting one's self as the Proposer of any useful Project that might be suppos'd to raise one's Reputation in the smallest degree above that of one's Neighbours, when one has need of their Assistance to accomplish that Project. I therefore put my self as much as I could out of sight, and stated it as a Scheme of *a Number of Friends,* who had requested me to go about and propose it to such as they thought Lovers of Reading. In this way my Affair went on more smoothly, and I ever after practis'd it on

---

140. Having negotiated the peace treaty with Britain (signed September 3, 1783), Franklin remained among his friends in Paris until July 1785.

such Occasions; and from my frequent Successes, can heartily recommend it. The present little Sacrifice of your Vanity will afterwards be amply repaid. If it remains a while uncertain to whom the Merit belongs, some one more vain than yourself will be encourag'd to claim it, and then even Envy will be dispos'd to do you Justice, by plucking those assum'd Feathers, & restoring them to their right Owner.

This Library afforded me the Means of Improvement by constant Study, for which I set apart an Hour or two each Day; and thus repair'd in some Degree the Loss of the Learned Education my Father once intended for me. Reading was the only Amusement I allow'd my self. I spent no time in Taverns, Games, or Frolicks of any kind. And my Industry in my Business continu'd as indefatigable as it was necessary. I was in debt for my Printing-house, I had a young Family coming on to be educated, and I had to contend with for Business two Printers who were establish'd in the Place before me. My Circumstances however grew daily easier: my original Habits of Frugality continuing. And My Father having among his Instructions to me when a Boy, frequently repeated a Proverb of Solomon, "*Seest thou a Man diligent in his Calling, he shall stand before Kings, he shall not stand before mean Men.*"[141] I from thence consider'd Industry as a Means of obtaining Wealth and Distinction, which encourag'd me; tho' I did not think that I should ever literally stand before Kings, which however has since happened.—for I have stood before five, & even had the honour of sitting down with one, the King of Denmark, to Dinner.[142]

We have an English Proverb that says,

He that would thrive
Must ask his Wife;

it was lucky for me that I had one as much dispos'd to Industry & Frugality as my self. She assisted me chearfully in my Business, folding & stitching Pamphlets, tending Shop, purchasing old Linen Rags for the Paper-makers, &c &c. We kept no idle Servants, our Table was plain & simple, our Furniture of the cheapest. For instance my Breakfast was a long time Bread & Milk, (no Tea,) and I

ate it out of a twopenny earthen Porringer with a Pewter Spoon. But mark how Luxury will enter Families, and make a Progress, in Spite of Principle. Being Call'd one Morning to Breakfast, I found it in a China Bowl with a Spoon of Silver. They had been bought for me without my Knowledge by my Wife, and had cost her the enormous Sum of three and twenty Shillings, for which she had no other Excuse or Apology to make, but that she thought *her* Husband deserv'd a Silver Spoon & China Bowl as well as any of his Neighbours. This was the first Appearance of Plate & China in our House, which afterwards in a Course of Years as our Wealth encreas'd, augmented gradually to several Hundred Pounds in Value.—

I had been religiously educated as a Presbyterian;[143] and tho' some of the Dogmas of that Persuasion, such as the Eternal Decrees of God, Election, Reprobation, &c. appear'd to me unintelligible, others doubtful, & I early absented myself from the Public Assemblies of the Sect, Sunday being my Studying-Day, I never was without some religious Principles; I never doubted, for instance, the Existance of the Deity, that he made the World, & govern'd it by his Providence; that the most acceptable Service of God was the doing Good to Man; that our Souls are immortal; and that all Crime will be punished & Virtue rewarded either here or hereafter; these I esteem'd the Essentials of every Religion, and being to be found in all the Religions we had in our Country I respected them all, tho' with different degrees of Respect as I found them more or less mix'd with other Articles which without any Tendency to inspire, promote or confirm Morality, serv'd principally to divide us & make us unfriendly to one another.—This Respect to all, with an Opinion that the worst had some good Effects, induc'd me to avoid all Discourse that might tend to lessen the good Opinion another might have of his own Religion; and as our Province increas'd in People and new Places of worship were continually wanted, & generally erected by voluntary Contribution, my Mite for such purpose, whatever might be the Sect, was never refused.—

Tho' I seldom attended any Public Worship, I had still an Opinion of its Propriety, and of its Utility when rightly

---

141. A paraphrase of Proverbs 22.29, but Franklin substituted "calling" for the word "business."

142. Louis XV and Louis XVI of France, George II and George III of Britain, and Christian VI of Denmark.

143. The Congregationalism practiced in Franklin's Boston was close to the Presbyterianism of Philadelphia, where Franklin claimed to belong to the Presbyterian church, although he also paid for his family's membership in Christ Church, an Anglican church. The Presbyterian minister mentioned later is Jedidiah Andrews.

conducted, and I regularly paid my annual Subscription for the Support of the only Presbyterian Minister or Meeting we had in Philadelphia. He us'd to visit me sometimes as a Friend, and admonish me to attend his Administrations, and I was now and then prevail'd on to do so, once for five Sundays successively. Had he been, *in my Opinion,* a good Preacher perhaps I might have continued, notwithstanding the occasion I had for the Sunday's Leisure in my Course of Study: But his Discourses were chiefly either polemic Arguments, or Explications of the peculiar Doctrines of our Sect, and were all to me very dry, uninteresting and unedifying, since not a single moral Principle was inculcated or enforc'd, their Aim seeming to be rather to make us Presbyterians than good Citizens. At length he took for his Text that Verse of the 4th Chapter of Philippians, *Finally, Brethren, Whatsoever Things are true, honest, just, pure, lovely, or of good report, if there be any virtue, or any praise, think on these Things;* & I imagin'd in a Sermon on such a Text, we could not miss of having some Morality: But he confin'd himself to five Points only as meant by the Apostle, viz. 1. Keeping holy the Sabbath Day. 2. Being diligent in Reading the Holy Scriptures. 3. Attending duly the Publick Worship. 4. Partaking of the Sacrament. 5. Paying a due Respect to God's Ministers.—These might be all good Things, but as they were not the kind of good Things that I expected from that Text, I despaired of ever meeting with them from any other, was disgusted, and attended his Preaching no more.—I had some Years before compos'd a little Liturgy or Form of Prayer for my own private Use, viz, in 1728. entitled, *Articles of Belief & Acts of Religion.*[144] I return'd to the Use of this, and went no more to the public Assemblies.—My Conduct might be blameable, but I leave it without attempting farther to excuse it, my present purpose being to relate Facts, and not to make Apologies for them.—

It was about this time that I conceiv'd the bold and arduous Project of arriving at moral Perfection. I wish'd to live without committing any Fault at any time; I would conquer all that either Natural Inclination, Custom, or Company might lead me into. As I knew, or thought I knew, what was right and wrong, I did not see why I might not *always* do the one and avoid the other. But I soon found I had undertaken a Task of more Difficulty than I had imagined: While my Care was employ'd in

guarding against one Fault, I was often surpriz'd by another. Habit took the Advantage of Inattention. Inclination was sometimes too strong for Reason. I concluded at length, that the mere speculative Conviction that it was our Interest to be compleatly virtuous, was not sufficient to prevent our Slipping, and that the contrary Habits must be broken and good Ones acquired and established, before we can have any Dependence on a steady uniform Rectitude of Conduct. For this purpose I therefore contriv'd the following Method.—

In the various Enumerations of the moral Virtues I had met with in my Reading, I found the Catalogue more or less numerous, as different Writers included more or fewer Ideas under the same Name. Temperance, for Example, was by some confin'd to Eating & Drinking, while by others it was extended to mean the moderating every other Pleasure, Appetite, Inclination or Passion, bodily or mental, even to our Avarice & Ambition. I propos'd to myself, for the sake of Clearness, to use rather more Names with fewer Ideas annex'd to each, than a few Names with more Ideas; and I included under Thirteen Names of Virtues all that at that time occurr'd to me as necessary or desirable, and annex'd to each a short Precept, which fully express'd the Extent I gave to its Meaning.—

These Names of Virtues with their Precepts were

1. TEMPERANCE.
   Eat not to Dulness
   Drink not to Elevation.
2. SILENCE.
   Speak not but what may benefit others or your self. Avoid trifling Conversation.
3. ORDER.
   Let all your Things have their Places. Let each Part of your Business have its Time.
4. RESOLUTION.
   Resolve to perform what you ought. Perform without fail what you resolve.
5. FRUGALITY.
   Make no Expence but to do good to others or yourself: i.e. Waste nothing.
6. INDUSTRY.
   Lose no Time.—Be always employ'd in something useful.—Cut off all unnecessary Actions.—
7. SINCERITY.
   Use no hurtful Deceit.
   Think innocently and justly; and, if you speak; speak accordingly.

---

144. The manuscript is dated Nov. 20, 1728.

8. JUSTICE.
   Wrong none, by doing Injuries or omitting the Benefits that are your Duty.
9. MODERATION.
   Avoid Extreams. Forbear resenting Injuries so much as you think they deserve.
10. CLEANLINESS
    Tolerate no Uncleanness in Body, Cloaths or Habitation.—
11. TRANQUILITY
    Be not disturbed at Trifles, or at Accidents common or unavoidable.
12. CHASTITY.
    Rarely use Venery but for Health or Offspring; Never to Dulness, Weakness, or the Injury of your own or another's Peace or Reputation.—
13. HUMILITY.
    Imitate Jesus and Socrates.—

My intention being to acquire the *Habitude* of all these Virtues, I judg'd it would be well not to distract my Attention by attempting the whole at once, but to fix it on one of them at a time, and when I should be Master of that, then to proceed to another, and so on till I should have gone thro' the thirteen. And as the previous Acquisition of some might facilitate the Acquisition of certain others, I arrang'd them with that View as they stand above. *Temperance* first, as it tends to procure that Coolness & Clearness of Head, which is so necessary where constant Vigilance was to be kept up, and Guard maintained, against the unremitting Attraction of ancient Habits, and the Force of perpetual Temptations. This being acquir'd & establish'd, *Silence* would be more easy, and my Desire being to gain Knowledge at the same time that I improv'd in Virtue, and considering that in Conversation it was obtain'd rather by the Use of the Ears than of the Tongue, & therefore wishing to break a Habit I was getting into of Prattling, Punning & Joking, which only made me acceptable to trifling Company, I gave *Silence* the second Place. This, and the next, *Order,* I expected would allow me more Time for attending to my Project and my Studies; RESOLUTION once become habitual, would keep me firm in my Endeavours to obtain all the subsequent Virtues; *Frugality & Industry,* by freeing me from my remaining Debt, & producing Affluence & Independance would make more easy the Practice of *Sincerity* and *Justice,* &c. &c.. Conceiving then that agreeable to the Advice of Pythagoras in his Golden

Verses,[145] daily Examination would be necessary, I contriv'd the following Method for conducting that Examination.

I made a little Book in which I allotted a Page for each of the Virtues. I rul'd each Page with red Ink so as to have seven Columns, one for each Day of the Week, marking each Column with a Letter for the Day. I cross'd these Columns with thirteen red Lines, marking the Beginning of each Line with the first Letter of one of the Virtues, on which Line & in its proper Column I might mark by a little black Spot every Fault I found upon Examination, to have been committed respecting that Virtue upon that Day.

I determined to give a Week's strict Attention to each of the Virtues successively. Thus in the first Week my great Guard was to avoid every the least Offence against Temperance, leaving the other Virtues to their ordinary Chance, only marking every Evening the Faults of the Day. Thus if in the first Week I could keep my first Line marked T clear of Spots, I suppos'd the Habit of that Virtue so much strengthen'd and its opposite weaken'd, that I might venture extending my Attention to include the next, and for the following Week keep both Lines clear of Spots. Proceeding thus to the last, I could go thro' a Course compleat in Thirteen Weeks, and four Courses in a Year.—And like him who having a Garden to weed,

---

145. Franklin noted that he wished the following verses, Nicholas Rowe's translation, to be printed in his memoir at this place. He had printed them in his "Letter from Father Abraham," published in *The New England Magazine of Knowledge and Pleasure,* August 1758:

> Let not the stealing God of Sleep surprize,
> Nor creep in slumbers on thy weary Eyes,
> Ere ev'ry Action of the former Day,
> Strictly thou dost, and righteously survey.
> With Rev'rence at thy own Tribunal stand,
> And answer justly to thy own Demand.
> Where have I been? In what have I transgrest?
> What Good or Ill has this Day's Life exprest?
> Where have I fail'd in what I ought to do?
> In what to GOD, to Man, or to myself I owe?
> Inquire severe whate'er from first to last,
> From Morning's Dawn till Ev'nings Gloom has past.
> If Evil were thy Deeds, repenting mourn,
> And let thy Soul with strong Remorse be torn:
> If Good, the Good with Peace of Mind repay,
> And to thy secret Self with Pleasure say,
> Rejoice, my Heart, for all went well to Day.

Form of the Pages

		S	M	T	W	T	F	S
	TEMPERANCE. *Eat not to Dulness. Drink not to Elevation.*							
T								
S		●●	●		●			
O		●	●	●			●	●
R					●			
F			●	●			●	
I					●			
S								
J								
M								
Cl.								
T								
Ch								
H								

does not attempt to eradicate all the bad Herbs at once, which would exceed his Reach and his Strength, but works on one of the Beds at a time, & having accomplish'd the first proceeds to a second; so I should have, (I hoped) the encouraging Pleasure of seeing on my Pages the Progress I made in Virtue, by clearing successively my Lines of their Spots, till in the End by a Number of Courses, I should be happy in viewing a clean Book after a thirteen Weeks daily Examination.

This my little Book had for its Motto these Lines from *Addison's Cato;*

Here will I hold: If there is a Pow'r above us,
(And that there is, all Nature cries aloud
Thro' all her Works) he must delight in Virtue,
And that which he delights in must be happy.[146]

Another from *Cicero.*

O Vita Philosophia Dux! O Virtutum indagatrix, expultrixque vitiorum! Unus dies bene, & ex preceptis tuis actus, peccanti immortalitati est anteponendus.[147]

Another from the Proverbs of Solomon speaking of Wisdom or Virtue;

Length of Days is in her right hand, and in her Left Hand Riches and Honours; Her Ways are Ways of Pleasantness, and all her Paths are Peace. III, 16, 17.

And conceiving God to be the Fountain of Wisdom, I thought it right and necessary to solicit his Assistance for obtaining it; to this End I form'd the following little Prayer, which was prefix'd to my Tables of Examination; for daily Use.

O Powerful Goodness! bountiful Father! merciful Guide! Increase in me that Wisdom which discovers my truest Interests; Strengthen my Resolutions to perform what that Wisdom dictates. Accept my kind Offices to thy other Children, as the only Return in my Power for thy continual Favours to me.

I us'd also sometimes a little Prayer which I took from *Thomson's* Poems. viz

Father of Light and Life, thou Good supreme,
O teach me what is good, teach me thy self!
Save me from Folly, Vanity and Vice,
From every low Pursuit, and fill my Soul
With Knowledge, conscious Peace, & Virtue pure,
Sacred, substantial, neverfading Bliss![148]

The Precept of *Order* requiring that *every Part of my Business should have its allotted Time,* one Page in my little Book contain'd the following Scheme of Employment for the Twenty-four Hours of a natural Day,[149]

I enter'd upon the Execution of this Plan for Self Examination, and continu'd it with occasional Intermissions for some time. I was surpriz'd to find myself so much fuller of Faults than I had imagined, but I had the Satisfaction of seeing them diminish. To avoid the Trouble of renewing now & then my little Book, which by scraping out the Marks on the Paper of old Faults to make room for new Ones in a new Course, became full of Holes: I transferr'd my Tables & Precepts to the Ivory Leaves of a Memorandum Book, on which the Lines were drawn with red Ink that made a durable Stain, and on those Lines I mark'd my Faults with a black Lead Pencil, which Marks I could easily wipe out with a wet Sponge. After a while I went thro' one Course only in a Year, and afterwards only one in several Years; till at length I omitted them entirely, being employ'd in Voyages & Business abroad with

---

146. Addison's *Cato* (1713), V.i.15–18.

147. From *Tusculum Disputations,* V.2.5: "O, Philosophy, guide of life! O teacher of virtue and corrector of vice. One day of virtue is better than an eternity of vice."

148. From James Thomson's poem *The Seasons.*

149. The figure on the next page appeared after this paragraph in the original.

The Morning Question, What Good shall I do this Day?	5	Rise, wash, and address *Powerful Goodness;* contrive Day's Business and take the Resolution of the Day; prosecute the present Study: and breakfast?—
	6	
	7	
	8	
	9	Work.
	10	
	11	
	12	Read, or overlook my Accounts, and dine.
	1	
	2	
	3	Work.
	4	
	5	
	6	Put Things in their Places, Supper, Musick, or Diversion, or Conversation, Examination of the Day.
	7	
Evening Question, What Good have I done to day?	8	
	9	
	10	
	11	
	12	
	1	Sleep.—
	2	
	3	
	4	

a Multiplicity of Affairs, that interfered. But I always carried my little Book with me. My Scheme of ORDER, gave me the most Trouble, and I found, that tho' it might be practicable where a Man's Business was such as to leave him the Disposition of his Time, that of a Journey-man Printer for instance, it was not possible to be exactly observ'd by a Master, who must mix with the World, and often receive People of Business at their own Hours.— *Order* too, with regard to Places for Things, Papers, & c. I found extremely difficult to acquire. I had not been early accustomed to it, & having an exceeding good Memory, I was not so sensible of the Inconvenience attending Want of Method. This Article therefore cost me so much painful Attention & my Faults in it vex'd me so much, and I made so little Progress in Amendment, & had such frequent Relapses, that I was almost ready to give up the Attempt, and content my self with a faulty Character in that respect. Like the Man who in buying an Ax of a Smith my Neighbour, desired to have the whole of its Surface as bright as the Edge; the Smith consented to grind it bright for him if he would turn the Wheel. He turn'd while the Smith press'd the broad Face of the Ax hard & heavily on the Stone, which made the Turning of it very fatiguing. The Man came every now & then from the Wheel to see how the Work went on; and at length would take his Ax as it was without farther Grinding. No, says the Smith, Turn on, turn on; we shall have it bright by and by; as yet 'tis only speckled. Yes, says the Man; but—*I think I like a speckled Ax best.*— And I believe this may have been the Case with many who having for want of some such Means as I employ'd found the Difficulty of obtaining good, & breaking bad Habits, in other Points of Vice & Virtue, have given up the Struggle, & concluded that *a speckled Ax was best.* For something that pretended to be Reason was every now and then suggesting to me, that such extream Nicety as I exacted of my self might be a kind of Foppery in Morals, which if it were known would make me ridiculous; that a perfect Character might be attended with the Inconvenience of being envied and hated; and that a benevolent Man should allow a few Faults in himself, to keep his Friends in Countenance. In Truth I found myself incorrigible with respect to *Order;* and now I am grown old, and my Memory bad, I feel very sensibly the want of it. But on the whole, tho' I never arrived at the Perfection I had been so ambitious of obtaining, but fell far short of it, yet I was by the Endeavour made a better and a happier Man than I otherwise should have been, if I had not attempted it; As those who aim at perfect Writing by imitating the engraved Copies, tho' they never reach the wish'd for Excellence of those Copies, their Hand is mended by the Endeavour, and is tolerable while it continues fair & legible.—

And it may be well my Posterity should be informed, that to this little Artifice, with the Blessing of God, their Ancestor ow'd the constant Felicity of his Life down to his 79th Year in which this is written. What Reverses may attend the Remainder is in the Hand of Providence: But if they arrive the Reflection on past Happiness enjoy'd ought to help his Bearing them with more Resignation. To *Temperance* he ascribes his long-continu'd Health, & what is still left to him of a good Constitution. To *Industry* and *Frugality* the early Easiness of his Circumstances, & Acquisition of his Fortune, with all that Knowledge which enabled him to be an useful Citizen, and obtain'd for him some Degree of Reputation among the Learned. To *Sincerity* & *Justice* the Confidence of his Country, and the honourable Employs it conferr'd upon him. And to the joint Influence of the whole Mass of the Virtues, even in their imperfect State he was able to acquire them, all that Evenness of Temper, & that Chearfulness in Conversation which makes his Company still sought for, & agreable even to his younger Acquaintance. I hope therefore that some of my Descendants may follow the Example & reap the Benefit.—

It will be remark'd that, tho' my Scheme was not wholly without Religion there was in it no Mark of any of the distinguishing Tenets of any particular Sect.—I had purposely avoided them; for being fully persuaded of the Utility and Excellency of my Method, and that it might be serviceable to People in all Religions, and intending some time or other to publish it, I would not have any thing in it that should prejudice any one of any Sect against it.—I purposed writing a little Comment on each Virtue, in which I would have shown the Advantages of possessing it, & the Mischiefs attending its opposite Vice; and I should have called my Book the ART *of Virtue,* because it would have shown the *Means & Manner* of obtaining Virtue; which would have distinguish'd it from the mere Exhortation to be good, that does not instruct & indicate the Means; but is like the Apostle's Man of verbal Charity, who only, without showing to the Naked & the Hungry *how* or where they might get Cloaths or Victuals, exhorted them to be fed & clothed. *James* II, 15, 16.—

But it so happened that my Intention of writing & publishing this Comment was never fulfilled. I did indeed, from time to time put down short Hints of the Sentiments, Reasonings, &c. to be made use of in it; some of which I have still by me: But the necessary close Attention to private Business in the earlier part of Life, and public Business since, have occasioned my postponing it. For it being connected in my Mind with a *great and extensive Project* that required the whole Man to execute, and which an unforeseen Succession of Employs prevented my attending to, it has hitherto remain'd unfinish'd.—

In this Piece it was my Design to explain and enforce this Doctrine, that vicious Actions are not hurtful because they are forbidden, but forbidden because they are hurtful, the Nature of Man alone consider'd: That it was therefore every ones Interest to be virtuous, who wish'd to be happy even in this World. And I should from this Circumstance, there being always in the World a Number of rich Merchants, Nobility, States and Princes, who have need of honest Instruments for the Management of their Affairs, and such being so rare, have endeavoured to convince young Persons, that no Qualities were so likely to make a poor Man's Fortune as those of Probity & Integrity.

My List of Virtues contain'd at first but twelve: But a Quaker Friend having kindly inform'd me that I was generally thought proud; that my Pride show'd itself frequently in Conversation; that I was not content with being in the right when discussing any Point, but was overbearing & rather insolent; of which he convinc'd me by mentioning several Instances;—I determined endeavouring to cure myself if I could of this Vice or Folly among the rest, and I added *Humility* to my List, giving an extensive Meaning to the Word.—I cannot boast of much Success in acquiring the *Reality* of this Virtue; but I had a good deal with regard to the *Appearance* of it.—I made it a Rule to forbear all direct Contradiction to the Sentiments of others, and all positive Assertion of my own. I even forbid myself agreable to the old Laws of our Junto, the Use of every Word or Expression in the Language that imported a fix'd Opinion; such as *certainly, undoubtedly,* &c. and I adopted instead of them, *I conceive, I apprehend,* or *I imagine* a thing to be so or so, or it so appears to me at present.—When another asserted something that I thought an Error, I deny'd my self the Pleasure of contradicting him abruptly, and of showing immediately some Absurdity in his Proposition; and in answering I began by observing that in certain Cases or Circumstances his Opinion would be right, but that in the present case there *appear'd* or *seem'd* to me some Difference, &c. I soon found the Advantage of this Change in my Manners. The Conversations I engag'd in went on more pleasantly. The modest way in which I propos'd my Opinions, procur'd them a readier Reception and less Contradiction; I had less Mortification when I was found to be in the wrong, and I more easily prevail'd with others to give up their Mistakes & join with me when I happen'd to be in the right. And this Mode, which I at first put on, with some violence to natural Inclination, became at length so easy & so habitual to me, that perhaps for these Fifty Years past no one has ever heard a dogmatical Expression escape me. And to this Habit (after my Character of Integrity) I think it principally owing, that I had early so much Weight with my Fellow Citizens, when I proposed new Institutions, or Alterations in the old; and so much Influence in public Councils when I became a Member.

For I was but a bad Speaker, never eloquent, subject to much Hesitation in my choice of Words, hardly correct in Language, and yet I generally carried my Points.—

In reality there is perhaps no one of our natural Passions so hard to subdue as *Pride*. Disguise it, struggle with it, beat it down, stifle it, mortify it as much as one pleases, it is still alive, and will every now and then peep out and show itself. You will see it perhaps often in this History. For even if I could conceive that I had compleatly overcome it, I should probably be proud of my Humility.—

Thus far written at Passy 1784

A Collection of Poems

As it had during the seventeenth century in British America, poetry was published in separate volumes, and it appeared as well in the public press. The vehicles of publication were more numerous during the eighteenth century than ever before, and poems appeared in a range of venues, including newspapers; almanacs; literary and general magazines; and broadsides, separately published sheets that one could pass around and post easily. The popularity of poetry remained as high during the eighteenth century as it did during the seventeenth, evidenced by the fact that even the era's better-known fictional publications and even its dramatic works often included poems inserted amid the prose or as epigraphs to chapters, as prefaces, or as prologues and epilogues to plays that did not otherwise employ verse.

Because of its wide general appeal and because it was being read and written by an ever-increasing number of people, poetry became a special concern of members of the elite and middling-level artisans, who sometimes sought to create a space apart for themselves and their poetic productions. Poetic materials, from formal verse to songs and ditties, often became the means by which groups identified themselves to one another. Men's clubs, for instance, used particular poems and songs to self-identify, as with John Leacock's *Song, The First of May, to St. Tammany,* which employed a well-known tune and served as a rallying and perhaps a drinking song for the members of the Society of the Sons of Saint Tammany, named after a legendary Indian chief of Pennsylvania. Some elite readers throughout the colonies sometimes considered—because publicity meant a sort of intellectual prostitution, implying social leveling, they thought—it was better not to publish their works but instead to circulate them in sheets and in whole manuscripts or copybooks only among friends. Thus, many men and women of the elite chose *not* to publish their works for those whom they considered to be the untalented masses; they instead selected who should be their recipients, sent (through private conveyance) their works in fair-copy manuscripts, and gained a status-driven sense of "publicity" in this way. This kind of situation is well represented by the poems of Annis Stockton, who saw that her poems were widely circulated among her friends and that certain of her poems, especially those on political affairs or on socially normative behavior, such as marriage, would reach print. Men likewise circulated their poems among friends, however, thus demarcating their sense of social lines and decorum, distinguishing characteristics of eighteenth-century "gentlemen."

Women, particularly of the elite, increasingly turned to writing poetry during the eighteenth century, although because they were not often trained to read Greek and Latin in the original, their poetry has a more generalized neoclassicism, the dominant mode of writers, than does men's poetry. That is, the men who were trained in the classics often composed poems that imitated classical models, reinforcing or critiquing the model in some way, even as they created new articulations along classical lines. Women, typically untrained in classical writings and readings, adapted their writings to a more generalized sense of meaning, tending to rely upon contemporary neoclassical writers, such as Pope and Dryden, and later in the century, James Thomson, for their poetic models.

To be sure, women were not as frequently encouraged in their literary pursuits as were men, and the writing of poetry was not an exception to this general cultural tendency. In some cases, women were actively discouraged and criticized by the men and even the women around them. Some women's poetry directly addressed the climate for women writers. In 1757, for example, Martha Brewster commented on the reaction she anticipated to the publication of her poetry, directly addressing her doubting readers, as Anne Bradstreet had done before her, with a statement indicating her belief, "most no doubt will call it Vanity; / Condemn the Stile you may without Offence, / Call it insipid, wanting Eloquence." Adapting the conventional apologies offered by many writers, especially women writers, Brewster concluded "Let me improve my Talents tho' but small, / And thus it humble waits upon you shall."

Men and women used literary circles, sometimes same-sex gatherings and sometimes mixed ones, to encourage one another and foster a sense of literate community with cultural links to England and Europe. The circles proved useful for sharing information, clarifying opinions, and circulating their work. Philadelphia poets Elizabeth Graeme Fergusson and Susanna Wright were, like their friend and contemporary Annis Boudinot Stockton in New Jersey, particularly well known for the literary salons they sponsored. Fergusson's salon at Graeme Park was a center for Philadelphia's literary and intellectual elite. It included, in addition to Stockton, her niece Anna Young Smith, Hannah Griffitts, Benjamin Rush, and Nathaniel Evans. Networks that developed among poets seem to have been particularly important for nurturing poets' creative talents, and they served as well to develop a sense of having a literate community for people who were all too aware that they were far away from what was considered the center of culture—London and, later, Edinburgh.

The selections that follow suggest the range of poetry circulated and printed by men and women of the British North American colonies and some of the ways these poets explored and tested the poetic conventions of their British counterparts. The works of these writers should be read alongside eighteenth-century poetic writings by James Grainger, Ebenezer Cook, Richard Lewis, Annis Boudinot Stockton, Jupiter Hammon, Phillis Wheatley, Mercy Otis Warren, Timothy Dwight, Judith Sargent Murray, Joel Barlow, and Philip Freneau presented elsewhere in this volume.

WILLIAM DAWSON (1704–1752)

Born in England and educated at Queen's College, Oxford, William Dawson was highly respected as a writer, clergyman, and public figure. After receiving his M.A. degree from Oxford in 1728, Dawson emigrated to Virginia, where he became a teacher, commissary, councilor, and college president at Virginia's College of William and Mary. Dawson published his poems on both sides of the Atlantic and contributed signed and unsigned verse to the *Virginia Gazette*. Dawson's poetry favored the neoclassical model of the pastoral, and his poems often include learned allusions to famed British poets of his day, including Milton, Pope, Shakespeare, and Rowe. His volume, *Poems on Several Occasions,* was first published anonymously in 1736 as the work of "a Gentleman of Virginia." The following poems, "To Sylvia, on Approach of Winter" and "Anacreontic," appeared in *Poems on Several Occasions*.

To Sylvia, On Approach of Winter

COME, my *Sylvia,* come away;
Youth and Beauty will not stay;
  Let's enjoy the present now.
Heark, tempestuous Winter's Roar,

How it blusters at the Door,
  Charg'd with Frosts, and Storms, and Snow.

SEATED near the crackling Fire,
Let's indulge our fond Desire,
  Careless of rough *Borea's* Blast:

Let us teach the blooming Youth,
What Joys attend on Love and Truth;
  How much they please, how long they last.

THE am'rous Warblers of the Grove,
That in sweet Carols chant their Love,
  Can only sing, whilst Spring inspires;
But let us show, no Age, no Time,
No warring Seasons, frozen Clime,
  Can damp the Warmth of our Desires.

Anacreontic[1]

OLD Poets sing the Dame, to Stone
Converted by *Jove's* radiant Son:[2]

---

1. This poem adapts stanzaic patterns employed by Greek poet, Anacreon, in the sixth century B.C. Anacreontic verse typically praises wine, women, and song.

2. This reference draws on the story of Niobe, wife of the king of Thebes, whose boasts of superiority angered Leto, mother of Apollo and Artemis. Leto asked Apollo to murder Niobe's sons and Artemis to murder Niobe's daughters. After the grieving Niobe prayed to the gods, they responded in pity and transformed her into a stone image.

How *Progne*[3] builds her clayey Cell
In Chimnies, where she once did dwell.
For me, (did Fate permit to use,
Whatever Form our Fancies chuse)
I'd be my lovely *Sylvia's* Glass,
Still to reflect her beauteous Face;
I'd be the pure and limpid Wave,
In which my Fair delights to lave;
I'd be her Garment, still to hide
Her snowy Limbs, with decent Pride;
I'd be the Girdle, to embrace
The gradual Taper of her Wast;
I'd be her Tippet, still to press
The snowy Velvet of her Breast;
But if the rigid Fates denied
Such Ornaments of Grace and Pride,
I'd be her very Shoe, that she
With scornful Tread might trample me.

---

3. Progne (frequently, Procne) Philoemela's sister, was changed into a swallow.

JANE COLMAN TURELL (1708–1735)

Massachusetts poet Jane Colman Turell was born into a family where women's education was valued highly. Her father, the Reverend Benjamin Colman of Boston's Brattle Street Church, offered his daughter an extensive education from her youth onward. A voracious reader, Turell relied upon the criticism of her father to assist her skill, and after she had moved from her family home, she wrote regularly to her father, requesting his comments on her poetry. In 1726, Turell married the Reverend Ebenezer Turell and moved to nearby Medford, Masssachusetts, where she gave birth to four children, only one of whom survived her.

Turell's topics and themes, relatively typical of women writers in her day, included spirituality, rural life, local affairs, childbirth, and death. She was a prolific writer. After her death, her husband prepared *Some Memoirs of the Life and Death of Mrs. Jane Turell* (1735), the source of the poems offered next. In presenting the volume, her husband explained that he excluded her "pieces of wit and humor" in order to focus on her more serious moral works.

An Invitation into the Country, in Imitation of Horace, Left Only in a Rough Copy

FROM the soft Shades, and from the balmy Sweets
Of *Medford's* flow'ry Vales, and green Retreats,
Your absent *Delia*[1] to her *Father* sends
And prays to see him 'ere the Summer ends.

  Now while the Earth's with beauteous Verdure dy'd,

And *Flora*[2] paints the Meads in all her Pride;
While laden Trees *Pomonia's* Bounty own,[3]
And *Ceres*[4] Treasures do the Fields adorn.
From the thick Smokes, and noisy *Town,* O come,
And in these *Plains* a while forget your Home.

---

2. Ancient Italian goddess of flowering plants.

3. Ancient Italian goddess of fruits.

4. Ancient Italian goddess of corn and harvest festivals.

---

1. Delia is Turell's pseudonym.

Tho' my small Incomes never can afford,
Like wealthy *Celsus*[5] to regale a Lord;
No Ivory Tables groan beneath the Weight
Of sumptuous Dishes, serv'd in massy Plate:
The Forest ne'r was search'd for Food for me,
Nor from my Hounds the timerous Hare does flee:
No leaden Thunder strikes the Fowl in Air,
Nor from my Shaft the winged Death do fear:
With silken Nets I ne're the Lake despoil,
Nor with my Bait the larger Fish beguile.
No luscious Sweet-Meats, by my Servants plac'd
In curious Order, 'ere my Table grac'd:
To please the Taste, no rich *Burgundian* Wine,
In chrystal Glasses on my Side-board shine;
The luscious Sweets of fair *Canaries* Isle
Ne'r fill'd my Casks, nor in my Flaggons smile:
No Wine, but what does from my Apples flow,
My frugal House on any can bestow:
Except when Cæsar's Birth-day does return,
And joyful Fires throughout the Village burn;
Then moderate each takes his chearful Glass,
And our good Wishes to *Augustus* pass.

But tho' rich Dainties never spread my Board,
Nor my cool Vaults *Calabrian* Wines afford;
Yet what is neat and wholesome I can spread,
My good fat Bacon, and our homely Bread,
With which my healthful Family is fed.
Milk from the Cow, and Butter newly churn'd,
And new fresh Cheese, with Curds and Cream just
    turn'd.
For a Desert upon my Table's seen
The Golden Apple, and the Melon green;
The blushing Peech and glossy Plumb there lies,
And with the *Mandrake* tempt your Hands and Eyes.

This I can give, and if you'l here repair,
To slake your Thirst a Cask of *Autumn Beer,*
Reserv'd on purpose for your drinking here.

Under the Spreading Elms our Limbs we'll lay,
While fragrant *Zephires* round our Temples play.
Retir'd from Courts, and Crouds, secure we'll set,
And freely feed upon our Country Treat.
No noisy Faction here shall dare intrude,
Or once disturb our peaceful Solitude.

No stately Beds my humble Roofs adorn
Of costly Purple, by carv'd *Panthers* born.
Nor can I boast *Arabia's* rich Perfumes,

Diffusing Odours thro' our stately Rooms.
For me no fair *Egyptian* plies the Loam,
But my fine Linnen all is made at Home.
Tho' I no Down or *Tapestry* can spread,
A clean soft *Pillow* shall support your Head,
Fill'd with the Wool from off my tender Sheep,
On which with Ease and Safety you may sleep.
The *Nightingale* shall lull You to your Rest,
And all be calm and still as is your Breast.

[Lines on Childbirth]

Phoebus[6] has thrice his Yearly Circuit run,
The Winter's over, and the Summer's done;
Since that *bright Day* on which our Hands were join'd,
And to *Philander*[7] I my All resign'd.

Thrice in my Womb I've found the pleasing Strife,
In the first Struggles of my Infants Life:
But O how soon by Heaven I'm call'd to mourn,
While from my Womb a *lifeless Babe* is torn?
Born to the Grave 'ere it had seen the Light,
Or with one Smile had chear'd my longing Sight.

Again in Travail Pains my Nerves are wreck'd.
My Eye-balls start, my Heart strings almost crack'd;
Now I forget my Pains, and now I press
Philander's Image to my panting Breast.
Ten Days I hold him in my joyful Arms,
And feast my Eyes upon his Infant Charms.
But then the King of Terrors does advance
To pierce it's Bosom with his Iron Lance.
It's Soul releas'd, upward it takes it's Flight,
Oh never more below to bless my Sight!
Farewell sweet *Babes* I hope to meet above,
And there with you Sing the Redeemer's Love.

And now O gracious Saviour lend thine Ear,
To this my earnest Cry and humble Prayer,
That when the Hour arrives with painful Throws,
Which shall my Burden to the World disclose;
I may Deliverance have, and joy to see
A living Child, to Dedicate to Thee.

[Lines on the Death of Mother][8]

She's gone! she's gone! I saw her rise
And quickly gain the distant Skies.

---

5. A distinguished Roman jurist and consul.

6. The Greek god of the sun.

7. Pseudonym for Ebenezer, Turell's husband.

8. Jane Clark Colman, Turell's mother, died on October 28,
1730.

Sudden from Heaven a sacred Mandate came,
Bro't by a Convoy of coelestial Flame.
She was prepar'd, the Summons did obey,
And joyful left her tottering House of Clay.
Her Pains, her Tears, her Fears, are all now past
In Joys unspeakable which ever last.
   Her Soul in Jesus Arms remain,
   The Grave her Body does detain.
Parted a while, her Joys will be compleat,
When in the Resurrection Morn they'l meet.

Ah *dearest, tenderest Parent!* must I mourn,

My heavy Loss, and bathe with Tears your Urn!
Since now no more to me you must return.

O *Quickening Spirit!* now perform thy Part,
Set up thy Glorious Kingdom in my Heart;
That when those Sands which in my Glass do run
Are spent and all my Work below is done,
I the *dear Saint* may then in Glory meet
Where Sin and Death lye vanquish'd at our Feet:
Where *Jesus* ever will improve
Our Souls with heavenly Grace and Love.

MARTHA WADSWORTH BREWSTER (1710–POST-1759)

Little is known about the life of Martha Brewster, a poet whose published volume, *Poems on Diverse Subjects* (1757), is the source of most of the information available about her. Brewster lived for a time in Goshen, Massachusetts, part of an evangelical community of that area, before she moved in 1745 to rural Lebanon, Massachusetts, perhaps to marry Oliver Brewster. She wrote in many of the standard religious genres common in her day, including scriptural paraphrases, but even though she wrote in fairly traditional genres for women writers, her skill as a writer who was also a woman was challenged by those around her. Brewster's collection is the source of the poems offered here.

[Prefatory Poem to the Reader][1]

Pardon her bold Attempt who has reveal'd
Her Thoughts to View, more fit to be conceal'd;
Since thus to do was urged vehemently,
Yet most no doubt will call it Vanity;
Condemn the Stile you may without Offence,
Call it insipid, wanting Eloquence.
I blush to Gaul[2] so delicate an Ear,
Which to sublimer Sonnets do adhere;
For why my Muse had but a single Aim,
Myself and nearest Friends to entertain;
But since some have a Gust[3] for Novelty,
I here presume upon your Clemency,
For rare it is to see a Female Bard,
Or that my Sex *in* Print *have e're appear'd:*
Let me improve my Talents tho' but small,
And thus it humbly waits upon you shall.

An Essay on the Four Ages of Man, Resembling the Four Seasons of the Year[4]

HAIL great Historians with your generous Fire,
Lay down your Books a while for to enquire,
A home-born Story, and discriminate,
Man's budding, blooming, ripening, withering State;
His first Approach is with a rufal[5] roar,
More senseless than a Beast, nor half the Pow'r;
But soon arrives to wear a graceful Smile,
Which gains him such Exceptance for a While,
That Weaponless he conquers ev'ry Foe,
Nor Cares, nor Fears, nor Malice Undergo.
Thus see the Resurrection of the Spring,
The Buds shoot forth the merry Birds do sing:
All Nature shouts, and ecchoes to their Song,
To reap the Favours waited for so long.
But to proceed the Infant grows a-pace,
When numerous Evils get upon his Chace,
All fully bent to crop him in the Bud,
And spill his Name, his Fortune, and his Blood;

---

1. This untitled poem appears opposite Brewster's "An Essay on the Four Ages of Man" and was first published in Martha Brewster's *Poems on Divers Subjects* (1757).

2. Gall, vex.

3. Taste.

---

4. This text is taken from Martha Brewster's *Poems on Divers Subjects* (1757).

5. That is, rueful.

The worst of all were in his Nature bred,
And thus the silly Creature is betray'd:
Some Friends he hath would fain his Good insure,
Yet many Ways his Evils they procure;
But there is one whose Pow'r and Grace extends,
Can save the Wretch, to whom we him commend.
The next we see advancing on the Stage
Is vig'rous Youth all in his blooming Age;
As *Flora*[6] in her Prime a Carpet spreads,
Of rich Imbroidery o'er the Hills and Meads,
While chearing Vines and Trees adorns the Bed
With curious Hangings each their Odours shed,
Which with their Fruits a double Blessing yield,
And Corn with growing Verdure decks the Field:
Even thus I say the gallant Youth appears,
In manly Features, and in graceful Airs;
His Front a stately Banner toward the Foe,
With noble Courage seated on his Brow;
His Eyes a penetrating Wit declare,
A Judgment found with artful Genious rare;
Here Beams of Love do gently dart their Rays,
And amorous Glances slide along his Face.
His Skin the Fair and Ruddy neatly met,
As Ruby's would in Alabaster set:
Polite his Carriage, and his Features gay,
His form Delectable, and his Array
Befitting well his every Exercise:
His Patrimony large, his Fortunes rise,
His Lips chant high in Academick Strains,
And healthful sanguine Juices fill his Veins:
His Temper mild, and a rare Symmetry
Runs through the whole attracting ev'ry Eye:
Come noble Youth, and wast along in Pleasure,
Taste all Delights without Restraint or Measure,
But know these Favours are so dearly bought.
The least Abuse must be to Judgment brought:
And there your Coin will not for Currant pass,
To pay the Debt, or Bail thee out, Alass!
Except your Judge your Advocate should be,
To pay the Debt and set the Prisoner free,
Which if he don't you'l love his Service more
Than all your Lust and Vanities before.
But lo, another rising on the Stage,
And by his Gravity 'tis middle-age;
As when bright *Sol*[7] withdraws his burning Rays.

The Summers Livery withers and decays,
And gentle *Autumn* with an Aspect mild,
Upon the painful Farmer casts a Smile,
The Earth her flow'ry Garb has cast away.
And now her summate Glory doth Display;
For now delightful, fruitful Stores abound,
And thus the Year is with God's goodness crown'd
So Middle-Age has shed her Frantick Airs,
Whereby her nobler Pow'rs more Bright appears;
As when bright *Phoebus*[8] Travails up the Sky,
The sparkling Gems of Heaven before him fly;
His Magnitude soon makes them dis-appear,
And radiant Blushes spread the Hemisphere.
Thus Reason fully ripe, the Judgment keen,
Each intellectual Faculty Serene:
His Schemes Computed, and his Goods procur'd,
His Seat erected, and his Lands manur'd;
A Consort Loyal, and with Virtue stor'd,
A pleasant Off-spring flourish round his Board;
A Thousand harmonising Blessings meet,
And all Concur to make his Breast their Seat,
Where such an ample source of Knowledge lies,
That all insipid, sordid Notions Dies,
Not envies, nor aspires a regal Throne,
He doth enjoy a Kingdom of his own.
Thus Middle-age exceeds what went before,
Both in his outward, and his inward Store;
The highest Topick that he ever sought,
Is now compleat, and to Perfection brought.
But turn another Leaf, and there you'l read
A dreadful Theme, 'twill make your Hearts to bleed
To see how Tyrant Sin doth fill the Throne,
Where Righteousness should dwell, and reign alone.
Sin ev'ry Cross, and ev'ry Evil breeds,
Yea Death, and Hell, are Paths to which it leads;
There's none but Giant Grace can Vict'ry get,
And when he doth, then is the Man compleat.
The fourth and last is venerable Age,
Leaning upon his Staff, his aspect Sage;
He on his Head a Crown of Glory wears;
Not made of sparkling Gems, but Silver Hairs:
Likewise the many Marks upon his Face,
Demands profound Respect in ev'ry Place:
His Head once richly stor'd with Knowlege sweet,
He has no Room for more, but doth repeat,
His past Experience to his numerous Seed,

---

6. Ancient Italian goddess of flowers and flowering plants.

7. Ancient Roman god of the sun.

---

8. Classical sun deity.

Who with a filial Reverence do him heed.
To whom their best Adherence now is due,
To their Procurer and Protector too;
Let anxious Care no more disturb his Head,
His provident, and frugal Hand has laid,
A Stock sufficient, as his Schemes were blest,
To feed himself and leave his Heirs the Rest:
Yet doth his Hand find some Imployment still,
Since they that nothing do, do always ill;
And when his Glass hath few more Sands behind,
More Vanity in human Things he finds;
But love of Friends, or more I scarce know what,
Still draws him back to Earth's inferior Spot.
The Winter Season shall an Emblem be,
The Leaves are shed, the Fruits all housed be;
The vived[9] Blood is chil'd in ev'ry Vein,

But still the Root doth Life and Growth retain;
A Snowy Robe adorns instead of Hairs,
And underneath a wither'd Face appears;
And thus she lies benum'd nor strives to rise,
Till the benign Influence of the Skies,
Destroy's her Foe and gently calls her forth,
In brighter Beauty and with larger Growth:
So may the Son of Righteousness arise,
And the celestial Dove descend the Skies,
And quicken ev'ry Age of mortal Dust,
And make this State more glorious than the first,
Nor let the aged Sinner die accurs'd;
Makes us to Grow 'till we advance so far,
To raise our Feet up high beyond the Stars;
There wholesome Fruit and living Water flows,
There we may bathe, and take a sweet Repose.

---

9. Vivid, living.

BRIDGET RICHARDSON FLETCHER (1726–1770)

Bridget Richardson Fletcher's poems celebrated the events of the lives led by many women in her circle. They centered upon issues related to proper conduct, marriage, and child rearing, and they featured a religious perspective frequently found among women who displayed their godliness to others even as they explored their own religious affections. Fletcher evidently did not intend that her poems would be published and instead circulated them among her friends and family. An unknown editor, probably a family member, prepared a collection of eighty-three of her writings in *Hymns and Spiritual Songs* (1773) a few years after Fletcher died and apparently in response to requests by friends that her writings be printed. This volume is the source of the present two poems.

Hymn XXXVI. The Greatest Dignity of a Woman, Christ Being Born of One

1

God's only son by woman came,
    To take away our shame;
And so thereby, to dignify,
    Also to raise our fame.

2

5 Did Christ our friend, thus condescend,
    Of woman to be born;
Did one so high, so dignify,
    Those that you treat with scorn?

3

What man is there, that shall thus dare
10   Woman to treat with scorn,
Since God's own son, from heav'n did come,
    Of such an one was born.

4

Did one so high, thus dignify,
    And here do such a thing;
Shall we now fear, those that live here,   15
    Although it was a king.

Hymn LXX. The Duty of Man and Wife

1

You gentlemen and who are friend
    To your own happiness,
Come now and hear or stop your ear,
    As it shall please you best.

2

To every head that is married,   5
    This song is now entail'd;
If any hiss, I say at this,
    Then let him be expell'd.

3

The matter here, which I'll declare
10   I hope will end much strife;
I wish it might, each man invite,
   To love and prize his wife.

4

Let women fair, also take care
   And see they do submit,
15 As reason there, shall say is fair,
   And as it shall seem fit.

5

Would man and wife, live free from strife,
   How happy might they be,
If they would try, in harmony
20   To live in unity.

6

As bone of bone, they should be one
   In heart so in pretence;

For 'tis a shame, if they are twain,
   Since join'd by providence.

7

Their hands and hearts, their skill and arts,   25
   Should combine together,
Thus join they must, and so one purse
   Hold all they do gather.

8

The poor that come you must give some,
   With kindness treat each friend;   30
And all your store, will be bless'd the more,
   Likewise the better spend.

9

Strict care pray take, least you do break,
   The bond of unity,
For if that's broke it makes sad work,   35
   Soon ends prosperity.

JOHN LEACOCK (1729–1802)

Born into a relatively prosperous artisan family in Philadelphia, John Leacock followed the trade of his father and became a gold- and silversmith and a merchant. He owned his own business by the middle of the 1750s, and he participated in a number of protests against British authorities at that time and later. He was related in various ways to significant leaders in the community of artisans and local political leaders, including printer David Hall, lawyer James Read, and printer and politician Benjamin Franklin. Leacock became prosperous himself and left the trade to apprentices, retiring to an estate in the country to write political propaganda, promote scientific study, and sponsor vineyards both public and private. He participated in the Revolutionary War when it reached Philadelphia by joining as an accounts keeper for the officers at Easton and Reading, where he signed bills of credit and took care of other matters related to supplies. After the war, he became Philadelphia's coroner and enjoyed local renown.

Leacock belonged to a few men's clubs, for which he probably wrote many songs and ditties. His best-known work, *The First Book of the American Chronicles of the Times*, a pamphlet series printed throughout the colonies from north to south between 1774 and 1775, was a biblical parodic satire that humorously but contentiously criticized Thomas Gage's seizure of Boston harbor and his takeover of the city of Boston. Leacock also wrote a propaganda play, *The Fall of British Tyranny*, which was probably used to while away the wartime winter hours in 1776, the year it reached print in Philadelphia. Leacock evidently wrote numerous songs, including the song to "Saint Tammany" included in *The Fall of British Tyranny* and printed in local newspapers on May 1, 1776.

Song, The First of May, to St. Tammany[1]

SONG

[Tune. The bounds are all out, etc.][2]

Of St. George, or St. Bute,[3] let the poet laureate sing,
Of Pharaoh or Pluto of old,
While he rhymes forth their praise, in false, flattering
   lays,
I'll sing of St. Tamm'ny the bold, my brave boys.

5 Let Hibernia's sons boast, make Patrick their toast;
And Scots Andrew's fame spread abroad.
Potatoes and oats, and Welch leeks for Welch goats,
Was never St. Tammany's food, my brave boys.

In freedom's bright cause, Tamm'ny pled with applause,
10 And reason'd most justly from nature;
For this, this was his song, all, all the day long:
Liberty's the right of each creature, brave boys.

Whilst under an oak his great parliament sat,
His throne was the crotch of the tree;
15 With Solomon's look, without statutes or book,
He widely sent forth his decree, my brave boys.

His subjects stood round, not the least noise or sound,
Whilst freedom blaz'd full in each face:
So plain were the laws, and each pleaded his cause;
20 That might BUTE, NORTH, and MANSFIELD[4] disgrace, my brave boys.

No duties, nor stamps, their blest liberty cramps,
A king, tho' no tyrant, was he;

He did oft 'times declare, nay sometimes wou'd swear,
The least of his subjects were free, my brave boys.

He, as king of the woods, of the rivers and floods,   25
Had a right all beasts to controul;
Yet, content with a few, to give nature her due:
So gen'rous was Tammany's soul, my brave boys.

In the morn he arose, and a-hunting he goes,
Bold Nimrod[5] his second was he.   30
For his breakfast he'd take a large venison stake,
And despis'd your flip-flops and tea, my brave boys.

While all in a row, with squaw, dog and bow,
Vermilion adorning his face,
With feathery head he rang'd the woods wide: 35
St. George sure had never such grace, my brave boys.

His jetty black hair, such as Buckskin saints wear,
Perfumed with bear's grease well smear'd,
Which illum'd the saints face, and ran down apace.
Like the oil from Aaron's old beard,[6] my brave boys.   40

The strong nervous deer, with amazing career,
In swiftness he'd fairly run down:
And, like Sampson, wou'd tear wolf, lion or bear.
Ne're was such a saint as our own, my brave boys.

When he'd run down a stag, he behind him wou'd lag;   45
For, so noble a soul had he!
He'd stop, tho' he lost it, tradition reports it,
To give him fresh chance to get free, my brave boys.

With a mighty strong arm, and a masculine bow,
His arrow he drew to the head,   50
And as sure as he shot, it was ever his lot,
His prey it fell instantly dead, my brave boys.

His table he spread where the venison bled,
Be thankful, he used to say;
He'd laugh and he'd sing, tho' a saint and a king,   55
And sumptuously dine on his prey, my brave boys.

Then over the hills, o'er the mountains and rills
He'd caper, such was his delight;
And ne'er in his days, Indian history says,
Did lack a good supper at night, my brave boys.   60

On an old stump he sat, without cap or hat,
When supper was ready to eat,

---

1. In the context of his play, *The Fall of British Tyranny* (1776), "Song to St. Tammany" offers a lighter tone to the highly oratorical action typical of the theater of his day. The song employs a common propagandist technique that was used during the war in its appropriation of American Indians to relay a message about the colonists' self-identification with the indigenous peoples of North America. The popular conceit was that Native Americans' war prowess had influenced the colonists, and they would, as a result, win any war against Britain. Tamanend was a noted chief of the Lenape peoples, and he became a namesake for a local prorebellion "society," or men's club. Leacock makes reference to a loyalist men's club in the first line, when he mentions the Society of St. George.

2. Songs, especially drinking songs, were typically composed to accompany popular ballads and tunes.

3. John Stuart, third earl of Bute, advised King George III to pursue repressive measures against the colonists.

4. Advisers to George III.

---

5. Nimrod, son of Cush in Genesis 10.8–9, is considered a mighty hunter.

6. Aaron had oil poured on his head, and it reached his beard, Psalms 113.2.

Snap, his dog, he stood by, and cast a sheep's eye;
For ven'son, the king of all meat, my brave boys.

65 Like Isaac of old, and both cast in one mould,
Tho' a wigwam was Tamm'ny's cottage,
He lov'd sav'ry meat, such that patriarch eat,
Of ven'son and squirrel made pottage, brave boys.

When fourscore years old, as I've oft'times been told,
70 To doubt it, sure, would not be right,
With a pipe in his jaw, he'd buss his old squaw,
And get a young saint ev'ry night, my brave boys.

As old age came on, he grew blind, deaf and dumb.
Tho' his sport, 'twere hard to keep from it,

Quite tired of life, bid adieu to his wife,   75
And blaz'd like the tail of a comet, brave boys.

What country on earth, then, did ever give birth
To such a magnanimous saint?
His acts far excel all that history tell,
And language too feeble to paint, my brave boys.   80

Now, to finish my song, a full flowing bowl
I'll quaff, and sing all the long day,
And with punch and wine paint my cheeks for my saint,
And hail ev'ry First of sweet May, my brave boys.

LUCY TERRY (1730–1821)

Lucy Terry, born in West Africa, was captured and enslaved while a young child and was brought, no doubt after a shocking and difficult middle passage, to Deerfield, Massachusetts. She lived in Deerfield during her early years, but after she married, she moved to Vermont with her husband, Abijah Prince, a free black man who purchased her freedom. In Vermont, she and her husband raised six children. Terry was well known as a poet within her Vermont community, so it is likely that more of her poetry will surface in the future. Until that time, however, Terry's only known poem remains "Bars Fight," a ballad that was passed down orally among people in Vermont for more than a century before it was published in Josiah Holland's *History of Western Massachusetts* (1885), the source of this text.

Bars Fight[1]

August, 'twas the twenty-fifth,
Seventeen hundred forty-six;
The Indians did in ambush lay,
Some very valiant men to slay,
5 The names of whom I'll not leave out.
Samuel Allen like a hero fout,[2]
And though he was so brave and bold,
His face no more shall we behold.
Eleazer Hawks was killed outright,
10 Before he had time to fight,—
Before he did the Indians see,
Was shot and killed immediately.
Oliver Amsden he was slain,

Which caused his friends much grief and pain.
Simeon Amsden they found dead,   15
Not many rods distant from his head.
Adonijah Gillett, we do hear,
Did lose his life which was so dear.
John Sadler fled across the water,
And thus escaped the dreadful slaughter.   20
Eunice Allen see the Indians coming,
And hopes to save herself by running,
And had not her petticoats stopped her,
The awful creatures had not catched her,
Nor tommy hawked her on her head,   25
And left her on the ground for dead.
Young Samuel Allen, Oh lackaday!
Was taken and carried to Canada.

---

1. "Bars" was a common term used to indicate a meadow.

2. Most likely "fought."

THOMAS GODFREY (1736–1763)

Born and educated in Philadelphia, Thomas Godfrey was part of a circle that included artisans and intellectuals in the area. A glazier by trade, Godfrey was a self-taught mathematician, and he invented a quadrant independent of the work of other scientists. He lodged with Benjamin Franklin for a time, but he annoyed Franklin when he took his *Godfrey's Almanac,* which Franklin had annually published for 1729, 1730, and 1731, to Franklin's Philadelphia printing rival, Andrew Bradford, for the year 1732. Franklin printed his *Poor Richard's Almanac,* in order to compete with them. Given the range of his talents, Godfrey was befriended by poets Francis Hopkinson, Nathaniel Evans, the Reverend Jacob Duché, and painter John Green and joined a group of writers who called themselves the "Swains of the Schuylkill," after the river that passes through Philadelphia. But he was often in poor finances because he neglected his work for his scientific pursuits. In 1758 he left Philadelphia and moved to Wilmington, North Carolina, to become a factor. He died in North Carolina in 1763.

During his lifetime, several of Godfrey's poems appeared in periodicals, such as the *American Magazine,* edited by his patron and friend, the College of Philadelphia Provost William Smith. Yet the bulk of Godfrey's writings did not appear in print until 1765, after his death, when William Smith and Nathaniel Evans organized and published Godfrey's work in the collection, *Juvenile Poems on Various Topics, With the Prince of Parthia, A Tragedy,* which serves as the source of the poems presented here.

A Dithyrambic on Wine[1]

I.

COME! let Mirth our hours employ,
The jolly God inspires;
The rosy juice our bosom fires,
And tunes our souls to joy.
5 See, great *Bacchus* now descending,
Gay, with blushing honours crown'd;
Sprightly *Mirth* and *Love* attending,
   Around him wait,
   In smiling state—
10 Let *Echo* resound,
Let *Echo* resound,
The joyful news all around.

II.

Fond Mortals come, if love perplex,
In *Wine* relief you'll find;

Who'd whine for womens giddy sex   15
More fickle than the wind?
If beauty's bloom thy fancy warms,
Here, see her shine,
Cloath'd in superior charms;
More lovely than the blushing morn,   20
When first the op'ning day
Bedecks the thorn,
And makes the meadows gay.
Here see her in her crystal shrine;
See and adore; confess her all divine,   25
The Queen of Love and Joy.
Heed not thy Chloe's scorn—
   This sparkling glass,
   With winning grace,
Shall ever meet thy fond embrace,   30
And never, never, never cloy,
   No never, never cloy.

III.

Here, POET! see, *Castalia's* spring—[2]
Come, give me a bumper, I'll mount to the skies,
Another, another—'Tis done! I arise;   35
   On fancy's wing,
   I mount, I sing,
   And now, sublime,

---

1. "The DITHYRAMBIC demands a greater boldness than any other poetical composition, and is indeed the only one in which a lyric irregularity may be happily indulged. [from] *Francis's* HORACE." [Au.] Godfrey's editors commented here: "As our Poet appears so warm on his subject, it may not be amiss to remark here, that *he never drank any wine,* and that his *bumpers* are all *ideal,* which may serve, perhaps, as a refutation of that noted adage, *that a water drinker can never be a good dithyrambic Poet.*" A dithyramb was a hymn to the god, Dionysis (who is later in the poem called by his Roman name, Bacchus), which took the form of a choral lyric.

2. Castalia's spring, located on the slopes of Mount Parnassus, was considered sacred by Apollo and the muses.

Parnassus' lofty top I climb—
40 But hark! what sounds are these I hear,
Soft as the dream of her in love,
Or *Zephyr's* whisp'ring thro' the Grove?
And now, more solemn far than fun'ral woe,
The heavy numbers flow!
45   And now again,
     The varied strain,
Grown louder and bolder, strikes quick on the ear,
And thrills thro' ev'ry vein.

IV.

'Tis *Pindar's* song![3]
50 His softer notes the fanning gales
Waft across the spicy vales,
    While, thro' the air,
    Loud whirlwinds bear
The harsher notes along.
55   Inspir'd by *Wine*,
He leaves the lazy croud below,
Who never dar'd to peep abroad,
And, mounting to his native sky,
For ever there shall shine.
60   No more I'll plod
    The beaten road;
Like him inspir'd, like him I'll moun[t] on high;
    Like his my strain shall flow.

V.

Haste, ye Mortals! leave your sorrow;
65 Let pleasure crown to-day—to morrow
    Yield to fate.
Join the universal chorus,
    Bacchus reigns,
    Ever great;
70   *Bacchus* reigns,
    Ever glorious—
Hark! the joyful groves rebound,
Sporting breezes catch the sound,
And tell to hill and dale around—
75   "*Bacchus* reigns"—
    While far away,
The busy *Echoes* die away.—

A Night-Piece

How awful is the Night! beneath whose shade,
   Calm mournful silence e'er serenely reigns;
And musing Meditation, heav'nly Maid!
   Unbends the mind, and sooth[e]s the heart-felt pains!

II.

What pleasing terrors strike upon the soul   5
   While hills and vales around dusk swims away;
While murmuring streams in plaintive numbers roll,
   And with their soft complainings close the day!

III.

While silver Cynthia with her pallid beams,
   Does clouded nature faintly re-illume,   10
Tips tops of trees, and dancing on the streams,
   Adds livelier horror to the rising gloom!

IV.

What hand can picture forth the solemn scene,
   The deepning shade and the faint glimm'ring light!
How much above th' expressive art of G——n[4]   15
   Are the dim beauties of [a] dewy night!

V.

How much this hour does noisy day excel
   To those who heav'nly contemplation love!—
Now nought is heard but pensive *Philomel*,[5]
   The wat'ry fall, or *Zephyr* in the grove.   20

VI.

Now searching thought unlimited may rove,
   And into nature's deep recesses pry;
Spread her fleet wings to mount the realms above,
   And gain the glowing glories of the sky.

VII.

Rich in expression, how sublimely bright,   25
   Those lucent arguments above us shine!
Now, Atheist! now lift up thy wondering sight,
   And own the great creating pow'r divine.

---

3. Pindar (518–483 B.C.), famous for his triumphal odes, is often considered the greatest Greek lyric poet.

4. The editors noted at this point, "Mr. JOHN GREEN, an ingenious Portrait Painter, a particular friend of Mr. GOD-FREY'S, and Author of the Elegy, that precedes these POEMS on Mr. G's death."

5. The nightingale.

VIII.

Heav'ns! what a throng, what a dread endless train,
30   Of complicated wonders yield surprize!
Systems on systems, systems yet again,
    And suns on suns, continually arise!

IX.

Too daring thought! give o'er thy vain emprize,
35   Nor rashly pry—at humble distance gaze!
Should heav'n unveil those beauties to our eyes
    The dazzled sense would sink beneath the blaze.

X.

But leave the glories of heavn's spangl'd dome,
    And thy slow-steps to dreary church-yards lead;
The[n] [l]ean attentive on yon marble tomb,
40   And learn instruction from the silent dead.

XI.

How dismal is this place! whilst round I gaze,
    What chilling fears my thoughtful soul invade!
Exaggerating Fancy shrubs doth raise,
    To dreadful spectres gliding cross the shade.

XII.

Pale sleep! thou emblem of eternal rest,   45
    When lock'd in thy coercive strong embrace,
Those of all-bounteous Nature's gifts possest,
    Are but as those whose gloomy haunts I trace.

XIII.

No objects now wide-straining eyes admit;
    Deaf is the ear, mute the persuasive tongue,   50
Discerning judgment, and keen piercing wit
    Are lost in thee, and warriors nerves unstrung!

XIV.

Still led by thee imagination roves,
    On tow'ring pinion seeks some distant world;
Or wanders pleas'd thro' soft enamel'd groves,   55
    Or down the dreadful precipice is hurl'd.

XV.

While sad reclining on this silent tomb,
    Surrounded with promiscuous dead I rest;
Thee, I invoke! sweet friendly sleep, O come!
    Lock up my sense, and lull my troubl'd breast!   60

MILCAH MARTHA HILL MOORE (1740–1829)

Milcah Martha Hill was born on the island of Madeira into a well-connected family affiliated with the Society of Friends and descended from some of the original Welsh settlers who had come to Pennsylvania in 1683. The Hill family moved to the Delaware Valley sometime during Milcah Martha Hill's youth, thus affording her many opportunities for circulating among family and friends situated between the greater Philadelphia area and Burlington, New Jersey. Milcah Martha Hill married her cousin, Dr. Charles Moore of Philadelphia, in 1767. The marriage caused a fracture in the community of Friends, which did not favor kinship marriages between even distant cousins. Moore and her husband were expelled from the Society of Friends, and this expulsion evidently caused them both some turmoil, but their reputation as a happy couple indicates the appropriateness of the match. After her husband died in 1801, Milcah Martha Hill Moore rejoined the Society of Friends and resided in Burlington, New Jersey, until her death.

Even when she was very young, Milcah Martha Hill wrote lengthy letters and poems to her friends and relatives. The range of her literary expertise appears in her collection, *Miscellanies, Moral and Instructive, in Prose and Verse* (1787), designed for "the improvement of Young Persons of Both Sexes." The volume went through numerous editions between its original publication date and the year of Moore's death. Moore used her profits from the miscellany to endow a school for indigent girls in Montgomery, Pennsylvania. Like many of the poets of the eighteenth century, Moore kept a copybook in which she recorded fair copies of admired pieces by friends among copies of her own poems. This copybook, *Milcah Martha Moore's Book,* edited by Catherine La Courreye Blecki and Karin A. Wulf, has recently been published.

The Female Patriots. Address'd to the Daughters of Liberty in America, 1768[1]

Since the men, from a party or fear of a frown,
Are kept by a sugar-plum quietly down,
Supinely asleep—and depriv'd of their sight,
Are stripp'd of their freedom, and robb'd of their right;
5 If the sons, so degenerate! the blessings despise,
Let the Daughters of Liberty nobly arise;
And though we've no voice but a negative here,
The use of the taxables, let us forbear:—
(Then merchants import till your stores are all full,
10 May the buyers be few, and your traffic be dull!)
Stand firmly resolv'd, and bid Grenville[2] to see,

That rather than freedom we part with our tea,
And well as we love the dear draught when a-dry,
As American Patriots our taste we deny—
Pennsylvania's gay meadows can richly afford   15
To pamper our fancy or furnish our board;
And paper sufficient at home still we have,
To assure the wiseacre, we will not sign slave;
When this homespun shall fail, to remonstrate our grief,
We can speak viva voce, or scratch on a leaf;   20
Refuse all their colors, though richest of dye,
When the juice of a berry our paint can supply,
To humor our fancy—and as for our houses,
They'll do without painting as well as our spouses;
While to keep out the cold of a keen winter morn,   25
We can screen the north-west with a well polished horn;
And trust me a woman, by honest invention,
Might give this state-doctor a dose of prevention.
    Join mutual in this—and but small as it seems,
We may jostle a Grenville, and puzzle his schemes;   30
But a motive more worthy our patriot pen,
Thus acting—we point out their duty to men;
And should the bound-pensioners tell us to hush,
We can throw back the satire, by biding them blush.

1. First published in the *Pennsylvania Chronicle,* December 25, 1769, the poem was introduced by the following letter to the editors: "Gentlemen, I send you the inclosed female performance for a place in your paper, if you think it may contribute any thing to the entertainment or reformation of your male readers, and am, Yours, &c. Q.R."

2. George Grenville (1712–70), British minister, suggested and supported taxing measures that contributed to the colonists' decision to rebel from Britain.

NATHANIEL EVANS (1742–1767)

The son of a Philadelphia merchant and his wife, Nathaniel Evans initially followed his parents' advice that he pursue a career in trade. Yet Evans found that he preferred spending his time among books, convinced as he was that the arts could flourish in North America as well as in Britain. He left his apprenticeship and, with the encouragement of friends and under the mentorship of the Reverend William Smith, enrolled in the College of Philadelphia. While there, he fell under Smith's tutelage and joined a group of poets, the "Swains of the Schuylkill," that included Francis Hopkinson, Jacob Duché, and Thomas Godfrey, among others.

After a brief return to the merchant trade, Evans completed his M.A. in 1765 and, under the auspices of William Smith, soon departed for London, where he studied for the Anglican ministry. He returned to serve a pastorate in Gloucester County, New Jersey. Evans died of tuberculosis at the age of twenty-five. William Smith, his primary supporter, gathered Evans's poems together and published them in a collection entitled *Poems on Several Occasions* (1772), the source of the following poems.

Hymn to May

I.

NOW had the beam of Titan gay
Usher'd in the blissful *May,*
Scatt'ring from his pearly bed,
Fresh dew on ev'ry mountain's head;
Nature mild and debonnair,
To thee, fair maid, yields up her care.
May, with gentle plastic hand,

Clothes in flow'ry robe the land;
O'er the vales the cowslips spreads,
And eglantine beneath the shades;
Violets blue befringe each fountain,
Woodbines lace each steepy mountain;
Hyacinths their sweets diffuse,
And the rose its blush renews;
With the rest of *Flora's* train,
Decking lowly dale or plain.

II.

Thro' creation's range, sweet *May!*
Nature's children own thy sway—
Whether in the chrystal flood,
Am'rous, sport the finny brood;
Or the feather'd tribes declare,
That they breathe thy genial air,
While they warble in each grove
Sweetest notes of artless love;
Or their wound the beasts proclaim,
Smitten with a fiercer flame;
Or the passion higher rise,
Sparing none beneath the skies,
But swaying soft the human mind
With feelings of extatic kind—
Thro' wide creation's range, sweet *May!*
All Nature's children own thy sway.

III.

Oft will I, (e'er *Phosphor's* light[1]
Quits the glimm'ring skirts of night)
Meet thee in the clover-field,
Where thy beauties thou shalt yield
To my fancy, quick and warm,
List'ning to the dawn's alarm,
Sounded loud by *Chanticleer*,[2]
In peals that sharply pierce the ear.
And, as *Sol* his flaming car
Urges up the vaulted air,
Shunning quick the scorching ray,
I will to some covert stray;
Coolly bow'rs or latent dells,
Where light-footed silence dwells,
And whispers to my heav'n-born dream,
Fair Schuylkill[3] by thy winding stream!
There I'll devote full many an hour,
To the still-finger'd Morphean-pow'r,
And entertain my thirsty soul
With draughts from *Fancy's* fairy bowl;
Or mount her orb of varied hue,
And scenes of heav'n and earth review.

IV.

Nor in milder *Eve's* decline,
As the sun forgets to shine,
And slopping down th' ætherial plain,

Plunges in the Western main,
Will I forbear due strain to pay
To the song-inspiring *May*
But as *Hesper*[4] 'gins to move
Round the radiant court of Jove,
(Leading thro' the azure sky
All the starry progeny,
Emitting prone their silver light,
To re-illume the shades of night)
Then, the dewy lawn along,
I'll carol forth my grateful song,
Viewing with transported eye
The blazing orbs that rolls on high,
Beaming lustre, bright and clear,
O'er the glowing hemisphere.
Thus from the early-blushing morn,
Till the dappled eve's return,
Will I, in free unlabour'd lay,
Sweetly sing the charming *May!*

An Ode, Attempted in the Manner of Horace, to My Ingenious Friend, Mr. Thomas Godfrey[5]

I.

WHILE you, dear TOM, are forc'd to roam,
In search of fortune, far from home,
 O'er bogs, o'er seas and mountains;
I too, debar'd the soft retreat
Of shady groves, and murmur sweet
 Of silver-prattling fountains,

II.

Must mingle with the bustling throng,
And bear my load of cares along,
 Like any other sinner:
For, where's the ecstasy in this,

---

1. "The Morning Star." [Au.]

2. "The Cock." [Au.]

3. The Schuylkill River, running through Philadelphia.

4. "The Evening Star." [Au.]

5. William Smith noted at this place, "See an account of the THOMAS GODFREYS, father and son, in the American Magazine. The above little ode is addressed to the son. Mr. *Evans* and he were intimate in *life,* and in *death* not long divided. They possessed a kind of congenial spirits, and their fates were not dissimilar. Both courted the Muses from their very infancy; and both were called from this world as they were but entering into their state of manhood. On Mr. Godfrey's death, Mr. *Evans* collected and published his pieces in a small volume, and soon afterwards left his *own* pieces to the like friendly care of others." Thomas Godfrey, Evans's friend, left Philadelphia for North Carolina.

To loiter in poetic bliss,
    And go without a dinner?

III.

FLACCUS,[6] we know, immortal bard!
With mighty kings and statesmen far'd,
    And liv'd in chearful plenty:
But now, in those degenerate days,
The slight reward of empty praise,
    Scarce one receives in twenty.

IV.

Well might the Roman swan, along
The pleasing Tiber,[7] pour his song,
    When blest with ease and quiet;
Oft did he grace Mæcenas' board,[8]
Who would for him throw by the lord,
    And in Falernian riot.

V.

But, dearest TOM! these days are past,
And we are in a climate cast
    Where few the muse can relish;
Where all the doctrine now that's told,
Is that a shining heap of gold
    Alone can man embellish.

VI.

Then since 'tis thus, my honest friend,
If you be wise, my strain attend,
    And counsel sage adhere to;
With me, henceforward, join the crowd,
And like the rest proclaim aloud,
    That MONEY is all VIRTUE!

VII.

Then may we both, in time, retreat
To some fair villa, sweetly neat,
    To entertain the muses;
And then life's noise and trouble leave—
Supremely blest, we'll never grieve
    At what the world refuses.

---

6. Horatius Flaccus, or Horace (65-8 B.C.), rose to great fame although he was born into a "low" position.

7. A river flowing through Rome into the Mediterranean.

8. Mæcenas (70?–8 B.C.), recognized as a literary patron to such figures as Horace.

Elegy, to the Memory of My Beloved Friend, Mr. Thomas Godfrey, Who died near *Wilmington, North-Carolina,* August 3d, 1763.

O DEATH! thou victor of the human frame!
The soul's poor fabric trembles at thy name!
How long shall man be urg'd to dread thy sway,
For those whom thou untimely tak'st away?
Life's blooming spring just opens to our eyes,
And strikes the senses with a sweet surprize,
When thy fierce arm uplifts the fatal blow
That hurls us breathless to the earth below.

Sudden, as darts the lightning thro' the sky,
Around the globe thy various weapons fly.
Here war's red engines heap the field with slain,
And pallid sickness there extends thy reign;
Here the soft virgin weeps her lover dead,
There maiden beauty sinks the graceful head;
Here infants grieve their parents are no more,
There rev'rend sires their childrens' deaths deplore
Here the sad friend—O! save the sacred name,
Yields half his soul to thy relentless claim;
O pardon, pardon the descending tear!
Friendship commands, and not the muses here.
O say, thou much lov'd dear departed shade,
To what celestial region hast thou stray'd?
Where is that vein of thought, that noble fire
Which fed thy soul, and bade the world admire?
That manly strife with fortune to be just,
That love of praise? an honourable thirst!
The Soul, alas! has fled to endless day,
And left its house a mould'ring mass of clay.

There, where no fears invade, nor ills molest,
Thy soul shall dwell immortal with the blest;
In that bright realm, where dearest friends no more
Shall from each other's throbbing breasts be tore,
Where all those glorious spirits sit enshrin'd,
The just, the good, the virtuous of mankind.
There shall fair angels in a radiant ring,
And the great SON of heav'n's eternal KING,
Proclaim thee welcome to the blissful skies,
And wipe the tears for ever from thy eyes.

How did we hope—alas! the hope how vain!
To hear thy future more enripen'd strain;
When fancy's fire with judgment had combin'd
To guide each effort of th' enraptur'd mind.
Yet are those youthful glowing lays of thine
The emanations of a soul divine;
Who heard thee sing but felt sweet music's dart
In thrilling transports pierce his captiv'd heart?

Whether soft melting airs attun'd thy song,
Or pleas'd to pour the thundring verse along,
Still nobly great, true offspring of the Nine,
Alas! how blasted in thy glorious prime!
So when first opes the eye-lids of the morn,
A radiant purple does the heav'ns adorn,
Fresh smiling glory streaks the skies around,
And gaily silvers each enamel'd mound,
Till some black storm o'erclouds the æther fair,
And all its beauties vanish into air.

Stranger, who e'er thou art, by fortune's hand
Tost on the baleful *Carolinian* strand,
Oh! if thou seest perchance the POET'S grave,
The sacred spot with tears of sorrow lave;
Oh! shade it, shade it with ne'er-fading bays.
Hallow'd's the place where gentle GODFREY lays.
(So may no sudden dart from death's dread bow
Far from the friends thou lov'st e'er lay thee low)
There may the weeping morn its tribute bring,
And angels shield it with their golden wing,
Till the last trump shall burst the womb of night,
And the purg'd atoms to their soul unite!

To Benjamin Franklin, Esq; L.L.D,
Occasioned by Hearing Him Play
on the Harmonica

IN grateful wonder lost, long had we view'd
Each gen'rous act thy patriot-soul pursu'd;
Our Little State resounds thy just applause,

And, pleas'd, from thee new fame and honour draws:
In thee those various virtues are combin'd,   5
That form the true pre-eminence of mind.

What wonder struck us when we did survey
The lambent lightnings innocently play,
And down thy rods[9] beheld the dreaded fire
In a swift flame descend—and then expire;   10
While the red thunders, roaring loud around,
Burst the black clouds, and harmless smite the ground.

Blest use of art! apply'd to serve mankind,
The noble province of the sapient mind!
For this the soul's best faculties were giv'n,   15
To trace great nature's laws from earth to heav'n!

Yet not these themes alone thy thoughts command,
Each softer *science* owns thy fostering hand;
Aided by thee, Urania's[10] heav'nly art,
With finer raptures charms the feeling heart;   20
Th' *Harmonica* shall join the sacred choir,
Fresh transports kindle, and new joys inspire—

Hark! the soft warblings, sounding smooth and clear,
Strike with celestial ravishment the ear,
Conveying inward, as they sweetly roll,   25
A tide of melting music to the soul;
And sure if aught of mortal-moving strain,
Can touch with joy the high angelic train,
'Tis this enchanting instrument of thine,
Which speaks in accents more than half divine!   30

---

9. Smith noted at this place, "Alluding to his noble discovery of the use of Pointed Rods of metal for saving houses from damage by lightning."

---

10. The muse of astronomy.

ANNIS BOUDINOT STOCKTON (1736–1801)

Annis Boudinot Stockton, poet, sponsor of literary salons, and host of important federal leaders during the era of confederation, was, next to Phillis Wheatley and Mercy Otis Warren, probably the best-known and most frequently published woman poet of her day. Born in Philadelphia to well-to-do merchant Elias Boudinot and his wife, Catherine Williams Boudinot, Annis Boudinot was raised in a household that offered her sufficient education and leisure time that she could pursue a literary career, even as a young woman. She associated in her youth with Elizabeth Graeme (later Fergusson) of Graeme Park and kept this friendship throughout her life, beginning from the time her father moved the family from Pennsylvania to Burlington, New Jersey, and then to Princeton, New Jersey.

Annis Boudinot quickly affiliated herself with the community of scholars and local leaders at the College of Princeton (later Princeton University), and she seems to have been courted by a tutor there before settling on Richard Stockton, whom she married in 1757. The Stocktons set up their home in an estate given to them by Richard's father. Publicizing her poetic notions from this early stage in their marriage, Annis Stockton renamed the estate "Morven," after a name used in the Ossianic poems. Richard Stockton, a well-educated lawyer and favorite of the royally appointed governor, William Franklin (Benjamin Franklin's son), had a difficult time deciding whether to support the rebellion against Britain, but once he signed the *Declaration of Independence,* he was fully into the war, serving in a number of capacities and indeed running materiel, at his own expense, to militia lines. He was captured by the British and held in one of their offshore boat-jails, off the coast of northern New Jersey. After his release, he was forced to sign an oath of noncombattance, meaning he could not assist the rebellion in any way thereafter. When her husband died of cancer in 1781, Annis Stockton sent many poems to press that indicated the family's full support of the war all along and sponsored, with her brother, Elias Boudinot, then president of the Congress, several meetings of the Continental Congress at Morven. She continued her role as a hostess at Morven through the 1780s and early 1790s, when, in increasing physical difficulty and from a sense that her son Richard's family needed their home (the Stockton family estate, Morven) to themselves, she moved in with a daughter. She died at her daughter's home in 1801.

Stockton was prolific, and like many men and women of her era, she kept a copybook of poems that were meant for circulation only among her friends. But she also published widely, before and after the American Revolution. Her family connections and her poetic abilities brought Stockton a public renown exceptional for a woman of her day. She drew the attention of significant statesmen in North America and Europe and published poems in some of the most widely circulated newspapers and magazines of her day, including the *Pennsylvania Chronicle,* the *New American Magazine,* the *Columbian Magazine,* and the *American Museum.* She wrote throughout her life. Her poems number over one hundred, with twenty-one of them published at least one time and most published more than once during her lifetime. Although most of her poems were published anonymously, she sometimes used her initials "A.S.," or a pen name, "Emilia" or "Amelia." Stockton was an accomplished writer whose energy and ability were well suited to the poetic norms of her day. Knowing the difficulties women faced in gaining an audience, she also assisted other poets, many of them friends or family members, to write. To be sure, she was advantaged by her status as a white woman and manager of an estate, but she was quite rightly described, even in her youth, by friend Esther Edwards Burr, daughter of Jonathan Edwards, as a "pretty, discreet, well-behaved girl. She has good sense and can talk very handsomely on almost any subject." Such seems to be the impression that Annis Stockton had most often on those she knew.

TO THE VISITANT, FROM A CIRCLE OF LADIES, ON READING HIS PAPER[1]

Hail candid, gen'rous man, whoe'er thou art;
Thy sentiments bespeak a noble heart.
With joy we Stile thee Censor of the fair,
To rectify their foibles be thy care.
5   Thee, who canst give to virtue praises due,

We safely trust to lash our errors too.
No keen reproach from satire's pen we fear,
Of little minds, or painted toys, to hear.
You, Sir, with better sense, will justly fix
Our faults on *education,* not our *sex;*   10
Will shew the source which makes the female mind
So oft appear but puerile and blind;
How many would surmount stern custom's laws,
And prove the want of *genius* not the cause;
But that the odium of a *bookish fair,*   15
Or *female pedant,* or "*they quit their sphere,*"
Damps all their views, and they must drag the chain,
And sigh for sweet instruction's page in vain.
But we commit our injur'd cause to you;
Point out the medium which we should pursue.   20
So may each scene of soft domestic peace
Heighten your joys, and animate your bliss.

---

1. The poem is a response to an essay serial published in the *Pennsylvania Chronicle,* in which the author, the "visitant" of this poem's title, offered remarks on women's conduct and the problem of having expectations of women that they are untrained to fulfill. The poem was published in the *Pennsylvania Chronicle* on March 14, 1768, and reprinted in other places thereafter.

BY A LADY IN AMERICA TO HER HUSBAND IN ENGLAND[1]

To thee whom Albion's distant shore detains,
And mirth and song accost in various strains,
I send all health—Oh hear my humble lay,
And with one smile my anxious love repay.

5   For me, not whispers of the rising gale,
Breath'd from the south to chear the frozen vale;
Nor gently sloping shores where naids lave,
And shells are polish'd by the lashing wave;
Nor rivers gliding by the flow'ry meads,
10 Whose silver currents sparkle thro' the reeds;
Nor sprightly spring, nor autumn fill'd with stores;
Nor summers coverts in sequester'd bow'rs,
Can yield a pleasure, while the dear lov'd youth,
For whom my soul preserves eternal truth,
15 Is absent from Cesaria's fertile plain,[2]
And gentle echo bears my sighs in vain.

The goat shall cease the mountains top to graze,
The fish for land shall leave their native seas,
The bees no more the flow'ry thyme shall taste,
20 Nor thirsty harts to limpid streams shall haste,
When I forget the sacred vow to bind,
Or put thy dear idea from my mind;
My mind—so late the seat of joy sincere,
Thy absence makes a prey to gloomy care.

25 My flowers—in vain they court my friendly hand,
Left in their beds the wintry blasts to stand;
For thee—the lily bloom'd, the garden's pride,
And blushing hyacinths with roses vied;
For thee—I tortur'd every fruit that grew,
30 To make the season ever smile anew:
But now untouch'd upon their boughs they die,
And lose their flavour ere they tempt my eye;
While pensive in each silent shade I mourn,
And count the tedious hours till thou return.

                                   EMELIA

---

1. Richard Stockton traveled to Britain, 1766–67, seeking John Witherspoon's agreement to become president of the College of New Jersey (later, Princeton University). The poem was printed in the *Pennsylvania Magazine; Or, American Monthly Museum* in June, 1775.

2. The name *Nova Cæsaria* was the name given the area between the Connecticut River valley and Philadelphia in the grant of land made by Charles II to his brother James, duke of York, at the time Britain wrested the territory from the Dutch. In ancient writings, *Cesaria* was the name given to two different cities in the Mediterranean.

A SUDDEN PRODUCTION OF MRS. STOCKTON'S IN ONE OF THOSE MANY ANXIOUS NIGHTS IN WHICH SHE WATCHED WITH MR. STOCKTON IN HIS LAST ILLNESS[1]

I.

SLEEP, balmy sleep, has clos'd the eyes of all
But me! ah me! no respite can I gain;
Tho' darkness reigns o'er the terrestrial ball,
Not one soft slumber cheats this vital pain.

II.

All day in secret sighs I've pour'd my soul,   5
My downy pillow, us'd to scenes of grief,
Beholds me now in floods of sorrow roll,
Without the power to yield his pains relief:

III.

While through the silence of this gloomy night,
My aching heart reverb'rates every groan;   10
And watching by that glimmering taper's light,
I make each sigh, each mortal pang my own.

IV.

But why should I implore sleep's friendly aid?
O'er me her poppies shed no ease impart;
But dreams of dear *departing joys* invade,   15
And rack with fears my sad prophetick heart.

V.

But vain is prophesy when death's approach,
Thro' years of pain, has sap'd a *dearer* life,
And makes me, coward like, myself reproach,
That e'er I knew the tender name of wife.   20

---

1. Richard Stockton had been a target during the war against Britain because he had been in the favor of the royally appointed New Jersey governor, William Franklin (Benjamin Franklin's son), and he signed the *Declaration of Independence*. During the Revolutionary War, he was seized and incarcerated by the British. According to family lore, he suffered sufficiently at that time to bring on the beginnings of the facial and throat cancer, from which he died, after a painful illness, in 1781. The poem was published under different titles, in separate places. The text is taken from the version published with Samuel Stanhope Smith's sermon, spoken at Richard Stockton's funeral as *A Funeral Sermon on the Death of the Hon. Richard Stockton, Esq., Princeton, March 2, 1781* (1781). The poem's title was given by Smith or the printer, Isaac Collins.

VI.

Oh! could I take the fate to him assign'd!
And leave the helpless family their head!
How pleas'd, how peaceful, to my lot resign'd,
I'd quit the nurse's station for the bed.

VII.

25 O death! thou canker-worm of human joy!
Thou cruel foe to sweet domestick peace!
He soon shall come, who shall thy shafts destroy,
And cause thy dreadful ravages to cease.

VIII.

Yes, the Redeemer comes to wipe the tears,
30 The briny tears, from every weeping eye.
And death and sin, and doubts, and gloomy fears,
Shall all be lost in endless victory.

A POETICAL EPISTLE, ADDRESSED BY A LADY OF NEW JERSEY TO HER NIECE, UPON HER MARRIAGE, IN THIS CITY[1]

Well! my lov'd Niece, I hear the bustle's o'er,
The wedding cake and visits are no more;
The gay ones buzzing round some other bride,
'While you with grave ones grace the fire's side.
5 Now with your usual sweetness deign to hear,
What from a heart most friendly flows sincere:
Nor do I fear a supercilious Smile—
To pay with gay contempt the muse's toil.
For be assur'd, I never will presume,
10 Superior sense or judgment to assume;
But barely that which long experience brings,
To men and women, those capricious things,
Nor do I once forget how very sage
Th'advice of Aunts has been in ev'ry age:
15 On matrimonial themes they all debate—

Wiseacres too who never try'd the state.
And 'twould, I own, appear as truly vain
For me, but to suppose I could attain
New light, upon a subject worn out quite;
And which both Aunts and Authors deem so trite.   20
But all the nuptial virtues in the class
Of spirit meek, and prudence, I shall pass;
Good nature—sense—of these you've ample store,
And Oeconomicks you have learnt before.
But there are lurking evils that do prove   25
Under the name of trifles—death to love.—
And from these trifles, all the jarring springs,
And trust me, child, they're formidable things.
First then—with rev'rence treat in ev'ry place,
The chosen patron of your future days;   30
For when you shew him but the least neglect,
Yourself you rifle of your due respect.—
But never let your fondness for him rise,
In words or actions to the prying eyes
Of witnesses—who claim a right to sneer   35
At all the honey'd words, "My life,—my love,—my
    dear."
Nor from your husband should you e'er require
Those epithets, which little minds admire—
Such short restraints will constantly maintain
That pow'r which fondness strives to reach in vain   40
And give new joy to the returning hour,
When sweet retirement bars the op'ning door.
Nor do nor say, before the man you love,—
What in its nature must offensive prove;
However closely drawn the mystic ties,   45
Yet men have always microscopic eyes;[2]
And easily advert to former time,
When nice reserve made females all divine.
"Would she to Damon or Alexis say,
"A thing so rude? and am I less than they?"   50
    Whene'er your husband means to stay at home,
Whate'er th'occasion—dont consent to roam;
For home's a solitary place to one
Who loves his wife, and finds her always gone.
At least consult the temper of his mind,   55
If vex'd abroad, he finds himself inclin'd
From public business to relax awhile;
How pleasing then the solace of a smile—

---

1. The poem was written upon the marriage of Susan Boudinot, daughter of Annis Stockton's brother, Elias, who married William Bradford on September 28, 1784. It was printed in *The Columbian Magazine,* November 1786.

2. An allusion to Alexander Pope's *Essay on Man* (1733–34), I.93–94, or perhaps to John Locke's *Essay on Human Understanding* (1690), I.23.12.

A soft companion to relieve his care,
60 His joy to heighten—or his grief to share?
    Unbend his thoughts and from the world retire,
Within his sacred home and round his chearful fire;
Nor let him know you've made a sacrifice,
He'll find it out himself: And then he'll prize
65 Your kind endeavours to promote his ease,
And make the study of your life to please.
    Another rule you'll find of equal weight,
When jars subside, never recriminate;
And when the cloud is breaking from his brow,
70 Repeat not *what* he said—nor *when* nor *how.*
If he's tenacious, gently give him way—
And tho' 'tis night, if he should say, 'tis day—
Dispute it not—but pass it with a smile;
He'll recollect himself—and pay your toil—
75 And shew he views it in a proper light;
And no Confusion seek—to do you right:
Just in his humour meet him—no debate,
And let it be your pleasure to forget.
His friends with kindness always entertain,
80 And tho' by chance he brings them, ne'er
    complain;
Whate'er's provided for himself and you,
With neatness serv'd, will surely please them too.
Nor e'er restrict him, when he would invite
His friends in form, to spend a day or night:
85 Some ladies think the trouble is so great,
That all such motions cause a high debate;
And madam pouts and says, I would not mind
How much to company you were inclin'd,
If I had things to entertain genteel;
90 And could but make my table look as well
As Mrs. A. and Mrs. B. can do;
I'd be as fond of company as you.—
And oft a richer service bribes the feast,
Than suits his purse, and makes himself a jest:
95 And tho' the good man gains his point at last,
It damps convivial mirth, and poisons the repast.
But you, my dear—if you would wish to shine,
Must always say, *your* friends are also *mine:*
The house is your's, and I will do the best,
00 To give a chearful welcome to each guest.
    Nor are those maxims difficult to cope
When stimulated by so fair a hope,
To reach the summit of domestic bliss;
And crown each day with ever smiling peace.
05   Now if these lines one caution should contain,
To gain that end, my labour's not in vain;

And be assur'd, my dear, while life endures
With every tender sentiment, I'm your's.

                EMELIA.

ADDRESSED TO GENERAL WASHINGTON, IN THE YEAR 1777, AFTER THE BATTLES OF TRENTON AND PRINCETON[1]

THE muse affrighted at the clash of arms,
And all the dire calamities of war,
From Morven's peaceful shades has long retir'd,
And left her faithful votary to mourn,
In sighs, not numbers, o'er her native land.   5
Dear native land, whom George's hostile slaves
Have drench'd with blood, and spread destruction round,
But thou, thy country's better genius come,
Heroic Washington, and aid my song!
While I the wonders of thy deeds relate,   10
Thy martial ardor, and thy temp'rate zeal—
Describe the fortitude, the saint like patience,
With which thou hast sustain'd the greatest load,
That ever guardian of his country bore.
What muse can sing the hardships thou endur'd;   15
Unarm'd, uncloth'd,[2] undisciplin'd thy men;
In winter's cold unhospitable reign;
And press'd by numerous hosts of veteran troops,
All well appointed for the hardy fight:
When quite deserted by the tatter'd bands   20
Which form'd thy camp (all but a chosen few,
Of spirits like thy own) was forced to fly

---

1. The New Jersey battles between Washington and armies in British support were fierce. New Jersey was an important territory to capture, especially as retaliation for what was perceived by Britain as its turncoat behavior (New Jersey had a significant number of people who sought neutrality or else loyalty to the Crown.) Hessian mercenary soldiers—called in the poem "George's hostile slaves"—were used in Britain's New Jersey campaign. The poem was printed in *The Columbian Magazine,* January 1787.

2. Stockton revived her husband's memory here: Richard Stockton had personally purchased clothing and shoes for the militias in New Jersey and New York, and he saw to their delivery at the lines of battle.

From Hudson's side before the victor foe.[3]
Ah! who can paint the horrors of that morn,
25 When fame, with brazen trumpet, sounded loud,
That Washington retreats! Caesaria's maids,[4]
Old men and matrons, children at the breast,
With hair dishevell'd, and with streaming eyes,
Implore the God of battles to protect
30 *Thee,* their best hope, and now their only care.
—Oh, greatly favour'd by the God of hosts!
He gave to thee to turn the battle's fate,[5]
And shew his power to potentates below:
While lines of Hessian captive slaves, announce
35 Thy triumph, and their haughty lords disgrace.
—Not good Æneas who his father bore,
And all his houshold gods from ruin'd Troy,
Was more the founder of the Latian realm,[6]
Than thou the basis of this mighty fabric,
40 Now rising to my view, of arms, of arts;
The seat of glory in the western world.
—For thee awaits the patriots shining crown;
The laurel blooms in blest elysian groves,
That twin'd by angel hands shall grace thy brow.
45 A vacant seat among the ancient heroes,
Of purple, amarynth and fragrant myrtle,
Awaits for thee—high rais'd above the rest,
By Cato,[7] Sydney,[8] and the sacred shades
Of bright illustrious line, from Greece and Rome,
50 Gallic,[9] American or British shores,
And long to hail thee welcome to the bower.
—Late may they lead thee to the blest abode,

---

3. Washington's militias were defeated on Long Island near the end of August 1776 and at White Plains, New York, in October.

4. That is, the women of New Jersey; *Nova Cæsaria* was New Jersey territory's name, under the charter granted by Charles II to his brother James, duke of York, at the time Britain wrested the territory from the Dutch.

5. Washington made important strategic maneuvers with troops in the area of Trenton, and so won several battles there.

6. In Virgil's *Aeneid,* the Latian realm was the settlement of Troy.

7. Marcus Porcius Cato of Utica (95–46 B.C.) was reputed to be a great upholder of republican liberties.

8. Sir Philip Sidney (1554–86), a courtier and poet during the reign of Elizabeth I.

9. That is, of Gaul (France).

And may'st thou meet the plaudit of thy God,
While future ages shall enroll thy name
In sacred annals of immortal fame.   55

EMELIA

TO THE PRESIDENT OF THE UNITED STATES[1]

Oft times, when rapture swells the heart,
Expressive silence can impart
    More full the joy sublime:
Thus WASHINGTON, my wond'ring mind,
In every grateful ardor join'd,   5
    Tho' words were out of time.

The muse of ******'s[2] peaceful shade,
Gave way to all the gay parade
    For transports of her own;
She felt the tear of pleasure flow,   10
And gratitude's delightful glow
    Was to her bosom known.

Triumphal arches—gratulating song,
And shouts of welcome from the mixed throng,
    Thy laurels can not raise.   15
We praise ourselves; exalt our name,
And in the scroll of time, we claim
    An int'rest in thy bays.

But erst on *Hudson's* whit'ned plain,
Where the blue mists enshroud the slain,   20
And Hero's spirits came;
    Anxious to seal thy future fate,
Each on his cloud, in awful state,
Pronounc'd thee good as well as great,
    And fill'd thy cup of fame.   25

While we the favorites of Heaven,
To whom these western climes are given,
    And halcyon days await
May bless our selves and bless our race
That God by his peculiar grace   30
    Sav'd thee to rule the state.

---

1. Printed in the federalist *Gazette of the United States,* May 1789.

2. In the manuscript, Stockton had supplied the name given her home, Morven, omitted in print.

Fame as she flies, her trump shall sound,
To all the admiring nations round,
   And millions yet unborn,
35 Will read the history of this day,
And as they read will pause—and say
   HERE NATURE TOOK A TURN.
For in the annals of mankind,
Who ever saw a compact bind
40   An empire's utmost bound;
Who ever saw ambition stand,
Without the power to raise her hand,
   While ONE the people crown'd.

                New-Jersey, May 1789.

THE VISION,
AN ODE TO WASHINGTON[1]

'TWAS in a beauteous verdant shade,
Deck'd by the genius of the glade,
   With Nature's fragrant stores;
Where Fairy Elves light trip'd the green—
5 Where Silvan Nymphs were often seen
   To strew the sweetest flowers.

Lethean air from tempes vale,
Wafted an aromatic gale,
   And lull'd my soul to rest:
10 I saw, or musing seem'd to see,
The future years of Destiny
   That brighten'd all the West.

The Muse array'd in heavenly grace,
Call'd up each actor in his place
15   Before my wondering eyes,
The magic of the Aonian Maid
The world of Vision wide display'd,
   And bid the scenes arise.

I saw great FABIUS[2] come in state,
20 I saw the British Lion's fate,

---

1. The poem, simply titled "The Vision" when originally printed, appeared after the following heading when it was published in the *Gazette of the United States* in May 1789: "Mr. Fenno, The following Ode was written and inscribed to General Washington, a short time after the surrender of York-Town."

2. Fabius, the name Stockton used for Washington.

The Unicorns dispair;
Conven'd in Secrecy's Divan,
The Chiefs contriv'd the fav'rite plan,
   And *York-Town* clos'd the war.

Nor could the dazzling triumph charm   25
The friends of faction, or its rage disarm—
   Fierce to divide, to weaken and subvert:
I saw the Imps of Discord rise—
Intrigue, with little arts, surprise,
   Delude—alarm—and then the State desert.   30

My soul grew sick of human things—
I took my Harp, and touch'd the strings,
   Full often set to woe;
Conjur'd the gentle Muse to take
The power of future knowledge back—   35
   No more I wish'd to know.

Rash Mortal stop! She cried with zeal,
One secret more I must reveal,
   That will renew your prime:
These storms will work the wish'd for cure,   40
And put the *State* in health so pure,
   As to resist old *Time.*

The free born mind will feel the force,
That Justice is the only source
   Of Laws concise and clear;   45
Their native rights, they will resign
To *Men,* who can those rights define,
   And every burthen bear.

The SACRED COMPACT, in a band
Of brothers, shall unite the land,   50
   And Envy's self be dead;
The Body one, and one the soul,
Virtue shall animate the whole,
   And FABIUS be the head.

Rous'd from the enthusiastic dream,   55
By the soft murmur of a stream,
   That glided thro' the meads,
I tun'd my lyre to themes refin'd,
While Nature's gentle voices join'd,
   To sing the glorious deeds.   60

When lo! HIMSELF, the CHIEF rever'd,
In native elegance appear'd,
   And all things smil'd around
Adorn'd with every pleasing art,
Enthron'd the Sov'reign of each heart,   65
   I saw the HERO crown'd.

                New-Jersey, May 1789

THOMAS PAINE (1737–1809)

If any single writer could be called the most outspoken spokesperson of the colonies' rebellion against Britain, it would be Thomas Paine. Paine's writings were widely read to an extent that was almost unimaginable in his day, and they helped to inspire and motivate the people who did the hard work of the war. Paine's interest in writing for common people might have come from his background working among laboring people. In many ways, he is the most appropriate representative of the most egalitarian ideals of the American Revolution.

Born in Thetford, England, the son of a Quaker staymaker and his Anglican wife, Thomas Paine was educated in the Thetford Grammar School, receiving a basic education that included the sciences but not the ancient languages typically used in preparing young men from wealthy families for a university education. He learned his father's trade and, for a brief time, practiced as a staymaker himself, but then shifted to work as a customs officer. He married twice. His first wife died soon after their marriage, and he separated from his second wife when the shop they ran together failed. In 1772, he wrote an essay arguing that customs officers should be paid more and was dismissed as a result. While unemployed but participating in the intellectual life of London in 1773, Paine met Benjamin Franklin, who encouraged him to emigrate to Philadelphia and provided him with letters of recommendation.

In late 1774, Paine took Franklin's advice and sailed for Philadelphia, where he quickly found a place for himself and his liberal political views. Working as the editor of the *Pennsylvania Magazine,* he published essays of a political nature and became a strong advocate for the importance of the colonies' separation from Britain. Paine published *Common Sense* in January 1776, a difficult time for the colonials who were facing an increased number of sanctions against them and who felt they had little recourse. The pamphlet was a forceful call for independence, written in a style designed to appeal to readers across different educational levels. Immensely popular, it sold over a hundred thousand copies the first year, a figure nearly unheard of for any publication in the British colonies at that time. The pamphlet brought Paine fame and political influence, and his devotion to the cause of revolution grew in the wake of his success as a revolutionary writer.

After independence was declared in July 1776, Paine enlisted in the army and was assigned as an aide to General Nathanael Greene. His real service to the revolutionary cause remained his pen, however. In December 1776, when Washington's army was forced to retreat across New Jersey, desperately reduced in number and supplies, Paine wrote and published an essay titled *The American Crisis* to call for support and perseverance. George Washington and congressional representatives considered Paine's "Crisis Paper," as it came to be called, a central part of the war effort. In 1777, Paine was appointed secretary for foreign affairs, which allowed him to be involved in the war but also to write about it, to serve as a voice for the revolutionary cause. He continued his essays in the *Crisis* series, writing sixteen in all by 1783.

At the end of the war, Paine found himself relatively unsettled financially. He had never taken money for his political writing, as a matter of principle. He was, however, granted three thousand dollars by the Congress for his wartime contributions, and the state of New York awarded him a confiscated Tory estate. He used his newly found leisure and financial security to pursue scientific and political interests. In 1787, he traveled to France. For several years he divided his time between France and England, where he associated with prominent liberal political figures, including Edmund Burke, Thomas Jefferson, and the marquis de Lafayette.

Paine was attracted by the success of the British Americans in overthrowing the monarchy. When French people went against the Bastille in 1789, he became a strong advocate of the revolution in France. Edmund Burke, shocked at the move to overthrow a monarchy so close to home, published *Reflections on the Revolution in France* (1790), and Paine responded with *Rights of Man* (1791). In this volume, Paine argued that people have the right to change government when it seems necessary, under the assumption that government "is for the living and not for the dead." Paine's strong defense of the French Revolution was read widely in British North America, Britain, and France. In the new United States, the work was accepted, but its endorsement by Jefferson, then secretary of state, gave the book a partisan status. In England, the book aroused resentment against Paine. In 1792, Paine published *Rights of Man: Part Second,* in which he more directly argued that monarchical governments were illegitimate, specifically pinpointing the British monarchy. *Rights of Man* was popular among British reformers, but it made of Paine a marked man: in September 1792, while in France, Paine was tried and declared guilty of sedition in England, and *Rights of Man* was suppressed there.

Paine was given important recognition in France during the French Revolution, but when he argued against the execution of the French royal family, he was imprisoned for obstructing the Revolution. After eighteen months in jail, Paine was released, narrowly escaping execution. After his release, he completed his last major work, *The Age of Reason* (1794, 1795), begun even before he was taken to prison. *The Age of Reason* explored deism, arguing that organized religion had supported oppressive governments. This was his most controversial work, turning many who had approved of or, at least, condoned Paine's earlier writings against him and causing many to label him, inaccurately, an atheist. Paine spent several more years in France, but he believed that those in the new government had moved away from the Revolution's ideals. In 1802, he returned to the United States, where he lived in relative penury on his estate in New Rochelle, New York. He spent the final years of his life in obscurity, having lost his political influence as he became more controversial.

The selections printed here are from Paine's two major texts of the American Revolution: *Common Sense* and *The Crisis.* These essays, with their enormous influence, present the arguments for British American independence as they seemed most compelling to many eighteenth-century Americans.

from COMMON SENSE[1]

Thoughts on the Present State of American Affairs

In the following pages I offer nothing more than simple facts, plain arguments, and common sense: and have no other preliminaries to settle with the reader, than that he will divest himself of prejudice and prepossession, and suffer his reason and his feelings to determine for themselves: that he will put on, or rather that he will not put off, the true character of a man, and generously enlarge his views beyond the present day.

Volumes have been written on the subject of the struggle between England and America. Men of all ranks have embarked in the controversy, from different motives, and with various designs; but all have been ineffectual, and the period of debate is closed. Arms as the last resource decide the contest; the appeal was the choice of the King, and the Continent has accepted the challenge.

It hath been reported of the late Mr. Pelham (who tho' an able minister was not without his faults) that on his being attacked in the House of Commons on the score that his measures were only of a temporary kind, replied, *"they will last my time."* Should a thought so fatal and unmanly possess the Colonies in the present contest, the name of ancestors will be remembered by future generations with detestation.

The Sun never shined on a cause of greater worth. 'Tis not the affair of a City, a County, a Province, or a Kingdom; but of a Continent—of at least one eighth part of the habitable Globe. 'Tis not the concern of a day, a year, or an age; posterity are virtually involved in the contest, and will be more or less affected even to the end of time, by the proceedings now. Now is the seed-time of Continental union, faith and honour. The least fracture now will be like a name engraved with the point of a pin on the tender rind of a young oak; the wound would enlarge with the tree, and posterity read it in full grown characters.

By referring the matter from argument to arms, a new æra for politics is struck—a new method of thinking hath arisen. All plans, proposals, &c. prior to the nineteenth of

---

1. "Thoughts on the Present State of Affairs" is Part Three of *Common Sense,* first published in 1776.

April, *i.e.* to the commencement of hostilities,[2] are like the almanacks of the last year; which tho' proper then, are superceded and useless now. Whatever was advanced by the advocates on either side of the question then, terminated in one and the same point, viz. a union with Great Britain; the only difference between the parties was the method of effecting it; the one proposing force, the other friendship; but it hath so far happened that the first hath failed, and the second hath withdrawn her influence.

As much hath been said of the advantages of reconciliation, which, like an agreeable dream, hath passed away and left us as we were, it is but right that we should examine the contrary side of the argument, and enquire into some of the many material injuries which these Colonies sustain, and always will sustain, by being connected with and dependant on Great-Britain. To examine that connection and dependance, on the principles of nature and common sense, to see what we have to trust to, if separated, and what we are to expect, if dependant.

I have heard it asserted by some, that as America has flourished under her former connection with Great-Britain, the same connection is necessary towards her future happiness, and will always have the same effect. Nothing can be more fallacious than this kind of argument. We may as well assert that because a child has thrived upon milk, that it is never to have meat, or that the first twenty years of our lives is to become a precedent for the next twenty. But even this is admitting more than is true; for I answer roundly, that America would have flourished as much, and probably much more, had no European power taken any notice of her. The commerce by which she hath enriched herself are the necessaries of life, and will always have a market while eating is the custom of Europe.

But she has protected us, say some. That she hath engrossed us is true, and defended the Continent at our expense as well as her own, is admitted; and she would have defended Turkey from the same motive, *viz.* for the sake of trade and dominion.

Alas! we have been long led away by ancient prejudices and made large sacrifices to superstition. We have boasted the protection of Great Britain, without considering, that her motive was *interest* not *attachment;* and that she did not protect us from *our enemies* on *our account;* but from *her enemies* on *her own account,* from those who had no quarrel with us on any *other account,* and

who will always be our enemies on the *same account.* Let Britain waive her pretensions to the Continent, or the Continent throw off the dependance, and we should be at peace with France and Spain, were they at war with Britain. The miseries of Hanover last war ought to warn us against connections.

It hath lately been asserted in parliament, that the Colonies have no relation to each other but through the Parent Country, *i.e.* that Pennsylvania and the Jerseys, and so on for the rest, are sister Colonies by the way of England; this is certainly a very roundabout way of proving relationship, but it is the nearest and only true way of proving enmity (or enemyship, if may so call it.) France and Spain never were, nor perhaps ever will be, our enemies as *Americans,* but as our being the *subjects of Great Britain.*

But Britain is the parent country, say some. Then the more shame upon her conduct. Even brutes do not devour their young, nor savages make war upon their families; Wherefore, the assertion, if true, turns to her reproach; but it happens not to be true, or only partly so, and the phrase *parent* or *mother country* hath been jesuitically adopted by the King and his parasites, with a low papistical design of gaining an unfair bias on the credulous weakness of our minds. Europe, and not England, is the parent country of America. This new World hath been the asylum for the persecuted lovers of civil and religious liberty from *every part* of Europe. Hither have they fled, not from the tender embraces of the mother, but from the cruelty of the monster; and it is so far true of England, that the same tyranny which drove the first emigrants from home, pursues their descendants still.

In this extensive quarter of the globe, we forget the narrow limits of three hundred and sixty miles (the extent of England) and carry our friendship on a larger scale; we claim brotherhood with every European Christian, and triumph in the generosity of the sentiment.

It is pleasant to observe by what regular gradations we surmount the force of local prejudices, as we enlarge our acquaintance with the World. A man born in any town in England divided into parishes, will naturally associate most with his fellow parishioners (because their interests in many cases will be common) and distinguish him by the name of *neighbour;* if he meet him but a few miles from home, he drops the narrow idea of a street, and salutes him by the name of *townsman;* if he travel out of the county and meet him in any other, he forgets the minor divisions of street and town, and calls him *countryman, i.e. countyman:* but if in their foreign excursions they

---

2. At Lexington, Massachusetts, in 1775, when armed British soldiers fired on members of the local community.

should associate in France, or any other part of *Europe,* their local remembrance would be enlarged into that of *Englishmen.* And by a just parity of reasoning, all Europeans meeting in America, or any other quarter of the globe, are *countrymen;* for England, Holland, Germany, or Sweden, when compared with the whole, stand in the same places on the larger scale, which the divisions of street, town, and county do on the smaller ones; Distinctions too limited for Continental minds. Not one third of the inhabitants, even of this province,[3] are of English descent. Wherefore, I reprobate the phrase of Parent or Mother Country applied to England only, as being false, selfish, narrow and ungenerous.

But, admitting that we were all of English descent, what does it amount to? Nothing. Britain, being now an open enemy, extinguishes every other name and title: and to say that reconciliation is our duty, is truly farcical. The first king of England, of the present line (William the Conqueror) was a Frenchman, and half the peers of England are descendants from the same country; wherefore, by the same method of reasoning, England ought to be governed by France.

Much hath been said of the united strength of Britain and the Colonies, that in conjunction they might bid defiance to the world: But this is mere presumption; the fate of war is uncertain, neither do the expressions mean any thing; for this continent would never suffer itself to be drained of inhabitants, to support the British arms in either Asia, Africa, or Europe.

Besides, what have we to do with setting the world at defiance? Our plan is commerce, and that, well attended to, will secure us the peace and friendship of all Europe; because it is the interest of all Europe to have America a free port. Her trade will always be a protection, and her barrenness of gold and silver secure her from invaders.

I challenge the warmest advocate for reconciliation to show a single advantage that this continent can reap by being connected with Great Britain. I repeat the challenge; not a single advantage is derived. Our corn will fetch its price in any market in Europe, and our imported goods must be paid for buy them where we will.

But the injuries and disadvantages which we sustain by that connection, are without number; and our duty to mankind at large, as well as to ourselves, instruct us to renounce the alliance: because, any submission to, or dependance on, Great Britain, tends directly to involve this Continent in European wars and quarrels, and set us at variance with nations who would otherwise seek our friendship, and against whom we have neither anger nor complaint. As Europe is our market for trade, we ought to form no partial connection with any part of it. It is true interest of America to steer clear of European contentions, which she never can do, while, by her dependance on Britain, she is made the make-weight in the scale of British politics.

Europe is too thickly planted with Kingdoms to be long at peace, and whenever a war breaks out between England and any foreign power, the trade of America goes to ruin, *because of her connection with Britain.* The next war may not turn out like the last, and should it not, the advocates for reconciliation now will be wishing for separation then, because neutrality in that case would be a safer convoy than a man of war. Everything that is right or reasonable pleads for separation. The blood of the slain, the weeping voice of nature cries, 'TIS TIME TO PART. Even the distance at which the Almighty hath placed England and America is a strong and natural proof that the authority of the one over the other, was never the design of Heaven. The time likewise at which the Continent was discovered, adds weight to the argument, and the manner in which it was peopled, encreases the force of it. The Reformation was preceded by the discovery of America: As if the Almighty graciously meant to open a sanctuary to the persecuted in future years, when home should afford neither friendship nor safety.

The authority of Great Britain over this continent, is a form of government, which sooner or later must have an end: And a serious mind can draw no true pleasure by looking forward, under the painful and positive conviction that what he calls "the present constitution" is merely temporary. As parents, we can have no joy, knowing that this government is not sufficiently lasting to ensure any thing which we may bequeath to posterity: And by a plain method of argument, as we are running the next generation into debt, we ought to do the work of it, otherwise we use them meanly and pitifully. In order to discover the line of our duty rightly, we should take our children in our hand, and fix our station a few years farther into life; that eminence will present a prospect which a few present fears and prejudices conceal from our sight.

Though I would carefully avoid giving unnecessary offence, yet I am inclined to believe, that all those who espouse the doctrine of reconciliation, may be included within the following descriptions.

---

3. That is, Pennsylvania.

Interested men, who are not to be trusted, weak men who *cannot* see, prejudiced men who will not see, and a certain set of moderate men who think better of the European world than it deserves; and this last class, by an ill-judged deliberation, will be the cause of more calamities to this Continent than all the other three.

It is the good fortune of many to live distant from the scene of present sorrow; the evil is not sufficiently brought to their doors to make them feel the precariousness with which all American property is possessed. But let our imaginations transport us a few moments to Boston; that seat of wretchedness will teach us wisdom, and instruct us for ever to renounce a power in whom we can have no trust. The inhabitants of that unfortunate city who but a few months ago were in ease and affluence, have now no other alternative than to stay and starve, or turn out to beg. Endangered by the fire of their friends if they continue within the city, and plundered by the soldiery if they leave it, in their present situation they are prisoners without the hope of redemption, and in a general attack for their relief they would be exposed to the fury of both armies.

Men of passive tempers look somewhat lightly over the offences of Great Britain, and, still hoping for the best, are apt to call out, *Come, come, we shall be friends again for all this.* But examine the passions and feelings of mankind: bring the doctrine of reconciliation to the touchstone of nature, and then tell me whether you can hereafter love, honour, and faithfully serve the power that hath carried fire and sword into your land? If you cannot do all these, then are you only deceiving yourselves, and by your delay bringing ruin upon posterity. Your future connection with Britain, whom you can neither love nor honour, will be forced and unnatural, and being formed only on the plan of present convenience, will in a little time fall into a relapse more wretched than the first. But if you say, you can still pass the violations over, then I ask, hath your house been burnt? Hath your property been destroyed before your face? Are your wife and children destitute of a bed to lie on, or bread to live on? Have you lost a parent or a child by their hands, and yourself the ruined and wretched survivor? If you have not, then are you not a judge of those who have. But if you have, and can still shake hands with the murderers, then are you unworthy the name of husband, father, friend, or lover, and whatever may be your rank or title in life, you have the heart of a coward, and the spirit of a sycophant.

This is not inflaming or exaggerating matters, but trying them by those feelings and affections which nature justifies, and without which we should be incapable of discharging the social duties of life, or enjoying the felicities of it. I mean not to exhibit horror for the purpose of provoking revenge, but to awaken us from fatal and unmanly slumbers, that we may pursue determinately some fixed object. 'Tis not in the power of Britain or of Europe to conquer America, if she doth not conquer herself by delay and timidity. The present winter is worth an age if rightly employed, but if lost or neglected the whole Continent will partake of the misfortune; and there is no punishment which that man doth not deserve, be he who, or what, or where he will, that may be the means of sacrificing a season so precious and useful.

'Tis repugnant to reason, to the universal order of things, to all examples from former ages, to suppose that this Continent can long remain subject to any external power. The most sanguine in Britain doth not think so. The utmost stretch of human wisdom cannot, at this time, compass a plan, short of separation, which can promise the continent even a year's security. Reconciliation is *now* a fallacious dream. Nature hath deserted the connection, and art cannot supply her place. For, as Milton wisely expresses, "never can true reconcilement grow where wounds of deadly hate have pierced so deep."

Every quiet method for peace hath been ineffectual. Our prayers have been rejected with disdain; and hath tended to convince us that nothing flatters vanity or confirms obstinacy in Kings more than repeated petitioning—and nothing hath contributed more than that very measure to make the Kings of Europe absolute. Witness Denmark and Sweden. Wherefore, since nothing but blows will do, for God's sake let us come to a final separation, and not leave the next generation to be cutting throats under the violated unmeaning names of parent and child.

To say they will never attempt it again is idle and visionary; we thought so at the repeal of the stamp act, yet a year or two undeceived us; as well may we suppose that nations which have been once defeated will never renew the quarrel.

As to government matters, 'tis not in the power of Britain to do this continent justice: the business of it will soon be too weighty and intricate to be managed with any tolerable degree of convenience, by a power so distant from us, and so very ignorant of us; for if they cannot conquer us, they cannot govern us. To be always running three or four thousand miles with a tale or a petition, waiting four or five months for an answer, which, when obtained, requires five or six more to explain it in, will in a few years be looked upon as folly and childishness. There was a time when it was proper, and there is a proper time for it to cease.

Small islands not capable of protecting themselves are the proper objects for government to take under their care; but there is something absurd, in supposing a Continent to be perpetually governed by an island. In no instance hath nature made the satellite larger than its primary planet; and as England and America, with respect to each other, reverse the common order of nature, it is evident that they belong to different systems. England to Europe: America to itself.

I am not induced by motives of pride, party, or resentment to espouse the doctrine of separation and independence; I am clearly, positively, and conscientiously persuaded that it is the true interest of this Continent to be so; that every thing short of *that* is mere patchwork, that it can afford no lasting felicity,—that it is leaving the sword to our children, and shrinking back at a time when a little more, a little further, would have rendered this Continent the glory of the earth.

As Britain hath not manifested the least inclination towards a compromise, we may be assured that no terms can be obtained worthy the acceptance of the Continent, or any ways equal to the expence of blood and treasure we have been already put to.

The object contended for, ought always to bear some just proportion to the expense. The removal of North, or the whole detestable junto, is a matter unworthy the millions we have expended. A temporary stoppage of trade was an inconvenience, which would have sufficiently balanced the repeal of all the acts complained of, had such repeals been obtained; but if the whole Continent must take up arms, if every man must be a soldier, 'tis scarcely worth our while to fight against a contemptible ministry only. Dearly, dearly do we pay for the repeal of the acts, if that is all we fight for; for, in a just estimation 'tis as great a folly to pay a Bunker-hill price for law as for land. As I have always considered the independency of this continent, as an event which sooner or later must arrive, so from the late rapid progress of the Continent to maturity, the event cannot be far off. Wherefore, on the breaking out of hostilities, it was not worth the while to have disputed a matter which time would have finally redressed, unless we meant to be in earnest: otherwise it is like wasting an estate on a suit at law, to regulate the trespasses of a tenant whose lease is just expiring. No man was a warmer wisher for a reconciliation than myself, before the fatal nineteenth of April, 1775, but the moment the event of that day was made known, I rejected the hardened, sullen-tempered Pharaoh of England for ever; and disdain the wretch, that with the pretended title of FA-THER OF HIS PEOPLE can unfeelingly hear of their slaughter, and composedly sleep with their blood upon his soul.

But admitting that matters were now made up, what would be the event? I answer, the ruin of the Continent. And that for several reasons.

First. The powers of governing still remaining in the hands of the King, he will have a negative over the whole legislation of this Continent. And as he hath shown himself such an inveterate enemy to liberty, and discovered such a thirst for arbitrary power, is he, or is he not, a proper person to say to these colonies, *You shall make no laws but what I please!?* And is there any inhabitant of America so ignorant as not to know, that according to what is called the *present constitution,* this Continent can make no laws but what the king gives leave to; and is there any man so unwise as not to see, that (considering what has happened) he will suffer no law to be made here but such as suits *his* purpose? We may be as effectually enslaved by the want of laws in America, as by submitting to laws made for us in England. After matters are made up (as it is called) can there be any doubt, but the whole power of the crown will be exerted to keep this continent as low and humble as possible? Instead of going forward we shall go backward, or be perpetually quarrelling, or ridiculously petitioning. We are already greater than the King wishes us to be, and will he not hereafter endeavor to make us less? To bring the matter to one point, Is the power who is jealous of our prosperity, a proper power to govern us? Whoever says *No,* to this question, is an Independant for independency means no more than this, whether we shall make our own laws, or, whether the King, the greatest enemy this continent hath, or can have, shall tell us *there shall be no laws but such as I like.*

But the King, you will say, has a negative in England; the people there can make no laws without his consent. In point of right and good order, it is something very ridiculous that a youth of twenty-one (which hath often happened) shall say to several millions of people older and wiser than himself, "I forbid this or that act of yours to be law." But in this place I decline this sort of reply, though I will never cease to expose the absurdity of it, and only answer that England being the King's residence, and America not so, makes quite another case. The King's negative here is ten times more dangerous and fatal than it can be in England; for there he will scarcely refuse his consent to a bill for putting England into as strong a state of defense as possible, and in America he would never suffer such a bill to be passed.

America is only a secondary object in the system of British politics. England consults the good of this country no further than it answers her own purpose. Wherefore, her own interest leads her to suppress the growth of ours in every case which doth not promote her advantage, or in the least interferes with it. A pretty state we should soon be in under such a second hand government, considering what has happened! Men do not change from enemies to friends by the alteration of a name: And in order to show that reconciliation now is a dangerous doctrine, I affirm, *that it would be policy in the King at this time to repeal the acts, for the sake of reinstating himself in the government of the provinces;* In order that HE MAY ACCOMPLISH BY CRAFT AND SUBTLETY, IN THE LONG RUN, WHAT HE CANNOT DO BY FORCE AND VIOLENCE IN THE SHORT ONE. Reconciliation and ruin are nearly related.

Secondly. That as even the best terms which we can expect to obtain can amount to no more than a temporary expedient, or a kind of government by guardianship, which can last no longer than till the Colonies come of age, so the general face and state of things in the interim will be unsettled and unpromising. Emigrants of property will not choose to come to a country whose form of government hangs but by a thread, and who is every day tottering on the brink of commotion and disturbance; and numbers of the present inhabitants would lay hold of the interval to dispose of their effects, and quit the Continent.

But the most powerful of all arguments is, that nothing but independence, *i.e.* a Continental form of government, can keep the peace of the Continent and preserve it inviolate from civil wars. I dread the event of a reconciliation with Britain now, as it is more than probable that it will be followed by a revolt some where or other, the consequences of which may be far more fatal than all the malice of Britain.

Thousands are already ruined by British barbarity; (thousands more will probably suffer the same fate.) Those men have other feelings than us who have nothing suffered. All they now possess is liberty; what they before enjoyed is sacrificed to its service, and having nothing more to lose they disdain submission. Besides, the general temper of the Colonies, towards a British government will be like that of a youth who is nearly out of his time; they will care very little about her: And a government which cannot preserve the peace is no government at all, and in that case we pay our money for nothing; and pray what is it that Britain can do, whose power will be wholly on paper, should a civil tumult break out the very day after

reconciliation? I have heard some men say, many of whom I believe spoke without thinking, that they dreaded an independance, fearing that it would produce civil wars: It is but seldom that our first thoughts are truly correct, and that is the case here; for there is ten times more to dread from a patched up connection than from independence. I make the sufferer's case my own, and I protest, that were I driven from house and home, my property destroyed, and my circumstances ruined, that as a man, sensible of injuries, I could never relish the doctrine of reconciliation, or consider myself bound thereby.

The Colonies have manifested such a spirit of good order and obedience to Continental government, as is sufficient to make every reasonable person easy and happy on that head. No man can assign the least pretence for his fears, on any other grounds, than such as are truly childish and ridiculous, viz., that one colony will be striving for superiority over another.

Where there are no distinctions there can be no superiority; perfect equality affords no temptation. The Republics of Europe are all (and we may say always) in peace. Holland and Switzerland are without wars, foreign or domestic: Monarchical governments, it is true, are never long at rest: the crown itself is a temptation to enterprising ruffians at home; and that degree of pride and insolence ever attendant on regal authority, swells into a rupture with foreign powers in instances where a republican government, by being formed on more natural principles, would negociate the mistake.

If there is any true cause of fear respecting independance, it is because no plan is yet laid down. Men do not see their way out. Wherefore, as an opening into that business I offer the following hints; at the same time modestly affirming, that I have no other opinion of them myself, than that they may be the means of giving rise to something better. Could the straggling thoughts of individuals be collected, they would frequently form materials for wise and able men to improve into useful matter. "Let the assemblies be annual, with a president only. The representation more equal, their business wholly domestic, and subject to the authority of a continental Congress."

Let each Colony be divided into six, eight, or ten, convenient districts, each district to send a proper number of Delegates to Congress, so that each Colony send at least thirty. The whole number in Congress will be at least 390. Each congress to sit and to choose a President by the following method. When the Delegates are met, let a Colony be taken from the whole thirteen Colonies by lot, after which let the Congress choose (by ballot) a president from out of the Delegates of that Province. In the next

Congress, let a Colony be taken by lot from twelve only, omitting that Colony from which the president was taken in the former Congress, and so proceeding on till the whole thirteen shall have had their proper rotation. And in order that nothing may pass into a law but what is satisfactorily just, not less than three fifths of the Congress to be called a majority. He that will promote discord, under a government so equally formed as this, would have joined Lucifer in his revolt.

But as there is a peculiar delicacy from whom, or in what manner, this business must first arise, and as it seems most agreeable and consistent that it should come from some intermediate body between the governed and the governors, that is, between the Congress and the People, let a Continental Conference be held in the following manner, and for the following purpose.

A Committee of twenty six members of congress, *viz.* Two for each Colony. Two Members from each House of Assembly, or Provincial Convention; and five Representatives of the people at large, to be chosen in the capital city or town of each Province, for, and in behalf of the whole Province, by as many qualified voters as shall think proper to attend from all parts of the Province for that purpose; or, if more convenient, the Representatives may be chosen in two or three of the most populous parts thereof. In this conference, thus assembled, will be united the two grand principles of business, *knowledge* and *power*. The Members of Congress, Assemblies, or Conventions, by having had experience in national concerns, will be able and useful counsellors, and the whole, being impowered by the people, will have a truly legal authority.

The conferring members being met, let their business be to frame a Continental Charter, or Charter of the United Colonies; (answering to what is called the Magna Charta of England) fixing the number and manner of choosing Members of Congress, Members of Assembly, with their date of sitting; and drawing the line of business and jurisdiction between them: Always remembering, that our strength is Continental, not Provincial. Securing freedom and property to all men, and above all things, the free exercise of religion, according to the dictates of conscience; with such other matter as it is necessary for a charter to contain. Immediately after which, the said conference to dissolve, and the bodies which shall be chosen conformable to the said charter, to be the Legislators and Governors of this Continent for the time being: Whose peace and happiness, may GOD preserve. AMEN.

Should any body of men be hereafter delegated for this or some similar purpose, I offer them the following extracts from that wise observer on Governments, Dragonetti. "The science," says he, "of the Politician consists in fixing the true point of happiness and freedom. Those men would deserve the gratitude of ages, who should discover a mode of government that contained the greatest sum of individual happiness, with the least national expense." (Dragonetti on "Virtues and Reward.")

But where, say some, is the King of America? I'll tell you, friend, he reigns above, and doth not make havoc of mankind like the Royal Brute of Great Britain. Yet that we may not appear to be defective even in earthly honours, let a day be solemnly set apart for proclaiming the Charter; let it be brought forth placed on the Divine Law, the Word of God; let a crown be placed thereon, by which the world may know, that so far as we approve of monarchy, that in America the law is king. For as in absolute governments the King is law, so in free countries the law ought to be king; and there ought to be no other. But lest any ill use should afterwards arise, let the Crown at the conclusion of the ceremony be demolished, and scattered among the people whose right it is.

A government of our own is our natural right: and when a man seriously reflects on the precariousness of human affairs, he will become convinced, that it is infinitely wiser and safer, to form a constitution of our own in a cool deliberate manner, while we have it in our power, than to trust such an interesting event to time and chance. If we omit it now, some Massanello[4] may hereafter arise, who, laying hold of popular disquietudes, may collect together the desperate and the discontented, and by assuming to themselves the powers of government, finally sweep away the liberties of the Continent like a deluge. Should the government of America return again into the hands of Britain, the tottering situation of things will be a temptation for some desperate adventurer to try his fortune; and in such a case, what relief can Britain give? Ere she could hear the news, the fatal business might be done; and ourselves suffering like the wretched Britons under the oppression of the Conqueror. Ye that oppose independance now, ye know not what ye do: ye are opening a door to eternal tyranny, by keeping vacant the seat of government. There are thousands and tens of thousands, who would think it glorious to expel from the Continent, that barbarous and hellish power, which hath stirred up the Indians and the Negroes to destroy us; the cruelty hath

---

4. "Thomas Anello, otherwise Massanello, a fisherman of Naples, who after spiriting up his countrymen in the public market place, against the oppression of the Spaniards, to whom the place was then subject, prompted them to revolt, and in the space of a day became King." [Au.]

a double guilt, it is dealing brutally by us, and treacherously by them.

To talk of friendship with those in whom our reason forbids us to have faith, and our affections wounded thro' a thousand pores instruct us to detest, is madness and folly. Every day wears out the little remains of kindred between us and them; and can there be any reason to hope, that as the relationship expires, the affection will encrease, or that we shall agree better when we have ten times more and greater concerns to quarrel over than ever?

Ye that tell us of harmony and reconciliation, can ye restore to us the time that is past? Can ye give to prostitution its former innocence? neither can ye reconcile Britain and America. The last cord now is broken, the people of England are presenting addresses against us. There are injuries which nature cannot forgive; she would cease to be nature if she did. As well can the lover forgive the ravisher of his mistress, as the Continent forgive the murders of Britain. The Almighty hath implanted in us these unextinguishable feelings for good and wise purposes. They are the Guardians of his Image in our hearts. They distinguish us from the herd of common animals. The social compact would dissolve, and justice be extirpated from the earth, or have only a casual existence were we callous to the touches of affection. The robber and the murderer would often escape unpunished, did not the injuries which our tempers sustain, provoke us into justice.

O! ye that love mankind! Ye that dare oppose not only the tyranny but the tyrant, stand forth! Every spot of the old world is overrun with oppression. Freedom hath been hunted round the Globe. Asia and Africa have long expelled her. Europe regards her like a stranger, and England hath given her warning to depart. O! receive the fugitive and prepare in time an asylum of mankind.

THE CRISIS[1]

I

These are the times that try men's souls. The summer soldier and the sunshine patriot will, in this crisis, shrink

from the service of their country; but he that stands it *now,* deserves the love and thanks of man and woman. Tyranny, like hell, is not easily conquered; yet we have this consolation with us, that the harder the conflict, the more glorious the triumph. What we obtain too cheap, we esteem too lightly: it is dearness only that gives every thing its value. Heaven knows how to put a proper price upon its goods; and it would be strange indeed if so celestial an article as FREEDOM should not be highly rated. Britain, with an army to enforce her tyranny, has declared that she has a right (*not only to* TAX) but "to BIND *us in* ALL CASES WHATSOEVER," and if being *bound in that manner,* is not slavery, then is there not such a thing as slavery upon earth. Even the expression is impious; for so unlimited a power can belong only to God.

Whether the independence of the continent was declared too soon, or delayed too long, I will not now enter into as an argument; my own simple opinion is, that had it been eight months earlier, it would have been much better. We did not make a proper use of last winter, neither could we, while we were in a dependant state. However, the fault, if it were one, was all our own[2]; we have none to blame but ourselves. But no great deal is lost yet. All that Howe[3] has been doing for this month past, is rather a ravage than a conquest, which the spirit of the Jerseys, a year ago, would have quickly repulsed, and which time and a little resolution will soon recover.

I have as little superstition in me as any man living, but my secret opinion has ever been, and still is, that God Almighty will not give up a people to military destruction, or leave them unsupportedly to perish, who have so earnestly and so repeatedly sought to avoid the calamities of war, by every decent method which wisdom could invent. Neither have I so much of the infidel in me, as to suppose that He has relinquishd the government of the world, and given us up to the care of devils; and as I do not, I cannot see on what grounds the king of Britain can look up to heaven for help against us: a common murderer, a highwayman, or a housebreaker, has a good a pretence as he.

---

1. Originally published in the *Pennsylvania Journal,* December 19, 1776, this paper was printed four days later in pamphlet form as *The American Crisis,* the source of the present text. Capitalizing on the success of his first pamphlet, *Common Sense,* Paine signed the Crisis Papers using "Common Sense" as his pen name.

2. "The present winter is worth an age, if rightly employed; but, if lost or neglected, the whole continent will partake of the evil; and there is no punishment that man does not deserve, be he who, or what, or where he will, that may be the means of sacrificing a season so precious and useful." [Au.]

3. Sir William Howe (1729–1814), British commander, was Washington's key opponent in battles during the 1776 and 1777 campaigns.

'Tis surprising to see how rapidly a panic will sometimes run through a country. All nations and ages have been subject to them: Britain has trembled like an ague at the report of a French fleet of flat bottomed boats; and in the fourteenth century the whole English army, after ravaging the kingdom of France, was driven back like men petrified with fear; and this brave exploit was performed by a few broken forces collected and headed by a woman, Joan of Arc.[4] Would that heaven might inspire some Jersey maid to spirit up her countrymen, and save her fair fellow sufferers from ravage and ravishment! Yet panics, in some cases, have their uses; they produce as much good as hurt. Their duration is always short; the mind soon grows through them, and acquires a firmer habit than before. But their peculiar advantage is, that they are the touchstones of sincerity and hypocrisy, and bring things and men to light, which might otherwise have lain forever undiscovered. In fact, they have the same effect on secret traitors, which an imaginary apparition would have upon a private murderer. They sift out the hidden thoughts of man, and hold them up in public to the world. Many a disguised tory has lately shown his head, that shall penitentially solemnize with curses the day on which Howe arrived upon the Delaware.

As I was with the troops at Fort Lee, and marched with them to the edge of Pennsylvania, I am well acquainted with many circumstances, which those who live at a distance know but little or nothing of. Our situation there was exceedingly cramped, the place being a narrow neck of land between the North River and the Hackensack. Our force was inconsiderable, being not one fourth so great as Howe could bring against us. We had no army at hand to have relieved the garrison, had we shut ourselves up and stood on our defence. Our ammunition, light artillery, and the best part of our stores, had been removed, on the apprehension that Howe would endeavor to penetrate the Jerseys, in which case fort Lee could be of no use to us; for it must occur to every thinking man, whether in the army or not, that these kind of field forts are only for temporary purposes, and last in use no longer than the enemy directs his force against the particular object, which such forts are raised to defend. Such was our situation and condition at fort Lee on the morning of the 20th of Novem-

ber, when an officer arrived with information that the enemy with 200 boats had landed about seven miles above: Major General Green,[5] who commanded the garrison, immediately ordered them under arms, and sent express to General Washington at the town of Hackensack, distant by the way of the ferry = six miles. Our first object was to secure the bridge over the Hackensack, which laid up the river between the enemy and us, about six miles from us, and three from them. General Washington arrived in about three quarters of an hour, and marched at the head of the troops towards the bridge, which place I expected we should have a brush for; however, they did not choose to dispute it with us, and the greatest part of our troops went over the bridge, the rest over the ferry, except some which passed at a mill on a small creek, between the bridge and the ferry, and made their way through some marshy grounds up to the town of Hackensack, and there passed the river. We brought off as much baggage as the wagons could contain, the rest was lost. The simple object was to bring off the garrison, and march them on till they could be strengthened by the Jersey or Pennsylvania militia, so as to be enabled to make a stand. We staid four days at Newark, collected our outposts with some of the Jersey militia, and marched out twice to meet the enemy, on being informed that they were advancing, though our numbers were greatly inferior to theirs. Howe, in my little opinion, committed a great error in generalship in not throwing a body of forces off from Staten Island through Amboy, by which means he might have seized all our stores at Brunswick, and intercepted our march into Pennsylvania; but if we believe the power of hell to be limited, we must likewise believe that their agents are under some providential controul.

I shall not now attempt to give all the particulars of our retreat to the Delaware; suffice it for the present to say, that both officers and men, though greatly harassed and fatigued, frequently without rest, covering, or provision, the inevitable consequences of a long retreat, bore it with a manly and martial spirit. All their wishes centred in one, which was, that the country would turn out and help them to drive the enemy back. Voltaire has remarked that king William never appeared to full advantage but in difficulties and in action; the same remark may be made on General Washington, for the character fits him. There is a natural firmness in some minds which cannot be unlocked by

---

4. Joan of Arc (1412–1431), said to have had divine inspiration, led the French against the English in several battles, defeating them in the battle over Orléans in 1429. She was captured by the English, sold to allies of her enemies, and burned at the stake as a heretic at Roven.

---

5. Nathanael Green (1742–86), a leading war general, fought the British at battles in Trenton and Brandywine, 1776–77.

trifles, but which, when unlocked, discovers a cabinet of fortitude; and I reckon it among those kind of public blessings, which we do not immediately see, that God hath blessed him with uninterrupted health, and given him a mind that can even flourish upon care.

I shall conclude this paper with some miscellaneous remarks on the state of our affairs; and shall begin with asking the following question, Why is it that the enemy have left the New-England provinces, and made these middle ones the seat of war? The answer is easy: New-England is not infested with tories, and we are. I have been tender in raising the cry against these men, and used numberless arguments to show them their danger, but it will not do to sacrifice a world either to their folly or their baseness. The period is now arrived, in which either they or we must change our sentiments, or one or both must fall. And what is a tory? Good God! what is he? I should not be afraid to go with a hundred whigs against a thousand tories, were they to attempt to get into arms. Every tory is a coward; for servile, slavish, self-interested fear is the foundation of toryism; and a man under such influence, though he may be cruel, never can be brave.

But, before the line of irrecoverable separation be drawn between us, let us reason the matter together: Your conduct is an invitation to the enemy, yet not one in a thousand of you has heart enough to join him. Howe is as much deceived by you as the American cause is injured by you. He expects you will all take up arms, and flock to his standard, with muskets on your shoulders. Your opinions are of no use to him, unless you support him personally, for 'tis soldiers, and not tories, that he wants.

I once felt all that kind of anger, which a man ought to feel, against the mean principles that are held by the tories: a noted one, who kept a tavern at Amboy, was standing at his door, with as pretty a child in his hand, about eight or nine years old, as I ever saw, and after speaking his mind as freely as he thought was prudent, finished with this unfatherly expression, "*Well! give me peace in my day.*" Not a man lives on the continent but fully believes that a separation must some time or other finally take place, and a generous parent should have said, "*If there must be trouble, let it be in my day, that my child may have peace;*" and this single reflection, well applied, is sufficient to awaken every man to duty. Not a place upon earth might be so happy as America. Her situation is remote from all the wrangling world, and she has nothing to do but to trade with them. A man can distinguish himself between temper and principle, and I am as confident, as I am that God governs the world, that America will never be happy till she gets clear of foreign dominion. Wars, without ceasing, will break out till that period arrives, and the continent must in the end be conqueror; for though the flame of liberty may sometimes cease to shine, the coal can never expire.

America did not, nor does not want force; but she wanted a proper application of that force. Wisdom is not the purchase of a day, and it is no wonder that we should err at the first setting off. From an excess of tenderness, we were unwilling to raise an army, and trusted our cause to the temporary defence of a well-meaning militia. A summer's experience has now taught us better; yet with those troops, while they were collected, we were able to set bounds to the progress of the enemy, and, thank God! they are again assembling. I always considered militia as the best troops in the world for a sudden exertion, but they will not do for a long campaign. Howe, it is probable, will make an attempt on this city;[6] should he fail on this side the Delaware, he is ruined: if he succeeds, our cause is not ruined. He stakes all on his side against a part on ours; admitting he succeeds, the consequence will be, that armies from both ends of the continent will march to assist their suffering friends in the middle states; for he cannot go everywhere, it is impossible. I consider Howe as the greatest enemy the tories have; he is bringing a war into their country, which, had it not been for him and partly for themselves, they had been clear of. Should he now be expelled, I wish with all the devotion of a Christian, that the names of whig and tory may never more be mentioned; but should the tories give him encouragement to come, or assistance if he come, I as sincerely wish that our next year's arms may expel them from the continent, and the congress appropriate their possessions to the relief of those who have suffered in well-doing. A single successful battle next year will settle the whole. America could carry on a two years war by the confiscation of the property of disaffected persons, and be made happy by their expulsion. Say not that this is revenge, call it rather the soft resentment of a suffering people, who, having no object in view but the *good* of *all,* have staked their *own all* upon a seemingly doubtful event. Yet it is folly to argue against determined hardness; eloquence may strike the ear, and the language of sorrow draw forth the tear of compassion, but nothing can reach the heart that is steeled with prejudice.

Quitting this class of men, I turn with the warm ardor

----

6. Philadelphia.

of a friend to those who have nobly stood, and are yet determined to stand the matter out: I call not upon a few, but upon all: not on *this* state or *that* state, but on *every* state: up and help us; lay your shoulders to the wheel; better have too much force than too little, when so great an object is at stake. Let it be told to the future world, that in the depth of winter, when nothing but hope and virtue could survive, that the city and the country, alarmed at one common danger, came forth to meet and to repulse it. Say not that thousands are gone, turn out your tens of thousands; throw not the burden of the day upon Providence, but *"show your faith by your works,"* that God may bless you. It matters not where you live, or what rank of life you hold, the evil or the blessing will reach you all. The far and the near, the home counties and the back, the rich and the poor, will suffer or rejoice alike. The heart that feels not now, is dead: the blood of his children will curse his cowardice, who shrinks back at a time when a little might have saved the whole, and made *them* happy. I love the man that can smile in trouble, that can gather strength from distress, and grow brave by reflection. 'Tis the business of little minds to shrink; but he whose heart is firm, and whose conscience approves his conduct, will pursue his principles unto death. My own line of reasoning is to myself as straight and clear as a ray of light. Not all the treasures of the world, so far as I believe, could have induced me to support an offensive war, for I think it murder; but if a thief breaks into my house, burns and destroys my property, and kills or threatens to kill me, or those that are in it, and to *"bind me in all cases whatsoever"*[7] to his absolute will, am I to suffer it? What signifies it to me, whether he who does it is a king or a common man; my countryman or not my countryman; whether it be done by an individual villain, or an army of them? If we reason to the root of things we shall find no difference; neither can any just cause be assigned why we should punish in the one case and pardon in the other. Let them call me rebel, and welcome, I feel no concern from it; but I should suffer the misery of devils, were I to make a whore of my soul by swearing allegiance to one whose character is that of a sottish, stupid, stubborn, worthless, brutish man. I conceive likewise a horrid idea in receiving mercy from a being, who at the last day shall be shrieking to the rocks and mountains to cover him, and fleeing with terror from the orphan, the widow, and the slain of America.

---

7. In the February 24, 1766, Declaratory Act, Parliament claimed authority over the colonies using this phrase.

There are cases which cannot be overdone by language, and this is one. There are persons, too, who see not the full extent of the evil which threatens them; they solace themselves with hopes that the enemy, if he succeed, will be merciful. It is the madness of folly, to expect mercy from those who have refused to do justice; and even mercy, where conquest is the object, is only a trick of war; the cunning of the fox is as murderous as the violence of the wolf, and we ought to guard equally against both. Howe's first object is, partly by threats and partly by promises, to terrify or seduce the people to deliver up their arms and receive mercy. The ministry recommended the same plan to Gage, and this is what the tories call making their peace, *"a peace which passeth all understanding"* indeed! A peace which would be the immediate forerunner of a worse ruin than any we have yet thought of. Ye men of Pennsylvania, do reason upon these things! Were the back counties to give up their arms, they would fall an easy prey to the Indians, who are all armed: this perhaps is what some tories would not be sorry for. Were the home counties to deliver up their arms, they would be exposed to the resentment of the back counties, who would then have it in their power to chastise their defection at pleasure. And were any one state to give up its arms, *that* state must be garrisoned by all Howe's army of Britons and Hessians to preserve it from the anger of the rest. Mutual fear is the principal link in the chain of mutual love, and woe be to that state that breaks the compact. Howe is mercifully inviting you to barbarous destruction, and men must be either rogues or fools that will not see it. I dwell not upon the vapours of imagination; I bring reason to your ears, and, in language as plain as A, B, C, hold up truth to your eyes.

I thank God, that I fear not. I see no real cause for fear. I know our situation well, and can see the way out of it. While our army was collected, Howe dared not risk a battle; and it is no credit to him that he decamped from the White Plains, and waited a mean opportunity to ravage the defenceless Jerseys; but it is great credit to us, that, with a handful of men, we sustained an orderly retreat for near an hundred miles, brought off our ammunition, all our field pieces, the greatest part of our stores, and had four rivers to pass. None can say that our retreat was precipitate, for we were near three weeks in performing it, that the country might have time to come in. Twice we marched back to meet the enemy, and remained out till dark. The sign of fear was not seen in our camp, and had not some of the cowardly and disaffected inhabitants spread false alarms through the country, the Jerseys had never been ravaged. Once more we are again collected and collecting; our new army at both ends of the continent is recruiting fast, and we shall be able to open the next campaign with sixty thousand men, well armed and clothed. This is our situation, and who will may know it. By perseverance and fortitude we have the prospect of a glorious issue; by cowardice and submission, the sad choice of a variety of evils—a ravaged country—a depopulated city—habitations without safety, and slavery without hope—our homes turned into barracks and bawdy-houses for Hessians, and a future race to provide for, whose fathers we shall doubt of. Look on this picture and weep over it! and if there yet remains one thoughtless wretch who believes it not, let him suffer it unlamented.

William Bartram (1739–1823)

William Bartram was one of the leading naturalists of his day, and he was renowned as a nature artist and author of *Travels through North and South Carolina, Georgia, East and West Florida* (1791). He was born in Kingsessing, Pennsylvania, to John Bartram, a renowned botanist and naturalist, and Ann Mendenhall, both members of the Society of Friends. John Bartram was self-taught in the natural sciences and botany. He had founded an important botanical garden in British America and corresponded extensively with European scientists, particularly Swedish botanist Carl von Linne, known as Carolus Linnaeus (1707–78). In 1754 John Bartram enrolled his son William in the Academy of Philadelphia, where William studied the classics, moral philosophy, mathematics, rhetoric, and science. Although William showed an early aptitude for scientific observation, in 1756 he was withdrawn from school by his father and apprenticed to a Philadelphia merchant. William struggled to find his vocation, while suffering from "melancholia" or depression. He spent several unsuccessful years running a trading store in North Carolina, and in 1765 he accompanied his father on a trip to St. John's River in Florida. William stayed behind in Florida and attempted to establish a rice plantation. His efforts failed, and a return to Philadelphia proved no more financially successful.

Finally, in 1772, William Bartram was able to pursue his own goals when Dr. John Fothergill, a wealthy British Quaker physician, became his patron and financed a return trip to Florida. Although Fothergill envisioned a trip of two to three years during which William would collect new plants and made illustrations and observations, the nearly four-year trip that Bartram began in March 1773, unfolded quite differently. Bartram traveled extensively, exploring Georgia, Florida, Alabama, and Louisiana from his base in Charleston, South Carolina. Although his patron was frustrated by Bartram's seemingly unfocused and costly travels, Bartram would not return to Philadelphia until January 1777.

Bartram's field journals became the basis of the two surviving versions of his *Travels*. Initially Bartram created a report for Fothergill, a rough transcription of his field notes, loosely written, using the common names of plants and animals. It described the land and recorded information about the plants and animals Bartram had observed. After returning to Philadelphia, Bartram wrote a second version in which he used Latin names. The manuscript of *Travels* was likely completed in the early 1780s, but it was not published until 1791. Although his book received relatively limited attention in the United States, it was well received abroad, and German, Dutch and French editions were published. Bartram's work attracted the attention of important writers, such as Wordsworth and Coleridge, and it gained renown among United States and Continental botanists and ornithologists. When Thomas Jefferson invited Bartram to join the Lewis and Clark expedition, Bartram turned him down, preferring to remain in Philadelphia. Bartram never fully recovered his health from his years in Florida. A private man who never married, Bartram remained in Philadelphia, living with family members, and he wrote little beyond his *Travels*.

from TRAVELS THROUGH NORTH AND SOUTH CAROLINA, GEORGIA, EAST AND WEST FLORIDA[1]

The little lake, which is an expansion of the river, now appeared in view; on the East side are extensive marshes, and on the other high forests and Orange groves, and then a bay, lined with vast Cypress swamps, both coasts gradually approaching each other, to the opening of the river again, which is in this place about three hundred yards wide; evening now drawing on, I was anxious to reach some high bank of the river, where I intended to lodge, and agreeably to my wishes, I soon after discovered on the West shore, a little promontory, at the turning of the river, contracting it here to about one hundred and fifty yards in width. This promontory is a peninsula, containing about three acres of high ground, and is one entire Orange grove, with a few Live Oaks, Magnolias and Palms. Upon doubling the point, I arrived at the landing, which is a circular harbour, at the foot of the bluff, the top of which is about twelve feet high; and back of it is a large Cypress swamp, that spreads each way, the right wing forming the West coast of the little lake, and the left stretching up the river many miles, and encompassing a vast space of low grassy marshes. From this promontory, looking Eastward across the river, we behold a landscape of low country, unparalleled as I think; on the left is the East coast of the little lake, which I had just passed, and from the Orange bluff at the lower end, the high forests begin, and increase in breadth from the shore of the lake, making a circular sweep to the right, and contain many hundred thousand acres of meadow, and this grand sweep of high forests encircles, as I apprehend, at least twenty miles of these green fields, interspersed with hommocks or islets of evergreen trees, where the sovereign Magnolia and lordly Palm stand conspicuous. The islets are high shelly knolls on the sides of creeks or branches of the river, which wind about and drain off the super-abundant waters that cover these meadows, during the winter season.

The evening was temperately cool and calm. The crocodiles began to roar and appear in uncommon numbers along the shores and in the river. I fixed my camp in an open plain, near the utmost projection of the promontory, under the shelter of a large Live Oak, which stood on the highest part of the ground and but a few yards from my boat. From this open, high situation, I had a free prospect of the river, which was a matter of no trivial consideration to me, having good reason to dread the subtle attacks of the alligators, who were crouding about my harbour. Having collected a good quantity of wood for the purpose of keeping up a light and smoke during the night, I began to think of preparing my supper, when, upon examining my stores, I found but a scanty provision, I thereupon determined, as the most expeditious way of supplying my necessities, to take my bob and try for some trout. About one hundred yards above my harbour, began a cove or bay of the river, out of which opened a large lagoon. The mouth or entrance from the river to it was narrow, but the waters soon after spread and formed a little lake, extending into the marshes, its entrance and shores within I observed to be verged with floating lawns of the Pistia[2] and Nymphea[3] and other aquatic plants; these I knew were excellent haunts for trout.

The verges and islets of the lagoon were elegantly embellished with flowering plants and shrubs; the laughing coots[4] with wings half spread were tripping over the little coves and hiding themselves in the tufts of grass; young broods of the painted summer teal,[5] skimming the still surface of the waters, and following the watchful parent unconscious of danger, were frequently surprised by the voracious trout, and he in turn, as often by the subtle, greedy alligator. Behold him rushing forth from the flags and reeds. His enormous body swells. His plaited tail brandished high, floats upon the lake. The waters like a cataract descend from his opening jaws. Clouds of smoke issue from his dilated nostrils. The earth trembles with his thunder. When immediately from the opposite coast of the lagoon, emerges from the deep his rival champion. They suddenly dart upon each other. The boiling surface of the lake marks their rapid course, and a terrific conflict commences. They now sink to the bottom folded together in horrid wreaths. The water becomes thick and dis-

---

1. Bartram's complete title read: *Travels through North and South Carolina, Georgia, East and West Florida, the Cherokee Country, the Extensive Territories of the Muscogulges, or Creek Confederacy, and the Country of the Chactaws, Containing an Account of the Soil and Natural Productions of Those Regions, Together with Observations on the Manners of the Indians.* It was originally published in Philadelphia in 1791.

---

2. Water lettuce.

3. Water chinquapin.

4. An aquatic bird.

5. Wood duck.

coloured. Again they rise, their jaws clap together, re-echoing through the deep surrounding forests. Again they sink, when the contest ends at the muddy bottom of the lake, and the vanquished makes a hazardous escape, hiding himself in the muddy turbulent waters and sedge on a distant shore. The proud victor exulting returns to the place of action. The shores and forests resound his dreadful roar, together with the triumphing shouts of the plaited tribes around, witnesses of the horrid combat.

My apprehensions were highly alarmed after being a spectator of so dreadful a battle; it was obvious that every delay would but tend to encrease my dangers and difficulties, as the sun was near setting, and the alligators gathered around my harbour from all quarters; from these considerations I concluded to be expeditious in my trip to the lagoon, in order to take some fish. Not thinking it prudent to take my fusee[6] with me, lest I might lose it overboard in case of a battle, which I had every reason to dread before my return, I therefore furnished myself with a club for my defence, went on board, and penetrating the first line of those which surrounded my harbour, they gave way; but being pursued by several very large ones, I kept strictly on the watch, and paddled with all my might towards the entrance of the lagoon, hoping to be sheltered there from the multitude of my assailants; but ere I had half-way reached the place, I was attacked on all sides, several endeavouring to overset the canoe. My situation now became precarious to the last degree: two very large ones attacked me closely, at the same instant, rushing up with their heads and part of their bodies above the water, roaring terribly and belching floods of water over me. They struck their jaws together so close to my ears, as almost to stun me, and I expected every moment to be dragged out of the boat and instantly devoured, but I applied my weapons so effectually about me, though at random, that I was so successful as to beat them off a little; when, finding that they designed to renew the battle, I made for the shore, as the only means left me for my preservation, for, by keeping close to it, I should have my enemies on one side of me only, whereas I was before surrounded by them, and there was a probability, if pushed to the last extremity, of saving myself, by jumping out of the canoe on shore, as it is easy to outwalk them on land, although comparatively as swift as lightning in the water. I found this last expedient alone could fully answer my expectations, for as soon as I gained the shore they drew off and kept aloof. This was a happy relief, as my confidence

was, in some degree, recovered by it. On recollecting myself, I discovered that I had almost reached the entrance of the lagoon, and determined to venture in, if possible to take a few fish and then return to my harbour, while daylight continued; for I could now, with caution and resolution, make my way with safety along shore, and indeed there was no other way to regain my camp, without leaving my boat and making my retreat through the marshes and reeds, which, if I could even effect, would have been in a manner throwing myself away, for then there would have been no hopes of ever recovering my bark, and returning in safety to any settlements of men. I accordingly proceeded and made good my entrance into the lagoon, though not without opposition from the alligators, who formed a line across the entrance, but did not pursue me into it, nor was I molested by any there, though there were some very large ones in a cove at the upper end. I soon caught more trout than I had present occasion for, and the air was too hot and sultry to admit of their being kept for many hours, even though salted or barbecued. I now prepared for my return to camp, which I succeeded in with but little trouble, by keeping close to the shore, yet I was opposed upon re-entering the river out of the lagoon, and pursued near to my landing (though not closely attacked) particularly by an old daring one, about twelve feet in length, who kept close after me, and when I stepped on shore and turned about, in order to draw up my canoe, he rushed up near my feet and lay there for some time, looking me in the face, his head and shoulders out of water; I resolved he should pay for his temerity, and having a heavy load in my fusee, I ran to my camp, and returning with my piece, found him with his foot on the gunwale of the boat, in search of fish, on my coming up he withdrew sullenly and slowly into the water, but soon returned and placed himself in his former position, looking at me and seeming neither fearful or any way disturbed. I soon dispatched him by lodging the contents of my gun in his head, and then proceeded to cleanse and prepare my fish for supper, and accordingly took them out of the boat, laid them down on the sand close to the water, and began to scale them, when, raising my head, I saw before me, through the clear water, the head and shoulders of a very large alligator, moving slowly towards me; I instantly stepped back, when, with a sweep of his tail, he brushed off several of my fish. It was certainly most providential that I looked up at that instant, as the monster would probably, in less than a minute, have seized and dragged me into the river. This incredible boldness of the animal disturbed me greatly, supposing there could now be no reasonable safety for me during the night, but by keeping

---

6. Flintlock gun.

continually on the watch; I therefore, as soon as I had prepared the fish proceeded to secure myself and effects in
the best manner I could: in the first place, I hauled my
bark upon the shore, almost clear out of the water, to prevent their oversetting or sinking her, after this every
moveable was taken out and carried to my camp, which
was but a few yards off; then ranging some dry wood in
such order as was the most convenient, cleared the ground
round about it, that there might be no impediment in my
way, in case of an attack in the night, either from the water
or the land; for I discovered by this time, that this small
isthmus, from its remote situation and fruitfulness, was
resorted to by bears and wolves. Having prepared myself
in the best manner I could, I charged my gun and proceeded to reconnoitre my camp and the adjacent grounds;
when I discovered that the peninsula and grove, at the distance of about two hundred yards from my encampment,
on the land side, were invested by a Cypress swamp, covered with water, which below was joined to the shore of
the little lake, and above to the marshes surrounding the
lagoon, so that I was confined to an islet exceedingly circumscribed, and I found there was no other retreat for me,
in case of an attack, but by either ascending one of the
large Oaks, or pushing off with my boat.

It was by this time dusk, and the alligators had nearly
ceased their roar, when I was again alarmed by a tumultuous noise that seemed to be in my harbour, and therefore
engaged my immediate attention. Returning to my camp I
found it undisturbed, and then continued on to the extreme
point of the promontory, where I saw a scene, new and surprising, which at first threw my senses into such a tumult,
that it was some time before I could comprehend what was
the matter; however, I soon accounted for the prodigious
assemblage of crocodiles at this place, which exceeded
every thing of the kind I had ever heard of.

How shall I express myself so as to convey an adequate idea of it to the reader, and at the same time avoid
raising suspicions of my want of veracity. Should I say,
that the river (in this place) from shore to shore, and perhaps near half a mile above and below me, appeared to be
one solid bank of fish, of various kinds, pushing through
this narrow pass of St. Juans[7] into the little lake, on their
return down the river, and that the alligators were in such
incredible numbers, and so close together from shore to
shore, that it would have been easy to have walked across
on their heads, had the animals been harmless. What expressions can sufficiently declare the shocking scene that

for some minutes continued, whilst this mighty army of
fish were forcing the pass? During this attempt, thousands, I may say hundreds of thousands of them were
caught and swallowed by the devouring alligators. I have
seen an alligator take up out of the water several great fish
at a time, and just squeeze them betwixt his jaws, while
the tails of the great trout flapped about his eyes and lips,
ere he had swallowed them. The horrid noise of their closing jaws, their plunging amidst the broken banks of fish,
and rising with their prey some feet upright above the
water, the floods of water and blood rushing out of their
mouths, and the clouds of vapour issuing from their wide
nostrils, were truly frightful. This scene continued at intervals during the night, as the fish came to the pass. After
this sight, shocking and tremendous as it was, I found myself somewhat easier and more reconciled to my situation,
being convinced that their extraordinary assemblage here,
was owing to this annual feast of fish, and that they were
so well employed in their own element, that I had little occasion to fear their paying me a visit.

It being now almost night, I returned to my camp,
where I had left my fish broiling, and my kettle of rice
stewing, and having with me, oil, pepper and salt, and excellent oranges hanging in abundance over my head (a
valuable substitute for vinegar) I sat down and regaled
myself chearfully; having finished my repast, I re-kindled
my fire for light, and whilst I was revising the notes of my
past day's journey, I was suddenly roused with a noise behind me toward the main land; I sprang up on my feet, and
listening, I distinctly heard some creature wading in the
water of the isthmus; I seized my gun and went cautiously
from my camp, directing my steps towards the noise;
when I had advanced about thirty yards, I halted behind a
coppice of Orange trees, and soon perceived two very
large bears, which had made their way through the water,
and had landed in the grove, about one hundred yards distance from me, and were advancing towards me. I waited
until they were within thirty yards of me, they there began
to snuff and look towards my camp, I snapped my piece,
but it flashed, on which they both turned about and gal-
loped off, plunging through the water and swamp, never
halting as I suppose, until they reached fast land, as I
could hear them leaping and plunging a long time; they
did not presume to return again, nor was I molested by
any other creature, except being occasionally awakened
by the whooping of owls, screaming of bitterns,[8] or the
wood-rats running amongst the leaves.

---

7. St. John's River.

8. Herons.

The wood-rat is a very curious animal, they are not half the size of the domestic rat; of a dark brown or black colour; their tail slender and shorter in proportion, and covered thinly with short hair; they are singular with respect to their ingenuity and great labour in the construction of their habitations, which are conical pyramids about three or four feet high, constructed with dry branches, which they collect with great labour and perseverance, and pile up without any apparent order, yet they are so interwoven with one another, that it would take a bear or wild-cat some time to pull one of these castles to pieces, and allow the animals sufficient time to secure a retreat with their young.

The noise of the crocodiles kept me awake the greater part of the night, but when I arose in the morning, contrary to my expectations, there was perfect peace; very few of them to be seen, and those were asleep on the shore, yet I was not able to suppress my fears and apprehensions of being attacked by them in future; and indeed yesterday's combat with them, notwithstanding I came off in a manner victorious, or at least made a safe retreat, had left sufficient impression on my mind to damp my courage, and it seemed too much for one of my strength, being alone in a very small boat to encounter such collected danger. To pursue my voyage up the river, and be obliged every evening to pass such dangerous defiles, appeared to me as perilous as running the gauntlet betwixt two rows of Indians armed with knives and fire brands; I however resolved to continue my voyage one day longer, if I possibly could with safety, and then return down the river, should I find the like difficulties to oppose. Accordingly I got every thing on board, charged my gun, and set sail cautiously along shore; as I passed by Battle lagoon, I began to tremble and keep a good look out, when suddenly a huge alligator rushed out of the reeds, and with a tremendous roar, came up, and darted as swift as an arrow under my boat, emerging upright on my lea quarter, with open jaws, and belching water and smoke that fell upon me like rain in a hurricane; I laid soundly about his head with my club and beat him off, and after plunging and darting about my boat, he went off on a strait line through the water, seemingly with the rapidity of lightning, and entered the cape of the lagoon; I now employed my time to the very best advantage in paddling close along shore, but could not forbear looking now and then behind me, and presently perceived one of them coming up again; the water of the river hereabouts, was shoal and very clear, the monster came up with the usual roar and menaces, and passed close by the side

of my boat, when I could distinctly see a young brood of alligators to the number of one hundred or more, following after her in a long train, they kept close together in a column without straggling off to the one side or the other, the young appeared to be of an equal size, about fifteen inches in length, almost black, with pale yellow transverse waved clouds or blotches, much like rattle snakes in colour. I now lost sight of my enemy again.

Still keeping close along shore; on turning a point or projection of the river bank, at once I beheld a great number of hillocks or small pyramids, resembling hay cocks, ranged like an encampment along the banks, they stood fifteen or twenty yards distant from the water, on a high marsh, about four feet perpendicular above the water; I knew them to be the nests of the crocodile, having had a description of them before, and now expected a furious and general attack, as I saw several large crocodiles swimming abreast of these buildings. These nests being so great a curiosity to me, I was determined at all events immediately to land and examine them. Accordingly I ran my bark on shore at one of their landing places, which was a sort of nick or little dock, from which ascended a slopping path or road up to the edge of the meadow, where their nests were, most of them were deserted, and the great thick whitish egg-shells lay broken and scattered upon the ground round about them.

The nests or hillocks are of the form of an obtuse cone, four feet high and four or five feet in diameter at their bases; they are constructed with mud, grass and herbage: at first they lay a floor of this kind of tempered mortar on the ground, upon which they deposit a layer of eggs, and upon this a stratum of mortar seven or eight inches in thickness, and then another layer of eggs, and in this manner one stratum upon another, nearly to the top: I believe they commonly lay from one to two hundred eggs in a nest: these are hatched I suppose by the heat of the sun, and perhaps the vegetable substances mixed with the earth, being acted upon by the sun, may cause a small degree of fermentation, and so increase the heat in those hillocks. The ground for several acres about these nests shewed evident marks of a continual resort of alligators; the grass was every where beaten down, hardly a blade or straw was left standing; whereas, all about, at a distance, it was five or six feet high, and as thick as it could grow together. The female, as I imagine, carefully watches her own nest of eggs until they are all hatched, or perhaps while she is attending her own brood, she takes under her care and protection, as many as she can get at one time, either from her own particular nest or others: but certain it is, that the young are not left to shift for themselves, having had frequent opportunities of seeing the female alligator, leading about the shores her train of young ones, just like a hen does her brood of chickens, and she is equally assiduous and courageous in defending the young, which are under their care, and providing for their subsistence; and when she is basking upon the warm banks, with her brood around her, you may hear the young ones continually whining and barking, like young puppies. I believe but few of a brood live to the years of full growth and magnitude, as the old feed on the young as long as they can make prey of them.

The alligator when full grown is a very large and terrible creature, and of prodigious strength, activity and swiftness in the water. I have seen them twenty feet in length, and some are supposed to be twenty-two or twenty-three feet; their body is as large as that of a horse; their shape exactly resembles that of a lizard, except their tail, which is flat or cuniform, being compressed on each side, and gradually diminishing from the abdomen to the extremity, which, with the whole body is covered with horny plates or squamae, impenetrable when on the body of the live animal, even to a rifle ball, except about their head and just behind their fore-legs or arms, where it is said they are only vulnerable. The head of a full grown one is about three feet, and the mouth opens nearly the same length, the eyes are small in proportion and seem sunk deep in the head, by means of the prominency of the brows; the nostrils are large, inflated and prominent on the top, so that the head in the water, resembles, at a distance, a great chunk of wood floating about. Only the upper jaw moves, which they raise almost perpendicular, so as to form a right angle with the lower one. In the fore part of the upper jaw, on each side, just under the nostrils, are two very large, thick, strong teeth or tusks, not very sharp, but rather the shape of a cone, these are as white as the finest polished ivory, and are not covered by any skin or lips, and always in sight, which gives the creature a frightful appearance; in the lower jaw are holes opposite to these teeth, to receive them; when they clap their jaws together it causes a surprising noise, like that which is made by forcing a heavy plank with violence upon the ground, and may be heard at a great distance.

But what is yet more surprising to a stranger, is the incredible loud and terrifying roar, which they are capable of making, especially in the spring season, their breeding time; it most resembles very heavy distant thunder, not only shaking the air and waters, but causing the earth to tremble; and when hundreds and thousands are roaring at the same time, you can scarcely be persuaded, but that the whole globe is violently and dangerously agitated.

An old champion, who is perhaps absolute sovereign of a little lake or lagoon (when fifty less than himself are obliged to content themselves with swelling and roaring in little coves round about) darts forth from the reedy coverts all at once, on the surface of the waters, in a right line; at first seemingly as rapid as lightning, but gradually more slowly until he arrives at the center of the lake, when he stops; he now swells himself by drawing in wind and water through his mouth, which causes a loud sonorous rattling in the throat for near a minute, but it is immediately forced out again through his mouth and nostrils, with a loud noise, brandishing his tail in the air, and the vapour ascending from his nostrils like smoke. At other times, when swollen to an extent ready to burst, his head and tail lifted up, he spins or twirls round on the surface of the water. He acts his part like an Indian chief when rehearsing his feats of war, and then retiring, the exhibition is continued by others who dare to step forth, and strive to excel each other, to gain the attention of the favourite female.

Having gratified my curiosity at this general breeding place and nursery of crocodiles, I continued my voyage up the river without being greatly disturbed by them: in my way I observed islets or floating fields of the bright green Pistia, decorated with other amphibious plants, as Senecio Jacobea,[9] Persicaria amphibia,[10] Coreopsis bidens,[11] Hydrocotile fluitans,[12] and many others of less note. . . .

---

9. Ragwort.

10. Smart weld.

11. Beggar ticks.

12. Water pennywort.

JUPITER HAMMON (1711–1806?)

The first published black American poet, Jupiter Hammon was born on the Henry Lloyd plantation at Oyster Bay, Long Island, New York. Limited information is available about Hammon's life. Hammon's parents were probably born in Africa and later captured, enslaved, and brought to the Americas. Hammon was owned by several generations of the Lloyd family, for whom he worked as a clerk and bookkeeper. He seems to have received some education while he was with the Lloyds, perhaps from the family itself or else from any one of a number of itinerant ministers in the area. Spirituality was evidently an important part of Hammon's life from an early age, and unlike many slaves in the area, he was a Christian. It is likely that he preached to audiences in New York and later in Connecticut. In 1760, when Hammon was nearly fifty, he published his first poem, "An Evening Thought: Salvation by Christ, with Penitential Cries."

After the death of Henry Lloyd, Hammon moved to Hartford, Connecticut, with his new master Joseph Lloyd, a revolutionary supporter who fled from the British on Long Island in 1776. While in Connecticut, Hammon published both poetry and prose. He later explained that these works "were well received, not only by those of my own colour, but by a number of white people, who thought they might do good among the servants." Once the Revolution ended, Hammon returned to New York, this time with his third master, John Lloyd. There he published his final work, *An Address to the Negroes in the State of New-York* (1787), which received significant praise from the Pennsylvania Society for Promoting the Abolition of Slavery. Hammon dedicated the *Address* to the African Society of New York, an African mutual aid society. Members of the Society of Friends (Quakers) seem to have supported Hammon's publication efforts, and after his death, both the Oyster Bay and Philadelphia Friends reprinted his *Address*.

All Hammon's writing is deeply religious, and it emphasizes the importance of spiritual and moral reformation for people of African descent. The fact that every one of his publications identifies him as a "servant" to the Lloyds reminds readers of the clear connection between Hammon's access to publication, his words, and his position as a slave. Thus his advice to Africans, in particular, must be understood in the context of circumstances surrounding his publication, as well as the context of the religious beliefs he expressed. Africans and those of African descent had few options regarding publication. All Hammon's writings reflect this complicated speaking, writing, and publishing position.

AN EVENING THOUGHT. SALVATION BY CHRIST, WITH PENETENTIAL CRIES

Composed by Jupiter Hammon, a Negro Belonging to Mr. Lloyd, of Queen's-Village, on Long-Island, the 25th of December, 1760.[1]

SALVATION comes by Jesus Christ alone,
  The only Son of God;
Redemption now to every one,
  That love his holy Word.

Dear Jesus we would fly to Thee,
  And leave off every Sin,
Thy tender Mercy well agree;
  Salvation from our King.
Salvation comes now from the Lord,
  Our victorious King;
His holy Name be well ador'd,
  Salvation surely bring.
Dear Jesus give thy Spirit now,
  Thy Grace to every Nation,
That han't the Lord to whom we bow,
  The Author of Salvation.
Dear Jesus unto Thee we cry,
  Give us thy Preparation;
Turn not away thy tender Eye;
  We seek thy true Salvation.
Salvation comes from God we know,

---

1. The poem was first published as a broadside, a single long sheet suitable for passing or posting.

The true and only One;
It's well agreed and certain true,
　He gave his only Son.
Lord hear our penetential Cry:
　Salvation from above;
It is the Lord that doth supply,
　With his Redeeming Love.
Dear Jesus by thy precious Blood,
　The World Redemption have:
Salvation comes now from the Lord,
　He being thy captive Slave.

Dear Jesus let the Nations cry,
　And all the People say,
Salvation comes from Christ on high,
　Haste on Tribunal Day.
We cry as Sinners to the Lord,
　Salvation to obtain;
It is firmly fixt his holy Word,
　Ye shall not cry in vain.
Dear Jesus unto Thee we cry,
　And make our Lamentation:
O let our Prayers ascend on high;
　We felt thy Salvation.
Lord turn our dark benighted Souls;
　Give us a true Motion,
And let the Hearts of all the World,
　Make Christ their Salvation.
Ten Thousand Angels cry to Thee,
　Yea louder than the Ocean.
Thou art the Lord, we plainly see;
　Thou art the true Salvation.
Now is the Day, excepted Time;
　The Day of Salvation;[2]
Increase your Faith, do not repine:
　Awake ye every Nation.
Lord unto whom now shall we go,
　Or seek a safe Abode;
Thou hast the Word Salvation too
　The only Son of God.
Ho! every one that hunger hath,
　Or pineth after me,
Salvation be thy leading Staff,
　To set the Sinner free.
Dear Jesus unto Thee we fly;
　Depart, depart from Sin,

Salvation doth at length supply,
　The Glory of our King.
Come ye Blessed of the Lord,
　Salvation gently given;
O turn your Hearts, accept the Word,
　Your Souls are fit for Heaven.
Dear Jesus we now turn to Thee,
　Salvation to obtain;
Our Hearts and Souls do meet again,
　To magnify thy Name.
Come holy Spirit, Heavenly Dove,
　The Object of our Care;
Salvation doth increase our Love;

　Our Hearts hath felt thy fear.
Now Glory be to God on High,
　Salvation high and low;
And thus the Soul on Christ rely,
　To Heaven surely go.
Come Blessed Jesus, Heavenly Dove,
　Accept Repentance here;
Salvation give, with tender Love;
　Let us with Angels share.

———

AN ADDRESS TO
MISS PHILLIS WHEATLY,
ETHIOPIAN POETESS

Hartford, August 4, 1778
AN ADDRESS to Miss PHILLIS WHEATLY,
Ethiopian Poetess, in Boston, who came from Africa
at eight years of age, and soon became acquainted
with the Gospel of Jesus Christ.[1]

Miss WHEATLY; pray give leave to express as follows:

1.

O Come you pious youth! adore
　The wisdom of thy God,　　　　　ECCLES. XII.
In bringing thee from distant shore,
　To learn his holy word.

2.

Thou mightst been left behind,
　Amidst a dark abode;　　　PSAL. CXXXV, 2, 3.

———

2. See 2 Corinthians 6:2.

1. "An Address to Miss Phillis Wheatly" was given a separate publication run in Hartford, Connecticut, August 4, 1778.

God's tender mercy still combin'd,
    Thou hast the holy word.

3.

Fair wisdom's ways are paths of peace,
    And they that walk therein,   PSAL. I. I, 2;
Shall reap the joys that never cease,   PROV. III, 7.
    And Christ shall be their king.

4.

God's tender mercy brought thee here,
    Tost o'er the raging main;   PSAL. CIII, I, 3, 4.
In Christian faith thou hast a share,
    Worth all the gold of Spain.[2]

5.

While thousands tossed by the sea,
    And others settled down,   DEATH.
God's tender mercy set thee free
    From dangers still unknown.

6.

That thou a pattern still might be,
    To youth of Boston town,   2 CORV, 10.
The blessed Jesus set thee free,
    From every sinful wound.

7.

The blessed Jesus, who came down,
    Unvail'd [sic] his sacred face,   ROM. V, 21.
To cleanse the soul of every wound,
    And give repenting grace.

8.

That we poor sinners may obtain
    The pardon of our sin;   PSAL. XXXIV, 6, 7, 8.
Dear blessed Jesus now constrain,
    And bring us flocking in.

9.

Come you, Phillis, now aspire,
    And seek the living God,   MATTH. VII, 7, 8.
So step by step thou mayst go higher,
    Till perfect in the word.

10.

While thousands mov'd to distant shore,
    And others left behind,   PSAL. LXXXIX, I.
The blessed Jesus still adore,
    Implant this in thy mind.

---

2. After Portugal, Spain's leadership in the slave trade and its responsibility for introducing slavery to the Western Hemisphere were well known to readers.

11.

Thou hast left the heathen shore,
    Thro' mercy of the Lord,   PSAL. XXXIV, I, 2, 3.
Among the heathen live no more,
    Come magnify thy God.

12.

I pray the living God may be,
    The shepherd of thy soul;   PSAL. LXXX, I, 2, 3.
His tender mercies still are free,
    His mysteries to unfold.

13.

Thou, Phillis, when thou hunger hast,
    Or pantest for thy God;   PSAL. XIII, I, 2, 3.
Jesus Christ is thy relief,
    Thou hast the holy word.

14.

The bounteous mercies of the Lord,
    Are hid beyond the sky,   PSAL. XIV, 10, 11.
And holy souls that love his word,
    Shall taste them when they die.

15.

These bounteous mercies are from God,
    The merits of his Son;   PSAL. XXXIV, 15.
The humble soul that loves his word,
    He chooses for his own.

16.

Come, dear Phillis, be advis'd,
    To drink Samaria's flood: JOHN IV, 13, 14.
There nothing is that shall suffice,
    But Christ's redeeming blood.

17.

While thousands muse with earthly toys,
    And range about the street,   MATTH. VI, 33.
Dear Phillis, seek for heaven's joys,
    Where we do hope to meet.

18.

When God shall send his summons down,
    And number saints together,   PSAL. CXVI, 15.
Blest angels chant, (triumphant sound)
    Come live with me for ever.

19.

The humble soul shall fly to God,
    And leave the things of time,   MATTH. V, 3, 8.
Start forth as 'twere at the first word,
    To taste things more divine.

20.

Behold! the soul shall waft away,
    Whene'er we come to die,   I COR. XV, 51, 52, 53.

And leave its cottage made of clay,
  In twinkling of an eye.

21.

Now glory be to the Most High,
  United praises given,   PSAL. CL, 6.
By all on earth, incessantly,
  And all the host of heav'n.

Composed by JUPITER HAMMON, a Negro Man belonging to Mr. Joseph Lloyd, of Queen's Village on Long-Island, now in Hartford.

The above lines are published by the Author, and a number of his friends, who desire to join with him in their best regards to Miss Wheatly.

———

A POEM FOR CHILDREN WITH THOUGHTS ON DEATH[1]

I

O Ye young and thoughtless youth,
  Come seek the living God,
The scriptures are a sacred truth,
  Ye must believe the word.

ECCLE. XII. I.

II

Tis God alone can make you wise,
  His wisdom's from above,
He fills the soul with sweet supplies
  By his redeeming love.

PROV. IV. 7.

III

Remember youth the time is short,
  Improve the present day
And pray that God may guide your thoughts,
  and teach your lips to pray.

PSALM XXX. 9.

IV

To pray unto the most high God,
  and beg restraining grace,
Then by the power of his word
  You'l see the Saviour's face.

V

Little children they may die,
  Turn to their native dust,
Their souls shall leap beyond the skies,
  And live among the just.

VI

Like little worms they turn and crawl,
  and gasp for every breath.
The blessed Jesus sends his call,
  and takes them to his rest.

VII

Thus the youth are born to die,
  The time is hastening on,
The Blessed Jesus rends the sky,
  and makes his power known.

PSALM CIII. 15.

VIII

Then ye shall hear the angels sing
  The trumpet give a sound,
Glory, glory to our King,
  The Saviour's coming down.

MATTH. XXVI. 64.

IX

Start ye saints from dusty beds,
  and hear a Saviour call,
Twas Jesus Christ that died and bled,
  and thus preserv'd thy soul.

X

This the portion of the just,
  Who lov'd to serve the Lord,
Their bodies starting from the dust,
  Shall rest upon their God.

XI

They shall join that holy word,
  That angels constant sing,
Glory, glory to the Lord,
  Hallelujahs to our King.

XII

Thus the Saviour will appear,
  With guards of heavenly host,
Those blessed Saints, shall then declare,
  Tis Father, Son and Holy Ghost.

REV. I. 7, 8.

XIII

Then shall ye hear the trumpet sound,
  The graves give up their dead,

---

1. "A Poem for Children with Thoughts on Death" was published January 1, 1782, in Hartford, Connecticut. The text is from *America's First Negro Poet: The Complete Works of Jupiter Hammon of Long Island*, ed. Stanley Austin Ransom, Jr. (1970).

Those blessed saints shall quick awake,
    and leave their dusty beds.

MATTH. XXVII. 51, 52.

XIV

Then shall you hear the trumpet sound,
    and rend the native sky,
Those bodies starting from the ground,
    In the twinkling of an eye.

I COR. XV. 51, 52, 53, 54.

XV

There to sing the praise of God,
    and join the angelic train,
And by the power of his word,
    Unite together again.

XVI

Where angels stand for to admit
    Their souls at the first word,
Cast sceptres down at Jesus feet
    Crying holy holy Lord.

XVII

Now glory be unto our God
    all praise be justly given,
Ye humble souls that love the Lord
    Come seek the joys of Heaven.

Hartford, January 1, 1782.

———

AN ADDRESS TO THE NEGROES OF THE STATE OF NEW-YORK[1]

When I am writing to you with a design to say something to you for your good, and with a view to promote your happiness, I can with truth and sincerity join with the apostle Paul, when speaking of his own nation the Jews, and say: *"That I have great heaviness and continual sorrow in my heart for my brethren, my kinsmen according to* the flesh."[2] Yes my dear brethren, when I think of you, which is very often, and of the poor, despised and miserable state you are in, as to the things of this world, and when I think of your ignorance and stupidity, and the great wickedness of the most of you, I am pained to the heart. It is at times, almost too much for human nature to bear, and I am obliged to turn my thoughts from the subject or endeavour to still my mind, by considering that it is permitted thus to be, by that God who governs all things, who setteth up one and pulleth down another. While I have been thinking on this subject, I have frequently had great struggles in my own mind, and have been at a loss to know what to do. I have wanted exceedingly to say something to you, to call upon you with the tenderness of a father and friend, and to give you the last, and I may say dying advice, of an old man, who wishes your best good in this world, and in the world to come. But while I have had such desires, a sense of my own ignorance, and unfitness to teach others, has frequently discouraged me from attempting to say any thing to you; yet when I thought of your situation, I could not rest easy.

When I was at Hartford in Connecticut, where I lived during the war, I published several pieces which were well received, not only by those of my own colour, but by a number of the white people, who thought they might do good among their servants. This is one consideration, among others, that emboldens me now to publish what I have written to you. Another is, I think you will be more likely to listen to what is said, when you know it comes from a negro, one of your own nation and colour, and therefore can have no interest in deceiving you, or in saying any thing to you, but what he really thinks is your interest, and duty to comply with. My age, I think, gives me some right to speak to you, and reason to expect you will hearken to my advice. I am now upwards of seventy years old, and cannot expect, though I am well, and able to do almost any kind of business, to live much longer. I have passed the common bounds set for man, and must soon go the way of all the earth. I have had more experience in the world than most of you, and I have seen a great deal of the vanity and wickedness of it, I have great reason to be thankful that my lot has been so much better than most slaves have had. I suppose I have had more advantages and privileges than most of you, who are slaves, have ever known, and I believe more than many white people have

———

1. *An Address to the Negroes of the State of New-York* was first published in New York in 1787. The text is from *America's First Negro Poet: The Complete Works of Jupiter Hammon of Long Island,* ed. Stanley Austin Ransom, Jr. (1970).

2. Compare with Romans 9:2–3.

enjoyed, for which I desire to bless God, and pray that he may bless those who have given them to me. I do not, my dear friends, say these things about myself, to make you think that I am wiser or better than others; but that you might hearken, without prejudice, to what I have to say to you on the following particulars.

1st. Respecting obedience to masters. Now whether it is right, and lawful, in the sight of God, for them to make slaves of us or not. I am certain that while we are slaves, it is our duty to obey our masters, in all their lawful commands, and mind them unless we are bid to do that which we know to be sin, or forbidden in God's word. The apostle Paul says: "Servants be obedient to them that are your masters according to the flesh, with fear and trembling in singleness in your heart as unto Christ: Not with eye service, as men pleasers, but as the servants of Christ doing the will of God from the heart: With good will doing service to the Lord, and not to men: Knowing that whatever thing a man doeth the same shall he receive of the Lord, whether he be bond or free."[3]—Here is a plain command of God for us to obey our masters. It may seem hard for us, if we think our masters wrong in holding us slaves, to obey in all things, but who of us dare dispute with God! He has commanded us to obey, and we ought to do it cheerfully, and freely. This should be done by us, not only because God commands, but because our own peace and comfort depend upon it. As we depend upon our masters, for what we eat and drink and wear, and for all our comfortable things in this world, we cannot be happay, unless we please them. This we cannot do without obeying them freely, without muttering or finding fault. If a servant strives to please his master and studies and takes pains to do it, I believe there are but few masters who would use such a servant cruelly. Good servants frequently make good masters. If your master is really hard, unreasonable and cruel, there is no way so likely for you to convince him of it, as always to obey his commands, and try to serve him, and take care of his interest, and try to promote it all in your power. If you are proud and stubborn and always finding fault, your master will think the fault lies wholly on your side; but if you are humble, and meek, and bear all things patiently, your master may think he is wrong; if he does not, his neighbours will be apt to see it, and will befriend you, and try to alter his conduct. If this does not do, you must cry to him, who has the hearts of all men in his hands, and turneth them as the rivers of waters are turned.

2nd. The particular I would mention, is honesty and faithfulness.

You must suffer me now to deal plainly with you, my dear brethren, for I do not mean to flatter or omit speaking the truth, whether it is for you, or against you. How many of you are there, who allow yourselves in stealing from your masters. It is very wicked for you not to take care of your masters' goods; but how much worse is it to pilfer and and steal from them, whenever you think you shall not be found out. This you must know is very wicked and provoking to God. There are none of you so ignorant but that you must know that this is wrong. Though you may try to excuse yourselves by saying that your masters are unjust to you, and though you may try to quiet your consciences in this way, yet if you are honest in owning the truth, you must think it is as wicked, and on some accounts more wicked to steal from your masters, than from others.

We cannot certainly have any excuse, either for taking any thing that belongs to our masters, without their leave, or for being unfaithful in their business. It is our duty to be faithful, *not with eye service as men pleasers.*[4] We have no right to stay, when we are sent on errands, any longer than to do the business we were sent upon. All the time spent idly is spent wickedly, and is unfaithfulness to our masters. In these things I must say, that I think many of you are guilty. I know that many of you endeavour to excuse yourselves, and say that you have nothing that you can call your own, and that you are under great temptations to be unfaithful and take from your masters. But this will not do; God will certainly punish you for stealing, and for being unfaithful. All that we have to mind, is our own duty. If God has put us in bad circumstances, that is not our fault, and he will not punish us for it. If any are wicked in keeping us so, we cannot help it; they must answer to God for it. Nothing will serve as an excuse to us for not doing our duty. The same God will judge both them and us. Pray then, my dear friends, fear to offend in this way, but be faithful to God, to your masters, and to your own souls.

The next thing I would mention and warn you against, is profaneness. This you know is forbidden by God. Christ tells us, "Swear not at all,"[5] and again it is said, "Thou shalt

---

3. Ephesians 6:5–8.

4. See Ephesians 6:6.

5. See Matthew 5:34.

not take the name of the Lord thy God in vain, for the Lord will not hold him guiltless that taketh his name in vain."[6] Now, though the great God has forbidden it, yet how dreadfully profane are many, and I don't know but I may say the most of you! How common is it to hear you take the terrible and awful name of the great God in vain!—To swear by it, and by Jesus Christ, his Son.—How common is it to hear you wish damnation to your companions, and to your own souls—and to sport with, in the name of Heaven and Hell, as if there were no such places for you to hope for or to fear. Oh my friends, be warned to forsake this dreadful sin of profaneness. Pray, my dear friends, believe and realize that there is a God—that he is great and terrible beyond what you can think—that he keeps you in life every moment—and that he can send you to that awful Hell that you laugh at, in an instant, and confine you there for ever; and that he will certainly do it, if you do not repent. You certainly do not believe that there is a God, or that there is a Heaven or Hell, or you would never trifle with them. It would make you shudder, if you hear others do it, if you believe them as much as you believe any thing you see with your bodily eyes.

I have heard some learned and good men say that the heathen, and all that worshipped false gods, never spoke lightly or irreverently of their gods; they never took their names in vain, or jested with those things which they held sacred. Now, why should the true God, who made all things, be treated worse in this respect than those false gods that were made of wood and stone? I believe it is because Satan tempts men to do it. He tried to make them love their false gods, and to speak well of them; but he wishes to have men think lightly of the true God, to take his holy name in vain, and to scoff at and make a jest of all things that are really good. You may think that Satan has not power to do so much, and have so great influence on the minds of men: But the Scripture says, "*He goeth about like a roaring Lion, seeking whom he may devour*[7]—*That he is the prince of the power of the air—and that he rules in the hearts of the children of disobedience*[8]—*and that*

wicked men are led captive by him, to do his will."[9] All those of you who are profane, are serving the Devil. You are doing what he tempts and desires you to do. If you could see him with your bodily eyes, would you like to make an agreement with him to serve him, and do as he bid you? I believe most of you would be shocked at this; but you may be certain that all of you who allow yourselves in this sin, are really serving him, and to just as good purpose, as if you met him and promised to dishonor God, and serve him with all your might. Do you believe this? It is true whether you believe it or not. Some of you to excuse yourselves, may plead the example of others, and say that you hear a great many white people, who know more than such poor ignorant Negroes as you are, and some who are rich and great gentlemen, swear, and talk profanely; and some of you may say this of your masters, and say no more than is true. But all this is not a sufficient excuse for you. You know that murder is wicked. If you saw your master kill a man, do you suppose this would be any excuse for you, if you should commit the same crime? You must know it would not; nor will your hearing him curse and swear, and take the name of God in vain, or any other man, be he ever so great or rich, excuse you. God is greater than all other beings, and him we are bound to obey. To him we must give an account for every *idle* word that we speak.[10] He will bring us all, rich and poor, white and black, to his judgment seat. If we are found among those who *feared his name,* and *trembled at his word,* we shall be called good and faithful servants. Our slavery will be at an end, and though ever so mean, low and despised in this world, we shall sit with God in his kingdom, as Kings and Priests, and rejoice for ever and ever. Do not then, my dear friends, take God's holy name in vain, or speak profanely in any way. Let not the example of others lead you into the sin, but reverence and fear that great *and fearful name, the Lord our God.*

I might now caution you against other sins to which you are exposed; but as I meant only to mention those you were exposed to, more than others, by your being slaves, I will conclude what I have to say to you, by advising you

---

6. Exodus 20:7.

7. See 1 Peter 5:8, "Be sober, be vigilant, because your adversary the devil, as a roaring lion, walketh about, seeking whom he may devour."

8. See Ephesians 2:2, "Wherein the time past ye walked according to the course of this world, according to the prince of the power of the air, the spirit that now worketh in the children of disobedience."

9. See 2 Timothy 2:26, "And *that* they may recover themselves out of the snare of the devil, who are taken captive by him at his will."

10. See Matthew 12:36, "But I say unto you, That every idle word that men shall speak, they shall give account thereof in the day of judgment."

to become religious, and to make religion the great business of your lives.

Now I acknowledge that liberty is a great thing, and worth seeking for, if we can get it honestly; and by our good conduct prevail on our masters to set us free: though for my own part I do not wish to be free, yet I should be glad if others, especially the young Negroes, were to be free; for many of us who are grown up slaves, and have always had masters to take care of us, should hardly know how to take care of ourselves; and it may be more for our own comfort to remain as we are. That liberty is a great thing we may know from our own feelings, and we may likewise judge so from the conduct of the white people in the late war. How much money has been spent, and how many lives have been lost to defend their liberty! I must say that I have hoped that God would open their eyes, when they were so much engaged for liberty, to think of the state of the poor blacks, and to pity us. He has done it in some measure, and has raised us up many friends; for which we have reason to be thankful, and to hope in his mercy. What may be done further, he only knows, for *known unto God are all his ways from the beginning.* But this, my dear brethren, is by no means the greatest thing we have to be concerned about. Getting our liberty in this world is nothing to our having the liberty of the children of God. Now the Bible tells us that we are all, by nature, sinners; that we are slaves to sin and Satan, and that unless we are converted, or born again, we must be miserable for ever. Christ says, except a man be born again, he cannot see the kingdom of God; and all that do not see the kingdom of God, must be in the kingdom of darkness. There are but two places where all go after death, white and black, rich and poor; those places are Heaven and Hell. Heaven is a place made for those who are born again, and who love God; and it is a place where they will be happy for ever. Hell is a place made for those who hate God, and are his enemies, and where they will be miserable to all eternity. Now you may think you are not enemies to God, and do not hate him: but if your heart has not been changed, and you have not become true Christians, you certainly are enemies to God, and have been opposed to him ever since you were born. Many of you, I suppose, never think of this, and are almost as ignorant as the beasts that perish. Those of you who can read, I must beg you to read the Bible; and whenever you can get time, study the Bible; and if you can get no other time, spare some of your time from sleep, and learn what the mind and will of God is. But what shall I say to them who cannot read? This lay with great weight on my mind, when I

thought of writing to my poor brethren; but I hope that those who can read will take pity on them, and read what I have to say to them. In hopes of this, I will beg of you to spare no pains in trying to learn to read. If you are once engaged, you may learn. Let all the time you can get be spent in trying to learn to read. Get those who can read, to learn you; but remember, that what you learn for, is to read the Bible. If there was no Bible, it would be no matter whether you could read or not. Reading other books would do you no good. But the Bible is the word of God, and tells you what you must do to please God; it tells you how you may escape misery, and be happy for ever. If you see most people neglect the Bible, and many that can read never look into it, let it not harden you, and make you think lightly of it, and that it is a book of no worth. All those who are really good love the Bible, and meditate on it day and night. In the Bible God has told us every thing it is necessary we should know, in order to be happy here and hereafter. The Bible is a revelation of the mind and will of God to men. Therein we may learn what God is. That he made all things by the power of his word; and that he made all things for his own glory, and not for our glory. That he is over all, and above all his creatures, and more above them than we can think or conceive—that they can do nothing without him—that he upholds them all, and will overrule all things for his own glory. In the Bible likewise we are told what man is. That he was at first made holy, in the image of God; that he fell from that state of holiness, and became an enemy to God; and that since the fall, *all the imaginations of the thoughts of his heart are evil, and only evil, and that continually. That the carnal mind is not subject to the law of God, neither indeed can be.*[11] And that all mankind were under the wrath and curse of God, and must have been for ever miserable, if they had been left to suffer what their sins deserved. It tells us that God, to save some of mankind, sent his Son into this world to die, in the room and stead of sinners; and that now God can save from eternal misery all that believe in his Son, and take him for their Saviour; and that all are called upon to repent, and believe in Jesus Christ. It tells us that those who do repent and believe, and are friends to Christ, shall have many trials and sufferings in this world, but that they shall be happy for ever, after death, and reign with Christ to all eternity. The Bible tells us that this world is a place of trial, and that there is no other time or

---

11. Hammon paraphrases several Bible verses. See Genesis 6:5, Jeremiah 7:24, and Romans 1:21, 8:7.

place for us to alter, but in this life. If we are Christians when we die, we shall awake to the resurrection of life; if not, we shall awake to the resurrection of damnation. It tells us we must all live in Heaven or Hell, be happy or miserable, and that without end. The Bible does not tell us of but two places, for all to go to. There is no place for innocent folks, that are not Christians. There is no place for ignorant folks, that did not know how to be Christians. What I mean is, that there is no place besides Heaven and Hell. These two places will receive all mankind; for Christ says, there are but two sorts, *he that is not with me is against me; and he that gathereth not with me, scattereth abroad.*[12]—The Bible likewise tells us that this world, and all things in it, shall be burnt up—and that "God has appointed a day in which he will judge the world; and that he will bring every secret thing, whether it be good or bad, into judgment—that which is done in secret shall be declared on the house top." I do not know, nor do I think any can tell, but that the day of judgment may last a thousand years. God could tell the state of all his creatures in a moment, but then every thing that every one has done, through his whole life, is to be told before the whole world of angels and men. Oh how solemn is the thought! You and I must stand, and hear every thing we have thought or done, however secret, however wicked and vile, told before all the men and women that ever have been, or ever will be, and before all the angels, good and bad.

Now, my dear friends, seeing the Bible is the word of God, and every thing in it is true, and it reveals such awful and glorious things, what can be more important than that you should learn to read it; and when you have learned to read, that you should study it day and night. There are some things very encouraging in God's word for such ignorant creatures as we are; for God hath not chosen the rich of this world. Not many rich, not many noble are called, but God hath chosen the weak things of this world, and things which are not, to confound the things that are. And when the great and the rich refused coming to the gospel feast, the servant was told to go into the highways and hedges, and compel those poor creatures that he found there, to come in. Now, my brethren, it seems to me that there are no people that ought to attend to the hope of happiness in another world so much as we. Most of us are cut off from comfort and happiness here in this world, and can expect nothing from it. Now seeing this is the case,

---

12. Matthew 12:30.

why should we not take care to be happy after death? Why should we spend our whole lives in sinning against God; and be miserable in this world, and in the world to come? If we do thus, we shall certainly be the greatest fools. We shall be slaves here, and slaves for ever. We cannot plead so great temptations to neglect religion as others. Riches and honours which drown the greater part of mankind, who have the gospel, in perdition, can be little or no temptations to us.

We have so little time in this world that it is no matter how wretched and miserable we are, if it prepares us for Heaven. What is forty, fifty, or sixty years, when compared to eternity? When thousands and millions of years have rolled away, this eternity will be no nigher coming to an end. Oh how glorious is an eternal life of happiness! And how dreadful an eternity of misery! Those of us who have had religious masters, and have been taught to read the Bible, and have been brought by their example and teaching to a sense of divine things, how happy shall we be to meet them in Heaven, where we shall join them in praising God for ever. But if any of us have had such masters, and yet have lived and died wicked, how will it add to our misery to think of our folly. If any of us, who have wicked and profane masters, should become religious, how will our estates be changed in another world. Oh, my friends, let me intreat of you to think on these things, and to live as if you believed them to be true. If you become Christians, you will have reason to bless God for ever, that you have been brought into a land where you have heard the gospel, though you have been slaves. If we should ever get to Heaven, we shall find nobody to reproach us for being black, or for being slaves. Let me beg of you, my dear African brethren, to think very little of your bondage in this life; for your thinking of it will do you no good. If God designs to set us free, he will do it in his own time and way; but think of your bondage to sin and Satan, and do not rest until you are delivered from it.

We cannot be happy, if we are ever so free or ever so rich, while we are servants of sin, and slaves to Satan. We must be miserable here, and to all eternity.

I will conclude what I have to say with a few words to those Negroes who have their liberty. The most of what I have said to those who are slaves, may be of use to you; but you have more advantages, on some accounts, if you will improve your freedom, as you may do, than they. You have more time to read God's holy word, and to take care of the salvation of your souls. Let me beg of you to spend your time in this way, or it will be better for you if you had always been slaves. If you think seriously of the matter, you must conclude that if you do not use your freedom to promote the salvation of your souls, it will not be of any lasting good to you. Besides all this, if you are idle, and take to bad courses, you will hurt those of your brethren who are slaves, and do all in your power to prevent their being free. One great reason that is given by some for not freeing us, I understand, is, that we should not know how to take care of ourselves, and should take to bad courses; that we should be lazy and idle, and get drunk and steal. Now all those of you who follow any bad courses, and who do not take care to get an honest living by your labour and industry, are doing more to prevent our being free than any body else. Let me beg of you then, for the sake of your own good and happiness, in time, and for eternity, and for the sake of your poor brethren, who are still in bondage, "*to lead quiet and peaceable lives in all Godliness and honesty,*"[13] and may God bless you, and bring you to his kingdom, for Christ's sake, Amen.

---

13. See 1 Timothy 2:2.

BRITON HAMMON (FLOURISHED 1760)

Briton Hammon's narrative is an important indicator that Africans in the Americas were telling their stories to one another all along, although few of these stories reached print in the way that Hammon's did in the middle of the eighteenth century. Some scholars have asserted that Hammon wrote the narrative independently, without anyone else's assistance, while others have concluded that some of the narrative or perhaps all of it was transcribed by an amanuensis. Hammon's status at the time his narrative was written down also remains a mystery. While some scholars have argued that the description of Hammon as "servant to General Winslow" indicates he was in the employ of John Winslow (1703–74), perhaps as an indentured servant, others assert that Hammon was indeed a slave to Winslow. The uncertainty surrounding this text and author reflect the complex social place inhabited by early African American writers.

Beyond what is available as background in his narrative, little is known about Hammon's life. In 1747, after leaving his master in Marshfield, Massachusetts, Hammon worked on a ship bound for Jamaica. Later, off the Florida coast, the ship was attacked by Native Americans, and Hammon, the only survivor, was taken captive. Hammon escaped from his Indian captors, only to be taken prisoner by the Spanish in Cuba for four and a half years. Once he escaped from the Spanish, he worked in Cuba and later on a ship bound for England. In London he was amazed to find his master, General Winslow, from whom he had been absent for thirteen years. The two returned together to Boston in 1760, where Hammon's narrative was soon published.

Why would the first prose text published in British North America by a person of African descent adopt methods used in Indian captivity narratives? Whether he was a servant or a slave, Hammon would have inhabited a low social position within the community. Indeed, in the narrative itself, Hammon refers repeatedly to his "low" status, yet only once—on the title page—does the narrative mention Hammon's race. In the year 1760, when Hammon's narrative reached print, the Seven Years War was taking place, and the stress of a wartime economy created a situation in which servants of all races assumed important roles. People like Hammon were being welcomed back to Boston, a city where the wartime population of men was limited, making laborers more scarce. Furthermore, Indian captivity narratives had remained popular in New England, especially during eras of economic and political uncertainty. They were particularly meaningful during such times because traditionally they had clearly identified an enemy and celebrated the return of the former captive to the community. Numerous questions about Hammon's narrative remain, however. The narrative imitates aspects of standard Indian captivity fare and spiritual autobiography, yet it also bears similarities with later slave narratives that served as evaluations and critiques of slavery. What would it mean to end a slave narrative, or an Indian captivity narrative, for that matter, with a happy reunion between the "servant" or slave and master? Hammon's narrative continues to challenge contemporary readers with questions about genre, authorship, and the accessibility of publication for people of African descent.

NARRATIVE OF THE UNCOMMON SUFFERINGS AND SURPRIZING DELIVERANCE OF BRITON HAMMON[1]

TO THE READER,

AS my capacities and Condition of Life are very low, it cannot be expected that I should make those Remarks on the Sufferings I have met with, or the kind Providence of a good GOD for my Preservation, as one in a higher Station: but shall leave that to the Reader as he goes along, and so I shall only relate Matters of Fact as they occur to my Mind—

On Monday, 25th Day of *December,* 1747, with the leave of my Master,[2] I went from *Marshfield,* with an Intention to go a Voyage to Sea, and the next Day, the 26th, got to *Plymouth,* where I immediately ship'd myself on board of a Sloop, Capt. *John Howland,* Master,[3] bound to *Jamaica* and the *Bay*—We sailed from *Plymouth* in a short Time, and after a pleasant Passage of about 30 Days, arrived at *Jamaica;* we was detain'd at *Jamaica* only 5 Days, from whence we sailed for the *Bay,* where we arrived safe' in 10 Days. We loaded our Vessel with Logwood, and sailed

from the *Bay* the 25th Day of May following, and the 15th Day of *June,* we were cast away on *Cape Florida,*[4] about 5 Leagues from the Shore; being now destitute of every Help, we knew not what to do or what Course to take in this our sad Condition:—The Captain was advised, intreated, and beg'd on, by every Person on board, to heave over but only 20 Ton of the *Wood,* and we should get clear, which if he had done, might have sav'd his Vessel and Cargo, and not only so, but his own Life, as well as the Lives of the Mate and Nine Hands, as I shall presently relate.

After being upon this Reef two Days, the Captain order'd the Boat to be hoisted out, and then ask'd who were willing to tarry on board? The whole Crew was for going on Shore at this Time, but as the Boat would not carry 12 persons at once, and to prevent any Uneasiness, the Captain, a Passenger, and one Hand tarry'd on board, while the Mate, with Seven Hands besides myself, were order'd to go on Shore in the Boat, which as soon as we had reached, one half were to be Landed, and the other four to return to the Sloop, to fetch the Captain and the others on Shore. The Captain order'd us to take with us our Arms, Ammunition, Provisions and Necessaries for Cooking, as also a Sail to make a Tent of, to shelter us from the Weather; after having left the Sloop we stood towards the Shore, and being within Two Leagues of the same, we espy'd a Number of Canoes, which we at first took to be Rocks, but soon found our Mistake, for we perceiv'd they moved towards us; we presently saw an English Colour hoisted in one of the Canoes, at the Sight of which we were not a little rejoiced, but on our advancing yet nearer, we found them, to our very great Surprize, to be *Indians* of which there were Sixty; being now so near them we could not possibly make our Escape; they soon came up with and boarded us, took away all our Arms, Ammunition, and Provision. The whole Number of Canoes (being about Twenty,) then made for the Sloop, except Two which they left to guard us, who order'd us to follow on with them; the Eighteen which made for the Sloop, went so much faster than we that they got on board above Three Hours before we came along side, and had kill'd Captain *Howland,* the Passenger and the other hand; we came to the Larboard[5] side of the Sloop, and they order'd us round to the Starboard,[6] and as we were passing round the Bow, we saw the whole Number of *Indians,* advancing forward and loading their Guns,

---

1. The complete title of the original Boston 1760 publication reprinted here reads: *NARRATIVE of the UNCOMMON SUFFERINGS AND Surprizing DELIVERANCE OF* BRITON HAMMON, *a Negro Man,—Servant to GENERAL WINSLOW, of* Marshfield, *in NEW-ENGLAND; Who returned to* Boston, *after having been absent almost Thirteen Years. CONTAINING An Account of the many Hardships he underwent from the Time he left his Master's House, in the Year 1747, to the Time of his Return to* Boston.—*How he was Cast away in the Capes of Florida;—the horrid Cruelty and inhuman Barbarity of the* Indians *in murdering the whole Ship's Crew;—the Manner of his being carry'd by them into Captivity. Also, An Account of his being Confined Four Years and Seven Months in a close Dungeon,—And the remarkable Manner in which he met with his good old Master in* London; *who returned to* New-England, *a Passenger, in the same Ship.*

2. Hammon's status as a slave or (perhaps indentured) servant to the man he called his "Master," General John Winslow (1703–74) remains uncertain. The difficulty arises because the word "master" at the time was used to indicate the holder of someone else's indenture, for whom the person labored some designated amount of time, and it was used, too, to identify someone who owned slaves.

3. Howland was captain of the ship, not Hammon's owner.

4. Florida was controlled by the Spanish.

5. Larboard: the left-hand side of the ship.

6. Starboard: the right-hand side of the ship.

upon which the Mate said, *"my Lads we are all dead Men,"* and before we had got round, they discharged their Small Arms upon us, and kill'd Three of our hands, viz. *Reuben Young of Cape-Cod,* Mate; *Joseph Little* and *Lemuel Doty* of *Plymouth,* upon which I immediately jump'd overboard, chusing rather to be drowned, than to be kill'd by those barbarous and inhuman Savages. In three or four Minutes after, I heard another Volley which dispatched the other five, viz. *John Nowland,* and *Nathaniel Rich,* both belonging to *Plymouth,* and *Elkanah Collymore,* and *James Webb,* Strangers, and *Moses Newmock,* Molatto. As soon as they had kill'd the whole of the People, one of the Canoes padled after me, and soon came up with me, hawled me into the Canoe, and beat me most terribly with a Cutlass, after that they ty'd me down, then this Canoe stood for the Sloop again and as soon as she came along side, the *Indians* on board the Sloop betook themselves to their Canoes, then set the Vessel on Fire, making a prodigious shouting and hallowing like so many Devils. As soon as the Vessel was burnt down to the Water's edge, the *Indians* stood for the Shore, together with our Boat, on board of which they put 5 hands. After we came to the Shore, they led me to their Hutts, where I expected nothing but immediate Death, and as they spoke broken English, were often telling me, while coming from the Sloop to the Shore, that they intended to roast me alive. But the Providence of God order'd it other ways, for He appeared for my Help, *in this Mount of Difficulty,* and they were better to me then my Fears, and soon unbound me, but set a Guard over me every Night. They kept me with them about five Weeks, during which Time they us'd me pretty well, and gave me boil'd Corn, which was what they often eat themselves. The Way I made my Escape from these Villains was this; A Spanish Schooner arriving there from *St. Augustine,* the Master of which, whose Name was *Romond,* asked the *Indians* to let me go on board his Vessel, which they granted, and the Captain[7] knowing me very well, weigh'd Anchor and carry'd me off to the *Havanna,*[8] and after being there four Days the *Indians* came after me, and insisted on having me again, as I was their Prisoner;— They made Application to the Governor,[9] and demanded

me again from him; in answer to which the Governor told them, that as they had put the whole Crew to Death, they should not have me again, and so paid them Ten Dollars for me, adding, that he would not have them kill any Person hereafter, but take as many of them as they could, of those that should be cast away, and bring them to him for which he would pay them Ten Dollars a-head. At the *Havanna* I lived with the Governor in the Castle about a Twelve-month, where I was walking thro' the Street, I met with a Press-Gang[10] who immediately prest me, and put me into Goal, and with a Number of others I was confin'd till next Morning, when we were all brought out, and ask'd who would go on board the King's Ships, four of which having been lately built, were bound to *Old-Spain,* and on my refusing to serve on board, they put me in a close Dungeon, where I was confin'd *Four Years and seven months;* during which time I often made application to the Governor, by Persons who came to see the Prisoners, but they never acquainted him with it, nor did he know all this Time what became of me, which was the means of my being confin'd there so long. But kind Providence so order'd it, that after I had been in this Place so long as the Time mention'd above the Captain of a Merchantman, belonging to *Boston,* having sprung a Leak was obliged to put into the *Havanna* to rest, and while he was at Dinner at Mrs. *Betty Howard's,* she told the Captain of my deplorable Condition, and said she would be glad, if he could by some means or other relieve me; The Captain told Mrs. *Howard* he would use his best Endeavours for my Relief and Enlargement.

Accordingly, after Dinner, [the Captain] came to the Prison, and ask'd the Keeper if he might see me; upon his Request I was brought out of the Dungeon, and after the Captain had Interrogated me, told me, he would intercede with the Governor for my Relief out of that miserable Place, which he did, and the next Day the Governor sent an order to release me; I lived with the Governor about a Year after I was delivered from the Dungeon, in which Time I endeavour'd three Times to make my Escape, the last of which proved effectual; the first Time I got on board of Captain *Marsh,* an *English* Twenty Gun Ship, with a Number of others, and lay on board conceal'd that Night; and the next Day the Ship being under sail, I thought myself safe, and so made my Appearance upon Deck, but as soon as we were discovered the Captain or-

---

7. "The Way I came to know this Gentleman was, by his being taken last War by an *English* Privateer, and brought into *Jamaica,* while I was there." [Au.]

8. Hammon traveled on a Spanish ship to Havanna, Cuba, from St. Augustine, Florida.

9. The governor of Cuba was Francisco Antonio Cagigal de la Vega (1695–1777).

10. Press-gangs are so-called because they impressed workers—that is, they were authorized by the government to take men, sometimes by force, into service in the navy.

dered the Boat out, and sent us all on Shore—I intreated the Captain to let me, in particular, tarry on board, begging, and crying to him, to commiserate my unhappy Condition, and added, that I had been confin'd almost five Years in a close Dungeon, but the Captain would not hearken to any Intreaties, for fear of having the Governor's Displeasure, and so I was obliged to go on Shore.

After being on Shore another Twelvemonth, I endeavour'd to make my Escape the second Time, by trying to get on board of a Sloop bound to *Jamaica,* and as I was going from the City to the Sloop, was unhappily taken by the Guard, and ordered back to the Castle, and there confined.—However, in a short Time I was set at Liberty, and order'd with a Number of others to carry the[11] Bishop from the Castle, thro' the Country, to confirm the old People, baptize Children, &c. for which he receives large Sums of Money.—I was employ'd in this Service about Seven Months, during which Time I lived very well, and then returned to the Castle again, where I had my Liberty to walk about the City, and do Work for my self;—The *Beaver,* an *English* Man of War then lay in the Harbour, and having been informed by some of the Ship's Crew that she was to sail in a few Days, I had nothing now to do, but to seek an Opportunity how I should make my Escape.

Accordingly one Sunday Night the Lieutenant of the Ship with a Number of the Barge Crew were in a Tavern, and Mrs. *Howard* who had before been a Friend to me, interceded with the Lieutenant to carry me on board: the Lieutenant said he would with all his Heart, and immediately I went on board in the Barge. The next Day the *Spaniards* came along side the *Beaver,* and demanded me again, with a Number of others who had made their Escape from them, and got on board the Ship, but just before I did; but the Captain, who was a true *Englishman,* refus'd them, and said he could not answer it, to deliver up any *Englishman* under *English* Colours.—In a few Days we set Sail for *Jamaica,* where we arrived safe, after a short and pleasant Passage.

After being at *Jamaica* a short Time we sail'd for *London,* as convoy to a Fleet of Merchantmen, who all arrived safe in the *Downs,* I was turned over to another Ship, the *Arcenceil,* and there remained about a Month. From this Ship I went on board the *Sandwich* of 90 Guns; on board the *Sandwich,* I tarry'd 6 Weeks, and then was order'd on

board the *Hercules,* Capt. *John Porter,* a 74 Gun Ship, we sail'd on a Cruize, and met with a *French* 84 Gun Ship, and had a very smart Engagement,[12] in which about 70 of our Hands were Kill'd and Wounded, the Captain lost his Leg in the Engagement, and I was Wounded in the Head by a small Shot. We should have taken this Ship, if they had not cut away the most of our Rigging; however, in about three Hours after, a 64 Gun Ship, came up with and took her— I was discharged from the *Hercules* the 12th Day of *May* 1759 (having been on board of that Ship 3 Months) on account of my being disabled in the Arm, and render'd incapable of Service, after being honourably paid the Wages due to me. I was put into the *Greenwich* Hospital where I stay'd and soon recovered.—I then ship'd myself a Cook on board Captain *Martyn,* an arm'd Ship in the King's Service. I was on board this Ship almost Two Months, and after being paid my Wages, was discharg'd in the Month of *October.*—After my discharge from Captain *Martyn,* I was taken sick in *London* of a Fever, and was confin'd about 6 Weeks, where I expended all my Money, and left in very poor Circumstances; and unhappy for me I knew nothing of my *good Master's* being in *London* at this my very difficult Time. After I got well of my sickness, I ship'd myself on board of a large Ship bound to *Guinea,*[13] and being in a publick House one Evening, I overheard a Number of Persons talking about Rigging a Vessel bound to *New-England,* I ask'd them to what Part of *New-England* this Vessel was bound? They told me, to *Boston;* and having ask'd them who was Commander? they told me, Capt. *Watt;* in a few Minutes after this the Mate of the Ship came in, and I ask'd him if Captain Watt did not want a Cook, who told me he did, and that the Captain would be in, in a few Minutes; and in about half an Hour the Captain came in, and then I ship'd myself at once, after begging off from the Ship bound to *Guinea;* I work'd on board Captain *Watt's* Ship almost Three Months, before she sail'd, and one Day being at Work in the Hold, I overheard some Persons on board mention the Name of *Winslow,* at the Name of which I was very inquisitive, and having ask'd what *Winslow* they were talking about? They told me it was *General Winslow;* and that he was one of the Passengers, I ask'd them what *General Winslow?* For I never knew *my good Master,* by that Title before; but after enquiring more particularly I found it must be *Master,* and in a few Days

---

11. "He is carried (by Way of Respect) in a large Two-arm Chair; the Chair is lin'd with crimson Velvet, and supported by eight Persons." [Au.] The Bishop was Pedro Augustín Morell de Santa Cruz (1694–1768). [Ed.]

---

12. "A particular Account of this Engagement, has been Publish'd in the *Boston* News-Papers." [Au.] The identity of the French ship is uncertain. [Ed.]

13. The ship was likely headed to Africa to acquire slaves.

Time the Truth was joyfully verify'd by a happy Sight of his Person, which so overcome me, that I could not speak to him for some Time—*My good Master* was exceeding glad to see me, telling me that I was like one arose from the Dead, for he thought I had been Dead a great many Years, having heard nothing of me for almost Thirteen Years.

I think I have not deviated from Truth, in any particular of this my Narrative, and tho' I have omitted a great many Things, yet what is wrote may suffice to convince the Reader, that I have been most grievously afflicted, and yet thro' the Divine Goodness, as miraculously preserved, and delivered out of many Dangers; of which I desire to retain a *grateful Remembrance,* as long as I live in the World.

And now, That in the Providence of that GOD, who delivered his Servant David *out of the Paw of the Lion and out of the Paw of the Bear,*[14] *I am freed from a* long *and* dreadful Captivity, among worse Savages than they; *And am return'd to my* own Native Land, to Shew how Great Things the Lord hath done for Me; *I would call upon all Men, and Say,* O Magnifie the Lord with Me, and let us Exalt his Name together![15]—O that Men would Praise the Lord for His Goodness, and for his Wonderful Works to the Children of Men!

---

14. See 1 Samuel 17:37.

15. See Psalm 34:4.

SAMSON OCCOM (1723–1792)

Born to Christianized Mohegans Joshua Tomacham and Sarah in New London, Connecticut, Samson Occom became a renowned schoolteacher and a renowned minister to his people. Occom experienced difficulty attempting to live a life between two worlds, one Indian and one white settler, among the Mohegans of New London. When he was sixteen years old, he was caught up in religious revivals in the area, and he fell under the influence of the missionaries who arrived to live and work among the Indians. Several years after his conversion to Christianity, he began to study with Reverend Eleazar Wheelock, who sought to train Indian men to become missionaries to their peoples.

After studying for four years with Wheelock, Occom became a missionary and a teacher. In 1749 he was sent to become the schoolmaster to the Montauk peoples of Long Island. There he married Mary Fowler, a Montauk, with whom he eventually had ten children. In the years that followed his marriage, Occom struggled to support his large family, supplementing his income by working as a bookbinder, a fisherman, a cooper, and a farmer. He was ordained in 1759 on Long Island, where he continued his ministry as an itinerant. It was during this time that Occom served as a missionary to the Oneidas living in the territory of eastern New York. He decided he wanted to develop his own Indian Charity School, and, following up on this goal, he moved his family to Mohegan, Connecticut, in 1764 in order to help the Reverend George Whitefield raise money for Wheelock's Indian school. Working with the evangelical Whitefield stimulated Occom. He developed his own method of delivering sermons and experienced great success in raising funds. On the basis of Occom's own success in raising funds and preaching, Wheelock and others asked Occom to travel to England with the Reverend Nathaniel Whitaker to raise more money for the school. The trip to England was tremendously productive. While abroad for two years in England and Scotland, Occom raised approximately £12,000, and he preached more than three hundred sermons.

After Occom returned home, however, his relationship with Wheelock rapidly deteriorated. While he was away, he had assumed that Wheelock was looking after his family, as Wheelock had promised to do, but instead, upon arriving back in Connecticut, Occom faced disappoinment after disappointment. Wheelock appropriated most of the funds Occom had obtained in Britain, so that Occom's school never materialized in the way that he had hoped, and Occom suffered personal financial difficulty. Occom's frustration reached its peak when Wheelock made clear his plans for the major part of the money Occom had raised: Wheelock determined to move the Indian charity school to Dartmouth. Soon, the school that became Dartmouth College enrolled only three Indian students, with the majority of the enrollees being young men from English farms and towns in Connecticut and Massachusetts. The schooling project thus drifted away from its original purpose. Occom had no alternative but to break from Wheelock. He wrote a ten-page autobiography, dated September 17, 1768, which shows the level of his frustration. Beginning as a spiritual autobiography, the narrative ends as a strong castigation of a leader and a system that had let Occom down.

Occom devoted the remainder of his life to preaching and assisting Native peoples. He traveled extensively to preach and gain financial support for resettling Christian Indians on Oneida lands in New York, a plan created and supported by the efforts of his son-in-law, Joseph Johnson. What became known as the Brotherton settlement in eastern New York was composed of Christian Indians from seven New England towns. Occom moved his family to Brotherton in 1789, and lived there the remainder of his life, amid ongoing turmoil surrounding land claims. When he died at age sixty-nine, Occom was working as a teacher among the Tuscarora of New York.

Occom saw two of his works published during his lifetime: *A Sermon Preached by Samson Occom . . . at the Execution of Moses Paul, an Indian* (1772), for which he is particularly well known today, and *Collection of Hymns and Spiritual Songs* (1774). Paul's story was sensational at the time because of the cause behind his execution. Moses Paul had been expelled from a Bethany, Connecticut, tavern, and he made a threat to kill the next person to leave the tavern, since he could not remain inside. Paul carried out his threat of revenge, killing Moses Cook, a prominent settler from Watertown. He was granted a three-month reprieve by the Connecticut General Assembly, so that he could ask Samson Occom to come and preach a sermon at his execution. Indeed, some scholars suggest that Moses Paul was urged by authorities to make the request of Occom. Both Indians and settler people crowded to Paul's hanging because it offered a unique chance to hear a renowned Indian minister preach at the execution of one of his people. Occom's rhetorical art becomes clear when one recalls that he was faced with the challenge of reaching three audiences—Moses Paul, the Indian people in the area, and the white settlers—all of whom had different expectations of the sermon. Because Occom's sermon, delivered in New Haven on September 1, 1771, created such an impact on the crowd, he was encouraged to publish it. Following its publication in Connecticut, the sermon became much admired, particularly among settlers who were concerned with the drunkenness of the Indians. At least nineteen editions of Occom's famous execution sermon were published.

A SHORT NARRATIVE OF MY LIFE[1]

From My Birth till I Received the Christian Religion

I was Born a Heathen and Brought up In Heathenism, till I was between 16 & 17 years of age, at a Place Calld Mohegan, in New London, Connecticut, in New England. My Parents Livd a wandering life, for did all the Indians at Mohegan, they Chiefly Depended upon Hunting, Fishing, & Fowling for their Living and had no Connection with the English, excepting to Traffic with them in their small Trifles; and they Strictly maintained and followed their Heathenish Ways, Customs & Religion, though there was Some Preaching among them. Once a Fortnight, in ye Summer Season, a Minister from New London used to come up, and the Indians to attend; not that they regarded the Christian Religion, but they had Blankets given to them every Fall of the Year and for these things they would attend and there was a Sort of School kept, when I was quite young, but I believe there never was one that ever Learnt to read any thing,—and when I was about 10 Years of age there was a man who went about among the Indian Wigwams, and wherever he Could find the Indian Children, would make them read; but the Children Used to take Care to keep out of his way;—and he used to Catch me Some times and make me

---

1. Occom's narrative was written in 1768. This text is taken from a typescript in Dartmouth College Library, Hanover, New Hampshire, as published in *The Elders Wrote: An Anthology of Early Prose by North American Indians, 1768–1931,* ed. Bernd Peyer (1982).

Say over my Letters; and I believe I learnt Some of them. But this was Soon over too; and all this Time there was not one amongst us, that made a Profession of Christianity——Neither did we Cultivate our Land, nor kept any Sort of Creatures except Dogs, which we used in Hunting; and we Dwelt in Wigwams. These are a Sort of Tents, Covered with Matts, made of Flags. And to this Time we were unacquainted with the English Tongue in general though there were a few, who understood a little of it.

From the Time of Our Reformation till I Left Mr. Wheelocks

When I was 16 years of age, we heard a Strange Rumor among the English, that there were Extraordinary Ministers Preaching from Place to Place and a Strange Concern among the White People. This was in the Spring of the Year. But we Saw nothing of these things, till Some Time in the Summer, when Some Ministers began to visit us and Preach the Word of God; and the Common People all Came frequently and exhorted us to the things of God, which it pleased the Lord, as I humbly hope, to Bless and accompany with Divine Influence to the Conviction and Saving Conversion of a Number of us; amongst whom I was one that was Imprest with the things we had heard. These Preachers did not only come to us, but we frequently went to their meetings and Churches. After I was awakened & converted, I went to all the meetings, I could come at; & Continued under Trouble of Mind about 6 months; at which time I began to Learn the English Letters; got me a Primer, and used to go to my English Neighbours frequently for Assistance in Reading, but went to no School. And when I was 17 years of age, I had, as I trust, a Discovery of the way of Salvation through Jesus Christ, and was enabl'd to put my trust in him alone for Life & Salvation. From this Time the Distress and Burden of my mind was removed, and I found Serenity and Pleasure of Soul, in Serving God. By this time I just began to Read in the New Testament without Spelling,— and I had a Stronger Desire Still to Learn to read the Word of God, and at the Same Time had un uncommon Pity and Compassion to my Poor Brethren According to the Flesh. I used to wish I was capable of Instructing my poor Kindred. I used to think, if I Could once Learn to Read I would Instruct the poor Children in Reading,—and used frequently to talk with our Indians Concerning Religion. This continued till I was in my 19th year: by this Time I Could Read a little in the Bible. At this Time my Poor Mother was going to Lebanon, and having had Some Knowledge of Mr. Wheelock and hearing he had a Number of English youth under his Tuition,[2] I had a great Inclination to go to him and be with him a week or a Fortnight, and Desired my Mother to Ask Mr. Wheelock whether he would take me a little while to Instruct me in Reading. Mother did so; and when She Came Back, She Said Mr. Wheelock wanted to See me as Soon as possible. So I went up, thinking I Should be back again in a few Days; when I got up there, he received me With kindness and Compassion and in Stead of Staying a Forthnight or 3 Weeks, I Spent 4 Years with him.—After I had been with him Some Time, he began to acquaint his Friends of my being with him, and of his Intentions of Educating me, and my Circumstances. And the good People began to give Some Assistance to Mr. Wheelock, and gave me Some old and Some New Clothes. Then he represented the Case to the Honorable Commissioners at Boston, who were Commission'd by the Honorable Society in London for Propagating the gospel among the Indians in New England and parts adjacent, and they allowed him 60 £ in old Tender, which was about 6 £ Sterling, and they Continu'd it 2 or 3 years, I can't tell exactly.—While I was at Mr. Wheelock's, I was very weakly and my Health much impaired, and at the End of 4 Years, I over Strained my Eyes to such a Degree, I Could not persue my Studies any Longer; and out of these 4 years I Lost Just about one year;—And was obliged to quit my Studies.

From the Time I Left Mr. Wheelock till I Went to Europe

As soon as I left Mr. Wheelock, I endeavored to find Some Employ among the Indians; went to Nahantuck,[3] thinking they may want a School Master, but they had one; then went to Narraganset, and they were Indifferent about a School, and went back to Mohegan, and heard a number of our Indians were going to Montauk, on Long Island, and I went with them, and the Indians there were very desirous to have me keep a School amongst them, and I Consented, and went back a while to Mohegan and Some time in November I went on the Island, I think it is 17 years ago last November. I agreed to keep School with them Half a Year, and left it with them to give me what they Pleased; and they took turns to Provide Food for me. I had near 30 Scholars this winter; I had an evening

---

2. Instruction.

3. Niantic.

School too for those that could not attend the Day School—and began to Carry on their meetings, they had a Minister, one Mr. Horton,[4] the Scotch Society's Missionary; but he Spent, I think two thirds of his Time at Sheenecock, 30 Miles from Montauk. We met together 3 times for Divine Worship every Sabbath and once on every Wednesday evening. I (used) to read the Scriptures to them and used to expound upon Some particular Passages in my own Tongue. Visited the Sick and attended their Burials.—When the half year expired, they Desired me to Continue with them, which I complied with, for another half year, when I had fulfilled that, they were urgent to have me Stay Longer, So I continued amongst them till I was Married, which was about 2 years after I went there. And Continued to Instruct them in the Same manner as I did before. After I was married a while, I found there was need of a Support more than I needed while I was Single,—and made my Case Known to Mr. Buell[5] and to Mr. Wheelock, and also the Needy Circumstances and the Desires of these Indians of my Continuing amongst them, and the Commissioners were so good as to grant £ 15 a year Sterling——And I kept on in my Service as usual, yea I had additional Service; I kept School as I did before and Carried on the Religious Meetings as often as ever, and attended the Sick and their Funerals, and did what Writings they wanted, and often Sat as a Judge to reconcile and Decide their Matters Between them, and had visitors of Indians from all Quarters; and, as our Custom is, we freely Entertain all Visitors. And was fetched often from my Tribe and from others to see into their Affairs Both Religious, Temporal,—Besides my Domestic Concerns. And it Pleased the Lord to Increase my Family fast—and Soon after I was Married, Mr. Horton left these Indians and the Shenecock & after this I was (alone) and then I had the whole care of these Indians at Montauk, and visited the Shenecock Indians often. Used to set out Saturdays towards Night and come back again Mondays. I have been obliged to Set out from Home after Sun Set, and Ride 30 Miles in the Night, to Preach to these Indians. And Some Indians at Shenecock Sent their Children to my School at Montauk, I kept one of them Some Time, and had a Young Man a half year from Mohegan, a Lad

from Nahantuck, who was with me almost a year; and had little or nothing for keeping them.

My Method in the School was, as Soon as the Children got together, and took their proper Seats, I Prayed with them, then began to hear them. I generally began (after some of them Could Spell and Read,) With those that were yet in their Alphabets, So around, as they were properly Seated till I got through and I obliged them to Study their Books, and to help one another. When they could not make out a hard word they Brought it to me—and I usually heard them, in the Summer Season 8 Times a Day 4 in the morning, and in ye after Noon.—In the Winter Season 6 Times a Day, As Soon as they could Spell, they were obliged to Spell when ever they wanted to go out. I concluded with Prayer; I generally heard my Evening Scholars 3 Times Round, And as they go out the School, every one, that Can Spell, is obliged to Spell a Word, and to go out Leisurely one after another. I Catechised 3 or 4 Times a Week according to the Assembly's Shout or Catechism, and many Times Proposed Questions of my own, and in my own Tongue. I found Difficulty with Some Children, who were Some what Dull, most of these can soon learn to Say over their Letters, they Distinguish the Sounds by the Ear, but their Eyes can't Distinguish the Letters, and the way I took to cure them was by making an Alphabet on Small bits of paper, and glued them on Small Chips of Cedar after this manner A B & C. I put these on Letters in order on a Bench then point to one Letter and bid a Child to take notice of it, and then I order the Child to fetch me the Letter from the Bench; if he Brings the Letter, it is well, if not he must go again and again till he brings ye right Letter. When they can bring any Letters this way, then I just Jumble them together, and bid them to set them in Alphabetical order, and it is a Pleasure to them; and they soon Learn their Letters this way.—I frequently Discussed or Exhorted my Scholars, in Religious matters.— My Method in our Religious Meetings was this; Sabbath Morning we Assemble together about 10 o'C and begin with Singing; we generally Sung Dr. Watt's[6] Psalms or Hymns. I distinctly read the Psalm or Hymn first, and then gave the meaning of it to them, after that Sing, then Pray, and Sing again after Prayer. Then proceed to Read from Suitable portion of Scripture, and so Just give the plain Sense of it in Familiar Discourse and apply it to them. So continued with Prayer and Singing. In the after Noon and Evening we Proceed in the Same Manner, and

---

4. The Reverend Azariah Horton (1715–77), missionary to the Shinnecock of Long Island.

5. The Reverend Samuel Buell (1716–98), a Presbyterian minister.

6. Isaac Watts (1674–1748), a famous English hymn writer.

so in Wednesday Evening. Some Time after Mr. Horton left these Indians, there was a remarkable revival of religion among these Indians and many were hopefully converted to the Saving knowledge of God in Jesus. It is to be observed before Mr. Horton left these Indians they had Some Prejudices infused in their minds, by Some Enthusiastical Exhorters from New England, against Mr. Horton, and many of them had left him; by this means he was Discouraged, and was disposed from these Indians. And being acquainted with the Enthusiasts in New England & the make and the Disposition of the Indians I took a mild way to reclaim them. I opposed them not openly but let them go on in their way, and whenever I had an opportunity, I would read Such pages of the Scriptures, and I thought would confound their Notions, and I would come to them with all Authority, Saying "these Saith the Lord"; and by this means, the Lord was pleased to Bless my poor Endeavours, and they were reclaimed, and Brought to hear almost any of the ministers.——I am now to give an Account of my Circumstances and manner of Living. I Dwelt in a Wigwam, a Small Hut with Small Poles and Covered with Matts made of Flags, and I was obligd to remove twice a Year, about 2 miles Distance, by reason of the Scarcity of wood, for in one Neck of Land they Planted their Corn, and in another, they had their wood, and I was obligd to have my Corn carted and my Hay also,—and I got my Ground Plow'd every year, which Cost me about 12 shillings an acre; and I kept a Cow and a Horse, for which I paid 21 shillings every year York currency, and went 18 miles to Mill for every Dust of meal we used in my family. I Hired or Joined with my Neighbours to go to Mill, with a Horse or ox Cart, or on Horse Back, and Some time went myself. My Family Increasing fast, and my Visitors also. I was obliged to contrive every way to Support my Family; I took all opportunities, to get Some thing to feed my Family Daily. I Planted my own Corn, Potatoes, and Beans; I used to be out hoeing my Corn Some times before Sun Rise and after my School is Dismist, and by this means I was able to raise my own Pork, for I was allowed to keep 5 Swine. Some mornings & Evenings I would be out with my Hook and Line to Catch fish, and in the Fall of Year and in the Spring, I used my gun, and fed my Family with Fowls. I Could more than pay for my Powder & Shot with Feathers. At other Times I Bound old Books for Easthampton People, made wooden Spoons and Ladles, Stocked Guns, & worked on Cedar to make Pails, (Piggins),[7] and Churns & C. Besides

all these Difficulties I met with advers Providence, I bought a Mare, had it but a little while, and she fell into the Quick Sand and Died, After a while Bought another, I kept her about half year, and she was gone, and I never have heard of nor Seen her from that Day to this; it was Supposed Some Rogue Stole her. I got another and Died with a Distemper, and last of all I Bought a Young Mare, and kept her till She had one Colt, and She broke her Leg and Died, and Presently after the Cold Died also. In the whole I Lost 5 Horse Kind; all these Losses helped to pull me down; and by this Time I got greatly in Debt, and acquainted my Circumstances to Some of my Friends, and they Represented my Case to the Commissioners of Boston, and Interceded with them for me, and they were pleased to vote 15 £ for my Help, and Soon after Sent a Letter to my good Friend at New London, acquainting him that they had Superseded[8] their Vote; and my Friends were so good as to represent my Needy Circumstances Still to them, and they were so good at Last, as to Vote £15 and Sent it, for which I am very thankful; and the Revd Mr. Buell was so kind as to write in my behalf to the gentlemen of Boston; and he told me they were much Displeased with him, and heard also once again that they blamed me for being Extravagant; I Can't Conceive how these gentlemen would have me Live. I am ready to (forgive) their Ignorance, and I would wish they had Changed Circumstances with me but one month, that they may know, by experience what my Case really was; but I am now fully convinced, that it was not Ignorance, For I believe it can be proved to the world that these Same Gentlemen gave a young Missionary a Single man, *one Hundred Pounds* for one year, and fifty Pounds for an Interpreter, and thirty Pounds for an Introducer; so it Cost them one Hundred & Eighty Pounds in one Single Year, and they Sent too where there was no Need of a Missionary.

Now you See what difference they made between me and other missionaries; they gave me 180 Pounds for 12 years Service, which they gave for one years Services in another Mission.—In my Service (I speak like a fool, but I am Constrained) I was my own Interpreter. I was both a School master and Minister to the Indians, yea I was their Ear, Eye & Hand, as Well as Mouth. I leave it with the World, as wicked as it is, to Judge, whether I ought not to have had half as much, they gave a young man Just mentioned which would have been but £ 50 a year; and if they

---

7. Small wooden pails.

8. Annulled.

ought to have given me that, I am not under obligations to them, I owe them nothing at all; what can be the Reason that they used me after this manner? I can't think of any thing, but this as a Poor Indian Boy Said, Who was Bound out to an English Family, and he used to Drive Plow for a young man, and he whipt and Beat him allmost every Day, and the young man found fault with him, and Complained of him to his master and the poor Boy was Called to answer for himself before his master, and he was asked, what it was he did, that he was So Complained of and beat almost every Day. He Said, he did not know, but he Supposed it was because he could not drive any better; but says he, I Drive as well as I know how; and at other Times he Beats me, because he is of a mind to beat me; but says he believes he Beats me for the most of the Time "because I am an Indian".

So I am *ready* to Say, they have used me thus, because I Can't Influence the Indians so well as other missionaries; but I can assure them I have endeavoured to teach them as well as I know how;—but I *must Say,* "I believe it is because I am a poor Indian". I Can't help that God has made me So; I did not make my self so.—

A SERMON PREACHED BY SAMSON OCCOM[1]

The sacred words that I have chosen to speak from, upon this undesirable occasion are found written in the Epistle of St. Paul to the ROMANS, VI. 23. For the Wages of Sin is Death, but the Gift of God is Eternal Life through Jesus Christ our Lord.

Death is called the king of terrors, and it ought to be the subject of every man and woman's thoughts daily; because it is that unto which they are liable every moment of their lives: And therefore it cannot be unreasonable to think, speak and hear of it at any time, and especially on this mournful occasion; for we must all come to it, how soon we cannot tell; whether we are prepared or not prepared, ready or not ready, whether death is welcome or not welcome, we must feel the force of it: Whether we

concern ourselves with death or not, it will concern itself with us. Seeing that this is the case with every one of us, what manner of persons ought we to be in all holy conversation and godliness; how ought men to exert themselves in preparation for death, continually; for they know not what a day or an hour may bring forth, with respect to them. But alas! according to the appearance of mankind in general; death is the least thought of. They go on from day to day as if they were to live here forever, as if this was the only life. They contrive, rack their inventions, disturb their rest, and even hazard their lives in all manner of dangers, both by sea and land; yea, they leave no stone unturned that they may live in the world, and at the same time have little or no contrivance to die well. God and their souls are neglected, and heaven and eternal happiness are disregarded; Christ and his religion are despised—yet most of these very men intend to be happy when they come to die, not considering that there must be great preparation in order to die well. Yea there is none so fit to live as those that are fit to die; those that are not fit to die are not fit to live. Life and death are nearly connected; we generally own that it is a great and solemn thing to die. If this be true, then it is a great and solemn thing to live, for as we live so we shall die. But I say again, how do mankind realize these things? They are busy about the things of this world as if there was no death before them. Dr. *Watts* pictures them out to the life in his psalms.[2]

> See the vain race of mortals move,
>   Like shadows o'er the plain,
> They rage and strive, desire and love,
>   But all the noise is vain.
>
> Some walk in honour's gaudy show,
>   Some dig for golden ore,
> They toil for heirs they know not who,
>   And strait are seen no more.

But on the other hand, life is the most precious thing, and ought to be the most desired by all rational creatures. It ought to be prized above all things; yet there is nothing so abused and despised as life, and nothing so neglected: I mean eternal life is shamefully disregarded by men in general, and eternal death is chosen rather than life. This is the general complaint of the Bible from the beginning

---

1. This sermon was first published in New Haven, Connecticut, in 1772. The text reprinted here is the tenth edition, published in Bennington, Vermont (n.d.).

2. Isaac Watts, *The Psalms of David Imitated in the Languages of the New Testament* (1719). Occom includes number 613.

to the end. As long as Christ is neglected, life is refused, as long as sin is cherished, death is chosen. And this seems to be the woful case of mankind of all nations, according to their appearance in these days: For it is too plain to be denied, that vice and immorality, and floods of iniquity are abounding every where amongst all nations, and all orders and ranks of men, and in every sect of people. Yea there is a great agreement and harmony among all nations, and from the highest to the lowest to practice sin and iniquity; and the pure religion of Jesus Christ is turned out of doors, and is dying without; or, in other words, the Lord Jesus Christ is turned out of doors by men in general, and even by his professed people. "He Came to his own, and his own received him not."[3] But the devil is admitted, he has free access to the houses and hearts of the children of men: Thus life is refused and death is chosen.

But in further speaking upon our text by divine assistance, I shall consider these two general propositions.

I. That sin is the cause of all the miseries that befall the children of men, both as to their bodies and souls, for time and eternity.

II. That eternal life and happiness is the gift of God through Jesus Christ our Lord.

In speaking to the first proposition, I shall first consider the nature of sin; and secondly I shall consider the consequences of sin or the wages of sin, which is death. First then, we are to describe the nature of sin.

Sin is the transgression of the law:—This is the scripture definition of sin.—Now the law of God being holy, just and good; sin must be altogether unholy, unjust and evil. If I was to define sin, I should call it a contrariety to God; and as such it must be the vilest thing in the world; it is full of all evil; it is the evil of evils; the only evil in which dwells no good thing; and it is most destructive to God's creation, wherever it takes effect. It was sin that transformed the very angels in heaven, into devils; and it was sin that caused hell to be made. If it had not been for sin, there never would have been such a thing as hell or devil, death or misery.

And if sin is such a thing as we have just described, it must be worse than the devils in hell itself.—Sin is full of deadly poison; it is full of malignity and hatred against God; against all his divine perfections and attributes, against his wisdom, against his power, against his holiness and goodness, against his mercy and justice, against his law and gospel; yea against his very being and existence. Were it in the power of sin, it would even dethrone God, and set itself on the throne.

When Christ the Son of the Most High came down from the glorious world above, into this wretched world of sin and sorrow, to seek and to save that which was lost, sin or sinners rose up against him, as soon as he entered our world, and pursued him with hellish malice, night and day, for above thirty years together, till they killed him.

Further, sin is against the Holy Ghost; it opposes all its good and holy operations upon the children of men. When, and wherever there is the out pouring of the Spirit of God, upon the children of men, in a way of conviction and conversion; sin will immediately prompt the devil and his children to rise up against it, and they will oppose the work with all their power, and in every shape. And if open opposition will not do, the devil will mimic the work and thus prevent the good effect.

Thus we find by the scripture accounts, that whenever God raises up men, and uses them as instruments of conviction and conversion, the devil and his instruments will rise up to destroy both the reformers and the reformed. Thus it has been from the early days of christianity to this day. We have found it so in our day. In the time of the out-pouring of the Spirit of God in these colonies, to the conviction and reformation of many; immediately sin and the devil influenced numbers to rise up against the good work of God, calling it a delusion, and work of the devil. And thus sin also opposes every motion of the Spirit of God, in the heart of every christian; this makes a warfare in the soul.

2. I shall endeavor to show the sad consequences or effects of sin upon the children of men.

Sin has poisoned them, and made them distracted or fools. The psalmist says, The fool hath said in his heart, there is no God.[4] And Solomon, through his proverbs, calls ungodly sinners fools; and their sin he calls their folly and foolishness.[5] The apostle James says, But the tongue can no man tame, it is an unruly evil, full of deadly poison.[6] It is the heart that is in the first place full of deadly poison. The tongue is only an interpreter of the

---

3. John 1:11.

4. Psalms 14:1.

5. See Proverbs 12:23, 14:8, 14:24, and 15:2.

6. James 3:8.

heart. Sin has vitiated the whole man, both soul and body; all the powers are corrupted; it has turned the minds of men against all good, towards all evil. So poisoned are they according to the prophet, Isa. v. 20. "Wo unto them that call evil good and good evil; that put darkness for light, and light for darkness; that put bitter for sweet, and sweet for bitter."[7] And Christ Jesus saith in John iii. 19, 20. "And this is the condemnation, that light has come into the world, and men have loved darkness rather than light, because their deeds were evil. For every one that doeth evil, hateth the light, neither cometh to the light lest his deeds should be reproved."[8] Sin hath stupified mankind, they are now ignorant of God their Maker; neither do they enquire after him. And they are ignorant of themselves, they know not what is good for them, neither do they understand their danger; and they have no fear of God before their eyes.

Further, sin hath blinded their eyes, so that they cannot discern spiritual things: neither do they see the way that they should go, and they are as deaf as adders, so that they cannot hear the joyful sound of the gospel that brings glad tidings of peace and pardon to sinners of mankind. Neither do they regard the charmer charming never so wisely.—Not only so, but sin has made man proud, though he has nothing to be proud of; for he has lost his excellency, his beauty and happiness; he is a bankrupt and is excommunicated from God; he was turned out of paradise by God himself, and became a vagabond in God's world, and as such he has no right or title to the least crumb of mercy, in the world: Yet he is proud, he is haughty, and exalts himself above God, though he is wretched and miserable, and poor and blind and naked. He glories in his shame. Sin has made him beastly and devilish; yea, he is sunk beneath the beasts, and is worse than the ravenous beasts of the wilderness. He is become ill-natured, cruel and murderous; he is contentious and quarrelsome. I said he is worse than the ravenous beasts, for wolves and bears don't devour their own kind, but man does; yea, we have numberless instances of women killing their own children; such women I think are worse than she-tygers.

Sin has made man dishonest, and deceitful, so that he goes about cheating and defrauding and deceiving his fellow-men in the world: Yea, he has become a cheat him-

self, he goes about in vain shew; we do not know where to find man.—Sometimes we find as an angel of God; and at other times we find as a devil, even one and the same man. Sin has made a man a liar even from the womb; so there is no believing nor trusting him. The royal psalmist says, "The wicked are estranged from the womb, they go astray as soon as they are born, speaking lies."[9] His language is also corrupted. Whereas he had a pure and holy language, in his innocency, to adore and praise God his Maker, he now curses and swears, and profanes, the holy name of God, and curses and damns his fellow creatures. In a word, man is a most unruly and ungovernable creature, and is become as the wild ass's colt, and is harder to tame than any of God's creatures in this world.—In short, man is worse than all the creatures in this lower world, his propensity is to evil and that continually; he is more like the devil than any creature we can think of: And I think it is not going beyond the word of God, to say man is the most devilish creature in the world. Christ said to his disciples, One of you is a devil;[10] to the Jews he said, Ye are of your father the devil, and the lusts of your father ye will do.[11] Thus every unconverted soul is a child of the devil, sin has made them so.

We have given some few hints of the nature of sin, and the effects of sin on mankind.

We shall in the next place consider the wages or the reward of sin, which is death.

Sin is the cause of all the miseries that attend poor sinful man, which will finally bring him to death, death temporal and eternal. I shall first consider his temporal death.

His temporal death then begins as soon as he is born. Though it seems to us that he is just beginning to live, yet in fact he is just entered into a state of death: St. Paul says, "W[h]erefore, as by one man sin entered into the world, and death by sin; and so death passed upon all men, for that all have sinned."[12] Man is surrounded with ten thousand instruments of death, and is liable to death every moment of his life; a thousand diseases await him on every side continually; the sentence of death has pass'd upon them as soon as they are born; yea they are struck with death as soon as they breathe. And it seems all the enjoyments of men in this world are also poisoned with sin; for

---

7. Isaiah 4:20.

8. Occom's citations are generally accurate. Exceptions are noted.

9. Psalms 58:3.

10. John 6:70.

11. John 8: 44.

12. Romans 5:12.

God said to Adam after he had sinned, "Cursed is the ground for thy sake, in sorrow shalt thou eat of it all the days of thy life."[13] By this we plainly see that every thing that grows out of the ground is cursed, and all creatures that God hath made for man are cursed also; and whatever God curses is a cursed thing indeed. Thus death and destruction is in all the enjoyments of men in this life, every enjoyment in this world is liable to misfortune in a thousand ways, both by sea and land.

How many ships, that have been loaded with the choicest treasures of the earth have been swallowed up in the ocean, many times just before they enter their desired haven. And vast treasures have been consumed by fire on the land, &c.—And the fruits of the earth are liable to many judgments. And the dearest and nearest enjoyments of men are generally balanced with equal sorrow and grief.—A man and his wife who have lived together in happiness for many years; that have comforted each other in various changes of life, must at last be separated; one or the other must be taken away first by death, and then the poor survivor is drowned in tears, in sorrow, mourning and grief. And when a child or children are taken away by death, the bereaved parents are bowed down with sorrow and deep mourning. When Joseph was sold by his brethren unto the Ishmaelites, they took his coat and rolled it in blood, and carried it to their father, and the good old patriarch knew it to be Joseph's coat, and he concluded that his dear Joseph was devoured by evil beasts; and he was plunged all over in sorrow and bitter mourning, and he refused to be comforted.[14] And so when tender parents are taken away by death, the children are left comfortless. All this is the sad effects of sin—These are the wages of sin.

And secondly we are to consider man's spiritual death, while he is here in this world. We find it thus written in the word of God, "And the Lord God commanded the man, saying of every tree of the garden thou mayst freely eat: but of the tree of knowledge of good and evil, thou shalt not eat of it, for in the day thou eatest thereof thou shalt surely die."[15] And yet he did eat of it, and so he and all his posterity are but dead men. And St. Paul to the Ephesians saith, "You hath he quickened who were dead in trespasses and sins."[16] The great Mr. Henry says, in this place,

that unregenerate souls are dead in trespasses and sins.[17] All those who are in their sins, are dead in sins; yea, in trespasses and sins; and which may signify all sorts of sins, habitual and actual; sins of heart and life. Sin is the death of the soul. Wherever that prevails, there is a privation of all spiritual life. Sinners are dead in state, being destitute of the principles and powers of spiritual life; and cut off from God, the fountain of life: and they are dead in law, as a condemned malefactor is said to be a dead man. Now a dead man, in a natural sense, is unactive, and is of no service to the living; there is no correspondence between the dead and the living: There is no agreement or union between them, no fellowship at all between the dead and the living. A dead man is altogether ignorant of the intercourse among the living:—Just so it is with men that are spiritually dead; they have no agreeable activity. Their activity in sin, is their deadness and inactivity towards God. They are of no service to God; and they have no correspondence with heaven; and there is no agreement or fellowship between them and the living God; and they are totally ignorant of the agreeable and sweet intercourse there is between God and his children here below: and they are ignorant, and know nothing of that blessed fellowship and union there is among the saints here below. They are ready to say indeed, behold how they love one another! But they know nothing of that love, that the children of God enjoy. As sin is in opposition to God; so sinners are at enmity against God; there is no manner of agreement between them.

Let us consider further. God is a living God, he is all life, the fountain of life; and a sinner is a dead soul; there is nothing but death in him. And now judge ye, what agreement can there be between them! God is a holy and pure God, and a sinner is an unholy and filthy creature;— God is a righteous Being, and a sinner is an unrighteous creature; God is light, and a sinner is darkness itself, &c. Further, what agreement can there be between God and a liar, a thief, a drunkard, a swearer, a profane creature, a whoremonger, an adulterer, an idolater, &c. No one that has any sense, dare say that there is any agreement. Further, as sinners are dead to God, as such, they have no delight in God, and godliness; they have no taste for the religion of Jesus Christ: they have no pleasure in the holy exercise of religion. Prayer is no pleasant work with

---

13. Genesis 3:17.

14. Genesis 37:27–28.

15. Genesis 2:16–17.

16. Ephesians 2:1.

---

17. Mathew Henry (1662–1714), *Exposition of the Old and New Testament* (1710).

them; or if they have any pleasure in it, it is not out of love to God, but out of self-love, like the Pharisees of old; they loved to pray in open view of men, that they might have praise from them. And perhaps, they were not careful to pray in secret. These were dead souls, they were unholy, rotten hypocrites, and so all their prayers and religious exercises were cold, dead, and abominable services to God. Indeed they are dead to all the duties that God requires of them, they are dead to the holy bible; to all the laws, commands, and precepts thereof; and to the ordinances of the gospel of the Lord Jesus Christ. When they read the book of God, it is like an old almanack to them, a dead book. But it is because they are dead, and as such, all their services are against God, even their best services are an abomination unto God; yea, sinners are so dead in sin, that the threatenings of God don't move them. All the thunderings and lightnings of Mount-Sinai don't stir them. All the curses of the law are out against them; yea, every time they read these curses in the bible, they are cursing them to their faces, and to their very eyes; yet they are unconcern'd, and go on in sin without fear. And lastly here, sin has so stupified the sinner, that he will not believe his own senses, he won't believe his own eyes, nor his own ears, he reads the book of God, but he does not believe what he reads. And he hears of God, and heaven, and eternal happiness, and of hell and eternal misery; but he believes none of these things; he goes on, as if there were no God, nor heaven and happiness; neither has he any fear of hell and eternal torments; and he sees his fellow-men dropping away daily on every side, yet he goes on carelessly in sin, as if he never was to die. And if he at any time thinks of dying, he hardly believes his own thoughts.——Death is at a great distance, so far off, that he dont concern himself about it, so as to prepare for it. God mournfully complains of his people, that they dont consider;—O that they were wise, that they understood this, that they would consider their latter end.

The next thing I shall consider, is the actual death of the body, or separation between soul and body. At the cessation of natural life, there is no more joy or sorrow; no more hope nor fear, as to the body; no more contrivance and carrying on of business; no more merchandizing and trading; no more farming; no more buying and selling; no more building of any kind, no more contrivance at all to live in the world; no more honor nor reproach; no more praise; no more good report, nor evil report; no more learning of any trades, arts or sciences in the world; no more sinful pleasures, they are all at an end; recreations, visiting, tavern-hunting, musick and dancing, chamber-

ing and carousing, playing at dice and cards, or any game whatsoever; cursing and swearing, and profaning the holy name of God, drunkeness, fighting, debauchery, lying and cheating, in this world must cease forever. Not only so, but they must bid an eternal farewell to all the world; bid farewell to all their beloved sins and pleasures; and the places and possessions that knew them once, shall know them no more forever. And further, they must bid adieu to all sacred and divine things. They are obliged to leave the bible, and all the ordinances thereof; and to bid farewell to preachers, and all sermons, and all christian people, and christian conversation; they must bid a long farewell to sabbaths and seasons, and opportunities of worship; yea an eternal farewell to all mercy and all hope; an eternal farewell to God the Father, Son and Holy Ghost, and adieu to heaven and all happiness, to saints and all the inhabitants of the upper world. At your leisure please to read the destruction of Babylon; you will find it written in the 18th of the Revelations.

On the other hand, the poor departed soul must take up its lodging in sorrow, wo and misery, in the lake that burns with fire and brimstone, were the worm dieth not and the fire is not quenched; where a multitude of frightful deformed devils dwell, and the damned ghosts of Adam's race; where darkness, horror and despair reigns, or where hope never comes, and where poor guilty naked souls will be tormented with exquisite torments, even the wrath of the Almighty poured out upon the damned souls; the smoke of their torments ascending up forever and ever; their mouths and nostrils streaming forth with living fire; and hellish groans, cries and shrieks all around them, and merciless devils upbraiding them for their folly and madness, and tormenting them incessantly. And there they must endure the most unsatiable, fruitless desire, and the most overwhelming shame and confusion and the most horrible fear, and the most doleful sorrow, and the most racking despair. When they cast their flaming eyes to heaven, with Dives in torments, they behold an angry GOD, whose eyes are as a flaming fire, and they are struck with ten thousand darts of pain; and the sight of the happiness of the saints above, adds to their pains and aggravates their misery. And when they reflect upon their past folly and madness in neglecting the great salvation in their day, it will pierce them with ten thousand inconceivable torments; it will as it were enkindle their hell afresh; and it will cause them to curse themselves bitterly, and curse the day in which they were born, and curse their parents that were the instruments of their being in the world; yea, they will curse, bitterly curse, and wish that very GOD that gave them their being to be in the same condition with them in hell torments. This is what is called the second death and it is the last death, and an eternal death to a guilty soul.

And O eternity, eternity, eternity! Who can measure it? Who can count the years thereof? Arithmetic must fail, the thoughts of men and angels are drowned in it; how shall we describe eternity? To what shall we compare it? Were it possible to employ a fly to carry off this globe by the small particles thereof, and to carry them to such a distance that it would return once in *ten thousand* years for another particle, and so continue till it has carried off all this globe, and framed them together in some unknown space, till it has made just such a world as this is: After all, eternity would remain the same unexhausted duration. This must be the unavoidable portion of all impenitent sinners, let them be who they will, great or small, honorable or ignoble, rich or poor, bond or free. Negroes, Indians, English, or of what nation soever; all that die in their sins must go to hell together; for the wages of sin is death.

The next thing that I was to consider is this:

That eternal life and happiness is the free gift of God through Jesus Christ our Lord.

Under this proposition I shall now endeavour to show that this life and happiness is.

The life that is mentioned in our text is a spiritual life, it is the life of the soul; from sin to holiness, from darkness to light, a translation from the kingdom and dominion of satan, to the kingdom of God's grace. In other words, it is being restored to the image of God and delivered from the image of satan. And this life consists in union of the soul to God, and communion with God; a real participation of the divine nature, or in the Apostle's words, is a Christ formed within us; I live says he, yet not I but Christ liveth in me.[18] And the Apostle John saith God is love and he that dwelleth in love, dwelleth in God, and God in him.[19] This is the life of the soul. It is called emphatically life, because it is a life that shall never have a period, a stable, a permanent, and unchangeable life, called in the scriptures everlasting life, or life eternal. And

the happiness of this life consists in communion with God, or in the spiritual enjoyment of God. As much as a soul enjoys of God in this life, just so much of life and happiness he enjoys or possesses; yea, just so much of heaven he enjoys. A true christian, desires no other heaven but the enjoyment of God; a full and perfect enjoyment of God, is a full and perfect heaven and happiness to a gracious soul.—Further, this life is called eternal life because God has planted a living principle in the soul; and whereas he was dead before, now he is made alive unto God; there is an active principle within him towards God, he now moves towards God in his religious devotions and exercises; is daily comfortably and sweetly walking with God, in all his ordinances and commands; his delight is in the ways of God; he breathes towards God, a living breath, in praises, prayers, adorations and thanksgivings; his prayers are now heard in the heavens, and his praises delight the ears of the Almighty, and his thanksgiving are accepted, so alive is he now to God, that it is his meat and drink, yea more than his meat and drink, to do the will of his heavenly Father. It is his delight, his happiness and pleasure to serve God. He does not drag himself to his duties now, but he does them out of choice, and with alacrity of soul. Yea, so alive is he to God, that he gives up himself and all that he has entirely to God, to be for him and no other; his whole aim is to glorify God, in all things, whether by life or death, all the same to him.

We have a bright example of this in St. Paul. After he was converted, he was all alive to God; he regarded not his life but was willing to spend and be spent in the service of his God; he was hated, revil'd, despised, laughed at, and called all manner of evil names; was scourged, stoned and imprisoned; and all could not stop his activity towards God. He would boldly and courageously go on in preaching the gospel of the Lord Jesus Christ, to poor lost and undone sinners; he would do the work God set him about, in spite of all opposition he met with either from men or devils, earth or hell; come death or come life, none of these things moved him, because he was alive unto God. Though he suffered hunger and thirst, cold and heat, poverty and nakedness by day and by night, by sea, and by land, and was in danger always; yet he would serve God amidst all these dangers. Read his amazing account in 2 Cor. 11. 23, and on.

Another instance of marvellous love towards God, we have in Daniel. When there was a proclamation of prohibition, sent by the king to all his subjects forbidding them to call upon their gods for 30 days; which was done by envious men, that they might find occasion against Daniel

---

18. Galatians 2:20. "I am crucified with Christ: nevertheless I live; yet not I, but Christ liveth in me: and the life which I now live in the flesh I live by the faith of the Son of God, who loved me, and gave himself for me."

19. 1 John 4:16.

the servant of the most high God; yet he having the life of God in his soul regarded not the king's decree, but made his petition to his God, as often as he used to do though death was threatened to the disobedient. But he feared not the hell they had prepared; for it seems, the den resembled hell, and the lions represented the devils. And when he was actually cast into the lions den, the ravenous beasts became meek and innocent as lambs, before the prophet, because he was alive unto God; the spirit of the Most High was in him, and the lions were afraid before him.[20] Thus it was with Daniel and Paul; they went through fire and water, as the common saying is, because they had eternal life in their souls in an eminent manner; and they regarded not this life for the cause and glory of God. And thus it has been in all ages with true Christians. Many of the fore-fathers of the English, in this country, had this life and are gone the same way, that the holy Prophets and Apostles went. Many of them went through all manner of sufferings for God; and a great number of them are gone home to heaven, in chariots of fire. I have seen the place in London, called Smithfield, where numbers were burnt to death for the religion of Jesus Christ. And there is the same life in true christians now in these days; and if there should persecutions arise in our day, I verily believe, true christians would suffer with the same spirit and temper of mind, as those did, who suffered in days past.—This is the life which our text speaks of.

We proceed in the next place to show, that this life, which we have described, is the free gift of God, through Jesus Christ our Lord.

Sinners have forfeited all mercy into the hands of divine justice and have merited hell and damnation to themselves; for the wages of sin is everlasting death, but heaven and happiness is a free gift; it comes by favor; and all merit is excluded; and especially if we consider that we are fallen sinful creatures, and there is nothing in us that can recommend us to the favour of God; and we can do nothing that is agreeable and acceptable to God; and the mercies we enjoy in this life are altogether from the pure mercy of God; we are unequal to them. Good old Jacob cried out, under the sense of his unworthiness, "I am less than the least of all thy mercies,"[21] and we have nothing to

give unto God if we essay to give all the service that we are capable of, we should give him nothing but what was his own, and when we give up ourselves unto God, both soul and body, we give him nothing; for we were his before; he had a right to do with us as he pleased, either to throw us into hell, or to save us.—There is nothing that we can call our own, but our sins; and who is he that dares to say, I expect to have heaven for my sins? for our text says, that the wages of sin is death. If we are thus unequal and unworthy of the least mercy in this life, how much more are we unworthy of eternal life? Yet God can find it in his heart to give it. And it is altogether unmerited; it is a free gift to undeserving and hell deserving sinners of mankind: it is altogether of God's sovereign good pleasure to give it. It is of free grace and sovereign mercy, and from the unbounded goodness of God; he was self-moved to it. And it is said that this life is given in and through our Lord Jesus Christ. It could not be given in any other way, but in and through the death and suffering of the Lord Jesus Christ; Christ himself is the gift, and he is the christian's life. "For God so loved the world that he gave his only begotten Son, that whosoever believed in him should not perish but have everlasting life."[22] The word says further, "For by grace ye are saved, through faith, and that not of yourselves it is the gift of God."[23] This is given through Jesus Christ our Lord; it is Christ that purchased it with his own blood; he prepared it with his divine and almighty power; and by the same power, and by the influence of his spirit, he prepares us for it; and by his divine grace preserves us to it. In a word, he is all in all in our eternal salvation; all this is the free gift of God.

I have now gone through what I proposed from my text. And I shall now make some application of the whole.

First to the criminal in particular; and then to the auditory in general.

My poor unhappy Brother MOSES,

As it was your own desire that I should preach to you this last discourse, so I shall speak plainly to you.—You are the bone of my bone, and flesh of my flesh. You are an Indian, a despised creature, but you have despised yourself; yea you have despised God more; you have trodden under foot his authority; you have despised his commands and precepts; And now as God says, be sure your

---

20. See Daniel 6.

21. Genesis 32:10. "I am not worthy of the least of all the mercies, and of all the truth, which thou hast shewed unto thy servant; for with my staff I passed over this Jordan; and now I am become two bands."

---

22. John 3:16.

23. Ephesians 2:8.

sins will find you out. And now, poor Moses, your sins have found you out, and they have overtaken you this day; the day of your death is now come; the king of terrors is at hand; you have but a very few moments to breathe in this world.—The just law of man, and the holy laws of Jehovah, call aloud for the destruction of your mortal life; God says, "Whoso sheddeth man's blood by man shall his blood be shed."[24] This is the ancient decree of heaven, and it is to be executed by man; nor have you the least gleam of hope of escape, for the unalterable sentence is past: The terrible day of execution is come; the unwelcome guard is about you; and the fatal instruments of death are now made ready; your coffin and your grave, your last lodging are open ready to receive you.

Alas! poor Moses, now you know by sad, by woful experience, the living truth of our text, that the wages of sin is death. You have been already dead; yea, twice dead: By nature spiritually dead. And since the awful sentence of death has been passed upon you, you have been dead to all the pleasures of this life; or all the pleasures, lawful or unlawful, have been dead to you: And death, which is the wages of sin, is standing even on this side of your grave ready to put a final period to your mortal life; and just beyond the grave, eternal death awaits your poor soul, and devils are ready to drag your miserable soul down to their bottomless den, where everlasting wo and horror reigns; the place is filled with doleful shrieks, howls and groans of the damned. Oh! to what a miserable, folorn, and wretched condition has your extravagance folly and wickedness brought you! i.e. if you die in your sins. And O! what manner of repentance ought you to manifest! How ought your heart to bleed for what you have done! How ought you to prostrate your soul before a bleeding God! And under self-condemnation, cry out ah Lord, ah Lord, what have I done?—Whatever partiality, injustice and error there may be among the judges of the earth, remember that you have deserved a thousand deaths, and a thousand hells, by reason of your sins, at the hands of a holy God. Should God come out against you in strict justice, alas! what could you say for yourself; for you have been brought up under the bright sunshine, and plain, and loud sound of the gospel; and you have had a good education; you can read and write well; and God has given you a good natural understanding: And therefore your sins are so much more aggravated. You have not sinned in such an ignorant manner as others have done; but you have sinned with both your eyes open as it were, under the light even the glorious light of the gospel of the Lord Jesus Christ.—You have sinned against the light of your own conscience, against your knowledge and understanding; you have sinned against the pure and holy laws of God, the just laws of men; you have sinned against heaven and earth; you have sinned against all the mercies and goodness of God; you have sinned against the whole bible, against the Old and New-Testament; you have sinned against the blood of Christ, which is the blood of the everlasting covenant. O poor Moses, see what you have done! And now repent, repent, I say again repent; see how the blood you shed cries against you, and the avenger of blood is at your heels. O fly, fly, to the blood of the Lamb of God for the pardon of all your aggravated sins.

But let us now turn to a more pleasant theme.— Though you have been a great sinner, a heaven-daring sinner; yet hark and hear the joyful sound from heaven, even from the King of kings, and Lord of lords; that the gift of God is eternal life, through Jesus Christ our Lord. It is the free gift offered to the greatest sinners, and upon their true repentance towards God and faith in the Lord Jesus Christ they shall be welcome to the life they have spoken of: it is offered upon free terms. He that hath no money may come; he that hath no righteousness, no goodness may come, the call is to poor undone sinners; the call is not to the righteous, but sinners calling them to repentance. Hear the voice of the Son of the Most High God, Come unto me all ye that labor and are heavy laden, and I will give you rest.[25] This is a call, a gracious call to you poor Moses, under your present burden and distresses. And Christ alone has a right to call sinners to himself. It would be presumption for a mighty angel to call a poor sinner in this manner; and were it possible for you to apply to all God's creatures, they would with one voice tell you, that it was not in them to help you. Go to all the means of grace, they would prove miserable helps without Christ himself. Yea, apply to all the ministers of the gospel in the world, they would all say, that it was not in them, but would only prove as indexes, to point out to you, the Lord Jesus Christ, the only Saviour of sinners of mankind. Yea, go to all the angels in heaven they would do the same. Yea, go to God the Father himself without Christ, he could not help you, to speak after the manner of

---

24. Genesis 9:6.

25. Matthew 11:28.

men, he would also point to the Lord Jesus Christ, and say this is my beloved Son, in whom I am well pleased hear ye him. Thus you see, poor Moses, that there is none in heaven, or earth, that can help you, but Christ; he alone has power to save, and to give life.—God the eternal Father appointed him, chose him, authorized and fully commissioned him to save sinners. He came down from heaven into this lower world, and became as one of us, and stood in our room. He was the second Adam. And as God demanded correct obedience of the first Adam; the second fulfil'd it; and as the first sinned and incurred the wrath and anger of God, the second endured it; he suffered in our room. As he became sin for us, he was a man of sorrows, and acquainted with grief; all our stripes were laid upon him; yea, he was finally condemned, because we were under condemnation; and at last was executed and put to death, for our sins; was lifted up between the heavens and the earth, and was crucified on the accursed tree; his blessed hands and feet were fastened there; there he died a shameful and ignominious death; There he finished the great work of our redemption: There his hearts blood was shed for our cleansing: There he fully satisfied the divine justice of God, for penitent, believing sinners, though they have been the chief of sinners.—O Moses! this is good news to you in this last day of your life; here is a crucified Saviour at hand for your sins; his blessed hands are outstretched, all in a gore of blood for you. This is the only Saviour, an Almighty Saviour, just such as you stand in infinite and perishing need of. O, poor Moses! hear the dying prayer of a gracious Saviour on the accursed tree. Father forgive them for they know not what they do. This was a prayer for his enemies and murderers; and it is for you, if you will now only repent and believe in him. O, why will you die eternally, poor Moses, since Christ has died for sinners? Why will you go to hell from beneath a bleeding Saviour as it were? This is the day of your execution, yet it is the accepted time, it is the day of salvation if you will now believe in the Lord Jesus Christ. Must Christ follow you into the prison by his servants and there intreat you to accept of eternal life, and will you refuse it? Must he follow you even to the gallows, and there beseech of you to accept of him, and will you refuse him? Shall he be crucified hard by your gallows, as it were, and will you regard him not. O poor Moses, now believe on the Lord Jesus Christ with all your heart, and thou shalt be saved eternally. Come just as you are, with all your sins and abominations, with all your filthiness, with all your blood-guiltiness, with all your condemnation, and lay hold of the hope set before you this day. This is the last day of salvation with your soul; you will be beyond the bounds of mercy in a few minutes more. O what a joyful day would it be if you would now openly believe in and receive the Lord Jesus Christ; it would be the beginning of heavenly days with your poor soul; instead of a melancholy day, it would be a wedding day to your soul: It would cause the very angels in heaven to rejoice, and the saints on earth to be glad; it would cause the angels to come down from the realms above, and wait hovering about your gallows, ready to convey your soul to the heavenly mansions. There to taste the possession of eternal glory and happiness, and join the heavenly choirs in singing the songs of Moses and the Lamb: There to set down forever with Abraham, Isaac and Jacob in the kingdom of God's glory; and your shame and guilt shall be forever banished from the place, and all sorrow and fear forever fly away, and tears be wiped from your face; and there shall you forever admire the astonishing and amazing and infinite mercy of God in Christ Jesus, in pardoning such a monstrous sinner as you have been; there you will claim the highest note of praise, for the riches of free grace in Christ Jesus. But if you will not except of a Saviour so freely offered to you in this last day of your life, you must this very day bid a farewell to God the Father Son and holy Ghost, to heaven and all the saints and angels that are there; and you must bid all the saints in this lower world an eternal farewell, and even the whole world. And so I must leave you in the hands of God; and I must turn to the whole auditory.

Sirs.—We may plainly see, from what we have heard, and from the miserable object before us, into what a doleful condition sin has brought mankind, even into a state of death and misery. We are by nature as certainly under the sentence of death from God, as this miserable man is by the just determination of man; for we are all dying creatures, and we are, or ought to be sensible of it; and this is the dreadful fruit of sin. O let us then fly from all appearance of sin; let us fight against it with all our might; let us repent and turn to God, and believe on the Lord Jesus Christ, that we may live for ever: Let us all prepare for death, for we know not how soon, nor how suddenly we may be called out of the world.

Permit me in particular, reverend gentlemen and fathers in Israel, to speak a few words to you, though I am very sensible that I need to be taught the first principles of the oracles of God, by the least of you. But since the Providence of God has so ordered it, that I must speak here on this occasion, I beg that you would not be offended nor be angry with me.

God has raised you up from among your brethren, and has qualified and authorized you to do his great work; and you are the servants of the Most High God, and ministers of the Lord Jesus Christ; you are Christ's ambassadors; you are called shepherds, watchmen overseers, or bishops, and you are rulers of the temples of God, or of the assemblies of God's people; you are God's angels, and as such you have nothing to do but to wait on God, and to do the work the Lord Jesus Christ your blessed Lord and Master has set you about, not fearing the face of any man, nor seeking to please men, but your Master. You are to declare the whole counsel of God, and to give a portion to every soul in due season; as a physician gives a portion to his patients, according to their diseases, so you are to give a portion to every soul in due season according to their spiritual maladies: Whether it be agreeable or not agreeable to them, you must give it to them; whether they will love you or hate you for it, you must do your work. Your work is to encounter sin and satan; this was the very end of the coming of Christ into the world, and the end of his death and sufferings; it was to make an end of sin and to destroy the works of the devil. And this is your work still, you are to fight the battles of the Lord. Therefore combine together, and be as terrible as an army with banners; attack this monster sin in all its shapes and windings, and lift up your voices as trumpets and not spare, call aloud, call your people to arms against this common enemy of mankind, that sin may not be their ruin. Call upon all orders ranks and degrees of people, to rise up against sin and satan. Arm your selves with fervent prayer continually, this is a terrible weapon against the kingdom of satan. And preach the death and sufferings, and the resurrection of Jesus Christ; for nothing is so destructive to the kingdom of the devil as this is. But what need I speak any more! Let us all attend, and hear the great Apostle of the Gentiles speak unto us in Eph. 6 ch. from the tenth verse and onward.[26] Finally my bretheren, be strong in the Lord, and in the power of his might; put on the whole armour of God, that ye may be able to stand against the wiles of the devil. For we wrestle not against flesh and blood, but against principalities, against powers, against the rulers of darkness of this world, against spiritual wickedness in high places. Wherefore take unto you the whole armour of God, that ye may be able to stand in the evil day, and having done all, to stand. Stand therefore, having your loins girt about with truth, and having on the breast-plate of righteousness; And your feet shod with the preparation of the gospel of peace: Above all, taking the shield of faith, wherewith ye shall be able to quench all the fiery darts of the wicked: And take the helmet of salvation, and the sword of the spirit, which is the word of God: Praying always with all prayer and supplication in the spirit, and watching therunto with all perseverance, and supplication for all saints.

I shall now address myself to the Indians, my bretheren and kindred according to the flesh.

My poor Kindred,

You see the woful consequences of sin, by seeing this our poor miserable countryman now before us, who is to die this day for his sins and great wickedness. And it was the sin of drunkenness that has brought this destruction and untimely death upon him. There is a dreadful wo denounced from the Almighty against drunkards; and it is this sin, this abominable, this beastly and accursed sin of drunkenness, that has stript us of every desirable comfort in this life; by this we are poor miserable and wretched; by this sin we have no name nor credit in the world among polite nations; for this sin we are despised in the world, and it is all right and just, for we despise ourselves more; and if we don't regard ourselves, who will regard us? And it is for our sins and especially for that accursed, that most devilish sin of drunkenness that we suffer every day. For the love of strong drink we spend all that we have, and every thing we can get. By this sin we can't have comfortable houses, nor any thing comfortable in our houses; neither food nor raiment, nor decent utensils. We are obliged to put up with any sort of shelter just to screen us from the severity of the weather, and we go about with very mean, ragged and dirty clothes, almost naked. And we are half-starved, for the most of the time obliged to pick up any thing to eat. And our poor children are suffering every day for want of the necessaries of life; they are very often crying for want of food, and we have nothing to give them; and in the cold weather they are shivering and crying, being pinched with cold. All this for the love of strong drink. And this is not all the misery and evil we bring on ourselves in this world; but when we are intoxicated with strong drink we drown our rational powers, by which we are distinguished from the brutal creation we unman ourselves, and bring ourselves not only level with the beasts of the field, but seven degrees beneath them; yea we bring ourselves level with the devils; I don't know but we make ourselves worse than devils, for I never heard of drunken devils.

---

26. Ephesians 6:10–18.

My poor kindred, do consider what a dreadful abominable sin drunkenness is. God made us men, and we chuse to be beasts and devils, God made us rational creatures, and we chuse to be fools. Do consider further, and behold a drunkard and see how he looks when he has drowned his reason; how deformed and shameful does he appear? He disfigures every part of him, both soul and body, which was made after the Image of God. He appears with awful deformity, and his whole visage is disfigured; if he attempts to speak he cannot bring out his words distinct, so as to be understood; if he walks he reels and staggers to and fro, and tumbles down. And see how he behaves, he is now laughing, and then he is crying, he is singing, and the next minute he is mourning, and is all love with every one, and anon he is raging and for fighting, and killing all before him, even the nearest and dearest relations and friends: Yea, nothing it too bad for a drunken man to do. He will do that which he would not do for the world, in his right mind; he may lie with his own sister or daughter as Lot did.

Further, when a person is drunk, he is just good for nothing in the world; he is of no service to himself, to his family, to his neighbours, or his country; and how much more unfit is he to serve God: Yet we are just fit for the service of the devil.

Again, a man in drunkenness is in all manner of dangers, he may be killed by his fellow-men, by wild beasts, and tame beasts; he may fall into the fire, into the water, or into a ditch; or he may fall down as he walks along, and break his bones or his neck; and he may cut him-self with edge-tools. Further if he has any money or any thing valuable, he may lose it all, or may be robbed, or he may make a foolish bargain and be cheated out of all he has.

I believe you know the truth of what I have just now said, many of you by sad experience; yet you will go on still in your drunkenness. Though you have been cheated over and over again, and you have lost your substance by drunkenness, yet you will venture to go on in this most destructive sin. O fools, when will ye be wise?—We all know the truth of what I have been saying, by what we have seen and heard of drunken deaths. How many have been drowned in our rivers, and how many frozen to death in the winter season! yet drunkards go on without fear and consideration: Alas, alas! What will become of all such drunkards? Without doubt they must all go to hell, except they truly repent and turn to God. Drunkenness is so common amongst us, that even our young men, (and what is still more shocking) *young women* are not ashamed to get drunk. Our young men will get drunk as soon as they will eat when they are hungry.—It is generally esteemed among men more abominable for a woman to be drunk than a man; and yet there is nothing more common amongst us than female drunkards. Women ought to be more modest than men; the holy scriptures recommend modesty to women in particular;—But drunken women have no modesty at all. It is more intolerable for a woman to get drunk, if we consider further, that she is in great danger of falling into the hands of the sons of Belial, or wicked men and being shamefully treated by them.

And here I cannot but observe, we find in sacred writ, a wo denounced against men who put their bottles to their neighbours mouth to make them drunk, that they may see their nakedness: And no doubt there are such devilish men now in our days, as there were in the days of old.

And to conclude, Consider my poor kindred, you that are drunkards, into what a miserable condition you have brought yourselves. There is a dreadful wo thundering against you every day, and the Lord says, That drunkards shall not inherit the kingdom of heaven.

And now let me exhort you all to break off from your drunkenness, by a gospel repentance, and believe on the Lord Jesus and you shall be saved. Take warning by this doleful sight before us, and by all the dreadful judgments that have befallen poor drunkards. O let us all reform our lives, and live as becomes dying creatures, in time to come. Let us be persuaded that we are accountable creatures to God, and we must be called to an account in a few days. You that have been careless all your days, now awake to righteousness, and be concerned for your poor never-dying souls. Fight against all sins, and especially the sin that easily besets you, and behave in time to come as becomes rational creatures; and above all things receive and believe on the Lord Jesus Christ, and you shall have eternal life; and when you come to die, your souls will be received into heaven, there to be with the Lord Jesus in eternal happiness, with all the saints in glory: Which God of his infinite mercy grant, through Jesus Christ our Lord.—Amen.

JOSEPH JOHNSON (1751–1776?)

Minister, teacher, and leader in a movement in the northeast for Indian unification, Joseph Johnson was born to Mohegans Joseph Johnson and Elizabeth Garrett in the village called Mohegan, Connecticut. The Johnsons' lives in this era were similar to the lives of many in the Indian communities: The indigenous peoples were forced by the wars of the Europeans in North America to choose sides in the Europeans' wars to take over the Indians' ancestral lands. In the case of Johnson's father, the decision was to join the British during the Seven Years War, known among British colonists as the French and Indian War. Johnson's father died in this war, leaving Elizabeth Johnson alone to tend to the interests of the family. Joseph Johnson thus was sent, at age seven, to the Reverend Eleazer Wheelock's Indian Charity School in Lebanon. There he spent the next eight years in a highly structured environment, studying religion, reading, and writing, and, when he was not being schooled, working at neighboring farms. For many Indian students, life at Christian schools meant lives of work, and Johnson's life was no different from this standard. Johnson found his experiences difficult at Wheelock's school, and he seems to have vacillated widely between his affections for Christianity (and the presumably settled life of English people) and the life he might have were he to remain "Indian." Johnson had gained some familiarity with Christianity while still a young child at home because his mother had been Christianized, as had many of their neighbors, and Johnson himself had been baptized. But the Christian way was, to Johnson and many Indians who attempted to live in two worlds, hard to follow.

Johnson's relationship with Wheelock and his experiences at Wheelock's school played a significant role in his life. Johnson was one of a number of Indian students whom Wheelock was working to convert fully and to educate in order to achieve his goal of converting the Iroquois (whom the British called the Six Nations) of New York. Wheelock believed that the Algonquian-speaking Natives were more quiescent with Christian faith practices and more familiar with the ways of British settlers, whereas the Six Nations people, living among Dutch, French, and British settlers, experienced lives of greater instability. With what he perceived as the necessary assistance of Samson Occom and the students he trained, Wheelock wanted to send students from New England to work as missionaries in Oneida territories. The challenges that participating in this project posed for Wheelock's students, such as Johnson, became clear when, at the age of fifteen, Johnson traveled to New York to become a schoolteacher among the Oneidas. Johnson struggled to meet the demands of the other teachers and Wheelock, even while he was negotiating for himself a speaking space among non-Christian peoples who had no kinship or cultural affiliations with his own people. Life in the middle was difficult. Amid his supervisor's charges that he had "turn'd pagan for about a week," Johnson lost his position in 1769, and his relationship with Wheelock faltered.

After working as a schoolteacher in Rhode Island and later on a whaling ship, Johnson returned to Mohegan in 1771 to work on his uncle's farm. During a religious revival in the area, Johnson experienced a spiritual conversion. He soon moved to an Indian community near Hartford, where he taught and preached. He developed a strong sense of religion and purpose while working in Farmington, Connecticut, which led to his decision to work with others who were preparing for a move to the Iroquois country. Johnson played a central role in attracting Indian peoples from around Farmington, Mohegan, Stonington, Lyme, Long Island, Groton, and Charlestown and encouraging them to migrate with him to Brotherton, New York, where they could live in a separate community of Indians, rather than dispersed among the settler peoples. To secure land from the Oneidas, they arranged trades and purchases of lands in order to establish their community at Brotherton.

In 1773 Johnson married Tabitha, the daughter of the renowned Mohegan preacher and former Wheelock student, Samson Occom. Johnson's travels on behalf of the Brotherton project and his work for his ministry meant that he had limited time to spend in Mohegan with his wife and two sons, William (b. 1774) and Joseph (b. 1776). Johnson died in 1776 or 1777 when he was only twenty-five.

Johnson's earliest surviving writings were letters addressed to Wheelock, his teacher. Two diaries, which address personal, religious, and community issues, cover the period between 1770 and 1773. Johnson also wrote a number of sermons and public letters directed to other Indians, benefactors, and political figures. Although only two pieces of his writing were published during his lifetime, a broad range of Johnson's writings survive and have recently been collected and published in a useful study of his life and writings by Laura Murray.

LETTER FROM J—H J—N

One of the Mohegan Tribe of Indians, to His Countryman, Moses Paul, Under Sentence of Death, in New-Haven Goal[1]

**Mohegan, in New-London County,
A.D. 1772, March 29**

My dear fellow traveller into a vast eternity; listen unto me a-while. I am an Indian, known by the name of J—h J—n, a native of this land and of the Mohegan tribe. I am one who am truly sorry for your misfortune, but so it was fore-ordained by an all-wise GOD; and so you see it is by woeful experience, but who knows what GOD has designed by it, perhaps to the good of your immortal soul.

My dear fellow mortal, it is too evident (that there is a GOD) for us to deny a being of a GOD, than we say we believe there is a GOD of almighty power, who has created all things by the word of his power, and he preserves all things both in heaven and earth; and he over-rules all things by his secret Providence, though we see him not, we do his will, and fulfil his word: Perhaps not designedly, yet he is glorified by us, or will be, either by our eternal salvation, or condemnation. And from this great GOD'S hands no one can deliver; whomsoever he sees fit to save, none can destroy or pluck out of his hands. And we hear likewise, that this great GOD is angry with the wicked every day. And he makes a dismal place of torments to put the wicked in, which is called HELL; a place prepared for the devil and his angels, and it burns with unquenchable fire and brimstone; there GOD Almighty

makes himself known by the displays of his eternal wrath which is poured upon the wicked, without the least mixture of mercy. I say we hear of such a place, but do we really believe it to be a sacred truth. If we do, should it not be our highest concern to know how we might escape that place of torments. Methinks you at once say yes, so do I too; well let us be sincere, and act the wiser part, and examine ourselves, until we convince ourselves that we are by nature the children of wrath, and more so by practice: and if we die as we were born, and as we have liv'd in times past, HELL must be our eternal home. And who that has a reasonable soul, can think of that dreadful place without horror and amazement? If there was no way found out, that we might escape this place of misery, then we must necessarily bear it as other unavoidable misfortunes. But glory be given to that GOD, who is good and gracious, in whom we believe; that he has in infinite wisdom found out a glorious way, not only to be saved from hell torments, but to give eternal life and glory that [passeth?] not away; and true happiness to every one, humble, penitent, believing soul, by the gift of his only begotten Son JESUS CHRIST.

You have heard of this JESUS CHRIST, the only Son of the ever living and true GOD; you was brought up in a Christian land where CHRIST was named and worshipped, and loved, trusted and adored. We have heard that GOD so loved the world, that he gave this CHRIST his only begotten Son, that whosoever believeth in him, should not perish, but have everlasting life. Well, come and let us believe in this Jesus Christ the glorious Son of GOD, that we may not perish, but have eternal life. I do really wish your soul well, and I hope that you will sincerely seek an interest in the Lord JESUS CHRIST.

Precious is your time indeed, if you did but know it: it is certain you have not a long continuance here, and the time is drawing nigh, when you must step out of time, into eternity. We hear that you are condemned by the Judges of this Colony, and that your life must be taken away by the execution of justice. Justice must, or ought to be done; and all that men can do is to kill the body: for our blessed Saviour said in the days of his flesh, Mat. x. 28. And fear

---

1. This letter was originally published in New London, Connecticut, in 1772, the edition that is the source of the present text. Moses Paul (1742–72), a Christian Mohegan, was executed for the killing of Moses Cook, a prominent man from Watertown. Samson Occom, Johnson's father-in-law, delivered Paul's execution sermon.

not them which kill the body, but are not able to kill the soul: but rather fear him, which is able to destroy both body and soul in hell,[2] that is GOD. If you are interested in the favour of God, and have his Son JESUS CHRIST for your friend and advocate, it will be well with you after death and the second death will have no power over you, that is spiritual and eternal death. I therefore, as a well wisher to your never dying soul, advise you to seek GOD's favour, and pray to him in the name of the Lord JESUS CHRIST to pardon, and forgive your soul, and give you his holy Spirit to sanctify, and purify your heart, and make you meet for the inheritance of the saints in light. Pray for true, and genuine conviction, such a conviction as GOD gives unto his true children; pray for true repentance, that which is unto life, and faith which purifies the heart; and pray for every grace of a true christian believer in the Lord Jesus Christ: Who knows but GOD will have mercy upon you, and hear you, and pardon and forgive you at last, for he is a merciful GOD, delighteth in forgiving iniquities, transgressions and sins, through the merits of his Son Jesus Christ. Perhaps you are not past hope as to your salvation, for Christ said in his day, in xii, 31 of Mat. Wherefore I say unto you, all manner of sin, and blasphemy, shall be forgiven unto men; but whosoever speaketh against the Holy Ghost, it shall not be forgiven him, neither in this world, neither in the world to come.[3] These are the words of him who cannot lie. Heaven and earth shall pass away before one jot, or tittle of his word shall pass; he has said this also, and may we not believe him? My spirit mourned within me, when I heard that you was unconcerned about your soul's eternal welfare. But I hope by this time you are of another mind, and things eternal your chiefest concern. Do you not desire to be made forever happy hereafter? Well, repent and believe, and bring forth fruit meet for repentance. Believe in the Lord Jesus Christ; believe that he is an all-sufficient Saviour, able to purge away thy sins, many and foul as they are; just such a one as you want and must have, or be eternally miserable. Except him for thy whole Saviour. Oh that you might be as happy as to have a true change wrought in you, and really obtain a full and free pardon, from the great GOD in Heaven, through Jesus Christ his beloved Son, in whom he is ever

well pleased. I say, if this was your happy case, I might pronounce you blessed indeed. And what joy and peace would it create in every heart of a true Christian, wherever you might be ever heard of! And what comfort and satisfaction would rest upon your soul, to think that in a few days I must remove from hence, and enter in those regions of bliss which are above, and there to dwell forever before a holy and pure GOD, who is at peace with me; and to be with Christ our Saviour in his kingdom, to behold his glory; the glory of an only begotten Son of GOD! O, what a pleasing prospect would consequently open! What must I, who am bound in these fetters, in this dark and lonesom prison, or dungeon, be set at liberty, and be admitted into that blessed company above! There angels of mighty power, in all their royal robes, with their golden harps, and starry crowns, are bowing and worshipping before our GOD and Saviour Jesus Christ. There likewise shall I see the spirits of just men made perfect; Moses and Aaron, and all the holy prophets and apostles and saints of every age, some of all nations, an innumerable company; and all exercised in one work of praise. What must I indeed enter into that holy city, the New-Jerusalem, which is described in the 21st chapter of Revelations! Methinks if this was your happy case, you would thus reason with yourself, and should be impatient, until that glorious hour should appear when that welcome messenger death should come, which shall carry you from hence, to the place of our GOD the Father, and to be received into the perfect enjoyment of him, which is a complete heaven. But if on the other hand, you have this great GOD, and Jesus Christ, his Son to be against you, you are, and must be eternally miserable. You cannot have any pleasing tho'ts of approaching death, judgment and eternity: neither of these can you escape. Death is certain, and so certain as death is, so is judgment and eternity; and there is but two places made known to us in the word of GOD, where all the children of men are to meet, that is heaven and hell; and in these two different places we must all find ourselves one day, sooner, or later. And be assured, if you fall short of heaven, into hell you must be turned: and I doubt not, but this is the earnest prayer and desire of many, who have a prejudice against the Indian nations, and wish no better of your soul, than to endure GOD's eternal wrath, and even rejoice that one of the devilish Indians, (as many express themselves) are suffered to act such a part; and wish that all were as nigh their end. But such as these it is to be feared, know but little of GOD, or have never had GOD's love shed abroad in their hearts;

---

2. Johnson accurately quotes Matthew 10:28. Unless noted otherwise, Johnson's biblical quotations and citations are generally accurate.

3. Compare with Matthew 12:31–32.

and therefore are liable to endure GOD's eternal wrath. But there are some, I doubt not, who know the great worth of souls, is praying from day to day to GOD [that] he would give you repentance, and faith in the Lord Jesus Christ; and their earnest desire is, that your soul may be saved from GOD's eternal wrath. It is the desire of my heart, that we might hear, that you have obtained GOD's forgiveness. And if you are not assured as yet, as to your state, I should be glad to hear that you were in earnest, seeking the favor of GOD. And it is the greatest happiness that we mortals can obtain in this life, to be assured of the favor of GOD, and JESUS CHRIST our Lord; then come what will, we are safe. If GOD is for us, who can be against us? My fellow traveller into a vast eternity, I want that you would put on consideration, and consider the word *eternity*. Think of heaven and hell—think of the great GOD against whom you have sinned, and Jesus Christ his Son. Also think of the devil; that is the serpent, that was the cause of the fall of our first parents; and brought GOD's wrath upon us. He is a deceiver, and the truth is not in him. He is miserable, and wants us to be miserable too.

I am far from discouraging you, that I will conclude this letter with a few passages out of the holy word of GOD, for your encouragement: first a glorious invitation, from Christ Jesus our Lord, which is in Mat. xi. 28. Christ saith, come unto me, all ye that labour, and are heavy laden, and I will give you rest. He does not say, may be I will give you rest, but I will give you rest. And he saith in another place; and he that cometh to me, I will in no way cast out, Joh. vi. 37. Is not this great encouragement when we consider that Christ spoke it, the Son of GOD that cannot lie. Let us then believe him. Again, he reasons with us in Isaiah i. 18. Come now and let us reason together, saith the Lord: though your sins be as scarlet, they shall be white as snow: though they be red like crimson, they shall be as wool. And further he says, in Mat, xii. chap. 31st ver. Wherefore I say unto you, all manner of sin and blasphemy, shall be forgiven unto men: but the blasphemy against the Holy Ghost, shall not be forgiven unto men. And also in Ezek. xviii. 23. Have I any pleasure at all, that the wicked should die? saith the LORD GOD: and not that he should return from his wicked ways and live? Again, Isa. xliii. chap. 24, 25, vers. Though thou hast made me to serve with thy sins; thou hast wearied me with thine iniquities. I, even I, am he that blotteth out thy transgressions, for my own sake, will not remember thy sins.[4] Also, in

Amos v.4.6. For thus saith the Lord, seek ye me, and ye shall live, seek the Lord and ye shall live, least he break out like fire, and there be none to quench it.[5] Seek him that made the seven Stars, and turneth the shadow of death into morning, and maketh the day dark with night, the Lord is his name. Luke vi.36.[6] A merciful GOD.

All I can say is, don't be discouraged, but resign yourself to that merciful GOD, and be willing to be disposed of by him, as seemeth him good; and ever say, Thy will be done. There is many precious promises, in GOD's book, called the holy scriptures, which I advise you to search diligently, there you may see the [Gospel?] terms of salvation. There you may learn, all those glorious characters of our exalted Lord and Saviour Jesus Christ. Neither doth he bear those blessed characters in vain. He said he came not for the righteous, but sinners to repentance. Mat. xi. 17.[7] They that are whole, need not a physician, but they that are sick; I came not to call the righteous, but sinners to repentance. Then Christ came for such as you and me, who are sinners, Should not we then rejoice that we have heard of the way of salvation in our day; which many have been, and are to this day denied, some who have never once heard of this blessed Jesus. It seems my soul delights to hear of his name! I desire you would take notice of what I have in so broken a manner hinted unto you. I mean to be sincere.—But I am uncapable of expressing myself, or writing as some may who have been favoured with great learning, and have had great experiences, and those who know all arts and sciences, neither can I speak as those who are acquainted with the deep mysteries of the kingdom of GOD. But this I know, that we must be born again, or never enter into the kingdom of GOD; for our exalted Lord Jesus Christ said in the days of his humiliation, John iii.5.7. Verily, verily, I say unto you, except a man be born of water, and of the Spirit, he can-

---

4. Compare with Isaiah 43:24–25.

5. Compare with Amos 5:4, 6.

6. Luke 6:36, "Be ye therefore merciful, as your Father also is merciful."

7. Johnson seems to be remembering another biblical passage here (not Matthew 11:17).

not enter into the kingdom of GOD. And soon after, he says, marvel not that I said unto thee, you must be born again. Take heed how you hear, and try to understand the meaning of these words, for they proceed from the mouth of our exalted Lord and Saviour Jesus Christ, the Son of GOD. But if you will not regard my advice, and truly repent before GOD, but hear all these warnings and encouragements, with indifference (for I trust and hope, these may be delivered you) remember that this letter, tho' it is in a broken manner wrote, will be a witness against you one day. But if you accept it, that is, whatever you find in it, that agrees with the holy word of GOD, and if it has effect upon your mind, try to lay it up in your heart, and practice it in your life; and if you receive any help from it, give GOD the glory; but what ever you find that is contrary to the word of GOD, reject it as an error. For we have a sure word of prophesy, which we do well to adhere, as unto a light that shineth in darkness.

I know that such a discourse, or letter, written to one, who is earthly minded, and has no spiritual understanding, I say, to such a one, it is nonsense; it appears to him to be foolishness, and idle story, not worth his notice; but rather ridicule it, and learn some of it to use it as a proverb, or as we say, a by-word. But one who is truly sensible, truly awakened, and sees his true condition by nature, that he is and must be lost eternally; to such a one, Jesus Christ is precious, and his ears, and heart is open to hear all advice, warnings and encouragements; the promises are precious unto him, and he seeks the favor of GOD, with his whole heart. I hope this is your disposition now. I have not much more to say, but I tell you that there is no other Name given unto men under heaven, whereby they may be saved but by the name of Jesus! That through his death and suffering alone, I say, through faith in his name, we must enter into rest. Therefore seek his favour, for the favour of man avails nothing before the sight of GOD; for it is said he has no respect of persons. Well I must conclude. I fear I have already wearied you! only if you will utterly refuse all the gospel invitations, you must hear Jesus Christ pronounce the word, Depart. Methinks he is pleading still with you, and says you will not come unto me, that you might have life. But I end.

I am your soul's well-wisher.

To Moses Paul,
New-Haven.   *J—h J—n,*
                    A native of the Mohegan tribe.

DEDICATION TO A LIFE OF THE SPIRIT[1]

Anno Domini 1772 May the 24th—

After a long time under the workings of Gods holy Spirit as I humbly trust—I this day have concluded that by the help of god I'll endeavour to dedicate my Self to him. It has long been my Souls desire to make a Publick dedication of my self to the liveing God who is the Creator, Preserver, & upholder of all things, & who is reconciling the world through his Son Jesus Christ, to himself. After many doubtings, trials & Difficulties, I think I can come to the Ordinances of Christ the Baptism, & the Lords Supper, with a clear Concience trusting I have found some clear Evidence of an interest in gods Eternal Son, Jesus Christ. Oh that when he Calls in his elect, that my worthless name might be found amongst them. This all my desire, no matter how the things of time passes with me, if at last I Shall meet the Lord of glory with Joy—let Sorrow fill my weary heart from day to day, in this life if then my Soul may leap for joy at his blessed appearance in the air. Shall that Blessed hour come when I shall leave this dark abode these weary limbs of mine and take a flight into the vissionary world to See the worship carried on in Perfection by the holy Angels of God & all the redeemed ones redeemed by the Precious blood of Christ? Not only See this Soul reviving Sight but to Join in Praising the wonders of redeeming Love. Can I entertain Such glorious hope & yet indulge Sin in my mortal body? O that I might have the grace of God to keep my Clay from iniquity. O that every corrupt inclination might be intirely rooted out from my corrupt nature. I know I am vile there is no natural good within me, but I trust that my vile nature Shall be changed, & be Subdued by the Same Power by which he Shall put all things under his feet, Subdue all things to himself.

Yet in this Life I do expect to war with my Corruptions, and I do expect many dark hours, lonsome nights, Seem destitute of all friends forsaken by my Acquaintance, despised, yea hated, & looked upon as an Enimy. But all these must be, the Sarvant is not greater than his

---

1. The text is taken from *To Do Good to My Indian Brethren: The Writings of Joseph Johnson, 1751–1776,* ed. Laura Murray (1998). Johnson did not sign his dedication.

Lord, and they are necessary they learn me that there is no happiness here below and if all things were well with me perhaps I Should place my happiness in them, and forget the Lord of Life at whose right hand there are Pleasures forevermore, without the least interruption, through out whole eternity.

I have Enimies within & without, and my flesh is weak. What am I over come by every Small wind of temptation? So frail am I, but I expect soon to pass thro this tempting wilderness whire temptations grow, and enter into the new world wherein dwelleth Rightiousness. Theither nothing Unclean Shall come, no temptation, no trouble, Sorrow is there all forgot. There Shall I look back and reflect the way wherin I walked through the wilderness; then Shall I See clearly, what all my various Stations, & Situations, which I now am in and have been in from my first birth to the moment of my resignation of my Soul & breath, I Say I Shall See clearly what all these mean, and with plaseing wonder Consider the goodness of God who has Safely Carried me through, and brought me to the happy Possession of the Promised Land—and is that blessed hour approaching when I Shall pass over the cold Streem of Jordan death, to the blessed land of Promise heaven? There on those glorious Shores of bliss Stands the Eternal Son of God the Saviour of men Smiling, waiting to receive the weary Passengers home to his fathers house where are many mansions. Amen. Farewell world with all your glory for it must come to an End neither hast thou any Joy like those in younder world to which I am Bound.

PHILLIS WHEATLEY (1754?–1784)

When she went on tour in London and the surrounding area, Phillis Wheatley became an overnight sensation. Given her literary gifts, the range of her reading, and the living testimony she offered as to the humanity, dignity, and superior intellectual gifts of African people, Wheatley was interviewed and entertained by important statesmen, such as Benjamin Franklin and William Legge, second earl of Dartmouth, and she was given tours and gifts of books that would prove immensely memorable to her when she returned to Massachusetts only to watch her friend and patron, Susanna Wheatley, suffer her last illness and die. Phillis Wheatley was the first African American poet to publish her writings, and the first to be so well received in London. She was, for those who followed Methodism and those who were members of the Society of Friends, the primary example available of the necessity of abolishing the dehumanizing practices of capturing and selling slaves.

Phillis Wheatley was born in Africa, most likely in present-day Gambia or Senegal. She was captured in 1761 and brought to Boston, where she was purchased by John Wheatley, a wealthy Boston tailor, for his wife Susanna. Given the name "Phillis" after the slave ship that brought her to Boston, Phillis Wheatley became a favored slave within the Wheatley household, enabled, because of her special talents, to lead a life quite different from the lives of most New England slaves. Recognizing her immense intellectual gifts, the Wheatleys offered Phillis access to an extensive education. She read classical writers in translation (including Ovid, Horace, and Virgil), several more-contemporary British poets (including Milton, Pope, and Gray), and the Bible. She studied history and geography, but her primary expertise resided in her literary expression. Although she was young and had lived only four years in Boston, Phillis Wheatley was sufficiently skilled in letters to begin a correspondence with the Mohegan minister Samson Occom. Phillis Wheatley's connection to the Wheatley family offered her the opportunity to meet many prominent Bostonians, some of whom would later testify to the authenticity of her poetry. Although little is known of Wheatley's early connections to the African American community in Boston, the location of the Wheatley home and Phillis Wheatley's access to local papers almost assured her knowledge of fellow African Americans who began to petition for their freedom during the 1770s.

Wheatley published her first poem in a Rhode Island paper when she was only thirteen years old. This publication was soon followed by additional publications of poems in newspapers and as broadsides, long sheets that could be passed readily from hand to hand. Poems like Wheatley's 1770 elegy to Reverend George Whitefield, a well-known Methodist evangelist, were quickly reprinted in New York, Boston, Newport, and Philadelphia. Patterned after the neoclassical verse of her contemporaries, Wheatley's poems addressed diverse topics and employed a variety of formal techniques. Although much of her poetry was religious in nature, she also wrote political poems, elegies, and occasional poetry.

Wheatley initially sought to publish a volume of her poetry in Boston in 1772, but she discovered that subscribers would not sign on for publishing her writings. With the support of Selina Hastings, the countess of Huntingdon (a philanthropist and patron of several early African American writers), Susanna Wheatley helped arrange to have Phillis Wheatley's volume, *Poems on Various Subjects, Religious and Moral* (1773), published in London. Wheatley's poetry received international praise, and her literary career was launched to a wide reading populace in Britain.

Wheatley's network of friends and acquaintances, including those who were represented within her correspondence, was strikingly diverse in racial background and social status, thus attesting to Wheatley's particular social and intellectual gifts. During her trip to London, for example, she met with the noted abolitionist Granville Sharp; with William Legge, the second earl of Dartmouth; and with Benjamin Franklin, among numerous other prominent figures. Wheatley's letter to David Wooster describes this visit and reveals something of the nature and extent of her transatlantic circle. Among Wheatley's most important correspondents was her close friend, Obour Tanner, a woman of African descent who was a servant to the John Tanner family in Newport. Wheatley's letters address religion, politics, colonization, and the publication of her works, as well as a range of other topics, and thus suggest the range of her interests, the importance of her goals, and the depth of her beliefs.

Shortly after Wheatley returned from London, and with her book of poems just published, she was granted her freedom. As she commented in a letter, it was only after she gained attention for her writing that John Wheatley decided, "at the desire of my friends in England" to "giv[e] me my freedom." Wheatley continued to live with and help care for John and Susanna Wheatley for a time, until 1778, when she married John Peters, a free black. The Peters family struggled financially, and Phillis's life as a free woman was difficult, owing to continued health problems and the deaths of her children. Although she proposed another volume of poetry and letters and advertised for subscribers in Boston papers in 1779 and again in 1784, her second project never came to fruition. Her last published poem appeared in the *Boston Magazine* in September 1784, just three months before her death at age thirty-one. The following selections are some of Wheatley's published and unpublished writings. Except where otherwise noted, many of the poems were first published in her volume, *Poems on Various Subjects, Religious and Moral* (1773), published in London.

from POEMS ON VARIOUS SUBJECTS, RELIGIOUS AND MORAL

To Mæcenas

MÆCENAS,[1] you, beneath the myrtle shade,
Read o'er what poets sung, and shepherds play'd.
What felt those poets but you feel the same?

---

1. Gaius Cilnius Mæcenas, a Roman statesman, was the patron of Horace and Virgil.

Does not your soul possess the sacred flame?
Their noble strains your equal genius shares
In softer language, and diviner airs.

While *Homer* paints lo! circumfus'd in air,
Celestial Gods in mortal forms appear;
Swift as they move hear each recess rebound,
Heav'n quakes, earth trembles, and the shores resound.
Great Sire of verse, before my mortal eyes,
The lightnings blaze across the vaulted skies,
And, as the thunder shakes the heav'nly plains,
A deep-felt horror thrills through all my veins.
When gentler strains demand thy graceful song,

The length'ning line moves languishing along.
When great *Patroclus*[2] courts *Achilles'* aid,
The grateful tribute of my tears is paid;
Prone on the shore he feels the pangs of love,
And stern *Pelides*[3] tend'rest passions move.

Great *Maro's* strain in heav'nly numbers flows,
The *Nine*[4] inspire, and all the bosom glows.
O could I rival thine and *Virgil's* page,
Or claim the *Muses* with the *Mantuan* Sage;[5]
Soon the same beauties should my mind adorn,
And the same ardors in my soul should burn;
Then should my song in bolder notes arise,
And all my numbers pleasingly surprise;
But here I sit, and mourn a grov'ling mind
That fain would mount and ride upon the wind.

Not you, my friend, these plaintive strains become,
Not you, whose bosom is the *Muses* home;
When they from tow'ring *Helicon*[6] retire,
They fan in you the bright immortal fire,
But I less happy, cannot raise the song,
The fault'ring music dies upon my tongue.

The happier *Terence*[7] all the choir inspir'd,
His soul replenish'd, and his bosom fir'd
But say, ye *Muses*, why this partial grace,
To one alone of *Afric's* sable race;
From age to age transmitting thus his name
With the first glory in the rolls of fame?

Thy virtues, great *Mæcenas!* shall be sung
In praise of him, from whom those virtues sprung:
While blooming wreaths around thy temples spread,
I'll snatch a laurel from thine honour'd head,
While you indulgent smile upon the deed.

As long as *Thames* in streams majestic flows,
Or *Naiads* in their oozy beds repose,
While *Phœbus*[8] reigns above the starry train,

While bright *Aurora*[9] purples o'er the main,
So long, great Sir, the muse thy praise shall sing,
So long thy praise shall make *Parnassus*[10] ring:
Then grant, *Mæcenas,* thy paternal rays,
Hear me propitious, and defend my lays.

To the University of Cambridge, in New-England[11]

WHILE an intrinsic ardor prompts to write,
The muses promise to assist my pen;
'Twas not long since I left my native shore
The land of errors, and *Egyptian* gloom:
Father of mercy, 'twas thy gracious hand
Brought me in safety from those dark abodes.

Students, to you 'tis giv'n to scan the heights
Above, to traverse the ethereal space,
And mark the systems of revolving worlds.
Still more, ye sons of science ye receive
The blissful news by messengers from heav'n,
How *Jesus'* blood for your redemption flows.
See him with hands out-stretcht upon the cross;
Immense compassion in his bosom glows;
He hears revilers, nor resents their scorn:
What matchless mercy in the Son of God!
When the whole human race by sin had fall'n,
He deign'd to die that they might rise again,
And share with him in the sublimest skies,
Life without death, and glory without end.

Improve your privileges while they stay,
Ye pupils, and each hour redeem, that bears
Or good or bad report of you to heav'n.
Let sin, that baneful evil to the soul,
By you be shunn'd, nor once remit your guard;
Suppress the deadly serpent in its egg.
Ye blooming plants of human race divine,
An *Ethiop* tells you 'tis your greatest foe;
Its transient sweetness turns to endless pain,
And in immense perdition sinks the soul.

On Being Brought from Africa to America

'TWAS mercy brought me from my *Pagan* land,
Taught my benighted soul to understand

---

2. The favorite companion of Achilles, Greek hero in the *Iliad.*

3. Achilles, son of Peleus.

4. The Muses responsible for serving literature and the arts.

5. The birthplace of Virgil was presumed to be Mantua.

6. According to legend, Mount Helicon is the home of the Muses.

7. "He was an *African* by birth." [Au.]

8. The Greek god of the sun.

---

9. The Roman goddess of the dawn.

10. A mountain ridge near ancient Delphi, celebrated as the haunt of Apollo and the Muses.

11. The title refers to Harvard College in Cambridge, Massachusetts.

That there's a God, that there's a *Saviour* too:
Once I redemption neither sought nor knew.
Some view our sable race with scornful eye,
"Their colour is a diabolic die."
Remember, *Christians, Negroes,* black as *Cain,*
May be refin'd, and join th' angelic train.

On the Death of the
Rev. Mr. George Whitefield[12]

HAIL, happy saint, on thine immortal throne,
Possest of glory, life, and bliss unknown;
We hear no more the music of thy tongue,
Thy wonted auditories cease to throng.
Thy sermons in unequall'd accents flow'd,
And ev'ry bosom with devotion glow'd;
Thou didst in strains of eloquence refin'd
Inflame the heart, and captivate the mind.
Unhappy we the setting sun deplore,
So glorious once, but ah! it shines no more.

  Behold the prophet in his tow'ring flight!
He leaves the earth for heav'n's unmeasur'd height,
And worlds unknown receive him from our sight.
There *Whitefield* wings with rapid course his way,
And sails to *Zion,* through vast seas of day.
Thy pray'rs, great saint, and thine incessant cries
Have pierc'd the bosom of thy native skies.
Thou moon hast seen, and all the stars of light,
How he has wrestled with his God by night.
He pray'd that grace in ev'ry heart might dwell,
He long'd to see *America* excel;
He charg'd its youth that ev'ry grace divine
Should with full lustre in their conduct shine;
That Savior, which his soul did first receive,
The greatest gift that ev'n a God can give,
He freely offer'd to the num'rous throng,
That on his lips with list'ning pleasure hung.

  "Take him, ye wretched, for your only good,
Take him ye starving sinners, for your food;
Ye thirsty, come to this life-giving stream,
Ye preachers, take him for your joyful theme;

Take him my dear *Americans,* he said,
Be your complaints on his kind bosom laid:
Take him, ye *Africans,* he longs for you,
Impartial Saviour is his title due;
Wash'd in the fountain of redeeming blood,
You shall be sons, and kings, and priests to God."

  Great *Countess,*[13] we *Americans* revere
Thy name, and mingle in thy grief sincere;
New England deeply feels, the *Orphans* mourn,[14]
Their more than father will no more return.

  But, though arrested by the hand of death,
Whitefield no more exerts his lab'ring breath,
Yet let us view him in th' eternal skies,
Let ev'ry heart to this bright vision rise;
While the tomb safe retains its sacred trust,
Till life divine re-animates his dust.

Thoughts on the Works of Providence

ARISE, my soul, on wings enraptur'd, rise
To praise the monarch of the earth and skies,
Whose goodness and beneficence appear
As round its centre moves the rolling year,
Or when the morning glows with rosy charms,
Or the sun slumbers in the ocean's arms:
Of light divine be a rich portion lent
To guide my soul, and favour my intent.
Celestial muse, my arduous flight sustain,
And raise my mind to a seraphic strain!

  Ador'd for ever be the God unseen,
Which round the sun revolves this vast machine,
Though to his eye its mass a point appears:
Ador'd the God that whirls surrounding spheres.
Which first ordain'd that mighty *Sol*[15] should reign
The peerless monarch of th' ethereal train:
Of miles twice forty millions is his height,
And yet his radiance dazzles mortal sight
So far beneath—from him th' extended earth
Vigour derives, and ev'ry flow'ry birth:
Vast through her orb she moves with easy grace

---

12. George Whitefield (1714–70) was a popular English Methodist and evangelist who participated in numerous revivals across Britain's North American colonies. The poem was published as a broadside and then revised slightly for publication in Wheatley's book.

---

13. "The Countess of *Huntingdon,* to whom Mr. *Whitefield* was Chaplain." [Au.]

14. Whitefield established an orphanage near Savannah, Georgia.

15. The sun.

Around her *Phœbus*[16] in unbounded space;
True to her course th' impetuous storm derides
Triumphant o'er the winds, and surging tides.

Almighty, in these wond'rous works of thine,
What *Pow'r,* what *Wisdom,* and what *Goodness* shine?
And are thy wonders, Lord, by men explor'd,
And yet creating glory unador'd!

Creation smiles in various beauty gay,
While day to night, and night succeeds to day:
That *Wisdom,* which attends *Jehovah's* ways,
Shines more conspicuous in the solar rays:
Without them, destitute of heat and light,
This world would be the reign of endless night:
In their excess how would our race complain,
Abhorring life! how hate its length'ned chain!
From air adust what num'rous ills would rise?
What dire contagion taint the burning skies?
What pestilential vapours, fraught with death,
Would rise, and overspread the lands beneath?

Hail, smiling morn, that from the orient main
Ascending dost adorn the heav'nly plain!
So rich, so various are thy beauteous dies
That spread through all the circuit of the skies,
That, full of thee, my soul in rapture soars,
And thy great God, the cause of all adores.

O'er beings infinite his love extends,
His *Wisdom* rules them, and his *Pow'r* defends.
When tasks diurnal tire the human frame,
The spirits faint, and dim the vital flame,
Then too that ever active bounty shines,
Which not infinity of space confines.
The sable veil, that *Night* in silence draws,
Conceals effects, but shews th' *Almighty Cause;*
Night seals in sleep the wide creation fair,
And all is peaceful but the brow of care.
Again, gay *Phœbus,* as the day before,
Wakes ev'ry eye, but what shall wake no more;
Again the face of nature is renew'd,
Which still appears harmonious, fair, and good.
May grateful strains salute the smiling morn,
Before its beams the eastern hills adorn!

Shall day to day and night to night conspire
To show the goodness of the Almighty Sire?
This mental voice shall man regardless hear,

And never, never rise the filial pray'r?
To-day, O hearken, nor your folly mourn
For time mispent, that never will return.

But see the sons of vegetation rise,
And spread their leafy banners to the skies.
All-wise Almighty Providence we trace
In trees, and plants, and all the flow'ry race;
As clear as in the nobler frame of man,
All lovely copies of the Maker's plan.
The pow'r the same that forms a ray of light,
That call'd creation from eternal night.
"Let there be light," he said: from his profound
Old *Chaos* heard, and trembled at the sound:
Swift as the word, inspir'd by pow'r-divine,
Behold the light around its maker shine,
The first fair product of th' omnific God,
And now through all his works diffus'd abroad.

As reason's pow'rs by day our God disclose,
So we may trace him in the night's repose:
Say what is sleep? and dreams how passing strange!
When action ceases, and ideas range
Licentious and unbounded o'er the plains,
When *Fancy's* queen in giddy triumph reigns.
Hear in soft strains the dreaming lover sigh
To a kind fair, or rave in jealousy;
On pleasure now, and now on vengeance bent,
The lab'ring passions struggle for a vent.
What pow'r, O man! thy *reason* then restores,
So long suspended in nocturnal hours?
What secret hand returns the mental train,
And gives improv'd thine active pow'rs again?
From thee, O man, what gratitude should rise!
And, when from balmy sleep thou op'st thine eyes,
Let thy first thoughts be praises to the skies.
How merciful our God who thus imparts
O'erflowing tides of joy to human hearts,
When wants and woes might be our righteous lot,
Our God forgetting, by our God forgot!

Among the mental pow'rs a question rose,
"What most the image of th' Eternal shows?"
When thus to *Reason* (so let *Fancy* rove)
Her great companion spoke immortal *Love.*

"Say, mighty pow'r, how long shall strife prevail,
And with its murmurs load the whisp'ring gale?
Refer the cause to *Recollection's* shrine,
Who loud proclaims, my origin divine,
The cause whence heav'n and earth began to be,
And is not man immortaliz'd by me?

---

16. The Greek god of the sun.

Reason let this most causeless strife subside."
Thus *Love* pronounc'd, and *Reason* thus reply'd.

"Thy birth, celestial queen! 'tis mine to own,
In thee resplendent is the Godhead shown;
Thy words persuade, my soul enraptur'd feels
Resistless beauty which thy smile reveals."
Ardent she spoke, and, kindling at her charms,
She clasp'd the blooming goddess in her arms.

Infinite *Love* where'er we turn our eyes
Appears: this ev'ry creature's wants supplies;
This most is heard in *Nature's* constant voice,
This makes the morn, and this the eve rejoice;
This bids the fost'ring rains and dews descend
To nourish all, to serve one gen'ral end,
The good of man: yet man ungrateful pays
But little homage, and but little praise.
To him, whose works array'd with mercy shine
What songs should rise, how constant, how divine!

On Recollection

MNEME begin.[17] Inspire, ye sacred nine,
Your vent'rous *Afric* in her great design.
Mneme, immortal pow'r, I trace thy spring:
Assist my strains, while I thy glories sing:
The acts of long departed years, by thee
Recover'd, in due order rang'd we see:
Thy pow'r the long-forgotten calls from night,
That sweetly plays before the *Fancy's* sight.

Mneme in our nocturnal visions pours
The ample treasure of her secret stores;
Swift from above she wings her silent flight
Through *Phœbe's* realms, fair regent of the night;
And, in her pomp of images display'd
To the high-raptur'd poet gives her aid,
Through the unbounded regions of the mind,
Diffusing light celestial and refin'd.
The heav'nly *phantom* paints the actions done
By ev'ry tribe beneath the rolling sun.

Mneme, enthron'd within the human breast,
Has vice condemn'd, and ev'ry virtue blest.
How sweet the sound when we her plaudit hear!
Sweeter than music to the ravish'd ear,
Sweeter than *Maro's*[18] entertaining strains

Resounding through the groves, and hills, and plains.
But how is *Mneme* dreaded by the race,
Who scorn her warnings, and despise her grace?
By her unveil'd each horrid crime appears,
Her awful hand a cup of wormwood bears.
Days, years misspent, O what a hell of woe!
Hers the worst tortures that our souls can know.

Now eighteen years their destin'd course have run,
In fast succession round the central sun.
How did the follies of that period pass
Unnotic'd, but behold them writ in brass!
In Recollection see them fresh return,
And sure 'tis mine to be asham'd, and mourn.

O *Virtue,* smiling in immortal green,
Do thou exert thy pow'r, and change the scene;
Be thine employ to guide my future days,
And mind to pay the tribute of my praise.

Of *Recollection* such the pow'r enthron'd
In ev'ry breast, and thus her pow'r is own'd.
The wretch, who dar'd the vengeance of the skies,
At last awakes in horror and surprize,
By her alarm'd, he sees impending fate,
He howls in anguish, and repents too late.
But O! what peace, what joys are hers t' impart
To ev'ry holy, ev'ry upright heart!
Thrice blest the man, who, in her sacred shrine,
Feels himself shelter'd from the wrath divine!

To the Right Honourable William, Earl of Dartmouth, His Majesty's Principal Secretary of State for North America, &c.

HAIL, happy day, when, smiling like the morn,
Fair *Freedom* rose *New-England* to adorn:
The northern clime beneath her genial ray,
Dartmouth,[19] congratulates thy blissful sway:
Elate with hope her race no longer mourns,
Each soul expands, each grateful bosom burns,

---

17. Wheatley is invoking Mneme, the Muse of memory, or remembrance, of Greek mythology.

18. Maro is the family name, often used in poetry, of Virgil.

19. William Legge (1731–1801), second earl of Dartmouth, was a friend of the countess of Huntingdon and a Methodist sympathizer. The colonists in British America hoped that, upon his appointment as secretary of state for the American colonies (1772–75), the colonists would find a sympathetic ear for their concerns. Wheatley was evidently impressed, too, that Dartmouth agreed to serve as president of the trustees of a fund collected in England for the Charity School that Samson Occom, Wheatley's friend, was working to establish for Eleazer Wheelock.

While in thine hand with pleasure we behold
The silken reins, and *Freedom's* charms unfold.
Long lost to realms beneath the northern skies
She shines supreme, while hated *faction* dies:
Soon as appear'd the *Goddess* long desir'd,
Sick at the view, she languish'd and expir'd;
Thus from the splendors of the morning light
The owl in sadness seeks the caves of night.

No more, *America,* in mournful strain
Of wrongs, and grievance unredress'd complain,
No longer shall thou dread the iron chain,
Which wanton *Tyranny* with lawless hand
Had made, and with it meant t' enslave the land.

Should you, my lord, while you peruse my song,
Wonder from whence my love of *Freedom* sprung,
Whence flow these wishes for the common good,
By feeling hearts alone best understood,
I, young in life, by seeming cruel fate
Was snatch'd from *Afric's* fancy'd happy seat:
What pangs excruciating must molest,
What sorrows labour in my parent's breast?
Steel'd was that soul and by no misery mov'd
That from a father seiz'd his babe belov'd:
Such, such my case. And can I then but pray
Others may never feel tyrannic sway?

For favours past, great Sir, our thanks are due,
And thee we ask thy favours to renew,
Since in thy pow'r, as in thy will before,
To sooth the griefs, which thou did'st once deplore.
May heav'nly grace the sacred sanction give
To all thy works, and thou for ever live
Not only on the wings of fleeting *Fame,*
Though praise immortal crowns the patriot's name,
But to conduct to heav'ns refulgent fane,
May fiery coursers sweep th' ethereal plain,
And bear thee upwards to that blest abode,
Where, like the prophet, thou shalt find thy God.

To S. M. a Young *African* Painter, on Seeing His Works[20]

TO show the lab'ring bosom's deep intent,
And thought in living characters to paint,
When first thy pencil did those beauties give,
And breathing figures learnt from thee to live,
How did those prospects give my soul delight,

A new creation rushing on my sight?
Still, wond'rous youth! each noble path pursue,
On deathless glories fix thine ardent view:
Still may the painter's and the poet's fire
To aid thy pencil, and thy verse conspire!
And may the charms of each seraphic theme
Conduct thy footsteps to immortal fame!
High to the blissful wonders of the skies
Elate thy soul, and raise thy wishful eyes.
Thrice happy, when exalted to survey
That splendid city, crown'd with endless day,
Whose twice six gates on radiant hinges ring:
Celestial *Salem* blooms in endless spring.

Calm and serene thy moments glide along,
And may the muse inspire each future song!
Still, with the sweets of contemplation bless'd,
May peace with balmy wings your soul invest!
But when these shades of time are chas'd away,
And darkness ends in everlasting day,
On what seraphic pinions shall we move,
And view the landscapes in the realms above?
There shall thy tongue in heav'nly murmurs flow,
And there my muse with heav'nly transport glow:
No more to tell of *Damon's* tender sighs,
Or rising radiance of *Aurora's*[21] eyes,
For nobler themes demand a nobler strain,
And purer language on th' ethereal plain.
Cease, gentle muse! the solemn gloom of night
Now seals the fair creation from my sight.

TO HIS EXCELLENCY GENERAL WASHINGTON[1]

[The following LETTER and VERSES, were written by the famous Phillis Wheatley, the African Poetess, and presented to his Excellency Gen. Washington.

---

20. S. M., Wheatley's friend Scipio Moorhead, was enslaved by the Reverend John Moorhead.

21. The Roman goddess of the dawn.

1. Wheatley had sent her poem to Washington in October 1775, when she was staying with her friend Obour Tanner in Providence because British forces were occupying Boston. Washington sent the poem to a friend early the following year, and his friend had the poem published. The poem first appeared in the *Virginia Gazette* on March 30, 1776, the source of the present text. It was printed in the *Virginia Gazette* (Dixon and Hunter) on March 30, 1776, and then in the *Pennsylvania Magazine* 17 (April 1776).

SIR,

I Have taken the freedom to address your Excellency in the enclosed poem, and entreat your acceptance, though I am not insensible of its inaccuracies. Your being appointed by the Grand Continental Congress to be Generalissimo of the armies of North America, together with the fame of your virtues, excite sensations not easy to suppress. Your generosity, therefore, I presume, will pardon the attempt. Wishing your Excellency all possible success in the great cause you are so generously engaged in. I am,

> *Your Excellency's most obedient humble servant,*
> *PHILLIS WHEATLEY. Providence, Oct. 26, 1775.*

His Excellency Gen. Washington.]

Celestial choir! enthron'd in realms of light,
Columbia's² scenes of glorious toils I write.
While freedom's cause her anxious breast alarms,
She flashes dreadful in refulgent arms.
5 See mother earth her offspring's fate bemoan,
And nations gaze at scenes before unknown!
See the bright beams of heaven's revolving light
Involved in sorrows and the veil of night!

The goddess comes, she moves divinely fair,
10 Olive and laurel binds her golden hair:
Wherever shines this native of the skies,
Unnumber'd charms and recent graces rise.

Muse! bow propitious while my pen relates
How pour her armies through a thousand gates,
15 As when Eolus³ heaven's fair face deforms,
Enwrapp'd in tempest and a night of storms;
Astonish'd ocean feels the wild uproar,
The refluent surges beat the sounding shore;
Or thick as leaves in Autumn's golden reign,
20 Such, and so many, moves the warrior's train.
In bright array they seek the work of war,
Where high unfurl'd the ensign waves in air.
Shall I to Washington their praise recite?
Enough thou know'st them in the fields of fight.
25 Thee, first in place and honours,—we demand
The grace and glory of thy martial band.
Fam'd for thy valour, for thy virtues more,
Hear every tongue thy guardian aid implore!

---

2. The name frequently applied to the North American colonies during the era of confederation.

3. The god of the winds.

One century scarce perform'd its destin'd round,
When Gallic powers Columbia's fury found;⁴   30
And so may you, whoever dares disgrace
The land of freedom's heaven-defended race!
Fix'd are the eyes of nations on the scales,
For in their hopes Columbia's arm prevails.
Anon Britannia droops the pensive head,   35
While round increase the rising hills of dead.
Ah! cruel blindness to Columbia's state!
Lament thy thirst of boundless power too late.

Proceed, great chief, with virtue on thy side,
Thy ev'ry action let the goddess guide.   40
A crown, a mansion, and a throne that shine,
With gold unfading, WASHINGTON! be thine.

LETTERS TO OBOUR TANNER¹

May 19, 1772

To Abour Tanner, in Newport

Boston, May 19th 1772

Dear Sister,—

I rec'd your favour of February 6th for which I give you my sincere thanks. I greatly rejoice with you in that realizing view, and I hope experience, of the saving change which you so emphatically describe. Happy were it for us if we could arrive to that evangelical Repentance, and the true holiness of heart which you mention. Inexpressibly happy should we be could we have a due sense of beauties and excellence of the crucified Saviour. In his Crucifixion may be seen marvellous displays of Grace and Love, sufficient to draw and invite us to the rich and endless treasures of his mercy; let us rejoice in and adore the

---

4. Wheatley refers to the Seven Years War in North America, during which British colonists defeated the French. Washington served British forces at the time, and he had victories that became important to the colonials during the era of the revolution against Britain.

1. The text is from *The Collected Works of Phillis Wheatley,* ed. John Shields (1988). Obour Tanner, a devoted friend of Wheatley, was a servant to the James Tanner family of Newport, Rhode Island.

wonders of God's infinite Love in bringing us from a land semblant of darkness itself, and where the divine light of revelation (being obscur'd) is as darkness. Here the knowledge of the true God and eternal life are made manifest; but there, profound ignorance overshadows the land. Your observation is true, namely, that there was nothing in us to recommend us to God. Many of our fellow creatures are pass'd by, when the bowels of divine love expanded towards us. May this goodness & long suffering of God lead us to unfeign'd repentance.

It gives me very great pleasure to hear of so many of my nation, seeking with eagerness the way to true felicity. O may we all meet at length in that happy mansion. I hope the correspondence between us will continue, (my being much indispos'd this winter past, was the reason of my not answering yours before now) which correspondence I hope may have the happy effect of improving our mutual friendship. Till we meet in the regions of consummate blessedness, let us endeavor by the assistance of divine grace, to live the life, and we shall die the death of the Righteous. May this be our happy case, and of those who are travelling to the region of Felicity, is the earnest request of your affectionate

Friend & humble servant, Phillis Wheatley

July 19, 1772

To Arbour Tanner, in Newport[1]
To the Care of Mr. Pease's Servant Rhode Island

Boston, July 19th 1772

Dear Friend,—
I rec'd your kind epistle a few days ago; much disappointed to hear that you had not rec'd my answer to your first letter. I have been in a very poor state of health all the past winter and spring, and now reside in the country for the benefit of its more wholesome air. I came to town this morning to spend the Sabbath with my master and mistress. Let me be interested in your prayers that God would please to bless to me the means us'd for my recovery, if agreeable to his holy will. While my outward man languishes under weakness and pa[in], may the inward be refresh'd and strengthen'd more abundantly by him who de-

clar'd from heaven that his strength was made perfect in weakness! May he correct our vitiated taste, that the meditation of him may be delightful to us. No longer to be so excessively charm'd with fleeting vanities: but pressing forward to the fix'd mark for the prize. How happy that man who is prepar'd for that night wherein no man can work! Let us be mindful of our high calling, continually on our guard, lest our treacherous hearts should give the adversary an advantage over us. O! who can think without horror of the snares of the Devil. Let us, by frequent meditation on the eternal Judgment, prepare for it. May the Lord bless to us these thoughts, and teach us by his Spirit to live to him alone, and when we leave this world may we be his. That this may be our happy case, is the sincere desire

of, your affectionate friend, & humble serv't,
Phillis Wheatley

I sent the letter to Mr. Whitwell's[2] who said he wou'd forward it.

October 30, 1773

To Obour Tanner, in New Port

Boston Oct. 30, 1773

Dear Obour,—I rec'd your most kind epistles of Augt. 27th, & Oct. 13th, by a young man of your acquaintance,[3] for which I am oblig'd to you. I hear of your welfare with pleasure; but this acquaints you that I am at present indispos'd by a cold, & since my arrival have been visited by the asthma.

Your observations on our dependence on the Deity, & your hopes that my wants will be supply'd from his fulness which is in Christ Jesus, is truly worthy of your self. I can't say but my voyage to England has conduced to the recovery (in a great measure) of my health. The friends I found there among the nobility and gentry, their benevolent conduct towards me, the unexpected and unmerited civility and complaisance with which I was treated by all, fills me with astonishment. I can scarcely realize it. This I humbly hope has the happy effect of lessening me in my

---

1. The text is from *The Collected Works of Phillis Wheatley*, ed. John Shields (1988).

2. William Whitwell (1714–95), a Boston merchant, was, like Wheatley, a member of Old South Church.

3. Possibly a reference to John Peters, Wheatley's future husband.

own esteem. Your reflections on the sufferings of the Son of God, & the inestimable price of our immortal souls, plainly demonstrate the sensations of a soul united to Jesus. What you observe of Esau is true of all mankind, who, (left to themselves) would sell their, heavenly birth rights for a few moments of sensual pleasure, whose wages at last (dreadful wages!) is eternal condemnation. Dear Obour, let us not sell our birthright for a thousand worlds, which indeed would be as dust upon the balance. The God of the seas and dry land, has graciously brought me home in safety. Join with me in thanks to him for so great a mercy, & that it may excite me to praise him with cheerfulness, to persevere in Grace & Faith, & in the knowledge of our Creator and Redeemer,—that my heart may be fill'd with gratitude. I should have been pleas'd greatly to see Miss West, as I imagine she knew you. I have been very busy ever since my arrival, or should have now wrote a more particular account of my voyage, but must submit that satisfaction to some other opportunity. I am Dear friend,

Most affectionately ever yours,
Phillis Wheatley

My mistress[4] has been very sick above 14 weeks, & confined to her bed the whole time, but is I hope somewhat better, now.

The young man by whom this is handed you seems to me to be a very clever man, knows you very well, & is very complaisant and agreeable.

I enclose Proposals for my book, and beg you'd use your interest to get subscriptions, as it is for my benefit.

LETTER TO SAMSON OCCOM

February 11, 1774

Reverend and Honoured Sir,[1]

I have this Day received your obliging kind Epistle, and am greatly satisfied with your Reasons respecting the

Negroes, and think highly reasonable what you offer in Vindication of their natural Rights: Those that invade them cannot be insensible that the divine Light is chasing away the thick Darkness which broods over the Land of Africa; and the Chaos which has reigned so long, is converting into beautiful Order, and reveals more and more clearly, the glorious Dispensation of civil and religious Liberty, which are so inseparably united, that there is little or no Enjoyment of one without the other: Otherwise, perhaps, the Israelites had been less solicitous for their Freedom from Egyptian Slavery; I do not say they would have been contented without it, by no Means, for in every human Breast, God has implanted a Principle, which we call Love of Freedom; it is impatient of Oppression, and pants for Deliverance; and by the Leave of our Modern Egyptians I will assert, that the same Principle lives in us. God grant Deliverance in his own way and Time, and get him honor upon all those whose Avarice impels them to countenance and help forward the Calamities of their Fellow Creatures. This I desire not for their Hurt, but to convince them of the strange Absurdity of their Conduct whose Words and Actions are so diametrically opposite. How well the Cry for Liberty, and the reverse Disposition for the Exercise of oppressive Power over others agree,—I humbly think it does not require the Penetration of a Philosopher to determine.

LETTERS TO SELINA HASTINGS, COUNTESS OF HUNTINGTON[1]

October 25, 1770

To the Rt. Hon'ble the Countess of Huntingdon
Most noble Lady,

The Occasion of my addressing your Ladiship will I hope, apologize for this my boldness in doing it. it is to enclose a few lines on the decease of your worthy chaplain, the Rev'd Mr. Whitefield, in the loss of whom I sin-

---

4. Susanna Wheatley.

1. Samson Occom, a Mohegan Indian, was, by the time Phillis Wheatley knew him, a renowned minister to the Indians. Wheatley's letter, originally written February 11, 1774, was published in the *Connecticut Gazette* on March 11, 1774, and it appeared subsequently in numerous New England newspapers. The text is from *The Collected Works of Phillis Wheatley,* ed. John Shields (1988).

1. Selina Hastings (1707–91), countess of Huntingdon, was a strong supporter of the Methodist movement and played a large role in establishing many Methodist chapels in England. She became Wheatley's sponsor during her trip to London and her literary patron. The text is from *The Collected Works of Phillis Wheatley,* ed. John Shields (1988).

cerely sympathize with your Ladiship; but your great loss which is his Greater gain, will, I hope, meet with infinite reparation, in the presence of God, the Divine Benefactor whose image you bear by filial imitation.

The Tongues of the Learned are insufficient, much less the pen of an untutor'd African, to paint in lively character, the excellencies of this Citizen of Zion! I beg an Interest in your Ladiship's Prayer and am,

> *With great humility*
> *your Ladiship's most*
> *obedient Humble Servant*
> *Phillis Wheatley*
> *Boston Octr. 25th 1770*

June 27, 1773

London
June 27, 1773

Madam,

It is with pleasure I acquaint your Ladyship of my safe arrival in London after a fine passage of 5 weeks in the Ship London with my young master[2] (advised by my physician for my Health) have Brought a letter from Richd. Carey Esqr.[3] but was Disappointed by your absence of the honour of waiting upon your Ladyship with it. I would have inclosed it, but was doubtful of the Safety of the conveyance.

I should think my self very happy in seeing your Ladyship, and if you was so desirous of the Image of the Author as to propose it for a Frontispiece I flatter myself that you would accept the Reality.

I conclude with thanking your Ladyship for permitting the dedication of my poems to you; and am not insinsible, that under the patronage of your Ladyship, not more eminent in the Station of Life than in your exemplary piety and virtues, my feeble efforts will be shielded from the severe trials of uppity Criticism and, being encourage'd by your Ladyship's Indulgence, I the more feebly resign

to the world these Juvenile productions, and am Madam, with greatest humility, your Dutiful Huml Ser't,

> *Phillis Wheatley*

LETTER TO WILLIAM LEGGE, SECOND EARL OF DARTMOUTH[1]

October 10, 1772

My Lord,

The Joyful occacion which has given me this Confidence in Addressing your Lordship in the inclosed peice will, I hope sufficiently apologize for this freedom in an African who with the now happy America exults with equal transport in the view of one of its greatest advocates presiding with the Special tenderness of a Fatherly Heart over that Department.

Nor can they my Lord be insensible of the Friendship so much exemplified in your Endeavours in their behalf during the late unhappy Disturbances.

I sincerely wish your Lordship all possible success in your Undertaking for the Interest of north America

That the united blessings of Heaven & Earth may attend you here and the endless Felicity of the invisible State in the presence of the divine Benefactor may be your portion hereafter is the hearty Desire of

> *My Lord*
> *Your Lordships*
> *Most Obedient*
> *H'ble Servant*
> *Phillis Wheatley*

Boston N. E. Octo. 10th 1772

---

2. Nathaniel Wheatley, son of Phillis Wheatley's master.

3. Richard Carey (1717–90) was one of the signers of the letter "To the Publick," the testimonial regarding Wheatley's authorship of her volume of poetry.

---

1. William Legge (1753–1801), second earl of Dartmouth, was recognized by the British colonists as their sympathizer. He was appointed to the position of secretary for the North American colonies in August 1772. This letter is the vehicle through which Wheatley sent Dartmouth her poem. The letter was not printed when the poems were published in her separate volume in 1773. The text is from *The Collected Works of Phillis Wheatley,* ed. John Shields (1988).

LETTER TO DAVID WOOSTER[1]

October 18, 1773

Sir

Having an opportunity by a Servant of Mr. Badcock's who lives near you, I am glad to learn you and your Family are well. I take the Freedom to transmit to you, a short Sketch of my voyage and return from London where I went for the recovery of my health as advis'd by my Physician. I was receiv'd in England with such kindness[,] Complaisance, and so many marks of esteem and real Friendship as astonishes me on the reflection, for I was no more than 6 weeks there. Was introduced to Lord Dartmouth and had near half an hour's conversation with his Lordship, with whom was Alderman Kirkman. Then to Lord Lincoln,[2] who visited me at my own Lodgings with the famous Dr. Solander who accompany'd Mr. Banks in his late expedition round the World. Then to Lady Cavendish, and Lady Carteret Webb,[3] Mrs. Palmer[4] a Poetess, an accomplished Lady. [To] Dr. Thos. Gibbons,[5] Rhetoric Professor. To Israel Mauduit[6] Esqr. [,] Benjamin Franklin[7] Esqr. F.R.S., Greenville Sharp[8] Esqr. who attended me to the Tower & show'd the Lions, Panthers, Tigers, &c. the Horse Armoury, Small Armoury, the Crowns, Sceptres, Diadems, the Fount for christening the Royal Family. Saw Westminster Abbey, British Museum

[,] Coxe's Museum, Saddler's wells, Greenwich Hospital, Park and Chapel, the royal Observatory at Greenwich, &c. &c. too many things and places to trouble you with in a Letter. The Earl of Dartmouth made me a Compliment of 5 guineas, and desired me to get the whole of Mr. Pope's Works,[9] as the best he could recommend to my perusal, this I did, also got Hudibrass, Don Quixot, & Gay's Fables[.] Was presented with a Folio Edition of Milton's Paradise Lost, printed on a Silver Type (so call'd from its elegance, I suppose) by Mr. Brook Watson Mercht, whose Coat of Arms is prefix'd. Since my return to America my Master, has at the desire of my friends in England given me my freedom. The Instrument is drawn, so as to secure me and my property from the hands of Executvs.[,] administrators, &c. of my master, and secure whatsoever should be given me as my Own. A Copy is sent to Isra. Mauduit Esqr. F.R.S.

I expect my Books which are publish'd in London in Capt. Hall, who will be here I believe in 8 or 10 days. I beg the favour that you would honour the enclos'd Proposals, & use your interest with Gentlemen & Ladies of your acquaintance to subscribe also, for the more subscribers there are, the more it will be for my advantage as I am to have half the Sale of the Books. This I am the more solicitous for, as I am now upon my own footing and whatever I get by this is entirely mine, & it is the Chief I have to depend upon. I must also request you would desire the Printers in New Haven, not to reprint that Book, as it will be a great hurt to me, preventing any further Benefit that I might receive from the Sale of my Copies from England. The price is 2/6d [two pounds six pence] Bound or 2/Sterling Sewed. If any should be so ungenerous as to reprint them the genuine Copy may be known, for it is sign'd in my own handwriting. My dutiful respects attend your Lady and Children and I am

ever respectfully your oblig'd Huml. sert.
Phillis Wheatley
Boston October
18th 1773

I found my mistress very sick on my return But she is somewhat better. We wish we could depend on it. She gives her compliments to you & your Lady.

---

1. David Wooster (1711–77) was a New Haven merchant with a military background. The text is from *The Collected Works of Phillis Wheatley,* ed. John Shields (1988).

2. Henry Fiennes Clinton, Lord Lincoln (1720–90), was a highly educated British politician.

3. Both Lady Cavendish and Lady Carteret Webb, sisters, supported the countess of Huntingdon's work in London.

4. Mary Palmer (1716–96) wrote two books on the dialect of Devonshire.

5. Dr. Thomas Gibbons (1720–85) was a tutor at Mile End Academy and a dissenting minister. He made contributions to Samson Occom while Occom was on his lecture tour in London.

6. Israel Mauduit (1708–87) was a wealthy scholar of classics and a London agent for the province of Massachusetts Bay.

7. Benjamin Franklin (1706–90) met with Wheatley during her visit. She later published proposals for a second volume of her work that she planned to dedicate to Franklin.

8. Granville Sharp (1735–1813) was a devoted abolitionist who founded the English Society for the Abolition of Slavery.

9. Wheatley received five volumes of Pope's translation of the *Iliad,* four volumes of Pope's translation of the *Odyssey* (1771) and nine volumes of Pope's own *Works* (1766).

LETTER TO SAMUEL HOPKINS[1]

February 9, 1774

Boston, Feb. 9, 1774

Rev'd Sir,—

I take with pleasure the opportunity by the Post, to acquaint you with the arrival of my books from London. I have sealed up a package containing 17 for you, and 2 for Mr. Tanner, and one for Mrs. Mason, and only wait for you to appoint some proper person, by whom I may convey them to you. I received some time ago 20s sterling upon them, by the hands of your son, in a letter from Abour Tanner. I received at the same time a paper, by which I understand there are two negro men,[2] who are desirous of returning to their native country, to preach the Gospel, but being much indisposed by the return of my asthmatic complaint, besides the sickness of my mistress, who has been long confined to her bed, and is not expected to live a great while; all these things render it impracticable for me to do anything at present with regard to that paper, but what I can do in influencing my Christian friends and acquaintances, to promote this laudable design, shall not be wanting. Me-thinks, Rev. Sir, this is the beginning of that happy period foretold by the Prophets, when all shall know the Lord from the least to the greatest, and that without the assistance of human Art of Eloquence. My heart expands with sympathetic joy to see at distant time the thick cloud of ignorance dispersing from the face of my benighted country. Europe and America have long been fed with the heavenly provision, and I fear they loath it, while Africa is perishing with a spiritual Famine. O that they could partake of the crumbs, the precious crumbs, which fall from the table of these distinguished children of the kingdom.[3]

---

1. Samuel Hopkins (1721–1803) was pastor of the First Congregational Church in Newport, Rhode Island. This letter was published in the *Pennsylvania Freeman,* an abolitionist newspaper edited by John Greenleaf Whittier, in May 1839. The text is from *The Collected Works of Phillis Wheatley,* ed. John Shields (1988).

2. According to William Robinson, the "two negro men" are Bristol Yamma (1744?–93) and John Quamine (1743?–99). Wheatley mentions them by name in her letter to John Thornton, October 30, 1774.

3. Compare with Matthew 15:27.

Their minds are unprejudiced against the truth, therefore 'tis to be hoped they would receive it with their whole heart. I hope that which the divine royal Psalmist says by inspiration is now on the point of being accomplished, namely, Ethiopia shall soon stretch forth her hands unto God.[4] Of this, Abour Tanner, and I trust many others within your knowledge, are living witnesses. Please to give my love to her, and I intend to write her soon. My best respects attend every kind inquiry after your obliged Humble servant,

Phillis Wheatley

LETTER TO JOHN THORNTON

October 30, 1774

Much Hon'd Sir[1]

I have the honour of your Obliging favour of August 1st by Mr. Wheatley[2] who arriv'd not before the 27th. Ultimo after a tedious passage of near two months; the obligations I am under to the family I desire to retain a grateful sense of and consequently rejoice in the bountiful dealings of providence towards him—

By the great loss I have sustain'd of my best friend, I feel like One forsaken by her parent in a desolate wilderness, for such the world appears to me, wandring thus without/my/friendly guide. I fear lest every step should lead me into error and confusion. She gave me many precepts and instructions; which I hope I shall never forget. Hon'd sir, pardon me if after the retrospect of such uncommon tenderness for thirteen years from my earliest youth—such unwearied diligence to instruct me in the principles of the true Religion, this in some degree Justifies me while I deplore my misery—/If/I readily join with you in wishing that you could in these respects supply her place, but this does not seem probable from the great distance of your residence. However I will endeavour to compensate it by a strict Observance of hers and your good ad-

---

4. See Psalm 68:31.

1. Samuel Hopkins had helped John Quamine reestablish contact with his mother and uncle in Anamaboe. The text is from *The Collected Works of Phillis Wheatley,* ed. John Shields (1988).

2. Nathaniel Wheatley and his wife had traveled from England to Boston.

vice from time/to/time, which you have given me encouragement to hope for—What a Blessed source of consolation that our greatest friend is an immortal God whose friendship is invariable! from whom I have all that is/*in me*/praise worthy in/mental/possession. This consideration humbles me much under ecomiums on the gifts of God, the fear that I should not improve them to his glory and the good of mankind, it almost hinders a commendable self estimation (at times) but quite beats down the boldness of presumption. The world is a severe schoolmaster, for its frowns are less dang'rous than its smiles and flatteries, and it is a difficult task to keep in the path of Wisdom. I attended, and find exactly true your thoughts on the behaviour of those who seem'd to respect me while under my mistresses patronage: you said right, for some of those have already put on a reserve; but I submit while God rules; who never forsakes any till they have ungratefully forsaken him—. My old master's generous behaviour in granting me my freedom, and still so kind to me I delight to acknowledge my great obligations to him, this he did about 3 months before the death of my dear mistress & at her desire, as well as his own humanity,/of w'ch/I hope ever to retain a grateful sense, and treat/him/with that respect which is ever due to a paternal friendship—If this had not been the Case, yet I hope I should willingly submit to servitude to be free in Christ.—But since it is thus—Let me be a *servant of Christ* and that is the most perfect freedom.—

You propose my returning to Africa with Bristol Yamma and John Quamine if either of them upon strict enquiry is such, as I dare give my heart and hand to, I believe they are either of them good enough if not too good for me, or they would not be fit for Missionaries; but why do you hon'd sir, wish those poor men so much trouble as to carry me so long a voyage? Upon my arrival, how like a Barbarian shou'd I look to the Natives; I can promise that my tongue shall be quiet/for a strong reason indeed/being an utter stranger to the language of Anamaboe.[3] Now to be serious, this undertaking appears too hazardous, and not sufficiently Eligible, to go—and leave my British & American Friends—I am also unacquainted with those Missionaries in Person. The reverend gentleman[4] who under [ta]kes their. Education has repeatedly inform'd me by Letters of their prospect in Learning also an account of John Quamine's family and [Kingdom? letter torn] But be that as it will I resign it all to God's all wise governance; I thank you heartily for your generous Offer With sincerity—

> *I am hon'd sir*
> *most gratefully your Devoted serv't*
> *Phillis Wheatley*
> *Boston October 30th 1774*

---

3. Anamaboe, a slave-trading town on the coast of Africa (today part of Ghana). Both Susanna Wheatley and Samson Occom had encouraged Wheatley to travel to Africa as a missionary.

4. Samuel Hopkins.

PRINCE HALL (1735?–1807)

Organizer and activist Prince Hall is best remembered as the founder of the world's first lodge of black Freemasons, a lodge that bears his name to this day. Hall rose to a prominent leadership position in Boston's black community during the final decades of the eighteenth century, a rather turbulent era for Africans and African-descended people. In his Masonic writings, letters, and petitions, Hall questioned the social, economic, and political position of people of African descent and set about challenging those institutions and practices that marginalized and subordinated Africans in America.

Because records concerning Hall's early years are scarce, myths about his life have abounded and continue to be retold. Although information about his birthplace and parents is unknown, we do know that by 1749 Hall was working as the slave of leather dresser William Hall of Boston. A self-educated man, Hall joined the Congregational Church at the age of twenty-seven and soon married the first of two wives. In 1770 William Hall presented Prince Hall with manumission papers certifying that he was "no longer Reckoned a slave, but [had] always been accounted as a free man." Thereafter, Hall worked on his own, laboring as a caterer and a leather dresser.

On March 6, 1775, just weeks before fighting broke out at Lexington and Concord, Hall and fourteen other black men became members of a lodge of Free and Accepted Masons, Army Lodge No. 441, attached to a British regiment composed primarily of Irish volunteers stationed in Boston. Within months, Hall petitioned Joseph Warren and John Hancock, both American Masons and key members of the Committee of Safety, to allow free and enslaved blacks to enlist in Revolutionary militias. Although his petition was initially rejected, George Washington later reconsidered the concerns Hall had raised and, perhaps in light of British recruitment of Africans, permitted free blacks to fight.

Hall encountered similar challenges when American Masons rejected his requests for support in establishing his own lodge after the British Masons left Boston. In 1787, three years after Hall turned to the London Masonic office to request a charter, the African Lodge gained official recognition. Hall moved quickly to establish additional lodges in cities, such as New York, Philadelphia, and Baltimore, thereby working to establish a national African organizational structure in the United States. Today the organization that Hall began remains active and maintains a substantial membership in the United States and elsewhere.

Hall's lodge was among the earliest of the African organizations (which also included churches and mutual aid societies) that were founded in the North for the moral, political, and economic benefit of Africans in America. The African lodges offered fraternity, fellowship, and support to the black men who constituted the lodges' membership. This was a time when the social formation was changing rapidly, creating a social divide among black working people, free and enslaved, and complications were emerging, too, because some but not all could read and write. Although it may be appropriate to talk about the lodges as cementing the differences between elite, free blacks (several of whom were lodge members) and middling and poorer ones, considering the impact of Hall's lodges and Masonry in general upon the African communities in North America, the importance of the lodges extends beyond any presumed borders between elite and nonelite blacks. The lodges offered leadership to the larger black community during an era of significant social change. Hall's important role received the attention and praise of prominent white Bostonian William Bentley, who described Hall as "an African and a person of great influence among his color in Boston, being Master of the African Lodge and a person, to whom they refer with confidence in their principal affairs."

From the 1770s through the late 1790s, Hall wrote and circulated numerous letters and petitions in support of Africans in Boston and elsewhere. As early as January 1777, Hall's name appeared on a petition to the General Court of Boston that challenged the presence of slavery in Massachusetts. In 1786 Hall offered the assistance of seven hundred blacks to quell the disturbance in rural western Massachusetts that eastern settlers and lawmakers called "Shays' rebellion" (using the name of the leader of the farmers). Hall's offer of assistance was rejected, but the offer itself suggests the degree of social agency that Hall assumed could follow from the establishment of lodges where Africans and African-descended men could meet. The following year Hall created a 1787 petition to the Massachusetts state legislature arguing that it was inequitable for blacks to be taxed to support schools while being denied the benefit of attending the same schools. His petition was rejected by the legislature, and in 1791 Hall appealed unsuccessfully to Boston selectmen to found a school for black children. Hall's efforts to organize resistance against the slave trade and the enslavement of three free black men in Massachusetts in 1788 were more successful.

Because the business of Masonic lodges was considered secret and was seldom circulated publicly, the publication of Hall's 1797 *Charge* is quite unusual. Hall used his *Charge* to challenge the African slave trade and to critique the treatment of African-descended peoples in Boston. He encouraged his black listeners, in part by alluding to the ongoing revolution in Saint Dominique, a revolution that would lead by 1804 to the founding of the first independent black republic in the Western hemisphere. At the same time, Hall's careful use of suggestive religious language reflects the concerns of wealthy white philanthropists, men whom Hall could not afford to alienate openly and who had befriended the black elite. Hall's writings reveal the marks of an orator who was skilled in public speech, one who was learned in classical and contemporary writings and legal matters, and one who founded his messages upon standing principles of a vaunted freedom understood by all around him but not applicable to him, in the minds of his white contemporaries.

For reasons that remain unclear, Hall appears to have faded from public life during the final decade of his life. Some speculate that he was pressured by the conservative white elite of Boston to speak less radically about blacks' position in the community. Long before his death in 1807, however, Hall's organizational activities had already laid the groundwork for a powerful and increasingly independent African community in Boston and elsewhere.

PETITION TO THE HONORABLE COUNCIL AND HOUSE OF REPRESENTATIVES FOR THE STATE OF MASSACHUSETTS-BAY, IN GENERAL COURT ASSEMBLED, JANUARY 13, 1777[1]

The Petition of a great number of Negroes who are detained in a state of Slavery in the Bowels of a free & Christian Country, Humbly showing

That your Petitioners apprehend that they have, in common with all other Men, a natural & unalienable right to that freedom, which the great Parent of the Universe hath bestowed equally on all Mankind, & which they have never forfeited by any compact or agreement whatever—But they were unjustly dragged, by the cruel hand of Power, from their dearest friends, & some of them even torn from the embraces of their tender Parents. From a populous, pleasant and plentiful Country—& in Violation of the Laws of Nature & of Nation & in defiance of all the tender feelings of humanity, brought hither to be sold like Beasts of Burden, & like them condemned to slavery for Life—Among a People professing the mild Religion of Jesus—A People not insensible of the sweets of rational freedom—Nor without spirit to resent the unjust endeavours of others to reduce them to a State of Bondage & Subjection—

Your Honors need not to be informed that a Life of Slavery, like that of your petitioners, deprived of every social privilege, of every thing requisite to render Life even tolerable, is far worse than Non-Existence—In imitation of the laudable example of the good People of these States, your Petitioners have long & patiently waited the event of Petition after Petition by them presented to the legislative Body of this State,[2] & can not but with grief reflect that their success has been but too similar—They can not but express their astonishment, that it has never been considered, that every principle from which America has acted in the course of her unhappy difficulties with Great-Britain, pleads stronger than a thousand arguments in favor of your Petitioners. They therefore humbly beseech your Honors, to give this Petition its due weight & consideration, & cause an Act of the Legislature to be passed, whereby they may be restored to the enjoyment of that freedom which is the natural right of all Men—& their Children (who were born in this Land of Liberty) may not be held as Slaves after they arrive at the age of twenty one years—So may the Inhabitants of this State (no longer chargeable with the inconsistency of acting, themselves, the part which they condemn & oppose in others) be prospered in their present glorious struggles for Liberty; & have those blessings secured to them by Heaven, of which benevolent minds can not wish to deprive their fellow Men.

---

1. Hall, who had received his manumission papers in 1770, was not a slave when this petition was submitted. The text was taken from an "improved" version of the petition, on file at the Massachusetts State Archives (volume 212).

2. Massachusetts slaves had submitted a series of petitions earlier in the 1770s. The level of Hall's involvement in the earlier petitions is unclear.

And your Petitioners, as in Duty Bound shall ever pray.

Lancaster Hill
Peter Bess
Brister Slenten

Prince Hall
Jack Purpont *his mark*

Nero Suneto *his mark*

Newport Symner *his mark*

Job Lock

Negroes Petition to the Hon[ble]
Gen[l] Assembly—Mass.
March 18
Judge Sargeant
M. Balton
M. Appleton
Coll. Brooks
M. Stony
W. Lowell
Matter Atlege
W. Davis

A CHARGE, DELIVERED TO THE BRETHREN OF THE AFRICAN LODGE, ON THE 25TH OF JUNE, 1792[1]

At the Hall of Brother William Smith, in Charlestown. By the Right Worshipful Master PRINCE HALL.

Dearly and well beloved Brethren of the African Lodge, as through the goodness and mercy of God, we are once more met together, in order to celebrate the Festival of St. John the Baptist;[2] it is requisite that we should on these public days, and when we appear in form, give some reason as a foundation for our so doing, but as this has been already done, in a discourse delivered in substance by our late Reverend Brother *John Marrant,*[3] and now in print, I shall at this time endeavour to raise part of the super-

structure, for howsoever good the foundation may be, yet without this it will only prove a Babel. I shall therefore endeavour to shew the duty of a Mason; and the first thing is, that he believes in one Supreme Being, that he is the great Architect of this visible world, and that he governs all things here below by his almighty power, and his watchful eye is over all our works. Again we must be good subjects to the laws of the land in which we dwell, giving honour to our lawful Governors and Magistrates, giving honour to whom honour is due; and that we have no hand in any plots or conspiracies or rebellion, or side or assist in them: for when we consider the blood-shed, the devastation of towns and cities that hath been done by them, what heart can be so hard as not to pity those our distrest brethren, and keep at the greatest distance from them. However just it may be on the side of the opprest, yet it doth not in the least, or rather ought not, abate that love and fellow-feeling which we ought to have for our brother fellow men.

The next thing is love and benevolence to all the whole family of mankind, as God's make and creation, therefore we ought to love them all, for love or hatred is of the whole kind, for if I love a man for the sake of the image of God which is on him, I must love all, for he made all, and upholds all, and we are dependant upon him for all we do enjoy and expect to enjoy in this world and that which is to come.—Therefore he will help and assist all his fellow-men in distress, let them be of what colour or nation they may, yea even our very enemies, much more a brother Mason. I shall therefore give you a few instances of this from Holy Writ, and first, how did Abraham prevent the storm, or rebellion that was rising between Lot's servants and his?[4] Saith Abraham to Lot, let there be no strife I pray thee between me and thee, for the land is before us, if you will go to the left, then I will go to the right, and if you will go to the right, then I will go to the left. They divided and peace was restored. I will mention the compassion of a blackman to a Prophet of the Lord, Ebedmelech, when he heard that Jeremiah was cast into the dungeon, he made intercession for him to the King, and got liberty to take him out from the jaws of death. See Jer. xxxviii, 7–13.[5]

Also the prophet Elisha after he had led the army of the Eramites blindfold into Samaria, when the King in a deriding manner said, my *Father* (not considering that he was as much their Father as his) shall I smite, or rather kill

---

1. The charge was printed as a pamphlet "at the Request of the Lodge" and sold at the Bible and Heart, Cornhill, Boston. *Early Negro Writing, 1760–1837,* ed. Dorothy Porter (1971), is the source of the present text.

2. John the Baptist (5 B.C.–A.D. 30) was the last of the Hebrew prophets and was considered a forerunner of Jesus.

3. John Marrant (1755–91), who met Prince Hall in the 1780s in Boston, published *A Sermon Preached on the 24th Day of June 1789* (1789), a sermon used during one of the Masons' celebrations of the festival of St. John.

4. See Genesis 19.27–29.

5. Here, and in the following sections, Hall accurately provides biblical references to the stories recounted.

them out of the way, as not worthy to live on the same earth, or draw the same air with himself; so eager was he to shed his brethren's blood, that he repeats his blood-thirsty demand, but the Prophet after reproaching him therefore, answers him no, but set bread and water before them; or in other words, give them a feast and let them go home in peace. See 2 Kings vi, 22–23.

I shall just mention the good deeds of the Samaritan, though at that time they were looked upon as unworthy to eat, drink or trade with their fellow-men, at least by the Jews; see the pity and compassion he had on a poor dis-trest and half dead stranger, see Luke x. from 30 to 37. See that you endeavour to do so likewise.—But when we consider the amazing condescending love and pity our blessed Lord had on such poor worms as we are, as not only to call us his friends, but his brothers, we are lost and can go no further in holy writ for examples to excite us to the love of our fellow-men.—But I am aware of an objec-tion that may arise (for some men will catch at any thing) that is that they were not all Masons; we allow it, and I say that they were not all Christians, and their benevolence to strangers ought to shame us both, that there is so little, so very little of it to be seen in these enlightened days.

Another thing which is the duty of a Mason is, that he pays a strict regard to the stated meetings of the Lodge, for masonry is of a progressive nature, and must be at-tended to if ever he intends to be a good Mason; for the man that thinks that because he hath been made a Mason, and is called so, and at the same time will wilfully neglect to attend his Lodge, he may be assured he will never make a good Mason, nor ought he to be looked upon as a good member of the craft. For if his example was followed, where would be the Lodge; and besides what a disgrace is it, when we are at our set meetings, to hear that one of our members is at a drinking house, or at a card table, or in some worse company, this brings disgrace on the Craft: Again there are some that attend the Lodge in such a man-ner that sometimes their absence would be better than their Company (I would not here be understood a brother in disguise, for such an one hath no business on a level floor) for if he hath been displeased abroad or at home, the least thing that is spoken that he thinks not right, or in the least offends him, he will raise his temper to such a height as to destroy the harmony of the whole Lodge; but we have a remedy and every officer ought to see it put in execution. Another thing a Mason ought to observe, is that he should lend his helping hand to a brother in dis-tress, and relieve him; this we may do various ways—for we may sometimes help him to a cup of cold water, and it

may be better to him than a cup of wine. Good advice may be sometimes better than feeding his body, helping him to some lawful employment, better than giving him money; so defending his case and standing by him when wrong-fully accused, may be better than clothing him; better to save a brother's house when on fire, than to give him one. Thus much may suffice.

I shall now cite some of our fore-fathers, for our imita-tion: and the first shall be Tertullian,[6] who defended the Christians against their heathen false accusations, whom they charged with treason against the empire and the Em-peror, because of their silent meetings: he proved that to be false for this reason, for in their meetings, they were wont to pray for the prosperity of the Empire, of Rome, and him also; and they were accused of being enemies to mankind, how can that be, said he, when their office is to love and pray for all mankind. When they were charged with worshipping the Sun, because they looked towards the East when they prayed; he defended them against this slander also, and proved that they were slandered, slighted and ill-treated, not for any desert of theirs, but only out of hatred of them and their profession. This friend of the distrest was born in Carthage in Africa, and died Anno Christi 202.

Take another of the same city, Cyprian,[7] for his fidelity to his profession was such, that he would rather suffer death than betray his trust and the truth of the gospel, or approve of the impious worship of the Gentiles: He was not only Bishop of Carthage, but of Spain and the east, west and northern churches, who died Anno Christi 259.

But I have not time to cite but one more (out of hun-dreds that I could count of our Fathers, who were not only examples to us, but to many of their nobles and learned); that is, Augustine,[8] who had engraven on his table these words

---

6. Tertullian, known as Quintus Septimus Florens Tertul-lianus (A.D. 150–230), defended Christianity, despite being per-secuted for his beliefs. A noted African writer of the early church, he was the center of a group of African men of spirit. Hall tells his story accurately, although the death date Hall men-tions differs from that in more recent records.

7. Cyprian, Thascius Cæcilius Cyprianus (d. A.D. 258), was another early African church leader, one advanced in age when he first converted to Christianity. He was persecuted and be-headed at Carthage.

8. St. Augustine (A.D. 354–430) was one of the most cele-brated leaders of the early church.

He that doth love an absent Friend to jeer,
May hence depart, no room is for him here.

His saying was that sincere and upright Prayer pierceth heaven, and returns not empty. That it was a shelter to the soul. A sacrifice to God and a scourge to the Devil. There is nothing, said he, more abateth pride and sin than the frequent meditation on death; he cannot die ill, that lives well, and seldom doth he die well, that lives ill: Again, if men want wealth, it is not to be unjustly gotten, if they have it they ought by good works to lay it up in heaven: And again, he that hath tasted the sweetness of divine love will not care for temporal sweetness. The reasonable soul made in the likeness of God may here find much distraction, but no full satisfaction; not to be without afflictions, but to overcome them, is blessedness. Love is as strong as death; as death kills the body, so love of eternal life kills worldly desires and affections. He called Ingratitude the Devil's sponge, wherewith he wipes out all the favours of the Almighty. His prayer was: Lord give first what thou requirest, and then require of me what thou wilt. This good man died Anno Christi 430.

The next is Fulgentius,[9] his speech was, why travel I in the world which can yield me no future, nor durable reward answerable to my pains? Thought it better to weep well, than to rejoice ill, yet if joy be our desire, how much more excellent is their joy, who have a good conscience before God, who dread nothing but sin, study to do nothing but to accomplish the precepts of Christ. Now therefore let me change my course, and as before I endeavoured amongst my noble friends to prove more noble, so now let my care and employment be among the humble and poor servants of Christ, and become more humble that I may help and instruct my poor and distrest brethren.

Thus, my brethren, I have quoted a few of your reverend fathers for your imitation, which I hope you will endeavour to follow, so far as your abilities will permit in your present situation and the disadvantages you labour under on account of your being deprived of the means of education in your younger days, as you see it is at this day with our children, for we see notwithstanding we are rated for that, and other Town charges, we are deprived of that blessing. But be not discouraged, have patience, and look forward to a better day; Hear what the great Architect of the universal world saith, *Aethippia shall stretch forth her hands unto me.* Hear also the strange but bold and confident language of *J. Husk,* who just before the executioner gave the last stroke, said, *I challenge you to meet me an hundred years hence.* But in the mean time let us lay by our recreations, and all superfluities, so that we may have that to educate our rising generation, which was spent in those follies. Make you this beginning, and who knows but God may raise up some friend or body of friends, as he did in *Philadelphia,* to open a School for the blacks here, as that friendly city has done there.[10]

I shall now shew you what progress Masonry hath made since the siege and taking of Jerusalem in the year 70, by Titus Vespasian; after a long and bloody siege, a million of souls having been slain or had perished in the city, it was taken by storm and the city set on fire. There was an order of men called the order of St. John, who besides their other engagements, subscribed to another, by which they bound themselves to keep up the war against the Turks. These men defended the temple when on fire, in order to save it, so long, that Titus was amazed and went to see the reason of it; but when he came so near as to behold the *Sanctum Sanctorum,* he was amazed, and shed tears, and said, no wonder these men should so long to save it. He honored them with many honors, and large contributions were made to that order from many kingdoms; and were also knighted. They continued 88 years in Jerusalem, till that city was again retaken by the Turks, after which they resided 104 years in the Cyrean city of Ptolemy, till the remains of the Holy Conquest were lost. Whereupon they settled on the Island of Cyprus, where they continued 18 years, till they found an opportunity to take the Island Rhodes; being masters of that, they maintained it for 213 years, and from thence they were called knights of Rhodes, till in the year 1530 they took their residence in the Island of Malta, where they have continued to this day, and are distinguished by the name of the knights of Malta.[11] Their first Master was Villaret in the year 1099. Fulco Villaret in the year 1322, took the Island

---

9. Fulgentius, known as Fabius Claudius Gordianus Fulgentius (A.D. 468–533), yet another persecuted African church leader, was known for leading a saintly life and for his eloquence.

10. William Sturgeon had opened a school for Africans in the 1760s, under the sponsorship of Philadelphia Quakers and others.

11. Titus Vespasian (A.D. 17–79), a military leader, became a Roman emperor and governor of Africa.

of Rhodes,[12] and was after that distinguished by the title of Grand-Master, which hath devolved to his Successors to this day.

Query, Whether at that day, when there was an African church, and perhaps the largest Christian church on earth, whether there was no African of that order; or whether, if they were all whites, they would refuse to accept them as their fellow Christians and brother Masons; or whether there were any so weak, or rather so foolish, as to say, because they were blacks, that would make their lodge or army too common or too cheap? Sure this was not our conduct in the late war; for then they marched shoulder to shoulder, brother soldier and brother soldier, to the field of battle; let who will answer; he that despises a black man for the sake of his colour, reproacheth his Maker, and he hath resented it, in the case of Aaron and Miriam. See for this Numbers xii.

But to return: In the year 1787 (the year in which we received our charter) there were 489 lodges under charge of his late Royal Highness the Duke of Cumberland; whose memory will always be esteemed by every good Mason.

And now, my African brethren, you see what a noble order you are members of. My charge to you is, that you make it your study to live up to the precepts of it, as you know that they are all good; and let it be known this day to the spectators that you have not been to a feast of Bacchus, but to a refreshment with Masons; and see to it that you behave as such, as well at home as abroad; always to keep in your minds the obligations you are under, both to God and your fellow men. And more so, you my dear brethren of Providence, who are at a distance from, and cannot attend the Lodge here but seldom; yet I hope you will endeavour to communicate to us by letters of your welfare; and remember your obligations to each other, and live in peace

and love as brethren.—We thank you for your attendance with us this day, and wish you a safe return.

If thus, we by the grace of God, live up to this our Profession; we may cheerfully go the rounds of the compass of this life, having lived according to the plumb line of uprightness, the square of justice, the level of truth and sincerity. And when we are come to the end of time, we may then bid farewell to that delightful Sun and Moon, and the other planets, that move so beautifully round her in their orbits, and all things here below, and ascend to that new Jerusalem, where we shall not want these tapers, for God is the Light thereof; where the Wicked cease from troubling, and where the weary are at rest.

> Then shall we hear and see and know,
> All we desir'd and wish'd below,
> And every power find sweet employ,
> In that eternal world of joy.
> Our flesh shall slumber in the ground,
> Till the last trumpet's joyful sound,
> Then burst the chains with sweet surprize,
> And in our Saviour's image rise.[13]

A CHARGE, DELIVERED TO THE AFRICAN LODGE, JUNE 24, 1797, AT MENOTOMY[1]

By the Right Worshipful PRINCE HALL. Published by the Desire of the Members of Said Lodge, 1797.

Beloved Brethren of the African Lodge,
'Tis now five years since I deliver'd a Charge[2] to you on some parts and points of Masonry. As one branch or su-

---

12. The Knights of Malta, perhaps better known as the Order of the Hospitallers of St. John of Jerusalem, their name until the early fourteenth century, were a military and religious order of monks of legendary fame even at the time Hall was writing. They were known as the Knights of Rhodes from 1309 to 1522, and they have been called the Knights of Malta since 1530. Christians, they took shelter at Malta during the territorial wars with Muslims. The most famous grand master of the order was La Vallette, who defended Malta against Turkish invasions in the 1560s. During the twelfth century, the order developed fleets to fight Muslims at sea, and they took over the island of Rhodes under Foulques de Villaret, who became the grand master. The takeover brought about a major transformation of the order from one that was primarily military to one that was increasingly religious, even as it developed a more formal system of authority.

13. Hall combines concluding lines from two different poems from the *Psalms* of Isaac Watts (1674–1748), taking the first four lines from the conclusion of Psalm 92, part one, "A Psalm for the Lord's Day," and the last four lines from Psalm 17, "The Sinner's Portion and Saint's Hope; or, the Heaven of Separate Souls, and the Resurrection," where they likewise serve as a conclusion to that poem.

1. Hall's charge was published as a pamphlet in 1797. *Early Negro Writing, 1760–1837,* ed. Dorothy Porter (1971), is the source of the present text.

2. *A Charge, Delivered to the Brethren of the African Lodge on the 25th of June, 1792, at the Hall of Brother William Smith, in Charlestown. By the Right Worshipful Master PRINCE HALL.*

perstructure on the foundation; when I endeavoured to shew you the duty of a Mason to a Mason, and charity or love to all mankind, as the mark and image of the great God, and the Father of the human race.

I shall now attempt to shew you that it is our duty to sympathise with our fellow men under their troubles, the families of our brethren who are gone: we hope to the Grand Lodge above, here to return no more. But the cheerfulness that you have ever had to relieve them, and ease their burdens, under their sorrows, will never be forgotten by them; and in this manner you will never be weary in doing good.

But my brethren, although we are to begin here, we must not end here; for only look around you and you will see and hear of numbers of our fellow men crying out with holy Job, Have pity on me, O my friends, for the hand of the Lord hath touched me.[3] And this is not to be confined to parties or colours; not to towns or states; not to a kingdom, but to the kingdoms of the whole earth, over whom Christ the king is head and grand master.

Among these numerous sons and daughters of distress, I shall begin with our friends and brethren; and first, let us see them dragg'd from their native country by the iron hand of tyranny and oppression, from their dear friends and connections, with weeping eyes and aching hearts, to a strange land and strange people, whose tender mercies are cruel;[4] and there to bear the iron yoke of slavery & cruelty till death as a friend shall relieve them. And must not the unhappy condition of these our fellow men draw forth our hearty prayer and wishes for their deliverance from these merchants and traders, whose characters you have in the xviii chap. of the Revelations 11, 12, & 13 verses, and who knows but these same sort of traders may in a short time, in the like manner, bewail the loss of the African traffick, to their shame and confusion: and if I mistake not, it now begins to dawn in some of the West-India islands;[5] which puts me in mind of a nation (that I have somewhere read of) called Ethiopeans, that cannot change their skin:[6] But God can and will change their conditions, and their hearts too; and let Boston and the world know, that He hath

no respect of persons;[7] and that that bulwark of envy, pride, scorn and contempt, which is so visible to be seen in some and felt, shall fall, to rise no more.

When we hear of the bloody wars which are now in the world, and thousands of our fellow men slain; fathers and mothers bewailing the loss of their sons; wives for the loss of their husbands; towns and cities burnt and destroy'd; what must be the heart-felt sorrow and distress of these poor and unhappy people! Though we cannot help them, the distance being so great, yet we may sympathize with them in their troubles, and mingle a tear of sorrow with them, and do as we are exhorted to—weep with those that weep.

Thus my brethren we see what a chequered world we live in. Sometimes happy in having our wives and children like olive-branches about our tables; receiving the bounties of our great Benefactor. The next year, or month, or week we may be deprived of some of them, and we go mourning about the streets, so in societies; we are this day to celebrate this Feast of St. John's, and the next week we might be called upon to attend a funeral of some one here, as we have experienced since our last in this Lodge. So in the common affairs of life we sometimes enjoy health and prosperity; at another time sickness and adversity, crosses and disappointments.

So in states and kingdoms; sometimes in tranquility, then wars and tumults; rich today, and poor tomorrow; which shews that there is not an independent mortal on earth, but dependent one upon the other, from the king to the beggar.

The great law-giver, Moses, who instructed by his father-in-law, Jethro, an Ethiopean, how to regulate his courts of justice and what sort of men to choose for the different offices; hear now my words, said he, I will give you counsel, and God shall be with you; be thou for the people to Godward, that thou mayest bring the causes unto God, and thou shall teach them ordinances and laws, and shall shew the way wherein they must walk, and the work that they must do: moreover thou shall provide out of all the people, able men, such as fear God, men of truth, hating covetousness, and place such over them, to be rulers of thousands, of hundreds and of tens.

So Moses hearkened to the voice of his father-in-law, and did all that he said. Exodus xviii. 22–24.[8]

---

3. Job 19:21.

4. See Proverbs 12:10.

5. Slave insurrections in the French colony of Saint Dominigue began in 1791 and led to the founding of the Republic of Haiti in 1804.

6. Hall echoes the language of Jeremiah 13:23.

7. Hall echoes the language of Acts 10:34.

8. Here, as elsewhere in the *Charge,* Hall's citation is accurate.

This is the first and grandest lecture that Moses ever received from the mouth of man; for Jethro understood geometry as well as laws, *that* a Mason may plainly see: so a little captive servant maid by whose advice Nomen, the great general of Syria's army, was healed of his leprosy; and by a servant his proud spirit was brought down: 2 Kings v. 3–14.[9] The feelings of this little captive for this great man, her captor, was so great, that she forgot her state of captivity, and felt for the distress of her enemy. Would to God (said she to her mistress) my lord were with the prophets in Samaria, he should be healed of his leprosy: So after he went to the prophet, his proud host was so haughty that he not only disdain'd the prophet's direction, but derided the good old prophet; and had it not been for his servant he would have gone to his grave with a double leprosy, the outward and the inward, in the heart, which is the worst of leprosies; a black heart is worse than a white leprosy.

How unlike was this great general's behaviour to that of as grand a character, and as well beloved by his prince as he was; I mean Obadiah, to a like prophet. See for this 1st Kings xviii. from 7 to the 16th.[10]

And as Obadiah was in the way, behold Elijah met him, and he knew him, and fell on his face, and said, Art not thou, my Lord, Elijah, and he told him, Yea, go and tell thy Lord, behold Elijah is here: and so on to the 16th verse. Thus we see that great and good men have, and always will have, a respect for ministers and servants of God. Another instance of this is in Acts viii. 27 to 31, of the Ethiopian Eunuch, a man of great authority, to Philip, the apostle: here is mutual love and friendship between them. This minister of Jesus Christ did not think himself too good to receive the hand, and ride in a chariot with a black man in the face of day; neither did this great monarch (for so he was) think it beneath him to take a poor servant of the Lord by the hand, and invite him into his carriage, though but with a staff, one coat, and no money in his pocket.[11] So our Grand Master, Solomon, was not asham'd to take the Queen of Sheba by the hand, and lead her into his court, at the hour of high twelve, and there converse with her on points of masonry (for if ever there was a female mason in the world she was one) and other curious matters; and gratified her, by shewing her all his riches and curious pieces of architecture in the temple, and in his house: After some time staying with her, he loaded her with much rich presents: he gave her the right hand of affection and parted in love.[12]

I hope that no one will dare openly (tho' in fact the behaviour of some implies as much) to say, as our Lord said on another occasion, Behold a greater than Solomon is here. But yet let them consider that our Grand Master Solomon did not divide the living child,[13] whatever he might do with the dead one, neither did he pretend to make a law to forbid the parties from having free intercourse with one another without the fear of censure, or be turned out of the synagogue.

Now my brethren, as we see and experience that all things here are frail and changeable and nothing here to be depended upon: Let us seek those things which are above, which are sure, and stedfast, and unchangeable, and at the same time let us pray to Almighty God, while we remain in the tabernacle, that he would give us the grace of patience and strength to bear up under all our troubles, which at this day God knows we have our share. Patience I say, for were we not possess'd of a great measure of it you could not bear up under the daily insults you meet with in the streets of Boston; much more on public days of recreation, how are you shamefully abus'd, and that at such a degree that you may truly be said to carry your lives in your hands, and the arrows of death are flying about your heads; helpless old women have their clothes torn off their backs, even to the exposing of their nakedness; and by whom are these disgraceful and abusive actions committed, not by the men born and bred in Boston, for they are better bred; but by a mob or horde of shameless, low-lived, envious, spiteful persons, some of them not long since, servants in gentlemen's kitchens, scouring knives, tending horses, and driving chaise. 'Twas said by a gentleman who saw that filthy behaviour in the common, that in all the places he had been in, he never saw so cruel behaviour in all his life, and that a slave in the West-Indies, on Sunday or holidays enjoys himself and friends without any molestation. Not only this man, but many in town who hath seen their

---

9. These verses offer a more detailed account of the events Hall describes here and throughout the paragraph.

10. Obadiah (whose name means "servant of God") readily agrees to seek the prophet Elijah. Hall continues this account in the following paragraph.

11. Hall glosses the biblical passage to emphasize its relevance to the eighteenth-century treatment of Africans in America, as he does throughout much of his oration.

---

12. Compare with 1 Kings 10:1–10.

13. 1 Kings 3:23–28.

behaviour to you, and that without any provocation—twenty or thirty cowards fall upon one man—have wonder'd at the patience of the Blacks: 'tis not for want of courage in you, for they know that they dare not face you man for man, but in a mob, which we despise, and had rather suffer wrong than to do wrong, to the disturbance of the community and the disgrace of our reputation: for every good citizen doth honor to the laws of the State where he resides.

My brethren, let us not be cast down under these and many other abuses we at present labour under: for the darkest is before the break of day. My brethren, let us remember what a dark day it was with our African brethren six years ago,[14] in the French West-Indies. Nothing but the snap of the whip was heard from morning to evening; hanging, broken on the wheel, burning, and all manner of tortures inflicted on those unhappy people for nothing else but to gratify their masters pride, wantonness, and cruelty: but blessed be God, the scene is changed; they now confess that God hath no respect of persons,[15] and therefore receive them as their friends, and treat them as brothers. Thus doth Ethiopia begin to stretch forth her hand, from a sink of slavery to freedom and equality.[16]

Although you are deprived of the means of education,[17] yet you are not deprived of the means of meditation; by which I mean thinking, hearing and weighing matters, men, and things in your own mind, and making that judgment of them as you think reasonable to satisfy your minds and give an answer to those who may ask you a question. This nature hath furnished you with, without letter learning; and some have made great progress therein, some of those I have heard repeat psalms and hymns, and a great part of a sermon, only by hearing it read or preached and why not in other things in nature: how many of this class of our brethren that follow the seas can foretell a storm some days before it comes; whether it will be a heavy or light, a long or short one; foretell a hurricane, whether it will be destructive or moderate, without any other means than observation and consideration.

So in the observation of the heavenly bodies, this same class without a telescope or other apparatus have through a smoak'd glass observed the eclipse of the sun: One being ask'd what he saw through his smoaked glass, said, Saw, saw, de clipsey, or de clipseys. And what do you think of it?—Stop, dere be two. Right, and what do they look like?—Look like, why if I tell you, they look like two ships sailing one bigger than tother; so they sail by one another, and make no noise. As simple as the answers are they have a meaning, and shew that God can out of the mouth of babes and Africans shew forth his glory,[18] let us then love and adore him as the God who defends us and supports us and will support us under our pressures, let them be ever so heavy and pressing. Let us by the blessing of God, in whatsoever state we are, or may be in, to be content; for clouds and darkness are about him; but justice and truth is his habitation; who hath said. Vengeance is mine and I will repay it, therefore let us kiss the rod and be still, and see the works of the Lord.

Another thing I would warn you against, is the slavish fear of man, which bringest a snare, saith Solomon.[19] This passion of fear, like pride and envy, hath slain its thousands.—What but this makes so many perjure themselves; for fear of offending them at home they are a little depending on for some trifles: A man that is under a panic of fear, is afraid to be alone; you cannot hear of a robbery or house broke open or set on fire, but he hath an accomplice with him, who must share the spoil with him; whereas if he was truly bold, and void of fear, he would keep the whole plunder to himself: so when either of them is detected and not the other, he may be call'd to oath to keep it secret, but through fear, (and that passion is so strong) he will not confess, till the fatal cord is put on his neck; then death will deliver him from the fear of man, and he will confess the truth when it will not be of any good to himself or the community: nor is this passion of fear only to be found in this class of men, but among the great.

What was the reason that our African kings and princes have plunged themselves and their peaceable kingdoms into bloody wars, to the destroying of towns and kingdoms, but the fear of the report of a great gun or the glittering of arms and swords, which struck these kings near the seaports with such a panic of fear, as not only to destroy the peace and happiness of their inland brethren, but

---

14. Hall refers to the era prior to the slave insurrections in Saint Dominigue.

15. Acts 10:34.

16. Hall adapts Psalm 68:31.

17. Children of African descent were typically not allowed to attend public schools, despite the fact that Africans were taxed as citizens. Hall challenged this policy unsuccessfully in a 1787 petition.

---

18. Hall adapts the language of Psalm 8:2.

19. Proverbs 29:25: "The fear of man bringeth a snare: but whoso putteth his trust in the Lord shall be safe."

plung'd millions of their fellow countrymen into slavery and cruel bondage.

So in other countries; see Felix trembling on his throne. How many Emperors and kings have left their kingdoms and best friends at the sight of a handful of men in arms: how many have we seen that have left their estates and their friends and ran over to the stronger side as they thought; all through the fear of men, who is but a worm, and hath no more power to hurt his fellow worm, without the permission of God, than a real worm.

Thus we see, my brethren, what a miserable condition it is to be under the slavish fear of men; it is of such a destructive nature to mankind, that the scriptures every where from Genesis to the Revelations warns us against it; and even our blessed Saviour himself forbids us from this slavish fear of man, in his sermon on the mount;[20] and the only way to avoid it is to be in the fear of God: let a man consider the greatness of his power, as the maker and upholder of all things here below, and that in Him we live, and move, and have our being, the giver of the mercies we enjoy here from day to day, and that our lives are in his hands, and that he made the heavens, the sun, moon and stars to move in their various orders; let us thus view the greatness of God, and then turn our eyes on mortal man, a worm, a shade, a wafer, and see whether he is an object of fear or not; on the contrary, you will think him in his best estate to be but vanity, feeble and a dependent mortal, and stands in need of your help, and cannot do without your assistance, in some way or other; and yet some of these poor mortals will try to make you believe they are Gods, but worship them not. My brethren, let us pay all due respect to all whom God hath put in places of honor over us: do justly and be faithful to them that hire you, and treat them with that respect they may deserve; but worship no man. Worship God, this much is your duty as christians and as masons.

We see then how becoming and necessary it is to have a fellow feeling for our distres'd brethren of the human race, in their troubles, both spiritual and temporal—How refreshing it is to a sick man, to see his sympathising friends around his bed, ready to administer all the relief in their power; although they can't relieve his bodily pain yet they may ease his mind by good instructions and cheer his heart by their company.

How doth it cheer up the heart of a man when his house is on fire, to see a number of friends coming to his relief; he is so transported that he almost forgets his loss and his danger, and fills him with love and gratitude; and their joys and sorrows are mutual.

So a man wreck'd at sea, how must it revive his drooping heart to see a ship bearing down for his relief.[21]

How doth it rejoice the heart of a stranger in a strange land to see the people cheerful and pleasant and are ready to help him.

How did it, think you, cheer the heart of those our poor unhappy African brethren, to see a ship commissioned from God, and from a nation that without flattery saith, that all men are free and are brethren; I say to see them in an instant deliver such a number from their cruel bolts and galling chains, and to be fed like men and treated like brethren. Where is the man that has the least spark of humanity, that will not rejoice with them; and bless a righteous God who knows how and when to relieve the oppressed, as we see he did in the deliverance of the captives among the Algerines; how sudden were they delivered by the sympathising members of the Congress of the United States, who now enjoy the free air of peace and liberty, to their great joy and surprize, to them and their friends.[22] Here we see the hand of God in various ways bringing about his own glory for the good of mankind, by the mutual help of their fellow men; which ought to teach us in all our straits, be they what they may, to put our trust in Him, firmly believing that he is able and will deliver us and defend us against all our enemies; and that no weapon form'd against us shall prosper; only let us be steady and uniform in our walks, speech and behaviour; always doing to all men as we wish and desire they would do to us in the like cases and circumstances.[23]

Live and act as Masons, that you may die as Masons; let those despisers see, altho' many of us cannot read, yet by our searches and researches into men and things, we have supplied that defect; and if they will let us we shall call ourselves a charter'd lodge of just and lawful Masons; be always ready to give an answer to those that ask you a question; give the right hand of affection and fellowship to whom it justly belongs; let their colour and

---

20. For the Sermon on the Mount, see Matthew 5:1–7:27.

21. Here and elsewhere Hall's metaphors reflect the experiences of Africans. During the eighteenth century, a large number of African men worked in the maritime industry. Thus Hall's frequent references to ships are particularly apt.

22. Congress's treaties (1786–97) with the Barbary states in the area of northern Africa promised annual payments of tribute in exchange for the end of piracy and the release of Americans taken captive and held in Africa.

23. Hall echoes the Golden Rule: Luke 6:31.

complexion be what it will, let their nation be what it may, for they are your brethren, and it is your indispensable duty so to do; let them as Masons deny this, and we & the world know what to think of them be they ever so grand: for we know this was Solomon's creed, Solomon's creed did I say, it is the decree of the Almighty, and all Masons have learnt it: tis plain market language, and plain and true facts need no apologies.

I shall now conclude with an old poem[24] which I found among some papers:

24. The lines reproduce the poem, "True Beauty," by the Reverend John Rawlet (1642–86), published in his *Poetick Miscellanies* (London, 1687).

Let blind admirers handsome faces praise,
And graceful features to great honor raise,
The glories of the red and white express,
I know no beauty but in holiness;
If God of beauty be the uncreate
Perfect idea, in this lower state,
The greatest beauties of an human mould
Who most resemble Him we justly hold;
Whom we resemble not in flesh and blood,
But being pure and holy, just and good:
May such a beauty fall but to my share,
For curious shape or face I'll never care.

OLAUDAH EQUIANO (1745–1797)

A former slave, mariner, trader, abolitionist, and author, Olaudah Equiano wrote and published an autobiography that became a motivating force behind abolitionism in Britain and helped bring about the end of the slave trade. Equiano's book was an international success because of its clear demonstration of its author's wide range of expertise. In preparing his story, Equiano drew upon a number of different trends in writings that were popular in his day. His narrative employs several complementary traditions, even as it tells a new story about the importance of ending slavery. Part spiritual autobiography, part episodic travel narrative, part seaman's tale, part sentimental novel, part abolitionist tract, the narrative is cast as a story also about religious faith. Equiano followed a tradition that dated back to St. Augustine and one that continued to be popular among writers and audiences of different backgrounds. His story of his spiritual progress is interwoven with a secular narrative in which Equiano describes his progress toward material and financial success. His telling of his story has been credited with establishing the prototype of the slave narrative, a genre that would prove central to United States debates about slavery during the nineteenth century.

Born around 1745 in the village of Esseke in present-day Nigeria, Equiano spent his childhood among the Ibo people before he was captured and sold to British slave traders in 1756. After experiencing the horrors of the Middle Passage, a journey that took him in the hold of a ship across the Atlantic from Africa to the West Indies, Equiano arrived in Barbados, the wealthiest of Britain's West Indian colonies. Soon afterward, he was taken to Virginia, where he was put to plantation work. But to his good fortune, as he describes it, Equiano was purchased by a British navy lieutenant, Michael Henry Pascal, in 1757, just as the Seven Year's War was beginning. It was at this point that Equiano's life as a slave became highly unusual for an African who was originally stolen to be a slave in the Americas.

Rather than spend his life on a plantation in the southern colonies or in the West Indies, Equiano was taken by his new owner to England, where he received some education and was introduced to Christianity. He later returned to sea as the British war effort against France was intensifying, and he took part in several key battles against the French. When the war ended, Equiano was sold and resold in the West Indies, eventually to a Philadelphia merchant, Robert King, who was also a member of the Society of Friends. It was in this capacity that he worked on slave ships in the Caribbean and took the opportunity to save money to purchase his own freedom. With some difficulty, Equiano gained his freedom on July 10, 1766, and decided to continue working at sea. He later traveled to England, where he worked as a hairdresser, expanded his education, experienced a religious conversion, and became a Methodist. He then returned to sea, traveling to the Arctic, to Turkey, and back to the West Indies and areas of Central America. His involvement in the slave trade continued, and in 1776 he managed a plantation in Central America.

Like many early writers of African descent whose lives were spent in Africa, England, and the Americas, Equiano identified himself with Britain, rather than British North America, and indeed it was in Britain where he eventually settled during the 1780s. Particularly after the 1772 Somerset case (in which Lord Mansfield ruled that slaves who arrived on British soil were free), many Africans and people of African descent considered Britain to be significantly more sympathetic to them and to the cause of freedom than they did British North America. Despite his misgivings about the plan, Equiano became involved in an unsuccessful Sierra Leone expedition to send poor blacks from Britain back to Africa. He later became active in the British campaign to abolish the slave trade. Upon his return to England, Equiano continued his abolitionism by writing letters to prominent figures and newspapers and by publishing his own life's story in 1789. In 1792 Equiano married a white Englishwoman, Susanna Cullen, with whom he had two daughters, and he died on March 31, 1797.

Equiano's narrative played a pivotal role in the British abolitionist movement because it linked diverse groups within the British public, among them white and mixed-race laborers, religious reformers, blacks, and elites. Although Equiano's descriptions of Africa are similar to and draw upon the writings of white abolitionists like Anthony Benezet, they are distinctive in that they focus on a single narrator who is seeking to bridge the gap between himself and his predominantly white audience. The diversity of his subscription list, which included people ranging from Africans living in Britain to the British royal family, reflects the breadth of Equiano's moral, religious, and economic appeals. Nine British editions were published between 1789 and 1794. When his narrative was published in the United States in 1791, it proved especially popular among artisans. By the time of his death, Equiano's autobiography was available in American, French, Dutch, and Russian editions and was already an international best-seller.

from THE INTERESTING NARRATIVE OF THE LIFE OF OLAUDAH EQUIANO, OR GUSTAVUS VASSA, THE AFRICAN[1]

CHAPTER 1

The Author's account of his country, and their manners and customs—Administration of justice— Embrenché—Marriage ceremony, and public entertainments—Mode of living—Dress— Manufactures—Buildings—Commerce— Agriculture—War and Religion—Superstition of the natives—Funeral ceremonies of the priests or magicians—Curious mode of discovering poison—

---

1. Equiano's autobiography was first published in London in 1789. This text is taken from the much-annotated ninth edition of Olaudah Equiano's *Interesting Narrative of the Life of Olaudah Equiano, or Gustavus Vassa, the African* (London, 1794).

Some hints concerning the origin of the author's countrymen, with the opinions of different writers on that subject.

I believe it is difficult for those who publish their own memoirs to escape the imputation of vanity; nor is this the only disadvantage under which they labour; it is also their misfortune, that whatever is uncommon is rarely, if ever, believed; and what is obvious we are apt to turn from with disgust, and to charge the writer with impertinence. People generally think those memoirs only worthy to be read or remembered which abound in great or striking events; those, in short, which in a high degree excite either admiration or pity: all others they consign to contempt and oblivion. It is, therefore, I confess, not a little hazardous, in a private and obscure individual, and a stranger too, thus to solicit the indulgent attention of the public; especially when I own I offer here the history of neither a saint, a hero, nor a tyrant. I believe there are a few events in my life which have not happened to many; it is true the incidents of it are numerous; and, did I consider myself an European, I might say my sufferings were great; but, when I compare my lot with that of most of my countrymen, I regard myself as a *particular favourite of Heaven,* and acknowledge the mercies of Providence in every oc-currence of my life. If, then, the following narrative does not appear sufficiently interesting to engage general at-tention, let my motive be some excuse for its publication. I am not so foolishly vain as to expect from it either im-mortality or literary reputation. If it afford any satisfac-tion to my numerous friends, at whose request it has been written, or in the smallest degree promotes the interest of humanity, the ends for which it was undertaken will be fully attained, and every wish of my heart gratified. Let it therefore be remembered that, in wishing to avoid cen-sure, I do not aspire to praise.

That part of Africa, known by the name of Guinea, to which the trade for slaves is carried on, extends along the coast above 3400 miles, from Senegal to Angola, and in-cludes a variety of kingdoms. Of these the most consider-able is the kingdom of Benin, both as to extent and wealth, the richness and cultivation of the soil, the power of its king, and the number and warlike disposition of the inhabitants. It is situated nearly under the line[2] and ex-tends along the coast about 170 miles, but runs back into the interior part of Africa to a distance hitherto I believe unexplored by any traveller; and seems only terminated at length by the empire of Abyssinia,[3] near 1500 miles from its beginning. This kingdom is divided into many provinces or districts: in one of the most remote and fer-tile of which, called Eboe,[4] I was born, in the year 1745, in a charming fruitful vale, named Essaka. The distance of this province from the capital of Benin and the sea coast must be very considerable; for I had never heard of white men or Europeans, nor of the sea; and our subjec-tion to the king of Benin was little more than nominal; for every transaction of the government, as far as my slender observation extended, was conducted by the chiefs or elders of the place. The manners and government of a people who have little commerce with other countries are generally very simple; and the history of what passes in one family or village may serve as a specimen of the whole nation. My father was one of those elders or chiefs I have spoken of, and was styled Embrenché; a term, as I remember, importing the highest distinction, and signify-ing in our language a mark of grandeur. This mark is con-ferred on the person entitled to it, by cutting the skin across at the top of the forehead, and drawing it down to the eye-brows; and, while it is in this situation, applying a warm hand, and rubbing it until it shrinks up into a thick *weal* across the lower part of the forehead. Most of the judges and senators were thus marked; my father had long borne it: I had seen it conferred on one of my brothers, and I was also *destined* to receive it by my parents. Those Embrenché, or chief men, decided disputes and punished crimes; for which purpose they always assembled to-gether. The proceedings were generally short; and in most cases the law of retaliation prevailed. I remember a man was brought before my father, and the other judges, for kidnapping a boy; and, although he was the son of a chief or senator, he was condemned to make recompense by a man or woman slave. Adultery, however, was sometimes punished with slavery or death; a punishment which I be-lieve is inflicted on it throughout most of the nations of Africa:[5] so sacred among them is the honour of the mar-riage bed, and so jealous are they of the fidelity of their wives. Of this I recollect an instance.—A woman was convicted before the judges of adultery, and delivered over, as the custom was, to her husband to be punished. Accordingly he determined to put her to death: but it being found, just before her execution, that she had an in-fant at her breast; and no woman being prevailed on to perform the part of a nurse, she was spared on account of the child. The men, however, do not preserve the same constancy to their wives, which they expect from them; for they indulge in a plurality, though seldom in more than two. Their mode of marriage is thus:—both parties are usually betrothed when young by their parents (though I have known the males to betroth themselves). On this occasion a feast is prepared, and the bride and bridegroom stand up in the midst of all their friends, who are assembled for the purpose, while he declares she is

---

2. The equator.

3. Abyssinia is the name for modern-day Ethiopia.

4. "See the Observations on a Guinea Voyage, in a series of letters, addressed to Rev. T. Clarkson, by Jas. Feild, Stanfield, in 1788, page 21—'I never saw a happier race of people than those of the kingdom of Benin, seated in ease and plenty, the Slave Trade, and its unavoidable bad effect excepted; everything bore the appearance of friendship, tranquillity, and primitive inde-pendence.'" [Au.]

5. "See Benezet's Account of Guinea throughout." [Au.] Equiano was referencing Anthony Benezet (1713–84), a re-former who wrote *Some Historical Account of Guinea, Its Situ-ation, Produce, and the General Disposition of Its Inhabitants. With an Inquiry into the Rise and Progress of the Slave Trade, Its Nature, and Lamentable Effects* (London, 1788).

thenceforth to be looked upon as his wife, and that no other person is to pay any addresses to her. This is also immediately proclaimed in the vicinity, on which the bride retires from the assembly. Some time after, she is brought home to her husband, and then another feast is made, to which the relations of both parties are invited: her parents then deliver her to the bridegroom, accompanied with a number of blessings, and at the same time they tie round her waist a cotton string of the thickness of a goose-quill, which none but married women are permitted to wear: she is now considered as completely his wife; and at this time the dowry is given to the new married pair, which generally consists of portions of land, slaves, and cattle, household goods, and implements of husbandry. These are offered by the friends of both parties; besides which the parents of the bridegroom present gifts to those of the bride, whose property she is looked upon before marriage; but after it she is esteemed the sole property of her husband. The ceremony being now ended, the festival begins, which is celebrated with bonfires, and loud acclamations of joy, accompanied with music and dancing.

We are almost a nation of dancers, musicians, and poets. Thus every great event, such as a triumphant return from battle, or other cause of public rejoicing, is celebrated in public dances, which are accompanied with songs and music suited to the occasion. The assembly is separated into four divisions, which dance either apart or in succession, and each with a character peculiar to itself. The first division contains the married men, who in their dances frequently exhibit feats of arms, and the representation of a battle. To these succeed the married women, who dance in the second division. The young men occupy the third; and the maidens the fourth. Each represents some interesting scene of real life, such as a great achievement, domestic employment, a pathetic story, or some rural sport; and as the subject is generally founded on some recent event, it is therefore ever new. This gives our dances a spirit and variety which I have scarcely seen elsewhere.[6] We have many musical instruments, particularly drums of different kinds, a piece of music which resembles a guitar,[7] and another much like a stickado. These last are chiefly used by betrothed virgins, who play on them on all grand festivals.

As our manners are simple, our luxuries are few. The dress of both sexes is nearly the same. It generally consists of a long piece of calico, or muslin, wrapped loosely round the body, somewhat in the form of a Highland plaid. This is usually dyed blue, which is our favourite colour. It is extracted from a berry, and is brighter and richer than any I have seen in Europe. Besides this, our women of distinction wear golden ornaments, which they dispose with some profusion on their arms and legs. When our women are not employed with the men in tillage, their usual occupation is spinning and weaving cotton, which they afterwards dye, and make into garments. They also manufacture earthen vessels, of which we have many kinds. Among the rest tobacco pipes, made after the same fashion, and used in the same manner, as those in Turkey.[8]

Our manner of living is entirely plain; for as yet the natives are unacquainted with those refinements in cookery which debauch the taste: bullocks, goats, and poultry supply the greatest part of their food. These constitute likewise the principal wealth of the country, and the chief articles of its commerce. The flesh is usually stewed in a pan. To make it savory, we sometimes use also pepper, and other spices, and we have salt made of wood ashes. Our vegetables are mostly plantains, eadas,[9] yams, beans, and Indian corn. The head of the family usually eats alone; his wives and slaves have also their separate tables. Before we taste food, we always wash our hands: indeed our cleanliness on all occasions is extreme; but on this it is an indispensable ceremony. After washing, libation is made, by pouring out a small portion of the drink on the floor, and tossing a small quantity of the food in a certain place, for the spirits of departed relations, which the natives suppose to preside over their conduct, and guard them from evil. They are totally unacquainted with strong or spiritous liquours; and their principal beverage is palm wine. This is got from a tree of that name, by tapping it at the top, and fastening a large gourd to it; and sometimes one tree will yield three or four gallons in a night. When just drawn it is of a most delicious sweetness; but in a few days it acquires a tartish and more spirituous flavour: though I never saw any one intoxicated by it. The same

---

6. "When I was in Smyrna, I have frequently seen the Greeks dance after this manner." [Au.]

7. "Xylophone." [Au.]

---

8. "The bowl is earthen, curiously figured, to which a long reed is fixed as a tube. This tube is sometimes so long as to be borne by one, and frequently, out of grandeur, by two boys." [Au.]

9. An edible, tuberous plant from the tropics.

tree also produces nuts and oil. Our principal luxury is in perfumes; one sort of these is an odoriferous wood of delicious fragrance: the other a kind of earth; a small portion of which thrown into the fire diffuses a most powerful odour.[10] We beat this wood into powder, and mix it with palm-oil; with which both men and women perfume themselves.

In our buildings we study convenience rather than ornament. Each master of a family has a large square piece of ground, surrounded with a moat or fence, or enclosed with a wall made of red earth tempered, which, when dry, is as hard as brick. Within this are his houses to accommodate his family and slaves; which, if numerous, frequently present the appearance of a village. In the middle stands the principal building, appropriated to the sole use of the master, and consisting of two apartments; in one of which he sits in the day with his family, the other is left apart for the reception of his friends. He has besides these a distinct apartment in which he sleeps, together with his male children. On each side are the apartments of his wives, who have also their separate day and night houses. The habitations of the slaves and their families are distributed throughout the rest of the enclosure. These houses never exceed one story in height; they are always built of wood, or stakes driven into the ground, crossed with wattles, and neatly plastered within, and without. The roof is thatched with reeds. Our dayhouses are left open at the sides; but those in which we sleep are always covered, and plastered in the inside, with a composition mixed with cow-dung, to keep off the different insects which annoy us during the night. The walls and floors also of these are generally covered with mats. Our beds consist of a platform, raised three or four feet from the ground, on which are laid skins, and different parts of a spungy tree called plaintain. Our covering is calico or muslin, the same as our dress. The usual seats are a few logs of wood; but we have benches, which are generally perfumed, to accommodate strangers; these compose the greater part of our household furniture. Houses so constructed and furnished require but little skill to erect them. Every man is a sufficient architect for the purpose. The whole neighbourhood afford their unanimous assistance in building them, and, in return, receive and expect no other recompense than a feast.

As we live in a country where nature is prodigal of her favours, our wants are few and easily supplied; of course we have few manufactures. They consist for the most part of calicoes, earthen ware, ornaments, and instruments of war and husbandry. But these make no part of our commerce, the principal articles of which, as I have observed, are provisions. In such a state money is of little use; however we have some small pieces of coin, if I may call them such. They are made something like an anchor; but I do not remember either their value or denomination. We have also markets, at which I have been frequently with my mother. These are sometimes visited by stout, mahogany-coloured men from the south west of us: we call them *Oye-Eboe,* which term signifies red men living at a distance. They generally bring us firearms, gun-powder, hats, beads, and dried fish. The last we esteemed a great rarity, as our waters were only brooks and springs. These articles they barter with us for odoriferous woods and earth, and our salt of wood-ashes. They always carry slaves through our land; but the strictest account is exacted of their manner of procuring them before they are suffered to pass. Sometimes indeed we sold slaves to them, but they were only prisoners of war, or such among us as had been convicted of kidnapping, or adultery, and some other crimes which we esteemed heinous. This practice of kidnapping induces me to think, that, notwithstanding all our strictness, their principal business among us was to trepan[11] our people. I remember too they carried great sacks along with them, which, not long after, I had an opportunity of fatally seeing applied to that infamous purpose.

Our land is uncommonly rich and fruitful, and produces all kinds of vegetables in great abundance. We have plenty of Indian corn, and vast quantities of cotton and tobacco. Our pine apples grow without culture; they are about the size of the largest sugarloaf, and finely flavoured. We have also spices of different kinds, particularly pepper; and a variety of delicious fruits which I have never seen in Europe; together with gums of various kinds, and honey in abundance. All our industry is exerted to improve those blessings of nature. Agriculture is our chief employment; and every one, even the children and women, are engaged in it. Thus we are all habituated to labour from our earliest years. Every one contributes something to the common stock; and as we are unacquainted with idleness, we have no beggars. The benefits of such a mode of living are obvious. The West-India

---

10. "When I was in Smyrna I saw the same kind of earth, and brought some of it with me to England; it resembles musk in strength, but is more delicious in scent, and is not unlike the smell of a rose." [Au.]

11. To ensnare or trick.

planters prefer the slaves of Benin or Eboe to those of any other part of Guinea, for their hardiness, intelligence, integrity, and zeal. Those benefits are felt by us in the general healthiness of the people, and in their vigour and activity; I might have added too in their comeliness. Deformity is indeed unknown amongst us, I mean that of shape. Numbers of the natives of Eboe now in London might be brought in support of this assertion; for, in regard to complexion, ideas of beauty are wholly relative. I remember while in Africa to have seen three negro children, who were tawny, and another quite white, who were universally regarded by myself and the natives in general, as far as related to their complexions, as deformed. Our women too were, in my eyes at least, uncommonly graceful, alert, and modest to a degree of bashfulness; nor do I remember to have ever heard of an instance of incontinence amongst them before marriage. They are also remarkably cheerful. Indeed cheerfulness and affability are two of the leading characteristics of our nation.

Our tillage is exercised in a large plain or common, some hours walk from our dwellings, and all the neighbours resort thither in a body. They use no beasts of husbandry; and their only instruments are hoes, axes, shovels, and beaks, or pointed iron to dig with. Sometimes we are visited by locusts, which come in large clouds, so as to darken the air, and destroy our harvest. This however happens rarely, but when it does, a famine is produced by it. I remember an instance or two wherein this happened. This common is oftimes the theatre of war; and therefore when our people go out to till their land, they not only go in a body, but generally take their arms with them, for fear of a surprise; and when they apprehend an invasion they guard the avenues to their dwellings, by driving sticks into the ground, which are so sharp at one end as to pierce the foot, and are generally dipt in poison. From what I can recollect of these battles, they appear to have been irruptions of one little state or district on the other, to obtain prisoners or booty. Perhaps they were incited to this by those traders who brought the European goods I mentioned amongst us. Such mode of obtaining slaves in Africa is common; and I believe more are procured this way, and by kidnapping, than any other.[12] When a trader wants slaves, he applies to a chief for them, and tempts him with his wares. It is not extraordinary, if on this occasion he yields to the temptation with as little firmness, and accepts the price of his fellow creature's liberty with as little reluctance, as the enlightened merchant. Accordingly, he falls on his neighbours, and a desperate battle ensues. If he prevails, and takes prisoners, he gratifies his avarice by selling them; but, if his party be vanquished, and he falls into the hands of the enemy, he is put to death: for, as he has been known to foment their quarrels, it is thought dangerous to let him survive, and no ransom can save him, though all other prisoners may be redeemed. We have firearms, bows and arrows, broad two-edged swords and javelins; we have shields also, which cover a man from head to foot. All are taught the use of the weapons. Even our women are warriors, and march boldly out to fight along with the men. Our whole district is a kind of militia: on a certain signal given, such as the firing of a gun at night, they all rise in arms and rush upon their enemy. It is perhaps something remarkable, that when our people march to the field, a red flag or banner is borne before them. I was once a witness to a battle in our common. We had been all at work in it one day as usual when our people were suddenly attacked. I climbed a tree at some distance, from which I beheld the fight. There were many women as well as men on both sides; among others my mother was there and armed with a broad sword. After fighting for a considerable time with great fury, and many had been killed, our people obtained the victory, and took their enemy's Chief prisoner. He was carried off in great triumph, and, though he offered a large ransom for his life, he was put to death. A virgin of note among our enemies had been slain in the battle, and her arm was exposed in our market-place, where our trophies were always exhibited. The spoils were divided according to the merit of the warriors. Those prisoners which were not sold or redeemed we kept as slaves: but how different was their condition from that of the slaves in the West-Indies! With us they do no more work than other members of the community, even their master. Their food, cloathing, and lodging were nearly the same as theirs, except that they were not permitted to eat with those who were free born and there was scarce any other difference between them, than a superior degree of importance which the head of a family possesses in our state, and that authority which, as such, he exercises over every part of his household. Some of these slaves have even slaves under them, as their own property, and for their own use.

As to religion, the natives believe that there is one Creator of all things, and that he lives in the sun, and is girded round with a belt, that he may never eat or drink; but, according to some, he smokes a pipe, which is our own

---

12. "See Benezet's Account of Africa throughout." [Au.] Equiano is probably referring to an earlier version of *Some Historical Account of Guinea* (Philadelphia, 1762).

favourite luxury. They believe he governs events, especially our deaths or captivity; but, as for the doctrine of eternity, I do not remember to have ever heard of it: some however believe in the transmigration of souls in a certain degree. Those spirits, which are not transmigrated, such as our dear friends or relations, they believe always attend them, and guard them from the bad spirits of their foes. For this reason, they always, before eating, as I have observed, put some small portion of the meat, and pour some of their drink, on the ground for them; and they often make oblations of the blood of beasts or fowls at their graves. I was very fond of my mother, and almost constantly with her. When she went to make these oblations at her mother's tomb, which was a kind of small solitary thatched house, I sometimes attended her. There she made her libations, and spent most of the night in cries and lamentations. I have been often extremely terrified on these occasions. The loneliness of the place, the darkness of the night, and the ceremony of libation, naturally awful and gloomy, were heightened by my mother's lamentations; and these, concurring with the doleful cries of birds, by which these places were frequented, gave an inexpressible terror to the scene.

We compute the year from the day on which the sun crosses the line, and, on its setting that evening, there is a general shout throughout the land; at least I can speak from my own knowledge throughout our vicinity. The people at the same time make a great noise with rattles, not unlike the basket rattles used by children here, though much larger, and hold up their hands to heaven for a blessing. It is then the greatest offerings are made; and those children whom our wise men foretell will be fortunate are then presented to different people. I remember many used to come to see me, and I was carried about to others for that purpose. They have many offerings, particularly at full moons; generally two at harvest, before the fruits are taken out of the ground: and, when any young animals are killed, sometimes they offer up part of them as a sacrifice. These offerings, when made by one of the heads of a family, serve for the whole. I remember we often had them at my father's and my uncle's, and their families have been present. Some of our offerings are eaten with bitter herbs. We had a saying among us to any one of a cross temper, "That if they were to be eaten, they should be eaten with bitter herbs."

We practised circumcision like the Jews, and made offerings and feasts on that occasion in the same manner as they did. Like them also, our children were named from some event, some circumstance, or fancied foreboding at the time of their birth. I was named *Olaudah,* which, in our language, signifies vicissitude, or fortunate also; one favoured, and having a loud voice and well spoken. I remember we never polluted the name of the object of our adoration; on the contrary, it was always mentioned with the greatest reverence; and we were totally unacquainted with swearing, and all those terms of abuse and reproach which find the way so readily and copiously into the languages of more civilized people. The only expressions of that kind I remember were "May you rot, or may you swell, or may a beast take you."

I have before remarked, that the natives of this part of Africa are extremely cleanly. This necessary habit of decency was with us a part of religion, and therefore we had many purifications and washings; indeed almost as many, and used on the same occasions, if my recollection does not fail me, as the Jews. Those that touched the dead at any time were obliged to wash and purify themselves before they could enter a dwelling-house. Every woman too, at certain times, was forbidden to come into a dwelling-house, or touch any person, or any thing we ate. I was so fond of my mother I could not keep from her, or avoid touching her at some of those periods, in consequence of which I was obliged to be kept out with her, in a little house made for that purpose, till offering was made, and then we were purified.

Though we had no places of public worship, we had priests and magicians, or wise men. I do not remember whether they had different offices, or whether they were united in the same persons but they were held in great reverence by the people. They calculated our time, and foretold events, as their name imported, for we called them Ah-affoe-way-cah, which signifies calculators, or yearly men, our year being called Ah-affoe. They wore their beards; and, when they died, they were succeeded by their sons. Most of their implements and things of value were interred along with them. Pipes and tobacco were also put into the grave with the corpse, which was always perfumed and ornamented; and animals were offered in sacrifice to them. None accompanied their funerals but those of the same profession or tribe. These buried them after sunset, and always returned from the grave by a different way from that which they went.

These magicians were also our doctors or physicians. They practised bleeding by cupping, and were very successful in healing wounds and expelling poisons. They had likewise some extraordinary method of discovering jealousy, theft, and poisoning; the success of which no doubt they derived from their unbounded influence over the credulity and superstition of the people. I do not remember what those methods were, except that as to poisoning. I recollect an instance or two, which I hope it will not be deemed impertinent here to insert, as it may serve as a kind of specimen of the rest, and is still used by the negroes in the West Indies. A young woman had been poisoned, but it was not known by whom; the doctors ordered the corpse to be taken up by some persons, and carried to the grave. As soon as the bearers had raised it on their shoulders, they seemed seized with some[13] sudden impulse, and ran to and fro', unable to stop themselves. At last, after having passed through a number of thorns and prickly bushes unhurt, the corpse fell from them close to a house, and defaced it in the fall: and the owner being taken up, he immediately confessed the poisoning.[14]

The natives are extremely cautious about poison. When they buy any eatable the seller kisses it all round before the buyer, to shew him it is not poisoned; and the same is done when any meat or drink is presented, particularly to a stranger. We have serpents of different kinds, some of which are esteemed ominous when they appear in our houses, and these we never molest. I remember two of those ominous snakes, each of which was as thick as the calf of a man's leg, and in colour resembling a dolphin in the water, crept at different times into my mother's night-house, where I always lay with her, and coiled themselves into folds, and each time they crowed like a cock. I was desired by some of our wise men to touch these, that I might be interested in the good omens, which I did, for they were quite harmless, and would tamely suffer themselves to be handled; and then they were put into a large open earthen pan, and set on one side of the highway. Some of our snakes, however, were poisonous: one of them crossed the road one day when I was standing on it, and passed between my feet, without offering to touch me, to the great surprise of many who saw it; and these incidents were accounted by the wise men, and likewise by my mother and the rest of the people, as remarkable omens in my favour.

Such is the imperfect sketch my memory has furnished me with of the manners and customs of a people among whom I first drew my breath. And here I cannot forbear suggesting what has long struck me very forcibly, namely, the strong analogy which even by this sketch, imperfect as it is, appears to prevail in the manners and customs of my countrymen, and those of the Jews, before they reached the Land of Promise, and particularly the patriarchs, while they were yet in that pastoral state which is described in Genesis—an analogy, which alone would induce me to think that the one people had sprung from the other.[15] Indeed this is the opinion of Dr. Gill, who, in his commentary on Genesis, very ably deduces the pedigree of the Africans from Afer and Afra, the descendants of Abraham by Keturah his wife and concubine, (for both these titles are applied to her).[16] It is also conformable to the sentiments of Dr. John Clarke, formerly Dean of Sarum, in his Truth of the Christian Religion: both these

---

13. "See Lieut. Matthew's Voyage, p. 123." [Au.] Equiano is refering to *A Voyage to the River Sierra-Leone, on the Coast of Africa; Containing an Account of the Trade and Productions of the Country, and of the Civil and Religious Customs and Manners of the People; in a Series of Letters to a Friend in England. By John Matthews, Lieutenant in the Royal Navy; During his Residence in that Country in the Years 1785, 1786, and 1787* (London, 1788).

14. "An instance of this kind happened at Montserrat, in the West Indies, in the year 1763. I then belonged to the ship Charming Sally, Capt. Doran.—The chief mate, Mr. Mansfield, and some of the crew being one day on shore, were present at the burying of a poisoned negro girl. Though they had often heard of the circumstance of the running in such cases, and had even seen it, they imagined it to be a trick of the corpse bearers. The mate therefore desired two of the sailors to take up the coffin, and carry it to the grave. The sailors, who were all of the same opinion, readily obeyed; but they had scarcely raised it to their shoulders before they began to run furiously about, quite unable to direct themselves, till at last, without intention, they came to the hut of him who had poisoned the girl. The coffin then immediately fell from their shoulders against the hut, and damaged part of the wall. The owner of the hut was taken into custody on this, and confessed the poisoning.—I give this story as it was related by the mate and crew on their return to the ship. The credit which is due to it I leave with the reader." [Au.]

15. "See 1 Chron. 1. 33. Also John Brown's Dictionary of the Bible [Edinburgh, 1788] on the same verse." [Au.]

16. John Gill, *An Exposition of the Old Testament, in which Are Recorded the Original of Mankind, of the Several Nations of the World, and of the Jewish Nation in Particular. . . .* (London, 1788), 158.

authors concur in ascribing to us this original.[17] The reasonings of these gentlemen are still further confirmed by the Scripture Chronology of the Rev. Arthur Bedford;[18] and if any further corroboration were required, this resemblance in so many respects is a strong evidence in support of the opinion. Like the Israelites in their primitive state, our government was conducted by our chiefs, our judges, our wise men, and elders; and the head of a family with us enjoyed a similar authority over his household with that which is ascribed to Abraham and the other patriarchs. The law of retaliation obtained almost universally with us as with them: and even their religion appeared to have shed upon us a ray of its glory, though broken and spent in its passage, or eclipsed by the cloud with which time, tradition, and ignorance might have enveloped it: for we had our circumcision (a rule I believe peculiar to that people): we had also our sacrifices and burnt-offerings, our washings and purifications, on the same occasions as they had.

As to the difference of colour between the Eboan Africans and the modern Jews, I shall not presume to account for it. It is a subject which has engaged the pens of men of both genius and learning, and is far above my strength. The most able and Reverend Mr. T. Clarkson, however, in his much-admired Essay on the Slavery and Commerce of the Human Species,[19] has ascertained the cause, in a manner that at once solves every objection on that account, and, on my mind at least, has produced the fullest conviction. I shall therefore refer to that performance for the theory,[20] contenting myself with extracting

a fact as related by Dr. Mitchel.[21] "The Spaniards, who have inhabited America, under the torrid zone, for any time, are become as dark coloured as our native Indians of Virginia, *of which I myself have been a witness.* There is also another instance[22] of a Portuguese settlement at Mitomba, a river in Sierra Leona, where the inhabitants are bred from a mixture of the first Portuguese discoverers with the natives, and are now become, in their complexion, and in the woolly quality of their hair, *perfect negroes,* retaining however a smattering of the Portuguese language."

These instances, and a great many more which might be adduced, while they shew how the complexions of the same persons vary in different climates, it is hoped may tend also to remove the prejudice that some conceive against the natives of Africa on account of their colour. Surely the minds of the Spaniards did not change with their complexions! Are there not causes enough to which the apparent inferiority of an African may be ascribed, without limiting the goodness of God, and supposing he forbore to stamp understanding on certainly his own image, because "carved in ebony?" Might it not naturally be ascribed to their situation? When they come among Europeans, they are ignorant of their language, religion, manners, and customs. Are any pains taken to teach them these? Are they treated as men? Does not slavery itself depress the mind, and extinguish all its fire, and every noble sentiment? But, above all, what advantages do not a refined people possess over those who are rude and uncultivated? Let the polished and haughty European recollect that *his* ancestors were once, like the Africans, uncivilized, and even barbarous. Did Nature make *them* inferior to their sons? and should *they too* have been made slaves? Every rational mind answers, No. Let such reflections as these melt the pride of their superiority into sympathy for the wants and miseries of their sable brethren, and compel them to acknowledge, that understanding is not confined to feature or colour. If, when they look round the world, they feel exultation, let it be tempered with benev-

17. *The Truth of the Christian Religion. In Six Books. By Hugo Grotius. Corrected and Illustrated with Notes by Mr. Le Clerc. To which Is Added, a Seventh Book, Concerning this Question, What Christian Church We Ought to Join Ourselves to? By the Said Mr. Le Clerc. Ninth Edition. Done into English by John Clarke* (London, 1786).

18. See Arthur Bedford (1688–1745), *The Scripture Chronology Demonstrated by Astronomical Calculations, and also by the Year of Jubilee, and the Sabbatical Year among the Jews; or, An Account of Time from the Creation of the World. . . .* (London, 1730), 229.

19. Thomas Clarkson (1760–1846), *Essay on the Slavery and Commerce of the Human Species, Particularly the African* (London, 1786).

20. "Page 178 to 216." [Au.]

21. "Philos. Trans. No. 476 Sect. 4. cited by the Rev. Mr. Clarkson, p. 205." [Au.] Clarkson quotes John Mitchel's "Causes of the Different Colours of Persons in Different Climates," published in The Philosophical Transactions (From the Year 1743 to the Year 1750) Abridged and Disposed under General Heads . . . By John Martyn [1699–1768] (London, 1756).

22. "Same page." [Au.]

olence to others, and gratitude to God, "who hath made of one blood all nations of men for to dwell on all the face of the earth;[23] and whose wisdom is not our wisdom, neither are our ways his ways."

CHAPTER 2

The Author's birth and parentage—His being kidnapped with his sister—Their separation—Surprise at meeting again—Are finally separated—Account of the different places and incidents the Author met with till his arrival on the coast—The effect the sight of a slave-ship had on him—He sails for the West-Indies—Horrors of a slave-ship—Arrives at Barbadoes, where the cargo is sold and dispersed.

I Hope the reader will not think I have trespassed on his patience in introducing myself to him with some account of the manners and customs of my country. They had been implanted in me with great care, and made an impression on my mind, which time could not erase, and which all the adversity and variety of fortune I have since experienced served only to rivet and record: for, whether the love of one's country be real or imaginary, or a lesson of reason, or an instinct of nature, I still look back with pleasure on the first scenes of my life, though that pleasure has been for the most part mingled with sorrow.

I have already acquainted the reader with the time and place of my birth. My father, besides many slaves, had a numerous family, of which seven lived to grow up, including myself and a sister, who was the only daughter. As I was the youngest of the sons, I became, of course, the greatest favourite with my mother, and was always with her; and she used to take particular pains to form my mind. I was trained up from my earliest years in the arts of agriculture and war: my daily exercise was shooting and throwing javelins; and my mother adorned me with emblems, after the manner of our greatest warriors. In this way I grew up till I was turned the age of eleven, when an end was put to my happiness in the following manner:— Generally, when the grown people in the neighbourhood were gone far in the fields to labour, the children assembled together in some of the neighbours' premises to play;

and commonly some of us used to get up a tree to look out for any assailant, or kidnapper, that might come upon us; for they sometimes took those opportunities of our parents' absence, to attack and carry off as many as they could seize. One day, as I was watching at the top of a tree in our yard, I saw one of those people come into the yard of our next neighbour but one, to kidnap, there being many stout young people in it. Immediately, on this, I gave the alarm of the rogue, and he was surrounded by the stoutest of them, who entangled him with cords, so that he could not escape till some of the grown people came and secured him. But, alas! ere long it was my fate to be thus attacked, and to be carried off, when none of the grown people were nigh. One day, when all our people were gone out to their works as usual, and only I and my dear sister were left to mind the house, two men and a woman got over our walls, and in a moment seized us both; and, without giving us time to cry out, or make resistance, they stopped our mouths, tied our hands, and ran off with us into the nearest wood: and continued to carry us as far as they could, till night came on, when we reached a small house, where the robbers halted for refreshment, and spent the night. We were then unbound, but were unable to take any food; and, being quite overpowered by fatigue and grief, our only relief was some sleep, which allayed our misfortune for a short time. The next morning we left the house, and continued travelling all the day. For a long time we had kept the woods, but at last we came into a road which I believed I knew. I had now some hopes of being delivered; for we had advanced but a little way before I discovered some people at a distance, on which I began to cry out for their assistance; but my cries had no other effect than to make them tie me faster, and stop my mouth, and then they put me into a large sack. They also stopped my sister's mouth, and tied her hands; and in this manner we proceeded till we were out of the sight of these people.—When we went to rest the following night they offered us some victuals; but we refused them; and the only comfort we had was in being in one another's arms all that night, and bathing each other with our tears. But, alas! we were soon deprived of even the smallest comfort of weeping together. The next day proved a day of greater sorrow than I had yet experienced; for my sister and I were then separated, while we lay clasped in each other's arms. It was in vain that we besought them not to part us: she was torn from me, and immediately carried away, while I was left in a state of distraction not to be described. I cried and grieved continually; and for several

---

23. "Acts xvii. 26." [Au.]

days I did not eat any thing but what they forced into my mouth. At length, after many days travelling, during which I had often changed masters, I got into the hands of a chieftain, in a very pleasant country. This man had two wives and some children, and they all used me extremely well, and did all they could to comfort me; particularly the first wife, who was something like my mother. Although I was a great many days journey from my father's house, yet these people spoke exactly the same language with us. This first master of mine, as I may call him, was a smith, and my principal employment was working his bellows, which were the same kind as I had seen in my vicinity. They were in some respects not unlike the stoves here in gentlemen's kitchens; and were covered over with leather; and in the middle of that leather a stick was fixed, and a person stood up, and worked it, in the same manner as is done to pump water out of a cask with a handpump. I believe it was gold he worked, for it was of a lovely bright yellow colour, and was worn by the women on their wrists and ancles. I was there I suppose about a month, and they at last used to trust me some little distance from the house. This liberty I used in embracing every opportunity to inquire the way to my own home: and I also sometimes, for the same purpose, went with the maidens, in the cool of the evenings, to bring pitchers of water from the springs for the use of the house. I had also remarked where the sun rose in the morning, and set in the evening, as I had travelled along; and I had observed that my father's house was towards the rising of the sun. I therefore determined to seize the first opportunity of making my escape, and to shape my course for that quarter; for I was quite oppressed and weighed down by grief after my mother and friends; and my love of liberty, ever great, was strengthened by the mortifying circumstance of not daring to eat with the free-born children, although I was mostly their companion.—While I was projecting my escape one day, an unlucky event happened, which quite disconcerted my plan, and put an end to my hopes. I used to be sometimes employed in assisting an elderly woman slave to cook and take care of the poultry; and one morning, while I was feeding some chickens, I happened to toss a small pebble at one of them, which hit it on the middle, and directly killed it. The old slave, having soon after missed the chicken, inquired after it; and on my relating the accident (for I told her the truth, because my mother would never suffer me to tell a lie) she flew into a violent passion, threatened that I should suffer for it; and, my master being out, she immediately went and told her mistress what I had done. This alarmed me very much,

and I expected an instant correction, which to me was uncommonly dreadful; for I had seldom been beaten at home. I therefore resolved to fly; and accordingly I ran into a thicket that was hard by, and hid myself in the bushes. Soon afterwards my mistress and the slave returned, and, not seeing me, they searched all the house, but, not finding me, and I not making answer when they called to me, they thought I had run away, and the whole neighbourhood was raised in the pursuit of me. In that part of the country (as well as ours) the houses and villages were skirted with woods, or shrubberies, and the bushes were so thick, that a man could readily conceal himself in them, so as to elude the strictest search. The neighbours continued the whole day looking for me, and several times many of them came within a few yards of the place where I lay hid. I expected every moment, when I heard a rustling among the trees, to be found out, and punished by my master; but they never discovered me, though they were often so near that I even heard their conjectures as they were looking about for me; and I now learned from them, that any attempt to return home would be hopeless. Most of them supposed I had fled towards home; but the distance was so great, and the way so intricate, that they thought I could never reach it, and that I should be lost in the woods. When I heard this I was seized with a violent panic, and abandoned myself to despair. Night too began to approach, and aggravated all my fears. I had before entertained hopes of getting home, and I had determined when it should be dark to make the attempt; but I was now convinced it was fruitless, and I began to consider that, if possibly I could escape all other animals, I could not those of the human kind; and that, not knowing the way, I must perish in the woods.—Thus was I like the hunted deer:

> Ev'ry leaf and ev'ry whisp'ring breath
> Convey'd a foe, and ev'ry foe a death.[24]

I heard frequent rustlings among the leaves; and, being pretty sure they were snakes, I expected every instant to be stung by them.—This increased my anguish, and the horror of my situation became now quite insupportable. I at length quitted the thicket, very faint and hungry, for I had not eaten or drank any thing all the day, and crept to my master's kitchen, from whence I set out at first, and

---

24. See Sir John Denham's (1615–99) *Cooper's Hill* (1643): "Now ev'ry leaf, and ev'ry moving breath/Presents a foe, and ev'ry foe a death" (lines 287–288).

which was an open shed, and laid myself down in the ashes, with an anxious wish for death to relieve me from all my pains. I was scarcely awake in the morning when the old woman slave, who was the first up, came to light the fire, and saw me in the fire-place. She was very much surprised to see me, and could scarcely believe her own eyes. She now promised to intercede for me, and went for her master, who soon after came, and, having slightly reprimanded me, ordered me to be taken care of, and not ill-treated.

Soon after this my master's only daughter and child by his first wife sickened and died, which affected him so much that for some time he was almost frantic, and really would have killed himself had he not been watched and prevented. However, in a small time afterwards he recovered, and I was again sold. I was now carried to the left of the sun's rising, through many dreary wastes and dismal woods, amidst the hideous roarings of wild beasts.—The people I was sold to used to carry me very often, when I was tired, either on their shoulders or on their backs. I saw many convenient well-built sheds along the roads, at proper distances, to accommodate the merchants and travellers, who lay in those buildings along with their wives, who often accompany them; and they always go well armed.

From the time I left my own nation I always found somebody that understood me till I came to the sea coast. The languages of different nations did not totally differ, nor were they so copious as those of the Europeans, particularly the English. They were therefore easily learned; and, while I was journeying thus through Africa, I acquired two or three different tongues. In this manner I had been travelling for a considerable time, when one evening, to my great surprise, whom should I see brought to the house where I was but my dear sister. As soon as she saw me she gave a loud shriek, and ran into my arms.—I was quite overpowered; neither of us could speak, but, for a considerable time, clung to each other in mutual embraces, unable to do any thing but weep. Our meeting affected all who saw us; and indeed I must acknowledge, in honour of those sable destroyers of human rights, that I never met with any ill treatment, or saw any offered to their slaves, except tying them, when necessary, to keep them from running away. When these people knew we were brother and sister they indulged us to be together; and the man, to whom I supposed we belonged, lay with us, he in the middle, while she and I held one another by the hands across his breast all night; and thus for a while we forgot our misfortunes in the joy of being to-gether: but even this small comfort was soon to have an end; for scarcely had the fatal morning appeared, when she was again torn from me for ever! I was now more miserable, if possible, than before. The small relief which her presence gave me from pain was gone, and the wretchedness of my situation was redoubled by my anxiety after her fate, and my apprehensions lest her sufferings should be greater than mine, when I could not be with her to alleviate them. Yes, thou dear partner of all my childish sports! thou sharer of my joys and sorrows! happy should I have ever esteemed myself to encounter every misery for you, and to procure your freedom by the sacrifice of my own. Though you were early forced from my arms, your image has been always rivetted in my heart, from which neither *time nor fortune* have been able to remove it: so that, while the thoughts of your sufferings have damped my prosperity, they have mingled with adversity, and increased its bitterness.—To that heaven which protects the weak from the strong, I commit the care of your innocence and virtues, if they have not already received their full reward; and if your youth and delicacy have not long since fallen victims to the violence of the African trader, the pestilential stench of a Guinea ship, the seasoning in the European colonies, or the lash and lust of a brutal and unrelenting overseer.

I did not long remain after my sister. I was again sold, and carried through a number of places, till, after travelling a considerable time, I came to a town called Tinmah, in the most beautiful country I had yet seen in Africa. It was extremely rich, and there were many rivulets which flowed through it; and supplied a large pond in the center of the town, where the people washed. Here I first saw and tasted cocoa nuts, which I thought superior to any nuts I had ever tasted before; and the trees, which were loaded, were also interspersed amongst the houses, which had commodious shades adjoining, and were in the same manner as ours, the insides being neatly plastered and whitewashed. Here I also saw and tasted for the first time sugar-cane. Their money consisted of little white shells, the size of the finger nail: they are known in this country by the name of *core*. I was sold here for one hundred and seventy-two of them by a merchant who lived and brought me there. I had been about two or three days at his house, when a wealthy widow, a neighbour of his, came there one evening, and brought with her an only son, a young gentleman about my own age and size. Here they saw me; and, having taken a fancy to me, I was bought of the merchant, and went home with them. Her house and premises were situated close to one of those rivulets I have mentioned, and were the finest I ever saw in Africa: they were very extensive, and she had a number of slaves to attend her. The next day I was washed and perfumed, and when meal-time came, I was led into the presence of my mistress, and ate and drank before her with her son. This filled me with astonishment: and I could scarce help expressing my surprise that the young gentleman should suffer me, who was bound,[25] to eat with him who was free; and not only so, but that he would not at any time either eat or drink till I had taken first, because I was the eldest, which was agreeable to our custom. Indeed every thing here, and all their treatment of me, made me forget that I was a slave. The language of these people resembled ours so nearly, that we understood each other perfectly. They had also the very same customs as we. There were likewise slaves daily to attend us, while my young master and I, with other boys, sported with our darts and bows and arrows, as I had been used to do at home. In this resemblance to my former happy state I passed about two months, and I now began to think I was to be adopted into the family, and was beginning to be reconciled to my situation, and to forget by degrees my misfortunes, when all at once the delusion vanished; for, without the least previous knowledge, one morning early, while my dear master and companion was still asleep, I was awakened out of my reverie to fresh sorrow, and hurried away even among the uncircumcised.

Thus, at the very moment I dreamed of the greatest happiness, I found myself most miserable: and it seemed as if fortune wished to give me this taste of joy only to render the reverse more poignant. The change I now experienced was as painful as it was sudden and unexpected. It was a change indeed from a state of bliss to a scene which is inexpressible by me, as it discovered to me an element I had never before beheld, and till then had no idea of, and wherein such instances of hardship and cruelty continually occurred as I can never reflect on but with horror.

All the nations and people I had hitherto passed through resembled our own in their manners, customs and language: but I came at length to a country, the inhabitants of which differed from us in all those particulars. I was very much struck with this difference, especially when I came among a people who did not circumcise, and eat without washing their hands. They cooked also in iron pots, and had European cutlasses and cross bows, which were unknown to us, and fought with their fists among themselves. Their women were not so modest as ours, for they eat, and drank, and slept with their men. But, above all, I was amazed to see no sacrifices or offerings among them. In some of those places the people ornamented themselves with scars, and likewise filed their teeth very sharp. They wanted sometimes to ornament me in the same manner, but I would not suffer them; hoping that I might some time be among a people who did not thus disfigure themselves, as I thought they did. At last, I came to the banks of a large river, which was covered with canoes, in which the people appeared to live with their household utensils and provisions of all kinds. I was beyond measure astonished at this, as I had never before seen any water larger than a pond or a rivulet; and my surprise was mingled with no small fear when I was put into one of these canoes, and we began to paddle and move along the river. We continued going on thus till night; and when we came to land, and made fires on the banks, each family by themselves, some dragged their canoes on shore, others staid and cooked in theirs, and laid in them all night. Those on the land had mats, of which they made tents, some in the shape of little houses: In these we slept; and after the morning meal we embarked again, and proceeded as before. I was often very much astonished to see some of the women, as well as the men, jump into the water, dive to the bottom, come up again, and swim about. Thus I continued to travel, sometimes by land, sometimes by water, through different countries, and various nations, till, at the end of six or seven months after I had been kidnapped, I arrived at the sea coast. It would be tedious and uninteresting to relate all the incidents which befel me during this journey, and which I have not yet forgotten; of the various hands I passed through, and the manners and customs of all the different people among whom I lived: I shall therefore only observe, that, in all the places where I was, the soil was exceedingly rich; the pomkins,[26] eadas, plantains, yams, &c. &c. were in great abundance, and of incredible size. There were also vast quantities of different gums, though not used for any purpose; and every where a great deal of tobacco. The cotton even grew quite wild; and there was plenty of red wood. I saw no mechanics whatever in all the way, except such as I have mentioned. The chief employment in all these countries was agriculture, and both the males and females, as with us, were brought up to it, and trained in the arts of war.

The first object which saluted my eyes when I arrived

---

25. Enslaved.

26. Pumpkins.

on the coast was the sea, and a slave-ship, which was then riding at anchor, and waiting for its cargo. These filled me with astonishment, which was soon converted into terror, which I am yet at a loss to describe, nor the then feelings of my mind. When I was carried on board I was immediately handled, and tossed up, to see if I were sound, by some of the crew; and I was now persuaded that I had gotten into a world of bad spirits, and that they were going to kill me. Their complexions too differing so much from ours, their long hair, and the language they spoke, which was very different from any I had ever heard, united to confirm me in this belief. Indeed, such were the horrors of my views and fears at the moment, that, if ten thousand worlds had been my own, I would have freely parted with them all to have exchanged my condition with that of the meanest slave in my own country. When I looked round the ship too, and saw a large furnace of copper boiling, and a multitude of black people of every description chained together, every one of their countenances expressing dejection and sorrow, I no longer doubted of my fate, and, quite overpowered with horror and anguish, I fell motionless on the deck and fainted. When I recovered a little, I found some black people about me, who I believed were some of those who brought me on board, and had been receiving their pay; they talked to me in order to cheer me, but all in vain. I asked them if we were not to be eaten by those white men with horrible looks, red faces, and long hair? They told me I was not; and one of the crew brought me a small portion of spirituous liquor in a wine glass; but, being afraid of him, I would not take it out of his hand. One of the blacks therefore took it from him and gave it to me, and I took a little down my palate, which, instead of reviving me, as they thought it would, threw me into the greatest consternation at the strange feeling it produced, having never tasted any such liquor before. Soon after this, the blacks who brought me on board went off, and left me abandoned to despair. I now saw myself deprived of all chance of returning to my native country, or even the least glimpse of hope of gaining the shore, which I now considered as friendly: and I even wished for my former slavery in preference to my present situation, which was filled with horrors of every kind, still heightened by my ignorance of what I was to undergo. I was not long suffered to indulge my grief; I was soon put down under the decks, and there I received such a salutation in my nostrils as I had never experienced in my life; so that with the loathsomeness of the stench, and crying together, I became so sick and low that I was not able to eat, nor had I the least desire to taste any thing. I now

wished for the last friend, Death, to relieve me; but soon, to my grief, two of the white men offered me eatables; and, on my refusing to eat, one of them held me fast by the hands, and laid me across, I think, the windlass, and tied my feet, while the other flogged me severely. I had never experienced any thing of this kind before; and although, not being used to the water, I naturally feared that element the first time I saw it; yet, nevertheless, could I have got over the nettings, I would have jumped over the side, but I could not; and, besides, the crew used to watch us very closely who were not chained down to the decks, lest we should leap into the water; and I have seen some of these poor African prisoners most severely cut for attempting to do so, and hourly whipped for not eating. This indeed was often the case with myself. In a little time after, amongst the poor chained men, I found some of my own nation, which in a small degree gave ease to my mind. I inquired of these what was to be done with us? they gave me to understand we were to be carried to these white people's country to work for them. I then was a little revived, and thought, if it were no worse than working, my situation was not so desperate: but still I feared I should be put to death, the white people looked and acted, as I thought, in so savage a manner; for I had never seen among any people such instances of brutal cruelty; and this not only shewn towards us blacks, but also to some of the whites themselves. One white man in particular I saw, when we were permitted to be on deck, flogged so unmercifully with a large rope near the foremast, that he died in consequence of it; and they tossed him over the side as they would have done a brute. This made me fear these people the more; and I expected nothing less than to be treated in the same manner. I could not help expressing my fears and apprehensions to some of my countrymen: I asked them if these people had no country, but lived in this hollow place the ship? they told me they did not, but came from a distant one. "Then," said I, "how comes it in all our country we never heard of them?" They told me, because they lived so very far off. I then asked where were their women? had they any like themselves! I was told they had: "And why," said I, "do we not see them?" they answered, because they were left behind. I asked how the vessel could go? they told me they could not tell; but that there were cloths put upon the masts by the help of the ropes I saw, and then the vessel went on; and the white men had some spell or magic[27] they put in

---

27. "Spell or magic" refers to the anchor.

the water when they liked in order to stop the vessel. I was exceedingly amazed at this account, and really thought they were spirits. I therefore wished much to be from amongst them, for I expected they would sacrifice me: but my wishes were vain; for we were so quartered that it was impossible for any of us to make our escape. While we staid on the coast I was mostly on deck; and one day, to my great astonishment, I saw one of these vessels coming in with the sails up. As soon as the whites saw it, they gave a great shout, at which we were amazed; and the more so as the vessel appeared larger by approaching nearer. At last she came to an anchor in my sight, and when the anchor was let go, I and my countrymen who saw it were lost in astonishment to observe the vessel stop; and were now convinced it was done by magic. Soon after this the other ship got her boats out, and they came on board of us, and the people of both ships seemed very glad to see each other. Several of the strangers also shook hands with us black people, and made motions with their hands, signifying, I suppose, we were to go to their country; but we did not understand them. At last, when the ship we were in had got in all her cargo, they made ready with many fearful noises, and we were all put under deck, so that we could not see how they managed the vessel. But this disappointment was the least of my sorrow. The stench of the hold while we were on the coast was so intolerably loathsome, that it was dangerous to remain there for any time, and some of us had been permitted to stay on the deck for the fresh air; but now that the whole ship's cargo were confined together, it became absolutely pestilential. The closeness of the place, and the heat of the climate, added to the number in the ship, which was so crowded that each had scarcely room to turn himself, almost suffocated us. This produced copious perspirations, so that the air soon became unfit for respiration, from a variety of loathsome smells, and brought on a sickness among the slaves, of which many died, thus falling victims to the improvident avarice, as I may call it, of their purchasers. This wretched situation was again aggravated by the galling of the chains, now become insupportable; and the filth of the necessary tubs,[28] into which the children often fell, and were almost suffocated. The shrieks of the women, and the groans of the dying, rendered the whole a scene of horror almost inconceiveable. Happily perhaps for myself I was soon reduced so low here that it was thought necessary to keep me almost al-

ways on deck; and from my extreme youth I was not put in fetters. In this situation I expected every hour to share the fate of my companions, some of whom were almost daily brought upon deck at the point of death, which I began to hope would soon put an end to my miseries. Often did I think many of the inhabitants of the deep much more happy than myself; I envied them the freedom they enjoyed, and as often wished I could change my condition for theirs. Every circumstance I met with served only to render my state more painful, and heighten my apprehensions, and my opinion of the cruelty of the whites. One day they had taken a number of fishes; and when they had killed and satisfied themselves with as many as they thought fit, to our astonishment who were on the deck, rather than give any of them to us to eat, as we expected, they tossed the remaining fish into the sea again, although we begged and prayed for some as well as we could, but in vain; and some of my countrymen, being pressed by hunger, took an opportunity, when they thought no one saw them, of trying to get a little privately; but they were discovered, and the attempt procured them some very severe floggings.

One day, when we had a smooth sea, and moderate wind, two of my wearied countrymen, who were chained together (I was near them at the time), preferring death to such a life of misery, somehow made through the nettings, and jumped into the sea: immediately another quite dejected fellow, who, on account of his illness, was suffered to be out of irons, also followed their example; and I believe many more would very soon have done the same, if they had not been prevented by the ship's crew, who were instantly alarmed. Those of us that were the most active were, in a moment, put down under the deck; and there was such a noise and confusion amongst the people of the ship as I never heard before, to stop her, and get the boat out to go after the slaves. However, two of the wretches were drowned, but they got the other, and afterwards flogged him unmercifully, for thus attempting to prefer death to slavery. In this manner we continued to undergo more hardships than I can now relate; hardships which are inseparable from this accursed trade.—Many a time we were near suffocation, from the want of fresh air, which we were often without for whole days together. This, and the stench of the necessary tubs, carried off many. During our passage I first saw flying fishes, which surprised me very much: they used frequently to fly across the ship, and many of them fell on the deck. I also now first saw the use of the quadrant. I had often with astonishment seen the mariners make observations with it,

---

28. Latrines.

and I could not think what it meant. They at last took notice of my surprise; and one of them, willing to increase it, as well as to gratify my curiosity, made me one day look through it. The clouds appeared to me to be land, which disappeared as they passed along. This heightened my wonder: and I was now more persuaded than ever that I was in another world, and that every thing about me was magic. At last we came in sight of the island of Barbadoes, at which the whites on board gave a great shout, and made many signs of joy to us. We did not know what to think of this; but as the vessel drew nearer we plainly saw the harbour, and other ships of different kinds and sizes: and we soon anchored amongst them off Bridge Town. Many merchants and planters now came on board, though it was in the evening. They put us in separate parcels,[29] and examined us attentively. They also made us jump, and pointed to the land, signifying we were to go there. We thought by this we should be eaten by these ugly men, as they appeared to us; and, when soon after we were all put down under the deck again, there was much dread and trembling among us, and nothing but bitter cries to be heard all the night from these apprehensions, insomuch that at last the white people got some old slaves from the land to pacify us. They told us we were not to be eaten, but to work, and were soon to go on land, where we should see many of our country people. This report eased us much; and sure enough, soon after we were landed, there came to us Africans of all languages. We were conducted immediately to the merchant's yard, where we were all pent up together like so many sheep in a fold, without regard to sex or age. As every object was new to me, every thing I saw filled me with surprise. What struck me first was, that the houses were built with bricks, in stories, and in every other respect different from those in I have seen in Africa: but I was still more astonished on seeing people on horseback. I did not know what this could mean; and indeed I thought these people were full of nothing but magical arts. While I was in this astonishment, one of my fellow prisoners spoke to a countryman of his about the horses, who said they were the same kind they had in their country. I understood them, though they were from a distant part of Africa, and I thought it odd I had not seen any horses there; but afterwards, when I came to converse with different Africans, I found they had many horses amongst them, and much larger than those I then saw. We were not many days in the merchant's custody before we were sold after their usual manner, which is this:—On a signal given, (as the beat of a drum), the buyers rush at once into the yard where the slaves are confined, and make choice of that parcel they like best. The noise and clamour with which this is attended, and the eagerness visible in the countenances of the buyers, serve not a little to increase the apprehensions of the terrified Africans, who may well be supposed to consider them as the ministers of that destruction to which they think themselves devoted.[30] In this manner, without scruple, are relations and friends separated, most of them never to see each other again. I remember in the vessel in which I was brought over, in the men's apartment, there were several brothers, who, in the sale, were sold in different lots; and it was very moving on this occasion to see and hear their cries at parting. O, ye nominal Christians! might not an African ask you, learned you this from your God? who says unto you, Do unto all men as you would men should do unto you? Is it not enough that we are torn from our country and friends to toil for your luxury and lust of gain? Must every tender feeling be likewise sacrificed to your avarice? Are the dearest friends and relations, now rendered more dear by their separation from their kindred, still to be parted from each other, and thus prevented from cheering the gloom of slavery with the small comfort of being together and mingling their sufferings and sorrows? Why are parents to lose their children, brothers their sisters, or husbands their wives? Surely this is a new refinement in cruelty, which, while it has no advantage to atone for it, thus aggravates distress, and adds fresh horrors even to the wretchedness of slavery.

---

29. Groups.

30. Devoted, doomed.

JOHN MARRANT (1755–1791)

John Marrant, author of one of the most popular captivity narratives of the eighteenth and nineteenth centuries, was born to a free black family in New York. As a child, he lived in Florida and Georgia before he moved to Charleston, South Carolina. There he worked for a music master for two years and learned to play the violin and French horn. During his early teens, Marrant worked with a carpenter and found work as a musician. Sometime in 1769 or 1770, Marrant met the evangelist George Whitefield, and his life changed significantly thereafter. Marrant was moved by Whitefield's preaching, and so he decided to leave home to engage in itinerant preaching among people in areas remote from British settlements. He spent two years preaching to the Chickasaws, Creeks, Cherokees, and Choctaws. During some of this time, he was held captive by the Cherokees. When he returned home, he worked with people in the Charleston area and established a church school that slaves attended. His work was cut short when he was taken by the British Royal Navy and pressed into service during the colonies' rebellion against Britain. He served the British on warships until 1782, when he was discharged because he was in poor health.

Marrant lived in London for the next few years, where he increasingly felt drawn to the ministry. His association with the countess of Huntington led to his ordination in her chapel in Bath on May 15, 1785. Soon after his ordination, he narrated his experiences to William Aldridge, a Methodist minister, who "arranged, corrected, and published" Marrant's narrative. The narrative was well received in Europe and later in the United States. Marrant traveled to Nova Scotia to minister to black Loyalists and the Micmacs, Algonquians who had been under the influence of French missionaries as well as British evangelists for two centuries. Despite some of the opposition he faced to his teaching, he spent several years working in southern Nova Scotia, where he organized and taught school, established a chapel in Birchtown, ordained two African ministers, and preached. The demands of his schedule, illness, and the lack of promised financial support from the countess of Huntington all finally wore Marrant down, and he eventually decided to move to Boston.

Once in Boston, Marrant met Prince Hall, recent founder of the first black Masonic lodge. Hall became Marrant's steady supporter, mentioning him in his speeches and introducing him to the circle of Africans who were working toward emancipation or, at least, equal rights before the law. Marrant preached sermons to black and whites, and he seems as well to have worked as a schoolteacher. One of Marrant's sermons for Hall's African lodge, *A Sermon Preached on the 24th Day of June 1789,* was delivered in celebration of the Festival of Saint John and published in the year of its delivery. Marrant eventually returned to London in 1790, where he published his account of his North American experiences in his *Journal* (1790). He died shortly afterward, in April 1791.

Many editions of Marrant's captivity narrative were published. The text that appears here is taken from the undated fourth edition of the narrative, which, according to Adam Potkay and Sandra Burr, Marrant caused to be printed so that he could include information about his family, Native American relations, and plantation culture. Aldridge, having his own purposes in seeing Marrant's materials published, evidently took a heavy editor's hand to Marrant's story. Of the many versions of his narrative, it seems that this version most expresses Marrant's personal concerns.

A NARRATIVE OF THE LORD'S WONDERFUL DEALINGS WITH JOHN MARRANT, A BLACK[1]

Preface

Reader

The following Narrative is as plain and artless, as it is surprising and extraordinary. Plausible reasonings may amuse and delight, but facts, and facts like these, strike, are felt, and go home to the heart. Were the power, grace and providence of God ever more eminently displayed, than in the conversion, success, and deliverances of John Marrant? *He and his companion enter the meeting at* Charles-Town[2] *together; but the one is taken, and the other is left. He is struck to the ground, shaken over the mouth of hell, snatched as a brand from the burning; he is pardoned and justified; he is washed in the atoning blood, and made happy in his God. You soon have another view of him, drinking into his master's cup; he is tried and perplext, opposed and despised; the neighbours hoot at him as he goes along; his mother, sisters, and brother, hate and persecute him; he is friendless and forsaken of all. These uneasy circumstances call forth the corruptions of his nature, and create a momentary debate, whether the pursuit of ease and pleasure was not to be preferred to the practice of religion, which he now found so sharp and severe? The stripling is supported and strengthened. He is persuaded to forsake his family and kindred altogether. He crosses the fence, which marked the boundary between the wilderness and the cultivated country; and prefers the habitations of brutal residence, to the less hospitable dwellings of enmity to God and godliness. He wanders, but Christ is his guide and protector.[3] Who can view him among the* Indian *tribes without wonder? He arrives among the* Cherokees, *where gross ignorance wore its rudest forms, and savage despotism exercised its most terrifying empire. Here the child just turned fourteen, without sling or stone, engages, and with the arrow of prayer pointed with faith, wounded* Goliah, *and conquers the King.[4]*

The untutor'd monarch feels the truth, and worships the God of the Christians; the seeds of the Gospel are disseminated among the Indians *by a youthful hand, and Jesus is received and obeyed.[5]*

The subsequent incidents related in this Narrative are great and affecting; but I must not anticipate the reader's pleasure and profit.

The novelty or magnitude of the facts contained in the following pages, may dispose some readers to question the truth of them. My answer to such is,—1. I believe it is clear to great numbers, and to some competent judges, that God is with the subject of them; but if he knowingly permitted an untruth to go abroad in the name of God, whilst it is confessed the Lord is with him, would it not follow, that the Almighty gave his sanction to a falsehood?—2. I have observed him to pay a conscientious regard to his word.—3. He appeared to me to feel most sensibly, when he related those parts of his Narrative, which describe his happiest moments with God, or the most remarkable interpositions of Divine Providence for him; and I have no reason to believe it was counterfeited.

I have always preserved Mr. Marrant's *ideas, tho' I could not his language; no more alterations, however, have been made, than were thought necessary.*

I now commit the whole to God.—That he may make it generally useful is the prayer of thy ready servant, for Christ's sake,

W. ALDRIDGE.[6]
London
July 19th, 1785.

A Narrative, &c.

I John Marrant, born June 15th, 1755, in New-York, in North-America, with these gracious dealings of the Lord with me to be published, in hopes they may be useful to others, to encourage the fearful, to confirm the wavering, and to refresh the hearts of true believers. My father died

---

1. John Marrant's narrative was first published in London in 1785. The text presented here is the fourth edition, undated but probably published in 1785, titled in its entirety, *A Narrative of the Lord's Wonderful Dealings with John Marrant, a Black, (Now Going to Preach the Gospel in Nova-Scotia) Born in New-York, in North-America.*

2. Charleston, South Carolina.

3. See Psalm 107.

4. See 1 Samuel 17 for the story of David and Goliath.

5. See the Parable of the Sower and the Seed in Matthew 13:18–30.

6. William Aldridge (1737–97), Methodist clergyman and minister of Jewry Street Chapel in London, assisted Marrant in London and edited the original publications of his narrative.

when I was little more than four years of age, and before I was five my mother removed from New-York to St. Augustine,[7] about seven hundred miles from that city. Here I was sent to school, and taught to read and spell; after we had resided here about eighteen months, it was found necessary to remove to Georgia, where we remained; and I was kept to school until I had attained my eleventh year. The Lord spoke to me in my early days, by these removes, if I could have understood him, and said, "Here we have no continuing city."[8] We left Georgia, and went to Charles-Town, where it was intended I should be put apprentice to some trade. Some time after I had been in Charles-Town, as I was walking one day, I passed by a school, and heard music and dancing, which took my fancy very much, and I felt a strong inclination to learn the music. I went home, and informed my sister, that I had rather learn to play upon music than go to a trade. She told me she could do nothing in it, until she had acquainted my mother with my desire. Accordingly she wrote a letter concerning it to my mother, which when she read, the contents were disapproved of by her, and she came to Charles-Town to prevent it. She persuaded me much against it, but her persuasions were fruitless. Disobedience either to God or man, being one of the fruits of sin,[9] grew out from me in early buds. Finding I was set upon it, and resolved to learn nothing else, she agreed to it, and went with me to speak to the man, and to settle upon the best terms with him she could. He insisted upon twenty pounds currency, which was paid, and I was engaged to stay with him eighteen months, and my mother to find me every thing during that term. The first day I went to him he put the violin into my hand, which pleased me much, and, applying close, I learned very fast, not only to play, but to dance also; so that in six months I was able to play for the whole school. In the evenings after the scholars were dismissed, I used to resort to the bottom of our garden, where it was customary for some musicians to assemble to blow the French-horn. Here my improvement was so rapid, that in a twelve-month's time I became master both of the violin and of the French-horn, and was much respected by the Gentlemen and Ladies whose children attended the school, as also by my master. This opened to me a large door of vanity and vice, for I was invited to all the balls and assemblies that were held in the town, and met with the general applause of the inhabitants. I was a stranger to want, being supplied with as much money as I had any occasion for; which my sister observing, said, "You have now no need of a trade." I was now in my thirteenth year, devoted to pleasure and drinking in iniquity like water; a slave to every vice suited to my nature and to my years. The time I had engaged to serve my master being expired, he persuaded me to stay with him, and offered me any thing or any money, not to leave him. His intreaties proving ineffectual, I quitted his service, and visited my mother in the country; with her I staid two months, living without God or hope in the world, fishing and hunting on the sabbath-day. Unstable as water, I returned to town, and wished to go to some trade. My sister's husband being informed of my inclination provided me with a master, who was a carpenter in that town, on condition that I should serve him one year and a half on trial, and afterwards be bound, if he approved of me. Accordingly I went, but every evening I was sent for to play on music, somewhere or another; and I often continued out very late, sometimes all night, so as to render me incapable of attending my master's business the next day; yet in this manner I served him a year and four months, and was much approved of by him. He wrote a letter to my mother to come and have me bound, and whilst my mother was weighing the matter in her own mind, the gracious purposes of God, respecting a perishing sinner, were now to be disclosed. One evening I was sent for in a very particular manner to go and play to some Gentlemen, which I agreed to do, and was on my way to fulfil my promise; and passing by a large meeting house I saw many lights in it, and crowds of people going in. I enquired what it meant, and was answered by my companion that a crazy man was hallooing there; this raised my curiosity to go in, that I might hear what he was hallooing about. He persuaded me not to go in, but in vain. He then said, "If you will do one thing I will go in with you." I asked him what that was? He replied, "Blow the French-horn among them." I liked the proposal well enough, but expressed my fears of being beaten for disturbing them; but upon his promising to stand by me and defend me, I agreed. So we went, and with much difficulty got within the doors. I was pushing the people to make room, to get

---

7. St. Augustine, Florida.

8. Compare with Hebrews 13:14, "For here we have no continuing city, but we seek one to come."

9. See Proverbs 10:16: "The labour of the righteous *tendeth* to life: the fruit of the wicked to sin."

the horn off my shoulder to blow it, just as Mr White-field[10] was naming his text, and looking round, as I thought, directly upon me, and pointing with his finger, he uttered these words, "PREPARE TO MEET THY GOD O IS-RAEL."[11] The Lord accompanied the word with such power, that I was struck to the ground, and lay both speechless and senseless near half an hour. When I was come a little too, I found two men attending me, and a woman throwing water in my face, and holding a smelling-bottle to my nose; and when something more recovered, every word I heard from the minister was like a parcel of swords thrust in to me, and what added to my distress, I thought I saw the devil on every side of me.[12] I was constrained in the bitterness of my spirit to halloo out in the midst of the congregation, which disturbing them, they took me away; but finding I could neither walk or stand, they carried me as far as the vestry, and there I remained till the service was over. When the people were dismissed Mr. Whitefield came into the vestry, and being told of my condition he came immediately, and the first word he said to me was, "JESUS CHRIST HAS GOT THEE AT LAST." He asked where I lived, intending to come and see me the next day; but recollecting he was to leave the town the next morning, he said he could not come himself, but would send another minister; he desired them to get me home, and then taking his leave of me, I saw him no more. When I reached my sister's house, being carried by two men, she was very uneasy to see me in so distressed a condition. She got me to bed, and sent for a doctor, who came immediately, and after looking at me, he went home, and sent me a bottle of mixture, and desired her to give me a spoonful every two hours; but I could not take anything the doctor sent, nor indeed keep in bed; this distressed my sister very much, and she cried out, "The lad will surely die." She sent for two other doctors, but no medicine they prescribed could I take. No, no; it may be asked, a wounded spirit who can cure? as well as who can bear? In this distress of soul I continued for three days without any food, only a little water now and then.[13] On the fourth day, the minister[14] Mr. Whitefield had desired to visit me came to see me, and being directed upstairs, when he entered the room, I thought he made my distress much worse. He wanted to take hold of my hand, but I durst not give it to him. He insisted upon taking hold of it, and I then got away from him on the other side of the bed; but being very weak I fell down, and before I could recover he came to me and took me by the hand, and lifted me up, and after a few words desired to go to prayer. So he fell upon his knees, and pulled me down also; after he had spent some time in prayer he rose up, and asked me how I did now; I answered, much worse; he then said, "Come, we will have the old thing over again," and so we kneeled down a second time, and after he had prayed earnestly we got up, and he said again, "How do you do now;" I replied worse and worse, and asked him if he intended to kill me? "No, no, said he, you are worth a thousand dead men, let us try the old thing over again," and so falling upon our knees, he continued in prayer a considerable time, and near the close of his prayer, the Lord was pleased to set my soul at perfect liberty, and being filled with joy I began to praise the Lord immediately; my sorrows were turned into peace, and joy, and love. The minister said, "How is it now?" I answered, all is well, all happy. He then took his leave of me; but called every day for several days afterwards, and the last time he said, "Hold fast that thou hast already obtained, 'till Jesus Christ come."[15] I now read the Scriptures very much. My master sent often to know how I did, and at last came himself, and finding me well, asked me if I would not come to work again? I answered no. He, asked me the reason, but receiving no answer he went away. I continued with my sister about three weeks, during which time she often asked me to play upon the violin for her, which I refused;

---

10. George Whitefield (1714–70), one of the founders of Methodism in the Church of England.

11. Amos 4:12.

12. Compare with Hebrews 4:12, "For the word of God *is* quick, and powerful, and sharper than any two-edged sword, piercing even to the dividing asunder of soul and spirit, and of the joints and marrow, and *is* a discerner of the thoughts and intents of the heart"; and Ephesians 6:17, "And take the helmet of salvation, and the sword of the Spirit, which is the word of God."

13. Compare with Acts 9:1–20.

14. "Mr. HART, a Baptist Minister at Charles-Town." [Au.]

15. Compare with Revelation 2:25, "But that which he have *already* hold fast till I come"; and 3:11, "Behold, I come quickly: hold that fast which thou hast, that no man take thy crown."

then she said I was crazy and mad, and so reported it among the neighbours, which opened the mouths of all around against me. I then resolved to go to my mother, which was eighty-four miles from Charles-Town. I was two days on my journey home, and enjoyed much communion with God on the road, and had occasion to mark the gracious interpositions of his kind Providence as I passed along. The third day I arrived at my mother's house, and was well received. At supper they sat down to eat without asking the Lord's blessing, which caused me to burst out into tears. My mother asked me what was the matter? I answered, I wept because they sat down to supper without asking the Lord's blessing. She bid me with much surprise, to ask a blessing. I remained with her fourteen days without interruption; the Lord pitied me, being a young soldier. Soon, however, Satan began to stir up my two sisters and brother, who were then at home with my mother; they called me every name but that which was good. The more they persecuted me, the stronger I grew in grace. At length my mother turned against me also, and the neighbours joined her, and there was not a friend to assist me, or that I could speak to; this made me earnest with God. In these circumstances, being the youngest but one of our family, and young in Christian experience, I was tempted so far as to threaten my life; but reading my Bible one day, and finding that if I did destroy myself I could not come where God was, I betook myself to the fields, and some days staid out from morning to night to avoid the persecutors. I staid one time two days without any food, but seemed to have clearer views into the spiritual things of God.

Not long after this I was sharply tried, and reasoned the matter within myself, whether I should turn to my old courses of sin and vice, or serve and cleave to the Lord; after prayer to God, I was fully persuaded in my mind, that if I turned to my old ways I should perish eternally. Upon this I went home, and finding them all as hardened, or worse than before, and every body saying I was crazy; but a little sister I had, about nine years of age, used to cry when she saw them persecute me, and continuing so about five weeks and three days, I thought it was better for me to die than to live among such people. I rose one morning very early, to get a little quietness and retirement, I went into the woods, and staid till eight o'clock in the morning; upon my return I found them all at breakfast; I passed by them, and went up-stairs without any interruption; I went upon my knees to the Lord, and returned him thanks; then I took up a small pocket Bible and one of Dr. Watts's hymn books,[16] and passing by them went out without one word spoken by any of us. After spending some time in the fields, I was persuaded to go from home altogether. Accordingly I went over the fence, about half a mile from our house, which divided the inhabited and cultivated parts of the country from the wilderness. I continued travelling in the desart all day without the least inclination of returning back. About evening I began to be surrounded with wolves; I took refuge from them on a tree, and remained there all night. About eight o'clock next morning I descended from the tree, and returned God thanks for the mercies of the night. I went on all this day without any thing to eat or drink.

The third day, taking my Bible out of my pocket, I read and walked for some time, and then being wearied and almost spent, I sat down, and after resting awhile I rose to go forward; but had not gone above a hundred yards when something tripped me up, and I fell down; I prayed to the Lord upon the ground that he would command the wild beasts to devour me, that I might be with him in glory. I made this request to God the third and part of the fourth day.

The fourth day in the morning, descending from my usual lodging, a tree, and having nothing all this time to eat, and but a little water to drink, I was so feeble that I tumbled half way down the tree, not being able to support myself, and lay upon my back on the ground about an hour and a half, praying and crying; after which, getting a little strength, and trying to stand upright to walk, I found myself not able; then I went upon my hands and knees, and so crawled till I reached a tree that was tumbled down, in order to get across it, and there I prayed with my body leaning upon it above an hour, that the Lord would take me to himself. Such nearness to God I then enjoyed, that I willingly resigned myself into his hands. After some time I thought I was strengthened, so I got across the tree without my feet or hands touching the ground; but struggling I fell over on the other side, and then thought the Lord will now answer my prayer, and take me home: But the time was not come. After laying there a little, I rose, and looking about, saw at some distance bunches of grass, called deer-grass; I felt a strong desire to get at it; though I rose, yet it was only on my hands and knees, being so

---

16. Rev. Isaac Watts (1674–1748), renowned English hymn writer, much admired by evangelicals and frequently cited by African writers.

feeble, and in this manner I reached the grass. I was about three-quarters of an hour going in this form twenty yards. When I reached it, I was unable to pull it up, so I bit it off like a horse, and prayed the Lord to bless it to me, and I thought it the best meal I ever had in my life, and I think so still, it was so sweet.[17] I returned my God hearty thanks for it, and then lay down about an hour. Feeling myself very thirsty, I prayed the Lord to provide me with some water. Finding I was something strengthened, I got up, and stood on my feet, and staggered from one tree to another, if they were near each other, otherwise the journey was too long for me. I continued moving so for some time, and at length passing between two trees, I happened to fall upon some bushes, among which were a few large hollow leaves, which had caught and contained the dews of the night, and lying low among the bushes, were not exhaled by the solar rays; this water in the leaves fell upon me as I tumbled down and was lost, I was now tempted to think the Lord had given me water from Heaven, and I had wasted it, I then prayed the Lord to forgive me.[18] What poor unbelieving creatures we are! though we are assured the Lord will supply all our needs. I was presently directed to a puddle of water very muddy, which some wild pigs had just left; I kneeled down, and asked the Lord to bless it to me, so I drank both mud and water mixed together, and being satisfied I returned the Lord thanks, and went on my way rejoicing. This day was much chequered with wants and supplies, with dangers and deliverances. I continued travelling on for nine days, feeding upon grass, and not knowing whither I was going; but the Lord Jesus Christ was very present, and that comforted me through the whole.

The next morning, having quitted my customary lodging, and returned thanks to the Lord for my preservation through the night, reading and travelling on, I passed between two bears, about twenty yards distance from each other. Both sat and looked at me, but I felt very little fear; and after I had passed them, they both went the same way from me without growling, or the least apparent uneasiness. I went and returned God thanks for my escape, who had tamed the wild beasts of the forest, and made them friendly to me: I rose from my knees and walked on,

singing hymns of praise to God, about five o'clock in the afternoon, and about fifty-five miles from home, right through the wilderness. As I was going on, and musing upon the goodness of the Lord, an Indian hunter, who stood at some distance, saw me; he hid himself behind a tree; but as I passed along he bolted out, and put his hands on my breast, which surprized me a few moments. He then asked me where I was going? I answered I did not know, but where the Lord was pleased to guide me. Having heard me praising God before I came up to him, he enquired who I was talking to? I told him I was talking to my Lord Jesus; he seemed surprized, and asked me where he was? for he did not see him there. I told him he could not be seen with bodily eyes. After a little more talk, he insisted upon taking me home; but I refused, and added, that I would die rather than return home. He then asked me if I knew how far I was from home? I answered, I did not know; you are fifty-five miles and a half, says he, from home. He farther asked me how I did to live? I said I was supported by the Lord. He asked me how I slept? I answered, the Lord provided me with a bed every night: he further enquired what preserved me from being devoured by the wild beasts? I replied, the Lord Jesus Christ kept me from them. He stood astonished, and said, you say the Lord Jesus Christ do this, and do that, and do every thing for you, he must be a very fine man, where is he? I replied, he is here present. To this he made me no answer, only said, I know you, and your mother and sister; and upon a little further conversation I found he did know them, having been used in winter to sell skins in our Town. This alarmed me, and I wept for fear he should take me home by force; but when he saw me so affected, he said he would not take me home if I would go with him. I objected against that, for fear he would rob me of my comfort and communion with God: But at last, being much pressed, I consented to go. Our employment for ten weeks and three days was killing deer, and taking off their skins by day, which we afterwards hung on the trees to dry till they were sent for; the means of defence and security against our nocturnal enemies, always took up the evenings: We collected a number of large bushes, and placed them nearly in a circular form, which uniting at the extremity, afforded us both a verdant covering, and a sufficient shelter from the night dews. What moss we could gather was strewed upon the ground, and this composed our bed. A fire was kindled in the front of our temporary lodging-room, and fed with fresh fuel all night, as we slept and watched by turns; and this was our defence from

---

17. Compare with Proverbs 27:7, "The full soul loatheth an honey-comb; but to the hungry soul every bitter thing is sweet."

18. Compare with Exodus 15:22–27.

the dreadful animals, whose shining eyes and tremendous roar we often saw and heard during the night.

By constant conversation with the hunter, I acquired a fuller knowledge of the Indian tongue: This, together with the sweet communion I enjoyed with God, I have since considered as a preparation for the great trial I was soon after to pass through.

The hunting season being now at an end, we left the woods, and directed our course towards a large Indian town, belonging to the Cherokee nation; and having reached it, I said to the hunter, they will not suffer me to enter in. He replied, as I was with him, nobody would interrupt me.

There was an Indian fortification all round the town, and a guard placed at each entrance. The hunter passed one of these without molestation, but I was stopped by the guard and examined. They asked me where I came from, and what was my business there? My companion of the woods attempted to speak for me, but was not permitted; he was taken away, and I saw him no more. I was now surrounded by about fifty men, and carried to one of their principal chiefs and Judge to be examined by him. When I came before him, he asked me what was my business there? I told him I came there with a hunter, whom I met with in the woods. He replied, "Did I not know that whoever came there without giving a better account of themselves than I did, was to be put to death?" I said I did not know it. Observing that I answered him so readily in his own language, he asked me where I learnt it? To this I returned no answer, but burst out into a flood of tears, and calling upon my Lord Jesus. At this he stood astonished, and expressed a concern for me, and said I was young. He asked me who my Lord Jesus was?—To this I gave him no answer, but continued praying and weeping. Addressing himself to the officer who stood by him, he said he was sorry; but it was the law, and it must not be broken. I was then ordered to be taken away, and put into a place of confinement. They led me from their court into a low dark place, and thrust me into it, very dreary and dismal; they made fast the door, and set a watch. The judge sent for the executioner, and gave him his warrant for my execution in the afternoon of the next day. The executioner came, and gave me notice of it, which made me very happy, as the near prospect of death made me hope for a speedy deliverance from the body: And truly this dungeon became my chapel, for the Lord Jesus did not leave me in this great trouble, but was very present, so that I continued blessing him, and singing his praises all night without ceasing: The watch hearing the noise, informed the executioner

that somebody had been in the dungeon with me all night; upon which he came in to see and to examine, with a great torch lighted in his hand, who it was I had with me; but finding nobody, he turned round, and asked me who it was? I told him it was the Lord Jesus Christ; but he made no answer, turned away, went out, and fastened the door. At the hour appointed for my execution I was taken out, and led to the destined spot, amidst a vast number of people. I praised the Lord all the way we went, and when we arrived at the place I understood the kind of death I was to suffer, yet blessed be God, at that instant none of those things moved me.

When the executioner shewed me a basket of turpentine wood, stuck full of small pieces like skewers; he told me I was to be stripped naked, and laid down on one side by the basket, and these sharp pegs were to be stuck into me, and then set on fire, and when they had burnt to my body, I was to be turned on the other side, and served in the same manner, and then to be taken by four men and thrown into the flame, which was to finish the execution; I burst into tears, and asked what I had done to deserve so cruel a death? To this he gave me no answer. I cried out, Lord, if it be thy will that it should be so, thy will be done:[19] I then asked the executioner to let me go to prayer; he asked me to whom? I answered, to the Lord my God; he seemed surprized, and asked me where he was? I told him he was present; upon which he gave me leave. I desired them all to do as I did, so I fell down upon my knees, and mentioned to the Lord his delivering of the three children in the fiery furnace,[20] and of Daniel in the Lion's den,[21] and had close communion with God. I prayed in English a considerable time, and about the middle of my prayer, the Lord impressed a strong desire upon my mind to turn into their language, and pray in their tongue. I did so, and with remarkable liberty, which wonderfully affected the people. One circumstance was very singular, and strikingly displays the power and grace of God. I believe the executioner was savingly converted to God. He rose from his knees, and embracing me round the middle was unable to speak for about five minutes; the first words he expressed, when he had utterance, were, "No man shall hurt thee till thou hast been to the king."[22]

---

19. See the Lord's Prayer in Matthew 6:9–13.

20. See Daniel 3:1–30.

21. See Daniel 6:1–29.

22. "The Office of Executioner there, in many respects resembles that of a High Sheriff in this country." [Au.]

I was taken away immediately, and as we passed along, and I was reflecting upon the deliverance which the Lord had wrought out for me, and hearing the praises which the executioner was singing to the Lord, I must own I was utterly at a loss to find words to praise him. I broke out in these words, what can't the Lord Jesus do! and what power is like unto his! I will thank thee for what is past, and trust thee for what is to come. I will sing thy praise with my feeble tongue whilst life and breath shall last, and when I fail to sound thy praises here, I hope to sing them round thy throne above: And thus with unspeakable joy, I sung two verses of Dr. Watts's hymns:

"My God, the spring of all my joys
    The life of my delights;
The glory of my brightest days,
    And comfort of my nights.
In darkest shades, if thou appear
    My dawning is begun;
Thou art my soul's bright morning star,
    And thou my rising sun."[23]

Passing by the judge's door, who had before examined and condemned me, he stopped us, and asked the executioner why he brought me back? The man fell upon his knees, and begged he would permit me to be carried before the king, which being granted, I went on, guarded by two hundred men with bows and arrows. After many windings I entered the king's outward chamber, and after waiting some time he came to the door, and his first question was, how came I there? I answered, I came with a hunter whom I met with in the woods, and who persuaded me to come there. He then asked me how old I was? I told him not fifteen. He asked me how I was supported before I met with this man? I answered, by the Lord Jesus Christ, which seemed to confound him. He turned round, and asked me if he lived where I came from? I answered, yes, and here also. He looked about the room, and said he did not see him; but I told him I felt him. The executioner fell upon his knees, and intreated the king in my behalf, and told him what he had felt of the same Lord. At this instant the king's eldest daughter came into the chamber, a person about nineteen years of age, and stood at my right hand. I had a Bible in my hand, which she took out of it, and having opened it, she kissed it, and seemed much delighted with it. When she had put it into my hand again, the king asked me what it was? And I told him the name of my God was recorded there; and after several questions, he bid me read it, which I did, particularly the fifty-third chapter of Isaiah, in the most solemn manner I was able; and also the twenty-sixth chapter of Matthew's Gospel;[24] and when I pronounced the name of Jesus, the particular effect it had upon me was observed by the king. When I had finished reading, he asked me why I read those names with so much reverence? I told him, because the Being to whom those names belonged made heaven and earth, and I and he; this he denied. I then pointed to the sun, and asked him who made the sun, and moon, and stars, and preserved them in their regular order; He said there was a man in their town that did it. I laboured as much as I could to convince him to the contrary. His daughter took the book out of my hand a second time; she opened it, and kissed it again; her father bid her give it to me, which she did; but said, with much sorrow, the book would not speak to her. The executioner then fell upon his knees again, and begged the king to let me go to prayer, which being granted, we all went upon our knees, and now the Lord displayed his glorious power. In the midst of the prayer some of them cried out, particularly the king's daughter, and the judge who ordered me to be executed, and several others seemed under deep conviction of sin: This made the king very angry; he called me a witch, and commanded me to be thrust into the prison, and to be executed the next morning. This was enough to make me think, as old Jacob once did, "All these things are against me;" for I was dragged away, and thrust into the dungeon again with much indignation,[25] but God, who never forsakes his people, was with me. Though I was weak in body, yet I was strong in spirit:[26] The executioner went to the king, and assured him, that if he put me to death, his daughter would never be well. They used the skill of all their doctors that afternoon and night; but physical prescriptions were useless. In the morning the executioner came to me, and, without opening the prison door, called to me, and hearing me answer, said, "Fear not, thy God who delivered thee yesterday, will deliver thee to-day." This comforted me very much, especially to

---

23. A somewhat altered version of Watts's Hymn 54.

24. Marrant's references here and elsewhere are accurate. Exceptions are noted.

25. See Genesis 42:36.

26. Compare with 2 Corinthians 12:10, "Therefore I take pleasure in infirmities, in reproaches, in necessities, in persecutions, in distresses for Christ's sake: for when I am weak, then am I strong."

find he could trust the Lord. Soon after I was fetched out; I thought it was to be executed; but they led me away to the king's chamber with much bodily weakness, having been without food two days. When I came into the king's presence, he said to me, with much anger, if I did not make his daughter and that man well, I should be laid down and chopped into pieces before him. I was not afraid, but the Lord tried my faith sharply. The king's daughter and the other person were brought out into the outer chamber, and we went to prayer; but the heavens were locked up to my petitions. I besought the Lord again, but received no answer: I cried again, and he was intreated. He said, "Be it to thee even as thou wilt;"[27] the Lord appeared most lovely and glorious; the king himself was awakened, and the others set at liberty. A great change took place among the people; the king's house became God's house; the soldiers were ordered away, and the poor condemned prisoner had perfect liberty, and was treated like a prince. Now the Lord made all my enemies to become my great friends. I remained nine weeks in the king's palace, praising God day and night: I was never out but three days all the time. I had assumed the habit of the country, and was dressed much like the king, and nothing was too good for me. The king would take off his golden ornaments, his chain and bracelets, like a child, if I objected to them, and lay them aside. Here I learnt to speak their tongue in the highest stile.

I began now to feel an inclination growing upon me to go farther on, but none to return home. The king being acquainted with this, expressed his fears of my being used ill by the next Indian nation, and to prevent it, sent fifty men, and a recommendation to the king, with me. The next nation was called the Creek Indians, at sixty miles distance. Here I was received with kindness, owing to the king's influence, from whom I had parted; here I staid five weeks. I next visited the Catawaw Indians,[28] at about fifty-five miles distance from the others; Lastly, I went among the Housaw Indians,[29] eighty miles distant from the last mentioned; here I staid seven weeks. These nations were then at peace with each other, and I passed

among them without danger, being recommended from one to the other. When they recollect, that the white people drove them from the American shores, they are full of resentment. These nations have often united, and murdered all the white people in the back settlements which they could lay hold of, men, women, and children. I had not much reason to believe any of these three nations were savingly wrought upon, and therefore I returned to the Cherokee nation, which took me up eight weeks. I continued with my old friends seven weeks and two days.

I now and then found, that my affections to my family and country were not dead; they were sometimes very sensibly felt, and at last strengthened into an invincible desire of returning home. The king was much against it; but feeling the same strong bias towards my country, after we had asked Divine direction, the king consented, and accompanied me sixty miles with one hundred and forty men. I went to prayer three times before we could part, and then he sent forty men with me a hundred miles farther; I went to prayer, and then took my leave of them, and passed on my way. I had seventy miles now to go to the back settlements of the white people. I was surrounded very soon with wolves again, which made my old lodging both necessary and welcome. However it was not long, for in two days I reached the settlements, and on the third I found a house: It was about dinner-time, and as I was coming to the door the family saw me, were frightened, and ran away. I sat down to dinner alone, and eat very heartily, and, after returning God thanks, I went to see what was become of the family. I found means to lay hold of a girl that stood peeping at me from behind a barn. She fainted away, and it was upwards of an hour before she recovered; it was nine o'clock before I could get them all to venture in, they were so terrified.

My dress was purely in the Indian stile; the skins of wild beasts composed my garments; my head was set out in the savage manner, with a long pendant down my back a sash round my middle, without breeches, and a tomahawk by my side. In about two days they became sociable. Having visited three or four other families at the distance of sixteen or twenty miles, I got them altogether to prayer on the Sabbath days, to the number of seventeen persons. I staid with them six weeks, and they expressed much sorrow when I left them. I was now one hundred and twelve miles from home. On the road I sometimes met with a house, then I was hospitably entertained; and when I met with none, a tree lent me the use of its friendly shelter and protection from the prowling beasts of the woods during the night. The God of mercy and grace sup-

---

27. Compare with Matthew 26:39, "And he went a little farther, and fell on his face, and prayed, saying, O my Father, if it be possible, let this cup pass from me: nevertheless not as I will, but as thou *wilt.*"

28. The Choctaws.

29. The Chickasaws.

ported me thus for eight days, and on the ninth I reached my uncle's house.

The following particulars, relating to the manner in which I was made known to my family, are less interesting; and yet, perhaps, some readers would not forgive their omission: I shall, however, be as brief as I can. I asked my uncle for a lodging, which he refused. I enquired how far the town was off; three quarters of a mile, said he. Do you know Mrs. Marrant and family, and how the children do? was my next question. He said he did, they were all well, but one was lately lost; at this I turned my head and wept. He did not know me, and upon refusing again to lodge me, I departed. When I reached the town it was dark, and passing by a house where one of my old school-fellows lived, I knocked at the door; he came out, and asked me what I wanted? I desired a lodging, which was granted: I went in, but was not known. I asked him if he knew Mrs. Marrant, and how the family were? He said, he had just left them, they were all well; but a young lad, with whom he went to school, who after he had quitted school, went to Charles-Town to learn some trade; but came home crazy, rambled in the woods, and was torn in pieces by the wild beasts.[30] How do you know, said I, that he was killed by wild beasts? I, and his brother, and uncle, and others, said he, went three days into the woods in search of him, and found his carcase torn, and brought it home and buried it. This affected me very much, and I wept; observing it, he said what is the matter? I made no answer. At supper they sat down without craving a blessing, for which I reproved them; this so affected the man, that I believe it ended in a sound conversion. Here is a wild man, says he, come out of the woods, to be a witness for God, and to reprove our ingratitude and stupefaction! After supper I went to prayer, and then to bed. Rising a little before day-light, and praising the Lord, as my custom was, the family were surprised, and got up: I staid with them till nine o'clock, and then went to my mother's house in the next street. The singularity of my dress drew every body's eyes upon me, yet none knew me. I knock'd at my mother's door, my sister opened it, and was startled at my appearance. Having expressed a desire to see Mrs. Marrant, I was answered, she was not very well, and that my business with her could be done by the person at the door, who also attempted to shut me out, which I prevented. My mother being called, I went in, and sat down, a mob of people being round the door. My mother asked, "what is your business;" only to see you, said I. She said she was much obliged to me, but did not know me. I asked, how are your children? how are your two sons? She replied, her daughters were in good health, of her two sons, one was well, and with her, but the other,—unable to contain, she burst into a flood of tears, and retired. I was overcome, and wept much; but nobody knew me.[31] This was an affecting scene! Presently my brother came in: He enquired, who I was, and what I was? My sister did not know; but being uneasy at my presence, they were contriving to get me out of the house, which, being over-heard by me, I resolved not to stir. My youngest sister, eleven years of age, came in from school, with a book under her arm. I was then sitting in the parlour, and as she passed by the parlour door, she peep'd in and seeing a strange person there, she recollected me; she goes into the kitchen, and tells the servants, her brother was come; but her report finding no credit, she came and peep'd again, that she might be certain it was me; and then passing into the next room, through the parlour where I was sitting, she made a running curtsy, and says to my eldest sister, who was there, it is my brother John! She called her a foolish girl, and threatened to beat her: Then she came again and peep'd at me, and being certain she was not mistaken, she went back, and insisted that it was me: Being then beat by my sister, she went crying upstairs to my mother, and told her; but neither would my mother believe her. At last they said to her, if it be your brother, go and kiss him, and ask him how he does? She ran and clasped me round the neck, and, looking me in the face, said, "Are not you my brother John?" I answered yes, and wept. I was then made known to all the family, to my friends, and acquaintances, who received me, and were glad and rejoiced: Thus the dead was brought to life again; thus the lost was found. I shall now close the Narrative, with only remarking a few incidents in my life, until my connection with my Right Honourable Patroness, the Countess of HUNTINGDON.[32]

I remained with my relations till the commencement of the American troubles.[33] I used to go and hear the word

---

30. Compare with Genesis 37, 39–47.

31. "I had been absent from them near twenty-three months." [Au.]

32. Selina Chirley Hastings, the countess of Huntingdon (1707–91), a British noble and Methodist.

33. That is, the rebellion against Great Britain, called in British North America the American Revolution, which concluded with the Treaty of Paris in 1783.

of God, if any Gospel ministers came into the country, though at a considerable distance, and thereby got acquainted with a few poor people, who feared God in Wills' Town, and Borough Town, Dorchester Town, and other places thereabouts; and in those places we used to meet and associate together for Christian Conversation, and at their request I frequently went to prayer with them, and at times enjoyed much of the Lord's presence among them.

About this time I went with my brother, who was a house-carpenter, to repair a plantation belonging to Mr. Jenkins, of Cumbee, about seventy miles from Charles-Town, where after I had done work in the evening, I used to spend my time in reading God's Word, singing Watts's Hymns and in Prayer, the little negro children would often come round the door with their pretty wishful looks, and finding my heart much drawn out in Love to their souls, I one evening called several of them in, and asked them if they could say the Lord's Prayer, &c. finding they were very ignorant, I told them, if they would come every evening I would teach them, which they did, and learned very fast, some of them in about four weeks could say the Lord's Prayer, and good part of the Catechism, after teaching, I used to go to prayer with them before we parted; this continued without interruption for three or four months, in which time, by the children acquainting their parents with it, I soon had my society increased to about thirty persons; and the Lord was pleased often to refresh us with a sense of his love and presence amongst us; one of the negro boys made a very great proficiency in that time, and could exercise in extemporary prayer much to my satisfaction. We are well advised in Ecclesiasticus, chap. ii. v. 1. *My Son, if thou come to serve the Lord, prepare thy heart for temptation:*[34] Nor was it long before they were made to pledge our dear Lord in the bitter cup of suffering; for now the old Lion began to roar,[35] their mistress became acquainted with our proceedings, and was full of rage at it, and determined to put a stop to it. She had two of the children brought before her to examine, and made them say the Lord's prayer to her, she then asked who taught them? and they told her the free Carpenter. She also enquired, how many he had instructed, and at what time he taught them; and they told her, it was

in the Evening after they had done work. She then stirred up her husband against us, who before had several times come in while I was instructing the children, and did not appear displeased with it: she told him it was the ready way to have all his negroes ruin'd, and made him promise to examine further into the matter, and break up our meeting; which he then very soon did, for a short space; for he, together with his overseer and negro-driver, and some of his neighbours, beset the place wherein we met, while we were at prayers; and as the poor creatures came out they caught them, and tied them together with cords, till the next morning, when all they caught, men, women, and children were strip'd naked and tied, their feet to a stake, their hands to the arm of a tree, and so severely flogg'd that the blood ran from their backs and sides to the floor, to make them promise they would leave off praying, &c. though several of them fainted away with the pain and loss of blood, and lay upon the ground as dead for a considerable time after they were untied. I did not hear that she obtained her end of any of them. She endeavoured to perswade her husband to flog me also, but he told her he did not dare to do it because I was free, and would take the law of him, and make him pay for it; which she told him, she had rather he should run the hazard of, than let me go without the benefit of a good flogging, and was afterwards very angry with him because he was afraid to gratify her. He told me afterwards that I had spoiled all his Negroes, but could not help acknowledging, that they did their tasks sooner than the others who were not instructed, and thereby had time after their tasks were done, to keep their own fields in better order than the others, who used to employ the Sabbath for that purpose, as is the common practice among the Negroes. He then said, I should make them so wise that he should not be able to keep them in subjection. I asked him whether he did not think they had Souls to be saved? He answered, yes. I asked him whether he thought they were in the way to save their Souls whilst they were ignorant of that God who made and preserved them. He made me no answer to that. I then told him that the blood of those poor negroes which he had spilt that morning would be required by God at his hands. He then left me. Soon after, meeting with his wife, I told her the same; but she laught at it, and was only sorry that she had not been able to get me flog'd with them. Finding I could not any longer live peaceably there, I encouraged the poor creatures to call upon God as well as they could, and returned home; where I afterwards heard that their Mistress continued to persecute them for meeting together as often as she discover'd them, and her husband for not being

---

34. Ecclesiastes 2:1: "I said in mine heart, Go to now, I will prove thee with mirth, therefore enjoy pleasures: and behold, this also *is* vanity."

35. The roaring lion represents the devil in 1 Peter 5:8.

more severe against them; they were then obliged to meet at midnight in different corners of the woods that were about the plantation, and were sure to be flog'd if ever she caught them, they nevertheless continued their meetings though in such imminent danger, and by what I have since heard, I believe it continues to this day, by which it appears that the work was of God; therefore neither the devil nor his servants could overthrow it; and to our faithful Covenant God be all the Glory.

In about two months after I left them, it pleased God to lay his hand upon their Mistress, and she was seized with a very violent fever, which no medicine that they could produce would remove, and in a very few days after she was taken ill, she died in a very dreadful manner, in great anger with her husband, for not preventing their meetings, which she had heard they continued, notwithstanding all her endeavours to stop it. After she was dead, her husband gave them liberty to meet together as before, and used sometimes to attend with them; and I have since heard that it was made very useful to him.

About this time I was an eye-witness of the remarkable conversion of a child seven and a half years old, named Mary Scott, which I shall here mention, in hopes the Lord may make it useful and profitable to my young readers.[36] Her parents lived in the house adjoining to my sister's. One day as I was returning from my work, and passing by the school where she was instructed, I saw the children coming out, and stop'd and looked among them for her, to take her home in my hand; but not seeing her among those that were coming out, I supposed she was gone before, and went on towards home; when passing by the church-yard which was in my way, I saw her very busy walking from one tomb to another, and went to her, and asked her what she was doing there? She told me, that in the lesson she had set her at school that morning, in the Twentieth of the Revelations, she read, "I saw the Dead, small and great, stand before God," &c.[37] and she had been measuring the graves, with a tape she then held in her hand, to see if there were any so small as herself among them; and that she had found six that were shorter. I then said, and what of that? She answered, "I will die, Sir." I told her I knew she would, but hoped she would live till she was grown a woman; but she continued to express

her desire to depart, and be with Christ, rather than to live till she was grown up. I then took her by the hand and brought her home with me. After this, she was observed to be always very solid and thoughtful, and that passage appeared always to be fresh upon her mind. I used frequently to be with her when in town, and at her request we often read and prayed together, and she appeared much affected. She never afterwards was seen out at play with other children; but spent her leisure time in reading God's word and prayer. In about four months after this, she was taken ill, and kept her room about three weeks; when first taken, she told me, she should never come down stairs alive. I frequently visited her during her illness, and made light of what she said about her dying so soon; but in the last week of her illness, she said to me in a very solemn manner, "Sir, I shall die before Saturday-night." The Physicians attended her, but she took very few if any medicines, and appeared quite calm and resigned to God's will. On Friday morning, which was the day she died, I visited her, and told her that I hoped she would not die so soon as she said, but she told me that she should certainly die before six o'clock that Evening. About five o'clock I visited her again. She was then sitting in a chair, and reading in her Bible, to all appearance pretty well recovered. After setting with her about a quarter of an hour, she got up, and desired me to go down, and send her mother up with a clean shift for her; which I did; and after a little time, when I went up again, I found her lying on the bed, with her eyes fixed up to heaven; when turning herself and seeing me, she said, "Mr. Marrant, don't you see that pretty town, and those fine people, how they shine like gold?—O how I long to be with my Lord and his redeemed Children in Glory!" and then turning to her parents and two sisters, (who were all present, having by her desire been called to her) she shook hands with them, and bade them farewell; desiring them not to lament for her when she was dead, for she was going to that fine place where God would wipe away all tears from her eyes, and she should sing Hallelujahs to God and to the Lamb for ever and ever, and where she hoped afterwards to meet them; and then turning again to me, she said—"Farewell, and God bless you." and then fell asleep in the arms of Jesus. This afterwards proved the conversion of her mother.

In those troublesome times, I was pressed on board the Scorpion sloop of war, as their musician, as they were told I could play on music.—I continued in his majesty's service six years and eleven months; and with shame confess, that a lamentable stupor crept over all my spiritual

---

36. Mary Scott's story, among others, is found in James Janeway's *A Token for Children: Being an Exact Account of the Conversion, Holy and Exemplary Lives, and Joyful Deaths, of Several Young Children* (London, 1672).

37. Revelation 20:18.

vivacity, life and vigour; I got cold and dead. What need, reader, have we to be continually mindful of our Lord's exhortation, *"What I say unto you, I say unto all, Watch."*[38] My gracious God, my dear Father in his dear Son, roused me every now and then by dangers and deliverances.—I was at the siege of Charles-Town,[39] and passed through many dangers. When the town was taken, my old royal benefactor and convert, the king of the Cherokee Indians, riding into the town with general Clinton, saw me, and knew me: He alighted off his horse,[40] and came to me; said he was glad to see me; that his daughter was very happy, and sometimes longed to get out of the body.

Some time after this I was cruising about in the American seas, and cannot help mentioning a singular deliverance I had from the most imminent danger, and the use the Lord made it of to me. We were overtaken by a violent storm; I was washed overboard, and thrown on again; dashed into the sea a second time, and tossed upon deck again. I now fastened a rope round my middle, as a security against being thrown in to the sea again; but, alas! forgot to fasten it to any part of the ship; being carried away the third time by the fury of the waves, when in the sea, I found the rope both useless and an incumbrance. I was in the sea the third time about eight minutes, and several sharks came round me; one of an enormous size, that could easily have taken me into his mouth at once, passed and rubbed against my side. I then cried more earnestly to the Lord than I had done for some time; and he who heard Jonah's prayer, did not shut out mine, for I was thrown aboard again;[41] these were the means the Lord used to revive me, and I began to set out afresh.

I was in the engagement with the Dutch off the Dogger bank,[42] on board the Princess-Amelia, of eighty-four guns.[43] We had a great number killed and wounded; the deck was running with blood; six men were killed and three wounded, stationed at the same gun with me; my head and face were covered with the blood and brains of the slain; I was wounded, but did not fall, till a quarter of an hour before the engagement ended, and was happy in my soul during the whole of it. After being in the hospital three months and sixteen days, I was sent to the West-Indies on board a ship of war, and, after cruising in those seas, we returned home as a convoy. Being taken ill of my old wounds, I was put into the hospital at Plymouth, and had not been there long, when the physician gave it as his opinion, that I should not be capable of serving the king again; I was therefore discharged, and came to London, where I lived with a respectable and pious merchant, near three years, who was unwilling to part with me. During this time, I saw my call to the ministry fuller and clearer; had a feeling concern for the salvation of my countrymen: I carried them constantly in the arms of prayer and faith to the throne of grace, and had continual sorrow in my heart for my brethren, for my kinsmen, according to the flesh.[44]—I wrote a letter to my brother, who returned me an answer, in which he prayed some ministers would come and preach to them, and desired me to shew it to the minister whom I attended. I used to exercise my gifts on a Monday evening in prayer and exhortation, in Spafields chapel, and was approved of, and sent down to Bath; where I was ordained, in Lady Huntingdon's Chapel. Her Ladyship having seen the letter from my brother in Nova Scotia, thought Providence called me there: To which place I am now bound, and expect to sail in a few days.

I have now only to intreat the earnest prayers of all my kind Christian friends, that I may be carried safe there; kept humble, made faithful, and successful; that strangers may hear of and run to Christ; that Indian tribes may stretch out their hands to God; that the black nations may be made white in the blood of the Lamb; that vast multitudes of hard tongues, and of a strange speech, may learn the language of Canaan, and sing the song of Moses, and of the Lamb; and, anticipating the glorious prospect, may we all with fervent hearts, and willing tongues, sing Hal-

---

38. Mark 13:37.

39. The colonists were defeated at the siege of Charleston, between February 11 and May 12, 1780.

40. "Though it is unusual for Indians to have a horse, yet the king accompanied the general on the present successful occasion riding on horseback.—If the king wished to serve me, there was no opportunity; the Town begin taken on Friday afternoon, Saturday an express arrived from the commander in chief at New York, for a large detachment, or the town would fall into the hands of the Americans, which hurried us away on Sunday morning." [Au.]

41. See Jonah 2.

42. An underwater sandbank in the North Sea, off the coast of England.

43. "This action was on the 5th of August, 1781." [Au.]

44. Compare with Romans 9:2–3, "That I have great heaviness and continual sorrow in my heart. For I could wish that myself were accursed from Christ for my brethren, my kinsmen according to the flesh."

lelujah; the kingdoms of the world are become the king-doms of our God, and of his Christ. Amen, and Amen.[45]

Nor can I take my leave of my very dear London Friends without intreating GOD to bless them with every blessing of the upper and nether Springs:[46]—May the good will of Him that dwelt in the bush ever preserve and lead them! is the fervent prayer of their affectionate and grateful Servant in the Gospel,

Mile-End Road

London, N° 69,
J. Marrant.
Aug. 18. 1785.

Psalm CVII. Dr. Watts.[47]

1 Give Thanks to God; He reigns above;
Kind are his Thoughts, his Name is Love;
His Mercy Ages past have known,
And Ages long to come shall own.

2 Let the Redeemed of the LORD
The Wonders of his Grace record;

Isr'el, the Nation whom he chose,
And rescu'd from their mighty Foes.

3 When GOD's Almighty Arm had broke
Their Fetters and th' Egyptian Yoke,
They trac'd the Desert, wand'ring round
A wild and solitary Ground!

4 There they could find no leading Road,
Nor City for a fix'd Abode;
Nor Food, nor Fountain to assuage
Their burning Thirst, or Hunger's Rage.

5 In their Distress to GOD they cry'd;
GOD was their Saviour and their Guide;
He led their March, far wand'ring round,
'Twas the right Path to Canaan's Ground.

6 Thus when our first Release we gain
From Sin's old Yoke, and Satan's Chain,
We have this desert World to pass,
A dang'rous and a tiresome Place.

7 He feeds and clothes us all the Way,
He guides our Footsteps lest we stray;
He guards us with a pow'rful Hand,
And brings us to the heav'nly Land.

8 O let the Saints with Joy record
The Truth and Goodness of the LORD!
How great his Works! how kind his Ways!
Let ev'ry Tongue pronounce his Praise.

FINIS.

---

45. Marrant alludes to Revelation 7:14, 11:15 17:15, and 15:3 in this paragraph.

46. See Joshua 15:19.

47. Isaac Watts's psalms went through numerous editions during the course of the eighteenth century.

10

CONFEDERATION AND THE FORMATION OF A BRITISH AMERICAN REPUBLIC

"The felicitations you offer on the present prospect of our public affairs," George Washington wrote in a letter to Annis Boudinot Stockton, August 31, 1788, "are highly acceptable to me." Washington was thanking Stockton for a poetic epistle (a letter, written in poetic form) she had just sent, congratulating him on the Constitution's ratification. Knowing that Annis Stockton had a wide circle with whom she shared her correspondence and that Stockton might use his letter as the thematic foundation of yet another poem about himself and affairs of state, Washington elaborated upon his sense of the importance of the moment to the future of government in the new British American republic. "I can never trace the concatenation of causes, which led to these events," Washington observed, "without acknowledging the mystery and admiring the goodness of Providence. To that superintending Power alone is our retraction from the brink of ruin to be attributed. A spirit of accommodation was happily infused into the leading characters of the Continent, and the minds of men were gradually prepared, by disappointment, for the reception of a good government. Nor would I rob the fairer sex of their share in the glory of a revolution so honorable to human nature, for, indeed, I think you Ladies are in the number of the best Patriots America can boast."

Washington strategically displayed his sense of honor and courage, generosity of spirit, and humility to his friend, speaking a language of "the nation" that would dominate federalist discourse about government for some time to come. He had yet to be called formally to the presidency, but all indications were that he would, by unanimous consent, be asked to stand as president. Linking the newly organizing government to providential history, a story of the past featuring the American Revolution against Great Britain as the fulfillment of his God's design for British North America, Washington was calling up a visual tableau of government by the people and for the people, according to their merits. "Leading characters," he wrote, enjoyed a "spirit of cooperation," thus bringing in "good government."

In Washington's view, there would be a place for women in this new government, not necessarily as the country's leaders in the political scene, but leaders nonetheless in a different and increasingly more powerful scene, the domestic one. "And now that I am speaking of your Sex," he continued in his letter, "I will ask whether they are not capable of doing something towards introducing fœderal fashions and national manners." The letter reveals Washington's significant insight into the ideological functioning of state systems, whereby the material representation of the government was central to forming, in the interior lives of its people, a felt experience of citizenship and an almost unquestioning acceptance of federal government. "A good general government," he explained to Stockton,

> without good morals and good habits, will not make us a happy People; and we shall deceive ourselves if we think it will. A good government will, unquestionably, tend to foster and confirm those qualities, on which public happiness must be engrafted. Is it not shameful that we should be the sport of European whims and caprices? Should we not blush to discourage our own industry and ingenuity; by purchasing foreign superfluities and adopting fantastic fashions, which are, at best, ill suited to our stage of Society?

Washington's comments show his distinct interest in encouraging people to imagine they were forming their own tastes, even as they were being told what their tastes should be. He wished to see inculcated the notion that the interest of the state should be the interest of its citizens. New "federal fashions" could be linked with what would be a "good government," one sponsoring "good morals and good habits." The self-conscious national self-construction, understood as such by the elites, Washington thought, could be sponsored for common people who needed to be instructed in what would be best for their nation. His letter is a remarkably telling reminder of the instability of the social and political formation at the time of the American Revolution against Great Britain and immediately after it, when it came to forming a federal republic.

Washington's comments to Annis Stockton reveal the standard assumptions behind federalism. Federalists believed that the people living in British North America in the thirteen newly forming states should be governed by those who were, in their view, most attuned to understanding the problems of state—the "leading characters of the nation." Their position was that government would be most effective if its power were in the hands of a few well-meaning (white) men who were authorized by the votes of the people to conduct national and international affairs, to tax all people for their lands and labor, and to organize a national banking system that would consolidate the debt of the United States and oversee its financial manipulation internally and externally. Many who became federalist in orientation believed that individuals could not be trusted to know what was in the best interest of the country because basic human instincts were acquisitive and debased. The strong federal arm could best control for the waywardness and self-interestedness of individuals, federalists thought.

The other key position held at the time was called the Democratic Republican position, favored by people like Thomas Jefferson, who believed that individuals, especially those in agriculture and farming, could be trusted to behave well. Democratic Republicans disliked the idea of a strong central government that oversaw the affairs of all people, preferring instead the idea of having a series of extended republics (the separate states) that would be protected by—but not run by—a central government. Opposing a national banking and taxing system, Democratic Republicans wanted the government to protect people and their property without, in their view, interfering in their lives. It is interesting that both attitudes about government were based on a concern about trade and commerce between nations. The Federalists believed that these issues should be in the hands of a few who understood what was at stake internationally; the Democratic Republicans believed that groups should be allowed to trade for themselves, according to what they conceived to be their best interest, without being taxed on their proceeds.

The publications of this era indicate the significant concern of most writers with how the government would operate and what its citizens would become. These were the questions of singular importance to leaders on both sides of the issue of confederation, just as they were the questions of great import to those who wrote about government and subject-citizens. Writers seeking to enter the literate cultural marketplace during the 1780s and 1790s were faced with the vexing problem of finding a readership in the numerous newspapers and periodicals that were springing up everywhere. Newspapers and readers came and went, with newspapers sometimes folding within the first year of operation. One way of obtaining readers was to provide them with didactic materials, materials that taught important and typically "moral" lessons that Federalists and Democratic Republicans alike could agree upon. Centering the gentility featured in standard British fare of an earlier day—as in the writings of Joseph Addison, Richard Steele, and later of Samuel Johnson—writers examined British American experiences for what they might offer middling-level readers as appropriate behavior. Only a few writers, most notably Charles Brockden Brown, concerned themselves with the interior life as it was being explored by writers of "gothic" fiction in Europe. Most writers stuck with conventional social or political concerns as the best way to gain a readership, and many were intensely interested, as their poems and fictions reveal, with the foundations of what would become the new "American" (meaning British American) character.

The most popular writers of the day featured stories about conduct, and their poems, essays, novels, and short pieces operated to clarify for readers the distinctions between good conduct and bad, vicious behavior and polite behavior. Women writers found that they would find a steady market of readers if they featured domestic concerns and the problem of living what was conceived of as a moral life. Several writers, both men and women, wished to test the gendered norms then developing for middling-level people—that men's work was outside the home, especially in business, and women's work at home, especially at needlework or family assistance. One way of doing so was by adopting a pen name or a leading character of the opposite sex. So Charles Brockden Brown, for instance, told his novel, *Wieland,* from the vantage point of a woman, and Judith Sargent Murray wrote many pieces from the position of Mr. Vigillius, or the Gleaner.

Even with the testing of cultural assumptions, however, writers seeking to make a living by their pens tended to remain close to the concerns of finding a putatively national literature for a new nation of readers. As we might expect, the issue of who "the nation" *was* became a major preoccupation of Africans and African-descended writers in this era. Prince Hall's Masons had a special understanding of themselves as African men, whose people and "nation" differed from their white counterparts. For Hall, the separate identity of Africans in America could enable them to succeed well, with the understanding that they would "worship no man," but worship their ancient African Christian leaders and the Christian God instead. Hall's Masons developed a cross-state solidarity sufficient to their becoming a new black elite in the newly organizing United States.

Other Africans and African-descended people followed a different road to achieve the same ends of public influence. Like Phillis Wheatley, they sought a wide audience for their work, and several became writers, orators, or religious leaders. As their private correspondence with one another attests, when African Americans read or heard of Thomas Jefferson's *Notes on the State of Virginia* (1787), they were made acutely aware of the attitudes of a leading statesman regarding the differences between Africans in America and their white counterparts. Jefferson derided Phillis Wheatley, the African-born poet, for not having an aesthetic appropriate to poetry (Jefferson linked her instead with religious sentimentalism), and Africans were said to lack the capacity for intellectual rigor. Benjamin Banneker, a self-taught astronomer and mathematician, took it upon himself to approach Washington's then secretary of state with his almanac, soon to be printed. Jefferson made a polite response to Banneker, but he seems not to have been willing to grant Banneker the same respect he might have granted to another self-taught scientist and almanac maker, Benjamin Franklin. Jefferson's expressed disregard for Africans and African-descended people belied his intimate experiences with at least one woman, Sally Hemings, and it brought him notoriety as a bigot among Africans and people of African descent, as well as among Methodists, members of the Society of Friends (Quakers), and others who were interested in abolishing slavery once and for all.

Yet despite their sense of the disparity of the treatment they received, even as free blacks, many African Americans chose to stay in the new United States and work to abolish slavery, rather than to live anywhere else. They concurred with Phillis Wheatley's position of 1774, expressed in a letter to her friend, Samson Occom, a Mohegan Christian missionary, about the "strange absurdity" that existed when some people would "cry for liberty" while at the same time having "the reverse disposition for the exercise of oppressive power over others." The option to remain in the new republic was not open to some others, those who had become loyal to the British Crown during the war, in an effort to buy their freedom by laboring in the war effort against the colonists. Black loyalists, even those born in the British colonies, felt unwelcome, and they formed separate communities in places like Nova Scotia or found ways to return to Africa, to the new state of Sierra Leone, to try a new life. For these writers especially, but really for all the writers of the era, the question of who the words "We the People" stood for in the new documents about the new nation would remain unanswered.

Thomas Jefferson (1743–1826)

Jefferson once said that of the many things he had done in his life, he wished to be remembered for three things primarily—drafting the Declaration of Independence, drafting and supporting the Virginia Statute for Religious Freedom, and founding the University of Virginia. Yet Jefferson's actions and writings had much wider significance, even in his own day, than these three accomplishments suggest. Jefferson served as the third president of the United States, the first secretary of state, and minister to France. A surveyor and architect of innovative designs, he worked on figures for the Virginia state capitol; for buildings at the university he was instrumental in founding; and for his own estate, Monticello. He created a significant library at his estate, one that would eventually serve as the basis for the Library of Congress, and he amassed one of the largest collections of paintings and sculptures known in British America. Jefferson participated in a wide correspondence with scientists and inventors, thus attesting to his own interest in experimental and natural philosophy. And he had a large plantation, served by enslaved Africans and African Americans, one of whom, Sally Hemings, he held in particular regard and with whom he had children.

Thomas Jefferson was born into a prestigious family in Albemarle County, Virginia. His father, a surveyor and local official, made what has been considered the first accurate map of Virginia, and his scant education probably contributed to Jefferson's own hungering after knowledge of all kinds. At the time he went to the College of William and Mary (1760), Jefferson already knew Latin and Greek, and he was, like many young Virginia gentlemen, a skilled horseman and musician. While in Williamsburg, Jefferson came to know the governor, Francis Fauquier, who had been named a fellow of the Royal Society; Dr. William Small, a recent emigrant from Scotland, who taught mathematics and philosophy; and George Wythe, a significant legal philosopher and teacher. After his graduation from college, Jefferson remained in Williamsburg to study law. He entered his distinguished public career in 1769, when he was elected to the House of Burgesses, the supreme local legal authority for Virginia.

His study of the law and of colonial Virginia history brought Jefferson to the important conclusion that the British Parliament, the supreme legislature of Great Britain, had no authority over Britain's colonies in North America. Jefferson concluded as well that King George III personally had no authority over the colonists, whose affiliation to the Crown was voluntary rather than requisite to their legal status. In that revolutionary era, such views brought him acclaim when he published and spoke them, and Jefferson became a delegate for Virginia to the Second Continental Congress meeting in Philadelphia in 1775. While listening to debates about forming continental armies and navies, finding foreign countries to assist their efforts, and developing formal ties to unite the colonies into a confederated system, Jefferson weighed the advantages of separating from Great Britain or remaining under British control. He concluded that King George III was responsible for the difficulties in the colonies, particularly with regard to what Jefferson considered to be the king's imposition of slavery, and, perhaps more important, he believed that the British people were themselves ultimately responsible for tolerating the corruption of the British ministry, Parliament, and king. Jefferson spoke ably about these matters, and on June 11, 1776, he was placed on the committee to draft the statement of separation from Britain. His statement, edited by his five committee colleagues and then the entire Congress together, became the Declaration of Independence. After the Declaration of Independence was passed and signed by Congress, Jefferson remained in Philadelphia, but not for long. He returned to Virginia in September.

Jefferson's career included serving as governor of Virginia (1779–81) until his resignation of that office in the face of unrest over his leadership during the war. He was blamed for the colonists' feelings of unpreparedness when the British military campaign reached Virginia. The legislature fled Richmond, which had been overtaken by the British military, only to be pursued by the British to Monticello. Jefferson resigned in the controversy over his lack of leadership and remained aloof from politics for several years, the key years during which he drafted the manuscript that became *Notes on the State of Virginia,* published in London in 1787. Jefferson's *Notes* was designed to address a series of questions he had received from the secretary of the French legation at Philadelphia, the marquis de Barbé-Marbois, regarding the geography and natural and social histories of Virginia. Understanding the political significance that would attach to his answers to these questions, Jefferson created useful summary analyses of the geological and manufacturing features of Virginia, knowing full well that they would be of concern to the French who had supported the colonists' war efforts and who would be interested in the international advantages of a strategic alliance with the new United States. Jefferson took up some of the major negative contentions offered by leading intellectuals in France and Europe about life in North America.

Of particular concern, in Jefferson's view, was the denigrating position offered by Georges Louis Leclerc, comte de Buffon (1707–88), renowned botanist and naturalist, that people in North America would degenerate physically and in terms of civil culture because of the climate. In refuting Buffon and others, Jefferson took the opportunity to offer his commentary and advice about matters of racial differences, the social polities and sexual practices of different racial groups in Virginia. In this regard, his obsession with the issue of slavery came to the fore again, as it had during the meetings of the Continental Congress, and Jefferson offered contradictory and, even in his day, offensive opinions about Native Americans and Africans in America that haunted him from the moment his book was published. While elucidating his points by engaging in what today is understood as a sacrilegious treatment of Native American remains, Jefferson romanticized Native people. While he made dehumanizing contentions about Africans and people of African descent in North America, he used their labor to build his houses and plantations and used at least one African woman to add to his estate. Now that Jefferson's intimate relations with his slave, Sally Hemings, and his parentage of at least one of her children are generally known, perhaps readers can come to a fuller recognition of the complicated, indeed troubling, contradictions in Jefferson's thinking on matters of slavery. Jefferson had a complicated, indeed inscrutable, response to the Africans and African-descended people who excelled in his midst, as evidenced by his exchange with Benjamin Banneker over Banneker's almanac, his scientific achievements, and his articulation of grievances about Jefferson's mistreatment of black people in *Notes on the State of Virginia.*

In 1784, Jefferson was appointed minister to France, and he joined Benjamin Franklin in the commission to create the Treaty of Paris, which, in terms of European and British North American law, put an end to the colonies' war against Britain. After he returned to Virginia, George Washington offered Jefferson the position of secretary of state, under the new powers granted by the Constitution. Jefferson accepted the post and served ably for three years, but he soon returned to Monticello. At the time Washington's term of appointment concluded, Jefferson ran against—and lost to—John Adams for the office of president. He served as Adams's vice president and was elected the third president of the United States, which post he served for two terms, from 1801 to 1809. Jefferson returned to Monticello thereafter, where he continued to run his plantation, study, and write for seventeen years.

from NOTES ON THE STATE OF VIRGINIA[1]

from QUERY 6 • A Notice of the Mines, and Other Subterraneous Riches

Animals

Our quadrupeds have been mostly described by Linnaeus and Mons. de Buffon.[2] Of these the Mammoth, or big buffalo, as called by the Indians, must certainly have been the largest. Their tradition is, that he was carnivorous, and still exists in the northern parts of America. A delegation of warriors from the Delaware tribe having visited the governor of Virginia, during the present revolution, on matters of business, after these had been discussed and settled in council, the governor asked them some questions relative to their country, and, among others, what they knew or had heard of the animal whose bones were found at the Saltlicks, on the Ohio. Their chief speaker immediately put himself into an attitude of oratory, and with a pomp suited to what he conceived the elevation of his subject, informed him that it was a tradition handed down from their fathers, "That in antient times a herd of these tremendous animals came to the Big-bone licks, and began an universal destruction of the bear, deer, elks, buffaloes, and other animals, which had been created for the use of the Indians: that the Great Man above, looking down and seeing this, was so enraged that he seized his lightning, descended on the earth, seated himself on a neighbouring mountain, on a rock, of which his seat and the print of his feet are still to be seen, and hurled his bolts among them till the whole were slaughtered, except the big bull, who presenting his forehead to the shafts, shook them off as they fell; but missing one at length, it wounded him in the side; whereon, springing round, he bounded over the Ohio, over the Wabash, the Illinois, and finally over the great lakes, where he is living at this day." It is well known that on the Ohio, and in many parts of America further north, tusks, grinders, and skeletons of unparalleled magnitude, are found in great numbers, some lying on the surface of the earth, and some a little below it. A Mr. Stanley, taken prisoner by the Indians near the mouth of the Tanissee, relates, that, after being transferred through several tribes, from one to another, he was at length carried over the mountains west of the Missouri to a river which runs westwardly; that these bones abounded there; and that the natives described to him the animal to which they belonged as still existing in the northern parts of their country; from which description he judged it to be an elephant. Bones of the same kind have been lately found, some feet below the surface of the earth, in salines opened on the North Holston, a branch of the Tanissee, about the latitude of $36\frac{1}{2}°$. North. From the accounts published in Europe, I suppose it to be decided, that these are of the same kind with those found in Siberia. Instances are mentioned of like animal remains found in the more southern climates of both hemispheres; but they are either so loosely mentioned as to leave a doubt of the fact, so inaccurately described as not to authorize the classing them with the great northern bones, or so rare as to found a suspicion that they have been carried thither as curiosities from more northern regions. So that on the whole there seem to be no certain vestiges of the existence of this animal further south than the salines last mentioned.[3] It is remarkable that the tusks and skeletons have been ascribed by the naturalists of Europe to the elephant, while the grinders have been given to the hippopotamus, or river-horse. Yet it is acknowledged, that the tusks and skeletons are much larger than those of the elephant, and the grinders many times greater than those

---

1. *Notes on the State of Virginia* was first published in Paris in a private edition in 1785. When he was in London in 1787, Jefferson hurried along an English edition because he was aware that an unauthorized edition was being prepared by a French publisher and bookseller, based on the earlier Paris edition and translated into French. The volume quickly reached an international audience. The text is adapted from *Notes on the State of Virginia,* ed. Frank Shuffelton (1998); only a selection of Jefferson's numerous notes have been reproduced.

2. Georges Louis Leclerc, comte de Buffon (1707–88), was a leading scientist and naturalist, keeper of the king's gardens and the Royal Museum in France. Buffon argued, according to contemporary theories about environmental effects upon human beings, that people in North America would degenerate because they were situated in a cold and damp climate, which was not conducive to physical stasis or, indeed, physical strength. In this section of his book, Jefferson takes up arguments to refute Buffon, quoting his French writings at length at strategic places in his own analysis.

---

3. That is, in a previous passage Jefferson had referenced Buffon.

of the hippopotamus, and essentially different in form. Wherever these grinders are found, there also we find the tusks and skeleton; but no skeleton of the hippopotamus nor grinders of the elephant. It will not be said that the hippopotamus and elephant came always to the same spot, the former to deposit his grinders, and the latter his tusks and skeleton. For what became of the parts not deposited there? We must agree then that these remains belong to each other, that they are of one and the same animal, that this was not a hippopotamus, because the hippopotamus had no tusks nor such a frame, and because the grinders differ in their size as well as in the number and form of their points. That it was not an elephant, I think ascertained by proofs equally decisive. I will not avail myself of the authority of the celebrated anatomist,[4] who, from an examination of the form and structure of the tusks, has declared they were essentially different from those of the elephant; because another anatomist,[5] equally celebrated, has declared, on a like examination, that they are precisely the same. Between two such authorities I will suppose this circumstance equivocal. But, 1. The skeleton of the mammoth (for so the incognitum has been called) bespeaks an animal of five or six times the cubic volume of the elephant, as Mons. de Buffon has admitted. 2. The grinders are five times as large, are square, and the grinding surface studded with four or five rows of blunt points: whereas those of the elephant are broad and thin, and their grinding surface flat. 3. I have never heard an instance, and suppose there has been none, of the grinder of an elephant being found in America. 4. From the known temperature and constitution of the elephant he could never have existed in those regions where the remains of the mammoth have been found. The elephant is a native only of the torrid zone and its vicinities: if, with the assistance of warm apartments and warm clothing, he has been preserved in life in the temperate climates of Europe, it has only been for a small portion of what would have been his natural period, and no instance of his multiplication in them has ever been known. But no bones of the mammoth, as I have before observed, have been ever found further south than the salines of the Holston, and they have been found as far north as the Arctic circle.

Those, therefore, who are of opinion that the elephant and mammoth are the same, must believe, 1. That the elephant known to us can exist and multiply in the frozen zone; or, 2. That an internal fire may once have warmed those regions, and since abandoned them, of which, however, the globe exhibits no unequivocal indications; or, 3. That the obliquity of the ecliptic, when these elephants lived, was so great as to include within the tropics all those regions in which the bones are found; the tropics being, as is before observed, the natural limits of habitation for the elephant. But if it be admitted that this obliquity has really decreased, and we adopt the highest rate of decrease yet pretended, that is, of one minute in a century, to transfer the northern tropic to the Arctic circle, would carry the existence of these supposed elephants 250,000 years back; a period far beyond our conception of the duration of animal bones left exposed to the open air, as these are in many instances. Besides, though these regions would then be supposed within the tropics, yet their winters would have been too severe for the sensibility of the elephant. They would have had too but one day and one night in the year, a circumstance to which we have no reason to suppose the nature of the elephant fitted. However, it has been demonstrated, that, if a variation of obliquity in the ecliptic takes place at all, it is vibratory, and never exceeds the limits of 9 degrees, which is not sufficient to bring these bones within the tropics. One of these hypotheses, or some other equally voluntary and inadmissible to cautious philosophy, must be adopted to support the opinion that these are the bones of the elephant.

For my own part, I find it easier to believe that an animal may have existed, resembling the elephant in his tusks, and general anatomy, while his nature was in other respects extremely different. From the 30th degree of South latitude to the 30th of North, are nearly the limits which nature has fixed for the existence and multiplication of the elephant known to us. Proceeding thence northwardly to $36\frac{1}{2}$ degrees, we enter those assigned to the mammoth. The further we advance North, the more their vestiges multiply as far as the earth has been explored in that direction; and it is as probable as otherwise, that this progression continues to the pole itself, if land extends so far. The center of the Frozen zone then may be the Achmé of their vigour, as that of the Torrid is of the elephant. Thus nature seems to have drawn a belt of separation between these two tremendous animals, whose breadth indeed is not precisely known, though at present we may suppose it about $6\frac{1}{2}$ degrees of latitude; to have assigned to the elephant the regions South of these con-

---

4. "Hunter" [Au.] Jefferson referred to John Hunter (1728–1793), Scottish scientist, physiologist and surgeon.

5. "D'Aubenton" [Au.] That is, LouisJean Marie Daubenton (1716–99), a French naturalist and associate of Buffon.

fines, and those North to the mammoth, founding the constitution of the one in her extreme of heat, and that of the other in the extreme of cold. When the Creator has therefore separated their nature as far as the extent of the scale of animal life allowed to this planet would permit, it seems perverse to declare it the same, from a partial resemblance of their tusks and bones. But to whatever animal we ascribe these remains, it is certain such a one has existed in America, and that it has been the largest of all terrestrial beings. It should have sufficed to have rescued the earth it inhabited, and the atmosphere it breathed, from the imputation of impotence in the conception and nourishment of animal life on a large scale: to have stifled, in its birth, the opinion of a writer, the most learned too of all others in the science of animal history, that in the new world, "La nature vivante est beaucoup moins agissante, beaucoup moins forte": that nature is less active, less energetic on one side of the globe than she is on the other. As if both sides were not warmed by the same genial sun; as if a soil of the same chemical composition, was less capable of elaboration into animal nutriment; as if the fruits and grains from that soil and sun, yielded a less rich chyle, gave less extension to the solids and fluids of the body, or produced sooner in the cartilages, membranes, and fibres, that rigidity which restrains all further extension, and terminates animal growth. The truth is, that a Pigmy and a Patagonian, a Mouse and a Mammoth, derive their dimensions from the same nutritive juices. The difference of increment depends on circumstances unsearchable to beings with our capacities. Every race of animals seems to have received from their Maker certain laws of extension at the time of their formation. Their elaborative organs were formed to produce this, while proper obstacles were opposed to its further progress. Below these limits they cannot fall, nor rise above them. What intermediate station they shall take may depend on soil, on climate, on food, on a careful choice of breeders. But all the manna of heaven would never raise the Mouse to the bulk of the Mammoth.

The opinion advanced by the Count de Buffon, is 1. That the animals common both to the old and new world, are smaller in the latter. 2. That those peculiar to the new, are on a smaller scale. 3. That those which have been domesticated in both, have degenerated in America: and 4. That on the whole it exhibits fewer species. And the reason he thinks is, that the heats of America are less; that more waters are spread over its surface by nature, and fewer of these drained off by the hand of man. In other words, that *heat* is friendly, and *moisture* adverse to the production and development of large quadrupeds. I will not meet this hypothesis on its first doubtful ground, whether the climate of America be comparatively more humid? Because we are not furnished with observations sufficient to decide this question. And though, till it be decided, we are as free to deny, as others are to affirm the fact, yet for a moment let it be supposed. The hypothesis, after this supposition, proceeds to another; that *moisture* is unfriendly to animal growth. The truth of this is inscrutable to us by reasonings a priori. Nature has hidden from us her modus agendi. Our only appeal on such questions is to experience; and I think that experience is against the supposition. It is by the assistance of *heat* and *moisture* that vegetables are elaborated from the elements of earth, air, water, and fire. We accordingly see the more humid climates produce the greater quantity of vegetables. Vegetables are mediately or immediately the food of every animal: and in proportion to the quantity of food, we see animals not only multiplied in their numbers, but improved in their bulk, as far as the laws of their nature will admit. Of this opinion is the Count de Buffon himself in another part of his work: "en general il paroit que les pays un peu *froids* conviennent mieux à nos boeufs que les pays chauds, et qu'ils sont d'autant plus gros et plus grands que le climat est plus *humide* et plus abondans en paturages. Les boeufs de Danemarck, de la Podolie, de l'Ukraine et de la Tartarie qu'bahitent les Calmouques sont les plus grands de tous."[6] Here then a race of animals, and one of the largest too, has been increased in its dimensions by *cold* and *moisture,* in direct opposition to the hypothesis, which supposes that these two circumstances diminish animal bulk, and that it is their contraries *heat* and *dryness* which enlarge it. But when we appeal to experience, we are not to rest satisfied with a single fact. Let us therefore try our question on more general ground. Let us take two portions of the earth, Europe and America for instance, sufficiently extensive to give operation to general causes; let us consider the circumstances peculiar to each, and observe their effect on animal nature. America, running through the torrid as well as temperate zone, has more *heat,* collectively taken, than Europe. But Europe,

---

6. "In general is seems that countries a bit cold better suit our oxen than hot countries, and they have all the more weight and size as the climate is damper and more abundant in pasturage. The oxen of Denmark, of Podolia, of the Ukraine, and of Tartary where the Kalmucks live are the largest of all."

according to our hypothesis, is the *dryest*. They are equally adapted then to animal productions; each being endowed with one of those causes which befriend animal growth, and with one which opposes it. If it be thought unequal to compare Europe with America, which is so much larger, I answer, not more so than to compare America with the whole world. Besides, the purpose of the comparison is to try an hypothesis, which makes the size of animals depend on the *heat* and *moisture* of climate. If therefore we take a region, so extensive as to comprehend a sensible distinction of climate, and so extensive too as that local accidents, or the intercourse of animals on its borders, may not materially affect the size of those in its interior parts, we shall comply with those conditions which the hypothesis may reasonably demand. The objection would be the weaker in the present case, because any intercourse of animals which may take place on the confines of Europe and Asia, is to the advantage of the former, Asia producing certainly larger animals than Europe. . . .

Of the Indian of South America I know nothing; for I would not honor with the appellation of knowledge, what I derive from the fables published of them. These I believe to be just as true as the fables of Aesop. This belief is founded on what I have seen of man, white, red, and black, and what has been written of him by authors, enlightened themselves, and writing amidst an enlightened people. The Indian of North America being more within our reach, I can speak of him somewhat from my own knowledge, but more from the information of others better acquainted with him, and on whose truth and judgment I can rely. From these sources I am able to say, in contradiction to this representation, that he is neither more defective in ardor, nor more impotent with his female, than the white reduced to the same diet and exercise: that he is brave, when an enterprize depends on bravery; education with him making the point of honor consist in the destruction of an enemy by stratagem, and in the preservation of his own person free from injury; or perhaps this is nature; while it is education which teaches us to honor force more than finesse:[7] that he will defend himself against an host of enemies, always chusing to be killed, rather than to surrender,[8] though it be to the whites, who he knows will treat him well: that in other situations also he meets death with more deliberation, and endures tortures with a firmness unknown almost to religious enthusiasm with us: that he is affectionate to his children, careful of them, and indulgent in the extreme: that his affections comprehend his other connections, weakening, as with us, from circle to circle, as they recede from the center: that his friendships are strong and faithful to the uttermost extremity: that his sensibility is keen, even the warriors weeping most bitterly on the loss of their children, though in general they endeavour to appear superior to human events: that his vivacity and activity of mind is equal to ours in the same situation; hence his eagerness for hunting, and for games of chance. The women are submitted to unjust drudgery. This I believe is the case with every barbarous people. With such, force is law. The stronger sex therefore imposes on the weaker. It is civilization alone which replaces women in the enjoyment of their natural equality. That first teaches us to subdue the selfish passions, and to respect those rights in others which we value in ourselves. Were we in equal barbarism, our females would be equal drudges. The man with them is less strong than with us, but their woman stronger than ours; and both for the same obvious reason; because our man and their woman is habituated to labour, and formed by it. With both races the sex which is indulged with ease is least athletic. An Indian man is small in the hand and wrist for the same reason for which a sailor is large and strong in the arms and shoulders, and a porter in the legs and thighs.—They raise fewer children than we do. The causes of this are to be found, not in a difference of nature, but of circumstance. The women very frequently attending the men in their parties of war and of hunting, child-bearing becomes extremely inconvenient to them. It is said, therefore, that they have learnt the practice of procuring abortion by the use of some vegetable; and that it even extends to prevent conception for a considerable time after. During these parties they are exposed to numerous hazards, to excessive exertions, to the greatest extremities of hunger. Even at their homes the nation depends for food, through a certain part of every year, on the

---

7. "Sol Rodomonte sprezza di venire / Se non, dove la via meno è sicura. Ariosto. 14. 117." [Au.] "Rodomont only scorns by any way / To wend, except by what is least secure," from *Orlando Furioso* by Lodovico Ariosto (1474–1533), 14, 117.

8. Jefferson made extended citations to Antonio de Ulloa (1716–95), who had published *Noticias Americanas* in 1772, based on his naturalist expeditions to South America. Ulloa also at the time he returned to Spain made a secret report on the American colonies, later published in English, designed to explain to Spanish leaders the causes behind the rebellion of the British American colonies.

gleanings of the forest: that is, they experience a famine once in every year. With all animals, if the female be badly fed, or not fed at all, her young perish: and if both male and female be reduced to like want, generation becomes less active, less productive. To the obstacles then of want and hazard, which nature has opposed to the multiplication of wild animals, for the purpose of restraining their numbers within certain bounds, those of labour and of voluntary abortion are added with the Indian. No wonder then if they multiply less than we do. Where food is regularly supplied, a single farm will shew more of cattle, than a whole country of forests can of buffaloes. The same Indian women, when married to white traders, who feed them and their children plentifully and regularly, who exempt them from excessive drudgery, who keep them stationary and unexposed to accident, produce and raise as many children as the white women. Instances are known, under these circumstances, of their rearing a dozen children. An inhuman practice once prevailed in this country of making slaves of the Indians. It is a fact well known with us, that the Indian women so enslaved produced and raised as numerous families as either the whites or blacks among whom they lived.—It has been said, that Indians have less hair than the whites, except on the head. But this is a fact of which fair proof can scarcely be had. With them it is disgraceful to be hairy on the body. They say it likens them to hogs. They therefore pluck the hair as fast as it appears. But the traders who marry their women, and prevail on them to discontinue this practice, say, that nature is the same with them as with the whites. Nor, if the fact be true, is the consequence necessary which has been drawn from it. Negroes have notoriously less hair than the whites; yet they are more ardent. But if cold and moisture be the agents of nature for diminishing the races of animals, how comes she all at once to suspend their operation as to the physical man of the new world, whom the Count acknowledges to be "à peu près de même stature que l'homme de notre monde,"[9] and to let loose their influence on his moral faculties? How has this "combination of the elements and other physical causes, so contrary to the enlargement of animal nature in this new world, these obstacles to the development and formation of great germs," been arrested and suspended, so as to permit the human body to acquire its just dimensions, and by what inconceivable process has their action been directed on his mind alone? To judge of the truth of this, to form a just estimate of their genius and mental

powers, more facts are wanting, and great allowance to be made for those circumstances of their situation which call for a display of particular talents only. This done, we shall probably find that they are formed in mind as well as in body, on the same module with the "Homo sapiens Europaeus."[10] The principles of their society forbidding all compulsion, they are to be led to duty and to enterprize by personal influence and persuasion. Hence eloquence in council, bravery and address in war, become the foundations of all consequence with them. To these acquirements all their faculties are directed. Of their bravery and address in war we have multiplied proofs, because we have been the subjects on which they were exercised. Of their eminence in oratory we have fewer examples, because it is displayed chiefly in their own councils. Some, however, we have of very superior lustre. I may challenge the whole orations of Demosthenes[11] and Cicero,[12] and of any more eminent orator, if Europe has furnished more eminent, to produce a single passage, superior to the speech of Logan, a Mingo chief, to Lord Dunmore, when governor of this state.[13] And, as a testimony of their tal-

9. That is, "almost the same size as the man of our world."

10. "Linn. Syst. Definition of Man." [Au.] The *Notes* refers frequently to the system of botanical classification developed by Carolus Linnaeus (1707–78), whose *Systema naturae, Species Plantarum,* and other works established a standard for the nomenclature used by botanists and other naturalists.

11. Demosthenes (384?–322 B.C.) has been considered the greatest of Greek orators, known particularly for his orations directed against the encroachment against Attica by Philip of Macedonia.

12. Marcus Tullius Cicero (106–43 B.C.), celebrated orator of the Romans, was renowned for the range of his oratorical and poetic performances.

13. Logan, known as Tah-gah-jute (1725?–80), was the son of a Cayuga Indian chief who married a Shawnee woman and went to live among her people on Yellow Creek on the Ohio River. Logan's story was an important feature of Jefferson's argument about the nobility of the Indian people, one well suited to French readers' predispositions to consider Indians as "noble savages." The story of Logan related to a series of skirmishes called "Dunmore's War" between Indians and whites in the border areas between western Virginia and Maryland and what was then considered "Indian Country." John Murray, earl of Dunmore (1730–1809), the last British-appointed governor of Virginia, attacked Indians in the area because of depredations they were causing settlers who had moved onto their land. Different versions of the causes of the contentions were raised over the years. Michael Cresap (1742–75) of Maryland was probably not responsible for the death of Logan's family, although he engaged in other attacks against Indian people in the area.

ents in this line, I beg leave to introduce it, first stating the incidents necessary for understanding it. In the spring of the year 1774, a robbery and murder were committed on an inhabitant of the frontiers of Virginia, by two Indians of the Shawanee tribe. The neighbouring whites, according to their custom, undertook to punish this outrage in a summary way. Col. Cresap, a man infamous for the many murders he had committed on those much-injured people, collected a party, and proceeded down the Kanhaway in quest of vengeance. Unfortunately a canoe of women and children, with one man only, was seen coming from the opposite shore, unarmed, and unsuspecting an hostile attack from the whites. Cresap and his party concealed themselves on the bank of the river, and the moment the canoe reached the shore, singled out their objects, and, at one fire, killed every person in it. This happened to be the family of Logan, who had long been distinguished as a friend of the whites. This unworthy return provoked his vengeance. He accordingly signalized himself in the war which ensued. In the autumn of the same year, a decisive battle was fought at the mouth of the Great Kanhaway, between the collected forces of the Shawanees, Mingoes, and Delawares, and a detachment of the Virginia militia. The Indians were defeated, and sued for peace. Logan however disdained to be seen among the suppliants. But, lest the sincerity of a treaty should be distrusted, from which so distinguished a chief absented himself, he sent by a messenger the following speech to be delivered to Lord Dunmore.

"I appeal to any white man to say, if ever he entered Logan's cabin hungry, and he gave him not meat; if ever he came cold and naked, and he clothed him not. During the course of the last long and bloody war, Logan remained idle in his cabin, an advocate for peace. Such was my love for the whites, that my countrymen pointed as they passed, and said, "Logan is the friend of white men." I had even thought to have lived with you, but for the injuries of one man. Col. Cresap, the last spring, in cold blood, and unprovoked, murdered all the relations of Logan, not sparing even my women and children. There runs not a drop of my blood in the veins of any living creature. This called on me for revenge. I have sought it: I have killed many: I have fully glutted my vengeance. For my country, I rejoice at the beams of peace. But do not harbour a thought that mine is the joy of fear. Logan never felt fear. He will not turn on his heel to save his life. Who is there to mourn for Logan?—Not one."

Before we condemn the Indians of this continent as wanting genius, we must consider that letters have not yet been introduced among them. Were we to compare them in their present state with the Europeans North of the Alps, when the Roman arms and arts first crossed those mountains, the comparison would be unequal, because, at that time, those parts of Europe were swarming with numbers; because numbers produce emulation, and multiply the chances of improvement, and one improvement begets another. Yet I may safely ask, How many good poets, how many able mathematicians, how many great inventors in arts or sciences, had Europe North of the Alps then produced? And it was sixteen centuries after this before a Newton could be formed. I do not mean to deny, that there are varieties in the race of man, distinguished by their powers both of body and mind. I believe there are, as I see to be the case in the races of other animals. I only mean to suggest a doubt, whether the bulk and faculties of animals depend on the side of the Atlantic on which their food happens to grow, or which furnishes the elements of which they are compounded? Whether nature has enlisted herself as a Cis[14] or Trans-Atlantic partisan? I am induced to suspect, there has been more eloquence than sound reasoning displayed in support of this theory; that it is one of those cases where the judgment has been seduced by a glowing pen: and whilst I render every tribute of honor and esteem to the celebrated Zoologist, who has added, and is still adding, so many precious things to the treasures of science, I must doubt whether in this instance he has not cherished error also, by lending her for a moment his vivid imagination and bewitching language.

So far the Count de Buffon has carried this new theory of the tendency of nature to belittle her productions on this side the Atlantic. Its application to the race of whites, transplanted from Europe, remained for the Abbé Raynal.[15] "On doit etre etonné (he says) que l'Amerique n'ait pas encore produit un bon poëte, un habile mathematicien, un homme de genie dans un seul art, ou une seule

---

14. *Cis* is a Latinism that translates as "on this side of." Jefferson asks whether "nature" has enlisted "herself" as a partisan of North America or of Europe.

15. Guillaume Thomas François Raynal (1713–96), a French historian and philosopher, wrote a philosophical and political history of commerce in the Indies, the *Histoire Philosophique et Politique,* that Jefferson referred to in the passage that follows. Jefferson quoted Raynal's statement: "One must be astonished . . . that America has not yet produced one good poet, one able mathematician, one man of genius in a single art or a single science."

science." 7. Hist. Philos. p. 92. ed. Maestricht. 1774. "America has not yet produced one good poet." When we shall have existed as a people as long as the Greeks did before they produced a Homer, the Romans a Virgil, the French a Racine and Voltaire, the English a Shakespeare and Milton, should this reproach be still true, we will enquire from what unfriendly causes it has proceeded, that the other countries of Europe and quarters of the earth shall not have inscribed any name in the roll of poets. But neither has America produced "one able mathematician, one man of genius in a single art or a single science." In war we have produced a Washington, whose memory will be adored while liberty shall have votaries, whose name will triumph over time, and will in future ages assume its just station among the most celebrated worthies of the world, when that wretched philosophy shall be forgotten which would have arranged him among the degeneracies of nature. In physics we have produced a Franklin, than whom no one of the present age has made more important discoveries, nor has enriched philosophy with more, or more ingenious solutions of the phaenomena of nature. We have supposed Mr. Rittenhouse[16] second to no astronomer living: that in genius he must be the first, because he is self-taught. As an artist he has exhibited as great a proof of mechanical genius as the world has ever produced. He has not indeed made a world; but he has by imitation approached nearer its Maker than any man who has lived from the creation to this day. As in philosophy and war, so in government, in oratory, in painting, in the plastic art, we might shew that America, though but a child of yesterday, has already given hopeful proofs of genius, as well of the nobler kinds, which arouse the best feelings of man, which call him into action, which substantiate his freedom, and conduct him to happiness, as of the subordinate, which serve to amuse him only. We therefore suppose, that this reproach is as unjust as it is unkind; and that, of the geniuses which adorn the present age, America contributes its full share. For comparing it with those countries, where genius is most cultivated, where are the most excellent models for art, and scaffoldings for the attainment of science, as France and England for instance, we calculate thus. The United States contain

three millions of inhabitants; France twenty millions; and the British islands ten. We produce a Washington, a Franklin, a Rittenhouse. France then should have half a dozen in each of these lines, and Great-Britain half that number, equally eminent. It may be true, that France has: we are but just becoming acquainted with her, and our acquaintance so far gives us high ideas of the genius of her inhabitants. It would be injuring too many of them to name particularly a Voltaire, a Buffon, the constellation of Encyclopedists, the Abbé Raynal himself, &c. &c. We therefore have reason to believe she can produce her full quota of genius. The present war having so long cut off all communication with Great-Britain, we are not able to make a fair estimate of the state of science in that country. The spirit in which she wages war is the only sample before our eyes, and that does not seem the legitimate offspring either of science or of civilization. The sun of her glory is fast descending to the horizon. Her philosophy has crossed the Channel, her freedom the Atlantic, and herself seems passing to that awful dissolution, whose issue is not given human foresight to scan.[17]

Having given a sketch of our minerals, vegetables, and quadrupeds, and being led by a proud theory to make a comparison of the latter with those of Europe, and to extend it to the Man of America, both aboriginal and emigrant, I will proceed to the remaining articles comprehended under the present query.

Between ninety and an hundred of our birds have been described by Catesby.[18] His drawings are better as to form and attitude, than colouring, which is generally too high. They are the following.

---

16. David Rittenhouse (1732–96), one of the most respected scientists of his era, was an astronomer, mathematician, and instrument maker who was later (1795) elected to the Royal Society of London.

---

17. "Has the world as yet produced more than two poets, acknowledged to be such by all nations? An Englishman, only, reads Milton with delight, an Italian Tasso, a Frenchman the Henriade, a Portuguese Camouens: but Homer and Virgil have been the rapture of every age and nation: they are read with enthusiasm in their originals by those who can read the originals, and in translations by those who cannot." [Au.] The poets Jefferson mentioned are John Milton; Torquato Tasso (1544–95), who wrote *Gerusalemme Liberata;* François Marie Arouet de Voltaire (1694–1778), who wrote *La Henriade* about Henri IV; and Luis de Camoens (1524–80), who wrote *Lusiads* about the Portuguese sailors of the fifteenth century.

18. Mark Catesby (1679–1749), a British naturalist who made several trips into North America and published several books about his discoveries.

from QUERY 11 • A Description of the Indians
Established in That State

Aborigines

When the first effectual settlement of our colony was
made, which was in 1607, the country from the sea-coast
to the mountains, and from Patowmac to the most southern waters of James river, was occupied by upwards of
forty different tribes of Indians. Of these the *Powhatans,*
the *Mannahoacs,* and *Monacans,* were the most powerful. Those between the sea-coast and falls of the rivers,
were in amity with one another, and attached to the
Powhatans as their link of union. Those between the falls
of the rivers and the mountains, were divided into two
confederacies; the tribes inhabiting the head waters of Patowmac and Rappahanoc being attached to the *Mannahoacs;* and those on the upper parts of James river to the
Monacans. But the *Monacans* and their friends were in
amity with the *Mannahoacs* and their friends, and waged
joint and perpetual war against the *Powhatans.* We are
told that the *Powhatans, Mannahoacs,* and *Monacans,*
spoke languages so radically different, that interpreters
were necessary when they transacted business. Hence we
may conjecture, that this was not the case between all the
tribes, and probably that each spoke the language of the
nation to which it was attached; which we know to have
been the case in many particular instances. Very possibly
there may have been anciently three different stocks, each
of which multiplying in a long course of time, had separated into so many little societies. This practice results
from the circumstance of their having never submitted
themselves to any laws, any coercive power, any shadow
of government. Their only controuls are their manners,
and that moral sense of right and wrong, which, like the
sense of tasting and feeling, in every man makes a part of
his nature. An offence against these is punished by contempt, by exclusion from society, or, where the case is serious, as that of murder, by the individuals whom it concerns. Imperfect as this species of coercion may seem,
crimes are very rare among them: insomuch that were it
made a question, whether no law, as among the savage
Americans, or too much law, as among the civilized Europeans, submits man to the greatest evil, one who has
seen both conditions of existence would pronounce it to
be the last: and that the sheep are happier of themselves,
than under care of the wolves. It will be said, that great societies cannot exist without government. The Savages
therefore break them into small ones.

The territories of the *Powhatan* confederacy, south of
the Patowmac, comprehended about 8000 square miles,
30 tribes, and 2400 warriors. Capt. Smith[19] tells us, that
within 60 miles of James town were 5000 people, of
whom 1500 were warriors. From this we find the proportion of their warriors to their whole inhabitants, was as 3
to 10. The *Powhatan* confederacy then would consist of
about 8000 inhabitants, which was one for every square
mile; being about the twentieth part of our present population in the same territory, and the hundredth of that of
the British islands.

Besides these, were the *Nottoways,* living on Nottoway river, the *Meherrins* and *Tuteloes* on Meherrin
river, who were connected with the Indians of Carolina,
probably with the Chowanocs. . . .

I know of no such thing existing as an Indian monument: for I would not honour with that name arrow points,
stone hatchets, stone pipes, and half-shapen images. Of
labour on the large scale, I think there is no remain as respectable as would be a common ditch for the draining of
lands: unless indeed it be the Barrows, of which many are
to be found all over this country. These are of different
sizes, some of them constructed of earth, and some of
loose stones. That they were repositories of the dead, has
been obvious to all: but on what particular occasion constructed, was matter of doubt. Some have thought they
covered the bones of those who have fallen in battles
fought on the spot of interment. Some ascribed them to the
custom, said to prevail among the Indians, of collecting, at
certain periods, the bones of all their dead, wheresoever
deposited at the time of death. Others again supposed them
the general sepulchres for towns, conjectured to have been
on or near these grounds; and this opinion was supported
by the quality of the lands in which they are found, (those
constructed of earth being generally in the softest and most
fertile meadow-grounds on river sides) and by a tradition,
said to be handed down from the Aboriginal Indians, that,
when they settled in a town, the first person who died was
placed erect, and earth put about him, so as to cover and
support him; that, when another died, a narrow passage
was dug to the first, the second reclined against him, and
the cover of earth replaced, and so on. There being one of
these in my neighbourhood, I wished to satisfy myself
whether any, and which of these opinions were just. For
this purpose I determined to open and examine it thor-

---

19. John Smith (1580–1631) became a leader in the original
Virginia colony and author of several books about his experiences there.

oughly. It was situated on the low grounds of the Rivanna, about two miles above its principal fork, and opposite to some hills, on which had been an Indian town. It was of a spheroidical form, of about 40 feet diameter at the base, and had been of about twelve feet altitude, though now reduced by the plough to seven and a half, having been under cultivation about a dozen years. Before this it was covered with trees of twelve inches diameter, and round the base was an excavation of five feet depth and width, from whence the earth had been taken of which the hillock was formed. I first dug superficially in several parts of it, and came to collections of human bones, at different depths, from six inches to three feet below the surface. These were lying in the utmost confusion, some vertical, some oblique, some horizontal, and directed to every point of the compass, entangled, and held together in clusters by the earth. Bones of the most distant parts were found together, as, for instance, the small bones of the foot in the hollow of a scull, many sculls would sometimes be in contact, lying on the face, on the side, on the back, top or bottom, so as, on the whole, to give the idea of bones emptied promiscuously from a bag or basket, and covered over with earth, without any attention to their order. The bones of which the greatest numbers remained, were sculls, jawbones, teeth, the bones of the arms, thighs, legs, feet, and hands. A few ribs remained, some vertebrae of the neck and spine, without their processes, and one instance only of the bone[20] which serves as a base to the vertebral column. The sculls were so tender, that they generally fell to pieces on being touched. The other bones were stronger. There were some teeth which were judged to be smaller than those of an adult; a scull, which, on a slight view, appeared to be that of an infant, but it fell to pieces on being taken out, so as to prevent satisfactory examination; a rib, and a fragment of the under-jaw of a person about half grown; another rib of an infant; and part of the jaw of a child, which had not yet cut its teeth. This last furnishing the most decisive proof of the burial of children here, I was particular in my attention to it. It was part of the right-half of the under-jaw. The processes, by which it was articulated to the temporal bones, were entire; and the bone itself firm to where it had been broken off, which, as nearly as I could judge, was about the place of the eye-tooth. Its upper edge, wherein would have been the sockets of the teeth, was perfectly smooth. Measuring it with that of an adult, by placing their hinder processes together, its bro-

ken end extended to the penultimate grinder of the adult. This bone was white, all the others of a sand colour. The bones of infants being soft, they probably decay sooner, which might be the cause so few were found here. I proceeded then to make a perpendicular cut through the body of the barrow, that I might examine its internal structure. This passed about three feet from its center, was opened to the former surface of the earth, and was wide enough for a man to walk through and examine its sides. At the bottom, that is, on the level of the circumjacent plain, I found bones; above these a few stones, brought from a cliff a quarter of a mile off, and from the river one-eighth of a mile off; then a large interval of earth, then a stratum of bones, and so on. At one end of the section were four strata of bones plainly distinguishable; at the other, three; the strata in one part not ranging with those in another. The bones nearest the surface were least decayed. No holes were discovered in any of them, as if made with bullets, arrows, or other weapons. I conjectured that in this barrow might have been a thousand skeletons. Every one will readily seize the circumstances above related, which militate against the opinion, that it covered the bones only of persons fallen in battle; and against the tradition also, which would make it the common sepulchre of a town, in which the bodies were placed upright, and touching each other. Appearances certainly indicate that it has derived both origin and growth from the accustomary collection of bones, and deposition of them together; that the first collection had been deposited on the common surface of the earth, a few stones put over it, and then a covering of earth, that the second had been laid on this, had covered more or less of it in proportion to the number of bones, and was then also covered with earth; and so on. The following are the particular circumstances which give it this aspect. 1. The number of bones. 2. Their confused position. 3. Their being in different strata. 4. The strata in one part having no correspondence with those in another. 5. The different states of decay in these strata, which seem to indicate a difference in the time of inhumation. 6. The existence of infant bones among them.

But on whatever occasion they may have been made, they are of considerable notoriety among the Indians: for a party passing, about thirty years ago, through the part of the country where this barrow is, went through the woods directly to it, without any instructions or enquiry, and having staid about it some time, with expressions which were constructed to be those of sorrow, they returned to the high road, which they had left about half a dozen miles to pay this visit, and pursued their journey. There is

---

20. "The os sacrum." [Au.]

another barrow, much resembling this in the low grounds of the South branch of Shenandoah, where it is crossed by the road leading from the Rock-fish gap to Staunton. Both of these have, within these dozen years, been cleared of their trees and put under cultivation, are much reduced in their height, and spread in width, by the plough, and will probably disappear in time. There is another on a hill in the Blue ridge of mountains, a few miles North of Wood's gap, which is made up of small stones thrown together. This has been opened and found to contain human bones, as the others do. There are also many others in other parts of the country.

Great question has arisen from whence came those aboriginal inhabitants of America? Discoveries, long ago made, were sufficient to shew that a passage from Europe to America was always practicable, even to the imperfect navigation of ancient times. In going from Norway to Iceland, from Iceland to Groenland, from Groenland to Labrador, the first traject is the widest: and this having been practised from the earliest times of which we have any account of that part of the earth, it is not difficult to suppose that the subsequent trajects may have been sometimes passed. Again, the late discoveries of Captain Cook,[21] coasting from Kamschatka to California, have proved that, if the two continents of Asia and America be separated at all, it is only by a narrow streight. So that from this side also, inhabitants may have passed into America: and the resemblance between the Indians of America and the Eastern inhabitants of Asia, would induce us to conjecture, that the former are the descendants of the latter, or the latter of the former: excepting indeed the Eskimaux, who, from the same circumstance of resemblance, and from identity of language, must be derived from the Groenlanders, and these probably from some of the northern parts of the old continent. A knowledge of their several languages would be the most certain evidence of their derivation which could be produced. In fact, it is the best proof of the affinity of nations which ever can be referred to. How many ages have elapsed since the English, the Dutch, the Germans, the Swiss, the Norwegians, Danes and Swedes have separated from

their common stock? Yet how many more must elapse before the proofs of their common origin, which exist in their several languages, will disappear? It is to be lamented then, very much to be lamented, that we have suffered so many of the Indian tribes already to extinguish, without our having previously collected and deposited in the records of literature, the general rudiments at least of the languages they spoke. Were vocabularies formed of all the languages spoken in North and South America, preserving their appellations of the most common objects in nature, of those which must be present to every nation barbarous or civilised, with the inflections of their nouns and verbs, their principles of regimen and concord, and these deposited in all the public libraries, it would furnish opportunities to those skilled in the languages of the old world to compare them with these, now, or at any future time, and hence to construct the best evidence of the derivation of this part of the human race.

But imperfect as is our knowledge of the tongues spoken in America, it suffices to discover the following remarkable fact. Arranging them under the radical ones to which they may be palpably traced, and doing the same by those of the red men of Asia, there will be found probably twenty in America, for one in Asia, of those radical languages, so called because, if they were ever the same, they have lost all resemblance to one another. A separation into dialects may be the work of a few ages only, but for two dialects to recede from one another till they have lost all vestiges of their common origin, must require an immense course of time; perhaps not less than many people give to the age of the earth. A greater number of those radical changes of language having taken place among the red men of America, proves them of greater antiquity than those of Asia.

from QUERY 14 • Laws

· · ·

Many of the laws which were in force during the monarchy being relative merely to that form of government, or inculcating principles inconsistent with republicanism, the first assembly which met after the establishment of the commonwealth appointed a committee to revise the whole code, to reduce it into proper form and volume, and report it to the assembly. This work has been executed by three gentlemen, and reported; but probably will not be taken up till a restoration of peace shall leave to the legislature leisure to go through such a work.

The plan of the revisal was this. The common law of

---

21. James Cook (1728–79) sailed the Pacific coastlines of North America and Asia. After he died, his command was taken up by Captain Charles Clerke, who visited Kamchatka while attempting to discover a northern pathway between the Pacific and Atlantic Oceans.

England, by which is meant, that part of the English law which was anterior to the date of the oldest statutes extant, is made the basis of the work. It was thought dangerous to attempt to reduce it to a text: it was therefore left to be collected from the usual monuments of it. Necessary alterations in that, and so much of the whole body of the British statutes, and of acts of assembly, as were thought proper to be retained, were digested into 126 new acts, in which simplicity of stile was aimed at, as far as was safe. The following are the most remarkable alterations proposed:

To change the rules of descent, so as that the lands of any person dying intestate shall be divisible equally among all his children, or other representatives, in equal degree.

To make slaves distributable among the next of kin, as other moveables.

To have all public expences, whether of the general treasury, or of a parish or county, (as for the maintenance of the poor, building bridges, court-houses, &c.) supplied by assessments on the citizens, in proportion to their property.

To hire undertakers for keeping the public roads in repair, and indemnify individuals through whose lands new roads shall be opened.

To define with precision the rules whereby aliens should become citizens, and citizens make themselves aliens.

To establish religious freedom on the broadest bottom.

To emancipate all slaves born after passing the act. The bill reported by the revisors does not itself contain this proposition; but an amendment containing it was prepared, to be offered to the legislature whenever the bill should be taken up, and further directing, that they should continue with their parents to a certain age, then be brought up, at the public expence, to tillage, arts or sciences, according to their geniusses, till the females should be eighteen, and the males twenty-one years of age, when they should be colonized to such place as the circumstances of the time should render most proper, sending them out with arms, implements of houshold and of the handicraft arts, feeds, pairs of the useful domestic animals, &c. to declare them a free and independant people, and extend to them our alliance and protection, till they shall have acquired strength; and to send vessels at the same time to other parts of the world for an equal number of white inhabitants; to induce whom to migrate hither, proper encouragements were to be proposed. It will probably be asked, Why not retain and incorporate the blacks into the state, and thus save the expence of supplying, by importation of white settlers, the vacancies they will leave? Deep rooted prejudices entertained by the whites; ten thousand recollections, by the blacks, of the injuries they have sustained; new provocations; the real distinctions which nature has made; and many other circumstances, will divide us into parties, and produce convulsions which will probably never end but in the extermination of the one or the other race.—To these objections, which are political, may be added others, which are physical and moral. The first difference which strikes us is that of colour. Whether the black of the negro resides in the reticular membrane between the skin and scarf-skin, or in the scarf-skin itself; whether it proceeds from the colour of the blood, the colour of the bile, or from that of some other secretion, the difference is fixed in nature, and is as real as if its seat and cause were better known to us. And is this difference of no importance? Is it not the foundation of a greater or less share of beauty in the two races? Are not the fine mixtures of red and white, the expressions of every passion by greater or less suffusions of colour in the one, preferable to that eternal monotony, which reigns in the countenances, that immoveable veil of black which covers all the emotions of the other race? Add to these, flowing hair, a more elegant symmetry of form, their own judgment in favour of the whites, declared by their preference of them, as uniformly as is the preference of the Oranootan for the black women over those of his own species. The circumstance of superior beauty, is thought worthy attention in the propagation of our horses, dogs, and other domestic animals; why not in that of man? Besides those of colour, figure, and hair, there are other physical distinctions proving a difference of race. They have less hair on the face and body. They secrete less by the kidnies, and more by the glands of the skin, which gives them a very strong and disagreeable odour. This greater degree of transpiration renders them more tolerant of heat, and less so of cold, than the whites. Perhaps too a difference of structure in the pulmonary apparatus, which a late ingenious experimentalist[22] has discovered to be the principal regulator of animal heat, may have disabled them from extricating, in the act of inspiration, so much of that fluid from the outer air, or obliged them in expiration, to part with more of it. They seem to require less sleep. A black, after hard labour through the

---

22. "Crawford." [Au.] Adair Crawford (1748–95), British physician and natural scientist.

day, will be induced by the slightest amusements to sit up till midnight, or later, though knowing he must be out with the first dawn of the morning. They are at least as brave, and more adventuresome. But this may perhaps proceed from a want of forethought, which prevents their seeing a danger till it be present. When present, they do not go through it with more coolness or steadiness than the whites. They are more ardent after their female: but love seems with them to be more an eager desire, than a tender delicate mixture of sentiment and sensation. Their griefs are transient. Those numberless afflictions, which render it doubtful whether heaven has given life to us in mercy or in wrath, are less felt, and sooner forgotten with them. In general, their existence appears to participate more of sensation than reflection. To this must be ascribed their disposition to sleep when abstracted from their diversions, and unemployed in labour. An animal whose body is at rest, and who does not reflect, must be disposed to sleep of course. Comparing them by their faculties of memory, reason, and imagination, it appears to me, that in memory they are equal to the whites; in reason much inferior, as I think one could scarcely be found capable of tracing and comprehending the investigations of Euclid; and that in imagination they are dull, tasteless, and anomalous. It would be unfair to follow them to Africa for this investigation. We will consider them here, on the same stage with the whites, and where the facts are not apocryphal on which a judgment is to be formed. It will be right to make great allowances for the difference of condition, of education, of conversation, of the sphere in which they move. Many millions of them have been brought to, and born in America. Most of them indeed have been confined to tillage, to their own homes, and their own society: yet many have been so situated, that they might have availed themselves of the conversation of their masters; many have been brought up to the handicraft arts, and from that circumstance have always been associated with the whites. Some have been liberally educated, and all have lived in countries where the arts and sciences are cultivated to a considerable degree, and have had before their eyes samples of the best works from abroad. The Indians, with no advantages of this kind, will often carve figures on their pipes not destitute of design and merit. They will crayon out an animal, a plant, or a country, so as to prove the existence of a germ in their minds which only wants cultivation. They astonish you with strokes of the most sublime oratory; such as prove their reason and sentiment strong, their imagination glowing and elevated. But never yet could I find that a black had uttered a thought above the level of plain narration; never see even an elementary trait of painting or sculpture. In music they are more generally gifted than the whites with accurate ears for tune and time, and they have been found capable of imagining a small catch. Whether they will be equal to the composition of a more extensive run of melody, or of complicated harmony, is yet to be proved. Misery is often the parent of the most affecting touches in poetry.—Among the blacks is misery enough, God knows, but no poetry. Love is the peculiar oestrum of the poet. Their love is ardent, but it kindles the senses only, not the imagination. Religion indeed has produced a Phyllis Whately;[23] but it could not produce a poet. The compositions published under her name are below the dignity of criticism. The heroes of the Dunciad are to her, as Hercules to the author of that poem.[24] Ignatius Sancho[25] has approached nearer to merit in composition; yet his letters do more honour to the heart than the head. They breathe the purest effusions of friendship and general philanthropy, and shew how great a degree of the latter may be compounded with strong religious zeal. He is often happy in the turn of his compliments, and his stile is easy and familiar, except when he affects a Shandean fabrication of words. But his imagination is wild and extravagant, escapes incessantly from every restraint of reason and taste, and, in the course of its vagaries, leaves a tract of thought as incoherent and eccentric, as is the course of a meteor through the sky. His subjects should often have led him to a process of sober reasoning: yet we find him always substituting sentiment for demonstration. Upon the whole, though we admit him to the first place among those of his own colour who have presented themselves to the public judgment, yet when we compare him with the writers of the race among whom he lived, and particularly with the epistolary class, in which he has taken his own

---

23. Phillis Wheatley (1754?–84) was well known and much admired as a poet in Britain and British North America at the time Jefferson wrote these lines.

24. Alexander Pope (1688–1744) wrote the *Dunciad,* a satiric poem that made fun of what he considered to be poor poetry.

25. Charles Ignatius Sancho (1729?–80), born on an African slave ship, was highly educated and patronized by leading British intellectuals, politicians, and artists, including Laurence Sterne and David Garrick. He and his writings were well known in European circles.

stand, we are compelled to enroll him at the bottom of the column. This criticism supposes the letters published under his name to be genuine, and to have received amendment from no other hand; points which would not be of easy investigation. The improvement of the blacks in body and mind, in the first instance of their mixture with the whites, has been observed by every one, and proves that their inferiority is not the effect merely of their condition of life. We know that among the Romans, about the Augustan age especially, the condition of their slaves was much more deplorable than that of the blacks on the continent of America. The two sexes were confined in separate apartments, because to raise a child cost the master more than to buy one. Cato, for a very restricted indulgence to his slaves in this particular, took from them a certain price.[26] But in this country the slaves multiply as fast as the free inhabitants. Their situation and manners place the commerce between the two sexes almost without restraint.—The same Cato, on a principle of oeconomy, always sold his sick and superannuated slaves. He gives it as a standing precept to a master visiting his farm, to sell his old oxen, old waggons, old tools, old and diseased servants, and every thing else become useless. "Vendat boves vetulos, plaustrum vetus, ferramenta vetera, servum senem, servum morbosum, & si quid aliud supersit vendat."[27] Cato de re rusticâ. c. 2. The American slaves cannot enumerate this among the injuries and insults they receive. It was the common practice to expose in the island of Aesculapius, in the Tyber, diseased slaves, whose cure was like to become tedious. The Emperor Claudius, by an edict, gave freedom to such of them as should recover, and first declared, that if any person chose to kill rather than to expose them, it should be deemed homicide. The exposing them is a crime of which no instance has existed with us; and were it to be followed by death, it would be punished capitally. We are told of a certain Vedius Pollio, who, in the presence of Augustus, would have given a slave as food to his fish, for having broken a glass. With the Romans, the regular method of taking the evidence of their slaves was under torture. Here it has been thought better never to resort to their evidence. When a master was murdered, all his slaves, in the same house, or within hearing, were condemned to death. Here punishment falls on the guilty only, and as precise proof is required against him as against a freeman. Yet notwithstanding these and other discouraging circumstances among the Romans, their slaves were often their rarest artists. They excelled too in science, insomuch as to be usually employed as tutors to their master's children. Epictetus, Terence, and Phaedrus,[28] were slaves. But they were of the race of whites. It is not their condition then, but nature, which has produced the distinction.— Whether further observation will or will not verify the conjecture, that nature has been less bountiful to them in the endowments of the head, I believe that in those of the heart she will be found to have done them justice. That disposition to theft with which they have been branded, must be ascribed to their situation, and not to any depravity of the moral sense. The man, in whose favour no laws of property exist, probably feels himself less bound to respect those made in favour of others. When arguing for ourselves, we lay it down as a fundamental, that laws, to be just, must give a reciprocation of right: that, without this, they are mere arbitrary rules of conduct, founded in force, and not in conscience: and it is a problem which I give to the master to solve, whether the religious precepts against the violation of property were not framed for him as well as his slave? And whether the slave may not as justifiably take a little from one, who has taken all from him, as he may slay one who would slay him? That a change in the relations in which a man is placed should change his ideas of moral right and wrong, is neither new, nor peculiar to the colour of the blacks. Homer tells us it was so 2600 years ago.

Ἥμιου, γαζ τ' ἀρετῆς ἀποαίνυ|αι εὐρύθπα Ζεὺς
Ἀνερος, ευτ' ἄν μιν κατὰ δόλιον ἡμαζ ἕλησιν.
OD. 17, 323.

Jove fix'd it certain, that whatever day
Makes man a slave, takes half his worth away.[29]

---

26. "He stipulated that the male slaves should pay a fixed price to consort with the females." [Au.] Jefferson refers to Marcus Porcius Cato (239–149 B.C.).

27. Jefferson provided the translation for this Latin from Cato's *De Re Rustica* in the preceding passage.

28. Jefferson names Epictetus, a celebrated philsopher who taught that one should desire nothing but freedom and contentment; Terence, a Roman poet born in Carthage and taken to Rome, where he was freed and Phaedrus, a Roman writer of fables.

29. The quotation is adapted from Alexander Pope's translation of Homer's *Odyssey*.

But the slaves of which Homer speaks were whites. Notwithstanding these considerations which must weaken their respect for the laws of property, we find among them numerous instances of the most rigid integrity, and as many as among their better instructed masters, of benevolence, gratitude, and unshaken fidelity.— The opinion, that they are inferior in the faculties of reason and imagination, must be hazarded with great diffidence. To justify a general conclusion, requires many observations, even where the subject may be submitted to the Anatomical knife, to Optical glasses, to analysis by fire, or by solvents. How much more then where it is a faculty, not a substance, we are examining; where it eludes the research of all the senses; where the conditions of its existence are various and variously combined; where the effects of those which are present or absent bid defiance to calculation; let me add too, as a circumstance of great tenderness, where our conclusion would degrade a whole race of men from the rank in the scale of beings which their Creator may perhaps have given them. To our reproach it must be said, that though for a century and a half we have had under our eyes the races of black and of red men, they have never yet been viewed by us as subjects of natural history. I advance it therefore as a suspicion only, that the blacks, whether originally a distinct race, or made distinct by time and circumstances, are inferior to the whites in the endowments both of body and mind. It is not against experience to suppose, that different species of the same genus, or varieties of the same species, may possess different qualifications. Will not a lover of natural history then, one who views the gradations in all the races of animals with the eye of philosophy, excuse an effort to keep those in the department of man as distinct as nature has formed them? This unfortunate difference of colour, and perhaps of faculty, is a powerful obstacle to the emancipation of these people. Many of their advocates, while they wish to vindicate the liberty of human nature, are anxious also to preserve its dignity and beauty. Some of these, embarrassed by the question "What further is to be done with them?" join themselves in opposition with those who are actuated by sordid avarice only. Among the Romans emancipation required but one effort. The slave, when made free, might mix with, without staining the blood of his master. But with us a second is necessary, unknown to history. When freed, he is to be removed beyond the reach of mixture.

QUERY 17 • The Different Religions Received into That State

Religion

The first settlers in this country were emigrants from England, of the English church, just at a point of time when it was flushed with complete victory over the religious of all other persuasions. Possessed, as they became, of the powers of making, administering, and executing the laws, they shewed equal intolerance in this country with their Presbyterian brethren, who had emigrated to the northern government. The poor Quakers were flying from persecution in England. They cast their eyes on these new countries as asylums of civil and religious freedom; but they found them free only for the reigning sect. Several acts of the Virginia assembly of 1659, 1662, and 1693, had made it penal in parents to refuse to have their children baptized; had prohibited the unlawful assembling of Quakers; had made it penal for any master of a vessel to bring a Quaker into the state; had ordered those already here, and such as should come thereafter, to be imprisoned till they should abjure the country; provided a milder punishment for their first and second return, but death for their third; had inhibited all persons from suffering their meetings in or near their houses, entertaining them individually, or disposing of books which supported their tenets. If no capital execution took place here, as did in New-England, it was not owing to the moderation of the church, or spirit of the legislature, as may be inferred from the law itself; but to historical circumstances which have not been handed down to us. The Anglicans retained full possession of the country about a century. Other opinions began then to creep in, and the great care of the government to support their own church, having begotten an equal degree of indolence in its clergy, two-thirds of the people had become dissenters at the commencement of the present revolution. The laws indeed were still oppressive on them, but the spirit of the one party had subsided into moderation, and of the other had risen to a degree of determination which commanded respect.

The present state of our laws on the subject of religion is this. The convention of May 1776, in their declaration of rights, declared it to be a truth, and a natural right, that the exercise of religion should be free; but when they proceeded to form on that declaration the ordinance of government, instead of taking up every principle declared in the bill of rights, and guarding it by legislative sanction, they passed over that which asserted our religious rights, leaving them as they found them. The same convention, however, when they met as a member of the general assembly in October 1776, repealed all *acts of parliament* which had rendered criminal the maintaining any opinions in matters of religion, the forbearing to repair to church, and the exercising any mode of worship; and suspended the laws giving salaries to the clergy, which suspension was made perpetual in October 1779. Statutory oppressions in religion being thus wiped away, we remain at present under those only imposed by the common law, or by our own acts of assembly. At the common law, *heresy* was a capital offence, punishable by burning. Its definition was left to the ecclesiastical judges, before whom the conviction was, till the statute of the 1 El. c. 1.[30] circumscribed it, by declaring, that nothing should be deemed heresy, but what had been so determined by authority of the canonical scriptures, or by one of the four first general councils, or by some other council having for the grounds of their declaration the express and plain words of the scriptures. Heresy, thus circumscribed, being an offence at the common law, our act of assembly of October 1777, c. 17. gives cognizance of it to the general court, by declaring, that the jurisdiction of that court shall be general in all matters at the common law. The execution is by the writ *De haeretico comburendo.*[31] By our own act of assembly of 1705, c. 30, if a person brought up in the Christian religion denies the being of a God, or the Trinity, or asserts there are more Gods than one, or denies the Christian religion to be true, or the scriptures to be of divine authority, he is punishable on the first offence by incapacity to hold any office or employment ecclesiastical, civil, or military; on the second by disability to sue, to take any gift or legacy, to be guardian, executor, or administrator, and by three years imprisonment, without bail. A father's right to the custody of his own children being founded in law on his right of guardianship, this being taken away, they may of course be severed from him, and put, by the authority of a court, into more orthodox hands. This is a summary view of that religious slavery, under which a people have been willing to remain,

who have lavished their lives and fortunes for the establishment of their civil freedom.[32] The error seems not sufficiently eradicated, that the operations of the mind, as well as the acts of the body, are subject to the coercion of the laws. But our rulers can have authority over such natural rights only as we have submitted to them. The rights of conscience we never submitted, we could not submit. We are answerable for them to our God. The legitimate powers of government extend to such acts only as are injurious to others. But it does me no injury for my neighbour to say there are twenty gods, or no god. It neither picks my pocket nor breaks my leg. If it be said, his testimony in a court of justice cannot be relied on, reject it then, and be the stigma on him. Constraint may make him worse by making him a hypocrite, but it will never make him a truer man. It may fix him obstinately in his errors, but will not cure them. Reason and free enquiry are the only effectual agents against error. Give a loose to them, they will support the true religion, by bringing every false one to their tribunal, to the test of their investigation. They are the natural enemies of error, and of error only. Had not the Roman government permitted free enquiry, Christianity could never have been introduced. Had not free enquiry been indulged, at the area of the reformation, the corruptions of Christianity could not have been purged away. If it be restrained now, the present corruptions will be protected, and new ones encouraged. Was the government to prescribe to us our medicine and diet, our bodies would be in such keeping as our souls are now. Thus in France the emetic was once forbidden as a medicine, and the potatoe as an article of food. Government is just as infallible too when it fixes systems in physics. Galileo was sent to the inquisition for affirming that the earth was a sphere: the government had declared it to be as flat as a trencher, and Galileo was obliged to abjure his error. This error however at length prevailed, the earth became a globe, and Descartes declared it was whirled round its axis by a vortex. The government in which he lived was wise enough to see that this was no question of civil jurisdiction, or we should all have been involved by authority in vortices. In fact, the vortices have been exploded, and the Newtonian principle of gravitation is now more

---

30. Jefferson uses legal shorthand to identify a law passed in the first year of the reign of Elizabeth I, 1558–59.

31. That is, "for burning a heretic."

32. "Furneaux passim." [Au.] A reference to the writings of Philip Furneaux (1723–86), who made observations on the laws established by Blackstone.

firmly established, on the basis of reason, than it would be were the government to step in, and to make it an article of necessary faith. Reason and experiment have been indulged, and error has fled before them. It is error alone which needs the support of government. Truth can stand by itself. Subject opinion to coercion: whom will you make your inquisitors? Fallible men; men governed by bad passions, by private as well as public reasons. And why subject it to coercion? To produce uniformity. But is uniformity of opinion desireable? No more than of face and stature. Introduce the bed of Procrustes then, and as there is danger that the large men may beat the small, make us all of a size, by lopping the former and stretching the latter. Difference of opinion is advantageous in religion. The several sects perform the office of a Censor morum over each other. Is uniformity attainable? Millions of innocent men, women, and children, since the introduction of Christianity, have been burnt, tortured, fined, imprisoned; yet we have not advanced one inch towards uniformity. What has been the effect of coercion? To make one half the world fools, and the other half hypocrites. To support roguery and error all over the earth. Let us reflect that it is inhabited by a thousand millions of people. That these profess probably a thousand different systems of religion. That ours is but one of that thousand. That if there be but one right, and ours that one, we should wish to see the 999 wandering sects gathered into the fold of truth. But against such a majority we cannot effect this by force. Reason and persuasion are the only practicable instruments. To make way for these, free enquiry must be indulged; and how can we wish others to indulge it while we refuse it ourselves. But every state, says an inquisitor, has established some religion. No two, say I, have established the same. Is this a proof of the infallibility of establishments? Our sister states of Pennsylvania and New York, however, have long subsisted without any establishment at all. The experiment was new and doubtful when they made it. It has answered beyond conception. They flourish infinitely. Religion is well supported; of various kinds, indeed, but all good enough; all sufficient to preserve peace and order: or if a sect arises, whose tenets would subvert morals, good sense has fair play, and reasons and laughs it out of doors, without suffering the state to be troubled with it. They do not hang more malefactors than we do. They are not more disturbed with religious dissensions. On the contrary, their harmony is unparalleled, and can be ascribed to nothing but their unbounded tolerance, because there is no other circum-

stance in which they differ from every nation on earth. They have made the happy discovery, that the way to silence religious disputes, is to take no notice of them. Let us too give this experiment fair play, and get rid, while we may, of those tyrannical laws. It is true, we are as yet secured against them by the spirit of the times. I doubt whether the people of this country would suffer an execution for heresy, or a three years imprisonment for not comprehending the mysteries of the Trinity. But is the spirit of the people an infallible, a permanent reliance? Is it government? Is this the kind of protection we receive in return for the rights we give up? Besides, the spirit of the times may alter, will alter. Our rulers will become corrupt, our people careless. A single zealot may commence persecutor, and better men be his victims. It can never be too often repeated, that the time for fixing every essential right on a legal basis is while our rulers are honest, and ourselves united. From the conclusion of this war we shall be going down hill. It will not then be necessary to resort every moment to the people for support. They will be forgotten, therefore, and their rights disregarded. They will forget themselves, but in the sole faculty of making money, and will never think of uniting to effect a due respect for their rights. The shackles, therefore, which shall not be knocked off at the conclusion of this war, will remain on us long, will be made heavier and heavier, till our rights shall revive or expire in a convulsion.

QUERY 18 • The Particular Customs and Manners That May Happen to Be Received in That State

Manners

It is difficult to determine on the standard by which the manners of a nation may be tried, whether *catholic,* or *particular.* It is more difficult for a native to bring to that standard the manners of his own nation, familiarized to him by habit. There must doubtless be an unhappy influence on the manners of our people produced by the existence of slavery among us. The whole commerce between master and slave is a perpetual exercise of the most boisterous passions, the most unremitting despotism on the one part, and degrading submissions on the other. Our children see this, and learn to imitate it; for man is an imitative animal. This quality is the germ of all education in him. From his cradle to his grave he is learning to do what he sees others do. If a parent could find no motive either in his philanthropy or his self-love, for restraining the intemperance of passion towards his slave, it should always be a sufficient one that his child is present. But generally it is not sufficient. The parent storms, the child looks on, catches the lineaments of wrath, puts on the same airs in the circle of smaller slaves, gives a loose to his worst of passions, and thus nursed, educated, and daily exercised in tyranny, cannot but be stamped by it with odious peculiarities. The man must be a prodigy who can retain his manners and morals undepraved by such circumstances. And with what execration should the statesman be loaded, who permitting one half the citizens thus to trample on the rights of the other, transforms those into despots, and these into enemies, destroys the morals of the one part, and the amor patriae of the other. For if a slave can have a country in this world, it must be any other in preference to that in which he is born to live and labour for another: in which he must lock up the faculties of his nature, contribute as far as depends on his individual endeavours to the evanishment of the human race, or entail his own miserable condition on the endless generations proceeding from him. With the morals of the people, their industry also is destroyed. For in a warm climate, no man will labour for himself who can make another labour for him. This is so true, that of the proprietors of slaves a very small proportion indeed are ever seen to labour. And can the liberties of a nation be thought secure when we have removed their only firm basis, a conviction in the minds of the people that these liberties are of the gift of God? That they are not to be violated but with his wrath? Indeed I tremble for my country when I reflect that God is just: that his justice cannot sleep for ever: that considering numbers, nature and natural means only, a revolution of the wheel of fortune, an exchange of situation, is among possible events: that it may become probable by supernatural interference! The Almighty has no attribute which can take side with us in such a contest.—But it is impossible to be temperate and to pursue this subject through the various considerations of policy, of morals, of history natural and civil. We must be contented to hope they will force their way into every one's mind. I think a change already perceptible, since the origin of the present revolution. The spirit of the master is abating, that of the slave rising from the dust, his condition mollifying, the way I hope preparing, under the auspices of heaven, for a total emancipation, and that this is disposed, in the order of events, to be with the consent of the masters, rather than by their extirpation.

LETTER TO FRANÇOIS JEAN, MARQUIS DE CHASTELLUX

September 2, 1785[1]

Dear Sir

You were so kind as to allow me a fortnight to read your journey through Virginia. But you should have thought of this indulgence while you were writing it, and have rendered it less interesting if you meant that your readers should have been longer engaged with it. In fact I devoured it at a single meal, and a second reading scarce allowed me sang froid enough to mark a few errors in the names of persons and places which I note on a paper herein inclosed, with an inconsiderable error or two in facts which I have also noted because I supposed you wished to state them correctly. From this general approbation however you must allow me to except about a dozen pages in the earlier part of the book which I read with a continued blush from beginning to end, as it presented me a lively picture of what I wish to be, but am not. No, my dear Sir, the thousand millionth part of what you there say, is more than I deserve. It might perhaps have passed in Europe at the time you wrote it, and the exaggeration might not have been detected. But consider that the animal is now brought there, and that every one will take his dimensions for himself. The friendly complexion of your mind has betrayed you into a partiality of which the European spectator will be divested. Respect to yourself therefore will require indispensably that you expunge the whole of those pages except your own judicious observations interspersed among them on Animal and physical subjects. With respect to my countrymen there is surely nothing which can render them uneasy, in the observations made on them. They know that they are not perfect, and will be sensible that you have viewed them with a philanthropic eye. You say much good of them, and less ill than they are conscious may be said with truth. I have studied their character with attention. I have thought them, as you found them, aristocratical, pompous, clan-

---

1. The marquis de Chastellux (1734–88) served during the Seven Years War and the Revolutionary War in North America. During the 1780s, he traveled through parts of North America. He sent Jefferson a copy of his remarks on northern Virginia; this letter is Jefferson's response. The text is from *The Papers of Thomas Jefferson,* vol. 8, ed. Julian P. Boyd (1953).

nish, indolent, hospitable, and I should have added, disinterested, but you say attached to their interest. This is the only trait in their character wherein our observations differ. I have always thought them so careless of their interests, so thoughtless in their expences and in all their transactions of business that I had placed it among the vices of their character, as indeed most virtues when carried beyond certain bounds degenerate into vices. I had even ascribed this to it's cause, to that warmth of their climate which unnerves and unmans both body and mind. While on this subject I will give you my idea of the characters of the several states.

In the North they are	In the South they are
cool	fiery
sober	Voluptuary
laborious	indolent
persevering	unsteady
independant	independant
jealous of their own liberties, and just to those of others	zealous for their own liberties, but trampling on those of others
interested	generous
chicaning	candid
superstitious and hypocritical in their religion	without attachment or pretentions to any religion but that of the heart.

These characteristics grow weaker and weaker by gradation from North to South and South to North, insomuch that an observing traveller, without the aid of the quadrant may always know his latitude by the character of the people among whom he finds himself. It is in Pennsylvania that the two characters seem to meet and blend and to form a people free from the extremes both of vice and virtue. Peculiar circumstances have given to New York the character which climate would have given had she been placed on the South instead of the North side of Pennsylvania. Perhaps too other circumstances may have occasioned in Virginia a transplantation of a particular vice foreign to it's climate. You could judge of this with more impartiality than I could, and the probability is that your estimate of them is the most just. I think it for their good that the vices of their character should be pointed out to them that they may amend them; for a malady of either body or mind once known is half cured.

I wish you would add to this peice your letter to Mr.

Madison on the expediency of introducing the arts into America. I found in that a great deal of matter, very many observations, which would be useful to the legislators of America, and to the general mass of citizens. I read it with great pleasure and analysed it's contents that I might fix them in my own mind. I have the honor to be with very sincere esteem Dear Sir Your most obedient & most humble servt.,

TH: JEFFERSON

LETTER TO MARIE JEAN ANTOINE NICOLAS CARITAT, MARQUIS DE CONDORCET

August 30, 1791[1]

Dear Sir

I am to acknolege the reciept of your favor on the subject of the element of measure adopted by France. Candor obliges me to confess that it is not what I would have approved. It is liable to the inexactitude of mensuration as to that part of the quadrant of the earth which is to be measured, that is to say as to one tenth of the quadrant, and as to the remaining nine tenths they are to be calculated on conjectural data, presuming the figure of the earth which has not yet been proved. It is liable too to the objection that no nation but your own can come at it; because yours is the only nation within which a meridian can be found of such extent crossing the 45th. degree and terminating at both ends in a level. We may certainly say then that this measure is uncatholic, and I would rather have seen you depart from Catholicism in your religion than in your Philosophy.

I am happy to be able to inform you that we have now in the United States a negro, the son of a black man born in Africa, and of a black woman born in the United States,

---

1. The marquis de Condorcet (1743–94) had sent Jefferson a report about a unit of measure by the French Academy of Sciences. Jefferson wrote in return about Benjamin Banneker, the African American mathematician and almanac maker. He wrote to Banneker at the same time he was writing Condorcet a polite letter. Banneker published Jefferson's letter along with his own letter to Jefferson (see the Banneker selections). The text is from *The Papers of Thomas Jefferson*, vol. 22, ed. Charles T. Cullen (1986).

who is a very respectable Mathematician. I procured him to be employed under one of our chief directors in laying out the new federal city on the Patowmac, and in the intervals of his leisure, while on that work, he made an Almanac for the next year, which he sent me in his own handwriting, and which I inclose to you. I have seen very elegant solutions of Geometrical problems by him. Add to this that he is a very worthy and respectable member of society. He is a free man. I shall be delighted to see these instances of moral eminence so multiplied as to prove that the want of talents observed in them is merely the effect of their degraded condition, and not proceeding from any difference in the structure of the parts on which intellect depends.

I am looking ardently to the completion of the glorious work in which your country is engaged. I view the general condition of Europe as hanging on the success or failure of France. Having set such an example of philosophical arrangement within, I hope it will be extended without your limits also, to your dependants and to your friends in every part of the earth.—Present my affectionate respects to Madame de Condorcet, and accept yourself assurance of the sentiments of esteem & attachment with which I have the honour to be Dear Sir Your most obedt & most humble servt,

TH: JEFFERSON

THE DECLARATION OF INDEPENDENCE

During the trying spring months of 1776, the Second Continental Congress meeting in Philadelphia, having resolved during the previous fall and winter to form a Continental Army and a Continental Navy, faced what had become the inevitable question of rebelling against Great Britain. In May, the Congress concluded that colonies governed by royal authority should have their governments replaced by authority from the people being governed, thus effectually undercutting the colonists' sense of obligation to the Crown. Richard Henry Lee (1732–94), who had been an early opponent of British administration in Virginia, his home region, proposed to the Congress on June 7, 1776, that "these united Colonies are, and of a right ought to be, free and independent states." Lee argued that as independent states, the colonies, under the new authority of the governed, would be able to create their own foreign alliances and confederate to protect and govern themselves.

Within days, a committee was named to draft a statement regarding the independence of the British colonies from Great Britain. The committee included John Adams (1735–1826) of Massachusetts, Benjamin Franklin (1706–90) of Pennsylvania, Roger Sherman (1721–93) of Connecticut, Robert Livingston of New York (1746–1813), and Thomas Jefferson (1743–1826) of Virginia. It was Jefferson who set out to draft the statement about the necessity of independence, while debates about declaring independence continued in Congress. He gave the draft to Adams and then to Franklin for review before showing it to others meeting in the Congress. Both editors of Jefferson's draft considered that some of Jefferson's statements regarding the tyranny of George III were too personal and perhaps inaccurate in terms of Jefferson's claim that George III had caused and supported slavery in the colonies. In becoming a personal attack against George III, the document could miss the point of the larger political issue before the committee—independence of the colonies—so they recommended excisions. The committee presented the draft formally to Congress on June 28, and by July 2, Lee's original analysis, now a resolution, was passed in Congress. The Declaration of Independence was adopted, with revisions Jefferson noted in his private writings, on July 4, 1776. The final copy of the paper document of the statement of independence, now called the Declaration of Independence, was prepared for signatures on August 2, and all but three delegates (who could not be present at this occasion) signed it that day. But the Declaration of Independence was already history when it was signed in August. It had been printed as a broadside, published in various newspapers, and reprinted throughout the colonies.

THE UNANIMOUS DECLARATION OF THE THIRTEEN UNITED STATES OF AMERICA,

Adopted in Congress, July 4, 1776[1]

In Congress, July 4, 1776

The Unanimous Declaration of the Thirteen United States of America

When in the Course of human events, it becomes necessary for one people to dissolve the political bands which have connected them with another, and to assume among the powers of the earth, the separate and equal station to which the Laws of Nature and of Nature's God entitle them, a decent respect to the opinions of mankind requires that they should declare the causes which impel them to the separation. We hold these truths to be self-evident, that all men are created equal, that they are endowed by their Creator with certain unalienable Rights, that among these are Life, Liberty and the pursuit of Happiness. That to secure these rights, Governments are instituted among Men, deriving their just powers from the consent of the governed. That whenever any Form of Government becomes destructive of these ends, it is the Right of the People to alter or to abolish it, and to institute new Government, laying its foundation on such principles and organizing its powers in such form, as to them shall seem most likely to effect their Safety and Happiness. Prudence, indeed, will dictate that Governments long established should not be changed for light and transient causes; and accordingly all experience hath shewn, that mankind are more disposed to suffer, while evils are sufferable, than to right themselves by abolishing the forms to which they are accustomed. But when a long train of abuses and usurpations, pursuing invariably the same Object evinces a design to reduce them under absolute Despotism, it is their right, it is their duty, to throw off such Government, and to provide New Guards for their future security. Such has been the patient sufferance of these Colonies; and such is now the necessity which constrains them to alter their former Systems of Government. The history of the present King of Great Britain[2] is a history of repeated injuries and usurpations, all having in direct object the establishment of an absolute Tyranny over these States. To prove this, let Facts be submitted to a candid world. He has refused his Assent to Laws, the most wholesome and necessary for the public good. He has forbidden his Governors to pass Laws of immediate and pressing importance, unless suspended in their operation till his Assent should be obtained; and when so suspended, he has utterly neglected to attend to them. He has refused to pass other Laws for the accommodation of large districts of people, unless these people would relinquish the right of Representation in the Legislature, a right inestimable to them and formidable to tyrants only. He has called together legislative bodies at places unusual, uncomfortable, and distant from the depository of their public Records, for the sole purpose of fatiguing them into compliance with his measures. He has dissolved Representative Houses repeatedly, for opposing with manly firmness his invasions on the right of the people. He has refused for a long time, after such dissolutions, to cause others to be elected; whereby the Legislative powers, incapable of Annihilation, have returned to the People at large for their exercise; the State remaining in the mean time exposed to all the dangers of invasion from without, and convulsions within. He has endeavoured to prevent the population of these States; for that purpose obstructing the Laws for Naturalization of Foreigners; refusing to pass others to encourage their migrations hither, and raising the conditions of new Appropriations of Lands. He has obstructed the Administration of Justice, by refusing his Assent to Laws for establishing Judiciary powers. He has made Judges dependent on his Will alone, for the tenure of their offices, and the amount and payment of their salaries. He has erected a multitude of New Offices, and sent hither swarms of Officers to harass our people, and eat out their substance. He has kept among us, in times of peace, standing Armies without the Consent of our legislatures. He has affected to render the Military independent of and superior to the Civil power. He has combined with others[3] to subject us to a jurisdiction foreign to our constitution, and unacknowledged by our laws; giving his Assent to their Acts of pretended Legislation: For Quartering large bodies of armed troops among us: For protecting them, by a mock Trial, from punishment for any Murders which they should commit on the Inhabitants of these States: For cutting off our Trade with all parts of the world: For impos-

---

1. The text is the Declaration of Independence as finally adopted in Congress, taken from *The Papers of Thomas Jefferson,* vol. 1, ed. Julian P. Boyd (1950).

2. King George III (1738–1820) reigned from 1760 to 1820.

3. British Parliament.

ing Taxes on us without our Consent: For depriving us in many cases of the benefits of Trial by Jury: For transporting us beyond Seas to be tried for pretended offences: For abolishing the free System of English Laws in a neighbouring Province,[4] establishing therein an Arbitrary government, and enlarging its Boundaries so as to render it at once an example and fit instrument for introducing the same absolute rule into these Colonies: For taking away our Charters, abolishing our most valuable Laws, and altering fundamentally the Forms of our Governments: For suspending our own Legislatures, and declaring themselves invested with power to legislate for us in all cases whatsoever. He has abdicated Government here, by declaring us out of his Protection and waging War against us. He has plundered our seas, ravaged our Coasts, burnt our towns, and destroyed the Lives of our people. He is at this time transporting large Armies of foreign Mercenaries[5] to compleat the works of death, desolation and tyranny, already begun with circumstances of Cruelty & perfidy scarcely paralleled in the most barbarous ages, and totally unworthy the Head of a civilized nation. He has constrained our fellow Citizens taken Captive on the high Seas to bear Arms against their Country, to become the executioners of their friends and Brethren, or to fall themselves by their Hands. He has excited domestic insurrections amongst us, and has endeavoured to bring on the inhabitants of our frontiers, the merciless Indian Savages, whose known rule of warfare, is an undistinguished destruction of all ages, sexes and conditions. In every stage of these Oppressions We have Petitioned for Redress in the most humble terms: Our repeated Petitions have been answered only by repeated injury. A Prince, whose character is thus marked by every act which may define a Tyrant, is unfit to be the ruler of a free people. Nor have We been wanting in attentions to our British brethren. We have warned them from time to time of attempts by their legislature to extend an unwarrantable jurisdiction over us. We have reminded them of the circumstances of our emigration and settlement here. We have appealed to their native justice and magnanimity, and we have conjured them by the ties of our common kindred to disavow these usurpations, which, would inevitably interrupt our connections and correspondence. They too have been deaf to the voice of justice and of consanguinity. We must, therefore, acquiesce in the necessity, which denounces our Separation, and hold them, as we hold the rest of mankind, Enemies in War, in Peace Friends.

We, therefore, the Representatives of the united States of America, in General Congress, Assembled, appealing to the Supreme Judge of the world for the rectitude of our intentions, do, in the Name, and by Authority of the good People of these Colonies, solemnly publish and declare, That these United Colonies are, and of right ought to be Free and Independent States; that they are Absolved from all Allegiance to the British Crown, and that all political connection between them and the State of Great Britain, is and ought to be totally dissolved; and that as Free and Independent States, they have full Power to levy War, conclude Peace, contract Alliances, establish Commerce, and to do all other Acts and Things which Independent States may of right do. And for the support of this Declaration, with a firm reliance on the protection of divine Providence, we mutually pledge to each other our Lives, our Fortunes and our sacred Honor.

---

4. Britain's Quebec Act of 1774 empowered the French in Quebec by restoring French civil law to the province, giving political recognition to Catholics, and formally extending the boundaries of the province to the Ohio River. The act was considered "intolerable" by the colonists, who considered that their territory had been circumscribed and their original motivations for settlement, to sponsor different forms of Protestantism, had been undermined.

5. The British government recruited soldiers from areas outside Britain to come to fight for the cause of Britain. German soldiers—all of whom were typically called "Hessians" although they came from different groups—were showing up in increasing numbers in the colonies. About one-third of Britain's soldiers were Germans, and they fought in nearly every important military campaign.

BRITISH LOYALISTS IN BRITISH NORTH AMERICA

John Adams once estimated that a third of the population of the British colonies of North America had opposed independence from Britain. Historians of the era have placed the estimate at a smaller number, about 500,000 loyalists, or about 20 percent of the white population. Whatever the number of loyalists (frequently called Tories), however, it is clear that only a small percentage of them, about 19,000, actually took up arms in behalf of Great Britain. Many others gave support in other ways—by not participating in local militia meetings or providing foodstuffs or clothing for colonials who were fighting; by writing anti-Revolutionary propaganda for the press; and less frequently but most notably, as in the case of William Franklin (Benjamin Franklin's son), by leading raiding parties against local men and their families who supported the cause of rebellion.

Deciding to enter the war against Britain was not easy. It was treason, first of all, and the penalty for treason was death. Also, entering the rebellion might lead to the total loss of any accumulated property if the war effort were lost. Loyalists who held much property, especially plantation-holding loyalists of the southern colonies who owned slaves, feared the loss of a whole way of life they had come to know and accept. Yet loyalists were not all large landholders, as one might assume, nor were they entirely from the south. Several loyalists were of Scottish descent, and these more recent immigrants were used to a colonial system (like the one in Scotland) that operated as England was attempting to operate in the North American colonies. So for these loyalists, not just landholders, the war had a particularly dangerous and radical edge that belied their Scottish and Scotch-Irish heritage. Loyalists came from all ranks. Wealthy merchants and royal officials were joined by independent farmers and shopkeepers.

Contributing factors, such as relative wealth and ethnic ties, influenced the thinking of loyalists, then. The relative length of time one's family had been in the colonies also influenced whether one would want to remain loyal or not. In many instances, loyalists were relative newcomers to North America, part of a great migration that had occurred in the first quarter of the eighteenth century. The pro-Revolution (Whig) colonists' sense of having original charter rights and their experiences of their purported accumulated wrongs over time did not always influence the newcomers sufficiently to encourage them to consider rebellion. Other ideological concerns also came to the fore for the loyalists. For instance, some loyalists did not share attitudes expressed by pro-Revolutionary propaganda about the equality of all people. Indeed, many believed that some degree of hierarchy (and, thus, some inequality) in society was necessary, a part of the Christian God's plan. Some loyalists, including many people who were affiliated with the Society of Friends (Quakers), shared the revolutionary agitators' complaints about Britain's treatment of the colonists, but they did not believe that political grievances justified violence and war.

The loyalists did not have an easy time of it during the American Revolution against Great Britain, and they had no better a time after the war was over. They lost their property, and they lost their lives. While some loyalists stalwartly remained in their homes during and after the Revolution, most others fled to Canada or back to Britain. Almost all those who fled had their property seized without compensation, according to standard wartime policy everywhere. Some returned after the war and attempted to regain their property, with mixed success, as in the case of Elizabeth Graeme Ferguson, whose husband finally fled during the Revolution and who, as a result of the system of coverture that held her rights to be subsidiary to her husband's, nearly lost her family's large homestead, despite her own neutrality during the war. The largest portion of loyalists went to Canada and remained there.

WILLIAM FRANKLIN (1730–1813)

William Franklin, the son of Benjamin Franklin whose mother remains unknown to this day, was raised in Franklin's household and given all the advantages of education and association that being Franklin's son could offer. He became an administrator and public official in North America and was the royally appointed governor of New Jersey at the time the Declaration of Independence was signed. As a young man, he had served as a captain among the Pennsylvania military forces in Canada, when the border was challenged by the French. He was first appointed to public office in 1754, when his father, then postmaster general, named him comptroller of the post office in Philadelphia. He also served as clerk of the Pennsylvania Assembly. In 1757, William accompanied his father to London, where he studied law and was admitted to the bar, and in 1763, he became New Jersey's governor. William, openly opposing his father's wishes and interests, remained a staunch supporter of royal authority, continuing his support during the Revolution by leading raids against local families who had joined the revolutionary cause and attempting to take over military stores. In 1776, William was arrested by order of the Provincial Congress of New Jersey and imprisoned for two years. In 1782 he returned to England, where he remained for the rest of his life. Although he might have wished for a reconciliation with his father after the war, such a reconciliation never occurred.

SPEECH BEFORE THE NEW JERSEY ASSEMBLY, JANUARY 13, 1775[1]

Gentlemen of the Council, and
Gentlemen of the Assembly,

It would argue not only a great Want of Duty to His Majesty, but of Regard to the good People of this Province, were I, on this Occasion, to pass over in Silence the late alarming Transactions in this and the neighbouring Colonies, or not endeavour to prevail on you to exert yourselves in preventing those Mischiefs to this Country, which, without your timely Interposition, will, in all Probability, be the Consequence.

It is not for me to decide on the particular Merits of the Dispute between Great-Britain and her Colonies, nor do I mean to censure those who conceive themselves aggrieved for aiming at a Redress of their Grievances. It is a Duty they owe themselves, their Country, and their Posterity. All that I would wish to guard you against, is the giving any Countenance or Encouragement to that destructive Mode of Proceeding which has been unhappily adopted in Part by some of the Inhabitants in this Colony, and has been carried so far in others as totally to subvert their former Constitution. It has already struck at the Authority of one of the Branches of the Legislature in a particular Manner. And, if you, Gentlemen of the Assembly, should give your Approbation to Transactions of this Nature, you will do as much as lies in your Power to destroy that Form of Government of which you are an important Part, and which it is your Duty by all lawful Means to preserve. To you your Constituents have intrusted a peculiar Guardianship of their Rights and Privileges. You are their legal Representatives, and you cannot, without a manifest Breach of your Trust, suffer any Body of Men, in this or any of the other Provinces, to usurp and exercise any of the Powers vested in you by the Constitution. It behoves you particularly, who must be constitutionally supposed to speak the Sense of the People at large, to be extremely cautious in consenting to any Act whereby you may engage them as Parties in, and make them answerable for Measures which may have a Tendency to involve them in Difficulties far greater than those they aim to avoid.

Besides, there is not, Gentlemen, the least Necessity, consequently there will not be the least Excuse for your running any such Risks on the present Occasion. If you are really disposed to represent to the King any Inconveniences you conceive yourselves to lie under, or to make any Propositions on the present State of *America,* I can assure you, from the best Authority, that such Representations or Propositions will be properly attended to, and certainly have greater Weight coming from each Colony in it's separate Capacity, than in a Channel, of the Propriety and Legality of which there may be much Doubt.

You have now pointed out to you, Gentlemen, two Roads—one evidently leading to Peace, Happiness, and a Restoration of the publick Tranquility—the other inevitably conducting you to Anarchy, Misery, and all the Horrors of a Civil War. Your Wisdom, your Prudence, your Regard for the true Interests of the People, will be best known when you have shewn to which Road you give the Preference. If to the former, you will probably afford Satisfaction to the moderate, the sober, and the discreet Part of your Constituents. If to the latter, you will, perhaps for a Time, give Pleasure to the warm, the rash, and the inconsiderate among them, who, I would willingly hope, violent as is the Temper of the present Times, are not even now the Majority. But it may be well for you to remember,

---

1. William Franklin convened his Assembly at Perth Amboy in January, 1775, in an effort to stave off the members' interest in joining the Continental Congress. He hoped the Assembly would submit a separate petition to the British Crown asking for the redress of colonial grievances. His argument hinged on a legal concern, that an unconstitutional congress was usurping the rights of the New Jersey Britons. His speech was first published in the New Jersey State Archives, in *Votes and Proceedings of the General Assembly of the Colony of New Jersey* (1775).

should any Calamity hereafter befal them from your Compliance with their Inclinations, instead of pursuing, as you ought, the Dictates of your own Judgment, that the Consequences of their returning to a proper Sense of their Conduct, may prove deservedly to yourselves.

I shall say no more at present on this disagreeable Subject, but only to repeat an Observation I made to a former Assembly on a similar Occasion. "Every Breach of the Constitution, whether it proceeds from the Crown or the People, is, in its Effects, equally destructive to the Rights of both. It is the Duty, therefore, of those who are intrusted with Government, to be equally careful in guarding against Encroachments from the one as the other. But *It is* (says one of the wisest of Men) *a most infallible Symptom of the dangerous State of Liberty, when the chief Men of a free Country shew a greater Regard to Popularity than to their own Judgment.*"

W. Franklin

HANNAH GRIFFITTS (1727–1817)

A lifelong resident of Philadelphia, Hannah Griffitts professed the beliefs of the Society of Friends (Quakers), which include a peace testimony that does not condone the taking of another's life for any reason. Griffitts, a single woman, spent her lifetime caring for her relatives. She wrote poetry throughout her long life, exchanging it through her wide network of female friends and relatives. Known among her literary friends as Fidelia, Griffitts received mentoring in her writing from her friend Susanna Wright, among others. Griffitts's ideas about the Revolution against Great Britain were influenced by her Quaker beliefs, but she expressed in her writings many of the ideas held by loyalists who were not Quakers, as well. This poem, a slur aimed at Thomas Paine, reveals in its biting criticism of Paine—that he had a venal pen, one that could be purchased for any price—the extent of Paine's general popularity. The poem was circulated widely among Griffitt's loyalist friends. The version that follows was copied into the copybook of her close friend, Milcah Martha Moore.

ON READING A FEW PARAGRAPHS IN "THE CRISIS," APRIL 1777[1]

Paine, tho' thy Tongue may now run glibber,
Warm'd with thy independent Glow,
Thou art indeed, the boldest Fibber,
I ever knew or wish to know.
5 Here Page & Page,[2] ev'n num'rous Pages,
Are void of Breeding, Sense or Truth,
I hope thou dont receive thy Wages,
As Tutor to our rising Youth.

Of female Manners never scribble,
Nor with thy Rudeness wound our Ear,   10
How e'er thy trimming Pen may quibble,
The Delicate—is not thy Sphere;
And now to prove how false thy Stories
By Facts,—which wont admit a Doubt
Know there are conscientious Tories
And one poor Whig at least without   15
Wilt thou permit the Muse to mention,
A Whisper circulated round,
"Let Howe[3] encrease the Scribblers Pension
"No more will Paine a Whig be found."—   20
For not from Principle, but Lucre,
He gains his Bread from out the Fire,
Let Court & Congress, both stand neuter,[4]
And the poor Creature must expire.—*Finis*

---

1. Griffitts's poem is a reaction to Thomas Paine's *Crisis* papers. Text is from *Milcah Martha Moore's Book: A Commonplace Book from Revolutionary America,* ed. Catherine La Courreye Blecki and Karin A. Wulf (1997).

2. Moore made a note at this place that Griffitts's poem cited some pages from Paine.

---

3. William Howe (1729–1814), English general who captured Philadelphia in 1777.

4. That is, neutral.

JACOB BAILEY (1731–1808)

Jacob Bailey was born in Massachusetts and educated for the ministry at Harvard. He served as a congregational minister briefly before going to England to be ordained as an Anglican (Church of England) minister. Bailey returned to North America in 1760 to serve an Anglican ministry in Maine among a largely congregationalist community that did not welcome members of the Church of England. In the 1770s, as tensions grew before the beginning of the Revolution, Bailey was persecuted by the local community for his loyalty to Britain. The pressure grew until 1779, when Bailey and his family fled to Nova Scotia, like many other loyalists. During the Revolution, Bailey wrote a number of political verse satires, including the lengthy poem "America." He also wrote prose descriptions of both Maine and Nova Scotia and a satiric poem about itinerant preachers, "The Adventures of Jack Ramble, the Methodist Preacher."

THE FACTIOUS DEMAGOGUE, A PORTRAIT[1]

As for his Religion, he could mix,
And blend it well with politics,
For 'twas his favourite opinion
In mobs was seated all dominion:
All pow'r and might he understood
Rose from the sov'reign multitude:
That right and wrong, that good and ill,
Were nothing but the rabble's will:
Tho' they renounce the truth for fiction,
In nonsense trust, and contradiction;
And tho' they change ten times a day
As fear or int'rest leads the way;
And what this hour is law and reason,
Declare, the next, revolt and treason;
Yet we each doctrine must receive,
And with a pious grin believe,
In ev'ry thing the people's choice
As true as God Almighty's voice.
'Tis all divine which they've aver'd
However foolish or absurd.
If in a tumult they agree
That men from all restraints are free,
At liberty to cut our throats;
'Tis sanctified by major votes;
To bathe the snow in kindred blood,
When it promotes the public good;
That is, when men of factious nature,

Aim with ambition to be greater.
Should they in mighty Congress plod
To set up *Hancock*[2] for a *God:*
A *God* in earnest he must be,
With all the forms of deity;
The high, the low, the rich, the poor,
Must quake and tremble at his pow'r;
And who denies him adoration,
Is sentenc'd straightway to damnation.
Yea, they have pow'r to godify
An onion, turnip, or a fly:
And some have even understood
To consecrate a pole of wood;
Then force their neighbours, great and small,
Before it on their knees to fall.
Since from the people only springs
The right of making Gods and Kings,
Whoe'er derives authority
From any Sov'reign Powers on high,
Is at the best a wicked dreamer,
A stupid *Tory,* and blasphemer.
From this we see, 'tis demonstration
There's no Supreme in the creation,
Except that mighty pow'r, the people:
That weather-cock which rides the steeple;
That noisy and licentious rabble,
Which storms e'en Heaven itself with gabble:
Should these give sanction to a lie,
'Tis plain that Heav'n must ratify!

---

1. This poem was first published in *Rivington's Gazette* (October 4, 1780) and later published in *The Loyalist Poetry of the Revolution,* ed. Winthrop Sargent (1857).

2. Wealthy merchant and shipowner John Hancock (1737–93) was influential in many events of the rebellion. On September 1, 1780, Hancock became the first governor of Massachusetts.

JOSEPH STANSBURY (1740–1809)

Joseph Stansbury emigrated to Philadelphia from England in 1767 and enjoyed several years of success as a merchant there. During the Revolution, Stansbury was outspoken in his opposition to the war, and in 1780 he was arrested as a spy, under the suspicion that he was working in behalf of Benedict Arnold. He sat out the war in New York, the base for many loyalists who remained in the colonies. Following the war, Stansbury moved to Nova Scotia, where he wrote the poem of exile printed next. He tried to return to Philadelphia, but he was received coldly among those whom he had known and returned to New York, where he lived for the remainder of his life.

TO CORDELIA[1]

Believe me, Love, this vagrant life
  O'er Nova Scotia's wilds to roam,
While far from children, friends, or wife,
  Or place that I can call a home
Delights not me;—another way
My treasures, pleasures, wishes lay.

In piercing, wet, and wintry skies,
  Where man would seem in vain to toil,
I see, where'er I turn my eyes,
  Luxuriant pasture, trees and soil.
Uncharm'd I see:—another way
My fondest hopes and wishes lay.

Oh could I through the future see
  Enough to form a settled plan,
To feed my infant train and thee
  And fill the rank and style of man:
I'd cheerful be the livelong day;
Since all my wishes point that way.

But when I see a sordid shed
  Of birchen bark, procured with care,
Design'd to shield the aged head
  Which British mercy placed there—
'Tis too, too much: I cannot stay,
But turn with streaming eyes away.

Oh! how your heart would bleed to view
  Six pretty prattlers like your own,
Expos'd to every wind that blew;
  Condemn'd in such a hut to moan.
Could this be borne, Cordelia, say?
Contented in your cottage stay.

'Tis true, that in this climate rude,
  The mind resolv'd may happy be;
And may, with toil and solitude,
Live independent and be free.
So the lone hermit yields to slow decay:
Unfriended lives—unheeded glides away.

If so far humbled that no pride remains,
  But moot indifference which way flows the stream;
Resign'd to penury, its cares and pains;
  And hope has left you like a painted dream;
Then here, Cordelia, bend your pensive way,
And close the evening of Life's wretched day.

---

1. The poem was written around 1784, while Stansbury was in exile in Nova Scotia. It was published in *The Loyal Verses of Joseph Stansbury and Doctor Jonathan Odell, Relating to the American Revolution,* ed. Winthrop Sargent (1860).

JONATHAN ODELL (1737–1818)

Like his close friend, Joseph Stansbury, Jonathan Odell was accused of spying during the situation surrounding Benedict Arnold, but unlike Stansbury, a newcomer to the colonies, Odell's family had long been settled in the British colonies of North America. A Princeton graduate, Odell studied medicine and became a surgeon, working for the British army in the West Indies for a time. After resigning his medical post, Odell went to England, where he studied for ministry with the Church of England. He returned to New Jersey as an Anglican chaplain and physician in 1767. Odell's loyalism during the years of revolutionary insurgency brought him sufficient attention that he was placed under a sort of house arrest, with severe restrictions upon his activities. Odell escaped to the British lines in 1776, and he served a variety of active roles in engagements against the colonial militias. When the war was over, he went back to England with his family for a time, but he returned to North America in 1784, where he and the family joined the loyalist settlement in Nova Scotia. *The American Times,* Odell's longest poem, reveals the bitterness with which many loyalists met the success of colonials' revolution against Great Britain.

from THE AMERICAN TIMES[1]

PART I.

When Faction, pois'nous as the scorpion's sting,
Infects the people and insults the King;
When foul Sedition skulks no more conceal'd,
But grasps the sword and rushes to the field;
5　When Justice, Law, and Truth are in disgrace,
And Treason, Fraud, and Murder fill their place;
Smarting beneath accumulated woes,
Shall we not dare the tyrants to expose?
We will, we must—tho' mighty Laurens[2] frown,
10　Or Hancock[3] with his rabble hunt us down;
Champions of virtue, we'll alike disdain
The guards of Washington, the lies of Payne;
And greatly bear, without one anxious throb,
The wrath of Congress, or its lords the mob.
15　Bad are the Times, almost too bad to paint;
The whole head sickens, the whole heart is faint;
The State is rotten, rotten to the core,
'Tis all one bruize, one putrefying sore.
Here Anarchy before the gaping crowd
20　Proclaims the people's majesty aloud;
There Folly runs with eagerness about,
And prompts the cheated populace to shout;
Here paper-dollars meagre Famine holds,

There votes of Congress Tyranny unfolds;
With doctrines strange in matter and in dress,　25
Here sounds the pulpit, and there groans the press;
Confusion blows her trump—and far and wide
The noise is heard—the plough is thrown aside;
The awl, the needle, and the shuttle drops;
Tools change to swords, and camps succeed to shops;　30
The doctor's glister-pipe, the lawyer's quill,
Transform'd to guns, retain the power to kill;
From garrets, cellars, rushing thro' the street,
The new-born statesmen in committee meet;
Legions of senators infest the land,　35
And mushroom generals thick as mushrooms stand.
Ye western climes, where youthful plenty smil'd,
Ye plains just rescued from the dreary wild,
Ye cities just emerging into fame,
Ye minds new ting'd with learning's sacred flame,　40
Ye people wondering at your swift increase,
Sons of united liberty and peace,
How are your glories in a moment fled?
See, Pity weeps, and Honour hangs his head.

O! for some magic voice, some pow'rful spell,　45
To call the Furies from profoundest hell;
Arise, ye Fiends, from dark Cocytus' brink;[4]
Soot all my paper; sulphurize my ink;
So with my theme the colours shall agree,
Brimstone and black, the livery of Lee.[5]　50

They come, they come!—convulsive heaves the ground,
Earth opens—Lo! they pour, they swarm around;
About me throng unnumber'd hideous shapes,
Infernal wolves, and bears, and hounds, and apes;
All Pandemonium stands reveal'd to sight;　55
Good monsters, give me leave, and let me write:
They will be notic'd—Memory, set them down,

----

1. *The American Times: A Satire in Three Parts* was originally printed as a pamphlet by New York printer, James Rivington, who at different times seems to have served as a spy for both the colonials and the supporters of the Crown. It was published in *The Loyal Verses of Joseph Stansbury and Doctor Jonathan Odell, Relating to the American Revolution,* ed. Winthrop Sargent (1860). The selection is taken from Part I of the poem.

2. Henry Laurens (1724–92) of South Carolina, a moderate in his stance regarding the Revolution, wrote pamphlets against the authority of the Crown and served in the Continental Congress.

3. John Hancock (1737–93).

4. Cocytus, the river of Hades, in Greek mythology.

5. Probably a reference to Richard Henry Lee (1732–94), who was influential in Virginia and, once the colonies united, an effectual leader in revolutionary agitation.

Tho' reason stand aghast, and order frown.[6]

. . .

185 Yet tho' the frantic populace applaud,
'Tis Satire's part to stigmatize the fraud.
Exult, ye jugglers, in your lucky tricks;
Yet on your fame the lasting brand we'll fix.
Cheat male and female, poison age and youth;
190 Still we'll pursue you with the goad of truth.
Whilst in mid-heav'n shines forth the golden flame,
Hancock and Adams shall be words of shame;
Whilst silver beams the face of night adorn,
Cooper of Boston shall be held in scorn.

195 Strike up, hell's music! roar, infernal drums!
Discharge the cannon—Lo! the warrior comes!
He comes, not tame as on Ohio's banks,
But rampant at the head of ragged ranks.
Hunger and itch are with him—Gates[7] and Wayne[8]—
200 And all the lice of Egypt in his train.
Sure these are Falstaff's soldiers,[9] poor and bare;
Or else the rotten regiments of Rag-fair:
Bid the French generals to their Chief advance,
And grace his suite—O shame! they're fled to France.
205 Wilt thou, great chief of Freedom's lawless sons,
Great captain of the western Goths and Huns,
Wilt thou for once permit a private man
To parley with thee, and thy conduct scan?
At Reason's bar has Catiline[10] been heard:
210 At Reason's bar e'en Cromwell[11] has appear'd:
Successless, or successful, all must stand
At her tribunal with uplifted hand.

Severe, but just, the case she fairly states;
And fame or infamy her sentence waits.

Hear thy indictment, Washington, at large;   215
Attend and listen to the solemn charge:
Thou hast supported an atrocious cause
Against thy King, thy Country, and the laws;
Committed perjury, encourag'd lies,
Forced conscience, broken the most sacred ties;   220
Myriads of wives and fathers at thy hand
Their slaughter'd husbands, slaughter'd sons demand;
That pastures hear no more the lowing kine,—
That towns are desolate, all—all is thine;
The frequent sacrilege that pain'd my sight: 225
The blasphemies my pen abhors to write;
Innumerable crimes on thee must fall—
For thou maintainest, thou defendest all.

Wilt thou pretend that Britain is in fault?
In Reason's court a falsehood goes for nought.   230
Will it avail, with subterfuge refin'd
To say, such deeds are foreign to thy mind?
Wilt thou assert that, generous and humane,
Thy nature suffers at another's pain?
He who a band of ruffians keeps to kill,   235
Is he not guilty of the blood they spill?
Who guards M'Kean, and Joseph Reed the vile,[12]
Help'd he not murder Roberts and Carlisle?
So, who protects committees in the chair,
In all their shocking cruelties must share.   240
What could, when half-way up the hill to fame,
Induce thee to go back, and link with shame?
Was it ambition, vanity, or spite,
That prompted thee with Congress to unite;
Or did all three within thy bosom roll,   245
"Thou heart of hero with a traitor's soul?"
Go, wretched author of thy country's grief,
Patron of villainy, of villains chief;
Seek with thy cursed crew the central gloom,
Ere Truth's avenging sword begin thy doom;   250
Or sudden vengeance of celestial dart
Precipitate thee with augmented smart.

---

6. In the section of Part I that is omitted, Odell takes up several revolutionary agitators who receive his castigation: Livingston, Jay, Chase, R. Morris, G. Morris, Duer, Duane, Cooper, Hancock, J. Adams, S. Adams.

7. Horatio Gates (1728–1806) of England, then Virginia, was a general in the Continental Army.

8. Anthony Wayne (1745–1796) was a Continental Army general from Pennsylvania.

9. Falstaff is a fat, sensual, and witty old knight in two plays by William Shakespeare.

10. Catiline (108–62 B.C.) was a Roman politician and conspirator, opposed by Cicero in the Roman senate.

11. Oliver Cromwell (1599–1658) Protestant leader and Lord Protector of England, Scotland, and Ireland during the middle of the seventeenth century.

---

12. Thomas McKean (1734–1817) and George Reed, both from Delaware, voted for and against the Declaration of Independence, causing Caesar Rodney to cast the tie-splitting vote for independence.

O Poet, seated on the lofty throne,
Forgive the bard who makes thy words his own;
255　Surpriz'd I trace in thy prophetic page
The crimes, the follies of the present age;
Thy scenery, sayings, admirable man,
Pourtray our struggles with the dark Divan.
What Michael to the first arch-rebel said,
260　Would well rebuke the rebel army's head;
What Satan to th' angelic Prince replied,

Such are the words of Continental pride.
I swear by Him, who rules the earth and sky,
The dread event shall equally apply;
That Clinton's[13] warfare is the war of God,　　　265
And Washington shall feel the vengeful rod.

---

13. Sir Henry Clinton (1730–1795) was second in command to Howe and a leading British military general.

J. Hector St. Jean de Crèvecoeur (1735–1813)

Born in Caen, France, in a family of minor nobility, J. Hector St. Jean de Crèvecoeur was educated at the Jesuit college there. At the age of twenty, he emigrated to the French colonies in Canada, where he made a living as a surveyor and cartographer. He served the French military during the Seven Years War, known by the British colonists as the French and Indian Wars, and was commissioned as a lieutenant in 1758. The following year, when he was wounded, he resigned his commission. He then moved to the British colonies, where he traveled through New York, Ohio, and Vermont, working as a surveyor. In 1769, he married and bought land in Orange County, New York. During the Revolution, Crèvecoeur attempted to remain neutral, but was suspected by both sides of spying. He was imprisoned by the British for several months. Crèvecoeur found life in British North America intolerable, and in 1780, he took his oldest son to Europe, while his wife remained on their farm with two younger children. He returned to America in 1783 as the French consul to New Jersey, Connecticut, and New York, discovering that in his absence his farm had been burned, his wife had died, and his two younger children were missing (they were later located). He remained in the United States as consul until 1790, when he returned to France, where he remained for the rest of his life.

Crèvecoeur used his experiences in British North America as the basis for several fictionalized accounts, written as separate essays but then published together as a book. The first and most famous of these volumes of essays was *Letters from an American Farmer,* which Crèvecoeur published in England in 1782; the book appeared in an American edition in 1793. Like popular novels and travel works of the day, Crèvecoeur's *Letters* used the epistolary narrative form, letting the reader read over his shoulder, as if he were writing letters to a friend. Crèvecoeur's *Letters* purported to be written by a British American, Quaker farmer in letters to a nobleman who had visited his farm. While in France, Crèvecoeur published a French adaptation of this work as *Letters d'un Cultivateur American,* which he enlarged in 1787. He also published an account of Pennsylvania and New York in French in 1801. Additional essays in English remained unpublished until 1923, when they appeared under the title *Sketches of Eighteenth-Century Life.*

Letters from an American Farmer appeared in only one American edition during the eighteenth century. Excerpts from the book, however, were published in periodicals, thus giving Crèvecoeur's work much greater circulation than it would have had otherwise. The following selections are published extracts of Crèvecoeur's *Letters,* and they give us a sense today of what editors of newspapers considered appealing to readers at that time.

ON THE SITUATION, FEELINGS, AND PLEASURES OF AN AMERICAN FARMER[1]

When young I entertained some thoughts of selling my farm. I thought it afforded but a dull repetition of the same labours and pleasures. I thought the former tedious and heavy, the latter few and insipid; but when I came to consider myself as divested of my farm, I then found the world so wide, and every place so full, that I began to fear lest there would be no room for me. My farm, my house, my barn, presented to my imagination, objects from which I adduced quite new ideas; they were more forcible than before. Why should not I find myself happy, said I, where my father was before? He left me no good books it is true, he gave me no other education than the art of reading and writing; but he left me a good farm, and his experience; he left me free from debts, and no kind of difficulties to struggle with. I married, and this perfectly reconciled me to my situation; my wife rendered my house all at once chearful and pleasing; it no longer appeared gloomy and solitary as before; when I went to work in my fields I worked with more alactrity and sprightliness; I felt that I did not work for myself alone, and this encouraged me much. My wife would often come with her knitting in her hand, and sit under the shady tree, praising the straightness of my furrows, and the docility of my horses; this swelled my heart and made every thing light and pleasant, and I regretted that I had not married before. I felt myself happy in my new situation, and where is that station which can confer a more substantial system of felicity than that of an American farmer, possessing freedom of action, freedom of thoughts, ruled by a mode of government which requires but little from us? I know no other landlord than the lord of all land, to whom I owe the most sincere gratitude. My father left me three hundred and seventy-one acres of land, forty-seven of which are good timothy meadow, and excellent orchard, a good house, and a substantial barn. It is my duty to think how happy I am that he lived to build and to pay for all these improvements; what are the labours which I have to undergo, what are my fatigues when compared to his, who had every thing to do from the first tree he felled to the finishing of his house? Every year I kill from 1500 to 2000 weight of pork, 1200 of beef, half a dozen of good weathers in harvest: of fowls my wife has always a great flock: what can I wish more? By a long series of industry and honest dealings, my father left behind him the name of a good man; I have but to tread his paths to be happy and a good man like him. I know enough of the law to regulate my little concerns with propriety, nor do I dread its power; these are the grand outlines of my situation, but as I can feel much more than I am able to express, I hardly know how to proceed. When my first son was born, the whole train of my ideas were suddenly altered; never was there a charm that acted so quickly and powerfully; I ceased to ramble in imagination through the wide world; my excursions since have not exceeded the bounds of my farm, and all my principal pleasures are now centered within its scanty limits: but at the same time there is not an operation belonging to it in which I do not find some food for useful reflections. This is the reason, I suppose, that when you was here, you used, in your refined stile, to denominate me the farmer of feelings; how rude must those feelings be in him who daily holds the axe or the plough, how much more refined on the contrary those of the European, whose mind is improved by education, example, books, and by every acquired advantage! Those feelings, however, I will delineate as well as I can, agreeably to your earnest request. When I contemplate my wife, by my fire-side, while she either spins, knits, darns, or suckles our child, I cannot describe the various emotions of love, of gratitude, of conscious pride which thrill in my heart, and often overflow in involuntary tears. I feel the necessity, the sweet pleasure of acting my part, the part of a husband and father, with an attention and propriety which may entitle me to my good fortune. It is true these pleasing images vanish with the smoke of my pipe, but though they disappear from my mind, the impression they have made on my heart is indelible. When I play with the infant, my warm imagination runs forward, and eagerly anticipates his future temper and constitution. I would willingly open the book of fate, and know in which page his destiny is delineated: alas! where is the father who in those moments of paternal extacy can delineate one half of the thoughts which dilate his heart? I am sure I cannot; then again I fear for the health of those who are become so dear to me, and in their sicknesses I severely pay for the joys I experienced while they were well. Whenever I go abroad it is always involuntary. I never return home without feeling some pleasing emotion, which I often suppress as useless and foolish. The

---

1. This essay was printed in the *Philadelphia Monthly Magazine* (June 1791). It is, in effect, an extract from the second letter of *Letters from an American Farmer.*

instant I enter on my own land, the bright idea of property, of exclusive right, of independence, exalts my mind. Precious soil, I say to myself, by what singular custom of law is it that thou wast made to constitute the riches of the free-holder? What should we American farmers be without the distinct possession of that soil? It feeds, it clothes us; from it we draw even a great exuberancy, our best meat, our richest drink, the very honey of our bees comes from this privileged spot. No wonder we should thus cherish its possession, no wonder that so many Europeans who have never been able to say that such portion of land was theirs, cross the Atlantic to realize that happiness. This formerly rude soil has been converted by my father into a pleasant farm, and in return it has established all our rights; on it is founded our rank, our freedom, our power as citizens, our importance as inhabitants of such a district. These images, I must confess, I always behold with pleasure, and extend them as far as my imagination can read: for this is what may be called the true and the only philosophy of an American farmer. Pray do not laugh in thus seeing an artless countryman tracing himself through the simple modifications of his life; remember that you have required it; therefore, with candour, though with diffidence, I endeavour to follow the thread of my feelings, but I cannot tell you all. Often when I plough my own ground, I place my little boy on a chair which screws to the beam of the plough; its motion, and that of the horses, please him, he is perfectly happy and begins to chat. As I lean over the handle, various are the thoughts which crowd into my mind. I am now doing for him, I say, what my father formerly did for me; may God enable him to live that he may perform the same operations for the same purposes when I am worn out and old! I relieve his mother of some trouble while I have him with me, the odoriferous furrow exhilarates his spirits, and seems to do the child a great deal of good, for he looks more blooming since I have adopted that practice: can more pleasure, more dignity be added to that primary occupation? The father thus ploughing with his child, and to feed his family, is inferior only to the emperor of China ploughing as an example to his kingdom. In the evening when I return home through my low grounds, I am astonished at the myriads of insects which I perceive dancing in the beams of the setting sun. I was before scarcely acquainted with their existence; they are so small that it is difficult to distinguish them; they are carefully improving this short evening space, not daring to expose themselves to the blaze of our meridian sun. I never see an egg brought on my table but I feel penetrated with the won-

derful change it would have undergone but for my gluttony; it might have been a gentle, useful hen leading her chickens with a care and vigilance which speaks shame to many women; a cock, perhaps, arrayed with the most majestic plumes, tender to its mate, bold, courageous, endowed with an astonishing instinct, with thoughts, with memory, and every distinguishing characteristic of the reason of man. I never see my trees drop their leaves and their fruit in the autumn, and bud again in the spring without wonder; the sagacity of those animals which have long been the tenants of my farm, astonished me: some of them seem to surpass even men in memory and sagacity. I could tell you singular instances of that kind. What then is this instinct which we so debase, and of which we are taught to entertain so diminutive an idea? My bees, above any other tenants of my farm, attract my attention and respect.

I draw a great fund of pleasure from the quails which inhabit my farm; they abundantly repay me, by their various notes and peculiar tameness, for the inviolable hospitality I constantly shew them in the winter. Instead of perfidiously taking advantage of their great and affecting distress, when nature offers nothing but a barren universal bed of snow, when irresistible necessity forces them to my barn doors, I permit them to feed unmolested; and it is not the least agreeable spectacle which that dreary season presents, when I see those beautiful birds, tamed by hunger, intermingling with all my cattle and sheep, seeking in security for the poor scanty grain which but for them would be useless and lost. Often in the angles of the fences where the motion of the wind prevents the snow from settling, I carry them both chaff and grain; the one to feed them, the other to prevent their tender feet from freezing fast to the earth as I have frequently observed them to do. I do not know an instance in which the singular barbarity of man is so strongly delineated, as in the catching and murdering those harmless birds, at that cruel season of the year. Mr. ****, one of the most famous and extraordinary farmers that have ever done honour to the province of Connecticut, by his timely and humane assistance in a hard winter, saved this species from being entirely destroyed. They perished all over the country, none of their delightful whistlings were heard the next spring, but upon this gentleman's farm; and to his humanity we owe the continuation of their music. When the severities of that season have dispirited all my cattle, no farmer ever attends them with more pleasure than I do; it is one of those duties which is sweetened with the most rational satisfaction. I assume myself in beholding their different tempers, actions, and the various effects of their instinct now powerfully impelled by the force of hunger. I trace their various inclinations, and the different effects of their passions, which are exactly the same as among men; the law is to us precisely what I am in my barn yard, a bridle and check to prevent the strong and greedy, from oppressing the timid and weak. Conscious of superiority they always strive to encroach on their neighbours; unsatisfied with their portion, they eagerly swallow it in order to have an opportunity of taking what is given to others, except they are prevented. Some I chide, others, unmindful of my admonitions, receive some blows. Could victuals thus be given to men without the assistance of any language, I am sure they would not behave better to one another, nor more philosophically than my cattle do. The same spirit prevails in the stable; but there I have to do with more generous animals, there my well known voice has immediate influence, and soon restores peace and tranquillity. Thus by superior knowledge I govern all my cattle as wise men are obliged to govern fools and the ignorant.

It is my bees, however, which afford me the most pleasing and extensive themes; let me look at them when I will, their government, their industry, their quarrels, their passions, always present me with something new; for which reason, when weary with labour, my common place of rest is under my locust-trees, close by my beehouse. By their movements I can predict the weather, and can tell the day of their swarming; but the most difficult point is, when on the wing, to know whether they want to go to the woods or not. If they have previously pitched in some hollow trees, it is not the allurements of salt and water, of fennel, hickory leaves, &c., nor the finest box, that can induce them to stay; they will prefer those rude, rough habitations to the best polished mahogany hive. When that is the case with mine, I seldom thwart their inclinations; it is in freedom that they work: were I to confine them, they would dwindle away and quit their labour. In such excursions we only part for a while; I am generally sure to find them again the following fall. This elopement of theirs only adds to my recreations: I know how to deceive even their superlative instinct; nor do I fear losing them, though eighteen miles from my house, and lodged in the most lofty trees, in the most impervious of our forests. I once took you along with me in one of those rambles, and yet you insist on my repeating the detail of our operations: it brings back into my mind many of the useful and entertaining reflections with which you so happily beguiled our tedious hours.

After I have done sowing, by way of recreation, I prepare for a week's jaunt in the woods, not to hunt either the deer or the bears, as my neighbours do, but to catch the more harmless bees. I cannot boast that this chase is so noble, or so famous among men, but I find it less fatiguing, and full as profitable; and the last consideration is the only one that moves me. I take with me my dog, as a companion, for he is useless as to this game; my gun, for no man you know ought to enter the woods without one; my blanket, some provisions, some wax, vermillion, honey, and a small pocket compass. With such implements I proceed to such woods as are at a considerable distance from any settlements. I carefully examine whether they abound with large trees; if so, I make a small fire on some flat stones, in a convenient place; on the fire I put some wax; close by this fire, on another stone I drop honey in distinct drops, which I surround with small quantities of vermillion, laid on the stone; and then I retire carefully to watch whether any bees appear. If there are any in that neighbourhood, I rest assured that the smell of the burnt wax will unavoidably attract them; they will soon find out the honey, for they are fond of preying on that which is not their own; and in their approach they will necessarily tinge themselves with some particles of vermillion, which will adhere long to their bodies. I next fix my compass, to find out their course, which they keep invariably strait, when they are returning home loaded. By the assistance of my watch, I observe how long those are returning which are marked with vermillion. Thus possessed of the course, and, in some measure, of the distance, which I can easily guess at I follow the first, and seldom fail of coming to the tree where those republics are lodged. I then mark it; and thus, with patience, I have found out sometimes eleven swarms in a season; and it is inconceivable what a quantity of honey these trees will sometimes afford. It entirely depends on the size of the hollow, as the bees never rest nor swarm till it is all replenished; for like men, it is only the want of room that induces them to quit the maternal hive. Next I proceed to some of the nearest settlements, where I procure proper assistance to cut down the trees, get all my prey secured, and then return home with my prize. The first bees I ever procured were thus found in the woods, by mere accident; for at that time I had no kind of skill in this method of tracing them. The body of the tree being perfectly found, they had lodged themselves in the hollow of one of its principal limbs, which I carefully sawed off, and with a good deal of labour and industry brought it home, where I fixed it up again in the same position in which I found it growing.

This was in April; I had five swarms that year, and they have been ever since very prosperous. This business generally takes up a week of my time every fall, and to me it is a week of solitary ease and relaxation.

HISTORY OF ANDREW, THE HEBRIDEAN[1]

Let historians give the detail of our charters, the succession of our several governors and of their administrations, of our political struggles, and of the foundation of our towns; let annalists amuse themselves with collecting anecdotes of the establishment of our modern provinces: eagles soar high—I, a feebler bird, cheerfully content myself with skipping from bush to bush and living on insignificant insects. I am so habituated to draw all my food and pleasure from the surface of the earth which I till that I cannot, nor indeed am I able to, quit it. I therefore present you with the short history of a simple Scotchman, though it contain not a single remarkable event to amaze the reader, no tragical scene to convulse the heart, or pathetic narrative to draw tears from sympathetic eyes. All I wish to delineate is the progressive steps of a poor man, advancing from indigence to ease, from oppression to freedom, from obscurity and contumely to some degree of consequence—not by virtue of any freaks of fortune, but by the gradual operation of sobriety, honesty, and emigration. These are the limited fields through which I love to wander, sure to find in some parts the smile of new-born happiness, the glad heart, inspiring the cheerful song, the glow of manly pride excited by vivid hopes and rising independence. I always return from my neighbourly excursions extremely happy because there I see good living almost under every roof and prosperous endeavours almost in every field. But you may say, "Why don't you describe some of the more ancient, opulent settlements of our country, where even the eye of an European has something to admire?" It is true, our American fields are in general pleasing to behold, adorned and intermixed as they are with so many substantial houses, flourishing orchards, and coppices of woodlands: the pride of our farms, the source of every good we possess. But what I might observe there is but natural and common; for to draw comfortable subsistence from well-fenced, cultivated fields is easy to conceive. A father dies and leaves a decent house and rich farm to his son; the son modernizes the one and carefully tills the other; he marries the daughter of a friend and neighbour: this is the common prospect; but though it is rich and pleasant, yet it is far from being so entertaining and instructive as the one now in my view.

I had rather attend on the shore to welcome the poor European when he arrives; I observe him in his first moments of embarrassment, trace him throughout his primary difficulties, follow him step by step until he pitches his tent on some piece of land and realizes that energetic wish which has made him quit his native land, his kindred, and induced him to traverse a boisterous ocean. It is there I want to observe his first thoughts and feelings, the first essays of an industry, which hitherto has been suppressed. I wish to see men cut down the first trees, erect their new buildings, till their first fields, reap their first crops, and say for the first time in their lives, "This is our own grain, raised from American soil; on it we shall feed and grow fat and convert the rest into gold and silver." I want to see how the happy effects of their sobriety, honesty, and industry are first displayed; and who would not take a pleasure in seeing these strangers settling as new countrymen, struggling with arduous difficulties, overcoming them, and becoming happy?

Landing on this great continent is like going to sea; they must have a compass, some friendly directing needle, or else they will uselessly err and wander for a long time, even with a fair wind. Yet these are the struggles through which our forefathers have waded, and they have left us no other records of them but the possession of our farms. The reflections I make on these new settlers recall to my mind what my grandfather did in his days; they fill me with gratitude to his memory as well as to that government which invited him to come and helped him when he arrived, as well as many others. Can I pass over these reflections without remembering thy name, O Penn, thou best of legislators, who by the wisdom of thy laws hast endowed human nature, within the bounds of thy province, with every dignity it can possibly enjoy in a civilized state and showed by this singular establishment what all men might be if they would follow thy example!

In the year 1770, I purchased some lands in the county of——, which I intended for one of my sons, and was obliged to go there in order to see them properly surveyed

---

1. This story was printed in the *New-York Magazine, or Literary Register,* in three installments, during February, March, and April 1797. It is an extract of the third letter published in *Letters from an American Farmer.*

and marked out: the soil is good, but the country has a very wild aspect. However, I observed with pleasure that land sells very fast, and I am in hopes when the lad gets a wife it will be a well-settled, decent country. Agreeable to our customs, which indeed are those of nature, it is our duty to provide for our eldest children while we live in order that our homesteads may be left to the youngest, who are the most helpless. Some people are apt to regard the portions given to daughters as so much lost to the family, but this is selfish and is not agreeable to my way of thinking; they cannot work as men do; they marry young: I have given an honest European a farm to till for himself, rent free, provided he clears an acre of swamp every year and that he quits it whenever my daughter shall marry. It will procure her a substantial husband, a good farmer— and that is all my ambition.

Whilst I was in the woods, I met with a party of Indians; I shook hands with them, and I perceived they had killed a cub; I had a little peach brandy; they perceived it also; we therefore joined company, kindled a large fire, and ate a hearty supper. I made their hearts glad, and we all reposed on good beds of leaves. Soon after dark, I was surprised to hear a prodigious hooting through the woods; the Indians laughed heartily. One of them, more skilful than the rest, mimicked the owls so exactly that a very large one perched on a high tree over our fire. We soon brought him down; he measured five feet seven inches from one extremity of the wings to the other. By Captain——I have sent you the talons, on which I have had the heads of small candlesticks fixed. Pray keep them on the table of your study for my sake.

Contrary to my expectation, I found myself under the necessity of going to Philadelphia in order to pay the purchase money and to have the deeds properly recorded. I thought little of the journey, though it was above two hundred miles, because I was well acquainted with many friends, at whose houses I intended to stop. The third night after I left the woods, I put up at Mr.——'s, the most worthy citizen I know; he happened to lodge at my house when you were there. He kindly inquired after your welfare and desired I would make a friendly mention of him to you. The neatness of these good people is no phenomenon, yet I think this excellent family surpasses everything I know. No sooner did I lie down to rest than I thought myself in a most odoriferous arbour, so sweet and fragrant were the sheets. Next morning I found my host in the orchard destroying caterpillars. "I think, friend B.," said I, "that thee art greatly departed from the good rules of the society; thee seemeth to have quitted that happy simplicity for which it hath hitherto been so remarkable." "Thy rebuke, friend James, is a pretty heavy one; what motive canst thee have for thus accusing us?" "Thy kind wife made a mistake last evening," I said; "she put me on a bed of roses instead of a common one; I am not used to such delicacies." "And is that all, friend James, that thee hast to reproach us with? Thee wilt not call it luxury I hope? Thee canst but know that it is the produce of our garden; and friend Pope sayeth that 'to enjoy is to obey.'" "This is a most learned excuse indeed, friend B., and must be valued because it is founded upon truth." "James, my wife hath done nothing more to thy bed than what is done all the year round to all the beds in the family; she sprinkles her linen with rose-water before she puts it under the press; it is her fancy, and I have nought to say. But thee shalt not escape so; verily I will send for her; thee and she must settle the matter whilst I proceed on my work before the sun gets too high.—Tom, go thou and call thy mistress, Philadelphia." "What," said I, "is thy wife called by that name? I did not know that before." "I'll tell thee, James, how it came to pass: her grandmother was the first female child born after William Penn landed with the rest of our brethren, and in compliment to the city he intended to build, she was called after the name he intended to give it; and so there is always one of the daughters of her family known by the name of Philadelphia." She soon came, and after a most friendly altercation. I gave up the point, breakfasted, departed, and in four days reached the city.

A week after, news came that a vessel was arrived with Scotch emigrants. Mr. C. and I went to the dock to see them disembark. It was a scene which inspired me with a variety of thoughts. "Here are," said I to my friend, "a number of people driven by poverty and other adverse causes to a foreign land in which they know nobody." The name of a stranger, instead of implying relief, assistance, and kindness, on the contrary, conveys very different ideas. They are now distressed; their minds are racked by a variety of apprehensions, fears, and hopes. It was this last powerful sentiment which has brought them here. If they are good people, I pray that heaven may realize them. Whoever were to see them thus gathered again in five or six years would behold a more pleasing sight, to which this would serve as a very powerful contrast. By their honesty, the vigour of their arms, and the benignity of government, their condition will be greatly improved; they will be well clad, fat, possessed of that manly confidence which property confers; they will become useful citizens. Some of the posterity may act conspicuous parts in our future American transactions. Most of them appeared pale and emaciated, from the length of the passage and the indifferent provision on which they had lived. The number of children seemed as great as that of the people; they had all paid for being conveyed here.

The captain told us they were a quiet, peaceable, and harmless people who had never dwelt in cities. This was a valuable cargo; they seemed, a few excepted, to be in the full vigour of their lives. Several citizens, impelled either by spontaneous attachments or motives of humanity, took many of them to their houses; the city, agreeable to its usual wisdom and humanity, ordered them all to be lodged in the barracks, and plenty of provisions to be given them. My friend pitched upon one also and led him to his house, with his wife and a son about fourteen years of age. The majority of them had contracted for land the year before, by means of an agent; the rest depended entirely upon chance; and the one who followed us was of this last class. Poor man, he smiled on receiving the invitation, and gladly accepted it, bidding his wife and son do the same, in a language which I did not understand. He gazed with uninterrupted attention on everything he saw: the houses, the inhabitants, the Negroes, and carriages—everything appeared equally new to him; and we went slow in order to give him time to feed on this pleasing variety. "Good God!" said he, "is this Philadelphia, that blessed city of bread and provisions of which we have heard so much? I am told it was founded the same year in which my father was born; why, it is finer than Greenock and Glasgow, which are ten times as old." "It is so," said my friend to him; "and when thee hast been here a month, thee will soon see that it is the capital of a fine province, of which thee art going to be a citizen. Greenock enjoys neither such a climate nor such a soil." Thus we slowly proceeded along, when we met several large Lancaster six-horse waggons, just arrived from the country. At this stupendous sight, he stopped short and with great diffidence asked us what was the use of these great moving houses, and where those big horses came from? "Have you none such at home?" I asked him. "Oh, no; these huge animals would eat all the grass of our island!" We at last reached my friend's house, who, in the glow of well-meant hospitality, made them all three sit down to a good dinner and gave them as much cider as they could drink. "God bless the country and the good people it contains," said he; "this is the best meal's victuals I have made a long time.—I thank you kindly."

"What part of Scotland dost thee come from, friend Andrew?" said Mr. C. "Some of us come from the main, some from the island of Barra," he answered; "I myself am a Barra man." I looked on the map, and by its latitude, easily guessed that it must be an inhospitable climate. "What sort of land have you got there?" I asked him. "Bad enough," said he; "we have no such trees as I see here, no wheat, no kine, no apples." Then, I observed that it must be hard for the poor to live. "We have no poor," he answered; "we are all alike, except our laird; but he cannot help everybody." "Pray what is the name of your laird?" "Mr. Neiel," said Andrew; "the like of him is not to be found in any of the isles; his forefathers have lived there thirty generations ago, as we are told. Now, gentlemen, you may judge what an ancient family estate it must be. But it is cold, the land is thin, and there were too many of us, which are the reasons that some are come to seek their fortunes here." "Well, Andrew, what step do you intend to take in order to become rich?" "I do not know, sir; I am but an ignorant man, a stranger besides; I must rely on the advice of good Christians: they would not deceive me, I am sure. I have brought with me a character from our Barra minister; can it do me any good here?" "Oh, yes; but your future success will depend entirely on your own conduct; if you are a sober man, as the certificate says, laborious, and honest, there is no fear but that you will do well. Have you brought any money with you, Andrew?" "Yes, sir, eleven guineas and an half." "Upon my word, it is a considerable sum for a Barra man; how came you by so much money?" "Why, seven years ago, I received a legacy of thirty-seven pounds from an uncle who loved me much; my wife brought me two guineas when the laird gave her to me for a wife; which I have saved ever since. I have sold all I had; I worked in Glasgow for some time." "I am glad to hear you are so saving and prudent; be so still; you must go and hire yourself with some good people; what can you do?" "I can thresh a little, and handle the spade." "Can you plough?" "Yes, sir, with the little breast plough I have brought with me." "These won't do here, Andrew; you are an able man; if you are willing, you will soon learn. I'll tell you what I intend to do: I'll send you to my house, where you shall stay two or three weeks; there you must exercise yourself with the axe; that is the principal tool the Americans want, and particularly the back-settlers. Can your wife spin?" "Yes, she can." "Well then, as soon as you are able to handle the axe, you shall go and live with Mr. P. R., a particular friend of mine, who will give you four dollars per month for the first six and the usual price of five as long as you remain with him. I shall place your wife in another house, where she shall receive half a dollar a week for spinning, and your son a dollar a month to drive the team. You shall have, besides, good victuals to eat and good beds to lie on; will all this satisfy you, Andrew?" He hardly understood what I said; the honest tears of gratitude fell from his eyes as he looked at me, and its expressions seemed to quiver on his lips. Though silent, this was saying a great deal; there was, besides, something extremely moving to see a man six feet high thus shed tears, and they did not lessen the good opinion I had entertained of him. At last he told me that my offers were more than he deserved and that he would first begin to work for his victuals. "No, no," said I; "if you are careful and sober and do what you can, you shall receive what I told you, after you have served a short apprenticeship at my house." "May God repay you for all your kindnesses," said Andrew; "as long as I live, I shall thank you and do what I can for you." A few days after, I sent them all three to——, by the return of some waggons, that he might have an opportunity of viewing and convincing himself of the utility of those machines which he had at first so much admired.

The farther descriptions he gave us of the Hebrides in general and of his native island in particular, of the customs and modes of living of the inhabitants, greatly entertained me. Pray, is the sterility of the soil the cause that there are no trees, or is it because there are none planted? What are the modern families of all the kings of the earth compared to the date of that of Mr. Neiel? Admitting that each generation should last but forty years, this makes a period of 1,200, an extraordinary duration for the uninterrupted descent of any family!

Agreeably to the description he gave us of those countries, they seem to live according to the rules of nature, which gives them but bare subsistence; their constitutions are uncontaminated by any excess or effeminacy, which their soil refuses. If their allowance of food is not too scanty, they must all be healthy by perpetual temperance and exercise; if so, they are amply rewarded for their poverty.

Could they have obtained but necessary food, they would not have left it; for it was not in consequence of oppression, either from their patriarch or the government, that they had emigrated. I wish we had a colony of these honest people settled in some parts of this province; their morals, their religion, seem to be as simple as their manners. This society would present an interesting spectacle could they be transported on a richer soil. But perhaps that soil would soon alter everything; for our opinions, vices, and virtues are altogether local: we are machines fashioned by every circumstance around us.

Andrew arrived at my house a week before I did, and I found my wife, agreeably to my instructions, had placed the axe in his hands as his first task. For some time, he was very awkward, but he was so docile, so willing, and grateful, as well as his wife, that I foresaw he would succeed. Agreeably to my promise, I put them all with different families, where they were well liked, and all parties were pleased. Andrew worked hard, lived well, grew fat, and every Sunday came to pay me a visit on a good horse, which Mr. P. R. lent him. Poor man, it took him a long time ere he could sit on the saddle and hold the bridle properly. I believe he had never before mounted such a beast, though I did not choose to ask him that question, for fear it might suggest some mortifying ideas. After having been twelve months at Mr. P. R.'s and having received his own and his family's wages, which amounted to eighty-four dollars, he came to see me on a weekday and told me that he was a man of middle age and would willingly have land of his own in order to procure him a home as a shelter against old age, that whenever this period should come, his son, to whom he would give his land, would then maintain him, and thus live altogether; he therefore required my advice and assistance. I thought his desire very natural and praiseworthy, and told him that I should think of it, but that he must remain one month longer with Mr. P. R., who had 3,000 rails to split. He immediately consented. The spring was not far advanced enough yet for Andrew to begin clearing any land, even supposing that he had made a purchase, as it is always necessary that the leaves should be out in order that this additional combustible may serve to burn the heaps of brush more readily. A few days after, it happened that the whole family of Mr. P. R. went to meeting, and left Andrew to take care of the house. While he was at the door, attentively reading the Bible, nine Indians just come from the mountains suddenly made their appearance and unloaded their packs of furs on the floor of the piazza. Conceive, if you can, what was Andrew's consternation at this extraordinary sight! From the singular appearance of these people, the honest Hebridean took them for a lawless band come to rob his master's house. He therefore, like a faithful guardian, precipitately withdrew and shut the doors; but as most of our houses are without locks, he was reduced to the necessity of fixing his knife over the latch, and then flew upstairs in quest of a broadsword he had brought from Scotland.

The Indians, who were Mr. P. R.'s particular friends, guessed at his suspicions and fears; they forcibly lifted the door and suddenly took possession of the house, got all the bread and meat they wanted, and sat themselves down by the fire. At this instant, Andrew, with his broadsword in his hand, entered the room, the Indians earnestly looking at him and attentively watching his motions. After a very few reflections, Andrew found that his weapon was useless when opposed to nine tomahawks, but this did not diminish his anger; on the contrary, it grew greater on observing the calm impudence with which they were devouring the family provisions. Unable to resist, he called them names in broad Scotch and ordered them to desist and be gone, to which the Indians (as they told me afterwards) replied in their equally broad idiom. It must have been a most unintelligible altercation between this honest Barra man and nine Indians who did not much care for anything he could say. At last he ventured to lay his hands on one of them in order to turn him out of the house. Here Andrew's fidelity got the better of his prudence, for the Indian, by his motions, threatened to scalp him, while the rest gave the war whoop. This horrid noise so effectually frightened poor Andrew that, unmindful of his courage, of his broadsword, and his intentions, he rushed out, left them masters of the house, and disappeared. I have heard one of the Indians say since that he never laughed so heartily in his life. Andrew, at a distance, soon recovered from the fears which had been inspired by this infernal yell and thought of no other remedy than to go to the meeting-house, which was about two miles distant. In the eagerness of his honest intentions, with looks of affright still marked on his countenance, he called Mr. P. R. out and told him with great vehemence of style that nine monsters were come to his house—some blue, some red, and some black; that they had little axes in their hands out of which they smoked; and that like highlanders, they had no breeches; that they were devouring all his victuals; and that God only knew what they would do more. "Pacify yourself," said Mr. P. R.; "my house is as safe with these people as if I was there myself; as for the victuals, they are heartily welcome, honest Andrew; they are not people of much ceremony; they help themselves thus whenever they are among their friends; I do so too in their wigwams, whenever I go to their village; you had better therefore step in and hear the remainder of the sermon, and when the meeting is over, we will all go back in the waggon together."

At their return, Mr. P. R., who speaks the Indian language very well, explained the whole matter; the Indians renewed their laugh and shook hands with honest Andrew, whom they made to smoke out of their pipes; and thus peace was made and ratified according to the Indian custom, by the calumet.

Soon after this adventure, the time approached when I had promised Andrew my best assistance to settle him; for that purpose, I went to Mr. A. V., in the county of——, who, I was informed, had purchased a track of land contiguous to——settlement. I gave him a faithful detail of the progress Andrew had made in the rural arts, of his honesty, sobriety, and gratitude; and pressed him to sell him a hundred acres. "This I cannot comply with," said Mr. A. V.; "but at the same time I will do better; I love to encourage honest Europeans as much as you do and to see them prosper; you tell me he has but one son; I will lease them a hundred acres for any term of years you please, and make it more valuable to your Scotchman than if he was possessed of the fee simple. By that means he may, with that little money he has, buy a plough, a team, and some stock; he will not be incumbered with debts and mortgages; what he raises will be his own; had he two or three sons as able as himself, then I should think it more eligible for him to purchase the fee simple." "I join with you in opinion, and will bring Andrew along with me in a few days."

"Well, honest Andrew," said Mr. A. V., "in consideration of your good name, I will let you have a hundred acres of good arable land that shall be laid out along a new road; there is a bridge already erected on the creek that passes through the land, and a fine swamp of about twenty acres. These are my terms; I cannot sell, but I will lease you the quantity that Mr. James, your friend, has asked; the first seven years you shall pay no rent; whatever you sow and reap, and plant and gather, shall be entirely your own; neither the king, government, nor church will have any claim on your future property. The remaining part of the time, you must give me twelve dollars and a half a year; and that is all you will have to pay me. Within the three first years, you must plant fifty apple trees and clear seven acres of swamp within the first part of the lease; it will be your own advantage; whatever you do more within that time, I will pay you for it, at the common rate of the country. The term of the lease shall be thirty years; how do you like it, Andrew?" "Oh, sir, it is very good, but I am afraid that the king or his ministers, or the governor, or some of our great men will come and take the land from me; your son may say to me, by and by, 'This is my father's land, Andrew, you must quit it.'" "No, no," said Mr. A. V.; "there is no such danger; the king and his ministers are too just to take the labour of a poor settler; here we have no great men, but what are subordinate to our laws; but to calm all your fears, I will give you a lease so that none can make you afraid. If ever you are dissatisfied with the land, a jury of your own neighbourhood shall value all your improvements, and you shall be paid agreeably to their verdict. You may sell the lease, or if you die, you may previously dispose of it as if the land was your own."

Expressive, yet inarticulate joy, was mixed in his countenance, which seemed impressed with astonishment and confusion. "Do you understand me well?" said Mr. A. V. "No, sir," replied Andrew; "I know nothing of what you mean about lease, improvement, will, jury, etc." "That is honest; we will explain these things to you by and by." It must be confessed that those were hard words, which he had never heard in his life; for by his own account, the ideas they convey would be totally useless in the island of Barra. No wonder, therefore, that he was embarrassed; for how could the man who had hardly a will of his own since he was born imagine he could have one after his death? How could the person who never possessed anything conceive that he could extend his new dominion over this land, even after he should be laid in his grave? For my part, I think Andrew's amazement did not imply any extraordinary degree of ignorance: he was an actor introduced upon a new scene; it required some time ere he could reconcile himself to the part he was to perform. However, he was soon enlightened and introduced into those mysteries with which we native Americans are but too well acquainted.

Here, then, is honest Andrew, invested with every municipal advantage they confer, become a freeholder, possessed of a vote, of a place of residence, a citizen of the province of Pennsylvania. Andrew's original hopes and the distant prospects he had formed in the island of Barra were at the eve of being realized; we therefore can easily forgive him a few spontaneous ejaculations, which would be useless to repeat. This short tale is easily told; few words are sufficient to describe this sudden change of situation; but in his mind it was gradual, and took him above a week before he could be sure that without disbursing any money he could possess lands. Soon after he prepared himself, I lent him a barrel of pork and 200-lb. weight of meal and made him purchase what was necessary besides.

He set out, and hired a room in the house of a settler who lived the most contiguous to his own land. His first work was to clear some acres of swamp, that he might have a supply of hay the following year for his two horses and cows. From the first day he began to work, he was indefatigable; his honesty procured him friends, and his industry the esteem of his new neighbours. One of them offered him two acres of cleared land whereon he might plant corn, pompions, squashes, and a few potatoes that very season. It is astonishing how quick men will learn when they work for themselves. I saw with pleasure, two months after, Andrew holding a two-horse plough and tracing his furrows quite straight; thus the spademan of the island of Barra was become the tiller of American soil. "Well done," said I; "Andrew, well done; I see that God speeds and directs your works; I see prosperity delineated in all your furrows and head-lands. Raise this crop of corn with attention and care, and then you will be master of the art."

As he had neither mowing nor reaping to do that year, I told him that the time was come to build his house; and that for the purpose I would myself invite the neighbourhood to a frolic; that thus he would have a large dwelling erected and some upland cleared in one day. Mr. P. R., his old friend, came at the time appointed, with all his hands, and brought victuals in plenty; I did the same. About forty people repaired to the spot; the songs and merry stories went round the woods from cluster to cluster, as the people had gathered to their different works; trees fell on all sides, bushes were cut up and heaped; and while many were thus employed, others with their teams hauled the big logs to the spot which Andrew had pitched upon for the erection of his new dwelling. We all dined in the woods; in the afternoon, the logs were placed with skids and the usual contrivances; thus the rude house was raised and above two acres of land cut up, cleared, and heaped.

Whilst all these different operations were performing, Andrew was absolutely incapable of working; it was to him the most solemn holiday he had ever seen; it would have been sacrilegious in him to have defiled it with menial labour. Poor man, he sanctified it with joy and thanksgiving and honest libations: he went from one to the other with the bottle in his hand, pressing everybody to drink, and drinking himself to show the example. He spent the whole day in smiling, laughing, and uttering monosyllables; his wife and son were there also, but as they could not understand the language, their pleasure must have been altogether that of the imagination. The powerful lord, the wealthy merchant, on seeing the superb mansion finished, never can feel half the joy and real happiness which was felt and enjoyed on that day by this honest Hebridean, though this new dwelling, erected in the midst of the woods, was nothing more than a square inclosure, composed of twenty-four large, clumsy logs, let in at the ends. When the work was finished, the company made the woods resound with the noise of their three cheers and the honest wishes they formed for Andrew's prosperity. He could say nothing, but with thankful tears he shook hands with them all. Thus, from the first day he had landed, Andrew marched towards this important event; this memorable day made the sun shine on that land on which he was to sow wheat and other grain. What swamp he had cleared lay before his door; the essence of future bread, milk, and meat were scattered all round him. Soon after, he hired a carpenter, who put on a roof and laid the floors; in a week more, the house was properly plastered and the chimney finished. He moved into it, and purchased two cows, which found plenty of food in the woods; his hogs had the same advantage. That very year, he and his son sowed three bushels of wheat, from which he reaped ninety-one and a half; for I had ordered him to keep an exact account of all he should raise. His first crop of other corn would have been as good had it not been for the squirrels, which were enemies not to be dispersed by the broad-sword. The fourth year, I took an inventory of the wheat this man possessed, which I send you. Soon after, farther settlements were made on that road, and Andrew, instead of being the last man towards the wilderness, found himself in a few years in the middle of a numerous society. He helped others as generously as others had helped him, and I have dined many times at his table with several of his neighbours. The second year, he was made overseer of the road and served on two petty juries, performing as a citizen all the duties required of him. The historiographer of some great prince or general does not bring his hero victorious to the end of a successful campaign with one half of the heart-felt pleasure with which I have conducted Andrew to the situation he now enjoys: he is independent and easy. Triumph and military honours do not always imply those two blessings. He is unencumbered with debts, services, rents, or any other dues; the successes of a campaign, the laurels of war, must be purchased at the dearest rate, which makes every cool, reflecting citizen to tremble and shudder. By the literal account hereunto annexed, you will easily be made acquainted with the happy effects which constantly flow, in this country, from sobriety and industry, when united with good land and freedom.

The account of the property he acquired with his own hands and those of his son, in four years, is as under:

	Dollars
The value of his improvements and lease	225
Six cows, at 13 dollars	78
Two breeding mares	50
The rest of the stock	100
Seventy-three bushels of wheat	66
Money due to him on notes	43
Pork and beef in his cellar	28
Wool and flax	19
Ploughs and other utensils of husbandry	<u>31</u>
£240 Pennsylvania currency—dollars	640

A SINGULAR PUNISHMENT[1]

I was not long since invited to dine with a planter who lived three miles from—, where he then resided. In order to avoid the heat of the sun, I resolved to go on foot, sheltered in a small path, leading through a pleasant wood. I was leisurely travelling along, attentively examining some peculiar plants which I had collected, when all at once I felt the air strongly agitated, though the day was perfectly calm and sultry. I immediately cast my eyes toward the cleared ground, from which I was but a small distance, in order to see whether it was not occasioned by a sudden shower; when at that instant a sound resembling a deep rough voice, uttered, as I thought, a few inarticulate monosyllables. Alarmed and surprised, I precipitately looked around, when I perceived about six rods distance something resembling a cage, suspended to the limbs of a tree, all the branches of which appeared covered with large birds of prey, fluttering about and anxiously endeavouring to perch on the cage. Actuated by an involuntary motion of my hands, more than by any

---

1. This story was printed in the *Rural Magazine* on September 17, 1798. It is a section from letter nine of *Letters from an American Farmer.*

design of my mind, I fired at them; they all flew to a short distance, with a most hideous noise; when, horrid to think and painful to repeat, I perceived a negro, suspended in the cage and left there to expire! I shudder when I recollect that the birds had already picked out his eyes; his cheek bones were bare; his arms had been attacked in several places, and his body seemed covered with a multitude of wounds. From the edges of the hollow sockets and from the lacerations with which he was disfigured, the blood slowly dropped and tinged the ground beneath. No sooner were the birds flown, than swarms of insects covered the whole body of this unfortunate wretch, eager to feed on his mangled flesh and to drink his blood. I found myself suddenly arrested by the power of affright and terror; my nerves were convulsed; I trembled; I stood motionless, involuntarily contemplating the fate of this Negro in all its dismal latitude. The living spectre though deprived of his eyes, could still distinctly hear, and in his uncouth dialect begged me to give him some water to allay his thirst. Humanity itself would have recoiled back with horror; she would have balanced whether to lessen such reliefless distress, or mercifully with one blow to end this dreadful scene of agonizing torture! Had I had a ball in my gun, I certainly should have dispatched him; but finding myself unable to perform so kind an office, I sought, though trembling, to relieve him as well as I could. A shell ready fixed to a pole, which had been used by some negroes, presented itself to me; I filled it with water, and with trembling hands I guided it to the quivering lips of the wretched sufferer. Urged by the irresistible power of thirst, he endeavoured to meet it, as he instinctively guessed its approach by the noise it made in passing through the bars of the cage. "Tankee you, white man; tankee you; puta some poison and give me." "How long have you been hanging there?" I asked him. "Two days, and me no die; the birds, the birds; aaah me!" Oppressed with the reflections which this shocking spectacle afforded me, I mustered strength enough to walk away, and soon reached the house at which I intended to dine. There I heard that the reason of this slave being thus punished, was on account of his having killed the overseer of the plantation. They told me that the laws of self-preservation rendered such executions necessary; and supported the doctrine of slavery with the arguments generally made use of to justify the practice; with the repetition of which I shall not trouble you at present.

from LETTERS FROM AN AMERICAN FARMER

from LETTER 12 • Distresses of a Frontier Man[1]

I wish for a change of place; the hour is come at last that I must fly from my house and abandon my farm! But what course shall I steer, inclosed as I am? The climate best adapted to my present situation and humour would be the polar regions, where six months' day and six months' night divide the dull year; nay, a simple aurora borealis would suffice me and greatly refresh my eyes, fatigued now by so many disagreeable objects. The severity of those climates, that great gloom where melancholy dwells, would be perfectly analogous to the turn of my mind. Oh, could I remove my plantation to the shores of the Obi, willingly would I dwell in the hut of a Samoyed; with cheerfulness would I go and bury myself in the cavern of a Laplander. Could I but carry my family along with me, I would winter at Pello, or Tobolsk, in order to enjoy the peace and innocence of that country. But let me arrive under the pole, or reach the antipodes, I never can leave behind me the remembrance of the dreadful scenes to which I have been witness; therefore, never can I be happy! Happy—why would I mention that sweet, that enchanting word? Once happiness was our portion; now it is gone from us, and I am afraid not to be enjoyed again by the present generation! Whichever way I look, nothing but the most frightful precipices present themselves to my view, in which hundreds of my friends and acquaintances have already perished; of all animals that live on the surface of this planet, what is man when no longer connected with society, or when he finds himself surrounded by a convulsed and a half-dissolved one? He cannot live in solitude; he must belong to some community bound by some ties, however imperfect. Men mutually support and add to the boldness and confidence of each other; the weakness of each is strengthened by the force of the whole. I had never before these calamitous times formed any such ideas; I lived on, laboured and prospered, without having ever studied on what the security of my life and the foundation of my prosperity were established; I perceived them just as they left me. Never was a situation so singularly terrible as mine, in every possible respect, as

---

1. The text is taken from the first edition of *Letters from an American Farmer* (1782).

a member of an extensive society, as a citizen of an inferior division of the same society, as a husband, as a father, as a man who exquisitely feels for the miseries of others as well as for his own! But alas! So much is everything now subverted among us that the very word *misery,* with which we were hardly acquainted before, no longer conveys the same ideas, or, rather, tired with feeling for the miseries of others, every one feels now for himself alone. When I consider myself as connected in all these characters, as bound by so many cords, all uniting in my heart, I am seized with a fever of the mind, I am transported beyond that degree of calmness which is necessary to delineate our thoughts. I feel as if my reason wanted to leave me, as if it would burst its poor weak tenement; again, I try to compose myself, I grow cool, and preconceiving the dreadful loss, I endeavour to retain the useful guest.

You know the position of our settlement; I need not therefore describe it. To the west it is inclosed by a chain of mountains, reaching to—; to the east, the country is as yet but thinly inhabited; we are almost insulated, and the houses are at a considerable distance from each other. From the mountains we have but too much reason to expect our dreadful enemy; the wilderness is a harbour where it is impossible to find them. It is a door through which they can enter our country whenever they please; and, as they seem determined to destroy the whole chain of frontiers, our fate cannot be far distant: from Lake Champlain, almost all has been conflagrated one after another. What renders these incursions still more terrible is that they most commonly take place in the dead of the night; we never go to our fields but we are seized with an involuntary fear, which lessens our strength and weakens our labour. No other subject of conversation intervenes between the different accounts, which spread through the country, of successive acts of devastation, and these, told in chimney-corners, swell themselves in our affrighted imaginations into the most terrific ideas! We never sit down either to dinner or supper but the least noise immediately spreads a general alarm and prevents us from enjoying the comfort of our meals. The very appetite proceeding from labour and peace of mind is gone; we eat just enough to keep us alive; our sleep is disturbed by the most frightful dreams; sometimes I start awake, as if the great hour of danger was come; at other times the howling of our dogs seems to announce the arrival of our enemy; we leap out of bed and run to arms; my poor wife, with panting bosom and silent tears, takes leave of me, as if we were to see each other no more; she snatches the youngest children from their beds, who, suddenly awak-

ened, increase by their innocent questions the horror of the dreadful moment. She tries to hide them in the cellar, as if our cellar was inaccessible to the fire. I place all my servants at the windows and myself at the door, where I am determined to perish. Fear industriously increases every sound; we all listen; each communicates to the other his ideas and conjectures. We remain thus sometimes for whole hours, our hearts and our minds racked by the most anxious suspense: what a dreadful situation, a thousand times worse than that of a soldier engaged in the midst of the most severe conflict! Sometimes feeling the spontaneous courage of a man, I seem to wish for the decisive minute; the next instant a message from my wife, sent by one of the children, puzzling me beside with their little questions, unmans me; away goes my courage, and I descend again into the deepest despondency. At last, finding that it was a false alarm, we return once more to our beds; but what good can the kind of sleep of Nature do to us when interrupted by such scenes! Securely placed as you are, you can have no idea of our agitations, but by hearsay; no relation can be equal to what we suffer and to what we feel. Every morning my youngest children are sure to have frightful dreams to relate; in vain I exert my authority to keep them silent; it is not in my power; and these images of their disturbed imagination, instead of being frivolously looked upon as in the days of our happiness, are on the contrary considered as warnings and sure prognostics of our future fate. I am not a superstitious man, but since our misfortunes, I am grown more timid and less disposed to treat the doctrine of omens with contempt.

Though these evils have been gradual, yet they do not become habitual like other incidental evils. The nearer I view the end of this catastrophe, the more I shudder. But why should I trouble you with such unconnected accounts; men secure and out of danger are soon fatigued with mournful details: can you enter with me into fellowship with all these afflictive sensations; have you a tear ready to shed over the approaching ruin of a once opulent and substantial family? Read this, I pray, with the eyes of sympathy, with a tender sorrow; pity the lot of those whom you once called your friends, who were once surrounded with plenty, ease, and perfect security, but who now expect every night to be their last, and who are as wretched as criminals under an impending sentence of the law.

As a member of a large society which extends to many parts of the world, my connexion with it is too distant to be as strong as that which binds me to the inferior division in the midst of which I live. I am told that the great nation of which we are a part is just, wise, and free beyond any other on earth, within its own insular boundaries, but not always so to its distant conquests; I shall not repeat all I have heard because I cannot believe half of it. As a citizen of a smaller society, I find that any kind of opposition to its now prevailing sentiments immediately begets hatred; how easily do men pass from loving to hating and cursing one another! I am a lover of peace; what must I do? I am divided between the respect I feel for the ancient connexion and the fear of innovations, with the consequence of which I am not well acquainted, as they are embraced by my own countrymen. I am conscious that I was happy before this unfortunate revolution. I feel that I am no longer so; therefore I regret the change. This is the only mode of reasoning adapted to persons in my situation. If I attach myself to the mother country, which is 3,000 miles from me, I become what is called an enemy to my own region; if I follow the rest of my countrymen, I become opposed to our ancient masters: both extremes appear equally dangerous to a person of so little weight and consequence as I am, whose energy and example are of no avail. As to the argument on which the dispute is founded, I know little about it. Much has been said and written on both sides, but who has a judgement capacious and clear enough to decide? The great moving principles which actuate both parties are much hid from vulgar eyes, like mine; nothing but the plausible and the probable are offered to our contemplation. The innocent class are always the victims of the few; they are in all countries and at all times the inferior agents on which the popular phantom is erected; they clamour and must toil and bleed, and are always sure of meeting with oppression and rebuke. It is for the sake of the great leaders on both sides that so much blood must be spilt; that of the people is counted as nothing. Great events are not achieved for us, though it is *by* us that they are principally accomplished, by the arms, the sweat, the lives of the people. Books tell me so much that they inform me of nothing. Sophistry, the bane of freemen, launches forth in all her deceiving attire! After all, most men reason from passions; and shall such an ignorant individual as I am decide and say this side is right, that side is wrong? Sentiment and feeling are the only guides I know. Alas, how should I unravel an argument in which Reason herself has given way to brutality and bloodshed! What then must I do? I ask the wisest lawyers, the ablest casuists, the warmest patriots; for I mean honestly. Great Source of wisdom! Inspire me with light sufficient to guide my benighted steps out of this intricate maze! Shall I discard all my ancient principles, shall I renounce that name, that nation which I held once so respectable? I feel the powerful attraction; the sentiments they inspired grew with my earliest knowledge and were grafted upon the first rudiments of my education. On the other hand, shall I arm myself against that country where I first drew breath, against the playmates of my youth, my bosom friends, my acquaintance? The idea makes me shudder! Must I be called a parricide, a traitor, a villain, lose the esteem of all those whom I love to preserve my own, be shunned like a rattlesnake, or be pointed at like a bear? I have neither heroism not magnanimity enough to make so great a sacrifice. Here I am tied, I am fastened by numerous strings, nor do I repine at the pressure they cause; ignorant as I am, I can pervade the utmost extent of the calamities which have already overtaken our poor afflicted country. I can see the great and accumulated ruin yet extending itself as far as the theatre of war has reached; I hear the groans of thousands of families now ruined and desolated by our aggressors. I cannot count the multitude of orphans this war has made nor ascertain the immensity of blood we have lost. Some have asked whether it was a crime to resist, to repel some parts of this evil. Others have asserted that a resistance so general makes pardon unattainable and repentance useless, and dividing the crime among so many renders it imperceptible. What one party calls meritorious, the other denominates flagitious. These opinions vary, contract, or expand, like the events of the war on which they are founded. What can an insignificant man do in the midst of these jarring contradictory parties, equally hostile to persons situated as I am? And after all, who will be the really guilty? Those most certainly who fail of success. Our fate, the fate of thousands, is, then, necessarily involved in the dark wheel of fortune. Why, then, so many useless reasonings; we are the sport of fate. Farewell education, principles, love of our country, farewell; all are become useless to the generality of us: he who governs himself according to what he calls his principles may be punished either by one party or the other for those very principles. He who proceeds without principle, as chance, timidity, or self-preservation directs, will not perhaps fare better, but he will be less blamed. What are *we* in the great scale of events, we poor defenceless frontier inhabitants? What is it to the gazing world whether we breathe or whether we die? Whatever virtue, whatever merit and disinterestedness we may exhibit in our secluded retreats, of what avail? We are like the pismires destroyed by the plough, whose destruction prevents not the future crop. Self-preservation, therefore, the rule of Nature, seems to be the best rule of conduct; what good can we do by vain resistance, by useless efforts? The cool, the distant spectator, placed in safety, may arraign me for ingratitude, may bring forth the principles of Solon or Montesquieu; he may look on me as wilfully guilty; he may call me by the most opprobrious names. Secure from personal danger, his warm imagination, undisturbed by the least agitation of the heart, will expatiate freely on this grand question and will consider this extended field but as exhibiting the double scene of attack and defence. To him the object becomes abstracted; the intermediate glares; the perspective distance and a variety of opinions, unimpaired by affections, present to his mind but one set of ideas. Here he proclaims the high guilt of the one, and there the right of the other. But let him come and reside with us one single month; let him pass with us through all the successive hours of necessary toil, terror, and affright; let him watch with us, his musket in his hand, through tedious, sleepless nights, his imagination furrowed by the keen chisel of every passion; let his wife and his children become exposed to the most dreadful hazards of death; let the existence of his property depend on a single spark, blown by the breath of an enemy; let him tremble with us in our fields, shudder at the rustling of every leaf; let his heart, the seat of the most affecting passions, be powerfully wrung by hearing the melancholy end of his relations and friends; let him trace on the map the progress of these desolations; let his alarmed imagination predict to him the night, the dreadful night when it may be his turn to perish, as so many have perished before. Observe, then, whether the man will not get the better of the citizen, whether his political maxims will not vanish! Yes, he will cease to glow so warmly with the glory of the metropolis; all his wishes will be turned toward the preservation of his family! Oh, were he situated where I am, were his house perpetually filled, as mine is, with miserable victims just escaped from the flames and the scalping knife, telling of barbarities and murders that make human nature tremble, his situation would suspend every political reflection and expel every abstract idea. My heart is full and involuntarily takes hold of any notion from whence it can receive ideal ease or relief. I am informed that the king has the most numerous, as well as the fairest, progeny of children of any potentate now in the world; he may be a great king, but he must feel as we common mortals do in the good

wishes he forms for their lives and prosperity. His mind no doubt often springs forward on the wings of anticipation and contemplates us as happily settled in the world. If a poor frontier inhabitant may be allowed to suppose this great personage the first in our system to be exposed but for one hour to the exquisite pangs we so often feel, would not the preservation of so numerous a family engross all his thoughts; would not the ideas of dominion and other felicities attendant on royalty all vanish in the hour of danger? The regal character, however sacred, would be superseded by the stronger, because more natural one of man and father. Oh! Did he but know the circumstances of this horrid war, I am sure he would put a stop to that long destruction of parents and children. I am sure that while he turned his ears to state policy, he would attentively listen also to the dictates of Nature, that great parent; for, as a good king, he no doubt wishes to create, to spare, and to protect, as she does. Must I then, in order to be called a faithful subject, coolly and philosophically say it is necessary for the good of Britain that my children's brains should be dashed against the walls of the house in which they were reared; that my wife should be stabbed and scalped before my face; that I should be either murthered or captivated; or that for greater expedition we should all be locked up and burnt to ashes as the family of the B—n was? Must I with meekness wait for that last pitch of desolation and receive with perfect resignation so hard a fate from ruffians acting at such a distance from the eyes of any superior, monsters left to the wild impulses of the wildest nature? Could the lions of Africa be transported here and let loose, they would no doubt kill us in order to prey upon our carcasses! But their appetites would not require so many victims. Shall I wait to be punished with death, or else to be stripped of all food and raiment, reduced to despair without redress and without hope? Shall those who may escape see everything they hold dear destroyed and gone? Shall those few survivors, lurking in some obscure corner, deplore in vain the fate of their families, mourn over parents either captivated, butchered, or burnt; roam among our wilds and wait for death at the foot of some tree, without a murmur or without a sigh, for the good of the cause? No, it is impossible! So astonishing a sacrifice is not to be expected from human nature; it must belong to beings of an inferior or superior order, actuated by less or by more refined principles. Even those great personages who are so far elevated above the common ranks of men, those, I mean, who wield and direct so many thunders, those who have let loose against us these demons of war, could they be transported here and metamorphosed into simple planters as we are—they would, from being the arbiters of human destiny, sink into miserable victims; they would feel and exclaim as we do, and be as much at a loss what line of conduct to prosecute. Do you well comprehend the difficulties of our situation? If we stay we are sure to perish at one time or another; no vigilance on our part can save us; if we retire, we know not where to go; every house is filled with refugees as wretched as ourselves; and if we remove, we become beggars. The property of farmers is not like that of merchants, and absolute poverty is worse than death. If we take up arms to defend ourselves, we are denominated rebels; should we not be rebels against Nature, could we be shamefully passive? Shall we, then, like martyrs, glory in an allegiance now become useless, and voluntarily expose ourselves to a species of desolation which, though it ruin us entirely, yet enriches not our ancient masters. By this inflexible and sullen attachment, we shall be despised by our countrymen and destroyed by our ancient friends; whatever we may say, whatever merit we may claim, will not shelter us from those indiscriminate blows, given by hired banditti, animated by all those passions which urge men to shed the blood of others; how bitter the thought! On the contrary, blows received by the hands of those from whom we expected protection extinguish ancient respect and urge us to self-defence—perhaps to revenge; this is the path which Nature herself points out, as well to the civilized as to the uncivilized. The Creator of hearts has himself stamped on them those propensities at their first formation; and must we then daily receive this treatment from a power once so loved? The fox flies or deceives the hounds that pursue him; the bear, when overtaken, boldly resists and attacks them; the hen, the very timid hen, fights for the preservation of her chicken, nor does she decline to attack and to meet on the wing even the swift kite. Shall man, then, provided both with instinct and reason, unmoved, unconcerned, and passive see his subsistence consumed and his progeny either ravished from him or murdered? Shall fictitious reason extinguish the unerring impulse of instinct? No; my former respect, my former attachment, vanishes with my safety; that respect and attachment were purchased by protection, and it has ceased. Could not the great nation we belong to have accomplished her designs by means of her numerous armies, by means of those fleets which cover the ocean? Must those who are masters of two thirds of the trade of the world, who have in their hands the power which almighty gold can give, who possess a

species of wealth that increases with their desires—must they establish their conquest with our insignificant, innocent blood!

Must I, then, bid farewell to Britain, to that renowned country? Must I renounce a name so ancient and so venerable? Alas, she herself, that once indulgent parent, forces me to take up arms against her. She herself first inspired the most unhappy citizens of our remote districts with the thoughts of shedding the blood of those whom they used to call by the name of friends and brethren. That great nation which now convulses the world, which hardly knows the extent of her Indian kingdoms, which looks toward the universal monarchy of trade, of industry, of riches, of power: why must she strew our poor frontiers with the carcasses of her friends, with the wrecks of our insignificant villages, in which there is no gold? When, oppressed by painful recollection, I revolve all these scattered ideas in my mind, when I contemplate my situation and the thousand streams of evil with which I am surrounded, when I descend into the particular tendency even of the remedy I have proposed, I am convulsed—convulsed sometimes to that degree as to be tempted to exclaim. "Why has the Master of the world permitted so much indiscriminate evil throughout every part of this poor planet, at all times, and among all kinds of people?" It ought surely to be the punishment of the wicked only. I bring that cup to my lips, of which I must soon taste, and shudder at its bitterness. What, then, is life, I ask myself; is it a gracious gift? No, it is too bitter; a gift means something valuable conferred, but life appears to be a mere accident, and of the worst kind: we are born to be victims of diseases and passions, of mischances and death; better not to be than to be miserable. Thus, impiously I roam, I fly from one erratic thought to another, and my mind, irritated by these acrimonious reflections, is ready sometimes to lead me to dangerous extremes of violence. When I recollect that I am a father and a husband, the return of these endearing ideas strikes deep into my heart. Alas! They once made it glow with pleasure and with every ravishing exultation; but now they fill it with sorrow. At other times, my wife industriously rouses me out of these dreadful meditations and soothes me by all the reasoning she is mistress of; but her endeavours only serve to make me more miserable by reflecting that she must share with me all these calamities the bare apprehensions of which I am afraid will subvert her reason. Nor can I with patience think that a beloved wife, my faithful helpmate, throughout all my rural schemes the principal hand which has assisted me in rearing the prosperous fabric of ease and independence I lately possessed, as well as my children, those tenants of my heart, should daily and nightly be exposed to such a cruel fate. Self-preservation is above all political precepts and rules, and even superior to the dearest opinions of our minds; a reasonable accommodation of ourselves to the various exigencies of the times in which we live is the most irresistible precept. To this great evil I must seek some sort of remedy adapted to remove or to palliate it; situated as I am, what steps should I take that will neither injure nor insult any of the parties, and at the same time save my family from that certain destruction which awaits it if I remain here much longer. Could I ensure them bread, safety, and subsistence, not the bread of idleness, but that earned by proper labour as heretofore; could this be accomplished by the sacrifice of my life, I would willingly give it up. I attest before heaven that it is only for these I would wish to live and toil, for these whom I have brought into this miserable existence. I resemble, methinks, one of the stones of a ruined arch, still retaining that pristine form which anciently fitted the place I occupied, but the centre is tumbled down; I can be nothing until I am replaced, either in the former circle or in some stronger one. I see one on a smaller scale, and at a considerable distance, but it is within my power to reach it; and since I have ceased to consider myself as a member of the ancient state now convulsed, I willingly descend into an inferior one. I will revert into a state approaching nearer to that of nature, unencumbered either with voluminous laws or contradictory codes, often galling the very necks of those whom they protect, and at the same time sufficiently remote from the brutality of unconnected savage nature. Do you, my friend, perceive the path I have found out? It is that which leads to the tenants of the great—village of—, where, far removed from the accursed neighbourhood of Europeans, its inhabitants live with more ease, decency, and peace than you imagine; who, though governed by no laws, yet find in uncontaminated simple manners all that laws can afford. Their system is sufficiently complete to answer all the primary wants of man and to constitute him a social being such as he ought to be in the great forest of Nature. There it is that I have resolved at any rate to transport myself and family: an eccentric thought, you may say, thus to cut asunder all former comexions and to form new ones with a people whom Nature has stamped with such different characteristics! But as the happiness of my family is the only object of my wishes, I care very little where we are or where we go, provided that we are safe and all united together. Our new calamities, being shared equally by all, will become lighter; our mutual affection for each other will in this great transmutation become the strongest link of our new society, will afford us every joy we can receive on a foreign soil, and preserve us in unity as the gravity and coherency of matter prevent the world from dissolution. Blame me not; it would be cruel in you, it would beside be entirely useless; for when you receive this, we shall be on the wing. When we think all hopes are gone, must we, like poor pusillanimous wretches, despair and die? No; I perceive before me a few resources, though through many dangers, which I will explain to you hereafter. It is not, believe me, a disappointed ambition which leads me to take this step; it is the bitterness of my situation, it is the impossibility of knowing what better measure to adopt: my education fitted me for nothing more than the most simple occupations of life; I am but a feller of trees, a cultivator of lands, the most honourable title an American can have. I have no exploits, no discoveries, no inventions to boast of; I have cleared about 370 acres of land, some for the plough, some for the scythe, and this has occupied many years of my life. I have never possessed or wish to possess anything more than what could be earned or produced by the united industry of my family. I wanted nothing more than to live at home independent and tranquil and to teach my children how to provide the means of a future ample subsistence, founded on labour, like that of their father. This is the career of life I have pursued and that which I had marked out for them and for which they seemed to be so well calculated by their inclinations and by their constitutions. But now these pleasing expectations are gone; we must abandon the accumulated industry of nineteen years; we must fly we hardly know whither, through the most impervious paths, and become members of a new and strange community. Oh, virtue! Is this all the reward thou hast to confer on thy votaries? Either thou art only a chimera, or thou art a timid, useless being; soon affrighted, when ambition, thy great adversary, dictates, when war re-echoes the dreadful sounds and poor helpless individuals are mowed down by its cruel reapers like useless grass. I have at all times generously relieved what few distressed people I have met with; I have encouraged the industrious; my house has always been opened to travellers; I have not lost a month in illness since I have been a man; I have caused upwards of a hundred and twenty families to remove hither. Many of them I have led by the hand in the days of their first trial; distant as I am from any places of worship or school of education, I have been the pastor of my family and the teacher of many of my neighbours. I have learnt them as well as I could the gratitude they owe to God, the Father of harvests, and their duties to man; I have been an useful subject, ever obedient to the laws, ever vigilant to see them respected and observed. My wife hath faithfully followed the same line within her province; no woman was ever a better economist or spun or wore better linen; yet we must perish, perish like wild beasts, included within a ring of fire!

Yes, I will cheerfully embrace that resource; it is a holy inspiration; by night and by day, it presents itself to my mind; I have carefully revolved the scheme; I have considered in all its future effects and tendencies the new mode of living we must pursue, without salt, without spices, without linen, and with little other clothing; the art of hunting we must acquire, the new manners we must adopt, the new language we must speak; the dangers attending the education of my children we must endure. These changes may appear more terrific at a distance perhaps than when grown familiar by practice; what is it to us whether we eat well-made pastry or pounded àlagrichés, well-roasted beef or smoked venison, cabbages or squashes? Whether we wear neat home-spun or good beaver, whether we sleep on feather-beds or on bearskins? The difference is not worth attending to. The difficulty of the language, the fear of some great intoxication among the Indians, finally the apprehension lest my younger children should be caught by that singular charm, so dangerous at their tender years, are the only considerations that startle me. By what power does it come to pass that children who have been adopted when young among these people can never be prevailed on to readopt European manners? Many an anxious parent have I seen last war who at the return of the peace went to the Indian villages where they knew their children had been carried in captivity, when to their inexpressible sorrow they found them so perfectly Indianized that many knew them no longer, and those whose more advanced ages permitted them to recollect their fathers and mothers absolutely refused to follow them and ran to their adoptive parents for protection against the effusions of love their unhappy real parents lavished on them! Incredible as this may appear, I have heard it asserted in a thousand instances, among persons of credit. In the village of———, where I purpose to go, there lived, about fifteen years ago, an Englishman and a Swede, whose history would appear moving had I time to relate it. They were grown to the age of men when they were taken; they happily escaped the great punishment of war captives and

were obliged to marry the squaws who had saved their lives by adoption. By the force of habit, they became at last thoroughly naturalized to this wild course of life. While I was there, their friends sent them a considerable sum of money to ransom themselves with. The Indians, their old masters, gave them their choice, and without requiring any consideration, told them that they had been long as free as themselves. They chose to remain, and the reasons they gave me would greatly surprise you: the most perfect freedom, the ease of living, the absence of those cares and corroding solicitudes which so often prevail with us, the peculiar goodness of the soil they cultivated, for they did not trust altogether to hunting—all these and many more motives which I have forgot made them prefer that life of which we entertain such dreadful opinions. It cannot be, therefore, so bad as we generally conceive it to be; there must be in their social bond something singularly captivating and far superior to anything to be boasted of among us; for thousands of Europeans are Indians, and we have no examples of even one of those aborigines having from choice become Europeans! There must be something more congenial to our native dispositions than the fictitious society in which we live; or else why should children, and even grown persons, become in a short time so invincibly attached to it? There must be something very bewitching in their manners, something very indelible and marked by the very hands of Nature. For, take a young Indian lad, give him the best education you possibly can, load him with your bounty, with presents, nay with riches, yet he would secretly long for his native woods, which you would imagine he must have long since forgot; and on the first opportunity he can possibly find, you will see him voluntarily leave behind all you have given him and return with inexpressible joy to lie on the mats of his fathers. Mr.———some years ago received from a good old Indian, who died in his house, a young lad of nine years of age, his grandson. He kindly educated him with his children and bestowed on him the same care and attention in respect to the memory of his venerable grandfather, who was a worthy man. He intended to give him a genteel trade, but in the spring season when all the family went to the woods to make their maple sugar, he suddenly disappeared, and it was not until seventeen months after that his benefactor heard he had reached the village of Bald Eagle, where he still dwelt. Let us say what we will of them, of their inferior organs, of their want of bread, etc., they are as stout and well made as the Europeans. Without temples, without priests, without kings, and without laws, they are in many instances superior to us; and the proofs of what I advance are that they live without care, sleep without inquietude, take life as it comes, bearing all its asperities with unparalleled patience, and die without any kind of apprehension for what they have done or for what they expect to meet with hereafter. What system of philosophy can give us so many necessary qualifications for happiness? They most certainly are much more closely connected with Nature than we are; they are her immediate children: the inhabitants of the woods are her undefiled offspring; those of the plains are her degenerated breed, far, very far removed from her primitive laws, from her original design. It is therefore resolved on. I will either die in the attempt or succeed; better perish all together in one fatal hour than to suffer what we daily endure. I do not expect to enjoy in the village of———an uninterrupted happiness; it cannot be our lot, let us live where we will; I am not founding my future prosperity on golden dreams. Place mankind where you will, they must always have adverse circumstances to struggle with; from nature, accidents, constitution; from seasons, from that great combination of mischances which perpetually leads us to diseases, to poverty, etc. Who knows but I may meet in this new situation some accident whence may spring up new sources of unexpected prosperity? Who can be presumptuous enough to predict all the good? Who can foresee all the evils which strew the paths of our lives? But after all, I cannot but recollect what sacrifice I am going to make, what amputation I am going to suffer, what transition I am going to experience. Pardon my repetitions, my wild, my trifling reflections; they proceed from the agitations of my mind and the fulness of my heart; the action of thus retracing them seems to lighten the burthen and to exhilarate my spirits; this is, besides, the last letter you will receive from me; I would fain tell you all, though I hardly know how. Oh! In the hours, in the moments of my greatest anguish, could I intuitively represent to you that variety of thought which crowds on my mind, you would have reason to be surprised and to doubt of their possibility. Shall we ever meet again? If we should, where will it be? On the wild shores of———. If it be my doom to end my days there, I will greatly improve them and perhaps make room for a few more families who will choose to retire from the fury of a storm, the agitated billows of which will yet roar for many years on our extended shores. Perhaps I may repossess my house, if it be not burnt down; but how will my improvements look? Why, half defaced, bearing the strong marks of abandonment and of the ravages of war. However, at present I give everything over for lost; I will bid a long farewell to what I leave behind. If ever I repossess it, I shall receive it as a gift, as a reward for my conduct and fortitude. Do not imagine, however, that I am a stoic—by no means: I must, on the contrary, confess to you that I feel the keenest regret at abandoning a house which I have in some measure reared with my own hands. Yes, perhaps I may never revisit those fields which I have cleared, those trees which I have planted, those meadows which, in my youth, were a hideous wilderness, now converted by my industry into rich pastures and pleasant lawns. If in Europe it is praiseworthy to be attached to paternal inheritances, how much more natural, how much more powerful must the tie be with us, who, if I may be permitted the expression, are the founders, the creators, of our own farms! When I see my table surrounded with my blooming offspring, all united in the bonds of the strongest affection, it kindles in my paternal heart a variety of tumultuous sentiments which none but a father and a husband in my situation can feel or describe. Perhaps I may see my wife, my children, often distressed, involuntarily recalling to their minds the ease and abundance which they enjoyed under the paternal roof. Perhaps I may see them want that bread which I now leave behind, overtaken by diseases and penury, rendered more bitter by the recollection of former days of opulence and plenty. Perhaps I may be assailed on every side by unforeseen accidents which I shall not be able to prevent or to alleviate. Can I contemplate such images without the most unutterable emotions? My fate is determined; but I have not determined it, you may assure yourself, without having undergone the most painful conflicts of a variety of passions—interest, love of ease, disappointed views, and pleasing expectations frustrated—I shuddered at the review! Would to God I was master of the stoical tranquillity of that magnanimous sect; oh, that I were possessed of those sublime lessons which Appollonius of Chalcis gave to the Emperor Antoninus! I could then with much more propriety guide the helm of my little bark, which is soon to be freighted with all that I possess most dear on earth, through this stormy passage to a safe harbour, and when there, become to my fellow-passengers a surer guide, a brighter example, a pattern more worthy of imitation, throughout all the new scenes they must pass and the new career they must traverse. I have observed, notwithstanding, the means hitherto made use of to arm the principal nations against our frontiers. Yet they have not, they will not take up the hatchet against a people who have done them no harm. The passions necessary to urge these people to war cannot be roused; they cannot feel the stings of vengeance, the thirst of which alone can impel them to shed blood: far superior in their motives of action to the Europeans who, for sixpence per day, may be engaged to shed that of any people on earth. They know nothing of the nature of our disputes; they have no ideas of such revolutions as this; a civil division of a village or tribe are events which have never been recorded in their traditions; many of them know very well that they have too long been the dupes and the victims of both parties, foolishly arming for our sakes, sometimes against each other, sometimes against our white enemies. They consider us as born on the same land, and, though they have no reasons to love us, yet they seem carefully to avoid entering into this quarrel, from whatever motives. I am speaking of those nations with which I am best acquainted; a few hundreds of the worst kind mixed with whites worse than themselves are now hired by Great Britain to perpetuate those dreadful incursions. In my youth I traded with the————, under the conduct of my uncle, and always traded justly and equitably; some of them remember it to this day. Happily their village is far removed from the dangerous neighbourhood of the whites; I sent a man last spring to it who understands the woods extremely well and who speaks their language; he is just returned, after several weeks' absence, and has brought me, as I had flattered myself, a string of thirty purple wampum as a token that their honest chief will spare us half of his wigwam until we have time to erect one. He has sent me word that they have land in plenty, of which they are not so covetous as the whites; that we may plant for ourselves, and that in the meantime he will procure us some corn and meat; that fish is plenty in the waters of————, and that the village to which he had laid open my proposals have no objection to our becoming dwellers with them. I have not yet communicated these glad tidings to my wife, nor do I know how to do it; I tremble lest she should refuse to follow me, lest the sudden idea of this removal rushing on her mind might be too powerful. I flatter myself I shall be able to accomplish it and to prevail on her; I fear nothing but the effects of her strong attachment to her relations. I would willingly let you know how I purpose to remove my family to so great a distance, but it would become unintelligible to you because you are not acquainted with the geographical situation of this part of the country. Suffice it for you to know that with about twenty-three miles land carriage, I am

enabled to perform the rest by water; and when once afloat, I care not whether it be two or three hundred miles. I propose to send all our provisions, furniture, and clothes to my wife's father, who approves of the scheme, and to reserve nothing but a few necessary articles of covering, trusting to the furs of the chase for our future apparel. Were we imprudently to encumber ourselves too much with baggage, we should never reach to the waters of————, which is the most dangerous as well as the most difficult part of our journey, and yet but a trifle in point of distance. I intend to say to my Negroes, "In the name of God, be free, my honest lads; I thank you for your past services; go, from henceforth, and work for yourselves; look on me as your old friend and fellow-labourer; be sober, frugal, and industrious, and you need not fear earning a comfortable subsistence." Lest my countrymen should think that I am gone to join the incendiaries of our frontiers, I intend to write a letter to Mr.————to inform him of our retreat and of the reasons that have urged me to it. The man whom I sent to———— village is to accompany us also, and a very useful companion he will be on every account.

You may therefore, by means of anticipation, behold me under the wigwam; I am so well acquainted with the principal manners of these people that I entertain not the least apprehension from them. I rely more securely on their strong hospitality than on the witnessed compacts of many Europeans. As soon as possible after my arrival, I design to build myself a wigwam, after the same manner and size with the rest in order to avoid being thought singular or giving occasion for any railleries, though these people are seldom guilty of such European follies. I shall erect it hard by the lands which they propose to allot me, and will endeavour that my wife, my children, and myself may be adopted soon after our arrival. Thus becoming truly inhabitants of their village, we shall immediately occupy that rank within the pale of their society, which will afford us all the amends we can possibly expect for the loss we have met with by the convulsions of our own. According to their customs, we shall likewise receive names from them, by which we shall always be known. My youngest children shall learn to swim and to shoot with the bow, that they may acquire such talents as will necessarily raise them into some degree of esteem among the Indian lads of their own age; the rest of us must hunt with the hunter. I have been for several years an expert marks-man; but I dread lest the imperceptible charm of Indian education may seize my younger children and give them such a propensity to that mode of life as may preclude their returning to the manners and customs of their parents. I have but one remedy to prevent this great evil, and that is to employ them in the labour of the fields as much as I can; I have even resolved to make their daily subsistence depend altogether on it. As long as we keep ourselves busy in tilling the earth, there is no fear of any of us becoming wild; it is the chase and the food it procures that have this strange effect. Excuse a simile—those hogs which range in the woods, and to whom grain is given once a week, preserve their former degree of tameness; but if, on the contrary, they are reduced to live on ground nuts and on what they can get, they soon become wild and fierce. For my part, I can plough, sow, and hunt, as occasion may require; but my wife, deprived of wool and flax, will have no room for industry; what is she then to do? Like the other squaws, she must cook for us the nasaump, the ninchickè, and such other preparations of corn as are customary among these people. She must learn to bake squashes and pompions under the ashes, to slice and smoke the meat of our own killing in order to preserve it; she must cheerfully adopt the manners and customs of her neighbours, in their dress, deportment, conduct, and internal economy, in all respects. Surely if we can have fortitude enough to quit all we have, to remove so far and to associate with people so different from us, these necessary compliances are but subordinate parts of the scheme. The change of garments, when those they carry with them are worn out, will not be the least of my wife's and daughter's concerns, though I am in hopes that self-love will invent some sort of reparation. Perhaps you would not believe that there are in the woods looking-glasses and paint of every colour; and that the inhabitants take as much pains to adorn their faces and their bodies, to fix their bracelets of silver, and plait their hair as our forefathers the Picts used to do in the time of the Romans. Not that I would wish to see either my wife or daughter adopt those savage customs; we can live in great peace and harmony with them without descending to every article; the interruption of trade hath, I hope, suspended this mode of dress. My wife understands inoculation perfectly well; she inoculated all our children one after another and has successfully performed the operation on several scores of people, who, scattered here and there through our woods, were too far removed from all medical assistance. If we can persuade but one family to submit to it, and it succeeds, we shall then be as happy as our situation will admit of; it will raise her into some degree of consideration, for whoever is useful in any society will always be respected. If we are so fortunate as to carry one family through a disorder, which is the plague among these peo-

ple, I trust to the force of example we shall then become truly necessary, valued, and beloved; we indeed owe every kind office to a society of men who so readily offer to admit us into their social partnership and to extend to my family the shelter of their village, the strength of their adoption, and even the dignity of their names. God grant us a prosperous beginning; we may then hope to be of more service to them than even missionaries who have been sent to preach to them a Gospel they cannot understand.

As to religion, our mode of worship will not suffer much by this removal from a cultivated country into the bosom of the woods; for it cannot be much simpler than that which we have followed here these many years, and I will with as much care as I can redouble my attention and twice a week retrace to them the great outlines of their duty to God and to man. I will read and expound to them some part of the decalogue, which is the method I have pursued ever since I married.

Half a dozen of acres on the shores of——, the soil of which I know well, will yield us a great abundance of all we want; I will make it a point to give the overplus to such Indians as shall be most unfortunate in their huntings; I will persuade them, if I can, to till a little more land than they do and not to trust so much to the produce of the chase. To encourage them still farther, I will give a quirn to every six families; I have built many for our poor back-settlers, it being often the want of mills which prevents them from raising grain. As I am a carpenter, I can build my own plough and can be of great service to many of them; my example alone may rouse the industry of some and serve to direct others in their labours. The difficulties of the language will soon be removed; in my evening conversations, I will endeavour to make them regulate the trade of their village in such a manner as that those pests of the continent, those Indian-traders, may not come within a certain distance; and there they shall be obliged to transact their business before the old people. I am in hopes that the constant respect which is paid to the elders, and shame, may prevent the young hunters from infringing this regulation. The son of——will soon be made acquainted with our schemes, and I trust that the power of love and the strong attachment he professes for my daughter may bring him along with us; he will make an excellent hunter; young and vigorous, he will equal in dexterity the stoutest man in the village. Had it not been for this fortunate circumstance, there would have been the greatest danger; for however I respect the simple, the inoffensive society of these people in their villages, the strongest prejudices would make me abhor any alliance with them in blood, disagreeable no doubt to Nature's intentions, which have strongly divided us by so many indelible characters. In the days of our sickness, we shall have recourse to their medical knowledge, which is well calculated for the simple diseases to which they are subject. Thus shall we metamorphose ourselves from neat, decent, opulent planters, surrounded with every conveniency which our external labour and internal industry could give, into a still simpler people divested of everything beside hope, food, and the raiment of the woods: abandoning the large framed house to dwell under the wigwam, and the featherbed to lie on the mat or bear's skin. There shall we sleep undisturbed by frightful dreams and apprehensions; rest and peace of mind will make us the most ample amends for what we shall leave behind. These blessings cannot be purchased too dear; too long have we been deprived of them. I would cheerfully go even to the Mississippi to find that repose to which we have been so long strangers. My heart sometimes seems tired with beating; it wants rest like my eyelids, which feel oppressed with so many watchings.

These are the component parts of my scheme, the success of each of which appears feasible, whence I flatter myself with the probable success of the whole. Still, the danger of Indian education returns to my mind and alarms me much; then again, I contrast it with the education of the times; both appear to be equally pregnant with evils. Reason points out the necessity of choosing the least dangerous, which I must consider as the only good within my reach; I persuade myself that industry and labour will be a sovereign preservative against the dangers of the former; but I consider, at the same time, that the share of labour and industry which is intended to procure but a simple subsistence, with hardly any superfluity, cannot have the same restrictive effects on our minds as when we tilled the earth on a more extensive scale. The surplus could be then realized into solid wealth, and at the same time that this realization rewarded our past labours, it engrossed and fixed the attention of the labourer and cherished in his mind the hope of future riches. In order to supply this great deficiency of industrious motives and to hold out to them a real object to prevent the fatal consequences of this sort of apathy, I will keep an exact account of all that shall be gathered and give each of them a regular credit for the amount of it, to be paid them in real property at the return of peace. Thus, though seemingly toiling for bare subsistence on a foreign land, they shall

entertain the pleasing prospect of seeing the sum of their labours one day realized either in legacies or gifts, equal if not superior to it. The yearly expense of the clothes which they would have received at home, and of which they will then be deprived, shall likewise be added to their credit; thus I flatter myself that they will more cheerfully wear the blanket, the matchcoat, and the moccasins. Whatever success they may meet with in hunting or fishing shall be only considered as recreation and pastime; I shall thereby prevent them from estimating their skill in the chase as an important and necessary accomplishment. I mean to say to them: "You shall hunt and fish merely to show your new companions that you are not inferior to them in point of sagacity and dexterity." Were I to send them to such schools as the interior parts of our settlements afford at present, what can they learn there? How could I support them there? What must become of me; am I to proceed on my voyage and leave them? That I never could submit to. Instead of the perpetual discordant noise of disputes so common among us, instead of those scolding scenes, frequent in every house, they will observe nothing but silence at home and abroad: a singular appearance of peace and concord are the first characteristics which strike you in the villages of these people. Nothing can be more pleasing, nothing surprises an European so much, as the silence and harmony which prevail among them, and in each family, except when disturbed by that accursed spirit given them by the wood rangers in exchange for their furs. If my children learn nothing of geometrical rules, the use of the compass, or of the Latin tongue, they will learn and practise sobriety, for rum can no longer be sent to these people; they will learn that modesty and diffidence for which the young Indians are so remarkable; they will consider labour as the most essential qualification, hunting as the second. They will prepare themselves in the prosecution of our small rural schemes, carried on for the benefit of our little community, to extend them farther when each shall receive his inheritance. Their tender minds will cease to be agitated by perpetual alarms, to be made cowards by continual terrors; if they acquire in the village of—such an awkwardness of deportment and appearance as would render them ridiculous in our gay capitals, they will imbibe, I hope, a confirmed taste for that simplicity which so well becomes the cultivators of the land. If I cannot teach them any of those professions which sometimes embellish and support our society, I will show them how to hew wood, how to construct their own ploughs, and with a few tools how to supply themselves with every necessary implement, both in the house and in the field. If they are hereafter obliged to confess that they belong to no one particular church, I shall have the consolation of teaching them that great, that primary worship which is the foundation of all others. If they do not fear God according to the tenets of any one seminary, they shall learn to worship Him upon the broad scale of nature. The Supreme Being does not reside in peculiar churches or communities; He is equally the great Manitou of the woods and of the plains; and even in the gloom, the obscurity of those very woods, His justice may be as well understood and felt as in the most sumptuous temples. Each worship with us hath, you know, its peculiar political tendency: there it has none but to inspire gratitude and truth: their tender minds shall receive no other idea of the Supreme Being than that of the Father of all men, who requires nothing more of us than what tends to make each other happy. We shall say with them: "Soungwanèha, èsa caurounkyawga, nughwonshauza neattèwek, nèsalanga." Our Father, be thy will done in earth as it is in great heaven.

Perhaps my imagination gilds too strongly this distant prospect; yet it appears founded on so few and simple principles that there is not the same probability of adverse incidents as in more complex schemes. These vague rambling contemplations which I here faithfully retrace carry me sometimes to a great distance; I am lost in the anticipation of the various circumstances attending this proposed metamorphosis! Many unforeseen accidents may doubtless arise. Alas! It is easier for me in all the glow of paternal anxiety, reclined on my bed, to form the theory of my future conduct than to reduce my schemes into practice. But when once secluded from the great society to which we now belong, we shall unite closer together, and there will be less room for jealousies or contentions. As I intend my children neither for the law nor the church, but for the cultivation of the land, I wish them no literary accomplishments; I pray heaven that they may be one day nothing more than expert scholars in husbandry: this is the science which made our continent to flourish more rapidly than any other. Were they to grow up where I am now situated, even admitting that we were in safety; two of them are verging toward that period of their lives when they must necessarily take up the musket and learn, in that new school, all the vices which are so common in armies. Great God! Close my eyes forever rather than I should live to see this calamity! May they rather become inhabitants of the woods.

Thus then in the village of———, in the bosom of that peace it has enjoyed ever since I have known it, connected with mild, hospitable people, strangers to *our* political disputes and having none among themselves; on the shores of a fine river, surrounded with woods, abounding with game, our little society, united in perfect harmony with the new adoptive one, in which we shall be incorporated, shall rest, I hope, from all fatigues, from all apprehensions, from our present terrors, and from our long watchings. Not a word of politics shall cloud our simple conversation; tired either with the chase or the labours of the field, we shall sleep on our mats without any distressing want, having learnt to retrench every superfluous one; we shall have but two prayers to make to the Supreme Being, that He may shed His fertilizing dew on our little crops and that He will be pleased to restore peace to our unhappy country. These shall be the only subject of our nightly prayers and of our daily ejaculations; and if the labour, the industry, the frugality, the union of men, can be an agreeable offering to Him, we shall not fail to receive His paternal blessings. There I shall contemplate Nature in her most wild and ample extent; I shall carefully study a species of society of which I have at present but very imperfect ideas; I will endeavour to occupy with propriety that place which will enable me to enjoy the few and sufficient benefits it confers. The solitary and unconnected mode of life I have lived in my youth must fit me for this trial; I am not the first who has attempted it; Europeans did not, it is true, carry to the wilderness numerous families; they went there as mere speculators, I as a man seeking a refuge from the desolation of war. They went there to study the manner of the aborigines, I to conform to them, whatever they are; some went as visitors, as travellers; I, as a sojourner, as a fellow-hunter and labourer, go determined industriously to work up among them such a system of happiness as may be adequate to my future situation and may be a sufficient compensation for all my fatigues and for the misfortunes I have borne: I have always found it at home; I may hope likewise to find it under the humble roof of my wigwam.

O Supreme Being! If among the immense variety of planets, inhabited by thy creative power, thy paternal and omnipotent care deigns to extend to all the individuals they contain, if it be not beneath thy infinite dignity to cast thy eye on us wretched mortals, if my future felicity is not contrary to the necessary effects of those secret causes which thou hast appointed, receive the supplications of a man to whom in thy kindness thou hast given a wife and an offspring; view us all with benignity, sanctify this strong conflict of regrets; wishes, and other natural passions; guide our steps through these unknown paths and bless our future mode of life. If it is good and well meant, it must proceed from thee; thou knowest, O Lord, our enterprise contains neither fraud nor malice nor revenge. Bestow on me that energy of conduct now become so necessary that it may be in my power to carry the young family thou hast given me through this great trial with safety and in thy peace. Inspire me with such intentions and such rules of conduct as may be most acceptable to thee. Preserve, O God, preserve the companion of my bosom, the best gift thou hast given me; endue her with courage and strength sufficient to accomplish this perilous journey. Bless the children of our love, those portions of our hearts; I implore thy divine assistance, speak to their tender minds and inspire them with the love of that virtue which alone can serve as the basis of their conduct in this world and of their happiness with thee. Restore peace and concord to our poor afflicted country; assuage the fierce storm which has so long ravaged it. Permit, I beseech thee, O Father of nature, that our ancient virtues and our industry may not be totally lost and that as a reward for the great toils we have made on this new land, we may be restored to our ancient tranquillity and enabled to fill it with successive generations that will constantly thank thee for the ample subsistence thou hast given them.

The unreserved manner in which I have written must give you a convincing proof of that friendship and esteem of which I am sure you never yet doubted. As members of the same society, as mutually bound by the ties of affection and old acquaintance, you certainly cannot avoid feeling for my distresses; you cannot avoid mourning with me over that load of physical and moral evil with which we are all oppressed. My own share of it I often overlook when I minutely contemplate all that hath befallen our native country.

THREE FEDERALIST PAPERS

The original agreement binding together the entities that had rebelled against Great Britain, called at the time the Articles of Confederation, was drafted rather hastily and during intense and sometimes heated debates in the Continental Congress between 1776 and 1777. The Articles of Confederation were not formally ratified by all the different states until 1781, and by that time, sentiment was growing that the Articles were insufficient as legal instruments, for they did not identify the individual powers or clarify the nature and operation of an executive power. Under the Articles of Confederation, Congress had the power to declare and make war and international treaties. But Congress lacked any measure to enable it to obtain funds for operations of the government because it lacked the power to tax. By 1780, the confederated government faced significant fiscal crises because it was unable to pay national debts or to secure the compliance of individual states with regard to international treaties.

The economic crisis was a crisis felt internally, as well. Within regions, people were feeling the stresses that a wartime economy—and the absence of wide farming—had brought. There were shortages of domestic goods and trade goods, and hard specie (i.e., hard currency, not paper money) was difficult to come by. Disturbances followed where stresses became the greatest. The civil disturbance, called Shays's Rebellion, in 1787 is a good case in point. The insurgency by farmers is called Shays's Rebellion because it was said to have been fostered by Daniel Shays, a Revolutionary War veteran. In this conflict, Massachusetts farmers surrounded local courthouses and federal arsenals to block the entrance of officials who would be ruling on their imprisonment or the foreclosures of their farms for lack of rental payments. The farmers were armed, and they felt justified in their complaints that they had not received sufficient time or assistance in taking care of their debt. The idea of being taxed or having the farms taken away was unconscionable to them. The armed standoff between approximately 1,500 farmers and 1,000 militia members ended in the deaths of four farmers.

Civil problems like the one caused in Massachusetts indicated an increasing economic crisis that was being felt within all the newly organizing states. Combined with the evident impotence of the national government, these problems prompted leaders to call for a Federal Convention. The Federal Convention was held outside the scrutiny of newspaper writers and public commentators between May and September 1787. It produced the new federal Constitution, which was then presented to the individual states for ratification.

Ratification of the Constitution was by no means an easy or uncontested process. Opponents of the Constitution argued that it concentrated too much power in the hands of a few individuals and that election to federal office would mean that the national government would be populated with aristocrats, rather than laboring and middling levels of people. The Federalists feared having a standing army because they thought conscription a dangerous instrument when it went into the hands of unscrupulous leaders. They argued that the new Constitution did nothing to guarantee the rights of individuals. (The Bill of Rights later attached to the Constitution was the eventual response to this last criticism.) Despite their general support for a loose confederation of states, these opponents of the Constitution came to be known as Anti-Federalists.

Those who supported the Constitution claimed the name Federalist for themselves, and when their opponents began publishing criticisms of the Constitution, especially in key states where ratification was hotly contested, the Federalists responded with their own statements supporting the new Constitutional measures. The most famous reply to the critics of the Constitution came in a series of essays published originally in New York (where the governor, George Clinton, opposed the Constitution). These essays, called simply "The Federalist" and signed "Publius," appeared in New York magazines between October 1787 and May 1788, but they were also reprinted in other states and were collected in book form in 1788.

The Federalist essays were the collaborative production of three members of the Federal Convention: Alexander Hamilton (1757–1804), John Jay (1745–1829), and James Madison (1751–1836). Hamilton, a New York lawyer who had been Washington's secretary during the war, had (using the pen name, Continentalist) published several letters beginning in 1781. Hamilton called for a strengthened national government in order to secure the future for posterity, given all that had been fought for during the Revolution. In 1787, when it seemed as though New York might not ratify the Constitution, Hamilton began the Federalist essays and then recruited Jay and Madison to assist him. Jay, also a New York lawyer, had been president of the Continental Congress. Madison, a Virginian, had been responsible for the "Virginia Plan" upon which much of the Constitution had been based. Madison had also made an intensive study of political theory in preparation for making that proposal.

The arguments that Hamilton, Madison, and Jay made in the Federalist Papers were eventually the views that prevailed. By 1789, ratification of the Constitution was guaranteed. In 1790, the last of the thirteen states (Rhode Island) ratified the document. With the exception of the Bill of Rights, the Anti-Federalists' concerns did not result in changes to the Constitution, which became and has remained the founding legal document of the United States.

THE FEDERALIST NO. 6[1]

November 14, 1787

To the People of the State of New York.
The three last numbers of this Paper have been dedicated to an enumeration of the dangers to which we should be exposed, in a state of disunion, from the arms and arts of foreign nations. I shall now proceed to delineate dangers of a different, and, perhaps, still more alarming kind, those which will in all probability flow from dissentions between the States themselves, and from domestic factions and convulsions. These have been already in some instances slightly anticipated, but they deserve a more particular and more full investigation.

A man must be far gone in Utopian speculations who can seriously doubt, that if these States should either be wholly disunited, or only united in partial confederacies, the subdivisions into which they might be thrown would have frequent and violent contests with each other. To presume a want of motives for such contests, as an argu-

---

1. The sixth federalist paper has been attributed to Alexander Hamilton. It was first published in *The Independent Journal* on November 14, 1787.

ment against their existence, would be to forget that men are ambitious, vindictive and rapacious. To look for a continuation of harmony between a number of independent unconnected sovereignties, situated in the same neighbourhood, would be to disregard the uniform course of human events, and to set at defiance the accumulated experience of ages.

The causes of hostility among nations are innumerable. There are some which have a general and almost constant operation upon the collective bodies of society: Of this description are the love of power or the desire of preeminence and dominion—the jealousy of power, or the desire of equality and safety. There are others which have a more circumscribed, though an equally operative influence, within their spheres: Such are the rivalships and competitions of commerce between commercial nations. And there are others, not less numerous than either of the former, which take their origin intirely in private passions; in the attachments, enmities, interests, hopes and fears of leading individuals in the communities of which they are members. Men of this class, whether the favourites of a king or of a people, have in too many instances abused the confidence they possessed; and assuming the pretext of some public motive, have not scrupled to sacrifice the national tranquility to personal advantage, or personal gratification.

The celebrated Pericles, in compliance with the resentments of a prostitute,[2] at the expense of much of the blood and treasure of his countrymen, attacked, vanquished and destroyed, the city of the *Samnians*. The same man, stimulated by private pique against the *Megarensians,*[3] another nation of Greece, or to avoid a prosecution with which he was threatened as an accomplice in a supposed theft of the statuary *Phidias,*[4] or to get rid of the accusations prepared to be brought against him for dissipating the funds of the State in the purchase of popularity,[5] or from a combination of all these causes, was the primitive author of that famous and fatal war, distinguished in the Grecian annals by the name of the *Pelopponesian* war; which, after various vicissitudes, intermissions and renewals, terminated in the ruin of the Athenian commonwealth.

The ambitious Cardinal,[6] who was Prime Minister to Henry VIIIth permitting his vanity to aspire to the Tripple-Crown[7] entertained hopes of succeeding in the acquisition of that splendid prize by the influence of the Emperor Charles Vth. To secure the favour and interest of this enterprising and powerful Monarch, he precipitated England into a war with France, contrary to the plainest dictates of Policy, and at the hazard of the safety and independence, as well of the Kingdom over which he presided by his councils, as of Europe in general. For if there ever was a Sovereign who bid fair to realise the project of universal monarchy it was the Emperor Charles Vth, of whose intrigues Wolsey was at once the instrument and the dupe.

The influence which the bigotry of one female,[8] the petulancies of another,[9] and the cabals of a third,[10] had in the cotemporary policy, ferments and pacifications of a considerable part of Europe are topics that have been too often descanted upon not to be generally known.[11]

To multiply examples of the agency of personal considerations in the production of great national events, either foreign or domestic, according to their direction would be an unnecessary waste of time. Those who have but a superficial acquaintance with the sources from which they are to be drawn will themselves recollect a variety of instances; and those who have a tolerable knowledge of human nature will not stand in need of such lights, to form their opinion either of the reality or extent of that agency. Perhaps however a reference, tending to illustrate the general principle, may with propriety be made to a case which has lately happened among ourselves. If SHAYS had not

---

2. "Aspasia, vide Plutarch's life of Pericles." [Au.]

3. "Idem." [Au.]

4. "Idem. Phidias was supposed to have stolen some public gold with the connivance of Pericles for the embellishment of the statue of Minerva." [Au.]

5. "Idem." [Au.]

6. Thomas Wolsey (c. 1475–1530).

7. The Pope's crown.

8. "Madame de Maintenon." [Au.]

9. "Dutchess of Marlborough." [Au.]

10. "Madame De Pompadoure." [Au.]

11. Madame de Maintenon, the wife of Louis XIV of France, was believed to have influenced him to persecute the Huguenots; the dutchess of Marlborough was an influential adviser to Queen Anne from 1702 to 1710; Madame de Pompadour was the mistress of Louis XV, infamous for her involvement in court intrigues.

been a *desperate debtor* it is much to be doubted whether Massachusetts would have been plunged into a civil war.[12]

But notwithstanding the concurring testimony of experience, in this particular, there are still to be found visionary, or designing men, who stand ready to advocate the paradox of perpetual peace between the States, though dismembered and alienated from each other. The genius of republics (say they) is pacific; the spirit of commerce has a tendency to soften the manners of men and to extinguish those inflammable humours which have so often kindled into wars. Commercial republics, like ours, will never be disposed to waste themselves in ruinous contentions with each other. They will be governed by mutual interest, and will cultivate a spirit of mutual amity and concord.

Is it not (we may ask these projectors in politics) the true interests of all nations to cultivate the same benevolent and philosophic spirit? If this be their true interest, have they in fact pursued it? Has it not, on the contrary, invariably been found, that momentary passions and immediate interests have a more active and imperious controul over human conduct than general or remote considerations of policy, utility or justice? Have republics in practice been less addicted to war than monarchies? Are not the former administered by men as well as the latter? Are there not aversions, predilections, rivalships and desires of unjust acquisition that affect nations as well as kings? Are not popular assemblies frequently subject to the impulses of rage, resentment, jealousy, avarice, and of other irregular and violent propensities? Is it not well known that their determinations are often governed by a few individuals, in whom they place confidence, and are of course liable to be tinctured by the passions and views of those individuals? Has commerce hitherto done anything more than change the objects of war? Is not the love of wealth as domineering and enterprising a passion as that of power or glory? Have there not been as many wars founded upon commercial motives, since that has become the prevailing system of nations, as were before occasioned b[y] the cupidity of territory or dominion? Has not the spirit of commerce in many instances administered new incentives to the appetite both for the one and for the other? Let experience, the least fallible guide of human opinions, be appealed to for an answer to these inquiries.

Sparta, Athens, Rome and Carthage were all Republics; two of them, Athens and Carthage, of the commercial kind. Yet were they as often engaged in wars, offensive and defensive, as the neighbouring Monarchies of the same times. Sparta was little better than a well regulated camp; and Rome was never sated of carnage and conquest.

Carthage, though a commercial Republic, was the aggressor in the very war that ended in her destruction. Hannibal had carried her arms into the heart of Italy and to the gates of Rome, before Scipio, in turn, gave him an overthrow in the territories of Carthage and made a conquest of the Commonwealth.

Venice in latter times figured more than once in wars of ambition; 'till becoming an object of terror to the other Italian States, Pope Julius the Second found means to accomplish that formidable league,[13] which gave a deadly blow to the power and pride of this haughty Republic.

The Provinces of Holland, 'till they were overwhelmed in debts and taxes, took a leading and conspicuous part in the wars of Europe. They had furious contests with England for the dominion of the sea; and were among the most persevering and most implacable of the opponents of Louis XIV.

In the government of Britain the representatives of the people compose one branch of the national legislature. Commerce has been for ages the predominant pursuit of that country. Few nations, nevertheless, have been more frequently engaged in war; and the wars, in which that kingdom has been engaged, have in numerous instances proceeded from the people.

There have been, if I may so express it, almost as many popular as royal wars. The cries of the nation and the importunities of their representatives have, upon various occasions, dragged their monarchs into war, or continued them in it contrary to their inclinations, and, sometimes, contrary to the real interests of the State. In that memorable struggle for superiority, between the rival Houses of Austria and Bourbon which so long kept Europe in a flame, it is well known that the antipathies of the English against the avarice of a favourite leader,[14] protracted the war beyond the limits marked out by sound policy and for

---

12. Shays's Rebellion of 1786–87, led by Revolutionary War veteran Daniel Shays, was an armed attempt to prevent legal action against debtors.

13. "The League of Cambray, comprehending the Emperor, the King of France, the King of Arragon, and most of the Italian Princes and States." [Au.]

14. "The Duke of Marlborough." [Au.]

a considerable time in opposition to the views of the Court.[15]

The wars of these two last mentioned nations have in a great measure grown out of commercial considerations—The desire of supplanting and the fear of being supplanted either in particular branches of traffic or in the general advantages of trade and navigation; and sometimes even the more culpable desire of sharing in the commerce of other nations, without their consent.

The last war but two between Britain and Spain sprang from the attempts of the English merchants, to prosecute an illicit trade with the Spanish main.[16] These unjustifiable practices on their part produced severities on the part of the Spaniards, towards the subjects of Great Britain, which were not more justifiable; because they exceeded the bounds of a just retaliation, and were chargeable with inhumanity and cruelty. Many of the English who were taken on the Spanish coasts were sent to dig in the mines of Potosi; and by the usual progress of a spirit of resentment, the innocent were after a while confounded with the guilty in indiscriminate punishment. The complaints of the merchants kindled a violent flame throughout the nation, which soon after broke out in the house of commons, and was communicated from that body to the ministry. Letters of reprisal were granted and a war ensued, which in its consequences overthrew all the alliances that but twenty years before had been formed, with sanguine expectations of the most beneficial fruits.[17]

From this summary of what has taken place in other countries, whose situations have borne the nearest resemblance to our own, what reason can we have to confide in those reveries, which would seduce us into an expectation of peace and cordiality between the members of the present confederacy, in a state of separation? Have we not already seen enough of the fallacy and extravagance of those idle theories which have amused us with promises of an exemption from the imperfections, weaknesses and evils incident to society in every shape? Is it not time to awake from the deceitful dream of a golden age, and to adopt as a practical maxim for the direction of our political conduct, that we, as well as the other inhabitants of the globe, are yet remote from the happy empire of perfect wisdom and perfect virtue?

Let the point of extreme depression to which our national dignity and credit have sunk—let the inconveniences felt everywhere from a lax and ill administration of government—let the revolt of a part of the State of North Carolina—the late menacing disturbances in Pennsylvania and the actual insurrections and rebellions in Massachusetts declare![18]

So far is the general sense of mankind from corresponding with the tenets of those, who endeavor to lull asleep our apprehensions of discord and hostility between the States, in the event of disunion, that it has from long observation of the progress of society become a sort of axiom in politics, that vicinity, or nearness of situation, constitutes nations natural enemies. An intelligent writer expresses himself on this subject to this effect—"NEIGHBOURING NATIONS (says he) are naturally ENEMIES of each other, unless their common weakness forces them to league in a CONFEDERATE REPUBLIC, and their constitution prevents the differences that neighbourhood occasions, extinguishing that secret jealousy, which disposes all States to aggrandise themselves at the expence of their neighbours."[19] This passage, at the same time points out the EVIL and suggests the REMEDY.

PUBLIUS.

THE FEDERALIST NO. 10[1]

November 22, 1787

To the People of the State of New York.
Among the numerous advantages promised by a well constructed Union, none deserves to be more accurately developed than its tendency to break and control the violence of faction. The friend of popular governments, never finds himself so much alarmed for their character

---

15. The War of the Spanish Succession, 1701–14.

16. The War of Jenkin's Ear of 1739.

17. The 1713 Treaty of Utrecht had established a balance of power on the European continent.

18. In 1784, citizens in North Carolina attempted to secede from that state; in 1787 a similar movement occurred in the Wyoming valley of Pennsylvania; Shays's Rebellion occurred in Massachusetts in 1786–87.

19. "Vede Principes des negotiations par L'Abbe de Mably." [Au.]

1. Federalist No. 10 has been attributed to James Madison. It was first published in the *Daily Advertiser* on November 22, 1787.

and fate, as when he contemplates their propensity to this dangerous vice. He will not fail therefore to set a due value on any plan which, without violating the principles to which he is attached, provides a proper cure for it. The instability, injustice and confusion introduced into the public councils, have in truth been the mortal diseases under which popular governments have every where perished; as they continue to be the favorite and fruitful topics from which the adversaries to liberty derive their most specious declamations. The valuable improvements made by the American Constitutions on the popular models, both antient and modern, cannot certainly be too much admired; but it would be an unwarrantable partiality, to contend that they have as effectually obviated the danger on this side as was wished and expected. Complaints are every where heard from our most considerate and virtuous citizens, equally the friends of public and private faith, and of public and personal liberty; that our governments are too unstable; that the public good is disregarded in the conflicts of rival parties; and that measures are too often decided, not according to the rules of justice, and the rights of the minor party; but by the superior force of an interested and over-bearing majority. However anxiously we may wish that these complaints had no foundation, the evidence of known facts will not permit us to deny that they are in some degree true. It will be found indeed, on a candid review of our situation, that some of the distresses under which we labour, have been erroneously charged on the operation of our governments; but it will be found at the same time, that other causes will not alone account for many of our heaviest misfortunes; and particularly, for that prevailing and increasing distrust of public engagements, and alarm for private rights, which are echoed from one end of the continent to the other. These must be chiefly, if not wholly, effects of the unsteadiness and injustice, with which a factious spirit has tainted our public administrations.

By a faction I understand a number of citizens, whether amounting to a majority or minority of the whole, who are united and actuated by some common impulse of passion, or of interest, adverse to the rights of other citizens, or to the permanent and aggregate interests of the community.

There are two methods of curing the mischiefs of faction: the one, by removing its causes; the other, by controling its effects.

There are again two methods of removing the causes of faction: the one by destroying the liberty which is essential to its existence; the other, by giving to every citizen the same opinions, the same passions, and the same interests.

It could never be more truly said than of the first remedy, that it is worse than the disease. Liberty is to faction, what air is to fire, an aliment without which it instantly expires. But it could not be a less folly to abolish liberty, which is essential to political life, because it nourishes faction, than it would be to wish the annihilation of air, which is essential to animal life, because it imparts to fire its destructive agency.

The second expedient is as impracticable, as the first would be unwise. As long as the reason of man continues fallible, and he is at liberty to exercise it, different opinions will be formed. As long as the connection subsists between his reason and his self-love, his opinions and his passions will have a reciprocal influence on each other; and the former will be objects to which the latter will attach themselves. The diversity in the faculties of men from which the rights of property originate, is not less an insuperable obstacle to a uniformity of interests. The protection of these faculties is the first object of Government. From the protection of different and unequal faculties of acquiring property, the possession of different degrees and kinds of property immediately results: And from the influence of these on the sentiments and views of the respective proprietors, ensues a division of the society into different interests and parties.

The latent causes of faction are thus sown in the nature of man; and we see them every where brought into different degrees of activity, according to the different circumstances of civil society. A zeal for different opinions concerning religion, concerning Government, and many other points, as well of speculation as of practice; an attachment to different leaders ambitiously contending for pre-eminence and power; or to persons of other descriptions whose fortunes have been interesting to the human passions, have in turn divided mankind into parties, inflamed them with mutual animosity, and rendered them much more disposed to vex and oppress each other, than to co-operate for their common good. So strong is this propensity of mankind to fall into mutual animosities, that where no substantial occasion presents itself, the most frivolous and fanciful distinctions have been sufficient to kindle their unfriendly passions, and excite their most violent conflicts. But the most common and durable source of factions, has been the various and unequal distribution of property. Those who hold, and those who are without property, have ever formed distinct interests in society. Those who are creditors, and those who are debtors, fall under a like discrimination. A landed interest, a manufacturing interest, a mercantile interest, a monied interest, with many lesser interests, grow up of necessity in civilized nations, and divide them into different classes, actuated by different sentiments and views. The regulation of these various and interfering interests forms the principal task of modern Legislation, and involves the spirit of party and faction in the necessary and ordinary operations of Government.

No man is allowed to be a judge in his own cause; because his interest would certainly bias his judgment, and, not improbably, corrupt his integrity. With equal, nay with greater reason, a body of men, are unfit to be both judges and parties, at the same time; yet, what are many of the most important acts of legislation, but so many judicial determinations, not indeed concerning the rights of single persons, but concerning the rights of large bodies of citizens; and what are the different classes of legislators, but advocates and parties to the causes which they determine? Is a law proposed concerning private debts? It is a question to which the creditors are parties on one side, and the debtors on the other. Justice ought to hold the balance between them. Yet the parties are and must be themselves the judges; and the most numerous party, or, in other words, the most powerful faction must be expected to prevail. Shall domestic manufactures be encouraged, and in what degree, by restrictions on foreign manufactures? are questions which would be differently decided by the landed and the manufacturing classes; and probably by neither, with a sole regard to justice and the public good. The apportionment of taxes on the various descriptions of property, is an act which seems to require the most exact impartiality, yet there is perhaps no legislative act in which greater opportunity and temptation are given to a predominant party, to trample on the rules of justice. Every shilling with which they over-burden the inferior number, is a shilling saved to their own pockets.

It is in vain to say, that enlightened statesman will be able to adjust these clashing interests, and render them all subservient to the public good. Enlightened statesmen will not always be at the helm: Nor, in many cases, can such an adjustment be made at all, without taking into view indirect and remote considerations, which will rarely prevail over the immediate interest which one party may find in disregarding the rights of another, or the good of the whole.

The inference to which we are brought, is, that the *causes* of faction cannot be removed; and that relief is only to be sought in the means of controling its *effects*.

If a faction consists of less than a majority, relief is supplied by the republican principle, which enables the majority to defeat its sinister views by regular vote: It may clog the administration, it may convulse the society; but it will be unable to execute and mask its violence under the forms of the Constitution. When a majority is included in a faction, the form of popular government on the other hand enables it to sacrifice to its ruling passion or interest, both the public good and the rights of other citizens. To secure the public good, and private rights, against the danger of such a faction, and at the same time to preserve the spirit and the form of popular government, is then the great object to which our enquiries are directed: Let me add that it is the great desideratum, by which alone this form of government can be rescued from the opprobrium under which it has so long labored, and be recommended to the esteem and adoption of mankind.

By what means is this object attainable? Evidently by one of two only. Either the existence of the same passion or interest in a majority at the same time, must be prevented; or the majority, having such co-existent passion or interest, must be rendered, by their number and local situation, unable to concert and carry into effect schemes of oppression. If the impulse and the opportunity be suffered to coincide, we well know that neither moral nor religious motives can be relied on as an adequate control. They are not found to be such on the injustice and violence of individuals, and lose their efficacy in proportion to the number combined together; that is, in proportion as their efficacy becomes needful.

From this view of the subject, it may be concluded, that a pure Democracy, by which I mean, a Society, consisting of a small number of citizens, who assemble and administer the Government in person, can admit of no cure for the mischiefs of faction. A common passion or interest will, in almost every case, be felt by a majority of the whole; a communication and concert results from the form of Government itself; and there is nothing to check the inducements to sacrifice the weaker party, or an obnoxious individual. Hence it is, that such Democracies have ever been spectacles of turbulence and contention; have ever been found incompatible with personal security, or the rights of property; and have in general been as short in their lives, as they have been violent in their deaths. Theoretic politicians, who have patronized this species of Government, have erroneously supposed, that by reducing mankind to a perfect equality in their political rights, they would, at the same time, be perfectly equalized and assimilated in their possessions, their opinions, and their passions.

A Republic, by which I mean a Government in which the scheme of representation takes place, opens a different prospect, and promises the cure for which we are seeking. Let us examine the points in which it varies from pure Democracy, and we shall comprehend both the nature of the cure, and the efficacy which it must derive from the Union.

The two great points of difference between a Democracy and a Republic, are first, the delegation of the Government, in the latter, to a small number of citizens elected by the rest; secondly, the greater number of citizens, and greater sphere of country, over which the latter may be extended.

The effect of the first difference is, on the one hand to refine and enlarge the public views, by passing them through the medium of a chosen body of citizens, whose wisdom may best discern the true interest of their country, and whose patriotism and love of justice, will be least likely to sacrifice it to temporary or partial considerations. Under such a regulation, it may well happen that the public voice pronounced by the representatives of the people, will be more consonant to the public good, than if pronounced by the people themselves convened for the purpose. On the other hand, the effect may be inverted. Men of factious tempers, of local prejudices, or of sinister designs, may by intrigue, by corruption or by other means, first obtain the suffrages, and then betray the interests of the people. The question resulting is, whether small or extensive Republics are most favourable to the election of proper guardians of the public weal: and it is clearly decided in favour of the latter by two obvious considerations.

In the first place it is to be remarked, that however small the Republic may be, the representatives must be raised to a certain number, in order to guard against the cabals of a few; and that however large it may be, they must be limited to a certain number, in order to guard against the confusion of a multitude. Hence the number of Representatives in the two cases not being in proportion to that of the Constituents, and being proportionally greatest in the small republic, it follows, that if the proportion of fit characters, be not less, in the large than in the small republic, the former will present a greater option, and consequently a greater probability of a fit choice.

In the next place, as each Representative will be chosen by a greater number of citizens in the large than in the small Republic, it will be more difficult for unworthy candidates to practise with success the vicious arts, by which elections are too often carried; and the suffrages of the people being more free, will be more likely to centre on men who possess the most attractive merit, and the most diffusive and established characters.

It must be confessed, that in this, as in most other cases, there is a mean, on both sides of which inconveniencies will be found to lie. By enlarging too much the number of electors, you render the representative too little acquainted with all their local circumstances and lesser interests; as by reducing it too much, you render him unduly attached to these, and too little fit to comprehend and pursue great and national objects. The Federal Constitution forms a happy combination in this respect; the great and aggregate interests being referred to the national, the local and particular to the state legislatures.

The other point of difference is, the greater number of citizens and extent of territory which may be brought within the compass of Republican, than of Democratic government; and it is this circumstance principally which renders factious combinations less to be dreaded in the former, than in the latter. The smaller the society, the fewer probably will be the distinct parties and interests composing it; the fewer the distinct parties and interests, the more frequently will a majority be found of the same party; and the smaller the number of individuals composing a majority, and the smaller the compass within which they are placed, the more easily will they concert and execute their plans of oppression. Extend the sphere, and you take in a greater variety of parties and interests; you make it less probable that a majority of the whole will have a common motive to invade the rights of other citizens; or if such a common motive exists, it will be more difficult for all who feel it to discover their own strength, and to act in unison with each other. Besides other impediments, it may be remarked, that where there is a consciousness of unjust or dishonourable purposes, communication is always checked by distrust, in proportion to the number whose concurrence is necessary.

Hence it clearly appears, that the same advantage, which a Republic has over a Democracy, in controling the effects of faction, is enjoyed by a large over a small republic—is enjoyed by the Union over the States composing it. Does this advantage consist in the substitution of Representatives, whose enlightened views and virtuous sentiments render them superior to local prejudices, and to schemes of injustice? It will not be denied, that the Representation of the Union will be most likely to possess these requisite endowments. Does it consist in the greater security afforded by a greater variety of parties, against the event of any one party being able to out-number and oppress the rest? In an equal degree does the encreased variety of parties, comprised within the Union, encrease this security. Does it, in fine, consist in the greater obstacles opposed to the concert and accomplishment of the secret wishes of an unjust and interested majority? Here, again, the extent of the Union gives it the most palpable advantage.

The influence of factious leaders may kindle a flame within their particular States, but will be unable to spread a general conflagration through the other States: A religious sect, may degenerate into a political faction in a part of the Confederacy; but the variety of sects dispersed over the entire face of it, must secure the national Councils against any danger from that source: a rage for paper money, for an abolition of debts, for an equal division of property, or for any other improper or wicked project, will be less apt to prevade the whole body of the Union, than a particular member of it; in the same proportion as such a malady is more likely to taint a particular county or district, than an entire State.

In the extent and proper structure of the Union, therefore, we behold a Republican remedy for the diseases most incident to Republican Government. And according to the degree of pleasure and pride, we feel in being Republicans, ought to be our zeal in cherishing the spirit, and supporting the character of Federalists.

Publius.

THE FEDERALIST NO. 51[1]

February 6, 1788

To the People of the State of New York.

To what expedient then shall we finally resort for maintaining in practice the necessary partition of power among the several departments, as laid down in the constitution? The only answer that can be given is, that as all these exterior provisions are found to be inadequate, the

---

1. Federalist No. 51 has been attributed to James Madison. It was first published in the *Independent Journal* on February 6, 1788. This essay was numbered "50" in the magazine, but given the number 51 in the collected 1788 edition, the number traditionally given it in succeeding years.

defect must be supplied, by so contriving the interior structure of the government, as that its several constituent parts may, by their mutual relations, be the means of keeping each other in their proper places. Without presuming to undertake a full development of this important idea, I will hazard a few general observations, which may perhaps place it in a clearer light, and enable us to form a more correct judgment of the principles and structure of the government planned by the convention.

In order to lay a due foundation for that separate and distinct exercise of the different powers of government, which to a certain extent, is admitted on all hands to be essential to the preservation of liberty, it is evident that each department should have a will of its own; and consequently should be so constituted that the members of each should have as little agency as possible in the appointment of the members of the others. Were this principle rigorously adhered to, it would require that all the appointments for the supreme executive, legislative and judiciary magistracies, should be drawn from the same fountain of authority, the people, through channels, having no communication whatever with one another. Perhaps such a plan of constructing the several departments would be less difficult in practice than it may in contemplation appear. Some difficulties however, and some additional expence, would attend the execution of it. Some deviations therefore from the principle must be admitted. In the constitution of the judiciary department in particular, it might be inexpedient to insist rigorously on the principle; first, because peculiar qualifications being essential in the members, the primary consideration ought to be to select that mode of choice, which best secures these qualifications, secondly, because the permanent tenure by which the appointments are held in that department, must soon destroy all sense of dependence on the authority conferring them.

It is equally evident that the members of each department should be as little dependent as possible on those of the others, for the emoluments annexed to their offices. Were the executive magistrate, or the judges, not independent of the legislature in this particular, their independence in every other would be merely nominal.

But the great security against a gradual concentration of the several powers in the same department, consists in giving to those who administer each department, the necessary constitutional means, and personal motives, to resist encroachments of the others. The provision for defence must in this, as in all other cases, be made commensurate to the danger of attack. Ambition must be made to counteract ambition. The interest of the man must be connected with the constitutional rights of the place. It may be a reflection on human nature, that such devices should be necessary to controul the abuses of government. But what is government itself but the greatest of all reflections on human nature? If men were angels, no government would be necessary. If angels were to govern men, neither external nor internal controuls on government would be necessary. In framing a government which is to be administered by men over men, the great difficulty lies in this: You must first enable the government to controul the governed; and in the next place, oblige it to controul itself. A dependence on the people is no doubt the primary controul on the government; but experience has taught mankind the necessity of auxiliary precautions.

This policy of supplying by opposite and rival interests, the defect of better motives, might be traced through the whole system of human affairs, private as well as public. We see it particularly displayed in all the subordinate distributions of power; where the constant aim is to divide and arrange the several offices in such a manner as that each may be a check on the other; that the private interest of every individual, may be a centinel over the public rights. These inventions of prudence cannot be less requisite in the distribution of the supreme powers of the state.

But it is not possible to give to each department an equal power of self-defence. In republican government the legislative authority, necessarily, predominates. The remedy for this inconveniency is, to divide the legislature into different branches; and to render them by different modes of election, and different principles of action, as little connected with each other, as the nature of their common functions, and their common dependence on the society, will admit. It may even be necessary to guard against dangerous encroachments by still further precautions. As the weight of the legislative authority requires that it should be thus divided, the weakness of the executive may require, on the other hand, that it should be fortified. An absolute negative, on the legislature, appears at first view to be the natural defence with which the executive magistrate should be armed. But perhaps it would be neither altogether safe, nor alone sufficient. On ordinary occasions, it might not be exerted with the requisite firmness; and on extraordinary occasions, it might be perfidiously abused. May not this defect of an absolute negative be supplied, by some qualified connection between this weaker department, and the weaker branch of the stronger department, by which the latter may be led to support the constitutional rights of the former, without being too much detached from the rights of its own department?

If the principles on which these observations are founded be just, as I persuade myself they are, and they be applied as a criterion, to the several state constitutions, and to the federal constitution, it will be found, that if the latter does not perfectly correspond with them, the former are infinitely less able to bear such a test.

There are moreover two considerations particularly applicable to the federal system of America, which place that system in a very interesting point of view.

First. In a single republic, all the power surrendered by the people, is submitted to the administration of a single government; and usurpations are guarded against by a division of the government into distinct and separate departments. In the compound republic of America, the power surrendered by the people, is first divided between two distinct governments, and then the portion allotted to each, subdivided among distinct and separate departments. Hence a double security arises to the rights of the people. The different governments will controul each other; at the same time that each will be controuled by itself.

Second. It is of great importance in a republic, not only to guard the society against the oppression of its rulers; but to guard one part of the society against the injustice of the other part. Different interests necessarily exist in different classes of citizens. If a majority be united by a common interest, the rights of the minority will be insecure. There are but two methods of providing against this evil: The one by creating a will in the community independent of the majority, that is, of the society itself; the other by comprehending in the society so many separate descriptions of citizens, as will render an unjust combination of a majority of the whole very improbable, if not impracticable. The first method prevails in all governments possessing an hereditary or self appointed authority. This at best is but a precarious security; because a power independent of the society may as well espouse the unjust views of the major, as the rightful interests, of the minor party, and may possibly be turned against both parties. The second method will be exemplified in the federal republic of the United States. Whilst all authority in it will be derived from and dependent on the society, the society itself will be broken into so many parts, interests and classes of citizens, that the rights of individuals or of the minority, will be in little danger from interested combinations of the majority. In a free government, the security for civil rights must be the same as that for religious rights. It consists in the one case in the multiplicity of interests, and in the other, in the multiplicity of sects. The degree of security in both cases will depend on the number of interests and sects; and this may be presumed to depend on the extent of country and number of people comprehended under the same government. This view of the subject must particularly recommend a proper federal system to all the sincere and considerate friends of republican government: Since it shews that in exact proportion as the territory of the union may be formed into more circumscribed confederacies or states, oppressive combinations of a majority will be facilitated, the best security under the republican form, for the rights of every class of citizens, will be diminished; and consequently, the stability and independence of some member of the government, the only other security must be proportionally increased. Justice is the end of government. It is the end of civil society. It ever has been, and ever will be pursued, until it be obtained, or until liberty be lost in the pursuit. In a society under the forms of which the stronger faction can readily unite and oppress the weaker, anarchy may as truly be said to reign, as in a state of nature where the weaker individual is not secured against the violence of the stronger. And as in the latter state even the stronger individuals are prompted by the uncertainty of their condition, to submit to a government which may protect the weak as well as themselves: So in the former state, will the more powerful factions or parties be gradually induced by a like motive, to wish for a government which will protect all parties, the weaker as well as the more powerful. It can be little doubted that if the state of Rhode Island was separated from the confederacy, and left to itself, the insecurity of rights under the popular form of government within such narrow limits, would be displayed by such reiterated oppressions of factious majorities, that some power altogether independent of the people would soon be called for by the voice of the very factions whose misrule had proved the necessity of it. In the extended republic of the United States, and among the great variety of interests, parties and sects which it embraces, a coalition of a majority of the whole society could seldom take place upon any other principles than those of justice and the general good: and there being thus less danger to a minor from the will of the major party, there must be less pretext also, to provide for the security of the former, by introducing into the government a will not dependent on the latter; or in other words, a will independent of the society itself. It is no less certain than it is important, notwithstanding the contrary opinions which have been entertained, that the larger the society, provided it lie within a practicable sphere, the more duly capable it will be of self government. And happily for the *republican cause,* the practicable sphere may be carried to a very great extent, by the judicious modification and mixture of the *federal principle.*

Publius.

MERCY OTIS WARREN (1728–1814)

Mercy Otis Warren was born into family and social circumstances that afforded her unusual opportunities in terms of education and leadership. Her family was deeply involved in Massachusetts politics, and she had an exemplary education. Her personal experiences as part of the generation that would come through the American Revolution combined with her intellectual gifts to give Warren a lasting reputation as a woman of letters. Warren's father, James Otis, was a prominent merchant. Along with Mercy's oldest brother James, he engaged in the political struggles of the 1760s that brought the British army to Massachusetts in the years preceding the open rebellion against Great Britain. Mercy received most of her education alongside her brother, who was tutored in preparation for attending Harvard. In 1754, Mercy Otis married James Warren, a Plymouth merchant and farmer who shared political views similar to those held by the Otis family. Warren wrote poetry during even the earliest years of her marriage, but she felt no particular compulsion to publish or circulate her writings widely. After her favorite brother James was severely beaten in a politically inspired attack in 1769, Warren became more active in her writing and decided to turn her attention to politics and society.

Beginning in 1772, Warren wrote a series of political satires that depicted Massachusetts's royally appointed government as corrupt and unworthy, opposed by native-born British Americans who were virtuous and motivated by the public good. *The Adulateur* (1772), *The Defeat* (1773), *The Blockheads* (1776), and *The Motley Assembly* (1779) were private dramas, intended for public or personal reading, but not to be acted. The royal governor Thomas Hutchinson and his political allies were thinly veiled in these works, and so the purpose of the plays was openly to inspire prorebellion attitudes and fortitude.

Warren's writings were ideologically founded upon a view of the original charters given the British people when they first came over, charters that allowed for, indeed were centered in, individual opportunity, as granted by right to all Britons. Thus it is that following the American Revolution, Warren found herself among the minority in wishing to forestall federalism. She became Anti-Federalist in her leanings, interested in retaining rights and privileges to local people, rather than permitting authority to go into the hands of a few leaders. In 1788, she published the pamphlet, *Observations on the New Constitution,* without signing her name to the work. Her Anti-Federalist argument was that the proposed Constitution did not leave power squarely enough in the hands of the people. Long thought to be the work of Warren's political ally, Elbridge Gerry, *Observations on the New Constitution* was one of the strongest arguments offered by those who held views that conflicted with the Federalist agendas.

During the years of the Revolution and its aftermath, Warren continued to write poetry, and in 1790, she brought out her first book-length work that was not solely political. *Poems, Dramatic and Miscellaneous* signaled Warren's effort to enter the debates about culture that were important especially to women in her day. The volume included advice to younger women, praise for other woman writers, and poems on domestic topics. It also included two historical dramas that had clear political messages, *The Sack of Rome* and *The Ladies of Castile.* The complicated messages conveyed by her work suggest that Warren was continually attempting to reason through the political and social events of her era in an effort to come to a better understanding of her culture and her new nation.

Part of the process she engaged in was developing an opinion on the Revolution in France. As Warren had parted with her friends over the issues of federalism, favoring greater local and state self-government above federal regulations, so she consistently held a position against monarchy. When the French Revolution entered the news scene in North America, Warren considered it an important event in behalf of new rights for all people around the globe. Her views favoring the Revolution did not square with her Federalist neighbors and friends and thus cut her off from the New England Federalists—including John and Abigail Adams—whom she had long known.

Warren had been at work for some time, perhaps since the 1770s, on a history of the American Revolution. She did not bring out her history until 1805, as a three-volume *History of the Rise, Progress, and Termination of the American Revolution.* Warren's history was overshadowed by the work of other historians, notably John Gordon's biography of Washington and David Ramsay's history of the war. Because she criticized her once-close friend John Adams, Warren caused increased resentment and strain in the relationship between the Adamses and the Warrens. Although her history is recognized today as a major achievement, in its day it had nothing like the impact of her early propaganda writings.

The selection of Warren's writings presented here ranges across genres and issues. Two poems from *Poems, Dramatic and Miscellaneous* reveal that despite her political focus, Warren took part in addressing many of the women's issues that were common in her day. Her letter on Chesterfield, a moralistic evaluation of rakish behavior, was reprinted in a number of magazines, and it became more popular with each reprinting. Finally, *Observations on the New Constitution* demonstrates Warren's cogent arguments against the Federalist arguments of Warren's day.

LETTER TO THE *INDEPENDENT CHRONICLE*, ON CHESTERFIELD[1]

My dear son,

I Perceive by your last you are enraptured with Lord Chesterfield, nor do I wonder at it; I should have no opinion of your taste, if you was not charmed with the correct stile, the elegant diction, the harmony of language, the thousand beauties of expression that run parrallel with the knowledge of the world, and the arts of life, through this compleat system of refinement.—This masterly writer has furnished the present generation with a code of politeness, which, perhaps, surpasses any thing of the kind in the English language. But when he sacrifices truth to convenience, probity to pleasure, virtue to the graces, generosity, gratitude, and all the finer feelings of the soul, to a momentary gratification, we cannot but pity the man, as much as we admire the author; and I never see this fascinating collection of letters, taken up by the youthful reader, but I tremble, least the honey'd poison, that lurks beneath the fairest flowers of fancy and Rhetoric, should leave a deeper tincture on the mind, than, even his documents for an external decency and the semblance of Morality.

I have no quarrel with the graces; I love the *Deuceurs* of civility, the placid manners, the *L-amiable,* and all the innocent arts of engaging the esteem, and alluring the affections of mankind.—The passion is laudable, and may be indulged to the highest pitch, consistent with the eternal law of rectitude; but I love better that frankness and sincerity, which bespeak a soul above dissimulation; that generous, resolute, manly fortitude, that equally despises and resists the temptations to vice in the Purlieu's of the Brothel, or the anti chamber of the Princess, in the arms of the emaciated, distemper'd prostitute, or beneath the smiles of the painted Courtezan, who decorates her guilty charms even with the blandishments of honour. And however ennobled by birth, dignify'd by rank, or justly admired for his literary productions, I must beg leave to differ from his Lordship, and think it, by no means, necessary that a gentleman, in order to be initiated into the science of good breeding, should drop his humanity; or to acquire a courtly mien and become an adept in politeness, that he should renounce the moral feelings; or to be master of the graces, that his life should be a contrast to every precept of Christianity.

Can there be a portrait more unnatural and deformed, or an object more completely ridiculous, than that of a father exerting all the powers of brilliant talents, aided by the chicanery of subtle politicians, the false reasonings of the infidel tribe, and the vulgar witticisms of all the voluptuaries from Julius Caesar to Borgia,[2] to arouse the corrupt passions in the bosom of his son, to enflame the desires, and to urge those loose gratifications, which it has been the work of ages to connteract, by all the arguments of reason, religion, and philosophy. And, if in the pangs of paternal anxiety, he had sometimes omitted the consonant S. and inculcated on his votary of pleasure, the necessity of a spark of *grace* in the heart, however exploded by *Les Beaux Esprit,* it might have produced a brighter embellishment of manners in the person, than all his Lordship's studied rules, his labour'd maxims, his machiavilian politicks, improved in the religious school of Voltaire, or supported by all the advocates for simulation, and dissimulation, that have lived since the Augustan age, when luxury was in its Zenith, till the more perfect model of education, exhibited by the noble Lord Chesterfield,—But I admire his sermon on *Suaviter* in *modo fortiter in re;*[3] yet, believe these happy emanations are, much oftener, the effects of a conscious moral principle, than the result of that finished turpitude, held up under a flimsy veil of deception, and urged on Mr. Stanhope[4] as the point of perfection; and I am persuaded, had the same brilliancy of thought, and the many masterly strokes of genius been played off, with a view to some higher motives of action; had his Lordship laid a little more stress on purity of sen-

---

1. Originally written as a private letter to her son in 1779, the letter was published in the *Independent Chronicle* in 1781. Philip Dormer (1694–1773), fourth earl of Chesterfield, was a British politician and writer noted for his fashionable ways. His letters to his son were not intended for publication, but they were published in 1774. He said of them that he hoped they succeeding in "uniting wickedness and the graces," and he endeavored to be renowned for his manners as a "man about town."

2. Julius Caesar (100–44 B.C.), known for imperial dignity; Cesare Borgia (1478–1507), duke of Valentinois, was reputed for his eloquence, wit, and learning. Warren evidently dislikes the aristocratic (or antidemocratic) leanings of Chesterfield and any high political leaders.

3. Sweetly in manner, strongly in matter.

4. Chesterfield's son, born out of wedlock, to whom Chesterfield's letters were addressed.

timent, and less on the efficacy of intrigue and gallantry, it might have corrected the errors of his raw traveller, and, perhaps, sooner have rubbed off the awkwardness inherent to his character, than *Un gout vif* about which the careful parent is so solicitous.—His Lordship's severity to the ladies only reminds me of the fable of the lion and the man:[5] I think his trite, hackney'd, vulgar observations, the contempt he affects to pour on so fair a part of the creation, are as much beneath the resentment of a woman of education and reflection, as derogatory to the candor and generosity of a writer of his acknowledged abilities and fame; and I believe in this age of refinement and philosophy, few men indulge a peculiar asperity with regard to the sex in general, but such as have been unfortunate in their acquaintance, unsuccessful in their address, or sowered from repeated disappointments; and however practicable, this connoiseur in the spirit of intrigue, might announce the conquest of the whole sex, it has been asserted by one of his biographers, that he was never known to be successful in any of his gallantries, but that which brought Mr. Stanhope into the world. I ever considered human nature as the same in both sexes, nor perhaps is the soul very differently modified by the vehicle in which it is placed; the foibles, the passions, the vices, and the virtues, appear to spring from the same scource, and under similar advantages, frequently reach the same degree of perfection, or sink to the same stages of pravity which so often stamp disgrace on the human form; yet custom in most countries has branded licentious manners in female life with peculiar marks of infamy; but we live in days happily adroit in the arts of removing every impediment to pleasure, when the bars of rectitude are systematically reasoned down, and no other distinction is necessary but a dextrous talent at concealment.

It may, perhaps, be deemed presumption for a woman to speak thus freely of so celebrated a work as Dormer's advice; but I shall yet venture to say more, as I have read his letters with attention, much more with a view to the happiness of some I love, than for my own pleasure or advantage—I think them crowded with the repetition of the most trifling injunctions, replete with observations, rules and precepts, exceedingly advantageous for the conduct

of younger life, but marked with the most atrocious licence of thought, and stained with insinuations subversive of every moral and religious principle; the utile is so studiously blended with the vile, that in some of his letters one would mistake Lord Chesterfield for a saint, was not his cloven step discovered by its precipitance to procure an arrangement for his noviciate.

I am happy in having a son, to whom I can disclose the full flow of sentiment and the mixture of indignation, that arises in the maternal bosom, when surveying such a specious digest of mischief, so artfully adapted to lead into error the most valuable part of society, the youth, adorn'd with native grace, and the rudiments of every excellence implanted in his heart.—I feel inexpressible pleasure in believing you to be a reader capable of investigating truth, while charm'd with the easy numbers sportively rang'd to disguise it; and though you admire the painted evil, the polished address, and melodious stile, you cannot be a proselyte of the modern Clodius.

It is the race of fops and fribbles, the half learn'd sceptic, the disciples of Hume and Bolingbroke,[6] who are the devotees of a man, bold enough to avow himself the champion of every species of vice, only cloathing it decently, that will subserve the guilty pleasure of the accomplish'd debauchee. Had I not made my letter so lengthy, I would add an observation or two from the celebrated Mr. Addison,[7] who did more to the improvement of the English language, and to correct the stile of the age, than, perhaps, any other man; and was a parrellel justly run, with regard to taste, manners, and even the graces, so far as they can be taught by letters, I believe Lord Chesterfield would drop in the comparison.

I expect the pleasure of seeing you here daily, but if you are prevented, you will answer some of my letters, as you are rather in arrears; when you recollect that circumstance, you will not be so deficient in *Les Bienseances,* as to neglect a point of politeness to a Lady, as well as duty to a most affectionate Mother.

———

5. In Aesop's story of the forester and the lion, a forester tells a lion that his strength is greater and shows the lion a statue of a man with a lion's head in his lap as proof; the lion responds that if lions made statues, the man would be shown with his head under the lion's feet.

6. David Hume (1711–76), Scottish philosopher and historian; Henry St. John, viscount Bolingbroke (1678–1751), a British statesman and political writer.

7. Joseph Addison (1672–1719), the famous British essayist, known for a variety of published essays that instructed in issues like manners and decorum.

OBSERVATIONS ON THE NEW CONSTITUTION, AND ON THE FEDERAL AND STATE CONVENTIONS[1]

Sic transit gloria Americana.[2]

Mankind may amuse themselves with theoretick systems of liberty, and trace its social and moral effects on sciences, virtue, industry, and every improvement of which the human mind is capable; but we can only discern its true value by the practical and wretched effects of slavery; and thus dreadfully will they be realized, when the inhabitants of the Eastern States are dragging out a miserable existence, *only* on the gleanings of their fields; and the Southern, blessed with a softer and more fertile climate, are languishing in hopeless poverty; and when asked, what is become of the flower of their crop, and the rich produce of their farms—they may answer in the hapless stile of the Man of *La Mancha.*—"The steward of my Lord has seized and sent it to *Madrid.*"—Or, in the more literal language of truth. The *exigencies* of government require that the collectors of the revenue should transmit it to the *Federal City.*

Animated with the firmest zeal for the interest of this country, the peace and union of the American States, and the freedom and happiness of a people who have made the most costly sacrifices in the cause of liberty.—who have braved the power of Britain, weathered the convulsions of war, and waded thro' the blood of friends and foes to establish their independence and to support the freedom of the human mind; I cannot silently witness this degradation without calling on them, before they are compelled to blush at their own servitude, and to turn back their languid eyes on their lost liberties—to consider, that the character of nations generally changes at the moment of revolution.—And when patriotism is discountenanced and publick virtue becomes the ridicule of the sycophant—when every man of liberality, firmness, and penetration, who cannot lick the hand stretched out to oppress, is deemed an enemy to the State—then is the gulph of despotism set open, and the grades to slavery, though

rapid, are scarce perceptible—then genius drags heavily its iron chain—science is neglected, and real merit flies to the shades for security from reproach—the mind becomes enervated, and the national character sinks to a kind of apathy with only energy sufficient to curse the breast that gave it milk, and as an elegant writer observes. "To bewail every new birth as an encrease of misery, under a government where the mind is necessarily debased, and talents are seduced to become the panegyrists of usurpation and tyranny." He adds, "that even sedition is not the most indubitable enemy to the publick welfare; but that its most dreadful foe is despotism, which always changes the character of nations for the worse, and is productive of nothing but vice, that the tyrant no longer excites to the pursuits of glory or virtue; it is not talents, it is baseness and servility that he cherishes, and the weight of arbitrary power destroys the spring of emulation."[3] If such is the influence of government on the character and manners, and undoubtedly the observation is just, must we not subscribe to the opinion of the celebrated *Abbé Mablé?* "That there are disagreeable sensons in the unhappy situation of human affairs, when policy requires both the intention and the power of doing mischief to be punished; and that when the senate proscribed the memory of *Caesar* they ought to have put *Anthony* to death, and extinguished the hopes of *Octavius.*[4] Self defence is a primary law of nature, which no subsequent law of society can abolish: this primœval principle, the immediate gift of the Creator, obliges every one to remonstrate against the strides of ambition, and a wanton lust of domination, and to resist the first approaches of tyranny, which at this day threaten to sweep away the rights for which the brave sons of America have fought with an heroism scarcely paralleled even in ancient republicks. It may be repeated, they have purchased it with their blood, and have gloried in their independence with a dignity of spirit, which has made them the admiration of philosophy, the pride of America, and the wonder of Europe. It has been observed, with great propriety, that "the virtues and vices of a people when a revolution happens in their government, are the measure of the liberty or slavery they ought to expect—An heroic love for the publick good, a

---

1. *Observations* was first published in Boston in 1788.

2. Thus goes the glory of America.

3. "Helvetius." [Au.]

4. This quotation and the next are from Gabriel Bonnot Mably, *Observations sur les Romains.*

profound reverence for the laws, a contempt of riches, and a noble haughtiness of soul, are the only foundations of a free government."[5] Do not their dignified principles still exist among us? Or are they extinguished in the breasts of Americans, whose fields have been so recently crimsoned to repel the potent arm of a foreign Monarch, who had planted his engines of slavery in every city, with design to erase the vestiges of freedom in this his last asylum. It is yet to be hoped, for the honour of human nature, that no combinations either foreign or domestick have thus darkened this Western hemisphere.—On these shores freedom has planted her standard, diped in the purple tide that flowed from the veins of her martyred heroes; and here every uncorrupted American yet hopes to see it supported by the vigour, the justice, the wisdom and unanimity of the people, in spite of the deep-laid plots, the secret intrigues, or the bold effrontery of those interested and avaricious adventurers for place, who intoxicated with the ideas of distinction and preferment, have prostrated every worthy principle beneath the shrine of ambition. Yet these are the men who tell us republicanism is dwindled into theory—that we are incapable of enjoying our liberties—and that we must have a master.—Let us retrospect the days of our adversity, and recollect who were then our friends; do we find them among the sticklers for aristocratick authority? No, they were generally the same men who now wish to save us from the distractions of anarchy on the one hand, and the jaws of tyranny on the other; where then were the class who now come forth importunately urging that our political salvation depends on the adoption of a system at which freedom spurns?—Were not some of them hidden in the corners of obscurity, and others wrapping themselves in the bosom of our enemies for safety? Some of them were in the arms of infancy; and others speculating for fortune, by sporting with public money; while a few, a very few of them were magnanimously defending their country, and raising a character, which I pray heaven may never be sullied by aiding measures derogatory to their former exertions. But the revolutions in principle which time produces among mankind, frequently exhibits the most mortifying instances of human weakness; and this alone can account for the extraordinary appearance of a few names, once distinguished in the honourable walks of patriotism, but now found on the list of the Massachusetts assent to the ratification of a Constitution, which, by the undefined mean-

ing of some parts, and the ambiguities of expression in others, is dangerously adapted to the purposes of an immediate *aristocratic tyranny;* that from the difficulty, if not impracticability of its operation, must soon terminate in the most *uncontrouled despotism.*

All writers on government agree, and the feelings of the human mind witness the truth of these political axioms, that man is born free and possessed of certain unalienable rights—that government is instituted for the protection, safety, and happiness of the people, and not for the profit, honour, or private interest of any man, family, or class of men—That the origin of all power is in the people, and that they have an incontestible right to check the creatures of their own creation, vested with certain powers to guard the life, liberty and property of the community: And if certain selected bodies of men, deputed on these principles, determine contrary to the wishes and expectations of their constituents, the people have an undoubted right to reject their decisions, to call for a revision of their conduct, to depute others in their room, or if they think proper, to demand further time for deliberation on matters of the greatest moment: it therefore is an unwarrantable stretch of authority or influence, if any methods are taken to preclude this reasonable, and peaceful mode of enquiry and decision. And it is with inexpressible anxiety, that many of the best friends to the Union of the States—to the peaceable and equal participation of the rights of nature, and to the glory and dignity of this country, behold the insidious arts, and the strenuous efforts of the partisans of arbitrary power, by their vague definitions of the best established truths, endeavoring to envelope the mind in darkness the concomitant of slavery, and to lock the strong chains of domestic despotism on a country, which by the most glorious and successful struggles is but newly emancipated from the sceptre of foreign dominion.—But there are certain seasons in the course of human affairs, when Genius, Virtue, and Patriotism, seems to nod over the vices of the times, and perhaps never more remarkably, than at the present period; or we should not see such a passive disposition prevail in some, who we must candidly suppose, have liberal and enlarged sentiments; while a supple multitude are paying a blind and idolatrous homage to the opinions of those who by the most precipitate steps are treading down their dear bought privileges; and who are endeavouring by all the arts of insinuation, and influence, to betray the people of the United States, into an acceptance of a most complicated system of government; marked on the one side with the *dark, secret* and *profound intrigues,* of the statesman,

---

5. "Abbé Mable." [Au.]

long practiced in the purlieus of despotism; and on the other, with the ideal projects of *young ambition,* with its wings just expanded to soar to a summit, which imagination has painted in such gawdy colours as to intoxicate the *inexperienced votary,* and send *him* rambling from State to State, to collect materials to construct the ladder of preferment.

But as a variety of objections to the *heterogeneous phantom,* have been repeatedly laid before the public, by men of the best abilities and intentions; I will not expatiate long on a Republican *form* of government, founded on the principles of monarchy—a democratick branch with the *features* of aristocracy—and the extravagance of nobility pervading the minds of many of the candidates for office, with the poverty of peasantry hanging heavily on them, and insurmountable, from their taste for expense, unless a generous provision should be made in the arrangement of the civil list, which may enable them with the champions of their cause to "*sail down the new pactolean channel.*" Some gentlemen with laboured zeal, have spent much time in urging the necessity of government, from the embarrassments of trade—the want of respectability abroad and confidence in the public engagements at home:—These are obvious truths which no one denies; and there are few who do not unite in the general wish for the restoration of public faith, the revival of commerce, arts, agriculture, and industry, under a lenient, peaceable and energetick government: But the most sagacious advocates for the party have not by fair discussion, and rational argumentation, evinced the necessity of adopting this many-headed monster; of such motley mixture, that its enemies cannot trace a feature of Democratick or Republican extract; nor have its friends the courage to denominate it a Monarchy, an Aristocracy, or an Oligarchy, and the favoured bantling must have passed through the short period of its existence without a name, had not Mr. *Wilson,* in the fertility of his genius, suggested the happy epithet of a *Federal Republic*—But I leave the field of general censure on the secrecy of its birth, the rapidity of its growth, and the fatal consequences of suffering it to live to the age of maturity, and will particularize some of the most weighty objections to its passing through this continent in a gigantic size.—It will be allowed by every one that the fundamental principle of a free government, is the equal representation of a free people—And I will *first* observe with a justly celebrated writer. "That the principal aim of society is to protect individuals in the absolute rights which were vested

in them by the immediate laws of nature, but which could not be preserved in peace, without the mutual intercourse which is gained by the institution of friendly and social communities."[6] And when society has thus deputed a certain number of their equals to take care of their personal rights, and the interest of the whole community, it must be considered that responsibility is the great security of integrity and honour; and that annual election is the basis of responsibility.—Man is not immediately corrupted, but power without limitation, or amenability, may endanger the brightest virtue—whereas a frequent return to the bar of their Constituents is the strongest check against the corruptions to which men are liable, either from the intrigues of others of more subtle genius, or the propensities of their own hearts.—and the gentlemen who have so warmly advocated in the late Convention of the Massachusetts, the change from annual to biennial elections; may have been in the same predicament, and perhaps with the same views that Mr. *Hutchinson* once acknowledged himself, when in a letter to *Lord Hillsborough,* he observed, "that the grand difficulty of making a change in government against the general bent of the people had caused him to turn his thoughts to a variety of plans, in order to find one that might be executed in spite of opposition," and the first he proposed was that, "instead of annual, the elections should be only once in three years:" but the Minister had not the hardiness to attempt such an innovation, even in the revision of colonial charters: nor has any one ever defended Biennial, Triennial, or Septennial, Elections, either in the British House of Commons, or in the debates of Provincial assemblies, on general and free principles: but it is unnecessary to dwell long on this article, as the best political writers have supported the principles of annual elections with a precision, that cannot be confuted, though they may be darkened, by the sophistical arguments that have been thrown out with design, to undermine all the barriers of freedom.

2. There is no security in the profered system, either for the rights of conscience, or the liberty of the Press: Despotism usually while it is gaining ground, will suffer men to think, say, or write what they please: but when once established, if it is thought necessary to subserve the purposes of arbitrary power, the most unjust restrictions may take place in the first instance, and an *imprimator* on

---

6. Blackstone's *Commentaries.*

the Press in the next, may silence the complaints, and forbid the most decent remonstrances of an injured and oppressed people.

3. There are no well defined limits of the Judiciary Powers, they seem to be left as a boundless ocean, that has broken over the chart of the Supreme Lawgiver *"thus far shalt thou go and no further,"* and as they cannot be comprehended by the clearest capacity, or the most sagacious mind, it would be an Herculean labour to attempt to describe the dangers with which they are replete.

4. The Executive and the Legislative are so dangerously blended as to give just cause of alarm, and every thing relative thereto, is couched in such ambiguous terms—in such vague and indefinite expression, as is a sufficient ground without any other objection, for the reprobation of a system, that the authors dare not hazard to a clear investigation.

5. The abolition of trial by jury in civil causes.—This mode of trial the learned Judge Blackstone observes, "has been coeval with the first rudiments of civil government, that property, liberty and life, depend on maintaining in its legal force the constitutional trial by jury." He bids his readers pause, and with Sir Matthew Hale observes, how admirably this mode is adapted to the investigation of truth beyond any other the world can produce.[7] Even the party who have been disposed to swallow, without examination, the proposals of the *secret conclave,* have started on a discovery that this essential right was curtailed; and shall a privilege, the origin of which may be traced to our Saxon ancestors—that has been a part of the law of nations, even in the fewdatory systems of France, Germany and Italy—and from the earliest records has been held so sacred, both in ancient and modern Britain, that it could never be shaken by the introduction of Norman customs, or any other conquests or change of government—shall this inestimable privilege be relinquished in America—either thro' the fear of inquisition for unaccounted thousands of public monies in the hands of some who have been officious in the fabrication of the *consolidated system,* or from the apprehension that some future delinquent possessed of more power than integrity, may be called to a trial by his peers in the hour of investigation?

6. Though it has been said by Mr. *Wilson* and many others, that a Standing-Army is necessary for the dignity and safety of America,[8] yet freedom revolts at the idea, when the Divan, or the Despot, may draw out his dragoons to suppress the murmurs of a few, who may yet cherish those sublime principles which call forth the exertions, and lead to the best improvement of the human mind. It is hoped this country may yet be governed by milder methods than are usually displayed beneath the bannerets of military law.—Standing armies have been the nursery of vice and the bane of liberty from the Roman legions, to the establishment of the artful Ximenes, and from the ruin of the Cortes of Spain, to the planting the British cohorts in the capitals of America:—By the edicts of authority vested in the sovereign power by the proposed constitution, the militia of the country, the bulwark of defence, and the security of national liberty is no longer under the controul of civil authority; but at the rescript of the Monarch, or the aristocracy, they may either be employed to extort the enormous sums that will be necessary to support the civil list—to maintain the regalia of power—and the splendour of the most useless part of the community, or they may be sent into foreign countries for the fulfilment of treaties, stipulated by the President and two thirds of the Senate.

7. Notwithstanding the delusory promise to guarantee a Republican form of government to every State in the Union—If the most discerning eye could discover any meaning at all in the engagement, there are no resources left for the support of internal government, or the liquidation of the debts of the State. Every source of revenue is in the monopoly of Congress, and if the several legislatures in their enfebled state, should against their own feelings be necessitated to attempt a dry tax for the payment of their debts, and the support of internal police, even this may be required for the purposes of the general government.

8. As the new Congress are empowered to determine their own salaries, the requisitions for this purpose may not be very moderate, and the drain for public moneys will probably rise past all calculation: and it is to be feared when America has consolidated its despotism, the world will witness the truth of the assertion—"that the pomp of an eastern monarch may impose on the vulgar who may estimate the force of a nation by the magnificence of its palaces; but the wise man, judges differently,

---

7. Blackstone's *Commentaries.*

8. James Wilson, "Address to the Citizens of Philadelphia," October 6, 1787.

it is by that very magnificence he estimates its weakness. He sees nothing more in the midst of this imposing pomp, where the tyrant sets enthroned, than a sumptuous and mournful decoration of the dead; the apparatus of a fastuous funeral, in the centre of which is a cold and lifeless lump of unanimated earth, a phantom of power ready to disappear before the enemy, by whom it is despised!"

9. There is no provision for a rotation, nor any thing to prevent the perpetuity of office in the same hands for life; which by a little well timed bribery, will probably be done, to the exclusion of men of the best abilities from their share in the offices of government.—By this neglect we lose the advantages of that check to the overbearing insolence of office, which by rendering him ineligible at certain periods, keeps the mind of man in equilibrio, and teaches him the feelings of the governed, and better qualifies him to govern in his turn.

10. The inhabitants of the United States, are liable to be draged from the vicinity of their own county, or state, to answer to the litigious or unjust suit of an adversary, on the most distant borders of the Continent: in short the appelate jurisdiction of the Supreme Federal Court, includes an unwarrantable stretch of power over the liberty, life, and property of the subject, through the wide Continent of America.

11. One Representative to thirty thousand inhabitants is a very inadequate representation; and every man who is not lost to all sense of freedom to his country, must reprobate the idea of Congress altering by law, or on any pretence whatever, interfering with any regulations for the time, places, and manner of choosing our own Representatives.

12. If the sovereignty of America is designed to be elective, the circumscribing the votes to only ten electors in this State, and the same proportion in all the others, is nearly tantamount to the exclusion of the voice of the people in the choice of their first magistrate. It is vesting the choice solely in an aristocratic junto, who may easily combine in each State to place at the head of the Union the most convenient instrument for despotic sway.

13. A Senate chosen for six years will, in most instances, be an appointment for life, as the influence of such a body over the minds of the people will be coequal to the extensive powers with which they are vested, and they will not only forget, but be forgotten by their constituents—a branch of the Supreme Legislature thus set beyond all responsibility is totally repugnant to every principle of a free government.

14. There is no provision by a bill of rights to guard against the dangerous encroachments of power in too many instances to be named but I cannot pass over in silence the insecurity in which we are left with regard to warrants unsupported by evidence—the daring experiment of granting *writs of assistance* in a former arbitrary administration is not yet forgotten in the Massachusetts; nor can we be so ungrateful to the memory of the patriots who counteracted their operation, as so soon after their many exertions to save us from such a detestable instrument of arbitrary power, to subject ourselves to the insolence of any petty revenue officer to enter our houses, search, insult, and seize at pleasure. We are told by a gentleman of too much virtue and real probity to suspect he has a design to deceive—"that the whole constitution is a declaration of rights"—but mankind must think for themselves, and to many very judicious and discerning characters, the whole constitution with very few exceptions appears to perversion of the rights of particular states, and of private citizens.—But the gentleman goes on to tell us, "that the primary object is the general government, and that the rights of individuals are only incidentally mentioned, and that there was a clear impropriety in being very particular about them."[9] But, asking pardon for dissenting from such respectable authority, who has been led into several mistakes, more from his prediliction in favour of certain modes of government, than from a want of understanding or veracity. The rights of individuals ought to be the primary object of all government, and cannot be too securely guarded by the most explicit declarations in their favor. This has been the opinion of the Hampdens, the Pyms, and many other illustrious names, that have stood forth in defence of English liberties; and even the Italian master in politicks, the subtle and renounced Machiavel acknowledges, that no republic ever yet stood on a stable foundation without satisfying the common people.

15. The difficulty, if not impracticability, of exercising the equal and equitable powers of government by a single legislature over an extent of territory that reaches from the Mississippi to the Western lakes, and from them to the Atlantic ocean, is an insuperable objection to the adoption of the new system.—Mr. *Hutchinson,* the great champion for arbitrary power, in the multitude of his

---

9. James Bowdoin, at the Massachusetts ratifying convention.

machinations to subvert the liberties of this country, was obliged to acknowledge in one of his letters, that, from the extent of country from north to south, the scheme of one government was impracticable." But if the authors of the present visionary project, can by the arts of deception, precipitation and address, obtain a majority of suffrages in the conventions of the states to try the hazardous experiment, they may then make the same inglorious boast with this insidious politician, who may perhaps be their model, that "the union of the colonies was pretty well broken, and that he hoped never to see it revewed."

16. It is an indisputed fact, that not one legislature in the United States had the most distant idea when they first appointed members for a convention, entirely commercial, or when they afterwards authorised them to consider on some amendments of the Federal union, that they would without any warrant from their constituents, presume on so bold and daring a stride, as ultimately to destroy the state governments, and offer a *consolidated system,* irreversible but on conditions that the smallest degree of penetration must discover to be impracticable.

17. The first appearance of the article which declares the ratification of nine states sufficient for the establishment of the new system, wears the face of dissention, is a subversion of the union of the Confederated States, and tends to the introduction of anarchy and civil convulsions, and may be a means of involving the whole country in blood.

18. The mode in which this constitution is recommended to the people to judge without either the advice of Congress, or the legislatures of the several states, is very reprehensible—it is an attempt to force it upon them before it could be thoroughly understood, and may leave us in that situation, that in the first moments of slavery the minds of the people agitated by the remembrance of their lost liberties, will be like the sea in a tempest, that sweeps down every mound of security.

But it is needless to enumerate other instances, in which the proposed constitution appears contradictory to the first principles which ought to govern mankind; and it is equally so to enquire into the motives that induced to so bold a step as the annihilation of the independence and sovereignty of the thirteen distinct states.—They are but too obvious through the whole progress of the business, from the first shutting up the doors of the federal convention and resolving that no member should correspond with gentlemen in the different states on the subject under discussion; till the trivial proposition of *recommending* a few amendments was artfully ushered into the convention of the Massachusetts. The questions that were then before that honorable assembly were profound and important, they were of such magnitude and extent, that the consequences may run parallel with the existence of the country; and to see them waved and hastily terminated by a measure too absurd to require a serious refutation, raises the honest indignation of every true lover of his country. Nor are they less grieved that the ill policy and arbitrary disposition of some of the sons of America has thus precipitated to the contemplation and discusion of questions that no one could rationally suppose would have been agitated among us, till time had blotted out the principles on which the late revolution was grounded; or till the last traits of the many political tracts, which defended the separation from Britain, and the rights of men were consigned to everlasting oblivion. After the severe conflicts this country has suffered, it is presumed that they are disposed to make every reasonable sacrifice before the altar of peace.—But when we contemplate the nature of men and consider them originally on an equal footing, subject to the same feelings, stimulated by the same passions, and recollecting the struggles they have recently made, for the security of their civil rights; it cannot be expected that the inhabitants of the Massachusetts, can be easily lulled into a fatal security, by the declamatory effusions of gentlemen, who, contrary to the experience of all ages would persuade them there is no danger to be apprehended, from vesting discretionary powers in the hands of man, which he may, or may not abuse. The very suggestion, that we ought to trust to the precarious hope of amendments and redress, after we have voluntarily fixed the shackles on our own necks should have awakened to a double degree of caution.—This people have not forgotten the artful insinuations of a former Governor, when pleading the unlimited authority of parliament before the legislature of the Massachusetts; nor that his arguments were very similar to some lately urged by gentlemen who boast of opposing his measures, "*with halters about their necks.*"

We were then told by him, in all the soft language of insinuation, that no form of government of human construction can be perfect—that we had nothing to fear—that we had no reason to complain—that we had only to acquiesce in their illegal claims, and to submit to the requisitions of parliament, and doubtless the lenient hand of government would redress all grievances, and remove the oppressions of the people:—Yet we soon saw armies of mercenaries encamped on our plains—our commerce ruined—our harbours blockaded—and our cities burnt. It may be replied, that this was in consequence of an obstinate defence of our privileges; this may be true; and when the *"ultima ratio"* is called to aid, the weakest must fall. But let the best informed historian produce an instance when bodies of men were intrusted with power, and the proper checks relinquished, if they were ever found destitute of ingenuity sufficient to furnish pretences to abuse it. And the people at large are already sensible, that the liberties which America has claimed, which reason has justified, and which have been so gloriously defended by the sword of the brave; are not about to fall before the tyranny of foreign conquest: it is native usurpation that is shaking the foundations of peace, and spreading the sable curtain of despotism over the United States. The banners of freedom were erected in the wilds of America by our ancestors, while the wolf prowled for his prey on the one hand, and more savage man on the other; they have been since rescued from the invading hand of foreign power, by the valor and blood of their posterity; and there was reason to hope they would continue for ages to illumine a quarter of the globe, by nature kindly seperated from the proud monarchies of Europe, and the infernal darkness of Asiatic slavery.—And it is to be feared we shall soon see this country rushing into the extremes of confusion and violence, in consequence of the proceedings of a set of gentlemen, who disregarding the purposes of their appointment, have assumed powers unauthorised by any commission, have unnecessarily rejected the confederation of the United States, and annihilated the sovereignty and independence of the individual governments.—The causes which have inspired a few men assembled for very different purposes with such a degree of temerity as to break with a single stroke the union of America, and disseminate the seeds of discord through the land may be easily investigated, when we survey the partizans of monarchy in the state conventions, urging the adoption of a mode of government that militates with the former professions and exertions of this country, and with all ideas of republicanism, and the equal rights of men.

Passion, prejudice, and error, are characteristics of human nature; and as it cannot be accounted for on any principles of philosophy, religion, or good policy; to these shades in the human character must be attributed the mad zeal of some, to precipitate to a blind adoption of the measures of the late federal convention, without giving opportunity for better information to those who are misled by influence or ignorance into erroneous opinions.—Litterary talents may be prostituted, and the powers of genius debased to subserve the purposes of ambition, or avarice: but the feelings of the heart will dictate the language of truth, and the simplicity of her accents will proclaim the infamy of those, who betray the rights of the people, under the specious, and popular pretence of *justice, consolidation,* and *dignity.*

It is presumed the great body of the people unite in sentiment with the writer of these observations, who most devoutly prays that public credit may rear her declining head, and remunerative justice pervade the land; nor is there a doubt if a free government is continued, that time and industry will enable both the public and private debtor to liquidate their arrearages in the most equitable manner. They wish to see the Confederated States bound together by the most indissoluble union, but without renouncing their seperate sovereignities and independence, and becoming tributaries to a consolidated fabrick of aristocratick tyranny.—They wish to see government established, and peaceably holding the reins with honour, energy and dignity; but they wish for no *federal city* whose *"cloud cap't towers"* may screen the state culprit from the hand of justice; while its exclusive jurisdiction may protect the riot of armies encamped within its limits.—They deprecate discord and civil convulsions, but they are not yet generally prepared with the ungrateful Israelites to ask a King, nor are their spirits sufficiently broken to yield the best of their olive grounds to his servants, and to see their sons appointed to run before his chariots—It has been observed by a zealous advocate for the new system, that most governments are the result of fraud or violence, and this with design to recommend its acceptance—but has not almost every step towards its fabrication been fraudulent in the extreme? Did not the prohibition strictly enjoined by the general Convention, that no member should make any communication to his Constituents, or to gentlemen of consideration and abilities in the other States, bear evident marks of fraudulent designs?—This circumstance is regretted in strong terms by Mr. Martin, a member from Maryland, who acknowledges "He had no idea that all the wisdom, integrity, and virtue of the States was contained in that Convention, and that he wished to have corresponded with gentlemen of eminent political characters abroad, and to give their sentiments due weight"—he adds, "so extremely solicitous were they, that their proceedings should not transpire, that the members were prohibited from taking copies of their resolutions, or extracts from the Journals, without express permission, by vote."—And the hurry with which it has been urged to the acceptance of the people, without giving time, by adjournments, for better information, and more unanimity has a deceptive appearance; and if finally driven to resistance, as the only alternative between that and servitude, till in the confusion of discord, the reins should be seized by the violence of some enterprizing genius, that may sweep down the last barrier of liberty, it must be added to the score of criminality with which the fraudulent usurpation at Philadelphia, may be chargeable.—Heaven avert such a tremendous scene! and let us still hope a more happy termination of the present ferment:—may the people be calm, and wait a legal redress; may the mad transport of some of our infatuated capitals subside; and every influential character through the States, make the most prudent exertions for a new general Convention, who may vest adequate powers in Congress, for all national purposes, without annihilating the individual governments, and drawing blood from every pore by taxes, impositions and illegal restrictions.—This step might again re-establish the Union, restore tranquility to the ruffled mind of the inhabitants, and save America from distresses, dreadful even in contemplation.—"The great art of governing is to lay aside all prejudices and attachments to particular opinions, classes or individual characters; to consult the spirit of the people; to give way to it; and in so doing, to give it a turn capable of inspiring those sentiments, which may induce them to relish a change, which an alteration of circumstances may hereafter make necessary."—The education of the advocates for monarchy should have taught them, and their memory should have suggested that "monarchy is a species of government fit only for a people too much corrupted by luxury, avarice, and a passion for pleasure, to have any love for their country, and whose vices the fear of punishment alone is able to restrain; but by no means calculated for a nation that is poor, and at the same time tenacious of their liberty—animated with a disgust to tyranny—and inspired with the generous feelings of patriotism and liberty, and at the same time, like the ancient Spartans have been hardened by temperance and manly exertions, and equally despising the fatigues of the field, and the fear of enemies,"—and while they change their ground they should recollect, that Aristocracy is still a more formidable foe to public virtue, and the prosperity of a nation—that under such a government her patriots become mercenaries—her soldiers, cowards, and the people slaves.—Though several State Conven-

tions have assented to, and ratified, yet the voice of the people appears at present strong against the adoption of the Constitution.—By the chicanery, intrigue, and false colouring of those who plume themselves, more on their education and abilities, than their political, patriotic, or private virtues—by the imbecility of some, and the duplicity of others, a majority of the Convention of Massachusetts have been flattered with the ideas of amendments, when it will be too late to complain—While several very worthy characters, too timid for their situation, magnified the hopeless alternative, between the dissolution of the bands of all government, and receiving the proffered system *in toto,* after long endeavouring to reconcile it to their consciences, swallowed the indigestible panacea, and in a kind of sudden desperation lent their signature to the dereliction of the houorable station they held in the Union, and have broken over the solemn compact, by which they were bound to support their own excellent constitution till the period of revision.—Yet Virginia, equally large and respectable, and who have done honour to themselves, by their vigorous exertions from the first dawn of independence, have not yet acted upon the question; they have wisely taken time to consider before they introduce innovations of a most dangerous nature:—her inhabitants are brave, her burgesses are free, and they have a Governor who dares to think for himself, and to speak his opinion (without first pouring libations on the altar of popularity) though it should militate with some of the most accomplished and illustrious characters.

Maryland, who has no local interest to lead her to adopt, will doubtless reject the system—I hope the same characters still live, and that the same spirit which dictated to them a wise and cautious care, against sudden revolutions in government, and made them the last State that acceded to the independence of America, will lead them to support what they so deliberately claimed.—Georgia apprehensive of a war with the Savages, has acceded in order to insure protection.—Pennsylvania has struggled through much in the same manner, as the Massachusetts, against the manly feelings, and the masterly reasonings of a very respectable part of the Convention: They have adopted the system, and seen some of its authors burnt in effigy—their towns thrown into riot and confusion, and the minds of the people agitated by apprehension and discord.

New-Jersey and Delaware have united in the measure, from the locality of their situation, and the selfish motives which too generally govern mankind; the Federal City, and the seat of government, will naturally attract the intercourse of strangers—the youth of enterprize, and the wealth of the nation to the central States.

Connecticut has pushed it through with the precipitation of her neighbour, with few dissentient voices:—but more from irritation and resentment to a sister State, perhaps partiality to herself in her commercial regulations, than from a comprehensive view of the system, as a regard to the welfare of all.—But New-York has motives, that will undoubtedly lead her to a rejection, without being afraid to appeal to the understanding of mankind, to justify the grounds of their refusal to adopt a Constitution, that even the framers dare not risque to the hazard of revision, amendment, or reconsideration, least the whole superstructure should be demolished by more skilful and discreet architects.—I know not what part the Carolinas will take; but I hope their determinations will comport with the dignity and freedom of this country— their decisions will have great weight in the scale.—But equally important are the small States of New-Hampshire and Rhode-Island:—New-York, the Carolinas, Virginia, Maryland, and these two lesser States may yet support the liberties of the Continent; if they refuse a ratification, or postpone their proceedings till the spirits of the community have time to cool, there is little doubt but the wise measure of another federal convention will be adopted, when the members would have the advantage of viewing, at large, through the medium of truth, the objections that have been made from various quarters; such a measure might be attended with the most salutary effects, and prevent the dread consequences of civil feuds.—But even if some of those large states should hastily accede, yet we have frequently seen in the story of revolution, relief spring from a quarter least expected.

Though the virtues of a Cato could not save Rome, nor the abilities of a Padilla defend the citizens of Castile from falling under the yoke of Charles; yet a *Tell* once suddenly rose from a little obscure city, and boldly rescued the liberties of his country.—Every age has its Bruti and its Deci, as well as its Caesars and Sejani:—The happiness of mankind depends much on the modes of government, and the virtues of the governors; and America may yet produce characters who have genius and capacity sufficient to form the manners and correct the morals of the people, and virtue enough to lead their country to freedom. Since her dismemberment from the British empire, America has, in many instances, resembled the conduct of a restless, vigorous, luxurious youth, prematurely emancipated from the authority of a parent, but without the experience necessary to direct him to act with dignity or discretion. Thus we have seen her break the shackles of foreign dominion, and all the blessings of peace restored on the most honourable terms: She acquired the liberty of framing her own laws, choosing her own magistrates, and adopting manners and modes of government the most favourable to the freedom and happiness of society. But how little have we availed ourselves of these superior advantages: The glorious fabric of liberty successfully reared with so much labour and assiduity totters to the foundation, and may be blown away as the bubble of fancy by the rude breath of military combinations, and politicians of yesterday.

It is true this country lately armed in opposition to regal despotism—impoverished by the expences of a long war, and unable immediately to fulfil their public or private engagements, have appeared in some instances, with a boldness of spirit that seemed to set at defiance all authority, government, or order, on the one hand; while on the other, there has been, not only a secret with, but an open avowal of the necessity of drawing the reins of government much too taught, not only for republicanism, but for a wise and limited monarchy.—But the character of this people is not averse to a degree of subordination: the truth of this appears from the easy restoration of tranquility, after a dangerous insurrection in one of the states: this also evinces the little necessity of a complete revolution of government throughout the union. But it is a republican principle that the majority should rule: and if a spirit of moderation could be cultivated on both sides, till the voice of the people at large could be fairly heard it should be held sacred—And if, on such a scrutiny, the proposed constitution should appear repugnant to their character and wishes; if they, in the language of a late elegant pen, should acknowledge that "no confusion in my mind, is more terrible to them than the stern disciplined regularity and vaunted police of arbitrary governments, where every heart is depraved by fear, where mankind dare not assume their natural characters, where the free spirit must crouch to the slave in office, where genius must repress her effusions, or like the Egyptian worshippers, offer them in sacrifice to the calves in power, and where the human mind, always in shackles, shrinks from every generous effort." Who would then have the effrontory to say, it ought not to be thrown out with indignation, however some respectable names have appeared to support it.—But if after all, on a dispassionate and fair discussion, the people generally give their voice for a voluntary dereliction of their privileges, let every individual who chooses the active scenes of life, strive to support the peace and unanimity of his country, though every other blessing may expire— And while the statesman is plodding for power, and the courtier practising the arts of dissimulation without check—while the rapacious are growing rich by oppression, and fortune throwing her gifts into the lap of fools, let the sublimer characters, the philosophic lovers of freedom who have wept over her exit, retire to the calm shades of contemplation, there they may look down with pity on the inconsistency of human nature, the revolutions of states, the rise of kingdoms, and the fall of empires.

from POEMS, DRAMATIC AND MISCELLANEOUS

To a Young Lady[1]

On shewing an excellent Piece of PAINTING, much faded.

Come, and attend, my charming maid;
See how the gayest colours fade;
As beauteous paintings lose their dye,
Age sinks the lustre of your eye.

Then seize the minutes as they pass;
Behold! how swift runs down the glass;
The hasty sands that measure time,
Point you to pleasures more sublime;
And bid you shun the flow'ry path,
That cheats the millions into death.

Snatch every moment time shall give,
And uniformly virtuous live;
Let no vain cares retard thy soul,
But strive to reach the happy goal;
When pale, when unrelenting Death,
Shall say, resign life's vital breath!
May you, swift as the morning lark
That stems her course to heav'n's high arch,
Leave every earthly care, and soar,
Where numerous seraphims adore;
Thy pinions spread and wafted high,
Beyond the blue etherial sky,
May you there chant the glorious lays,
The carols of eternal praise,
To that exhaustless source of light,

Who rules the shadows of the night,
Who lends each orb its splendid ray,
And points the glorious beams of day.

Time and eternity he holds;
Nor all eternity unfolds,
The glories of Jehovah's name;
Nor highest angels can proclaim,
The wonders of his boundless grace,
They bow, and veil before his face.

What then shall mortals of an hour,
But bend submissive to his power;
And learn at wisdom's happy lore,
Nature's great author to adore.

To Mrs. Montague, Author of "Observations on the Genius and Writings of Shakespeare"[2]

Will Montague, whose critic pen adds praise,
Ev'n to a Shakespeare's bold exalted lays;
Who points the faults in sweet Corneille's[3] page,

Sees all the errors of the Gallic stage—
Corrects Voltaire[4] with a superior hand,
Or traces genius in each distant land?
Will she across the Atlantic stretch her eye,
Look o'er the main, and view the western sky;
And there Columbia's infant drama see—
Reflect that Britain taught us to be free;
Survey with candor what she can't approve;
Let local fondness yield to gen'rous love;
And, if fair truth forbids her to commend,
Then let the critic soften to the friend.

The bard of Avon justly bears the meed
Of fond applause, from Tyber to the Tweed;[5]
Each humbler muse at distance may admire,
But none to Shakespeare's fame e'er dare aspire.
And if your isle, where he so long has charm'd,
If Britain's sons, when by his mantle warm'd,
Have soar'd in vain to reach his lofty quill,
Nature to paint with true Shakespearean skill—

---

2. Elizabeth Robinson Montagu (1720–1800) was a well-known British woman of letters.

3. Pierre Corneille (1606–84), the French dramatist.

4. Francois Marie Arouet (1694–1778), the French philosopher.

5. The Tiber in Italy and the Tweed in Scotland represented the ends of the Roman empire.

---

1. The texts for this poem and the next are taken from *Poems, Dramatic and Miscellaneous* (1790).

A sister's hand may wrest a female pen,
From the bold outrage of imperious men.

  If gentle Montague my chaplet raise,
Critics may frown, or mild good nature praise;

Secure I'll walk, and placid move along,
And heed alike their censure or their song;
I'll take my stand by fam'd Parnassus' side,
And for a moment feel a poet's pride.

JOHN ADAMS (1735–1826)

The first vice president and second president of the United States, John Adams was both an important political figure and a significant contributor to the literature of the American Revolution against Great Britain. Born into a Massachusetts family that was descended from early Puritan settlers, Adams was educated at Harvard, graduating in 1755. He was admitted to the Boston bar within three years and slowly began to build up his law practice. He married Abigail Smith in 1764, forming a happy union that brought with it Abigail's family ties to people who were prominent in Massachusetts affairs. The following year, with the passage of the Stamp Act in 1765, Adams became involved in the political controversies that would lead to the Revolution and therafter determine the shape of the rest of his career.

Adams agreed with his contemporaries that stamp duties were unfair forms of taxation, but he thought his friends and relatives unwise to turn to violence and rioting in making their protests known. As he would throughout his career, Adams turned to the law, to legal reasoning and the articulation of legal statutes, to base his opposition to Britain in what he considered to be sound legal principles. In 1765, he published a series of essays in the *Boston Gazette* that were later collected under the title *A Dissertation on the Canon and Feudal Law.* Adams argued for the existence of a largely unwritten British constitution, which had, at some time long ago, replaced medieval church-based law. Through the 1760s and 1770s, Adams continued to participate in political writings in American periodicals that defended British Americans' complaints against Great Britain and their legal right to resist royal forces. While serving in the Continental Congress in 1776, he published *Thoughts on Government,* which advocated a bicameral legislature. In 1779, Adams was sent to Great Britain to negotiate peace and trade. He helped negotiate and then signed the Treaty of Paris in 1783. Adams remained in England as the first ambassador of the United States. He returned to North America in 1788.

Adams continued to argue that any new policies should be based in historical legal justifications. He published a three-volume *Defense of the Constitutions of Government of the United States of America* (1787) as debates were taking place at the Constitutional Convention. Adams's *Defense* advocated a tripartite government with a careful system of checks and balances. The *Defense* had a significant influence on the Constitution, but it was later used by Adams's opponents to argue that he had aristocratic tendencies because of his concern about the "undue influence" of popular movements. Adams had said of the Senate that it should be composed of "the rich, the well-born and the able."

A year after his return from England, Adams was elected vice president in Washington's administration, an office he told Abigail Adams was "the most insignificant office that ever the invention of man contrived or his imagination conceived." Within seven years, he would defeat Thomas Jefferson for the office of president, and he took office in 1797. During his presidency, Adams worked to keep the United States out of war with France and Britain; he dealt with the XYZ Affair, in which French agents had demanded bribes; and the Alien and Sedition Acts, seen by many as a serious threat to individual liberty, were passed. In 1800, Adams lost the presidency to Thomas Jefferson and retired from politics, embittered by the squabbling over policy matters and foreign affairs that had, in his view, marred his presidency. In his retirement, Adams wrote several more essays and an autobiography that defended his political career. He published *Discourses on Davila,* an extended statement reacting to the French Revolution and warning against "unlimited democracy." This work added to Adams's opponents' belief that he was at heart a monarchist, but it gave Adams an opportunity to explore his lifelong concern about the problems that can emerge when individuals all seek opportunity without sufficient knowledge or training to justify their assessments of their own wants and needs. Adams also engaged in his later years in an extensive correspondence with Jefferson. Together, they discovered that their political differences were not as extensive as they had supposed when they were younger men. The correspondence must have been gratifying to Adams, who felt during most of his later life that his politics and writings had been largely misunderstood.

A DISSERTATION ON THE CANON AND THE FEUDAL LAW NO. 4[1]

WE have been afraid to think. We have felt a reluctance to examining into the grounds of our privileges, and the extent in which we have an indisputable right to demand them against all the power and authority, on earth. And many who have not scrupled to examine for themselves, have yet for certain prudent reasons been cautious, and diffident of declaring the result of their enquiries.

The cause of this timidity is perhaps hereditary and to be traced back in history, as far as the cruel treatment the first settlers of this country received, before their embarkation for America, from the government at Home. Every body knows how dangerous it was to speak or write in favour of any thing in those days, but the triumphant system of religion and politicks. And our fathers were particularly, the objects of the persecutions and proscriptions of the times. It is not unlikely therefore, that, although they were inflexibly steady in refusing their positive assent to any thing against their principles, they might have contracted habits of reserve, and a cautious diffidence of asserting their opinions publickly. These habits they probably brought with them to America, and have transmitted down to us. Or, we may possibly account for this appearance, by the great affection and veneration, Americans have always entertained for the country from whence they sprang—or by the quiet temper for which they have been remarkable, no country having been less disposed to discontent than this—or by a sense they have, that it is their duty to acquiesce, under the administration of government, even when in many smaller matters gravaminous to them, and until the essentials of the great compact are destroy'd or invaded. These peculiar causes might operate upon them; but without these we

all know, that human nature itself, from indolence, modesty, humanity or fear, has always too much reluctance to a manly assertion of its rights. Hence perhaps it has happened that nine tenths of the species, are groaning and gasping in misery and servitude.

But whatever the cause has been, the fact is certain, we have been excessively cautious of giving offence by complaining of grievances. And it is as certain that American governors, and their friends and all the crown officers have avail'd themselves of this disposition in the people. They have prevailed on us to consent to many things, which were grosly injurious to us, and to surrender many others with voluntary tameness, to which we had the clearest right. Have we not been treated formerly, with abominable insolence, by officers of the navy? I mean no insinuation against any gentleman now on this station, having heard no complaint of any one of them to his dishonor. Have not some generals, from England, treated us like servants, nay more like slaves than like Britons? Have we not been under the most ignominious contribution, the most abject submission, the most supercilious insults of some custom house officers? Have we not been trifled with, browbeaten, and trampled on, by former governors, in a manner which no king of England since James the second has dared to indulge towards his subjects? Have we not raised up one family,[2] in them placed an unlimited confidence, and been soothed and battered and intimidated by their influence, into a great part of this infamous tameness and submission? "These are serious and alarming questions, and deserve a dispassionate consideration."

This disposition has been the great wheel and the mainspring in the American machine of court politicks. We have been told that "the word 'Rights' is an offensive expression." That "the King his ministry and parliament will not endure to hear Americans talk of their Rights." That "Britain is the mother and we the children, that a fil-

---

1. Originally published in the *Boston Gazette,* on October 21, 1765.

2. Relatives of Lieutenant Governor Thomas Hutchinson held a large number of public offices in Massachusetts.

ial duty and submission is due from us to her," and that "we ought to doubt our own judgment, and presume that she is right, even when she seems to us to shake the foundations of government." That "Britain is immensely rich and great and powerful, has fleets and armies at her command, which have been the dread and terror of the universe, and that she will force her own judgment into execution, right or wrong." But let me intreat you Sir to pause and consider. Do you consider your self as a missionary of loyalty or of rebellion? Are you not representing your King his ministry and parliament as tyrants, imperious, unrelenting tyrants by such reasoning as this? Is not this representing your most gracious sovereign, as endeavouring to destroy the foundations of his own throne? Are you not putting language into the royal mouth, which if fairly pursued will shew him to have no right to the crown on his own sacred head? Are you not representing every member of parliament as renouncing the transactions at Runningmede,[3] and as repealing in effect the bill of rights, when the Lords and Commons asserted and vindicated the rights of the people and their own rights, and insisted on the King's assent to that assertion and vindication? Do you not represent them as forgetting that the prince of Orange, was created King William by the People, on purpose that their rights might be eternal and inviolable? Is there not something extremely fallacious, in the commonplace images of mother country and children colonies? Are we the children of Great-Britain, any more than the cities of London, Exeter and Bath? Are we not brethren and fellow subjects, with those in Britain, only under a somewhat different method of legislation, and a totally different method of taxation? But admitting we are children; have not children a right to complain when their parents are attempting to break their limbs, to administer poison, or to sell them to enemies for slaves? Let me intreat you to consider, will the mother, be pleased, when you represent her as deaf to the cries of her children? When you compare her to the infamous miscreant, who lately stood on the gallows for starving her child? When you resemble her to Lady Macbeth in Shakespear, (I cannot think of it without horror)

Who "had given suck, and knew
How tender 'twas to love the Babe that milk'd her."
But yet, who could

"Even while 'twas smiling in her Face,
Have pluck'd her Nipple from the boneless Gums,
And dash'd the Brains out."

Let us banish forever from our minds, my countrymen, all such unworthy ideas of the King, his ministry and parliament. Let us not suppose, that all are become luxurious effeminate and unreasonable, on the other side the water, as many designing persons would insinuate. Let us presume, what is in fact true, that the spirit of liberty is as ardent as ever among the body of the nation, though a few individuals may be corrupted. Let us take it for granted, that the same great spirit, which once gave Cæsar so warm a reception; which denounced hostilities against John 'till Magna Charta was signed; which severed the head of Charles the first from his body, and drove James the second from his kingdom; the same great spirit (may heaven preserve it till the earth shall be no more) which first seated the great grand father of his present most gracious Majesty, on the throne of Britain, is still alive and active and warm in England; and that the same spirit in America, instead of provoking the inhabitants of that country, will endear us to them for ever and secure their good will.

This spirit however without knowledge, would be little better than a brutal rage. Let us tenderly and kindly cherish, therefore the means of knowledge. Let us dare to read, think, speak and write. Let every order and degree among the people rouse their attention and animate their resolution. Let them all become attentive to the grounds and principles of government, ecclesiastical and civil. Let us study the law of nature; search into the spirit of the British constitution; read the histories of ancient ages; contemplate the great examples of Greece and Rome; set before us, the conduct of our own British ancestors, who have defended for us, the inherent rights of mankind, against foreign and domestic tyrants and usurpers, against arbitrary kings and cruel priests, in short against the gates of earth and hell. Let us read and recollect and impress upon our souls, the views and ends, of our own more immediate forefathers, in exchanging their native country for a dreary, inhospitable wilderness. Let us examine into the nature of that power and the cruelty of that oppression which drove them from their homes. Recollect their amazing fortitude, their bitter sufferings! The hunger, the nakedness, the cold, which they patiently endured! The severe labours of clearing their grounds, building their houses, raising their provisions amidst dangers from wild beasts and savage men, before they had time or money or

---

3. The location where the Magna Carta, the traditional source of British liberties, was signed.

materials for commerce! Recollect the civil and religious principles and hopes and expectations, which constantly supported and carried them through all hardships, and patience and resignation! Let us recollect it was liberty! The hope of liberty for themselves and us and ours, which conquered all discouragements, dangers and trials! In such researches as these let us all in our several departments chearfully engage! But especially the proper patrons and supporters of law, learning and religion.

Let the pulpit resound with the doctrines and sentiments of religious liberty. Let us hear the danger of thraldom to our consciences, from ignorance, extream poverty and dependance, in short from civil and political slavery. Let us see delineated before us, the true map of man. Let us hear the dignity of his nature, and the noble rank he holds among the works of God! that consenting to slavery is a sacriligious breach of trust, as offensive in the sight of God, as it is derogatory from our own honor or interest or happiness; and that God almighty has promulgated from heaven, liberty, peace, and good-will to man!

Let the Bar proclaim, "the laws, the rights, the generous plan of power," delivered down from remote antiquity; inform the world of the mighty struggles, and numberless sacrifices, made by our ancestors, in defence of freedom. Let it be known, that British liberties are not the grants of princes or parliaments, but original rights, conditions of original contracts, coequal with prerogative and coeval with government.—That many of our rights are inherent and essential, agreed on as maxims and establish'd as preliminaries, even before a parliament existed. Let them search for the foundations of British laws and government in the frame of human nature, in the constitution of the intellectual and moral world. There let us see, that truth, liberty, justice and benevolence, are its everlasting basis; and if these could be removed, the superstructure is overthrown of course.

Let the colleges join their harmony in the same delightful concern. Let every declamation turn upon the beauty of liberty and virtue, and the deformity, turpitude and malignity of slavery and vice. Let the public disputations become researches into the grounds and nature and ends of government, and the means of preserving the good and demolishing the evil. Let the dialogues and all the exercises, become the instruments of impressing on the tender mind, and of spreading and distributing, far and wide, the ideas of right and the sensations of freedom.

In a word, let every sluice of knowledge be open'd and set a flowing. The encroachments upon liberty, in the reigns of the first James and the first Charles, by turning the general attention of learned men to government, are said to have produced the greatest number of consummate statesmen, which has ever been seen in any age, or nation. Your Clarendons, Southamptons, Seldens, Hampdens, Faulklands, Sidneys, Locks, Harringtons, are all said to have owed their eminence in political knowledge, to the tyrannies of those reigns. The prospect, now before us, in America, ought in the same manner to engage the attention of every man of learning to matters of power and of right, that we may be neither led nor driven blindfolded to irretrievable destruction. Nothing less than this seems to have been meditated for us, by somebody or other in Great-Britain. There seems to be a direct and formal design on foot, to enslave all America. This however must be done by degrees. The first step that is intended seems to be an entire subversion of the whole system of our Fathers, by an introduction of the cannon and feudal law, into America. The cannon and feudal systems tho' greatly mutilated in England, are not yet destroy'd. Like the temples and palaces, in which the great contrivers of them, once worship'd and inhabited, they exist in ruins; and much of the domineering spirit of them still remains. The designs and labours of a certain society,[4] to introduce the former of them into America, have been well exposed to the public by a writer of great abilities,[5] and the further attempts to the same purpose that may be made by that society, or by the ministry or parliament, I leave to the conjectures of the thoughtful. But it seems very manifest from the S—p A-t itself, that a design is form'd to strip us in a great measure of the means of knowledge, by loading the Press, the Colleges, and even an Almanack and a News-Paper, with restraints and duties; and to introduce the inequalities and dependances of the feudal system, by taking from the poorer sort of people all their little subsistance, and conferring it on a set of stamp officers, distributors and their deputies. But I must proceed no further at present. The sequel, whenever I shall find health and leisure to pursue it, will be a "disquisition of the policy of the stamp act." In the mean time however let me add, These are not the vapours of a melancholly mind, nor the effusions of envy, disappointed ambition, nor of a spirit of opposition to government: but the emanations of an heart

---

4. The Society for the Propagation of the Gospel in Foreign Parts.

5. Jonathan Mayhew (1720–66), a noted clergyman and political liberalist.

that burns, for its country's welfare. No one of any feeling, born and educated in this once happy country, can consider the numerous distresses, the gross indignities, the barbarous ignorance, the haughty usurpations, that we have reason to fear are meditating for ourselves, our children, our neighbours, in short for all our countrymen and all their posterity, without the utmost agonies of heart, and many tears.

LETTER TO MERCY OTIS WARREN[1]

April 16, 1776

Madam

Not untill Yesterdays Post, did your agreable Favour of March the Tenth, come to my Hands. It gave me great Pleasure and altho in the distracted Kind of Life, I am obliged to lead, I cannot promise to deserve a Continuance of So excellent a Correspondence yet I am determined by Scribbling Something or other, be it what it may, to provoke it.

The Ladies I think are the greatest Politicians, that I have the Honour to be acquainted with, not only because they act upon the Sublimest of all the Principles of Policy, vizt. the Honesty is the best Policy but because they consider Questions more coolly than those who are heated with Party Zeal, and inflamed with the bitter Contentions of active, public Life.

I know of no Researches in any of the sciences more ingenious than those which have been made after the best Forms of Government nor can there be a more agreable Employment to a benevolent Heart. The Time is now approaching, when the Colonies, will find themselves under a Necessity, of engaging in Earnest in this great and indispensable Work. I have ever Thought it the most difficult and dangerous Part of the Business, Americans have to do, in this mighty Contest, to contrive some Method for the Colonies to glide insensibly, from under the old Government, into a peaceable and contented Submission to new ones. It is a long Time since this opinion was conceived, and it has never been out of my Mind. My constant Endeavour has been to convince, Gentlemen of the

Necessity of turning their Thoughts to those subjects. At present, the sense of this Necessity seems to be general, and Measures are taking which must terminate in a compleat Revolution. There is a Danger of Convulsions. But I hope, not great ones.

The Form of Government, which you admire, when its Principles are pure, is admirable indeed. It is productive of every Thing, which is great and excellent among Men. But its Principles are as easily destroyed, as human Nature is corrupted. Such a Government is only to be supported by pure Religion, or Austere Morals. Public Virtue cannot exist in a Nation without private, and public Virtue is the only Foundation of Republics. There must be a possitive Passion for the public good, the public Interest, Honour, Power, and Glory, established in the Minds of the People, or there can be no Republican Government, nor any real Liberty. And this public Passion must be Superior to all private Passions. Men must be ready, they must pride themselves, and be happy to sacrifice their private Pleasures, Passions, and Interests, nay their private Friendships and dearest Connections, when they Stand in Competition with the Rights of society.

Is there in the World a Nation, which deserves this Character. There have been several, but they are no more. Our dear Americans perhaps have as much of it as any Nation now existing, and New England perhaps has more than the rest of America. But I have seen all along my Life, Such Selfishness, and Littleness even in New England, that I sometimes tremble to think that, altho We are engaged in the best Cause that ever employed the Human Heart, yet the Prospect of success is doubtfull not for Want of Power or of Wisdom, but of Virtue.

The Spirit of Commerce, Madam, which even insinuates itself into Families, and influences holy Matrimony, and thereby corrupts the Morals of Families as well as destroys their Happiness, it is much to be feared is incompatible with that purity of Heart, and Greatness of soul which is necessary for an happy Republic. This Same Spirit of Commerce is as rampant in New England as in any Part of the World. Trade is as well understood and as passionately loved there as any where. Even the Farmers, and Tradesmen are addicted to Commerce, and it is too true, that Property is generally the standard of Respect there as much as any where. While this is the Case, there is great Danger that a Republican Government, would be very factious and turbulent there. Divisions in Elections are much to be dreaded. Every Man must seriously set himself to root out his Passions, Prejudices and Attachments, and to get the better of his private Interest. The

---

1. The text is taken from *Papers of John Adams,* ed. Robert J. Taylor, vol. 4 (1979).

only reputable Principle and Doctrine must be that all Things must give Way to the public.

This is very grave and solemn Discourse to a Lady. True, and I thank God, that his Providence has made me Acquainted with two Ladies at least, who can bear it.

I think Madam, that the Union of the Colonies, will continue and be more firmly cemented, But We must move slowly. Patience, Patience, Patience! I am obliged to invoke thee every Morning of my Life, every Noon, and every Evening.

It is Surprising to me that any among you should flatter themselves with an Accommodation. Every Appearance is against it, to an Attentive observer. The Story of Commissioners is a Bubble. Their real Errand is an Insult. But popular Passions and Fancies will have their Course, you may as well reason down a Gale of Wind.

You expect, if a certain Bargain Should be complied with, to be made acquainted with noble and Royal Characters. But in this you will be disappointed. Your Correspondent, has neither Principles, nor Address, nor Abilities, for such Scenes, and others are as sensible of it, I assure you as he is. They must be Persons of more Complaisance and Ductility of Temper as well as better Accomplishments for such great Things.

He wishes for nothing less. He wishes for nothing more than to retire from all public stages, and public Characters, great and small, to his Farm and his Attorneys office. And to both these he must return.

LETTER TO THOMAS JEFFERSON[1]

July 29, 1791

Dear Sir

Yesterday, at Boston, I received your friendly Letter of July 17th. with great pleasure. I give full credit to your relation of the manner in which your note was written and prefixed to the Philadelphia edition of Mr. Paines pamphlet on the rights of Man: but the misconduct of the person, who committed this breach of your confidence, by making it publick, whatever were his intentions, has sown the Seeds of more evils, than he can ever attone for. The

Pamphlet, with your name, to so striking a recommendation to it, was not only industriously propogated in New York and Boston; but, that the recommendation might be known to every one, was reprinted with great care in the Newspapers, and was generally considered as a direct and open personal attack upon me, by countenancing the false interpretation of my Writings as favouring the Introduction of hereditary Monarchy and Aristocracy into this Country. The Question every where was, What Heresies are intended by the Secretary of State?[2] The answer in the Newspapers was, The Vice Presidents[3] notions of a Limited Monarchy, an hereditary Government of King and Lords, with only elective commons. Emboldened by these murmurs, soon after appeared the Paragraphs of an unprincipled Libeller in the New Haven Gazette, carefully reprinted in the Papers of New York, Boston and Philadelphia, holding up the Vice President to the ridicule of the World for his meanness, and to their detestation for wishing to subjugate the People to a few Nobles. These were soon followed by a formal Speech of the Lieutenant Governor of Massachusetts[4] very solemnly holding up the Idea of hereditary Powers, and cautioning the Publick against them, as if they were at that moment in the most imminent danger of them. These Things were all accompanied with the most marked neglect both of the Governor[5] and Lieutenant Governor of this State towards me; and alltogether opperated as an Hue and Cry to all my Ennemies and Rivals, to the old constitutional faction of Pensilvania in concert with the late Insurgents of Massachusetts, both of whom consider my Writings as the Cause of their overthrow, to hunt me down like a hare, if they could. In this State of Things, Publicola, who, I suppose, thought that Mr. Paines Pamphlet was made Use of as an Instrument to destroy a Man, for whom he had a regard, he thought innocent, and in the present moment [o]f some importance to the Publick, came forward.

You declare very explicitly that you never did, by yourself or by any other, have a Sentence of yours, inserted in a Newspaper without your name to it. And I, with equal frankness declare that I never did, either by my self or by any other, have a Sentence of mine inserted in any Newspaper since I left Philadelphia. I neither wrote

---

1. The text is taken from *The Adams-Jefferson Letters,* ed. Lester J. Cappon, vol. 1 (1959).

2. Jefferson.

3. John Adams himself.

4. Samuel Adams.

5. John Hancock.

nor corrected Publicola. The Writer in the Composition of his Pieces followed his own Judgment, Information and discretion, without any assistance from me.

You observe "That You and I differ in our Ideas of the best form of Government is well known to us both." But, my dear Sir, you will give me leave to say, that I do not know this. I know not what your Idea is of the best form of Government. You and I have never had a serious conversation together that I can recollect concerning the nature of Government. The very transient hints that have ever passed between Us have been jocular and superficial, without ever coming to any explanation. If You suppose that I have or ever had a design or desire, of attempting to introduce a Government of King, Lords and Commons, or in other Words an hereditary Executive, or an hereditary Senate, either into the Government of the United States or that of any Individual State, in this Country, you are wholly mistaken. There is not such a Thought expressed or intimated in any public writing or private Letter of mine, and I may safely challenge all Mankind to produce such a passage and quote the Chapter and Verse. If you have ever put such a Construction on any Thing of mine, I beg you would mention it to me, and I will undertake to convince you, that it has no such meaning. Upon this occasion I will venture to say that my unpolished Writings, although they have been read by a sufficient Number of Persons to have assisted in crushing the Insurrection of the Massachusetts, in the formation of the new Constitutions of Pennsylvania, Georgia and South Carolina, and in procuring the Assent of all the States to the new national Constitution, yet they have not been read by great Numbers. Of the few who have taken the pains to read them, some have misunderstood them and others have willfully misrepresented them, and these misunderstandings and misrepresentations have been made the pretence for overwhelming me with floods and Whirlwinds of tempestuous Abuse, unexampled in the History of this Country.

It is thought by some, that Mr. Hancock's friends are preparing the Way, by my destruction, for his Election to the Place of Vice President, and that of Mr. Samuel Adams to be Governor of this Commonwealth, and then the Stone House Faction[6] will be sure of all the Loaves and Fishes, in the national Government and the State Government as they hope. The Opposers of the present Constitution of Pensilvania, the promoters of Shases Rebellion and County Resolves, and many of the Detesters of the present national Government, will undoubtedly aid them. Many People think too that no small Share of a foreign Influence, in revenge for certain untractable conduct at the Treaty of Peace, is and will be intermingled. The Janizaries of this goodly Combination, among whom are three or four, who hesitate at no falshood, have written all the Impudence and Impertinence which have appeared in the Boston Papers upon this memorable Occasion.

I must own to you that the daring Traits of Ambition and Intrigue, and those unbridled Rivalries which have already appeared, are the most melancholly and alarming Symptoms that I have ever seen in this Country: and if they are to be encouraged to proceed in their Course, the sooner I am relieved from the Competition the happier I shall be.

I thank you, Sir very sincerely for writing to me upon this Occasion. It was high time that you and I should come to an explanation with each other. The friendship that has subsisted for fifteen Years between Us without the smallest interruption, and untill this occasion without the slightest Suspicion, ever has been and still is, very dear to my heart. There is no office which I would not resign, rather than give a just occasion to one friend to forsake me. Your motives for writing to me, I have not a doubt were the most pure and the most friendly; and I have no suspicion that you will not receive this explanation from me in the same candid Light.

I thank You Sir for the foreign Intelligence and beg leave to present You with the friendly compliments of Mrs. Adams, as well as the repeated Assurances of the friendship, Esteem and respect of Dear Sir Your most obedient and most humble Servant

John Adams

---

6. Hancock and his supporters (the name refers to Hancock's granite mansion).

ABIGAIL ADAMS (1744–1818)

Although she never published her writing during her lifetime, Abigail Adams was among the best known women correspondents of her day, and she was proficient in the two key genres commonly used in her day: letter writing and journal narratives. In both letters and travel narratives, women were expected not merely to describe the events of their days, but to create evaluations of the events according to timely affairs or domestic norms. Adams's letters and journals reveal her steady awareness of the role she played as an author, but they also reveal a degree of both wittiness and detail that is unusual in such writing.

Abigail Smith was the daughter of a Massachusetts clergyman and the descendant of families that had long been in New England. When she was twenty, she married John Adams, a young lawyer. During the first ten years of her marriage, Abigail Adams bore five children, while her husband became involved in the controversies leading to the Revolution. John Adams became a delegate to the Continental Congress, which forced him to travel often and remain away for long periods. When her husband was away, and increasingly even when he was home, Adams ran the family farm, managed business dealings, and served as the head of the household, roles she held for the major part of their lives together. During these absences, the Adamses corresponded frequently, creating an exchange noted for its liveliness, domestic honesty, and sensitivity to the events all around them.

John Adams's work in behalf of the new United States took him to England and Europe in the 1780s. Abigail Adams traveled to England in 1784, to join her husband, who had remained in Europe after signing the Treaty of Paris. During this trip, she kept brief travel journals that served to record the trip and provide readers with her impressions of England and Paris. After John Adams was appointed ambassador to Great Britain, the couple moved to London, where they remained until 1788, when he returned home, having asked to be recalled from service. John Adams became vice president of the United States the next year, and the Adamses went to live in New York City (then the capital). During her husband's tenure in national office, Abigail Adams divided her time between the national capital (which soon changed to Philadelphia) and their home in Massachusetts. When John Adams became the second president, Abigail took on the social duties of the first lady in Philadelphia and then Washington. After Jefferson's election in 1801, Abigail and John Adams returned to Massachusetts, where they lived for the remainder of their lives.

The selections that follow reveal Abigail Adams's interests in social matters, her engagement in politics, and her views of domestic issues. While the letter to John in which Abigail Adams requests that the new Congress "Remember the Ladies" during its deliberations is perhaps her most famous piece of writing, it does not reveal the range of Adams's intellect and the issues of importance that she regularly discussed with her husband. The letter to her friend, Mercy Otis Warren, provides a complementary view of the comment she had sent to John Adams about the new Continental Congress.

from THE TRAVEL DIARIES OF ABIGAIL ADAMS[1]

[Boston to Deal]

Embarked on Board the ship Active Capt. Lyde commander, with my daughter and 2 servants for London. To go back to the painfull Scenes I endured in taking leave of my Friends and Neighbours will but excite them over again. Suffice it to say that I left my own House the 18 of june. Truly a house of mourning; full of my Neighbours. Not of unmeaning complimenters, but the Honest yeomanary, their wifes and daughters like a funeral procession, all come to wish me well and to pray for a speedy return.—Good Heaven, what were my sensations? Heitherto I had fortified my mind. Knowing I had to act my little part alone, I had possessd myself with calmness, but this was too much for me, so I shook them by the hand

---

1. Abigail Adams's travel diary is excerpted from *Diary and Autobiography of John Adams,* ed. L. H. Butterfield, vol. 3 (1961).

mingling my tears with theirs, and left them. I had after this to bid my neices, adieu. And then another scene still more afflictive, an aged Parent from whom I had kept the day of my departure a secret knowing the agony she would be in.[2] I calld at her door. As soon as the good old Lady beheld me, the tears rolled down her aged check, and she cried out O! why did you not tell me you was going so soon? Fatal day! I take my last leave; I shall never see you again. Carry my last blessing to my son.— I was obliged to leave her in an agony of distress, myself in no less. My good Sister Cranch who accompanied me to Town endeavourd to amuse me and to console me. I was glad to shut myself up the remainder of the day and to be denied to company. Saturday I had recoverd some from my fatigue and employed the day in writing to several of my Friends and in getting my baggage on Board. Several of the Passengers calld upon me, amongst whom was a Col. Norton from Marthas Vinyard a Member of our Senate, a grave sedate Man about 50 Years of age. A Mr. Green an english Gentleman who was Seeceretary to Admiral Arbuthnot when he was at Charlestown, a high monarckcal man you may easily discover but he behaves like a Gentleman. A Dr. Clark and Mr. Foster, Mr. Spear and a Capt. Mellicot make up the number of our male passengers. We have one Lady a name sake of mine, Mrs. Adams Daughter of the late Revd. Mr. Laurence of Lincoln whose Husband has been absent ever since the War, is a physician and setled abroad. A modest, amiable woman well educated with whom I had a passing acquaintance before I came on Board. Sund[ay] at 12 oclock Mr. Foster sent his carriage for myself and daughter. We bid adieu to our Friends and were drove to Rows Wharf, from whence we allighted amidst an 100 Gentlemen who were upon the Wharf, to receive us. Mr. Smith handed me from the Carriage and I hastned into the ship from amidst the throng. The ship was soon under sail and we went of with a fine wind. About 2 oclock we reachd the light when the Capt. sent word to all the Ladies to put on their Sea cloaths and prepare for sickness. We had only time to follow his directions before we found ourselves all sick. To those who have never been at Sea or experienced this disspiriting malady tis impossible to discribe it, the Nausia arising from the smell of the Ship, the continual rolling, tossing and tumbling contribute to keep up this Disorder, and when once it seazeis a person it levels Sex and condition. My Servant Man was very attentive the first day, not sick at all, made our beds and did what I should not have put him upon in any other Situation for my maid was wholy useless and the sickest of either. Monday mor[nin]g very fogy every Body on Board Sick except the Dr. and 3 or 4 old sea men. My Servant as bad as any. I was obliged to send a petition to the Capt. to release to me Jobe Feild whose place on board the ship I had procured for him. He came and amply supplied the others place. Handy, attentive, obligeing and kind, an excellent Nurse, we all prized him. He continued untill tuesday when we had a fine mor'g. Our sickness abated and we went upon Deck, beheld the vast and boundless ocean before us with astonishment, and wonder. How great, how Excellent, how stupendous He who formed, governs, and directs it.

Sunday June 27

I have been so sick that I could not be regular in my journal. We have had two days calm since we came to Sea. The rest of the time good winds which have brought us on our Way rejoiceing, for we have not had any bad weather except rain, thunder and lightning one evening which was not severe. I have been surprized at myself to find that I can sleep notwithstanding the lasshing of the waves; and the tumbling of the vessel. This is the 8th day of our imprisonment. We are now about 200 and 50 leagues from Boston. Our Gentleman all civil and polite. This Mr. G———n mentiond in the former part of this journal as an englishman, I rather think is Scotch, and appears to have inflamibility enough to furnish a Waggon load of Baloons. He talks much. His countanance planly speaks the ruleing passions of his mind. He governs himself as he appears to know what belongs to a Gentleman. Our Captain appears more amiable at sea than on shore, his men all still and quiet, nothing severe towards them has yet appear'd. The mate a droll being; swears for all the rest of the Ship. A Good deal in his manners like Captn. Newcombe, has been several time[s] taken during the war, and has many a sad as well as diverting Story to tell which he does with a countanance as droll as you please. He is a right Tar in his manners.

Monday Mor'g 28 JUNE

A very dissagreeable Night. Wind at the southard near the Banks of Newfoundland. The morning damp. A most voilent Headack. Sick every one of us. Our Ship goes at about nine and 8 knots an hour. No going upon deck.

---

2. Adams's mother-in-law, Susannah Adams Hall.

Their is so much confinement on Board a Ship and such a Sameness that one knows not what to do. I have been reading since I came on Board Buchan Domestick Medicine. He appears a sensible, judicious and rational writer.[3]

I endeavour to bear my voyage with patience. It was at the request of my dear long absent Friend that I undertook it. I expected it would be dissagreable to be at sea. I can bear every thing I meet with better than the Nausias Smells: it is utterly impossible to keep nice and clean. I strive for Decency, and that can hardly be obtained. How flattering is attention and how agreeable does it render a person when it appears the result of a good Heart, disposed to make every one happy. This Dr. Clark is a very agreable Man. His kindness is of that Benevolent nature which extends to all: to the Servant as well as the Master. He has renderd our passage much pleasenter than it could have been without him, and we have been so sick, that his advise has been of great use to us. By tomorrow we hope to make a quarter part of our passage. When may I begin to look forward to the joyfull day of meeting my long absent partner. Heaven grant it may be a joy, without alloy.

Thursday July 1 1784

> "And thou, Majestick, Main,
> A Secret World of Wonders in thyself
> Sound his stupendous praise; whose greater voice
> Or bids you roar, or bids your roarings fall."[4]

I have not been able to write a line since Monday when a North east Storm came on and held till Wednesday Mor'g. It was with the utmost difficulty that we could set or lie only by holding by each other with our feet against a table braced with ropes, that we could keep up; and when in bed I was obliged to hold fast by the sides till my hands and wrists aked to keep in: only conceive a great cradle rocking with amaizing force from side, to side, whilst a continual creek from every part of the Ship responded to the roll: not a wink of Sleep to be had, bottles, mugs, plates, every thing crashing to peices.

The Sailors call it a Breize only. But if it was only of that kind: good heaven defend me from a storm. Tho they all allow that it is very unusual at this Season of the year to meet with such a *Breize* there is no time when the vessel does not roll like the moderate rocking of a cradle; it is easily accounted for. The writing shews the constant motion of the Vessel when not one letter in ten, can be made in its proper Shape.

I am more and more of the mind that a Lady ought not to go to sea. It is impossible to preserve that Decency and Cleanliness which ought to be an inherint principal in every female. Even those times which by Gentlemen are Esteemed fine and pleasent cannot fail to be dissagreable to a Lady. I have reflected upon Mrs. Hayley['s] observation to me, that altho she was surrounded with every accommodation that could be obtained on Board a fine large Ship, with agreable company, yet it was a terrible thing for a Lady to attempt, and nothing but the ardent desire she had to visit a Country so distinguished for its noble and ardent defence of the rights of Mankind, could have tempted her at her advanced age to have undertaken a sea voyage. What ever curiosity might prompt, I think I should content myself with the page of the Historian if I had no superiour inducement to visit foreign climes, but when I reflect that for ten years past I have been cut of from a large Share of Domestick happiness by a Seperation from my partner, I think my Sufferings small when I look forward to the recompence and the reward.

> Unutterable happiness! which Love
> alone bestows, and on a *favour few*
> those sacred feelings of the Heart, informed
> by reasons purest ray.[5]

We have on Board a Mr. Spear, the only single Gentleman of all the passengers. He is a droll mortal and keeps us in good Spirits, which is very necessary on board a Ship. Change of Ideas, says the medical writer, is as necessary for Health, as change of posture. Learned Men often contract a contempt for what they call trilling company. They are ashamed to be seen with any but philosophers. This however is no proof of their being philosophers themselves. No Man deserves that Name who is ashamed to unbend his mind, by associating with the cheerfull and gay. Even the Society of children will relieve the mind, and expell the Gloom which application to study is too apt to occasion.

I transcribe this passage because I think the Health of my best Friend has suffered from too intense application to study and the perplexing Science of politicks in which he

---

3. William Buchan, *Domestic Medicine; or, the Family Physician* (1769).

4. The lines are from "Hymn," published after the poem "Winter," in James Thomson's *The Seasons*.

5. The lines are from "Spring" in James Thomson's *The Seasons*.

has been constantly engaged. I believe he has sufferd greatly; for Want of his family and a thousand little attentions which sooth the mind and warm the heart. Of all happiness domestick is the sweetest. It is the sun shine of the Heart.

I have great satisfaction in the behaviour of my daughter. The Struggle of her mind was great, her passions strong, never before calld into opposition; the parting of two persons strongly attached to each other is only to be felt; discription fails.

Yet when once the struggle was over, she has obtaind a Calmness and a degree of cheerfulness which I feard she would not be able to acquire. To this the kindness and attention of Dr. Clark has contributed, tho he knew not that there was more than ordinary occasion for them. His manners are soothing and cheerfull. I do not however esteem him as a Man of superiour parts but he has the art of making Men happy and keeping them so. Says Buchan all that is necessary for Man to know in order to be happy, is easily obtaind and the rest like the forbiden fruit serves only to encrease his misiry.

This if true is no great compliment to Learning, but it is certain that your deep thinkers seldom enjoy Health, or Spirits.

Saturday 3 July

A fine morning. Rose by six o clock. Went upon deck. None of the Gentlemen up; our Second Mate, a grand son of the Revd. Dr. Chauncy of Boston. He was upon deck and handed me out. A likely young fellow whose countanance is a good Letter of recommendation. We were all prejudiced in his favour as soon as we saw him; he told me to day that he was taken a prisoner during the War, and carried to Plimouth jail in England where after being confined a Year he made his escape and got to Holland, where he saw Mr. Adams, who gave him money and a letter to Commodore Gillion but that he had sailed for America before he reached the Vessel. He said there were several other prisoners with him at that time who received Money from Mr. Adams. It always give me pleasure when I hear of the kindness of my best Friend to the poor and the needy. The Blessing of him that is ready to perish come upon him. By this said our Blessed saviour shall all Men know that ye are my diciples, if ye have Love to one an other; how many inducements does the Christian Religion offer to excite us to universal Benevolence and Good will towards each other, and yet how often do we suffer the vilest of passions to Dominer over us and extinguish from our Bosoms every generous principal.

This afternoon saw a sail. She bore down to speak with us. Said she was from Abberdeen bound to Novia Scotia, was full of Emigrants—men, women and children. Capt. Cullen in the brigg John, designd afterward for Philadelphia, wanted to put some Letters on Board of us. Our Capt. offerd to lay too, if she would higst out her Boat, but instead of that they attempted to come so near as to throw them on Board, and by that means were in danger of running on Board of us. The Capt. was allarmed, and gave them a hearty broad side: obliged to croud all our sails to keep clear; and tho I was first pleased with the sight of her, I was so much allarmed by our danger, that I wished her many leagues of. We put away as fast as possible without her Letters.—We suppose ourselves in Latitude 42.

Sunday July 4th 1784

This is the Anniversary of our Glorious Independance.

> O thou! by whose Almighty Nod the Scale,
> of Empires rises, or alternate falls,
> Send forth the Saveing virtues round our land
> In bright patrol; white peace, and social Love,
> The tender looking Charity, intent
> on Gentle Deeds, and sheding tears through Smiles,
> Undaunted Truth, and Dignity of mind
> Courage composed and keen; sound temperance
> Healthfull in Heart and look; Clear Chastity
> with blushes reddening as she moves along
> Disordered at the deep regard she draws;
> Rough Industery; Activity untir'd,
> With copious Life informed and all awake;
> While in the Radient front, superiour shines
> That first parental virtue, publick Zeal;
> Who throws o'er all an equal wide survey;
> And ever museing on the common Weal,
> Still Labours glorious with some great design;[6]

Whilst the Nations of Europe are enveloped in Luxery and dissipation; and a universal venality prevails throughout Britain, may the new empire, Gracious Heaven, become the Guardian and protector of Religion and Liberty, of universal Benevolence and Phylanthropy. May those virtues which are banished from the land of our Nativity, find a safe Assylum with the inhabitants of this new world.

We have a fine wind and a clear sky. We go at 7 knots an hour; I hope two Sundays more, will bring us safe to land but we have all conquerd our Sea Sickness, and are

---

6. The lines are from "Summer" in Thomson's *Seasons*.

able to do much better than for the first ten days. It is said of Cato, that one of the three things which he regreted at the close of Life; was that he had once gone by sea when he might have made his journey by land; alass poor Cato! I fancy thy Philosophy was not proof against this dispiriting disease.

Saturday 17 of July

I have neglected my journal for a week. During that time we have had 3 calm days, some wet weather but nothing worth remarking has occur'd. I have been several days sick of the Rheumatisim, occasiond I suppose by the dampness of the Ship, which made my Bed so too. I had the precaution to take some medicine on Board proper for the Disease, which the Dr. administerd, and I have in a great measure got the better of it. This day makes 27 since we came to Sea. From observation to day we were in Latitude 49 and a half, Long[itude] 6. We have seen a great Number of Vessels to day which lead us to think we are not far from the Channel. A small Sail Boat spoke with us out 3 days from Morlay, told us we were nearer the channel than we imagind, upon which the Capt. sounded and found bottom 55 fathom.

We have a head wind, but go at about 4 knots an hour. Hope to make land to morrow. Can it be that I have past this great ocean with no more inconvenience, with such favourable weather upon the whole. Am I so near the land of my fore Fathers? And am I Gracious Heaven; there to meet, the Dear long absent partner of my Heart? How many how various how complicated my Sensations! Be it unto me according to my wishes.

Sunday July 18th

This Day about 2 oclock made land. It is almost a Calm, so that we shall gain but little. We hope to land at Portsmouth a tuesday; this is doing very well; I have great reason to be thankfull for so favourable a passage. The mate caught a shark this morning but he got away, after receiving several wounds with a harpoon. I believe I could continue on Board this Ship 8 or ten days more, and find it less urksome than the first 8 or ten hours, so strong is habit and so easily do we become reconciled to the most dissagreeable Situation.

Monday Morning July 19th

A calm. The vessel rolling: the wind freshning towards Night. We hope for a speedy passage up the Channel.

Tuesday a fine wind but squally. We have seen land supposed to be Dover cliffs.

[London to Plymouth]

Fryday July 20 1787 London

This day three years I landed at Deal. Since that time I have travelled to France, to Holland and several parts of England but have never kept any journal, or record except what my Letters to my Friends may furnish nor have I ever perused this Book since it was first written till this Day when looking into the first page, it excited all my former emotions and made the Tears flow affresh. I have now determined on this journey to keep a journal. This Day we set out from Grosvenour Square on a Tour to Plimouth. Mr. Adams, myself, Mrs. Smith and Son about 3 months old, her Nursery maid, Esther my own maid and Edward Farmer a footman, our own Coachman and a postilion. Our first Stage was to Epsom in the county of Surry where we dinned. This place is famous for the races which are held there. From Epsom we proceeded to Guilford where we put up for the Night. This is a agreeable road and a highly cultivated Country.

21

We set out about 9 in the morning, stoped and baited at Farnham, dinned at Alton and reached Winchester about 8 oclock. Robert Quincy Earl of Winchester formerly resided here and was I presume an ancestor of my mothers, bearing the same arms. There is a Cathedral Church here, it being a Bishops See. The present Bishop of Winchester is Brother to Lord North whose Seat and park is in Farnham. There is a remarkable high Hill calld Catharine Hill just after you quit Guilford near two miles long from which one has a good view of the Town which seems to be placed between 2 Hills. The Houses are very old. In further examining respecting this earl of Winchester, I find that Saar de Quincy was created first Earl of Winchester by King John in 1224 and signed Magna Charta. In 1321 the title is said to be extinct, but this I do not believe as my Ancestors who went to America bore the same Name and Arms. And I well remember seeing when I was a child a parchment containing the Descent of the families in the possession of my Grandfather and that it was traced back to William the conquerer who came from Normandy. Saer de Quincy was a French Marquiss. Mr. Edmund Quincy borrowed this Genealogicall Table of my Grandmother for some purpose and lost it as he says. If the Tittle had been

extinct for want of Male Heirs, it is not probable that an illegitimate ospring would have taken pains to have preserved the Geneoligy. These matters have heitherto been
of so little consideration in America that scarcely any person traces their desent beyond the third Generation by
which means the Britains sometimes twit us of being descended from the refuse of their Goals and from transported convicts. But it is well known that the first setlers
of New England were no such persons, but worthy conscientious people who fled from Religious percecution to
a New World and planted themselves amidst Savages that
they might enjoy their Religion unmolested.

July [24–]25

We left this village and proceeded on our way to Blanford
where we put up for the Night. Saw nothing striking in this
place and met with poor accommodations oweing chiefly
to the Assizes, which were to commence the next Day and
the House was nearly occupied when we arrived. We stayd
only untill the next morning and then persued our route.
Arrived at diner time at Dorchester an other very old Town.
It is famous for Beer and Butter. It resembles Dorchester
in New England, in the Hills and in the appearence of the
Land. About four miles from the middle of the Town on the
road to Weymouth is a very Regular entrenchment upon a
very high Hill: this must have been the encampment of
some Army. Some say it was a Danish encampment, others that it was a Roman. There is an Amphitheatre in the
middle of a mile circumference and a castle calld Maiden
Castle. Weymouth lies 8 miles from Dorchester, is a Sea
port and esteemed a very Healthey Situation, a Noted
Bathing place and much resorted to during the Summer
Months. The whole Town draws its Support from the company which frequent it. It is a small place and little Land
which is not occupied by Buildings for the conveniency of
the company. It has no Manufactory of any kind. Some
vessels are built here. We tarried here only one Night.

LETTER TO JOHN ADAMS[1]

Braintree March 31 1776

I wish you would ever write me a Letter half as long as I
write you; and tell me if you may where your Fleet are
gone? What sort of Defence Virginia can make against
our common Enemy? Whether it is so situated as to make
an able Defence? Are not the Gentery Lords and the common people vassals, are they not like the uncivilized Natives Brittain represents us to be? I hope their Riffel Men
who have shewen themselves very savage and even Blood
thirsty; are not a specimen of the Generality of the people.

I am willing to allow the Colony great merit for having produced a Washington but they have been shamefully duped by a Dunmore.

I have sometimes been ready to think that the passion
for Liberty cannot be Eaqually Strong in the Breasts of
those who have been accustomed to deprive their fellow
Creatures of theirs. Of this I am certain that it is not
founded upon that generous and christian principal of
doing to others as we would that others should do unto us.

Do not you want to see Boston; I am fearfull of the
small pox, or I should have been in before this time. I got
Mr. Crane to go to our House and see what state it was in.
I find it has been occupied by one of the Doctors of a Regiment, very dirty, but no other damage has been done to it.
The few things which were left in it are all gone. Cranch
has the key which he never deliverd up. I have wrote to
him for it and am determined to get it cleand as soon as
possible and shut it up. I look upon it a new acquisition of
property, a property which one month ago I did not value
at a single Shilling, and could with pleasure have seen it
in flames.

The Town in General is left in a better state than we expected, more oweing to a percipitate flight than any Regard to the inhabitants, tho some individuals discoverd a
sense of honour and justice and have left the rent of the
Houses in which they were, for the owners and the furniture unhurt, or if damaged sufficient to make it good.

Others have committed abominable Ravages. The
Mansion House of your President[2] is safe and the furniture unhurt whilst both the House and Furniture of the
Solisiter General[3] have fallen a prey to their own merciless party. Surely the very Fiends feel a Reverential awe
for Virtue and patriotism, whilst they Detest the paricide
and traitor.

I feel very differently at the approach of spring to what
I did a month ago. We knew not then whether we could
plant or sow with safety, whether when we had toild we
could reap the fruits of our own industry, whether we

---

1. The text is taken from *Adams Family Correspondence,*
ed. L. H. Butterfield (1963).

2. John Hancock.

3. Samuel Quincy.

could rest in our own Cottages, or whether we should not be driven from the sea coasts to seek shelter in the wilderness, but now we feel as if we might sit under our own vine and eat the good of the land.

I feel a gaieti de Coar[4] to which before I was a stranger. I think the Sun looks brighter, the Birds sing more melodiously, and Nature puts on a more chearfull countanance. We feel a temporary peace, and the poor fugitives are returning to their deserted habitations.

Tho we felicitate ourselves, we sympathize with those who are trembling least the Lot of Boston should be theirs. But they cannot be in similar circumstances unless pusilanimity and cowardise should take possession of them. They have time and warning given them to see the Evil and shun it.—I long to hear that you have declared an independancy—and by the way in the new Code of Laws which I suppose it will be necessary for you to make I desire you would Remember the Ladies, and be more generous and favourable to them than your ancestors. Do not put such unlimited power into the hands of the Husbands. Remember all Men would be tyrants if they could. If perticuliar care and attention is not paid to the Laidies we are determined to foment a Rebelion, and will not hold ourselves bound by any Laws in which we have no voice, or Representation.

That your Sex are Naturally Tyrannical is a Truth so thoroughly established as to admit of no dispute, but such of you as wish to be happy willingly give up the harsh title of Master for the more tender and endearing one of Friend. Why then, not put it out of the power of the vicious and the Lawless to use us with cruelty and indignity with impunity. Men of Sense in all Ages abhor those customs which treat us only as the vassals of your Sex. Regard us then as Beings placed by providence under your protection and in immitation of the Supreem Being make use of that power only for our happiness.

April 5

Not having an opportunity of sending this I shall add a few lines more; tho not with a heart so gay. I have been attending the sick chamber of our Neighbour Trot whose affliction I most sensibly feel but cannot discribe, striped of two lovely children in one week. Gorge the Eldest died on wednesday and Billy the youngest on fryday, with the Canker fever, a terible disorder so much like the thr[o]at

distemper, that it differs but little from it. Betsy Cranch has been very bad, but upon the recovery. Becky Peck they do not expect will live out the day. Many grown person[s] are now sick with it, in this [street?] 5. It rages much in other Towns. The Mumps too are very frequent. Isaac is now confined with it. Our own little flock are yet well. My Heart trembles with anxiety for them. God preserve them.

I want to hear much oftener from you than I do. March 8 was the last date of any that I have yet had.—You inquire of whether I am making Salt peter. I have not yet attempted it, but after Soap making believe I shall make the experiment. I find as much as I can do to manufacture cloathing for my family which would else be Naked. I know of but one person in this part of the Town who has made any, that is Mr. Tertias Bass as he is calld who has got very near an hundred weight which has been found to be very good. I have heard of some others in the other parishes. Mr. Reed of Weymouth has been applied to, to go to Andover to the mills which are now at work, and has gone. I have lately seen a small Manuscrip de[s]cribing the proportions for the various sorts of powder, fit for cannon, small arms and pistols. If it would be of any Service your way I will get it transcribed and send it to you.— Every one of your Friend[s] send their Regards, and all the little ones. Your Brothers youngest child lies bad with convulsion fitts. Adieu. I need not say how much I am

Your ever faithfull Friend.

LETTER TO MERCY OTIS WARREN[1]

April 27, 1776

Braintree April 27 1776

I set myself down to comply with my Friends request, who I think seem's rather low spiritted.

I did write last week, but not meeting with an early conveyance I thought the Letter of But little importance and tos'd it away. I acknowledge my Thanks due to my Friend for the entertainment she so kindly afforded me in

---

4. Adams's attempt to write French, for "gaiety at heart."

1. The text is taken from *Adams Family Correspondence,* ed. L. H. Butterfield (1963).

the Characters drawn in her Last Letter, and if coveting my Neighbours Goods was not prohibited by the Sacred Law, I should be most certainly tempted to envy her the happy talant she possesses above the rest of her Sex, by adorning with her pen even trivial occurances, as well as dignifying the most important. Cannot you communicate some of those Graces to your Friend and suffer her to pass them upon the World for her own that she may feel a little more upon an Eaquality with you?—Tis true I often receive large packages from P[hiladelphi]a. They contain as I said before more News papers than Letters, tho they are not forgotton. It would be hard indeed if absence had not some alleviations.

I dare say he writes to no one unless to Portia oftner than to your Friend, because I know there is no one besides in whom he has an eaquel confidence. His Letters to me have been generally short, but he pleads in Excuse the critical state of affairs and the Multiplicity of avocations and says further that he has been very Busy, and writ near ten Sheets of paper, about some affairs which he does not chuse to Mention for fear of accident.

He is very sausy to me in return for a List of Female Grievances which I transmitted to him. I think I will get you to join me in a petition to Congress. I thought it was very probable our wise Statesmen would erect a New Government and form a new code of Laws. I ventured to speak a word in behalf of our Sex, who are rather hardly dealt with by the Laws of England which gives such unlimitted power to the Husband to use his wife Ill.

I requested that our Legislators would consider our case and as all Men of Delicacy and Sentiment are averse to Exercising the power they possess, yet as there is a natural propensity in Humane Nature to domination, I thought the most generous plan was to put it out of the power of the Arbitary and tyranick to injure us with impunity by Establishing some Laws in our favour upon just and Liberal principals.

I believe I even threatned fomenting a Rebellion in case we were not considerd, and assured him we would not hold ourselves bound by any Laws in which we had neither a voice, nor representation.

In return he tells me he cannot but Laugh at My Ex-

trodonary Code of Laws. That he had heard their Struggle had loosned the bands of Government, that children and apprentices were dissabedient, that Schools and Colledges were grown turbulant, that Indians slighted their Guardians, and Negroes grew insolent to their Masters. But my Letter was the first intimation that another Tribe more numerous and powerfull than all the rest were grown discontented. This is rather too coarse a complement, he adds, but that I am so sausy he wont blot it out.

So I have help'd the Sex abundantly, but I will tell him I have only been making trial of the Disintresstedness of his Virtue, and when weigh'd in the balance have found it wanting.

It would be bad policy to grant us greater power say they since under all the disadvantages we Labour we have the assendancy over their Hearts

And charm by accepting, by submitting sway.[2]

I wonder Apollo and the Muses could not have indulged me with a poetical Genious. I have always been a votary to her charms but never could assend Parnassus myself.

I am very sorry to hear of the indisposition of your Friend. I am affraid it will hasten his return, and I do not think he can be spaired.

"Though certain pains attend the cares of State
A Good Man owes his Country to be great
Should act abroad the high distinguishd part
or shew at least the purpose of his heart."[3]

Good Night my Friend. You will be so good as to remember me to our worthy Friend Mrs. W———e[4] when you see her and write soon to your

Portia

---

2. The source is not identified.

3. The lines are from Lady Mary Wortley Montagu's poem, "Epistle to Lord *B*———," published in her *Poetical Works* (1768).

4. Mrs. John Winthrop.

TIMOTHY DWIGHT (1752–1817)

A grandson of Jonathan Edwards (Dwight's mother was Edwards's daughter), Dwight tended to follow the conservative Congregationalist practices of his forebears. He was born in Massachusetts to a merchant family and educated at Yale College. He studied law for a time, but he gave it up to become a tutor at Yale until 1777, when he resigned his post to serve as a chaplain at West Point. From 1779 to 1783, Dwight preached at Northampton, Massachusetts, his birthplace, and then took a twelve-year post as pastor of the Congregational Church at Greenfield Hill, Connecticut. He then became president of Yale College, a position he held until his death in 1817.

With Joel Barlow and other Yale friends, Dwight spent his early years writing pro-Federalist verse and becoming known as one of the "Connecticut Wits." His poem, "African Address," and his 1794 antislavery speech before the Connecticut Society for the Promotion of Freedom are both suggestive of the sympathy Dwight felt for nondominant groups whose lives were inalterably interrupted by whites. This sympathy is apparent as well in Part IV of *Greenfield Hill: A Poem in Seven Parts* (published in New York in 1794), in which Dwight attempted to address British American guilt over the murder of the Pequot Indians during the war that the colonists called the Pequot War, 1635–36. Although in today's light, Dwight's position seems to be a rationalization of the fate of North Americans, his comments are interesting for their implication of a motif typical of British Americans of his (and later) generations—that the Native Americans are, by necessity, vanishing before more energetic and organized forces. Indeed, the motif of the "vanishing American" is one that found immense popularity in the early nineteenth century, perhaps spurred by the success of writers like Dwight.

In *Greenfield Hill*, Dwight adopted the pastoral and elegiac modes of Augustan writers, such as John Denham (*Cooper's Hill*), Alexander Pope (*Windsor Forest*), and Oliver Goldsmith (*The Deserted Village*). The pastoral mode was appropriate to the farming ideal Dwight was fond of from Goldsmith's poem, and he used it, as in Book II of *Greenfield Hill*, to offer the example of Connecticut as the ideal society that the new nation could become. By adopting neoclassical poetic norms, Dwight constructed his poem along traditional and admired models, and he was thus able to cast the problems faced by the British American colonists in an appropriately stylized past while offering an idealized vision of their future.

from GREENFIELD HILL[1]

Part II
The Flourishing Village

Fair Verna! loveliest village of the west;
Of every joy, and every charm, possess'd;
How pleas'd amid thy varied walks I rove,
Sweet, cheerful walks of innocence, and love,
5 And o'er thy smiling prospects cast my eyes,
And see the seats of peace, and pleasure, rise,
And hear the voice of Industry resound,
And mark the smile of Competence, around!
Hail, happy village! O'er the cheerful lawns,

With earliest beauty, spring delighted dawns;   10
The northward sun begins his vernal smile;
The spring-bird carols o'er the cressy rill:
The shower, that patters in the ruffled stream,
The ploughboy's voice, that chides the lingering team,
The bee, industrious, with his busy song,   15
The woodman's axe, the distant groves among,
The wagon, rattling down the rugged steep,
The light wind, lulling every care to sleep,
All these, with mingled music, from below,
Deceive intruding sorrow, as I go.   20

How pleas'd, fond Recollection, with a smile,
Surveys the varied round of wintery toil!
How pleas'd, amid the flowers, that scent the plain,
Recalls the vanish'd frost, and sleeted rain;
The chilling damp, the ice-endangering street,   25
And treacherous earth that slump'd beneath the feet.

---

1. The text is from *Greenfield Hill: A Poem in Seven Parts*, published in Hartford, 1794.

Yet even stern winter's glooms could joy inspire:
Then social circles grac'd the nutwood fire;
The axe resounded, at the sunny door;
30 The swain, industrious, trimm'd his flaxen store;
Or thresh'd, with vigorous flail, the bounding wheat,
His poultry round him pilfering for their meat;
Or slid his firewood on the creaking snow;
Or bore his produce to the main below;
35 Or o'er his rich returns exulting laugh'd;
Or pledg'd the healthful orchard's sparkling draught:
While, on his board, for friends and neighbors spread,
The turkey smok'd, his busy housewife fed;
And Hospitality look'd smiling round,
40 And Leisure told his tale, with gleeful sound.

Then too, the rough road hid beneath the sleigh,
The distant friend despis'd a length of way,
And join'd the warm embrace, and mingling smile,
And told of all his bliss, and all his toil;
45 And, many a month elaps'd, was pleas'd to view
How well the household far'd, the children grew;
While tales of sympathy deceiv'd the hour,
And Sleep, amus'd, resign'd his wonted power.

Yes! let the proud despise, the rich deride,
50 These humble joys, to Competence allied:
To me, they bloom, all fragrant to my heart,
Nor ask the pomp of wealth, nor gloss of art.
And as a bird, in prison long confin'd,
Springs from his open'd cage, and mounts the wind,
55 Thro' fields of flowers, and fragrance, gaily flies,
Or reassumes his birth-right, in the skies:
Unprison'd thus from artificial joys,
Where pomp fatigues, and fussful fashion cloys,
The soul, reviving, loves to wander free
60 Thro' native scenes of sweet simplicity;
Thro' Peace' low vale, where Pleasure lingers long,
And every songster tunes his sweetest song,
And Zephyr hastes, to breathe his first perfume,
And Autumn stays, to drop his latest bloom:
65 'Till grown mature, and gathering strength to roam,
She lifts her lengthen'd wings, and seeks her home.

But now the wintery glooms are vanish'd all;
The lingering drift behind the shady wall;
The dark-brown spots, that patch'd the snowy field;
70 The surly frost, that every bud conceal'd;
The russet veil, the way with slime o'erspread,
And all the saddening scenes of March are fled.

Sweet-smiling village! loveliest of the hills!
How green thy groves! How pure thy glassy rills!

With what new joy, I walk thy verdant streets! 75
How often pause, to breathe thy gale of sweets,
To mark thy well-built walls! thy budding fields!
And every charm, that rural nature yields;
And every joy, to Competence allied,
And every good, that Virtue gains from Pride! 80

No griping landlord here alarms the door,
To halve, for rent, the poor man's little store.
No haughty owner drives the humble swain
To some far refuge from his dread domain;
Nor wastes, upon his robe of useless pride, 85
The wealth, which shivering thousands want beside;
Nor in one palace sinks a hundred cots;
Nor in one manor drowns a thousand lots;
Nor, on one table, spread for death and pain,
Devours what would a village well sustain. 90

O Competence, thou bless'd by Heaven's decree,
How well exchang'd is empty pride for thee!
Oft to thy cot my feet delighted turn,
To meet thy cheerful smile, at peep of morn;
To join thy toils, that bid the earth look gay; 95
To mark thy sports, that hail the eve of May;
To see thy ruddy children, at thy board,
And share thy temperate meal, and frugal hoard;
And every joy, by winning prattlers giv'n,
And every earnest of a future Heaven. 10

There the poor wanderer finds a table spread,
The fireside welcome, and the peaceful bed.
The needy neighbor, oft by wealth denied,
There finds the little aids of life supplied;
The horse, that bears to mill the hard-earn'd grain; 1C
The day's work given, to reap the ripen'd plain;
The useful team, to house the precious food,
And all the offices of real good.

There too, divine Religion is a guest,
And all the Virtues join the daily feast. 1
Kind Hospitality attends the door,
To welcome in the stranger and the poor;
Sweet Chastity, still blushing as she goes;
And Patience smiling at her train of woes;
And meek-eyed Innocence, and Truth refin'd, 1
And Fortitude, of bold, but gentle mind.

Thou pay'st the tax, the rich man will not pay;
Thou feed'st the poor, the rich man drives away.
Thy sons, for freedom, hazard limbs, and life,
While pride applauds, but shuns the manly strife: 1
Thou prop'st religion's cause, the world around,
And show'st thy faith in works, and not in sound.

Say, child of passion! while, with idiot stare,
Thou seest proud grandeur wheel her sunny car;
125 While kings, and nobles, roll bespangled by,
And the tall palace lessens in the sky;
Say, while with pomp thy giddy brain runs round,
What joys, like these, in splendor can be found?
Ah, yonder turn thy wealth-enchanted eyes,
130 Where that poor, friendless wretch expiring lies!
Hear his sad partner shriek, beside his bed,
And call down curses on her landlord's head,
Who drove, from yon small cot, her household sweet,
To pine with want, and perish in the street.
135 See the pale tradesman toil, the livelong day,
To deck imperious lords, who never pay!
Who waste, at dice, their boundless breadth of soil,
But grudge the scanty meed of honest toil.
See hounds and horses riot on the store,
140 By Heaven created for the hapless poor!
See half a realm one tyrant scarce sustain,
While meager thousands round him glean the plain!
See, for his mistress' robe, a village sold,
Whose matrons shrink from nakedness and cold!
145 See too the Farmer prowl around the shed,
To rob the starving household of their bread;
And seize, with cruel fangs, the helpless swain,
While wives, and daughters, plead, and weep, in vain;
Or yield to infamy themselves, to save
150 Their sire from prison, famine, and the grave.

There too foul luxury taints the putrid mind,
And slavery there imbrutes the reasoning kind:
There humble worth, in damps of deep despair,
Is bound by poverty's eternal bar:
155 No motives bright the ethereal aim impart,
Nor one fair ray of hope allures the heart.

But, O sweet Competence! how chang'd the scene,
Where thy soft footsteps lightly print the green!

Where Freedom walks erect, with manly port,
And all the blessings to his side resort,   160
In every hamlet, Learning builds her schools,
And beggars, children gain her arts, and rules;
And mild Simplicity o'er manners reigns,
And blameless morals Purity sustains.

From thee the rich enjoyments round me spring,   165
Where every farmer reigns a little king;
Where all to comfort, none to danger, rise;
Where pride finds few, but nature all supplies;
Where peace and sweet civility are seen,
And meek good-neighborhood endears the green.   170
Here every class (if classes those we call,
Where one extended class embraces all,
All mingling, as the rainbow's beauty blends,
Unknown where every hue begins or ends)
Each following, each, with uninvidious strife,   175
Wears every feature of improving life.
Each gains from other comeliness of dress,
And learns, with gentle mein to win and bless,
With welcome mild the stranger to receive,
And with plain, pleasing decency to live.   180
Refinement hence even humblest life improves;
Not the loose fair, that form and frippery loves;
But she, whose mansion is the gentle mind,
In thought, and action, virtuously refin'd.
Hence, wives and husbands act a lovelier part,   185
More just the conduct, and more kind the heart;
Hence brother, sister, parent, child, and friend,
The harmony of life more sweetly blend;
Hence labor brightens every rural scene;
Hence cheerful plenty lives along the green;   190
Still Prudence eyes her hoard, with watchful care,
And robes of thrift and neatness, all things wear.

JUDITH SARGENT MURRAY (1751–1820)

Born into a prosperous mercantile family in Gloucester, Massachusetts, Judith Sargent received an early education unusual for a woman, even a woman of her standing, during the eighteenth century. Studying with her brother Winthrop while he prepared for college, Sargent studied Latin and Greek, as well as the sciences. At the age of eighteen, she married John Stevens, a merchant and sea captain. During the seventeen years they were married (they had no children), Judith Stevens began publishing essays and poetry in Boston periodicals. In addition, her family became acquainted with John Murray, an English minister who was advocating Universalism in North America. After the death of John Stevens in 1786, Judith Stevens and John Murray developed a closer relationship, and they married in 1788.

After her second marriage, Judith Murray published even more frequently, contributing essays under various pseudonyms to local newspapers and magazine. For one series, she adopted the mask, or persona, of a man, "The Gleaner," publishing over thirty essays. Murray eventually published a total of one hundred Gleaner essays in book form (1798). She also published frequently under the pseudonym Constantia. Murray wrote a number of plays, two of which appeared in *The Gleaner* series. After 1800, she turned her attention to finishing the memoir of John Murray that he was no longer able to continue writing. After his death in 1815, Murray moved to Mississippi, where she lived with her daughter Julia until her own death.

Murray's writings engaged a range of her concerns—religious, social, political, domestic—and reveal a remarkable wit and learning. Much of Murray's formal prose was about women, their education, and their equality with men, at least in spiritual and mental capacities. But she was also interested in developing virtuous people, both men and women, and a virtuous society as a whole. Her essays show Murray's familiarity with the conventions of the occasional essay as practiced by the best English writers. Murray also worked other genres, including short fiction, plays, and history, into the character sketches and other musings that formed the staple of the occasional essay.

ON THE EQUALITY OF THE SEXES[1]

That minds are not alike, full well I know,
This truth each day's experience will show;
To heights surprising some great spirits soar,
With inborn strength mysterious depths explore;
Their eager gaze surveys the path of light,
Confest it stood to Newton's piercing sight.
Deep science, like a bashful maid retires,
And but the *ardent* breast her worth inspires;
By perserverance the coy fair is won.
And Genius, led by Study, wears the crown.
But some there are who wish not to improve,
Who never can the path of knowledge love,
Whose souls almost with the dull body one,
With anxious care each mental pleasure shun;
Weak is the level'd, enervated mind,
And but while here to vegetate design'd.
The torpid spirit mingling with its clod,
Can scarcely boast its origin from God;
Stupidly dull—they move progressing on—
They eat, and drink, and all their work is done.
While others, emulous of sweet applause,
Industrious seek for each event a cause,
Tracing the hidden springs whence knowledge flows,
Which nature all in beauteous order shows.

Yet cannot I their sentiments imbibe,
Who this distinction to the sex ascribe,
As if a woman's form must needs enrol,
A weak, servile, an inferiour soul;
And that the guise of man must still proclaim,
Greatness of mind, and him, to be the same:
Yet as the hours revolve fair proofs arise,
Which the bright wreath of growing fame supplies;
And in past times some men have *sunk so low,*
That female records nothing *less* can show.
But imbecility is still confin'd,
And by the lordly sex to us consign'd;
They rob us of the power t' improve,
And then declare we only trifles love;
Yet haste the era, when the world shall know,
That such distinctions only dwell below;
The soul unfetter'd, to no sex confin'd,
Was for the abodes of cloudless day design'd.
Mean time we emulate their manly fires,
Though erudition all their thoughts inspires,
Yet nature with *equality* imparts,
And *noble passions,* swell e'en *female hearts.*

Is it upon mature consideration we adopt the idea, that nature is thus partial in her distributions? Is it indeed a fact, that she hath yielded to one half of the human species so unquestionable a mental superiority? I know that to both sexes elevated understandings, and the reverse, are common. But, suffer me to ask, in what the minds of females are so notoriously deficient, or unequal. May not the intellectual powers be ranged under these four heads—

---

1. Originally published in the *Massachusetts Magazine* in two parts, March and April 1790.

imagination, reason, memory and judgment. The province of imagination hath long since been surrendered up to us, and we have been crowned undoubted sovereigns of the regions of fancy. Invention is perhaps the most arduous effort of the mind; this branch of imagination hath been particularly ceded to us, and we have been time out of mind invested with that creative faculty. Observe the variety of fashions (here I bar the contemptuous smile) which distinguish and adorn the female world; how continually are they changing, insomuch that they almost render the wise man's assertion problematical, and we are ready to say, *there is something new under the sun.* Now what a playfulness, what an exuberance of fancy, what strength of inventive imagination, doth this continual variation discover? Again, it hath been observed, that if the turpitude of the conduct of our sex, hath been ever so enormous, so extremely ready are we, that the very first thought presents us with an apology, so plausible, as to produce our actions even in an amiable light. Another instance of our creative powers, is our talent for slander; how ingenious are we at inventive scandal? what a formidable story can we in a moment fabricate merely from the force of a prolifick imagination? how many reputations, in the fertile brain of a female, have been utterly despoiled? how industrious are we at improving a hint? suspicion how easily do we convert into conviction, and conviction, embellished by the power of eloquence, stalks abroad to the surprise and confusion of unsuspecting innocence. Perhaps it will be asked if I furnish these facts as instances of excellency in our sex. Certainly not; but as proofs of a creative faculty, of a lively imagination. Assuredly great activity of mind is thereby discovered, and was this activity properly directed, what beneficial effects would follow. Is the needle and kitchen sufficient to employ the operations of a soul thus organized? I should conceive not. Nay, it is a truth that those very departments leave the intelligent principle vacant, and at liberty for speculation. Are we deficient in reason? we can only reason from what we know, and if an opportunity of acquiring knowledge hath been denied us, the inferiority of our sex cannot fairly be deduced from thence. Memory, I believe, will be allowed us in common, since every one's experience must testify, that a loquacious old woman is as frequently met with, as a communicative old man; their subjects are alike drawn from the fund of other times, and the transactions of their youth, or of maturer life, entertain, or perhaps fatigue you, in the evening of their lives. "But our judgment is not so strong—we do not distinguish so well."—Yet it may be questioned, from what doth this superiority, in this determining faculty of the soul, proceed.

May we not trace its source in the difference of education, and continued advantages? Will it be said that the judgment of a male of two years old, is more sage than that of a female's of the same age? I believe the reverse is generally observed to be true. But from that period what partiality! how is the one exalted, and the other depressed, by the contrary modes of education which are adopted! the one is taught to aspire, and the other is early confined and limited. As their years increase, the sister must be wholly domesticated, while the brother is led by the hand through all the flowery paths of science. Grant that their minds are by nature equal, yet who shall wonder at the *apparent* superiority, if indeed custom becomes *second nature;* nay if it taketh place of nature, and that it doth the experience of each day will evince. At length arrived at womanhood, the uncultivated fair one feels a void, which the employments allotted her are by no means capable of filling. What can she do? to books she may not apply; or if she doth, *to those only of the novel kind,* lest she merit the appellation of a *learned lady;* and what ideas have been affixed to this term, the observation of many can testify. Fashion, scandal, and sometimes what is still more reprehensible, are then called in to her relief; and who can say to what lengths the liberties she takes may proceed. Meantime she herself is most unhappy; she feels the want of a cultivated mind. Is she single, she in vain seeks to fill up time from sexual employments or amusements. Is she united to a person whose soul nature made equal to her own, education hath set him so far above her, that in those entertainments which are productive of such rational felicity, she is not qualified to accompany him. She experiences a mortifying consciousness of inferiority, which embitters every enjoyment. Doth the person to whom her adverse fate hath consigned her, posses a mind incapable of improvement, she is equally wretched, in being so closely connected with an individual whom she cannot but despise. Now, was she permitted the same instructors as her brother, (with an eye however to their particular departments) for the employment of a rational mind an ample field would be opened. In astronomy she might catch a glimpse of the immensity of the Deity, and thence she would form amazing conceptions of the august and supreme Intelligence. In geography she would admire Jehovah in the midst of his benevolence; thus adapting this globe to the various wants and amusements of its inhabitants. In natural philosophy she would adore the infinite majesty of heaven, clothed in condescension; and as she traversed the reptile world, she would hail the goodness of a creating God. A mind, thus filled, would have little room for the trifles with which our sex are, with too much justice, accused of amusing themselves, and they would thus be rendered fit companions for those, who should one day wear them as their crown. Fashions, in their variety, would then give place to conjectures, which might perhaps conduce to the improvement of the literary world; and there would be no leisure for slander or detraction. Reputation would not then be blasted, but serious speculations would occupy the lively imaginations of the sex. Unnecessary visits would be precluded, and that custom would only be indulged by way of relaxation, or to answer the demands of consanguinity and friendship. Females would become discreet, their judgments would be invigorated, and their partners for life being circumspectly chosen, an unhappy Hymen would then be as rare, as is now the reverse.

Will it be urged that those acquirements would supersede our domestick duties. I answer that every requisite in female economy is easily attained; and, with truth I can add, that when once attained, they require no further *mental attention.* Nay, while we are pursuing the needle, or the superintendency of the family, I repeat, that our minds are at full liberty for reflection; that imagination may exert itself in full vigor; and that if a just foundation is early laid, our ideas will then be worthy of rational beings. If we were industrious we might easily find time to arrange them upon paper, or should avocations press too hard for such an indulgence, the hours allotted for conversation would at least become more refined and rational. Should it still be vociferated, "Your domestick employments are sufficient"—I would calmly ask, is it reasonable, that a candidate for immortality, for the joys of heaven, an intelligent being, who is to spend an eternity in contemplating the works of Deity, should at present be so degraded, as to be allowed no other ideas, than those which are suggested by the mechanism of a pudding, or the sewing the seams of a garment? Pity that all such censurers of female improvement do not go one step further, and deny their future existence; to be consistent they surely ought.

Yes, ye lordly, ye haughty sex, our souls are by nature *equal* to yours; the same breath of God animates, enlivens, and invigorates us; and that we are not fallen lower than yourselves, let those witness who have greatly towered above the various discouragements by which they have been so heavily oppressed; and though I am unacquainted with the list of celebrated characters on either side, yet from the observations I have made in the contracted circle in which I have moved, I dare confidently believe, that from the commencement of time to the pres-

ent day, there hath been as many females, as males, who, by the *mere force of natural powers,* have merited the crown of applause; who, *thus unassisted,* have seized the wreath of fame. I know there are who assert, that as the animal powers of the one sex are superior, of course their mental faculties also must be stronger; thus attributing strength of mind to the transient organization of this earth born tenement. But if this reasoning is just, man must be content to yield the palm to many of the brute creation, since by not a few of his brethren of the field, he is far surpassed in bodily strength. Moreover, was this argument admitted, it would prove too much, for occular demonstration evinceth, that there are many robust masculine ladies, and effeminate gentlemen. Yet I fancy that Mr. Pope, though clogged with an enervated body, and distinguished by a diminutive stature, could nevertheless lay claim to greatness of soul; and perhaps there are many other instances which might be adduced to combat so unphilosophical an opinion. Do we not often see, that when the clay built tabernacle is well nigh dissolved, when it is just ready to mingle with the parent soil, the immortal inhabitant aspires to, and even attaineth heights the most sublime, and which were before wholly unexplored. Besides, were we to grant that animal strength proved any thing, taking into consideration the accustomed impartiality of nature, we should be induced to imagine, that she had invested the female mind with superior strength as an equivalent for the bodily powers of man. But waving this however palpable advantage, for *equality only,* we wish to contend.

I am aware that there are many passages in the sacred oracles which seem to give the advantage to the other sex; but I consider all these as wholly metaphorical. Thus David was a man after God's own heart, yet see him enervated by his licentious passions! behold him following Uriah to the death, and shew me wherein could consist the immaculate Being's complacency. Listen to the curses which Job bestoweth upon the day of his nativity, and tell me where is his perfection, where his patience—*literally* it existed not. David and Job were types of him who was to come; and the superiority of man, as exhibited in scripture, being also emblematical, all arguments deduced from thence, of course fall to the ground. The exquisite delicacy of the female mind proclaimeth the exactness of its texture, while its nice sense of honour announceth its innate, its native grandeur. And indeed, in one respect, the preeminence seems to be tacitly allowed us, for after an education which limits and confines, and employments and recreations which naturally tend to enervate the body, and debilitate the mind; after we have from early youth been adorned with ribbons, and other gewgaws, dressed out like the ancient victims previous to a sacrifice, being taught by the care of our parents in collecting the most showy materials that the ornamenting our exteriour ought to be the principal object of our attention; after, I say, fifteen years thus spent, we are introduced into the world, amid the united adulation of every beholder. Praise is sweet to the soul; we are immediately intoxicated by large draughts of flattery, which being plentifully administered, is to the pride of our hearts the most acceptable incense. It is expected that with the other sex we should commence immediate war, and that we should triumph over the machinations of the most artful. We must be constantly upon our guard; prudence and discretion must be our characteristicks; and we must rise superiour to, and obtain a complete victory over those who have been long adding to the native strength of their minds, by an unremitted study of men and books, and who have, moreover, conceived from the loose characters which they have been portrayed in the extensive variety of their reading, a most contemptible opinion of the sex. Thus unequal, we are, notwithstanding, forced to the combat, and the infamy which is consequent upon the smallest deviation in our conduct, proclaims the high idea which was formed of our native strength: and thus, indirectly at least, is the preference acknowledged to be our due. And if we are allowed an equality of acquirement, let serious studies equally employ our minds, and we will bid our souls arise to equal strength. We will meet upon even ground, the despot man; we will rush with alacrity to the combat, and, crowned by success, we shall then answer the exalted expectations which are formed. Though sensibility, soft compassion, and gentle commiseration, are inmates in the female bosom, yet against every deep laid art, altogether fearless of the event, we will set them in array; for assuredly the wreath of victory will encircle the spotless brow. If we meet an equal, a sensible friend, we will reward him with the hand of amity, and through life we will be assiduous to promote his happiness; but from every deep laid scheme for our ruin, retiring into ourselves, amid the flowery paths of science, we will indulge in all the refined and sentimental pleasures of contemplation. And should it still be urged, that the studies thus inlisted upon would interfere with our more peculiar department, I must further reply, that *early hours,* and close application, will do wonders; and to her who is from the first dawn of reason taught to fill up time rationally, both the requisites will be easy. I grant that niggard fortune is too

generally unfriendly to the mind; and that much of that valuable treasure, time, is necessarily expended upon the wants of the body; but it should be remembered, that in embarrassed circumstances our companions have as little leisure for literary improvement, as is afforded to us; for most certainly their provident care is at least as requisite as our exertions. Nay, we have even more leisure for sedentary pleasures, as our avocations are more retired, much less laborious, and, as hath been observed, by no means require that avidity of attention which is proper to the employments of the other sex. In high life, or, in other words, where the parties are in possession of affluence, the objection respecting time is wholly obviated, and of course falls to the ground; and it may also be repeated, that many of those hours which are at present swallowed up in fashion and scandal, might be redeemed, were we habituated to useful reflections. But in one respect, O ye arbiters of our fate! we confess that the superiority is indubitably yours; you are by nature formed for our protectors; we pretend not to vie with you in bodily strength; upon this point we will never contend for victory. Shield us then, we beseech you, from external evils, and in return we will transact *your* domestick affairs. Yes, *your,* for are you not equally interested in those matters with ourselves? Is not the elegancy of neatness as agreeable to your sight as to ours; is not the well favoured viand equally delightful to your taste; and doth not your sense of hearing suffer as much, from the discordant sounds prevalent in an ill regulated family, produced by the voices of children and many *et ceteras?*

Constantia.

By way of supplement to the foregoing pages, I subjoin the following extract from a letter, wrote to a friend in the December of 1780.

And now assist me, O thou genius of my sex, while I undertake the arduous task of endeavouring to combat that vulgar, that almost universal errour, which hath, it seems, enlisted even Mr. P———under its banners. The superiority of your sex hath, I grant, been time out of mind esteemed a truth incontrovertible; in consequence of which persuasion, every plan of education hath been calculated to establish this favourite tenet. Not long since; weak and presuming as I was, I amused myself with selecting some arguments from nature, reason, and experience, against this so generally received idea. I confess that to sacred testimonies I had not recourse. I held them to be merely metaphorical, and thus regarding them, I could not persuade myself that there was any propriety in bringing them to decide in this *very important debate*. However, as you, sir, confine yourself entirely to the sacred oracles, I mean to bend the whole of my artillery against those supposed proofs, which you have from thence provided, and from which you have formed an intrenchment *apparently* so invulnerable. And first, to begin with our great progenitors; but here, suffer me to premise, that it is for mental strength I mean to contend, for with respect to animal powers, I yield them undisputed to that sex, which enjoys them in common with the lion, the tyger, and many other beasts of prey; therefore your observations respecting the *rib under the arm, at a distance from the head, &c. &c.* in no sort militate against my view. Well, but the woman was first in the transgression. Strange how blind *self love* renders you men; were you not wholly absorbed in a partial admiration of your own abilities, you would long since have acknowledged the force of what I am now going to urge. It is true some ignoramuses have absurdly enough informed us, that the beauteous fair of paradise, was seduced from her obedience, by a malignant demon, *in the guise of a baleful serpent;* but we, who are better informed, know that the fallen spirit presented himself to her view, *a shining angel still;* for thus, saith the criticks in the Hebrew tongue, ought the word to be rendered. Let us examine her motive—Hark! the seraph declares that she shall attain a perfection of knowledge; for is there aught which is not comprehended under one or other of the terms *good* and *evil*. It doth not appear that she was governed by any one sensual appetite; but merely by a desire of adorning her mind; a laudable ambition fired her soul, and a thirst for knowledge impelled the predilection so fatal in its consequences. Adam could not plead the same deception; assuredly he was not deceived; nor ought we to admire his superior strength, or wonder at his sagacity, when we so often confess that example is much more influential than precept. His gentle partner stood before him, a melancholy instance of the direful effects of disobedience; he saw her not possessed of that wisdom which she had fondly hoped to obtain, but he beheld the once blooming female, disrobed of that innocence, which had heretofore rendered her so lovely. To him then deception became impossible, as he had proof positive of the fallacy of the argument, which the deceiver had suggested. What then could be his inducement to burst the barriers, and to fly directly in the face of that command, which *immediately* from the mouth of deity *he* had received, since, I say, he could not plead that fascinating stimulus, the accumulation of knowledge, as indis-

putable conviction was so visibly portrayed before him. What mighty cause impelled him to sacrifice myriads of beings yet unborn, and by one impious act, which *he saw* would be productive of such fatal effects, entail undistinguished ruin upon a race of beings, which he was yet to produce. Blush, ye vaunters of fortitude; ye boasters of resolution; ye haughty lords of the creation; blush when ye remember, that he was influenced by no other motive than a bare pusillanimous attachment to a woman! by sentiments so exquisitely soft, that all his sons have, from that period, when they have designed to degrade them, described as highly feminine. Thus it should seem, that all the arts of the grand deceiver (since means adequate to the purpose are, I conceive, invariably pursued) were requisite to mislead our general mother, while the father of mankind forfeited his own, and relinquished the happines of posterity, merely in compliance with the blandishments of a female. The subsequent subjection the apostle Paul explains as a figure; after enlarging, upon the subject, he adds, *"This is a great mystery; but I speak concerning Christ and the church."* Now we know with what consummate wisdom the unerring father of eternity hath formed his plans; all the types which he hath displayed, he hath permitted *materially* to fail, in the very virtue for which *they* were famed. The reason for this is obvious, we might otherwise mistake his economy, and render that honour to the creature, which is due only to the creator. I know that Adam was a figure of him who was to come. The grace contained in his figure, is the reason of my rejoicing, and while I am very far from prostrating before the shadow, I yield joyfully in all things the preeminence to the second federal head. Confiding faith is prefigured by Abraham, yet he exhibits a contrast to affiance, when he says of his fair companion, she is my sister. Gentleness was the characteristick of Moses, yet he hesitated not to reply to Jehovah himself, with unsaintlike tongue he murmured at the waters of strife, and with rash hands he break the tables, which were inscribed by the finger of divinity. David, dignified with the title of the man after God's own heart, and yet how stained was his life. Solomon was celebrated for wisdom, but folly is wrote in legible characters upon his almost every action. Lastly, let us turn our eyes to man in the aggregate. He is manifested as the figure of strength, but that we may not regard him as any thing more than a figure, his soul is formed in no sort superiour, but every way equal to the mind of her, who is the emblem of weakness, and whom he hails the gentle companion of his better days.

———

DESULTORY THOUGHTS UPON THE UTILITY OF ENCOURAGING A DEGREE OF SELF-COMPLACENCY, ESPECIALLY IN FEMALE BOSOMS[1]

Self estimation, kept within due bounds,
However oddly the assertion sounds,
May, of the fairest efforts be the root,
May yield the embow'ring shade—the mellow fruit;
May stimulate to most exalted deeds,
Direct the soul where blooming honor leads;
May give her there, to act a noble part,
To virtuous pleasures yield the willing heart.
Self-estimation will debasement shun,
And, in the path of wisdom, joy to run;
An unbecoming act in fears to do,
And still, its exaltation keeps in view.
"To rev'rence self," a Bard long since directed,
And, on each moral truth HE well reflected;
But, lost to conscious worth, to decent pride,
Compass nor helm there is, our course to guide:
Nor may we anchor cast, for rudely tost
In an unfathom'd sea, each motive's lost.
Wildly amid contending waves we're beat,
And rocks and quick sands, shoals and depths we meet;
'Till, dash'd in pieces, or, till found'ring, we
One common wreck of all our prospects see!
Nor, do we mourn, for we were lost to fame,
And never hap'd to reach a tow'ring name;
Ne'er taught to "rev'rence self," or to aspire;
Our bosoms never caught ambition's fire;
An indolence of virtue still prevail'd,
Nor the sweet gale of praise was e'er inhal'd;
Rous'd by a new stimulus, no kindling glow.
No soothing emulations gentle flow,
We judg'd that nature, not to us inclin'd,
In narrow bounds our progress had confin'd,
And, that our forms, to say the very best,
Only, not frightful, were by all confest.

---

1. Originally published in the *Gentleman and Lady's Town and Country Magazine,* October 1794.

I think, to teach young minds to aspire, ought to be the ground work of education: many a laudable achievement is lost, from a persuasion that our efforts are unequal to the arduous attainment. Ambition is a noble principle, which properly directed, may be productive of the most valuable consequences. It is amazing to what heights the mind by exertion may tow'r: I would, therefore, have my pupils believe, that every thing in the compass of mortality, was placed within their grasp, and that, the avidity of application, the intenseness of study, were only requisite to endow them with every external grace; and mental accomplishment. Thus I should impel them to progress on, if I could not lead them to the heights I would wish them to attain. It is too common with parents to expatiate in their hearing, upon all the foibles of their children, and to let their virtues pass, in appearance, unregarded: this they do, least they should, (were they to commend) swell their little hearts to pride, and implant in their tender minds, undue conceptions of their own importance. Those, for example, who have the care of a beautiful female, they assiduously guard every avenue, they arrest the stream of due admiration, and endeavour to divest her of all idea of the bounties of nature: what is the consequence? She grows up, and of course mixes with those who are self interested: strangers will be sincere; she encounters the tongue of the flatterer, he will exaggerate, she finds herself possessed of accomplishments which have been studiously concealed from her, she throws the reins upon the neck of fancy, and gives every encomiast full credit for his most extravagant eulogy. Her natural connections, her home is rendered disagreeable, and she hastes to the scenes, whence arise the sweet perfume of adulation, and when she can obtain the regard due to a merit, which she supposes altogether uncommon. Those who have made her acquainted with the dear secret, she considers as her best friends; and it is more than probable, that she will soon fall a sacrifice to some worthless character, whose interest may lead him to the most hyperbolical lengths in the round of flattery. Now, I should be solicitous that my daughter should possess for me the fondest love, as well as that respect which gives birth to duty; in order to promote this wish of my soul, from my lips she should be accustomed to hear the most pleasing truths, and, as in the course of my instructions, I should doubtless find myself but too often impelled to wound the delicacy of youthful sensibility. I would therefore, be careful to avail myself of this exuberating balance: I would, from the early dawn of reason, address her as a rational being; hence, I apprehend, the most valuable consequences would result in some such language as this, she might from time to time be accosted. A pleasing form is undoubtedly advantageous. Nature, my dear, hath furnished you with an agreeable person, your glass, was I to be silent, would inform you that you are pretty, your appearance will sufficiently recommend you to a stranger, the flatterer will give a more than mortal finishing to every feature; but, it must be your part, my sweet girl, to render yourself worthy respect from higher motives: you must learn "to reverence yourself," that is, your intellectual existance; you must join my efforts, in endeavouring to adorn your mind, for, it is from the proper furnishing of that, you will become indeed a valuable person, you will, as I said, give birth to the most favorable impressions at first sight: but, how mortifying should this be all, if, upon a more extensive knowledge you should be discovered to possess no one mental charm, to be fit only at best, to be hung up as a pleasing picture among the paintings of some spacious hall. The FLATTERER, indeed, will still pursue you, but it will be from interested views, and he will smile at your undoing! Now, then, my best Love, is the time for you to lay in such a fund of useful knowledge as shall continue, and augment every kind sentiment in regard to you, as shall set you above the snares of the artful betrayer.

Thus, that sweet form, shall serve but as a polished casket, which will contain a most beautiful gem, highly finished, and calculated for advantage, as well as ornament. Was she, I say, habituated thus to reflect, she would be taught to aspire; she would learn to estimate every accomplishment, according to its proper value; and, when the voice of adulation should assail her ear, as she had early been initiated into its true meaning, and from youth been accustomed to the language of praise; her attention would not be captivated, the Siren's song would not borrow the aid of novelty, her young mind would not be enervated or intoxicated, by a delicious surprise, she would possess her soul in serenity, and by that means, rise superior to the deep laid schemes which, too commonly, encompass the steps of beauty.

Neither should those to whom nature had been parsimonious, be tortured by me with degrading comparisons; every advantage I would expatiate upon, and there are few who possess not some personal charms. I would teach them to gloss over their imperfections, inasmuch as, I do think, an agreeable form, a very necessary introduction to society, and of course it behoves us to render our appearance as pleasing as possible: I would, I must repeat, by all means guard them against a low estimation of self. I would leave no charm undiscovered or unmarked, for the penetrating eye of the pretended admirer, to make unto himself a merit by holding up to her view; thus, I would destroy the weapons of flattery, or render them useless, by leaving not the least room for their operation.

A young lady, growing up with the idea, that she possesses few, or no personal attractions, and that her mental abilities are of an inferior kind, imbibing at the same time, a most melancholly idea of a female, descending down the vale of life in an unprotected state; taught also to regard her character ridiculously contemptible, will, too probably, throw herself away upon the first who approaches her with tenders of love, however indifferent may be her chance of happiness, least if she omits the present day of grace, she may never be so happy as to meet a second offer, and must then inevitably be stigmatized with that dreaded title, an Old Maid, must rank with a class whom she has been accustomed to regard as burthens upon society, and objects whom she might with impunity turn into ridicule! Certainly love, friendship and esteem, ought to take place of marriage, but, the woman thus circumstanced, will seldom regard these previous requisites to felicity, if she can but insure the honors, which she, in idea, associates with a matrimonial connection—to prevent which great evil, I would early impress under proper regulations, a reverence of self; I would endeavour to rear to worth, and a consciousness thereof: I would be solicitous to inspire the glow of virtue, with that elevation of soul, that dignity, which is ever attendant upon self-approbation, arising from the genuine source of innate rectitude. I must be excused for thus insisting upon my hypothesis, as I am, from observation, persuaded, that many have suffered materially all their life long, from a depression of soul, early inculcated, in compliance to a false maxim, which hath supposed pride would thereby be eradicated. I know there is a contrary extreme, and I would, in almost all cases, prefer the happy medium. However, if these fugitive hints may induce some abler pen to improve thereon, the exemplification will give pleasure to the heart of CONSTANTIA.

———

OBSERVATIONS ON FEMALE ABILITIES[1]

PART III

Tis joy to tread the splendid paths of fame,
Where countless myriads mental homage claim;
Time honour'd annals careful to explore,
And mark the heights which intellect can soar.

. . . In the thirteenth century, a young lady of Bologna, pursuing, with avidity, the study of the Latin language, and the legislative institutions of her country, was able, at the age of twenty-three, to deliver, in the great church of Bologna, a Latin oration, in praise of a deceased person, eminent for virtue; nor was she indebted for the admiration she received, to the indulgence granted to her youth, or Sex. At the age of twenty-six, she took the degree of a Doctor of Laws, and commenced her career in this line, by public expositions of the doctrines of Justinian: At the age of thirty, her extraordinary merit raised her to the chair, where she taught the law to an astonishing number of pupils, collected from various nations. She joined to her profound knowledge, sexual modesty, and every feminine accomplishment; yet her personal attractions were absorbed in the magnitude and splendor of her intellectual abilities; and the charms of her exterior only commanded attention, when she ceased to speak. The fourteenth century produced, in the same city, a like example; and the fifteenth continued, and acknowledged the pretensions of the Sex, insomuch that a learned chair was appropriated to illustrious women.

Issotta Nogarolla[2] was also an ornament of the fifteenth century; and Sarochisa of Naples was deemed worthy of comparison with Tasso. Modesta Pozzo's[3] defense of her Sex did her honour; she was, herself, an example of excellence. Gabrielle, daughter of a king, found leisure to devote to her pen; and her literary pursuits contributed to her usefulness and her happiness. Mary de Gournai[4] rendered herself famous by her learning. Guyon,[5] by her writings and her sufferings, have evinced the justice of her title to immortality. Anna Maria Schuman of Cologne, appears to have been mistress of all the useful and ornamental learning of the age which she adorned: She was born in 1607; her talents unfolded with extraordinary brilliancy: In the bud of her life, at the age of six years, she cut, with her scissors, the most striking resemblances of every figure which was presented to her view, and they were finished with astonishing neatness. At ten, she was but three hours in learning to embroider. She studied music, painting, sculpture and engraving, and made an admirable proficiency in all those arts. The Hebrew, Greek and Latin languages were familiar to her; and she made some progress in the oriental tongues. She perfectly understood French, English and Italian, and expressed herself eloquently in all those languages; and she appropriated a portion of her time, to the acquirement of an extensive acquaintance with geography, astronomy, philosophy, and the other sciences: Yet she possessed so much feminine delicacy, and retiring modesty, that her talents and acquirements had been consigned to oblivion, if Vassius, and other amateurs of literature, had not ushered her, in opposition to her wishes upon the theatre of the world: But when she was once known, persons of erudition, of every description, corresponded with her; and those in the most elevated stations, assiduously sought opportunities of seeing and conversing with her.

Mademoiselle Scudery,[6] stimulated by necessity, rendered herself eminent by her writings. Anna de Parthenay[7] possessed great virtues, great talents, and great learning; she read, with facility and pleasure, authors in the Greek and Latin languages; she was a rationale theologician; she was a perfect mistress of music; and was as remarkable for her vocal powers, as for her execution of the various instruments which she attempted. Catharine de Parthenay,[8] niece to Anna, married to Renatus de Rohan, signalized herself by her attention to the education of her children; and her maternal cares were crowned with abundant success: Her eldest son was the illustrious Duke of Rohan, who obtained immortal honour by his zeal and exertions in the Protestant cause; and she was

---

1. Originally published in Murray's *The Gleaner* (1798).

2. A poet and letter writer (ca. 1420–66).

3. A dramatist and essayist (1555–92).

4. Marie de Jars Gournay (1565–1645), an essayist who advocated equality between the sexes.

5. A religious writer (1648–1717).

6. Marie-Madeleine du Moncel de Martinval Scudery (1627–1711), a novelist and letter writer.

7. A poet and musical composer of the sixteenth century.

8. A poet, dramatist, and translator (d. 1631).

also mother to Anna de Rohan, who was as illustrious for her genius and piety, as for her birth. She was mistress of the Hebrew language; her numbers were beautifully elegant; and she supported, with heroic firmness, the calamities consequent upon the siege of Rochelle.

Mademoiselle le Fevre,[9] celebrated in the literary world by the name of Madame Dacier, gave early testimonies of that fine genius which her father delighted to cultivate. Her edition of Callimachus was received with much applause. At the earnest request of the Duke of de Montansier, she published an edition of Florus, for the use of the dauphin; she exchanged letters with Christina, queen of Sweden; she devoted herself to the education of her son and daughter, whose progress were proportioned to the abilities of their interested preceptress: Greek and Latin were familiar to her, and she was often addressed in both those languages, by the literati of Europe. Her translation of the Iliad was much admired. She is said to have possessed great firmness, generosity, and equality of temper, and to have been remarkable for her piety. Marie de Sevigne[10] appropriated her hours to the instruction of her son and daughter; she has enriched the world with eight volumes of letters, which will be read with pleasure by every critic in the French language. The character of Mary II. Queen of England, and consort to William of Nassau,[11] is transcendently amiable. She is delineated as a princess, endowed with uncommon powers of mind, and beauty of person. She is extensively acquainted with history, was attached to poetry, and possessed a good taste in compositions of this kind. She had a considerable knowledge in architecture and gardening; and her dignified condescension, and consistent piety, were truly admirable and praiseworthy—Every reader of history and lover of virtue, will lament her early exit. The Countess of Pembroke[12] translated from the French, a dramatic piece; she gave a metrical edition of the Book of Psalms, and supported an exalted character.

Anna Killigrew, and Anna Wharton, were eminent, both for poetry and painting; and their unblemished virtue, and exemplary piety, pointed and greatly enhanced the value of their other accomplishments. Catharine Phillips[13] was, from early life, a lover of the Muses; she translated Corneille's Tragedy of Pompey into English; and in this, as well as the poems which she published, she was successful. Lady Burleigh, Lady Bacon, Lady Russell,[14] and Mrs. Killigrew, daughters of Sir Anthony Cook, received from their father a masculine education; and their prodigious improvement was an ample compensation for his paternal indulgence: They were eminent for genius and virtue, and obtained an accurate knowledge of the Greek and Latin languages. The writings of the Dutchess of Newcastle[15] were voluminous; she is produced as the first English lady who attempted what has since been termed polite literature. Lady Halket[16] was remarkable for her erudition; she was well skilled, both in physic and divinity. Lady Masham, and Mary Astell,[17] reasoned accurately on the most abstract particulars in divinity, and in metaphysics. Lady Grace Gethin[18] was happy in natural genius and a cultivated understand; she was a woman of erudition; and we are informed that, at the age of twenty, "*she treated of life and morals, with the discernment of Socrates, and the elegance of Xenophon*"—Mr. Congreve has done justice to her merit. Chudleigh, Winchelsea, Monk, Bovey, Stella, Montague[19]—these all possess their respective claims. Catharine Macauley[20] wielded successfully the historic pen; nor were her exertions confined to this line—But we

---

9. Anne Le Fevre Dacier (1651–1720), an editor and pamphlet writer.

10. A letter writer (1626–96).

11. Mary II (1662–94), who ruled jointly with William of Orange.

12. Mary Sidney, countess of Pembroke (1561–1621), a translator.

13. Katherine Fowler Philips (1631–64), a dramatist and translator.

14. Mildred Burghley, wife of Lord Burghley; Anne Cooke Bacon (1528–1610), a translator and letter writer; Elizabeth Cooke Russell (1540–1609), a poet and translator.

15. Margaret Lucas Cavendish (1623–73), a philosopher and essayist.

16. Ann Halkett (1623–99), a memoirist.

17. Lady Masham (1658–1708), a religious writer; Mary Astell (1666–1731), a poet and political essayist.

18. An essayist (1676–97).

19. Mary Lee, Lady Chudleigh (1656–1710), a poet; Anne Kingsmill Finch, countess of Winchilsea (1661–1720), a poet; Mary Molesworth (d. 1715), a poet; Catharina Bovey (1669–1726), philanthropist; Lady Mary Wortley Montagu (1689–1762), a letter writer and essayist.

20. Catharine Macaulay (1731–91), a historian and philosopher who advocated women's education.

have already multiplied our witnesses far beyond our original design; and it is proper that we apologize to our readers, for a transgression of that brevity which we had authorized them to expect.

PART IV

Nor are the modern Fair a step behind,
In the transcendent energies of mind:
Their worth conspicuous swells the ample roll,
While emulous they reach the splendid goal.

. . . But while we do homage to the women of other times, we feel happy that nature is no less bountiful to the females of the present day. We cannot, indeed, obtain a list of the names that have done honour to their Sex, and to humanity, during the period now under observation: The lustre of those minds, still enveloped in a veil of mortality, is necessarily muffled and obscure; but the curtain will be thrown back, and posterity will contemplate, with admiration, their manifold perfections. Yet, in many instances, fame has already lifted her immortalizing trump. Madame de Genlis[21] has added new effulgence to the literary annals of France. This lady unites, in an astonishing degree, both genius and application! May her indefatigable exertions be crowned with the success they so richly merit—May no illiberal prejudices obstruct the progress of her multiplied productions; but, borne along the stream of time, may they continue pleasurable vehicles of instruction, and confer on their ingenious author that celebrity to which she is indisputably entitled. France may also justly place among her list of illustrious personages, the luminous name of Roland.[22] Madame Roland comprised, in her own energetic and capacious mind, all those appropriate virtues, which are characterized as masculine and feminine. She not only dignified the Sex, but human nature in the aggregate; and her memory will be held in veneration, wherever talents, literature, patriotism, and uniform heroism, are properly appreciated.

The British Isle is at this moment distinguished by a constellation of the first magnitude. Barbauld, Seward, Cowley, Inchbald, Burney, Smith, Radcliffe, Moore, Williams, Wollstonecraft, &c. &c.[23]—these ladies, celebrated for brilliancy of genius and literary attainments, have rendered yet more illustrious the English name.

Nor is America destitute of females, whose abilities and improvements give them an indisputable claim to immortality. It is a fact, established beyond all controversy, that we are indebted for the discovery of our country, to female enterprize, decision, and generosity. The great Columbus, after having in vain solicited the aid of Genoa, France, England, Portugal, and Spain—after having combated, for a period of eight years, with every objection that a want of knowledge could propose, found, at last, his only resource in the penetration and magnanimity of Isabella of Spain, who furnished the equipment, and raised the sums necessary to defray the expenses, on the sale of her own jewels; and while we conceive an action, so honourable to the Sex, hath not been sufficiently applauded, we trust, that the equality of the female intellect to that of their brethren, who have so long usurped an unmanly and unfounded superiority, will never, in this younger world, be left without a witness. We cannot ascertain the number of ingenious women, who at present adorn our country. In the shade of solitude they perhaps cultivate their own minds, and superintend the education of their children. Our day, we know, is only dawning—But when we contemplate a Warren, a Philenia,[24] an Antonia, a Euphelia, &c. &c. we gratefully acknowledge, that genius and application, even in the female line, already gild, with effulgent radiance, our blest Aurora.

But women are calculated to shine in other characters than those adverted to, in the preceding Essays; and with proper attention to their education, and subsequent habits, they might easily attain that independence, for which a Wollstonecraft hath so energetically contended; the term, *helpless widow,* might be rendered as unfrequent and inapplicable as that of *helpless widower;* and although we

---

21. Comtesse de Genlis (1746–1830), a novelist, dramatist, and memoirist.

22. Marion Philipon Roland (1754–93), a letter writer, essayist, memoirist.

23. Anna Laetitia Aikin Barbauld (1743–1825), a poet and essayist; Anna Seward (1742–1809), a poet, novelist, and letter writer; Hannah Parkhouse Cowley (1743–1809), a poet and dramatist; Elizabeth Inchbald (1753–1821), a dramatist, essayist, and novelist; Fanny Burney (1752–1850), a novelist; Charlotte Turner Smith (1749–1806), a novelist, Ann Radcliffe (1764–1823), a novelist; Jane Elizabeth Moore (1738–?), a poet; Helen Maria Williams (1762–1827), a poet, novelist, and translator; Mary Wollstonecraft (1759–97), an essayist and novelist.

24. Mercy Otis Warren (1728–1814), a historian, dramatist, and poet; Philenia was the pen name of Sarah Wentworth Morton (1759–1846), a poet.

should undoubtedly continue to mourn the dissolution of wedded amity, yet we should derive consolation from the knowledge, that the infant train had still a remaining prop, and that a mother could *assist* as well as *weep* over her offspring.

That women have a talent—a talent which, duly cultivated, would confer that independence, which is demonstrably of incalculable utility, every attentive observer will confess. The Sex should be taught to depend on their own efforts, for the procurement of an establishment in life. The chance of a matrimonial còadjutor, is no more than a probable contingency; and if they were early accustomed to regard this *uncertain* event with suitable *indifference,* they would make elections with that deliberation, which would be calculated to give a more rational prospect of tranquility. All this we have repeatedly asserted, and all this we do invariably believe. To neglect polishing a gem, or obstinately to refuse bringing into action a treasure in our possession, when we might thus accumulate a handsome interest, is surely egregiously absurd, and the height of folly. The *united efforts of male and female* might rescue many a family from destruction, which, notwithstanding the efforts of its *individual* head, is now involved in all the calamities attendant on a dissipated fortune and augmenting debts. It is not possible to educate children in a manner which will render them *too beneficial* to society; and the more we multiply aids to a family, the greater will be the security, that its individuals will not be thrown a burden on the public.

An instance of *female capability,* this moment occurs to memory. In the State of Massachusetts, in a small town, some miles from the metropolis, resides a woman, who hath made astonishing improvements in agriculture. Her mind, in the early part of her life, was but penuriously cultivated, and she grew up almost wholly uneducated: But being suffered, during her childhood, to rove at large among her native fields, her limbs expanded, and she acquired a height of stature above the common size; her mind also became invigorated; and her understanding snatched sufficient information, to produce a consciousness of the injury she sustained in the want of those aids, which should have been furnished in the beginning of her years. She however applied herself diligently to remedy the evil, and soon made great proficiency in writing, and in arithmetic. She read every thing she could procure; but the impressions adventitiously made on her infant mind still obtained the ascendency. A few rough acres constituted her patrimonial inheritance; these she has brought into a state of high cultivation; their productions are every

year both useful and ornamental; she is mistress of agricolation, and is at once a botanist and a florist. The most approved authors in the English language, on these subjects, are in her hands, and she studies them with industry and success.

She has obtained such a considerable knowledge in the nature of soils, the precise manure which they require, and their particular adaptation to the various fruits of the earth, that she is become the oracle of all the farmers in her vicinity; and when laying out, or appropriating their grounds, they uniformly submit them to her inspection. Her gardens are the resort of all strangers who happen to visit her village; and she is particularly remarkable for a growth of trees, from which, gentlemen, solicitous to enrich their fruit-gardens, or ornament their parterres, are in the habit of supplying themselves; and those trees are, to their ingenious cultivator, a considerable income. Carefully attentive to her nursery, she knows when to transplant, and when to prune; and she perfectly understands the various methods of inoculating and ingrafting. In short, she is a complete *husbandwoman;* and she has, besides, acquired a vast stock of general knowledge, while her judgment has attained such a degree of maturity, as to justify the confidence of the villagers, who are accustomed to consult her on every perplexing emergency.

In the constant use of exercise, she is not corpulent; and she is extremely active, and wonderfully athletic. Instances, almost incredible, are produced of her strength. Indeed, it is not surprising that she is the idol and standing theme of the village, since, with all her uncommon qualifications, she combines a tenderness of disposition not to be exceeded. Her extensive acquaintance with herbs, contributes to render her a skilful and truly valuable nurse; and the world never produced a more affectionate, attentive, or faithful woman: Yet, while she feelingly sympathizes with every invalid, she is not herself subject to imaginary complaints; nor does she easily yield to real illness. . . .

Although far advanced in years, without a matrimonial connexion, yet, constantly engaged in useful and interesting pursuits, she manifests not that peevishness and discontent, so frequently attendant on *old maids;* she realizes all that independence which is proper to humanity; and she knows how to set a just value on the blessings she enjoys.

From my treasury of facts, I produce a second instance, equally in point. I have seen letters, written by a lady, an inhabitant of St. Sebastian, (a Spanish emporium) that breathed the true spirit of commerce, and evinced the writer to possess all the integrity, punctuality and dispatch, which are such capital requisites in the mercantile career. This lady is at the head of a firm, of which herself and daughters make up the individuals—Her name is *Birmingham.* She is, I imagine, well known to the commercial part of the United States. She was left a widow in the infancy of her children, who were numerous; and she immediately adopted the most vigorous measures for their emolument. Being a woman of a magnanimous mind, she devoted her sons to the profession of arms; and they were expeditiously disposed of, in a way the best calculated to bring them acquainted with the art of war. Her daughters were educated for business; and, arriving at womanhood, they have long since established themselves into a capital trading-house, of which, as has been observed, their respectable mother is the head. She is, in the hours of business, invariably to be found in her compting-house; there she takes her morning repast; her daughters act as clerks, (and they are adepts in their office) regularly preparing the papers and letters, which pass in order under her inspection. She signs herself, in all accounts and letters, *Widow Birmingham;* and this is the address by which she is designated. I have conversed with one of our captains, who has often negociated with her the disposal of large and valuable cargoes. Her consignments, I am told, are to a great amount; and one of the principal merchants in the town of Boston asserts, that he receives from no house in Europe more satisfactory returns. Upright in their dealings, and unwearied in their application, these ladies possess a right to prosperity; and we trust that their circumstances are as easy, as their conduct is meritorious. . . .

JOEL BARLOW (1754–1812)

Joel Barlow was the celebrated diplomat who negotiated the release of English-speaking prisoners held captive in Algiers and the first epic poet to publish a poem on America in English. A friend of President Thomas Jefferson and noted French scientists and philosophers, he became, alongside Thomas Paine, a "citizen" of the new French Republic in the first flush of revolution against monarchy in France and an outcast in England when the French Revolution turned into a bloodbath. Barlow's life would forever be linked with France from that time, for it was Barlow who was sent in 1811–12 to attempt to negotiate with Napoleon, who, having agreed to a settlement of peace, continued to elude peace treaty negotiator Barlow who followed him from town to town as Napoleon faced disaster on the Russian steppes. That journey killed Barlow, who died of pneumonia caught during the rough sled and carriage rides across the ice.

Barlow celebrated America in his writings, from poems on hasty pudding to disquisitions on the new British American nation's constitution and legal system. But Barlow's celebration was always in the context of his knowledge of countries other than America, such as France, England, Germany, and Algiers,—countries that he hoped would achieve free representative governments—knowledge that he gained during the seventeen years he spent away from America as an international statesman.

Joel Barlow was born on a farm in Connecticut and educated by a local minister before he was sent to Moor's Indian school (later Dartmouth) in Hanover, New Hampshire, in 1772. His father's sudden death made it necessary (and financially possible) for Barlow to return home briefly and then to matriculate at Yale College with the class of 1778. It was at Yale that Barlow began to evidence his interest in poetry, moral philosophy, and science as the key to the improvement of the human condition.

Barlow's college years were interrupted by the Revolutionary War, in which he took part during 1780–81 as a chaplain to the Third Massachusetts Brigade. The chaplain's post enabled Barlow to continue writing poetry at the encouragement of his family and friends. His secret engagement (secret engagements were punishable by Connecticut law) to Ruth Baldwin in 1779 led to their eventual (and enduring) marriage in 1781. Newly married, and with the war over in the early 1780s, Barlow sought patrons for his writing and opened a printing and stationer's store in Hartford, Connecticut. Upon the publication of *The Vision of Columbus* (1787), an epic poem about the history and promise of the Americas, Barlow was selected by the Scioto Associates, a group of businessmen interested in land sales, to be their European representative. Barlow sailed for Europe in 1788.

Barlow's seventeen years abroad gave him the intellectual freedom and impetus to pursue projects that would not have been condoned, even by his friends, in Federalist America. With the onset of the French Revolution in 1789, Barlow wrote social and political propaganda, moving from England to France and back again as the currents of the revolution ebbed and flowed. When the Reign of Terror brought a bloodbath to some of his closest friends in 1793, Barlow made plans to leave France with his wife Ruth (who had joined him in Europe in 1790). He took part in a shipping business in Hamburg, 1794–95, and became minister to Algiers in 1796. Barlow's Algerian mission—to create treaties that would free the Mediterranean of piracy and to ensure the release of prisoners taken captive by the pirates—lasted until late 1797, when he returned to Ruth in France. The Barlows bought a house in Paris and became patrons of the arts and sciences—and of Robert Fulton, who lived with them for many months.

By 1805, when the intellectual climate in America had shifted so that it might accommodate the liberal Republican tendencies of Joel Barlow, the Barlows returned to the United States and established themselves in the Washington, D.C., community made inviting by the presidency of their friend Thomas Jefferson. The Barlows remained in Washington in social and intellectual prominence. Barlow proposed, too much before its time, a national institution for the arts and sciences, and his friends Jefferson, Monroe, and Madison encouraged him to write a history of America. But Barlow never completed his projects signaled by the republication of *The Vision of Columbus* (1787) as a much-altered poem, *The Columbiad* (1807). He was called upon for diplomacy once again, this time by President Madison in 1811, to negotiate the treaty with Napoleon.

Barlow's poem, *The Vision of Columbus,* was published in Hartford, Connecticut, in 1787, thanks to subscriptions he had received from people as distinguished as King Louis XVI of France, the marquis de Lafayette, and George Washington. Barlow's goal—to deliver a poem that would extol the past as a mere prelude to the promise of "America"—appropriated the Spanish and Portuguese efforts into his own story, as if they were preludes to the necessary war that would occur in the British North American colonies because such was the course of empire, to establish arts and sciences in a putatively free and confederated band of states. Barlow adopted stories of the Portuguese and Spanish historians, blended them with some of the stories told by William Robertson, and came up with his own millennial version of American history that would speak to Columbus, were he alive, "Behold the fruits of thy unwearied toil. / To yon far regions of descending day, / Thy swelling pinions led the untrodden way, / And taught mankind adventurous deeds to dare, / To trace new seas and peaceful empires rear." Part of the effort of the poem was didactic, to instruct citizens of the newly confederated states about the social and political history and the geographic and topographical sites of the land they had, in Barlow's view, inherited as theirs. Toward this end, Barlow created a global view of the Americas, identifying and defining the courses of rivers and streams, the highest mountain peaks, the widest waterways between islands, and so forth. The result is a new vision of the Americas that could be claimed as one peculiarly "American," a vision that was, in Barlow's story, prophesied prior to the moment of Columbus's first landing on the soil of the Americas.

from THE VISION OF COLUMBUS; A POEM IN NINE BOOKS.[1]

[Dedication to King Louis XVI of France]

To His most Christian Majesty, Louis the Sixteenth, King of France and Navarre.

Sire,

In recounting the numerous blessings which have arisen to mankind from the discovery of America, the mind dwells with particular pleasure and gratitude upon those Characters, from whose hands these blessings have immediately flowed. That change in the political face of Europe, that liberality of sentiment, that enlargement of commercial, military and philosophical knowledge, which contrast the present with the fifteenth century, are but so many consequences of this great event; an event which laid open all parts of the earth to the range of the liberal mind. The illustrious line of your royal Ancestors have been conspicuous in seizing those advantages and diffusing their happy effects. The great Father of the House of Bourbon will be held in the highest veneration, till his favourite political system shall be realized among the nations of Europe, and extended to all mankind. But it was left to his more glorious Descendant, to accelerate the progress of society, by disregarding the temporary interests and local policies of other Monarchs, reaching the hand of beneficence to another hemisphere, and raising an infant empire, in a few years, to a degree of importance, which several ages were scarcely thought sufficient to produce.

This is the sublime of humanity, to feel for future ages and distant nations; to act those things, as a Monarch, which another can only contemplate as a Philosopher, or image in the flights of poetry. America acknowledges her obligations to the Guardian of her rights; mankind, who survey your conduct, and posterity, for whom you act, will see that the tribute of gratitude is paid.

If to patronize the Arts can add to the praise of these more glorious actions, your Majesty's fame in this respect will be ever sacred; as there are none, who can feel the subject so strongly as those who are the particular objects of your royal condescension.

The following work, which may be considered in part, as the offspring of those reflections which your Majesty's conduct has taught me to make, possesses one advantage scarcely to be expected in a Poem written in a foreign language. Your Majesty's permission, that the unfortunate Columbus may once more enjoy the protection of a royal benefactor, has added a new obligation to those I before felt—in common with a grateful country. It is the policy of wise Princes to encourage the liberal arts among their subjects; and, as the human race are the objects of your extended administration, they may all in some measure claim the privilege of subjects, in seeking your literary as well as political protection.

With the deepest sense of your Majesty's royal munificence to my country, and gracious condescension to myself, I have the honour to be,

Sire, YOUR MAJESTY's *Most humble and Most devoted Servant, Joel Barlow.*

INTRODUCTION

Every circumstance relating to the discovery and settlement of America, is an interesting object of enquiry. Yet it is presumed, from the present state of literature in this country, that many persons, who might be entertained with an American production of this kind, are but slightly acquainted with the life and character of that great man, whose extraordinary genius led him to the discovery of the continent, and whose singular sufferings ought to excite the indignation of the world.

The Spanish historians, who treat of the discovery and settlement of South-America, are very little known in the United States; and Doctor Robertson's history[2] of that country, which, as is usual in the works of that judicious writer, contains all that is valuable on the subject, is not yet reprinted in America, and therefore cannot be supposed to be in the hands of American readers in general: and perhaps no other writer in the English language has

---

1. Barlow sought the patronage of French King Louis XVI by asking him to subscribe to the publication of his poem and then dedicating the poem to him. The long poem was published in Hartford in 1787, the edition that is the source of the present text.

2. The *History of America* (1777) by William Robertson (1721–93), a historian and principal of the University of Edinburgh, was a frequently cited resource by writers who were influenced by the Scottish Enlightenment.

given a sufficient account of the life of Columbus to enable them to understand many of the necessary allusions in the following Poem.

Christopher Columbus was born in the republic of Genoa about the year 1447; at a time when the navigation of Europe was scarcely extended beyond the limits of the Mediterranean. The mariner's compass had been invented and in common use for more than a century; yet with the help of this sure guide, prompted by the most ardent spirit of discovery, and encouraged by the patronage of princes, the mariners of those days rarely ventured from the sight of land. They acquired great applause by sailing along the coast of Africa and discovering some of the neighbouring islands; and after pushing their researches with the greatest industry and perseverance for more than half a century, the Portuguese, who were the most fortunate and enterprising, extended their discoveries southward no farther than the equator.

The rich commodities of the East had for several ages been brought into Europe by the way of the Red Sea and the Mediterranean; and it had now become the object of the Portuguese to find a passage to India, by sailing round the southern extremity of Africa and then taking an eastern course. This great object engaged the general attention of mankind, and drew into the Portuguese service adventurers from every maritime nation in Europe. Every year added to their experience in navigation and seemed to promise a reward to their industry. The prospect however of arriving at the Indies was extremely distant; fifty years perseverance in the same track, had brought them only to the equator, and it was probable that as many more would elapse before they could accomplish their purpose. But Columbus, by an uncommon exertion of genius, formed a design no less astonishing to the age in which he lived, than beneficial to posterity. This design was to sail to India by taking a western direction. By the accounts of travellers who had visited India, that country seemed almost without limits on the east; and by attending to the spherical figure of the earth, Columbus drew this conclusion, that the Atlantic ocean must be bounded on the west either by India itself, or by some great continent not far distant from it.

This extraordinary man, who was now about twenty-seven years of age, appears to have united in his character every trait, and to have possessed every tallant, requisite to form and execute the greatest enterprizes. He was early educated in all the useful sciences that were taught in that day. He had made great proficiency in geography, astronomy and drawing, as they were necessary to his favourite pursuit of navigation. He had now been a number of years in the service of the Portuguese, and had acquired all the experience that their voyages and discoveries could afford. His courage and perseverance had been put to the severest test, and the exercise of every amiable and heroic virtue rendered him universally known and respected. He had married a Portuguese lady by whom he had two sons, Diego and Fardinand; the younger of whom is the historian of his life.

Such was the situation of Columbus, when he formed and thoroughly digested a plan, which, in its operation and consequences, unfolded to the view of mankind one half of the globe, diffused wealth and dignity over the other, and extended commerce and civilization through the whole. To corroborate the theory which he had formed of the existence of a western continent, his descerning mind, which always knew the application of every circumstance that fell in his way, had observed several facts which by others would have passed unnoticed. In his voyages to the African islands he had found, floating ashore after a long western storm, pieces of wood carved in a curious manner, canes of a size unknown in that quarter of the world, and human bodies with very singular features. Fully confirmed in the opinion that a considerable portion of the earth was still undiscovered, his genius was too vigorous and persevering to suffer an idea of this importance to rest merely in speculation, as it had done in the minds of Plato and Seneca, who appear to have had conjectures of a similar nature. He determined therefore to bring his favourite theory to the test of actual experiment. But an object of that magnitude required the patronage of a Prince; and a design so extraordinary met with all the obstructions, delays and disappointments, which an age of superstition could invent, and which personal jealousy and malice could magnify and encourage. Happily for mankind, in this instance, a genius, capable of devising the greatest undertakings, associated in itself a degree of patience and enterprize, modesty and confidence, which rendered him superior, not only to these misfortunes, but to all the future calamities of his life. Prompted by the most ardent enthusiasm to be the discoverer of new continents, and fully sensible of the advantages that would result to mankind from such discoveries, he had the mortification to waste away eighteen years of his life, after his system was well established in his own mind, before he could obtain the means of executing his designs. The greatest part of this period was spent in successive and fruitless solicitations, at Genoa, Portugal and Spain. As a duty to his native country, he made his first proposal to the

Senate of Genoa; where it was soon rejected. Conscious of the truth of his theory, and of his own abilities to execute his design, he retired without dejection from a body of men who were incapable of forming any just ideas upon the subject; and applied with fresh confidence to John the second, King of Portugal, who had distinguished himself as the great patron of navigation, and in whose service Columbus had acquired a reputation which entitled him and his project to general confidence and approbation. But here he suffered an insult much greater than a direct refusal. After referring the examination of his scheme to the council who had the direction of naval affairs, and drawing from him his general ideas of the length of the voyage and the course he meant to take, that great monarch had the meanness to conspire with this council to rob Columbus of the glory and advantage he expected to derive from his undertaking. While Columbus was amused with this negotiation, in hopes of having his scheme adopted and patronized, a vessel was secretly dispatched, by order of the king, to make the intended discovery. Want of skill and perseverance in the pilot rendered the plot unsuccessful; and Columbus, on discovering the treachery, retired with an ingenuous indignation from a court capable of such duplicity.

Having now performed what was due to the country that gave him birth and to the one that had adopted him as a subject, he was at liberty to court the patronage of any prince who should have the wisdom and justice to accept his proposals. He had communicated his ideas to his brother Bartholomew, whom he sent to England to negotiate with Henry seventh; at the same time that he went himself into Spain to apply in person to Fardinand and Isabella, who governed the united kingdoms of Aragon and Castile.[3] The circumstances of his brother's application in England, which appears to have been unsuccessful, is not to my purpose to relate; and the limits prescribed to this introduction will prevent the detail of all the particulars relating to his own negociation in Spain. In this negociation Columbus spent eight years, in the various agitations of suspence, expectation and disappointment; till, at length his scheme was adopted by Isabella, who undertook, as Queen of Castile, to destroy the ex-

pences of the expedition; and declared herself, ever after, the friend and patron of the hero who projected it.

Columbus, who, during all his ill success in the negotiation, never abated any thing of the honours and emoluments which he expected to acquire in the expedition, obtained from Fardinand and Isabella a full stipulation of every article contained in his first proposals. He was constituted high Admiral and Viceroy of all the Seas, Islands and Continents which he should discover; with power to receive one tenth of the profits arising from their productions and commerce. These offices and emoluments were to be hereditary in his family.

These articles being adjusted, the preparations for the voyage were brought forward with rapidity; but they were by no means adequate to the importance of the expedition. Three small vessels, scarcely sufficient in size to be employed in the coasting business, were appointed to traverse the vast Atlantic; and to encounter the storms and currents that might be expected in so lengthy a voyage, through distant and unknown seas. These vessels, as might be expected in the infancy of navigation, were ill constructed, in a poor condition, and manned by seamen unaccustomed to distant voyages. But the tedious length of time which Columbus had spent in solicitation and suspence, and the prospect of being able soon, to obtain the object of his wishes, induced him to overlook what he could not easily remedy, and led him to disregard those circumstances which would have intimidated any other mind. He accordingly equiped his small squadron with as much expedition as possible, manned with ninety men and victualled for one year. With these, on the 3d of August 1492, amidst a vast croud of anxious spectators, he set sail on an enterprize, which, if we consider the ill condition of his ships, the inexperience of his sailors, the length and uncertainty of his voyage, and the consequences that flowed from it, was the most daring and important that ever was undertaken. He touched at some of the Portuguese settlements in the Canary Isles; where, although he had had but a few days run, he found his vessels needed refitting. He soon made the necessary repairs, and took his departure from the westermost Islands that had hitherto been discovered. Here he left the former track of navigation and steered his course due west.

Not many days after he had been at sea, he began to experience a new scene of difficulty. The sailors now began to contemplate the dangers and uncertain issue of a voyage, the nature and length of which was left entirely open to conjecture. Besides the fickleness and timidity natural to men unaccustomed to the discipline of a seafaring life,

---

3. Ferdinand V (Ferdinand II of Aragon, 1452–1516) and Isabella I (1451–1504) united the provinces of Aragon and Castile when they married in 1469.

several circumstances contributed to inspire an obstinate and mutinous disposition, which required the most consummate art as well as fortitude in the admiral to controul. Having been three weeks at sea, and experienced the uniform course of the trade winds, which always blow in a western direction, they contended that, should they continue the same course for a longer period, the same winds would never permit them to return to Spain. The magnetic needle began to vary its direction. This being the first time that phenomenon was ever discovered, it was viewed by the sailors with astonishment, and considered as an indication that nature itself had changed her course, and that Providence was determined to punish their audacity, in venturing so far beyond the ordinary bounds of man. They declared that the commands of their sovereign had been fully obeyed, in their proceeding so many days in the same direction, and so far surpassing the attempts of all former navigators, in quest of new discoveries. Every talent, requisite for governing, soothing and tempering the passions of men, is conspicuous in the conduct of Columbus on this occasion. The dignity and affability of his manners, his surprising knowledge and experience in naval affairs, his unwearied and minute attention to the duties of his command gave him a complete ascendant over the minds of his men, and inspired that degree of confidence which would have maintained his authority in almost any possible circumstances. But here, from the nature of the undertaking, every man had leisure to feed his imagination with all the gloominess and uncertainty of the prospect. They found, every day, that the same steady gales carried them with great rapidity from their native country, and indeed from all countries of which they had any knowledge. Notwithstanding all the variety of management with which Columbus addressed himself to their passions, sometimes by soothing them with the prognostics of discovering land, sometimes by flattering their ambition and feasting their avarice with the glory and wealth they would acquire from discovering those rich countries beyond the Atlantic, and sometimes by threatening them with the displeasure of their sovereign, should their timidity and disobedience defeat so great an object, their uneasiness still increased. From secret whisperings, it arose to open mutiny and dangerous conspiracy. At length they determined to rid themselves of the remonstrances of Columbus, by throwing him into the sea. The infection spread from ship to ship, and involved Officers as well as common sailors. They finally lost all sense of subordination, and addressed their commander in an insolent manner, demanding to be conducted immediately back to Spain; or, they assured him, they would seek their own safety by taking away his life.

Columbus, whose sagacity and penetration had discovered every symptom of the disorder, was prepared for this last stage of it, and was sufficiently apprized of the danger that awaited him. He found it vain to contend with passions he could no longer controul. He therefore proposed that they should obey his orders for three days longer; and, should they not discover land in that time, he would then direct his course for Spain. They complied with his proposal; and, happily for mankind, in three days they discovered Land. This was a small Island, to which Columbus gave the name of San Salvador. Their first interview with the natives was a scene of amusement and compassion on the one part, and of astonishment and adoration on the other. The natives were entirely naked, simple and timorous, and they viewed the Spaniards as a superior order of beings, descended from the Sun, which, in that Island and in most parts of America, was worshiped as a Deity. By this it was easy for Columbus to perceive the line of conduct proper to be observed toward that simple and inoffensive people. Had his companions and successors, of the Spanish nation possessed the wisdom and humanity of that great discoverer, the benevolent mind would feel no sensations, of regret, in contemplating the extensive advantages arising to mankind from the discovery of America.

In this voyage, Columbus discovered the Islands of Cuba and Hispaniola; on the latter of which, he erected a small fort, and having left a garrison of thirty-eight men, under the command of an Officer by the name of Arada, he set sail for Spain. Returning across the Atlantic, he was overtaken by a violent storm, which lasted several days and increased to such a degree, as baffled all his naval skill and threatened immediate destruction. In this situation, when all were in a state of despair, and it was expected that every sea would swallow up the crazy vessel, he manifested a serenity and presence of mind, perhaps never equalled in cases of like extremity. He wrote a short account of his voyage and of the discoveries he had made, wrapped it in an oiled cloth, enclosed it in a cake of wax, put it into an empty cask and threw it overboard; in hopes that some accident might preserve a deposit of so much importance to the world.

The storm however abated, and he at length arrived in Spain, after having been driven by stress of weather into the Port of Lisbon, where he had opportunity in an interview with the King of Portugal, to prove the truth of his system by arguments more convincing than those he had before advanced, in the character of an humble and unsuccessful suitor. He was received every where in Spain with Royal honours, his family was ennobled, and his former stipulation respecting his offices and emoluments was ratified in the most solemn manner, by Fardinand and Isabella; while all Europe resounded his praises and reciprocated their joy and congratulations on the discovery of a new world.

The immediate consequence of this was a second voyage; in which Columbus took charge of a squadron of seventeen Ships of considerable burthen. Volunteers of all ranks and conditions solicited to be employed in this expedition. He carried over fifteen hundred persons, together with all the necessaries for establishing a Colony and extending his discoveries. In this voyage he explored most of the West-India Islands; but, on his arrival at Hispaniola, he found the garrison he had left there had been totally destroyed by the natives, and the fort demolished. He however proceeded in the planting of his colony; and, by his prudent and humane conduct towards the natives, he effectually established the Spanish authority in that Island. But while he was thus laying the foundation of their future grandeur in South America, some discontented persons, who had returned from the colony to Spain, together with his former enemies in that Kingdom, conspired to accomplish his ruin.

They represented his conduct in such a light at court, as to create uneasiness and distrust in the jealous mind of Fardinand, and made it necessary for Columbus again to return to Spain, in order to counteract their machinations, and to obtain such farther supplies as were necessary to his great political and benevolent purposes. On his arriving at court, and stating with his usual dignity and confidence the whole history of his transactions abroad, every thing wore a favourable appearance. He was received with usual honours, and again solicited to take charge of another squadron, to carry out farther supplies, to pursue his discoveries, and in every respect to use his discretion in extending the Spanish Empire in the new World. In this third voyage he discovered the Continent of America at the mouth of the river Oronoque. He rectified many disorders in his government of Hispaniola which had happened in his absence; and every thing was going on in a prosperous train, when an event was announced to him, which completed his own ruin, and gave a fatal turn to the Spanish policy and conduct in America. This was the arrival of Francis de Bovadilla, with a commission to supercede Columbus in his government; and with power to arraign him as a criminal, and to judge of his former administration.

It seems that by this time the enemies of Columbus, despairing to complete his overthrow by groundless insinuations of mal-conduct, had taken the more effectual method of exciting the jealousy of their Sovereigns. From the promising samples of Gold and other valuable commodities brought from America, they took occasion to represent to the King and Queen, that the prodigious wealth and extent of the countries he had discovered would soon throw such power into the hands of the Viceroy, that he would trample on the Royal Authority and bid defiance to the Spanish power. These arguments were well calculated for the cold and suspicious temper of Fardinand, and they must have had some effect upon the mind of Isabella. The consequence was the appointment of Bavadilla,[4] who had been the inveterate enemy of Columbus, to take the government from his hands. This first tyrant of the Spanish nation in America began his administration by ordering Columbus to be put in chains on board a ship, and sending him prisoner to Spain. By relaxing all discipline he introduced disorder and licenciousness throughout the colony. He subjected the unhappy natives to a most miserable servitude, and apportioned them out in large numbers among his adherents. Under this severe treatment perished in a short time many thousands of those innocent people.

Columbus was carried in his fetters to the Spanish court, where the King and Queen either feigned or felt a sufficient regret at the conduct of Bovadilla towards this illustrious prisoner. He was not only released from confinement, but treated with all imaginable respect. But, although the king endeavoured to expiate the offence by censuring and recalling Bovadilla, yet we may judge of his sincerity from his appointing Nicholas de Ovando,[5] another bitter enemy of Columbus, to succeed in the government, and from his ever after refusing to reinstate Columbus, or to fulfil any of the conditions on which the

---

4. Francisco de Bobadilla (d. 1502) was sent to Hispaniola (now Haiti) by Ferdinand and Isabella to investigate rumors about Columbus. When he arrived, he had Columbus imprisoned and set himself up as governor of the colony.

5. Nicolás de Ovando (1460–1518) was appointed governor of the Spanish colonies in 1501.

discoveries were undertaken. After two years solicitation for this or some other employment, he at length obtained a squadron of four small vessels to attempt new discoveries. He now set out, with the ardour and enthusiasm of a young adventurer, in quest of what was always his favourite object, a passage into the South Sea, by which he might sail to India. He touched at Hispaniola, where Ovando, the governor, refused him admittance on shore even to take shelter during a hurricane, the prognostics of which his experience had taught him to discern. By putting into a small creek, he rode out the storm, and then bore away for the continent. Several months, in the most boisterous season of the year, he spent in exploring the coast round the gulph of Mexico in hopes of finding the intended navigation to India. At length he was shipwrecked, and driven ashore on the Island of Jamaica.

His cup of calamities seemed now completely full. He was cast upon an island of savages, without provisions, without any vessel, and thirty leagues from any Spanish settlement. But the greatest providential misfortunes are capable of being imbittered by the insults of our fellow creatures. A few of his hardy companions generously offered, in two Indian canoes, to attempt a voyage to Hispaniola, in hopes of obtaining a vessel for the relief of the unhappy crew. After suffering every extremity of danger and hardship, they arrived at the Spanish colony in ten days. Ovando, through personal malice and jealousy of Columbus, after having detained these messengers eight months, dispatched a vessel to Jamaica, in order to spy out the condition of Columbus and his crew; with positive instructions to the Captain not to afford them any relief. This order was punctually executed. The Captain approached the shore, delivered a letter of empty compliment from Ovando to the Admiral, received his answer and returned. About four months afterwards a vessel came to their relief; and Columbus, worn out with fatigues and broken with misfortunes, returned for the last time to Spain. Here a new distress awaited him, which he considered as one of the greatest he had suffered, in his whole life. This was the death of Queen Isabella, his last and greatest friend.

He did not suddenly abandon himself to despair. He called upon the gratitude and justice of the King; and, in terms of dignity, demanded the fulfilment of his former contract. Notwithstanding his age and infirmities, he even solicited to be farther employed in extending the career of discovery, without a prospect of any other reward but the consciousness of doing good to mankind. But Fardinand,

cold, ungrateful and timid, dared not to comply with a single proposal of this kind, lest he should encrease his own obligations to a man, whose services he thought it dangerous to reward. He therefore delayed and avoided any decision on these subjects, in hopes that the declining health of Columbus would soon rid the court of the remonstrances of a man, whose extraordinary merit was, in their opinion, a sufficient occasion of destroying him. In this they were not disappointed. Columbus languished a short time, and gladly resigned a life, which had been worn out in the most essential services perhaps that were ever rendered, by any human character, to an ungrateful world.

Sometime in this gloomy interval, before his death, the Vision is supposed to have been presented to him; in order to satisfy his benevolent mind, by unfolding to him the importance of his discoveries, in their extensive influence upon the interest and happiness of mankind, in the progress of society.

The Author has indulged a small anachronism in the opening of the Poem, for the sake of grouping the misfortunes of the hero; as the time of his actual imprisonment was previous to his last voyage and to the death of Isabella.

The Author, at first, formed an idea of attempting a regular Epic Poem, on the discovery of America. But on examining the nature of that event, he found that the most brilliant subjects incident to such a plan would arise from the consequences of the discovery, and must be represented in vision. Indeed to have made it a patriotic Poem, by extending the subject to the settlement and revolutions of North America and their probable effect upon the future progress of society at large, would have protracted the vision to such a degree as to render it disproportionate to the rest of the work. To avoid an absurdity of this kind, which he supposed the critics would not pardon, he rejected the idea of a regular Epic form, and has confined his plan to the train of events which might be represented to the hero in vision. This form he considers as the best that the nature of the subject would admit; and the regularity of the parts will appear by observing, that there is a single poetical design constantly kept in view, which is to gratify and sooth the desponding mind of the hero: It being the greatest possible reward of his services, and the only one that his situation would permit him to enjoy, to convince him that his labours had not been bestowed in vain, and that he was the author of such extensive happiness to the human race.

BOOK I • Argument

*Condition and soliloquy of Columbus. Appearance
and speech of the Angel. They ascend the Mount of
Vision. Continent of America draws into view, and is
described by the mountains, rivers, lakes, soil,
temperature and some of the natural productions.*

Long had the Sage, the first who dared to brave
The unknown dangers of the western wave,
Who taught mankind where future empires lay
In these fair confines of descending day,
With cares o'erwhelm'd, in life's distressing gloom,
Wish'd from a thankless world a peaceful tomb;
While kings and nations, envious of his name,
Enjoy'd his toils and triumph'd o'er his fame,
And gave the chief, from promised empire hurl'd,
Chains for a crown, a prison for a world.
Now night and silence held their lonely reign,
The half-orb'd moon declining to the main;
Descending clouds, o'er varying ether driven,
Obscured the stars and shut the eye from heaven;
Cold mists through opening grates the cell invade,
And deathlike terrors haunt the midnight shade;
When from a visionary, short repose,
That raised new cares and temper'd keener woes,
Columbus woke, and to the walls address'd
The deep-felt sorrows of his manly breast.

Here lies the purchase, here the wretched spoil,
Of painful years and persevering toil:
For these dread walks, this hideous haunt of pain,
I traced new regions o'er the pathless main,
Dared all the dangers of the dreary wave,
Hung o'er its clefts and topp'd the surging grave,
Saw billowy seas, in swelling mountains roll,
And bursting thunders rock the reddening pole,
Death rear his front in every dreadful form,
Gape from beneath and blacken in the storm;
Till, tost far onward to the skirts of day,
Where milder suns dispens'd a smiling ray,
Through brighter skies my happier sails descry'd
The golden banks that bound the western tide,
And gave the admiring world that bounteous shore
Their wealth to nations and to kings their power.
Oh land of transport! dear, delusive coast,
To these fond, aged eyes forever lost!
No more thy gladdening vales I travel o'er,
For me thy mountains rear the head no more,

For me thy rocks no sparkling gems unfold,
Or streams luxuriant wear their paths in gold;
From realms of promised peace forever borne,
I hail dread anguish, and in secret mourn.

But dangers past, fair climes explored in vain,
And foes triumphant shew but half my pain.
Dissembling friends, each earlier joy who gave,
And fired my youth the storms of fate to brave,
Swarm'd in the sunshine of my happier days,
Pursued the fortune and partook the praise,
Bore in my doubtful cause a twofold part,
The garb of friendship and the viper's heart,
Pass my loath'd cell with smiles of sour disdain,
Insult my woes and triumph in my pain.

One gentle guardian Heaven indulgent gave,
And now that guardian slumbers in the grave.
Hear from above, thou dear departed shade,
As once my joys, my present sorrows aid,
Burst my full heart, afford that last relief,
Breathe back my sighs and reinspire my grief;
Still in my sight thy royal form appears,
Reproves my silence and demands my tears.
On that blest hour my soul delights to dwell,
When thy protection bade the canvass swell,
When kings and courtiers found their factions vain,
Blind Superstition shrunk beneath her chain,
The sun's glad beam led on the circling way,
And isles rose beauteous in the western day.
But o'er those silvery shores, that fair domain,
What crouds of tyrants fix their horrid reign!
Again fair Freedom seeks her kindred skies,
Truth leaves the world, and Isabella dies.

Oh, lend thy friendly shroud to veil my sight,
That these pain'd eyes may dread no more the light,
These welcome shades conclude my instant doom,
And this drear mansion moulder to a tomb.

Thus mourn'd the hapless chief; a thundering sound
Roll'd round the shuddering walls and shook the
    ground;
O'er all the dome, where solemn arches bend,
The roofs unfold and streams of light descend;
The growing splendor fill'd the astonish'd room,
And gales etherial breathed a glad perfume;
Mild in the midst a radiant seraph shone,
Robed in the vestments of the rising sun;
Tall rose his stature, youth's primeval grace
Moved o'er his limbs and wanton'd in his face,

His closing wings, in golden plumage drest,
With gentle sweep came folding o'er his breast,
His locks in rolling ringlets glittering hung,
And sounds melodious moved his heavenly tongue.

Rise, trembling Chief, to scenes of rapture, rise,
This voice awaits thee from the approving skies;
Thy just complaints, in heavenly audience known
Call mild compassion from the indulgent throne;
Let grief no more awake the piteous strain,
Nor think thy piety or toils are vain.
Tho' faithless men thy injured worth despise,
Depress all virtue and insult the skies,
Yet look thro' nature, Heaven's own conduct trace,
What power divine sustains the unthankful race!
From that great Source, that life-inspiring Soul,
Suns drew their light and systems learn'd to roll,
Time walk'd the silent round, and life began,
And God's fair image stamp'd the mind of man.
Down the long vale, where rolling years descend,
To thy own days, behold his care extend;
From one eternal Spring, what love proceeds!
Smiles in the seraph, in the Saviour bleeds,
Shines through all worlds, that fill the bounds of space,
And lives and brightens in thy favour'd race.
Yet no return the almighty Power can know,
From earth to heaven no just reward can flow,
Men spread their wants, the all-bounteous hand supplies,
And gives the joys that mortals dare despise.
In these dark vales where blinded faction sways,
Wealth pride and conquest claim the palm of praise,
Aw'd into slaves, while groping millions groan,
And blood-stain'd steps lead upwards to a throne.

Far other wreaths thy virtuous temples claim,
Far nobler honours build thy sacred name,
Thine be the joys the immortal mind that grace
Pleas'd with the toils, that bless thy kindred race,
Now raise thy ravish'd soul to scenes more bright,
The glorious fruits ascending on thy sight;
For, wing'd with speed, from brighter worlds I came,
To sooth thy grief and show thy distant fame.
As that great Seer,[6] whose animating rod
Taught Israel's sons the wonder-working God,
Who led, thro' dreary wastes, the murmuring band
To the fair confines of the promised land,

Oppress'd with years, from Pisgah's beauteous height,
O'er boundless regions cast the raptured sight;
The joys of unborn nations warm'd his breast,
Repaid his toils and sooth'd his soul to rest;
Thus, o'er thy subject wave, shalt thou behold
Far happier realms their future charms unfold,
In nobler pomp another Pisgah rise,
Beneath whose foot thine own Canäan lies;
There, rapt in vision, hail the distant clime,
And taste the blessings of remotest time.

The Seraph spoke; and now before them lay
(The doors unbarr'd) a steep ascending way,
That, through disparting shades, arose on high,
Reach'd o'er the hills and lengthen'd up the sky,
Oped a fair summit, graced with rising flowers,
Sweet odours breathing through celestial bowers,
O'er proud Hispanian spires, it looks sublime,
Subjects the Alps and levels all the clime.
Led by the Power, the hero gain'd the height,
A touch from heaven sublimed his mortal sight,
And, calm beneath them, flow'd the western main,
Far stretch'd, immense, a sky-encircled plain;
No sail, no isle, no cloud invests the bound,
Nor billowy surge disturbs the unvaried round;
Till, deep in distant heavens, the sun's dim ray
Topp'd unknown cliffs and call'd them up to day;
Slow glimmering into sight wide regions drew,
And rose and brighten'd on the expanding view;
Fair sweep the waves, the lessening ocean smiles,
And breathes the fragrance of a thousand isles;
Near and more near the long-drawn coasts arise,
Bays stretch their arms and mountains lift the skies,
The lakes, unfolding, point the streams their way,
The plains the hills their lengthening skirts display,
The vales draw forth, high walk the approaching groves,
And all the majesty of nature moves.

O'er the wild climes his eyes delighted rove,
Where lands extend and glittering waters move;
He saw through central realms, the winding shore
Spread the deep gulph, his sail had traced before,
The rocky isthmus meet the raging tide,
Join distant lands and neighbouring seas divide,
On either side the shores unbounded bend,
Push wide their waves and to the poles ascend;
While two fair continents united rise,
Broad as the main and lengthen'd with the skies.

Such views around them spread, when thus the Guide,
Here bounteous earth displays her noblest pride,

---

6. In the Bible, Moses viewed Canaan from one of the summits of the mountain of Pisgah.

Ages unborn shall bless the happy day,
When thy bold streamers steer'd the trackless way,
O'er these delightful realms thy sons shall tread.
And following millions trace the path you led.
Behold yon isles, where first the flag, unfurl'd,
Waved peaceful triumph o'er the newfound world,
Where, aw'd to silence, savage bands gave place,
And hail'd with joy the sun-descended race.

See there the banks that purest waters lave,
Swift Oronoque rolls back the ocean's wave,
The well known current cleaves the lofty coast,
Where Paria's walks thy former footsteps boast.
These scanty shores no more thy joys shall bound,
See nobler prospects lead their swelling round,
Nature's sublimest scenes before thee roll,
And years and empires open on thy soul.
High to yon seats exalt thy roving view,
Where Quito's lofty plains o'erlook Peru,
On whose broad base, like clouds together driven,
A world exalted props the skirts of heaven.
From south to north what long, blue fronts arise!
Ridge over ridge, and lost in ambient skies!
Approaching near, they heave expanding bounds,
The yielding concave bends sublimer rounds,
Earth's loftiest towers there lift the daring height,
And all the Andes fill the bounded sight.

Round the low base what sloping breaches bend!
Hills form on hills and trees o'er trees extend,
Ascending, whitening, how the craggs are lost!
O'erwhelm'd with summits of eternal frost;
Broad fields of ice give back the morning ray,
Like walls of suns or heaven's perennial day.

There folding storms on eastern pinions ride,
Veil the black heavens and wrap the mountain's side,
The thunders rake the craggs, the rains descend,
And the long lightnings o'er the vallies bend,
While blasts unburden'd sweep the cliffs of snow,
The whirlwinds wheel above, the floods convolve below.
There molten rocks, explosive rend their tomb,
And dread volcanoes ope the nations' doom,
Wild o'er the regions pour the floods of fire,
The shores heave backward and the seas retire.
There slumbering vengeance waits the Almighty call,
Long ages hence to shake some guilty wall;
Thy pride, O Lima, swells the sulph'rous wave,
And fanes and priests and idols croud thy grave.

But cease, my son, these dread events to trace,
Nor learn the woes that wait thy kindred race.

Beyond those glimmering hills, in lands unknown,
O'er the wide gulph, beyond the flaming zone,
Thro' milder climes, see gentler mountains rise,
Where yon dim regions bound the northern skies.
Back from the shore ascending champaigns run,
And lift their heights to hail the eastern sun,
Through all the midland realm, to yon blue pole,
The green hills lengthen and the rivers roll.

So spoke the blest Immortal; when, more near,
The northern climes in various pomp appear;
Lands yet unknown, and streams without a name
Rise into vision and demand their fame.
As when some saint, in heaven's sublime abode,
Extends his views o'er all the works of God;
While earth's fair circuit in his presence rolls,
Here glows the centre and there point the poles;
O'er land and sea his eyes sublimely rove,
And joys of mortals kindle heaven with love;
With equal glance the great Observer's sight
Ranged the low vale or climb'd the cloudly height,
As, led by heaven's own light, his raptured mind,
Explored the realms that here await mankind.

Now the still morn had tinged the mountain's brow
And rising radiance warm'd the plains below;
Stretch'd o'er Virginian hills, in long array,
The beauteous Alleganies met the day.
From sultry Mobile's rich Floridian shore,
To where Ontario bids hoarse Laurence roar,
O'er the clear mountain-tops and winding streams,
Rose a pure azure, streak'd with orient beams;
Fair spread the scene, the hero gazed sublime,
And thus in prospect hail'd the happy clime.

Blest shores of fame, conceal'd in earlier days
To lure my steps to trace the untempted seas!
And blest the race my guardian Saint shall lead,
Where these tall forests wave the beckoning head.
Thro' each wide ridge what various treasures shine!
Sleep there ye diamonds, and ye ores refine.
Exalt your heads ye oaks, ye pines ascend.
Till future navies bid your branches bend,
Then spread the canvass o'er the subject sea,
Explore new worlds and teach the old your sway.

He said, and northward cast his wondering eyes,
Where other cliffs, in other climes, arise,
Where bleak Acadia spreads the dangerous coast,
And isles and shoals their latent horrors boast,
High in the distant heaven, the hoary height
Heaves the glad sailor an eternal light.

Nor could those hills, unnoticed, raise their head,
That look sublime o'er Hudson's winding bed;
Tho' no bold fiction rear them to the skies,
And neighbouring summits far superior rise,
Yet the blue Kaatskill, where the storms divide,
Would lift the heavens from Atlas' labouring pride.

Awhile the ridgy heights his notice claim,
And hills unnumber'd rose without a name,
Which placed, in pomp, on any eastern shore,
Taurus would shrink, the Alps be sung no more;
For here great nature, more exalted show'd
The last ascending footsteps of her God.

He saw those mountains ope their watery store,
Floods leave their caves and seek the distant shore,
Down the long hills and through the subject plain,
Roll the delightful currents to the main;
Whose numerous channels cleave the lengthening
    strand,
And heave their banks where future towns must stand;
He stretch'd his eager glance from pole to pole.
Traced all their sources and explored the whole.

First, from the dreadful Andes' opening side,
He saw Maranon lead his sovereign tide.
A thousand hills for him dissolve their snow,
A thousand streams obedient bend below,
From distant lands their devious courses wind,
Sweep beds of ore and leave their gold behind,
In headlong cataracts indignant heave,
Rush to his opening banks and swell the sweeping wave.

Ucayla, chief of all his mighty sons,
From Cusco's bounds a lengthening circuit runs;
Yutay moves gently in a shorter course,
And rapid Yatva pours a gathering force;
Far in a wild, by nameless tributes fed,
The silent Chavar wears a lonely bed;
Aloft, where northern Quito sits on high,
The roaring Napo quits his misty sky,
Down the long steeps, in whitening torrents driven,
Like Nile descending from his fabled heaven.
While other waves and lakes unknown to fame,
Discharge their urns and fill the swelling stream,
That, far, from clime to clime, majestic goes,
Enlarging widening deepening as it flows;
Approaching ocean hears the distant roar,
Moves up the bed, nor finds the expected shore;
His freshening waves, with high and hoary tide,
Whelm back the flood, and isles and champaigns hide,

Till mingling waters lead the downward sweep,
And waves and trees and banks roll whirling to the deep.

Now, where the sun in milder glory beams,
Brazilia's hills pour down their spreading streams,
The smiling lakes their opening sides display,
And winding vales prolong the devious way;
He saw Xaraya's diamond banks unfold,
And Paraguay's deep channel paved with gold,
Saw proud Potosi lift his glittering head,
Whence the clear Plata wears his tinctur'd bed;
Rich with the spoils of many a distant mine,
In one broad silver sea their floods combine;
Wide o'er the realms its annual bounties spread,
By nameless streams from various mountains fed;
The thirsty regions wait its glad return,
And drink their future harvests from its urn.

Round the cold climes, beneath the southern sky,
Thy path, Magellan,[7] caught the hero's eye;
The long cleft ridges oped the widening way
Fair gleaming westward to the Placid Sea.[8]
Soon as the distant wave was seen to roll,
His ancient wishes[9] fill'd his rising soul,
Warm from his heaving heart an anxious sigh
Breathed o'er his lips; he turn'd his moisten'd eye,
And thus besought the Angel. Speak, my guide,
Where leads the pass? and whence yon purple tide?
Deep in the blue horizon, widely spread,
What liquid realms in blending ether fade!
How the dim waters skirt the bounds of day!
No lands behind them rise, no streamers in them play.
In those low skies extends the boundless main,
I sought so long, and sought, alas, in vain.
Restore, celestial Power, my youthful morn,
Call back my years and bid my fame return;
Grant me to trace, beyond that pathless sea,
Some happier shore from lust of empire free;

---

7. Ferdinand Magellan (1480–1521) sailed around the southern tip of Brazil in his effort to sail to Asia from the Spanish Americas.

8. Barlow's poetic name for the Pacific Ocean.

9. "The great object of Columbus in most of his voyages was to discover a western passage to India. For this purpose he navigated the gulph of Mexico, with great care, and was much disappointed in not finding a pass into the South Sea. The view he is here supposed to have of that ocean would therefore naturally recall his former desire of sailing round the world." [Au.]

In that far world to fix a peaceful bower,
From envy safe, and curst Ovando's power.
Since joys of mortals claim thy guardian care,
Oh bless the nations and regard my prayer:
There rest forever kingdoms unexplored,
A God creating, and no God adored.
Earth's happiest realms shall endless darkness hide?
And seas forever roll their useless tide?
Grant, heavenly guide, the welcome task to dare,
One venturous bark, and be my life thy care.

The hero spoke; the Seraph mild replies,
While warm compassion soften'd in his eyes;
Though still to virtuous deeds thy mind aspires,
And heavenly visions kindle new desires;
Yet hear with reverence what attends thy state,
Nor pass the confines of eternal fate.
Led by this sacred light thy soul shall see,
That half mankind shall owe their bliss to thee,
And joyous empires claim their future birth,
In these fair bounds of sea-encircled earth;
While unborn times, by thine example prest,
Shall call forth heroes to explore the rest.

Beyond those seas, the well-known climes arise,
Where morning splendors gild the eastern skies.
The circling course to India's happy shores,
Round Afric's coast, bold Gamma now explores;
Another pass these opening straits provide,
Nor long shall rest the daring search untry'd;
This watery glade shall open soon to fame,
Here a lost hero fix his lasting name,
From that new main in furious waves be tost,
And fall neglected on the barbarous coast.

But see the chief from Albion's strand arise,
Speed in his pinions, fame before his eyes;
Hither, O Drake,[10] display the hastening sails,
Widen ye passes, and awake ye gales,
Move thou before him, heaven-revolving sun,
Wind his long course, and teach him where to run,
Earth's distant shores in circling bands unite,
Lands, learn your fame, and oceans, roll in light,

---

10. Francis Drake (1540–96) sailed for England. He challenged Spain's holdings in the West Indies, crossed through the isthmus of Panama, and saw and sailed the Pacific Ocean along the coast of present-day California.

Round all the beauteous globe his flag be hurl'd,
A new Columbus to the astonish'd world.

He spoke; and silent tow'rd the northern sky,
Wide o'er the realms the hero cast his eye;
Saw the long floods pour forth their watery stores,
And wind their currents to the opening shores;
While midland seas and lonely lakes display
Their glittering glories to the beams of day.
Thy capes, Virginia, towering from the tide,
Raised up their arms and branch'd their borders wide;
Whose broad embrace in circling extent lay,
Round the calm bosom of thy beauteous bay.
Where commerce since has wing'd her channel'd flight
Each spreading stream lay brightening to the light;
York led his wave, imbank'd in mazy pride,
And nobler James fell winding by his side;
Back tow'rd the distant hills, through many a vale,
Wild Rappahanock seem'd to lure the sail,
While, far o'er all, in sea-like azure spread,
The great Potowmac swept his lordly bed.

When thus he saw the mingling waters play,
And seas, in lost disorder, idly stray,
Where frowning forests stretch the dusky wing,
And deadly damps forbid the flowers to spring,
No seasons clothe the field with beauteous grain,
No buoyant ship attempt the useless main,
With fond impatience, Heavenly Seer, he cry'd,
When shall my children cross the lonely tide?
Here, here, my sons, the hand of culture bring,
Here teach the lawns to smile, the groves to sing;
Ye sacred floods, no longer vainly glide,
Ye harvests, load them, and ye forests, ride,
Bear the deep burden from the joyous swain,
And tell the world where peace and plenty reign.

Now round the coast, where other floods invite,
He fondly turn'd; they fill'd his eager sight:
Here Del'ware's waves the yielding shores invade,
And here bold Hudson oped a glassy glade;
Thy parent stream, fair Hartford, met his eye,
Far lessening upward to the northern sky;
No watery gleams thro' happier valleys shine,
Nor drinks the sea a lovlier wave than thine.
Bright Charles and Mystick laved their bloomy isles,
And gay Piscatuway caught his passing smiles;
Swift Kenebeck, descending from on high,
Swept the tall hills and lengthen'd down the sky;
When hoarse resounding through the gaping shore,

He heard cold Laurence' dreadful surges roar.
Tho' softening May had waked the vernal blade,
And happier climes her fragrant garb display'd,
Yet howling winter, in this bleak domain,
Shook the wide waste and held his gloomy reign;
Still groans the flood, in frozen fetters bound,
And isles of ice his threatening front surround,
Clothed in white majesty, the foaming main
Leads up the tide and tempts the wintery chain,
Billows on billows lift the maddening brine,
And seas and clouds in battling conflict join,
The dash'd wave struggling heaves in swelling sweep,
Wide crash the portals of the frozen deep,
Till forced alost, high-bounding in the air,
Moves the blear ice and sheds a hideous glare,
The torn foundations on the surface ride,
And wrecks of winter load the downward tide.

When now the stream had oped its northern course,
He traced the current to its milder source;
There, far retired, the Angellic Power displays
Earth's sweetest charms, her own imbosom'd seas.
Ontario's banks, fair opening on the north,
With sweep majestic, pour'd his Laurence forth;
Above, bold Erie's wave sublimely stood,
Look'd o'er the cliff and heaved the headlong flood,
Far circling in the north, great Huron spread,
And Michigan o'erwhelm'd a western bed;
While, stretch'd in circling majesty away,
The deep Superior closed the setting day.

Here all the midland seas their waves unite,
And gleam in grandeur to the hero's sight;
Wide opening round them lands delightful spread,
Deep groves innumerous cast a solemn shade;
Slow moved the settling mist in lurid streams,
And dusky radiance brown'd the glimmering beams;
O'er all the great Discoverer wondering stood,
And thus address'd the messenger of good.

What lonely walks, what wonderous wilds are these?
What branching vales run smiling to their seas?
The peaceful seats, reserved by Heaven to grace,
The virtuous toils of some illustrious race.
But why these regions form'd so fair in vain?
And why so distant rolls the unconscious main?
These desert fountains must forever rest,
Of man unseen, by native beasts possest;
For, see, no ship can point the streamer here,
No opening pass, no spreading ocean near;
Eternal winter clothes the shelvy shores,

Where yon far northern son[11] of ocean roars;
Or should some bark the daring entrance brave,
And climes by culture warm his lessening wave,
Yon frightful cataract exalts the brow,
And frowns defiance to the world below.

To whom the Seraph. Here extended lies
The happiest realm that feels the fostering skies;
Led by this arm thy sons shall hither come,
And streams obedient yield the heroes room;
Nor think no pass can find the distant main,
Or heaven's last polish touch'd these climes in vain.
Behold, from yon fair lake, the current led,
And silent waves adorn its infant head;
Far south thro' happy regions see it wind,
By gathering floods and nobler fountains join'd,
Yon opening gulph receive the beauteous wave,
And thy known isles its freshening current lave;
There lies the path some future ship shall trace,
And waft to these wide vales thy kindred race.

The hero saw the blooming isles ascend
And round the gulph the circling shore extend,
He saw fair Missisippi wind his way,
Through all the western boundless tracts of day;
Where Alleganies stretch the morning shade,
From lone Oswago to the gulphy glade,
Where absent suns their midnight circles ride,
Pours the long current of his rushing tide.
Unnumber'd branches from the channel stray,
Akansa here, and there Missouri lay,
Rouge roll'd his wave along the western wild,
And broad Ohio's northern beauties smiled.

Retiring far round Hudson's frozen bay,
Where lessening circles shrink beyond the day,
The shivering shrubs scarce brave the dismal clime,
Snows ever-rising with the years of time;
The beasts all whitening roam the lifeless plain,
And caves unfrequent scoop the couch for man.

Where Spring's coy steps, in cold Canadia, stray,
And joyless seasons hold unequal sway,
He saw the pine its daring mantle rear,
Break the rude blast and mock the inclement year,
Secure the limits of the angry skies,
And bid all southern vegetation rise.
Wild o'er the vast, impenetrable round,
The untrod bowers of shadowy nature frown'd;

---

11. "St. Laurence." [Au.]

The neighbouring cedar waved its honours wide,
The fir's tall boughs, the oak's resistless pride,
The branching beach, the aspin's trembling shade,
Veil'd the dim heavens and brown'd the dusky glade.
Here in huge crouds those sturdy sons of earth,
In frosty regions, claim a nobler birth;
Where heavy trunks the sheltering dome requires,
And copious fuel feeds the wintery fires.
While warmer suns, that southern climes emblaze,
A cool deep umbrage o'er the woodland raise;
Floridia's blooming shores around him spread,
And Georgian hills erect their shady head;
Beneath tall trees, in livelier verdure gay,
Long level walks a humble garb display;
The infant corn, unconscious of its worth,
Points the green spire and bends the foliage forth;
Sweeten'd on flowery banks, the passing air
Breathes all the untasted fragrance of the year;
Unbidden harvests o'er the regions rise,
And blooming life repays the genial skies.
Where circling shores around the gulph extend,
the bounteous groves with richer burdens bend;
Spontaneous fruits the uplifted palms unfold,
The beauteous orange waves a load of gold,
The untaught vine, the wildly-wanton cane
Bloom on the waste, and clothe the enarbour'd plain,
The rich pimento scents the neighbouring skies,
And woolly clusters o'er the cotton rise.
Here, in one view, the same glad branches bring
The fruits of autumn and the flowers of spring;
No wintery blasts the unchanging year deform,
Nor beasts unshelter'd fear the pinching storm;
But vernal breezes o'er the blossoms rove,
And breathe the ripen'd juices thro' the grove.
Beneath the crystal wave's inconstant light,
Pearls undistinguish'd sparkle on the sight;
From opening earth, in living lustre, shine
The various treasures of the blazing mine;
Hills, cleft before him, all their stores unfold,
The quick mercurius and the burning gold;
Gems of unnumber'd hues, in bright array,
Illume the changing rocks and shed the beams of day

When now the Chief had travel'd with his eye,
O'er each fair clime that meets the incumbent sky;
The stream, the mountain, forest, vale and plain,
And isle and coast, and wide untravers'd main;
He cast, o'er all, the immeasurable glance,
And all past views in one broad vision dance.

Skirting the western heavens and each far pole,
With blending skies Pacific oceans roll,
Atlantic surges lead their swelling round,
and distant straits the polar confines bound.
The western coasts their long, high summits heave,
And look majestic o'er the subject wave;
While, on the lowly east, the winding strand
Draws from the silent sea and gently steals to land.

BOOK II • Argument

*Natives of America appear in vision. Their manners
and characters. Columbus enquires the cause of the
dissimilarity of nations. The Angel replies—That the
human body is composed of a due proportion of the
elements suited to the place of its first creation—that
these elements, differently proportioned, produce all
the changes of health, sickness, growth and decay;
and will likewise produce any other changes which
occasion the diversity of men—that these elemental
proportions are varied, not more by climate, than
temperature, and many other local accidents—that
the mind is likewise in a state of change, and will take
its physical character from the body and from external
objects: examples. Enquiry and answer concerning
the first peopling of America. View of Mexico. Its
destruction by Cortez. View of Cusco and Quito,
cities of Peru. Tradition of Capac and Oella,
founders of the Peruvian empire. Columbus enquires
their real history. The Angel gives an account of their
origin, and relates the stratagems they used in
establishing that empire.*

High o'er the changing scene, as thus he gazed,
The indulgent Power his arm sublimely raised;
When round the realms superior lustre flew,
And call'd new wonders to the hero's view.

He saw, at once, as far as eye could rove,
Like scattering herds, the swarthy people move,
In tribes innumerable; all the waste,
Beneath their steps, a varying shadow cast.
As airy shapes, beneath the moon's pale eye,
When broken clouds sail o'er the curtain'd sky,
Spread thro' the grove and flit along the glade,
And cast their grisly phantoms thro' the shade;
So move the hordes, in thickers half conceal'd,
Or vagrant stalking o'er the open field.
Here ever-restless tribes, despising home,

O'er shadowy streams and trackless deserts roam;
While others there, thro' downs and hamlets stray,
And rising domes a happier state display.

The painted chiefs, in death's grim terrors drest,
Rise fierce to war, and beat the savage breast;
Dark round their steps collecting warriors pour,
And dire revenge begins the hideous roar;
While to the realms around the signal flies,
And tribes on tribes, in dread disorder, rise,
Track the mute foe and scour the distant wood,
Wide as a storm, and dreadful as a flood;
Now deep in groves the silent ambush lay,
Or wing the flight or sweep the prize away,
Unconscious babes and reverend sires devour,
Drink the warm blood and paint their cheeks with gore.

While all their mazy movements fill the view.
Where'er they turn his eager eyes pursue;
He saw the same dire visage thro' the whole,
And mark'd the same fierce savageness of soul:
In doubt he stood, with anxious thoughts oppress'd,
And thus his wavering mind the Power address'd.

Say, from what source, O Voice of wisdom, sprung
The countless tribes of this amazing throng?
Where human frames and brutal souls combine,
No force can tame them and no arts refine.
Can these be fashion'd on the social plan?
Or boast a lineage with the race of man?
In yon fair isle, when first my wandering view
Ranged the glad coast and met the savage crew;
A timorous herd, like harmless roes, they ran,
Hail'd us as Gods from whom their race began,
Supply'd our various wants, relieved our toil,
And oped the unbounded treasures of their isle.
But when, their fears allay'd, in us they trace
The well-known image of a mortal race;
When Spanish blood their wondering eyes beheld,
Returning rage their changing bosoms swell'd;
Their jaws the crimson dainty long'd to taste,
And spread, with foreign flesh, the rich repast.
My homeward sail, far distant on the main,
Incautious left a small unguarded train,
When, in their horrid power, bereft of aid,
That train with thee, O lost Arada,[12] bled.
No faith no treaty calms their maddening flame,

---

12. Perhaps a reference to Diego de Arana, who was Columbus's bailiff during the first voyage.

Rage all their joy, and slaughter all their aim;
How the dread savage bands with fury burn'd,
When o'er the wave our growing host return'd!
Now, mild with joy, a friendly smile they show'd,
And now their dark-red visage frown'd in blood;
Till, call'd afar, from all the circling shore,
Swift thro' the groves the yelling squadrons pour,
The wide wings stretching sweep the unbounded plain,
That groans beneath the innumerable train.
Our scanty files, ascending o'er the strand,
Tread the bold champaign and the fight demand;
With steeds and hounds the dreadful onset moves,
And thundering batteries rend the distant groves;
Swift fly the scattering foes, like shades of night,
When orient splendors urge their rapid flight.
Our proffer'd friendship bade the discord cease,
Spared the grim host and gave the terms of peace.
The arts of civil life we strove to lend,
Their lands to culture and their joys extend,
Sublime their views, fair virtue's charms display,
And point their passage to eternal day.

Still proud to rove, our offers they disdain,
Insult our friendship and our rites prophane.
In that blest island, still the myriads rest,
Bask in the sunshine, wander with the beast,
Feed on the foe, or from the victor fly,
Rise into life, exhaust their rage, and die.

Tell then, my Seer, from what dire sons of earth
The brutal people drew their ancient birth?
Whether in realms, the western heavens that close,
A tribe distinct from other nations rose,
Born to subjection; when, in happier time,
A nobler race should hail their fruitful clime.
Or, if a common source all nations claim,
Their lineage, form, and reasoning powers the same,
What sovereign cause, in secret wisdom laid,
This wonderous change in God's own work has made?
Why various powers of soul and tints of face
In different climes diversify the race?

To whom the Guide; Unnumber'd causes lie
In earth and sea and round the varying sky,
That fire the soul, or damp the genial flame,
And work their wonders on the human frame.
See beauty, form and colour change with place—
Here charms of health the blooming visage grace;
There pale diseases float in every wind,
Deform the figure, and degrade the mind.

From earth's own elements, thy race at first
Rose into life, the children of the dust;
These kindred elements, by various use,
Nourish the growth and every change produce;
Pervade the pores, awake the infant bloom,
Lead life along, and ope the certain tomb;
In each ascending stage the man sustain,
His breath, his food, his physic and his bane.
In due proportions, where these virtues lie,
A perfect form their equal aids supply;
And, while unchanged the efficient causes reign,
Age following age the unvaried race maintain.
But where crude elements distemper'd rise,
And cast their sickening vapours round the skies,
Unlike that harmony of human frame,
Where God's first works and nature's were the same,
The unconscious tribes, attempering to the clime,
Still vary downward with the years of time;
Till fix'd, at last, their characters abide,
And local likeness feeds their local pride.
The soul too varying with the changing clime,
Feeble or fierce, or groveling or sublime,
Forms with the body to a kindred plan,
And lives the same, a nation or a man.

Yet think not clime alone, or height of poles,
On every shore, the springs of life controuls;
A different cast the glowing zone demands,
In Paria's blooms, from Tombut's burning sands.
Internal causes, thro' the earth and skies,
Blow in the breeze or on the mountain rise,
Thro' air and ocean, with their changes run,
Breathe from the ground or circle with the sun.
Where these long shores their boundless regions spread
See the same form all different tribes pervade;
Thro' all, alike, the fertile forests bloom,
And all, uncultured, shed a solemn gloom;
Thro' all great nature's boldest features rise,
Sink into vales and tower amid the skies;
Streams, darkly-winding, stretch a broader sway,
The groves and mountains bolder walks display:
A dread sublimity informs the whole,
And wakes a dread sublimity of soul.

Yet time and art shall other changes find,
And open still and vary still the mind;
The countless swarms that tread these dank abodes,
Who glean spontaneous fruits and range the woods,
Fix'd here for ages, in their swarthy face,

Display the wild complexion of the place.
Yet when their tribes to happy nations rise,
And earth by culture warms the genial skies,
A fairer tint and more majestic grace
Shall flush their features and exalt the race;
While milder arts, with social joys refined,
Inspire new beauties in the growing mind.

Thy followers too, fair Europe's noblest pride,
When future gales shall wing them o'er the tide,
A ruddier hue[13] and deeper shade shall gain,
And stalk, in statelier figures, o'er the plain.
While nature's grandeur lifts the eye abroad
O'er these dread footsteps of the forming God;
Wing'd on a wider glance the venturous soul
Bids greater powers and bolder thoughts unroll;
The sage, the chief, the patriot, unconfined,
Shield the weak world and counsel for mankind.

But think not thou, in all the race of man,
That different pairs, in different climes, began;
Or tribes distinct, by signal marks confest,
Were born to serve or subjugate the rest.

The hero heard; But say, celestial Guide,
Who led the wanderers o'er the billowy tide?
Could these dark bands, unskill'd the paths to gain,
To build the bark, or cross the extended main,
Descry the coast, or tread the blest abode,
Unled, unguided by the hand of God?

When first thy roving race, the Power reply'd,
Learn'd by the stars the devious sail to guide,
From stormy Hellespont explored the way,
And sought the bound'ries of the midland sea;
Ere great Alcides[14] form'd the impious plan,
To bound the sail and fix the range of man,
Driven from those rocky straits, a hapless train
Roll'd on the waves that sweep the western main,
While eastern storms the billowing skies o'ershade,
Nor sun nor stars afford their wonted aid.
For many a darksome day, o'erwhelm'd and tost,
Their sails, their oars in swallowing surges lost;

---

13. The complexion of the inhabitants of North America, who are descended from the English and Dutch, is evidently darker and their stature is taller than those of the English and Dutch in Europe.

14. Heracles, Hercules.

At length, the clouds withdrawn, they sad descry
Their course directing from their native sky;
No hope remains; while, o'er the flaming zone,
The winds still bear them with the circling sun;
Till the wild walks of this delightful coast
Receive to lonely seats the suffering host.
The fruitful plains invite their steps to roam,
Renounce their sorrows and forget their home;
Revolving years their ceaseless wanderings led,
And from their sons descending nations spread.

These round the south and middle regions stray,
Where cultured fields their growing arts display;
While northern tribes a later source demand,
And snow their wanderers from the Asian strand.
Far tow'rd the distant pole thy view extend;
See isles and shores and seas Pacific blend;
And that blue coast, where Amur's currents glide,
From thy own world a narrow frith divide;
There Tartar hosts for countless years, have sail'd,
And changing tribes the alternate regions hail'd.

He look'd: the opening shores beneath him spread,
And moving nations on the margin tread.
As, when autumnal storms awake their force,
The storks foreboding tempt their southern course;
From all the fields collecting throngs arise,
Mount on the wing and croud along the skies;
Thus, to his eye, from far Siberia's shore,
O'er isles and seas, the gathering people pour;
From those cold regions hail a happier strand,
Leap from the wave and tread the welcome land;
The growing tribes extend their southern sway,
And widely wander to a milder day.

But why; the chief return'd, if ages past
Have led these vagrants o'er the wilder'd waste—
If human souls, for social compact given,
Inform their nature with the stamp of heaven,
Why the dread glooms forever must they rove?
And no mild joys their temper'd passions move?
Ages remote and dark thou bring'st to light,
When the first leaders dared the western flight;
On other shores, in every eastern clime,
Since that unletter'd, distant tract of time,
What arts have shone! what empires found their place,
What golden sceptres sway'd the human race!
What guilt and grandeur from their seats been hurl'd,
And dire divulsions shook the changing world.
Ere Rome's bold eagle clave the affrighted air,

Ere Sparta form'd her death-like sons of war,
Ere proud Chaldea saw her greatness rise,
Or Memphian columns heaved against the skies;
These tribes have stray'd beneath the fruitful zone,
Their souls unpolish'd and their name unknown.

The Voice of heaven reply'd; A scanty band,
In that far age, approach'd the untrodden land.
Prolific wilds, with game and fruitage crown'd,
Supply'd their wishes from the uncultured ground.
By nature form'd to rove, the restless mind,
Of freedom fond, will ramble unconfined,
Till all the realm is fill'd, and rival right
Restrains their steps, and bids their force unite;
When common safety builds a common cause,
Conforms their interests and inspires their laws;
By mutual checks their different manners blend,
Their fields bloom joyous and their walls ascend.

Here, to their growing hosts, no bounds arose,
They claim'd no safeguard, as they fear'd no foes;
Round all the land their scattering sons must stray,
Ere arts could rise, or power extend the sway.
And what a world their mazy wanderings led!
What streams and wilds in boundless order spread!
See the shores lengthen, see the waters roll,
To each far main and each extended pole!

Yet circling years the destined course have run,
The realms are peopled and their arts begun.
Behold, where that mid region strikes the eyes,
A few fair cities glitter to the skies;
There move, in eastern pomp, the scenes of state,
And temples heave, magnificently great.

The hero look'd; when from the varying height,
Three growing splendors, rising on the sight,
Flamed like a constellation: high in view,
Ascending near, their opening glories drew;
In equal pomp, beneath their roofs of gold,
Three spiry towns, in blazing pride, unfold.
So, led by visions of the guiding God,
The sacred Seer, in Patmos' waste who trod,[15]
Saw the dim vault of heaven its folds unbend,
And gates and spires and streets and domes descend;
With golden skies, and suns and rainbows crown'd,
The new-form'd city lights the world around.

---

15. The biblical apostle John is said to have had visions at
Patmos.

Fair on the north, bright Mexico, arose,
A mimic morn her sparkling towers disclose,
An ample range the opening streets display,
Give back the sun and shed internal day;
The circling wall with sky-built turrets frown'd,
And look'd defiance to the realms around;
A glimmering lake, without the walls, retires,
Inverts the trembling towers and seems a grove of spires.

Bright, o'er the midst, on columns lifted high,
A rising structure claims a loftier sky;
O'er the tall gates sublimer arches bend,
Courts larger lengthen, bolder walks ascend,
Starr'd with superior gems, the porches shine,
And speak the royal residence within.

There, robed in state, high on a golden throne,
Mid suppliant kings, dread Montezuma[16] shone:
Mild in his eye a temper'd grandeur sate,
Great seem'd his soul, with conscious power elate;
In aspect open, haughty and sincere,
Untamed by crosses and unknown to fear,
Of fraud incautious, credulous and vain,
Enclosed with favourites and of friends unseen.

Round the rich throne, with various lustre bright,
Gems undistinguish'd, cast a changing light;
Sapphires and emeralds deck the splendent scene,
Sky-tinctures mingling with the vernal green;
The ruby's blush, the amber's flames unfold,
And diamonds brighten from the burning gold;
Through all the dome the living blazes blend,
And cast their rainbows where the arches bend.
Wide round the walls, with mimic action gay,
In order ranged, historic figures stray,
And show, in Memphian style, with rival grace,
Their boasted chiefs and all their regal race.

Thro' the full gates, and round each ample street,
Unnumber'd throngs, in various concourse, meet,
Ply different toils, new walls and structures rear,
Or till the fields, or train the ranks of war.
Thro' spreading realms the skirts of empire bend,
New temples rise and other plains extend;
Thrice ten fair provinces, in culture gay,
Bless the same monarch and enlarge his sway.
A smile benignant kindling in his eyes,

Oh happy clime! the exulting hero cries;
Far in the midland, safe from foreign foes,
Thy joys shall ripen as thy grandeur grows,
To future years thy rising fame extend,
And sires of nations from thy sons descend.
May no gold-thirsty race thy temples tread,
Nor stain thy streams nor heap thy plains with dead;
No Bovadilla sieze the tempting spoil,
Ovando dark, or sacrilegious Boyle,[17]
In mimic priesthood grave, or robed in state,
O'erwhelm thy glories in oblivious fate.

Vain are thy fondest hopes, the Power reply'd,
These rich abodes from ravening hosts to hide;
Teach harden'd guilt and cruelty to spare
The guardless prize, and check the waste of war.
Think not the vulture, o'er the field of slain,
Where base and brave promiscuous strow the plain,
Where the young hero, in the pride of charms,
Pours deeper crimson o'er his spotless arms,
Will pass the tempting prey, and glut his rage
On harder flesh, and carnage black with age;
O'er all alike he darts his eager eye,
Whets the dire beak and hovers down the sky,
From countless corses picks the dainty food,
And screams and fattens in the purest blood.
So the dire hosts, that trace thy daring way,
By gold allured to sail the unfathom'd sea,
Power all their aim and avarice all their joy,
Seize brightest realms and happiest tribes destroy.
Thine the dread task, O Cortez,[18] here to show
What unknown crimes can heighten human woe,
On these fair fields the blood of realms to pour,
Tread sceptres down and print thy steps in gore,
With gold and carnage swell thy sateless mind,
And live and die the blackest of mankind.

Now see, from yon fair isle, his murdering band
Stream o'er the wave and mount the sated strand;
On the wild shore behold his fortress rise,
The fleet in flames ascends the darken'd skies.
The march begins; the nations, from afar,

---

16. Montezuma (1477–1520) was the war leader and respected chief at the time Cortés captured Mexico.

17. Robert Boyle (1627–91), scientist and natural philosopher.

18. Hernando Cortés or Cortéz (1485–1547) conquered Montezuma at Mexico City; he was made governor of New Spain in 1523.

Quake in his sight, and wage the fruitless war;
O'er the rich provinces he bends his way,
Kings in his chain, and kingdoms for his prey;
While, robed in peace, great Montezuma stands,
And crowns and treasures sparkle in his hands,
Proffers the empire, yields the sceptred sway,
Bids vassal'd millions tremble and obey;
And plies the victor, with incessant prayer,
Thro' ravaged realms the harmless race to spare.
But prayers and tears and sceptres plead in vain,
Nor threats can move him, nor a world restrain;
While blest religion's prostituted name,
And monkish fury guides the sacred flame:
O'er fanes and altars, fires unhallow'd bend,
Climb o'er the walls and up the towers ascend,
Pour, round the lowering skies, the smoky flood,
And whelm the fields, and quench their rage in blood.

The hero heard; and, with a heaving sigh,
Dropp'd the full tear that started in his eye,
Oh hapless day! his trembling voice reply'd,
That saw my wandering streamer mount the tide!
Oh! had the lamp of heaven, to that bold sail,
Ne'er mark'd the passage nor awaked the gale,
Taught eastern worlds these beauteous climes to find,
Nor led those tygers forth to curse mankind.
Then had the tribes, beneath these bounteous skies,
Seen their walls widen and their spires arise;
Down the long tracts of time their glory shone,
Broad as the day and lasting as the sun:
The growing realms, beneath thy shield that rest,
O hapless monarch, still thy power had blest,
Enjoy'd the pleasures that surround thy throne,
Survey'd thy virtues and sublimed their own.
Forgive me, prince; this impious arm hath led
The unseen storm that blackens o'er thy head;
Taught the dark sons of slaughter where to roam,
To seize thy crown and seal thy nation's doom.
Arm, sleeping empire, meet the daring band,
Drive back the terrors, save the sinking land—
Yet vain the strife! behold the sweeping flood!
Forgive me nature, and forgive me God.

Thus, from his heart, while speaking sorrows roll,
The Power, reproving, sooth'd his tender soul.
Father of this new world, thy tears give o'er,
Let virtue grieve and Heaven be blamed no more.
Enough for man, with persevering mind,
To act his part and strive to bless his kind;
Enough for thee, o'er thy dark age to rise,
With genius warm'd, and favour'd of the skies.

For this my guardian care thy youth inspired,
To virtue raised thee, and with glory fired,
Bade in thy plan each distant world unite,
And wing'd thy streamer for the adventurous flight.

Nor think no blessings shall thy toils attend,
Or these fell tyrants can defeat their end.
Such impious deeds, in Heaven's all-ruling plan,
Lead in disguise the noblest bliss of man.
Long have thy race, to narrow shores confined,
Trod the same round that cramp'd the roving mind;
Now, borne on bolder wings, with happier flight,
The world's broad bounds unfolding to the sight,
The mind shall soar; the nations catch the flame,
Enlarge their counsels and extend their fame;
While mutualities the social joys enhance,
And the last stage of civil rule advance.

Tho' impious ruffians spread their crimes abroad,
And o'er these empires pour the purple flood;
Tis thus religious rage, its own dire bane,
Shall fall at last, with all its millions slain,
And buried gold, drawn bounteous from the mine,
Give wings to commerce and the world refine.

Now to yon southern walls extend thy view,
And mark the rival seats of rich Peru.
There Quito's airy plains, exalted high,
With loftier temples rise along the sky;
And elder Cusco's richer roofs unfold,
Flame on the day and shed their suns of gold.

Another range, in these delightful climes,
Spreads a broad theatre for unborn crimes.
Another Cortez shall the treasures view,
The rage rekindle and the guilt renew;
His treason, fraud, and every dire decree,
O curst Pizarro,[19] shall revive in thee.

There reigns a prince, whose hand the sceptre claims,
Thro' a long lineage of imperial names;
Where the brave roll of following Incas trace
The distant father of their realm and race,
Immortal Capac.[20] He in youthful pride,

---

19. Francisco Pizarro (1471–1541) conquered Peru.

20. Manco Capac, the traditional founder of the Inca monarchy of Peru, was, according to legend, the father of the sun and was sent to unify, civilize, and rule the Indians of Peru with his sister and wife, Mama Occlo Huaco. Barlow tells the story of Manco Capac in the lines that follow and in the "dissertation" inserted in *The Vision of Columbus* at the end of Book II.

With fair Oella, his illustrious bride,
In virtuous guile, proclaim'd their birth begun,
From the pure splendors of their God, the sun;
With power and dignity a throne to found,
Fix the mild sway and spread their arts around;
Crush the dire Gods that human victims claim,
And point all worship to a nobler name;
With cheerful rites, the due devotions pay
To the bright beam, that gives the changing day.

On this fair plan, the children of the skies
Bade, in the wild, a growing empire rise;
Beneath their hand, and sacred to their fame,
Rose yon fair walls, that meet the solar flame.
Succeeding sovereigns spread their bounds afar,
By arts of peace and temper'd force of war;
Till these surrounding realms the sceptre own,
And grateful millions hail the genial sun.

Behold, in yon fair lake, a beauteous isle,
Where fruits and flowers, in rich profusion smile;
High in the midst a sacred temple rise,
Seat of the sun, and pillar of the skies.
The roofs of burnish'd gold, the blazing spires
Light the glad heavens and lose their upward fires;
Fix'd in the flaming front, with living ray,
A diamond circlet gives the rival day;
In whose bright face forever looks abroad
The radiant image of the beaming God.
Round the wide courts, and in the solemn dome,
A white-robed train of holy virgins bloom;
Their pious hands the sacred rites require,
To grace the offerings, and preserve the fire.

On this blest isle, with flowery garlands crown'd,
That ancient pair, in charms of youth, were found,
Whose union'd souls the mighty plan design'd,
To bless the nations[21] and reform mankind.

---

21. Barlow wrote a long note at this place:

From the traditions of Capac and Oella, mentioned by the
Spanish historians, they appear to have been very great
and distinguished characters. About three centuries previous to the discovery of that country by the Spaniards,
the natives of Peru were as rude savages as any in America. They had no fixed habitations, no ideas of permanent
property; they wandered naked like the beasts, and, like
them, depended on the events of each day for a precarious subsistence. At this period, Manco Capac and his
wife Mama Oella appeared on a small island in the lake
Titiaca; near which the city of Cusco was afterwards
erected. These persons, in order to establish a belief of

---

their divinity, in the minds of the people, were clothed in
white garments of cotton; and declared themselves descended from the Sun, who was their father and the God
of that country. They affirmed that he was offended at
their cruel and perpetual wars, their barbarous modes of
worship, and their neglecting to make the best use of the
blessings he was constantly bestowing, in fertilizing the
earth and producing vegetation; that he pitied their
wretched state, and had sent his own children to instruct
them, and to establish a number of wise regulations, by
which they might be rendered happy.

By some extraordinary method of persuasion, these
persons drew together a number of the savage tribes, laid
the foundations of the city of Cusco, and established
what was called the kingdom of the Sun, or the Peruvian
empire. In the reign of the Manco Capac, the dominion
was extended about eight leagues from the city; and at the
end of three centuries, it was established fifteen hundred
miles on the coast of the Pacific ocean; and from that
ocean to the mountains of the Andes. During this period,
through a succession of twelve monarchs, the original
constitution, established by the first Inca, remained unaltered; and was at last overturned by an accident, which no
human wisdom could foresee or prevent.

For a more particular disquisition on the character and
institutions of this great Legislator, the Reader is referred
to a dissertation prefixed to the third Book.

Mama Oella is said to have invented many of the domestic arts, particularly that of making garments of cotton and other vegetable substances.

In the passage preceding this reference, I have alluded
to most of the traditions, relating to the manner of their
introducing themselves, and establishing their dominion.
In the remainder of the second, and through the whole of
the third Book, I have given what may be supposed a
probable narrative of their real origin and conduct. I have
thrown the episode into an epic form, and given it so considerable a place in the Poem, for the purpose of exhibiting *in action* the characters, manners and sentiments of
the different tribes of savages, that inhabit the mountains
of South-America.

In reviewing this part of my subject, I have to lament,
that so extraordinary and meritorious a Poem, as the
Araucana of don Alonso de Ercilla, of the sixteenth century, has never yet appeared in our language. The account
given of that work by Voltaire excited my curiosity at an
early day; as I conceived the manners and characters of
the mountain savages of Chile, as described by that
heroic Spaniard, must have opened a new field of Poetry,
rich with uncommon ornaments.

That elegant and concise sketch of it lately given to the
public by Mr. Hayley, has come into my hands, since I
have been writing these notes, and but a few days previ-

The hero heard, and thus the Power besought;
What arts unknown the wonderous blessings wrought?
What human skill, in that benighted age,
In savage souls could quell the barbarous rage?
With leagues of peace combine the wide domain?
And teach the virtues in their laws to reign?

Long is their story, said the Power divine,
The labours great and glorious the design;
And tho' to earthly minds, their actions rest,
By years obscured, in flowery fiction drest,
Yet my glad voice shall wake their honour'd name,
And give their virtues to immortal fame.

Led by his father's wars, in early prime,
Young Capac wander'd from a northern clime;
Along these shores, with livelier verdure gay,
Thro' fertile vales, the adventurous armies stray.
He saw the tribes unnumber'd range the plain,
And rival chiefs, by rage and slaughter, reign;
He saw the sires their dreadful Gods adore,
Their altars staining with their children's gore;
Yet mark'd their reverence for the Sun, whose beam
Proclaims his bounties and his power supreme;

---

ous to the Poem's being put to the press. Yet it gives me
reason to hope, with every friend of literature, that the
whole of that great work will ere long be presented to the
English Reader by the same hand.

It is usually presumed, that every Author must have
read all that have gone before him, at least on subjects
similar to what he attempts; yet the Lusiad of Camoens,
a Poem of great merit on the expedition of Gama, I had
sought for in vain in different parts of America, and even
sent to Europe without being able to obtain it; till, a few
days since, it came to hand in the majestic and spirited
translation of Mr. Mickle. The extensive and sublime objects opened to our view in a work which celebrates the
discovery of one part of the globe, may well be thought
worthy the contemplation of a writer, who endeavours to
trace the consequences of a similar event in another. Of
this I was before sensible; but these are not the only disadvantages that an Author, in a new country, and in moderate circumstances, must have to encounter. [Au.]

Alonso de Ercilla y Zuñiga (1533–94) wrote La Araucana, a
heroic poem in three parts. François Marie Arouet Voltaire
(1694–1778) was a French Enlightenment philosopher and prolific writer, much admired in Europe. William Hayley (1745–
1820) was an English poet. Luiz de Camoens (1524?–80), a Portuguese poet banished from Lisbon for falling in love with a
woman at court, wrote the Lusiad during his banishment. Thirty-
eight editions were published in Lisbon before 1700; William
Mickle (1735–88) published an English translation in 1775.

Who sails in happier skies, diffusing good,
Demands no victim and receives no blood.

In peace returning with his conquering sire,
Fair glory's charms his youthful soul inspire;
With virtue warm'd, he fix'd the generous plan,
To build his greatness on the bliss of man.

By nature formed to daring deeds of fame,
Tall, bold and beauteous rose his stately frame;
Strong moved his limbs, a mild majestic grace
Beam'd from his eyes and open'd in his face;
O'er the dark world his mind superior shone,
And, soaring, seem'd the semblance of the sun.
Now fame's prophetic visions lift his eyes,
And future empires from his labours rise;
Yet softer fires his daring views controul,
Sway the warm wish and fill the changing soul.
Shall the bright genius, kindled from above,
Bend to the milder, gentler voice of love;
That bounds his glories, and forbids to part
From that calm bower, that held his glowing heart?
Or shall the toils, imperial heroes claim,
Fire his bold bosom with a patriot flame?
Bid sceptres wait him on the distant shore?
And blest Oella meet his eyes no more?

Retiring pensive, near the wonted shade,
His unseen steps approach the beauteous maid.
Her raven-locks roll on her heaving breast,
And wave luxuriant round her slender waist,
Gay wreaths of flowers her lovely brows adorn,
And her white raiment mocks the pride of morn.
Her busy hand sustains a bending bough,
Where woolly clusters spread their robes of snow,
From opening pods, unbinds the fleecy store,
And culls her labours for the evening bower.
Her sprightly soul, by deep invention led,
Had found the skill to turn the twisting thread,
To spread the woof, the shuttle to command,
Till various garments graced her forming hand.
Here, while her thoughts with her own Capac rove,
O'er former scenes of innocence and love,
Through many a field his fancied dangers share,
And wait him glorious from the distant war;
Blest with the ardent wish, her glowing mind
A snowy vesture for the prince design'd;
She seeks the purest wool, to web the fleece,
The sacred emblem of returning peace.
Sudden his near approach her breast alarms;
He flew enraptured to her yielding arms,
And lost, dissolving in a softer name,

The distant empire and the fire of fame.
At length, retiring o'er the homeward field,
Their mutual minds to happy converse yield,
O'er various scenes of blissful life they ran,
When thus the warrior to the fair began.

Joy of my life, thou know'st my roving mind,
With these grim tribes, in dark abodes, confined,
With grief hath mark'd what vengeful passions sway
The bickering bands, and sweep the race away.
Where late my distant steps the war pursued,
The fertile plains grew boundless as I view'd;
Increasing nations trod the waving wild,
And joyous nature more delightful smiled.
No changing seasons there the flowers deform,
No dread volcano, and no mountain storm;
Rains ne'er invade, nor livid lightnings play,
Nor clouds obscure the radiant Power of day.
But, while the God, in ceaseless glory bright,
Rolls o'er the day and fires his stars by night,
Unbounded fulness flows beneath his reign,
Seas yield their treasures, fruits adorn the plain;
Warm'd by his beam, their mountains pour the flood,
And the cool breezes wake beneath the God.
My anxious thoughts indulge the great design,
To form those nations to a sway divine;
Destroy the rights of every dreadful Power,
Whose crimson altars glow with human gore;
To laws and mildness teach the realms to yield,
And nobler fruits to grace the cultured field.

But great, my charmer, is the task of fame,
The countless tribes to temper and to tame.
Full many a spacious wild my soul must see,
Spread dreary bounds between my joys and me;
And yon bright Godhead circle many a year;
Each lonely evening number'd with a tear.
Long robes of white[22] my shoulders must embrace,
To speak my lineage of etherial race;
That wondering tribes may tremble, and obey
The radiant offspring of the Power of day.

And when thro' cultured fields their bowers encrease,
And streams and plains survey the works of peace,

---

22. "As the art of spinning is said to have been invented by Oella; it is no improbable fiction, to suppose they first assumed these white garments of cotton, as an emblem of the sun; in order to inspire that reverence for their persons which was necessary to their success; and that such a dress should be continued in the family, as a badge of royalty." [Au.]

When these glad hands the rod of nations claim,
And happy millions bless thy Capac's name,
Then shall he feign a journey to the Sun,
To bring the partner of the peaceful throne;
So shall descending kings the line sustain,
And unborn ages bloom beneath their reign.

Will then my fair, in that delightful hour,
Forsake these wilds and hail a happier bower?
And now consenting, with approving smiles,
Bid the young warrior tempt the daring toils?
And, sweetly patient, wait the flight of days,
That crown our labours with immortal praise?

Silent the fair one heard; her moistening eye
Spoke the full soul, nor could her voice reply;
Till softer accents sooth'd her listening ear,
Composed her tumult and allay'd her fear.
Think not, enchanting maid, my steps would part,
While silent sorrows heave that tender heart:
More dear to me are blest Oella's joys,
Than all the lands that bound the bending skies;
Nor thou, bright Sun, should'st bribe my soul to rest,
And leave one struggle in her lovely breast.
Yet think in those vast climes, my gentle fair,
What hapless millions claim our guardian care;
How age to age leads on the dreadful gloom,
And rage and slaughter croud the untimely tomb;
No social joys their wayward passions prove,
Nor peace nor pleasure treads the savage grove;
Mid thousand heroes and a thousand fair,
No fond Oella meets her Capac there.
Yet, taught by thee each nobler joy to prize,
With softer charms the virgin race shall rise,
Awake new virtues, every grace improve,
And form their minds for happiness and love.

Behold, where future years, in pomp, descend,
How worlds and ages on thy voice depend!
And, like the Sun, whose all-delighting ray
O'er those mild borders sheds serenest day,
Diffuse thy bounties, give my steps to rove,
A few short months the noble task to prove,
And, swift return'd from glorious toils, declare
What realms submissive wait our fostering care.

And will my prince, my Capac, borne away,
Thro' those dark wilds, in quest of empire, stray?
Where tygers fierce command the howling wood,
And men like tygers thirst for human blood.
Think'st thou no dangerous deed the course attends?
Alone, unaided by thy sire and friends?

Even chains and death may meet my rover there,
Nor his last groan could reach Oella's ear.
But chains, nor death, nor groans shall Capac prove,
Unknown to her, while she has power to rove.
Close by thy side where'er thy wanderings stray,
My equal steps shall measure all the way;
With borrow'd soul each dire event I'll dare,
Thy toils to lessen and thy dangers share.

Command, blest chief, since virtue bids thee go
To rule the realms and banish human woe,
Command these hands two snowy robes to weave,
The Sun to mimic and the tribes deceive;
Then let us range, and spread the peaceful sway,
The radiant children of the Power of day.

The lovely counsel pleased. The smiling chief
Approved her courage and dispel'd her grief;
Then to the distant bower in haste they move,
Begin their labours and prepare to rove.

Soon grow the robes beneath her forming care,
And the fond parents wed the noble pair;
But, whelm'd in grief, beheld, the approaching dawn,
Their joys all vanish'd, and their children gone.
Nine changing days, thro' southern wilds, they stray'd,
Now wrapp'd in glooms, now gleaming thro' the glade,
Till the tenth morning, with an orient smile,
Beheld them blooming in the happy isle.
The toil begins; to every neighbouring band,
They speak the message and their faith demand;
With various art superior powers display,
To prove their lineage and confirm their sway.
The astonish'd tribes behold with glad surprize,
The Gods descended from the favouring skies;
Adore their persons, robed in shining white,
Receive their laws and leave each horrid rite;
Build with assisting toil, the golden throne,
And hail and bless the sceptre of the Sun.

Philip Freneau (1752–1832)

Philip Freneau was born into a successful Manhattan tradesman's family, so as a young man, he was the recipient of many advantages, including an education with tutors and then at the College of New Jersey (now Princeton University). At age fifteen, when Freneau entered college, he became the associate of young men from the leading families of all the British colonies of North America, including James Madison, Freneau's roommate, who would become president one day. Like many men of his generation, Freneau was interested in the arts and sciences, and he was trained to considered belletristic writing a high art. But as it was for Benjamin Franklin, so it was for Philip Freneau—writing poems would not necessarily pay the bills, as Franklin's father had told the young Franklin. When he finished college, Freneau became a teacher.

Through family connections, Freneau was offered a position as secretary on a plantation in the West Indies in 1776, and he accepted it. He sailed to Santa Cruz that year and remained in his job for three years. He loved the islands, the landscape and peoples, but he was deeply troubled by witnessing the injustices of the plantation slave economy, which bought luxury for a few based on the submission, efforts, and struggles of enslaved people. He returned home in 1778 and enlisted as a seaman on a blockade-running ship during the Revolutionary War against Britain. When his ship was captured, Freneau was treated brutally while he was imprisoned on board a prison ship held by the British. After he was freed from his incarceration, and after he had recovered from these wartime ordeals—his family had feared for his life when they first saw him after his release—Freneau worked in the post office in Philadelphia and wrote repeatedly and rapidly for newspapers and magazines. He edited the *Freemans Journal* and wrote stunning verse supporting the American Revolution and archly satirizing anyone who could support Great Britain. Yet the seafaring life called to Freneau, and he went to sea again, this time as a merchant shipman in the mid-1780s. He returned in 1791 to the offer of a position from Thomas Jefferson, then secretary of state, to work as a translator in his department. Freneau took the post, and he took on the editorship of the *National Gazette* as well. He used the newspaper to support the French Revolution and its vaunted democracy and to critique Federalist policies and Federalism's major supporters, President George Washington and Alexander Hamilton.

Shortly after Jefferson resigned his office, the *National Gazette* stopped publication, Freneau left Philadelphia and spent the next decades alternating his activities among the shipping trade, newspaper editing in New Jersey and New York, and farming his father's land in New Jersey, which he had inherited. The summary of Freneau's career attests to his difficulty staying with any laboring position for long. Freneau failed to make his farming produce an income sufficient to sustain him, and he ended up selling off parcels of his father's land to avoid running into debt. He finally decided to apply to the federal government for the pension owed him for his efforts during the American Revolution. He died in penury.

Despite his dwindling resources and his continual change of posts, Freneau wrote an abundance of verse of various kinds—satires, lyrics, odes, and ditties—and a voluminous amount of journalism, particularly political journalism. His themes ranged from a romanticized and nostalgic sense of the loss of a whole way of life shared by Native Americans to the difficulties and injustices endured by slaves to the loss of personal liberty for citizens because of a federal system that supported the interests of the rich on the backs of laboring people everywhere. His liberal attitudes shifted over time, especially as he hit hard times in his own life, but his poems are memorable for Freneau's linguistic variation and for the sense of beauty, the feelings of indignation and alienation, or the sentiments of sympathy that he, at various times, attempted to evoke in his readers.

ACCOUNT OF THE ISLAND OF SANTA CRUZ, CONTAINING AN ORIGINAL POEM ON THE BEAUTIES OF THAT ISLAND[1]

As I resided a considerable time on the island of Santa Cruz, it is but natural I should say something concerning it. The appearance of this island, as you approach it from the ocean, is inexpressibly beautiful. The whole isle is divided into square plantations cutting each other every way at right angles. The verdure of the canes, which are of a most lively green, affords a pleasure to the eye which is not so striking in any northern country. Santa Cruz is about 28 or 30 miles in length from east to west; and at most is not more than 4 miles broad, and in general much less: The latitude of this most delicious island is 17: 50 N., its longitude between 63 and 64 West—Although in a clear sky you may see several other islands from this, yet there are no soundings between, and when you are but a mile from the shore the sea appears as blue and bottomless as any part of the main ocean; but at the distance of half a mile from the land and inwards you can see the bottom with the greatest perspicuity, which is of a fine bright sand, and various kinds of fish sporting above it, some the

most beautiful that the eye ever beheld, particularly the angel fish, which is streaked over with circles near half an inch in breadth, which glow with all the lustre of the most brilliant diamond.

From this island as I mentioned before, you have a prospect of several others in clear weather, viz. the east end of Porto Rico, and in particular Cape Malapasco—2. St. Thomas, St. John, Tortola, and the Virgin Gorda, these being some of the Virgin islands—you may also see Boriquain, otherwise Crab Island, not far from Porto Rico.— There are two towns on St. Cruz, Bassend or Bassin, so called formerly by the French, *i.e.* Bason, in respect to the harbour, and a smaller town at the west end called by the Danes Frederickstadt; at the other is Christianstadt. Bassend is situate upon a pretty level spot at the foot of a mountain close to the water side; it may contain 5 or 600 houses, some of them very handsome buildings of stone, but in general of wood—The harbour is defended from the sea by a continued reef of rocks upon which the sea breaks with a continual roar. There are only two narrow passages through this reef into the harbour, one for ships, the other for sloops and vessels of a moderate draught of water. This harbour will contain 2 or 300 sail of vessels, and is always as smooth as a mill-pond, with excellent anchoring ground in one, two, three, or four fathoms, but not much more, I believe. Within the harbour is a small island containing three or four acres of ground, upon which is built an elegant edifice for the use of the king's pilot, who

---

1. Published in the *United States Magazine,* February 1779.

keeps his look-out from hence for all vessels that heave in sight. The pilot is here a man of consequence, being ranked as a king's officer, and keeps only one small sloop-rigged boat with a deputy, who, with three or four Negroes, conducts all the business: There is a town wharf here, but not water enough for any thing but boats to come along side; all the shipping are obliged to lie at anchor. Within a stone throw of this wharf to the eastward stands a handsome fort, called Christianswaern, which commands the whole harbour. Bassend is twelve miles from the most eastwardly part of the island, and as well as Frederickstadt, is situated upon the north side. From this town up to the east end the island is generally laid out in plantations of cotton, or else pasture lands for keeping mules, sheep, neat cattle and the like: But when you travel from Bassend down towards the west, the scene is inexpressibly charming, and even those that have no taste to admire the beauties of nature would at the view be forced to confess that the vales of Paradise were now displayed in their primaeval beauty. From the summits of the hills which rise with an easy ascent, you look forward as far as the eye can reach over the most enchanting plains and little vallies. On the right hand towards the north are high mountains bordering on the sea covered with wood. To use the words of Milton,

"Mountains on whose barren breast,
The labouring clouds do often rest."[2]

Towards the south the land slopes away with a gentle descent towards the sea, which you have in sight all the way. The square plantations of sugar cane with their regular intervals; the tall cocoa-nut trees, with the planters' habitations surrounded with orange and other fruit trees; the exact straightness of the road and the charming mildness of the climate give one the idea of an inchanted island, or such as we read of in romance—Too much cannot be said of the happy climate of this and the neighbouring islands: The sky is ever serene and unclouded in comparison to that of the northern countries; there are never any heavy continued rains; the land is watered by gentle showers, and it is the rarest thing in the world to lose sight of the sun for two hours together after he is above the horizon. The days and nights are pretty equally divided, each never being much more or less than twelve hours. From ten o'clock in the morning till four in the afternoon the heat

is somewhat troublesome, but even then you are fanned with a brisk dry wind always from the eastward, which renders it at least tolerable. The evenings and nights are cool and refreshing. The moon and stars shine with an extraordinary brightness, owing I suppose to their reflection on the water of the ocean, which surrounds these happy lands. The town at the west end is but mean and ordinary, consisting of a fort, and perhaps 80 or 90 wooden houses. The harbour is nothing but an open road, where however ships lie in the utmost security at their moorings, the bottom being good for anchorage, and the wind always offshore. About two miles to the eastward of this town along the sea shore is the estate of capt. Hanson, into which the sea has formed a beautiful little bay, called Buttler's Bay, about 100 yards across; it has a sandy shore and an excellent landing, though all the rest of the shore is sharp craggy rocks. My agreeable residence at this place, for above two years off and on during the wars in America, renders the idea of it but too pleasing, and makes me feel much the same anxiety at a distance from it as Adam did after he was banished from the bowers of Eden.

The only disagreeable circumstance attending this island, which it has in common with the rest, is the cruel and detestable slavery of the Negroes. "If you have tears prepare to shed them now."[3] A description of the slavery they endure would be too irksome and unpleasant to me; and to those who have not beheld it, would be incredible. Sufficient be it to say, that no class of mankind in the known world undergo so complete a servitude as the common Negroes in the West-Indies. It casts a shade over the native charms of the country; it blots out the beauties of the eternal spring which Providence has there ordained to reign, and amidst all the profusion of bounties which nature has scattered, the brightness of heaven, the mildness of the air, and the luxuriancy of the vegetable kingdom, it leaves me melancholy and disconsolate, convinced that there is no pleasure in this world without its share of pain. And thus the earth, which, were it not for the lust of pride and dominion, might be an earthly paradise, is, by the ambition and overbearing nature of mankind, rendered an eternal scene of desolation, woe, and horror; the weak goes to the wall, while the strong

---

2. Lines from "L'Allegro," published in the 1645 *Poems* by John Milton (1608–74).

3. The line was used twice in British verse drama of the earlier eighteenth century: Act 3 of William Davenant's and John Dryden's *The Tragedy of Julius Caesar, with the Death of Brutus and Cassius* (1719), and Act 5 of John Sheffield's *The Tragedy of Julius Caesar* (1723).

prevails; and after our ambitious phrenzy has turned the world upside down, we are contented with a narrow spot, and leave our follies and cruelties to be acted over again, by every succeeding generation. But to return: the only natural failing I know of here is the hurricanes, which are storms of wind that blow with an inconceivable fury, and often carry away all before them. They are so much the more dangerous, as they do not blow steadily from one point, but often go round the compass in less than half an hour. There are melancholy remains in Santa Cruz of the havoc they made in 1772. There was also one on Sept. 7, 1776, while I was on the island. It exceeded any thing I had ever seen before, but however did not do much damage, the strongest of it not lasting above six hours. I believe the best thing I can do with the rest of this paper is to transcribe a few dull heavy lines which I composed near two years ago on the spot.

Sick of thy northern glooms, come shepherd seek
Less rigorous climes, and a more friendly sky:
Why shouldst thou toil amidst that frozen ground,
Where half year snows a barren prospect lie?

When thou mayst go where never frost was seen,
Or north-west winds with cutting fury blow;
Where never ice congeal'd the limpid stream,
Where never mountain crown'd its head with snow.

Two weeks, with prospersous gales, thy barque shall bear
To isles that flourish in perpetual green,
Where richest herbage glads each shady vale,
And ever-verdant plants on every hill are seen.

Nor dread the dangers of the billowy deep:
Autumnal gales shall safely waft thee o'er:
Put off the timid heart, or man unblest,
Ne'er shalt thou reach this gay enchanting shore.

So some dull minds, in spite of age and care,
Are grown so wedded to this globe below,
They never wish to cross death's dusky main
That parting them and happiness, doth flow.

Tho' reason's voice must whisper *to the soul*
That nobler climes for man the Gods design.
Come shepherd haste the rising breezes blow:
No more the slumbering winds thy barque confine.

From the vast caverns of *old* Ocean's bed,
St. Cruz arising laves her humed waist:
The threatening waters roar on every side;
For every side by ocean is embrac'd.

Sharp craggy rocks repel the surging brine,
Whose cavern'd sides by restless ocean wore,
Resemblance claim to that remoter isle,
Where once the prince of winds the sceptre bore.

Betwixt the Tropick and the Midway Line,
In happiest climate lies this envy'd isle;
Trees bloom throughout the year, flowers ever blow,
And fragment Flora wears a lasting smile.

No lowering skies are here; the neighbouring sun,
Clear and unveil'd his brilliant journey goes;
Each morn emerging from the azure main,
And sinking there each evening to repose.

In June's fair month, the spangled traveller gains
The utmost limits of his northern way,
And blesses with his beams cold lands remote,
Sad Greenland's coast and Hudson's frozen bay.

The shivering swains of those unhappy climes
Behold the mid-way monarch thro' the trees:
We feel his friendly heat, his zenith beams
Temper'd with cooling showers and trade-wind breeze.

No threatening tides upon our island rise:
Gay Cynthia[4] scarce disturbs the ocean here:
No waves approach her orb, and she as kind
Attracts no water to her silver sphere.

The happy waters boast, of various kinds,
Unnumber'd myriads of the scaly race:
Sportive they play above the delug'd sand,
(Gay as their clime) in ocean's ample vase.

Some streak'd with burnish'd gold resplendent glare;
Some cleave the limpid deep all silver'd o'er;
Some clad in living green delight the eye;
Some red, some blue, of mingled colours more.

Here glides the spangled dolphin through the deep;
Here bulky, spouting whales more distant stray;
The huge green turtles wallow through the wave,
Well pleas'd alike with land or water they.

The rainbow cuts the deep of varied green;
The well fed grouper lurks remote below;
The swift bonetta swims and flies by turns;
The diamond coated angels kindle as they go.

Delicious to the taste, salubrious food,
Which might some frugal Samian sage allure,
To curse the fare of his abstemious school,
And turn for once a cheerful Epicure!

---

4. In Roman mythology, the goddess of the moon.

Hail, verdant isle! through thy dark woods I rove,
And learn the nature of each native tree—
The rustic hard, the poisonous manchineal,
Which for its fragrant apple pleaseth thee.

Enticing to the smell, fair to the eye,
But deadly poison in the taste is found:
O shun the dangerous fruit, nor taste, like Eve
This interdicted fruit in Eden's ground.

The lowly mangrove fond of wat'ry soil;
The white bark'd gregory rising high in air;
The mastic in the woods you may descry;
Tamarinds and lofty plumb trees flourish there.

Sweet orange groves in lonely vallies rise,
And drop their fruits unnotic'd and unknown:
The cooling acid limes in hedges grow;
The juicy lemons swell in shades their own.

Sweet spungy plumbs on trees wide spreading hang;
The happy flavour'd pine grows crested from the
    ground;
Plump grenadillo's and guava's small,
With melons in each wood and lawn abound.

The conic form'd cashew, of juicy kind,
Which bears at once an apple and a nut;
Whose poison coat indignant to the lips,
Doth in its cell a wholesome kernel shut.

The plaintain and banana flourish here,
Of hasty growth, and love to fix their root,
Where some soft stream of ambling water goes,
To give full moisture to their clustered fruit.

No other trees so vast a leaf can boast,
So broad, so long—through these refresh'd I stray;
And tho' fierce Sol[5] his beams directly shed,
Those friendly leaves shall shade me all the way.

And tempt the cooling breeze to hasten there,
With its sweet odorous breath to charm the grove,
High shades and cooling air, while underneath,
A little stream by mossy banks doth rove.

Where once the indian dames inchanted slept,
Or fondly kiss'd the moon light eves away:
The lovers fled, the tearful stream remains,
And only I console it with my lay.

Pomegranates grace yon vale, and sweet-sops there

Ready to fall, require thy helping hand;
Nor yet neglect the papaw or mammee,
Whose slighted trees with fruit unheeded stand.

Those shaddocks juicy shall thy taste delight;
And yon high fruits that over-top the wood,
And cling in clusters to the mother tree—
The cocoa nut, rich milky healthful food.

Cassada shrubs abound, whose poison root,
Supplies the want of snow-white northern flour:
This grated fine, and steep'd in water fair,
Forsakes each particle of noxious power.

But the chief, the glory of these Indian isles,
Springs from the sweet uncloving sugar cane:
Hence comes the planter's wealth: Hence commerce
    sends
Such floating piles beyond the western main.

Who'er thou art, that leav'st thy native shore,
And shalt to fair West-India climates come,
Taste not the enchanting plant—to taste forbear,
If ever thou wouldst reach thy much-lov'd home.

Ne'er through the isle permit thy feet to rove,
Or if thou dost, let prudence lead the way;
Forbear to taste the magic sugar-cane;
Forebear to taste what will complete thy stay.

Whoever sips of this inchanting juice—
Delicious nectar, fit for Jove's own hall,
Returns no more from his lov'd Santa Cruz,
But quits his friends, his country, and his all.

And thinks no more of home—Ulysses[6] so
Dragg'd off by force, his sailors from that shore,
Where Lotos grew; and had not force prevailed,
They never would have sought their country more.

No annual toil inters this juicy plant,
The stalks lopp'd off, the fresh'ning showers prolong,
To future years, unfading and secure,
The root so vig'rous, and the juice so strong.

On yonder peaked hill fresh harvests rise,
Where wretched he—the Ethiopian swain,
Oft o'er the ocean turns his wishful eyes,
To isles remote high luming o'er the main.

He pants a land of freedom and repose,
Where cruel slavery never sought to reign.

---

5. The sun.

6. Ulysses, hero of Homer's *Odyssey,* had to drag off his sailors from a lovely island coast because they ate lotus blossoms and did not want to sail farther.

O quit thee them, my muse, and tell me why
You abject trees lie scatter'd o'er the plain?

These climes, lest nature should have been too kind,
And man have sought his happiest heaven below,
Are torn with mighty winds, fierce hurricanes,
Nature convuls'd in every form of woe.

Scorn not yon lonely vale of trees to rest:
There plaintain groves late grew of lovely green—
The orange flourish'd and the lemon bore—
The genius of the isle dwelt there unseen.

Wild were the skies, affrighted nature groan'd,
As though approach'd the last decisive day—
Skies blaz'd around, and bellowing winds had nigh
Dislodg'd those cliffs and tore those hills away.

And how, alas! could these fair trees withstand,
The killing fury of so fierce a blast,
That storm'd along the plain, seiz'd every grove,
And delug'd with a sea yon mournful waste?

But now the winds are past, the storm subsides,
All nature smiles again serenely gay,
The beauteuous groves renew'd—how shall I leave
My green retreat at Butler's verdant bay.

Fain would I view my native climes again,
But murder marks the cruel Briton there—
Contented here I rest, in spite of pain,
And quaff the enlivening juice in spite of care.

Winter and winter's gloom are far remov'd,
Eternal spring with smiling summer join'd.
Absence and death, or heart carroding care,
Why should they cloud the sunshine of the mind?

The drowsy pelican wings home his way,
The misty night sits heavy on the sea,
Yon lagging sail drags slowly o'er the main.
Night and its kindred glooms are nought to me.

To-morrow's sun new paints the faded scene;
Though deep in ocean sink his western beams,
His spangled chariot shall ascend more clear,
More radiant from the drowsy land of dreams.

Then shepherd haste, and leave behind thee far,
Thy bloody plains and iron glooms above,
Quit thy cold northern star, and here enjoy.
Beneath the smiling skies this land of love.

Soon shall the genius of the fertile soil,
A new creation to thy view unfold,
Admire the works of nature's liberal hand,
And scorn that vulgar bait, all-potent gold.

Yet if persuaded by no lay of mine,
You still admire your climes of frost and snow,
And pleas'd prefer above our southern groves,
The darksome forests that around thee grow,—

Still there remain—thy native air enjoy,
Repel the tyrant who thy peace invades,
While pleas'd I trace the vales of Santa Cruz,
And sing with rapture her inspiring shades.

THE PROPHECY OF KING TAMMANY[1]

THE Indian chief who, fam'd of yore,
Saw Europe's sons advent'ring here,
    Look'd sorrowing to the crowded shore,
    And sighing dropt a tear:
He saw them half his world explore,
He saw them draw the shining blade,
He saw their hostile ranks display'd,
And cannons blazing thro' that shade
    Where only peace was known before.

"Ah, what unequal arms!" he cry'd,
How art thou fall'n, my country's pride,
    The rural, sylvan reign!
Far from our pleasing shores to go
To western rivers, winding slow,—
Is this the boon the gods bestow?
What have we done, great patrons, say,
That strangers seize our woods away,
    And drive us naked from our native plain!

Rage and revenge inspire my soul,
And passion burns without controul;
    Hence, strangers, to your native shore!
Far from our Indian shades retire,
Remove these *gods* that vomit fire,
    And stain with blood these ravag'd glades no more.

In vain I weep, in vain I sigh,
These strangers all our arms defy,
As they advance our chieftains die!—

---

1. Tammany, the common British name for a renowned Lenape, Tamanend, was often appropriated at this time for the creation of political or social messages, and a Society of the Sons of Saint Tammany was formed in Philadelphia. Published in *Freeman's Journal* on December 11, 1782.

What can their hosts oppose?
The bow has left its wonted spring,
The arrow faulters on the wing,
Nor carries ruin from the string
   To end their being and our woes:

Yes, yes,—I see our nation bends;
The gods no longer are our friends,
   But why these weak complaints and sighs?
Are there not gardens in the west,
Where all our far fam'd Sachems rest?—
I'll go, an unexpected guest,
   And the dark horrors of the way despise.

Ev'n now the thundering peals draw nigh,
'Tis theirs to triumph, ours to die!
But mark me, Christian, ere I go—
Thou too shalt have thy share of woe,
The time rolls on, not moving slow,
When hostile squadrons for your blood shall come,
   And ravage all your shore!
Your warriors and your children slay,
And some in dismal dungeons lay,
Or lead them captive far away
   To climes unknown, thro' seas untry'd before.

When struggling long, at last with pain
You break a cruel tyrant's chain,
That never shall be join'd again,
   When half your foes are homeward fled,
   And hosts on hosts in triumph led,
   And hundreds maim'd and thousands dead,
   A timid race shall then succeed,
Shall slight the virtues of the firmer race,
That brought your tyrant to disgrace,
Shall give your honours to an odious train,
Who shun'd all conflicts on the main
And dar'd no battles on the bloody plain,
   Whose little souls sunk in the gloomy day
   When *virtue only* could support the fray
And sunshine friends kept off—or ran away."

So spoke the chief, and rais'd his funeral pyre—
   Around him soon the crackling flames ascend;
He smil'd amid the fervours of the fire
   To think his troubles were so near their end,
Till the freed soul, her debt to nature paid,
Rose from the ashes that her prison made,
And sought the world unknown, and dark oblivion's
    shade.

———

LINES WRITTEN AT
THE PALLISADES,

Near Port-Royal, in the Island of Jamaica—
September, 1784[1]

HERE, by the margin of the murmuring main,
While her proud remnants I explore in vain,
Though abject now, *Port Royal* claims a sigh,
Nor shall the muse the unenvied gift deny.

   Of all the towns that grac'd Jamaica's isle,
This was her glory, and the proudest pile;
Where toils on toils bade wealth's gay structures rise,
And commerce swell'd that glory to the skies:
St. Jago seated on a distant plain,
Ne'er saw the tall ship entering from the main;
Unnotic'd streams her *Cobre's* margin lave
Where yon' tall plaintains cool her glowing wave,
And burning sands, or rock-surrounded hill
Confess its founder's fears—or want of skill.

   While o'er these wastes with pensive step I go,
Past scenes of death return with all their woe,—
Here opening gulphs confess'd the Almighty hand,[2]
Here, the dark ocean roll'd across the land;
Here, domes on domes a moment tore away—
Here, crowds on crowds in mingled ruin lay,
Whom fate scarce gave to end their noon-day feast,
Or time to call the sexton or the priest.

   Where you proud barque, with all her ponderous load,
Commits her anchor to its dark abode;
Eight fathoms down, where unseen waters flow
To quench the sulphur of the caves below;
There, midnight sounds torment the sailor's ear,
And drums and fifes play drowsy concerts there;
Dull songs of woe prevent the hours of sleep,
While fancy hears the fiddlers of the deep.

   What now is left of all thy boasted pride;
Lost are thy splendours that were spread so wide;
A spit of sand is thine, by fate's decree,
And mouldering mounds that scarce oppose the sea;

---

1. Published in the *Columbian Herald* on February 2, 1786.

2. "June 7, 1692." [Au.]

No sprightly lads, or gay, bewitching maids
Walk on these wastes, or wander in these shades;
To other shores past time beheld them go,
And some are fiddling in the groves below:—
A negro tribe but ill their place supply,
With bending back, short hair, and downcast eye,—
A feeble rampart guards the wretched town
Where banish'd *Tories*[3] come to seek renown,—
Where worn-out slaves their drams of gin retail,
And hungry Scotsmen watch the distant sail.

To these dull scenes with eager haste I came
To find some reliques in this sink of fame—
Not worth the search, what domes are left to fall,
Guns, fires, and earthquakes shall destroy them all.
Where shall I go, what *Lethe*[4] shall I find,
To drink these dark ideas from my mind!—
A tatter'd roof o'er every hut appears,
And mouldering brick-work prompts the stranger's
     fears:
A church without a priest I grieve to see,
Grass round its door, and rust upon its key;
One only inn, with weary search I found,
Where parson *Lovegrog* deal'd the porter round,
And gay *Quadroons*[5] their *killing* glances stole,
Watch'd at the bar, or drain'd the passing bowl.

K.

THE ISLAND FIELD NEGRO[1]

[*Written some years ago, on a
Sugar Plantation in Jamaica.*]

IF there exists a Hell, (the case is clear,)
Sir *Toby's* slaves enjoy that portion here:
Here are no burning brimstone lakes, 'tis true,

But kindled rum, full often burns as blue;
In which some fiend, half serious, half in jest,
Steeps *Toby's* name, and brands poor Cudjoe's breast.

Here whips on whips excite a thousand fears,
And mingled howlings vibrate through my ears;
Here Nature's plagues abound, of all degrees,
Snakes, scorpions, despots, lizards, centipedes—
No art, no care escapes the busy lash,
All have their dues, and paid in ready cash:
The lengthy cart-whip guards this tyrant's reign,
And cracks, like pistols from the fields of cane.
Ye powers that form'd these wretched tribes relate,
What have they done to merit such a fate!—
Why were they brought from Eboe's sultry waste
To see the plenty that they must not taste?
Food which they cannot buy, and dare not steal;
Yams and potatoes—many a scanty meal!

One with a gibbet wakes his negroe's fears,
One to the wind-mill nails him by the ears;
One keeps his slave in dismal dens unfed,
One puts the wretch in pickle, ere he's dead;
This, to a tree suspends him by the thumbs,
That, from his table grudges even crumbs!

O'er yon rough hills a tribe of females go,
Each with her gourd, her infant, and her hoe,
Scorch'd by a sun, that has no mercy here,
Driven by a devil, that men call *Overseer:*
In chains twelve wretches to their labor haste,
Thrice twelve I see with iron collars grac'd—
Are these the joys that flow from vast domains,
Is gold thus got, Sir Toby, worth your pains;
Who would your wealth on terms like these possess,
Where all we see is pregnant with distress?—

Talk not of blossoms, and your endless spring,
No joy to me these scenes of misery bring,
Hell's Picture, I this rich plantation call;
And you the Beezlebub[2]—that rule it all.

---

3. People who wished to remain loyal to the British Crown during the American Revolution against Great Britain.

4. In Greek mythology, the river of forgetfulness in Hades.

5. A person of one-fourth African ancestry.

1. Published in the *Daily Advertiser,* on February 1, 1791, with the dateline, "January 31" at its conclusion. Freneau used the image of a fat Sir Toby, a generalized British figure of self-satisfaction, in several poems.

2. The devil.

SPEECH OF THE INDIAN HEAD OF THE SHIP *DELAWARE*[1]

[All our curious dock-walkers must have taken notice of the fine Indian head of the ship Delaware, belonging to this port. Whether it was from a late attentive survey of that figure (which is a model of perfection in its kind) or from what other cause I know not, but upon my retiring to rest a few nights ago, I no sooner fell asleep, than I imagined myself standing upon one of the wharves, with the carved Indian figure full in my front; when it instantly assumed the mien and attitude of an orator, and with a menacing frown, uttered the following speech to a crowd that had collected upon this extraordinary occasion.]

"I have every reason to believe, gentlemen, that I was placed here as the emblem of valor, activity, perseverance, industry, and cunning. So far, therefore, have your countrymen testified in favour of an opinion, almost universally exploded, that the inhabitants of the western forests have some affinity with the human species. I wish they had gone a little farther, and in their general conduct towards our tribes, in peace and war, treated us as being possessed of reason, and practicing some few of the inferior virtues. Alas, it is too evident from their actions, that they place us upon a footing, with the beasts of the wilderness, and consider an Indian and a buffaloe as alike entitled by nature to property or possession.

"My heart bleeds within me, when I reflect upon the wrongs of my countrymen, the insignificant rank they appear to hold in the scale of animated being, and their probable extirpation from the continent of America.

"Nature is cruel in all her works. She successively destroys not only the individuals of a species, but at certain periods a whole class of a species; nay, even the species itself sometimes totally disappears. This cruel mother is nevertheless so merciful, as, for the most part, to bring about such events imperceptibly and gradually. Why then would you anticipate her designs, and by every means in your power hurry us in a moment from this earth, before Nature has said, there is an end to the children of the forest?

"Our habitations were once on the borders of the rivers of the ocean, and in the pleasant vicinity of its shores. The sails of Columbus, and Cabot, and Raleigh appeared. With grief we saw your superior skill, your surprising preeminence in art, your machines of death, before which our arrows and darts were no more than the toys of children. In dread of your superior power, we retreated from the shore to the Allegany to the Ohio; we have bid an everlasting adieu to the pleasant land of Kentucky; you have at length followed us over the Ohio—you meditate to drive us beyond the Mississippi—to the lake of the woods—to the frozen deserts of the north, and to the regions of darkness and desolation. But, how unreasonable, how cruel, are your designs! Compelling us to remove farther into the forests is the same to us as death and ruin. We must there fight for the possession of the soil, before we can hunt in safety, as independent possessors; and as we retreat before you, remember, that foes of our own colour and kindred increase upon us, like swarms from the hollow tree—nations, extremely tenacious of their hunting grounds, less enervated with your baneful liquors than ourselves, and consequently more warlike, more robust, and even gods, in comparison to the feeble tribes who yet exist between you and them.

"You detest us for having the feelings of men; you despise, in us, the virtues of patriotism, so natural to all mankind, and so extolled by yourselves. But what were your feelings, when, only a few years ago, the great king on the other side of the water, intruded upon your rights? You filled the world with your clamours—heaven and earth were called to witness, that you were determined to defend those rights which had been bestowed upon you by the Great Man above, and for the preservation of which you prayed him to smile upon your warfare. He heard your prayers, and you were successful: the enemy retired with shame, and your warfare was crowned with an honourable peace.

"You yourselves are now, in your turn, become the oppressors. Do not blame us, then, for possessing the same feelings with yourselves, on the same occasion. Your desperation carried all before it: and why should not ours do the same, when we are obliged to act against you, from the same motives?

"Say not, that you have purchased our territory. Was a keg of whiskey, some bundles of laced coats, or a few packages of blankets, an equivalent for the extent of a kingdom? or was a bargain with some drunken chiefs, of one or two nations, an obligation upon an hundred tribes?

"How much do you stand in your own light, you free white men of America? How are you duped by the deep and designing! Not a single soldier need be sent to act offensively in the Indian country. Our commercial intercourse with you would effectually destroy us as fast as you could advance your frontier by cultivation and natu-

---

1. First published in the *American Museum,* March 1792.

ral population. Your neighborhood is death to us. We cannot exist among you—but suffer us, we beseech you, to disappear gradually from this miserable stage of human existence, and not, like a taper, by a sudden blast, be extinguished in a moment!

"You have, at different times, been at much expense in sending among us religious missionaries to effect our conversion to your faith. I wish those gentlemen had been as assiduous in inculcating the practice of the moral and social virtues as they were busy with pestering us with mysteries. They have, however, said enough upon the virtue of temperance, to persuade us not to destroy ourselves with rum, brandy, or New England whiskey, during the remainder of the present century. These good men have now quit us entirely, and given us up to the God of nature—you send armies in their room, not to convert, but to destroy us; to burn our towns, and turn us out naked to the mercy of the elements; to shoot us down, wherever they can see us, and propagate a principle as disgraceful to your pretended age of philosophy, as it is repugnant to truth and reason, *that the rights of an Indian are not the rights of a man!*—"

Being suddenly awakened by the yelpings of a spaniel, that constantly sleeps at the foot of my bed, I lost the remainder of this extraordinary speech.

ON DEBORAH GANNET[1]

The American heroine, who on Tuesday last presented a petition to Congress, for a pension in consideration of services rendered during the whole of the late war, in the character of a common soldier, in the regular armies of America.

Ye Congress-men, and men of weight,
   Who fill the public chairs,
Who many a favour have conferr'd,
   On men unknown to Mars—
      And ye, that on the lofty bench
   Decide by vote our great affairs,
    Ah, turn a calm attentive ear
      To *her,* who never war did fear—
        —Relieve this gallant wench.

With the same generous heat inspir'd
   As Joan of Arc,[2] of old;
With zeal against the Briton fir'd,
   A spirit warm and bold,
She march'd to meet her country's foes.
      Disguis'd in man's attire—
   Where'er they fled, through field or town,
   With steady step she follow'd on,
   Resolv'd fair Freedom to maintain
   She met them on the embattled plain,
      And hurl'd the blasting fire.

Oh!—for such generous toils endur'd,
   So many dangers run,
In life's decline at length reward,
   This gallant Amazon,
Who for no splendid pension sues,
   She asks no proud triumphal car,
No pompous flattery of the muse,
   No pageantries of war,

But something in the wane of days
   To cheer her heart and keep her warm;
A cottage—such as I would raise,
   To guard her from the storm;
And whate'er else in Reason's view
   Your bounty may afford,
To her who did our foes pursue
   With bayonet, gun and sword.

Reflect—how many tender ties
   A woman must forego
Ere to the field of war she flies,
   To meet a savage foe—
How many bars has nature plac'd,
   And custom many more
That women never should be grac'd,
   With honours won from war.
All these she nobly overcame,
   And taught by reason sage,
Check'd not her military flame,
   But scorn'd a censuring age,
And men that with contracted mind,
   All arrogant, condemn
And make disgrace in woman kind,
   What honour is in them.

---

1. Deborah Gannet dressed as a man and joined the militias during the American Revolution against Great Britain. When the war was over, she asked for a pension like that given other soldiers, with whom she had served. The poem was published under an editorial heading—"A soldier should be made of sterner stuff!"—in the *Time-Piece* on December 4, 1797.

2. Joan of Arc (1412–31), said to have had divine inspiration, led the French against the English in several battles, defeating them in the battle over Orléans in 1429. She was captured by the English, sold to allies of her enemies, and burned at the state as a heretic at Roven.

WILLIAM HILL BROWN (1765–1793)

William Hill Brown, reputedly the first published novelist in British America, was probably introduced early to the literary life by a relative, Catharine Byles, who saw that some of his writings reached print. He was born into the home of a clock maker and carver in Boston and probably spent his youth working sometimes in his father's clock-making shop and more often with books, under the direction of Byles or a local schoolmaster. Brown's writings—poems, dramatic works, and novels—make it clear that Brown knew most of the then well-known writers of his day in Boston and that he was well read in classical, English, and American writings. It is clear, too, that like many of his generation, Brown wanted the new United States to have a national literature and believed a conscious effort could be made to create such a literature. In *The Power of Sympathy,* his first novel, Brown cited Noah Webster, Joel Barlow, and Timothy Dwight, three of the most admired scholar-poets of his day.

Brown began his publishing career in April 1787, with the printing of a poem related to the uprising called Shays's Rebellion in the *Massachusetts Centinel.* Brown continued to write and publish poetry and drama throughout his brief life. Indeed, shortly after *The Power of Sympathy* reached print in 1789, Brown published (also with Isaiah Thomas) a ballad opera called *The Better Sort: Or, The Girl of Spirit, An Operatical, Comical Farce.* The year 1789, then, was probably the high point in his publishing career, but Brown nonetheless continued to write sporadically. He published literary and political essays in Boston's *Columbian Centinel* from September to December 1790, under the title "The Yankee." In 1792, he moved from New England to the home of his married sister, Elizabeth Brown Hinchborne, in Murfreesborough, North Carolina. Although his sister died (from complications in pregnancy) in January 1793, Brown stayed on in North Carolina to study law with General William Richardson Davie in Halifax, North Carolina. Indeed, his last publication—called "Education" and signed "Columbus" in the *North Carolina Journal* on July 10, 1793—supported a movement of which his legal mentor Davie was fond: the establishment of the University of North Carolina. Brown died on September 2, 1793, from an unknown cause, perhaps associated with the malaria epidemic that hit his area in the fall of that year. It seems that he never married.

At the time he died, Brown left among his papers a number of writings that later saw print and dramatic performance. His play *West-Point Preserved; or, the Treason of Arnold* (now lost) seems to have been performed in Boston in 1797 and then again in 1800, to critical acclaim. In addition, Samuel T. Armstrong and Joshua Belcher (Brown's cousin) brought out several of his works between 1805 and 1807, including a number of prose pieces, several poems, and a group of verse fables. These pieces, along with Brown's "Original Maxims" after the manner of Rochefoucault (whom Brown admired and mentioned in *The Power of Sympathy*), brought Brown an audience sufficient to warrant Armstrong's and Belcher's publication of his second novel, *Ira and Isabella: or, The Natural Children* (1807). The latter was a second try, with a happier ending, on the themes taken up in *The Power of Sympathy.* Ironically, the credit Brown received during his lifetime for his wit and his observations about human foibles came from the numerous verses and essays he wrote, rather than from his novel-writing. Today, however, Brown—who once dubbed himself "a warm, good fed'ralist at heart"—is best known as the first British American novelist.

The selections that follow provide a glimpse into the reading fare available in local newspapers and magazines in Brown's day. Brown's story, "Harriot, or the Domestick Reconciliation," appeared in printer Isaiah Thomas's *Massachusetts Magazine* in 1789. Because there were no copyright laws, publishers regularly published selections taken from other newspapers and books. Thus it is that Brown's popular novel, *The Power of Sympathy,* supplied printers with several selections, printed in different places throughout British America. The short story, "Seduction," a small piece taken from one of the novel's many commentaries on this theme, appeared as an item in the *New York Magazine, or Literary Repository* in 1795.

HARRIOT

Or, The Domestick Reconciliation.
Sketched from the Life[1]

The benevolence of the heart is an inexhausted source of pleasure to the possessor, and of happiness to the world. Other pleasures are unstable and transitory, and perhaps the recollection of them may sometimes upbraid us with mispent time; but the conscious pride of having done a good action, will always be remembered with repeated satisfaction. To fulfil the duties of our station in life—to extend the hand of liberality to the indigent; to regulate the passions of others by our precept and example; and to appear as a mediator in affairs of a domestick nature, are moral duties which every one is willing to acknowledge, to admire and to praise. But it is a truth that few are ambitious of excelling in these duties, or storing in their hearts the joy that arises from this true goodness.

Of the few, however, who are not ashamed to declare their love of virtue by shielding the head of the distrest, and who have the courage to interpose in the most delicate cases, we introduce the amiable Harriot. Her natural genius has been cultivated by a polite education, and reading the best authors—She has a most refined sensibility, with an uncommon share of prudence—It is this prudence that checks the sallies of a too sympathetick heart, and which characterizes her as the principal agent to the subsequent story.

The juvenile days of Mr. Oldham were distinguished by the volitility and dissipation which often mark men of strong passions. Amidst the hurry of which he still posset what is commonly called a good heart; but it is not to be supposed it was free from errours of impurity—he has passed through many scenes of debauchery, and often borne a considerable part in the execution of midnight revelry. The waters that have wandered through a country of mines will retain some tincture or contamination: the maxim, therefore, that a reformed rake makes the best husband, is not founded in truth.

At the age of seven and twenty, Mr. Oldham paid his addresses to Myranda. She was a young lady of amiable manners, of considerable fortune, and was called handsome. There was, she imagined, a peculiar power in her charms, which could lay prostrate at her feet the man who had conquered and triumphed over many artless females; the suit of Oldham, therefore, succeeded, and Myranda was persuaded to receive him as a husband "With all his imperfections on his head."

Notwithstanding the attempt we have made to explode the proverbial expression of a reformed rake making the best husband, too often unguardedly repeated by young girls, we suppose there is nothing, which has a greater tendency to bring about such an event than the company of an amiable wife—at the same time, we are compelled, by the moral of our story, to add, that nothing can sooner break the bonds of connubial happiness than the conversation of women of loose morals.

Mr. Oldham was for several years happy; but domestick quietude, without a regular system of conduct, is extremely mutable. He again experienced that rage for pleasure, which robs a man of himself, and was doomed to suffer once more, the tyranny of the passions.

Starting into life with the possession of a competency, and as deeply engaging in the gaieties of fashion, as a republican government will admit, the sole object of Oldham was the pursuit of pleasure—He was *irregularly* bred a merchant, and kept a store of English goods, which he did not attend, being always satisfied with looking at such parts of the ledger as his clerk was pleased to shew him.

Gaming, inebriety, and the company of our modern Massinellas, nearly at once destroyed his fortune, his health, and his conscience. Ambitious of gaining the laudable renown of being acknowledged a legitimate heir of pleasure, he mounted the car of dissipation like another son of Phebus.

We will not pretend to trace him through his mad career, but take that part of his conduct only which is connected with our story.

One evening at a tavern, having had a bad run of luck at play, he thought to drown his mortification in wine; which proving inefficient, he retreated from the company to hide his sorrow in the bosom of his Thais.

Thais, with arts peculiar to women of her profession, had moulded the heart of Oldham to her wishes, and was now plotting a scheme, against him, which if carried into execution, would terminate his ruin.

Oldham had imprudently wasted away the greater part of his estate, but of what remained was a genteel house in Boston, which he did not occupy. This house was very convenient for Madam Thais, and she was planning matters to get it into her possession. She observed his head a little giddy, and insisted upon a deed of his tenement. You

---

1. Published in Isaiah Thomas's *Massachusetts Magazine,* 1 (January 1789). It is signed "Q.S." in its original appearance but known, from Brown's manuscript, to have been Brown's story.

must give me a deed of that estate, said she—"Impossible! my affairs are now in a very deranged state—I am worth nothing, I am ruined already—what will become of my family if—"

And what will become of me too—is it for this, I have sacrificed my honour, and my reputation?

"*You* talk of honour—were you not a mother before I knew you, and were you not lately found out?"—

Thais, finding Oldham was not to be easily frightened, thought proper to lower her tone, and change her style—did you never know, said she, that all women were honest till they were found out?—and you pretend to talk to me of your family.

"Think, replied he, of my wife, my virtuous wife and child"—a very *virtuous child,* I dare say, answered she—"And is not the epithet equally applicable to the other?"

Do you pretend to talk to me, rejoined Thais, perceiving the muscles of his face begin to dilate—do you pretend to talk to me of your wife's virtue after I have told you that *we* are *all* honest, until we are discovered slipping? Now there is Mrs. Brittle made poor Mr. Brittle believe he was a father, before he was a husband, and Mrs. Cornnter plants a very handsome pair of horns on her husband's head, and he dandles children on his knee that are none of his own. I could tell you many stories of this kind—Do you think then, I am unacquainted with the weaknesses, the frailties and artifices of my own sex?—All these affairs glide on smoothly and unknown; and no doubt your wife is as secret in her amours as most of us—

"*What* did you say?"

I do not love to call out names, but—

"But what? Say quick—"

No, no—save your estate, accumulate a fortune, debar yourself of expenses and all the pleasures of life, and leave your estate to a *virtuous wife.*

"You keep me on the rack—speak—Speak *out* and let me sacrifice to my honour—" By no means—consider your loving wife, your *virtuous child.* However, the deed is drawn, and you may put your name to it, and get it properly authenticated, and after that—

Distracted with the suggestions of the cunning Thais, Oldham, perplexed and enraged, rushed out of the house without hearing the end of her speech, and walked home with great speed.

As soon as he had entered the door he inquired for his wife, and was answered by the maid that she was expected home every minute—At that instant Mrs. Oldham came into the entry with her daughter—Chagrined at his loss at the gaming table, and prejudiced against his wife by the machination of the artful Thais, he abruptly demanded where she had been—The answer she gave would have satisfied any one who had a mind to be satisfied, but blinded by rage and the fumes of intoxication, he determined on the contrary—not to see the light of reason—Give me leave to observe, Madam, said he, trembling, with rage, you behave very *different* from what you did—

And give me the liberty to remark, said she, that you behave very *indifferent*—and made an attempt to pass up the stairs. At any other time he would have smiled at this turn, but now it increased his rage, and intercepting her flight, took hold of her arm, and precipitately hurried her and her child into the street and shut the door.

With remarkable presence of mind, she appeased her little daughter and walked into the next street. She thought it imprudent to trouble those persons with a recital of her misfortunes, who are generally called neighbours, and she wished her troubles might be kept secret—her particular friends, whom she could call upon with propriety lived at the most remote part of the town. Her situation was now deplorable—her spirits failed her—seeing a door open and several ladies in the house, and recollecting the countenance of one, she immediately entered but, opprest with the horrours of her condition, she fainted away as soon as she stepped into the house.

We now introduce Harriot in the exercise of benevolence. She had formerly been acquainted with Myranda, and it was Harriot whom she had seen, and whose friendly countenance had encouraged her to stop here, where, by the by, Harriot was only on a visit—she instantly made the cause of the fair stranger her own, while another lady took care of the child.

When the unfortunate Myranda opened her eyes, she was welcomed to life by the harmonious voice of her young friend—little ceremony was necessary at this critical junction—Harriot, therefore, made but a faint inquiry into the cause of her calamity, but conducted her to her own house where she was made acquainted with the particulars, and determined to endeavour to obtain justice for her injured friend. She was sensible she had undertaken the management of a very delicate point, but the suggestion of this observation but armed her with more prudence, perseverance and resolution.

Leaving Myranda and her little daughter to the care of the benevolent Harriot, we will return to Oldham.

After wasting away a restless night, he began to consider the adventure of the preceding evening. The insinuations of Thais against his wife's honour exceedingly disturbed him—He did not know but it might have been an artifice to inveigle him to assign that estate to her—If he had recollected that it was a governing principle with those women, who have no reputation to loose, to destroy the character of the whole sex—he would have wisely concluded that this was no more than a cunning trick to raise his jealousy and curiosity—the short of his soliloquy was this—he resolved to satisfy the demand of Thais in order to arrive at the truth—he rose with the determination of visiting her, but was detained by the following letter:

"To Mr. Oldham.

"DOMESTICK misunderstandings are seldom reconciled by the casual intervention of a third person—it is a hazardous matter to interpose at any time, but when one is impressed with *that* truth, it becomes temerity. Forgive me, Sir, if I, though personally unknown to you, dare remind you of *your imprudence* by pleading the cause of an innocent woman—I am the friend of your wife. But why do I arraign you *imprudence?* I have inquired the state of your affairs—I see they are in a desperate situation—I see the measures you take to prevent reflection, and now stretch out the arm of friendship, to pluck you from the gulph of perdition. Can the losses of the gaming table afford you entertainment? Can the solacing conversation of a diabolical Thais, who would delight in your ruin, quiet your apprehensions of approaching poverty? Awake from your stupor—put on the man—think, determine, and execute for yourself, with judgment and stability. Be not deceived by the lure of an unprincipled woman—Will you sacrifice your wife, your most faithful friend, to the caprice of a prostitute? And shall your last dollar satiate her avarice?—Harken to the advice of a sincere well wisher to your happiness, and do her the justice to believe when she tells you that the happiness of a married man depends materially upon his attention to the cultivation of domestick felicity. Let me *advise* you therefore (for you stand in need of advice) immediately to banish from your presence the detestable Thais; to abjure play; and to receive to your bosom the dishonoured, the highly injured Myranda; I have then no doubt of the completion of your happiness; repentance will succeed to misconduct, and industry to dissipation.

"If you have any farther particulars to inquire, the bearer will inform you where you may have an interview with your humble servant,

"HARRIOT—."

To this uncommon address Mr. Oldham returned a polite answer, acknowledging he was penetrated with the most lively grief at the representation of his own case; he confessed his eyes were now open to his misfortune, and that he saw the danger into which he was running; such a life, he owned, was the most unhappy, and nothing gave him so much pleasure as the hope of an alteration in his life; he knew nothing that could reclaim him so soon as the pointed and spirited manner in which she had analyzed his conduct, and concluded by desiring the promised interview might take place.

The fair interposer finding the heart of Oldham not totally depraved, imagined it most prudent to reconcile the family difference with all speed. She accordingly managed her hand with such adroitness, as to hasten the scene which is represented in the prefixed plate.

Oldham seized the hand of the injured Myranda, and on the bended knee of repentance and contrition implored her forgiveness of his temerity, neglect and insult. She immediately arose and received him with tears of unfeigned affection; he took his child in his arms, who was unconscious of this new instance of paternal tenderness. Harriot was no unconcerned spectator of this pathetick scene. She felicitated herself as the agent of this happy meeting, and strove not to conceal the tear of joy that glistened in her eye. She felt the divine sensation which can only be experienced by one who has done a good action.

Several months have elapsed since this domestick reconciliation, and Mr. Oldham enjoys unknown pleasures in an easy, equable life, the effects of a happy reformation; a reformation which includes the uniform practice of temperance, politeness, economy and morality; a reformation which is not so much owing to a self conviction, as to the amiable remonstrance of the fair mediator.

Q.S.

SEDUCTION[1]

Behold the youthful virgin arrayed in all the delightful charms of vivacity, modesty and sprightliness—Behold even while she is rising in beauty and dignity, like a lily of the valley, in the full blossom of her graces, she is cut off suddenly by the rude hand of the Seducer. Unacquainted with his baseness and treachery, and too ready to

---

1. The story is taken verbatim from Brown's novel, *The Power of Sympathy,* originally published by Isaiah Thomas in 1789. Selections were taken from the novel and published by different printers throughout the new United States, once the novel appeared. This selection was published in the *New York Magazine, or Literary Repository,* 6 (November 1795).

repose confidence in him—she is deluded by the promises and flattery of the man who professes the greatest love and tenderness for her welfare:—But did she understand the secret villainy of his intentions, would she appear thus elate and joyous? Would she assent to her ruin? Would she subscribe her name to the catalogue of infamy? Would she kiss the hand of the atrocious dastard, already raised to give the final wound to her reputation and peace?

O! Why is there not an adequate punishment for this crime, when that of a common traitor is marked with its deserved iniquity and abhorrence!

Is it necessary to depicture the state of this deluded young creature after her fall from virtue? Stung with remorse, and frantick with despair, does she not fly from the face of day, and secrete her conscious head in the bosom of eternal forgetfulness? Melancholy and guilt transfix her heart, and she sighs out her miserable existence—the prey of poverty, ignominy and reproach! Lost to the world, to her friends, and to herself, she blesses the approach of death in whatever shape he may appear, that terminates a life, no longer a blessing to its possessor, or a joy to those around her.

Behold her stretched upon the mournful bier!—Behold her silently descend to the grave!—Soon the wild weeds spring afresh round the *little hillock,* as if to shelter the remains of betrayed innocence—and the friends of her youth shun even the spot which conceals her relicks.

Such is the consequence of SEDUCTION, but it is not the only consequence. Peace and happiness fly the nuptial couch which is unattended by love and fidelity. The mind no longer enjoys its quiet, while it ceases to cherish sentiments of truth and gratitude. The sacred *ties* of conubial duty are not to be violated with impunity; for though a violation of those *ties* may be overlooked by the eye of justice, the heart shall supply a *monitor,* who will not fail to correct those, who are hardy enough to burst them asunder.

Hannah Webster Foster (1758–1840)

Hannah Webster Foster's novels *The Coquette* and *The Boarding School* were immensely popular in her own day, bringing Foster a reputation that exceeded most other writers of her generation. *The Coquette* alone went through thirteen editions—and probably thirty printings—before the end of the nineteenth century. Yet Hannah Webster Foster was probably better known among her acquaintance as a well-read women and an apt conversationalist, an overall "notable woman" (that is, a modest housewife and mother). These would have been the qualities for which a woman of her station would have wished to remain known.

Hannah Webster was born in Salisbury, Massachusetts, into the family of a prosperous Boston merchant. She was sent to a boarding school when she was only four years old, after her mother died. Beyond this information, little is known of her youth. In 1771 she was living in Boston, where her literary career took shape and where she began publishing political pieces in newspapers in the 1780s. Webster married the Reverend John Foster, a graduate of Dartmouth College and pastor of the First Church in Brighton, Massachusetts. The year after she married, she bore her first child, who seems to have died just after birth. Thereafter, between 1789 and 1796, she bore five children.

Somehow amid her daily activities, Foster found time to write her first novel, *The Coquette; or, the History of Eliza Wharton, A Novel, Founded on Fact,* published anonymously as written "By a Lady of Massachusetts" (1797). Her publisher republished the novel in 1802, the same year it received a dramatization by J. Horatio Nichols as *The New England Coquette.* Throughout the nineteenth century, *The Coquette* remained popular; indeed, just between 1824 and 1828, the novel was reprinted eight times.

Foster's second novel, *The Boarding School; or, Lessons of a Preceptress to Her Pupils,* published in 1798, never achieved the acclaim that *The Coquette* realized. Designed to assist in forming the characters and manners of young women, *The Boarding School* is written in the guise of a series of farewell talks between a school's teacher and her young women students who will soon leave the school and enter society.

Like most advice books of the day, this one offered advice about needlework, reading, composition, dance, and "sentimental song." Probably the most interesting feature of this book (with regard to a reading of Foster's novel, *The Coquette*) lies in the preceptress's contention that seducers of women should be punished and their victims treated with a greater degree of tolerance.

In the first decade of the nineteenth century, Foster contributed anonymously to *The Monthly Anthology or Magazine of Polite Literature,* later known as the *North American Review.* She saw two of her children reach their own literary success in the first quarter of the century: Her daughter Elizabeth Foster (under her married name Eliza Lanesford Cushing) published two novels (in 1824 and 1826) and coedited a monthly magazine in Montreal, Canada, called *The Literary Garland,* and her daughter Harriet Foster (under her married name Harriet Vaughan Cheney) published two popular books (1824 and 1827). Foster had a long life. In her later years, she went to live in Montreal with her daughter Eliza Cushing; she died in Montreal on April 17, 1840. Although she wrote a great deal during her lifetime, she remains best known to literary scholars for having published one of the most popular American novels of the eighteenth century.

Part of the popularity of *The Coquette* certainly arose from its interesting use of epistolarity, so that the events of the novel are revealed in letters written by and to the central and surrounding characters. Foster's characters express themselves in ways suggestive of feelings and attitudes that provide for a useful examination of the complexity of motivations. And yet part of the novel's renown is probably also attributable to the story upon which it is indeed "Founded on Fact." Like William Hill Brown, who used a scandalous story of his friends the Mortons only faintly veiled in his novel, *The Power of Sympathy,* Foster developed her fiction around the story of a woman known to her and her family, friends, and acquaintances, substituting the name "Eliza Wharton" for the real-life person, Elizabeth Whitman (1752–88). The story of Elizabeth Whitman's life is ultimately an unhappy one. Having been born into a long line of families prominent in the clergy and in Hartford, Connecticut, society, Whitman was well educated in most fields where women sought accomplishment, and she was admired for her wit and her poetic accomplishments. After two engagements to ministers that ended unhappily, Whitman became involved with someone whose identity remains unknown, and she bore a child away from her home, attempting to remain in anonymity throughout her pregnancy and dying in the process of the delivery. Her contemporaries frowned upon her situation—being unwed and bearing the child in a strange town—even in the death notices written about her, and her situation became a moral and monitory tale for young women and men for years to come.

Foster embellished what she knew about Whitman's situation and developed the story of *The Coquette* around Whitman's unhappy circumstances. Literary historians frequently speak about the narrative as if it provides advice for the conduct of women primarily. This is one aspect, an important one, of the epistolary narrative, but the book also reveals the problems in Foster's era regarding gender codes and masculinity, how masculinity should be defined and how it would operate in a society that frequently seemed to prize gaiety and monetary worth above the attempt to retain good character, a reputation for ethical conduct. The selection that follows gives readers today some insight into the reading norms and expectations of Foster's day. It is interesting that while the popularity of the novel might have rested upon it being a "tale of truth" about a woman, the editor of the *New York Magazine, of Literary Repository,* which published this selection from the novel, in 1797, selected from the novel the letter from the man who fell in love with Wharton and whose baby Wharton died while delivering. Peter Sanford had married to relieve his debt; he lost his Eliza Wharton in the process.

PICTURE OF A LIBERTINE[1]

Confusion, horror and despair are the portion of your wretched, unhappy friend! Oh, Deighton, I am undone! Misery irremediable is my future lot! She is gone—yes, she is gone for ever! The darling of my soul, the centre of all my wishes and enjoyments is no more! Cruel Fate has snatched her from me; and she is irretrievably lost! I rave, and then reflect: I reflect, and then rave! I have not patience to bear this calamity, nor power to remedy it! Where shall I fly from the upbraidings of my mind, which accuses me as the murderer of my Eliza? I would fly to death, and seek a refuge in the grave; but the forebodings of a retribution to come, I cannot away with! Oh, that I had seen her, that I had once more asked her forgiveness! But even that privilege, that consolation was denied me! The day on which I meant to visit her, most of my property was attached, and, to secure the rest, I was obliged to shut my doors, and become a prisoner in my own house! High living and old debts, incurred by extravagance, had reduced the fortune of my wife to very little, and I could not satisfy the clamorous demands of my creditors.

I would have given millions, had I possessed them, to have been at liberty to see, and to have had power to preserve Eliza from death! But in vain was my anxiety; it could not relieve, it could not liberate me. When I first heard the dreadful tidings of her exit, I believe I acted like a madman! Indeed, I am little else now!

I have compounded with my creditors, and resigned the whole of my property.

Thus, that splendor and equipage, to secure which I have sacrificed a virtuous woman, is taken from me; that property, the dread of which prevented my forming an honorable connection with an amiable and accomplished girl, the only one I ever loved, has fallen, with redoubled vengeance, upon my guilty head; and I must become a vagabond in the earth!

---

1. When printing this piece from Foster's novel, the newspaper editor indicated it was "From the Coquette, or the History of Eliza Wharton." The selection is a letter written by Peter Sanford, the "rake" or "libertine" of the novel, to his friend, Deighton, who serves as a sounding board for Sanford's problems. The piece appeared in the *New York Magazine, or Literary Repository,* n.s. 2 (September 1797).

I shall fly my country as soon as possible; I shall go from every object which reminds me of my departed Eliza! But never, never shall I eradicate from my bosom, the idea of her excellence; or the painful remembrance of the injuries I have done her! Her shade will perpetually haunt me! The image of her, as she appeared when mounting the carriage which conveyed her for ever from my sight, she waved her hand in token of a last adieu, will always be present to my imagination! The solemn counsel she gave me before we parted, never more to meet, will not cease to resound in my ears!

While my being is prolonged, I must feel the disgraceful, and torturing effects of my guilt in seducing her! How madly have I deprived her of happiness, of reputation, of life! Her friends, could they know the pangs of contrition, and the horror of conscience which attend me, would be amply revenged.

It is said, she quitted the world with composure and peace. Well she might! She had not that insupportable weight of iniquity, which sinks me to despair! She found consolation in that religion which I have ridiculed as priestcraft and hypocrisy! But whether it be true or false, would to heaven I could now enjoy the comforts which its votaries evidently feel.

My wife has left me. As we lived together without love, we parted without regret.

Now, Charles, I am to bid you a long, perhaps, a last farewell. Where I shall roam in future, I neither know nor care—I shall go where the name of Sanford is unknown, and his person and sorrows unnoticed.

In this happy clime I have nothing to induce my stay. I have not money to support me with my profligate companions; nor have I any relish, at present, for their society. By the virtuous part of the community I am shunned as the pest and bane of social enjoyment. In short, I am debarred from every kind of happiness. If I look back, I recoil with horror from the black catalogue of vices which have stained my past life, and reduced me to indigence and contempt. If I look forward, I shudder at the prospects which my foreboding mind presents to view, both in this and a coming world! This is a deplorable, yet just picture of myself! How totally the reverse of what I once appeared!

Let it warn you, my friend, to shun the dangerous paths which I have trodden, that you may never be involved in the hopeless ignominy and wretchedness of

Peter Sanford.

SUSANNA HASWELL ROWSON (1762–1824)

Of the many writers who attempted fictional stories and novels, none achieved the fame of Susanna Haswell Rowson, whose novel *Charlotte, a Tale of Truth,* first published in London in 1791, soon became a best-seller in the new British American Republic. *Charlotte, a Tale of Truth,* which came to be known as *Charlotte Temple,* went through approximately two hundred editions in its heyday. Yet despite the immense popularity of her novel, Rowson was better known in the first part of her adult life as an actor and in the second part as a successful educator who sponsored young women's academies.

Susanna Haswell was both in Portsmouth, England, but her father moved the family to Massachusetts while she was young. Her father served in the British royal navy, which compromised the stability of his family during the years leading to the rebellion against Great Britain. In 1775 the Haswell family was imprisoned and held under house arrest for three years. They were later taken to Nova Scotia and exchanged for prisoners of war. They returned to England thereafter.

In England Susanna Haswell became involved in the arts and the theater, and she met and married a fellow actor, William Rowson. They could not succeed in making a living as actors, so the Rowsons turned to other trades. William Rowson became a hardware merchant, and Susanna Rowson, a writer. She published *A Trip to Parnassus,* a poetic critique of the stage, and a novel, *The Inquisitor,* both in 1788, and she began to think of other stories that would lend themselves to current reading interests. William Rowson's drinking interfered with his work, and the marriage appears to have been a difficult one. Rowson continued to write extensively, and she also continued to work in the theater to support herself and her husband. The couple joined Thomas Wignell's theater company, to venture onstage in North America. In 1793 they formally established themselves with a troupe called the Philadelphia Theatre Company, and they toured areas between Philadelphia and Boston.

Even though she continued to act, Rowson kept up her writing career, and shortly after her arrival in Philadelphia, Matthew Carey published an American edition of her *Charlotte, a Tale of Truth* (1794). But Rowson earned little money from her novel because no copyright laws existed at the time in the new United States, and printers could just republish works for their own financial gain alone. Thus, despite the overwhelming, ongoing popularity of her novel, Rowson earned relatively little from her novel, which was easily pirated. Rowson published songs and lyrics, two plays, and two novels in addition to *Charlotte* before turning to a different effort for the next part of her life.

In 1797 Rowson capitalized on her immense literary and social accomplishments by founding Mrs. Rowson's Young Ladies' Academy in Boston. Her heavy involvement in the administration of the school took time away from her writing, but even during the last two decades of her life, Rowson continued her career as a prolific writer. She published columns in the *Boston Weekly Magazine,* as well as poems, textbooks, and fiction. Her final years were made difficult by health problems, ongoing financial struggles, an unhappy marriage, and the loss of family members and close friends. Yet she had a remarkably prolific and interesting career, and she died with significant renown.

Rowson's best-known writings had didactic goals; they were intended as instructions on behavior, piety, and the acceptance of one's station in life. The selections that follow exemplify the kinds of writing typical of the day in most newspapers and magazines, and they indicate, too, the range of treatments a prolific author could give the themes of piety and good conduct. Many of her shorter works were printed with the notation that Rowson was the author, thus capitalizing on her standing reputation as a novelist and literary exemplar. Two of the selections were extracted by editors from Rowson's novel, *The Inquisitor* (1788). The third selection was taken from Rowson's best-selling novel *Charlotte, a Tale of Truth* (1791). In all three instances, it is clear that the editors understood that these stories would be well received by their readership. Indeed, a readership could be secured easily if one simply advertised that the work was by "Mrs. Rowson."

THE HAPPY PAIR[1]

It was a neat little house, by the side of the fields—a pretty looking woman, drest by Simplicity, the handmaid of Nature, was laying the table cloth and trimming her little parlour; her looks were cheerful and serene, and with a voice pleasing, though untutored, she sung the following stanza,

> Here beneath my humble cot,
> Tranquil peace and pleasures dwell,
> If contented with our lot,
> Smiling joy can grace a cell.
>
> Nature's wants are all supply'd,
> Food and raiment, house and fire.
> Let others swell the courts of pride.
> This is all that I require.

Just as she had finished, a genteel young man entered the gate: she ran eagerly to meet him.

My dear Charles she cried you are too late to night.

It was near ten o clock—I had taken the advantage of my ring, which had the peculiar quality of rendering me invisible to mortal view, and followed them into the house.

I am weary, Betsey, said he, leaning his head upon her shoulder.

I am sorry for it my love, but rest is welcome to the weary, and refreshment sweet when earnt by virtuous toil. Let us eat our supper and retire to rest. Recline your head upon my bosom, and lull your cares to rest—

Their frugal meal was bread and butter and sallad—

If to be content is to be happy, my dear, said she, how superlatively blest am I:—I have no wish beyond what our little income will afford me; my home is to me a palace, thy love my estate. I envy not the rich dames who shine in costly array; I please my Charles in my plain, simple attire; I wish to please no other.

Thou dear reward of all my toils, said he, embracing her, how can I have a wish ungratified, while possessed of thee—I have never desired wealth but for thy sake, and thy cheerful contented disposition makes even wealth unnecessary.

It is by no means necessary to happiness, said I, as I left the house—Charles and Betsey seem perfectly happy

with only a bare competence,—I ask but a competence, cries the luxurious or avoricious wretch; the very exclamation convinces us that a trifle is adequate to the wants of the humble, frugal mind, while thousands cannot supply the inordinate desires of the prodigal, or satisfy the grasping disposition of the miser.

THE INGRATE[1]

Do you see that beautiful woman in that splendid equipage, surrounded by a train of servants? 'tis the thoughtless, ungrateful Amelia!

Behold that poor old woman, who toils through the dirt, unattended by any but two lovely daughters, sweet as opening flowers, and innocent as new-born infants; see on her venerable countenance, what grief and despondency is imprinted! see the big tears roll down her furrowed cheeks! see she enters an obscure apartment, and a scanty meal is divided between her children and herself!

She looks at them by turns with such maternal tenderness, such anguish of heart, that she seems to say, what will become of you, my sweet children? how will you pass through life, when I am gone?

That poor old woman was Amelia's benefactress—but it is fit I should tell my tale methodically.

Amelia was the daughter of a gentleman of small fortune, who, besides her, had nine other children: Mrs. Ellwin was a distant relation of the family; she was the wife of an opulent merchant, and their habitation was the habitation of philanthropy.

Amelia had received a tolerable education—she was pretty in her person, cheerful in her disposition, and had a good share of understanding; with these accomplishments Mrs. Ellwin thought it would be a pity for Amelia to be buried in obscurity; she gave her an invitation to her house, cloathed her genteely, and introduced her into such company as she thought would be most conducive to her future advancement in life. It was not long before Amelia's charms made a conquest of a gentleman of large fortune— he loved her; and her virtues were so kindly brought forward by Mrs. Ellwin, and her little faults buried in obliv-

---

1. "The Happy Pair" is a selection made from Rowson's novel, *The Inquisitor,* originally published in 1788. The piece appeared in the *Monthly Miscellany* 1 (July 1794)

---

1. "The Ingrate," a selection taken from Rowson's novel, *The Inquisitor* (1788), appeared in *New York Magazine, or Literary Repository,* n.s. 1 (April 1796). The story was prefaced by the editor's heading note, "From the Inquisitor, or Invisible Rambler. By Mrs. Rowson."

ion, that he overlooked her want to fortune, made her his wife, and settled upon her 500 £ per annum, jointure. Amelia had not long enjoyed this advancement, before Mr. Ellwin, having placed too great a dependence on the honor of a friend, lost a large sum of money; of consequence his payments were not punctual, and he became a bankrupt.

He struggled for some time against his adverse fate, but at length died of a broken heart, and left his wife and lovely daughters no inheritance but poverty.

About this time Amelia became a widow,—but Amelia was now a fine lady—she had no time to spend with poor relations; no money to spare to relieve the distresses of Mrs. Ellwin, though her wedding cloaths were purchased by that generous friend, and cost near five hundred pounds, and that sum had never been repaid.

Amelia is now just married again, and flying about in all the gaity of heart which wealth and splendor can inspire in a giddy mortal, while poor Mrs. Ellwin is sinking under a load of anguish, unpitied and unthought of. Her once blooming, amiable daughters dropping like frost-nipped blossoms, and neither Friendship, Humanity, nor Gratitude will reach forth a hand to cheer, revive, or save them.

MATERNAL SORROW[1]

SLOW and heavy passed the time while the carriage was conveying Mr. Eldridge home—and yet, when he came in sight of the house, he wished a longer reprieve from the dreadful task of informing Mr. and Mrs. Temple of their daughter's elopement.

It is easy to judge the anxiety of these affectionate parents, when they found the return of their father delayed so much beyond the expected time. They were now met in the dining parlour, and several of the young people who had been invited were already arrived. Each different part of the company was employed in the same manner, looking out at the windows which faced the road. At length the long expected chaise appeared. Mrs. Temple ran out to receive and welcome her darling; her young companions flocked round the door, each one eager to give her joy on

the return of her birth day. The door of the chaise was opened; Charlotte was not there. "Where is my child?" cried Mrs. Temple, in breathless agitation.

Mr. Eldridge could not answer: he took hold of his daughter's hand and led her into the house; and, sinking on the first chair he came to, burst into tears, and sobbed aloud.

"She is dead!" cried Mrs. Temple. "Oh my dear Charlotte!" and clasping her hands in an agony of distress, fell into strong hysterics.

Mr. Temple, who had stood speechless with surprize and fear, now ventured to inquire if indeed his Charlotte was no more. Mr. Eldridge led him into another apartment, and putting the fatal note into his hand, cried— "Bear it like a christian," and turned from him, endeavoring to suppress his own too visible emotions.

It would be vain to attempt describing what Mr. Temple felt whilst he hastily ran over the dreadful lines: when he had finished, the paper dropt from his unnerved hand. "Gracious heaven!" said he, "could Charlotte act thus?" Neither tear nor sigh escaped him; and he sat the image of mute sorrow, till roused from his stupor by the repeated shrieks of Mrs. Temple. He rose hastily, and rushing into the apartment where she was, folded his arms about her; and saying, "Let us be patient, my dear Lucy," nature relieved his almost bursting heart by a friendly gush of tears.

Should any one, presuming on his own philosophic temper, look with an eye of contempt on the man who could indulge a woman's weakness, let him remember that man was a father, and he will then pity the misery which wrung those drops from a noble, generous heart.

Mrs. Temple beginning to be a little more composed, but still imagining her child was dead, her husband, gently taking her hand, cried, "You are mistaken, my love—Charlotte is not dead."

"Then she is very ill, else why did she not come? But I will to her: the chaise is still at the door; let me go instantly to the dear girl. If I was ill she would fly to attend me, to alleviate my sufferings, and cheer me with her love."

"Be calm my dearest Lucy, and I will tell you all," said Mr. Temple. "You must not go, indeed you must not; it will be of no use."

"Temple," said she, assuming a look of firmness and composure, "tell me the truth I beseech you: I cannot bear this dreadful suspence. What misfortune has befallen my child? Let me know the worst, and I will endeavor to bear it as I ought."

---

1. "Maternal Sorrow" is a selection from Rowson's novel, *Charlotte, or, A Tale of Truth* (1791). It was published in the *New York Magazine, or Literary Repository,* n.s. 1 (May 1796), with the editor's comment, "From Mrs. Rowson's 'Tale of Truth.'"

"Lucy," replied Mr. Temple, "imagine your daughter alive, and in no danger of death; what misfortune would you then dread?"

"There is one misfortune which is worse than death—But I know my child too well to suspect—"

"Be not too confident, Lucy."

"O heavens!" said she, "what horrid images do you start! Is it possible she should forget—"

"She has forgot us all, my love; she has preferred the love of a stranger to the affectionate protection of her friends."

"Not eloped!" cried she eagerly.

Mr. Temple was silent.

"You cannot contradict it," said she. "I see my fate in those tearful eyes. Oh Charlotte! Charlotte! how ill have you requited our tenderness!—But Father of Mercies, continued she, sinking on her knees and raising her streaming eyes and clasped hands to heaven, "this once vouchsafe to hear a fond, a distracted mother's prayer:—Oh! let thy bounteous providence watch over and protect the dear thoughtless girl—save her from the miseries which I fear will be her portion—and oh! of thine infinite mercy make her not a mother, less she should one day feel what I now suffer!"

The last words faultered on her tongue, and she fell fainting into the arms of her husband, who had involuntarily dropped on his knees beside her.

A mother's anguish, when disappointed in her tenderest hopes, none but a mother can conceive. Yet, my dear young readers, I would have you read this scene with attention, and reflect, that you may yourselves one day be mothers. Oh my friends! as you value your eternal happiness, wound not, by thoughtless ingratitude, the peace of the mother who bore you: remember the tenderness, the care, the unremitting anxiety with which she has attended to all your wants and wishes, from earliest infancy to the present day: behold the mild ray of affectionate applause, that beams from her eye on the performance of your duty; listen to her reproofs with silent attention, they proceed from a heart anxious for your future felicity: you must love her; nature, all powerful nature, has planted the seeds of filial affection in your bosoms.

Then once more read over the sorrows of poor Mrs. Temple, and remember, the mother whom you so dearly love and venerate will feel the same, when you, forgetful of the respect due to your Maker and yourself, forsake the paths to virtue for those of vice and folly.

CHARLES BROCKDEN BROWN (1771–1810)

Novelist, essayist, and editor, Charles Brockden Brown was born in Philadelphia into a prosperous family. With both his parents affiliated with the Society of Friends (Quakers), Brown was well educated at the Friends Latin School of Philadelphia. When he reached age sixteen, he reluctantly followed his family's wishes and became apprenticed to a lawyer, so he could better observe and study the law. But he did not like the work any more than he had enjoyed working in his father's business. While studying the law, Brown joined the Belles-Letters Club, a group of educated young men who had similar literary interests and wanted to become established writers, although they pursued different trades. Brown enjoyed the issues raised by his club and liked having literary friendship. He grew unhappy with the legal profession and finally abandoned it in 1793, determined to earn a living as a writer.

Brown considered that in the era of progaganda writing; increased newspaper publication; and concern about issues, such as citizenship and conduct, he might be able to make a reputation and thus an income as a writer. He formed a lasting acquaintance with members of a New York City literary circle made up of Federalists and moved to New York City for a brief time in order to nurture his writing career. His conversations with Federalist-oriented associates, including Timothy Dwight and Elihu Hubbard Smith, along with his reading the works of such figures as Mary Wollstonecraft and William Godwin would have an impact upon much of Brown's writing in the years that followed.

Brown struggled to support himself in New York, but he finally returned to Philadelphia, to join two of his brothers in an importing business. In Philadelphia, Brown began "The Man at Home" series in *The Weekly Magazine,* a series that drew on his experiences with yellow fever while he lived in New York City. After publishing a series of short writings, Brown turned his attention to *Alcuin* (1798), an exploration of women's rights. The late 1790s were intense and creative years for Brown. He published several major novels: *Wieland,* an exploration of the effects of ventriloquism and scientific phenomena and a critique of religious delusion; *Ormond,* the celebration of a woman of character who struggled against the title character, a seducer; *Edgar Huntly,* an unusual tale about a sleepwalker; and *Arthur Mervyn,* which took as its focal point the yellow fever epidemic in Philadelphia in 1793.

Brown gradually shifted his focus from fiction writing to journalism. He took on three different editorships in succession. He founded and edited *The Monthly Magazine and American Review* at the turn into the new century (1799–1800) and then took up the *Literary Magazine and American Register* (1803–06) and *The American Register, or General Repository of History, Politics, and Science* (1806–10). The last periodical he edited had a distinctive social and political vein not present in the earlier publications, thus signaling a shift toward different fare than that of the imagination during his last years. Brown died of tuberculosis early in 1810.

Running literary newspapers and magazines was time intensive, for it usually meant that the editor was both the author and type compositor at the same time, and he (or sometimes she) typically ran a print shop in addition to printing the periodical or newspaper. Most editors tired of the steady labor that brought in relatively low remuneration for such a competitive labor market. Although magazines were gradually growing in popularity during Brown's day, most folded quickly because editors simply could not sustain the labor burdens and the costs. The relative longevity of two of Brown's magazines reflects Brown's commitment to his projects, amid the challenges of obtaining contributions or writing them himself, while remaining financially afloat.

In his heyday as a writer of imaginative pieces, Brown tested the limits of fiction and fact, whether he was employing ventriloquists, dreamers, or women of high moral character for his central figures. In many of his writings, he used what has been called the "gothic" mode, including mysterious events, episodes of terror, nighttime settings, and forested or cavernous places or ruins. Brown also used devices typical of what is called "sentimental" fiction, fiction that relied for its effects upon a presumed heightening of emotion and that clarified questions of conduct between people. Brown's oeuvre is quite large. He contributed essays, literary criticism, and short fiction to the three magazines he edited, as well as to several other magazines, as the following three selections attest. These readings have narrative surprises that are common features in Brown's work. Often described as the first professional writer in the British American republic, Brown devoted much of his adult life to writing, critiquing, and encouraging the publication of what might become a distinctly "American" literature.

THE MAN AT HOME, NO. XI[1]

What a series of calamities is the thread of human existence? I have heard of men who, though free themselves from any uncommon distress, were driven to suicide by reflecting on the misery of others. They employed their imagination in running over the catalogue of human woes, and were so affected by the spectacle, that they willingly resorted to death to shut it from their view. No doubt their minds were constituted after a singular manner. We are generally prone, when objects chance to present to us their gloomy side, to change their position, till we hit upon the brightest of its aspects.

I was lately perusing, in company with my friends Harrington and Wallace, the history of intestine commotions, in one of the ancient republics. It was one of the colonies of Magna Graecia. The nation comprehended a commercial city, peopled by eighty thousand persons, with a small territory annexed. Two factions were for a long time contending for the sovereignty. On one occasion, the party that had hitherto been undermost, obtained the upper place. The maxims by which they intended to deport themselves were, for some time, unknown. That they would revenge themselves upon their adversaries, in any signal or atrocious way, was, by no means, expected. Time, however, soon unfolded their characters and views.

---

1. "The Man at Home, No. XI" appeared in the *Weekly Magazine of Original Essays,* April 14, 1798.

The annal [o]ft proceeds to describe the subsequent events with great exactness of time, place, and number; but exhibits none of those general views which fill the reader's imagination, and translate him to the scene of action. His details, however, are, on that account, the more valuable, since the dullest reader, when possessed of these materials, will stand in no need of foreign aid to *circumstantialize* the picture.

The ordinary course and instruments of judicature were esteemed inadequate to their purposes. These would not allow them to select their victims, in sufficient numbers, and with sufficient dispatch. They therefore erected a secret tribunal, and formed a band of three hundred persons, who should execute, implicitly, the decrees of this tribunal. These judges were charged with the punishment of those who had been guilty of crimes against the state. They set themselves to the vigorous performance of their office.

On other occasions it has been usual to subject to some appearance of trial, the objects of persecution; to furnish them with an intelligible statement of their offences; to summon them to an audience of their judges; and to found their sentence on some evidence real or pretended; but these rulers were actuated by no other impulse than vengeance. The members of this tribunal were convened, daily, for no other purpose than to form a catalogue of those who should be forthwith sacrificed.

The avenues to the hall where they assembled were guarded by the troop before mentioned. Having executed the business of the day, the officers of this band of executioners were summoned, and the fatal list was put into their hands. The work of death began at night-fall. This season was adopted to render their proceedings more terrible. For this end, likewise, it was ordered that no warning should be given to the men whose names were inscribed upon this roll, but by the arrival of the messengers at their door.

These, dressed in peculiar uniform, marched by night to the sound of harsh and lamentable music, through the streets of the mute and affrighted city. They stopped at the appointed door, and admission being gained, peaceably or by violence, they proceeded, in silence, to the performance of their commission. The bow-string was displayed; the victim torn from his bed, from the arms of his wife, from the embraces of his children, was strangled in an instant; and the breathless corpse, left upon the spot where it had fallen. They retired, without any interruption to their silence, and ended not their circuit till the catalogue was finished.

To inflict punishment was the intention of these judges, but they considered that our own death is not, in all instances, the greatest evil that we can suffer. We would sometimes willingly purchase the safety of others at the price of our own existence. The tribunal therefore conducted itself by a knowledge of the characters of those whom its malice had selected. Sometimes the criminal remained untouched, but he was compelled to witness the destruction of some of his family. Sometimes his wife, sometimes his children were strangled before his eyes. Sometimes, after witnessing the agonies of all that he loved, the sentence was executed on himself.

The nature of this calamity was adapted to inspire the utmost terror. No one was apprized of his fate. The list was inscrutable to every eye but that of the tribunal. The adherents to the ruling faction composed about one third of the inhabitants. These of course were secure. If they did not triumph in the confusion of their foes, they regarded it with unconcern.

The rage and despair which accompanied the midnight progress of the executioners, scarcely excited their attention. Their revels and their mirth suffered no interruption or abatement.

It was asked in vain, by the sufferers, when the power which thus scattered death and dismay was to end. No answer was returned. They were left to form their judgment on the events that arose. Night succeeded night; but the murders, instead of lessening, increased in number. Many admitted the persuasion that a total extermination of the fallen party was intended. For a considerable period every circumstance contributed to heighten this persuasion. It was observed that the list continued gradually to swell, till the number of executions in a single night amounted to no less than two hundred.

It were worthy of some eloquent pen to describe this state of things. Surely never did the depravity of human passions more conspicuously display itself than on this stage. The most vigorous efforts were made to shake off this dreadful yoke, but the tyrants had previously armed their adherents, and guarded every avenue to a revolution, with the utmost care. The city-walls and gates served to stop the fugitives, and none but the members of the triumphant faction were suffered to go out. Policy required that those who furnished the city with provisions should be unmolested in their entrances and exits. In no variation of circumstances, indeed, had the wretched helots any thing to fear. No change in their condition could possibly be for the worse.

It will hardly be believed that this state of things continued for so long a period as four months. During this time vengeance did not pause for a single night. At the expiration of this period, suddenly, and without warning, the nightly visitations ceased, and, the tribunal was dissolved. The world were permitted to discover what limits had been assigned to the destruction. On counting up the slain, it appeared that six thousand persons had perished, and, consequently, that the purpose of the tyrants had been, not the indiscriminate massacre, but, merely the decimation of their adversaries.

Having finished the perusal of this tale, I could not forbear expatiating to my friends on the enormity of these evils, and thanking the destiny that had reserved us for a milder system of manners—"Not so fast," said Harrington. "You forget that the very city of which we are inhabitants, no longer ago than 1793, suffered evils, considerably parallel to those that are here described. In some respects the resemblance is manifest and exact. In the inscrutableness of the causes that produced death; the duration of the calamity; and the proportional number of the slain, the cases are parallel. Our condition was worse inasmuch as the lingerings and agonies of fever are worse than the expeditious operation of the bow-string. We had to encounter the miseries of neglect and want. The cessation of all lucrative business, and the sealing up of most of the sources of subsistence, were disadvantages peculiar to ourselves. Against these may be put in the balance the misery which haunts the oppressors, and those aggravations of distress flowing from a knowledge that the authors of our calamities are men like ourselves, whom, perhaps, our own folly, has armed against us. The evils which infest human society flow either from causes beyond our power to scrutinize, or from the licence of malignant passions. It would require a delicate hand to adjust truly the balance between these opposite kinds of evil. Suppose tyranny and plague, as in these cases, to destroy the same numbers in the same time, which has produced the greatest quantity of suffering? It is not easy to decide, but I am apt to think that the miseries of plague must be allowed to preponderate."

"The cases," said Wallace, "seem to me to have very little resemblance. If I had been an inhabitant of the Greek colony, I see not how I should have been benefited by this state of affairs, whereas the Yellow Fever was, to me, the most fortunate event that could have happened. I kept a store, as you know, in Water Street. I am young, and was then so poor that my stock, small as it was, was obtained upon credit. I was obliged to exert the most unremitting industry to procure myself the means of living, and the

very means, by which I sought to live, had like to have destroyed me. My frail constitution could not support the inconveniences of inactivity and bad air. My health was rapidly declining, and I could not afford to relinquish my business. The Yellow Fever, however, compelled me to relinquish it for a while.

"I took cheap lodgings in the neighbourhood of Lancaster. Country air and exercises completely reinstated me in the possession of health, but this was not all, for I formed an acquaintance with a young lady, who added three hundred pounds a year, to youth, beauty, and virtue. This acquaintance soon ripened into love, and now you see me one of the happiest of men. A lovely wife, a plentiful fortune, health, and leisure are the ingredients of my present lot, and for all these am I indebted to the Yellow Fever."

A LESSON ON SENSIBILITY[1]

Archibald was a youth of very lively parts. His sensibility had become diseased by an assiduous study of those Romancers and Poets, who make love the basis of their fictions. He has scarcely grown up, when he contracted a passion for a woman, whose chief merit consisted in her beauty. A new object quickly succeeded: Though he loved for a time with every appearance of ardour, it was perceived that his affections were easily transferred to a new object, and easily dissolved by absence. Love however, was his element: He could not exist without it. To sigh, to muse, to frame elegies, was the business of his life. Provided there was some object to receive his amourous devoirs, it seemed nearly indifferent what the real qualifications of the object were.

His friends prevailed upon him to put himself under the care of a merchant in Ireland. His situation required that he should qualify himself for some profession. That of a merchant was chosen by him as liable to fewest objections. After some time, however, he was brought back to his friends a maniac. A phrenzy at first furious and terrible, subsided into a melancholy, harmless to others, but invincibly silent and motionless, with scarcely a change of attitude; without opening his lips except to converse on his own misfortunes or the events that caused his despair. He has remained for some years, an example of the fatal

---

1. "A Lesson on Sensibility" appeared in the *Weekly Magazine of Original Essays* on May 19, 1798.

effects of addicting the undisciplined mind to books, in which Nature is so fantastically and egregiously belied. These were the circumstances that produced an effect so mournful.

He had scarcely been settled in his new abode at Corke, when he became enamoured of the daughter of a family more distinguished for their pride of birth, than their wealth. The Butlers claimed an alliance with the House of Ormond. There was honour in this descent, which, in the opinion of those who partook of it, survived, and was almost a counterbalance to the disasters that follow an attainder.

The daughter was carefully instructed in that creed which her parents valued so highly; but whether the inconveniences, the formality, and restraint to which this prejudice subjected her; or whether the books which she had an opportunity of consulting, and which, when they are admitted into any plan of education, always possess the largest portion of influence, exhibited human nature in its true colours, her sentiments were of a cast wholly opposite to those that actuated her kindred.

Her love of simplicity and independence appeared to gain new strength from contemplating the pomp and indolence that encumbered her steps. These qualities, however, were not suspected to exist, till the occasion presented itself, that called them into action. She was first seen by Archibald, in a shop where they accidentally met.

On the subjects of gracefulness and beauty, the youth was the most ardent of critics. He fancied himself profoundly skilled in the languages of features and looks. Among the numerous attempts that he had made to interpret this language, some had luckily succeeded. On these as on so many demonstrative deductions, had he built his theory; and the aid of certain German writers, had enabled him to give it an air of completeness and consistency. On this occasion he instantly formed his conclusions. He had the imagination and hand of a painter. By means of these he supplied himself with a portrait of the lady. He collected all the information respecting her which the stately reserve and unsocial habits of the family admitted. In brooding over what is imperfectly known and seldom seen, enthusiasm is apt to be awakened. No wonder, in such a fancy as that of Archibald, this image should at length be idolized, and his passion, fostered by incessant meditation, should break out into the utmost extravagances. In a rational mind the difficulties that attended this pursuit would have induced him to relinquish it: In Archibald those difficulties, which were all but insuperable, had no other effect than to stimulate his ardour.

For some time he had full employment in contriving and executing expedients for obtaining the great object of his wishes. His memory was fraught with the wiles and stratagems of lovers' such as have afforded a theme to the poets of all ages: But his own fertile invention, contemplating the circumstances peculiar to his situation, enabled him to surpass them all in subtlety and perseverance.

The efforts of a strenuous mind constitute sometimes a pleasing, but always an instructive spectacle. Instances of a powerful understanding laying out its strength upon trivial or base purposes, are by far too common in the world. They cannot be considered without regret, nor, may I add, without benefit. The misery which misguided endeavours produce, is no less real, than the happiness which would reward a different application of them; but there is pleasure in reflecting that the time may come when our faculties will not be able to vary from a true direction, and the errors of the present race, by the magnitude and extent of their effects, enable us, in some degree, to appreciate the good which may be hoped from a different condition of society.

The case of Archibald afforded a signal example of a powerful but misdirected capacity. I shall not mention the various contrivances which his ruling passion suggested to him. It is sufficient to say that after a due period of industry, and hope, and suspense, a good correspondence was established between him and the lady. She was sufficiently aware of the prejudices of her friends; but the rectitude of her own mind did not allow her to foresee all the effects of their prejudices: She could never apprehend the benefits of a clandestine connection: She rejected disguise, without a moment's hesitation: She discoursed without scruple, on those tokens and suggestions which Archibald, like an hovering genius, laid in her way without allowing her to distinguish the agent: She spoke with the same unreserve when the true agent was discovered.

The family were of course alarmed. The sincerity of the lady's attachment, and the energy of her principles, were quickly put to the test. Their remonstrances and arguments, though urged with all the advantages of numbers, age, and authority, availed nothing. They taught her neither to disguise nor relinquish her principles. She naturally imagined that this was a question on which no one had a right to decide but herself.

Archibald had sprung from obscurity and indigence. The last defect was of slight importance in the apprehension of the Butlers. An objection on this ground alone had never been made. A noble descent would have expiated every fault, but that of baseness and profligacy. Without this requisite no merit would suffice. That which was of greatest moment in the eyes of her friends, was of least, or rather was of no moment at all in those of the lady. She vindicated her choice with simplicity and mildness, and not with the zeal of one, the gratification of whose wishes depends on the success of her arguments in inspiring conviction; but with the collectedness of one who is merely desirous of evincing the propriety of a step that is inevitable. She did not suffer debate and opposition to ruffle her temper, or destroy her tranquility.

Her parents finding arguments ineffectual, deemed themselves justified, in order to obviate an evil of such magnitude, in resorting to force. All intercourse between the lovers was prohibited. She was condemned to a rigorous confinement. Her constancy, however, was not to be shaken: She reserved herself for better times: She yielded to personal restraints, because it was in vain to resist them; but she retained the freedom of her mind. She was insensible to menaces and persuasions; denied every parental claim, and the obligations of filial duty. She could by no means be induced to part with the independence of a reasonable being.

The behaviour of Archibald was, in many respects, a contrast to that of the lady. They with equal clearness perceived the injustice of those pretensions in her family; with equal strenuousness they refused to be controlled by them; but, while the latter displayed all the calmness of fortitude, the former was tormented by impatience and resentment.

The friends of Archibald endeavoured to persuade him to make a voyage to the West Indies. There being no room to hope for a change in the determinations of the lady's family, this expedient was chosen as most likely to dissolve a connection which, while it lasted, could only be productive of mutual distress. But it could hardly be expected that Archibald would admit the reasonableness of such ideas, or be induced by such arguments, to embrace this proposal. Many endeavours were made to vanquish the reluctance which he entertained for this scheme. None of them succeeded, till at length, the lady herself became its advocate.

She was fully acquainted with the character of her lover. His absence appeared to her to be desirable, as furnishing a useful trial to his constancy, as well as allowing scope to her own exertions to remove those obstacles to their union, which the prejudices of her family created. When every conceivable expedient has failed, time, alone, may work the most happy revolutions. She was not inclined to despair of the efficacy of perseverance and sincerity, in any cause. Here indeed they had hitherto been tried in vain; but great and unexpected changes in the temper and views of those around her might take place in the lapse of a year: meanwhile the presence of her lover tended only to exasperate their evil passions, and retard the event which they both so much desired. Influenced by these considerations she exerted herself to overcome his aversion to this voyage, and after many delays and struggles on his part, she at length effected her end.

The scheme, however plausible, proved unfortunate. The family after exhausting the obvious expedients, resorted to more atrocious ones. The longer we pursue a favorite end, the more enamoured we become of it, and the less scrupulous we are about the means that we use. The strictness of our morality relaxes while we mistake the instigations of passion for the enlargement of knowledge. I shall not dwell on the progress of their minds from the state in which, that which they finally embraced with eagerness, would have been rejected with horror. A plan was devised of deceiving the lady into an opinion that her lover was false; that he had made his address to a lady in the island to which he had gone, and was on the point of marriage.

Her sagacity was equal to her fortitude; but the craft with which she had to contend was consummate. Suspicion had not put her on her guard against that degree of depravity, to whose machinations it was her lot to be exposed. She was deceived, and at the same moment she was forsaken by the fortitude which had hitherto accompanied her.

A young man, to whom none of the objections made against Archibald were incident, had applied for the lady's favour, previously to her acquaintance with the latter. He was well-born and opulent, young and elegant in his figure and deportment, and intimately allied to the family. He entitled himself to the friendship of Miss Butler, but could not gain her affections.

The family approved of this match; but, partly from a sense of injustice, and partly from a persuasion that time and the lover's assiduities would ultimately prevail, allowed her to be governed in this respect by her own inclination. On the claims of Archibald, however, they altered their measures, and were no less anxious to prevail with her to discard Archibald than to accept his competitor. To neither proposal would she give any countenance; but whatever she should determine with respect to the former, she was irreconcilably averse to the latter. The belief of the inconstancy of Archibald seemed to have wrought a total revolution in her sentiments; but her secret resolutions were widely different from those with which she allowed her family to flatter themselves, as the fruits of their schemes.

Misfortune had turned a being of no common excellence into one capable of harbouring the most dreadful purposes. Though it be the property of injustice to propagate itself, to make its subjects not only miserable, but vicious, it would not be easy to account for the change that now took place in the mind of this lady. That she should start out into no excess of anger or grief on hearing of her lover's perfidy; that she should sustain the disappointment of her hopes, with unwavering magnanimity, was to be expected from the tenor of her former life, and the principles she had so steadily avowed; but it was not easy to comprehend how she could reconcile, at least so suddenly, her mind to an union with his rival.

These reflections did not hinder her family from eagerly profiting by this compliance, and making immediate preparations for the nuptials. The interval had passed without any thing to cloud their prospect. Every hour produced new tokens of the entire satisfaction with which the lady adopted her new measures. On the evening preceding the appointed day, she parted with her mother with every appearance of happiness and good humour. The morning arrived. She delayed her departure from her chamber beyond her customary hour. Her parent went thither to discover the reason and found her, not asleep, but dead.

Whether some sudden or unforeseen stroke had overtaken her; or, whether she was the author of her own death could never be certainly determined. On the whole the latter opinion was most probable.

It is remarkable that an event which the lady's parents had imposed upon their child, without believing it themselves, had really taken place. Absence had produced the usual effect upon the lover. He had seen a new object which had quickly supplanted the old. His ingenuity furnished an opiate to his conscience. He laid his heart at the feet of his new mistress; the present was accepted; she gave her own in return; and a distant day was assigned for ratifying the exchange: before it arrived, however, tidings reached him, by what means I shall not mention, of the fate of the Irish lady; of her voluntary death in consequence of the belief of his inconstancy. Of the groundlessness of this belief, and of the means by which it had been produced, he was wholly ignorant. As his inconstancy was real, he supposed she was apprized of no more than the truth.

The effect of this information may be easily conceived. He broke off his present connection, and immediately embarked for Europe. He arrived at Cork, and without delay procured an interview with the lady's family. His purpose was to obtain their assent to a proposal sufficiently singular—it was no other than that the vault, in which the body had been interred, should be opened, and himself permitted to take a last view of the corpse. He urged his demand with the energy of frenzy, and at length succeeded.

The solemn period of midnight was selected. The vault was opened in the presence of the desperate lover and some of the family of the deceased. They descended the stair-case: I shudder to describe the object that saluted their sight. They beheld the lady, not decently reposing in her coffin, and shrouded with a snow-white mantle, but—naked, ghastly, stretched on the floor at the foot of the stair-case, with indubitable tokens of having died, a second time, a victim of terror and famine.

It is not to be wondered at, that a spectacle like this plunged the unhappy lover into a frenzy the most outrageous. He was torn from the spot and speedily delivered to the care of his friends.

NOAH WEBSTER (1758–1843)

Noah Webster is best known as a lexicographer, the author and compiler of the first spelling book, grammar, and reader in the United States, published as *Grammatical Institutes of the English Language* (1783–85). Webster was remarkably well read, however, and keenly interested in the public affairs of his country. He was born in Hartford, Connecticut, and educated at Yale College during the American Revolution against Great Britain. He studied law after the war, after he completed college, and established himself as a lawyer in 1781. After practicing the law and teaching in several different places, he moved to New York in 1788, where his primary interests were in writing on linguistic and political matters. In addition to his *Grammatical Institutes,* he published *Dissertations on the English Language* (1789), and two separate grammars and dictionaries. He had long been involved in educational issues. He moved from New

York to New Haven in 1798 and to Amherst, Massachusetts, in 1828, where he took part in founding the college there.

Readers today probably know best the fact that Webster published an *American Dictionary of the English Language* (1828). Webster was well aware of the extent to which learning affected one's status in society, and he considered that individuals could best represent themselves before the law if they understood that the way the law was written down would have an influence over their actions as citizens. In addition to writing works on the English language, Webster published *Rights of Neutrals* (1802), a legal tract; a brief history of the United States (1823); and a compendium, *Collection of Papers on Political, Literary, and Moral Subjects* (1843). One of the lesser known but important papers Webster published was his pamphlet, *The Effects of Slavery, on Morals and Industry* (1793). The title of the pamphlet identifies Webster as counselor at law for the state of Connecticut and a member of the Connecticut Society for the Promotion of Freedom. In publishing an announcement of his pamphlet in the *American Minerva,* Webster said his essay was "designed to exhibit in a new point of view, its [slavery's] effects on morals, industry, and the peace of society." He announced: "Some facts and calculations are offered to prove the labor of freemen to be much more productive than that of slaves; that countries are rich, powerful and happy in proportion as the laboring people enjoy the fruits of their own Labor; and hence the necessary conclusion, that slavery is impolitic as well as unjust." Webster's argument hinged on an analysis that there was no innate inferiority in being black, something that had been under discussion for years, and he attributed any indications of inferior intelligence to the slaves' "depressed condition." Webster finally came out in behalf of the colonization of Africans, a move that would preserve the social and financial status of white people while drastically altering the lives of the many people of African descent. It was not, in other words, the more liberal and enlightened view of emancipation and political equality readers today would have hoped for, but Webster nonetheless spoke, at a time when his comments would not be welcome, on behalf of the illegitimacy and immorality of keeping people in subjection.

from EFFECTS OF SLAVERY, ON MORALS AND INDUSTRY[1]

It is evidently the will of heaven that men should be prompted to action by a regard to their own benefit and happiness. Whenever by the positive institutions of society, or by external force, men are stripped of the power of exerting themselves for their own benefit, the mind, having lost its spring or stimulus, either ceases to act, and men become mere machines, moving only when impelled by some extraneous power; or if the mind acts at all, it is at the impulse of violent passions, struggling to throw off an unnatural restraint, and to revenge the injury. Hence it is, that slaves, with few exceptions, may be divided into two classes, the *indolent* and the *villanous.*

In America the laziness of slaves has become proverbial: indeed the blacks are so remarkable for their inac-

tion, their want of foresight and their disinclination to improvement, as to create very great doubts in the minds of some men of a philosophical cast, whether they are not a distinct and inferior race of beings.[2] But on examining this subject, and comparing the blacks of this country, with the slaves of other countries, who are confessedly of the same race with the most improved European nation, it will probably be found that, making the usual allowances for the effects of their native climate, all the peculiar features in the character of the African race in America, may justly be ascribed to their depressed condition.

The indolence of the slaves in the southern states, must indeed approach almost to stupidity. It is said by gentlemen, well informed on this subject, that three blacks will not perform more labor than one free white in the northern states.[3] And it is well known that on every plantation, a

---

1. *Effects of Slavery, on Morals and Industry* was published in Hartford, Connecticut, in 1793. The text is from *Racial Thought in America,* ed. Louis Ruchames (1969).

2. "See Hume's *Essays* vol. 1. p. 550. Note M. Jefferson's Notes on Virginia, p. 237." [Au.]

3. "Letter from the Hon. Dr. Ramsay, Charleston, South Carolina." [Au.]

negro driver is required, with his whip and his cane, to compel the reluctant slave to perform his daily task. But are American slaves only distinguished for their aversion to labor? History teaches us a very different doctrine. Among the ancient Germans, who, by their vigor and bravery, conquered half the world, slavery had the same debasing stupifying influence: and it is remarkable that the word *lazzi,* which among our Saxon ancestors, was the denomination of the lowest order of bondmen or servants, is the origin of our English word *lazy,* a word expressive of that indolence and aversion to labor, which remarkably characterize the negroes in America. If slavery had this effect upon our own ancestors, the warlike heroes of the *north,* surely modern philosophers need not resort to an original difference of race, for the cause of that dullness and want of mental vigor, remarkable in the enslaved natives of the *torrid zone* and their degenerate descendants.

But if we turn our eyes upon the present nations of Europe, we shall find multiplied proofs of this important truth, that slavery necessarily enervates the vigor of the human mind, in all climates and among all nations. . . .

That freedom is the sacred right of every man whatever be his color, who has not forfeited it by some violation of municipal law, is a truth established by God himself in the very creation of human beings. No time, no circumstances, no human power or policy can change the nature of this truth, nor repeal the fundamental laws of society by which every man's right to liberty is guaranteed. The first act therefore of enslaving men is always a violation of those great primary laws of society, by which alone the master himself holds every particle of his own freedom.

But are there not cases when it is necessary to make a distinction between *abstract right and political expedience?* Is it not true that *political expedience,* properly understood, is the foundation of all *public right and justice?* The African slave trade originated when political and social rights were not generally understood, and when the few philosophers who understood and attempted to defend them could make a very feeble resistance to the suggestions of private avarice and the tyrannical policy of nations.[4] Under such circumstances, the business was begun and continued, till about 40 years ago when the society of Quakers, under the auspices of the benevolent Anthony

Benezet, remonstrated against the shameful traffic. From that period powerful efforts have been made by numerous societies as well as individuals, to procure the emancipation of those already reduced to slavery, and to put a stop to further importations from Africa. These efforts have been attended with great success. In some of the northern states of America, all the slaves have been set free by constitutional declarations of rights; in almost all of them provision has been made by law to introduce a gradual abolition of the existing slavery, and the further importation is strictly prohibited. At the same time we may remark that by a late act of the British Parliament, the slave trade is to cease in the year 1796; and the revolution in France has already produced very important changes in that trade and in the condition of the slaves in some of the French Islands. What will be the final result of these measures and events in the West Indies, no man can predict with any degree of assurance.

With respect to the United States of America, no great difficulties or inconveniences occur in gradually abolishing slavery in all the States north of Delaware. In the 8 States north and east of Delaware, the number of slaves is comparatively small; being to the free inhabitants in the proportion of only *one to forty four;* but in the six southern States, where the slaves make nearly *one third* of the inhabitants, the liberation of them is a matter of very serious consequence.[5]

To give freedom at once to almost 700,000 slaves, would reduce perhaps 20,000 white families to beggary. It would impoverish the country south of Pennsylvania; all cultivation would probably cease for a time; a famine would ensue; and there would be extreme danger of insurrections which might deluge the country in blood and perhaps depopulate it. Such calamities would be deprecated by every benevolent man and good citizen; and that zeal which some persons discover to effect a *total sudden abolition* of slavery in the United States, appears to be very intemperate. Indeed it is a zeal which counteracts its own purposes; for a sudden emancipation of such a number of slaves, instead of bettering their condition would render it worse, and inevitably expose them to perish with cold and famine. Whatever have been the means and however unjustifiable the policy by which slavery has been in-

---

4. "I have heard elderly people remark, that in the early part of their lives it never once occurred to them that it was unjust and iniquitous to enslave Africans. It is within a few years only that the question has been generally discussed." [Au.]

5. "Of 40,384 Slaves in the States north of Delaware, 32,777 are in New-York and New-Jersey: the slaves in Pennsylvania Vermont and the four New-England States amounting only to 7607. . . ." [Au.]

troduced and encouraged, the evil has taken such deep root, and is so widely spread in the southern States, that an attempt to eradicate it at a single blow would expose the whole political body to dissolution. In these ideas I shall probably be seconded by a great proportion of thinking men throughout the United States.

It has been suggested that the country may gradually be delivered from its black inhabitants by transporting a certain number of them to Africa every year, furnished with the necessary means of subsistence. A settlement of this kind has been already begun by a colony from Great-Britain, under the superintendance of Mr. Clarkson.[6] Indeed if colonial establishments of this kind could be effected, without great injury to the United States, humanity and philosophy would exult at the prospect of seeing the arts of civilized nations introduced into the heart of Africa. But the practicability of this plan of colonization seems to be yet problematical. It seems not yet decided by the experiments made, whether such colonies would not dwindle away by disease, and be perpetually exposed to the hostility of the surrounding natives. Indeed, it may be an important question, whether even well civilized blacks placed in the torrid zone, where little labor is requisite to procure their necessary food and clothing, would not neglect all arts and labor, beyond what are necessary to supply immediate wants, and gradually revert back to a savage state. How far a commercial intercourse with such colonies, by exciting a taste for luxuries and the love of wealth and splendor, would tend to preserve their habits of industry and prompt them to encourage arts and manufactures, we have perhaps no certain data from which we can draw even a probable conclusion.

But other objections oppose themselves to the project of African colonization. Who is to pay the expense? The master will think the loss of his slaves a sacrifice on his part sufficiently great, without furnishing them with food, utensils, and shipping for their transportation; and the slaves are not able to furnish themselves with these articles. The funds therefore must be raised by private subscriptions, or supplied by government; and these resources cannot be relied on in the present state of America. Besides it is not certain that the slaves themselves would be willing to risk such a change of situation;

as most of them are born in this country and are total strangers to Africa and its inhabitants. In this case, to compel them to quit the country, and encounter the dangers of the sea, an insalubrious climate and the hostile tribes of Africa; together with the risk of starving, would be a flagrant act of injustice, inferior only to the first act of enslaving their ancestors.

The objection that the unhealthiness of the climate renders it impossible for whites to cultivate rice and indigo plantations, and therefore it is necessary to perform this business by blacks, seems to be of little weight; or at least, it cannot be of permanent duration. It is commonly supposed that the insalubrity of the air in the southern states, arises in great measure, from the stagnant waters which cover the rice and indigo plantations. These waters indeed increase the evil; but the principal cause is a much more extensive one; the large marshes and vast tracts of uncleared land in the flat country. Marshes and stagnant waters, in which vegetable substances putrify and dissolve, produce pestilential exhalations; and when a country is mostly covered with forests, the air itself becomes stagnant and does not carry off the noxious effluvia generated in low grounds. It is with the air as with water; its purity depends on its motion. To render any flat country healthy, it must be cleared of its forests, and laid open on all sides to the action of the wind. It is not sufficient to open here and there a plantation, and leave four fifths of the earth covered with wood. Besides the advantage of giving motion to the air on an extended plain, the clearing and cultivation of the earth lays it open to the sun, whose heat warms and dries the surface, and by removing the moisture, prevents the generation of noxious exhalations. Thus whenever most of the land in the southern states shall be cleared, the principal cause of epidemic diseases will be destroyed; and the free circulation of air near the surface of the earth will render the putrid exhalations from the plantations and marsh ground which cannot be drained, much less fatal. The New-England States, sixty years ago, were infested with the same annual fevers, which now prove so troublesome to the southern states; but by the clearing and cultivation of the earth, those diseases no longer prevail. The rice fields in Italy and Spain are all cultivated by white people, and tho they render the air about them less salubrious than it is in other parts of the country, yet it is not so fatal to the health of the people as to discourage the culture of that useful grain.

There is therefore no question that a general and high state of cultivation will, to a great degree, correct the insalubrity of the low flat country in the southern States, so

---

6. Thomas Clarkson (1760–1846), British abolitionist, devoted his life to abolishing the slave trade and slavery in the British colonies of North America.

as to render it cultivable with white laborers; except perhaps in the vicinity of such saltmarshes as cannot be drained. But the obstacles that present themselves to the project of *colonization,* and to that of a *general sudden abolition* of slavery, appear to be equally insurmountable. The blacks in the southern States must, it is presumed, continue there, for a great number of years, perhaps forever; government at least will not undertake the herculean task of exporting them to a foreign country, and repeopling five or six States with white inhabitants.[7]

What then can be done? What method can be devised for meliorating the condition of the blacks, without essentially injuring the slave, the master and the public. This is the great desideratum. There appears to me only one plan or expedient for effecting this desirable object, which, in its operation, will combine the three several interests which are to be consulted; this is, to raise the slaves, by gradual means, to the condition of free tenants.

7. "The project of exporting all the blacks in the United States, would, if practicable, be attended with many desireable effects. The separation of the whites from all mixture of colour, would remove the causes of much jealousy and dissention, which will otherwise prevail among the whites and blacks. But should colonization ever be attempted, the exportation of the slaves from the southern States must be slow and gradual, to

prevent the impoverishment of the country. The sudden explusion of 700,000 morescoes from Spain, in the reign of Philip 3, gave a blow to the agriculture and manufactures of that kingdom which the efforts of almost two centuries have scarcely repaired. . . . Many of the wealthiest people in Spain were reduced to poverty and distress!—Perhaps a more eligible scheme would be to assign the blacks a portion of land in the United States, and remove them all thither by slow degrees, furnishing them with means of cultivation." [Au.]

BENJAMIN BANNEKER (1731–1806)

A self-taught mathematician and astronomer, Benjamin Banneker achieved international acclaim for his almanacs, and he was part of the surveying team that worked to establish the coordinates for the new federal city called the District of Columbia. Banneker was cited by the the Reverend Henri Grégoire in France in a pamphlet about Africans and slavery, and in the House of Commons, he was hailed as a preeminent example of the unbelievable injustices of holding Africans and their descendants as slaves. As part of the surveying team mapping out the quadrants for the new federal district in 1792, Banneker logged the survey's progress, calculated coordinates by using the astronomical instruments provided the team, and established the base points from which the survey would be drawn. He spent most of his time in the observatory tent, where he slept, but on the walks through the countryside, Banneker was the one being watched. People were fascinated with his accomplishments—and with his status on the team, as a black man. The *Georgetown Weekly Ledger* reported about the surveying team in March 1792, that they had arrived under the leadership of Andrew Ellicott (a relative of Banneker's farming neighbor and friend from Baltimore County, Maryland). Ellicott was attended, the newspaper reported, "by *Benjamin Banneker,* an Ethiopian, whose abilities, as a surveyor, and an astronomer, clearly prove that Mr. Jefferson's concluding that race of men void of mental endowments, was without foundation." The slighting reference to Jefferson came from his *Notes on the State of Virginia.* Jefferson's name at this time would be remarkably intertwined with Banneker's. Jefferson himself had an exchange of letters with Banneker that would become famous because Banneker saw that their exchange was published.

Benjamin Banneker was the oldest child of Mary and Robert Banneker, free blacks who owned a sizable farm north of Baltimore, Maryland. Taught by his grandmother to read, Banneker was sent to a local school run by the Society of Friends (Quakers) for the rural children. Although he disliked the labor on his father's tobacco farm, he enjoyed the tabulations and calculations that being a farmer required of him. From his earliest days, he was interested in science and mathematics. He continued to work on the family farm after his parents' death, dividing his time between agricultural work and mathematical and scientific pursuits. It was Banneker's friendship with his new neighbors (particularly George Ellicott) in the early 1770s, that would draw him into more a formal study of astronomy and related sciences. The Ellicotts noticed Banneker's talents and lent him some books and some calculating instruments, so that he could further his own education. Banneker used these resources to teach himself to calculate the positions of the sun, moon, and planets each year. From his calculations of the positions of these bodies, Banneker learned to forecast the rising and setting of the sun and moon, solar and lunar eclipses, and the ocean's tides. The first ephemeris (a twelve-month table of forecastings, based on astronomical calculations) Banneker constructed was the essential part of an almanac maker's labor. He sought a publisher to no avail in 1791, but he had learned a lot, and he continued his work with the intention of finding a publisher for his work the following year.

In the meantime, however, Banneker was called upon for the important surveying project in behalf of the new federal government. The work of the survey took place during the spring of 1792. After completing the necessary part of his own work with Ellicott, Banneker returned home and wrote a letter to Thomas Jefferson, enclosing with it a manuscript copy of his ephemeris. Banneker challenged Jefferson's low opinion of Africans, as expressed in his *Notes on the State of Virginia,* saying that he had heard that Jefferson was "measurably friendly" toward blacks, people "of my complexion." When Jefferson wrote a brief letter in response to Banneker, Banneker's first thought was to get their letters printed in his first almanac, but when this did not occur, Banneker decided upon a separate printing. The pamphlet was made up of Banneker's letter and Jefferson's reply, along with a descriptive attestation regarding the life of Benjamin Banneker by Dr. James McHenry of Baltimore. McHenry helped Banneker because, he said, "I cannot but wish on this occasion to see the Public patronage keep pace with my black friend's merit." The pamphlet was printed in 1792 in Philadelphia, a city with a strong Quaker abolitionist community. So that he could pursue his almanac making thereafter, Banneker retired from his work as a farmer and focused his attention on mathematical puzzles and astronomical calculations. Between 1792 and 1797, Banneker's almanacs were published in Baltimore, Philadelphia, Wilmington, Trenton, Petersburg, and Richmond. His almanacs were used widely, and his work became known on both sides of the Atlantic. Banneker lived his final years alone on his farm, writing in his journal and studying his bees, the stars, and mathematics.

COPY OF A LETTER FROM BENJAMIN BANNEKER TO THE SECRETARY OF STATE, WITH HIS ANSWER[1]

Maryland, Baltimore County, **August 19, 1791**

SIR,

I am fully sensible of the greatness of that freedom which I take with you on the present occasion, a liberty which seemed to me scarcely allowable, when I reflected on that distinguished and dignified station in which you stand, and

---

1. *Copy of a Letter from Benjamin Banneker, to the Secretary of State, with His Answer* (Philadelphia, 1792) is the source of the present text. The pamphlet included Banneker's letter to Jefferson, Jefferson's response, and the statement by James McHenry.

the almost general prejudice and prepossession, which is so prevalent in the world against those of my complexion.

I suppose it is a truth too well attested to you, to need a proof here, that we are a race of beings that have long labored under the abuse and censure of the world; that we have long been looked upon with an eye of contempt; and that we have long been considered rather as brutish than human, and scarcely capable of mental endowments.

Sir, I hope I may safely admit, in consequence of that report which has reached me, that you are a man far less inflexible in sentiments of this nature, than many others; that you are measurably friendly and well disposed towards us; and that you are willing and ready to lend your aid and assistance to our relief from those many distresses and numerous calamities to which we are reduced.

Now Sir, if this is founded in truth, I apprehend you will embrace every opportunity to eradicate that train of absurd and false ideas and opinions which so generally prevails with respect to us; and that your sentiments are concurrent with mine, which are, that one universal Father has given being to us all; and that he hath not only made us all of one flesh, but that he hath also, without partiality, afforded us all the same sensations and endowed us all with the same faculties; and that however variable we may be in society or religion, however diversified in situation or color, we are all of the same family, and stand in the same relation to him.

Sir, if these are sentiments of which you are fully persuaded, I hope you cannot but acknowledge that it is the indispensable duty of those who maintain for themselves the rights of human nature, and who possess the obligations of Christianity, to extend their power and influence to the relief of every part of the human race from whatever burden or oppression they may unjustly labor under; and this, I apprehend, a full conviction of the truth and obligation of these principles should lead all to.

Sir, I have long been convinced that if your love for yourselves, and for those inestimable laws which preserved to you the rights of human nature, was founded on sincerity, you could not but be solicitous that every individual, of whatever rank or distinction, might with you equally enjoy the blessings thereof; neither could you rest satisfied short of the most active effusion of your exertions, in order to their promotion from any state of degradation, to which the unjustifiable cruelty and barbarism of men may have reduced them.

Sir, I freely and cheerfully acknowledge that I am of the African race, and in that color which is natural to them of the deepest dye; and it is under a sense of the most profound gratitude to the Supreme Ruler of the Universe that I now confess to you that I am not under that state of tyrannical thraldom and inhuman captivity to which many of my brethren are doomed, but that I have abundantly tasted of the fruition of those blessings, which proceed from that free and unequalled liberty with which you are favored; and which, I hope, you will willingly allow you have mercifully received from the immediate hand of that Being from whom proceedeth every good and perfect gift.

Sir, suffer me to recall to your mind that time in which the arms and tyranny of the British crown were exerted, with every powerful effort, in order to reduce you to a state of servitude: look back, I entreat you, on the variety of dangers to which you were exposed; reflect on that time in which every human aid appeared unavailable, and in which every hope and fortitude wore the aspect of inability to the conflict, and you cannot but be led to a serious and grateful sense of your miraculous and providential preservation; you cannot but acknowledge, that the

present freedom and tranquillity which you enjoy you have mercifully received, and that it is the peculiar blessing of Heaven.

This, Sir, was a time when you clearly saw into the injustice of a state of slavery, and in which you had just apprehensions of the horrors of its condition. It was now that your abhorrence thereof was so excited, that you publicly held forth this true and invaluable doctrine, which is worthy to be recorded and remembered in all succeeding ages: "We hold these truths to be self-evident, that all men are created equal; that they are endowed by their Creator with certain inalienable rights, and that among these are, life, liberty, and the pursuit of happiness."[2]

Here was a time, in which your tender feelings for yourselves had engaged you thus to declare you were then impressed with proper ideas of the great violation of liberty, and the free possession of those blessings to which you were entitled by nature; but, Sir, how pitiable is it to reflect, that although you were so fully convinced of the benevolence of the Father of Mankind, and of his equal and impartial distribution of these rights and privileges which he hath conferred upon them, that you should at the same time counteract his mercies, in detaining by fraud and violence so numerous a part of my brethren under groaning captivity and cruel oppression, that you should at the same time be found guilty of that most criminal act, which you professedly detested in others, with respect to yourselves.

I suppose that your knowledge of the situation of my brethren is too extensive to need a recital here; neither shall I presume to prescribe methods by which they may be relieved, otherwise than by recommending to you and all others, to wean yourselves from those narrow prejudices which you have imbibed with respect to them, and as Job proposed to his friends, "put your soul in their souls' stead";[3] thus shall your hearts be enlarged with kindness and benevolence towards them; and thus shall you need neither the direction of myself or others, in what manner to proceed herein.

And now, Sir, although my sympathy and affection for my brethren hath caused my enlargement thus far, I ardently hope that your candor and generosity will plead with you in my behalf, when I make known to you, that it was not originally my design; but having taken up my pen in order to direct to you, as a present, a copy of an Al-

---

2. The first lines of the *Declaration of Independence* (1776).

3. See Job 16:4.

manac which I have calculated for the succeeding year, I was unexpectedly and unavoidably led thereto.

This calculation is the production of my arduous study, in this my advanced stage of life; for having long had unbounded desires to become acquainted with the secrets of nature, I have had to gratify my curiosity herein, through my own assiduous application to Astronomical Study, in which I need not recount to you the many difficulties and disadvantages, which I have had to encounter.

And although I had almost declined to make my calculation for the ensuing year, in consequence of that time which I had allotted therefor, being taken up at the Federal Territory, by the request of Mr. Andrew Ellicott;[4] yet finding myself under several engagements to Printers of this state, to whom I had communicated my design, on my return to my place of residence, I industriously applied myself thereto, which I hope I have accomplished with correctness and accuracy; a copy of which I have taken the liberty to direct to you, and which I humbly request you will favorably receive; and although you may have the opportunity of perusing it after its publication, yet I choose to send it to you in manuscript previous thereto, that thereby you might not only have an earlier inspection, but that you might also view it in my own hand writing.

And now, Sir, I shall conclude, and subscribe myself, with the most profound respect,

Your most obedient humble servant,
BENJAMIN BANNEKER

To, Mr. BENJAMIN BANNEKER
Philadelphia, August 30, 1791

SIR,

I THANK you, sincerely, for your letter of the 19th instant,[5] and for the Almanac it contained. Nobody wishes more than I do, to see such proofs as you exhibit, that nature has given to our black brethren talents equal to those of the other colors of men; and that the appearance of the want of them is owing merely to the degraded condition of their existence, both in Africa and America. I can add with truth, that nobody wishes more ardently to see a

good system commenced for raising the condition, both of their body and mind, to what it ought to be, as far as the imbecility of their present existence, and other circumstances, which cannot be neglected, will admit.

I have taken the liberty of sending your Almanac to Monsieur de Condozett,[6] Secretary of the Academy of Sciences at Paris, and Member of the Philanthropic Society, because I considered it as a document to which your whole color had a right for their justification, against the doubts which have been entertained of them.

I am with great esteem, Sir,
Your most obedient
Humble Servant,
THOMAS JEFFERSON.

The following Account, taken from BANNEKER'S Almanac, is inserted here, for the Information of the Public.[7]

Baltimore, August 20, 1791

BENJAMIN BANNEKER, a free Black, is about 59 years of age; he was born in Baltimore county; his father an African, and his mother the offspring of African parents. His father and mother having obtained their freedom, were able to send him to an obscure school, where he learned, when a boy, reading, writing, and arithmetic, as far as double position; and to leave him, at their deaths, a few acres of land, upon which he has supported himself ever since, by means of economy and constant labor, and preserved a fair reputation. To struggle incessantly against want, is no ways favorable to improvement: what he had learned, however, he did not forget; for as some hours of leisure will occur in the most toilsome life, he availed himself of these, not to read and acquire knowledge from writings of genius and discovery, for of such he had none, but to digest and apply, as occasions presented, the few principles of the few rules of mathematics he had been taught at school. This kind of mental exercise formed his chief amusement, and soon gave him a facility in calculation that was often serviceable to his neighbours, and at length

---

4. Andrew Ellicott (1754–1820), a cousin of Banneker's neighbor George Ellicott, directed the 1791–93 survey of the lands that would become the District of Columbia.

5. That is, August 19.

6. Marie Jean Antoine Nicolas Caritat, marquis de Condorcet (1743–94), a French philosopher and mathematician, was also president of the French legislative assembly of the new French Republic after the start of the French Revolution, at the time Jefferson transmitted Banneker's almanac. Condorcet joined ranks with the Gironde and was sought for arrest at the time he poisoned himself to escape the guillotine.

7. At the time he wrote this attestation, James McHenry (1753–1816) was a member of the Maryland Senate.

attracted the attention of the Messrs. Ellicott, a family remarkable for their ingenuity and turn to the useful mechanics. It is about three years since Mr. George Ellicott lent him Mayer's Tables, Ferguson's Astronomy, Leadbeater's Lunar Tables,[8] and some Astronomic Instruments, but without accompanying them with either hint or instruction, that might further his studies, or lead him to apply them to any useful result. These books and instruments, the first of the kind he had ever seen, opened a new world to Benjamin, and from thenceforward he employed his leisure in Astronomical Researches.

He now took up the idea of the calculations for an Almanac, and actually completed an entire set for the last year, upon his original stock of Arithmetic. Encouraged by his first attempt, he entered upon his calculation for 1792 which, as well as the former, he began and finished without the least information or assistance from any person, or other books than those I have mentioned; so that whatever merit is attached to his present performance, is exclusively and peculiarly his own.

I have been the more careful to investigate those particulars, and to ascertain their reality, as they form an interesting fact in the History of Man; and as you may want them to gratify curiosity, I have no objection to your selecting them for your account of Benjamin.

---

8. Banneker was lent other books as well. McHenry refers to the solar and lunar tables by Tobias Mayer (1723–62), published in a translation from Latin in 1770; *Astronomy Explained upon Sir Isaac Newton's Principles* by James Ferguson (1710–70); and *A Compleat System of Astronomy* by Charles Leadbetter (fl. 1728).

THE NATIVE PEOPLES OF
EASTERN NORTH AMERICA AND
THE SETTLERS WHO REMAINED

The study of the written records created by the British and European settlers who came over to the Americas, but particularly to North America, dominates any attempt to comprehend how the United States was formed as a literary, cultural, and political entity. But by focusing attention on the writings of the settler people or those whom they culturally or socially influenced, whether for good or ill, it can be easy to lose sight of the many Native peoples who remained in their own lands, spoke about the injustices of the takeover that was continuing to occur, and attempted to negotiate in peaceful and persistent ways with the competing British and European powers so that they could retain their ancestral lands.

Given the rampant overtaking of Indian lands that occurred especially during the eighteenth century in North America, it may be easy to assume that Native peoples silently or quietly acquiesced, that they just moved farther inland or died from diseases brought by Europeans or became culturally assimilated in the face of the relentless pursuit of land and the clear cultural aggressiveness of the people who settled in North America. Native people did employ many different methods to accommodate themselves to the intruders on their lands, and they did face biological agents brought from Europe that caused a diminution of their numbers. But Native peoples during the eighteenth century did not just fade or die away, leaving the woods uninhabited, as many writers, particularly the writers of the early republic, may lead us to believe. Instead, they were persistently at council with the settlers; cogently arguing their cases before listeners, both Indians and settlers; and actively seeking redress for their grievances. Narratives of captivity among Indian peoples may tend to make it seem today as if Indians were always the aggressors against British and European settlers. By examining Native Americans' speeches, recorded at treaty councils and in narratives by those who lived among Native Americans, we gain a different perspective about who the aggressors were and what happened to the Indian peoples whose lands were being taken, whether by theft or purchase. Native peoples had then, as they have now, much to say about what happened to their ancestral lands and their peoples.

THE MAHICANS

The Mahicans lived along the lower end of the Hudson River area, and during the colonial era, they learned to negotiate well among the different settler groups—Dutch, French, Swedish, German, and English—who passed through or came to live in their area. Their first experiences with Europeans occurred when Dutch settlers arrived in their territory during the early seventeenth century, and as time wore on, they faced continual and competing incursions by Europeans on their lands. Like other Indian peoples in other areas, the

Mahicans understood that they were living among different cultural and ethnic populations, people who came to their lands from somewhere else to the east and who were not themselves from the same culture.

What the Mahicans persistently reported that they did not understand was the extent to which the different groups would say one thing and do something else. Their complaints about the inconsistency of the settlers' behaviors are like complaints by many Indian peoples. Indians were told by missionaries or political leaders to behave in certain ways, and they were expected to adhere to what they were told. But Indians were also subjected to settlers living among them who did not adhere to the settlers' community polity defined by the people with whom the Indians were negotiating at any given time. That is, the settlers' activity was uncontrolled: Trappers, traders, and individuals or family groups also came to Indian lands and lived outside the communities whose leaders were engaging in negotiations with the Indians.

This situation is evident in the selection presented next. Governor William Burnet of New York met with the Mahicans, whom the British called the River Indians because of their location on the southern end of the Hudson River, in late August 1722. The goal of the council was an attestation of amity between the two cultures, Indian and English, which the Mahicans, like their Iroquois neighbors, considered a renewal of the Covenant Chain of friendship. The Convenant Chain was important to the polity of the Indian peoples of New York, for it served as a symbol of friendship among people who, presumably, understood that they were equal parties creating a chain of amity together. For the Mahicans, the Covenant Chain was most clearly renewed by the dispersal of gifts, wampum (aesthetically devised and complicated strings of shells), or pelts, which marked the importance of the thing just spoken while also conferring obligations upon the listener to understand and behave according to what was said. Such gifts conferred obligations of partnership; they were not tribute, but instead were signs of the Indians' understanding of their own equal power in council.

The method of delivery of the spoken words, even down to the time taken for laying down the goods—in effect, the punctuating of the meeting—was perceived by many of the colonist-negotiators as necessary to continue the friendship but time consuming and sometimes incomprehensible. They often misunderstood the obligation imposed by the gift giving as, instead, tribute given to the settlers that indicated a sense of submission to their superior power. Such an interpretation, when it occurred, was a total misapprehension of Indian diplomacy.

When the Mahicans met with Governor Burnet in 1722, the meeting was to renew the chain of friendship and amity, the Covenant Chain, so that the two groups would continue to respect one another. Their negotiations were conducted through Dutch translators who had learned the Mahicans' language and who could thus relay the messages between the Mahicans and the English leaders. During the meeting, the governor commented that the Mahicans were wasting their precious goods, pelts and corn, in trade for rum. He advised the Mahicans to resist rum and be more sober. What follows is the response given to Burnet's comments.

SPEECH OF THE MAHICANS TO GOV. WILLIAM BURNET OF NEW YORK, 1722[1]

Father

We are sensible that you are much in the right, that Rum does a great deal of Harm, we approve of all that you

1. The text is from *Documents Relative to the Colonial History of the State of New York,* 15 vols., ed. E. B. O'Callaghan (1855), vol. 5.

said on that Point, but the matter is this, When our people come from Hunting to the Town or Plantations and acquaint the Traders & People that we want Powder and Shot & Clothing, they first give us a large cup of Rum, and after we get the Taste of it crave for more so that in fine all the Beaver & Peltry we have hunted goes for drink, and we are left destitute either of Clothing or Ammunition, Therefore we desire our father to order the Tap or Crane to be shut & to prohibit ye selling of Rum, for as long as the Christians will sell Rum, our People will drink it, do give 3 Beavers

Father

We acknowledge that our Father is very much in the right to tell us that we squander away our Indian Corn which should subsist our Wives & Children but one great cause of it is y^t many of our People are obliged to hire Land of the Christians at a very dear Rate, to give half the Corn for Rent & the other half they are tempted by Rum to sell, & so the Corn goes, y^t ye Poor women & children are left to shift as well as the can do give 3 Beavers

Father

We have no more Land the Christians when they buy a small spot of Land of us, ask us if we have no more Land & when we say yes they enquire the name of the Land & take in a greater Bounds than was intended to be sold them & the Indians not understanding what is writ in the Deed or Bill of Sale sign it and are so deprived of Part of their Lands—Give 3 Beavers

Father

In former days when the Christians came to settle this Country they came with a ship & desired to fasten their Cable to the Hills near Hosak above Albany, which we readily granted & ever since we have lived in Friendship & Amity together, which we hope will continue so long as Sun & Moon endure Gave 3 Beavers

STUNG SERPENT

Stung Serpent, whom Antoine Le Page du Pratz reported was considered the "brother to the Great Sun, and Chief of the Warriors of the Natchez," was the cultural leader of the Natchez peoples who resided at Natchez, on the southern part of the Mississippi River in present-day Mississippi, then part of the Louisiana territory. The Natchez formed a small confederacy of Indian groups on both sides of the Mississippi, and as a result of their confederacy, they controlled the traffic on Indian goods along that southern portion of the river. When the French moved into Natchez territory, the relationship arranged between the groups was an uneasy friendship, but a peaceful one nonetheless, until the number of settlers invading Natchez lands reached a proportion that the Indians could no longer tolerate.

At the beginning of the eighteenth century, the Natchez peoples met with less frequency among the settlers, and they consolidated culturally for defensive purposes. Open hostilities broke out when the Natchez started to make small raids on those in outlying areas. The French retaliated by attacking the Natchez fortification in 1728–29, killing many Natchez but not totally wiping out the people as historians formerly supposed. The Natchez went to live among the Chicasaws and Cherokees, who were also concerned about French incursions in the area, and they scattered themselves among other Indian groups, forsaking their territory as lost to the French.

Antoine Le Page du Pratz, who lived among the Natchez peoples for five years, came to know and highly respect Stung Serpent, the Natchez leader. He reported in his history that in 1723, Stung Serpent passed him by in the street, foregoing the greetings that formerly had been exchanged between them. The following is the response he received from Stung Serpent.

SPEECH TO ANTOINE LE PAGE DU PRATZ, 1723[1]

Why did the French come into our country? We did not go to seek them. They asked land of us, because their country was too little for all the men that were in it. We told them they might take land where they pleased, there was enough for them and for us; that it was good the same sun should enlighten us both, and that we should walk as friends, in the same path, and that we would give them of our provisions, assist them to build, and to labor in their fields. We have done so; is not this true? What occasion, then, had we for Frenchmen? Before they came, did we not live better than we do, seeing we deprive ourselves of a part of our corn, our game, and fish, to give a part to them? In what respect, then, had we occasion for them? Was it for their

---

1. The text is from Antoine Le Page du Pratz, *The History of Louisiana,* translated from the French for the English edition of 1774.

guns? The bows and arrows, which we used, were sufficient to make us live well. Was it for their white, blue, and red blankets? We can do well enough with buffalo skins which are warmer; our women wrought feather blankets for the winter, and mulberry mantles for the summer; which indeed were not so beautiful, but our women were more laborious and less vain than they are now. In fine, before the arrival of the French we lived like men who can be satisfied with what they have; whereas at this day we are like slaves, who are not suffered to do as they please.

CANASATEGO

The treaty parties meeting at Lancaster in the Pennsylvania territory engaged in what would become an important meeting, given the outcome of the Seven Years War in North America and, later, of the Revolution of the British colonies against Great Britain. The treaty council, which took place during two weeks, was designed to settle territorial complaints made by Virginia, Maryland, and the Iroquois. The complaints were negotiated through the services of Johann Conrad Weiser (1696–1760), an Indian agent and interpreter who had been born in Germany but came to the New York area with his family in 1710. Soon after his arrival, Weiser went to live among the Iroquois, and he married a Mohawk woman in 1720. He maintained close, lifelong ties with Indian peoples. It should be acknowledged that several of Weiser's negotiations between the Indian and white worlds ended up benefiting the settlers significantly. Yet Weiser is to be credited with retaining the interests of both groups in his attempt to keep to the fore the idea that peaceful negotiations could occur, rather than wholesale land wars.

At the time of the treaty at Lancaster, the Iroquois were engaging in a struggle to retain and enlarge their territory so as to create a greater cooperative alliance among Indian peoples in the face of encroachments by the settlers. Internally, the Iroquois were facing their own struggles, however, as well. In Iroquoian culture, the Onandaga peoples were traditionally the keepers of the council fires, and all important negotiations were traditionally to have taken place at Onandaga, at the geographic center of Iroquoia. When the Dutch and then the English settled in the eastern part of Iroquoia, they developed trading alliances with the Mohawks, traditionally the keepers of the eastern gate of Iroquoia but not, in terms of Iroquoian polity, the people who would make treaties for the Iroquois peoples. The Mohawks' trading and land negotiations with the settlers brought complications into Iroquoian polity, and the Onandagas struggled to retain their traditional leadership roles as chief negotiators for all the Iroquoian peoples, according to the confederacy's time-honored and traditional way. For the Onandagas, the treaty at Lancaster, although it took place outside Onandaga, the traditional center for negotiations with outsiders, was very important, because it gave them the opportunity to reassert their right—by way of the conference leader, the Onandaga chief Canasatego—as the primary negotiators for Iroquoia. Whereas in recent years the outsiders had been negotiating with the Mohawks, the Onandagas regained control, intraculturally, as the major negotiators and speakers of the Iroquois. So the treaty accomplished much in terms of internal Iroquoian affairs.

According to those representing Virginia and Maryland, the Iroquois were engaging in an unjustified territorial expansion. The Virginians had wanted the meeting to take place in Williamsburg, but the Iroquois refused to meet there. The Iroquois might have preferred the treaty talks to have occurred at Albany or at Onandaga, but Virginia refused. Meeting at Lancaster was a middle ground, then, as historian Francis Jennings has indicated, and it suited the Pennsylvania settlers' wishes to be centrally included in whatever negotiations would take place. About 250 Indians attended the two weeks of talks in June 1744, accompanying several leading speakers of the Iroquois, or Six Nations peoples (as they were called by the British). The governor of Pennsylvania, George Thomas, was there, along with commissioners representing Virginia and Maryland. The Lancaster courthouse was the site of the talks. Although the Virginians would have preferred a different negotiator than Conrad Weiser, the Pennsylvanians, who had a crucial concern about Germans in inland areas, insisted that he perform the interpreting tasks.

The Iroquois claimed that they had conquered the Susquehannocks, who had joined them as tributary peoples of the Iroquois. The Marylanders knew well that the Susquehannocks actually had been driven out of their homelands as a result of battles with Maryland settlers. The Iroquois nonetheless, in the thinking of Canasatego, had a right to lay claim to Susquehannock ancestral territory. Maryland disputed such a claim, based on Maryland's possession and use of the land for over a century. Canasatego responded with his interpretation of the history of Indian and European contact in the area. On the final day of the conference, Canasatego was offered the opportunity to have Iroquois men sent to school at Williamsburg. He responded politely that he considered this unnecessary and impractical. He concluded his part of the council by offering advice to the many different leaders who represented different interests of British and Europeans in his land. They had much to learn from the Iroquois, he thought.

SPEECH AT THE TREATY OF LANCASTER, 1744[1]

Brother, the Governor of Maryland,

When you mentioned the Affair of the Land Yesterday, you went back to old Times, and told us, you had been in Possession of the Province of *Maryland* above One Hundred Years; but what is One Hundred Years in Comparison of the Length of Time since our Claim began? since we came out of this Ground? For we must tell you, that long before One Hundred Years our Ancestors came out of this very Ground, and their Children have remained here ever since. You came out of the Ground in a Country that lies beyond the Seas, there you may have a just Claim, but here you must allow us to be your elder Brethren, and the Lands to belong to us long before you knew any thing of them. It is true, that above One Hundred Years ago the *Dutch* came here in a Ship, and brought with them several Goods; such as Awls, Knives, Hatchets, Guns, and many other Particulars, which they gave us; and when they had taught us how to use their Things, and we saw what sort of People they were, we were so well pleased with them, that we tied their Ship to the Bushes on the Shore; and afterwards, liking them still better the longer they staid with us, and thinking the Bushes too slender, we removed the Rope, and tied it to the Trees; and as the Trees were liable to be blown down by high winds, or to decay of themselves, we from the Af-

fection we bore them, again removed the Rope, and tied it to a strong and big Rock (*here the Interpreter said, They mean the* Oneido *Country*) and not content with this, for its further Security we removed the Rope to the big Mountain (*here the Interpreter says they mean the* Onandago *Country*) and there we tied it very fast, and rowlled Wampum about it; and, to make it still more secure, we stood upon the Wampum, and sat down upon it, to defend it, and to prevent any Hurt coming to it, and did our best Endeavours that it might remain uninjured for ever. During all this Time the New-comers, the *Dutch,* acknowledged our Right to the Lands, and sollicited us, from Time to Time, to grant them Parts of our Country, and enter into League and Covenant with us, and to become one People with us.

After this the *English* came into the Country, and, as we were told, became one People with the *Dutch.* About two Years after the Arrival of the *English,* an *English* Governor came to *Albany* and finding what great Friendship subsisted between us and the *Dutch,* he approved it mightily, and desired to make as strong a League, and to be upon as good Terms with us as the *Dutch* were, with whom he was united, and to become one People with us: And by his further Care in looking into what had passed between us, he found that the Rope which tied the Ship to the great Mountain was only fastened with Wampum, which was liable to break and rot, and to perish in a Course of Years; he therefore told us, he would give us a Silver Chain, which would be much stronger, and would last for ever. This we accepted, and fastened the Ship with it, and it has lasted ever since. Indeed we have had some small Differences with the *English,* and, during these Misunderstanding, some of their young Men would, by way of Reproach, be every now and then telling us, that

---

1. The text is from *Colonial Records of Pennsylvania* (also known as *Minutes of the Provincial Council of Pennsylvania*), ed. Samuel Hazard (1841), vol. 4. The italics in the text appear in the minutes as originally recorded.

we should have perished if they had not come into the Country and furnished us with Strowds[2] and Hatchets, and Guns, and other Things necessary for the Support of Life; but we always gave them to understand that they were mistaken, that we lived before they came amongst us, and as well, or better, if we may believe what our Forefathers have told us. We had then Room enough, and Plenty of Deer, which was easily caught; and tho' we had not Knives, Hatchets, or Guns, such as we have now, yet we had Knives of Stone, and Hatchets of Stone, and Bows and Arrows, and those served our Uses as well then as the *English* ones do now. We are now straitened, and sometimes in want of Deer, and liable to many other inconveniencies since the *English* came among us, and particularly from that Pen-and-Ink Work that is going on at the Table (*pointing to the Secretary*) and we will give you an Instance of this. Our Brother *Onas,* a great while ago, came to *Albany* to buy the *Sasquahannah* Lands of us, but our Brother, the Governor of *New York,* who, as we suppose, had not a good Understanding with our Brother *Onas,* advised us not to sell him any Land, for he would make an ill Use of it; and, pretending to be our good Friend, he advised us, in order to prevent *Onas's,* or any other Person's imposing upon us, and that we might always have our Land when we should want it, to put it into his Hands; and told us, he would keep it for our Use, and never open his Hands, but keep them close shut, and not part with any of it, but at our Request. Accordingly we trusted him, and put our Land into his Hands, and charged him to keep it safe for our Use; but, some Time after, he went to *England,* and carried our Land with him, and there sold it to our Brother *Onas,* for a large Sum of Money; and when, at the Instance of our Brother *Onas,* we were minded to sell him some Lands, he told us, we had sold the *Sasquahannah* Lands already to the Governor of *New-York,* and that he had bought them from him in *England;* tho', when he came to understand how the Governor of *New-York* had deceived us, he very generously paid us for our Lands over again.

Tho' we mention this Instance of an Imposition put upon us by the Governor of *New-York,* yet we must do the *English* the Justice to say, we have had their hearty Assistances in our Wars with the *French,* who were no sooner arrived amongst us than they began to render us uneasy, and to provoke us to War, and we have had several Wars with them; during all which we constantly received Assistance from the *English,* and, by their Means, we have always been able to keep up our Heads against their Attacks.

We now come nearer home. We have had your Deeds interpreted to us, and we acknowledge them to be good and valid, and that the *Conestogoe* or *Sasquahannah Indians* had a Right to sell those Lands to you, for they were then theirs; but since that Time we have conquered them, and their Country now belongs to us, and the Lands we demanded Satisfaction for are no Part of the Lands comprized in those Deeds; they are the *Cohongoroutas*[3] Lands; those, we are sure, you have not possessed One Hundred Years, no, nor above Ten Years, and we made our Demands so soon as we knew your People were settled in those Parts. These have never been sold, but remain still to be disposed of; and we are well pleased to hear you are provided with Goods, and do assure you of our Willingness to treat with you for those unpurchased Lands; in Confirmation whereof, we present you with this Belt of Wampum. . . .

Brother Assaragoa;[4]

You told us Yesterday, that all Disputes with you being now at an End; you desired to confirm all former Treaties between *Virginia* and us, and to make our Chain of Union as bright as the Sun.

We agree very heartily with you in these Propositions; we thank you for your good Inclinations; we desire you will pay no Regard to any idle Stories that may be told to our Prejudice. And, as the Dispute about the Land is now intirely over, and we perfectly reconciled, we hope, for the future, we shall not act towards each other but as becomes Brethren and hearty Friends.

We are very willing to renew the Friendship with you, and to make it as firm as possible, for us and our Children with you and your Children to the latest Generation, and we desire you will imprint these Engagements on your Hearts in the Strongest Manner; and, in Confirmation that we shall do the same, we give you this Belt of Wampum. . . .

---

2. Clothing made from cheaply made cloth manufactured in Stroud, England. By this time, the term had come to represent all cheap cloth used in the Indian trade between British settlers and Indians.

3. The note attached to the original document indicates that this term represents "Potomack."

4. *Assaraquoa* was the title commonly used for the governors of Virginia, a term describing them as "sword" or "big knife."

Brother Assaragoa;

You told us likewise, you had a great House provided for the Education of Youth, and that there were several white People and *Indians* Children there to learn Languages, and to write and read, and invited us to send some of our Children amongst you, &c.

We must let you know we love our Children too well to send them so great a Way, and the *Indians* are not inclined to give their Children Learning. We allow it to be good, and we thank you for your Invitation; but our Customs differing from yours, you will be so good as to excuse us. . . .

Brother Onas, Assaragoa, and Tocarry-hogan;[5]

At the Close of your respective Speeches Yesterday, you made us very handsome Presents, and we should return you something suitable to your Generosity; but, alas, we are poor, and shall ever remain so, as long as there are so many *Indian* Traders among us. Theirs and the white Peoples Cattle have eat up all the Grass, and made Deer scarce. However, we have provided a small Present for you, and tho' some of you gave us more than others, yet, as you are all equally our Brethren, we shall leave it to you to divide it as you please.—And then presented three Bundles of Skins, which were received with the usual Ceremony from the three Governments.

We have one Thing further to say, and that is, We heartily recommend Union and a good Agreement between you our Brethren. Never disagree, but preserve a strict Friendship for one another, and thereby you, as well as we, will become the stronger.

Our wise Forefathers established Union and Amity between the *Five Nations;* this has made us formidable; this has given us great Weight and Authority with our neighbouring Nations.

We are a powerful Confederacy; and, by your observing the same Methods our wise Forefathers have taken, you will acquire fresh Strength and Power; therefore whatever befals you, never fall out one with another.

---

5. That is, Maryland.

GACHRADODOW

Like Canasatego, Gachradodow was an impressive speaker. Witham Marshe, who made his own journal at the Lancaster treaty meeting, said of this noted Cayuga leader, "This Gachradodon is a very celebrated warrior, and one of the Cahuga chiefs, about forty years of age, tall, straight-limbed, and a graceful person, but not so fat as Cannasateego. His action, when he spoke, was certainly the most graceful, as well as bold, that any person ever saw; without the buffoonery of the French, or the over-solemn deportment of the haughty Spaniards." Commissioner Edmund Jennings of Maryland remarked, Marshe said, "that he had never seen so just an action in any of the most celebrated orators he had heard speak."

When he spoke at the treaty meeting at Lancaster, Gachradodow (also sometimes called Gachadow) illustrated the problems caused in the Indians' country by the presence of settlers who took different sides with different peoples at different times. He took the opportunity of speaking to the Virginia commissioners to make them understand that the Iroquois had issues of their own to settle with the southern Indians, issues he preferred the Virginians would not interfere with. Feuding over territory had long been taking place among the eastern Native peoples of North America. It was exacerbated by the colonists, and the territorial claims received a whole new set of metaphors when the colonists remained in the Indians' midst and began to claim the Indians' lands as their own.

Gachradodow crafted his statement using a language of the justification of Iroquoian attitudes and behaviors that employed the same alienating perspective typically used among the settlers of their Indian neighbors whom they feared. By calling the Catawbas "treacherous," Gachradodow effectively constructed an implied justification for Iroquoian aggression against their neighbors to the south, using a term often used to describe the Iroquois by the French-allied Hurons, who lived to the north of Iroquoia.

SPEECH AT THE TREATY OF LANCASTER, 1744[1]

Brother Assaraquoa:[2]

The World at the first was made on the other side of the Great water different from what it is on this side, as may be known from the different Colour of Our Skin and of Our Flesh, and that which you call Justice may not be so amongst us. You have your Laws and Customs and so have we. The Great King might send you over to Conquer the Indians, but looks to us that God did not approve of it, if he had, he would not have Placed the Sea where it is, as the Limits between us and you.

Brother Assaraquoa:

Tho' great things are well remembered among Us, Yet we don't remember that we were ever Conquered by the Great King, or that we have been employ'd by that Great King to conquer others; if it was so it is beyond our Memory. We do remember we were employed by Maryland to Conquer the Conestogo's,[3] and that the Second time we were at War with them we carry'd them all off.

Brother Assaraquoa:

You Charge us with not acting agreeable to our Peace with the Catawbas; we will repeat truly to you what was done: The Governor of New York at Albany, in behalf of Assaraquoa, gave us several Belts from the Cherickees and Catawbas, and we agreed to a Peace if those Nations would send some of their Great men to Us to confirm it face to face, and that they would Trade with us, and desired that they would appoint a time to meet at Albany for this Purpose, but they never came.

----

1. The text is from *Colonial Records of Pennsylvania* (also known as *Minutes of the Provincial Council of Pennsylvania*), ed. Samuel Hazard (1841), vol. 4.

2. *Assaraquoa* meant "sword" or "big knife," and it was used for the Virginia commissioners.

3. Conestogas, another name for the Susquehannocks.

Brother Assaraquoa:

We then desired a Letter might be sent to the Catawbas and Cherikees to desire them to come and confirm the Peace. It was long before an Answer came, but we met the Cherikees and Confirmd the Peace, and sent some of Our People to take care of them untill they returned to their own Country.

The Catawbas refused to come, and sent us word that we were but Women; that they were men and double men for they had two P—s; that they could make Women of Us, and would be always at War with us. They are a deceitful People; Our Brother Assaraquoa is deceived by him; we don't blame him for it, but are sorry he is so deceived. . . .

Brother Assaraquoa:

We have confirm'd the Peace with the Cherikees, but not with the Catawbas. They have been Treacherous, and know it, so that the War must continue till one of Us is destroyed. This we think Proper to tell you, that you may not be Troubled at what we do to the Catawbas.

Brother Assaraquoa:

We will now Speak to the Point between us. You say you will agree with us to the Road. We desire that may be the Road which was last made (the Waggon Road). It is always a custom among Brethren or Strangers to use each other kindly. You have some very ill-natured People living up there, so that we desire the Persons in Power may know that we are to have reasonable Victuals when we are in want.

You know very well when the White People came first here they were poor; but now they have got our Lands and are by them become Rich, and we are Now poor. What little we had for the Land goes soon away, but the Land lasts forever. You told us you had brought with you a Chest of Goods, and that you have the Key in your Pockets; But we have never seen the Chest nor the Goods that are said to be in it. It may be smal and the Goods few. We want to see them, and are desirous to come to some Conclusion. We have been sleeping here these Ten Days past, and have not done any thing to the Purpose.

THE CHICKASAWS

During the eighteenth century, the Chickasaws lived in a series of villages along the Mississippi River, in the area of the present-day state of Mississippi, and they claimed as their hunting territory areas of present-day Mississippi, Alabama, Tennessee, and Kentucky. Their main landing site along the Mississippi River was at the present location of Memphis, Tennessee. They successfully routed Hernando de

Soto in the early 1540s, when he came to live among them and demanded the use of Chickasaw people for labor, and they held onto their territory long after the arrival of the French in the area. For this reason, they came to be known as fierce peoples among the settlers in the area.

By the middle of the eighteenth century, with the help of neighboring groups of Indians, particularly the Choctaws, the French began to undermine the Chickasaws' hold on their lands. The continued warfare meant that supplies like ammunition became scarce and the population, particularly of men, diminished to such a serious extent that their numbers were significantly reduced. Yet until the end of the Revolution against Great Britain, the British settlers in the Carolinas considered the Chickasaws important allies for Britain. The Chicasaws remained so until they were forced to move, during the 1830s period of federally forced removals of Native peoples, to territory in the federally designated Indian Country west of the Mississippi that was already inhabited by their old enemies, the Choctaws.

SPEECH OF THE CHICKASAWS TO THE GOVERNOR OF SOUTH CAROLINA, 1756[1]

From the Headmen and Warriours of the Chekesaws Nation to the King of Carolina and His Beloved Men, This is to let you know we are daily cut oft by our Enemies the French and their Indians who seems to be resolved to drive us from this Land. Therefore we beg of you, our best Friends, to send back our People that are living in other Nations in order to enable us to keep our Lands from the French and their Indians. We hope you will think on us in our Poverty as we have not had the Liberty of Hunting these 3 Years but have had enough to do to defend our Lands and prevent our Women and Children from being Slaves to the French. Our Traders that come here are not willing to trust us Gun Powder and Bulletts to hunt and defend ourselves from our Enemies, neither are we able to buy from them. Many of our Women are without Flaps and many of our young Men without Guns which renders them uncapable of making any Defence against such a powerful Enemy. We are very thankful to you for your last Presents without which it would not have been possible for us to keep Possession of this Land. We have not forgotten all your old good Talks, they are stil fresh in our Minds and we shall always look upon the English as our best Friends and will always endeavour to hinder the French from incroaching on our Lands either to build Forts or make any other Improvments. We will never give up this Land but with the Loss of our Lives. We look upon your Enemies as ours and your Friends as our Friends. The Day shall never come while Sun shines and Water runs that we will join any other Nation but the English. We hope you will stil take Pity on us and give us a Supply of Powder and Bullets and Guns &c. to enable us to outlive our Enemies and revive a dying Friend. We have had no less than four Armies against us this Winter and have lost 20 of our Warriours and many of our Wives and Children carried of alive, our Towns sett on Fire in the Night and burnt down, many of our Houses &c. destroyed our Blanketts &c. We were out a hunting at the Time where we was all attacked by the Back Enemy at our Hunting Camp where we lost several of our Warriours, Women and Children so that we were obliged to leave our Hunting Camps and return to our Nation. Our Traders can tell you all this is true, if you think we tell Lies. We have told you the greatest of our Wants and are in hopes you will not forget us and leave us to be cutt of by our Enemies. Pray send all our People that lives amongst you to our Nation for we think they must be troublesome to you and would be of great Service to us for we are now reduced to small a Number we can hardly spare Men to guard our Traders to and from our Nation. We have no more to say at Present but hope you will pity us for we are very poor.

Tuska Chickamobbey (his Mark)

Pia Hagego (his Mark)

Tiske Omastabey (his Mark)

Mucklassau Mingo (his Mark)

Mingo Opya (his Mark)

Pia Mattaha (his Mark)

Tanna Puskemingo (his Mark)

War King (his Mark)

Pia Haggo (his Mark)

Funne Mingo Mas Habey (his Mark)

---

1. The text is from *Colonial Records of South Carolina: Documents Relating to Indian Affairs, 1754–1765,* ed. W. L. McDowell, Jr. (1970).

JOHN KILLBUCK

John Killbuck became a key spokesman for the Lenapes (called the Delawares in most British records of the era) during the decades when serious encroachment by settlers overtook the Lenape villages established among their allies, the Shawnees, along the Ohio River. As his speech, presented next, indicates, several treaty instruments had been drawn up and agreed to between the Lenapes (Delawares) and their allied groups and the British. One of the central instruments was not a treaty, however, but a proclamation by King George III. The Proclamation of 1763, by which the British government claimed it would restrict settlement to the eastern side of any headwaters that began at the Allegheny Mountains, purportedly left the western side of the mountains as an Indian reserve that would be protected from settlers' encroachments. Settlers were already on Indian lands, however, at the time the Proclamation of 1763 was made, and merely informing settlers of the new proclamation did nothing to prevent them from remaining in the area or attempting further removes to the west.

The treaty made at Fort Stanwix in 1768 was another instrument the British government drew up to lay claim to Indian lands. At this treaty negotiation, Iroquois headmen, meeting with the British Indian superintendent Sir William Johnson, agreed to confer a large cession of land held by the Shawnees, their neighbors, that took British-held territory all the way to the Ohio River. Despite the Shawnees' objections, the land cession was permanent. The Shawnees and Delawares were greatly outnumbered among the land speculators, traders, missionaries, and governors who attended the Fort Stanwix treaty negotiations. Their protests and concerns went almost entirely unheeded, and the British representatives and settlers were happier to deal with the allies they were hoping to secure—the Iroquois—in any case. The Shawnees and Delawares were, as historian Randolph Downes once put it, lost in the crowd.

Sir William Johnson was told at that 1768 meeting that news had reached the Shawnees that both the Spanish and French were urging the western peoples to rise up against the English and had invited the Indians to a council for that purpose. The English authorities had more immediate concerns, though, and given that they had been hearing similar things for years, they ignored the appeals made by the Shawnees and Delawares. It was easy to disregard such protests because they had all along been disregarded. The result in the Indian territory in the Ohio River valley was that, especially among the Lenapes and as early as the mid-eighteenth century, a series of prophets emerged beginning with Neolin in the early 1760s, who instructed the Lenape people and their allies to return to Indian lifeways, urging that they drop their guns and return to using bows and arrows; live entirely on dried meats and traditional cooking; abhor the use of alcohol; abandon commerce with all the white people; and clothe themselves in their traditional costumes, skins and furs. This return to traditional ways worked for a time to consolidate the Lenapes and their western allies culturally and, indeed, became a critical cultural impetus behind the war that the settlers called Pontiac's Rebellion in 1763.

During the 1760s and early part of the 1770s, the western peoples became aware that the British government was negotiating a consolidation of its forces with the Cherokees to the south and the Iroquois to the north. The western peoples were incensed. The attempt to consolidate British interests with much larger Indian groups compromised the situation of the Lenapes who were living in villages in the Ohio area, for it caught them between their Iroquois associates and their friends, the Shawnees. Killbuck was sent to express his people's concerns to the British. He knew that the Shawnees were preparing to make a final retaliatory effort against British settlers in attacks on western areas of Virginia, attacks that eventually gave John Murray, earl of Dunmore and governor of Virginia, an excuse to send out a military force against the Shawnees in 1774.

SPEECH TO THE GOVERNORS OF PENNSYLVANIA, MARYLAND, AND VIRGINIA, 1771[1]

Brethren, in former times our forefathers and yours lived in great friendship together and often met to strengthen the chain of their friendship. As your people grew numerous we made room for them and came over the Great Mountains to Ohio. And some time ago when you were at war with the French your soldiers came into this country, drove the French away and built forts. Soon after a number of your people came over the Great Mountains and settled on our lands. We complained of their encroachments into our country, and, brethren, you either could not or would not remove them. As we did not choose to have any disputes with our brethren, the English, we agreed to make a line and the Six Nations at Fort Stanwix three years ago sold the King all the lands on the east side of the Ohio down to the Cherokee[2] River, which lands were the property of our confederacy, and gave a deed to Sir William Johnson as he desired. Since that time great numbers more of your people have come over the Great Mountains and settled throughout this country. And we are sorry to tell you that several quarrels have happened between your people and ours, in which people have been killed on both sides, and that we now see the nations round us and your people ready to embroil in a quarrel, which gives our nation great concern, as we on our parts want to live in friendship with you, as you have always told us you have laws to govern your people by (but we do not see that you have). Therefore, brethren, unless you can fall upon some method of governing your people who live between the Great Mountains and the Ohio River and who are now very numerous, it will be out of the Indians' power to govern their young men, for we assure you the black clouds begin to gather fast in this country. And if something is not soon done those clouds will deprive us of seeing the sun. We desire you to give the greatest attention to what we now tell you as it comes from our hearts and a desire we have to live in peace and friendship with our brethren the English. And therefore it grieves us to see some of the nations about us and your people ready to strike each other. We find your people are very fond of our rich land. We see them quarrelling every day about land and burning one another's houses. So that we do not know how soon they may come over the River Ohio and drive us from our villages, nor do we see you brethren take any care to stop them. It's now several years since we have met together in council, which all nations are surprised and concerned at. What is the reason you kindled a fire at Ohio for us to meet you (which we did and talked friendly together) that you have let your fire go out for some years past? This makes all nations jealous about us as we also frequently hear of our brethren the English meeting with Cherokees and with the Six Nations to strengthen their friendship, which gives us cause to think you are forming some bad designs against us who lives between the Ohio and Lakes. I have now told you everything that is in my heart and desire you will write what I have said and send it to the Great King. A belt.

Killbuck, speaker.

1. Killbuck's speech is taken from *Documents of the American Revolution*, ed. K. G. Davies, (1977–81), vol. 3.

2. The name commonly given to the Tennessee River because the Cherokees lived in the area.

CORNPLANTER

The Seneca chief, Cornplanter (1732?–1836), was among the most renowned orators of his day, a leading negotiator at councils with the British American colonists, the British war leaders, and the Indian peoples who were troubled by the events taking place all around them, whether between the British and French or the British and the colonists who became known as the Americans. Cornplanter was born to a full-blood Seneca woman and an Albany Dutch trader named Abeel, (who also had a white wife back in the settlements), and he lived among the western New York and Allegheny River Senecas as a young man. Because of his mixed parentage, Cornplanter was known among the Indians as Kayantwahkeh Gyantwaia (sometimes spelled as Gayentwahga) and among the settler peoples as Cornplanter, or John O'Bail (or

O'Beale, an Irishism made of his father's name, Abeel). Cornplanter took part in several of the major treaty meetings, including the ones at Fort Stanwix (1784) and Fort Harmar (1789), before he met with George Washington and other military and political leaders in Philadelphia in 1790.

Of the many Indian men whose lives were caught up in the confused wrangling over loyalties during the era of the Revolution against Great Britain, Cornplanter stood nearly alone in consistently and quietly remaining neutral or else supporting the British American colonists with whom his people had come to agreements earlier in the century. At an important meeting in the summer of 1777 at Irondequoit (near present-day Rochester, New York, on the south shore of Lake Ontario), for instance, Cornplanter vigorously opposed having the Senecas, then sitting in council with British military leaders headed by Major John Butler, take part in any of the British military campaigns against the Americans. The Senecas agreed to attempt to take no side in the conflict, as they had promised the American colonists, thus refusing to take sides with British forces in the havoc of the American Revolution against Great Britain.

As the war was concluding and settlements were being laid for agreements among all the parties, the new American government faced the challenge of figuring out how to assert its newly won authority over the Indians of the Pennsylvania, Ohio, and New York territories. Cornplanter and his people got caught between the confusion over who had jurisdiction over the Iroquois in western New York and Pennsylvania, the state governments or the federal government. One of the points the Pennsylvania government insisted upon was the Iroquois cession of Iroquoian lands, a large tract that comprised most of the northwestern section of the state of Pennsylvania. On behalf of the Six Nations peoples, Cornplanter protested to the Pennsylvania commissioners at council at Fort Stanwix in October 1784, that the Indians loved their land and would not part with their hunting grounds. They could not agree to such a gift of their lands, he said. The commissioners responded that the land was already lost because it had been long ago ceded in Britain's treaty with Pennsylvania. They told the Indians to make their agreement quickly—offering assorted goods that equaled about four thousand dollars in payment—because they wanted to return to their homes back in the eastern area, and the next day would be a Sunday, when they could not carry on their negotiations. The Indians considered a bit, apart from the commissioners, then returned to council stating that they wanted one thousand more dollars' worth in goods, to be paid the following year. They signed the agreement on October 23, 1784.

When the Senecas started to get caught in the buffer zone between western Indians, such as the Miamis, who were interested in raiding colonists' encroaching settlements, and the larger colonial settlements to the east, Cornplanter attempted to draw the warring parties into treaty councils, to save lives and, he evidently hoped, create a better understanding among all the peoples involved. The council at Fort Harmar, on the southern end of the Muskingum River in Ohio, in January 1789, was a fiasco from the start. The western Indians refused to come to the meetings, and none of the chiefs who were present were leading headmen of their nations, thus undermining, from the Indians' point of view, any sense of the validity of the treaties that might be conducted. But the treaty negotiations were opened nonetheless. The agreements at Fort Harmar confirmed those of Fort Stanwix, this time with Cornplanter agreeing to the same land cessions made at Stanwix with the federal government, rather than with the state government of Pennsylvania. Cornplanter made a separate agreement with the state of Pennsylvania that ceded territory near Erie to the state in exchange for Seneca-occupied lands running east of the Conewango Creek and Chautauqua Lake. It had seemed to Cornplanter that there was nothing to do but to make these agreements because the settlers would take over the lands anyway. He asked that a system of trade be established and monitored, and he asked for agricultural instruments. "We shall want our hoes and other Articles mended," he said, "and for that purpose we would wish to have a Blacksmith settled amongst us." Indian agent George Morgan remarked of the whole negotiation that "Few of the natives attended, and none were fully represented; here the treaty was negotiated and speeches and explanations to the Indians made by our superintendent in the French language through a Canadian interpreter who had to guess at his meaning for he can neither write nor speak the language so as to make himself understood in any matter of that importance."

When he went to Philadelphia in late October 1790, Cornplanter carried the burden of the memory of that Fort Stanwix agreement and other treaties that were weighing heavily with him and his people. With several other Indian chiefs, he complained to George Washington about the treatment the Iroquois had received at the council meetings with Pennsylvanians and also with New York leaders. Washington's reply was sympathetic, for Indian policy was yet to be made and tested, and Washington always argued for the full powers of the federal government over state governments. Washington told Cornplanter and the others that treaties between individual groups like this, which took place apart from officers of the new federal government, would not hold under the newly adopted Constitution, which gave supreme power to the federal government, rather than to the states. Washington's concern seems to have been genuine, although, to be sure, Washington was worried that these buffer Indian peoples who lived between the settlers' and western Indians' worlds might just as easily go over to the side of the British in Canada and the western Indians beyond their immediate territories. "The General Government," he told Cornplanter, "will never consent to your being defrauded, but it will protect you in all your just Rights."

SPEECH IN COUNCIL AT PHILADELPHIA, 1790[1]

The Fathers of the Quaker State, Obeale or Cornplanter, returns thanks to God for the pleasure he has in meeting you this day with six of his people.

Fathers: Six years ago I had the pleasure of making peace with you, and at that time a hole was dug in the earth, and all contentions between my nation and you ceased and were buried there.

At a treaty then held at Fort Stanwix between the six nations of Indians and the Thirteen Fires,[2] three friends from the Quaker State came to me and treated with me for the purchase of a large tract of land upon the northern boundary of Pennsylvania, extending from Tioga to Lake Erie for the use of their warriors. I agreed to sale of the same, and sold it to them for four thousand dollars. I begged of them to take pity on my nation and not buy it forever. They said they would purchase it forever, but that they would give me further one thousand dollars in goods when the leaves were ready to fall, and when I found that they were determined to have it, I agreed that they should have it. I then requested, as they were determined to have the land to permit my people to have the game and hunt upon the same, which request they complied with, and promised me to have it put upon record, that I and my people should have that privilege.

Fathers: The six nations then requested that another talk might be held with the Thirteen Fires, which was agreed to, and a talk afterwards held between them at Muskingum.[3] Myself with three of my chiefs attended punctually, and were much fatigued in endeavoring to procure the attendance of the other nations, but none of them came to the council fire except the Delawares and the Wyandots.

Fathers: At the same treaty the Thirteen Fires asked me on which side I would die, whether on their side, or the side on those nations who did not attend the council fire. I replied, listen to me fathers of the Thirteen Fires, I hope you will consider how kind your fathers were treated by our fathers, the six nations, when they first came into this country, since which time you have become strong, insomuch, that I now call you fathers.

In former days when you were young and weak, I used to call you brother, but now I call you father. Father, I hope you will take pity on your children, for now I inform you that I'll die on your side. Now, father, I hope you will make my bed strong.

Fathers of the Quaker State: I speak but little now, but will speak more when the Thirteen Fires meet, I will only inform you further, that when I had finished my talk with the Thirteen Fires, General Gibson, who was sent by the Quaker State, came to the fire, and said that the Quaker State had bought of the Thirteen Fires a tract of land extending from the northern boundary of Pennsylvania at Connewango River to Buffaloe Creek on Lake Erie, and thence along the said lake to the northern boundary of Pennsylvania aforesaid. Hearing this I run to my father,

---

1. The text is from *Colonial Records of Pennsylvania,* ed. Samuel Hazard (1853), vol. 16.

2. A reference to the Fort Stanwix treaty of 1784.

3. A reference to the Fort Harmar treaty of 1789.

and said to him, father have you sold this land to the Quaker State, and he said he did not know, it might have been done since he came there. I then disputed with Gibson and Butler,[4] who was with him about the same, and told them I would be satisfied if the line was run from Connewango River through Chatochque Lake to Lake Erie, for Gibson and Butler had told me that the Quaker State had purchased the land from the Thirteen Fires, but that notwithstanding the Quaker State had given to me one thousand dollars in fine prime goods which were ready for me and my people at Fort Pitt, we then agreed that the line should be run from Connewango River through Chatochque Lake into Lake Erie, and that one-half of the fish in Chatochque Lake should be mine and one-half theirs.

They then said as the Quaker State had purchased the whole from the Thirteen Fires, that the Thirteen Fires must pay back to the Quaker State the value of the remaining land. When I heard this my mind was at ease, and I was satisfied.

I then proposed to give a half mile square of land upon the line so agreed upon to a Mr. Hartzhorn who was an ensign in General Harmar's army out to a Mr. Britt, a cadet who acted as a clerk upon occasion, and who I well know by the name of Half-Town,[5] for the purpose of their settling there to prevent any mischief being committed in future upon my people's lands, and I hoped that the Quaker State would in addition thereto give them another half mile square on their side of the line so agreed upon for the same purpose, expecting thereby that the line so agreed upon would be known with sufficient certainty and that no disputes would thereafter arise between my people and the Quaker State concerning it. I then went to my father of the Thirteen Fires and told him I was satisfied, and the coals being covered up I said to my children you must take your course right through the woods to Fort Pitt. When I was leaving Muskingum my own son who re-

mained a little while behind to warm himself at the fire was robbed of a rifle by one of the white men, who, I believe, to have been a Yankee. Myself with Mr. Joseph Nicholson[6] and a Mr. Morgan[7] then travelled three days together through the wilderness, but the weather being very severe they were obliged to separate from me, and I sent some of my own people along with Mr. Nicholson and Mr. Morgan as guides to conduct them on to Wheelen.

After I had separated from Mr. Nicholson and Mr. Morgan, I had under my charge one hundred and seventy persons of my own nation, consisting of men, women and children to conduct through the wilderness through heaps of briars, and having lost our way, we, with great difficulty reached Wheelen. When arrived there being out of provision I requested of a Mr. Zanes to furnish me and my people with bacon and flour to the amount of seventeen dollars, to be paid for out of goods belonging to me and my people at Fort Pitt. Having obtained my request, I proceeded on my journey for Pittsburg, and about ten miles from Wheelen[8] my party were fired upon by three white people, and one of my people in the rear of my party received two shot through his blanket.

Fathers: It was a constant practice with me throughout the whole journey to take great care of my people, and not suffer them to commit any outrages or drink more than their necessities required. During the whole of my journey only one accident happened which was owing to the kindness of the people of the town called Catfish, in the Quaker State, who, while I was talking with the head men of the town, gave to my people more liquor than was proper, and some of them got drunk, which obliged me to continue there with my people all night, and in the night my people were robbed of three rifles and one shot gun; and though every endeavor was used by the head men of the town upon complaint made to them to discover the perpetrators of the robbery, they could not be found; and on my people's complaining to me I told them it was their own fault by getting drunk.

---

4. Richard Butler (1743–91), who was born in Ireland, served the militias in Pennsylvania and Virginia during the American Revolution and then took part in Indian affairs, representing the federal government at Fort Pitt, in present-day Pittsburgh, Pennsylvania.

5. Gahgeote, or Half Town, an Allegheny Seneca, worked with Cornplanter during both wartime and peacetime to retain as much power as possible for the Allegheny Senecas.

6. Joseph Nicholson was a steady friend of Cornplanter and the other Senecas who formed his party.

7. Colonel George Morgan replaced Richard Butler at Fort Pitt. He was distinctly concerned about the potential of Indian alliances with British forces to the west.

8. Wheeling, in present-day West Virginia.

Fathers: Upon my arrival at Fort Pitt I saw the goods which I had been informed of at Muskingum, and one hundred of the blankets were all moth eaten and good for nothing, I was advised not to take the blankets, but the blankets which I and my people then had being all torn by the briars in our passage through the wilderness, we were under the necessity of taking them to keep ourselves warm; and what most surprised me, was that after I had received the goods they extinguished the fire and swept away the ashes, and having no interpreter there I could talk with no one upon the subject. Feeling myself much hurt upon the occasion, I wrote a letter to you Fathers of the Quaker State, complaining of the injury, but never received any answer. Having waited a considerable time, and having heard that my letter got lost, I wrote a second time to you Fathers of the Quaker State and then I received an answer.

I am very thankful to have received that answer, and as the answer intreated me to come and speak for myself, I thank God that I have this opportunity, I therefore speak to you as follows. I hope that you, the Fathers of the Quaker State, will fix some person at Fort Pitt to take care of me and my people. I wish, and it is the wish of my people if agreeable to you that my present interpreter, Joseph Nicholson, may be the person, as I and my people have a confidence in him, and are satisfied that he will always exert himself to preserve peace and harmony between you and us. My reasons for wishing an interpreter to be placed there, are that often times when my hunters and people come there, their canoes and other things are stolen, and they can obtain no redress, not having any person there on whom they can rely to interpret for them and see justice done to them.

Fathers of the Quaker State: About a year ago a young man, one of my tribe who lived among the Shawanese, was one of a party who had committed some outrages and stolen a quantity of skins the property of David Duncan, being at Fort Pitt, was seized by the white people there who would have put him into confinement and perhaps to death had not some of the chiefs of the Seneca Nation interfered and bound themselves to the said David Duncan, who insisted upon satisfaction, for payment of the sum of five hundred and thirty dollars for the said skins so stolen, upon which the young man aforesaid was released and delivered up to them.

Fathers of the Quaker State: I wish now to acquaint you with what happened to one of my people about four years ago, four miles above Fort Pitt: A young man who was married to my wife's sister, when he was hunting, was murdered by a white man. There were three reasons for his being killed: In the first place he had a very fine riding horse; secondly, he was very richly dressed, and had about him a good deal of silver; and thirdly, he had with him a very fine rifle. The white man invited him to his house, to light from his horse, and as he was getting off his horse, his head being rather down, the white man struck him with a tomahawk on the head and killed him, and having plundered him dragged him into the river. Upon discovery of the murder, my people, with Mr. Nicholson and Mr. Duncan, had a great deal of trouble, and took a great deal of pains to find out the person who had committed the murder, and after three days' searching, they discovered him.

Father of the Quaker State: About five years ago, one of my chiefs, name Half Town, was sent to Fort Pitt to deliver up into your hands your own flesh and blood who were taken in the war, and before he returned two horses were stolen from him by the white people. Now, Fathers, I will inform you of another accident which happened to my people last winter, fifteen miles below Fort Pitt. My nephew, with a hunting party, being there, was shot through the head in Mr. Nicholson's camp, the particulars of which Mr. Nicholson, who is here present, can inform you.

Well, Fathers, I beg of you once more not to let such bad people be 'longside of me. And, Fathers, you must not think I or any of my people are bad or wish evil to you and yours, nor must you blame us for mischiefs that have been committed by the other nations. Fathers, consider me and my people, and the many injuries we have sustained by the repeated robberies, and in the murders and depredations committed by the whites against us.

It is my wish and the wishes of my people to live peaceably and quietly with you and yours, but the losses we have sustained require some compensation. I have, with the consent of my people, agreed to receive from you eight hundred and thirty dollars, as a satisfaction for all losses and injuries I and my people have sustained, and this being paid me by you, to enable me to satisfy such of my people as have sustained those losses and suffered those injuries, we shall, I hope, in future live peaceable together, and bury in the earth all ill will and enmity to each other.

Fathers of the Quaker State: I have now had the pleasure to meet you with six of my people. We have come a great way, by your desire, to talk with you and to show to you the many injuries my nation has sustained. It now remains with you to do with me and my people what you please, on account of the present trouble which I and my people have taken for your satisfaction, and in compliance with your request.

Fathers, having come this great way at your request, and as it is necessary for some of us to remain here to talk with the Thirteen Fires when they meet, I have concluded to send back four of my people, and to remain here myself with Half Town and my interpreter, Mr. Nicholson, until that time, which I hope you will approve of. But should you not approve of it, I must be under the necessity of returning with the whole of my people, which will be attended with a considerable expense.

Fathers of the Quaker State: You have now got the most of our lands, and have taken the game upon the same. We have only the privilege of hunting and fishing thereon. I, therefore, would make this further request, that a store may be established at Fort Pitt for the accommodation of my people and the other nations when they go out to hunt; and where they may purchase goods at a reasonable price. For, believe me, Fathers, you yourselves would be frightened were you to know the extravagant prices we are obliged to pay for the goods we purchase.

There is a man (Esquire Wilkie) in Pittsburg, who has taken a great deal of pains to serve my people, and has pitied them; my people, when there, are very kindly treated by him, and give him a great deal of trouble, but he thinks nothing of it; he is the man my people wish should have charge of the store.

Fathers of the Quaker State: I have heard that you have been pleased to present to me a tract of land,[9] but as yet I have not seen no writings for the same; well, Fathers, if it is true that you have given me this tract of land, I can only thank you for the same, but I hope you will also give me tools and materials for working the same.

Fathers of the Quaker State: Five years ago, when I used to be with my present interpreter, Joseph Nicholson, he took care of me and my people. Considering his services and the difficulties he underwent in his journey from Muskingum to Fort Pitt, the Six Nations wished to have him seated upon a tract of land of six miles square, lying in the forks of Allegany River, and Broken Straw creek, and accordingly patented the same to him, this being the place where the battle was fought between my people and yours, and where about thirty of my people were beaten by him and twenty-five of your people, and where he was shot through the thigh. Now, Fathers, it is my wish, and I tell you it is the wish of the whole Six Nations, in behalf of whom and myself, I request that you would grant and confirm to our brother and friend, the before named Joseph Nicholson, the aforesaid tract of land, as described in our patent or grant to him.

This, Fathers, is all I have to say to the Quaker State, and I hope you will consider well all I have mentioned.

---

9. Cornplanter received, during the treaty, a promise by a land company for a tract of 640 acres in Marietta. According to Seneca tradition, the signed treaty paper was stolen from him. Cornplanter received, after that, a personal grant of land in western Pennsylvania, taken back during the twentieth century, when the state flooded the reserve to form the Kinsua Dam.

INDEX

1125